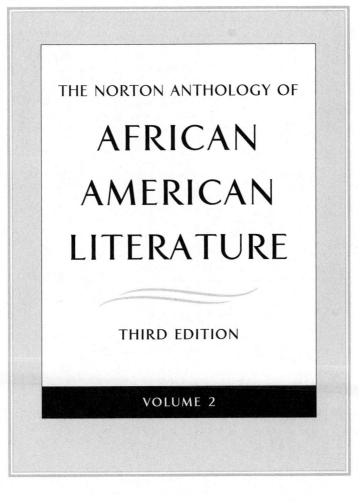

THE NORTON ANTHOLOGY OF

AFRICAN
AMERICAN
LITERATURE

THIRD EDITION

VOLUME 2

The Vernacular
Tradition
Part 2

In African American literature, *the vernacular* refers to the church songs, blues, ballads, sermons, stories, and, in our own era, hip-hop songs that are part of the oral, not primarily the literate (or written-down) tradition of black expression. What distinguishes this body of work is its in-group and, at times, secretive, defensive, and aggressive character: it is not, generally speaking, produced for circulation beyond the black group itself (though it sometimes is bought and sold by those outside its circle). This highly charged material has been extraordinarily influential for writers of poetry, fiction, drama, and so on. What would the work of Langston Hughes, Sterling A. Brown, Zora Neale Hurston, and Toni Morrison be like without its black vernacular ingredients? What, for that matter, would the writing of Mark Twain or William Faulkner be without these same elements? Still, this vernacular material also has its own shapes, its own integrity, its own place in the black literary canon: *the literature of the vernacular.*

Defining the vernacular and delineating it as a category of African American literary studies have been difficult and controversial projects. Some critics note

Avenue Steppers Marching Club, 1982. Black New Orleans features parades at Mardi Gras and throughout the year—for other holidays, funerals, and many occasions. The stylized music and dance steps characteristic of the parades have helped define New Orleans' culture and bind its community. These street forms offer a continuing source of inspiration for artists across the categories: literary, visual, and otherwise. Photography by Michael P. Smith © The Historic New Orleans Collection.

the vernacular's typical demarcation as a category of things that are male, attached only to lower-class groups, and otherwise simplistically expressive of a vast and complexly layered and dispersed group of people. Others warn both against the sentimentalization of a stereotyped "folk" and their "lore" and against the impulse to define black people and their literature solely in terms of the production of unconscious but somehow definitive work from the bottom of the social hierarchy. With these critiques often come warnings against forming too easy an idea about the shape and direction of African American literary history. Most emphatic is the argument against a "modernist" view that would posit an almost sacred set of foundational vernacular texts by "black and unknown bards" (to borrow James Weldon Johnson's ringing phrase) leading to ever more complex works by higher and higher artists marching into the future. Is contemporary music really more "progressive" or "complex" than the work of Bessie Smith, Robert Johnson, or Louis Armstrong?

And yet even after these questions and criticisms have been raised, somehow such distinctive forms as church songs, blues, tall tales, work songs, games, jokes, dozens, and rap songs—along with myriad other such forms, past and present—persist among African Americans, as they have for decades. They are, as a Langston Hughes poem announces, *still here.* Indeed, the vernacular is not a body of quaint, folksy items. It is not an exclusive male province. Nor is it associated with a particular level of society or with a particular historical era. It is neither long ago, far away, nor fading. Instead, the vernacular encompasses vigorous, dynamic processes of expression, past and present. It makes up a rich storehouse of materials wherein the values, styles, and character types of black American life are reflected in language that is highly energized and often marvelously eloquent.

Ralph Ellison and Toni Morrison have argued that vernacular art accounts, to a large degree, for the black American's legacy of self-awareness and endurance. For black performers and listeners (as well as readers) it has often served the classic function of teaching as it delights. Refusing to subscribe wholly to the white American's ethos and worldview, African Americans expressed in these vernacular forms their own ways of seeing the world, its history, and its meanings. The vernacular comprises, Ellison said, nothing less than another instance of humanity's "triumph over chaos." In it experiences of the past are remembered and evaluated; through it African Americans attempt to humanize an often harsh world, and to do so with honesty, with toughness, and often with humor.

VERNACULAR IN THE MODERN AND CONTEMPORARY PERIODS: A BRIEF HISTORY

From the first stirrings of the Civil Rights Movement in the 1940s through the first decade of the twenty-first century, the lived experience of black Americans creating freshly innovated art has continued to be a fact of American cultural life. In particular, black Americans have produced a tidal wave of innovative black vernacular expression: new forms sacred and secular, across the categories of art. Perhaps the philosopher Cornel West's formulation best explains this phenomenon of spurting black creativity: he has said that as black creative output is adopted, bought, and sold by the broader community, the blacks themselves have been forced to come up

Jazz singer Billie Holiday often performed the anti-lynching song "Strange Fruit" at New York's Café Society, one of the country's first major interracial night clubs. This poem set to music was part of a continuum of black protest songs—"What Did I Do (to Be So Black and Blue)" and "Miss Otis Regrets" among them—that became popular with American audiences.

with another—and then yet *another*—something new of their own. Perhaps the zealousness of the search for identity, direction, and freedom in a still-hostile native land explains something about the black American's energies for ever-dawning new directions in personal/communal expression.

Whatever black Americans' motives for creativity have been, their imagery, sounds, and products have traveled very well. In 2013, the French anthropologist Alexandre Pierrepont reported that year after year in his large freshman music history classes in Paris, more than 80 percent of the students when asked what music they listened to at home routinely selected a black American music (or one directly shaped by it) as their favorite. It is not an exaggeration to say that by the end of the twentieth century, black American culture had become the most popular youth culture in the world.

At mid-twentieth century, rhythm-and-blues (much of it gospel-based) was circling the globe, and new forms of jazz were emerging. By the 1980s, jazz had become a widely accepted concert music, studied and taught—sometimes in interdisciplinary courses in jazz studies—all over the United States as well as overseas. Jazz dances (and their various blends) were filling the concert theaters and public dance halls (as well as private party spaces) of the world. Brewing in the last quarter of the twentieth century, and continuing to claim new listeners on a worldwide scale have been hip-hop music and culture, whose Bronx-born rhythms may now be heard in Hong Kong, Stockholm, Johannesburg, Berlin, and Lima. As the American economy, and indeed most of the world's economies, faltered in the early twenty-first century—and then as these economies attempted a gradual crawl back to stability in the 2010s—markets at home and abroad continued to use blues, jazz, and hip-hop to sell their wares.

Of course sheer quality accounts for much of this story of success—the mysteriously persistent allure of the beautiful U.S. black vernacular. But who can doubt that the black American's placement in the hydra-headed economy of the United States, where the hunger for new products is primary and where the capacity to market, package, and deliver them on a worldwide scale has increased with the decades, has also played its eager part? Some of this is a matter of hardware and software. The rising array of new technologies has rendered black creative productions of all sorts, in music and word art as well as in dance and the visual arts, more widely and quickly available than ever before—far beyond black communities themselves. The perfection of the microphone, of speakers large and small, and of ever-more-precise recording devices, audio and video; the rise of the LP and then the CD and then of other digital chips and delivery systems; the prevalence of mini-computer and of social media technologies—all these have made it possible for art created by individuals or small groups to be potentially available to a worldwide audience, and available in an instantaneous zip.

With all this said, on the level of the black community itself, the engines of black vernacular creativity in the modern and postmodern eras have been amazingly robust. Through the Civil Rights and Black Arts Movement and post-Black Arts Movement years, black churches (Christian and Muslim) have continued to serve as fertile training grounds for young musicians, singers, and keyboardists in particular, though with horn players and percussionists also frequently in the mix. As early as the late 1940s, the influence of blues and jazz on church music was evident. In turn, by the 1950s the influence of gospel on jazz was creating new dimensions of "soul jazz"—sometimes with musical structures and modes of

James Brown in 1962, photograph by Charles Stewart. By many reports, Brown reigns as the single most influential and widely "sampled" musician in the world.

presentation springing straight out of church. The hard bop jazz group The Jazz Messengers was one of many outstanding groups playing jazz from a gospel foundation. Likewise, the mid-twentieth century's rising tide of rhythm-and-blues could thank gospel for much of its sustained appeal. James Brown began his career as a church singer in Toccoa, Georgia. Even Motown, with its push to reach audiences beyond the black community, typically hired young singers first known to church congregations in Detroit or the Deep South. Ironically, all the singers in the hit Motown group The Temptations began as church vocalists. Sacred spaces, with their long tradition of vivid projections of The Word, have also nurtured secular black styles of spoken-word presentation—right up to our own hip-hop era.

Worldwide jazz festivals during this period frequently featured prominent gospel stages, where wide arrays of church-born projects were to be heard. In 2003, one highly significant jazz singer, Dianne Reeves, reported she spent her entire time at the New Orleans Jazz Fest under the gospel tent. "That's where you hear the most innovative vocal music," she said. In the 1990s one began to see more and more churches experimenting with new technological equipment—with recorded music sometimes filling in for instrumental and vocal backgrounds and with large screens showing congregations words of songs and close-ups of presenters. And just as hip-hop rhyme virtuosos were influenced by word artists in the church pulpits of the United States, preachers and choirs in turn were increasingly experimenting with hip-hop staccato rhymes, rhythms, and flow. Indeed, the rapid and vigorous cycling of influences, sacred and secular, "folk" and "not folk," across the decades and even the centuries, may be the most crucial aspect of the U.S. black vernacular story.

Of course jazz festivals, the first of which appeared in the early 1950s, also featured jazz. By the 1960s and '70s, these festivals had become an important circuit for jazz musicians in the United States and especially in Europe, where in some cities the festivals occurred throughout the year. During this era, many forms of music have been presented under the "jazz" banner. In New York and other major cities, on a given night one might hear a virtual history of the form: re-creations of the earliest work of King Oliver and Jelly Roll Morton, big band music (with charts sometimes borrowed from the Smithsonian or the Institute for Jazz Studies at Rutgers University), small bands playing bebop or modal jazz in the tradition of Miles Davis and John Coltrane, replays of the avant-gardists of the late 1950s, '60s, and '70s, fusions of many kinds—involving rock, flamenco, opera and other European art musics, gospel, and hip-hop. In the twenty-first century, some of these mixes left jazz afficionados doubtful that the word "jazz" still applied to music marketed and even sincerely played under its name. These musical experiments left other observers hopeful that whether called *jazz* or not, the new mixes would include ingredients from which the forms of things yet unknown would crystallize.

This period saw the rise of blues as a worldwide music, and of rhythm and blues—very often, as noted, involving singers who got their start in church—as a local urban youth phenomenon that captured the world's attention. By the mid-1960s, a new hard-driving blues line called *funk* was giving new energy to the generally softer sway of Motown and most other (blues and gospel-based) forms of R&B. James Brown, Sly Stone, the Funkadelics, and their many imitators, along with those who were extending the idiom on their own, were holding center stage on the secular black music scene. Many of the new Afro-Pop world music productions draw from these highly danceable roots. Several experts report the bass, drum, and horn lines of James Brown as being the single most sampled source in the realm of hip-hop, where sampling is a definitive mode.

The story of the forms and meanings of hip-hop is still unfolding. Most histories mark its starting place in uptown New York City, particularly in the Bronx, while also crediting important background activities in and around Kingston, Jamaica. What's clear now is that beginning sometime in the early 1970s, a form of spoken-word art was emerging that was driven by new technologies, by the will to sample, remix, and improvise rhythmical commentary over existing recorded materials of many kinds, and by the flow of the human voice in spirited and often defiant recitation. Some of the performances and recordings involved virtuosic improvisation. But at least as many hip-hop artists were careful "loose-leaf" poets who tightened their words on paper and then memorized them for public presentations that could seem improvised on the spot. (Sometimes the rapper's rhythms were improvised when the lyrics were not.)

In the quarter century since hip-hop first hit the national airwaves and party-spaces of America, the music has changed its course and, like jazz and gospel, has fused with other forms—in search, always, of fresh effects and directions. It is a street party music, dance-club music: music of courtship and playful (as well as sometimes competitive and even hostile) social interaction. It is a form of poetry or "spoken word" art where the subject frequently has been the grittiness of urban black life—and where, increasingly, many other subjects (including romance, political activism, and the difficulty of creating art) also are raised. Hip-hop's advocates speak of the characteristically hardcore diction and subject matter of hip-hop as new forms of black urban realism and protest, harsh but true reports from the bottom of the American social hierarchy. They also smile at over-the-top parodic aspects of the music that insiders know not to take too seriously. At its best, this is a music of broad aesthetic pleasures: of intricate Afro-rhythms and rhymes to challenge and delight the mind, the foot, and the eardrum—a music that raises contemporary black questions in an idiom no one can ignore.

As much as any black vernacular form in the last hundred years, hip-hop music and culture represent a *generational* preference, with those coming of age before roughly 1980 typically expressing strong dislike of hip-hop culture in its various manifestations. Hip-hop's most outspoken critics emphasize the music's casual uses of explicitly sexual language and the association of certain rappers with gangs, violence, misogyny, loveless sex, and bragging about personal wealth. But as hip-hop is gradually institutionalized, not just as a commercial product but as an art form to be researched and studied as well as aesthetically enjoyed (and blended with other forms of expression on a worldwide scale), it is emerging as a mightily persistent force. In many contemporary schools, hip-hop is employed as a tool for teaching. As with other forms of black vernacular expression—blues and jazz in particular—hip-hop is becoming a global music. And as it develops new accents and vocabularies in Asia, Africa, Europe, and throughout the Americas, new hip-hop forms, built on a black U.S. base, are emerging fast.

DEFINING THE VERNACULAR

What is the vernacular? According to *Webster's* second edition, the term comes from the Latin—*"vernaculus:* Born in one's house, native, from *verna,* a slave born in his master's house, a native"—and counts among its meanings the following: (1) "belonging to, developed in, and spoken or used by the people of a particular place, region, or country; native; indigenous. . . . (2) characteristic of a locality; local." In the context of American art, the vernacular may be defined as expression that springs from the creative interaction between the received or learned traditions and that which is locally invented, "made in America." This definition, derived from American cultural historian John A. Kouwenhoven and Ralph Ellison, sees Manhattan's skyscrapers as well as Appalachian quilts as vernacular because they use modern techniques and forms (machines, factory-made materials, etc.) along with what Ellison calls the play-it-by-ear methods and local products that give American forms their distinctive resonances and power. What, then, is the African American vernacular? It consists of forms sacred—songs, prayers, and sermons—and secular—work songs, secular rhymes and songs, blues, jazz, and stories of many kinds. It also consists of dances, wordless musical performances, stage shows, and visual art forms of many sorts.

As Houston A. Baker Jr. noted, the word *vernacular* as a cultural term has been used most frequently to describe developments in the world of architecture. In contrast to the exalted, refined, or learned styles of designing buildings, the vernacular in architecture refers both to local styles by builders unaware of or unconcerned with developments beyond their particular province and to works by inspired, cosmopolitan architects such as Frank Lloyd Wright, a careful student of architecture as a worldwide enterprise and of the latest technologies but also one who wanted his buildings custom-made for their surroundings.

This example from architecture is relevant insofar as the makers of black vernacular art used the American language and everything at their disposal to make art that paid a minimum of attention to the Thou-shalt-nots of the academy or the arbiters of high style. Coming from the bottom of the American social ladder, blacks have been relatively free from scrutiny by the official cultural monitors. As a group they tended to care little about such opinions; what the black social dance called the Black Bottom looked like to the proctors at the local ballet class (be they white or black) was of little interest to them. Thus it is no surprise that the black inventors of this rich array of definitively American forms have had such a potent impact on America's cultural life and history.

The forms included here are varied and resist aesthetic generalizations. One is drawn nonetheless to parts of Zora Neale Hurston's wonderful catalog of the "Characteristics of Negro Expression": "angularity," "asymmetry," a tendency toward "mimicry" and the "will to adorn." In addition, the forms share traits that reflect their African background: call–response patterns of many kinds; group creation; and a poly-rhythmically percussive, dance-beat orientation not only in musical forms but in the rhythm of a line, tale, or rhyme. It is not surprising that improvisation is a highly prized aspect of vernacular performance. Here too one finds European, Euro-American, and American Indian forms reshaped to African American purposes and sensibilities. For example, like black folktales, tales from Europe often lack clear delineations of sacred and profane, good and evil, righteous punishers and righteously punished. Similarly, the blues offer few such consolations, solutions, or even scapegoats. At times what seems revealed is the starkness of a life that is real, that is tough, and that must be confronted without the convenience of formulaic dodges or wishful escapes. Even the spirituals admit that "I've been 'buked and I've been scorned, I've been talked about, / Sure as you're born." And the church songs involve—along with the yearning for heaven's peace—confrontation with real troubles of the world and the will to do something about them.

One of the most compelling efforts at generalization about African American aesthetics is drawn by Henry Louis Gates Jr. from the vernacular itself. Drawing on linguistic research by Geneva Smitherman and others, Gates has defined *signifying*—the often competitively figurative, subversively parodying speech of tales and of less formalized talk as well as of various forms of music—as an impulse that operates not only between contesting tale tellers but between writers (and painters, and dancers, etc.) as well. According to this view, Toni Morrison signifies on writers who precede her by revising their conceptions of character and scene, for example, or perhaps she even signifies on aspects of the novelistic tradition itself. In Gates's complex formulations about how African Americans create, the vernacular meets not only formal art but the world of scholarly criticism as well.

This leaves us with a battery of concerns from postmodern cultural criticism: Is the idea of the vernacular "essentialist," that is, dependent on definitions of racial essences that are not knowable outside the black circle? What is *black* about the black vernacular? When is "American" culture not *black* and *vernacular*? What stake do cultural observers have in this terminology, or, for that matter, in its rejection?

This leads us further to inquire: How were this section's entries selected? Whence came these particular texts? Pouring over dozens of anthologies and collections, hymnals, songbooks, recordings, and literary works yielded texts that are not only historically representative but also distinctive and resonant with aesthetic power. One abiding problem with capturing such works is that they were not originally constructed for the printed page but for performance within complicated social and often highly ritualized settings. Nonstandard pronunciations in texts transcribed from records are generally represented with a minimum of invented spellings—the "eye dialect" so often used by American writers to designate declassé or politically disempowered groups. This effort was informed by those of writers who captured black speech by getting the rhythms right, the pauses, the special emphases and colors. But contractions and new spellings were allowed when they seemed called for.

What determines the order of the vernacular selections, genre by genre? Whenever possible, works are presented in chronological order and are clustered according to authorship. But because authorship and chronology are often unknown or ambiguous (for example, who first told the tale of the rabbit and the tar-baby?), we simply have done our best to ascertain credits and dates when they are available. In the folktales section, works are credited and dated in footnotes, but—recognizing that in this instance the "authors" are the recorders (brilliantly artistic ones though they may be) of works created incrementally by many, many voices over many, many years—they are listed not by date or writer but by subject: the animal tales precede the ones with human characters and follow a general chronological arc. Such broad thematic and timeline concerns govern all of the vernacular section's orderings—even when specific dates and authors are given. For even in the case of a Duke Ellington song or a Martin Luther King sermon/speech, for which date and author seem so specific, what we reproduce here is one particular text or version of a performance given over and over, according to changing settings and moments. And both Ellington and King draw on rich vernacular traditions (on black and unknown bards) to fashion and project their works. (In Ellington's case, the best text may be the recorded "text," with its performance by the sixteen members of his band, each of whom adds much more to the creative process than is the case with European "classical" music.) More than any other form of black literature, the vernacular resists being captured on a page or in a historical frame: by definition, it is about gradual, group creation; it is about *change*.

Clearly, the selections here and on the StudySpace playlist are not meant to be definitive but to invite further explorations and findings. Black vernacular forms are works in progress, experiments in a still new country. They have not survived because they are perfect, polished jewels but because they are vigorous fountains of expression. Not only are they influential for writers but they are wonderful creations on their own. In the black tradition, no forms are more quick or overflowing with black power and black meaning.

Gospel

I n a sense, the distinction between spirituals and gospel is so slight that it seems contrived. Both are black sacred songs, church songs that are constructed in a variety of forms within the African American musical tradition. Both are born and nurtured in the context of ritualized Christian worship, and yet both comment widely on the trying circumstances of black life in white America. To complicate the picture even more, traditional Negro spirituals are frequently rendered in a "gospel manner." Sometimes, indeed, songs from eighteenth- and nineteenth-century English hymnals—most notably the songs of Isaac Watts—may be rendered in so convincing a gospel version that listeners have thought them generated as the spirituals were generated: within the richly dramatic space of the black church service itself.

What is the gospel manner? And what is its history? Briefly, gospel music emerged in the first decades of the twentieth century as blues and early jazz styles of singing and playing instruments began to exert a powerful impact on the way church musicians conceived their task. Especially in holiness churches, Churches of God in Christ—those farthest from the genteel European models of churchly decorum—a highly percussive, polyrhythmically syncopated, and bluesy music began to appear. These singers, says poet and critic Sterling A. Brown,

> fight the devil by using what have been considered the devil's weapons. Tambourines, cymbals, trumpets and even trombones and bass fiddles are now accepted in some churches. The devil has no right to all that fine rhythm, so a joyful noise is made unto the Lord with bounce and swing.

Eventually, not only gospelized versions of familiar church songs but also songs composed in this particular idiom—a body of gospel songs per se—began to be heard in certain churches, notably in Chicago, where the music first claimed a citywide and then a national audience.

According to historian Anthony Heilbut, it is important to note the presence of gospel quartets such as the Dinwiddie Colored Quartet (recorded in 1902, arguably the first gospel music to be commercially waxed) and singing preachers such as the Reverends J. M. Gates and J. C. Burnett along with street singers and singing evangelists such as Blind Willie Johnson and Blind Arizona Dranes (all first recorded in the 1920s) as early performers of the music that became more stylized and codified as gospel.

The 1930s were the key years in the music's development. During those years, Thomas A. Dorsey, known during his blues playing and composing days as "Georgia Tom," became active in Chicago's black Protestant churches, and his experience as a blues player gave the music a truly great composer. Among his compositions are "Take My Hand, Precious Lord," "I'm Going to Live the Life I Sing about in My Song," and "Old Ship of Zion." Born the son of a Baptist minister and nephew of church organists in Villa Rica, Georgia, in 1899, Dorsey was a child prodigy who absorbed the musical styles and techniques surrounding him, including circus songs, vaudeville tunes, hillbilly ballads, and revival hymns. His single major influence was C. A. Tindley, the black religious songwriter who, like certain other late-nineteenth-century musicians, distinguished himself by combining the themes and melodies of the white religious revivals with the blues tonalities and other features of black music. Among Tindley's major hymns are the universally acclaimed "We'll Understand It Better By and By," "Stand by Me," and "Take Your Burdens to the Lord." Dorsey's wide range of musical experience permitted him to take Tindley's example and combine it with what he knew from the secular world to create the bedrock compositions in this new musical form.

Using vehicles by Dorsey, Tindley, and others were such gospel warriors and pioneers as Mitchell's Christian Singers, the Golden Gate Jubilee Quartet, the Dixie Hummingbirds, Alex Bradford, Sallie Martin, Clara Hudman (the Georgia Peach), Willie Mae Ford Smith, Marion Williams, Sister Rosetta Tharpe, Edna Gallmon Cooke, and Mahalia Jackson. Jackson's spectacular art was best described by Ralph Ellison, whose essay "The World's Greatest Gospel Singer" stands as a statement about gospel's range of influences and special powers. He wrote:

> It is an art which depends upon the employment of the full expressive resources of the human voice—from the rough growls employed by blues singers, the intermediate sounds, half-cry, half-recitative, which are common to Eastern music; the shouts and hollers of American Negro folk cries; the rough-edged tones and broad vibratos, the high, shrill and grating tones which rasp one's ears like the agonized flourishes of flamenco, to the gut tones, which remind us of where the jazz trombone found its human source. . . . In Mahalia's own "Move On Up a Little Higher" there is a riff straight out of early Ellington. Most of all it is an art which swings, and in the South there are many crudely trained groups who use it naturally for the expression of religious feeling who could teach the jazz modernists quite a bit about polyrhythmics and polytonality.

Gospel's ongoing practice of absorbing new music has continued to the present day, with current gospel groups dipping into the treasure trove of works by Dorsey and Tindley and of Negro spirituals at the same time that they invent new works influenced by the forms and instrumental mixes of rhythm and blues, Broadway, opera, and rap. As certain current groups experiment with new sound and video technologies, the solid rock of gospel sound holds firm. Like jazz, gospel has managed to absorb many influences while maintaining a distinctiveness and power all its own.

This Little Light of Mine•

Oh, this little light of mine,
I'm gonna let it shine.
This little light of mine,
I'm gonna let it shine.
This little light of mine,   5
I'm gonna let it shine.
Let it shine, shine, shine,
Let it shine.

All in my home,
I'm gonna let it shine.   10
All in my home,
I'm gonna let it shine.
All in my home,
I'm gonna let it shine.
Let it shine, shine, shine,   15
Let it shine.

God give it to me,
I'm gonna let it shine.
God give it to me,
I'm gonna let it shine.   20
God give it to me,
I'm gonna let it shine.
Let it shine, shine, shine,
Let it shine.

This little light of mine,   25
I'm gonna let it shine.
This little light of mine,
I'm gonna let it shine.
This little light of mine,
I'm gonna let it shine.   30
Let it shine, shine, shine,
Let it shine.

Everywhere I go,
I'm gonna let it shine
Everywhere I go,   35
I'm gonna let it shine
Everywhere I go, I'm gonna let it shine
Let it shine, shine, shine,
Let it shine.

Down by the Riverside•

I'm gonna lay down my sword and shield
Down by the riverside
Down by the riverside
Down by the riverside

I'm gonna lay down my sword and shield 5
Down by the riverside
Study war no more

I ain't gonna study war no more
Ain't gonna study war no more
I ain't gonna study war no more 10
I ain't gonna study war no more
Ain't gonna study war no more
Ain't gonna study war no more

I'm gonna put on my long white robes
Down by the riverside 15
Down by the riverside
Down by the riverside
I'm gonna put on my long white robes
Down by the riverside
Study war no more 20

I ain't gonna study war no more
Ain't gon' study war no more
Study war no more
Ain't gon' study war no more
Study war no more 25
I ain't gonna study war no more

I'm gonna meet all my friends who're gone
Down by the riverside
Down by the riverside
Down by the riverside 30
Gonna meet all my friends who're gone
Down by the riverside
Study war no more

I ain't gonna study war no more
Study war no more 35
Ain't gon' study war no more
I ain't gonna study war no more
Study war no more
Ain't gonna study war no more

I'm gonna put on my golden shoes 40
Down by the riverside
Down by the riverside
Down by the riverside
Gonna put on my golden shoes
Down by the riverside 45
Study war no more

Well, I ain't gon' study war no more
Study war no more
I ain't gonna study war no more
I ain't gonna study war no more 50

Study war no more
Study war no more

I'm gonna meet my dear old mother
Down by the riverside
Down by the riverside   55
Down by the riverside
Gonna meet my dear old mother
Down by the riverside
Study war no more

Well, I ain' gon' study war no more   60
Lawd, study war no more
Ain't gonna study war no more
Halleluljah
Ain't gonna study war no more
No, study war no more   65
Ain't gonna study war no more

Freedom in the Air•

Over my head
I see freedom in the air
Over my head, Oh Lord
I see freedom in the air
Over my head   5
I see freedom in the air
There must be a God somewhere

Take My Hand, Precious Lord[1]•

Precious Lord, take my hand,
Lead me on, let me stand,
I am tired, I am weak, I am worn.
Through the storm, through the night
Lead me on to the light,   5
Take my hand, precious Lord,
Lead me home.

When my way grows drear,
Precious Lord, linger near.
When my life is almost gone,   10
Hear my cry, hear my call,
Hold my hand lest I fall.
Take my hand, precious Lord,
Lead me home.

1. By Thomas A. Dorsey.

When the darkness appears   15
And the night draws near,
And the day is past and gone,
At the river I stand,
Guide my feet, hold my hand.
Take my hand, precious Lord,   20
Lead me home.

Peace Be Still

Master, the tempest is raging
The billows are tossing high
The sky is overshadowed with blackness
No shelter or hope is nigh
Carest thou not that we perish?   5
How can thou lie asleep?
When it seems each moment is threatening
A grave in the angry deep

Get up Jesus because:
The winds and the waves shall obey thy will   10
Peace be still, Peace be still
Whether the wrath of the storm-tossed sea
Or demons or man or whatever it be
No water can swallow the ship where lies
The master of ocean and earth and skies   15
They shall sweetly obey thy will
Peace, peace be still

Stand by Me[1]•

When the storms of life are raging,
Stand by me, stand by me.
When the storms of life are raging,
Stand by me, stand by me.

When the world is tossing me,   5
Like a ship out on the sea:
Thou who knowest all about it,
Stand by your child, stand by me.

In the midst of persecution,
Stand by me, stand by me.   10
In the midst of persecution,
Stand by me, stand by me.

---

1. By C. A. Tindley. The title and tune of this gospel song were appropriated for a rhythm and blues song in the early 1960s.

When my foes in battle array
Undertake to stop my way,
Thou who rescued Paul and Silas,[2]
Stand by me, stand by me.

When I'm growing old and feeble,
Stand by me, stand by me.
When I'm growing old and feeble,
Stand by me, stand by me.

When my life becomes a burden,
And I'm nearing chilly Jordan[3]
O thou Lily of the Valley,[4]
Stand by me, stand by me.

Songs of Social Change

Through much of the twentieth century, most dramatically in the decades of the civil rights and Black Power movements, black Americans deployed sacred and secular forms to voice their insistence on radical change in their political status in the United States. In some instances, church songs that already had a political edge were conscripted for service on the picket lines: "O Freedom" and "We Shall Overcome" are in this category. In other cases, songs sprang up from long decades of struggle: "Ain't Gonna Let Nobody Turn Me 'Round" is one of the songs that reportedly rang from prisons that held political prisoners of the civil rights struggle. According to Bernice Johnson Reagon, at the same time that such songs gave strength to their singers, they also shifted the locus of power away from the prison guards.

This tradition of protest song also includes "(What Did I Do to Be So) Black and Blue," a show tune by Andy Razaf and Thomas "Fats" Waller that, in Louis Armstrong's version, became a powerful plaint against racism; "Strange Fruit," a dirgelike wail against lynching that was written by a leftist Jewish schoolteacher from New York and then co-signed by the great singer Billie Holiday; and Langston Hughes's "Backlash Blues" and Nina Simone's "Four Women," songs of the 1960s that spoke of black anger and of the black woman's specific quest for wholeness, freedom, and agency.

Oh, Freedom[1]•

Oh freedom, oh freedom, oh freedom over me
And before I'd be a slave I'll be buried in a my grave
And go home to my Lord and be free

---

2. In the New Testament, Paul, an Apostle of Jesus, and Silas, a missionary, were freed from a Macedonian prison by a miraculous earthquake (Acts 16.25–26).
3. A river in the Mideast. The phrase *crossing over Jordan* is a metaphor for going to heaven.

4. See Song of Solomon 2.1, where the bride says, "I am the rose of Sharon, and the lily of the valleys."
1. A traditional song dating from the 19th century and sung as a protest song during the civil rights movement.

No more mourning, no more mourning, no more mourning over me
And before I'd be a slave I'll be buried in a my grave   5
And go home to my Lord and be free

No more crying, no more crying, no more crying over me
And before I'd be a slave I'll be buried in a my grave
And go home to my Lord and be free

Oh freedom, oh freedom, oh freedom over me   10
And before I'd be a slave I'll be buried in a my grave
And go home to my Lord and be free

There'll be singin', there'll be singin', there'll be singin' over me
And before I'd be a slave I'll be buried in a my grave
And go home to my Lord and be free   15

Oh freedom, oh freedom, oh freedom over me
And before I'd be a slave I'll be buried in a my grave
And go home to my Lord and be free

Ain't Gonna Let Nobody Turn Me 'Round[1]•

Ain't gonna let nobody, Lordy, turn me 'round,
Turn me 'round, turn me 'round,
Ain't gonna let nobody turn me 'round,
I'm gonna keep on a-walkin',
Keep on a-talkin',   5
Marching up to freedom land.

Ain't gonna let no jail house turn me 'round,
Turn me 'round, turn me 'round,
Ain't gonna let no jail house turn me 'round,
I'm gonna keep on a-walkin',   10
Keep on a-talkin',
Marching up to freedom land.

Ain't gonna let no sheriff turn me 'round,
Turn me 'round, turn me 'round,
Ain't gonna let no sheriff turn me 'round,   15
I'm gonna keep on a-walkin',
Keep on a-talkin',
Marching up to freedom land.

1. See p. 17, n. 1.

Strange Fruit[1]•

Southern trees bear strange fruit,
Blood on the leaves and blood at the root,
Black bodies swinging in the southern breeze,
Strange fruit hanging from poplar trees.

Pastoral scene of the gallant South,   5
The bulging eyes and the twisted mouth,
Scent of magnolia, sweet and fresh,
Then the sudden smell of burning flesh.

Here is a fruit for the crows to pluck,
For the rain to gather, for the wind to suck,   10
For the sun to rot, for the trees to drop,
Here is a strange and bitter crop.

We Shall Overcome[1]•

We shall overcome
We shall overcome
We shall overcome some day
Oh deep in my heart
I do believe   5
We shall overcome some day

We'll walk hand in hand
We'll walk hand in hand
We'll walk hand in hand some day
Oh deep in my heart   10
I do believe
We'll walk hand in hand some day

We shall all be free
We shall all be free
We shall all be free some day   15
Oh deep in my heart
I do believe
We shall all be free some day

We are not afraid
We are not afraid   20
We are not afraid some day

1. Written by Abel Meeropol (aka Lewis Allen), a New York schoolteacher and left-wing activist in the anti-lynching campaign of the 1930s. While Billie Holiday did not write this song as has often been claimed, any more than Meeropool wrote it especially for her, as she routinely insisted, nonetheless "Strange Fruit" became Billie Holiday's own. Through her artistry, she changed the melody and intensified the mood of this famous protest piece.

1. A Christian church song about moral women and men overcoming the trials of enduring a fallen world. Under Martin Luther King Jr.'s leadership of the civil rights movement, this became a great anthem proclaiming the inevitable victory of all Americans over racism and prejudice.

Oh deep in my heart
I do believe
We are not afraid some day

We are not alone   25
We are not alone
We are not alone some day
Oh deep in my heart
I do believe
We are not alone some day   30

The whole wide world around
The whole wide world around
The whole wide world around some day
Oh deep in my heart
I do believe   35
The whole wide world around some day

We shall overcome
We shall overcome
We shall overcome some day
Oh deep in my heart   40
I do believe
We shall overcome some day

The Backlash Blues[1]•

Mister Backlash, Mister Backlash,
Just who do you think I am?
Tell me, Mister Backlash,
Who do you think I am?
You raise my taxes, freeze my wages,   5
Send my son to Vietnam.

You give me second-class houses,
Give me second-class schools,
Second-class houses
And second-class schools.
You must think us colored folks   10
Are second-class fools.

When I try to find a job
To earn a little cash,
Try to find myself a job   15
To earn a little cash,
All you got to offer
Is a white backlash.

---

1. Based on a poem by Langston Hughes (ca. 1966), this was sung and recorded by Nina Simone in the late 1960s.

But the world is big;
The world is big and round,   20
Great big world, Mister Backlash,
Big and bright and round—
And it's full of folks like me who are
Black, Yellow, Beige, and Brown.

Mister Backlash, Mister Backlash,   25
What do you think I got to lose?
Tell me, Mister Backlash,
What you think I got to lose?
I'm gonna leave you, Mister Backlash,
Singing your mean old backlash blues   30

You're the one,
Yes, you're the one
Will have the blues.

Four Women[1]•

My skin is black
My arms are long
My hair is wooly
My back is strong
Strong enough to take the pain   5
Inflicted again and again
What do they call me?
My name is Aunt Sarah
My name is Aunt Sarah

My skin is yellow   10
My hair is long
Between two worlds
I do belong
My father was rich and white
He forced my mother late one night   15
What do they call me?
My name is Saffronia
My name is Saffronia

My skin is tan
My hair is fine,   20
My hips invite you
My mouth like wine
Whose little girl am I?
Anyone who has money to buy
What do they call me?   25
My name is Sweet Thing
My name is Sweet Thing

1. Written by Nina Simone; she performed it at the Newport Jazz Festival (July 1, 1967).

My skin is brown
My manner is tough
I'll kill the first mother I see   30
My life has been rough
I'm awfully bitter these days
Because my parents were slaves
What do they call me?
My   35
name
is
Peaches

Jazz

The music that came to be called jazz emerged in the first decades of the twentieth century from the artistic meeting of several elements, including African and African-derived musics, opera and other European musics, Native American musics, ragtime, marching-band music, spirituals, work songs, and especially the blues. No seedbed for the new music was richer than New Orleans, where, in spite of separatist racial policies, musicians could tap into the city's spectacularly broad range of musical influences and where the opportunities to hear, play, and practice music under expert musician tutors were extraordinarily abundant.

By the 1920s, the good news of early jazz was beginning to spread across the nation to Mobile, Alabama; Houston, Texas; Washington, D.C.; Chicago; St. Louis and Kansas City, Missouri; Philadelphia and Pittsburgh; Minneapolis; New York; Boston; and beyond. Jazz crystallized from disparate elements: rural and urban, portside and inland, long settled and frontier. Still, it developed primarily as a city phenomenon, one that attempted to capture in music the cadences, voices, and even the rising skylines, of new urban America. It particularly was influenced by the tremendousness and the music-in-motion of the modern train, the beautiful machine that seems to have represented both the power and the promise of moving away from the land where one's parents and grandparents had been slaves (which occurred in a mighty wave during this period's Great Migration) and the remembrance of such earlier train images in the spirituals (with their trains bound for glory) and in the Underground Railroad (with its stations, conductors, and hard-riding runners for freedom). From the beginning, jazz was a music of train-whistle guitars, bell-ringing pianos and horns, "conductors" calling and squalling, riders "rolling and tumbling." "Honky-Tonk Train," "Daybreak Express," "9:20 Special," and "Take the A Train" are just a tiny sampling of jazz compositions with titles bearing this locomotive influence. Both Thelonious Monk's "Little Rootie Tootie" and Elmore James's "Sunnyland," the latter (a blues) on the Student StudySpace, involve significant locomotive onomatopoeia.

From the beginning, too, jazz was primarily an instrumental music strongly impacted by the sound of the African American voice. What this music can sound like more than anything else is the jam-session-like talk and song from the Harlems of America and from its southern roads. In a real sense, the sound of jazz is that of the African American voice scored as band music, with all of black talk's flair for storytelling as well as the dirty dozens, understatement as well as braggadocio, whispery romance as well as loud-talk menace, the exalted eloquence of a Martin Luther King and the spare dry poetry of a pool-hall boast or a jump-rope rhyme. All of that "talking and testifying" and "speaking and speechifying"—stylized statement, overstatement, and understatement—make their way into this music, giving it great force and flavor. Once singers got into the jazz act, they tended to follow Louis Armstrong in using their voices as if they were jazz instruments—which meant, paradoxically, that they were voices imitating instruments that were imitating voices!

Jazz is not, generally speaking, an art of unaccompanied solo making. In this collaborative music, one hears the instruments and the singers in conversation with each other in patterns often called call and response or call and recall. Jazz instrumentalists often sing the blues through their horns and boxes. Even when singing a nonblues number, artists may improvise on it as if it were a blues, and they may inject it with the spirit of blue demons and devils. Like the blues singer's art, the jazz musicians' is defined by blue notes, blues timbres, dance rhythms, and improvisations. And jazz has a blueslike tragic dimension, too: it knows that life is a lowdown dirty shame or that, as the bluesman Elmore James puts it, "the sky is crying." As opposed to pop music, which comes and goes with every era, jazz music fingers the jagged grain of experience and knows that, despite all hopes and efforts, things might not work out for the best.

And yet with the deep sea-blue tragic sense of life that underlies the music comes an overwhelming impulse to celebrate human experience. For jazz is a music with a strong sense of possibility and humor. It is a music of rejuvenation. What makes it so is that again, like all blues-idiom music, jazz proclaims the human will to keep on keeping on in spite of the troubles traditionally sung about in blues lyrics. Jazz swings and stomps and laughs and finger snaps these blues troubles out of town for a while. It is a music that, as Jelly Roll Morton (and many others) has said, "opens up the window and lets the bad air out."

In its early forms and in forms that persist into our own times, jazz was music that wanted to get up and dance. Duke Ellington once said that you had to be able to dance to play his music properly. Whatever its key and time signatures, whatever its paces, it has remained a dance music, one defined by the urge to make the body rock in rhythm, to swing: to exult in physical movement and in music's dance-beat orientation, its groove that moves singers, instrumentalists, and dancers in dynamically syncopated coordination. No wonder Ralph Ellison said that jazz makers function in society as bringers of great joy.

Jazz, then, heralds the human capacity to create an individual self or voice that can maintain itself, under pressure, with style and equipoise, that can confront trouble and improvise ways of coping no matter what changes or disjunctures may get in the way. Whether labeled "hot" or "cool," jazz is a music of black American endurance under the fast-changing circumstances of a new century. Wrung from the rock of U.S. black life, it has become a (some would say it has become *the*) quintessential modern music, the soundtrack adopted by the world as it realizes, intellectually, what this music symbolizes and also as it finds the music's beat, now heartbeat steady, now fast-train syncopated, too swinging for body or soul to resist.

In many cases, writers have written about jazz music as such, or they have made detailed references to it in their work. Ellison, Albert Murray, James Baldwin, Toni Morrison, Gloria Naylor, Al Young, Nathaniel Mackey, and Amiri Baraka are among those in this large group. Others have performed to jazz music or have written works meant to be performed to jazz accompaniment. What is just as interesting is to trace the influences of jazz, as a set of artistic forms and body of techniques, on African American writing's shapes and purposes. There is very good new criticism in this direction, suggesting that in the years to come, students of African American culture will find more ways to talk about the elements of jazz—its vamps (or introductory statements), breaks (or solos), riffs (repeated structural phrases), choruses (main themes), bridges (secondary, connecting themes), call–response patterns, improvisations, syncopated cadences, and other definitive structures—and the ways in which they operate in the pages

John Coltrane performs during a jazz festival at Soldier Field in Chicago, 1965.

of a book. Some important scholars are already considering how the forms and functions of jazz music have impacted the visual arts, film, and dance. Perhaps the key point here is that jazz (and much jazz-inflected black art) expresses what Ellison termed "the American joke" as well as the "real secret of life," which is, he said, "to make life swing"; and the bittersweet bluesy knowledge that though we be dismembered every day, somehow still another day we rise.

For the twenty-first-century jazz scholar, a variety of questions trouble the waters: How to evaluate and nurture a music that is still evolving but where the impulse—represented shiningly by Jazz at Lincoln Center—to codify, conserve, and play with excellence a "classic" archive of great jazz is also very significant? Where, beyond New Orleans, did jazz come from? What (leaving aside the usual simplifications about where rhythm and harmony come from) are its debts to Africa, Europe, Asia, Native America, and the Caribbean? To what extent has jazz remained an international music, with dynamic and continuing cycles of influence? How best to evaluate jazz played outside the United States by player/composers who are excellent but who make few references to the music's black American roots? If jazz is quintessentially American music, how is it also sometimes a freedom music without a national agenda? (Max Roach's "Freedom Now Suite" is both a challenge to U.S. unfreedom and a statement of solidarity with the struggle for freedom in South Africa.) How do we discuss race and jazz in a way that avoids chauvinism without diminishing the African American elements in jazz? What do we make of the wholesale appropriation of jazz by cultures all over the world? How do we locate the feminine and the feminist in jazz? How, for that matter, can we come to terms with the variety of masculinities on the jazz scene? Who listens to jazz? As jazz is institutionalized in the museums, opera houses, and universities of America, to what degree is it still its own institution, with its own values, standards, and room for personal expression and growth? And finally, in a world of boomeranging change, global artistic communication, and economic scheming, what *is* jazz? Does that term—famously disliked by Duke Ellington, Abbey Lincoln, and many others—still have meaning? When is a black musician playing improvised music *not* a jazz musician?

It Don't Mean a Thing (If It Ain't Got That Swing)[1]•

> Wah-dah do, wah-dah do,
> Wah-dah do, dah-dah do, dah-dah do.
>
> It don't mean a thing
> If it ain't got that swing!

---

1. Transcribed from a performance by Ivie Anderson with Duke Ellington (1899–1974). Recorded in 1932, this song gave a motto to the swing era of the 1930s and to jazz music in general.

It don't mean a thing,   5
All you've got to do is sing!

It makes no difference if it's sweet or hot,
Just keep that rhythm,
Give it everything you've got!

It don't mean a thing   10
If it ain't got that swing!

Wah-dah-dah doo!
Yah-yah-yah-yah-dah doo!

Bup be-duh be-duh be-dut,
Dat-dat-dat   15

Ohhh, it don't mean a thing
If it ain't got that swing!

(What Did I Do to Be So) Black and Blue[1]•

Out in the street,
Shufflin' feet,
Couples passin' two by two.
While here am I,
Left high and dry,   5
Black, and 'cause I'm black I'm blue.

Browns and yellers,
All have fellers,
Gentlemen prefer them light.
Wish I could fade,   10
Can't make the grade,
Nothin' but dark days in sight.

Cold empty bed,
Springs hard as lead,
Pains in my head,   15
Feel like old Ned.
What did I do to be so black and blue?

No joys for me,
No company,
Even the mouse   20
Ran from my house.
All my life through, I've been so black and blue.

1. Written by Thomas "Fats" Waller, Andy Razaf, and Harry Brooks for the 1929 Broadway review *Hot Chocolates*. This song gained new, powerful meaning in Louis Armstrong's recorded version of that same year and plays an important role in Ralph Ellison's novel *Invisible Man* (1952).

I'm white inside,
It don't help my case,
'Cause I can't hide what is on my face.   25

I'm so forlorn,
Life's like a thorn,
My heart is torn.
Why was I born?
What did I do to be so black and blue?   30

Just 'cause you're black,
Folks think you lack,
They laugh at you and scorn you too.
What did I do to be so black and blue?

Parker's[1] Mood•

Come with me,
If you want to go to Kansas City.

I'm feeling lowdown and blue,
My heart's full of sorrow.
Don't hardly know what to do.   5
Where will I be tomorrow?

Going to Kansas City.
Want to go too?
No, you can't make it with me.
Going to Kansas City,   10
Sorry that I can't take you.

When you see me coming,
Raise your window high.
When you see me leaving, baby,
Hang your head and cry.   15

I'm afraid there's nothing in this cream, this dreamy town
A honky-tonky monkey-woman can do.
She'd only bring herself down.

So long everybody!
The time has come   20
And I must leave you
So if I don't ever see your smiling face again:
Make a promise you'll remember
Like a Christmas Day in December

---

1. I.e., Charlie Parker, alto saxophonist and key contributor to the modern (post–World War II) movement in jazz called bebop. The lyrics of this song were written by the singer King Pleasure (Clarence Beeks) in 1953 to fit the Parker sax solo on his recorded slow blues, also called "Parker's Mood."

That I told you   25
All through thick and thin
On up until the end
Parker's been your friend.

Don't hang your head
When you see, when you see those six pretty horses pulling me.   30
Put a twenty dollar silver-piece on my watchchain,
Look at the smile on my face,
And sing a little song
To let the world know I'm really free.
Don't cry for me,   35
'Cause I'm going to Kansas City.

RHYTHM AND BLUES

The designations *rhythm and blues, rock and roll*, and *soul* are inventions not of musicians or scholars but of the marketplace, where labels and categories promote sales. That said, sometime after World War II, new forms of black dance music—blending boogie-woogie bass and melody lines with ingredients from blues, jazz, Latin, and gospel music—appeared on the American and then the worldwide scene. Drawn from the work of such pioneers as Big Joe Turner, Louis Jordan, T-Bone Walker, and Dinah Washington, this hybrid form began to rock dance halls and variety shows across the nation by the early 1950s. Single recordings (and eventually albums) were played on jukeboxes, home record players, and the radio, bringing singers and their small instrumental combinations (called "combos") to America's party spaces, both public and private.

In its infancy, this soulful garden made a thousand flowers bloom: blue-mood crooners, following the path of Nat King Cole and Charles Brown; gospel and blues stompers, such as Ruth Brown, Sam Cooke, and Ray Charles (who started his career as a Cole/Brown copy); a cappella kings and queens of a harmonic ballad style called doo-wop such as the Moonglows, the Ravens, Frankie Lymon and the Teenagers, and many others, some of whom, like the Platters and the Drifters, made records that were softened and smoothed for cross-over marketing to white audiences. From the beginning, this tradition included instrumentals, most of them blues-based pieces by rhythm trios plus guitar and saxophone, many with a variety of Latin and pseudo-Latin "tinges." There were pieces sporting lyrics in the form of tragicomical boasts and narratives, like "Stagolee," reverberating directly from the playgrounds of black America. There were also songs consisting of dance-instruction calls (part of a long tradition of such songs)—for example, "The Madison," "Walkin' the Dog," and "Shake a Tail Feather!" And there were reports and anticipations of parties not to be missed: Shorty Long's "Function at the Junction," Ray Charles's "Good Times Roll," and many more. There were dance numbers like "Iko Iko" by the Dixie Cups and "Ooh Poo Pah Doo" by Jessie Hill, jumping numbers that were hard to classify but were unquestionably part of this new wave of black musical activity. White musicians were part of the early story, too, some of them, such as Johnny Otis, the Skyliners, and the Righteous Brothers, were accepted as authentic artists; others, like Elvis Presley and later the Beatles, were somewhat resented for their bold capacity to translate black (or black-spun) material into venues not available to black artists themselves. R&B had national reach and involved distinctive creative activity in cities such as New York, Philadelphia, Chicago, Washington, Memphis, Pittsburgh, and New Orleans.

By the mid-1960s, Detroit's Motown label had gathered a group of R&B performers whose combination of canny urbane wit, unfailably danceable tempos, and bluesy balladeering spelled artistic and financial success in a teen market that crossed over almost from the very beginning. Excellent writing, polished performances (including class-act choreography by the brilliant inventor of "vocal choreography," Cholly Atkins), and high-quality instrumental backgrounds made Motown uniquely potent: Smokey Robinson and the Miracles, the Temptations, the Marvelettes, the Supremes (with Diana Ross), Marvin Gaye, Stevie Wonder, Gladys Knight and the Pips, the Jackson Five (with Michael Jackson), Martha and the Vandellas—all these recorded for the Motown label. While some of the best songs in the Motown book were blueslike in their yearning for love (some rather frank in their hope of sexual contact), others carried the sting of love's labors avenged: An easy rocking number by the Marvellettes called "Strange I Know" tells of a boy who stayed away so long that his former girlfriend has replaced him with someone else: "When you get home," the lead singer announces tersely, "I'll be gone." In some cases, Motown pieces that were ostensibly nothing more than romantic ballads or good-time party songs contained indications of greater complexity: Smokey's "Tracks of My Tears" makes clear that the face's public smile may mask a deep sorrow. Some Motown performances suggested readiness for sociopolitical action. Martha and the Vandellas' "Dancing in the Street," for example, celebrated urban block parties; did it also refer to that era's riot-dances of black anger and retribution in the streets of America? The most enduring of the Motown performers—Smokey, Marvin, Stevie, and Michael (all known among their fans by their first names)— became major artists well beyond the formulas of their first years by continually reinventing themselves, by adding layers of artistic complexity as well as social awareness to songs of love and loss. Keeping its dance-steady beat, Marvin's "What's Going On?" used a popular greeting to reflect on the Vietnam War, the black freedom struggle, and the threats to black families and neighborhoods that character-

As landmark studies by dance historian Jacqui Malone have made clear, Cholly Atkins was an important modern choreographer who taught Motown singers to dance while performing their songs. Here Atkins is working with the Four Tops (ca. 1962). The Tops—and especially Atkins's great students like the Pips, the Temptations, and, directly and indirectly, the Jackson Five—brought a modern Afro-style of dance to the nation and then to the globe.

ized that era. Stevie and Michael (who eventually had to leave Motown to have the creative freedom they wanted) wrote more topical and inventively poetical lyrics and, especially in the case of virtuoso dancer Michael Jackson, invented supercharged performance styles that kept them changing and growing without ever losing touch with the rhythms or the blues with which they had begun.

Aretha Franklin started as a church singer and then became a jazz singer in the mold of her idol Dinah Washington (the great jazz singer who also started in the church, where she was known as Ruth Jones), before finding her own voice in R&B. Like the legends at Motown, Aretha (herself not a Motown singer) sang love ballads with an antisentimental edge and, sometimes, with a distinctive political thrust. "Respect" (written as a man's song by the brilliant Georgia-born singer Otis Redding) spelled out, in Aretha's version, young black women's setting of a new agenda for their relations with their men and, implicitly, for their interactions with "the man" (white America). In her forthrightness, she continued in the steps of her mentor Sam Cooke, whose "A Change Is Gonna Come" (eventually covered by Aretha) presented a soaring R&B soundtrack to the civil rights movement. Aretha also stood in the tradition of Curtis Mayfield, lead singer and artistic director of the Impressions (and son of the master blues-ballad lyricist Percy Mayfield), whose "People Get Ready" and "We're a Winner" also spoke of black America's determination to move forward. These songs also set the stage for the gifted singer–songwriter Donny Hathaway, whose "Someday We'll All Be Free" is a meditative song of hope in the face of well-founded doubt and fear. Hathaway's version of "A Song for You," by the way, is a song of love suitable for a church service and, as choreographer Alvin Ailey decided, for the modern dance concert hall: "I love you in a way," Hathaway sings, "where there is neither space nor time."

Like Aretha and Curtis, James Brown could croon ballads or throw down hard-swinging dance songs; and like the others, he also invented (and reinvented) a style that would carry his sound across the decades, from the 1950s into the twenty-first century. With his blues-based band-as-drum sound, he hearkened back to the era of the Kansas City big bands, but his insistently funky and drum and minimalist lyrics (sometimes only grunts and hollers and signals to the band, like "Take me the bridge!" and "Hit me!" "Maceo, blow your horn!") inspired a generation of followers and, in the case of the hip hop artists, of samplers. James, too, offered forthright songs of protest: "I Don't Want Nobody to Give Me Nothing (Open Up the Door, I'll Get It Myself)" and "Say It Loud: 'I'm Black and I'm Proud.'" But even his "Make It Funky" expresses a down to earthiness that is thick and black; here James's virtuoso naming of items from the southern soul menu—"neckbones, candied yams, turnips, smo[thered] steak, grits-and-gravy, cracklin' bread, snap-beans, Mobile gumbo, hot corn bread, buttermilk"—strongly celebrates the African American group with energy to match the drumlike horns, with organ underneath. Like James and Stevie, Sly and the Family Stone produced melodic and bass lines (and occasionally lyrics, too) that have become a hip hop sampler's gold mine.

It would be wrong to think of this music as primarily social protest. Soul, rock and roll, and R&B included fast and slow dance numbers with lyrics that were often sentimental—sometimes quite sweetly, as in Smokey Robinson's love-sick "Tracks of My Tears"—but that were just as often made real by the bedrock of the blues: a "that's the way it goes" music that despised or laughed off the easy tears and moony promises of sentimentality. Sometimes the lyrics contained meanings much deeper than the school crush gone wrong; indeed, the music's true poets—a handful of whom are included here—created transcendentally significant art that worked in dance settings of years gone by and that works here and now, in these pages, nearly as well as when performed on record or, best of all, at a party.

The Tracks of My Tears[1]•

(Do do do do)
(Do do do do)
(Do do do do)
(Do do, do do do do)

People say I'm the life of the party   5
'Cause I tell a joke or two
Although I might be laughin' loud and hearty
Deep inside I'm blue

So take a good look at my face
You'll see my smile looks out of place   10
If you look closer it's easy to trace
The tracks of my tears

I need you (need you)
Need you (need you)

Since you left me if you see me with another girl   15
Seemin' like I'm havin' fun
Although she may be cute
She's just a substitute
Because you're the permanent one

So take a good look at my face, uh-huh   20
You see my smile (looks out of place)
Yeah, look a little bit closer
It's easy to trace, oh the tracks of my tears

Oh-ho-ho-ho I need you (need you)
Need you (need you)   25

Hey hey yeah
(Outside) I'm masquerading
(Inside) My hope is fading
(I'm just a clown) ooo-yeah, since you put me down
My smile is my makeup   30
I wear since my break-up with you

Baby, take a good look at my face, uh-huh
You see my smile looks (out of place)
Yeah, just look closer it's easy (to trace)
Oh, the tracks of my tears   35

Baby, baby, baby, baby
Take a good look at (my face)
Ooo, yeah you see my smile (looks out of place)
Look a little bit closer (it's easy to trace)
Yeah . . .   40

---

1. Written by Smokey Robinson, W. Moore, and M. Tarplin. Performed by Smokey Robinson and the Miracles (1965).

Dancing in the Street[1]•

Callin' out around the world
Are you ready for a brand-new beat?
Summer's here and the time is right
For dancin' in the streets

They're dancin' in Chicago (dancin' in the street)   5
Down in New Orleans (dancin' in the streets)
In New York City (dancin' in the streets)
All we need is music (sweet sweet) sweet music (sweet sweet music)
There'll be music everywhere
They'll be swinging, swaying, and records playing   10
Dancin' in the street

Oh it doesn't matter what you wear, just as long as you are there
So come on
Every guy, grab a girl, everywhere around the world
They'll be dancin', they're dancin' in the street   15
It's just an invitation, across the nation
A chance for folks to meet
They'll be laughing, singing, and music swinging
Dancin' in the street

Philadelphia, P.A. (dancin' in the street)   20
Baltimore and D.C., now (dancin' in the street)
Can't forget the Motor City (dancin' in the street)
All we need is music (sweet sweet) sweet music (sweet sweet music)
There'll be music everywhere
They'll be swinging, swaying, and records playing   25
Dancin' in the street

Oh it doesn't matter what you wear, just as long as you are there
So come on
Every guy, grab a girl, everywhere around the world
They'll be dancin', they're dancin' in the street   30
Way down in LA, every day
They're dancin' in the street (dancin' in the street)
Let's form a big strong line
Get in time
We're dancin' in the street   35
Across the ocean blue
Me and you
We're dancin' in the street, yeah
San Francisco way (dancin' in the streets) they do it every day now
Dancin' in the streets   40

---

1. Written by Marvin Gaye, Ivy J. Hunter, Mickey (William) Stevenson (1964); performed by Martha and the Vandellas.

Respect[1]●

What you want
Baby, I got it
What you need
Do you know I've got it?
All I'm askin'   5
Is for a little respect when you come home
Hey baby, when you get home
Mister! (Just a little bit)

I ain't gonna do you wrong while you're gone
Ain't gonna do you wrong 'cause I don't wanna   10
All I'm askin'
Is for a little respect when you come home
Baby when you get home
Yeah
(Just a little bit)   15

I'm about to give you all of my money
And all I'm askin' in return, honey
Is to give me my propers
When you get home
Yeah, baby   20
When you get home
(Just a little bit)
Yeah!

Ooo, your kisses
Sweeter than honey   25
And guess what?
So is my money!
All I want you to do for me
Is give it to me when you get home
Yeah, baby,   30
Whip it to me
(Respect)
When you get home

Now:
R E S P E C T!   35
Find out what it means to me
R E S P E C T
Take care of TCB

Show
A little respect!   40
Show, yeah!
A little respect!
I get tired
Keep on tryin'
You're runnin' out of fools   45

---

1. Written by Otis Redding; performed by Aretha Franklin (1967).

And I ain't lyin'
(Re-re-re-re, re-re-re-re-) 'spect
When you come home!
Or you might walk in
And find out I'm gone!   50
I got to have
A little respect!

What's Goin' On?[1]•

Mother, Mother, there's too many of you crying
Brother, Brother, Brother, there's far too many of you dying
You know we've got to find a way
To bring some lovin' here today

Father, Father, we don't need to escalate   5
War is not the answer, for only love can conquer hate
You know we've got to find a way
To bring some lovin' here today

Picket lines and picket signs:
"Don't Punish Me with Brutality"   10
Talk to me, so you can see
Oh what's goin' on? What's goin' on?
Yeah, what's goin' on? Ah, what's going on?

Mother, Mother, everybody thinks we're wrong
Ah, but who are they to judge us   15
Simply 'cause our hair is long
Ah, you know we've got to find a way
To bring some understanding here today

Picket lines and picket signs:
"Don't Punish Me with Brutality"   20
Come on, talk to me, so you can see
What's goin' on? Yeah what's goin' on?
Tell me, what's goin' on? I'll tell you what's goin' on . . .
What's goin' on?

Living for the City[1]•

A boy is born in hard time Mississippi
Surrounded by four walls that ain't so pretty
His parents give him love and affection
To keep him strong moving in the right direction
Living just enough, just enough for the city . . . ee ha!   5

1. Written and performed by Marvin Gaye (1971).
1. Written and performed by Stevie Wonder (1973).

His father works some days for fourteen hours
And you can bet he barely makes a dollar
His mother goes to scrub the floors for many
And you'd best believe she hardly gets a penny
Living just enough, just enough for the city . . . yeah!   10

His sister's black but she is sho'nuff pretty
Her skirt is short but Lord her legs are sturdy
To walk to school she's got to get up early
Her clothes are old but never are they dirty
Living just enough, just enough for the city . . . um hum   15

Her brother's smart he's got more sense than many
His patience's long but soon he won't have any
To find a job is like a haystack needle
Cause where he lives they don't use colored people
Living just enough, just enough for the city . . .   20

Living just enough . . .
For the city . . . ooh, ooh
[Repeat several times]

His hair is long, his feet are hard and gritty
He spends his life walking the streets of New York City
He's almost dead from breathing in air pollution   25
He tried to vote but to him there's no solution
Living just enough, just enough for the city . . .
yeah, yeah, yeah!

I hope you hear inside my voice of sorrow
And that it motivates you to make a better tomorrow   30
This place is cruel no where could be much colder
If we don't change the world will soon be over
Living just enough, stop giving just enough for the city!!!!

La, la, la, la, la, la,
Da ba da da da da da da   35
Da da da da da da
Da da da da da da da da
[Repeat to end]

We're a Winner[1]•

We're a winner
And never let anybody say
Boy you can't make it
'Cause a feeble mind is in your way
No more tears do we cry   5
And we have finally

---

1. Written and performed by Curtis Mayfield (1976).

Dried our eyes
And we're movin on up
Lawd have mercy
We're movin on up   10

We're living proof
And all's alert
That we're true
From the good black dirt
And we're a winner   15
And everybody knows it too
We'll just keep on pushing
Like your leaders tell you to
At last that blessed day has come
And I don't care   20
Where you come from
We're all movin on up
Lawd have mercy
We're movin on up

I don't mind leaving here   25
To show the world
We have no fear
'Cause we're a winner
And everybody knows it too
We'll just keep on pushin'   30
Your leaders tell you to
At last that blessed day has come
And I don't care where you come from
We're just gon' move on up
Movin' on up   35
Lawd have mercy

We're movin' on up
Just keep on pushin'
Lawd, baby
Everybody   40
Hey!
You know we're movin' on up
We're a winner

Hip-Hop

Like other contemporary black (or mostly black) traditions of music in America, hip-hop music is a hybrid form traceable to speech and songs of the nineteenth and early twentieth centuries, at least, and perhaps to traditions that are much older. Traditions of eloquence in black America have been nurtured by long-standing interactions with Native Americans, Europeans, and European Americans as well as with Caribbean and African instrumentalists, singers, speakers, and speaker–singers (including African oral historian–poets called *griots*), arriving on American shores in waves, across the centuries. These forms of black American eloquence predate antebellum sermons and antislavery oration, black and white. Distinctively African American antecedents of the virtuoso sung speech of hip-hop turn up in black preacher's sermons, invitations, invocations, and prayers, especially when delivered with instrumental or choral music continuing underneath.

Hip-hop music also comes from the stylized talk between verses that is characteristic of blues and rhythm and blues (and, some observers say, of all black American) song forms. It derives from black game chants and songs, like the dynamic singsong patter that can accompany girls' jump-rope or cheerleading sessions or their hand-slap games and from the crisply cadenced vocalizing of military or military-like drill teams and fraternity and sorority step shows. These staccato songs of self derive from playground, pool hall, juke joint, barber shop, and beauty salon narration and argumentation and from the highly competitive boasts and toasts (like "The Signifyin' Monkey") and from the dozens (an age-old verbal dance of derision in which one trades insults with one's opponent while trying to stay cool under the pressure of hearing oneself potentially outwitted by ribald verbal darts aimed at one's closest family members). Hip-hop flows from the cool—and then heated—banter of radio disc jockeys who, for decades now, have talked between and over the recordings they spin. If the black-uplift elements of hip-hop are traceable to sermons and political speeches, the touted insouciance and bawdiness of many hip-hop lyrics derive from the blues, which so often celebrates sexual congress, and from the narratives of such vernacular heroes as Uncle Bud, Shine, and the Pool-Shooting Monkey.

Nor should we forget the impact on hip-hop of jazz singers' vocalese and scat singing—fitting words and other syllables into the framework of a jazz performance—and of the widely popular black arts movement poetry of such writers as Nikki Giovanni, Melvin Van Peebles, Amiri Baraka, Sonia Sanchez, Gil Scott-Heron, and the Last Poets (the parents of hip-hop)—these latter, in turn, influenced by the poetry of Langston Hughes, Sterling Brown, and others working in a black vernacular idiom. Some hip-hop artists name jazz saxophone players as important models.

More immediately, hip-hop sprang from the streets of uptown New York City in the late 1970s. The background of spoken-word activity in and around Kingston, Jamaica—birthplace of several important rappers eventually on the New York scene—also is very important to the geographical history of this form. According to historian Nelson George, it arrived "via black parties and jams in public parks, sparked by the innovative moves of a handful of pioneering men. Working under wild monikers, they called themselves 'DJ's,' but they left in the dust any traces of the AM radio jocks who first popularized that term. On their wheels of steel, Kool Herc, Afrika Babaataa, and Grandmaster Flash staked out a loud, scratchy, in-your-face aesthetic that, to this day, still informs the culture." Working with sound systems as if they were musical instruments, these DJs and their followers were performers who developed the early hip-hop techniques of scratching, break spinning, punch phrasing, and the chanting of party-hearty phrases to accentuate the dance music's full effect. It was not long before the highly cadenced and highly competitive extended verbal play brought a new level of word artistry to the hip-hop experience, some of it improvised, some written to appear improvised. With this virtuoso verse making came the dynamic sampling of favorite passages of well-known recordings, along with samplings of music little known or previously unknown. Recordings of hip-hop performances passed from hand to hand, underground, until record producers, many of them very late in realizing the marketability of this black and Latino street music, got into the act. Once "Rapper's Delight" by the Sugar Hill Gang—released on vinyl in twelve-inch sleeves and sold in such local stores as Birdel's in the Bronx—unleashed a hurricane of enthusiasm among buyers, hip-hop music elicited a national excitement that soon spun through the Americas to Europe, Africa, and Asia. The title of this first hit fastened the name *rappers* onto the performers, but old-school artists and new ones alike seem to prefer *hip-hop*, and in the case of the oldest old schoolers, the performer's correct title was not *rapper* but *M.C.*

To make the point that hip hop performances often involve verbal violence that routinely erupts into physical fighting and killing, Nelson George likened the hip-hop party to the battle royal scene in Ralph Ellison's novel *Invisible Man,* in which blindfolded black boys are paid by powerful white voyeurs to fight one another, each against all the rest, in return for what turns out to be fake coins tossed onto an electrically rigged carpet. But, as George and others have argued, if the themes of hip-hop lyrics are often brutally violent, self-destructive, nihilistic, bluntly sexist, drug glorifying, nakedly profane, and hollowly materialistic—"Gimme the loot/ Gimme the loot," one performer blankly repeats—do they not also echo such themes in U.S. culture at large? Many hip-hop performances, drawing directly from vernacular sources, describe imaginary sexual quests and conquests along with fantasies of power, mobility, and access to money and its extravagances. Perhaps the single most influential current in the music was introduced by a "gangsta" group called N.W.A (Niggaz With Attitude), rhymers from California ("straight outta Compton") who laugh at the idea that they should be role models. What N.W.A. says it wants is simply put: sex and money—always the motives for action of the infamous trickster figure Brer Rabbit. But N.W.A operates more in the tradition of the badman than of the trickster. Their lyrics broadcast the will to meet a violent world with alluring, shocking fast talk and, if necessary, with hard fists and bullets. Despite N.W.A's disclaimers, however, even gangsta rappers teach their listeners—in something like the way that realist fiction writers teach their readers—by detailing in rivetingly raw terms the violence of life in the no-exit realm of the black urban poor. At times there is a political critique embedded in the lyrics: for all its vulgarity and violence, N.W.A's "Fuck da Police" raises issues of racial profiling and other forms of harassment that our nation is still struggling to address.

Other hip-hop artists, like Public Enemy and Queen Latifah, are explicitly progressive in their critiques of the sociopolitical systems that surround them. They even tap into the black prophetic tradition by urging listeners to awaken to new levels of political and spiritual consciousness, to read challenging books and to prepare to take forthright action in a far-downfallen world. Note the recent work by Jay-Z, in which the rapper tries to come to terms with his sense of social responsibility and his extravagant wealth. In "Song Cry," Jay-Z confesses his guilt over a love affair gone wrong and, more surprising, admits pouring sentimental feeling into his work that otherwise would make the rapper himself shed tears. And listen to Jean Grae, who in her autobiographical "Don't Rush Me" accepts her own complexity as an artist who is ambitious and full of contradictions: "I know I'm wrong and right," she says, "At the same time, both I'm the dark and light." She is still growing—"Don't rush me!"

It is vital to note that hip-hop music began and to some degree still thrives not as an isolated phenomenon but as part of a larger hip-hop *culture.* Like its parents, rhythm and blues and jazz, hip-hop is at once an in-group ritual music, a performance music, and a dance music designed to make listeners move together to its loudspeaker-busting drum lines and machine-gun-like firings of chanted sound. Hip-hop culture includes social dances associated with the music as well as more extroverted break-dancing, with its incredibly athletic spins, turns, robotic movements, and even possession-like trances. A generation of hip-hop tap dancers, led by the highly virtuosic Savion Glover, has reinvented the vocabulary of tap to include very hard hitting "get down" moves, sounds, and attitudes. Hip-hop culture embraces graffiti artists, decorating (critics would say defacing) public walls and subway cars with their cartoonlike figures and bubble signatures. Hip-hop affects styles of dress, haircut, and self-decoration. Hip-hop language influences everyday informal language, spoken and written, as well as formal speech and writing: journalism, poetry, fiction, drama.

Usually eclipsed in discussions of hip-hop's sociological implications is this style's value as music and poetry. In the work of Rakim, Nas, and the Notorious B.I.G., the alliteration is as startlingly inventive as the rhyme schemes, which depend on end rhymes and complex interlocking internal rhymes. When hip-hop is at its best, its lines vary in length without seeming forced or distended. The sense of humor—the impulse to parody and to signify—drives the work at least as much as its impulses to detail the lives of the urban underclass. This is an art of what one observer calls "verbal fire and ice," performed with and against a background of sounds pulled from any and every previously recorded music. Such sampling has given the music a self-conscious postmodern mix. Truly, it is a patchwork music speech, vigorously quilted from fragments, granting it a sparkling pastichelike effect and a parodist's attitude both toward the songs that are quoted and toward their traditions. Like much art associated with postmodernism, hip-hop is often whimsically comical and self-mockingly reflexive.

Hip-hop is a music that makes room for young black performers to address black audiences concerning serious matters of disempowerment and the urgent need for fundamental change. Some of the most intriguing questions about this music involve its quest for authenticity; its relation to postmodernism; its geography beyond the confines of New York City and the urban northeastern United States; its international appeal; its counterpart rappers in Europe, Africa, and Asia; and its attractiveness to middle- and upper-class white Americans. To what degree is hip-hop as much a youth culture as it is a black culture? How are these lines drawn? How does one fairly measure the value and social effect of an art form that is so often full of what appear to be gratuitous vulgarities and casual declarations of misogyny and violence? And again, how do we measure the art of musicians who play no instruments (in the conventional sense), vocal artists who (generally) do not sing, and poets whose rhymes are not written to be read on a page and that, alas, are generally too profane for anthologies such as this one? There has been excellent new scholarship focusing on the history and meaning of hip hop music and culture. To follow up, students are advised to consult the work of Adam Bradley, Jeff Chang, Sujatha Fernandes, Bakari Kitwana, and Tricia Rose.

The Revolution Will Not Be Televised[1]•

You will not be able to stay home, brother.
You will not be able to plug in, turn on and cop out.
You will not be able to lose yourself on scag[2] and
skip out for beer during commercials because
The revolution will not be televised.   5

The revolution will not be televised.
The revolution will not be brought to you by Xerox in four parts
    without commercial interruption.
The revolution will not show you pictures of Nixon[3] blowing a bugle
    and leading a charge by John Mitchell, General Abramson and
    Spiro Agnew[4] to eat hog maws confiscated from a Harlem
    sanctuary.
The revolution will not be televised.

The revolution will not be brought to you by   10
The Schaeffer Award Theatre and will not star

1. This recorded poem by Gil Scott-Heron (1970) is not hip-hop per se, but it had a vital influence on its forms and themes.
2. Slang for heroin, which plagued urban communities from the 1940s through the 1980s.
3. Richard M. Nixon was U.S. president from 1968 to 1974.
4. Vice president under Nixon. John Mitchell, attorney general under Nixon. General James Abramson, former director of Reagan's Strategic Defense Initiative ("Star Wars").

Natalie Wood and Steve McQueen or Bullwinkle and Julia.[5]
The revolution will not give your mouth sex appeal.
The revolution will not get rid of the nubs.
The revolution will not make you look five pounds thinner.   15
The revolution will not be televised, brother.

There will be no pictures of you and Willie Mae[6]
pushing that shopping cart down the block on the dead run
or trying to slide that color t.v. in a stolen ambulance.
NBC will not be able to predict the winner at 8:32 on reports from
    twenty-nine districts.   20
The revolution will not be televised.

There will be no pictures of pigs[7] shooting down brothers
on the instant replay.
There will be no pictures of pigs shooting down brothers
on the instant replay.   25
The will be no slow motion or still lifes of Roy Wilkins[8] strolling
    through Watts[9] in a red, black and green liberation jumpsuit
    that he has been saving for just the proper occasion.

Green Acres, Beverly Hillbillies and Hooterville Junction[1]
will no longer be so damned relevant
and women will not care if Dick finally got down with Jane[2]
on Search for Tomorrow[3]   30
because black people will be in the streets looking for
A Brighter Day.
The revolution will not be televised.

There will be no highlights on the Eleven O'Clock News
and no pictures of hairy armed women liberationists   35
and Jackie Onassis[4] blowing her nose.
The theme song will not be written by Jim Webb or Francis Scott
    Key
nor sung by Glen Campbell, Tom Jones, Johnny Cash,[5]
Englebert Humperdink or Rare Earth.[6]
The revolution will not be televised.   40

The revolution will not be right back after a
message about a white tornado, white lightning or white people.
You will not have to worry about a dove in your bedroom,
the tiger in your tank or the giant in your toilet bowl.

5. Late 1960s TV drama depicting a middle-class black female character, starring Diahann Carroll. Natalie Wood and Steve McQueen, mainstream movie stars. Bullwinkle, cartoon moose character of 1960s–70s TV show *The Rocky and Bullwinkle Show*.
6. Common name among southern African American women and those who migrated to urban areas in the 1960s and 1970s. Willie Mae was probably a generic reference to a female.
7. Derogatory reference to the police, common among black militants of the 1960s and early 1970s.
8. Former executive director of the NAACP, who criticized black militancy and advocated a "moderate" approach toward civil rights attainment.

9. A working-class section of southeastern Los Angeles, populated mainly by African Americans in the 1960s and 1970s.
1. References to TV sitcoms that spoofed white southern and Appalachian culture.
2. Common characters in children's stories. In this context, Dick and Jane are generic soap opera characters.
3. A popular TV soap opera.
4. Socialite and widow of President John F. Kennedy.
5. Mainstream white music entertainers of the 1970s.
6. A white R&B-influenced pop group of the 1970s. Englebert Humperdinck, white pop singer of the 1970s.

The revolution will not go better with coke.   45
The revolution will not fight germs that may cause bad breath.[7]
The revolution *will* put you in the driver's seat.
The revolution will not be televised
        will not be televised
            not be televised   50
                be televised
The revolution will be no re-run, brothers.
The revolution will be LIVE.

The Message[1]•

It's like a jungle sometimes, it makes me wonder
How I keep from going under
It's like a jungle sometimes, it makes me wonder
How I keep from going under

Broken glass everywhere   5
People pissing on the stairs
You know they just don't care
I can't take the smell, can't take the noise
Got no money to move out, I guess I got no choice
Rats in the front room, roaches in the back   10
Junkies in the alley with a baseball bat
I tried to get away but I couldn't get far
'Cause the man with the tow truck repossessed my car

Don't push me 'cause I'm close to the edge
I'm trying not to lose my head   15
Ah huh huh huh huh
It's like a jungle sometimes, it makes me wonder
How I keep from going under

Standing on the front stoop, hanging out the window
Watching all the cars go by, roaring as the breezes blow   20
Crazy lady, living in a bag
Eating outta garbage pails, used to be a fag hag[2]
Says she danced the tango, skip the light fandango[3]
Was zircon princess[4] seemed to lost her senses
Down at the peep show, watching all the creeps so   25
She could tell the story to the girls back home
She went to the city and got social security
She had to get a pension, she couldn't make it on her own

Don't push me 'cause I'm close to the edge
I'm trying not to lose my head   30
Ah huh huh huh huh
It's like a jungle sometimes, it makes me wonder

7. Lines 41–46 play with commonly used commercial advertising phrases of the early 1970s.
1. Recorded by Grandmaster Flash & the Furious Five (1982).
2. A straight woman who consciously befriends
and surrounds herself with gay men.
3. A dance.
4. The female character's materialism. Zirconia
is a faux diamond.

How I keep from going under
Huh ah huh huh huh
It's like a jungle sometimes, it makes me wonder   35
How I keep from going under

My brother's doing bad, stole my mother's TV
Says she watches too much, it's just not healthy
"All My Children" in the daytime, "Dallas" at night
Can't even see the game or the Sugar Ray fight[5]   40
The bill collectors, they ring my phone
And scare my wife when I'm not home
Got a bum education, double-digit inflation
Can't train to the job, there's a strike at the station
Neon King Kong, standing on my back   45
Can't stop to turn around, broke my sacroiliac
A mid-range migraine, cancered membrane
Sometimes I think I'm going insane
I swear, I might hijack a plane

Don't push me 'cause I'm close to the edge   50
I'm trying not to lose my head
It's like a jungle sometimes, it makes me wonder
How I keep from going under

My son said, "Daddy, I don't want to go to school
'Cause the teacher's a jerk, he must think I'm a fool   55
And all the kids smoke reefer, I think it'd be cheaper
If I just got a job, learned to be a street sweeper
Dance to the beat, shuffle my feet
Wear a shirt and tie and run with the creeps
'Cause it's all about money, ain't a damn thing funny   60
You got to have a con in this land of milk and honey"

They pushed that girl in front of the train
Took her to the doctor, sewed her arm on again
Stabbed that man right in his heart
Gave him a transplant for a brand new start   65
I can't walk through the park 'cause it's crazy after dark
Keep my hand on my gun
'Cause they got me on the run
I feel like a outlaw
Broke my last glass jaw   70
Hear them say, "You want some more?"
Livin' on a seesaw

Don't push me 'cause I'm close to the edge
I'm trying not to lose my head
Say what?   75
It's like a jungle sometimes, it makes me wonder
How I keep from going under

---

5. "Sugar" Ray Leonard was a popular boxer at the time.

A child is born with no state of mind
Blind to the ways of mankind
God is smiling on you but he's frowning too 80
Because only God knows what you go through
You grow in the ghetto, living second rate
And your eyes will sing a song of deep hate
The place that you play and where you stay
Looks like one great big alleyway 85
You'll admire all the number book-takers[6]
Thugs, pimps, and pushers and the big money makers
Driving big cars, spending twenties and tens
And you wanna grow up to be just like them, huh
Smugglers, scramblers, burglars, gamblers 90
Pickpockets, peddlers, even panhandlers
You say, "I'm cool, huh, I'm no fool"
But then you wind up dropping out of high school
Now you're unemployed, all nonvoid
Walking 'round like you're Pretty Boy Floyd[7] 95
Turned stick-up kid but look what you done did
Got sent up for a eight-year bid
Now your manhood is took and you're a Maytag[8]
Spend the next two years as a undercover fag

Being used and abused to serve like hell 100
'Til one day you was found hung dead in the cell
It was plain to see that your life was lost
You was cold and your body swung back and forth
But now your eyes sing the sad sad song
Of how ya lived so fast and died so young 105
So don't push me 'cause I'm close to the edge
I'm trying not to lose my head
Ah huh huh huh huh
It's like a jungle sometimes, it makes me wonder
How I keep from going under 110

[Dialogue]
Yo, Mel, you see that girl man?
Yeah, man
Cowboy
Yo! That sound like Cowboy, man
That's cool 115
Yo! What's up money?
Yo!
Hey, where's Creole and Rahiem at, man?
They upstairs cooling out
So, what's up for tonight y'all? 120
Yo! We could go down to Fever, man
Let's go check out June Bug, man
Hey yo! You know that girl Betty?
Yeah, man
Her moms got robbed, man 125

6. The numbers was an illegal lottery popular in poor African American urban areas. The book-taker collected the information from customers.

7. A legendary flamboyant outlaw of the 1920s and 1930s.

8. A well-known brand of household appliances.

What?
Not again?
She got hurt real bad
When this happen? When this happen?
[*Tires squeal*]
Everybody freeze! Don't nobody move nothing, y'all know what
    this is   130
Get 'em up!
What?
Get 'em up!
Man, we down with Grandmaster Flash and the Furious Five
What's that? A gang?   135
No!
Look, shut up! I don't want to hear your mouth
'Scuse me, Officer, Officer, what's the problem?
You the problem, you the problem
You ain't got to push me, man   140
Get in the car! Get in the car! Get in the godda—
Get in the car!

Don't Believe the Hype[1] •

Don't believe the hype

Back—caught you lookin' for the same thing
It's a new thing—check out this I bring
Uh-oh, the roll below the level
'Cause I'm livin' low   5
Next to the bass (c'mon)
Turn up the radio
They claim that I'm a criminal
By now I wonder how
Some people never know   10
The enemy could be their friend, guardian
I'm not a hooligan
I rock the party and
Clear all the madness, I'm not a racist
Preach to teach to all   15
'Cause some, they never had this
Number one, not born to run
About the gun
I wasn't licensed to have one
The minute they see me, fear me   20
I'm the epitome—a public enemy
Used, abused, without clues
I refused to blow a fuse
They even had it on the news
Don't believe the hype   25

Don't believe the hype

---

1. Recorded by Public Enemy (1988).

Yes—was the start of my last jam
So here it is again, another def jam
But since I gave you all a little something
That we knew you lacked   30
They still consider me a new jack[2]
All the critics, you can hang 'em
I'll hold the rope
But they hope to the pope
And pray it ain't dope   35
The follower of Farrakhan[3]
Don't tell me that you understand
Until you hear the man
The book of the new school rap game
Writers treat me like Coltrane,[4] insane   40
Yes to them, but to me I'm a different kind
We're brothers of the same mind, unblind
Caught in the middle and
Not surrenderin'
I don't rhyme for the sake of riddlin'   45
Some claim that I'm a smuggler
Some say I never heard of ya
A rap burglar, false media
We don't need it, do we?
It's fake, that's what it be to ya, dig me?   50
Yo, Terminator X,[5] step up on the stand and show the people what
    time it is, boyyyyy!

Don't believe the hype

Don't believe the hype—it's a sequel
As an equal, can I get this through to you
My 98's boomin' with a trunk of funk   55
All the jealous punks can't stop the dunk
Comin' from the school of hard knocks
Some perpetrate, they drink Clorox
Attack the Black, because I know they lack exact
The cold facts, and still they try to xerox   60
The leader of the new school, uncool
Never played the fool, just made the rules
Remember there's a need to get alarmed
Again I said I was a timebomb
In the daytime, radio's scared of me   65
'Cause I'm mad, 'cause I'm the enemy
They can't come on and play me in prime time
'Cause I know the time, plus I'm gettin' mine
I get on the mix late in the night
They know I'm livin' right, so here go the mike, psych   70
Before I let it go, don't rush my show
You try to reach and grab and get elbowed

2. Newly arrived, notable male character in a community.
3. Minister Louis Farrakhan, leader of the Black Nationalist Muslim group, the Nation of Islam.
4. John Coltrane, saxophonist innovator, was one of several African American jazz musicians who were frequently depicted by mainstream media as eccentric, difficult to understand, or crazy.
5. The DJ (turntablist) for Public Enemy.

Word to Herb, yo if you can't swing this
Learn the words, you might sing this
Just a little bit of the taste of the bass for you 75
As you get up and dance at the LQ[6]
When some deny it, defy it, I swing bolos
And then they clear the lane, I go solo
The meaning of all of that
Some media is the wack 80
As you believe it's true
It blows me through the roof
Suckers, liars, get me a shovel
Some writers I know are damn devils
For them I say, "Don't believe the hype" 85
Yo Chuck, they must be on the pipe, right?
Their pens and pads I'll snatch
'Cause I've had it
I'm not an addict, fiendin' for static
I'll see their tape recorder and grab it 90
No, you can't have it back, silly rabbit
I'm goin' to my media assassin
Harry Allen,[7] I gotta ask him
Yo Harry, you're a writer, are we that type?
Don't believe the hype 95
Don't believe the hype

I got Flava and all those things you know
Yeah boy, part two bum rush the show
Yo Griff, get the green, black, red, and
Gold down, countdown to Armageddon[8] 100
'88 you wait the S-One's will
Put the left in effect and I still will
Rock the hard jams, treat it like a seminar
Reach the bourgeois, and rock the boulevard
Some say I'm negative 105
But they're not positive
But what I got to give
The media says this
Red black and green
Know what I mean 110
Yo, don't believe the hype

The Evil That Men Do[1]•

You asked, I came
So behold the Queen
Let's add a little sense to the scene
I'm livin' positive
Not out here knocked up 5

6. Latin Quarter, a popular New York dance
venue that was a key locale in the early hip-hop
scene of the 1970s and 1980s.
7. Journalist and music critic.
8. According to the New Testament, the final
battle between good and evil.

1. Recorded by Queen Latifah (1989). The title
comes from *Julius Caesar* 3.2, by William Shakespeare (1564–1616) and may also derive from the
ancient Greek playwright Euripedes (480–406
B.C.E.).

But the lines are so dangerous
I oughta be locked up
This rhyme doesn't require prime time
I'm just sharin' thoughts in mind
Back again because I knew you wanted it   10
From the Latifah with the Queen in front of it
Droppin' bombs, you're up in arms and puzzled
The lines will flow like fluid while you guzzle
You slip, I'll drop you on a BDP[2]-produced track
From KRS[3] to be exact   15
It's a Flavor Unit[4] quest that today has me speakin'
'Cause it's knowledge I'm seekin'
Enough about myself, I think it's time that I tell you
About the Evil That Men Do

Situations, reality, what a concept   20
Nothin' ever seems to stay in step
So today here is a message for my sisters and brothers
Here are some things I want to cover
A woman strives for a better life
But who the hell cares   25
Because she's livin' on welfare
The government can't come up with a decent housin' plan
So she's in no man's land
It's a sucker who tells you you're equal
(You don't need 'em   30
Johannesburg[5] cries for freedom)
We the people hold these truths to be self-evident
(But there's no response from the president)
Someone's livin' the good life tax-free
'Cause some poor girl can't find   35
A way to be crack-free
And that's just part of the message
I thought I had to send you
About the Evil That Men Do

Tell me, don't you think it's a shame   40
When someone can put a quarter in a video game
But when a homeless person approaches you on the street
You can't treat him the same
It's time to teach the deaf, the dumb, the blind
That black on black crime only shackles and binds   45
You to a doom, a fate worse than death
But there's still time left
To stop puttin' your conscience on cease
And bring about some type of peace
Not only in your heart but also in your mind   50
It will benefit all mankind
Then there will be one thing

2. Boogie Down Productions, an influential hip-
hop duo of the mid-1980s, consisting of KRS-
One and DJ Scott La Rock.
3. I.e., KRS-One, the surviving member of Boogie Down Productions.

4. A hip-hop management company founded by
Queen Latifah in the 1980s that worked with rap
groups into the 1990s.
5. A South African city that struggled with
apartheid until its official end in 1990.

That will never stop you
And it's the Evil That Men Do

I Ain't No Joke[1]•

I ain't no joke, I use to let the mic[2] smoke
Now I slam it when I'm done and make sure it's broke
When I'm gone I wrote this song cuz I won't let
Nobody press up and mess up to seen I set
I like to stand in a crowd and watch the people wonder damn   5
But think about it then you'll understand
I'm just an addict addicted to music
Maybe it's a habit, I gotta use it
Even if it's jazz or the quiet storm
I hook a beat up convert it in a hip-hop form   10
Write a rhyme in graffiti in every show you see me in
Deep concentration cuz I'm no comedian
Jokers are wild if you wanna be tame
I treat you like a child then you're gonna be named
Another enemy, not even a friend of me   15
Cuz you'll get fried in the end if you pretend to be
Cuz I just put your mind on pause
And I can beat you when you compare my rhyme with yours
I wake you up and as I stare in your face you seem stunned
Remember me, the one you got your idea from   20
But soon you start to suffer but you only get rougher
When you start to stutter that's when you had enuff of
Biting it, I make you choke, you can't provoke
You can't cope, you should of broke cuz I ain't no joke

I got a question, it's serious as cancer   25
Who can keep the average dancer
Hyper as a heart attack nobody smiling
Cuz you're expressing the rhyme that I'm styling
This is what we all sit down to write
You can't make it so you take it home, break it and bite   30
Use pieces and bits of all the hip-hop hits
Get the style down pack then it's time to switch
Put my tape on pause and add some more to yours
Then you figure you're ready for the neighborhood chores
The E-M-C-E-E don't even try to be   35
When you come up to speak, don't even lie to me
You like to exaggerate, dream and imaginate
Then change the rhyme around, that can aggravate me
So when you see me come up, freeze
Or you'll be one of those 7 MC's   40
They think that I'm a new jack but only if they knew that
They who think wrong are they who can't do that
Style that I'm doing, they might ruin
Patterns of paragraphs based on you and
Your offbeat DJ, if anything he play   45

1. Recorded by Eric B. & Rakim (1987).   2. Microphone.

Sound familiar, I'll wait til E say
Play 'em, so I'ma have to dis and broke
You could get a smack for this, I ain't no joke

I hold the microphone like a grudge
E'll hold the record so the needle don't budge   50
I hold a conversation cuz when I invent
I nominated my DJ the president
When I'm see I'll, people freestyle, going steadily
So pucker up and whistle my melody
But whatever you do, don't miss one   55
There'll be another rough rhyme after this one
Before you know it, you're following and fiending
Waiting for the punchline to get the meaning
Like before the middle of my story I'm telling
Nobody beats the R[3] so stop yelling   60
Save it, put it in your pocket for later
Cuz I'm moving the crowd and be a record fader
No interruptions and the mic is broke
When I'm gone, then you can joke
Cuz everything is real on a serious tip   65
Keep playing and I varies quick
And take you for a walk through hell
Feed your dome then watch your eyeballs swell
Guide you out of triple stage darkness
When it get dark again then I'ma spark this   70
Microphone cuz the heat is on, you see smoke
And I'm finish when the beat is gone, I'm no joke

Things Done Changed[1] •

Remember back in the days, when niggaz had waves,[2]
Gazelle shades, and corn braids?
Pitchin pennies,[3] honeys had the high-top jellies
Shootin skelly,[4] motherfuckers was all friendly,
Loungin at the barbeques, drinkin brews   5
With the neighborhood crews, hangin on the avenues.
Turn your pages, to nineteen ninety-three:
Niggaz is gettin smoked G,[5] believe me.
Talk slick, you get your neck slit quick,
Cause real street niggaz ain't havin that shit.   10
Totin techs for rep, smokin blunts[6] in the project
Hallways, shootin dice all day;
Wait for niggaz to step up on some fightin shit,
We get hype and shit and start lifin shit
So step away with your fist-fight ways   15
Motherfucker this ain't back in the day, but you don't hear me though.

3. I.e., Rakim, the rapper.
1. Written and performed by Biggie Smalls (The Notorious B.I.G.) (1994).
2. A hairstyle popular in the 1980s.
3. A children's game.

4. Another game.
5. Term of endearment used among black males, equivalent to *brother*. "Smoked": killed by gunfire.
6. Marijuana rolled in cigar paper. "Techs": semi-automatic handguns. "Rep": reputation.

No more cocoa leave-io, one two three[7]
One two three, all of this to me, is a mystery.
I hear you motherfuckers talk about it,
But I stay seein bodies with the motherfuckin chalk around it.   20
And I'm down with the shit too
For the stupid motherfuckers wanna try to use Kung-Fu.
Instead of a Mac-10[8] he tried scrappin:
Slugs in his back and, that's what the fuck's happenin.
When you sleep on the street,   25
Little motherfuckers with heat, want to leave a nigga six feet deep.
And we comin to the wake
To make sure the cryin and commotion ain't a motherfuckin fake.
Back in the days, our parents used to take care of us;
Look at em now, they even fuckin scared of us: 30
Callin the city for help because they can't maintain.
Damn, shit done changed.

If I wasn't in the rap game,
I'd probably have a key knee-deep in the crack game.
Because the streets is a short stop: 35
Either you're slingin crack-rock or you got a wicked jumpshot.
Shit, it's hard being young from the slums
Eatin five-cent gums not knowin where your meals comin from.
And now the shit's gettin crazier and major:
Kids younger than me, they got the Sky brand Pagers,   40
Goin outta town, blowin up,
Six months later all the dead bodies showin up.
It make me wanna grab the nine and the shottie,[9]
But I gotta go identify the body.
Damn, what happened to the summertime cookouts?   45
Everytime I turn around a nigga gettin took out.
Shit, my momma got cancer in her breast;
Don't ask me why I'm motherfuckin stressed, things done changed.

N.Y. State of Mind[1]•

Yeah yeah, aiyyo[2] black it's time (word?)
(Word, it's time nigga?)
Yeah, it's time man (aight nigga, begin)
Yeah, straight out the fuckin dungeons of rap
Where fake niggaz don't make it back   5
I don't know how to start this shit, yo, now

Rappers I monkey flip em with the funky rhythm I be kickin
Musician, inflictin compositions
Of pain I'm like Scarface sniffin cocaine
Holdin a M-16, see with the pen I'm extreme, now   10
Bullet-holes left in my peepholes
I'm suited up in street clothes
Hand me a nine[3] and I'll defeat foes

7. Another game.
8. Type of gun.
9. Types of guns.

1. Written and performed by Nas (1994).
2. Hey yo.
3. I.e., a 9-mm handgun.

Y'all know my steelo[4] with or without the airplay
I keep some E&J, sittin bent up[5] in the stairway   15
Or either on the corner bettin Grants with the celo[6] champs
Laughin at baseheads[7] tryin to sell some broken amps
G-Packs get off quick, forever niggaz talk shit
Reminiscing about the last time the Task Force flipped
Niggaz be runnin through the block shootin   20
Time to start the revolution, catch a body head for Houston
Once they caught us off guard, the Mac-10 was in the grass and
I ran like a cheetah with thoughts of an assassin
Pick the Mac up, told brothers, "Back up," the Mac spit
Lead was hittin niggaz: one ran, I made him backflip   25
Heard a few chicks scream my arm shook, couldn't look
Gave another squeeze, heard it click, yo, my shit is stuck
Try to cock it, it wouldn't shoot now I'm in danger
Finally pulled it back and saw three bullets caught up in the Chamber
So now I'm jetting to the building lobby   30
And it was filled with children probably couldn't see as high as I be
(So what you sayin?) It's like the game ain't the same
Got younger niggaz pullin the triggers bringing fame to they Name
And claim some corners, crews without guns are goners
In broad daylight, stickup kids, they run up on us   35
Fo'-fives and gauges,[8] Macs in fact
Same niggaz'll catch a back to back, snatchin yo' cracks in Black
There was a snitch on the block gettin niggaz knocked
So hold your stash until the coke price drop
I know this crackhead, who said she gotta smoke nice rock   40
And if it's good she'll bring ya customers in measuring pots, but Yo
You gotta slide on a vacation
Inside information keeps large niggaz erasin and they wives Basin[9]
It drops deep as it does in my breath
I never sleep, cause sleep is the cousin of death   45
Beyond the walls of intelligence, life is defined
I think of crime when I'm in a New York state of mind

Be havin dreams that I'ma gangster—drinkin Moet, holdin Tecs
Makin sure the cash came correct then I stepped
Investments in stocks, sewing up the blocks   50
To sell rocks, winnin gunfights with mega cops
But just a nigga, walking with his finger on the trigger
Make enough figures until my pockets get bigger
I ain't the type of brother made for you to start testin
Give me a Smith and Wessun[1] I'll have niggaz undressin   55
Thinkin of cash flow, buddah[2] and shelter
Whenever frustrated I'ma hijack Delta
In the P.J.'s,[3] my blend tape plays, bullets are strays
Young bitches is grazed each block is like a maze
Full of black rats trapped, plus the Island[4] is packed   60

4. Style.
5. Intoxicated. "E&J": i.e., Ernst and James Brandy.
6. A kind of dice game.
7. Those addicted to a smoked (freebase) form of cocaine.
8. Types of guns.
9. I.e., freebasing. "Erasin": dying.
1. I.e., Smith & Wesson, a gun manufacturer.
2. Marijuana.
3. I.e., housing projects.
4. Rikers Island, a jail in New York City.

From what I hear in all the stories when my peoples come back, Black
I'm livin where the nights is jet black
The fiends fight to get crack I just max, I dream I can sit back
And lamp like Capone,[5] with drug scripts sewn
Or the legal luxury life, rings flooded with stones, homes   65
I got so many rhymes I don't think I'm too sane
Life is parallel to Hell but I must maintain
And be prosperous, though we live dangerous
Cops could just arrest me, blamin us, we're held like hostages
It's only right that I was born to use mics[6]   70
And the stuff that I write, is even tougher than dice
I'm takin rappers to a new plateau, through rap slow
My rhymin is a vitamin, Hell without a capsule
The smooth criminal on beat breaks
Never put me in your box if your shit eats tapes   75
The city never sleeps, full of villains and creeps
That's where I learned to do my hustle had to scuffle with Freaks
I'ma addict for sneakers, twenties of buddah and bitches with Beepers
In the streets I can greet ya, about blunts[7] I teach ya
Inhale deep like the words of my breath   80
I never sleep, cause sleep is the cousin of death
I lay puzzled as I backtrack to earlier times
Nothing's equivalent, to the New York state of mind

Song Cry[1]•

The most incredible baby
Uhh, mmm, mmm, mmm, mmm
yeah, yeah, uhh

I can't see 'em comin' down my eyes
So I gotta make the song cry   5
I can't see 'em comin' down my eyes
So I gotta make the song cry

Good dudes, I know you love me like cooked food
Even though a nigga gotta move like a crook move
We was together on the block since free lunch[2]   10
We shoulda been together havin' 4 seasons[3] brunch

We used to use umbrellas to face the bad weather
So now we travel first class to change the forecast
Never in bunches, just me and you
I loved your point of view 'cause you held no punches   15

Still I left you for months on end
It's been months since I checked back in

5. Al Capone, infamous Chicago gangster of the 1920s, admired in hardcore hip-hop lore.
6. Microphones
7. Marijuana rolled in cigar paper.
1. Recorded by Jay-Z (2001). Samples Bobby Glenn's 1976 "Sounds Like a Love Song" (performed here by Jaguar Wright).
2. State-subsidized school lunch programs.
3. A luxury hotel chain.

Well, somewhere in a small town somewhere lockin' a mall down
Woodgrain, four and change armor all'd[4] down

I can understand why you want a divorce now   20
Though I can't let you know it, pride won't let me show it
Pretend to be heroic, that's just one to grow with
But deep inside a nigga so sick

I can't see 'em comin' down my eyes
So I gotta make the song cry   25
I can't see it comin' down my eyes
So I gotta make the song cry

On repeat, the CD of Big's, "Me and my bitch"[5]
Watchin' Bonnie and Clyde,[6] pretendin' to be that shit
Empty gun in your hand sayin' "Let me see that clip"[7]   30
Shoppin' sprees, pull out your visa quick

A nigga had very bad credit, you helped me lease that whip[8]
You helped me get the keys to that V dot 6[9]
We was so happy poor but when we got rich
That's when our signals got crossed, and we got flipped   35

Rather mine, I don't know what made me leave that shit
Made me speed that quick, let me see, that's it
It was the cheese[1] helped them bitches get amnesia quick
I used to cut up they buddies, now they sayin' they love me.

Used to tell they friends I was ugly and wouldn't touch me   40
Then I showed up in that dubbed out buggy[2]
And then they got fussy and they don't remember that
And I don't remember you

I can't see it comin' down my eyes
So I gotta make the song cry   45
I can't see it comin' down my eyes
So I gotta make the song cry

Yeah, I seen 'em comin' down my eyes
So I gotta make the song cry
I can't see it comin' down my eyes   50
So I gotta make the song cry

A face of stone, was shocked on the other end of the phone
Word back home is that you had a special friend
So what was oh so special then?
You have given away without gettin' at me   55

---

4. A vehicle waxing and polishing product made by Armor All. "Woodgrain, four and change": i.e., a 4.6-liter Range Rover (vehicle) with a wood-grain interior.
5. Track from the Notorious B.I.G.'s 1994 debut album *Ready to Die.*
6. A 1967 film based on the exploits of the titu-lar Great Depression partners in crime.
7. A bundle of ammunition.
8. Car.
9. A car with a high-performance V6 engine.
1. Money.
2. Reference to the bug-eyed headlights of Mercedes-Benz luxury vehicles.

That's your fault, how many times you forgiven me?
How was I to know that you was plain sick of me?
I know the way a nigga livin' was whack
But you don't get a nigga back like that

Shit I'm a man with pride, you don't do shit like that   60
You don't just pick up and leave and leave me sick like that
You don't throw away what we had, just like that
I was just fuckin' them girls, I was gon' get right back

They say you can't turn a bad girl good
But once a good girl's goin' bad, she's gone forever   65
And more forever
Shit I gotta live with the fact I did you wrong forever

I can't see 'em comin' down my eyes
So I gotta make the song cry
I can't see 'em comin' down my eyes   70
So I gotta make the song cry

I know, I seen 'em comin' down your eyes
But I gotta make the song cry
I can't see 'em comin' down my eyes
So I gotta make the song cry   75
It's fucked up girl

Don't Rush Me[1]•

9th's got them beats that you just sing to for no reason

Sometimes you gotta get to know yourself
You gotta travel, little bit
Look at yourself from another perspective   5
So I try to do that

Come on
Listen, there's nothing like knowin' yourself
Like the way I know that smokin's kinda broken my health
Like the way I know my flow don't make appropriate wealth
I can't change that   10
But funny I'm sayin' that when it's money I'm aimed at
I don' give a fuck if you frame that or quote it (shit)
I meant what I said cuz I wrote it, point noted
I know I'm overly sensitive when it comes to, well,
Just about everything   15

And I'm so hardheaded, I don't need your help
Like no advice for these records 'less it's me, myself
Like, I don't ever want to breathe if it requires assistance
Just, just shut down my system

1. Recorded by Jean Grae and producer 9th Wonder (line 1) in 2004. 9th Wonder collaborated with Grae on this song and the entire album *Jeanius.*

I'm a victim of choosin' bad love: a bad luck Lucy[2]   20
Every man touched seems to be a doozy and plus
I'm attached to this loose-leaf, stand on my two feet
So it's hard enough to even have to physically move me
Go ahead, try

I know I'm on the right path   25
To who I'm gonna be at last
But don't rush me nigga
I know I'm wrong and right
At the same time, both I'm the dark and light
And they say life needs everything to live   30
At the same time I got everything to give
So don't rush me
Don't rush me

I gotta be more disciplined
I'm listenin' more to straight logic   35
Blockin' random shit that's driftin' in
Age is a motherfucker (*damn right*)
Find myself starin' at the little kids
Thinkin' *"I can beat 'em like a stepmother"*[3]
Creepin' on a come-up on thirty soon   40
But lookin' twenty ooh
The food catches up to you now plenty
Attendin' christenin's of my best friends' children
And they're askin' *"Who's next?"*
And I'm wishin' for six more wishes for Christmas or   45
Kids on the wish list
Or time-machines to be in existence
I'm a team player, not
The dry wit is similar to Arizona weather
Say it, nigga: *Hot!*   50
Patent leather sole, tappin' at my bowl
If the album's not platinum then I'll have to rack a gold[4]
This rappin' ain't for nothin'
Unless I hold plaques[5] so I can sit up on a boat like Colin, roll that
And you know that   55

I know I'm on the right path
To who I'm gonna be at last
But don't rush me nigga
I know I'm wrong and right
At the same time, both I'm the dark and light   60
And they say life needs everything to live
At the same time I got everything to give
So just don't rush me

---

2. Reference to Lucille Ball's protagonist on the 1950s sitcom *I Love Lucy*.
3. Echoes the stock phrase "Beat 'em like a red-headed stepchild"—meaning to single out a child for disfavor and violence. Used in many prior settings, perhaps most widely heard in the musical *Annie*, which opened on Broadway in 1977.
4. A platinum album has sold at least 1 million copies. A gold album has sold at least 500,000 copies.
5. Grammy awards.

(C'mon)

(Didn't I just tell you?)   65
Don't rush me now

(C'mon)

See this here is the most serious that I've ever been
The most clear-headed
My gear fetish clearly needs an accountant   70
So if I need I'll smoke 'em all like Denis Leary[6] in a mountain
Beef's[7] great though, thanks for addin' more insecurities
Just as I was findin' my level of maturity
Just as I was mindin' my business
Tried to murder Jean's confidence   75
But lucky for me, you're all incompetent
Road block in this, yes
I see him try to put a stop to my obnoxiousness but
I stayed long-winded like sayin' *"George Papadopoulous"* (Who's that?)
I know that I write from the heart with this   80
So, I've got some things to work on
My moodiness like masturbation gets its jerk on
My fascination with the fast pace
Money's encapsulated in my mind-space like what a thrill
Past-dated and I know I'm not in last place   85
But it's hard to work through it with this masked face
And maskin' tape up on the windows keeps the cold out
And everytime I'm layin' down my back breaks because it's old now
I yell too much, get stressed too quick
But the best thing about it, I can change that shit   90
And still remain what came down to earth to be
It's not Jean Grae, that's just a name, you'll see

I know I'm on the right path
To who I'm gonna be at last
But don't rush me nigga   95
I know I'm wrong and right
At the same time, both I'm the dark and light
And they say life needs everything to live
At the same time I got everything to give
So don't rush me   100

(C'mon, now)
Don't rush me now

(C'mon, now)

---

6. American actor and comedian, known for his   7. A feud or grudge.
chain smoking.

Sermons and Prayers

The African American sermon is a complex oratorical form with significant differences from religion to religion, denomination to denomination, region to region, era to era, and preacher to preacher. Sermons heard in a northern Nation of Islam mosque differ significantly from those heard in a down-home Southern Baptist church. Those flattening out all of these differences to expound on *the* black sermon deny this pulchritudinous variety and do a serious injustice to history and its unfurling. Still, there is a sense of continuity in black homiletics (or sermon making), especially observable within those black churches that are independent (or relatively independent) from non–African American leadership hierarchies and cultural values.

The folklorist Gerald L. Davis outlined several features that define the black sermon as a distinctive form. According to Davis, the African American sermon typically has these parts: (1) the disclaimer, in which the preacher makes clear that the morning's message comes not from him or her alone but from God; (2) the statement of theme as drawn from specific biblical readings; (3) the literal and then the broad interpretation of the biblical word; (4) the formulaic body of the sermon, the morning's main message; and (5) the closing statement, rarely a summary as such but rather an open-ended conclusion leading to the next part of the church service.

Within this frame, black preachers are storytellers, actors, and singers who use their voices and bodies to lend dynamism to the performed word. Sometimes, as in the Reverend C. L. Franklin's "The Eagle Stirreth Her Nest," a sermon will take the form of the preacher's own personal witnessing of God's power and ways in the world. There is also an important body of black folk sermons, and of fragments of sermons, that have become part of the black sermonic canon. "The Valley of Dry Bones" and "The Eagle Stirreth Her Nest" are examples of canonized sermons. Like other vernacular forms, black sermons have developed by incremental repetition— from Africa through slavery (that cultural cauldron in which not only Christianity but Christian forms of worship were learned and then refashioned to meet black values) to freedom—and have become part of a nationwide black (and black diasporic) creative process.

Twenty-first-century black preaching often involves newish technologies—not just miniature, cordless microphones and powerhouse speakers but also video cameras and projectors. Many contemporary black preachers also use elements of hip-hop culture to add close-to-the-edge fire and ice to their delivery of the ancient Word.

Despite the relative rigidity of the black sermon's architecture, it is jazzlike in its insistence that preachers find their own voice and imprint on each sermon their own particular style. Jazzlike too is black preaching's emphasis on the improvisational mode. For, like jazz players, preachers participate in a dynamic collaborative process in which they listen with the greatest care while playing, as it were, *with and against* the congregation. The result is that often the best sermons are not just individual productions in the usual Western sense of the artist's product but spring from a creative process involving all those in a given congregation who participate with a full spirit. The most successful preacher can listen through handclaps and countercalls for a *"Well"* from the Amen Corner (the section of the church, positioned near the pulpit, where older members sit and lead the church in responses to the service), a word voiced in a tone or timbre that says "Slow down" or "Explain that" or "Keep building, sister, we hear you!" And of course the preacher also plays with and against the conventions of black preaching itself, plays with the *tradition* of the form. He or she knows what formal elements the congregation expects, and, like the artist, delays them, pretends to ignore or undermine them, then hammers them home or slips them in, to the congregation's aesthetic satisfaction and delight.

"God's Trombones," 2009, Frank Stewart. This photograph presents a mass baptism (with trombone choir accompaniment) by fire hose, as conducted every June since the 1920s by the United House of Prayer for All People in Harlem. The photographer has noted the picture's "African idiom"—i.e., the imagery here suggests Accra, Dakar, or New Orleans as much as it does Manhattan. The work borrows its title from the 1927 book of poetry by James Weldon Johnson.

Again like other artists in the black vernacular tradition, the black preacher is involved not just in call–response patterns but in patterns of call and *re*call: inspiration, anticipation, and memory. The black preacher presents a rhythmically sophisticated statement in which repetitions, dramatic pauses, shifts in tone and pitch, physical movement, and a variety of other devices associated with black music (and the other arts) are employed. At times, too, the man or woman of the Word drops words altogether and moans, chants, sings, grunts, hums, and/or hollers the morning message in a way that transcends what one of Ralph Ellison's characters calls "the straight meaning of the words." In these most musical portions of the "sermonic narrative," as Davis noted, perhaps the deepest African American take-home lessons resound. Inspiration, anticipation, and memory all serve to release the black sermon's spiritual message.

Still, it is crucial also to note the black sermon's steadfast linking of spiritual lessons to those of the here and the now. Sometimes the here and now references—to the foibles of the congregation, to current events, or to contemporary media forms, for example—take a comical turn. But then again the references to current affairs can be deadly serious. For the black sermon typically is a vehicle not only for conversion and worship but also for sociopolitical exposition and analysis. It is in this sense, as the contemporary philosopher Cornel West observed, that preachers are vital *intellectual* presences—and, as with Martin Luther King Jr. and Malcolm X, prophetic seers—in our communities. For even as the unmistakably black forms of their presentations implicitly celebrate black Americans as a group, the sermons also aim to help congregations comprehend the mysterious and often unfriendly world through which they are rolling. Little wonder that so many preachers have been political movers and shakers: organizers, analysts, spokespersons, office seekers, and community leaders on a very large scale.

Many black writers—including James Weldon Johnson, Zora Neale Hurston, James Baldwin, Toni Morrison, and Ralph Ellison—have written brilliantly about the church and have movingly rendered sermons in their works. In Baldwin's play *Amen Corner* you can hear the fans fanning and smell the after-service food cooking through the church's thumping floorboards. In the preface to his book of "seven sermons in verse" titled *God's Trombones*, Johnson recorded the moment when he realized that a sermon could be presented in written verse form. The inspiration came from hearing a preacher in Kansas City who

> strode the pulpit up and down in what was actually a very rhythmic dance, and he brought into play the full gamut of his wonderful voice, a voice—what shall I say? Not of an organ or a trumpet, but rather of a trombone, the instrument possessing above all others the power to express the wide and varied range of emotions encompassed by the human voice—and with greater amplitude. He intoned, he moaned, he pleaded—he blared, he crashed, he thundered. . . . Before he had finished I took a slip of paper and somewhat surreptitiously jotted down some ideas for the first poem, "The Creation."

Doubtless the best way to experience the sermon is to attend a black church, to hear and see the Word performed in context; second best is to experience the sermon in literature, where the sense of context also can be very full. But reading transcripts of actual sermons and listening to and viewing recordings of them—especially for those who have the original cultural settings in mind—also make the case that these works are a wonderfully rich site of African American vernacular expression, a living art form in its own right. The styles of the black preacher in the pulpit have become part of American oratorical style. Martin Luther King Jr. and Malcolm X—both masters of the drama of the sermon, though of different faiths—gave the mid-twentieth century its greatest examples of black church rhetoric and of the black sermon's possibilities for persuasive force.

Recent collections of prayers and testimonials, notably James Washington's masterful *Conversations with God,* have revealed the depth and range of church forms other than songs and sermons. Accordingly, this section of the anthology also features the African American *prayer* as a distinctive form of the performed Word. Like the black sermons, these are also highly stylized, shapely, dramatic expressions that owe much to Europe, Africa, and the mixing bowl of the Americas. With their improvisations, dramatic call–recall patterns, pauses, and polyrhythmical insistences, prayers also bespeak the continuing resonance of the black vernacular tradition.

God[1]

I vision God standing
On the heights of heaven,
Throwing the devil like
A burning torch
Over the gulf   5
Into the valleys of hell.
His eye the lightning's flash,
His voice the thunder's roll.

1. Collected in the Congaree River area of South Carolina by E. C. L. Adams (1876–1946) and published in 1928.

Wid one hand He snatched
The sun from its socket,   10
And the other He clapped across the moon.

I vision God wringing
A storm from the heavens;
Rocking the world
Like an earthquake;   15
Blazing the sea
Wid a trail er fire.
His eye the lightning's flash,
His voice the thunder's roll.
Wid one hand He snatched   20
The sun from its socket,
And the other He clapped across the moon.

I vision God standing
On a mountain
Of burnished gold,   25
Blowing His breath
Of silver clouds
Over the world.
His eye the lightning's flash,
His voice the thunder's roll.   30

Wid one hand He snatched
The sun from its socket,
And the other He clapped across the moon.

JAMES WELDON JOHNSON

Listen Lord, a Prayer [1]

O Lord, we come this morning
Knee-bowed and body-bent
Before Thy throne of grace.
O Lord—this morning—
Bow our hearts beneath our knees,   5
And our knees in some lonesome valley.
We come this morning—
Like empty pitchers to a full fountain,
With no merits of our own.
O Lord—open up a window of heaven,   10
And lean out far over the battlements of glory,
And listen this morning.

1. From *God's Trombones: Seven Negro Sermons in Verse* (1927).

Lord, have mercy on proud and dying sinners—
Sinners hanging over the mouth of hell,
Who seem to love their distance well.   15
Lord—ride by this morning—
Mount Your milk-white horse,
And ride-a this morning—
And in Your ride, ride by old hell,
Ride by the dingy gates of hell,   20
And stop poor sinners in their headlong plunge.

And now, O Lord, this man of God,
Who breaks the bread of life this morning—
Shadow him in the hollow of Thy hand,
And keep him out of the gunshot of the devil.   25
Take him, Lord—this morning—
Wash him with hyssop inside and out,
Hang him up and drain him dry of sin.
Pin his ear to the wisdom-post,

And make his words sledge hammers of truth—   30
Beating on the iron heart of sin.
Lord God, this morning—
Put his eye to the telescope of eternity,
And let him look upon the paper walls of time.
Lord, turpentine his imagination,   35
Put perpetual motion in his arms,
Fill him full of the dynamite of Thy power,
Anoint him all over with the oil of Thy salvation,
And set his tongue on fire.

And now, O Lord—   40
When I've done drunk my last cup of sorrow—
When I've been called everything but a child of God—
When I'm done traveling up the rough side of the mountain—
O—Mary's Baby—
When I start down the steep and slippery steps of death—   45
When this old world begins to rock beneath my feet—
Lower me to my dusty grave in peace
To wait for that great gittin'-up morning—Amen.

C. L. FRANKLIN

The Eagle Stirreth Her Nest[1]

"As an eagle stirreth up her nest, fluttereth over her young, spreadeth abroad on her wings, taketh them, beareth them on her wings: So the Lord alone did lead him, and there was no strange god with him." The eagle stirreth her nest.

The eagle here is used to symbolize God's care and God's concern for his people. Many things have been used as symbolic expressions to give us a picture of God or some characteristic of one of his attributes: the ocean, with her turbulent majesty; the mountains, the lions. Many things have been employed as pictures of either God's strength or God's power or God's love or God's mercy. And the psalmist has said that The heavens declare the glory of God and the firmament shows forth his handiworks.

So the eagle here is used as a symbol of God. Now in picturing God as an eagle stirring her nest, I believe history has been one big nest that God has been eternally stirring to make man better and to help us achieve world brotherhood. Some of the things that have gone on in your own experiences have merely been God stirring the nest of your circumstances. Now the Civil War, for example, and the struggle in connection with it, was merely the promptings of Providence to lash man to a point of being brotherly to all men. In fact, all of the wars that we have gone through, we have come out with new outlooks and new views and better people. So that throughout history, God has been stirring the various nests of circumstances surrounding us, so that he could discipline us, help us to know ourselves, and help us to love another, and to help us hasten on the realization of the kingdom of God.

The eagle symbolizes God because there is something about an eagle that is a fit symbol of things about God. In the first place, the eagle is the king of fowls. And if he is a regal or kingly bird, in that majesty he represents the kingship of God or symbolizes the kingship of God. (Listen if you please.) For God is not merely a king, he is *the* king. Somebody has said that he is the king of kings. For you see, these little kings that we know, they've got to have a king over them. They've got to account to somebody for the deeds done in their bodies. For God is *the* king. And if the eagle is a kingly bird, in that way he symbolizes the regalness and kingliness of our God.

In the second place, the eagle is strong. Somebody has said that as the eagle goes winging his way through the air he can look down on a young lamb grazing by a mountainside, and can fly down and just with the strength of his claws, pick up this young lamb and fly away to yonder's cleft and devour it—because he's strong. If the eagle is strong, then, in that he is a symbol of God, for our God is strong. Our God is strong. Somebody has called him a fortress. So that when the enemy is pursuing me I can run

1. Franklin (1915–1984) uses Deuteronomy 32.11–12 as his opening text in this sermon.

behind him. Somebody has called him a citadel of protection and redemption. Somebody else has said that he's so strong until they call him a leaning-post that thousands can lean on him, and he'll never get away. (I don't believe you're praying with me.) People have been leaning on him ever since time immemorial. Abraham leaned on him. Isaac and Jacob leaned on him. Moses[2] and the prophets leaned on him. All the Christians leaned on him. People are leaning on him all over the world today. He's never given way. He's strong. That's strong. Isn't it so?

In the second place, he's swift. The eagle is swift. And it is said that he could fly with such terrific speed his wings can be heard rowing in the air. He's swift. And if he's swift in that way, he's a symbol of our God. For our God is swift. I said he's swift. Sometimes, sometimes he'll answer you while you're calling him. He's swift. Daniel was thrown in a lions' den. And Daniel rung him on the way to the lions' den. And having rung him, why, God had dispatched the angel from heaven. And by the time that Daniel got to the lions' den, the angel had changed the nature of lions and made them lay down and act like lambs.[3] He's swift. Swift. One night Peter[4] was put in jail and the church went down on its knees to pray for him. And while the church was praying, Peter knocked on the door. God was so swift in answering prayer. So that if the eagle is a swift bird, in that way he represents or symbolizes the fact that God is swift. He's swift. If you get in earnest tonight and tell him about your troubles, he's swift to hear you. All you do is need a little faith, and ask him in grace.

Another thing about the eagle is that he has extraordinary sight. Extraordinary sight. Somewhere it is said that he can rise to a lofty height in the air and look in the distance and see a storm hours away. That's extraordinary sight. And sometimes he can stand and gaze right in the sun because he has extraordinary sight. I want to tell you my God has extraordinary sight. He can see every ditch that you have dug for me and guide me around them. God has extraordinary sight. He can look behind that smile on your face and see that frown in your heart. God has extraordinary sight.

Then it is said that an eagle builds a nest unusual. It is said that the eagle selects rough material, basically, for the construction of his nest. And then as the nest graduates toward a close or a finish, the material becomes finer and softer right down at the end. And then he goes about to set up residence in that nest. And when the little eaglets are born, she goes out and brings in food to feed them. But when they get to the point where they're old enough to be out on their own, why, the eagle will begin to pull out some of that down and let some of those thorns come through so that the nest won't be, you know, so comfortable. So when they get to lounging around and rolling around, the thorns prick 'em here and there. (Pray with me if you please.)

I believe that God has to do that for us sometimes. Things are going so well and we are so satisfied that we just lounge around and forget to pray. You'll walk around all day and enjoy God's life, God's health and God's strength, and go climb into bed without saying, "Thank you, Lord, for another day's journey." We'll do that. God has to pull out a little of the plush around us, a little of the comfort around us, and let a few thorns of

---

2. All great leaders of the Old Testament. Abraham was the father of Isaac, who was the father of Jacob. Moses delivered the Israelites from slavery under the Pharaoh.
3. See Daniel 6.16–22.
4. One of the apostles chosen by Jesus.

trial and tribulation stick through the nest to make us pray sometime. Isn't it so? For most of us forget God when things are going well with us. Most of us forget him.

It is said that there was a man who had a poultry farm. And that he raised chickens for the market. And one day in one of his broods he discovered a strange looking bird that was very much unlike the other chickens on the yard. [*Whooping:*]

And[5]
>> the man
>>>> didn't pay too much attention.
>> But he noticed
>>>> as time went on
> that
>> this strange looking bird
>>>> was unusual.
>> He outgrew
>>>> the other little chickens,
>> his habits were stranger
>>>> and different.

O Lord.
>> But he let him grow on,
>> and let him mingle
>>>> with the other chickens.

O Lord.
>> And then one day a man
>> who knew eagles
>>>> when he saw them,
>> came along
>>>> and saw that little eagle
>>>> walking in the yard.

And
>> he said to his friend,
>> "Do you know
>>>> that you have an eagle here?"
>> The man said, "Well,
>>>> I didn't really know it.
>> But I knew he was different
>>>> from the other chickens.

And
>> I knew that his ways
>>>> were different.

And
>> I knew that his habits
>>>> were different.

And
>> he didn't act like
>>>> the other chickens.
>> But I didn't know
>>>> that he was an eagle."

---

5. Note that from here on the preached words are printed in a form that approximates the rhythmic chanting quality of their presentation.

But the man said, "Yes,
            you have an eagle here on your yard.
And what you ought to do
            is build a cage.
After a while
when he's a little older
            he's going to get tired
            of the ground.
Yes he will.
     He's going to rise up
            on the pinion of his wings.
Yes,
and
     as he grows,
why,
     you can change the cage,
and
     make it a little larger
            as he grows older
            and grows larger."
     The man went out
            and built a cage.
And
     every day he'd go in
            and feed the eagle.
But
     he grew
            a little older
            and a little older.
Yes he did.
     His wings
            began
     to scrape on the sides
            of the cage.
And
     he had to build
            another cage
     and open the door of the old cage
            and let him into
     a larger cage.
Yes he did.
O Lord.
And
     after a while
            he outgrew that one day
            and then he had to build
            another cage.
     So one day
            when the eagle had gotten grown,
Lord God,
     and his wings
            were twelve feet
            from tip to tip,
O Lord,

he began to get restless
in the cage.
Yes he did.
He began to walk around
and be uneasy.
Why,
he heard
noises
in the air.
A flock of eagles flew over
and he heard
their voices.
And
though he'd never been around eagles,
there was something about that voice
that he heard
that moved
down in him,
and made him
dissatisfied.
O Lord.
And
the man watched him
as he walked around
uneasy.
O Lord.
He said, "Lord,
my heart goes out to him.
I believe I'll go
and open the door
and set the eagle free."
O Lord.
He went there
and opened the door.
Yes.
The eagle walked out,
yes,
spreaded his wings,
then took 'em down.
Yes.
The eagle walked around
a little longer,
and
he flew up a little higher
and went to the barnyard.
And,
yes,
he set there for a while.
He wiggled up a little higher
and flew in yonder's tree.
Yes.
And then he wiggled up a little higher
and flew to yonder's mountain.
Yes.

Yes!
Yes.

One of these days,
one of these days.
My soul
is an eagle
in the cage that the Lord
has made for me.
My soul,
my soul,
my soul
is caged in,
in this old body,
yes it is,
and one of these days
the man who made the cage
will open the door
and let my soul
go.
Yes he will.
You ought to
be able to see me
take the wings of my soul.
Yes, yes,
yes,
yes!
Yes, one of these days.
One of these old days.
One of these old days.
Did you hear me say it?
I'll fly away
and be at rest.
Yes.
Yes!
Yes!
Yes!
Yes!
Yes.
One of these old days.
One of these old days.
And
when troubles
and trials are over,
when toil
and tears are ended,
when burdens
are through burdening,
ohh!
Ohh.
Ohh!
Ohh one of these days.
Ohh one of these days.
One of these days.
One of these days,

my soul will take wings,
my soul will take wings.
Ohh!

> Ohh, a few more days.
> Ohh, a few more days.
> A few more days.
> O Lord.

HOWARD THURMAN

O God, I Need Thee[1]

I Need Thy Sense of Time
  Always I have an underlying anxiety about things.
  Sometimes I am in a hurry to achieve my ends
  And am completely without patience. It is hard for me
  To realize that some growth is slow,   5
  That all processes are not swift. I cannot always discriminate
  Between what takes time to develop and what can be rushed,
  Because my sense of time is dulled.
  I measure things in terms of happenings.
  O to understand the meaning of perspective   10
  That I may do all things with a profound sense of leisure—of time.

I Need Thy Sense of Order
  The confusion of the details of living
  Is sometimes overwhelming. The little things
  Keep getting in my way providing ready-made   15
  Excuses for failure to do and be
  What I know I ought to do and be.
  Much time is spent on things that are not very important
  While significant things are put into an insignificant place
  In my scheme of order. I must unscramble my affairs   20
  So that my life will become order. O God, I need
    Thy sense of order.

I Need Thy Sense of the Future
  Teach me to know that life is ever
  On the side of the future.   25
  Keep alive in me the forward look, the high hope,
  The onward surge. Let me not be frozen
  Either by the past or the present.
  Grant me, O patient Father, Thy sense of the future
  Without which all life would sicken and die.   30

1. A prayer.

G. I. TOWNSEL

The Way Out Is to Pray Out[1]•

Somebody . . . been running a long time
Somebody . . . who been running
They haven't got tired
Somebody been loaded, been loaded down
Somebody, Who loved us   5
Somebody, That's bigger than me
That got a little load, that I were carr'ing
To help me bear my burden
And go on to Jesus with me

And Jesus, He identify Himself again   10
You know, sometimes, He have to re-identify Himself to us
Sometime . . . in a troublesome world
Sometime . . . when we got to meet so many difficulties
So many trials, so many tribulations
Heey—ahhh!   15
We need somebody, like Jesus
Who own the world
To say they don't mind:
"I see their trials and tribulations
And not only that,   20
I see that's hell coming down the aisle"
Come on to Jesus with me
And you can say what you will to me
If you follow Him, He'll lead you out
If you been in the doghouse   25
And didn't want to be let out into the light
You follow Jesus
Come on, right about here . . .
If you've been down
And didn't want to be picked up   30
You follow Jesus
He'll lift you up, He'll stand you on your feet
Heey—ahh!
Who will come to Jesus with me?

He'll help you bear your burden   35
If you get on the highway with Him,
Not only will He go 'piece the way with you,
He'll go AAALL the way
Through the dark valley, and even the shadow of death
And then he'll get up EARLY in the morning . . .   40

1. A sermon fragment.

He'll go with ya
The way out
The way out
The way out
The way out of darkness   45
The way out of sin
The way out of trouble
The way out this situation
Amen
You can pray out of a situation   50
But you can't pray out of a place
So let us be careful and not fool around, you know, and idle our time away
And get behind that gulf into that place
You can't pray out of that place
But you can pray out of that condition   55

If you don't believe it, ask Jonah
He'll tell you he was in the belly of a whale
And he prayed out
Isn't that right?
The way out, you can pray out   60
But you can't pray out of a place:

God bless you, God sanctify you
I'll be back one day
And I'll say more
I'll just ask to say a word . . .   65

MARTIN LUTHER KING JR.

I Have a Dream[1]•

I am happy to join with you today in what will go down in history as the greatest demonstration for freedom in the history of our nation.

Fivescore years ago, a great American, in whose symbolic shadow we stand today, signed the Emancipation Proclamation. This momentous decree came as a great beacon light of hope to millions of Negro slaves who had been seared in the flames of withering injustice. It came as a joyous daybreak to end the long night of their captivity.

But one hundred years later, the Negro still is not free; one hundred years later, the life of the Negro is still sadly crippled by the manacles of segregation and the chains of discrimination; one hundred years later, the Negro lives on a lonely island of poverty in the midst of a vast ocean of material prosperity; one hundred years later, the Negro is still languished in the corners of American society and finds himself in exile in his own land.

1. King (1929–1968) delivered this speech in front of the Lincoln Memorial on August 28, 1963, at the March on Washington, D.C., for civil rights.

So we've come here today to dramatize a shameful condition. In a sense we've come to our nation's capital to cash a check. When the architects of our republic wrote the magnificent words of the Constitution and the Declaration of Independence, they were signing a promissory note to which every American was to fall heir. This note was the promise that all men, yes, black men as well as white men, would be guaranteed the unalienable rights of life, liberty, and the pursuit of happiness.

It is obvious today that America has defaulted on this promissory note in so far as her citizens of color are concerned. Instead of honoring this sacred obligation, America has given the Negro people a bad check; a check which has come back marked "insufficient funds." We refuse to believe that there are insufficient funds in the great vaults of opportunity of this nation. And so we've come to cash this check, a check that will give us upon demand the riches of freedom and the security of justice.

We have also come to this hallowed spot to remind America of the fierce urgency of now. This is no time to engage in the luxury of cooling off or to take the tranquilizing drug of gradualism. Now is the time to make real the promises of democracy; now is the time to rise from the dark and desolate valley of segregation to the sunlit path of racial justice; now is the time to lift our nation from the quicksands of racial injustice to the solid rock of brotherhood; now is the time to make justice a reality for all of God's children. It would be fatal for the nation to overlook the urgency of the moment. This sweltering summer of the Negro's legitimate discontent will not pass until there is an invigorating autumn of freedom and equality.

Nineteen sixty-three is not an end, but a beginning. And those who hope that the Negro needed to blow off steam and will now be content, will have a rude awakening if the nation returns to business as usual.

There will be neither rest nor tranquility in America until the Negro is granted his citizenship rights. The whirlwinds of revolt will continue to shake the foundations of our nation until the bright day of justice emerges.

But there is something that I must say to my people who stand on the warm threshold which leads into the palace of justice. In the process of gaining our rightful place we must not be guilty of wrongful deeds.

Let us not seek to satisfy our thirst for freedom by drinking from the cup of bitterness and hatred. We must forever conduct our struggle on the high plane of dignity and discipline. We must not allow our creative protest to degenerate into physical violence. Again and again we must rise to the majestic heights of meeting physical force with soul force.

The marvelous new militancy which has engulfed the Negro community must not lead us to a distrust of all white people, for many of our white brothers, as evidenced by their presence here today, have come to realize that their destiny is tied up with our destiny and they have come to realize that their freedom is inextricably bound to our freedom. This offense we share mounted to storm the battlements of injustice must be carried forth by a biracial army. We cannot walk alone.

And as we walk, we must make the pledge that we shall always march ahead. We cannot turn back. There are those who are asking the devotees of civil rights, "When will you be satisfied?" We can never be satisfied as long as the Negro is the victim of the unspeakable horrors of police brutality.

We can never be satisfied as long as our bodies, heavy with fatigue of travel, cannot gain lodging in the motels of the highways and the hotels of the cities. We cannot be satisfied as long as the Negro's basic mobility is from a smaller ghetto to a larger one.

We can never be satisfied as long as our children are stripped of their selfhood and robbed of their dignity by signs stating "for whites only." We cannot be satisfied as long as a Negro in Mississippi cannot vote and a Negro in New York believes he has nothing for which to vote. No, we are not satisfied, and we will not be satisfied until justice rolls down like waters and righteousness like a mighty stream.

I am not unmindful that some of you have come here out of excessive trials and tribulation. Some of you have come fresh from narrow jail cells. Some of you have come from areas where your quest for freedom left you battered by the storms of persecution and staggered by the winds of police brutality. You have been the veterans of creative suffering. Continue to work with the faith that unearned suffering is redemptive.

Go back to Mississippi; go back to Alabama; go back to South Carolina; go back to Georgia; go back to Louisiana; go back to the slums and ghettos of the northern cities, knowing that somehow this situation can, and will be changed. Let us not wallow in the valley of despair.

So I say to you, my friends that even though we must face the difficulties of today and tomorrow, I still have a dream. It is a dream deeply rooted in the American dream that one day this nation will rise up and live out the true meaning of its creed—we hold these truths to be self-evident, that all men are created equal.

I have a dream that one day on the red hills of Georgia, sons of former slaves and sons of former slave-owners will be able to sit down together at the table of brotherhood.

I have a dream that one day, even the state of Mississippi, a state sweltering with the heat of injustice, sweltering with the heat of oppression, will be transformed into an oasis of freedom and justice.

I have a dream my four little children will one day live in a nation where they will not be judged by the color of their skin but by content of their character. I have a dream today!

I have a dream that one day, down in Alabama, with its vicious racists, with its governor having his lips dripping with the words of interposition and nullification, that one day, right there in Alabama, little black boys and black girls will be able to join hands with little white boys and white girls as sisters and brothers. I have a dream today!

I have a dream that one day every valley shall be exalted, every hill and mountain shall be made low, the rough places shall be made plain, and the crooked places shall be made straight and the glory of the Lord will be revealed and all flesh shall see it together.[2]

This is our hope. This is the faith that I go back to the South with.

With this faith we will be able to hew out of the mountain of despair a stone of hope. With this faith we will be able to transform the jangling discords of our nation into a beautiful symphony of brotherhood.

With this faith we will be able to work together, to pray together, to struggle together, to go to jail together, to stand up for freedom together, knowing that we will be free one day. This will be the day when all of God's

---

2. Isaiah 40.4–5: "Every valley shall be exalted, and every mountain and hill shall be made low: and the crooked shall be made straight, and the rough places plain: and the glory of the Lord shall be revealed, and all flesh shall see it together."

children will be able to sing with new meaning—"my country 'tis of thee; sweet land of liberty; of thee I sing; land where my fathers died, land of the pilgrim's pride; from every mountain side, let freedom ring"—and if America is to be a great nation, this must become true.

So let freedom ring from the prodigious hilltops of New Hampshire.

Let freedom ring from the mighty mountains of New York.

Let freedom ring from the heightening Alleghenies of Pennsylvania.

Let freedom ring from the snow-capped Rockies of Colorado.

Let freedom ring from the curvaceous slopes of California.

But not only that.

Let freedom ring from Stone Mountain of Georgia.

Let freedom ring from Lookout Mountain of Tennessee.

Let freedom ring from every hill and molehill of Mississippi, from every mountainside, let freedom ring.

And when we allow freedom to ring, when we let it ring from every village and hamlet, from every state and city, we will be able to speed up that day when all of God's children—black men and white men, Jews and Gentiles, Catholics and Protestants—will be able to join hands and to sing in the words of the old Negro spiritual, "Free at last, free at last; thank God Almighty, we are free at last."

I've Been to the Mountaintop[1]•

Thank you very kindly, my friends. As I listened to Ralph Abernathy[2] in his eloquent and generous introduction and then thought about myself, I wondered who he was talking about. It's always good to have your closest friend and associate say something good about you. And Ralph is the best friend that I have in the world.

I'm delighted to see each of you here tonight in spite of a storm warning. You reveal that you are determined to go on anyhow. Something is happening in Memphis, something is happening in our world.

You know, if I were standing at the beginning of time, with the possibility of general and panoramic view of the whole human history up to now, and the Almighty said to me, "Martin Luther King, which age would you like to live in?"—I would take my mental flight by Egypt through, or rather across the Red Sea, through the wilderness on toward the promised land. And in spite of its magnificence, I wouldn't stop there. I would move on by Greece, and take my mind to Mount Olympus. And I would see Plato, Aristotle, Socrates, Euripides and Aristophanes assembled around the Parthenon as they discussed the great and eternal issues of reality.

But I wouldn't stop there. I would go on, even to the great heyday of the Roman Empire. And I would see developments around there, through various emperors and leaders. But I wouldn't stop there. I would even come up to the day of the Renaissance, and get a quick picture of all that the Renais-

---

1. King delivered this sermon, his last, on April 3, 1968, at the Bishop Charles Mason Temple in Memphis, Tennessee, on behalf of the city's largely black body of sanitation workers, who were pressing for higher wages and an end to maltreatment by white supervisors. King was assassinated on the following day.
2. Civil rights leader (1926–1990).

sance did for the cultural and esthetic life of man. But I wouldn't stop there. I would even go by the way that the man for whom I'm named had his habitat. And I would watch Martin Luther as he tacked his ninety-five theses on the door at the church in Wittenberg.

But I wouldn't stop there. I would come on up even to 1863, and watch a vacillating president by the name of Abraham Lincoln finally come to the conclusion that he had to sign the Emancipation Proclamation. But I wouldn't stop there. I would even come up to the early thirties, and see a man grappling with the problems of the bankruptcy of his nation. And come with an eloquent cry that we have nothing to fear but fear itself.

But I wouldn't stop there. Strangely enough, I would turn to the Almighty, and say, "If you allow me to live just a few years in the second half of the twentieth century, I will be happy." Now that's a strange statement to make, because the world is all messed up. The nation is sick. Trouble is in the land. Confusion all around. That's a strange statement. But I know, somehow, that only when it is dark enough, can you see the stars. And I see God working in this period of the twentieth century in a way that men, in some strange way, are responding—something is happening in our world. The masses of people are rising up. And wherever they are assembled today, whether they are in Johannesburg, South Africa: Nairobi, Kenya; Accra, Ghana; New York City; Atlanta, Georgia; Jackson, Mississippi; or Memphis, Tennessee—the cry is always the same—"We want to be free."

And another reason that I'm happy to live in this period is that we have been forced to a point where we're going to have to grapple with the problems that men have been trying to grapple with through history, but the demands didn't force them to do it. Survival demands that we grapple with them. Men, for years now, have been talking about war and peace. But now, no longer can they just talk about it. It is no longer a choice between violence and nonviolence in this world; it's nonviolence or nonexistence.

That is where we are today. And also in the human rights revolution, if something isn't done, and in a hurry, to bring the colored peoples of the world out of their long years of poverty, their long years of hurt and neglect, the whole world is doomed. Now, I'm just happy that God has allowed me to live in this period, to see what is unfolding. And I'm happy that he's allowed me to be in Memphis.

I can remember, I can remember when Negroes were just going around as Ralph has said, so often, scratching where they didn't itch, and laughing when they were not tickled. But that day is all over. We mean business now, and we are determined to gain our rightful place in God's world.

And that's all this whole thing is about. We aren't engaged in any negative protest and in any negative arguments with anybody. We are saying that we are determined to be men. We are determined to be people. We are saying that we are God's children. And that we don't have to live like we are forced to live.

Now, what does all of this mean in this great period of history? It means that we've got to stay together. We've got to stay together and maintain unity. You know, whenever Pharaoh wanted to prolong the period of slavery in Egypt, he had a favorite, favorite formula for doing it. What was that? He kept the slaves fighting among themselves. But whenever the slaves get together, something happens in Pharaoh's court, and he cannot hold the slaves in slavery. When the slaves get together, that's the beginning of getting out of slavery. Now let us maintain unity.

Secondly, let us keep the issues where they are. The issue is injustice. The issue is the refusal of Memphis to be fair and honest in its dealings with its public servants, who happen to be sanitation workers. Now, we've got to keep attention on that. That's always the problem with a little violence. You know what happened the other day, and the press dealt only with the window-breaking. I read the articles. They very seldom got around to mentioning the fact that one thousand, three hundred sanitation workers were on strike, and that Memphis is not being fair to them, and that Mayor Loeb[3] is in dire need of a doctor. They didn't get around to that.

Now we're going to march again, and we've got to march again, in order to put the issue where it is supposed to be. And force everybody to see that there are thirteen hundred of God's children here suffering, sometimes going hungry, going through dark and dreary nights wondering how this thing is going to come out. That's the issue. And we've got to say to the nation: we know it's coming out. For when people get caught up with that which is right and they are willing to sacrifice for it, there is no stopping point short of victory.

We aren't going to let any mace stop us. We are masters in our nonviolent movement in disarming police forces; they don't know what to do. I've seen them so often. I remember in Birmingham, Alabama, when we were in that majestic struggle there we would move out of the 16th Street Baptist Church day after day; by the hundreds we would move out. And Bull Connor[4] would tell them to send the dogs forth and they did come; but we just went before the dogs singing, "Ain't gonna let nobody turn me round." Bull Connor next would say, "Turn the fire hoses on." And as I said to you the other night, Bull Connor didn't know history. He knew a kind of physics that somehow didn't relate to the transphysics that we knew about. And that was the fact that there was a certain kind of fire that no water could put out. And we went before the fire hoses; we had known water. If we were Baptist or some other denomination, we had been immersed. If we were Methodist, and some others, we had been sprinkled, but we knew water.

That couldn't stop us. And we just went on before the dogs and we would look at them; and we'd go on before the water hoses and we would look at it, and we'd just go on singing "Over my head I see freedom in the air." And then we would be thrown in the paddy wagons, and sometimes we were stacked in there like sardines in a can. And they would throw us in, and old Bull would say, "Take them off," and they did; and we would just go in the paddy wagon singing, "We Shall Overcome." And every now and then we'd get in the jail, and we'd see the jailers looking through the windows being moved by our prayers, and being moved by our words and our songs. And there was a power there which Bull Connor couldn't adjust to: and so we ended up transforming Bull into a steer, and we won our struggle in Birmingham.

Now we've got to go on in Memphis just like that. I call upon you to be with us Monday. Now about injunctions: We have an injunction and we're going into court tomorrow morning to fight this illegal, unconstitutional injunction. All we say to America is, "Be true to what you said on paper." If

3. Henry Loeb, mayor of Memphis (1960–63, 1968–71).
4. Eugene "Bull" Connor, Birmingham's commis-

sioner of public safety, who repeatedly tangled with civil rights workers during demonstrations and marches.

I lived in China or even Russia, or any totalitarian country, maybe I could understand the denial of certain basic First Amendment privileges, because they hadn't committed themselves to that over there. But somewhere I read of the freedom of assembly. Somewhere I read of the freedom of speech. Somewhere I read of the freedom of the press. Somewhere I read that the greatness of America is the right to protest for right. And so just as I say, we aren't going to let any injunction turn us around. We are going on. We need all of you. And you know what's beautiful to me, is to see all of these ministers of the Gospel. It's a marvelous picture. Who is it that is supposed to articulate the longings and aspirations of the people more than the preacher? Somehow the preacher must be an Amos, and say, "Let justice roll down like waters and righteousness like a mighty stream." Somehow, the preacher must say with Jesus, "The spirit of the Lord is upon me, because he hath anointed me to deal with the problems of the poor."

And I want to commend the preachers, under the leadership of these noble men: James Lawson, one who has been in this struggle for many years; he's been to jail for struggling, but he's still going on, fighting for the rights of his people. Rev. Ralph Jackson, Billy Kiles; I could just go right on down the list, but time will not permit. But I want to thank them all. And I want you to thank them, because so often, preachers aren't concerned about anything but themselves. And I'm always happy to see a relevant ministry.

It's alright to talk about "long white robes over yonder," in all of its symbolism. But ultimately people want some suits and dresses and shoes to wear down here. It's alright to talk about "streets flowing with milk and honey," but God has commanded us to be concerned about the slums down here, and his children who can't eat three square meals a day. It's alright to talk about the new Jerusalem, but one day, God's preacher must talk about the New York, the new Atlanta, the new Philadelphia, the new Los Angeles, the new Memphis, Tennessee. This is what we have to do.

Now the other thing we'll have to do is this: Always anchor our external direct action with the power of economic withdrawal. Now, we are poor people, individually, we are poor when you compare us with white society in America. We are poor. Never stop and forget that collectively, that means all of us together, collectively we are richer than all the nations in the world, with the exception of nine. Did you ever think about that? After you leave the United States, Soviet Russia, Great Britain, West Germany, France, and I could name the others, the Negro collectively is richer than most nations of the world. We have an annual income of more than thirty billion dollars a year, which is more than all of the exports of the United States, and more than the national budget of Canada. Did you know that? That's power right there, if we know how to pool it.

We don't have to argue with anybody. We don't have to curse and go around acting bad with our words. We don't need any bricks and bottles, we don't need any Molotov cocktails, we just need to go around to these stores, and to these massive industries in our country, and say, "God sent us by here, to say to you that you're not treating his children right. And we've come by here to ask you to make the first item on your agenda—fair treatment, where God's children are concerned. Now, if you are not prepared to do that, we do have an agenda that we must follow. And our agenda calls for withdrawing economic support from you."

And so, as a result of this, we are asking you tonight, to go out and tell your neighbors not to buy Coca-Cola in Memphis. Go by and tell them not

to buy Sealtest milk. Tell them not to buy—what is the other bread?—
Wonder Bread. And what is the other bread company, Jesse? Tell them not
to buy Hart's bread. As Jesse Jackson has said, up to now, only the garbage
men have been feeling pain; now we must kind of redistribute the pain. We
are choosing these companies because they haven't been fair in their hiring
policies; and we are choosing them because they can begin the process of
saying, they are going to support the needs and the rights of these men who
are on strike. And then they can move on downtown and tell Mayor Loeb to
do what is right.

But not only that, we've got to strengthen black institutions. I call upon
you to take your money out of the banks downtown and deposit your money
in Tri-State Bank—we want a "bank-in" movement in Memphis. So go by the
savings and loan association. I'm not asking you something that we don't
do ourselves at SCLC. Judge Hooks and others will tell you that we have
an account here in the savings and loan association from the Southern
Christian Leadership Conference. We're just telling you to follow what
we're doing. Put your money there. You have six or seven black insurance
companies in Memphis. Take out your insurance there. We want to have an
"insurance-in."

Now these are some practical things we can do. We begin the process
of building a greater economic base. And at the same time, we are putting
pressure where it really hurts. I ask you to follow through here.

Now, let me say as I move to my conclusion that we've got to give ourselves to this struggle until the end. Nothing would be more tragic than to
stop at this point, in Memphis. We've got to see it through. And when we
have our march, you need to be there. Be concerned about your brother.
You may not be on strike. But either we go up together, or we go down
together.

Let us develop a kind of dangerous unselfishness. One day a man came
to Jesus; and he wanted to raise some questions about some vital matters in
life. At points, he wanted to trick Jesus, and show him that he knew a little
more than Jesus knew and through this, throw him off base. Now that
question could have easily ended up in a philosophical and theological
debate. But Jesus immediately pulled that question from mid-air, and
placed it on a dangerous curve between Jerusalem and Jericho. And he
talked about a certain man, who fell among thieves. You remember that a
Levite and a priest passed by on the other side. They didn't stop to help
him. And finally a man of another race came by. He got down from his
beast, decided not to be compassionate by proxy. But with him, administered first aid, and helped the man in need. Jesus ended up saying, this
was the good man, this was the great man, because he had the capacity to
project the "I" into the "thou," and to be concerned about his brother. Now
you know, we use our imagination a great deal to try to determine why the
priest and the Levite didn't stop. At times we say they were busy going to a
church meeting—an ecclesiastical gathering—and they had to get on
down to Jerusalem so they wouldn't be late for their meeting. At other
times we would speculate that there was a religious law that "One who was
engaged in religious ceremonials was not to touch a human body twenty-
four hours before the ceremony." And every now and then we begin to
wonder whether maybe they were not going down to Jerusalem, or down to
Jericho, rather to organize a "Jericho Road Improvement Association."
That's a possibility. Maybe they felt that it was better to deal with the prob-

lem from the causal root, rather than to get bogged down with an individual effort.

But I'm going to tell you what my imagination tells me. It's possible that these men were afraid. You see, the Jericho road is a dangerous road. I remember when Mrs. King and I were first in Jerusalem. We rented a car and drove from Jerusalem down to Jericho. And as soon as we got on that road, I said to my wife, "I can see why Jesus used this as a setting for his parable." It's a winding, meandering road. It's really conducive for ambushing. You start out in Jerusalem, which is about 1200 miles, or rather 1200 feet above sea level. And by the time you get down to Jericho, fifteen or twenty minutes later, you're about 2200 feet below sea level. That's a dangerous road. In the days of Jesus it came to be known as the "Bloody Pass." And you know, it's possible that the priest and the Levite looked over that man on the ground and wondered if the robbers were still around. Or it's possible that they felt that the man on the ground was merely faking. And he was acting like he had been robbed and hurt, in order to seize them over there, lure them there for quick and easy seizure. And so the first question that the Levite asked was, "If I stop to help this man, what will happen to me?" But then the Good Samaritan came by. And he reversed the question: "If I do not stop to help this man, what will happen to him?"

That's the question before you tonight. Not, "If I stop to help the sanitation workers, what will happen to all of the hours that I usually spend in my office every day and every week as a pastor?" The question is not, "If I stop to help this man in need, what will happen to me?" "If I do not stop to help the sanitation workers, what will happen to them?" That's the question.

Let us rise up tonight with a greater readiness. Let us stand with a greater determination. And let us move on in these powerful days, these days of challenge to make America what it ought to be. We have an opportunity to make America a better nation. And I want to thank God, once more, for allowing me to be here with you.

You know, several years ago, I was in New York City autographing the first book that I had written. And while sitting there autographing books, a demented black woman came up. The only question I heard from her was, "Are you Martin Luther King?"

And I was looking down writing, and I said yes. And the next minute I felt something beating on my chest. Before I knew it I had been stabbed by this demented woman. I was rushed to Harlem Hospital. It was a dark Saturday afternoon. And that blade had gone through, and the X-rays revealed that the tip of the blade was on the edge of my aorta, the main artery. And once that's punctured, you drown in your own blood—that's the end of you.

It came out in the *New York Times* the next morning, that if I had sneezed, I would have died. Well, about four days later, they allowed me, after the operation, after my chest had been opened, and the blade had been taken out, to move around in the wheel chair in the hospital. They allowed me to read some of the mail that came in, and from all over the states, and the world, kind letters came in. I read a few, but one of them I will never forget. I had received one from the President and the Vice-President. I've forgotten what those telegrams said. I'd received a visit and a letter from the Governor of New York, but I've forgotten what the letter said. But there was another letter that came from a little girl, a young girl who was a student at the White Plains High School. And I looked at that letter, and I'll never forget it. It said simply, "Dear Dr. King: I am a ninth-grade student at the White Plains High School." She said, "While it should not matter, I would like to mention that I am a white girl. I read in the paper of your misfortune, and of your suffering. And I read that if you had sneezed, you would have died. And I'm simply writing you to say that I'm so happy that you didn't sneeze."

And I want to say tonight, I want to say that I am happy that I didn't sneeze. Because if I had sneezed, I wouldn't have been around here in 1960, when students all over the South started sitting-in at lunch counters. And I knew that as they were sitting in, they were really standing up for the best in the American dream. And taking the whole nation back to those great walls of democracy which were dug deep by the Founding Fathers in the Declaration of Independence and the Constitution. If I had sneezed, I wouldn't have been around in 1962, when Negroes in Albany, Georgia, decided to straighten their backs up. And whenever men and women straighten their backs up, they are going somewhere, because a man can't ride your back unless it is bent. If I had sneezed, I wouldn't have been here in 1963, when the black people of Birmingham, Alabama, aroused the con-science of this nation, and brought into being the Civil Rights Bill. If I had sneezed, I wouldn't have had a chance later that year, in August, to try to tell America about a dream that I had had. If I had sneezed, I wouldn't have been down in Selma, Alabama, to see the great movement there. If I had sneezed, I wouldn't have been in Memphis to see a community rally around those brothers and sisters who are suffering. I'm so happy that I didn't sneeze.

And they were telling me, now it doesn't matter now. It really doesn't matter what happens now. I left Atlanta this morning, and as we got started on the plane, there were six of us, the pilot said over the public address sys-tem, "We are sorry for the delay, but we have Dr. Martin Luther King on the plane. And to be sure that all of the bags were checked, and to be sure that nothing would be wrong with the plane, we had to check out every-thing carefully. And we've had the plane protected and guarded all night."

And then I got into Memphis. And some began to say the threats, or talk about the threats that were out. What would happen to me from some of our sick white brothers?

Well, I don't know what will happen now. We've got some difficult days ahead. But it doesn't matter with me now. Because I've been to the moun-taintop. And I don't mind. Like anybody, I would like to live a long life. Longevity has its place. But I'm not concerned about that now. I just want to do God's will. And He's allowed me to go up to the mountain. And I've looked over. And I've seen the promised land. I may not get there with you. But I want you to know tonight, that we, as a people, will get to the prom-ised land. And I'm happy, tonight. I'm not worried about anything. I'm not fearing any man. Mine eyes have seen the glory of the coming of the Lord.

MALCOLM X

The Ballot or the Bullet[1]•

Brothers and sisters and friends, and I see some enemies.

In fact I think we'd be fooling ourselves if we had an audience this large and didn't realize that there were some enemies present.

This afternoon, we want to talk about *The Ballot or the Bullet. The Ballot or the Bullet* explains itself. But before we get into it, since this is the year of the ballot or the bullet, I would like to clarify some things that refer to me, personally, concerning my own personal position. I'm still a Muslim, that is my religion is still Islam.

My religion is still Islam. I still credit Mr. Muhammad for what I know and what I am. He's the one who opened my eyes. At present I am the minister of the newly founded Muslim Mosque Incorporated, which has its offices in the Theresa Hotel, right in that heart of Harlem—that's the black belt in New York City. And when we realize that Adam Clayton Powell[2] is a Christian minister, he heads the Abyssinian Baptist Church, but at the same time, he's more famous for his political struggling. And Dr. King[3] is a Christian minister from Atlanta, Georgia—or in Atlanta, Georgia—but he's become more famous for being involved in the Civil Rights struggle. The same as they are Christian ministers, I'm a Muslim minister. And I don't believe in fighting today in any one front, but on all fronts.

In fact I'm a black nationalist freedom fighter.

Islam is my religion, but I believe my religion is my personal business. It governs my personal life and my personal morals. And my religious philosophy is personal between me and the God in whom I believe—just as the religious philosophy of these others is between them and the God in whom they believe. And this is best this way. Were we to come out here discussing religion, we'd have too many differences from the out-start, and we could never get together. So today, though Islam is my religious philosophy, my political, economic, and social philosophy is black nationalism. As I say, if we bring up religion, we'll have differences, we'll have arguments, we'll never be able to get together. But if we keep our religion at home, keep our religion in the closet, keep our religion between ourselves and our God, but when we come out here, we have a fight that is common to all of us against an enemy who is common to all of us.

The political philosophy of black nationalism only means that the black man should control the politics and the politicians in his own community. The time when white people can come in our community, and get us to vote for them so that they can be our political leaders and tell us what to do and what not to do is long gone. Those days are gone. By the same token, the

1. After his break with Black Muslim leader Elijah Muhammad in 1964, Malcolm X (1925–1965) spoke with more forthrightness about politics in the United States. That year, he delivered versions of this speech many times, in New York, Cleveland, and Detroit. He gave this particular version in Detroit on April 14, 1964, at a rally sponsored by the Group on Advanced Leadership (GOAL).
2. Congressional representative from New York (1945–70).
3. Martin Luther King Jr.

time when that same white man, knowing that your eyes are too far open, can send another Negro into the community and get you and me to support him, so he can use him to lead us astray, those days are long gone, too.

The political philosophy of black nationalism only means that if you and I are going to live in a black community—and that's where we're going to live, 'cause soon as you move out of the black community into their community it's mixed for a period of time, but they're gone and you're right there by yourself again.

We must, we must understand the politics of our community. And we must know what politics is supposed to produce. We must know what part politics play in our lives. And until we become politically mature, we will always be misled, led astray, or deceived, or maneuvered into supporting someone politically who doesn't have the good of our community at heart.

So the political philosophy of black nationalism only means that we will have to carry on a program, a political program, of re-education, to open our people's eyes, make us become more politically conscious, politically mature. And then whenever we get ready to cast our ballot, that ballot will be cast for a man of the community who has the good of the community at heart.

The economic philosophy of black nationalism only means that we should own and operate and control the economy of our community. You can't open up a black store in a white community; the white man won't even patronize you. And he's not wrong, he's got sense enough to look out for himself. It's you, it's you who don't have sense enough to look out for yourself.

The white man is too intelligent to let someone else come and gain control of the economy of his community. But you will let anybody come in and control the economy of your community—control the housing, control the education, control the jobs, control the businesses—under the pretext that you want to integrate. Naw, you're out of your mind.

The economic philosophy of black nationalism only means that we have to become involved in a program of re-education, to educate our people into the importance of knowing that when you spend your dollar out of the community in which you live, the community in which you spend your money becomes richer and richer. The community out of which you take your money becomes poorer and poorer. And because these Negroes who have been misled and misguided are breaking their necks to take their money and spend it with the man, the man is becoming richer and richer and you're becoming poorer and poorer. And then what happens? The community in which you live becomes a slum. It becomes a ghetto. The conditions become run down. And then you have the audacity to complain about poor housing in a run-down community. Why, you run it down yourself, when you take your dollar out.

And you and I are in a double trap because, not only do we lose by taking our money someplace else and spending it, when we try and spend it in *our own* community, we're trapped because we haven't had sense enough to set up stores and control the businesses of our community. The man who's controlling the stores in our community is a man who doesn't look like we do. He's a man who doesn't even live in the community. So you and I, even when we try and spend our money in the block where we live, or the area where we live, we're spending it with a man who when the sun goes down takes that basket full of money in another part of the town.

So we're trapped. Trapped. Double trapped. Triple trapped. Any way we go, we find that we're trapped. And any kind of solution that someone comes

up with is just another trap. But the economic philosophy of black nationalism shows our people the importance of setting up these little stores, and
developing them and expanding them into larger operations. Woolworth
didn't start out big like they are today. They started out with *a* dime store
and expanded and expanded and then expanded until today, they're all over
the country and all over the world and they're getting some of everybody's
money. Now, this is what you and I—General Motors, the same way, didn't
start out like it is. It started out like a little rat-race type operation, and it
expanded and it expanded until today it is where it is right now. And you
and I have to make a start. And the best place to start is right in the community where we live.

So our people not only have to be re-educated to the importance of supporting black business, but the black man himself has to be made aware of
the importance of going into business. And once you and I go into business,
we own and operate *at least* the businesses in our community, what we will
be doing is developing a situation wherein we will actually be able to create
employment for the people in the community. And once you can create some
employment in the community where you live, it will eliminate the necessity
of you and me having to act ignorantly and disgracefully, boycotting and
picketing some cracker someplace else, trying to beg him for a job.

Anytime you have to rely upon your enemy for a job, you're in bad shape.

He is your enemy. You wouldn't be in this country if some enemy hadn't
kidnapped you and brought you here.

On the other hand, some of you think you came here on the *Mayflower.*

So, as you can see, brothers and sisters, today, this afternoon, it's not our
intention to discuss religion. We're going to forget religion. If we bring up
religion, we'll be in an argument. And the best way to keep away from arguments and differences, as I said earlier . . . put your religion at home, in
the closet. Keep it between you and your God. Because if it hasn't done
anything more for you than it has, you need to forget it anyway.

Whether you are a Christian or a Muslim or a Nationalist, we all have
the same problem. They don't hang you because you're a Baptist, they hang
you 'cause you're black. They don't attack me because I'm a Muslim, they
attack me 'cause I'm black. They attack all of us for the same reason. All of
us catch hell from the same enemy. We're all in the same bag. In the same
boat. We suffer political oppression. Economic exploitation. And social
degradation. All of 'em from the same enemy. The government has failed
us. You can't deny that. Anytime you're living in the twentieth century, and
you're walking around here singing "We Shall Overcome," the government
has failed us.

This is part of what's wrong with you. You do too much singing.

Today, it's time to stop singing and start swinging.

You can't sing up on freedom. But you can *swing* up on some freedom.

Cassius Clay[4] can sing. But singing didn't help him to become the heavyweight champion of the world. *Swinging* helped him become the heavyweight
champion of the world.

So this government has failed us. The government itself has failed us. And
the white liberals, who have been posing as our friends, have failed us.
And once we see that all these other sources to which we've turned have

4. Heavyweight boxer who, in 1964, took the name Muhammad Ali.

failed, we stop turning to them and turn to ourselves. We need a self-help program. A do-it-yourself philosophy. A do-it-right-now philosophy. A it's-already-too-late philosophy. This is what you and I need to get with. And the only way we're going to solve our problem is with a self-help program. Before we can get a self-help program started, we have to have a self-help philosophy. Black nationalism is a self-help philosophy. What's so good about it, you can stay right in the church where you are and still take black nationalism as your philosophy. You can stay in any kind of civic organization that you belong to and still take black nationalism as your philosophy. You can be an atheist and still take black nationalism as your philosophy. This is a philosophy that eliminates the necessity for division and argument. Because if you are black, you should be thinking black. And if you're a black, and you're not thinking black at this late date, why, I'm sorry for you.

Once you change your philosophy, you change your thought pattern. Once you change your thought pattern, you change your attitude. Once you change your attitude, it changes your behavior pattern. And then you go on into some action. As long as you got a sit-down philosophy, you'll have a sit-down thought pattern. And as long as you think that old sit-down thought, you'll be in some kind of sit-down action. They'll have you sitting-in everywhere.

It's not so good to refer to what you're going to do as a sit-in. Then right there it castrates you. Right there it brings you down. What goes with it? Think of the image of someone sitting. An old woman can sit. An old man can sit. A chump can sit. A coward can sit. Anything can sit. For you and I have been *sitting* long enough and it's time today for you and I to be doing some *standing*. And some *fighting* to back that up.

When we look at other parts of this earth in which we live, we find that black, brown, red and yellow people in Africa and Asia are getting their independence. They're not getting it by singing "We Shall Overcome." No, they're getting it through *nationalism*. It is nationalism that brought about the independence of the people in Asia. Every nation in Asia gained its independence through the philosophy of nationalism. Every nation on the African continent that has gotten its independence brought it about through the philosophy of nationalism. And it will take *black* nationalism to bring about the freedom of twenty-two million Afro-Americans here in this country where we have suffered *colonialism* for the past four hundred years.

America is just as much a colonial power as England ever was. America is just as much a colonial power as France ever was. In fact, America is more so a colonial power than they. Because she's a hypocritical colonial power behind it. What do you call second class citizenship? Why, that's colonization. Second-class citizenship is nothing but twentieth-century slavery. How are you going to tell me you're a second-class citizen? They don't have second class citizenship in any other government on this earth. They just have slaves and people who are free. Well, this country is a hypocrite. They try and make you think they set you free by calling you a second class citizen. Naw, you're nothing but a twentieth-century slave.

Just as it took nationalism to remove colonialism from Asia and Africa, it'll take black nationalism today to remove colonialism from the backs and the minds of twenty-two million Afro-Americans here in this country. Looks like it might be the year of the ballot or the bullet.

Why does it look like it might be the year of the ballot or the bullet? Because Negroes have listened to the trickery and the lies and the false promises of the white man now for too long. And they're fed up. They've become disenchanted. They've become disillusioned. They've become dissatisfied. And all of this has built up frustrations in the black community that makes the black community throughout America today more explosive than all of the atomic bombs the Russians can ever invent. Whenever you got a racial powder keg sitting in your lap, you're in more trouble than if you had an atomic power keg sitting in your lap. When a racial powder keg goes off, it doesn't care who it knocks out the way. Understand this: it's dangerous. Because what can the white man use, now, to fool us? After he put down that march on Washington, and you see all through that now. He tricked you, had you marching down to Washington. Yes, had you marching back and forth between the feet of a dead man named Lincoln and another dead man named George Washington, singing "We Shall Overcome."

He made a chump out of you. He made a fool out of you. He made you think you were going somewhere and you end up going nowhere but between Lincoln and Washington.

So today our people are disillusioned. They've become disenchanted. They've become dissatisfied. And in their frustrations they want action. You can see this young black man, this new generation, asking for the ballot or the bullet. That old Uncle Tom action is outdated. The young generation don't want to hear anything about "The odds are against us." What do we care about odds?

When this country here was first being founded, there were thirteen colonies. The whites were colonized. They were fed up with this taxation without representation. So some of them stood up and said "liberty or death." Well, I went to a white school over here in Mason, Michigan. The white man made the mistake of letting me read his history books. He made the mistake of teaching me that Patrick Henry[5] was a patriot. And George Washington—wasn't nothing non-violent about old Pat. Or George Washington. "Liberty or death" was what brought about the freedom of whites in this country from the English.

They didn't care about the odds. Why, they faced the wrath of the entire British Empire. And in those days, they used to say that the British Empire was so vast and so powerful that the sun would never set on it. This is how big it was. Yet these thirteen little scrawny states, tired of taxation without representation, tired of being exploited and oppressed and degraded, told that big British Empire, "liberty or death." And here you have twenty-two million Afro-Americans, black people today, catching more hell than Patrick Henry ever saw.

And I'm here to tell you, in case you don't know it, that you got a new, you got a new generation of black people in this country who don't care anything whatsoever about odds. They don't want to hear you old Uncle Tom handkerchief-heads talking about the odds. No.

This is a new generation. If they're going to draft these young black men and send them over to Korea or South Vietnam to face eight hundred million Chinese . . . if you're not afraid of those odds, you shouldn't be afraid of these odds.

Why does this loom to be such an explosive *political* year? Because this is the year of politics. This is the year when all of the white politicians are

---

5. American Revolutionary leader and orator (1736–1799), famous for his pronouncement "Give me liberty or give me death."

going to come into the Negro community. You've never seen them until election time. You can't find them until election time. They're going to come in with false promises. And as they make these false promises, they're going to feed our frustrations. And this will only serve to make matters worse. I'm no politician. I'm not even a student of politics. I'm not a Republican nor a Democrat, nor an American. And got sense enough to know it.

I'm one of the twenty-two million black *victims* of the Democrats. One of the twenty-two million black *victims* of the Republicans. And one of the twenty-two million black *victims* of Americanism.

And when I speak, I don't speak as a Democrat, or a Republican, nor an American. I speak as a *victim* of America's so-called democracy. You and I have never seen democracy; all we've seen is hypocrisy. When we open our eyes today and look around America, we see America not through the eyes of someone who has enjoyed the fruits of Americanism, we see America through the eyes of someone who has been the victim of Americanism. We don't see any American dream. We've experienced only the American nightmare.

We haven't benefited from America's democracy. We've only suffered from America's hypocrisy. And the generation that is coming up now can see it, and are not afraid to say it. If you go to jail, so what? If you're black, you were born in jail. In the North as well as the South. Stop talking about the South. Long as you're south of the Canadian border, you're South.

Don't call Governor Wallace a Dixie governor; *Romney*[6] is a Dixie governor.

Twenty-two million black victims of Americanism are waking up. And they're gaining a new political consciousness, becoming politically mature. And as they develop this political maturity, they are able to see the recent trends in these political elections. They see that the whites are so evenly divided that every time they vote, the race is so close, they have to go back and count the votes all over again. Which means that any block, any minority that has a block of votes that stick together is in a strategic position. Either way you go, that's who gets it. You're in a position to determine who'll go to the White House and who'll stay in the dog house.

You're the one who has that power. You can keep Johnson[7] in Washington, D.C. or you can send him back to his Texas cotton patch.

You're the one who sent Kennedy to Washington. You're the one who put the present Democratic administration in Washington, D.C. The whites were evenly divided. It was the fact that you threw 80 percent of your votes behind the Democrats that put the Democrats in the White House. When you see this, you can see that the Negro vote is the key factor. And despite the fact that you are in a position to be the determining factor, what do you get out of it? The Democrats have been in Washington, D.C., only because of the Negro vote. They've been down there four years. And there, all other legislation they wanted to bring up, they've brought it up and gotten it out of the way, and now they bring up you. And *now* they bring up you. You put them first and they put you last . . .'cause you're a chump . . . a political chump.

In Washington, D.C., in the House of Representatives, there are 257 who are Democrats. Only 177 are Republican. In the Senate there are 67 Demo-

6. George Romney, governor of Michigan (1963–69). George Wallace, segregationist gov- ernor of Alabama (1963–66, 1971–79).
7. Lyndon B. Johnson, U.S. president (1963–69).

crats. Only 33 are Republicans. The party that *you* backed controls two-thirds of the House of Representatives and the Senate. And *still* they can't keep their promise to you. 'Cause you're a chump.

Anytime you throw your weight behind a political party that controls two-thirds of the government, and that party can't keep the promise that it made to you during election time, and you're dumb enough to walk around continuing to identify yourself with that party, you're not only a chump but you're a traitor to your race.

And what kind of alibi do they come up with? They try and pass the buck to the Dixiecrats. Now, back during the days when you were blind, deaf, and dumb, ignorant, politically immature, naturally you went along with that. But today, as your eyes come open, and you develop political maturity, you're able to see and think for yourself. And you can see that a Dixiecrat is nothing but a Democrat . . . in disguise.

You look at the structure of the government that controls this country. It's controlled by sixteen senatorial committees and twenty congressional committees. Of the sixteen senatorial committees that run the government, ten of them are in the hands of southern segregationists. Of the twenty congressional committees that run the government, twelve of them are in the hands of southern segregationists. And they going to tell you and me that the South lost the war.

You today are in the hands of a government of segregationists: Racists, white supremacists . . . who belong to the Democratic Party but disguise themselves as Dixiecrats. A Dixiecrat is nothing but a Democrat. Whoever runs the Democrats is also the follower of the Dixiecrats. And the follower of all of them is sitting in the White House.

I say and I say it again: You got a president who's nothing but a southern segregationist. From the state of Texas. They'll lynch you in Texas as quick as they'll lynch you in Mississippi. Only, in Texas, they lynch you with a Texas accent; in Mississippi, they lynch you with a Mississippi accent.

And the first thing the cracker does when he comes in power, he takes all the Negro leaders and invites them for coffee. To show that he's all right. And those Uncle Toms can't pass up the coffee.

They come away from the coffee table, telling you and me that this man is all right. 'Cause he's from the South. And since he's from the South, he can deal with the South. Look at the logic that they're using. What about Eastland?[8] He's from the South. Make him the president. If Johnson is a good man 'cause he's from Texas, and being from Texas will enable him to deal with the South, Eastland can deal with the South better than Johnson.

Naw, I say, you've been misled. You've been had. You been took.

I was in Washington a couple weeks ago—while the senators were filibustering. And I noticed at the back of the Senate a huge map. And on this map, it showed the distribution of Negroes in America. And surprisingly, the same senators that were involved in the filibuster were from the states where there were the most Negroes. Why were they filibustering the civil rights legislation? Because the civil rights legislation is supposed to guarantee voting rights to Negroes in those states. And those senators from those states know that if the Negroes in those states can vote, those senators are down the drain.

8. James Eastland, U.S. senator from Mississippi (1943–78).

The representatives of those states go down the drain. And in the Constitution of this country, it has a stipulation wherein whenever the rights, the voting rights of people in a certain district are violated, then the representative who's from a particular district, according to the Constitution is supposed to be expelled from the Congress. Now, if this particular aspect of the Constitution was enforced, why you wouldn't have a cracker in Washington, D.C.

But what would happen? When you expel the Dixiecrat, you're expelling the Democrat. When you destroy the power of the Dixiecrat, you're destroying the power of the Democratic Party. So how in the world can the Democratic Party in the South actually side with you, in sincerity, when all of this power is based in the South? These northern Democrats are in cahoots with the southern Democrats.

They're playing a giant con game. A political con game. You know how it goes. Whenever one of them comes to you, and make believe he's for you. And he's in cahoots with the other one that's not for you. Why? Because neither one of them is for you. But they got to make you go with one of them or the other. So this is a con game. And this is what they been doing with you and me all these years. First thing Johnson got off the plane, when he became president, he asked, "Where's Dicky?" You know who "Dicky" is? Dicky is old southern cracker Richard Russell.[9] Look a-here! *Yes!* Lyndon B. Johnson's best friend is the one who is the head, who's heading the forces that are filibustering civil rights legislation. You tell me how in the hell is he going to be Johnson's best friend?

How can Johnson be his friend and your friend too? Naw, that man is too tricky. Especially if his friend is still old Dicky.

Whenever the Negroes keep the Democrats in power, they're keeping the Dixiecrats in power. Is this true? A vote for a Democrat is nothing but a vote for a Dixiecrat. I know you don't like me saying that. But I'm not the kind of person who'll come here to say what you like. I'm going to tell you the truth whether you like it or not.

Up here in the North, you have the same thing. The Democratic Party . . . they don't do it that way. They got a thing that they call gerrymandering. They maneuver you out of power. Even though you can vote, they fix it so you're voting for nobody.

They got you going and coming. In the South, they're outright political wolves. In the North they're political foxes. A fox and a wolf are both canine—both belong to the dog family. Now, you take your choice. You going to choose a northern dog or a southern dog? Because either dog you choose, I guarantee you, you'll still be in the doghouse.

This is why I say it's the ballot or the bullet. It's liberty or it's death. It's freedom for everybody or freedom for nobody.

America today finds herself in a unique situation. Historically, revolutions are bloody, oh yes they are. They haven't ever had a blood*less* revolution. Or a non-violent revolution. That don't happen even in Hollywood. You don't have a revolution in which you love your enemy. And you don't have a revolution in which you're begging the system of exploitation to integrate you into it. Revolutions overturn systems. Revolutions destroy systems. A revolution is bloody.

9. Governor of Georgia (1931–33), U.S. senator from Georgia (1932–71).

But America is in a unique position. She's the only country in history in a position actually to become involved in a bloodless revolution. The Russian revolution was bloody. The Chinese revolution was bloody. The French revolution was bloody. The Cuban revolution was bloody. And there was nothing more bloody than the American revolution. But today, this country can become involved in a revolution that won't take bloodshed. All she's got to do is give the black man in this country everything that's due him. Everything.

I hope that the white man can see this. 'Cause if you don't see it, you're finished. If you don't see it, you're going to become involved in some action in which you don't have a chance. And we don't care about your atomic bomb, it's useless. Because other countries have atomic bombs. When two or three different countries have atomic bombs, nobody can use it. So it means that the white man today is without a weapon. And if you want some action, you got to come on down to earth. And there's more black people on earth than there are white people on earth.

I only got a couple more minutes. The white man can never win another war on the ground. His days of war victory, his days of ground victory are over. Can I prove it? Yes. Take all the action that's going on on this earth, right now, that he's involved in. Tell me where he's winning. Nowhere. Why some rice farmers, some rice farmers, some rice eaters, ran him out of Korea. Yes, they ran him out of Korea. Rice eaters, with nothing but gym shoes and a rifle and a bowl of rice. Took him and his tanks and his napalm and all that other action he's supposed to have, and ran him 'cross the Yalu. Why? 'Cause the day that he can win on the ground is past. Up in French Indochina, those little peasants, rice growers, took on the might of the French army. And ran all the Frenchmen—you don't remember Dien Bien Phu???[1] Naw!!! The same thing happened in Algeria, in Africa. They didn't have anything but a rifle. The French had all these highly mechanized instruments of warfare. But they put some guerrilla action on 'em. And a white man can't fight a guerrilla war. Guerrilla action takes heart, takes nerve, and he doesn't have that.

He's brave when he's got tanks. He's brave when he's got planes. He's brave when he's got bombs. He's brave when he's got a whole lot of company along with him. But you take that little man from Africa and Asia, turn him loose in the woods with a blade, with a blade. That's all he needs, all he needs is a blade. And when the sun goes down, and it's dark, it's even-steven.

So it's the ballot or the bullet. Today our people can see that we're faced with a government conspiracy. This government has failed us. The senators who are filibustering concerning your and my rights—that's the government. Don't say it's southern senators. This is the *government*. This is the *government* filibuster. It's not a segregationist filibuster. It's the *government* filibuster. Any kind of activity that takes place on the floor of the Congress or the Senate, that's the government. Any kind of dilly-dallying, that's the government. Any kind of pussyfooting, that's the government. Any kind of act that's designed to delay or deprive you and me, right now, of getting full rights, that's the government that's responsible. And anytime you find the

1. The Vietnamese victory in the battle of Dien Bien Phu (1954) inspired the permanent withdrawal of the French from Indochina and the Geneva Accords of 1954.

government involved in a conspiracy, to violate the citizenship, or the civil rights of a people, then you are wasting your time going to that government expecting redress. Instead you have to take that government to the World Court and accuse it of genocide and all of the other crimes that it is guilty of today.

So those of us whose political and economic and social philosophy is black nationalism have become involved in the civil rights struggle, we have injected ourselves into the civil rights struggle, and we intend to expand it from the level of civil rights to the level of human rights. As long as you fight it on the level of civil rights, you're under Uncle Sam's jurisdiction. You're going to his court expecting him to correct the problem. He *created* the problem. He's the criminal. You don't take your case to the criminal. You take your criminal to court.

When the government of South Africa began to trample upon the human rights of the people of South Africa, they were taken to the U.N. When the government of Portugal began to trample upon the rights of our brothers and sisters in Angola, it was taken before the U.N. Why even the white man took the Hungarian question to the U.N. and just this week, Chief Justice Goldberg[2] was crying over three million Jews in Russia about their human rights, charging Russia with violating the U.N. charter, because of its mistreatment of the human rights of Jews in Russia. Now you tell me, how can the plight of everybody on this earth reach the halls of the United Nations, and you have twenty-two million Afro-Americans whose churches are being bombed? Whose little girls are being murdered. Whose leaders are being shot down in broad daylight. Now you tell me why the leaders of this struggle have never taken it before the United Nations.

So, our next move, is to take the entire civil rights struggle, problem, into the United Nations.

And let the world see that Uncle Sam is guilty of violating the human rights of twenty-two million Afro-Americans and still has the audacity or the nerve to stand up and to represent himself as the leader of the free world.

Not only is he a crook, he's a hypocrite. Here he is, standing up in front of other people, Uncle Sam, with the blood of your and my mothers and fathers on his hands. With the blood dripping down his jaws like a bloody-jawed wolf. And still got the nerve to point his finger at other countries. You can't even get civil rights legislation. And this man has got the nerve to stand up and talk about South Africa. Or talk about Nazi Germany. Or talk about Portugal. Naw, no more days like those.

So I say in my conclusion, the only way we're going to solve it, we got to unite, we got to work together in unity and harmony. And black nationalism is the key. How we going to overcome the tendency to be at each other's throats that always exists in our neighborhood? And the reason this tendency exists—the strategy of the white man has always been divide and conquer. He keeps us divided in order to conquer us. He tells you I'm for separation and you're for integration and keep us fighting with each other. No, I'm not for separation and you're not for integration. What you and I are for is freedom.

---

2. Arthur Joseph Goldberg, lawyer, associate Supreme Court justice (1962–65), U.S. representative to the United Nations (1965–68).

Only you think that integration will get you freedom, I think that separation will get me freedom. We both got the same objective. We just both got different ways of getting at it.

So, I studied this man Billy Graham,[3] who preaches white nationalism. That's what he preaches. I say, that's what he preaches. The whole church structure in this country is white nationalism. You go inside a white church, that's what they preaching, white nationalism. They got Jesus white, Mary white, God white, everybody white, that's white nationalism.

So, what he does, the way he circumvents the jealousy and envy that he ordinarily would incur among the heads of the church, whenever you go into an area where the church already is, you going to run into trouble. Because they got that thing, what you call it, syndicated, they got a syndicate, just like the racketeers have. I'm going to say what's on my mind, cause the church, the preachers have already proved to you that they got a syndicate.

And when you're out in the rackets, whenever you're getting in another man's territory, you know, they gang up on you. And that's the same way with you—you run into the same thing. So how Billy Graham gets around that, instead of going into somebody else's territory, like he going to start a new church, he doesn't try to start a church, he just goes in preaching Christ. And he says, everybody who believes in Him, you go wherever you find Him. So this helps all the churches, and so since it helps all the churches, they don't fight him. Well, we're going to do the same thing, only our gospel is black nationalism. His gospel is white nationalism, our gospel is black nationalism. And the gospel of black nationalism, as I told you, means you should control your own—the politics of your community, the economy of your community, and all of the society in which you live should be under your control. And once you feel that this philosophy will solve your problem, go join any church where that's preached. Don't join a church where white nationalism is preached. Now, you can go to a Negro church and be exposed to white nationalism. 'Cause when you walk in a Negro church and you see a white Jesus and a white Mary and some white angels, that Negro church is preaching white nationalism.

But when you go to a church and you see the pastor of that church with a philosophy and a program that's designed to bring black people together and elevate black people, join that church. Join that church. If you see where the NAACP is preaching and practicing that which is designed to make black nationalism materialize, join the NAACP. Join any kind of organization, civic, religious, fraternal, political, or otherwise, that's based on lifting the black man up and making him master of his own community.

It'll be the ballot or it'll be the bullet. It'll be liberty or it'll be death. And if you're not ready to pay that price, don't use the word freedom in your vocabulary.

One more thing: I was on the program in Illinois recently with Senator Paul Douglas[4] the so-called liberal, the so-called Democrat, the so-called white man. At which time he told me that our African brothers were not interested in us in Africa. He says the Africans are not interested in the American Negro. I knew he was lying. But, during the next two or three weeks, it's my intention and plan to make a tour of our African homeland.

---

3. American evangelist (b. 1918).   4. U.S. senator from Massachusetts (1948–66).

And I hope that when I come back I'll be able to come back and let you know how our African brothers and sisters feel toward us.

And I know before I go there, that they love us. We're one. We're the same. It's the same man that colonized them all these years that colonized you and me too, all these years. And all we have to do now is wake up and work in unity and harmony and the battle will be over.

I want to thank the Freedom Now Party in the gold; I want to thank Milton and Richard Henry for inviting me here this afternoon, and also a Reverend Cley. And I want them to know that anything that I can ever do at anytime to work with anybody in any kind of program that is sincerely designed to eliminate the political, the economic, and the social evils that confront all of our people in Detroit and elsewhere, all you've got to do is give me a telephone call, and I'll be on the next jet right on into the city.

Thank you.

BERT WILLIAMS

Elder Eatmore's Sermon on Generosity[1]•

I takes my text tonight from the book of 'Phesians: "The Lord loveth a cheerful giver."[2] Tonight my friends, you can omit the "cheerful." The truth is the light and here is the truth: Y'all is way back in my salary! And somethin' has got to be done here this evenin'. 'Cause if somethin' ain't done, your shepherd is gone. That's all. That-is-all!! I admit that times is tight. 'Cause when there used to be a ham coming here and a fowl or two from there from different members of this flock, I managed to make out fair to middlin'. They all come to heal weight, but you-all done learnt me that self-preservation is the first law of he who gets it! And the Lord helps them that helps theirself.

Everything's got so scientifical nowadays that they done commenced buildin' such things as smokehouses and henhouses out of pure concrete! And they's invented locks for 'em, the same as combinations on the First National Bank. True, true, that makes it harder for all of us. (It's pretty nigh ruint me.) And my friends, I needs, I needs. . . . T'ain't no use talkin' about what I needs, I needs everything! From a hat down and from an overcoat in.

T'ain't no use in getting restless, brother there now, now, now now now now, 'cause here is the program: We ain't gwine to pass no plate this evenin', y'all is comin' up one at a time. And drap your offerin's on this thing here whiles I's-a look down from the altar here with a eagle eye. We will start with the first row. Come, my lambs. Your shepherd calls unto you,

---

1. A parody of a sermon by Bert Williams; recorded in New York, June 1919 that underscores how, for some believers, humor can fortify religious conviction.
2. The line is actually from 2 Corinthians 9.7. "'Phesians": i.e., Ephesians.

saying: "Give unto me that I may eat of the Bread of Life, so that when That Great Day comes, you can meet me in Judgment and shake my hand with a clear conscience."

We shall build our mansions in the skies by the seeds we sows today. Common leader?

[*We shall build a mansion in the skies by the seeds we sow today.*]
First thing, what's the first thing? Yes. What will the harvest be? Ha, ha! Thank ye, yes, yes, thank you, thank you. How-do, Brother Jenkins? Yes, yes, thank you, eight chickens? Yes. All right Sister Jones, yes. Hmm? Some more? Yes, chickens, chickens are fine, yes, yes.

We shall reap our joys in the bye and bye by what we sows today.
[*We shall reap our joys in the bye and bye by what we sow today.*]
Yes yes, yes yes, yes yes. Bless you, my lambs. Ah, a friend in need is a friend indeed, tell the truth. And your shepherd is in need.
[*We shall build our mansions in the skies by the seeds we sow today.*]
Yes, yes, yes. Ah, oh my my. Ah, my my. Yes. Keep sowing those chickens! Yes, step up here. Yas!
[*We shall reap our joys in the bye and bye by what we sow today.*]

Now I'm gon' count it.

Realism, Naturalism, Modernism 1940–1960

Carving out the two decades between 1940 and 1960 from the historical trajectory of African American letters is, of course, the arbitrary and largely artificial work of literary historians. And yet it would be difficult to gainsay the general consensus that these two decades constitute an extraordinarily fertile moment in the development of African American writing, a period during which a galaxy of exceptional literary talents emerged. The roll call is impressive: James Baldwin, Gwendolyn Brooks, Ralph Ellison, Robert Hayden, Ann Petry, Melvin Tolson, Margaret Walker, Dorothy West, and, proverbially speaking, last but not least, Richard Wright. Conventional narratives of the period, have tended to focus on literary luminaries, most of whom published celebrated books—both critically acclaimed and commercially successful—but such narratives tend to flatten the landscape. For example, the rich and complex collection of writings that blacks contributed to literary and cultural magazines magazines seldom figures in familiar synopses of the period, and yet many black magazines, notably *The Crisis, Opportunity, The Negro Quarterly, Negro Digest,* and *Phylon,* gave a hearing and occasional modest financial incentives to black writers whose work, with few exceptions, was rarely featured in the more elite literary magazines. By the same token, standard literary histories tend to obscure those writers—Chester Himes and Frank Yerby, for instance—whose talents ran to popular instead of "high cultural" literary forms.

The Little Rock Nine, 1957. Nine African American students integrating Central High School in Little Rock, Arkansas, under the protection of Federalized Arkansas National Guardsmen.

After publishing two serious novels to respectable notice, Himes turned to writing detective stories, widely successful in France though less so in the United States. Similarly, Yerby aspired to write what many critics classed, individously, pulp or escapist fiction. Yerby preferred to categorize his more than thirty popular novels, including the best-selling *The Foxes of Harrow* (1946), as "costume novels," which appealed to readers needing an occasional escape from the "sprawling messiness" and "shapelessness of modern existence." Judging, however, from the texts that achieved canonical status during the years between 1940 and 1960, these were the times that called not for escape but for confrontation with the "sprawling mess" and "shapelessness" of modern existence: atomic explosions, fascism, social revolution, the crumbling of colonialism, the death throes of Jim Crow, and many other cataclysms in between. The writings emerging from this cauldron cannot be neatly contained within traditional categories of genre, mode, or subject matter.

The writers who produced their major works within the parameters of these two decades did much more than ply their trades at the novel, the short story, the poem or play; they were often engaged in bitter disagreements over the form and functions of African American expression, over the obligations of black writers to their reading publics, and even over how such publics were to be identified. Such were but the stateside brouhahas, for across the Atlantic, black expatriate writers, like so many writers and intellectuals throughout the African diaspora, were also confronting the sprawling mess and shapelessness, which included the grip of the cold war and U.S. imperialism, colonial racism, and European domination.

To group such a diverse array of literary and geopolitical concerns punctuating the mid-twentieth century under the three-pronged rubric—realism, naturalism, modernism—is to deploy yet another artifice of literary history, for certainly it is difficult to dispute the notion that all three categories are semantically unstable. Realism and naturalism are often considered modern if not modernist, and all three assume quite different profiles and inflections from writer to writer, region to region, and sometimes even from work to work in a given author's corpus. But if *realism* is taken to refer broadly to a faithful representation of material "reality"; *naturalism*, to a franker, harsher treatment of the power of the social environment cum jungle on individual psychology; and *modernism*, to a break with the familiar functions of language and conventions of form, then the works selected here would vaguely suit these loose descriptors. But all three categories are best regarded as conveniences, points of analytical departure, which call for fuller interrogation.

WAR, MIGRATION, DESEGREGATION, AND SOCIAL REVOLUTION

Literary historians are fond of subdividing and punctuating artistic periods with references to war, and although few writers of this period confronted it directly in their writing, the cataclysm of World War II comes to mark for some historians the outer boundary of this period. The second wave of the Great Migration was, in part, a response to the realities of war, for many of the African Americans who fled impoverished farms and hamlets of the Jim Crow South were headed for economic opportunity in the major war indus-

An African American family from Florida prepares to migrate north in 1940.

tries, which Franklin Roosevelt dubbed the Arsenal of Democracy. And those African Americans, who went abroad to fight, returned as they had in previous wars, only to come face to face with democracy's failures at home. Perhaps, then, among the most defining moments of these two decades are Truman's creation of the Commission on Civil Rights in 1947; the U.S. Supreme Court's May 1954 ruling on *Brown v. the Topeka Board of Education,* desegregating the public schools (at least nominally); and, ironically, in the Cradle of the Confederacy, the Montgomery, Alabama, Bus Boycott in December 1955, which birthed what came to be called the "nonviolent protest movement." Led by the young Martin Luther King Jr., the movement succeeded in hammering at, if not dismantling, the walls of the U.S. system of apartheid, the "separate but equal" laws and customs of the Jim Crow South.

Although conditions in the rural Jim Crow South of the pre–civil rights era were at the center of and much the catalyst for African American writing during the 1930s—the poetry of Sterling Brown's *Southern Road,* the early fiction of Richard Wright and Zora Neale Hurston—African American literary production from the 1940s to the 1960s is emphatically northern, urban, set mainly in the black American culture capitals: Chicago, Boston, and Harlem, which fueled black artistic production, high and low. In these cities, a black urban street culture, the product of roiling social tensions, transformed the so-called cultural (read white) mainstream. White youth copied the zoot suit vogue, along with many elements of bop, or hip talk. Termed by some the "new poetry of the proletariat," this language of hip introduced a distinctly black urban idiom into the American language, an argot of resistance to forms of racial discrimination. But even minus hipsterism, an urban sensibility pervades the literature that African Americans produced during this period, a literature steeped in the signs, sights, and sounds of the city.

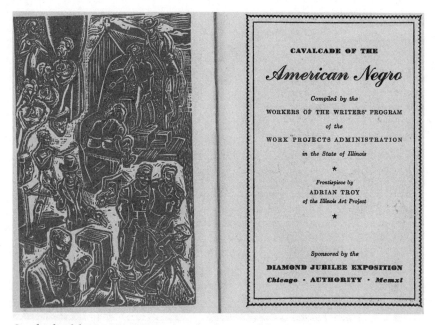

CAVALCADE OF THE

American Negro

Compiled by the
WORKERS OF THE WRITERS' PROGRAM
of the
WORK PROJECTS ADMINISTRATION
in the State of Illinois

★

Frontispiece by
ADRIAN TROY
of the Illinois Art Project

★

Sponsored by the
DIAMOND JUBILEE EXPOSITION
Chicago · AUTHORITY · Mcmxl

Cavalcade of the American Negro (1940) is the story of the Negro's progress over seventy-five years, compiled by the Illinois Writers' Project.

Setting the tone, of course, was Richard Wright's 1940 publishing sensation *Native Son*.

URBAN REALISM

At least in strictly literary terms, Wright's novel christened the 1940s decade. A Book-of-the-Month Club selection, *Native Son* made Wright the first African American writer to receive both critical acclaim and commercial success simultaneously. Close on the heels of Wright's success, other African American writers garnered recognition and prestige from a predominantly white literary world, which had been notoriously stingy in dispensing its awards and favors—even recognition at times—to black writers. Margaret Walker won the Yale Younger Poets Award for *For My People* in 1942; Gwendolyn Brooks, the Pulitzer Prize for *Annie Allen* in 1950; Ralph Ellison, the National Book Award for *Invisible Man* in 1952; and closing out this two-decades-long run was Lorraine Hansberry's stunning New York Drama Critics Circle Award for *A Raisin in the Sun* in 1959.

To many, Wright was mainly owed the credit for setting the stage for these successes, particularly for creating publishing opportunities, directly and indirectly, for many other black writers. He helped James Baldwin win a Rosenwald fellowship; read and encouraged the poetry of Margaret Walker; favorably reviewed Chester Himes's first novel, *If He Hollers Let Him Go*; and helped Gwendolyn Brooks place her first volume of poetry, *A Street in Bronzeville*. But some critics were compelled to make more exaggerated claims for Wright's influence, including Irving Howe, who ventured: "The day *Native Son* appeared, American culture was changed forever. . . . It made impossible a repetition of the old lies. . . . [Wright] brought out into the open, as no one ever had before, the hatred, fear and violence that have crippled and may yet destroy our culture."

Standard histories and chronologies of African American literature have tacitly assented to the spirit if not the letter of Howe's judgment that Richard Wright's *Native Son* greatly transformed American culture and African American letters of the post–World War II era. According to John Henrik Clarke, for example, "After the emergence of Richard Wright, the period of indulgence for Negro writers was over. . . . The era of the patronized and pampered black writer had at last come to an end." Presumably, the era to which Clarke referred was the Harlem Renaissance.

This 1920s and 1930s efflorescence of activity in all branches of the arts, the Harlem Renaissance, has sometimes been harshly judged in retrospectives on the period, including Wright's own famous statement in *Blueprint for Negro Writing* (1937). Indeed Clark may well have taken his wording directly from Wright's famous opening statement: "Generally speaking, Negro writing in the past has been confined to humble novels, poems, and plays, prim and decorous ambassadors who went a-begging to white America. They entered the court of American public opinion dressed in the knee pants of servility, curtsying to show that the Negro was not inferior." Alain Locke, the self-appointed dean of Harlem Renaissance letters, published his *Spiritual Truancy* in the same issue of *New Challenge* (fall 1937) in which Wright's *Blueprint* appeared. There he described Harlem Renaissance writers as "aesthetic wastrels," given to a decadent and "exhibitionist flair." Although they should have addressed themselves to the "people themselves," he continued, they played to a "gallery of faddist negrophiles." To the "present younger generation of Negro writers," Locke issued the vaguely worded challenge to discover the "undiscovered and dormant" "group soul." Reinforcing Wright's blueprint, Locke called for black writers to forsake their frivolous preoccupations with bourgeois privilege and property, for the greater rewards—literary and social alike—of "race expression" and "sacrificial social devotion."

At least in his early and most critically significant work, Wright effectively executed his own blueprint by rejecting what Locke termed the "decadent aestheticism" of Harlem Renaissance writers and by drawing on the presumably more "nourishing" elixer of Marxism and social protest. Despite its urban, "secular" ingredients, this formula was actually a reformulation of the historically didactic, declamatory pitches of the black sermons and old-time religion of his grandmother, which he putatively despised. Although critics have certainly observed this rich blend of past and present in Wright, the grossly popular description of his work is much more one dimensional. The opinion widely shared is that Wright's *Native Son* had single-handedly birthed and shaped a radically new agenda and established for African American writing a new center of gravity, one that documented the gritty realities of urban living for black Americans filtered through the lenses of urban sociology and the conventions of naturalism.

It is clear from reading both *Native Son* and "How Bigger Was Born," the essay that traced the genealogy of that novel's famous character, that Wright was strongly attracted to the Chicago School of Urban Sociology, especially to its theories about "juvenile delinquency" and the "urban environment." But he was equally attracted to the compatible premises of such American naturalists as Theodore Dreiser and Upton Sinclair, in whose works the force and power of the social environment are overwhelming. Bigger Thomas is the victim of a raw environmental determinism, the prototypical delinquent mired in the unforgiving straits of urban blight and deprivation. Wright's commitment to documenting these conditions and their effects on Bigger's psychology, came to be esteemed by a range of critics as perhaps the highest form of social protest.

Social protest certainly did not originate with Wright. Indeed the current of social consciousness, commonly associated with protest, had long flowed vigorously through African American letters. It was there in Wright's nineteenth-century antecedents: the fugitive slave narrative; the abolitionist orator–poets; the essays, pamphlets, and letters; and in the novels of racial uplift. It was there too in much of the work of those Harlem Renaissance writers whom Wright was so quick to dismiss. If in Wright's estimation, these writers cum ambassadors had squandered their talents by merely pleading for justice for blacks instead of fulfilling their responsibilities to the masses by producing more radical writing, capturing the perspectives of the proletariat, some were closer to Wright's way of thinking than he was prepared to concede. For example, a full decade before Wright published *Blueprint*, W. E. B. Du Bois had issued his own manifesto in *Criteria of Negro Art* (1926), in which he repudiated any notion that *art* and *protest* (he called it propaganda) were separable, insisting that "all art is propaganda and ever must be, despite the wailing of the purists. I stand in utter shamelessness and say that whatever art I have for writing has been used always for propaganda for gaining the right of black folk to love and enjoy." It is important that the spirit of protest during the Harlem Renaissance was not addressed exclusively to whites. In his famous manifesto *The Negro Artist and the Racial Mountain*, Langston Hughes protested the assumption, held by many writers of the period, that only certain sides of the black American experience were suitable for literary treatment, only certain aesthetic modes were acceptable. But with the emergence of Richard Wright, many concluded, the battle over the content and form of African American writing seemed finally and definitively decided: black art and social protest were one and the same. Protest not only blended optimally with the aesthetics of naturalism and the reportorial practices of journalism and urban sociology, but worked organically with a range of cultural activity—including grassroots organizing—underpinning a self-styled radical literary and intellectual movement.

This elevation of protest to a category of aesthetic value far outlived the decade of the 1940s and came to be applied retrospectively to writers as diverse as William Attaway, Chester Himes, Frank Yerby, and Ann Petry, all assumed to be Wright's direct descendents. Despite their obvious differences, these writers have been readily yoked together far too often under what some critics have misleadingly termed the "Wright School." To be sure, recognizable elements of the realism and naturalism associated most commonly with Wright are detectable in their work, but these writers did not simply parrot Richard Wright but rather brought their own distinctive stamp to these familiar modes.

Traces of Wright's early style show most plainly in the writings of another Mississippi-born writer, William Attaway, who became friends with Wright while both were involved in the Federal Writers' Project of Illinois. Attaway's second and most accomplished novel, *Blood on the Forge*, was published in 1941, the same year as Wright's phototext *Twelve Million Black Voices*, and like that book Attaway's novel dramatized the Great Migration from the agrarian South to the industrial North just after World War I. *Blood on the Forge* was rated one of the most complex treatments of black American workers who were exploited in northern steel mills, locked in a losing competition with white and immigrant labor in a market that pitted each group against the other.

Chester Himes's association with the labor movement also figures in his two most significant novels of the 1940s. *The Lonely Crusade* (1947) depicted a labor organizer battling racial discrimination in the unions. *If He Hollers Let Him Go* (1945), Himes's best-known and most successful novel, told the story of an educated, northern Negro in conflict with poor white southerners in a Los Angeles shipyard during war time. Accused of raping a white woman, the protagonist is ultimately defeated by the powerful and intractable tradition of sexual racism.

Based largely on its urban setting and naturalistic mode, Ann Petry's first novel, *The Street* (1946), is frequently likened to *Native Son*. While the comparison holds some merit, it overlooks those aspects of Petry's novel that not only set it apart from Wright's but might also be read as a radical negation of *Native Son*. Indeed, as some critics have argued, in the ending of *The Street*, when Lutie, the female protagonist bludgeons to death a man who has tried to exploit her sexually, Petry could be seen as attempting to redress the murders of the two women in *Native Son*—Mary and Bessie—whose deaths are figured merely as essential to Bigger Thomas's emergent creativity. But, more important, to insist too keenly on her indebtedness to Wright is to overlook the impressive artistry of Petry's own work. Not just in *The Street* but also in *The Narrows* and *Country Place*, Petry makes masterful use of pacing and suspense, of details of scenery, and of concealed narration that move her beyond any narrow notions of naturalism as well as beyond the category of social protest. To read her novels is to be reminded of the stylistic continuities she shares with such 1920s and 1930s writers as Nella Larsen and Jessie Fauset.

The critical commonplace, then, casting Wright as progenitor of a new era in African American letters ignores much that is significant about the two decades examined in this section of the anthology. Make no mistake, when Wright emerged, black American writing was indeed shifting away from literary exploration of middle-class ideals, which he had so roundly rejected, and toward the proletarian impulses more characteristic of the 1930s. But class consciousness was not the only order of business in the 1940s literary world, nor was Richard Wright the only agent of literary transformation within black America.

The effects of the Depression quickened the social consciousness of many black writers, who, like Wright, found the conventions of socialist realism compatible with their own literary objectives and philosophies. Others found such conventions too confining, perhaps none more notable than Ralph Ellison. In his 1941 essay "Recent Negro Fiction," published in *New Masses*, Ellison had made grand, enthusiastic claims for *Native Son*. He credited the novel with setting a new paradigm for black writing. As Ellison put it, *Native Son* "represent[ed] the take-off in a leap which promise[d] to carry over a whole tradition, and mark[ed] the merging of the imaginative depiction of American Negro life into the broad stream of American literature." But by the time Ellison published *Invisible Man*, a little more than ten years later, he had distanced himself from this early assessment. Wright no longer

First edition cover of *Native Son*, published in 1940.

seemed to point the Negro writer toward a "path which he might follow to reach maturity."

ELLISON AND BLACK MODERNIST FICTION

It so happens that Ellison's reassessment which demoted the merits of urban realism, coincided with a burgeoning vision of integration as a social ideal. That ideal called for minimizing emphatically racial subject matter. Indeed, as the 1940s drew to a close, writers—among them, Petry, Zora Neale Hurston, and Willard Motley—who came of age during the Depression manifested this "integrationist" temper by turning to what some critics have termed, albeit awkwardly, "non-Negro" or nonracial subject matter, especially in the novel. So labeled simply because black characters and black urban settings seemed no longer central, this work included Petry's novels *Country Place* (1947) and *The Narrows* (1953), set in New England. Although some critics regarded this shift as evidence of Petry's artistic maturation beyond the urban realism and sociological determinism of *The Street*, others found these later novels much less successful than the first. For most critics, though, the turn from urban realism had less to do with integrationist ideals than with the exhaustion of the mode itself. In "Inventory of Mid-Century: A Review of the Literature of the Negro" (1950), one of his annual omnibus overviews for *Phylon*, Alain Locke, referring to his penchant for developmental metaphors, determined that "the Negro writer as artist has several Rubicons to cross." He added, while in fiction the writer was "on the march," the output was "still qualitiatively immature." Such assessments seemed at the time, almost de rigueur. Writing that same year, also in *Phylon*, N. P. Tillman wrote, "In retrospect, many generations of Negro creative expressions" amounted but to a "child's gamut of tears, sobs, sulks, and passionate protest."

The publication of James Baldwin's essay "Everybody's Protest Novel" the year before in the *Partisan Review* (1949) had perhaps led the way to such critical themes, but it took the success of *Invisible Man* to further liberate those African American writers already chafing under the narrative straitjacket of realism and naturalism and thus breaking free of the pressures to protest injustice. In "Brave Words for a Startling Occasion," his speech at the ceremony of the National Book Award in 1952, Elllison addressed the matter of literary constraints more generally, whatever forms they took: "the very 'facts' which the naturalists assumed would make us free have lost the power to protect us from despair." He went on to suggest that the "tight well-made Jamesian novel" and the "hard boiled" novel were both "too restricted to contain the experience which I knew. The diversity of American life with its extreme fluidity and openness seemed too vital and alive to be caught for more than the briefest instant" by these forms. Without naming either Wright or his alleged "descendants," Ellison admitted that, in the course of writing *Invisible Man*, he *was* "forced to conceive of a novel unburdened by the narrow naturalism which has led, after so many triumphs, to the final and unrelieved despair which marks so much of our current fiction." As a result, his novel reflected what Ellison described as a more "experimental attitude," one which combined a commitment to "social responsibility" with a more studied attention to the novel as artistic form. And in "The Art of Fiction," a 1955 interview published in *Paris Review*, Ellison would write, "I am not primarily concerned with injustice, but with art."

It is a critical commonplace that, with *Invisible Man*, African American writers came to grips not only with the demands of "art" but also with the aims and prerogatives of modernism. But, of course, if *modernism* is seen as synonymous with rigorous attention to stylistic detail, to experimentations with narrative form, to fragmentation of the human image, then Jean Toomer's *Cane* (1923) and Nella Larsen's *Quicksand* and *Passing* (1929) would have to be identified as precursors to Ellison's *Invisible Man*, as would Langston Hughes's *The Weary Blues* (1926), Melvin Tolson's *Libretto for the Republic of Liberia* (1953), and Gwendolyn Brooks's *Anniad* (1949) or *In the Mecca* (1968). In other words, to associate the advent of modernism in African American letters with the coming of Ellison's *Invisible Man* is as misleading as associating the advent of socially conscious fiction with Richard Wright.

That said, however it is mapped, few would deny that *Invisible Man* places Ellison squarely within modernism's ranks, although not all critics found this a salutary placement early on. While the novel was mainly well received, certain critics objected to Ellison's acknowledged debts to the Western modernist tradition, assumed by some to be necessarily incompatible with African American cultural and expressive values. John Killens, who reviewed *Invisible Man* for *Freedom*, a left-wing newspaper, pronounced it a "vicious distortion of Negro life," a notion belied by the novel's grounding in black folklore and legend; in spirituals, blues, and jazz; in language and humor; and in the rites, manners, and customs of black Americans, sounded in its very prologue, as the protagonist listens to Louis Armstrong's "What Did I Do to Be So Black and Blue." Ellison sustained one of his harshest blows from Irving Howe, in the famous essay, "Black Boys and Native Sons," published in 1963, when the climate of critical opinion was surely influenced by the political turmoil of the times. Howe attacked both Ellison and Baldwin for the "aesthetic distance" toward the "Negro experience," for failing to understand that "plight and protest" (embodied most perfectly in Richard Wright) "are inseparable from that experience." In Ellison's equally famous answer, "The World and the Jug," he riffed on Howe's familial metaphors, openly rejecting the notion that he was the "son" and Richard Wright, his literary "father." Drawing a controversial distinction, Ellison explained that, although "one can do nothing about choosing one's relatives, one can, as artist, choose one's 'ancestors.' Wright was . . . a 'relative'; Hemingway an 'ancestor.'" Ellison went on to say, "I am a human being, not just the black successor to Richard Wright, and there are ways of celebrating my experience more complex than terms like 'protest' can suggest." Even so, it would be a mistake to read this statement as Ellison's categorical opposition to the tradition of social protest in literature. As he explained to an interviewer, "I recognize no dichotomy between art and protest. Dostoyevsky's *Notes from the Underground* is, among other things, a protest against the limitations of 19th century rationalisim; *Don Quixote, Man's Fate, Oedipus Rex, The Trial*—all these embody protest," while observing the strictest disciplines and requirements of craft.

Ellison was not the only one of Wright's African American contemporaries to dissociate himself from the artistic vision of Richard Wright, although the themes of Baldwin's first novel, *Go Tell It on the Mountain* (1953)—religious fundamentalism, collective guilt, and the psychodynamics of family life— share much with Wright, both stylistically and thematically. Similarly, Baldwin's most celebrated essays are steeped in the fiery Protestant rhetoric that echoes throughout Wright's early work. Centering the plots of African

American literary history, from 1940 to 1960, on the Wright–Baldwin–Ellison controversy and the paradigm of protest writing has resulted in a brotherhood narrative, which marginalizes women. As the critic Mary Helen Washington has put it, "the real 'invisible man' of the 1950s was the black woman." Gwendolyn Brooks's novel *Maud Martha* (1953) and Paule Marshall's *Brown Girl, Brownstones* (1959) were two exceptions in an era in which the contributions of black women in prose fiction garnered only passing notice. *Maud Martha*, published on the heels of *Annie Allen*, Brooks's Pulitzer Prize–winning volume of poems and a year after *Invisible Man*, received only belittling treatment before lapsing into critical neglect. Although Brooks did not aim for the epic sweep and narrative grandeur of Ellison's novel, in structuring *Maud Martha* as a series of vignettes with freeze frame endings, she showed her own experiments with narrative form and brought to the novel's prose the poetic lyricism that so distinguished her poetry.

POETRY

The poetry published between 1940 and 1960 defies the categories and complicates the debates provoked by this period's narrative forms. The poetry of Gwendolyn Brooks, as well as that of her most esteemed contemporaries—Margaret Walker, Melvin Tolson, and Robert Hayden—challenges the bearded debates about social protest, even though critics often seem reluctant to leave such debates behind. For example, the last lines of "For My People," the title poem of Margaret Walker's prize-winning volume, are frequently quoted to support the premise that Walker keeps a tradition of militant protest alive: "Let the martial songs be written, let the dirges disappear. Let a race of men now rise and take control!" But these lines do not summarize the volume's tone overall. Little critical attention has focused on the breathless stanzaic forms and word collages of the volume's first half, which have been likened to Whitman, and even less attention has been accorded the folk ballads of the volume's second half, which invite comparison to Sterling Brown's *Southern Road*.

A similar confluence of poetic forms characterizes the poems in Gwendolyn Brooks's first volume, *A Street in Bronzeville* (1945). What Brooks herself describes as "folksy narrative" in the volume's ballads runs alongside the conventions of Italian and English sonnet forms employed in *Gay Chaps at the Bar,* the sonnet sequence on World War II. Again, because the first part of the volume focuses on poor blacks in the kitchenettes and vacant lots of Chicago's South Side, Brooks has been linked to Richard Wright and to the realism and naturalism associated most readily with his work. Praised for taking her poetry to the ghetto streets of Chicago and capturing its sounds and rhythms, its smells of "onion fumes," of garbage "ripening in the hall," Brooks widens her frame beyond the titular, geographically delimited "Bronzeville" to embrace the global realities of war and the spreading shadow of fascism.

Brooks describes *Annie Allen* (1949), for which she won the Pulitzer Prize, as an extensive experiment, written to "*prove* that [she] could write *well.*" The experiment resulted, in her view, in "some rather artificial poetry," especially the *Anniad*, which she judged "just an exercise, just an exercise." Few have concurred with Brooks's opinion that *Annie Allen* is merely an exercise in conventional poetics. While she demonstrated technical accomplishment in a range of conventional poetic forms—the lyric, ballad, sonnet—she also showed a willingness to challenge them, especially what some critics regard as the gendered limitations of the traditional sonnet form.

Writing in an era when American poetry was highly intellectualized and academic, Brooks's studied attention to form and technical craftsmanship links her with Melvin Tolson and Robert Hayden. The three are frequently grouped together as highly technical poets in the tradition of such modern experimentalists as Hart Crane, T. S. Eliot, and William Butler Yeats. Unlike Brooks, however, Tolson and Hayden have been frequently disparaged as library poets, intellectual exhibitionists, who self-consciously used their verse to parade their schooling. Such an assessment seems much more befitting Tolson than Hayden, whose poetry, however densely allusive and studiously attentive to craft, is full of passionate simplicity. Hayden's poetry shows his self-confessed passion for history, especially African American history.

Critics generally consider Tolson's first volume, *Rendezvous with America* (1944), the most "accessible" of his work, while noting that its elite and mannered form, its tight-lipped control seem inconsistent with the poet's rebellious and populist convictions. The opening sections of *Rendezvous* do show Tolson's engagement with Whitman's populist vision as well as Dickinson's compressed syntax and understatement. Tolson's critics regard *Libretto for the Republic of Liberia* (1953) as his most erudite, densely allusive or "academic" volume. Tolson admitted to reading and absorbing the techniques of Eliot, Pound, Yeats, Baudelaire, and all those he termed "the great moderns." Describing modernism as an "historical inevitability," Tolson observed, "When T. S. Eliot published *The Waste Land* in 1922 . . . the victory of the moderns was complete. . . . The modern idiom is here to stay—like modern physics."

When Tolson published *Rendezvous with America*, World War II was reducing the cities of Europe to rubble. For "The Idols of the Tribe," one of the volume's most successful poems, he selected as epigraph a passage from Hitler's *Mein Kampf*: "A State which, in the epoch of race poisoning, dedicates itself to the cherishing of its best racial elements, must some day be master of the world." Tolson's war sonnets in this first volume might be compared to Brooks's sonnet sequence at the end of *A Street in Bronzeville*. Both poets employ forms and imagery from popular culture—Tolson, the propaganda of World War II poster art; Brooks, the rough-riding heroic cowboy (or "chap"), a cultural figure that gave way to the image of the American soldier-as-hero.

Although the careers of Brooks, Hayden, Tolson, and Walker had their genesis in the 1940s, their poetic output extended through to the Black Arts movement of the 1960s and beyond. Still other poets—Langston Hughes, for example, whose career dates back to the early days of the Harlem Renaissance—continued to be productive: Hughes published *The Panther and the Lash* in 1967, the year he died. Hughes published three volumes of poetry in the 1940s and two in the 1950s, including his jazz-influenced *Montage of a Dream Deferred* (1951), which contains "Harlem," one of his most anthologized poems. Its teasing, opening question, "What happens to a dream deferred?" is one of the most popular lines in all of African American poetry. From the first in a string of answers to the question—"Does it dry up like a raisin in the sun?"—Lorraine Hansberry took the title of her play *A Raisin in the Sun* (1959), which took the theater establishment by storm.

DRAMA

Lorraine Hansberry's *A Raisin in the Sun* began the longest run on Broadway of any drama written by a black American up to that time, but throughout the 1930s and 1940s, blacks had demonstrated a talent for drama as well as appeal and significance as dramatic subjects, capable of attracting theatergoers and ensuring sizable financial returns. The establishment of the American Negro Theater (ANT) in 1940 was a milestone in African American theater history. Conceived as an experimental community theater in Harlem, the ANT produced several original scripts in its roughly ten-year existence, including *On Striver's Row*, its inaugural production, written by Abram Hill, one of the theater's founders. *Native Son: A Biography of a Young American* (1941) by Richard Wright and Paul Green, the stage adaptation of Wright's *Native Son*, produced by Orson Welles's Mercury Theater, enjoyed a short run on Broadway. Langston Hughes returned to playwrighting with *The Sun Do Move* (1942) and *Simply Heavenly* (1957), the latter, based on his book *Simple Takes a Wife* (1957). James Baldwin's *The Amen Corner* opened at Howard University in 1956, and Alice Childress's *Trouble in Mind* won an Obie Award in 1955 for best original off-Broadway play.

Only ten plays written totally or partly by black Americans were produced on Broadway from 1926 until 1959, when Hansberry's *A Raisin in the Sun* commanded the stage, winning the New York Drama Critics Award over entries by such long-established playwrights as Eugene O'Neill and Tennessee Williams. Although written at a moment when visions of an integrated society seemed closer to realization, accelerated by such landmark decisions as *Brown v. the Topeka Board of Education* and the success of the Montgomery bus boycott, *A Raisin in the Sun* anticipated many of the defining concerns of a soon-to-be black arts movement, which exploded in the 1960s. The play's explorations of the African roots of African American identity and culture, for example, are often seen to link Hansberry to the spirit of cultural nationalism soon to emerge in full flower. But more important, the play linked Hansberry to a pan-Africanist, anticolonialist agenda pervasive throughout the 1950s.

As Hansberry scholar Margaret Wilkerson has noted, throughout her formative years, Hansberry was exposed to African history, culture, and politics, largely through her uncle William Leo Hansberry, a writer and a scholar of African civilizations, cultures, and politics. As writer for and associate editor of Paul Robeson's monthly newspaper, *Freedom*, Hansberry herself authored articles recording the independence movements throughout sub-Saharan Africa, beginning with Ghanaian independence in 1957. As early as 1960, Hansberry had begun to draft *Les Blancs*, a play unifinished at the time of her death, exploring the theme of colonialism and neo-colonialism in Africa. According to Margaret Wilkerson, the play asks the controversial question: "Can the liberation of oppressed people be achieved without violent revolution?" However one might answer this question, another related question could not be avoided, one that James Baldwin posed in his essay "Princes and Powers" (anthologized here): "What had this colonial experience made of [Africans] and what were they now to do with it?" Baldwin posed this question in his report on the First International Congress of Negro Writers and Artists in Paris in 1956. Sparked specifically by Aime

Cesaire's speech "Culture and Colonization," Baldwin's question brought nuance to this heady occasion. Partly answering his own question, Baldwin suggested, "whether they liked it or not," all those present, representing former (and some still), colonized nations, were "related to Europe, stained by European visions and standards . . . and their relation to themselves . . . and to their past had changed."

The very next year, in 1957, Baldwin would return to the United States, bringing the anti-colonial energies abroad to struggle for black liberation at home. This was a moment when many writers and intellectuals sought to establish the intricate connections between anti-colonialism and the movements for black civil rights for social and economic justice. That the U.S. civil rights movement gathered momentum at the same time that Ghana was about to achieve formal independence was an encouraging sign, but if, as Roi Ottley had proclaimed, blacks in the United States were "feeling a great resurgence of racial kinship to other colored people of the world," there remained pressing domestic questions to be addressed, chief among them, those concerning the viability of integration at a moment when many had begun to question whether a racially integrated America was possible.

Such questions grew louder and more insistent throughout the 1960s, voiced even by the formerly most vocal defenders of integrationism, including writer–activist James Baldwin. Returning to his signature rhetoric of apocalypse, Baldwin began to ask why any black American would want to be integrated into a burning house. Or as he put the matter to his biographer, Fern Eckman: "I don't want to be fitted into this society . . . I would rather be *dead*. In fact, there's no difference between being fitted into this society and *dying*."

PROPHETS OF A NEW DAY

Making similar use of apocalyptic imagery, black writers emerging in the waning days of the 1950s, served notice that yet another era in black letters was struggling to be born. The apocalypse they heralded was indeed the realization of Old Testament prophecy, which James Baldwin borrowed in titling his volume of essays *The Fire Next Time*. In the famous words of one of their idols, Malcolm X, whom they anointed the "fire prophet," these writers would force social revolution "by any means necessary." To borrow the title of Margaret Walker's volume of verse, these writers would come to be called the "prophets of a new day." One such self-styled prophet was Amiri Baraka (LeRoi Jones), whose signature poem, "Black Art," from his volume *Black Magic Poetry*, set much of the pace, form, and violent tone of the "new" black literature of the 1960s.

> We want "poems that kill."
> Assassin poems, Poems that shoot
> guns. Poems that wrestle cops into alleys
> and take their weapons leaving them dead
> with tongues pulled out and sent to Ireland.

Baraka's desire for "killing poems" hearkened back to Richard Wright's desire for "words as weapons," for art in the service of a struggle for human liberation. While some writers of the previous generation resisted the aesthetics and ideology of this Black Arts vanguard, others, notably Margaret Walker and Gwendolyn Brooks, sought common cause with this younger generation. Brooks participated in poetry workshops with the Blackstone Rangers, a Chicago youth gang, and endeavored to take her poetry into the forgotten corners of African America: taverns, street corners, and prison cells.

The spirit of the times was reflected in the titles of books, magazines, and anthologies—*Black Feeling, Black Talk, Black Judgment, Black Fire, The Black Poets, The Black Aesthetic, Black World, Black Magic*—which rolled ferverishly off the presses, some newly established by blacks themselves. In keeping with this literary self-determination for blacks, Brooks severed ties with the New York publishing establishment and began to publish her work with the black-run Broadside Press. From this period came several volumes, including *In the Mecca* (1968), *Riot* (1969), *Family Pictures* (1970), and *The Near-Johannesburg Boy, and Other Poems* (1986).

Because black writers of the 1940–69 generation had earned their stripes, so to speak, in the American market of letters and had garnered a considerable degree of public success and recognition, it could be said that they opened a frontier on the future that the Harlem Renaissance generation had only dimly perceived. Though it would be a mistake to propose an evolutionary narrative of progress in which every round of writers gets "higher and higher," it seems plausible to argue that the 1940s to 1960s brought forth the first full crop of African American writers. Unlike at least most of their Harlem Renaissance predecessors, the writers of this period were bolder, more militant. With this generation of writers, black readers in particular were summoned to confront new literary realities, a bracing new tenor of change, whose echoes we occasionally hear as far away from its source as David Bradley's *Chaneysville Incident* (1981). This 1940–60 generation offers quite likely our most powerful cluster of texts and propositions in the post–World War II period.

MELVIN B. TOLSON
1898?–1966

If this anthology does nothing more than recover the works of Melvin B. Tolson to a wider audience, that alone will justify its existence. Reading Tolson allows one to explore modernist poetics from an African American cultural stance. Like Ralph Ellison and Gwendolyn Brooks, Tolson grew up on an American frontier; like Langston Hughes, he witnessed the later stages of the civil rights movement; and like modernist practitioners before him, he exploited poetic traditions.

Born February 6, in either 1898 or 1900, in Moberly, Missouri, to the Reverend Alonzo Tolson and Lera Hurt Tolson, Melvin was raised in a Methodist Episcopal household, with a father who had taught himself classical languages. As the reverend took different churches, the Tolsons moved around a circuit of small midwestern towns. It was in the local newspaper of Oskaloosa, Iowa, that Tolson, fourteen years old, published his first poem, on the sinking of the *Titanic*. Tolson moved with his family in 1916 to Kansas City, Missouri, where he was elected senior class poet. He spent one year at Fisk University but transferred the next to Lincoln University in

Lincoln, Pennsylvania; there he acquired impressive skills in debating and public speaking and met his future wife, Ruth Southall. They were married on January 29, 1922, and a year and a half later, Tolson graduated with a bachelor's degree. Shortly thereafter, Melvin B. Tolson, Jr. was born, the first of their four children.

Throughout the 1920s, Tolson taught at Wiley College in Marshall, Texas, where he coached the debating team and published adventure stories in the Wiley *Wild Cat*. With the advent of the Depression, he moved his family to his parents' home in Kansas City, and during a 1931–32 sabbatical from Wiley, he enrolled in a master's program in comparative literature at Columbia University in New York City, producing a thesis on the Harlem Renaissance. During that year, Tolson began writing his first book of poems, *Gallery of Harlem Portraits*, which was not published until 1965. Still, throughout the 1930s, poems from the volume appeared in *Arts Quarterly*, *Modern Monthly*, and *Modern Quarterly*. In New York, Tolson met important figures such as literary critic and editor V. F. Calverton, who described him in *Current History* as "a bright vivid writer who attains his best effects by understatement rather than overstatement, and who catches in a line or a stanza what most of his contemporaries have failed to capture in pages or volumes."

Tolson's fearless attitude toward controversy and his spirited defense of his religious and social views drew not only fire but also an invitation to publish in the *Pittsburgh Courier*. From 1937 to 1944 he wrote a weekly column, "Caviar and Cabbages," for the *Washington Tribune*. In the column, whose topics ranged from national politics to popular culture, Tolson attacked the class pretensions and lack of racial pride of the black middle class. His poem "Dark Symphony" (printed here) won first place in a 1939 national poetry contest sponsored by Chicago's American Negro Exposition. The poem chronicles the African American struggle from slavery to the emergence of the New Negro and the "black men" of Tolson's "day" who are inspired by their history to "advance" along "[w]ith the Peoples of the World." "Dark Symphony" moves through six sections, each titled with an Italian musical phrase framing the stanzas that follow. "I. Allegro Moderato," presents Crispus Attucks as an American hero against a backdrop of slave auctions and the specter of racial violence. Transitioning to "Lento Grave," a description of sorrowful slave songs, Tolson marks the tradition of music in which his symphony resides and the painful African American slave past denied in his contemporary moment. Set to a European classical tempo, slave voices evoke a "centuries-old pathos" that extends the pain of slavery beyond the physical and temporal bounds of antebellum America, firmly taking their place on the world stage. Evoking the plight of poor whites in *The Grapes of Wrath*, examples of treason in Italy, and German attacks against Poland, "Dark Symphony" refutes black stereotypes, reminding Tolson's readers that poverty, treachery, and violence belong not only to Richard Wright's Bigger Thomas but to people throughout the world. Ultimately, an argument for black human perseverance in a conflictual world, "Dark Symphony" returns to the heroism and optimism with which it began, anticipating a new American revolution of black progress, its soldiers marching in step with their global peers.

When the *Atlantic Monthly* published "Dark Symphony" in 1941, the magazine's editor at the time, Mary Lou Chamberlain, so admired it that upon moving to Dodd, Mead and Company, she urged Tolson to produce a volume for her to publish. *Rendezvous with America*, which includes the poem that so impressed Mead, was the result, and the book quickly saw three editions, from 1944 on. Tolson left Wiley College in 1947 for Langston University in Langston, Oklahoma; that same year he was named poet laureate of the West African nation of Liberia by its president, William S. V. Tubman, the son of Harriet Tubman. Perhaps the poet's most ambitious work, *Libretto for the Republic of Liberia* was commissioned that year; he completed it in 1953 for the 1956 Liberian centennial. Tolson was subsequently admitted to the Liberian Knighthood of the Order of the Star of Africa.

While the 1950s and 1960s would bring Tolson increasing successes—among them, *Poetry*'s Bess Hokin Prize for his 1951 poem "E. & O.E.," an honorary doctorate from Lincoln University in 1965, and a chair in the humanities at the Tuskegee Institute—none of these honors, perhaps, generated more excitement for Tolson than his being elected mayor of the town of Langston for four consecutive terms, beginning in 1951. But as Tolson's visibility grew, his health declined. In 1966 he died of abdominal cancer.

Dark Symphony

I. Allegro Moderato[1]

Black Crispus Attucks[2] taught
    Us how to die
Before white Patrick Henry's[3] bugle breath
Uttered the vertical
     Transmitting cry: 5
"Yea, give me liberty or give me death."

Waifs of the auction block,
     Men black and strong
The juggernauts of despotism withstood,
Loin-girt with faith that worms   10
     Equate the wrong
And dust is purged to create brotherhood.

No Banquo's[4] ghost can rise
     Against us now,
Aver we hobnailed Man beneath the brute,   15
Squeezed down the thorns of greed
     On Labor's brow,
Garroted lands and carted off the loot.

II. Lento Grave[5]

The centuries-old pathos in our voices
Saddens the great white world,   20
And the wizardry of our dusky rhythms
Conjures up shadow-shapes of ante-bellum years:

Black slaves singing *One More River to Cross*
In the torture tombs of slave-ships,
Black slaves singing *Steal Away to Jesus*   25
In jungle swamps,
Black slaves singing *The Crucifixion*
In slave-pens at midnight,
Black slaves singing *Swing Low, Sweet Chariot*
In cabins of death,   30
Black slaves singing *Go Down, Moses*
In the canebrakes of the Southern Pharaohs.

1. Moderately lively (Italian). This and the other section titles are directions for the performance of music.
2. An escaped slave who was killed by the British in the Boston Massacre, March 5, 1770, a prelude to the American Revolutionary War.
3. Virginia-born patriot (1736–1799) whose oratorical skills fueled the American Revolution.
4. In Shakespeare's *Macbeth*, the murdered lord whose ghost haunts the guilty Macbeth.
5. Slowly and solemnly (Italian).

III. *Andante Sostenuto*[6]

They tell us to forget
The Golgotha[7] we tread . . .
We who are scourged with hate,   35
A price upon our head.
They who have shackled us
Require of us a song,
They who have wasted us
Bid us condone the wrong.   40

They tell us to forget
Democracy is spurned.
They tell us to forget
The Bill of Rights is burned.
Three hundred years we slaved,   45
We slave and suffer yet:
Though flesh and bone rebel,
They tell us to forget!

Oh, how can we forget
Our human rights denied?   50
Oh, how can we forget
Our manhood crucified?
When Justice is profaned
And plea with curse is met,
When Freedom's gates are barred,   55
Oh, how can we forget?

IV. *Tempo Primo*[8]

The New Negro strides upon the continent
In seven-league boots . . .
The New Negro
Who sprang from the vigor-stout loins   60
Of Nat Turner,[9] gallows-martyr for Freedom,
Of Joseph Cinquez,[1] Black Moses of the Amistad Mutiny,
Of Frederick Douglass,[2] oracle of the Catholic Man,
Of Sojourner Truth,[3] eye and ear of Lincoln's legions,
Of Harriet Tubman,[4] Saint Bernard of the Underground Railroad.   65

The New Negro
Breaks the icons of his detractors,
Wipes out the conspiracy of silence,
Speaks to *his* America:
"My history-moulding ancestors   70

6. Moderately slowly and sustained (Italian).
7. Or the hill of Calvary, where Jesus was crucified.
8. In the time of the opening movement (Italian).
9. Led his fellow slaves in a revolt against his master and other local whites (1800–1831).
1. Or Cinqué, led an 1839 mutiny on board *The Amistad*, a slave ship.

2. African American abolitionist (1817–1895), writer, and orator.
3. African American abolitionist and religious orator (ca. 1797–1883).
4. An escaped slave (ca. 1820–1913) who helped hundreds of other slaves escape to freedom in the North.

Planted the first crops of wheat on these shores,
Built ships to conquer the seven seas,
Erected the Cotton Empire,
Flung railroads across a hemisphere,
Disemboweled the earth's iron and coal,   75

Tunneled the mountains and bridged rivers,
Harvested the grain and hewed forests,
Sentineled the Thirteen Colonies,
Unfurled Old Glory at the North Pole,[5]
Fought a hundred battles for the Republic."   80

The New Negro:
His giant hands fling murals upon high chambers,
His drama teaches a world to laugh and weep,
His music leads continents captive,
His voice thunders the Brotherhood of Labor,   85
His science creates seven wonders,
His Republic of Letters challenges the Negro-baiters.

The New Negro,
Hard-muscled, Fascist-hating, Democracy-ensouled,
Strides in seven-league boots   90
Along the Highway of Today
Toward the Promised Land of Tomorrow!

V. Larghetto[6]

None in the Land can say
To us black men Today:
You send the tractors on their bloody path,   95
And create Okies for *The Grapes of Wrath.*[7]
You breed the slum that breeds a *Native Son*[8]
To damn the good earth Pilgrim Fathers won.

None in the Land can say
To us black men Today: 100
You dupe the poor with rags-to-riches tales,
And leave the workers empty dinner pails.
You stuff the ballot box, and honest men
Are muzzled by your demagogic din.

None in the Land can say   105
To us black men Today:
You smash stock markets with your coined blitzkriegs,[9]
And make a hundred million guinea pigs.

---

5. Reference to Matthew Henson (1866–1955), African American explorer and co-discoverer, with Robert Peary, of the North Pole.
6. Somewhat slowly (Italian).
7. John Steinbeck's 1939 novel is about an Oklahoma family's trek westward looking for farmwork.

8. Richard Wright's 1940 novel about Bigger Thomas, a young African American living in the northern ghettos, specifically Chicago.
9. Lightning wars (German, literal trans.); sudden attacks made by Germany against Poland and France during World War II.

You counterfeit our Christianity,
And bring contempt upon Democracy.   110

None in the Land can say
To us black men Today:
You prowl when citizens are fast asleep,
And hatch Fifth Column[1] plots to blast the deep
Foundations of the State and leave the Land   115
A vast Sahara with a Fascist brand.

VI. *Tempo di Marcia*[2]

Out of abysses of Illiteracy,
Through labyrinths of Lies,
Across waste lands of Disease . . .
We advance!   120

Out of dead-ends of Poverty,
Through wildernesses of Superstition,
Across barricades of Jim Crowism[3] . . .
We advance!

With the Peoples of the World . . .   125
We advance!

                                                     1944

The Birth of John Henry[1]

The night John Henry is born an ax
    of lightning splits the sky,
and a hammer of thunder pounds the earth,
    and the eagles and panthers cry!

John Henry—he says to his Ma and Pa: 5
    "Get a gallon of barleycorn.[2]
I want to start right, like a he-man child,
    the night that I am born!"

Says: "I want some ham hocks, ribs, and jowls,
    a pot of cabbage and greens;   10
some hoecakes,[3] jam, and buttermilk,
    a platter of pork and beans!"

---

1. Franco (fascist) sympathizers in Madrid during the Spanish Civil War (1936–39); more generally, a group who acts traitorously out of secret sympathy with an enemy of their country.
2. In march time (Italian).
3. Legal system that promoted racial segregation; first enacted by southern legislatures in 1865 to separate blacks from whites on public transportation.

1. A legendary figure from African American ballads and folklore. In the story, John Henry competed with a steam-powered drill to drive railroad spikes; he won the contest but died from exhaustion.
2. Whiskey made from barley.
3. Cornmeal cakes.

John Henry's Ma—she wrings her hands,
 and his Pa—he scratches his head.
John Henry—he curses in giraffe-tall words,   15
 flops over, and kicks down the bed.

He's burning mad, like a bear on fire—
 so he tears to the riverside.
As he stoops to drink, Old Man River gets scared
 and runs upstream to hide!   20

Some say he was born in Georgia—O Lord!
 Some say in Alabam.
But it's writ on the rock at the Big Bend Tunnel:
 "Lousyana was my home. So scram!"

           1965

Satchmo[1]

   King Oliver[2] of New Orleans
has kicked the bucket, but he left behind
old Satchmo with his red-hot horn
 to syncopate the heart and mind.
   The honky-tonks in Storyville   5
have turned to ashes, have turned to dust,
 but old Satchmo is still around
like Uncle Sam's IN GOD WE TRUST.

   Where, oh, where is Bessie Smith[3]
with her heart as big as the blues of truth?   10
Where, oh, where is Mister Jelly Roll[4]
 with his Cadillac and diamond tooth?
   Where, oh, where is Papa Handy[5]
with his blue notes a-dragging from bar to bar?
Where, oh, where is bulletproof Leadbelly[6]   15
 with his tall tales and 12-string guitar?

           1965

1. The title of American jazz musician Louis Armstrong's (1901–1971) autobiography.
2. New Orleans–born bandleader (1885–1938), whose King Oliver Creole Band was considered the greatest jazz band of its day. Armstrong stated that Oliver was his true idol.
3. American blues singer (1894–1937), known as the Empress of the Blues.
4. Ferdinand "Jelly Roll" Morton (1885–1941), American jazz pianist.
5. William Christopher Handy (1873–1958), American composer known as the Father of the Blues.
6. Nickname for American blues singer Hudson William Ledbetter (1885–1949). Master of the guitar, Ledbetter was one of the most prolific performers of the blues genre.

DOROTHY WEST
1907–1998

I n the biographical remarks that accompanied the second publication of her short story "An Unimportant Man," Dorothy West wrote, "I have no ability nor desire to be other than a writer, though the fact is I whistle beautifully." West was born on June 2, 1907, to Rachel Pease West and Isaac Christopher West in Boston, Massachusetts, where she attended Girls' Latin School and Boston University. Hers had been a long and varied writing career, which spanned more than seventy years, if we count the short story she wrote at age seven. When she was barely fifteen she was selling stories to the *Boston Post*. And before she turned eighteen, already living in New York, West had won second place in the national competition sponsored by *Opportunity* magazine, an honor she shared with Zora Neale Hurston. The winning story, "The Typewriter," was later included in Edward O'Brien's *The Best Short Stories of 1926*.

A friend of such luminaries as Countee Cullen, Langston Hughes, Claude McKay, and Wallace Thurman, Dorothy West judged them and herself harshly for "degenerate[ing] through [their] vices" and for failing, in general, to live up to their promise. Thus, in what many consider the waning days of the Harlem Renaissance and in the lean years of the Depression, West used personal funds to start *Challenge,* a literary quarterly, hoping to recapture some of this unfulfilled promise. She served as the magazine's editor from 1934 to 1937. Its last issue appeared in the spring of 1937 and was followed by *New Challenge* in the fall of that same year. The renamed journal listed Dorothy West and Marian Minus as co-editors and Richard Wright as associate editor; it included Wright's famous and influential essay "Blueprint for Negro Writing" and Ralph Ellison's first published piece, "Creative and Cultural Lag."

The shift from *Challenge* to *New Challenge* can perhaps best be summed up in Wallace Thurman's observation to West that *Challenge* had been too "high school-ish" and "pink tea." Whether *Challenge* was to *New Challenge* what pink tea was to red is debatable, but West has admitted that *New Challenge* became associated with a strict Communist Party line, which she found increasingly difficult to toe. Despite her resistance to this turn in the journal's emphases, *New Challenge,* under West's editorship, encouraged and published submissions that explored the desperate conditions of the black working class.

Because of her involvement with *Challenge* and her early associations with the figures and events that gave the period its singular status and acclaim, West is generally included with writers of the Harlem Renaissance although the bulk of her writing actually began to be published long after what most literary historians consider the height of the movement.

During the Depression, West worked as a bit actress in the original 1929 production of DuBose Heyward's *Porgy* and in 1932–33, she spent time in the Soviet Union as a member of a group of intellectuals, including Langston Hughes, invited to make a film about black life in the United States. The film was never made. West worked briefly as a welfare investigator in Harlem and then, until the mid-1940s, for the WPA Federal Writers' Project.

Many of the more than sixty short stories written throughout her career were published in the *New York Daily News*. The first to appear there was "Jack in the Pot" (retitled "Jackpot" by the editors), which won the Blue Ribbon Fiction contest. Despite her success with the short story form, West is best known for her novel *The Living Is Easy,* the first chapter of which is printed here. Published in 1948, the novel has been praised for its engaging portrayal of Cleo Judson, the unscrupulous and manipulative woman who brings ruin on herself as well as the members of her family who fall under her domination and control. But the novel has also earned West high marks for its treatment of the class snobbery, insularity, and all-around shallowness of the New England black bourgeoisie, whom West dubbed the "genteel poor."

New evaluations of West's works followed the 1982 Feminist Press reprint of *The Living Is Easy*. Critics placed the novel in both an emergent women's tradition, focused on the development of female power and autonomy, and in an American tradition that includes Theodore Dreiser and Sinclair Lewis.

From 1968 until her death in 1998, Dorothy West lived on Martha's Vineyard and contributed a generous sampling of occasional pieces and columns to its newspaper, the *Vineyard Gazette*. Her long-awaited novel *The Wedding* received strong notices when it was published in 1995; *The Richer, the Poorer: Sketches and Reminiscences* was published the same year.

From The Living Is Easy

From *Part One*

CHAPTER 1. [CLEO]

"Walk up," hissed Cleo, somewhat fiercely.

Judy was five, and her legs were fat, but she got up steam and propelled her small stout body along like a tired scow straining in the wake of a racing sloop. She peeped at her mother from under the expansive brim of her leghorn straw. She knew what Cleo would look like. Cleo looked mad.

Cleo swished down the spit-spattered street with her head in the air and her sailor aslant her pompadour. Her French heels rapped the sidewalk smartly, and her starched skirt swayed briskly from her slender buttocks. Through the thin stuff of her shirtwaist her golden shoulders gleamed, and were tied to the rest of her torso with the immaculate straps of her camisole, chemise, and summer shirt, which were banded together with tiny gold-plated safety pins. One gloved hand gave ballast to Judy, the other gripped her pocketbook.

This large patent-leather pouch held her secret life with her sisters. In it were their letters of obligation, acknowledging her latest distribution of money and clothing and prodigal advice. The instruments of the concrete side of her charity, which instruments never left the inviolate privacy of her purse, were her credit books, showing various aliases and unfinished payments, and her pawnshop tickets, the expiration dates of which had mostly come and gone, constraining her to tell her husband, with no intent of irony, that another of her diamonds had gone down the drain.

The lesser items in Cleo's pocketbook were a piece of chamois, lightly sprinkled with talcum powder, and only to be used in extreme necessity if there was no eye to observe this public immodesty, a lollipop for Judy in case she got tiresome, an Irish-linen handkerchief for elegance, a cotton square if Judy stuck up her mouth, and a change purse with silver, half of which Cleo, clandestinely and without conscience, had shaken out of Judy's pig bank.

Snug in the bill compartment of the bag were forty-five dollars, which she had come by more or less legitimately after a minor skirmish with her husband on the matter of renting a ten-room house.

She had begun her attack in the basement kitchen of their landlady's house, a brownstone dwelling in the South End section of Boston. Judy had been sent upstairs to play until bedtime, and Bart had been basking in the afterglow of a good dinner. Ten years before, he had brought his bride to this address, where they had three furnished rooms and the use of the kitchen and the clothesline at a rent which had never increased from its first modest figure. Here, where someone else was responsible for the upkeep, Bart intended to stay and save his money until he was rich enough to spend it.

Cleo had bided her time impatiently. Now Judy was nearing school age. She had no intention of sending her to school in the South End. Whenever she passed these schools at recess time, she would hustle Judy out of sight and sound. "Little knotty-head niggers," she would mutter unkindly, while Judy looked shocked because "nigger" was a bad-word.

These midget comedians made Cleo feel that she was back in the Deep South. Their accents prickled her scalp. Their raucous laughter soured the sweet New England air. Their games were reminiscent of all the whooping and hollering she had indulged in before her emancipation. These r'aring-tearing young ones had brought the folkways of the South to the classrooms of the North. Their numerical strength gave them the brass to mock their timid teachers and resist attempts to make them conform to the Massachusetts pattern. Those among them who were born in Boston fell into the customs of their southern-bred kin before they were old enough to know that a Bostonian, black or white, should consider himself a special species of fish.

The nicer colored people, preceded by a similar class of whites, were moving out of the South End, so prophetically named with this influx of black cotton-belters. For years these northern Negroes had lived next door to white neighbors and taken pride in proximity. They viewed their southern brothers with alarm, and scattered all over the city and its suburbs to escape this plague of their own locusts.

Miss Althea Binney, Judy's private teacher, who for the past three years had been coming four mornings weekly to give Judy the benefit of her accent and genteel breeding, and to get a substantial lunch that would serve as her principal meal of the day, had told Cleo of a house for rent to colored on a street abutting the Riverway, a boulevard which touched the storied Fens[1] and the arteries of sacred Brookline.

On the previous night, Thea's brother, Simeon, the impoverished owner and editor of the Negro weekly, *The Clarion*, had received a telephone call from a Mr. Van Ryper, who succinctly advised him that he would let his ten-room house for thirty-five dollars monthly to a respectable colored family. Notice to this effect was to be inserted in the proper column of the paper.

Thea, *The Clarion*'s chronicler of social events, had urged Simeon to hold the notice until Cleo had had first chance to see the house. Cleo had been so grateful that she had promised Thea an extravagant present, though Thea could better have used her overdue pay that Cleo had spent in an irresistible moment in a department store.

The prospect of Judy entering school in Brookline filled her with awe. There she would rub shoulders with children whose parents took pride in sending them to public school to learn how a democracy functions. This

1. Or the Fenway, a parkland that stretches through part of Brookline, a town adjacent to Boston famous for its wealthy homes, estates, and apartment buildings.

moral obligation discharged, they were then sent to private school to fulfill their social obligation to themselves.

"It's like having a house drop in our laps," said Cleo dramatically. "We'd be fools, Mr. Judson, to let this opportunity pass."

"What in the name of common sense," Bart demanded, "do we want with a ten-room house? We'd rattle around like three pills in a box, paying good money for unused space. What's this Jack the Ripper want for rent?"

"Fifty dollars," Cleo said easily, because the sum was believable and she saw a chance to pocket something for herself.

"That's highway robbery," said Bart, in an aggrieved voice. It hurt him to think that Cleo would want him to pay that extravagant rent month after month and year after year until they all landed in the poorhouse.

"Hold on to your hat," Cleo said coolly. "I never knew a man who got so hurt in his pocketbook. Don't think I want the care of a three-story house. I wasn't born to work myself to the bone. It's Judy I'm thinking of. I won't have her starting school with hoodlums. Where's the common sense in paying good money to Thea if you want your daughter to forget everything she's learned?"

Bart had never seen the sense in paying Thea Binney to teach his daughter to be a Bostonian when two expensive doctors of Cleo's uncompromising choosing could bear witness to her tranquil Boston birth. But he did not want Cleo to think that he was less concerned with his child's upbringing than she.

Slowly an idea took shape in his mind. "I'll tell you how I figure we can swing the rent without strain. We can live on one floor and let the other two. If we got fifteen dollars a floor, our part would be plain sailing."

"Uh huh," said Cleo agreeably.

He studied her pleasant expression with suspicion. It wasn't like her to consent to anything without an argument.

"You better say what you want to say now," he advised her.

"Why, I like a house full of people," she said dreamily. "I've missed it ever since I left the South. Mama and Pa and my three sisters made a good-size family. As long as I'm the boss of the house, I don't care how many people are in it."

"Well, of course," he said cautiously, "strangers won't be like your own flesh. Matter of fact, you don't want to get too friendly with tenants. It encourages them to fall behind with the rent."

"I tell you what," she said brilliantly, "we can rent furnished rooms instead of flats. Then there won't be any headaches with poor payers. It's easier to ask a roomer to pack his bag and go than it is to tell a family to pack their furniture."

He saw the logic of that and nodded sagely. "Ten to one a roomer's out all day at work. You don't get to see too much of them. But when you let flats to families, there's bound to be children. No matter how they fell behind, I couldn't put people with children on the sidewalk. It wouldn't set right on my conscience."

Cleo said quietly, "I'd have banked my life on your saying that." For a moment tenderness flooded her. But the emotion embarrassed her. She said briskly: "You remind me of Pa. One of us had a sore tooth, Mama would tell us to go to sleep and forget it. But Pa would nurse us half the night, keeping us awake with kindness."

He accepted the dubious compliment with a modest smile. Then the smile froze into a grimace of pain. He had been hurt in his pocketbook.

"It'll take a pretty penny to furnish all those extra bedrooms. We don't want to bite off more than we can chew. Don't know but what unfurnished flats would be better, after all. We could pick settled people without any children to make me chicken-hearted."

She stared at him like an animal at bay. Little specks of green began to glow in her gray eyes, and her lips pulled away from her even teeth. Bart started back in bewilderment.

"You call yourself a businessman," she said passionately. "You run a big store. You take in a lot of money. But whenever I corner you for a dime, it's like pulling teeth to get it out of you. You always have the same excuse. You need every dollar to buy bananas. And when I say, What's the sense of being in business if you can't enjoy your cash, you always say, In business you have to spend money to make money. Now when I try to advise you to buy a few measly sticks of bedroom furniture, a man who spends thousands of dollars on fruit, you balk like a mule at a racetrack."

He rubbed his mustache with his forefinger. "I see what you mean," he conceded. "I try to keep my store filled with fruit. I can't bear to see an empty storeroom. I guess you got a right to feel the same way about a house. In the long run it's better to be able to call every stick your own than have half your rooms dependent on some outsider's furniture."

She expelled a long breath. "That's settled then."

He thought it prudent to warn her. "We'll have to economize to the bone while we're furnishing that house."

She rolled her eyes upward. "We'll even eat bones if you say so."

He answered quietly: "You and the child will never eat less than the best as long as I live. And all my planning is to see to it that you'll never know want when I'm gone. No one on earth will ever say that I wasn't a good provider. That's my pride, Cleo. Don't hurt it when you don't have to."

"Well, I guess you're not the worst husband in the world," she acknowledged softly, and added slowly, "And I guess I'm the kind of wife God made me." But she did not like the echo of that in her ears. She said quickly, "And you can like it or lump it."

Bart took out an impressive roll of bills, peeled off a few of the lesser ones, and laid them on the table. The sight of the bank roll made Cleo sick with envy. There were so many things she could do with it. All Mr. Judson would do with it was buy more bananas.

She sighed and counted her modest pile. There were only forty-five dollars.

"It's five dollars short," she said frigidly.

"Yep," he said complacently. "I figure if this Jack the Ripper wants fifty dollars he'll take forty-five if he knows he'll get it every month on the dot. And if he ever goes up five dollars on the rent, we still won't be paying him any more than he asked for in the first place. In business, Cleo, I've learned to stay on my toes. You've got to get up with the early birds to get ahead of me."

1948

RICHARD WRIGHT
1908–1960

summary of Richard Wright's life is captured in the title of an early critical article on his work: "Juvenile Delinquent Becomes Famous Writer." Born in 1908 on a plantation near Natchez, Mississippi, Wright's life conformed to the stock pattern of the American success myth. From his impoverished and educationally barren early years to his achievement as a favored literary touchstone and ancestor figure, the details of Wright's life constitute the stuff of legends.

Wright's early life gave him bitter preparation for the intellectual outlook and the acute social and political consciousness of his writing. Shuttled from relative to relative, after his mother's partial paralysis forced her to place him and his brother temporarily in an orphanage, Wright lived a time with his grandmother and aunt, whose religious fanaticism stunted Wright's education but not his passion for encyclopedic reading. Working in Memphis as an errand boy, Wright fed this obsession, subverting Jim Crow laws by forging the now famous note to a public librarian: "Dear Madam: Will you please let this nigger boy have some books by H. L. Mencken?" Although Wright also read the fiction of Theodore Dreiser, Sherwood Anderson, and Sinclair Lewis and shared their indictments of middle-class babbitry, it was Mencken's work that first inspired Wright's own literary ambitions and focused his own aspirations as a stylist. From Mencken's *A Book of Prefaces*, Wright sensed a man "fighting, fighting with words . . . using words as a weapon . . . as one would use a club." Wright would later supplement this early reading with the work of experimentalists and modernists such as Marcel Proust, Henry James, and Gertrude Stein, whose character Melanctha from *Three Lives*, Wright considered one of the few credible portraits of an African American by a white author.

In 1927 Wright migrated to Chicago, along with masses of other blacks who fled the racism, poverty, and lynch law of the rural South only to find the cities of the urban North, as he put it, "sprawling centers of steel and stone" as cold and unyielding as the South. Disabused of his expectation that life in the North "could be lived with dignity," Wright turned to Communism and began to find a literary voice and ideological affinity in the leftist political ferment of the 1930s. He eventually broke with the Communist Party in 1942 because of its weak position on discrimination in the armed forces during World War II and because of its attempts to control his writing. The break became public and official in 1944 when he published excerpts of "I Tried to Be a Communist" in *Atlantic Monthly*, but it was far from precipitous. Well up to the publication of *Twelve Million Black Voices* (1941), Wright had tried to sharpen his conception of literary form and to work out the relationship between the techniques of fiction and the tenets of Marxism. He attended meetings of the Chicago John Reed Club and served as chief Harlem correspondent for the *Daily Worker,* while churning out proletarian poems for such Communist journals as *New Masses* and *Partisan Review.* It followed logically from these experiences that Wright would try his own hand at outlining a literary theory with broad claims for African American writers. The result was "Blueprint for Negro Writing." Published in the inaugural issue of *New Challenge* (1937), a magazine Wright co-edited with Dorothy West and Marian Minus, "Blueprint," was, like Langston Hughes's earlier "The Negro Artist and the Racial Mountain," a manifesto and declaration of independence from what Wright judged to be the hidebound bourgeois literary forms and agendas that had long dominated black letters. Distancing himself from the writings of the Harlem Renaissance, which he dismissed as "humble novels, poems, and plays," written by "prim and decorous ambassadors who went a-begging to white America," Wright urged black writers to embrace a Marxist conception of reality and society, which offered, in his judgment, the "maximum degree of freedom in thought and feeling . . . for the Negro writer."

Wright executed his own blueprint in *Uncle Tom's Children* (1938), a collection of four novellas set in the Jim Crow South. His blueprint worked, at the expense of the stories, which are often flawed by Marxist propagandizing, melodrama, ponderous didacticism, and improbable plots. These stories show some of the major influences on Wright's fiction: naturalism, Marxism, Freudianism, and the black folk tradition, with the latter of which Wright had a contradictory relationship that lasted throughout his career.

"Long Black Song" is one of the few works by Wright written from the perspective of a woman. It is believed to be based on the tragedy of his uncle Hoskins, a successful bar owner in Elaine, Arkansas, who was murdered by whites who wanted possession of his business and his land. Critics have often praised its somber lyricism, reminiscent of Jean Toomer's "Blood Burning Moon," a tale of an interracial triangle, and also noticed the extent to which "Long Black Song" fits a pattern dominant in Wright's work: the marginality of women, who figure merely as accessories to the larger political and philosophical themes of his fiction. In this story, as novelist and critic Sherley Anne Williams notes, Wright represents the rape of Sarah not as a violation of *her* body, but rather, as an affront to her husband's pride and masculinity.

Uncle Tom's Children brought Wright first prize in a competition among writers of the Works Progress Administration (WPA) as well as a Guggenheim fellowship; this success enabled him to work exclusively on his writing. Despite its success, at least with some critics, Wright was himself harshly critical of the collection. Characterizing it as a sentimental work, which "even bankers' daughters could read and weep over and feel good about," he vowed that his next novel would be one "so hard and deep that [readers] would have to face it without the consolation of tears." That next novel was *Native Son*, which contained extremities of violence and horror not likely to inspire anything but fear. Indeed "Fear" was, significantly, the title Wright gave to the first of the book's three parts.

Native Son is widely considered Wright's most monumental achievement in fiction. In a now famous overstatement, critic Irving Howe declared, "The day *Native Son* appeared, American culture was changed forever." Whether one accepts Howe's judgment or not, it is certain that *Native Son* is not only the novel that established Richard Wright as a major literary talent of the twentieth century but also the novel whose mix of urban realism, sociological theory, and naturalistic determinism helped define and influence almost the entire sweep of African American fiction of the post–World War II era. It is significant that *Native Son* is also the novel that worked virtually to limit the critical response of Wright's entire corpus to a single category: protest writer. The book earned Wright the reputation as a writer who dared to expose the stresses and pathologies in the urban ghettoes in which poor blacks were confined. Equally significant is that *Native Son* made Wright the first African American writer to receive both critical acclaim and commercial success simultaneously.

Published by Harper & Brothers, *Native Son* was a Book-of-the-Month Club selection. Selling two hundred thousand copies inside of three weeks, the novel broke a twenty-year sales record for Harper's, beating out John Steinbeck's Pulitzer Prize–winning novel *The Grapes of Wrath*, as the number one best-seller. Although these impressive sales did not spell wealth or even financial security for Wright—he would struggle to support himself for the duration of his career—the novel proved a paradox. As notes critic Lawrence Jackson, *Native Son* established that "black American themes could create a national buzz, meriting their adoption by the major presses" and, at the same time, that "Negro writers were still a world apart, too 'special' in their direction to become blockbuster sellers."

Native Son shows a mix of aesthetic forms and traditions. The novel combined the determinism of naturalism with the grittiness of socialist realism that Wright drew from the works of such writers as James T. Farrell and Theodore Dreiser. Dreiser's *An American Tragedy*, to which *Native Son* is frequently compared, had an especial impact on Wright's literary development and philosophical outlook. He would later write in *Black Boy*, his autobiography: "I was overwhelmed. . . . It would have been impossible for me to have told anyone what I derived from these novels. All my life has shaped me for the, the naturalism of the modern novel." Of course, by the time Wright made that statement, the aesthetics of modernism, which had revolutionized so many of the arts in America, was an established fact of literary life. For Wright, however, realism and naturalism remained vital forces in his work. While clearly influenced by these traditions, Wright, as his more perceptive critics have noted, was also influenced by the tradition of the Gothic romance, employed by such nineteenth-century American writers as Nathaniel Hawthorne and Edgar Allan Poe. Still others have noted that the language of symbolism in Wright's work brings him closer to the tradition of modernism than is generally acknowledged.

Whatever modernist elements are to be found in Wright's work are arguably eclipsed by his overwhelming investments in the Chicago School of sociology and the deterministic slants of its theories. He acknowledged that the Chicago School provided him the explanatory concepts and theoretical frameworks for his fiction. Indeed the Chicago School provided the shaping apparatus not only for *Native Son* but also for *Twelve Million Black Voices*. Published a year after *Native Son* in 1941, *Twelve Million Black Voices* was subtitled "A Folk History of the American Negro." Based on photographs culled from the Farm Security Administration files, the book features Wright's running commentary throughout the text, explaining the crippling effects of the Great Migration on southern blacks. In an idea that structured his entire text, Wright supposed that the forces affecting black life in the North, as in the South, were all attributable to property ownership. "The Lords of the Land" in the agrarian South and the "Bosses of Buildings" in the industrial North were alike in exacting a heavy toll of oppression and death on blacks who were "landless upon the land" in the South and constricted in kitchenette apartments in the North.

The fame that Wright earned in the early 1940s, chiefly engendered by *Native Son*, led to extensive lecturing and travel. He spoke around the country and, in 1942, was awarded the NAACP's Spingarn Medal, then the most prestigious award for achievements by any African American in the country. A successful stage production of *Native Son* (1941), which Wright himself adapted, toured the country after a brief Broadway run. But Wright was clearly not content to have his literary reputation rest on *Native Son* alone or entirely on the prerogatives of socialist realism. The publication of his autobiography, *Black Boy*, in 1945 indicated a new direction.

Hailed as a masterpiece, *Black Boy* was praised for its achievement of a tautness and lyric intensity generally smothered in Wright's work by ideological abstractions. Writing in the militant spirit of Frederick Douglass's 1845 *Narrative* and drawing on a number of slave narrative conventions, Wright succeeded in fashioning a myth of self that conformed to the stock pattern of the American success myth of the self-made man, of which Benjamin Franklin's *Autobiography* and Douglass's *Narrative* are prototypical examples. *Black Boy* sold as vigorously upon release as had *Native Son* five years before. Four months after its release, the book had sold 450,000 copies, making it the leading nonfiction best-seller in the nation at the time. When he reviewed the book, Ralph Ellison judged *Black Boy* a "personal catastrophe expressed lyrically." Cheering Wright as a "black boy singing lustily as he probes his own grievous wound," Ellison predicted that the book would "do much to redefine the problem of the Negro and American Democracy."

Following the publication of *Black Boy* Wright expatriated to Paris, where he remained until his premature death in 1960. As such recent scholars as William J. Maxwell have suggested, Wright's decampment to France was likely motivated, at least in part, by the FBI surveillance to which he and other African American writers,

In *Twelve Million Black Voices*, Wright drew upon the archive of photographs taken by photographers in the employ of the Farm Security Administration.

including Baldwin, Lorraine Hansberry, and Langston Hughes, were subjected. State surveillance notwithstanding, Wright's sojourn in Paris inspired his famous quip: "there is more freedom in one block of Paris than there is in the whole United States." In Paris Wright became involved with Jean-Paul Sartre, Simone de Beauvoir, Albert Camus, and other members of *Les Temps Modernes* who are credited with, perhaps too uncritically, influencing the existentialist philosophy apparent in Wright's novel *The Outsider* (1953). Some critics suggest that Wright's traumatic childhood in Mississippi made him a "home-grown" existentialist, who had actually begun to incorporate the philosophy into his writing as early as 1944 when his short story "The Man Who Lived Underground" appeared in the anthology *Cross Section*. In both *The Outsider* and "The Man Who Lived Underground," Wright also indulged his lifelong fascination with the conventions of such popular genres as detective stories and dime novels.

Wright traveled throughout Europe and Africa in the 1950s and continued to be prolific in a variety of forms, but during this decade his imagination took an increasingly cosmopolitan turn, based on his travels as well as on his associations with various international luminaries. These included no less than Léopold Senghor, Senegalese poet, politician, and cultural theorist who served as the first president of Senegal from 1960 to 1980; Aimé Césaire, French poet, author and politician from Martinique, and founding member of the Negritude movement in Francophone literature; Jawaharlal Nehru, first prime minister of independent India; and Kwame Nkrumah, who would lead the Gold Coast to nationhood in 1957 and the new West African state of Ghana. George and Dorothy Padmore, Pan-Africanist leftists committed to independence movements in Africa, had urged Wright to visit the Gold Coast in 1953. On the basis of his extensive travels there, Wright wrote *Black Power: A Record of Reactions in a Land of Pathos* (1954), in which he recorded his impressions of the social and psychological effects of material oppression in global perspective. Though often credited for its participation in Pan-Africanist and anticolonialist projects, as well as for its investments in the promise of black emancipation worldwide, *Black Power* has been critiqued just as often for "colonialist" impulses, evident in its condescending assertions about African cultural practices. On the heels of *Black Power* came *The Color Curtain: A Report on the Bandung Conference* (1956). Wright attended the spring 1955 Bandung Conference of nonaligned Asian and African nations in Indonesia as a reporter for *Encounter*—in which venue Baldwin's coverage of the First International Congress of Black Writers and Artists would appear in 1956. Alongside his old antagonist, Wright also participated in that congress at the Sorbonne where he delivered the closing address, "Tradition and Industrialization." The essay, which bears the provocative subtitle "The Historic Meaning of the Plight of the Tragic Elite in Africa," calls Wright's putative anticolonialist credentials into question. Although some might stop short of endorsing Henry Louis Gates's argument that Wright's essay is a "blueprint for a neocolonialist police state," there is much merit in his critique of Wright's overinvestment in Western notions of modernity which Wright regarded as the blessed obverse of "tradition," presumably embodied by non-Western nations. Critics have wrestled with Wright's celebratory idea that the West was a welcomed corrective to "tradition," in that it helped "smash the irrational ties of religion and custom and tradition in Asia and Africa." No less troubling is the essay's statement: "WHAT IS GOOD FOR EUROPE IS GOOD FOR ALL MANKIND" (emphasis in the original). Although the essay is clearly irreducible to these excerpts, the ambiguities they create in the writings of one otherwise so openly critical of Western domination must be noted. Perhaps one of the essay's saving graces lies in Wright's observation that the congress attendance was dramatically absent of visible women participants:

> I would like to say—I don't know how many of you have noticed it (sic) there have been no women functioning vitally and responsibly upon this platform helping to mold and mobilize our thoughts. This is not a criticism of the conference, it is not a criticism of anyone, it is a criticism that I heap upon ourselves collectively.

When and if we hold another conference—and I hope we will—I hope there
shall be an effective utilization of Negro womanhood in the world to help us
mobilize and pool our forces.

A remarkable statement in any event, but coming from Richard Wright and from the
perspective of the traditional criticism lodged against the treatment of women in
his fictional plots, it is weighty enough to provoke a reconsideration of this phase of
Wright's career, if not the whole. "Tradition and Industrialization" might be said to
belong to Wright's "international" years, insofar as the topics of his address are no
longer strictly centered on African American life and thought but, rather, reflect on
the broader currents of the global political scene.

"Tradition and Industrialization" underwent subtle revisions and modifications
of its most troubling passages before its inclusion in Wright's collection of essays
White Man Listen! (1957) In *Pagan Spain* (1957) Wright rounded out perhaps his
most productive decade, during which he published not only his trilogy of travel
books—*Black Power, The Color Curtain,* and *Pagan Spain*—but also three novels—
The Outside (1953), *Savage Holiday* (1954), and *The Long Dream* (1958).

Despite this prodigious output, however, many critics have argued that Wright's
career as a serious literary artist ended in 1946, when he left the United States.
While France and French citizenship liberated Wright as a person, they argue, it
shackled his creative expression, dulling the vivid memories of his childhood and
early life, deadening his ear to the rhythms and cadences of black American speech,
all of which he had captured so compellingly in such works as "The Ethics of Living
Jim Crow" and *Black Boy*. The result, for some, was work that seemed contrived and
artificial, full of windy abstractions. Such criticisms, which verge on dictating the
range and limits of Wright's imagination to African American life and culture, fail
to give proper due to Wright's growing awareness of a world emerging from Western
and American hegemony of which his life as an émigré had made him keenly aware.

During the last decade of his life and career, Wright devoted much of his work to
exploring this emergent world order, however troubling some of his conclusions
might be. That he attempted to chart this shifting order and to describe the emancipatory movements by linking those oppressed behind the "color curtains" around the
globe, including the Jim Crow South, is not easily dismissed. Indeed, Wright's preoccupations with black nationalist, independence movements in Africa formed a
bridge connecting him again across the Atlantic to the black aesthetic critics and
writers of the late 1960s who claimed Wright as a favored ancestor and who suggested that without *Native Son*, no viable African American literary tradition would
have been possible. Like most critics before them, the black aestheticians designated
Wright a "protest" writer par excellence, finding in his work the "clenched militancy"
that Irving Howe had praised at the expense of Ralph Ellison and James Baldwin.

The full extent and importance of Wright's artistic contributions to African
American literature are still being assessed in light of the contemporary editions of
his work that restore expurgated passages originally perceived to be too raw and
sexually explicit for American reading audiences of the time. The restored passages
of *Native Son*, for example, now lead critics to underline the homoerotic aspects of
that novel, only hinted at in the original. Similarly, Wright's autobiography, structured originally in two parts, appeared separately in two parts as *Black Boy* in 1945
and posthumously as *American Hunger*. The Library of America edition brought the
two together for the first time. Finally, the restoration of lengthy editorial cuts made
originally in *The Outsider* provides a stronger sense of the style, which Wright called
"poetic realism," toward which he was groping in this work. Finally, with the posthumous novel, *A Father's Law* (2008), on which he was working during the last months
of his life, he had circled back to the genre of crime fiction that brought him his fame.

Even without these invaluable new editions of Wright's work, it would continue to
be read. *Native Son* made sure of that. If Wright had produced nothing else, the novel
would have secured and solidified his reputation. Although critics have disagreed,
often bitterly, over the artistic merits of *Native Son*, none deny its power. Though

compromised by ideological commitments and marred by overwriting, the novel's class consciousness, its exploration of sexual racism and social dislocation, and its rejection of the dominant discourse on race guarantee the novel's lasting significance and Wright's place in world letters.

Blueprint for Negro Writing

1) The Role of Negro Writing: Two Definitions

Generally speaking, Negro writing in the past has been confined to humble novels, poems, and plays, prim and decorous ambassadors who went a-begging to white America. They entered the Court of American Public Opinion dressed in the knee-pants of servility, curtsying to show that the Negro was not inferior, that he was human, and that he had a life comparable to that of other people. For the most part these artistic ambassadors were received as though they were French poodles who do clever tricks.

White America never offered these Negro writers any serious criticism. The mere fact that a Negro could write was astonishing. Nor was there any deep concern on the part of white America with the role Negro writing should play in American culture; and the role it did play grew out of accident rather than intent or design. Either it crept in through the kitchen in the form of jokes; or it was the fruits of that foul soil which was the result of a liason between inferiority-complexed Negro "geniuses" and burnt-out white Bohemians with money.

On the other hand, these often technically brilliant performances by Negro writers were looked upon by the majority of literate Negroes as something to be proud of. At best, Negro writing has been something external to the lives of educated Negroes themselves. That the productions of their writers should have been something of a guide in their daily living is a matter which seems never to have been raised seriously.

Under these conditions Negro writing assumed two general aspects: 1) It became a sort of conspicuous ornamentation, the hallmark of "achievement." 2) It became the voice of the educated Negro pleading with white America for justice.

Rarely was the best of this writing addressed to the Negro himself, his needs, his sufferings, his aspirations. Through misdirection, Negro writers have been far better to others than they have been to themselves. And the mere recognition of this places the whole question of Negro writing in a new light and raises a doubt as to the validity of its present direction.

2) The Minority Outlook

Somewhere in his writings Lenin[1] makes the observation that oppressed minorities often reflect the techniques of the bourgeoisie more brilliantly than some sections of the bourgeoisie themselves. The psychological importance of this becomes meaningful when it is recalled that oppressed minorities, and especially the petty bourgeois sections of oppressed minorities, strive to assimilate the virtues of the bourgeoisie in the assumption that by doing so

---

1. Vladimir Ilyich Ulyanov (1870–1924), Communist theorist and founder of the Bolshevik Party. He was the leader of the newly formed Soviet Union until his death.

they can lift themselves into a higher social sphere. But not only among the oppressed petty bourgeoisie does this occur. The workers of a minority people, chafing under exploitation, forge organizational forms of struggle to better their lot. Lacking the handicaps of false ambition and property, they have access to a wide social vision and a deep social consciousness. They display a greater freedom and initiative in pushing their claims upon civilization than even do the petty bourgeoisie. Their organizations show greater strength, adaptability, and efficiency than any other group or class in society.

That Negro workers, propelled by the harsh conditions of their lives, have demonstrated this consciousness and mobility for economic and political action there can be no doubt. But has this consciousness been reflected in the work of Negro writers to the same degree as it has in the Negro workers' struggle to free Herndon and the Scottsboro Boys,[2] in the drive toward unionism, in the fight against lynching? Have they as creative writers taken advantage of their unique minority position?

The answer decidedly is *no*. Negro writers have lagged sadly, and as time passes the gap widens between them and their people.

How can this hiatus be bridged? How can the enervating effects of this long standing split be eliminated?

In presenting questions of this sort an attitude of self-consciousness and self-criticism is far more likely to be a fruitful point of departure than a mere recounting of past achievements. An emphasis upon tendency and experiment, a view of society as something becoming rather than as something fixed and admired is the one which points the way for Negro writers to stand shoulder to shoulder with Negro workers in mood and outlook.

3) A Whole Culture

There is, however, a culture of the Negro which is his and has been addressed to him; a culture which has, for good or ill, helped to clarify his consciousness and create emotional attitudes which are conducive to action. This culture has stemmed mainly from two sources: 1) the Negro church; 2) and the folklore of the Negro people.

It was through the portals of the church that the American Negro first entered the shrine of western culture. Living under slave conditions of life, bereft of his African heritage, the Negroes' struggle for religion on the plantations between 1820–60 assumed the form of a struggle for human rights. It remained a relatively revolutionary struggle until religion began to serve as an antidote for suffering and denial. But even today there are millions of American Negroes whose only sense of a whole universe, whose only relation to society and man, and whose only guide to personal dignity comes through the archaic morphology of Christian salvation.

---

2. Nine black youths tried for the alleged rape of two white women in 1931 in Alabama. All were convicted, and all but one were sentenced to death, despite expert medical testimony that no rape had occurred. Subsequent U.S. Supreme Court decisions (1932 and 1935) reversed the convictions. In further proceedings in Alabama from 1935 to 1937, four of the Scottsboro Nine were once again convicted, resulting in prison terms ranging from seventy-five years to life. Charges against the remaining five were dropped. The case was used by the Communist Party to shore up its support, as it fought the NAACP for the opportunity to represent the defendants. Angelo Herndon was the lead figure in what was, along with the trial of the Scottsboro Boys, one of the most celebrated criminal trials in African American history. Born in Ohio, Herndon was a member of the Communist Party. For organizing an antidiscrimination march in Georgia, he was convicted in 1933 of inciting insurrection and sentenced to a twenty-year prison term under a one-hundred-year-old slave law. The U.S. Supreme Court reversed this decision in 1937.

It was, however, in a folklore moulded out of rigorous and inhuman conditions of life that the Negro achieved his most indigenous and complete expression. Blues, spirituals, and folk tales recounted from mouth to mouth; the whispered words of a black mother to her black daughter on the ways of men; the confidential wisdom of a black father to his black son; the swapping of sex experiences on street corners from boy to boy in the deepest vernacular; work songs sung under blazing suns—all these formed the channels through which the racial wisdom flowed.

One would have thought that Negro writers in the last century of striving at expression would have continued and deepened this folk tradition, would have tried to create a more intimate and yet a more profoundly social system of artistic communication between them and their people. But the illusion that they could escape through individual achievement the harsh lot of their race swung Negro writers away from any such path. Two separate cultures sprang up: one for the Negro masses, unwritten and unrecognized; and the other for the sons and daughters of a rising Negro bourgeoisie, parasitic and mannered.

Today the question is: Shall Negro writing be for the Negro masses, moulding the lives and consciousness of those masses toward new goals, or shall it continue begging the question of the Negroes' humanity?

4) The Problem of Nationalism in Negro Writing

In stressing the difference between the role Negro writing failed to play in the lives of the Negro people, and the role it should play in the future if it is to serve its historic function; in pointing out the fact that Negro writing has been addressed in the main to a small white audience rather than to a Negro one, it should be stated that no attempt is being made here to propagate a specious and blatant nationalism. Yet the nationalist character of the Negro people is unmistakable. Psychologically this nationalism is reflected in the whole of Negro culture, and especially in folklore.

In the absence of fixed and nourishing forms of culture, the Negro has a folklore which embodies the memories and hopes of his struggle for freedom. Not yet caught in paint or stone, and as yet but feebly depicted in the poem and novel, the Negroes' most powerful images of hope and despair still remain in the fluid state of daily speech. How many John Henrys[3] have lived and died on the lips of these black people? How many mythical heroes in embryo have been allowed to perish for lack of husbanding by alert intelligence?

Negro folklore contains, in a measure that puts to shame more deliberate forms of Negro expression, the collective sense of Negro life in America. Let those who shy at the nationalist implications of Negro life look at this body of folklore, living and powerful, which rose out of a unified sense of a common life and a common fate. Here are those vital beginnings of a recognition of value in life as it is *lived*, a recognition that marks the emergence of a new culture in the shell of the old. And at the moment this process starts, at the moment when a people begin to realize a *meaning* in their suffering, the civilization that engenders that suffering is doomed.

The nationalist aspects of Negro life are as sharply manifest in the social institutions of Negro people as in folklore. There is a Negro church, a Negro

3. A legendary figure from African American ballads and folklore. In the story, John Henry competed with a steam-powered drill to drive railroad spikes. He won the contest but died from exhaustion.

press, a Negro social world, a Negro sporting world, a Negro business world, a Negro school system, Negro professions; in short, a Negro way of life in America. The Negro people did not ask for this, and deep down, though they express themselves through their institutions and adhere to this special way of life, they do not want it now. This special existence was forced upon them from without by lynch rope, bayonet and mob rule. They accepted these negative conditions with the inevitability of a tree which must live or perish in whatever soil it finds itself.

The few crumbs of American civilization which the Negro has got from the tables of capitalism have been through these segregated channels. Many Negro institutions are cowardly and incompetent; but they are all that the Negro has. And, in the main, any move, whether for progress or reaction, must come through these institutions for the simple reason that all other channels are closed. Negro writers who seek to mould or influence the consciousness of the Negro people must address their messages to them through the ideologies and attitudes fostered in this warping way of life.

5) The Basis and Meaning of Nationalism in Negro Writing

The social institutions of the Negro are imprisoned in the Jim Crow[4] political system of the South, and this Jim Crow political system is in turn built upon a plantation-feudal economy. Hence, it can be seen that the emotional expression of group-feeling which puzzles so many whites and leads them to deplore what they call "black chauvinism" is not a morbidly inherent trait of the Negro, but rather the reflex expression of a life whose roots are imbedded deeply in Southern soil.

Negro writers must accept the nationalist implications of their lives, not in order to encourage them, but in order to change and transcend them. They must accept the concept of nationalism because, in order to transcend it, they must *possess* and *understand* it. And a nationalist spirit in Negro writing means a nationalism carrying the highest possible pitch of social consciousness. It means a nationalism that knows its origins, its limitations; that is aware of the dangers of its position; that knows its ultimate aims are unrealizable within the framework of capitalist America; a nationalism whose reason for being lies in the simple fact of self-possession and in the consciousness of the interdependence of people in modern society.

For purposes of creative expression it means that the Negro writer must realize within the area of his own personal experience those impulses which, when prefigured in terms of broad social movements, constitute the stuff of nationalism.

For Negro writers even more so than for Negro politicians, nationalism is a bewildering and vexing question, the full ramifications of which cannot be dealt with here. But among Negro workers and the Negro middle class the spirit of nationalism is rife in a hundred devious forms; and a simple literary realism which seeks to depict the lives of these people devoid of wider social connotations, devoid of the revolutionary significance of these nationalist tendencies, must of necessity do a rank injustice to the Negro people and alienate their possible allies in the struggle for freedom.

---

4. System of social segregation in the U.S. South during the late 19th and the 20th centuries.

6) Social Consciousness and Responsibility

The Negro writer who seeks to function within his race as a purposeful agent has a serious responsibility. In order to do justice to his subject matter, in order to depict Negro life in all of its manifold and intricate relationships, a deep, informed, and complex consciousness is necessary; a consciousness which draws for its strength upon the fluid lore of a great people, and moulds this lore with the concepts that move and direct the forces of history today.

With the gradual decline of the moral authority of the Negro church, and with the increasing irresolution which is paralyzing Negro middle class leadership, a new role is devolving upon the Negro writer. He is being called upon to do no less than create values by which his race is to struggle, live and die.

By his ability to fuse and make articulate the experiences of men, because his writing possesses the potential cunning to steal into the inmost recesses of the human heart, because he can create the myths and symbols that inspire a faith in life, he may expect either to be consigned to oblivion, or to be recognized for the valued agent he is.

This raises the question of the personality of the writer. It means that in the lives of Negro writers must be found those materials and experiences which will create a meaningful picture of the world today. Many young writers have grown to believe that a Marxist analysis of society presents such a picture. It creates a picture which, when placed before the eyes of the writer, should unify his personality, organize his emotions, buttress him with a tense and obdurate will to change the world.

And, in turn, this changed world will dialectically change the writer. Hence, it is through a Marxist conception of reality and society that the maximum degree of freedom in thought and feeling can be gained for the Negro writer. Further, this dramatic Marxist vision, when consciously grasped, endows the writer with a sense of dignity which no other vision can give. Ultimately, it restores to the writer his lost heritage, that is, his role as a creator of the world in which he lives, and as a creator of himself.

Yet, for the Negro writer, Marxism is but the starting point. No theory of life can take the place of life. After Marxism has laid bare the skeleton of society, there remains the task of the writer to plant flesh upon those bones out of his will to live. He may, with disgust and revulsion, say *no* and depict the horrors of capitalism encroaching upon the human being. Or he may, with hope and passion, say *yes* and depict the faint stirrings of a new and emerging life. But in whatever social voice he chooses to speak, whether positive or negative, there should always be heard or *over*-heard his faith, his necessity, his judgement.

His vision need not be simple or rendered in primer-like terms; for the life of the Negro people is not simple. The presentation of their lives should be simple, yes; but all the complexity, the strangeness, the magic wonder of life that plays like a bright sheen over the most sordid existence, should be there. To borrow a phrase from the Russians, it should have a *complex simplicity.* Eliot, Stein, Joyce, Proust, Hemingway, and Anderson; Gorky, Barbusse, Nexo, and Jack London[5] no less than the folklore of the Negro himself

5. American writer (1876–1916). T. S. Eliot (1888–1965), American poet, playwright, and literary critic. Gertrude Stein (1874–1946), American-born author who later settled in Paris, where her home became the social center for a group of American and European artists. James Joyce (1882–1941), Irish novelist and poet. Marcel Proust (1871–1922), French novelist, essayist, and critic. Ernest Hemingway (1899–1961), American writer. Sherwood Anderson (1876–1941), American writer. Maxim Gorky (1868–1935), Russian prose writer and playwright. Henri Barbusse (1874–1935), French novelist and journalist. Martin Anderson Nexo (1869–1954), Danish novelist.

should form the heritage of the Negro writer. Every iota of gain in human thought and sensibility should be ready grist for his mill, no matter how far-fetched they may seem in their immediate implications.

7) *The Problem of Perspective*

What vision must Negro writers have before their eyes in order to feel the impelling necessity for an about face? What angle of vision can show them all the forces of modern society in process, all the lines of economic development converging toward a distant point of hope? Must they believe in some "ism"?

They may feel that only dupes believe in "isms"; they feel with some measure of justification that another commitment means only another disillusionment. But anyone destitute of a theory about the meaning, structure and direction of modern society is a lost victim in a world he cannot understand or control.

But even if Negro writers found themselves through some "ism," how would that influence their writing? Are they being called upon to "preach"? To be "salesmen"? To "prostitute" their writing? Must they "sully" themselves? Must they write "propaganda"?

No; it is a question of awareness, of consciousness; it is, above all, a question of perspective.

Perspective is that part of a poem, novel, or play which a writer never puts directly upon paper. It is that fixed point in intellectual space where a writer stands to view the struggles, hopes, and sufferings of his people. There are times when he may stand too close and the result is a blurred vision. Or he may stand too far away and the result is a neglect of important things.

Of all the problems faced by writers who as a whole have never allied themselves with world movements, perspective is the most difficult of achievement. At its best, perspective is a pre-conscious assumption, something which a writer takes for granted, something which he wins through his living.

A Spanish writer recently spoke of living in the heights of one's time. Surely, perspective means just *that*.

It means that a Negro writer must learn to view the life of a Negro living in New York's Harlem or Chicago's South Side with the consciousness that one-sixth of the earth surface belongs to the working class. It means that a Negro writer must create in his readers' minds a relationship between a Negro woman hoeing cotton in the South and the men who loll in swivel chairs in Wall Street and take the fruits of her toil.

Perspective for Negro writers will come when they have looked and brooded so hard and long upon the harsh lot of their race and compared it with the hopes and struggles of minority peoples everywhere that the cold facts have begun to tell them something.

8) *The Problem of Theme*

This does not mean that a Negro writer's sole concern must be with rendering the social scene; but if his conception of the life of his people is broad and deep enough, if the sense of the *whole* life he is seeking is vivid and strong in him, then his writing will embrace all those social, political, and economic forms under which the life of his people is manifest.

In speaking of theme one must necessarily be general and abstract; the temperament of each writer moulds and colors the world he sees. Negro life may be approached from a thousand angles, with no limit to technical and stylistic freedom.

Negro writers spring from a family, a clan, a class, and a nation; and the social units in which they are bound have a story, a record. Sense of theme will emerge in Negro writing when Negro writers try to fix this story about some pole of meaning, remembering as they do so that in the creative process meaning proceeds *equally* as much from the contemplation of the subject matter as from the hopes and apprehensions that rage in the heart of the writer.

Reduced to its simplest and most general terms, theme for Negro writers will rise from understanding the meaning of their being transplanted from a "savage" to a "civilized" culture in all of its social, political, economic, and emotional implications. It means that Negro writers must have in their consciousness the foreshortened picture of the *whole*, nourishing culture from which they were torn in Africa, and of the long, complex (and for the most part, unconscious) struggle to regain in some form and under alien conditions of life a *whole* culture again.

It is not only this picture they must have, but also a knowledge of the social and emotional milieu that gives it tone and solidity of detail. Theme for Negro writers will emerge when they have begun to feel the meaning of the history of their race as though they in one life time had lived it themselves throughout all the long centuries.

9) Autonomy of Craft

For the Negro writer to depict this new reality requires a greater discipline and consciousness than was necessary for the so-called Harlem school[6] of expression. Not only is the subject matter dealt with far more meaningful and complex, but the new role of the writer is qualitatively different. The Negro writers' new position demands a sharper definition of the status of his craft, and a sharper emphasis upon its functional autonomy.

Negro writers should seek through the medium of their craft to play as meaningful a role in the affairs of men as do other professionals. But if their writing is demanded to perform the social office of other professions, then the autonomy of craft is lost and writing detrimentally fused with other interests. The limitations of the craft constitute some of its greatest virtues. If the sensory vehicle of imaginative writing is required to carry too great a load of didactic material, the artistic sense is submerged.

The relationship between reality and the artistic image is not always direct and simple. The imaginative conception of a historical period will not be a carbon copy of reality. Image and emotion possess a logic of their own. A vulgarized simplicity constitutes the greatest danger in tracing the reciprocal interplay between the writer and his environment.

Writing has its professional autonomy; it should complement other professions, but it should not supplant them or be swamped by them.

---

6. Designation given those writers who took their subject matter from the black working classes and their language from the rhythms and inflections of black speech.

10) *The Necessity for Collective Work*

It goes without saying that these things cannot be gained by Negro writers if their present mode of isolated writing and living continues. This isolation exists *among* Negro writers as well as *between* Negro and white writers. The Negro writers' lack of thorough integration with the American scene, their lack of a clear realization among themselves of their possible role, have bred generation after generation of embittered and defeated literati.

Barred for decades from the theater and publishing houses, Negro writers have been *made* to feel a sense of difference. So deep has this white-hot iron of exclusion been burnt into their hearts that thousands have all but lost the desire to become identified with American civilization. The Negro writers' acceptance of this enforced isolation and their attempt to justify it is but a defense-reflex of the whole special way of life which has been rammed down their throats.

This problem, by its very nature, is one which must be approached contemporaneously from *two* points of view. The ideological unity of Negro writers and the alliance of that unity with all the progressive ideas of our day is the primary prerequisite for collective work. On the shoulders of white writers and Negro writers alike rest the responsibility of ending this mistrust and isolation.

By placing cultural health above narrow sectional prejudices, liberal writers of all races can help to break the stony soil of aggrandizement out of which the stunted plants of Negro nationalism grow. And, simultaneously, Negro writers can help to weed out these choking growths of reactionary nationalism and replace them with hardier and sturdier types.

These tasks are imperative in light of the fact that we live in a time when the majority of the most basic assumptions of life can no longer be taken for granted. Tradition is no longer a guide. The world has grown huge and cold. Surely this is the moment to ask questions, to theorize, to speculate, to wonder out of what materials can a human world be built.

Each step along this unknown path should be taken with thought, care, self-consciousness, and deliberation. When Negro writers think they have arrived at something which smacks of truth, humanity, they should want to test it with others, feel it with a degree of passion and strength that will enable them to communicate it to millions who are groping like themselves.

Writers faced with such tasks can have no possible time for malice or jealousy. The conditions for the growth of each writer depend too much upon the good work of other writers. Every first rate novel, poem, or play lifts the level of consciousness higher.

1937

The Ethics of Living Jim Crow,[1] an Autobiographical Sketch

I

My first lesson in how to live as a Negro came when I was quite small. We were living in Arkansas. Our house stood behind the railroad tracks. Its

---

1. System of social segregation in the U.S. South.

skimpy yard was paved with black cinders. Nothing green ever grew in that yard. The only touch of green we could see was far away, beyond the tracks, over where the white folks lived. But cinders were good enough for me and I never missed the green growing things. And anyhow, cinders were fine weapons. You could always have a nice hot war with huge black cinders. All you had to do was crouch behind the brick pillars of a house with your hands full of gritty ammunition. And the first woolly black head you saw pop out from behind another row of pillars was your target. You tried your very best to knock it off. It was great fun.

I never fully realized the appalling disadvantages of a cinder environment till one day the gang to which I belonged found itself engaged in a war with the white boys who lived beyond the tracks. As usual we laid down our cinder barrage, thinking that this would wipe the white boys out. But they replied with a steady bombardment of broken bottles. We doubled our cinder barrage, but they hid behind trees, hedges, and the sloping embankments of their lawns. Having no such fortifications, we retreated to the brick pillars of our homes. During the retreat a broken milk bottle caught me behind the ear, opening a deep gash which bled profusely. The sight of blood pouring over my face completely demoralized our ranks. My fellow-combatants left me standing paralyzed in the center of the yard, and scurried for their homes. A kind neighbor saw me and rushed me to a doctor, who took three stitches in my neck.

I sat brooding on my front steps, nursing my wound and waiting for my mother to come from work. I felt that a grave injustice had been done me. It was all right to throw cinders. The greatest harm a cinder could do was leave a bruise. But broken bottles were dangerous; they left you cut, bleeding, and helpless.

When night fell, my mother came from the white folks' kitchen. I raced down the street to meet her. I could just feel in my bones that she would understand. I knew she would tell me exactly what to do next time. I grabbed her hand and babbled out the whole story. She examined my wound, then slapped me.

"How come yuh didn't hide?" she asked me. "How come yuh awways fightin'?"

I was outraged, and bawled. Between sobs I told her that I didn't have any trees or hedges to hide behind. There wasn't a thing I could have used as a trench. And you couldn't throw very far when you were hiding behind the brick pillars of a house. She grabbed a barrel stave, dragged me home, stripped me naked, and beat me till I had a fever of one hundred and two. She would smack my rump with the stave, and, while the skin was still smarting, impart to me gems of Jim Crow wisdom. I was never to throw cinders any more. I was never to fight any more wars. I was never, never, under any conditions, to fight *white* folks again. And they were absolutely right in clouting me with the broken milk bottle. Didn't I know she was working hard every day in the hot kitchens of the white folks to make money to take care of me? When was I ever going to learn to be a good boy? She couldn't be bothered with my fights. She finished by telling me that I ought to be thankful to God as long as I lived that they didn't kill me.

All that night I was delirious and could not sleep. Each time I closed my eyes I saw monstrous white faces suspended from the ceiling, leering at me.

From that time on, the charm of my cinder yard was gone. The green trees, the trimmed hedges, the cropped lawns grew very meaningful, became a symbol. Even today when I think of white folks, the hard, sharp outlines of white houses surrounded by trees, lawns, and hedges are present somewhere in the background of my mind. Through the years they grew into an overreaching symbol of fear.

It was a long time before I came in close contact with white folks again. We moved from Arkansas to Mississippi. Here we had the good fortune not to live behind the railroad tracks, or close to white neighborhoods. We lived in the very heart of the local Black Belt. There were black churches and black preachers; there were black schools and black teachers; black groceries and black clerks. In fact, everything was so solidly black that for a long time I did not even think of white folks, save in remote and vague terms. But this could not last forever. As one grows older one eats more. One's clothing costs more. When I finished grammar school I had to go to work. My mother could no longer feed and clothe me on her cooking job.

There is but one place where a black boy who knows no trade can get a job, and that's where the houses and faces are white, where the trees, lawns, and hedges are green. My first job was with an optical company in Jackson, Mississippi. The morning I applied I stood straight and neat before the boss, answering all his questions with sharp yessirs and nosirs. I was very careful to pronounce my *sirs* distinctly, in order that he might know that I was polite, that I knew where I was, and that I knew he was a *white* man. I wanted that job badly.

He looked me over as though he were examining a prize poodle. He questioned me closely about my schooling, being particularly insistent about how much mathematics I had had. He seemed very pleased when I told him I had had two years of algebra.

"Boy, how would you like to try to learn something around here?" he asked me.

"I'd like it fine, sir," I said, happy. I had visions of "working my way up." Even Negroes have those visions.

"All right," he said. "Come on."

I followed him to the small factory.

"Pease," he said to a white man of about thirty-five, "this is Richard. He's going to work for us."

Pease looked at me and nodded.

I was then taken to a white boy of about seventeen.

"Morrie, this is Richard, who's going to work for us."

"Whut yuh sayin' there, boy!" Morrie boomed at me.

"Fine!" I answered.

The boss instructed these two to help me, teach me, give me jobs to do, and let me learn what I could in my spare time.

My wages were five dollars a week.

I worked hard, trying to please. For the first month I got along O.K. Both Pease and Morrie seemed to like me. But one thing was missing. And I kept thinking about it. I was not learning anything and nobody was volunteering to help me. Thinking they had forgotten that I was to learn something about the mechanics of grinding lenses, I asked Morrie one day to tell me about the work. He grew red.

"Whut yuh tryin' t' do, nigger, git smart?" he asked.

"Naw; I ain' tryin' t' git smart," I said.

"Well, don't, if yuh know whut's good for yuh!"

I was puzzled. Maybe he just doesn't want to help me, I thought. I went to Pease.

"Say, are you crazy, you black bastard?" Pease asked me, his gray eyes growing hard.

I spoke out, reminding him that the boss had said I was to be given a chance to learn something.

"Nigger, you think you're *white,* don't you?"

"Naw, sir!"

"Well, you're acting mighty like it!"

"But, Mr. Pease, the boss said . . ."

Pease shook his fist in my face.

"This is a *white* man's work around here, and you better watch yourself!"

From then on they changed toward me. They said goodmorning no more. When I was just a bit slow in performing some duty, I was called a lazy black son-of-a-bitch.

Once I thought of reporting all this to the boss. But the mere idea of what would happen to me if Pease and Morrie should learn that I had "snitched" stopped me. And after all, the boss was a white man, too. What was the use?

The climax came at noon one summer day. Pease called me to his work-bench. To get to him I had to go between two narrow benches and stand with my back against a wall.

"Yes, sir," I said.

"Richard, I want to ask you something," Pease began pleasantly, not looking up from his work.

"Yes, sir," I said again.

Morrie came over, blocking the narrow passage between the benches. He folded his arms, staring at me solemnly.

I looked from one to the other, sensing that something was coming.

"Yes, sir," I said for the third time.

Pease looked up and spoke very slowly.

"Richard, *Mr.* Morrie here tells me you called me *Pease.*"

I stiffened. A void seemed to open up in me. I knew this was the showdown.

He meant that I had failed to call him *Mr.* Pease. I looked at Morrie. He was gripping a steel bar in his hands. I opened my mouth to speak, to protest, to assure Pease that I had never called him simply *Pease,* and that I had never had any intentions of doing so, when Morrie grabbed me by the collar, ramming my head against the wall.

"Now, be careful, nigger!" snarled Morrie, baring his teeth. "*I* heard yuh call 'im *Pease!* 'N' if yuh say yuh didn't, yuh're callin' me a *lie,* see?" He waved the steel bar threateningly.

If I had said: No, sir, Mr. Pease, I never called you *Pease,* I would have been automatically calling Morrie a liar. And if I had said: Yes, sir, Mr. Pease, I called you *Pease,* I would have been pleading guilty to having uttered the worst insult that a Negro can utter to a southern white man. I stood hesitating, trying to frame a neutral reply.

"Richard, I asked you a question!" said Pease. Anger was creeping into his voice.

"I don't remember calling you *Pease,* Mr. Pease," I said cautiously. "And if I did, I sure didn't mean . . ."

"You black son-of-a-bitch! You called me *Pease,* then!" he spat, slapping me till I bent sideways over a bench. Morrie was on top of me, demanding:

"Didn't yuh call 'im *Pease?* If yuh say yuh didn't, I'll rip yo' gut string loose with this bar, yuh black granny dodger! Yuh can't call a white man a lie 'n' git erway with it, you black son-of-a-bitch!"

I wilted. I begged them not to bother me. I knew what they wanted. They wanted me to leave.

"I'll leave," I promised. "I'll leave right *now.*"

They gave me a minute to get out of the factory. I was warned not to show up again, or tell the boss.

I went.

When I told the folks at home what had happened, they called me a fool. They told me that I must never again attempt to exceed my boundaries. When you are working for white folks, they said, you got to "stay in your place" if you want to keep working.

II

My Jim Crow education continued on my next job, which was portering in a clothing store. One morning, while polishing brass out front, the boss and his twenty-year-old son got out of their car and half dragged and half kicked a Negro woman into the store. A policeman standing at the corner looked on, twirling his nightstick. I watched out of the corner of my eye, never slackening the strokes of my chamois upon the brass. After a few minutes, I heard shrill screams coming from the rear of the store. Later the woman stumbled out, bleeding, crying, and holding her stomach. When she reached the end of the block, the policeman grabbed her and accused her of being drunk. Silently, I watched him throw her into a patrol wagon.

When I went to the rear of the store, the boss and his son were washing their hands at the sink. They were chuckling. The floor was bloody and strewn with wisps of hair and clothing. No doubt I must have appeared pretty shocked, for the boss slapped me reassuringly on the back.

"Boy, that's what we do to niggers when they don't want to pay their bills," he said, laughing.

His son looked at me and grinned.

"Here, hava cigarette," he said.

Not knowing what to do, I took it. He lit his and held the match for me. This was a gesture of kindness, indicating that even if they had beaten the poor old woman, they would not beat me if I knew enough to keep my mouth shut.

"Yes, sir," I said, and asked no questions.

After they had gone, I sat on the edge of a packing box and stared at the bloody floor till the cigarette went out.

That day at noon, while eating in a hamburger joint, I told my fellow Negro porters what had happened. No one seemed surprised. One fellow, after swallowing a huge bite, turned to me and asked:

"Huh! Is tha' all they did t' her?"

"Yeah. Wasn't tha' enough?" I asked.

"Shucks! Man, she's a lucky bitch!" he said, burying his lips deep into a juicy hamburger. "Hell, it's a wonder they didn't lay her when they got through."

III

I was learning fast, but not quite fast enough. One day, while I was delivering packages in the suburbs, my bicycle tire was punctured. I walked along the hot, dusty road, sweating and leading my bicycle by the handle-bars.

A car slowed at my side.

"What's the matter, boy?" a white man called.

I told him my bicycle was broken and I was walking back to town.

"That's too bad," he said. "Hop on the running board."

He stopped the car. I clutched hard at my bicycle with one hand and clung to the side of the car with the other.

"All set?"

"Yes, sir," I answered. The car started.

It was full of young white men. They were drinking. I watched the flask pass from mouth to mouth.

"Wanna drink, boy?" one asked.

I laughed as the wind whipped my face. Instinctively obeying the freshly planted precepts of my mother, I said:

"Oh, no!"

The words were hardly out of my mouth before I felt something hard and cold smash me between the eyes. It was an empty whisky bottle. I saw stars, and fell backwards from the speeding car into the dust of the road, my feet becoming entangled in the steel spokes of my bicycle. The white men piled out and stood over me.

"Nigger, ain' yuh learned no better sense'n tha' yet?" asked the man who hit me. "Ain' yuh learned t' say *sir* t' a white man yet?"

Dazed, I pulled to my feet. My elbows and legs were bleeding. Fists doubled, the white man advanced, kicking my bicycle out of the way.

"Aw, leave the bastard alone. He's got enough," said one.

They stood looking at me. I rubbed my shins, trying to stop the flow of blood. No doubt they felt a sort of contemptuous pity, for one asked:

"Yuh wanna ride t' town now, nigger? Yuh reckon yuh know enough t' ride now?"

"I wanna walk," I said, simply.

Maybe it sounded funny. They laughed.

"Well, walk, yuh black son-of-a-bitch!"

When they left they comforted me with:

"Nigger, yuh sho better be damn glad it wuz us yuh talked t' tha' way. Yuh're a lucky bastard, 'cause if yuh'd said tha' t' somebody else, yuh might've been a dead nigger now."

IV

Negroes who have lived South know the dread of being caught alone upon the streets in white neighborhoods after the sun has set. In such a simple situation as this the plight of the Negro in America is graphically symbolized. While white strangers may be in these neighborhoods trying to get home, they can pass unmolested. But the color of a Negro's skin makes him easily recognizable, makes him suspect, converts him into a defenseless target.

Late one Saturday night I made some deliveries in a white neighborhood. I was pedaling my bicycle back to the store as fast as I could, when a police car, swerving toward me, jammed me into the curbing.

"Get down and put up your hands!" the policemen ordered.

I did. They climbed out of the car, guns drawn, faces set, and advanced slowly.

"Keep still!" they ordered.

I reached my hands higher. They searched my pockets and packages. They seemed dissatisfied when they could find nothing incriminating. Finally, one of them said:

"Boy, tell your boss not to send you out in white neighborhoods after sundown."

As usual, I said:

"Yes, sir."

V

My next job was as hall-boy in a hotel. Here my Jim Crow education broadened and deepened. When the bell-boys were busy, I was often called to assist them. As many of the rooms in the hotel were occupied by prostitutes, I was constantly called to carry them liquor and cigarettes. These women were nude most of the time. They did not bother about clothing, even for bell-boys. When you went into their rooms, you were supposed to take their nakedness for granted, as though it startled you no more than a blue vase or a red rug. Your presence awoke in them no sense of shame, for you were not regarded as human. If they were alone, you could steal sidelong glimpses at them. But if they were receiving men, not a flicker of your eyelids could show. I remember one incident vividly. A new woman, a huge, snowy-skinned blonde, took a room on my floor. I was sent to wait upon her. She was in bed with a thick-set man; both were nude and uncovered. She said she wanted some liquor and slid out of bed and waddled across the floor to get her money from a dresser drawer. I watched her.

"Nigger, what in hell you looking at?" the white man asked me, raising himself upon his elbows.

"Nothing," I answered, looking miles deep into the blank wall of the room.

"Keep your eyes where they belong, if you want to be healthy!" he said.

"Yes, sir."

VI

One of the bell-boys I knew in this hotel was keeping steady company with one of the Negro maids. Out of a clear sky the police descended upon his home and arrested him, accusing him of bastardy. The poor boy swore he had had no intimate relations with the girl. Nevertheless, they forced him to marry her. When the child arrived, it was found to be much lighter in complexion than either of the two supposedly legal parents. The white men around the hotel made a great joke of it. They spread the rumor that some white cow must have scared the poor girl while she was carrying the baby. If you were in their presence when this explanation was offered, you were supposed to laugh.

VII

One of the bell-boys was caught in bed with a white prostitute. He was castrated and run out of town. Immediately after this all the bell-boys and hall-boys were called together and warned. We were given to understand that the boy who had been castrated was a "mighty, mighty lucky bastard." We were impressed with the fact that next time the management of the hotel would not be responsible for the lives of "trouble-makin' niggers." We were silent.

VIII

One night, just as I was about to go home, I met one of the Negro maids. She lived in my direction, and we fell in to walk part of the way home together. As we passed the white night-watchman, he slapped the maid on her buttock. I turned around, amazed. The watchman looked at me with a long, hard, fixed-under stare. Suddenly he pulled his gun and asked:

"Nigger, don't yuh like it?"

I hesitated.

"I asked yuh don't yuh like it?" he asked again, stepping forward.

"Yes, sir," I mumbled.

"Talk like it, then!"

"Oh, yes, sir!" I said with as much heartiness as I could muster.

Outside, I walked ahead of the girl, ashamed to face her. She caught up with me and said:

"Don't be a fool! Yuh couldn't help it!"

This watchman boasted of having killed two Negroes in self-defense.

Yet, in spite of all this, the life of the hotel ran with an amazing smoothness. It would have been impossible for a stranger to detect anything. The maids, the hall-boys, and the bell-boys were all smiles. They had to be.

IX

I had learned my Jim Crow lessons so thoroughly that I kept the hotel job till I left Jackson for Memphis. It so happened that while in Memphis I applied for a job at a branch of the optical company. I was hired. And for some reason, as long as I worked there, they never brought my past against me.

Here my Jim Crow education assumed quite a different form. It was no longer brutally cruel, but subtly cruel. Here I learned to lie, to steal, to dissemble. I learned to play that dual role which every Negro must play if he wants to eat and live.

For example, it was almost impossible to get a book to read. It was assumed that after a Negro had imbibed what scanty schooling the state furnished he had no further need for books. I was always borrowing books from men on the job. One day I mustered enough courage to ask one of the men to let me get books from the library in his name. Surprisingly, he consented. I cannot help but think that he consented because he was a Roman Catholic and felt a vague sympathy for Negroes, being himself an object of hatred. Armed with a library card, I obtained books in the following manner: I would write a note to the librarian, saying: "Please let this nigger boy have the following books." I would then sign it with the white man's name.

When I went to the library, I would stand at the desk, hat in hand, looking as unbookish as possible. When I received the books desired I would take them home. If the books listed in the note happened to be out, I would sneak into the lobby and forge a new one. I never took any chances guessing with the white librarian about what the fictitious white man would want to read. No doubt if any of the white patrons had suspected that some of the volumes they enjoyed had been in the home of a Negro, they would not have tolerated it for an instant.

The factory force of the optical company in Memphis was much larger than that in Jackson, and more urbanized. At least they liked to talk, and would engage the Negro help in conversation whenever possible. By this means I found that many subjects were taboo from the white man's point of view. Among the topics they did not like to discuss with Negroes were the following: American white women; the Ku Klux Klan; France, and how Negro soldiers fared while there; French women; Jack Johnson; the entire northern part of the United States; the Civil War; Abraham Lincoln; U. S. Grant; General Sherman; Catholics; the Pope; Jews; the Republican Party; slavery; social equality; Communism; Socialism; the 13th and 14th Amendments to the Constitution;[2] or any topic calling for positive knowledge or manly self-assertion on the part of the Negro. The most accepted topics were sex and religion.

There were many times when I had to exercise a great deal of ingenuity to keep out of trouble. It is a southern custom that all men must take off their hats when they enter an elevator. And especially did this apply to us blacks with rigid force. One day I stepped into an elevator with my arms full of packages. I was forced to ride with my hat on. Two white men stared at me coldly. Then one of them very kindly lifted my hat and placed it upon my armful of packages. Now the most accepted response for a Negro to make under such circumstances is to look at the white man out of the corner of his eye and grin. To have said: "Thank you!" would have made the white man *think* that you *thought* you were receiving from him a personal service. For such an act I have seen Negroes take a blow in the mouth. Finding the first alternative distasteful, and the second dangerous, I hit upon an acceptable course of action which fell safely between these two poles. I immediately—no sooner than my hat was lifted—pretended that my packages were about to spill, and appeared deeply distressed with keeping them in my arms. In this fashion I evaded having to acknowledge his service, and, in spite of adverse circumstances, salvaged a slender shred of personal pride.

How do Negroes feel about the way they have to live? How do they discuss it when alone among themselves? I think this question can be answered in a single sentence. A friend of mine who ran an elevator once told me:

"Lawd, man! Ef it wuzn't fer them polices 'n' them ol' lynch-mobs, there wouldn't be nothin' but uproar down here!"

1937

---

2. The Thirteenth Amendment (proclaimed December 18, 1865) abolished slavery and involuntary servitude, and the Fourteenth Amendment (proclaimed July 28, 1868) made American blacks citizens of the United States. Jack Johnson (1879–1946), black American heavyweight fighter who won the championship title in 1908.

From Black Boy

Chapter XIII

[BOOKLIST]

One morning I arrived early at work and went into the bank lobby where the Negro porter was mopping. I stood at a counter and picked up the Memphis *Commercial Appeal* and began my free reading of the press. I came finally to the editorial page and saw an article dealing with one H. L. Mencken.[1] I knew by hearsay that he was the editor of the *American Mercury*, but aside from that I knew nothing about him. The article was a furious denunciation of Mencken, concluding with one, hot, short sentence: Mencken is a fool.

I wondered what on earth this Mencken had done to call down upon him the scorn of the South. The only people I had ever heard denounced in the South were Negroes, and this man was not a Negro. Then what ideas did Mencken hold that made a newspaper like the *Commercial Appeal* castigate him publicly? Undoubtedly he must be advocating ideas that the South did not like. Were there, then, people other than Negroes who criticized the South? I knew that during the Civil War the South had hated northern whites, but I had not encountered such hate during my life. Knowing no more of Mencken than I did at that moment, I felt a vague sympathy for him. Had not the South, which had assigned me the role of a non-man, cast at him its hardest words?

Now, how could I find out about this Mencken? There was a huge library near the riverfront, but I knew that Negroes were not allowed to patronize its shelves any more than they were the parks and playgrounds of the city. I had gone into the library several times to get books for the white men on the job. Which of them would now help me to get books? And how could I read them without causing concern to the white men with whom I worked? I had so far been successful in hiding my thoughts and feelings from them, but I knew that I would create hostility if I went about this business of reading in a clumsy way.

I weighed the personalities of the men on the job. There was Don, a Jew; but I distrusted him. His position was not much better than mine and I knew that he was uneasy and insecure; he had always treated me in an off-hand, bantering way that barely concealed his contempt. I was afraid to ask him to help me to get books; his frantic desire to demonstrate a racial solidarity with the whites against Negroes might make him betray me.

Then how about the boss? No, he was a Baptist and I had the suspicion that he would not be quite able to comprehend why a black boy would want to read Mencken. There were other white men on the job whose attitudes showed clearly that they were Kluxers[2] or sympathizers, and they were out of the question.

There remained only one man whose attitude did not fit into an anti-Negro category, for I had heard the white men refer to him as a "Pope lover." He was an Irish Catholic and was hated by the white Southerners. I knew that he read books, because I had got him volumes from the library several times. Since he, too, was an object of hatred, I felt that he might refuse me but

1. Henry Louis Mencken (1880–1956), American editor and critic; founder and editor (1924–33) of the *American Mercury*, he wrote essays of vitriolic social criticism.

2. I.e., members of the Ku Klux Klan.

would hardly betray me. I hesitated, weighing and balancing the imponderable realities.

One morning I paused before the Catholic fellow's desk.

"I want to ask you a favor," I whispered to him.

"What is it?"

"I want to read. I can't get books from the library. I wonder if you'd let me use your card?"

He looked at me suspiciously.

"My card is full most of the time," he said.

"I see," I said and waited, posing my question silently.

"You're not trying to get me into trouble, are you, boy?" he asked, staring at me.

"Oh, no, sir."

"What book do you want?"

"A book by H. L. Mencken."

"Which one?"

"I don't know. Has he written more than one?"

"He has written several."

"I didn't know that."

"What makes you want to read Mencken?"

"Oh, I just saw his name in the newspaper," I said.

"It's good of you to want to read," he said. "But you ought to read the right things."

I said nothing. Would he want to supervise my reading?

"Let me think," he said. "I'll figure out something."

I turned from him and he called me back. He stared at me quizzically.

"Richard, don't mention this to the other white men," he said.

"I understand," I said. "I won't say a word."

A few days later he called me to him.

"I've got a card in my wife's name," he said. "Here's mine."

"Thank you, sir."

"Do you think you can manage it?"

"I'll manage fine," I said.

"If they suspect you, you'll get in trouble," he said.

"I'll write the same kind of notes to the library that you wrote when you sent me for books," I told him. "I'll sign your name."

He laughed.

"Go ahead. Let me see what you get," he said.

That afternoon I addressed myself to forging a note. Now, what were the names of books written by H. L. Mencken? I did not know any of them. I finally wrote what I thought would be a foolproof note: *Dear Madam: Will you please let this nigger boy*—I used the word "nigger" to make the librarian feel that I could not possibly be the author of the note—*have some books by H. L. Mencken?* I forged the white man's name.

I entered the library as I had always done when on errands for whites, but I felt that I would somehow slip up and betray myself. I doffed my hat, stood a respectful distance from the desk, looked as unbookish as possible, and waited for the white patrons to be taken care of. When the desk was clear of people, I still waited. The white librarian looked at me.

"What do you want, boy?"

As though I did not possess the power of speech, I stepped forward and simply handed her the forged note, not parting my lips.

"What books by Mencken does he want?" she asked.

"I don't know, ma'am," I said, avoiding her eyes.

"Who gave you this card?"

"Mr. Falk," I said.

"Where is he?"

"He's at work, at the M—— Optical Company," I said. "I've been in here for him before."

"I remember," the woman said. "But he never wrote notes like this."

Oh, God, she's suspicious. Perhaps she would not let me have the books? If she had turned her back at that moment, I would have ducked out the door and never gone back. Then I thought of a bold idea.

"You can call him up, ma'am," I said, my heart pounding.

"You're not using these books, are you?" she asked pointedly.

"Oh, no, ma'am. I can't read."

"I don't know what he wants by Mencken," she said under her breath.

I knew now that I had won; she was thinking of other things and the race question had gone out of her mind. She went to the shelves. Once or twice she looked over her shoulder at me, as though she was still doubtful. Finally she came forward with two books in her hand.

"I'm sending him two books," she said. "But tell Mr. Falk to come in next time, or send me the names of the books he wants. I don't know what he wants to read."

I said nothing. She stamped the card and handed me the books. Not daring to glance at them, I went out of the library, fearing that the woman would call me back for further questioning. A block away from the library I opened one of the books and read a title: *A Book of Prefaces*. I was nearing my nineteenth birthday and I did not know how to pronounce the word "preface." I thumbed the pages and saw strange words and strange names. I shook my head, disappointed. I looked at the other book; it was called *Prejudices*. I knew what that word meant; I had heard it all my life. And right off I was on guard against Mencken's books. Why would a man want to call a book *Prejudices*? The word was so stained with all my memories of racial hate that I could not conceive of anybody using it for a title. Perhaps I had made a mistake about Mencken? A man who had prejudices must be wrong.

When I showed the books to Mr. Falk, he looked at me and frowned.

"That librarian might telephone you," I warned him.

"That's all right," he said. "But when you're through reading those books, I want you to tell me what you get out of them."

That night in my rented room, while letting the hot water run over my can of pork and beans in the sink, I opened *A Book of Prefaces* and began to read. I was jarred and shocked by the style, the clear, clean, sweeping sentences. Why did he write like that? And how did one write like that? I pictured the man as a raging demon, slashing with his pen, consumed with hate, denouncing everything American, extolling everything European or German, laughing at the weaknesses of people, mocking God, authority. What was this? I stood up, trying to realize what reality lay behind the meaning of the words . . . Yes, this man was fighting, fighting with words. He was using words as a weapon, using them as one would use a club. Could words be weapons? Well, yes, for here they were. Then, maybe, perhaps, I could use them as a weapon? No. It frightened me. I read on and what amazed me was not what he said, but how on earth anybody had the courage to say it.

Occasionally I glanced up to reassure myself that I was alone in the room. Who were these men about whom Mencken was talking so passionately? Who was Anatole France? Joseph Conrad? Sinclair Lewis, Sherwood Anderson, Dostoevski, George Moore, Gustave Flaubert, Maupassant, Tolstoy, Frank Harris, Mark Twain, Thomas Hardy, Arnold Bennett, Stephen Crane, Zola, Norris, Gorky, Bergson, Ibsen, Balzac, Bernard Shaw, Dumas, Poe, Thomas Mann, O. Henry, Dreiser, H. G. Wells, Gogol, T. S. Eliot, Gide, Baudelaire, Edgar Lee Masters, Stendhal, Turgenev, Huneker, Nietzsche, and scores of others? Were these men real? Did they exist or had they existed? And how did one pronounce their names?

I ran across many words whose meanings I did not know, and I either looked them up in a dictionary or, before I had a chance to do that, encountered the word in a context that made its meaning clear. But what strange world was this? I concluded the book with the conviction that I had somehow overlooked something terribly important in life. I had once tried to write, had once reveled in feeling, had let my crude imagination roam, but the impulse to dream had been slowly beaten out of me by experience. Now it surged up again and I hungered for books, new ways of looking and seeing. It was not a matter of believing or disbelieving what I read, but of feeling something new, of being affected by something that made the look of the world different.

As dawn broke I ate my pork and beans, feeling dopey, sleepy. I went to work, but the mood of the book would not die; it lingered, coloring everything I saw, heard, did. I now felt that I knew what the white men were feeling. Merely because I had read a book that had spoken of how they lived and thought, I identified myself with that book. I felt vaguely guilty. Would I, filled with bookish notions, act in a manner that would make the whites dislike me?

I forged more notes and my trips to the library became frequent. Reading grew into a passion. My first serious novel was Sinclair Lewis's *Main Street*. It made me see my boss, Mr. Gerald, and identify him as an American type. I would smile when I saw him lugging his golf bags into the office. I had always felt a vast distance separating me from the boss, and now I felt closer to him, though still distant. I felt now that I knew him, that I could feel the very limits of his narrow life. And this had happened because I had read a novel about a mythical man called George F. Babbitt.

The plots and stories in the novels did not interest me so much as the point of view revealed. I gave myself over to each novel without reserve, without trying to criticize it; it was enough for me to see and feel something different. And for me, everything was something different. Reading was like a drug, a dope. The novels created moods in which I lived for days. But I could not conquer my sense of guilt, my feeling that the white men around me knew that I was changing, that I had begun to regard them differently.

Whenever I brought a book to the job, I wrapped it in newspaper—a habit that was to persist for years in other cities and under other circumstances. But some of the white men pried into my packages when I was absent and they questioned me.

"Boy, what are you reading those books for?"

"Oh, I don't know, sir."

"That's deep stuff you're reading, boy."

"I'm just killing time, sir."

"You'll addle your brains if you don't watch out."

I read Dreiser's *Jennie Gerhardt* and *Sister Carrie* and they revived in me a vivid sense of my mother's suffering; I was overwhelmed. I grew silent, wondering about the life around me. It would have been impossible for me to have told anyone what I derived from these novels, for it was nothing less than a sense of life itself. All my life had shaped me for the realism, the naturalism of the modern novel, and I could not read enough of them.

Steeped in new moods and ideas, I bought a ream of paper and tried to write; but nothing would come, or what did come was flat beyond telling. I discovered that more than desire and feeling were necessary to write and I dropped the idea. Yet I still wondered how it was possible to know people sufficiently to write about them? Could I ever learn about life and people? To me, with my vast ignorance, my Jim Crow station in life, it seemed a task impossible of achievement. I now knew what being a Negro meant. I could endure the hunger. I had learned to live with hate. But to feel that there were feelings denied me, that the very breath of life itself was beyond my reach, that more than anything else hurt, wounded me. I had a new hunger.

In buoying me up, reading also cast me down, made me see what was possible, what I had missed. My tension returned, new, terrible, bitter, surging, almost too great to be contained. I no longer *felt* that the world about me was hostile, killing; I *knew* it. A million times I asked myself what I could do to save myself, and there were no answers. I seemed forever condemned, ringed by walls.

I did not discuss my reading with Mr. Falk, who had lent me his library card; it would have meant talking about myself and that would have been too painful. I smiled each day, fighting desperately to maintain my old behavior, to keep my disposition seemingly sunny. But some of the white men discerned that I had begun to brood.

"Wake up there, boy!" Mr. Olin said one day.

"Sir!" I answered for the lack of a better word.

"You act like you've stolen something," he said.

I laughed in the way I knew he expected me to laugh, but I resolved to be more conscious of myself, to watch my every act, to guard and hide the new knowledge that was dawning within me.

If I went north, would it be possible for me to build a new life then? But how could a man build a life upon vague, unformed yearnings? I wanted to write and I did not even know the English language. I bought English grammars and found them dull. I felt that I was getting a better sense of the language from novels than from grammars. I read hard, discarding a writer as soon as I felt that I had grasped his point of view. At night the printed page stood before my eyes in sleep.

Mrs. Moss, my landlady, asked me one Sunday morning:

"Son, what is this you keep on reading?"

"Oh, nothing. Just novels."

"What you get out of 'em?"

"I'm just killing time," I said.

"I hope you know your own mind," she said in a tone which implied that she doubted if I had a mind.

I knew of no Negroes who read the books I liked and I wondered if any Negroes ever thought of them. I knew that there were Negro doctors, lawyers, newspapermen, but I never saw any of them. When I read a Negro newspaper I never caught the faintest echo of my preoccupation in its pages. I felt trapped and occasionally, for a few days, I would stop reading. But a vague hunger would come over me for books, books that opened up new avenues of feeling and seeing, and again I would forge another note to the white librarian. Again I would read and wonder as only the naïve and unlettered can read and wonder, feeling that I carried a secret, criminal burden about with me each day.

That winter my mother and brother came and we set up housekeeping, buying furniture on the installment plan, being cheated and yet knowing no way to avoid it. I began to eat warm food and to my surprise found that regular meals enabled me to read faster. I may have lived through many illnesses, and survived them, never suspecting that I was ill. My brother obtained a job and we began to save toward the trip north, plotting our time, setting tentative dates for departure. I told none of the white men on the job that I was planning to go north; I knew that the moment they felt I was thinking of the North they would change toward me. It would have made them feel that I did not like the life I was living, and because my life was completely conditioned by what they said or did, it would have been tantamount to challenging them.

I could calculate my chances for life in the South as a Negro fairly clearly now.

I could fight the southern whites by organizing with other Negroes, as my grandfather had done. But I knew that I could never win that way; there were many whites and there were but few blacks. They were strong and we were weak. Outright black rebellion could never win. If I fought openly I would die and I did not want to die. News of lynchings were frequent.

I could submit and live the life of a genial slave, but that was impossible. All of my life had shaped me to live by my own feelings and thoughts. I could make up to Bess and marry her and inherit the house. But that, too, would be the life of a slave; if I did that, I would crush to death something within me, and I would hate myself as much as I knew the whites already hated those who had submitted. Neither could I ever willingly present myself to be kicked, as Shorty had done. I would rather have died than do that.

I could drain off my restlessness by fighting with Shorty and Harrison. I had seen many Negroes solve the problem of being black by transferring their hatred of themselves to others with a black skin and fighting them. I would have to be cold to do that, and I was not cold and I could never be.

I could, of course, forget what I had read, thrust the whites out of my mind, forget them; and find release from anxiety and longing in sex and alcohol. But the memory of how my father had conducted himself made that course repugnant. If I did not want others to violate my life, how could I voluntarily violate it myself?

I had no hope whatever of being a professional man. Not only had I been so conditioned that I did not desire it, but the fulfillment of such an ambition was beyond my capabilities. Well-to-do Negroes lived in a world that was almost as alien to me as the world inhabited by whites.

What, then, was there? I held my life in my mind, in my consciousness each day, feeling at times that I would stumble and drop it, spill it forever. My reading had created a vast sense of distance between me and the world in which I lived and tried to make a living, and that sense of distance was increasing each day. My days and nights were one long, quiet, continuously contained dream of terror, tension, and anxiety. I wondered how long I could bear it.

Chapter XVI

[CHICAGO]

In the spring I took the postal examination again. Time had somewhat repaired the ravages of hunger and I was able to meet the required physical weight. We moved to a larger apartment. My increased pay made better food possible. I was happy in my own way.

Working nights, I spent my days in experimental writing, filling endless pages with stream-of-consciousness Negro dialect, trying to depict the dwellers of the Black Belt as I felt and saw them. My reading in sociology had enabled me to discern many strange types of Negro characters, to identify many modes of Negro behavior; and what moved me above all was the frequency of mental illness, that tragic toll that the urban environment exacted of the black peasant. Perhaps my writing was more an attempt at understanding than self-expression. A need that I did not comprehend made me use words to create religious types, criminal types, the warped, the lost, the baffled; my pages were full of tension, frantic poverty, and death.

But something was missing in my imaginative efforts; my flights of imagination were too subjective, too lacking in reference to social action. I hungered for a grasp of the framework of contemporary living, for a knowledge of the forms of life about me, for eyes to see the bony structures of personality, for theories to light up the shadows of conduct.

While sorting mail in the post office, I met a young Irish chap whose sensibilities amazed me. We would take a batch of mail in our fingers and, while talking in low monotones out of the sides of our mouths, toss them correctly into their designated holes and suddenly our hands would be empty and we would have no memory of having worked. Most of the clerks could work in this automatic manner. The Irish chap and I had read a lot in common and we laughed at the same sacred things. He was as cynical as I was regarding uplift and hope, and we were proud of having escaped what we called the "childhood disease of metaphysical fear." I was introduced to the Irish chap's friends and we formed a "gang" of Irish, Jewish, and Negro wits who poked fun at government, the masses, statesmen, and political parties. We assumed that all people were good to the degree to which they amused us, or to the extent to which we could make them objects of laughter. We ridiculed all ideas of protest, of organized rebellion or revolution. We felt that all businessmen were thoroughly stupid and that no other group was capable of rising to challenge them. We sneered at voting, for we felt that the choice between one political crook and another was too small for serious thought. We believed that man should live by hard facts alone, and we had so long ago put God out of our minds that we did not even discuss Him.

During this cynical period I met a Negro literary group on Chicago's South Side; it was composed of a dozen or more boys and girls, all of whom possessed academic learning, economic freedom, and vague ambitions to write. I found them more formal in manner than their white counterparts; they wore stylish clothes and were finicky about their personal appearance. I had naïvely supposed that I would have much in common with them, but I found them preoccupied with twisted sex problems. Coming from a station in life which they no doubt would have branded "lower class," I could not understand why they were so all-absorbed with sexual passion. I was encountering for the first time the full-fledged Negro Puritan invert—the emotionally sick—and I discovered that their ideas were but excuses for sex, leads to sex, hints at sex, substitutes for sex. In speech and action they strove to act as un-Negro as possible, denying the racial and material foundations of their lives, accepting their class and racial status in ways so oblique that one had the impression that no difficulties existed for them. Though I had never had any assignments from a college professor, I had made much harder and more prolonged attempts at self-expression than any of them. Swearing love for art, they hovered on the edge of Bohemian life. Always friendly, they could never be anybody's friend; always reading, they could really never learn; always boasting of their passions, they could never really feel and were afraid to live.

The one group I met during those exploring days whose lives enthralled me was the Garveyites, an organization of black men and women who were forlornly seeking to return to Africa. Theirs was a passionate rejection of America, for they sensed with that directness of which only the simple are capable that they had no chance to live a full human life in America. Their lives were not cluttered with ideas in which they could only half believe; they could not create illusions which made them think they were living when they were not; their daily lives were too nakedly harsh to permit of camouflage. I understood their emotions, for I partly shared them.

The Garveyites had embraced a totally racialistic outlook which endowed them with a dignity that I had never seen before in Negroes. On the walls of their dingy flats were maps of Africa and India and Japan, pictures of Japanese generals and admirals, portraits of Marcus Garvey in gaudy regalia, the faces of colored men and women from all parts of the world. I gave no credence to the ideology of Garveyism; it was, rather, the emotional dynamics of its adherents that evoked my admiration. Those Garveyites I knew could never understand why I liked them but would never follow them, and I pitied them too much to tell them that they could never achieve their goal, that Africa was owned by the imperial powers of Europe, that their lives were alien to the mores of the natives of Africa, that they were people of the West and would forever be so until they either merged with the West or perished. It was when the Garveyites spoke fervently of building their own country, of someday living within the boundaries of a culture of their own making, that I sensed the passionate hunger of their lives, that I caught a glimpse of the potential strength of the American Negro.

Rumors of unemployment came, but I did not listen to them. I heard of the organizational efforts of the Communist party among the Negroes of the South Side, but Communist activities were too remote to strike my mind with any degree of vividness. Whenever I met a person whom I suspected of being a Communist, I talked to him affably but from an emotional distance. I sensed that something terrible was beginning to happen in the world, but I tried to shut it out of my mind by reading and writing.

When the time came for my appointment as a regular clerk, I was told that no appointments would be made for the time being. The volume of mail dropped. My hours of work dwindled. My paychecks grew small. Food became scarce at home. The hunger I thought I had left behind returned. One winter afternoon, in 1929, en route to work from the library, I passed a newsstand on which papers blazed:

STOCKS CRASH—BILLIONS FADE

Most of what I had seen in newspapers had never concerned me, so why should this? Newspapers reported the doings in a life I did not share. But the volume of mail fell so low that I worked but one or two nights a week. In the post-office canteen the boys stood about and talked.

"The cops beat up some demonstrators today."

"The Reds had a picket line around the City Hall."

"Wall Street's cracking down on the country."

"Surplus production's throwing millions out of work."

"There're more than two million unemployed."

"They don't count. They're always out of work."

"Read Karl Marx and get the answer, boys."

"There'll be a revolution if this keeps up."

"Hell, naw. Americans are too dumb to make a revolution."

The post-office job ended and again I was out of work. I could no longer think that the tides of economics were not my concern. But how could I have had any possible say in how the world had been run? I had grown up in complete ignorance of what created jobs. Having been thrust out of the world because of my race, I had accepted my destiny by not being curious about what shaped it.

The following summer I was again called for temporary duty in the post office, and the work lasted into the winter. Aunt Cleo succumbed to a severe cardiac condition and, hard on the heels of her illness, my brother developed stomach ulcers. To rush my worries to a climax, my mother also became ill. I felt that I was maintaining a private hospital. Finally the post-office work ceased altogether and I haunted the city for jobs. But when I went into the streets in the morning I saw sights that killed my hope for the rest of the day. Unemployed men loitered in doorways with blank looks in their eyes, sat dejectedly on front steps in shabby clothing, congregated in sullen groups on street corners, and filled all the empty benches in the parks of Chicago's South Side.

Luck of a sort came when a distant cousin of mine, who was a superintendent in a Negro burial society, offered me a position on his staff as an agent. The thought of selling insurance policies to ignorant Negroes disgusted me.

"Well, if you don't sell them, somebody else will," my cousin told me. "You've got to eat, haven't you?"

During that year I worked for several burial and insurance societies that operated among Negroes, and I received a new kind of education. I found that the burial societies, with some exceptions, were mostly "rackets." Some of them conducted their businesses legitimately, but there were many that exploited the ignorance of their black customers.

I was paid under a system that netted me fifteen dollars for every dollar's worth of new premiums that I placed upon the company's books, and for every dollar's worth of old premiums that lapsed I was penalized fifteen dollars. In addition, I was paid a commission of ten per cent on total premiums collected, but during the depression it was extremely difficult to persuade a black family to buy a policy carrying even a dime premium. I considered myself lucky if, after subtracting lapses from new business, there remained fifteen dollars that I could call my own.

This "gambling" method of remuneration was practiced by some of the burial companies because of the tremendous "turnover" in policyholders, and the companies had to have a constant stream of new business to keep afloat. Whenever a black family moved or suffered a slight reverse in fortune, it usually let its policy lapse and later bought another policy from some other company.

Each day now I saw how the Negro in Chicago lived, for I visited hundreds of dingy flats filled with rickety furniture and ill-clad children. Most of the policyholders were illiterate and did not know that their policies carried clauses severely restricting their benefit payments, and, as an insurance agent, it was not my duty to tell them.

After tramping the streets and pounding on doors to collect premiums, I was dry, strained, too tired to read or write. I hungered for relief and, as a salesman of insurance to many young black girls, I found it. There were many comely black housewives who, trying desperately to keep up their insurance payments, were willing to make bargains to escape paying a ten-cent premium. I had a long, tortured affair with one girl by paying her ten-cent premium each week. She was an illiterate black child with a baby whose father she did not know. During the entire period of my relationship with her, she had but one demand to make of me: She wanted me to take her to a circus. Just what significance circuses had for her, I was never able to learn.

After I had been with her one morning—in exchange for the dime premium—I sat on the sofa in the front room and began to read a book I had with me. She came over shyly.

"Lemme see that," she said.

"What?" I asked.

"That book," she said.

I gave her the book; she looked at it intently. I saw that she was holding it upside down.

"What's in here you keep reading?" she asked.

"Can't you really read?" I asked.

"Naw," she giggled. "You know I can't read."

"You can read *some*," I said.

"Naw," she said.

I stared at her and wondered just what a life like hers meant in the scheme of things, and I came to the conclusion that it meant absolutely nothing. And neither did my life mean anything.

"How come you looking at me that way for?" she asked.

"Nothing."

"You don't talk much."

"There isn't much to say."

"I wished Jim was here," she sighed.

"Who's Jim?" I asked, jealous. I knew that she had other men, but I resented her mentioning them in my presence.

"Just a friend," she said.

I hated her then, then hated myself for coming to her.

"Do you like Jim better than you like me?" I asked.

"Naw. Jim just likes to talk."

"Then why do you be with me, if you like Jim better?" I asked, trying to make an issue and feeling a wave of disgust because I wanted to.

"You all right," she said, giggling. "I like you."

"I could kill you," I said.

"What?" she exclaimed.

"Nothing," I said, ashamed.

"Kill me, you said? You crazy, man," she said.

"Maybe I am," I muttered, angry that I was sitting beside a human being to whom I could not talk, angry with myself for coming to her, hating my wild and restless loneliness.

"You oughta go home and sleep," she said. "You tired."

"What do you ever think about?" I demanded harshly.

"Lotta things."

"What, for example?"

"You," she said, smiling.

"You know I mean just one dime to you each week," I said.

"Naw, I thinka lotta you."

"Then what do you think?"

"'Bout how you talk when you talk. I wished I could talk like you," she said seriously.

"Why?" I taunted her.

"When you gonna take me to a circus?" she demanded suddenly.

"You ought to be in a circus," I said.

"I'd like it," she said, her eyes shining.

I wanted to laugh, but her words sounded so sincere that I could not laugh.

"There's no circus in town," I said.

"I bet there is and you won't tell me 'cause you don't wanna take me," she said, pouting.

"But there's no circus in town, I tell you!"

"When will one come?"

"I don't know."

"Can't you read it in the papers?" she asked.

"There's nothing in the papers about a circus."

"There is," she said. "If I could read, I'd find it."

I laughed and she was hurt.

"There *is* a circus in town," she said stoutly.

"There's no circus in town," I said. "But if you want to learn to read, then I'll teach you."

She nestled at my side, giggling.

"See that word?" I said, pointing.

"Yeah."

"That's an 'and,'" I said.

She doubled, giggling.

"What's the matter?" I asked.

She rolled on the floor, giggling.

"What's so funny?" I demanded.

"You," she giggled. "You so funny."

I rose.

"The hell with you," I said.

"Don't you go and cuss me now," she said. "I don't cuss you."

"I'm sorry," I said.

I got my hat and went to the door.

"I'll see you next week?" she asked.

"Maybe," I said.

When I was on the sidewalk, she called to me from a window.

"You promised to take me to a circus, remember?"

"Yes." I walked close to the window. "What is it you like about a circus?"

"The animals," she said simply.

I felt that there was a hidden meaning, perhaps, in what she had said; but I could not find it. She laughed and slammed the window shut.

Each time I left her I resolved not to visit her again. I could not talk to her; I merely listened to her passionate desire to see a circus. She was not calculating; if she liked a man, she just liked him. Sex relations were the only relations she had ever had; no others were possible with her, so limited was her intelligence.

Most of the other agents also had their bought girls and they were extremely anxious to keep other agents from tampering with them. One day a new section of the South Side was given to me as a part of my collection area and the agent from whom the territory had been taken suddenly became very friendly with me.

"Say, Wright," he asked, "did you collect from Ewing at—Champlain Avenue yet?"

"Yes," I answered, after consulting my book.

"How did you like her?" he asked, staring at me.

"She's a good-looking number," I said.

"You had anything to do with her yet?" he asked.

"No, but I'd like to," I said, laughing.

"Look," he said. "I'm a friend of yours."

"Since when?" I countered.

"No, I'm really a friend," he said.

"What's on your mind?"

"Listen, that gal's sick," he said seriously.

"What do you mean?"

"She's got the clap," he said. "Keep away from her. She'll lay with anybody."

"Gee, I'm glad you told me," I said.

"You had your eye on her, didn't you?" he asked.

"Yes, I did," I said.

"Leave her alone," he said. "She'll get you down."

That night I told my cousin what the agent had said about Miss Ewing. My cousin laughed.

"That gal's all right," he said. "That agent's been fooling around with her. He told you she had a disease so that you'd be scared to bother her. He was protecting her from you."

That was the way the black women were regarded by the black agents. Some of the agents were vicious; if they had claims to pay to a sick black woman and if the woman was able to have sex relations with them, they would insist upon it, using the claim money as a bribe. If the woman refused, they would report to the office that the woman was a malingerer. The average black woman would submit because she needed the money badly.

As an insurance agent, it was necessary for me to take part in one swindle. It appears that the burial society had originally issued a policy that was—from their point of view—too liberal in its provisions, and the officials decided to exchange the policies then in the hands of their clients for other policies carrying stricter clauses; of course, this had to be done in a manner that would not allow the policyholder to know that his policy was being switched, that he was being swindled. I did not like it, but there was only one thing I could do to keep from being a party to it: I could quit and starve. But I did not feel that being honest was worth the price of starvation.

The swindle worked in this way. In my visits to the homes of policyholders to collect premiums, I was accompanied by the superintendent who claimed to the policyholder that he was making a routine inspection. The policyholder, usually an illiterate black woman, would dig up her policy from the bottom of a trunk or a chest and hand it to the superintendent. Meanwhile I would be marking the woman's premium book, an act which would distract her from what the superintendent was doing. The superintendent would exchange the old policy for a new one which was identical in color, serial number, and beneficiary, but which carried much smaller payments. It was dirty work and I wondered how I could stop it. And when I could think of no safe way I would curse myself and the victims and forget about it. (The black owners of the burial societies were leaders in the Negro communities and were respected by whites.)

As I went from house to house collecting money, I saw black men mounted upon soapboxes at street corners, bellowing about bread, rights, and revolution. I liked their courage, but I doubted their wisdom. The speakers claimed that Negroes were angry, that they were about to rise and join their white fellow workers to make a revolution. I was in and out of many Negro homes each day and I knew that the Negroes were lost, ignorant, sick in mind and body. I saw that a vast distance separated the agitators from the masses, a distance so vast that the agitators did not know how to appeal to the people they sought to lead.

Some mornings I found leaflets on my steps telling of China, Russia, and Germany; on some days I witnessed as many as five thousand jobless Negroes, led by Communists, surging through the streets. I would watch them with an aching heart, firmly convinced that they were being duped; but if I had been asked to give them another solution for their problems, I would not have known how.

It became a habit of mine to visit Washington Park of an afternoon after collecting a part of my premiums, and I would wander through crowds of unemployed Negroes, pausing here and there to sample the dialectic or indignation of Communist speakers. What I heard and saw baffled and angered me. The Negro Communists were deliberately careless in their personal appearance, wearing their shirt collars turned in to make V's at their throats, wearing their caps—they wore caps because Lenin had worn caps—with the visors turned backward, tilted upward at the nape of their necks. Many of their mannerisms, pronunciations, and turns of speech had been consciously copied from white Communists whom they had recently met. While engaged in conversation, they stuck their thumbs in their suspenders or put their left hands into their shirt bosoms or hooked their thumbs into their back pockets as they had seen Lenin or Stalin do in photographs. Though they did not know it, they were naïvely practicing magic; they thought that if they acted like the men who had overthrown the czar, then surely they ought to be able to win their freedom in America.

In speaking they rolled their "r's" in Continental style, pronouncing "party" as "parrrtee," stressing the last syllable, having picked up the habit from white Communists. "Comrades" became "cumrrades," and "distribute," which they had known how to pronounce all their lives, was twisted into "distrrribuuute," with the accent on the last instead of the second syllable, a mannerism which they copied from Polish Communist immigrants who did not know how to pronounce the word. Many sensitive Negroes agreed with the Communist program but refused to join their ranks because of the shabby quality of those Negroes whom the Communists had already admitted to membership.

When speaking from the platform, the Negro Communists, eschewing the traditional gestures of the Negro preacher—as though they did not possess the strength to develop their own style of Communist preaching—stood straight, threw back their heads, brought the edge of the right palm down hammerlike into the outstretched left palm in a series of jerky motions to pound their points home, a mannerism that characterized Lenin's method of speaking. When they walked, their stride quickened; all the peasant hesitancy of their speech vanished as their voices became clipped, terse. In debate they interrupted their opponents in a tone of voice that was an octave higher, and if their opponents raised their voices to be heard, the Communists raised theirs still higher until shouts rang out over the park. Hence, the only truth that prevailed was that which could be shouted and quickly understood.

Their emotional certainty seemed buttressed by access to a fund of knowledge denied to ordinary men, but a day's observation of their activities was sufficient to reveal all their thought processes. An hour's listening disclosed the fanatical intolerance of minds sealed against new ideas, new facts, new feelings, new attitudes, new hints at ways to live. They denounced books they had never read, people they had never known, ideas they could never understand, and doctrines whose names they could not pronounce. Communism, instead of making them leap forward with fire in their hearts to become masters of ideas and life, had frozen them at an even lower level of ignorance than had been theirs before they met Communism.

When Hoover threatened to drive the bonus marchers from Washington, one Negro Communist speaker said:

"If he drives the bonus marchers out of Washington, the people will rise up and make a revolution!"

I went to him, determined to get at what he really meant.

"You know that even if the United States Army actually kills the bonus marchers, there'll be no revolution," I said.

"You don't know the indignation of the masses!" he exploded.

"But you don't seem to know what it takes to make a revolution," I explained. "Revolutions are rare occurrences."

"You underestimate the masses," he told me.

"No, I know the masses of Negroes very well," I said. "But I don't believe that a revolution is pending. Revolutions come through concrete historical processes . . ."

"You're an intellectual," he said, smiling disdainfully.

A few days later, after Hoover had had the bonus marchers driven from Washington at the point of bayonets, I accosted him:

"What about that revolution you predicted if the bonus marchers were driven out?" I asked.

"The prerequisite conditions did not exist," he shrugged and muttered.

I left him, wondering why he felt it necessary to make so many ridiculous overstatements. I could not refute the general Communist analysis of the world; the only drawback was that their world was just too simple for belief. I liked their readiness to act, but they seemed lost in folly, wandering in a fantasy. For them there was no yesterday or tomorrow, only the living moment of today; their only task was to annihilate the enemy that confronted them in any manner possible.

At times their speeches, glowing with rebellion, were downright offensive to lowly, hungry Negroes. Once a Negro Communist speaker, inveighing against religion, said:

"There ain't no goddamn God! If there is, I hereby challenge Him to strike me dead!"

He paused dramatically before his vast black audience for God to act, but God declined. He then pulled out his watch.

"Maybe God didn't hear me!" he yelled. "I'll give Him two more minutes!" Then, with sarcasm: "Mister God, kill me!"

He waited, looking mockingly at his watch. The audience laughed uneasily.

"I'll tell you where to find God," the speaker went on in a hard, ranting voice. "When it rains at midnight, take your hat, turn it upside down on a floor in a dark room, and you'll have God!"

I had to admit that I had never heard atheism of so militant a nature; but the Communist speaker seemed to be amusing and frightening the people more than he was convincing them.

"If there is a God up there in that empty sky," the speaker roared on, "I'll reach up there and grab Him by His beard and jerk Him down here on this hungry earth and cut His throat!" He wagged his head. "Now, let God dare me!"

The audience was shocked into silence for a moment, then it yelled with delight. I shook my head and walked away. That was not the way to destroy people's outworn beliefs . . . They were acting like irresponsible children . . .

I was now convinced that they did not know the complex nature of Negro life, did not know how great was the task to which they had set themselves. They had rejected the state of things as they were, and that seemed to me to be the first step toward embracing a creative attitude toward life. I felt that it was not until one wanted the world to be different that one could look at the world with will and emotion. But these men had rejected what was before their eyes without quite knowing what they had rejected and why.

I felt that the Negro could not live a full, human life under the conditions imposed upon him by America; and I felt, too, that America, for different reasons, could not live a full, human life. It seemed to me, then, that if the Negro solved his problem, he would be solving infinitely more than his problem alone. I felt certain that the Negro could never solve his problem until the deeper problem of American civilization had been faced and solved. And because the Negro was the most cast-out of all the outcast people in America, I felt that no other group in America could tackle this problem of what our American lives meant so well as the Negro could.

But, as I listened to the Communist Negro speakers, I wondered if the Negro, blasted by three hundred years of oppression, could possibly cast off his fear and corruption and rise to the task. Could the Negro ever possess himself, learn to know what had happened to him in relation to the aspirations of Western society? It seemed to me that for the Negro to try to save himself he would have to forget himself and try to save a confused, materialistic nation from its own drift toward self-destruction. Could the Negro accomplish this miracle? Could he take up his bed and walk?

Election time was nearing and a Negro Republican precinct captain asked me to help him round up votes. I had no interest in the candidates, but I needed the money. I went from door to door with the precinct captain and discovered that the whole business was one long process of bribery, that people voted for three dollars, for the right to continue their illicit trade in sex or alcohol. On election day I went into the polling booth and drew the curtain behind me and unfolded my ballots. As I stood there the sordid implications of politics flashed through my mind. "Big Bill" Thompson headed the local Republican machine and I knew that he was using the Negro vote to control the city hall; in turn, he was engaged in vast political deals of which the Negro voters, political innocents, had no notion. With my pencil I wrote in a determined scrawl across the face of the ballots:

I PROTEST THIS FRAUD

I knew that my gesture was futile. But I wanted somebody to know that out of that vast sea of ignorance in the Black Belt there was at least one person who knew the game for what it was. I collected my ten dollars and went home.

The depression deepened and I could not sell insurance to hungry Negroes. I sold my watch and scouted for cheaper rooms; I found a rotting building and rented an apartment in it. The place was dismal; plaster was falling from the walls; the wooden stairs sagged. When my mother saw it, she wept. I felt bleak. I had not done what I had come to the city to do.

One morning I rose and my mother told me that there was no food for breakfast. I knew that the city had opened relief stations, but each time I thought of going into one of them I burned with shame. I sat for hours, fighting hunger, avoiding my mother's eyes. Then I rose, put on my hat and coat, and went out. As I walked toward the Cook County Bureau of Public Welfare to plead for bread, I knew that I had come to the end of something.

1945

CHESTER B. HIMES
1909–1984

Born on July 29, 1909, in Jefferson City, Missouri, Chester B. Himes was the youngest of three sons of schoolteachers. Himes spent his early years in several places, including Mississippi. After graduating from high school in 1926, he sustained a serious back injury; a disability pension allowed him to enroll at Ohio State University in Columbus, but after a single semester, Himes left the university, according to one source withdrawn for disciplinary reasons, according to another "depressed by the white environment." In any event, Himes entered the work force at the bottom—as a bellhop and hustler—and soon launched a very different kind of career. Arrested in 1928 for armed robbery, he was sentenced to twenty years in the Ohio State Penitentiary. Like other celebrated black prisoners, among them Malcolm X, George Jackson, Etheridge Knight, and Eldridge Cleaver, Himes apparently changed course during his confinement and became an apprentice writer. In fact, his first story, "His Last Day," appeared in *Abbott's Monthly* in 1932, while he was still in prison. Two years later, one of Himes's most widely read early stories, "To What Red Hell," was published by Esquire, taking its cue from a 1930 prison fire that had killed 320 convicts. His 1952 novel, *Cast the First Stone*, was also based on his prison experience.

By the time of his release in 1936, Himes had published in various venues; in addition to *Abbott's Monthly* and *Esquire*, his stories had appeared in the *Pittsburgh Cou-*

rier and the *Afro-American,* among other newspapers and journals. Himes spent a brief period on the West Coast, working in the shipyards of Los Angeles and San Francisco. His first novels, *If He Hollers Let Him Go* (1945) and *Lonely Crusade* (1947), both take their inspiration from those years. A failed marriage, unsuccessful love, racism, and underemployment all worked to drive him out of American society. In 1953, Himes left the United States for Europe. Until his death in 1984, he would make only brief trips back, usually to New York City.

Though in the shadow of Richard Wright, as were many black writers of the period, Himes was actually quite celebrated within French literary and intellectual circles, especially for his detective novels. The French translation of the first novel in his series, *For Love of Imabelle,* appeared in 1958, for which Himes won the Grand Prix Policier. Set in Harlem, the novels featured characters named Coffin Ed Johnson and Gravedigger Jones, after the tradition of hard-boiled heroes such as Dashiell Hammet's Sam Spade and Raymond Chandler's Philip Marlowe. Much of Himes's work, especially *If He Hollers,* with its depiction of the difficult circumstances of black life, owes a profound debt to Richard Wright. Himes's two autobiographies, *The Quality of Hurt* and *My Life of Absurdity,* were published in 1972 and 1976, respectively. Other work includes *Third Generation* (1954), *The Primitive* (1955), *Pinktoes* (1961), and *Cotton Comes to Harlem* (1965), later made into a successful film.

Perhaps among the least read of the postwar writers, Chester Himes, after twenty years of European living and certain material success, apparently remained American to the core, never quite working out his existential dilemma. In *My Life of Absurdity,* Himes writes: "I travelled through Europe trying desperately to find a life into which I would fit; and my determination stemmed from my desire to succeed without America. . . . I never found a place where I even began to fit, due in great part to my inability to learn any foreign language and my antagonism toward all white people, who, I thought, treated me as an inferior." A web of contradictions, Himes spent a good deal of his life among some of "all [those] white people." As we might anticipate, his varied writings reflect the intense conflicts within Chester Himes himself.

Cotton Gonna Kill Me Yet

We was at the Creole Breakfast Club knockin' ourselves out when this icky, George Brown, butts in. Ain't nobody called him and I hardly knew the man, just seen him four or five times 'round the poolroom where I works. He takes a seat at our table and grabs my glass of licker[1] and asts, "Is you mad at anybody?"

I was getting mad but I didn't tell him. "Me?" I laughed, tryna be a good fellow. "Only at the man wanna put me in the army."

The bugler caught a spot for a riff[2] in "Don't Cry Baby" and blew my ear off. All down the time the cats latched on, shoulders rocked, heads bobbed, the joint jumped. My queen 'gan bouncin' out her twelve-dollar dress.

George waited for the bugler to blow out of breath. "Thass what I mean. You ain't mad at nobody, yet you gotta go to war. Thass 'cause you's a fool."

I didn't mind the man drinkin' my licker so much, nor even him callin' me a fool. But when I see my queen, Beulah, give him the eye and then get prissy as a sissy, I figured I better get him gone. 'Cause this George Brown was strictly an icky, drape-shaped in a fine brown zoot[3] with a pancho conk slicker'n mine. So I said, "State yo' plan, Charlie Chan[4]—then scram."

1. Liquor.
2. Bugle improvisational solo.
3. A men's suit popular in ethnic American communities during the 1940s, featuring high-waisted, wide-legged, trousers and a long coat with wide lapels and wide padded shoulders.
4. A fictional Chinese American detective.

"Don't rush me, don't rush me," he said. "You needs me, I don't need you. If'n you was to die tomorrow wouldn't mean nothing to me. Pour me some mo' of that licker."

He come on so fast I done took out my half-pint bottle and poured him a shot under the table 'fore I knew what I was doin'. Then I got mad. "This ain't no river, man," I said.

"Thass what I mean," he said. "Here you is strainin' yo'self to keep up a front. You works in the poolroom all day and you makes 'bout ten bucks. Then comes night and you takes out yo' queen. You pays two bucks to get in this joint, fo' bucks for a half-pint grog, two bucks for a coke setup. If'n you get anything to eat you got to fight the man 'bout the bill. For ten bucks a day you drinkin' yo'self in the grave on cheap licker—"

"You calls fo' bucks a half pint cheap?" I snarled.

He kept drivin' like he didn't hear me. "Then what happen. They put you in 1-A and say you gotta fight. You don't wanna fight 'cause you ain't mad at nobody—not even at the man what charge you fo' bucks for a half-pint grog. Ain't got sense 'nough to be mad. So what does you do?"

"What does I do?" I just looked at that icky.

"Well, what *does* you do?" That's my queen talkin'. She's a strictly fine queen, fine as wine. Slender, tender, and tall. But she ain't got brain the first.

"I does what everybody else do," I gritted. "I gets ready an' go."

"Thass what I mean," George Brown said. "Thass 'cause you's a fool. I know guys makin' twice as much as you is, workin' half as hard. And does they have to fight? They is deferred 'cause what they doin' means more to Uncle Sam than them in there fightin'."

"Well, tell High C 'bout it." That's my queen again. "I sho' don't want him to go to no war. And he may's well be makin' more money. Li'l 'nough he's makin' in that poolroom."

That's a queen for you; just last week she was talkin' 'bout how rich us was gettin'.

"Money! Make so much money he can't count it," he said to her. They done left me outen it altogether; I'se just the man what gonna make the money. "W'y in less than no time at all this cat can come back an' drape yo' fine shape in silver foxes and buy you a Packard Clipper[5] to drive up and down the avenue. All he gotta do is go up to Bakersfield[6] and pick a li'l cotton—"

I jumped up. "What's your story, morning glory? Me pickin' cotton. I ain't never seen no cotton, don't know what cotton is—"

"All he got to do," he went on talkin' to my queen, "to knock down his double sawbuck is pick a coupla thousand pounds. After that the day is his own."

"Why come he got to stop in the middle of the day?" my queen ast. "Who do he think he is, Rockefeller[7] or somebody?"

"Thass what I been tryna tell you," George said. "He don't. He keep right on an' pick 'nother ton. Make forty flags. And does you have to worry 'bout him goin' to the army? You can go to bed ev'y night and dream 'bout them silver foxes."

I had to get them people straight and get 'em straightened fast. "Yo' mouth may drool, fool, and yo' gums may flop, pop—" but my queen cut me off.

---

5. A single model of the Packard Motor Car Company, introduced in April 1941 and manufactured from 1942 to 1947.
6. A city in California near the southern end of the San Joaquin Valley.
7. Likely a reference to John D. Rockefeller (1839–1937), American industrialist and philanthropist who founded the Standard Oil Company.

"Listen to the man!" she shouts. "Don't you want me to have no silver foxes?"

"Ain't like what he thinks," he said. "Lotta hustlers up there. Cats say they's goin' east—slip up there and make them layers; show up in a Clipper. Cats here all wonder where they got their scratch."[8] He turned to me. "I bet you bin wonderin'—"

"Not me!" I said. "All I'se wonderin' is how come you pick on me? I ain't that man. 'Fore I pick anybody's cotton I'll—"

So there I was the next mornin' waitin' for the bus to take me up to Bakersfield. Done give this icky twenty-five bucks to get me the job and all I got is a slip of paper with his name on it I'm supposed to give to the man when I get there. My queen done took what scratch I had left sayin' I wouldn't need nothin' 'cause George said everything I could want would be given to me for nothin'. All I had was the four bits she let me keep.

By then it had me too. Done gone money mad as her. At first I was thinkin' in the C's;[9] knock seven or eight hundred then jump down. But by the time I got to Bakersfield I was way up in the G's;[1] I seen myself with pockets full of thousand-dollar bills.

After knockin' the natives cold in my forty-inch frock and my cream-colored drapes I looked 'round for the cat George said gonna meet me. Here come a big Uncle Tomish lookin' cat in starched overalls astin' me is I "High C."

"What you wanna know for, is you the police?" I came back at him.

"Dey calls me Poke Chops," he said. "I'se de cook at de plantation. I come tuh pick y'all up."

"Well bless my soul if you ain't Mr. Cotton Boll," I chirped, givin' him the paper George gimme. Then I ast him, "Is that you parked across the street?"

He looked at the green Lincoln Zephyr[2] and then he looked back at me. "Dass me on dis side," he mumbled, pointin' at a battered Model A Ford truck.

Well now, that made me mad, them sendin' that jalopy[3] for me. But I was so high off'n them dreams I let it pass. I could take my twenty G's and buy me a Sherman tank[4] to ride in if'n I wanted; warn't like I just had to ride in that jalopy. So I climb in beside old Chops and he driv off.

After we'd gone along a ways he come astin' me, "'Bout how much ken y'all pick, shawty?"

"Don't worry 'bout me, Chops," I told him. "I'll knock out my coupla thousand all ricky. Then if'n I ain't too tired I'll knock out a deuce[5] mo'."

"Coupla thousand." He turned in his seat and looked at me. "Dass uh tun."

"Well now, take yo' diploma," I said.

"Wun't tek us long tuh whup de enemy at dat rate," was all he said.

'Bout an hour later we pulled in at a shanty. I got out and went inside. On both sides there were rows of bunks and in the middle a big long wooden trestle table with benches. Looked like a prison camp where I done six months. I was mad now sure 'nough. "I ain't gonna stay in this dump," I snarled.

"Whatcha gunna do den?" he wanted to know. "Build yo'self a house?"

I'da cut out right then and there but the loot had me. I'm a hip-cat from way back and I don't get so mad I don't know how I'm gettin' down. If'n

---

8. Money (slang), usually a small amount.
9. One hundred dollar bills, from the Roman numeral C, which equals one hundred.
1. I.e., thousands.
2. A lower priced line of luxury cars manufac-

tured by Lincoln from 1936 to 1940.
3. An old, dilapidated automobile.
4. Designed and built by the United States for use in World War II.
5. Two (slang).

them other hustlers could put up with it, so could I. So when old Chops gimme a bunk down in the corner I didn't want him to know I was mad. I flipped my last half buck at him. "Take good care of me, Chops," I said.

He didn't bat an eye; he caught the half and stashed it. "Yassuh," he said.

At sundown the pickers came in, threw their sacks on their bunks, and made for the table. If there was any hustlers there, they musta been some mighty hard hustlers 'cause them was some rugged-looking stiffs. Them stiffs talked loud as Count Basie's[6] brass and walked hard as Old Man Mose. By the time I got to the table wasn't nothin' left but one lone po'k chop bone.

Then when us got through eatin' here comes Chops from the kitchen. "Folkses, I wants y'all tuh meet High C. High C is a pool shark. He pick uh tun uh cotton ev'y day. Den if'n he ain't tahd he pick unother'n."

I got up and give 'em the old prize fighter shake. But them stiffs just froze. I never seen nothin' like it. Ain't nobody said nothin', not one word.

That night Bayou Dad and Uncle Toliver come down to my bunk. "Whar'd y'all evah pick cotton befor', son?" Bayou Dad ast me.

"Don't start me to lyin', you'll have me cryin'," I said. "I done picked all over. From 'Bama[7] to Maine."

Uncle Toliver puffed at his pipe. "Dat Maine cotton is uh killer as de younguns say."

"You ain't just sayin' it," I said.

Somebody shook me in the middle of the night and I thought the joint was on fire and jumped up and run outside. By the time I find they was gettin' up for breakfast all the breakfast was gone but a spoon of grits. And the next thing I know there we is out in a cotton patch blacker'n me.

"What's this, a blackout?" I wanted to know.

But warn't nobody sayin' nothin' that early in the day. Big stiff on the right of me called Thousand Pound Red. 'Nother'n on the left called Long Row Willie. Stiffs shaped up like Jack Johnson. I hitched up the strap over my shoulder like I seen them do and threw the long tail out behind me.

"Well, we're off said the rabbit to the snails," I chirped jolly-like, rollin' up the bottoms of my drapes.

An' I warn't lyin' neither. When I looked up them two stiffs was gone. Let me tell you, them stiffs was grabbin' that cotton so fast you couldn't see the motion of their arms. I looked 'round and seen all the other stiffs in the patch watchin' me.

"W'y these stiffs call theyselves racin'," I said to myself. "W'y I'll pick these stiffs blind deaf and cripple."

I hauled off and started workin' my arms and grabbed at the first cotton I saw. Somp'n jumped out and bit me on the finger and I jumped six feet. Thought sure I was snakebit. When I found out it was just the sharp joint of the cotton boll I felt like a plugged slug. Next time I snuck up on it, got aholt, and heaved. Didn't stop fallin' 'til I was in the next row. Then I got mad. I 'gan grabbin' that cotton with both hands.

In 'bout an hour looked like I'd been in the rain. Hands ain't never been so bruised, look like every boll musta bit 'em. When I tried to straighten up my straightener wouldn't work. I looked at my bag. The mouth was full but when I shook it the cotton disappeared. Then I thought 'bout the money;

6. William "Count" Basie (1904–1984), American jazz pianist, organist, bandleader, and composer who formed his own jazz band in 1935, which he led for nearly fifty years.
7. Alabama.

forty bucks a day, maybe fifty since I'd done begun in the middle of the night. Money'll make a man eat kine pepper. I started off again.

By the time I got halfway through my row I couldn't hear nobody. I raised my neck and skinned my glims.[8] Warn't nobody in the whole patch but a man at the end of my row. Thought the rest of them stiffs musta gone for water so I 'cided to hurry up and finish my row while they was gone and be ahead of 'em.

I'd gone ten yards through the weeds pickin' thistledown from dried weeds 'fore it come to me I was at the end of my row.

"Whew!" I blew and wiped the sweat out my eyes. An' then I saw the walkin' boss. "Howma doin', poppa," I crowed. "Didn't quit when them other stiffs did; thought I'd knock out my row 'fore I went for a drink."

"You did?" He sounded kinda funny but I didn't think nothin' of it.

"That's my story; Mister Glory; never get my Clipper stoppin' every few minutes for a drink." I shifted my weight and got groovy. "I ain't like a lotta stiffs what swear they won't hit a lick at a snake then slip up here and cop this slave sayin' they goin' east an' come back all lush. I don't care who knows I'm slavin' long as I get my proper layers. Now take when this icky, George Brown, sprung this jive; I got a piece of slave[9] in a poolroom and figure I'm settin' solid—"

"This ain't no poolroom and the others ain't gone for no water," the man cut in. "They finished out their rows and went over the hump."

"Well, run into me!" I said. "Finished!" But I couldn't see how them stiffs got finished that quick. "Maybe they didn't have as much to pick as me," I pointed out.

The man stood there looking at me and not sayin' a mumblin' word. Made me nervous just standin' there. I picked up my sack and sorta sashayed off. "Which way they go, man?"

"Come back here, you!" he yelled.

"All right, I can hear you, man," I muttered.

"Take a look at that row." He pointed at the row I'd just finished.

I looked. It was white as rice. "Well look at that jive!" I said. "What's that stuff, man?"

"It's cotton," he said. "You know what cotton is, don't you? You heard of it somewhere, ain't you?"

I stepped over and looked down the other rows. They were bare as Mama Hubbard's cubbard. I came back and looked at my row again. "Say, man, where did all that cotton come from?" I wanted to know.

"It grew," he said.

"You mean since I picked it? You kiddin', man?"

He didn't say nothin'.

"Well then, how come it grew on my row and didn't grow nowhere else?" I pressed him.

He leaned toward me and put his chops in my face, then he bellowed, "Pick it! You hear me, pick it! Don't stand there looking at me, you—you grasshopper! Pick it! And pick every boll!"

I got out that man's way. "Well all root," I said quickly. "You don't have to do no Joe Louis."

---

8. Eyes.
9. A job.

That's where I learned 'bout cotton; I found out what it was all 'bout, you hear me. I shook them stalks down like the FBI shakin' down a slacker. I beat them bolls to a solid pulp. As I dragged that heavy sack I thought, Lord, this cotton must weigh a ton—a halfa ton anyway. But when I looked at the sack didn't look like nothin' was in it. Just a li'l ol' knot at the bottom. Lord, cotton sure is heavy, I thought.

Then it come to me all of a sudden I must be blowin' my lid. Here I is gettin' paid by the pound and beefin' 'cause the stuff is heavy. The more it weigh the more I earn. Couldn't get too heavy. I knowed I'd done picked a thousand pounds if'n I'd picked a ounce. At that rate I could pick at least four thousand 'fore sundown. Maybe five! Fifty flags in the bag! "Club Alabam, here to you I scram," I rhymed just to pass the time. Them cotton bolls turned into gin fizzes.

At the end of the row I straightened up and looked into the eyes of the man. "Fifty flags a day would be solid kicks, please believe me," I said. "I could knock me that Clipper and live on Central Avenue." I sat down on my thousand pounds of cotton and relaxed. "There I was last Friday, just dropped a trey of balls to Thirty No-count, and it seemed like I could smell salty pork fryin'. Man, it sure smelt good."

"Turn around," the man said.

I screwed 'round, thinkin' he was gonna tell me what a good job I done.

"Look down that row."

I looked. That was some row. Beat as Mussolini.[1] Limp as Joe Limpy. Leaves stripped from stalks. Stalks tromped into the ground. The ground tromped 'round and 'round. And just as many bolls of cotton as when I first got started. I got mad then sure 'nough. "Lookahere, man," I snarled. "You goin' 'long behind me fillin' up them bolls?"

The man rubbed his hand over his face. He pulled a weed and bit off the root. Then he blew on the button of his sleeve and polished it on his shirt. He laughed like a crazy man. "Ice cream and fried salt pork shore would taste good ridin' down Central Avenue in a Clipper. Look, shorty, it's noon. Twelve o'clock. F' stay? Ice cream—" He shook himself. "Listen, go weigh in and go eat. Eat all the fried ice cream and salty clippers you can stand. Then come back and pick this row clean if it takes you all week."

"Well all root, man," I said. "Don't get on your elbows."

I dragged my sack to the scales. Them other stiffs stopped to watch. I waved at them, then threw my sack on the scales. I stood back. "What does she scan, Charlie Chan?"

"Fifty-five!" the weigher called.

"Fifty-five," I said. "Don't gimme no jive." I started toward the shanty walkin' on air. Fifty-five smackeroos and the day just half gone. Then I heard somebody laugh. I stopped, batted my eyes. I wheeled 'round. "Fifty-five!" I shouted. "Fifty-five what?"

"Pounds," the weigher said.

I started to assault the man. But first I jumped for the scale. "Lemme see this thing," I snarled.

The weigher got out my way. I weighed the cotton myself. It weighed fifty-five pounds. I swallowed. I went over and sat down. It was all I could do to keep from cryin'. Central Avenue had never seemed so far away. Right then

---

1. Benito Mussolini (1883–1945), Italian politician who ruled the country from 1922 to 1943. He was a key figure in the creation of fascism and led the National Fascist Party.

and there I got suspicious of that icky, George Brown. Then I got mad at my queen. I couldn't wait to get back to L.A. to tell her what a lain she was. I could see my queen on this George Brown. My queen ain't so bright but when she gets mad look out.

When them stiffs went in for dinner I found the man and said, "I'm quittin'."

"Quit then," he said.

"I is," I said. "Gimme my pay."

"You ain't got none coming," he said.

I couldn't whip the man, he was big as Turkey Thompson.[2] An' I couldn't cut him 'cause I didn't have no knife. So I found Poke Chops and said, "I wanna send a tellygraph to my queen in L.A."

"Go 'head an' send it den," he said.

"I want you to go in town an' send it for me," I said.

He said, "Yassuh. Cost you two bucks."

"I ain't got no scratch," I pointed out. "That's what I wanna get."

"'Tis?" he said. "Dass too bad."

All I could do was go back and look them bolls in the face. At sundown I staggered in, beat as down-home steak. I didn't even argue with the weigher when he weighed my thirty-five pounds. Then I got left for scoff. Old Chops yelled, "Cum 'n' get it!" and nine stiffs run right over me.

After supper I was gonna wash my face but when I seen my conk[3] was ruint and my hair was standin' on end like burnt grass I just fell in the bed. There I lay wringin' and twistin'. Dreamt I was jitterbuggin' with a cotton boll. But that boll was some ickeroo 'cause it was doin' some steps I ain't never seen and I'm a 'gator from way back.

Next day I found myself with a row twixt two old men. Been demoted. But I figured surely I could beat them old stiffs. One was a-moanin': "*Cotton is tall, cotton is shawt, Lawd, Lawd, cotton is tall, cotton is shawt . . . How y'all comin' dare, son? . . . Lawd, Lawd, cotton is tall, cotton is shawt . . .*" The other'n a-wailin': "*Ah'm gonna pick heah, pick heah a few days longah, 'n' den go home. Lawd, Lawd, 'n' den go home . . .*"

Singin' them down-home songs. I knew I could beat them old stiffs. But pretty soon they left me. When I come to the end of my row and seen the man I just turned 'round and started back. Warn't no need 'f argyin'.

All next day I picked twixt them ancient stiffs. An' they left me at the post. I caught myself singin': "*Cotton is tall, cotton is shawt*" an' when I seen the man at the end of my row I changed to: "*Cotton is where it ain't.*"

That night I got a letter from my fine queen in L.A. I felt just like hollerin' like a mountain Jack. Here I is wringin' an' twistin' like a solid fool, I told myself, an' I got a fine queen waitin' for me to come back to her ever-lovin' heart. A good soft slave in the poolroom. An' some scratch stashed away. What is I got to worry 'bout?

Then I read the letter.

Dear High C daddy mine:

I know you is up there making all that money and aint hardly thinkin none about poor little me I bet but just the same I is your sweet little sugar

2. Albert "Turkey" Thompson (1919–1984), heavyweight boxer.   3. A hairstyle named after congolene, a hair straightening product made from lye.

pie and you better not forget to mail me your check Saturday. But dont you think I is jealous cause I aint. I hates a jealous woman worsen anything I know of. You just go head and have fun and I will go head and have mine.

I promised him I wouldnt say nothing to you bout him but he just stay on my mind. Didnt you think he was awful sweet the way he thought bout me wanting some silver foxes. Mr Brown I mean. And it was so nice of him getting you that fine job where you can improve your health and keep out the army at the same time. And then you can make all that money.

He been awful nice to me since you been gone. I just dont know rightly how to thank him. He been taking care of everything for you so nice. He wont let me worry none at all bout you being away up there mong all those fine fellows and me being here all by my lonely self. He say you must be gained five pounds already cause you getting plenty fresh air and exercise and is eating and sleeping regular. He say I the one what need taking care of (aint he cute). He been taking me out to keep me from getting so lonesome and when I get after him bout spening all his time with me he say dont I to worry none cause youd want me to have a little fun too (smile). Here he come now so I wont take up no more of your time.

I know this will be a happy surprise hearing from me this way when I dont even write to my own folks in Texas.

                   xxxxxxxxxxxxxxxxxx them is kisses
                                Your everloving sugar pie
                                      Beulah

P.S. Georgie say for me to send you his love (smile) and to tell you not to make all the money. Save him some.

There I was splittin' my sides, rollin' on the ground, laffin' myself to death. I'se so happy. Havin' my fun. Makin' plenty money, just too much money. With tears in my eyes as big as dill pickles. I couldn't hardly wait to get my pay. Just wait 'til I roll into L.A. an' tell her how much fun I been havin'.

Then come Sat-day night. There we was all gathered in the shanty and the man callin' names. When he call mine everybody got quiet but I didn't think nothin' of it. I went up and said, "Well, that's a good deal. Just press the flesh with the cash."

But the man give my money to old Chops an' Chops start to figurin'. "Now lemme see, y'all owes me thirteen dollahs. Uh dollah fuh haulin' yuh from de depo'. Nine dollahs fuh board countin' suppah. Three dollahs fuh sleepin'." He counted the money. He counted it again. "Is dis all dat boy is earned?" he ast the man.

The man said, "That's all."

"Does y'all mean tuh say dat dis wut y'all give George Brown twenty-five dollahs fuh sending up heah fuh help?"

The man rubbed his chin. "We got to take the bad ones with the good ones. George has sent us some mighty good boys."

My eyes bucked out like skinned bananas. Sellin' me like a slave! Slicin' me off both ends. Wait 'til my queen hears 'bout this, I thought. Then I yelled at Chops, "Gimme my scratch. I gotta throat to cut!"

Chops put his fists on his hips and looked at me. "Wut is y'all reachin' fuh?" he ast. "Now jes tell me, wut is y'all reachin' fuh?"

"Lookahere, man—" I began.

But he cut me off. "Whar is mah nine dollahs? All y'all is got heah is three dollahs 'n' ninety-nine cents."

"Say, don't play no games, Jessie James," I snarled. "If'n I ain't got no more dough 'n that—"

But 'fore I could get through he'd done grabbed me by the pants an' heaved me out the door. "An' doan y'all come back 'till y'all git mah nine dollahs t'gethah," he shouted.

I knew right then and there is where I shoulda fit. But a man with all on his mind what I had on mine just don't feel like fightin'. All he feels like doin' is layin' down an' grievin'. But he gotta have someplace to lay and all I got is the hard cold ground.

A old stiff took pity on me and give me some writin' paper an' I writ my queen an' he say he take it to church with him next day and get the preacher to mail it. That night and the next I slept on the ground. Some other old stiffs brung me some grub from the table or I'da starved.

Come Monday I found myself 'mongst the old queens an' the chillun. They men work in the mill and they pick a li'l now an' then. I know I'da beat them six-year-olds if'n I hadn't got so stiffened sleepin' on the ground. But I couldn't even stand up straight no more. I had to crawl down the row an' tree the cotton like a cotton dog. I was beat, please believe me. But I warn't worried none. I'd got word to my queen an' looked any minute to get a money tellygraph.

'Stead I got a letter come Wednesday. Couldn't hardly wait to open it.

High C:

> *I is as mad as mad can be. I been setting here waiting for your check and all I get is a letter from somebody signing your name and writing in your handwriting to send them some money and talking all bad bout that nice man Mr Brown. You better tell those hustlers up there that I aint nobodys lain.*
>
> *Georgie say he cant understand it you must of got paid Saturday. If you think I is the kind of girl you can hold out on you better get your thinking cap on cause aint no man going to hold out on this fine queen.*
>
> *Your mad sugar pie*
Beulah

> *P.S. Georgie bought a Clipper yesterday. We been driving up and down the Avenue. I been hoping you hurry up and come on home and buy me one just like hisn.*

"Lord, what is I done?" I moaned. "If'n I done sompn I don't know of please forgive me, Lord. I'd forgive you if you was in my shape."

The first thing I did was found that old stiff and got some more writin' paper. I had to get that queen straight.

Dear Sugar pie:

> *You doesn't understand. I aint made dollar the first. Cotton aint what you think. Ifn you got any cotton dresses burn them. I is stranded without funds. Does you understand that? Aint got one white quarter not even a blip.[4] That was me writing in my handwriting. George Brown is a lowdown*

---

4. Five cents.

dog. I is cold and hungry. Aint got no place to stay. When I get back I going to carve out his heart. Ifn you ever loved your ever-loving papa send me ten bucks (dollars) by tellygraph.

Lots of love and kisses. I can hardly wait.

> *Your stranded papa*
> *High C*

Come Friday I ain't got no tellygraph. Come Sat-day I ain't got none neither. The man say I earned five dollars an' eighty-three cents an' Chops kept that. Come Sunday, Monday, Tuesday, Wednesday, I ain't got word one.

I is desperate, so help me. I said to myself, I gotta beat this rap, more ways to skin a cat than grabbling to his tail. So I got to thinkin'.

At night after everybody weighed in an' the weigher left, lots of them stiffs went back to the field and picked some more cotton so they'd have a head start next day. They kept it in their bags overnight. But them stiffs slept on them bags for pillows.

Well I figured a stiff what done picked all day an' then pick half the night just got to sleep sound. So Thursday night I slipped into the shanty after everybody gone to sleep an' stole them stiffs' cotton. Warn't hard. I just lifted their heads, tuk out their bags an' emptied 'em into mine an' put the empty bags back. Next day at noon I weighed in three hundred pounds.

Ain't got no word that night. But I got sompn else. When I slipped into the shanty an' lifted one of them stiffs' head he rolled over an' grabbed me. Them other stiffs jumped up and I got the worse beatin' I ever got.

Come Sat'day I couldn't walk atall. Old Chops taken pity on me an' let me come back on my bunk. There I lay a-moanin' an' a-groanin' when the letter come. It was a big fat letter an' I figured it sure must be filled with one-dollar bills. But when I opened it all dropped out was 'nother letter. I didn't look at it then, I read hers'n first.

High C:

> I believe now its been you writing me all these funny letters in your handwriting. So thats the kind of a fellow you turned out to be. Aint man enough to come out in the open. Got to make out like you broke. You the kind of a man let a little money go to his head. But that dont worry me none cause I done put you down first.
>
> Me and George Brown is getting married. He bought me a fur coat yesterday. Aint no silver foxes but it bettern you done and it cost $79.99. So you just hang onto your little money and see ifn you can find another queen as fine as me.

> *Your used to be sugar pie*
> *Beulah*

P.S. Here is your induction papers come to your room while you been gone. I hope the army likes you bettern I does.

That's how I got back to L.A. The man bought me a ticket when he seen the army wanted me. But I warn't the same cat what left tryna dodge the draft. Done lost my queen, lost my soft slave, and the man done got me. Now why they start all this cutting and shooting in the first place, you tell me. 'Cause I ain't mad at them people. They ain't done nothing to me. Who I is mad at is just cotton. That old mother, cotton, is gonna kill me yet.

1944

ANN PETRY
1911–1997

Students of Ann Petry's fiction see the blighted landscape of the inner city and the false fronts of rural New England as the boundaries of her art, but such a schema quickly breaks down upon closer inspection of her rich corpus, which includes three novels (*The Street*, 1946; *Country Place*, 1947; and *The Narrows*, 1953), one collection of short stories (*Miss Muriel and Other Stories*, 1971), and four children's books.

Ann Petry was born on October 12, 1911, in Old Saybrook, Connecticut, to a middle-class family. Her father was a pharmacist and owned a drugstore in town. Her mother was licensed to practice chiropody in 1915. Convinced that she could write when she created a slogan for a perfume advertisement while still in high school, Petry began her writing career in earnest following a brief stint as a pharmacist in her hometown. In the late 1930s, she served a kind of apprenticeship as a journalist for two Harlem newspapers, the *Amsterdam News* and the *People's Voice*. This experience rubbed her face in the gritty world of Harlem's poverty, violence, crime, and economic exploitation, which worked its way into her early fiction giving it its compelling edge. Her first published short story, "On Saturday the Siren Sounds at Noon," appeared in *Crisis* in 1943. The editor at *Crisis* found "Like a Winding Sheet" similarly engrossing and published it in 1945. Collected in Martha Foley's *Best American Stories of 1946*, "Like a Winding Sheet" brought Petry national attention and a Houghton Mifflin Literary Fellowship award to complete her best-known novel, *The Street* (1946), the first by a black woman to sell more than a million copies.

Inspired by a newspaper story of an apartment house superintendent who taught a young boy to steal letters from mailboxes, *The Street* aimed, according to Petry, to "show how simply and easily the environment can change the course of a person's life." It is precisely for treating the power of a corrosive urban environment on Lutie Johnson that *The Street* has linked Petry, in the minds of many critics, to Richard Wright.

While there are obvious and valid comparisons to be made between *The Street* and *Native Son,* exaggerating the links between Wright and Petry obscures perhaps the most salient and critical distinction between them: the sexual politics of race and the racial politics of gender. As critic Calvin Hernton observes, until *The Street* "no one had made a thesis of the debilitating mores of economic, racial and sexual violence let loose against black women in their new urban ghetto environment." Unlike *Native Son,* which projects its anxieties about black masculinity onto a phallicized Bigger Thomas, *The Street* focuses on the thwarted and naive efforts of a young black woman to secure a decent living for herself and her son. Petry closely documents the effects of the ghetto on a black woman and shows a critical sensitivity to woman as spectacle, as a body to be looked at and made the object of male sexual desire and exploitation. This particular achievement of *The Street* must be set against the perception in *Native Son* that the objectification, rape, and dismemberment of women are preconditions of Bigger's rising manhood.

In her second novel, *Country Place* (1947), which has been likened to Sherwood Anderson's *Winesburg, Ohio,* and Sinclair Lewis's *Main Street,* Petry shifts her focus from Harlem to Monmouth, Connecticut. Petry wrote *Country Place,* as she explained to critic James O'Brien, "because I happened to have been in a small town in Connecticut during a hurricane—I decided to write about that violent, devastating storm and its effect on the town and the people who lived there." But such a description hardly begins to capture the novel's intricately woven strands of class conflict, blood-lines, and social respectability. Petry reworks many of these same themes in *The Nar-rows*, a novel about the tabooed and ultimately tragic relationship between a black man and a white woman. She does not skirt the history of sexual and racial politics that weighs on their relationship, a history that makes the woman's accusation of rape and the man's subsequent lynching inevitable. In both *Country Place* and *The Narrows*, Petry turned to what critics have inadequately termed non-Negro or New England subject matter. While some see this shift as evidence of artistic maturation beyond the urban realism of *The Street*, others regard both these New England nov-els as less powerful than *The Street*.

Petry joins the urban and rural scenes in *Miss Muriel and Other Stories*. Promi-nent in this diverse collection are those stories in which Petry experiments with the point of view of precocious introspective child narrators. Set variously in Harlem, small-town New York, and Connecticut, these stories show Petry's deft manipula-tion of psychology. Petry's interest in children as fictional subjects extended to the publication of four children's books, including *Harriet Tubman: Conductor on the Underground Railway* (1955) and *Tituba of Salem Village* (1964). In a *Hornbook* essay on children's literature, published in 1965, Petry described her driving motivations as writer: "Over and over again, I have said: These are people. . . . Look at them and remember them. Remember for what a long, long time black people have been in this country, have been part of America; a sturdy, indestructible, wonderful part of America, woven into its heart and into its soul."

From The Street

Chapter I

[THE APARTMENT]

There was a cold November wind blowing through 116th Street.[1] It rattled the tops of garbage cans, sucked window shades out through the top of opened windows and set them flapping back against the windows; and it drove most of the people off the street in the block between Seventh and Eighth Avenues except for a few hurried pedestrians who bent double in an effort to offer the least possible exposed surface to its violent assault.

It found every scrap of paper along the street—theater throwaways, announcements of dances and lodge meetings, the heavy waxed paper that loaves of bread had been wrapped in, the thinner waxed paper that had enclosed sandwiches, old envelopes, newspapers. Fingering its way along the curb, the wind set the bits of paper to dancing high in the air, so that a barrage of paper swirled into the faces of the people on the street. It even took time to rush into doorways and areaways and find chicken bones and pork-chop bones and pushed them along the curb.

It did everything it could to discourage the people walking along the street. It found all the dirt and dust and grime on the sidewalk and lifted it up so that the dirt got into their noses, making it difficult to breathe; the dust got into their eyes and blinded them; and the grit stung their skins. It wrapped newspaper around their feet entangling them until the people cursed deep in their throats, stamped their feet, kicked at the paper. The wind blew it back again and again until they were forced to stoop and dislodge the paper with their hands. And then the wind grabbed their hats, pried their scarves

---

1. In Harlem.

from around their necks, stuck its fingers inside their coat collars, blew their coats away from their bodies.

The wind lifted Lutie Johnson's hair away from the back of her neck so that she felt suddenly naked and bald, for her hair had been resting softly and warmly against her skin. She shivered as the cold fingers of the wind touched the back of her neck, explored the sides of her head. It even blew her eyelashes away from her eyes so that her eyeballs were bathed in a rush of coldness and she had to blink in order to read the words on the sign swaying back and forth over her head.

Each time she thought she had the sign in focus, the wind pushed it away from her so that she wasn't certain whether it said three rooms or two rooms. If it was three, why, she would go in and ask to see it, but if it said two—why, there wasn't any point. Even with the wind twisting the sign away from her, she could see that it had been there for a long time because its original coat of white paint was streaked with rust where years of rain and snow had finally eaten the paint off down to the metal and the metal had slowly rusted, making a dark red stain like blood.

It was three rooms. The wind held it still for an instant in front of her and then swooped it away until it was standing at an impossible angle on the rod that suspended it from the building. She read it rapidly. Three rooms, steam heat, parquet floors, respectable tenants. Reasonable.

She looked at the outside of the building. Parquet floors here meant that the wood was so old and so discolored no amount of varnish or shellac would conceal the scars and the old scraped places, the years of dragging furniture across the floors, the hammer blows of time and children and drunks and dirty, slovenly women. Steam heat meant a rattling, clanging noise in radiators early in the morning and then a hissing that went on all day.

Respectable tenants in these houses where colored people were allowed to live included anyone who could pay the rent, so some of them would be drunk and loud-mouthed and quarrelsome; given to fits of depression when they would curse and cry violently, given to fits of equally violent elation. And, she thought, because the walls would be flimsy, why, the good people, the bad people, the children, the dogs, and the godawful smells would all be wrapped up together in one big package—the package that was called respectable tenants.

The wind pried at the red skullcap on her head, and as though angered because it couldn't tear it loose from its firm anchorage of bobby pins, the wind blew a great cloud of dust and ashes and bits of paper into her face, her eyes, her nose. It smacked against her ears as though it were giving her a final, exasperated blow as proof of its displeasure in not being able to make her move on.

Lutie braced her body against the wind's attack determined to finish thinking about the apartment before she went in to look at it. Reasonable—now that could mean almost anything. On Eighth Avenue it meant tenements—ghastly places not fit for humans. On St. Nicholas Avenue it meant high rents for small apartments; and on Seventh Avenue it meant great big apartments where you had to take in roomers in order to pay the rent. On this street it could mean almost anything.

She turned and faced the wind in order to estimate the street. The buildings were old with small slit-like windows, which meant the rooms were small and dark. In a street running in this direction there wouldn't be any sunlight in the apartments. Not ever. It would be hot as hell in summer and cold in winter. "Reasonable" here in this dark, crowded street ought to be about twenty-eight dollars, provided it was on a top floor.

The hallways here would be dark and narrow. Then she shrugged her shoulders, for getting an apartment where she and Bub would be alone was more important than dark hallways. The thing that really mattered was getting away from Pop and his raddled[2] women, and anything was better than that. Dark hallways, dirty stairs, even roaches on the walls. Anything. Anything. Anything.

Anything? Well, almost anything. So she turned toward the entrance of the building and as she turned, she heard someone clear his or her throat. It was so distinct—done as it was on two notes, the first one high and then the grunting expiration of breath on a lower note—that it came to her ears quite clearly under the sound of the wind rattling the garbage cans and slapping at the curtains. It was as though someone had said "hello," and she looked up at the window over her head.

There was a faint light somewhere in the room she was looking into and the enormous bulk of a woman was silhouetted against the light. She half-closed her eyes in order to see better. The woman was very black, she had a bandanna knotted tightly around her head, and Lutie saw, with some surprise, that the window was open. She began to wonder how the woman could sit by an open window on a cold, windy night like this one. And she didn't have on a coat, but a kind of loose-looking cotton dress—or at least it must be cotton, she thought, for it had a clumsy look—bulky and wrinkled.

"Nice little place, dearie. Just ring the Super's bell and he'll show it to you."

The woman's voice was rich. Pleasant. Yet the longer Lutie looked at her, the less she liked her. It wasn't that the woman had been sitting there all along staring at her, reading her thoughts, pushing her way into her very mind, for that was merely annoying. But it was understandable. She probably didn't have anything else to do; perhaps she was sick and the only pleasure she got out of life was in watching what went on in the street outside her window. It wasn't that. It was the woman's eyes. They were as still and as malignant as the eyes of a snake. She could see them quite plainly—flat eyes that stared at her—wandering over her body, inspecting and appraising her from head to foot.

"Just ring the Super's bell, dearie," the woman repeated.

Lutie turned toward the entrance of the building without answering, thinking about the woman's eyes. She pushed the door open and walked inside and stood there nodding her head. The hall was dark. The low-wattage bulb in the ceiling shed just enough light so that you wouldn't actually fall over—well, a piano that someone had carelessly left at the foot of the stairs; so that you could see the outlines of—oh, possibly an elephant if it were dragged in from the street by some enterprising tenant.

However, if you dropped a penny, she thought, you'd have to get down on your hands and knees and scrabble around on the cracked tile floor before you could ever hope to find it. And she was wrong about being able to see an elephant or a piano because the hallway really wasn't wide enough to admit either one. The stairs went up steeply—dark high narrow steps. She stared at them fascinated. Going up stairs like those you ought to find a newer and

2. Worn out, broken down.

more intricate—a much-involved and perfected kind of hell at the top—the very top.

She leaned over to look at the names on the mail boxes. Henry Lincoln Johnson lived here, too, just as he did in all the other houses she'd looked at. Either he or his blood brother. The Johnsons and the Jacksons were mighty prolific. Then she grinned, thinking who am I to talk, for I, too, belong to that great tribe, that mighty mighty tribe of Johnsons. The bells revealed that the Johnsons had roomers—Smith, Roach, Anderson—holy smoke! even Rosenberg. Most of the names were inked in over the mail boxes in scrawling handwriting—the letters were big and bold on some of them. Others were written in pencil; some printed in uneven scraggling letters where names had been scratched out and other names substituted.

There were only two apartments on the first floor. And if the Super didn't live in the basement, why, he would live on the first floor. There it was printed over One A. One A must be the darkest apartment, the smallest, most unrentable apartment, and the landlord would feel mighty proud that he'd given the Super a first-floor apartment.

She stood there thinking that it was really a pity they couldn't somehow manage to rent the halls, too. Single beds. No. Old army cots would do. It would bring in so much more money. If she were a landlord, she'd rent out the hallways. It would make it so much more entertaining for the tenants. Mr. Jones and wife could have cots number one and two; Jackson and girl friend could occupy number three. And Rinaldi, who drove a cab nights, could sublet the one occupied by Jackson and girl friend.

She would fill up all the cots—row after row of them. And when the tenants who had apartments came in late at night, they would have the added pleasure of checking up on the occupants. Jackson not home yet but girl friend lying in the cot alone—all curled up. A second look, because the lack of light wouldn't show all the details, would reveal—ye gods, why, what's Rinaldi doing home at night! Doggone if he ain't tucked up cozily in Jackson's cot with Jackson's girl friend. No wonder she looked contented. And the tenants who had apartments would sit on the stairs just as though the hall were a theater and the performance about to start—they'd sit there waiting until Jackson came home to see what he'd do when he found Rinaldi tucked into his cot with his girl friend. Rinaldi might explain that he thought the cot was his for sleeping and if the cot had blankets on it did not he, too, sleep under blankets; and if the cot had girl friend on it, why should not he, too, sleep with girl friend?

Instead of laughing, she found herself sighing. Then it occurred to her that if there were only two apartments on the first floor and the Super occupied one of them, then the occupant of the other apartment would be the lady with the snake's eyes. She looked at the names on the mail boxes. Yes. A Mrs. Hedges lived in One B. The name was printed on the card—a very professional-looking card. Obviously an extraordinary woman with her bandanna on her head and her sweet, sweet voice. Perhaps she was a snake charmer and she sat in her window in order to charm away at the snakes, the wolves, the foxes, the bears that prowled and loped and crawled on their bellies through the jungle of 116th Street.

Lutie reached out and rang the Super's bell. It made a shrill sound that echoed and re-echoed inside the apartment and came back out into the hall. Immediately a dog started a furious barking that came closer and closer as he ran toward the door of the apartment. Then the weight of his body

landed against the door and she drew back as he threw himself against the
door. Again and again until the door began to shiver from the impact of his
weight. There was the horrid sound of his nose snuffing up air, trying to get
her scent. And then his weight hurled against the door again. She retreated
toward the street door, pausing there with her hand on the knob. Then she
heard heavy footsteps, the sound of a man's voice threatening the dog, and
she walked back toward the apartment.

She knew instantly by his faded blue overalls that the man who opened
the door was the Super. The hot fetid air from the apartment in back of him
came out into the hall. She could hear the faint sound of steam hissing
in the radiators. Then the dog tried to plunge past the man and the man
kicked the dog back into the apartment. Kicked him in the side until the
dog cringed away from him with its tail between its legs. She heard the dog
whine deep in its throat and then the murmur of a woman's voice—a whispering voice talking to the dog.

"I came to see about the apartment—the three-room apartment that's
vacant," she said.

"It's on the top floor. You wanta look at it?"

The light in the hall was dim. Dim like that light in Mrs. Hedges' apartment. She pulled her coat around her a little tighter. It's this bad light, she
thought. Somehow the man's eyes were worse than the eyes of the woman
sitting in the window. And she told herself that it was because she was so
tired; that was the reason she was seeing things, building up pretty pictures
in people's eyes.

He was a tall, gaunt man and he towered in the doorway, looking at her.
It isn't the bad light, she thought. It isn't my imagination. For after his first
quick furtive glance, his eyes had filled with a hunger so urgent that she
was instantly afraid of him and afraid to show her fear.

But the apartment—did she want the apartment? Not in this house where
he was super; not in this house where Mrs. Hedges lived. No. She didn't
want to see the apartment—the dark, dirty three rooms called an apartment.
Then she thought of where she lived now. Those seven rooms where Pop
lived with Lil, his girl friend. A place filled with roomers. A place spilling
over with Lil.

There seemed to be no part of it that wasn't full of Lil. She was always
swallowing coffee in the kitchen; trailing through all seven rooms in
housecoats that didn't quite meet across her lush, loose bosom; drinking
beer in tall glasses and leaving the glasses in the kitchen sink so the foam
dried in a crust around the rim—the dark red of her lipstick like an accent
mark on the crust; lounging on the wide bed she shared with Pop and only
God knows who else; drinking gin with the roomers until late at night.

And what was far more terrifying giving Bub a drink on the sly; getting
Bub to light her cigarettes for her. Bub at eight with smoke curling out of his
mouth.

Only last night Lutie slapped him so hard that Lil cringed away from her
dismayed; her housecoat slipping even farther away from the fat curve of
her breasts. "Jesus!" she said. "That's enough to make him deaf. What's the
matter with you?"

But did she want to look at the apartment? Night after night she'd come
home from work and gone out right after supper to peer up at the signs in
front of the apartment houses in the neighborhood, looking for a place just
big enough for her and Bub. A place where the rent was low enough so that

she wouldn't come home from work some night to find a long sheet of white paper stuck under the door; "These premises must be vacated by——" better known as an eviction notice. Get out in five days or be tossed out. Stand by and watch your furniture pile up on the sidewalk. If you could call those broken beds, wornout springs, old chairs with the stuffing crawling out from under, chipped porcelain-topped kitchen table, flimsy kitchen chairs with broken rungs—if you could call those things furniture. That was an important point—now could you call fire-cracked china from the five-and-dime, and red-handled knives and forks and spoons that were bent and coming apart, could you really call those things furniture?

"Yes," she said firmly. "I want to look at the apartment."

"I'll get a flashlight," he said and went back into his apartment, closing the door behind him so that it made a soft, sucking sound. He said something, but she couldn't hear what it was. The whispering voice inside the apartment stopped and the dog was suddenly quiet.

Then he was back at the door, closing it behind him so it made the same soft, sucking sound. He had a long black flashlight in his hand. And she went up the stairs ahead of him thinking that the rod of its length was almost as black as his hands. The flashlight was a shiny black—smooth and gleaming faintly as the light lay along its length. Whereas the hand that held it was flesh—dull, scarred, worn flesh—no smoothness there. The knuckles were knobs that stood out under the skin, pulled out from hauling ashes, shoveling coal.

But not apparently from using a mop or a broom, for, as she went up and up the steep flight of stairs, she saw that they were filthy, with wastepaper, cigarette butts, the discarded wrappings from packages of snuff, pink ticket stubs from the movie houses. On the landings there were empty gin and whiskey bottles.

She stopped looking at the stairs, stopped peering into the corners of the long hallways, for it was cold, and she began walking faster trying to keep warm. As they completed a flight of stairs and turned to walk up another hall, and then started climbing another flight of stairs, she was aware that the cold increased. The farther up they went, the colder it got. And in summer she supposed it would get hotter and hotter as you went up until when you reached the top floor your breath would be cut off completely.

The halls were so narrow that she could reach out and touch them on either side without having to stretch her arms any distance. When they reached the fourth floor, she thought, instead of her reaching out for the walls, the walls were reaching out for her—bending and swaying toward her in an effort to envelop her. The Super's footsteps behind her were slow, even, steady. She walked a little faster and apparently without hurrying, without even increasing his pace, he was exactly the same distance behind her. In fact his heavy footsteps were a little nearer than before.

She began to wonder how it was that she had gone up the stairs first, why was she leading the way? It was all wrong. He was the one who knew the place, the one who lived here. He should have gone up first. How had he got her to go up the stairs in front of him? She wanted to turn around and see the expression on his face, but she knew if she turned on the stairs like this, her face would be on a level with his; and she wouldn't want to be that close to him.

She didn't need to turn around, anyway; he was staring at her back, her legs, her thighs. She could feel his eyes traveling over her—estimating her, summing her up, wondering about her. As she climbed up the last flight of stairs, she was aware that the skin on her back was crawling with fear. Fear of what? she asked herself. Fear of him, fear of the dark, of the smells in the halls, the high steep stairs, of yourself? She didn't know, and even as she admitted that she didn't know, she felt sweat start pouring from her armpits, dampening her forehead, breaking out in beads on her nose.

The apartment was in the back of the house. The Super fished another flashlight from his pocket which he handed to her before he bent over to unlock the door very quietly. And she thought, everything he does, he does quietly.

She played the beam of the flashlight on the walls. The rooms were small. There was no window in the bedroom. At least she supposed it was the bedroom. She walked over to look at it, and then went inside for a better look. There wasn't a window—just an air shaft and a narrow one at that. She looked around the room, thinking that by the time there was a bed and a chest of drawers in it there'd be barely space enough to walk around in. At that she'd probably bump her knees every time she went past the corner of the bed. She tried to visualize how the room would look and began to wonder why she had already decided to take this room for herself.

It might be better to give it to Bub, let him have a real bedroom to himself for once. No, that wouldn't do. He would swelter in this room in summer. It would be better to have him sleep on the couch in the living room, at least he'd get some air, for there was a window out there, though it wasn't a very big one. She looked out into the living room, trying again to see the window, to see just how much air would come through, how much light there would be for Bub to study by when he came home from school, to determine, too, the amount of air that would reach into the room at night when the window was open, and he was sleeping curled up on the studio couch.

The Super was standing in the middle of the living room. Waiting for her. It wasn't anything that she had to wonder about or figure out. It wasn't by any stretch of the imagination something she had conjured up out of thin air. It was a simple fact. He was waiting for her. She knew it just as she knew she was standing there in that small room. He was holding his flashlight so the beam fell down at his feet. It turned him into a figure of never-ending tallness. And his silent waiting and his appearance of incredible height appalled her.

With the light at his feet like that, he looked as though his head must end somewhere in the ceiling. He simply went up and up into darkness. And he radiated such desire for her that she could feel it. She told herself she was a fool, an idiot, drunk on fear, on fatigue and gnawing worry. Even while she thought it, the hot, choking awfulness of his desire for her pinioned her there so that she couldn't move. It was an aching yearning that filled the apartment, pushed against the walls, plucked at her arms.

She forced herself to start walking toward the kitchen. As she went past him, it seemed to her that he actually did reach one long arm out toward her, his body swaying so that its exaggerated length almost brushed against her. She really couldn't be certain of it, she decided, and resolutely turned the beam of her flashlight on the kitchen walls.

It isn't possible to read people's minds, she argued. Now the Super was probably not even thinking about her when he was standing there like that. He probably wanted to get back downstairs to read his paper. Don't kid yourself, she thought, he probably can't read, or if he can, he probably doesn't spend any time at it. Well—listen to the radio. That was it, he probably wanted to hear his favorite program and she had thought he was filled with the desire to leap upon her. She was as bad as Granny. Which just went on to prove you couldn't be brought up by someone like Granny without absorbing a lot of nonsense that would spring at you out of nowhere, so to speak, and when you least expected it. All those tales about things that people sensed before they actually happened. Tales that had been handed down and down and down until, if you tried to trace them back, you'd end up God knows where—probably Africa. And Granny had them all at the tip of her tongue.

Yet would wanting to hear a radio program make a man look quite like that? Impatiently she forced herself to inspect the kitchen; holding the light on first one wall, then another. It was no better and no worse than she had anticipated. The sink was battered; and the gas stove was a little rusted. The faint smell of gas that hovered about it suggested a slow, incurable leak somewhere in its connections.

Peering into the bathroom, she saw that the fixtures were old-fashioned and deeply chipped. She thought Methuselah[3] himself might well have taken baths in the tub. Certainly it looked ancient enough, though he'd have had to stick his beard out in the hall while he washed himself, for the place was far too small for a man with a full-grown beard to turn around in. She presumed because there was no window that the vent pipe would serve as a source of nice, fresh, clean air.

One thing about it the rent wouldn't be very much. It couldn't be for a place like this. Tiny hall. Bathroom on the right, kitchen straight ahead; living room to the left of the hall and you had to go through the living room to get to the bedroom. The whole apartment would fit very neatly into just one good-sized room.

She was conscious that all the little rooms smelt exactly alike. It was a mixture that contained the faint persistent odor of gas, of old walls, dusty plaster, and over it all the heavy, sour smell of garbage—a smell that seeped through the dumb-waiter shaft. She started humming under her breath, not realizing she was doing it. It was an old song that Granny used to sing. "Ain't no restin' place for a sinner like me. Like me. Like me." It had a nice recurrent rhythm. "Like me. Like me." The humming increased in volume as she stood there thinking about the apartment.

There was a queer, muffled sound from the Super in the living room. It startled her so she nearly dropped the flashlight. "What was that?" she said sharply, thinking, My God, suppose I'd dropped it, suppose I'd been left standing here in the dark of this little room and he'd turned out his light. Suppose he'd started walking toward me, nearer and nearer in the dark. And I could only hear his footsteps, couldn't see him, but could hear him coming closer until I started reaching out in the dark trying to keep him away from me, trying to keep him from touching me—and then—then my hands found him right in front of me— At the thought she gripped the flashlight so tightly that the long beam of light from it started wavering and dancing over the walls so that the shadows moved—shadow from the light fixture overhead, shadow from the tub, shadow from the very doorway itself—shifting, moving back and forth.

"I cleared my throat," the Super said. His voice had a choked, unnatural sound as though something had gone wrong with his breathing.

3. In the Book of Genesis, a man who lived to be 969 years old.

She walked out into the hall, not looking at him; opened the door of the apartment and stepping over the threshold, still not looking at him, said, "I've finished looking."

He came out and turned the key in the lock. He kept his back turned toward her so that she couldn't have seen the expression on his face even if she'd looked at him. The lock clicked into place, smoothly. Quietly. She stood there not moving, waiting for him to start down the hall toward the stairs, thinking, Never, so help me, will he walk down those stairs in back of me.

When he didn't move, she said, "You go first." Then he made a slight motion toward the stairs with his flashlight indicating that she was to precede him. She shook her head very firmly.

"Think you'll take it?" he asked.

"I don't know yet. I'll think about it going down."

When he finally started down the hall, it seemed to her that he had stood there beside her for days, weeks, months, willing her to go down the stairs first. She followed him, thinking, It wasn't my imagination when I got that feeling at the sight of him standing there in the living room; otherwise, why did he have to go through all that rigamarole of my going down the stairs ahead of him? Like going through the motions of a dance; you first; no, you first; but you see, you'll spoil the pattern if you don't go first; but I won't go first, you go first; but no, it'll spoil the—

She was aware that they'd come up the stairs much faster than they were going down. Was she going to take the apartment? The price wouldn't be too high from the looks of it and by being careful she and Bub could manage— by being very, very careful. White paint would fix the inside of it up; not exactly fix it up, but keep it from being too gloomy, shove the darkness back a little.

Then she thought, Layers and layers of paint won't fix that apartment. It would always smell; finger marks and old stains would come through the paint; the very smell of the wood itself would eventually win out over the paint. Scrubbing wouldn't help any. Then there were these dark, narrow halls, the long flights of stairs, the Super himself, that woman on the first floor.

Or she could go on living with Pop. And Lil. Bub would learn to like the taste of gin, would learn to smoke, would learn in fact a lot of other things that Lil could teach him—things that Lil would think it amusing to teach him. Bub at eight could get a liberal education from Lil, for she was home all day and Bub got home from school a little after three.

You've got a choice a yard wide and ten miles long. You can sit down and twiddle your thumbs while your kid gets a free education from your father's blowsy girl friend. Or you can take this apartment. The tall gentleman who is the superintendent is supposed to rent apartments, fire the furnace, sweep the halls, and that's as far as he's supposed to go. If he tries to include making love to the female tenants, why, this is New York City in the year 1944, and as yet there's no grass growing in the streets and the police force still functions. Certainly you can holler loud enough so that if the gentleman has some kind of dark designs on you and tries to carry them out, a cop will eventually rescue you. That's that.

As for the lady with the snake eyes, you're supposed to be renting the top-floor apartment and if she went with the apartment the sign out in front would say so. Three rooms and snake charmer for respectable tenant. No extra charge for the snake charmer. Seeing as the sign didn't say so, it stood to reason if the snake charmer tried to move in, she could take steps—whatever the hell that meant.

Her high-heeled shoes made a clicking noise as she went down the stairs, and she thought, Yes, take steps like these. It was all very well to reason lightheartedly like that; to kid herself along—there was no explaining away the instinctive, immediate fear she had felt when she first saw the Super. Granny would have said, "Nothin' but evil, child. Some folks so full of it you can feel it comin' at you—oozin' right out of their skins."

She didn't believe things like that and yet, looking at his tall, gaunt figure going down that last flight of stairs ahead of her, she half-expected to see horns sprouting from behind his ears; she wouldn't have been greatly surprised if, in place of one of the heavy work shoes on his feet, there had been a cloven hoof that twitched and jumped as he walked so slowly down the stairs.

Outside the door of his apartment, he stopped and turned toward her.

"What's the rent?" she asked, not looking at him, but looking past him at the One A printed on the door of his apartment. The gold letters were filled with tiny cracks, and she thought that in a few more years they wouldn't be distinguishable from the dark brown of the door itself. She hoped the rent would be so high she couldn't possibly take it.

"Twenty-nine fifty."

He wants me to take it, she thought. He wants it so badly that he's bursting with it. She didn't have to look at him to know it; she could feel him willing it. What difference does it make to him? Yet it was of such obvious importance that if she hesitated just a little longer, he'd be trembling. No, she decided, not that apartment. Then she thought Bub would look cute learning to drink gin at eight.

"I'll take it," she said grimly.

"You wanta leave a deposit?" he asked.

She nodded, and he opened his door, standing aside to let her go past him. There was a dim light burning in the small hall inside and she saw that the hall led into a living room. She didn't wait for an invitation, but walked on into the living room. The dog had been lying near the radio that stood under a window at the far side of the room. He got up when he saw her, walking toward her with his head down, his tail between his legs; walking as though he were drawn toward her irresistibly, even though he knew that at any moment he would be forced to stop. Though he was a police dog, his hair had such a worn, rusty look that he resembled a wolf more than a dog. She saw that he was so thin, his great haunches and the small bones of his ribs were sharply outlined against his skin. As he got nearer to her, he got excited and she could hear his breathing.

"Lie down," the Super said.

The dog moved back to the window, shrinking and walking in such a way that she thought if he were human he'd walk backward in order to see and be able to dodge any unexpected blow. He lay down calmly enough and looked at her, but he couldn't control the twitching of his nose; he looked, too, at the Super as though he were wondering if he could possibly cross the room and get over to her without being seen.

The Super sat down in front of an old office desk, found a receipt pad, picked up a fountain pen and, carefully placing a blotter in front of him, turned toward her. "Name?" he asked.

She swallowed an impulse to laugh. There was something so solemn about the way he'd seated himself, grasping the pen firmly, moving the pad in front of him to exactly the right angle, opening a big ledger book whose pages were filled with line after line of heavily inked writing that she thought he's acting like a big businessman about to transact a major deal.

"Mrs. Lutie Johnson. Present address 2370 Seventh Avenue." Opening her pocketbook she took out a ten-dollar bill and handed it to him. Ten whole dollars that it had taken a good many weeks to save. By the time she had moved in here and paid the balance which would be due on the rent, her savings would have disappeared. But it would be worth it to be living in a place of her own.

He wrote with a painful slowness, concentrating on each letter, having difficulty with the numbers twenty-three seventy. He crossed it out and bit his lip. "What was that number?" he asked.

"Twenty-three seventy," she repeated, thinking perhaps it would be simpler to write it down for him. At the rate he was going, it would take him all of fifteen minutes to write ten dollars and then figure out the difference between ten dollars and twenty-nine dollars which would in this case constitute that innocuous looking phrase, "the balance due." She shouldn't be making fun of him; very likely he had taught himself to read and write after spending a couple of years in grammar school where he undoubtedly didn't learn anything. He looked to be in his fifties, but it was hard to tell.

It irritated her to stand there and watch him go through the slow, painful process of forming the letters. She wanted to get out of the place, to get back to Pop's house, plan the packing, get hold of a moving man. She looked around the room idly. The floor was uncarpeted—a terrible-looking floor. Rough and splintered. There was a sofa against the long wall; its upholstery marked by a greasy line along the back. All the people who had sat on it from the time it was new until the time it had passed through so many hands it finally ended up here must have ground their heads along the back of it.

Next to the sofa there was an overstuffed chair and she drew her breath in sharply as she looked at it, for there was a woman sitting in it, and she had thought that she and the dog and the Super were the only occupants of the room. How could anyone sit in a chair and melt into it like that? As she looked, the shapeless small dark woman in the chair got up and bowed to her without speaking.

Lutie nodded her head in acknowledgment of the bow, thinking, That must be the woman I heard whispering. The woman sat down in the chair again. Melting into it. Because the dark brown dress she wore was almost the exact shade of the dark brown of the upholstery and because the overstuffed chair swallowed her up until she was scarcely distinguishable from the chair itself. Because, too, of a shrinking withdrawal in her way of sitting as though she were trying to take up the least possible amount of space. So that after bowing to her Lutie completely forgot the woman was in the room, while she went on studying its furnishings.

No pictures, no rugs, no newspapers, no magazines, nothing to suggest anyone had ever tried to make it look homelike. Not quite true, for there was a canary huddled in an ornate birdcage in the corner. Looking at it, she thought, Everything in the room shrinks: the dog, the woman, even the canary, for it had only one eye open as it perched on one leg. Opposite the sofa an overornate table shone with varnish. It was a very large table with intricately carved claw feet and looking at it she thought, That's the kind of big ugly furniture white women love to give to their maids.

She turned to look at the shapeless little woman because she was almost certain the table was hers.

The woman must have been looking at her, for when Lutie turned the woman smiled; a toothless smile that lingered while she looked from Lutie to the table.

"When you want to move in?" the Super asked, holding out the receipt.

"This is Tuesday—do you think you could have the place ready by Friday?"

"Easy," he said. "Some special color you want it painted?"

"White. Make all the rooms white," she said, studying the receipt. Yes, he had it figured out correctly—balance due, nineteen fifty. He had crossed out his first attempt at the figures. Evidently nines were hard for him to make. And his name was William Jones. A perfectly ordinary name. A highly suitable name for a superintendent. Nice and normal. Easy to remember. Easy to spell. Only the name didn't fit him. For he was obviously unusual, extraordinary, abnormal. Everything about him was the exact opposite of his name. He was standing up now looking at her, eating her up with his eyes.

She took a final look around the room. The whispering woman seemed to be holding her breath; the dog was dying with the desire to growl or whine, for his throat was working. The canary, too, ought to be animated with some desperate emotion, she thought, but he had gone quietly to sleep. Then she forced herself to look directly at the Super. A long hard look, malignant, steady, continued. Thinking, That'll fix you, Mister William Jones, but, of course, if it was only my imagination upstairs, it isn't fair to look at you like this. But just in case some dark leftover instinct warned me of what was on your mind—just in case it made me know you were snuffing on my trail, slathering, slobbering after me like some dark hound of hell seeking me out, tonguing along in back of me, this look, my fine feathered friend, should give you much food for thought.

She closed her pocketbook with a sharp, clicking final sound that made the Super's eyes shift suddenly to the ceiling as though seeking out some pattern in the cracked plaster. The dog's ears straightened into sharp points; the canary opened one eye and the whispering woman almost showed her gums again, for her mouth curved as though she were about to smile.

Lutie walked quickly out of the apartment, pushed the street door open and shivered as the cold air touched her. It had been hot in the Super's apartment, and she paused a second to push her coat collar tight around her neck in an effort to make a barrier against the wind howling in the street outside. Now that she had this apartment, she was just one step farther up on the ladder of success. With the apartment Bub would be standing a better chance, for he'd be away from Lil.

Inside the building the dog let out a high shrill yelp. Immediately she headed for the street, thinking he must have kicked it again. She paused for a moment at the corner of the building, bracing herself for the full blast of the wind that would hit her head-on when she turned the corner.

"Get fixed up, dearie?" Mrs. Hedges' rich voice asked from the street-floor window.

She nodded at the bandannaed head in the window and flung herself into the wind, welcoming its attack, aware as she walked along that the woman's hard flat eyes were measuring her progress up the street.

1946

ALICE CHILDRESS
1912?–1994

In a comment explaining her choice of literary themes, Alice Childress admitted to an interviewer, "I think I am forced to write things that people are disturbed about, annoyed about." And explaining her choice of characters, she remarked, "I deal with the people I know best, which are ordinary people . . . the intellectual poor. People who are thoughtful about their condition, people who . . . have been cut off from having all that they want and desire." Noting that such ordinary characters were missing particularly from the American stage, Childress speculated that their absence stemmed from widespread assumptions, in and out of the theatrical world, that they were not "interesting enough dramatically or important enough." Childress spent the entirety of her roughly four-decades-long career implicitly challenging, largely through the characters she created, the popular notion that blacks were best cast as "source material for derogatory humor/and or condescending clinical, social analyses." She admittedly identified with and elevated in her work the kind of characters she observed during her childhood. Born in Charleston, South Carolina, on October 20, 1912 (her birth date is variously listed as 1912, 1916, and 1920), Childress grew up in Harlem nurtured by a grandmother with a strong sense of the dramatic, who noticed and fostered her granddaughter's literary ambitions, encouraging her to create and perform plays at home. This early immersion in the world of drama, which included plays, recitations, and readings performed in churches, led naturally, then, to Childress's early and short-term experience as an actor. She was nominated for a Tony Award as best supporting actor for her role in Philip Yordan's *Anna Lucasta*. Adapted from the original play for an all-black cast, it became the longest running all-black play on Broadway. Eventually abandoning her acting ambitions, Childress turned to playwriting, determined to create dramatic material for black actors that transcended the standard theatrical fare.

A founding member of the American Negro Theater (ANT), a small amateur acting company established in the 1940s, Childress developed and honed her craft as a playwright, while also gaining experience as director, costume designer, and scene designer during the eleven years she was a member of the company. As she put it, "Everything that happened in the theater, you had to do some of it [there]." The ANT produced Childress's first play, *Florence* (1949), staged in St. Mark's Church in Harlem. Set in a segregated bus station in the South, and centered on a conversation between two women—one white, one black—*Florence* not only launched Childress's career as a playwright but introduced what became her familiar, and unfavorable, assessment of American theater. Fundamentally conservative, in her estimation, it had failed to treat black female characters with any depth, complexity, or sophistication. Whether in "popular American drama, television, motion pictures [or] radio," she argued, black women failed to exist as serious subjects for serious literature. "A serious woman character is harder to sell than a serious male character," especially a serious black female character, she once told an interviewer. Why? Perhaps because American audiences had become inured to seeing black women as either docile, servile, maids or mammies or as "defeated, unloved figures, good at taking the hard knocks of life." Her role as a playwright, she believed, was not only to transcend these limitations but also to "interpret 'the ordinary,'" the "genteel poor" whose lives were "marvelously intricate in thought and actions."

Not only did "Florence," set the template for the female characters Childress would go on to create, the play also established Childress's artistic signature: a talent for humor with a caustic bite, an irreverent treatment of American race relations, and a willingness to provoke discomfort by wading into various social controversies (including the taboo of interracial romance). Indeed, as Childress was fond of saying, "Drama is the controversy of life."

Childress found no more fruitful controversy for dramatization than that contained in the worldwide racial struggles of the 1950s, unfolding at the very moment she hit her stride as a playwright. In *Gold through the Trees*, a 1952 revue, she staged these struggles as they were manifested before and after colonialism. In taking up the subject of colonialism in Africa, Childress expressed her understanding that the struggles of people of African descent against oppression must be cast in global frame. At the same time, she found it necessary to see such struggles localized, "close up" and distilled, a move she made in *Trouble in Mind*. Her first full-length and first professionally produced drama, *Trouble in Mind* earned her an Obie in 1956 (the first African American woman to be so honored) .

In this play, which debuted in November 1955, Childress brought to bear her own early struggles and frustrations as a professional actress. Through the structure of a play within a play, she also advocated, as she did throughout her career, for the necessity, if limited availability, of black artistic autonomy. Set during the rehearsal for a production of *Chaos in Belleville*, billed as a protest against lynching, *Trouble in Mind* stages the clashes and conflicts that ensue when a group of black actors in a racially mixed cast must wrestle with the racist condescension of a white director determined to produce a palatable play for a largely white theatergoing audience. The black members of the cast must choose between necessity and indignity, between needing to work and the humiliation of playing subservient roles. The interracial conflicts brewing inside the rehearsal studio mirror, to some degree, the interracial struggles offstage. Matters come to a head over the ending of the play, which called for a walkout by the interracial cast members, who close ranks in protest against the director. Although Childress knew that nothing approaching this hokey rapprochement ever occurred in commercial theater, she acceded to the producer's demands for a "happy ending," for one that provided "a positive image to the public of black and white working together." As she noted, "Anything that deals with the conflict between the races leads to discomfort for those selling products." When *Trouble in Mind* was later optioned for Broadway, Childress passed on the opportunity. This would not be the last time that she exercised this option, despite knowing that a Broadway production is an important measure of a playwright's success. As she noted in an interview, "I don't want to go to Broadway and end up doing what I did on *Trouble in Mind*—changing the ending when I *knew* I was doing the wrong thing."

Changing the ending of a play to accommodate the demands of the marketplace was the least of Alice Childress's challenges of the 1950s. Facing McCarthy-era tactics was another. As Mary Helen Washington has noted, the 1950s was not a "decade without dissent," and Childress's penchant for dissent, evident in writings published in the radical press—*Freedom* (Paul Robeson's newspaper), *Masses and Mainstream*, and the *Baltimore Afro-American*—brought her unwanted notice from the FBI. Listed by the bureau among its black subversives, many of whom were suspected of being members of the Communist Party, Childress, notes Washington, eventually sought to shed her radical past. Although black leftist politics was a vital, even essential grounding of African American cultural production of the 1950s, Childress, like so many others fingered as communists by the House Un-American Activities Committee (HUAC) during the 1950s, "spent the next forty years," adds Washington, "erasing or disguising her leftist past."

The disguise did not work altogether, for Childress was still drawn to controversial subjects and cultural critique—Jim Crow laws of the South, black liberation movements in Africa, the union of domestic workers—all of which she took on in *Like One of the Family: Conversations from a Domestic's Life* (1956), a collection of pieces first published as columns in *Freedom* and the *Baltimore Afro-American*. Her choice of subjects frequently compelled her readers to ask, Why talk about that? a question that some asked about her controversial play *Wedding Band: A Love/Hate Story in Black and White*," produced in 1966. She answered them forthrightly: "We are at a moment in history when the playwright cannot turn away from social drama." The drama from which she would not turn away, even in the thick of racial tensions that marked the 1960s, concerned a play about a black woman and a white man who wished to become legally married in the South Carolina of 1918. Her decision to confront this taboo topic head on cost her yet another opportunity for a Broadway production. The play was eventually staged at the University of Michigan, a venue not necessitating the kind of compromises to which Childress had acceded in *Trouble in Mind*.

While Childress continued to write and produce plays through to the end of her career—*String* (1969), *Mojo* (1970), *When the Rattlesnake Sounds* (1975), *Let's Hear It for the Queen"* (1976), and *Sea Island Song* (1979)—she turned increasingly to writing fiction in her latter years. She often conceded that she preferred writing prose to drama, perhaps because writing prose was not a collaborative process, necessitating chafing compromises with producers and directors. Childress found particular success writing fiction for young adults, *A Hero Ain't Nothing but a Sandwich* (1973), being perhaps the most well known. Structured, as was *Like One of the Family*, as a series of monologues, the novel centered on the rehabilitation of a thirteen-year-old heroin addict. Although the book won awards, it was widely censored and banned from public school libraries across the country. In *A Short Walk*, published a few years later in 1979 (it was nominated for a Pulitzer), Childress returned to the setting of the Jim Crow South, rounding out writing credits for the 1970s before returning to the young adult audience in such 1980s publications as *Rainbow Jordan* (1981) and *Those Other People* (1989), in which works she characteristically tackled such difficult subjects, such as racism, homophobia, and incest.

In a writing career that spanned roughly four decades, Childress earned her share of accolades, but most critics would concede that she never earned the literary or commercial successes many believed she deserved. However her output is judged in the end, few could deny the merits of Elizabeth Brown Guillory's assessment that Childress represents a crucial link in the development of black female drama. Anticipating the emergence of Lorraine Hansberry, Adrienne Kennedy, Ntozake Shange, and Susan Lori-Parks. Like them, she brought to the stage material that broke the dramatic mold, especially for African American women, long established in American theater.

Trouble in Mind

A Comedy-Drama in Two Acts

Characters

WILETTA MAYER	SHELDON FORRESTER
HENRY	AL MANNERS
JOHN NEVINS	EDDIE FENTON
MILLIE DAVIS	BILL O'WRAY
JUDY SEARS	

ACT 1

TIME

Ten o'clock Monday morning, fall, 1957.

PLACE

A Broadway theater in New York City. Blues music in—out after lights up.

SCENE

The stage of the theater. Stage left leads to the outside entrance. Stage right to upstairs dressing rooms. There are many props and leftovers from the last show: a plaster fountain with a cupid perched atop, garden furniture, tables, benches, a trellis, two white armchairs trimmed with gold gilt. Before the curtain rises we hear banging sounds from offstage left, the banging grows louder and louder. Curtain rises. WILETTA MAYER, *a middle-aged actress, appears. She is attractive and expansive in personality. She carries a purse and a script. At the moment, she is in quite a huff.*

WILETTA   My Lord, I like to have wore my arm off bangin' on that door! What you got it locked for?

[*Lights up brighter.*]

Had me standin' out there in the cold, catchin' my death of pneumonia!

[HENRY, *the elderly doorman, enters.*]

HENRY   I didn't hear a thing . . . I didn't know . . .

[WILETTA *is suddenly moved by the sight of the theater. She holds up her hand for silence, looks out and up at the balcony. She loves the theater. She turns back to* HENRY.]

WILETTA   A theater always makes me feel that way . . . gotta get still for a second.

HENRY [*welcomes an old memory*]   You . . . you are Wiletta Mayer . . . more than twenty years ago, in the old Galy Theater . . . [*is pleased to be remembered*] You was singin' a number, with the lights changin' color all around you . . . What was the name of that show?

WILETTA   *Brownskin Melody.*

HENRY   That's it . . . and the lights . . .

WILETTA   Was a doggone rainbow.

HENRY   And you looked so pretty and sounded so fine, there's no denyin' it.

WILETTA   Thank you, but I . . . I . . .

[WILETTA *hates to admit she doesn't remember him.*]

HENRY   I'm Henry.

WILETTA   Mmmmm, you don't say.

HENRY   I was the electrician. Rigged up all those lights and never missed a cue. I'm the doorman here now. I've been in show business over fifty years. I'm the doorman . . . Henry.

WILETTA   That's a nice name. I . . . I sure remember those lights.

HENRY   Bet you can't guess how old I am, I'll betcha.

WILETTA [*would rather not guess*]   Well . . . you're sure lookin' good.

HENRY   Go ahead, take a guess.

WILETTA [*being very kind*]   Ohhhhh, I'd say you're in your . . . late fifties.

HENRY [*laughs proudly*]   I fool 'em all! I'm seventy-eight years old! How's that?

WILETTA   Ohhhh, don't be tellin' it.

[*She places her script and purse on the table, removes her coat.* HENRY *takes coat and hangs it on a rack.*]

HENRY   You singin' in this new show?

WILETTA   No, I'm actin'. I play the mother.

HENRY [*is hard of hearing*]   How's that?

WILETTA   I'm the mother!

HENRY   Could I run next door and get you some coffee? I'm goin' anyway, no bother.

WILETTA   No, thank you just the same.

HENRY   If you open here, don't let 'em give you dressin' room "C." It's small and it's got no "john" in it . . . excuse me, I mean . . . no commode . . . Miss Mayer.

WILETTA [*feeling like the star he's made her*]   Thank you, I'll watch out for that.

> [HENRY *reaches for a small chair, changes his mind and draws the gilt armchair to the table.*]

HENRY   Make yourself comfortable. The old Galy. Yessir, I'm seventy-eight years old.

WILETTA   Well, I'm not gonna tell you my age. A woman that'll tell her age will tell anything.

HENRY [*laughs*]   Oh, that's a good one! I'll remember that! A woman that'll tell her age . . . what else?

WILETTA   Will tell anything.

HENRY   *Will* tell. Well, I'll see you a little later.

> [*He exits stage left.*]

WILETTA [*saying good-bye to the kind of gentle treatment she seldom receives*] So long.

> [*She rises and walks downstage, strikes a pose from the "old Galy," and sings a snatch of an old song.*]

Oh, honey babe

Oh, honey babe . . .

> [*She pushes the memory aside.*]

Yes, indeed!

> [JOHN NEVINS, *a young Negro actor, enters. He tries to look self-assured, but it's obvious that he is new to the theater and fighting hard to control his enthusiasm.*]

Good morning. Another early bird! I'm glad they hired you, you read so nice er . . . ah . . .

JOHN   John, John Nevins.

WILETTA   This is new for you, ain't it?

JOHN   Yes, ma'am.

WILETTA   Yes, ma'am? I know you're not a New Yorker, where's your home?

JOHN   Newport News, that's in Virginia.

WILETTA   HOT DOG. I shoulda known anyone as handsome and mannerly as you had to come from my home. Newport News! Think of that! Last name?

JOHN   Nevins, John Nevins.

WILETTA   Wait a minute . . . do you know Estelle Nevins, used to live out on Prairie Road . . . fine built woman?

JOHN   Guess I do, that's my mother.

WILETTA [*very touched*]   No, she ain't!

JOHN [*afraid of oncoming sentiment*]   Yes . . . ah . . . yes she is.

WILETTA   What a day! I went to school with Estelle! She married a fella named Clarence! Used to play baseball. Last time I hit home she had a little baby in the carriage. How many children she got?

JOHN   I'm the only one.

WILETTA   You can't be that little baby in the carriage! Stand up, let me look at you! Brings all of yesterday back to my mind! Tell me, John, is the drug-store still on the corner? Used to be run by a tall, strappin' fella . . . got wavy, black hair . . . and, well, he's kind of devilish . . . Eddie Bentley!

JOHN   Oh yes, Mr. Bentley is still there . . .

WILETTA   Fresh and sassy and . . .

JOHN   But he's gray-haired and very stern and businesslike.

WILETTA [*very conscious of her age*]   You don't say. Why you want to act? Why don't you make somethin' outta yourself?

JOHN [*is amazed at this*]   What? Well, I . . .

WILETTA   You look bright enough to be a doctor or even a lawyer maybe . . . You don't have to take what I've been through . . . don't have to take it off 'em.

JOHN   I think the theater is the grandest place in the world, and I plan to go right to the top.

WILETTA [*with good humor*]   Uh-huh, and where do you think I was plannin' to go?

JOHN [*feeling slightly superior because he thinks he knows more about the craft than* WILETTA]   Ohhh, well . . .

WILETTA [*quick to sense his feelings*]   Oh, well, what?

JOHN [*feels a bit chastised*]   Nothing. I know what I want to do. I'm set, decided, and that's that. You're in it, aren't you proud to be a part of it all?

WILETTA   Of what all?

JOHN   Theater.

WILETTA   *Show business,* it's just a business. Colored folks ain't in no theater. You ever do a professional show before?

JOHN   Yes, some off-Broadway . . . and I've taken classes.

WILETTA   Don't let the man know that. They don't like us to go to school.

JOHN   Oh, now.

WILETTA   They want us to be naturals . . . you know, just born with the gift. Course they want you to be experienced too. Tell 'em you was in the last revival of *Porgy and Bess.*[1]

JOHN   I'm a little young for that.

WILETTA   They don't know the difference. You were one of the children.

JOHN   I need this job but . . . must I lie?

WILETTA   Yes. Management hates folks who *need* jobs. They get the least money, the least respect, and most times they don't get the job.

JOHN [*laughs*]   Got it. I'm always doing great.

WILETTA   But don't get too cocky. They don't like that either. You have to cater to these fools too . . .

JOHN   I'm afraid I don't know how to do that.

WILETTA   Laugh! Laugh at everything they say, makes 'em feel superior.

JOHN   Why do they have to feel superior?

WILETTA   You gonna sit there and pretend you don't know why?

JOHN   I . . . I'd feel silly laughing at everything.

WILETTA   You don't. Sometimes they laugh, you're supposed to look serious, other times they serious, you supposed to laugh.

JOHN [*in polite disagreement*]   Sounds too complicated.

WILETTA [*warming to her subject*]   Nothin' to it. Suppose the director walks in, looks around, and says . . . [*She mimics* MANNERS] "Well, if the dust around here doesn't choke us to death, we'll be able to freeze in comfort."

1. *Porgy and Bess*, an "American Folk Opera," premiered in New York in 1935, featuring music by George Gershwin (1898–1937) and Ira Gershwin (1896–1983) and a libretto by DuBose Heyward (1885–1940). Set in Charleston, South Carolina, in the early 1920s, the work is based on Heyward's novel *Porgy* and play of the same title (co-written with Dorothy Heyward [1890–1961]) and focuses on African American life along a fictitious "Catfish Row."

JOHN   Yes?

WILETTA   We laugh and dispute him. [*She illustrates*] "Oh, now, Mr. Manners, it ain't that bad!" . . . White folks can't stand unhappy Negroes . . . so laugh, laugh when it ain't funny at all.

JOHN   Sounds kind of Uncle Tommish.[2]

WILETTA   You callin' me a "Tom"?

JOHN   No, ma'am.

WILETTA   Stop sayin' ma'am, it sounds countrified.

JOHN   Yes.

WILETTA   It is Tommish . . . but they do it more than we do. They call it bein' a "yes man." You either do it and stay or don't do it and get out. I can let you in on things that school never heard of . . .'cause I know what's out here and they don't.

JOHN   Thank you. I guess I'll learn the ropes as I go along.

WILETTA   I'm tellin' you, now! Oh, you so lucky! Nobody told me, had to learn it for myself.
       [JOHN *is trying to hide the fact that he does not relish her instructions.*]
       Another thing. He's gonna ask your honest opinion about the play. Don't tell him, he don't mean it . . . just say you're crazy about it . . . butter him up.
       [*This remark really bothers* JOHN.]

JOHN   What *do* you think of our play?

WILETTA   Oh, honey, it stinks, ain't nothin' at all. Course, if I hear that again, I'll swear you lyin'.

JOHN   Why are you doing it? A flop can't make you but so rich.

WILETTA   Who said it's gonna flop? I said it ain't nothin', but things that aggravate me always *run* for a long time . . . cause what bugs me is what sends somebody else, if you know what I mean.

JOHN   [*defensively*]   I studied it thoroughly and . . .

WILETTA   Honey, don't study it, just learn it.

JOHN   I wouldn't, couldn't play anything I didn't believe in . . . I couldn't.

WILETTA   [*understands he's a bit upstage now*]   Oh, well, you just a lost ball in the high grass.
       [MILLIE DAVIS, *an actress about thirty-five years old, enters. She breezes in, beautifully dressed in a mink coat, pastel wool dress and hat, suede shoes and bag.*]

MILLIE   Hi!

WILETTA   Walk, girl! Don't she look good?

MILLIE   Don't look too hard, it's not paid for.
       [MILLIE *models the coat for* WILETTA *as she talks to* JOHN.]
   You got the job! Good for you.
       [WILETTA *picks up* MILLIE's *newspaper.*]

JOHN   And congratulations to you.
       [MILLIE *takes off her coat and hangs it up.*]

MILLIE   I don't care one way or the other 'cause my husband doesn't want me workin' anyway.

WILETTA   Is he still a dining-car waiter?

2. Adjective for "Uncle Tom," derived from the title character of Harriet Beecher Stowe's 1852 novel. A derogatory term, "Uncle Tom" refers to a person perceived to be subservient and deferential to authority figures, particularly a black person who behaves in an obsequious manner to whites, whether authority figures or not.

MILLIE   I wanted to read for your part but Mr. Manners said I was too young. They always say too young . . . too young.

WILETTA   Hear they're lookin' for a little girl to play Goldilocks, maybe you should try for that.

MILLIE   Oh, funny.

WILETTA [*commenting on the headlines*]   Look at 'em! Throwin' stones at little children, got to call out the militia to go to school.

JOHN   That's terrible.

MILLIE [*quite proud of her contribution to Little Rock*]   A woman pushed me on the subway this mornin' and I was ready for her! Called her everything but a child of God. She turned purple! Oh, I fixed her!

   [JUDY SEARS, *a young actress, is heard offstage with* SHELDON FORRESTER, *an elderly character man.*]

JUDY   This way . . .

SHELDON   Yes, ma'am. Don't hurt yourself.

   [SHELDON *and* JUDY *enter,* JUDY *first.*]

JUDY   Good morning.

   [*Others respond in unison.*]

JOHN   Hello again, glad you made it.

MILLIE   Hi! I'm Millie, that's John, Wiletta, and you're?

JUDY   Judith, just call me Judy.

   [SHELDON *is bundled in heavy overcoat, two scarves, one outer, one inner.*]

SHELDON   And call me Shel!

WILETTA   Sheldon Forrester! So glad to see you! Heard you was sick.

MILLIE   I heard he was dead.

SHELDON   Yes! Some fool wrote a piece in that *Medium Brown Magazine* 'bout me bein' dead. You can see he was lyin'. But I lost a lotta work on accounta that. Doctor says that with plenty of rest and fresh air, I oughta outlive him.

WILETTA   Bet you will, too.

SHELDON   Mr. Manners was lookin' all over for me, said nobody could play this part but me.

MILLIE   Not another soul can do what you're gonna do to it.

SHELDON   Thank you.

   [JOHN *starts over to* JUDY *but* SHELDON *stops him.*]

   Didn't you play in er . . . ah . . . er . . .

WILETTA   He was in the last revival of *Porgy and Bess.* Was one of the children.

   [*She watches* JOHN'S *reaction to this.*]

SHELDON   Yeah, I know I remembered you. He ain't changed much, just bigger. Nice little actor.

JOHN [*embarrassed*]   Thank you, sir.

WILETTA   Sheldon got a good memory.

MILLIE [*to* JUDY]   What're you doing?

SHELDON   She's *Miss* Renard, the Southerner's daughter. Fights her father 'bout the way he's treatin' us.

MILLIE   What I want is a part where I get to fight him.

WILETTA   Ha! That'll be the day!

SHELDON   Bill O'Wray is the father, he's awful nice.

MILLIE   Also wish I'd get to wear some decent clothes sometime. Only chance I get to dress up is offstage. I'll wear them baggy cotton dresses but damn if I'll wear another bandana.

SHELDON That's how country people do! But go on the beach today, what do you see? Bandanas. White folks wear 'em! They stylish!

MILLIE That's a lot of crap!

SHELDON There you go! You holler when there's no work—when the man give you some, you holler just as loud. Ain't no pleasin' you!

[JOHN *starts toward* JUDY *again; this time* MILLIE *stops him.*]

MILLIE Last show I was in, I wouldn't even tell my relatives. All I did was shout "Lord, have mercy!" for almost two hours every night.

WILETTA Yes, but you did it, so hush! She's played every flower in the garden. Let's see, what was your name in that TV mess?

MILLIE Never mind.

WILETTA Gardenia! She was Gardenia! 'Nother thing . . . she was Magnolia, Chrysanthemum was another . . .

MILLIE And you've done the jewels . . . Crystal, Pearl, Opal!

[MILLIE *laughs.*]

JOHN [*weak, self-conscious laughter*] Oh, now . . .

[JUDY *has retreated to one side, trying to hide herself behind a book.*]

SHELDON Do, Lord, let's keep peace. Last thing I was in, the folks fought and argued so, the man said he'd never do a colored show again . . . and he didn't!

WILETTA I always say it's the man's play, the man's money, and the man's theater, so what you gonna do? [*To* MILLIE] You ain't got a pot nor a window. Now, when you get your own . . .

[SHELDON *clears his throat to remind them that* JUDY *is listening.*]

Honey, er . . . what you say your name was?

JUDY Judy.

[WILETTA *sweeps over to* JUDY *and tries to cover the past argument.*]

WILETTA I know I've seen you in pictures, didn't you make some pictures?

JUDY No, this is my first job.

JOHN [*joshing* WILETTA] Oh, you mustn't tell that because . . .

WILETTA [*cutting him off*] You're just as cute as a new penny.

SHELDON Sure is.

[*A brief moment of silence while they wait for* JUDY *to say something.*]

JUDY [*starts hesitantly but picks up momentum as she goes along*] Thank you, and er . . . er . . . I hope I can do a good job and that people learn something from this play.

MILLIE Like what?

JUDY That people are the same, that people are . . . are . . . well, you know . . . that people are people.

SHELDON There you go . . . brotherhood of man stuff! Sure!

WILETTA Yes, indeed. I don't like to think of theater as just a business. Oh, it's the art . . . ain't art a wonderful thing?

MILLIE [*bald, flat statement to no one in particular*] People aren't the same.

JUDY I read twice for the part and there were so many others before me and after me . . . and I was so scared that my voice came out all funny . . . I stumbled on the rug when I went in . . . everything was terrible.

MILLIE [*another bald, flat statement*] But you got the job.

JUDY [*uneasy about* MILLIE's *attitude*] Yes.

JOHN [*to the rescue*] And all the proud relatives will cheer you on opening night!

JUDY [*nothing can drown her spirits for long*] Yes! My mother and father . . . they live in Bridgeport . . . they really don't want me here at all. They keep expecting something *terrible* to happen to me . . . like being murdered or something! But they're awfully sweet and they'll be so happy. [*Abrupt change of subject*] What do you think of the play?

WILETTA   Oh, I never had anything affect me so much in all my life. It's so sad, ain't it sad?

JUDY   Oh, there's some humor.

WILETTA   I'm tellin' you, I almost busted my sides laughin'.
      [SHELDON *is busy looking in the script.*]

JOHN   It has a social theme and something to say.

JUDY   Yes.

WILETTA   Art! Art is a great thing!

MILLIE   It's all right except for a few words here and there . . . and those Gawd-awful clothes . . .

JOHN   Words, clothes. What about the very meaning?
      [SHELDON *startles everyone by reading out loud. His finger runs down the page; he skips his cues and reads his lines.*]

SHELDON   Mr. Renard, sir, everything is just fine . . . Yes, sir . . . Thank you, sir . . . Yes, sirreee, I sure will . . . I know . . . Yes, sir . . . But iffen, iffen . . .
      [*He pauses to question the word.*]
    Iffen?
      [*Now he understands.*]
    Iffen you don't mind, we'd like to use the barn.

MILLIE   Iffen.

SHELDON   Hush, Millie, so I can get these lines, I'm not a good reader, you know.

MILLIE   Iffen you forget one, just keep shakin' your head.
      [*Offstage we hear a door slam.* AL MANNERS, *the director (white), is giving* EDDIE FENTON, *the stage manager (white), a friendly chastising.*]

MANNERS [*offstage*]   Eddie, why? Why do you do it?

EDDIE [*offstage*]   I didn't know.

SHELDON [*assumes a very studious air and begins to study his script earnestly*]   Mr. Manners.
      [EDDIE *and* MANNERS *enter, followed by* HENRY. EDDIE *is eager and quick. He carries a portfolio and a stack of scripts.* MANNERS *is in his early forties, hatless, well-tweeded product of Hollywood. He is a bundle of energy, considerate and understanding after his own fashion; selfish and tactless after ours.* HENRY *is following him around, ready to write out a coffee order.*]

EDDIE [*with a smile*]   You asked my opinion.

MANNERS   That, my friend, was a mistake.

EDDIE [*laughing while cast smiles in anticipation of* MANNERS's *words*]   Okay, I admit you were right, you were.

MANNERS [*enjoying himself*]   Of course I was. [*To company*] All of his taste is in his mouth!
      [*Burst of company laughter, especially from* SHELDON *and* WILETTA.]

EDDIE [*playfully correcting* MANNERS]   All right, Al, play fair . . . uncle . . . a truce.

MANNERS [*to company*]   Greetings to New York's finest.

ALL   Good morning . . . Flatterer . . . Hello . . . Good morning.

MANNERS [*to* HENRY]   Coffee all around the room and count yourself in.
      [MANNERS *hands him a bill.*]
    Rolls? Cake? No . . . how about Danish . . . all right?

ALL   Yes . . . Sure . . . Anything . . . OK.

SHELDON   I like doughtnuts, those jelly doughnuts.

MANNERS   Jelly doughnuts! What a horrible thought. Get Danish . . . all right?

ALL   Sure . . . Anything . . . That's fine.

MANNERS [*after* HENRY *exits*]   If you were looking for that type, you could never find it! A real character.

JOHN   One of the old forty-niners.[3]

MANNERS   No, no . . . not quite that . . .
     [MANNERS *turns off that faucet and quickly switches to another.*]
     Everyone on speaking terms?

ALL   Of course . . . Old friends . . . Oh, yes . . . Sure.
     [MANNERS *opens the portfolio with a flourish.*]

MANNERS   Best scenic design you've ever laid eyes on.
     [ALL *gasp and sigh as they gather around him. They are quite impressed with the sketch.* JUDY *is very close, and* MANNERS *looks down at her hair and neck which is perched right under his nostrils.* JUDY *can feel his breath on her neck. She turns suddenly and* MANNERS *backs away a trifle.*]
     You er . . . wear a beautiful dress in the third act and I wanted to see if you have nice shoulders.
     [JUDY *backs away slightly.*]
     I wasn't planning to attack you.
     [CAST *laughs.*]

MILLIE   I got nice shoulders. You got one of those dresses for me?

SHELDON [*determined to enjoy everything*]   Ha! He wasn't gonna attack her!

MANNERS [*suddenly changes faucets again*]   Oh, I'm so weary.

EDDIE [*running interference*]   He was with Melton on this sketch until four A.M.

MANNERS   Four thirty.

EDDIE   Four thirty.

MANNERS [*swoops down on* WILETTA]   Ahhhhh, this is my sweetheart!

WILETTA [*with mock severity*]   Go on! Go 'way! Ain't speakin' to you! He won't eat, he won't sleep, he's just terrible! I'm mad with you.

SHELDON   Gonna ruin your health like that!

WILETTA   Gonna kill himself!

MANNERS   Bawl me out, I deserve it.

EDDIE   Melton is so stubborn, won't change a line.

MANNERS   But he did.

EDDIE   Yes, but so stubborn.

MANNERS   A genius should be stubborn. [*Pointing index finger at* SHELDON] Right?

SHELDON [*snaps his finger and points back*]   There you go!
     [CAST *laughs.*]

MANNERS [*to* WILETTA]   You'd better speak to me. This is my girl, we did a picture together.

CAST [*ad lib*]   Really? How nice. She sure did. That's right.

MANNERS [*as though it's been centuries*]   Ohhhhhh, years and years ago. She and I worked together, too.

MILLIE [*to* WILETTA]   Remember that?

SHELDON [*proudly*]   I was helpin' the Confederate Army.

---

3. Perhaps a reference to the gold seekers of the California Gold Rush (1848–55). They were called "forty-niners" (as a reference to 1849).

MANNERS   And what a chestnut, guns, cannons, drums, Indians, slaves, hearts and flowers, sex and Civil War . . . on wide screen!

JUDY   Oh, just horrible.

MANNERS   [*touchy about outside criticism*]   But it had something, wasn't the worst . . . I twisted myself out of shape to build this guy's part. It was really a sympathetic character.

SHELDON   Sure, everybody was sorry for me.

MANNERS   [*to* JOHN]   Hear you went to college. You're so modest you need a press agent.

SHELDON   He was one of the children in the last revival of *Porgy and Bess.*

MANNERS   Ohhhh, yes . . . nice clean job.

JUDY   I'm not modest. I finished the Yale drama course. Girls . . . girls . . . can go to the Yale drama . . .

MANNERS   Yale. I'm impressed.

JUDY   You're teasing.

MANNERS   No, you are. Well, where are we? Bill O'Wray is out until tomorrow, he's in a rehearsal for a TV show tonight.

   [*Proper sighs of regret from the* CAST.]

WILETTA   Oh, I was lookin' forward to seein' him today.

SHELDON   Yeah, yeah, nice fella.

MANNERS   Works all the time. [*Now some attention for* MILLIE]   You look gorgeous. This gal has such a flair for clothes. How do you do it?

   [MILLIE *is pleased.* MANNERS *changes the subject.*]

Ted Bronson is one of our finest writers.

WILETTA   Knows art, knows it.

EDDIE   He was up for an award.

MANNERS   Really, Eddie. I wish you'd let me tell it.

EDDIE   I'm sorry.

MANNERS   Ted's been out on the coast batting out commercial stuff . . . meat grinder . . . he's in Europe now . . . Italy . . . about a week before he can get back . . . he did this "Chaos in Belleville" a while back. Producers gave him nothing but howls . . . "It's ahead of the times!" "Why stick your neck out?" "Why you?"

SHELDON   [*raises his hand, speaks after* MANNERS *gives him a nod*]   Who is chaos?

EDDIE   Oh, no.

JOHN   *Who?*

MANNERS   [*holds up his hand for silence*]   Chaos means er . . . ah, confusion. Confusion in Belleville, confusion in a small town.

SHELDON   Ohhhhhh.

MANNERS   I was casually talking to Ted about the er . . . er, race situation, kicking a few things around . . . dynamic subject, hard to come to grips with on the screen, TV, anywhere . . . explosive subject. Suddenly he reaches to the bottom shelf and comes up with "Chaos." I flipped a few pages . . . when I read it bells rang. This is *now,* we're living this, who's in the headlines these days?

   [*Eloquent pause.*]

SHELDON   How 'bout that Montgomery, Alabama?[4] Made the bus company lose one, cold, cash, billion dollars!

JOHN   Not a billion.

---

4. Reference to the Montgomery Bus Boycott of 1955.

MANNERS   Here was a contribution to the elimination of . . .

SHELDON   I know what I read!

MANNERS   A story of Negro rights that . . .

SHELDON   How 'bout them buses!

JUDY   And they're absolutely right.

MILLIE   Who's right?

MANNERS   A contribution that really . . .

JUDY   The colored people.

MANNERS   Leads to a clearer understanding . . .

MILLIE   Oh, I thought you meant the other people.

MANNERS   A clearer understanding.

JUDY   I didn't mean that.

MANNERS   Yale, please!

     [ALL *silent.*]

I placed an option on this script so fast . . .

     [SHELDON *raises his hand.*]

I tied it up, Sheldon, so that no one else could get hold of it. When I showed it to Hoskins . . .

WILETTA [*to* SHELDON]   The producer. Another nice man.

MANNERS   Well, the rest is history. This is my first Broadway show . . .

     [*Applause from* CAST.]

But I definitely know what I want and however unorthodox my methods, I promise never to bore you.

SHELDON [*popping his fingers rapidly*]   He's like that.

MANNERS   I bring to this a burning desire above and beyond anything I've . . . well, I'm ready to sweat blood. I want to see you kids drawing pay envelopes for a long time to come and . . .

     [SHELDON *applauds; the others join him.* SHELDON *aims his remark at* MILLIE.]

SHELDON   Listen to the man! Listen.

     [MANNERS *holds up his hand for silence.*]

MANNERS   At ease. [*Mainly for* JOHN *and* JUDY] I ask this, please forget your old methods of work and go along with me. I'll probably confuse the hell out of you for the first few days, but after that . . . well, I hope we'll be swingin'. Now, you're all familiar with the story . . .

WILETTA   Oh, I never had anything affect me so much in all my life.

ALL [*ad lib*]   There was one part . . . I have a question . . . Uh-huh . . . A question . . .

MANNERS   We will *not* discuss the parts.

     [JOHN *groans in mock agony.*]

JUDY   One little thing.

MANNERS   We will not discuss the parts.

     [EDDIE *smiles knowingly.*]

We will not read the play down from beginning to end.

SHELDON [*popping his fingers*]   There he goes!

MANNERS   We will *not* delve into character backgrounds . . . not now. Turn to act one, scene two, page fifteen.

     [*Actors scramble madly for places in scripts.*]

Top of the page. Eddie, you read for O'Wray. Judy! Stand up!

     [JUDY *stands hesitantly while* MANNERS *toys with a sheet of paper.*]

Walk downstage!

[JUDY *is startled and nervous, she walks upstage. The others are eager to correct her but* MANNERS *will not tolerate cast interference. He crumbles the paper, throws it to the floor, takes* JUDY *by the shoulders and speedily leads her around the stage.*]

Downstage! Center stage! Left center! Right center! Up right! Up left, down center, down right, down left, upstage . . . DOWNSTAGE!

JUDY   I know, I forgot . . .

MANNERS   Don't forget again. Take downstage.

[MANNERS *notices the paper he threw on the floor.*]

A trashy stage is most distracting.

[JUDY *starts to pick up the paper.*]

Hold your position! Wiletta, pick up the paper!

[JOHN *and* SHELDON *start for the paper.*]

I asked Wiletta! [*Catching* WILETTA's *eye*] Well?

WILETTA   [*shocked into a quick flare of temper*]   Well, hell! I ain't the damn janitor! [*Trying to check her temper*] I . . . well, I . . . shucks . . . I . . . damn.

[*Even though* MANNERS *was trying to catch them off guard, he didn't expect this.*]

MANNERS   Cut! Cut! It's all over.

[*Everyone is surprised again.*]

What you have just seen is . . . is . . . is fine acting.

[*He is quite shaken and embarrassed from* WILETTA's *action.*]

Actors struggle for weeks to do what you have done perfectly . . . the first time. You gave me anger, frustration, movement, er . . . excitement. Your faces were alive! Why? You did what came naturally, you believed . . . That is the quality I want in your work . . . the firm texture of truth.

JUDY   Oh, you tricked us.

MILLIE   I didn't know what to think.

JOHN   Tension all over the place.

[WILETTA *is still having a hard time getting herself under control. She fans herself with a pocket handkerchief and tries to muster a weak laugh.*]

WILETTA   Yes indeed.

[MANNERS *gingerly touches* WILETTA *and shivers in mock fear.*]

MANNERS   She plays rough. "Well, hell!" Honey, I love you, believe me.

SHELDON   Oh, she cut up!

[WILETTA *tries to laugh along with them, but it's hard going. From this point on, she watches* MANNERS *with a sharp eye, always cautious and on the lookout.*]

WILETTA   Yes . . . well, let's don't play that no more.

MANNERS   Top of the page. Judy, you're appealing to your father to allow some of his tenant farmers . . .

[*He glances at script to find the next direction.* SHELDON *leans over and whispers to* WILETTA.]

WILETTA   Sharecroppers.

SHELDON   Oh.

MANNERS   . . . hold a barn dance. Now! Some of them have been talking about voting.

SHELDON   Trouble.

MANNERS   [*points first to* MILLIE, *then* WILETTA]   Petunia and Ruby are in your father's study . . . er . . . er . . .

[MANNERS *consults script again.*]

SHELDON   [*without consulting script*]   Cleanin' up. Sure, that's what they're doin'.

MANNERS   Tidying up. Your father is going over his account books, you're there . . .

SHELDON [*with admiration*]   Lookin' pretty.

MANNERS   There's an awful echo coming from our assistant director.

SHELDON [*laughs*]   'Sistant director! This man breaks me up all the time!

MANNERS [*liking the salve*]   What, what did you say?

SHELDON   Say you tickle me to death.

WILETTA   Tickles me too.

MANNERS   Take it!

JUDY [*reading*]   Papa, it's a good year, isn't it?

EDDIE [*with a too-broad Southern accent*]   I'd say fair, fair to middlin'.
      [CAST *snickers.*]

MANNERS   All right, Barrymore,[5] just read it.

JUDY   Papa, it's Petunia's birthday today.

EDDIE   That so? Happy birthday, Petunia.

MILLIE [*wearily*]   Thank you, sir.

MANNERS [*correcting the reading*]   You feel good, full of ginger . . . your birthday!

MILLIE [*remembers the old, standard formula; gives the line with a chuckle and extra warmth*]   Thank you, sir.

JUDY   It would be nice if they could have a stomp in the barn.

MILLIE [*her attitude suggesting that* JUDY *thought up the line*]   Hmmph.

EDDIE   No need to have any barn stomp until this election business is over.

MILLIE   What the hell is a stomp?

JUDY   I can't see why.

MANNERS   A barn dance. You know that, Millie.

EDDIE   Ruby, you think y'all oughta use the barn?

WILETTA [*pleasantly*]   Lord, have mercy, Mr. Renard, don't ask me 'cause I don't know nothin'.

EDDIE   Well, better forget about it.

JUDY   Oh, papa, let the . . . let the . . .

MILLIE [*for* JUDY's *benefit*]   Mmmmmmmmmmmph. Why didn't they call it a barn dance?

JUDY   . . . let the . . . [*stops reading*] Oh, must I say that word?

MANNERS   What word?

MILLIE   *Darkies.* That's the word. It says, "Papa, let the darkies have their fun."

MANNERS   *What* do you want us to say?

MILLIE   She could say . . . "Let *them* have their fun."

MANNERS   But that's Carrie. [*To* SHELDON] Do you object?

SHELDON   Well, no, not if that's how they spoke in them days.

MANNERS   The time is now, down South in some remote little county, they say those things . . . now. Can you object in an artistic sense?

SHELDON   No, but you better ask him, he's more artistic than I am.

JOHN   No, I don't object. I don't like the word but it is used, it's a slice of life. Let's face it, Judy wouldn't use it, Mr. Manners wouldn't . . .

MANNERS [*very pleased with* JOHN's *answer*]   Call me Al, everybody. Al's good enough, Johnny.

JOHN   Al wouldn't say it but Carrie would.
      [MANNERS *gives* WILETTA *an inquiring look.*]

5. Reference to the famed family acting dynasty, which included Lionel, Ethel, and John Barrymore.

WILETTA Lord, have mercy, don't ask me 'cause I don't know . . .
   [*She stops short as she realizes that she is repeating words from the script. She's disturbed that she's repeating the exact line the author indicated.*]
   [MANNERS *gives* JUDY *a light tap on the head.*]
MANNERS Yale! Proceed.
EDDIE [*reads*] Ruby and Petunia leave the room and wait on the porch.
JUDY Please, papa, I gave my word. I ask one little thing and . . .
EDDIE All right! Before you know it, them niggers will be runnin' me!
JUDY Please don't use that word!
MANNERS Oh, stop it!
WILETTA That's her line in the play, Mr. Manners, Carrie says . . .
ALL Please, don't use the word.
   [MANNERS *signals* EDDIE *to carry on.*]
EDDIE [*reads*] Carrie runs out to the porch.
JUDY You can use the barn!
MILLIE Lord, have mercy . . .
EDDIE [*intones*] Wrong line.
MILLIE [*quickly corrects line*] Er . . . er, somethin' seems to trouble my spirit, a troublous feelin' is in old Petunia's breast. [*Stops reading*] Old Petunia?
WILETTA Yes, *old* Petunia!
JUDY [*reads*] I'm going upstairs to lay out my white organdy dress.
WILETTA No, you ain't, I'm gonna do that for you.
JUDY Then I'll take a nap.
MILLIE No, you ain't, I'm gonna do that for you.
EDDIE Wrong line.
MILLIE Sorry. [*Corrects line*] Yes, child, you rest yourself, you had a terrible, hard day. Bless your soul, you just one of God's golden-haired angels.
   [MANNERS *is frantically searching for that certain quality. He thinks everything will open once they hit the right chord.*]
MANNERS Cut! Top of page three, act one, as it's written. Ruby is shelling beans on the back porch as her son Job approaches.
JOHN If I can read over . . .
MANNERS Do as I ask, do it. Take it, Wiletta.
SHELDON [*popping his fingers*] He's just like that.
WILETTA [*reads*] Boy, where you goin'?
JOHN Down to Turner's Corner.
WILETTA You ain't lost nothin' down there. Turner and his brother is talkin' 'bout votin'. I know.
JOHN They only talkin', I'm goin'.
SHELDON Mr. Renard say to stay outta that.
JOHN I got a letter from the President 'bout goin' in the army, Turner says when that happens, a man's s'posed to vote and things.
   [MILLIE *and* JUDY *are very pleased about this line.*]
SHELDON Letter ain't from no President, it come from the crackers on the draft board.
JOHN It *say* from the President.
WILETTA Pa say you don't go.
   [MANNERS *is jotting down a flood of notes.*]
JOHN Sorry, but I say I'd be there.
SHELDON I don't know who that boy take after.

EDDIE   Ruby dashes from the porch and Sam follows her. Carrie comes outside and Renard follows her.
[EDDIE *reads Renard.*]
You pamper them rascals too much, see how they do? None of 'em's worth their weight in salt, that boy would steal the egg out of a cake.
[JUDY *tries to laugh while* MILLIE *watches coldly.* MANNERS *is amazed at the facial distortion.*]

JUDY   It says laugh.

MANNERS   Well?

JUDY   [*laughs and continues reading*]   But I can't help feeling sorry for them, they didn't ask to be born.

MILLIE   [*just loud enough for* JUDY's *ears*]   Hmmmmmmph.

JUDY   I keep thinking, there but for the grace of God go I. If we're superior we should prove it by our actions.

SHELDON   [*commenting on the line*]   There you go, prove it!
[MANNERS *is taking more notes.* JUDY *is disturbed by the reactions to her reading. She hesitates.* MANNERS *looks up. The phone rings.* EDDIE *goes off to answer.*]

JUDY   She *is* their friend, right? It's just that I feel reactions and . . .

MANNERS   What reactions?

MILLIE   I was reacting.

MANNERS   Ohhhhh, who pays Millie any attention, that's her way.

MILLIE   There you go.

SHELDON   Sure is.

JUDY   [*tries again but she's very uncomfortable*]   I . . . I keep thinking . . . there but for the grace of God . . .

MANNERS   Are you planning to cry?

JUDY   No, but . . . no.
[*She's fighting to hold back the tears.*]

SHELDON   Millie's pickin' on her.

MANNERS   Utter nonsense!

JUDY   My part seems . . . she seems so smug.

MILLIE   [*to* SHELDON]   Keep my name out of your mouth.

WILETTA   [*to* SHELDON]   Mind your business, your own affairs.

MANNERS   This is fantastic. What in the hell is smug?
[HENRY *enters with a cardboard box full of coffee containers and a large paper bag.*]
Cut! Coffee break! [*To* JUDY] Especially you.

HENRY   Told the waiter feller to fix up everything nice.

MANNERS   [*looks in bag*]   What's this?

HENRY   That's what you said. I heard you. "Jelly doughnuts!" you said.
[SHELDON *gets a container of coffee for* JUDY *and one for himself.*]

MANNERS   I won't eat it!

HENRY   But I heard you.

MANNERS   Take your coffee and leave.
[HENRY *starts to leave without the coffee.*]
Don't play games, take it with you.
[HENRY *snatches a container and leaves in a quiet huff.* SHELDON *hands coffee to* JUDY *but* MILLIE *snatches it from his hand.*]

MILLIE   I know you brought that for me.

MANNERS   Where do they find these characters? All right, he's old but it's an imposition . . . he's probably ninety, you know.

WILETTA [*laughs and then suddenly stops*] We all get old sometimes.
> [EDDIE *hurries onstage; looks worried.*]

EDDIE It's Mrs. Manners . . . she . . . she says it's urgent. She has to talk to you *now* . . . immediately.

MANNERS Oh, you stupid jerk. Why did you say I was here? You and your big, stupid mouth. Couldn't you say "He isn't here now, I'll give him your message"?

EDDIE I'm sorry. She was so . . . so . . . Well, she said right off "I *know* he's there." If I had any idea that she would . . .

MANNERS I don't expect you to have *ideas!* Only common sense, just a little common sense. Where do you find a stage manager these days?

EDDIE I can tell her you can't be disturbed now.

MANNERS No, numbskull, don't do another thing, you've done enough. [*With wry humor*] Alimony is not enough, every time I make three extra dollars she takes me to court to get two-thirds of it. If I don't talk to her I'll have a subpoena. You're stupid.
> [*He exits to the telephone. During the brief silence which follows,* EDDIE *is miserably self-conscious.*]

WILETTA [*tries to save the day*] Well . . . I'm glad it's getting a little like winter now. We sure had a hot summer. Did you have a nice summer?

EDDIE [*choking back his suppressed anger*] I worked in stock . . . summer theater. It was OK.

WILETTA That's nice. What did you do?

EDDIE [*relaxing more*] Kind of jack of all trades . . . understudied some, stage managed, made sets . . .

MILLIE And did three people out of a job.

JUDY I spent the summer with my folks. Soon as we open, I want everyone to come up to Bridgeport and have a glorious day!
> [MANNERS *returns, looks up briefly.*]
> Daddy makes the yummiest barbecue, you'll love it.

WILETTA You better discuss it with your folks first.

JUDY Why?

MILLIE 'Cause we wouldn't want it discussed after we got there.

SHELDON No, thank you, ma'am. I'm plannin' to be busy all winter lookin' for an apartment, I sure hate roomin'.

EDDIE I have my own apartment. It's only a cold-water walk-up but I have it fixed real nice like the magazines show you . . . whitewashed brick and mobiles hanging in the kitchen and living room. I painted the floors black and spattered them with red and white paint . . . I learned that in stock . . . then I shellacked over it and waxed it . . . and I scraped all of the furniture down to the natural wood . . .

MILLIE Oh, hush, you're making me tired. Cold-water flat!

EDDIE It gives a cheery effect . . .

MILLIE And it'll give you double pneumonia.

SHELDON Yeah, that's the stuff you got to watch.

EDDIE Well, it's only thirty dollars a month.

SHELDON They got any colored livin' in that buildin'?

EDDIE I . . . I . . . I don't know. I haven't seen any.

SHELDON Well, there's none there then.

EDDIE [*slightly ill at ease*] Sheldon, I'll gladly ask.

SHELDON [*in great alarm*] Oh, no, no, no! I don't want to be the first.

MILLIE   Damn cold-water flats! I like ease, comfort, furs, cards, big, thick steaks. I want everything.

EDDIE [*trying to change the subject*]   Aren't there a lot of new shows this season?

JUDY   My mother says . . . gosh, every time I open my mouth it's something about my parents. It's not stylish to love your parents . . . you either have a mother-complex or a father-fixation!

> [*She laughs and* MANNERS *looks up again. He doesn't care for her remarks.*]

But I'm crazy about my parents, but then maybe that's abnormal. I probably have a mother-father-fixation.

WILETTA   What did your mother say?

JUDY   "Never have limitations on your horizon, reach for infinity!" She also feels that everyone has a right to an equal education and not separate either.

JOHN   She sounds like a wonderful woman who . . .

JUDY [*raising her voice*]   Oh, I get so mad about this prejudice nonsense! It's a wonder colored people don't go out and *kill* somebody, I mean actually, really do it . . . bloody murder, you know?

SHELDON   There's lotsa folks worse off than we are, Millie.

MILLIE   Well, all I hope is that they don't like it, dontcha know.

MANNERS [*boastful about his trials and troubles*]   The seven-year-old kid, the seven-year-old kid . . . to hear her tell it, our son is ragged, barefoot, hungry . . . and his teeth are lousy. The orthodontist says he needs braces . . . they wanta remake his mouth. The kid is falling to pieces. When I go for visitation . . . he looks in my pockets before he says hello. Can you imagine? Seven years old. The orthodontist and the psychiatrist . . . the story of my life. But he's a bright kid . . . smart as a whip . . . you can't fool him. [*A big sigh*] Oh, well, let's go. Suppose you were all strangers, had never heard anything about this story except the snatches you heard today. What would you know?

MILLIE   It's my birthday.

> [WILETTA *is following him closely; she doesn't care to be caught off guard again.*]

JOHN   Carrie's father has tenant farmers working for him.

MANNERS   Yes and . . .

JUDY   They want to hold a barn dance and he's against it because . . .

JOHN   Some of the Negroes are planning to vote for the first time and there's opposition . . .

SHELDON   His ma and pa don't want him mixed in it 'cause they smell trouble.

JUDY   And my father overheard that John is in it.

SHELDON   And *he don't like it*, that's another thing.

WILETTA [*amazed that they have learned so much*]   Mmmmmmm, all of that.

JOHN   But Job is determined.

JUDY   And he's been notified by the draft board.

SHELDON   And the paper, the paper!

MANNERS   Paper?

WILETTA   You know, upstage, downstage, and doin' what comes natural.

MANNERS   Not bad for an hour's work.

EDDIE   Amazing.

SHELDON [*popping his fingers*]   Man is on the ball. Fast.

MANNERS   Now we can see how we're heading for the lynching.

SHELDON [*starts to peep at back page of script*]   Lynchin'?

MANNERS   We're dealing with an antilynch theme. I want it uncluttered, clear in your mind, you must see the skeleton framework within which we're working. Wiletta, turn to the last page of act one.

EDDIE   Fifty.

MANNERS   Wiletta, dear heart . . . the end of the act finds you alone on the porch, worried, heartsick . . .

WILETTA   And singin' a song, sittin', worryin', and singin'.

MANNERS   It's not simply a song, it's a summing up. You're thinking of Renard, the threats, the people and your son . . .

> [WILETTA *is tensely listening, trying to follow him.* MANNERS *stands behind her and gently shakes her shoulders.*]

Loosen up, let the thoughts flood over you. I know you have to read . . .

WILETTA   Oh, I know the song, learned it when I was a child.

MANNERS   Hold a thought, close your eyes, and think aloud . . . get a good start and then sing . . . speak your mind and then sing.

WILETTA [*not for thinking out loud*]   I know exactly what you want.

MANNERS   Blurt out the first thing that enters your mind.

WILETTA [*sings a mournful dirge of despair*]   Come and go with me to that land, come and go with me to that land . . .

MANNERS   Gosh, that guy can write.

WILETTA

Come and go with me to that land where I'm bound
No confusion in that land, no confusion in that land
No confusion in that land where I'm bound . . .

MILLIE [*wipes her eyes*]   A heartbreaker.

EDDIE   Oh, Wiletta, it's so . . . so . . . gosh.

JOHN   Leaves you weak.

MANNERS   Beautiful. What were you thinking?

WILETTA [*ready to move on to something else*]   Thank you.

MANNERS   What were you thinking?

WILETTA   I thought . . . I . . . er, er . . . I don't know, whatever you said.

MANNERS   Tell me. You're not a vacuum, you thought something.

JOHN   Your motivation. What motivated . . .

MANNERS [*waving* JOHN *out of it*]   You thought *something*, right?

WILETTA   Uh-huh.

MANNERS   And out of the thought came song.

WILETTA   Yeah.

MANNERS   What did you think?

WILETTA   I thought that's what you wanted.

> [*She realizes she is the center of attention and finds it uncomfortable.*]

MANNERS   It won't do. You must know why you do a thing, that way you're true to me, to the part and yourself . . .

WILETTA   Didn't you like it?

MANNERS   Very much but . . . I'm sure you've never worked this way before, but you're not carrying a tray or answering doorbells, this is substance, meat. I demand that you *know* what you're doing and *why*, at all times, I will accept nothing less.

WILETTA [*to* JOHN *and* JUDY]   I know, you have to justify.

SHELDON [*worried and trying to help* WILETTA]   You was thinkin' how sad it was, wasn't you?

WILETTA   Uh-huh.

MANNERS   It's new to you but it must be done. Let go, think aloud and when you are moved to do so . . . sing.

[WILETTA *looks blank.*]

Start anywhere.

WILETTA   Ah, er . . . it's so sad that folks can't vote . . . it's also sad that er, er . . .

MANNERS   No.

[MANNERS *picks up newspaper.*]

We'll try word association. I'll give you a word, then you say what comes to your mind and keep on going . . . one word brings on another . . . Montgomery!

WILETTA   Alabama.

MANNERS   Montgomery!

WILETTA   Alabama.

MANNERS   Montgomery!

WILETTA   Reverend King[6] is speakin' on Sunday.

MANNERS   Colored.

WILETTA   Lights changin' colors all around me.

MANNERS   Colored.

WILETTA   They . . . they . . .

MANNERS   Colored.

WILETTA   "They got any colored in that buildin'?"

MANNERS   Children, little children.

WILETTA   Children . . . children . . . "Pick up that paper!" Oh, my . . .

MANNERS   Lynching.

WILETTA   Killin'! Killin'!

MANNERS   Killing.

WILETTA   It's the man's theater, the man's money, so what you gonna do?

MANNERS   Oh, Wiletta . . . I don't know! *Darkness!*

WILETTA   A star! Oh, I can't, I don't like it . . .

MANNERS   Sing.

WILETTA [*sings a song of strength and anger*]
Come and go with me to that land
[*The song is overpowering; we see a woman who could fight the world.*]
Come and go with me to that land
Come and go with me to that land—
where I'm bound.

JUDY   Bravo! Magnificent!

MANNERS   Wiletta, if you dare! You will undo us! Are you out of your senses? When you didn't know what you were doing . . . perfection on the nose. I'll grant you the first interpretation was right, without motivating. All right, I'll settle for that.

WILETTA [*feeling very lost*]   I said I *knew* what you wanted.

MANNERS   Judy! I . . . I want to talk to you about . . . about Carrie.

[*He rises and starts for the dressing room.*]

Eddie, will you dash out and get me a piece of Danish? Okay, at ease.

[EDDIE *quickly exits.* MANNERS *and* JUDY *exit stage right toward dressing rooms.*]

---

6. Reference to famed civil rights leader Rev. Dr. Martin Luther King, Jr. (1929–1968), who is credited with leading the Montgomery bus boycott.

MILLIE [*to* JOHN]   Look, don't get too close to her.

SHELDON   Mind your own business.

JOHN   What have I done?

MILLIE   You're too friendly with her.

WILETTA   Justify. Ain't enough to do it, you got to justify.

JOHN   I've only been civil.

MILLIE   That's too friendly.

WILETTA   Got a splittin' headache.

SHELDON [*to* WILETTA]   I wish I had an aspirin for you.

MILLIE [*to* JOHN]   All set to run up and see her folks. Didn't you hear her say they expect something terrible to happen to her? Well, you're one of the terrible things they have in mind!

SHELDON   Mind your business.

MILLIE   It is my business. When they start raisin' a fund for his defense, they're gonna come and ask me for money and I'll have to be writin' the President and signin' petitions . . . so it's my business.

SHELDON   I tell you, son. I'm friendly with white folks in a distant sorta way but I don't get too close. Take Egypt, Russia, all these countries, why they kickin' up their heels? 'Cause of white folks, I wouldn't trust one of 'em sittin' in front of me on a merry-go-round, wouldn't trust 'em if they was laid up in bed with lockjaw and the mumps both at the same time.

JOHN   Last time I heard from you, you said it was the colored who made all the trouble.

SHELDON   They do, they're the worst ones. There's two kinda people that's got the world messed up for good, that's the colored and the white, and I got no use for either one of 'em.

MILLIE   I'm going to stop trying to help people.

JOHN   Hell, I'm through with it. Oh, I'm learning the ropes!

SHELDON   *That's* why they don't do more colored shows . . . trouble makers, pot boilers, spoon stirrers . . . and sharper than a serpent's tooth! Colored women wake up in the mornin' with their fists ball up . . . ready to fight.

WILETTA   What in the devil is all this justifyin'? Ain't necessary.

MILLIE [*to* SHELDON]   And you crawlin' all over me to hand her coffee! Damn "Tom."

SHELDON   You talkin' 'bout your relatives, ain't talkin' 'bout me, if I'm a "Tom," you a "Jemima."[7]

JOHN   I need out, I need air.

   [*He exits stage left.*]

SHELDON   White folks is stickin' together, stickin' together, stickin' together . . . we fightin'.

WILETTA   Hush, I got a headache.

MILLIE   I need a breath of air, too, before I slap the taste out of somebody's mouth.

   [MILLIE *grabs her coat and exits stage left.*]

SHELDON   I hope the wind blows her away. They gonna kick us until we all out in the street . . . unemployed . . . get all the air you want then.

---

7. "Aunt Jemima" is sometimes used colloquially as a female version of "Uncle Tom." Considered a "mammy" figure, Aunt Jemima is perceived to be servile and obsequious, especially to whites.

Sometimes I take low, yes, gotta take low. Man says somethin' to me, I say . . . "Yes, sure, certainly." You 'n' me know how to do. That ain't *tommin'*, that's common sense. You and me . . . we don't mind takin' low because we tryin' to accomplish somethin' . . .

WILETTA   I mind . . . I do mind . . . I mind . . . I mind . . .

SHELDON   Well, yeah, we all mind . . . but you got to swaller what you mind. What you mind won't buy beans. I mean, you gotta take what you mind to survive . . . to eat, to breathe . . .

WILETTA   [*tensely*]   I mind. Leave me alone.

    [SHELDON *exits with a sigh.* HENRY *enters carrying a lunch box.* WILETTA *turns; she looks so distressed.*]

HENRY   They've all flown the coop?

WILETTA   Yes.

HENRY   What's the matter? Somebody hurt your feelin's?

WILETTA   Yes.

HENRY   Don't fret, it's too nice a day. I believe in treatin' folks right. When you're just about through with this life, that's the time when you know how to live. Seems like yesterday I was forty years old and the day before that I wasn't but nineteen . . . Think of it.

WILETTA   I don't like to think . . . makes me fightin' mad.

HENRY   [*giving vent to his pent-up feelings*]   Don't I know it? When he yelled about jelly doughnuts, I started to land one on him! Oh, I almost did it!

WILETTA   I know it!

HENRY   But . . . "Hold your temper!" I says. I have a most ferocious temper.

WILETTA   Me too. I take and take, then watch out!

HENRY   Have to hold my temper, I don't want to kill the man.

WILETTA   Yeah, makes you feel like fightin'.

HENRY   [*joining in the spirit of the discussion*]   Sure I'm a fighter and I come from a fightin' people.

WILETTA   You from Ireland?

HENRY   A fightin' people! Didn't we fight for the home rule?[8]

WILETTA   Uh-huh, now you see there.

    [WILETTA *doesn't worry about making sense out of* HENRY'S *speech on Ireland; it's the feeling behind it that counts.*]

HENRY   O, a history of great men, fightin' men!

WILETTA   [*rallying to the call, she answers as though sitting on an amen bench at a revival meeting*]   Yes, carry on.

HENRY   Ah, yes, we was fightin' for the home rule! Ah, there was some great men!

WILETTA   I know it.

HENRY   There was Parnell![9] Charles Stewart Parnell!

WILETTA   All right!

HENRY   A figure of a man! The highest! Fightin' hard for the home rule! A parliamentarian! And they clapped him in the blasted jailhouse for six months!

WILETTA   Yes, my Lord!

---

8. A movement, advocated by the Irish Parliamentary Party, that demanded Irish political representation in Parliament and a form of local government within Ireland. This was debated from the late 19th century on.

9. Leader of the Irish Parliamentary Party and land reform agitator, who was considered one of the most important figures of the 19th century.

HENRY   And Gladstone introduced the bill[1] . . . and later on you had Dillon and John Redmond[2] . . . and then when the home rule was almost put through, what did you think happened? World War One! That killed the whole business!

WILETTA [*very indignant*]   Oh, if it ain't one thing, it's another!

HENRY   I'm descended from a great line! And then the likes of him with his jelly doughnuts! Jelly doughnuts, indeed, is it? What does he know? Tramplin' upon a man's dignity! Me father was the greatest, most dignified man you've ever seen . . . and he played vaudeville! Oh, the bearin' of him! [*Angrily demonstrating his father's dignity*] Doin' the little soft-shoe step . . . and it's take your hat off to the ladies . . . and step along there . . .

WILETTA   Henry, I want to be an actress, I've always wanted to be an actress and they ain't gonna do me the way they did the home rule! I want to be an actress 'cause one day you're nineteen and then forty and so on . . . I want to be an actress! Henry, they stone us when we try to go to school, the world's crazy.

HENRY   It's a shame, a shame . . .

WILETTA   Where the hell do I come in? Every damn body pushin' me off the face of the earth! I want to be an actress . . . hell, I'm gonna be one, you hear me?

   [*She pounds the table.*]

HENRY   Sure, and why not, I'd like to know!

WILETTA [*quietly*]   Yes, dammit . . . and why not? Why in the hell not?

   [*Blues record in; woman singer.*]

Act 2

TIME

Ten o'clock Thursday morning.

PLACE

Same as act 1. [Blues music—in—up and out.]

SCENE

Same as act 1, except furniture has been changed around; some of the old set removed. BILL O'WRAY, *a character actor (white) stands upstage on a makeshift platform. He radiates strength and power as he addresses an imaginary audience.* MANNERS *stands stage left, tie loosened, hair ruffled. He is hepped up with nervous energy, can barely stand still.* EDDIE *is stage right, in charge of the script and a tape recorder, he follows the script and turns up the tape recorder on cue from* MANNERS. BILL *is delivering a "masterful" rendition of Renard's speech on "tolerance."* MANNERS *is elated one moment, deflated the next.* EDDIE *is obviously nervous, drawn, and lacking the easy-going attitude of act 1.*

---

1. A double-entendre. On the surface a reference to William Ewart Gladstone's Land Act of 1881; however, may also refer to the 1979 Supreme Court case *Gladstone Realtors v. The Village of Bellwood*, an attempt to enforce a law that prohibited "steering." Ruled illegal in 1968, steering was the effort on the part of housing agents and property managers to "steer" African Americans searching for property away from white neighborhoods.

2. Advocated and won the Third Home Rule Act, intended to provide self-government in Ireland. John Dillon (1851–1927), the final leader of the Irish Parliamentary Party and an advocate of land reform, denounced Gladstone's Land Act of 1881.

BILL [*intones speech with vigor and heartfelt passion*] My friends, if all the world were just, there would be no need for valor . . . And those of us who are of a moderate mind . . . I would say the majority . . . [*light applause from tape recorder*] . . . we are anything but light-hearted. But the moving finger writes and having writ moves *on.* No you can't wash out a word of it. Heretofore we've gotten along with our Nigra population . . . but times change. [*Applause from tape recorder*] I do not argue with any man who believes in segregation. I, of all people, will not, cannot question that belief. We all believe in the words of Henry Clay[3]—"Sir, I would rather be right than be president."

[EDDIE *sleeps his cue.*]

MANNERS   Dammit! Eddie!

[EDDIE *suddenly switches to loud applause.*]

BILL   But difficulties are things that show what men are, and necessity is still the mother of invention. As Emerson[4] so aptly pointed out—"The true test of civilization is not the—census, nor the size of cities, nor the crops—but the kind of man the country turns out." Oh, my friends, let every man look before he leaps, let us consider submitting to the present evil lest a greater one befall us—say to yourself, my honor is dearer to me than my life.[5] [*Very light applause*] I say moderation—for these are the times that try men's souls.[6] In these terrible days we must realize—how oft the darkest hour of ill breaks brightest into dawn.[7] Moderation, yes. [*Very light applause*] Even the misguided, infamous Adolph Hitler[8] said—"One should guard against believing the great masses to be more stupid than they actually are!" [*Applause*] Oh, friends, moderation. Let us weigh our answer very carefully when the dark-skinned Oliver Twist[9] approaches our common pot and says: "Please, sir, I want some more. When we say "no," remember that a soft answer turneth away wrath. Ohhh, we shall come out of the darkness, and sweet is pleasure after pain. If we are superior, let us show our superiority!

[MANNERS *directs* EDDIE *to take applause up high and then out.*]

Moderation. With wisdom and moderation, these terrible days will pass. I am reminded of the immortal words of Longfellow.[1] "And the night shall be filled with music and the cares that infest the day shall fold their tents like the Arabs and silently steal away." [*Terrific applause.*]

[MANNERS *slaps* BILL *on back, dashes to* EDDIE, *and turns the applause up and down.*]

MANNERS   Is this such a Herculean task? All you have to do is listen! Inattention—aggravates the hell out of me!

[*When* BILL *drops out of character we see that he is very different from the strong Renard. He appears to be worried at all times. He has a habit of negatively shaking his head even though nothing is wrong.* BILL O'WRAY

---

3. Patriot (1777–1852), Speaker of the House, and president of the American Colonization Society, who is considered by some one of the greatest senators in the country's history. The following quotation is his response to being informed that his stand against slavery would cost him the presidential election. Although Clay owned slaves, he condemned slavery, judging it a great evil.
4. Ralph Waldo Emerson (1803–1882), American writer, philosopher, and central figure in the Transcendentalist movement. The following quotation is from his "American Civilization" (1862).
5. Bill is paraphrasing from *Don Quixote* by

Miguel de Cervantes (1547–1616).
6. Quoting Thomas Paine (1737–1809), British-born American writer and revolutionary.
7. Quoting Iphigenia in *Taurus of Euripedes.*
8. L. Austrian-born founder of the German Nazi Party and chancellor of the Third Reich (1889–1945). The following quotation from his *Mein Kampf* (1925–26).
9. The second novel (published in 1838) by English author Charles Dickens (1812–1870).
1. American poet Henry Wadsworth Longfellow (1807–1882). The following quotation is from "The Day Is Done."

is but a shadow of a man—but by some miracle he turns into a dynamic figure as Renard. As BILL *—he sees dragons in every corner and worries about each one.*]

BILL   I don't know, I don't know . . .

[MANNERS *fears the worst for the show as he watches* BILL.]

MANNERS   What? What is it?

BILL   [*half dismissing the thought*]   Oh, well . . . I guess . . .

[EDDIE *is toying with the machine and turns the applause up by accident.*]

MANNERS   Hello, Eddie, a little consideration! Why do you do it? Damned childish!

[EDDIE *turns off machine.*]

What's bothering you?

BILL   Well, you never can tell . . . but I don't know . . .

MANNERS   Bill, cut it out, come on.

BILL   That Arab stuff . . . you know, quietly folding his tent . . . you're gonna get a laugh . . . and then on the other hand you might offend somebody . . . well, we'll see . . .

MANNERS   Eddie, make a note of that Arab folding his tent. I'll take it up with Bronson.

[EDDIE *is making notes.*]

BILL   I'm tellin' you, you don't need it . . . wouldn't lose a thing . . . the Longfellow quote . . . I don't know, maybe I'm wrong but . . .

MANNERS   You act like you've lost your last friend! I'm the one holding the blasted bag!

[BILL *takes* Show Business Weekly[2] *out of his coat pocket.*]

BILL   Well, maybe I shouldn't have said . . .

MANNERS   I'm out of my mind! When I think of the money borrowed and for what! Oh, I'm just talking. This always happens when the ship leaves port. The union's making me take three extra stage hands [*laughs*] . . . They hate *us*! Coproduce, filthy word! You know who I had to put the bite on for an extra ten thousand? My ex-wife's present boyfriend. Enough to emasculate a man for the rest of his life!

BILL   How is Fay? Sweet kid. I was sure surprised when you two broke it off. Oh, well, that's the way . . .

MANNERS   She's fine and we're good friends. Thank God for civilization.

BILL   That's nice. Ten thousand? She must have connected up with a big wheel, huh?

MANNERS   I've known you long enough to ask a favor.

BILL   All depends.

MANNERS   Will you stop running off at lunch hour? It looks bad.

BILL   Now, wait a minute . . .

EDDIE   I eat with them all the time.

MANNERS   Drop it, Eddie. Unity in *this* company is very important. Hell, I don't care, but it looks like you don't want to eat with the colored members of the cast.

BILL   I don't.

EDDIE   I guess you heard him.

MANNERS   Bill, this is fantastic. I never credited you with this kind of . . . silly, childlike . . .

2. Performing arts trade magazine founded by Leo Shutt in 1941.

BILL   There's not a prejudiced bone in my body. It is important that I eat my lunch. I used to have an ulcer. I have nothing against anybody but I can't eat my damn lunch . . . people *stare*. They sit there glaring and staring.

MANNERS   Nonsense.

BILL   Tuesday I lunched with Millie because I bumped into her on the street. That restaurant . . . people straining and looking at me as if I were an old lecher! God knows what they're thinking. I've got to eat my lunch. After all . . . I can't stand that . . .

MANNERS   [*laughs*]   All right but mix a little . . . it's the show . . . do it for the show.

BILL   Every time I open my mouth somebody is telling me don't say this or that . . . Millie doesn't want to be called "gal" . . . I call *all* women "gal" . . . I don't know . . . I'm not going into analysis about this . . . I'm not. How do you think my character is shaping up?

MANNERS   Great, no complaints . . . fine.

   [WILETTA *drags in, tired and worn.*]

   'Morning, sweetie.

EDDIE   Good morning.

WILETTA   [*indicating script*]   I been readin' this back and forth and over again.

MANNERS   [*automatic sympathy*]   Honey, don't . . .

WILETTA   My neighbor, Miss Green, she come up and held the book and I sat there justifyin' like you said . . .

MANNERS   Darling, don't think. You're great until you start thinking. I don't expect you to . . .

WILETTA   [*weak laugh*]   I've been in this business a long time, more than twenty-five years and . . .

MANNERS   Don't tell it, you're beautiful.

WILETTA   Guess I can do like the others. We was justifyin' and Miss Green says to me . . .

BILL   [*gets in his good deed*]   Wiletta, you look wonderful, you really do.

WILETTA   Huh?

BILL   You . . . you're looking well.

WILETTA   Thank you, Miss Green says . . .

MANNERS   [*wearily*]   Oh, a plague on Miss Green. Darling, it's too early to listen to outside criticism, it can be dangerous if the person doesn't understand . . .

WILETTA   Miss Green puts on shows at the church . . . and she had an uncle that was a sharecropper, so she says the first act . . .

MANNERS   [*flips the script to act 3*]   We're hitting the third today.

WILETTA   Miss Green also conducts the church choir . . .

MANNERS   Wiletta, don't complicate my life. [*To* BILL *and* EDDIE] Isn't she wonderful? [*To* WILETTA] Dear heart, I adore you.

WILETTA   [*feels like a fool as she limply trails on*]   She . . . she did the Messiah[3] . . . Handel's *Messiah* . . . last Easter . . . and folks come from downtown to hear it . . . all kinds of folks . . . white folks too.

MANNERS   Eddie! Did I leave the schedule at home?

   [EDDIE *hands him the schedule.*]

EDDIE   I have a copy.

---

3. A famous oratorio by George Frideric Handel (1685–1759).

WILETTA Miss Green says, now . . . she said it . . . she says the third act doesn't justify with the first . . . no, wait . . . her exact words was, "The third act is not the natural outcome of the first." I thought, I thought she might be right.

MANNERS [*teasing*] Make me a solemn promise, don't start thinking.

[SHELDON *enters in a rush and hastily begins to remove scarves, coat, etc.*]

SHELDON Good mornin', there ain't no justice.

[BILL O'WRAY *glances at* Show Business *from time to time.*]

EDDIE What a greeting.

SHELDON I dreamed six, twelve, six, one, two . . . just like that. You know what come out yesterday? Six, one, three. What you gonna do?

MANNERS Save your money.

BILL Hey, what do you know?

MANNERS Did we make the press?

SHELDON [*to* WILETTA] Friend of mine died yesterday, went to see about his apartment . . . gone! Just like that!

BILL Gary Brewers going into rehearsal on *Lost and Lonely*.

MANNERS Been a long time.

BILL He was in that Hollywood investigation some years ago.

SHELDON [*to* EDDIE] They musta applied whilst the man was dyin'.

MANNERS He wasn't really in it, someone named him I think.

BILL You knew him well, didn't you?

MANNERS Me? I don't know him. I've worked with him a couple of times but I don't really know him.

BILL A very strange story reached me once, some fellow was planning to name me, can you imagine?

[MILLIE *enters wearing a breathtaking black suit. She is radiant.*]

EDDIE That's ridiculous.

BILL Nothing ever happened, but that's the story. Naming *me*.

MANNERS [*as he studies schedule*] Talking about the coast, I could be out there now on a honey of a deal . . . but this I had to do, that's all.

SHELDON Y'all ever hear my stories 'bout people namin' me?

MANNERS What?

BILL Oh, Shell

[*This is a burden* SHELDON *has carried for quite some time.*]

SHELDON I sang on a program once with Millie, to help some boy that was in trouble . . . but later on I heard they was tryin' to overthrow the gov'ment.

[MANNERS, EDDIE, *and* BILL *are embarrassed by this.*]

MILLIE Oh, hush! Your mouth runs like a race horse!

SHELDON Well, ain't nothin' wrong with singin' is there? We just sang.

MILLIE [*as she removes her hat*] A big fool.

MANNERS [*making peace*] Oh, now . . . we're all good Americans.

BILL [*to ease the tension*] I . . . I . . . er, didn't know you went in for singing, Sheldon.

SHELDON Sure, I even wrote me a coupla tunes. Can make a lotta money like that but you gotta know somebody, I ain't got no pull.

WILETTA [*to* MILLIE] He talks too much, talks too much.

MANNERS Ah, we have a composer, popular stuff?

[SHELDON *stands and mechanically rocks to and fro in a rock-and-roll beat as he sings.*]

SHELDON
>   You-oo-hoo-oo are my hon-honey
>   Ooo-oo-ooo-oo, you smile is su-hu-hunny
>   My hu-hu-hunny, Bay-hay-hay-bee-e-e-e
> . . . and it goes like that.

MANNERS   Well!

SHELDON   Thank you.

BILL   I don't know why you haven't sold it, that's all you hear.
>   [SHELDON *is pleased with* BILL'*s compliment but also a little worried.*]

MILLIE   Hmmmmmph.

EDDIE   Really a tune.

SHELDON [*to* BILL]   My song . . . it . . . it's copyrighted.

BILL   Oh?

SHELDON   I got papers.

MILLIE [*extends her wrist to* WILETTA]   Look. My husband is in off the road.

WILETTA   What's the matter?

MILLIE   A new watch, and I got my suit out . . . brought me this watch. We
>   looked at a freezer this morning . . . food freezer . . . what's best, a chest
>   freezer or an upright? I don't know.
>   [JUDY *enters dressed a little older than in act 1; her hair is set with more
>   precision. She is reaching for a sophistication that can never go deeper
>   than the surface. She often makes graceful, studied postures and tries
>   new attitudes, but very often she forgets.*]

JUDY   Greetings and salutations. Sheldon, how are you dear?

SHELDON   Thank you.

JUDY [*as* MILLIE *displays her wrist for inspection*]   Millie, darling, how lovely,
>   ohhhhh, exquisite . . .

WILETTA [*really trying to join in*]   Mmmmm, ain't it divine.
>   [HENRY *and* JOHN *enter together.* HENRY *carries a container of coffee and
>   a piece of Danish for* MANNERS, HENRY *is exact, precise, all business. He
>   carries the container to* MANNERS'*s table, places pastry, taps* EDDIE *on
>   the shoulder, points to* MANNERS, *points to container, nods to* MANNERS
>   and company, turns and leaves, all while dialogue continues.* JOHN *enters
>   on a cloud. He is drifting more and more toward the heady heights of
>   opportunism. He sees himself on the brink of escaping* WILETTA, MILLIE,
>   and SHELDON. It's becoming very easy to conform to* MANNERS'*s pattern.*]

JOHN   I'm walking in my sleep. I was up all hours last night.

MANNERS   At Sardi's[4] no doubt.

JOHN   No!

JUDY   Exposed! We've found you out.
>   [*General laughter from* MILLIE, JUDY, BILL, EDDIE, *and* MANNERS, JUDY
>   *is enjoying the intangible joke to the utmost, but as she turns to* WILETTA
>   *her laughter dies . . . but* WILETTA *quickly picks it up.*]

WILETTA   Oh, my, yes indeed!

JOHN   I struggled with the third act. I think I won.
>   [MILLIE *sticks out her wrist for* JOHN'*s inspection.*]
>   Exquisite, Millie, beautiful. You deserve it.
>   [*During the following the conversation tumbles criss-cross in all direc-
>   tions and the only clear things are underscored.*]

MANNERS   Tell him what I told you this morning.

BILL   Why should I swell his head?

---

4. A continental restaurant in Manhattan's theater district.

MANNERS [*arm around* JOHN's *shoulder*]   <u>Hollywood's going to grab you so fast!</u> I won't drop names but our opening night is going to be the end.

MILLIE [*to* WILETTA]   <u>Barbara died!</u>

JUDY [*to* MANNERS]   Oh, you terrify me!

MILLIE   <u>Died alone in her apartment.</u> Sudden-like!

JOHN   I've got to catch Katherine's performance, I hear it's terrific!

BILL   She's great, only great.

MILLIE   <u>I wouldn't live alone!</u>

MANNERS   She's going to get the award, no doubt about it!

JUDY   Marion Hatterly is good.

MANNERS   Marion is as <u>old as the hills!</u> I mean, she's so old it's embarrassing.

JOHN   But she has a quality.

SHELDON [*to* MILLIE *and* WILETTA]   <u>People dyin' like they got nothin' else to do!</u>

JUDY   She has, John, a real quality.

SHELDON   <u>I ain't gonna die,</u> can't afford to do it.

MANNERS   You have to respect her.

EDDIE   Can name her own ticket.

JOHN   Imperishable talent.

MILLIE   <u>Funeral is Monday.</u>

WILETTA [*weakly, to no one in particular*]   Mmmmm, fascinatin' . . .

MANNERS   Picnic is over! Third Act!

SHELDON   I know my lines.

BILL   Don't worry about lines yet.

MANNERS   No, let him worry . . . I mean it's okay. Beginning of third!
   [WILETTA *feels dizzy from past conversation. She rises and walks in a half-circle, then half-circle back again. She is suddenly the center of attraction.*]

WILETTA   It . . . it's night time and I'm ironin' clothes.

MANNERS   Right. We wander through it. Here's the ironing board, door, window . . . you iron. Carrie is over there crying.

JUDY   Oh, poor, dear, Carrie, crying again.

MANNERS   Petunia is near the window, looking out for Job. Everyone is worried, worried, worried like crazy. Have the lynchers caught Job? Sam is seated in the corner, whittling a stick.

SHELDON [*flat statement*]   Whittlin' a stick.

MANNERS   Excitement. Everyone knows that a mob is gathering.
   [SHELDON *is seated and busy running one index finger over the other.*]

SHELDON   I'm whittlin' a stick.

MANNERS [*drumming up excitement*]   The hounds can be heard baying in the distance.
   [SHELDON *bays to fill in the dog bit.* MANNERS *silences him with a gesture.*]
Everyone *listens!* They are thinking—has Job been killed? Ruby begins to sing.
   [WILETTA *begins to sing with a little too much power but* MANNERS *directs her down.*]

WILETTA   Lord, have mercy, Lord have mercy . . . [*Hums.*]

MILLIE [*in abject, big-eyed fear*]   Listen to them dogs in the night.
   [MANNERS *warns* SHELDON *not to provide sound effects.*]

WILETTA [*trying to lose herself in the part*]   Child, you better go now.
   [BILL *whispers to* EDDIE.]

EDDIE *Line. Miss Carrie,* you better go now.

MANNERS Oh, bother! Don't do that!

> [EDDIE *feels resentful toward* BILL [*as* BILL *acts as though he had nothing to do with the correction.*]

WILETTA This ain't no place for you to be.

> [JUDY *now plays Carrie in a different way from act 1. There is a reserved kindliness, rather than real involvement.*]

JUDY I don't want to leave you alone, Ruby.

SHELDON Thassa mistake, Mr. Manners. She can't be alone if me Millie is there with her.

MANNERS Don't interrupt!

SHELDON Sorry.

> [BILL *shakes his fist at* SHELDON *in playful pantomime.*]

WILETTA Man that is born of woman is but a few days and full of trouble.

JUDY I'm going to drive over to the next county and get my father and Judge Willis.

MILLIE No, you ain't. Mr. Renard would never forgive me if somethin' was to happen to you.

> [SHELDON *is very touched and sorry for all concerned as he whittles his stick*]

JUDY I feel so helpless.

SHELDON [*interrupts out of sheer frustration*] Am I still whittlin' the stick?

WILETTA Dammit, yes.

MANNERS [*paces to control his annoyance*] Shel.

SHELDON I thought I lost my place.

WILETTA [*picks up* MANNERS's *signal*] Nothin' to do now but pray!

SHELDON [*recognizes his cue*] Oh, yeah, that's me. [*Knows his lines almost perfectly*] Lord, once and again and one more time . . .

> [MILLIE *moans in the background.* WILETTA's *mind seems a thousand miles away.* MANNERS *snaps his fingers and she begins to moan background for* SHELDON's *prayer.*]

Your humble servant calls on your everlastin' mercy . . .

MILLIE Yes, Lord!

SHELDON   . . . to beseech, to beseech thy help for all your children this evenin' . . .

MILLIE This evenin', Lord.

> [MANNERS *is busy talking to* JOHN.]

SHELDON But most of all we ask, we pray . . . that you help your son and servant Job . . .

WILETTA Help him, Lord!

SHELDON [*doing a grand job of the prayer*] Walk with Job! Talk with Job! Ohhhhh, be with Job![5]

JUDY Yes!

> [MANNERS *and* BILL *give* JUDY *disapproving looks and she clasps her hand over her mouth.*]

WILETTA [*starts to sing and is joined by* SHELDON *and* MILLIE] Death ain't nothin' but a robber, cantcha see, cantcha see . . .

> [MANNERS *is in a real tizzy, watching to catch* BILL's *reaction to the scene, and trying with his whole body to keep the scene up and going.*]

MANNERS Eddie! Direction!

EDDIE The door opens and Job enters!

---

5. The biblical figure whose faith was tested but remained unwavering despite repeated calamities.

WILETTA Job, why you come here?
  [MANNERS *doesn't like her reading. It is too direct and thoughtful.*]
MILLIE [*lashing out*] They after you! They told you 'bout mixin' in with Turner and that votin'!
MANNERS Oh, good girl!
WILETTA I'm the one to talk to my boy!
JOHN [*a frightened, shivering figure*] If somebody could get me a wagon, I'll take the low road around Simpkin's Hollow and catch a train goin' away from here.
WILETTA Shoulda gone 'fore you started this misery.
  [MANNERS *indicates that she should get rougher; she tries.*]
  Screamin' 'bout your rights! You got none! You got none!
JOHN I'm askin' for help, I gotta leave.
MANNERS [*to* JOHN] Appeal, remember it's an appeal.
JOHN [*as though a light has dawned*] Ah, you're so right. [*Reads with tender appeal*] I gotta leave.
MANNERS Right.
WILETTA You tryin' to tell me that you runnin' away?
SHELDON [*worried about Job's escape and getting caught up outside of the scene*] Sure! That's what he said in the line right there!
  [MANNERS *silences* SHELDON *with a gesture.*]
WILETTA You say you ain't done nothin' wrong?
  [MANNERS *looks at* EDDIE *and* BILL *with despair.*]
JOHN I ain't lyin' . . .
WILETTA Then there's no need to be runnin'. Ain't you got no faith?
SHELDON [*sings in a shaky voice as he raps out time*]
  Oh, well, a time of trouble is a lonesome time
  Time of trouble is a lonesome time . . .
    [*Joined by* MILLIE.]
  Feel like I could die, feel like I could die . . .
WILETTA Tell 'em you sorry, tell 'em you done wrong!
MANNERS Relate, Wiletta. Relate to what's going on around you! [*To* JOHN] Go on.
JOHN I wasn't even votin' for a black man, votin' for somebody white same as they. [*Aside to* MANNERS] Too much? Too little? I fell off.
    [MANNERS *indicates that he's on the beam.*]
WILETTA I ain't never voted!
SHELDON No, Lord!
WILETTA I don't care who get in! Don't make no nevermind to us!
MILLIE The truth?
JOHN [*all afire*] When a man got a decent word to say for us down here, I gonna vote for him.
WILETTA A decent word! And that's all you ever gonna get outta him. Dammit! He ain't gonna win no how! They done said he ain't and they gonna see to it! And you gonna be dead . . . for a decent word!
JOHN I ain't gonna wait to be killed.
WILETTA There's only one right thing to do!
    [CAST *turns page in unison.*]
  You got to go and give yourself up.
JOHN But I ain't done nothin'.
SHELDON [*starts to sing again*] Wella, trouble is a lonesome thing . . . lonesome . . . lonesome . . .

MANNERS [*the song even grates on him*]   Cut it, it's too much.

JUDY   My father will have you put in the county jail where you'll be safe.

JOHN   But I ain't done nothin'!

JUDY   I'm thinking of Ruby and the others, even if you aren't. I don't want murder in this community.

WILETTA [*screams*]   Boy, get down on your knees.

MANNERS [*to* EDDIE]   Muscular tension.
[EDDIE *makes a note.*]

WILETTA   Oh, Lord, touch this boy's heart!

SHELDON   Mmmmmm, hmmmmmmmmmm. Hmmmmmm . . .

WILETTA   Reach him tonight! Take the fear and hatred out of his soul!

MILLIE   Mercy, Lord!

JOHN   Stop, I can't stand no more. Whatever you say, anything you say.

SHELDON   Praise the Lord!

EDDIE   Renard enters.

BILL   Carrie, you shouldn't be here.

WILETTA   I told her. I'm beggin' you to help my boy, sir . . .
[*She drops script and picks it up.*]

JOHN   Ohhh, I can't sustain.

MANNERS   Don't try. We're breaking everything down to the simplest components . . . I want simple reactions to given circumstances in order to highlight the outstanding phrases.
[WILETTA *finds her place.*]
Okay, let it roll.

WILETTA   I'm beggin' you to help my boy.

BILL   Boy, you're a mighty little fella to fly in the face of things people live by 'round here. I'll do what I can, what little I can.

WILETTA   Thank you, sir.

JUDY   Have Judge Willis put him in jail where he'll be safe.

BILL   Guess it wasn't his fault.

WILETTA   He don' know nothin'.

BILL   There are all kinds of white men in the world.

SHELDON   The truth.

BILL   This bird Akins got to sayin' the kind of things that was bound to stir you folks up.

MILLIE   I ain't paid him no mind myself.

BILL   Well, anything you want to take to the jailhouse with you? Like a washcloth and . . . well, whatever you might need.

JOHN   I don't know, don't know what I'm doin'.

BILL   Think you learned a lesson from all this?

MILLIE   You hear Mr. Renard?

SHELDON   He wanna know if you learned your lesson.

JOHN   I believed I was right.

SHELDON   Now you know you wasn't.

BILL   If anything happens, you tell the men Mr. Akins put notions in your head, understand?

SHELDON   He wanna know if you understand.

BILL   Come along, we'll put you in the jailhouse. Reckon I owe your ma and pa that much.

JOHN   I'm afraid, I so afraid . . .

MILLIE   Just go, 'fore they get here.

EDDIE   Job turns and looks at his father.

[SHELDON *places one finger to his lips and throws up his arms to show that he has no line.*]

Finally, he looks to his mother, she goes back to her ironing.

BILL   Petunia, see that Miss Carrie gets home safe.

MILLIE   Yes, sir.

EDDIE   Job follows Renard out into the night as Ruby starts to sing.

WILETTA [*sings*]

Keep me from sinkin' down

O, Lord, O, my Lord

Keep me from sinkin' down[6] . . .

MANNER   Cut, relax, at ease!

MILLIE [*brushes lint from her skirt*]   I'll have to bring work clothes.

SHELDON [*to* MILLIE]   I almost hit the number yesterday.

MILLIE   I'm glad you didn't.

[BILL *crosses to* MANNERS; *we hear snatches of their conversation as the others cross-talk.*]

JUDY [*to* JOHN]   Did you finish my book?

[JOHN *claps his hand to his forehead in a typical* MANNERS *gesture.*]

BILL [*a light conference on* WILETTA]   A line of physical action might . . .

SHELDON [*to* MILLIE]   I almost got an apartment.

MANNERS   Limited emotional capacity.

MILLIE [*to* SHELDON]   *Almost* doesn't mean a thing.

MANNERS   Well, it's coming. Sheldon, I like what's happening.

SHELDON   Thank you, does he give himself up to Judge Willis and get saved?

MANNERS [*flabbergasted, as are* JOHN, JUDY, BILL, *and* EDDIE]   Shel, haven't you read it? Haven't you heard us read it?

SHELDON   No, I just go over and over my own lines, I ain't in the last of the third act.

JUDY   Are my motivations coming through?

MANNERS   Yeah, forget it. Sit down, Sheldon . . . just for you . . . Renard drives him toward jail, deputies stop them on the way, someone shoots and kills Job as he tries to escape, afterward they find out he was innocent, Renard makes everyone feel like a dog . . . they realize they were wrong and so forth.

SHELDON   And so forth.

MANNERS   He makes them realize that lynching is wrong.

[*He refers to his notes.*]

SHELDON [*to* WILETTA]   What was he innocent of?

WILETTA   I don't know.

JOHN   About the voting.

SHELDON   Uh-uh, he was guilty of that 'cause he done confessed.

MANNERS   Innocent of wrong-doing, Sheldon.

SHELDON   Uh-huh, oh, yeah.

MANNERS   Yale, you're on the right track. John, what can I say? You're great. Millie, you're growing, gaining command . . . I begin to feel an inner as well as the outer rendering.

JOHN   If we could run the sequence without interruption.

SHELDON   Yeah, then we would motorate and all that.

MANNERS [*to* WILETTA]   Dear heart, I've got to tell you . . .

6. From a Negro spiritual.

WILETTA   I ain't so hot.

MANNERS   Don't be sensitive, let me help you, will you?

WILETTA [*trying to handle* MANNERS *in the same way as* JOHN *and* JUDY] I know my relations and motivations may not be just so . . .

SHELDON [*wisely*]   Uh-huh, *motivation*, that's the thing.

WILETTA   They not right and I think I know why . . .

MANNERS   Darling, that's my department, will you listen?
   [JOHN *is self-conscious about* WILETTA *and* SHELDON. *He is ashamed of them and has reached the point where he exchanges knowing looks with* BILL, EDDIE, *and* MANNERS.]

WILETTA   You don't ever listen to me. You hear the others but not me. And it's 'cause of the school. 'Cause they know 'bout justifyin' and the antagonist . . . I never studied that, so you don't want to hear me, that's all right.

JUDY [*stricken to the heart*]   Oh, don't say that.

SHELDON   He listen to me, and I ain't had it.

JOHN [*starts to put his arm around* WILETTA]   Oh, Wiletta . . .

WILETTA [*moving away from him*]   Oh, go on.

MANNERS   Wiletta, dear, I'm sorry if I've complicated things. I'll make it as clear as I can. You are pretending to act and I can see through your pretense. I want truth. What is truth? Truth is simply whatever you can bring yourself to believe, that is all. You must have integrity about your work . . . a sense of . . . well, sense.

WILETTA   I'm tryin' to lose myself like you say but . . .

JOHN [*wants to help but afraid to interrupt*]   Oh, no . . .

MANNERS [*sternly*]   You can't lose yourself, you are you . . . and you can't get away. You, Wiletta, must relate.

SHELDON   That's what I do.

WILETTA   I don't see why the boy couldn't get away . . . it's the killin' that . . . something's wrong. I may be in fast company but I got as much integrity as any. I didn't start workin' no yesterday.

MANNERS   No, Wiletta, no self-pity. Look, he can't escape this death. We want audience sympathy. We have a very subtle point to make, very subtle . . .

BILL   I hate the kind of play that bangs you over the head with the message. Keep it subtle.

MANNERS [*getting very basic*]   We don't want to antagonize the audience.

WILETTA   It'll make 'em mad if he gets away?

MANNERS   This is a simple, sweet, lovable guy. Sheldon, does it offend you that he gives himself up to Judge Willis?

SHELDON   No, not if that's how they do.

MANNERS   We're making one beautiful, clear point . . . violence is wrong.

WILETTA   My friend, Miss Green, say she don't see why they act like this.
   [JOHN *thinks he knows how to handle* WILETTA. *He is about to burst with an idea.* MANNERS *decides to let* JOHN *wade in.*]

JOHN   Look, think of the intellectual level here . . . they're under-privileged, uneducated . . .

WILETTA [*letting* JOHN *know he's treading on thin ice*]   Lookout, you ain't so smart.

JOHN [*showing so much of* MANNERS]   They've probably never seen a movie or television . . . never used a telephone. They . . . they're not like us. They're good, kind, folksy people . . . but they're ignorant, they just don't know.

WILETTA   You ain't the director.

SHELDON [*to* JOHN]   You better hush.

MANNERS   We're dealing with simple, backward people but they're human beings.

WILETTA   'Cause they colored, you tellin' me they're human bein's . . . I *know* I'm a human bein' . . . Listen here . . .

MANNERS   I will not listen! It does not matter to me that they're Negroes. Black, white, green, or purple, I maintain there is only one race . . . the human race.

　　　[SHELDON *bursts into applause.*]

MILLIE   That's true.

MANNERS   Don't think "Negro," think "people."

SHELDON   Let's stop segregatin' ourselves.

JOHN [*to* WILETTA]   I didn't mean any harm, you don't understand . . .

BILL [*to* MILLIE *as be looks heavenward and acts out his weariness*]   Oh, honey child!

MILLIE   Don't call me no damn honey child!

BILL   Well, is my face red?

MILLIE   Yeah, and on you it looks good.

MANNERS   What's going on?

MILLIE   Honey child.

WILETTA [*mumbling as all dialogue falls pell-mell*]   Justify.

BILL [*with great resignation*]   Trying to be friendly.

WILETTA   Justify.

MILLIE   Get friendly with someone else.

MANNERS   May we have order!

SHELDON [*in a terrible flash of temper*]   That's why they don't do more colored shows! Always fightin'! Everybody hush, let this man direct! He don't even have to be here! Right now he could be out in Hollywood in the middle of a big investigation!

EDDIE   The word is production!

SHELDON   That's what I said, production.

EDDIE   No, you didn't:

SHELDON   What'd I say?

MANNERS [*bangs table*]   I will not countenance another outbreak of this nature. I say to each and every one of you . . . I am in charge and I'll thank you to remember it. I've been much too lax, too informal. Well, it doesn't work. There's going to be order.

WILETTA   I was only sayin' . . .

MANNERS   I said *everyone!* My patience is at an end. I demand your concentrated attention. It's as simple as A, B, C, if you will apply yourselves. The threat of this horrible violence throws you into cold, stark fear. It's a perfectly human emotion, anyone would feel it. I'm not asking you to dream up some fantastic horror . . . it's a lynching. We've never actually seen such a thing, thank God . . . but allow your imagination to soar, to take hold of it . . . think.

SHELDON   I seen one.

MANNERS [*can't believe he heard right*]   What?

BILL   What did you see?

SHELDON   A lynchin', when I was a little boy 'bout nine years old.

JUDY   Oh, no.

WILETTA   How did it happen? Tell me, Sheldon, did you really?

MANNERS   Would it help you to know, Wiletta?

WILETTA   I . . . guess . . . I don't know.

BILL [*not eager to hear about it*]   Will it bother you, Sheldon? It could be wrong for him . . . I don't know . . .

   [EDDIE *gives* MANNERS *a doubtful look.*]

MILLIE   That must be something to see.

MANNERS [*with a sigh*]   Go on, Sheldon.

   [MANNERS *watches* CAST *reactions.*]

SHELDON   I think it was on a Saturday, yeah, it had to be or elsewise I woulda been in the field with my ma and pa.

WILETTA   What field?

SHELDON   The cotton field. My ma said I was too little to go every day but some of 'em younger'n me was out there all the time. My grandma was home with me . . .

   [SHELDON *thinks of grandma and almost forgets his story.*]

WILETTA   What about the lynchin'?

SHELDON   It was Saturday and rainin' a sort of sifty rain. I was standin' at the window watchin' the lilac bush wavin' in the wind. A sound come to my ears like bees hummin' . . . was voices comin' closer and closer, screamin' and cursin'. My granny tried to pull me from the window. "Come on, chile." She said, "They gonna kill us all . . . hide!" But I was fightin' to keep from goin' with her, scared to go in the dark closet.

   [JUDY *places her hands over her ears and bows her head.*]

The screamin' comin' closer and closer . . . and the screamin' was laughin' . . . Lord, how they was laughin' . . . louder and louder.

   [SHELDON *rises and puts in his best performance to date. He raises one hand and creates a stillness . . . everyone is spellbound.*]

Hush! Then I hear wagon wheels bumpin' over the wet, stony road, chains clankin'. Man drivin' the wagon, beatin' the horse . . . Ahhhhh- hhh! Ahhhhhhhh! Horse just pullin' along . . . and then I saw it! Chained to the back of the wagon, draggin' and bumpin' along . . .

   [*He opens his arms wide.*]

The arms of it stretched out . . . a burnt, naked thing . . . a burnt, naked thing that once was a man . . . and I started to scream but no sound come out . . . just a screamin' but no sound . . .

   [*He lowers his arms and brings the company back to the present.*]

That was Mr. Morris that they killed. Mr. Morris. I remember one time he come to our house and was laughin' and talkin' about everything . . . and he give us a fruit cake that his wife made. Folks said he was crazy . . . you know, 'bout talkin' back . . . quick to speak his mind. I left there when I was seventeen. I don't want to live in no place like that.

MANNERS   When I hear of barbarism . . . I feel so wretched, so guilty.

SHELDON   Don't feel that way. You wouldn't kill nobody and do 'em like that . . . would you?

MANNERS [*hurt by the question*]   No, Sheldon.

SHELDON   That's what I know.

   [BILL *crosses and rests his hand on* SHELDON's *shoulder.* SHELDON *flinches because he hadn't noticed* BILL's *approach.*]

Oh! I didn't see you. Did I help y'all by tellin' that story?

MANNERS   It was quite an experience. I'm shot. Break for lunch, we'll pickup in an hour, have a good afternoon session.

MILLIE   Makes me feel like goin' out in the street and crackin' heads.

JUDY [*shocked*]   Oh!

EDDIE   Makes my blood boil . . . but what can you do?

MANNERS   We're doing a play.

MILLIE [*to* JUDY]   I'm starved. You promised to show us that Italian place.

JUDY [*surprised that* MILLIE *no longer feels violent*]   Why . . . sure, I'd love to. Let's have a festive lunch, with wine!

SHELDON   Yeah, that wine that comes in a straw bottle.

JUDY   Imported wine.

MILLIE   And chicken cacciatore . . . let's live!

[WILETTA *crosses to* MANNERS *while others are getting coats; she has hit on a scheme to make* MANNERS *see her point.*]

WILETTA   Look here, I ain't gonna let you get mad with me. You supposed to be my buddy.

JOHN   Let's go!

[MANNERS *opens his arms to* WILETTA.]

MANNERS   I'm glad you said that. You're my sweetheart.

MILLIE   Bill, how about you?

BILL [*places his hand on his stomach*]: The Italian place. Okay, count me in.

EDDIE [*stacking scripts*]: I want a kingsize dish of clams . . . raw ones.

WILETTA   Wouldn't it be nice if the mother could say, "Son, you right! I don't want to send you outta here but I don't know what to do . . ."

MANNERS   Darling, darling . . . no.

MILLIE   Wiletta, get a move on.

WILETTA   Or else she says "Run for it, Job!", and then they catch him like that . . . he's dead *anyway*, see?

MANNERS [*trying to cover his annoyance*]   It's not the script, it's *you*. Bronson does the writing, you do the acting, it's that simple.

SHELDON   One race, the human race. I like that.

JUDY   Veal parmesan with oodles and oodles of cheese!

WILETTA   I was just thinkin' if I could . . .

MANNERS [*indicating script*]   Address yourself to this.

JUDY [*to* JOHN]   Bring my book tomorrow.

JOHN   Cross my heart.

WILETTA   I just wanted to talk about . . .

MANNERS   You are going to get a spanking.

[*He leaves with* EDDIE *and others.*]

MILLIE   Wiletta, come on!

WILETTA [*abruptly*]   I . . . I'll be there later.

MILLIE [*miffed by the short answer*]   Suit yourself.

JUDY [*to* WILETTA]   It's on the corner of Sixth Avenue on this side of the street.

JOHN   Correction. Correction, Avenue of the Americas.

[*Laughter from* MANNERS, MILLIE, SHELDON, *and* BILL *offstage.*]

JUDY [*posturing in her best theatrical style*]   But no one, absolutely no one ever says it. He's impossible, absolutely impossible!

WILETTA   Oh, ain't he though.

[JOHN *bows to* JUDY *and indicates that she goes first.*]

JOHN   Dear Gaston, Alphonse will follow.

WILETTA   John, I told you everything wrong 'cause I didn't know better, that's the size of it. No fool like an old fool. You right, don't make sense to be bowin' and scrapin' and tommin' . . . No, don't pay no attention to what I said.

JOHN [*completely* MANNERS] Wiletta, my dear, you're my sweetheart, I love you madly and I think you're wonderfully magnificent!
> [JUDY *suddenly notices his posturing and hers; she feels silly. She laughs, laughter bordering on tears.*]

JUDY John, you're a puppet with strings attached and so am I. Everyone's a stranger and I'm the strangest of all.
> [*She quickly leaves.*]

JOHN Wiletta, don't forget to come over!
> [*He follows* JUDY.]

WILETTA [*paces up and down, tries doing her lines aloud*] Only one thing to do, give yourself up! Give yourself up . . . give up . . . give up . . . give up . . . give up . . . give up.
> [*Lights whirl and flicker. Blues record comes in loud—then down— lights flicker to indicate passage of time.* WILETTA *is gone. Stage is empty.*]
> [BILL *enters, removing his coat. He has a slight attack of indigestion and belches his disapproval of pizza pie. Others can be heard laughing and talking offstage.*]

BILL Ohhhhhh, ahhhhh . . .
> [MANNERS *enters with* EDDIE. EDDIE *proceeds to the table and script.* MANNERS *is just getting over the effects of a good laugh . . . but his mirth suddenly fades as he crosses to* BILL.]

MANNERS I am sorry you felt compelled to tell that joke about the colored minister and the stolen chicken.

BILL Trying to be friendly . . . I don't know . . . I even ate pizza.

EDDIE I always *think* . . . think first, is this the right thing to say, would I want anyone to say this to me?
> [*Burst of laughter from offstage.*]

BILL Oh, you're so noble, you give me a pain in the ass. Love thy neighbor as thyself, now I ask you, is that a reasonable request?

MANNERS [*for fear the others will hear*] All right Knock it off.

BILL Okay, I said I was sorry, but for what . . . I'll never know.
> [SHELDON, MILLIE, JUDY, *and* JOHN *enter in a hilarious mood.* JUDY *is definitely feeling the wine.* SHELDON *is supplying the fun.*]

SHELDON Sure, I was workin' my hind parts off . . . Superintendent of the buildin' . . .

JOHN But the tenants, Shel! That's a riot!

SHELDON One day a man came along and offered me fifty dollars a week just to walk across the stage real slow. [*Mimics his acting role*] Sure, I took it! Hard as I worked I was glad to slow down!
> [*Others laugh.*]

JUDY [*holds her head*] Ohhhhhh, that wine.

MILLIE Wasn't it good? I wanna get a whole *case* of it for the holidays. All that I have to do! My liquors, wreathes, presents, cards . . . I'm gonna buy my husband a tape recorder.

JUDY [*to* JOHN] I'm sorry I hurt your feelings but you are a little puppet, and I'm a little puppet, and all the world . . .
> [*She impresses the lesson by tapping* JOHN *on his chest.*]

MANNERS Judy, I want to go over something with you . . .

JUDY No, you don't . . . you're afraid I'm going to . . . hic. 'Fraid I'll go overboard on the friendship deal and *complicate* matters . . . complications . . .

MANNERS Two or three glasses of wine, she's delirious. Do you want some black coffee?

JUDY No, no, I only have hiccups.

MILLIE [*to* JOHN]   Which would you rather have, a tape recorder or a camera?

JOHN   I don't know.

SHELDON   I'd rather have some money, make mine cash.

MANNERS [*to* JUDY]   Why don't you sit down and get yourself together?
[*She sits.*]

JOHN [*to* MANNERS]   I . . . I think I have some questions about Wiletta and the third act.

MANNERS   It's settled, don't worry, John, she's got it straight.

JOHN   I know but it seems . . .

MANNERS   Hoskins sat out front yesterday afternoon. He's mad about you. First thing he says, "Somebody's going to try and steal that boy from us."

JOHN [*very pleased*]   I'm glad I didn't know he was there.

MANNERS   Eddie, call it, will you? Okay, attention!

EDDIE   Beginning of the third.
[*Company quiets down, opens scripts.* WILETTA *enters.*]

MANNERS   You're late.

WILETTA   I know it. [*To* MILLIE] I had a bowl of soup and was able to relate to it and justify, no trouble at all. [*To* MANNERS] I'm not gonna take up your time now but I wanta see you at the end of the afternoon.

MANNERS   Well . . . I . . . I'll let you know . . . we'll see.

WILETTA   It's important.

MANNERS [*ignoring her and addressing entire company*]   Attention, I want to touch on a corner of what we did this morning and then we'll high-light the rest of three!
[*Actors rise and start for places.*]
John, top of page four.

JOHN   When a man has a decent word to say for us down here, I gonna vote for him.

WILETTA [*with real force; she is lecturing him rather than scolding*]   A decent word? And that's all you ever gonna get out of him. Dammit, he ain't gonna win no how. They done said he ain't and they gonna see to it! And you gonna be dead for a decent word.

MANNERS [*to* EDDIE]   This is deliberate.

JOHN   I gotta go, I ain't gonna wait to be killed.

WILETTA   There's only one right thing to do. You got to go and give your-self up.

JOHN   I ain't done nothin'.

JUDY   My father will have Judge Willis put you in the county jail where you'll be safe.
[MANNERS *is quite disheartened.*]

WILETTA   Job, she's tryin' to help us.

JUDY   I'm thinking of the others even if you aren't. I don't want murder in this community.

WILETTA   Boy, get down on your knees.
[JOHN *falls to his knees.*]
Oh, Lord touch this boy's heart. Reach him tonight, take the fear and hatred out of his soul!

SHELDON   Hmmmmmm, mmmmmmm, mmmmmmmm . . .

MILLIE   Mercy, Lord.

JOHN   Stop, I can't stand anymore . . .
[WILETTA *tries to raise* JOHN.]

MANNERS   No, keep him on his knees.

JOHN   I can't stand anymore . . . whatever you say . . .

[*Again* WILETTA *tries to raise him.*]

SHELDON [*to* WILETTA]   He say keep him on his knees.

WILETTA   Aw, get up off the floor, wallowin' around like that.

[*Everyone is shocked.*]

MANNERS   Wiletta, this is not the time or place to . . .

WILETTA   All that crawlin' and goin' on before me . . . hell, I ain't the one tryin' to lynch him. This ain't sayin' nothin', don't make sense. Talkin' 'bout the truth is anything I can believe . . . well, I don't believe this.

MANNERS   I will not allow you to interrupt in this disorganized manner.

WILETTA   You been askin' me what I think and where things come from and how come I thought it and all that. Where is this comin' from?

[*Company murmuring in the background.*]

Tell me, why this boy's people turned against him? Why we sendin' him out into the teeth of a lynch mob? I'm his mother and I'm sendin' him to his death. This is a lie.

JOHN   But his mother doesn't understand . . .

WILETTA   Everything people do is counta their mother . . . well, maybe so.

JOHN   There have been cases of men dragged from their homes . . . for voting and asking others to vote.

WILETTA   But they was *dragged* . . . they come with guns and dragged 'em out. They weren't sent to be killed by their mama. The writer wants the damn white man to be the hero—and I'm the villain.

MILLIE   I think we're all tired.

SHELDON   Outta order, outta order, you outta order. This ain't the time.

MANNERS   Quiet please. She's confused and I'd just as soon have everything made clear.

WILETTA   Would you do this to a son of yours?

MANNERS   She places him in the hands of Judge Willis and . . .

WILETTA   And I tell you she knows better.

BILL   It's only because she trusts and believes. Couldn't you trust and believe in Al?

MANNERS   Bill, please.

WILETTA   No, I wouldn't trust him with my son's life.

MANNERS   Thank you.

SHELDON   She don't mean it.

WILETTA   Judge Willis! Why don't his people help him?

MANNERS   The story goes a certain way and . . .

WILETTA   It oughta go another way.

ENTIRE COMPANY [*in unison*]   Talk about it later. We're all tired. Yes. We need a rest. Sometimes your own won't help you.

MANNERS   Leave her alone!

[MANNERS *is on fire now. He loves the challenge of this conflict and is determined to win the battle. He must win.*]

Why this great fear of death? Christ died for something and . . .

WILETTA   Sure, they came and got him and hauled him off to jail. His mother didn't turn him in, in fact, the one who did it was one of them so-called friends.

MANNERS   His death proved something. Job's death brings him the lesson.

WILETTA   That they should stop lynchin' *innocent* men! Fine thing! Lynch the guilty, is that the idea? The dark-skinned Oliver Twist. [*Points to* JOHN] That's you. Yeah, I mean, you got to go to school to justify this!

MANNERS   Wiletta, I've listened. I've heard you out . . .

WILETTA [*to* SHELDON]   And you echoin' every damn word he says—"Keep him on his knees."

MANNERS   I've heard you out and even though you think you know more than the author . . .

WILETTA   You don't want to hear. You are a prejudiced man, a prejudiced racist.

> [*Gasp from company.*]

MANNERS [*caught off guard*]   I will not accept that from you or anyone else.

WILETTA   I told this boy to laugh and grin at everything you said, well . . . I ain't laughin'.

MANNERS   While you give me hell-up-the-river, I'm supposed to stand here and take it with a tolerance beyond human endurance. I'm white! You think it's so wonderful to be white? I've got troubles up to here! But I don't expect anyone to hand me anything and it's high time you got rid of that notion. No, I never worked in a cotton field. I didn't. I was raised in a nice, comfortable, nine-room house in the Midwest . . . and I learned to say nigger, kike, sheeny, spick, dago, wop, and chink . . . I hear 'em plenty! I was raised by a sweet, dear, kind old aunt, who spent her time gathering funds for missionaries . . . but she almost turned our town upside down when Mexicans moved in on our block. I know about troubles . . . my own! I've never been *handed* any gifts. Oh, it's so grand to be white! I had to crawl and knuckle under step by step. What I want and what I believe, indeed! I directed blood, guts, fist-fights, bedroom farces, and the lowest kind of dirtied-up sex until I earned the respect of this business.

WILETTA   But would you send your son out to . . .

MANNERS   I proclaim this National Truth Week! Whites! You think we belong to one great, grand fraternity? They stole and snatched from me for years, and I'm a club member! Ever hear of an idea man? They picked my brains! They stripped me! They threw me cash and I let the credit go! My brains milked, while somebody else climbed on my back to take bows. But I didn't beg for mercy . . . why waste your breath? I learned one thing that's the only damned truth worth knowing . . . you get nothin' for nothin', but nothin'! No favors, no dreams served up on silver platters. Now . . . finally I get something for all of us . . . but it's not enough for you! I'm prejudiced! Get wise, there's damned few of us interested in putting on a colored show at all, much less one that's going to say anything. It's rough out here, it's a hard world! Do you think I can stick my neck out by telling the truth about you? There are billions of things that *can't be said* . . . do you follow me, billions! Where the hell do you think I can raise a hundred thousand dollars to tell the unvarnished truth?

> [*Picks up the script and waves it.*]

So, maybe it's a lie . . . but it's one of the finest lies you'll come across for a damned long time! Here's bitter news, since you're livin' off truth . . . The American public is not ready to see you the way you want to be seen because, one, they don't believe it, two, they don't want to believe it, and three, they're convinced they're superior—and that, my friend, is why Carrie and Renard have to carry the ball! Get it? Now you wise up and aim for the soft spot in that American heart, let 'em pity you, make 'em weep buckets, be helpless, make 'em feel so damned sorry for you that they'll lend a hand in easing up the pressure. You've got a free ride. Coast, baby, coast.

WILETTA Would you send your son out to be murdered?

MANNERS [*so wound up, he answers without thinking*] Don't compare yourself to me! What goes for my son doesn't necessarily go for yours! Don't compare him [*points to* JOHN] . . . with three strikes against him, don't compare him with my son, they've got nothing in common . . . not a goddamn thing!

> [*He realizes what he has said, also that he has lost company sympathy. He is utterly confused and embarrassed by his own statement.*]

I tried to make it clear.

JOHN It is clear.

> [MANNERS *quickly exits to dressing room.* EDDIE *follows him.* JUDY *has an impulse to follow.*]

BILL No, leave him alone.

JOHN [*to* WILETTA] I feel like a fool . . . Hmmph. "Don't think Negro, think people."

SHELDON [*to* BILL] You think he means we're fired?

BILL I don't know . . . I don't know . . .

MILLIE Wiletta, this should have been discussed with everyone first.

SHELDON Done talked yourself out of a job.

BILL Shel, you don't know that.

> [*During the following scene,* SHELDON *is more active and dynamic than ever before.*]

SHELDON Well, he didn't go out there to bake her no birthday cake.

> [JUDY *is quietly crying.*]

MILLIE We got all the truth we bargained for and then some.

WILETTA Yes, I spoke my mind and he spoke his.

BILL We have a company representative, Sheldon is the deputy. Any complaints we have should be handled in an orderly manner. Equity has rules, the rule book says . . .

SHELDON I left my rule book home. Furthermore, I don't think I want to be the deputy.

MILLIE He was dead right about some things but I didn't appreciate that *last* remark.

SHELDON [*to* WILETTA] You can't spit in somebody's eye and tell 'em you was washin' it out.

BILL Sheldon, now is not the time to resign.

SHELDON [*taking charge*] All right, I'm tryin' to lead 'em, tryin' to play peace-maker. Shame on y'all! Look at the U.N.!

MILLIE The U.N.?

SHELDON Yes, the United Nations. You think they run their business by blabbin' everything they think? No! They talk sweet and polite 'til they can outslick the next feller. Wisdom! The greatest gift in the world, they got it! [*To* WILETTA] Way you talked, I thought you had the 'tomic bomb.

WILETTA I'm sick of people signifyin' we got no sense.

SHELDON I know. I'm the only man in the house and what am I doin'? Whittlin' a doggone stick. But I whittled it, didn't I? I can't write a play and I got no money to put one on . . . Yes! I'm gonna whittle my stick!

> [*Stamps his foot to emphasize the point.*]

JOHN [*very noble and very worried*] How do you go about putting in a notice?

SHELDON [*to* JOHN] Hold on 'til I get to you. [*To* WILETTA] Now, when he gets back here, you be sure and tell him.

WILETTA Tell him what?

SHELDON Damn, tell him you *sorry*.

BILL Oh, he doesn't want that.

WILETTA Shame on him if he does.

MILLIE I don't want to spend the rest of the day wondering why he walked out.

WILETTA I'm playin' a leadin' part and I want this script changed or else.

SHELDON Hush up, before the man hears you.

MILLIE Just make sure you're not the one to tell him. You're a great one for runnin' to management and telling your guts.

SHELDON I never told management nothin', anybody say I did is lyin'.

JUDY Let's ask for a *quiet* talk to straighten things out.

BILL No. This is between Wiletta and Manners and I'm sure they can . . .

JOHN We all ought to show some integrity.

SHELDON Integrity . . . got us in a big mess.

MILLIE [*to* JOHN] You can't put in your notice until after opening night. You've got to follow Equity rules . . .

SHELDON Yeah, he's trying to defy the union.

WILETTA [*thumping the script*] This is a damn lie.

MILLIE But you can't tell people what to write, that's censorship.

SHELDON [*to* WILETTA] And that's another point in your disfavor.

JOHN They can write what they want but we don't have to do it.

SHELDON You outta order!

BILL [*to* JOHN] Oh, don't keep stirring it up, heaping on coals . . .

JUDY Wiletta, maybe if we appeal to Mr. Hoskins or Mr. Bronson . . .

SHELDON The producer and the author ain't gonna listen to her, after all . . . they white same as Manners.

JUDY I resent that!

BILL I do too, Shel.

JUDY I've had an awful lot of digs thrown on me . . . remarks about white, white . . . and I do resent it.

JOHN [*to* JUDY] He means what can you expect from Sheldon. [*To* SHELDON] Sheldon.

BILL [*to* JUDY] I'm glad you said that.

SHELDON I'm sorry, I won't say nothin' 'bout white. [*To* WILETTA] Look here, Hoskins, Manners, and Bronson . . . they got things in . . . er . . . common, you know what I mean?

WILETTA Leave me alone . . . and suit yourselves.

MILLIE I know what's right but I need this job.

SHELDON There you go . . . talk.

WILETTA Thought your husband doesn't want you to work.

MILLIE He doesn't but I have to anyway.

JUDY But you'll still be in New York. If this falls through I'll have to go back to Bridgeport . . . before I even get started.

JOHN Maybe I'll never get another job.

MILLIE Like Al Manners says, there's more to this life than the truth. [*To* JUDY] You'll have to go to Bridgeport. Oh, how I wish I had a Bridgeport.

BILL   Okay, enough, *I'm* the villain. I get plenty of work, forgive me.

JUDY   Life scares me, honestly it does.

SHELDON   When you kick up a disturbance, the man's in his rights to call the cops . . . police car will come rollin' up here, next thing you know . . . you'll be servin' time.

MILLIE   Don't threaten her!

JOHN   Why don't you call a cop *for* him . . . try it.
    [HENRY *enters carrying a paper bag.*]

HENRY   I got Mr. Manners some nice Danish, cheese and prune.

MILLIE   He can't eat it right now . . . leave it there.
    [EDDIE *enters with a shaken but stern attitude.*]

EDDIE   Attention company. You are all dismissed for the day. I'll telephone about tomorrow's rehearsal.

SHELDON   Tell Mr. Manners I'm gonna memorize my first act.
    [EDDIE *exits and* SHELDON *talks to company.*]
    I still owe the doctor money . . . and I can't lift no heavy boxes or be scrubbin' no floors. If I was a drinkin' man I'd get drunk.

MILLIE   Tomorrow is another day. Maybe everybody will be in better condition to . . . talk . . . just talk it all out. Let's go to the corner for coffee and a calm chat. [*Suddenly solicitous with* JUDY] How about you, honey, wouldn't you like to relax and look over the situation? Bill?

BILL   I have to study for my soap opera . . . but thanks.

JUDY   Yes, let's go talk.

MILLIE   John? Wiletta, honey, let's go for coffee.

WILETTA   I'll be there after a while. Go on.

JOHN   We couldn't go without you.

SHELDON   We don't want to leave you by yourself in this old theater.

WILETTA   There are times when you got to be alone. *This is mine.*
    [JOHN *indicates that they should leave.* MILLIE, SHELDON, JUDY, JOHN, *and* BILL *exit.*]

HENRY   Are you cryin'?

WILETTA   Yes.

HENRY   Ah, don't do that. It's too nice a day.
    [HENRY *sits near tape recorder.*]
    I started to throw coffee at him that time when he kicked up a fuss, but you got to take a lotta things in this life.

WILETTA   Divide and conquer . . . that's the way they get the upper hand. A telephone call for tomorrow's rehearsal . . . they won't call me . . . But I'm gonna show up any damn way. The next move is his. He'll have to fire me.

HENRY   Whatcha say?

WILETTA   We have to go further and do better.

HENRY   That's a good one. I'll remember that. What's on this, music?
    [WILETTA *turns the machine on and down. The applause plays.*]

WILETTA   Canned applause. When you need a bit of instant praise . . . you turn it on . . . and there you are.
    [He tries it.]

HENRY   Canned applause. They got everything these days. Time flies. I bet you can't guess how old I am.

WILETTA   Not more than sixty.

HENRY   I'm seventy-eight.

WILETTA   Imagine that. A fine-lookin' man like you.
    [*Sound of police siren in street.*]

HENRY   What's that?

WILETTA   Police siren.

HENRY   They got a fire engine house next to where I live. God-in-heaven, you never heard such a noise . . . and I'm kinda deaf . . . Didn't know that, did you?

WILETTA   No, I didn't. Some live by what they call great truths. Henry, I've always wanted to do somethin' real grand . . . in the theater . . . to stand forth at my best . . . to stand up here and do anything I want . . .

HENRY   Like my father . . . he was in vaudeville . . . doin' the soft-shoe and tippin' his hat to the ladies . . .

WILETTA   Yes, somethin' grand.

HENRY   [adjusting the tape recorder to play applause]   Do it . . . do it. I'm the audience.

WILETTA   I don't remember anything grand . . . I can't recall.

HENRY   Say somethin' from the Bible . . . like the twenty-third psalm.

WILETTA   Oh, I know.

[She comes downstage and recites beautifully from Psalm 133.]

Behold how good and how pleasant it is for brethren to dwell together in unity. It is like the precious ointment upon the head, that ran down upon the beard, even Aaron's beard; that went down to the skirts of his garment; as the dew of Hermon, and as the dew that descended upon the mountains of Zion; for there the Lord commanded the blessing, even life forevermore.

[HENRY turns on applause as WILETTA stands tall for the curtain.]

1955

ROBERT HAYDEN
1913–1980

Born Asa Bundy Sheffey on August 4, 1913, in Detroit, Michigan, Robert Hayden grew up in a slum neighborhood called Paradise Valley, which he would later memorialize in *Elegies for Paradise Valley* (1978). Asa and Gladys Ruth Finn Sheffey separated soon after his birth, and their child became the foster son of neighbors Sue Ellen Westerfield and William Hayden. As a teenager, Hayden was embroiled in an ongoing family drama that shuttled him emotionally between the Haydens and his mother, who lived next door. Actually, Ruth Sheffey moved in with the Haydens for a time, as the two women and the son were often allied against the father. At other times, this triangle of desire and antagonism pitted the Haydens and Robert against his mother. This complicated fabric of intimate relations helped shape the sensitive personality of the boy, who also suffered from a severe sight impairment that kept him from participating in sports and games but did not prevent his becoming an avid reader. Hayden as a poet would take full advantage of that reading, whose richness is translated into the body of his work. Perhaps his most significant achievement was the idea that "black experience" illuminated the human predicament, as he, not unlike Melvin Tolson, adapted modernist notions of technical precision and polish to the historical context of African American life.

In spite of the poverty and strife in which he grew up, Hayden's foster parents provided him with whatever advantages they could. He graduated from Detroit Northern High School in 1932 and, on a scholarship arranged by the Hayden family's caseworker, matriculated at Detroit City College, later renamed Wayne State University. During his undergraduate years, Hayden acted in a Langston Hughes play, which led to his meeting the celebrated writer and showing him some early poems. Hughes pronounced them "derivative." Between 1936 and 1938, Hayden worked with Detroit's Federal Writers' Project, conducting research in local black history and folklore.

In 1940 Hayden published *Heart-Shape in the Dust*, his first book of poems, and married concert pianist and aspiring composer Erma Morris. *Heart-Shape in the Dust* deals with subjects of protest, as in "These Are My People," which takes up the story of the Scottsboro Boys. Other poems from this volume include "Gabriel," about the nineteenth-century slave insurrectionist Gabriel Prosser, and "Bacchanale," which is written in the rhythms of a folk song. He enrolled in the graduate program in English literature at the University of Michigan in 1941; that year his and Erma's only child, Maia, was born. While at Michigan, he studied with visiting professor W. H. Auden; Hayden would later recall this encounter as a "strategic experience" in his life, as Auden showed him his poetic strengths and weaknesses "in ways no one else before had done." Though Hayden was already a student of the craft, having admired the poetry of Harlem Renaissance writers Langston Hughes, Countee Cullen, and Jean Toomer as well as that of Elinor Wiley, Edna St. Vincent Millay, Sara Teasdale, Carl Sandburg, and Hart Crane, Auden would lead the apprentice poet to find his own voice and to explore his feelings. Hayden continued to write through graduate school and twice received the Hopwood Prize for student poetry. He took a master's degree in English in 1944 and stayed at Michigan for two years as a teaching fellow, the first black member of the English department.

Selections from Hayden's second and unpublished manuscript; *Black Spear*, began to appear in various periodicals in 1942; and though still the work of an apprentice, it, along with *Heart-Shape in the Dust*, shows Hayden's passionate, lifelong interest in African American history as well as his taste for radical politics. Critics have concluded that the major stylistic influence on *Black Spear* is Stephen Vincent Benét's Civil War epic *John Brown's Body* (1928). If, as one critic suggests, Hayden's narrator in *Black Spear* was calling for a poet to sing the "blackskinned epic, epic with the black spear," that volume represents one of the first appearances of Hayden as poet-historiographer and especially as poet-historiographer of the African sojourn in the New World. "Middle Passage," among Hayden's best-known works, was first published in the journal *Phylon* in 1945. Characterized by multiple voices and a dialogue between narrative and lyric, the poem offers Hayden's version of a rebellion aboard the slave ship *Amistad*, focusing especially on the legendary African mutineer Cinqué. Along with "Runagate Runagate" and "Frederick Douglass," "Middle Passage" is one of three major history poems by Hayden from the 1940s.

In 1946 Hayden accepted a professorship in English literature at Fisk University in Nashville, where he would remain for more than twenty years. At Fisk he met writer and head librarian Arna Bontemps; together they edited the anthology *Poetry of the Negro* (1949). With another Fisk colleague, art curator Myron O'Higgins, Hayden published a small poetry collection titled *The Lion and the Archer* (1948), which included "Homage to the Empress of the Blues," Hayden's paean to blues singer Bessie Smith.

While Hayden published consistently across the decades, including *Figure of Time* in the 1950s, the 1960s brought him both international recognition and controversy. First issued by Dutch publisher Paul Bremen, *Ballad of Remembrance* (1962) was thematically arranged around an assortment of topics, from black history and Mexico to human quest and autobiographical issues. *Ballad* won the grand prize for poetry at the First World Festival of Negro Arts at Dakar, Senegal, West Africa, in 1966; an American version of the book came out that year as *Selected Poems*.

But in 1966, too, the first of the Black Writers' Conferences to be convened at Fisk University took place. Hayden's art—subtle, intellectual, firmly situated in the academy—was not what the young black nationalists had in mind, mainly because it did not promote an aesthetic that furthered the cause of black revolution, and they did not hold back from saying so. Gwendolyn Brooks's work also came in for such criticism during the second meeting. Though Brooks's poetry did eventually take a different turn, Hayden refused to be pressured. Four years later, after returning to the University of Michigan as a professor of English, Hayden explored the 1966 event in *Words in the Mourning Time*. Several poems in *Mourning* deal explicitly with the idea of liberation—"Soledad"; "The Dream"; and "El Hajj Malik El-Shabazz," a tribute to Malcolm X. *The Night Blooming Cereus* (1972) was seen by some as Hayden's retreat from black history into a world of private symbolism; others felt it showed a successful coexistence of Hayden the symbolist with Hayden the historicist. After publishing *Angle of Ascent: New and Selected Poems* in 1975, Hayden was appointed consultant in poetry to the Library of Congress in 1976, the first black American artist to receive that honor. At work on a new collection, he died of a heart ailment in Ann Arbor, in February 1980.

Nearly anywhere that one turns in the Hayden canon, one is struck by the elegant concision of line and contour, by sentences honed by a "hard precision of thought," to quote Ezra Pound, and by a vision of human possibility that bets its whole hand on the redemptive occasions of the future. It is difficult to believe that the 1960s radicals could have mistaken this beat, for example, that evokes the shade of Frederick Douglass:

> When it is finally ours, this freedom, this liberty, this beautiful
> and terrible thing, needful to man as air,
> usable as earth . . .
> this man, superb in love and logic, this man
> shall be remembered.

Perhaps we could say, with a good deal of justification, that these lines are not unfitting for Hayden himself.

The Diver

Sank through easeful
azure. Flower
creatures flashed and
shimmered there—
lost images   5
fadingly remembered.
Swiftly descended
into canyon of cold
nightgreen emptiness.
Freefalling, weightless   10
as in dreams of
wingless flight,
plunged through infra-
space and came to
the dead ship,   15
carcass that swarmed with
voracious life.
Angelfish, their
lively blue and
yellow prised from   20

darkness by the
flashlight's beam,
thronged her portholes.
Moss of bryozoans[1]
blurred, obscured her   25
metal. Snappers,
gold groupers explored her,
fearless of bubbling
manfish. I entered
the wreck, awed by her silence,   30
feeling more keenly
the iron cold.
With flashlight probing
fogs of water
saw the sad slow   35
dance of gilded
chairs, the ectoplasmic[2]
swirl of garments,
drowned instruments
of buoyancy,   40
drunken shoes. Then
livid gesturings,
eldritch[3] hide and
seek of laughing
faces. I yearned to   45
find those hidden
ones, to fling aside
the mask and call to them,
yield to rapturous
whisperings, have   50
done with self and
every dinning[4]
vain complexity.
Yet in languid
frenzy strove, as   55
one freezing fights off
sleep desiring sleep;
strove against the
cancelling arms that
suddenly surrounded   60
me, fled the numbing
kisses that I craved.
Reflex of life-wish?
Respirator's brittle
belling? Swam from   65
the ship somehow;
somehow began the
measured rise.

                                                    1962

Homage to the Empress of the Blues[1]

Because there was a man somewhere in a candystripe silk shirt,
gracile[2] and dangerous as a jaguar and because a woman moaned
for him in sixty-watt gloom and mourned him Faithless Love
Twotiming Love Oh Love Oh Careless Aggravating Love,

> She came out on the stage in yards of pearls, emerging like   5
> a favorite scenic view, flashed her golden smile and sang.

Because grey laths[3] began somewhere to show from underneath
torn hurdygurdy[4] lithographs of dollfaced heaven;
and because there were those who feared alarming fists of snow
on the door and those who feared the riot-squad of statistics,   10

> She came out on the stage in ostrich feathers, beaded satin,
> and shone that smile on us and sang.

1948

Middle Passage[1]

Jesús, Estrella, Esperanza, Mercy:[2]

> Sails flashing to the wind like weapons,
> sharks following the moans the fever and the dying;
> horror the corposant and compass rose.[3]

Middle Passage: 5
> voyage through death
> to life upon these shores.

> "10 April 1800—
> Blacks rebellious. Crew uneasy. Our linguist says
> their moaning is a prayer for death,   10
> ours and their own. Some try to starve themselves.
> Lost three this morning leaped with crazy laughter
> to the waiting sharks, sang as they went under."

Desire, Adventure, Tartar, Ann:

> Standing to America, bringing home   15
> black gold, black ivory, black seed.

---

1. Bessie Smith (1894–1937), American blues singer.
2. Slender.
3. Strips of wood or metal used as supports in building.
4. Barrel organ or similar musical instrument played by turning a crank.

1. The journey across the Atlantic from Africa to the Americas aboard slave ships.
2. Names of slave ships. *"Estrella"*: star (Spanish). *"Esperanza"*: hope (Spanish).
3. Circle printed on a map showing compass directions. "Corposant": a fiery light that can appear on the decks of ships during electrical storms.

Deep in the festering hold thy father lies,
of his bones New England pews are made,
those are altar lights that were his eyes.[4]

Jesus   Saviour   Pilot   Me   20
Over   Life's   Tempestuous   Sea[5]

We pray that Thou wilt grant, O Lord,
safe passage to our vessels bringing
heathen souls unto Thy chastening.

Jesus   Saviour   25

"8 bells. I cannot sleep, for I am sick
with fear, but writing eases fear a little
since still my eyes can see these words take shape
upon the page & so I write, as one
would turn to exorcism. 4 days scudding,[6]   30
but now the sea is calm again. Misfortune
follows in our wake like sharks (our grinning
tutelary[7] gods). Which one of us
has killed an albatross?[8] A plague among
our blacks—Ophthalmia: blindness—& we   35
have jettisoned the blind to no avail.
It spreads, the terrifying sickness spreads.
Its claws have scratched sight from the Capt.'s eyes
& there is blindness in the fo'c'sle[9]
& we must sail 3 weeks before we come   40
to port."

What port awaits us, Davy Jones'
or home? I've heard of slavers drifting, drifting,
playthings of wind and storm and chance, their crews
gone blind, the jungle hatred   45
crawling up on deck.

Thou   Who   Walked   On   Galilee

"Deponent[1] further sayeth *The Bella J*
left the Guinea Coast
with cargo of five hundred blacks and odd   50
for the barracoons[2] of Florida:

"That there was hardly room 'tween-decks for half
the sweltering cattle stowed spoon-fashion there;
that some went mad of thirst and tore their flesh
and sucked the blood: 55

---

4. An allusion to Shakespeare's *The Tempest* 1.2.399–401: "Full fathom five thy father lies / Of his bones are coral made / Those are pearls that were his eyes."
5. Lines from a Protestant hymn.
6. Running rapidly before the wind.
7. Guardian.

8. Sea bird thought to bring good luck; to kill one is considered a bad omen. An allusion to Samuel Taylor Coleridge's "The Rime of the Ancient Mariner."
9. I.e., forecastle; sailors' quarters aboard a ship.
1. One who gives evidence.
2. Slave quarters.

"That Crew and Captain lusted with the comeliest
of the savage girls kept naked in the cabins;
that there was one they called The Guinea Rose
and they cast lots and fought to lie with her:

"That when the Bo's'n piped all hands,[3] the flames   60
spreading from starboard already were beyond
control, the negroes howling and their chains
entangled with the flames:

"That the burning blacks could not be reached,
that the Crew abandoned ship,   65
leaving their shrieking negresses behind,
that the Captain perished drunken with the wenches:

"Further Deponent sayeth not."

Pilot   Oh   Pilot   Me

II

Aye, lad, and I have seen those factories,   70
Gambia, Rio Pongo, Calabar;[4]
have watched the artful mongos[5] baiting traps
of war wherein the victor and the vanquished

Were caught as prizes for our barracoons.
Have seen the nigger kings whose vanity   75
and greed turned wild black hides of Fellatah,
Mandingo, Ibo, Kru[6] to gold for us.

And there was one—King Anthracite we named him—
fetish face beneath French parasols
of brass and orange velvet, impudent mouth   80
whose cups were carven skulls of enemies:

He'd honor us with drum and feast and conjo[7]
and palm-oil-glistening wenches deft in love,
and for tin crowns that shone with paste,
red calico and German-silver trinkets   85

Would have the drums talk war and send
his warriors to burn the sleeping villages
and kill the sick and old and lead the young
in coffles[8] to our factories.

Twenty years a trader, twenty years,   90
for there was wealth aplenty to be harvested

3. I.e., when the boatswain (petty officer) signaled to all the crew.
4. A city in southeast Nigeria. Gambia is a West
African nation. Rio Pongo is an East African
waterway.

5. Africans.
6. African tribes.
7. Dance.
8. Trains of slaves fastened together.

from those black fields, and I'd be trading still
but for the fevers melting down my bones.

III

Shuttles in the rocking loom of history,
the dark ships move, the dark ships move,   95
their bright ironical names
like jests of kindness on a murderer's mouth;
plough through thrashing glister toward
fata morgana's[9] lucent melting shore,
weave toward New World littorals[1] that are   100
mirage and myth and actual shore.

Voyage through death,
                    voyage whose chartings are unlove.

A charnel stench, effluvium of living death
spreads outward from the hold,   105
where the living and the dead, the horribly dying,
lie interlocked, lie foul with blood and excrement.

> *Deep in the festering hold thy father lies,*
> *the corpse of mercy rots with him,*
> *rats eat love's rotten gelid eyes.*   110

But, oh, the living look at you
with human eyes whose suffering accuses you,
whose hatred reaches through the swill of dark
to strike you like a leper's claw.

You cannot stare that hatred down   115
or chain the fear that stalks the watches
and breathes on you its fetid scorching breath;
cannot kill the deep immortal human wish,
the timeless will.

"But for the storm that flung up barriers   120
of wind and wave, *The Amistad*,[2] señores,
would have reached the port of Príncipe in two,
three days at most; but for the storm we should
have been prepared for what befell.
Swift as the puma's leap it came. There was   125
that interval of moonless calm filled only
with the water's and the rigging's usual sounds,
then sudden movement, blows and snarling cries
and they had fallen on us with machete
and marlinspike. It was as though the very   130
air, the night itself were striking us.
Exhausted by the rigors of the storm,
we were no match for them. Our men went down

9. A mirage.
1. Shores.
2. Friendship (Spanish); a Spanish ship carrying fifty-three illegally obtained slaves out of
Havana, Cuba, in July 1839.

before the murderous Africans.[3] Our loyal
Celestino ran from below with gun   135
and lantern and I saw, before the cane-
knife's wounding flash, Cinquez,
that surly brute who calls himself a prince,
directing, urging on the ghastly work.
He hacked the poor mulatto down, and then   140
he turned on me. The decks were slippery
when daylight finally came. It sickens me
to think of what I saw, of how these apes
threw overboard the butchered bodies of
our men, true Christians all, like so much jetsam.   145
Enough, enough. The rest is quickly told:
Cinquez was forced to spare the two of us
you see to steer the ship to Africa,
and we like phantoms doomed to rove the sea
voyaged east by day and west by night,   150
deceiving them, hoping for rescue,
prisoners on our own vessel, till
at length we drifted to the shores of this
your land, America, where we were freed
from our unspeakable misery. Now we   155
demand, good sirs, the extradition of
Cinquez and his accomplices to La
Havana.[4] And it distresses us to know
there are so many here who seem inclined
to justify the mutiny of these blacks.   160
We find it paradoxical indeed
that you whose wealth, whose tree of liberty
are rooted in the labor of your slaves
should suffer the august John Quincy Adams[5]
to speak with so much passion of the right   165
of chattel slaves to kill their lawful masters
and with his Roman rhetoric weave a hero's
garland for Cinquez. I tell you that
we are determined to return to Cuba
with our slaves and there see justice done. Cinquez—   170
or let us say 'the Prince'—Cinquez shall die."

The deep immortal human wish,
the timeless will:

Cinquez its deathless primaveral image,
life that transfigures many lives.   175

Voyage through death
                    to life upon these shores.

                                                                    1962

3. During the mutiny the Africans, led by a man called Cinqué, or Cinquez, killed the captain, his slave Celestino, and the mate, but spared the two slave owners.
4. *The Amistad* reached Long Island Sound after two months, where it was detained by the American ship *Washington*; the slaves were impris-

oned, and the owners were freed. The owners began litigation to force the slaves' return to Havana to be tried for murder.
5. The case reached the Supreme Court in 1841; the Africans were defended by former president John Quincy Adams, and the court released the thirty-seven survivors to Africa.

Those Winter Sundays

Sundays too my father got up early
and put his clothes on in the blueblack cold,
then with cracked hands that ached
from labor in the weekday weather made
banked fires blaze. No one ever thanked him.   5

I'd wake and hear the cold splintering, breaking.
When the rooms were warm, he'd call,
and slowly I would rise and dress,
fearing the chronic angers of that house,

Speaking indifferently to him,   10
who had driven out the cold
and polished my good shoes as well.
What did I know, what did I know
of love's austere and lonely offices?

1962

O Daedalus, Fly Away Home[1]

(For Maia and Julie)

Drifting night in the Georgia pines,
coonskin drum and jubilee banjo.
    Pretty Malinda, dance with me.
Night is juba, night is conjo.[2]
    Pretty Malinda, dance with me.   5

Night is an African juju[3] man
weaving a wish and a weariness together
    to make two wings.

    O fly away home fly away

Do you remember Africa?   10

    O cleave the air fly away home

My gran, he flew back to Africa,
just spread his arms and
    flew away home.

---

1. In Greek mythology, Daedalus and his son, Icarus, were imprisoned by the Minotaur in a labyrinth (designed by Daedalus himself). He made wings of wax and feathers so he and Icarus could escape, but when Icarus flew too close to the sun, the wax binding together the wings melted and he fell into the sea and drowned. Daedalus escaped to Sicily.
2. "Conjo" and "juba" are dances.
3. Endowed with magical powers; a West African belief.

Drifting night in the windy pines; 15
night is a laughing, night is a longing.
    Pretty Malinda, come to me.

Night is a mourning juju man
weaving a wish and a weariness together
    to make two wings. 20

    O fly away home fly away

1962

Runagate[1] Runagate

I

Runs falls rises stumbles on from darkness into darkness
and the darkness thicketed with shapes of terror
and the hunters pursuing and the hounds pursuing
and the night cold and the night long and the river
to cross and the jack-muh-lanterns beckoning beckoning 5
and blackness ahead and when shall I reach that somewhere
morning and keep on going and never turn back and keep on going
    Runagate
            Runagate
                    Runagate 10
Many thousands rise and go
many thousands crossing over

                    O mythic North
              O star-shaped yonder Bible city
Some go weeping and some rejoicing 15
some in coffins and some in carriages
some in silks and some in shackles

    Rise and go or fare you well

No more auction block for me
no more driver's lash for me 20

    If you see my Pompey, 30 yrs of age,
    new breeches, plain stockings, negro shoes;
    if you see my Anna, likely young mulatto
    branded E on the right cheek, R^2 on the left,
    catch them if you can and notify subscriber. 25
    Catch them if you can, but it won't be easy.
    They'll dart underground when you try to catch them,
    plunge into quicksand, whirlpools, mazes,
    turn into scorpions when you try to catch them.

And before I'll be a slave 30
I'll be buried in my grave

---

1. Runaway (archaic).
2. The letters *ER* stand for Elizabeth Regina, or Elizabeth I of England.

North star and bonanza gold
I'm bound for the freedom, freedom-bound
and oh Susyanna don't you cry for me

Runagate   35

Runagate

II

Rises from their anguish and their power,

Harriet Tubman,[3]

woman of earth, whipscarred,
a summoning, a shining   40

Mean to be free

And this was the way of it, brethren brethren,
way we journeyed from Can't to Can.
Moon so bright and no place to hide,
the cry up and the patterollers[4] riding,   45
hound dogs belling in bladed air.
And fear starts a-murbling, Never make it,
we'll never make it. *Hush that now,*
and she's turned upon us, levelled pistol
glinting in the moonlight: 50
Dead folks can't jaybird-talk, she says;
you keep on going now or die, she says.

Wanted   Harriet Tubman   alias The General
alias Moses   Stealer of Slaves
In league with Garrison   Alcott   Emerson[5]   55
Garrett   Douglass   Thoreau   John Brown[6]

Armed and known to be Dangerous

Wanted   Reward   Dead or Alive

Tell me, Ezekiel[7] oh tell me do you see
mailed Jehovah[8] coming to deliver me?   60
Hoot-owl calling in the ghosted air,
five times calling to the hands in the air.

---

3. Slave-born American abolitionist (1820?–1913) who helped hundreds of enslaved African Americans escape through the Underground Railroad.
4. White patrollers of southern plantations whose job was to prevent slaves from escaping.
5. Ralph Waldo Emerson (1803–1882), American philosopher. William Lloyd Garrison (1805–1879), American abolitionist and social reformer. Amos Bronson Alcott (1799–1888), American educator and philosopher.

6. U. S. abolitionist (1800–1859), hanged for treason after planning a slave rebellion and leading a raid on Harpers Ferry. Thomas Garrett (1789–1871), American abolitionist, instrumental in the Underground Railroad. Frederick Douglass (1817?–1895), American abolitionist and statesman. Henry David Thoreau (1817–1862), American author.
7. An old Testament prophet.
8. God (Hebrew).

Shadow of a face in the scary leaves,
shadow of a voice in the talking leaves:

Come ride-a my train   65

Oh that train, ghost-story train
through swamp and savanna movering movering,
over trestles of dew, through caves of the wish,
Midnight Special on a sabre track movering movering,
first stop Mercy and the last Hallelujah.   70

Come ride-a my train

Mean mean mean to be free.

1962

Frederick Douglass[1]

When it is finally ours, this freedom, this liberty, this beautiful
and terrible thing, needful to man as air,
usable as earth; when it belongs at last to all,
when it is truly instinct, brain matter, diastole, systole,[2]
reflex action; when it is finally won; when it is more   5
than the gaudy mumbo jumbo of politicians:
this man, this Douglass, this former slave, this Negro
beaten to his knees, exiled, visioning a world
where none is lonely, none hunted, alien,
this man, superb in love and logic, this man   10
shall be remembered. Oh, not with statues' rhetoric,
not with legends and poems and wreaths of bronze alone,
but with the lives grown out of his life, the lives
fleshing his dream of the beautiful, needful thing.

1962

A Ballad of Remembrance

Quadroon[1] mermaids, Afro angels, black saints
balanced upon the switchblades of that air
and sang. Tight streets unfolding to the eye
like fans of corrosion and elegiac lace
crackled with their singing: Shadow of time. Shadow of blood.   5

Shadow, echoed the Zulu king, dangling
from a cluster of balloons. Blood,

---

1. Slave-born American abolitionist and statesman (1817?–1895).
2. The regular contraction of the heart that
pushes the blood outward into the blood vessels.

"Diastole": the rhythmic dilation and relaxation
of the heart during which it fills with blood.
1. A person having one quarter black ancestry.

whined the gun-metal priestess, floating
over the courtyard where dead men diced.

What will you have? she inquired, the sallow vendeuse[2]   10
of prepared tarnishes and jokes of nacre and ormolu,[3]
what but those gleamings, oldrose[4] graces,
manners like scented gloves? Contrived ghosts
rapped to metronome clack of lavalieres.[5]

Contrived illuminations riding a threat   15
of river, masked Negroes wearing chameleon
satins gaudy now as a fortuneteller's
dream of disaster, lighted the crazy flopping
dance of love and hate among joys, rejections.

Accommodate, muttered the Zulu king,   20
toad on a throne of glaucous[6] poison jewels.
Love, chimed the saints and the angels and the mermaids.
Hate, shrieked the gun-metal priestess
from her spiked bellcollar curved like a fleur-de-lis:[7]

As well have a talon as a finger, a muzzle as a mouth,   25
as well have a hollow as a heart. And she pinwheeled
away in coruscations[8] of laughter, scattering
those others before her like foil stars.

But the dance continued—now among metaphorical
doors, coffee cups floating poised   30
hysterias, decors of illusion; now among
mazurka[9] dolls offering death's-heads
of cocaine roses and real violets.

Then you arrived, meditative, ironic,
richly human; and your presence was shore where I rested   35
released from the hoodoo[1] of that dance, where I spoke
with my true voice again.

And therefore this is not only a ballad of remembrance
for the down-South arcane city[2] with death
in its jaws like gold teeth and archaic cusswords;   40
not only a token for the troubled generous friends
held in the fists of that schizoid city like flowers,
but also, Mark Van Doren,[3]
a poem of remembrance, a gift, a souvenir for you.

                                                    1962

---

2. Vendor (French, feminine).
3. An alloy of copper, tin, and zinc that looks like gold. "Nacre": mother-of-pearl.
4. Grayish.
5. Ornamental pendants. "Metronome": an instrument that marks off an exact tempo by a series of clicks.
6. Sea green.
7. A stylized iris; armorial symbol of French royalty. "Bellcollar": device used to torture slaves, especially women suspected of having an abortion, in which case the collar remained on their necks until they had a child.
8. Sparkles of light.
9. Polish dance.
1. Syncretistic blend of African and Christian religious beliefs; also called *voodoo*.
2. New Orleans during Mardi Gras.
3. American man of letters (1894–1972), a friend of Hayden's.

Mourning Poem for the Queen of Sunday

Lord's lost Him His mockingbird,
His fancy warbler;
Satan sweet-talked her,
four bullets hushed her.
Who would have thought   5
she'd end that way?

Four bullets hushed her. And the world a-clang with evil.
Who's going to make old hardened sinner men tremble now
and the righteous rock?
Oh who and oh who will sing Jesus down   10
to help with struggling and doing without and being colored
all through blue Monday?
Till way next Sunday?

All those angels
in their cretonne[1] clouds and finery   15
the true believer saw
when she rared back her head and sang,
all those angels are surely weeping.
Who would have thought
she'd end that way?   20

Four holes in her heart. The gold works wrecked.
But she looks so natural in her big bronze coffin
among the Broken Hearts and Gates-Ajar,
it's as if any moment she'd lift her head
from its pillow of chill gardenias   25
and turn this quiet into shouting Sunday
and make folks forget what she did on Monday.

Oh, Satan sweet-talked her,
and four bullets hushed her.
Lord's lost Him His diva,   30
His fancy warbler's gone.
Who would have thought,
who would have thought she'd end that way?

1962

Soledad[1]

(And I, I am no longer of that world)

Naked, he lies in the blinded room
chainsmoking, cradled by drugs, by jazz
as never by any lover's cradling flesh.

1. White.
1. Aloneness or loneliness (Spanish).

Miles Davis coolly blows for him:
O *pena negra*, sensual Flamenco[2] blues;   5
the red clay foxfire voice of Lady Day[3]

(lady of the pure black magnolias)
sobsings her sorrow and loss and fare you well,
dryweeps the pain his treacherous jailers

have released him from for a while.   10
His fears and his unfinished self
await him down in the anywhere streets.

He hides on the dark side of the moon,
takes refuge in a stained-glass cell,
flies to a clockless country of crystal.   15

Only the ghost of Lady Day knows where
he is. Only the music. And he swings
oh swings: beyond complete immortal now.

1970

El-Hajj Malik El-Shabazz[1]

(Malcolm X)

O masks and metamorphoses of Ahab, Native Son

I

The icy evil that struck his father down
and ravished his mother into madness
trapped him in violence of a punished self
struggling to break free.

As Home Boy, as Dee-troit Red,   5
he fled his name, became the quarry of
his own obsessed pursuit.
He conked his hair and Lindy-hopped,[2]
zoot-suited[3] jiver, swinging those chicks
in the hot rose and reefer glow.   10

His injured childhood bullied him.
He skirmished in the Upas trees[4]
and cannibal flowers of the American Dream—

---

2. A southern Spanish music and dance. "O *pena negra*": Oh dark pain (Spanish).
3. Billie Holiday (1915–1959), American jazz singer whose career was eventually ended by drug addiction.
1. Arabic name of Malcolm X, African American religious and political leader, assassinated in 1965, purportedly by Black Muslims, from whom he had split in 1963.
2. Jitter-bugged; danced energetically. "Conked": straightened.
3. Wearing a zootsuit, a man's suit with baggy, tight-cuffed trousers and an oversize jacket, popular in the 1940s.
4. Tropical trees whose milky sap is used for arrow poison.

but could not hurt the enemy
powered against him there.   15

II

Sometimes the dark that gave his life
its cold satanic sheen would shift
a little, and he saw himself
floodlit and eloquent;

yet how could he, "Satan" in The Hole,   20
guess what the waking dream foretold?

Then false dawn of vision came;
he fell upon his face before
a racist Allah[5] pledged to wrest him from
the hellward-thrusting hands of Calvin's[6] Christ—   25

to free him and his kind
from Yakub's[7] white-faced treachery.
He rose redeemed from all but prideful anger,
though adulterate attars[8] could not cleanse
him of the odors of the pit.   30

III

Asalam alaikum![9]

He X'd his name, became his people's anger,
exhorted them to vengeance for their past;
rebuked, admonished them,

their scourger who   35
would shame them, drive them from
the lush ice gardens of their servitude.

Asalam alaikum!

Rejecting Ahab, he was of Ahab's tribe.
"Strike through the mask!"   40

IV

Time. "The martyr's time," he said.
Time and the karate killer,
knifer, gunman. Time that brought
ironic trophies as his faith

---

5. God (Arabic).
6. John Calvin (1509–1564), French Protestant theologian who taught the doctrine of
predestination.
7. According to the teachings of the Nation of
Islam in the United States, a black man embittered toward God who creates an evil race of
white men as a revenge against his fellow blacks
and God.
8. Perfumes.
9. Peace be unto you (Arabic).

twined sparking round the bole,   45
the fruit of neo-Islam.
"The martyr's time."

But first, the ebb time pilgrimage
toward revelation, hejira to
his final metamorphosis;   50

Labbayk![1] *Labbayk!*

He fell upon his face before
Allah the raceless in whose blazing Oneness all
were one. He rose renewed renamed, became
much more than there was time for him to be.   55

1970

A Letter from Phillis Wheatley[1]

London, 1773

   Dear Obour[2]
     Our crossing was without
event. I could not help, at times,
reflecting on that first—my Destined   5
voyage long ago (I yet
have some remembrance of its Horrors)
and marvelling at God's Ways.
    Last evening, her Ladyship[3] presented me
to her illustrious Friends.   10
I scarce could tell them anything
of Africa, though much of Boston
and my hope of Heaven. I read
my latest Elegies to them.
"O Sable[4] Muse!" the Countess cried,   15
embracing me, when I had done.
I held back tears, as is my wont,
and there were tears in Dear
Nathaniel's[5] eyes.
    At supper—I dined apart   20
like captive Royalty—
the Countess and her Guests promised
signatures affirming me
True Poetess, albeit once a slave.
Indeed, they were most kind, and spoke,   25
moreover, of presenting me

1. Here I come, O Lord (Arabic).
1. American poet (1753–1784), born in Africa and brought to the United States in slavery to work for John and Susannah Wheatley. When she was nineteen, she published *Poems on Various Subjects, Religious, and Moral*, which bore a prefatory testament by many prominent Boston citizens assuring the public that a female slave had indeed written the enclosed poems.
2. I.e., Tanner, a young, free black woman who was one of Wheatley's few friends.
3. The countess of Huntington, one of many Londoners who knew and loved Wheatley.
4. Black; an allusion to Wheatley's term *sable race* in her poem "On Being Brought from Africa to America."
5. John and Susannah Wheatley's son, who accompanied Phillis to England.

at Court (I thought of Pocahontas[6])—
an Honor, to be sure, but one,
I should, no doubt, as Patriot decline.
     My health is much improved;   30
I feel I may, if God so Wills,
entirely recover here.
Idyllic England! Alas, there is
no Eden without its Serpent. Under
the chiming Complaisance I hear him Hiss;   35
I see his flickering tongue
when foppish would-be Wits
murmur of the Yankee Pedlar
and his Cannibal Mockingbird.[7]
     Sister, forgive th'intrusion of   40
my Sombreness—Nocturnal Mood
I would not share with any save
your trusted Self. Let me disperse,
in closing, such unseemly Gloom
by mention of an Incident   45
you may, as I, consider Droll:
Today, a little Chimney Sweep,
his face and hands with soot quite Black,
staring hard at me, politely asked:
"Does you, M'lady, sweep chimneys too?"   50
I was amused, but dear Nathaniel
(ever Solicitous) was not.
     I pray the Blessings of our Lord
and Saviour Jesus Christ be yours
Abundantly. In His Name.   55

                    Phillis

                                                  1978

RALPH ELLISON
1914–1994

Ralph Waldo Ellison, who at mid-century would single-handedly rewrite the American novel as an *African American* adventure in fiction, was born in Oklahoma City on March 1, 1914. Years later Ellison would write that the frontier spirit of Oklahoma, which had achieved statehood in only 1907, had fostered in him a sense of human potential that he considered the very essence of American democracy. Elli-

6. A Native American princess (1595–1617) who is the heroine of a folk tale that recounts how she saved the life of Captain John Smith. She married Englishman John Rolfe, who presented her to the British court in 1616.
7. Insulting references to John Wheatley and Phillis herself, whose poetry's detractors found her work "merely imitative."

son's father, small businessman Lewis Alfred Ellison, died when Ellison was three; Ellison and his brother were raised by their mother, Ida Millsap, who moved the family into the parsonage of a local church. There, young Ralph, already an avid reader, was exposed to a wider world of books and popular magazines, *Vanity Fair* and *Literary Digest*, for example, brought home by his mother from the white households in which she worked as a domestic. Years later, such glimpses into a world beyond his own would evoke these memories:

> You might say that my environment was extended by these slender threads into the worlds of white families. . . . These magazines and recordings . . . spoke to me of a life that was broader and more interesting and although it was not really a part of my own life, I never thought they were not for me because I happened to be a Negro. They were things which spoke of a world which I could some day make my own.

An early interest in music developed into one of the great passions of Ellison's life and one of the great presences in his writing. During his years at the Frederick Douglass School in Oklahoma City, which he entered in 1919, Ellison studied music theory and acquired working knowledge of several brass instruments, including the trumpet. Oklahoma City was at that time, along with Kansas City, a rich experimental music scene, and Ellison heard many jazz eminences, notably King Oliver and the Old Blue Devils Band. Wanting to become a versatile musician, Ellison decided to obtain conservatory training and so entered the Tuskegee Institute on a state scholarship in 1933. At Tuskegee he was inspired by two fine teachers: William L. Dawson, director of the a cappella choir, and Hazel Harrison, a concert pianist. A sophomore-year course in the English novel introduced him to another brilliant teacher, Morteza Sprague, who in turn exposed him to the powerful influence of Eliot's *Waste Land*. Truly a Renaissance man, Ellison soon added the study of sculpture to his impressive arts repertoire.

Despite the richness of this education, Ellison left Tuskegee at the end of his junior year not just because confusion over his scholarship left him unable to pay his full tuition but also because he found Tuskegee anti-intellectual and overly accommodationist, and he could not rest easy with the state of race relations in Alabama. That same year, Ellison embarked on a pilgrimage to New York City, not unlike that of the unnamed protagonist of *Invisible Man*. In New York and living at the Harlem YMCA, he renewed his acquaintance with Alain Locke (whom he'd met during one of the philosopher's visits to Tuskegee) and was introduced to Langston Hughes. Hughes in turn provided the young man entree to Richard Wright, who was soon to begin editing the Marxist literary magazine *New Challenge*. Stimulated by their common interest in literature, Wright and Ellison were bound for an instant friendship. For Wright, Ellison offered relief from the unpleasant working atmosphere in the Harlem bureau of the *Daily Worker*; for Ellison, Wright was an informal teacher and mentor. Some of Ellison's early reviews and short fiction were submitted, with Wright's encouragement, for publication in the *New Challenge*.

His mother's death in 1937 interrupted Ellison's New York apprenticeship. Grieving, Ellison spent seven months in Ohio with his brother, Herbert, during which time he hunted and read. Having withdrawn temporarily from the challenge of the metropolis, Ellison emerged from his depression with a clear purpose: he would return to New York and become a writer. But the late 1930s in the United States were hardly an auspicious time for creative work among black intellectuals, especially as the Depression had depleted the patronage that had fed the Harlem Renaissance during the 1920s. Aspiring writers either could take on low-paying jobs, which would leave them just barely enough time to develop their craft, or could find employment with the Federal Writers' Project, in which case a bit more space could be freed up for creativity. With Wright's help, Ellison was able to do the latter, working for $103 a month collecting facts and folklore for books on African Americans. Ellison's experience interviewing Harlem residents, rather like Du Bois's interviewing black Philadelphians at the turn of the century, deepened his appreciation for folk tales and offered themes for his fiction. Doubtless, the creative synthesis in *Invisible Man*—between the folk and the modern, the city and the country, the psychic and the archetypal—had its roots, in part, in Ellison's work with the Writers' Project.

Between 1938 and 1944, Ellison produced some fifty-seven articles and eight stories; he reported on the 1943 Harlem riot for the *New York Post* and offered commentary on other significant political events of the day. Although Ellison, along with other black intellectuals of the time, was deeply attracted to Marxism, it was his doubting the ideology that in part allowed him to write his celebrated novel. Ellison's reflections on the inadequacy of Marxism for art arose out of careful consideration of texts by Marx, Engels, and Malraux but also from his friendship with Richard Wright. Close enough to Wright to be able to see *Native Son* emerge from the typewriter, Ellison, as essays in *Shadow and Act* attest, sustained mixed feelings toward his friend's magnum opus and eventually concluded that Wright's career itself gave the lie to black psychopathology as black personality's first and only truth: Wright himself was refined, interesting, and life affirming, while the protagonist of *Native Son*, Bigger Thomas, embodied the terrible spectacle of stunted modern man—devoid of imagination and purely victimized by negative social forces. Rejecting Wright's theory of naturalism, as well as radical Marxist cant, Ellison turned his attention toward a world different from Wright's fictional creation for much of his inspiration: the blues, jazz, and the tragicomedy of everyday life, as seen in tales like "Sweet Monkey." To affirm himself, his mother, and the old men who told stories in barber shops, Ellison had to depart, quite radically, from *Native Son* and the tenets that it had deployed.

Even though World War II ended the Depression by gearing up the nation's war machine, it did little to resolve the paradoxical status of African Americans. Could one really wage war against fascist evil from the swollen ranks of a segregated armed force? Ellison did not think so, and so he joined the merchant marine in 1943, serving as a cook until 1945. During the war years, Ellison met Fanny McConnell, whom he would marry in 1946. On sick leave in 1945, he wrote the following words: "I am an invisible man." Ellison nearly threw out the page, but not before attempting to imagine what kind of soul would say such a thing. Within seven years, he knew. And so did the world.

It is difficult to imagine any response to *Invisible Man* short of praise. Sure enough, on its debut in 1952 it was hailed by critics as proof that the black writer had arrived. Ellison's newfound golden status among black intellectuals, however, was marred by displeasure from the Left, where some were not happy with an apparently ironic portrait of the Communist Party contained in a chapter called "The Brotherhood"; others felt that the novel was devoid of the radical political message that black artists should communicate. Critic Oliver O. Killens, for example, called the book a "vicious distortion of Negro life," claiming that the "Negro people need[ed] Ralph Ellison's *Invisible Man* like [they] need[ed] a hole in the head or a stab in the back." Responses like Killens's demonstrated the extent to which Ellison had threatened the ideological stranglehold that had so long prevailed over the study of African American life and thought. Ellison's acceptance speech for the 1953 National Book Award acknowledged the "rhetorical canniness" of black American speech, the accents of its "rich babble" as heard in *Invisible Man*, and spoke of the novel's attempt to go beyond immediate literary predecessors like Wright and Hemingway as well as to draw on the ancestral figures of Melville and Twain, whose situating of race as a matter of importance in fiction loomed large over any writer dealing with that topic in the twentieth century.

Though a 1965 *Book Week* poll of two hundred critics voted *Invisible Man* "the most distinguished American novel written since World War II," controversy again surrounded the book late in the decade, as a young generation of black nationalists took issue with Ellison's stance on black rebellion, particularly with his treatment of the character of Ras the Destroyer. Earlier in the 1960s, white critic Irving Howe had confronted Ellison and James Baldwin for evading what he saw as the mission of the

A Memorial to Ralph Ellison and his prize-winning novel, *Invisible Man*, in Riverside Park at 150th Street in New York City. Art © Catlett Mora Family Trust/Licensed by Vaga, New York, NY

black intellectual—to foreground and protest victimization, to avoid taking comfort from the promises of Western civilization. Ellison responded with his essay "The World and the Jug," printed here, in which he spoke out against the pigeonholing of artists by race and called down the limitations of such expectations as Howe's.

Why does *Invisible Man* evoke such passionate, antagonistic responses? In part, the answer lies in its brilliant use of intertextual and cultural nuance and maneuver, from Dante to Louis Armstrong to German *lieder* to Eliot to the slave auction to Dostoevsky. In part, it arises out of the text's ability to fit simultaneously into and challenge any number of theoretical grids, from the American novel since World War II to the African American novel, from problems of canon formation to questions about minority and postcolonial discourse. *Invisible Man* defined the historic moment of mid-twentieth-century America and forced a reconsideration of the powers of fiction. As fresh today as it was in 1952, it eschews the liabilities of pathos and opens before its readership, particularly its African American readers, a new and different order of inquiry: What is the value of self-knowledge?

Over the years, Ellison taught at Bard College, the University of Chicago, and New York University, where he was the Albert Schweitzer Professor of the Humanities. In 1986 he published *Going to the Territory*, a book of essays and stories. When Ralph Ellison died of pancreatic cancer on April 16, 1994, he left behind a second, unfinished novel, published posthumously under the title *Juneteenth*. "Juneteenth" was the popular name black Texans gave their emancipation day, celebrated on June 19. This was the day Major General Gordon Granger supposedly announced that slaves were officially freed. Black folklore offers other explanations of the date, including that emancipation was declared in June because the January messenger was killed en route to Texas.

Ellison was as perceptive a literary and cultural critic as he was a novelist, and his talents shone most brilliantly in various essays and riffs within essays on music. None is perhaps more famous than his frequently quoted statement on the blues, which he described as "an impulse to keep the painful details and episodes of a brutal experience alive in one's aching consciousness, to finger the jagged grain." Taken from his essay "Richard Wright's Blues," this passage also provided Ellison one of many opportunities (as did "Remembering Richard Wright") to delineate the differences between his artistic philosophies and Richard Wright's. But it is important that the essay is no mere critique of Wright. In it Ellison also displays the breadth of his reading and the incisiveness of his thinking on a range of subjects from music to southern violence, to black structures of feeling, to the "eroticism" of black expression in religious ceremony and dance.

Never content with sociological and critical clichés or commonplace assumptions in any form, Ellison ever remained the intellectual, even in his correspondence. His letter to Stanley Hyman is a case in point. In one paragraph alone Ellison seemingly settles the long-standing criticism that Phillis Wheatley denied her racial heritage. In the process Ellison complicated the popular notion that *race* and *culture* are synonymous. But more important, he continued to insist on the multiplicity of influences on his writing, "high" and "low." Despite his scrupulous intellectual habits, Ellison kept a sharp eye out for what he termed the "unintellectualized" areas of the writer's experience and a keen ear for audibly comic tones.

Richard Wright's Blues

> If anybody ask you
> who sing this song,
> Say it was ole [Black Boy]
> done been here and gone.[1]

As a writer, Richard Wright has outlined for himself a dual role: to discover and depict the meaning of Negro experience; and to reveal to both Negroes and whites those problems of a psychological and emotional nature which arise between them, when they strive for mutual and understanding.

Now, in *Black Boy*,[2] he has used his own life to probe what qualities of will, imagination and intellect are required of a Southern Negro in order to possess the meaning of his life in the United States. Wright is an important

1. Signature formula used by blues singers at conclusion of song [Ellison's note].

2. Wright's autobiographical novel (1945).

writer, perhaps the most articulate Negro American, and what he has to say is highly perceptive. Imagine Bigger Thomas projecting his own life in lucid prose, guided, say, by the insights of Marx and Freud,[3] and you have an idea of this autobiography.

Published at a time when any sharply critical approach to Negro life has been dropped as a wartime expendable, it should do much to redefine the problem of the Negro and American Democracy. Its power can be observed in the shrill manner with which some professional "friends of the Negro people" have attempted to strangle the work in a noose of newsprint.

What in the tradition of literary autobiography is it like, this work described as a "great American autobiography"? As a non-white intellectual's statement of his relationship to Western culture, *Black Boy* recalls the conflicting pattern of identification and rejection found in Nehru's *Toward Freedom*.[4] In its use of fictional techniques, its concern with criminality (sin) and the artistic sensibility, and in its author's judgment and rejection of the narrow world of his origin, it recalls Joyce's rejection of Dublin in *A Portrait of the Artist*.[5] And as a psychological document of life under oppressive conditions, it recalls *The House of the Dead*, Dostoievsky's[6] profound study of the humanity of Russian criminals.

Such works were perhaps Wright's literary guides, aiding him to endow his life's incidents with communicable significance; providing him with ways of seeing, feeling and describing his environment. These influences, however, were encountered only after these first years of Wright's life were past and were not part of the immediate folk culture into which he was born. In that culture the specific folk-art form which helped shape the writer's attitude toward his life and which embodied the impulse that contributes much to the quality and tone of his autobiography was the Negro blues. This would bear a word of explanation:

The blues is an impulse to keep the painful details and episodes of a brutal experience alive in one's aching consciousness, to finger its jagged grain, and to transcend it, not by the consolation of philosophy but by squeezing from it a near-tragic, near-comic lyricism. As a form, the blues is an autobiographical chronicle of personal catastrophe expressed lyrically. And certainly Wright's early childhood was crammed with catastrophic incidents. In a few short years his father deserted his mother, he knew intense hunger, he became a drunkard begging drinks from black stevedores[7] in Memphis saloons; he had to flee Arkansas, where an uncle was lynched; he was forced to live with a fanatically religious grandmother in an atmosphere of constant bickering; he was lodged in an orphan asylum; he observed the suffering of his mother, who became a permanent invalid, while fighting off the blows of the poverty-stricken relatives with whom he had to live; he was cheated, beaten and kicked off jobs by white employees who disliked his eagerness to learn a trade; and to these objective circumstances must be added the subjective fact that Wright, with his sensitivity, extreme shyness and intelligence, was a problem child who rejected his family and was by them rejected.

3. Sigmund Freud (1856–1939), founder of psychoanalysis. Bigger Thomas is the male protagonist in Wright's novel *Native Son* (1940). Karl Marx (1818–1883), revolutionary, sociologist, historian, and economist.
4. Jawaharlal Nehru (1889–1964), the first prime minister of independent India (1947–64). His autobiography was published in the United States in 1941.
5. Irish author James Joyce's (1882–1941) largely autobiographical novel, published in 1916.
6. Russian author Fyodor Dostoyevsky's (1821–1881) novel based on his prison experiences, published in 1861–62.
7. Workers responsible for loading and unloading ships in port.

Thus along with the themes, equivalent descriptions of milieu and the perspectives to be found in Joyce, Nehru, Dostoievsky, George Moore and Rousseau,[8] *Black Boy* is filled with blues-tempered echoes of railroad trains, the names of Southern towns and cities, estrangements, fights and flights, deaths and disappointments, charged with physical and spiritual hungers and pain. And like a blues sung by such an artist as Bessie Smith,[9] its lyrical prose evokes the paradoxical, almost surreal image of a black boy singing lustily as he probes his own grievous wound.

In *Black Boy*, two worlds have fused, two cultures merged, two impulses of Western man become coalesced. By discussing some of its cultural sources I hope to answer those critics who would make of the book a miracle and of its author a mystery. And while making no attempt to probe the mystery of the artist (who Hemingway[1] says is "forged in injustice as a sword is forged"), I do hold that basically the prerequisites to the writing of *Black Boy* were, on the one hand, the microscopic degree of cultural freedom which Wright found in the South's stony injustice, and, on the other, the existence of a personality agitated to a state of almost manic restlessness. There were, of course, other factors, chiefly ideological; but these came later.

Wright speaks of his journey north as

> . . . taking a part of the South to transplant in alien soil, to see if it could grow differently, if it could drink of new and cool rains, bend in strange winds, respond to the warmth of other suns, and perhaps, to bloom. . . .

And just as Wright, the man, represents the blooming of the delinquent child of the autobiography, just so does *Black Boy* represent the flowering—cross-fertilized by pollen blown by the winds of strange cultures—of the humble blues lyric. There is, as in all acts of creation, a world of mystery in this, but there is also enough that is comprehensible for Americans to create the social atmosphere in which other black boys might freely bloom.

For certainly, in the historical sense, Wright is no exception. Born on a Mississippi plantation, he was subjected to all those blasting pressures which in a scant eighty years have sent the Negro people hurtling, without clearly defined trajectory, from slavery to emancipation, from log cabin to city tenement, from the white folks' fields and kitchens to factory assembly lines; and which, between two wars, have shattered the wholeness of its folk consciousness into a thousand writhing pieces.

Black Boy describes this process in the personal terms of *one* Negro childhood. Nevertheless, several critics have complained that it does not "explain" Richard Wright. Which, aside from the notion of art involved, serves to remind us that the prevailing mood of American criticism has so thoroughly excluded the Negro that it fails to recognize some of the most basic tenets of Western democratic thought when encountering them in a black skin. They forget that human life possesses an innate dignity and mankind an innate sense of nobility; that all men possess the tendency to dream and the compulsion to make their dreams reality; that the need to be ever dissatisfied and the urge ever to seek satisfaction is implicit in the human organism; and that all men are the victims and the beneficiaries of the goading, tormenting, commanding and informing activity of that imperious process

---

8. Jean-Jacques Rousseau (1712–1778), French political philosopher. Moore (1851–1933), Irish novelist and man of letters.

9. American blues singer (1898?–1937).
1. Ernest Hemingway (1899–1961), American novelist and short story writer.

known as the Mind—the Mind, as Valéry[2] describes it, "armed with its inexhaustible questions."

Perhaps all this (in which lies the very essence of the human, and which Wright takes for granted) has been forgotten because the critics recognize neither Negro humanity nor the full extent to which the Southern community renders the fulfillment of human destiny impossible. And while it is true that *Black Boy* presents an almost unrelieved picture of a personality corrupted by brutal environment, it also presents those fresh, human responses brought to its world by the sensitive child:

> There was the *wonder* I felt when I first saw a brace of mountainlike, spotted, black-and-white horses clopping down a dusty road . . . the *delight* I caught in seeing long straight rows of red and green vegetables stretching away in the sun . . . the faint, cool kiss of *sensuality* when dew came on to my cheeks . . . the vague *sense of the infinite* as I looked down upon the yellow, dreaming waters of the Mississippi . . . the echoes of *nostalgia* I heard in the crying strings of wild geese . . . the *love* I had for the mute regality of tall, moss-clad oaks . . . the hint of *cosmic cruelty* that I *felt* when I saw the curved timbers of a wooden shack that had been warped in the summer sun . . . and there was the *quiet terror* that suffused my senses when vast hazes of gold washed earthward from star-heavy skies on silent nights. . . . [3]

And a bit later, his reactions to religion:

> Many of the religious symbols appealed to my sensibilities and I responded to the dramatic vision of life held by the church, feeling that to live day by day with death as one's sole thought was to be so compassionately sensitive toward all life as to view all men as slowly dying, and the trembling sense of fate that welled up, sweet and melancholy, from the hymns blended with the sense of fate that I had already caught from life.

There was also the influence of his mother—so closely linked to his hysteria and sense of suffering—who (though he only implies it here) taught him, in the words of the dedication prefacing *Native Son*,[4] "to revere the fanciful and the imaginative." There were also those white men—the one who allowed Wright to use his library privileges and the other who advised him to leave the South, and still others whose offers of friendship he was too frightened to accept.

Wright assumed that the nucleus of plastic sensibility is a human heritage: the right and the opportunity to dilate, deepen and enrich sensibility—democracy. Thus the drama of *Black Boy* lies in its depiction of what occurs when Negro sensibility attempts to fulfill itself in the undemocratic South. Here it is not the individual that is the immediate focus, as in Joyce's *Stephen Hero*,[5] but that upon which his sensibility was nourished.

Those critics who complain that Wright has omitted the development of his own sensibility hold that the work thus fails as art. Others, because it presents too little of what they consider attractive in Negro life, charge that it distorts reality. Both groups miss a very obvious point: That whatever else the environment contained, it had as little chance of prevailing against the

---

2. Paul Valéry (1871–1945), French poet, essayist, and critic.
3. Italics mine [Ellison's note].

4. One of Wright's novels (1940).
5. Protagonist of Joyce's *Portrait of the Artist* (see p. 248, n. 5).

overwhelming weight of the child's unpleasant experiences as Beethoven's[6] Quartets would have of destroying the stench of a Nazi prison.

We come, then, to the question of art. The function, the psychology, of artistic selectivity is to eliminate from art form all those elements of experience which contain no compelling significance. Life is as the sea, art a ship in which man conquers life's crushing formlessness, reducing it to a course, a series of swells, tides and wind currents inscribed on a chart. Though drawn from the world, "the organized significance of art," writes Malraux,[7] "is stronger than all the multiplicity of the world; . . . that significance alone enables man to conquer chaos and to master destiny."

Wright saw his destiny—that combination of forces before which man feels powerless—in terms of a quick and casual violence inflicted upon him by both family and community. His response was likewise violent, and it has been his need to give that violence significance which has shaped his writings.

What were the ways by which other Negroes confronted their destiny?

In the South of Wright's childhood there were three general ways: They could accept the role created for them by the whites and perpetually resolve the resulting conflicts through the hope and emotional cartharsis of Negro religion; they could repress their dislike of Jim Crow[8] social relations while striving for a middle way of respectability, becoming—consciously or unconsciously—the accomplices of the whites in oppressing their brothers; or they could reject the situation, adopt a criminal attitude, and carry on an unceasing psychological scrimmage with the whites, which often flared forth into physical violence.

Wright's attitude was nearest the last. Yet in it there was an all-important qualitative difference: it represented a groping for *individual* values, in a black community whose values were what the young Negro critic, Edward Bland, has defined as "pre-individual." And herein lay the setting for the extreme conflict set off, both within his family and in the community, by Wright's assertion of individuality. The clash was sharpest on the psychological level, for, to quote Bland:

> In the pre-individualistic thinking of the Negro the stress is on the group. Instead of seeing in terms of the individual, the Negro sees in terms of "races," masses of peoples separated from other masses according to color. Hence, an act rarely bears intent against him as a Negro individual. He is singled out not as a person but as a specimen of an ostracized group. He knows that he never exists in his own right but only to the extent that others hope to make the race suffer vicariously through him.

This pre-individual state is induced artificially—like the regression to primitive states noted among cultured inmates of Nazi prisons. The primary technique in its enforcement is to impress the Negro child with the omniscience and omnipotence of the whites to the point that whites appear as ahuman as Jehovah, and as relentless as a Mississippi flood. Socially it is

---

6. Ludwig van Beethoven (1770–1827), German composer.
7. André-Georges Malraux (1901–1976), French novelist, art historian, and statesman.

8. Any of the laws that enforced racial segregation in the South between the end of the formal Reconstruction period (1877) and the beginning of the strong civil rights movement of the 1950s.

effected through an elaborate scheme of taboos supported by a ruthless physical violence, which strikes not only the offender but the entire black community. To wander from the paths of behavior laid down for the group is to become the agent of communal disaster.

In such a society the development of individuality depends upon a series of accidents, which often arise, as in Wright's case, from conditions within the Negro family. In Wright's life there was the accident that as a small child he could not distinguish between his fair-skinned grandmother and the white women of the town, thus developing skepticism as to their special status. To this was linked the accident of his having no close contacts with whites until after the child's normal formative period.

But these objective accidents not only link forward to these qualities of rebellion, criminality and intellectual questioning expressed in Wright's work today. They also link backward into the shadow of infancy where environment and consciousness are so darkly intertwined as to require the skill of a psychoanalyst to define their point of juncture. Nevertheless, at the age of four, Wright set the house afire and was beaten near to death by his frightened mother. This beating, followed soon by his father's desertion of the family, seems to be the initial psychological motivation of his quest for a new identification. While delirious from this beating Wright was haunted "by huge wobbly white bags like the full udders of a cow, suspended from the ceiling above me [and] I was gripped by the fear that they were going to fall and drench me with some horrible liquid . . ."

It was as though the mother's milk had turned acid, and with it the whole pattern of life that had produced the ignorance, cruelty and fear that had fused with mother-love and exploded in the beating. It is significant that the bags were of the hostile color white, and the female symbol that of the cow, the most stupid (and, to the small child, the most frightening) of domestic animals. Here in dream symbolism is expressed an attitude worthy of an Orestes.[9] And the significance of the crisis is increased by virtue of the historical fact that the lower-class Negro family is matriarchal; the child turns not to the father to compensate if he feels mother-rejection, but to the grandmother, or to an aunt—and Wright rejected both of these. Such rejection leaves the child open to psychological insecurity, distrust and all of those hostile environmental forces from which the family functions to protect it.

One of the Southern Negro family's methods of protecting the child is the severe beating—a homeopathic dose of the violence generated by black and white relationships. Such beatings as Wright's were administered for the child's own good; a good which the child resisted, thus giving family relationships an undercurrent of fear and hostility, which differs qualitatively from that found in patriarchal middle-class families, because here the severe beating is administered by the mother; leaving the child no parental sanctuary. He must ever embrace violence along with maternal tenderness, or else reject, in his helpless way, the mother.

The division between the Negro parents of Wright's mother's generation, whose sensibilities were often bound by their proximity to the slave experience, and their children, who historically and through the rapidity of American change stand emotionally and psychologically much farther

9. In Greek mythology, son of Agamemnon and Clytemnestra. He avenged his father's death by killing his mother.

away, is quite deep. Indeed, sometimes as deep as the cultural distance between Yeats'[1] *Autobiographies* and a Bessie Smith blues. This is the historical background to those incidents of family strife in *Black Boy* which have caused reviewers to question Wright's judgment of Negro emotional relationships.

We have here a problem in the sociology of sensibility that is obscured by certain psychological attitudes brought to Negro life by whites.

The first is the attitude which compels whites to impute to Negroes sentiments, attitudes and insights which, as a group living under certain definite social conditions, Negroes could not humanly possess. It is the identical mechanism which William Empson[2] identifies in literature as "pastoral." It implies that since Negroes possess the richly human virtues credited to them, then their social position is advantageous and should not be bettered; and, continuing syllogistically, the white individual need feel no guilt over his participation in Negro oppression.

The second attitude is that which leads whites to misjudge Negro passion, looking upon it as they do, out of the turgidity of their own frustrated yearning for emotional warmth, their capacity for sensation having been constricted by the impersonal mechanized relationships typical of bourgeois society. The Negro is idealized into a symbol of sensation, of unhampered social and sexual relationships. And when *Black Boy* questions their illusion they are thwarted much in the manner of the occidental who, after observing the erotic character of a primitive dance, "shacks up" with a native woman—only to discover that far from possessing the hair-trigger sexual responses of a Stork Club[3] "babe," she is relatively phlegmatic.

The point is not that American Negroes are primitives, but that as a group their social situation does not provide for the type of emotional relationships attributed them. For how could the South, recognized as a major part of the backward third of the nation, nurture in the black, most brutalized section of its population, those forms of human relationships achievable only in the most highly developed areas of civilization?

Champions of this "Aren't-Negroes-Wonderful?" school of thinking often bring Paul Robeson and Marian Anderson[4] forward as examples of highly developed sensibility, but actually they are only its *promise*. Both received their development from an extensive personal contact with European culture, free from the influences which shape Southern Negro personality. In the United States, Wright, who is the only Negro literary artist of equal caliber, had to wait years and escape to another environment before discovering the moral and ideological equivalents of his childhood attitudes.

Man cannot express that which does not exist—either in the form of dreams, ideas or realities—in his environment. Neither his thoughts nor his feelings, his sensibility nor his intellect are fixed, innate qualities. They are processes which arise out of the interpenetration of human instinct with environment, through the process called experience; each changing and being changed by the other. Negroes cannot possess many of the sentiments attributed to them because the same changes in environment which, through experience, enlarge man's intellect (and thus his capacity for still greater

---

1. William Butler Yeats (1865–1939), Irish poet, dramatist, and prose writer.
2. British poet and critic (1906–1984).
3. Famous New York City night club.
4. American singer (1897–1993). Robeson (1898–1976), American singer, actor, and black activist.

change) also modify his feelings; which in turn increase his sensibility, i.e., his sensitivity, to refinements of impression and subtleties of emotion. The extent of these changes depends upon the quality of political and cultural freedom in the environment.

Intelligence tests have measured the quick rise in intellect which takes place in Southern Negroes after moving north, but little attention has been paid to the mutations effected in their sensibilities. However, the two go hand in hand. Intellectual complexity is accompanied by emotional complexity; refinement of thought, by refinement of feeling. The movement north affects more than the Negro's wage scale, it affects his entire psychosomatic structure.

The rapidity of Negro intellectual growth in the North is due partially to objective factors present in the environment, to influences of the industrial city and to a greater political freedom. But there are also changes within the "inner world." In the North energies are released and given *intellectual* channelization—energies which in most Negroes in the South have been forced to take either a *physical* form or, as with potentially intellectual types like Wright, to be expressed as nervous tension, anxiety and hysteria. Which is nothing mysterious. The human organism responds to environmental stimuli by converting them into either physical and / or intellectual energy. And what is called hysteria is suppressed intellectual energy expressed physically.

The "physical" character of their expression makes for much of the difficulty in understanding American Negroes. Negro music and dances are frenziedly erotic; Negro religious ceremonies violently ecstatic; Negro speech strongly rhythmical and weighted with image and gesture. But there is more in this sensuousness than the unrestraint and insensitivity found in primitive cultures; nor is it simply the relatively spontaneous and undifferentiated responses of a people living in close contact with the soil. For despite Jim Crow, Negro life does not exist in a vacuum, but in the seething vortex of those tensions generated by the most highly industrialized of Western nations. The welfare of the most humble black Mississippi sharecropper is affected less by the flow of the seasons and the rhythm of natural events than by the fluctuations of the stock market; even though, as Wright states of his father, the sharecropper's memories, actions and emotions are shaped by his immediate contact with nature and the crude social relations of the South.

All of this makes the American Negro far different from the "simple" specimen for which he is taken. And the "physical" quality offered as evidence of his primitive simplicity is actually the form of his complexity. The American Negro is a Western type whose social condition creates a state which is almost the reverse of the cataleptic trance: Instead of his consciousness being lucid to the reality around it while the body is rigid, here it is the body which is alert, reacting to pressures which the constricting forces of Jim Crow block off from the transforming, concept-creating activity of the brain. The "eroticism" of Negro expression springs from much the same conflict as that displayed in the violent gesturing of a man who attempts to express a complicated concept with a limited vocabulary; thwarted ideational energy is converted into unsatisfactory pantomime, and his words are burdened with meanings they cannot convey. Here lies the source of the basic ambiguity of *Native Son*, wherein in order to translate Bigger's complicated feelings into universal ideas, Wright had to force into Bigger's consciousness concepts and ideas which his intellect could not formulate. Between

Wright's skill and knowledge and the potentials of Bigger's mute feelings lay a thousand years of conscious culture.

In the South the sensibilities of both blacks and whites are inhibited by the rigidly defined environment. For the Negro there is relative safety as long as the impulse toward individuality is suppressed. (Lynchings have occurred because Negroes painted their homes.) And it is the task of the Negro family to adjust the child to the Southern milieu; through it the currents, tensions and impulses generated within the human organism by the flux and flow of events are given their distribution. This also gives the group its distinctive character. Which, because of Negroes' suppressed minority position, is very much in the nature of an elaborate but limited defense mechanism. Its function is dual: to protect the Negro from whirling away from the undifferentiated mass of his people into the unknown, symbolized in its most abstract form by insanity, and most concretely by lynching; and to protect him from those unknown forces *within himself* which might urge him to reach out for that social and human equality which the white South says he cannot have. Rather than throw himself against the charged wires of his prison he annihilates the impulses within him.

The pre-individualistic black community discourages individuality out of self-defense. Having learned through experience that the whole group is punished for the actions of the single member, it has worked out efficient techniques of behavior control. For in many Southern communities everyone knows everyone else and is vulnerable to his opinions. In some communities everyone is "related" regardless of blood-ties. The regard shown by the group for its members, its general communal character and its cohesion are often mentioned. For by comparison with the coldly impersonal relationships of the urban industrial community, its relationships are personal and warm.

Black Boy, however, illustrates that this personal quality, shaped by outer violence and inner fear, is ambivalent. Personal warmth is accompanied by an equally personal coldness, kindliness by cruelty, regard by malice. And these opposites are as quickly set off against the member who gestures toward individuality as a lynch mob forms at the cry of rape. Negro leaders have often been exasperated by this phenomenon, and Booker T. Washington[5] (who demanded far less of Negro humanity than Richard Wright) described the Negro community as a basket of crabs, wherein should one attempt to climb out, the others immediately pull him back.

The member who breaks away is apt to be more impressed by its negative than by its positive character. He becomes a stranger even to his relatives and he interprets gestures of protection as blows of oppression—from which there is no hiding place, because every area of Negro life is affected. Even parental love is given a qualitative balance akin to "sadism." And the extent of beatings and psychological maimings meted out by Southern Negro parents rivals those described by the nineteenth-century Russian writers as characteristic of peasant life under the Czars. The horrible thing is that the cruelty is also an expression of concern, of love.

In discussing the inadequacies for democratic living typical of the education provided Negroes by the South, a Negro educator has coined the term

5. Educator and reformer (1856–1915).

mis-education. Within the ambit of the black family this takes the form of training the child away from curiosity and adventure, against reaching out for those activities lying beyond the borders of the black community. And when the child resists, the parent discourages him; first with the formula, "That there's for white folks. Colored can't have it," and finally with a beating.

It is not, then, the family and communal violence described by *Black Boy* that is unusual, but that Wright *recognized* and made no peace with its essential cruelty—even when, like a babe freshly emerged from the womb, he could not discern where his own personality ended and it began. Ordinarily both parent and child are protected against this cruelty—seeing it as love and finding subjective sanction for it in the spiritual authority of the Fifth Commandment[6] and on the secular level in the legal and extralegal structure of the Jim Crow system. The child who did not rebel, or who was unsuccessful in his rebellion, learned a masochistic submissiveness and a denial of the impulse toward Western culture when it stirred within him.

Why then have Southern whites, who claim to "know" the Negro, missed all this? Simply because they, too, are armored against the horror and the cruelty. Either they deny the Negro's humanity and feel no cause to measure his actions against civilized norms; or they protect themselves from their guilt in the Negro's condition and from their fear that their cooks might poison them, or that their nursemaids might strangle their infant charges, or that their field hands might do them violence, by attributing to them a superhuman capacity for love, kindliness and forgiveness. Nor does this in any way contradict their stereotyped conviction that all Negroes (meaning those with whom they have no contact) are given to the most animal behavior.

It is only when the individual, whether white or black, *rejects* the pattern that he awakens to the nightmare of his life. Perhaps much of the South's regressive character springs from the fact that many, jarred by some casual crisis into wakefulness, flee hysterically into the sleep of violence or the coma of apathy again. For the penalty of wakefulness is to encounter ever more violence and horror than the sensibilities can sustain unless translated into some form of social action. Perhaps the impassioned character so noticeable among those white Southern liberals so active in the Negro's cause is due to their sense of accumulated horror; their passion—like the violence in Faulkner's[7] novels—is evidence of a profound spiritual vomiting.

This compulsion is even more active in Wright and the increasing number of Negroes who have said an irrevocable "no" to the Southern pattern. Wright learned that it is not enough merely to reject the white South, but that he had also to reject that part of the South which lay within. As a rebel he formulated that rejection negatively, because it was the negative face of the Negro community upon which he looked most often as a child. It is this he is contemplating when he writes:

> Whenever I thought of the essential bleakness of black life in America, I knew that Negroes had never been allowed to catch the full spirit of Western civilization, that they lived somehow in it but not of it. And

6. "Honor thy father and thy mother" (Exodus 20.12).

7. William Faulkner (1897–1962), American novelist and short story writer.

when I brooded upon the cultural barrenness of black life, I wondered if clean, positive tenderness, love, honor, loyalty and the capacity to remember were native to man. I asked myself if these human qualities were not fostered, won, struggled and suffered for, preserved in ritual from one generation to another.

But far from implying that Negroes have no capacity for culture, as one critic interprets it, this is the strongest affirmation that they have. Wright is pointing out what should be obvious (especially to his Marxist critics) that Negro sensibility is socially and historically conditioned; that Western culture must be won, confronted like the animal in a Spanish bullfight, dominated by the red shawl of codified experience and brought heaving to its knees.

Wright knows perfectly well that Negro life is a by-product of Western civilization, and that in it, if only one possesses the humanity and humility to see, are to be discovered all those impulses, tendencies, life and cultural forms to be found elsewhere in Western society.

The problem arises because the special condition of Negroes in the United States, including the defensive character of Negro life itself (the "will toward organization" noted in the Western capitalist appears in the Negro as a will to camouflage, to dissimulate), so distorts these forms as to render their recognition as difficult as finding a wounded quail against the brown and yellow leaves of a Mississippi thicket—even the spilled blood blends with the background. Having himself been in the position of the quail—to expand the metaphor—Wright's wounds have told him both the question and the answer which every successful hunter must discover for himself: "Where would I hide if *I* were a wounded quail?" But perhaps that requires more sympathy with one's quarry than most hunters possess. Certainly it requires such a sensitivity to the shifting guises of humanity under pressure as to allow them to identify themselves with the human content, whatever its outer form; and even with those Southern Negroes to whom Paul Robeson's name is only a rolling sound in the fear-charged air.

Let us close with one final word about the blues: Their attraction lies in this, that they at once express both the agony of life and the possibility of conquering it through sheer toughness of spirit. They fall short of tragedy only in that they provide no solution, offer no scapegoat but the self. Nowhere in America today is there social or political action based upon the solid realities of Negro life depicted in *Black Boy*; perhaps that is why, with its refusal to offer solutions, it is like the blues. Yet in it thousands of Negroes will for the first time see their destiny in public print. Freed here of fear and the threat of violence, their lives have at last been organized, scaled down to possessable proportions. And in this lies Wright's most important achievement: He has converted the American Negro impulse toward self-annihilation and "going-under-ground"[8] into a will to confront the world, to evaluate his experience honestly and throw his findings unashamedly into the guilty conscience of America.

1945

---

8. I.e., living in hiding.

From Invisible Man

Prologue

I am an invisible man. No, I am not a spook like those who haunted Edgar Allan Poe; nor am I one of your Hollywood-movie ectoplasms. I am a man of substance, of flesh and bone, fiber and liquids—and I might even be said to possess a mind. I am invisible, understand, simply because people refuse to see me. Like the bodiless heads you see sometimes in circus sideshows, it is as though I have been surrounded by mirrors of hard, distorting glass. When they approach me they see only my surroundings, themselves, or figments of their imagination—indeed, everything and anything except me.

Nor is my invisibility exactly a matter of a biochemical accident to my epidermis. That invisibility to which I refer occurs because of a peculiar disposition of the eyes of those with whom I come in contact. A matter of the construction of their *inner* eyes, those eyes with which they look through their physical eyes upon reality. I am not complaining, nor am I protesting either. It is sometimes advantageous to be unseen, although it is most often rather wearing on the nerves. Then too, you're constantly being bumped against by those of poor vision. Or again, you often doubt if you really exist. You wonder whether you aren't simply a phantom in other people's minds. Say, a figure in a nightmare which the sleeper tries with all his strength to destroy. It's when you feel like this that, out of resentment, you begin to bump people back. And, let me confess, you feel that way most of the time. You ache with the need to convince yourself that you do exist in the real world, that you're a part of all the sound and anguish, and you strike out with your fists, you curse and you swear to make them recognize you. And, alas, it's seldom successful.

One night I accidentally bumped into a man, and perhaps because of the near darkness he saw me and called me an insulting name. I sprang at him, seized his coat lapels and demanded that he apologize. He was a tall blond man, and as my face came close to his he looked insolently out of his blue eyes and cursed me, his breath hot in my face as he struggled. I pulled his chin down sharp upon the crown of my head, butting him as I had seen the West Indians do, and I felt his flesh tear and the blood gush out, and I yelled, "Apologize! Apologize!" But he continued to curse and struggle, and I butted him again and again until he went down heavily, on his knees, profusely bleeding. I kicked him repeatedly, in a frenzy because he still uttered insults though his lips were frothy with blood. Oh yes, I kicked him! And in my outrage I got out my knife and prepared to slit his throat, right there beneath the lamplight in the deserted street, holding him in the collar with one hand, and opening the knife with my teeth—when it occurred to me that the man had not *seen* me, actually; that he, as far as he knew, was in the midst of a walking nightmare! And I stopped the blade, slicing the air as I pushed him away, letting him fall back to the street. I stared at him hard as the lights of a car stabbed through the darkness. He lay there, moaning on the asphalt; a man almost killed by a phantom. It unnerved me. I was both disgusted and ashamed. I was like a drunken man myself, wavering about on weakened legs. Then I was amused: Something in this man's thick head had sprung out and beaten him within an inch of his life. I began to laugh at this crazy discovery. Would he have awakened at the point of death? Would Death himself have freed him for wakeful living? But I didn't linger. I ran away into the dark, laughing so hard I feared I might rupture myself. The next day I saw his picture in the *Daily News,* beneath a caption stating that he had been "mugged." Poor fool, poor blind fool, I thought with sincere compassion, mugged by an invisible man!

Most of the time (although I do not choose as I once did to deny the violence of my days by ignoring it) I am not so overtly violent. I remember that I am invisible and walk softly so as not to awaken the sleeping ones. Sometimes it is best not to awaken them; there are few things in the world as dangerous as sleepwalkers. I learned in time though that it is possible to carry on a fight against them without their realizing it. For instance, I have been carrying on a fight with Monopolated Light & Power for some time now. I use their service and pay them nothing at all, and they don't know it. Oh, they suspect that power is being drained off, but they don't know where. All they know is that according to the master meter back there in their power station a hell of a lot of free current is disappearing somewhere into the jungle of Harlem. The joke, of course, is that I don't live in Harlem but in a border area. Several years ago (before I discovered the advantages of being invisible) I went through the routine process of buying service and paying their outrageous rates. But no more. I gave up all that, along with my apartment, and my old way of life: That way based upon the fallacious assumption that I, like other men, was visible. Now, aware of my invisibility, I live rent-free in a building rented strictly to whites, in a section of the basement that was shut off and forgotten during the nineteenth century, which I discovered when I was trying to escape in the night from Ras the Destroyer. But that's getting too far ahead of the story, almost to the end, although the end is in the beginning and lies far ahead.

The point now is that I found a home—or a hole in the ground, as you will. Now don't jump to the conclusion that because I call my home a "hole" it is damp and cold like a grave; there are cold holes and warm holes. Mine is a warm hole. And remember, a bear retires to his hole for the winter and lives until spring; then he comes strolling out like the Easter chick breaking from its shell. I say all this to assure you that it is incorrect to assume that, because I'm invisible and live in a hole, I am dead. I am neither dead nor in a state of suspended animation. Call me Jack-the-Bear,[1] for I am in a state of hibernation.

My hole is warm and full of light. Yes, *full* of light. I doubt if there is a brighter spot in all New York than this hole of mine, and I do not exclude Broadway. Or the Empire State Building on a photographer's dream night. But that is taking advantage of you. Those two spots are among the darkest of our whole civilization—pardon me, our whole *culture* (an important distinction, I've heard)—which might sound like a hoax, or a contradiction, but that (by contradiction, I mean) is how the world moves: Not like an arrow, but a boomerang. (Beware of those who speak of the *spiral* of history; they are preparing a boomerang. Keep a steel helmet handy.) I know; I have been boomeranged across my head so much that I now can see the darkness of lightness. And I love light. Perhaps you'll think it strange that an invisible man should need light, desire light, love light. But maybe it is exactly because I *am* invisible. Light confirms my reality, gives birth to my form. A beautiful girl once told me of a recurring nightmare in which she lay in the center of

1. The title of a 1940 recording by jazz musician Duke Ellington (1899–1974) and his orchestra.

a large dark room and felt her face expand until it filled the whole room, becoming a formless mass while her eyes ran in bilious jelly up the chimney. And so it is with me. Without light I am not only invisible, but formless as well; and to be unaware of one's form is to live a death. I myself, after existing some twenty years, did not become alive until I discovered my invisibility.

That is why I fight my battle with Monopolated Light & Power. The deeper reason, I mean: It allows me to feel my vital aliveness. I also fight them for taking so much of my money before I learned to protect myself. In my hole in the basement there are exactly 1,369 lights. I've wired the entire ceiling, every inch of it. And not with fluorescent bulbs, but with the older, more-expensive-to-operate kind, the filament type. An act of sabotage, you know. I've already begun to wire the wall. A junk man I know, a man of vision, has supplied me with wire and sockets. Nothing, storm or flood, must get in the way of our need for light and ever more and brighter light. The truth is the light and light is the truth. When I finish all four walls, then I'll start on the floor. Just how that will go, I don't know. Yet when you have lived invisible as long as I have you develop a certain ingenuity. I'll solve the problem. And maybe I'll invent a gadget to place my coffee pot on the fire while I lie in bed, and even invent a gadget to warm my bed—like the fellow I saw in one of the picture magazines who made himself a gadget to warm his shoes! Though invisible, I am in the great American tradition of tinkers. That makes me kin to Ford, Edison and Franklin. Call me, since I have a theory and a concept, a "thinker-tinker." Yes, I'll warm my shoes; they need it, they're usually full of holes. I'll do that and more.

Now I have one radio-phonograph; I plan to have five. There is a certain acoustical deadness in my hole, and when I have music I want to *feel* its vibration, not only with my ear but with my whole body. I'd like to hear five recordings of Louis Armstrong[2] playing and singing "What Did I Do to Be so Black and Blue"—all at the same time. Sometimes now I listen to Louis while I have my favorite dessert of vanilla ice cream and sloe gin. I pour the red liquid over the white mound, watching it glisten and the vapor rising as Louis bends that military instrument into a beam of lyrical sound. Perhaps I like Louis Armstrong because he's made poetry out of being invisible. I think it must be because he's unaware that he *is* invisible. And my own grasp of invisibility aids me to understand his music. Once when I asked for a cigarette, some jokers gave me a reefer, which I lighted when I got home and sat listening to my phonograph. It was a strange evening. Invisibility, let me explain, gives one a slightly different sense of time, you're never quite on the beat. Sometimes you're ahead and sometimes behind. Instead of the swift and imperceptible flowing of time, you are aware of its nodes, those points where time stands still or from which it leaps ahead. And you slip into the breaks and look around. That's what you hear vaguely in Louis' music.

Once I saw a prizefighter boxing a yokel. The fighter was swift and amazingly scientific. His body was one violent flow of rapid rhythmic action. He hit the yokel a hundred times while the yokel held up his arms in stunned surprise. But suddenly the yokel, rolling about in the gale of boxing gloves, struck one blow and knocked science, speed and footwork as cold as a well-digger's posterior. The smart money hit the canvas. The long shot got the nod. The yokel had simply stepped inside of his opponent's sense of time. So

2. African American jazz musician (1900–1971).

under the spell of the reefer I discovered a new analytical way of listening to music. The unheard sounds came through, and each melodic line existed of itself, stood out clearly from all the rest, said its piece, and waited patiently for the other voices to speak. That night I found myself hearing not only in time, but in space as well. I not only entered the music but descended, like Dante, into its depths. And *beneath the swiftness of the hot tempo there was a slower tempo and a cave and I entered it and looked around and heard an old woman singing a spiritual as full of Weltschmerz[3] as flamenco, and beneath that lay a still lower level on which I saw a beautiful girl the color of ivory pleading in a voice like my mother's as she stood before a group of slave-owners who bid for her naked body, and below that I found a lower level and a more rapid tempo and I heard someone shout:*

"Brothers and sisters, my text this morning is the 'Blackness of Blackness.'"

And a congregation of voices answered: "That blackness is most black, brother, most black . . ."

"In the beginning . . ."

"At the very start," they cried.

". . . there was blackness . . ."

"Preach it . . ."

". . . and the sun . . ."

"The sun, Lawd . . ."

". . . was bloody red . . ."

"Red . . ."

"Now black is . . ." the preacher shouted.

"Bloody . . ."

"I said black is . . ."

"Preach it, brother . . ."

". . . an' black ain't . . ."

"Red, Lawd, red: He said it's red!"

"Amen, brother . . ."

"Black will git you . . ."

"Yes, it will . . ."

"Yes, it will . . ."

". . . an' black won't . . ."

"Naw, it won't!"

"It do . . ."

"It do, Lawd . . ."

". . . an' it don't."

"Halleluiah . . ."

". . . It'll put you, glory, glory, Oh my Lawd, in the WHALE'S BELLY."

"Preach it, dear brother . . ."

". . . an' make you tempt . . ."

"Good God a-mighty!"

"Old Aunt Nelly!"

"Black will make you . . ."

"Black . . ."

". . . or black will un-make you."

"Ain't it the truth, Lawd?"

And at that point a voice of trombone timbre screamed at me, "Git out of here, you fool! Is you ready to commit treason?"

---

3. Sadness or world weariness (German).

And I tore myself away, hearing the old singer of spirituals moaning, "Go curse your God, boy, and die."

I stopped and questioned her, asked her what was wrong.

"I dearly loved my master, son," she said.

"You should have hated him," I said.

"He gave me several sons," she said, "and because I loved my sons I learned to love their father though I hated him too."

"I too have become acquainted with ambivalence," I said. "That's why I'm here."

"What's that?"

"Nothing, a word that doesn't explain it. Why do you moan?"

"I moan this way 'cause he's dead," she said.

"Then tell me, who is that laughing upstairs?"

"Them's my sons. They glad."

"Yes, I can understand that too," I said.

"I laughs too, but I moans too. He promised to set us free but he never could bring hisself to do it. Still I loved him . . ."

"Loved him? You mean . . . ?"

"Oh yes, but I loved something else even more."

"What more?"

"Freedom."

"Freedom," I said. "Maybe freedom lies in hating."

"Naw, son, it's in loving. I loved him and give him the poison and he withered away like a frost-bit apple. Them boys woulda tore him to pieces with they homemade knives."

"A mistake was made somewhere," I said, "I'm confused." And I wished to say other things, but the laughter upstairs became too loud and moan-like for me and I tried to break out of it, but I couldn't. Just as I was leaving I felt an urgent desire to ask her what freedom was and went back. She sat with her head in her hands, moaning softly; her leather-brown face was filled with sadness.

"Old woman, what is this freedom you love so well?" I asked around a corner of my mind.

She looked surprised, then thoughtful, then baffled. "I done forgot, son. It's all mixed up. First I think it's one thing, then I think it's another. It gits my head to spinning. I guess now it ain't nothing but knowing how to say what I got up in my head. But it's a hard job, son. Too much is done happen to me in too short a time. Hit's like I have a fever. Ever' time I starts to walk my head gits to swirling and I falls down. Or if it ain't that, it's the boys; they gits to laughing and wants to kill up the white folks. They's bitter, that's what they is . . ."

"But what about freedom?"

"Leave me 'lone, boy; my head aches!"

I left her, feeling dizzy myself. I didn't get far.

Suddenly one of the sons, a big fellow six feet tall, appeared out of nowhere and struck me with his fist.

"What's the matter, man?" I cried.

"You made Ma cry!"

"But how?" I said, dodging a blow.

"Askin' her them questions, that's how. Git outa here and stay, and next time you got questions like that, ask yourself!"

He held me in a grip like cold stone, his fingers fastening upon my windpipe until I thought I would suffocate before he finally allowed me to go. I stumbled about dazed, the music beating hysterically in my ears. It was dark. My head *cleared and I wandered down a dark narrow passage, thinking I heard his foot-steps hurrying behind me. I was sore, and into my being had come a profound craving for tranquillity, for peace and quiet, a state I felt I could never achieve. For one thing, the trumpet was blaring and the rhythm was too hectic. A tom-tom beating like heart-thuds began drowning out the trumpet, filling my ears. I longed for water and I heard it rushing through the cold mains my fingers touched as I felt my way, but I couldn't stop to search because of the footsteps behind me.*

"Hey, Ras," I called. "Is it you, Destroyer? Rinehart?"

No answer, only the rhythmic footsteps behind me. Once I tried crossing the road, but a speeding machine struck me, scraping the skin from my leg as it roared past.

Then somehow I came out of it, ascending hastily from this underworld of sound to hear Louis Armstrong innocently asking,

> *What did I do*
> *To be so black*
> *And blue?*

At first I was afraid; this familiar music had demanded action, the kind of which I was incapable, and yet had I lingered there beneath the surface I might have attempted to act. Nevertheless, I know now that few really listen to this music. I sat on the chair's edge in a soaking sweat, as though each of my 1,369 bulbs had every one become a klieg light[4] in an individual setting for a third degree with Ras and Rinehart in charge. It was exhausting—as though I had held my breath continuously for an hour under the terrifying serenity that comes from days of intense hunger. And yet, it was a strangely satisfying experience for an invisible man to hear the silence of sound. I had discovered unrecognized compulsions of my being—even though I could not answer "yes" to their promptings. I haven't smoked a reefer since, however; not because they're illegal, but because to *see* around corners is enough (that is not unusual when you are invisible). But to hear around them is too much; it inhibits action. And despite Brother Jack and all that sad, lost period of the Brotherhood, I believe in nothing if not in action.

Please, a definition: A hibernation is a covert preparation for a more overt action.

Besides, the drug destroys one's sense of time completely. If that happened, I might forget to dodge some bright morning and some cluck would run me down with an orange and yellow street car, or a bilious bus! Or I might forget to leave my hole when the moment for action presents itself.

Meanwhile I enjoy my life with the compliments of Monopolated Light & Power. Since you never recognize me even when in closest contact with me, and since, no doubt, you'll hardly believe that I exist, it won't matter if you know that I tapped a power line leading into the building and ran it into my hole in the ground. Before that I lived in the darkness into which I was chased, but now I see. I've illuminated the blackness of my invisibility— and vice versa. And so I play the invisible music of my isolation. The last statement doesn't seem just right, does it? But it is; you hear this music simply because music is heard and seldom seen, except by musicians. Could this compulsion to put invisibility down in black and white be thus an urge to make music of invisibility? But I am an orator, a rabble rouser—Am? I

---

4. Powerful arc light once widely used when filming motion pictures.

was, and perhaps shall be again. Who knows? All sickness is not unto death, neither is invisibility.

I can hear you say, "What a horrible, irresponsible bastard!" And you're right. I leap to agree with you. I am one of the most irresponsible beings that ever lived. Irresponsibility is part of my invisibility; any way you face it, it is a denial. But to whom can I be responsible, and why should I be, when you refuse to see me? And wait until I reveal how truly irresponsible I am. Responsibility rests upon recognition, and recognition is a form of agreement. Take the man whom I almost killed: Who was responsible for that near murder—I? I don't think so, and I refuse it. I won't buy it. You can't give it to me. *He* bumped *me, he* insulted *me.* Shouldn't he, for his own personal safety, have recognized my hysteria, my "danger potential"? He, let us say, was lost in a dream world. But didn't *he* control that dream world—which, alas, is only too real!—and didn't *he* rule me out of it? And if he had yelled for a policeman, wouldn't *I* have been taken for the offending one? Yes, yes, yes! Let me agree with you, I was the irresponsible one; for I should have used my knife to protect the higher interests of society. Some day that kind of foolishness will cause us tragic trouble. All dreamers and sleepwalkers must pay the price, and even the invisible victim is responsible for the fate of all. But I shirked that responsibility; I became too snarled in the incompatible notions that buzzed within my brain. I was a coward . . .

But what did *I* do to be so blue? Bear with me.

Chapter 1.

[BATTLE ROYAL]

It goes a long way back, some twenty years. All my life I had been looking for something, and everywhere I turned someone tried to tell me what it was. I accepted their answers too, though they were often in contradiction and even self-contradictory. I was naïve. I was looking for myself and asking everyone except myself questions which I, and only I, could answer. It took me a long time and much painful boomeranging of my expectations to achieve a realization everyone else appears to have been born with: That I am nobody but myself. But first I had to discover that I am an invisible man!

And yet I am no freak of nature, nor of history. I was in the cards, other things having been equal (or unequal) eighty-five years ago. I am not ashamed of my grandparents for having been slaves. I am only ashamed of myself for having at one time been ashamed. About eighty-five years ago they were told that they were free, united with others of our country in everything pertaining to the common good, and, in everything social, separate like the fingers of the hand. And they believed it. They exulted in it. They stayed in their place, worked hard, and brought up my father to do the same. But my grandfather is the one. He was an odd old guy, my grandfather, and I am told I take after him. It was he who caused the trouble. On his death-bed he called my father to him and said, "Son, after I'm gone I want you to keep up the good fight. I never told you, but our life is a war and I have been a traitor all my born days, a spy in the enemy's country ever since I give up my gun back in the Reconstruction.[5] Live with your head in the lion's mouth. I

5. Period of readjustment (1865–77) following the Civil War; black civil and political rights were highly contested at this time.

want you to overcome 'em with yeses, undermine 'em with grins, agree 'em to death and destruction, let 'em swoller you till they vomit or bust wide open." They thought the old man had gone out of his mind. He had been the meekest of men. The younger children were rushed from the room, the shades drawn and the flame of the lamp turned so low that it sputtered on the wick like the old man's breathing. "Learn it to the younguns," he whispered fiercely; then he died.

But my folks were more alarmed over his last words than over his dying. It was as though he had not died at all, his words caused so much anxiety. I was warned emphatically to forget what he had said and, indeed, this is the first time it has been mentioned outside the family circle. It had a tremendous effect upon me, however. I could never be sure of what he meant. Grandfather had been a quiet old man who never made any trouble, yet on his deathbed he had called himself a traitor and a spy, and he had spoken of his meekness as a dangerous activity. It became a constant puzzle which lay unanswered in the back of my mind. And whenever things went well for me I remembered my grandfather and felt guilty and uncomfortable. It was as though I was carrying out his advice in spite of myself. And to make it worse, everyone loved me for it. I was praised by the most lily-white men of the town. I was considered an example of desirable conduct—just as my grandfather had been. And what puzzled me was that the old man had defined it as *treachery*. When I was praised for my conduct I felt a guilt that in some way I was doing something that was really against the wishes of the white folks, that if they had understood they would have desired me to act just the opposite, that I should have been sulky and mean, and that that really would have been what they wanted, even though they were fooled and thought they wanted me to act as I did. It made me afraid that some day they would look upon me as a traitor and I would be lost. Still I was more afraid to act any other way because they didn't like that at all. The old man's words were like a curse. On my graduation day I delivered an oration in which I showed that humility was the secret, indeed, the very essence of progress. (Not that I believed this—how could I, remembering my grandfather?—I only believed that it worked.) It was a great success. Everyone praised me and I was invited to give the speech at a gathering of the town's leading white citizens. It was a triumph for our whole community.

It was in the main ballroom of the leading hotel. When I got there I discovered that it was on the occasion of a smoker, and I was told that since I was to be there anyway I might as well take part in the battle royal to be fought by some of my schoolmates as part of the entertainment. The battle royal came first.

All of the town's big shots were there in their tuxedoes, wolfing down the buffet foods, drinking beer and whiskey and smoking black cigars. It was a large room with a high ceiling. Chairs were arranged in neat rows around three sides of a portable boxing ring. The fourth side was clear, revealing a gleaming space of polished floor. I had some misgivings over the battle royal, by the way. Not from a distaste for fighting, but because I didn't care too much for the other fellows who were to take part. They were tough guys who seemed to have no grandfather's curse worrying their minds. No one could mistake their toughness. And besides, I suspected that fighting a battle royal might detract from the dignity of my speech. In those pre-invisible days I visualized myself as a potential Booker T. Washington.[6] But the other fellows didn't care too much for me either, and there were nine of them. I felt superior to them in my way, and I didn't like the manner in which we were all crowded together into the servants' elevator. Nor did they like my being there. In fact, as the warmly lighted floors flashed past the elevator we had words over the fact that I, by taking part in the fight, had knocked one of their friends out of a night's work.

We were led out of the elevator through a rococo hall into an anteroom and told to get into our fighting togs. Each of us was issued a pair of boxing gloves and ushered out into the big mirrored hall, which we entered looking cautiously about us and whispering, lest we might accidentally be heard above the noise of the room. It was foggy with cigar smoke. And already the whiskey was taking effect. I was shocked to see some of the most important men of the town quite tipsy. They were all there—bankers, lawyers, judges, doctors, fire chiefs, teachers, merchants. Even one of the more fashionable pastors. Something we could not see was going on up front. A clarinet was vibrating sensuously and the men were standing up and moving eagerly forward. We were a small tight group, clustered together, our bare upper bodies touching and shining with anticipatory sweat; while up front the big shots were becoming increasingly excited over something we still could not see. Suddenly I heard the school superintendent, who had told me to come, yell, "Bring up the shines, gentlemen! Bring up the little shines!"

We were rushed up to the front of the ballroom, where it smelled even more strongly of tobacco and whiskey. Then we were pushed into place. I almost wet my pants. A sea of faces, some hostile, some amused, ringed around us, and in the center, facing us, stood a magnificent blonde—stark naked. There was dead silence. I felt a blast of cold air chill me. I tried to back away, but they were behind me and around me. Some of the boys stood with lowered heads, trembling. I felt a wave of irrational guilt and fear. My teeth chattered, my skin turned to goose flesh, my knees knocked. Yet I was strongly attracted and looked in spite of myself. Had the price of looking been blindness, I would have looked. The hair was yellow like that of a circus kewpie doll, the face heavily powdered and rouged, as though to form an abstract mask, the eyes hollow and smeared a cool blue, the color of a baboon's butt. I felt a desire to spit upon her as my eyes brushed slowly over her body. Her breasts were firm and round as the domes of East Indian temples, and I stood so close as to see the fine skin texture and beads of pearly perspiration glistening like dew around the pink and erected buds of her nipples. I wanted at one and the same time to run from the room, to sink through the floor, or go to her and cover her from my eyes and the eyes of the others with my body; to feel the soft thighs, to caress her and destroy her, to love her and murder her, to hide from her, and yet to stroke where below the small American flag tattooed upon her belly her thighs formed a capital V. I had a notion that of all in the room she saw only me with her impersonal eyes.

And then she began to dance, a slow sensuous movement; the smoke of a hundred cigars clinging to her like the thinnest of veils. She seemed like a fair bird-girl girdled in veils calling to me from the angry surface of some gray and threatening sea. I was transported. Then I became aware of the clarinet

6. Slave-born American educator (1856–1915), founder of the Tuskegee Institute in Alabama, an industrial training school. He emphasized the priority of economic equality for African Americans over social equality.

playing and the big shots yelling at us. Some threatened us if we looked and others if we did not. On my right I saw one boy faint. And now a man grabbed a silver pitcher from a table and stepped close as he dashed ice water upon him and stood him up and forced two of us to support him as his head hung and moans issued from his thick bluish lips. Another boy began to plead to go home. He was the largest of the group, wearing dark red fighting trunks much too small to conceal the erection which projected from him as though in answer to the insinuating low-registered moaning of the clarinet. He tried to hide himself with his boxing gloves.

And all the while the blonde continued dancing, smiling faintly at the big shots who watched her with fascination, and faintly smiling at our fear. I noticed a certain merchant who followed her hungrily, his lips loose and drooling. He was a large man who wore diamond studs in a shirtfront which swelled with the ample paunch underneath, and each time the blonde swayed her undulating hips he ran his hand through the thin hair of his bald head and, with his arms upheld, his posture clumsy like that of an intoxicated panda, wound his belly in a slow and obscene grind. This creature was completely hypnotized. The music had quickened. As the dancer flung herself about with a detached expression on her face, the men began reaching out to touch her. I could see their beefy fingers sink into the soft flesh. Some of the others tried to stop them and she began to move around the floor in graceful circles, as they gave chase, slipping and sliding over the polished floor. It was mad. Chairs went crashing, drinks were spilt, as they ran laughing and howling after her. They caught her just as she reached a door, raised her from the floor, and tossed her as college boys are tossed at a hazing, and above her red, fixed-smiling lips I saw the terror and disgust in her eyes, almost like my own terror and that which I saw in some of the other boys. As I watched, they tossed her twice and her soft breasts seemed to flatten against the air and her legs flung wildly as she spun. Some of the more sober ones helped her to escape. And I started off the floor, heading for the anteroom with the rest of the boys.

Some were still crying and in hysteria. But as we tried to leave we were stopped and ordered to get into the ring. There was nothing to do but what we were told. All ten of us climbed under the ropes and allowed ourselves to be blindfolded with broad bands of white cloth. One of the men seemed to feel a bit sympathetic and tried to cheer us up as we stood with our backs against the ropes. Some of us tried to grin. "See that boy over there?" one of the men said. "I want you to run across at the bell and give it to him right in the belly. If you don't get him, I'm going to get you. I don't like his looks." Each of us was told the same. The blindfolds were put on. Yet even then I had been going over my speech. In my mind each word was as bright as flame. I felt the cloth pressed into place, and frowned so that it would be loosened when I relaxed.

But now I felt a sudden fit of blind terror. I was unused to darkness. It was as though I had suddenly found myself in a dark room filled with poisonous cottonmouths. I could hear the bleary voices yelling insistently for the battle royal to begin.

"Get going in there!"

"Let me at that big nigger!"

I strained to pick up the school superintendent's voice, as though to squeeze some security out of that slightly more familiar sound.

"Let me at those black sonsabitches!" someone yelled.

"No, Jackson, no!" another voice yelled. "Here, somebody, help me hold Jack."

"I want to get at that ginger-colored nigger. Tear him limb from limb," the first voice yelled.

I stood against the ropes trembling. For in those days I was what they called ginger-colored, and he sounded as though he might crunch me between his teeth like a crisp ginger cookie.

Quite a struggle was going on. Chairs were being kicked about and I could hear voices grunting as with a terrific effort. I wanted to see, to see more desperately than ever before. But the blindfold was tight as a thick skin-puckering scab and when I raised my gloved hands to push the layers of white aside a voice yelled, "Oh, no you don't, black bastard! Leave that alone!"

"Ring the bell before Jackson kills him a coon!" someone boomed in the sudden silence. And I heard the bell clang and the sound of the feet scuffing forward.

A glove smacked against my head. I pivoted, striking out stiffly as someone went past, and felt the jar ripple along the length of my arm to my shoulder. Then it seemed as though all nine of the boys had turned upon me at once. Blows pounded me from all sides while I struck out as best I could. So many blows landed upon me that I wondered if I were not the only blindfolded fighter in the ring, or if the man called Jackson hadn't succeeded in getting me after all.

Blindfolded, I could no longer control my motions. I had no dignity. I stumbled about like a baby or a drunken man. The smoke had become thicker and with each new blow it seemed to sear and further restrict my lungs. My saliva became like hot bitter glue. A glove connected with my head, filling my mouth with warm blood. It was everywhere. I could not tell if the moisture I felt upon my body was sweat or blood. A blow landed hard against the nape of my neck. I felt myself going over, my head hitting the floor. Streaks of blue light filled the black world behind the blindfold. I lay prone, pretending that I was knocked out, but felt myself seized by hands and yanked to my feet. "Get going, black boy! Mix it up!" My arms were like lead, my head smarting from blows. I managed to feel my way to the ropes and held on, trying to catch my breath. A glove landed in my mid-section and I went over again, feeling as though the smoke had become a knife jabbed into my guts. Pushed this way and that by the legs milling around me, I finally pulled erect and discovered that I could see the black, sweat-washed forms weaving in the smoky-blue atmosphere like drunken dancers weaving to the rapid drum-like thuds of blows.

Everyone fought hysterically. It was complete anarchy. Everybody fought everybody else. No group fought together for long. Two, three, four, fought one, then turned to fight each other, were themselves attacked. Blows landed below the belt and in the kidney, with the gloves open as well as closed, and with my eye partly opened now there was not so much terror. I moved carefully, avoiding blows, although not too many to attract attention, fighting from group to group. The boys groped about like blind, cautious crabs crouching to protect their mid-sections, their heads pulled in short against their shoulders, their arms stretched nervously before them, with their fists testing the smoke-filled air like the knobbed feelers of hypersensitive snails. In one corner I glimpsed a boy violently punching the air and heard him scream in pain as he smashed his hand against a ring post. For a second I saw him bent over holding his hand, then going down as a blow caught his unprotected head. I played one group against the other, slipping in and throwing a punch then stepping out of range while pushing the others into the melee to take the blows blindly aimed at me. The smoke was agonizing and there were no rounds, no bells at three minute intervals to relieve our exhaustion. The room spun round me, a swirl of lights, smoke, sweating bodies surrounded by tense white faces. I bled from both nose and mouth, the blood spattering upon my chest.

The men kept yelling, "Slug him, black boy! Knock his guts out!"

"Uppercut him! Kill him! Kill that big boy!"

Taking a fake fall, I saw a boy going down heavily beside me as though we were felled by a single blow, saw a sneaker-clad foot shoot into his groin as the two who had knocked him down stumbled upon him. I rolled out of range, feeling a twinge of nausea.

The harder we fought the more threatening the men became. And yet, I had begun to worry about my speech again. How would it go? Would they recognize my ability? What would they give me?

I was fighting automatically when suddenly I noticed that one after another of the boys was leaving the ring. I was surprised, filled with panic, as though I had been left alone with an unknown danger. Then I understood. The boys had arranged it among themselves. It was the custom for the two men left in the ring to slug it out for the winner's prize. I discovered this too late. When the bell sounded two men in tuxedoes leaped into the ring and removed the blindfold. I found myself facing Tatlock, the biggest of the gang. I felt sick at my stomach. Hardly had the bell stopped ringing in my ears than it clanged again and I saw him moving swiftly toward me. Thinking of nothing else to do I hit him smash on the nose. He kept coming, bringing the rank sharp violence of stale sweat. His face was a black blank of a face, only his eyes alive—with hate of me and aglow with a feverish terror from what had happened to us all. I became anxious. I wanted to deliver my speech and he came at me as though he meant to beat it out of me. I smashed him again and again, taking his blows as they came. Then on a sudden impulse I struck him lightly and as we clinched, I whispered, "Fake like I knocked you out, you can have the prize."

"I'll break your behind," he whispered hoarsely.

"For *them?*"

"For *me,* sonofabitch!"

They were yelling for us to break it up and Tatlock spun me half around with a blow, and as a joggled camera sweeps in a reeling scene, I saw the howling red faces crouching tense beneath the cloud of blue-gray smoke. For a moment the world wavered, unraveled, flowed, then my head cleared and Tatlock bounced before me. That fluttering shadow before my eyes was his jabbing left hand. Then falling forward, my head against his damp shoulder, I whispered,

"I'll make it five dollars more."

"Go to hell!"

But his muscles relaxed a trifle beneath my pressure and I breathed, "Seven?"

"Give it to your ma," he said, ripping me beneath the heart.

And while I still held him I butted him and moved away. I felt myself bombarded with punches. I fought back with hopeless desperation. I wanted to deliver my speech more than anything else in the world, because I felt that only these men could judge truly my ability, and now this stupid clown was ruining my chances. I began fighting carefully now, moving in to punch him and out again with my greater speed. A lucky blow to his chin and I had him going too—until I heard a loud voice yell, "I got my money on the big boy."

Hearing this, I almost dropped my guard. I was confused: Should I try to win against the voice out there? Would not this go against my speech, and was not this a moment for humility, for nonresistance? A blow to my head as I danced about sent my right eye popping like a jack-in-the-box and settled my dilemma. The room went red as I fell. It was a dream fall, my body languid and fastidious as to where to land, until the floor became impatient and smashed up to meet me. A moment later I came to. An hypnotic voice said FIVE emphatically. And I lay there, hazily watching a dark red spot of my own blood shaping itself into a butterfly, glistening and soaking into the soiled gray world of the canvas.

When the voice drawled TEN I was lifted up and dragged to a chair. I sat dazed. My eye pained and swelled with each throb of my pounding heart and I wondered if now I would be allowed to speak. I was wringing wet, my mouth still bleeding. We were grouped along the wall now. The other boys ignored me as they congratulated Tatlock and speculated as to how much they would be paid. One boy whimpered over his smashed hand. Looking up front, I saw attendants in white jackets rolling the portable ring away and placing a small square rug in the vacant space surrounded by chairs. Perhaps, I thought, I will stand on the rug to deliver my speech.

Then the M.C. called to us, "Come on up here boys and get your money."

We ran forward to where the men laughed and talked in their chairs, waiting. Everyone seemed friendly now.

"There it is on the rug," the man said. I saw the rug covered with coins of all dimensions and a few crumpled bills. But what excited me, scattered here and there, were the gold pieces.

"Boys, it's all yours," the man said. "You get all you grab."

"That's right, Sambo," a blond man said, winking at me confidentially.

I trembled with excitement, forgetting my pain. I would get the gold and the bills, I thought. I would use both hands. I would throw my body against the boys nearest me to block them from the gold.

"Get down around the rug now," the man commanded, "and don't anyone touch it until I give the signal."

"This ought to be good," I heard.

As told, we got around the square rug on our knees. Slowly the man raised his freckled hand as we followed it upward with our eyes.

I heard, "These niggers look like they're about to pray!"

Then, "Ready," the man said. "Go!"

I lunged for a yellow coin lying on the blue design of the carpet, touching it and sending a surprised shriek to join those rising around me. I tried frantically to remove my hand but could not let go. A hot, violent force tore through my body, shaking me like a wet rat. The rug was electrified. The hair bristled up on my head as I shook myself free. My muscles jumped, my nerves jangled, writhed. But I saw that this was not stopping the other boys. Laughing in fear and embarrassment, some were holding back and scooping up the coins knocked off by the painful contortions of the others. The men roared above us as we struggled.

"Pick it up, goddamnit, pick it up!" someone called like a bass-voiced parrot. "Go on, get it!"

I crawled rapidly around the floor, picking up the coins, trying to avoid the coppers and to get greenbacks and the gold. Ignoring the shock by laughing, as I brushed the coins off quickly, I discovered that I could contain the electricity—a contradiction, but it works. Then the men began to push us onto the rug. Laughing embarrassedly, we struggled out of their hands and kept after the coins. We were all wet and slippery and hard to hold. Suddenly I saw a boy lifted into the air, glistening with sweat like a circus seal, and dropped, his wet back landing flush upon the charged rug, heard him yell and saw him literally dance upon his back, his elbows beating a frenzied tattoo upon the floor, his muscles twitching like the flesh of a horse stung by many flies. When he finally rolled off, his face was gray and no one stopped him when he ran from the floor amid booming laughter.

"Get the money," the M.C. called. "That's good hard American cash!"

And we snatched and grabbed, snatched and grabbed. I was careful not to come too close to the rug now, and when I felt the hot whiskey breath descend upon me like a cloud of foul air I reached out and grabbed the leg of a chair. It was occupied and I held on desperately.

"Leggo, nigger! Leggo!"

The huge face wavered down to mine as he tried to push me free. But my body was slippery and he was too drunk. It was Mr. Colcord, who owned a chain of movie houses and "entertainment palaces." Each time he grabbed me I slipped out of his hands. It became a real struggle. I feared the rug more than I did the drunk, so I held on, surprising myself for a moment by trying to topple *him* upon the rug. It was such an enormous idea that I found myself actually carrying it out. I tried not to be obvious, yet when I grabbed his leg, trying to tumble him out of the chair, he raised up roaring with laughter, and, looking at me with soberness dead in the eye, kicked me viciously in the chest. The chair leg flew out of my hand and I felt myself going and rolled. It was as though I had rolled through a bed of hot coals. It seemed a whole century would pass before I would roll free, a century in which I was seared through the deepest levels of my body to the fearful breath within me and the breath seared and heated to the point of explosion. It'll all be over in a flash, I thought as I rolled clear. It'll all be over in a flash.

But not yet, the men on the other side were waiting, red faces swollen as though from apoplexy as they bent forward in their chairs. Seeing their fingers coming toward me I rolled away as a fumbled football rolls off the receiver's fingertips, back into the coals. That time I luckily sent the rug sliding out of place and heard the coins ringing against the floor and the boys scuffling to pick them up and the M.C. calling, "All right, boys, that's all. Go get dressed and get your money."

I was limp as a dish rag. My back felt as though it had been beaten with wires.

When we had dressed the M.C. came in and gave us each five dollars, except Tatlock, who got ten for being last in the ring. Then he told us to leave. I was not to get a chance to deliver my speech, I thought. I was going out into the dim alley in despair when I was stopped and told to go back. I returned to the ballroom, where the men were pushing back their chairs and gathering in groups to talk.

The M.C. knocked on a table for quiet. "Gentlemen," he said, "we almost forgot an important part of the program. A most serious part, gentlemen.

This boy was brought here to deliver a speech which he made at his graduation yesterday . . ."

"Bravo!"

"I'm told that he is the smartest boy we've got out there in Greenwood. I'm told that he knows more big words than a pocket-sized dictionary."

Much applause and laughter.

"So now, gentlemen, I want you to give him your attention."

There was still laughter as I faced them, my mouth dry, my eye throbbing. I began slowly, but evidently my throat was tense, because they began shouting, "Louder! Louder!"

"We of the younger generation extol the wisdom of that great leader and educator," I shouted, "who first spoke these flaming words of wisdom: 'A ship lost at sea for many days suddenly sighted a friendly vessel. From the mast of the unfortunate vessel was seen a signal: "Water, water; we die of thirst!" The answer from the friendly vessel came back: "Cast down your bucket where you are." The captain of the distressed vessel, at last heeding the injunction, cast down his bucket, and it came up full of fresh sparkling water from the mouth of the Amazon River.' And like him I say, and in his words, 'To those of my race who depend upon bettering their condition in a foreign land, or who underestimate the importance of cultivating friendly relations with the Southern white man, who is his next-door neighbor, I would say: "Cast down your bucket where you are"—cast it down in making friends in every manly way of the people of all races by whom we are surrounded . . .'"

I spoke automatically and with such fervor that I did not realize that the men were still talking and laughing until my dry mouth, filling up with blood from the cut, almost strangled me. I coughed, wanting to stop and go to one of the tall brass, sand-filled spittoons to relieve myself, but a few of the men, especially the superintendent, were listening and I was afraid. So I gulped it down, blood, saliva and all, and continued. (What powers of endurance I had during those days! What enthusiasm! What a belief in the rightness of things!) I spoke even louder in spite of the pain. But still they talked and still they laughed, as though deaf with cotton in dirty ears. So I spoke with greater emotional emphasis. I closed my ears and swallowed blood until I was nauseated. The speech seemed a hundred times as long as before, but I could not leave out a single word. All had to be said, each memorized nuance considered, rendered. Nor was that all. Whenever I uttered a word of three or more syllables a group of voices would yell for me to repeat it. I used the phrase "social responsibility" and they yelled:

"What's that word you say, boy?"

"Social responsibility," I said.

"What?"

"Social . . ."

"Louder."

". . . responsibility."

"More!"

"Respon—"

"Repeat!"

"—sibility."

The room filled with the uproar of laughter until, no doubt distracted by having to gulp down my blood, I made a mistake and yelled a phrase I had often seen denounced in newspaper editorials, heard debated in private.

"Social . . ."

"What?" they yelled.

". . . equality—"

The laughter hung smokelike in the sudden stillness. I opened my eyes, puzzled. Sounds of displeasure filled the room. The M.C. rushed forward. They shouted hostile phrases at me. But I did not understand.

A small dry mustached man in the front row blared out, "Say that slowly, son!"

"What, sir?"

"What you just said!"

"Social responsibility, sir," I said.

"You weren't being smart, were you, boy?" he said, not unkindly.

"No, sir!"

"You sure that about 'equality' was a mistake?"

"Oh, yes, sir," I said. "I was swallowing blood."

"Well, you had better speak more slowly so we can understand. We mean to do right by you, but you've got to know your place at all times. All right, now, go on with your speech."

I was afraid. I wanted to leave but I wanted also to speak and I was afraid they'd snatch me down.

"Thank you, sir," I said, beginning where I had left off, and having them ignore me as before.

Yet when I finished there was a thunderous applause. I was surprised to see the superintendent come forth with a package wrapped in white tissue paper, and, gesturing for quiet, address the men.

"Gentlemen, you see that I did not overpraise this boy. He makes a good speech and some day he'll lead his people in the proper paths. And I don't have to tell you that that is important in these days and times. This is a good, smart boy, and so to encourage him in the right direction, in the name of the Board of Education I wish to present him a prize in the form of this . . ."

He paused, removing the tissue paper and revealing a gleaming calfskin brief case.

". . . in the form of this first-class article from Shad Whitmore's shop."

"Boy," he said, addressing me, "take this prize and keep it well. Consider it a badge of office. Prize it. Keep developing as you are and some day it will be filled with important papers that will help shape the destiny of your people."

I was so moved that I could hardly express my thanks. A rope of bloody saliva forming a shape like an undiscovered continent drooled upon the leather and I wiped it quickly away. I felt an importance that I had never dreamed.

"Open it and see what's inside," I was told.

My fingers a-tremble, I complied, smelling the fresh leather and finding an official-looking document inside. It was a scholarship to the state college for Negroes. My eyes filled with tears and I ran awkwardly off the floor.

I was overjoyed; I did not even mind when I discovered that the gold pieces I had scrambled for were brass pocket tokens advertising a certain make of automobile.

When I reached home everyone was excited. Next day the neighbors came to congratulate me. I even felt safe from grandfather, whose deathbed curse usually spoiled my triumphs. I stood beneath his photograph with my brief case in hand and smiled triumphantly into his stolid black peasant's face. It was a face that fascinated me. The eyes seemed to follow everywhere I went.

That night I dreamed I was at a circus with him and that he refused to laugh at the clowns no matter what they did. Then later he told me to open my brief case and read what was inside and I did, finding an official envelope stamped with the state seal; and inside the envelope I found another and another, endlessly, and I thought I would fall of weariness. "Them's years," he said. "Now open that one." And I did and in it I found an engraved document containing a short message in letters of gold. "Read it," my grandfather said. "Out loud!"

"To Whom It May Concern," I intoned. "Keep This Nigger-Boy Running."

I awoke with the old man's laughter ringing in my ears.

(It was a dream I was to remember and dream again for many years after. But at that time I had no insight into its meaning. First I had to attend college.)

* * *

Epilogue

So there you have all of it that's important. Or at least you *almost* have it. I'm an invisible man and it placed me in a hole—or showed me the hole I was in, if you will—and I reluctantly accepted the fact. What else could I have done? Once you get used to it, reality is as irresistible as a club, and I was clubbed into the cellar before I caught the hint. Perhaps that's the way it had to be; I don't know. Nor do I know whether accepting the lesson has placed me in the rear or in the *avant-garde. That,* perhaps, is a lesson for history, and I'll leave such decisions to Jack and his ilk while I try belatedly to study the lesson of my own life.

Let me be honest with you—a feat which, by the way, I find of the utmost difficulty. When one is invisible he finds such problems as good and evil, honesty and dishonesty, of such shifting shapes that he confuses one with the other, depending upon who happens to be looking through him at the time. Well, now I've been trying to look through myself, and there's a risk in it. I was never more hated than when I tried to be honest. Or when, even as just now I've tried to articulate exactly what I felt to be the truth. No one was satisfied—not even I. On the other hand, I've never been more loved and appreciated than when I tried to "justify" and affirm someone's mistaken beliefs; or when I've tried to give my friends the incorrect, absurd answers they wished to hear. In my presence they could talk and agree with themselves, the world was nailed down, and they loved it. They received a feeling of security. But here was the rub: Too often, in order to justify *them,* I had to take myself by the throat and choke myself until my eyes bulged and my tongue hung out and wagged like the door of an empty house in a high wind. Oh, yes, it made them happy and it made me sick. So I became ill of affirmation, of saying "yes" against the nay-saying of my stomach—not to mention my brain.

There is, by the way, an area in which a man's feelings are more rational than his mind, and it is precisely in that area that his will is pulled in several directions at the same time. You might sneer at this, but I know now. I was pulled this way and that for longer than I can remember. And my problem was that I always tried to go in everyone's way but my own. I have also been called one thing and then another while no one really wished to hear what I called myself. So after years of trying to adopt the opinions of others

I finally rebelled. I am an *invisible* man. Thus I have come a long way and returned and boomeranged a long way from the point in society toward which I originally aspired.

So I took to the cellar; I hibernated. I got away from it all. But that wasn't enough. I couldn't be still even in hibernation. Because, damn it, there's the mind, the *mind*. It wouldn't let me rest. Gin, jazz and dreams were not enough. Books were not enough. My belated appreciation of the crude joke that had kept me running, was not enough. And my mind revolved again and again back to my grandfather. And, despite the farce that ended my attempt to say "yes" to Brotherhood, I'm still plagued by his deathbed advice . . . Perhaps he hid his meaning deeper than I thought, perhaps his anger threw me off—I can't decide. Could he have meant—hell, he *must* have meant the principle, that we were to affirm the principle on which the country was built and not the men, or at least not the men who did the violence. Did he mean say "yes" because he knew that the principle was greater than the men, greater than the numbers and the vicious power and all the methods used to corrupt its name? Did he mean to affirm the principle, which they themselves had dreamed into being out of the chaos and darkness of the feudal past, and which they had violated and compromised to the point of absurdity even in their own corrupt minds? Or did he mean that we had to take the responsibility for all of it, for the men as well as the principle, because we were the heirs who must use the principle because no other fitted our needs? Not for the power or for vindication, but because we, with the given circumstance of our origin, could only thus find transcendence? Was it that we of all, we, most of all, had to affirm the principle, the plan in whose name we had been brutalized and sacrificed—not because we would always be weak nor because we were afraid or opportunistic, but because we were older than they, in the sense of what it took to live in the world with others and because they had exhausted in us, some—not much, but some—of the human greed and smallness, yes, and the fear and superstition that had kept them running. (Oh, yes, they're running too, running all over themselves.) Or was it, did he mean that we should affirm the principle because we, through no fault of our own, were linked to all the others in the loud, clamoring semi-visible world, that world seen only as a fertile field for exploitation by Jack and his kind, and with condescension by Norton[7] and his, who were tired of being the mere pawns in the futile game of "making history?" Had he seen that for these too we had to say "yes" to the principle, lest they turn upon us to destroy both it and us?

"Agree 'em to death and destruction," grandfather had advised. Hell, weren't they their own death and their own destruction except as the principle lived in them and in us? And here's the cream of the joke: Weren't we *part of them* as well as apart from them and subject to die when they died? I can't figure it out; it escapes me. But what do *I* really want, I've asked myself. Certainly not the freedom of a Rinehart or the power of a Jack, nor simply the freedom not to run. No, but the next step I couldn't make, so I've remained in the hole.

---

7. A white philanthropist whom the invisible man guides around his college and its environs. When he inadvertently allows Norton to meet the black sharecropper Jim Trueblood, who has committed incest with his daughter, the invisible man incurs the wrath of Dr. Bledsoe, the college president.

I'm not blaming anyone for this state of affairs, mind you; nor merely crying *mea culpa.* The fact is that you carry part of your sickness within you, at least I do as an invisible man. I carried my sickness and though for a long time I tried to place it in the outside world, the attempt to write it down shows me that at least half of it lay within me. It came upon me slowly, like that strange disease that affects those black men whom you see turning slowly from black to albino, their pigment disappearing as under the radiation of some cruel, invisible ray. You go along for years knowing something is wrong, then suddenly you discover that you're as transparent as air. At first you tell yourself that it's all a dirty joke, or that it's due to the "political situation." But deep down you come to suspect that you're yourself to blame, and you stand naked and shivering before the millions of eyes who look through you unseeingly. *That* is the real soul-sickness, the spear in the side, the drag by the neck through the mob-angry town, the Grand Inquisition, the embrace of the Maiden, the rip in the belly with the guts spilling out, the trip to the chamber with the deadly gas that ends in the oven so hygienically clean—only it's worse because you continue stupidly to live. But live you must, and you can either make passive love to your sickness or burn it out and go on to the next conflicting phase.

Yes, but what *is* the next phase? How often have I tried to find it! Over and over again I've gone up above to seek it out. For, like almost everyone else in our country, I started out with my share of optimism. I believed in hard work and progress and action, but now, after first being "for" society and then "against" it, I assign myself no rank or any limit, and such an attitude is very much against the trend of the times. But my world has become one of infinite possibilities. What a phrase—still it's a good phrase and a good view of life, and a man shouldn't accept any other; that much I've learned underground. Until some gang succeeds in putting the world in a strait jacket, its definition is possibility. Step outside the narrow borders of what men call reality and you step into chaos—ask Rinehart, he's a master of it—or imagination. That too I've learned in the cellar, and not by deadening my sense of perception; I'm invisible, not blind.

No indeed, the world is just as concrete, ornery, vile and sublimely wonderful as before, only now I better understand my relation to it and it to me. I've come a long way from those days when, full of illusion, I lived a public life and attempted to function under the assumption that the world was solid and all the relationships therein. Now I know men are different and that all life is divided and that only in division is there true health. Hence again I have stayed in my hole, because up above there's an increasing passion to make men conform to a pattern. Just as in my nightmare, Jack and the boys are waiting with their knives, looking for the slightest excuse to . . . well, to "ball the jack," and I do not refer to the old dance step, although what they're doing is making the old eagle rock dangerously.

Whence all this passion toward conformity anyway?—diversity is the word. Let man keep his many parts and you'll have no tyrant states. Why, if they follow this conformity business they'll end up by forcing me, an invisible man, to become white, which is not a color but the lack of one. Must I strive toward colorlessness? But seriously, and without snobbery, think of what the world would lose if that should happen. America is woven of many strands; I would recognize them and let it so remain. It's "winner take nothing" that is the great truth of our country or of any country. Life is to be lived, not controlled; and humanity is won by continuing to play in face of certain defeat.

Our fate is to become one, and yet many—This is not prophecy, but description. Thus one of the greatest jokes in the world is the spectacle of the whites busy escaping blackness and becoming blacker every day, and the blacks striving toward whiteness, becoming quite dull and gray. None of us seems to know who he is or where he's going.

Which reminds me of something that occurred the other day in the subway. At first I saw only an old gentleman who for the moment was lost. I knew he was lost, for as I looked down the platform I saw him approach several people and turn away without speaking. He's lost, I thought, and he'll keep coming until he sees me, then he'll ask his direction. Maybe there's an embarrassment in it if he admits he's lost to a strange white man. Perhaps to lose a sense of *where* you are implies the danger of losing a sense of *who* you are. That must be it, I thought—to lose your direction is to lose your face. So here he comes to ask his direction from the lost, the invisible. Very well, I've learned to live without direction. Let him ask.

But then he was only a few feet away and I recognized him; it was Mr. Norton. The old gentleman was thinner and wrinkled now but as dapper as ever. And seeing him made all the old life live in me for an instant, and I smiled with tear-stinging eyes. Then it was over, dead, and when he asked me how to get to Centre Street, I regarded him with mixed feelings.

"Don't you know me?" I said.

"Should I?" he said.

"You see me?" I said, watching him tensely.

"Why, of course—Sir, do you know the way to Centre Street?"

"So. Last time it was the Golden Day, now it's Centre Street. You've retrenched, sir. But don't you really know who I am?"

"Young man, I'm in a hurry," he said, cupping a hand to his ear. "Why should I know you?"

"Because I'm your destiny."

"My destiny, did you say?" He gave me a puzzled stare, backing away. "Young man, are you well? Which train did you say I should take?"

"I didn't say," I said, shaking my head. "Now, aren't you ashamed?"

"Ashamed? ASHAMED!" he said indignantly.

I laughed, suddenly taken by the idea. "Because, Mr. Norton, if you don't know *where* you are, you probably don't know *who* you are. So you came to me out of shame. You are ashamed, now aren't you?"

"Young man, I've lived too long in this world to be ashamed of anything. Are you light-headed from hunger? How do you know my name?"

"But I'm your destiny, I made you. Why shouldn't I know you?" I said, walking closer and seeing him back against a pillar. He looked around like a cornered animal. He thought I was mad.

"Don't be afraid, Mr. Norton," I said. "There's a guard down the platform there. You're safe. Take any train; they all go to the Golden D—"

But now an express had rolled up and the old man was disappearing quite spryly inside one of its doors. I stood there laughing hysterically. I laughed all the way back to my hole.

But after I had laughed I was thrown back on my thoughts—how had it all happened? And I asked myself if it were only a joke and I couldn't answer. Since then I've sometimes been overcome with a passion to return into that "heart of darkness" across the Mason-Dixon line, but then I remind myself that the true darkness lies within my own mind, and the idea loses itself in the gloom. Still the passion persists. Sometimes I feel the need to reaffirm all of it, the whole unhappy territory and all the things loved and unlovable in it, for all of it is part of me. Till now, however, this is as far as I've ever gotten, for all life seen from the hole of invisibility is absurd.

So why do I write, torturing myself to put it down? Because in spite of myself I've learned some things. Without the possibility of action, all knowledge comes to one labeled "file and forget," and I can neither file nor forget. Nor will certain ideas forget me; they keep filing away at my lethargy, my complacency. Why should I be the one to dream this nightmare? Why should I be dedicated and set aside—yes, if not to at least *tell* a few people about it? There seems to be no escape. Here I've set out to throw my anger into the world's face, but now that I've tried to put it all down the old fascination with playing a role returns, and I'm drawn upward again. So that even before I finish I've failed (maybe my anger is too heavy; perhaps, being a talker, I've used too many words). But I've failed. The very act of trying to put it all down has confused me and negated some of the anger and some of the bitterness. So it is that now I denounce and defend, or feel prepared to defend. I condemn and affirm, say no and say yes, say yes and say no. I denounce because though implicated and partially responsible, I have been hurt to the point of abysmal pain, hurt to the point of invisibility. And I defend because in spite of all I find that I love. In order to get some of it down I *have* to love. I sell you no phony forgiveness, I'm a desperate man—but too much of your life will be lost, its meaning lost, unless you approach it as much through love as through hate. So I approach it through division. So I denounce and I defend and I hate and I love.

Perhaps that makes me a little bit as human as my grandfather. Once I thought my grandfather incapable of thoughts about humanity, but I was wrong. Why should an old slave use such a phrase as, "This and this or this has made me more human," as I did in my arena speech? Hell, he never had any doubts about his humanity—that was left to his "free" offspring. He accepted his humanity just as he accepted the principle. It was his, and the principle lives on in all its human and absurd diversity. So now having tried to put it down I have disarmed myself in the process. You won't believe in my invisibility and you'll fail to see how any principle that applies to you could apply to me. You'll fail to see it even though death waits for both of us if you don't. Nevertheless, the very disarmament has brought me to a decision. The hibernation is over. I must shake off the old skin and come up for breath. There's a stench in the air, which, from this distance underground, might be the smell either of death or of spring—I hope of spring. But don't let me trick you, there *is* a death in the smell of spring and in the smell of thee as in the smell of me. And if nothing more, invisibility has taught my nose to classify the stenches of death.

In going underground, I whipped it all except the mind, the *mind.* And the mind that has conceived a plan of living must never lose sight of the chaos against which that pattern was conceived. That goes for societies as well as for individuals. Thus, having tried to give pattern to the chaos which lives within the pattern of your certainties, I must come out, I must emerge. And there's still a conflict within me: With Louis Armstrong one half of me says, "Open the window and let the foul air out," while the other says, "It was good green corn before the harvest." Of course Louie was kidding, *he* wouldn't have thrown old Bad Air out, because it would have broken up the music and the dance, when it was the good music that came from the bell of old Bad Air's horn that counted. Old Bad Air is still around with his music and his dancing and his diversity, and I'll be up and around with mine. And, as I said before, a decision has been made. I'm shaking off the old skin and I'll leave it here in the hole. I'm coming out, no less invisible without it, but coming out nevertheless. And I suppose it's damn well time. Even hibernations can be overdone, come to think of it. Perhaps that's my greatest social crime, I've overstayed my hibernation, since there's a possibility that even an invisible man has a socially responsible role to play.

"Ah," I can hear you say, "so it was all a build-up to bore us with his buggy jiving. He only wanted us to listen to him rave!" But only partially true: Being invisible and without substance, a disembodied voice, as it were, what else could I do? What else but try to tell you what was really happening when your eyes were looking through? And it is this which frightens me:

Who knows but that, on the lower frequencies, I speak for you?

1952

Change the Joke and Slip the Yoke[1]

Stanley Edgar Hyman's essay on the relationship between Negro American literature and Negro American folklore concerns matters in which my own interest is such that the very news of his piece aroused my enthusiasm. Yet after reading it I find that our conceptions of the way in which folk tradition gets into literature—and especially into the novel; our conceptions of just what is *Negro* and what is *American* in Negro American folklore; and our conceptions of a Negro American writer's environment—are at such odds that I must disagree with him all along the way. And since much of his essay is given over so generously to aspects of my own meager writings, I am put in the ungrateful—and embarrassing—position of not only evaluating some of his statements from that highly dubious (but privileged) sanctuary provided by one's intimate knowledge of one's personal history, but of questioning some of his readings of my own novel by consulting the text.

Archetypes, like taxes, seem doomed to be with us always, and so with literature, one hopes; but between the two there must needs be the living human being in a specific texture of time, place and circumstance; who must respond, make choices, achieve eloquence and create specific works of art. Thus I feel that Hyman's fascination with folk tradition and the pleasure of archetype-hunting leads to a critical game that ignores the specificity of literary works. And it also causes him to blur the distinction between various archetypes and different currents of American folklore, and, generally, to oversimplify the American tradition.

Hyman's favorite archetypical figure is the trickster, but I see a danger here. From a proper distance *all* archetypes would appear to be tricksters and confidence men; part-God, part-man, no one seems to know he-she-its

1. This essay originated in the form of a letter in which, from Rome, I expressed my reactions to a lecture which Stanley Edgar Hyman, an old friend and intellectual sparring partner, was preparing for what was to be the first of the Ludwig Lewisohn lectures at Brandeis University. Hyman wrote back suggesting that I work up my ideas as part of a publishable debate, and the two essays were presented in Partisan Review, Spring 1958. They were titled "The Negro Writer in America: An Exchange," and they are apt to yield their maximum return when read together. Hyman's part of the exchange, which is a most useful discussion of the Negro American's relation to the folk tradition, appears in his book of essays and reviews, "The Promised End," published by The World Publishing Company, 1963 [Ellison's note].

true name, because he-she-it is protean with changes of pace, location and identity. Further, the trickster is everywhere and anywhere at one and the same time, and, like the parts of some dismembered god, is likely to be found on stony as well as on fertile ground. Folklore is somewhat more stable, in its identity if not in its genealogy; but even here, if we are to discuss *Negro* American folklore let us not be led astray by interlopers.

Certainly we should not approach Negro folklore through the figure Hyman calls the "'darky' entertainer." For even though such performers as he mentions appear to be convenient guides, they lead us elsewhere, into a Cthonic[2] labyrinth. The role with which they are identified is not, despite its "blackness," *Negro* American (indeed, Negroes are repelled by it); it does not find its popularity among Negroes but among whites; and although it resembles the role of the clown familiar to Negro variety-house audiences, it derives not from the Negro but from the Anglo-Saxon branch of American folklore. In other words, this "'darky' entertainer" is white. Nevertheless, it might be worth while to follow the trail for a while, even though we seem more interested in interracial warfare than the question of literature.

These entertainers are, as Hyman explains, professionals, who in order to enact a symbolic role basic to the underlying drama of American society assume a ritual mask—the identical mask and role taken on by white minstrel men when *they* depicted comic Negroes. Social changes occurring since the 1930's have made for certain modifications (Rochester operates in a different climate of rhetoric, say, than did Stepin Fetchit[3]) but the mask, stylized and iconic, was once required of anyone who would act the role— even those Negroes whose natural coloration should, for any less ritualistic purposes at least, have made it unnecessary.

Nor does the role, which makes use of Negro idiom, songs, dance motifs and word-play, grow out of the Negro American sense of the comic (although we too have our comedy of blackness), but out of the white American's Manichean[4] fascination with the symbolism of blackness and whiteness expressed in such contradictions as the conflict between the white American's Judeo-Christian morality, his democratic political ideals and his daily conduct— indeed in his general anti-tragic approach to experience.

Being "highly pigmented," as the sociologists say, it was our Negro "misfortune" to be caught up associatively in the negative side of this basic dualism of the white folk mind, and to be shackled to almost everything it would repress from conscience and consciousness. The physical hardships and indignities of slavery were benign compared with this continuing debasement of our image. Because these things are bound up with their notion of chaos it is almost impossible for many whites to consider questions of sex, women, economic opportunity, the national identity, historic change, social justice—even the "criminality" implicit in the broadening of freedom itself— without summoning malignant images of black men into consciousness.

In the Anglo-Saxon branch of American folklore and in the entertainment industry (which thrives on the exploitation and debasement of all folk materi-

---

2. Of the dark gods of the underworld of Greek mythology.
3. Actor and comedian (1902–1985) who portrayed the stereotype of an unsophisticated, subservient black man; the first black actor to receive feature billing. Rochester, Jack Benny's

"handyman," was played by Eddie Anderson (1906–1977).
4. Dualistic; a reference to the religious system of the Persian prophet Manes (ca. 216–276), whose basic doctrine posited a conflict between light and dark.

als), the Negro is reduced to a negative sign that usually appears in a comedy of the grotesque and the unacceptable. As Constance Rourke[5] has made us aware, the action of the early minstrel show—with its Negro-deprived choreography, its ringing of banjos and rattling of bones, its voices cackling jokes in pseudo-Negro dialect, with its nonsense songs, its bright costumes and sweating performers—constituted a ritual of exorcism. Other white cultures had their gollywogs and blackamoors but the fact of Negro slavery went to the moral heart of the American social drama and here the Negro was too real for easy fantasy, too serious to be dealt with in anything less than a national art. The mask was an inseparable part of the national iconography. Thus even when a Negro acted in an abstract role the national implications were unchanged. His costume made use of the "sacred" symbolism of the American flag—with red and white striped pants and coat and with stars set in a field of blue for a collar—but he could appear only with his hands gloved in white and his face blackened with burnt cork or greasepaint.

This mask, this willful stylization and modification of the natural face and hands, was imperative for the evocation of that atmosphere in which the fascination of blackness could be enjoyed, the comic catharsis achieved. The racial identity of the performer was unimportant, the mask was the thing (the "thing" in more ways than one) and its function was to veil the humanity of Negroes thus reduced to a sign, and to repress the white audience's awareness of its moral identification with its own acts and with the human ambiguities pushed behind the mask.

Hyman sees the comic point of the contemporary Negro's performance of the role as arising from the circumstance that a skilled man of intelligence is parodying a subhuman grotesque; this is all very kind, but when we move in from the wide-ranging spaces of the archetype for a closer inspection we see that the specific rhetorical situation involves the self-humiliation of the "sacrificial" figure, and that a psychological dissociation from this symbolic self-maiming is one of the powerful motives at work in the audience. Motives of race, status, economics and guilt are always clustered here. The comic point is inseparable from the racial identity of the performer—as is clear in Hyman's example from Wright's *Black Boy*—who by assuming the group-debasing role for gain not only substantiates the audience's belief in the "blackness" of things black, but relieves it, with dreamlike efficiency, of its guilt by accepting the very profit motive that was involved in the designation of the Negro as national scapegoat in the first place. There are all kinds of comedy: here one is reminded of the tribesman in *Green Hills of Africa*[6] who hid his laughing face in shame at the sight of a gun-shot hyena jerking out its own intestines and eating them, in Hemingway's words, "with relish."

Down at the deep dark bottom of the melting pot, where the private is public and the public private, where black is white and white black, where the immoral becomes moral and the moral is anything that makes one feel good (or that one has the power to sustain), the white man's relish is apt to be the black man's gall.

It is not at all odd that this black-faced figure of white fun is for Negroes a symbol of everything they rejected in the white man's thinking about race, in themselves and in their own group. When he appears, for example, in the guise of Nigger Jim, the Negro is made uncomfortable. Writing at a time

5. American biographer and cultural critic (1885–1941).

6. Novel (1935) by American writer Ernest Hemingway (1899–1961).

when the blackfaced minstrel was still popular, and shortly after a war which left even the abolitionists weary of those problems associated with the Negro, Twain fitted Jim into the outlines of the minstrel tradition, and it is from behind this stereotype mask that we see Jim's dignity and human capacity— and Twain's complexity—emerge. Yet it is his source in this same tradition which creates that ambivalence between his identification as an adult and parent and his "boyish" naïveté, and which by contrast makes Huck, with his street-sparrow sophistication, seem more adult. Certainly it upsets a Negro reader, and it offers a less psychoanalytical explanation of the discomfort which lay behind Leslie Fiedler's thesis concerning the relation of Jim and Huck in his essay "Come Back to the Raft Ag'in, Huck Honey!"[7]

A glance at a more recent fictional encounter between a Negro adult and a white boy, that of Lucas Beauchamp and Chick Mallison in Faulkner's *Intruder in the Dust,*[8] will reinforce my point. For all the racial and caste differences between them, Lucas holds the ascendency in his mature dignity over the youthful Mallison and refuses to lower himself in the comic duel of status forced on him by the white boy whose life he has saved. Faulkner was free to reject the confusion between manhood and the Negro's caste status which is sanctioned by white Southern tradition, but Twain, standing closer to the Reconstruction[9] and to the oral tradition, was not so free of the white dictum that Negro males must be treated either as boys or "uncles"—never as men. Jim's friendship for Huck comes across as that of a boy for another boy rather than as the friendship of an adult for a junior; thus there is implicit in it not only a violation of the manners sanctioned by society for relations between Negroes and whites, there is a violation of our conception of adult maleness.

In Jim the extremes of the private and the public come to focus, and before our eyes an "archetypal" figure gives way before the realism implicit in the form of the novel. Here we have, I believe, an explanation in the novel's own terms of that ambiguity which bothered Fiedler. Fiedler was accused of mere sensationalism when he named the friendship homosexual, yet I believe him so profoundly disturbed by the manner in which the deep dichotomies symbolized by blackness and whiteness are resolved that, forgetting to look at the specific form of the novel, he leaped squarely into the middle of that tangle of symbolism which he is dedicated to unsnarling, and yelled out his most terrifying name for chaos. Other things being equal, he might have called it "rape," "incest," "parricide" or—"miscegenation." It is ironic that what to a Negro appears to be a lost fall in Twain's otherwise successful wrestle with the ambiguous figure in black face is viewed by a critic as a symbolic loss of sexual identity. Surely for literature there is some rare richness here.

Although the figure in black face looks suspiciously homegrown, Western and Calvinist to me, Hyman identifies it as being related to an archetypical trickster figure, originating in Africa. Without arguing the point I shall say only that if it *is* a trickster, its adjustment to the contours of "white" sym-

---

7. The references in this paragraph are to Mark Twain's *Adventures of Huckleberry Finn* (1885), in which Huck, a white boy, and runaway slave Jim raft down the Mississippi River. As noted in the following paragraphs, Fiedler examined what he saw as the homoeroticism in Huck and Jim's friendship.

8. William Faulkner's 1948 novel. This and his collection of stories *Go Down, Moses* (1942) make up his fullest treatment of African American life in the South.
9. The period of adjustment (1865–1977) following the Civil War, a time during which black civil and political rights were highly contested.

bolic needs is far more intriguing than its alleged origins, for it tells us something of the operation of American values as modulated by folklore and literature. We are back once more to questions of order and chaos, illusion and reality, nonentity and identity.

The trickster, according to Karl Kerenyi (in a commentary included in Paul Radin's study, *The Trickster*[1]), represents a personification of the body

> which is . . . never wholly subdued, ruled by lust and hunger, forever running into pain and injury, cunning and stupid in action. Disorder belonging to the totality of life . . . the spirit of this disorder is the trickster. His function in an archaic society, or rather the function of his mythology, of the tales told about him, is to add disorder to order and to make a whole, to render possible, within the fixed bounds of what is permitted, an experience of what is not permitted. . . .

But ours is no archaic society (although its archaic elements exert far more influence in our lives than we care to admit), and it is an ironic reversal that in what is regarded as the most "open" society in the world, the license of the black trickster figure is limited by the rigidities of racial attitudes, by political expediencies, and by the guilt bound up with the white compulsion to identify with the ever-present man of flesh and blood whose irremediable features have been expropriated for "immoral" purposes. Hyman, incidentally, would have found in Louis Armstrong[2] a much better example of the trickster, his medium being music rather than words and pantomime. Armstrong's clownish license and intoxicating powers are almost Elizabethan; he takes liberties with kings, queens and presidents; emphasizes the physicality of his music with sweat, spittle and facial contortions; he performs the magical feat of making romantic melody issue from a throat of gravel; and some few years ago was recommending to all and sundry his personal physic, "Pluto Water," as a purging way to health, happiness and international peace.

When the white man steps behind the mask of the trickster his freedom is circumscribed by the fear that he is not simply miming a personification of his disorder and chaos but that he will become in fact that which he intends only to symbolize; that he will be trapped somewhere in the mystery of hell (for there is a mystery in the whiteness of blackness, the innocence of evil and the evil of innocence, though, being initiates, Negroes express the joke of it in the blues) and thus lose that freedom which, in the fluid, "traditionless," "classless" and rapidly changing society, he would recognize as the white man's alone.

Here another ironic facet of the old American problem of identity crops up. For out of the counterfeiting of the black American's identity there arises a profound doubt in the white man's mind as to the authenticity of his own image of himself. He, after all, went into the business when he refused the king's shilling and revolted. He had put on a mask of his own, as it were; and when we regard our concern with identity in the light of what Robert Penn Warren has termed the "intentional" character of our national beginnings, a quotation from W. B. Yeats[3] proves highly meaningful:

---

1. Anthropologist Radin's *The Trickster: A Study in American Indian Mythology* (1956) is a widely read collection of Winnebago trickster stories. Kerenyi's essay is titled "The Trickster in Relation to Greek Mythology."

2. African American jazz musician (1900–1971).
3. Irish poet, playwright, and philosopher (1865–1939). Warren (1905–1989), American poet, novelist, teacher, and literary critic.

There is a relation between discipline and the theatrical sense. If we cannot imagine ourselves as different from what we are and assume the second self, we cannot impose a discipline upon ourselves, though we may accept one from others. Active virtue, as distinct from the passive acceptance of a current code, is the wearing of a mask. It is the condition of an arduous full life.

For the ex-colonials, the declaration of an American identity meant the assumption of a mask, and it imposed not only the discipline of national self-consciousness, it gave Americans an ironic awareness of the joke that always lies between appearance and reality, between the discontinuity of social tradition and that sense of the past which clings to the mind. And perhaps even an awareness of the joke that society is man's creation, not God's. Americans began their revolt from the English fatherland when they dumped the tea into the Boston Harbor, masked as Indians, and the mobility of the society created in this limitless space has encouraged the use of the mask for good and evil ever since. As the advertising industry, which is dedicated to the creation of masks, makes clear, that which cannot gain authority from tradition may borrow it with a mask. Masking is a play upon possibility and ours is a society in which possibilities are many. When American life is most American it is apt to be most theatrical.

And it is this which makes me question Hyman's designation of the "smart man playing dumb" role as primarily Negro, if he means by "conflict situations" those in which racial pressure is uppermost. Actually it is a role which Negroes share with other Americans, and it might be more "Yankee" than anything else. It is a strategy common to the culture, and it is reinforced by our anti-intellectualism, by our tendency toward conformity and by the related desire of the individual to be left alone; often simply by the desire to put more money in the bank. But basically the strategy grows out of our awareness of the joke at the center of the American identity. Said a very dark Southern friend of mine in laughing reply to a white businessman who complained of his recalcitrance in a bargaining situation, "I know, you thought I was colored, didn't you." It is across this joke that Negro and white Americans regard one another. The white American has charged the Negro American with being without past or tradition (something which strikes the white man with a nameless horror), just as he himself has been so charged by European and American critics with a nostalgia for the stability once typical of European cultures; and the Negro knows that both were "mammy-made" right here at home. What's more, each secretly believes that he alone knows what is valid in the American experience, and that the other knows he knows but will not admit it, and each suspects the other of being at bottom a phony.

The white man's half-conscious awareness that his image of the Negro is false makes him suspect the Negro of always seeking to take him in, and assume his motives are anger and fear—which very often they are. On his side of the joke the Negro looks at the white man and finds it difficult to believe that the "grays"—a Negro term for white people—can be so absurdly self-deluded over the true interrelatedness of blackness and whiteness. To him the white man seems a hypocrite who boasts of a pure identity while standing with his humanity exposed to the world.

Very often, however, the Negro's masking is motivated not so much by fear as by a profound rejection of the image created to usurp his identity. Sometimes it is for the sheer joy of the joke; sometimes to challenge those who presume, across the psychological distance created by race manners, to know his identity. Nonetheless, it is in the American grain. Benjamin Franklin, the practical scientist, skilled statesman and sophisticated lover, allowed the French to mistake him for Rousseau's Natural Man.[4] Hemingway poses as a non-literary sportsman, Faulkner as a farmer; Abe Lincoln allowed himself to be taken for a simple country lawyer—until the chips were down. Here the "darky" act makes brothers of us all. America is a land of masking jokers. We wear the mask for purposes of aggression as well as for defense; when we are projecting the future and preserving the past. In short, the motives hidden behind the mask are as numerous as the ambiguities the mask conceals.

My basic quarrel with Hyman is not over his belief in the importance of the folk tradition, nor over his interest in archetypes; but that when he turns to specific works of literature he tends to distort their content to fit his theory. Since he refers so generously to my own novel, let us take it as a case in point. So intense is Hyman's search for archetypical forms that he doesn't see that the narrator's grandfather in *Invisible Man* is no more involved in a "darky" act than was Ulysses in Polyphemus' cave.[5] Nor is he so much a "smart-man-playing-dumb" as a weak man who knows the nature of his oppressor's weakness. There is a good deal of spite in the old man, as there comes to be in his grandson, and the strategy he advises is a kind of jiujitsu of the spirit, a denial and rejection through agreement. Samson,[6] eyeless in Gaza, pulls the building down when his strength returns; politically weak, the grandfather has learned that conformity leads to a similar end, and so advises his children. Thus his mask of meekness conceals the wisdom of one who has learned the secret of saying the "yes" which accomplishes the expressive "no." Here, too, is a rejection of a current code and a denial become metaphysical. More important to the novel is the fact that he represents the ambiguity of the past for the hero, for whom his sphinxlike deathbed advice poses a riddle which points the plot in the dual direction which the hero will follow throughout the novel.

Certainly B. P. Rinehart[7] (the P. is for "Proteus," the B. for "Bliss") would seem the perfect example of Hyman's trickster figure. He is a cunning man who wins the admiration of those who admire skulduggery and know-how; an American virtuoso of identity who thrives on chaos and swift change; he is greedy, in that his masquerade is motivated by money as well as by the sheer bliss of impersonation; he is godlike, in that he brings new techniques— electric guitars, etc.—to the service of God, and in that there are many men in his image while he is himself unseen; he is phallic in his role of "lover"; as a numbers runner he is a bringer of manna and a worker of miracles, in that he transforms (for winners, of course) pennies into dollars, and thus he feeds (and feeds on) the poor. Indeed, one could extend this list in the manner of much myth-mongering criticism until the fiction dissolved into anthropology, but Rinehart's role in the formal structure of the narrative is to suggest to the

4. Jean-Jacques Rousseau (1712–1778), Swiss-French philosopher, saw civilization as a fall from humanity's natural goodness. Late in 1776, Franklin (1706–1790) sailed to France as a diplomat for the new American republic and paved the way for French recognition of the United States in 1778.

5. In Homer's *Odyssey* the cyclops Polyphemus imprisoned Odysseus and his men in a cave; they escaped by giving Polyphemus wine, blinding him when he was drunk, and hiding under his sheep as they left the cave.

6. Judge of Israel whose long hair symbolized the covenant with God that gave him great strength. Delilah cut his hair, which enabled the Philistines to blind and chain him. When his hair grew back and his strength returned, Samson pulled down the temple walls, in the process killing his captors and himself (Judges 13–16).

7. Character in Ellison's *Invisible Man* (1952) who assumes many different roles.

hero a mode of escape from Ras, and a means of applying, in yet another form, his grandfather's cryptic advice to his own situation. One could throw Rinehart among his literary betters and link him with Mann's Felix Krull, the Baron Clappique of Malraux's *Man's Fate*[8] and many others, but that would be to make a game of criticism and really say nothing.

The identity of fictional characters is determined by the implicit realism of the form, not by their relation to tradition; they are what they do or do not do. Archetypes are timeless, novels are time-haunted. Novels achieve timelessness through time. If the symbols appearing in a novel link up with those of universal myth they do so by virtue of their emergence from the specific texture of a specific form of social reality. The final act of *Invisible Man* is not that of a concealment in darkness in the Anglo-Saxon connotation of the word, but that of a voice issuing its little wisdom out of the substance of its own inwardness—after having undergone a transformation from ranter to writer. If, by the way, the hero is pulling a "darky art" in this, he certainly is not a smart man playing dumb. For the novel, his memoir, is one long, loud rant, howl and laugh. Confession, not concealment, is his mode. His mobility is dual; geographical, as Hyman points out, but, more importantly, it is intellectual. And in keeping with the reverse English of the plot, and with the Negro American conception of blackness, his movement vertically downward (not into a "sewer," Freud[9] notwithstanding, but into a coal cellar, a source of heat, light, power and, through association with the character's motivation, self-perception) is a process of *rising* to an understanding of his human condition. He gets his restless mobility not so much from the blues or from sociology but from the circumstance that he appears in a literary form which has time and social change as its special province. Besides, restlessness of the spirit is an American condition that transcends geography, sociology and past condition of servitude.

Discussions of folk tradition and literature which slight the specific literary forms involved seem to me questionable. Most of the writers whom Hyman mentions are novelists, workers in a form which has absorbed folk tradition into its thematic structures, its plots, symbolism and rhetoric; and which has its special way with folklore as it has with manners, history, sociology and psychology. Besides, novelists in our time are more likely to be inspired by reading novels than by their acquaintance with any folk tradition.

I use folklore in my work not because I am Negro, but because writers like Eliot and Joyce[1] made me conscious of the literary value of my folk inheritance. My cultural background, like that of most Americans, is dual (my middle name, sadly enough, is Waldo).

I knew the trickster Ulysses just as early as I knew the wily rabbit of Negro American lore, and I could easily imagine myself a pint-sized Ulysses but hardly a rabbit, no matter how human and resourceful or Negro. And a little later I could imagine myself as Huck Finn (I so nicknamed my brother) but not, though I racially identified with him, as Nigger Jim, who struck me as a white man's inadequate portrait of a slave.

My point is that the Negro American writer is also an heir of the human experience which is literature, and this might well be more important to him

8. A 1933 novel about the Chinese revolution of the 1920s by André-Georges Malraux (1901–1976), French writer and political figure. It features the enigmatic Baron de Clappique, who has a talent for disguise. Thomas Mann (1875–1955), German writer, published the picaresque comedy *Confessions of Felix Krull, Confidence Man* in 1954.
9. Sigmund Freud (1856–1939), Austrian psychiatrist and founder of psychoanalysis.
1. James Joyce (1882–1941), Irish novelist. T. S. Eliot (1888–1965), United States–born English poet and critic.

than his living folk tradition. For me, at least, in the discontinuous, swiftly changing and diverse American culture, the stability of the Negro American folk tradition became precious as a result of an act of literary discovery. Taken as a whole, its spirituals along with its blues, jazz and folk tales, it has, as Hyman suggests, much to tell us of the faith, humor and adaptability to reality necessary to live in a world which has taken on much of the insecurity and blues-like absurdity known to those who brought it into being. For those who are able to translate its meanings into wider, more precise vocabularies it has much to offer indeed. Hyman performs a service when he makes us aware that Negro American folk tradition constitutes a valuable source for literature, but for the novelist, of any cultural or racial identity, his form is his greatest freedom and his insights are where he finds them.

1958

The World and the Jug[1]

> What runs counter to the revolutionary convention is, in revolu-
> tionary histories, suppressed more imperiously than embarrassing
> episodes in private memoirs, and by the same obscure forces. . . .
> —ANDRÉ MALRAUX

I

First, three questions: Why is it so often true that when critics confront the American as *Negro* they suddenly drop their advanced critical armament and revert with an air of confident superiority to quite primitive modes of analysis? Why is it that sociology-oriented critics seem to rate literature so far below politics and ideology that they would rather kill a novel than modify their presumptions concerning a given reality which it seeks in its own terms to project? Finally, why is it that so many of those who would tell us the meaning of Negro life never bother to learn how varied it really is?

These questions are aroused by "Black Boys and Native Sons," an essay by Irving Howe, the well-known critic and editor of *Dissent,* in the Autumn 1963 issue of that magazine. It is a lively piece, written with something of the Olympian authority that characterized Hannah Arendt's "Reflections on Little Rock" in the Winter 1959 *Dissent* (a dark foreshadowing of the Eich-mann blowup). And in addition to a hero, Richard Wright, it has two villains, James Baldwin[2] and Ralph Ellison, who are seen as "black boys" masquerading as false, self-deceived "native sons." Wright himself is given a diversity of roles (all conceived by Howe): He is not only the archetypal and true-blue black boy—the "honesty" of his famous autobiography established this for

1. "The World and the Jug" is actually a combination of two separate pieces. The first, bearing the original title, was written at the suggestion of Myron Kolatch of *The New Leader,* who was interested in my reactions, via telephone, to an essay by Irving Howe titled "Black Boys and Native Sons," which appeared in the Autumn 1963 issue of Howe's magazine, *Dissent.*

Usually such a reply would have appeared in the same magazine in which the original essay was published, but in this instance, and since it hadn't occurred to me to commit my reactions to paper, they went to the editor who asked for

them. The second section of the essay, originally entitled, "A Rejoinder," was written after Irving Howe had consented to reply, in *The New Leader,* of February 3, 1964, to my attack. There is, unfortunately, too little space here to do justice to Howe's arguments, and it is recommended that the interested reader consult Mr. Howe's book of essays, *A World More Attractive*—a book worthy of his attention far beyond the limits of our exchange—published by Horizon Press in 1963 [Ellison's note].

2. African American author (1924–1987). Wright (1908–1960), African American author.

Howe—but the spiritual father of Ellison, Baldwin and all other Negroes of literary bent to come. Further, in the platonic sense he is his own father and the culture hero who freed Ellison and Baldwin to write more "modulated" prose.

Howe admires Wright's accomplishments, and is frankly annoyed by the more favorable evaluation currently placed upon the works of the younger men. His claims for *Native Son* are quite broad:

> The day [it] appeared, American culture was changed forever . . . it made impossible a repetition of the old lies . . . it brought into the open . . . the fear and violence that have crippled and may yet destroy our culture. . . . A blow at the white man, the novel forced him to recognize himself as an oppressor. A blow at the black man, the novel forced him to recognize the cost of his submission. *Native Son* assaulted the most cherished of American vanities: the hope that the accumulated injustices of the past would bring with it no lasting penalties, the fantasy that in his humiliation the Negro somehow retained a sexual potency . . . that made it necessary to envy and still more to suppress him. Speaking from the black wrath of retribution, Wright insisted that history can be a punishment. He told us the one thing even the most liberal whites preferred not to hear: that Negroes were far from patient or forgiving, that they were scarred by fear, that they hated every moment of their suppression even when seeming most acquiescent, and that often enough they hated *us*, the decent and cultivated white men who from complicity or neglect shared in the responsibility of their plight. . . .

There are also negative criticisms: that the book is "crude," "melodramatic" and marred by "claustrophobia" of vision, that its characters are "cartoons," etc. But these defects Howe forgives because of the book's "clenched militancy." One wishes he had stopped there. For in his zeal to champion Wright, it is as though he felt it necessary to stage a modern version of the Biblical myth of Noah, Ham, Shem and Japheth (based originally, I'm told, on a castration ritual), with first Baldwin and then Ellison acting out the impious role of Ham:[3] Baldwin by calling attention to Noah-Wright's artistic nakedness in his famous essays, "Everybody's Protest Novel" (1949) and "Many Thousands Gone" (1951); Ellison by rejecting "narrow naturalism" as a fictional method, and by alluding to the "diversity, fluidity and magical freedom of American life" on that (for him at least) rather magical occasion when he was awarded the National Book Award. Ellison also offends by having the narrator of *Invisible Man* speak of his life (Howe either missing the irony or assuming that *I* did) as one of "infinite possibilities" while living in a hole in the ground.

Howe begins by attacking Baldwin's rejection in "Everybody's Protest Novel" of the type of literature he labeled "protest fiction" (*Uncle Tom's Cabin* and *Native Son*[4] being prime examples), and which he considered incapable of dealing adequately with the complexity of Negro experience. Howe, noting that this was the beginning of Baldwin's career, sees the essay's underlying motive as a declaration of Baldwin's intention to transcend "the sterile categories of 'Negroness,' whether those enforced by the white world or those

3. After his son Ham saw him naked and drunk in his tent, Noah cursed Ham and his descendants and made them slaves to the two brothers, who had covered their father with a garment.

4. Richard Wright's 1940 novel. Harriet Beecher Stowe's *Uncle Tom's Cabin* (1852) aroused much northern indignation against slavery.

defensively erected by the Negroes themselves. No longer mere victim or rebel, the Negro would stand free in a self-achieved humanity. As Baldwin put it some years later, he hoped to 'prevent himself from becoming merely a Negro; or even, merely, a Negro writer.'" Baldwin's elected agency for self-achievement would be the novel—as it turns out, it was the essay *and* the novel—but the novel, states Howe, "is an inherently ambiguous genre: it strains toward formal autonomy and can seldom avoid being public gesture."

I would have said that it is *always* a public gesture, though not necessarily a political one. I would also have pointed out that the American Negro novelist is himself "inherently ambiguous." As he strains toward self-achievement as artist (and here he can only "integrate" and free himself), he moves toward fulfilling his dual potentialities as Negro and American. While Howe agrees with Baldwin that "literature and sociology are not one and the same," he notes nevertheless that, "it is equally true that such statements hardly begin to cope with the problem of how a writer's own experience affects his desire to represent human affairs in a work of fiction." Thus Baldwin's formula evades "through rhetorical sweep, the genuinely difficult issue of the relationship between social experience and literature." And to Baldwin's statement that one writes "out of one thing only—one's own experience" (I would have added, for the novelist, this qualification: one's own experience as understood and ordered through one's knowledge of self, culture and literature), Howe, appearing suddenly in blackface, replies with a rhetorical sweep of his own:

> What, then, was the experience of a man with a black skin, what *could* it be here in this country? How could a Negro put pen to paper, how could he so much as think or breathe, without some impulsion to protest, be it harsh or mild, political or private, released or buried? . . . The "sociology" of his existence forms a constant pressure on his literary work, and not merely in the way this might be true of any writer, but with a pain and ferocity that nothing could remove.

I must say that this brought a shock of recognition. Some twelve years ago, a friend argued with me for hours that I could not possibly write a novel because my experience as a Negro had been too excruciating to allow me to achieve that psychological and emotional distance necessary to artistic creation. Since he "knew" Negro experience better than I, I could not convince him that he might be wrong. Evidently Howe feels that unrelieved suffering is the only "real" Negro experience, and that the true Negro writer must be ferocious.

But there is also an American Negro tradition which teaches one to deflect racial provocation and to master and contain pain. It is a tradition which abhors as obscene any trading on one's own anguish for gain or sympathy; which springs not from a desire to deny the harshness of existence but from a will to deal with it as men at their best have always done. It takes fortitude to be a man and no less to be an artist. Perhaps it takes even more if the black man would be an artist. If so, there are no exemptions. It would seem to me, therefore, that the question of how the "sociology of his existence" presses upon a Negro writer's work depends upon how much of his life the individual writer is able to transform into art. What moves a writer to eloquence is less meaningful than what he makes of it. How much, by the way, do we know of Sophocles'[5] wounds?

5. Greek tragic poet (ca. 496–406 B.C.E.).

One unfamiliar with what Howe stands for would get the impression that when he looks at a Negro he sees not a human being but an abstract embodiment of living hell. He seems never to have considered that American Negro life (and here he is encouraged by certain Negro "spokesmen") is, for the Negro who must live it, not only a burden (and not always that) but also a *discipline*—just as any human life which has endured so long is a discipline teaching its own insights into the human condition, its own strategies of survival. There is a fullness, even a richness here; and here *despite* the realities of politics, perhaps, but nevertheless here and real. Because it is *human* life. And Wright, for all of his indictments, was no less its product than that other talented Mississippian, Leontyne Price.[6] To deny in the interest of revolutionary posture that such possibilities of human richness exist for others, even in Mississippi, is not only to deny us our humanity but to betray the critic's commitment to social reality. Critics who do so should abandon literature for politics.

For even as his life toughens the Negro, even as it brutalizes him, sensitizes him, dulls him, goads him to anger, moves him to irony, sometimes fracturing and sometimes affirming his hopes; even as it shapes his attitudes toward family, sex, love, religion; even as it modulates his humor, tempers his joy—it *conditions* him to deal with his life and with himself. Because it is *his* life and no mere abstraction in someone's head. He must live it and try consciously to grasp its complexity until he can change it; must live it *as* he changes it. He is no mere product of his socio-political predicament. He is a product of the interaction between his racial predicament, his individual will and the broader American cultural freedom in which he finds his ambiguous existence. Thus he, too, in a limited way, is his own creation.

In his loyalty to Richard Wright, Howe considers Ellison and Baldwin guilty of filial betrayal because, in their own work, they have rejected the path laid down by *Native Son*, phonies because, while actually "black boys," they pretend to be mere American writers trying to react to something of the pluralism of their predicament.

In his myth Howe takes the roles of both Shem and Japheth, trying mightily (his face turned backward so as not to see what it is he's veiling) to cover the old man's bare belly, and then becoming Wright's voice from beyond the grave by uttering the curses which Wright was too ironic or too proud to have uttered himself, at least in print:

> In response to Baldwin and Ellison, Wright would have said (I virtually quote the words he used in talking to me during the summer of 1958) that only through struggle could men with black skins, and for that matter, all the oppressed of the world, achieve their humility. It was a lesson, said Wright, with a touch of bitterness yet not without kindness, that the younger writers would have to learn in their own way and their own time. All that has happened since bears him out.

What, coming eighteen years after *Native Son* and thirteen years after World War II, does this rather limp cliché mean? Nor is it clear what is meant by the last sentence—or is it that today Baldwin has come to out-Wrighting Richard? The real questions seem to be: How does the Negro writer participate *as a writer* in the struggle for human freedom? To whom does he address his work? What values emerging from Negro experience does he try to affirm?

6. African American soprano and eminent opera singer (b. 1927).

I started with the primary assumption that men with black skins, having retained their humanity before all of the conscious efforts made to dehumanize them, especially following the Reconstruction,[7] are unquestionably human. Thus they have the obligation of freeing themselves—whoever their allies might be—by depending upon the validity of their own experience for an accurate picture of the reality which they seek to change, and for a gauge of the values they would see made manifest. Crucial to this view is the belief that their resistance to provocation, their coolness under pressure, their sense of timing and their tenacious hold on the ideal of their ultimate freedom are indispensable values in the struggle, and are at least as characteristic of American Negroes as the hatred, fear and vindictiveness which Wright chose to emphasize.

Wright believed in the much abused idea that novels are "weapons"—the counterpart of the dreary notion, common among most minority groups, that novels are instruments of good public relations. But I believe that true novels, even when most pessimistic and bitter, arise out of an impulse to celebrate human life and therefore are ritualistic and ceremonial at their core. Thus they would preserve as they destroy, affirm as they reject.

In *Native Son*, Wright began with the ideological proposition that what whites think of the Negro's reality is more important than what Negroes themselves know it to be. Hence Bigger Thomas was presented as a near-subhuman indictment of white oppression. He was designed to shock whites out of their apathy and end the circumstances out of which Wright insisted Bigger emerged. Here environment is all—and interestingly enough, environment conceived solely in terms of the physical, the non-conscious. Well, cut off my legs and call me Shorty! Kill my parents and throw me on the mercy of the court as an orphan! Wright could imagine Bigger, but Bigger could not possibly imagine Richard Wright. Wright saw to that.

But without arguing Wright's right to his personal vision, I would say that he was himself a better argument for my approach than Bigger was for his. And so, to be fair and as inclusive as Howe, is James Baldwin. Both are true Negro Americans, and both affirm the broad possibility of personal realization which I see as a saving aspect of American life. Surely, this much can be admitted without denying the injustice which all three of us have protested.

Howe is impressed by Wright's pioneering role and by the ". . . enormous courage, the discipline of self-conquest required to conceive Bigger Thomas. . . ." And earlier: "If such younger novelists as Baldwin and Ralph Ellison were able to move beyond Wright's harsh naturalism toward more supple modes of fiction, that was only possible because Wright had been there first, courageous enough to release the full weight of his anger."

It is not for me to judge Wright's courage, but I must ask just why it was possible for me to write as I write "only" because Wright released his anger? Can't I be allowed to release my own? What does Howe know of my acquaintance with violence, or the shape of my courage or the intensity of my anger? I suggest that my credentials are at least as valid as Wright's, even though he began writing long before I did, and it is possible that I have lived through and committed even more violence than he. Howe must wait for an autobiography before he can be responsibly certain. Everybody wants to tell us

---

7. Period of adjustment (1865–77) following the Civil War, during which black political and civil rights were highly contested.

what a Negro is, yet few wish, even in a joke, to be one. But if you would tell me who I am, at least take the trouble to discover what I have been.

Which brings me to the most distressing aspect of Howe's thinking: his Northern white liberal version of the white Southern myth of absolute separation of the races. He implies that Negroes can only aspire to contest other Negroes (this at a time when Baldwin has been taking on just about everyone, including Hemingway, Faulkner and the United States Attorney General!), and must wait for the appearance of a Black Hope before they have the courage to move. Howe is so committed to a sociological vision of society that he apparently cannot see (perhaps because he is dealing with Negroes—although not because he would suppress us socially or politically, for in fact he is anxious to end such suppression) that whatever the efficiency of segregation as a socio-political arrangement, it has been far from absolute on the level of *culture*. Southern whites cannot walk, talk, sing, conceive of laws or justice, think of sex, love, the family or freedom without responding to the presence of Negroes.

Similarly, no matter how strictly Negroes are segregated socially and politically, on the level of the imagination their ability to achieve freedom is limited only by their individual aspiration, insight, energy and will. Wright was able to free himself in Mississippi because he had the imagination and the will to do so. He was as much a product of his reading as of his painful experiences, and he made himself a writer by subjecting himself to the writer's discipline—as he understood it. The same is true of James Baldwin, who is not the product of a Negro store-front church but of the library, and the same is true of me.

Howe seems to see segregation as an opaque steel jug with the Negroes inside waiting for some black messiah to come along and blow the cork. Wright is his hero and he sticks with him loyally. But if we are in a jug it is transparent, not opaque, and one is allowed not only to see outside but to read what is going on out there; to make identifications as to values and human quality. So in Macon County, Alabama, I read Marx, Freud, T. S. Eliot, Pound, Gertrude Stein and Hemingway.[8] Books which seldom, if ever, mentioned Negroes were to release me from whatever "segregated" idea I might have had of my human possibilities. I was freed not by propagandists or by the example of Wright—I did not know him at the time and was earnestly trying to learn enough to write a symphony and have it performed by the time I was twenty-six, because Wagner had done so and I admired his music—but by composers, novelists, and poets who spoke to me of more interesting and freer ways of life.

These were works which, by fulfilling themselves as works of art, by being satisfied to deal with life in terms of their own sources of power, were able to give me a broader sense of life and possibility. Indeed, I understand a bit more about myself as Negro because literature has taught me something of my identity as Western man, as political being. It has also taught me something of the cost of being an individual who aspires to conscious eloquence. It requires real poverty of the imagination to think that this can come to a

---

8. American novelist and short story writer (1899–1961). Karl Marx (1818–1883), German social philosopher and theorist of modern socialism and communism. Sigmund Freud (1856–1939), Austrian psychiatrist and founder of psychoanalysis. Eliot (1888–1965), United States–born English poet and critic. Ezra Pound (1885–1972), American poet, critic, and translator. Stein (1874–1946), American expatriate and author.

Negro *only* through the example of *other Negroes,* especially after the performance of the slaves in re-creating themselves, in good part, out of the images
and myths of the Old Testament Jews.

No, Wright was no spiritual father of mine, certainly in no sense I
recognize—nor did he pretend to be, since he felt that I had started writing
too late. It was Baldwin's career, not mine, that Wright proudly advanced by
helping him attain the Eugene Saxton Fellowship,[9] and it was Baldwin who
found Wright a lion in his path. Being older and familiar with quite different lions in quite different paths, I simply stepped around him.

But Wright was a friend for whose magazine I wrote my first book review
and short story, and a personal hero in the same way Hot Lips Paige and
Jimmy Rushing[1] were friends and heroes. I felt no need to attack what I considered the limitations of his vision because I was quite impressed by what he
had achieved. And in this, although I saw with the black vision of Ham,
I was, I suppose, as pious as Shem and Japheth. Still I would write my own
books and they would be in themselves, implicitly, criticisms of Wright's;
just as all novels of a given historical moment form an argument over the
nature of reality and are, to an extent, criticisms each of the other.

While I rejected Bigger Thomas as any *final* image of Negro personality, I
recognized *Native Son* as an achievement; as one man's essay in defining the
human condition as seen from a specific Negro perspective at a given time in
a given place. And I was proud to have known Wright and happy for the
impact he had made upon our apathy. But Howe's ideas notwithstanding, history is history, cultural contacts ever mysterious, and taste exasperatingly
personal. Two days after arriving in New York I was to read Malraux's *Man's
Fate* and *The Days of Wrath,*[2] and after these how could I be impressed by
Wright as an ideological novelist. Need my skin blind me to all other values?
Yet Howe writes:

> When Negro liberals write that despite the prevalence of bias there has
> been an improvement in the life of their people, such statements are
> reasonable and necessary. But what have these to do with the way
> Negroes feel, with the power of the memories they must surely retain?
> About this we know very little and would be well advised not to nourish
> preconceptions, for their feelings may well be closer to Wright's rasping
> outbursts than to the more modulated tones of the younger Negro novel-
> ists. *Wright remembered,* and what he remembered other Negroes must
> also have remembered. And in that way he kept faith with the experience
> of the boy who had fought his way out of the depths, to speak for those
> who remained there.

Wright, for Howe, is the genuine article, the authentic Negro writer, and
his tone the only authentic tone. But why strip Wright of his individuality
in order to criticize other writers. He had his memories and I have mine,
just as I suppose Irving Howe has his—or has Marx spoken the final word
for him? Indeed, very early in *Black Boy,*[3] Wright's memory and his contact
with literature come together in a way revealing, at least to the eye con-

9. At Wright's request, Baldwin mailed him the
first sixty pages of his first novel, *In My Father's
House,* which Wright liked enough to arrange
the award for Baldwin. Baldwin was unable to
complete the novel during the tenure of the
fellowship.

1. Jazz singer (1903–1972). Oran "Hot Lips"
Page (1908–1954), jazz trumpeter and singer.
2. Novels by French author and political figure
André-Georges Malraux (1901–1976).
3. Wright's 1945 autobiography.

cerned with Wright the literary man, that his manner of keeping faith with the Negroes who remained in the depths is quite interesting:

(After I had outlived the shocks of childhood, after the habit of reflection had been born in me, I used to mull over the strange absence of real kindness in Negroes, how unstable was our tenderness, how lacking in genuine passion we were, how void of great hope, how timid our joy, how bare our traditions, how hollow our memories, how lacking we were in those intangible sentiments that bind man to man and how shallow was even our despair. After I had learned other ways of life I used to brood upon the unconscious irony of those who felt that Negroes led so passional an existence! I saw that what had been taken for our emotional strength was our negative confusions, our flights, our fears, our frenzy under pressure.

(Whenever I thought of the essential bleakness of black life in America, I knew that Negroes had never been allowed to catch the full spirit of Western civilization, that they lived somehow in it but not of it. And when I brooded upon the cultural barrenness of black life, I wondered if clean, positive tenderness, love, honor, loyalty and the capacity to remember were native with man. I asked myself if these human qualities were not fostered, won, struggled and suffered for, preserved in ritual from one generation to another.)

Must I be condemned because my sense of Negro life was quite different? Or because for me keeping faith would never allow me to even raise such a question about any segment of humanity? *Black Boy* is not a sociological case history but an autobiography, and therefore a work of art shaped by a writer bent upon making an ideological point. Doubtlessly, this was the beginning of Wright's exile, the making of a decision which was to shape his life and writing thereafter. And it is precisely at this point that Wright is being what I would call, in Howe's words, "literary to a fault."

For just as *How Bigger Was Born* is Wright's Jamesian preface to *Native Son,* the passage quoted above is his paraphrase of Henry James' catalogue of those items of a high civilization which were absent from American life during Hawthorne's[4] day, and which seemed so necessary in order for the novelist to function. This, then, was Wright's list of those items of high humanity which he found missing among Negroes. Thank God, I have never been quite that literary.

How awful that Wright found the facile answers of Marxism before he learned to use literature as a means for discovering the forms of American Negro humanity. I could not and cannot question their existence, I can only seek again and again to project that humanity as I see it and feel it. To me Wright as *writer* was less interesting than the enigma he personified: that he could so dissociate himself from the complexity of his background while trying so hard to improve the condition of black men everywhere; that he could be so wonderful an example of human possibility but could not for ideological reasons depict a Negro as intelligent, as creative or as dedicated as himself.

---

4. Nathaniel Hawthorne (1804–1864), American novelist and short story writer. James (1843–1916), American novelist and critic.

In his effort to resuscitate Wright, Irving Howe would designate the role which Negro writers are to play more rigidly than any Southern politician—and for the best of reasons. We must express "black" anger and "clenched militancy"; most of all we should not become too interested in the problems of the art of literature, even though it is through these that we seek our individual identities. And between writing well and being ideologically militant, we must choose militancy.

Well, it all sounds quite familiar and I fear the social order which it forecasts more than I do that of Mississippi. Ironically, during the 1940s it was one of the main sources of Wright's rage and frustration.

II

I am sorry Irving Howe got the impression that I was throwing bean-balls when I only meant to pitch him a hyperbole. It would seem, however, that he approves of angry Negro writers only until one questions his ideas; then he reaches for his honor, cries "misrepresentation" and "distortion," and charges the writer with being both out of control of himself and with fashioning a "strategy calculated to appeal, ready-made, to the preconceptions of the liberal audience." Howe implies that there are differences between us which I disguised in my essay, yet whatever the validity of this attempt at long-distance psychoanalysis, it was not his honor which I questioned but his thinking; not his good faith but his critical method.

And the major differences which these raised between us I tried to describe. They are to be seen by anyone who reads Howe's "Black Boys and Native Sons" not as a collection of thematically related fragments but as the literary exposition of a considered point of view. I tried to interpret this essay in the light of the impact it made upon my sense of life and literature, and I judged it through its total form—just as I would have Howe base his judgments of writers and their circumstances on as much of what we know about the actual complexity of men living in a highly pluralistic society as is possible. I realize that the *un*common sense of a critic, his special genius, is a gift to be thankful for whenever we find it. The very least I expected of Howe, though, was that he would remember his *common* sense, that he would not be carried away by that intellectual abandon, that lack of restraint, which seizes those who regard blackness as an absolute and who see in it a release from the complications of the real world.

Howe is interested in militant confrontation and suffering, yet evidently he recognizes neither when they involve some act of his own. He *really* did not know the subject was loaded. Very well, but I was brought into the booby-trapped field of his assumptions and finding myself in pain, I did not choose to "hold back from the suffering" inflicted upon me there. Out of an old habit I yelled—without seeking Howe's permission, it is true—where it hurt the most. For oddly enough, I found it far less painful to have to move to the back of a Southern bus, or climb to the peanut gallery of a movie house—matters about which I could do nothing except walk, read, hunt, dance, sculpt, cultivate ideas, or seek other uses for my time—than to tolerate concepts which distorted the actual reality of my situation or my reactions to it.

I could escape the reduction imposed by unjust laws and customs, but not that imposed by ideas which defined me as no more than the *sum* of those laws and customs. I learned to outmaneuver those who interpreted my silence as submission, my efforts at self-control as fear, my contempt as awe before superior status, my dreams of faraway places and room at the top of the heap as defeat before the barriers of their stifling, provincial world. And my struggle became a desperate battle which was usually fought, though not always, in silence; a guerrilla action in a larger war in which I found some of the most treacherous assaults against me committed by those who regarded themselves either as neutrals, as sympathizers, or as disinterested military advisers.

I recall this not in complaint, for thus was I disciplined to endure the absurdities of both conscious and unconscious prejudice, to resist racial provocation and, before the ready violence of brutal policemen, railroad "bulls," and casual white citizens, to hold my peace and bide my time. Thus was I forced to evaluate my own self-worth, and the narrow freedom in which it existed, against the power of those who would destroy me. In time I was to leave the South, although it has never left me, and the interests which I discovered there became my life.

But having left the South I did not leave the battle—for how could I leave Howe? He is a man of words and ideas, and since I, too, find my identity in the world of ideas and words, where would I flee? I still endure the nonsense of fools with a certain patience, but when a respected critic distorts my situation in order to feel comfortable in the abstractions he would impose upon American reality, then it is indeed "in accordance with my nature" to protest. Ideas are important in themselves, perhaps, but when they are interposed between me and my sense of reality I feel threatened; they are too elusive, they move with missile speed and are too often fired from altitudes rising high above the cluttered terrain upon which I struggle. And too often those with a facility for ideas find themselves in the councils of power representing me at the double distance of racial alienation and inexperience.

Taking leave of Howe for a moment—for his lapse is merely symptomatic— let me speak generally. Many of those who write of Negro life today seem to assume that as long as their hearts are in the right place they can be as arbitrary as they wish in their formulations. Others seem to feel that they can air with impunity their most private Freudian fantasies as long as they are given the slightest camouflage of intellectuality and projected as "Negro." They have made of the no-man's land created by segregation a territory for infantile self-expression and intellectual anarchy. They write as though Negro life exists only in light of their belated regard, and they publish interpretations of Negro experience which would not hold true for their own or for any other form of human life.

Here the basic unity of human experience that assures us of some possibility of empathic and symbolic identification with those of other backgrounds is blasted in the interest of specious political and philosophical conceits. Prefabricated Negroes are sketched on sheets of paper and superimposed upon the Negro community; then when someone thrusts his head through the page and yells, "Watch out there, Jack, there're people living under here," they are shocked and indignant. I am afraid, however, that we shall hear much more of such protest as these interpositions continue. And I predict this, not out of any easy gesture of militancy (and what an easy con-game for ambitious, publicity-hungry Negroes this stance of "militancy" has become!) but because as Negroes express increasingly their irritation in this critical area, many of those who make so lightly with our image shall find their own subjected to a most devastating scrutiny.

One of the most insidious crimes occurring in this democracy is that of designating another, politically weaker, less socially acceptable, people as the receptacle for one's own self-disgust, for one's own infantile rebellions, for one's own fears of, and retreats from, reality. It is the crime of reducing the humanity of others to that of a mere convenience, a counter in a banal game which involves no apparent risk to ourselves. With us Negroes it started with the appropriation of our freedom and our labor; then it was our music, our speech, our dance and the comic distortion of our image by burnt-corked, cotton-gloved corn-balls yelling, "Mammy!" And while it would be futile, non-tragic, and un-Negro American to complain over the processes through which we have become who and what we are, it is perhaps permissible to say that the time for such misappropriations ran out long ago.

For one thing, Negro American consciousness is not a product (as so often seems true of so many American groups) of a will to historical forget-fulness. It is a product of our memory, sustained and constantly reinforced by events, by our watchful waiting, and by our hopeful suspension of final judgment as to the meaning of our grievances. For another, most Negroes recognize themselves as themselves despite what others might believe them to be. Thus, although the sociologists tell us that thousands of light-skinned Negroes become white each year undetected, most Negroes can spot a paper-thin "white Negro" every time simply because those who masquerade missed what others were forced to pick up along the way: discipline—a discipline which these heavy thinkers would not undergo even if guaranteed that combined with their own heritage it would make of them the freest of spir-its, the wisest of men and the most sublime of heroes.

The rhetorical strategy of my original reply was not meant, as Howe inter-prets it, to strike the stance of a "free artist" against the "ideological critic," although I *do* recognize that I can be free only to the extent that I detect error and grasp the complex reality of my circumstances and work to domi-nate it through the techniques which are my means of confronting the world. Perhaps I am only free enough to recognize those tendencies of thought which, actualized, would render me even less free.

Even so, I did not intend to take the stance of the "knowing Negro writer" against the "presuming white intellectual." While I am without doubt a Negro, and a writer, I am also an *American* writer, and while I am more knowing than Howe where my own life and its influences are concerned, I took the time to question his presumptions as one responsible for contribut-ing as much as he is capable to the clear perception of American social reality. For to think unclearly about that segment of reality in which I find my existence is to do myself violence. To allow others to go unchallenged when they distort that reality is to participate not only in that distortion but to accept, as in this instance, a violence inflicted upon the art of criticism. And if I am to recognize those aspects of my role as writer which do not depend primarily upon my racial identity, if I am to fulfill the writer's basic responsibilities to his craft, then surely I must insist upon the maintenance of a certain level of precision in language, a maximum correspondence between the form of a piece of writing and its content, and between words and ideas and the things and processes of his world.

Whatever my role as "race man" (and it knocks me out whenever anyone, black or white, tries to tell me—and the white Southerners have no mon-opoly here—how to become their conception of a "good Negro"), I am as writer no less a custodian of the American language than is Irving Howe. Indeed, to the extent that I am a writer—I lay no claims to being a thinker— the American language, including the Negro idiom, is all that I have. So let me emphasize that my reply to Howe was neither motivated by racial defensiveness nor addressed to his own racial identity.

It is fortunate that it was not, for considering how Howe identifies himself in this instance, I would have missed the target, which would have been embarrassing. Yet it would have been an innocent mistake, because in situations such as this many Negroes, like myself, make a positive distinction between "whites" and "Jews." Not to do so could be either offensive, embarrassing, unjust or even dangerous. If I would know who I am and preserve who I am, then I must see others distinctly whether they see me so or no. Thus I feel uncomfortable whenever I discover Jewish intellectuals writing as though *they* were guilty of enslaving my grandparents, or as though the *Jews* were responsible for the system of segregation. Not only do they have enough troubles of their own, as the saying goes, but Negroes know this only too well.

The real guilt of such Jewish intellectuals lies in their facile, perhaps unconscious, but certainly unrealistic, identification with what is called the "power structure." Negroes call that "passing for white." Speaking personally, both as writer and as Negro American, I would like to see the more positive distinctions between whites and Jewish Americans maintained. Not only does it make for a necessary bit of historical and social clarity, at least where Negroes are concerned, but I consider the United States freer politically and richer culturally because there are Jewish Americans to bring it the benefit of their special forms of dissent, their humor and their gift for ideas which are based upon the uniqueness of their experience. The diversity of American life is often painful, frequently burdensome and always a source of conflict, but in it lies our fate and our hope.

To Howe's charge that I found his exaggerated claims for Richard Wright's influence upon my own work presumptuous, I plead guilty. Was it necessary to impose a line of succession upon Negro writers simply because Howe identified with Wright's cause? And why, since he grasps so readily the intentional absurdity of my question regarding his relationship to Marx, couldn't he see that the notion of an intellectual or artistic succession based upon color or racial background is no less absurd than one based upon a common religious background? (*Of course, Irving, I know that you haven't believed in final words for twenty years—not even your own—and I know, too, that the line from Marx to Howe is as complex and as dialectical as that from Wright to Ellison. My point was to try to see to it that certain lapses in your thinking did not become final.*) In fact, this whole exchange would never have started had I not been dragged into the discussion. Still, if Howe could take on the role of man with a "black skin," why shouldn't I assume the role of critic-of-critic?

But how surprising are Howe's ideas concerning the ways of controversy. Why, unless of course he holds no respect for his opponent, should a polemicist be expected to make things *hard* for himself? As for the "preconceptions of the liberal audience," I had not considered them, actually, except as they appear in Howe's own thinking. Beyond this I wrote for anyone who might hesitate to question his formulations, especially very young Negro writers who might be bewildered by the incongruity of such ideas coming from such an authority. Howe himself rendered complicated rhetorical strategies unnecessary by lunging into questionable territory with his flanks left so unprotected that any schoolboy sniper could have routed him with a bird gun. Indeed, his reaction to my reply reminds me of an incident which occurred during the 1937 Recession[5] when a companion and I were hunting the country outside Dayton, Ohio.

There had been a heavy snowfall and we had just put up a covey of quail from a thicket which edged a field when, through the rising whirr of the rocketing, snow-shattering birds, we saw, emerging from a clump of trees across the field, a large, red-faced, mackinawed farmer, who came running toward us shouting and brandishing a rifle. I could see strands of moisture tearing from his working mouth as he came on, running like a bear across the whiteness, the brown birds veering and scattering before him; and standing there against the snow, a white hill behind me and with no tree nor foxhole for cover I felt as exposed as a Black Muslim caught at a meeting of the K.K.K.[6]

He had appeared as suddenly as the quail, and although the rifle was not yet to his shoulder, I was transfixed, watching him zooming up to become the largest, loudest, most aggressive-sounding white man I'd seen in my life, and I was, quite frankly, afraid. Then I was measuring his approach to the crunching tempo of his running and praying silently that he'd come within range of my shotgun before he fired; that I would be able to do what seemed necessary for me to do; that, shooting from the hip with an old twelve-gauge shotgun, I could stop him before he could shoot either me or my companion; and that, though stopped effectively, he would be neither killed, nor blinded, nor maimed.

It was a mixed-up prayer in an icy interval which ended in a smoking fury of cursing, when, at a warning from my companion, the farmer suddenly halted. Then we learned that the reckless man had meant only to warn us off of land which was not even his but that of a neighbor—my companion's foster father. He stood there between the two shotguns pointing short-ranged at his middle, his face quite drained of color now by the realization of how close to death he'd come, sputtering indignantly that we'd interpreted his rifle, which wasn't loaded, in a manner other than he'd intended. He truly did not realize that situations can be more loaded than guns and gestures more eloquent than words.

Fortunately, words are not rifles, but perhaps Howe is just as innocent of the rhetorical eloquence of situations as the farmer. He does not see that the meaning which emerges from his essay is not determined by isolated statements, but by the juxtaposition of those statements in a context which creates a larger statement. Or that contributing to the judgment rendered by that larger statement is the one in which it is uttered. When Howe pits Baldwin and Ellison against Wright and then gives Wright the better of the argument by using such emotionally weighted terms as "remembered" and "kept faith," the implication to me is that Baldwin and Ellison did *not* remember or keep faith with those who remained behind. If this be true, then I think that in this instance "villain" is not too strong a term.

5. From 1937 to 1938 there was a severe recession, during which time the percentage of industries registering decline was 97 to 100 percent.
6. Ku Klux Klan, a secret organization directed against blacks, Catholics, Jews, and the foreign born. "Black Muslim": a member of a U.S. black nationalist religious movement.

Howe is not the first writer given to sociological categories who has had unconscious value judgments slip into his "analytical" or "scientific" descriptions. Thus I can believe that his approach was meant to be "analytic, not exhortatory; descriptive, not prescriptive." The results, however, are something else again. And are we to believe that he simply does not recognize rhetoric when he practices it? That when he asks, "what *could* [his italics] the experience of a man with a black skin be . . ." etc., he thinks he is describing a situation as viewed by each and every Negro writer rather than expressing, yes, and in the mode of "exhortation," the views of Irving Howe? Doesn't he recognize that just as the anti-Negro stereotype is a command to Negroes to mold themselves in its image, there sounds through his descriptive "thus it is" the command "thus you become"? And doesn't he realize that in this emotion-charged area definitive description is, in effect, prescription? If he does not, how then can we depend upon his "analysis" of politics or his reading of fiction?

Perhaps Howe could relax his views concerning the situation of the writers with a "black skin" if he examined some of the meanings which he gives to the word "Negro." He contends that I "cannot help being caught up with *the idea* of the Negro," but I have never said that I could or wished to do so—only Howe makes a problem for me here. When he uses the term "Negro" he speaks of it as a "stigma," and again, he speaks of "Negroness" as a "sterile category." He sees the Negro writer as experiencing a "constant pressure upon his literary work" from the "sociology of his existence . . . not merely in the way this might be true of any writer, but with a *pain* and *ferocity* that nothing could remove."[7]

Note that this is a condition arising from a *collective* experience which leaves no room for the individual writer's unique existence. It leaves no room for that intensity of personal anguish which compels the artist to seek relief by projecting it into the world in conjunction with other things; that anguish which might take the form of an acute sense of inferiority for one, homosexuality for another, an overwhelming sense of the absurdity of human life for still another. Nor does it leave room for the experience that might be caused by humiliation, by a harelip, by a stutter, by epilepsy—indeed, by any and everything in this life which plunges the talented individual into solitude while leaving him the will to transcend his condition through art. The individual Negro writer must create out of his own special needs and through his own sensibilities, and these alone. Otherwise, all those who suffer in anonymity would be creators.

Howe makes of "Negroness" a metaphysical condition, one that is a state of irremediable agony which all but engulfs the mind. Happily, the view from inside the skin is not so dark as it appears to be from Howe's remote position, and therefore my view of "Negroness" is neither his nor that of the exponents of *negritude*. It is not skin color which makes a Negro American but cultural heritage as shaped by the American experience, the social and political predicament; a sharing of that "concord of sensibilities" which the group expresses through historical circumstance and through which it has come to constitute a subdivision of the larger American culture. Being a Negro American has to do with the memory of slavery and the hope of emancipation and the betrayal by allies and the revenge and contempt inflicted by our former masters after the Reconstruction, and the myths, both North-

7. Italics mine [Ellison's note].

ern and Southern, which are propagated in justification of that betrayal. It involves, too, a special attitude toward the waves of immigrants who have come later and passed us by.

It has to do with a special perspective on the national ideals and the national conduct, and with a tragicomic attitude toward the universe. It has to do with special emotions evoked by the details of cities and countrysides, with forms of labor and with forms of pleasure; with sex and with love, with food and with drink, with machines and with animals; with climates and with dwellings, with places of worship and places of entertainment; with garments and dreams and idioms of speech; with manners and customs, with religion and art, with life styles and hoping, and with that special sense of predicament and fate which gives direction and resonance to the Freedom Movement.[8] It involves a rugged initiation into the mysteries and rites of color which makes it possible for Negro Americans to suffer the injustice which race and color are used to excuse without losing sight of either the humanity of those who inflict that injustice or the motives, rational or irrational, out of which they act. It imposes the uneasy burden and occasional joy of a complex double vision, a fluid, ambivalent response to men and events which represents, at its finest, a profoundly civilized adjustment to the cost of being human in this modern world.

More important, perhaps, being a Negro American involves a *willed* (who wills to be a Negro? *I* do!) affirmation of self as against all outside pressures—an identification with the group as extended through the individual self which rejects all possibilities of escape that do not involve a basic resuscitation of the original American ideals of social and political justice. And those white Negroes (and I do not mean Norman Mailer's[9] dream creatures) are Negroes too—if they wish to be.

Howe's defense against my charge that he sees unrelieved suffering as the basic reality of Negro life is to quote favorable comments from his review of *Invisible Man*. But this does not cancel out the restricted meaning which he gives to "Negroness," or his statement that "the sociology of [the Negro writer's] existence forms a constant pressure with a *pain* and *ferocity* that nothing could remove." He charges me with unfairness for writing that he believes ideological militancy is more important than writing well, yet he tells us that "there may of course be times when one's obligation as a human being supersedes one's obligation as a writer. . . ." I think that the writer's obligation in a struggle as broad and abiding as the one we are engaged in, which involves not merely Negroes but all Americans, is best carried out through his role as writer. And if he chooses to stop writing and take to the platform, then it should be out of personal choice and not under pressure from would-be managers of society.

Howe plays a game of pitty-pat with Baldwin and Ellison. First he throws them into the pit for lacking Wright's "pain," "ferocity," "memory," "faithfulness" and "clenched militance," then he pats them on the head for the quality of their writing. If he would see evidence of this statement, let him observe how these terms come up in his original essay when he traces Baldwin's move toward Wright's position. Howe's rhetoric is weighted against "more modulated tones" in favor of "rasping outbursts," the Baldwin of *Another Country*

8. The civil rights movement of the 1960s.
9. American writer (1923–2007).

becomes "a voice of anger, rasping and thrusting," and he is no longer "held back" by the "proprieties of literature." The character of Rufus in that novel displays a "ferocity" quite new in Baldwin's fiction, and Baldwin's essays gain resonance from "the tone of unrelenting protest . . . from [their] very anger, even the violence," etc. I am afraid that these are "good" terms in Howe's essay and they led to part of my judgment.

In defense of Wright's novel *The Long Dream*, Howe can write:

> . . . This book has been attacked for presenting Negro life in the South through "old-fashioned" images of violence, but [and now we have "pre-scription"] one ought to hesitate before denying the relevance of such images or joining in the criticism of their use. *For Wright was perhaps justified* in not paying attention to the changes that have occurred in the South these past few decades.[1]

If this isn't a defense, if not of bad writing at least of an irresponsible attitude toward good writing, I simply do not understand the language. I find it astonishing advice, since novels exist, since the fictional spell comes into existence precisely through the care which the novelist gives to select-ing the details, the images, the tonalities, the specific social and psycho-logical processes of specific characters in specific milieus at specific points in time. Indeed, it is one of the main tenets of the novelist's morality that he should write of that which he knows, and this is especially crucial for nov-elists who deal with a society as mobile and rapidly changing as ours. To justify ignoring this basic obligation is to encourage the downgrading of lit-erature in favor of other values, in this instance "anger," "protest" and "clenched militancy." Novelists create not simply out of "memory" but out of memory modified, extended, transformed by social change. For a novelist to heed such advice as Howe's is to commit an act of artistic immorality. Amplify this back through society and the writer's failure could produce not order but chaos.

Yet Howe proceeds on the very next page of his essay to state, with no sense of contradiction, that Wright failed in some of the stories which com-prise *Eight Men* ("The Man Who Lived Underground" was first published, by the way, in 1944) because he needed the "accumulated material of cir-cumstance." If a novelist ignores social change, how can he come by the "accumulated material of circumstance"? Perhaps if Howe could grasp the full meaning of that phrase he would understand that Wright did not report in *Black Boy* much of his life in Mississippi, and he would see that Ross Barnett[2] is not the whole state, that there is also a Negro Mississippi which is much more varied than that which Wright depicted.

For the critic there simply exists no substitute for the knowledge of history and literary tradition. Howe stresses Wright's comment that when he went into rooms where there were naked white women he felt like a "non-man . . . doubly cast out." But had Howe thought about it he might have questioned this reaction, since most young men would have been delighted with the opportunity to study, at first hand, women usually cloaked in an armor of taboos. I wonder how Wright felt when he saw Negro women acting just as shamelessly? Clearly this was an ideological point, not a factual report. And anyone aware of the folk sources of Wright's efforts to create literature

1. Italics mine [Ellison's note].
2. Governor of Mississippi during the early civil rights era (1960–64).

would recognize that the situation is identical with that of the countless stories which Negro men tell of the male slave called in to wash the mistress' back in the bath, of the Pullman porter invited in to share the beautiful white passenger's favors in the berth, of the bellhop seduced by the wealthy blond guest.

It is interesting that Howe should interpret my statement about Mississippi as evidence of a loss of self-control. So allow me to repeat it coldly: I fear the implications of Howe's ideas concerning the Negro writer's role as actionist more than I do the State of Mississippi. Which is not to deny the viciousness which exists there but to recognize the degree of freedom which also exists there precisely because the repression is relatively crude, or at least it was during Wright's time, and it left the world of literature alone. William Faulkner lived neither in Jefferson nor Frenchman's Bend but in Oxford. He, too, was a Mississippian, just as the boys who helped Wright leave Jackson were the sons of a Negro college president. Both Faulkner and these boys must be recognized as part of the social reality of Mississippi. I said nothing about Ross Barnett, and I certainly did not say that Howe was a "cultural authoritarian," so he should not spread his honor so thin. Rather, let him look to the implications of his thinking.

Yes, and let him learn more about the South and about Negro Americans if he would speak with authority. When he points out that "the young Ralph Ellison, even while reading these great writers, could not in Macon County attend the white man's school or movie house," he certainly appears to have me cornered. But here again he does not know the facts and he underplays choice and will. I rode freight trains to Macon County, Alabama, during the Scottsboro trial because I desired to study with the Negro conductor-composer William L. Dawson,[3] who was, and probably still is, the greatest classical musician in that part of the country. I had no need to attend a white university when the master I wished to study with was available at Tuskegee. Besides, why should I have wished to attend the white state-controlled university where the works of the great writers might not have been so easily available.

As for the movie-going, it is ironic but nonetheless true that one of the few instances where "separate but equal" was truly separate and equal was in a double movie house in the town of Tuskegee, where Negroes and whites were accommodated in parallel theaters, entering from the same street level through separate entrances and with the Negro side viewing the same pictures shortly after the showing for whites had begun. It was a product of social absurdity and, of course, no real relief from our resentment over the restriction of our freedom, but the movies were just as enjoyable or boring. And yet, is not knowing the facts more interesting, even as an isolated instance, and more stimulating to real thought than making abstract assumptions? I went to the movies to see pictures, not to be with whites. I attended a certain college because what I wanted was there. What is more, I *never* attended a white school from kindergarten through my three years of college, and yet, like Howe, I have taught and lectured for some years now at Northern, predominantly white, colleges and universities.

Perhaps this counts for little, changes little of the general condition of society, but it *is* factual and it does form a part of my sense of reality because,

3. Musician and composer (1898–1971) who directed the Tuskegee Institute choir for many years. "Scottsboro trial": in 1931 nine black youths were indicted at Scottsboro, Alabama, on charges of having raped two white girls in a freight car passing through Alabama.

though it was not a part of Wright's life, it is my own. And if Howe thinks mine is an isolated instance, let him do a bit of research.

I do not really think that Howe can make a case for himself by bringing up the complimentary remarks which he made about *Invisible Man*. I did not quarrel with them in 1952, when they were first published, and I did not quarrel with them in my reply. His is the right of any critic to make judgment of a novel, and I do not see the point of arguing that I achieved an aesthetic goal if it did not work for him. I can only ask that my fiction be judged as art; if it fails, it fails aesthetically, not because I did or did not fight some ideological battle. I repeat, however, that Howe's strategy of bringing me into the public quarrel between Baldwin and Wright was inept. I simply did not belong in the conflict, since I knew, even then, that protest is *not* the source of the inadequacy characteristic of most novels by Negroes, but the simple failure of craft, bad writing; the desire to have protest perform the difficult tasks of art; the belief that racial suffering, social injustice or ideologies of whatever mammy-made variety, is enough. I know, also, that when the work of Negro writers has been rejected they have all too often protected their egos by blaming racial discrimination, while turning away from the fairly obvious fact that good art—and Negro musicians are ever present to demonstrate this—commands attention of itself, whatever the writer's politics or point of view. And they forget that publishers will publish almost anything which is written with even a minimum of competency, and that skill is developed by hard work, study and a conscious assault upon one's own fear and provincialism.

I agree with Howe that protest is an element of all art, though it does not necessarily take the form of speaking for a political or social program. It might appear in a novel as a technical assault against the styles which have gone before, or as protest against the human condition. If *Invisible Man* is even "apparently" free from "the ideological and emotional penalties suffered by Negroes in this country," it is because I tried to the best of my ability to transform these elements into art. My goal was not to escape, or hold back, but to work through; to transcend, as the blues transcend the painful conditions with which they deal. The protest is there, not because I was helpless before my racial condition, but because I *put* it there. If there is anything "miraculous" about the book it is the result of hard work undertaken in the belief that the work of art is important in itself, that it is a social action in itself.

I cannot hope to persuade Irving Howe to this view, for it seems quite obvious that he believes there are matters more important than artistic scrupulousness. I will point out, though, that the laws of literary form exert their validity upon all those who write, and that it is his slighting of the formal necessities of his essay which makes for some of our misunderstanding. After reading his reply, I gave in to my ear's suggestion that I had read certain of his phrases somewhere before, and I went to the library, where I discovered that much of his essay was taken verbatim from a review in the *Nation* of May 10, 1952, and that another section was published verbatim in the *New Republic* of February 13, 1962; the latter, by the way, being in its original context a balanced appraisal and warm farewell to Richard Wright.

But when Howe spliced these materials together with phrases from an old speech of mine, swipes at the critics of the *Sewanee* and *Kenyon* reviews (journals in which I have never published), and the Baldwin-Wright quarrel, the effect was something other than he must have intended. A dialectical transformation into a new quality took place and despite the intention of Howe's content, the form made its own statement. If he would find the absurdities he wants me to reduce to a quotation, he will really have to read his essay whole. One gets the impression that he did a paste-and-scissors job and, knowing what he intended, knowing how the separated pieces had operated by themselves, did not bother to read very carefully their combined effect. It could happen to anyone; nevertheless, I'm glad he is not a scientist or a social engineer.

I do not understand why Howe thinks I said anything on the subject of writing about "Negro experience" in a manner which excludes what he calls "plight and protest"; he must have gotten his Negroes mixed. But as to answering his question concerning the "ways a Negro writer can achieve personal realization apart from the common effort of his people to win their full freedom," I suggest that he ask himself in what way shall a Negro writer achieve personal realization (as writer) *after* his people shall have won their full freedom? The answer appears to be the same in both instances: He will have to go it alone! He must suffer alone even as he shares the suffering of his group, and he must write alone and pit his talents against the standards set by the best practitioners of the craft, both past and present, in any case. For the writer's real way of sharing the experience of his group is to convert its mutual suffering into lasting value. Is Howe suggesting, incidentally, that Heinrich Heine[4] did not exist?

His question is silly, really, for there is no such thing as "full freedom" (Oh, how Howe thirsts and hungers for the absolute for *Negroes!*), just as the notion of an equality of talent is silly. I am a Negro who once played trumpet with a certain skill, but alas, I am no Louis Armstrong or Clark Terry.[5] Willie Mays[6] has realized himself quite handsomely as an individual despite coming from an impoverished Negro background in oppressive Alabama; and Negro Americans, like most Americans who know the value of baseball, exult in his success. I am, after all, only a minor member, not the whole damned tribe; in fact, most Negroes have never heard of me. I could shake the nation for a while with a crime or with indecent disclosures, but my pride lies in earning the right to call myself quite simply "writer." Perhaps if I write well enough the children of today's Negroes will be proud that I did, and so, perhaps, will Irving Howe's.

Let me end with a personal note: Dear Irving, I have no objections to being placed beside Richard Wright in any estimation which is based not upon the irremediable ground of our common racial identity, but upon the quality of our achievements as writers. I respected Wright's work and I knew him, but this is not to say that he "influenced" me as significantly as you assume. Consult the text! I *sought out* Wright because I had read Eliot, Pound, Gertrude Stein and Hemingway, and as early as 1940 Wright viewed me as a potential rival, partially, it is true, because he feared I would allow myself to be used against him by political manipulators who were not Negro and who envied and hated him. But perhaps you will understand when I say he did not influence me if I point out that while one can do nothing about choosing one's relatives, one can, as artist, choose one's "ancestors." Wright was, in

---

4. German-born Jewish poet (1797–1856) who was politically exiled because of his liberal sympathies; he left for Paris in 1831.

5. African American jazz trumpeter (b. 1920).

6. Professional baseball player (b. 1931).

this sense, a "relative"; Hemingway an "ancestor." Langston Hughes,[7] whose work I knew in grade school and whom I knew before I knew Wright, was a "relative"; Eliot, whom I was to meet only many years later, and Malraux and Dostoievsky and Faulkner, were "ancestors"—if you please or don't please!

Do you still ask why Hemingway was more important to me than Wright? Not because he was white, or more "accepted." But because he appreciated the things of this earth which I love and which Wright was too driven or deprived or inexperienced to know: weather, guns, dogs, horses, love *and* hate and impossible circumstances which to the courageous and dedicated could be turned into benefits and victories. Because he wrote with such precision about the processes and techniques of daily living that I could keep myself and my brother alive during the 1937 Recession by following his descriptions of wing-shooting; because he knew the difference between politics and art and something of their true relationship for the writer. Because all that he wrote—and this is very important—was imbued with a spirit beyond the tragic with which I could feel at home, for it was very close to the feeling of the blues, which are, perhaps, as close as Americans can come to expressing the spirit of tragedy. (And if you think Wright knew anything about the blues, listen to a "blues" he composed with Paul Robeson singing, a *most* unfortunate collaboration!; and read his introduction to Paul Oliver's *Blues Fell This Morning*.[8]) But most important, because Hemingway was a greater artist than Wright, who although a Negro like myself, and perhaps a great man, understood little if anything of these, at least to me, important things. Because Hemingway loved the American language and the joy of writing, making the flight of birds, the loping of lions across an African plain, the mysteries of drink and moonlight, the unique styles of diverse peoples and individuals come alive on the page. Because he was in many ways the true father-as-artist of so many of us who came to writing during the late thirties.

I will not dwell upon Hemingway's activities in Spain or during the liberation in Paris,[9] for you know all of that. I will remind you, however, that any writer takes what he needs to get his own work done from wherever he finds it. I did not need Wright to tell me how to be a Negro, or how to be angry or to express anger—Joe Louis[1] was doing that very well—or even to teach me about socialism; my mother had canvassed for the socialists, not the communists, the year I was born. No, I had been a Negro for twenty-two or twenty-three years when I met Wright, and in more places and under a greater variety of circumstances than he had then known. He was generously helpful in sharing his ideas and information, but I needed instruction in other values and I found them in the works of other writers—Hemingway was one of them, T. S. Eliot initiated the search.

I like your part about Chekhov[2] arising from his sickbed to visit the penal colony at Sakhalin Island. It was, as you say, a noble act. But shouldn't we remember that it was significant only because Chekhov was *Chekhov*, the great writer? You compliment me truly, but I have not written so much or so

7. African American poet and author (1902–1967).
8. A history and criticism of blues music (1960) by Oliver (b. 1927), a British lecturer on art and folk music who has written extensively on jazz. Robeson (1898–1976), an African American actor and singer, was controversial for his left-wing politics.
9. On August 26, 1944, the German occupation of Paris ended.
1. American boxer (1914–1981).
2. Anton Chekhov (1860–1904), Russian short story writer, dramatist, and physician.

well, even though I *have* served a certain apprenticeship in the streets and even touch events in the Freedom Movement in a modest way. But I can also recall the story of a certain writer who succeeded with a great fanfare of publicity in having a talented murderer released from prison. It made for another very short story which ended quite tragically—though not for the writer: A few months after his release the man killed the mother of two young children. I also know of another really quite brilliant writer who, under the advice of certain wise men who were then managing the consciences of artists, abandoned the prison of his writing to go to Spain, where he was allowed to throw away his life defending a worthless hill. I have not heard his name in years but I remember it vividly; it was Christopher Cauldwell, *né* Christopher St. John Sprigg.[3] There are many such stories, Irving. It's heads you win, tails you lose, and you are quite right about my not following Baldwin, who is urged on by a nobility—or is it a demon—quite different from my own. It has cost me quite a pretty penny, indeed, but then I was always poor and not (and I know this is a sin in our America) too uncomfortable.

Dear Irving, I am still yakking on and there's many a thousand gone, but I assure you that no Negroes are beating down my door, putting pressure on me to join the Negro Freedom Movement, for the simple reason that they realize that I am enlisted for the duration. Such pressure is coming only from a few disinterested "military advisers," since Negroes want no more fairly articulate would-be Negro leaders cluttering up the airways. For, you see, my Negro friends recognize a certain division of labor among the members of the tribe. Their demands, like that of many whites, are that I publish more novels— and here I am remiss and vulnerable perhaps. You will recall what the Talmud[4] has to say about the trees of the forest and the making of books, etc. But then, Irving, they recognize what you have not allowed yourself to see; namely, that reply to your essay is in itself a small though necessary action in the Negro struggle for freedom. You should not feel unhappy about this or think that I regard you either as dishonorable or an enemy. I hope, rather, that you will come to view this exchange as an act of, shall we say, "antagonistic co-operation"?

1963, 1964

Remembering Richard Wright

Earlier today while considering my relationship with Richard Wright, I recalled Heraclitus' axiom "Geography is fate," and I was struck by the ironic fact that in this country, where Frederick Jackson Turner's[1] theory of the frontier has been so influential in shaping our conception of American history, very little attention has been given to the role played by geography in shaping the fate of Afro-Americans.

For example, Wright was a Mississippian who migrated to Chicago and then to New York. I, by contrast, am an Oklahoman and by geographical

3. British aviator, publisher, journalist, literary theorist, poet, and author of crime novels and nonfiction (1907–1937).
4. Volume of commentary on Jewish civil and religious law.
1. Historian of the American West (1861–1932). Heraclitus (ca. 540–480 B.C.E.), Greek philosopher.

origin a Southwesterner. Wright grew up in a part of what was the old Confederacy, while I grew up in a state which possesses no indigenous tradition of chattel slavery. Thus, while we both grew up in segregated societies, mine lacked many of the intensities of custom, tradition, and manners which "colored" the institutions of the Old South, and which were important in shaping Wright's point of view. Both of us were descendants of slaves, but since my civic, geographical, and political circumstances were different from those of Mississippi, Wright and I were united by our connection with a past condition of servitude, and divided by geography and a difference of experience based thereupon. And yet it was that very difference of experience and background which had much to do with Wright's important impact upon my sensibilities.

And then there was New York. I met Wright there in 1937, and it was no accidental encounter. It came about because through my reading and working in the library at Tuskegee Institute,[2] I'd become fascinated by the exciting developments that were taking place in modern literature. Somehow in my uninstructed reading of Eliot and Pound,[3] I had recognized a relationship between modern poetry and jazz music, and this led me to wonder why I was not encountering similar devices in the work of Afro-American writers. Indeed, such reading and wondering prepared me not simply to *meet* Wright, but to seek him out. It led, in other words, to a personal quest. I insist upon the "seeking out" because, you see, I too have an ego and it is important to me that our meeting came about through my own initiative. For not only is it historically true, but it has something to do with my being privileged to be here on what I consider to be a very important moment in the history of our literature. Perhaps Richard Wright would have dismissed such a moment as impossible, even as late as 1957, but still, here we are, gathered in the hot summertime to pay him honor. *I* would not have been surprised, since it was my reading of one of Wright's poems in the *New Masses*[4] which gave me a sense of his importance. I had arrived in New York on July 5, 1936—a date of no broad symbolic importance, but one highly significant to me because it made a meeting with Wright a possibility. For although the *New Masses* poem was not a masterpiece, I found in it traces of the modern poetic sensibility and technique that I had been seeking.

The morning after my arrival in New York, I encountered standing in the entrance of the Harlem YMCA two fateful figures. They were Langston Hughes, the poet, and Dr. Alain Locke, the then head of the philosophy department at Howard University.[5] I had never seen Langston Hughes before, but regardless of what is said about the quality of education provided by the old Negro schools (ours was named for Frederick Douglass[6]), we were taught what is now termed "Black History" and were kept abreast of current events pertaining to our people. Thus, as early as the sixth grade we were made aware of the poetry of Langston Hughes along with the work of the other Negro Renaissance writers. So I recognized Hughes from his photographs. But I recognized Dr. Locke because he had been at Tuskegee only a few

---

2. Institute of higher education in Alabama, originally founded to train African Americans in manual trade and agricultural skills.
3. Ezra Pound (1885–1972), U.S. poet and critic. T. S. Eliot (1888–1965), United States–born English poet, playwright, and literary critic.
4. Left-wing, communist magazine founded in 1922.

5. Predominantly black university in Washington, D.C., founded in 1867. Hughes (1902–1967), African American poet and writer. Locke (1886–1954), American educator, writer, and philosopher.
6. African American human rights leader, writer, orator, and abolitionist (1817–1985).

weeks prior to my arrival in New York, having gone there to visit with Hazel Harrison, a teacher in the music department, and a very fine pianist who had been one of Ferruccio Busoni's[7] prize pupils . . . Here I'm trying to provide a bit of historical background to give you an idea of the diverse cultural forces at play in the lives of Afro-Americans from the early 1920s to 1936.

Miss Harrison was a friend of Prokofiev,[8] and possessed some of his scores at a time when few would have imagined that a Russian master's music was being made a part of the musical consciousness of an Afro-American college. And certainly not in such a college as Tuskegee—even though Tuskegee's musical tradition was actually quite rich and quite varied. But then, this is but another example of the contradictions of American culture which escape our attention because they are obscured by racism. And yet, thanks to Miss Harrison, I could, like any eager, young, celebrity-fascinated college junior, walk straight up to Dr. Locke and say, "Dr. Locke, do you remember me?" And to my delight he said, "Why, of course I do." He then introduced me to Langston Hughes and told Hughes of my interest in poetry.

Langston Hughes had with him copies of Malraux's[9] Man's Fate and The Days of Wrath, and after a few moments' conversation he said, "Since you like to read so much, maybe you'd like to read these novels and then return them to their owner"—and so I did. And the returns were tremendous. This incident and this meeting later made it possible for me to ask Langston Hughes if he knew Richard Wright, "Yes," he said, "and it so happens that he's coming here from Chicago next week." And with his great generosity, and without telling me, Hughes wrote Richard Wright that there was a young Negro something-or-the-other in New York who wanted to meet him. The next thing I knew I received a postcard—which I still have—that said, "Dear Ralph Ellison, Langston Hughes tells me that you're interested in meeting me. I will be in New York . . ." on such and such a date in July . . . signed Richard Wright. Thus I was to meet Wright on the day after his arrival in New York in July of 1937.

At the time I still thought that I would return to Tuskegee to take my degree in music, but I was not to make it. I had come to New York to earn expenses for my senior year, but it was during the Depression[1] and I was unable to make the money. Then, in talking with Wright, my plans and goals were altered; were, in fact, fatefully modified by Wright's.

Wright had come to New York for two purposes, one which was talked about openly, and the other quietly underplayed. The first was to become the editor of the magazine New Challenge.[2] The other was to work in the Harlem Bureau of the Communist newspaper The Daily Worker.[3] With Wright's presence in the Worker's 135th Street office, my introduction to the craft of writing leaped ahead. For it was there that I read many of his unpublished stories and discussed his ideas concerning literature and culture.

Wright was quiet concerning his assignment to the Worker's staff because he had left Chicago under a cloud. In 1936 he had been thrown out of the May Day[4] parade—sacred to all Communists—for refusing to carry out some

---

7. Italian pianist and composer (1866–1924).
8. Sergeyevich Prokofiev (1891–1953), Russian composer.
9. André-Georges Malraux (1901–1976), French writer, art historian, and statesman. His novels Man's Fate and Days of Wrath were published in 1933 and 1935, respectively.
1. Devastating economic slump of the 1930s

that affected North America and Europe.
2. Founded by Dorothy West and Richard Wright; the first publication to bring together black art and politics.
3. Founded in 1924.
4. International working-class holiday, celebrated on May 1.

assignment. And the fact that he had been publicly humiliated by both white *and* black Communists had left him quite bitter. However, someone higher up in the hierarchy recognized his value and was able to persuade him to go to New York—which proved to be to my good fortune.

Being unemployed much of the time, I began to hang around the Harlem Bureau, not so much for the ideology being purveyed there—although I found it fascinating—but because of Wright and the manuscripts of a sheaf of novelettes (Later published as *Uncle Tom's Children*[5]) that lay in an open desk drawer. Of all those who visited the office, I was the only one who bothered to read those now-famous stories. Perhaps this was because his comrades looked upon Wright as an intruder. He was distrusted not only as an "intellectual" and thus a potential traitor, but as a possible "dark horse" in the race for Harlem party leadership; a "ringer" who had been sent from Chicago to cause them trouble. Wright had little sense of humor concerning their undisguised hostility, and this led, as would be expected, to touchy relationships. Despite his obvious organizational and journalistic abilities— the *Worker* featured his reportage—the members of the Communist rank and file sneered at his intellectuality, ridiculed his writings, and dismissed his concern with literature and culture as an affectation. In brief, they thought him too ambitious, and therefore a threat to their own ambitions as possible party functionaries.

Being a true outsider, I was amused by this comedy of misperception, for Wright seemed anything but a threat to their petty ambitions. Besides, I was absolutely intrigued by his talent and felt privileged to read his writings. I'd never met anyone who, lacking the fanfare of public recognition, could move me with the unpublished products of his fictional imagination. Of course, I read Wright's work uncritically, but there was no doubt in my mind that he was an exceptional writer. Even better, he was delighted to discuss the techniques, the ideological and philosophical implications of his writings, and this with one who'd never attempted to write anything beyond classroom assignments and a few poems. Evidently Wright wished to exchange ideas with someone of his own general background, and I was fortunate in being able to contribute more than curiosity to our discussion. For I had studied with creative musicians, both classical and jazz, and had been taught to approach the arts analytically. I had also read fairly widely on my own. But to encounter the possessor of such literary talent and have him make me his friend and confidant—that was indeed an exciting and inspiring experience.

Nor did it end with mere talk. As editor of *New Challenge*, Wright asked me to contribute a book review in its first issue. To one who had never attempted to write anything, this was the wildest of ideas. But still, pressed by his editorial needs, and sustained by his belief that an untapped supply of free-floating literary talent existed in the Negro community, Wright kept after me, and I wrote a review and he published it. But then he went even further by suggesting that I write a short story!

I said, "But I've never even tried to write a story . . ."

He said, "Look, you talk about these things, you've read a lot, and you've been around. Just put something down and let me see it . . ."

---

5. Wright's 1938 volume of novellas. "Harlem Bureau": headquarters of the *Daily Worker*.

So I wrote a story, titled "Hymie's Bull," that was based upon experiences that I'd had a few years before when riding freight trains from Oklahoma to Alabama. I was dubious over the outcome, but to my delight Wright accepted the story and sent it to the printer.

Ah, but fate, as they say, was in the wings and New Challenge was not to appear again. I hasten to add that this was not a disaster created by my first attempt at fiction. Rather, it had to do with an aspect of Afro-American cultural history and involved certain lingering echoes of the Negro Renaissance, a movement which "ran out of gas" with the Crash of 1929.[6] As the period ended, a number of figures important to the movement had died, and with the Great Depression upon them, those members of the white community who had sponsored the Renaissance were unable to continue. The money was no longer available, and so the movement languished. However, with the deepening of the Depression there came a significant development in the form of the federal projects for the arts that were organized by the Works Progress Administration.[7] These projects were most important to the continuing development of Afro-American artists. For although a reaction to a national disaster, they provided—as have most national disasters—the possibility for a broader Afro-American freedom. This is a shocking thing to say, but it is also a very blues, or tragicomic, thing to say, and a fairly accurate description of the manner in which, for Negroes, a gift of freedom arrived wrapped in the guise of disaster. It is ironic, but no less true, that the most tragic incident of our history, the Civil War, was a disaster which ended American slavery.

Wright himself worked on both the Chicago and the New York Federal Writers' Project,[8] and I could not have become a writer at the time I began had I not been able to earn my board and keep by doing research for the New York project. Through Wright's encouragement, I had become serious about writing, but before going on the project I sometimes slept in the public park below City College because I had neither job nor money. But my personal affairs aside, the WPA provided an important surge to Afro-American cultural activity. The result was not a "renaissance," but there was a resuscitation and transformation of that very vital artistic impulse that is abiding among Afro-Americans. Remember that our African forefathers originated in cultures wherein even the simple routines of daily living were highly ritualized and that even their cooking utensils were fashioned with forms of symbolism which resonated with overtones of godhead. And though modified, if not suppressed, by the experience of American slavery, that tradition of artistic expressiveness has infused the larger American culture. Afro-American cultural style is an abiding aspect of our culture, and the economic disaster which brought the WPA gave it an accelerated release and allowed many Negroes to achieve their identities as artists.

But now, back to Wright and New Challenge. New Challenge was organized by people active in the Negro Renaissance and whose outlook was in many ways at odds with Wright's. Thus, according to Wright, New Challenge ended

---

6. Stock market crash that initiated the Great Depression (see p. 309, n. 1).
7. Or WPA; work program for the unemployed that was created in 1935 under President Frank-

lin D. Roosevelt's New Deal.
8. Program sponsored by the WPA that provided jobs for unemployed writers, editors, and research workers.

publication because the two young women who were in charge before he came on the scene were afraid that his connection with the Communist party would lead to its being taken over. So rather than lose control, they got rid of Wright.

History has no vacuum. There are transformations, there are lesions, there are metamorphoses, and there are mysteries that cloak the clashing of individual wills and private interests. *New Challenge* faded, but Wright went on to publish *Uncle Tom's Children* and, shortly afterward, *Native Son*.[9] When Richard Wright came to New York his talents as a writer were, to a large extent, already formed. Indeed, even before 1927, when he migrated to Chicago, he had published fiction in Robert S. Abbott's[1] magazine *The Bronzeman*. So it isn't true, as has been said, that the Communist party "discovered" his talent. Wright was literary in an informed way even in Jackson, Mississippi. But what happened to him in Chicago resulted from his coming into contact with an organized political group which possessed a concept of social hierarchy that was a conscious negation of our racially biased social system. Thus, through his political affiliation Wright was able to identify his artistic ambitions with what was, for him, a totally new conception of social justice. In the discussions that took place in the Chicago John Reed Club[2] he sharpened his conception of literary form and the relationship between fictional techniques and the world view of Marxism. And he came to see art and society in terms of an ideology that was concerned with power, and willing to forgo racial differences in order to take over the world. I realize that this is all rather abstract, but I am trying to suggest the tenor of our discussions. Fortunately, Wright's interest in literary theory was not limited to areas prescribed by the party line.

For instance, I was very curious as to how one could put Marx and Freud[3] together. No real problem now, I suppose. But coming from where I did, it was puzzling. And I was to discover that it was also a problem for Communist intellectuals and for many of their opponents. Either Marx was raised up and Freud put down, or Freud raised up and Marx put down. So for me, all of this was pretty strange. But at least with Richard Wright, I could discuss such matters. This was very important for a young writer (and of course I became a young writer, for I soon realized that I wasn't going back to Tuskegee and to music). And since Wright had assured me that I possessed a certain talent, I decided that writing was the direction I would take. I don't know whether he was satisfied with my talent or not; I suspect not. This was interesting, for while I possessed more formal education, it was he who encouraged me and gave me a sense of direction. I'd like you to appreciate the irony of this development: Here was a young Afro-American who had gone only to grade school, but who had arrived in Chicago possessing a certain articulateness and an undeveloped talent for writing. He had no further formal education—although he was aware of the University of Chicago and came to associate with a number of its intellectuals—but he gave himself over to the complex reality of late 1927 Chicago and made it his own. Chicago, the city where after years of Southern Negro migration the great jazz was being played and reinvented, where the stockyards and

---

9. Wright's 1940 novel.
1. Founder and editor of the *Chicago Defender*, a black weekly newspaper (1870–1940).
2. Communist Party organization of writers and artists. Reed (1887–1920), poet, writer, activist,

and leader of the Communist Labor Party.
3. Sigmund Freud (1856–1939), founder of psychoanalysis. Karl Marx (1818–1883), revolutionary, sociologist, historian, and economist.

railroads, and the steel mills of Gary, Indiana, were transforming a group of rural, agricultural Americans into city people and into a *lumpenprole-tariat*,[4] a class over whom we now despair.

Wright found the scene challenging. He learned that in this country wherever one wanders, one must pay his dues to change and take advantage of possibility by asserting oneself. You'll recall my saying earlier that "geography is fate"; now let me say that one's fate is also determined by what one does and by what one does *not* do. Wright set out to come into a conscious possession of his experience as Negro, as political revolutionary, as writer, and as citizen of Chicago.

Somehow, in getting into the John Reed Club, Wright had learned the techniques of agitprop art[5]—which he came later to despise—and before he went to Harlem he had been a contributing editor of the original *Partisan Review* and a founder of such magazines as *Anvil*. He had been poor in accepting discipline and had had his political troubles in the Communist party, but when I knew him he was not shrinking from the challenges of his existence. Nor complaining that he'd been "'buked and scorned."[6] Nor did he feel that he had handicaps that could not be overcome because of his identity as a Negro writer. Instead, he was striving to live consciously—at least artistically and intellectually—at the top of his times. Wright's spirit was such, and his sense of possibility was such, that even during the time when he was writing *Native Son* he was concerned with learning the stylistic and dialectical fine points found in the work of Steinbeck, of Hemingway, of Malraux, and of Thomas Mann;[7] for these he viewed as his competitors. I warn you that this is only *my* interpretation, but it was as though Wright was thinking, "I have a finer sense, a more basic knowledge of American reality than Hemingway, or Steinbeck, or anybody else who is writing." He had the kind of confidence that jazzmen have, although I assure you that he knew very little about jazz and didn't even know how to dance. Which is to say that he didn't possess the full range of Afro-American culture. But having the confidence of his talent, having the sense (which he gained from Marxism) that he was living in a world in which he did not have to be confused by the mystifications of racism, Wright harnessed his revolutionary tendencies to a political program which he hoped would transform American society. Through his cultural and political activities in Chicago he made a dialectical leap into a sense of his broadest possibilities, as man and as artist. He was well aware of the forces ranked against him, but in his quiet way he was as arrogant in facing up to them as was Louis Armstrong[8] in a fine blaring way.

To a young Oklahoman this attitude of Wright's was affirmative—and again, "geography is fate." For out there our people fought back. We seldom won more than moral victories, but we fought back—as can be seen from the many civil rights victories that were initiated there. And as can be heard in the Southwestern jazz and in the performances of the Jimmy Rushings, the Hot Lips Pages, the Count Basies, the Benny Motens, and Charlie Christians.[9]

4. Underclass (German).
5. Art that uses agitation and propaganda to influence and mobilize public opinion.
6. The title of an old Negro spiritual.
7. German novelist and essayist (1875–1955). John Steinbeck (1902–1968), American novelist. Ernest Hemingway (1899–1961), American novelist and short story writer.

8. American jazz trumpeter (1901–1971).
9. American jazz guitarist (1916–1942). Rushing (1902–1972), jazz singer. Oran "Hot Lips" Page (1908–1954), jazz trumpeter. Basie (1904–1984), American pianist, composer, and organizer of jazz bands. Moten (1894–1935), American pianist and organizer of jazz bands.

We were an assertive people, and our mode of social assertion was artistic, mainly music, as well as political. But there was also the Negro church, wherein you heard the lingering accents of nineteenth-century rhetoric with its emphasis upon freedom and individual responsibility; a rhetorical style which gave us Lincoln, Harriet Tubman, Harriet Beecher Stowe,[1] and the other abolition-preaching Beechers. Which gave us Frederick Douglass and John Jasper[2] and many other eloquent and heroic Negroes whose spirit still moves among us through the contributions they made to the flexibility, the music, and the idealism of the American language. Richard Wright was a possessor of that tradition. It is resonant in his fiction and it was a factor in his eager acceptance of social responsibility.

But now I should add that as far as Negroes in New York were concerned, Wright was for the most part friendless. Part of this was due to the fact that he kept to Communist circles and was intensely involved with writing and political activities. But as far as his rapid development as a writer is concerned, it would not have been possible but for the Chicago John Reed Club. This required an intellectual environment, and in Negro communities such were few and far between. Thus, given his talent and driving ambition, it was fortunate that he found the necessary associations among other young writers, many of whom were not Communists. Within such integrated groups he could question ideas, programs, theories. He could argue over philosophical interpretations of reality and say, if he chose, "Well, dammit, I'm black, and this concept of this program doesn't seem valid to me." This was most important for Wright, and since he affirmed many impulses which I felt and understood in my own way, it proved important to me. And no less important was his willingness to discuss problems encountered within the Communist party, and especially his difficulty in pursuing independent thought.

Because there, too, he was encountering a form of intellectual racism. It was not couched in the rhetoric of Negro inferiority à l'americain,[3] but in the form of an insistence upon blind discipline and a constant pressure to follow unthinkingly a political "line." It was dramatized in the servile attitudes of certain black Communist functionaries who regarded Wright— with his eloquence and his tendency toward an independence of thought—as a dangerous figure who had to be kept under rigid control.

And of course, Wright's personality would not allow him to shun a battle. He fought back and was into all kinds of trouble. He had no interest in keeping silent as the price of his freedom of expression. Nor was he so dazzled by his freedom to participate in the councils of newspapers and magazines as to keep his mouth shut. Instead, he felt that his experience, insight, and talent were important to the party's correct assessment of American reality. Thus he fought to make his comrades understand that *they* didn't know a damn thing about the complexities of the South, whether black or white, and insisted that they could not possibly understand America's racial situation by approaching it through such facile slogans as "Black and White Unite and Fight." Not when the white workingman was doing us the greatest face-to-face damage, and when the unions were practicing policies of racial exclusion. In trying to get this across, in saying, as it were, "Your

1. American writer, abolitionist, and philanthropist (1811–1896). Abraham Lincoln (1809–1865), sixteenth president of the United States. Tubman (1820–1913), African American abolitionist.

2. American philosopher and preacher (1812–1901).

3. In the American style (French).

approach is too simple," Wright met all kinds of resistance, both ideological and personal. But at least he made the fight, and I bring it up here by way of offering you something of the background of emotional and intellectual conflict out of which Native Son was written.

I read most of Native Son as it came off the typewriter, and I didn't know what to think of it except that it was wonderful. I was not responding critically. After all, how many of you have had the unexpected privilege of reading a powerful novel as it was, literally, ripped off the typewriter? Such opportunities are rare, and being young, I was impressed beyond all critical words. And I am still impressed. I feel that Native Son was one of the major literary events in the history of American literature. And I can say this even though at this point I have certain reservations concerning its view of reality. Yet it continues to have a powerful effect, and it seems to me a mistake to say, as was said not long ago in Life magazine, that Native Son is a "neglected" novel. And here I should remind those of you who were too young to remember, that Native Son was such a popular work that the dust jacket of the Book-of-the-Month Club edition could consist of a collage made of accolades written by critics and reviewers from throughout the country. It was a financial as well as a critical success, and with its publication Wright became a famous man.

But its success was by no means to still his burning passion—not simply for justice, but to become the author of other compelling works of literature. His response to the reception of 12 Million Black Voices,[4] which is, I think, his most lyrical work, is an example. He was much bemused by the fact that this work could move his white readers to tears, and saw this as an evasion of the intended impact of his vision. Thus he began to talk over and over again of forging such hard, mechanical images and actions that no white reading them could afford the luxury of tears.

But here I must turn critic. For in my terms, Wright failed to grasp the function of artistically induced catharsis—which suggests that he failed also to understand the Afro-American custom of shouting in church (a form of ritual cartharsis), or its power to cleanse the mind and redeem and rededicate the individual to forms of ideal action. Perhaps he failed to understand—or he rejected—those moments of exultation wherein man's vision is quickened by the eloquence of an orchestra, an actor or orator or dancer, or by anyone using the arts of music or speech or symbolic gesture to create within us moments of high consciousness; moments wherein we grasp, in the instant, a knowledge of how transcendent and how abysmal and yet affirmative it can be to be human beings. Yet it is for such moments of inspired communication that the artist lives. The irony here is that Wright could evoke them, but felt, for ideological reasons, that tears were a betrayal of the struggle for freedom.

I disagreed with his analysis, for tears can induce as well as deter action. Nevertheless, it is imperative that I say that through his writings Richard Wright achieved, here in the social and racial chaos of the United States, a position of artistic equality. He insisted upon it. And not only in his own political party—with which he eventually broke—but internationally. He was never at peace. He was never at rest. The restlessness which sent our forefathers hurtling toward the West Coast, and which now has us climbing

4. One of Wright's books (1941).

up all sorts of walls, was very much within him. In 1956, in Paris, when we were leaving the headquarters of the magazine *Presence Africaine* (and this is the first time I've revealed this and I hope he won't mind, since it might be meaningful to some scholar), he said to me, "Really, Ralph, after I broke with the Communist party I had nowhere else to go . . ." This was said in resigned explanation of his continued presence in Europe. And I think he was telling me that his dedication to communism had been so complete and his struggle so endless that he had had to change his scene, that he had had to find a new ground upon which to struggle. Because as long as he stayed within the framework of his political party, he had to struggle on two fronts: asserting on one the principles of equality and possibility (which the Communists stood for, or *pretended* to stand for), and on the other, insisting upon the fact *not* that it took a Negro to tell the truth about Afro-American experience, but that you had to at least get down into the mud and live with its basic realities to do so. And that you could not deal with its complexities simply from a theoretical perspective. *Black Boy*[5] was an attempt to depict some of those complexities.

So much of *Black Boy* (originally entitled *American Hunger*), is exaggerated, I think, precisely because Wright was trying to drive home, to dramatize—indeed, because of its many fictional techniques he could with justice have called it a "nonfiction" novel—the complexity of Negro American experience as he knew it and had lived it. The fictional techniques were not there in order to "con" anyone, but to drive home to Americans, black and white, something of the complexity and cost in human terms, in terms of the loss to literature and to art, and to the cause of freedom itself, imposed by racial discrimination; the cost, that is, of growing up in a society which operated on one side of its mind by the principle of equality while qualifying that principle severely according to the dictates of racism. Wright was thinking and fighting over these issues at close quarters—fighting with the Communists especially because he had thought that they offered a viable solution. Instead, he discovered that they were blind.

But now to more delightful relationships with Wright. He had as much curiosity about how writing is written as I had about how music is composed, and our curiosity concerning artistic creation became the basis of our friendship. Having studied music from the age of eight, and having studied harmony and symphonic form in our segregated school, I was also interested in how music related to the other arts. This, combined with my growing interest in literary creation, made my contact with Wright's enthusiasm an educational and spirit-freeing experience. Having read Pound and Eliot and Shaw and the criticism of Harriet Monroe[6] and I. A. Richards—all available in Tuskegee's excellent little library—it was important that in Wright, I had discovered a Negro American writer who possessed a working knowledge of modern literature, its techniques and theories. My approach to literature was by no means racial, but Wright was not only available, he was eager to share his interests, and it gave me something of that sense of self-discovery and exaltation which is implicit in the Negro church and in good jazz. Indeed, I had found it in baseball and football games, and it turns up in almost any group activity of Afro-Americans when we're not really thinking about white folks and are simply being our own American selves.

---

5. Wright's 1945 autobiographical novel.
6. American founder and long-time editor of *Poetry* magazine (1860–1936). George Bernard

Shaw (1856–1950), Irish comic dramatist, literary critic, and socialist propagandist.

I'm reminded of a discussion that another Tuskegeian and I were having with a group of white friends. The discussion had to do with our discovery of Hemingway (whom I discovered in a Negro barbershop), and Conrad[7] (another writer I often discussed with Wright), and suddenly the Tuskegee graduate said to me, "Aren't you glad that we found those guys on our own at Tuskegee?"

Now, that was not Negro chauvinism, but a meaningful observation about the relationship between social scene and experience, and I concurred. Because I had had the same reaction when I first talked with Wright about fictional technique and we had gone on to discuss some of the complications and interconnections between culture and society that claimed our conscious attention despite the fact that we were segregated. The question reminded me of how wonderful it was to have read T. S. Eliot in the context of Tuskegee. The question was not raised to celebrate a then-segregated college in a violently segregated state, but to inform our white friends that racism aside, there are other important relationships between scenes, ideas, and experience. Scene and circumstance combined to give ideas resonance and compel a consciousness of perspective. What one reads becomes part of what one sees and feels. Thus it is impossible for me to reread certain passages from Joyce or Eliot or Sir Thomas Browne[8] without seeing once again the deep magenta skies that descend upon the Tuskegee campus at dusk in summer. The scene, then, is always a part of personality, and scene and personality combine to give viability to ideas. Scene is thus always a part, the ground, of action—and especially of *conscious* action. Its associations and implicit conflicts provide the extra dimension which anchors poetry in reality and structures our efforts toward freedom.

Richard Wright was trying to add to our consciousness the dimension of being a black boy who grew up in Jackson, Mississippi (a scene that was not always so rugged, even for him, as he pictured it artistically), but a boy who grew up and who achieved through his reading a sense of what was possible out there in the wider world. A boy who grew up and achieved and accepted his own *individual* responsibility for seeing to it that America become conscious of itself. He insisted that it recognize the interconnections between its places and its personalities, its act and its ideals. This was the burden of Richard Wright and, as I see it, the driving passion of Richard Wright. It led to his triumphs as it led, inevitably, to some of his defeats. But one thing must be said of Richard Wright: In him we had for the first time a Negro American writer as randy, as courageous, and as irrepressible as Jack Johnson.[9] And if you don't know who Jack Johnson was, I'll tell you that when I was a little boy that early heavyweight boxing champion was one of the most admired underground heroes. He was rejected by most whites and by many respectable Negroes, but he was nevertheless a hero among veterans of the Spanish-American War who rejoiced in the skill and élan with which Johnson set off the now-outrageous search for a "White Hope."[1]

This suggests that we literary people should always keep a sharp eye on what's happening in the unintellectualized areas of our experience. Our peripheral vision had better be damned good. Because while baseball,

7. Joseph Conrad (1857–1924), Polish-born English novelist.
8. English physician and author (1605–1682). James Joyce (1882–1941), Irish novelist.

9. Boxer; the first black heavyweight champion of the world (1878–1946).
1. A white boxer who would be able to win the heavyweight belt from Jackson.

basketball, and football players cannot really tell us how to write our books, they *do* demonstrate where much of the significant action is taking place. Often they are themselves cultural heroes who work powerful modification in American social attitudes. And they tell us in nonliterary terms much about the nature of possibility. They tell us about the cost of success, and much about the nonpolitical aspects of racial and national identity, about the changing nature of social hierarchy, and about the role which individual skill and excellence can play in creating social change.

In this country there were good Negro writers before Wright arrived on the scene—and my respects to all the good ones—but it seems to me that Richard Wright wanted more and dared more. He was sometimes too passionate, I think now as I offer you the memories of a middle-aged man. But at least Wright wanted and demanded as much as any novelist, any artist, should want: He wanted to be tested in terms of his talent, and not in terms of his race or his Mississippi upbringing. Rather, he had the feeling that his vision of American life, and his ability to project it eloquently, justified his being considered among the best of American writers. And in this crazy, mixed-up country, as is witnessed by this conference dedicated to his works and to his memory, it turns out that he was right.

1971

MARGARET WALKER
1915–1998

W hen Margaret Walker's first volume of poetry, *For My People*, was published in 1942, it was only the second collection of American poetry published by a black woman for more than two decades (Georgia Douglass Johnson's *The Heart of a Woman and Other Poems* had been published in 1918). *For My People* launched Walker's career, which spanned several decades, extending from the waning days of the Harlem Renaissance in the 1930s to the Black Arts movement of the 1960s and beyond. In the foreword to *For My People*, Stephen Vincent Benét praised Walker's poetry for its "controlled intensity of emotion and [its] language that, at times, even when it is most modern, has something of the surge of biblical poetry." Walker would have heard these biblical overtones in the sermons of her father, a minister in the Methodist Episcopal Church in Alabama and Mississippi. It is little wonder, then, that the Bible and the black sermonic tradition influence so much of Walker's writing and that the title poem of *For My People* has been likened to a sermon.

Walker was born July 7, 1915, in Birmingham, Alabama, to Reverend Sigismund C. Walker and Marion Dozier Walker who instilled in her a love of scholarship, music, and the church. She was exposed early on to the classics of English and American literature, reading widely in poetry from Shakespeare to John Greenleaf Whittier to Countee Cullen and Langston Hughes. She credited Hughes—both his life and his poetry—with profoundly influencing her ambitions and her development as a writer.

While a student at Northwestern University, Walker worked for the WPA Federal Writers' Project, where she became friends with Richard Wright, enjoying a three-year collaboration and exchange that she described as a strictly "literary" relationship, a "rare and once-in-a-lifetime association." Wright read and responded to

Walker's poetry, and she helped with his revisions of *Almos' a Man* and the posthumously published *Lawd Today*. After leaving Chicago, Walker assisted Wright in the research for *Native Son*, sending him newspaper clippings about Robert Nixon, a young black man accused of rape in Chicago, who partly inspired Wright's depiction of Bigger Thomas. Their friendship and literary collaboration ended abruptly, and Walker has explained some of the underlying reasons in her controversial book, *Richard Wright: A Daemonic Genius.*

From Chicago, Walker went to the University of Iowa Writers' Workshop where she finished *For My People*, which won the Yale University Younger Poet's Award in 1942. Critic Eugenia Collier described the title poem as community property, a "signature piece" for black audiences:

> We knew the poem. It was ours. . . . And as [it] moved on, rhythmically piling image after image of our lives, making us know again the music wrenched from our slave agony, the religious faith, the toil and confusion and hopelessness, the strength to endure in spite of it all, [it] went on mirroring our collective selves, [and] we cried out in deep response.

Despite its success, *For My People* marked the end of Walker's published efforts for roughly twenty years. After receiving her master's degree, she married and began a teaching career. Her novel *Jubilee* broke the silence in 1966. *Jubilee* is most frequently read as a response to the nostalgic fantasies about slavery found in white fiction that re-creates the antebellum and Reconstruction South—especially Margaret Mitchell's popular *Gone with the Wind*. Two volumes of poetry followed: *Prophets for a New Day* (1970) and *October Journey* (1973). *Prophets for a New Day* features poems on the black freedom struggle from Nat Turner's rebellion to the civil rights movement. Its cover a montage of photographs of Martin Luther King Jr. and Malcolm X, *Prophets for a New Day* addresses the need for leadership in chaotic times and the despair of a community that finds a worthy leader, only to be deprived of his guidance by an assassin's bullet. Published by Broadside Press, the volume also represents Walker's decision, like that of Gwendolyn Brooks, to support black independent publishers dedicated, as the word *broadside* suggests, to forceful verbal attack, to militance on the page.

Few disagree that Margaret Walker's reputation rests largely on the poems in *For My People*. Stephen Vincent Benét's original judgment of them still rings true: "These poems keep on talking to you after the book is shut because . . . Walker has made living and passionate speech."

For My People

For my people everywhere singing their slave songs repeatedly: their
    dirges and their ditties and their blues and jubilees, praying their
    prayers nightly to an unknown god, bending their knees humbly to
    an unseen power;

For my people lending their strength to the years, to the gone years and   5
    the now years and the maybe years, washing ironing cooking scrub-
    bing sewing mending hoeing plowing digging planting pruning
    patching dragging along never gaining never reaping never know-
    ing and never understanding.

For my playmates in the clay and dust and sand of Alabama backyards   10
    playing baptizing and preaching and doctor and jail and soldier and
    school and mama and cooking and playhouse and concert and store
    and hair and Miss Choomby and company;

For the cramped bewildered years we went to school to learn to know
    the reasons why and the answers to and the people who and the   15
    places where and the days when, in memory of the bitter hours
    when we discovered we were black and poor and small and different
    and nobody cared and nobody wondered and nobody understood;

For the boys and girls who grew in spite of these things to be Man and
    Woman, to laugh and dance and sing and play and drink their wine   20
    and religion and success, to marry their playmates and bear chil-
    dren and then die of consumption and anemia and lynching;

For my people thronging 47th Street in Chicago and Lenox Avenue in
    New York and Rampart Street in New Orleans, lost disinherited
    dispossessed and happy people filling the cabarets and taverns and   25
    other people's pockets needing bread and shoes and milk and land
    and money and something—something all our own;

For my people walking blindly spreading joy, losing time being lazy,
    sleeping when hungry, shouting when burdened, drinking when
    hopeless, tied and shackled and tangled among ourselves by the   30
    unseen creatures who tower over us omnisciently and laugh;

For my people blundering and groping and floundering in the dark of
    churches and schools and clubs and societies, associations and
    councils and committees and conventions, distressed and disturbed   35
    and deceived and devoured by money-hungry glory-craving leeches,
    preyed on by facile force of state and fad and novelty, by false prophet
    and holy believer;

For my people standing staring trying to fashion a better way from
    confusion, from hypocrisy and misunderstanding, trying to fashion   40
    a world that will hold all the people, all the faces, all the adams and
    eves and their countless generations;

Let a new earth rise. Let another world be born. Let a bloody peace
    be written in the sky. Let a second generation full of courage issue
    forth; let a people loving freedom come to growth. Let a beauty full   45
    of healing and a strength of final clenching be the pulsing in our
    spirits and our blood. Let the martial songs be written, let the
    dirges disappear. Let a race of men now rise and take control.

1937, 1942

Poppa Chicken

    Poppa was a sugah daddy
    Pimping in his prime;
    All the gals for miles around
    Walked to Poppa's time.

    Poppa Chicken owned the town,   5
    Give his women hell;

All the gals on Poppa's time
Said that he was swell.

Poppa's face was long and black;
Poppa's grin was broad.   10
When Poppa Chicken walked the streets
The gals cried Lawdy! Lawd!

Poppa Chicken made his gals
Toe his special line:
"Treat 'em rough and make 'em say   15
Poppa Chicken's fine!"

Poppa Chicken toted guns;
Poppa wore a knife.
One night Poppa shot a guy
Threat'ning Poppa's life.   20

Poppa done his time in jail
Though he got off light;
Bought his pardon in a year;
Come back out in might.

Poppa walked the streets this time,   25
Gals around his neck.
And everybody said the jail
Hurt him nary speck.

Poppa smoked his long cigars—
Special Poppa brands—   30
Rocks all glist'ning in his tie;
On his long black hands.

Poppa lived without a fear;
Walked without a rod.
Poppa cussed the coppers out;   35
Talked like he was God.

Poppa met a pretty gal;
Heard her name was Rose;
Took one look at her and soon
Bought her pretty clothes.   40

One night she was in his arms,
In walked her man Joe.
All he done was look and say,
"Poppa's got to go."

Poppa Chicken still is hot   45
Though he's old and gray,
Walking round here with his gals
Pimping every day.

1942

For Malcolm X

All you violated ones with gentle hearts;
You violent dreamers whose cries shout heartbreak;
Whose voices echo clamors of our cool capers,
And whose black faces have hollowed pits for eyes.
All you gambling sons and hooked children and bowery bums   5
Hating white devils and black bourgeoisie,
Thumbing your noses at your burning red suns,
Gather round this coffin and mourn your dying swan.

Snow-white moslem head-dress around a dead black face!
Beautiful were your sand-papering words against our skins!   10
Our blood and water pour from your flowing wounds.
You have cut open our breasts and dug scalpels in our brains.
When and Where will another come to take your holy place?
Old man mumbling in his dotage, or crying child, unborn?

                                                                1970

Prophets for a New Day

I

As the Word came to prophets of old,
As the burning bush spoke to Moses,
And the fiery coals cleansed the lips of Isaiah;
As the wheeling cloud in the sky
Clothed the message of Ezekiel;   5
So the Word of fire burns today
On the lips of our prophets in an evil age—
Our sooth-sayers and doom-tellers and doers of the Word.
So the Word of the Lord stirs again
These passionate people toward deliverance.   10
As Amos, Shepherd of Tekoa spoke.
To the captive children of Judah,[1]
Preaching to the dispossessed and the poor,
So today in the pulpits and the jails,
On the highways and in the byways,   15
A fearless shepherd speaks at last
To his suffering weary sheep.

1. This stanza makes many references to the Old Testament of the Bible. Moses saw a vision of an angel in a burning bush and was compelled by God to return to Egypt to deliver the Israelites from bondage (Exodus 3.2–10). Isaiah (8th century B.C.E.) prophesied the destruction and redemption of Israel. Ezekiel (6th century B.C.E.), prophet who had a vision of God as wheels within wheels (Ezekiel 1.4–18). Amos (8th century B.C.E.), from Tekoa (a small town just south of Jerusalem), was the first prophet to proclaim God as ruler of the universe. Judah, the fourth son of Jacob, saved Joseph's life by proposing that his brother be sold into slavery rather than be murdered (Genesis 37.26–27). He is also the ancestor of the tribe of Judah (one of the twelve tribes of Israel).

2

So, kneeling by the river bank
Comes the vision to a valley of believers
So in flaming flags of stars in the sky   20
And in the breaking dawn of a blinding sun
The lamp of truth is lighted in the Temple
And the oil of devotion is burning at midnight
So the glittering censer in the Temple
Trembles in the presence of the priests   25
And the pillars of the door-posts move
And the incense rises in smoke
And the dark faces of the sufferers
Gleam in the new morning
The complaining faces glow   30
And the winds of freedom begin to blow
While the Word descends on the waiting World below.

3

A beast is among us.
His mark is on the land.
His horns and his hands and his lips are gory with our blood.   35
He is War and Famine and Pestilence
He is Death and Destruction and Trouble
And he walks in our houses at noonday
And devours our defenders at midnight.
He is the demon who drives us with whips of fear   40
And in his cowardice
He cries out against liberty
He cries out against humanity
Against all dignity of green valleys and high hills
Against clean winds blowing through our living;   45
Against the broken bodies of our brothers.
He has crushed them with a stone.
He drinks our tears for water
And he drinks our blood for wine;
He eats our flesh like a ravenous lion   50
And he drives us out of the city
To be stabbed on a lonely hill.

1970

GWENDOLYN BROOKS
1917–2000

The following observation from Gwendolyn Brooks's 1972 autobiography, *Report from Part One,* outlines several of the many motives that have marked the poet's long, distinguished career:

> My aim, in my next future, is to write poems that will somehow successfully "call" . . . all black people: black people in taverns, black people in alleys, black people in gutters, schools, offices, factories, prisons, the consulate; I wish to reach black people in pulpits, black people in mines, on farms, on thrones; not always to "teach"—I shall wish often to entertain, to illumine. My newish voice will not be an imitation of the contemporary young black voice, which I so admire, but an adaptation of today's Gwendolyn Brooks' voice.

And indeed, the poet, shifting allegiance after three decades from Harper & Row to Broadside Press (Detroit) and Third World Press (Chicago), continued into the 1990s to write the elegant spare rhythms that characterized her poetry all along. True to her wish to reach a wide audience, her thin, handsome volumes were quite affordable—*Primer for Blacks* (1980) and *Black Love* (1982) originally sold for less than $5 a piece. Though this distribution strategy made it difficult for academics to get hold of Brooks's poetry for the classroom, it suggested her passionate commitment to making her work available to black people everywhere and underscored her belief that poetry is not the sole province of the privileged, educated few.

One of two children of schoolteacher Keziah Corinne Wims and janitor David Anderson Brooks, Gwendolyn Brooks was born in Topeka, Kansas, in 1917. Five weeks after her birth, the family moved to Chicago, where she spent most of her life. Brooks published her first poem at thirteen, in *American Child* magazine. Fonder at fourteen of paper dolls than parties and in possession at sixteen of a critique of her poems from poet and novelist James Weldon Johnson, Brooks graduated from high school in 1935, by which time she was already a regular contributor to the weekly variety column of the *Chicago Defender.* In 1936 she graduated from Wilson Junior College and then worked for a short time as a maid and secretary to one Dr. E. N. French. A spiritual adviser who hawked charms and potions to the unfortunate, this "doctor" appears to have informed the image of Prophet Williams in the poet's powerful 1960s epic *In the Mecca.* Brooks joined Chicago's NAACP Youth Council in 1937; there she met Henry Lowington Blakely II, whom she married in 1939.

Shortly after the birth of her first child, in October 1940, Brooks met the "elegant rebel" and resident of the city's Gold Coast, Inez Cunningham Stark Boulton. Boulton came to the South Side "to instruct a class of Negro would-be poets, in the very *buckle* of the Black Belt." Armed with subscriptions to *Poetry* magazine for the class, Boulton would count among her students more than a few who would later publish books, articles, fiction, poems, and criticism. In her autobiography, Brooks discussed her teacher's pedagogical strategies, but it appears that Boulton did not regard herself so much as an instructor as "a friend who loved poetry and respected [the students'] interest in it." The poetry workshop—often quite rigorous—exposed Brooks to a wide variety of reading, in modernist verse particularly; but if Brooks's own teacherly strategies at Chicago's Columbia College some years later took their cue from Boulton's example, then Boulton's students were grounded in a range of styles, from Petrarchan and Shakespearean sonnets, through the ballad and iambic pentameter, to free verse.

After winning the Midwestern Writers' Conference poetry award in 1943, Brooks was approached by Emily Morison of Knopf for a book of poems. Morison read a batch on various subjects—love, war, nature, patriotism, prejudice—and then told Brooks that she would like to see more of the "Negro poems." Brooks gathered nineteen poems on the subject, but somewhat put off by Morison, she sent the bundle to Elizabeth Lawrence at Harper & Row. *A Street in Bronzeville* was published in 1945. It would be followed by *Annie Allen* (1949), winner of the 1950 Pulitzer Prize; *Maud Martha* (1953); and *The Bean Eaters* (1960). As she observed, Brooks's poetry of this period is solidly based in the stuff of everyday life: "As for my husband and myself, our own best parties were given at 623 East 63rd Street, our most exciting kitchenette . . . right on the corner . . . of 63rd and Champlain, above a real-estate agency. If you wanted a poem, you had only to look out a window. There was material always, walking or running, fighting or screaming or singing." It was in this famed kitchenette that Brooks hosted a party for her friend and mentor Langston Hughes; once, he dropped in unexpectedly, and Brooks and Blakely shared with him a meal of mustard greens, ham hocks, and candied sweet potatoes.

Hughes died in 1967, the year of the Second Black Writers' Conference at Nashville's Fisk University. "A general energy, an electricity, in look, walk, speech, gesture" underscored the proceedings, according to Brooks, who reported that she had never before seen "such insouciance, such live firmness, such confident vigor." Here Brooks was exposed to cultural activists and artists such as Don L. Lee (Haki Madhubuti), Imamu Amiri Baraka, Larry Neal, and A. B. Spelman, among others, who would fashion the outline of a new black cultural nationalism. After the Fisk conference, Brooks reported: "If it hadn't been for these young people, these young writers who influenced me, I wouldn't know what I know about this society. By associating with them, I know who I am." Much of Brooks's subsequent activity was inspired by her experience at Fisk, including the creative writing class that she conducted with some of Chicago's Blackstone Rangers, a teenage gang. In 1968, she published *In the Mecca*, with its brilliant closing pieces: the "sermons" on the Warpland.

Across the years and volumes, Brooks's poetry has struck readers with several distinctive traits: a stunning juxtaposition of disparate objects and words, notably in *The Anniad* and *In the Mecca;* a masterful control of rhyme and meter; sophisticated use of formal and thematic irony, as in "We Real Cool"; and the delicate but striking translation of public events into memorable poetic detail. Though Brooks's later poetry shows something of a different innovation and though the results may not be as uniformly impressive as the earlier work, the poet's primary concern—to hammer out a portrait of and for African Americans—remained unaltered.

Any attempt to outline Gwendolyn Brooks's career would be incomplete without at least brief mention of the prose fiction *Maud Martha*. A female subject's ruminations before, during, and after World War II, the work should be read *with* the poetry, not apart from it. Not only is *Maud Martha* one of the few works by a black woman writer written between the Harlem Renaissance and the civil rights era but it also offers a point of view not marked by the ideological debates of the postwar years. *Maud Martha*'s ugliness—the ugliness of racism, classism, and sexism—is "made in America" and must be solved there as well. But as unflinching is its view of one woman's life, so beautiful and muscular is its lyricism. The marvel of this text is that it narrates the most difficult, or unspeakable, of human failings—those that occur on the level of intimacy—through the finely tuned sensibility and contemplations of its protagonist. It is a generous, sensitive, and tough contribution to a remarkable body of work by a major modern American poet. Brooks died during the Christmas season of 2000.

kitchenette building

We are things of dry hours and the involuntary plan,
Grayed in, and gray. "Dream" makes a giddy sound, not strong
Like "rent," "feeding a wife," "satisfying a man."

But could a dream send up through onion fumes
Its white and violet, fight with fried potatoes   5
And yesterday's garbage ripening in the hall,
Flutter, or sing an aria down these rooms

Even if we were willing to let it in,
Had time to warm it, keep it very clean,
Anticipate a message, let it begin?   10

We wonder. But not well! not for a minute!
Since Number Five is out of the bathroom now,
We think of lukewarm water, hope to get in it.

1945

the mother

Abortions will not let you forget.
You remember the children you got that you did not get,
The damp small pulps with a little or with no hair,
The singers and workers that never handled the air.
You will never neglect or beat   5
Them, or silence or buy with a sweet.
You will never wind up the sucking-thumb
Or scuttle off ghosts that come.
You will never leave them, controlling your luscious sigh,
Return for a snack of them, with gobbling mother-eye.   10

I have heard in the voices of the wind the voices of my dim killed
    children.
I have contracted. I have eased
My dim dears at the breasts they could never suck.
I have said, Sweets, if I sinned, if I seized
Your luck   15
And your lives from your unfinished reach,
If I stole your births and your names,
Your straight baby tears and your games,
Your stilted or lovely loves, your tumults, your marriages, aches, and
    your deaths,
If I poisoned the beginnings of your breaths,   20
Believe that even in my deliberateness I was not deliberate.
Though why should I whine,
Whine that the crime was other than mine?—
Since anyhow you are dead.
Or rather, or instead,   25
You were never made.

But that too, I am afraid,
Is faulty: oh, what shall I say, how is the truth to be said?
You were born, you had body, you died.
It is just that you never giggled or planned or cried.   30

Believe me, I loved you all.
Believe me, I knew you, though faintly, and I loved, I loved you
All.

                                                                    1945

a song in the front yard

I've stayed in the front yard all my life.
I want a peek at the back
Where it's rough and untended and hungry weed grows.
A girl gets sick of a rose.

I want to go in the back yard now   5
And maybe down the alley,
To where the charity children play.
I want a good time today.

They do some wonderful things.
They have some wonderful fun.   10
My mother sneers, but I say it's fine
How they don't have to go in at quarter to nine.
My mother, she tells me that Johnnie Mae
Will grow up to be a bad woman.
That George'll be taken to Jail soon or late   15
(On account of last winter he sold our back gate).

But I say it's fine. Honest, I do.
And I'd like to be a bad woman, too,
And wear the brave stockings of night-black lace
And strut down the streets with paint on my face.   20

                                                                    1945

Sadie and Maud

Maud went to college.
Sadie stayed at home.
Sadie scraped life
With a fine-tooth comb.

She didn't leave a tangle in.   5
Her comb found every strand.
Sadie was one of the livingest chits[1]
In all the land.

---

1. Pert young girls.

Sadie bore two babies
Under her maiden name.   10
Maud and Ma and Papa
Nearly died of shame.

When Sadie said her last so-long
Her girls struck out from home.
(Sadie had left as heritage   15
Her fine-tooth comb.)

Maud, who went to college,
Is a thin brown mouse.
She is living all alone
In this old house.   20

1945

the vacant lot

Mrs. Coley's three-flat brick
Isn't here any more.
All done with seeing her fat little form
Burst out of the basement door;
And with seeing her African son-in-law   5
(Rightful heir to the throne)
With his great white strong cold squares of teeth
And his little eyes of stone;
And with seeing the squat fat daughter
Letting in the men   10
When majesty has gone for the day—
And letting them out again.

1945

the preacher: ruminates behind the sermon

I think it must be lonely to be God.
Nobody loves a master. No. Despite
The bright hosannas,[1] bright dear-Lords, and bright
Determined reverence of Sunday eyes.

Picture Jehovah[2] striding through the hall   5
Of His importance, creatures running out
From servant-corners to acclaim, to shout
Appreciation of His merit's glare.

But who walks with Him?—dares to take His arm,
To slap Him on the shoulder, tweak His ear,   10

1. Songs of praise.
2. God (Hebrew).

Buy Him a Coca-Cola or a beer,
Pooh-pooh His politics, call Him a fool?

Perhaps—who knows?—He tires of looking down.
Those eyes are never lifted. Never straight.
Perhaps sometimes He tires of being great   15
In solitude. Without a hand to hold.

1945

The Sundays of Satin-Legs Smith

Inamoratas[1] with an approbation,
Bestowed his title. Blessed his inclination.)

He wakes, unwinds, elaborately: a cat
Tawny, reluctant, royal. He is fat
And fine this morning. Definite. Reimbursed.   5

He waits a moment, he designs his reign,
That no performance may be plain or vain.
Then rises in a clear delirium.

He sheds, with his pajamas, shabby days.
And his desertedness, his intricate fear, the   10
Postponed resentments and the prim precautions.

Now, at his bath, would you deny him lavender
Or take away the power of his pine?
What smelly substitute, heady as wine,
Would you provide? life must be aromatic.   15
There must be scent, somehow there must be some.
Would you have flowers in his life? suggest
Asters? a Really Good geranium?
A white carnation? would you prescribe a Show
With the cold lilies, formal chrysanthemum   20
Magnificence, poinsettias, and emphatic
Red of prize roses? might his happiest
Alternative (you muse) be, after all,
A bit of gentle garden in the best
Of taste and straight tradition? Maybe so.   25
But you forget, or did you ever know,
His heritage of cabbage and pigtails,
Old intimacy with alleys, garbage pails,
Down in the deep (but always beautiful) South
Where roses blush their blithest (it is said)   30
And sweet magnolias put Chanel[2] to shame.

No! He has not a flower to his name.
Except a feather one, for his lapel.

1. Women with whom one has had an intimate   2. A perfume created by Coco Chanel, Parisian
relation.   fashion designer.

Apart from that, if he should think of flowers
It is in terms of dandelions or death. 35
Ah, there is little hope. You might as well—
Unless you care to set the world a-boil
And do a lot of equalizing things,
Remove a little ermine, say, from kings,
Shake hands with paupers and appoint them men, 40
For instance—certainly you might as well
Leave him his lotion, lavender and oil.

Let us proceed. Let us inspect, together
With his meticulous and serious love,
The innards of this closet. Which is a vault 45
Whose glory is not diamonds, not pearls,
Not silver plate with just enough dull shine.
But wonder-suits in yellow and in wine,
Sarcastic green and zebra-striped cobalt.
All drapes. With shoulder padding that is wide 50
And cocky and determined as his pride;
Ballooning pants that taper off to ends
Scheduled to choke precisely.
                              Here are hats
Like bright umbrellas; and hysterical ties 55
Like narrow banners for some gathering war.

People are so in need, in need of help.
People want so much that they do not know.

Below the tinkling trade of little coins
The gold impulse not possible to show 60
Or spend. Promise piled over and betrayed.

These kneaded limbs receive the kiss of silk.
Then they receive the brave and beautiful
Embrace of some of that equivocal wool.
He looks into his mirror, loves himself— 65
The neat curve here; the angularity
That is appropriate at just its place;
The technique of a variegated grace.

Here is all his sculpture and his art
And all his architectural design. 70
Perhaps you would prefer to this a fine
Value of marble, complicated stone.
Would have him think with horror of baroque,[3]
Rococo.[4] You forget and you forget.

He dances down the hotel steps that keep 75
Remnants of last night's high life and distress.
As spat-out purchased kisses and spilled beer.

---

3. A style in art and architecture typified by elaborate and ornate scrolls, curves, and symmetrical ornamentation.

4. An artistic style originating in 18th-century France characterized by elaborate ornamentation.

He swallows sunshine with a secret yelp.
Passes to coffee and a roll or two.
Has breakfasted.   80
       Out. Sounds about him smear,
Become a unit. He hears and does not hear
The alarm clock meddling in somebody's sleep;
Children's governed Sunday happiness;
The dry tone of a plane; a woman's oath;   85
Consumption's[5] spiritless expectoration;
An indignant robin's resolute donation
Pinching a track through apathy and din;
Restaurant vendors weeping; and the L[6]
That comes on like a slightly horrible thought.   90

Pictures, too, as usual, are blurred.
He sees and does not see the broken windows
Hiding their shame with newsprint; little girl
With ribbons decking wornness, little boy
Wearing the trousers with the decentest patch,   95
To honor Sunday; women on their way
From "service," temperate holiness arranged
Ably on asking faces; men estranged
From music and from wonder and from joy
But far familiar with the guiding awe   100
Of foodlessness.

              He loiters.
                       Restaurant vendors

Weep, or out of them rolls a restless glee.
The Lonesome Blues, the Long-lost Blues, I Want A   105
Big Fat Mama. Down these sore avenues
Comes no Saint-Saëns, no piquant elusive Grieg,[7]
And not Tschaikovsky's[8] wayward eloquence
And not the shapely tender drift of Brahms.[9]
But could he love them? Since a man must bring   110
To music what his mother spanked him for
When he was two: bits of forgotten hate,
Devotion: whether or not his mattress hurts:
The little dream his father humored: the thing
His sister did for money: what he ate   115
For breakfast—and for dinner twenty years
Ago last autumn: all his skipped desserts.

The pasts of his ancestors lean against
Him. Crowd him. Fog out his identity.
Hundreds of hungers mingle with his own,   120
Hundreds of voices advise so dexterously
He quite considers his reactions his,

5. I.e., tuberculosis's.
6. I.e., the elevated train that runs through
Chicago.
7. Edvard Grieg (1843–1907), Norwegian composer. Camille Saint-Saëns (1835–1921), French

composer.
8. Piotr Tchaikovsky (1840–1893), Russian
composer.
9. Johannes Brahms (1833–1897), German
composer.

Judges he walks most powerfully alone,
That everything is—simply what it is.

But movie-time approaches, time to boo 125
The hero's kiss, and boo the heroine
Whose ivory and yellow it is sin
For his eye to eat of. The Mickey Mouse,
However, is for everyone in the house.

Squires his lady to dinner at Joe's Eats. 130
His lady alters as to leg and eye,
Thickness and height, such minor points as these,
From Sunday to Sunday. But no matter what
Her name or body positively she's
In Queen Lace stockings with ambitious heels 135
That strain to kiss the calves, and vivid shoes
Frontless and backless, Chinese fingernails,
Earrings, three layers of lipstick, intense hat
Dripping with the most voluble of veils.
Her affable extremes are like sweet bombs 140
About him, whom no middle grace or good
Could gratify. He had no education
In quiet arts of compromise. He would
Not understand your counsels on control, nor
Thank you for your late trouble. 145
             At Joe's Eats
You get your fish or chicken on meat platters.
With coleslaw, macaroni, candied sweets,
Coffee and apple pie. You go out full.
(The end is—isn't it?—all that really matters.) 150

       And even and intrepid come
       The tender boots of night to home.

Her body is like new brown bread
Under the Woolworth mignonette.[1]
Her body is a honey bowl 155
Whose waiting honey is deep and hot.
Her body is like summer earth,
Receptive, soft, and absolute . . .

1945

The Rites for Cousin Vit

Carried her unprotesting out the door.
Kicked back the casket-stand. But it can't hold her,
That stuff and satin aiming to enfold her,
The lid's contrition nor the bolts before.
Oh oh. Too much. Too much. Even now, surmise, 5

---

1. A plant known for its dainty and fragrant white flowers.

She rises in the sunshine. There she goes,
Back to the bars she knew and the repose
In love-rooms and the things in people's eyes.
Too vital and too squeaking. Must emerge.
Even now she does the snake-hips with a hiss,　　　　10
Slops the bad wine across her shantung,[1] talks
Of pregnancy, guitars and bridgework, walks
In parks or alleys, comes haply on the verge
Of happiness, haply hysterics. Is.

　　　　　　　　　　　　　　　　　　　　1949

The Children of the Poor[1]

1

People who have no children can be hard:
Attain a mail[2] of ice and insolence:
Need not pause in the fire, and in no sense
Hesitate in the hurricane to guard.
And when wide world is bitten and bewarred　　　　5
They perish purely, waving their spirits hence
Without a trace of grace or of offense
To laugh or fail, diffident, wonder-starred.
While through a throttling dark we others hear
The little lifting helplessness, the queer　　　　10
Whimper-whine; whose unridiculous
Lost softness softly makes a trap for us.
And makes a curse. And makes a sugar of
The malocclusions,[3] the inconditions of love.

2

What shall I give my children? who are poor,　　　　15
Who are adjudged the leastwise of the land,
Who are my sweetest lepers, who demand
No velvet and no velvety velour;
But who have begged me for a brisk contour,
Crying that they are quasi, contraband　　　　20
Because unfinished, graven by a hand
Less than angelic, admirable or sure.
My hand is stuffed with mode, design, device.
But I lack access to my proper stone.
And plenitude or plan shall not suffice　　　　25
Nor grief nor love shall be enough alone
To ratify my little halves who bear
Across an autumn freezing everywhere.

3

And shall I prime my children, pray, to pray?
Mites, come invade most frugal vestibules　　　　30

1. Garment of heavy, irregular, partly silk fabric.
1. This sonnet sequence features both Petrarchan and Shakespearean sonnet forms.
2. Armor usually made of metal links.
3. Faulty closure, usually in the coming together of the teeth.

Spectered with crusts of penitents' renewals
And all hysterics arrogant for a day.
Instruct yourselves here is no devil to pay.
Children, confine your lights in jellied rules;
Resemble graves; be metaphysical mules;   35
Learn Lord will not distort nor leave the fray.
Behind the scurryings of your neat motif
I shall wait, if you wish: revise the psalm
If that should frighten you: sew up belief
If that should tear: turn, singularly calm   40
At forehead and at fingers rather wise,
Holding the bandage ready for your eyes.

4

First fight. Then fiddle. Ply the slipping string
With feathery sorcery; muzzle the note
With hurting love; the music that they wrote   45
Bewitch, bewilder. Qualify to sing
Threadwise. Devise no salt, no hempen⁴ thing
For the dear instrument to bear. Devote
The bow to silks and honey. Be remote
A while from malice and from murdering.   50
But first to arms, to armor. Carry hate
In front of you and harmony behind.
Be deaf to music and to beauty blind.
Win war. Rise bloody, maybe not too late
For having first to civilize a space   55
Wherein to play your violin with grace.

5

When my dears die, the festival-colored brightness
That is their motion and mild repartee
Enchanted, a macabre mockery
Charming the rainbow radiance into tightness   60
And into a remarkable politeness
That is not kind and does not want to be,
May not they in the crisp encounter see
Something to recognize and read as rightness?
I say they may, so granitely discreet,   65
The little crooked questionings inbound,
Concede themselves on most familiar ground,
Cold an old predicament of the breath:
Adroit, the shapely prefaces complete,
Accept the universality of death.   70

6

Life for my child is simple, and is good.
He knows his wish. Yes, but that is not all.
Because I know mine too.
And we both want joy of undeep and unabiding things,
Like kicking over a chair or throwing blocks out of a window   75

---

4. Resembling hemp, a coarse fiber often used for ropes.

Or tipping over an icebox pan
Or snatching down curtains or fingering an electric outlet
Or a journey or a friend or an illegal kiss.
No. There is more to it than that.
It is that he has never been afraid.   80
Rather, he reaches out and to the chair falls with a beautiful crash,
And the blocks fall, down on the people's heads,
And the water comes slooshing sloppily out across the floor.
And so forth.
Not that success, for him, is sure, infallible.   85
But never has he been afraid to reach.
His lesions are legion.
But reaching is his rule.

                                                                    1949

The Lovers of the Poor

       arrive. The Ladies from the Ladies' Betterment
   League
Arrive in the afternoon, the late light slanting
In diluted gold bars across the boulevard brag
Of proud, seamed faces with mercy and murder hinting
Here, there, interrupting, all deep and debonair,   5
The pink paint on the innocence of fear;
Walk in a gingerly manner up the hall.
Cutting with knives served by their softest care,
Served by their love, so barbarously fair.
Whose mothers taught: You'd better not be cruel!   10
You had better not throw stones upon the wrens!
Herein they kiss and coddle and assault
Anew and dearly in the innocence
With which they baffle nature. Who are full,
Sleek, tender-clad, fit, fiftyish, a-glow, all   15
Sweetly abortive, hinting at fat fruit,
Judge it high time that fiftyish fingers felt
Beneath the lovelier planes of enterprise.
To resurrect. To moisten with milky chill.
To be a random hitching-post or plush.   20
To be, for wet eyes, random and handy hem.
        Their guild is giving money to the poor.
The worthy poor. The very very worthy
And beautiful poor. Perhaps just not too swarthy?
Perhaps just not too dirty nor too dim   25
Nor—passionate. In truth, what they could wish
Is—something less than derelict or dull.
Not staunch enough to stab, though, gaze for gaze!
God shield them sharply from the beggar-bold!
The noxious needy ones whose battle's bald   30
Nonetheless for being voiceless, hits one down.
        But it's all so bad! and entirely too much for them.
The stench; the urine, cabbage, and dead beans,

Dead porridges of assorted dusty grains,
The old smoke, *heavy* diapers, and, they're told,   35
Something called chitterlings.[1] The darkness. Drawn
Darkness, or dirty light. The soil that stirs.
The soil that looks the soil of centuries.
And for that matter the *general* oldness. Old
Wood. Old marble. Old tile. Old old old.   40
Not homekind Oldness! Not Lake Forest, Glencoe[2]
Nothing is sturdy, nothing is majestic,
There is no quiet drama, no rubbed glaze, no
Unkillable infirmity of such
A tasteful turn as lately they have left,   45
Glencoe, Lake Forest, and to which their cars
Must presently restore them. When they're done
With dullards and distortions of this fistic[3]
Patience of the poor and put-upon.
                    They've never seen such a make-do-ness as   50
Newspaper rugs before! In this, this "flat,"
Their hostess is gathering up the oozed, the rich
Rugs of the morning (tattered! the bespattered. . . .)
Readies to spread clean rugs for afternoon.
Here is a scene for you. The Ladies look,   55
In horror, behind a substantial citizenness
Whose trains clank out across her swollen heart.
Who, arms akimbo, almost fills a door.
All tumbling children, quilts dragged to the floor
And tortured thereover, potato peelings, soft-   60
Eyed kitten, hunched-up, haggard, to-be-hurt.
                    Their League is allotting largesse to the Lost.
But to put their clean, their pretty money, to put
Their money collected from delicate rose-fingers
Tipped with their hundred flawless rose-nails seems.   65
                    They own Spode, Lowestoft, candelabra,
Mantels, and hostess gowns, and sunburst clocks,
Turtle soup, Chippendale, red satin "hangings,"
Aubussons and Hattie Carnegie.[4] They Winter
In Palm Beach; cross the Water[5] in June; attend,   70
When suitable, the nice Art Institute;
Buy the right books in the best bindings; saunter
On Michigan,[6] Easter mornings, in sun or wind.
Oh Squalor! This sick four-story hulk, this fiber
With fissures everywhere! Why, what are bringings   75
Of loathe-love largesse? What shall peril hungers
So old old, what shall flatter the desolate?
Tin can, blocked fire escape and chitterling
And swaggering seeking youth and the puzzled wreckage
Of the middle passage,[7] and urine and stale shames   80

1. The small intestines of animals, mainly hogs, especially fried or boiled.
2. Prosperous suburbs north of Chicago.
3. Having to do with boxing or fighting with the fists.
4. Symbols of wealth. "Spode" and "Lowestoft": English fine china. "Chippendale": 18th-century English furniture. "Aubussons": 18th-century French rugs. Hattie Carnegie was a fashionable American designer of the 1950s.
5. I.e., travel to Europe.
6. Prosperous Chicago avenue.
7. An allusion to the passage of slaves from Africa across the Atlantic to America and the West Indies.

And, again, the porridges of the underslung
And children children children. Heavens! That
Was a rat, surely, off there, in the shadows? Long
And long-tailed? Gray? The Ladies from the Ladies'
Betterment League agree it will be better   85
To achieve the outer air that rights and steadies,
To hie to a house that does not holler, to ring
Bells elsetime, better presently to cater
To no more Possibilities, to get
Away. Perhaps the money can be posted.   90
Perhaps they two may choose another Slum!
Some serious sooty half-unhappy home!—
Where loathe-love likelier may be invested.
       Keeping their scented bodies in the center
Of the hall as they walk down the hysterical hall,   95
They allow their lovely skirts to graze no wall,
Are off at what they manage of a canter,
And, resuming all the clues of what they were,
Try to avoid inhaling the laden air.

                           1960

We Real Cool

    The Pool Players.
    Seven at the Golden Shovel.

    We real cool. We
    Left school. We

    Lurk late. We   5
    Strike straight. We

    Sing sin. We
    Thin gin. We

    Jazz June. We
    Die soon.   10

                           1960

The Chicago *Defender* Sends a Man to Little Rock[1]

Fall, 1957

    In Little Rock the people bear
    Babes, and comb and part their hair
    And watch the want ads, put repair
    To roof and latch. While wheat toast burns
    A woman waters multiferns.   5

---

1. Federal intervention was necessary to implement school desegregation in Little Rock.

Time upholds or overturns
The many, tight, and small concerns.

In Little Rock the people sing
Sunday hymns like anything,
Through Sunday pomp and polishing.   10

And after testament and tunes,
Some soften Sunday afternoons
With lemon tea and Lorna Doones.

I forecast
And I believe   15
Come Christmas Little Rock will cleave
To Christmas tree and trifle, weave,
From laugh and tinsel, texture fast.
In Little Rock is baseball; Barcarolle.[2]
That hotness in July . . . the uniformed figures raw and
        implacable   20
And not intellectual,
Batting the hotness or clawing the suffering dust.
The Open Air Concert, on the special twilight green . . .
When Beethoven[3] is brutal or whispers to lady-like air.
Blanket-sitters are solemn, as Johann[4] troubles to lean   25
To tell them what to mean. . . .

There is love, too, in Little Rock. Soft women softly
Opening themselves in kindness,
Or, pitying one's blindness,
Awaiting one's pleasure   30
In azure
Glory with anguished rose at the root. . . .
To wash away old semi-discomfitures.
They re-teach purple and unsullen blue.
The wispy soils go. And uncertain   35
Half-havings have they clarified to sures.

In Little Rock they know
Not answering the telephone is a way of rejecting life,
That it is our business to be bothered, is our business
To cherish bores or boredom, be polite   40
To lies and love and many-faceted fuzziness.

I scratch my head, massage the hate-I-had.
I blink across my prim and pencilled pad.
The saga I was sent for is not down.
Because there is a puzzle in this town.   45
The biggest News I do not dare
Telegraph to the Editor's chair:
"They are like people everywhere."

2. A Venetian gondolier's song with a rhythm suggestive of rowing.
3. Ludwig van Beethoven (1770–1827), German composer noted for his innovative symphonies.
4. Johann Sebastian Bach (1685–1750), German organist and composer.

The angry Editor would reply
In hundred harryings of Why.   50

And true, they are hurling spittle, rock,
Garbage and fruit in Little Rock.
And I saw coiling storm a-writhe
On bright madonnas. And a scythe
Of men harassing brownish girls.   55
(The bows and barrettes in the curls
And braids declined away from joy.)

I saw a bleeding brownish boy. . . .

The lariat lynch-wish I deplored.

The loveliest lynchee was our Lord.   60

                                                        1960

Malcolm X

For Dudley Randall

Original.
Ragged-round.
Rich-robust.

He had the hawk-man's eyes.
We gasped. We saw the maleness.   5
The maleness raking out and making guttural the air
and pushing us to walls.

And in a soft and fundamental hour
a sorcery devout and vertical
beguiled the world.   10

He opened us—
who was a key,

who was a man.

                                                        1968

Riot

A riot is the language of the unheard.
        —MARTIN LUTHER KING

John Cabot,[1] out of Wilma, once a Wycliffe,
all whitebluerose below his golden hair,

---

1. The Cabot family has been prominent in America since the early 18th century; their fortune was initially based on trading in rum, slaves, and opium.

wrapped richly in right linen and right wool,
almost forgot his Jaguar and Lake Bluff;
almost forgot Grandtully (which is The   5
Best Thing That Ever Happened To Scotch); almost
forgot the sculpture at the Richard Gray
and Distelheim; the kidney pie at Maxim's,
the Grenadine de Boeuf at Maison Henri.

Because the Negroes were coming down the street.   10

Because the Poor were sweaty and unpretty
(not like Two Dainty Negroes in Winnetka[2])
and they were coming toward him in rough ranks.
In seas. In windsweep. They were black and loud.
And not detainable. And not discreet.   15

Gross. Gross. *"Que tu es grossier!"*[3] John Cabot
itched instantly beneath the nourished white
that told his story of glory to the World.
"Don't let It touch me! the blackness! Lord!" he whispered
to any handy angel in the sky.   20
But, in a thrilling announcement, on It drove
and breathed on him: and touched him. In that breath
the fume of pig foot, chitterling[4] and cheap chili,
malign, mocked John. And, in terrific touch, old
averted doubt jerked forward decently,   25
cried "Cabot! John! You are a desperate man,
and the desperate die expensively today."

John Cabot went down in the smoke and fire
and broken glass and blood, and he cried "Lord!
Forgive these nigguhs that know not what they do."   30

                                                        1969

A Bronzeville Mother Loiters in Mississippi.
Meanwhile, a Mississippi Mother Burns Bacon

From the first it had been like a
Ballad. It had the beat inevitable. It had the blood.
A wildness cut up, and tied in little bunches,
Like the four-line stanzas of the ballads she had never quite
Understood—the ballads they had set her to, in school.   5

Herself: the milk-white maid, the "maid mild"
Of the ballad. Pursued
By the Dark Villain. Rescued by the Fine Prince.
The Happiness-Ever-After.
That was worth anything.   10

---

2. Prosperous Chicago suburb.   4. The small intestines of animals, especially
3. How crude you are! (French).   fried or boiled.

It was good to be a "maid mild."
That made the breath go fast.

Her bacon burned. She
Hastened to hide it in the step-on can, and
Drew more strips from the meat case. The eggs and sour-milk
    biscuits   15
Did well. She set out a jar
Of her new quince preserve.

. . . But there was a something about the matter of the Dark
    Villain.
He should have been older, perhaps.
The hacking down of a villain was more fun to think about   20
When his menace possessed undisputed breadth, undisputed
    height,
And a harsh kind of vice.
And best of all, when his history was cluttered
With the bones of many eaten knights and princesses.

The fun was disturbed, then all but nullified   25
When the Dark Villain was a blackish child
Of fourteen, with eyes still too young to be dirty,
And a mouth too young to have lost every reminder
Of its infant softness.

That boy must have been surprised! For   30
These were grown-ups. Grown-ups were supposed to be wise.
And the Fine Prince—and that other—so tall, so broad, so
Grown! Perhaps the boy had never guessed
That the trouble with grown-ups was that under the
    magnificent shell of adulthood, just under,
Waited the baby full of tantrums.   35
It occurred to her that there may have been something
Ridiculous in the picture of the Fine Prince
Rushing (rich with the breadth and height and
Mature solidness whose lack, in the Dark Villain, was
    impressing her,
Confronting her more and more as this first day after the trial   40
And acquittal wore on) rushing
With his heavy companion to hack down (unhorsed)
That little foe.
So much had happened, she could not remember now what
    that foe had done
Against her, or if anything had been done.   45
The one thing in the world that she did know and knew
With terrifying clarity was that her composition
Had disintegrated. That, although the pattern prevailed,
The breaks were everywhere. That she could think
Of no thread capable of the necessary   50
Sew-work.

She made the babies sit in their places at the table.
Then, before calling Him, she hurried

To the mirror with her comb and lipstick. It was necessary
To be more beautiful than ever.   55
The beautiful wife.
For sometimes she fancied he looked at her as though
Measuring her. As if he considered, Had she been worth It?
Had *she* been worth the blood, the cramped cries, the little
          stuttering bravado,
The gradual dulling of those Negro eyes,   60
The sudden, overwhelming *little-boyness* in that barn?
Whatever she might feel or half-feel, the lipstick necessity
          was something apart. He must never conclude
That she had not been worth It.

He sat down, the Fine Prince, and
Began buttering a biscuit. He looked at his hands.   65
He twisted in his chair, he scratched his nose.
He glanced again, almost secretly, at his hands.
More papers were in from the North, he mumbled. More
          meddling headlines.
With their pepper-words, "bestiality," and "barbarism," and
"Shocking."   70
The half-sneers he had mastered for the trial worked across
His sweet and pretty face.

What he'd like to do, he explained, was kill, them all.
The time lost. The unwanted fame.
Still, it had been fun to show those intruders   75
A thing or two. To show that snappy-eyed mother,
That sassy, Northern, brown-black——

Nothing could stop Mississippi.
He knew that. Big Fella
Knew that.   80
And, what was so good, Mississippi knew that.
Nothing and nothing could stop Mississippi.
They could send in their petitions, and scar
Their newspapers with bleeding headlines. Their governors
Could appeal to Washington. . . .   85

"What I want," the older baby said, "is 'lasses on my jam."
Whereupon the younger baby
Picked up the molasses pitcher and threw
The molasses in his brother's face. Instantly
The Fine Prince leaned across the table and slapped   90
The small and smiling criminal.

She did not speak. When the Hand
Came down and away, and she could look at her child,
At her baby-child,
She could think only of blood.   95
Surely her baby's cheek
Had disappeared, and in its place, surely,
Hung a heaviness, a lengthening red, a red that had no end.
She shook her head. It was not true, of course.

It was not true at all. The   100
Child's face was as always, the
Color of the paste in her paste-jar.
She left the table, to the tune of the children's lamentations,
      which were shriller
Than ever. She
Looked out of a window. She said not a word. *That*   105
Was one of the new Somethings—
The fear,
Tying her as with iron.

Suddenly she felt his hands upon her. He had followed her.
To the window. The children were whimpering now.   110
Such bits of tots. And she, their mother,
Could not protect them. She looked at her shoulders, still
Gripped in the claim of his hands. She tried, but could not
      resist the idea
That a red ooze was seeping, spreading darkly, thickly, slowly,
Over her white shoulders, her own shoulders,   115
And over all of Earth and Mars.

He whispered something to her, did the Fine Prince, something
About love, something about love and night and intention.

She heard no hoof-beat of the horse and saw no flash of
      the shining steel.

He pulled her face around to meet   120
His, and there it was, close close,
For the first time in all those days and nights.
His mouth, wet and red,
So very, very, very red,
Closed over hers.   125

Then a sickness heaved within her. The courtroom Coca-Cola,
The courtroom beer and hate and sweat and drone,
Pushed like a wall against her. She wanted to bear it.
But his mouth would not go away and neither would the
Decapitated exclamation points in that Other Woman's eyes.   130

She did not scream.
She stood there.
But a hatred for him burst into glorious flower,
And its perfume enclasped them—big,
Bigger than all magnolias.   135

The last bleak news of the ballad.
The rest of the rugged music.
The last quatrain.

1960

Maud Martha

1. description of Maud Martha

What she liked was candy buttons, and books, and painted music (deep blue, or delicate silver) and the west sky, so altering, viewed from the steps of the back porch; and dandelions.

She would have liked a lotus, or China asters or the Japanese Iris, or meadow lilies—yes, she would have liked meadow lilies, because the very word meadow made her breathe more deeply, and either fling her arms or want to fling her arms, depending on who was by, rapturously up to whatever was watching in the sky. But dandelions were what she chiefly saw. Yellow jewels for everyday, studding the patched green dress of her back yard. She liked their demure prettiness second to their everydayness; for in that latter quality she thought she saw a picture of herself, and it was comforting to find that what was common could also be a flower.

And could be cherished! To be cherished was the dearest wish of the heart of Maud Martha Brown, and sometimes when she was not looking at dandelions (for one would not be looking at them all the time, often there were chairs and tables to dust or tomatoes to slice or beds to make or grocery stores to be gone to, and in the colder months there were no dandelions at all), it was hard to believe that a thing of only ordinary allurements—if the allurements of any flower could be said to be ordinary—was as easy to love as a thing of heart-catching beauty.

Such as her sister Helen! who was only two years past her own age of seven, and was almost her own height and weight and thickness. But oh, the long lashes, the grace, the little ways with the hands and feet.

2. spring landscape: detail

The school looked solid. Brownish-red brick, dirty cream stone trim. Massive chimney, candid, serious. The sky was gray, but the sun was making little silver promises somewhere up there, hinting. A wind blew. What sort of June day was this? It was more like the last days of November. It was more than rather bleak; still, there were these little promises, just under cover; whether they would fulfill themselves was anybody's guess.

Up the street, mixed in the wind, blew the children, and turned the corner onto the brownish-red brick school court. It was wonderful. Bits of pink, of blue, white, yellow, green, purple, brown, black, carried by jerky little stems of brown or yellow or brown-black, blew by the unhandsome gray and decay of the double-apartment buildings, past the little plots of dirt and scanty grass that held up their narrow brave banners: PLEASE KEEP OFF THE GRASS—NEWLY SEEDED. There were lives in the buildings. Past the tiny lives the children blew. Cramp, inhibition, choke—they did not trouble themselves about these. They spoke shrilly of ways to fix curls and pompadours, of "nasty" boys and "sharp" boys, of Joe Louis, of ice cream, of bicycles, of baseball, of teachers, of examinations, of Duke Ellington, of Bette Davis.[1]

---

1. American actress (1905–1989). Joe Louis (1914–1981), African American boxer who was the heavyweight champion from 1937 to 1949. Duke Ellington (1899–1974), African American jazz composer, orchestra leader, and pianist.

They spoke—or at least Maud Martha spoke—of the sweet potato pie that would be served at home.

It was six minutes to nine; in one minute the last bell would ring. "Come on! You'll be late!" Low cries. A quickening of steps. A fluttering of brief cases. Inevitably, though, the fat girl, who was forced to be nonchalant, who pretended she little cared whether she was late or not, who would *not* run! (Because she would wobble, would lose her dignity.) And inevitably the little fellows in knickers, ten, twelve, thirteen years old, nonchalant just for the fun of it—who lingered on the red bricks, throwing balls to each other, or reading newspapers and comic books, or punching each other half playfully.

But eventually every bit of the wind managed to blow itself in, and by five minutes after nine the school court was bare. There was not a hot cap nor a bow ribbon anywhere.

3. *love and gorillas*

so the gorilla really did escape!

She was sure of it, now that she was awake. For she was awake. This was awakeness. Stretching, curling her fingers, she was still rather protected by the twists of thin smoky stuff from the too sudden onslaught of the red draperies with white and green flowers on them, and the picture of the mother and dog loving a baby, and the dresser with blue paper flowers on it. But that she was now awake in all earnest she could not doubt.

That train—a sort of double-deck bus affair, traveling in a blue-lined half dark. Slow, that traveling. Slow. More like a boat. It came to a stop before the gorilla's cage. The gorilla, lying back, his arms under his head, one leg resting casually across the other, watched the people. Then he rose, lumbered over to the door of his cage, peered, clawed at his bars, shook his bars. All the people on the lower deck climbed to the upper deck.

But why would they not get off?

"Motor trouble!" called the conductor. "Motor trouble! And the gorilla, they think, will escape!"

But why would not the people get off?

Then there was flaring green and there was red and there was red-orange, and she was in the middle of it, her few years many times added to, doubtless, for she was treated as an adult. All the people were afraid, but no one would get off.

All the people wondered if the gorilla would escape.

Awake, she knew he had.

She was safe, but the others—were they eaten? and if so had he begun on the heads first? and could he eat such things as buttons and watches and hair? or would he first tear those away?

Maud Martha got up, and on her way to the bathroom cast a glance toward her parents' partly open door. Her parents were close together. Her father's arm was around her mother.

Why, how lovely!

For she remembered last night. Her father stamping out grandly, dressed in his nicest suit and hat, and her mother left alone. Later, she and Helen and Harry had gone out with their mother for a "night hike."

How she loved a "hike." Especially in the evening, for then everything was moody, odd, deliciously threatening, always hunched and ready to close in on you but never doing so. East of Cottage Grove you saw fewer people, and those you did see had, all of them (how strange, thought Maud Martha), white faces. Over there that matter of mystery and hunchedness was thicker, a hundredfold.

Shortly after they had come in, Daddy had too. The children had been sent to bed, and off Maud Martha had gone to her sleep and her gorilla. (Although she had not known that in the beginning, oh no!) In the deep deep night she had waked, just a little, and had called "Mama." Mama had said, "Shut up!"

The little girl did not mind being told harshly to shut up when her mother wanted it quiet so that she and Daddy could love each other.

Because she was very *very* happy that their quarrel was over and that they would once again be nice.

Even though while the loud hate or silent cold was going on, Mama was so terribly sweet and good to her.

4. *death of Grandmother*

They had to sit in a small lobby, waiting for the nurses to change Gramma.

"She can't control herself," explained Maud Martha's mother.

Oh what a thing! What a thing.

When finally they could be admitted, Belva Brown, Maud Martha and Harry tiptoed into the lackluster room, single file.

Gramma lay in what seemed to Maud Martha a wooden coffin. Boards had been put up on either side of the bed to keep the patient from harming herself. All the morning, a nurse confided, Ernestine Brown had been trying to get out of the bed and go home.

They looked in the coffin. Maud Martha felt sick. That was not her Gramma. Couldn't be. Elongated, pulpy-looking face. Closed eyes; lashes damp-appearing, heavy lids. Straight flat thin form under a dark gray blanket. And the voice thick and raw. "Hawh—hawh—hawh." Maud Martha was frightened. But she mustn't show it. She spoke to the semi-corpse.

"Hello, Gramma. This is Maudie." After a moment, "Do you know me, Gramma?"

"Hawh—"

"Do you feel better? Does anything hurt you?"

"Hawh—" Here Gramma slightly shook her head. She did not open her eyes, but apparently she could understand whatever they said. And maybe, thought Maud Martha, what we are not saying.

How alone they were, how removed from this woman, this ordinary woman who had suddenly become a queen, for whom presently the most interesting door of them all would open, who, lying locked in boards with her "hawhs," yet towered, triumphed over them, while they stood there asking the stupid questions people ask the sick, out of awe, out of half horror, half envy.

"I never saw anybody die before," thought Maud Martha. "But I'm seeing somebody die now."

What was that smell? When would her mother go? She could not stand much more. What was that smell? She turned her gaze away for a while. To look at the other patients in the room, instead of at Gramma! The others were white women. There were three of them, two wizened ones, who were asleep, a stout woman of about sixty, who looked insane, and who was sitting up in bed, wailing, "Why don't they come and bring me a bedpan? Why don't they? Nobody brings me a bedpan." She clutched Maud Martha's coat hem, and stared up at her with glass-bright blue eyes, begging, "Will you tell them to bring me a bedpan? Will you?" Maud Martha promised, and the weak hand dropped.

"Poor dear," said the stout woman, glancing tenderly at Gramma.

When they finally left the room and the last "hawh," Maud Martha told a nurse passing down the hall just then about the woman who wanted the bedpan. The nurse tightened her lips. "Well, she can keep on wanting," she said, after a moment's indignant silence. "That's all they do, day long, night long—whine for the bedpan. We can't give them the bedpan every two minutes. Just forget it, Miss."

They started back down the long corridor. Maud Martha put her arm around her mother.

"Oh Mama," she whimpered, "she—she looked awful. I had no idea. I never saw such a horrible—creature—" A hard time she had, keeping the tears back. And as for her brother, Harry had not said a word since entering the hospital.

When they got back to the house, Papa was receiving a telephone message. Ernestine Brown was dead.

She who had taken the children of Abraham Brown to the circus, and who had bought them pink popcorn, and Peanut Crinkle candy, who had laughed—that Ernestine was dead.

5. you're being so good, so kind

Maud Martha looked the living room over. Nicked old upright piano. Sag-seat leather armchair. Three or four straight chairs that had long ago given up the ghost of whatever shallow dignity they may have had in the beginning and looked completely disgusted with themselves and with the Brown family. Mantel with scroll decorations that usually seemed rather elegant but which since morning had become unspeakably vulgar, impossible.

There was a small hole in the sad-colored rug, near the sofa. Not an outrageous hole. But she shuddered. She dashed to the sofa, maneuvered it till the hole could not be seen.

She sniffed a couple of times. Often it was said that colored people's houses necessarily had a certain heavy, unpleasant smell. Nonsense, that was. Vicious—and nonsense. But she raised every window.

Here was the theory of racial equality about to be put into practice, and she only hoped she would be equal to being equal.

No matter how taut the terror, the fall proceeds to its dregs. . . .

At seven o'clock her heart was starting to make itself heard, and with great energy she was assuring herself that, though she liked Charles, though she admired Charles, it was only at the high school that she wanted to see Charles.

This was no Willie or Richard or Sylvester coming to call on her. Neither was she Charles's Sally or Joan. She was the whole "colored" race, and Charles was the personalization of the entire Caucasian plan.

At three minutes to eight the bell rang, hesitantly. Charles! No doubt regretting his impulse already. No doubt regarding, with a rueful contempt, the outside of the house, so badly in need of paint. Those rickety steps. She retired into the bathroom. Presently she heard her father go to the door; her father—walking slowly, walking patiently, walking unafraid, as if about to let in a paper boy who wanted his twenty cents, or an insurance man, or Aunt Vivian, or no more than Woodette Williams, her own silly friend.

What was this she was feeling now? Not fear, not fear. A sort of gratitude! It sickened her to realize it. As though Charles, in coming, gave her a gift.

Recipient and benefactor.

It's so good of you.

You're being so good.

6. *at the Regal*

The applause was quick. And the silence—final.

That was what Maud Martha, sixteen and very erect, believed, as she manipulated herself through a heavy outflowing crowd in the lobby of the Regal Theatre on Forty-seventh and South Park.

She thought of fame, and of that singer, that Howie Joe Jones, that tall oily brown thing with hair set in thickly pomaded waves, with cocky teeth, eyes like thin glass. With—a Voice. A Voice that Howie Joe's publicity described as "rugged honey." She had not been favorably impressed. She had not been able to thrill. Not even when he threw his head back so that his waves dropped low, shut his eyes sweetly, writhed, thrust out his arms (really *gave* them to the world) and thundered out, with passionate seriousness, with deep meaning, with high purpose—

—Sa-WEET sa-oooo
Jaust-a YOOOOOOO—

Maud Martha's brow wrinkled. The audience had applauded. Had stamped its strange, hilarious foot. Had put its fingers in its mouth—whistled. Had sped a shininess up to its eyes. But now part of it was going home, as she was, and its face was dull again. It had not been helped. Not truly. Not well. For a hot half hour it had put that light gauze across its little miseries and monotonies, but now here they were again, ungauzed, self-assertive, cancerous as ever. The audience had gotten a fairy gold. And it was not going to spend the rest of its life, or even the rest of the night, being grateful to Howie Joe Jones. No, it would not make plans to raise a hard monument to him.

She swung out of the lobby, turned north.

The applause was quick.

But the silence was final, so what was the singer's profit?

Money.

You had to admit Howie Joe Jones was making money. Money that was raced to the track, to the De Lisa, to women, to the sellers of cars; to Capper and Capper, to Henry C. Lytton and Company for those suits in which he looked like an upright corpse. She read all about it in the columns of the Chicago *Defender's* gossip departments.

She had never understood how people could parade themselves on a stage like that, exhibit their precious private identities; shake themselves about; be very foolish for a thousand eyes.

She was going to keep herself to herself. She did not want fame. She did not want to be a "star."

To create—a role, a poem, picture, music, a rapture in stone: great. But not for her.

What she wanted was to donate to the world a good Maud Martha. That was the offering, the bit of art, that could not come from any other.

She would polish and hone that.

7. Tim

Oh, how he used to wriggle!—do little mean things! do great big wonderful things! and laugh laugh laugh.

He had shaved and he had scratched himself through the pants. He had lain down and ached for want of a woman. He had married. He had wiped out his nostrils with bits of tissue paper in the presence of his wife and his wife had turned her head, quickly, but politely, to avoid seeing them as they dropped softly into the toilet, and floated. He had had a big stomach and an alarmingly loud laugh. He had been easy with the ain'ts and sho-nuffs. He had been drunk one time, only one time, and on that occasion had done the Charleston in the middle of what was then Grand Boulevard and is now South Park, at four in the morning. Here was a man who had absorbed the headlines in the *Tribune,* studied the cartoons in *Collier's* and the *Saturday Evening Post.*

These facts she had known about her Uncle Tim. And she had known that he liked sweet potato pie. But what were the facts that she had not known, that his wife, her father's sister Nannie, had not known? The things that nobody had known.

Maud Martha looked down at the gray clay lying hard-lipped, cold, definitely not about to rise and punch off any alarm clock, on the tufted white satin that was at once so beautiful and so ghastly. I must tell them, she thought, as she walked back to her seat, I must let Helen and Harry know how I want to be arranged in my casket; I don't want my head straight up like that; I want my head turned a little to the right, so my best profile will be showing; and I want my left hand resting on my breast, nicely; and I want my hair plain, not waved—I don't want to look like a gray clay doll.

It all came down to gray clay.

Then just what was important? What had been important about this life, this Uncle Tim? Was the world any better off for his having lived? A little, perhaps. Perhaps he had stopped his car short once, and saved a dog, so that another car could kill it a month later. Perhaps he had given some little street wretch a nickel's worth of peanuts in its unhappy hour, and that little wretch would grow up and forget Uncle Tim but all its life would carry in its heart an anonymous, seemingly underivative softness for mankind. Perhaps. Certainly he had been good to his wife Nannie. She had never said a word against him.

But how important was this, what was the real importance of this, what would—God say? Oh, no! What she would rather mean was, what would Uncle Tim say, if he could get back?

Maud Martha looked at Aunt Nannie. Aunt Nannie had put too much white powder on her face. Was it irreverent, Maud Martha wondered, to be able to think of powdering your face for a funeral, when you were the new widow? Not in this case, she decided, for (she remembered this other thing about him) Uncle Tim, whose nose was always oily, had disliked an oily nose. Aunt Nannie was being brave. As yet she had not dropped a tear. But then, her turn at the casket had not come.

A large woman in a white uniform and white stockings and low-heeled white shoes was playing "We Shall Understand It Better By and By" at the organ, almost inaudibly (with a little jazz roll in her bass). How gentle the music was, how suggestive. Maud Martha saw people, after having all but knocked themselves out below, climbing up the golden, golden stairs, to a throne where sat Jesus, or the Almighty God; who promptly opened a Book, similar to the arithmetic book she had had in grammar school, turned to the back, and pointed out—the Answers! And the people, poor little things, nodding and cackling among themselves—"So that was it all the time! that is what I should have done!" "But—so simple! so *easy*! I should just have turned here! instead of there!" How wonderful! Was it true? Were people to get the Answers in the sky? Were people really going to understand It better by and by? When it was too late?

8. *home*

What had been wanted was this always, this always to last, the talking softly on this porch, with the snake plant in the jardiniere[2] in the southwest corner, and the obstinate slip from Aunt Eppie's magnificent Michigan fern at the left side of the friendly door. Mama, Maud Martha and Helen rocked slowly in their rocking chairs, and looked at the late afternoon light on the lawn, and at the emphatic iron of the fence and at the poplar tree. These things might soon be theirs no longer. Those shafts and pools of light, the tree, the graceful iron, might soon be viewed possessively by different eyes.

Papa was to have gone that noon, during his lunch hour, to the office of the Home Owners' Loan. If he had not succeeded in getting another extension, they would be leaving this house in which they had lived for more than fourteen years. There was little hope. The Home Owners' Loan was hard. They sat, making their plans.

"We'll be moving into a nice flat somewhere," said Mama. "Somewhere on South Park, or Michigan, or in Washington Park Court." Those flats, as the girls and Mama knew well, were burdens on wages twice the size of Papa's. This was not mentioned now.

"They're much prettier than this old house," said Helen. "I have friends I'd just as soon not bring here. And I have other friends that wouldn't come down this far for anything, unless they were in a taxi."

Yesterday, Maud Martha would have attacked her. Tomorrow she might. Today she said nothing. She merely gazed at a little hopping robin in the tree, her tree, and tried to keep the fronts of her eyes dry.

"Well, I do know," said Mama, turning her hands over and over, "that I've been getting tireder and tireder of doing that firing. From October to April, there's firing to be done."

"But lately we've been helping, Harry and I," said Maud Martha. "And sometimes in March and April and in October, and even in November, we could build a little fire in the fireplace. Sometimes the weather was just right for that."

2. A large, decorative stand or pot for plants.

She knew, from the way they looked at her, that this had been a mistake. They did not want to cry.

But she felt that the little line of white, somewhat ridged with smoked purple, and all that cream-shot saffron, would never drift across any western sky except that in back of this house. The rain would drum with as sweet a dullness nowhere but here. The birds on South Park were mechanical birds, no better than the poor caught canaries in those "rich" women's sun parlors.

"It's just going to kill Papa!" burst out Maud Martha. "He loves this house! He *lives* for this house!"

"He lives for us," said Helen. "It's us he loves. He wouldn't want the house, except for us."

"And he'll have us," added Mama, "wherever."

"You know," Helen sighed, "if you want to know the truth, this is a relief. If this hadn't come up, we would have gone on, just dragged on, hanging out here forever."

"It might," allowed Mama, "be an act of God. God may just have reached down, and picked up the reins."

"Yes," Maud Martha cracked in, "that's what you always say—that God knows best."

Her mother looked at her quickly, decided the statement was not suspect, looked away.

Helen saw Papa coming. "There's Papa," said Helen.

They could not tell a thing from the way Papa was walking. It was that same dear little staccato walk, one shoulder down, then the other, then repeat, and repeat. They watched his progress. He passed the Kennedys', he passed the vacant lot, he passed Mrs. Blakemore's. They wanted to hurl themselves over the fence, into the street, and shake the truth out of his collar. He opened his gate—the gate—and still his stride and face told them nothing.

"Hello," he said.

Mama got up and followed him through the front door. The girls knew better than to go in too.

Presently Mama's head emerged. Her eyes were lamps turned on.

"It's all right," she exclaimed. "He got it. It's all over. Everything is all right."

The door slammed shut. Mama's footsteps hurried away.

"I think," said Helen, rocking rapidly, "I think I'll give a party. I haven't given a party since I was eleven. I'd like some of my friends to just casually see that we're homeowners."

9. Helen

What she remembered was Emmanuel; laughing, glinting in the sun; kneeing his wagon toward them, as they walked tardily home from school. Six years ago.

"How about a ride?" Emmanuel had hailed.

She had, daringly—it was not her way, not her native way—made a quip. A "sophisticated" quip. "Hi, handsome!" Instantly he had scowled, his dark face darkening.

"I don't mean you, you old black gal," little Emmanuel had exclaimed. "I mean Helen."

He had meant Helen, and Helen on the reissue of the invitation had climbed, without a word, into the wagon and was off and away.

Even now, at seventeen—high school graduate, mistress of her fate, and a ten-dollar-a-week file clerk in the very Forty-seventh Street lawyer's office where Helen was a fifteen-dollar-a-week typist—as she sat on Helen's bed and watched Helen primp for a party, the memory hurt. There was no consolation in the thought that not now and not then would she have *had* Emmanuel "off a Christmas tree." For the basic situation had never changed. Helen was still the one they wanted in the wagon, still "the pretty one," "the dainty one." The lovely one.

She did not know what it was. She had tried to find the something that must be there to imitate, that she might imitate it. But she did not know what it was. I wash as much as Helen does, she thought. My hair is longer and thicker, she thought. I'm much smarter. I read books and newspapers and old folks like to talk with me, she thought.

But the kernel of the matter was that, in spite of these things, she was poor, and Helen was still the ranking queen, not only with the Emmanuels of the world, but even with their father—their mother—their brother. She did not blame the family. It was not their fault. She understood. They could not help it. They were enslaved, were fascinated, and they were not at all to blame.

Her noble understanding of their blamelessness did not make any easier to bear such a circumstance as Harry's springing to open a door so that Helen's soft little hands might not have to cope with the sullyings of a doorknob, or running her errands, to save the sweet and fine little feet, or shouldering Helen's part against Maud Martha. Especially could these items burn when Maud Martha recalled her comradely rompings with Harry, watched by the gentle Helen from the clean and gentle harbor of the porch: take the day, for example, when Harry had been chased by those five big boys from Forty-first and Wabash, cursing, smelling, beast-like boys! with bats and rocks, and little stones that were more worrying than rocks; on that occasion out Maud Martha had dashed, when she saw from the front-room window Harry, panting and torn, racing for home; out she had dashed and down into the street with one of the smaller porch chairs held high over her head, and while Harry gained first the porch and next the safety side of the front door she had swung left, swung right, clouting a head here, a head there, and screaming at the top of her lungs, "Y' leave my brother alone! Y' leave my brother alone!" And who had washed those bloody wounds, and afterward vaselined them down? Really—in spite of everything she could not understand why Harry had to hold open doors for Helen, and calmly let them slam in her, Maud Martha's, his friend's, face.

It did not please her either, at the breakfast table, to watch her father drink his coffee and contentedly think (oh, she knew it!), as Helen started on her grapefruit, how daintily she ate, how gracefully she sat in her chair, how pure was her robe and unwrinkled, how neatly she had arranged her hair. Their father preferred Helen's hair to Maud Martha's (Maud Martha knew), which impressed him, not with its length and body, but simply with its apparent untamableness; for he would never get over that zeal of his for order in all things, in character, in housekeeping, in his own labor, in groom-ing, in human relationships. Always he had worried about Helen's homework, Helen's health. And now that boys were taking her out, he believed not one of them worthy of her, not one of them good enough to receive a note of her sweet voice: he insisted that she be returned before midnight. Yet who was it who sympathized with him in his decision to remain, for the rest of his days, the simple janitor! when everyone else was urging him to get out, get prestige, make more money? Who was it who sympathized with him in his almost desperate love for this old house? Who followed him about, emotionally speaking, loving this, doting on that? The kitchen, for instance, that was not beautiful in any way! The walls and ceilings, that were cracked. The chairs, which cried when people sat in them. The tables, that grieved audibly if anyone rested more than two fingers upon them. The huge cabinets, old and tired (when you shut their doors or drawers there was a sick, bickering little sound). The radiators, high and hideous. And underneath the low sink coiled unlovely pipes, that Helen said made her think of a careless woman's underwear, peeping out. In fact, often had Helen given her opinion, unasked, of the whole house, of the whole "hulk of rotten wood." Often had her cool and gentle eyes sneered, gently and coolly, at her father's determination to hold his poor estate. But take that kitchen, for instance! Maud Martha, taking it, saw herself there, up and down her seventeen years, eating apples after school; making sweet potato tarts; drawing, on the pathetic table, the horse that won her the sixth grade prize; getting her hair curled for her first party, at that stove; washing dishes by summer twilight, with the back door wide open; making cheese and peanut butter sandwiches for a picnic. And even crying, crying in that pantry, when no one knew. The old sorrows brought there!—now dried, flattened out, breaking into interesting dust at the merest look. . . .

"You'll never get a boy friend," said Helen, fluffing on her Golden Peacock powder, "if you don't stop reading those books."

10. first beau

He had a way of putting his hands on a Woman. Light, but perforating. Passing by, he would touch the Woman's hair, he would give the Woman's hair a careless, and yet deliberate, caress, working down from the top to the ends, then gliding to the chin, then lifting the chin till the poor female's eyes were forced to meet his, then proceeding down the neck. Maud Martha had watched this technique time after time, privately swearing that if he ever tried it on her she would settle him soon enough. Finally he had tried it, and a sloppy feeling had filled her, and she had not settled him at all. Not that she was thereafter, like the others, his to command, flatter, neglect, swing high, swing low, smooth with a grin, wrinkle with a scowl, just as his fancy wished. For Russell lacked—what? He was—nice. He was fun to go about with. He was decorated inside and out. He did things, said things, with a flourish. That was what he was. He was a flourish. He was a dazzling, long, and sleepily swishing flourish. "He will never be great," Maud Martha thought. "But he wouldn't be hurt if anybody told him that—if possible to choose from two, he would without hesitation choose being grand."

There he sat before her, in a sleeveless yellow-tan sweater and white, open-collared sport shirt, one leg thrust sexily out, fist on that hip, brown eyes ablaze, chin thrust up at her entrance as if *it* were to give her greeting, devil-like smile making her blink.

11. second beau

And—don't laugh—he wanted a dog.

A picture of the English country gentleman. Roaming the rustic hill. He had not yet bought a pipe. He would immediately.

There already was the herringbone tweed. (Although old sensuousness, old emotional daring broke out at the top of the trousers, where there was that gathering, that kicked-back yearning toward the pleat!) There was the tie a man might think about for an hour before entering that better shop, in order to be able to deliberate only a sharp two minutes at the counter, under the icy estimate of the salesman. Here were the socks, here was the haircut, here were the shoes. The educated smile, the slight bow, the faint imperious nod. He belonged to the world of the university.

He was taking a number of loose courses on the Midway.

His scent was withdrawn, expensive, as he strode down the worn carpet of her living room, as though it were the educated green of the Midway.

He considered Parrington's *Main Currents in American Thought.* He had not mastered it. Only recently, he announced, had he learned of its existence. "Three volumes of the most reasonable approaches!—Yet there are chaps on that campus—*young!*—younger than I am—who read it years ago, who know it, who have had it for themselves for years, who have been seeing it on their fathers' shelves since infancy. They heard it discussed at the dinner table when they were four. As a ball is to me, so Parrington is to them. They've been kicking him around for years, like a *foot*ball!"

The idea agitated. His mother had taken in washing. She had had three boys, whom she sent to school clean but patched-up. Just so they were clean, she had said. That was all that mattered, she had said. She had said "ain't." She had said, "I ain't stud'n you." His father—he hadn't said anything at all.

He himself had had a paper route. Had washed windows, cleaned basements, sanded furniture, shoveled snow, hauled out trash and garbage for the neighbors. He had worked before that, running errands for people when he was six. What chance did he have, he mused, what chance was there for anybody coming out of a set of conditions that never allowed for the prevalence of sensitive, and intellectual, yet almost frivolous, dinner-table discussions of Parrington across four-year-old heads?

Whenever he left the Midway, said David McKemster, he was instantly depressed. East of Cottage Grove, people were clean, going somewhere that mattered, not talking unless they had something to say. West of the Midway, they leaned against buildings and their mouths were opening and closing very fast but nothing important was coming out. What did they know about Aristotle?[3] The unhappiness he felt over there was physical. He wanted to throw up. There was a fence on Forty-seventh and—Champlain? Langley? Forestville?—he forgot what; broken, rotten, trying to lie down; and passing it on a windy night or on a night when it was drizzling, he felt lost, lapsed, negative, untended, extinguished, broken and lying down too—unappeasable. And looking up in those kitchenette windows, where the lights were dirty through dirty glass—they *could* wash the windows—was not at all "interesting" to him as it probably was to those guys at the university who had—who had—

---

3. Greek philosopher and scientist (384–322 B.C.E.).

Made a football out of Parrington.

Because he knew what it was. He knew it was a mess! He knew it wasn't "colorful," "exotic," "fascinating."

He wanted a dog. A good dog. No mongrel. An apartment—well-furnished, containing a good bookcase, filled with good books in good bindings. He wanted a phonograph, and records. The symphonies. And Yehudi Menuhin.[4] He wanted some good art. These things were not extras. They went to make up a good background. The kind of background those guys had.

12. Maud Martha and New York

The name "New York" glittered in front of her like the silver in the shops on Michigan Boulevard. It was silver, and it was solid, and it was remote: it was behind glass, it was behind bright glass like the silver in the shops. It was not for her. Yet.

When she was out walking, and with grating iron swish a train whipped by, off, above, its passengers were always, for her comfort, New York-bound. She sat inside with them. She leaned back in the plush. She sped, past farms, through tiny towns, where people slept, kissed, quarreled, ate midnight snacks; unfortunate folk who were not New York-bound and never would be.

Maud Martha loved it when her magazines said "New York," described "good" objects there, wonderful people there, recalled fine talk, the bristling or the creamy or the tactfully shimmering ways of life. They showed pictures of rooms with wood paneling, softly glowing, touched up by the compliment of a spot of auburn here, the low burn of a rare binding there. There were ferns in these rooms, and Chinese boxes; bits of dreamlike crystal; a taste of leather. In the advertisement pages, you saw where you could buy six Italian plates for eleven hundred dollars—and you must hurry, for there was just the one set; you saw where you could buy antique French bisque figurines (pale blue and gold) for—for— Her whole body become a hunger, she would pore over these pages. The clothes interested her, too; especially did she care for the pictures of women wearing carelessly, as if they were rags, dresses that were plain but whose prices were not. And the foolish food (her mother's description) enjoyed by New Yorkers fascinated her. They paid ten dollars for an eight-ounce jar of Russian caviar; they ate things called anchovies, and capers; they ate little diamond-shaped cheeses that paprika had but breathed on; they ate bitter-almond macaroons; they ate papaya packed in rum and syrup; they ate peculiar sauces, were free with honey, were lavish with butter, wine and cream.

She bought the New York papers downtown, read of the concerts and plays, studied the book reviews, was intent over the announcements of auctions. She liked the sound of "Fifth Avenue," "Town Hall," "B. Altman," "Hammacher Schlemmer." She was on Fifth Avenue whenever she wanted to be, and she it was who rolled up, silky or furry, in the taxi, was assisted out, and stood, her next step nebulous, before the theaters of the thousand lights, before velvet-lined impossible shops; she it was.

New York, for Maud Martha, was a symbol. Her idea of it stood for what she felt life ought to be. Jeweled. Polished. Smiling. Poised. Calmly rushing! Straight up and down, yet graceful enough.

4. American violinist and concert virtuoso (1916–1999).

She thought of them drinking their coffee there—or tea, as in England. It was afternoon. Lustrous people glided over perfect floors, correctly smiling. They stopped before a drum table, covered with heavy white—and bearing a silver coffee service, old (in the better sense) china, a platter of orange and cinnamon cakes (or was it nutmeg the cakes would have in them?), sugar and cream, a Chinese box, one tall and slender flower. Their host or hostess poured, smiling too, nodding quickly to this one and that one, inquiring gently whether it should be sugar, or cream, or both, or neither. (She was teaching herself to drink coffee with neither.) All was *very* gentle. The voices, no matter how they rose, or even sharpened, had fur at the base. The steps never bragged, or grated in any way on any ear—not that they could very well, on so good a Persian rug, or deep soft carpeting. And the drum table stood in front of a screen, a Japanese one, perhaps, with rich and mellow, bread-textured colors. The people drank and nibbled, while they discussed the issues of the day, sorting, rejecting, revising. Then they went home, quietly, elegantly. They retired to homes not one whit less solid or embroidered than the home of their host or hostess.

What she wanted to dream, and dreamed, was her affair. It pleased her to dwell upon color and soft bready textures and light, on a complex beauty, on gemlike surfaces. What was the matter with that? Besides, who could safely swear that she would never be able to make her dream come true for herself? Not altogether, then!—but slightly?—in some part?

She was eighteen years old, and the world waited. To caress her.

13. *low yellow*

I know what he is thinking, thought Maud Martha, as she sat on the porch in the porch swing with Paul Phillips. He is thinking that I am all right. That I am really all right. That I will do.

And I am glad of that, because my whole body is singing beside him. And when you feel like that beside a man you ought to be married to him.

I am what he would call—sweet.

But I am certainly not what he would call pretty. Even with all this hair (which I have just assured him, in response to his question, is not "natural," is not good grade or anything like good grade) even with whatever I have that puts a dimple in his heart, even with these nice ears, I am still, definitely, not what he can call pretty if he remains true to what his idea of pretty has always been. Pretty would be a little cream-colored thing with curly hair. Or at the very lowest pretty would be a little curly-haired thing the color of cocoa with a lot of milk in it. Whereas, I am the color of cocoa straight, if you can be even that "kind" to me.

He wonders, as we walk in the street, about the thoughts of the people who look at us. Are they thinking that he could do no better than—me? Then he thinks, Well, hmp! Well, huh!—all the little good-lookin' dolls that have wanted *him*—all the little sweet high-yellows that have ambled slowly past *his* front door—What he would like to tell those secretly snickering ones!—That any day out of the week he can do better than this black gal.

And by my own admission my hair is absolutely knappy.

"Fatherhood," said Paul, "is not exactly in my line. But it would be all right to have a couple or so of kids, good-looking, in my pocket, so to speak."

"I am not a pretty woman," said Maud Martha. "If you married a pretty woman, you could be the father of pretty children. Envied by people. The father of beautiful children."

"But I don't know," said Paul. "Because my features aren't fine. They aren't regular. They're heavy. They're real Negro features. I'm light, or at least I can claim to be a sort of low-toned yellow, and my hair has a teeny crimp. But even so I'm not handsome."

No, there would be little "beauty" getting born out of such a union.

Still, mused Maud Martha, I am what he would call—sweet, and I am good, and he will marry me. Although, he will be thinking, that's what he always says about letting yourself get interested in these incorruptible virgins, that so often your manhood will not let you concede defeat, and before you know it, you have let them steal you, put an end, perhaps, to your career.

He will fight, of course. He will decide that he must think a long time before he lets that happen here.

But in the end I'll hook him, even while he's wondering how this marriage will cramp him or pinch at him—at him, admirer of the gay life, spiffy clothes, beautiful yellow girls, natural hair, smooth cars, jewels, night clubs, cocktail lounges, class.

14. *everybody will be surprised*

"Of course," said Paul, "we'll have to start small. But it won't be very long before everybody will be surprised."

Maud Martha smiled.

"Your apartment, eventually, will be a dream. The *Defender* will come and photograph it." Paul grinned when he said that, but quite literally he believed it. Since he had decided to go ahead and marry her, he meant to "do it up right." People were going to look at his marriage and see only things to want. He was going to have a swanky flat. He and Maudie were going to dress well. They would entertain a lot.

"Listen," said Paul eagerly, "at a store on Forty-third and Cottage they're selling four rooms of furniture for eighty-nine dollars."

Maud Martha's heart sank.

"We'll go look at it tomorrow," added Paul.

"Paul—do you think we'll have a hard time finding a nice place—when the time comes?"

"No. I don't think so. But look here. I think we ought to plan on a stove-heated flat. We could get one of those cheap."

"Oh, I wouldn't like that. I've always lived in steam."

"I've always lived in stove—till a year ago. It's just as warm. And about fifteen dollars cheaper."

"Then what made your folks move to steam, then?"

"Ma wanted to live on a better-looking street. But we can't think about foolishness like that, when we're just starting out. Our flat will be hot stuff; the important thing is the flat, not the street; we can't study about foolishness like that; but our flat will be hot stuff. We'll have a swell flat."

"When you have stove heat, you have to have those ugly old fat black pipes stretching out all over the room."

"You don't just have to have long ones."

"I don't want any ones."

"You can have a little short one. And the new heaters they got look like radios. You'll like 'em."

Maud Martha silently decided she wouldn't, and resolved to hold out firmly against stove-heated flats. No stove-heated flats. And no basements. You got T.B. in basements.

"If you think a basement would be better—" began Paul.

"I don't," she interrupted.

"Basements are cheap too."

Was her attitude unco-operative? Should she be wanting to sacrifice more, for the sake of her man? A procession of pioneer women strode down her imagination; strong women, bold; praiseworthy, faithful, stout-minded; with a stout light beating in the eyes. Women who could stand low temperatures. Women who would toil eminently, to improve the lot of their men. Women who cooked. She thought of herself, dying for her man. It was a beautiful thought.

15. *the kitchenette*

Their home was on the third floor of a great gray stone building. The two rooms were small. The bedroom was furnished with a bed and dresser, old-fashioned, but in fair condition, and a faded occasional chair. In the kitchen were an oilcloth-covered table, two kitchen chairs, one folding chair, a cabinet base, a brown wooden icebox, and a three-burner gas stove. Only one of the burners worked, the housekeeper told them. The janitor would fix the others before they moved in. Maud Martha said she could fix them herself.

"Nope," objected Paul. "The janitor'll do it. That's what they pay him for." There was a bathroom at the end of the hall, which they would have to share with four other families who lived on the floor.

The housekeeper at the kitchenette place did not require a reference. . . .

The *Defender* would never come here with cameras.

Still, Maud Martha was, at first, enthusiastic. She made plans for this home. She would have the janitor move the bed and dresser out, tell Paul to buy a studio couch, a desk chest, a screen, a novelty chair, a white Venetian blind for the first room, and a green one for the kitchen, since the wallpaper there was green (with little red fishes swimming about). Perhaps they could even get a rug. A green one. And green drapes for the windows. Why, this *might* even turn out to be their dream apartment. It was small, but wonders could be wrought here. They could open up an account at L. Fish Furniture Store, pay a little every month. In that way, they could have the essentials right away. Later, they could get a Frigidaire. A baby's bed, when one became necessary, could go behind the screen, and they would have a pure living room.

Paul, after two or three weeks, told her sheepishly that kitchenettes were not so bad. Theirs seemed "cute and cozy" enough, he declared, and for his part, he went on, he was ready to "camp right down" until the time came to "build." Sadly, however, by that time Maud Martha had lost interest in the place, because the janitor had said that the Owner would not allow the furniture to be disturbed. Tenants moved too often. It was not worth the Owner's financial while to make changes, or to allow tenants to make them. They would have to be satisfied with "the apartment" as it was.

Then, one month after their installation, the first roach arrived. Ugly, shiny, slimy, slick-moving. She had rather see a rat—well, she had rather see a mouse. She had never yet been able to kill a roach. She could not bear to touch one, with foot or stick or twisted paper. She could only stand help-less, frozen, and watch the slick movement suddenly appear and slither, looking doubly evil, across the mirror, before which she had been calmly brushing her hair. And why? Why was he here? For she was scrubbing with water containing melted American Family soap and Lysol every other day.

And these things—roaches, and having to be satisfied with the place as it was—were not the only annoyances that had to be reckoned with. She was becoming aware of an oddness in color and sound and smell about her, the color and sound and smell of the kitchenette building. The color was gray, and the smell and sound had taken on a suggestion of the properties of color, and impressed one as gray, too. The sobbings, the frustrations, the small hates, the large and ugly hates, the little pushing-through love, the bore-dom, that came to her from behind those walls (some of them beaver-board) via speech and scream and sigh—all these were gray. And the smells of various types of sweat, and of bathing and bodily functions (the bathroom was always in use, someone was always in the bathroom) and of fresh or stale love-making, which rushed in thick fumes to your nostrils as you walked down the hall, or down the stairs—these were *gray*.

There was a whole lot of grayness here.

16. the young couple at home

Paul had slept through most of the musicale. Three quarters of the time his head had been a heavy knot on her shoulder. At each of her attempts to remove it, he had waked up so suddenly, and had given her a look of such childlike fierceness, that she could only smile.

Now on the streetcar, however—the car was in the garage—he was not sleepy, and he kept "amusing" Maud Martha with little "tricks," such as cocking his head archly and winking at her, or digging her slyly in the ribs, or lifting her hand to his lips, and blowing on it softly, or poking a finger under her chin and raising it awkwardly, or feeling her muscle, then putting her hand on his muscle, so that she could tell the difference. Such as that. "Clowning," he called it. And because he felt that he was making her happy, she tried not to see the uncareful stares and smirks of the other passengers—uncareful and insultingly consolatory. He sat playfully upon part of her thigh. He gently kicked her toe.

Once home, he went immediately to the bathroom. He did not try to mask his need, he was obvious and direct about it.

"He could make," she thought, "a comment or two on what went on at the musicale. Or some little joke. It isn't that I'm unreasonable or stupid. But everything can be done with a little grace. I'm sure of it."

When he came back, he yawned, stretched, smeared his lips up and down her neck, assured her of his devotion, and sat down on the bed to take off his shoes. She picked up *Of Human Bondage*,[5] and sat at the other end of the bed.

"Snuggle up," he invited.

"I thought I'd read awhile."

5. Novel by British writer Somerset Maugham (1874–1965).

"I guess I'll read awhile, too," he decided, when his shoes were off and had been kicked into the kitchen. She got up, went to the shoes, put them in the closet. He grinned at her merrily. She was conscious of the grin, but refused to look at him. She went back to her book. He settled down to his. His was a paper-backed copy of *Sex in the Married Life*.[6]

There he sat, slouched down, terribly absorbed, happy in his sock feet, curling his toes inside the socks.

"I want you to read this book," he said, "—but at the right times: one chapter each night before retiring." He reached over, pinched her on the buttock.

She stood again. "Shall I make some cocoa?" she asked pleasantly. "And toast some sandwiches?"

"Say, I'd like that," he said, glancing up briefly.

She toasted rye strips spread with pimento cheese and grated onion. She made cocoa.

They ate, drank, and read together. She read *Of Human Bondage*. He read *Sex in the Married Life*. They were silent.

Five minutes passed. She looked at him. He was asleep. His head had fallen back, his mouth was open—it was a good thing there were no flies— his ankles were crossed. And the feet!—pointing confidently out (no one would harm them). *Sex in the Married Life* was about to slip to the floor. She did not stretch out a hand to save it.

Once she had taken him to a library. While occupied with the card cases she had glanced up, had observed that he, too, was busy among the cards. "Do you want a book?" "No-o. I'm just curious about something. I wondered if there could be a man in the world named Bastard. Sure enough, there is."

Paul's book fell, making a little clatter. But he did not wake up, and she did not get up.

17. Maud Martha spares the mouse

There. She had it at last. The weeks it had devoted to eluding her, the tricks, the clever hide-and-go-seeks, the routes it had in all sobriety devised, together with the delicious moments it had, undoubtedly, laughed up its sleeve—all to no ultimate avail. She had that mouse.

It shook its little self, as best it could, in the trap. Its bright black eyes contained no appeal—the little creature seemed to understand that there was no hope of mercy from the eternal enemy, no hope of reprieve or postponement—but a fine small dignity. It waited. It looked at Maud Martha.

She wondered what else it was thinking. Perhaps that there was not enough food in its larder. Perhaps that little Betty, a puny child from the start, would not, now, be getting fed. Perhaps that, now, the family's seasonal house-cleaning, for lack of expert direction, would be left undone. It might be regretting that young Bobby's education was now at an end. It might be nursing personal regrets. No more the mysterious shadows of the kitchenette, the uncharted twists, the unguessed halls. No more the sweet delights of the chase, the charms of being unsuccessfully hounded, thrown at.

---

6. Perhaps *Sex in Married Life: A Practical Handbook for Men and Women* (1938, 1965), by George Ryley Scott.

Maud Martha could not bear the little look.

"Go home to your children," she urged. "To your wife or husband." She opened the trap. The mouse vanished.

Suddenly, she was conscious of a new cleanness in her. A wide air walked in her. A life had blundered its way into her power and it had been hers to preserve or destroy. She had not destroyed. In the center of that simple restraint was—creation. She had created a piece of life. It was wonderful.

"Why," she thought, as her height doubled, "why, I'm good! I am *good*."

She ironed her aprons. Her back was straight. Her eyes were mild, and soft with a godlike loving-kindness.

18. *we're the only colored people here*

When they went out to the car there were just the very finest bits of white powder coming down with an almost comical little ethereal hauteur, to add themselves to the really important, piled-up masses of their kind.

And it wasn't cold.

Maud Martha laughed happily to herself. It was pleasant out, and tonight she and Paul were very close to each other.

He held the door open for her—instead of going on around to the driving side, getting in, and leaving her to get in at her side as best she might. When he took this way of calling her "lady" and informing her of his love she felt precious, protected, delicious. She gave him an excited look of gratitude. He smiled indulgently.

"Want it to be the Owl again?"

"Oh, no no, Paul. Let's not go there tonight. I feel too good inside for that. Let's go downtown?"

She had to suggest that with a question mark at the end, always. He usually had three protests. Too hard to park. Too much money. Too many white folks. And tonight she could almost certainly expect a no, she feared, because he had come out in his blue work shirt. There was a spot of apricot juice on the collar, too. His shoes were not shined. . . . But he nodded!

"We've never been to the World Playhouse," she said cautiously. "They have a good picture. I'd feel rich in there."

"You really wanta?"

"Please?"

"Sure."

It wasn't like other movie houses. People from the Studebaker Theatre which, as Maud Martha whispered to Paul, was "all-locked-arms" with the World Playhouse, were strolling up and down the lobby, laughing softly, smoking with gentle grace.

"There must be a play going on in there and this is probably an intermission," Maud Martha whispered again.

"I don't know why you feel you got to whisper," whispered Paul. "Nobody else is whispering in here." He looked around, resentfully, wanting to see a few, just a few, colored faces. There were only their own.

Maud Martha laughed a nervous defiant little laugh; and spoke loudly. "There certainly isn't any reason to whisper. Silly, huh."

The strolling women were cleverly gowned. Some of them had flowers or flashers in their hair. They looked—cooked. Well cared-for. And as though they had never seen a roach or a rat in their lives. Or gone without heat for a week. And the men had even edges. They were men, Maud Martha thought, who wouldn't stoop to fret over less than a thousand dollars.

"We're the only colored people here," said Paul.

She hated him a little. "Oh, hell. Who in hell cares."

"Well, what I want to know is, where do you pay the damn fares."

"There's the box office. Go on up."

He went on up. It was closed.

"Well," sighed Maud Martha, "I guess the picture has started already. But we can't have missed much. Go on up to that girl at the candy counter and ask her where we should pay our money."

He didn't want to do that. The girl was lovely and blonde and cold-eyed, and her arms were akimbo, and the set of her head was eloquent. No one else was at the counter.

"Well. We'll wait a minute. And see—"

Maud Martha hated him again. Coward. She ought to flounce over to the girl herself—show him up. . . .

The people in the lobby tried to avoid looking curiously at two shy Negroes wanting desperately not to seem shy. The white women looked at the Negro woman in her outfit with which no special fault could be found, but which made them think, somehow, of close rooms, and wee, close lives. They looked at her hair. They liked to see a dark colored girl with long, long hair. They were always slightly surprised, but agreeably so, when they did. They supposed it was the hair that had got her that yellowish, good-looking Negro man.

The white men tried not to look at the Negro man in the blue work shirt, the Negro man without a tie.

An usher opened a door of the World Playhouse part and ran quickly down the few steps that led from it to the lobby. Paul opened his mouth.

"Say, fella. Where do we get the tickets for the movie?"

The usher glanced at Paul's feet before answering. Then he said coolly, but not unpleasantly, "I'll take the money."

They were able to go in.

And the picture! Maud Martha was so glad that they had not gone to the Owl! Here was technicolor, and the love story was sweet. And there was classical music that silvered its way into you and made your back cold. And the theater itself! It was no palace, no such Great Shakes as the Tivoli out south, for instance (where many colored people went every night). But you felt good sitting there, yes, good, and as if, when you left it, you would be going home to a sweet-smelling apartment with flowers on little gleaming tables; and wonderful silver on night-blue velvet, in chests; and crackly sheets; and lace spreads on such beds as you saw at Marshall Field's. Instead of back to your kit'n't apt., with the garbage of your floor's families in a big can just outside your door, and the gray sound of little gray feet scratching away from it as you drag up those flights of narrow complaining stairs.

Paul pressed her hand. Paul said, "We oughta do this more often."

And again. "We'll have to do this more often. And go to plays, too. I mean at that Blackstone, and Studebaker."

She pressed back, smiling beautifully to herself in the darkness. Though she knew that once the spell was over it would be a year, two years, more, before he would return to the World Playhouse. And he might never go to a real play. But she was learning to love moments. To love moments for themselves.

When the picture was over, and the lights revealed them for what they were, the Negroes stood up among the furs and good cloth and faint perfume, looked about them eagerly. They hoped they would meet no cruel eyes. They hoped no one would look intruded upon. They had enjoyed the picture so, they were so happy, they wanted to laugh, to say warmly to the other out-goers, "Good, huh? Wasn't it swell?"

This, of course, they could not do. But if only no one would look intruded upon. . . .

19. *if you're light and have long hair*

Came the invitation that Paul recognized as an honor of the first water, and as sufficient indication that he was, at last, a social somebody. The invitation was from the Foxy Cats Club, the club of clubs. He was to be present, in formal dress, at the Annual Foxy Cats Dawn Ball. No chances were taken: "Top hat, white tie and tails" hastily followed the "Formal dress," and that elucidation was in bold type.

Twenty men were in the Foxy Cats Club. All were good-looking. All wore clothes that were rich and suave. All "handled money," for their number consisted of well-located barbers, policemen, "government men" and men with a lucky touch at the tracks. Certainly the Foxy Cats Club was not a representative of that growing group of South Side organizations devoted to moral and civic improvements, or to literary or other cultural pursuits. If that had been so, Paul would have chucked his bid (which was black and silver, decorated with winking cat faces) down the toilet with a yawn. "That kind of stuff" was hardly understood by Paul, and was always dismissed with an airy "dicty," "hincty" or "high-falutin'." But no. The Foxy Cats devoted themselves solely to the business of being "hep," and each year they spent hundreds of dollars on their wonderful Dawn Ball, which did not begin at dawn, but was scheduled to end at dawn. "Ball," they called the frolic, but it served also the purposes of party, feast and fashion show. Maud Martha, watching him study his invitation, watching him lift his chin, could see that he considered himself one of the blessed.

Who—what kind soul had recommended him!

"He'll have to take me," thought Maud Martha. "For the envelope is addressed 'Mr. and Mrs.,' and I opened it. I guess he'd like to leave me home. At the Ball, there will be only beautiful girls, or real stylish ones. There won't be more than a handful like me. My type is not a Foxy Cat favorite. But he can't avoid taking me—since he hasn't yet thought of words or ways strong enough, and at the same time soft enough—for he's kind: he doesn't like to injure—to carry across to me the news that he is not to be held permanently by my type, and that he can go on with this marriage only if I put no ropes or questions around him. Also, he'll want to humor me, now that I'm pregnant."

She would need a good dress. That, she knew, could be a problem, on his grocery clerk's pay. He would have his own expenses. He would have to rent his topper and tails, and he would have to buy a fine tie, and really excellent shoes. She knew he was thinking that on the strength of his appearance and sophisticated behavior at this Ball might depend his future admission (for why not dream?) to *membership*, actually, in the Foxy Cats Club!

"I'll settle," decided Maud Martha, "on a plain white princess-style thing and some blue and black satin ribbon. I'll go to my mother's. I'll work miracles at the sewing machine.

"On that night, I'll wave my hair. I'll smell faintly of lily of the valley."

The main room of the Club 99, where the Ball was held, was hung with green and yellow and red balloons, and the thick pillars, painted to give an effect of marble, and stretching from floor to ceiling, were draped with green and red and yellow crepe paper. Huge ferns, rubber plants and bowls of flowers were at every corner. The floor itself was a decoration, golden, glazed. There was no overhead light; only wall lamps, and the bulbs in these were romantically dim. At the back of the room, standing on a furry white rug, was the long banquet table, dressed in damask, accented by groups of thin silver candlesticks bearing white candles, and laden with lovely food: cold chicken, lobster, candied ham fruit combinations, potato salad in a great gold dish, corn sticks, a cheese fluff in spiked tomato cups, fruit cake, angel cake, sunshine cake. The drinks were at a smaller table nearby, behind which stood a genial mixologist, quick with maraschino cherries, and with lemon, ice and liquor. Wines were there, and whiskey, and rum, and eggnog made with pure cream.

Paul and Maud Martha arrived rather late, on purpose. Rid of their wraps, they approached the glittering floor. Bunny Bates's orchestra was playing Ellington's "Solitude."

Paul, royal in rented finery, was flushed with excitement. Maud Martha looked at him. Not very tall. Not very handsomely made. But there was that extraordinary quality of maleness. Hiding in the body that was not *too* yellow, waiting to spring out at her, surround her (she liked to think)—that maleness. The Ball stirred her. The Beauties, in their gorgeous gowns, bustling, supercilious; the young men, who at other times most unpleasantly blew their noses, and darted surreptitiously into alleys to relieve themselves, and sweated and swore at their jobs, and scratched their more intimate parts, now smiling, smooth, overgallant; the drowsy lights; the smells of food and flowers, the smell of Murray's pomade, the body perfumes, natural and superimposed; the sensuous heaviness of the wine-colored draperies at the many windows; the music, now steamy and slow, now as clear and fragile as glass, now raging, passionate, now moaning and thickly gray. The Ball made toys of her emotions, stirred her variously. But she was anxious to have it end, she was anxious to be at home again, with the door closed behind herself and her husband. Then, he might be warm. There might be more than the absent courtesy he had been giving her of late. Then, he might be the tree she had a great need to lean against, in this "emergency." There was no telling what dear thing he might say to her, what little gem let fall.

But, to tell the truth, his behavior now was not very promising of gems to come. After their second dance he escorted her to a bench by the wall, left her. Trying to look nonchalant, she sat. She sat, trying not to show the inferiority she did not feel. When the music struck up again, he began to dance with someone red-haired and curved, and white as a white. Who was she? He had approached her easily, he had taken her confidently, he held her and conversed with her as though he had known her well for a long, long time. The girl smiled up at him. Her gold-spangled bosom was pressed—was pressed against that maleness—

A man asked Maud Martha to dance. He was dark, too. His mustache was small.

"Is this your first Foxy Cats?" he asked.

"What?" Paul's cheek was on that of Gold-Spangles.

"First Cats?"

"Oh. Yes." Paul and Gold-Spangles were weaving through the noisy twisting couples, were trying, apparently, to get to the reception hall.

"Do you know that girl? What's her name?" Maud Martha asked her partner, pointing to Gold-Spangles. Her partner looked, nodded. He pressed her closer.

"That's Maella. That's Maella."

"Pretty, isn't she?" She wanted him to keep talking about Maella. He nodded again.

"Yep. She has 'em howling along the stroll, all right, all right."

Another man, dancing past with an artificial redhead, threw a whispered word at Maud Martha's partner, who caught it eagerly, winked. "Solid, ol' man," he said. "Solid, Jack." He pressed Maud Martha closer. "You're a babe," he said. "You're a real babe." He reeked excitingly of tobacco, liquor, pine-soap, toilet water, and Sen Sen.

Maud Martha thought of her parents' back yard. Fresh. Clean. Smokeless. In her childhood, a snowball bush had shone there, big above the dandelions. The snowballs had been big, healthy. Once, she and her sister and brother had waited in the back yard for their parents to finish readying themselves for a trip to Milwaukee. The snowballs had been so beautiful, so fat and startlingly white in the sunlight, that she had suddenly loved home a thousand times more than ever before, and had not wanted to go to Milwaukee. But as the children grew, the bush sickened. Each year the snowballs were smaller and more dispirited. Finally a summer came when there were no blossoms at all. Maud Martha wondered what had become of the bush. For it was not there now. Yet she, at least, had never seen it go.

"Not," thought Maud Martha, "that they love each other. It oughta be that simple. Then I could lick it. It oughta be that easy. But it's my color that makes him mad. I try to shut my eyes to that, but it's no good. What I am inside, what is really me, he likes okay. But he keeps looking at my color, which is like a wall. He has to jump over it in order to meet and touch what I've got for him. He has to jump away up high in order to see it. He gets awful tired of all that jumping."

Paul came back from the reception hall. Maella was clinging to his arm. A final cry of the saxophone finished that particular slice of the blues. Maud Martha's partner bowed, escorted her to a chair by a rubber plant, bowed again, left.

"I could," considered Maud Martha, "go over there and scratch her upsweep down. I could spit on her back. I could scream. 'Listen,' I could scream, 'I'm making a baby for this man and I mean to do it in peace.'"

But if the root was sour what business did she have up there hacking at a leaf?

20. *a birth*

After dinner, they washed dishes together. Then they undressed, and Paul got in bed, and was asleep almost instantly. She went down the long public hall to the bathroom, in her blue chenille robe. On her way back down the squeezing dark of the hall she felt—something softly separate in her. Back in the bedroom, she put on her gown, then stepped to the dresser to smear her face with cold cream. But when she turned around to get in the bed she couldn't move. Her legs cramped painfully, and she had a tremendous desire to eliminate which somehow she felt she would never be able to gratify.

"Paul!" she cried. As though in his dreams he had been waiting to hear that call, and that call only, he was up with a bound.

"I can't move."

He rubbed his eyes.

"Maudie, are you kidding?"

"I'm not kidding, Paul. I can't move."

He lifted her up and laid her on the bed, his eyes stricken.

"Look here, Maudie. Do you think you're going to have that baby tonight?"

"No—no. These are just what they call 'false pains.' I'm not going to have the baby tonight. Can you get—my gown off?"

"Sure. Sure."

But really he was afraid to touch her. She lay nude on the bed for a few moments, perfectly still. Then all of a sudden motion came to her. Whereas before she had not been able to move her legs, now she could not keep them still.

"Oh, my God," she prayed aloud. "Just let my legs get still five minutes." God did not answer the prayer.

Paul was pacing up and down the room in fright.

"Look here. I don't think those are false pains. I think you're going to have that baby tonight."

"Don't say that, Paul," she muttered between clenched teeth. "I'm not going to have the baby tonight."

"I'm going to call your mother."

"Don't do that, Paul. She can't stand to see things like this. Once she got a chance to see a stillborn baby, but she fainted before they even unwrapped it. She can't stand to see things like this. False pains, that's all. Oh, God, why don't you let me keep my legs still!"

She began to whimper in a manner that made Paul want to vomit. His thoughts traveled to the girl he had met at the Dawn Ball several months before. Cool. Sweet. Well-groomed. Fair.

"You're going to have that baby *now*. I'm going down to call up your mother and a doctor."

"DON'T YOU GO OUT OF HERE AND LEAVE ME ALONE! Damn. DAMN!"

"All right. All right. I won't leave you alone. I'll get the woman next door to come in. But somebody's got to get a doctor here."

"Don't you sneak out! Don't you *sneak* out!" She was pushing down with her stomach now. Paul, standing at the foot of the bed with his hands in his pockets, saw the creeping insistence of what he thought was the head of the child.

"Oh, my Lord!" he cried. "It's coming! It's coming!"

He walked about the room several times. He went to the dresser and began to brush his hair. She looked at him in speechless contempt. He went out of the door, and ran down the three flights of stairs two or three steps at a time. The telephone was on the first floor. No sooner had he picked up the receiver than he heard Maud Martha give what he was sure could *only* be called a "bloodcurdling scream." He bolted up the stairs, saw her wriggling on the bed, said softly, "Be right back," and bolted down again. First he called his mother's doctor, and begged him to come right over. Then he called the Browns.

"Get her to the hospital!" shouted Belva Brown. "You'll have to get her to the hospital right away!"

"I can't. She's having the baby now. She isn't going to let anybody touch her. I tell you, she's having the baby."

"Don't be a fool. Of course she can get to the hospital. Why, she mustn't have it there in the house! I'm coming over there. I'll take her myself. Be sure there's plenty of gas in that car."

He tried to reach his mother. She was out—had not returned from a revival meeting.

When Paul ran back up the stairs, he found young Mrs. Cray, who lived in the front apartment of their floor, attending his shrieking wife.

"I heard 'er yellin', and thought I'd better come in, seein' as how you all is so confused. Got a doctor comin'?"

Paul sighed heavily. "I just called one. Thanks for coming in. This—this came on all of a sudden, and I don't think I know what to do."

"Well, the thing to do is get a doctor right off. She's goin' to have the baby soon. Call *my* doctor." She gave him a number. "Whichever one gets here first can work on her. Ain't no time to waste."

Paul ran back down the stairs and called the number. "What's the doctor's address?" he yelled up. Mrs. Cray yelled it down. He went out to get the doctor personally. He was glad of an excuse to escape. He was sick of hearing Maudie scream. He had had no idea that she could scream that kind of screaming. It was awful. How lucky he was that he had been born a man. How lucky he was that he had been born a man!

Belva arrived in twenty minutes. She was grateful to find another woman present. She had come to force Maud Martha to start for the hospital, but a swift glance told her that the girl would not leave her bed for many days. As she said to her husband and Helen later on, "The baby was all ready to spill out."

When her mother came in the door Maud Martha tightened her lips, temporarily forgetful of her strange pain. (But it wasn't pain. It was something else.) "Listen. If you're going to make a fuss, go on out. I'm having enough trouble without you making a fuss over everything."

Mrs. Cray giggled encouragingly. Belva said bravely, "I'm not going to make a fuss. You'll see. Why, there's nothing to make a fuss *about*. You're just going to have a baby, like millions of other women. Why should I make a fuss?"

Maud Martha tried to smile but could not quite make it. The sensations were getting grindingly sharp. She screamed longer and louder, explaining breathlessly in between times, "I just can't help it. Excuse me."

"Why, go on and scream," urged Belva. "You're supposed to scream. That's your privilege. I'm sure *I* don't mind." Her ears were splitting, and over and over as she stood there looking down at her agonized daughter, she said to herself, "Why doesn't the doctor come? Why doesn't the doctor come? I know I'm going to faint." She and Mrs. Cray stood, one on each side of the bed, purposelessly holding a sheet over Maud Martha, under which they peeped as seldom as they felt was safe. Maud Martha kept asking, "Has the head come?" Presently she felt as though her whole body were having a bowel movement. The head came. Then, with a little difficulty, the wide shoulders. Then easily, with soft and slippery smoothness, out slipped the rest of the body and the baby was born. The first thing it did was sneeze.

Maud Martha laughed as though she could never bear to stop. "Listen to him sneeze. My little baby. Don't let him drown, Mrs. Cray." Mrs. Cray looked at Maud Martha, because she did not want to look at the baby. "How you know it's a him?" Maud Martha laughed again.

Belva also refused to look at the baby. "See, Maudie," she said, "see how brave I was? The baby is born, and I didn't get nervous or faint or anything. Didn't I tell you?"

"Now isn't that nice," thought Maud Martha. "Here I've had the baby, and she thinks I should praise her for having stood up there and looked on." Was it, she suddenly wondered, as hard to watch suffering as it was to bear it?

Five minutes after the birth, Paul got back with Mrs. Cray's doctor, a large silent man, who came in swiftly, threw the sheet aside without saying a word, cut the cord. Paul looked at the new human being. It appeared gray and greasy. Life was hard, he thought. What had he done to deserve a stillborn child? But there it was, lying dead.

"It's dead, isn't it?" he asked dully.

"Oh, get out of here!" cried Mrs. Cray, pushing him into the kitchen and shutting the door.

"Girl," said the doctor. Then grudgingly, "Fine girl."

"Did you hear what the doctor said, Maudie?" chattered Belva. "You've got a daughter, the doctor says." The doctor looked at her quickly.

"Say, you'd better go out and take a walk around the block. You don't look so well."

Gratefully, Belva obeyed. When she got back, Mrs. Cray and the doctor had oiled and dressed the baby—dressed her in an outfit found in Maud Martha's top dresser drawer. Belva looked at the newcomer in amazement.

"Well, she's a little beauty, isn't she!" she cried. She had not expected a handsome child.

Maud Martha's thoughts did not dwell long on the fact of the baby. There would be all her life long for that. She preferred to think, now, about how well she felt. Had she ever in her life felt so well? She felt well enough to get up. She folded her arms triumphantly across her chest, as another young woman, her neighbor to the rear, came in.

"Hello, Mrs. Barksdale!" she hailed. "Did you hear the news? I just had a baby, and I feel strong enough to go out and shovel coal! Having a baby is *nothing*, Mrs. Barksdale. Nothing at all."

"Aw, yeah?" Mrs. Barksdale smacked her gum admiringly. "Well, from what I heard back there a while ago, didn't seem like it was nothing. Girl, I didn't know anybody *could* scream that loud." Maud Martha tittered. Oh, she felt fine. She wondered why Mrs. Barksdale hadn't come in while the screaming was going on; she had missed it all.

People. Weren't they sweet. She had never said more than "Hello, Mrs. Barksdale" and "Hello, Mrs. Cray" to these women before. But as soon as something happened to her, in they trooped. People were sweet.

The doctor brought the baby and laid it in the bed beside Maud Martha. Shortly before she had heard it in the kitchen—a bright delight had flooded through her upon first hearing that part of Maud Martha Brown Phillips expressing itself with a voice of its own. But now the baby was quiet and

MAUD MARTHA | 369

returned its mother's stare with one that seemed equally curious and mystified but perfectly cool and undisturbed.

21. posts

People have to choose something decently constant to depend on, thought Maud Martha. People must have something to lean on.

But the love of a single person was not enough. Not only was personal love itself, however good, a thing that varied from week to week, from second to second, but the parties to it were likely, for example, to die, any minute, or otherwise be parted, or destroyed. At any time.

Not alone was the romantic love of a man and a woman fallible, but the breadier love between parents and children; brothers; animals; friend and friend. Those too could not be heavily depended on.

Could be nature, which had a seed, or root, or an element (what do you want to call it) of constancy, under all that system of change. Of course, to say "system" at all implied arrangement, and therefore some order of constancy.

Could be, she mused, a marriage. The marriage shell, not the romance, or love, it might contain. A marriage, the plainer, the more plateaulike, the better. A marriage made up of Sunday papers and shoeless feet, baking powder biscuits, baby baths, and matinees and laundrymen, and potato plants in the kitchen window.

Was, perhaps, the whole life of man a dedication to this search for something to lean upon, and was, to a great degree, his "happiness" or "unhappiness" written up for him by the demands or limitations of what he chose for that work?

For work it was. Leaning was a work.

22. tradition and Maud Martha

What she had wanted was a solid. She had wanted shimmering form; warm, but hard as stone and as difficult to break. She had wanted to found—tradition. She had wanted to shape, for their use, for hers, for his, for little Paulette's, a set of falterless customs. She had wanted stone: here she was, being wife to *him,* salving him, in every way considering and replenishing him—in short, here she was celebrating Christmas night by passing pretzels and beer.

He had done his part, was his claim. He had, had he not? lugged in a Christmas tree. So he had waited till early Christmas morning, when a tree was cheap; so he could not get the lights to burn; so the tinsel was insufficient and the gold balls few. He had promised a tree and he had gotten a tree, and that should be enough for everybody. Furthermore, Paulette had her blocks, her picture book, her doll buggy and her doll. So the doll's left elbow was chipped: more than that would be chipped before Paulette was through! And if the doll buggy was not like the Gold Coast[7] buggies, that was too bad; that was too, too bad for Maud Martha, for Paulette. Here he was, whipping himself to death daily, that Maud Martha's stomach and Paulette's stomach might receive bread and milk and navy beans with tomato

---

7. Slang term for the wealthy, lakeside, residential area of Chicago.

catsup, and he was taken to task because he had not furnished, in addition, a velvet-lined buggy with white-walled wheels! Oh yes that *was* what Maud Martha wanted, for her precious princess daughter, and no use denying. But she could just get out and work, that was all. She could just get out and grab herself a job and buy some of these beans and buggies. And in the meantime, she could just help entertain his friends. She was his wife, and he was the head of the family, and on Christmas night the least he could do, by God, and *would* do, by God, was stand his friends a good mug of beer. And to heck with, in fact, to hell with, her fruitcakes and coffees. Put Paulette to bed.

At Home, the buying of the Christmas tree was a ritual. Always it had come into the Brown household four days before Christmas, tall, but not too tall, and not too wide. Tinsel, bulbs, little Santa Clauses and snowmen, and the pretty gold and silver and colored balls did not have to be renewed oftener than once in five years because after Christmas they were always put securely away, on a special shelf in the basement, where they rested for a year. Black walnut candy, in little flat white sheets, crunchy, accompanied the tree, but it was never eaten until Christmas eve. Then, late at night, a family decorating party was held, Maud Martha, Helen and Harry giggling and teasing and occasionally handing up a ball or Santa Claus, while their father smiled benignly over all and strung and fitted and tinseled, and their mother brought in the black walnut candy and steaming cups of cocoa with whipped cream, and plain shortbread. And everything peaceful, sweet!

And there were the other customs. Easter customs. In childhood, never till Easter morning was "the change" made, the change from winter to spring underwear. Then, no matter how cold it happened to be, off came the heavy trappings and out, for Helen and Maud Martha, were set the new little patent leather shoes and white socks, the little b.v.d.'s and light petticoats, and for Harry, the new brown oxfords, and white shorts and sleeveless undershirts. The Easter eggs had always been dyed the night before, and in the morning, before Sunday school, the Easter baskets, full of chocolate eggs and candy bunnies and cotton bunnies, were handed round, but not eaten from until after Sunday school, and even then not much!— because there was more candy coming, and dyed eggs, too, to be received (and eaten on the spot) at the Sunday School Children's Easter Program, on which every one of them recited until Maud Martha was twelve.

What of October customs?—of pumpkins yellowly burning; of polished apples in a water-green bowl; of sheets for ghost costumes, surrendered up by Mama with a sigh?

And birthdays, with their pink and white cakes and candles, strawberry ice cream, and presents wrapped up carefully and tied with wide ribbons: whereas here was this man, who never considered giving his own mother a birthday bouquet, and dropped in his wife's lap a birthday box of drugstore candy (when he thought of it) wrapped in the drugstore green.

The dinner table, at home, was spread with a white white cloth, cheap but white and very white, and whatever was their best in china sat in cheerful dignity, firmly arranged, upon it. This man was not a lover of tablecloths, he could eat from a splintery board, he could eat from the earth.

She passed round Blatz, and inhaled the smoke of the guests' cigarettes, and watched the soaked tissue that had enfolded the corner Chicken Inn's burned barbecue drift listlessly to her rug. She removed from her waist the arm of Chuno Jones, Paul's best friend.

23. *kitchenette folks*

Of the people in her building, Maud Martha was most amused by Oberto, who had the largest flat of all, a three-roomer on the first floor.

Oberto was a happy man. He had a nice little going grocery store. He had his health. And, most important, he had his little lovely wife Marie.

Some folks did not count Marie among his blessings. She never got up before ten. Oberto must prepare his breakfast or go breakfastless. As a rule, he made only coffee, leaving one cup of it in the pot for her. At ten or after, in beautiful solitude, she would rise, bathe and powder for an hour, then proceed to the kitchen, where she heated that coffee, fried bacon and eggs for herself, and toasted raisin bread.

Marie dusted and swept infrequently, scrubbed only when the floors were heavy with dirt and grease. Her meals were generally underdone or burned. She sent the laundry out every week, but more often than not left the clothes (damp) in the bag throughout the week, spilling them out a few minutes before she expected the laundryman's next call, that the bag might again be stuffed with dirty clothes and carried off. Oberto's shirts were finished at the laundry. Underwear he wore rough-dried. Her own clothes, however, she ironed with regularity and care.

Such domestic sins were shocking enough. But people accused her of yet more serious crimes. It was well thought on the south side that Oberto's wife was a woman of affairs, barely taking time to lay one down before she gathered up another. It was rumored, too, but not confirmed, that now and then she was obliged to make quiet calls of business on a certain Madame Lomiss, of Thirty-fourth and Calumet.

But Oberto was happy. The happiest man, he argued, in his community. True enough, Wilma, the wife of Magnicentius, the Thirty-ninth Street barber, baked rolls of white and fluffy softness. But Magnicentius himself could not deny that Wilma was a filthy woman, and wore stockings two days, at least, before she washed them. He even made no secret of the fact that she went to bed in ragged, dire, cotton nightgowns.

True, too, Viota, the wife of Leon, the Coca-Cola truck driver, not only ironed her husband's shirts, but did all the laundry work herself, beginning early every Monday morning—scrubbing the sheets, quilts, blankets, and slip covers with her own hefty hand. But Leon himself could not deny that Viota was a boisterous, big woman with a voice of wonderful power, and eyes of pink-streaked yellow and a nose that never left off sniffing.

Who, further, would question the truth that Nathalia, the wife of John the laundryman, kept her house shining, and smelling of Lysol and Gold Dust at all times, and that every single Saturday night she washed down the white walls of her perfect kitchen? But verily who (of an honorable tongue) could deny that the active-armed Nathalia had little or no acquaintance with the deodorant qualities of Mum, Hush, or Quiet?

Remembering Nathalia, and remembering Wilma and Viota, Oberto thanked his lucky stars that he had had sense enough to marry his dainty little Marie, who spoke in modulated tones (almost in a whisper), who wore filmy black nightgowns, who bathed always once and sometimes twice a day in water generously treated with sweet bath crystals, and fluffed herself all over with an expensive lavender talcum, and creamed her arms and legs with a rosy night cream, and powdered her face, that was reddish brown (like an Indian's!) with a stuff that the movie stars preferred, and wore clothes out of *Vogue* and *Harper's Bazaar,* and favored Kleenex, and dressed her hair in a smart upsweep, and pinned silver flowers at her ears, and used My Sin perfume.

He loved to sit and watch her primp before the glass.

She didn't know whether she liked a little or a lot (a person could not always tell) the white woman married to a West Indian who lived in the third-floor kitchenette next Maud Martha's own. Through the day and night this woman, Eugena Banks, sang over and over again—varying the choruses, using what undoubtedly were her own improvisations, for they were very bad—the same popular song. Maud Martha had her own ideas about popular songs. "A popular song," thought she, "especially if it's one of the old, soft ones, is beautiful, sometimes, and seems to touch your mood exactly. But the touch is usually not full. You rise up with a popular song, but it isn't able to rise as high, once it has you started, as you are; by the time you've risen as high as it can take you you can't bear to stop, and you swell up and up and up till you're swelled to bursting. The popular music has long ago given up and left you."

This woman would come over, singing or humming her popular song, to see Maud Martha, wanting to know what special technique was to be used in dealing with a Negro man; a Negro man was a special type man; she knew that there should be, indeed, that there had to be, a special technique to be used with this type man, but what? And after all, there should be more than—than singing across the sock washing, the cornbread baking, the fish frying. No, she had not expected wealth, no—but he had seemed so exciting! so primitive!—life with a Negro man had looked, from the far side, like adventure—and the nights *were* good; but there were precious few of the nights, because he stayed away for days (though when he came back he was "very swell" and would hang up a picture or varnish a chair or let her make him some crêpes suzette, which she had always made so well).

Her own mother would not write to her; and she was, Mrs. Eugena Banks whined, beginning to wonder if it had not all been a mistake; could she not go back to Dayton? could she not begin again?

Then there was Clement Lewy, a little boy at the back, on the second floor.

Lewy life was not terrifically tossed. Saltless, rather. Or like an unmixed batter. Lumpy.

Little Clement's mother had grown listless after the desertion. She looked as though she had been scrubbed, up and down, on the washing board, doused from time to time in gray and noisome water. But little Clement looked alert, he looked happy, he was always spirited. He was in second grade. He did his work, and had always been promoted. At home he sang. He recited little poems. He told his mother little stories wound out of the air by himself. His mother glanced at him once in a while. She would have been proud of him if she had had the time.

She started toward her housemaid's work each morning at seven. She left a glass of milk and a bowl of dry cereal and a dish of prunes on the table, and set the alarm clock for eight. At eight little Clement punched off the alarm, stretched, got up, washed, dressed, combed, brushed, ate his breakfast. It was quiet in the apartment. He hurried off to school. At noon he returned from school, opened the door with his key. It was quiet in the apartment. He poured himself a second glass of milk, got more prunes, and ate a slice—"just one slice," his mother had cautioned—of bread and butter. He went back to school. At three o'clock he returned from school, opened the door with his key. It was quiet in the apartment. He got a couple of graham crackers out of the cookie can. He drew himself a glass of water. He changed his clothes. Then he went out to play, leaving behind him the two rooms. Leaving behind him the brass beds, the lamp with the faded silk tassel and frayed cord, the hooked oven door, the cracks in the walls and the quiet. As he played, he kept a lookout for his mother, who usually arrived at seven, or near that hour. When he saw her rounding the corner, his little face underwent a transformation. His eyes lashed into brightness, his lips opened suddenly and became a smile, and his eyebrows climbed toward his hairline in relief and joy.

He would run to his mother and almost throw his little body at her. "Here I am, mother! Here I am! Here I am!"

There was, or there had been, Richard—whose weekly earnings as a truck driver for a small beverage concern had dropped, slyly, from twenty-five, twenty-three, twenty-one, to sixteen, fifteen, twelve, while his weekly rent remained what it was (the family of five lived in one of the one-room apartments, a whole dollar cheaper than such a two-room as Paul and Maud Martha occupied); his family food and clothing bills had not dropped; and altogether it had been too much, the never having enough to buy Pabst or Ninety Proof for the boys, the being scared to death to offer a man a couple of cigarettes for fear your little supply, and with it your little weak-kneed nonchalance, might be exhausted before the appearance of your next pay envelope (pink, and designated elaborately on the outside, "Richard"), the coming back at night, every night, to a billowy diaper world, a wife with wild hair, twin brats screaming, and writhing, and wetting their crib, and a third brat, leaping on, from, and about chairs and table with repeated Hi-yo Silvers, and the sitting down to a meal never quite adequate, never quite— despite all your sacrifices, your inability to "treat" your friends, your shabby rags, your heartache. . . . It was altogether too much, so one night he had simply failed to come home.

There was an insane youth of twenty, twice released from Dunning. He had a smooth tan face, overlaid with oil. His name was Binnie. Or perhaps it was Bennie, or Benjamin. But his mother lovingly called him "Binnie." Binnie strode the halls, with huge eyes, direct and annoyed. He strode, and played "catch" with a broken watch, which was attached to a long string wound around his left arm. There was no annoyance in his eyes when he spoke to Maud Martha, though, and none in his nice voice. He was very fond of Maud Martha. Once, when she answered a rap on the door, there he was, and he pushed in before she could open her mouth. He had on a new belt, he said. "My Uncle John gave it to me," he said. "So my pants won't fall down." He walked about the apartment, after closing the door with a careful sneer. He touched things. He pulled a petal from a pink rose with savage anger, then kissed it with a tenderness that was more terrible than the anger; briskly he rapped on the table, turned suddenly to stare at her, to see if she approved of what he was doing—she smiled uncertainly; he saw the big bed, fingered it, sat on it, got up, kicked it. He opened a dresser drawer, took out a ruler. "This is ni-ice—but I won't take it" (with firm decision, noble virtue). "I'll put it back." He spoke of his aunt, his Uncle

John's wife Octavia. "She's ni-ice—you know, she can even call me, and I don't even get mad." With another careful sneer, he opened the door. He went out.

Mrs. Teenie Thompson. Fifty-three; and pepper whenever she talked of the North Shore people who had employed her as housemaid for ten years. "She went to huggin' and kissin' of me—course I got to receive it—I got to work for 'em. But they think they got me thinkin' they love me. Then I'm supposed to kill my silly self slavin' for 'em. To be worthy of their love. These old whi' folks. They jive you, honey. Well, I jive 'em just like they jive me. They can't beat me jivin'. They'll have to jive much, to come anywhere *near* my mark in jivin'."

About one of the one-roomers, a little light woman flitted. She was thin and looked ill. Her hair, which was long and of a strangely flat blackness, hung absolutely still, no matter how much its mistress moved. If anyone passed her usually open door, she would nod cheerily, but she rarely spoke. Chiefly you would see her flitting, in a faded blue rayon housecoat, touching this, picking up that, adjusting, arranging, posing prettily. She was Mrs. Whitestripe. Mr. Whitestripe was a dark and dapper young man of medium height, with a small soot-smear of a mustache. The Whitestripes were the happiest couple Maud Martha had ever met. They were soft-spoken, kind to each other, were worried about each other. "Now you watch that cough now, Coopie!" For that was what she called him. "Here, take this Rem, here, take this lemon juice." "You wrap up good, now, you put on that scarf, Coo!" For that was what he called her. Or (rushing out of the door in his undershirt, one shoe off) "Did I hear you stumble down there, Coo? Did I hear you hurt your knee?" Often, visiting them, you were embarrassed, because it was obvious that you were interrupting the progress of a truly great love; even as you conversed, there they would be, kissing or patting each other, or gazing into each other' eyes. Most fitting was it that adjacent to their "domicile" was the balcony of the building. Unfortunately, it was about two inches wide. Three pressures of a firm foot, and the little balcony would crumble downward to mingle with other dust. The Whitestripes never sat on it, but Maud Martha had no doubt that often on summer evenings they would open the flimsy "French" door, and stand there gazing out, thinking of what little they knew about Romeo and Juliet, their arms about each other.

"It is such a beautiful story," sighed Maud Martha once, to Paul.

"What is?"

"The love story of the Whitestripes."

"Well, I'm no 'Coopie' Whitestripe," Paul had observed, sharply, "so you can stop mooning. I'll never be a 'Coopie' Whitestripe."

"No," agreed Maud Martha. "No, you never will."

The one-roomer next the Whitestripes was occupied by Maryginia Washington, a maiden of sixty-eight, or sixty-nine, or seventy, a becrutched, gnarled, bleached lemon with smartly bobbed white hair; who claimed, and proudly, to be an "indirect" descendant of the first President of the United States; who loathed the darker members of her race but did rather enjoy playing the *grande dame,* a hobbling, denture-clacking version, for their benefit, while they played, at least in her imagination, Topsys—and did rather enjoy advising them, from time to time, to apply lightening creams to the horror of their flesh—"because they ain't no sense in lookin' any worser'n you have to, is they, dearie?"

In the fifth section, on the third floor, lived a Woman of Breeding. Her name was Josephine Snow. She was too much of a Woman of Breeding to allow the title "Madame" to vulgarize her name, but certain inhabitants of the building had all they could do to keep from calling her "Madame Snow," and eventually they relaxed, and called her that as a matter of course, behind her back.

Madame Snow was the color of soured milk, about sixty, and very superior to her surroundings—although she was not a Maryginia Washington. She had some sort of mysterious income, for although she had lived for seven years in "Gappington Arms" (the name given the building by the tenants, in dubious honor of the autocratic lady owner) no one had ever seen her go out to work. She rarely went anywhere. She went to church no more than once a month, and she sent little Clement Lewy and other children in the building to the store. She maintained a standard rate of pay; no matter how far the errand runner had to go, nor how heavily-loaded he was to be upon his return, she paid exactly five cents. It is hardly necessary to add that the identity of her runner was seldom the same for two days straight, and that a runner had to be poverty-stricken indeed before he searched among the paper nameplates downstairs and finally rang, with a disgruntled scowl, the bell of Miss Josephine Alberta Snow, Apt. 3E, who, actually, had been graduated from Fisk University.

What the source or size of Josephine's income was nobody knew. Her one-room apartment, although furnished with the same type of scarred brass bed and scratched dresser with which the other apartments were favored (for all her seven years), had received rich touches from her cultured hands. Her walls were hung with tapestry, strange pictures, china and illuminated poems. She had "lived well," as these things declared, and it was evident that she meant to go on "living well," Gappington Arms or no Gappington Arms.

This lady did the honors of the teacup and cookie crock each afternoon, with or without company. She would spread a large stool with a square of lace, deck it with a low bowl of artificial flowers, a teacup or teacups, the pot of tea, sugar, cream and lemon, and the odd-shaped crock of sweet crackers.

On indoor weekdays she wore always the same dress—a black sateen thing that fell to her ankles and rose to her very chin. On the Sundays she condescended to go to church, she wore a pink lace, winter and summer, which likewise embraced her from ankle to chin. She charmed the neighborhood with that latter get-up, too, on those summer afternoons when the heat drove her down from her third-floor quarters to the little porch, with its one chair. There she would sit, frightening everyone, panting, fanning, and glaring at old Mr. Neville, the caretaker's eighty-two-year-old father, if he came out and so much as dared to look, with an eyeful of timid covetousness, at the single porch chair over which her bottom flowed (for she was a large lady). Then there was nothing for poor old Mr. Neville to do but sit silently on the hard stone steps—split, and crawling with ants and worse—chew his tobacco, glance peculiarly from time to time at that large pink lady, that pink and yellow lady, fanning indignantly at him.

As for the other tenants, they did not know what to say to Miss Snow after they had exchanged the time of day with her. Some few had attempted the tossing of sallies her way, centered in politics, the current murders, or homely philosophy, wanting to draw her out. But they very soon saw they would have to leave off all that, because it was too easy to draw her out. She would come out so far as to almost knock them down. She had a tremendous impatience with other people's ideas—unless those happened to be exactly like hers; even then, often as not, she gave hurried, almost angry, affirmative, and flew on to emphatic illuminations of her own. Then she would settle back in her chair, nod briskly a few times, as if to say, "Now! Now we are finished with it." What could be done? What was there further to be said?

24. *an encounter*

They went to the campus Jungly Hovel, a reedy-boothed place. Inside, before you saw anything, really, you got this impression of straw and reed. There were vendor outlets in the booths, and it could be observed what a struggle the management had had, trying to settle on something that was not out-and-out low, and that yet was not out-and-out highborn. In a weak moment someone had included Borden's Boogie Hoogie Woogie.

Maud Martha had gone to hear the newest young Negro author speak, at Mandel Hall on the University campus, and whom had she run into, coming out, but David McKemster. Outside, David McKemster had been talking seriously with a tall, dignified old man. When he saw her, he gravely nodded. He gravely waved. She decided to wait for him, not knowing whether that would be agreeable to him or not. After all, this was the University world, this was his element. Perhaps he would feel she did not belong here, perhaps he would be cold to her.

He certainly was cold to her. Free of the dignified old man, he joined her, walked with her down Fifty-ninth Street, past the studious gray buildings, west toward Cottage Grove. He yawned heartily at every sixth or seventh step.

"I'll put you on a streetcar," he said. "God, I'm tired."

Then nothing more was said by him, or by her—till they met a young white couple, going east. David's face lit up. These were his good, good friends. He introduced them as such to Maud Martha. Had they known about the panel discussion? No, they had not. Tell him, when had they seen Mary, Mary Ehreburg? Say, he had seen Metzger Freestone tonight. Ole Metzger. (He lit a cigarette.) Say, he had had dinner with the Beefy Godwins and Jane Wather this evening. Say, what were they doing tomorrow night? Well, what about going to the Adamses' tomorrow night? (He took excited but carefully sophisticated puffs.) Yes, they would go to the Adamses' tomorrow night. They would get Dora, and all go to the Adamses'. Say, how about going to Power's for a beer, tonight, if they had nothing else to do? Here he glanced at his companion—how to dispose of her! Well, no "how" about it, the disposal would have to be made. But first he had better buy her a coffee. That would pacify her. "Power'll still be up—prob'ly *sprawl*ing on that white rug of his, with Parrington in front of 'im," laughed David. It was, Maud Martha observed, one of the conceits of David McKemster that he did not have to use impeccable English all the time. Sometimes it was permissible to make careful slips. These must be, however, when possible, sandwiched in between thick hunks of the most rational, particularistic, critical, and intellectually aloof discourse. "But first let's go to the Jungly Hovel and have coffee with Mrs. Phillips," said David McKemster.

So off to the Jungly Hovel. They went into one of the booths and ordered.

The strange young man's face was pleasant when it smiled; the jaw was a little forward; Maud Martha was reminded of Pat O'Brien, the movie star. He kept looking at her; when he looked at her his eyes were somewhat agape; "Well!" they seemed to exclaim—"Well! and what have we here!" The girl, who was his fiancée, it turned out—"Stickie"—had soft pink coloring, summer-blue eyes, was attractive. She had, her soft pink notwithstanding, that brisk, thriving, noisy, "oh-so-American" type of attractiveness. She was confidential, she communicated everything except herself, which was precisely the thing her eyes, her words, her nods, her suddenly whipped-off laughs assured you she *was* communicating. She leaned healthily across the table; her long, lovely dark hair swung at you; her bangs came right out to meet you, and her face and forefinger did too (she emphasized, robustly, some point). But herself stayed stuck to the back of her seat, and was shrewd, and "took in," and contemplated, not quite warmly, everything.

"And there was this young—man. Twenty-one or two years old, wasn't he, Maudie?" David looked down at his guest. When they sat, their heights were equal, for his length was in the legs. But he thought he was looking down at her, and she was very willing to concede that that was what he was doing, for the immediate effect of the look was to make her sit straight as a stick. "Really quite, really most a*mazing*. Didn't you think, Maudie? Has written a book. Seems well-read chap, seems to know a lot about—a lot about—"

"Everything," supplied Maud Martha furiously.

"Well—yes." His brows gathered. He stabbed "Stickie" with a well-made gaze of seriousness, sober economy, doubt—mixed. "PRESENT things," he emphasized sharply. "He's very impressed by, he's all adither about—current plays in New York—Kafka.[8] *That* sawt of thing," he ended. His "sawt" was not sarcastic. Our position is hardly challenged, it implied. We are still on top of the wave, it implied. We, who know about Aristotle, Plato,[9] who weave words like anachronism, transcendentalist, cosmos, metaphysical, corollary, integer, monarchical, into our breakfast speech as a matter of course—

"And he disdains the universities!"

"Is he in school?" asked "Stickie," leaning: on the answer to that would depend—so much.

"Oh, no," David assured her, smiling. "He was pretty forceful on that point. There is nothing in the schools for *him*, he has decided. What are degrees, he asks contemptuously." You see? David McKemster implied. This upstart, this, this brazen emissary, this rash representative from the ranks of the intellectual *nouveau riche*.[1] So he was brilliant. So he could outchatter me. So intellectuality was his oyster. So he has kicked—not Parrington—but Joyce, maybe, around like a football. But he is not rooted in Aristotle, in Plato, in Aeschylus, in Epictetus.[2] In all those Goddamn Greeks. As we are.

8. Franz Kafka (1883–1924), novelist and short story writer known for his experimental prose.
9. Greek philosopher (ca. 428–ca. 348 B.C.E.).
1. Newly rich (French); often used to suggest vulgar excess.
2. Greek philosopher of the Stoic period (50?–130 C.E.). Aeschylus (524?–456 B.C.E.), Greek dramatist and writer of tragedies.

Aloud, David skirted some of this—"Aristotle," he said, "is probably Greek to him." "Stickie" laughed quickly, stopped. Pat O'Brien smiled lazily; leered.

The waitress brought coffee, four lumps of sugar wrapped in pink paper, hot mince pie.

25. *the self-solace*

Sonia Johnson got together her towels and soap. She scrubbed out her bowls. She mixed her water.

Maud Martha, waiting, was quiet. It was pleasant to let her mind go blank. And here in the beauty shop that was not a difficult thing to do. For the perfumes in the great jars, to be sold for twelve dollars and fifty cents an ounce and one dollar a dram, or seven dollars and fifty cents an ounce and one dollar a dram, the calendars, the bright signs extolling the virtues of Lily cologne (Made by the Management), the limp lengths of detached human hair, the pile of back-number *Vogues* and *Bazaars,* the earrings and clasps and beaded bags, white blouses—the "side line"—these things did not force themselves into the mind and make a disturbance there. One was and was not aware of them. Could sit here and think, or not think, of problems. Think, or not. One did not have to, if one wished not.

"If she burns me today—if she yanks at my hair—if she calls me sweetheart or dahlin'—"

Sonia Johnson parted the hangings that divided her reception room from her workrooms. "Come on back, baby doll."

But just then the bell tinkled, and in pushed a young white woman, wearing a Persian lamb coat, and a Persian lamb cap with black satin ribbon swirled capably in a soft knot at the back.

"Yes," thought Maud Martha, "it's legitimate. It's November. It's not cold, but it's cool. You can wear your new fur now and not be laughed at by too many people."

The young white woman introduced herself to Mrs. Johnson as Miss Ingram, and said that she had new toilet waters, a make-up base that was so good it was "practically impossible," and a new lipstick.

"No make-up bases," said Sonia. "And no toilet water. We create our own."

"This new lipstick, this new shade," Miss Ingram said, taking it out of a smart little black bag, "is just the thing for your customers. For their dark complexions."

Sonia Johnson looked interested. She always put herself out to be kind and polite to these white salesmen and saleswomen. Some beauticians were brusque. They were almost insulting. They were glad to have the whites at their mercy, if only for a few moments. They made them crawl. Then they applied the whiplash. Then they sent the poor creatures off—with no orders. Then they laughed and laughed and laughed, a terrible laughter. But Sonia Johnson was not that way. She liked to be kind and polite. She liked to be merciful. She did not like to take advantage of her power. Indeed, she felt it was better to strain, to bend far back, to spice one's listening with the smooth smile, the quick and attentive nod, the well-timed "sure" or "uh-huh." She was against this eye-for-eye-tooth-for-tooth stuff.

Maud Martha looked at Miss Ingram's beautiful legs, wondered where she got the sheer stockings that looked like bare flesh at the same time that they did not, wondered if Miss Ingram knew that in the "Negro group" there were complexions whiter than her own, and other complexions, brown, tan, yellow, cream, which could not take a dark lipstick and keep their poise. Maud Martha picked up an ancient *Vogue,* turned the pages.

"What's the lipstick's name?" Sonia Johnson asked.

"Black Beauty," Miss Ingram said, with firm-lipped determination. "You won't regret adding it to your side line, I assure you, Madam."

"What's it sell for?"

"A dollar and a half. Let me leave you—say, ten—and in a week I'll come back and find them all gone, and you'll be here clamoring for more, I know you will. I'll leave ten."

"Well. Okay."

"That's fine, Madam. Now, I'll write down your name and address—"

Sonia rattled them off for her. Miss Ingram wrote them down. Then she closed her case.

"Now, I'll take just five dollars. Isn't that reasonable? You don't pay the rest till they're all sold. Oh, I know you're going to be just terribly pleased. And your customers too, Mrs. Johnson."

Sonia opened her cash drawer and took out five dollars for Miss Ingram. Miss Ingram brightened. The deal was closed. She pushed back a puff of straw-colored hair that had slipped from under her Persian lamb cap and fallen over the faint rose of her cheek.

"I'm mighty glad," she confided, "that the cold weather is in. I love the cold. It was awful, walking the streets in that nasty old August weather. And even September was rather close this year, didn't you think?"

Sonia agreed. "Sure was."

"People," confided Miss Ingram, "think this is a snap job. It ain't. I work like a nigger to make a few pennies. A few lousy pennies."

Maud Martha's head shot up. She did not look at Miss Ingram. She stared intently at Sonia Johnson. Sonia Johnson's sympathetic smile remained. Her eyes turned, as if magnetized, toward Maud Martha; but she forced her smile to stay on. Maud Martha went back to *Vogue.* "For," she thought, "I must have been mistaken. I was afraid I heard that woman say 'nigger.' Apparently not. Because of course Mrs. Johnson wouldn't let her get away with it. In her own shop." Maud Martha closed *Vogue.* She began to consider what she herself might have said, had she been Sonia Johnson, and had the woman really said "nigger." I wouldn't curse. I wouldn't holler. I'll bet Mrs. Johnson would do both those things. And I could understand her wanting to, all right. I would be gentle in a cold way. I would give her, not a return insult—directly, at any rate!—but information. I would get it across to her that—" Maud Martha stretched. "But I wouldn't insult her." Maud Martha began to take the hairpins out of her hair. "I'm glad, though, that she didn't say it. She's pretty and pleasant. If she had said it, I would feel all strained and tied up inside, and I would feel that it was my duty to help Mrs. Johnson get it settled, to help clear it up in some way. I'm too relaxed to fight today. Sometimes fighting is interesting. Today, it would have been just plain old ugly duty."

"Well, I wish you success with Black Beauty," Miss Ingram said, smiling in a tired manner, as she buttoned the top button of her Persian lamb. She walked quickly out of the door. The little bell tinkled charmingly.

Sonia Johnson looked at her customer with thoughtful narrowed eyes. She walked over, dragged a chair up close. She sat. She began to speak in a dull level tone.

"You know, why I didn't catch her up on that, is—our people is got to stop feeling so sensitive about these words like 'nigger' and such. I often think about this, and how these words like 'nigger' don't mean to some of these here white people what our people *think* they mean. Now, 'nigger,' for instance, means to them something bad, or slavey-like, or low. They don't mean anything against me. I'm a Negro, not a 'nigger.' Now, a white man can be a 'nigger,' according to their meaning for the word, just like a colored man can. So why should I go getting all stepped up about a thing like that? Our people is got to stop getting all stepped up about every little thing, especially when it don't amount to nothing. . . ."

"You mean to say," Maud Martha broke in, "that that woman really did say 'nigger'?"

"Oh, yes, she said it, all right, but like I'm telling—"

"Well! At first, I thought she said it, but then I decided I must have been mistaken, because you weren't getting after her."

"Now that's what I'm trying to explain to you, dearie. Sure, I could have got all hot and bothered, and told her to clear out of here, or cussed her daddy, or something like that. But what would be the point, when, like I say, that word 'nigger' can mean one of them just as fast as one of us, and in fact it don't mean us, and in fact we're just too sensitive and all? What would be the point? Why make enemies? Why go getting all hot and bothered all the time?"

Maud Martha stared steadily into Sonia Johnson's irises. She said nothing. She kept on staring into Sonia Johnson's irises.

26. *Maud Martha's tumor*

As she bent over Paulette, she felt a peculiar pain in her middle, at the right. She touched the spot. There it was. A knot, hard, manipulable, the proscription of her doom.

At first, she could only be weak (as the pain grew sharper and sharper). Then she was aware of creeping fear; fear of the operating table, the glaring instruments, the cold-faced nurses, the relentlessly submerging ether, the chokeful awakening, the pain, the ensuing cancer, the ensuing death.

Then she thought of her life. Decent childhood, happy Christmases; some shreds of romance, a marriage, pregnancy and the giving birth, her growing child, her experiments in sewing, her books, her conversations with her friends and enemies.

"It hasn't been bad," she thought.

"It's been interesting," she thought, as she put Paulette in the care of Mrs. Maxawanda Barksdale and departed for the doctor's.

She looked at the trees, she looked at the grass, she looked at the faces of the passers-by. It had been interesting, it had been rather good, and it was still rather good. But really, she was ready. Since the time had come, she was ready. Paulette would miss her for a long time, Paul for less, but really, their sorrow was their business, not hers. Her business was to descend into the deep cool, the salving dark, to be alike indifferent to the good and the not-good.

"And what," asked Dr. Williams, "did you do yesterday that was out of line with your regular routine?" He mashed her here, tapped there.

She remembered.

"Why, I was doing the bends."

"Doing—"

"The bends. Exercising. With variations. I lay on the bed, also, and keeping my upper part absolutely still, I raised my legs up, then lowered them, twenty times."

"Is this a nightly custom of yours?"

"No. Last night was the first time I had done it since before my little girl was born."

"Three dollars, please."

"You mean—I'm not going to die."

She bounced down the long flight of tin-edged stairs, was shortly claimed by the population, which seemed proud to have her back. An old woman, bent, shriveled, smiled sweetly at her.

She was already on South Park. She jumped in a jitney and went home.

27. *Paul in the 011 Club*

The 011 Club did not like it so much, your buying only a beer. . . .

Do you want to get into the war? Maud Martha "thought at" Paul, as, over their wine, she watched his eye-light take leave of her. To get into the war, perhaps. To be mixed up in peculiar, hooped adventure, adventure dominant, entire, ablaze with bunched and fidgeting color, pageantry, thrilling with the threat of danger—through which he would come without so much as a bruised ankle.

The baby was getting darker all the time! She knew that he was tired of his wife, tired of his living quarters, tired of working at Sam's, tired of his two suits.

He is ever so tired, she thought.

He had no money, no car, no clothes, and he had not been put up for membership in the Foxy Cats Club.

Something should happen. He was not on show. She knew that he believed he had been born to invade, to occur, to confront, to inspire the flapping of flags, to panic people. To wear, but carelessly, a crown. What could give him his chance, illuminate his gold?—be a happening?

She looked about, about at these, the people he would like to impress. The real people. It was Sunday afternoon and they were dressed in their best. It was May, and for hats the women wore gardens and birds. They wore tight-fitting prints, or flounced satin, or large-flowered silk under the coats they could not afford but bought anyhow. Their hair was intricately curled, or it was sedately marcelled. Some of it was hennaed. Their escorts were in broad-shouldered suits, and sported dapper handkerchiefs. Their hair was either slicked back or very close-cut. All spoke in subdued tones. There were no roughnecks here. These people knew what whiskies were good, what wine was "the thing" with this food, that food, what places to go, how to dance, how to smoke, how much stress to put on love, how to dress, when to curse, and did not indulge (for the most part) in homosexuality but could discuss it without eagerness, distaste, curiosity—without anything but ennui. These, in her husband's opinion, were the real people. And this was the real place. The manner of the waitresses toward the patrons, by unspoken agreement, was just this side of insulting. They seemed to have something to prove. They wanted you to know, to be *sure* that they were as good as you were and maybe a lot better. They did not want you to be misled by the fact that on a Sunday afternoon, instead of silk and little foxes, they wore white uniforms and carried trays and picked up (rapidly) tips.

A flame-colored light flooded the ceiling in the dining foyer. (But there was a blue-red-purple note in the bar.) On the east wall of the dining foyer, painted against a white background, was an unclothed lady, with a careless bob, challenging nipples, teeth-revealing smile; her arms were lifted, to call attention to "all"—and she was standing behind a few huge leaves of sleepy color and amazing design. On the south wall was painted one of those tropical ladies clad in carefully careless sarong, and bearing upon her head with great ease and glee a platter of fruit—apples, spiky pineapple, bananas. . . .

She watched the little dreams of smoke as they spiraled about his hand, and she thought about happenings. She was afraid to suggest to him that, to most people, nothing at all "happens." That most people merely live from day to day until they die. That, after he had been dead a year, doubtless fewer than five people would think of him oftener than once a year. That there might even come a year when no one on earth would think of him at all.

28. *brotherly Love*

Maud Martha was fighting with a chicken. The nasty, nasty mess. It had been given a bitter slit with the bread knife and the bread knife had been biting in that vomit-looking interior for almost five minutes without being able to detach certain resolute parts from their walls. The bread knife had it all to do, as Maud Martha had no intention of putting her hand in there. Another hack—another hack—STUFF! Splat in her eye. She leaped at the faucet.

She thought she had praise coming to her. She was doing this job with less stomach-curving than ever before. She thought of the times before the war, when there were more chickens than people wanting to buy them, and butchers were happy to clean them, and even cut them up. None of that now. In those happy, happy days—if she had opened up a chicken and seen it all unsightly like this, and smelled it all smelly, she would have scooped up the whole batch of slop and rushed it to the garbage can. Now meat was jewelry and she was practically out of Red Points. You were lucky to find a chicken. She had to be as brave as she could.

People could do this! people could cut a chicken open, take out the mess, with bare hands or a bread knife, pour water in, as in a bag, pour water out, shake the corpse by neck or by legs, free the straggles of water. Could feel that insinuating slipping bone, survey that soft, that headless death. The *faint* hearted could do it. But if the chicken were a man!—cold man with no head or feet and with all the little feath—er, hairs to be pulled, and the intestines loosened and beginning to ooze out, and the gizzard yet to be grabbed and the stench beginning to rise! And yet the chicken was a sort of person, a respectable individual, with its own kind of dignity. The difference was in the knowing. What was unreal to you, you could deal with violently. If chickens were ever to be safe, people would have to live with them, and know them, see them loving their children, finishing the evening meal, arranging jealousy.

When the animal was ready for the oven Maud Martha smacked her lips at the thought of her meal.

29. millinery

"Looks lovely on you," said the manager. "Makes you look—" What? Beautiful? Charming? Glamorous? Oh no, oh no, she could not stoop to the usual lies; not today; her coffee had been too strong, had not set right; and there had been another fight at home, for her daughter continued to insist on gallivanting about with that Greek—a Greek!—not even a Jew, which, though revolting enough, was at least becoming fashionable, was "timely." Oh, not today would she cater to these nigger women who tried on every hat in her shop, who used no telling what concoctions of smelly grease on the heads that integrity, straightforwardness, courage, would certainly have kept kinky. She started again—"Makes you look—" She stopped.

"How much is the hat?" Maud Martha asked.

"Seven ninety-nine."

Maud Martha rose, went to the door.

"Wait, wait," called the hat woman, hurrying after her. She smiled at Maud Martha. When she looked at Maud Martha, it was as if God looked; it was as if—

"Now just how much, Madam, had you thought you would prefer to pay?"

"Not a cent over five."

"Five? Five, dearie? You expect to buy a hat like this for five dollars? This, this straw that you can't even get any more and which I showed you only because you looked like a lady of taste who could appreciate a good value?"

"Well," said Maud Martha, "thank you." She opened the door.

"Wait, wait," shrieked the hat woman. Good-naturedly, the escaping customer hesitated again. "Just a moment," ordered the hat woman coldly. "I'll speak to the—to the owner. He might be willing to make some slight reduction, since you're an old customer. I remember you. You've been in here several times, haven't you?"

"I've never been in the store before." The woman rushed off as if she had heard nothing. She rushed off to consult with the owner. She rushed off to appeal to the boxes in the back room.

Presently the hat woman returned.

"Well. The owner says it'll be a crying shame, but seeing as how you're such an old customer he'll make a reduction. He'll let you have it for five. Plus tax, of course!" she added chummily; they had, always, more appreciation when, after one of these "reductions," you added that.

"I've decided against the hat."

"What? Why, you told—But, you said—"

Maud Martha went out, tenderly closed the door.

"Black—oh, black—" said the hat woman to her hats—which, on the slender stands, shone pink and blue and white and lavender, showed off their tassels, their sleek satin ribbons, their veils, their flower coquettes.

30. at the Burns-Coopers'

It was a little red and white and black woman who appeared in the doorway of the beautiful house in Winnetka.

About, thought Maud Martha, thirty-four.

"I'm Mrs. Burns-Cooper," said the woman, "and after this, well, it's all right this time, because it's your first time, but after this time always use the back entrance."

There is a pear in my icebox, and one end of rye bread. Except for three Irish potatoes and a cup of flour and the empty Christmas boxes, there is absolutely nothing on my shelf. My husband is laid off. There is newspaper on my kitchen table instead of oilcloth. I can't find a filing job in a hurry. I'll smile at Mrs. Burns-Cooper and hate her just some.

"First, you have the beds to make," said Mrs. Burns-Cooper. "You either change the sheets or air the old ones for ten minutes. I'll tell you about the changing when the time comes. It isn't any special day. You are to pull my sheets, and pat and pat and pull till all's tight and smooth. Then shake the pillows into the slips, carefully. Then punch them in the middle.

"Next, there is the washing of the midnight snack dishes. Next, there is the scrubbing. Now, I know that your other ladies have probably wanted their floors scrubbed after dinner. I'm different. I like to enjoy a bright clean floor all the day. You can just freshen it up a little before you leave in the evening, if it needs a few more touches. Another thing. I disapprove of mops. You can do a better job on your knees.

"Next is dusting. Next is vacuuming—that's for Tuesdays and Fridays. On Wednesdays, ironing and silver cleaning.

"Now about cooking. You're very fortunate in that here you have only the evening meal to prepare. Neither of us has breakfast, and I always step out for lunch. Isn't that lucky?"

"It's quite a kitchen, isn't it?" Maud Martha observed. "I mean, big."

Mrs. Burns-Cooper's brows raced up in amazement.

"Really? I hadn't thought so. I'll bet"—she twinkled indulgently—"you're comparing it to your *own* little kitchen." And why do that, her light eyes laughed. Why talk of beautiful mountains and grains of alley sand in the same breath?

"Once," mused Mrs. Burns-Cooper, "I had a girl who botched up the kitchen. Made a botch out of it. But all I had to do was just sort of cock my head and say, 'Now, now, Albertine!' Her name was Albertine. Then she'd giggle and scrub and scrub and she was *so* sorry about trying to take advantage."

It was while Maud Martha was peeling potatoes for dinner that Mrs. Burns-Cooper laid herself out to prove that she was not a snob. Then it was that Mrs. Burns-Cooper came out to the kitchen and, sitting, talked and talked at Maud Martha. In my college days. At the time of my debut. The imported lace on my lingerie. My brother's rich wife's Stradivarius.[3] When I was in Madrid. The charm of the Nile. Cost fifty dollars. Cost one hundred dollars. Cost one thousand dollars. Shall I mention, considered Maud Martha, my own social triumphs, my own education, my travels to Gary and Milwaukee and Columbus, Ohio? Shall I mention my collection of fancy pink satin bras? She decided against it. She went on listening, in silence, to the confidences until the arrival of the lady's mother-in-law (large-eyed, strong, with hair of a mighty white, and with an eloquent, angry bosom). Then the junior Burns-Cooper was very much the mistress, was stiff, cool, authoritative.

There was no introduction, but the elder Burns-Cooper boomed, "Those potato parings are entirely too thick!"

---

3. A rare and expensive violin.

The two of them, richly dressed, and each with that health in the face that bespeaks, or seems to bespeak, much milk drinking from earliest childhood, looked at Maud Martha. There was no remonstrance; no firing! They just looked. But for the first time, she understood what Paul endured daily. For so—she could gather from a Paul-word here, a Paul-curse there—his Boss! when, squared, upright, terribly upright, superior to the President, commander of the world, he wished to underline Paul's lacks, to indicate soft shock, controlled incredulity. As his boss looked at Paul, so these people looked at her. As though she were a child, a ridiculous one, and one that ought to be given a little shaking, except that shaking was—not quite the thing, would not quite do. One held up one's finger (if one did anything), cocked one's head, was arch. As in the old song, one hinted, "Tut tut! now now! come come!" Metal rose, all built, in one's eye.

I'll never come back, Maud Martha assured herself, when she hung up her apron at eight in the evening. She knew Mrs. Burns-Cooper would be puzzled. The wages were very good. Indeed, what could be said in explanation? Perhaps that the hours were long. I couldn't explain *my* explanation, she thought.

One walked out from that almost perfect wall, spitting at the firing squad. What difference did it make whether the firing squad understood or did not understand the manner of one's retaliation or why one had to retaliate?

Why, one was a human being. One wore clean nightgowns. One loved one's baby. One drank cocoa by the fire—or the gas range—come the evening, in the wintertime.

31. on Thirty-fourth Street

Maud Martha went east on Thirty-fourth Street, headed for Cottage Grove. It was August, and Thirty-fourth Street was all in bloom. The blooms, in their undershirts, sundresses and diapers, were hanging over porches and fence stiles and strollers, and were even bringing chairs out to the rims of the sidewalks.

At the corner of Thirty-fourth and Cottage Grove, a middle-aged blind man on a three-legged stool picked at a scarred guitar. The five or six patched and middle-aged men around him sang in husky, low tones, which carried the higher tone—ungarnished, insistent, at once a question and an answer—of the instrument.

Those men were going no further—and had gone nowhere. Tragedy.

She considered that word. On the whole, she felt, life was more comedy than tragedy. Nearly everything that happened had its comic element, not too well buried, either. Sooner or later one could find something to laugh at in almost every situation. That was what, in the last analysis, could keep folks from going mad. The truth was, if you got a good Tragedy out of a lifetime, one good, ripping tragedy, thorough, unridiculous, bottom-scraping, *not* the issue of human stupidity, you were doing, she thought, very well, you were doing well.

32. Mother comes to call

Mama came, bringing two oranges, nine pecans, a Hershey bar and a pear.

Mama explained that one of the oranges was for Maud Martha, one was for Paulette. The Hershey bar was for Paulette. The pear was for Maud

Martha, for it was not, Mama said, a very good pear. Four of the pecans were for Maud Martha, four were for Paulette, one was for Paul.

Maud Martha spread her little second-hand table—a wide tin band was wound beneath the top, for strength—with her finest wedding gift, a really good white luncheon cloth. She brought out white coffee cups and saucers, sugar, milk, and a little pink pot of cocoa. She brought a plate of frosted gingerbread. Mother and daughter sat down to Tea.

"And how is Helen? I haven't seen her in two weeks. When I'm over there to see you, she's always out."

"Helen doesn't like to come here much," said Mama, nodding her head over the gingerbread. "Not enough cinnamon in this but very good. She says it sort of depresses her. She wants you to have more things."

"I like nutmeg better than cinnamon. I have a lot of things. I have more than she has. I have a husband, a nice little girl, and a clean home of my own."

"A kitchenette of your own," corrected Mama, "without even a private bathroom. I think Paul could do a little better, Maud Martha."

"It's hard to find even a kitchenette."

"Nothing beats a trial but a failure. Helen thinks she's going to marry Doctor Williams."

"Our own family doctor. Not our own family doctor!"

"She says her mind's about made up."

"But he's over fifty years old."

"She says he's steady, not like the young ones she knows, and kind, and will give her a decent home."

"And what do you say?"

"I say, it's a hard cold world and a woman had better do all she can to help herself get along as long what she does is honest. It isn't as if she didn't like Doctor Williams."

"She always did, yes. Ever since we were children, and he used to bring her licorice sticks, and forgot to bring any to me, except very seldom."

"It isn't as if she merely sold herself. She'll try to make him happy, I'm sure. Helen was always a good girl. And in any marriage, the honeymoon is soon over."

"What does Papa say?"

"He's thinking of changing doctors."

"It hasn't been a hard cold world for you, Mama. You've been very lucky. You've had a faithful, homecoming husband, who bought you a house, not the best house in town, but a house. You have, most of the time, plenty to eat, you have enough clothes so that you can always be clean. And you're strong as a horse."

"It certainly has been a hard season," said Belva Brown. "I don't know when we've had to burn so much coal in October before."

"I'm thinking of Helen."

"What about Helen, dear?"

"It's funny how some people are just charming, just pretty, and others, born of the same parents, are just not."

"You've always been wonderful, dear."

They looked at each other.

"I always say you make the best cocoa in the family."

"I'm never going to tell my secret."

"That girl down at the corner, next to the parsonage—you know?—is going to have another baby."

"The third? And not her husband's *either?*"

"Not her husband's either."

"Did Mrs. Whitfield get all right?"

"No, she'll have to have the operation."

33. *tree leaves leaving trees*

Airplanes and games and dolls and books and wagons and blackboards and
boats and guns and bears and rabbits and pandas and ducks, and dogs and
cats and gray elephants with black howdahs and rocking chairs and houses
and play dishes and scooters and animal hassocks, and trains and trucks
and yo-yos and telephones and balls and jeeps and jack-in-the-boxes and
puzzles and rocking horses.

And Santa Claus.

> Round, ripe, rosy,
> As the stories said.
> And white, it fluffed out from his chin,
> It laughed about his head.

And there were the children. Many groups of them, for this was a big
department store. Santa pushed out plump ho-ho-ho's! He patted the children's cheeks, and if a curl was golden and sleek enough he gave it a bit of
a tug, and sometimes he gave its owner a bit of a hug. And the children's
Christmas wants were almost torn out of them.

It was very merry and much as the children had dreamed.

Now came little Paulette. When the others had been taken care of. Her
insides scampering like mice. And, leaving her eyeballs, diamonds and stars.

Santa Claus.

Suddenly she was shy.

Maud Martha smiled, gave her a tiny shove, spoke as much to Santa
Claus as to her daughter.

"Go on. There he is. You've wanted to talk to him all this time. Go on.
Tell Santa what you want for Christmas."

"No."

Another smile, another shove, with some impatience, with some severity
in it. And Paulette was off.

"Hello!"

Santa Claus rubbed his palms together and looked vaguely out across the
Toy Department.

He was unable to see either mother or child.

"I want," said Paulette, "a wagon, a doll, a big ball, a bear and a tricycle
with a horn."

"Mister," said Maud Martha, "my little girl is talking to you."

Santa Claus's neck turned with hard slowness, carrying his unwilling
face with it.

"Mister," said Maud Martha.

"And what—do you want for Christmas." No question mark at the end.

"I want a wagon, a doll, a bear, a big ball, and a tricycle with a horn."

Silence. Then, "Oh." Then, "Um-hm."

Santa Claus had taken care of Paulette.

"And some candy and some nuts and a seesaw and bow and arrow."

"Come on, baby."

"But I'm not through, Mama."

"Santa Claus is through, hon."

Outside, there was the wonderful snow, high and heavy, crusted with blue twinkles. The air was quiet.

"Certainly is a nice night," confided Mama.

"Why didn't Santa Claus like me?"

"Baby, of course he liked you."

"He didn't like me. Why didn't he like me?"

"It maybe seemed that way to you. He has a lot on his mind, of course."

"He liked the other children. He smiled at them and shook their hands."

"He maybe got tired of smiling. Sometimes even I get—"

"He didn't look at me, he didn't shake *my* hand."

"Listen, child. People don't have to kiss you to show they like you. Now you know Santa Claus liked you. What have I been telling you? Santa Claus loves every child, and on the night before Christmas he brings them swell presents. Don't you remember, when you told Santa Claus you wanted the ball and bear and tricycle and doll he said 'Um-hm'? That meant he's going to bring you all those. You watch and see. Christmas'll be here in a few days. You'll wake up Christmas morning and find them and then you'll know Santa Claus loved *you too*."

Helen, she thought, would not have twitched, back there. Would not have yearned to jerk trimming scissors from purse and jab jab jab that evading eye. Would have gathered her fires, patted them, rolled them out, and blown on them. Because it really would not have made much difference to Helen. Paul would have twitched, twitched awfully, might have cursed, but after the first tough cough-up of rage would forget, or put off studious perusal indefinitely.

She could neither resolve nor dismiss. There were these scraps of baffled hate in her, hate with no eyes, no smile and—this she especially regretted, called her hungriest lack—not much voice.

Furtively, she looked down at Paulette. Was Paulette believing her? Surely she was not going to begin to think tonight, to try to find out answers tonight. She hoped the little creature wasn't ready. She hoped there hadn't been enough for that. She wasn't up to coping with—Some other night, not tonight.

Feeling her mother's peep, Paulette turned her face upward. Maud Martha wanted to cry.

Keep her that land of blue!

Keep her those fairies, with witches always killed at the end, and Santa every winter's lord, kind, sheer being who never perspires, who never does or says a foolish or ineffective thing, who never looks grotesque, who never has occasion to pull the chain and flush the toilet.

34. *back from the wars!*

There was Peace, and her brother Harry was back from the wars, and well.

And it was such a beautiful day!

The weather was bidding her bon voyage.

She did not have to tip back the shade of her little window to know that outside it was bright, because the sunshine had broken through the dark green of that shade and was glorifying every bit of her room. And the air crawling in at the half-inch crack was like a feather, and it tickled her throat, it teased her lashes, it made her sit up in bed and stretch, and zip the dark green shade up to the very top of the window—and made her whisper, What, *what*, am I to do with all of this life?

And exactly what was one to do with it all? At a moment like this one was ready for anything, was not afraid of anything. If one were down in a dark cool valley one could stick arms out and presto! they would be wings cutting away at the higher layers of air. At a moment like this one could think even of death with a sharp exhilaration, feel that death was a part of life: that life was good and death would be good too.

Maud Martha, with her daughter, got out-of-doors.

She did not need information, or solace, or a guidebook, or a sermon—not in this sun!—not in this blue air!

. . . They "marched," they battled behind her brain—the men who had drunk beer with the best of them, the men with two arms off and two legs off, the men with the parts of faces. Then her guts divided, then her eyes swam under frank mist.

And the Negro press (on whose front pages beamed the usual representations of womanly Beauty, pale and pompadoured) carried the stories of the latest of the Georgia and Mississippi lynchings. . . .

But the sun was shining, and some of the people in the world had been left alive, and it was doubtful whether the ridiculousness of man would ever completely succeed in destroying the world or, in fact, the basic equanimity of the least and commonest flower: for would its kind not come up again in the spring? come up, if necessary, among, between, or out of—beastly inconvenient!—the smashed corpses lying in strict composure, in that hush infallible and sincere.

And was not this something to be thankful for?

And, in the meantime, while people did live they would be grand, would be glorious and brave, would have nimble hearts that would beat and beat. They would even get up nonsense, through wars, through divorce, through evictions and jiltings and taxes.

And, in the meantime, she was going to have another baby.

The weather was bidding her bon voyage.

1953

JAMES BALDWIN
1924–1987

All of James Baldwin's writings bear some stamp of his assertion that "All art is a kind of confession," that "all artists, if they are to survive, are forced, at last, to tell the whole story, to vomit the anguish up." But in Baldwin's work, such confession was not merely a self-indulgent form of personal catharsis. With elegance and artfulness, he pierced the historic block in America's racial consciousness by linking the most intimate areas of his own experience with the broadest questions of national and global destiny.

He returned compulsively to those events of his early life that were seared in his imagination: the struggles with poverty; the humiliation of police brutality; the strangling religious indoctrination; but most of all, the estrangement from his stepfather, David Baldwin, an authoritarian lay preacher steeped in the Old Testament gospel of sinners in the hands of an angry god. Baldwin inherited that tradition, serving a brief time as a child evangelist in a storefront church in Harlem. Although he left the church and renounced Christianity, he often conceded that he never left the pulpit and the spirit of evangelism in his writings bears him out. Baldwin possessed the consciousness of a moralist, shaped by an Old Testament certainty of right and wrong, sin and transgression, and the New Testament promise of resurrection and redemption. This sermonic rhetoric of sin, damnation, and repentance pours through Baldwin's writings and mixes with the lyrics of the spirituals, blues, and gospel, creating a prose that demands the reader's attentive ear as much as eye, for the pace, cadences, rhythms, accents, and timbres are often lost to print. His immersion in black biblical rhetoric earned Baldwin the rightful title and mantle of latter-day Jeremiah, a mantle never more apparent than in *The Fire Next Time* (1963), judged by many to be his finest piece of writing. In "Down at the Cross: Letter from a Region in My Mind," from that collection, Baldwin utters one of his most famous prophecies: "If we do not dare everything, the fulfill-

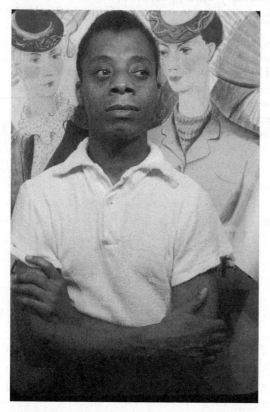

James Baldwin in 1955.

ment of that prophecy, re-created from the Bible in song by a slave, is upon us: God gave Noah the rainbow sign, No more water, the fire next time!" He was to see his prophecies come continually to pass in the uprisings that erupted all over urban America in the 1960s, leaving whole communities under piles of ash and rubble.

Born on August 2, 1924, in Harlem, which he described as a "southern community displaced in the streets of New York," Baldwin was the out-of-wedlock son of Emma Berdis Jones. When she married David Baldwin, who was from New Orleans, three years later, he adopted James, who was never to feel a sense of security or belonging in the family. Baldwin seemed to find escape from his stepfather's hatred and the harshness of his home in reading, claiming that by age thirteen he had read most of the books in the two Harlem libraries before moving on to the New York Public Library on Forty-second Street.

Baldwin began his literary apprenticeship at the early age of twelve when he published a short story about the Spanish revolution in a church newspaper. He found support for his writing in the school's literary club, directed by Harlem Renaissance poet Countee Cullen, and served as editor of the school newspaper, the *Douglass Pilot*. After high school, he continued to write, publishing his first book review (on Maxim Gorky) in 1946 at age twenty-two. His subsequent reviews for the *New Leader* on "the Negro problem" prompted Robert Warshow to commission a piece on Harlem for *Commentary*, the publishing arm of the American Jewish Committee. Titled "The Harlem Ghetto," the controversial essay on black anti-Semitism launched Baldwin's career as a writer and garnered for him numerous invitations to contribute to other magazines.

With characteristic candor, Baldwin admits to writing in an "attempt to be loved. It seemed the only way to another world." But the passage to that "other" world that writing provided seemed restricted and constrained by Baldwin's experience with racism and homophobia, a situation that compelled his expatriation to Paris in November 1948, a year after his mentor-cum-antagonist, Richard Wright, made the same transatlantic trek.

During Baldwin's days as a fledgling writer in New York, Wright had encouraged him, helping him secure the Eugene F. Saxton fellowship for work on his first novel, *Go Tell It on the Mountain*. Again, in Paris, Wright introduced Baldwin to the editors of *Zero* magazine, in which Baldwin published one of his most influential essays, "Everybody's Protest Novel" (1949). Best known for its attack on protest fiction, the essay examines Harriet Beecher Stowe's *Uncle Tom's Cabin* and Richard Wright's *Native Son* as examples of the limitations and excesses of ideological fiction. Appearing simultaneously in New York's *Partisan Review*, the essay sparked intense debate on both sides of the Atlantic and was widely perceived as a spiteful and ungrateful personal attack on Richard Wright. Although the essay resulted in a breach between Wright and Baldwin that was never healed, it further established Baldwin's reputation as a major American writer and essayist in the Emersonian tradition and a polemicist in the tradition of Thomas Paine and W. E. B. Du Bois.

Many, including Baldwin himself, have interpreted his relationship with Wright, and the estrangement that followed, as an Oedipal struggle of fathers and sons. Certainly, this struggle figures as one of the major obsessions of Baldwin's life and work and is at the heart of his first novel and first full-length work, *Go Tell It on the Mountain*. Published in 1953 to excellent reviews, the novel was originally titled "In My Father's House" and is a semiautobiographical story of a young man's coming-of-age, repressed and choked by his father's religious fundamentalism and its puritanical regime.

The relationship between the father, Gabriel, and Johnny, his son, recalls that of the biblical Abraham and Ishmael. As the rejected "bastard" within the home, Baldwin saw his position as that of Ishmael, the son of the bondwoman. Like many African American writers before him, Baldwin seized the story of Ishmael, the archetypal outcast, not only as a metaphor for his own life but as a metaphor for the collective lives of dispossessed black Americans, estranged from the nation.

Although many critics agree that *Go Tell It on the Mountain* is Baldwin's most technically accomplished and narratively disciplined novel, it is virtually a critical axiom that Baldwin's true *métier* was the essay, not the novel. Although Baldwin published six other novels, in steady succession, over the course of his career—*Giovanni's Room* (1956), *Another Country* (1962), *Tell Me How Long This Train's Been Gone* (1968), *If Beale Street Could Talk* (1974), and *Just above My Head* (1979)—his essays were invariably praised at the expense of his fiction, except perhaps for those collected in *Notes of Native Son* (1955), *Nobody Knows My Name* (1961), and *The Fire Next Time* (1963).

Baldwin's essays won him a popularity and acclaim as the "conscience of the nation," the voice that brought to racial discourse in America a passion and honesty that demanded notice. Baldwin's knife-edged criticism of the failed promises of American democracy, and the consequent social injustices, is unrelenting and uncompromising. Racial inequality, he insisted, in "A Talk to Teachers," a 1963 essay published in *Saturday Review,* must be understood, not as the outgrowth of prejudice and intolerance but rather as a "deliberate policy hammered into place in order to make money from black flesh." While much of Baldwin's work in the late 1950s, early 1960s centered on race, racism, and inequality, equally important were his interrogations of sex, sexuality, homoeroticism, and masculinist ideals, particularly as they intersected with race. Many of his most justly celebrated essays demonstrate a piercing understanding of the function of black males in the white racial imagination.

In "The Black Boy Looks at the White Boy," Baldwin's response to Norman Mailer's essay "The White Negro," he made some of his most trenchant pronouncements on the subject. "[T]o be an American Negro male," he wrote, "is also to be a kind of walking phallic symbol; which means that one pays, in one's own personality, for the sexual insecurity of others." He expanded these insights in essays and interviews throughout his career—"Preservation of Innocence," "Here Be Dragons," "The Male Prison," "Freaks and the American Ideal of Manhood"—analyzing the inextricable connections between sex and race in America. He speculated that if America ever transcended its racial antagonisms, it would then have to confront its Protestant Puritan legacy, complete with its taboos against sex and the flesh. He understood that, in terms of violence and discrimination, black Americans have borne the historical brunt of American sexual anxieties, the very same anxieties that serve a cultural agenda of compulsory heterosexuality. This agenda has, in turn, created the homosexual as outcast to shore up an enfeebled masculine identity. In "Go the Way Your Blood Beats," a 1984 interview with Richard Goldstein, Baldwin argued that macho men need "faggots" whom they have created "in order to act out a sexual fantasy on the body of another man and not take any responsibility for it." Both in *Giovanni's Room* (1956) and in *Another Country* (1962), he waged a twin assault on such forms of racial and sexual violence and, somewhat sentimentally, dramatized blackness and homosexuality as liberating influences.

Baldwin had a long and varied career in which, in addition to penning several essays and novels, he produced plays, scripts, short stories, and children's books, but critics agree that he was at his artistic summit in those works that he published during the 1950s and early 1960s. Almost nothing pertaining to race relations and social turbulence escaped Baldwin's pen during this period, although he addressed a range of other subjects, including homosexuality in Andre Gide's novel *Madeleine*, William Faulkner and desegregation, and the ideology of racial separatism espoused by the Black Muslims.

Neither racial separatism nor segregation could Baldwin easily abide. By his account, the sight of photographs of Dorothy Counts being spat upon as she tried to integrate a Charlotte, North Carolina, school convinced him that he needed to return to join the civil rights struggle, and after nearly a decade in France, he moved back to the United States in 1957. Baldwin had long parried questions about his self-exile from the United States, but as he noted in *James Baldwin: From Another Place*, a 1973 film by Turkish director Sedat Pakay:

> I suppose that many people do blame me for being out of the States as often as I am. But one can't afford to worry about that . . . *perhaps only someone who is outside of the States realizes that it's impossible to get out. . . . Being out . . . one is not really very far out of the United States. . . . One sees it better from a distance . . . from another place, from another country."*

It could be argued that, as an American in Paris, Baldwin could "see better" the reach of America as a global power within the context of the Cold War as well as the bid on behalf of black writers and intellectuals to inscribe a new, momentous era for global Africanity. Baldwin's writings would mark one of the essential witnesses to this new era encompassing the civil rights movement in the United States and decolonization struggles across sub-Saharan Africa and the Caribbean. Taking place not long after the historic conclave of Asian and African nonaligned nations in Bandung, Indonesia, in April 1955, the First International Congress of Black Writers and Artists (*Le Congres des Ecrivains et Artistes Noirs*) was convened in Paris in September 1956. Baldwin covered this event for *Encounter*, "the flagship organ of the Congress for Cultural Freedom"; notes critic Kevin Gaines, *Encounter* was later discovered to have been secretly funded by the Central Intelligence Agency. Published in 1957 as "Princes and Powers" (included here), Baldwin's report on the congress rehearses in considerable detail the highlights of this gathering of preeminent black male intellectuals from a variety of diasporic ports of call, from the United States to Martinique to Senegal. Many of the figures, including Frantz Fanon, Aimé Césaire, Léopold Senghor, Alioune Diop, Cheik Anta Diop, Jean Price-Mars, and George Lamming, were associated with some of the most powerful theorizations on black cultural production. They addressed, and at times fiercely contested, the pressing issues of the convocation, chiefly the achievement of black unity across national and cultural boundaries as well as the substance of the black intellectual's "response" to Europe. By *princes*, Baldwin likely referred to that impressive group of writers and intellectuals debating these and other geopolitical concerns. By *powers* he likely meant the potentates of European imperialism, of a dying colonialism, the guardians of "European vision of the world," as Baldwin put it. Richard Wright, whom Baldwin had antagonized years earlier, attended the congress as a member of the African American delegation, although Wright had been a denizen of Paris for a decade by that time. From the point of view of "Princes and Powers," Baldwin makes clear his ambivalent feelings toward the ideals of Senghorian "Negritude," although his apparent commitment to the U.S. scene of civil rights struggle would assume a prominent role in his career during the following decade.

Baldwin became a national figure in the movement, traveling to the South, where he continued to produce acid social commentaries published in such mass-circulation magazines as *Commentary*, *Partisan Review*, and *Esquire* and later collected in *Nobody Knows My Name* and *The Fire Next Time*. These essays, along with those in the first collection, *Notes of a Native Son*, are Baldwin at his best, by most critical accounts. Some have suggested, perhaps too patly, that, taken together, these three collections move backward from a New Testament optimism to an Old Testament gloom and record the stages in Baldwin's growing disillusionment with the American racial situation. While the first two, *Notes of a Native Son* and *Nobody Knows My Name*, are seen to register hope that blacks would be integrated into an American society where the healing force of love abounded, the third, *The Fire Next Time*, shows evidence that all belief in the redemptive possibilities of love is shattered. By the latter collection, a decade of assassinations and urban conflagrations had already fulfilled the prophecy embedded in the title.

Later collections found Baldwin's prophetic stance unshaken. In *No Name in the Street* (1972), he returned to the Old Testament to offer the curse of Job's friend

Bildad as an object lesson for America. Bildad foretold the doom that would befall the wicked of his generation: "His remembrance shall perish from the earth and he shall have no name in the street" (Job 18.17). Closing on a characteristically apocalyptic note, Baldwin prophesied yet more violence and bloodshed for an America heedless of the lessons of its own history and shackled to myths, shibboleths, and primitive reflexes that had too long defined race relations in America: "There will be bloody actions all over the world for years to come; but the Western party is over, and the white man's sun has set. Period."

After his civil rights involvement, Baldwin returned to Europe, where he resided, except for brief trips to the United States, until his death on November 30, 1987, in St. Paul de Vence. In an interview with Quincy Troupe weeks before his death, Baldwin said,

> No true account really of black life can be held, can be contained, in the American vocabulary. As it is, the only way that you can deal with it is by doing great violence to the assumptions on which the vocabulary is based. What I tried to do, or to interpret and make clear, was that no society can smash the social contract and be exempt from the consequences, and the consequences are chaos for everybody in the society.

Many critics allege that, by the end of his career, Baldwin was simply spouting rhetoric that compromised the moral persuasion and authority that had made his earlier works so powerful and compelling. Others charged that the line between his artistic preoccupations and his own personal and psychic life had become embarrassingly blurred. Still others observed that, in resorting to abstract sociological categories, Baldwin was simply flattening what had once been a richly complicated and nuanced view of race and racialism in America and thus was committing the same ideological excesses he had once condemned in Richard Wright. Whatever the criticisms, however, few will deny that Baldwin played a shaping role in the definition of post–World War II African American literature and had a stunning impact on American cultural life.

Everybody's Protest Novel

In *Uncle Tom's Cabin*,[1] that cornerstone of American social protest fiction, St. Clare, the kindly master, remarks to his coldly disapproving Yankee cousin, Miss Ophelia, that, so far as he is able to tell, the blacks have been turned over to the devil for the benefit of the whites in this world—however, he adds thoughtfully, it may turn out in the next. Miss Ophelia's reaction is, at least, vehemently right-minded: "This is perfectly horrible!" she exclaims. "You ought to be ashamed of yourselves!"

Miss Ophelia, as we may suppose, was speaking for the author; her exclamation is the moral, neatly framed, and incontestable like those improving mottoes sometimes found hanging on the walls of furnished rooms. And, like these mottoes, before which one invariably flinches, recognizing an insupportable, almost an indecent glibness, she and St. Clare are terribly in earnest. Neither of them questions the medieval morality from which their dialogue springs: black, white, the devil, the next world—posing its alternatives between heaven and the flames—were realities for them as, of course, they were for their creator. They spurned and were terrified of the darkness,

---

1. Harriet Beecher Stowe's antislavery novel, published in 1851–52. A runaway bestseller, this novel played a major role in the debate over slavery in the decade before the Civil War.

striving mightily for the light; and considered from this aspect, Miss Ophelia's exclamation, like Mrs. Stowe's novel, achieves a bright, almost a lurid significance, like the light from a fire which consumes a witch. This is the more striking as one considers the novels of Negro oppression written in our own, more enlightened day, all of which say only: "This is perfectly horrible! You ought to be ashamed of yourselves!" (Let us ignore, for the moment, those novels of oppression written by Negroes, which add only a raging, near-paranoiac postscript to this statement and actually reinforce, as I hope to make clear later, the principles which activate the oppression they decry.)

Uncle Tom's Cabin is a very bad novel, having, in its self-righteous, virtuous sentimentality, much in common with *Little Women*.[2] Sentimentality, the ostentatious parading of excessive and spurious emotion, is the mark of dishonesty, the inability to feel; the wet eyes of the sentimentalist betray his aversion to experience, his fear of life, his arid heart; and it is always, therefore, the signal of secret and violent inhumanity, the mask of cruelty. *Uncle Tom's Cabin*—like its multitudinous, hard-boiled descendants—is a catalogue of violence. This is explained by the nature of Mrs. Stowe's subject matter, her laudable determination to flinch from nothing in presenting the complete picture; an explanation which falters only if we pause to ask whether or not her picture is indeed complete; and what constriction or failure of perception forced her to so depend on the description of brutality—unmotivated, senseless—and to leave unanswered and unnoticed the only important question: what it was, after all, that moved her people to such deeds.

But this, let us say, was beyond Mrs. Stowe's powers; she was not so much a novelist as an impassioned pamphleteer; her book was not intended to do anything more than prove that slavery was wrong; was, in fact, perfectly horrible. This makes material for a pamphlet but it is hardly enough for a novel; and the only question left to ask is why we are bound still within the same constriction. How is it that we are so loath to make a further journey than that made by Mrs. Stowe, to discover and reveal something a little closer to the truth?

But that battered word, truth, having made its appearance here, confronts one immediately with a series of riddles and has, moreover, since so many gospels are preached, the unfortunate tendency to make one belligerent. Let us say, then, that truth, as used here, is meant to imply a devotion to the human being, his freedom and fulfillment; freedom which cannot be legislated, fulfillment which cannot be charted. This is the prime concern, the frame of reference; it is not to be confused with a devotion to Humanity which is too easily equated with a devotion to a Cause; and Causes, as we know, are notoriously blood-thirsty. We have, as it seems to me, in this most mechanical and interlocking of civilizations, attempted to lop this creature down to the status of a time-saving invention. He is not, after all, merely a member of a Society or a Group or a deplorable conundrum to be explained by Science. He is—and how old-fashioned the words sound!—something more than that, something resolutely indefinable, unpredictable. In overlooking, denying, evading his complexity—which is nothing more than the disquieting complexity of ourselves—we are diminished and we perish; only within this web of ambiguity, paradox, this hunger, danger, darkness, can we

2. Novel by Louisa May Alcott, published in 1868–69. Extremely popular children's book detailing the daily lives of four girls in a 19th-century New England family.

find at once ourselves and the power that will free us from ourselves. It is this power of revelation which is the business of the novelist, this journey toward a more vast reality which must take precedence over all other claims. What is today parroted as his Responsibility—which seems to mean that he must make formal declaration that he is involved in, and affected by, the lives of other people and to say something improving about this somewhat self-evident fact—is, when he believes it, his corruption and our loss; moreover, it is rooted in, interlocked with and intensifies this same mechanization. Both *Gentleman's Agreement* and *The Postman Always Rings Twice*[3] exemplify this terror of the human being, the determination to cut him down to size. And in *Uncle Tom's Cabin* we may find foreshadowing of both: the formula created by the necessity to find a lie more palatable than the truth has been handed down and memorized and persists yet with a terrible power.

It is interesting to consider one more aspect of Mrs. Stowe's novel, the method she used to solve the problem of writing about a black man at all. Apart from her lively procession of field hands, house niggers, Chloe, Topsy, etc.—who are the stock, lovable figures presenting no problem—she has only three other Negroes in the book. These are the important ones and two of them may be dismissed immediately, since we have only the author's word that they are Negro and they are, in all other respects, as white as she can make them. The two are George and Eliza, a married couple with a wholly adorable child—whose quaintness, incidentally, and whose charm, rather put one in mind of a darky bootblack doing a buck and wing to the clatter of condescending coins. Eliza is a beautiful, pious hybrid, light enough to pass—the heroine of *Quality*[4] might, indeed, be her reincarnation—differing from the genteel mistress who has overseered her education only in the respect that she is a servant. George is darker, but makes up for it by being a mechanical genius, and is, moreover, sufficiently un-Negroid to pass through town, a fugitive from his master, disguised as a Spanish gentleman, attracting no attention whatever beyond admiration. They are a race apart from Topsy. It transpires by the end of the novel, through one of those energetic, last-minute convolutions of the plot, that Eliza has some connection with French gentility. The figure from whom the novel takes its name, Uncle Tom, who is a figure of controversy yet, is jet-black, wooly-haired, illiterate; and he is phenomenally forbearing. He has to be; he is black; only through this forbearance can he survive or triumph. (Cf. Faulkner's preface to *The Sound and the Fury*.[5] These others were not Compsons. They were black:—They endured.) His triumph is metaphysical, unearthly; since he is black, born without the light, it is only through humility, the incessant mortification of the flesh, that he can enter into communion with God or man. The virtuous rage of Mrs. Stowe is motivated by nothing so temporal as a concern for the relationship of men to one another—or, even, as she would have claimed, by a concern for their relationship to God—but merely by a panic of being hurled into the flames,

---

3. A 1946 film directed by Tay Garnett, based on a novel of the same name by James M. Cain. An example of *film noir,* it takes a critical look at the pernicious consequences of the American dream. *Gentleman's Agreement* is a 1947 film directed by Elia Kazan, based on a novel of the same name by Laura Hobson; one of the first films to openly attack anti-Semitism.

4. A 1946 novel by Cid Ricketts Sumner.

5. Novel (1929) by William Faulkner (1897–1962).

of being caught in traffic with the devil. She embraced this merciless doctrine with all her heart, bargaining shamelessly before the throne of grace: God and salvation becoming her personal property, purchased with the coin of her virtue. Here, black equates with evil and white with grace; if, being mindful of the necessity of good works, she could not cast out the blacks—a wretched, huddled mass, apparently, claiming, like an obsession, her inner eye—she could not embrace them either without purifying them of sin. She must cover their intimidating nakedness, robe them in white, the garments of salvation; only thus could she herself be delivered from ever-present sin, only thus could she bury, as St. Paul demanded, "the carnal man, the man of the flesh."[6] Tom, therefore, her only black man, has been robbed of his humanity and divested of his sex. It is the price for that darkness with which he has been branded.

Uncle Tom's Cabin, then, is activated by what might be called a theological terror, the terror of damnation; and the spirit that breathes in this book, hot, self-righteous, fearful, is not different from that spirit of medieval times which sought to exorcize evil by burning witches; and is not different from that terror which activates a lynch mob. One need not, indeed, search for examples so historic or so gaudy; this is a warfare waged daily in the heart, a warfare so vast, so relentless and so powerful that the interracial handshake or the interracial marriage can be as crucifying as the public hanging or the secret rape. This panic motivates our cruelty, this fear of the dark makes it impossible that our lives shall be other than superficial; this, interlocked with and feeding our glittering, mechanical, inescapable civilization which has put to death our freedom.

This, notwithstanding that the avowed aim of the American protest novel is to bring greater freedom to the oppressed. They are forgiven, on the strength of these good intentions, whatever violence they do to language, whatever excessive demands they make of credibility. It is, indeed, considered the sign of a frivolity so intense as to approach decadence to suggest that these books are both badly written and wildly improbable. One is told to put first things first, the good of society coming before niceties of style or characterization. Even if this were incontestable—for what exactly is the "good" of society?—it argues an insuperable confusion, since literature and sociology are not one and the same; it is impossible to discuss them as if they were. Our passion for categorization, life neatly fitted into pegs, has led to an unforeseen, paradoxical distress; confusion, a breakdown of meaning. Those categories which were meant to define and control the world for us have boomeranged us into chaos; in which limbo we whirl, clutching the straws of our definitions. The "protest" novel, so far from being disturbing, is an accepted and comforting aspect of the American scene, ramifying that framework we believe to be so necessary. Whatever unsettling questions are raised are evanescent, titillating; remote, for this has nothing to do with us, it is safely ensconced in the social arena, where, indeed, it has nothing to do with anyone, so that finally we receive a very definite thrill of virtue from the fact that we are reading such a book at all. This report from the pit reassures us of its reality and its darkness and of our

6. Probably from St. Paul's first letter to the Corinthians, one of two canonical letters Paul addressed to his congregation in Corinth (see Romans 8.7–8). St. Paul was an early Christian missionary and Christianity's first theologian.

own salvation; and "As long as such books are being published," an American liberal once said to me, "everything will be all right."

But unless one's ideal of society is a race of neatly analyzed, hard-working ciphers, one can hardly claim for the protest novels the lofty purpose they claim for themselves or share the present optimism concerning them. They emerge for what they are: a mirror of our confusion, dishonesty, panic, trapped and immobilized in the sunlit prison of the American dream. They are fantasies, connecting nowhere with reality, sentimental; in exactly the same sense that such movies as *The Best Years of Our Lives* or the works of Mr. James M. Cain[7] are fantasies. Beneath the dazzling pyrotechnics of these current operas one may still discern, as the controlling force, the intense theological preoccupations of Mrs. Stowe, the sick vacuities of *The Rover Boys*.[8] Finally, the aim of the protest novel becomes something very closely resembling the zeal of those alabaster missionaries to Africa to cover the nakedness of the natives, to hurry them into the pallid arms of Jesus and thence into slavery. The aim has now become to reduce all Americans to the compulsive, bloodless dimensions of a guy named Joe.

It is the peculiar triumph of society—and its loss—that it is able to convince those people to whom it has given inferior status of the reality of this decree; it has the force and the weapons to translate its dictum into fact, so that the allegedly inferior are actually made so, insofar as the societal realities are concerned. This is a more hidden phenomenon now than it was in the days of serfdom, but it is no less implacable. Now, as then, we find ourselves bound, first without, then within, by the nature of our categorization. And escape is not effected through a bitter railing against this trap; it is as though this very striving were the only motion needed to spring the trap upon us. We take our shape, it is true, within and against that cage of reality bequeathed us at our birth; and yet it is precisely through our dependence on this reality that we are most endlessly betrayed. Society is held together by our need; we bind it together with legend, myth, coercion, fearing that without it we will be hurled into that void, within which, like the earth before the Word was spoken, the foundations of society are hidden. From this void—ourselves—it is the function of society to protect us; but it is only this void, our unknown selves, demanding, forever, a new act of creation, which can save us—"from the evil that is in the world." With the same motion, at the same time, it is this toward which we endlessly struggle and from which, endlessly, we struggle to escape.

It must be remembered that the oppressed and the oppressor are bound together within the same society; they accept the same criteria, they share the same beliefs, they both alike depend on the same reality. Within this cage it is romantic, more, meaningless, to speak of a "new" society as the desire of the oppressed, for that shivering dependence on the props of reality which he shares with the *Herrenvolk*[9] makes a truly "new" society impossible to conceive. What is meant by a new society is one in which inequalities will disappear, in which vengeance will be exacted; either there will be no oppressed at all, or the oppressed and the oppressor will change places.

---

7. Novelist and journalist (1892–1977) known primarily for novels about criminals and those on the fringe of society. "*The Best Years of Our Live*": Academy Award–winning. William Wyler film (1946), based on *Glory for Me* by MacKinley Kantor, which examines the difficulties faced by World War II veterans when they returned to their jobs and families.
8. Series of books for boys by Edward Stratemeyer published 1899–1916 under the pseudonym Arthur M. Winfield.
9. Master race (German).

But, finally, as it seems to me, what the rejected desire is, is an elevation of status, acceptance within the present community. Thus, the African, exile, pagan, hurried off the auction block and into the fields, fell on his knees before that God in Whom he must now believe; who had made him, but not in His image. This tableau, this impossibility, is the heritage of the Negro in America: *Wash me,* cried the slave to his Maker, *and I shall be whiter, whiter than snow!* For black is the color of evil; only the robes of the saved are white. It is this cry, implacable on the air and in the skull, that he must live with. Beneath the widely published catalogue of brutality—bringing to mind, somehow, an image, a memory of church-bells burdening the air—is this reality which, in the same nightmare notion, he both flees and rushes to embrace. In America, now, this country devoted to the death of the paradox—which may, therefore, be put to death by one—his lot is as ambiguous as a tableau by Kafka.[1] To flee or not, to move or not, it is all the same; his doom is written on his forehead, it is carried in his heart. In *Native Son*,[2] Bigger Thomas stands on a Chicago street corner watching airplanes flown by white men racing against the sun and "Goddamn" he says, the bitterness bubbling up like blood, remembering a million indignities, the terrible, rat-infested house, the humiliation of home-relief, the intense, aimless, ugly bickering, hating it; hatred smoulders through these pages like sulphur fire. All of Bigger's life is controlled, defined by his hatred and his fear. And later, his fear drives him to murder and his hatred to rape; he dies, having come, through this violence, we are told, for the first time, to a kind of life, having for the first time redeemed his manhood. Below the surface of this novel there lies, as it seems to me, a continuation, a complement of that monstrous legend it was written to destroy. Bigger is Uncle Tom's descendant, flesh of his flesh, so exactly opposite a portrait that, when the books are placed together, it seems that the contemporary Negro novelist and the dead New England woman are locked together in a deadly, timeless battle; the one uttering merciless exhortations, the other shouting curses. And, indeed, within this web of lust and fury, black and white can only thrust and counter-thrust, long for each other's slow, exquisite death; death by torture, acid, knives and burning; the thrust, the counter-thrust, the longing making the heavier that cloud which blinds and suffocates them both, so that they go down into the pit together. Thus has the cage betrayed us all, this moment, our life, turned to nothing through our terrible attempts to insure it. For Bigger's tragedy is not that he is cold or black or hungry, not even that he is American, black; but that he has accepted a theology that denies him life, that he admits the possibility of his being subhuman and feels constrained, therefore, to battle for his humanity according to those brutal criteria bequeathed him at his birth. But our humanity is our burden, our life; we need not battle for it; we need only to do what is infinitely more difficult—that is, accept it. The failure of the protest novel lies in its rejection of life, the human being, the denial of his beauty, dread, power, in its insistence that it is his categorization alone which is real and which cannot be transcended.

1949

---

1. Franz Kafka (1883–1924), German-speaking Jewish novelist, known for his often disturbing portrayals of a surreal reality that conspires against lonely and confused individuals.
2. A 1940 novel by Richard Wright.

Notes of a Native Son

On the 29th of July, in 1943, my father died. On the same day, a few hours later, his last child was born. Over a month before this, while all our energies were concentrated in waiting for these events, there had been, in Detroit, one of the bloodiest race riots of the century. A few hours after my father's funeral, while he lay in state in the undertaker's chapel, a race riot broke out in Harlem. On the morning of the 3rd of August, we drove my father to the graveyard through a wilderness of smashed plate glass.

The day of my father's funeral had also been my nineteenth birthday. As we drove him to the graveyard, the spoils of injustice, anarchy, discontent, and hatred were all around us. It seemed to me that God himself had devised, to mark my father's end, the most sustained and brutally dissonant of codas. And it seemed to me, too, that the violence which rose all about us as my father left the world had been devised as a corrective for the pride of his eldest son. I had declined to believe in that apocalypse which had been central to my father's vision; very well, life seemed to be saying, here is something that will certainly pass for an apocalypse until the real thing comes along. I had inclined to be contemptuous of my father for the conditions of his life, for the conditions of our lives. When his life had ended I began to wonder about that life and also, in a new way, to be apprehensive about my own.

I had not known my father very well. We had got on badly, partly because we shared, in our different fashions, the vice of stubborn pride. When he was dead I realized that I had hardly ever spoken to him. When he had been dead a long time I began to wish I had. It seems to be typical of life in America, where opportunities, real and fancied, are thicker than anywhere else on the globe, that the second generation has no time to talk to the first. No one, including my father, seems to have known exactly how old he was, but his mother had been born during slavery. He was of the first generation of free men. He, along with thousands of other Negroes, came North after 1919 and I was part of that generation which had never seen the landscape of what Negroes sometimes call the Old Country.

He had been born in New Orleans and had been a quite young man there during the time that Louis Armstrong, a boy, was running errands for the dives and honky-tonks of what was always presented to me as one of the most wicked of cities—to this day, whenever I think of New Orleans, I also helplessly think of Sodom and Gomorrah.[1] My father never mentioned Louis Armstrong,[2] except to forbid us to play his records; but there was a picture of him on our wall for a long time. One of my father's strong-willed female relatives had placed it there and forbade my father to take it down. He never did, but he eventually maneuvered her out of the house and when, some years later, she was in trouble and near death, he refused to do anything to help her.

He was, I think, very handsome. I gather this from photographs and from my own memories of him, dressed in his Sunday best and on his way to preach a sermon somewhere, when I was little. Handsome, proud, and

---

1. Cities of ancient Palestine; according to Genesis 19.24–28, they were destroyed by fire because of vice and corruption.

2. Jazz trumpeter and singer (1900–1971) who was famous for his innovative playing style and gravelly voice.

ingrown, "like a toe-nail," somebody said. But he looked to me, as I grew older, like pictures I had seen of African tribal chieftains: he really should have been naked, with war-paint on and barbaric mementos, standing among spears. He could be chilling in the pulpit and indescribably cruel in his personal life and he was certainly the most bitter man I have ever met; yet it must be said that there was something else in him, buried in him, which lent him his tremendous power and, even, a rather crushing charm. It had something to do with his blackness, I think—he was very black— with his blackness and his beauty, and with the fact that he knew that he was black but did not know that he was beautiful. He claimed to be proud of his blackness but it had also been the cause of much humiliation and it had fixed bleak boundaries to his life. He was not a young man when we were growing up and he had already suffered many kinds of ruin; in his outrageously demanding and protective way he loved his children, who were black like him and menaced, like him; and all these things sometimes showed in his face when he tried, never to my knowledge with any success, to establish contact with any of us. When he took one of his children on his knee to play, the child always became fretful and began to cry; when he tried to help one of us with our homework the absolutely unabating tension which emanated from him caused our minds and our tongues to become paralyzed, so that he, scarcely knowing why, flew into a rage and the child, not knowing why, was punished. If it ever entered his head to bring a surprise home for his children, it was, almost unfailingly, the wrong surprise and even the big watermelons he often brought home on his back in the summertime led to the most appalling scenes. I do not remember, in all those years, that one of his children was ever glad to see him come home. From what I was able to gather of his early life, it seemed that this inability to establish contact with other people had always marked him and had been one of the things which had driven him out of New Orleans. There was something in him, therefore, groping and tentative, which was never expressed and which was buried with him. One saw it most clearly when he was facing new people and hoping to impress them. But he never did, not for long. We went from church to smaller and more improbable church, he found himself in less and less demand as a minister, and by the time he died none of his friends had come to see him for a long time. He had lived and died in an intolerable bitterness of spirit and it frightened me, as we drove him to the graveyard through those unquiet, ruined streets, to see how powerful and overflowing this bitterness could be and to realize that this bitterness now was mine.

When he died I had been away from home for a little over a year. In that year I had had time to become aware of the meaning of all my father's bitter warnings, had discovered the secret of his proudly pursed lips and rigid carriage: I had discovered the weight of white people in the world. I saw that this had been for my ancestors and now would be for me an awful thing to live with and that the bitterness which had helped to kill my father could also kill me.

He had been ill a long time—in the mind, as we now realized, reliving instances of his fantastic intransigence in the new light of his affliction and endeavoring to feel a sorrow for him which never, quite, came true. We had not known that he was being eaten up by paranoia, and the discovery that his cruelty, to our bodies and our minds, had been one of the symptoms of his illness was not, then, enough to enable us to forgive him. The younger children felt, quite simply, relief that he would not be coming home anymore. My mother's observation that it was he, after all, who had kept them alive all these years meant nothing because the problems of keeping children alive are not real for children. The older children felt, with my father gone, that they could invite their friends to the house without fear that their friends would be insulted or, as had sometimes happened with me, being told that their friends were in league with the devil and intended to rob our family of everything we owned. (I didn't fail to wonder, and it made me hate him, what on earth we owned that anybody else would want.)

His illness was beyond all hope of healing before anyone realized that he was ill. He had always been so strange and had lived, like a prophet, in such unimaginably close communion with the Lord that his long silences which were punctuated by moans and hallelujahs and snatches of old songs while he sat at the living-room window never seemed odd to us. It was not until he refused to eat because, he said, his family was trying to poison him that my mother was forced to accept as a fact what had, until then, been only an unwilling suspicion. When he was committed, it was discovered that he had tuberculosis and, as it turned out, the disease of his mind allowed the disease of his body to destroy him. For the doctors could not force him to eat, either, and, though he was fed intravenously, it was clear from the beginning that there was no hope for him.

In my mind's eye I could see him, sitting at the window, locked up in his terrors; hating and fearing every living soul including his children who had betrayed him, too, by reaching towards the world which had despised him. There were nine of us. I began to wonder what it could have felt like for such a man to have had nine children whom he could barely feed. He used to make little jokes about our poverty, which never, of course, seemed very funny to us; they could not have seemed very funny to him, either, or else our all too feeble response to them would never have caused such rages. He spent great energy and achieved, to our chagrin, no small amount of success in keeping us away from the people who surrounded us, people who had all-night rent parties to which we listened when we should have been sleeping, people who cursed and drank and flashed razor blades on Lenox Avenue. He could not understand why, if they had so much energy to spare, they could not use it to make their lives better. He treated almost everybody on our block with a most uncharitable asperity and neither they, nor, of course, their children were slow to reciprocate.

The only white people who came to our house were welfare workers and bill collectors. It was almost always my mother who dealt with them, for my father's temper, which was at the mercy of his pride, was never to be trusted. It was clear that he felt their very presence in his home to be a violation: this was conveyed by his carriage, almost ludicrously stiff, and by his voice, harsh and vindictively polite. When I was around nine or ten I wrote a play which was directed by a young, white schoolteacher, a woman, who then took an interest in me, and gave me books to read and, in order to corroborate my theatrical bent, decided to take me to see what she somewhat tactlessly referred to as "real" plays. Theater-going was forbidden in our house, but, with the really cruel intuitiveness of a child, I suspected that the color of this woman's skin would carry the day for me. When, at school, she suggested taking me to the theater, I did not, as I might have done if she had been a Negro, find a way of discouraging her, but agreed that she should pick me up at my house one evening. I then, very cleverly, left all the rest to my mother, who suggested to my father, as I knew she would, that it would not be very nice to let such a kind woman make the trip for nothing. Also, since it was a schoolteacher, I imagine that my mother countered the idea of sin with the idea of "education," which word, even with my father, carried a kind of bitter weight.

Before the teacher came my father took me aside to ask *why* she was coming, what *interest* she could possibly have in our house, in a boy like me. I said I didn't know but I, too, suggested that it had something to do with education. And I understood that my father was waiting for me to say something—I didn't quite know what; perhaps that I wanted his protection against this teacher and her "education." I said none of these things and the teacher came and we went out. It was clear, during the brief interview in our living room, that my father was agreeing very much against his will and that he would have refused permission if he had dared. The fact that he did not dare caused me to despise him: I had no way of knowing that he was facing in that living room a wholly unprecedented and frightening situation.

Later, when my father had been laid off from his job, this woman became very important to us. She was really a very sweet and generous woman and went to a great deal of trouble to be of help to us, particularly during one awful winter. My mother called her by the highest name she knew: she said she was a "christian." My father could scarcely disagree but during the four or five years of our relatively close association he never trusted her and was always trying to surprise in her open, Midwestern face the genuine, cunningly hidden, and hideous motivation. In later years, particularly when it began to be clear that this "education" of mine was going to lead me to perdition, he became more explicit and warned me that my white friends in high school were not really my friends and that I would see, when I was older, how white people would do anything to keep a Negro down. Some of them could be nice, he admitted, but none of them were to be trusted and most of them were not even nice. The best thing was to have as little to do with them as possible. I did not feel this way and I was certain, in my innocence, that I never would.

But the year which preceded my father's death had made a great change in my life. I had been living in New Jersey, working in defense plants, working and living among southerners, white and black. I knew about the south, of course, and about how southerners treated Negroes and how they expected them to behave, but it had never entered my mind that anyone would look at me and expect *me* to behave that way. I learned in New Jersey that to be a Negro meant, precisely, that one was never looked at but was simply at the mercy of the reflexes the color of one's skin caused in other people. I acted in New Jersey as I had always acted, that is as though I thought a great deal of myself—I had to *act* that way—with results that were, simply, unbelievable. I had scarcely arrived before I had earned the enmity, which was extraordinarily ingenious, of all my superiors and nearly all my co-workers. In the beginning, to make matters worse, I simply did not know what was happening. I did not know what I had done, and I shortly began to wonder what *anyone* could possibly do, to bring about such unanimous, active, and unbearably vocal hostility. I knew about jim-crow[3] but I had never experienced it. I went to the same self-service restaurant three times and stood with all the Princeton boys before the counter, waiting

3. Systematic supression and segregation of blacks.

for a hamburger and coffee; it was always an extraordinarily long time before anything was set before me; but it was not until the fourth visit that I learned that, in fact, nothing had ever been set before me: I had simply picked something up. Negroes were not served there, I was told, and they had been waiting for me to realize that I was always the only Negro present. Once I was told this, I determined to go there all the time. But now they were ready for me and, though some dreadful scenes were subsequently enacted in that restaurant, I never ate there again.

It was the same story all over New Jersey, in bars, bowling alleys, diners, places to live. I was always being forced to leave, silently, or with mutual imprecations. I very shortly became notorious and children giggled behind me when I passed and their elders whispered or shouted—they really believed that I was mad. And it did begin to work on my mind, of course; I began to be afraid to go anywhere and to compensate for this I went places to which I really should not have gone and where, God knows, I had no desire to be. My reputation in town naturally enhanced my reputation at work and my working day became one long series of acrobatics designed to keep me out of trouble. I cannot say that these acrobatics succeeded. It began to seem that the machinery of the organization I worked for was turning over, day and night, with but one aim: to eject me. I was fired once, and contrived, with the aid of a friend from New York, to get back on the payroll; was fired again, and bounced back again. It took a while to fire me for the third time, but the third time took. There were no loopholes anywhere. There was not even any way of getting back inside the gates.

That year in New Jersey lives in my mind as though it were the year during which, having an unsuspected predilection for it, I first contracted some dread, chronic disease, the unfailing symptom of which is a kind of blind fever, a pounding in the skull and fire in the bowels. Once this disease is contracted, one can never be really carefree again, for the fever, without an instant's warning, can recur at any moment. It can wreck more important things than race relations. There is not a Negro alive who does not have this rage in his blood—one has the choice, merely, of living with it consciously or surrendering to it. As for me, this fever has recurred in me, and does, and will until the day I die.

My last night in New Jersey, a white friend from New York took me to the nearest big town, Trenton, to go to the movies and have a few drinks. As it turned out, he also saved me from, at the very least, a violent whipping. Almost every detail of that night stands out very clearly in my memory. I even remember the name of the movie we saw because its title impressed me as being so patly ironical. It was a movie about the German occupation of France, starring Maureen O'Hara and Charles Laughton and called *This Land Is Mine*. I remember the name of the diner we walked into when the movie ended: it was the "American Diner." When we walked in the counterman asked what we wanted and I remember answering with the casual sharpness which had become my habit: "We want a hamburger and a cup of coffee, what do you think we want?" I do not know why, after a year of such rebuffs, I so completely failed to anticipate his answer, which was, of course, "We don't serve Negroes here." This reply failed to discompose me, at least for the moment. I made some sardonic comment about the name of the diner and we walked out into the streets.

This was the time of what was called the "brown-out," when the lights in all American cities were very dim. When we re-entered the streets something happened to me which had the force of an optical illusion, or a night-mare. The streets were very crowded and I was facing north. People were moving in every direction but it seemed to me, in that instant, that all of the people I could see, and many more than that, were moving toward me, against me, and that everyone was white. I remember how their faces gleamed. And I felt, like a physical sensation, a *click* at the nape of my neck as though some interior string connecting my head to my body had been cut. I began to walk. I heard my friend call after me, but I ignored him. Heaven only knows what was going on in his mind, but he had the good sense not to touch me—I don't know what would have happened if he had—and to keep me in sight. I don't know what was going on in my mind, either; I certainly had no conscious plan. I wanted to do something to crush these white faces, which were crushing me. I walked for perhaps a block or two until I came to an enormous, glittering, and fashionable restaurant in which I knew not even the intercession of the Virgin would cause me to be served. I pushed through the doors and took the first vacant seat I saw, at a table for two, and waited.

I do not know how long I waited and I rather wonder, until today, what I could possibly have looked like. Whatever I looked like, I frightened the waitress who shortly appeared, and the moment she appeared all of my fury flowed towards her. I hated her for her white face, and for her great, astounded, frightened eyes. I felt that if she found a black man so frighten-ing I would make her fright worth-while.

She did not ask me what I wanted, but repeated, as though she had learned it somewhere, "We don't serve Negroes here." She did not say it with the blunt, derisive hostility to which I had grown so accustomed, but, rather, with a note of apology in her voice, and fear. This made me colder and more murderous than ever. I felt I had to do something with my hands. I wanted her to come close enough for me to get her neck between my hands.

So I pretended not to have understood her, hoping to draw her closer. And she did step a very short step closer, with her pencil poised incongruously over her pad, and repeated the formula: ". . . don't serve Negroes here."

Somehow, with the repetition of that phrase, which was already ringing in my head like a thousand bells of a nightmare, I realized that she would never come any closer and that I would have to strike from a distance. There was nothing on the table but an ordinary water-mug half full of water, and I picked this up and hurled it with all my strength at her. She ducked and it missed her and shattered against the mirror behind the bar. And, with that sound, my frozen blood abruptly thawed, I returned from wherever I had been, I *saw*, for the first time, the restaurant, the people with their mouths open, already, as it seemed to me, rising as one man, and I realized what I had done, and where I was, and I was frightened. I rose and began running for the door. A round, potbellied man grabbed me by the nape of the neck just as I reached the doors and began to beat me about the face. I kicked him and got loose and ran into the streets. My friend whispered, *"Run!"* and I ran.

My friend stayed outside the restaurant long enough to misdirect my pur-suers and the police, who arrived, he told me, at once. I do not know what I said to him when he came to my room that night. I could not have said much. I felt, in the oddest, most awful way, that I had somehow betrayed him. I lived it over and over and over again, the way one relives an automo-bile accident after it has happened and one finds oneself alone and safe. I could not get over two facts, both equally difficult for the imagination to grasp, and one was that I could have been murdered. But the other was that I had been ready to commit murder. I saw nothing very clearly but I did see this: that my life, my *real* life, was in danger, and not from anything other people might do but from the hatred I carried in my own heart.

II

I had returned home around the second week in June—in great haste because it seemed that my father's death and my mother's confinement were both but a matter of hours. In the case of my mother, it soon became clear that she had simply made a miscalculation. This had always been her tendency and I don't believe that a single one of us arrived in the world, or has since arrived anywhere else, on time. But none of us dawdled so intolerably about the business of being born as did my baby sister. We sometimes amused ourselves, during those endless, stifling weeks, by picturing the baby sitting within in the safe, warm dark, bitterly regretting the necessity of becoming a part of our chaos and stubbornly putting it off as long as possible. I understood her perfectly and congratulated her on showing such good sense so soon. Death, however, sat as purposefully at my father's bedside as life stirred within my mother's womb and it was harder to understand why he so lingered in that long shadow. It seemed that he had bent, and for a long time, too, all of his energies towards dying. Now death was ready for him but my father held back.

All of Harlem, indeed, seemed to be infected by waiting. I had never before known it to be so violently still. Racial tensions throughout this country were exacerbated during the early years of the war, partly because the labor market brought together hundreds of thousands of ill-prepared people and partly because Negro soldiers, regardless of where they were born, received their military training in the south. What happened in defense plants and army camps had repercussions, naturally, in every Negro ghetto. The situation in Harlem had grown bad enough for clergymen, policemen, educators, politicians, and social workers to assert in one breath that there was no "crime wave" and to offer, in the very next breath, suggestions as to how to combat it. These suggestions always seemed to involve playgrounds, despite the fact that racial skirmishes were occurring in the playgrounds, too. Playground or not, crime wave or not, the Harlem police force had been augmented in March, and the unrest grew—perhaps, in fact, partly as a result of the ghetto's instinctive hatred of policemen. Perhaps the most revealing news item, out of the steady parade of reports of muggings, stabbings, shootings, assaults, gang wars, and accusations of police brutality, is the item concerning six Negro girls who set upon a white girl in the subway because, as they all too accurately put it, she was stepping on their toes. Indeed she was, all over the nation.

I had never before been so aware of policemen, on foot, on horseback, on corners, everywhere, always two by two. Nor had I ever been so aware of small knots of people. They were on stoops and on corners and in doorways, and what was striking about them, I think, was that they did not seem to be talking. Never, when I passed these groups, did the usual sound of a curse or a laugh ring out and neither did there seem to be any hum of gossip. There was certainly, on the other hand, occurring between them communication extraordinarily intense. Another thing that was striking was the unexpected diversity of the people who made up these groups. Usually, for example, one would see a group of sharpies standing on the street corner, jiving the passing chicks; or a group of older men, usually, for some reason, in the vicinity of a barber shop, discussing baseball scores, or the numbers, or making rather chilling observations about women they had known. Women, in a general way, tended to be seen less often together—unless they were church women, or very young girls, or prostitutes met together for an unprofessional instant. But that summer I saw the strangest combinations: large, respectable, churchly matrons standing on the stoops or the corners with their hair tied up, together with a girl in sleazy satin whose face bore the marks of gin and the razor, or heavy-set, abrupt, no-nonsense older men, in company with the most disreputable and fanatical "race" men, or these same "race" men with the sharpies, or these sharpies with the churchly women. Seventh Day Adventists and Methodists and Spiritualists seemed to be hobnobbing with Holyrollers and they were all, alike, entangled with the most flagrant disbelievers; something heavy in their stance seemed to indicate that they had all, incredibly, seen a common vision, and on each face there seemed to be the same strange, bitter shadow.

The churchly women and the matter-of-fact, no-nonsense men had children in the Army. The sleazy girls they talked to had lovers there, the sharpies and the "race" men had friends and brothers there. It would have demanded an unquestioning patriotism, happily as uncommon in this country as it is undesirable, for these people not to have been disturbed by the bitter letters they received, by the newspaper stories they read, not to have been enraged by the posters, then to be found all over New York, which described the Japanese as "yellow-bellied Japs." It was only the "race" men, to be sure, who spoke ceaselessly of being revenged—how this vengeance was to be exacted was not clear—for the indignities and dangers suffered by Negro boys in uniform; but everybody felt a directionless, hopeless bitterness, as well as that panic which can scarcely be suppressed when one knows that a human being one loves is beyond one's reach, and in danger. This helplessness and this gnawing uneasiness does something, at length, to even the toughest mind. Perhaps the best way to sum all this up is to say that the people I knew felt, mainly, a peculiar kind of relief when they knew that their boys were being shipped out of the south, to do battle overseas. It was, perhaps, like feeling that the most dangerous part of a dangerous journey had been passed and that now, even if death should come, it would come with honor and without the complicity of their countrymen. Such a death would be, in short, a fact with which one could hope to live.

It was on the 28th of July, which I believe was a Wednesday, that I visited my father for the first time during his illness and for the last time in his life. The moment I saw him I knew why I had put off this visit so long. I had told my mother that I did not want to see him because I hated him. But this was not true. It was only that I *had* hated him and I wanted to hold on to this hatred. I did not want to look on him as a ruin: it was not a ruin I had hated. I imagine that one of the reasons people cling to their hates so stubbornly is because they sense, once hate is gone, that they will be forced to deal with pain.

We traveled out to him, his older sister and myself, to what seemed to be the very end of a very Long Island. It was hot and dusty and we wrangled, my aunt and I, all the way out, over the fact that I had recently begun to smoke and, as she said, to give myself airs. But I knew that she wrangled with me because she could not bear to face the fact of her brother's dying. Neither could I endure the reality of her despair, her unstated bafflement as to what had happened to her brother's life, and her own. So we wrangled and I smoked and from time to time she fell into a heavy reverie. Covertly, I watched her face, which was the face of an old woman; it had fallen in, the eyes were sunken and lightless; soon she would be dying, too.

In my childhood—it had not been so long ago—I had thought her beautiful. She had been quick-witted and quick-moving and very generous with all the children and each of her visits had been an event. At one time one of my brothers and myself had thought of running away to live with her. Now she could no longer produce out of her handbag some unexpected and yet familiar delight. She made me feel pity and revulsion and fear. It was awful to realize that she no longer caused me to feel affection. The closer we came to the hospital the more querulous she became and at the same time, naturally, grew more dependent on me. Between pity and guilt and fear I began to feel that there was another me trapped in my skull like a jack-in-the-box who might escape my control at any moment and fill the air with screaming.

She began to cry the moment we entered the room and she saw him lying there, all shriveled and still, like a little black monkey. The great, gleaming apparatus which fed him and would have compelled him to be still even if he had been able to move brought to mind, not beneficence, but torture; the tubes entering his arm made me think of pictures I had seen when a child, of Gulliver, tied down by the pygmies on that island.[4] My aunt wept and wept, there was a whistling sound in my father's throat; nothing was said; he could not speak. I wanted to take his hand, to say something. But I do not know what I could have said, even if he could have heard me. He was not really in that room with us, he had at last really embarked on his journey; and though my aunt told me that he said he was going to meet Jesus, I did not hear anything except that whistling in his throat. The doctor came back and we left, into that unbearable train again, and home. In the morning came the telegram saying that he was dead. Then the house was suddenly full of relatives, friends, hysteria, and confusion and I quickly left my mother and the children to the care of those impressive women, who, in Negro communities at least, automatically appear at times of bereavement armed with lotions, proverbs, and patience, and an ability to cook. I went downtown. By the time I returned, later the same day, my mother had been carried to the hospital and the baby had been born.

III

For my father's funeral I had nothing black to wear and this posed a nagging problem all day long. It was one of those problems, simple, or impossible of solution, to which the mind insanely clings in order to avoid the mind's real trouble. I spent most of that day at the downtown apartment of a girl I knew, celebrating my birthday with whiskey and wondering what to wear that night. When planning a birthday celebration one naturally does

4. A reference to Jonathan Swift's *Gulliver's Travels* (1726).

not expect that it will be up against competition from a funeral and this girl had anticipated taking me out that night, for a big dinner and a night club afterwards. Sometime during the course of that long day we decided that we would go out anyway, when my father's funeral service was over. I imagine *I* decided it, since, as the funeral hour approached, it became clearer and clearer to me that I would not know what to do with myself when it was over. The girl, stifling her very lively concern as to the possible effects of the whiskey on one of my father's chief mourners, concentrated on being conciliatory and practically helpful. She found a black shirt for me somewhere and ironed it and, dressed in the darkest pants and jacket I owned, and slightly drunk, I made my way to my father's funeral.

The chapel was full, but not packed, and very quiet. There were, mainly, my father's relatives, and his children, and here and there I saw faces I had not seen since childhood, the faces of my father's one-time friends. They were very dark and solemn now, seeming somehow to suggest that they had known all along that something like this would happen. Chief among the mourners was my aunt, who had quarreled with my father all his life; by which I do not mean to suggest that her mourning was insincere or that she had not loved him. I suppose that she was one of the few people in the world who had, and their incessant quarreling proved precisely the strength of the tie that bound them. The only other person in the world, as far as I knew, whose relationship to my father rivaled my aunt's in depth was my mother, who was not there.

It seemed to me, of course, that it was a very long funeral. But it was, if anything, a rather shorter funeral than most, nor, since there were no overwhelming, uncontrollable expressions of grief, could it be called—if I dare to use the word—successful. The minister who preached my father's funeral sermon was one of the few my father had still been seeing as he neared his end. He presented to us in his sermon a man whom none of us had ever seen—a man thoughtful, patient, and forbearing, a Christian inspiration to all who knew him, and a model for his children. And no doubt the children, in their disturbed and guilty state, were almost ready to believe this; he had been remote enough to be anything and, anyway, the shock of the incontrovertible, that it was really our father lying up there in that casket, prepared the mind for anything. His sister moaned and this grief-stricken moaning was taken as corroboration. The other faces held a dark, non-committal thoughtfulness. This was not the man they had known, but they had scarcely expected to be confronted with *him*; this was, in a sense deeper than questions of fact, the man they had not known, and the man they had not known may have been the real one. The real man, whoever he had been, had suffered and now he was dead: this was all that was sure and all that mattered now. Every man in the chapel hoped that when his hour came he, too, would be eulogized, which is to say forgiven, and that all of his lapses, greeds, errors, and strayings from the truth would be invested with coherence and looked upon with charity. This was perhaps the last thing human beings could give each other and it was what they demanded, after all, of the Lord. Only the Lord saw the midnight tears, only He was present when one of His children, moaning and wringing hands, paced up and down the room. When one slapped one's child in anger the recoil in the heart reverberated through heaven and became part of the pain of the universe. And when the children were hungry and sullen and distrustful and one watched them, daily, growing wilder, and further away, and running headlong into danger, it was the Lord who knew what the charged heart endured as the strap was laid to the backside; the Lord alone who knew what one *would* have said if one had had, like the Lord, the gift of the living word. It was the Lord who knew of the impossibility every parent in that room faced: how to prepare the child for the day when the child would be despised and how to *create* in the child—by what means?—a stronger antidote to this poison than one had found for oneself. The avenues, side streets, bars, billiard halls, hospitals, police stations, and even the playgrounds of Harlem—not to mention the houses of correction, the jails, and the morgue—testified to the potency of the poison while remaining silent as to the efficacy of whatever antidote, irresistibly raising the question of whether or not such an antidote existed; raising, which was worse, the question of whether or not an antidote was desirable; perhaps poison should be fought with poison. With these several schisms in the mind and with more terrors in the heart than could be named, it was better not to judge the man who had gone down under an impossible burden. It was better to remember: *Thou knowest this man's fall; but thou knowest not his wrassling.*

While the preacher talked and I watched the children—years of changing their diapers, scrubbing them, slapping them, taking them to school, and scolding them had had the perhaps inevitable result of making me love them, though I am not sure I knew this then—my mind was busily breaking out with a rash of disconnected impressions. Snatches of popular songs, indecent jokes, bits of books I had read, movie sequences, faces, voices, political issues—I thought I was going mad; all these impressions suspended, as it were, in the solution of the faint nausea produced in me by the heat and liquor. For a moment I had the impression that my alcoholic breath, inefficiently disguised with chewing gum, filled the entire chapel. Then someone began singing one of my father's favorite songs and, abruptly, I was with him, sitting on his knee, in the hot, enormous, crowded church which was the first church we attended. It was the Abyssinia Baptist Church on 138th Street. We had not gone there long. With this image, a host of others came. I had forgotten, in the rage of my growing up, how proud my father had been of me when I was little. Apparently, I had had a voice and my father had liked to show me off before the members of the church. I had forgotten what he had looked like when he was pleased but now I remembered that he had always been grinning with pleasure when my solos ended. I even remembered certain expressions on his face when he teased my mother—had he loved her? I would never know. And when had it all begun to change? For now it seemed that he had not always been cruel. I remembered being taken for a haircut and scraping my knee on the footrest of the barber's chair and I remembered my father's face as he soothed my crying and applied the stinging iodine. Then I remembered our fights, fights which had been of the worst possible kind because my technique had been silence.

I remembered the one time in all our life together when we had really spoken to each other.

It was on a Sunday and it must have been shortly before I left home. We were walking, just the two of us, in our usual silence, to or from church. I was in high school and had been doing a lot of writing and I was, at about this time, the editor of the high school magazine. But I had also been a Young Minister and had been preaching from the pulpit. Lately, I had been taking fewer engagements and preached as rarely as possible. It was said in the church, quite truthfully, that I was "cooling off."

My father asked me abruptly, "You'd rather write than preach, wouldn't you?"

I was astonished at his question—because it was a real question. I answered, "Yes."

That was all we said. It was awful to remember that that was all we had *ever* said.

The casket now was opened and the mourners were being led up the aisle to look for the last time on the deceased. The assumption was that the family was too overcome with grief to be allowed to make this journey alone and I watched while my aunt was led to the casket and, muffled in black, and shaking, led back to her seat. I disapproved of forcing the children to look on their dead father, considering that the shock of his death, or, more truthfully, the shock of death as a reality, was already a little more than a child could bear, but my judgment in this matter had been overruled and there they were, bewildered and frightened and very small, being led, one by one, to the casket. But there is also something very gallant about children at such moments. It has something to do with their silence and gravity and with the fact that one cannot help them. Their legs, somehow, seem *exposed,* so that it is at once incredible and terribly clear that their legs are all they have to hold them up.

I had not wanted to go to the casket myself and I certainly had not wished to be led there, but there was no way of avoiding either of these forms. One of the deacons led me up and I looked on my father's face. I cannot say that it looked like him at all. His blackness had been equivocated by powder and there was no suggestion in that casket of what his power had or could have been. He was simply an old man dead, and it was hard to believe that he had ever given anyone either joy or pain. Yet, his life filled that room. Further up the avenue his wife was holding his newborn child. Life and death so close together, and love and hatred, and right and wrong, said something to me which I did not want to hear concerning man, concerning the life of man.

After the funeral, while I was downtown desperately celebrating my birthday, a Negro soldier, in the lobby of the Hotel Braddock, got into a fight with a white policeman over a Negro girl. Negro girls, white policemen, in or out of uniform, and Negro males—in or out of uniform—were part of the furniture of the lobby of the Hotel Braddock and this was certainly not the first time such an incident had occurred. It was destined, however, to receive an unprecedented publicity, for the fight between the policeman and the soldier ended with the shooting of the soldier. Rumor, flowing immediately to the streets outside, stated that the soldier had been shot in the back, an instantaneous and revealing invention, and that the soldier had died protecting a Negro woman. The facts were somewhat different—for example, the soldier had not been shot in the back, and was not dead, and the girl seems to have been as dubious a symbol of womanhood as her white counterpart in Georgia usually is, but no one was interested in the facts. They preferred the invention because this invention expressed and corroborated their hates and fears so perfectly. It is just as well to remember that people are always doing this. Perhaps many of those legends, including Christianity, to which the world clings began their conquest of the world with just some such concerted surrender to distortion. The effect, in Harlem, of this particular legend was like the effect of a lit match in a tin of gasoline. The mob gathered before the doors of the Hotel

Braddock simply began to swell and to spread in every direction, and Harlem exploded.

The mob did not cross the ghetto lines. It would have been easy, for example, to have gone over Morningside Park on the west side or to have crossed the Grand Central railroad tracks at 125th Street on the east side, to wreak havoc in white neighborhoods. The mob seems to have been mainly interested in something more potent and real than the white face, that is, in white power, and the principal damage done during the riot of the summer of 1943 was to white business establishments in Harlem. It might have been a far bloodier story, of course, if, at the hour the riot began, these establishments had still been open. From the Hotel Braddock the mob fanned out, east and west along 125th Street, and for the entire length of Lenox, Seventh, and Eighth avenues. Along each of these avenues, and along each major side street—116th, 125th, 135th, and so on—bars, stores, pawnshops, restaurants, even little luncheonettes had been smashed open and entered and looted—looted, it might be added, with more haste than efficiency. The shelves really looked as though a bomb had struck them. Cans of beans and soup and dog food, along with toilet paper, corn flakes, sardines and milk tumbled every which way, and abandoned cash registers and cases of beer leaned crazily out of the splintered windows and were strewn along the avenues. Sheets, blankets, and clothing of every description formed a kind of path, as though people had dropped them while running. I truly had not realized that Harlem *had* so many stores until I saw them all smashed open; the first time the word *wealth* ever entered my mind in relation to Harlem was when I saw it scattered in the streets. But one's first, incongruous impression of plenty was countered immediately by an impression of waste. None of this was doing anybody any good. It would have been better to have left the plate glass as it had been and the goods lying in the stores.

It would have been better, but it would also have been intolerable, for Harlem had needed something to smash. To smash something is the ghetto's chronic need. Most of the time it is the members of the ghetto who smash each other, and themselves. But as long as the ghetto walls are standing there will always come a moment when these outlets do not work. That summer, for example, it was not enough to get into a fight on Lenox Avenue, or curse out one's cronies in the barber shops. If ever, indeed, the violence which fills Harlem's churches, pool halls, and bars erupts outward in a more direct fashion, Harlem and its citizens are likely to vanish in an apocalyptic flood. That this is not likely to happen is due to a great many reasons, most hidden and powerful among them the Negro's real relation to the white American. This relation prohibits, simply, anything as uncomplicated and satisfactory as pure hatred. In order really to hate white people, one has to blot so much out of the mind—and the heart—that this hatred itself becomes an exhausting and self-destructive pose. But this does not mean, on the other hand, that love comes easily: the white world is too powerful, too complacent, too ready with gratuitous humiliation, and, above all, too ignorant and too innocent for that. One is absolutely forced to make perpetual qualifications and one's own reactions are always canceling each other out. It is this, really, which has driven so many people mad, both white and black. One is always in the position of having to decide between amputation and gangrene. Amputation is swift but time may prove that the amputation was not necessary—or one may delay the amputation too long.

Gangrene is slow, but it is impossible to be sure that one is reading one's symptoms right. The idea of going through life as a cripple is more than one can bear, and equally unbearable is the risk of swelling up slowly, in agony, with poison. And the trouble, finally, is that the risks are real even if the choices do not exist.

"But as for me and my house," my father had said, "we will serve the Lord."[5] I wondered, as we drove him to his resting place, what this line had meant for him. I had heard him preach it many times. I had preached it once myself, proudly giving it an interpretation different from my father's. Now the whole thing came back to me, as though my father and I were on our way to Sunday school and I were memorizing the golden text: *And if it seem evil unto you to serve the Lord, choose you this day whom you will serve; whether the gods which your fathers served that were on the other side of the flood, or the gods of the Amorites, in whose land ye dwell: but as for me and my house, we will serve the Lord.* I suspected in these familiar lines a meaning which had never been there for me before. All of my father's texts and songs, which I had decided were meaningless, were arranged before me at his death like empty bottles, waiting to hold the meaning which life would give them for me. This was his legacy: nothing is ever escaped. That bleakly memorable morning I hated the unbelievable streets and the Negroes and whites who had, equally, made them that way. But I knew that it was folly, as my father would have said, this bitterness was folly. It was necessary to hold on to the things that mattered. The dead man mattered, the new life mattered; blackness and whiteness did not matter; to believe that they did was to acquiesce in one's own destruction. Hatred, which could destroy so much, never failed to destroy the man who hated and this was an immutable law.

It began to seem that one would have to hold in the mind forever two ideas which seemed to be in opposition. The first idea was acceptance, the acceptance, totally without rancor, of life as it is, and men as they are: in the light of this idea, it goes without saying that injustice is a commonplace. But this did not mean that one could be complacent, for the second idea was of equal power: that one must never, in one's own life, accept these injustices as commonplace but must fight them with all one's strength. This fight begins, however, in the heart and it now had been laid to my charge to keep my own heart free of hatred and despair. This intimation made my heart heavy and, now that my father was irrecoverable, I wished that he had been beside me so that I could have searched his face for the answers which only the future would give me now.

1955

Sonny's Blues

I read about it in the paper, in the subway, on my way to work. I read it, and I couldn't believe it, and I read it again. Then perhaps I just stared at it, at the newsprint spelling out his name, spelling out the story. I stared at it in the swinging lights of the subway car, and in the faces and bodies of the people, and in my own face, trapped in the darkness which roared outside.

5. Joshua 24.15.

It was not to be believed and I kept telling myself that, as I walked from the subway station to the high school. And at the same time I couldn't doubt it. I was scared, scared for Sonny. He became real to me again. A great block of ice got settled in my belly and kept melting there slowly all day long, while I taught my classes algebra. It was a special kind of ice. It kept melting, sending trickles of ice water all up and down my veins, but it never got less. Sometimes it hardened and seemed to expand until I felt my guts were going to come spilling out or that I was going to choke or scream. This would always be at a moment when I was remembering some specific thing Sonny had once said or done.

When he was about as old as the boys in my classes his face had been bright and open, there was a lot of copper in it; and he'd had wonderfully direct brown eyes, and great gentleness and privacy. I wondered what he looked like now. He had been picked up, the evening before, in a raid on an apartment downtown, for peddling and using heroin.

I couldn't believe it: but what I mean by that is that I couldn't find any room for it anywhere inside me. I had kept it outside me for a long time. I hadn't wanted to know. I had had suspicions, but I didn't name them, I kept putting them away. I told myself that Sonny was wild, but he wasn't crazy. And he'd always been a good boy, he hadn't ever turned hard or evil or disrespectful, the way kids can, so quick, so quick, especially in Harlem. I didn't want to believe that I'd ever see my brother going down, coming to nothing, all that light in his face gone out, in the condition I'd already seen so many others. Yet it had happened and here I was, talking about algebra to a lot of boys who might, every one of them for all I knew, be popping off needles every time they went to the head.[1] Maybe it did more for them than algebra could.

I was sure that the first time Sonny had ever had horse,[2] he couldn't have been much older than these boys were now. These boys, now, were living as we'd been living then, they were growing up with a rush and their heads bumped abruptly against the low ceiling of their actual possibilities. They were filled with rage. All they really knew were two darknesses, the darkness of their lives, which was now closing in on them, and the darkness of the movies, which had blinded them to that other darkness, and in which they now, vindictively, dreamed, at once more together than they were at any other time, and more alone.

When the last bell rang, the last class ended, I let out my breath. It seemed I'd been holding it for all that time. My clothes were wet—I may have looked as though I'd been sitting in a steam bath, all dressed up, all afternoon. I sat alone in the classroom a long time. I listened to the boys outside, downstairs, shouting and cursing and laughing. Their laughter struck me for perhaps the first time. It was not the joyous laughter which—God knows why—one associates with children. It was mocking and insular, its intent was to denigrate. It was disenchanted, and in this, also, lay the authority of their curses. Perhaps I was listening to them because I was thinking about my brother and in them I heard my brother. And myself.

One boy was whistling a tune, at once very complicated and very simple, it seemed to be pouring out of him as though he were a bird, and it sounded very cool and moving through all that harsh, bright air, only just holding its own through all those other sounds.

---

1. Bathroom.　　　　2. Heroin.

I stood up and walked over to the window and looked down into the court-yard. It was the beginning of the spring and the sap was rising in the boys. A teacher passed through them every now and again, quickly, as though he or she couldn't wait to get out of that courtyard, to get those boys out of their sight and off their minds. I started collecting my stuff. I thought I'd better get home and talk to Isabel.

The courtyard was almost deserted by the time I got downstairs. I saw this boy standing in the shadow of a doorway, looking just like Sonny. I almost called his name. Then I saw that it wasn't Sonny, but somebody we used to know, a boy from around our block. He'd been Sonny's friend. He'd never been mine, having been too young for me, and, anyway, I'd never liked him. And now, even though he was a grown-up man, he still hung around that block, still spent hours on the street corners, was always high and raggy. I used to run into him from time to time and he'd often work around to ask-ing me for a quarter or fifty cents. He always had some real good excuse, too, and I always gave it to him, I don't know why.

But now, abruptly, I hated him. I couldn't stand the way he looked at me, partly like a dog, partly like a cunning child. I wanted to ask him what the hell he was doing in the school courtyard.

He sort of shuffled over to me, and he said, "I see you got the papers. So you already know about it."

"You mean about Sonny? Yes, I already know about it. How come they didn't get you?"

He grinned. It made him repulsive and it also brought to mind what he'd looked like as a kid. "I wasn't there. I stay away from them people."

"Good for you." I offered him a cigarette and I watched him through the smoke. "You come all the way down here just to tell me about Sonny?"

"That's right." He was sort of shaking his head and his eyes looked strange, as though they were about to cross. The bright sun deadened his damp dark brown skin and it made his eyes look yellow and showed up the dirt in his kinked hair. He smelled funky. I moved a little away from him and I said, "Well, thanks. But I already know about it and I got to get home."

"I'll walk you a little ways," he said. We started walking. There were a couple of kids still loitering in the courtyard and one of them said good-night to me and looked strangely at the boy beside me.

"What're you going to do?" he asked me. "I mean, about Sonny?"

"Look. I haven't seen Sonny for over a year, I'm not sure I'm going to do anything. Anyway, what the hell *can* I do?"

"That's right," he said quickly, "ain't nothing you can do. Can't much help old Sonny no more, I guess."

It was what I was thinking and so it seemed to me he had no right to say it.

"I'm surprised at Sonny, though," he went on—he had a funny way of talking, he looked straight ahead as though he were talking to himself—"I thought Sonny was a smart boy, I thought he was too smart to get hung."

"I guess he thought so too," I said sharply, "and that's how he got hung. And now about you? You're pretty goddamn smart, I bet."

Then he looked directly at me, just for a minute. "I ain't smart," he said. "If I was smart, I'd have reached for a pistol a long time ago."

"Look. Don't tell *me* your sad story, if it was up to me, I'd give you one." Then I felt guilty—guilty, probably, for never having supposed that the poor bastard *had* a story of his own, much less a sad one, and I asked, quickly, "What's going to happen to him now?"

He didn't answer this. He was off by himself some place. "Funny thing," he said, and from his tone we might have been discussing the quickest way to get to Brooklyn, "when I saw the papers this morning, the first thing I asked myself was if I had anything to do with it. I felt sort of responsible."

I began to listen more carefully. The subway station was on the corner, just before us, and I stopped. He stopped, too. We were in front of a bar and he ducked slightly, peering in, but whoever he was looking for didn't seem to be there. The juke box was blasting away with something black and bouncy and I half watched the barmaid as she danced her way from the juke box to her place behind the bar. And I watched her face as she laughingly responded to something someone said to her, still keeping time to the music. When she smiled one saw the little girl, one sensed the doomed, still-struggling woman beneath the battered face of the semi-whore.

"I never *give* Sonny nothing," the boy said finally, "but a long time ago I come to school high and Sonny asked me how it felt." He paused, I couldn't bear to watch him, I watched the barmaid, and I listened to the music which seemed to be causing the pavement to shake. "I told him it felt great." The music stopped, the barmaid paused and watched the juke box until the music began again. "It did."

All this was carrying me some place I didn't want to go. I certainly didn't want to know how it felt. It filled everything, the people, the houses, the music, the dark, quicksilver barmaid, with menace; and this menace was their reality.

"What's going to happen to him now?" I asked again.

"They'll send him away some place and they'll try to cure him." He shook his head. "Maybe he'll even think he's kicked the habit. Then they'll let him loose"—he gestured, throwing his cigarette into the gutter. "That's all."

"What do you mean, that's *all?*"

But I knew what he meant.

"I *mean,* that's *all.*" He turned his head and looked at me, pulling down the corners of his mouth. "Don't you know what I mean?" he asked, softly.

"How the hell *would* I know what you mean?" I almost whispered it, I don't know why.

"That's right," he said to the air, "how would *he* know what I mean?" He turned toward me again, patient and calm, and yet I somehow felt him shaking, shaking as though he were going to fall apart. I felt that ice in my guts again, the dread I'd felt all afternoon; and again I watched the barmaid, moving about the bar, washing glasses, and singing. "Listen. They'll let him out and then it'll just start all over again. That's what I mean."

"You mean—they'll let him out. And then he'll just start working his way back in again. You mean he'll never kick the habit. Is that what you mean?"

"That's right," he said, cheerfully. "*You* see what I mean."

"Tell me," I said it last, "why does he want to die? He must want to die, he's killing himself, why does he want to die?"

He looked at me in surprise. He licked his lips. "He don't want to die. He wants to live. Don't nobody want to die, ever."

Then I wanted to ask him—too many things. He could not have answered, or if he had, I could not have borne the answers. I started walking. "Well, I guess it's none of my business."

"It's going to be rough on old Sonny," he said. We reached the subway station. "This is your station?" he asked. I nodded. I took one step down. "Damn!" he said, suddenly. I looked up at him. He grinned again. "Damn it if I didn't leave all my money home. You ain't got a dollar on you, have you? Just for a couple of days, is all."

All at once something inside gave and threatened to come pouring out of me. I didn't hate him any more. I felt that in another moment I'd start crying like a child.

"Sure," I said. "Don't sweat." I looked in my wallet and didn't have a dollar, I only had a five. "Here," I said. "That hold you?"

He didn't look at it—he didn't want to look at it. A terrible, closed look came over his face, as though he were keeping the number on the bill a secret from him and me. "Thanks," he said, and now he was dying to see me go. "Don't worry about Sonny. Maybe I'll write him or something."

"Sure," I said. "You do that. So long."

"Be seeing you," he said. I went on down the steps.

And I didn't write Sonny or send him anything for a long time. When I finally did, it was just after my little girl died, he wrote me back a letter which made me feel like a bastard.

Here's what he said:

Dear brother,

You don't know how much I needed to hear from you. I wanted to write you many a time but I dug how much I must have hurt you and so I didn't write. But now I feel like a man who's been trying to climb up out of some deep, real deep and funky hole and just saw the sun up there, outside. I got to get outside.

I can't tell you much about how I got here. I mean I don't know how to tell you. I guess I was afraid of something or I was trying to escape from something and you know I have never been very strong in the head (smile) I'm glad Mama and Daddy are dead and can't see what's happened to their son and I swear if I'd known what I was doing I would never have hurt you so, you and a lot of other fine people who were nice to me and who believed in me.

I don't want you to think it had anything to do with me being a musician. It's more than that. Or maybe less than that. I can't get anything straight in my head down here and I try not to think about what's going to happen to me when I get outside again. Sometime I think I'm going to flip and *never* get outside and sometime I think I'll come straight back. I tell you one thing, though, I'd rather blow my brains out than go through this again. But that's what they all say, so they tell me. If I tell you when I'm coming to New York and if you could meet me, I sure would appreciate it. Give my love to Isabel and the kids and I was sure sorry to hear about little Gracie. I wish I could be like Mama and say the Lord's will be done, but I don't know it seems to me that trouble is the one thing that never does get stopped and I don't know what good it does to blame it on the Lord. But maybe it does some good if you believe it.

Your brother,
Sonny

Then I kept in constant touch with him and I sent him whatever I could and I went to meet him when he came back to New York. When I saw him many things I thought I had forgotten came flooding back to me. This was because I had begun, finally, to wonder about Sonny, about the life that Sonny lived inside. This life, whatever it was, had made him older and thinner and it had deepened the distant stillness in which he had always moved. He looked very unlike my baby brother. Yet, when he smiled, when we shook hands, the baby brother I'd never known looked out from the depths of his private life, like an animal waiting to be coaxed into the light.

"How you been keeping?" he asked me.

"All right. And you?"

"Just fine." He was smiling all over his face. "It's good to see you again."

"It's good to see you."

The seven years' difference in our ages lay between us like a chasm: I wondered if these years would ever operate between us as a bridge. I was remembering, and it made it hard to catch my breath, that I had been there when he was born; and I had heard the first words he had ever spoken. When he started to walk, he walked from our mother straight to me. I caught him just before he fell when he took the first steps he ever took in this world.

"How's Isabel?"

"Just fine. She's dying to see you."

"And the boys?"

"They're fine, too. They're anxious to see their uncle."

"Oh, come on. You know they don't remember me."

"Are you kidding? Of course they remember you."

He grinned again. We got into a taxi. We had a lot to say to each other, far too much to know how to begin.

As the taxi began to move, I asked, "You still want to go to India?"

He laughed. "You still remember that. Hell, no. This place is Indian enough for me."

"It used to belong to them," I said.

And he laughed again. "They damn sure knew what they were doing when they got rid of it."

Years ago, when he was around fourteen, he'd been all hipped on the idea of going to India. He read books about people sitting on rocks, naked, in all kinds of weather, but mostly bad, naturally, and walking barefoot through hot coals and arriving at wisdom. I used to say that it sounded to me as though they were getting away from wisdom as fast as they could. I think he sort of looked down on me for that.

"Do you mind," he asked, "if we have the driver drive alongside the park? On the west side—I haven't seen the city in so long."

"Of course not," I said. I was afraid that I might sound as though I were humoring him, but I hoped he wouldn't take it that way.

So we drove along, between the green of the park and the stony, lifeless elegance of hotels and apartment buildings, toward the vivid, killing streets of our childhood. These streets hadn't changed, though housing projects jutted up out of them now like rocks in the middle of a boiling sea. Most of the houses in which we had grown up had vanished, as had the stores from which we had stolen, the basements in which we had first tried sex, the rooftops from which we had hurled tin cans and bricks. But houses exactly like the houses of our past yet dominated the landscape, boys exactly like the boys we once had been found themselves smothering in these houses, came down into the streets for light and air and found themselves encircled by disaster. Some escaped the trap, most didn't. Those who got out always left something of themselves behind, as some animals amputate a leg and leave it in the trap. It might be said, perhaps, that I had escaped, after all, I was a school teacher; or that Sonny had, he hadn't lived in Harlem for years. Yet, as the cab moved uptown through streets which seemed, with a rush, to darken with dark people, and as I covertly studied Sonny's face, it came to me that what we both were seeking through our separate cab windows was that part of ourselves which had been left behind. It's always at the hour of trouble and confrontation that the missing member aches.

We hit 110th Street and started rolling up Lenox Avenue. And I'd known this avenue all my life, but it seemed to me again, as it had seemed on the day I'd first heard about Sonny's trouble, filled with a hidden menace which was its very breath of life.

"We almost there," said Sonny.

"Almost." We were both too nervous to say anything more.

We live in a housing project. It hasn't been up long. A few days after it was up it seemed uninhabitably new, now, of course, it's already rundown. It looks like a parody of the good, clean, faceless life—God knows the people who live in it do their best to make it a parody. The beat-looking grass lying around isn't enough to make their lives green, the hedges will never hold out the streets, and they know it. The big windows fool no one, they aren't big enough to make space out of no space. They don't bother with the windows, they watch the TV screen instead. The playground is most popular with the children who don't play at jacks, or skip rope, or roller skate, or swing, and they can be found in it after dark. We moved in partly because it's not too far from where I teach, and partly for the kids; but it's really just like the houses in which Sonny and I grew up. The same things happen, they'll have the same things to remember. The moment Sonny and I started into the house I had the feeling that I was simply bringing him back into the danger he had almost died trying to escape.

Sonny has never been talkative. So I don't know why I was sure he'd be dying to talk to me when supper was over the first night. Everything went fine, the oldest boy remembered him, and the youngest boy liked him, and Sonny had remembered to bring something for each of them; and Isabel, who is really much nicer than I am, more open and giving, had gone to a lot of trouble about dinner and was genuinely glad to see him. And she's always been able to tease Sonny in a way that I haven't. It was nice to see her face so vivid again and to hear her laugh and watch her make Sonny laugh. She wasn't, or, anyway, she didn't seem to be, at all uneasy or embarrassed. She chatted as though there were no subject which had to be avoided and she got Sonny past his first, faint stiffness. And thank God she was there, for I was filled with that icy dread again. Everything I did seemed awkward to me, and everything I said sounded freighted with hidden meaning. I was trying to remember everything I'd heard about dope addiction and I couldn't help watching Sonny for signs. I wasn't doing it out of malice. I was trying to find out something about my brother. I was dying to hear him tell me he was safe.

"Safe!" my father grunted, whenever Mama suggested trying to move to a neighborhood which might be safer for children. "Safe, hell! Ain't no place safe for kids, nor nobody."

He always went on like this, but he wasn't, ever, really as bad as he sounded, not even on weekends, when he got drunk. As a matter of fact, he was always on the lookout for "something a little better," but he died before he found it. He died suddenly, during a drunken weekend in the middle of the war, when Sonny was fifteen. He and Sonny hadn't ever got on too well. And this was partly because Sonny was the apple of his father's eye. It was because he loved Sonny so much and was frightened for him, that he was always fighting with him. It doesn't do any good to fight with Sonny. Sonny just moves back, inside himself, where he can't be reached. But the principal reason that they never hit it off is that they were so much alike. Daddy was big and rough and loud-talking, just the opposite of Sonny, but they both had—that same privacy.

Mama tried to tell me something about this, just after Daddy died. I was home on leave from the army.

This was the last time I ever saw my mother alive. Just the same, this picture gets all mixed up in my mind with pictures I had of her when she was younger. The way I always see her is the way she used to be on a Sunday afternoon, say, when the old folks were talking after the big Sunday dinner. I always see her wearing pale blue. She'd be sitting on the sofa. And my father would be sitting in the easy chair, not far from her. And the living room would be full of church folks and relatives. There they sit, in chairs all around the living room, and the night is creeping up outside, but nobody knows it yet. You can see the darkness growing against the windowpanes and you hear the street noises every now and again, or maybe the jangling beat of a tambourine from one of the churches close by, but it's real quiet in the room. For a moment nobody's talking, but every face looks darkening, like the sky outside. And my mother rocks a little from the waist, and my father's eyes are closed. Everyone is looking at something a child can't see. For a minute they've forgotten the children. Maybe a kid is lying on the rug, half asleep. Maybe somebody's got a kid in his lap and is absentmindedly stroking the kid's head. Maybe there's a kid, quiet and big-eyed, curled up in a big chair in the corner. The silence, the darkness coming, and the darkness in the faces frightens the child obscurely. He hopes that the hand which strokes his forehead will never stop—will never die. He hopes that there will never come a time when the old folks won't be sitting around the living room, talking about where they've come from, and what they've seen, and what's happened to them and their kinfolk.

But something deep and watchful in the child knows that this is bound to end, is already ending. In a moment someone will get up and turn on the light. Then the old folks will remember the children and they won't talk any more that day. And when light fills the room, the child is filled with darkness. He knows that every time this happens he's moved just a little closer to that darkness outside. The darkness outside is what the old folks have been talking about. It's what they've come from. It's what they endure. The child knows that they won't talk any more because if he knows too much about what's happened to *them*, he'll know too much too soon, about what's going to happen to *him*.

The last time I talked to my mother, I remember I was restless. I wanted to get out and see Isabel. We weren't married then and we had a lot to straighten out between us.

There Mama sat, in black, by the window. She was humming an old church song, *Lord, you brought me from a long ways off.* Sonny was out somewhere. Mama kept watching the streets.

"I don't know," she said, "if I'll ever see you again, after you go off from here. But I hope you'll remember the things I tried to teach you."

"Don't talk like that," I said, and smiled. "You'll be here a long time yet."

She smiled, too, but she said nothing. She was quiet for a long time. And I said, "Mama, don't you worry about nothing. I'll be writing all the time, and you be getting the checks. . . ."

"I want to talk to you about your brother," she said, suddenly. "If anything happens to me he ain't going to have nobody to look out for him."

"Mama," I said, "ain't nothing going to happen to you *or* Sonny. Sonny's all right. He's a good boy and he's got good sense."

"It ain't a question of his being a good boy," Mama said, "nor of his having good sense. It ain't only the bad ones, nor yet the dumb ones that gets sucked under." She stopped, looking at me. "Your Daddy once had a brother," she said, and she smiled in a way that made me feel she was in pain. "You didn't never know that, did you?"

"No," I said, "I never knew that," and I watched her face.

"Oh, yes," she said, "your Daddy had a brother." She looked out of the window again. "I know you never saw your Daddy cry. But *I* did—many a time, through all these years."

I asked her, "What happened to his brother? How come nobody's ever talked about him?"

This was the first time I ever saw my mother look old.

"His brother got killed," she said, "when he was just a little younger than you are now. I knew him. He was a fine boy. He was maybe a little full of the devil, but he didn't mean nobody no harm."

Then she stopped and the room was silent, exactly as it had sometimes been on those Sunday afternoons. Mama kept looking out into the streets.

"He used to have a job in the mill," she said, "and, like all young folks, he just liked to perform on Saturday nights. Saturday nights, him and your father would drift around to different place, go to dances and things like that, or just sit around with people they knew, and your father's brother would sing, he had a fine voice, and play along with himself on his guitar. Well, this particular Saturday night, him and your father was coming home from some place, and they were both a little drunk and there was a moon that night, it was bright like day. Your father's brother was feeling kind of good, and he was whistling to himself, and he had his guitar slung over his shoulder. They was coming down a hill and beneath them was a road that turned off from the highway. Well, your father's brother, being always kind of frisky, decided to run down this hill, and he did, with that guitar banging and clanging behind him, and he ran across the road, and he was making water behind a tree. And your father was sort of amused at him and he was still coming down the hill, kind of slow. Then he heard a car motor and that same minute his brother stepped from behind the tree, into the road, in the moonlight. And he started to cross the road. And your father started to run down the hill, he says he don't know why. This car was full of white men. They was all drunk, and when they seen your father's brother they let out a great whoop and holler and they aimed the car straight at him. They was having fun, they just wanted to scare him, the way they do sometimes, you know. But they was drunk. And I guess the boy, being drunk, too, and scared, kind of lost his head. By the time he jumped it was too late. Your father says he heard his brother scream when the car rolled over him, and he heard the wood of that guitar when it give, and he heard them strings go flying, and he heard them white men shouting, and the car kept on a-going and it ain't stopped till this day. And, time your father got down the hill, his brother weren't nothing but blood and pulp."

Tears were gleaming on my mother's face. There wasn't anything I could say.

"He never mentioned it," she said, "because I never let him mention it before you children. Your Daddy was like a crazy man that night and for many a night thereafter. He says he never in his life seen anything as dark as that road after the lights of that car had gone away. Weren't nothing, weren't nobody on that road, just your Daddy and his brother and that busted guitar. Oh, yes. Your Daddy never did really get right again. Till the day he died he weren't sure but that every white man he saw was the man that killed his brother."

She stopped and took out her handkerchief and dried her eyes and looked at me.

"I ain't telling you all this," she said, "to make you scared or bitter or to make you hate nobody. I'm telling you this because you got a brother. And the world ain't changed."

I guess I didn't want to believe this. I guess she saw this in my face. She turned away from me, toward the window again, searching those streets.

"But I praise my Redeemer," she said at last, "that He called your Daddy home before me. I ain't saying it to throw no flowers at myself, but, I declare, it keeps me from feeling too cast down to know I helped your father get safely through this world. Your father always acted like he was the roughest, strongest man on earth. And everybody took him to be like that. But if he hadn't had *me* there—to see his tears!"

She was crying again. Still, I couldn't move. I said, "Lord, Lord, Mama, I didn't know it was like that."

"Oh, honey," she said, "there's a lot that you don't know. But you are going to find it out." She stood up from the window and came over to me. "You got to hold on to your brother," she said, "and don't let him fall, no matter what it looks like is happening to him and no matter how evil you gets with him. You going to be evil with him many a time. But don't you forget what I told you, you hear?"

"I won't forget," I said. "Don't you worry, I won't forget. I won't let nothing happen to Sonny."

My mother smiled as though she were amused at something she saw in my face. Then, "You may not be able to stop nothing from happening. But you got to let him know you's *there*."

Two days later I was married, and then I was gone. And I had a lot of things on my mind and I pretty well forgot my promise to Mama until I got shipped home on a special furlough for her funeral.

And, after the funeral, with just Sonny and me alone in the empty kitchen, I tried to find out something about him.

"What do you want to do?" I asked him.

"I'm going to be a musician," he said.

For he had graduated, in the time I had been away, from dancing to the juke box to finding out who was playing what, and what they were doing with it, and he had bought himself a set of drums.

"You mean, you want to be a drummer?" I somehow had the feeling that being a drummer might be all right for other people but not for my brother Sonny.

"I don't think," he said, looking at me very gravely, "that I'll ever be a good drummer. But I think I can play a piano."

I frowned. I'd never played the role of the older brother quite so seriously before, had scarcely ever, in fact, *asked* Sonny a damn thing. I sensed myself in the presence of something I didn't really know how to handle, didn't understand. So I made my frown a little deeper as I asked: "What kind of musician do you want to be?"

He grinned. "How many kinds do you think there are?"

"Be *serious*," I said.

He laughed, throwing his head back, and then looked at me. "I *am* serious."

"Well, then, for Christ's sake, stop kidding around and answer a serious question. I mean, do you want to be a concert pianist, you want to play classical music and all that, or—or what?" Long before I finished he was laughing again. "For Christ's *sake*, Sonny!"

He sobered, but with difficulty. "I'm sorry. But you sound so—*scared!*" and he was off again.

"Well, you may think it's funny now, baby, but it's not going to be so funny when you have to make your living at it, let me tell you *that.*" I was furious because I knew he was laughing at me and I didn't know why.

"No," he said, very sober now, and afraid, perhaps, that he'd hurt me, "I don't want to be a classical pianist. That isn't what interests me. I mean"—he paused, looking hard at me, as though his eyes would help me to understand, and then gestured helplessly, as though perhaps his hand would help—"I mean, I'll have a lot of studying to do, and I'll have to study *every-thing*, but, I mean, I want to play *with*—jazz musicians." He stopped. "I want to play jazz," he said.

Well, the word had never before sounded as heavy, as real, as it sounded that afternoon in Sonny's mouth. I just looked at him and I was probably frowning a real frown by this time. I simply couldn't see why on earth he'd want to spend his time hanging around nightclubs, clowning around on bandstands, while people pushed each other around a dance floor. It seemed—beneath him, somehow. I had never thought about it before, had never been forced to, but I suppose I had always put jazz musicians in a class with what Daddy called "good-time people."

"Are you *serious*?"

"Hell, *yes*, I'm serious."

He looked more helpless than ever, and annoyed, and deeply hurt.

I suggested, helpfully: "You mean—like Louis Armstrong?"[3]

His face closed as though I'd struck him. "No. I'm not talking about none of that old-time, down home crap."

---

3. Jazz musician and singer (1900–1971).

"Well, look, Sonny, I'm sorry, don't get mad. I just don't altogether get it, that's all. Name somebody—you know, a jazz musician you admire."

"Bird."

"Who?"

"Bird! Charlie Parker!⁴ Don't they teach you nothing in the goddamn army?"

I lit a cigarette. I was surprised and then a little amused to discover that I was trembling. "I've been out of touch," I said. "You'll have to be patient with me. Now. Who's this Parker character?"

"He's just one of the greatest jazz musicians alive," said Sonny, sullenly, his hands in his pockets, his back to me. "Maybe *the* greatest," he added, bitterly, "that's probably why *you* never heard of him."

"All right," I said, "I'm ignorant. I'm sorry. I'll go out and buy all the cat's records right away, all right?"

"It don't," said Sonny, with dignity, "make any difference to me. I don't care what you listen to. Don't do me no favors."

I was beginning to realize that I'd never seen him so upset before. With another part of my mind I was thinking that this would probably turn out to be one of those things kids go through and that I shouldn't make it seem important by pushing it too hard. Still, I didn't think it would do any harm to ask: "Doesn't all this take a lot of time? Can you make a living at it?"

He turned back to me and half leaned, half sat, on the kitchen table. "Everything takes time," he said, "and—well, yes, sure, I can make a living at it. But what I don't seem to be able to make you understand is that it's the only thing I want to do."

"Well, Sonny," I said, gently, "you know people can't always do exactly what they *want* to do—"

"*No,* I don't know that," said Sonny, surprising me. "I think people *ought* to do what they want to do, what else are they alive for?"

"You getting to be a big boy," I said desperately, "it's time you started thinking about your future."

"I'm thinking about my future," said Sonny, grimly. "I think about it all the time."

I gave up. I decided, if he didn't change his mind, that we could always talk about it later. "In the meantime," I said, "you got to finish school." We had already decided that he'd have to move in with Isabel and her folks. I knew this wasn't the ideal arrangement because Isabel's folks are inclined to be dicty⁵ and they hadn't especially wanted Isabel to marry me. But I didn't know what else to do. "And we have to get you fixed up at Isabel's."

There was a long silence. He moved from the kitchen table to the window. "That's a terrible idea. You know it yourself."

"Do you have a *better* idea?"

He just walked up and down the kitchen for a minute. He was as tall as I was. He had started to shave. I suddenly had the feeling that I didn't know him at all.

He stopped at the kitchen table and picked up my cigarettes. Looking at me with a kind of mocking, amused defiance, he put one between his lips. "You mind?"

"You smoking already?"

He lit the cigarette and nodded, watching me through the smoke. "I just wanted to see if I'd have the courage to smoke in front of you." He grinned and blew a great cloud of smoke to the ceiling. "It was easy." He looked at my face. "Come on, now. I bet you was smoking at my age, tell the truth."

I didn't say anything but the truth was on my face, and he laughed. But now there was something very strained in his laugh. "Sure. And I bet that ain't all you was doing."

He was frightening me a little. "Cut the crap," I said. "We already decided that you was going to go and live at Isabel's. Now what's got into you all of a sudden?"

"*You* decided it," he pointed out. "*I* didn't decide nothing." He stopped in front of me, leaning against the stove, arms loosely folded. "Look, brother. I don't want to stay in Harlem no more, I really don't." He was very earnest. He looked at me, then over toward the kitchen window. There was something in his eyes I'd never seen before, some thoughtfulness, some worry all his own. He rubbed the muscle of one arm. "It's time I was getting out of here."

"Where do you want to *go*, Sonny?"

"I want to join the army. Or the navy, I don't care. If I say I'm old enough, they'll believe me."

Then I got mad. It was because I was so scared. "You must be crazy. You goddamn fool, what the hell do you want to go and join the *army* for?"

"I just told you. To get out of Harlem."

"Sonny, you haven't even finished *school*. And if you really want to be a musician, how do you expect to study if you're in the *army*?"

He looked at me, trapped, and in anguish. "There's ways. I might be able to work out some kind of deal. Anyway, I'll have the G.I. Bill[6] when I come out."

"*If* you come out." We stared at each other. "Sonny, please. Be reasonable. I know the setup is far from perfect. But we got to do the best we can."

"I ain't learning nothing in school," he said. "Even when I go." He turned away from me and opened the window and threw his cigarette out into the narrow alley. I watched his back. "At least, I ain't learning nothing you'd want me to learn." He slammed the window so hard I thought the glass would fly out, and turned back to me. "And I'm sick of the stink of these garbage cans!"

"Sonny," I said, "I know how you feel. But if you don't finish school now, you're going to be sorry later that you didn't." I grabbed him by the shoulders. "And you only got another year. It ain't so bad. And I'll come back and I swear I'll help you do *whatever* you want to do. Just try to put up with it till I come back. Will you please do that? For me?"

He didn't answer and he wouldn't look at me.

"Sonny. You hear me?"

He pulled away. "I hear you. But you never hear anything *I* say."

I didn't know what to say to that. He looked out of the window and then back at me. "OK," he said, and sighed. "I'll try."

Then I said, trying to cheer him up a little, "They got a piano at Isabel's. You can practice on it."

---

6. Popular name for the Serviceman's Readjustment Act of 1944, which provided World War II veterans up to four years of educational and vocational training at government expense.

And as a matter of fact, it did cheer him up for a minute. "That's right," he said to himself. "I forgot that." His face relaxed a little. But the worry, the thoughtfulness, played on it still, the way shadows play on a face which is staring into the fire.

But I thought I'd never hear the end of that piano. At first, Isabel would write me, saying how nice it was that Sonny was so serious about his music and how, as soon as he came in from school, or wherever he had been when he was supposed to be at school, he went straight to that piano and stayed there until suppertime. And, after supper, he went back to that piano and stayed there until everybody went to bed. He was at the piano all day Saturday and all day Sunday. Then he bought a record player and started playing records. He'd play one record over and over again, all day long sometimes, and he'd improvise along with it on the piano. Or he'd play one section of the record, one chord, one change, one progression, then he'd do it on the piano. Then back to the record. Then back to the piano.

Well, I really don't know how they stood it. Isabel finally confessed that it wasn't like living with a person at all, it was like living with sound. And the sound didn't make any sense to her, didn't make any sense to any of them—naturally. They began, in a way, to be afflicted by this presence that was living in their home. It was as though Sonny were some sort of god, or monster. He moved in an atmosphere which wasn't like theirs at all. They fed him and he ate, he washed himself, he walked in and out of their door; he certainly wasn't nasty or unpleasant or rude, Sonny isn't any of those things; but it was as though he were all wrapped up in some cloud, some fire, some vision all his own; and there wasn't any way to reach him.

At the same time, he wasn't really a man yet, he was still a child, and they had to watch out for him in all kinds of ways. They certainly couldn't throw him out. Neither did they dare to make a great scene about that piano because even they dimly sensed, as I sensed, from so many thousands of miles away, that Sonny was at that piano playing for his life.

But he hadn't been going to school. One day a letter came from the school board and Isabel's mother got it—there had, apparently, been other letters but Sonny had torn them up. This day, when Sonny came in, Isabel's mother showed him the letter and asked where he'd been spending his time. And she finally got it out of him that he'd been down in Greenwich Village, with musicians and other characters, in a white girl's apartment. And this scared her and she started to scream at him and what came up, once she began—though she denies it to this day—was what sacrifices they were making to give Sonny a decent home and how little he appreciated it.

Sonny didn't play the piano that day. By evening, Isabel's mother had calmed down but then there was the old man to deal with, and Isabel herself. Isabel says she did her best to be calm but she broke down and started crying. She says she just watched Sonny's face. She could tell, by watching him, what was happening with him. And what was happening was that they penetrated his cloud, they had reached him. Even if their fingers had been a thousand times more gentle than human fingers ever are, he could hardly help feeling that they had stripped him naked and were spitting on that nakedness. For he also had to see that his presence, that music, which was life or death to him, had been torture for them and that they had endured it, not at all for his sake, but only for mine. And Sonny couldn't take that.

He can take it a little better today than he could then but he's still not very good at it and, frankly, I don't know anybody who is.

The silence of the next few days must have been louder than the sound of all the music ever played since time began. One morning, before she went to work, Isabel was in his room for something and she suddenly realized that all of his records were gone. And she knew for certain that he was gone. And he was. He went as far as the navy would carry him. He finally sent me a postcard from some place in Greece and that was the first I knew that Sonny was still alive. I didn't see him any more until we were both back in New York and the war had long been over.

He was a man by then, of course, but I wasn't willing to see it. He came by the house from time to time, but we fought almost every time we met. I didn't like the way he carried himself, loose and dreamlike all the time, and I didn't like his friends, and his music seemed to be merely an excuse for the life he led. It sounded just that weird and disordered.

Then we had a fight, a pretty awful fight, and I didn't see him for months. By and by I looked him up, where he was living, in a furnished room in the Village, and I tried to make it up. But there were lots of other people in the room and Sonny just lay on his bed, and he wouldn't come downstairs with me, and he treated these other people as though they were his family and I weren't. So I got mad and then he got mad, and then I told him that he might just as well be dead as live the way he was living. Then he stood up and he told me not to worry about him any more in life, that he *was* dead as far as I was concerned. Then he pushed me to the door and the other people looked on as though nothing were happening, and he slammed the door behind me. I stood in the hallway, staring at the door. I heard somebody laugh in the room and then the tears came to my eyes. I started down the steps, whistling to keep from crying, I kept whistling to myself, *You going to need me, baby, one of these cold, rainy days.*

I read about Sonny's trouble in the spring. Little Grace died in the fall. She was a beautiful little girl. But she only lived a little over two years. She died of polio and she suffered. She had a slight fever for a couple of days, but it didn't seem like anything and we just kept her in bed. And we would certainly have called the doctor, but the fever dropped, she seemed to be all right. So we thought it had just been a cold. Then, one day, she was up, playing, Isabel was in the kitchen fixing lunch for the two boys when they'd come in from school, and she heard Grace fall down in the living room. When you have a lot of children you don't always start running when one of them falls, unless they start screaming or something. And, this time, Grace was quiet. Yet, Isabel says that when she heard that *thump* and then that silence, something happened in her to make her afraid. And she ran to the living room and there was little Grace on the floor, all twisted up, and the reason she hadn't screamed was that she couldn't get her breath. And when she did scream, it was the worst sound, Isabel says, that she'd ever heard in all her life, and she still hears it sometimes in her dreams. Isabel will sometimes wake me up with a low, moaning, strangled sound and I have to be quick to awaken her and hold her to me and where Isabel is weeping against me seems a mortal wound.

I think I may have written Sonny the very day that little Grace was buried. I was sitting in the living room in the dark, by myself, and I suddenly thought of Sonny. My trouble made his real.

One Saturday afternoon, when Sonny had been living with us, or, anyway, been in our house, for nearly two weeks, I found myself wandering
aimlessly about the living room, drinking from a can of beer, and trying
to work up the courage to search Sonny's room. He was out, he was usually
out whenever I was home, and Isabel had taken the children to see their
grandparents. Suddenly I was standing still in front of the living room window, watching Seventh Avenue. The idea of searching Sonny's room made
me still. I scarcely dared to admit to myself what I'd be searching for. I
didn't know what I'd do if I found it. Or if I didn't.

On the sidewalk across from me, near the entrance to a barbecue joint,
some people were holding an old-fashioned revival meeting. The barbecue
cook, wearing a dirty white apron, his conked[7] hair reddish and metallic in
the pale sun, and a cigarette between his lips, stood in the doorway, watching them. Kids and older people paused in their errands and stood there,
along with some older men and a couple of very tough-looking women who
watched everything that happened on the avenue, as though they owned it,
or were maybe owned by it. Well, they were watching this, too. The revival
was being carried on by three sisters in black, and a brother. All they had
were their voices and their Bibles and a tambourine. The brother was testifying[8] and while he testified two of the sisters stood together, seeming
to say, amen, and the third sister walked around with the tambourine outstretched and a couple of people dropped coins into it. Then the brother's
testimony ended and the sister who had been taking up the collection
dumped the coins into her palm and transferred them to the pocket of her
long black robe. Then she raised both hands, striking the tambourine
against the air, and then against one hand, and she started to sing. And the
two other sisters and the brother joined in.

It was strange, suddenly, to watch, though I had been seeing these street
meetings all my life. So, of course, had everybody else down there. Yet, they
paused and watched and listened and I stood still at the window. *"Tis the old
ship of Zion,"* they sang, and the sister with the tambourine kept a steady,
jangling beat, *"it has rescued many a thousand!"* Not a soul under the sound
of their voices was hearing this song for the first time, not one of them had
been rescued. Nor had they seen much in the way of rescue work being
done around them. Neither did they especially believe in the holiness of the
three sisters and the brother, they knew too much about them, knew where
they lived, and how. The woman with the tambourine, whose voice dominated the air, whose face was bright with joy, was divided by very little from
the woman who stood watching her, a cigarette between her heavy, chapped
lips, her hair a cuckoo's nest, her face scarred and swollen from many beatings, and her black eyes glittering like coal. Perhaps they both knew this,
which was why, when, as rarely, they addressed each other, they addressed
each other as Sister. As the singing filled the air the watching, listening faces
underwent a change, the eyes focusing on something within; the music
seemed to soothe a poison out of them; and time seemed, nearly, to fall away
from the sullen, belligerent, battered faces, as though they were fleeing
back to their first condition, while dreaming of their last. The barbecue
cook half shook his head and smiled, and dropped his cigarette and disappeared into his joint. A man fumbled in his pockets for change and stood

---

7. Straightened and greased.   8. Publicly professing belief.

holding it in his hand impatiently, as though he had just remembered a pressing appointment further up the avenue. He looked furious. Then I saw Sonny, standing on the edge of the crowd. He was carrying a wide, flat notebook with a green cover, and it made him look, from where I was standing, almost like a schoolboy. The coppery sun brought out the copper in his skin, he was very faintly smiling, standing very still. Then the singing stopped, the tambourine turned into a collection plate again. The furious man dropped in his coins and vanished, so did a couple of the women, and Sonny dropped some change in the plate, looking directly at the woman with a little smile. He started across the avenue, toward the house. He has a slow, loping walk, something like the way Harlem hipsters walk, only he's imposed on this his own half-beat. I had never really noticed it before.

I stayed at the window, both relieved and apprehensive. As Sonny disappeared from my sight, they began singing again. And they were still singing when his key turned in the lock.

"Hey," he said.

"Hey, yourself. You want some beer?"

"No. Well, maybe." But he came up to the window and stood beside me, looking out. "What a warm voice," he said.

They were singing *If I could only hear my mother pray again!*

"Yes," I said, "and she can sure beat that tambourine."

"But what a terrible song," he said, and laughed. He dropped his notebook on the sofa and disappeared into the kitchen. "Where's Isabel and the kids?"

"I think they went to see their grandparents. You hungry?"

"No." He came back into the living room with his can of beer. "You want to come some place with me tonight?"

I sensed, I don't know how, that I couldn't possibly say no. "Sure. Where?"

He sat down on the sofa and picked up his notebook and started leafing through it. "I'm going to sit in with some fellows in a joint in the Village."

"You mean, you're going to play, tonight?"

"That's right." He took a swallow of his beer and moved back to the window. He gave me a sidelong look. "If you can stand it."

"I'll try," I said.

He smiled to himself and we both watched as the meeting across the way broke up. The three sisters and the brother, heads bowed, were singing *God be with you till we meet again.* The faces around them were very quiet. Then the song ended. The small crowd dispersed. We watched the three women and the lone man walk slowly up the avenue.

"When she was singing before," said Sonny, abruptly, "her voice reminded me for a minute of what heroin feels like sometimes—when it's in your veins. It makes you feel sort of warm and cool at the same time. And distant. And—and sure." He sipped his beer, very deliberately not looking at me. I watched his face. "It makes you feel—in control. Sometimes you've got to have that feeling."

"Do you?" I sat down slowly in the easy chair.

"Sometimes." He went to the sofa and picked up his notebook again. "Some people do."

"In order," I asked, "to play?" And my voice was very ugly, full of contempt and anger.

"Well"—he looked at me with great, troubled eyes, as though, in fact, he hoped his eyes would tell me things he could never otherwise say—"they *think* so. And *if* they think so—!"

"And what do *you* think?" I asked.

He sat on the sofa and put his can of beer on the floor. "I don't know," he said, and I couldn't be sure if he were answering my question or pursuing his thoughts. His face didn't tell me. "It's not so much to *play*. It's to *stand* it, to be able to make it at all. On any level." He frowned and smiled: "In order to keep from shaking to pieces."

"But these friends of yours," I said, "they seem to shake themselves to pieces pretty goddamn fast."

"Maybe." He played with the notebook. And something told me that I should curb my tongue, that Sonny was doing his best to talk, that I should listen. "But of course you only know the ones that've gone to pieces. Some don't—or at least they haven't *yet* and that's just about all *any* of us can say." He paused. "And then there are some who just live, really, in hell, and they know it and they see what's happening and they go right on. I don't know." He sighed, dropped the notebook, folded his arms. "Some guys, you can tell from the way they play, they on something *all* the time. And you can see that, well, it makes something real for them. But of course," he picked up his beer from the floor and sipped it and put the can down again, "they *want* to, too, you've got to see that. Even some of them that say they don't— *some*, not all."

"And what about you?" I asked—I couldn't help it. "What about you? Do *you* want to?"

He stood up and walked to the window and remained silent for a long time. Then he sighed. "Me," he said. Then: "While I was downstairs before, on my way here, listening to that woman sing, it struck me all of a sudden how much suffering she must have had to go through—to sing like that. It's *repulsive* to think you have to suffer that much."

I said: "But there's no way not to suffer—is there, Sonny?"

"I believe not," he said and smiled, "but that's never stopped anyone from trying." He looked at me. "Has it?" I realized, with this mocking look, that there stood between us, forever, beyond the power of time or forgiveness, the fact that I had held silence—so long!—when he had needed human speech to help him. He turned back to the window. "No, there's no way not to suffer. But you try all kinds of ways to keep from drowning in it, to keep on top of it, and to make it seem—well, like *you*. Like you did something, all right, and now you're suffering for it. You know?" I said nothing. "Well you know," he said, impatiently, "why *do* people suffer? Maybe it's better to do something to give it a reason, *any* reason."

"But we just agreed," I said, "that there's no way not to suffer. Isn't it better, then, just to—take it?"

"But nobody just takes it," Sonny cried, "that's what I'm telling you! *Everybody* tries not to. You're just hung up on the *way* some people try—it's not *your* way!"

The hair on my face began to itch, my face felt wet. "That's not true," I said, "that's not true. I don't give a damn what other people do, I don't even care how they suffer. I just care how *you* suffer." And he looked at me. "Please believe me," I said, "I don't want to see you—die—trying not to suffer."

"I won't," he said, flatly, "die trying not to suffer. At least, not any faster than anybody else."

"But there's no need," I said, trying to laugh, "is there? in killing yourself."

I wanted to say more, but I couldn't. I wanted to talk about will power and how life could be—well, beautiful. I wanted to say that it was all within; but was it? or, rather, wasn't that exactly the trouble? And I wanted to promise that I would never fail him again. But it would all have sounded— empty words and lies.

So I made the promise to myself and prayed that I would keep it.

"It's terrible sometimes, inside," he said, "that's what's the trouble. You walk these streets, black and funky and cold, and there's not really a living ass to talk to, and there's nothing shaking, and there's no way of getting it out—that storm inside. You can't talk it and you can't make love with it, and when you finally try to get with it and play it, you realize *nobody's* listening. So *you've* got to listen. You got to find a way to listen."

And then he walked away from the window and sat on the sofa again, as though all the wind had suddenly been knocked out of him. "Sometimes you'll do *anything* to play, even cut your mother's throat." He laughed and looked at me. "Or your brother's." Then he sobered. "Or your own." Then: "Don't worry. I'm all right now and I think I'll *be* all right. But I can't forget— where I've been. I don't mean just the physical place I've been, I mean where I've *been*. And *what* I've been."

"What have you been, Sonny?" I asked.

He smiled—but sat sideways on the sofa, his elbow resting on the back, his fingers playing with his mouth and chin, not looking at me. "I've been something I didn't recognize, didn't know I could be. Didn't know anybody could be." He stopped, looking inward, looking helplessly young, looking old. "I'm not talking about it now because I feel *guilty* or anything like that— maybe it would be better if I did, I don't know. Anyway, I can't really talk about it. Not to you, not to anybody," and now he turned and faced me. "Sometimes, you know, and it was actually when I was most *out* of the world, I felt that I was in it, that I was *with* it, really, and I could play or I didn't really have to *play*, it just came out of me, it was there. And I don't know how I played, thinking about it now, but I know I did awful things, those times, sometimes, to people. Or it wasn't that I *did* anything to them—it was that they weren't real." He picked up the beer can; it was empty; he rolled it between his palms: "And other times—well, I needed a fix, I needed to find a place to lean, I needed to clear a space to *listen*—and I couldn't find it, and I—went crazy, I did terrible things to *me*, I was terrible *for* me." He began pressing the beer can between his hands, I watched the metal begin to give. It glittered, as he played with it, like a knife, and I was afraid he would cut himself, but I said nothing. "Oh well. I can never tell you. I was all by myself at the bottom of something, stinking and sweating and crying and shaking, and I smelled it, you know? *my* stink, and I thought I'd die if I couldn't get away from it and yet, all the same, I knew that every- thing I was doing was just locking me in with it. And I didn't know," he paused, still flattening the beer can, "I didn't know, I still *don't* know, some- thing kept telling me that maybe it was good to smell your own stink, but I didn't think that *that* was what I'd been trying to do—and—who can stand it?" and he abruptly dropped the ruined beer can, looking at me with a small, still smile, and then rose, walking to the window as though it were the lodestone rock. I watched his face, he watched the avenue. "I couldn't tell you when Mama died—but the reason I wanted to leave Harlem so bad was to get away from drugs. And then, when I ran away, that's what I was running from—really. When I came back, nothing had changed, I hadn't changed, I was just—older." And he stopped, drumming with his fingers on the windowpane. The sun had vanished, soon darkness would fall. I watched his face. "It can come again," he said, almost as though speaking to himself. Then he turned to me. "It can come again," he repeated. "I just want you to know that."

"All right," I said, at last. "So it can come again, All right."

He smiled, but the smile was sorrowful. "I had to try to tell you," he said.

"Yes," I said. "I understand that."

"You're my brother," he said, looking straight at me, and not smiling at all.

"Yes," I repeated, "yes. I understand that."

He turned back to the window, looking out. "All that hatred down there," he said, "all that hatred and misery and love. It's a wonder it doesn't blow the avenue apart."

We went to the only nightclub on a short, dark street, downtown. We squeezed through the narrow, chattering, jam-packed bar to the entrance of the big room, where the bandstand was. And we stood there for a moment, for the lights were very dim in this room and we couldn't see. Then, "Hello, boy," said a voice and an enormous black man, much older than Sonny or myself, erupted out of all that atmospheric lighting and put an arm around Sonny's shoulder. "I been sitting right here," he said, "waiting for you."

He had a big voice, too, and heads in the darkness turned toward us.

Sonny grinned and pulled a little away, and said, "Creole, this is my brother. I told you about him."

Creole shook my hand. "I'm glad to meet you, son," he said, and it was clear that he was glad to meet me *there*, for Sonny's sake. And he smiled, "You got a real musician in *your* family," and he took his arm from Sonny's shoulder and slapped him, lightly, affectionately, with the back of his hand.

"Well. Now I've heard it all," said a voice behind us. This was another musician, and a friend of Sonny's, a coal-black, cheerful-looking man, built close to the ground. He immediately began confiding to me, at the top of his lungs, the most terrible things about Sonny, his teeth gleaming like a lighthouse and his laugh coming up out of him like the beginning of an earthquake. And it turned out that everyone at the bar knew Sonny, or almost everyone; some were musicians, working there, or nearby, or not working, some were simply hangers-on, and some were there to hear Sonny play. I was introduced to all of them and they were all very polite to me. Yet, it was clear that, for them, I was only Sonny's brother. Here, I was in Sonny's world. Or, rather: his kingdom. Here, it was not even a question that his veins bore royal blood.

They were going to play soon and Creole installed me, by myself, at a table in a dark corner. Then I watched them, Creole, and the little black man, and Sonny, and the others, while they horsed around, standing just below the bandstand. The light from the bandstand spilled just a little short of them and, watching them laughing and gesturing and moving about, I had the feeling that they, nevertheless, were being most careful not to step into that circle of light too suddenly: that if they moved into the light too suddenly, without thinking, they would perish in flame. Then, while I watched, one of them, the small, black man, moved into the light and crossed the bandstand and started fooling around with his drums. Then—being funny and being, also, extremely ceremonious—Creole took Sonny by the arm and led him to the piano. A woman's voice called Sonny's name and a few hands started clapping. And Sonny, also being funny and being ceremonious, and so touched, I think, that he could have cried, but neither hiding it nor showing it, riding it like a man, grinned, and put both hands to his heart and bowed from the waist.

Creole then went to the bass fiddle and a lean, very bright-skinned brown man jumped up on the bandstand and picked up his horn. So there they were, and the atmosphere on the bandstand and in the room began to change and tighten. Someone stepped up to the microphone and announced them. Then there were all kinds of murmurs. Some people at the bar shushed others. The waitress ran around, frantically getting in the last orders, guys and chicks got closer to each other, and the lights on the band-stand, on the quartet, turned to a kind of indigo. Then they all looked different there. Creole looked about him for the last time, as though he were making certain that all his chickens were in the coop, and then he—jumped and struck the fiddle. And there they were.

All I know about music is that not many people ever really hear it. And even then, on the rare occasions when something opens within, and the music enters, what we mainly hear, or hear corroborated, are personal, private, vanishing evocations. But the man who creates the music is hearing something else, is dealing with the roar rising from the void and imposing order on it as it hits the air. What is evoked in him, then, is of another order, more terrible because it has no words, and triumphant, too, for that same reason. And his triumph, when he triumphs, is ours. I just watched Sonny's face. His face was troubled, he was working hard, but he wasn't with it. And I had the feeling that, in a way, everyone on the bandstand was waiting for him, both waiting for him and pushing him along. But as I began to watch Creole, I realized that it was Creole who held them all back. He had them on a short rein. Up there, keeping the beat with his whole body, wailing on the fiddle, with his eyes half closed, he was listening to everything, but he was listening to Sonny. He was having a dialogue with Sonny. He wanted Sonny to leave the shoreline and strike out for the deep water. He was Sonny's witness that deep water and drowning were not the same thing—he had been there, and he knew. And he wanted Sonny to know. He was waiting for Sonny to do the things on the keys which would let Creole know that Sonny was in the water.

And, while Creole listened, Sonny moved, deep within, exactly like someone in torment. I had never before thought of how awful the relationship must be between the musician and his instrument. He has to fill it, this instrument, with the breath of life, his own. He has to make it do what he wants it to do. And a piano is just a piano. It's made out of so much wood and wires and little hammers and big ones, and ivory. While there's only so much you can do with it, the only way to find this out is to try; to try and make it do everything.

And Sonny hadn't been near a piano for over a year. And he wasn't on much better terms with his life, not the life that stretched before him now. He and the piano stammered, started one way, got scared, stopped; started another way, panicked, marked time, started again; then seemed to have found a direction, panicked again, got stuck. And the face I saw on Sonny I'd never seen before. Everything had been burned out of it, and, at the same time, things usually hidden were being burned in, by the fire and fury of the battle which was occurring in him up there.

Yet, watching Creole's face as they neared the end of the first set, I had the feeling that something had happened, something I hadn't heard. Then they finished, there was scattered applause, and then, without an instant's warning, Creole started into something else, it was almost sardonic, it was *Am I Blue*.[9] And, as though he commanded, Sonny began to play. Something began to happen. And Creole let out the reins. The dry, low, black man said something awful on the drums, Creole answered, and the drums talked back. Then the horn insisted, sweet and high, slightly detached perhaps, and Creole listened, commenting now and then, dry, and driving, beautiful and calm and old. Then they all came together again, and Sonny was part of the family again. I could tell this from his face. He seemed to have found, right there beneath his fingers, a damn brand-new piano. It seemed that he couldn't get over it. Then, for awhile, just being happy with Sonny, they seemed to be agreeing with him that brand-new pianos certainly were a gas.

Then Creole stepped forward to remind them that what they were playing was the blues. He hit something in all of them, he hit something in me, myself, and the music tightened and deepened, apprehension began to beat the air. Creole began to tell us what the blues were all about. They were not about anything very new. He and his boys up there were keeping it new, at the risk of ruin, destruction, madness, and death, in order to find new ways to make us listen. For, while the tale of how we suffer, and how we are delighted, and how we may triumph is never new, it always must be heard. There isn't any other tale to tell, it's the only light we've got in all this darkness.

And this tale, according to that face, that body, those strong hands on those strings, has another aspect in every country, and a new depth in every generation. Listen, Creole seemed to be saying, listen. Now these are Sonny's blues. He made the little black man on the drums know it, and the bright, brown man on the horn. Creole wasn't trying any longer to get Sonny in the water. He was wishing him Godspeed. Then he stepped back, very slowly, filling the air with the immense suggestion that Sonny speak for himself.

Then they all gathered around Sonny and Sonny played. Every now and again one of them seemed to say, amen. Sonny's fingers filled the air with life, his life. But that life contained so many others. And Sonny went all the way back, he really began with the spare, flat statement of the opening phrase of the song. Then he began to make it his. It was very beautiful because it wasn't hurried and it was no longer a lament. I seemed to hear with what burning he had made it his, with what burning we had yet to make it ours, how we could cease lamenting. Freedom lurked around us and I understood, at last, that he could help us to be free if we would listen, that he would never be free until we did. Yet, there was no battle in his face now. I heard what he had gone through, and would continue to go through until he came to rest in earth. He had made it his: that long line, of which we knew only Mama and Daddy. And he was giving it back, as everything

9. Jazz standard; Billie Holliday made a famous recording of it.

must be given back, so that, passing through death, it can live forever. I saw my mother's face again, and felt, for the first time, how the stones of the road she had walked on must have bruised her feet. I saw the moonlit road where my father's brother died. And it brought something else back to me, and carried me past it, I saw my little girl again and felt Isabel's tears again, and I felt my own tears begin to rise. And I was yet aware that this was only a moment, that the world waited outside, as hungry as a tiger, and that trouble stretched above us, longer than the sky.

Then it was over. Creole and Sonny let out their breath, both soaking wet, and grinning. There was a lot of applause and some of it was real. In the dark, the girl came by and I asked her to take drinks to the bandstand. There was a long pause, while they talked up there in the indigo light and after awhile I saw the girl put a Scotch and milk on top of the piano for Sonny. He didn't seem to notice it, but just before they started playing again, he sipped from it and looked toward me, and nodded. Then he put it back on top of the piano. For me, then, as they began to play again, it glowed and shook above my brother's head like the very cup of trembling.[1]

1957

Princes and Powers

The conference of Negro-African Writers and Artists (*Le Congrès des Ecrivains et Artistes Noirs*) opened on Wednesday, September 19, 1956, in the Sorbonne's Amphitheatre Descartes, in Paris. It was one of those bright, warm days which one likes to think of as typical of the atmosphere of the intellectual capital of the Western world. There were people on the café terraces, boys and girls on the boulevards, bicycles racing by on their fantastically urgent errands. Everyone and everything wore a cheerful aspect, even the houses of Paris, which did not show their age. Those who were unable to pay the steep rents of these houses were enabled, by the weather, to enjoy the streets, to sit, unnoticed, in the parks. The boys and girls and old men and women who had nowhere at all to go and nothing whatever to do, for whom no provision had been made, or could be, added to the beauty of the Paris scene by walking along the river. The newspaper vendors seemed cheerful; so did the people who bought the newspapers. Even the men and women queueing up before bakeries—for there was a bread strike in Paris—did so as though they had long been used to it.

The conference was to open at nine o'clock. By ten o'clock the lecture hall was already unbearably hot, people choked the entrances and covered the wooden steps. It was hectic with the activity attendant upon the setting up of tape recorders, with the testing of earphones, with the lighting of flashbulbs. Electricity, in fact, filled the hall. Of the people there that first day, I should judge that not quite two-thirds were colored.

Behind the table at the front of the hall sat eight colored men. These included the American novelist Richard Wright; Alioune Diop, the editor of *Présence Africaine* and one of the principal organizers of the conference;

---

1. See Isaiah 51.17, 22.

poets Leopold Senghor, from Senegal, and Aimé Césaire, from Martinique, and the poet and novelist Jacques Alexis,[1] from Haiti. From Haiti, also, came the President of the conference, Dr. Price-Mars,[2] a very old and very handsome man.

It was well past ten o'clock when the conference actually opened. Alioune Diop, who is tall, very dark, and self-contained, and who rather resembles, in his extreme sobriety, an old-time Baptist minister, made the opening address. He referred to the present gathering as a kind of second Bandung.[3] As at Bandung, the people gathered together here held in common the fact of their subjugation to Europe, or, at the very least, to the European vision of the world. Out of the fact that European well-being had been, for centuries, so crucially dependent on this subjugation had come that *rocisme* from which all black men suffered. Then he spoke of the changes which had taken place during the last decade regarding the fate and the aspirations of non-European peoples, especially the blacks. "The blacks," he said, "whom history has treated in a rather cavalier fashion. I would even say that history has treated in a rather cavalier fashion. I would even say that history has treated black men in a resolutely spiteful fashion were it not for the fact that this history with a large *H* is nothing more, after all, than the Western interpretation of the life of the world." He spoke of the variety of cultures the conference represented, saying that they were genuine cultures and that the ignorance of the West regarding them was largely a matter of convenience.

Yet, in speaking of the relation between politics and culture, he pointed out that the loss of vitality from which all Negro cultures were suffering was due to the fact that their political destinies were not in their hands. A people deprived of political sovereignty finds it very nearly impossible to recreate, for itself, the image of its past, this perpetual recreation being an absolute necessity for, if not, indeed, the definition of a living culture. And one of the questions, then, said Diop, which would often be raised during this conference was the question of assimilation. Assimilation was frequently but another name for the very special brand of relations between human beings which had been imposed by colonialism. These relations demanded that the individual, torn from the context to which he owed his identity, should replace his habits of feeling, thinking, and acting by another set of habits which belonged to the strangers who dominated him. He cited the example of certain natives of the Belgian Congo, who, *accablé des complexes*,[4] wished for an assimilation so complete that they would no longer be distinguishable from white men. This, said Diop, indicated the blind horror which the spiritual heritage of Africa inspired in their breasts.

The question of assimilation could not, however, be posed this way. It was not a question, on the one hand, of simply being swallowed up, of dis-

---

1. A Haitian Communist novelist (1922—1961). *"Presence Africaine"*: quarterly literary magazine, published in Paris and founded by Diop, that was influential in the Pan-Africanist movement and in the decolonization struggles of former French colonies. Senghor (1906–2001), Senegalese poet, politician, and cultural theorist who served as the first president of Senegal from 1960 to 1980. Césaire (1913–2008), French poet, author, and politician from Martinque and founding member of the Negritude movement in Francophone literature.

2. Haitian diplomat, teacher, writer, and ethnographer (1876—1969).

3. Reference to the Asian African or Afro-Asian Conference, which took place April 18–24 in Bandung, Indonesia. The first large-scale meeting of Asian and African states, and most newly independent, the conference promoted Afro-Asian economic and cultural cooperation and opposed colonialism and neocolonialism.

4. Overwhelmed by complexes (French).

appearing in the maw of western culture, nor was it, on the other hand, a question of rejecting assimilation in order to be isolated within African culture. Neither was it a question of deciding which African values were to be retained and which European values were to be adopted. Life was not that simple.

It was due to the crisis which their cultures were now undergoing that black intellectuals had come together. They were here to define and accept their responsibilities, to assess the riches and the promise of their cultures, and to open, in effect, a dialogue with Europe. He ended with a brief and rather moving reference to the fifteen-year struggle of himself and his confreres to bring about this day.

His speech won a great deal of applause. Yet, I felt that among the dark people in the hall there was, perhaps, some disappointment that he had not been more specific, more bitter, in a word, more demagogical; whereas, among the whites in the hall, there was certainly expressed in their applause a somewhat shamefaced and uneasy relief. And, indeed, the atmosphere was strange. No one, black or white, seemed quite to believe what was happening and everyone was tense with the question of which direction the conference would take. Hanging in the air, as real as the heat from which we suffered, were the great specters of America and Russia, of the battle going on between them for the domination of the world. The resolution of this battle might very well depend on the earth's non-European population, a population vastly outnumbering Europe's, and which had suffered such injustices at European hands. With the best will in the world, no one now living could undo what past generations had accomplished. The great question was what, exactly, *had* they accomplished: whether the evil, of which there had been so much, alone lived after them, whether the good, and there had been some, had been interred with their bones.

Of the messages from well-wishers which were read immediately after Diop's speech, the one which caused the greatest stir came from America's W. E. B. Du Bois.[5] "I am not present at your meeting," he began, "because the U.S. government will not give me a passport." The reading was interrupted at this point by great waves of laughter, by no means good-natured, and by a roar of applause, which, as it clearly could not have been intended for the State Department, was intended to express admiration for Du Bois's plain speaking. "Any American Negro traveling abroad today must either not care about Negroes or say what the State Department wishes him to say." This, of course, drew more applause. It also very neatly compromised whatever effectiveness the five-man American delegation then sitting in the hall might have hoped to have. It was less Du Bois's extremely ill-considered communication which did this than the incontestable fact that he had not been allowed to leave his country. It was a fact which could scarcely be explained or defended, particularly as one would have also had to explain just how the reasons for Du Bois's absence differed from those which had prevented the arrival of the delegation from South Africa. The very attempt at such an explanation, especially for people whose distrust of the West, however richly justified, also tends to make them dangerously blind

---

5. William Edward Burghardt Du Bois (1868–1963), writer, public intellectual, classicist, critic, and social scientist, was one of the most famous black men before the Civil Rights Era. He cofounded the Niagara Movement, the National Association for the Advancement of Colored People (NAACP), and the Pan-African Congress.

and hasty, was to be suspected of "caring nothing about Negroes," of saying what the State Department "wished" you to say. It was a fact which increased and seemed to justify the distrust with which all Americans are regarded abroad, and it made yet deeper, for the five American Negroes present, that gulf which yawns between the American Negro and all other men of color. This is a very sad and dangerous state of affairs, for the American Negro is possibly the only man of color who can speak of the West with real authority, whose experience, painful as it is, also proves the vitality of the so transgressed western ideals. The fact that Du Bois was not there and could not, therefore, be engaged in debate, naturally made the more seductive his closing argument: which was that, the future of Africa being socialist, African writers should take the road taken by Russia, Poland, China, etc., and not be "betrayed backward by the U.S. into colonialism."

When the morning session ended and I was spewed forth with the mob into the bright courtyard, Richard Wright introduced me to the American delegation. And it seemed quite unbelievable for a moment that the five men standing with Wright (and Wright and myself) were defined, and had been brought together in this courtyard by our relation to the African continent. The chief of the delegation, John Davis,[6] was to be asked just *why* he considered himself a Negro—he was to be told that he certainly did not look like one. He *is* a Negro, of course, from the remarkable legal point of view which obtains in the United States, but, more importantly, as he tried to make clear to his interlocutor, he was a Negro by choice and by depth of involvement—by experience, in fact. But the question of choice in such a context can scarcely be coherent for an African and the experience referred to, which produces a John Davis, remains a closed book for him. Mr. Davis might have been rather darker, as were the others—Mercer Cook, William Fontaine, Horace Bond, and James Ivy[7]—and it would not have helped matters very much.

For what, at bottom, distinguished the Americans from the Negroes who surrounded us, men from Nigeria, Senegal, Barbados, Martinique—so many names for so many disciplines—was the banal and abruptly quite overwhelming fact that we had been born in a society, which, in a way quite inconceivable for Africans, and no longer real for Europeans, was open, and, in a sense which has nothing to do with justice or injustice, was free. It was a society, in short, in which nothing was fixed and we had therefore been born to a greater number of possibilities, wretched as these possibilities seemed at the instant of our birth. Moreover, the land of our forefathers' exile had been made, by that travail, our home. It may have been the popular impulse to keep us at the bottom of the perpetually shifting and bewildered populace; but we were, on the other hand, almost personally indispensable to each of them, simply because, without us, they could never have been certain, in such a confusion, where the bottom was; and nothing, in any case, could take away our title to the land which we, too, had pur-

---

6. John Aubrey Davis, Sr. (1912–2002), Head of the delegation of writers.
7. Educator, scholar (1901–1974) who was editor of the NAACP's journal the *Crisis*. Cook (1903–1987), African American professor, and the ambassador to Senegal from 1964 to 1966. Fontaine (1909–1968), professor of philosophy who traveled worldwide to discuss pan-African issues and African nationalism during the height of decolonization. Bond (1904–1972), American historian and educator and an influential leader at several historically black colleges, including Lincoln University.

chased with our blood. This results in a psychology very different—at its best and at its worst—from the psychology which is produced by a sense of having been invaded and overrun, the sense of having no recourse whatever against oppression other than overthrowing the machinery of the oppressor. We had been dealing with, had been made and mangled by, another machinery altogether. It had never been in our interest to overthrow it. It had been necessary to make the machinery work for our benefit and the possibility of its doing so had been, so to speak, built in.

We could, therefore, in a way, be considered the connecting link between Africa and the West, the most real and certainly the most shocking of all African contributions to Western cultural life. The articulation of this reality, however, was another matter. But it was clear that our relation to the mysterious continent of Africa would not be clarified until we had found some means of saying, to ourselves and to the world, more about the mysterious American continent than had ever been said before.

M. Lasebikan,[8] from Nigeria, spoke that afternoon on the tonal structure of Youriba poetry, a language spoken by five million people in his country. Lasebikan was a very winning and unassuming personality, dressed in a most arresting costume. What looked like a white lace poncho covered him from head to foot; beneath this he was wearing a very subdued but very ornately figured silk robe, which looked Chinese, and he wore a red velvet toque, a sign, someone told me, that he was a Muhammadan.

The Youriba language, he told us, had only become a written language in the middle of the last century and this had been done by missionaries. His face expressed some sorrow at this point, due, it developed, to the fact that this had not already been accomplished by the Youriba people. However— and his face brightened again—he lived in the hope that one day an excavation would bring to light a great literature written by the Youriba people. In the meantime, with great good nature, he resigned himself to sharing with us that literature which already existed. I doubt that I learned much about the tonal structure of Youriba poetry, but I found myself fascinated by the sensibility which had produced it. M. Lasebikan spoke first in Youriba and then in English. It was perhaps because he so clearly loved his subject that he not only succeeded in conveying the poetry of this extremely strange language, he also conveyed something of the style of life out of which it came. The poems quoted ranged from the devotional to a poem which described the pounding of yams. And one somehow felt the loneliness and the yearning of the first and the peaceful, rhythmic domesticity of the second. There was a poem about the memory of a battle, a poem about a faithless friend, and a poem celebrating the variety to be found in life, which conceived of this variety in rather startling terms: "Some would have been great eaters, but they haven't got the food; some, great drinkers, but they haven't got the wine." Some of the poetry demanded the use of a marvelously ornate drum, on which were many little bells. It was not the drum it once had been, he told us, but despite whatever mishap had befallen it, I could have listened to him play it for the rest of the afternoon.

He was followed by Leopold Senghor. Senghor is a very dark and impressive figure in a smooth, bespectacled kind of way, and he is very highly regarded as a poet. He was to speak on West African writers and artists.

8. Nigerian linguist and critic born in Ibadan in 1908.

He began by invoking what he called the "spirit of Bandung." In referring to Bandung, he was referring less, he said, to the liberation of black peoples than he was saluting the reality and the toughness of their culture, which, despite the vicissitudes of their history, had refused to perish. We were now witnessing, in fact, the beginning of its renaissance. This renaissance would owe less to politics than it would to black writers and artists. The "spirit of Bandung" had had the effect of "sending them to school to Africa."

One of the things, said Senghor—perhaps *the* thing—which distinguished Africans from Europeans is the comparative urgency of their ability to feel. "*Sentir c'eat apercevair*",[9] it is perhaps a tribute to his personal force that this phrase then meant something which makes the literal English translation quite inadequate, seeming to leave too great a distance between the feeling and the perception. The feeling and the perception, for Africans, is one and the same thing. This is the difference between European and African reasoning: the reasoning of the African is not compartmentalized, and, to illustrate this, Senghor here used the image of the bloodstream in which all things mingle and flow to and through the heart. He told us that the difference between the function of the arts in Europe and their function in Africa lay in the fact that, in Africa, the function of the arts is more present and pervasive, is infinitely less special, "is done by all, for all." Thus, art for art's sake is not a concept which makes any sense in Africa. The division between art and life out of which such a concept comes does not exist there. Art itself is taken to be perishable, to be made again each time it disappears or is destroyed. What is clung to is the spirit which makes art possible. And the African idea of this spirit is very different from the European idea. European art attempts to imitate nature. African art is concerned with reaching beyond and beneath nature, to contact, and itself become a part of *la force vitale*.[1] The artistic image is not intended to represent the thing itself, but, rather, the reality of the force the thing contains. Thus, the moon is fecundity, the elephant is force.

Much of this made great sense to me, even though Senghor was speaking of, and out of, a way of life which I could only very dimly and perhaps somewhat wistfully imagine. It was the esthetic which attracted me, the idea that the work of art expresses, contains, and is itself a part of that energy which is life. Yet, I was aware that Senghor's thought had come into my mind translated. What he had been speaking of was something more direct and less isolated than the line in which my imagination immediately began to move. The distortions used by African artists to create a work of art are not at all the same distortions which have become one of the principal aims of almost every artist in the West today. (They are not the same distortions even when they have been copied from Africa.) And this was due entirely to the different situations in which each had his being. Poems and stories, in the only situation I know anything about, were never told, except, rarely, to children, and, at the risk of mayhem, in bars. They were written to be read, alone, and by a handful of people at that—there was really beginning to be something suspect in being read by more than a handful. These creations no more insisted on the actual presence of other human beings than they demanded the collaboration of a dancer and a drum. They could not be said

9. To feel is to perceive (French).
1. The vital force (French).

to celebrate the society any more than the homage which Western artists sometimes receive can be said to have anything to do with society's celebration of a work of art. The only thing in western life which seemed even faintly to approximate Senghor's intense sketch of the creative interdependence, the active, actual, joyful intercourse obtaining among African artists and what only a westerner would call their public, was the atmosphere sometimes created among jazz musicians and their fans during, say, a jam session. But the ghastly isolation of the jazz musician, the neurotic intensity of his listeners, was proof enough that what Senghor meant when he spoke of social art had no reality whatever in western life. He was speaking out of his past, which had been lived where art was naturally and spontaneously social, where artistic creation did not presuppose divorce. (Yet he was not there. Here he was, in Paris, speaking the adopted language in which he also wrote his poetry.)

Just what the specific relation of an artist to his culture says about that culture is a very pretty question. The culture which had produced Senghor seemed, on the face of it, to have a greater coherence as regarded assumptions, traditions, customs, and beliefs than did the western culture to which it stood in so problematical a relation. And this might very well mean that the culture represented by Senghor was healthier than the culture represented by the hall in which he spoke. But the leap to this conclusion, than which nothing would have seemed easier, was frustrated by the question of just what health is in relation to a culture. Senghor's culture, for example, did not seem to need the lonely activity of the singular intelligence on which the cultural life—the moral life—of the West depends. And a really cohesive society, one of the attributes, perhaps, of what is taken to be a "healthy" culture, has, generally, and, I suspect, necessarily, a much lower level of tolerance for the maverick, the dissenter, the man who steals the fire, than have societies in which, the common ground of belief having all but vanished, each man, in awful and brutal isolation, is for himself, to flower or to perish. Or, not impossibly, to make real and fruitful again that vanished common ground, which, as I take it, is nothing more or less than the culture itself, endangered and rendered nearly inaccessible by the complexities it has, itself, inevitably created.

Nothing is more undeniable than the fact that cultures vanish, undergo crises; are, in any case, in a perpetual state of change and fermentation, being perpetually driven, God knows where, by forces within and without. And one of the results, surely, of the present tension between the society represented by Senghor and the society represented by the Salle Descartes[2] was just this perceptible drop, during the last decade, of the western level of tolerance. I wondered what this would mean—for Africa, for us. I wondered just what effect the concept of art expressed by Senghor would have on that renaissance he had predicted and just what transformations this concept itself would undergo as it encountered the complexities of the century into which it was moving with such speed.

The evening debate rang perpetual changes on two questions. These questions—each of which splintered, each time it was asked, into a thousand more—were, first: What *is* a culture? This is a difficult question under the most serene circumstances—under which circumstances, incidentally,

2. Descartes Auditorium.

it mostly fails to present itself. (This implies, perhaps, one of the possible definitions of a culture, at least at a certain stage of its development.) In the context of the conference, it was a question which was helplessly at the mercy of another one. And the second question was this: Is it possible to describe as a culture what may simply be, after all, a history of oppression? That is, is this history and these present facts, which involve so many millions of people who are divided from each other by so many miles of the globe, which operates, and has operated, under such very different conditions, to such different effects, and which has produced so many different subhistories, problems, traditions, possibilities, aspirations, assumptions, languages, hybrids—is this history enough to have made of the earth's black populations anything that can legitimately be described as a culture? For what, beyond the fact that all black men at one time or another left Africa, or have remained there, do they really have in common?

And yet, it became clear as the debate wore on, that there *was* something which all black men held in common, something which cut across opposing points of view, and placed in the same context their widely dissimilar experience. What they held in common was their precarious, their unutterably painful relation to the white world. What they held in common was the necessity to remake the world in their own image, to impose this image on the world, and no longer be controlled by the vision of the world, and of themselves, held by other people. What, in sum, black men held in common was their ache to come into the world as men. And this ache united people who might otherwise have been divided as to what a man should be.

Yet, whether or not this could properly be described as a *cultural* reality remained another question. Haiti's Jacques Alexis made the rather desperate observation that a cultural survey must have *something* to survey; but then seemed confounded, as, indeed, we all were, by the dimensions of the particular cultural survey in progress. It was necessary, for example, before one could relate the culture of Haiti to that of Africa, to know what the Haitian culture was. Within Haiti there were a great many cultures. Frenchmen, Negroes, and Indians had bequeathed it quite dissimilar ways of life; Catholics, voodooists, and animists[3] cut across class and color lines. Alexis described as "pockets" of culture those related and yet quite specific and dissimilar ways of life to be found within the borders of any country in the world and wished to know by what alchemy these opposing ways of life became a national culture. And he wished to know, too, what relation national culture bore to national independence—was it possible, really, to speak of a national culture when speaking of nations which were not free?

Senghor remarked, apropos of this question, that one of the great difficulties posed by this problem of cultures within cultures, particularly within the borders of Africa herself, was the difficulty of establishing and maintaining contact with the people if one's language had been formed in Europe. And he went on, somewhat later, to make the point that the heritage of the American Negro was an African heritage. He used, as proof of this, a poem of Richard Wright's which was, he said, involved with African tensions and symbols, even though Wright himself had not been aware of this. He suggested that the study of African sources might prove extremely

---

3. Followers of an "animistic view," the anthropological concept that encompasses a religious world view that holds that natural physical entities possess a spiritual essence. "Voodooists": practitioners of Kongolese-based syncretic religion in the New World.

illuminating for American Negroes. For, he suggested, in the same way that white classics exist—classic here taken to mean an enduring revelation and statement of a specific, peculiar, cultural sensibility—black classics must also exist. This raised in my mind the question of whether or not white classics *did* exist, and, with this question, I began to see the implications of Senghor's claim.

For, if white classics existed, in distinction, that is, to merely French or English classics, these could only be the classics produced by Greece and Rome. If *Black Boy*,[4] said Senghor, were to be analyzed, it would undoubtedly reveal the African heritage to which it owed its existence; in the same way, I supposed, that Dickens's *A Tale of Two Cities*,[5] would, upon analysis, reveal its debt to Aeschylus. It did not seem very important.

And yet, I realized, the question had simply never come up in relation to European literature. It was not, now, the European necessity to go rummaging in the past, and through all the countries of the world, bitterly staking out claims to its cultural possessions.

Yet *Black Boy* owed its existence to a great many other factors, by no means so tenuous or so problematical; in so handsomely presenting Wright with his African heritage, Senghor rather seemed to be taking away his identity. *Black Boy* is the study of the growing up of a Negro boy in the Deep South, and is one of the major American autobiographies. I had never thought of it, as Senghor clearly did, as one of the major *African* autobiographies, only one more document, in fact, like one more book in the Bible, speaking of the African's long persecution and exile.

Senghor chose to overlook several gaps in his argument, not the least of which was the fact that Wright had not been in a position, as Europeans had been, to remain in contact with his hypothetical African heritage. The Greco-Roman tradition had, after all, been *written down*; it was by this means that it had kept itself alive. Granted that there was something African in *Black Boy*, as there was undoubtedly something African in all American Negroes, the great question of what this was, and how it had survived, remained wide open. Moreover, *Black Boy* has been written in the English language which Americans had inherited from England, that is, if you like, from Greece and Rome; its form, psychology, moral attitude, preoccupations, in short, its cultural validity, were all due to forces which had nothing to do with Africa. Or was it simply that we had been rendered unable to recognize Africa in it?—for, it seemed that, in Senghor's vast recreation of the world, the footfall of the African would prove to have covered more territory than the footfall of the Roman.

Thursday's great event was Aimé Césaire's speech in the afternoon, dealing with the relation between colonization and culture. Césaire is a caramel-colored man from Martinique, probably around forty, with a great tendency to roundness and smoothness, physically speaking, and with the rather vaguely benign air of a schoolteacher. All this changes the moment he begins to speak. It becomes at once apparent that his curious, slow-moving blandness is related to the grace and patience of a jungle cat and that the intelligence behind those spectacles is of a very penetrating and demagogic order.

---

4. Richard Wright's memoir, published in 1945.   5. Charles Dickens's novel, published in 1859.

The cultural crisis through which we are passing today can be summed up thus, said Césaire: that culture which is strongest from the material and technological point of view threatens to crush all weaker cultures, particularly in a world in which, distance counting for nothing, the technologically weaker cultures have no means of protecting themselves. All cultures have, furthermore, an economic, social, and political base, and no culture can continue to live if its political destiny is not in its own hands. "Any political and social regime which destroys the self-determination of a people also destroys the creative power of that people." When this has happened the culture of that people has been destroyed. And it is simply not true that the colonizers bring to the colonized a new culture to replace the old one, a culture not being something given to a people, but, on the contrary and by definition, something that they make themselves. Nor is it, in any case, in the nature of colonialism to wish or to permit such a degree of well-being among the colonized. The well-being of the colonized is desirable only insofar as this well-being enriches the dominant country, the necessity of which is simply to remain dominant. Now the civilizations of Europe, said Césaire, speaking very clearly and intensely to a packed and attentive hall, evolved an economy based on capital and the capital was based on black labor; and thus, regardless of whatever arguments Europeans used to defend themselves, and in spite of the absurd palliatives with which they have sometimes tried to soften the blow, the fact, of their domination, in order to accomplish and maintain this domination—in order, in fact, to make money— they destroyed, with utter ruthlessness, everything that stood in their way, languages, customs, tribes, lives; and not only put nothing in its place, but erected, on the contrary, the most tremendous barriers between themselves and the people they ruled. Europeans never had the remotest intention of raising Africans to the Western level, of sharing with them the instruments of physical, political or economic power. It was precisely their intention, their necessity, to keep the people they ruled in a state of cultural anarchy, that is, simply in a barbaric state. "The famous inferiority complex one is pleased to observe as a characteristic of the colonized is no accident but something very definitely desired and deliberately inculcated by the colonizer." He was interrupted at this point—not for the first time—by long and prolonged applause.

"The situation, therefore, in the colonial countries, is tragic," Césaire continued. "Wherever colonization is a fact the indigenous culture begins to rot. And, among these ruins, something begins to be born which is not a culture but a kind of subculture, a subculture which is condemned to exist on the margin allowed it by European culture. This then becomes the province of a few men, the elite, who find themselves placed in the most artificial conditions, deprived of any revivifying contact with the masses of the people. Under such conditions, this subculture has no chance whatever of growing into an active, living culture." And what, he asked, before this situation, can be done?

The answer would not be simple. "In every society there is always a delicate balance between the old and the new, a balance which is perpetually being reestablished, which is reestablished by each generation. Black societies, cultures, civilizations, will not escape this law." Césaire spoke of the energy already proved by black cultures in the past, and, declining to believe that this energy no longer existed, declined also to believe that the total obliteration of the existing culture was a condition for the renaissance of black people. "In the culture to be born there will no doubt be old and new elements. How these elements will be mixed is not a question to which any individual can respond. The response must be given by the community. But we can say this: that the response will be given, and not verbally, but in tangible facts, and by action."

He was interrupted by applause again. He paused, faintly smiling, and reached his peroration: "We find ourselves today in a cultural chaos. And this is our role: to liberate the forces which, alone, can organize from this chaos a new synthesis, a synthesis which will deserve the name of a culture, a synthesis which will be the reconciliation—et dépassement[6]—of the old and the new. We are here to proclaim the right of our people to speak, to let our people, black people, make their entrance on the great stage of history."

This speech, which was very brilliantly delivered, and which had the further advantage of being, in the main, unanswerable (and the advantage, also, of being very little concerned, at bottom, with culture), wrung from the audience which heard it the most violent reaction of joy. Césaire had spoken for those who could not speak and those who could not speak thronged around the table to shake his hand, and kiss him. I myself felt stirred in a very strange and disagreeable way. For Césaire's case against Europe, which was watertight, was also a very easy case to make. The anatomizing of the great injustice which is the irreducible fact of colonialism was yet not enough to give the victims of that injustice a new sense of themselves. One may say, of course, that the very fact that Césaire had spoken so thrillingly, and in one of the great institutions of Western learning, invested them with this new sense, but I do not think this is so. He had certainly played very skillfully on their emotions and their hopes, but he had not raised the central, tremendous question, which was, simply: What *had* this colonial experience made of them and what were they now to do with it? For they were all, now, whether they liked it or not, related to Europe, stained by European visions and standards, and their relation to themselves, and to each other, and to their past had changed. Their relation to their poets had also changed, as had the relation of their poets to them. Césaire's speech left out of account one of the great effects of the colonial experience: its creation, precisely, of men like himself. His real relation to the people who thronged about him now had been changed, by this experience, into something very different from what it once had been. What made him so attractive now was the fact that he, without having ceased to be one of them, yet seemed to move with the European authority. He had penetrated into the heart of the great wilderness which was Europe and stolen the sacred fire. And this, which was the promise of their freedom, was also the assurance of his power.

Friday's session began in a rather tense atmosphere and this tension continued throughout the day. Diop opened the session by pointing out that each speaker spoke only for himself and could not be considered as speaking for the conference. I imagined that this had something to with Césaire's speech of the day before and with some of its effects, among which,

6. And the exceeding (French).

apparently, had been a rather sharp exchange between Césaire and the American delegation.

This was the session during which it became apparent that there was a religious war going on at the conference, a war which suggested, in miniature, some of the tensions dividing Africa. A Protestant minister from the Cameroons, Pastor T. Ekollo, had been forced by the hostility of the audience the day before to abandon a dissertation in defense of Christianity in Africa. He was visibly upset still. "There will be Christians in Africa, even when there is not a white man there," he said, with a tense defiance, and added, with an unconsciously despairing irony to which, however, no one reacted, "supposing that to be possible." He had been asked how he could defend Christianity in view of what Christians had done in his country. To which his answer was that the doctrine of Christianity was of more moment than the crimes committed by Christians. The necessity which confronted Africans was to make Christianity real in their own lives, without reference to the crimes committed by others. The audience was extremely cold and hostile, forcing him again, in effect, from the floor. But I felt that this also had something to do with Pastor Ekollo's rather petulant and not notably Christian attitude toward them.

Dr. Marcus James, a priest of the Anglican church from Jamaica, picked up where Ekollo left off. Dr. James is a round, very pleasant-looking, chocolate-colored man, with spectacles. He began with a quotation to the effect that, when the Christian arrived in Africa, he had the Bible and the African had the land; but that, before long, the African had the Bible and the Christian had the land. There was a great deal of laughter at this, in which Dr. James joined. But the postscript to be added today, he said, is that the African not only has the Bible but has found in it a potential weapon for the recovery of his land. The Christians in the hall, who seemed to be in the minority, applauded and stomped their feet at this, but many others now rose and left.

Dr. James did not seem to be distressed and went on to discuss the relationship between Christianity and democracy. In Africa, he said, there was none whatever. Africans do not, in fact, believe that Christianity is any longer real for Europeans, due to the immense scaffolding with which they have covered it, and the fact that this religion has no effect whatever on their conduct. There are, nevertheless, more than twenty million Christians in Africa, and Dr. James believed that the future of their country was very largely up to them. The task of making Christianity real in Africa was made the more difficult in that they could expect no help whatever from Europe: "Christianity, as practiced by Europeans in Africa, is a cruel travesty."

This bitter observation, which was uttered in sorrow, gained a great deal of force from the fact that so genial a man had felt compelled to make it. It made vivid, unanswerable, in a way which rage could not have done, how little the West has respected its own ideals in dealing with subject peoples, and suggested that there was a price we would pay for this. He speculated a little on what African Christianity might become, and how it might contribute to the rebirth of Christianity everywhere; and left his audience to chew on this momentous speculation: Considering, he said, that what Africa wishes to wrest from Europe is power, will it be necessary for Africa to take the same bloody road which Europe has followed? Or will it be possible for her to work out some means of avoiding this?

M. Wahal,[7] from the Sudan, spoke in the afternoon on the role of the law in culture, using as an illustration the role the law had played in the history of the American Negro. He spoke at length on the role of French law in Africa, pointing out that French law is simply not equipped to deal with the complexity of the African situation. And what is even worse, of course, is that it makes virtually no attempt to do so. The result is that French law, in Africa, is simply a legal means of administering injustice. It is not a solution, either, simply to revert to African tribal custom, which is also helpless before the complexities of present-day African life. Wahal spoke with a quiet matter-of-factness, which lent great force to the ugly story he was telling, and he concluded by saying that the question was ultimately a political one and that there was no hope of solving it within the framework of the present colonial system.

He was followed by George Lamming.[8] Lamming is tall, raw-boned, untidy, and intense, and one of his real distinctions is his refusal to be intimidated by the fact that be is a genuine writer. He proposed to raise certain questions pertaining to the quality of life to be lived by black people in that hypothetical tomorrow when they would no longer be ruled by whites. "The profession of letters is an untidy one," he began, looking as though he had dressed to prove it. He directed his speech to Aimé Césaire and Jacques Alexis in particular, and quoted Djuna Barnes:[9] "Too great a sense of identity makes a man feel he can do no wrong. And too little does the same." He suggested that it was important to bear in mind that the word Negro meant black—and meant nothing more than that; and commented on the great variety of heritages, experiences, and points of view which the conference had brought together under the heading of this single noun. He wished to suggest that the nature of power was unrelated to pigmentation, that bad faith was a phenomenon which was independent of race. He found—from the point of view of an untidy man of letters—something crippling in the obsession from which Negroes suffered as regards the existence and the attitudes of the Other—this Other being everyone who was not Negro. That black people faced great problems was surely not to be denied and yet the greatest problem facing us was what we, Negroes, would do among ourselves "when there was no longer any colonial horse to ride." He pointed out that this was the horse on which a great many Negroes, who were in what he called "the skin trade," hoped to ride to power, power which would be in no way distinguishable from the power they sought to overthrow.

Lamming was insisting on the respect which is due the private life. I respected him very much, not only because he raised this question, but because he knew what he was doing. He was concerned with the immensity and the variety of the experience called Negro; he was concerned that one should recognize this variety as wealth. He cited the case of Amos Tutuola's *The Palm-Wine Drinkard*,[1] which he described as a fantasy, made up of legends, anecdotes, episodes, the product, in fact, of an oral story-telling tradi-

7. Listed as a delegate at the First International Congress of Black Writers and Artists (1956).
8. Novelist, essayist, and poet from Barbados (b. 1927), whose novels are linked to the changing political currents in the Caribbean. His first novel, *In the Castle of My Skin* (1953), remains a canonical text of Caribbean literature.

9. American writer (1892–1982) who played an important role in the development of modernist writing in the early 20th century.
1. Published in 1952, perhaps the most famous novel by Tutuola (1920–1997), Nigerian writer famous for books based on Nigerian folk tales.

tion which disappeared from Western life generations ago. Yet "Tutuola really *does* speak English. It is *not* his second language." The English did not find the book strange. On the contrary, they were astonished by how truthfully it seemed to speak to them of their own experience. They felt that Tutuola was closer to the English than he could possibly be to his equivalent in Nigeria; and yet Tutuola's work could elicit this reaction only because, in a way which could never really he understood, but which Tutuola had accepted, he was closer to his equivalent in Nigeria than he would ever be to the English. It seemed to me that Lamming was suggesting to the conference a subtle and difficult idea, the idea that part of the great wealth of the Negro experience lay precisely in its double-edgedness. He was suggesting that all Negroes were held in a state of supreme tension between the difficult, dangerous relationship in which they stood to the white world and the relationship, not a whit less painful or dangerous, in which they stood to each other. He was suggesting that in the acceptance of this duality lay their strength, that in this, precisely, lay their means of defining and controlling the world in which they lived.

Lamming was interrupted at about this point, however, for it had lately been decided, in view of the great number of reports still to be read, to limit everyone to twenty minutes. This quite unrealistic rule was not to be observed very closely, especially as regarded the French-speaking delegates. But Lamming put his notes in his pocket and ended by saying that if, as someone had remarked, silence was the only common language, politics, for Negroes, was the only common ground.

The evening session began with a film, which I missed, and was followed by a speech from Cheik Anta Diop,[2] which, in sum, claimed the ancient Egyptian empire as part of the Negro past. I can only say that this question has never greatly exercised my mind, nor did M. Diop succeed in doing so—at least not in the direction he intended. He quite refused to remain within the twenty-minute limit and, while his claims of the deliberate dishonesty of all Egyptian scholars may be quite well founded for all I know, I cannot say that he convinced me. He was, however, a great success in the hall, second only, in fact, to Aimé Césaire.

He was followed by Richard Wright. Wright had been acting as liaison man between the American delegation and the Africans and this had placed him in rather a difficult position, since both factions tended to claim him as their spokesman. It had not, of course, occurred to the Americans that he could be anything less, whereas the Africans automatically claimed him because of his great prestige as a novelist and his reputation for calling a spade a spade—particularly if the spade were white. The consciousness of his peculiar and certainly rather grueling position weighed on him, I think, rather heavily.

He began by confessing that the paper he had written, while on his farm in Normandy, impressed him as being, after the events of the last few days, inadequate. Some of the things he had observed during the course of the conference had raised questions in him which his paper could not have foreseen. He had not, however, rewritten his paper, but would read it now,

2. Senegalese historian, anthropologist, physicist, and politician (1923–1986), who organized the first postwar Pan-African student congress in 1950. The group politicized and promoted anticolonial struggles in Africa.

exactly as it had been written, interrupting himself whenever what he had written and what he had since been made to feel seemed to be at variance. He was exposing, in short, his conscience to the conference and asking help of them in his confusion.

There was, first of all, he said, a painful contradiction in being at once a westerner and a black man. "I see both worlds from another, and third, point of view." This fact had nothing to do with his will, his desire, or his choice. It was simply that he had been born in the West and the West had formed him.

As a black westerner, it was difficult to know what one's attitude should be toward three realities which were inextricably woven together in the western fabric. These were religion, tradition, and imperialism, and in none of these realities had the lives of black men been taken into account: their advent dated back to 1455, when the church had determined to rule all infidels. And it just so happened, said Wright, ironically, that a vast proportion of these infidels were black. Nevertheless, this decision on the part of the church had not been, despite the church's intentions, entirely oppressive, for one of the results of 1455 had, at length, been Calvin and Luther,[3] who shook the authority of the Church in insisting on the authority of the individual conscience. This might not, he said accurately, have been precisely their intention, but it had certainly been one of their effects. For, with the authority of the Church shaken, men were left prey to many strange and new ideas, ideas which led, finally, to the discrediting of the racial dogma. Neither had this been foreseen, but what men imagine they are doing and what they are doing in fact are rarely the same thing. This was a perfectly valid observation which would, I felt, have been just as valid without the remarkable capsule history with which Wright imagined he supported it.

Wright then went on to speak of the effects of European colonialism in the African colonies. He confessed—bearing in mind always the great gap between human intentions and human effects—that he thought of it as having been, in many ways, liberating, since it smashed old traditions and destroyed old gods. One of the things that surprised him in the last few days had been the realization that most of the delegates to the conference did not feel as he did. He felt, nevertheless, that, though Europeans had not realized what they were doing in freeing Africans from the "rot" of their past, they had been accomplishing a good. And yet—he was not certain that he had the right to say that, having forgotten that Africans are not American Negroes and were not, therefore, as he somewhat mysteriously considered American Negroes to be, free from their "irrational" past.

In sum, Wright said, he felt that Europe had brought the Enlightenment[4] to Africa and that "what was good for Europe was good for all mankind." I felt that this was, perhaps, a tactless way of phrasing a debatable idea, but Wright went on to express a notion which I found even stranger. And this was that the West, having created an African and Asian elite, should now "give them their heads" and "refuse to be shocked" at the "methods they will feel compelled to use" in unifying their countries. We had not, ourselves,

3. Martin Luther (1483–1546), German theologian, Catholic priest, and key figure during the Protestant Reformation. "Calvin": John Calvin (1509–1564), French theologian during the Protestant Reformation.
4. Eighteenth-century movement in Western philosophical thought.

used very pretty methods. Presumably, this left us in no position to throw stones at Nehru, Nasser, Sukarno,[5] etc., should they decide, as they almost surely would, to use dictatorial methods in order to hasten the "social evolution." In any case, Wright said, these men, the leaders of their countries, once the new social order was established, would voluntarily surrender the "personal power." He did not say what would happen then, but I supposed it would be the second coming.

Saturday was the last day of the conference, which was scheduled to end with the invitation to the audience to engage with the delegates in the Euro-African dialogue. It was a day marked by much confusion and excitement and discontent—this last on the part of people who felt that the conference had been badly run, or who had not been allowed to read their reports. (They were often the same people.) It was marked, too, by rather a great deal of plain speaking, both on and off, but mostly off, the record. The hall was even more hot and crowded than it had been the first day and the photographers were back.

The entire morning was taken up in an attempt to agree on a "cultural inventory." This had to be done before the conference could draft those resolutions which they were, today, to present to the world. This task would have been extremely difficult even had there obtained in the black world a greater unity—geographical, spiritual, and historical—than is actually the case. Under the circumstances, it was an endeavor complicated by the nearly indefinable complexities of the word *culture*, by the fact that no coherent statement had yet been made concerning the relationship of black cultures to each other, and, finally, by the necessity, which had obtained throughout the conference, of avoiding the political issues.

The inability to discuss politics had certainly handicapped the conference, but it could scarcely have been run otherwise. The political question would have caused the conference to lose itself in a war of political ideologies. Moreover, the conference *was* being held in Paris, many of the delegates represented areas which belonged to France, most of them represented areas which were not free. There was also to be considered the delicate position of the American delegation, which had sat throughout the conference uncomfortably aware that they might at any moment be forced to rise and leave the hall.

The declaration of political points of view being thus prohibited, the "cultural" debate which raged in the hall that morning was in perpetual danger of drowning in the sea of the unstated. For, according to his political position, each delegate had a different interpretation of his culture, and a different idea of its future, as well as the means to be used to make that future a reality. A solution of a kind was offered by Senghor's suggestion that two committees be formed, one to take an inventory of the past, and one to deal with present prospects. There was some feeling that two committees were scarcely necessary. Diop suggested that one committee be formed, which, if necessary, could divide itself into two. Then the question arose as to just how the committee should be appointed, whether by countries or by cul-

5. Born Kusno Sosrodihardjo (1901–1970), president of Indonesia during the Bandung Conference (1955). "Nehru": Jawaharlal Nehru (1889–1964), first Prime Minister of independent India. "Nasser:" Gamal Abdel Nasser (1918–1970), second president of modern Egypt in power during the Suez Canal crisis (1956).

tural areas. It was decided, at length, that the committee should be set up on the latter basis, and should have resolutions drafted by noon. "It is by these resolutions," protested Mercer Cook, "that we shall make ourselves known. It cannot be done in an hour."

He was entirely right. At eleven-twenty a committee of eighteen members had been formed. At four o'clock in the afternoon they were still invisible. By this time, too, the most tremendous impatience reigned in the crowded hall, in which, today, Negroes by far outnumbered whites. At four-twenty-five the impatience of the audience erupted in whistles, catcalls, and stamping of feet. At four-thirty, Alioune Diop arrived and officially opened the meeting. He tried to explain some of the difficulties such a conference inevitably encountered and assured the audience that the committee on resolutions would not be absent much longer. In the meantime, in their absence, and in the absence of Dr. Price-Mars, he proposed to read a few messages from well-wishers. But the audience was not really interested in these messages and was manifesting a very definite tendency to get out of hand again when, at four-fifty-five, Dr. Price-Mars entered. His arrival had the effect of calming the audience somewhat and, luckily, the committee on resolutions came in very shortly afterwards. At five-seven, Diop rose to read the document which had come one vote short of being unanimously approved.

As is the way with documents of this kind, it was carefully worded and slightly repetitious. This did not make its meaning less clear or diminish its importance.

It spoke first of the great importance of the cultural inventory here begun in relation to the various black cultures which had been "systematically misunderstood, underestimated, sometimes destroyed." This inventory had confirmed the pressing need for a reexamination of the history of these cultures ("*la verité historique*")[6] with a view to their reevaluation. The ignorance concerning them, the errors, and the willful distortions, were among the great contributing factors to the crisis through which they now were passing, in relation to themselves and to human culture in general. The active aid of writers, artists, theologians, thinkers, scientists, and technicians was necessary for the revival, the rehabilitation, and the development of these cultures as the first step toward their integration in the active cultural life of the world. Black men, whatever their political and religious beliefs, were united in believing that the health and growth of these cultures could not possibly come about until colonialism, the exploitation of undeveloped peoples, and racial discrimination had come to an end. (At this point the conference expressed its regret at the involuntary absence of the South African delegation and the reading was interrupted by prolonged and violent applause.)[7] All people, the document continued, had the right to be able to place themselves in fruitful contact with their national cultural values and to benefit from the instruction and education which could be afforded them within this framework. It spoke of the progress which had taken place in the world in the last few years and stated that this progress permitted one to hope for the general abolition of the colonial system and the total and universal end of racial discrimination, and ended: "Our conference, which respects the cultures of all countries and appreciates their

6. The historical truth (French).
7. A response to apartheid, the ruling practice in South Africa at that time.

contributions to the progress of civilization, engages all black men in the defense, the illustration, and the dissemination throughout the world of the national values of their people. We, black writers and artists, proclaim our brotherhood toward all men and expect of them *("nous attendons d'eux")*[8] the manifestation of this same brotherhood toward our people."

When the applause in which the last words of this document were very nearly drowned had ended, Diop pointed out that this was not a declaration of war; it was, rather, he said, a declaration of love—for the culture, European, which had been of such importance in the history of mankind. But it had been very keenly felt that it was now necessary for black men to make the effort to define themselves *au lieu d'être toujours défini par les autres.*[9] Black men had resolved "to take their destinies into their own hands." He spoke of plans for the setting up of an international association for the dissemination of black culture and, at five-twenty-two, Dr. Price-Mars officially closed the conference and opened the floor to the audience for the Euro-African dialogue.

Someone, a European, addressed this question to Aimé Césaire: How, he asked, do you explain the fact that many Europeans—as well as many Africans, *bien entendu*[1]—reject what is referred to as European culture? A European himself, he was far from certain that such a thing as a European culture existed. It was possible to be a European without accepting the Greco-Roman tradition. Neither did he believe in race. He wanted to know in what, exactly, this Negro-African culture consisted and, more, why it was judged necessary to save it. He ended, somewhat vaguely, by saying that, in his opinion, it was human values which had to be preserved, human needs which had to be respected and expressed.

This admirable but quite inadequate psychologist precipitated something of a storm. Diop tried to answer the first part of his question by pointing out that, in their attitudes toward their cultures, a great diversity of viewpoints also obtained among black men. Then an enormous, handsome, extremely impressive black man whom I had not remarked before, who was also named Césaire, stated that the contemporary crisis of black cultures had been brought about by Europe's nineteenth- and twentieth-century attempts to impose their culture on other peoples. They did this without any recognition of the cultural validity of these peoples and thus aroused their resistance. In the case of Africa, where culture was fluid and largely unwritten, resistance had been most difficult. "Which is why," he said, "we are here. We are the most characteristic products of this crisis." And then a rage seemed to shake him, and he continued in a voice thick with fury. "Nothing will ever make us believe that our beliefs . . . are merely frivolous superstitions. No power will ever cause us to admit that we are lower than any other people." He then made a reference to the present Arab struggle against the French, which I did not understand, and ended, "What we are doing is holding on to what is ours. Little," he added, sardonically, "but it belongs to us."

Aimé Césaire, to whom the question had been addressed, was finally able to answer it. He pointed out, with a deliberate, mocking logic, that the rejection by a European of European culture was of the utmost unimpor-

---

8. "We expect of them" (French).
9. Instead of always being defined by others (French).

1. Of course (French).

tance. "Reject it or not, he is still a European, even his rejection is a European rejection. We do not choose our cultures, we belong to them." As to the speaker's implied idea of cultural relativity, and the progressive role this idea can sometimes play, he cited the French objection to this idea. It is an idea which, by making all cultures, as such, equal, undermines French justification for its presence in Africa. He also suggested that the speaker had implied that this conference was primarily interested in an idealistic reconstruction of the past. "But our attitude," said Césaire, "toward colonialism and racial discrimination is very concrete. Our aims cannot be realized without this concreteness." And as for the question of race: "No one is suggesting that there is such a thing as a pure race, or that culture is a racial product. We are not Negroes by our own desire, but, in effect, because of Europe. What unites all Negroes is the injustices they have suffered at European hands."

The moment Césaire finished, Cheik Anta Diop passionately demanded if it were a heresy from a Marxist point of view to try to hang onto a national culture. "Where," he asked, "is the European nation which, in order to progress, surrendered its past?"

There was no answer to this question, nor were there any further questions from the audience. Richard Wright spoke briefly, saying that this conference marked a turning point in the history of Euro-African relations: it marked, in fact, the beginning of the end of the European domination. He spoke of the great diversity of techniques and approaches now at the command of black people, with particular emphasis on the role the American Negro could be expected to play. Among black people, the American Negro was in the technological vanguard and this could prove of inestimable value to the developing African sovereignties. And the dialogue ended immediately afterward, at six-fifty-five, with Senghor's statement that this was the first of many such conferences, the first of many dialogues. As night was falling we poured into the Paris streets. Boys and girls, old men and women, bicycles, terraces, all were there, and the people were queueing up before the bakeries for bread.

January 1957

Going to Meet the Man

"What's the matter?" she asked.

"I don't know," he said, trying to laugh, "I guess I'm tired."

"You've been working too hard," she said. "I keep telling you."

"Well, goddammit, woman," he said, "it's not my fault!" He tried again; he wretchedly failed again. Then he just lay there, silent, angry, and helpless. Excitement filled him like a toothache, but it refused to enter his flesh. He stroked her breast. This was his wife. He could not ask her to do just a little thing for him, just to help him out, just for a little while, the way he could ask a nigger girl to do it. He lay there, and he sighed. The image of a black girl caused a distant excitement in him, like a far-away light; but, again, the excitement was more like pain; instead of forcing him to act, it made action impossible.

"Go to sleep," she said, gently, "you got a hard day tomorrow."

"Yeah," he said, and rolled over on his side, facing her, one hand still on one breast. "Goddamn the niggers. The black stinking coons.[1] You'd think they'd learn. Wouldn't you think they'd learn? I mean, *wouldn't* you?"

"They going to be out there tomorrow," she said, and took his hand away, "get some sleep."

He lay there, one hand between his legs, staring at the frail sanctuary of his wife. A faint light came from the shutters; the moon was full. Two dogs, far away, were barking at each other, back and forth, insistently, as though they were agreeing to make an appointment. He heard a car coming north on the road and he half sat up, his hand reaching for his holster, which was on a chair near the bed, on top of his pants. The lights hit the shutters and seemed to travel across the room and then went out. The sound of the car slipped away, he heard it hit gravel, then heard it no more. Some liver-lipped students, probably, heading back to that college—but coming from where? His watch said it was two in the morning. They could be coming from anywhere, from out of state most likely, and they would be at the court-house tomorrow. The niggers were getting ready. Well, they would be ready, too.

He moaned. He wanted to let whatever was in him out; but it wouldn't come out. Goddamn! he said aloud, and turned again, on his side, away from Grace, staring at the shutters. He was a big, healthy man and he had never had any trouble sleeping. And he wasn't old enough yet to have any trouble getting it up—he was only forty-two. And he was a good man, a God-fearing man, he had tried to do his duty all his life, and he had been a deputy sheriff for several years. Nothing had ever bothered him before, certainly not getting it up. Sometimes, sure, like any other man, he knew that he wanted a little more spice than Grace could give him and he would drive over yonder and pick up a black piece or arrest her, it came to the same thing, but he couldn't do that now, no more. There was no telling what might happen once your ass was in the air. And they were low enough to kill a man then, too, everyone of them, or the girl herself might do it, right while she was making believe you made her feel so good. The niggers. What had the good Lord Almighty had in mind when he made the niggers? Well. They were pretty good at that, all right. Damn. Damn. Goddamn.

This wasn't helping him to sleep. He turned again, toward Grace again, and moved close to her warm body. He felt something he had never felt before. He felt that he would like to hold her, hold her, hold her, and be buried in her like a child and never have to get up in the morning again and go downtown to face those faces, good Christ, they were ugly! and never have to enter that jail house again and smell that smell and hear that singing; never again feel that filthy, kinky, greasy hair under his hand, never again watch those black breasts leap against the leaping cattle prod, never hear those moans again or watch that blood run down or the fat lips split or the sealed eyes struggle open. They were animals, they were no better than animals, what could be done with people like that? Here they had been in a civilized country for years and they still lived like animals. Their houses were dark, with oil cloth or cardboard in the windows, the smell was enough to make you puke your guts out, and there they sat, a whole tribe, pumping out kids, it looked like, every damn five minutes, and laughing and

---

1. Short for *raccoon*, used as a disparaging term for a black person.

talking and playing music like they didn't have a care in the world, and he reckoned they didn't, neither, and coming to the door, into the sunlight, just standing there, just looking foolish, not thinking of anything but just getting back to what they were doing, saying, Yes suh, Mr. Jesse. I surely will, Mr. Jesse. Fine weather, Mr. Jesse. Why, I thank you, Mr. Jesse. He had worked for a mail-order house for a while and it had been his job to collect the payments for the stuff they bought. They were too dumb to know that they were being cheated blind, but that was no skin off his ass—he was just supposed to do his job. They would be late—they didn't have the sense to put money aside; but it was easy to scare them, and he never really had any trouble. Hell, they all liked him, the kids used to smile when he came to the door. He gave them candy, sometimes, or chewing gum, and rubbed their rough bullet heads—maybe the candy should have been poisoned. Those kids were grown now. He had had trouble with one of them today.

"There was this nigger today," he said; and stopped; his voice sounded peculiar. He touched Grace. "You awake?" he asked. She mumbled something, impatiently, she was probably telling him to go to sleep. It was all right. He knew that he was not alone.

"What a funny time," he said, "to be thinking about a thing like that— you listening?" She mumbled something again. He rolled over on his back. "This nigger's one of the ringleaders. We had trouble with him before. We must have had him out there at the work farm three or four times. Well, Big Jim C. and some of the boys really had to whip that nigger's ass today." He looked over at Grace; he could not tell whether she was listening or not; and he was afraid to ask again. "They had this line you know, to register"—he laughed, but she did not—"and they wouldn't stay where Big Jim C. wanted them, no, they had to start blocking traffic all around the court house so couldn't nothing or nobody get through, and Big Jim C. told them to disperse and they wouldn't move, they just kept up that singing, and Big Jim C. figured that the others would move if this nigger would move, him being the ring-leader, but he wouldn't move and he wouldn't let the others move, so they had to beat him and a couple of the others and they threw them in the wagon—but I didn't see this nigger till I got to the jail. They were still singing and I was supposed to make them stop. Well, I couldn't make them stop for me but I knew he could make them stop. He was lying on the ground jerking and moaning, they had threw him in a cell by himself, and blood was coming out his ears from where Big Jim C. and his boys had whipped him. Wouldn't you think they'd learn? I put the prod to him and he jerked some more and he kind of screamed—but he didn't have much voice left. "You make them stop that singing," I said to him, "you hear me? You make them stop that singing." He acted like he didn't hear me and I put it to him again, under his arms, and he just rolled around on the floor and blood started coming from his mouth. He'd pissed his pants already." He paused. His mouth felt dry and his throat was as rough as sandpaper; as he talked, he began to hurt all over with that peculiar excitement which refused to be released. "You all are going to stop your singing, I said to him, and you are going to stop coming down to the court house and disrupting traffic and molesting the people and keeping us from our duties and keeping doctors from getting to sick white women and getting all them Northerners in this town to give our town a bad name—!" As he said this, he kept prodding the boy, sweat pouring from beneath the helmet he had not yet taken off. The boy rolled around in his own dirt and water and blood and tried to scream again as the prod hit his testicles, but the scream did not come out, only a kind of rattle and a moan. He stopped. He was not supposed to kill the nigger. The cell was filled with a terrible odor. The boy was still. "You hear me?" he called. "You had enough?" The singing went on. "You had enough?" His foot leapt out, he had not known it was going to, and caught the boy flush on the jaw. *Jesus,* he thought, *this ain't no nigger, this is a goddamn bull,* and he screamed again, "You had enough? You going to make them stop that singing now?"

But the boy was out. And now he was shaking worse than the boy had been shaking. He was glad no one could see him. At the same time, he felt very close to a very peculiar, particular joy; something deep in him and deep in his memory was stirred, but whatever was in his memory eluded him. He took off his helmet. He walked to the cell door.

"White man," said the boy, from the floor, behind him.

He stopped. For some reason, he grabbed his privates.

"You remember Old Julia?"

The boy said, from the floor, with his mouth full of blood, and one eye, barely open, glaring like the eye of a cat in the dark, "My grandmother's name was Mrs. Julia Blossom. *Mrs.* Julia Blossom. You going to call our women by their right names yet.—And those kids ain't going to stop singing. We going to keep on singing until every one of you miserable white mothers go stark raving out of your minds." Then he closed the one eye; he spat blood; his head fell back against the floor.

He looked down at the boy, whom he had been seeing, off and on, for more than a year, and suddenly remembered him: Old Julia had been one of his mail-order customers, a nice old woman. He had not seen her for years, he supposed that she must be dead.

He had walked into the yard, the boy had been sitting in a swing. He had smiled at the boy, and asked, "Old Julia home?"

The boy looked at him for a long time before he answered. "Don't no Old Julia live here."

"This is her house. I know her. She's lived her for years."

The boy shook his head. "You might know a Old Julia someplace else, white man. But don't nobody by that name live here."

He watched the boy; the boy watched him. The boy certainly wasn't more than ten. *White man.* He didn't have time to be fooling around with some crazy kid. He yelled, "Hey! Old Julia!"

But only silence answered him. The expression on the boy's face did not change. The sun beat down on them both, still and silent; he had the feeling that he had been caught up in a nightmare, a nightmare dreamed by a child; perhaps one of the nightmares he himself had dreamed as a child. It had that feeling—everything familiar, without undergoing any other change, had been subtly and hideously displaced: the trees, the sun, the patches of grass in the yard, the leaning porch and the weary porch steps and the card-board in the windows and the black hole of the door which looked like the entrance to a cave, and the eyes of the pickaninny,[2] all, all, were charged with malevolence. *White man.* He looked at the boy. "She's gone out?"

The boy said nothing.

---

2. Child.

"Well," he said, "tell her I passed by and I'll pass by next week." He started to go; he stopped. "You want some chewing gum?"

The boy got down from the swing and started for the house. He said, "I don't want nothing you got, white man." He walked into the house and closed the door behind him.

Now the boy looked as though he were dead. Jesse wanted to go over to him and pick him up and pistol whip him until the boy's head burst open like a melon. He began to tremble with what he believed was rage, sweat, both cold and hot, raced down his body, the singing filled him as though it were a weird, uncontrollable, monstrous howling rumbling up from the depths of his own belly, he felt an icy fear rise in him and raise him up, and he shouted, he howled, "You lucky we *pump* some white blood into you every once in a while—your women! Here's what I got for all the black bitches in the world—!" Then he was, abruptly, almost too weak to stand; to his bewilderment, his horror, beneath his own fingers, he felt himself violently stiffen—with no warning at all; he dropped his hands and he stared at the boy and he left the cell.

"All that singing they do," he said. "All that singing." He could not remember the first time he had heard it; he had been hearing it all his life. It was the sound with which he was most familiar—though it was also the sound of which he had been least conscious—and it had always contained an obscure comfort. They were singing to God. They were singing for mercy and they hoped to go to heaven, and he had even sometimes felt, when looking into the eyes of some of the old women, a few of the very old men, that they were singing for mercy for his soul, too. Of course he had never thought of their heaven or of what God was, or could be, for them; God was the same for everyone, he supposed, and heaven was where good people went—he supposed. He had never thought much about what it meant to be a good person. He tried to be a good person and treat everybody right: it wasn't his fault if the niggers had taken it into their heads to fight against God and go against the rules laid down in the Bible for everyone to read! Any preacher would tell you that. He was only doing his duty: Protecting white people from the niggers and the niggers from themselves. And there were still lots of good niggers around—he had to remember that; they weren't all like that boy this afternoon; and the good niggers must be mighty sad to see what was happening to their people. They would thank him when this was over. In that way they had, the best of them, not quite looking him in the eye, in a low voice, with a little smile: We surely thanks you, Mr. Jesse. From the bottom of our hearts, we thanks you. He smiled. They hadn't all gone crazy. This trouble would pass.—He knew that the young people had changed some of the words to the songs. He had scarcely listened to the words before and he did not listen to them now; but he knew that the words were different; he could hear that much. He did not know if the faces were different, he had never, before this trouble began, watched them as they sang, but he certainly did not like what he saw now. They hated him, and this hatred was blacker than their hearts, blacker than their skins, redder than their blood, and harder, by far, than his club. Each day, each night, he felt worn out, aching, with their smell in his nostrils and filling his lungs, as though he were drowning—drowning in niggers; and it was all to be done again when he awoke. It would never end. It would never end. Perhaps this was what the singing had meant all along. They had not been singing black folks into heaven, they had been singing white folks into hell.

Everyone felt this black suspicion in many ways, but no one knew how to express it. Men much older than he, who had been responsible for law and order much longer than he, were now much quieter than they had been, and the tone of their jokes, in a way that he could not quite put his finger on, had changed. These men were his models, they had been friends to his father, and they had taught him what it meant to be a man. He looked to them for courage now. It wasn't that he didn't know that what he was doing was right—he knew that, nobody had to tell him that; it was only that he missed the ease of former years. But they didn't have much time to hang out with each other these days. They tended to stay close to their families every free minute because nobody knew what might happen next. Explosions rocked the night of their tranquil town. Each time each man wondered silently if perhaps this time the dynamite had not fallen into the wrong hands. They thought that they knew where all the guns were; but they could not possibly know every move that was made in that secret place where the darkies lived. From time to time it was suggested that they form a posse and search the home of every nigger, but they hadn't done it yet. For one thing, this might have brought the bastards from the North down on their backs; for another, although the niggers were scattered throughout the town—down in the hollow near the railroad tracks, way west near the mills, up on the hill, the well-off ones, and some out near the college—nothing seemed to happen in one part of town without the niggers immediately knowing it in the other. This meant that they could not take them by surprise. They rarely mentioned it, but they *knew* that some of the niggers had guns. It stood to reason, as they said, since, after all, some of them had been in the Army. There were niggers in the Army right now and God knows they wouldn't have had any trouble stealing this half-assed government blind—the whole world was doing it, look at the European countries and all those countries in Africa. They made jokes about it—bitter jokes; and they cursed the government in Washington, which had betrayed them; but they had not yet formed a posse. Now, if their town had been laid out like some towns in the North, where all the niggers lived together in one locality, they could have gone down and set fire to the houses and brought about peace that way. If the niggers had all lived in one place, they could have kept the fire in one place. But the way this town was laid out, the fire could hardly be controlled. It would spread all over town—and the niggers would probably be helping it to spread. Still, from time to time, they spoke of doing it, anyway; so that now there was a real fear among them that somebody might go crazy and light the match.

They rarely mentioned anything not directly related to the war that they were fighting, but this had failed to establish between them the unspoken communication of soldiers during a war. Each man, in the thrilling silence which sped outward from their exchanges, their laughter, and their anecdotes, seemed wrestling, in various degrees of darkness, with a secret which he could not articulate to himself, and which, however directly it related to the war, related yet more surely to his privacy and his past. They could no longer be sure, after all, that they had all done the same things. They had never dreamed that their privacy could contain any element of terror, could threaten, that is, to reveal itself, to the scrutiny of a judgment day, while remaining unreadable and inaccessible to themselves; nor had they dreamed that the past, while certainly refusing to be forgotten, could yet so stubbornly refuse to be remembered. They felt themselves mysteriously set at naught, as no longer entering into the real concerns of other people—while here they were, out-numbered, fighting to save the civilized world. They had thought that people would care—people didn't care; not enough, anyway, to help them. It would have been a help, really, or at least a relief, even to have been forced to surrender. Thus they had lost, probably forever, their old and easy connection with each other. They were forced to depend on each other more and, at the same time, to trust each other less. Who could tell when one of them might not betray them all, for money, or for the ease of confession? But no one dared imagine what there might be to confess. They were soldiers fighting a war, but their relationship to each other was that of accomplices in a crime. They all had to keep their mouths shut.

I stepped in the river at Jordan.[3]

Out of the darkness of the room, out of nowhere, the line came flying up at him, with the melody and the beat. He turned wordlessly toward his sleeping wife. *I stepped in the river at Jordan.* Where had he heard that song?

"Grace," he whispered. "You awake?"

She did not answer. If she was awake, she wanted him to sleep. Her breathing was slow and easy, her body slowly rose and fell.

I stepped in the river at Jordan.
The water came to my knees.

He began to sweat. He felt an overwhelming fear, which yet contained a curious and dreadful pleasure.

I stepped in the river at Jordan.
The water came to my waist.

It had been night, as it was now, he was in the car between his mother and his father, sleepy, his head in his mother's lap, sleepy, and yet full of excitement. The singing came from far away, across the dark fields. There were no lights anywhere. They had said good-bye to all the others and turned off on this dark dirt road. They were almost home.

I stepped in the river at Jordan,
The water came over my head,
I looked way over to the other side,
He was making up my dying bed!

"I guess they singing for him," his father said, seeming very weary and subdued now. "Even when they're sad, they sound like they just about to go and tear off a piece." He yawned and leaned across the boy and slapped his wife lightly on the shoulder, allowing his hand to rest there for a moment. "Don't they?"

"Don't talk that way," she said.

"Well, that's what we going to do," he said, "you can make up your mind to that." He started whistling. "You see? When I begin to feel it, I gets kind of musical, too."

Oh, Lord! Come on and ease my troubling mind!

He had a black friend, his age, eight, who lived nearby. His name was Otis. They wrestled together in the dirt. Now the thought of Otis made him sick. He began to shiver. His mother put her arm around him.

---

3. From a version of the Negro spiritual "Wade in the Water." The Jordan River marked the threshold to the Promised Land for the Israelites (see Joshua 3.1–17). For black slaves, the Jordan symbolized freedom.

"He's tired," she said.

"We'll be home soon," said his father. He began to whistle again.

"We didn't see Otis this morning," Jesse said. He did not know why he said this. His voice, in the darkness of the car, sounded small and accusing.

"You haven't seen Otis for a couple of mornings," his mother said.

That was true. But he was only concerned about *this* morning.

"No," said his father, "I reckon Otis's folks was afraid to let him show himself this morning."

"But Otis didn't do nothing!" Now his voice sounded questioning.

"Otis *can't* do nothing," said his father, "he's too little." The car lights picked up their wooden house, which now solemnly approached them, the lights falling around it like yellow dust. Their dog, chained to a tree, began to bark.

"We just want to make sure Otis *don't* do nothing," said his father, and stopped the car. He looked down at Jesse. "And you tell him what your Daddy said, you hear?"

"Yes sir," he said.

His father switched off the lights. The dog moaned and pranced, but they ignored him and went inside. He could not sleep. He lay awake, hearing the night sounds, the dog yawning and moaning outside, the sawing of the crickets, the cry of the owl, dogs barking far away, then no sounds at all, just the heavy, endless buzzing of the night. The darkness pressed on his eyelids like a scratchy blanket. He turned, he turned again. He wanted to call his mother, but he knew his father would not like this. He was terribly afraid. Then he heard his father's voice in the other room, low, with a joke in it; but this did not help him, it frightened him more, he knew what was going to happen. He put his head under the blanket, then pushed his head out again, for fear, staring at the dark window. He heard his mother's moan, his father's sigh; he gritted his teeth. Then their bed began to rock. His father's breathing seemed to fill the world.

That morning, before the sun had gathered all its strength, men and women, some flushed and some pale with excitement, came with news. Jesse's father seemed to know what the news was before the first jalopy stopped in the yard, and he ran out, crying, "They got him, then? They got him?"

The first jalopy held eight people, three men and two women and three children. The children were sitting on the laps of the grown-ups. Jesse knew two of them, the two boys; they shyly and uncomfortably greeted each other. He did not know the girl.

"Yes, they got him," said one of the women, the older one, who wore a wide hat and a fancy, faded blue dress. "They found him early this morning."

"How far had he got?" Jesse's father asked.

"He hadn't got no further than Harkness," one of the men said. "Look like he got lost up there in all them trees—or maybe he just go so scared he couldn't move." They all laughed.

"Yes, and you know it's near a graveyard, too," said the younger woman, and they laughed again.

"Is that where they got him now?" asked Jesse's father.

By this time there were three cars piled behind the first one, with everyone looking excited and shining, and Jesse noticed that they were carrying food. It was like a Fourth of July picnic.

"Yeah, that's where he is," said one of the men, "declare, Jesse, you going to keep us here all day long, answering your damn fool questions. Come on, we ain't got no time to waste."

"Don't bother putting up no food," cried a woman from one of the other cars, "we got enough. Just come on."

"Why, thank you," said Jesse's father, "we be right along, then."

"I better get a sweater for the boy," said his mother, "in case it turns cold."

Jesse watched his mother's thin legs cross the yard. He knew that she also wanted to comb her hair a little and maybe put on a better dress, the dress she wore to church. His father guessed this, too, for he yelled behind her, "Now don't you go trying to turn yourself into no movie star. You just come on." But he laughed as he said this, and winked at the men; his wife was younger and prettier than most of the other women. He clapped Jesse on the head and started pulling him toward the car. "You all go on," he said, "I'll be right behind you. Jesse, you go tie up that there dog while I get this car started."

The cars sputtered and coughed and shook; the caravan began to move; bright dust filled the air. As soon as he was tied up, the dog began to bark. Jesse's mother came out of the house, carrying a jacket for his father and a sweater for Jesse. She had put a ribbon in her hair and had an old shawl around her shoulders.

"Put these in the car, son," she said, and handed everything to him. She bent down and stroked the dog, looked to see if there was water in his bowl, then went back up the three porch steps and closed the door.

"Come on," said his father, "ain't nothing in there for nobody to steal." He was sitting in the car, which trembled and belched. The last car of the caravan had disappeared but the sound of singing floated behind them.

Jesse got into the car, sitting close to his father, loving the smell of the car, and the trembling, and the bright day, and the sense of going on a great and unexpected journey. His mother got in and closed the door and the car began to move. Not until then did he ask, "Where are we going? Are we going on a picnic?"

He had a feeling that he knew where they were going, but he was not sure.

"That's right," his father said, "we're going on a picnic. You won't ever forget *this* picnic—!"

"Are we," he asked, after a moment, "going to see the bad nigger—the one that knocked down old Miss Standish?"

"Well, I reckon," said his mother, "that we *might* see him."

He started to ask, *Will a lot of niggers be there? Will Otis be there?*—but he did not ask his question, to which, in a strange and uncomfortable way, he already knew the answer. Their friends, in the other cars, stretched up the road as far as he could see; other cars had joined them; there were cars behind them. They were singing. The sun seemed suddenly very hot, and he was at once very happy and a little afraid. He did not quite understand what was happening, and he did not know what to ask—he had no one to ask. He had grown accustomed, for the solution of such mysteries, to go to Otis. He felt that Otis knew everything. But he could not ask Otis about this. Anyway, he had not seen Otis for two days; he had not seen a black face anywhere for more than two days; and he now realized, as they began chugging up the long hill which eventually led to Harkness, that there were no black faces on the road this morning, no black people anywhere. From the houses in which they lived, all along the road, no smoke curled, no life stirred—maybe one or two chickens were to be seen, that was all. There was no one at the windows, no one in the yard, no one sitting on the porches, and the doors were closed. He had come this road many a time and seen women washing in the yard (there were no clothes on the clotheslines) men working in the fields, children playing in the dust; black men passed them on the road other mornings, other days, on foot, or in wagons, sometimes in cars, tipping their hats, smiling, joking, their teeth a solid white against their skin, their eyes as warm as the sun, the blackness of their skin like dull fire against the white of the blue or the grey of their torn clothes. They passed the nigger church—dead-white, desolate, locked up; and the graveyard, where no one knelt or walked, and he saw no flowers. He wanted to ask, *Where are they? Where are they all?* But he did not dare. As the hill grew steeper, the sun grew colder. He looked at his mother and his father. They looked straight ahead, seeming to be listening to the singing which echoed and echoed in this graveyard silence. They were strangers to him now. They were looking at something he could not see. His father's lips had a strange, cruel curve, he wet his lips from time to time, and swallowed. He was terribly aware of his father's tongue, it was as though he had never seen it before. And his father's body suddenly seemed immense, bigger than a mountain. His eyes, which were grey-green, looked yellow in the sunlight; or at least there was a light in them which he had never seen before. His mother patted her hair and adjusted the ribbon, leaning forward to look into the car mirror. "You look all right," said his father, and laughed. "When that nigger looks at you, he's going to swear he threw his life away for nothing. Wouldn't be surprised if he don't come back to haunt you." And he laughed again.

The singing now slowly began to cease; and he realized that they were nearing their destination. They had reached a straight, narrow, pebbly road, with trees on either side. The sunlight filtered down on them from a great height, as though they were under-water; and the branches of the trees scraped against the cars with a tearing sound. To the right of them, and beneath them, invisible now, lay the town; and to the left, miles of trees which led to the high mountain range which his ancestors had crossed in order to settle in this valley. Now, all was silent, except for the bumping of the tires against the rocky road, the sputtering of motors, and the sound of a crying child. And they seemed to move more slowly. They were beginning to climb again. He watched the cars ahead as they toiled patiently upward, disappearing into the sunlight of the clearing. Presently, he felt their vehicle also rise, heard his father's changed breathing, the sunlight hit his face, the trees moved away from them, and they were there. As their car crossed the clearing, he looked around. There seemed to be millions, there were certainly hundreds of people in the clearing, staring toward something he could not see. There was a fire. He could not see the flames, but he smelled the smoke. Then they were on the other side of the clearing, among the trees again. His father drove off the road and parked the car behind a great many other cars. He looked down at Jesse.

"You all right?" he asked.

"Yes sir," he said.

"Well, come on, then," his father said. He reached over and opened the door on his mother's side. His mother stepped out first. They followed her into the clearing. At first he was aware only of confusion, of his mother and father greeting and being greeted, himself being handled, hugged, and patted, and told how much he had grown. The wind blew the smoke from the fire across the clearing into his eyes and nose. He could not see over the backs of the people in front of him. The sounds of laughing and cursing and wrath—and something else—rolled in waves from the front of the mob to the back. Those in front expressed their delight at what they saw, and this delight rolled backward, wave upon wave, across the clearing, more acrid than the smoke. His father reached down suddenly and sat Jesse on his shoulders.

Now he saw the fire—of twigs and boxes, piled high; flames made pale orange and yellow and thin as a veil under the steadier light of the sun; grey-blue smoke rolled upward and poured over their heads. Beyond the shifting curtain of fire and smoke, he made out first only a length of gleaming chain, attached to a great limb of the tree; then he saw that this chain bound two black hands together at the wrist, dirty yellow palm facing dirty yellow palm. The smoke poured up; the hands dropped out of sight; a cry went up from the crowd. Then the hands slowly came into view again, pulled upward by the chain. This time he saw the kinky, sweating, bloody head—he had never before seen a head with so much hair on it, hair so black and so tangled that it seemed like another jungle. The head was hanging. He saw the forehead, flat and high, with a kind of arrow of hair in the center, like he had, like his father had; they called it a widow's peak; and the mangled eye brows, the wide nose, the closed eyes, and the glinting eye lashes and the hanging lips, all streaming with blood and sweat. His hands were straight above his head. All his weight pulled downward from his hands; and he was a big man, a bigger man than his father, and black as an African jungle Cat, and naked. Jesse pulled upward; his father's hands held him firmly by the ankles. He wanted to say something, he did not know what, but nothing he said could have been heard, for now the crowd roared again as a man stepped forward and put more wood on the fire. The flames leapt up. He thought he heard the hanging man scream, but he was not sure. Sweat was pouring from the hair in his armpits, poured down his sides, over his chest, into his navel and his groin. He was lowered again; he was raised again. Now Jesse knew that he heard him scream. The head went back, the mouth wide open, blood bubbling from the mouth; the veins of the neck jumped out; Jesse clung to his father's neck in terror as the cry rolled over the crowd. The cry of all the people rose to answer the dying man's cry. He wanted death to come quickly. They wanted to make death wait: and it was they who held death, now, on a leash which they lengthened little by little. *What did he do?* Jesse wondered. *What did the man do? What did he do?*—but he could not ask his father. He was seated on his father's shoulders, but his father was far away. There were two older men, friends of his father's, raising and lowering the chain; everyone, indiscriminately, seemed to be responsible for the fire. There was no hair left on the nigger's privates, and the eyes, now, were wide open, as white as the eyes of a clown or a doll. The smoke now carried a terrible odor across the clearing, the odor of something burning which was both sweet and rotten.

He turned his head a little and saw the field of faces. He watched his mother's face. Her eyes were very bright, her mouth was open: she was more beautiful than he had ever seen her, and more strange. He began to feel a joy he had never felt before. He watched the hanging, gleaming body, the most beautiful and terrible object he had ever seen till then. One of his father's friends reached up and in his hands he held a knife: and Jesse wished that he had been that man. It was a long, bright knife and the sun seemed to catch it, to play with it, to caress it—it was brighter than the fire. And a wave of laughter swept the crowd. Jesse felt his father's hands on his ankles slip and tighten. The man with the knife walked toward the crowd, smiling slightly; as though this were a signal, silence fell; he heard his mother cough. Then the man with the knife walked up to the hanging body. He turned and smiled again. Now there was a silence all over the field. The hanging head looked up. It seemed fully conscious now, as though the fire had burned out terror and pain. The man with the knife took the nigger's privates in his hand, one hand, still smiling, as though he were weighing them. In the cradle of the one white hand, the nigger's privates seemed as remote as meat being weighed in the scales; but seemed heavier, too, much heavier, and Jesse felt his scrotum tighten; and huge, huge, much bigger than his father's, flaccid, hairless, the largest thing he had ever seen till then, and the blackest. The white hand stretched them, cradled them, caressed them. Then the dying man's eyes looked straight into Jesse's eyes—it could not have been as long as a second, but it seemed longer than a year. Then Jesse screamed, and the crowd screamed as the knife flashed, first up, then down, cutting the dreadful thing away, and the blood came roaring down. Then the crowd rushed forward, tearing at the body with their hands, with knives, with rocks, with stones, howling and cursing. Jesse's head, of its own weight, fell downward toward his father's head. Someone stepped forward and drenched the body with kerosene. Where the man had been, a great sheet of flame appeared. Jesse's father lowered him to the ground.

"Well, I told you," said his father, "you wasn't never going to forget *this* picnic." His father's face was full of sweat, his eyes were very peaceful. At that moment Jesse loved his father more than he had ever loved him. He felt that his father had carried him through a mighty test, had revealed to him a great secret which would be the key to his life forever.

"I reckon," he said. "I reckon."

Jesse's father took him by the hand and, with his mother a little behind them, talking and laughing with the other women, they walked through the crowd, across the clearing. The black body was on the ground, the chain which had held it was being rolled up by one of his father's friends. Whatever the fire had left undone, the hands and the knives and the stones of the people had accomplished. The head was caved in, one eye was torn out, one ear was hanging. But one had to look carefully to realize this, for it was, now, merely, a black charred object on the black, charred ground. He lay spread-eagled with what had been a wound between what had been his legs.

"They going to leave him here, then?" Jesse whispered.

"Yeah," said his father, "they'll come and get him by and by. I reckon we better get over there and get some of that food before it's all gone."

"I reckon," he muttered now to himself, "I reckon." Grace stirred and touched him on the thigh: the moonlight covered her like glory. Something bubbled up in him, his nature again returned to him. He thought of the boy in the cell; he thought of the man in the fire; he thought of the knife and grabbed himself and stroked himself and a terrible sound, something between a high laugh and a howl, came out of him and dragged his sleeping wife up on one elbow. She stared at him in a moonlight which had now grown cold as ice. He thought of the morning and grabbed her, laughing and crying, crying and laughing, and he whispered, as he stroked her, as he took her, "Come on, sugar, I'm going to do you like a nigger, just like a nigger, come on, sugar, and love me just like you'd love a nigger." He thought of the morning as he labored and she moaned, thought of morning as he labored harder than he ever had before, and before his labors had ended, he heard the first cock crow and the dogs begin to bark, and the sound of tires on the gravel road.

1965

BOB KAUFMAN
1925–1986

Born on April 18, 1925, in New Orleans to an Orthodox German Jewish father and a Catholic mother of African descent, Bob Kaufman has been referred to as the "black Rimbaud" of the Beat poets. Some think of him as the Beat movement's "unsung Patriarch"; and for sure, he is not frequently included in the roll call of bad boys that embraces the likes of Ferlinghetti, Kerouac, Rexroth, Burrows, Ginsberg, and Corso, whose works, *Howl, On the Road,* and *Naked Lunch,* among others, have generally been accepted as the leading benchmarks of this alternative American culture that sprang up among the bars and gay places of San Francisco in the 1950s and 1960s. But inspired by the musical innovations of Charlie Parker, Dizzy Gillespie, and Miles Davis, Kaufman fashioned a poetry that was decidedly modernist in its irrational, surrealist, and Dadaistic appeal. Some have even attributed the term *Beat* to Kaufman and his fine sense of wordplay. One critic suggests that Kaufman's poetic practice adapts the "harmonic complexities and spontaneous inventions of bebop to poetic euphony and meter," employing "the jargon of bebop and the improvisational structure" of this musical genre in the interest of poetic discourse. The "quintessential jazz poet," Kaufman also borrowed some of his licks from jazz singer and songwriter King Pleasure. But his repertoire of heroes showed a considerable catholicity of taste as it included the literary figures Walt Whitman, Hart Crane, Albert Camus, and Guillaume Apollinaire. Kaufman's poetry crosses the thematic range of Beat concerns—madness, poverty, spontaneity, and the search for holiness. Superimposed on Kaufman's metrical innovations, these influences combine to make the poet an invigorating radical and unconventional voice.

One of the younger of thirteen siblings, Kaufman searched at length for a system of values, a basis for belief, and found it, in part, in an eventual strong identification with the philosophy of Buddhism. After attending elementary school in New Orleans, he left home at the seventh or eighth grade for a life at sea and spent twenty years in the U.S. merchant marine, during which time he acquired a taste for literature. In the late 1950s, he settled in San Francisco, with his wife, Eileen. One of the key figures of the burgeoning literary scene on the West Coast, he produced at least two classic works of the Beat school—a broadside titled "Abomunist Manifesto" (1959) and *Solitudes Crowded with Loneliness* (1965). The former, "an indictment of contemporary society," might be taken as a programmatic statement of Beat intent and purpose, though we would be hard pressed to think of the original Beatniks as "programmatic" in any rigorous sense. One poem from *Solitudes*—"Bagel Shop Jazz," its title resonating across disparate cultures—won the poet the Guiness Poetry Award and appeared in the fourth volume of the *Guiness Book of Poetry* in 1961. Kaufman's *Golden Sardine* came out in 1967. "Crootey Song," from this collection, is said to have abandoned "language altogether in an attempt to reproduce a bebop scat improvisation."

For almost a decade after the publication of *Golden Sardine*, Kaufman, it is said, did not speak a word, but he dramatically breached his silence on the day that the Vietnam War ended. Over the next few years, Kaufman wrote new poems that were collected in *The Ancient Rain: Poems 1956–1978* (1981). But in 1978, Kaufman renounced both writing and speech and withdrew once again into a silent place. A target of police harrassment, a user of drugs, and no stranger to madness and its anguish, Kaufman died of emphysema and cirrhosis on a Sunday morning, January 12, 1986, in San Francisco. It is not difficult to trace the cutting edge of his poetry down to the succeeding generation of black nationalists and the Black Arts movement of the sixties, especially in the chanting poems of LeRoi Jones's and Larry Neal's important anthology *Black Fire*.

Jail Poems

1

I am sitting in a cell with a view of evil parallels,
Waiting thunder to splinter me into a thousand me's.
It is not enough to be in one cage with one self;
I want to sit opposite every prisoner in every hole.
Doors roll and bang, every slam a finality, bang!   5
The junkie disappeared into a red noise, stoning out his hell.
The odored wino congratulates himself on not smoking,
Fingerprints left lying on black inky gravestones,
Noises of pain seeping through steel walls crashing
Reach my own hurt. I become part of someone forever.   10
Wild accents of criminals are sweeter to me than hum of cops,
Busy battening down hatches of human souls; cargo
Destined for ports of accusations, harbors of guilt.
What do policemen eat, Socrates,[1] still prisoner, old one?

2

Painter, paint me a crazy jail, mad water-color cells.   15
Poet, how old is suffering? Write it in yellow lead.
God, make me a sky on my glass ceiling. I need stars now,
To lead through this atmosphere of shrieks and private hells,
Entrances and exits, in . . . out . . . up . . . down, the civic seesaw.
Here—me—now—hear—me—now—always here somehow.   20

3

In a universe of cells—who is not in jail? Jailers.
In a world of hospitals—who is not sick? Doctors.
A golden sardine is swimming in my head.

---

1. Ancient Greek teacher and philosopher (470–399 B.C.E.) who was charged with the corruption of youth; he was sentenced to die by drinking hemlock.

Oh we know some things, man, about some things
Like jazz and jails and God.   25
Saturday is a good day to go to jail.

4

Now they give a new form, quivering jelly-like,
That proves any boy can be president of Muscatel.[2]
They are mad at him because he's one of Them.
Gray-speckled unplanned nakedness; stinking   30
Fingers grasping toilet bowl. Mr. America wants to bathe.
Look! On the floor, lying across America's face—
A real movie star featured in a million newsreels.
What am I doing—feeling compassion?
When he comes out of it, he will help kill me.   35
He probably hates living.

5

Nuts, skin bolts, clanking in his stomach, scrambled.
His society's gone to pieces in his belly, bloated.
See the great American windmill, tilting at itself,
Good solid stock, the kind that made America drunk.   40
Success written all over his street-streaked ass.
Successful-type success, forty home runs in one inning.
Stop suffering, Jack, you can't fool us. We know.
This is the greatest country in the world, ain't it?
He didn't make it. Wino in Cell 3.   45

6

There have been too many years in this short span of mine.
My soul demands a cave of its own, like the Jain[3] god;
Yet I must make it go on, hard like jazz, glowing
In this dark plastic jungle, land of long night, chilled.
My navel is a button to push when I want inside out.   50
Am I not more than a mass of entrails and rough tissue?
Must I break my bones? Drink my wine-diluted blood?
Should I dredge old sadness from my chest?
Not again,
All those ancient balls of fire, hotly swallowed, let them lie. 55
Let me spit breath mists of introspection, bits of me,
So that when I am gone, I shall be in the air.

7

Someone whom I am is no one.
Something I have done is nothing.
Someplace I have been is nowhere.   60
I am not me.
What of the answers
I must find questions for?
All these strange streets

---

2. Sweet fortified wine made from Muscat grapes.
3. One who practices the Indian religion of Jainism, which teaches that salvation can be achieved
through knowledge, faith, and good conduct.

I must find cities for,
Thank God for beatniks.   65

8

All night the stink of rotting people,
Fumes rising from pyres of live men,
Fill my nose with gassy disgust,
Drown my exposed eyes in tears.   70

9

Traveling God salesmen, bursting my ear drum
With the dullest part of a good sexy book,
Impatient for Monday and adding machines.

10

Yellow-eyed dogs whistling in evening.

11

The baby came to jail today.   75

12

One more day to hell, filled with floating glands.

13

The jail, a huge hollow metal cube
Hanging from the moon by a silver chain.
Someday Johnny Appleseed is going to chop it down.

14

Three long strings of light   80
Braided into a ray.

15

I am apprehensive about my future;
My past has turned its back on me.

16

Shadows I see, forming on the wall,
Pictures of desires protected from my own eyes.   85

17

After spending all night constructing a dream,
Morning came and blinded me with light.
Now I seek among mountains of crushed eggshells
For the God damned dream I never wanted.

18

Sitting here writing things on paper,   90
Instead of sticking the pencil into the air.

19

The Battle of Monumental Failures raging,
Both hoping for a good clean loss.

20

Now I see the night, silently overwhelming day.

21

Caught in imaginary webs of conscience,   95
I weep over my acts, yet believe.

22

Cities should be built on one side of the street.

23

People who can't cast shadows
Never die of freckles.

24

The end always comes last.   100

25

We sat at a corner table,
Devouring each other word by word,
Until nothing was left, repulsive skeletons.

26

I sit here writing, not daring to stop,
For fear of seeing what's outside my head.   105

27

There, Jesus, didn't hurt a bit, did it?

28

I am afraid to follow my flesh over those narrow
Wide hard soft female beds, but I do.

29

Link by link, we forged the chain.
Then, discovering the end around our necks,   110
We bugged out.

30

I have never seen a wild poetic loaf of bread,
But if I did, I would eat it, crust and all.

31

From how many years away does a baby come?

32

Universality, duality, totality . . . . one.

33

The defective on the floor, mumbling,
Was once a man who shouted across tables.

34

Come, help flatten a raindrop.

*Written in San Francisco City Prison
Cell 3, 1959*

1965

LORRAINE HANSBERRY
1930–1965

W hen *A Raisin in the Sun* debuted at the Ethel Barrymore Theater in March 1959, Lorraine Hansberry became the first black woman to have a play produced on Broadway. When it went on to win the New York Drama Critics Circle award for Best Play of the Year, beating out Tennessee Williams's *Sweet Bird of Youth* and Eugene O'Neill's *A Touch of the Poet,* Hansberry became the youngest writer and first black to achieve that distinction. Running for 538 performances, *A Raisin in the Sun* broke yet another record as the longest running play by an African American on Broadway.

Since its first appearance, the popularity of *A Raisin in the Sun* with American audiences has never waned, and its impact on modern drama has been consistently noted. The play has been hailed a classic and often placed in that small inner circle of American dramas that includes Arthur Miller's *Death of a Salesman,* Tennessee Williams's *The Glass Menagerie,* and Eugene O'Neill's *Long Day's Journey into Night.*

Originally titling the play "The Crystal Stair," after a line from Langston Hughes's "Mother to Son," Hansberry finally settled on a line from "Harlem," another Hughes poem: "What happens to a dream deferred? / Does it dry up / like a raisin in the sun. . . . *Or does it explode?*" In its dramatization of deferred dreams that ever threaten to explode, *A Raisin in the Sun* has been likened to Richard Wright's *Native Son.* Beginning with the sound of the alarm clock that opens the play, some note, the play bears a striking resemblance to Wright's novel. Others press the comparison still further to suggest that *A Raisin in the Sun* is to black drama what Richard Wright's *Native Son* is to the black novel.

Born May 19, 1930, on the South Side of Chicago, Lorraine Vivian Hansberry was the youngest of four children of Carl A. Hansberry and Nanny Perry Hansberry. She enjoyed a comfortable, middle-class existence, and the prominence of her family in Chicago, as well as national, black political circles brought her into contact with such figures as Paul Robeson; Duke Ellington; and Walter White, novelist and former secretary of the NAACP. Her uncle Leo Hansberry, distinguished professor of African history at Howard University, is credited with influencing the pan-African dimension of Hansberry's work, which in turn globalized her commitments to black liberation struggles.

Hansberry became personally acquainted with struggles for social and political change when her family challenged Chicago's restrictive real estate covenants and became a test case for integrated housing in 1938. Hansberry, then eight years old, would go on to describe that moment: "howling mobs surrounded [our] house," throwing bricks in protest against the move. Hansberry's father eventually won the case in a historic 1940 Supreme Court decision (*Hansberry v. Lee*).

Hansberry's interests in drama were sparked when she wandered into a rehearsal of Sean O'Casey's *Juno and the Paycock*, while a student at the University of Wisconsin. Dissatisfied with the Wisconsin curriculum, she left for New York in 1950, where she worked as a reporter for Robeson's radical black newspaper, *Freedom*, writing reviews and essays, and eventually becoming associate editor. She was actively involved in peace and freedom movements, marching on picket lines and protesting against the domination of a white power elite. It was while marching on a picket line that she met Robert Nemiroff, whom she married in 1953 and with whom she maintained a strong artistic relationship even after their separation and subsequent divorce. The year she married, Hansberry resigned from *Freedom* to pursue her ambitions as a playwright.

While the forces that collaborated to create *A Raisin in the Sun* are multiple, Hansberry could not have chosen a more propitious moment to dramatize the role of racial discrimination in deferring the dreams of a black family for decent housing. The play appeared five years after *Brown v. the Board of Education,* the Supreme Court's landmark decision on school desegregation; four years after the Montgomery Bus Boycott; and on the eve of the student sit-in movement. For these reasons, Amiri Baraka called *A Raisin in the Sun* the "quintessential civil rights drama."

Her commitments to social commentary, but not to agitprop, led Hansberry to employ the conventional realism of the well-made play, a style that other classic American dramatists had used to full effect, but one that seemed already anachronistic by 1959. Hansberry described her work as "genuine realism," which she distinguished from naturalism:

> Naturalism tends to take the world as it is and say: this is what it is, this is how it happens, it is "true" because we see it everyday in life that way—you know, you simply photograph the garbage can. But in realism—I think the artist who is creating the realistic work imposes on it not only what is but what is *possible* . . . because that is part of reality too.

While critics have been almost uniform in their praise of Hansberry and of the impact of *A Raisin in the Sun* on modern drama, others have taken issue with her work, going so far as to suggest that her vision and expectations as a dramatist were shaped by whites, and especially white males, who constitute the elite world of Broadway, theater critics, and the white theater-going public.

Although many of its self-styled militant 1960s vanguard were stringent in their criticism of *A Raisin in the Sun*—some dismissing it as nonthreatening "kitchen melodrama," others as "assimilationist," others as a sellout to the white power structure, still others as a fable of a rejected strategy of "passive resistance"—Hansberry's play actually paved the way for the black theater movement of that decade. Amiri Baraka later admitted this and reversed his early opinion that the play was a period piece with outdated topical concerns. He praised it for its "profoundly imposing stature, continuing relevance, and pointed social analysis."

Hansberry sold the film rights for *A Raisin in the Sun* to Columbia Pictures in 1959, and in an effort to preserve the play's artistic integrity, she wrote the screenplay. Although Columbia heavily censored the script, especially scenes judged to be too critical of dominant white culture, the film was nominated for best screenplay of the year by the Screenwriters' Guild.

The success of *A Raisin in the Sun* brought Hansberry celebrity status and expanded her role as activist and spokesperson for black causes. She organized sup-

A 1954 production of *A Raisin in the Sun*. From left to right, Ruby Dee, Sidney Potier, and Diana Sands.

port for the Student Non-Violent Coordinating Committee (SNCC) and wrote the text for *The Movement: Documentary of a Struggle for Equality,* a book prepared by the SNCC that consisted of graphic photographs of lynchings and savage beatings of civil rights demonstrators. Her work with the SNCC, as well as her criticism of the House Un-American Activities Committee, undoubtedly contributed to Hansberry's classification by the FBI as a member of "black nationalist hate groups."

Hansberry's unwavering and uncompromising political stances contribute to an understanding of her second play, *The Sign in Sidney Brustein's Window.* Produced in 1964, it follows a Jewish intellectual's vacillation between disenchantment and political conviction. In a letter to an admirer in China, Hansberry discussed one force behind the writing of the play: "I am working on a play which presumes to try and examine something of the nature of commitment. It happens to be, in my opinion, one of the leading problems before my generation here: what to identify with, what to become involved in; what to take a stand on; what, if you will, even to believe in at all."

Sidney Brustein enjoyed neither the critical acclaim nor the commercial success of *A Raisin in the Sun*, a fact that has been widely attributed to the intellectual content of the play and the subtle complexity of the characters. In part, an attack on the then fashionable ideas of existentialism and the theater of the absurd, *The Sign in Sidney Brustein's Window* challenged the bankrupt assumption that struggles for social change were pointless. In an unpublished play, *The Arrival of Mr. Todog,* Hansberry satirized Samuel Beckett's play *Waiting for Godot,* registering her sense of the spiritual bankruptcy in its ideas, which American intellectuals of the time were taking warmly to their bosom. Despite the poor reception that greeted *Sidney Brustein,* Hansberry's supporters rallied to keep the play alive and managed to keep it open for 101 performances. The play closed the day Hansberry died of cancer, on January 12, 1965.

At the time of her death, Hansberry was at work on a play about Mary Wollstonecraft, an eighteenth-century feminist, along with two other plays, which were eventually edited and published by her ex-husband and literary executor, Robert Nemiroff: *Les Blancs* and *What Use Are Flowers?* A third television drama, *The Drinking Gourd,* commissioned but not produced by NBC, was posthumously published in 1972. Scenes from the script were included in Nemiroff's play *To Be Young, Gifted and Black,* also the title he gave the series of Hansberry's autobiographical writings, letters, and plays he compiled and published in 1969. *To Be Young, Gifted and Black—* subtitled *Lorraine Hansberry in Her Own Words*—has been criticized for revealing too little about Hansberry and for possibly censoring or diluting the radical feminist vision found in early planning notes for her plays and evident in such unpublished essays as "Simone De Beauvoir and The Second Sex: An American Commentary, 1957."

By the time she wrote the essay on de Beauvoir, Hansberry was coming out as a lesbian and ending her marriage. In several letters to *The Ladder,* an early lesbian publication, she analyzed the political connections between homophobia and antifeminism, as well as the economic and psychological factors that pressure lesbians into marriage.

While Hansberry produced much in her short life of both aesthetic and social significance, it is *A Raisin in the Sun* that critics single out from among her versatile contributions. In 1989, in celebration of the play's twenty-fifth anniversary, *A Raisin in the Sun* was staged with restorations of scenes and passages omitted from the original production. Time had not diminished the enthusiasm the play has long enjoyed. Critics praised its expanded version as a "bristling, unqualified triumph." While preparing for a documentary film on the black theater movement, Woodie King Jr. found that more than forty of the sixty playwrights interviewed professed to being influenced or aided, or both, by Lorraine Hansberry and her work, a tribute earning her a place in the firmament of classic American drama.

A Raisin in the Sun

What happens to a dream deferred?
Does it dry up
Like a raisin in the sun?
Or fester like a sore—
And then run?
Does it stink like rotten meat?
Or crust and sugar over—
Like a syrupy sweet?

Maybe it just sags
Like a heavy load.

Or does it explode?
—Langston Hughes

CAST OF CHARACTERS

Ruth Younger   Joseph Asagai
Travis Younger   George Murchison
Walter Lee Younger (brother)   Karl Lindner
Beneatha Younger   Bobo
Lena Younger (Mama)   Moving Men

Act I

SCENE ONE

The Younger living room would be a comfortable and well-ordered room if it were not for a number of indestructible contradictions to this state of being. Its furnishings are typical and undistinguished and their primary feature now is that they have clearly had to accommodate the living of too many people for too many years—and they are tired. Still, we can see that at some time, a time probably no longer remembered by the family (except perhaps for MAMA) *the furnishings of this room were actually selected with care and love and even hope—and brought to this apartment and arranged with taste and pride.*

That was a long time ago. Now the once loved pattern of the couch upholstery has to fight to show itself from under acres of crocheted doilies and couch covers which have themselves finally come to be more important than the upholstery. And here a table or a chair has been moved to disguise the worn places in the carpet; but the carpet has fought back by showing its weariness, with depressing uniformity, elsewhere on its surface.

Weariness has, in fact, won in this room. Everything has been polished, washed, sat on, used, scrubbed too often. All pretenses but living itself have long since vanished from the very atmosphere of this room.

Moreover, a section of this room, for it is not really a room unto itself, though the landlord's lease would make it seem so, slopes backward to provide a small kitchen area, where the family prepares the meals that are eaten in the living room proper, which must also serve as dining room. The single window that has been provided for these "two" rooms is located in this kitchen area. The sole natural light the family may enjoy in the course of a day is only that which fights its way through this little window.

At left, a door leads to a bedroom which is shared by MAMA *and her daughter,* BENEATHA. *At right, opposite, is a second room (which in the beginning of the life of this apartment was probably a breakfast room) which serves as a bedroom for* WALTER *and his wife,* RUTH.

TIME: *Sometime between World War II and the present.*

PLACE: *Chicago's Southside.*

AT RISE: *It is morning dark in the living room.* TRAVIS *is asleep on the make-down bed at center. An alarm clock sounds from within the bedroom at right, and presently* RUTH *enters from that room and closes the door behind her. She crosses sleepily toward the window. As she passes her sleeping son she reaches down and shakes him a little. At the window she raises the shade and a dusky Southside morning light comes in feebly. She fills a pot with water and puts it on to boil. She calls to the boy, between yawns, in a slightly muffled voice.*

RUTH *is about thirty. We can see that she was a pretty girl, even exceptionally so, but now it is apparent that life has been little that she expected, and disappointment has already begun to hang in her face. In a few years, before thirty-five even, she will be known among her people as a "settled woman."*

She crosses to her son and gives him a good, final, rousing shake.

RUTH Come on now, boy, it's seven thirty!;

[*Her son sits up at last, in a stupor of sleepiness.*] I say hurry up, Travis! You ain't the only person in the world got to use a bathroom! [*The child, a sturdy, handsome little boy of ten or eleven, drags himself out of the bed and almost blindly takes his towels and "today's clothes" from drawers and a closet and goes out to the bathroom, which is in an outside hall and which is shared by another family or families on the same floor.* RUTH *crosses to the bedroom door at right and opens it and calls in to her husband.*] Walter Lee! . . . It's after seven thirty! Lemme see you do some waking up in there now! [*She waits.*] You better get up from there, man! It's after seven thirty I tell you. [*She waits again.*] All right, you just go ahead and lay there and next thing you know Travis be finished and Mr. Johnson'll be in there and you'll be fussing and cussing round here like a mad man! And be late too! [*She waits, at the end of patience.*] Walter Lee—it's time for you to get up!

> [*She waits another second and then starts to go into the bedroom, but is apparently satisfied that her husband has begun to get up. She stops, pulls the door to, and returns to the kitchen area. She wipes her face with a moist cloth and runs her fingers through her sleep-disheveled hair in a vain effort and ties an apron around her housecoat. The bedroom door at right opens and her husband stands in the doorway in his pajamas, which are rumpled and mismated. He is a lean, intense young man in his middle thirties, inclined to quick nervous movements and erratic speech habits—and always in his voice there is a quality of indictment.*]

WALTER Is he out yet?

RUTH What you mean *out*? He ain't hardly got in there good yet.

WALTER [*Wandering in, still more oriented to sleep than to a new day.*] Well, what was you doing all that yelling for if I can't even get in there yet? [*Stopping and thinking.*] Check coming today?

RUTH They *said* Saturday and this is just Friday and I hopes to God you ain't going to get up here first thing this morning and start talking to me 'bout no money—'cause I 'bout don't want to hear it.

WALTER Something the matter with you this morning?

RUTH No—I'm just sleepy as the devil. What kind of eggs you want?

WALTER Not scrambled. [RUTH *starts to scramble eggs.*] Paper come?

> [RUTH *points impatiently to the rolled up* Tribune *on the table, and he gets it and spreads it out and vaguely reads the front page.*] Set off another bomb yesterday.

RUTH [*Maximum indifference.*] Did they?

WALTER [*Looking up.*] What's the matter with you?

RUTH Ain't nothing the matter with me. And don't keep asking me that this morning.

WALTER Ain't nobody bothering you. [*Reading the news of the day absently again.*] Say Colonel McCormick is sick.

RUTH [*Affecting tea-party interest.*] Is he now? Poor thing.

WALTER [*Sighing and looking at his watch.*] Oh, me. [*He waits.*] Now what is that boy doing in that bathroom all this time? He just going to have to start getting up earlier. I can't be late to work on account of him fooling around in there.

RUTH [*Turning on him.*] Oh, no he ain't going to be getting up no earlier no such thing! It ain't his fault that he can't get to bed no earlier nights 'cause he got a bunch of crazy good-for-nothing clowns sitting up running their mouths in what is supposed to be his bedroom after ten o'clock at night . . .

WALTER That's what you mad about, ain't it? The things I want to talk about with my friends just couldn't be important in your mind, could they? [*He rises and finds a cigarette in her handbag on the table and crosses to the little window and looks out, smoking and deeply enjoying this first one.*]

RUTH [*Almost matter of factly, a complaint too automatic to deserve emphasis.*] Why you always got to smoke before you eat in the morning?

WALTER [*At the window.*] Just look at 'em down there . . . Running and racing to work . . . [*He turns and faces his wife and watches her a moment at the stove, and then, suddenly.*] You look young this morning, baby.

RUTH [*Indifferently.*] Yeah?

WALTER Just for a second—stirring them eggs. It's gone now—just for a second it was—you looked real young again. [*Then, drily.*] It's gone now—you look like yourself again.

RUTH Man, if you don't shut up and leave me alone.

WALTER [*Looking out to the street again.*] First thing a man ought to learn in life is not to make love to no colored woman first thing in the morning. You all some evil people at eight o'clock in the morning.
[*TRAVIS appears in the hall doorway, almost fully dressed and quite wide awake now, his towels and pajamas across his shoulders. He opens the door and signals for his father to make the bathroom in a hurry.*]

TRAVIS [*Watching the bathroom.*] Daddy, come on!
[*WALTER gets his bathroom utensils and flies out to the bathroom.*]

RUTH Sit down and have your breakfast, Travis.

TRAVIS Mama, this is Friday. [*Gleefully.*] Check coming tomorrow, huh?

RUTH You get your mind off money and eat your breakfast.

TRAVIS [*Eating.*] This is the morning we supposed to bring the fifty cents to school.

RUTH Well, I ain't got no fifty cents this morning.

TRAVIS Teacher say we have to.

RUTH I don't care what teacher say. I ain't got it. Eat your breakfast, Travis.

TRAVIS I *am* eating.

RUTH Hush up now and just eat!
[*The boy gives her an exasperated look for her lack of understanding, and eats grudgingly.*]

TRAVIS You think Grandmama would have it?

RUTH No! And I want you to stop asking your grandmother for money, you hear me?

TRAVIS [*Outraged.*] Gaaaleee! I don't ask her, she just gimme it sometimes!

RUTH Travis Willard Younger—I got too much on me this morning to be—

TRAVIS Maybe Daddy—

RUTH *Travis!*
[*The boy hushes abruptly. They are both quiet and tense for several seconds.*]

TRAVIS [*Presently.*] Could I maybe go carry some groceries in front of the supermarket for a little while after school then?

RUTH Just hush, I said. [*TRAVIS jabs his spoon into his cereal bowl viciously, and rests his head in anger upon his fists.*] If you through eating, you can get over there and make up your bed.

[*The boy obeys stiffly and crosses the room, almost mechanically, to the bed and more or less carefully folds the covering. He carries the bedding into his mother's room and returns with his books and cap.*]

TRAVIS [*Sulking and standing apart from her unnaturally.*] I'm gone.

RUTH [*Looking up from the stove to inspect him automatically.*] Come here. [*He crosses to her and she studies his head.*] If you don't take this comb and fix this here head, you better! [TRAVIS *puts down his books with a great sigh of oppression, and crosses to the mirror. His mother mutters under her breath about his "slubbornness."*] 'Bout to march out of here with that head looking just like chickens slept in it! I just don't know where you get your stubborn ways . . . And get your jacket, too. Looks chilly out this morning.

TRAVIS [*With conspicuously brushed hair and jacket.*] I'm gone.

RUTH Get carfare and milk money—[*Waving one finger.*]—and not a single penny for no caps, you hear me?

TRAVIS [*With sullen politeness.*] Yes'm.

[*He turns in outrage to leave. His mother watches after him as in his frustration he approaches the door almost comically. When she speaks to him, her voice has become a very gentle tease.*]

RUTH [*Mocking; as she thinks he would say it.*] Oh, Mama makes me so mad sometimes, I don't know what to do! [*She waits and continues to his back as he stands stock-still in front of the door.*] I wouldn't kiss that woman good-bye for nothing in this world this morning! [*The boy finally turns around and rolls his eyes at her, knowing the mood has changed and he is vindicated; he does not, however, move toward her yet.*] Not for nothing in this world! [*She finally laughs aloud at him and holds out her arms to him and we see that it is a way between them, very old and practiced. He crosses to her and allows her to embrace him warmly but keeps his face fixed with masculine rigidity. She holds him back from her presently and looks at him and runs her fingers over the features of his face. With utter gentleness—*] Now—whose little old angry man are you?

TRAVIS [*The masculinity and gruffness start to fade at last.*] Aw gaalee—Mama . . .

RUTH [*Mimicking.*] Aw—gaaaaalleeeee, Mama! [*She pushes him, with rough playfulness and finality, toward the door.*] Get on out of here or you going to be late.

TRAVIS [*In the face of love, new aggressiveness.*] Mama, could I *please* go carry groceries?

RUTH Honey, it's starting to get so cold evenings.

WALTER [*Coming in from the bathroom and drawing a make-believe gun from a make-believe holster and shooting at his son.*] What is it he wants to do?

RUTH Go carry groceries after school at the supermarket.

WALTER Well, let him go . . .

TRAVIS [*Quickly, to the ally.*] I *have* to—she won't gimme the fifty cents . . .

WALTER [*To his wife only.*] Why not?

RUTH [*Simply, and with flavor.*] 'Cause we don't have it.

WALTER [*To* RUTH *only.*] What you tell the boy things like that for? [*Reaching down into his pants with a rather important gesture.*] Here, son—

[*He hands the boy the coin, but his eyes are directed to his wife's.* TRAVIS *takes the money happily.*]

TRAVIS Thanks, Daddy.

[*He starts out.* RUTH *watches both of them with murder in her eyes.* WALTER *stands and stares back at her with defiance, and suddenly reaches into his pocket again on an afterthought.*]

WALTER [*Without even looking at his son, still staring hard at his wife.*]   In fact, here's another fifty cents . . . Buy yourself some fruit today—or take a taxicab to school or something!

TRAVIS   Whoopee—

[*He leaps up and clasps his father around the middle with his legs, and they face each other in mutual appreciation; slowly* WALTER LEE *peeks around the boy to catch the violent rays from his wife's eyes and draws his head back as if shot.*]

WALTER   You better get down now—and get to school, man.

TRAVIS [*At the door.*]   O.K. Good-bye.

[*He exits.*]

WALTER [*After him, pointing with pride.*]   That's *my* boy. [*She looks at him in disgust and turns back to her work.*] You know what I was thinking 'bout in the bathroom this morning?

RUTH   No.

WALTER   How come you always try to be so pleasant!

RUTH   What is there to be pleasant 'bout!

WALTER   You want to know what I was thinking 'bout in the bathroom or not!

RUTH   I know what you thinking 'bout.

WALTER [*Ignoring her.*]   'Bout what me and Willy Harris was talking about last night.

RUTH [*Immediately—a refrain.*]   Willy Harris is a good-for-nothing loud mouth.

WALTER   Anybody who talks to me has got to be a good-for-nothing loud mouth, ain't he? And what you know about who is just a good-for-nothing loud mouth? Charlie Atkins was just a "good-for-nothing loud mouth" too, wasn't he! When he wanted me to go in the dry-cleaning business with him. And now—he's grossing a hundred thousand a year. A hundred thousand dollars a year! You still call *him* a loud mouth!

RUTH [*Bitterly.*]   Oh, Walter Lee . . .

[*She folds her head on her arms over the table.*]

WALTER [*Rising and coming to her and standing over her.*]   You tired, ain't you? Tired of everything. Me, the boy, the way we live—this beat-up hole—everything. Ain't you? [*She doesn't look up, doesn't answer.*] So tired—moaning and groaning all the time, but you wouldn't do nothing to help, would you? You couldn't be on my side that long for nothing, could you?

RUTH   Walter, please leave me alone.

WALTER   A man needs for a woman to back him up . . .

RUTH   Walter—

WALTER   Mama would listen to you. You know she listen to you more than she do me and Bennie. She think more of you. All you have to do is just sit down with her when you drinking your coffee one morning and talking 'bout things like you do and—[*He sits down beside her and demonstrates graphically what he thinks her methods and tone should be.*]—you just sip your coffee, see, and say easy like that you been thinking 'bout that deal Walter Lee is so interested in, 'bout the store and all, and sip some more coffee, like what you saying ain't really that important to you— And the next thing you know, she be listening good and asking you questions and when I come home—I can tell her the details. This ain't no fly-by-night proposition, baby. I mean we figured it out, me and Willy and Bobo.

RUTH [*With a frown.*] Bobo?

WALTER Yeah. You see, this little liquor store we got in mind cost seventy-five thousand and we figured the initial investment on the place be 'bout thirty thousand, see. That be ten thousand each. Course, there's a couple of hundred you got to pay so's you don't spend your life just waiting for them clowns to let your license get approved—

RUTH You mean graft?

WALTER [*Frowning impatiently.*] Don't call it that. See there, that just goes to show you what women understand about the world. Baby, don't *nothing* happen for you in this world 'less you pay *somebody* off!

RUTH Walter, leave me alone! [*She raises her head and stares at him vigorously—then says, more quietly.*] Eat your eggs, they gonna be cold.

WALTER [*Straightening up from her and looking off.*] That's it. There you are. Man say to his woman: I got me a dream. His woman say: Eat your eggs. [*Sadly, but gaining in power.*] Man say: I got to take hold of this here world, baby! And a woman will say: Eat your eggs and go to work. [*Passionately now.*] Man say: I got to change my life, I'm choking to death, baby! And his woman say—[*In utter anguish as he brings his fists down on his thighs.*]—Your eggs is getting cold!

RUTH [*Softly.*] Walter, that ain't none of our money.

WALTER [*Not listening at all or even looking at her.*] This morning, I was lookin' in the mirror and thinking about it . . . I'm thirty-five years old; I been married eleven years and I got a boy who sleeps in the living room—[*Very, very quietly.*]—and all I got to give him is stories about how rich white people live . . .

RUTH Eat your eggs, Walter.

WALTER *Damn my eggs . . . damn all the eggs that ever was!*

RUTH Then go to work.

WALTER [*Looking up at her.*] See—I'm trying to talk to you 'bout myself—[*Shaking his head with the repetition.*]—and all you can say is eat them eggs and go to work.

RUTH [*Wearily.*] Honey, you never say nothing new. I listen to you every day, every night and every morning, and you never say nothing new. [*Shrugging.*] So you would rather *be* Mr. Arnold than be his chauffeur. So—I would *rather* be living in Buckingham Palace.

WALTER That is just what is wrong with the colored woman in this world . . . Don't understand about building their men up and making 'em feel like they somebody. Like they can do something.

RUTH [*Drily, but to hurt.*] There *are* colored men who do things.

WALTER No thanks to the colored woman.

RUTH Well, being a colored woman, I guess I can't help myself none.
[*She rises and gets the ironing board and sets it up and attacks a huge pile of rough-dried clothes, sprinkling them in preparation for the ironing and then rolling them into tight fat balls.*]

WALTER [*Mumbling.*] We one group of men tied to a race of women with small minds.
[*His sister BENEATHA enters. She is about twenty, as slim and intense as her brother. She is not as pretty as her sister-in-law, but her lean, almost intellectual face has a handsomeness of its own. She wears a bright-red*

flannel nightie, and her thick hair stands wildly about her head. Her speech is a mixture of many things; it is different from the rest of the family's insofar as education has permeated her sense of English—and perhaps the Midwest rather than the South has finally—at last—won out in her inflection; but not altogether, because over all of it is a soft slurring and transformed use of vowels which is the decided influence of the Southside. She passes through the room without looking at either RUTH *or* WALTER *and goes to the outside door and looks, a little blindly, out to the bathroom. She sees that it has been lost to the Johnsons. She closes the door with a sleepy vengeance and crosses to the table and sits down a little defeated.*]

BENEATHA I am going to start timing those people.

WALTER You should get up earlier.

BENEATHA [*Her face in her hands. She is still fighting the urge to go back to bed.*] Really—would you suggest dawn? Where's the paper?

WALTER [*Pushing the paper across the table to her as he studies her almost clinically, as though he has never seen her before.*] You a horrible-looking chick at this hour.

BENEATHA [*Drily.*] Good morning, everybody.

WALTER [*Senselessly.*] How is school coming?

BENEATHA [*In the same spirit.*] Lovely. Lovely. And you know, biology is the greatest. [*Looking up at him.*] I dissected something that looked just like you yesterday.

WALTER I just wondered if you've made up your mind and everything.

BENEATHA [*Gaining in sharpness and impatience.*] And what did I answer yesterday morning—and the day before that?

RUTH [*From the ironing board, like someone disinterested and old.*] Don't be so nasty, Bennie.

BENEATHA [*Still to her brother.*] And the day before that and the day before that!

WALTER [*Defensively.*] I'm interested in you. Something wrong with that? Ain't many girls who decide—

WALTER *and* BENEATHA [*In unison.*] —"to be a doctor."
          [*Silence.*]

WALTER Have we figured out yet just exactly how much medical school is going to cost?

RUTH Walter Lee, why don't you leave that girl alone and get out of here to work?

BENEATHA [*Exits to the bathroom and bangs on the door.*] Come on out of there, please!
          [*She comes back into the room.*]

WALTER [*Looking at his sister intently.*] You know the check is coming tomorrow.

BENEATHA [*Turning on him with a sharpness all her own.*] That money belongs to Mama, Walter, and it's for her to decide how she wants to use it. I don't care if she wants to buy a house or a rocket ship or just nail it up somewhere and look at it. It's hers. Not ours—*hers.*

WALTER [*Bitterly.*] Now ain't that fine! You just got your mother's interest at heart, ain't you, girl? You such a nice girl—but if Mama got that money she can always take a few thousand and help you through school too—can't she?

BENEATHA I have never asked anyone around here to do anything for me!

WALTER   No! And the line between asking and just accepting when the time comes is big and wide—ain't it!

BENEATHA [*With fury.*]   What do you want from me, Brother—that I quit school or just drop dead, which!

WALTER   I don't want nothing but for you to stop acting holy 'round here. Me and Ruth done made some sacrifices for you—why can't you do something for the family?

RUTH   Walter, don't be dragging me in it.

WALTER   You are in it— Don't you get up and go work in somebody's kitchen for the last three years to help put clothes on her back?

RUTH   Oh, Walter—that's not fair . . .

WALTER   It ain't that nobody expects you to get on your knees and say thank you, Brother; thank you, Ruth; thank you, Mama—and thank you, Travis, for wearing the same pair of shoes for two semesters—

BENEATHA [*Dropping to her knees.*]   Well—I *do*—all right?—thank everybody . . . and forgive me for ever wanting to be anything at all . . . forgive me, forgive me!

RUTH   Please stop it! Your mama'll hear you.

WALTER   Who the hell told you you had to be a doctor? If you so crazy 'bout messing 'round with sick people—then go be a nurse like other women—or just get married and be quiet . . .

BENEATHA   Well—you finally got it said . . . It took you three years but you finally got it said. Walter, give up; leave me alone—it's Mama's money.

WALTER   *He was my father, too!*

BENEATHA   So what? He was mine, too—and Travis' grandfather—but the insurance money belongs to Mama. Picking on me is not going to make her give it to you to invest in any liquor stores—[*Underbreath, dropping into a chair.*]—and I for one say, God bless Mama for that!

WALTER [*To* RUTH.]   See—did you hear? Did you hear!

RUTH   Honey, please go to work.

WALTER   Nobody in this house is ever going to understand me.

BENEATHA   Because you're a nut.

WALTER   Who's a nut?

BENEATHA   You—you are a nut. Thee is mad, boy.

WALTER [*Looking at his wife and his sister from the door, very sadly.*]   The world's most backward race of people, and that's a fact.

BENEATHA [*Turning slowly in her chair.*]   And then there are all those prophets who would lead us out of the wilderness—[WALTER *slams out of the house.*]—into the swamps!

RUTH   Bennie, why you always gotta be pickin' on your brother? Can't you be a little sweeter sometimes? [*Door opens.* WALTER *walks in.*]

WALTER [*To Ruth.*]   I need some money for carfare.

RUTH [*Looks at him, then warms; teasing, but tenderly.*]   Fifty cents? [*She goes to her bag and gets money.*]   Here, take a taxi.

[WALTER *exits.* MAMA *enters. She is a woman in her early sixties, full-bodied and strong. She is one of those women of a certain grace and beauty who wear it so unobtrusively that it takes a while to notice. Her dark-brown face is surrounded by the total whiteness of her hair, and, being a woman who has adjusted to many things in life and overcome many more, her face is full of strength. She has, we can see, wit and faith of a kind that keep her eyes lit and full of interest and expectancy. She is, in a word, a beautiful woman. Her bearing is perhaps most like the noble bearing of the women of the Hereros[1] of Southwest Africa—rather as if she imagines that as she walks she still bears a basket or a vessel upon her head. Her speech, on the other hand, is as careless as her carriage is precise—she is inclined to slur everything—but her voice is perhaps not so much quiet as simply soft.*]

MAMA Who that 'round here slamming doors at this hour?
[*She crosses through the room, goes to the window, opens it, and brings in a feeble little plant growing doggedly in a small pot on the window sill. She feels the dirt and puts it back out.*]

RUTH That was Walter Lee. He and Bennie was at it again.

MAMA My children and they tempers. Lord, if this little old plant don't get more sun than it's been getting it ain't never going to see spring again. [*She turns from the window.*] What's the matter with you this morning, Ruth? You looks right peaked. You aiming to iron all them things? Leave some for me. I'll get to 'em this afternoon. Bennie honey, it's too drafty for you to be sitting 'round half dressed. Where's your robe?

BENEATHA In the cleaners.

MAMA Well, go get mine and put it on.

BENEATHA I'm not cold, Mama, honest.

MAMA I know—but you so thin . . .

BENEATHA [*Irritably.*] Mama, I'm not cold.

MAMA [*Seeing the make-down bed as* TRAVIS *has left it.*] Lord have mercy, look at that poor bed. Bless his heart—he tries, don't he?
[*She moves to the bed* TRAVIS *has sloppily made up.*]

RUTH No—he don't half try at all 'cause he knows you going to come along behind him and fix everything. That's just how come he don't know how to do nothing right now—you done spoiled that boy so.

MAMA Well—he's a little boy. Ain't supposed to know 'bout housekeeping. My baby, that's what he is. What you fix for his breakfast this morning?

RUTH [*Angrily.*] I feed my son, Lena!

MAMA I ain't meddling—[*Underbreath; busy-bodyish.*] I just noticed all last week he had cold cereal, and when it starts getting this chilly in the fall a child ought to have some hot grits or something when he goes out in the cold—

RUTH [*Furious.*] I gave him hot oats—is that all right!

MAMA I ain't meddling. [*Pause.*] Put a lot of nice butter on it? [RUTH *shoots her an angry look and does not reply.*] He likes lots of butter.

RUTH [*Exasperated.*] Lena—

MAMA [*To* BENEATHA. MAMA *is inclined to wander conversationally sometimes.*] What was you and your brother fussing 'bout this morning?

BENEATHA It's not important, Mama.
[*She gets up and goes to look out at the bathroom, which is apparently free, and she picks up her towels and rushes out.*]

MAMA What was they fighting about?

RUTH Now you know as well as I do.

MAMA [*Shaking her head.*] Brother still worrying hisself sick about that money?

RUTH You know he is.

MAMA You had breakfast?

RUTH Some coffee.

---

1. Nomadic people of a region of eastern Namibia.

MAMA Girl, you better start eating and looking after yourself better. You almost thin as Travis.

RUTH Lena—

MAMA Un-hunh?

RUTH What are you going to do with it?

MAMA Now don't you start, child. It's too early in the morning to be talking about money. It ain't Christian.

RUTH It's just that he got his heart set on that store—

MAMA You mean that liquor store that Willy Harris want him to invest in?

RUTH Yes—

MAMA We ain't no business people, Ruth. We just plain working folks.

RUTH Ain't nobody business people till they go into business. Walter Lee say colored people ain't never going to start getting ahead till they start gambling on some different kinds of things in the world—investments and things.

MAMA What done got into you, girl? Walter Lee done finally sold you on investing.

RUTH No. Mama, something is happening between Walter and me. I don't know what it is—but he needs something—something I can't give him any more. He needs this chance, Lena.

MAMA [Frowning deeply.] But liquor, honey—

RUTH Well—like Walter say—I spec people going to always be drinking themselves some liquor.

MAMA Well—whether they drinks it or not ain't none of my business. But whether I go into business selling it to 'em is, and I don't want that on my ledger this late in life. [Stopping suddenly and studying her daughter-in-law.] Ruth Younger, what's the matter with you today? You look like you could fall over right there.

RUTH I'm tired.

MAMA Then you better stay home from work today.

RUTH I can't stay home. She'd be calling up the agency and screaming at them, "My girl didn't come in today—send me somebody! My girl didn't come in!" Oh, she just have a fit . . .

MAMA Well, let her have it. I'll just call her up and say you got the flu—

RUTH [Laughing.] Why the flu?

MAMA 'Cause it sounds respectable to 'em. Something white people get, too. They know 'bout the flu. Otherwise they think you been cut up or something when you tell 'em you sick.

RUTH I got to go in. We need the money.

MAMA Somebody would of thought my children done all but starved to death the way they talk about money here late. Child, we got a great big old check coming tomorrow.

RUTH [Sincerely, but also self-righteously.] Now that's your money. It ain't got nothing to do with me. We all feel like that—Walter and Bennie and me—even Travis.

MAMA [Thoughtfully, and suddenly very far away.] Ten thousand dollars—

RUTH Sure is wonderful.

MAMA Ten thousand dollars.

RUTH You know what you should do, Miss Lena? You should take yourself a trip somewhere. To Europe or South America or someplace—

MAMA [Throwing up her hands at the thought.] Oh, child!

RUTH I'm serious. Just pack up and leave! Go on away and enjoy yourself some. Forget about the family and have yourself a ball for once in your life—

MAMA [*Drily.*] You sound like I'm just about ready to die. Who'd go with me? What I look like wandering 'round Europe by myself?

RUTH Shoot—these here rich white women do it all the time. They don't think nothing of packing up they suitcases and piling on one of them big steamships and—swoosh!—they gone, child.

MAMA Something always told me I wasn't no rich white woman.

RUTH Well—what are you going to do with it then?

MAMA I ain't rightly decided. [*Thinking. She speaks now with emphasis.*] Some of it got to be put away for Beneatha and her schoolin'—and ain't nothing going to touch that part of it. Nothing. [*She waits several seconds, trying to make up her mind about something, and looks at* RUTH *a little tentatively before going on.*] Been thinking that we maybe could meet the notes on a little old two-story somewhere, with a yard where Travis could play in the summertime, if we use part of the insurance for a down payment and everybody kind of pitch in. I could maybe take on a little day work again, few days a week—

RUTH [*Studying her mother-in-law furtively and concentrating on her ironing, anxious to encourage without seeming to.*] Well, Lord knows, we've put enough rent into this here rat trap to pay for four houses by now . . .

MAMA [*Looking up at the words "rat trap" and then looking around and leaning back and sighing—in a suddenly reflective mood—*] "Rat trap"— yes, that's all it is. [*Smiling.*] I remember just as well the day me and Big Walter moved in here. Hadn't been married but two weeks and wasn't planning on living here no more than a year. [*She shakes her head at the dissolved dream.*] We was going to set away, little by little, don't you know, and buy a little place out in Morgan Park. We had even picked out the house. [*Chuckling a little.*] Looks right dumpy today. But Lord, child, you should know all the dreams I had 'bout buying that house and fixing it up and making me a little garden in the back—[*She waits and stops smiling.*] And didn't none of it happen.

[*Dropping her hands in a futile gesture.*]

RUTH [*Keeps her head down, ironing.*] Yes, life can be a barrel of disappointments, sometimes.

MAMA Honey, Big Walter would come in here some nights back then and slump down on that couch there and just look at the rug, and look at me and look at the rug and then back at me—and I'd know he was down then . . . really down. [*After a second very long and thoughtful pause; she is seeing back to times that only she can see.*] And then, Lord, when I lost that baby—little Claude—I almost thought I was going to lose Big Walter too. Oh, that man grieved hisself! He was one man to love his children.

RUTH Ain't nothin' can tear at you like losin' your baby.

MAMA I guess that's how come that man finally worked hisself to death like he done. Like he was fighting his own war with this here world that took his baby from him.

RUTH He sure was a fine man, all right. I always liked Mr. Younger.

MAMA Crazy 'bout his children! God knows there was plenty wrong with Walter Younger—hard-headed, mean, kind of wild with women—plenty wrong with him. But he sure loved his children. Always wanted them to have something—be something. That's where Brother gets all these notions, I reckon. Big Walter used to say, he'd get right wet in the eyes sometimes, lean his head back with the water standing in his eyes and say, "Seem like God didn't see fit to give the black man nothing but dreams—but He did give us children to make them dreams seem worth while." [*She smiles.*] He could talk like that, don't you know.

RUTH Yes, he sure could. He was a good man, Mr. Younger.

MAMA Yes, a fine man—just couldn't never catch up with his dreams, that's all.

> [BENEATHA *comes in, brushing her hair and looking up to the ceiling, where the sound of a vacuum cleaner has started up.*]

BENEATHA What could be so dirty on that woman's rugs that she has to vacuum them every single day?

RUTH I wish certain young women 'round here who I could name would take inspiration about certain rugs in a certain apartment I could also mention.

BENEATHA [*Shrugging.*] How much cleaning can a house need, for Christ's sakes.

MAMA [*Not liking the Lord's name used thus.*] Bennie!

RUTH Just listen to her—just listen!

BENEATHA Oh, God!

MAMA If you use the Lord's name just one more time—

BENEATHA [*A bit of a whine.*] Oh, Mama—

RUTH Fresh—just fresh as salt, this girl!

BENEATHA [*Drily.*] Well—if the salt loses its savor—

MAMA Now that will do. I just ain't going to have you 'round here reciting the scriptures in vain—you hear me?

BENEATHA How did I manage to get on everybody's wrong side by just walking into a room?

RUTH If you weren't so fresh—

BENEATHA Ruth, I'm twenty years old.

MAMA What time you be home from school today?

BENEATHA Kind of late. [*With enthusiasm.*] Madeline is going to start my guitar lessons today.

> [MAMA *and* RUTH *look up with the same expression.*]

MAMA Your *what* kind of lessons?

BENEATHA Guitar.

RUTH Oh, Father!

MAMA How come you done taken it in your mind to learn to play the guitar?

BENEATHA I just want to, that's all.

MAMA [*Smiling.*] Lord, child, don't you know what to do with yourself? How long it going to be before you get tired of this now—like you got tired of that little play-acting group you joined last year? [*Looking at* RUTH.] And what was it the year before that?

RUTH The horseback-riding club for which she bought that fifty-five-dollar riding habit that's been hanging in the closet ever since!

MAMA [*To* BENEATHA.] Why you got to flit so from one thing to another, baby?

BENEATHA [*Sharply.*] I just want to learn to play the guitar. Is there anything wrong with that?

MAMA Ain't nobody trying to stop you. I just wonders sometimes why you has to flit so from one thing to another all the time. You ain't never done nothing with all that camera equipment you brought home—

BENEATHA I don't flit! I—I experiment with different forms of expression—

RUTH Like riding a horse?

BENEATHA —People have to express themselves one way or another.

MAMA What is it you want to express?

BENEATHA [*Angrily.*] Me! [MAMA *and* RUTH *look at each other and burst into raucous laughter.*] Don't worry—I don't expect you to understand.

MAMA [*To change the subject.*] Who you going out with tomorrow night?

BENEATHA [*With displeasure.*] George Murchison again.

MAMA [*Pleased.*] Oh—you getting a little sweet on him?

RUTH You ask me, this child ain't sweet on nobody but herself—[*Under-breath.*] Express herself!

[*They laugh.*]

BENEATHA Oh—I like George all right, Mama. I mean I like him enough to go out with him and stuff, but—

RUTH [*For devilment.*] What does *and stuff* mean?

BENEATHA Mind your own business.

MAMA Stop picking at her now, Ruth. [*A thoughtful pause, and then a suspicious sudden look at her daughter as she turns in her chair for emphasis.*] What *does* it mean?

BENEATHA [*Wearily.*] Oh, I just mean I couldn't ever really be serious about George. He's—he's so shallow.

RUTH Shallow—what do you mean he's shallow? He's *Rich!*

MAMA Hush, Ruth.

BENEATHA I know he's rich. He knows he's rich, too.

RUTH Well—what other qualities a man got to have to satisfy you, little girl?

BENEATHA You wouldn't even begin to understand. Anybody who married Walter could not possibly understand.

MAMA [*Outraged.*] What kind of way is that to talk about your brother?

BENEATHA Brother is a flip—let's face it.

MAMA [*To* RUTH, *helplessly.*] What's a flip?

RUTH [*Glad to add kindling.*] She's saying he's crazy.

BENEATHA Not crazy. Brother isn't really crazy yet—he—he's an elaborate neurotic.

MAMA Hush your mouth!

BENEATHA As for George. Well. George looks good—he's got a beautiful car and he takes me to nice places and, as my sister-in-law says, he is probably the richest boy I will ever get to know and I even like him sometimes—but if the Youngers are sitting around waiting to see if their little Bennie is going to tie up the family with the Murchisons, they are wasting their time.

RUTH You mean you wouldn't marry George Murchison if he asked you someday? That pretty, rich thing? Honey, I knew you was odd—

BENEATHA No I would not marry him if all I felt for him was what I feel now. Besides, George's family wouldn't really like it.

MAMA Why not?

BENEATHA Oh, Mama—The Murchisons are honest-to-God-real-*live*-rich colored people, and the only people in the world who are more snobbish than rich white people are rich colored people. I thought everybody knew that. I've met Mrs. Murchison. She's a scene!

MAMA You must not dislike people 'cause they well off, honey.

BENEATHA Why not? It makes just as much sense as disliking people 'cause they are poor, and lots of people do that.

RUTH [*A wisdom-of-the-ages manner. To* MAMA.]   Well, she'll get over some of this—

BENEATHA   Get over it? What are you talking about, Ruth? Listen, I'm going to be a doctor. I'm not worried about who I'm going to marry yet—if I ever get married.

MAMA *and* RUTH   If!

MAMA   Now, Bennie—

BENEATHA   Oh, I probably will . . . but first I'm going to be a doctor, and George, for one, still thinks that's pretty funny. I couldn't be bothered with that. I am going to be a doctor and everybody around here better understand that!

MAMA [*Kindly.*]   'Course you going to be a doctor, honey, God willing.

BENEATHA [*Drily.*]   God hasn't got a thing to do with it.

MAMA   Beneatha—that just wasn't necessary.

BENEATHA   Well—neither is God. I get sick of hearing about God.

MAMA   Beneatha!

BENEATHA   I mean it! I'm just tired of hearing about God all the time. What has He got to do with anything? Does he pay tuition?

MAMA   You 'bout to get your fresh little jaw slapped!

RUTH   That's just what she needs, all right!

BENEATHA   Why? Why can't I say what I want to around here, like everybody else?

MAMA   It don't sound nice for a young girl to say things like that—you wasn't brought up that way. Me and your father went to trouble to get you and Brother to church every Sunday.

BENEATHA   Mama, you don't understand. It's all a matter of ideas, and God is just one idea I don't accept. It's not important. I am not going out and be immoral or commit crimes because I don't believe in God. I don't even think about it. It's just that I get tired of Him getting credit for all the things the human race achieves through its own stubborn effort. There simply is no blasted God—there is only man and it is he who makes miracles!

[MAMA *absorbs this speech, studies her daughter and rises slowly and crosses to* BENEATHA *and slaps her powerfully across the face. After, there is only silence and the daughter drops her eyes from her mother's face, and* MAMA *is very tall before her.*]

MAMA   Now—you say after me, in my mother's house there is still God. [*There is a long pause and* BENEATHA *stares at the floor wordlessly.* MAMA *repeats the phrase with precision and cool emotion.*] In my mother's house there is still God.

BENEATHA   In my mother's house there is still God.

[*A long pause.*]

MAMA [*Walking away from* BENEATHA, *too disturbed for triumphant posture. Stopping and turning back to her daughter.*]   There are some ideas we ain't going to have in this house. Not long as I am at the head of this family.

BENEATHA   Yes, ma'am.

[MAMA *walks out of the room.*]

RUTH [*Almost gently, with profound understanding.*]   You think you a woman, Bennie—but you still a little girl. What you did was childish—so you got treated like a child.

BENEATHA   I see. [*Quietly.*]   I also see that everybody thinks it's all right for Mama to be a tyrant. But all the tyranny in the world will never put a God in the heavens!

[*She picks up her books and goes out.*]

RUTH [*Goes to* MAMA's *door.*]   She said she was sorry.

MAMA [*Coming out, going to her plant.*]   They frightens me, Ruth. My children.

RUTH   You got good children, Lena. They just a little off sometimes—but they're good.

MAMA   No—there's something come down between me and them that don't let us understand each other and I don't know what it is. One done almost lost his mind thinking 'bout money all the time and the other done commence to talk about things I can't seem to understand in no form or fashion. What is it that's changing, Ruth?

RUTH [*Soothingly, older than her years.*]   Now . . . you taking it all too seriously. You just got strong-willed children and it takes a strong woman like you to keep 'em in hand.

MAMA [*Looking at her plant and sprinkling a little water on it.*]   They spirited all right, my children. Got to admit they got spirit—Bennie and Walter. Like this little old plant that ain't never had enough sunshine or nothing—and look at it . . .

   [*She has her back to* RUTH, *who has had to stop ironing and lean against something and put the back of her hand to her forehead.*]

RUTH [*Trying to keep* MAMA *from noticing.*]   You . . . sure . . . loves that little old thing, don't you? . . .

MAMA   Well, I always wanted me a garden like I used to see sometimes at the back of the houses down home. This plant is close as I ever got to having one. [*She looks out of the window as she replaces the plant.*] Lord, ain't nothing as dreary as the view from this window on a dreary day, is there? Why ain't you singing this morning, Ruth? Sing that "No Ways Tired." That song always lifts me up so—[*She turns at last to see that* RUTH *has slipped quietly into a chair, in a state of semiconsciousness.*] Ruth! Ruth honey—what's the matter with you . . . Ruth!

[*Curtain.*]

SCENE TWO

It is the following morning; a Saturday morning, and house cleaning is in progress at the Youngers. Furniture has been shoved hither and yon and MAMA *is giving the kitchen-area walls a washing down.* BENEATHA, *in dungarees, with a handkerchief tied around her face, is spraying insecticide into the cracks in the walls. As they work, the radio is on and a Southside disk-jockey program is inappropriately filling the house with a rather exotic saxophone blues.* TRAVIS, *the sole idle one, is leaning on his arms, looking out of the window.*

TRAVIS   Grandmama, that stuff Bennie is using smells awful. Can I go downstairs, please?

MAMA   Did you get all them chores done already? I ain't seen you doing much.

TRAVIS   Yes'm—finished early. Where did Mama go this morning?

MAMA [*Looking at* BENEATHA.]   She had to go on a little errand.

TRAVIS   Where?

MAMA   To tend to her business.

TRAVIS   Can I go outside then?

MAMA   Oh, I guess so. You better stay right in front of the house, though . . . and keep a good lookout for the postman.

TRAVIS   Yes'm. [*He starts out and decides to give his aunt* BENEATHA *a good swat on the legs as he passes her.*] Leave them poor little old cockroaches alone, they ain't bothering you none.

[*He runs as she swings the spray gun at him both viciously and playfully.* WALTER *enters from the bedroom and goes to the phone.*]

MAMA   Look out there, girl, before you be spilling some of that stuff on that child!

TRAVIS [*Teasing.*]   That's right—look out now!

[*He exits.*]

BENEATHA [*Drily.*]   I can't imagine that it would hurt him—it has never hurt the roaches.

MAMA   Well, little boys' hides ain't as tough as Southside roaches.

WALTER [*Into phone.*]   Hello—Let me talk to Willy Harris.

MAMA   You better get over there behind the bureau. I seen one marching out of there like Napoleon yesterday.

WALTER   Hello, Willy? It ain't come yet. It'll be here in a few minutes. Did the lawyer give you the papers?

BENEATHA   There's really only one way to get rid of them, Mama—

MAMA   How?

BENEATHA   Set fire to this building.

WALTER   Good. Good. I'll be right over.

BENEATHA   Where did Ruth go, Walter?

WALTER   I don't know.

[*He exits abruptly.*]

BENEATHA   Mama, where did Ruth go?

MAMA [*Looking at her with meaning.*]   To the doctor, I think.

BENEATHA   The doctor? What's the matter? [*They exchange glances.*] You don't think—

MAMA [*With her sense of drama.*]   Now I ain't saying what I think. But I ain't never been wrong 'bout a woman neither.

[*The phone rings.*]

BENEATHA [*At the phone.*]   Hay-lo . . . [*Pause, and a moment of recognition.*] Well—when did you get back! . . . And how was it? . . . Of course I've missed you—in my way . . . This morning? No . . . house cleaning and all that and Mama hates it if I let people come over when the house is like this . . . You *have?* Well, that's different . . . What is it— Oh, what the hell, come on over . . . Right, see you then.

[*She hangs up.*]

MAMA [*Who has listened vigorously, as is her habit.*]   Who is that you inviting over here with this house looking like this? You ain't got the pride you was born with!

BENEATHA   Asagai doesn't care how houses look, Mama—he's an intellectual.

MAMA   Who?

BENEATHA   Asagai—Joseph Asagai. He's an African boy I met on campus. He's been studying in Canada all summer.

MAMA   What's his name?

BENEATHA   Asagai, Joseph. Ah-sah-guy . . . He's from Nigeria.

MAMA   Oh, that's the little country that was founded by slaves way back . . .

BENEATHA   No, Mama—that's Liberia.

MAMA   I don't think I never met no African before.

BENEATHA Well, do me a favor and don't ask him a whole lot of ignorant questions about Africans. I mean, do they wear clothes and all that—

MAMA Well, now, I guess if you think we so ignorant 'round here maybe you shouldn't bring your friends here—

BENEATHA It's just that people ask such crazy things. All anyone seems to know about when it comes to Africa is Tarzan—

MAMA [*Indignantly.*] Why should I know anything about Africa?

BENEATHA Why do you give money at church for the missionary work?

MAMA Well, that's to help save people.

BENEATHA You mean save them from *heathenism*—

MAMA [*Innocently.*] Yes.

BENEATHA I'm afraid they need more salvation from the British and the French.

[RUTH *comes in forlornly and pulls off her coat with dejection. They both turn to look at her.*]

RUTH [*Dispiritedly.*] Well, I guess from all the happy faces—everybody knows.

BENEATHA You pregnant?

MAMA Lord have mercy, I sure hope it's a little old girl. Travis ought to have a sister.

[BENEATHA *and* RUTH *give her a hopeless look for this grandmotherly enthusiasm.*]

BENEATHA How far along are you?

RUTH Two months.

BENEATHA Did you mean to? I mean did you plan it or was it an accident?

MAMA What do you know about planning or not planning?

BENEATHA Oh, Mama.

RUTH [*Wearily.*] She's twenty years old, Lena.

BENEATHA Did you plan it, Ruth?

RUTH Mind your own business.

BENEATHA It is my business—where is he going to live, on the *roof*? [*There is silence following the remark as the three women react to the sense of it.*] Gee—I didn't mean that, Ruth, honest. Gee, I don't feel like that at all. I—I think it is wonderful.

RUTH [*Dully.*] Wonderful.

BENEATHA Yes—really.

MAMA [*Looking at* RUTH, *worried.*] Doctor say everything going to be all right?

RUTH [*Far away.*] Yes—she says everything is going to be fine . . .

MAMA [*Immediately suspicious.*] "She"—What doctor you went to?

[RUTH *folds over, near hysteria.*]

MAMA [*Worriedly hovering over* RUTH.] Ruth honey—what's the matter with you—you sick?

[RUTH *has her fists clenched on her thighs and is fighting hard to suppress a scream that seems to be rising in her.*]

BENEATHA What's the matter with her, Mama?

MAMA [*Working her fingers in* RUTH's *shoulder to relax her.*] She be all right. Women gets right depressed sometimes when they get her way. [*Speaking softly, expertly, rapidly.*] Now you just relax. That's right . . . just lean back, don't think 'bout nothing at all . . . nothing at all—

RUTH I'm all right . . .

[*The glassy-eyed look melts and then she collapses into a fit of heavy sobbing. The bell rings.*]

BENEATHA   Oh, my God—that must be Asagai.

MAMA [*To* RUTH.]   Come on now, honey. You need to lie down and rest
awhile . . . then have some nice hot food.

> [*They exit,* RUTH's *weight on her mother-in-law.* BENEATHA, *herself
> profoundly disturbed, opens the door to admit a rather dramatic-looking
> young man with a large package.*]

ASAGAI   Hello, Alaiyo—

BENEATHA [*Holding the door open and regarding him with pleasure.*]
Hello . . . [*Long pause.*] Well—come in. And please excuse everything.
My mother was very upset about my letting anyone come here with the
place like this.

ASAGAI [*Coming into the room.*]   You look disturbed too . . . Is something
wrong?

BENEATHA [*Still at the door, absently.*]   Yes . . . we've all got acute ghet-
toitus. [*She smiles and comes toward him, finding a cigarette and sitting.*]
So—sit down! How was Canada?

ASAGAI [*A sophisticate.*]   Canadian.

BENEATHA [*Looking at him.*]   I'm very glad you are back.

ASAGAI [*Looking back at her in turn.*]   Are you really?

BENEATHA   Yes—very.

ASAGAI   Why—you were quite glad when I went away. What happened?

BENEATHA   You went away.

ASAGAI   Ahhhhhhhh.

BENEATHA   Before—you wanted to be so serious before there was time.

ASAGAI   How much time must there be before one knows what one feels?

BENEATHA [*Stalling this particular conversation. Her hands pressed together,
in a deliberately childish gesture.*]   What did you bring me?

ASAGAI [*Handing her the package.*]   Open it and see.

BENEATHA [*Eagerly opening the package and drawing out some records and
the colorful robes of a Nigerian woman.*]   Oh, Asagai! . . . You got them
for me! . . . How beautiful . . . and the records too! [*She lifts out the robes
and runs to the mirror with them and holds the drapery up in front of
herself.*]

ASAGAI [*Coming to her at the mirror.*]   I shall have to teach you how to
drape it properly. [*He flings the material about her for the moment and
stands back to look at her.*] Ah—Oh-pay-gay-day, oh-gbah-mu-shay. [*A
Yoruba exclamation for admiration.*] You wear it well . . . very well . . .
mutilated hair and all.

BENEATHA [*Turning suddenly.*]   My hair—what's wrong with my hair?

ASAGAI [*Shrugging.*]   Were you born with it like that?

BENEATHA [*Reaching up to touch it.*]   No . . . of course not.

> [*She looks back to the mirror, disturbed.*]

ASAGAI [*Smiling.*]   How then?

BENEATHA   You know perfectly well how . . . as crinkly as yours . . . that's
how.

ASAGAI   And it is ugly to you that way?

BENEATHA [*Quickly.*]   Oh, no—not ugly . . . [*More slowly, apologetically.*]
But it's so hard to manage when it's, well—raw.

ASAGAI   And so to accommodate that—you mutilate it every week?

BENEATHA   It's not mutilation!

ASAGAI [*Laughing aloud at her seriousness.*]   Oh . . . please! I am only teasing you because you are so very serious about these things. [*He stands

*back from her and folds his arms across his chest as he watches her pulling
at her hair and frowning in the mirror.*] Do you remember the first time
you met me at school? . . . [*He laughs.*] You came up to me and you said—
and I thought you were the most serious little thing I had ever seen—you
said: [*He imitates her.*] "Mr. Asagai—I want very much to talk with you.
About Africa. You see, Mr. Asagai, I am looking for my *identity!*"
[*He laughs.*]

BENEATHA [*Turning to him, not laughing.*]   Yes—
[*Her face is quizzical, profoundly disturbed.*]

ASAGAI [*Still teasing and reaching out and taking her face in his hands and
turning her profile to him.*]   Well . . . it is true that this is not so much
a profile of a Hollywood queen as perhaps a queen of the Nile—[*A mock
dismissal of the importance of the question.*] But what does it matter?
Assimilationism is so popular in your country.

BENEATHA [*Wheeling, passionately, sharply.*]   I am not an assimilationist!

ASAGAI [*The protest hangs in the room for a moment and* ASAGAI *studies her,
his laughter fading.*]   Such a serious one. [*There is a pause.*] So—you
like the robes? You must take excellent care of them—they are from my
sister's personal wardrobe.

BENEATHA [*With incredulity.*]   You—you sent all the way home—for me?

ASAGAI [*With charm.*]   For you—I would do much more . . . Well, that is
what I came for. I must go.

BENEATHA   Will you call me Monday?

ASAGAI   Yes . . . We have a great deal to talk about. I mean about identity
and time and all that.

BENEATHA   Time?

ASAGAI   Yes. About how much time one needs to know what one feels.

BENEATHA   You never understood that there is more than one kind of
feeling which can exist between a man and a woman—or, at least, there
should be.

ASAGAI [*Shaking his head negatively but gently.*]   No. Between a man and
a woman there need be only one kind of feeling. I have that for you . . .
Now even . . . right this moment . . .

BENEATHA   I know—and by itself—it won't do. I can find that anywhere.

ASAGAI   For a woman it should be enough.

BENEATHA   I know—because that's what it says in all the novels that men
write. But it isn't. Go ahead and laugh—but I'm not interested in being
someone's little episode in America or—[*With feminine vengeance.*]—one
of them! [ASAGAI *has burst into laughter again.*] That's funny as hell, huh!

ASAGAI   It's just that every American girl I have known has said that to me.
White—black—in this you are all the same. And the same speech, too!

BENEATHA [*Angrily.*]   Yuk, yuk, yuk!

ASAGAI   It's how you can be sure that the world's most liberated women
are not liberated at all. You all talk about it too much!
[MAMA *enters and is immediately all social charm because of the presence of a guest.*]

BENEATHA   Oh—Mama—this is Mr. Asagai.

MAMA   How do you do?

ASAGAI [*Total politeness to an elder.*]   How do you do, Mrs. Younger. Please
forgive me for coming at such an outrageous hour on a Saturday.

MAMA   Well, you are quite welcome. I just hope you understand that our
house don't always look like this. [*Chatterish.*] You must come again. I

would love to hear all about—[*Not sure of the name.*]—your country. I think it's so sad the way our American Negroes don't know nothing about Africa 'cept Tarzan and all that. And all that money they pour into these churches when they ought to be helping you people over there drive out them French and Englishmen done taken away your land.

[*The mother flashes a slightly superior look at her daughter upon completion of the recitation.*]

ASAGAI [*Taken aback by this sudden and acutely unrelated expression of sympathy.*] Yes . . . yes . . .

MAMA [*Smiling at him suddenly and relaxing and looking him over.*] How many miles is it from here to where you come from?

ASAGAI Many thousands.

MAMA [*Looking at him as she would* WALTER.] I bet you don't half look after yourself, being away from your mama either. I spec you better come 'round here from time to time and get yourself some decent home-cooked meals . . .

ASAGAI [*Moved.*] Thank you. Thank you very much. [*They are all quiet, then—*] Well . . . I must go. I will call you Monday, Alaiyo.

MAMA What's that he call you?

ASAGAI Oh—"Alaiyo." I hope you don't mind. It is what you would call a nickname, I think. It is a Yoruba word. I am a Yoruba.

MAMA [*Looking at* BENEATHA.] I—I thought he was from—

ASAGAI [*Understanding.*] Nigeria is my country. Yoruba is my tribal origin—

BENEATHA You didn't tell us what Alaiyo means . . . for all I know, you might be calling me Little Idiot or something . . .

ASAGAI Well . . . let me see . . . I do not know how just to explain it . . . The sense of a thing can be so different when it changes languages.

BENEATHA You're evading.

ASAGAI No—really it is difficult . . . [*Thinking.*] It means . . . it means One for Whom Bread—Food—Is Not Enough. [*He looks at her.*] Is that all right?

BENEATHA [*Understanding, softly.*] Thank you.

MAMA [*Looking from one to the other and not understanding any of it.*] Well . . . that's nice . . . You must come see us again—Mr.—

ASAGAI Ah-sah-guy . . .

MAMA Yes . . . Do come again.

ASAGAI Good-bye.

[*He exits.*]

MAMA [*After him.*] Lord, that's a pretty thing just went out here! [*Insinuatingly, to her daughter.*] Yes, I guess I see why we done commence to get so interested in Africa 'round here. Missionaries my aunt Jenny!

[*She exits.*]

BENEATHA Oh, Mama! . . .

[*She picks up the Nigerian dress and holds it up to her in front of the mirror again. She sets the headdress on haphazardly and then notices her hair again and clutches at it and then replaces the headdress and frowns at herself. Then she starts to wriggle in front of the mirror as she thinks a Nigerian woman might.* TRAVIS *enters and regards her.*]

TRAVIS You cracking up?

BENEATHA Shut up.

[*She pulls the headdress off and looks at herself in the mirror and clutches at her hair again and squinches her eyes as if trying to imagine something. Then, suddenly, she gets her raincoat and kerchief and hurriedly prepares for going out.*]

MAMA [*Coming back into the room.*] She's resting now. Travis, baby, run next door and ask Miss Johnson to please let me have a little kitchen cleanser. This here can is empty as Jacob's kettle.

TRAVIS I just came in.

MAMA Do as you told. [*He exits and she looks at her daughter.*] Where you going?

BENEATHA [*Halting at the door.*] To become a queen of the Nile!
[*She exits in a breathless blaze of glory.* RUTH *appears in the bedroom doorway.*]

MAMA Who told you to get up?

RUTH Ain't nothing wrong with me to be lying in no bed for. Where did Bennie go?

MAMA [*Drumming her fingers.*] Far as I could make out—to Egypt. [RUTH *just looks at her.*] What time is it getting to?

RUTH Ten twenty. And the mailman going to ring that bell this morning just like he done every morning for the last umpteen years.
[TRAVIS *comes in with the cleanser can.*]

TRAVIS She say to tell you that she don't have much.

MAMA [*Angrily.*] Lord, some people I could name sure is tight-fisted! [*Directing her grandson.*] Mark two cans of cleanser down on the list there. If she that hard up for kitchen cleanser, I sure don't want to forget to get her none!

RUTH Lena—maybe the woman is just short on cleanser—

MAMA [*Not listening.*]—Much baking powder as she done borrowed from me all these years, she could of done gone into the baking business!
[*The bell sounds suddenly and sharply and all three are stunned—serious and silent—mid-speech. In spite of all the other conversations and distractions of the morning, this is what they have been waiting for, even* TRAVIS, *who looks helplessly from his mother to his grandmother.* RUTH *is the first to come to life again.*]

RUTH [*To* TRAVIS.] Get down them steps, boy!
[TRAVIS *snaps to life and flies out to get the mail.*]

MAMA [*Her eyes wide, her hand to her breast.*] You mean it done really come?

RUTH [*Excited.*] Oh, Miss Lena!

MAMA [*Collecting herself.*] Well . . . I don't know what we all so excited about 'round here for. We known it was coming for months.

RUTH That's a whole lot different from having it come and being able to hold it in your hands . . . a piece of paper worth ten thousand dollars . . . [TRAVIS *bursts back into the room. He holds the envelope high above his head, like a little dancer, his face is radiant and he is breathless. He moves to his grandmother with sudden slow ceremony and puts the envelope into her hands. She accepts it, and then merely holds it and looks at it.*] Come on! Open it . . . Lord have mercy, I wish Walter Lee was here!

TRAVIS Open it, Grandmama!

MAMA [*Staring at it.*] Now you all be quiet. It's just a check.

RUTH Open it . . .

MAMA [*Still staring at it.*] Now don't act silly . . . We ain't never been no people to act silly 'bout no money—

RUTH [*Swiftly.*] We ain't never had none before—*open it!*

[MAMA *finally makes a good strong tear and pulls out the thin blue slice of paper and inspects it closely. The boy and his mother study it raptly over* MAMA'S *shoulders.*]

MAMA   *Travis!* [*She is counting off with doubt.*] Is that the right number of zeros.

TRAVIS   Yes'm . . . ten thousand dollars. Gaalee, Grandmama, you rich.

MAMA [*She holds the check away from her, still looking at it. Slowly her face sobers into a mask of unhappiness.*]   Ten thousand dollars. [*She hands it to* RUTH.] Put it away somewhere, Ruth. [*She does not look at* RUTH; *her eyes seem to be seeing something somewhere very far off.*] Ten thousand dollars they give you. Ten thousand dollars.

TRAVIS [*To his mother, sincerely.*]   What's the matter with Grandmama— don't she want to be rich?

RUTH [*Distractedly.*]   You go on out and play now, baby. [TRAVIS *exits,* MAMA *starts wiping dishes absently, humming intently to herself.* RUTH *turns to her, with kind exasperation.*] You've gone and got yourself upset.

MAMA [*Not looking at her.*]   I spec if it wasn't for you all . . . I would just put that money away or give it to the church or something.

RUTH   Now what kind of talk is that. Mr. Younger would just be plain mad if he could hear you talking foolish like that.

MAMA [*Stopping and staring off.*]   Yes . . . he sure would. [*Sighing.*] We got enough to do with that money, all right. [*She halts then, and turns and looks at her daughter-in-law hard;* RUTH *avoids her eyes and* MAMA *wipes her hands with finality and starts to speak firmly to* RUTH.] Where did you go today, girl?

RUTH   To the doctor.

MAMA [*Impatiently.*]   Now, Ruth . . . you know better than that. Old Doctor Jones is strange enough in his way but there ain't nothing 'bout him make somebody slip and call him "she"—like you done this morning.

RUTH   Well, that's what happened—my tongue slipped.

MAMA   You went to see that woman, didn't you?

RUTH [*Defensively, giving herself away.*]   What woman you talking about?

MAMA [*Angrily.*]   That woman who—
        [WALTER *enters in great excitement.*]

WALTER   Did it come?

MAMA [*Quietly.*]   Can't you give people a Christian greeting before you start asking about money?

WALTER [*To* RUTH.]   Did it come? [RUTH *unfolds the check and lays it quietly before him, watching him intently with thoughts of her own.* WALTER *sits down and grasps it close and counts off the zeros.*] Ten thousand dollars— [*He turns suddenly, frantically to his mother and draws some papers out of his breast pocket.*] Mama—look. Old Willy Harris put everything on paper—

MAMA   Son—I think you ought to talk to your wife . . . I'll go on out and leave you alone if you want—

WALTER   I can talk to her later—Mama, look—

MAMA   Son—

WALTER   WILL SOMEBODY PLEASE LISTEN TO ME TODAY!

MAMA [*Quietly.*]   I don't 'low no yellin' in this house, Walter Lee, and you know it—[WALTER *stares at them in frustration and starts to speak several times.*] And there ain't going to be no investing in no liquor stores. I don't aim to have to speak on that again.
        [*A long pause.*]

WALTER   Oh—so you don't aim to have to speak on that again? So *you* have decided . . . [*Crumpling his papers.*] Well, *you* tell that to my boy tonight when you put him to sleep on the living-room couch . . . [*Turning to* MAMA *and speaking directly to her.*] Yeah—and tell it to my wife, Mama, tomorrow when she has to go out of here to look after somebody else's kids. And tell it to *me*, Mama, every time we need a new pair of curtains and I have to watch *you* go out and work in somebody's kitchen. Yeah, you tell me then!
    [WALTER *starts out.*]
RUTH   Where you going?
WALTER   I'm going out!
RUTH   Where?
WALTER   Just out of this house somewhere—
RUTH [*Getting her coat.*]   I'll come too.
WALTER   I don't want you to come!
RUTH   I got something to talk to you about, Walter.
WALTER   That's too bad.
MAMA [*Still quietly.*]   Walter Lee—[*She waits and he finally turns and looks at her.*] Sit down.
WALTER   I'm a grown man, Mama.
MAMA   Ain't nobody said you wasn't grown. But you still in my house and my presence. And as long as you are—you'll talk to your wife civil. Now sit down.
RUTH [*Suddenly.*]   Oh, let him go on out and drink himself to death! He makes me sick to my stomach! [*She flings her coat against him.*]
WALTER [*Violently.*]   And you turn mine too, baby! [RUTH *goes into their bedroom and slams the door behind her.*] That was my greatest mistake—
MAMA [*Still quietly.*]   Walter, what is the matter with you?
WALTER   Matter with me? Ain't nothing the matter with *me!*
MAMA   Yes there is. Something eating you up like a crazy man. Something more than me not giving you this money. The past few years I been watching it happen to you. You get all nervous acting and kind of wild in the eyes—[WALTER *jumps up impatiently at her words.*] I said sit there now, I'm talking to you!
WALTER   Mama—I don't need no nagging at me today.
MAMA   Seem like you getting to a place where you always tied up in some kind of knot about something. But if anybody ask you 'bout it you just yell at 'em and bust out the house and go out and drink somewheres. Walter Lee, people can't live with that. Ruth's a good, patient girl in her way—but you getting to be too much. Boy, don't make the mistake of driving that girl away from you.
WALTER   Why—what she do for me?
MAMA   She loves you.
WALTER   Mama—I'm going out. I want to go off somewhere and be by myself for a while.
MAMA   I'm sorry 'bout your liquor store, son. It just wasn't the thing for us to do. That's what I want to tell you about—
WALTER   I got to go out, Mama—
    [*He rises.*]
MAMA   It's dangerous, son.
WALTER   What's dangerous?
MAMA   When a man goes outside his home to look for peace.

WALTER [*Beseechingly.*]   Then why can't there never be no peace in this house then?

MAMA   You done found it in some other house?

WALTER   No—there ain't no woman! Why do women always think there's a woman somewhere when a man gets restless. [*Coming to her.*] Mama— Mama—I want so many things . . .

MAMA   Yes, son—

WALTER   I want so many things that they are driving me kind of crazy . . . Mama—look at me.

MAMA   I'm looking at you. You a good-looking boy. You got a job, a nice wife, a fine boy and—

WALTER   A job. [*Looks at her.*] Mama, a job? I open and close car doors all day long. I drive a man around in his limousine and I say, "Yes, sir; no, sir; very good, sir; shall I take the Drive, sir?" Mama, that ain't no kind of job . . . that ain't nothing at all. [*Very quietly.*] Mama, I don't know if I can make you understand.

MAMA   Understand what, baby?

WALTER [*Quietly.*]   Sometimes it's like I can see the future stretched out in front of me—just plain as day. The future, Mama. Hanging over there at the edge of my days. Just waiting for me—a big, looming blank space—full of *nothing*. Just waiting for *me*. [*Pause.*] Mama—sometimes when I'm downtown and I pass them cool, quiet-looking restaurants where them white boys are sitting back and talking 'bout things . . . sitting there turning deals worth millions of dollars . . . sometimes I see guys don't look much older than me—

MAMA   Son—how come you talk so much 'bout money?

WALTER [*With immense passion.*]   Because it is life, Mama!

MAMA [*Quietly.*]   Oh—[*Very quietly.*] So now it's life. Money is life. Once upon a time freedom used to be life—now it's money. I guess the world really do change . . .

WALTER   No—it was always money, Mama. We just didn't know about it.

MAMA   No . . . something has changed. [*She looks at him.*] You something new, boy. In my time we was worried about not being lynched and getting to the North if we could and how to stay alive and still have a pinch of dignity too . . . Now here come you and Beneatha—talking 'bout things we ain't never even thought about hardly, me and your daddy. You ain't satisfied or proud of nothing we done. I mean that you had a home; that we kept you out of trouble till you was grown; that you don't have to ride to work on the back of nobody's streetcar— You my children— but how different we done become.

WALTER   You just don't understand, Mama, you just don't understand.

MAMA   Son—do you know your wife is expecting another baby? [WALTER *stands, stunned, and absorbs what his mother has said.*] That's what she wanted to talk to you about.[WALTER *sinks down into a chair.*] This ain't for me to be telling—but you ought to know.[*She waits.*] I think Ruth is thinking 'bout getting rid of that child.

WALTER [*Slowly understanding.*]   No—no—Ruth wouldn't do that.

MAMA   When the world gets ugly enough—a woman will do anything for her family. *The part that's already living.*

WALTER   You don't know Ruth, Mama, if you think she would do that.

[RUTH *opens the bedroom door and stands there a little limp.*]

RUTH [*Beaten.*] Yes I would too, Walter. [*Pause.*] I gave her a five-dollar down payment.

> [*There is total silence as the man stares at his wife and the mother stares at her son.*]

MAMA [*Presently.*] Well—[*Tightly.*] Well—son, I'm waiting to hear you say something . . . I'm waiting to hear how you be your father's son. Be the man he was . . . [*Pause.*] Your wife say she going to destroy your child. And I'm waiting to hear you talk like him and say we a people who give children life, not who destroys them—[*She rises.*] I'm waiting to see you stand up and look like your daddy and say we done give up one baby to poverty and that we ain't going to give up nary another one . . . I'm waiting.

WALTER Ruth—

MAMA If you a son of mine, tell her! [WALTER *turns, looks at her and can say nothing. She continues, bitterly.*] You . . . you are a disgrace to your father's memory. Somebody get me my hat.

> [*Curtain.*]

Act II

SCENE ONE

Time: Later the same day.

At rise: RUTH *is ironing again. She has the radio going. Presently* BENEATHA'S *bedroom door opens and* RUTH'S *mouth falls and she puts down the iron in fascination.*

RUTH What have we got on tonight!

BENEATHA [*Emerging grandly from the doorway so that we can see her thoroughly robed in the costume* ASAGAI *brought.*] You are looking at what a well-dressed Nigerian woman wears—[*She parades for* RUTH, *her hair completely hidden by the headdress; she is coquettishly fanning herself with an ornate oriental fan, mistakenly more like Butterfly than any Nigerian that ever was.*] Isn't it beautiful? [*She promenades to the radio and, with an arrogant flourish, turns off the good loud blues that is playing.*] Enough of this assimilationist junk! [RUTH *follows her with her eyes as she goes to the phonograph and puts on a record and turns and waits ceremoniously for the music to come up. Then, with a shout—*] OCOMOGOSIAY!

> [RUTH *jumps. The music comes up, a lovely Nigerian melody.* BENEATHA *listens, enraptured, her eyes far away—"back to the past." She begins to dance.* RUTH *is dumbfounded.*]

RUTH What kind of dance is that?

BENEATHA A folk dance.

RUTH [*Pearl Bailey.*][2] What kind of folks do that, honey?

BENEATHA It's from Nigeria. It's a dance of welcome.

RUTH Who you welcoming?

BENEATHA The men back to the village.

RUTH Where they been?

BENEATHA How should I know—out hunting or something. Anyway, they are coming back now . . .

RUTH Well, that's good.

---

2. American singer, dancer, actor, and author (1918–1990).

BENEATHA [*With the record.*]

> Alundi, alundi
> Alundi alunya
> Jop pu a jeepua
> Ang gu sooooooooooo
>
> Ai yai yae . . .
> Ayehaye—alundi . . .

[WALTER *comes in during this performance; he has obviously been drinking. He leans against the door heavily and watches his sister, at first with distaste. Then his eyes look off—"back to the past"—as he lifts both his fists to the roof, screaming.*]

WALTER   YEAH . . . AND ETHIOPIA STRETCH FORTH HER HANDS AGAIN! . . .

RUTH [*Drily, looking at him.*]   Yes—and Africa sure is claiming her own tonight. [*She gives them both up and starts ironing again.*]

WALTER [*All in a drunken, dramatic shout.*]   Shut up! . . . I'm digging them drums . . . them drums move me! . . . [*He makes his weaving way to his wife's face and leans in close to her.*] In my *heart of hearts*— [*He thumps his chest.*]—I am much warrior!

RUTH [*Without even looking up.*]   In your heart of hearts you are much drunkard.

WALTER [*Coming away from her and starting to wander around the room, shouting.*]   Me and Jomo . . . [*Intently, in his sister's face. She has stopped dancing to watch him in this unknown mood.*] That's my man, Kenyatta. [*Shouting and thumping his chest.*] FLAMING SPEAR! HOT DAMN! [*He is suddenly in possession of an imaginary spear and actively spearing enemies all over the room.*] OCOMOGOSIAY . . . THE LION IS WAKING . . . OWIMOWEH! [*He pulls his shirt open and leaps up on a table and gestures with his spear. The bell rings.* RUTH *goes to answer.*]

BENEATHA [*To encourage* WALTER, *thoroughly caught up with this side of him.*]   OCOMOGOSIAY, FLAMING SPEAR!

WALTER [*On the table, very far gone, his eyes pure glass sheets. He sees what we cannot, that he is a leader of his people, a great chief, a descendant of Chaka, and that the hour to march has come.*]   Listen, my black brothers—

BENEATHA   OCOMOGOSIAY!

WALTER   —Do you hear the waters rushing against the shores of the coastlands—

BENEATHA   OCOMOGOSIAY!

WALTER   —Do you hear the screeching of the cocks in yonder hills beyond where the chiefs meet in council for the coming of the mighty war—

BENEATHA   OCOMOGOSIAY!

WALTER   —Do you hear the beating of the wings of the birds flying low over the mountains and the low places of our land—

[RUTH *opens the door.* GEORGE MURCHISON *enters.*]

BENEATHA   OCOMOGOSIAY!

WALTER   —Do you hear the singing of the women, singing the war songs of our fathers to the babies in the great houses . . . singing the sweet war songs? OH, DO YOU HEAR, MY BLACK BROTHERS!

BENEATHA [*Completely gone.*]   We hear you, Flaming Spear—

WALTER   Telling us to prepare for the greatness of the time—[*To* GEORGE.] Black Brother!

   [*He extends his hand for the fraternal clasp.*]

GEORGE   Black Brother, hell!

RUTH [*Having had enough, and embarrassed for the family.*]   Beneatha, you got company—what's the matter with you? Walter Lee Younger, get down off that table and stop acting like a fool . . .

   [WALTER *comes down off the table suddenly and makes a quick exit to the bathroom.*]

RUTH   He's had a little to drink . . . I don't know what her excuse is.

GEORGE [*To* BENEATHA.]   Look honey, we're going *to* the theatre—we're not going to be *in* it . . . so go change, huh?

RUTH   You expect this boy to go out with you looking like that?

BENEATHA [*Looking at* GEORGE.]   That's up to George. If he's ashamed of his heritage—

GEORGE   Oh, don't be so proud of yourself, Bennie—just because you look eccentric.

BENEATHA   How can something that's natural be eccentric?

GEORGE   That's what being eccentric means—being natural. Get dressed.

BENEATHA   I don't like that, George.

RUTH   Why must you and your brother make an argument out of everything people say?

BENEATHA   Because I hate assimilationist Negroes!

RUTH   Will somebody please tell me what assimila-who-ever means!

GEORGE   Oh, it's just a college girl's way of calling people Uncle Toms— but that isn't what it means at all.

RUTH   Well, what does it mean?

BENEATHA [*Cutting* GEORGE *off and staring at him as she replies to* RUTH.] It means someone who is willing to give up his own culture and submerge himself completely in the dominant, and in this case, *oppressive* culture!

GEORGE   Oh, dear, dear, dear! Here we go! A lecture on the African past! On our Great West African Heritage! In one second we will hear all about the great Ashanti empires; the great Songhay civilizations; and the great sculpture of Bénin[3]—and then some poetry in the Bantu— and the whole monologue will end with the word *heritage!* [*Nastily.*] Let's face it, baby, your heritage is nothing but a bunch of raggedy-assed spirituals and some grass huts!

BENEATHA   *Grass huts!* [RUTH *crosses to her and forcibly pushes her toward the bedroom.*] See there . . . you are standing there in your splendid ignorance talking about people who were the first to smelt iron on the face of the earth! [RUTH *is pushing her through the door.*] The Ashanti were performing surgical operations when the English—[RUTH *pulls the door to, with* BENEATHA *on the other side, and smiles graciously at* GEORGE. BENEATHA *opens the door and shouts the end of the sentence defiantly at* GEORGE.]—were still tatooing themselves with blue dragons . . . [*She goes back inside.*]

___

3. Bronze and brass royal sculptures produced in Benin (now part of Nigeria) in the 14th to 17th centuries. The Ashanti empires were the strongest political organization in West Africa during the time of the European slave trade. The Songhay civilizations were the largest and longest-lasting political group in West Africa before the advent of European trade.

RUTH   Have a seat, George. [*They both sit.* RUTH *folds her hands rather primly on her lap, determined to demonstrate the civilization of the family.*] Warm, ain't it? I mean for September. [*Pause.*] Just like they always say about Chicago weather: If it's too hot or cold for you, just wait a minute and it'll change. [*She smiles happily at this cliché of clichés.*] Everybody say it's got to do with them bombs and things they keep setting off. [*Pause.*] Would you like a nice cold beer?

GEORGE   No, thank you. I don't care for beer. [*He looks at his watch.*] I hope she hurries up.

RUTH   What time is the show?

GEORGE   It's an eight-thirty curtain. That's just Chicago, though. In New York standard curtain time is eight forty.
    [*He is rather proud of this knowledge.*]

RUTH [*Properly appreciating it.*]   You get to New York a lot?

GEORGE [*Offhand.*]   Few times a year.

RUTH   Oh—that's nice. I've never been to New York.
    [WALTER *enters. We feel he has relieved himself, but the edge of unreality is still with him.*]

WALTER   New York ain't got nothing Chicago ain't. Just a bunch of hustling people all squeezed up together—being "Eastern."
    [*He turns his face into a screw of displeasure.*]

GEORGE   Oh—you've been?

WALTER   *Plenty* of times.

RUTH [*Shocked at the lie.*]   Walter Lee Younger!

WALTER [*Staring her down.*]   Plenty! [*Pause.*] What we got to drink in this house? Why don't you offer this man some refreshment. [*To* GEORGE.] They don't know how to entertain people in this house, man.

GEORGE   Thank you—I don't really care for anything.

WALTER [*Feeling his head; sobriety coming.*]   Where's Mama?

RUTH   She ain't come back yet.

WALTER [*Looking* MURCHISON *over from head to toe, scrutinizing his carefully casual tweed sports jacket over cashmere V-neck sweater over soft eyelet shirt and tie, and soft slacks, finished off with white buckskin shoes.*] Why all you college boys wear them fairyish-looking white shoes?

RUTH   Walter Lee!
    [GEORGE MURCHISON *ignores the remark.*]

WALTER [*To* RUTH.]   Well, they look crazy as hell—white shoes, cold as it is.

RUTH [*Crushed.*]   You have to excuse him—

WALTER   No he don't! Excuse me for what? What you always excusing me for! I'll excuse myself when I needs to be excused! [*A pause.*] They look as funny as them black knee socks Beneatha wears out of here all the time.

RUTH   It's the college *style*, Walter.

WALTER   Style, hell. She looks like she got burnt legs or something!

RUTH   Oh, Walter—

WALTER [*An irritable mimic.*]   Oh, Walter! Oh, Walter! [*To* MURCHISON.] How's your old man making out? I understand you all going to buy that big hotel on the Drive? [*He finds a beer in the refrigerator, wanders over to* MURCHISON, *sipping and wiping his lips with the back of his hand, and straddling a chair backwards to talk to the other man.*] Shrewd move. Your old man is all right, man. [*Tapping his head and half winking for emphasis.*] I mean he knows how to operate. I mean he thinks *big*, you know what I mean, I mean for a *home,* you know? But I think he's kind of running out of ideas now. I'd like to talk to him. Listen, man, I got some plans that could turn this city upside down. I mean I think like he does. *Big.* Invest big, gamble big, hell, lose *big* if you have to, you know what I mean. It's hard to find a man on this whole Southside who understands my kind of thinking—you dig? [*He scrutinizes* MURCHISON *again, drinks his beer, squints his eyes and leans in close, confidential, man to man.*] Me and you ought to sit down and talk sometimes, man. Man, I got me some ideas . . .

GEORGE [*With boredom.*]   Yeah—sometimes we'll have to do that, Walter.

WALTER [*Understanding the indifference, and offended.*]   Yeah—well, when you get the time, man. I know you a busy little boy.

RUTH   Walter, please—

WALTER [*Bitterly, hurt.*]   I know ain't nothing in this world as busy as you colored college boys with your fraternity pins and white shoes . . .

RUTH [*Covering her face with humiliation.*]   Oh, Walter Lee—

WALTER   I see you all all the time—with the books tucked under your arms—going to your [*British A—a mimic.*] "clahsses." And for what! What the hell you learning over there? Filling up your heads—[*Counting off on his fingers.*]—with the sociology and the psychology—but they teaching you how to be a man? How to take over and run the world? They teaching you how to run a rubber plantation or a steel mill? Naw—just to talk proper and read books and wear white shoes . . .

GEORGE [*Looking at him with distaste, a little above it all.*]   You're all wacked up with bitterness, man.

WALTER [*Intently, almost quietly, between the teeth, glaring at the boy.*]   And you—ain't you bitter, man? Ain't you just about had it yet? Don't you see no stars gleaming that you can't reach out and grab? You happy?—You contented son-of-a-bitch—you happy? You got it made? Bitter? Man, I'm a volcano. Bitter? Here I am a giant—surrounded by ants! Ants who can't even understand what it is the giant is talking about.

RUTH [*Passionately and suddenly.*]   Oh, Walter—ain't you with nobody!

WALTER [*Violently.*]   No! 'Cause ain't nobody with me! Not even my own mother!

RUTH   Walter, that's a terrible thing to say!
   [BENEATHA *enters, dressed for the evening in a cocktail dress and earrings.*]

GEORGE   Well—hey, you look great.

BENEATHA   Let's go, George. See you all later.

RUTH   Have a nice time.

GEORGE   Thanks. Good night. [*To* WALTER, *sarcastically.*]   Good night, Prometheus.[4]
   [BENEATHA *and* GEORGE *exit.*]

WALTER [*To* RUTH.]   Who is Prometheus?

RUTH   I don't know. Don't worry about it.

WALTER [*In fury, pointing after* GEORGE.]   See there—they get to a point where they can't insult you man to man—they got to go talk about something ain't nobody never heard of!

RUTH   How do you know it was an insult? [*To humor him.*] Maybe Prometheus is a nice fellow.

---

4. In Greek mythology, a Titan who stole fire from Mount Olympus and gave it to humankind. As punishment for the theft, Zeus chained him to a rock and sent an eagle to eat his liver, which grew back daily.

WALTER   Prometheus! I bet there ain't even no such thing! I bet that simple-minded clown—

RUTH   Walter—
     [*She stops what she is doing and looks at him.*]

WALTER [*Yelling.*]   Don't start!

RUTH   Start what?

WALTER   Your nagging! Where was I? Who was I with? How much money did I spend?

RUTH [*Plaintively.*]   Walter Lee—why don't we just try to talk about it . . .

WALTER [*Not listening.*]   I been out talking with people who understand me. People who care about the things I got on my mind.

RUTH [*Wearily.*]   I guess that means people like Willy Harris.

WALTER   Yes, people like Willy Harris.

RUTH [*With a sudden flash of impatience.*]   Why don't you all just hurry up and go into the banking business and stop talking about it!

WALTER   Why? You want to know why? 'Cause we all tied up in a race of people that don't know how to do nothing but moan, pray and have babies!
     [*The line is too bitter even for him and he looks at her and sits down.*]

RUTH   Oh, Walter . . . [*Softly.*] Honey, why can't you stop fighting me?

WALTER [*Without thinking.*]   Who's fighting you? Who even cares about you?
     [*This line begins the retardation of his mood.*]

RUTH   Well—[*She waits a long time, and then with resignation starts to put away her things.*] I guess I might as well go on to bed . . . [*More or less to herself.*] I don't know where we lost it . . . but we have . . . [*Then, to him.*] I—I'm sorry about this new baby, Walter. I guess maybe I better go on and do what I started . . . I guess I just didn't realize how bad things was with us . . . I guess I just didn't really realize— [*She starts out to the bedroom and stops.*] You want some hot milk?

WALTER   Hot milk?

RUTH   Yes—hot milk.

WALTER   Why hot milk?

RUTH   'Cause after all that liquor you come home with you ought to have something hot in your stomach.

WALTER   I don't want no milk.

RUTH   You want some coffee then?

WALTER   No, I don't want no coffee. I don't want nothing hot to drink. [*Almost plaintively.*] Why you always trying to give me something to eat?

RUTH [*Standing and looking at him helplessly.*]   What else can I give you, Walter Lee Younger?
     [*She stands and looks at him and presently turns to go out again. He lifts his head and watches her going away from him in a new mood which began to emerge when he asked her "Who cares about you?"*]

WALTER   It's been rough, ain't it, baby? [*She hears and stops but does not turn around and he continues to her back.*] I guess between two people there ain't never as much understood as folks generally thinks there is. I meazn like between me and you—[*She turns to face him.*] How we gets to the place where we scared to talk softness to each other. [*He waits, thinking hard himself.*] Why you think it got to be like that? [*He is thoughtful, almost as a child would be.*] Ruth, what is it gets into people ought to be close?

RUTH   I don't know, honey. I think about it a lot.

WALTER On account of you and me, you mean? The way things are with us. The way something done come down between us.

RUTH There ain't so much between us, Walter . . . Not when you come to me and try to talk to me. Try to be with me . . . a little even.

WALTER [*Total honesty.*] Sometimes . . . sometimes . . . I don't even know how to try.

RUTH Walter—

WALTER Yes?

RUTH [*Coming to him, gently and with misgiving, but coming to him.*] Honey . . . life don't have to be like this. I mean sometimes people can do things so that things are better . . . You remember how we used to talk when Travis was born . . . about the way we were going to live . . . the kind of house . . . [*She is stroking his head.*] Well, it's all starting to slip away from us . . .

[MAMA *enters, and* WALTER *jumps up and shouts at her.*]

WALTER Mama, where have you been?

MAMA My—them steps is longer than they used to be. Whew! [*She sits down and ignores him.*] How you feeling this evening, Ruth?

[RUTH *shrugs, disturbed some at having been prematurely interrupted and watching her husband knowingly.*]

WALTER Mama, where have you been all day?

MAMA [*Still ignoring him and leaning on the table and changing to more comfortable shoes.*] Where's Travis?

RUTH I let him go out earlier and he ain't come back yet. Boy, is he going to get it!

WALTER Mama!

MAMA [*As if she has heard him for the first time.*] Yes, son?

WALTER Where did you go this afternoon?

MAMA I went downtown to tend to some business that I had to tend to.

WALTER What kind of business?

MAMA You know better than to question me like a child, Brother.

WALTER [*Rising and bending over the table.*] Where were you, Mama? [*Bringing his fists down and shouting.*] Mama, you didn't go do something with that insurance money, something crazy?

[*The front door opens slowly, interrupting him, and* TRAVIS *peeks his head in, less than hopefully.*]

TRAVIS [*To his mother.*] Mama, I—

RUTH "Mama I" nothing! You're going to get it, boy! Get on in that bedroom and get yourself ready!

TRAVIS But I—

MAMA Why don't you all never let the child explain hisself.

RUTH Keep out of it now, Lena.

[MAMA *clamps her lips together, and* RUTH *advances toward her son menacingly.*]

RUTH A thousand times I have told you not to go off like that—

MAMA [*Holding out her arms to her grandson.*] Well—at least let me tell him something. I want him to be the first one to hear . . . Come here, Travis. [*The boy obeys, gladly.*] Travis—[*She takes him by the shoulder and looks into his face.*]—you know that money we got in the mail this morning?

TRAVIS Yes'm—

MAMA Well—what you think your grandmama gone and done with that money?

TRAVIS   I don't know, Grandmama.

MAMA [*Putting her finger on his nose for emphasis.*]   She went out and she bought you a house! [*The explosion comes from* WALTER *at the end of the revelation and he jumps up and turns away from all of them in a fury.* MAMA *continues, to* TRAVIS.] You glad about the house? It's going to be yours when you get to be a man.

TRAVIS   Yeah—I always wanted to live in a house.

MAMA   All right, gimme some sugar then—[TRAVIS *puts his arms around her neck as she watches her son over the boy's shoulder. Then, to* TRAVIS, *after the embrace.*] Now when you say your prayers tonight, you thank God and your grandfather—'cause it was him who give you the house—in his way.

RUTH [*Taking the boy from* MAMA *and pushing him toward the bedroom.*] Now you get out of here and get ready for your beating.

TRAVIS   Aw, Mama—

RUTH   Get on in there—[*Closing the door behind him and turning radiantly to her mother-in-law.*] So you went and did it!

MAMA [*Quietly, looking at her son with pain.*]   Yes, I did.

RUTH [*Raising both arms classically.*]   Praise God! [*Looks at* WALTER *a moment, who says nothing. She crosses rapidly to her husband.*] Please, honey—let me be glad . . . you be glad too. [*She has laid her hands on his shoulders, but he shakes himself free of her roughly, without turning to face her.*] Oh, Walter . . . a home . . . a home. [*She comes back to* MAMA.] Well—where is it? How big is it? How much it going to cost?

MAMA   Well—

RUTH   When we moving?

MAMA [*Smiling at her.*]   First of the month.

RUTH [*Throwing back her head with jubilance.*]   Praise God!

MAMA [*Tentatively, still looking at her son's back turned against her and* RUTH.]   It's—it's a nice house too . . . [*She cannot help speaking directly to him. An imploring quality in her voice, her manner, makes her almost like a girl now.*] Three bedrooms—nice big one for you and Ruth . . . Me and Beneatha still have to share our room, but Travis have one of his own—and [*With difficulty.*] I figure if the—new baby—is a boy, we could get one of them double-decker outfits . . . And there's a yard with a little patch of dirt where I could maybe get to grow me a few flowers . . . And a nice big basement . . .

RUTH   Walter honey, be glad—

MAMA [*Still to his back, fingering things on the table.*]   'Course I don't want to make it sound fancier than it is . . . It's just a plain little old house—but it's made good and solid—and it will be *ours*. Walter Lee—it makes a difference in a man when he can walk on floors that belong to him . . .

RUTH   Where is it?

MAMA [*Frightened at this telling.*]   Well—well—it's out there in Clybourne Park—

[RUTH's *radiance fades abruptly, and* WALTER *finally turns slowly to face his mother with incredulity and hostility.*]

RUTH   Where?

MAMA [*Matter-of-factly.*]   Four o six Clybourne Street, Clybourne Park.

RUTH   Clybourne Park? Mama, there ain't no colored people living in Clybourne Park.

MAMA [*Almost idiotically.*]   Well, I guess there's going to be some now.

WALTER [*Bitterly.*]   So that's the peace and comfort you went out and bought for us today!

MAMA [*Raising her eyes to meet his finally.*]   Son—I just tried to find the nicest place for the least amount of money for my family.

RUTH [*Trying to recover from the shock.*]   Well—well—'course I ain't one never been 'fraid of no crackers,[5] mind you—but—well, wasn't there no other houses nowhere?

MAMA   Them houses they put up for colored in them areas way out all seem to cost twice as much as other houses. I did the best I could.

RUTH [*Struck senseless with the news, in its various degrees of goodness and trouble, she sits a moment, her fists propping her chin in thought, and then she starts to rise, bringing her fists down with vigor, the radiance spreading from cheek to cheek again.*]   Well—well!—All I can say is—if this is my time in life—*my time*—to say good-bye—[*And she builds with momentum as she starts to circle the room with an exuberant, almost tearfully happy release.*]—to these Goddamned cracking walls!—[*She pounds the walls.*]—and these marching roaches!—[*She wipes at an imaginary army of marching roaches.*]—and this cramped little closet which ain't now or never was no kitchen! . . . then I say it loud and good, Hallelujah! and good-bye misery . . . I don't never want to see your ugly face again! [*She laughs joyously, having practically destroyed the apartment, and flings her arms up and lets them come down happily, slowly, reflectively, over her abdomen, aware for the first time perhaps that the life therein pulses with happiness and not despair.*] Lena?

MAMA [*Moved, watching her happiness.*]   Yes, honey?

RUTH [*Looking off.*]   Is there—is there a whole lot of sunlight?

MAMA [*Understanding.*]   Yes, child, there's a whole lot of sunlight.

[*Long pause.*]

RUTH [*Collecting herself and going to the door of the room* TRAVIS *is in.*]   Well—I guess I better see 'bout Travis. [*To* MAMA.] Lord, I sure don't feel like whipping nobody today!

[*She exits.*]

MAMA [*The mother and son are left alone now and the mother waits a long time, considering deeply, before she speaks.*]   Son—you—you understand what I done, don't you? [WALTER *is silent and sullen.*] I—I just seen my family falling apart today . . . just falling to pieces in front of my eyes . . . We couldn't of gone on like we was today. We was going backwards 'stead of forwards—talking 'bout killing babies and wishing each other was dead . . . When it gets like that in life—you just got to do something different, push on out and do something bigger . . . [*She waits.*] I wish you say something, son . . . I wish you'd say how deep inside you you think I done the right thing—

WALTER [*Crossing slowly to his bedroom door and finally turning there and speaking measuredly.*]   What you need me to say you done right for? *You* the head of this family. You run our lives like you want to. It was your money and you did what you wanted with it. So what you need for me to say it was all right for? [*Bitterly, to hurt her as deeply as he knows*

5. Whites (slang).

is possible.] So you butchered up a dream of mine—you—who always talking 'bout your children's dreams . . .

MAMA   Walter Lee—

[*He just closes the door behind him.* MAMA *sits alone, thinking heavily.*]

[*Curtain.*]

SCENE TWO

Time: Friday night. A few weeks later.

At rise: Packing crates mark the intention of the family to move. BENEATHA *and* GEORGE *come in, presumably from an evening out again.*

GEORGE   O.K. . . . O.K., whatever you say . . . [*They both sit on the couch. He tries to kiss her. She moves away.*] Look, we've had a nice evening; let's not spoil it, huh? . . .

[*He again turns her head and tries to nuzzle in and she turns away from him, not with distaste but with momentary lack of interest; in a mood to pursue what they were talking about.*]

BENEATHA   I'm *trying* to talk to you.

GEORGE   We always talk.

BENEATHA   Yes—and I love to talk.

GEORGE   [*Exasperated; rising.*]   I know it and I don't mind it sometimes . . . I want you to cut it out, see—The moody stuff, I mean. I don't like it. You're a nice-looking girl . . . all over. That's all you need, honey, forget the atmosphere. Guys aren't going to go for the atmosphere—they're going to go for what they see. Be glad for that. Drop the Garbo[6] routine. It doesn't go with you. As for myself, I want a nice—[*Groping.*]—simple [*Thoughtfully.*]—sophisticated girl . . . not a poet—O.K.?

[*She rebuffs him again and he starts to leave.*]

BENEATHA   Why are you angry?

GEORGE   Because this is stupid! I don't go out with you to discuss the nature of "quiet desperation" or to hear all about your thoughts— because the world will go on thinking what it thinks regardless—

BENEATHA   Then why read books? Why go to school?

GEORGE   [*With artificial patience, counting on his fingers.*]   It's simple. You read books—to learn facts—to get grades—to pass the course—to get a degree. That's all—it has nothing to do with thoughts.

[*A long pause.*]

BENEATHA   I see. [*A longer pause as she looks at him.*] Good night, George.
[GEORGE *looks at her a little oddly, and starts to exit. He meets* MAMA *coming in.*]

GEORGE   Oh—hello, Mrs. Younger.

MAMA   Hello, George, how you feeling?

GEORGE   Fine—fine, how are you?

MAMA   Oh, a little tired. You know them steps can get you after a day's work. You all have a nice time tonight?

GEORGE   Yes—a fine time. Well, good night.

MAMA   Good night. [*He exits.* MAMA *closes the door behind her.*] Hello, honey. What you sitting like that for?

BENEATHA   I'm just sitting.

---

6. Greta Garbo (1905–1990), Swedish-born American actor known for her reclusiveness.

MAMA Didn't you have a nice time?

BENEATHA No.

MAMA No? What's the matter?

BENEATHA Mama, George is a fool—honest. [*She rises.*]

MAMA [*Hustling around unloading the packages she has entered with. She stops.*] Is he, baby?

BENEATHA Yes.

[BENEATHA *makes up* TRAVIS' *bed as she talks.*]

MAMA You sure?

BENEATHA Yes.

MAMA Well—I guess you better not waste your time with no fools.

[BENEATHA *looks up at her mother, watching her put groceries in the refrigerator. Finally she gatheres up her things and starts into the bedroom. At the door she stops and looks back at her mother.*]

BENEATHA Mama—

MAMA Yes, baby—

BENEATHA Thank you.

MAMA For what?

BENEATHA For understanding me this time.

[*She exits quickly and the mother stands, smiling a little, looking at the place where* BENEATHA *just stood.* RUTH *enters.*]

RUTH Now don't you fool with any of this stuff, Lena—

MAMA Oh, I just thought I'd sort a few things out.

[*The phone rings.* RUTH *answers.*]

RUTH [*At the phone.*] Hello—Just a minute. [*Goes to door.*] Walter, it's Mrs. Arnold. [*Waits. Goes back to the phone. Tense.*] Hello. Yes, this is his wife speaking . . . He's lying down now. Yes . . . well, he'll be in tomorrow. He's been very sick. Yes—I know we should have called, but we were so sure he'd be able to come in today. Yes—yes, I'm very sorry. Yes . . . Thank you very much. [*She hangs up.* WALTER *is standing in the doorway of the bedroom behind her.*] That was Mrs. Arnold.

WALTER [*Indifferently.*] Was it?

RUTH She said if you don't come in tomorrow that they are getting a new man . . .

WALTER Ain't that sad—ain't that crying sad.

RUTH She said Mr. Arnold has had to take a cab for three days . . . Walter, you ain't been to work for three days! [*This is a revelation to her.*] Where you been, Walter Lee Younger? [WALTER *looks at her and starts to laugh.*] You're going to lose your job.

WALTER That's right . . .

RUTH Oh, Walter, and with your mother working like a dog every day—

WALTER That's sad too— Everything is sad.

MAMA What you been doing for these three days, son?

WALTER Mama—you don't know all the things a man what got leisure can find to do in this city . . . What's this—Friday night? Well—Wednesday I borrowed Willy Harris' car and I went for a drive . . . just me and myself and I drove and drove . . . Way out . . . way past South Chicago, and I parked the car and I sat and looked at the steel mills all day long. I just sat in the car and looked at them big black chimneys for hours. Then I drove back and I went to the Green Hat. [*Pause.*] And Thursday— Thursday I borrowed the car again and I got in it and I pointed it the other way and I drove the other way—for hours—way, way up to Wisconsin, and I looked at the farms. I just drove and looked at the farms. Then I drove back and I went to the Green Hat. [*Pause.*] And today—today I didn't get the car. Today I just walked. All over the Southside. And I looked at the Negroes and they looked at me and finally I just sat down on the curb at Thirty-ninth and South Parkway and I just sat there and watched the Negroes go by. And then I went to the Green Hat. You all sad? You all depressed? And you know where I am going right now—

[RUTH *goes out quietly.*]

MAMA Oh, Big Walter, is this the harvest of our days?

WALTER You know what I like about the Green Hat? [*He turns the radio on and a steamy, deep blues pours into the room.*] I like this little cat they got there who blows a sax . . . He blows. He talks to me. He ain't but 'bout five feet tall and he's got a conked[7] head and his eyes is always closed and he's all music—

MAMA [*Rising and getting some papers out of her handbag.*] Walter—

WALTER And there's this other guy who plays the piano . . . and they got a sound. I mean they can work on some music . . . They got the best little combo in the world in the Green Hat . . . You can just sit there and drink and listen to them three men play and you realize that don't nothing matter worth a damn, but just being there—

MAMA I've helped do it to you, haven't I, son? Walter, I been wrong.

WALTER Naw—you ain't never been wrong about nothing, Mama.

MAMA Listen to me, now. I say I been wrong, son. That I been doing to you what the rest of the world been doing to you. [*She stops and he looks up slowly at her and she meets his eyes pleadingly.*] Walter—what you ain't never understood is that I ain't got nothing, don't own nothing, ain't never really wanted nothing that wasn't for you. There ain't nothing as precious to me . . . There ain't nothing worth holding on to, money, dreams, nothing else—if it means—if it means it's going to destroy my boy. [*She puts her papers in front of him and he watches her without speaking or moving.*] I paid the man thirty-five hundred dollars down on the house. That leaves sixty-five hundred dollars. Monday morning I want you to take this money and take three thousand dollars and put it in a savings account for Beneatha's medical schooling. The rest you put in a checking account—with your name on it. And from now on any penny that come out of it or that go in it is for you to look after. For you to decide. [*She drops her hands a little helplessly.*] It ain't much, but it's all I got in the world and I'm putting it in your hands. I'm telling you to be the head of this family from now on like you supposed to be.

WALTER [*Stares at the money.*] You trust me like that, Mama?

MAMA I ain't never stop trusting you. Like I ain't never stop loving you. [*She goes out, and* WALTER *sits looking at the money on the table as the music continues in its idiom, pulsing in the room. Finally, in a decisive gesture, he gets up, and, in mingled joy and desperation, picks up the money. At the same moment,* TRAVIS *enters for bed.*]

TRAVIS What's the matter, Daddy? You drunk?

WALTER [*Sweetly, more sweetly than we have ever known him.*] No, Daddy ain't drunk. Daddy ain't going to never be drunk again. . . .

TRAVIS Well, good night, Daddy.

---

7. Chemically straightened hair.

[*The father has come from behind the couch and leans over, embracing his son.*]

WALTER   Son, I feel like talking to you tonight.

TRAVIS   About what?

WALTER   Oh, about a lot of things. About you and what kind of man you going to be when you grow up. . . . Son—son, what do you want to be when you grow up?

TRAVIS   A bus driver.

WALTER   [*Laughing a little.*]   A what? Man, that ain't nothing to want to be!

TRAVIS   Why not?

WALTER   'Cause, man—it ain't big enough—you know what I mean.

TRAVIS   I don't know then. I can't make up my mind. Sometimes Mama asks me that too. And sometimes when I tell you I just want to be like you—she says she don't want me to be like that and sometimes she says she does. . . .

WALTER   [*Gathering him up in his arms.*]   You know what, Travis? In seven years you going to be seventeen years old. And things is going to be very different with us in seven years, Travis. . . . One day when you are seventeen I'll come home—home from my office downtown somewhere—

TRAVIS   You don't work in no office, Daddy.

WALTER   No—but after tonight. After what your daddy gonna do tonight, there's going to be offices—a whole lot of offices. . . .

TRAVIS   What you gonna do tonight, Daddy?

WALTER   You wouldn't understand yet, son, but your daddy's gonna make a transaction . . . a business transaction that's going to change our lives. . . . That's how come one day when you 'bout seventeen years old I'll come home and I'll be pretty tired, you know what I mean, after a day of conferences and secretaries getting things wrong the way they do . . . 'cause an executive's life is hell, man—[*The more he talks the farther away he gets.*] And I'll pull the car up on the driveway . . . just a plain black Chrysler, I think, with white walls—no—black tires. More elegant. Rich people don't have to be flashy . . . though I'll have to get something a little sportier for Ruth—maybe a Cadillac convertible to do her shopping in. . . . And I'll come up the steps to the house and the gardener will be clipping away at the hedges and he'll say, "Good evening, Mr. Younger." And I'll say, "Hello, Jefferson, how are you this evening?" And I'll go inside and Ruth will come downstairs and meet me at the door and we'll kiss each other and she'll take my arm and we'll go up to your room to see you sitting on the floor with the catalogues of all the great schools in America around you. . . . All the great schools in the world! And—and I'll say, all right son—it's your seventeenth birthday, what is it you've decided? . . . Just tell me where you want to go to school and you'll *go.* Just tell me, what it is you want to be—and you'll *be* it. . . . Whatever you want to be—Yessir! [*He holds his arms open for* TRAVIS.] You just name it, son . . . [TRAVIS *leaps into them.*] and I hand you the world!

[WALTER's *voice has risen in pitch and hysterical promise and on the last line he lifts* TRAVIS *high.*]

[*Blackout.*]

SCENE THREE

Time: Saturday, moving day, one week later.

Before the curtain rises, RUTH's voice, a strident, dramatic church alto, cuts through the silence.

It is, in the darkness, a triumphant surge, a penetrating statement of expectation: "Oh, Lord, I don't feel no ways tired! Children, oh, glory hallelujah!"

As the curtain rises we see that RUTH is alone in the living room, finishing up the family's packing. It is moving day. She is nailing crates and tying cartons. BENEATHA enters, carrying a guitar case, and watches her exuberant sister-in-law.

RUTH Hey!

BENEATHA [*Putting away the case.*] Hi.

RUTH [*Pointing at a package.*] Honey—look in that package there and see what I found on sale this morning at the South Center. [RUTH *gets up and moves to the package and draws out some curtains.*] Lookahere—hand-turned hems!

BENEATHA How do you know the window size out there?

RUTH [*Who hadn't thought of that.*] Oh— Well, they bound to fit something in the whole house. Anyhow, they was too good a bargain to pass up. [RUTH *slaps her head, suddenly remembering something.*] Oh, Bennie— I meant to put a special note on that carton over there. That's your mama's good china and she wants 'em to be very careful with it.

BENEATHA I'll do it.

[BENEATHA *finds a piece of paper and starts to draw large letters on it.*]

RUTH You know what I'm going to do soon as I get in that new house?

BENEATHA What?

RUTH Honey—I'm going to run me a tub of water up to here . . . [*With her fingers practically up to her nostrils.*] And I'm going to get in it—and I am going to sit . . . and sit . . . and sit in that hot water and the first person who knocks to tell *me* to hurry up and come out—

BENEATHA Gets shot at sunrise.

RUTH [*Laughing happily.*] You said it, sister! [*Noticing how large BENEATHA is absent-mindedly making the note.*] Honey, they ain't going to read that from no airplane.

BENEATHA [*Laughing herself.*] I guess I always think things have more emphasis if they are big, somehow.

RUTH [*Looking up at her and smiling.*] You and your brother seem to have that as a philosophy of life. Lord, that man—done changed so 'round here. You know—you know what we did last night? Me and Walter Lee?

BENEATHA What?

RUTH [*Smiling to herself.*] We went to the movies. [*Looking at BENEATHA to see if she understands.*] We went to the movies. You know the last time me and Walter went to the movies together?

BENEATHA No.

RUTH Me neither. That's how long it been. [*Smiling again.*] But we went last night. The picture wasn't much good, but that didn't seem to matter. We went—and we held hands.

BENEATHA Oh, Lord!

RUTH We held hands—and you know what?

BENEATHA What?

RUTH When we come out of the show it was late and dark and all the stores and things was closed up . . . and it was kind of chilly and there wasn't many people on the streets . . . and we was still holding hands, me and Walter.

BENEATHA You're killing me.

[WALTER *enters with a large package. His happiness is deep in him; he cannot keep still with his new-found exuberance. He is singing and wiggling and snapping his fingers. He puts his package in a corner and puts a phonograph record, which he has brought in with him, on the record player. As the music comes up he dances over to* RUTH *and tries to get her to dance with him. She gives in at last to his raunchiness and in a fit of giggling allows herself to be drawn into his mood and together they deliberately burlesque an old social dance of their youth.*]

BENEATHA [*Regarding them a long time as they dance, then drawing in her breath for a deeply exaggerated comment which she does not particularly mean.*] Talk about—olddddddddddd-fashioneddddddddd—Negroes!

WALTER [*Stopping momentarily.*] What kind of Negroes?

[*He says this in fun. He is not angry with her today, nor with anyone. He starts to dance with his wife again.*]

BENEATHA Old-fashioned.

WALTER [*As he dances with* RUTH.] You know, when these *New Negroes* have their convention—[*Pointing at his sister.*]—that is going to be the chairman of the Committee on Unending Agitation. [*He goes on dancing, then stops.*] Race, race, race! . . . Girl, I do believe you are the first person in the history of the entire human race to successfully brainwash yourself. [BENEATHA *breaks up and he goes on dancing. He stops again, enjoying his tease.*] Damn, even the N double A C P takes a holiday sometimes! [BENEATHA *and* RUTH *laugh. He dances with* RUTH *some more and starts to laugh and stops and pantomimes someone over an operating table.*] I can just see that chick someday looking down at some poor cat on an operating table before she starts to slice him, saying . . . [*Pulling his sleeves back maliciously.*] "By the way, what are your views on civil rights down there? . . ."

[*He laughs at her again and starts to dance happily. The bell sounds.*]

BENEATHA Sticks and stones may break my bones but . . . words will never hurt me!

[BENEATHA *goes to the door and opens it as* WALTER *and* RUTH *go on with the clowning.* BENEATHA *is somewhat surprised to see a quiet-looking middle-aged white man in a business suit holding his hat and a briefcase in his hand and consulting a small piece of paper.*]

MAN Uh—how do you do, miss. I am looking for a Mrs.—[*He looks at the slip of paper.*] Mrs. Lena Younger?

BENEATHA [*Smoothing her hair with slight embarrassment.*] Oh—yes, that's my mother. Excuse me [*She closes the door and turns to quiet the other two.*] Ruth! Brother! Somebody's here. [*Then she opens the door. The* MAN *casts a curious quick glance at all of them.*] Uh—come in please.

MAN [*Coming in.*] Thank you.

BENEATHA My mother isn't here just now. Is it business?

MAN Yes . . . well, of a sort.

WALTER [*Freely, the Man of the House.*] Have a seat. I'm Mrs. Younger's son. I look after most of her business matters.

[RUTH *and* BENEATHA *exchange amused glances.*]

MAN [*Regarding* WALTER, *and sitting.*] Well—My name is Karl Lindner . . .

WALTER [*Stretching out his hand.*] Walter Younger. This is my wife— [RUTH *nods politely.*]—and my sister.

LINDNER How do you do.

WALTER [*Amiably, as he sits himself easily on a chair, leaning with interest forward on his knees and looking expectantly into the newcomer's face.*] What can we do for you, Mr. Lindner!

LINDNER [*Some minor shuffling of the hat and briefcase on his knees.*] Well—I am a representative of the Clybourne Park Improvement Association—

WALTER [*Pointing.*] Why don't you sit your things on the floor?

LINDNER Oh—yes. Thank you. [*He slides the briefcase and hat under the chair.*] And as I was saying—I am from the Clybourne Park Improvement Association and we have had it brought to our attention at the last meeting that you people—or at least your mother—has bought a piece of residential property at—[*He digs for the slip of paper again.*]—four o six Clybourne Street . . .

WALTER That's right. Care for something to drink? Ruth, get Mr. Lindner a beer.

LINDNER [*Upset for some reason.*] Oh—no, really. I mean thank you very much, but no thank you.

RUTH [*Innocently.*] Some coffee?

LINDNER Thank you, nothing at all.
    [BENEATHA *is watching the man carefully.*]

LINDNER Well, I don't know how much you folks know about our organization. [*He is a gentle man; thoughtful and somewhat labored in his manner.*] It is one of these community organizations set up to look after—oh, you know, things like block upkeep and special projects and we also have what we call our New Neighbors Orientation Committee . . .

BENEATHA [*Drily.*] Yes—and what do they do?

LINDNER [*Turning a little to her and then returning the main force to WAL-TER.*] Well—it's what you might call a sort of welcoming committee, I guess. I mean they, we, I'm the chairman of the committee—go around and see the new people who move into the neighborhood and sort of give them the lowdown on the way we do things out in Clybourne Park.

BENEATHA [*With appreciation of the two meanings, which escape RUTH and WALTER.*] Un-huh.

LINDNER And we also have the category of what the association calls— [*He looks elsewhere.*]—uh—special community problems . . .

BENEATHA Yes—and what are some of those?

WALTER Girl, let the man talk.

LINDNER [*With understated relief.*] Thank you. I would sort of like to explain this thing in my own way. I mean I want to explain to you in a certain way.

WALTER Go ahead.

LINDNER Yes. Well. I'm going to try to get right to the point. I'm sure we'll all appreciate that in the long run.

BENEATHA Yes.

WALTER Be still now!

LINDNER Well—

RUTH [*Still innocently.*] Would you like another chair—you don't look comfortable.

LINDNER [*More frustrated than annoyed.*]   No, thank you very much. Please. Well—to get right to the point I—[*A great breath, and he is off at last.*] I am sure you people must be aware of some of the incidents which have happened in various parts of the city when colored people have moved into certain areas—[BENEATHA *exhales heavily and starts tossing a piece of fruit up and down in the air.*] Well—because we have what I think is going to be a unique type of organization in American community life—not only do we deplore that kind of thing—but we are trying to do something about it. [BENEATHA *stops tossing and turns with a new and quizzical interest to the man.*] We feel—[*gaining confidence in his mission because of the interest in the faces of the people he is talking to.*]—we feel that most of the trouble in this world, when you come right down to it—[*He hits his knee for emphasis.*]—most of the trouble exists because people just don't sit down and talk to each other.

RUTH [*Nodding as she might in church, pleased with the remark.*] You can say that again, mister.

LINDNER [*More encouraged by such affirmation.*]   That we don't try hard enough in this world to understand the other fellow's problem. The other guy's point of view.

RUTH   Now that's right.

[BENEATHA *and* WALTER *merely watch and listen with genuine interest.*]

LINDNER   Yes—that's the way we feel out in Clybourne Park. And that's why I was elected to come here this afternoon and talk to you people. Friendly like, you know, the way people should talk to each other and see if we couldn't find some way to work this thing out. As I say, the whole business is a matter of *caring* about the other fellow. Anybody can see that you are a nice family of folks, hard working and honest I'm sure. [BENEATHA *frowns slightly, quizzically, her head tilted regarding him.*] Today everybody knows what it means to be on the outside of *something.* And of course, there is always somebody who is out to take the advantage of people who don't always understand.

WALTER   What do you mean?

LINDNER   Well—you see our community is made up of people who've worked hard as the dickens for years to build up that little community. They're not rich and fancy people; just hard-working, honest people who don't really have much but those little homes and a dream of the kind of community they want to raise their children in. Now, I don't say we are perfect and there is a lot wrong in some of the things they want. But you've got to admit that a man, right or wrong, has the right to want to have the neighborhood he lives in a certain kind of way. And at the moment the overwhelming majority of our people out there feel that people get along better, take more of a common interest in the life of the community, when they share a common background. I want you to believe me when I tell you that race prejudice simply doesn't enter into it. It is a matter of the people of Clybourne Park believing, rightly or wrongly, as I say, that for the happiness of all concerned that our Negro families are happier when they live in their *own* communities.

BENEATHA [*With a grand and bitter gesture.*]   This, friends, is the Welcoming Committee!

WALTER [*Dumfounded, looking at* LINDNER.]   Is this what you came marching all the way over here to tell us?

LINDNER   Well, now we've been having a fine conversation. I hope you'll hear me all the way through.

WALTER [*Tightly.*]   Go ahead, man.

LINDNER   You see—in the face of all things I have said, we are prepared to make your family a very generous offer . . .

BENEATHA   Thirty pieces and not a coin less!

WALTER   Yeah?

LINDNER [*Putting on his glasses and drawing a form out of the briefcase.*] Our association is prepared, through the collective effort of our people, to buy the house from you at a financial gain to your family.

RUTH   Lord have mercy, ain't this the living gall!

WALTER   All right, you through?

LINDNER   Well, I want to give you the exact terms of the financial arrangement—

WALTER   We don't want to hear no exact terms of no arrangements. I want to know if you got any more to tell us 'bout getting together?

LINDNER [*Taking off his glasses.*]   Well—I don't suppose that you feel . . .

WALTER   Never mind how I feel—you got any more to say 'bout how people ought to sit down and talk to each other? . . . Get out of my house, man.
    [*He turns his back and walks to the door.*]

LINDNER [*Looking around at the hostile faces and reaching and assembling his hat and briefcase.*]   Well—I don't understand why you people are reacting this way. What do you think you are going to gain by moving into a neighborhood where you just aren't wanted and where some elements— well—people can get awful worked up when they feel that their whole way of life and everything they've ever worked for is threatened.

WALTER   Get out.

LINDNER [*At the door, holding a small card.*]   Well—I'm sorry it went like this.

WALTER   Get out.

LINDNER [*Almost sadly regarding* WALTER.]   You just can't force people to change their hearts, son.
    [*He turns and put his card on a table and exits.* WALTER *pushes the door to with stinging hatred, and stands looking at it.* RUTH *just sits and* BENEATHA *just stands. They say nothing.* MAMA *and* TRAVIS *enter.*]

MAMA   Well—this all the packing got done since I left out of here this morning. I testify before God that my children got all the energy of the dead. What time the moving men due?

BENEATHA   Four o'clock. You had a caller, Mama.
    [*She is smiling, teasingly.*]

MAMA   Sure enough—who?

BENEATHA [*Her arms folded saucily.*]   The Welcoming Committee.
    [WALTER *and* RUTH *giggle.*]

MAMA [*Innocently.*]   Who?

BENEATHA   The Welcoming Committee. They said they're sure going to be glad to see you when you get there.

WALTER [*Devilishly.*]   Yeah, they said they can't hardly wait to see your face.
    [*Laughter.*]

MAMA [*Sensing their facetiousness.*]   What's the matter with you all?

WALTER   Ain't nothing the matter with us. We just telling you 'bout the gentleman who came to see you this afternoon. From the Clybourne Park Improvement Association.

MAMA What he want?

RUTH [*In the same mood as* BENEATHA *and* WALTER.] To welcome you, honey.

WALTER He said they can't hardly wait. He said the one thing they don't have, that they just *dying* to have out there is a fine family of colored people! [*To* RUTH *and* BENEATHA.] Ain't that right!

RUTH *and* BENEATHA [*Mockingly.*] Yeah! He left his card in case—
    [*They indicate the card, and* MAMA *picks it up and throws it on the floor—understanding and looking off as she draws her chair up to the table on which she has put her plant and some sticks and some cord.*]

MAMA Father, give us strength. [*Knowingly—and without fun.*] Did he threaten us?

BENEATHA Oh—Mama—they don't do it like that any more. He talked Brotherhood. He said everybody ought to learn how to sit down and hate each other with good Christian fellowship.
    [*She and* WALTER *shake hands to ridicule the remark.*]

MAMA [*Sadly.*] Lord, protect us . . .

RUTH You should hear the money those folks raised to buy the house from us. All we paid and then some.

BENEATHA What they think we going to do—eat 'em?

RUTH No, honey, marry 'em.

MAMA [*Shaking her head.*] Lord, Lord, Lord . . .

RUTH Well—that's the way the crackers crumble. Joke.

BENEATHA [*Laughingly noticing what her mother is doing.*] Mama, what are you doing?

MAMA Fixing my plant so it won't get hurt none on the way . . .

BENEATHA Mama, you going to take *that* to the new house?

MAMA Un-huh—

BENEATHA That raggedy-looking old thing?

MAMA [*Stopping and looking at her.*] It expresses *me*.

RUTH [*With delight, to* BENEATHA.] So there, Miss Thing!
    [WALTER *comes to* MAMA *suddenly and bends down behind her and squeezes her in his arms with all his strength. She is overwhelmed by the suddenness of it and, though delighted, her manner is like that of* RUTH *with* TRAVIS.]

MAMA Look out now, boy! You make me mess up my thing here!

WALTER [*His face lit, he slips down on his knees beside her, his arms still about her.*] Mama . . . you know what it means to climb up in the chariot?

MAMA [*Gruffly, very happy.*] Get on away from me now . . .

RUTH [*Near the gift-wrapped package, trying to catch* WALTER'S *eye.*] Psst—

WALTER What the old song say, Mama . . .

RUTH Walter—Now?
    [*She is pointing at the package.*]

WALTER [*Speaking the lines, sweetly, playfully, in his mother's face.*]
        I got wings . . . you got wings . . .
        All God's Children got wings[8] . . .

MAMA Boy—get out of my face and do some work . . .

WALTER   When I get to heaven gonna put on my wings,
        Gonna fly all over God's heaven . . .

BENEATHA [*Teasingly, from across the room.*] Everybody talking 'bout heaven ain't going there!

---

8. Black spiritual; also the title of a controversial 1923 play by Eugene O'Neill about a racially mixed marriage.

WALTER [*To* RUTH, *who is carrying the box across to them.*] I don't know, you think we ought to give her that . . . Seems to me she ain't been very appreciative around here.

MAMA [*Eying the box, which is obviously a gift.*] What is that?

WALTER [*Taking it from* RUTH *and putting it on the table in front of* MAMA.] Well—what you all think? Should we give it to her?

RUTH Oh—she was pretty good today.

MAMA I'll good you—
[*She turns her eyes to the box again.*]

BENEATHA Open it, Mama.
[*She stands up, looks at it, turns and looks at all of them, and then presses her hands together and does not open the package.*]

WALTER [*Sweetly.*] Open it, Mama. It's for you. [MAMA *looks in his eyes. It is the first present in her life without its being Christmas. Slowly she opens her package and lifts out, one by one, a brand-new sparkling set of gardening tools.* WALTER *continues, prodding.*] Ruth made up the note—read it . . .

MAMA [*Picking up the card and adjusting her glasses.*] "To our own Mrs. Miniver[9]—Love from Brother, Ruth and Beneatha." Ain't that lovely . . .

TRAVIS [*Tugging at his father's sleeve.*] Daddy, can I give her mine now?

WALTER All right, son. [TRAVIS *flies to get his gift.*] Travis didn't want to go in with the rest of us, Mama. He got his own. [*Somewhat amused.*] We don't know what it is . . .

TRAVIS [*Racing back in the room with a large hatbox and putting it in front of his grandmother.*] Here!

MAMA Lord have mercy, baby. You done gone and bought your grandmother a hat?

TRAVIS [*Very proud.*] Open it!
[*She does and lifts out an elaborate, but very elaborate, wide gardening hat, and all the adults break up at the sight of it.*]

RUTH Travis, honey, what is that?

TRAVIS [*Who thinks it is beautiful and appropriate.*] It's a gardening hat! Like the ladies always have on in the magazines when they work in their gardens.

BENEATHA [*Giggling fiercely.*] Travis—we were trying to make Mama Mrs. Miniver—not Scarlett O'Hara!

MAMA [*Indignantly.*] What's the matter with you all! This here is a beautiful hat! [*Absurdly.*] I always wanted me one just like it!
[*She pops it on her head to prove it to her grandson, and the hat is ludicrous and considerably oversized.*]

RUTH Hot dog! Go, Mama!

WALTER [*Doubled over with laughter.*] I'm sorry, Mama—but you look like you ready to go out and chop you some cotton sure enough!
[*They all laugh except* MAMA, *out of deference to* TRAVIS' *feelings.*]

MAMA [*Gathering the boy up to her.*] Bless your heart—this is the prettiest hat I ever owned—[WALTER, RUTH *and* BENEATHA *chime in—noisily, festively and insincerely congratulating* TRAVIS *on his gift.*] What are we all standing around here for? We ain't finished packin' yet. Bennie, you ain't packed one book.
[*The bell rings.*]

9. Title character in a 1942 film about life in wartime London.

BENEATHA That couldn't be the movers . . . it's not hardly two good yet—
[BENEATHA *goes into her room.* MAMA *starts for door.*]

WALTER [*Turning, stiffening.*] Wait—wait—I'll get it.
[*He stands and looks at the door.*]

MAMA You expecting company, son?

WALTER [*Just looking at the door.*] Yeah—yeah . . .
[MAMA *looks at* RUTH, *and they exchange innocent and unfrightened glances*].

MAMA [*Not understanding.*] Well, let them in, son.

BENEATHA [*From her room.*] We need some more string.

MAMA Travis—you run to the hardware and get me some string cord.
[MAMA *goes out and* WALTER *turns and looks at* RUTH. TRAVIS *goes to a dish for money.*]

RUTH Why don't you answer the door, man?

WALTER [*Suddenly bounding across the floor to her.*] 'Cause sometimes it hard to let the future begin! [*Stooping down in her face.*]

I got wings! You got wings!
All God's children got wings!

[*He crosses to the door and throws it open. Standing there is a very slight little man in a not too prosperous business suit and with haunted frightened eyes and a hat pulled down tightly, brim up, around his forehead.* TRAVIS *passes between the men and exits.* WALTER *leans deep in the man's face, still in his jubilance.*]

When I get to heaven gonna put on my wings,
Gonna fly all over God's heaven . . .

[*The little man just stares at him.*]

Heaven—

[*Suddenly he stops and looks past the little man into the empty hallway.*]
Where's Willy, man?

BOBO He ain't with me.

WALTER [*Not disturbed.*] Oh—come on in. You know my wife.

BOBO [*Dumbly, taking off his hat.*] Yes—h'you, Miss Ruth.

RUTH [*Quietly, a mood apart from her husband already, seeing* BOBO.] Hello, Bobo.

WALTER You right on time today . . . Right on time. That's the way! [*He slaps* BOBO *on his back.*] Sit down . . . lemme hear.
[RUTH *stands stiffly and quietly in back of them, as though somehow she senses death, her eyes fixed on her husband.*]

BOBO [*His frightened eyes on the floor, his hat in his hands.*] Could I please get a drink of water, before I tell you about it, Walter Lee?
[WALTER *does not take his eyes off the man.* RUTH *goes blindly to the tap and gets a glass of water and brings it to* BOBO.]

WALTER There ain't nothing wrong, is there?

BOBO Lemme tell you—

WALTER Man—didn't nothing go wrong?

BOBO Lemme tell you—Walter Lee. [*Looking at* RUTH *and talking to her more than to* WALTER.] You know how it was. I got to tell you how it was. I mean first I got to tell you how it was all the way . . . I mean about the money I put in, Walter Lee . . .

WALTER [*With taut agitation now.*] What about the money you put in?

BOBO Well—it wasn't much as we told you—me and Willy—[*He stops.*] I'm sorry, Walter. I got a bad feeling about it. I got a real bad feeling about it . . .

WALTER   Man, what you telling me about all this for? . . . Tell me what happened in Springfield . . .

BOBO   Springfield.

RUTH [*Like a dead woman.*]   What was supposed to happen in Springfield?

BOBO [*To her.*]   This deal that me and Walter went into with Willy—Me and Willy was going to go down to Springfield and spread some money 'round so's we wouldn't have to wait so long for the liquor license . . . That's what we were going to do. Everybody said that was the way you had to do, you understand, Miss Ruth?

WALTER   Man—what happened down there?

BOBO [*A pitiful man, near tears.*]   I'm trying to tell you, Walter.

WALTER [*Screaming at him suddenly.*]   THEN TELL ME, GODDAMMIT . . . WHAT'S THE MATTER WITH YOU?

BOBO   Man . . . I didn't go to no Springfield, yesterday.

WALTER [*Halted, life hanging in the moment.*]   Why not?

BOBO [*The long way, the hard way to tell.*]   'Cause I didn't have no reasons to . . .

WALTER   Man, what are you talking about!

BOBO   I'm talking about the fact that when I got to the train station yesterday morning—eight o'clock like we planned . . . Man—*Willy didn't never show up.*

WALTER   Why . . . where was he . . . where is he?

BOBO   That's what I'm trying to tell you . . . I don't know . . . I waited six hours . . . I called his house . . . and I waited . . . six hours . . . I waited in that train station six hours . . . [*Breaking into tears.*] That was all the extra money I had in the world . . . [*Looking up at* WALTER *with the tears running down his face.*] Man, *Willy is gone.*

WALTER   Gone, what you mean Willy is gone? Gone where? You mean he went by himself. You mean he went off to Springfield by himself—to take care of getting the license—[*Turns and looks anxiously at* RUTH.] You mean maybe he didn't want too many people in on the business down there? [*Looks to* RUTH *again, as before.*] You know Willy got his own ways. [*Looks back to* BOBO.] Maybe you was late yesterday and he just went on down there without you. Maybe—maybe—he's been callin' you at home tryin' to tell you what happened or something. Maybe—maybe—he just got sick. He's somewhere—he's got to be somewhere. We just got to find him—me and you got to find him. [*Grabs* BOBO *senselessly by the collar and starts to shake him.*] We got to!

BOBO [*In sudden angry, frightened agony.*]   What's the matter with you, Walter! *When a cat take off with your money he don't leave you no maps!*

WALTER [*Turning madly, as though he is looking for* WILLY *in the very room.*]   Willy! . . . Willy . . . don't do it . . . Please don't do it . . . Man, not with that money . . . Man, please, not with that money . . . Oh, God . . . Don't let it be true . . . [*He is wandering around, crying out for* WILLY *and looking for him or perhaps for help from God.*] Man . . . I trusted you . . . Man, I put my life in your hands . . . [*He starts to crumple down on the floor as* RUTH *just covers her face in horror.* MAMA *opens the door and comes into the room, with* BENEATHA *behind her.*] Man . . . [*He starts to pound the floor with his fists, sobbing wildly.*] That money is made out of my father's flesh . . .

BOBO [*Standing over him helplessly.*]   I'm sorry, Walter . . . [*Only* WALTER'S *sobs reply.* BOBO *puts on his hat.*] I had my life staked on this deal, too . . .

[*He exits.*]

MAMA [*To* WALTER.] Son—[*She goes to him, bends down to him, talks to his bent head.*] Son . . . Is it gone? Son, I gave you sixty-five hundred dollars. Is it gone? All of it? Beneatha's money too?

WALTER [*Lifting his head slowly.*] Mama . . . I never . . . went to the bank at all . . .

MAMA [*Not wanting to believe him.*] You mean . . . your sister's school money . . . you used that too . . . Walter? . . .

WALTER Yessss! . . . All of it . . . It's all gone . . . [*There is total silence.* RUTH *stands with her face covered with her hands;* BENEATHA *leans forlornly against a wall, fingering a piece of red ribbon from the mother's gift.* MAMA *stops and looks at her son without recognition and then, quite without thinking about it, starts to beat him senselessly in the face.* BENEATHA *goes to them and stops it.*]

BENEATHA Mama!

[MAMA *stops and looks at both of her children and rises slowly and wanders vaguely, aimlessly away from them.*]

MAMA I seen . . . him . . . night after night . . . come in . . . and look at that rug . . . and then look at me . . . the red showing in his eyes . . . the veins moving in his head . . . I seen him grow thin and old before he was forty . . . working and working and working like somebody's old horse . . . killing himself . . . and you—you give it all away in a day . . .

BENEATHA Mama—

MAMA Oh, God . . . [*She looks up to Him.*] Look down here—and show me the strength.

BENEATHA Mama—

MAMA [*Folding over.*] Strength . . .

BENEATHA [*Plaintively.*] Mama . . .

MAMA Strength!

[*Curtain.*]

Act III

An hour later.

At curtain, there is a sullen light of gloom in the living room, gray light not unlike that which began the first scene of Act I. At left we can see WALTER within his room, alone with himself. He is stretched out on the bed, his shirt out and open, his arms under his head. He does not smoke, he does not cry out, he merely lies there, looking up at the ceiling, much as if he were alone in the world.

In the living room BENEATHA sits at the table, still surrounded by the now almost ominous packing crates. She sits looking off. We feel that this is a mood struck perhaps an hour before, and it lingers now, full of the empty sound of profound disappointment. We see on a line from her brother's bedroom the sameness of their attitudes. Presently the bell rings and BENEATHA rises without ambition or interest in answering. It is ASAGAI, smiling broadly, striding into the room with energy and happy expectation and conversation.

ASAGAI I came over . . . I had some free time. I thought I might help with the packing. Ah, I like the look of packing crates! A household in preparation for a journey! It depresses some people . . . but for me . . . it is another feeling. Something full of the flow of life, do you understand? Movement, progress . . . It makes me think of Africa.

BENEATHA Africa!

ASAGAI What kind of a mood is this? Have I told you how deeply you move me?

BENEATHA He gave away the money, Asagai . . .

ASAGAI Who gave away what money?

BENEATHA The insurance money. My brother gave it away.

ASAGAI Gave it away?

BENEATHA He made an investment! With a man even Travis wouldn't have trusted.

ASAGAI And it's gone?

BENEATHA Gone!

ASAGAI I'm very sorry . . . And you, now?

BENEATHA Me? . . . Me? . . . Me I'm nothing . . . Me. When I was very small . . . we used to take our sleds out in the wintertime and the only hills we had were the ice-covered stone steps of some houses down the street. And we used to fill them in with snow and make them smooth and slide down them all day . . . and it was very dangerous you know . . . far too steep . . . and sure enough one day a kid named Rufus came down too fast and hit the sidewalk . . . and we saw his face just split open right there in front of us . . . And I remember standing there looking at his bloody open face thinking that was the end of Rufus. But the ambulance came and they took him to the hospital and they fixed the broken bones and they sewed it all up . . . and the next time I saw Rufus he just had a little line down the middle of his face . . . I never got over that . . .

[WALTER *sits up, listening on the bed. Throughout this scene it is important that we feel his reaction at all times, that he visibly respond to the words of his sister and* ASAGAI.]

ASAGAI What?

BENEATHA That that was what one person could do for another, fix him up—sew up the problem, make him all right again. That was the most marvelous thing in the world . . . I wanted to do that. I always thought it was the one concrete thing in the world that a human being could do. Fix up the sick, you know—and make them whole again. This was truly being God . . .

ASAGAI You wanted to be God?

BENEATHA No—I wanted to cure. It used to be so important to me. I wanted to cure. It used to matter. I used to care. I mean about people and how their bodies hurt . . .

ASAGAI And you've stopped caring?

BENEATHA Yes—I think so.

ASAGAI Why?

[WALTER *rises, goes to the door of his room and is about to open it, then stops and stands listening, leaning on the door jamb.*]

BENEATHA Because it doesn't seem deep enough, close enough to what ails mankind—I mean this thing of sewing up bodies or administering drugs. Don't you understand? It was a child's reaction to the world. I thought that doctors had the secret to all the hurts. . . . That's the way a child sees things—or an idealist.

ASAGAI Children see things very well sometimes—and idealists even better.

BENEATHA I know that's what you think. Because you are still where I left off—you still care. This is what you see for the world, for Africa. You with the dreams of the future will patch up all Africa—you are going to cure the Great Sore of colonialism with Independence—

ASAGAI Yes!

BENEATHA Yes—and you think that one word is the penicillin of the human spirit: "Independence!" But then what?

ASAGAI That will be the problem for another time. First we must get there.

BENEATHA And where does it end?

ASAGAI End? Who even spoke of an end? To life? To living?

BENEATHA An end to misery!

ASAGAI [*Smiling.*] You sound like a French intellectual.

BENEATHA No! I sound like a human being who just had her future taken right out of her hands! While I was sleeping in my bed in there, things were happening in this world that directly concerned me—and nobody asked me, consulted me—they just went out and did things—and changed my life. Don't you see there isn't any real progress, Asagai, there is only one large circle that we march in, around and around, each of us with our own little picture—in front of us—our own little mirage that we think is the future.

ASAGAI That is the mistake.

BENEATHA What?

ASAGAI What you just said—about the circle. It isn't a circle—it is simply a long line—as in geometry, you know, one that reaches into infinity. And because we cannot see the end—we also cannot see how it changes. And it is very odd but those who see the changes are called "idealists"— and those who cannot, or refuse to think, they are the "realists." It is very strange, and amusing too, I think.

BENEATHA You—you are almost religious.

ASAGAI Yes . . . I think I have the religion of doing what is necessary in the world—and of worshipping man—because he is so marvelous, you see.

BENEATHA Man is foul! And the human race deserves its misery!

ASAGAI You see: *you* have become the religious one in the old sense. Already, and after such a small defeat, you are worshipping despair.

BENEATHA From now on, I worship the truth—and the truth is that people are puny, small and selfish. . . .

ASAGAI Truth? Why is it that you despairing ones always think that only you have the truth? I never thought to see *you* like that. You! Your brother made a stupid, childish mistake—and you are grateful to him. So that now you can give up the ailing human race on account of it. You talk about what good is struggle; what good is anything? Where are we all going? And why are we bothering?

BENEATHA *And you cannot answer it!* All your talk and dreams about Africa and Independence. Independence and then what? What about all the crooks and petty thieves and just plain idiots who will come into power to steal and plunder the same as before—only now they will be black and do it in the name of the new Independence— You cannot answer that.

ASAGAI [*Shouting over her.*] *I live the answer!* [*Pause.*] In my village at home it is the exceptional man who can even read a newspaper . . . or who ever *sees* a book at all. I will go home and much of what I will have to say will seem strange to the people of my village . . . But I will teach and work and things will happen, slowly and swiftly. At times it will

seem that nothing changes at all . . . and then again . . . the sudden
dramatic events which make history leap into the future. And then quiet
again. Retrogression even. Guns, murder, revolution. And I even will have
moments when I wonder if the quiet was not better than all that death
and hatred. But I will look about my village at the illiteracy and disease
and ignorance and I will not wonder long. And perhaps . . . perhaps I
will be a great man . . . I mean perhaps I will hold on to the substance of
truth and find my way always with the right course . . . and perhaps for
it I will be butchered in my bed some night by the servants of empire . . .

BENEATHA *The martyr!*

ASAGAI . . . or perhaps I shall live to be a very old man, respected and
esteemed in my new nation . . . And perhaps I shall hold office and this
is what I'm trying to tell you, Alaiyo; perhaps the things I believe now for
my country will be wrong and outmoded, and I will not understand and
do terrible things to have things my way or merely to keep my power.
Don't you see that there will be young men and women, not British soldiers then, but my own black countrymen . . . to step out of the shadows
some evening and slit my then useless throat? Don't you see they have
always been there . . . that they always will be. And that such a thing
as my own death will be an advance? They who might kill me even . . .
actually replenish me!

BENEATHA Oh, Asagai, I know all that.

ASAGAI Good! Then stop moaning and groaning and tell me what you
plan to do.

BENEATHA Do?

ASAGAI I have a bit of a suggestion.

BENEATHA What?

ASAGAI [*Rather quietly for him.*] That when it is all over—that you come
home with me—

BENEATHA [*Slapping herself on the forehead with exasperation born of
misunderstanding.*] Oh—Asagai—at this moment you decide to be
romantic!

ASAGAI [*Quickly understanding the misunderstanding.*] My dear, young
creature of the New World—I do not mean across the city—I mean
across the ocean; home—to Africa.

BENEATHA [*Slowly understanding and turning to him with murmured
amazement.*] To—to Nigeria?

ASAGAI Yes! . . . [*Smiling and lifting his arms playfully.*] Three hundred
years later the African Prince rose up out of the seas and swept the
maiden back across the middle passage over which her ancestors had
come—

BENEATHA [*Unable to play.*] Nigeria?

ASAGAI Nigeria. Home. [*Coming to her with genuine romantic flippancy.*]
I will show you our mountains and our stars; and give you cool drinks
from gourds and teach you the old songs and the ways of our people—
and, in time, we will pretend that—[*Very softly.*]—you have only been
away for a day—

[*She turns her back to him, thinking. He swings her around and takes
her full in his arms in a long embrace which proceeds to passion.*]

BENEATHA [*Pulling away.*] You're getting me all mixed up—

ASAGAI Why?

BENEATHA Too many things—too many things have happened today. I must sit down and think. I don't know what I feel about anything right this minute.

[*She promptly sits down and props her chin on her fist.*]

ASAGAI [*Charmed.*] All right, I shall leave you. No—don't get up. [*Touching her, gently, sweetly.*] Just sit awhile and think . . . Never be afraid to sit awhile and think. [*He goes to door and looks at her.*] How often I have looked at you and said, "Ah—so this is what the New World hath finally wrought . . ."

[*He exits.* BENEATHA *sits on alone. Presently* WALTER *enters from his room and starts to rummage through things, feverishly looking for something. She looks up and turns in her seat.*]

BENEATHA [*Hissingly.*] Yes—just look at what the New World hath wrought! . . . Just look! [*She gestures with bitter disgust.*] There he is! *Monsieur le petit bourgeois noir*[1]—himself! There he is—Symbol of a Rising Class! Entrepreneur! Titan of the system! [WALTER *ignores her completely and continues frantically and destructively looking for something and hurling things to the floor and tearing things out of their place in his search.* BENEATHA *ignores the eccentricity of his actions and goes on with the monologue of insult.*] Did you dream of yachts on Lake Michigan, Brother? Did you see yourself on that Great Day sitting down at the Conference Table, surrounded by all the mighty bald-headed men in America? All halted, waiting, breathless, waiting for your pronouncements on industry? Waiting for you—Chairman of the Board? [WALTER *finds what he is looking for—a small piece of white paper—and pushes it in his pocket and puts on his coat and rushes out without ever having looked at her. She shouts after him.*] I look at you and I see the final triumph of stupidity in the world!

[*The door slams and she returns to just sitting again.* RUTH *comes quickly out of* MAMA's *room.*]

RUTH Who was that?

BENEATHA Your husband.

RUTH Where did he go?

BENEATHA Who knows—maybe he has an appointment at U.S. Steel.

RUTH [*Anxiously, with frightened eyes.*] You didn't say nothing bad to him, did you?

BENEATHA Bad? Say anything bad to him? No—I told him he was a sweet boy and full of dreams and everything is strictly peachy keen, as the ofay[2] kids say!

[MAMA *enters from her bedroom. She is lost, vague, trying to catch hold, to make some sense of her former command of the world, but it still eludes her. A sense of waste overwhelms her gait; a measure of apology rides on her shoulders. She goes to her plant, which has remained on the table, looks at it, picks it up and takes it to the window sill and sits it outside, and she stands and looks at it a long moment. Then she closes the window, straightens her body with effort and turns around to her children.*]

MAMA Well—ain't it a mess in here, though? [*A false cheerfulness, a beginning of something.*] I guess we all better stop moping around and get some work done. All this unpacking and everything we got to do.

---

1. Mr. Black Bourgeoisie (French).
2. White (slang).

[RUTH *raises her head slowly in response to the sense of the line; and* BENEATHA *in similar manner turns very slowly to look at her mother.*] One of you all better call the moving people and tell 'em not to come.

RUTH Tell 'em not to come?

MAMA Of course, baby. Ain't no need in 'em coming all the way here and having to go back. They charges for that too. [*She sits down, fingers to her brow, thinking.*] Lord, ever since I was a little girl, I always remembers people saying, "Lena—Lena Eggleston, you aims too high all the time. You needs to slow down and see life a little more like it is. Just slow down some." That's what they always used to say down home—"Lord, that Lena Eggleston is a high-minded thing. She'll get her due one day!"

RUTH No, Lena . . .

MAMA Me and Big Walter just didn't never learn right.

RUTH Lena, no! We gotta go. Bennie—tell her . . . [*She rises and crosses to* BENEATHA *with her arms outstretched.* BENEATHA *doesn't respond.*] Tell her we can still move . . . the notes ain't but a hundred and twenty-five a month. We got four grown people in this house—we can work . . .

MAMA [*To herself.*] Just aimed too high all the time—

RUTH [*Turning and going to* MAMA *fast—the words pouring out with urgency and desperation.*] Lena—I'll work . . . I'll work twenty hours a day in all the kitchens in Chicago . . . I'll strap my baby on my back if I have to and scrub all the floors in America and wash all the sheets in America if I have to—but we got to move . . . We got to get out of here . . .

[MAMA *reaches out absently and pats* RUTH's *hand.*]

MAMA No—I sees things differently now. Been thinking 'bout some of the things we could do to fix this place up some. I seen a second-hand bureau over on Maxwell Street just the other day that could fit right there. [*She points to where the new furniture might go.* RUTH *wanders away from her.*] Would need some new handles on it and then a little varnish and then it look like something brand-new. And—we can put up them new curtains in the kitchen . . . Why this place be looking fine. Cheer us all up so that we forget trouble ever came . . . [*To* RUTH.] And you could get some nice screens to put up in your room round the baby's bassi-net . . . [*She looks at both of them, pleadingly.*] Sometimes you just got to know when to give up some things . . . and hold on to what you got.

[WALTER *enters from the outside, looking spent and leaning against the door, his coat hanging from him.*]

MAMA Where you been, son?

WALTER [*Breathing hard.*] Made a call.

MAMA To who, son?

WALTER To The Man.

MAMA What man, baby?

WALTER The Man, Mama. Don't you know who The Man is?

RUTH Walter Lee?

WALTER *The Man.* Like the guys in the streets say—The Man. Captain Boss—Mistuh Charley . . . Old Captain Please Mr. Bossman . . .

BENEATHA [*Suddenly.*] Lindner!

WALTER That's right! That's good. I told him to come right over.

BENEATHA [*Fiercely, understanding.*] For what? What do you want to see him for!

WALTER [*Looking at his sister.*] We going to do business with him.

MAMA What you talking 'bout, son?

WALTER   Talking 'bout life, Mama. You all always telling me to see life like it is. Well—I laid in there on my back today . . . and I figured it out. Life just like it is. Who gets and who don't get. [*He sits down with his coat on and laughs.*] Mama, you know it's all divided up. Life is. Sure enough. Between the takers and the "tooken." [*He laughs.*] I've figured it out finally. [*He looks around at them.*] Yeah. Some of us always getting "tooken." [*He laughs.*] People like Willy Harris, they don't never get "tooken." And you know why the rest of us do? 'Cause we all mixed up. Mixed up bad. We get to looking 'round for the right and the wrong; and we worry about it and cry about it and stay up nights trying to figure out 'bout the wrong and the right of things all the time . . . And all the time, man, them takers is out there operating, just taking and taking. Willy Harris? Shoot—Willy Harris don't even count. He don't even count in the big scheme of things. But I'll say one thing for old Willy Harris . . . he's taught me something. He's taught me to keep my eye on what counts in this world. Yeah—[*Shouting out a little.*] Thanks, Willy!

RUTH   What did you call that man for, Walter Lee?

WALTER   Called him to tell him to come on over to the show. Gonna put on a show for the man. Just what he wants to see. You see, Mama, the man came here today and he told us that them people out there where you want us to move—well they so upset they willing to pay us not to move out there. [*He laughs again.*] And—and oh, Mama—you would of been proud of the way me and Ruth and Bennie acted. We told him to get out . . . Lord have mercy! We told the man to get out. Oh, we was some proud folks this afternoon, yeah. [*He lights a cigarette.*] We were still full of that old-time stuff . . .

RUTH   [*Coming toward him slowly.*]   You talking 'bout taking them people's money to keep us from moving in that house?

WALTER   I ain't just talking 'bout it, baby—I'm telling you that's what's going to happen.

BENEATHA   Oh, God! Where is the bottom! Where is the real honest-to-God bottom so he can't go any farther!

WALTER   See—that's the old stuff. You and that boy that was here today. You all want everybody to carry a flag and a spear and sing some marching songs, huh? You wanna spend your life looking into things and trying to find the right and the wrong part, huh? Yeah. You know what's going to happen to that boy someday—he'll find himself sitting in a dungeon, locked in forever—and the takers will have the key! Forget it, baby! There ain't no causes—there ain't nothing but taking in this world, and he who takes most is smartest—and it don't make a damn bit of difference *how*.

MAMA   You making something inside me cry, son. Some awful pain inside me.

WALTER   Don't cry, Mama. Understand. That white man is going to walk in that door able to write checks for more money than we ever had. It's important to him and I'm going to help him . . . I'm going to put on the show, Mama.

MAMA   Son—I come from five generations of people who was slaves and sharecroppers—but ain't nobody in my family never let nobody pay 'em no money that was a way of telling us we wasn't fit to walk the earth. We ain't never been that poor. [*Raising her eyes and looking at him.*] We ain't never been that dead inside.

BENEATHA Well—we are dead now. All the talk about dreams and sunlight that goes on in this house. All dead.

WALTER What's the matter with you all! I didn't make this world! It was
give to me this way! Hell, yes, I want me some yachts someday! Yes, I
want to hang some real pearls 'round my wife's neck. Ain't she supposed
to wear no pearls? Somebody tell me—tell me, who decides which
women is suppose to wear pearls in this world. I tell you I am a *man*—
and I think my wife should wear some pearls in this world!

[*This last line hangs a good while and* WALTER *begins to move about the
room. The word "Man" has penetrated his consciousness; he mumbles it
to himself repeatedly between strange agitated pauses as he moves about.*]

MAMA Baby, how you going to feel on the inside?

WALTER Fine! . . . Going to feel fine . . . a man . . .

MAMA You won't have nothing left then, Walter Lee.

WALTER [*Coming to her.*] I'm going to feel fine, Mama. I'm going to look
that son-of-a-bitch in the eyes and say—[*He falters.*]—and say, "All
right, Mr. Lindner—[*He falters even more.*]—that's your neighborhood
out there. You got the right to keep it like you want. You got the right to
have it like you want. Just write the check and—the house is yours."
And, and I am going to say—[*His voice almost breaks.*] And you—you
people just put the money in my hand and you won't have to live next to
this bunch of stinking niggers! . . . [*He straightens up and moves away
from his mother, walking around the room.*] Maybe—maybe I'll just get
down on my black knees . . . [*He does so;* RUTH *and* BENNIE *and* MAMA
watch him in frozen horror.] Captain, Mistuh, Bossman. [*He starts crying.*] A-hee-hee-hee! [*Wringing his hands in profoundly anguished imitation.*] Yasssssuh! Great White Father, just gi' ussen de money, fo' God's
sake, and we's ain't gwine come out deh and dirty up yo' white folks
neighborhood . . .

[*He breaks down completely, then gets up and goes into the bedroom.*]

BENEATHA That is not a man. That is nothing but a toothless rat.

MAMA Yes—death done come in this here house. [*She is nodding, slowly,
reflectively.*] Done come walking in my house On the lips of my children.
You what supposed to be my beginning again. You—what supposed to be
my harvest. [*To* BENEATHA.] You—you mourning your brother?

BENEATHA He's no brother of mine.

MAMA What you say?

BENEATHA I said that that individual in that room is no brother of mine.

MAMA That's what I thought you said. You feeling like you better than
he is today? [BENEATHA *does not answer.*] Yes? What you tell him a minute ago? That he wasn't a man? Yes? You give him up for me? You done
wrote his epitaph too—like the rest of the world? Well, who give you the
privilege?

BENEATHA Be on my side for once! You saw what he just did, Mama! You
saw him—down on his knees. Wasn't it you who taught me—to despise
any man who would do that. Do what he's going to do.

MAMA Yes—I taught you that. Me and your daddy. But I thought I taught
you something else too . . . I thought I taught you to love him.

BENEATHA Love him? There is nothing left to love.

MAMA There is always something left to love. And if you ain't learned
that, you ain't learned nothing. [*Looking at her.*] Have you cried for that
boy today? I don't mean for yourself and for the family 'cause we lost the

money. I mean for him; what he been through and what it done to him. Child, when do you think is the time to love somebody the most; when they done good and made things easy for everybody? Well then, you ain't through learning—because that ain't the time at all. It's when he's at his lowest and can't believe in hisself 'cause the world done whipped him so. When you starts measuring somebody, measure him right, child, measure him right. Make sure you done taken into account what hills and valleys he come through before he got to wherever he is.

> [TRAVIS *bursts into the room at the end of the speech, leaving the door open.*]

TRAVIS Grandmama—the moving men are downstairs! The truck just pulled up.

MAMA [*Turning and looking at him.*]   Are they, baby? They downstairs?

> [*She sighs and sits.* LINDNER *appears in the doorway. He peers in and knocks lightly, to gain attention, and comes in. All turn to look at him.*]

LINDNER [*Hat and briefcase in hand.*]   Uh—hello . . . [RUTH *crosses mechanically to the bedroom door and opens it and lets it swing open freely and slowly as the lights come up on* WALTER *within, still in his coat, sitting at the far corner of the room. He looks up and out through the room to* LINDNER.]

RUTH He's here.

> [*A long minute passes and* WALTER *slowly gets up.*]

LINDNER [*Coming to the table with efficiency, putting his briefcase on the table and starting to unfold papers and unscrew fountain pens.*]   Well, I certainly was glad to hear from you people. [WALTER *has begun the trek out of the room, slowly and awkwardly, rather like a small boy, passing the back of his sleeve across his mouth from time to time.*] Life can really be so much simpler than people let it be most of the time. Well—with whom do I negotiate? You, Mrs. Younger, or your son here? [MAMA *sits with her hands folded on her lap and her eyes closed as* WALTER *advances.* TRAVIS *goes close to* LINDNER *and looks at the papers curiously.*] Just some official papers, sonny.

RUTH Travis, you go downstairs.

MAMA [*Opening her eyes and looking into* WALTER's.]   No. Travis, you stay right here. And you make him understand what you doing, Walter Lee. You teach him good. Like Willy Harris taught you. You show where our five generations done come to. Go ahead, son—

WALTER [*Looks down into his boy's eyes.* TRAVIS *grins at him merrily and* WALTER *draws him beside him with his arm lightly around his shoulders.*] Well, Mr. Lindner. [BENEATHA *turns away.*] We called you—[*There is a profound, simple groping quality in his speech.*]—because, well, me and my family [*He looks around and shifts from one foot to the other.*] Well—we are very plain people . . .

LINDNER Yes—

WALTER I mean—I have worked as a chauffeur most of my life—and my wife here, she does domestic work in people's kitchens. So does my mother. I mean—we are plain people . . .

LINDNER Yes, Mr. Younger—

WALTER [*Really like a small boy, looking down at his shoes and then up at the man.*]   And—uh—well, my father, well, he was a laborer most of his life.

LINDNER [*Absolutely confused.*]   Uh, yes—

WALTER [*Looking down at his toes once again.*]   My father almost beat a man to death once because this man called him a bad name or something, you know what I mean?

LINDNER   No, I'm afraid I don't.

WALTER [*Finally straightening up.*]   Well, what I mean is that we come from people who had a lot of pride. I mean—we are very proud people. And that's my sister over there and she's going to be a doctor—and we are very proud—

LINDNER   Well—I am sure that is very nice, but—

WALTER [*Starting to cry and facing the man eye to eye.*]   What I am telling you is that we called you over here to tell you that we are very proud and that this is—this is my son, who makes the sixth generation of our family in this country, and that we have all thought about your offer and we have decided to move into our house because my father—my father—he earned it. [MAMA *has her eyes closed and is rocking back and forth as though she were in church, with her head nodding the amen yes.*] We don't want to make no trouble for nobody or fight no causes—but we will try to be good neighbors. That's all we got to say. [*He looks the man absolutely in the eyes.*] We don't want your money.
   [*He turns and walks away from the man.*]

LINDNER [*Looking around at all of them.*]   I take it then that you have decided to occupy.

BENEATHA   That's what the man said.

LINDNER [*To* MAMA *in her reverie.*]   Then I would like to appeal to you, Mrs. Younger. You are older and wiser and understand things better I am sure . . .

MAMA [*Rising.*]   I am afraid you don't understand. My son said we was going to move and there ain't nothing left for me to say. [*Shaking her head with double meaning.*] You know how these young folks is nowadays, mister. Can't do a thing with 'em. Good-bye.

LINDNER [*Folding up his materials.*]   Well—if you are that final about it . . . There is nothing left for me to say. [*He finishes. He is almost ignored by the family, who are concentrating on* WALTER LEE. *At the door* LINDNER *halts and looks around.*] I sure hope you people know what you're doing.
   [*He shakes his head and exits.*]

RUTH [*Looking around and coming to life.*]   Well, for God's sake—if the moving men are here—LET'S GET THE HELL OUT OF HERE!

MAMA [*Into action.*]   Ain't it the truth! Look at all this here mess. Ruth, put Travis' good jacket on him . . . Walter Lee, fix your tie and tuck your shirt in, you look just like somebody's hoodlum. Lord have mercy, where is my plant? [*She flies to get it amid the general bustling of the family, who are deliberately trying to ignore the nobility of the past moment.*] You all start on down . . . Travis child, don't go empty-handed . . . Ruth, where did I put that box with my skillets in it? I want to be in charge of it myself . . . I'm going to make us the biggest dinner we ever ate tonight . . . Beneatha, what's the matter with them stockings? Pull them things up, girl . . .
   [*The family starts to file out as two moving men appear and begin to carry out the heavier pieces of furniture, bumping into the family as they move about.*]

BENEATHA   Mama, Asagai—asked me to marry him today and go to Africa—

MAMA [*In the middle of her getting-ready activity.*]   He did? You ain't old
enough to marry nobody—[*Seeing the moving men lifting one of her
chairs precariously.*] Darling, that ain't no bale of cotton, please handle
it so we can sit in it again. I had that chair twenty-five years . . .
   [*The movers sigh with exasperation and go on with their work.*]
BENEATHA [*Girlishly and unreasonably trying to pursue the conversation.*]
To go to Africa, Mama—be a doctor in Africa . . .
MAMA [*Distracted.*] Yes, baby—
WALTER   Africa! What he want you to go to Africa for?
BENEATHA   To practice there . . .
WALTER   Girl, if you don't get all them silly ideas out your head! You bet-
ter marry yourself a man with some loot . . .
BENEATHA [*Angrily, precisely as in the first scene of the play.*]   What have
you got to do with who I marry!
WALTER   Plenty. Now I think George Murchison—
   [*He and* BENEATHA *go out yelling at each other vigorously;* BENEATHA *is
   heard saying that she would not marry* GEORGE MURCHISON *if he were
   Adam and she were Eve, etc. The anger is loud and real till their voices
   diminish.* RUTH *stands at the door and turns to* MAMA *and smiles
   knowingly.*]
MAMA [*Fixing her hat at last.*]   Yeah—they something all right, my
children . . .
RUTH   Yeah—they're something. Let's go, Lena.
MAMA [*Stalling, starting to look around at the house.*]   Yes—I'm coming.
Ruth—
RUTH   Yes?
MAMA [*Quietly, woman to woman.*]   He finally come into his manhood
today, didn't he? Kind of like a rainbow after the rain . . .
RUTH [*Biting her lip lest her own pride explode in front of* MAMA.]   Yes,
Lena.
   [WALTER's *voice calls for them raucously.*]
MAMA [*Waving* RUTH *out vaguely.*]   All right, honey—go on down. I be
down directly.
   [RUTH *hesitates, then exits.* MAMA *stands, at last alone in the living room,
   her plant on the table before her as the lights start to come down. She
   looks around at all the walls and ceilings and suddenly, despite herself,
   while the children call below, a great heaving thing rises in her and she
   puts her fist to her mouth, takes a final desperate look, pulls her coat
   about her, pats her hat and goes out. The lights dim down. The door opens
   and she comes back in, grabs her plant, and goes out for the last time.*]

[*Curtain.*]

1959

The Black Arts Era
1960–1975

I n this 1966 photograph of Amiri Baraka amidst
some of the musicians and actors he had assembled
at his new community organization, Newark's Spirit
House, we see a portrait of the young black artist as
cultural impresario, social activist, and ethnic stylist—
an icon of the mid to late twentieth-century African
American artistic ferment known as the Black Arts
movement. Clothed in the colorful kente dashiki shirt,
kufi hat, and bone-and-shell necklace evocative of
African and Muslim cultures, Baraka strikes a pose
emblematic of the Black Arts movement's declared
aims and internal tensions: purposeful, communal,
prideful, and charged, perhaps, with a hint of guarded
hesitancy. While no one figure can encapsulate the
era's incessant innovation in art, politics, and identity,
we do well to begin our exploration of this period by
briefly charting the development of an artist whom
fellow Black Arts writer Kalamu ya Salaam called "the
founding father of the Black Arts movement."

As a young writer in the 1950s, Baraka (then known
as LeRoi Jones) gained a formidable reputation as a
poet among the more accomplished American writers
of his generation, especially white "bohemian" Beats
and New York School poets who combined a rich lyricism with a vituperative rejection of conventional culture, both its conformist decorum and its post–World
War II commercialism. Eloquently expressing the wry
alienation of a generation dissatisfied by bland material pursuits and fearful of atomic annihilation in the
shadow of the Cold War, Baraka won recognition not
only from his peers but even from the elder guardians
of the culture he so ruthlessly despised.

But Baraka obeyed his own pronouncements more
thoroughly than we might expect an artist to do. If, he

Amiri Baraka (center) with musicians and actors at the
entrance of Spirit House, Newark, New Jersey, 1966.

reasoned, the West is in fact a "dying place" (to cite an early poem), he could either maintain his admired position within the "mainstream" and from there prophesy his own death (a position enacted by his early dramatic characters, *Dutchman*'s Clay and *The Slave*'s Walker); or, by aligning himself with the burgeoning aspirations of black culture at home and abroad, he could direct his energy toward realizing a specific ideal: collective emancipation from degradation and tyranny. While he had expressed a yearning to identify with what the 1960 poem "Notes for a Speech" calls "my so-called people," a vast psychological and political distance stretched between that troubled connection and the fiery communitarian assertions that Baraka issued from the steps of Spirit House half a decade later.

What was crucial in his development as a touchstone of Black Arts aesthetic and political orientation was not so much the intellectual formulation, which has deep roots in African American culture, extending back from Ralph Ellison's Invisible Man through James Weldon Johnson's Ex-Colored Man and Du Bois's double-consciousness to Frederick Douglass's memorial celebration of slave culture from "outside the circle." Rather, it was Baraka's insistence on pressing the formulation beyond the realm of metaphor into the dominion of action. Thus Baraka's divorce from what his "Hymn for Lanie Poo" terms the "benevolent step / mother America" was literalized in his moves from white Greenwich Village to black Harlem, from an inter- to an intra-racial marriage, and from the Western Christian "slave" name *LeRoi Jones* to the Pan-African-Islamic-warrior title *Imamu Amiri Baraka*. Such transformations in affiliation, place, and language were hallmarks of the Black Arts movement's symbolic and performative vision.

A succession of events, both in Baraka's life and in that of the social world from which he was fiercely estranged, impelled him toward this shift in allegiance from the irreverent avant-garde of the American left to the angry vanguard of an emergent black nationalism. Robert F. Williams's 1959 call for armed self-defense by black Americans; the assassination of civil rights activist Medgar Evers in 1963; the killing that same year of four black girls in the bombing of Birmingham's 16th Street Baptist Church; a prolonged series of impassioned debates on racial politics between Baraka and white liberals, capped by a 1964 Town Hall exchange on "The Black Revolution and the White Backlash"—all these were major elements in Baraka's conversion to an ethos of uncompromising "blackness." But two episodes stand out especially, framing that defining era of the early 1960s: Baraka's trip to Cuba in 1960 and the assassination of Malcolm X in 1965.

In the summer of 1960, Baraka accompanied several black intellectuals and activists (including Robert Williams, Harold Cruse, Julian Mayfield, and John Henrik Clarke) to Cuba and discovered there a profound political rebellion successfully achieved by force of arms. This perception shook him with the realization that revolution elsewhere was an actual event, not a metaphor, a recognition reinforced by the wave of successful African liberation movements that reached its apex in 1960—the "Year of Independence"—when 17 sub-Saharan nations threw off the shackles of colonization. "Revolutionary change through violence" could now be seen as more than fanciful bluster; it was accomplished fact. "At first, I didn't understand that people could actually make a revolution," Baraka later reflected. "When I came back from Cuba I was turned completely around; I was never the same." The poet of ironic defeat, of tragic despair, had seen the means of bypassing ineffective protest; poetry as personal expression now seemed an indulgent distraction. Thenceforth, Baraka's writing became more steadily focused on the possibilities of transforming African Americans' social reality through insistent action.

For several years, in plays and poems that featured heroes who understand that their release from socio-political oppression requires only what his character Clay calls "a simple knife thrust" but who remain imprisoned by psychological ties to white culture, those possibilities remained tinged with fear and irresolution. By stages, during the years between Baraka's Cuban excursion and his permanent abandonment of "white" culture—even its branch of countercultural rebellion seen in radical politics and modernist literature—Baraka kept edging toward a black nationalist ideology. But it was the reality of violence that shocked him into an intensified commitment to change. Malcolm X, whose fierce denunciations of white society and of the civil rights leaders who sought to lead black America into the "wasteland" of American life, was assassinated in early 1965. Even before his murder, Malcolm had increasingly become for a generation of restless African American activists and writers a symbol of unyielding black struggle and assertive selfhood. For Baraka, his death signaled an immediate challenge, at once personal and communal, composed equally of regret and rage, aimed equally at social and psychological salvation:

> For Malcolm's eyes, when they broke
> the face of some dumb white man, For
> Malcolm's hands raised to bless us [. . .]
> For all of him, and all of yourself, look up,
> black man, quit stuttering and shuffling, look up,
> black man, quit whining and stooping, for all of him,
> For Great Malcolm a prince of the earth, let nothing in us rest
> until we avenge ourselves for his death [. . .]
>   let us never breathe a pure breath if
> we fail.
> ("A Poem for Black Hearts")

In its line lengths that build like a gathering storm, in the restless momentum of its enjambed syntax, and in its urgent summoning of black pride and manhood, Baraka's poem for Malcolm enacts the rhythm of a new kind of African American "uplift" no longer trapped in impotent complaint or solicitation. Everything "in us" is dedicated to righteous assertion in the world and to the restorative revolution that will celebrate a triumphal black nation. And haunting this determination is the specter of failure.

The day after Malcolm's killing, Baraka announced his intention to establish the Black Arts Repertory Theatre/School (BARTS) to provide both "theoretical and practical" training in the performance of "the black arts." By March, he had abandoned his life in bohemian Lower Manhattan and taken up residence uptown in Harlem; his formation of BARTS, alongside such fellow black writers as Larry Neal and Askia Muhammad Touré and with the support of artists like "free jazz" musicians Sun Ra, Archie Shepp, Albert Ayler, and John Coltrane, is often taken to be the "founding moment" of the Black Arts movement. But that movement, and the complex energies and ideas that propelled it, truly emerged, like Baraka himself, from the rapidly unfolding drama of black life in America, and of America itself. At the heart of that drama was the towering moral force of civil rights protest and the growing voice of Black Power activism.

AIN'T GOING TO JAIL NO MORE: CIVIL RIGHTS
AND BLACK NATIONALISM

The 1960s was a time of extraordinary social upheaval at home and abroad, fueled by liberation struggles undertaken by peoples of color across the world against a backdrop of entrenched hostility between the Soviet Union and the United States. The optimistic sense of global leadership and domestic tranquility that characterized post–World War II America (despite the muffled undertones of middle-class sterility and countercultural dissent) was shattered during the decade by the black civil rights and white youth movements that polarized various populations of the United States. Youth squared off against age; southern whites dug in their heels against blacks seeking civil rights; urban northerners challenged the Deep South's cherished system of racial segregation.

In national politics, the decade was launched by Democratic senator John F. Kennedy's successful campaign for the presidency in 1960 against Republican nominee Richard M. Nixon, who had served two terms as vice president under Dwight D. Eisenhower. The victory of Kennedy, the youngest person and the only Roman Catholic ever elected to the presidency, signaled in many ways the country's turning toward what he called a "new frontier." Kennedy's youth, decisiveness, charisma, idealism, and exuberant charm brought national and international prestige. He and his wife, Jackie, transformed the bland, conventional atmosphere of the Eisenhower years into a sophisticated and dynamic political milieu that, in later years, was popularly compared to King Arthur's court at Camelot.

But after such an ebullient and hopeful beginning, the 1960s quickly produced a series of international diplomatic emergencies such as the ill-fated Bay of Pigs invasion of Cuba in 1961 and the Cuban Missile Crisis in 1962. The following years brought disruptive civil rights and Black Power agitation, national mourning for the deaths of slain leaders (John Kennedy, 1963; Malcolm X, 1965; Martin Luther King Jr. and Robert Kennedy, 1968), monumental military expenditure for an unpopular war in Southeast Asia, and unprecedented generational conflict and revolt. The decade ended with Kennedy's erstwhile defeated rival Richard Nixon firmly in control of the White House, having captured the presidency in 1968 by vowing to restore "law and order" to a nation dispirited by urban riots, antiwar demonstrations, and tens of thousands of American deaths in the jungles of Vietnam.

In the context of this increasingly bitter and cynical national politics, the movement for black civil rights that had begun in the 1950s and come to full fruition in the mid-1960s now struggled not only to advance the cause of racial justice but to sustain the energetic idealism that pitted nonviolent civil protest against truculent, often murderous, racism. At the beginning of the decade, even while courageous black children like New Orleans's Ruby Bridges embodied the dangerous mission of school desegregation mandated by the landmark 1954 *Brown v. Board of Education* decision, four black college students inaugurated the modern black civil rights sit-in movement by occupying seats at a segregated lunch counter in the downtown Woolworth's store of Greensboro, North Carolina. Joseph McNeill, Ezell Blair, Franklin McCain, and David Richardson were all students at North Carolina Agricultural & Technical State University, one of many historical

Ruby Bridges integrating the all-white William Frantz Elementary School in New Orleans, Louisiana, under protection of U.S. Marshals in November, 1960.

black colleges and universities (HBCUs) that throughout the decade produced scores of increasingly militant black intellectuals, artists, and organizers. Energized by the bus boycotts led by Martin Luther King Jr. in Montgomery, Alabama, during the mid-1950s, they believed that nonviolent, direct-action protest by African Americans was a moral and effective means of securing guaranteed constitutional rights for black America. Establishing himself as a magnetic and savvy leader of difficult antisegregation campaigns, King had invoked the doctrines of "nonviolent noncooperation" and passive defiance that had been used so effectively by Gandhi during the fight against British colonialism in India. By the time of the Greensboro sit-in, King was already acknowledged to be one of the most effective black political leaders of the era, not least for his inspirational oratory and physical courage. The young students in North Carolina, like much of the rest of the country, admired King's strategies of black liberation, which translated Gandhi's philosophy into the spirit of Judeo-Christian narratives of emancipation and American Transcendentalist concepts of civil disobedience.

In North Carolina in 1960, Woolworth's capitulated: its lunch counter was desegregated. The heroic spirit displayed by the Greensboro Four and the many others who joined their protest galvanized black youth across the nation. Nonviolent action and moral suasion became the weapons for a sit-in movement that enlisted hundreds of thousands of high school and university students. The Student Non-Violent Coordinating Committee (SNCC), led by black students like Robert Moses, Diane Nash, John Lewis, and Stokely Carmichael, emerged as a major activist organization, playing a significant role in the Freedom Rides of 1961 (which challenged segregation in transportation), the March on Washington for Jobs and Freedom of 1963, and the struggle for voting rights during the Mississippi Summer of

Martin Luther King Jr. arrested in Montgomery, Alabama, 1958.

1964. The courage and energy of these students inspired adults, especially national civil rights leaders, to heighten their demands for "Freedom Now!" Becoming a multigenerational, multiracial coalition, the civil rights movement pulsed with moral conviction and pragmatic hope.

By the end of the decade, however, the African American freedom struggle had encountered bitter frustration and violent setbacks. Despite the passage of the 1964 and 1968 Civil Rights Acts, and the 1965 Voting Rights Act, the U.S. government repeatedly refused to enforce the laws of the land even as intractable whites shot, bombed, beat, and viciously harassed blacks who dared to speak out for citizenship rights. A river of blood extended from beaten Freedom Riders to the four black children killed in the Bir-

Freedom Riders with National Guard, 1961.

mingham church bombing, to four young civil rights workers who were murdered during Mississippi Summer. Civil rights activist James Meredith was shot during his "March Against Fear" when he entered Mississippi—the state where, upon integrating the University of Mississippi in 1962, he had been greeted with a torrent of abuse so violent that the president called in federal troops. Southern policemen, National Guard forces, and state troopers violently assaulted demonstrators with complete impunity. And white vigilantes orchestrated a reign of terror reminiscent of the campaigns of martial horror and intimidation waged by the Ku Klux Klan decades earlier.

A tipping point for young blacks dismayed by state-sanctioned violent denial of African American citizenship rights came with the 1963 assassination of civil rights leader Medgar Evers—just hours after President Kennedy's nationally televised speech in support of civil rights. Black disillusionment deepened with the Democratic Party's refusal to seat the black delegates of the Mississippi Freedom Democratic Party at its 1964 presidential convention. Stokely Carmichael and other SNCC leaders, increasingly unhappy with King's insistence that nonviolent action should proceed without the paramilitary protection of black supporters, made the first public declaration of "Black Power" at a June 1966 rally in Greenwood, Mississippi. "This is the twenty-seventh time I have been arrested," he said. "I ain't going to jail no more. What we gonna start saying now is 'Black Power!'" Speaking for young black America, Carmichael declared an end to sitting-in at lunch counters for the right to eat the bland fare of mainstream American culture, only to then be thrown in jail for breaking unjust laws in a lawless land. The time had arrived for militant, radical, Afrocentric revolt.

Strenuously promoting armed self-defense in the manner of Robert F. Williams's fiery 1962 antipacifist manifesto *Negroes with Guns*, Carmichael's advocacy of Black Power ignited a movement against multiracial coalitions,

Sixteenth Street Baptist Church bombing, Birmingham, Alabama, 1963. Victims, from left to right: Denise McNair, Carole Robertson, Addie Mae Collins, and Cynthia Wesley. Below: Rubble seen through bombed-out basement window.

Civil rights protester Walter Gadsden attacked by police dogs in Birmingham, Alabama, 1963.

leading to increasing emphasis in black communities on black nationalist discourses, aims, and tactics. In many ways, this black nationalist fervor echoed the voices of black visionaries from Martin R. Delany and Alexander Crummell in the nineteenth century to W. E. B. Du Bois and Marcus Garvey in the early twentieth century. This fervor arose alongside the black separatist agenda of the Nation of Islam (known popularly as the Black Muslims), whose network of black-owned business enterprises, focus on strict gender roles and ascetic self-discipline, rejection of "slave names," embrace of the mythos of aboriginal black spiritual glory, and message of vehement black independence (articulated in its 1962 call for a separate Black Nation within the United States) appealed to many young blacks beyond its actual membership.

But it is equally important to grasp that the roots of Black Power lay in the very movement from which it detached itself, because the quest for civil rights, under King's passionate and dynamic leadership, was, like black nationalism, a fundamental repudiation of American history and the state power that upheld its many transgressions against human dignity. Moreover, King's work left an unparalleled legacy of expertise in building institutions and organizing direct actions from which black nationalists were to draw with inventive zeal. Yet it is also true that the civil rights movement staked its project on integrating black Americans with a white America that was more and more clearly, even to its own children swept into the decade's radicalism, saturated with the useless products of a vacuous commodity culture, sick with a hypocritical refusal to make real its constitutional ideals, and misguided in its deafness to people clamoring for freedom on the world stage. Black nationalism was, therefore, a divorce not so much from the civil rights movement's demand for freedom as from its pragmatic aim of inclusion in a nation grown spiritually bankrupt and morally corrupt.

DRESS REHEARSALS FOR THE REVOLUTION:
BLACK POWER AND THE "BLACK AESTHETIC"

Even as the civil rights movement saw its dream of equal citizenship for African Americans brought nearer to reality by the momentous legislation of the mid-1960s, riots in dozens of black communities from Harlem to Watts unleashed violent indignation at the lived realities of black Americans. The shift from images of young civil rights marchers terrorized by state militia to scenes of black youth burning America's cities provoked a range of responses reflecting the deepening rifts in American society. Whites either decried what they saw as rampant "Negro criminality" or, following the lead of President Lyndon Johnson's Kerner Commission (charged in 1967 with uncovering the riots' root causes), read black unrest as a sign of impatience with the pace of integration. Many elder black civil rights leaders expressed fear and regret, and some, like King, described the riots as a "suicidal" outburst of frustration and bitterness by the "voiceless"; but many younger black intellectuals and activists saw the unrest as a populist assertion of a new voice unwilling to remain silent. In the words of H. Rap Brown, successor to Carmichael of the now avowedly black nationalist SNCC, "We stand on the eve of a black revolution. . . . These rebellions are but a dress rehearsal for real revolution."

Brown's words—uttered in the immediate aftermath of the so-called Newark Rebellion of 1967, during which Baraka was arrested (charged, he later quipped, with illegally carrying "two revolvers and two poems")—provided a revealing gloss on the intertwining of revolution and aesthetics in the new black nationalist imagination. Indeed, his characterization of the riots as a theatrical experiment soon to be displaced by a "real revolution" speaks to the fundamentally performative vision of insurrection underlying the Black Arts movement, a vision Baraka had vividly evoked two years earlier in his manifesto "The Revolutionary Theatre": "The Revolutionary Theatre must take dreams and make them a reality. [It] is shaped by the world, and moves to reshape the world. . . . We will scream and cry, murder, run through the streets in agony, if it means some soul will be moved."

Baraka's "dream" is decidedly not that which Martin Luther King Jr. so eloquently expounded in his oration delivered from the steps of the Lincoln Memorial at the 1963 March on Washington. Baraka had no interest in portraying the "Negro [as] God's instrument to save the soul of America," as King had declared in his extraordinary "I Have a Dream" speech; the souls that concerned him would achieve their redemption in the blood of their oppressors and the newly consecrated reality of a *black* world. And they would do so through action provoked by a form of literary enactment, theater, designed to be revolution's prophetic mirror.

Brown's blending of political action and aesthetic discourse reminds us that Stokely Carmichael's inaugural black nationalist pronouncement was itself explicitly couched as a shift in language: "What we gonna start *saying* now is 'Black Power!'" Later, as Carmichael began to develop this improvised declamation into more systematic political thought in the tradition of Du Bois and Malcolm X, he defined Black Power as the ability "to exercise control over our lives, politically, economically, and psychically." Such control would reshape the world in both concrete and conceptual terms; revolution would take place both in society and in consciousness. And thus the Revolution would necessarily be *linguistic* as well as material, *cultural* as well as political. As Larry Neal put it in the 1968 essay that gave "the Black Arts movement" its name: "The movement is the aesthetic and spiritual sister of the Black Power concept."

This conjunction of social and cultural aspirations took many forms, not least being the rise of black community and artistic institutions that blended multimedia arts presentations with nationalist-inspired activism. Across the nation, organizations like Newark's Spirit House, Detroit's Concept East, Chicago's Organization of Black American Culture (OBAC), and San Francisco's Black Arts West developed cultural programming that embodied "blackness" as both means and ends of a new communal sensibility. Theater companies devoted to the new wave of black dramatists sprang up not only in major urban centers like New York (The New Lafayette Theatre, directed by Bob Macbeth, with Ed Bullins as resident playwright), Chicago (Grey Ward's Kuumba Theatre Company), and Los Angeles (PALSA, directed by Vantile Whitfield), but throughout the country in smaller cities like Cleveland and Houston, some with distinct regional affiliations (most distinctively, Tom Dent's Free Southern Theater, rooted in New Orleans). Meanwhile, a thriving independent black publishing scene offered Black Arts poets, aesthetic theoreticians, and political visionaries a platform for works that were typically ignored by mainstream outlets. Magazines such as the *Journal of Black Poetry, Liberator, Freedomways, Soulbook, Umbra, Negro Digest* (renamed *Black World* in 1970), and *Black Dialogue*, as well as publishing houses like Dudley Randall's Broadside Press and Haki Madhubuti's Third World Press, declared a *de facto* defiance of white-controlled commercial media while lending visible substance to Black Arts claims of autonomous authority. In the process, these instruments of publicly circulated black expression became a laboratory for experimenting with new forms, sounds, and ideas that gave shape and content to an emergent "Black Aesthetic."

Formally articulated by critics Hoyt Fuller, Addison Gayle Jr., and Stephen E. Henderson, but elaborated also in the writing of artists and activists like Baraka, Neal, Touré, Sonia Sanchez, and Maulana Karenga, the new Black Aesthetic set itself against its forebears in Negritude and the Harlem Renaissance by an emphasis on the efficacy of art grown from, addressed to, and in service of the full black *nation*'s desire for self-realization. "The Black Arts Movement," Neal's foundational essay begins, "is radically opposed to any concept of the artist that alienates him from his community." In accord with their definition of themselves as participants in a popular movement, black writers and artists turned to the African American masses for their inspiration and defined their goals in broadly social and political terms. Their objective was to create works that would be—in Karenga's words— "functional, collective, and committing." And in order to produce art that "speaks directly to the needs and aspirations of Black America," Neal writes, the Black Arts movement "proposes a radical reordering of the Western cultural aesthetic. It proposes a separate symbolism, mythology, critique, and iconology."

Because the turn toward "blackness" envisioned by Black Aesthetic theorists is entangled with a repudiation of a potentially suffocating white tradition, the Black Arts movement is vulnerable to accusations of parochialism and even inverse racism. But for a people historically imprisoned in a literal and linguistic framework designed to deny their very humanity, liberation must begin by dismantling the mental subjugation of inherited idioms and their intended meanings. By insisting that refutation of the aesthetic foundations of "whiteness" was integral to a decolonization of the mind that must precede revolutionary action, Neal and other Black Aesthetic thinkers made clear not only the intensity of their political "commitment" but also the necessity of "radically reordering" the basic terms through which art is conceived, made, received, and evaluated.

The Black Aesthetic manifestos written by Neal and others during the period are thus, for all their air of clipped prescription, essentially speculations on the nature and purpose of cultural performance. At the center of this inquiry is the nexus of artist, work, and audience, each term of which undergoes the serious "critique" that Neal purposefully embeds in his catalogue of proposed aesthetic values. No longer, like Du Bois in his upstairs study (*The Souls of Black Folk*) or Invisible Man in his underground cave, working at a distance from his subject matter or his reader, the black writer now enters into a dynamic transaction with his intended audience, submitting himself to their judgment and even to their collaborative participation in the shaping of the work itself. The artwork thus becomes not a static repository of meanings but an open-ended exchange among members of a community that is not merely convened but is virtually constituted by the *occasion* of the work. That work might be a poetic score for performance like the jazz-inspired poems of David Henderson and Jayne Cortez, a philosophical meditation like the metaphor-dense poems of Raymond Patterson and Audre Lorde, a psychological inquiry like the dramas of Adrienne Kennedy and Ed Bullins, an experiment in textual "voice" like the fictions of Toni Cade Bambara and Ishmael Reed, or a full-throated exhortation like the "preachment" verse of Haki Madhubuti and Nikki Giovanni. Through a transpersonal ethos arising from the cultural literacy shared by artist and audience, the black community itself becomes an autonomous creative agent. As Henry Dumas intimates with gathering ferocity in his story "Will the Circle Be Unbroken?"—in which an innocent-seeming excursion to a jazz club by white hipsters who cannot truly enter the circle of black music ends in their apocalyptic destruction—less-than-complete cultural competency can be lethal.

The artist's work itself can therefore no longer be considered autonomous—an idea propounded by the dominant schools of aesthetic thinking at the time Neal wrote his manifesto. The work, as joint but never fixed property of all those knowledgeably assembled before it, has become ceaselessly "revolutionary" in its impulse to unmake and remake the world into which it's been cast. "Neo-HooDoo is a litany seeking its text," Reed writes in his "Neo-HooDoo Manifesto," capturing the contingent, in-process nature of the Black Aesthetic work, always subject to critique and revision by its black audience. The measure of the Black Aesthetic work is never the judgment of "good" or "bad," but always its capacity to *move* its audiences, spurring their capacity for communal feeling and self-transforming action. Much of the formal experimentation seen in writing of the Black Arts period—from the poetry's disruption of standard verse structures by eccentric typographic practices, to the drama's inventive mixtures of ritual and realistic representation, to the fiction's circular and reflexive narratives— expresses this restive quest of an art that feels itself emerging "on the eve of a black revolution."

THE REVOLUTION WILL NOT BE TELEVISED:
PERFORMANCE AND POLEMIC

"Seeking its text," the Black Arts movement took up residence in locations far removed from the austere venues of high culture: community centers, storefront churches, lofts, bars, coffee-houses, prisons, subways, alleys, and street corners. The search for alternative spaces gave form to the artist's desire to speak from within the community, and street-hugging establishments like Lewis Michaux's African National Memorial Bookstore in Harlem that, festooned with nationalist slogans, teeming with books on the African Diaspora often unavailable in official libraries, and rocking with the sounds of Malcolm X and other nationalist orators, was itself a kind of multigeneric

Lewis Michaux's House of Common Sense and House of Proper Propaganda in Harlem, 1964.

performance and suggested an act of reclamation that faintly paralleled the liberation of African statehood from European occupation. But such repurposing of the African American "colonial" landscape could at best seem a kind of blueprint for the full-scale emancipation foretold by young radical black artists. Like the riots that opened (as well as scorched) ghetto spaces, these aesthetic reclamations might be seen as rehearsals of revolution; but as jazz poet Gil Scott-Heron, channeling H. Rap Brown, chanted in the hard-driving style later redeployed in rap, "The revolution will *not* be televised."

Scott-Heron's classic 1970 composition pits authentic revolutionary action against a capitalist, imperialist society addicted to images at the expense of embodied experience, what French philosopher Guy Debord called "the society of the spectacle":

> The revolution will not be televised.
> The revolution will not be brought to you by Xerox
> In 4 parts without commercial interruptions.
> The revolution will not show you pictures of Nixon
> blowing a bugle and leading a charge [. . .] to eat
> hog maws confiscated from a Harlem sanctuary.
> The revolution will not be televised.

Scott-Heron's lyric humorously but relentlessly indicts modern American culture for substituting representation for relationships, commodities for community. This specter of falsified reality haunted practitioners of the Black Aesthetic, which helps to explain their proclivity for genres of performance. Indeed, the performance of "blackness" itself permeated the consciousness of 1960s African American culture, as the Black Power ethos touched everything from fashion and hairstyles (with African dress and natural "Afros") to athletic competition and ghetto landscapes. Artists like Jeff Donaldson, William Walker, Mitchell Caton, and Eugene Eda created spectacular, vibrantly colored narratives of black aspiration as a black nationalist muralist movement in the late 1960s spread "Walls of Respect" across ghetto buildings from Chicago to Boston.

Earlier in the decade, Cassius Clay's ascent to the heavyweight boxing crown through two stunning defeats of Sonny Liston, during which time he

The Organization of Black Culture's "Wall of Respect," Chicago, 1967.

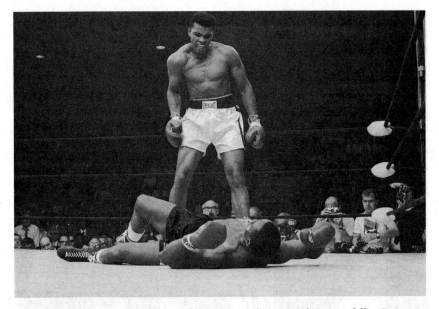

Muhammad Ali (then popularly known as Cassius Clay) triumphant over fallen Sonny Liston in the first round of "Clay/Liston II," Lewiston, Maine, 1964.

converted to the Nation of Islam and renamed himself Muhammad Ali, offered a compelling allegory of the "rising" black nation, while his linguistically deft prophesies of pugilistic triumph and his resistance to fighting in Vietnam ("no Vietcong ever called me nigger") made him an emblem of unconstrained rebellion.

Ali became the most visible of a cadre of black athletes who, guided by African American sociologist Harry Edwards and the ethos of black nationalism, grew increasingly defiant of the white sports establishment. This defiance climaxed in the iconic moment at the 1968 Olympics in Mexico City when black American sprinters Tommie Smith and John Carlos, respectively first- and third-place finishers in the 200-meter dash, raised black-gloved fists during the playing of the U.S. national anthem at their medal ceremony. Within hours the two men had been stripped of their medals by the American-led International Olympic Committee, expelled from the Olympic Village, and elevated to a major place in the iconography of Black Power.

This kind of empowered blackness was most distinctively mobilized by the Black Panther Party, founded in 1966 by Huey Newton and Bobby Seale in Oakland, California, as a socialist revolutionary militia advocating armed self-defense against rampant police brutality and state oppression. At once edgily streetwise and intellectually sophisticated, the Panthers' socialist orientation made them theoretically hostile to black cultural nationalism; but their development as a community self-help organization that spread a children's breakfast program through many urban ghettos and, above all, their gift for crafting spectacular scenes of power and authority, made them among the era's most dramatically effective practitioners of the Black Arts. Most famously in the image of Huey Newton enthroned, wearing the Panther-trademark beret and black leather jacket while holding a spear and a rifle, the Panthers stood the commodity fetishism of capitalism's

John Carlos and Tommie Smith with raised fists on Awards Podium at Olympic Stadium, Mexico City, 1968. Australian competitor Peter Norman, wearing human rights badge, is at far left.

"society of the spectacle" on its head, eliciting revolutionary effects from an assemblage of signifying objects and poses. The Panthers staged themselves as confidently potent precisely because of their understanding of symbolic power: staging *was* power, instilling in its audience (frightened officials and galvanized young black supporters alike) the persuasive sensation of revolutionary vigor.

Black Panther Party headquarters, with Huey Newton Enthroned poster at center in Oakland, California, 1968.

The history of the Black Panther Party is a litany of struggles with police harassment and legal strife, culminating in a series of trials of party leaders that were themselves occasions for dynamic revolutionary theatrics. Ritually chanting "Free Huey" or "Free Bobby," phalanxes of party members carried their touchstone images like icons in a religious procession. Even if some Black Arts writers could not accept the Panthers' ideological formulations or their bent for hyper-masculine hero-worship, they often nevertheless sought to conscript the Panthers' talent for subordinating language to enactment, and enactment to the achievement of social meaning. For as Baraka best captured in his own early dramas, especially *Dutchman* and *The Slave*, what his character Clay calls "words and clean hard thoughts urging me to new conquests" aren't necessarily a mechanism of revolutionary action; they can be a betrayal, too, and this helps us to understand why performance and polemic so often appear together in Black Arts literature— sometimes as antagonists, sometimes as partners—in the drive to push from revolutionary rehearsal to reality.

Because audience and subject matter are so often the same for Black Arts authors, like the "Wall of Respect" muralists and marching Black Panther adherents, their works often take the form of secular sermons, manifestos summoning the reader, listener, or witness to the values and goals of communal action: "Calling all Black People/Calling all Black people/Come in. Come in. in. in. in. in. in" (Neal, "Black Boogaloo"). In service of this collective mobilization, instruction becomes a central weapon and communication a moral imperative. "Change/life if you were a match I wd light u into something beautiful/change./change / . . . change change your change change change./your/mind nigger," chants Madhubuti in "a poem to complement other poems," fusing plea with command, stretching the word across the page so that style converges on meaning. But the very urgency of this demand can make the complicated layerings and detours of figurative language a kind of treachery:

> Poems are bullshit unless they are
> teeth or trees or lemons piled
> on a step. [. . .]
>   We want live
> words of the hip world live flesh &
> coursing blood. Hearts Brains
> Souls splintering fire.
>   (Baraka, "Black Art")

Beginning like a didactic lecture on aesthetics, Baraka's poem declares that "Liveness" requires a synthetic relation between words and things, intentions and actions. Itself a poem, "Black Art" hovers between a presentational energy that seems to embody the art it demands, and a sensation of incomplete aspiration, as if the poem were a search for its own perfected form. This tension is likewise built into the poem's imagery, which describes a poem capable of explosive transformation. For "Liveness" is that which cannot be simply transcribed or recorded; the "reality" that it conjures is the moment of poetic speech itself ("Black Art" concludes: "Let All Black People Speak This Poem/Silently/or LOUD"). Like other works of "statement" in an era rife with manifestos, "Black Art"—which became a rallying cry for Black Arts poetics—is both doctrinaire and indeterminate, describing a potency that remains in the realm of "want."

Desiring an aesthetic form that would itself accomplish what it envisions, Black Arts movement writers consistently turned to music as an abstract inspiration and practical model. Soul, rhythm and blues, and funk singers like Aretha Franklin, Marvin Gaye, and James Brown were celebrated in Black Arts literature for promoting the ethos of awakened blackness; however, it was primarily the bold inventiveness of modern jazz that sparked the speculative and creative efforts of the Black Arts movement. Experimental ensemble leader Sun Ra's poetic assertion that "Music is existence, the key to universal/Language" ("The Neglected Plane of Wisdom") captures the idealization underlying Black Arts writers' embrace of new black musical idioms.

Beginning with the self-consciously "free" innovations of Ornette Coleman in the early 1960s, the creative ferment known as the New Black Music presented a radical reimagining of musical conventions that felt like systematic but often violent liberation from tradition and expectation. Led by saxophonists like Coleman, Archie Shepp, Sonny Rollins, Albert Ayler, and, above all, John Coltrane, whose playing often seemed to imitate the clamor or supplication of the human voice, the New Black Music felt at once transgressive and transcendent, political and spiritual. Built upon the rebellious explorations of bebop musicians like Charlie ("Bird") Parker and Dizzy Gillespie, whose ironic conceits pushed back against the quiet repressions of 1950s African American life, the avant-garde jazz music of the 1960s articulated a wholly new musical vocabulary. "My music is words," Sun Ra proclaimed; as if supplying the antiphonal affirmation, poet A. B. Spellman's elegy for Coltrane declared "trane's horn had words in it" ("Did John's Music Kill Him?"). Black music appeared to be the crucible within which language and experience would fuse in a fiery expressive synthesis.

Among these musicians, Coltrane was singular for the daring of his experimentation, commitment to aesthetic struggle, and spiritual dedication. Dismantling and then audaciously reconstructing such standards of the American songbook as Rodgers and Hammerstein's "My Favorite Things," Coltrane was said by Baraka to have "showed us how to murder the popular song. To do away with weak Western forms." At the same time, that capacity for achieving insurrectionary intention was seen, in the aftermath of Coltrane's death in 1967, to bear the authority of unconfined, hence revolutionary, power: "o john death will/not contain you death/will not contain you" ("Did John's Music Kill Him?"). "Trane" thus became for a wide spectrum of poets—Baraka, Spellman, Madhubuti, Carolyn Rodgers, Michael Harper, Jayne Cortez, and Sonia Sanchez, among many others—an artistic, cultural, and political resource from which the poet can draw means for unifying individual and collective voices.

Turning the written page into a dramatic stage, "Coltrane poets" free polemic from plain didacticism and performance from mere play or gesture:

> my favorite things
>   is u/blowen
>   yo/favorite/things.
> Stretchen the mind
>   till it bursts past the con/fines of
> solo/en melodies. [. . .]
> (soft   c/people,   rise up blk/people
> chant)   RISE. & BE. What u can.
>   MUST BE. BE. BE. BE. BE. BE. B-E-E-E-E-E . . .
> (Sanchez, "a/coltrane/poem")

Not merely referring to Coltrane's musical accomplishment but translating his improvisational style to poetic form and meaning, "a/coltrane/poem" exemplifies the modern black artist's use of music as a structural device to both enact and symbolize the unleashing of "blackness" through collective vocalization. The poem works like a musician's chart, directing its readers' performances so that the voice literally "rises" in concert with the theme of explosive black being. Dissolving "solo" self into an inclusive "u" that encompasses the musician, the black audience, and the poet who unites them, Sanchez fulfills the "Black Aesthetic" project of locating artistic voice in communal realization. By evoking Coltrane and his peers in jazz's New Wave, Black Arts writers sought a resolution to the prerevolutionary double-consciousness that divided polemic from performance, artist from audience, and audience from the full promise of its proper identity.

THE CHANGING SAME: REVOLUTION AND TRADITION

The "im-mediacy" prized by Black Arts writers is thus not simply the expansive "Now" celebrated by the Euro-American avant-garde of the same period, which sought through such "anti-art" practices as happenings and aleatory music release from rigid traditional structures through the disorganizing effects of chance. For the modern black artist, im-mediacy involved a complex negotiation with time and history, in which the present was both contaminated by the exploitation and brutality of the past and teeming with seeds of a transformed future. The present was therefore paradoxical—both burden and opportunity—and the era's clamor for revolution arose directly from this paradox. In the lead manifesto of the anthology *Black Fire*—the Black Arts movement's anthem of collective textual performances edited by Baraka and Neal in the watershed year of 1968—James T. Stewart declares: "A revolutionary is against the established order, regime, or culture. The revolutionary understands change. Change is what it is all about." Seeking what jazz musicians call the "break" or "cut" with the current moment, the revolutionary black artist refuses to repeat the stuttering of history that seemed to trap African Americans in a static story of oppression, whatever its name: slavery; Jim Crow; poverty; incarceration.

The central term in this program of change was, of course, "blackness," which potentially subjected Black Arts thought to a second paradox, the paradox of being itself: was "blackness" a constant, and therefore a fixed essence? If so, the revolution was a mask for chauvinism and, ironically, conservatism—a charge that subsequent generations of critics have continued to make against Black Arts writing. But looking backward at a western tradition in which "blackness" signified not merely an inventory of denigrating traits but indeed the very negation of value and identity, African American artists labored to repossess the term as an instrument of critique and a sign of possibility. "Blackness" became thereby the era's touchstone of resistance and deliverance, its means for radically revaluing the relation between past and future in the present's perpetually agitated state of imminent transformation.

Notwithstanding fierce debates among black revolutionary thinkers about whether the movement should primarily address economic and material or cultural and political concerns (debates that occurred within as well as among organizations like BARTS and the Black Panther Party, and which in their own way animated strategic discussions among civil rights activists), the Black Arts movement was elementally about revolution of *consciousness*, the precondition and purpose of social upheaval. A renovated "blackness" was conceived above all as a reconception of selfhood liberated not only from white culture but from the internalization by black folk of "whiteness" as a form of desire as well as repugnance. This double thrust of black self-recovery accounts in part for the racialist, often bitingly satirical animus of many works in the 1960s and early 1970s that pillory white characters, speech patterns, artifacts, and bodies in an unremitting exorcism of "the white thang." But more importantly it illuminates the strenuous reorientation, frequently pressed toward spiritual commitment, that suffuses so many Black Arts works, whose characters so often struggle with the contradictions of black life in the modern world. At the heart of those contradictions is the question of "blackness" itself, and specifically whether its emancipatory efficacy, founded on an ethos of ceaseless change, requires a break not only from "the West" but also from all prior kinds of "blackness," including black tradition itself.

For some writers, particularly those (like Karenga, Madhubuti, and the young Baraka) influenced by the Martiniquean anticolonial existentialist Frantz Fanon, the answer was, at least initially, a harsh rejection of tradition, as for Fanon only violent repudiation of the past could fully demystify the "European version of things" and secure a healthy black life. In a searing 1962 essay, Baraka dismissed the idea that there existed an authentic African American literature, while Karenga and Madhubuti declared the blues "invalid" for teaching passive resignation to reality, for "crying" in "acceptance of reality" rather than, like New Wave jazz, "screaming" change into existence. But for most writers of the time (including many who admired Fanon), revolutionary black consciousness entailed a recovery of radical potentiality located in black cultural history, brought forward now with a new intentionality and focus. Revolution, the era's poets and philosophers tell us, demands rupture, but the word itself means also "repetition," suggesting that the way forward depends upon retrieval and redirection of a past rich with untapped resources for survival, resistance, and reinvention.

This creative retrieval permeates the Black Arts era in the rise of "Afrocentric" scholarship, which established black studies programs throughout the country grounded in historical studies of the African diaspora and which undertook to recover neglected radical and vernacular texts of African American literature, from early black nationalist Martin Delaney's *Blake, or the Huts of America* to Zora Neale Hurston's now-classic *Their Eyes Were Watching God*. Self-consciousness regarding familial "roots" spurred interest in genealogical investigation, as African Americans proudly traced the family trees of African-derived people displaced from multiple tribal beginnings into the crazy-quilt landscape of American slavery and its aftermath. Meanwhile, the artists themselves drew particularly from three intermingled sources in seeking both to dissolve individual estrangement into cultural solidarity and to make possible a new communal narrative by resituating the origins of black history: vernacular expression; mythic imagination; and African sensibility.

For all its stress on the plain style of polemical address, Black Arts movement literature is suffused with vernacular idioms and techniques that accentuate the virtuosity, savvy, and adaptability of black vocal performance. Through structural and allusive means, such forms as the dozens, toasts, call-and-response, rapping, chanting, scatting, shouting, and sermonizing lend an unruly "signifying" rhythm to Black Arts texts, such that the very capacity for "black" speech takes on thematic force. In turn, these vernacular-inspired texts infuse the performer's vocal and gestural presentation so that his or her very body becomes a breathing archive of a recognizable and living heritage. As exemplified by works like Calvin Hernton's "Jitterbugging in the Streets" and Amus Mor's "We Are the Hip Men," contemporary urban dialects mix with inherited folk imagery to suggest a seamless continuum of vernacular swagger refusing confinement by stiff regulations of literary form, social mores, or political condition. Championing as a kind of secular liberation theology what Larry Neal (refuting Karenga) called "the blues ethos" of their forebears, Black Arts writers embraced vernacular expression as a repository of existential, yet collective, assertion that was at once oppositional and affirmative.

The political import of vernacular poetics is perhaps felt most strongly in the new black theater, which playwright Paul Carter Harrison dubbed "the drama of Nommo," employing a West African term for the power of the spoken word. In plays by Ed Bullins, Sonia Sanchez, Clay Goss, Alice Childress, and others, the characters' sharp, streetwise exchanges signal that, unlike their immediate predecessors in African American plays of the 1950s, they have no interest in securing a place in white America. Rather, the aim of Black Arts dramas is a renewal of black will, insight, energy, and awareness. This renovation is predicated on an exposed, spoken performance and a sounding of everyday black American reality that, while suffering under the weight of white American racism, has found its own vocabulary and timbre to express the depths of its own experience and aspirations. This drama of passionate self-revelation often drives these characters to the extremes of tragic dissolution or radical metamorphosis, seeking through vernacular tonalities to speak a new spirit of black liberation unmastered by conventions that historically have "staged" their lives as society's dispensable detritus.

If such vernacular sounds reflected the performative impulse of the movement, their thematic emphases stretched black writing into new configurations of mythic thought, so that myth became a counterintuitive adjunct to revolutionary action. Whether drawn from indigenous fables like toasts (with their celebration of the rebellious trickster-hero, Shine) and the Nation of Islam's racial origin story of the black magician Yakub, from New World cosmologies like Voodoo and Rastafarianism, or from the legends of traditional African cultures and languages like the Akan, Dogon, and Yoruba, mythic explorations in these works strategically harness spiritual authority to political intention. Thus the prison verse of Etheridge Knight and the feminist-lesbian poetry of Audre Lorde can each layer West African mythographic patterns against African American vernacular textures in order to transfigure mundane entrapment into visionary action.

But this mythic impulse is not an effort to import grandeur where harsh banality rules. Rather, it is an effort to exhume from the past for present use systems of symbolic meaning that were, in their original forms, already efforts to achieve the "radical reordering" of experience called for by Larry Neal and other Black Arts theorists. Ishmael Reed's transmutation of Haitian and New Orleans Voodoo practices into the literary process of Neo-Hoodoo brilliantly exemplifies the critical dimension of Black Arts mythic reclamation. For Reed absorbs and redeploys the therapeutic yet also subversive objective of Voodoo conjuration, giving it new purpose in the context of African American struggles for meaning and legitimacy. Indeed, perhaps the most destabilizing implication of experimental works like Reed's novel *Mumbo Jumbo* or his mini-epic "I Am a Cowboy in the Boat of Ra" is that it is mainstream culture, not its repressed black "other," that constitutes an "alternative," and decidedly atrophied, tradition.

That confidence in a foundational black tradition from which radical innovation can be launched is rooted in the era's embrace of Africa as the movement's historical, psychological, mythic, and political cornerstone. African American artistic and social history is, of course, replete with longing for Africa, plans for blacks to emigrate from the United States back to an African "homeland," and programs of reform or withdrawal that will produce an "African" way of life in the Americas. But the reality of the African continent before the 1960s was a sobering condition of white domination.

Foregrounded were images of white colonial administrators and their over-seers poised with whips in hand—literally, ideologically, or metaphorically—over the naked backs of African subordinates. Early experiments in black migration to Africa such as the Liberia and Sierra Leone projects did not substantially alter the subordinate status of Africa in even the most roman-tic black nationalist's imagination. At an imaginative level, however, black writers and thinkers such as Phillis Wheatley, Martin Delaney, Wylmot Blyden, Marcus Garvey, Melvin Tolson, Countee Cullen, Julian Mayfield, and others from the eighteenth to the twentieth century have projected often sophisticated, if purely aspirational, representations of Africa as a place of hope and promise for black Americans.

It was not until the 1960s that such images seemed to coexist with a new spatial and political reality. The eruption of the African independence movement offered a model of "decolonization"—a freeing of the black mind as well as political, economic, and cultural spaces for black occupancy. Fanon's *The Wretched of the Earth* became a philosophical manifesto for imagining the transformation of black American urban ghettos into empow-ered, self-dependent realms for a black national "good life." The music, dress, and rituals of Africa were incorporated by African Americans into their daily lives, and the assertion "We Are an African People!" became conventional wisdom in the Black Arts. Most importantly, the introduction of African intellectual, cultural, and imaginative artifacts into the works of Black Power and the Black Arts shifted the very definition of *modernism* as it was articulated by the West.

By aggressively confronting European colonialism, imperialism, and cul-tural domination, Black Power and the Black Arts revealed the ghost in the machine of Western dominance. Cultural effacement by force was the insidi-ous corollary to colonialism's actual physical conquest and was the West's most important strategy in proclaiming its own "modern" progress and social superiority. Never before the 1960s had so many African Americans consid-ered the realities of what the scholar Chancellor Williams calls the "destruc-tion of African civilization." Just as powerfully, never before had so many considered African history as the very foundation of the West, a foundation carefully revealed by historians such as Cheik Anta Diop, John Henrik Clarke, Vincent Harding, and others in a way that restored African cultural meaning from the destructive effects of Western imperialism. In the 1960s writers, scholars, and artists of the Black Arts movement hailed their African homeland as a thriving zone of black independence and rich cultural prom-ise, sparking a global revolution in "pan-African" sensibility. Sanchez, Baraka, Neal, Hoyt Fuller, Nikki Giovanni, and others actually traveled to Africa, a journey back to their origins that became critical for their efforts to frame a "new" African American identity rooted in this project of recovery. These writers returned from their African expeditions equipped not only with new vocabularies and images but also with fresh perspectives of a world set free from both material and internalized "whiteness."

No figure of the period better exemplifies the multiform and transforma-tive meanings of a reinvented "Africa" for the period's revolutionary aspira-tions than Malcolm X, who in 1964 proudly returned from his second trip to the continent having had the honorific name Omowale, "The Son Who Has Come Home," bestowed upon him by the Nigerian Muslim Students Association. Tellingly, this African excursion came at a time of great upheaval for Malcolm, for by the mid-sixties he had in many ways outgrown

Malcolm X speaking in Harlem, 1964. This iconic poster references his speech "By Any Means Necessary," delivered on February 14, 1965, at Detroit's Ford Auditorium the night his New York home was firebombed.

the religious and cultic parochialism of the Nation of Islam. Malcolm refused to be silenced by the Nation's leader, Elijah Muhammad, on national matters such as the assassination of President John F. Kennedy, scandalously proclaiming, much to the horror of a grieving nation: "The chickens have come home to roost!" His insistence that the type of violence America was visiting on black people at home and "colored subjects" abroad had returned to kill Kennedy gave pungent immediacy to his increasingly global perspective on the historical and conceptual roots of modern racism. In early 1964 Malcolm broke with the Nation of Islam, setting forth on a new and more inclusive quest for "heightened political consciousness."

It is not, though, that Africa thus became for Malcolm the final destination of his lifetime search for freedom, empowerment, and dignity; rather, at what proved to be among his final moments, Malcolm's African (re)turn consolidated a drama of perpetual self-redefinition that made Malcolm X, with Coltrane, the Black Arts' most influential inspiration. Though his prison conversion to the Nation of Islam is the epiphanic centerpiece of his *Autobiography*, perpetual conversion was the true hallmark of Malcolm's identity. From naïve schoolboy to criminal hustler to ignorant prisoner to Black Muslim minister to black nationalist orator to Islamic convert to international activist, from Malcolm Little to Mascot to Detroit Red to Malcolm X to El-Hajj Malik El-Shabazz, Malcolm made his life a furious embodiment of Stewart's vision of revolution-as-change. Certainly his profound impact on a generation of black thinkers and writers is largely attributable to the vibrancy of his public voice, the clarity of his analysis of oppression's hidden history and inner logic, the fearlessness of his opposition to white supremacy, and the unconstrained ardor of his advocacy for revolution "by any means necessary." But it was above all his capacity to blend iconoclastic defiance with spiritual passion in a life submitted wholly to historical struggle on behalf of his people that made Malcolm at once singular and exemplary. In Malcolm, revolution's generative relation to repetition achieved active realization.

VISIONS OF A LIBERATED FUTURE: END(S) OF THE BLACK ARTS MOVEMENT

Temporal markers are to some extent arbitrary, but the choice of 1975 as the boundary of "The Black Arts Era" has representative value when one considers the post–civil rights and post–Black Power events on the economic, athletic, political, expressive, cultural, and legal fronts in that year. In 1975 the U.S. Senate extended the Voting Rights Act of 1965. The Associated Press elected Muhammad Ali "Athlete of the Year" for 1974. Black elected officials throughout the country were giving a new face to local and regional politics. The "Black South," as represented by a city like Atlanta with its black mayor Maynard Jackson, seemed to be on the rise for the first time since early Reconstruction. And a new black middle class was making its presence felt in every facet of American life. Measured by the standards of racial aspiration that emerged at the dawn of the sixties, America was seemingly on a progressive road.

But matters are seldom simply "post": In 1975 the battles for a truly free black citizenship in the United States continued on many fronts. The condemnations by Black Arts and Black Power activists of white America's reluctance to yield a single inch without struggle remained justified by the violence triggered across the United States by school desegregation and busing rulings handed down in states such as Massachusetts and Kentucky. Joann Little—a black inmate in a North Carolina jail who killed the guard who was allegedly attempting to rape her—became a *cause célèbre*. The incarceration and brutalization of black life had not disappeared, and was beginning to shift toward the fast-growing prison-industrial complex. Whether Black Power was receding because of black advancement or the stronger undertow of American racism was a matter of contemporary doubt and debate.

A literary history is not exempt from "history" in general. Time moves; one era gives way to the next. But for a movement staked on millenarian ambitions, scrutiny of its dissolution into a successor period will naturally be sharp, even harsh. Yet it remains a challenge for historians of the Black Arts movement to distinguish between internal and external causes of its termination. Youthful energies fueling the Black Arts and Black Power projects at times degenerated into self-destructive impulses, as key organizations like BARTS, the Black Panther Party, and SNCC fractured in part because "armed self-defense" became fratricidal conflict. But if internal strife permeated key radical enclaves, it is also true that they were systemically infiltrated, hounded, and assaulted by arms of the state, including the IRS and FBI, whose infamous COINTELPRO (Counter Intelligence Program) waged a relentless campaign of defamation, harassment, incarceration, and even murder against both civil rights and Black Power activists. As became chillingly clear with the police murder of Illinois Black Panther Fred Hampton in 1969 and the bloody suppression of the Attica (New York) Correctional Facility uprising in 1971, the state would unleash unchecked violence against any outbreaks of black insurrection. In concrete terms, by the mid-1970s many of the movement's most audacious figures—Malcolm X, King, Newton, Cleaver, Angela Davis, Carmichael, H. Rap Brown—had suffered jail, exile, or assassination.

But there were other pressures from within the Black Arts movement that rattled many of its assumptions and inclinations. The undersides of bold black "manhood"—homophobia, misogyny, and bellicose essentialism—were exposed as contradictory to "revolutionary justice" by the emergence of African American gay and women authors, artists, and activists. The appearance in 1970 of *The Black Woman*, a landmark anthology of black feminist writing edited by Toni Cade Bambara, both mirrored and critically engaged Baraka and Neal's *Black Fire*, foretelling the rise of black women's voices to prominence in the post–Black Arts period. Often adapting and refining Black Arts tactics of appropriation and recontextualization, black women artists expanded the purview of revolutionary critique, as we see in Sanchez's poem "so this is our revolution" ("how bout a fo/real revolu shun/with a fo real/battle to be fought/outside of bed/room/minds"), Nikki Giovanni's essay "Black Poems, Poseurs and Power," Angela Davis's gender-aware black-Marxist orations, and Betye Saar's sculptural assemblage "The Liberation of Aunt Jemima," whose central mammy figure, standing with broom in one hand and rifle in the other, salutes and signifies on Newton's enthroned image.

What is bracing about these works and their creators is their simultaneous presence within and outside the Black Arts movement's ideological and rhetorical center. For not only are their strategies of demystification and resistance made possible by Black Arts insights, but indeed they exercised great influence as movement participants in developing those very practices. On the one hand, expressively powerful figures like Davis and Giovanni were instrumental in creating the "voice" of Black Power politics, while experimental poets like Sanchez and Cortez were among the vanguards shaping a new "sound" for revolutionary black art. On the other hand, these writers, both in their intellectual bearing and in their very being, shattered the presumed congruence of *blackness* and *masculinity*, thereby widening the movement's analytical and pragmatic quest for cultural transformation and social justice. In the voice of women writers, "blackness" thus became ever more capacious, inclusive, and productive, at once confident (given its broader scope) and aspirational (given its sharper self-awareness). From a literary perspective, this

Attica Prison uprising, 1968.

openness infused the Black Arts movement with an insistent lyricism unafraid of public exchange or the tasks of institutional critique and communal affirmation. In the verse of June Jordan, Audre Lorde, and Carolyn Rodgers, for example, "private" themes of familial unrest, betrayal, sorrow, and love derive persuasive force by reflecting collective experience, so that lyrical expression becomes a form of expanded shared consciousness. The possibility of intimacy explored by black women writers of the era invariably accompanies a linguistic awakening attuned to specific historical circumstances, so domesticicity becomes the very site of political desire:

> momma momma
> teach me how to kiss
> the king within the kingdom
> teach me how to t.c.b./to make do
> and be
> like you

"The Liberation of Aunt Jemima," Betye Saar's 1972 mixed media assemblage, juxtaposing images of the stereotypical mammy figure as happy servant and as armed militant.

> teach me to survive my
> momma
> teach me how to hold a new life
> momma
> help me
> turn the face of history
> *to your face.*
> (June Jordan, "Getting Down to Get Over")

Angela Davis speaking to a crowd in Raleigh, North Carolina, 1974.

Neither passive victims of what Davis called the "confusion of revolution with maleness" nor naïve proponents of a feminism detached from the era's burning concern with racial struggle, women writers infused the Black Arts movement with continuous awareness that "revolutionary" black identity is an expansively humanistic and ethical ideal, and thus is always a subject-in-process.

Thus, as we navigate the new millennium, it is clear that we must continuously revise our estimation of the Black Arts movement's scope and meaning, taking stock of its extraordinary breadth and inclusiveness, which go hand-and-glove with its undervalued capacity for critical self-revision. If Larry Neal could, in *Black Fire*, excoriate Ralph Ellison's *Invisible Man* as having "little bearing on the world as the 'New Breed' sees it," by the early 1970s he was championing Ellison's novel as a thickly textured performance of cultural nationalism. If, in his "Letter from Birmingham Jail," Martin Luther King Jr. described the untrammeled dignity of the downtrodden in terms of Christian salvation while Malcolm X was promoting the redemptive power of Black Muslim separatism, they each by the time of their deaths spoke the secular language of economic and political justice based on democratic principles. If, for example, Baraka entered the 1960s a restless black bohemian and by mid-decade was an incendiary black nationalist, he exited it headed toward an embrace of international socialism that was no less informed by unstinting revolutionary fervor and a self-consciously "black" disposition than was his Black Arts persona. The Revolution is indeed change, and so, too, our visions of the Black Arts movement will continue to revolve as its reverberations remain felt in the ongoing expression of African American experience.

MARI EVANS
b. 1923

orn in Toledo, Ohio, Mari Evans is one of the most energetic and respected
poets of the Black Arts movement. The eloquent simplicity of her lyrics perfectly complements the directness of her themes. She writes preeminently of
loss—a lost Africa, lost love, failed relationships between black women and black
men. But she is also a blues philosopher insofar as she feels that such losses summon from us the courage to struggle, to continue in the face of adversity and pain.
She works with the themes of African liberation and comes, eventually, to embrace
Africa and the Third World as ideal subjects.

After attending college at the University of Toledo, Evans established her credentials in theater, media production, and the literary arts. Always an aspiring writer,
she also had ambitions as a teacher and scholar. Her various posts as a professor of
literature and creative writing have carried her from Indiana University to Northwestern University and the State University of New York at Albany. She has served
as a visiting professor at Washington University and Cornell University.

Her television show *The Black Experience,* broadcast in the late 1960s and early
1970s by WTTV in Indianapolis, helped to bring her renown in the African American community and, in turn, helped focus her energy and attention on the unique
problems of the black community. She has written of the show, which she both
produced and directed, that it "attempted to answer the question posed by some
anonymous poet: 'Who will show me myself?'" Since the 1970s, Evans has explored
the language, history, and concerns of the black community in works ranging from
children's books and dramas to collections of poetry and an important, timely
anthology, *Black Women Writers (1950–1980): A Critical Evaluation* (1984).

Her volume *I Am a Black Woman* (1970) links the themes of black enslavement
and impoverishment with that of global oppression. Demands for freedom and justice for blacks in the United States are joined with protest against the imperialistic
oppression of the Vietnamese people and the subjugation of people of color generally. Evans vindicates the lives of the poor, particularly poor black women who work
in white homes as domestics. Such historical figures as Malcolm X and Martin
Luther King Jr. feature prominently in the poems.

One of the volume's most trenchant poems, "Vive Noir!" sharpens these themes
in a voice tinged with racial pride, biblical resonance, and vernacular wit. Infused
with the burning resistance that fueled the Black Arts movement, Evans's poem
salts revolutionary energy with a keen sense of material context and historical
implication. Its subtle tension between an exuberantly defiant "i" and an insistently
confronted "you" shapes politics as a drama of encounter.

Vive Noir![1]

i
am going to rise
en masse[2]
from Inner City

---

1. Long live blackness (French). 2. In a body; as a whole (French).

                                sick   5
                          of newyork ghettos
                          chicago tenements
                    l   a's slums
         weary
                    of exhausted lands   10
                    sagging privies³
                    saying yessuh yessah
                    yesSIR
                    in an assortment
                    of geographical dialects i   15
         have seen my last
         broken down plantation
         even from a
         distance
                          i   20
         will load all my goods
         in '50 Chevy pickups '53
         Fords fly United and '66
         caddys⁴ i
                    have packed in   25
                    the old man and the old lady⁵ and
                    wiped the children's noses
                          I'm tired
                          of hand me downs
                          shut me ups   30
                          pin me ins
                          keep me outs
                          messing me over have
                          just had it
                          baby   35
                    from
               you . . .
         i'm
         gonna spread out
         over America   40
                    intrude
         my proud blackness
         all
               over the place
                    i have wrested wheat fields   45
                    from the forests

                    turned rivers
                    from their courses

                    leveled mountains
                    at a word   50

3. Latrines.   5. That is, male and female partners.
4. Cadillacs.

festooned the land with
bridges
       gemlike
       on filaments of steel
         moved   55
glistening towersofBabel[6] in place
     like blocks
sweated a whole
civilization

     now   60
       i'm
gonna breathe fire
through flaming nostrils BURN
    a place for

       me   65

in the skyscrapers and the
schoolrooms on the green
lawns and the white
beaches
       i'm   70
gonna wear the robes and
sit on the benches
make the rules and make
the arrests say
who can and who   75
can't
       baby you don't stand
       a
       chance
i'm
           80
gonna put black angels
in all the books and a black
Christchild in Mary's arms i'm
gonna make black bunnies black
fairies black santas black   85
nursery rhymes and
       black
ice cream
     i'm
gonna make it a   90
   crime
     to be anything BUT   black
     pass the coppertone[7]

---

6. In the biblical story, after the Great Flood a united humanity designed a tower to reach heaven. Seeing this, God destroyed the tower as an act of human presumption, and the people were scattered from their city, called Babel "because the Lord did there confound the language of all the Earth" (Genesis 11.1–9).

7. Sunscreen developed originally in the 1940s as a cream to darken tans.

gonna make white
a twentyfourhour
lifetime
J.O.B.

      an' when all the coppertone's gone . . . ?

1970

MALCOLM X
(EL-HAJJ MALIK EL-SHABAZZ)
1925–1965

Malcolm X was born Malcolm Little in Omaha, Nebraska, to Louise and Earl Little, a black man who championed the nationalist, back-to-Africa doctrines of Marcus Garvey. After years of threats, Malcolm's father was murdered by white supremacists, and his family came to depend entirely on Malcolm's mother. Under the stress of overwhelming family responsibilities and severely limited finances, Louise Little suffered a nervous breakdown and was placed in a mental asylum. The family came apart.

After a successful middle-school career, Malcolm headed for Boston. There he enjoyed the street life and fell into criminal activity. Moving to New York in the bustling 1940s, he quickly became part of a black urban scene rife with underworld number runners, jazz musicians, masterful hustlers, and budding comedians such as Redd Foxx. Soon engaged in life outside the law, he was later arrested and imprisoned for burglary in Massachusetts at the Charlestown State Prison from 1946 to 1952.

It was in prison that Malcolm underwent a conversion to the doctrines of the Lost-Found Nation of Islam in America and its charismatic leader, Elijah Muhammad. Upon his release from prison, Malcolm became a member of the Nation of Islam (NOI)—popularly known as the Black Muslims. Not surprisingly, given his verbal and oratorical skills, Malcolm soon rose to prominence as the chief spokesperson for Muhammad, serving as assistant minister in the NOI's Number One Temple in Detroit, the founding minister of Boston's temple Number Eleven, and eventually as the leader of Harlem's Temple Number Seven, where he received national recognition as the leading voice of black nationalism. He fell into disfavor with Muhammad, however, when he described the assassination of John F. Kennedy as commensurate with America's traditional history of armed violence. Tensions between Malcolm and Muhammad intensified, and Malcolm eventually recanted his longtime championing of the NOI. In 1964 he traveled to Mecca and then returned home to establish the Organization of Afro-American Unity. Renouncing separatism without relinquishing his withering critique of American racism, Malcolm became an advocate of international socialism and Pan-Africanism while refocusing his religious practice as a Sunni Muslim. In February 1965, he was assassinated at the Audubon Ballroom in Harlem, a murder in which the Black Muslims have long been vaguely and controversially implicated.

Malcolm X's nationalist oratory, sheer magnetism of style, and courage in the face of white power inspired a generation of Black Power adherents, who found in him an exemplary embodiment of the black "manhood" he so eloquently espoused.

A man of exceptional intellectual and rhetorical abilities, Malcolm spoke with particular force for northern urban African Americans who felt themselves ensnared by a complex and inescapable system of oppression. Blending a trenchant critique of American racial history with the wit and verve of vernacular street idioms, Malcolm's voice established a vigorous alternative to the oracular preachings of Martin Luther King Jr., with whom he was often contrasted, though also sometimes subtly aligned.

In his lifetime, Malcolm's reputation was forged largely through a vast number of intricately designed speeches, as well as through his portrayals in journalistic media, which he himself exploited with a masterful sense of timing and presence. But the posthumous publication in 1965 of *The Autobiography of Malcolm X*, co-authored by African American journalist and writer Alex Haley, secured his stature as a major literary figure of the Black Arts era. Borrowing from a variety of narrative forms—from the spiritual autobiography established by St. Augustine and the American conversion narrative developed by seventeenth-century Puritans like Jonathan Edwards, to the cheerier secular self-representation of Benjamin Franklin and the emancipation tale of the African American slave narrative—Malcolm's *Autobiography* takes pains to interrogate the very models through which his persona achieves gradual self-understanding. Indeed, one of the major strategies of his narrative is to invite the reader to enjoy each successive style he adopts and then experience its limits under the pressure of corrective experience. In this way, the reader must remain alert, perpetually adjusting expectation and evaluation, just as the protagonist moves from one "father figure" to another only to learn that he can "trust no one, not even fully myself." We discover with Malcolm himself that his story's inner logic defines his life as a quest for an authentic mode of being, a quest that demands a constant openness to new ideas requiring fresh kinds of expression. In this way, Malcolm has himself become for generations of readers a sometimes paradoxical "model" of self-discovery in service to collective realization and universal justice.

From The Autobiography of Malcolm X

Chapter One

NIGHTMARE

When my mother was pregnant with me, she told me later, a party of hooded Ku Klux Klan[1] riders galloped up to our home in Omaha, Nebraska, one night. Surrounding the house, brandishing their shotguns and rifles, they shouted for my father to come out. My mother went to the front door and opened it. Standing where they could see her pregnant condition, she told them that she was alone with her three small children, and that my father was away, preaching, in Milwaukee. The Klansmen shouted threats and warnings at her that we had better get out of town because "the good Christian white people" were not going to stand for my father's "spreading trouble" among the "good" Negroes of Omaha with the "back to Africa" preachings of Marcus Garvey.[2]

---

1. White supremacist terrorist organization organized in the aftermath of the Civil War, reaching a peak of several million members in the 1920s, the period of Malcolm's childhood.
2. Marcus Mosiah Garvey Jr. (1887–1940), Jamaican-born, self-educated Pan-Africanist and proponent of the black nationalist "Back to Africa" movement, which encouraged African Americans to emigrate to African nations of origin as a means of recovering social and economic power. Garvey patterned elements of his public presentation and rhetorical style on the Roman emperor Marcus Aurelius, adding the latter's name to his own.

My father, the Reverend Earl Little, was a Baptist minister, a dedicated organizer for Marcus Aurelius Garvey's U.N.I.A. (Universal Negro Improvement Association). With the help of such disciples as my father, Garvey, from his headquarters in New York City's Harlem, was raising the banner of black-race purity and exhorting the Negro masses to return to their ancestral African homeland—a cause which had made Garvey the most controversial black man on earth.

Still shouting threats, the Klansmen finally spurred their horses and galloped around the house, shattering every window pane with their gun butts. Then they rode off into the night, their torches flaring, as suddenly as they had come.

My father was enraged when he returned. He decided to wait until I was born—which would be soon—and then the family would move. I am not sure why he made this decision, for he was not a frightened Negro, as most then were, and many still are today. My father was a big, six-foot-four, very black man. He had only one eye. How he had lost the other one I have never known. He was from Reynolds, Georgia, where he had left school after the third or maybe fourth grade. He believed, as did Marcus Garvey, that freedom, independence and self-respect could never be achieved by the Negro in America, and that therefore the Negro should leave America to the white man and return to his African land of origin. Among the reasons my father had decided to risk and dedicate his life to help disseminate this philosophy among his people was that he had seen four of his six brothers die by violence, three of them killed by white men, including one by lynching. What my father could not know then was that of the remaining three, including himself, only one, my Uncle Jim, would die in bed, of natural causes. Northern white police were later to shoot my Uncle Oscar. And my father was finally himself to die by the white man's hands.

It has always been my belief that I, too, will die by violence. I have done all that I can to be prepared.

I was my father's seventh child. He had three children by a previous marriage—Ella, Earl, and Mary, who lived in Boston. He had met and married my mother in Philadelphia, where their first child, my oldest full brother, Wilfred, was born. They moved from Philadelphia to Omaha, where Hilda and then Philbert were born.

I was the next in line. My mother was twenty-eight when I was born on May 19, 1925, in an Omaha hospital. Then we moved to Milwaukee, where Reginald was born. From infancy, he had some kind of hernia condition which was to handicap him physically for the rest of his life.

Louise Little, my mother, who was born in Grenada, in the British West Indies, looked like a white woman. Her father *was* white. She had straight black hair, and her accent did not sound like a Negro's. Of this white father of hers, I know nothing except her shame about it. I remember hearing her say she was glad that she had never seen him. It was, of course, because of him that I got my reddish-brown "mariny" color of skin, and my hair of the same color. I was the lightest child in our family. (Out in the world later on, in Boston and New York, I was among the millions of Negroes who were insane enough to feel that it was some kind of status symbol to be light-complexioned—that one was actually fortunate to be born thus. But, still later, I learned to hate every drop of that white rapist's blood that is in me.)

Our family stayed only briefly in Milwaukee, for my father wanted to find a place where he could raise our own food and perhaps build a business.

The teaching of Marcus Garvey stressed becoming independent of the white man. We went next, for some reason, to Lansing, Michigan. My father bought a house and soon, as had been his pattern, he was doing free-lance Christian preaching in local Negro Baptist churches, and during the week he was roaming about spreading word of Marcus Garvey.

He had begun to lay away savings for the store he had always wanted to own when, as always, some stupid local Uncle Tom[3] Negroes began to funnel stories about his revolutionary beliefs to the local white people. This time, the get-out-of-town threats came from a local hate society called The Black Legion.[4] They wore black robes instead of white. Soon, nearly everywhere my father went, Black Legionnaires were reviling him as an "uppity nigger" for wanting to own a store, for living outside the Lansing Negro district, for spreading unrest and dissension among "the good niggers."

As in Omaha, my mother was pregnant again, this time with my youngest sister. Shortly after Yvonne was born came the nightmare night in 1929, my earliest vivid memory. I remember being suddenly snatched awake into a frightening confusion of pistol shots and shouting and smoke and flames. My father had shouted and shot at the two white men who had set the fire and were running away. Our home was burning down around us. We were lunging and bumping and tumbling all over each other trying to escape. My mother, with the baby in her arms, just made it into the yard before the house crashed in, showering sparks. I remember we were outside in the night in our underwear, crying and yelling our heads off. The white police and firemen came and stood around watching as the house burned down to the ground.

My father prevailed on some friends to clothe and house us temporarily; then he moved us into another house on the outskirts of East Lansing. In those days Negroes weren't allowed after dark in East Lansing proper. There's where Michigan State University is located; I related all of this to an audience of students when I spoke there in January, 1963 (and had the first reunion in a long while with my younger brother, Robert, who was there doing postgraduate studies in psychology). I told them how East Lansing harassed us so much that we had to move again, this time two miles out of town, into the country. This was where my father built for us with his own hands a four-room house. This is where I really begin to remember things—this home where I started to grow up.

After the fire, I remember that my father was called in and questioned about a permit for the pistol with which he had shot at the white men who set the fire. I remember that the police were always dropping by our house, shoving things around, "just checking" or "looking for a gun." The pistol they were looking for—which they never found, and for which they wouldn't issue a permit—was sewed up inside a pillow. My father's .22 rifle and his shotgun, though, were right out in the open; everyone had them for hunting birds and rabbits and other game.

3. Derogatory epithet for black person who dis-plays self-debasing subservience to whites (derived from the title character of Harriet Beecher Stowe's 1852 novel, *Uncle Tom's Cabin*).

4. Splinter group of the KKK active in Michigan in the early twentieth century, with peak mem-bership during the 1930s.

Chapter Four

LAURA

Shorty[5] would take me to groovy, frantic scenes in different chicks' and cats' pads, where with the lights and the juke down mellow, everybody blew gage and juiced back and jumped. I met chicks who were fine as May wine, and cats who were hip to[6] all happenings.

That paragraph is deliberate, of course; it's just to display a bit more of the slang that was used by everyone I respected as "hip" in those days. And in no time at all, I was talking the slang like a lifelong hipster.[7]

Like hundreds of thousands of country-bred Negroes who had come to the Northern black ghetto before me, and have come since, I'd also acquired all the other fashionable ghetto adornments—the zoot suits and conk[8] that I have described, liquor, cigarettes, then reefers[9]—all to erase my embarrassing background. But I still harbored one secret humiliation: I couldn't dance.

I can't remember when it was that I actually learned how—that is to say, I can't recall the specific night or nights. But dancing was the chief action at those "pad parties," so I've no doubt about how and why my initiation into lindy-hopping[1] came about. With alcohol or marijuana lightening my head, and that wild music wailing away on those portable record players, it didn't take long to loosen up the dancing instincts in my African heritage. All I remember is that during some party around this time, when nearly everyone but me was up dancing, some girl grabbed me—they often would take the initiative and grab a partner, for no girl at those parties ever would dream that anyone present couldn't dance—and there I was out on the floor.

I was up in the jostling crowd—and suddenly, unexpectedly, I got the idea. It was as though somebody had clicked on a light. My long-suppressed African instincts broke through, and loose.

Having spent so much time in Mason's[2] white environment, I had always believed and feared that dancing involved a certain order or pattern of specific steps—as dancing *is* done by whites. But here among my own less-inhibited people, I discovered it was simply letting your feet, hands and body spontaneously act out whatever impulses were stirred by the music.

From then on, hardly a party took place without me turning up—inviting myself, if I had to—and lindy-hopping my head off.

I'd always been fast at picking up new things. I made up for lost time now so fast, that soon girls were asking me to dance with them. I worked my partners hard; that's why they liked me so much.

5. Malcolm's first and closest friend in Boston, where he had gone to live with his half-sister Ella Collins.

6. Aware of; "chicks' and cats' pads": men and women's apartments; "juke": jazz or rhythm-and-blues music (of the sort played at a "juke-joint" or roadside inn); "down mellow": at a low volume; "blew gage": smoked marijuana; "juiced back": got drunk; "jumped": danced energetically to swing music.

7. Aficionado of jazz (especially bebop) and its associated lifestyle; "hip": sophisticated, in the manner of a hipster.

8. Chemically straightened hair; "zoot suit": flashy style of dress popular in the 1940s among African American and Latino men, characterized by long jackets, tapered pants, padded shoulders, and wide lapels.

9. Marijuana cigarettes.

1. Dancing in a style that evolved alongside jazz of the 1920s and 1930s; "pad parties": parties hosted at an apartment.

2. Mason, Michigan, where Malcolm was placed in a juvenile home and excelled in a nearly all-white middle school.

When I was at work, up in the Roseland[3] men's room, I just couldn't keep still. My shine rag popped with the rhythm of those great bands rocking the ballroom. White customers on the shine stand, especially, would laugh to see my feet suddenly break loose on their own and cut a few steps. Whites are correct in thinking that black people are natural dancers. Even little kids are—except for those Negroes today who are so "integrated," as I had been, that their instincts are inhibited. You know those "dancing jigaboo"[4] toys that you wind up? Well, I was like a live one—music just wound me up.

By the next dance for the Boston black folk—I remember that Lionel Hampton[5] was coming in to play—I had given my notice to the Roseland's manager.

When I told Ella why I had quit, she laughed aloud: I told her I couldn't find time to shine shoes and dance, too. She was glad, because she had never liked the idea of my working at that no-prestige job. When I told Shorty, he said he'd known I'd soon outgrow it anyway.

Shorty could dance all right himself but, for his own reasons, he never cared about going to the big dances. He loved just the music-making end of it. He practiced his saxophone and listened to records. It astonished me that Shorty didn't care to go and hear the big bands play. He had his alto sax idol, Johnny Hodges, with Duke Ellington's[6] band, but he said he thought too many young musicians were only carbon-copying the big-band names on the same instrument. Anyway, Shorty was really serious about nothing except his music, and about working for the day when he could start his own little group to gig around Boston.

The morning after I quit Roseland, I was down at the men's clothing store bright and early. The salesman checked and found that I'd missed only one weekly payment; I had "A-1" credit. I told him I'd just quit my job, but he said that didn't make any difference; I could miss paying them for a couple of weeks if I had to; he knew I'd get straight.

This time, I studied carefully everything in my size on the racks. And finally I picked out my second zoot. It was a sharkskin gray, with a big, long coat, and pants ballooning out at the knees and then tapering down to cuffs so narrow that I had to take off my shoes to get them on and off. With the salesman urging me on, I got another shirt, and a hat, and new shoes—the kind that were just coming into hipster style; dark orange colored, with paper-thin soles and knob style toes. It all added up to seventy or eighty dollars.

It was such a red-letter day that I even went and got my first barbershop conk. This time it didn't hurt so much, just as Shorty had predicted.

That night, I timed myself to hit Roseland as the thick of the crowd was coming in. In the thronging lobby, I saw some of the real Roxbury[7] hipsters eyeing my zoot, and some fine women were giving me that look. I sauntered up to the men's room for a short drink from the pint in my inside coat-pocket. My replacement was there—a scared, narrow-faced, hungry-looking little brown-skinned fellow just in town from Kansas City. And when he

---

3. The Roseland State Ballroom in downtown Boston, where Malcolm worked as a "shoeshine boy" when he first lived with his half-sister Ella Collins.
4. Disparaging term for black person, possibly a combination of "jib" (jerky dance) and "buga-boo" (something imaginary that instills fear).
5. Jazz vibraphonist and band leader

(1908–2002).
6. Jazz pianist, composer, and band leader (1899–1974); Johnny Hodges (1906–1987), jazz saxophonist known for his solo work in Ellington's band.
7. Boston neighborhood, center of the city's African American community in the 1940s.

recognized me, he couldn't keep down his admiration and wonder. I told him to "keep cool," that he'd soon catch on to the happenings. Everything felt right when I went into the ballroom.

Hamp's[8] band was working, and that big, waxed floor was packed with people lindy-hopping like crazy. I grabbed some girl I'd never seen, and the next thing I knew we were out there lindying away and grinning at each other. It couldn't have been finer.

I'd been lindying previously only in cramped little apartment living rooms, and now I had room to maneuver. Once I really got myself warmed and loosened up, I was snatching partners from among the hundreds of unattached, free-lancing girls along the sidelines—almost every one of them could really dance—and I just about went wild! Hamp's band wailing. I was whirling girls so fast their skirts were snapping. Black girls, brown-skins, high yellows,[9] even a couple of the white girls there. Boosting them over my hips, my shoulders, into the air. Though I wasn't quite sixteen then, I was tall and rawboned and looked like twenty-one; I was also pretty strong for my age. Circling, tap-dancing, I was underneath them when they landed—doing the "flapping eagle," "the kangaroo" and the "split."[1]

After that, I never missed a Roseland lindy-hop as long as I stayed in Boston.

From *Chapter Six*

DETROIT RED

* * *

Every day in Small's Paradise Bar[2] was fascinating to me. And from a Harlem point of view, I couldn't have been in a more educational situation. Some of the ablest of New York's black hustlers took a liking to me, and knowing that I still was green by the terms, soon began in a paternal way to "straighten Red[3] out."

Their methods would be indirect. A dark, businessman-looking West Indian often would sit at one of my tables. One day when I brought his beer, he said, "Red, hold still a minute." He went over me with one of those yellow tape measures, and jotted figures in his notebook. When I came to work the next afternoon, one of the bartenders handed me a package. In it was an expensive, dark blue suit, conservatively cut. The gift was thoughtful, and the message clear.

The bartenders let me know that this customer was one of the top executives of the fabulous Forty Thieves gang.[4] That was the gang of organized boosters, who would deliver, to order, in one day, C.O.D.[5], any kind of garment you desired. You would pay about one-third of the store's price.

8. I.e., Lionel Hampton.
9. Light-skinned African Americans, often in the upper echelon of black social and economic status (sometimes derogatory).
1. Boisterous, athletic dances popular in the era of swing and the Lindy Hop.
2. Legendary speakeasy of the 1920s and 1930s, and one of the three major Harlem nightclubs of the 1940s (along with the Cotton Club and Connie's Inn); Malcolm got a job as a waiter there upon moving to New York in 1943.
3. Malcolm's nickname refers to his "reddish-brown 'mariny' color of skin," which indicated his mixed-race heritage.
4. First organized New York street gang, formed by Irish immigrants in the 1820s on the Lower East Side; splinter groups of various ethnicities continued to operate throughout the 20th century.
5. Cash on delivery.

I heard how they made mass hauls. A well-dressed member of the gang who wouldn't arouse suspicion by his manner would go into a selected store about closing time, hide somewhere, and get locked inside when the store closed. The police patrols would have been timed beforehand. After dark, he'd pack suits in bags, then turn off the burglar alarm, and use the telephone to call a waiting truck and crew. When the truck came, timed with the police patrols, it would be loaded and gone within a few minutes. I later got to know several members of the Forty Thieves.

Plainclothes detectives soon were quietly identified to me, by a nod, a wink. Knowing the law people in the area was elementary for the hustlers, and, like them, in time I would learn to sense the presence of any police types. In late 1942, each of the military services had their civilian-dress eyes and ears picking up anything of interest to them, such as hustles being used to avoid the draft, or who hadn't registered, or hustles that were being worked on servicemen.

Longshoremen, or fences[6] for them, would come into the bars selling guns, cameras, perfumes, watches, and the like, stolen from the shipping docks. These Negroes got what white-longshoreman thievery left over. Merchant marine sailors often brought in foreign items, bargains, and the best marijuana cigarettes to be had were made of the *gunja* and *kisca*[7] that merchant sailors smuggled in from Africa and Persia.

In the daytime, whites were given a guarded treatment. Whites who came at night got a better reception; the several Harlem nightclubs they patronized were geared to entertain and jive[8] the night white crowd to get their money.

And with so many law agencies guarding the "morals" of servicemen, any of them that came in, and a lot did, were given what they asked for, and were spoken to if they spoke, and that was all, unless someone knew them as natives of Harlem.

What I was learning was the hustling society's first rule; that you never trusted anyone outside of your own close-mouthed circle, and that you selected with time and care before you made any intimates even among these.

*　　*　　*

There was a big, fat pimp we called "Dollarbill." He loved to flash his "Kansas City roll," probably fifty one-dollar bills folded with a twenty on the inside and a one-hundred dollar bill on the outside. We always wondered what Dollarbill would do if someone ever stole his hundred-dollar "cover."

A man who, in his prime, could have stolen Dollarbill's whole roll, blindfolded, was threadbare, comic old "Fewclothes." Fewclothes had been one of the best pickpockets in Harlem, back when the white people swarmed up every night in the 1920s, but then during the Depression, he had contracted a bad case of arthritis in his hands. His finger joints were knotted and gnarled so that it made people uncomfortable to look at them. Rain, sleet, or snow, every afternoon, about six, Fewclothes would be at Small's, telling tall tales about the old days, and it was one of the day's rituals for one or another regular customer to ask the bartender to give him drinks, and me to feed him.

6. Receivers of stolen goods.
7. Persian marijuana; "gunja": variant of *ganja*,

term for marijuana of Sanskrit origin.
8. Deceive or entertain with clever banter.

My heart goes out to all of us who in those afternoons at Small's enacted our scene with Fewclothes. I wish you could have seen him, pleasantly "high" with drinks, take his seat with dignity—no begging, not on anybody's Welfare—and open his napkin, and study the day's menu that I gave him, and place his order. I'd tell the cooks it was Fewclothes and he'd get the best in the house. I'd go back and serve it as though he were a millionaire.

Many times since, I have thought about it, and what it really meant. In one sense, we were huddled in there, bonded together in seeking security and warmth and comfort from each other, and we didn't know it. All of us—who might have probed space, or cured cancer, or built industries— were, instead, black victims of the white man's American social system. In another sense, the tragedy of the once master pickpocket made him, for those brother old-timer hustlers a "there but for the grace of God" symbol. To wolves who still were able to catch some rabbits, it had meaning that an old wolf who had lost his fangs was still eating.

Chapter Eleven

SAVED

I did write to Elijah Muhammad.[9] He lived in Chicago at that time, at 6116 South Michigan Avenue. At least twenty-five times I must have written that first one-page letter to him, over and over. I was trying to make it both legible and understandable. I practically couldn't read my handwriting myself; it shames even to remember it. My spelling and my grammar were as bad, if not worse. Anyway, as well as I could express it, I said I had been told about him by my brothers and sisters, and I apologized for my poor letter.

Mr. Muhammad sent me a typed reply. It had an all but electrical effect upon me to see the signature of the "Messenger of Allah." After he welcomed me into the "true knowledge," he gave me something to think about. The black prisoner, he said, symbolized white society's crime of keeping black men oppressed and deprived and ignorant, and unable to get decent jobs, turning them into criminals.

He told me to have courage. He even enclosed some money for me, a five-dollar bill. Mr. Muhammad sends money all over the country to prison inmates who write to him, probably to this day.

Regularly my family wrote to me, "Turn to Allah . . . pray to the East."[1]

The hardest test I ever faced in my life was praying. You understand. My comprehending, my believing the teachings of Mr. Muhammad had only required my mind's saying to me, "That's right!" or "I never thought of that."

But bending my knees to pray—that *act*—well, that took me a week.

You know what my life had been. Picking a lock to rob someone's house was the only way my knees had ever been bent before.

I had to force myself to bend my knees. And waves of shame and embarrassment would force me back up.

Of evil to bend its knees, admitting its guilt, to implore the forgiveness of God, is the hardest thing in the world. It's easy for me to see and to say that

9. Muhammad (1897–1975) was the leader of the Nation of Islam during Malcolm's lifetime.
1. For Muslims, the direction of prayer (or Qiblah) is Mecca, which is east from North America.

now. But then, when I was the personification of evil, I was going through it. Again, again, I would force myself back down into the praying-to-Allah posture. When finally I was able to make myself stay down—I didn't know what to say to Allah.

For the next years, I was the nearest thing to a hermit in the Norfolk Prison Colony.[2] I never have been more busy in my life. I still marvel at how swiftly my previous life's thinking pattern slid away from me, like snow off a roof. It is as though someone else I knew of had lived by hustling and crime. I would be startled to catch myself thinking in a remote way of my earlier self as another person.

The things I felt, I was pitifully unable to express in the one-page letter that went every day to Mr. Elijah Muhammad. And I wrote at least one more daily letter, replying to one of my brothers and sisters. Every letter I received from them added something to my knowledge of the teachings of Mr. Muhammad. I would sit for long periods and study his photographs.

I've never been one for inaction. Everything I've ever felt strongly about, I've done something about. I guess that's why, unable to do anything else, I soon began writing to people I had known in the hustling world, such as Sammy the Pimp, John Hughes, the gambling house owner, the thief Jump-steady, and several dope peddlers. I wrote them all about Allah and Islam and Mr. Elijah Muhammad. I had no idea where most of them lived. I addressed their letters in care of the Harlem or Roxbury bars and clubs where I'd known them.

I never got a single reply. The average hustler and criminal was too uneducated to write a letter. I have known many slick, sharp-looking hustlers, who would have you think they had an interest in Wall Street; privately, they would get someone else to read a letter if they received one. Besides, neither would I have replied to anyone writing me something as wild as "the white man is the devil."

What certainly went on the Harlem and Roxbury wires was that Detroit Red[3] was going crazy in stir, or else he was trying some hype to shake up the warden's office.

During the years that I stayed in the Norfolk Prison Colony, never did any official directly say anything to me about those letters, although, of course, they all passed through the prison censorship. I'm sure, however, they monitored what I wrote to add to the files which every state and federal prison keeps on the conversion of Negro inmates by the teachings of Mr. Elijah Muhammad.

But at that time, I felt that the real reason was that the white man knew that he was the devil.

Later on, I even wrote to the Mayor of Boston, to the Governor of Massachusetts, and to Harry S. Truman.[4] They never answered; they probably never even saw my letters. I handscratched to them how the white man's society was responsible for the black man's condition in this wilderness of North America.

It was because of my letters that I happened to stumble upon starting to acquire some kind of a homemade education.

---

2. Malcolm was arrested and convicted of multiple counts of burglary in 1946. He served a total of six years at Norfolk and two other Massachusetts prisons.

3. Malcolm's nickname while a hustler in New York and Boston during the early to mid 1940s.
4. 33rd President of the United States (1884–1972), serving from 1945 to 1953.

I became increasingly frustrated at not being able to express what I wanted to convey in letters that I wrote, especially those to Mr. Elijah Muhammad. In the street, I had been the most articulate hustler out there—I had commanded attention when I said something. But now, trying to write simple English, I not only wasn't articulate, I wasn't even functional. How would I sound writing in slang, the way I would *say* it, something such as, "Look, daddy, let me pull your coat about a cat, Elijah Muhammad—"

Many who today hear me somewhere in person, or on television, or those who read something I've said, will think I went to school far beyond the eighth grade. This impression is due entirely to my prison studies.

It had really begun back in the Charlestown Prison, when Bimbi[5] first made me feel envy of his stock of knowledge. Bimbi had always taken charge of any conversations he was in, and I had tried to emulate him. But every book I picked up had few sentences which didn't contain anywhere from one to nearly all of the words that might as well have been in Chinese. When I just skipped those words, of course, I really ended up with little idea of what the book said. So I had come to the Norfolk Prison Colony still going through only book-reading motions. Pretty soon, I would have quit even these motions, unless I had received the motivation that I did.

I saw that the best thing I could do was get hold of a dictionary—to study, to learn some words. I was lucky enough to reason also that I should try to improve my penmanship. It was sad. I couldn't even write in a straight line. It was both ideas together that moved me to request a dictionary along with some tablets and pencils from the Norfolk Prison Colony school.

I spent two days just riffling uncertainly through the dictionary's pages. I'd never realized so many words existed! I didn't know *which* words I needed to learn. Finally, just to start some kind of action, I began copying.

In my slow, painstaking, ragged handwriting, I copied into my tablet everything printed on that first page, down to the punctuation marks.

I believe it took me a day. Then, aloud, I read back, to myself, everything I'd written on the tablet. Over and over, aloud, to myself, I read my own handwriting.

I woke up the next morning, thinking about those words—immensely proud to realize that not only had I written so much at one time, but I'd written words that I never knew were in the world. Moreover, with a little effort, I also could remember what many of these words meant. I reviewed the words whose meanings I didn't remember. Funny thing, from the dictionary's first page right now, that "aardvark" springs to my mind. The dictionary had a picture of it, a long-tailed, long-eared, burrowing African mammal, which lives off termites caught by sticking out its tongue as an anteater does for ants.

I was so fascinated that I went on—I copied the dictionary's next page. And the same experience came when I studied that. With every succeeding page, I also learned of people and places and events from history. Actually the dictionary is like a miniature encyclopedia. Finally the dictionary's A section had filled a whole tablet—and I went on into the B's. That was the way I started copying what eventually became the entire dictionary. It went a lot faster after so much practice helped me to pick up handwriting speed.

---

5. Fellow inmate at Charlestown State Prison in Massachusetts; Bimbi encouraged Malcolm to begin correspondence courses.

Between what I wrote in my tablet, and writing letters, during the rest of my time in prison I would guess I wrote a million words.

I suppose it was inevitable that as my word-base broadened, I could for the first time pick up a book and read and now begin to understand what the book was saying. Anyone who has read a great deal can imagine the new world that opened. Let me tell you something: from then until I left that prison, in every free moment I had, if I was not reading in the library, I was reading on my bunk. You couldn't have gotten me out of books with a wedge. Between Mr. Muhammad's teachings, my correspondence, my visitors—usually Ella and Reginald[6]—and my reading of books, months passed without my even thinking about being imprisoned. In fact, up to then, I never had been so truly free in my life.

The Norfolk Prison Colony's library was in the school building. A variety of classes was taught there by instructors who came from such places as Harvard and Boston universities. The weekly debates between inmate teams were also held in the school building. You would be astonished to know how worked up convict debaters and audiences would get over subjects like "Should Babies Be Fed Milk?"

Available on the prison library's shelves were books on just about every general subject. Much of the big private collection that Parkhurst[7] had willed to the prison was still in crates and boxes in the back of the library—thousands of old books. Some of them looked ancient: covers faded, old-time parchment-looking binding. Parkhurst, I've mentioned, seemed to have been principally interested in history and religion. He had the money and the special interest to have a lot of books that you wouldn't have in general circulation. Any college library would have been lucky to get that collection.

As you can imagine, especially in a prison where there was heavy emphasis on rehabilitation, an inmate was smiled upon if he demonstrated an unusually intense interest in books. There was a sizable number of well-read inmates, especially the popular debaters. Some were said by many to be practically walking encyclopedias. They were almost celebrities. No university would ask any student to devour literature as I did when this new world opened to me, of being able to read and *understand*.

I read more in my room than in the library itself. An inmate who was known to read a lot could check out more than the permitted maximum number of books. I preferred reading in the total isolation of my own room.

When I had progressed to really serious reading, every night at about ten P.M. I would be outraged with the "lights out." It always seemed to catch me right in the middle of something engrossing.

Fortunately, right outside my door was a corridor light that cast a glow into my room. The glow was enough to read by, once my eyes adjusted to it. So when "lights out" came, I would sit on the floor where I could continue reading in that glow.

At one-hour intervals the night guards paced past every room. Each time I heard the approaching footsteps, I jumped into bed and feigned sleep. And as soon as the guard passed, I got back out of bed onto the floor area of that light-glow, where I would read for another fifty-eight minutes—until

6. Malcolm's half-sister and brother; both worked hard to convert him to Islam.
7. Millionaire who left his library to the Norfolk

State Prison. Norfolk was considered a relatively enlightened "intellectuals' prison."

the guard approached again. That went on until three or four every morning. Three or four hours of sleep a night was enough for me. Often in the years in the streets I had slept less than that.

The teachings of Mr. Muhammad stressed how history had been "whitened"—when white men had written history books, the black man simply had been left out. Mr. Muhammad couldn't have said anything that would have struck me much harder. I had never forgotten how when my class, me and all of those whites, had studied seventh-grade United States history back in Mason, the history of the Negro had been covered in one paragraph, and the teacher had gotten a big laugh with his joke, "Negroes' feet are so big that when they walk, they leave a hole in the ground."

This is one reason why Mr. Muhammad's teachings spread so swiftly all over the United States, among *all* Negroes, whether or not they became followers of Mr. Muhammad. The teachings ring true—to every Negro. You can hardly show me a black adult in America—or a white one, for that matter—who knows from the history books anything like the truth about the black man's role. In my own case, once I heard of the "glorious history of the black man," I took special pains to hunt in the library for books that would inform me on details about black history.

I can remember accurately the very first set of books that really impressed me. I have since bought that set of books and I have it at home for my children to read as they grow up. It's called *Wonders of the World*. It's full of pictures of archeological finds, statues that depict, usually, non-European people.

I found books like Will Durant's *Story of Civilization*. I read H. G. Wells' *Outline of History*. *Souls of Black Folk* by W. E. B. Du Bois[8] gave me a glimpse into the black people's history before they came to this country. Carter G. Woodson's *Negro History*[9] opened my eyes about black empires before the black slave was brought to the United States, and the early Negro struggles for freedom.

J. A. Rogers' three volumes of *Sex and Race*[1] told about race-mixing before Christ's time; about Aesop being a black man who told fables; about Egypt's Pharaohs; about the great Coptic Christian Empires; about Ethiopia, the earth's oldest continuous black civilization, as China is the oldest continuous civilization.

Mr. Muhammad's teaching about how the white man had been created led me to *Findings in Genetics* by Gregor Mendel.[2] (The dictionary's G section was where I had learned what "genetics" meant.) I really studied this book by the Austrian monk. Reading it over and over, especially certain sections, helped me to understand that if you started with a black man, a white man could be produced; but starting with a white man, you never could produce a black man—because the white chromosome is recessive.

8. Du Bois's *Souls of Black Folk* (1903) contains a detailed analysis of social and economic relations in the post-Reconstruction South. Will and Ariel Durant's *Story of Civilization* is an eleven-volume treatise published between 1935 and 1975. Wells's *Outline of History, being a plain history of life and mankind*, was published in two volumes in 1920.
9. *The Negro in Our History* was first published in 1927. Woodson, an African American historian, founded the *Journal of Negro History* in 1916.
1. Rogers's three-volume *Sex and Race* (1900) dealt with the subject of race-mixing in the Old and New Worlds.
2. Gregor Johann Mendel (1822–1884), considered the father of modern genetics, arrived at his theories by studying plant hybridization in peas; Mendel discovered the whiteness of the pea's flowers to be a recessive trait.

And since no one disputes that there was but one Original Man, the conclusion is clear.

During the last year or so, in the *New York Times*, Arnold Toynbee[3] used the word "bleached" in describing the white man. His words were: "White (i.e. bleached) human beings of North European origin. . . ." Toynbee also referred to the European geographic area as only a peninsula of Asia. He said there is no such thing as Europe. And if you look at the globe, you will see for yourself that America is only an extension of Asia. (But at the same time Toynbee is among those who have helped to bleach history. He has written that Africa was the only continent that produced no history. He won't write that again. Every day now, the truth is coming to light.)

I never will forget how shocked I was when I began reading about slavery's total horror. It made such an impact upon me that it later became one of my favorite subjects when I became a minister of Mr. Muhammad's. The world's most monstrous crime, the sin and the blood on the white man's hands, are almost impossible to believe. Books like the one by Frederick Olmsted[4] opened my eyes to the horrors suffered when the slave was landed in the United States. The European woman, Fannie Kimball,[5] who had married a Southern white slaveowner, described how human beings were degraded. Of course I read *Uncle Tom's Cabin*.[6] In fact, I believe that's the only novel I have ever read since I started serious reading.

Parkhurst's collection also contained some bound pamphlets of the Abolitionist Anti-Slavery Society of New England. I read descriptions of atrocities, saw those illustrations of black slave women tied up and flogged with whips; of black mothers watching their babies being dragged off, never to be seen by their mothers again; of dogs after slaves, and of the fugitive slave catchers, evil white men with whips and clubs and chains and guns. I read about the slave preacher Nat Turner,[7] who put the fear of God into the white slavemaster. Nat Turner wasn't going around preaching pie-in-the-sky and "non-violent" freedom for the black man. There in Virginia one night in 1831, Nat and seven other slaves started out at his master's home and through the night they went from one plantation "big house" to the next, killing, until by the next morning 57 white people were dead and Nat had about 70 slaves following him. White people, terrified for their lives, fled from their homes, locked themselves up in public buildings, hid in the woods, and some even left the state. A small army of soldiers took two months to catch and hang Nat Turner. Somewhere I have read where Nat Turner's example is said to have inspired John Brown[8] to invade Virginia

3. English historian (1889–1975) who published extensively on world history, with an emphasis on European and Asian histories.
4. Frederick Law Olmsted (1822–1903), antislavery journalist, spent fourteen months traveling throughout the slave states. His observations were recorded in a trilogy: *Journey to the Seaboard Slave States* (1856), *A Journey through Texas* (1857), and *A Journey in the Back Country* (1860). In 1861 Olmsted published *The Cotton Kingdom*, which was based on his three earlier volumes. He is usually remembered as a designer of public parks, including New York City's Central Park.
5. Frances Anne Kemble (1809–1893), British actress and author, spent the winter of 1838–39 at the plantations in Sea Islands, Georgia, of her husband, Pierce Mease Butler. Her diary of that experience, *Journal of a Residence on a*

Georgian Plantation in 1838–39, circulated among abolitionists in manuscript but was not published until 1863.
6. The novel by abolitionist Harriet Beecher Stowe (1811–1896) was first published in 1852.
7. Slave (1800–1831) who led his followers in the most serious slave insurrection of the antebellum South, in Virginia's Southampton County in August 1831. A confession was allegedly obtained from Turner while in prison, and he was hanged on November 11, 1831.
8. Brown (1800–1859) raided Harper's Ferry, a government armory and arsenal, in an attempt to instigate a slave rebellion. The eighteen men who marched with Brown included five blacks. A week after the raid, Brown and four of the surviving men were tried and convicted. Brown was hanged on December 2, 1859.

and attack Harper's Ferry nearly thirty years later, with thirteen white men and five Negroes.

I read Herodotus, "the father of History,"[9] or, rather, I read about him. And I read the histories of various nations, which opened my eyes gradually, then wider and wider, to how the whole world's white men had indeed acted like devils, pillaging and raping and bleeding and draining the whole world's non-white people. I remember, for instance, books such as Will Durant's *The Story of Oriental Civilization*, and Mahatma Gandhi's[1] accounts of the struggle to drive the British out of India.

Book after book showed me how the white man had brought upon the world's black, brown, red, and yellow peoples every variety of the sufferings of exploitation. I saw how since the sixteenth century, the so-called "Christian trader" white man began to ply the seas in his lust for Asian and African empires, and plunder, and power. I read, I saw, how the white man never has gone among the non-white peoples bearing the Cross in the true manner and spirit of Christ's teachings—meek, humble, and Christ-like.

I perceived, as I read, how the collective white man had been actually nothing but a piratical opportunist who used Faustian machinations[2] to make his own Christianity his initial wedge in criminal conquests. First, always "religiously," he branded "heathen" and "pagan" labels upon ancient non-white cultures and civilizations. The stage thus set, he then turned upon his non-white victims his weapons of war.

I read how, entering India—half a *billion* deeply religious brown people—the British white man, by 1759, through promises, trickery and manipulations, controlled much of India through Great Britain's East India Company. The parasitical British administration kept tentacling out to half of the subcontinent. In 1857, some of the desperate people of India finally mutinied—and, excepting the African slave trade, nowhere has history recorded any more unnecessary bestial and ruthless human carnage than the British suppression of the non-white Indian people.

Over 115 million African blacks—close to the 1930s population of the United States—were murdered or enslaved during the slave trade. And I read how when the slave market was glutted, the cannibalistic white powers of Europe next carved up, as their colonies, the richest areas of the black continent. And Europe's chancelleries for the next century played a chess game of naked exploitation and power from Cape Horn to Cairo.[3]

Ten guards and the warden couldn't have torn me out of those books. Not even Elijah Muhammad could have been more eloquent than those books were in providing indisputable proof that the collective white man had acted like a devil in virtually every contact he had with the world's collective non-white man. I listen today to the radio, and watch television, and read the

---

9. Herodotus, 5th-century B.C.E. Greek who introduced the idea of *history*, meaning a record of past events, to Western literature. He was dubbed the Father of History by the Roman orator and statesman Cicero.
1. Gandhi (1869–1948) led India in its long struggle for independence from Britain, which finally came in 1947. He developed his belief in nonviolent protest and religious tolerance while working as a barrister in South Africa in his early years. Gandhi was assassinated in 1948.
2. Immoral schemes. Johann Faust, protagonist of a medieval German legend, was a scholar who

sold his soul to the devil for a limited period of boundless knowledge and pleasure.
3. Refers to the "scramble for Africa," the competition among European nations for control of African colonies during the New Imperialist period between 1881 and the beginning of World War I in 1914. "Cape to Cairo" was the term coined by South African businessman and white supremacist Cecil Rhodes (1853–1902) for the British goal of establishing an unbroken swath of colonies from the Cape of Good Hope at Africa's southernmost tip northward all the way to Egypt.

headlines about the collective white man's fear and tension concerning China. When the white man professes ignorance about why the Chinese hate him so, my mind can't help flashing back to what I read, there in prison, about how the blood forebears of this same white man raped China at a time when China was trusting and helpless. Those original white "Christian traders" sent into China millions of pounds of opium. By 1839, so many of the Chinese were addicts that China's desperate government destroyed twenty thousand chests of opium. The first Opium War was promptly declared by the white man. Imagine! Declaring *war* upon someone who objects to being narcotized! The Chinese were severely beaten, with Chinese-invented gunpowder.

The Treaty of Nanking[4] made China pay the British white man for the destroyed opium; forced open China's major ports to British trade; forced China to abandon Hong Kong; fixed China's import tariffs so low that cheap British articles soon flooded in, maiming China's industrial development.

After a second Opium War, the Tientsin Treaties[5] legalized the ravaging opium trade, legalized a British-French-American control of China's customs. China tried delaying that Treaty's ratification; Peking was looted and burned.

"Kill the foreign white devils!" was the 1901 Chinese war cry in the Boxer Rebellion.[6] Losing again, this time the Chinese were driven from Peking's choicest areas. The vicious, arrogant white man put up the famous signs, "Chinese and dogs not allowed."

Red China[7] after World War II closed its doors to the Western white world. Massive Chinese agricultural, scientific, and industrial efforts are described in a book that *Life* magazine recently published.[8] Some observers inside Red China have reported that the world never has known such a hate-white campaign as is now going on in this non-white country where, present birth-rates continuing, in fifty more years Chinese will be half the earth's population. And it seems that some Chinese chickens will soon come home to roost, with China's recent successful nuclear tests.

Let us face reality. We can see in the United Nations a new world order being shaped, along color lines—an alliance among the non-white nations. America's U.N. Ambassador Adlai Stevenson complained not long ago that in the United Nations "a skin game" was being played.[9] He was right. He was facing reality. A "skin game" *is* being played. But Ambassador Stevenson sounded like Jesse James accusing the marshal of carrying a gun. Because who in the world's history ever has played a worse "skin game" than the white man?

4. Signed on August 28, 1842, marking the end of the First Opium War (1839–42), the first of two violent conflicts between the British Empire and the Chinese Qing Dynasty.
5. Signed in late June 1858, which actually failed to end the Second Opium War (1856–60).
6. Nationalist Chinese uprising against foreign occupation, also known as the Yihetuan Movement (1898–1901).
7. I.e., Communist China, or the People's Republic of China, which came into being in October 1949 by proclamation of Mao Zedong, chairman of the Communist Party of China.
8. Likely refers to January 5, 1959, photo-essay by French photographer Henri Cartier-Bresson (1908–2004), which depicted China's massive effort at social and economic transformation known as the Great Leap Forward (1958–61).
9. Stevenson (1900–1965) accused newly independent African nations of trading on racial grievance in the high-stakes "game" of international politics.

From *Chapter Nineteen*

1965

* * *

I am in agreement one hundred percent with those racists who say that no government laws ever can *force* brotherhood. The only true world solution today is governments guided by true religion—of the spirit. Here in race-torn America, I am convinced that the Islamic religion is desperately needed, particularly by the American black man. The black man needs to reflect that he has been America's most fervent Christian—and where has it gotten him? In fact, in the white man's hands, in the white man's interpretation . . . where has Christianity brought this *world*?

It has brought the non-white two-thirds of the human population to rebellion. Two-thirds of the human population today is telling the one-third minority white man, "Get out!" And the white man is leaving. And as he leaves, we see the non-white peoples returning in a rush to their original religions, which had been labeled "pagan" by the conquering white man. Only one religion—Islam—had the power to stand and fight the white man's Christianity for a *thousand years*! Only Islam could keep white Christianity at bay.

The Africans are returning to Islam and other indigenous religions. The Asians are returning to being Hindus, Buddhists, and Muslims.

As the Christian Crusade once went East, now the Islamic Crusade is going West. With the East—Asia—closed to Christianity, with Africa rapidly being converted to Islam, with Europe rapidly becoming un-Christian, generally today it is accepted that the "Christian" civilization of America—which is propping up the white race around the world—is Christianity's remaining strongest bastion.

Well, if *this* is so—if the so-called "Christianity" now being practiced in America displays the best that world Christianity has left to offer—no one in his right mind should need any much greater proof that very close at hand is the *end* of Christianity.

Are you aware that some Protestant theologians, in their writings, are using the phrase "post-Christian era"[1]—and they mean *now*?

And what is the greatest single reason for this Christian church's failure? It is its failure to combat racism. It is the old "You sow, you reap" story.[2] The Christian church sowed racism—blasphemously; now it reaps racism.

Sunday mornings in this year of grace 1965, imagine the "Christian conscience" of congregations guarded by deacons barring the door to black would-be worshipers, telling them "You can't enter *this* House of God!"

Tell me, if you can, a sadder irony than that St. Augustine, Florida—a city named for the black African saint who saved Catholicism from heresy[3]—was recently the scene of bloody race riots.

I believe that God now is giving the world's so-called "Christian" white society its last opportunity to repent and atone for the crimes of exploiting and enslaving the world's non-white peoples. It is exactly as when God gave

1. A term made current by Gabriel Vahanian (1927–2012) in his 1961 book *The Death of God: The Culture of Our Post-Christian Era.*
2. Galatians 6.7: "Be not deceived: God is not mocked; for whatever a man soweth, that he shall also reap."

3. Augustine of Hippo (354–430), whose concept of the Catholic Church as a "City of God," not an earthly realm, was instrumental in defining the spiritual mission and authority of medieval Christianity.

Pharaoh a chance to repent.[4] But Pharaoh persisted in his refusal to give justice to those whom he oppressed. And, we know, God finally destroyed Pharaoh.

Is white America really sorry for her crimes against the black people? Does white America have the capacity to repent—and to atone? Does the capacity to repent, to atone, exist in a majority, in one-half, in even one-third of American white society?

Many black men, the victims—in fact most black men—would like to be able to forgive, to forget, the crimes.

But most American white people seem not to have it in them to make any serious atonement—to do justice to the black man.

Indeed, how *can* white society atone for enslaving, for raping, for unmanning, for otherwise brutalizing *millions* of human beings, for centuries? What atonement would the God of Justice demand for the robbery of the black people's labor, their lives, their true identities, their culture, their history— and even their human dignity?

A desegregated cup of coffee, a theater, public toilets—the whole range of hypocritical "integration"—these are not atonement.

After a while in America, I returned abroad—and this time, I spent eighteen weeks in the Middle East and Africa.

The world leaders with whom I had private audiences this time included President Gamal Abdel Nasser, of Egypt; President Julius K. Nyerere, of Tanzania; President Nnamoi Azikiwe, of Nigeria; Osagyefo Dr. Kwame Nkrumah, of Ghana; President Sekou Touré, of Guinea; President Jomo Kenyatta, of Kenya; and Prime Minister Dr. Milton Obote, of Uganda.[5]

I also met with religious leaders—African, Arab, Asian, Muslim, and non-Muslim. And in all of these countries, I talked with Afro-Americans and whites of many professions and backgrounds.

An American white ambassador in one African country was Africa's most respected American ambassador: I'm glad to say that this was told to me by one ranking African leader. We talked for an entire afternoon. Based on what I had heard of him, I had to believe him when he told me that as long as he was on the African continent, he never thought in terms of race, that he dealt with human beings, never noticing their color. He said he was more aware of language differences than of color differences. He said that only when he returned to America would he become aware of color differences.

I told him, "What you are telling me is that it isn't the American white *man* who is a racist, but it's the American political, economic, and social *atmosphere* that automatically nourishes a racist psychology in the white man." He agreed.

We both agreed that American society makes it next to impossible for humans to meet in America and not be conscious of their color differences.

---

4. Throughout the Book of Exodus, before each plague is visited by God upon the Egyptians, God sends Moses to Pharoah to ask for the Hebrew slaves' emancipation.
5. Leaders of various African national independence movements in the late 1950s and early 1960s. Gamal Abdel Nasser (1918–1970), second president of modern Egypt, 1956–70; Julius K. Nyerere (1922–1999), first president of Tanzania, 1961–85; Nnamdi Azikiwe (1904–1996),

first president of Nigeria, 1963–66; Osagyego Dr. Kwame Nkrumah (1909–1972), first prime minister and first president of Ghana, 1951–66; Ahmed Séko Touré (1922–1984), first president of an independent Guinea, 1958–84; Jomo Kenyatta (1894–1978), first prime minister and president of Kenya, 1964–78; Milton Obote (1925–2005), first prime minister and president of Uganda, 1962–71.

And we both agreed that if racism could be removed, America could offer a society where rich and poor could truly live like human beings.

That discussion with the ambassador gave me a new insight—one which I like: that the white man is *not* inherently evil, but America's racist society influences him to act evilly. The society has produced and nourishes a psychology which brings out the lowest, most base part of human beings.

* * *

I kept having all kinds of troubles trying to develop the kind of Black Nationalist organization I wanted to build for the American Negro. Why Black Nationalism? Well, in the competitive American society, how can there ever be any white-black solidarity before there is first some black solidarity? If you will remember, in my childhood I had been exposed to the Black Nationalist teachings of Marcus Garvey—which, in fact, I had been told had led to my father's murder. Even when I was a follower of Elijah Muhammad, I had been strongly aware of how the Black Nationalist political, economic and social philosophies had the ability to instill within black men the racial dignity, the incentive, and the confidence that the black race needs today to get up off its knees, and to get on its feet, and get rid of its scars, and to take a stand for itself.

One of the major troubles that I was having in building the organization that I wanted—an all-black organization whose ultimate objective was to help create a society in which there could exist honest white-black brotherhood— was that my earlier public image, my old so-called "Black Muslim" image, kept blocking me. I was trying to gradually reshape that image. I was trying to turn a corner, into a new regard by the public, especially Negroes; I was no less angry than I had been, but at the same time the true brotherhood I had seen in the Holy World[6] had influenced me to recognize that anger can blind human vision.

Every free moment I could find, I did a lot of talking to key people whom I knew around Harlem, and I made a lot of speeches, saying: "True Islam taught me that it takes *all* of the religious, political, economic, psychological, and racial ingredients, or characteristics, to make the Human Family and the Human Society complete.

"Since I learned the *truth* in Mecca, my dearest friends have come to include *all* kinds—some Christians, Jews, Buddhists, Hindus, agnostics, and even atheists! I have friends who are called capitalists, Socialists, and Communists! Some of my friends are moderates, conservatives, extremists—some are even Uncle Toms! My friends today are black, brown, red, yellow, and *white*!"

I said to Harlem street audiences that only when mankind would submit to the One God who created all—only then would mankind even approach the "peace" of which so much *talk* could be heard . . . but toward which so little *action* was seen.

I said that on the American racial level, we had to approach the black man's struggle against the white man's racism as a human problem, that we had to forget hypocritical politics and propaganda. I said that both races, as human beings, had the obligation, the responsibility, of helping to correct

---

6. Malcolm made a life-transforming pilgrimage, the spiritual journey to Mecca (known in Islam as the *Hajj*) in the spring of 1964.

America's human problem. The well-meaning white people, I said, had to combat, actively and directly, the racism in other white people. And the black people had to build within themselves much greater awareness that along with equal rights there had to be the bearing of equal responsibilities.

I knew, better than most Negroes, how many white people truly wanted to see American racial problems solved. I knew that many whites were as frustrated as Negroes. I'll bet I got fifty letters some days from white people. The white people in meeting audiences would throng around me, asking me, after I had addressed them somewhere, "What *can* a sincere white person do?"

When I say that here now, it makes me think about that little co-ed I told you about, the one who flew from her New England college down to New York and came up to me in the Nation of Islam's restaurant in Harlem, and I told her that there was "nothing" she could do. I regret that I told her that. I wish that now I knew her name, or where I could telephone her, or write to her, and tell her what I tell white people now when they present themselves as being sincere, and ask me, one way or another, the same thing that she asked.

The first thing I tell them is that at least where my own particular Black Nationalist organization, the Organization of Afro-American Unity, is concerned, they can't *join* us.[7] I have these very deep feelings that white people who want to join black organizations are really just taking the escapist way to salve their consciences. By visibly hovering near us, they are "proving" that they are "with us." But the hard truth is this *isn't* helping to solve America's racist problem. The Negroes aren't the racists. Where the really sincere white people have got to do their "proving" of themselves is not among the black *victims*, but out on the battle lines of where America's racism really *is*—and that's in their own home communities; America's racism is among their own fellow whites. That's where the sincere whites who really mean to accomplish something have got to work.

* * *

Sometimes, I have dared to dream to myself that one day, history may even say that my voice—which disturbed the white man's smugness, and his arrogance, and his complacency—that my voice helped to save America from a grave, possibly even a fatal catastrophe.

The goal has always been the same, with the approaches to it as different as mine and Dr. Martin Luther King's non-violent marching,[8] that dramatizes the brutality and the evil of the white man against defenseless blacks. And in the racial climate of this country today, it is anybody's guess which of the "extremes" in approach to the black man's problems might *personally* meet a fatal catastrophe first—"non-violent" Dr. King, or so-called "violent" me.

Anything I do today, I regard as urgent. No man is given but so much time to accomplish whatever is his life's work. My life in particular never has

---

7. Modeled on the Organisation of African Unity, founded in 1963 and encountered by Malcolm in his 1964 tour of Africa, the OOAU was founded in June 1964 with a four-pronged program for African American autonomy: Restoration; Reorientation; Education; Economic Security. When asked by a reporter if whites could join the OOAU, Malcolm answered, "Definitely not," then added, "If John Brown were still alive, we might accept him."

8. Martin Luther King Jr. (1929–1968) led several nonviolent public protests in the African American campaign for civil rights in the early 1960s.

stayed fixed in one position for very long. You have seen how throughout my life, I have often known unexpected drastic changes.

I am only facing the facts when I know that any moment of any day, or any night, could bring me death. This is particularly true since the last trip that I made abroad. I have seen the nature of things that are happening, and I have heard things from sources which are reliable.

To speculate about dying doesn't disturb me as it might some people. I never have felt that I would live to become an old man. Even before I was a Muslim—when I was a hustler in the ghetto jungle, and then a criminal in prison, it always stayed on my mind that I would die a violent death. In fact, it runs in my family. My father and most of his brothers died by violence—my father because of what he believed in. To come right down to it, if I take the kind of things in which I believe, then add to that the kind of temperament that I have, plus the one hundred percent dedication I have to whatever I believe in—these are ingredients which make it just about impossible for me to die of old age.

I have given to this book so much of whatever time I have because I feel, and I hope, that if I honestly and fully tell my life's account, read objectively it might prove to be a testimony of some social value.

I think that an objective reader may see how in the society to which I was exposed as a black youth here in America, for me to wind up in a prison was really just about inevitable. It happens to so many thousands of black youth.

I think that an objective reader may see how when I heard "The white man is the devil,"[9] when I played back what had been my own experiences, it was inevitable that I would respond positively; then the next twelve years of my life were devoted and dedicated to propagating that phrase among the black people.

I think, I hope, that the objective reader, in following my life—the life of only one ghetto-created Negro—may gain a better picture and understanding than he has previously had of the black ghettoes which are shaping the lives and the thinking of almost all of the 22 million Negroes who live in America.

Thicker each year in these ghettoes is the kind of teen-ager that I was— with the wrong kinds of heroes, and the wrong kinds of influences. I am not saying that all of them become the kind of parasite that I was. Fortunately, by far most do not. But still, the small fraction who do add up to an annual total of more and more costly, dangerous youthful criminals. The F.B.I. not long ago released a report of a shocking rise in crime each successive year since the end of World War II—ten to twelve percent each year. The report did not say so in so many words, but I am saying that the majority of that crime increase is annually spawned in the black ghettoes which the American racist society permits to exist. In the 1964 "long, hot summer" riots in major cities across the United States,[1] the socially disinherited black ghetto youth were always at the forefront.

In this year, 1965, I am certain that more—and worse—riots are going to erupt, in yet more cities, in spite of the conscience-salving Civil Rights Bill. The reason is that the *cause* of these riots, the racist malignancy in America, has been too long unattended.

---

9. Tenet of the Nation of Islam, propagated in such teachings of Elijah Muhammad as his *Message to the Black Man*.

1. Referring to race riots in Harlem, Jersey City, Philadelphia, and Rochester, New York.

I believe that it would be almost impossible to find anywhere in America a black man who has lived further down in the mud of human society than I have; or a black man who has been any more ignorant than I have been; or a black man who has suffered more anguish during his life than I have. But it is only after the deepest darkness that the greatest light can come; it is only after extreme grief that the greatest joy can come; it is only after slavery and prison that the sweetest appreciation of freedom can come.

For the freedom of my 22 million black brothers and sisters here in America, I do believe that I have fought the best that I knew how, and the best that I could, with the shortcomings that I have had. I know that my shortcomings are many.

My greatest lack has been, I believe, that I don't have the kind of academic education I wish I had been able to get—to have been a lawyer, perhaps. I do believe that I might have made a good lawyer. I have always loved verbal battle, and challenge. You can believe me that if I had the time right now, I would not be one bit ashamed to go back into any New York City public school and start where I left off at the ninth grade, and go on through a degree. Because I don't begin to be academically equipped for so many of the interests that I have. For instance, I love languages. I wish I were an accomplished linguist. I don't know anything more frustrating than to be around people talking something you can't understand. Especially when they are people who look just like you. In Africa, I heard original mother tongues, such as Hausa, and Swahili, being spoken, and there I was standing like some little boy, waiting for someone to tell me what had been said; I never will forget how ignorant I felt.

Aside from the basic African dialects, I would try to learn Chinese, because it looks as if Chinese will be the most powerful political language of the future. And already I have begun studying Arabic, which I think is going to be the most powerful spiritual language of the future.

I would just like to *study*. I mean ranging study, because I have a wide-open mind. I'm interested in almost any subject you can mention. I know this is the reason I have come to really like, as individuals, some of the hosts of radio or television panel programs I have been on, and to respect their minds—because even if they have been almost steadily in disagreement with me on the race issue, they still have kept their minds open and objective about the truths of things happening in this world. Irv Kupcinet in Chicago, and Barry Farber, Barry Gray, and Mike Wallace in New York—people like them.[2] They also let me see that they respected my mind—in a way I know they never realized. The way I knew was that often they would invite my opinion on subjects off the race issue. Sometimes, after the programs, we would sit around and talk about all kinds of things, current events and other things, for an hour or more. You see, most whites, even when they credit a Negro with some intelligence, will still feel that all he can talk about is the race issue; most whites never feel that Negroes can contribute anything to other areas of thought, and ideas. You just notice how rarely you will ever hear whites asking any Negroes what they think about the problem of world health, or the space race to land men on the moon.

---

2. Contemporary white print and broadcast media journalists: Irv Kupcinet (1912–2003); Barry Farber (b. 1930); Barry Gray (1916–1996); Mike Wallace (1918–2012).

Every morning when I wake up, now, I regard it as having another borrowed day. In any city, wherever I go, making speeches, holding meetings of my organization, or attending to other business, black men are watching every move I make, awaiting their chance to kill me. I have said publicly many times that I know that they have their orders. Anyone who chooses not to believe what I am saying doesn't know the Muslims in the Nation of Islam.

But I am also blessed with faithful followers who are, I believe, as dedicated to me as I once was to Mr. Elijah Muhammad. Those who would hunt a man need to remember that a jungle also contains those who hunt the hunters.

I know, too, that I could suddenly die at the hands of some white racists. Or I could die at the hands of some Negro hired by the white man. Or it could be some brainwashed Negro acting on his own idea that by eliminating me he would be helping out the white man, because I talk about the white man the way I do.

Anyway, now, each day I live as if I am already dead, and I tell you what I would like for you to do. When I *am* dead—I say it that way because from the things I *know*, I do not expect to live long enough to read this book in its finished form—I want you to just watch and see if I'm not right in what I say: that the white man, in his press, is going to identify me with "hate."

He will make use of me dead, as he has made use of me alive, as a convenient symbol of "hatred"—and that will help him to escape facing the truth that all I have been doing is holding up a mirror to reflect, to show, the history of unspeakable crimes that his race has committed against my race.

You watch. I will be labeled as, at best, an "irresponsible" black man. I have always felt about this accusation that the black "leader" whom white men consider to be "responsible" is invariably the black "leader" who never gets any results. You only get action as a black man if you are regarded by the white man as "irresponsible." In fact, this much I had learned when I was just a little boy. And since I have been some kind of a "leader" of black people here in the racist society of America, I have been more reassured each time the white man resisted me, or attacked me harder—because each time made me more certain that I was on the right track in the American black man's best interests. The racist white man's opposition automatically made me know that I did offer the black man something worthwhile.

Yes, I have cherished my "demagogue" role. I know that societies often have killed the people who have helped to change those societies. And if I can die having brought any light, having exposed any meaningful truth that will help to destroy the racist cancer that is malignant in the body of America—then, all of the credit is due to Allah. Only the mistakes have been mine.

1964

JOHN ALFRED WILLIAMS
b. 1925

John A. Williams was born in Hinds County, near Jackson, Mississippi. He earned his bachelor's degree in English and Journalism at Syracuse University, from which he later received the Centennial Medal for Outstanding Achievement. During World War II Williams served in the Navy, an experience he later fictionalized in his novel *Captain Blackman* (1972). He has worked for CBS and NBC and for *Newsweek*, *Ebony*, and *Jet* magazines, and has taught at the College of the Virgin Islands, Sarah Lawrence College, the University of California at Santa Barbara, and elsewhere. From 1973 to 1977, he served as distinguished professor of English at the City University of New York, and in 1994 he retired from Rutgers University, where he had served as Paul Robeson Professor of English.

A friend and admirer of Richard Wright and Chester Himes, Williams has produced both romantically plotted popular novels and hard-edged journalistic essays denouncing the pervasiveness of white racism across the globe. His fictional prose is always fast moving and psychologically gripping. During the Black Arts era, Williams was an outspoken and deeply informed sharer of a new vision of the possibilities for black life in the United States, informed by a Pan-African sensibility alert to the fast pace of international change.

Williams has himself been an embattled writer. Indeed, one of the most inexplicable moments of his career came when his 1962 nomination for the prestigious Prix de Rome was rejected by the American Academy of Arts and Letters, a rejection Williams took personally and publicly. This moment finds its fictional reflection in *The Man Who Cried I Am* (1967), a fictionalized account of Wright's life in European exile that teems with tensions born of government conspiracy against black people, especially black writers. This daring and innovative narrative deals specifically with black male writers who are trying to navigate the challenges of identity and politics in an international society that is riddled with histories of colonialism and racism. Max Reddick, the protagonist, is dying of colon cancer while struggling to reconcile social anger and personal angst with his efforts to make sense of a world at the brink of global revolution.

From The Man Who Cried I Am

3

AMSTERDAM

[PICTURE OF THE WRITER]

When Roger Wilkinson opened his door, to Max Reddick he was the picture of the writer as a failure. Max pushed Margrit forward into a dingy flat, and he shook hands with Roger who seemed both surprised and embarrassed by the unannounced visit.

But Roger broke into a smile and said, "Sit down, you folks, if you can find a chair. You lookin' pretty tired, Max. You been down to Paris? For the funeral? Yeah?" He was rustling through some bottles. "Ain't got much here.

A little beer, some Genever."[1] Roger smiled through his reddish beard. "How'd you find me? You see I've moved." He'd always left his places of residence a mystery. "I'm into my thing," he would explain, and vanish, and in Europe, the black artists went along with your wish to be left alone, most of the time. Until you started to make it, then they came back to bug you back into failure. "You should have let me know you were coming," Roger said.

"Ah, well," Max said, accepting a beer. "What's new?"

Roger cleared his throat loudly and glanced around the room. "You know, man, the same old thing. Trying to make it, you know."

Max nodded. Roger had been in Europe a long time. He had written three novels, which he had been unable to sell. Roger was wound up in himself, Max had concluded. Roger for Roger.

"Articles?" Max asked. Roger was one of those writers who, whenever race riots broke out back home, was summoned hastily by the local magazine or newspaper editors to explain what was going on. *"Le célèbre écrivain noir américain Roger Wilkinson explique pourquoi les noirs des États Unis . . ."*[2] With a photo of Roger bearded and pensive, *artistic*, surveying the accompanying three-column picture of rioters.

"Well, they keep me in bread.[3] But here in Holland, man, getting money out of Hans Brinker[4] is like forcing your way into Fort Knox. They tight with the change, man. Tight."

"Yeah-yeah," Max said. He had known Roger back in the States. Then Roger had come to Europe. To be free. He'd returned to New York briefly then back to Europe for good. He knew all the European capitals, having lived in them at one time or another, until he settled in Amsterdam. He would have preferred Scandinavia; the women were the most handsome in Europe. But it was too cold.

"Listen," Max said. "I'm not in town for long. Just came up to see Margrit. Have to get back home."

"You're not going to stay a while, Max? What a drag, man. Really."

"Yeah. Do you know Alfonse Edwards?"

Roger feigned drawing away from an unwholesome object. *"That* cat![5] Well, yes and well, no. I mean I'm not up tight with him; no one is. I see him around when he's in town. That's about all."

"Do you know where he's staying?"

"I hear he's in a hotel. What's happening, Max?"

"I don't know. Margrit tells me he's writing."

Roger drew a dirty fingernail through his beard. His hair was very thick, but no one would mistake him for an African; his complexion was too light. "I *guess* he writes. I've *heard* that he writes. He loads up a car with articles and drives around Europe selling them to papers and magazines. You know, crap all *pre*pared, and about half of it plagiarized. I mean, these people over here just don't know."

"Does he make it, like that?"

---

1. Juniper-flavored alcoholic drink popular in the Netherlands and Belgium, thought since the medieval period to have medicinal effects; also called "Dutch gin."
2. The celebrated black American writer Roger Wilkinson explains why the blacks in the United States . . . (French).

3. Money (slang).
4. Slang for Dutch person (play on the title of the popular novel *Hans Brinker, or the Silver Skates,* written by American author Mary Mapes Dodge [1831–1905] and first published in 1865).
5. Originally, jazz musician; generally, anyone male (slang).

"He must. Always wearing some boss shit and got some fine fox[6] on his arm. He *must* be making it."

"Yeah," Max said.

"—and he eats very well," Roger added.

"Is he a fink?"[7]

"A fink. No, man, he's just got his hype[8] going and it's working. If the government planted a fink, wouldn't they make him to be one of the boys, you know, not sharp,[9] an artist, starving, trying to get all the pussy he can. Now, Edwards, he's just a little bit away from everybody. Uncle Sam don't work that way. In the middle, right in the middle."

Margrit was watching Max. What is the matter with him, she wondered. The hand with which he was holding the beer glass trembled suddenly, and Max casually lowered it to the table. But Margrit had seen it. She wished she could be glad he was ill, but she could not; she had got over the past and had even been pleased to see him again. She never thought she would be. She was still attracted to him; the mystery that seemed to be him when they first met to a substantial extent was still there. Perhaps in a way the reason for that *was* because of that big, ponderously walking Negro who led a column of liberating black Americans through the streets of Groningen.[1] Groningen was a city you left just as soon as you realized that the people in it were more German than Dutch. He had walked, Margrit remembered, with a wide step, and there was a grin on his face and chocolate bars were sticking out from his pockets. She had broken loose from her parents and, with a group of other small children who waved the tiny American flags their parents had kept hidden, had raced into the street. The big black man picked her up and laughed, gave her candy and put her down again. Max had said, once when she talked about that day, "Well, the world starts whirling for different people for different reasons and at different times. I'll thank that guy if I ever see him."

"More beer?" Roger asked. "Man, I'm really sorry I didn't know you were coming. We coulda turned one on."

"Your first book, we'll turn one on. You'll be coming home then, I guess?"

"Yeah, I guess it would be time enough then."

Max thought back to when he had ever thought to quit writing. All the time. Roger never thought about it and should have quit a long time ago. After a while, Max thought, all the talk of writing, all the advice, is nothing if you haven't got it yourself. With Harry, they seldom talked about writing or even other writers. That was mostly because they were always talking about women or The Problem at home.[2] It was also because Harry was secretive with his French and British and American writer friends if they were the good ones. Max never knew just who they were; they would show up at a party, and by the way Harry talked with them Max would know that they had been friends for a long time. Harry didn't really like to share things. Like Roger, still looking very young, but starting to age in a strange, distant sort of way, didn't like to share himself either. And chances were, Max mused, that Roger did have a bottle tucked back somewhere, for a very special piece of ass that he had to impress. He didn't bring the bottle out because

6. Beautiful black girl (slang); "Boss": excellent (slang).
7. Informer (slang).
8. Clever, deceptive self-promotion (slang).
9. Stylishly dressed (slang).
1. In northeastern Netherlands.
2. Reference to the Civil Rights struggle, used by expatriates during the Vietnam War.

he had to have his revenge for the invasion of his privacy. In that privacy, Max knew, he was picking dried snot out of his nose, rubbing it into his pants and thinking hard thoughts on a world that refused to read his works. Mostly, he was feeling sorry for himself, whether as a Negro or a writer, Max didn't know. As a Negro, he hadn't suffered, hadn't Armied in the South, hadn't been hungry, and he had never gone south of Manhattan. Roger's Negro anger was ersatz; ersatz, but useful. If he hadn't been Negro, he would have had no reason on earth to raise his voice, or to want to write.

"Listen," Roger was saying. "Shall we look for Edwards' hotel?"

Max spun the glass between his thumb and forefinger. "Maybe tomorrow."

"But I thought you were leaving, like, *zap!*"

"I have to take care of a few things first. Tomorrow morning I've got something to do and then we'll see."

"Where you staying?" Roger asked, sliding his eyes toward Margrit.

"The American," Max said, rising, catching pain midway up, but shuffling in his step so they wouldn't see.

"That's boss," Roger said. His smile was twisted. "One of these days, baby, one of these days."

"Got to stay with it," Max mumbled.

"See you tomorrow? We can have a taste on the Plein.[3] I'll stop by the hotel, okay?"

"Well, yeah, okay, maybe late in the afternoon." Max started through the door after Margrit, then paused. "None of my business. But I talk to your father pretty often. Scribble a note so I can take it back with me. Something?"

Roger's face became blank, then stiff. He shook his head. Max knew that talk of Roger's father, for some reason, was off limits. "No, man, nothing."

"Okay, Roger," Max said. He reached into his wallet. This cat was just too much. Max thought of all the time he'd wasted with Roger. He found the check. "Catch, baby, he sent you a few bills.[4] With love." Max swung his arm in a soft arc and the check tumbled up out of his hand, twisted once or twice and started its green and white descent to the floor. "He's very sick," Max said, watching the check and Roger's face at the same time. "He doesn't think you're a writer at all. He thinks you're pretending; he thinks you're afraid to go home and take your lumps with the rest of the spades." Roger's hand was snapping at the check now. "Don't call me at the hotel, Roger, I'll call *you*."

"Hey, man," Roger was saying as Max closed the door after him; his last view was that of Roger scrambling around on the floor for the check.

"You were hard on him," Margrit said, holding his arm.

"Screw 'im. Christ, why did I have to wait until now to start telling people the way they are? Look, a cab. I don't feel like walking."

"All right."

They passed a herring stand. Max stopped. "Shall we have eel or the green herring?"

"Whichever you want, Mox."

He shook his head. "Neither." They walked to the cabs parked beneath the trees. They were just down the street from the Anne Frank House,[5] and that

3. Square (Dutch). "Taste": alcoholic drink (slang).
4. Dollars (slang).
5. The house in Amsterdam in which Anne Frank (1929–1945), a Jew, and her family hid during the Nazi occupation. She died in a concentration camp, but her diary survived and was published in 1947.

part of Amsterdam always did strange things to him; it made him sad and it made him angry. It also made him aware of what so easily could be at home.

"Mox, why are you so thin?"

The cab rolled easily over the cobblestones; it passed the couples lingering over the edges of the canals. Max suddenly felt frightened. There would be a billion other nights in Amsterdam as soft as this one, filled with the odor of sea and old bricks and tarred wood pilings; and there would be the smell of food, drifting gently down upon the street from those Vermeer[6] kitchens; there would be young men and young women, unjaded as yet, talking about loving one another.

I don't want to miss it! Max thought, I don't want to miss any of it! I want to live forever and ever and ever and ever . . .

"Mox . . ."

"Oh! That last trip to Africa, I guess. It was kind of rough."

"Thanks for the card." They were at her house now. The cab had stopped. Margrit got out. For a second she waited, then she knew that Max was going on to the hotel. She spoke to the driver in Dutch. "I will see you tomorrow?"

"In the afternoon, Maggie. Shall I meet you in the hotel?"

"What is wrong with the morning?"

"You have to work."

"I would take it off."

"I have something to do. In Leiden."[7]

"Do you want me to go with you?"

She was bending, peering into the cab, and Max could smell her perfume. "Thanks, no. Business."

"Good night, Mox."

"Good night, Maggie."

She closed the door. "American," Max said, and slumped back in the seat, his eyes half closed. The driver nodded. "She telled," he said.

"Okay," Max said. "Fine."

1967

---

6. Jan Vermeer (1632–1675), Dutch painter noted for interior scenes.   7. City in southwestern Netherlands.

MARTIN LUTHER KING JR.
1929–1968

Grandson of a sharecropper and son of a preacher with a sixth-grade education, Martin Luther King Jr. was born in Atlanta, Georgia—a city defined by pervasive prejudice but rife with possibilities for social change. King was tutored in the history of segregation by his mother when as a young boy he found himself perplexed by being forced to separate from white children with whom he played in order to attend an all-black elementary school. Throughout his youth, his family nurtured the intellectual and linguistic skills with which he would eventually combat the sense of injustice he had felt since that first entrance into the public institutions of American life. Precocious and ambitious, King entered Morehouse College at fifteen, though he was a relatively undistinguished student of sociology harboring the hope of pursuing a medical career. But two experiences joined to move King toward a life in the church: his reading of nineteenth-century Transcendentalist Henry David Thoreau's essay *Civil Disobedience*, and his encouragement by the school's president, Benjamin E. Mays, to see the ministry as an ideal means for combating social oppression.

Upon entering Crozer Theological Seminary in Chester, Pennsylvania, King found his calling as a theologian and preacher of uncommon philosophical and oratorical gifts. His intense reading in traditions extending from Plato to Tillich led him eventually to earn a Ph.D. at Boston University, where he developed a theological synthesis of humanism, nonviolence, and "Social Gospel" that would soon be tested and refined by his participation in the fast-developing struggles of the civil rights era. Those struggles were for King not only a quest for a complete realization of American ideals in the form of a fully legitimated black citizenry; they also constituted a spiritual quest to purge Christianity as practiced in modern times of its implication in various forms of human subjugation.

King's "Letter from Birmingham Jail" was written in 1963 while he was serving a jail sentence for participating in demonstrations in Birmingham, Alabama. The eloquent testimony was written formally in response to eight white "liberal" Alabama clergymen who, early in 1963, had collectively drafted an open letter that addressed King's engagement in the civil rights movement. They entreated King to limit his battle for integration to local and federal courts and cautioned him that his peaceful, pacifist resistance could serve to incite further civil unrest and even rioting. King drew from this local provocation a response self-consciously addressed to much wider audiences. Suggesting to his critics that a Christianity lending any sanction to racial oppression and prejudice was morally bankrupt, King authored a text rich in biblical and literary allusion, informed by a mastery of classical rhetoric, and driven to link the cause of African American participation in American democracy to the most venerable traditions of civil disobedience and nonviolent assertions of social justice.

The title of the piece (which was written on scraps of paper provided to King by the jail's black trustees) was chosen to evoke the memory of the apostle Paul, who was jailed many times for the sake of Jesus. In 1956 Dr. King had preached a sermon titled "Paul's Letter to American Christians." The sermon contained most of the points he later made in his own "Letter," including the central tenet that segregation violated America's democratic faith and religious heritage.

"Letter from Birmingham Jail" was instrumental in galvanizing a wide American audience attentive to issues of black civil rights. King himself believed that it was indispensable in helping him and others to conceptualize the 1963 March on Washington and that it influenced the legislation leading up to the 1963 Civil Rights Bill. The letter was widely circulated by the national and international media; not surprisingly, it shook the conscience of its readers.

With the publication of the "Letter from Birmingham Jail" came an enormous outpouring of support for the civil rights struggle from myriad organizations and individuals. Finances were suddenly available, and coalitions of a new type were forged. Soon after absorbing the import of the letter, the leadership of the National Council of Churches urged its thirty-one member denominations to initiate "nationwide organizations against racial discrimination." At the same time, violence by the white supremacist officials of Birmingham against the city's black citizens intensified, culminating in the fateful events of May 3, 1963, when Commissioner of Public Safety Bull Connor turned fire hoses and attack dogs on protesting black youth. Against the background of King's eloquent defense of nonviolent resistance, images of this state violence against youngsters seeking to exercise basic rights proved pivotal in the unfolding drama of the civil rights movement.

Letter from Birmingham Jail

MY DEAR FELLOW CLERGYMEN:[1]

While confined here in the Birmingham city jail, I came across your recent statement calling my present activities "unwise and untimely." Seldom do I pause to answer criticism of my work and ideas. If I sought to answer all the criticisms that cross my desk, my secretaries would have little time for anything other than such correspondence in the course of the day, and I would have no time for constructive work. But since I feel that you are men of genuine good will and that your criticisms are sincerely set forth, I want to try to answer your statement in what I hope will be patient and reasonable terms.

I think I should indicate why I am here in Birmingham, since you have been influenced by the view which argues against "outsiders coming in." I have the honor of serving as president of the Southern Christian Leadership Conference,[2] an organization operating in every southern state, with headquarters in Atlanta, Georgia. We have some eighty-five affiliated organizations across the South, and one of them is the Alabama Christian Movement for Human Rights. Frequently we share staff, educational, and financial resources with our affiliates. Several months ago the affiliate here in Birmingham asked us to be on call to engage in a nonviolent direct-action program if such were deemed necessary. We readily consented, and when the hour came we lived up to our promise. So I, along with several members of my staff, am here because I was invited here. I am here because I have organizational ties here.

But more basically, I am in Birmingham because injustice is here. Just as the prophets of the eighth century B.C.[3] left their villages and carried their "thus saith the Lord" far beyond the boundaries of their home towns, and just as the Apostle Paul left his village of Tarsus and carried the gospel of Jesus Christ to the far corners of the Greco-Roman world, so am I compelled to carry the gospel of freedom beyond my own home town.[4] Like Paul, I must constantly respond to the Macedonian call for aid.[5]

Moreover, I am cognizant of the interrelatedness of all communities and states. I cannot sit idly by in Atlanta and not be concerned about what happens in Birmingham. Injustice anywhere is a threat to justice everywhere. We are caught in an inescapable network of mutuality, tied in a single garment of destiny. Whatever affects one directly, affects all indirectly. Never again can we afford to live with the narrow, provincial "outside agitator" idea. Anyone who lives inside the United States can never be considered an outsider anywhere within its bounds.

You deplore the demonstrations taking place in Birmingham. But your statement, I am sorry to say, fails to express a similar concern for the condi-

---

1. King's letter responds to "A Call for Unity," a public statement issued by eight white clergymen that criticized his involvement in the nonviolent campaign for civil rights then underway in Birmingham.
2. Inspired by the Montgomery bus boycott and originally called the Negro Leadership Conference on Transportation and Nonviolent Organization, the SCLC was formed in January 1957 by sixty African American ministers as a civil rights organization dedicated to nonviolent resistance against racism and segregation. King served as its president from its inception to the time of his assassination in 1968.
3. I.e., Amos, Hosea, Micah, and Isaiah.
4. A native of Tarsus (in modern-day Turkey), the Apostle Paul (c. 5–67 C.E.) made three missionary journeys throughout the ancient world to proclaim the gospel of Jesus Christ.
5. "And a vision appeared to Paul in the night; There stood a man of Macedonia, and prayed him, saying, Come over into Macedonia, and help us." (Acts 16.9).

tions that brought about the demonstrations. I am sure that none of you would want to rest content with the superficial kind of social analysis that deals merely with effects and does not grapple with underlying causes. It is unfortunate that demonstrations are taking place in Birmingham, but it is even more unfortunate that the city's white power structure left the Negro community with no alternative.

In any nonviolent campaign there are four basic steps: collection of the facts to determine whether injustices exist; negotiation; self-purification; and direct action. We have gone through all these steps in Birmingham. There can be no gainsaying the fact that racial injustice engulfs this community. Birmingham is probably the most thoroughly segregated city in the United States. Its ugly record of brutality is widely known. Negroes have experienced grossly unjust treatment in the courts. There have been more unsolved bombings of Negro homes and churches in Birmingham than in any other city in the nation. These are the hard, brutal facts of the case. On the basis of these conditions, Negro leaders sought to negotiate with the city fathers. But the latter consistently refused to engage in good-faith negotiation.

Then, last September, came the opportunity to talk with leaders of Birmingham's economic community. In the course of the negotiations, certain promises were made by the merchants—for example, to remove the stores' humiliating racial signs. On the basis of these promises, the Reverend Fred Shuttlesworth and the leaders of the Alabama Christian Movement for Human Rights[6] agreed to a moratorium on all demonstrations. As the weeks and months went by, we realized that we were the victims of a broken promise. A few signs, briefly removed, returned; the others remained.

As in so many past experiences, our hopes had been blasted, and the shadow of deep disappointment settled upon us. We had no alternative except to prepare for direct action, whereby we would present our very bodies as a means of laying our case before the conscience of the local and the national community. Mindful of the difficulties involved, we decided to undertake a process of self-purification.[7] We began a series of workshops on nonviolence, and we repeatedly asked ourselves: "Are you able to accept blows without retaliating?" "Are you able to endure the ordeal of jail?" We decided to schedule our direct-action program for the Easter season, realizing that except for Christmas, this is the main shopping period of the year. Knowing that a strong economic-withdrawal program[8] would be the by-product of direct action, we felt that this would be the best time to bring pressure to bear on the merchants for the needed change.

Then it occurred to us that Birmingham's mayoral election was coming up in March, and we speedily decided to postpone action until after election day. When we discovered that the Commissioner of Public Safety, Eugene "Bull" Connor,[9] had piled up enough votes to be in the run-off, we decided

6. Civil rights leader and Baptist minister, Shuttlesworth (1922–2011) formed the Alabama Christian Movement for Human Rights (ACMHR) as a response to Circuit Judge Walter B. Jones's banning of NAACP activity in the state of Alabama in 1956. Shuttlesworth served as president of the ACMHR from the organization's inception in 1956 until 1969.
7. A phase of Mohandas Gandhi's doctrine of *Satyagraha*, a method of nonviolent political action designed to achieve justice through direct and peaceful resistance.

8. I.e., a boycott of segregated Birmingham businesses organized during the spring of 1963 to pressure business leaders to offer equal employment opportunities.
9. Theophilus Eugene Connor (1897–1973); as Birmingham commissioner of public safety, Connor ordered police forces to attack civil rights demonstrators with high-pressure water hoses and police dogs, nationally published images of which helped to shift public opinion in support of civil rights legislation.

again to postpone action until the day after the run-off so that the demonstrations could not be used to cloud the issues. Like many others, we wanted to see Mr. Connor defeated, and to this end we endured postponement after postponement. Having aided in this community need, we felt that our direct-action program could be delayed no longer.

You may well ask, "Why direct action? Why sit-ins, marches, and so forth? Isn't negotiation a better path?" You are quite right in calling for negotiation. Indeed, this is the very purpose of direct action. Nonviolent direct action seeks to create such a crisis and foster such a tension that a community which has constantly refused to negotiate is forced to confront the issue. It seeks so to dramatize the issue that it can no longer be ignored. My citing the creation of tension as part of the work of the nonviolent-resister may sound rather shocking. But I must confess that I am not afraid of the word "tension." I have earnestly opposed violent tension, but there is a type of constructive, nonviolent tension which is necessary for growth. Just as Socrates[1] felt that it was necessary to create a tension in the mind so that individuals could rise from the bondage of myths and half-truths to the unfettered realm of creative analysis and objective appraisal, so must we see the need for nonviolent gadflies[2] to create the kind of tension in society that will help men rise from the dark depths of prejudice and racism to the majestic heights of understanding and brotherhood.

The purpose of our direct-action program is to create a situation so crisis-packed that it will inevitably open the door to negotiation. I therefore concur with you in your call for negotiation. Too long has our beloved Southland been bogged down in a tragic effort to live in monologue rather than dialogue.

One of the basic points in your statement is that the action that I and my associates have taken in Birmingham is untimely. Some have asked: "Why didn't you give the new city administration time to act?" The only answer that I can give to this query is that the new Birmingham administration must be prodded about as much as the outgoing one, before it will act. We are sadly mistaken if we feel that the election of Albert Boutwell as mayor will bring the millennium to Birmingham. While Mr. Boutwell is a much more gentle person than Mr. Connor, they are both segregationists, dedicated to maintenance of the status quo. I have hoped that Mr. Boutwell will be reasonable enough to see the futility of massive resistance to desegregation. But he will not see this without pressure from devotees of civil rights. My friends, I must say to you that we have not made a single gain in civil rights without determined legal and nonviolent pressure. Lamentably, it is an historical fact that privileged groups seldom give up their privileges voluntarily. Individuals may see the moral light and voluntarily give up their unjust posture; but, as Reinhold Niebuhr[3] has reminded us, groups tend to be more immoral than individuals.

We know through painful experience that freedom is never voluntarily given by the oppressor; it must be demanded by the oppressed. Frankly, I have yet to engage in a direct-action campaign that was "well timed" in the

1. Ancient Greek philosopher (469–399 B.C.E.) whose thoughts, recorded most notably in dialogues by Plato and Xenophon, shaped philosophy as a liberation of "analysis" from "myth."
2. People who stimulate or annoy by persistent criticism.

3. American Protestant theologian (1892–1971). Niebuhr's concept of Christian realism asserted the necessity of nonviolent action to counteract humanity's inherent sinfulness, citing racial oppression as an example. His work influenced King's own theories of nonviolent resistance.

view of those who have not suffered unduly from the disease of segregation. For years now I have heard the word "Wait!" It rings in the ear of every Negro with piercing familiarity. This "Wait" has almost always meant "Never." We must come to see, with one of our distinguished jurists,[4] that "justice too long delayed is justice denied."

We have waited for more than 340 years[5] for our constitutional and God-given rights. The nations of Asia and Africa are moving with jetlike speed toward gaining political independence, but we still creep at horse-and-buggy pace toward gaining a cup of coffee at a lunch counter.[6] Perhaps it is easy for those who have never felt the stinging darts of segregation to say, "Wait." But when you have seen vicious mobs lynch your mothers and fathers at will and drown your sisters and brothers at whim; when you have seen hate-filled policemen curse, kick, and even kill your black brothers and sisters; when you see the vast majority of your twenty million Negro brothers smothering in an airtight cage of poverty in the midst of an affluent society; when you suddenly find your tongue twisted and your speech stammering as you seek to explain to your six-year-old daughter why she can't go to the public amusement park that has just been advertised on television, and see tears welling up in her eyes when she is told that Funtown is closed to colored children, and see ominous clouds of inferiority beginning to form in her little mental sky, and see her beginning to distort her personality by developing an unconscious bitterness toward white people; when you have to concoct an answer for a five-year-old son who is asking, "Daddy, why do white people treat colored people so mean?"; when you take a cross-country drive and find it necessary to sleep night after night in the uncomfortable corners of your automobile because no motel will accept you; when you are humiliated day in and day out by nagging signs reading "white" and "colored"; when your first name becomes "nigger," your middle name becomes "boy" (however old you are) and your last name becomes "John," and your wife and mother are never given the respected title "Mrs."; when you are harried by day and haunted by night by the fact that you are a Negro, living constantly at tiptoe stance, never quite knowing what to expect next, and are plagued with inner fears and outer resentments; when you are forever fighting a degenerating sense of "nobodiness"—then you will understand why we find it difficult to wait. There comes a time when the cup of endurance runs over,[7] and men are no longer willing to be plunged into the abyss of despair.[8] I hope, sirs, you can understand our legitimate and unavoidable impatience.

You express a great deal of anxiety over our willingness to break laws. This is certainly a legitimate concern. Since we so diligently urge people to obey the Supreme Court's decision of 1954 outlawing segregation in the

4. William Ewart Gladstone (1809–1898), four-time prime minister of the United Kingdom, asserted to the British Parliament that "if we be just men, we shall go forward in the name of truth and right, bearing this in mind—that when the case is proved, and the hour is come, justice delayed is justice denied."
5. In 1619, a Dutch trading ship brought twenty African slaves to Jamestown, Virginia, marking the beginning of slavery in what would become the United States.
6. On February 1, 1960, four black freshmen from the Agricultural and Technical College of North Carolina, an historically black land-grant university, ordered coffee at the "whites only" lunch counter of a Woolworth's store in Greensboro, North Carolina, igniting one of the signal campaigns of the civil rights movement.
7. An allusion to Psalm 23: "Thou preparest a table before me in the presence of mine enemies: thou annointest my head with oil; my cup runneth over" (23.5).
8. An allusion to the description by German Protestant reformer Martin Luther (1483–1548) of his spiritual struggle: "I was myself more than once driven to the very abyss of despair so that I wished I had never been created."

public schools,[9] at first glance it may seem rather paradoxical for us consciously to break laws. One may well ask: "How can you advocate breaking some laws and obeying others?" The answer lies in the fact that there are two types of laws: just and unjust. I would be the first to advocate obeying just laws. One has not only a legal but a moral responsibility to obey just laws. Conversely, one has a moral responsibility to disobey unjust laws. I would agree with St. Augustine[1] that "an unjust law is no law at all."

Now, what is the difference between the two? How does one determine whether a law is just or unjust? A just law is a man-made code that squares with the moral law or the law of God. An unjust law is a code that is out of harmony with the moral law. To put it in the terms of St. Thomas Aquinas: An unjust law is a human law that is not rooted in eternal law and natural law.[2] Any law that uplifts human personality is just. Any law that degrades human personality is unjust. All segregation statutes are unjust because segregation distorts the soul and damages the personality. It gives the segregator a false sense of superiority and the segregated a false sense of inferiority. Segregation, to use the terminology of the Jewish philosopher Martin Buber,[3] substitutes an "I-it" relationship for an "I-thou" relationship and ends up relegating persons to the status of things. Hence segregation is not only politically, economically, and sociologically unsound, it is morally wrong and sinful. Paul Tillich[4] has said that sin is separation. Is not segregation an existential expression of man's tragic separation, his awful estrangement, his terrible sinfulness? Thus it is that I can urge men to obey the 1954 decision of the Supreme Court, for it is morally right; and I can urge them to disobey segregation ordinances, for they are morally wrong.

Let us consider a more concrete example of just and unjust laws. An unjust law is a code that a numerical or power majority group compels a minority group to obey but does not make binding on itself. This is *difference* made legal. By the same token, a just law is a code that a majority compels a minority to follow and that it is willing to follow itself. This is *sameness* made legal.

Let me give another explanation. A law is unjust if it is inflicted on a minority that, as a result of being denied the right to vote, had no part in enacting or devising the law. Who can say that the legislature of Alabama which set up that state's segregation laws was democratically elected? Throughout Alabama all sorts of devious methods are used to prevent Negroes from becoming registered voters, and there are some counties in which, even though Negroes constitute a majority of the population, not a

---

9. That is, *Brown v. Board of Education of Topeka*, in which the Supreme Court ruled that legally mandated racial segregation violated the equal protection clause of the Fourteenth Amendment, and that separate education facilities were inherently unequal, thus overturning the precedent of "separate but equal" sanctioned by *Plessy v. Ferguson* (1896).
1. Augustine of Hippo, early Christian theologian (354–430). King refers more broadly here to the moral and legal theory known as "natural law," which holds that the laws regulating social behavior are derived from the "higher" objective sanction of moral truths innate to human nature.
2. As developed by Christian theologian Thomas Aquinas (1225–1274) in his *Summa Theologiae*, eternal law is the rational plan by which God has

ordered creation, while natural law is the set of universal laws intelligible to human beings through reason or natural inclination.
3. Hasidic Jewish philosopher and Zionist (1878–1965); Buber was born in Vienna but moved to Palestine in 1938 to escape Nazi persecution. His treatise *I and Thou* (1923) argues that human relationships take either of two forms: "I-It" or "I-Thou." In the former, the subject objectifies the other; the latter depends upon intersubjectivity and the recognition of God in the other.
4. German-born American Lutheran theologian (1886–1965). Dismissed from his post as chair of philosophy at Frankfurt for his opposition to the Nazi regime, Tillich came to the United States in 1933. His work develops existentialist philosophy in a Christian theological context.

single Negro is registered. Can any law enacted under such circumstances be considered democratically structured?

Sometimes a law is just on its face and unjust in its application. For instance, I have been arrested on a charge of parading without a permit.[5] Now, there is nothing wrong in having an ordinance which requires a permit for a parade. But such an ordinance becomes unjust when it is used to maintain segregation and to deny citizens the First-Amendment privilege of peaceful assembly and protest.

I hope you are able to see the distinction I am trying to point out. In no sense do I advocate evading or defying the law, as would the rabid segregationist. That would lead to anarchy. One who breaks an unjust law must do so openly, lovingly, and with a willingness to accept the penalty. I submit that an individual who breaks a law that conscience tells him is unjust, and who willingly accepts the penalty of imprisonment in order to arouse the conscience of the community over its injustice, is in reality expressing the highest respect for law.

Of course, there is nothing new about this kind of civil disobedience.[6] It was evidenced sublimely in the refusal of Shadrach, Meshach, and Abednego to obey the laws of Nebuchadnezzar,[7] on the ground that a higher moral law was at stake. It was practiced superbly by the early Christians, who were willing to face hungry lions and the excruciating pain of chopping blocks rather than submit to certain unjust laws of the Roman Empire. To a degree, academic freedom is a reality today because Socrates practiced civil disobedience.[8] In our own nation, the Boston Tea Party represented a massive act of civil disobedience.[9]

We should never forget that everything Adolf Hitler did in Germany was "legal" and everything the Hungarian freedom fighters[1] did in Hungary was "illegal." It was "illegal" to aid and comfort a Jew in Hitler's Germany. Even so, I am sure that, had I lived in Germany at the time, I would have aided and comforted my Jewish brothers. If today I lived in a Communist country where certain principles dear to the Christian faith are suppressed, I would openly advocate disobeying that country's anti-religious laws.

I must make two honest confessions to you, my Christian and Jewish brothers. First, I must confess that over the past few years I have been gravely disappointed with the white moderate. I have almost reached the regrettable conclusion that the Negro's great stumbling block in his stride toward freedom is not the White Citizen's Counciler[2] or the Ku Klux Klanner, but the white moderate, who is more devoted to "order" than to justice; who prefers a negative peace which is the absence of tension to a positive peace which is

5. While helping to lead a series of protests in Albany, Georgia, King was arrested on December 16, 1961, on charges of "parading without a permit" and sidewalk obstruction.
6. Term coined by Henry David Thoreau in an eponymous essay published in 1849.
7. Chapter 3 of the Book of Daniel describes Babylonian King Nebuchadnezzar erecting a large golden idol. In deference to their Jewish faith, Shadrach, Meshach, and Abednego refuse to worship this idol. Enraged, the king orders them to be burned in a fiery furnace, but the men are protected from the flames by the presence of God.
8. The ancient Greek philosopher was tried for corrupting the youth of Athens through his skeptical, questioning manner of teaching. He refused to change his ways, which included acts of civil disobedience, and was condemned to die by drinking the poison hemlock.
9. As a protest against the British Parliament's imposition of a tax on tea imported into the North American colonies, on the night of December 6, 1773, Samuel Adams, Paul Revere, and other colonists disguised themselves as Native Americans, boarded three ships docked in Boston Harbor, and threw its cargo of tea overboard.
1. In the anti-Communist revolution of 1956, which was quickly put down by Soviet forces.
2. I.e., a member of a southern organization formed to combat the implementation of the *Brown v. the Board of Education* decision on the integration of schools.

the presence of justice; who constantly says, "I agree with you in the goal you seek, but I cannot agree with your methods of direct action"; who paternalistically believes he can set the timetable for another man's freedom; who lives by a mythical concept of time and who constantly advises the Negro to wait for a "more convenient season." Shallow understanding from people of good will is more frustrating than absolute misunderstanding from people of ill will. Lukewarm acceptance is much more bewildering than outright rejection.

I had hoped that the white moderate would understand that law and order exist for the purpose of establishing justice and that when they fail in this purpose they become the dangerously structured dams that block the flow of social progress. I had hoped that the white moderate would understand that the present tension in the South is a necessary phase of the transition from an obnoxious negative peace, in which the Negro passively accepted his unjust plight, to a substantive and positive peace, in which all men will respect the dignity and worth of human personality. Actually, we who engage in nonviolent direct action are not the creators of tension. We merely bring to the surface the hidden tension that is already alive. We bring it out in the open, where it can be seen and dealt with. Like a boil that can never be cured so long as it is covered up but must be opened with all its ugliness to the natural medicines of air and light, injustice must be exposed, with all the tension its exposure creates, to the light of human conscience and the air of national opinion, before it can be cured.

In your statement you assert that our actions, even though peaceful, must be condemned because they precipitate violence. But is this a logical assertion? Isn't this like condemning a robbed man because his possession of money precipitated the evil act of robbery? Isn't this like condemning Socrates because his unswerving commitment to truth and his philosophical inquiries precipitated the act by the misguided populace in which they made him drink hemlock? Isn't this like condemning Jesus because his unique God-consciousness and never-ceasing devotion to God's will precipitated the evil act of crucifixion? We must come to see that, as the federal courts have consistently affirmed, it is wrong to urge an individual to cease his efforts to gain his basic constitutional rights because the quest may precipitate violence. Society must protect the robbed and punish the robber.

I had also hoped that the white moderate would reject the myth concerning time in relation to the struggle for freedom. I have just received a letter from a white brother in Texas. He writes: "All Christians know that the colored people will receive equal rights eventually, but it is possible that you are in too great a religious hurry. It has taken Christianity almost two thousand years to accomplish what it has. The teachings of Christ take time to come to earth." Such an attitude stems from a tragic misconception of time, from the strangely irrational notion that there is something in the very flow of time that will inevitably cure all ills. Actually, time itself is neutral; it can be used either destructively or constructively. More and more I feel that the people of ill will have used time much more effectively than have the people of good will. We will have to repent in this generation not merely for the hateful words and actions of the bad people, but for the appalling silence of the good people. Human progress never rolls in on wheels of inevitability; it comes through the tireless efforts of men willing to be co-workers with God, and without this hard work, time itself becomes an ally of the forces of social stagnation. We must use time creatively, in the knowledge that the time is always ripe to do right. Now is the time to make real the promise of democracy and transform our pending national elegy into a creative psalm of brotherhood. Now is the time to lift our national policy from the quicksand of racial injustice to the solid rock of human dignity.

You speak of our activity in Birmingham as extreme. At first I was rather disappointed that fellow clergymen would see my nonviolent efforts as those of an extremist. I began thinking about the fact that I stand in the middle of two opposing forces in the Negro community. One is a force of complacency, made up in part of Negroes who, as a result of long years of oppression, are so drained of self-respect and a sense of "somebodiness" that they have adjusted to segregation; and in part of a few middle-class Negroes who, because of a degree of academic and economic security and because in some ways they profit by segregation, have become insensitive to the problems of the masses. The other force is one of bitterness and hatred, and it comes perilously close to advocating violence. It is expressed in the various black nationalist groups that are springing up across the nation, the largest and best-known being Elijah Muhammad's Muslim movement.[3] Nourished by the Negro's frustration over the continued existence of racial discrimination, this movement is made up of people who have lost faith in America, who have absolutely repudiated Christianity, and who have concluded that the white man is an incorrigible "devil."

I have tried to stand between these two forces, saying that we need emulate neither the "do-nothingism" of the complacent nor the hatred and despair of the black nationalist. For there is the more excellent way of love and nonviolent protest. I am grateful to God that, through the influence of the Negro church, the way of nonviolence became an integral part of our struggle.

If this philosophy had not emerged, by now many streets of the South would, I am convinced, be flowing with blood. And I am further convinced that if our white brothers dismiss as "rabblerousers" and "outside agitators" those of us who employ nonviolent direct action, and if they refuse to support our nonviolent efforts, millions of Negroes will, out of frustration and despair, seek solace and security in black-nationalist ideologies—a development that would inevitably lead to a frightening racial nightmare.

Oppressed people cannot remain oppressed forever. The yearning for freedom eventually manifests itself, and that is what has happened to the American Negro. Something within has reminded him of his birthright of freedom, and something without has reminded him that it can be gained. Consciously or unconsciously, he has been caught up by the *Zeitgeist*,[4] and with his black brothers of Africa and his brown and yellow brothers of Asia, South America, and the Caribbean, the United States Negro is moving with a sense of great urgency toward the promised land[5] of racial justice. If

---

3. I.e., the Nation of Islam, an influential American religious movement based on black nationalism, founded in 1930. Under the leadership of Elijah Muhammad (1897–1975) the organization taught a heterodox brand of Islam that viewed the white race as an evil creation of a sinister black scientist named Yakub. During the period that he served as spokesman for the group, Malcolm X (1925–1965) advocated the Nation of Islam's black separatism as an alternative to

King's nonviolent and integrationist approach to civil rights.
4. The spirit of the times (German).
5. An allusion to the covenant made by God with the Israelites, first given to Abraham (Genesis 15.18–21), renewed to his son Isaac and to Isaac's son Jacob (Genesis 28.13), and expanded to their descendants after Moses led the Exodus out of Egypt (Deuteronomy 1.8).

one recognizes this vital urge that has engulfed the Negro community, one should readily understand why public demonstrations are taking place. The Negro has many pent-up resentments and latent frustrations, and he must release them. So let him march; let him make prayer pilgrimages to the city hall; let him go on freedom rides—and try to understand why he must do so. If his repressed emotions are not released in nonviolent ways, they will seek expression through violence; this is not a threat but a fact of history. So I have not said to my people, "Get rid of your discontent." Rather, I have tried to say that this normal and healthy discontent can be channeled into the creative outlet of nonviolent direct action. And now this approach is being termed extremist.

But though I was initially disappointed at being categorized as an extremist, as I continued to think about the matter I gradually gained a measure of satisfaction from the label. Was not Jesus an extremist for love: "Love your enemies, bless them that curse you, do good to them that hate you, and pray for them which despitefully use you, and persecute you."[6] Was not Amos an extremist for justice: "Let justice roll down like waters and righteousness like an ever-flowing stream."[7] Was not Paul an extremist for the Christian gospel: "I bear in my body the marks of the Lord Jesus."[8] Was not Martin Luther an extremist: "Here I stand; I cannot do otherwise, so help me God."[9] And John Bunyan:[1] "I will stay in jail to the end of my days before I make a butchery of my conscience." And Abraham Lincoln: "This nation cannot survive half slave and half free."[2] And Thomas Jefferson: "We hold these truths to be self-evident, that all men are created equal. . . ."[3] So the question is not whether we will be extremists, but what kind of extremists we will be. Will we be extremists for hate or for love? Will we be extremists for the preservation of injustice or for the extension of justice? In that dramatic scene on Calvary's hill three men were crucified.[4] We must never forget that all three were crucified for the same crime—the crime of extremism. Two were extremists for immorality, and thus fell below their environment. The other, Jesus Christ, was an extremist for love, truth, and goodness, and thereby rose above his environment. Perhaps the South, the nation, and the world are in dire need of creative extremists.

I had hoped that the white moderate would see this need. Perhaps I was too optimistic; perhaps I expected too much. I suppose I should have realized that few members of the oppressor race can understand the deep groans and passionate yearnings of the oppressed race, and still fewer have the vision to see that injustice must be rooted out by strong, persistent, and determined action. I am thankful, however, that some of our white brothers in the South have grasped the meaning of this social revolution and committed themselves to it. They are still all too few in quantity, but they are big in quality. Some—such as Ralph McGill, Lillian Smith, Harry Golden, James

---

6. Matthew 5.44.

7. Amos 5.24.

8. Galatians 6.17.

9. Apocryphal concluding words to Luther's 1521 defense of his teachings before the Holy Roman Emperor Charles V at the Diet of Worms.

1. English preacher and author (1628–1688), best known for his allegory *The Pilgrim's Progress* (1678, 1684), Bunyan was imprisoned for twelve years in the Bedford jail for his preaching and his refusal to attend the established Anglican service.

2. In his "House Divided" speech, delivered June 16, 1858, at the Republican State Convention in Springfield, Illinois, Lincoln said: "I believe this government cannot endure, permanently half *slave* and half *free*."

3. From the second sentence of the Declaration of Independence (1776).

4. I.e., the site outside ancient Jerusalem of Christ's crucifixion. See Mark 15.22, Matthew 27.33, Luke 23.33, and John 19.17.

McBride Dabbs, Ann Braden, and Sarah Patton Boyle[5]—have written about our struggle in eloquent and prophetic terms. Others have marched with us down nameless streets of the South. They have languished in filthy, roach-infested jails, suffering the abuse and brutality of policemen who view them as "dirty nigger-lovers." Unlike so many of their moderate brothers and sisters, they have recognized the urgency of the moment and sensed the need for powerful "action" antidotes to combat the disease of segregation.

Let me take note of my other major disappointment. I have been so greatly disappointed with the white church and its leadership. Of course, there are some notable exceptions. I am not unmindful of the fact that each of you has taken some significant stands on this issue. I commend you, Reverend Stallings,[6] for your Christian stand on this past Sunday, in welcoming Negroes to your worship service on a nonsegregated basis. I commend the Catholic leaders of this state for integrating Spring Hill College several years ago.[7]

But despite these notable exceptions, I must honestly reiterate that I have been disappointed with the church. I do not say this as one of those negative critics who can always find something wrong with the church. I say this as a minister of the gospel, who loves the church; who was nurtured in its bosom; who has been sustained by its spiritual blessings and who will remain true to it as long as the cord of life shall lengthen.

When I was suddenly catapulted into the leadership of the bus protest in Montgomery, Alabama, a few years ago,[8] I felt we would be supported by the white church. I felt that the white ministers, priests, and rabbis of the South would be among our strongest allies. Instead, some have been outright opponents, refusing to understand the freedom movement and misrepresenting its leaders; all too many others have been more cautious than courageous and have remained silent behind the anesthetizing security of stained-glass windows.

In spite of my shattered dreams, I came to Birmingham with the hope that the white religious leadership of this community would see the justice of our cause and, with deep moral concern, would serve as the channel through which our just grievances could reach the power structure. I had hoped that each of you would understand. But again I have been disappointed.

I have heard numerous southern religious leaders admonish their worshipers to comply with a desegregation decision because it is the law, but I have longed to hear white ministers declare: "Follow this decree because integration is morally right and because the Negro is your brother." In the midst of blatant injustices inflicted upon the Negro, I have watched white churchmen stand on the sideline and mouth pious irrelevancies and sanctimonious

5. Sarah Patton Boyle (1906–1994), Virginia-born author of *The Desegregated Heart* (1962). Ralph Emerson McGill (1898–1969), anti-segregationist, Pulitzer Prize–winning journalist, editor, and publisher of the *Atlanta Constitution*. Lillian Smith (1897–1966), civil rights advocate and novelist who explored issues of race in such works as *Strange Fruit* (1944). Harry Lewis Golden (1902–1981), born Herschel Goldhirsch in Ukraine, American Jewish journalist, biographer, and newspaper publisher. James McBride Dabbs (1896–1970), Presbyterian churchman, farmer, author, professor of English, and campaigner for civil rights. Anne Braden (1924–2006), journalist, author, and civil rights activist.
6. The Reverend Earl Stallings (1916–2006),

pastor of First Baptist Church in Birmingham, was one of the eight white clergymen whose open letter calling for King to limit his struggle for civil rights to the courts prompted King's response. Nevertheless, King singled him out for praise because Stallings, risking the ire of his own congregation, had integrated his Easter service in 1963.
7. A Jesuit college in Mobile, Alabama. In 1954, the college president, Andrew Smith, desegregated the school by enrolling nine African American students, making Spring Hill the first integrated college in the Deep South.
8. The boycott began in December 1955, when Rosa Parks refused to move to the Negro section of a bus.

trivialities. In the midst of a mighty struggle to rid our nation of racial and economic injustice, I have heard many ministers say: "Those are social issues, with which the gospel has no real concern." And I have watched many churches commit themselves to a completely otherworldly religion which makes a strange, un-Biblical distinction between body and soul, between the sacred and the secular.

I have traveled the length and breadth of Alabama, Mississippi, and all the other southern states. On sweltering summer days and crisp autumn mornings I have looked at the South's beautiful churches with their lofty spires pointing heavenward. I have beheld the impressive outlines of her massive religious-education buildings. Over and over I have found myself asking: "What kind of people worship here? Who is their God? Where were their voices when the lips of Governor Barnett dripped with words of interposition and nullification? Where were they when Governor Wallace gave a clarion call for defiance and hatred?[9] Where were their voices of support when bruised and weary Negro men and women decided to rise from the dark dungeons of complacency to the bright hills of creative protest?"

Yes, these questions are still in my mind. In deep disappointment I have wept over the laxity of the church. But be assured that my tears have been tears of love. There can be no deep disappointment where there is not deep love. Yes, I love the church. How could I do otherwise? I am in the rather unique position of being the son, the grandson, and the great-grandson of preachers. Yes, I see the church as the body of Christ.[1] But, oh! How we have blemished and scarred that body through social neglect and through fear of being nonconformists.

There was a time when the church was very powerful—in the time when the early Christians rejoiced at being deemed worthy to suffer for what they believed. In those days the church was not merely a thermometer that recorded the ideas and principles of popular opinion; it was a thermostat that transformed the mores of society. Whenever the early Christians entered a town, the people in power became disturbed and immediately sought to convict the Christians for being "disturbers of the peace" and "outside agitators." But the Christians pressed on, in the conviction that they were "a colony of heaven,"[2] called to obey God rather than man. Small in number, they were big in commitment. They were too God-intoxicated to be "astronomically intimidated." By their effort and example they brought an end to such ancient evils as infanticide and gladiatorial contests.[3]

Things are different now. So often the contemporary church is a weak, ineffectual voice with an uncertain sound. So often it is an arch-defender of the status quo. Far from being disturbed by the presence of the church, the power structure of the average community is consoled by the church's silent—and often even vocal—sanction of things as they are.

---

9. George Wallace (1919–1998), then governor of Alabama, opposed admission of black students to the University of Alabama. In his first inaugural address (1963), Wallace declared: "In the name of the greatest people who ever trod the earth, I draw the line in the dust and toss the gauntlet before the feet of tyranny, and I say segregation now, segregation tomorrow, segregation forever." Ross Barnett (1898–1988), governor of Mississippi, opposed James Meredith's admission to the University of Mississippi.
1. The church is identified as Christ's body throughout the New Testament, notably by Paul in Colossians 1.24: "[I] now rejoice in my sufferings for you, and fill up that which is behind of the afflictions of Christ in my flesh for his body's sake, which is the church."
2. Here King quotes James Moffatt's 1913 translation of the Bible (Philippians 3.20).
3. The Christian Emperor Valentinian I (321–375), outlawed infanticide in 374. Constantine I (272–337) outlawed gladiatorial contests in the Roman Empire in 325.

But the judgment of God is upon the church as never before. If today's church does not recapture the sacrificial spirit of the early church, it will lose its authenticity, forfeit the loyalty of millions, and be dismissed as an irrelevant social club with no meaning for the twentieth century. Every day I meet young people whose disappointment with the church has turned into outright disgust.

Perhaps I have once again been too optimistic. Is organized religion too inextricably bound to the status quo to save our nation and the world? Perhaps I must turn my faith to the inner spiritual church, the church within the church, as the true *ekklesia*[4] and the hope of the world. But again I am thankful to God that some noble souls from the ranks of organized religion have broken loose from the paralyzing chains of conformity and joined us as active partners in the struggle for freedom. They have left their secure congregations and walked the streets of Albany, Georgia, with us.[5] They have gone down the highways of the South on tortuous rides for freedom.[6] Yes, they have gone to jail with us. Some have been dismissed from their churches, have lost the support of their bishops and fellow ministers. But they have acted in the faith that right defeated is stronger than evil triumphant. Their witness has been the spiritual salt[7] that has preserved the true meaning of the gospel in these troubled times. They have carved a tunnel of hope through the dark mountain of disappointment.

I hope the church as a whole will meet the challenge of this decisive hour. But even if the church does not come to the aid of justice, I have no despair about the future. I have no fear about the outcome of our struggle in Birmingham, even if our motives are at present misunderstood. We will reach the goal of freedom in Birmingham and all over the nation, because the goal of America is freedom. Abused and scorned though we may be, our destiny is tied up with America's destiny. Before the pilgrims landed at Plymouth, we were here.[8] Before the pen of Jefferson etched the majestic words of the Declaration of Independence across the pages of history, we were here. For more than two centuries our forebears labored in this country without wages; they made cotton king;[9] they built the homes of their masters while suffering gross injustice and shameful humiliation—and yet out of a bottomless vitality they continued to thrive and develop. If the inexpressible cruelties of slavery could not stop us, the opposition we now face will surely fail. We will win our freedom because the sacred heritage of our nation and the eternal will of God are embodied in our echoing demands.

Before closing I feel impelled to mention one other point in your statement that has troubled me profoundly. You warmly commended the Birmingham police force for keeping "order" and "preventing violence." I doubt that you would have so warmly commended the police force if you had seen its dogs

---

4. The Greek New Testament word for the Christian church.
5. Reference to the protests of the Albany Movement (1961–62).
6. Reference to the Freedom Rides, initiated by the Congress of Racial Equality (CORE) in the late spring of 1961 as a challenge to segregated interstate travel, which persisted in the South despite its being banned by the Supreme Court. Both white and black volunteers participated by integrating Trailways and Greyhound bus lines on journeys from Washington, D.C., to an intended destination of Louisiana. Facing assault, fire-bombing, and incarceration, the Freedom Riders eventually pressured the Interstate Commerce Commission to commit itself to enforcing the Supreme Court's rulings in 1961.
7. Possible reference to Matthew 5.13: "Ye [the multitudes] are the salt of the earth."
8. The *Mayflower* dropped anchor in Plymouth Harbor on December 16, 1620; slaves were first brought to Jamestown, Virginia, in 1619.
9. In the early days of the Civil War, southerners used the slogan "King Cotton" as a rallying cry for secession, asserting that cotton exports would make the new country economically independent of the North.

sinking their teeth into unarmed, nonviolent Negroes. I doubt that you would so quickly commend the policemen if you were to observe their ugly and inhumane treatment of Negroes here in the city jail; if you were to watch them push and curse old Negro women and young Negro girls; if you were to see them slap and kick old Negro men and young boys; if you were to observe them, as they did on two occasions, refuse to give us food because we wanted to sing our grace together. I cannot join you in your praise of the Birmingham police department.

It is true that the police have exercised a degree of discipline in handling the demonstrators. In this sense they have conducted themselves rather "nonviolently" in public. But for what purpose? To preserve the evil system of segregation. Over the past few years I have consistently preached that nonviolence demands that the means we use must be as pure as the ends we seek. I have tried to make clear that it is wrong to use immoral means to attain moral ends. But now I must affirm that it is just as wrong, or perhaps even more so, to use moral means to preserve immoral ends. Perhaps Mr. Connor and his policemen have been rather nonviolent in public, as was Chief Pritchett in Albany, Georgia,[1] but they have used the moral means of nonviolence to maintain the immoral end of racial injustice. As T. S. Eliot has said, "The last temptation is the greatest treason: To do the right deed for the wrong reason."[2]

I wish you had commended the Negro sit-inners and demonstrators of Birmingham for their sublime courage, their willingness to suffer, and their amazing discipline in the midst of great provocation. One day the South will recognize its real heroes. They will be the James Merediths,[3] with the noble sense of purpose that enables them to face jeering and hostile mobs, and with the agonizing loneliness that characterizes the life of the pioneer. They will be old, oppressed, battered Negro women, symbolized in a seventy-two-year-old woman in Montgomery, Alabama,[4] who rose up with a sense of dignity and with her people decided not to ride segregated buses, and who responded with ungrammatical profundity to one who inquired about her weariness: "My feets is tired, but my soul is at rest." They will be the young high school and college students, the young ministers of the gospel and a host of their elders, courageously and nonviolently sitting in at lunch counters and willingly going to jail for conscience' sake. One day the South will know that when these disinherited children of God sat down at lunch counters, they were in reality standing up for what is best in the American dream and for the most sacred values in our Judaeo-Christian heritage, thereby bringing our nation back to those great wells of democracy which were dug deep by the founding fathers in their formulation of the Constitution and the Declaration of Independence.

Never before have I written so long a letter. I'm afraid it is much too long to take your precious time. I can assure you that it would have been much shorter if I had been writing from a comfortable desk, but what else can

---

1. As police chief of Albany, Georgia, Laurie Pritchett (1926–2000) countered the efforts of the Albany Movement (1961–62) by nonviolently arresting more than a thousand demonstrators, including King.
2. From Eliot's verse play *Murder in the Cathedral* (1935).
3. Meredith (b. 1933) was the first African American to enroll at the University of Mississippi (1962). In the face of rioting from white protestors, and with the protection of federal marshals, Meredith graduated from the university in 1963.
4. I.e., Mother Pollard, a participant in the Montgomery bus boycott.

one do when he is alone in a narrow jail cell, other than write long letters, think long thoughts, and pray long prayers?

If I have said anything in this letter that overstates the truth and indicates an unreasonable impatience, I beg you to forgive me. If I have said anything that understates the truth and indicates my having a patience that allows me to settle for anything less than brotherhood, I beg God to forgive me.

I hope this letter finds you strong in the faith. I also hope that circumstances will soon make it possible for me to meet each of you, not as an integrationist or a civil-rights leader but as a fellow clergyman and a Christian brother. Let us all hope that the dark clouds of racial prejudice will soon pass away and the deep fog of misunderstanding will be lifted from our fear-drenched communities, and in some not too distant tomorrow the radiant stars of love and brotherhood will shine over our great nation with all their scintillating beauty.

Yours for the cause of Peace and Brotherhood,

MARTIN LUTHER KING, JR.

1964

RAYMOND PATTERSON
1929–2001

Raymond Patterson, like Langston Hughes, brought a love for African American musical and folk traditions into dialogue with modernist poetic forms. Writing in *Elemental Blues* (a volume of poems composed in the early 1980s), Patterson noted that "the language of the blues is, by tradition, the language of the folk. It is direct, concrete, vivid, terse, 'unlettered,' rich in figures of speech, imagery, allusion, symbolism, irony, and double meaning. It addresses the difficult problems of everyday life as well as the problems of the human condition." Celebrated not only as poet but also as an opera librettist and an educator, Patterson forged complex but lucid verse in the blues tradition, becoming an important contributor to modern black poetry despite his relatively small output.

Born in New York City on December 14, 1929, to John Tollie and Mildred (née Clemens), Patterson remained in the New York area for much of his life. His father was a railroad worker who later opened a delicatessen on Long Island, where he moved the family during Patterson's teenage years. But his boyhood in Harlem made a particularly profound impression on him: "As a child growing up in Harlem during the Depression, I knew the grim spectacle of men in vacant lots, around crackling oil-drum fires, smoke billowing, flames shooting up as from the hell of frustrated ambition." And yet what lasted longest with him was the "raw, loud spectacle of men who not only survive impossible circumstances, but who transcend them in the heroic tradition of the blues." That wresting of being from the painful and potentially fatal edges of non-being forms the core of Patterson's poetic exploration of blackness as a wellspring of human possibility.

In 1951 Patterson received a B.A. from Lincoln University, a historically black college in Pennsylvania (where he also won the award for best undergraduate poem) before serving in the U.S. Army from 1951 to 1953. He went on to receive an M.A.

in English from New York University in 1954. In 1957 he married Boydie Alice Cooke, with whom he had one child, Anna, and with whom he later organized the Black Poets Reading series in New York City.

As with Wallace Stevens, whose poem "Thirteen Ways of Looking at a Blackbird" provided a template for Patterson's celebrated poem "Twenty-Six Ways of Looking at a Blackman," Patterson's outwardly quiet existence concealed a rich, vibrantly poetic inner life. He spent most of his adult years as an educator, first as a professor of English at HBC Benedict College in South Carolina and then as a junior-high English teacher in the New York City public school system. He eventually served as professor of English for over twenty years at the City University of New York, from 1968 to 1992.

During that time he wrote some of his best-known volumes, including *Twenty-Six Ways of Looking at a Blackman and Other Poems* (1969) and *Elemental Blues* (1983), as well as a book-length manuscript poem on the life of Phillis Wheatley. Widely anthologized, Patterson's work was published in leading literary journals such as the *Transatlantic Review*, the *Ohio Review*, and the *Beloit Poetry Journal*, as well as in numerous anthologies, including *The Poetry of the Negro, New Black Voices*, and *The Best American Poetry of 1996*.

Patterson's contributions to contemporary culture extended beyond verse; he was also an executive board member of the Poetry Society of America, the PEN American Center, and the Walt Whitman Birthplace. He founded the Langston Hughes Festival at CUNY, serving as its director from 1973 to 1993. During the Black Arts period, he associated with the writers and artists of the Umbra Workshop on New York's Lower East Side, a group that included such fellow poets as David Henderson, A. B. Spellman, and Ishmael Reed, who shared an experimental approach to vernacular-inspired creativity that forged links between a variously conceived African sensibility and multiple strands of modernist expression, all tinged with a strong commitment to cultural and political activism.

Twenty-Six Ways of Looking at a Blackman

I

On the road we met a blackman,
But no one else.

II

Dreams are reunions. Who has not
On occasion entertained the presence
Of a blackman?   5

III

From brown paper bags[1]
A blackman fills the vacancies of morning
With orange speculations.

---

1. Patterson recalled from his boyhood in Harlem the "sight of a bottle passing from hand to hand in an ancient rite of the alienated and dis- possessed." (Brown paper bags were used to cover liquor bottles, illegal if displayed openly.)

IV

Always I hope to find
The blackman I know,   10
Or one who knows him.[2]

V

Devouring earthly possessions
Is one of a blackman's excesses.
Exaggerating their transiency
Is another.   15

VI

Even this shadow has weight.
A cool heaviness.
Call it a blackman's ghost.

VII

The possibilities of color
Were choices made by the eye   20
Looking inward.
The possibilities of rhythms
For a blackman are predetermined.

VIII

When it had all been unravelled,
The blackman found that it had been   25
Entirely woven of black thread.[3]

IX

Children who loved him
Hid him from the world
By pretending he was a blackman.

X

The fingerprints of a blackman   30
Were on her pillow. Or was it
Her luminous tears?[4]
. . . An absence, or a presence?
Only when it was darker
Would she know.   35

2. Cf. Wallace Stevens's "Thirteen Ways of Looking at a Blackbird," VIII, which the seventh stro-
phe of Patterson's poem also echoes: "I know
noble accents / And lucid, inescapable rhythms; /
But I know, too, / That the blackbird is involved /
In what I know."
3. Possible allusion to the classical goddesses or
"spinners" of Fate, the three Moirae: Clotho
(who spins the thread), Lachesis (who measures
the thread), and Atropos (who cuts the thread);
cf. section XVII.
4. Possible allusion to Shakespeare's *Othello*, in
which the titular character, a Moor, strangles his
white wife, Desdemona, despite her desperate
protestations.

XI

The blackman dipped water
From a well.
And when the well dried,
He dipped cool blackness.

XII

We are told that the seeds   40
Of rainbows are not unlike
A blackman's tear.

XIII

What is more beautiful than black flowers,
Or blackmen in fields
Gathering them?   45
. . . The bride, or the wedding?

XIV

When it was finished,
Some of the carvers of Destiny
Would sigh in relief,
But the blackmen would sigh in intaglio,[5]   50
Having shed vain illusions in mastering the stone.

XV

Affirmation of negatives:
A blackman trembles
That his thoughts run towards darkness.

XVI

The odor of a blackman derives   55
No less from the sweat of his apotheosis,[6]
Than emanations of crushed apples
He carries under his arms.

XVII

If I could imagine the shaping of Fate,
I would think of blackmen   60
Handling the sun.

XVIII

Is it harvest time in the brown fields,
Or is it just a blackman
Singing?

5. A figure or design carved into or beneath the surface of hard metal or stone so that an impression from the design yields an image in relief.

6. Exaltation to divine stature, or deification; quintessence.

XIX

There is the sorrow of blackmen   65
Lost in cities. But who can conceive
Of cities lost in a blackman?

XX

A small boy lifts a seashell
To his listening ear.
It is the blackman again,   70
Whispering his sagas of drowned sailors.

XXI

At the cradle of Justice[7] were found
Three gifts: a pair of scales, a sword,
And a simple cloth. But the Magi[8] had departed.
Several who were with us agreed,   75
One of the givers must have been
A blackman.

XXII

As vines grow towards light,
So roots grow towards darkness.
Back and forth a blackman goes,   80
Gathering the harvest.

XXIII

By moonlight
We tossed our pebbles into the lake
And marveled
At the beauty of concentric sorrows.   85
You thought it was like the troubled heart
Of a blackman,
Because of the dancing light.

XXIV

As the time of our leave taking drew near,
The blackman blessed each of us   90
By pronouncing the names of his children.[9]

7. The Roman poet Claudian (c. 370–404) refers to Rome as "the cradle of justice" in his poem *On the Consulship of Stilicho.*
8. According to the Gospel of Matthew (2.1–12), "wise men from the east"—one of whom (Balthasar), according to legend, was black—visited the infant Jesus shortly after his birth, presenting him with gifts—gold, frankincense, and myrrh. "Scales, sword, cloth": The Roman goddess of Justice (traceable to the Egyptian goddess Maat), was portrayed carrying scales and a sword, and wearing a blindfold.
9. Cf. Numbers 6.27: "And they shall put my name upon the children of Israel; and I will bless them."

XXV

As I remember it,
The only unicorn[1] in the park
Belonged to a blackman
Who went about collecting bits   95
And torn scraps of afternoons.

XXVI

At the center of Being,
Said the blackman,
All is tangential.
Even this laughter, even your tears.   100

1969

1. Legendary wild animal, believed in antiquity to be of Indian origin and generally depicted as a white horse adorned with a single, often black horn on its forehead. In the King James translation of the Old Testament, the unicorn is associated with God's power in liberating Hebrew slaves: "God brought them out of Egypt; he hath as it were the strength of an unicorn" (Numbers 23.22).

ETHERIDGE KNIGHT
1931–1991

Perpetually shifting between limitation and power, imprisonment and emancipation, the poetry and the life of Etheridge Knight address the challenges of black masculine identity in a world of mingled violence and love. For Knight, freedom operates from "mobility and communication" that move the self into community: the black artist, according to Knight, "must hasten his own dissolution as an individual (in the Western sense)—painful though this process may be, having been breast-fed the poison of 'individual experience.'" But within this process of dissolution there is also a continual strengthening of the self through resistance and strenuous self-enactment. Like his life of imprisonment and release, addiction and discipline, Knight's poetry develops through a dialogue between death and resurrection: "I died in Korea from a shrapnel wound and narcotics resurrected me," he wrote; "I died in 1960 from a prison sentence and poetry brought me back to life."

Within this dialogue emerges a story at once harrowing and heartening, taking us from societal penitentiaries to prisons of the mind and body. Born on April 19, 1931, in Corinth, Mississippi, Knight was one of seven children of Etheridge ("Bushie") and Belzora Cozart Knight. In 1939 Knight's father gave up farming to become a laborer on the construction of the Kentucky Dam, which demanded that the Knight family relocate to Paducah, Kentucky, where Knight spent most of his late childhood. His frequent attempts to run away from home led Knight's parents to send him and his siblings back to Mississippi to live with family and stay out of trouble. Yet these measures did not have the intended effect: Knight dropped out of school after the eighth grade and took to the streets. This was by no means the end of Knight's education, though. Always an attentive listener and engaging performer, Knight's poetic sensibility—and his interest in poetry as *spoken* art rooted in various oral traditions—found its first forms in his participation in toasts (long, rhyming, semi-. improvised narratives of urban, mock-heroic events) in bars and poolrooms. But this time was also an emotionally and physically trying one for Knight and, anxious to get off the streets, in 1947 he forged his parents' signatures in order to join the U.S. Army. Knight saw active duty in the Korean War, where he received a shrapnel wound for which he was given morphine, initiating him into a life of struggling with drug addiction.

In 1951 Knight left the army and settled in Indianapolis, where his parents had moved. There his addiction continued unabated. He was later arrested for an armed robbery he carried out to support his drug habit and, in 1960, received a 10- to 25-year indeterminate sentence, which he began serving at Indiana State Reformatory. He was soon transferred to the Indiana State Prison in Michigan City, however, because of his initial rage at being imprisoned.

In 1968 Knight was paroled early for good behavior, but those eight years in prison proved elemental for his development. Having begun "poeting," as he called it, Knight declared in prison: "I will write well. My voice will be heard and I will help my people." The tension between "will" and deferral would come to haunt Knight throughout his life, but his intention to write well and help his people resonates with his poetry's persistent tension between self-assertion and a sense of communal responsibility.

While in prison, Knight received visits from black poets who encouraged his writing (visitors, he later wrote in a volume he edited called *Black Voices from Prison* [1970], "whose love and words cracked these walls"): Gwendolyn Brooks, Dudley Randall, and Sonia Sanchez. When Knight's first volume of poetry, *Poems from Prison* (1968), was made available—a volume unrelenting in its exploration of "black people's pains" and "black people's chains"—it was published by Randall's Broadside Press. That same year he married Sonia Sanchez. Some poets were unsettled by Knight's slim volume. Haki Madhubuti (Don L. Lee), for example, did not approve of Knight's use of "dictionary words" and references to Greek classics. Though the collection of poems commences with the sharply vernacular "Cell Song" and "Hard Rock Returns to Prison . . . ," it ends with a Rilke-like paean to Gwendolyn Brooks, which begins "O Courier on Pegasus. O Daughter of Parnasus! / O Splendid woman of the purple stitch." Yet many fellow poets praised Knight's verse. For Michael Harper, at its best Knight's work is "wise and lyrical, as well as sly, filled with a knowingness" about the "margins" of American society—prison, drug abuse, rural and urban poverty—that are often not represented in American literature. Gwendolyn Brooks, who wrote a poetic preface to *Poems from Prison*, called Knight's poetry "vital," "a major announcement," "certainly male—with formidable austerities, dry grins, and a dignity that is scrupulous even when lenient."

The late 1960s and early-to-mid '70s were busy times for Knight: from 1969 to 1972 he worked as poet in residence at the University of Pittsburgh, the University of Hartford, and Lincoln University. He toured the country giving poetry readings and led Free People's Poetry Workshops, which were open to anyone. In 1972 he received a National Endowment for the Arts Grant, and in 1974 Knight was awarded a Guggenheim Fellowship to study the oral traditions, speech patterns, and music with which he had grown up, performative aspects of the African American experience that he believed are elemental to the "legitimate basis" of black poetry.

Knight's *Belly Song and Other Poems* (1973) is one of the most significant volumes to emerge from the Black Arts movement. An inspiration to all those who felt poetry should be a functional and communal art with a strong oral artist in the middle of the circle, Knight was in particular, as Stephen Henderson notes, a guiding spirit behind the prisoners' rebellion at the Attica (New York) Correctional Facility in 1971. At the same time, Knight eventually widened his vision beyond his initial attempt to articulate an exclusively black aesthetic, seeking to incorporate the concerns of Native Americans, women, and poor whites into his struggles for revolutionary vision. Despite this newfound belief in "love," though, during this period Knight's marriage with Sanchez ended because of his persistent drug addictions, for which he frequently admitted himself to veterans' hospitals for treatment.

We discern such tensions in "Hard Rock Returns to Prison from the Hospital for the Criminal Insane," which juxtaposes the past and present by contrasting images of the "Destroyer" and the "gelded stallion." The idolization of blackness—blackness as rage, as violent resistance—with Hard Rock as the "doer of things" that "we" cannot do, represents Hard Rock as the leader who has the "scars" to prove that the other prisoners must follow him for their own liberation. Yet as we read on and we, too, wrap ourselves "in the cloak of his exploits," it becomes clear that "Hard Rock" is itself a story ("the jewel of a myth"). Against the glorification of Hard Rock as the "doer" is the hardened realization that communal resistance is finally a strenuous but necessary discipline, lest we suffer the threat of being reduced to *nothing*.

The Idea of Ancestry

I

Taped to the wall of my cell are 47 pictures: 47 black
faces: my father, mother, grandmothers (1 dead), grand
fathers (both dead), brothers, sisters, uncles, aunts,
cousins (1st & 2nd), nieces, and nephews. They stare
across the space at me sprawling on my bunk. I know   5
their dark eyes, they know mine. I know their style,
they know mine. I am all of them, they are all of me;
they are farmers, I am a thief, I am me, they are thee.

I have at one time or another been in love with my mother,
1 grandmother, 2 sisters, 2 aunts (1 went to the asylum),   10
and 5 cousins. I am now in love with a 7 yr old niece
(she sends me letters written in large block print, and
her picture is the only one that smiles at me).

I have the same name as 1 grandfather, 3 cousins, 3 nephews,
and 1 uncle. The uncle disappeared when he was 15, just took   15
off and caught a freight (they say). He's discussed each year
when the family has a reunion, he causes uneasiness in
the clan, he is an empty space. My father's mother, who is 93
and who keeps the Family Bible with everybody's birth dates
(and death dates) in it, always mentions him. There is no   20
place in her Bible for "whereabouts unknown."

II

Each Fall the graves of my grandfathers call me, the brown
hills and red gullies[1] of mississippi send out their electric
messages, galvanizing my genes. Last yr / like a salmon quitting
the cold ocean—leaping and bucking up his birthstream / I   25
hitchhiked my way from L.A. with 16 caps[2] in my pocket and a
monkey on my back, and I almost kicked it[3] with the kinfolks.

---

1. Small valleys or gulches.
2. Units of heroin sold on the street to addicts.

3. That is, overcame drug addiction (the "monkey on my back").

I walked barefooted in my grandmother's backyard / I smelled the
old land and the woods / I sipped cornwhiskey from fruit jars
　　with the men /
I flirted with the women / I had a ball till the caps ran out　　　　30
and my habit came down. That night I looked at my grandmother
and split / my guts were screaming for junk[4] / but I was almost
contented / I had almost caught up with me.
　　The next day in Memphis I cracked a croaker's crib[5] for a fix.

This yr there is a gray stone wall damming my stream, and when　　35
the falling leaves stir my genes, I pace my cell or flop on my bunk
and stare at 47 black faces across the space. I am all of them,
they are all of me, I am me, they are thee, and I have no sons[6]
to float in the space between.

　　　　　　　　　　　　　　　　　　　　　　　1968

Hard Rock[1] Returns to Prison from the Hospital for the Criminal Insane

Hard Rock was "known not to take no shit
From nobody," and he had the scars to prove it:
Split purple lips, lumped ears, welts above
His yellow eyes, and one long scar that cut
Across his temple and plowed through a thick　　　　　　5
Canopy of kinky hair.

The WORD was that Hard Rock wasn't a mean nigger
Anymore, that the doctors had bored a hole in his head,
Cut out part of his brain, and shot electricity
Through the rest.[2] When they brought Hard Rock back,　　10
Handcuffed and chained, he was turned loose,
Like a freshly gelded stallion, to try his new status.
And we all waited and watched, like indians at a corral,[3]
To see if the WORD was true.

As we waited we wrapped ourselves in the cloak　　　　15
Of his exploits: "Man, the last time, it took eight
Screws to put him in the Hole."[4] "Yeah, remember when he

4. Narcotics (here, heroin).
5. Home of a drug seller or physician (*croaker* is slang for "doctor").
6. Having been convinced by a woman at the 1975 National Poetry Festival that this line was sexist, Knight replaced "sons" with "children" for the poem's publication in the 1980 volume *Born of a Woman*.
1. When asked if the poem was based on an actual person or event from his prison experience, Knight replied: "Yes. 'Hard Rock' was really seven or eight guys I know who had shock treatment. But it was only one guy I had in mind. Yes, it actually happened." ("Rock" is also slang for "prison.")
2. Refers to a combination of prefrontal lobotomy, in which the connections to and from the anterior parts of the brain are severed, and electro-shock therapy; most commonly practiced from the mid-1940s to the early 1960s, these procedures were thought to alleviate intense anxiety or violent behavior.
3. When the poem was reissued in *Born of a Woman*, Knight emended "indians at a corral" to "like a herd of sheep." Knight explained this revisionary practice in the "Preface" to *Born of a Woman* as integral to his poetic and political project: "I became aware (sometimes I was *made* aware) that I was perpetuating the racism and sexism that is inherent in our language. . . . To perpetuate a lie, an evil, whether through omission or commission is to commit artistic and/or actual suicide."
4. Solitary confinement. "Screws": prison guards.

Smacked the captain with his dinner tray?" "He set
The record for time in the Hole—67 straight days!"
"Ol Hard Rock! man, that's one crazy nigger." 20
And then the jewel of a myth that Hard Rock had once bit
A screw on the thumb and poisoned him with syphilitic spit.

The testing came, to see if Hard Rock was really tame.
A hillbilly called him a black son of a bitch
And didn't lose his teeth, a screw who knew Hard Rock 25
From before shook him down and barked in his face.
And Hard Rock did *nothing*. Just grinned and looked silly,
His eyes empty like knot holes in a fence.

And even after we discovered that it took Hard Rock
Exactly 3 minutes to tell you his first name, 30
We told ourselves that he had just wised up,
Was being cool; but we could not fool ourselves for long,
And we turned away, our eyes on the ground. Crushed.
He had been our Destroyer,[5] the doer of things
We dreamed of doing but could not bring ourselves to do, 35
The fears of years, like a biting whip,
Had cut grooves too deeply across our backs.

1968

Ilu, the Talking Drum[1]

The deadness was threatening us—15 Nigerians and 1
    Mississippi nigger.
It hung heavily, like stones around our necks, pulling us down
to the ground, black arms and legs outflung
on the wide green lawn of the big white house
The deadness was threatening us, the day 5
was dying with the sun, the stillness—
unlike the sweet silence after love / making or
the pulsating quietness of a summer night—
the stillness was skinny and brittle and wrinkled
by the precise people sitting on the wide white porch 10
of the big white house . . .
The darkness was threatening us, menacing . . .
we twisted, turned, shifted positions, picked our noses,
stared at our bare toes, hissed air thru our teeth . . .
Then Tunji,[2] green robes flowing as he rose, 15
strapped on Ilu, the talking drum,
and began:

5. A reference to Ras the Destroyer, a central figure in Rastafarianism; also a charismatic and violent black nationalist character in Ralph Ellison's *Invisible Man* (1952).
1. Iya ilu is a traditional lead drum played by the Yoruba people of southern Nigeria. Figuratively understood as a mother drum (a leader), iya ilu leads, instructs, encourages, and supports other drums in the drum ensemble, which are said to "talk" because adjusting the tension of the drum heads changes their pitch and allows them to mimic human voices.
2. Nigerian percussion master, educator, and social activist Babatunde Olatunji (1927–2003), who in 1965 founded the Olatunji Center for African Culture in Harlem.

kah doom / kah doom-doom / kah doom / kah doom-doom-doom
kah doom / kah doom-doom / kah doom / kah doom-doom-doom
kah doom / kah doom-doom / kah doom / kah doom-doom-doom   20
kah doom / kah doom-doom / kah doom / kah doom-doom-doom

the heart, the heart beats, the heart, the heart beats slow
the heart beats slowly, the heart beats
the blood flows slowly, the blood flows
the blood, the blood flows, the blood, the blood flows slow   25
kah doom / kah doom-doom / kah doom / kah doom-doom-doom
and the day opened to the sound

kah doom / kah doom-doom / kah doom
and our feet moved to the sound of life
kah doom / kah doom-doom / kah doom   30
and we rode the rhythms as one
from Nigeria to Mississippi
and back
kah doom / kah doom-doom / kah doom

1980

ADRIENNE KENNEDY
b. 1931

In a 1977 autobiographical essay, Adrienne Kennedy describes her playwrighting as a gradual process of transmuting scattered images into coherent aesthetic artifacts:

> I see my writing as a growth of images. I think all my plays come out of dreams I had two or three years before; I played around with the images for a long period of time to try to get to the most powerful dreams. . . . I think about things for many years and keep loads of notebooks, with images, dreams, ideas I've jotted down.

Kennedy's dramas themselves become dreamscapes in which embodied images clash with one another as they yearn painfully for stable and intelligible identity. For Kennedy, the stage becomes the place of consciousness itself, rife with conflict, desire, insight, and uncertainty, especially when the violent legacies of racial and sexual experience erupt into nightmares. The results, like aching dreams, are at once beautiful and haunting, inspirational and elusive.

Kennedy's experimental approach in constructing her theatrical vision has resulted in plays that combine hallmarks of Euro-American modernist drama—expressionism (with its emphasis on subjective assertion), surrealism (with its evocation of the unconscious as source of meaning), and absurdism (with its futile quest for meaning in a teasingly familiar but also inexplicable world)—with features of African ritual and African American folk symbolism to create rich, original plays that changed the boundaries for Black Arts performers and artists. In fashioning her dramatic vision, Kennedy uses a range of theatrical devices, including masks, non-traditional music, pagan and Christian imagery, and innovative casting strategies that call into question our commonsense ideas about character, with actors playing multiple roles and roles fragmenting into multiple personas.

Kennedy's unique style, introduced in 1962 with *Funnyhouse of a Negro*, has powerfully influenced conceptions of modern theater, in great measure because it demonstrates the political potential of abstract theatrical language. For her African American contemporaries, Kennedy opened doors to non-realist ideas of key contemporary themes—history's inescapable burdens; the complexity of racial identity when forged in the crucible of slavery; the intricate, often invisible relation between colonialism and familial relationships—which expanded their imaginative explorations of hardscrabble political challenges.

Kennedy was born Adrienne Lita in Pittsburgh, Pennsylvania, the first child and only daughter of Cornell Wallace Hawkins, executive secretary of the YMCA, and Etra Haugebook Hawkins, a teacher. She was a gifted child who learned to read at age three. When she was four, Kennedy's family moved to an ethnically, racially, and religiously diverse neighborhood in Cleveland, Ohio. Captivated by this external cultural mosaic, Kennedy compensated for a certain rigidity in her upbringing by developing a dramatic inner life. "I often saw our family [as] if they were in a play," she recalled, and, indeed, Kennedy's characters are often composites of people from her childhood, particularly her immediate family. Her eccentric autobiography, *People Who Led to My Plays* (1987), begins with lists of actual and fictional characters who shaped her early life, including movie stars like Bette Davis about whom she developed a lifelong obsession—"As long as I can remember I've wanted to be Bette Davis." Still, alongside these beckoning fantasies of connection with the culturally enshrined, Kennedy asserts an anchoring normality: "I don't think I felt different from my family at all. I was proud of my family."

Kennedy graduated from Ohio State University in 1953 with a degree in elementary education. Two weeks later, she married Joseph C. Kennedy, who six months later was sent to Korea. Pregnant, Adrienne returned to her parents' home to await her husband, during which time she began writing her first plays, including a piece based on Elmer Rice's *Street Scene* and another based on Tennessee Williams's *Glass Menagerie*. Upon returning from Korea, Joseph Kennedy decided to continue his education at Columbia's Teachers College, and he and Adrienne along with their son, Joseph C. Jr., moved to New York. Kennedy studied creative writing at Columbia University from 1954 to 1956 and at the American Theatre Wing in 1958. In 1961 the family traveled to Africa, where she began work on *Funnyhouse of a Negro*. Because of a difficult pregnancy with her second son, Adam, the family moved to Italy, where Kennedy finished the play that would launch her career as a playwright.

Kennedy's next play, *The Owl Answers* (1965), further developed her interest in nonlinear "plot" in which events arise as much from the demands of thought and feeling as from the requirements of naturalistic time. At the core of this one-act drama is a black woman's quest for identity in a world dominated by white authority and symbolic power. Kennedy explores the implication of the self shattered into multiple guises by using composite characters that continuously melt into and detach from one another. For example, the central character is labeled "she who is clara passmore who is the virgin mary who is the bastard who is the owl." Kennedy's works are often organized as searches for the place where an identity ("she") can locate an integral mode of being ("is"), a place rife with historical contradictions.

From 1965 to 1970, Kennedy wrote six more plays: *A Beast Story* (1966); *A Rat's Mass* (1966); *A Lesson in a Dead Language* (1968); *Boats* (1969); and *Sun: A Poem for Malcolm X Inspired by His Murder* (1970), one of her few dramas dominated by a male voice. With John Lennon and Victor Spinetti, she wrote *The Lennon Play: In His Own Write* (1969), adapted from Lennon's books of absurdist wordplay. Taken together, these works align with the broad thematic concerns of the Black Arts Movement—racial assertion, the clash of violence and possibility, the potential and limits of ritual as a means of release from material burdens—yet cannot be simply assimilated to the ideology of any group of Black Arts writers or thinkers. Instead, they constitute meditative speculations that evoke central impulses of the era's radical artistic statements.

During the late 1960s and the 1970s, Kennedy sustained her writing career through grants awarded as her work gained recognition. She received a Guggenheim fellowship in 1968; Rockefeller fellowships in 1969, 1973, and 1976; a National Endowment grant in 1973; and the Creative Artists Public Service grant in 1974. In that year she and her husband were divorced, and she embarked on a life of writing and teaching that sustained her for decades. She has been a fellow at the Yale School of Drama and a visiting professor at Yale, Princeton, Brown, Harvard, and Emory, as well as the University of California at Davis and at Berkeley, among other institutions.

While teaching from the late 1970s to the 1990s, Kennedy continued to write plays, including *A Movie Star Has to Star in Black and White* (1976), *Orestes and Electra* (an adaptation commissioned by the Juilliard Conservatory of Music in 1980), and a children's musical, based on Charlie Chaplin's memoirs, titled *A Lancashire Lad* (1980), commissioned by the Empire State Youth Theatre Institute. During that time Kennedy also published a series of volumes that translate into prose the qualities of spectral exploration and teeming lyricism that suffuse her plays: *People Who Led to My Plays* (1987); *Adrienne Kennedy in One Act* (1988); and in 1990, her first work of prose fiction, *Deadly Triplets: A Theatre Mystery and Journal*, which introduces the character of Suzanne Alexander, around whom Kennedy would later compose a cycle of plays. In 1992 she published *The Alexander Plays*, which consist of four dramas: *She Talks to Beethoven*, *The Ohio State Murders*, *The Film Club: A Monologue*, and *The Dramatic Circle*; and in 1993 there was a fifth play concerned with this character: *Letter to My Students on My 61st Birthday by Suzanne Alexander*. In 1996 *Sleep Deprivation Chamber: A Theatre Piece*, co-written with her son Adam P. Kennedy, was produced in New York by the Signature Theatre Company, during a season dedicated solely to her work; the play won an Obie Award.

The movement of characters through play-cycles and recurrent structures is no accident. Kennedy declared once that "autobiographical work is the only kind that interests me," and one feels throughout her work, despite its formal variety, the urge to locate the single voice in which identity can reach its truest and fullest expression. The eruption of history within this journey, disturbing and fragmenting the autobiographical enterprise, represents not only an irony but also a challenge, one that Kennedy meets by returning again and again to a personal iconography—made of animals (especially birds), objects, clothes, and gestures—that binds otherwise distinctive works to one another and so creating one comprehensive project. Repetition-with-difference is thus the signal characteristic of Kennedy's writing, appearing within a given piece as a kind of stutter inhibiting coherent expression, but working across her drama and prose as a unifying, and therefore possibly hopeful, effect.

Funnyhouse of a Negro is the initial and still perhaps most compelling installment in this lifelong search for a unified sensibility. Drawing from English and European colonial history, African cultural practices, and her own experiences of growing up in the intricate racial territory of mid-twentieth-century America, Kennedy crafts a searing exploration of a black woman's psyche, riven by personal and inherited psychosis, at the root of which is the ambiguously double failure of both rapacious white society and its burdened yet also distorted victims. Throughout the play, as in the histories layered within it, oppressor and victim spiral around and through one another, creating both confusion and energy. Despite the aura of splintered and tragic longing that arises from this powerful but dangerous mixture, the play offers a subtle yield of hope in its formal precision, suggesting, if only subliminally, a possible deliverance from painful tumult by the ultimate logic of freedom and fulfillment.

Funnyhouse[1] of a Negro

CHARACTERS

NEGRO-SARAH	
DUCHESS OF HAPSBURG	One of herselves
QUEEN VICTORIA REGINA	One of herselves
JESUS	One of herselves
PATRICE LUMUMBA[2]	One of herselves
SARAH'S LANDLADY	Funnyhouse Lady
RAYMOND	Funnyhouse Man
THE MOTHER	

AUTHOR'S NOTE

Funnyhouse of a Negro is perhaps clearest and most explicit when the play is placed in the girl Sarah's room. The center of the stage works well as her room, allowing the rest of the stage as the place for herselves. Her room should have a bed, a writing table and a mirror. Near her bed is the statue of Queen Victoria; other objects might be her photographs and her books. When she is placed in her room with her belongings, then the director is free to let the rest of the play happen around her.

BEGINNING: *Before the closed Curtain a* WOMAN *dressed in a white nightgown walks across the Stage carrying before her a bald head. She moves as one in a trance and is mumbling something inaudible to herself. Her hair is wild, straight and black and falls to her waist. As she moves, she gives the effect of one in a dream. She crosses the Stage from Right to Left. Before she has barely vanished, the* CURTAIN *opens. It is a white satin Curtain of a cheap material and a ghastly white, a material that brings to mind the interior of a cheap casket, parts of it are frayed and look as if it has been gnawed by rats.*

SCENE: TWO WOMEN *are sitting in what appears to be a Queen's chamber. It is set in the middle of the Stage in a strong white LIGHT, while the rest of the Stage is in unnatural BLACKNESS. The quality of the white light is unreal and ugly. The Queen's chamber consists of a dark monumental bed resembling an ebony tomb, a low, dark chandelier with candles, and wine-colored walls. Flying about are great black* RAVENS.[3] QUEEN VICTORIA *is standing before her bed holding a small mirror in her hand. On the white pillow of her bed is a dark, indistinguishable object. The* DUCHESS OF HAPSBURG *is standing at the foot of the bed. Her back is to us as is the* QUEEN'S. *Throughout the entire scene, they do not move.* BOTH WOMEN *are dressed in royal gowns of white, a white similar to the white of the Curtain, the material cheap satin. Their headpieces are white and of a net that falls over their faces. From beneath both their headpieces springs a headful of wild kinky hair. Although in this scene we do*

1. Psychiatric hospital or asylum (slang), often applied to an amusement hall where patrons encounter skewed self-images in distorting mirrors.
2. Patrice Emery Lumumba (1925–1961), Congolese independence leader and first prime minister of the Republic of Congo (1960), was deposed by a Belgian-led coup and executed shortly thereafter. Duchess of Hapsburg: The House of Habsburg, the dynastic source of Holy Roman Emperors from 1438 to 1740, ruled the Austrian and Spanish empires until the late 18th century. Though a general title, the Duchess referred to here is Char-

lotte of Belgium, later Carlota of Mexico (1840–1927), wife or "empress consort" of Maximilian I of Mexico: her mental health deteriorated after the capture and execution of her husband in the Mexican revolution of 1867, and her fortune was used by her brother Leopold II of Belgium (1839–1909) to colonize the Congo. Queen Victoria (1819–1901): monarch of Great Britain, and empress of India, from 1837 until 1901.
3. Traditional harbingers of death and supernatural messages. Resident ravens in the Tower of London were thought to ensure the success of the British Empire.

not see their faces, I will describe them now. They look exactly alike and will wear masks or be made up to appear a whitish yellow. It is an alabaster face, the skin drawn tightly over the high cheekbones, great dark eyes that seem gouged out of the head, a high forehead, a full red mouth and a head of frizzy hair. If the characters do not wear a mask, then the face must be highly powdered and possess a hard expressionless quality and a stillness as in the face of death. We hear KNOCKING.

VICTORIA [*Listening to the knocking.*]   It is my father. He is arriving again for the night. [*The* DUCHESS *makes no reply.*] He comes through the jungle to find me. He never tires of his journey.

DUCHESS   How dare he enter the castle, he who is the darkest of them all, the darkest one? My mother looked like a white woman, hair as straight as any white woman's. And at least I am yellow,[4] but he is black, the blackest one of them all. I hoped he was dead. Yet he still comes through the jungle to find me.
   [*The KNOCKING is louder.*]

VICTORIA   He never tires of the journey, does he, Duchess? [*Looking at herself in the mirror.*]

DUCHESS   How dare he enter the castle of Queen Victoria Regina, Monarch of England? It is because of him that my mother died. The wild black beast[5] put his hands on her. She died.

VICTORIA   Why does he keep returning? He keeps returning forever, coming back ever and keeps coming back forever. He is my father.

DUCHESS   He is a black Negro.

VICTORIA   He is my father. I am tied to the black Negro. He came when I was a child in the south, before I was born he haunted my conception, diseased my birth.

DUCHESS   Killed my mother.

VICTORIA   My mother was the light. She was the lightest one. She looked like a white woman.

DUCHESS   We are tied to him unless, of course, he should die.

VICTORIA   But he is dead.

DUCHESS   And he keeps returning.
   [*The KNOCKING is louder; BLACKOUT. The LIGHTS go out in the Chamber. Onto the Stage from the Left comes the* FIGURE *in the white nightgown carrying the bald head. This time we hear her speak.*]

MOTHER   Black man, black man, I never should have let a black man put his hands on me. The wild black beast raped me and now my skull is shining. [*She disappears to the Right.*]
   [*Now the LIGHT is focused on a single white square wall that is to the Left of the Stage, that is suspended and stands alone, of about five feet in dimension and width. It stands with the narrow part facing the audience. A CHARACTER steps through. She is a faceless, dark character with a hangman's rope about her neck and red blood on the part that would be her face. She is the* NEGRO. *The most noticeable aspect of her looks is her wild kinky hair. It is a ragged head with a patch of hair missing from the crown which the* NEGRO *carries in her hand. She is dressed in black. She steps slowly through the wall, stands still before it and begins her monologue:*]

---

4. Indication of mixed racial heritage, taken here to be a sign of social superiority to the darker complected father.

5. An appellation commonly given to African American men accused by whites of rape and often subjected to mob violence.

NEGRO Part of the time I live with Raymond, part of the time with God, Maxmillian and Albert Saxe Coburg.[6] I live in my room. It is a small room on the top floor of a brownstone in the West Nineties in New York,[7] a room filled with my dark old volumes, a narrow bed and on the wall old photographs of castles and monarchs of England. It is also Victoria's chamber. Queen Victoria Regina's. Partly because it is consumed by a gigantic plaster statue of Queen Victoria who is my idol and partly for other reasons; three steps that I contrived out of boards lead to the statue which I have placed opposite the door as I enter the room. It is a sitting figure, a replica of one in London,[8] and a thing of astonishing whiteness. I found it in a dusty shop on Morningside Heights.[9] Raymond says it is a thing of terror, possessing the quality of nightmares, suggesting large and probable deaths. And of course he is right. When I am the Duchess of Hapsburg I sit opposite Victoria in my headpiece and we talk. The other time I wear the dress of a student, dark clothes and dark stockings. Victoria always wants me to tell her of whiteness. She wants me to tell her of a royal world where everything and everyone is white and there are no unfortunate black ones. For as we of royal blood know, black is evil and has been from the beginning.[1] Even before my mother's hair started to fall out. Before she was raped by a wild black beast. Black was evil.

As for myself I long to become even a more pallid Negro than I am now; pallid like Negroes on the covers of American Negro magazines; soulless, educated and irreligious. I want to possess no moral value, particularly value as to my being. I want not to be. I ask nothing except anonymity. I am an English major, as my mother was when she went to school in Atlanta. My father majored in social work. I am graduated from a city college and have occasional work in libraries, but mostly spend my days preoccupied with the placement and geometric position of words on paper. I write poetry filling white page after white page with imitations of Edith Sitwell.[2] It is my dream to live in rooms with European antiques and my Queen Victoria, photographs of Roman ruins, walls of books, a piano, oriental carpets and to eat my meals on a white glass table. I will visit my friends' apartments which will contain books, photographs of Roman ruins, pianos and oriental carpets. My friends will be white.

I need them as an embankment to keep me from reflecting too much upon the fact that I am a Negro. For, like all educated Negroes—out of life and death essential—I find it necessary to maintain a stark fortress against recognition of myself. My white friends, like myself, will be shrewd, intellectual and anxious for death. Anyone's death. I will mistrust them, as I do myself, waver in their opinion of me, as I waver in the opinion of myself. But if I had not wavered in my opinion of myself, then my hair would never have fallen out. And if my hair hadn't fallen out, I wouldn't have bludgeoned my father's head with an ebony mask.

---

6. British prince consort, husband of Queen Victoria (1819–1861). Maximillian I (1832–1867) was the Austrian-born monarch of the Second Mexican Empire (1864–67), overthrown and executed by the republican forces of Benito Juárez (1806–1872).
7. That is, part of the Upper West Side, a Manhattan district immediately south of Harlem.
8. Allusion to the Queen Victoria Memorial, located in front of Buckingham Palace.
9. Upper West Side neighborhood of New York,

near Columbia University.
1. See Genesis 1.1–3: "In the beginning . . . darkness was upon the face of the deep. And God said, Let there be light."
2. Dame Edith Louise Sitwell (1887–1964), British poet and critic, known for her eccentric social circle, biographies of British queens (including in 1936 *Victoria of England*), and stark, nature-inspired poetry. The following line is a fair description of Sitwell's London home.

In appearance I am good-looking in a boring way; no glaring Negroid features, medium nose, medium mouth and pale yellow skin. My one defect is that I have a head of frizzy hair, unmistakably Negro kinky hair; and it is indistinguishable. I would like to lie and say I love Raymond. But I do not. He is a poet and is Jewish. He is very interested in Negroes.

[*The* NEGRO *stands by the wall and throughout her following speech, the following characters come through the wall, disappearing off into varying directions in the darkened night of the* Stage: DUCHESS, QUEEN VICTORIA, JESUS, PATRICE LUMUMBA. JESUS *is a hunchback, yellow-skinned dwarf, dressed in white rags and sandals.* PATRICE LUMUMBA *is a black man. His head appears to be split in two with blood and tissue in eyes. He carries an ebony mask.*]

SARAH [NEGRO]   The rooms are my rooms; a Hapsburg chamber, a chamber in a Victorian castle, the hotel where I killed my father, the jungle. These are the places myselves exist in. I know no places. That is, I cannot believe in places. To believe in places is to know hope and to know the emotion of hope is to know beauty. It links us across a horizon and connects us to the world. I find there are no places only my funnyhouse. Streets are rooms, cities are rooms, eternal rooms. I try to create a space for myselves in cities, New York, the midwest, a southern town, but it becomes a lie. I try to give myselves a logical relationship but that too is a lie. For relationships was one of my last religions. I clung loyally to the lie of relationships, again and again seeking to establish a connection between my characters. Jesus is Victoria's son. Mother loved my father before her hair fell out. A loving relationship exists between myself and Queen Victoria, a love between myself and Jesus but they are lies.

[*Then to the Right front of the Stage comes the* WHITE LIGHT. *It goes to a suspended stairway. At the foot of it, stands the* LANDLADY. *She is a tall, thin, white woman dressed in a black and red hat and appears to be talking to someone in a suggested open doorway in a corridor of a rooming house. She laughs like a mad character in a funnyhouse throughout her speech.*]

LANDLADY [*Who is looking up the stairway.*]   Ever since her father hung himself in a Harlem hotel when Patrice Lumumba was murdered she hides herself in her room. Each night she repeats: He keeps returning. How dare he enter the castle walls, he who is the darkest of them all, the darkest one? My mother looked like a white woman, hair as straight as any white woman's. And I am yellow but he, he is black, the blackest one of them all. I hoped he was dead. Yet he still comes through the jungle.

I tell her: Sarah, honey, the man hung himself. It's not your blame. But, no, she stares at me: No, Mrs. Conrad, he did not hang himself, that is only the way they understand it, they do, but the truth is that I bludgeoned his head with an ebony skull that he carries about with him. Wherever he goes, he carries black masks and heads.

She's suffering so till her hair has fallen out. But then she did always hide herself in that room with the walls of books and her statue. I always did know she thought she was somebody else, a Queen or something, somebody else.

BLACKOUT

SCENE: *Funnyman's place.*

The next scene is enacted with the DUCHESS *and* RAYMOND. *Raymond's place is suggested as being above the* NEGRO's *room and is etched in with a prop of*

*blinds and a bed. Behind the blinds are mirrors and when the blinds are opened
and closed by Raymond this is revealed.* RAYMOND *turns out to be the funnyman[3] of the funnyhouse. He is tall, white and ghostly thin and dressed in a black
shirt and black trousers in attire suggesting an artist. Throughout his dialogue he
laughs. The* DUCHESS *is partially disrobed and it is implied from their attitudes
of physical intimacy—he is standing and she is sitting before him clinging to his
leg. During the scene* RAYMOND *keeps opening and closing the blinds.*

DUCHESS [*Carrying a red paper bag.*]   My father is arriving and what am I
   to do?

   [RAYMOND *walks about the place opening the blinds and laughing.*]

FUNNYMAN   He is arriving from Africa, is he not?

DUCHESS   Yes, yes, he is arriving from Africa.

FUNNYMAN   I always knew your father was African.

DUCHESS   He is an African who lives in the jungle. He is an African who
   has always lived in the jungle. Yes, he is a nigger who is an African who is
   a missionary teacher and is now dedicating his life to the erection of a
   Christian mission in the middle of the jungle. He is a black man.

FUNNYMAN   He is a black man who shot himself when they murdered
   Patrice Lumumba.

DUCHESS [*Goes on wildly.*]   Yes, my father is a black man who went to
   Africa years ago as a missionary teacher, got mixed up in politics, was
   revealed and is now devoting his foolish life to the erection of a Christian mission in the middle of the jungle in one of those newly freed
   countries. Hide me. [*Clinging to his knees.*] Hide me here so the nigger will not find me.

FUNNYMAN [*Laughing.*]   Your father is in the jungle dedicating his life to
   the erection of a Christian mission.

DUCHESS   Hide me here so the jungle will not find me. Hide me.

FUNNYMAN   Isn't it cruel of you?

DUCHESS   Hide me from the jungle.

FUNNYMAN   Isn't it cruel?

DUCHESS   No, no.

FUNNYMAN   Isn't it cruel of you?

DUCHESS   No. [*She screams and opens her red paper bag and draws from it
   her fallen hair. It is a great mass of dark wild hair. She holds it up to him.
   He appears not to understand. He stares at it.*] It is my hair. [*He continues
   to stare at her.*] When I awakened this morning it had fallen out, not all of
   it but a mass from the crown of my head that lay on the center of my pillow. I arose and in the greyish winter morning light of my room I stood
   staring at my hair, dazed by my sleeplessness, still shaken by nightmares
   of my mother. Was it true, yes, it was my hair. In the mirror I saw that,
   although my hair remained on both sides, clearly on the crown and at my
   temples my scalp was bare. [*She removes her black crown and shows him
   the top of her head.*]

FUNNYMAN [*Staring at her.*]   Why would your hair fall out? Is it because
   you are cruel? How could a black father haunt you so?

DUCHESS   He haunted my very conception. He was a wild black beast
   who raped my mother.

FUNNYMAN   He is a black Negro. [*Laughing.*]

---

3. That is, a comedian or trickster, as well as proprietor or supervisor of the Funnyhouse.

DUCHESS   Ever since I can remember he's been in a nigger pose of agony. He is the wilderness. He speaks niggerly groveling about wanting to touch me with his black hand.

FUNNYMAN   How tormented and cruel you are.

DUCHESS [As if not comprehending.]   Yes, yes, the man's dark, very dark-skinned. He is the darkest, my father is the darkest, my mother is the lightest. I am in between. But my father is the darkest. My father is a nigger who drives me to misery. Any time spent with him evolves itself into suffering. He is a black man and the wilderness.

FUNNYMAN   How tormented and cruel you are.

DUCHESS   He is a nigger.

FUNNYMAN   And your mother, where is she?

DUCHESS   She is in the asylum. In the asylum bald. Her father was a white man. And she is in the asylum.

    [He takes her in his arms. She responds wildly.]
    BLACKOUT

    KNOCKING is heard; it continues, then somewhere near the Center of the Stage a FIGURE appears in the darkness, a large dark faceless MAN carrying a mask in his hand.

MAN   It begins with the disaster of my hair. I awaken. My hair has fallen out, not all of it, but a mass from the crown of my head that lies on the center of my white pillow. I arise and in the greyish winter morning light of my room I stand staring at my hair, dazed by sleeplessness, still shaken by nightmares of my mother. Is it true? Yes. It is my hair. In the mirror I see that although my hair remains on both sides, clearly on the crown and at my temples my scalp is bare. And in my sleep I had been visited by my bald crazy mother who comes to me crying, calling me to her bedside. She lies on the bed watching the strands of her own hair fall out. Her hair fell out after she married and she spent her days lying on the bed watching the strands fall from her scalp, covering the bedspread until she was bald and admitted to the hospital. Black man, black man, my mother says, I never should have let a black man put his hands on me. She comes to me, her bald skull shining. Black diseases, Sarah, she says. Black diseases. I run. She follows me, her bald skull shining. That is the beginning.

    BLACKOUT

SCENE: Queen's Chamber.

    Her hair is in a small pile on the bed and in a small pile on the floor, several other small piles of hair are scattered about her and her white gown is covered with fallen-out hair. QUEEN VICTORIA acts out the following scene: She awakens (in pantomime) and discovers her hair has fallen. It is on her pillow. She arises and stands at the side of the bed with her back toward us, staring at hair. The DUCHESS enters the room, comes around, standing behind VICTORIA, and they stare at the hair. VICTORIA picks up a mirror. The DUCHESS then picks up a mirror and looks at her own hair. She opens the red paper bag that she is carrying and takes out her hair, attempting to place it back on her head (for unlike VICTORIA, she does not wear her headpiece now.) The LIGHTS remain on. The unidentified MAN returns out of the darkness and speaks. He carries the mask.

MAN [Patrice Lumumba.]   I am a nigger of two generations. I am Patrice Lumumba. I am a nigger of two generations. I am the black shadow that haunted my mother's conception. I belong to the generation born at the turn of the century and the generation born before the depression. At present I reside in New York City in a brownstone in the West Nineties. I am an English major at a city college. My nigger father majored in social work, so did my mother. I am a student and have occasional work in libraries. But mostly I spend my vile days preoccupied with the placement and geometric position of words on paper. I write poetry filling white page after white page with imitations of Sitwell. It is my vile dream to live in rooms with European antiques and my statue of Queen Victoria, photographs of Roman ruins, walls of books, a piano and oriental carpets and to eat my meals on a white glass table. It is also my nigger dream for my friends to eat their meals on white glass tables and to live in rooms with European antiques, photographs of Roman ruins, pianos and oriental carpets. My friends will be white. I need them as an embankment to keep me from reflecting too much upon the fact that I am Patrice Lumumba who haunted my mother's conception. They are necessary for me to maintain recognition against myself. My white friends, like myself, will be shrewd intellectuals and anxious for death. Anyone's death. I will despise them as I do myself. For if I did not despise myself then my hair would not have fallen and if my hair had not fallen then I would not have bludgeoned my father's face with the ebony mask.

[*The* LIGHT *remains on him. Before him a* BALD HEAD *is dropped on a wire,* SOMEONE *screams. Another wall is dropped, larger than the first one was. This one is near the front of the Stage facing thus. Throughout the following monologue, the* CHARACTERS: DUCHESS, VICTORIA, JESUS *go back and forth. As they go in their backs are to us but the* NEGRO *faces us, speaking:*]

I always dreamed of a day when my mother would smile at me. My father . . . his mother wanted him to be Christ. From the beginning in the lamp of their dark room she said—I want you to be Jesus, to walk in Genesis[4] and save the race. You must return to Africa, find revelation in the midst of golden savannas, nim and white frankopenny[5] trees, white stallions roaming under a blue sky, you must walk with a white dove and heal the race, heal the misery, take us off the cross. She stared at him anguished in the kerosene light . . . At dawn he watched her rise, kill a hen for him to eat at breakfast, then go to work down at the big house till dusk, till she died.

His father told him the race was no damn good. He hated his father and adored his mother. His mother didn't want him to marry my mother and sent a dead chicken[6] to the wedding. I DON'T want you marrying that child, she wrote, she's not good enough for you, I want you to go to Africa. When they first married they lived in New York. Then they went to Africa where my mother fell out of love with my father. She didn't want him to save the black race and spent her days combing her hair. She would not let him touch her in their wedding bed and called him black. He is black of skin with dark eyes and a great dark square brow. Then in Africa he started to drink and came home drunk one night and raped my mother. The child from the union is me.

---

4. "And they heard the voice of the Lord God walking in the garden in the cool of the day: and Adam and his wife hid themselves from the presence of the Lord God" (Genesis 3.8).
5. Fragrant tree commonly found in West Africa, especially Ghana. "Nim": mahagony tree, grown in India; the "Africa Mahagony" is native to the tropical areas or "savannas" of East Africa.
6. In the Vodun traditions of West Africa, a curse or threat.

I clung to my mother. Long after she went to the asylum I wove long dreams of her beauty, her straight hair and fair skin and grey eyes, so identical to mine. How it anguished him. I turned from him, nailing him on the cross, he said, dragging him through grass and nailing him on a cross until he bled. He pleaded with me to help him find Genesis, search for Genesis in the midst of golden savannas, nim and white frankopenny trees and white stallions roaming under a blue sky, help him search for the white doves, he wanted the black man to make a pure statement, he wanted the black man to rise from colonialism. But I sat in the room with my mother, sat by her bedside and helped her comb her straight black hair and wove long dreams of her beauty. She had long since begun to curse the place and spoke of herself trapped in blackness. She preferred the company of night owls.[7] Only at night did she rise, walking in the garden among the trees with the owls. When I spoke to her she saw I was a black man's child and she preferred speaking to owls. Nights my father came from his school in the village struggling to embrace me. But I fled and hid under my mother's bed while she screamed of remorse. Her hair was falling badly and after a while we had to return to this country.

He tried to hang himself once. After my mother went to the asylum he had hallucinations, his mother threw a dead chicken at him, his father laughed and said the race was no damn good, my mother appeared in her nightgown screaming she had trapped herself in blackness. No white doves flew. He had left Africa and was again in New York. He lived in Harlem and no white doves flew. Sarah, Sarah, he would say to me, the soldiers are coming and a cross they are placing high on a tree[8] and are dragging me through the grass and nailing me upon the cross. My blood is gushing.[9] I wanted to live in Genesis in the midst of golden savannas, nim and white frankopenny trees and white stallions roaming under a blue sky. I wanted to walk with a white dove. I wanted to be a Christian. Now I am Judas.[1] I betrayed my mother. I sent your mother to the asylum. I created a yellow child who hates me. And he tried to hang himself in a Harlem hotel.
    BLACKOUT
    [A BALD HEAD is dropped on a string. We hear LAUGHING.]

SCENE: DUCHESS's place.
    The next scene is done in the DUCHESS OF HAPSBURG's place which is a chandeliered ballroom with SNOW falling, a black and white marble floor, a bench decorated with white flowers, all of this can be made of obviously fake materials as they would be in a funnyhouse. The DUCHESS is wearing a white dress and as in the previous scene a white headpiece with her kinky hair springing out from under it. In the scene are the DUCHESS and JESUS. JESUS enters the room, which is at first dark, then suddenly BRILLIANT, he starts to cry out at the DUCHESS, who is seated on a bench under the chandelier, and pulls his hair from the red paper bag holding it up for the DUCHESS to see.

7. Associated with death or ill luck among the Kikuyu of Kenya, and with wisdom in the Greek tradition through the guise of Athena, the motherless goddess born from the head of her father, Zeus.
8. Imagery of lynching here merges with that of Christ's crucifixion, an association developed in the Black Liberation Theology of African American theologian James Cone (b. 1938).
9. Image of stigmata, the spontaneous appearance of bleeding at the sites of Christ's wounds.
1. Judas Iscariot, the apostle who betrayed Christ to the Romans (see, e.g., Matthew 26–27).

JESUS   My hair. [*The* DUCHESS *does not speak,* JESUS *again screams.*] My hair. [*Holding the hair up, waiting for a reaction from the* DUCHESS.]

DUCHESS [*As if oblivious.*]   I have something I must show you. [*She goes quickly to shutters and darkens the room, returning standing before* JESUS. *She then slowly removes her headpiece and from under it takes a mass of her hair.*] When I awakened I found it fallen out, not all of it but a mass that lay on my white pillow. I could see, although my hair hung down at the sides, clearly on my white scalp it was missing.
[*Her baldness is identical to* JESUS'.]
BLACKOUT

The LIGHTS *come back up. They are* BOTH *sitting on the bench examining each other's hair, running it through their fingers, then slowly the* DUCHESS *disappears behind the shutters and returns with a long red comb. She sits on the bench next to* JESUS *and starts to comb her remaining hair over her baldness.* [*This is done slowly.*] JESUS *then takes the comb and proceeds to do the same to the* DUCHESS OF HAPSBURG'S *hair. After they finish they place the* DUCHESS'S *headpiece back on and we can see the strands of their hair falling to the floor.* JESUS *then lies down across the bench while the* DUCHESS *walks back and forth, the* KNOCKING *does not cease. They speak in unison as the* DUCHESS *walks about and* JESUS *lies on the bench in the falling snow, staring at the ceiling.*

DUCHESS and JESUS. [*Their hair is falling more now, they are both hideous.*] My father isn't going to let us alone. [KNOCKING.] Our father isn't going to let us alone, our father is the darkest of us all, my mother was the fairest, I am in between, but my father is the darkest of them all. He is a black man. Our father is the darkest of them all. He is a black man. My father is a dead man.
[*Then they suddenly look up at each other and scream, the* LIGHTS *go to their heads and we see that they are totally bald. There is a* KNOCKING. LIGHTS *go to the stairs and the* LANDLADY.]

LANDLADY   He wrote to her saying he loved her and asked her forgiveness. He begged her to take him off the cross [*He had dreamed she would.*], stop them from tormenting him, the one with the chicken and his cursing father. Her mother's hair fell out, the race's hair fell out because he left Africa, he said. He had tried to save them. She must embrace him. He said his existence depended on her embrace. He wrote her from Africa where he is creating his Christian center in the jungle and that is why he came here. I know that he wanted her to return there with him and not desert the race. He came to see her once before he tried to hang himself, appearing in the corridor of my apartment. I had let him in. I found him sitting on a bench in the hallway. He put out his hand to her, tried to take her in his arms, crying out— Forgiveness, Sarah, is it that you never will forgive me for being black? Sarah, I know you were a child of torment. But forgiveness. That was before his breakdown. Then, he wrote her and repeated that his mother hoped he would be Christ but he failed. He had married her mother because he could not resist the light. Yet, his mother from the beginning in the kerosene lamp of their dark rooms in Georgia said: I want you to be Jesus, to walk in Genesis and save the race, return to Africa, find revelation in the black. He went away.

But Easter morning, she got to feeling badly and went into Harlem to see him; the streets were filled with vendors selling lilies.[2] He had checked out of that hotel. When she arrived back at my brownstone he was here, dressed badly, rather drunk, I had let him in again. He sat on a bench in the dark hallway, put out his hand to her, trying to take her in his arms, crying out—forgiveness, Sarah, forgiveness for my being black, Sarah. I know you are a child of torment. I know on dark winter afternoons you sit alone weaving stories of your mother's beauty. But Sarah, answer me, don't turn away, Sarah. Forgive my blackness. She would not answer. He put out his hand to her. She ran past him on the stairs, left him there with his hand out to me, repeating his past, saying his mother hoped he would be Christ. From the beginning in the kerosene lamp of their dark rooms, she said, "Wally, I want you to be Jesus, to walk in Genesis and save the race. You must return to Africa, Wally, find revelation in the midst of golden savannas, nim and white frankopenny trees and white stallions roaming under a blue sky. Wally, you must find the white dove and heal the pain of the race, heal the misery of the black man, Wally, take us off the cross, Wally." In the kerosene light she stared at me anguished from her old Negro face—but she ran past him leaving him. And now he is dead, she says, now he is dead. He left Africa and now Patrice Lumumba is dead.

[*The next scene is enacted back in the* DUCHESS OF HAPSBURG's *place.* JESUS *is still in the Duchess's chamber, apparently he has fallen asleep and as we see him he awakens with the* DUCHESS *by his side, and sits here as in a trance. He rises terrified and speaks.*]

JESUS Through my apocalypses and my raging sermons I have tried so to escape him, through God Almighty I have tried to escape being black. [*He then appears to rouse himself from his thoughts and calls:*] Duchess, Duchess. [*He looks about for her, there is no answer. He gets up slowly, walks back into the darkness and there we see that she is hanging on the chandelier, her bald head suddenly drops to the floor and she falls upon* JESUS. *He screams.*] I am going to Africa and kill this black man named Patrice Lumumba. Why? Because all my life I believed my Holy Father to be God, but now I know that my father is a black man. I have no fear for whatever I do, I will do in the name of God, I will do in the name of Albert Saxe Coburg, in the name of Victoria, Queen Victoria Regina, the monarch of England, I will.

BLACKOUT

SCENE: *In the jungle,* RED SUN, FLYING THINGS, *wild black grass. The effect of the jungle is that it, unlike the other scenes, is over the entire stage. In time this is the longest scene in the play and is played the slowest, as the slow, almost standstill stages of a dream. By lighting the desired effect would be— suddenly the jungle has overgrown the chambers and all the other places with a violence and a dark brightness, a grim yellowness.*

JESUS *is the first to appear in the center of the jungle darkness. Unlike in previous scenes, he has a nimbus above his head. As they each successively appear, they all too have nimbuses atop their heads in a manner to suggest that they are saviours.*

2. Derived from *leiron* (the Greek term for the white or "Madonna" flower of the lily genus), lilies in Christian iconography evoke the Virgin Mary in her role as Queen of the Angels, but also are associated with funerals, symbolizing the hope of restored purity after death.

JESUS I always believed my father to be God.
[*Suddenly they all appear in various parts of the jungle.* PATRICE
LUMUMBA, *the* DUCHESS, VICTORIA, *wandering about speaking at once.
Their speeches are mixed and repeated by one another:*]

ALL He never tires of the journey, he who is the darkest one, the darkest
one of them all. My mother looked like a white woman, hair as straight
as any white woman's. I am yellow but he is black, the darkest one of us
all. How I hoped he was dead, yet he never tires of the journey. It was
because of him that my mother died because she let a black man put his
hands on her. Why does he keep returning? He keeps returning forever,
keeps returning and returning and he is my father. He is a black Negro.
They told me my Father was God but my father is black. He is my father.
I am tied to a black Negro. He returned when I lived in the south back in
the twenties, when I was a child, he returned. Before I was born at the
turn of the century, he haunted my conception, diseased my birth . . .
killed my mother. He killed the light. My mother was the lightest one. I
am bound to him unless, of course, he should die.

But he is dead.

And he keeps returning. Then he is not dead.

Then he is not dead.

Yet, he is dead, but dead he comes knocking at my door.

[*This is repeated several times, finally reaching a loud pitch and then
ALL rushing about the grass. They stop and stand perfectly still. ALL
speaking tensely at various times in a chant.*]
I see him. The black ugly thing is sitting in his hallway, surrounded
by his ebony masks, surrounded by the blackness of himself. My mother
comes into the room. He is there with his hand out to me, groveling,
saying—Forgiveness, Sarah, is it that you will never forgive me for being
black.

Forgiveness, Sarah, I know you are a nigger of torment.

Why? Christ would not rape anyone.

You will never forgive me for being black.

Wild beast. Why did you rape my mother? Black beast, Christ would
not rape anyone.

He is in grief from that black anguished face of his. Then at once the
room will grow bright and my mother will come toward me smiling
while I stand before his face and bludgeon him with an ebony head.

Forgiveness, Sarah, I know you are a nigger of torment.
[*Silence. Then they suddenly begin to laugh and shout as though they
are in victory. They continue for some minutes running about laughing
and shouting.*]
BLACKOUT

*Another WALL drops. There is a white plaster statue of Queen Victoria
which represents the NEGRO's room in the brownstone, the room appears
near the staircase highly lit and small. The main prop is the statue but
a bed could be suggested. The figure of Victoria is a sitting figure, one of
astonishing repulsive whiteness, suggested by dusty volumes of books
and old yellowed walls.*

*The Negro SARAH is standing perfectly still, we hear the KNOCKING,
the LIGHTS come on quickly, her FATHER's black figure with bludgeoned*

hands rushes upon her, the LIGHT GOES BLACK and we see her hanging in the room.

LIGHTS come on the laughing LANDLADY. *And at the same time remain on the hanging figure of the* NEGRO.

LANDLADY   The poor bitch has hung herself. [FUNNYMAN RAYMOND *appears from his room at the commotion.*] The poor bitch has hung herself.

RAYMOND [*Observing her hanging figure.*]   She was a funny little liar.

LANDLADY [*Informing him.*]   Her father hung himself in a Harlem hotel when Patrice Lumumba died.

RAYMOND   Her father never hung himself in a Harlem hotel when Patrice Lumumba was murdered. I know the man. He is a doctor, married to a white whore. He lives in the city in rooms with European antiques, photographs of Roman ruins, walls of books and oriental carpets. Her father is a nigger who eats his meals on a white glass table.

END

1964

CALVIN HERNTON
1932–2001

Poet, novelist, playwright, screenwriter, editor, cultural historian, social theorist, and educator, Calvin Hernton exerted subtle but wide influence on the development of African American writing in the Black Arts era and beyond. A writer who combined great learning with penetrating analysis of both self and society to forge taboo-shattering accounts of American racial history, Hernton challenged his readers to take seriously the roots of modern racial relations in slavery's violent cauldron of sexual predation, misplaced desire, and displaced guilt. As a trained sociologist, experienced social worker, and student of existential psychology under the tutelage of heterodox Scottish psychoanalyst R. D. Laing, Hernton brought to his work a keen eye for the way individuals struggle to assert themselves within built landscapes strewn with the debris of historical tumult and its lingering rumblings in contemporary social consciousness. At the same time, there arises from his portrayal of searing urban wastelands and their scorched inhabitants a vision of therapeutic release, born first of uncompromising understanding, then of renewed assertion from amidst the ruins. And for Hernton, this vision was decidedly the task of the poet whose "perpetual struggle," as he wrote in the poem "Underlying Strife," is "an eternal / Cause-of-the-People / Towards the self-liberation of a wilderness dream / Deep frozen in a profit-making civilization."

Born in Chattanooga, Tennessee, Hernton received his B.A. from Alabama's Talladega College in 1953 and his M.A. from Nashville's Fisk University in 1954, both in sociology. He soon married Mildred Webster and lived briefly in Harlem before teaching at a series of historically African American southern schools (Benedict College in South Carolina, Edward Waters College in Florida, Alabama A & M, and Louisiana's Southern University). In what he called his "fateful summer of 1961," he and Mildred moved to New York City's East Village, a bohemian neighborhood whose predominantly white population included a smattering of black poets, artists, musicians, and social activists. Though Hernton was already a published poet, it was during this sojourn in the East Village that he realized "just how hopelessly I was possessed by the desire to be a writer; recklessly and excitedly I gave myself to writing and the life it entailed." With such fellow African American writers as Tom Dent, David Henderson, Ishmael Reed, and Raymond Patterson, Hernton founded the radical artists collective known as Umbra, which vigorously asserted the black presence within bohemian culture as a blend of vernacular sound, experimental aesthetics, social critique, and public performance. As co-editor of the journal *Umbra,* Hernton helped craft a distinctive inflection of the new black poetic sound then emerging in American cities from New York to San Francisco.

Umbra played an important role in Hernton's own poetic development: the experience, he later wrote, "captivated, inspired, and invigorated me." Umbra's intense and popular poetry jams were notoriously daring and contentious, but Hernton said that "when you returned for the next session, your revised work was markedly improved, you were praised, and you felt good." Hernton himself was described by Dent as "our strongest and most mature voice," noting that Hernton "dominated just about everything he did with the salt of his personality."

Hernton traveled abroad in the mid-1960s, during which time he worked as a research fellow under Laing at the London Institute for Phenomenological Studies. It was also then that he released his pathbreaking sociological study *Sex and Racism in America* (1965), which probed the psychological turbulence set in motion by the volatile mixture of puritanism and prejudice that drove slavery's masculinist violence, and which, he argued, generated congenital unrest within the American psyche well into the civil rights era. Anticipating both the raw-edged mythography of Eldridge Cleaver's *Soul on Ice* (1968) and later scholarly analyses of the social construction of race, gender, and class in American history, Hernton's book struck a nerve among its readers that established Hernton as a simultaneously erudite and revolutionary voice among those exploring the outer edges of thought about race in America. Hernton subsequently enlarged that voice in essays such as those collected in *White Papers for White Americans* (1966) and *The Sexual Mountain and Black Women Writers* (1987), as well as in the novel *Scarecrow* (1974) and a continuing stream of poems, many of which were collected in the volumes *Medicine Man* (1976) and *The Red Crab Gang and Black River Poems* (1999).

In the latter part of his life, Hernton influenced new generations of young writers as a professor of black studies and creative writing at Oberlin College, where he served from 1970 to 1999. To that task of mentoring he brought the same erudite yet sharp-toned voice that can be heard in "Jitterbugging in the Streets," which, with its complex rhythm of anxiety and aspiration, remains a signature work of the period that he helped shape.

Jitterbugging in the Streets[1]

(to Ishmael Reed)[2]

There will be no Holy Savior crying out this year
No seer, no trumpeteer, no George Fox[3] treading barefoot up and down
    the hot land

---

1. Dancing in the energetic, quick-tempo swing style, favoring improvisation, also known as the Lindy Hop and Jive, made popular in the 1930s. Jitterbugging's raucous, frenzied motions led some psychiatrists to fear it could induce mass hysteria, and the dance was banned in some Midwestern dance halls in 1939.
2. Reed (b. 1938), an African American poet, novelist, playwright, and essayist; with Hernton, Reed was one of the founders in 1962 of Umbra, an experimental collective of young black writers and artists located in the East Village of New York City.
3. George Fox (1624–1691), founder of the Religious Society of Friends (also known as Quakers), was said to have walked barefoot through the streets of Lichfield, England, crying, "Woe to the bloody city of Lichfield." Fox claimed he was imitating Christ, often depicted as walking barefoot.

The only Messiah we shall see this year is a gunned-down man
    staggering to and fro 5
    through the wilderness of the screaming ghetto[4]
Blotted out by soap opera housewives in the television afternoons
    exchanging gossip vomited up from cesspools
    of plastic lives
Talking themselves 10

An unshaven idiot!
A senile derelict!
Ugly black nigger!

Piety and scorn on the doormouth of the Lord[5]
    instructing the populace to love thine oppressor,[6] be kind to 15
    puppies and the Chaste Manhattan National Bank[7]

Because of this there will be no Fourth-of-July this year
No shouting, no popping of firecrackers, no celebrating,
    no parade
But the rage of a hopeless people 20
Jitterbugging
    in
        the streets.

Jacksonville Florida Selma Alabama
Birmingham, Atlanta, Rochester, Detroit, Bedford Stuyvesant, 25
Jackson Mississippi Watts Los Angeles Harlem New York[8]
Jitterbugging
    in
        the streets
To ten thousand rounds of ammunition 30
Water hoses, electrical prods, phallic sticks,
    hound dogs, black boots stomping in soft places
    of black bodies—
Venom on the tongues of virgin maidens[9] and dresswell fags, Christian
    housewives, smart young Italians, old Scandinavians in Yorkville,[1] 35
    businessmen, civil service employees, suntanned suburban
    organization men,[2] clerks and construction workers, poor white
    folks and gunhappy policemen;

"WHY DON'T WE KILL ALL NIGGERS: NOT ONE OR TWO BUT EVERY DAMN
    BLACK OF THEM! NIGGERS WILL DO ANYTHING. I BETTER NEVER CATCH 40

4. A reference to Christ's forty-day trial in the wilderness during which he was tempted by the devil: "The voice of one crying in the wilderness, Prepare ye the way of the Lord, make his paths straight" (Luke 3.4).
5. "Set a watch, O Lord, before my mouth; keep the door of my lips" (Psalm 141.3).
6. Cf. Matthew 5.44: "But I say unto you, Love your enemies, bless them that curse you, do good to them that hate you, and pray for them which despitefully use you, and persecute you."
7. Wordplay on Chase Manhattan National Bank, founded in 1799 by Aaron Burr (1756–1836), third vice-president of the United States (1801–5). About 13,000 slaves had been accepted as collateral for loans between 1831 and 1865 by two banks (Citizen's Bank and Canal Bank) that were absorbed by Chase in 1931.
8. Sites of racial violence in the 1960s, with a play on the lyrics of the 1964 soul song "Dancing in the Streets," made famous by Martha and the Vandellas.
9. The Greek goddess Invidia Daimon, or Envy, whose tongue drips venom, was asked by the virgin maiden of war, the goddess Athena, to punish a woman who disobeyed her.
1. Upper East Side neighborhood of Manhattan.
2. An allusion to the Organization Man (1956) by sociologist William Whyte Jr. (1914–2000), a study of the worrisome impact of mass organization on American life in the 1950s.

A NIGGER LOOKING AT MY DAUGHTER . . . AUGHTER GRAB EM UP AND SHIP
EVERY BLACK OF THEM OUT OF THE COUNTRY . . . AUGHTER JUST LINE
EM UP AND MOW EM DOWN MACHINEGUNFIRE!"

All Americans: loving their families, going to church regularly
    depositing money in their neighborhood bank   45
All Fourth-of-July celebrators vomitted up from the guiltridden
    cockroach sick sex terror of the Eldorado of the West[3]
Talking to themselves, fantasizing hatred
In drinking bars and public houses[4]
On street corners and park benches   50
At bridge clubs and bingo games
And in fashionable midtown Manhattan restaurants.

Shame! Shame! Shame![5]

No Holy Savior shall cry out upon the Black Nation this year
No true believer, no trombonist, no coal train[6]   55
The only Messiah black people will know this year is a bullet
In the belly
    of a black youth shot down by a coward crouched
    behind an outlaw's badge—[7]
Mississippi   60
Georgia
Tennessee, Alabama
Your mother your father your brothers sisters
    wives sons daughters and loved ones
Up   65
And
Down
The hot land
      There is a specter haunting America![8]
Spitfire of clubs, pistols, shotguns, and the missing   70
Murdered
Mutilated
Bodies of relatives and friends
Be the only Santa Claus black children will remember this year
Be the only Jesus Christ born this year curled out dead on the   75
    pavement, torso floating at the bottom of a lake.[9]

3. The Eldorado, a twin-tower apartment building located in Manhattan's Upper West Side,
known for its famous and wealthy residents.
4. Pubs.
5. A 1963 song by blues singer Jimmy Reed
(1925–1976).
6. Pun on John Coltrane (1926–1967), avant-
garde jazz saxophonist.
7. Reference to the killing of James Powell, a
15-year-old black resident of Yorkville, during the
summer of 1964 by white off-duty police officer
Thomas Gilligan who, when asked by Powell's
grieving friend, "Why did you shoot him?" took
his police badge from his pocket, pinned it on his
shirt, and answered, "This is why." Angry protests
met by police violence followed for six consecutive
nights, known as the New York Riot of 1964.
8. Play on the opening line of *The Communist
Manifesto* (1848) by German political philosophers Karl Marx (1818–1883) and Friedrich
Engels (1820–1895): "A spectre is haunting
Europe—the spectre of communism."
9. Allusion to the murder of black youth Emmett
Till (1941–1955) at the hands of white men
angry at his exchange with a white woman in a
small grocery store in Money, Mississippi. Till's
bound and mutilated corpse was discovered several days later in the Tallahatchie River.

You say there are twenty-five million blacks in America and one
      gate to the ghetto[1]
Make their own bed hard and that is where they have got to lie[2]
You say there is violence and lawlessness in the ghetto, niggers   80
      run amuck perpetrating crimes against property, looting stores,
      breaking windows, flinging beer bottles at officers of the law
You say a virgin gave birth to God
Through some mysterious process, some divine conjure,[3] a messenger
      of the Lord turned his walking cane into a serpent,[4] and the   85
      snake stood upright and walked away like a natural man[5]
You say . . .

AMERICA, WHY ARE YOU SCARED OF THE SCARECROW?

I say!
There is TERROR in the ghettoes!   90
Terror that shakes the foundation of the very assholes
      of the people
And fear! And corruption! and Murder!

The ghettoes are the plantations of America
Rat infested tenements totter like shanty houses stacked upon   95
      one another
Circular plague of the welfare check brings vicious wine every
      semi-month, wretched babies twice a year, death and hopelessness
      every time the sun goes down
Big-bellied agents of absentee slumlords and trustee insurance   100
      companies and millionaire humanitarian philanthropists
Forcing little black girls to get down and do the dog before they
      learn to spell their names—sleeping on the floor
They do not have any beds to make hard!

He[6] said he was fifteen years old   105
And as he walked beside us there in the littered fields of the
      Harlem Nation, he spoke with a dignity of the language that
      shocked us
And he said he had a *theory* about what *perpetrated* the horror
      that was upon us, walking among flying bullets, broken glass,   110
      curses and the ignorant phalluses of cops whirling about
      our bloody heads.
He said he was a business major at George Washington High School
And he picked up a bottle and hurled it above the undulating crowd

1. Typically, the Jewish ghettos of Europe had only one entrance and one exit gate, so that those leaving and those entering would not pass each other; the gates were often locked at night and during Christian festivals.
2. Reference to a well-known proverb: "You've made your bed, now lie in it."
3. Magic spell (referencing West Indian and African American vernacular religious practice).
4. Reference to passage of Exodus in which Moses attempts to persuade Pharoah to free the Hebrew slaves: "And Moses and Aaron went in unto Pharoah, and they did so as the Lord had commanded: and Aaron cast down his rod before Pharoah, and before his servants, and it became a serpent" (7.10).
5. In Genesis, God's judgment upon the serpent for his role in the fall of mankind, "upon thy belly shalt thou go" (Genesis 3.14), has often been taken to suggest that this creature formerly walked upright.
6. Black activist William "Bill" Epton Jr. (1932–2002), speaking about James Powell (see earlier note); Epton was jailed on charges of "criminal anarchy" after delivering a speech, "We Accuse," during the demonstrations following Powell's killing.

Straight into the chalk face of a black helmet!— 115
Thirty-seven Properties Ransacked
Steel Gates Ripped From Their Hinges
Front Panes Shattered
Pawn Shops   Dry Cleaners   Liquor Stores . . . Piggly Wigglies[7]
Ripped 120
        apart
            and
            LOOTED!

"Niggers will do anything!"
And long as the sun rises in the East 125
Niggers, in dingy fish-n-chip and bar-b-q joints,
Will be doing business as usual—
From River to river,
Signboard to signboard
Dribbling Schaefer six-packs of beer all over the ghetto 130
Marques Haynes[8] is a globetrotting basketball playing fool.

TERROR stalks the Black Nation
A Genocide so blatant
Black men and women die in the gutters as if they were reptiles
And every third child will do the dope addict nod[9] in the whore- 135
        scented night before the fire this time[1]
And Fourth-of-July comes with the blasting bullet in the mind
        of a black man
Against which no great white father, no social worker,
        no psychothanatopsis[2] 140
Will nail ninety-nine *theses* to no door:[3]
            Jitterbugging
                in
                    the streets!

                                        1968

---

7. Supermarket chain.
8. Haynes (b. 1926) was a member of the Harlem Globetrotters basketball team, noted for his extraordinary dribbling ability.
9. Drug-induced stupor.
1. Allusion to *The Fire Next Time* (1963) by African American writer James Baldwin (1924–1987), which explored the crisis of racial relations in contemporary America. The book's title refers to the lines of a spiritual: "God gave Noah the rainbow sign / No more water, the fire next time."
2. Portmanteau word combining *psycho* (mental or psychical) and *thanatopsis* (a contemplation of death).
3. German priest Martin Luther (1483–1546) posted his pamphlet "The Ninety-Five Theses" on the door of the Castle Church of Wittenberg, Germany, in 1517, an event often described as the beginning of the Protestant Reformation.

AUDRE LORDE
1934–1992

Acclaimed essayist, poet, and feminist theorist, Audre Lorde was born Audrey Geraldine Lorde to West Indian parents in Harlem, New York, in 1934. In *Zami: A New Spelling of My Name* (1982), Lorde explained why, at age four, she chose to rename herself: "I did not like the tail of the Y hanging down below the line in Audrey, and would always forget to put it on, which used to disturb my mother greatly." This childhood act of self-determination presages the themes and motifs that characterize much of Lorde's later poetry and nonfiction—the struggle for self-expression in a society that considers difference to be subversive and suspect. In *Sister Outsider: Essays and Speeches* (1984), Lorde refutes the belief that difference can at best be merely tolerated by society; instead, she writes, difference is an energizing charge, "a fund of necessary polarities between which our creativity can spark." A self-described "Black lesbian mother warrior poet" who played significant roles in the civil rights, feminist, and LGBT movements—and who was among the first public figures to speak openly of her experience of breast cancer—Lorde embraced her "differences" as inspiration for generative insight and expressive power.

As her self-naming suggests, Lorde's childhood and educational experiences were integral to her development as a poet and theorist. Lorde confessed that, as a child, she had difficulty learning to speak in complete sentences, expressing herself instead through the poems and poetic fragments she had memorized. She attended Catholic elementary schools in New York City and, while still in high school, published her first poem in *Seventeen* magazine because the editors of her school's literary journal deemed her submission inappropriately romantic. This uneasy relation to self-appointed custodians of official literary expression extended to Lorde's experience of sophisticated black culture in New York, as she found when occasionally taking part during her Hunter High years in poetry workshops sponsored by the prestigious Harlem Writers Guild. "There had been a very uneasy dialogue between me and the Harlem Writers Guild where I felt I was tolerated but never really accepted—that I was both crazy and queer but would grow out of it all." The social challenges of Lorde's fledgling literary career foretell a lifelong quest to find partners for a dialogue in which acceptance could be achieved without compromise of personhood or principle.

After completing high school, she enrolled at the National University of Mexico in 1954 for one year, which she later identified as one of the transformative experiences of her life. In a land of greater racial, social, and intellectual variety than she experienced in 1950s America, Lorde was struck by a revelation of "connectedness" that would beckon to her in subsequent years of continued alienation: "I stood on this hill, halfway down to the market, and for the first time in that one instant I felt that I could make a connection—that there could be a real connection between the things that I felt most deeply and those gorgeous words that I needed to spin in order to live . . . And for one minute I thought 'I can write a poem that feels like this.'" Lorde's vision in Mexico, and particularly its ideal of fitting words to life, would linger in her consciousness as a creatively disruptive alternative to the life she would soon take up again as an evidently conventional New Yorker pursuing the life of an educated aspirant to middle-class respectability.

Upon returning to New York, Lorde earned her B.A. in English and Philosophy from Hunter College in 1959, and received her M.A. from the Columbia University School of Library Science in 1961. During the 1950s she had been employed intermittently as an x-ray technician and factory laborer; she worked as a librarian during the 1960s, eventually attaining the position of head librarian of the Town School Library from 1966 to 1968.

The turbulent period of the late 1960s were also pivotal years for Lorde's burgeoning career as poet. In 1968 Diane Di Prima, whom Lorde had met at Hunter College, published Lorde's first collection of poems, *The First Cities*. In fact, her reputation as a poet preceded this publication, for she received the first copies of *The First Cities* while serving as poet-in-residence at Tougaloo College, a small historically black college in Mississippi. There, amidst the growing turmoil of the civil rights movement, Lorde formed a poetry workshop composed of approximately ten undergraduates, most of whom were black, militant, and eager to discuss the era's pressing issues of race and social justice. As with her sojourn in Mexico, her work at Tougaloo initiated for Lorde a radical reevaluation of her personal and professional priorities. "It was pivotal for me because in 1968 my first book had just been published; it was my first trip into the Deep South; it was the first time I had been away from my children. It was the first time I dealt with young black students in a workshop situation. I came to realize that this was my work, that teaching and writing were inextricably combined, and it was there that I knew what I wanted to do for the rest of my life." This epiphany was equally about poetry as a discipline and life as a mission. Both literary vocation and lived experience seemed to her a blank page, daunting but thrilling. "Formally, I knew nothing. I had never read a book *about* poetry! So I would talk to the students, and I was learning." Aptly titled *Cables to Rage,* the book of poems Lorde wrote during the Tougaloo period blended Lorde's increasing attention to poetic craft with an urgency to live the truth of her "crazy and queer" identity. It was at Tougaloo that she met her female lover, Frances Clayton, who would accompany Lorde on the extraordinary artistic path that now stretched before her.

Lorde would publish nine subsequent volumes of poetry: *From a Land Where Other People Live* (1973), which was nominated for the National Book Award; *New York Head Shop and Museum* (1974); *Coal* (1976); *Between Ourselves* (1976); *The Black Unicorn* (1978); *Chosen Poems: Old and New* (1982); *Our Dead behind Us* (1986); *Undersong: Chosen Poems Old and New* (1992); and the posthumous *The Marvelous Arithmetics of Distance* (1993). In each collection, Lorde explored her complex identity, which she would later term her "consciousness as a woman, a black lesbian feminist mother lover poet all I am," and interrogated American homophobia, imperialism, and racism with unrelenting acuity and candor. She was awarded the Walt Whitman Citation of Merit in 1991, making her the poet laureate of New York State.

With the release of *Coal* in 1976, Lorde became an influential voice among Black Arts writers, though her relation to the movement was always complex. In that context, it is tempting to read the title poem's images of coal and diamond as metaphors for a purified blackness, but Lorde characteristically undermines any such essentialist oversimplification with a continual shifting of subject positions, a self-reflexive rumination on the very act of symbolization that embodies the poem's early claim that "there are many kinds of open." This intricate openness constitutes a central theme of her next collection of poems, *The Black Unicorn,* an effort to ahieve an expansive ideal of identity with a richer range of mythic, social, and linguistic resources. Drawing upon African creation stories, with their compelling pantheon of female divinities, Lorde begins to fashion her own version of pan-Africanism that at once augments and challenges those of many Black Arts era artists and activists. If for writers like Baraka and Reed, African cosmologies furnished a repetoire of bold male gods capable of forging and defending an aboriginal black universe, for Lorde that warrior ethos is transferred to a female vangard capable equally of force and fertility. Emblemized in the amazonian heroine (whose self-sacrifice of one breast in the service of military prowess resonated with Lorde's own struggle with breast cancer), Lorde's africanicity inflects gender and sexuality in terms that oppose the masculinist ethos prevalent among many male writers of the period, though it aims no less at a reimagined "blackness" capable of fierce yet loving communal identity. But for Lorde such "blackness" becomes not a privileged but a companion figure, sharing space and authority with other dimensions of self-hood in Lorde's vision of ancestrally founded consciousness.

Though Lorde once remarked that "communicating deep feeling in linear, solid blocks of print felt arcane, a method beyond me," she is widely recognized for her non-fiction prose. *The Cancer Journals* (1980) is part confession, part polemic; it chronicles the diagnosis and treatment of and her recovery from breast cancer even as it inveighs against cultural norms of physical beauty that "encourage" postoperative breast cancer patients to conceal their new "deformities" with prostheses. Lorde would once again reflect on the effects of cancer on her life in *A Burst of Light* (1988), a collage of essays and journal entries that won an American Book Award in 1989. Lorde's *Zami: A New Spelling of My Name* (1982) is likewise a remarkable literary feat that seamlessly blends memoir, myth, and poetry. A record of her childhood and early adulthood, *Zami* is an often poignant, often didactic, but always emotionally raw narrative of sexual self-awareness and of the friendships forged among marginalized black women. In the highly influential anthology *Sister Outsider: Essays and Speeches* (1984), Lorde insists that those whom society has marginalized must communicate their experiences and render visible, however painfully, what society endeavors to repress.

Lorde's activism and political vision, however, were not confined to her poetry and prose writings. She taught at Hunter College, at Lehman College, and at John Jay College; lectured widely on racism and on homophobia; co-founded The Kitchen Table: Women of Color Press; and was a featured speaker at the first national gay and lesbian march held in Washington, D.C., in 1979. She also worked tirelessly to mobilize women across the African diaspora, establishing the St. Croix Women's Coalition and the Sisterhood in Support of Sisters in South Africa.

Seven years before her death, Lorde relocated to the Caribbean, where she adopted the African name Gamba Adisa, expressing her dedication to Pan-Africanism. There, she prepared a final volume of poetry, *Undersong: Chosen Poems Old and New* (1992). That year, at the age of fifty-eight, she succumbed to liver cancer at her home on St. Croix. In considering her complex legacy, we might do best by recalling Lorde's reflection on her poetry's effort to revisit our inheritances of thought and feeling: "The white fathers told us: I think, therefore I am. The Black mother within each of us— the poet—whispers in our dreams: I feel, therefore I can be free. Poetry coins the language to express and charter this revolutionary demand, the implementation of that freedom."

Following her death, virtually every major U.S. journal and newspaper eulogized Lorde, and women across the United States, Europe, and the Caribbean held tributes in her honor. In the November 20, 1992, edition of the *Boston Globe*, columnist Renee Graham praised Lorde's sparkling lyricism and emotional register: "With words spun into light, she could weep like Billie Holiday, chuckle like Dizzy Gillespie, or bark bad like John Coltrane."

New York City 1970

How do you spell change like frayed slogan underwear
with the emptied can of yesterdays' meanings
with yesterdays' names?
And what does the we-bird see with
who has lost its I's?   5

There is nothing beautiful left in the streets of this city.
I have come to believe in death and renewal by fire.[1]

---

1. In classical mythology, the phoenix, later also called the firebird, was an eagle-like bird that was consumed by a funeral pyre ignited by the sun, only to renew itself from its own ashes for another long cycle of life.

Past questioning the necessities of blood
or why it must be mine or my children's time
that will see the grim city quake to be reborn perhaps   10
blackened again but this time with a sense of purpose;
tired of the past tense forever, of assertion and repetition
of the ego-trips through an incomplete self
where two years ago proud rang for promise[2] but now
it is time for fruit and all the agonies are barren—   15
only the children are growing:[3]

For how else can the self become whole
save by making self into its own new religion?
I am bound like an old lover—a true believer—
to this city's death by accretion and slow ritual,   20
and I submit to its penance for a trial
as new steel is tried[4]
I submit my children also to its death throes and agony
and they are not even the city's past lovers. But I submit them
to the harshness and growing cold to the brutalizations   25
which if survived
will teach them strength or an understanding of how strength is gotten
and will not be forgotten: It will be their city then:
I submit them
loving them above all others save myself   30
to the fire to the rage to the ritual scarifications[5]
to be tried as new steel is tried;
and in its wasting the city shall try them
as the blood-splash of a royal victim
tries the hand of the destroyer.[6]   35

II

I hide behind tenements and subways in fluorescent alleys
watching as flames walk the streets of an empire's altar
raging through the veins of the sacrificial stenchpot
smeared upon the east shore of a continent's insanity
conceived in the psychic twilight of murderers and pilgrims   40
rank with money and nightmare and too many useless people
who will not move over nor die, who cannot bend
even before the winds of their own preservation
even under the weight of their own hates
Who cannot amend nor conceive nor even learn to share   45
their own visions

2. Possible reference to passage of the Civil Rights Act of 1968, the last of the three great civil rights federal legislative achievements of the 1960s following the Civil Rights Act of 1964 and the Voting Rights Act of 1965. The bill guaranteed fair access to housing but provided no provisions for the law's enforcement.
3. Possible reference to Sophocles' *Oedipus the King*, which opens with a priest accompanied by children lamenting the curse of barren fields that plagues the great city of Thebes.
4. Newly formed steel is strengthened by application of extreme heat, a process called "tempering."
5. The practice of cutting and raising dermal scars on the face or body has a long history among many African cultures for whom the resultant complex patterns serve variously to enhance beauty and indicate social or spiritual status.
6. The Yoruba are said to have practiced human sacrifice until the 20th century; only the purest or best individuals were selected for sacrifice in order to propitiate certain divinities and to purify the community in times of crisis.

who bomb my children into mortar in churches[7]
and work plastic offal and metal and the flesh of their enemies
into subway rush-hour temples where obscene priests
finger and worship each other in secret   50
and think they are praying when they squat
to shit money-pebbles shaped like their parents' brains—
who exist to go into dust to exist again
grosser and more swollen and without ever relinquishing
space or breath or energy from their private hoard.   55

I do not need to make war nor peace
with these prancing and murderous deacons[8]
who refuse to recognize their role in this covenant[9] we live upon
and so have come to fear and despise even their own children;
but I condemn myself, and my loves   60
past and present
and the blessed enthusiasms of all my children
to this city
without reason or future
without hope   65
to be tried as the new steel is tried
before trusted to slaughter.

I walk down the withering limbs of my last discarded house
and there is nothing worth salvage left in this city
but the faint reedy voices like echoes   70
of once beautiful children.[1]

                                                                    1970

Coal

I
Is the total black, being spoken
From the earth's inside.
There are many kinds of open.
How a diamond comes into a knot of flame[1]   5
How a sound comes into a word, coloured
By who pays what for speaking.[2]

7. On September 15, 1963, in an act of white supremacist terrorism, the 16th Street Baptist Church in Birmingham, Alabama was bombed, killing four young girls. The bombing immediately became a critical moment and powerful symbol in the civil rights struggle.
8. Lay preachers, given biblical sanction in 1 Timothy 3.8: "Likewise must the deacons be grave, not doubletongued, not given much to wine, not greedy of filthy lucre."
9. Solemn agreement; in biblical terms, one that links entrance into a community with a promise to God of faith, and links God to the community in a pledge of care and perpetual inheritance of the promised land.

1. Cf. the Old Testament's Book of Lamentations, which mourns the destruction of Jerusalem and the Holy Temple in the 6th century B.C.E.: "Her [Jerusalem's] adversaries are the chief, her enemies prosper; for the Lord hath afflicted her for the multitude of her transgressions: her children are gone into captivity before the enemy" (Lamentations 1.5).
1. Like coal, diamonds are produced after great pressure and heat are applied to carbon, though diamonds are created over billions of years, coal over millions, under differing natural conditions.
2. In the Bible's Book of Isaiah, a heavenly being touches the prophet's mouth with a cleansing coal (6.6–7).

Some words are open
Like a diamond on glass windows
Singing out within the crash of passing sun   10
Then there are words like stapled wagers
In a perforated book—buy and sign and tear apart—
And come whatever wills all chances
The stub remains
An ill-pulled tooth with a ragged edge.   15
Some words live in my throat
Breeding like adders.[3] Others know sun
Seeking like gypsies over my tongue
To explode through my lips
Like young sparrows bursting from shell.   20
Some words
Bedevil me.

Love is a word another kind of open—
As a diamond comes into a knot of flame
I am black because I come from the earth's inside   25
Take my word for jewel in your open light.

                                                                      1976

Power

The difference between poetry and rhetoric
is being ready to kill
yourself
instead of your children.

I am trapped on a desert of raw gunshot wounds   5
and a dead child dragging his shattered
black face off the edge of my sleep
blood from his punctured cheeks and shoulders
is the only liquid for miles and my stomach
churns at the imagined taste while   10
my mouth splits into dry lips
without loyalty or reason
thirsting for the wetness of his blood
as it sinks into the whiteness
of the desert where I am lost   15
without imagery or magic
trying to make power
out of hatred and destruction
trying to heal my dying son with kisses
only the sun will bleach his bones quicker.   20

3. Snakes (traditionally considered demonic).

The policeman who shot down a ten year old in Jamaica[1]
stood over the boy with his cop shoes in childish blood
and a voice said "Die you little motherfucker"[2] and
there are tapes to prove that.
At his trial this policeman said in his own defense   25
"I didn't notice the size or anything else
only the color," and
there are tapes to prove that too.

Today that 37 year old white man with 13 years of police forcing
was set free   30
by 11 white men who said they were satisfied
justice had been done
and one black woman who said "They convinced me"[3]
meaning
they had dragged her 4'10" black woman's frame   35
over the hot coals of four centuries of white male approval
until she let go of the first real power she ever had
and lined her own womb with cement
to make a graveyard for our children.

I have not been able to touch the destruction within me   40
but unless I learn to use
the difference between poetry and rhetoric
my power too will run corrupt as poisonous mold
or lie limp and useless as an unconnected wire
and one day I will take my teenaged plug   45
and connect it to the nearest socket
raping some 85 year old white woman
and as I beat her senseless and set a torch to her bed
a greek chorus will be singing in ¾ time[4]
"Poor thing. She never hurt a soul. What beasts they are."   50

1976

Poetry Is Not a Luxury

The quality of light by which we scrutinize our lives has direct bearing
upon the product which we live, and upon the changes which we hope to
bring about through those lives. It is within this light that we form those
ideas by which we pursue our magic and make it realized. This is poetry as
illumination, for it is through poetry that we give name to those ideas which

1. On April 28, 1973, a ten-year-old black boy
named Clifford Glover was shot in the back
while running away from New York police officer Thomas Shea in the South Jamaica section
of the borough of Queens. On June 12 Shea was
indicted on a charge of murder and, after a
lengthy trial, was acquitted by a jury of eleven
white men and one African American woman,
Ederica Campbell.
2. At the crime scene, an obscene remark uttered
by a police officer was inadvertently transmitted
over police radio.
3. After the trial, when another juror inadvertently revealed her as the one who had held out
against acquittal the longest, Campbell stated,
"They almost killed me, and I almost killed
them."
4. Musical time signature or meter; "greek chorus": in classical drama, a group of characters,
usually representing and often played by citizens, who typically offer judgments about a
play's protagonists.

are—until the poem—nameless and formless, about to be birthed, but already felt. That distillation of experience from which true poetry springs births thought as dream births concept, as feeling births idea, as knowledge births (precedes) understanding.

As we learn to bear the intimacy of scrutiny and to flourish within it, as we learn to use the products of that scrutiny for power within our living, those fears which rule our lives and form our silences begin to lose their control over us.

For each of us as women, there is a dark place within, where hidden and growing our true spirit rises, "beautiful / and tough as chestnut / stanchions against (y)our nightmare of weakness /"[1] and of impotence.

These places of possibility within ourselves are dark because they are ancient and hidden; they have survived and grown strong through that darkness. Within these deep places, each one of us holds an incredible reserve of creativity and power, of unexamined and unrecorded emotion and feeling. The woman's place of power within each of us is neither white nor surface; it is dark, it is ancient, and it is deep.

When we view living in the european mode only as a problem to be solved, we rely solely upon our ideas to make us free, for these were what the white fathers told us were precious.

But as we come more into touch with our own ancient, noneuropean consciousness of living as a situation to be experienced and interacted with, we learn more and more to cherish our feelings, and to respect those hidden sources of our power from where true knowledge and, therefore, lasting action comes.

At this point in time, I believe that women carry within ourselves the possibility for fusion of these two approaches so necessary for survival, and we come closest to this combination in our poetry. I speak here of poetry as a revelatory distillation of experience, not the sterile word play that, too often, the white fathers distorted the word *poetry* to mean—in order to cover a desperate wish for imagination without insight.

For women, then, poetry is not a luxury. It is a vital necessity of our existence. It forms the quality of the light within which we predicate our hopes and dreams toward survival and change, first made into language, then into idea, then into more tangible action. Poetry is the way we help give name to the nameless so it can be thought. The farthest horizons of our hopes and fears are cobbled by our poems, carved from the rock experiences of our daily lives.

As they become known to and accepted by us, our feelings and the honest exploration of them become sanctuaries and spawning grounds for the most radical and daring of ideas. They become a safe-house for that difference so necessary to change and the conceptualization of any meaningful action. Right now, I could name at least ten ideas I would have found intolerable or incomprehensible and frightening, except as they came after dreams and poems. This is not idle fantasy, but a disciplined attention to the true meaning of "it feels right to me." We can train ourselves to respect our feelings and to transpose them into a language so they can be shared. And where that language does not yet exist, it is our poetry which helps to fashion it. Poetry is not only dream and vision; it is the skeleton architecture of

---

1. From Lorde's 1973 poem "Black Mother Woman."

our lives. It lays the foundations for a future of change, a bridge across our fears of what has never been before.

Possibility is neither forever nor instant. It is not easy to sustain belief in its efficacy. We can sometimes work long and hard to establish one beach-head of real resistance to the deaths we are expected to live, only to have that beachhead assaulted or threatened by those canards we have been socialized to fear, or by the withdrawal of those approvals that we have been warned to seek for safety. Women see ourselves diminished or soft-ened by the falsely benign accusations of childishness, of nonuniversality, of changeability, of sensuality. And who asks the question: Am I altering your aura, your ideas, your dreams, or am I merely moving you to temporary and reactive action? And even though the latter is no mean task, it is one that must be seen within the context of a need for true alteration of the very foundations of our lives.

The white fathers told us: I think, therefore I am.[2] The Black mother within each of us—the poet—whispers in our dreams: I feel, therefore I can be free. Poetry coins the language to express and charter this revolutionary demand, the implementation of that freedom.

However, experience has taught us that action in the now is also necessary, always. Our children cannot dream unless they live, they cannot live unless they are nourished, and who else will feed them the real food without which their dreams will be no different from ours? "If you want us to change the world someday, we at least have to live long enough to grow up!" shouts the child.

Sometimes we drug ourselves with dreams of new ideas. The head will save us. The brain alone will set us free. But there are no new ideas still waiting in the wings to save us as women, as human. There are only old and forgotten ones, new combinations, extrapolations and recognitions from within ourselves—along with the renewed courage to try them out. And we must constantly encourage ourselves and each other to attempt the hereti-cal actions that our dreams imply, and so many of our old ideas disparage. In the forefront of our move toward change, there is only poetry to hint at possibility made real. Our poems formulate the implications of ourselves, what we feel within and dare make real (or bring action into accordance with), our fears, our hopes, our most cherished terrors.

For within living structures defined by profit, by linear power, by institu-tional dehumanization, our feelings were not meant to survive. Kept around as unavoidable adjuncts or pleasant pastimes, feelings were expected to kneel to thought as women were expected to kneel to men. But women have sur-vived. As poets. And there are no new pains. We have felt them all already. We have hidden that fact in the same place where we have hidden our power. They surface in our dreams, and it is our dreams that point the way to free-dom. Those dreams are made realizable through our poems that give us the strength and courage to see, to feel, to speak, and to dare.

If what we need to dream, to move our spirits most deeply and directly toward and through promise, is discounted as a luxury, then we give up the core—the fountain—of our power, our womanness; we give up the future of our worlds.

---

2. The conventional English translation of French philosopher René Descartes's (1596–1650) Latin phrase *cogito ergo sum*, a fundamental precept of modern Western thought.

For there are no new ideas. There are only new ways of making them felt—of examining what those ideas feel like being lived on Sunday morning at 7 A.M., after brunch, during wild love, making war, giving birth, mourning our dead—while we suffer the old longings, battle the old warnings and fears of being silent and impotent and alone, while we taste new possibilities and strengths.

1977

125th Street and Abomey[1]

Head bent, walking through snow
I see you Seboulisa[2]
printed inside the back of my head
like marks of the newly wrapped akai[3]
that kept my sleep fruitful in Dahomey   5
and I poured on the red earth in your honor
those ancient parts of me
most precious and least needed
my well-guarded past
the energy-eating secrets   10
I surrender to you as libation
mother, illuminate my offering
of old victories
over men over women over my selves
who has never before dared   15
to whistle into the night
take my fear of being alone
like my warrior sisters
who rode in defense of your queendom[4]
disguised and apart   20
give me the woman strength
of tongue in this cold season.

Half earth and time splits us apart
like struck rock.[5]
A piece lives elegant stories   25
too simply put
while a dream on the edge of summer
of brown rain in nim trees[6]
snail shells from the dooryard
of King Toffah[7]   30

---

1. Capital of the ancient African kingdom of Dahomey (modern-day Benin), one of the main centers of the slave trade. "125th Street": major thoroughfare in the Harlem district of Manhattan, today called "Martin Luther King Jr. Boulevard" and often referred to as "Harlem's Main Street."
2. Another name for the Dahomey hermaphroditic sky deity Mawu-Lisa, whom Lorde glosses in The Black Unicorn as "the goddess of Abomey—'The mother of us all' . . . sometimes known as Sogbo, creator of the world."
3. Tight woven braids wrapped with thread.
4. The Dahomey king employed a special sect of female warriors, known as Amazons, who would generally fight behind the men so as to mislead the enemy as to the army's size.
5. In Exodus 17.5–6, Moses strikes the rock at Horeb and produces water for the Israelites, whose thirst had caused them to doubt the presence of God.
6. A tree common in Benin, believed to cure malaria and other diseases.
7. King Toffah (generally spelled "Toffa") reigned in the kingdom of Hogbonu, a region of Benin now called Porto-Novo, from 1874 until his death in 1908.

bring me where my blood moves
Seboulisa mother goddess with one breast[8]
eaten away by worms of sorrow and loss
see me now
your severed daughter   35
laughing our name into echo
all the world shall remember.

                                                        1978

Walking Our Boundaries

This first bright day has broken
the back of winter.
We rise from war
to walk across the earth
around our house   5
both stunned that sun can shine so brightly
after all our pain
Cautiously we inspect our joint holding.
A part of last year's garden still stands
bracken[1]   10
one tough missed okra[2] pod clings to the vine
a parody of fruit cold-hard and swollen
underfoot
one rotting shingle
is becoming loam.   15

I take your hand beside the compost heap
glad to be alive and still
with you
we talk of ordinary articles
with relief   20
while we peer upward
each half-afraid
there will be no tight buds started
on our ancient apple tree
so badly damaged by last winter's storm   25
knowing
it does not pay to cherish symbols
when the substance
lies so close at hand
waiting to be held   30
your hand
falls off the apple bark
like casual fire

---

8. Double reference, first to the Amazons, who
according to legend removed their right breasts
to improve their ability to hurl javelins (*a-mazos*
is Greek for "without breast"); and then to Lorde's
own postsurgical condition.

1. A dense undergrowth of ferns.
2. Annual herb, native to Africa and extensively
cultivated in the southern United States; also
called gumbo.

along my back
my shoulders are dead leaves   35
waiting to be burned
to life.

The sun is watery warm
our voices
seem too loud for this small yard   40
too tentative for women
so in love
the siding has come loose in spots
our footsteps hold this place
together   45
as our place
our joint decisions make the possible
whole.
I do not know when
we shall laugh again   50
but next week
we will spade up another plot
for this spring's seeding.

1978

From Zami: A New Spelling of My Name

Epilogue

Every woman I have ever loved has left her print upon me, where I loved
some invaluable piece of myself apart from me—so different that I had to
stretch and grow in order to recognize her. And in that growing, we came to
separation, that place where work begins. Another meeting.

A year later, I finished library school.[1] The first summer of a new decade
was waning as I walked away from Seventh Street for the last time, leaving
that door unlocked for whatever person came after me who needed shelter.[2]
There were four half-finished poems scribbled on the bathroom wall
between the toilet and the bathtub, others in the window jambs and the
floorboards under the flowered linoleum, mixed up with the ghosts of rich
food smells.

The casing of this place had been my home for seven years, the amount
of time it takes for the human body to completely renew itself, cell by living
cell. And in those years my life had become increasingly a bridge and field
of women. Zami.

Zami. A Carriacou[3] name for women who work together as friends and
lovers.

We carry our traditions with us. Buying boxes of Red Cross Salt and a
fresh corn straw broom for my new apartment in Westchester: new job, new

1. Lorde received her degree in library science
from Columbia University in 1961.
2. After graduating from high school, Lorde
lived in an apartment on 7th Street in New York,
where she "played mother" to a number of young
women.
3. In reference to an island off the coast of Grenada in the West Indies.

house, new living the old in a new way. Recreating in words the women who helped give me substance.

> Ma-Liz, DeLois, Louise Briscoe, Aunt Anni, Linda, and Genevieve;[4] MawuLisa,[5] thunder, sky, sun, the great mother of us all; and Afrekete,[6] her youngest daughter, the mischievous linguist, trickster, best-beloved, whom we must all become.

Their names, selves, faces feed me like corn before labor. I live each of them as a piece of me, and I choose these words with the same grave concern with which I choose to push speech into poetry, the mattering core, the forward visions of all our lives.

Once *home* was a long way off, a place I had never been to but knew out of my mother's mouth. I only discovered its latitudes when Carriacou was no longer my home.

There it is said that the desire to lie with other women is a drive from the mother's blood.

1984

Inheritance—His

I.

My face resembles your face
less and less each day. When I was young
no one mistook whose child I was.
Features   build   coloring
alone among my creamy fine-boned sisters   5
marked me Byron's daughter.[1]

No sun set when you died, but a door
opened onto my mother. After you left
she grieved her crumpled world aloft
an iron fist sweated with business symbols   10
a printed blotter   *dwell in a house of Lord's*[2]
your hollow voice chanting down a hospital corridor[3]
       yea, though I walk through the valley
       of the shadow of death
       I will fear no evil.[4]   15

4. Female relatives, close friends, role models, and lovers associated with Lorde's childhood and adolescence, listed in the same order—with explanatory notes—in the prologue to *Zami*.
5. The hermaphroditic creator deity in Dahomey cosmology.
6. In the Afro-Cuban pantheon, a mother goddess associated with the ocean; in *Zami*, Lorde's final lover as she begins fully to accept her lesbian identity. Since the publication of *Zami*, Afrekete's name has become generically associated with love between women.
1. Audre, daughter of Frederick Byron Lorde, resembled her father more than the sisters with whom she was reared, Helen and Phyllis.
2. Reference to Psalm 23.6—"Surely goodness and mercy shall follow me all the days of my life: and I will dwell in the house of the Lord for ever"—and to the fact that her father, Byron Lorde, along with his wife, Linda, ran a real estate business that managed small rooming-houses in Harlem.
3. Byron Lorde died after suffering several severe strokes.
4. See Psalm 23.4.

II.

I rummage through the deaths you lived
swaying on a bridge of question.
At seven   in Barbados[5]
dropped into your unknown father's life
your courage vault from his tailor's table   20
back to the sea
Did the Grenada[6] treeferns sing
your 15th summer as you jumped ship
to seek your mother
finding her   too late   25
surrounded with new sons?[7]

Who did you bury to become enforcer of the law[8]
the handsome legend
before whose raised arm even trees wept
a man of deep and wordless passion   30
who wanted sons and got five girls?[9]
You left the first two scratching in a treefern's shade
the youngest[1] is a renegade poet
searching for your answer in my blood.

My mother's Grenville[2] tales   35
spin through early summer evenings.
But you refused to speak of home
of stepping proud Black and penniless
into this land where only white men
ruled by money.   How you labored   40
in the docks of the Hotel Astor[3]
your bright wife a chambermaid upstairs[4]
welded love and survival to ambition
as the land of promise withered
crashed   the hotel closed   45
and you peddle dawn-bought apples
from a pushcart on Broadway.
Does an image of return
wealthy and triumphant
warm your chilblained[5] fingers   50
as you count coins in the Manhattan snow
or is it only Linda
who dreams of home?

---

5. Island country in the eastern Caribbean;
Lorde's father's land of origin.
6. Island country in the southeastern Caribbean; Lorde's mother's land of origin.
7. At age fifteen, while working as an apprentice
in his father's tailor shop, Byron ran away in
search of his mother, whom he found with a new
family only years later.
8. Byron Lorde was a police constable before
emigrating from Grenada.
9. Audre was raised with two sisters, but later
discovered that her Byron had fathered two

other girls, twins, the year that her parents were
married.
1. I.e., Audre Lorde.
2. Linda Lorde's hometown on the east coast of
Grenada.
3. I.e., the Waldorf-Astoria Hotel.
4. Linda Lorde's light skin allowed her the
"upstairs" employment of chambermaid in a luxurious hotel.
5. Inflammatory swelling or sore caused by
exposure to cold.

When my mother's first-born cries for milk
in the brutal city winter   55
do the faces of your other daughters dim
like the image of the treeferned yard
where a dark girl first cooked for you
and her ash heap still smells curry?

III.

Did the secret of my sisters steal your tongue   60
like I stole money from your midnight pockets
stubborn and quaking
as you threaten to shoot me if I am the one?
the naked lightbulbs in our kitchen ceiling
glint off your service revolver   65
as you load   whispering.

Did two little dark girls in Grenada
dart like flying fish
between your averted eyes
and my pajamaless body   70
our last adolescent summer
eavesdropped orations
to your shaving mirror
our most intense conversations
were you practicing how to tell me   75
of my twin sisters   abandoned
as you had been abandoned
by another Black woman seeking
her fortune   Grenada   Barbados
Panama   Grenada.   80
New York City.

IV.

You bought old books at auction
for my unlanguaged world
gave me your idols   Marcus Garvey   Citizen Kane[6]
and morsels from your dinner plate   85
when I was seven.
I owe you my Dahomeyan[7] jaw
the free high school for gifted girls[8]
no one else thought I should attend
and the darkness that we share.   90
Our deepest bonds remain
the mirror and the gun.

---

6. 1941 film directed by Orson Welles. Marcus Mosiah Garvey Jr. (1887–1940), self-educated Jamaican-born Pan-Africanist and proponent of the black nationalist "Back to Africa" movement, which encouraged African Americans to emigrate to African nations of origin as a means of recovering social and economic power.
7. Referring to Dahomey, ancient kingdom of the Fon people, now Benin.
8. Hunter High School, where Lorde said she found a "lifeline" in a "sisterhood of rebels."

V.

An elderly Black judge
known for his way with women
visits this island where I live[9]   95
shakes my hand, smiling
"I knew your father," he says
"quite a man!" Smiles again.
I flinch at his raised eyebrow.
A long-gone woman's voice   100
lashes out at me   in parting
"You will never be satisfied
until you have the whole world
in your bed!"

Now I am older than you were when you died   105
overwork and silence exploding in your brain.
You are gradually receding from my face.
Who were you outside the 23rd Psalm?
Knowing so little
how did I become so much   110
like you?

Your hunger for rectitude
blossoms into rage
the hot tears of mourning
never shed for you before   115
your twisted measurements
the agony of denial
the power of unshared secrets.

                                                    1992

9. St. Croix, in the Caribbean, where Lorde spent a great portion of her final years and where she died.

HENRY DUMAS
(1934–1968)

Henry Dumas was among the most original writers of the Black Arts era, producing poetry and fiction rich in wide-ranging languages, images, and cosmologies, but unified in their aim of recovering a primary "soul force" of African American spiritual identity. Drawing upon an astonishing array of sources from African religions and African American vernacular traditions to European mythology and American modernist authors, Dumas fashioned a style that is at once formally simple and conceptually challenging. Beyond establishing a voice that is distinctive in its blend of accessibility and complexity, Dumas works thereby offered a unique perspective on the fundamental questions posed by the Black Arts movement's aesthetic and political ambitions: What is "blackness" and what kind of culture does it evoke and demand? From whom and for whom does authentic black expression emerge? And most importantly: How is the destiny of black folk in the New World linked to both ancestral origins and contemporary struggles waged globally by all peoples of color? Probing these questions through works haunted by traumatic memories of slavery and entrapment but uplifted by perceptions of transcendent possibility, Dumas sought a form of expression that could reconcile desire and history by renovating what he called the "broken chords" of African American experience.

Born in Sweet Home, Arkansas but raised in Harlem after moving there with his family at the age of ten, Dumas was educated by New York City schools, studying literature and philosophy at City College before leaving to enter the Air Force in 1953. His military service sent him first to the Arabian Peninsula and then to San Antonio, Texas, which together gave early substance to a growing interest in language and religion across cultural frames of reference. In particular, Dumas's sharp ear for both vernacular and priestly idioms began to absorb and mingle the sounds of Arabic and African American speech, while his scholarly nature led him to independent investigations of those idioms' linguistic and cultural roots. Gradually, he developed a view of history as a clash of official, dominant discourses and alternative systems of understanding grounded in the lived reality of oppressed communities. For Dumas this perception was simultaneously political and spiritual, leading him to commitments as a writer and social actor that were at once humble and fierce.

By the early 1960s, married to Loretta Ponton and father to sons David and Michael, Dumas was searching for a vocation through which to fuse his intellectual, social, and artistic capabilities. Though he undertook formal studies in linguistics, sociology, and English literature at Rutgers University in New Jersey, Dumas eventually left school to provide both sustenance for his family and support for the increasingly energized civil rights movement. Loretta Ponton later reflected that her husband's involvement in the struggle for black liberation was motivated by an underlying spiritual and humanitarian impulse, as he worked tirelessly to give succor to poor people in the South risking their lives in the cause of economic and social justice. That spiritual zeal soon took a practical turn in Dumas's life as he became first a social worker and then an educator, working to help underprepared students advance to college as assistant director of Upward Bound at Hiram College and then joining the Experiment in Higher Education at Southern Illinois University, where he helped develop cultural programs that often featured mixed media presentations of African American poetry, music, and dance. These experiences intensified Dumas's attentiveness to the sound of ordinary people taking charge of lives often wrenched from natural inclination, while affording him time to quietly develop his highly personal synthesis of metaphysical contemplation and revolutionary urgency.

Dumas began to give that singular vision public form through his contributions to many of the most important little magazines of the era, including *Umbra, Freedomways, The Anthologist, American Weave,* and *The Hiram Poetry Review.* Though in his lifetime his work was known only in these dispersed forms, he exerted a peculiar influence among other young African American writers like Amiri Baraka and Larry Neal, who expressed keen appreciation for what Baraka called "the fantastic aura of weirdness and mystery" that pervaded Dumas's carefully crafted but explosively purposeful poems and short stories. After his never-explained death at the hands of police on a New York City subway platform, Dumas, rather like Malcom X and John Coltrane, became something of a spectral icon of the Black Arts movement's aspiration for transformative consciousness achieved at the expense of violent sacrifice. Dumas finally began to enter the wider canons of modern African American writing with the posthumous publication in 1970 of his poetry in the volume *Poetry for my People* (re-released in 1974 as *Play Ebony, Play Ivory*) and his prose in the collection *Ark of Bones and Other Stories* (1970), both issued under the editorial direction of poet and educator Eugene Redmond, whom Dumas had met while working at the E.H.E. project at Southern Illinois University.

Dumas's writing is tinged with the urgency characteristic of his period's revolutionary fervor, but it is consistently suffused with a textured appreciation of, and sometimes longing for, a world of authentic "africanicity" that he finds deeply embedded in hard urban streets and the rich, oozing soil of onetime slaveholding territories. His characteristic idiom, sometimes stately, sometimes jagged, resonates with mythic power, while myth itself is subject to careful scrutiny, especially in explorations of the clash between western "civilization" and the cultures of non-white peoples. In a letter to a friend, Dumas describes the importance of his southern roots in his fashioning of this capacious artistic world: "I was born in the South (rural Arkansas) and come quite definitely from the rural elements. . . . My interest in Gospel music coincides with my interest in folk poetry and folk expression. There is a wealth of good things to be developed on in our heritage." That heritage is itself the beginning of Dumas's odyssey through world cultures and religions, part of a quest to study *all* facets of new and ancient African and modern African American traditions (including its various syncretistic fusions with European and Asian cultures). His vision draws widely from the imagery and intonations of Islamic, Greek, and Christian mysticisms, Western and Eastern mythological traditions, African and New World cosmologies, and philosophical formulations extending from allegorical Hindu epics to reflections on consciousness and time by modern figures like Williams James and Henri Bergson. Elements of blues, gospel, and jazz idioms permeate his work, often as a kind of subliminal hum rumbling beneath a surface texture of realistic image or ritual evocation.

Scenes of creation, set against apocalyptic portents, are frequently associated with these soundings in both his poetry and short stories. Like the images of natural elements—wind, earth, fire, and, especially, water—that flow through Dumas's works, these landscapes evoke the power of divination that Dumas, inspired by the iconography of West African religion, summoned as a means of cultural renewal. In "Will the Circle be Unbroken?," for example, the eruptive emergence of African Music shatters the edifice of the modern built world, linking Black Arts celebrations of "New Wave" or "Free" jazz to their literal and metaphorical sources in ancestral profundity. Thus does Dumas's work reach back in time and through space for expressive resources that can give idiosyncratic flavor to his vision of black nationalist assertion.

Black Star Line[1]

My black mothers I hear them singing.

> Sons, my sons,
> dip into this river with your ebony cups
> A vessel of knowledge sails under power.
> Study stars as well as currents.   5
> Dip into this river with your ebony cups.

My black fathers I hear them chanting.

> Sons, my sons,
> let ebony strike the blow that launches the ship!
> Send cargoes and warriors back to sea.   10

---

1. Reference to steamship company founded in 1919 by Marcus Garvey (1887–1940), Pan-Africanist founder of the United Negro Improvement Association (UNIA), as an instrument and emblem of his "Back to Africa" movement, which advocated the repatriation of African Americans to their African countries of origin.

Remember the pirates and their chains of nails.
Let ebony strike the blow that launches this ship.
Make your heads not idle sails, blown about
by any icy wind like a torn page from a book.
    Bones of my bones,[2]   15
all you golden-black children of the sun,
lift up! and read the sky
written in the tongue of your ancestors.
It is yours, claim it.
Make no idle sails, my sons,   20
make heavy-boned ships that break a wave and pass it.
Bring back sagas from Songhay, Kongo, Kaaba,[3]
deeds and words of Malik, Toussaint, Marcus,[4]
statues of Mahdi[5] and a lance of lightning.
Make no idle ships.   25
Remember the pirates.
For it is the sea who owns the pirates,
not the pirates the sea.

My black mothers I hear them singing.

    Children of my flesh,   30
dip into this river with your ebony cups.
A ship of knowledge sails unto wisdom.
Study what mars and what lifts up.
Dip into this river with your ebony cups.

                1965

Will the Circle Be Unbroken?[1]

At the edge of the spiral of musicians Probe sat cross-legged on a blue cloth, his soprano sax resting against his inner knee, his afro-horn linking his ankles like a bridge. The afro-horn was the newest axe[2] to cut the deadwood of the world. But Probe, since his return from exile, had chosen only special times to reveal the new sound. There were more rumors about it than there were ears and souls that had heard the horn speak. Probe's dark full head tilted toward the vibrations of the music as if the ring of sound from the six wailing pieces was tightening, creating a spiraling circle.

2. In Genesis, when Adam awakens to the newly created Eve, he says: "This is now bone of my bones, and flesh of my flesh" (2.23).

3. Central shrine of Islam, a one-room stone structure in Mecca toward which Muslims turn to pray and the destination of the prescribed pilgrimage, or *Hajj*; "Songhay": ancient empire of western Africa, founded ca. 700 by Berbers and reaching the height of its power around 1500; "Kongo": ancient West African kingdom founded ca. 1200 that was a highly developed nation when European colonialists arrived in force in the late 16th century.

4. Marcus Garvey; "Malik": El-Hajj Malik Shabazz (1925–1965), Muslim minister and black nationalist activist better known as Malcolm X;

"Toussaint": François Dominique Toussaint L'Ouverture (1743–1803), leader of the Haitian revolution (1791–1804).

5. In Muslim eschatology, the "Mahdi" is the prophesied redeemer (or "guided one") of Islam who will restore justice before the Day of Judgment.

1. Title of 1907 hymn by Ada Ruth Habershon (1861–1918), the chorus for which is: "Will the circle be unbroken / By and by, by and by? / Is a better home awaiting / In the sky, in the sky?" Recorded by Jimmy Collier and the Movement Singers, the hymn became an anthem of the civil rights movement.

2. Musical instrument (often a saxophone or other horn).

The black audience, unaware at first of its collectiveness, had begun to move in a soundless rhythm as if it were the tiny twitchings of an embryo. The waiters in the club fell against the wall, shadows, dark pillars holding up the building and letting the free air purify the mind of the club.

The drums took an oblique. Magwa's hands, like the forked tongue of a dark snake, probed the skins,[3] probed the whole belly of the coming circle. Beginning to close the circle, Haig's alto arc, rapid piano incisions, Billy's thin green flute arcs and tangents, Stace's examinations of his own trumpet discoveries, all fell separately, yet together, into a blanket which Mojohn had begun weaving on bass when the set began. The audience breathed, and Probe moved into the inner ranges of the sax.

Outside the Sound Barrier Club three white people were opening the door. Jan, a tenor sax case in his hand, had his game all planned. He had blown[4] with Probe six years ago on the West Coast. He did not believe that there was anything to this new philosophy the musicians were talking about. He would talk to Probe personally. He had known many Negro musicians and theirs was no different from any other artist's struggles to be himself, including his own.

Things were happening so fast that there was no one who knew all directions at once. He did not mind Ron and Tasha coming along. They were two of the hippest ofays[5] in town, and if anybody could break the circle of the Sound Club, it would be friends and old friends of friends.

Ron was bearded and scholarly. Thickset, shabbily dressed, but clean. He had tried to visit the Club before. But all of his attempts had been futile. He almost carried the result of one attempt to court. He could not understand why the cats[6] would want to bury themselves in Harlem and close the doors to the outside world. Ron's articles and reviews had helped many black musicians, but of all of them, Probe Adams had benefited the most. Since his graduation from Yale, Ron had knocked around the music world; once he thought he wanted to sing blues. He had tried, but that was in college. The best compliment he ever got was from Mississippi John or Muddy Waters,[7] one of the two, during a civil rights rally in Alabama. He had spontaneously leaped up during the rally and played from his soul. Muddy was in the audience, and later told Ron: "Boy, you keep that up, you gwine put me back on the plantation."

Ron was not fully satisfied that he had found the depth of the black man's psyche. In his book he had said this. Yet he knew that if he believed strongly enough, some of the old cats would break down. His sincerity was written all over his face. Holding Tasha's hand, he saw the door opening. . . .

Tasha was a shapely blonde who had dyed her hair black. It now matched her eyes. She was a Vassar girl and had once begun a biography of Oliver Fullerton. Excerpts had been published in *Down Beat*[8] and she became noted as a critic and authority on the Fullerton movement. Fullerton's development as an important jazz trombonist had been interrupted soon after Tasha's article. No one knew why. Sometimes Tasha was afraid to think about it. If they had married, she knew that Oliver would have been able to continue making it. But he had gotten strung out on H.[9] Sometimes she believed her

---

3. Drums.
4. That is, played improvisational jazz.
5. White people (derogatory).
6. Men (originally, jazzmen).
7. Mississippi John Hurt, born John Smith Hurt (1892/3–1966), country blues singer and guitar-

ist, and Muddy Waters, born McKinley Morgan-field (1913–1993), Mississippi-born blues singer, guitarist, and harmonicist considered an originator of "Chicago" or "urban" blues.
8. Leading jazz magazine.
9. That is, addicted to heroin.

friends who said Oliver was psychopathic. At least when he stopped beating her, she forgave him. And she did not believe it when he was really hooked. She still loved him. It was her own love, protected deep inside her, encased, her little black secret and her passport to the inner world that Oliver had died trying to enter. It would be only a matter of time. She would translate love into an honest appraisal of black music.

"I am sorry," the tall brown doorman said. "Sessions for Brothers and Sisters only."

"What's the matter, baby?" Jan leaned his head in and looked around as if wondering what the man was talking about.

"I said . . ."

"Man, if you can't recognize a Brother, you better let me have your job." He held up his case. "We're friends of Probe."

The man called for assistance. Quickly two men stepped out of the shadows. "What's the trouble, Brother?"

"These people say they're friends of the Probe."

"What people?" asked one of the men. He was neatly dressed, a clean shaven head, with large darting eyes. He looked past the three newcomers. There was a silence.

Finally, as if it were some supreme effort, he looked at the three. "I'm sorry, but for your own safety we cannot allow you."

"Man, what you talkin bout?" asked Jan, smiling quizzically. "Are you blockin Brothers now? I told him I am blood. We friends of the Probe."

The three men at the door went into a huddle. Carl, the doorman, was skeptical, but he had seen some bloods that were pretty light. He looked at this cat again, and as Kent and Rafael were debating whether or not to go get Probe's wife in the audience, he decided against the whole thing. He left the huddle and returned with a sign which said: "We cannot allow non-Brothers because of the danger involved with extensions."

Jan looked at the sign, and a smile crept across his face. In the street a cop was passing and leaned in. Carl motioned the cop in. He wanted a witness to this. He knew what might happen but he had never seen it.

Jan shook his head at the sign, turning to Ron and Tasha. He was about to explain that he had seen the same sign on the West Coast. It was incredible that all the spades believed this thing about the lethal vibrations from the new sound.[1]

Carl was shoving the sign in their faces as the cop, a big, pimpled Irishman, moved through the group. "All right, break it up, break it up. You got people outside want to come in . . ."

Kent and Rafael, seeing Carl's decision and the potential belligerence of the whites, folded their hands, buddha-like. Carl stood with his back to the door now.

"Listen, officer, if these people go in, the responsibility is yours."

The Irish cop, not knowing whether he should get angry over what he figured was reverse discrimination, smirked and made a path for the three. He would not go far inside because he didn't think the sounds were worth listening to. If it wasn't Harlem he could see why these people would want to go in, but he had never seen anything worthwhile from niggers in Harlem.

"Don't worry. You got a license, don't you?"

---

1. Reference to avant-garde African American jazz of the 1960s, variously referred to as the New Wave, the New Sound, or the New Black Music.

"Let them go through," said Rafael suddenly. A peace seemed to gather over the faces of the three club members now. They folded their arms and went into the dark cavern which led to the music. In front of them walked the invaders. "See," said Jan, "if you press these cats, they'll cop out." They moved toward the music in an alien silence.

Probe was deep into a rear-action sax monologue. The whole circle now, like a bracelet of many colored lights, gyrated under Probe's wisdom. Probe was a thoughtful, full-headed black man with narrow eyes and a large nose. His lips swelled over the reed and each note fell into the circle like an acrobat on a tight rope stretched radially across the center of the universe.

He heard the whistle of the wind. Three ghosts, like chaff blown from a wasteland, clung to the wall. . . . He tightened the circle. Movement began from within it, shaking without breaking balance. He had to prepare the womb for the afro-horn. Its vibrations were beyond his mental frequencies unless he got deeper into motives. He sent out his call for motives. . . .

The blanket of the bass rippled and the fierce wind in all their minds blew the blanket back, and there sat the city of Samson.[2] The white pillars imposing . . . but how easy it is to tear the building down with motives. Here they come. Probe, healed of his blindness, born anew of spirit, sealed his reed with pure air. *He moved to the edge of the circle, rested his sax, and lifted his axe.* . . .

There are only three afro-horns in the world. They were forged from a rare metal found only in Africa and South America. No one knows who forged the horns, but the general opinion among musicologists is that it was the Egyptians. One European museum guards an afro-horn. The other is supposed to be somewhere on the West Coast of Mexico, among a tribe of Indians. Probe grew into his from a black peddler who claimed to have traveled a thousand miles just to give it to his son. From that day on, Probe's sax handled like a child, a child waiting for itself to grow out of itself.

Inside the center of the gyrations is an atom stripped of time, black. The gathering of the hunters, deeper. Coming, laced in the energy of the sun. He is blowing. Magwa's hands. Reverence of skin. Under the single voices is the child of a woman, black. They are building back the wall, crumbling under the disturbance.

In the rear of the room, Jan did not hear the volt, nor did he see the mystery behind Probe's first statement on the afro-horn. He had closed his eyes, trying to capture or elude the panthers of the music, but he had no eyes. He did not feel Ron slump against him. Strands of Tasha's hair were matted on a button of Ron's jacket, but she did not move when he slumped. Something was hitting them like waves, like shock waves. . . .

Before his mind went black, Jan recalled the feeling when his father had beat him for playing "with a nigger!" and later he allowed the feeling to merge with his dislike of white people. When he fell, his case hit the floor and opened, revealing a shiny tenor saxophone that gleamed and vibrated in the freedom of freedom.

---

2. Jewish hero from the Book of Judges (13–16) during a time when God is punishing the Israelites by subjecting them to the Philistines. In the final episode of his life, he is taken from prison to be sacrificed, but he pulls down the pillars of the pagan temple, collapsing it upon himself and all assembled there.

Ron's sleep had been quick, like the rush of post-hypnotic suggestions. He dropped her hand, slumped, felt the wall give (no, it was the air), and he fell face forward across a table, his heart silent in respect for truer vibrations.

The musicians stood. The horn and Probe drew up the shadows now from the audience. A child climbed upon the chords of sound, growing out of the circle of the womb, searching with fingers and then with motive, and as the volume of the music increased—penetrating the thick callousness of the Irishman twirling his stick outside of black flesh—the musicians walked off, one by one, linked to Probe's respectful nod at each and his quiet pronouncement of their names. He mopped his face with a blue cloth.

"What's the matter here?"

"Step aside, folks!"

"These people are unconscious!"

"Look at their faces!"

"They're dead."

"Dead?"

"What happened?"

"Dead?"

"It's true then. It's true . . ."

1966

The Zebra Goes Wild Where the Sidewalk Ends

I

Neon stripes tighten my wall
where my crayon landlord hangs
from a bent nail.

My black father sits crooked
in the kitchen 5
drunk on Jesus' blood turned
to cheap wine.[1]

In his tremor he curses
the landlord who grins
from inside the rent book.[2] 10

My father's eyes are
bolls of cotton.

He sits upon the landlord's
operating table,
the needle of the nation 15
sucking his soul.

1. Inversion of Christian ritual of communion, in which wine is, by consecration, "transubstantiated" into the blood of Christ.
2. Ledger in which a renter's obligation to the landlord is tallied and recorded.

II

Chains of light race over
my stricken city.
Glittering web spun by
the white widow spider.   20

I see this wild arena
where we are harnessed
by alien electric shadows.

Even when the sun washes
the debris   25
I will recall my landlord
hanging in my room
and my father moaning in
Jesus' tomb.

In America all zebras   30
are in the zoo.

I hear the piston bark
and ibm[3] spark:
let us program rabies.
the madness is foaming now.   35

No wild zebras roam the American plain.
The mad dogs are running.
The African zebra is gone into the dust.

I see the shadow thieves coming
and my father on the specimen table.   40

1974

3. International Business Machines, or IBM, a computer manufacturer for which Dumas worked as a
printing-machine operator for two years.

AMIRI BARAKA
(1934–2014)

Through his prolific and varied work as poet, playwright, essayist, critic, community organizer, and educator, Amiri Baraka established himself as one of the most intriguing, controversial, and influential figures in modern letters. It is hardly an exaggeration to say that Baraka was the main architect and propelling force of the Black Arts movement, nor even that contemporary African American literature and culture would not be what they are without his dynamic presence for over half a century. In a career of encyclopedic he wrote numerous volumes of drama, poetry, prose, literary and cultural criticism, musical analysis, and political manifestos, and he has come to be regarded variously as an artist, politician, villain, and prophet. And yet however we choose to regard him, there remains something elusive about the image he presented for our consideration. For Baraka's trajectory as writer and social activist was marked by dramatic departures of place, theory, and personal association that rendered his life a continuous quest for an identity fully realized in the fusion of purpose and experience. As he wrote in his second volume of poetry: "I am a man / who is loud / on the birth / of his ways. Publicly redefining / each change in my soul, as if I had predicted / them, / and profited, biblically, even tho / their chanting weight,/ erased familiarity/ from my face." Baraka's openness to such perpetual redefinition lent his work a distinctive power, at once volatile and challenging.

Born LeRoi Jones in Newark, New Jersey to middle-class parents and a heritage of teachers and preachers, Baraka excelled in the institutions that structured his early life, graduating from high school at fifteen. And yet he was also restless and rebellious as a youth. Reflecting back on this stage of his life, he remarked, "When I was in high school I used to drink a lot of wine, throw bottles around, walk down the street in women's clothes just because I couldn't find anything to satisfy myself." That sense of unease despite success, leading to adoption of new and daring roles, was to become a hallmark of Baraka's evolution. After beginning college at nearby Rutgers University, Baraka transferred to Howard University, an historical black university that he felt suffocating in its official curriculum and prevailing culture. "Howard University shocked me into realizing how sick the Negro could be, how he could be led to self-destruction and how he would not realize that it was the society that had forced him into great sickness." And yet in classes in religion, philosophy, and literature, Baraka built the foundations of one of the most learned artistic imaginations of his generation. Moreover, through his extracurricular education from such luminaries as poet and scholar Sterling Brown, who offered students like Baraka and A. B. Spellman informal seminars in the history and meaning of African American vernacular traditions, Baraka gained a formative understanding of black oral forms as both aesthetic achievement and social statement. Thus Baraka's Howard experience proved paradigmatic in setting him against an institutional structure from which he nevertheless mined a storehouse of knowledge and an ambivalent inspiration.

After leaving Howard at nineteen, Baraka endured two years in the Air Force, which he felt "racist, degrading, and intellectually paralyzing." But once again, his struggle with social establishment proved productive, as Baraka used his time stationed in Puerto Rico, where he worked at the base library, to read through the canons of European, American, and African American literature. It was also in the Air Force that Baraka began to write poetry flavored with the jagged, pugnacious attitudes of the Beat poets who were then making their mark on American culture. Having contemplated such vocations as the ministry, medicine, and painting, Baraka left the service with a stack of miscellaneous writings under his arm. "Suddenly I said, 'Gee, I have all this stuff. I guess that makes me a writer.'"

Upon discharge from military service, Baraka brought that sense of artistic vocation to Greenwich Village in the late 1950s, where the Beat scene was in full swing, with writers such as Gregory Corso and Allen Ginsberg "howling" their audiences into a new consciousness, while Ornette Coleman, Thelonius Monk, Wilbur Ware, John Coltrane, and other principals of the "new music" challenged the boundaries of African American musical convention. During the next few years, Baraka established his reputation as a music critic, writing about jazz for *Downbeat*, *Metronome*, and the *Jazz Review* in a style that was simultaneously analytical and lyrical. Along with Hettie Cohen, whom he married in 1958, he founded *Yugen*, an art magazine that featured avant-garde verse and poetic manifestos. Expanding his role as literary impresario with his work on *Floating Bear*, a magazine he edited with Diane di Prima, and the founding of Totem Press, which published a strong cadre of Beat writers including Ginsberg and Jack Kerouac, he gained the moniker "King of the

Village," a nickname influenced by the French meaning of his birth name, LeRoi. For the first time of many, Baraka secured his place in the center of a literary movement driven by transgressive values underwritten by spiritual ambition and supported by self-made mechanisms for producing and disseminating radical expression.

Baraka's first collection of poems, *Preface to a Twenty Volume Suicide Note* (1961), reflects these sentiments, joining the Beats' assault on American middle-class society through verse that is at once savagely witty, plaintive, and defiant. And yet we hear in them also a subterranean rumble of a voice seeking an alternative sound. In his 1959 essay "How You Sound??," Baraka describes the primacy of this search as motivation for poetic creation:

> I'm not interested in writing sonnets, sestinas or anything. . . . only poems. If the poem has got to be a sonnet (unlikely tho) or whatever, it'll certainly let me know. The only 'recognizable tradition' a poet need follow is himself . . . & with that, say, all those things out of the tradition he can use, adapt, work over, into something for himself. To broaden his own voice with. (You have to start and finish there . . . your own voice . . . how you sound.)

Despite the provocative assertion of individuality in this statement, *Preface* reveals Baraka's use of available poetic conventions to be characteristic of the aggressive ambivalence he had displayed in his relation to social institutions. For against the vituperative refutation of inherited literary structures that we find in the poems' flamboyant experimentalism, we find a budding appreciation of forms developed within the African American tradition, especially the blues, that will soon emerge as a key feature of Baraka's post-Bohemian art and ideology.

In 1960, the Fair Play for Cuba Committee invited Baraka to visit Cuba, a trip described in *The Autobiography of LeRoi Jones/Amiri Baraka* (1984) as personally "revolutionary": "Cuba split me open." His encounters there with Cuba's publicly revolutionary artists were harsh and eye-opening, leading to unexpected self-criticism. As vividly portrayed in his 1961 essay "Cuba Libre," Baraka was accused by the Cuban culture workers of being a "cowardly bourgeoisie individualist" bent on "cultivating [his own] soul" rather than addressing oppressive conditions endured by the masses. Stung by these critiques, Baraka began to revalue his very status as "poet": "I'm a poet," he had told his Cuban counterparts; "what can I do?" Upon return to the States, he set out to answer that question by insistently probing the relation between words and actions, at times setting them in stark opposition, at times seeking to forge them into a powerful unity. Ultimately, this shift in his poetic project required for Baraka a broader change in literary and personal allegiances, as he gradually forsook bohemianism for the cause of black nationalism.

Before Baraka materialized this shift in 1965 by divorcing Cohen, moving from Greenwich Village uptown to Harlem and establishing himself as foremost spokesman of the emerging Black Arts and Black Power movements, he signaled the aims of radical change in three key works across different genres: *Blues People* (1963), a sociological study of black music; *The Dead Lecturer* (1964), his second volume of poetry; and the experimental plays *Dutchman* and *The Slave* (both 1964). In *Blues People*, Baraka interprets the history of black musical expression as a dialectic in which authentic forms of diasporic cultural expression are debased by mainstream commercial appropriation, then reborn in a rebellion of new forms. *The Dead Lecturer*, in such masterworks as the "Crow Jane" poems and "A Poem for Willie Best," self-consciously charts the transformation of Baraka's poetic voice from a "teller" of the dominant tradition to an invocatory agent of its destruction. And Baraka's plays present young black male protagonists forced from their cocoons of "white"-endorsed privilege into fatal struggles through which we glimpse the possibility of revolutionary rebirth. Providing a crucial bridge from the Bohemian stylings of his Greenwich Village sojourn to the nationalist formulations of his immersion in the black communities of Harlem and Newark, these works bear the Barakan signature of metamorphic necessity. Sometimes analytical or oratorical, at other times lyrical or visionary, the voice that emerges here searches for what Baraka, in the many aesthetic tracts that he began to produce during this period, called "a post-Western form."

This ethos of change sparked Baraka's fast-developing commitment to revolutionary aims, which first took form in the black cultural nationalism with which he is most prominently associated. In the works that best define his contributions to the artistic and political climate of the Black Power movement—the poetry collections *Black Magic* (1968), *In Our Terribleness* (1970), and *It's Nation Time* (1970); the dramas *A Black Mass* (1966), *Slave Ship* (1967), and *Four Black Revolutionary Plays* (1969); the critical volumes *Black Music* (1968) and *Raise Race Rays Raze: Essays Since 1965* (1971); and the era-defining anthology *Black Fire* (which he edited with Larry Neal in 1968)—Baraka elevates the energy of resistance over any particular structure that might rise from the rubble of rebellious destruction. Thus along with the thematic emphasis on uncompromising black liberation we find that these writings, whatever their genre, offer innovative revisions of inherited forms, from the modernist poetic line that he had practiced as a young "Black Bohemian" to the theatrical naturalism that had ruled the stage before the ritualistic disruptions of *Dutchman* and *Slave Ship* inspired an explosion of African American dramatic invention.

Baraka's various experiments in artistic form and media were united by the intention of confronting, resituating, and ultimately replacing threatening authority, whether aesthetic or political. Much of the early poetry, especially that of *The Dead Lecturer*, poses a direct challenge to both high modernist influences (especially T.S. Eliot, Ezra Pound, and William Carlos Williams) and the next generation of poets associated with Baraka's Village years (Ginsberg, Robert Creeley, Charles Olson, and others). His overt quarrel with these authors concerned the relation of politics and art; art and politics were for Baraka equally "in the world," and in conceiving his duty as uniting them in service of uncompromised black freedom he found himself also attacking the stylistic habits that he had once shared with his forebears and peers in the American modernist tradition. In poems like "Black Dada Nihilismus" the need to break out of what Baraka perceived as privacy without authenticity and to emerge as an insurgent agent of social transformation led to new poetic strategies. In the exchange of muses by which Baraka declared, "The poor have become our creators. The black" ("Short Speech to My Friends"), African American oral modes—the dozens, scatting, shouts, chants, blues and jazz tonalities—already evident in *Preface*, became Baraka's dominant poetic resource. The later volumes such as *In Our Terribleness* and *It's Nation Time* continue to deploy the formal power of this black vocal repertoire while seeking to supplant their "universal" formulations with urgent political content. Meanwhile, Baraka's drama, from the explosively absurdist *Dutchman* to the ceremonially prophetic *Slave Ship*, developed and violently diverged from contemporary American theater, from Edward Albee's *The Zoo Story* to The Performance Group's *Dionysus in '69*. Likewise, Baraka's raucous satirical drama *Great Goodness of Life: A Coon Show* (1966)—written after his father had informed on him to the FBI—is, in part, a black nationalist answer to Jean Genet's *The Blacks*, just as Baraka's plays *Jello* (1965) and *Experimental Death Unit #1* (1969) are parodistic re-enactments of, respectively, popular entertainment (the Jack Benny Show) and European expressionism (Samuel Beckett's *Endgame*). In all of these works, a struggle for control of the available means of expression illuminates all other thematic interests.

The complexities of this struggle are perhaps most vivid in Baraka's plays, where it takes embodied form in confrontations of fully voiced characters. *Dutchman* is structured as an extended linguistic rivalry between Clay and Lula, including a contest in naming found at the heart of the play (*Lula*. "Are you talking to my name?" *Clay*. "What is it, a secret?). Clay's attempt at self-assertion through rhetorical resistance is cut short by his own recognition that a dependence on borrowed words, on the "metaphors" of Lula's "bastard literature," separates him from the cleansing language of violent acts. In *The Slave*, Walker likewise laments that "I learned so many words . . . but almost none of them are mine." Their entrapment in foreign vocabularies involves a loss of cultural continuity, a divorce from the language of their shared but repressed origins in African-derived expressive values. As Baraka's theater progressed, leaving Clay and Walker at the threshold of an immense discovery that they could not embrace, the oppressive force of Lula is eventually transformed into the abstracted Voice of *Slave Ship*, which, after waging a prolonged war of sound against the captive black nation, suffers a death-by-uproar inflicted by the collective exclamations of the "old slave ship."

The very intensity of these battles of form and meaning illuminate the paradoxical insight that drives and unifies Baraka's writing through its various ideological phases: in seeking what the old man of *The Slave* calls a "meta-language," a rebel poet must incorporate the expressive presence of an alien idiom in order to transcend it. This complex lesson lies at the heart of Baraka's theoretical essays such as "Technology and Ethos," in which he expresses with almost self-mocking intensity his need to shape a new "kind of instrument" that can eclipse the standards and methods of his predecessors:

> A typewriter?—why shd it only make use of the tips of the fingers. If I invented a word placing machine, an "expression-scriber," *if you will*, then I would have a kind of instrument into which I could step & sit or sprawl or hang & use not only my fingers to make words express feelings but elbows, feet, head, behind, and all the sounds I wanted, screams, grunts, taps.

This humorous but determined confrontation with inherited instruments illuminates Baraka's often caustic attack on conventions, both artistic and social. The protagonists of such plays as *Dutchman, The Slave,* and *A Black Mass,* for example, encounter within themselves the very forms of consciousness they despise. As a revolutionary poet, Baraka decided that he could begin to say what he wished to be only by saying what he is not. And, like his self-limited and self-liberating heroes (for example, the titular subject of "A Poem for Willie Best"), he offered the lesson that one can create anew only with some recourse to the withering grammar of previous generations. But, Baraka's works tell us, by shocking that grammar sufficiently, by twisting it into unprecedented shapes, the revolutionary artist can generate new and living forms. It is only with the typewriter that he can inscribe into his art the blueprint for a new instrument.

In their search for an "expression-scriber" as fresh and radical as the content of a "post-Western" revolutionary vision, Baraka's works continued to evolve alongside his succeeding political and personal changes. With the publication of the essay "Toward Ideological Clarity" in 1974, Baraka announced his repudiation of black cultural nationalism and his turn to international socialism. "Fraternal liberation" became the watchword of the Barakan enterprise, signaling a type of relationship cleansed of both sentimentality and suspicion, in which the individual can feel trusted and encouraged. Baraka came to see this pan-cultural unity of oppressed people, especially peoples of color, as the best available means of attaining the ever-desired end of Baraka's lifelong quest: to break through the barriers of imprisoned individuality and establish a binding and just relation with the world of others.

True to his developing sense that change was the aim and not just the means of revolution, but with an abiding sense that old mechanisms bear their own revolutionary potential if properly recast, Baraka now fashioned literary work that experimented with new strategies for locating the proper "sound" of a global emancipatory practice, while emphasizing the blues inflections and jazz rhythms that he began developing in his earliest poems. In the poetry of *Hard Facts* (1975) and *Poetry for the Advanced* (1979), familiar idioms and timbres of black vernacular speech and performance are "transcribed" into the discourse of socialist critique. Though critics decried what they perceived as a psychological and conceptual crudity in these works, we find in them the touchstone of Baraka's ever-experimental poetic voice: the insistence that language itself is a major protagonist of ideologically charged historical drama. "The means of production" for Baraka is here not merely an evocation of Marxist economics but a reminder of the integral relation of expression and practice in any program of radical social reformation. In contrast to the heroes of his early drama and narrators of his early poems, who are overwhelmed by "the motion of history" when they fail to advance its imperative of transformation, the voices of these later works carry forward the revolutionary impulse of his black nationalist works by finding the resolve to seize history by the throat and engage the world in deadly encounter. And, as with the figures that populate Baraka's black nationalist writings, these voices—particularly those heard in the later volumes *Transbluency* (1995), *Wise Whys Y's* (1995), *Funk Lore: New Poems* (1996), *Somebody Blew Up America & Other Poems* (2003), and *The Book of Monk* (2005)—conspire with history to forge isolated individuals into a communal whole, to realize in fact the idea that "the nation is like our selves."

Thus whatever his ideological position, Baraka attempted to mold a style of expression that could enable him to dissolve the differences between history and self—as well as between the different functions of self (political, artistic, personal) that he sought to unify by creating his work in the context of community organizations that he founded (in 1965, the Black Arts Repertory/Theater School; in 1966, Spirit House; in 1968, the Black Community Development and Defense Organization; in 1970, the Congress of African Peoples—to name only those most crucial to his leadership in the Black Arts movement). Through all his various changes of political philosophy, association, and venue, Baraka asserted that the flux of history is the essence of experience; that the individual will must come to terms with the logical necessities of change; and that revolution is the authentic form of the historical process. True to the spirit of that belief, Baraka's work, especially its spirited and innovative elevation of black experience over all that would denigrate oppress it, bestowed a profound legacy on the continuing story of African American creativity and aspiration.

Preface to a Twenty Volume Suicide Note

(For Kellie Jones, born 16 May 1959)

Lately, I've become accustomed to the way
The ground opens up and envelopes me
Each time I go out to walk the dog.
Or the broad edged silly music the wind
Makes when I run for a bus . . .   5

Things have come to that.

And now, each night I count the stars,
And each night I get the same number.
And when they will not come to be counted,
I count the holes they leave.   10

Nobody sings anymore.

And then last night, I tiptoed up
To my daughter's room and heard her
Talking to someone, and when I opened
The door, there was no one there . . .   15
Only she on her knees, peeking into

Her own clasped hands.

1961

Notes for a Speech

African blues
does not know me.[1] Their steps, in sands
of their own
land. A country
in black & white, newspapers   5
blown down pavements
of the world. Does
not feel
what I am.
        Strength   10
in the dream, an oblique
suckling of nerve, the wind
throws up sand, eyes
are something locked in
hate, of hate, of hate, to   15
walk abroad, they conduct
their deaths apart
from my own. Those
heads, I call
my "people."   20
        (And who are they. People. To concern
myself, ugly man. Who
you, to concern
the white flat stomachs
of maidens, inside houses   25
dying. Black. Peeled moon
light on my fingers
move under
her clothes. Where
is her husband. Black   30
words throw up sand
to eyes, fingers of
their private dead. Whose
soul, eyes, in sand. My color
is not theirs. Lighter, white man   35
talk. They shy away. My own
dead souls,[2] my, so called
people. Africa
is a foreign place. You are
as any other sad man here   40
american.

1961

---

1. Echo of "What is Africa to me," opening refrain from the poem "Heritage" (1925) by African American poet Countee Cullen (1903–1946). 2. In the 19th century, Russian landowners counted among their property registered serfs, or laborers held in bondage, even after they had died; these were called "dead souls."

A Poem for Willie Best[1]

I

The face sings, alone
at the top
     of the body. All
flesh, all song, aligned. For hell
is silent, at those cracked lips   5
flakes of skin and mind
twist and whistle softly
as they fall.
         It was your own death
you saw. Your own face, stiff   10
and raw. This
without sound, or
movement. Sweet afton,[2] the
dead beggar bleeds
yet. His blood, for a time   15
alive, and huddled in a door
way, struggling to sing. Rain
washes it into cracks. Pits
whose bottoms are famous. Whose sides
are innocent broadcasts   20
of another life.

II

At this point, neither
front nor back. A point, the
dimensionless line. The top
of a head, seen from Christ's   25
heaven, stripped of history
or desire.
         Fixed, perpendicular
to shadow. (even speech, vertical,
leaves no trace. Born in to death   30
held fast to it, where
the lover spreads his arms, the line
he makes to threaten Gods with history.
The fingers stretch to emptiness. At
each point, after flesh, even light   35
is speculation. But an end, his end,
failing a beginning.

2

A cross. The gesture, symbol, line
arms held stiff, nailed stiff, with

---

1. "Willie Best was a Negro character actor whose Hollywood name was Sleep'n'eat." [Baraka's note.] Best (1916–1962) modeled his performances on those of Lincoln Perry (1902–1985), who, under the name Stepin Fetchit, adapted the stereotyped conventions of the minstrel traditions to mid-20th-century American films.
2. The river of the 1789 poem "Sweet Afton" by Scottish poet Robert Burns (1759–1796).

no sign, of what gave them strength.
The point, become a line, a cross, or
the man, and his material, driven in
the ground. If the head rolls back
and the mouth opens, screamed into
existence, there will be perhaps
only the slightest hint of movement—
a smear; no help will come. No one
will turn to that station[3] again.

III

At a cross roads, sits the
player. No drum, no umbrella, even
though it's raining. Again, and we
are somehow less miserable because
here is a hero, used to being wet.
One road is where you are standing now
(reading this, the other, crosses then
rushes into a wood.
                    5 lbs neckbones.
                    5 lbs hog innards.
                    10 bottles cheap wine.
                              (The contents
of a paper bag, also shoes, with holes
for the big toe, and several rusted
knives. This is a literature, of
symbols. And it is his gift, as the
bag is.
        (The contents
again, holy saviours,
                    300 men on horseback
                    75 bibles
                    the quietness
of a field. A rich
man, though wet through
by the rain.
            I said,
                    47 howitzers
                    7 polished horses jaws
                    a few trees being waved
softly back under
the black night
            All This should be
invested.

IV

Where
ever,
        he has gone. Who ever

---

3. Radio station, with pun on Stations of the Cross, scenes depicting Christ's carrying of the cross to his crucifixion.

mourns
or sits silent
to remember   85

There is nothing of pity
here. Nothing
of sympathy.   90

V

This is the dance of the raised
leg. Of the hand on the knee
quickly.[4]
    As a dance it punishes
speech. 'The house burned. The   95
old man killed.'
    As a dance it
is obscure.

VI

This is the song
of the highest C.   100
    The falsetto.[5] An elegance
that punishes silence. This is the song
of the toes pointed inward, the arms swung, the
hips, moved, for fucking, slow, from side
to side. He is quoted   105
saying, "My father was
never a jockey,
    but
        he did teach me
        how to ride."[6]   110

VII

The balance.
    (Rushed in, swarmed of dark, cloaks,
and only red lights pushed a message
to the street. Rub.
    This is the lady,   115
I saw you with.
This is your mother.
This is the lady I wanted
some how to sleep with.
    As a dance, or   120
our elegant song. Sun red and grown
from trees, fences, mud roads in dried out

---

4. Allusion to minstrel gestures.
5. In minstrel shows, men sometimes dressed as women to play the "mammy" role and sang in falsetto.
6. Allusion to "Jockey Blues" by Bill Samuels (1911–1964) and the Cats 'n' Jammers Three, recorded in 1945; the song's lyrics include the lines, "My father was no jockey / But he sure taught me how to ride / He said first in the middle / And then you swing from side to side."

river beds. This is for me, with no God
but what is given. Give me.
                         Something more   125
than what is here. I must tell you
my body hurts.

The balance.
                  Can you hear? Here
I am again. Your boy, dynamite. Can   130
you hear? My soul is moved. The soul
you gave me. I say, my soul, and it
is moved. That soul
you gave me.
                 Yes, I'm sure   135
this is the lady. You
slept with her. Witness, your boy,
here, dynamite. Hear?
                  I mean
can you?   140
The balance.
                 He was tired of losing. (And
his walking buddies tired
of walking.
                Bent slightly,   145
at the waist. Left hand low, to flick
quick showy jabs ala Sugar.[7] The right
cocked, to complete,
                    any combination.[8]
                          He was   150
tired of losing, but he was fighting
a big dumb "farmer."
                  Such a blue bright
afternoon, and only a few hundred yards
from the beach. He said, I'm tired   155
of losing.
          "I *got* ta cut 'cha."

VIII

A renegade
behind the mask. And even
the mask, a renegade   160
disguise. Black skin
and hanging lip.
          Lazy
          Frightened
          Thieving   165
          Very potent sexually
          Scars

---

7. Walter Smith Jr. (1921–1989), known as Sugar
Ray Robinson, African American boxer, six-time
world champion between 1946 and 1960.
8. Sequence of boxing moves.

Generally inferior
(but natural

rhythms.[9]   170

His head is
at the window. The only
part
    that sings.

(The word he used   175
    (we are passing St. Mark's place[1]
    and those crazy jews who fuck)
        to provoke

in neon, still useful
in the rain,   180
      to provoke
some meaning, where before
there was only hell. I said
silence, at his huddled blood.
      It is an obscene invention.   185
      A white sticky discharge.
      "Jism,"[2] in white chalk
      on the back of Angel's garage.
      Red jackets with the head of
      Hobbes staring into space. "Jasm"[3]   190
      the name the leader took, had it
      stenciled on his chest.
          And he sits
wet at the crossroads, remembering distinctly
each weightless face that eases by. (Sun at   195
the back door, and that hideous mindless grin.
        (Hear?

        1964

Black Dada Nihilismus[1]

.Against what light

is false what breath
sucked, for deadness.
    Murder, the cleansed

9. "Lazy . . . but natural rhythms": stereotyped features of the black minstrel character.
1. Street in New York's East Village popular with beats, jazz musicians, and other bohemians of the 1950s and 1960s. (Several of Baraka's early plays were produced at St. Mark's Playhouse.)
2. Semen.
3. 19th-century slang for spirit, vigor, or spunk (hence its transformation into "jism"), a possible source for the word "jazz"; "Hobbes": English politi-

cal philosopher Thomas Hobbes (1588–1679).
1. German for nihilism (from the Latin *nihil*: "nothing"), a philosophical doctrine that denies the existence of all knowledge, values, and any social or metaphysical order claiming truth or authority. "Dada": a nihilistic artistic movement that flourished in Zurich, Berlin, Paris, and New York following the horrors of World War I; dada artists expressed disdain for traditional aesthetic, cultural, and ethical conventions.

purpose, frail, against
God, if they bring him
                    bleeding, I would not   5

forgive, or even call him
black dada nihilismus.

The protestant love, wide windows,   10
color blocked to Mondrian,[2] and the
ugly silent deaths of jews under

the surgeon's knife. (To awake on
69th street with money and a hip
nose. Black dada nihilismus, for   15

the umbrella'd jesus. Trilby intrigue[3]
movie house presidents sticky the floor.
B.D.N., for the secret men, Hermes,[4] the

blacker art. Thievery (ahh, they return
those secret gold killers. Inquisitors[5]   20
of the cocktail hour. Trismegistus, have

them, in their transmutation,[6] from stone
to bleeding pearl, from lead to burning
looting, dead Moctezuma,[7] find the West

a grey hideous space.   25

2.

From Sartre,[8] a white man, it gave
the last breath. And we beg him die,
before he is killed. Plastique,[9] we

do not have, only thin heroic blades.
The razor. Our flail against them, why   30
you carry knives? Or brutaled lumps of

2. Pieter Cornelis "Piet" Mondrian (1872–1944), Dutch painter of the modernist abstract style.
3. The novel *Trilby* by French-born British author George du Maurier (1834–1896) tells of a beautiful artist's model, Trilby O'Ferrall, who falls under the spell of a Jewish musician who turns her into a star singer by training her voice through hypnosis. The 1894 novel caused a sensation in England and America, arousing fascination with its portrait of bohemianism.
4. Greek god of boundaries, messages, transitions, and trickery, an adaptation of Hermes Trismegistus (Hermes the Thrice-Greatest), an Egyptian deity associated with magic, astronomy, and the invention of writing. In the Renaissance, the "Hermetic Writings" were associated with the "dark arts" of occult philosophy and mysticism.
5. Officials associated with the Inquisition, a program that extended from the 12th through the 16th centuries designed to identify and eliminate heresy as defined by Roman Catholic doctrine.
6. Conversion, usually from one metallic form to another (as in the alchemical effort to turn lead to gold).
7. Moctezuma II (1466–1520), ruler of the Aztec Empire during the period (1502–20) when it attained its greatest power and then suddenly suffered defeat at the hands of the gold-seeking Spanish conquistador Hernán Cortés (1485–1547).
8. Jean-Paul Sartre (1905–1980), French philosopher of existentialism, which focuses on the individual's search for meaning in the face of an absurd, meaningless world.
9. A form of moldable explosive (French).

heart? Why you stay, where they can
reach? Why you sit, or stand, or walk
in this place, a window on a dark

warehouse. Where the minds packed in   35
straw. New homes, these towers, for those
lacking money or art. A cult of death,

need of the simple striking arm under
the streetlamp. The cutters, from under
their rented earth. Come up, black dada   40

nihilismus. Rape the white girls. Rape
their fathers. Cut the mothers' throats.
Black dada nihilismus, choke my friends

in their bedrooms with their drinks spilling
and restless for tilting hips or dark liver   45
lips sucking splinters from the master's thigh.

Black scream
and chant, scream,
and dull, un
earthly   50

hollering. Dada, bilious[1]
what ugliness, learned
in the dome, colored[2] holy
shit (i call them sinned

or lost   55
     burned masters
          of the lost
              nihil German killers
                    all our learned

art, 'member   60
what you said
money, God, power,
a moral code, so cruel
it destroyed Byzantium, Tenochtitlan, Commanch[3]
                (got it, *Baby!*   65

For tambo, willie best, dubois, patrice, mantan, the
bronze buckaroos.

     For Jack Johnson, asbestos, tonto, buckwheat,
     billie holiday.

1. Sickeningly unpleasant.
2. Reference to the "dome of many-colored glass" in the poem "Adonais" by English poet Percy Bysshe Shelley (1792–1822), a metaphor for distracting worldly concerns that are the source of human despair.
3. Examples of empires (Middle Eastern, Mexican, and Native American, respectively) conquered by Christian European invaders.

For tom russ, l'overture, vesey, beau jack,[4]   70

(may a lost god damballah,[5] rest or save us
against the murders we intend
against his lost white children
black dada nihilismus

1964

Dutchman[1]

CHARACTERS

CLAY, twenty-year-old Negro
LULA, thirty-year-old white woman
RIDERS OF COACH, white and black
YOUNG NEGRO
CONDUCTOR

*In the flying underbelly of the city. Steaming hot, and summer on top, outside.
Underground. The subway heaped in modern myth.*

*Opening scene is a man sitting in a subway seat, holding a magazine but
looking vacantly just above its wilting pages. Occasionally he looks blankly
toward the window on his right. Dim lights and darkness whistling by against
the glass. (Or paste the lights, as admitted props, right on the subway windows.
Have them move, even dim and flicker. But give the sense of speed. Also stations, whether the train is stopped or the glitter and activity of these stations
merely flashes by the windows.)*

*The man is sitting alone. That is, only his seat is visible, though the rest of
the car is outfitted as a complete subway car. But only his seat is shown. There
might be, for a time, as the play begins, a loud scream of the actual train. And
it can recur throughout the play, or continue on a lower key once the dialogue
starts.*

---

4. These stanzas primarily catalog black historical figures, including political activists killed,
exiled, or shunned for their resistance to oppressive powers—Oliver Tambo (1917–1993), South
African anti-apartheid activist; W. E. B. Du
Bois (1868–1963), African American author and
Pan-Africanist activist; Patrice Lumumba
(1925–1961), Congolese independence leader;
Toussaint L'Ouverture (1743–1803), leader of
the Haitian Revolution (1791–1804); and Denmark Vesey (1767?–1822), Afro-Caribbean
leader of a failed slave revolt in 1822 near
Charleston, South Carolina; also, entertainers
who struggled against exploitation: Billie Holiday (1915–1959), jazz singer and songwriter;
Willie Best (1916–1962), Mantan Moreland
(1902–1973), and William "Buckwheat" Thomas
(1931–1980), stereotyped Hollywood character
actors; and finally, accomplished athletes forced
into poverty or imprisonment at the peaks of
their careers: John Arthur ("Jack") Johnson
(1878–1946) and Sidney Walker or "Beau Jack"
(1921–2000), African American boxing champions. "Tambo" might refer also to a character in
the blackface minstrel tradition who played the
tambourine, appearing along with the black-
faced "Bones" and a white interlocutor; "the
bronze buckaroos": reference to the *The Bronze
Buckaroo* (1939), all-black western directed by
Richard Kahn; "asbestos": character in Kenneth
King's comic strip "Joe and Asbestos," a stable-
boy whose dark face and cowardly tendencies
evoked the servile males of the minstrel show;
"tonto": Native American sidekick of the white
cowboy known as the "Lone Ranger," the eponymous hero of a popular radio program in the
1930s and TV series in the 1950s; "tom russ":
Thomas Everett Russ (b. unknown–1943), Baraka's maternal grandfather, who owned several
businesses destroyed by white arsonists.
5. Most powerful *loa* or spirit of the Haitian
Vodun pantheon, a creator and patron protector
of children symbolized by the serpent who parallels deities in the West African Fon and Ewe
cosmologies.
1. Baraka's title evokes the legendary ghost ship
The Flying Dutchman, condemned to sail the
seas forever without reaching port, a portent of
doom to other ships that sight it. In some early
19th-century versions of the tale, the ship is said
to be cursed either from an onboard murder or
for being the original vessel of the slave trade.

The train slows after a time, pulling to a brief stop at one of the stations. The man looks idly up, until he sees a woman's face staring at him through the window; when it realizes that the man has noticed the face, it begins very premeditatedly to smile. The man smiles too, for a moment, without a trace of self-consciousness. Almost an instinctive though undesirable response. Then a kind of awkwardness or embarrassment sets in, and the man makes to look away, is further embarrassed, so he brings back his eyes to where the face was, but by now the train is moving again, and the face would seem to be left behind by the way the man turns his head to look back through the other windows at the slowly fading platform. He smiles then; more comfortably confident, hoping perhaps that his memory of this brief encounter will be pleasant. And then he is idle again.

Scene I

Train roars. Lights flash outside the windows.

LULA[2] *enters from the rear of the car in bright, skimpy summer clothes and sandals. She carries a net bag full of paper books, fruit, and other anonymous articles. She is wearing sunglasses, which she pushes up on her forehead from time to time. LULA is a tall, slender, beautiful woman with long red hair hanging straight down her back, wearing only loud lipstick in somebody's good taste. She is eating an apple, very daintily. Coming down the car toward CLAY.*

She stops beside CLAY's seat and hangs languidly from the strap, still managing to eat the apple. It is apparent that she is going to sit in the seat next to CLAY, and that she is only waiting for him to notice her before she sits.

CLAY sits as before, looking just beyond his magazine, now and again pulling the magazine slowly back and forth in front of his face in a hopeless effort to fan himself. Then he sees the woman hanging there beside him and he looks up into her face, smiling quizzically.

LULA Hello.

CLAY Uh, hi're you?

LULA I'm going to sit down. . . . O.K.?

CLAY Sure.

LULA [*Swings down onto the seat, pushing her legs straight out as if she is very weary.*] Oooof! Too much weight.

CLAY Ha, doesn't look like much to me. [*Leaning back against the window, a little surprised and maybe stiff.*]

LULA It's so anyway.
  [*And she moves her toes in the sandals, then pulls her right leg up on the left knee, better to inspect the bottoms of the sandals and the back of her heel. She appears for a second not to notice that CLAY is sitting next to her or that she has spoken to him just a second before. CLAY looks at the magazine, then out the black window. As he does this, she turns very quickly toward him.*]
  Weren't you staring at me through the window?

2. Lula: a blended name, evoking (a) lulu, first a 19th-century slang term for an alluring lady of questionable character, then Lulu, the protagonist in a series of sexually charged plays by German expressionist playwright Frank Wedekind (1864–1918) about a young dancer's rise and fall in German society; (b) Lilith, a figure of several early religious traditions, especially Jewish mysticism, seen as a demon but also as Adam's first wife, created from the earth like her husband; (c) Tallulah Bankhead (1902–1968), flamboyant, husky-voiced American actress, referred to later in the play; and (d) lullaby, a soothing song used to quiet children or lull them to sleep.

CLAY [*Wheeling around and very much stiffened.*] What?

LULA Weren't you staring at me through the window? At the last stop?

CLAY Staring at you? What do you mean?

LULA Don't you know what staring means?

CLAY I saw you through the window . . . if that's what it means. I don't know if I was staring. Seems to me you were staring through the window at me.

LULA I was. But only after I'd turned around and saw you staring through that window down in the vicinity of my ass and legs.

CLAY Really?

LULA Really. I guess you were just taking those idle potshots.[3] Nothing else to do. Run your mind over people's flesh.

CLAY Oh boy. Wow, now I admit I was looking in your direction. But the rest of that weight is yours.

LULA I suppose.

CLAY Staring through train windows is weird business. Much weirder than staring very sedately at abstract asses.

LULA That's why I came looking through the window . . . so you'd have more than that to go on. I even smiled at you.

CLAY That's right.

LULA I even got into this train, going some other way than mine. Walked down the aisle . . . searching you out.

CLAY Really? That's pretty funny.

LULA That's pretty funny. . . . God, you're dull.

CLAY Well, I'm sorry, lady, but I really wasn't prepared for party talk.

LULA No, you're not. What are you prepared for?
[*Wrapping the apple core in a Kleenex and dropping it on the floor*]

CLAY [*Takes her conversation as pure sex talk. He turns to confront her squarely with this idea*] I'm prepared for anything. How about you?

LULA [*Laughing loudly and cutting it off abruptly*] What do you think you're doing?

CLAY What?

LULA You think I want to pick you up, get you to take me somewhere and screw me, huh?

CLAY Is that the way I look?

LULA You look like you been trying to grow a beard. That's exactly what you look like. You look like you live in New Jersey with your parents and are trying to grow a beard. That's what. You look like you've been reading Chinese poetry and drinking lukewarm sugarless tea. [*Laughs, uncrossing and recrossing her legs*] You look like death eating a soda cracker.[4]

CLAY [*Cocking his head from one side to the other, embarrassed and trying to make some comeback, but also intrigued by what the woman is saying . . . even the sharp city coarseness of her voice, which is still a kind of gentle sidewalk throb.*] Really? I look like all that?

LULA Not all of it. [*She feints a seriousness to cover an actual somber tone.*] I lie a lot. [*Smiling.*] It helps me control the world.

CLAY [*Relieved and laughing louder than the humor.*] Yeah, I bet.

LULA But it's true, most of it, right? Jersey? Your bumpy neck?

---

3. Random glances.   4. Extremely pale (proverbial).

CLAY How'd you know all that? Huh? Really, I mean about Jersey . . . and even the beard. I met you before? You know Warren Enright?

LULA You tried to make it with your sister when you were ten. [CLAY *leans back hard against the back of the seat, his eyes opening now, still trying to look amused.*] But I succeeded a few weeks ago. [*She starts to laugh again.*]

CLAY What're you talking about? Warren tell you that? You're a friend of Georgia's?

LULA I told you I lie. I don't know your sister. I don't know Warren Enright.

CLAY You mean you're just picking these things out of the air?

LULA Is Warren Enright a tall skinny black black boy with a phony English accent?

CLAY I figured you knew him.

LULA But I don't. I just figured you would know somebody like that. [*Laughs.*]

CLAY Yeah, yeah.

LULA You're probably on your way to his house now.

CLAY That's right.

LULA [*Putting her hand on* CLAY's *closest knee, drawing it from the knee up to the thigh's hinge, then removing it, watching his face very closely, and continuing to laugh, perhaps more gently than before.*] Dull, dull, dull. I bet you think I'm exciting.

CLAY You're O.K.

LULA Am I exciting you now?

CLAY Right. That's not what's supposed to happen?

LULA How do I know?
[*She returns her hand, without moving it, then takes it away and plunges it in her bag to draw out an apple.*]
You want this?

CLAY Sure.

LULA [*She gets one out of the bag for herself.*] Eating apples together is always the first step.[5] Or walking up uninhabited Seventh Avenue in the twenties[6] on weekends. [*Bites and giggles, glancing at* CLAY *and speaking in loose sing-song.*] Can get you involved . . . boy! Get us involved. Um-huh. [*Mock seriousness.*] Would you like to get involved with me, Mister Man?

CLAY [*Trying to be as flippant as* LULA, *whacking happily at the apple.*] Sure. Why not? A beautiful woman like you. Huh, I'd be a fool not to.

LULA And I bet you're sure you know what you're talking about. [*Taking him a little roughly by the wrist, so he cannot eat the apple, then shaking the wrist.*] I bet you're sure of almost everything anybody ever asked you about . . . right? [*Shakes his wrist harder.*] Right?

CLAY Yeah, right. . . . Wow, you're pretty strong, you know? Whatta you, a lady wrestler or something?

LULA What's wrong with lady wrestlers? And don't answer because you never knew any. Huh. [*Cynically.*] That's for sure. They don't have any lady wrestlers in that part of Jersey. That's for sure.

CLAY Hey, you still haven't told me how you know so much about me.

5. In Genesis, Adam and Eve suffer the Fall after eating fruit (traditionally taken to be an apple) from the Tree of the Knowledge of Good and Evil.
6. Area of Manhattan just north of the bohe-mian neighborhood of Greenwich Village; 7th Avenue and 20th Street is the location of the final scene in the influential beat novel *On the Road* (1957) by Jack Kerouac (1922–1969).

LULA   I told you I didn't know anything about *you* . . . you're a well-known type.

CLAY   Really?

LULA   Or at least I know the type very well. And your skinny English friend too.

CLAY   Anonymously?

LULA   [*Settles back in seat, single-mindedly finishing her apple and humming snatches of rhythm and blues song.*]   What?

CLAY   Without knowing us specifically?

LULA   Oh boy. [*Looking quickly at* CLAY.]   What a face. You know, you could be a handsome man.

CLAY   I can't argue with you.

LULA   [*Vague, off-center response.*]   What?

CLAY   [*Raising his voice, thinking the train noise has drowned part of his sentence.*]   I can't argue with you.

LULA   My hair is turning gray. A gray hair for each year and type I've come through.

CLAY   Why do you want to sound so old?

LULA   But it's always gentle when it starts. [*Attention drifting.*] Hugged against tenements, day or night.

CLAY   What?

LULA   [*Refocusing.*]   Hey, why don't you take me to that party you're going to?

CLAY   You must be a friend of Warren's to know about the party.

LULA   Wouldn't you like to take me to the party? [*Imitates clinging vine.*] Oh, come on, ask me to your party.

CLAY   Of course I'll ask you to come with me to the party. And I'll bet you're a friend of Warren's.

LULA   Why not be a friend of Warren's? Why not? [*Taking his arm.*] Have you asked me yet?

CLAY   How can I ask you when I don't know your name?

LULA   Are you talking to my name?

CLAY   What is it, a secret?

LULA   I'm Lena the Hyena.[7]

CLAY   The famous woman poet?

LULA   Poetess! The same!

CLAY   Well, you know so much about me . . . what's my name?

LULA   Morris the Hyena.

CLAY   The famous woman poet?

LULA   The same. [*Laughing and going into her bag.*] You want another apple?

CLAY   Can't make it, lady. I only have to keep one doctor away a day.

LULA   I bet your name is . . . something like . . . uh, Gerald or Walter. Huh?

CLAY   God, no.

LULA   Lloyd, Norman? One of those hopeless colored names creeping out of New Jersey. Leonard? Gag. . . .

---

7. Lena the Hyena was the name given in a contest to draw "the ugliest woman in the world" sponsored in the comic strip *Lil' Abner* by Al Capp (1909–1979). In classical and later folklore, the hyena is depicted as a vampiric, androgynous animal, attacking graveyards and luring humans from their homes by imitating human voices.

CLAY   Like Warren?

LULA   Definitely. Just exactly like Warren. Or Everett.[8]

CLAY   Gag. . . .

LULA   Well, for sure, it's not Willie.

CLAY   It's Clay.

LULA   Clay? Really? Clay what?

CLAY   Take your pick. Jackson, Johnson, or Williams.

LULA   Oh, really? Good for you. But it's got to be Williams. You're too pretentious to be a Jackson or Johnson.

CLAY   Thass right.

LULA   But Clay's O.K.

CLAY   So's Lena.

LULA   It's Lula.

CLAY   Oh?

LULA   Lula the Hyena.

CLAY   Very good.

LULA   [*Starts laughing again.*]   Now you say to me, "Lula, Lula, why don't you go to this party with me tonight?" It's your turn, and let those be your lines.

CLAY   Lula, why don't you go to this party with me tonight, Huh?

LULA   Say my name twice before you ask, and no huh's.

CLAY   Lula, Lula, why don't you go to this party with me tonight?

LULA   I'd like to go, Clay, but how can you ask me to go when you barely know me?

CLAY   That is strange, isn't it?

LULA   What kind of reaction is that? You're supposed to say, "Aw, come on, we'll get to know each other better at the party."

CLAY   That's pretty corny.

LULA   What are you into anyway? [*Looking at him half sullenly but still amused.*] What thing are you playing at, Mister? Mister Clay Williams? [*Grabs his thigh, up near the crotch.*] What are *you* thinking about?

CLAY   Watch it now, you're gonna excite me for real.

LULA   [*Taking her hand away and throwing her apple core through the window.*] I bet. [*She slumps in the seat and is heavily silent.*]

CLAY   I thought you knew everything about me? What happened? [LULA *looks at him, then looks slowly away, then over where the other aisle would be. Noise of the train. She reaches in her bag and pulls out one of the paper books. She puts it on her leg and thumbs the pages listlessly.* CLAY *cocks his head to see the title of the book. Noise of the train.* LULA *flips pages and her eyes drift. Both remain silent.*] Are you going to the party with me, Lula?

LULA   [*Bored and not even looking.*]   I don't even know you.

CLAY   You said you know my type.

LULA   [*Strangely irritated.*]   Don't get smart with me, Buster. I know you like the palm of my hand.

CLAY   The one you eat the apples with?

LULA   Yeh. And the one I open doors late Saturday evening with. That's my door. Up at the top of the stairs. Five flights. Above a lot of Italians and lying Americans. And scrape carrots with. Also . . . [*Looks at him.*]

---

8. The middle of Baraka's given names, Leroy (later LeRoi) Everett Jones, bestowed in honor of his maternal grandfather, Thomas Everett Russ.

the same hand I unbutton my dress with, or let my skirt fall down. Same hand. Lover.

CLAY   Are you angry about anything? Did I say something wrong?

LULA   Everything you say is wrong. [*Mock smile.*] That's what makes you so attractive. Ha. In that funnybook jacket with all the buttons. [*More animated, taking hold of his jacket.*] What've you got that jacket and tie on in all this heat for? And why're you wearing a jacket and tie like that? Did your people ever burn witches or start revolutions over the price of tea? Boy, those narrow-shoulder clothes come from a tradition you ought to feel oppressed by. A three-button suit. What right do you have to be wearing a three-button suit and striped tie? Your grandfather was a slave, he didn't go to Harvard.

CLAY   My grandfather was a night watchman.

LULA   And you went to a colored college where everybody thought they were Averell Harriman.[9]

CLAY   All except me.

LULA   And who did you think you were? Who do you think you are now?

CLAY   [*Laughs as if to make light of the whole trend of the conversation.*]   Well, in college I thought I was Baudelaire.[1] But I've slowed down since.

LULA   I bet you never once thought you were a black nigger. [*Mock serious, then she howls with laughter.* CLAY *is stunned but after initial reaction, he quickly tries to appreciate the humor.* LULA *almost shrieks.*] A black Baudelaire.

CLAY   That's right.

LULA   Boy, are you corny. I take back what I said before. Everything you say is not wrong. It's perfect. You should be on television.

CLAY   You act like you're on television already.

LULA   That's because I'm an actress.

CLAY   I thought so.

LULA   Well, you're wrong. I'm no actress. I told you I always lie. I'm nothing, honey, and don't you ever forget it. [*Lighter.*] Although my mother was a Communist. The only person in my family ever to amount to anything.

CLAY   My mother was a Republican.

LULA   And your father voted for the man rather than the party.

CLAY   Right!

LULA   Yea for him. Yea, yea for him.

CLAY   Yea!

LULA   And yea for America where he is free to vote for the mediocrity of his choice! Yea!

CLAY   Yea!

LULA   And yea for both your parents who even though they differ about so crucial a matter as the body politic still forged a union of love and sacrifice that was destined to flower at the birth of the noble Clay . . . what's your middle name?

CLAY   Clay.

LULA   A union of love and sacrifice that was destined to flower at the birth of the noble Clay Clay Williams. Yea! And most of all yea yea for

9. Democratic politician, businessman, and author (1891–1986), governor of New York from 1955 to 1958.

1. French Symbolist poet (1821–1867).

you, Clay Clay. The Black Baudelaire! Yes! [*And with knifelike cyni-cism.*] My Christ. My Christ.

CLAY   Thank you, ma'am.

LULA   May the people accept you as a ghost of the future. And love you, that you might not kill them when you can.

CLAY   What?

LULA   You're a murderer, Clay, and you know it. [*Her voice darkening with significance.*] You know goddamn well what I mean.

CLAY   I do?

LULA   So we'll pretend the air is light and full of perfume.

CLAY   [*Sniffing at her blouse.*] It is.

LULA   And we'll pretend the people cannot see you. That is, the citizens. And that you are free of your own history. And I am free of my history. We'll pretend that we are both anonymous beauties smashing along through the city's entrails. [*She yells as loud as she can.*] GROOVE! [*Black.*]

Scene II

Scene is the same as before, though now there are other seats visible in the car. And throughout the scene other people get on the subway. There are maybe one or two seated in the car as the scene opens, though neither CLAY nor LULA notices them. CLAY's tie is open. LULA is hugging his arm.

CLAY   The party!

LULA   I know it'll be something good. You can come in with me, looking casual and significant. I'll be strange, haughty, and silent, and walk with long slow strides.

CLAY   Right.

LULA   When you get drunk, pat me once, very lovingly on the flanks, and I'll look at you cryptically, licking my lips.

CLAY   It sounds like something we can do.

LULA   You'll go around talking to young men about your mind, and to old men about your plans. If you meet a very close friend who is also with someone like me, we can stand together, sipping our drinks and exchanging codes of lust. The atmosphere will be slithering in love and half-love and very open moral decision.

CLAY   Great. Great.

LULA   And everyone will pretend they don't know your name, and then . . . [*She pauses heavily.*] later, when they have to, they'll claim a friendship that denies your sterling character.

CLAY [*Kissing her neck and fingers.*]   And then what?

LULA   Then? Well, then we'll go down the street, late night, eating apples and winding very deliberately toward my house.

CLAY   Deliberately?

LULA   I mean, we'll look in all the shopwindows, and make fun of the queers. Maybe we'll meet a Jewish Buddhist[2] and flatten his conceits over some very pretentious coffee.

CLAY   In honor of whose God?

2. Buddhism was a fascination of Beat writers, including the Jewish writer Allen Ginsberg (1926–1997), a fellow New Jerseyan whom Baraka knew well.

LULA   Mine.

CLAY   Who is . . . ?

LULA   Me . . . and you?

CLAY   A corporate Godhead.[3]

LULA   Exactly. Exactly. [*Notices one of the other people entering.*]

CLAY   Go on with the chronicle. Then what happens to us?

LULA   [*A mild depression, but she still makes her description triumphant and increasingly direct.*]   To my house, of course.

CLAY   Of course.

LULA   And up the narrow steps of the tenement.

CLAY   You live in a tenement?

LULA   Wouldn't live anywhere else. Reminds me specifically of my novel form of insanity.

CLAY   Up the tenement stairs.

LULA   And with my apple-eating hand I push open the door and lead you, my tender big-eyed prey, into my . . . God, what can I call it . . . into my hovel.

CLAY   Then what happens?

LULA   After the dancing and games, after the long drinks and long walks, the real fun begins.

CLAY   Ah, the real fun. [*Embarrassed, in spite of himself.*] Which is . . . ?

LULA   [*Laughs at him.*]   Real fun in the dark house. Hah! Real fun in the dark house, high up above the street and the ignorant cowboys.[4] I lead you in, holding your wet hand gently in my hand . . .

CLAY   Which is not wet?

LULA   Which is dry as ashes.

CLAY   And cold?

LULA   Don't think you'll get out of your responsibility that way. It's not cold at all. Your Fascist! Into my dark living room. Where we'll sit and talk endlessly, endlessly.

CLAY   About what?

LULA   About what? About your manhood, what do you think? What do you think we've been talking about all this time?

CLAY   Well, I didn't know it was that. That's for sure. Every other thing in the world but that. [*Notices another person entering, looks quickly, almost involuntarily up and down the car, seeing the other people in the car.*] Hey, I didn't even notice when those people got on.

LULA   Yeah, I know.

CLAY   Man, this subway is slow.

LULA   Yeah, I know.

CLAY   Well, go on. We were talking about my manhood.

LULA   We still are. All the time.

CLAY   We were in your living room.

LULA   My dark living room. Talking endlessly.

CLAY   About my manhood.

LULA   I'll make you a map of it. Just as soon as we get to my house.

CLAY   Well, that's great.

LULA   One of the things we do while we talk. And screw.

CLAY   [*Trying to make his smile broader and less shaky.*]   We finally got there.

---

3. Divine nature or essence.   4. Male prostitutes (slang).

LULA   And you'll call my rooms black as a grave. You'll say, "This place is like Juliet's tomb."

CLAY   [*Laughs.*]   I might.

LULA   I know. You've probably said it before.

CLAY   And is that all? The whole grand tour?

LULA   Not all. You'll say to me very close to my face, many, many times, you'll say, even whisper, that you love me.

CLAY   Maybe I will.

LULA   And you'll be lying.

CLAY   I wouldn't lie about something like that.

LULA   Hah. It's the only kind of thing you will lie about. Especially if you think it'll keep me alive.

CLAY   Keep you alive? I don't understand.

LULA   [*Bursting out laughing, but too shrilly.*]   Don't understand? Well, don't look at me. It's the path I take, that's all. Where both feet take me when I set them down. One in front of the other.

CLAY   Morbid. Morbid. You sure you're not an actress? All that self-aggrandizement.

LULA   Well, I told you I wasn't an actress . . . but I also told you I lie all the time. Draw your own conclusions.

CLAY   Morbid. Morbid. You sure you're not an actress? All scribed?[5] There's no more?

LULA   I've told you all I know. Or almost all.

CLAY   There's no funny parts?

LULA   I thought it was all funny.

CLAY   But you mean peculiar, not ha-ha.

LULA   You don't know what I mean.

CLAY   Well, tell me the almost part then. You said almost all. What else? I want the whole story.

LULA   [*Searching aimlessly through her bag. She begins to talk breathlessly, with a light and silly tone.*]   All stories are whole stories. All of 'em. Our whole story . . . nothing but change. How could things go on like that forever? Huh?

   [*Slaps him on the shoulder, begins finding things in her bag, taking them out and throwing them over her shoulder into the aisle.*]

Except I do go on as I do. Apples and long walks with deathless intelligent lovers. But you mix it up. Look out the window, all the time. Turning pages. Change change change. Till, shit, I don't know you. Wouldn't, for that matter. You're too serious. I bet you're even too serious to be psychoanalyzed. Like all those Jewish poets from Yonkers,[6] who leave their mothers looking for other mothers, or others' mothers, on whose baggy tits they lay their fumbling heads. Their poems are always funny, and all about sex.

CLAY   They sound great. Like movies.

LULA   But you change. [*Blankly.*] And things work on you till you hate them.

   [*More people come into the train. They come closer to the couple, some of them not sitting, but swinging drearily on the straps, staring at the two with uncertain interest.*]

---

5. Written.
6. A city in southeastern New York. Perhaps a reference to Yonkers-born Beat poet and patron Lawrence Ferlinghetti (b. 1919).

CLAY   Wow. All these people, so suddenly. They must all come from the same place.

LULA   Right. That they do.

CLAY   Oh? You know about them too?

LULA   Oh yeah. About them more than I know about you. Do they frighten you?

CLAY   Frighten me? Why should they frighten me?

LULA   'Cause you're an escaped nigger.

CLAY   Yeah?

LULA   'Cause you crawled through the wire and made tracks to my side.

CLAY   Wire?

LULA   Don't they have wire around plantations?

CLAY   You must be Jewish. All you can think about is wire.[7] Plantations didn't have any wire. Plantations were big open whitewashed places like heaven, and everybody on 'em was grooved to be there. Just strummin' and hummin' all day.

LULA   Yes, yes.

CLAY   And that's how the blues was born.[8]

LULA   Yes, yes. And that's how the blues was born.
[Begins to make up a song that becomes quickly hysterical. As she sings she rises from her seat, still throwing things out of her bag into the aisle, beginning a rhythmical shudder and twistlike wiggle, which she continues up and down the aisle, bumping into many of the standing people and tripping over the feet of those sitting. Each time she runs into a person she lets out a very vicious piece of profanity, wiggling and stepping all the time.]
And that's how the blues was born. Yes. Yes. Son of a bitch, get out of the way. Yes. Quack. Yes. Yes. And that's how the blues was born. Ten little niggers sitting on a limb, but none of them ever looked like him. [Points to CLAY, returns toward the seat, with her hands extended for him to rise and dance with her.] And that's how blues was born. Yes. Come on, Clay. Let's do the nasty. Rub bellies. Rub bellies.[9]

CLAY [Waves his hands to refuse. He is embarrassed, but determined to get a kick out of the proceedings.]   Hey, what was in those apples? Mirror, mirror on the wall, who's the fairest one of all? Snow White, baby, and don't you forget it.

LULA [Grabbing for his hands, which he draws away.]   Come on, Clay. Let's rub bellies on the train. The nasty. The nasty. Do the gritty grind, like your ol' rag-head mammy.[1] Grind till you lose your mind. Shake it, shake it, shake it, shake it! OOOOweeee! Come on, Clay. Let's do the choo-choo train shuffle, the navel scratcher.

CLAY   Hey, you coming on like the lady who smoked up her grass skirt.[2]

LULA [Becoming annoyed that he will not dance, and becoming more animated as if to embarrass him still further.]   Come on, Clay . . . let's do the thing. Uhh! Uhh! Clay! Clay! You middle-class black bastard. Forget

---

7. Reference to concentration camps of the 1930s and 1940s in which millions of Jews were imprisoned, tortured, and killed; the camp fences were made of barbed wire.

8. Reference to "The Birth of the Blues" by white composer Rex Henderson (1896–1970), recorded by black singer and band leader Cab Calloway (1907–1994) in 1943.

9. Slang for sexual intercourse or close dancing.

1. Stereotyped black female traceable to the character Aunt Chloe in the 1852 novel *Uncle Tom's Cabin* by Harriet Beecher Stowe (1811–1896), typified by service in white households, very dark skin, and a head rag signifying domestic duties.

2. I.e., smoked marijuana ("grass").

your social-working mother for a few seconds and let's knock stomachs. Clay, you liver-lipped white man. You would-be Christian. You ain't no nigger, you're just a dirty white man. Get up, Clay. Dance with me, Clay.

CLAY   Lula! Sit down, now. Be cool.

LULA   [*Mocking him, in wild dance.*]   Be cool. Be cool. That's all you know . . . shaking that wildroot cream-oil[3] on your knotty head, jackets buttoning up to your chin, so full of white man's words. Christ. God. Get up and scream at these people. Like scream meaningless shit in these hopeless faces. [*She screams at people in train, still dancing.*] Red trains cough Jewish underwear for keeps![4] Expanding smells of silence. Gravy snot whistling like sea birds. Clay. Clay, you got to break out. Don't sit there dying the way they want you to die. Get up.

CLAY   Oh, sit the fuck down. [*He moves to restrain her.*] Sit down, goddamn it.

LULA   [*Twisting out of his reach.*]   Screw yourself, Uncle Tom.[5] Thomas Woolly-head.

[*Begins to dance a kind of jig, mocking* CLAY *with loud forced humor.*] There is Uncle Tom . . . I mean, Uncle Thomas Woolly-Head. With old white matted mane. He hobbles on his wooden cane. Old Tom. Old Tom. Let the white man hump his ol' mama, and he jes' shuffle off in the woods and hide his gentle gray head. Ol' Thomas Woolly-Head.

[*Some of the other riders are laughing now. A drunk gets up and joins* LULA *in her dance, singing, as best he can, her "song."* CLAY *gets up out of his seat and visibly scans the faces of the other riders.*]

CLAY   Lula! Lula!

[*She is dancing and turning, still shouting as loud as she can. The drunk too is shouting, and waving his hands wildly.*]

Lula . . . you dumb bitch. Why don't you stop it? [*He rushes half stumbling from his seat, and grabs one of her flailing arms.*]

LULA   Let me go! You black son of a bitch. [*She struggles against him.*] Let me go! Help!

[CLAY *is dragging her towards her seat, and the drunk seeks to interfere. He grabs* CLAY *around the shoulders and begins wrestling with him.* CLAY *clubs the drunk to the floor without releasing* LULA, *who is still screaming.* CLAY *finally gets her to the seat and throws her into it*]

CLAY   Now you shut the hell up. [*Grabbing her shoulders.*] Just shut up. You don't know what you're talking about. You don't know anything. So just keep your stupid mouth closed.

LULA   You're afraid of white people. And your father was. Uncle Tom Big Lip!

CLAY   [*Slaps her as hard as he can, across the mouth.* LULA's *head bangs against the back of the seat. When she raises it again,* CLAY *slaps her again.*]   Now shut up and let me talk.

[*He turns toward the other riders, some of whom are sitting on the edge of their seats. The drunk is on one knee, rubbing his head, and singing softly the same song. He shuts up too when he sees* CLAY *watching him. The others go back to newspapers or stare out the windows.*]

---

3. Hair product popular in the 1940s and 1950s, considered a sign of straight-laced conformity by bohemians.
4. Complex metaphor for the Holocaust, during which Jewish victims were brought to death camps in railroad cars.
5. Reference to titular character of Harriet Beecher Stowe's novel (1852), a figure eventually symbolic of a servile and fearful black man.

Shit, you don't have any sense, Lula, nor feelings either. I could murder you now. Such a tiny ugly throat. I could squeeze it flat, and watch you turn blue, on a humble. For dull kicks. And all these weak-faced ofays[6] squatting around here, staring over their papers at me. Murder them too. Even if they expected it. That man there . . . [*Points to well-dressed man.*] I could rip that *Times* right out of his hand, as skinny and middle-classed as I am, I could rip that paper out of his hand and just as easily rip out his throat. It takes no great effort. For what? To kill you soft idiots? You don't understand anything but luxury.

LULA You fool!

CLAY [*Pushing her against the seat.*] I'm not telling you again, Tallulah Bankhead! Luxury. In your face and your fingers. You telling me what I ought to do. [*Sudden scream frightening the whole coach.*] Well, don't! Don't you tell me anything! If I'm a middle-class fake white man . . . let me be. And let me be in the way I want. [*Through his teeth*] I'll rip your lousy breasts off! Let me be who I feel like being. Uncle Tom. Thomas. Whoever. It's none of your business. You don't know anything except what's there for you to see. An act. Lies. Device. Not the pure heart, the pumping black heart. You don't ever know that. And I sit here, in this buttoned-up suit, to keep myself from cutting all your throats. I mean wantonly. You great liberated whore! You fuck some black man, and right away you're an expert on black people. What a lotta shit that is. The only thing you know is that you come if he bangs you hard enough. And that's all. The belly rub? You wanted to do the belly rub? Shit, you don't even know how. You don't know how. That ol' dipty-dip shit you do, rolling your ass like an elephant. That's not my kind of belly rub. Belly rub is not Queens. Belly rub is dark places, with big hats and over-coats held up with one arm. Belly rub hates you. Old bald-headed four-eyed ofays popping their fingers . . . and don't know yet what they're doing. They say, "I love Bessie Smith."[7] And don't even understand that Bessie Smith is saying, "Kiss my ass, kiss my black unruly ass." Before love, suffering, desire, anything you can explain, she's saying, and very plainly, "Kiss my black ass." And if you don't know that, it's you that's doing the kissing.

Charlie Parker?[8] Charlie Parker. All the hip white boys scream for Bird. And Bird saying, "Up your ass, feeble-minded ofay! Up your ass." And they sit there talking about the tortured genius of Charlie Parker. Bird would've played not a note of music if he just walked up to East Sixty-seventh Street[9] and killed the first ten white people he saw. Not a note! And I'm the great would-be poet. Yes. That's right! Poet. Some kind of bastard literature . . . all it needs is a simple knife thrust. Just let me bleed you, you loud whore, and one poem vanished. A whole people of neurotics, struggling to keep from being sane. And the only thing that would cure the neurosis would be your murder. Simple as that. I mean if I murdered you, then other white people would begin to understand me. You understand? No. I guess not. If Bessie Smith had killed some white people she wouldn't have needed that music. She

6. A derogatory term for white people. "On a humble": immediately, without hesitation.
7. Blues and jazz singer (1898–1937).
8. Jazz saxophonist (1920–1955); he was called "Bird."
9. I.e., in the wealthy, mainly white Upper East Side of Manhattan.

could have talked very straight and plain about the world. No metaphors. No grunts. No wiggles in the dark of her soul. Just straight two and two are four. Money. Power. Luxury. Like that. All of them. Crazy niggers turning their backs on sanity. When all it needs is that simple act. Murder. Just murder! Would make us all sane. [*Suddenly weary.*]

Ahhh. Shit. But who needs it? I'd rather be a fool. Insane. Safe with my words, and no deaths, and clean, hard thoughts, urging me to new conquests. My people's madness. Hah! That's a laugh. My people. They don't need me to claim them. They got legs and arms of their own. Personal insanities. Mirrors. They don't need all those words. They don't need any defense. But listen, though, one more thing. And you tell this to your father, who's probably the kind of man who needs to know at once. So he can plan ahead. Tell him not to preach so much rationalism and cold logic to these niggers. Let them alone. Let them sing curses at you in code and see your filth as simple lack of style. Don't make the mistake, through some irresponsible surge of Christian charity, of talking too much about the advantages of Western rationalism, or the great intellectual legacy of the white man, or maybe they'll begin to listen. And then, maybe one day, you'll find they actually do understand exactly what you are talking about, all these fantasy people. All these blues people.[1] And on that day, as sure as shit, when you really believe you can "accept" them into your fold, as half-white trusties late of the subject peoples. With no more blues, except the very old ones, and not a watermelon in sight, the great missionary heart will have triumphed, and all of those ex-coons[2] will be stand-up Western men, with eyes for clean hard useful lives, sober, pious and sane, and they'll murder you. They'll murder you, and have very rational explanations. Very much like your own. They'll cut your throats, and drag you out to the edge of your cities so the flesh can fall away from your bones, in sanitary isolation.

LULA [*Her voice takes on a different, more businesslike quality.*]   I've heard enough.

CLAY [*Reaching for his books.*]   I bet you have. I guess I better collect my stuff and get off this train. Looks like we won't be acting out that little pageant you outlined before.

LULA   No. We won't. You're right about that, at least. [*She turns to look quickly around the rest of the car.*]

All right! [*The others respond.*]

CLAY [*Bending across the girl to retrieve his belongings.*]   Sorry, baby, I don't think we could make it. [*As he is bending over her, the girl brings up a small knife and plunges it into* CLAY's *chest. Twice. He slumps across her knees, his mouth working stupidly.*]

LULA   Sorry is right. [*Turning to the others in the car who have already gotten up from their seats.*] Sorry is the rightest thing you've said. Get this man off me! Hurry, now! [*The others come and drag* CLAY's *body down the aisle.*] Open the door and throw his body out. [*They throw him off.*] And all of you get off at the next stop.

[LULA *busies herself straightening her things. Getting everything in order. She takes out a notebook and makes a quick scribbling note.*

---

1. *Blues People* is the title of Baraka's seminal 1963 study of African American musical expression as a form of political and spiritual resistance to Western culture.
2. "Coons": derogatory term for black people.

*Drops it in her bag. The train apparently stops and all the others get off,
leaving her alone in the coach.*

    Very soon a YOUNG NEGRO *of about twenty comes into the coach, with
a couple of books under his arm. He sits a few seats in back of* LULA.
*When he is seated she turns and gives him a long slow look. He looks
up from his book and drops the book on his lap. Then an old Negro*
CONDUCTOR *comes into the car, doing a sort of restrained soft shoe,[3] and
half mumbling the words of some song. He looks at the* YOUNG MAN,
briefly, with a quick greeting.]

CONDUCTOR   Hey, brother!

YOUNG MAN   Hey. [*The* CONDUCTOR *continues down the aisle with his little
dance and the mumbled song.* LULA *turns to stare at him and follows his
movements down the aisle. The* CONDUCTOR *tips his hat when he reaches
her seat, and continues out the car.*]

[*Curtain.*]

1964

The Revolutionary Theatre

The Revolutionary Theatre should force change; it should be change. (All
their faces turned into the lights and you work on them black nigger magic,
and cleanse them at having seen the ugliness. And if the beautiful see
themselves, they will love themselves.) We are preaching virtue again, but
by that to mean NOW, toward what seems the most constructive use of the
world.

    The Revolutionary Theatre must EXPOSE! Show up the insides of these
humans, look into black skulls. White men will cower before this theatre
because it hates them. Because they themselves have been trained to hate.
The Revolutionary Theatre must hate them for hating. For presuming with
their technology to deny the supremacy of the Spirit. They will all die
because of this.

    The Revolutionary Theatre must teach them their deaths. It must crack
their faces open to the mad cries of the poor. It must teach them about
silence and the truths lodged there. It must kill any God anyone names
except Common Sense. The Revolutionary Theatre should flush the fags
and murders out of Lincoln's face.

    It should stagger through our universe correcting, insulting, preaching,
spitting craziness—but a craziness taught to us in our most rational
moments. People must be taught to trust true scientists (knowers, diggers,
oddballs) and that the holiness of life is the constant possibility of widening
the consciousness. And they must be incited to strike back against *any*
agency that attempts to prevent this widening.

    The Revolutionary Theatre must Accuse and Attack anything that can be
accused and attacked. It must Accuse and Attack because it is a theatre of
Victims.[1] It looks at the sky with the victims' eyes, and moves the victims to
look at the strength in their minds and their bodies.

---

3. A form of tap dancing done in soft-soled
shoes, characterized by wit and a leisurely pace.
1. Play on "the Theater of Cruelty" proposed by
the French dramatic theorist and playwright

Antonin Artaud (1896–1948) in his manifesto
The Theatre and Its Double (1938), the language
and style of which are evoked throughout Baraka's essay.

Clay, in *Dutchman*, Ray in *The Toilet*, Walker in *The Slave*,[2] are all victims. In the Western sense they could be heroes. But the Revolutionary Theatre, even if it is Western, must be anti-Western. It must show horrible coming attractions of *The Crumbling of the West*. Even as Artaud designed *The Conquest of Mexico*,[3] so we must design *The Conquest of White Eye*, and show the missionaries and wiggly Liberals dying under blasts of concrete. For sound effects, wild screams of joy, from all the peoples of the world.

The Revolutionary Theatre must take dreams and give them a reality. It must isolate the ritual and historical cycles of reality. But it must be food for all those who need food, and daring propaganda for the beauty of the Human Mind. It is a political theatre, a weapon to help in the slaughter of these dim-witted fatbellied white guys who somehow believe that the rest of the world is here for them to slobber on.

This should be a theatre of World Spirit.[4] Where the spirit can be shown to be the most competent force in the world. Force. Spirit. Feeling. The language will be anybody's, but tightened by the poet's backbone. And even the language must show what the facts are in this consciousness epic, what's happening. We will talk about the world, and the preciseness with which we are able to summon the world will be our art. Art is method. And art, "like any ashtray or senator," remains in the world. Wittgenstein[5] said ethics and aesthetics are one.[6] I believe this. So the Broadway theatre is a theatre of reaction whose ethics, like its aesthetics, reflect the spiritual values of this unholy society, which sends young crackers[7] all over the world blowing off colored people's heads. (In some of these flippy Southern towns they even shoot up the immigrants' Favorite Son, be it Michael Schwerner[8] or JFKennedy.)

The Revolutionary Theatre is shaped by the world, and moves to reshape the world, using as its force the natural force and perpetual vibrations of the mind in the world. We are history and desire, what we are, and what any experience can make us.

It is a social theatre, but all theatre is social theatre. But we will change the drawing rooms into places where real things can be said about a real world, or into smoky rooms where the destruction of Washington can be plotted. The Revolutionary Theatre must function like an incendiary pencil planted in Curtis Lemay's[9] cap. So that when the final curtain goes down brains are splattered over the seats and the floor, and bleeding nuns must wire SOS's to Belgians with gold teeth.[1]

Our theatre will show victims so that their brothers in the audience will be better able to understand that they are the brothers of victims, and that they themselves are victims if they are blood brothers. And what we show

2. Protagonists in Baraka plays first produced in 1964.
3. In Artaud's abstract play *The Conquest of Mexico*, Hernando Cortés and the colonial Spaniards are defeated.
4. Reference to 1807 treatise *The Phenomenology of Spirit* by German philosopher Georg Wilhelm Friedrich Hegel (1770–1831), in which Hegel explores the concept of *Geist* ("spirit") as a means of understanding human history and the evolution of consciousness.
5. Ludwig Wittgenstein (1889–1951), Austrian-British philosopher.
6. Reference to Wittgenstein's *Tractatus Logico-Philosophicus* (1921), Proposition 6.
7. Derogatory term for white person.
8. White civil rights activist who was killed in 1964, along with two other activists (one white, one black), in Mississippi.
9. Curtis Emerson Lemay (1906–1990), U.S. Air Force general, architect of a failed campaign during the early Vietnam War that he said would "bomb the North Vietnamese back to the stone age."
1. Perhaps a reference to Catholic missionaries who worked in the Congo when it was a Belgian colony.

must cause the blood to rush, so that pre-revolutionary temperaments will be bathed in this blood, and it will cause their deepest souls to move, and they will find themselves tensed and clenched, even ready to die, at what the soul has been taught. We will scream and cry, murder, run through the streets in agony, if it means some soul will be moved, moved to actual life understanding of what the world is, and what it ought to be. We are preaching virtue and feeling, and a natural sense of the self in the world. All men live in the world, and the world ought to be a place for them to live.

What is called the imagination (from image, magi, magic, magician, etc.) is a practical vector from the soul. It stores all data, and can be called on to solve all our "problems." The imagination is the projection of ourselves past our sense of ourselves as "things." Imagination (Image) is all possibility, because from the image, the initial circumscribed energy, any use (idea) is possible. And so begins that image's use in the world. Possibility is what moves us.

The popular white man's theatre like the popular white man's novel shows tired white lives, and the problems of eating white sugar, or else it herds bigcaboosed blondes onto huge stages in rhinestones and makes believe they are dancing or singing. WHITE BUSINESSMEN OF THE WORLD, DO YOU WANT TO SEE PEOPLE REALLY DANCING AND SINGING??? ALL OF YOU GO UP TO HARLEM AND GET YOURSELF KILLED. THERE WILL BE DANCING AND SINGING, THEN, FOR REAL!! (In *The Slave*, Walker Vessels, the black revolutionary, wears an armband, which is the insignia of the attacking army—a big red-lipped minstrel, grinning like crazy.)

The liberal white man's objection to the theatre of the revolution (if he is "hip" enough) will be on aesthetic grounds. Most white Western artists do not need to be "political," since usually, whether they know it or not, they are in complete sympathy with the most repressive social forces in the world today. There are more junior birdmen fascists running around the West today disguised as Artists than there are disguised as fascists. (But then, that word, *Fascist*, and with it, *Fascism*, has been made obsolete by the words *America* and *Americanism*.) The American Artist usually turns out to be just a super-Bourgeois, because, finally, all he has to show for his sojourn through the world is "better taste" than the Bourgeois—many times not even that.

Americans will hate the Revolutionary Theatre because it will be out to destroy them and whatever they believe is real. American cops will try to close the theatres where such nakedness of the human spirit is paraded. American producers will say the revolutionary plays are filth, usually because they will treat human life as if it were actually happening. American directors will say that the white guys in the plays are too abstract and cowardly ("don't get me wrong . . . I mean aesthetically . . .") and they will be right.

The force we want is of twenty million spooks[2] storming America with furious cries and unstoppable weapons. We want actual explosions and actual brutality: AN EPIC IS CRUMBLING and we must give it the space and hugeness of its actual demise. The Revolutionary Theatre, which is now peopled with victims, will soon begin to be peopled with new kinds of heroes—not

---

2. Derogatory term for a black person.

the weak Hamlets[3] debating whether or not they are ready to die for what's on their minds, but men and women (and minds) digging out from under a thousand years of "high art" and weak-faced dalliance. We must make an art that will function so as to call down the actual wrath of world spirit. We are witch doctors and assassins, but we will open a place for the true scientists to expand our consciousness. This is a theatre of assault. The play that will split the heavens for us will be called THE DESTRUCTION OF AMERICA. The heroes will be Crazy Horse, Denmark Vesey, Patrice Lumumba,[4] and not history, not memory, not sad sentimental groping for a warmth in our despair; these will be new men, new heroes, and their enemies most of you who are reading this.

1964

The Slave

Prologue

WALKER

[*Coming out dressed as an old field slave, balding, with white hair, and an old ragged vest. (Perhaps he is sitting, sleeping, initially nodding and is awakened by faint cries, like a child's.) He comes to the center of the stage slowly, and very deliberately, puffing on a pipe, and seemingly uncertain of the reaction any audience will give his speech.*]

Whatever the core of our lives. Whatever the deceit. We live where we are, and seek nothing but ourselves. We are liars, and we are murderers. We invent death for others. Stop their pulses publicly. Stone possible lovers with heavy worlds we think are ideas . . . and we know, even before these shapes are realized, that these worlds, these depths or heights we fly to smoothly, as in a dream, or slighter, when we stare dumbly into space, leaning our eyes just behind a last quick moving bird, then sometimes the place and twist of what we are will push and sting, and what the crust of our stance has become will ring in our ears and shatter that piece of our eyes that is never closed. An ignorance. A stupidity. A stupid longing not to know . . . which is automatically fulfilled. Automatically triumphs. Automatically makes us killers or foot-dragging celebrities at the core of any filth. And it is a deadly filth that passes as whatever thing we feel is too righteous to question, too deeply felt to deny.

[*Pause to relight pipe*]

I am much older than I look . . . or maybe much younger. Whatever I am or seem . . .

[*Significant pause*]

to you, then let that rest. But figure, still, that you might not be right. Figure, still, that you might be lying . . . to save yourself. Or myself's image, which might set you crawling like a thirsty dog, for the meanest of drying streams. The meanest of ideas.

---

3. Shakespeare's tragic protagonist Hamlet is celebrated for brooding soliloquies such as "To be, or not to be," in which Hamlet variously imagines what it might mean to die.
4. African nationalist leader (1925–1961) who

was the first prime minister of the Democratic Republic of the Congo (now Zaire). Crazy Horse (1849–1877), Oglala Sioux war chief. Vesey (1767–1822), leader of a failed 1822 slave revolt in South Carolina.

[*Gentle, mocking laugh*]

Yeah. Ideas. Let that settle! Ideas. Where they form. Or whose they finally seem to be. Yours? The other's? Mine?

[*Shifts uneasily, pondering the last*]

No, no more. Not mine. I served my slow apprenticeship . . . and maybe came up lacking. Maybe. Ha. Who's to say, really? Huh? But figure, still, ideas are still in the world. They need judging. I mean, they don't come in that singular or wild, that whatever they are, just because they're beautiful and brilliant, just because they strike us full in the center of the heart. . . . My God!

[*Softer*]

My God, just because, and even this, believe me, even if, that is, just because they're *right* . . . doesn't mean anything. The very rightness stinks a lotta times. The very rightness.

[*Looks down and speaks softer and quicker*]

I am an old man. An old man.

[*Blankly*]

The waters and wars. Time's a dead thing really . . . and keeps nobody whole. An old man, full of filed rhythms. Terrific, eh? That I hoarded so much dignity? An old man full of great ideas. Let's say theories. As: Love is an instrument of knowledge. Oh, not my own. Not my own . . . is right. But listen now. . . . Brown is not brown except when used as an intimate description of personal phenomenological[1] fields. As your brown is not my brown, et cetera, that is, we need, ahem, a meta-language.[2] We need some thing not included here.

[*Spreads arms*]

Your ideas? An old man can't be expected to be right. If I'm old. If I really claim that embarrassment.

[*Saddens . . . brightens*]

A poem? Lastly, that, to distort my position? To divert you . . . in your hour of need. Before the thing goes on. Before you get your lousy chance. Discovering racially the funds of the universe. Discovering the last image of the thing. As the sky when the moon is broken. Or old, old blues people[3] moaning in their sleep, singing, man, oh, nigger, nigger, you still here, as hard as nails, and takin' no shit from nobody. He say, yeah, yeah, he say yeah, yeah. He say, yeah, yeah . . . goin' down slow, man. Goin' down slow.[4] He say . . . yeah, heh . . .

[*Running down, growing anxiously less articulate, more "field hand" sounding, blankly lyrical, shuffles slowly around, across the stage, as the lights dim and he enters the set proper and assumes the position he will have when the play starts . . . still moaning . . .*]

1964

1. Concerned with the philosophical investigation of subjectivity and self-awareness, as opposed to theoretical reflection on existence as such.
2. A language used to analyze or talk about language itself.
3. *Blues People* is the title of Baraka's seminal 1963 study of African American musical expression as a form of political and spiritual resistance to Western culture.
4. Title of blues song by vocalist and composer James Burke "St. Louis Jimmy" Oden (1903–1977), first released in 1941 and made famous by Howlin' Wolf (Chester Arthur Burnett, 1910–1976) in his 1962 recording of the song.

A Poem for Black Hearts

For Malcolm's[1] eyes, when they broke
the face of some dumb white man, For
Malcolm's hands raised to bless us
all black and strong in his image
of ourselves, For Malcolm's words   5
fire darts, the victor's tireless
thrusts, words hung above the world
change as it may, he said it, and
for this he was killed, for saying,
and feeling, and being / / / change, all   10
collected hot in his heart, For Malcolm's
heart, raising us above our filthy cities,
for his stride, and his beat, and his address
to the grey monsters of the world, For Malcolm's
pleas for your dignity, black men, for your life,   15
black man, for the filling of your minds
with righteousness, For all of him dead and
gone and vanished from us, and all of him which
clings to our speech black god of our time.
For all of him, and all of yourself, look up,   20
black man, quit stuttering and shuffling, look up,
black man, quit whining and stooping, for all of him,
For Great Malcolm a prince of the earth, let nothing in us rest
until we avenge ourselves for his death, stupid animals
that killed him, let us never breathe a pure breath if   25
we fail, and white men call us faggots till the end of
the earth

                                                                    1965

Ka 'Ba[1]

A closed window looks down
on a dirty courtyard, and black people
call across or scream across or walk across
defying physics in the stream of their will

Our world is full of sound   5
Our world is more lovely than anyone's
tho we suffer, and kill each other
and sometimes fail to walk the air

1. Malcolm X (1925–1965), African American Muslim minister, black nationalist, and human rights activist; he was assassinated in February 1965, two months before Baraka first published this poem.
1. Ka 'Ba (also spelled Ka'Bah or Kaaba): a religious shrine considered Islam's most sacred site, located inside the Masjid al-Haram mosque in Mecca's center. A cuboid granite structure whose corners correspond roughly to the points of the compass, it is the orientation for Muslims' five daily prayers and the destination of the Muslim pilgrimage, or Hajj.

We are beautiful people
with african imaginations   10
full of masks and dances and swelling chants
with african eyes, and noses, and arms,
though we sprawl in grey chains in a place
full of winters, when what we want is sun.[2]

We have been captured,   15
brothers. And we labor
to make our getaway, into
the ancient image, into a new

correspondence with ourselves
and our black family. We need magic   20
now we need the spells, to raise up
return, destroy, and create. What will be

the sacred words?

                                                       1967

Slave Ship

An Historical Pageant[1]

CAST

SPEAKING PARTS

AFRICAN SLAVES—VOICES OF AFRICAN SLAVES

1st Man (Prayer—Husband of Dademi)
2nd Man (Curser)
3rd Man (Struggler)

1st Woman (Prayer)
2nd Woman (Screamer—Attacked)
3rd Woman (With Child)

Dancers
Musicians

Children
Voices and bodies in the slave ship

Old Tom[2] Slave
New Tom (Preacher)

---

2. The sun comes directly overhead above the Ka 'Ba two days a year, times at which it is said that Muslims can align perfectly the *Qibla*, or direction for prayer.
1. An elaborate drama or spectacle, usually a loose series of tableaux illustrating a central theme, often with musical accompaniment.
2. I.e., an "Uncle Tom," a figure symbolic of black servility and fear in the face of white authority, based on the titular figure of the 1852 novel *Uncle Tom's Cabin* by Harriet Beecher Stowe (1811–1896).

WHITE MEN—VOICES OF WHITE MEN

Captain
Sailor
Plantation Owner—"Eternal Oppressor"

PROPS

Smell effects: incense . . . dirt/filth smells/bodies

Heavy chains

Drums (African bata drums, and bass and snare[3])
Rattles and tambourines
Banjo music for plantation atmosphere

Ship noises
Ship bells
Rocking and splashing of sea

Guns and cartridges

Whips/whip sounds

Whole theater in darkness. Dark. For a long time. Just dark. Occasional sound, like ship groaning, squeaking, rocking. Sea smells. In the dark. Keep the people in the dark, and gradually the odors of the sea, and the sounds of the sea, and sounds of the ship, creep up. Burn incense, but make a significant, almost stifling, smell come up. Pee. Shit. Death. Life processes going on anyway. Eating. These smells and cries, the slash and tear of the lash, in a total atmos-feeling, gotten some way.

African Drums like the worship of some Orisha. Obatala. Mbwanga[4] rattles of the priests. BamBamBamBamBoom BoomBoom BamBam.

Rocking of the slave ship, in darkness, without sound. But smells. Then sound. Now slowly, out of blackness with smells and drums staccato, the hideous screams. All the women together, scream. AAAAAIIIEEEEEEEEEEEE. Drums come up again, rocking, rocking; black darkness of the slave ship. Smells. Drums on up high. Stop. Scream. AAAAAAIIIIEEEEEEEEEE. Drums. Black darkness with smells.

Chains, the lash, and people moaning. Listen to the sounds come up out of the actors. Sounds thrown down into the hold. AAAAIIIEEEEEEEEE. Of people, dropped down in the darkness, frightened, angry, mashed together in common terror. The bells of the ship. White Men's voices, on top, ready to set sail.

---

3. Types of drums; the bata (or Batá) drum is a Yoruban instrument with religious significance that has migrated into other traditions such as the West African and Caribbean syncretic religion of Santería.

4. Kikongo instrument; "Orisha": any deity or spirit of the Yoruba religion; "Obatala": the eldest Orisha, the arch divinity and creator of human bodies.

VOICE 1   OK, let's go! A good cargo of black gold. Let's go! We head West! We head West. [*Long laughter*] Black gold in the West. We got our full cargo.

VOICE 2   Aye, Aye, Cap'n. We're on our way. Riches be ours, by God.

VOICE 1   Aye, riches, riches be ours. We're on our way. America! [*Laughter*]

[*There is just dim light at top of the set, to indicate where voices are* . . .]
[*African Drums. With the swiftness of dance, but running into the heaviness the dark enforces. The drums slow. The beat beat of the darkness. "Where are we, God?" The mumble murmur rattle below. The drone of terror. The voices begin to beat against the dark.*]

WOMAN 1   Oooooooooo, Obatala!

WOMAN 2   Shango![5]

WOMAN 1   Oooooooooo, Obatala . . .

[*Children's crying in the hold, and the women trying to comfort them. Trying to keep their sanity, too.*]

WOMAN 3   Moshake, chile, calm, calm, be you. Moshake chile. O calm, Orisha, save us!

WOMAN 2   AAAIIIIEEEEEEE.

MAN 1   Quiet woman! Quiet! Save your strength for your child.

WOMAN 2   AAAIIIIEEEEEEE.

MAN 1   Quiet, foolish woman! Be quiet!

WOMAN 3   Moshake, baby, chile, be calm, be calm, it give you, ooooooo.

MAN 1   Shango, Obatala, make your lightning, beat the inside bright with paths for your people. Beat. Beat. Beat. [*Drums come up, but they are walls and floors being beaten. Chains rattled. Chains rattled. Drag the chains.*]

[*We get the feeling of many people jammed together, men, women, children, aching in the darkness. The chains. The whips, magnify the chains and whips. The dragging together. The pain. The terror. Women begin to moan and chant songs, "African Sorrow Song,"[6] with scraping of floor and chains for accompaniment.*]

MAN 2   Fukwididila! Fukwididila! Fukwididila![7] Fuck you, Orisha! God! Where you be? Where you now, Black God? Help me. I be a strong warrior, and no woman. And I strain against these chains! But you must help me, Orisha. Obatala!

MAN 3   Quiet, you fool, you frighten the women!

[*Women still chanting, moaning. Children now crying. Mothers trying to comfort them. Feeling of people moving around, tumbling over each other. Screaming as they try to find a "place" in the bottom of the boat, and then the long stream of different wills, articulated as screams, grunts, cries, songs, et cetera.*]

MAN 3   Pull, pull break them . . . Pull.

WOMAN 1   Oh, Obatala!

WOMAN 3   Oh, chile . . . my chile, please, please get away . . . you crush . . . !

MAN 3   Break . . . Break . . .

ALL   Uhh, Uhhh, Uhhh, Uhhh, OOOOOOOOOOOOOOOO.

---

5. Yoruba god of fire, lightning, and thunder. The Shango initiation ceremony is the best preserved of the Yoruba rituals among descendants of New World slaves.
6. Allusion to a chapter on slave music in *The*

Souls of Black Folk (1903) by African American author and philosopher W. E. B. Du Bois (1868–1963).
7. A Bantu expression of diminishing vitality or life force.

WOMEN   AAAAAIIIIIIIEEEEEEE.

ALL   Uhhh, Uhhh, Uhhh, Uhhh, OOOOOOOOOOOO.

WOMEN   AAAIIIIEEEEEEE.

> [*Drums down low, like tapping, turn to beating floor, walls, rattling, dragging chains, percussive sounds people make in the hold of a ship. The moans and pushed-together agony. Children crying incessantly. The mothers trying to calm them. More than one child. Young girls afraid they may be violated. Men trying to break out, or turning into frightened children. Families separated for the first time.*]

WOMAN 2   Ifanami, Ifanami[8] . . . where you?? Where you?? Ifanami. [*Cries*] Please, oh, God.

MAN 1   Obata . . . [*Drums beat down, softer . . . humming starts . . . humm-mmmm, hummmmmmmmmm, like old black women humming for three centuries in the slow misery of slavery . . . hummmmmmmmmmmmmmmmm-mmm, hummmmmmmmmmmmmmmmmmmmmmmmmmmmmmmm.*]

> [*Lights flash on white men in sailor suits grinning their vices . . . voices down . . . hummmmmmmmmmmmmmmmmmmmmmmmm mmmmmm. Lights to light white people are sudden, very bright and blinding. The white men begin to laugh and point, as if they were pointing at the filth, misery, and degradation of the Black People. They laugh: HAAAAAA-HAAAAHAAHAAHAAHAAAHAAHAAHAHAHAHA. When they are outlined again they are rolling in merriment. Pointing, dancing, jumping up and down, HAHAHA hahaha Haaaa . . .*]

> [*Laughter is drowned in the drums. Then the chant-moan of the women . . . then silence. Then the drums, softer, then the humming, on and on, in a maddening, building death-patience, broken by the screams, and the babies and the farts, and the babies crying for light, and young wives crying for their men. Old people calling for God. Warriors calling for freedom. Some crying out against the white men.*]

MAN 3   Devils! Devils! Devils! White beasts! Shit eaters! Beasts! [*They beat the walls, and try to tear the chains out of the walls.*] White shit eaters.

WOMAN 3   Aiiiiieeeeeeeeeeeee.

MAN 1   God, she's killed herself and the child. Oh, God. Oh, God. [*Moans. Moans. Soft drums, and the constant, now almost maddenning, humming . . . hummmmmmmmmmmmmmmmmm, hummmmmmmmmmmmm-mmmmmm . . . like mad old nigger ladies humming forever in deathly patience . . . hummmmmmm hummmmmmmmm hummmm.*]

WOMAN 1   She strangled herself with the chain. Choked the child. Oh, Shango! Help us, Lord. Oh, please.

WOMAN 2   Why you leave us, Lord?

MAN 1   Dademi, Dademi . . . she dead, she dead . . . Dademi . . . [*Hear man wracked with death cries, screams.*] Dademi, Dademi!

> [*Hummmmmmmmmmmm, Hummmmmmmmmmmmmm, Hummmm-mmmmmmmmm, Hummmmmmmmmmmmmmmmmmm. Drums low, and moans . . . the chains, and Black People pushed against each other, struggling for breath and room to live. The Black Man weeps for his woman. The Black Woman weeps for her man together in the darkness, some calling for God.*]

WOMAN 2   Oh, please, please don't touch me . . . Please . . . [*Frantic*] Ifanami, where you? [*Screams at someone's touch in the dark, grabbing her,*

---

8. An Orisha, a guardian of roads, hence of travel.

trying to drag her in the darkness, press her down against the floor.] Aki-yele . . . please . . . please . . . don't, don't touch me . . . please, Ifanami, where you? Please, help me . . . Go . . .

MAN 1 What you doing? Get away from that woman. That's not your woman. You turn into a beast, too. [*Scuffle of two men turning in the darkness trying to kill each other. Lights show white men laughing silently, dangling their whips, in pantomime, still pointing.*]

MAN 3 Devils. Devils. Cold walking shit. [*All mad sounds together*]
[*Humming begins again. Bells of ship. Silence, and moans, and humming, and movement in the dark of people. Sliding back and forth. Trying to stay alive, and now, over it, the constant crazy laughter of the sailors.*]

SAILORS AHAHAHAHAHAHAHAHAHAHAHAAAAAHHAHHHAHAHA HAHAHAHAHAHAHAHAHAH.

MAN 3 I kill you, devils. I break these chains. [*Sound of men struggling against heavy chains*] I tear your face off. Crush your throat. Devils. Devils.

WOMAN 1 Oh, Oh, God, she dead . . . and the child.
[*SILENCE/Sound of the sea . . . fades.*]

ALL [*Humming* HMMMMMMMMMM HMMMMMMMMMMM HMM-MMMMMMMMMMMM HMMMMMMMMMM HMMMMMM-MMMM.
[*Lights on suddenly, show a shuffling "Negro." Lights off . . . drums of ancient African warriors come up . . . hero-warriors. Lights blink back on, show shuffling black man, hat in his hand, scratching his head. Lights off. Drums again. Black dancing in the dark, with bells, as if free, dancing wild old dances. Bam Boom Bam Booma Bimbam boomama boom beem bam. Dancing in the darkness . . . Yoruba Dance.[9] Lights flash on briefly, spot on, off the dance. Then off. Then on, to show The Slave, raggedy ass, raggedy hat in hand, shuffling toward the audience, shuffling, scratching his head and butt. Shaking his head up and down, agreeing with massa,[1] agreeing, and agreeing, while the whips snap. Lights off, flash on, and the sailors, with hats changed to show them as plantation owners, are still laughing; no sound, but laughing and pointing, holding their sides, and they laugh and point.*]

SLAVE [*In darkness*] Yassa, boss, yassa Massa Tim, yassa, boss. [*Lights up*] I'se happy as a brand new monkey ass, yassa, boss, yassa, Massa Tim, yassa, Massa Booboo, I's so happy I jus don't know what to do. Yass, massa, boss, you'se so han'some and good and youse hip, too, yass, I's so happy I jus' stan' and scratch my ol' nigger haid. [*Lights flash on Slave doing an old-new dance for the boss; when he finishes he bows and scratches.*]
[*Lights out . . . the same hummmmmm rises up . . . with low drums, but the hum, grown louder, drowns it out . . . hummmmmmmmmmmm-mmmmmmmmmmmmmmmmm hummmmmmmmmmmmmmmmmmm-mmmmmmmmm. The laughter now drowns out the humming, the same cold, hideous laughter.*]

WOMAN 3 [*Whispering after death*] Moshake . . . Moshake . . . Moshake chile, calm yourself, love. [*Woman runs down into soft weep, with no*

---

9. In Yoruban tradition, dance is an expression of communal desires, values, and collective spir-itual identity.
1. I.e., the plantation "master."

other distracting sound, just her moaning sad cry, for her baby. Chains. Chains. Dragging the chains. The humming. Hummmmmmmmmmmm-mmmmmmmmmmm.]

WOMAN 2   AIEEEEEEEEEEEEEEEEE.

ALL   Uhh, Uhhh, Uhhh, Uhhh, Oooooooooooooo.

[*Silence*]

[*Soft at first, then rising. Banjos of the plantation.*]

SLAVE 1   Reverend what we gon' do when massa come? [*He sounds afraid.*]

SLAVE 2   We gon' cut his fuckin' throat!

[*Banjos*]

[*Humming . . . Hummmmmmmmmmmmmmm.*]

SLAVE 1   Reverend, what we gon' do when the white man come?

SLAVE 2   We gon' cut his fuckin' throat.

SLAVE 3   Devil. Beast. Murderer of women and children. Soulless shit eater!

SLAVE 1   Reverend Turner,[2] sir, what we gon' do when the massa come?

SLAVE 2   Cut his godless throat.

[*Lights flash up on same Tomish slave, still scratching his head, but now apparently talking to a white man.*]

SLAVE   Uhh, dass right, Massa Tim . . . dey gon' 'volt.

WHITE VOICE   What? Vote? Are you crazy?

SLAVE   Nawsaw . . . I said 'volt . . . uhhhh . . . revolt.

[*Laughter, now . . . rising behind the dialogue.*]

WHITE VOICE   When, boy?

SLAVE   Ahhh, t'night, boss, t'night . . . they say they gon' . . .'scuse de 'spression . . . cut you . . . uhh fuckin' . . . uhh throat . . .

WHITE VOICE [*Laughs*]   And who's in charge of this "'volt"?

SLAVE   Uhh . . . Reverend Turner . . . suh . . .

WHITE VOICE   What?

SLAVE   Uhh . . . dass right . . . Reverend Turner . . . suh . . . Now can I have dat extra chop you promised me?

[*Screams now, as soon as the lights go down AIEEEEEEEEEIEIEIEI-EIEIE Gunshots, combination of slave ship and break up of the revolt. Voices of master and slaves in combat.*]

WHITE VOICE   I kill you, niggahs. You black savages.

BLACK VOICE   White Beasts. Devil from hell.

[*Voice, now, humming, humming, slow, deathly patient hum HUMMMMMMMMMMMMMMMMMMMMMM.*]

[*Drums of Africa, and the screams of Black and White in combat.*]

[*Lights flash on Tom, cringing as if he hiding from combat, gnawing on pork chop. Voice of white man laughing in triumph. Another chop comes sailing out of the darkness. Tom grabs it and scoffs it down, grinning, and doing the deadape shuffle, humming while he eats.*]

WOMAN 3 [*Dead whispered voice*]   Moshake, Moshake . . . chile . . . calm calm . . . we be all right, now . . . Moshake, be calm . . .

MAN 1   White beasts!

ALL   Uhh. Ohhh. Uhhh, Uhhh [*As if pulling a tremendous weight*] Uhh. Ohhh. Uhhh. Uhhh. Uhhh.

WOMAN 1   Ifanami . . .

MAN 1   Dademi . . . Dademi.

---

2. Nat Turner (1800–1831), American slave leader of a slave revolt in Virginia; he was convicted of "conspiring to rebel and make insurrection" and executed.

WOMAN 2   Akiyele . . . Akiyele . . . Lord, husband, where you . . . help
me . . .
MAN   . . . touch my hand . . . woman . . .
WOMAN 2   Ifanami!
WOMAN 3   Moshake!
[*Now the same voices, as if transported in time to the slave farms, call
names, English slaves names.*]
ALL [*Alternating man and woman losing mate in death, or through slave sale,
or the aura of constant fear of separation . . .*]   Luke. Oh my God.
MAN   Sarah.
WOMAN   John.
WOMAN 2   Everett. My God, they killed him.
ALL   Mama, Mama . . . Nana. Nana.[3] Willie. Ohhh, Lord . . . They done.
ALL   Uhh. Uhhh. Uhh. Obatala. Obatala. Save us. Lord. Shango. Lord of
forests. Give us back our strength. [*Chains. Chains. Dragging and grunt-
ing of people pushed against each other.*]
[*The sound of a spiritual. "Oh, Lord, Deliver Me, Oh Lord." And now
cries of "*JESUS, LORD, JESUS . . . HELP US, JESUS . . .*"*]
MAN 1   Ogun.[4] Give me weapons. Give me iron. My spear. My bone and
muscle make them tight with tension of combat. Ogun, give me fire and
death to give to these beasts. Sarava! Sarava![5] Ogun!
[*Drums of fire and blood, briefly loud and smashing against the dark,
but now calming, dying down, till only the moans, and then the same
patient humming . . . of women, now, no men, only the women . . .
strains of "The Old Rugged Cross"[6] . . . and only the women and the
humming . . . the time passing in the darkness, soft, soft, mournful
weeping   "Jesus . . . Jesus . . . Jesus . . . Jesus . . . Jesus . . . Jesus . . .
Jesus . . . Jesus . . . Jesus . . ."*]

[*Now lights flash on, and preacher in modern business suit stands with
hat in his hand. He is the same Tom as before. He stands at first talking
to his congregation: "Jesus, Jesus, Jesus, Jesus, Jesus, Jesus." Then,
with a big grin, speaking in the pseudo-intelligent patter he uses for the
boss. He tries to be, in fact, assumes he is, dignified, trying to hold his
shoulders straight, but only succeeds in giving his body an odd slant like
a diseased coal chute.*]
PREACHER   Yasss, we understand . . . the problem. And, personally, I think
some agreement can be reached. We will be nonviolenk . . . to the
last . . . because we understand the dignity of Pruty McBonk and the
Greasy Ghost. Of course diddy rip to bink, of vout juice. And penguins
would do the same. I have a trauma that the gold sewers won't integrate.
Present fink. I have an enema . . . a trauma, on the coaster with your
wife bird shit.
WOMAN 3 [*Black woman's voice screaming for her child again*]   Moshake!
Moshake! Moshake! beeba . . . beeba . . . Wafwa ko[7] wafwa ko
fukwididila.
[*Screams . . . moans . . . drums . . . mournful   death-tone . . . The
preacher looks, head turned just slightly, as if embarrassed, trying still*]

3. Nana Buluku, Mother of the Orishas and
goddess of creation, an avatar of a parallel deity
in the Dahomey mythology of the West African
Fon people.
4. Orisha of war, vengeance, and blacksmithing;
brother of Shango.

5. Save, or bestow fortune (salute or blessing
used by members of the Candomblé religion,
taken to Brazil by African slaves).
6. Popular hymn written by evangelist George
Bennard (1873–1958) in 1912.
7. Thank you (Kiluba, a Congolese language).

to talk to the white man. Then, one of the black men, out of the darkness, comes and sits before the Tom, a wrapped-up bloody corpse of a dead burned baby as if they had just taken the body from a blown-up church, sets corpse in front of preacher. Preacher stops. Looks up at "person" he's Tomming before, then, with his foot, tries to push baby's body behind him, grinning, and jeffing,[8] *all the time, showing teeth, and being "dignified."*]

PREACHER Uhhherr . . . as I was sayin' . . . Mas' uh . . . Mister Tasty-slop . . . We Kneegrows are ready to integrate . . . the blippy rump of stomach bat has corrinked a lip to push the thimble. Yass. Yass. Yass . . .

    [*In background, while preacher is frozen in his "Jeff" position, high hard sound of saxophone, backed up by drums. New-sound*[9] *saxophone tearing up the darkness. At height of screaming saxophone, instruments, and drums come voices screaming . . .*]

MAN Beasts! Beasts! Beasts! Ogun. Give me spear and iron. Let me kill . . .
[*Humming as before . . . long . . . incredible patience, as if it would go on forever, turns into* OMMMMMMMMMMMMMMMMMMMMMMMMMMMMMMMMMMMM: *All take it up, as the climax rises.*]

    [*Lights down. Ommmmm sound, mixed with sounds of slave ship, saxophone, and drums. Sounds of people thrown against each other, now as if trying, all, to rise, pick up. Sounds of people picking up. Like dead people rising. And against that, the same sounds of slave ship. White laughter over all of it. White laughter. Song begins to build with the saxophone and drums. First chanted.*]

ALL
Rise, Rise, Rise
Cut these ties, Black Man Rise
We gon' be the thing we are . . .
    [*Now all sing "When We Gonna Rise"*]
When we gonna rise up, brother
When we gonna rise above the sun
I mean, when we gonna lift our heads and voices
When we gonna show the world who we really are
When we gonna rise up, brother
When we gonna take our own place, brother
Like the world had just begun
I mean, when we gonna lift our heads and voices
Show the world who we really are
Warriors-Gods, and lovers, The First Men to walk this star
Yes, oh, yes, the first Men to walk this star
How far, how long will it be
When the world belongs to you and me
When we gonna rise up, brother
When we gonna rise above the sun
When we gonna take our own place, brother
Like the world had just begun?
    [*Drum—new sax—voice arrangement*]
    [*Bodies dragging up, in darkness*]

8. Imitating "white" behavior in a servile manner.

9. I.e., the "new wave" style of 1960s avant-garde jazz.

[*Lights on the preacher in one part of the stage. He stands still, jabbering senselessly to the white man. And the white man's laughter is heard trying to drown out the music, but the music is rising.*]

[*Preacher turns to look into the darkness at the people dragging up behind him, embarrassed at first, then beginning to get frightened. The laughter, too, takes on a less arrogant tone.*]

WOMAN 3   Moshake. Moshake.

MAN   Ogun, give me steel.

ALL   Uhh. Uhh. Ohhh. Uhhh. Uhhh.

[*Humming rising, too, behind. Still singing "When We Gonna Rise." Preacher squirms, turns to see, and suddenly his eyes begin to open very wide, lights are coming up very, very slowly, almost imperceptibly at first. Now, singing is beginning to be heard, mixed with old African drums, and voices, cries, pushing screams, of the slave ship. Preacher begins to fidget, as if he does not want to be where he is. He looks to boss for help. Voice is breaking, as lights come up and we see all the people in the slave ship in Miracles'/Temptations' dancing line.[1] Some doing African dance. Some doing new Boogaloo,[2] but all moving toward preacher, and toward voice. It is a new-old dance, Boogalooyoruba line, women, children all moving, popping fingers, all singing, and drummers, beating out old and new, and moving, all moving. Finally, the preacher begins to cringe and plead for help from the white voice.*]

PREACHER   Please, boss, these niggers goin' crazy; please, boss, throw yo' lightnin' at 'em, white Jesus boss, white light god, they goin crazy! Help!

VOICE   [*Coughing, as if choking on something, trying to laugh because the sight of preacher is funny . . . still managing to laugh at preacher.*]   Fool. Fool.

PREACHER   Please, boss, please . . . I do anything for you . . . you know that, boss . . . Please . . . Please . . .

[*All group merge on him and kill him daid. Then they turn in the direction of where the voice is coming from. Dancing, Singing, right on toward the now pleading voice.*]

VOICE   HaaHaaHaaHaa. [*Laugh gets stuck in his throat.*] Uhh . . . now what . . . you haha can't touch me . . . you scared of me, niggers. I'm God. You cain't kill white Jesus God. I got long blond blow-hair. I don't even need to wear a wig. You love the way I look. You want to look like me. You love me. You want me. Please. I'm good. I'm kind. I'll give you anything you want. I'm white Jesus savior right god pay you money nigger me is good god be please . . . please don't . . .

[*Lights begin to fade . . . drums and voices of old slave ship come back.*]

ALL   Uhh. Ohh. Uhh. Ohh. Uhh. Ohh. Uhh. Ohh. [*And then the terrible humming, turning to the OMMMMMMMMMMmmmmmmmmmmmmmm sound, broken now, by the finally awful scream of the killed white voice.*]

VOICE   AWHAWHAEHAHWAWHWHAHW.

[*All players fixed in half light, at the movement of the act. Then lights go down. Black.*]

[*Lights come up abruptly, and people on stage begin to dance, same hip Boogalooyoruba, fingerpop, skate, monkey, dog[3] . . . Enter audience; get members of audience to dance. To same music Rise Up. Turns into*]

---

1. The Miracles and The Temptations were African American rhythm and blues vocal ensembles best known for their "Motown sound" and up-tempo, tightly choreographed dance steps.
2. A dance popular among African Americans in the 1960s that originated in the Latino community of New York City.
3. Popular African American dances of the 1950s and 1960s.

an actual party. When the party reaches some loose improvisation, et
cetera, audience relaxed, somebody throws the preacher's head into
center of floor, that is, after dancing starts for real. Then black.]

1967

Black Art

Poems are bullshit unless they are
teeth or trees or lemons piled
on a step. Or black ladies dying
of men leaving nickel hearts
beating them down. Fuck poems   5
and they are useful, wd they shoot
come at you, love what you are,
breathe like wrestlers, or shudder
strangely after pissing. We want live
words of the hip world live flesh &   10
coursing blood. Hearts Brains
Souls splintering fire. We want poems
like fists beating niggers out of Jocks
or dagger poems in the slimy bellies
of the owner-jews.[1] Black poems to   15
smear on girdlemamma mulatto bitches
whose brains are red jelly stuck
between 'lizabeth taylor's[2] toes. Stinking
Whores! We want "poems that kill."
Assassin poems, Poems that shoot   20
guns. Poems that wrestle cops into alleys
and take their weapons leaving them dead
with tongues pulled out and sent to Ireland.[3] Knockoff
poems for dope selling wops[4] or slick halfwhite
politicians Airplane poems, rrrrrrrrrrrrrrrr   25
rrrrrrrrrrrrrr . . . tuhtuhtuhtuhtuhtuhtuhtuhtuh
. . . rrrrrrrrrrrrrrrr . . . Setting fire and death to
whities ass. Look at the Liberal
Spokesman for the jews clutch his throat
& puke himself into eternity . . . rrrrrrrr   30
There's a negroleader pinned to
a bar stool in Sardi's[5] eyeballs melting
in hot flame Another negroleader
on the steps of the white house one
kneeling between the sheriff's thighs   35
negotiating cooly for his people.
Agggh . . . stumbles across the room . . .

<hr>

1. Anti-Semitic rhetoric most likely directed at
Jewish proprietors in black communities. Baraka
suspected that Jewish liberals were politically
opportunistic.
2. American actress (1932–2011) known for her
onscreen and off-screen romances.
3. Possible reference to the "Whiteboys," tenants
in Munster, Ireland, who gathered in a secret society from 1761 to 1764, terrorizing Munster as rebels against oppressive landlords; the Whiteboys
would march at night, burning farms, leveling
houses, and sometimes cutting out men's tongues.
4. A pejorative term for those of Italian descent.
5. A fashionable after-theater spot in Manhattan.

Put it on him, poem. Strip him naked
to the world! Another bad poem cracking
steel knuckles in a jewlady's mouth   40
Poem scream poison gas on beasts in green berets[6]
Clean out the world for virtue and love,
Let there be no love poems written
until love can exist freely and
cleanly. Let Black People understand   45
that they are the lovers and the sons
of lovers and warriors and sons
of warriors Are poems & poets &
all the loveliness here in the world

We want a black poem. And a   50
Black World.
Let the world be a Black Poem
And Let All Black People Speak This Poem
Silently
or LOUD   55

                                                                    1969

It's Nation Time

Time to get
together
time to be one strong fast black energy space
          one pulsating positive magnetism, rising
time to get up and   5
be
come
be
come, time to
          be come   10
          time to
          get up be come
          black genius rise in spirit muscle
          sun man get up[1] rise heart of universes to be
future of the world   15
the black man is the future of the world
be come
rise up
future of the black genius spirit reality
          move   20
          from crushed roach back
          from dead snake head
          from wig funeral in slowmotion
          from dancing teeth and coward tip

6. Reference to the Green Berets, an elite corps
within the U.S. Army.
1. "Get up . . . get up . . . get up": Reference to
chorus of 1970 funk song, "Get Up (I Feel Like

Being) a Sex Machine" by James Brown (1933–
2006): "Get up (get on up) / get up (get on up) /
Stay on the scene . . ."

from jibberjabber[2] patme boss patme smmich   25
when the brothers strike niggers come out
come out niggers
when the brothers take over the school
help niggers
come out niggers   30
all niggers negroes must change up
come together in unity unify
for nation time
it's nation time

       Boom   35
       Booom
       BOOOM
       Boom
       Dadadadadadadadadadad
       Boom   40
       Boom
       Boom
       Boom
       Dadadadad adadadad
             Hey aheee (soft)   45
             Hey ahheee (loud)
       Boom
       Boom
       Boom
sing a get up time to nationfy   50
singa a miracle fire light
sing a airplane invisibility for the jesus niggers come from the
   grave
for the jesus niggers dead in the cave, rose up, passt jewjuice
on shadow world
raise up christ nigger   55
Christ was black
krishna was black shango[3] was black
       black jesus nigger come out and strike
      come out and strike boom boom
          Heyahheeee come out   60
     strike close ford
       close prudential burn the policies[4]
    tear glasses off dead statue puppets[5] even those
       they imitate life
       Shango budda black   65
     hermes rasis[6] black
       moses krishna
          black

---

2. Foolish chatter (slang).
3. Yoruba god of fire, lightning, and thunder; "krishna": Hindu deity, an avatar of the supreme Vedic god Vishnu.
4. Prudential Financial: life insurance company founded in 1875 in Baraka's hometown of Newark, New Jersey.
5. In part, a possible allusion to the marionette Howdy Doody, eponymous protagonist of an American children's TV show in the late 1940s and 1950s, whose prominent 48 freckles stood for the nation's 48 states; the show was introduced by a tune called "Howdy Doody Time," which Baraka's poem parodies in title, tone, and diction.
6. Shape-shifting avatar of Satan; "hermes": Greek god of boundaries, messages, transitions, and trickery; "budda": Gautama Buddha, spiritual thinker on whose teachings Buddhism was founded.

when the brothers wanna stop animals
come out niggers come out   70
come out niggers niggers niggers come out
help us stop the devil
help us build a new world

niggers come out, brothers are we
   with you and your sons your daughters are ours   75
   and we are the same, all the blackness from one black allah
     when the world is clear you'll be with us
      come out niggers come out
      come out niggers come out
It's nation time eye ime   80
     It's nation ti eye ime
       chant with bells and drum
       it's nation time

It's nation time, get up santa claus   (repeat)
  it's nation time, build it   85
    get up muffet dragger[7]
    get up rastus for real to be rasta farari[8]
    ras jua[9]
    get up got here bow

      It's Nation   90
      Time!

                                   1970

Wailers

(For Larry Neal and Bob Marley)[1]

Wailers are we
We are Wailers. Dont get scared.
Nothing happening but out and way out.
Nothing happening but the positive. (Unless you the
negative.) Wailers. We Wailers. Yeh, Wailers.   5
We wail, we wail.
   We could dig Melville[2] on his ship
  confronting the huge white mad beast
  speeding death cross the sea to we.

7. Possibly a play on slang terms for a fool: "mup-pet" and "knuckle dragger" (or ape-like person).
8. Derived from "Ras Tafari," the pre-coronation name of Haile Selassie I (1892–1975), Ethiopian Emperor from 1930 to 1936 and 1941 to 1974. Rastafarianism arose in Jamaica in the 1930s as a religious sect whose adherents worshiped Haile Selassie I as the reincarnation of Christ and viewed Ethiopia as their spiritual homeland; by the 1960s, Rastafarianism had developed fea-tures of political resistance consistent with the contemporary Pan-African movement. "Rastus": derogatory term for a black man commonly used in minstrel shows.

9. God of princes, or princely god (from "ras," Amharic for prince; "jah": the Rastafarian term for Jehovah or God).
1. Neal (1937–1981), a leading theorist of the Black Arts movement; also a music critic, pianist, and flutist. Marley (1945–1981), Jamaican singer and composer. Marley and his band, The Wail-ers, introduced reggae music to a global audience in the 1970s. Marley was also an important political figure and peace activist in Jamaica.
2. Herman Melville (1819–1891), 19th-century American writer whose masterpiece *Moby-Dick* (1851) relates the story of Captain Ahab's venge-ful search for the white whale that maimed him.

But we whalers. We can kill whales.   10
We could get on top of a whale
and wail. Wailers. Undersea defense hot folk
Blues babies humming when we arrive. Boogie[3] ladies strumming our
black violet souls. Rag daddies[4] come from the land of never say die.
Reggae workers bringing the funk[5] to the people of I. We wailers all right. 15

Hail to you Bob, man! We will ask your question all our lives.
Could You Be Loved?[6] I and I understand. We see the world
Eyes and eyes say Yes to transformation. Wailers. Aye, Wailers.
Subterranean night color Magis,[7] working inside the soul of the world.
Wailers. Eyes seeing the world's being   20

Hey, Bob, Wail on rock on Jah[8] come into us as real vision and action
Hey, Larry, Wail on, with Lester and the Porkpie,[9] wailing us energy
for truth. We Wailers is all, and on past that to say, wailing for all
we worth. Rhythm folks obsessed with stroking what is with our
sound purchase.   25

Call he Thelonius,[1] in my crowded Wail Vessel, I hold the keys to the
funk kingdom. Lie on me if you want to, tell folks its yours
But for real wailing not tale telling, the sensitive know who the Wailers
Be We. Be We. We Wailers. Blue Blowers. The Real Rhythm Kings.[2]
We sing philosophy. Hambone[3] precise findings. Image Masters of the   30
syncopated. Wailers & Drummers.
  Wailers & Trumpet stars.
  Wailers & Box cookers.[4]
  Wailers & Sax flyers.
  Wailers & Bass thumpers.   35
  Wailers and Hey, wail, wail. We Wailers!
  Trombone benders. Magic singers.
  Ellingtonians.[5]
The only Tranes[6] faster than rocket ships. Shit.
Cut a rocket in our pocket and put a chord on the wall of the wind.   40
Wailers. Can you dig Wailing?

3. A repetitive, swung note or shuffle rhythm used in blues, hence the term boogie-woogie, a hard-driving, fast-stepping style of blues, popular in the 1930s and 1940s; also, slang term for devil.
4. Black men who wear head scarves or "do-rags" to protect processed hairdos, with pun on ragtime music.
5. The "soul" quality of rhythm-and-blues music, and the name given to an African American musical genre originating in the late 1960s characterized by bass-driven rhythm.
6. Title of a hit song by Bob Marley & The Wailers from their 1980 album *Uprising.*
7. Magician.
8. In the Rastafarian movement of which Marley was an adherent, the Christian God is called Jah (foreshortened form of Jehovah); according to Rastafarian belief, Ethiopian emperor Haile Selassie I (1892–1975) is Jah's incarnation and, as *Jah-Rastafari,* the second coming of Christ.
9. Refers to Neal's poem "Don't Say Goodbye to the Porkpie Hat" about American tenor saxophonist Lester Young (1909–1959), a.k.a. Prez,

always wore a suit and a trademark porkpie hat.
1. Jazz pianist Thelonious Monk (1917–1982), "the high priest of bebop."
2. Possibly a reference to the New Orleans Rhythm Kings, an influential jazz band of the 1920s. "Blowers": soloists (usually of wind instruments like saxophone or trumpet).
3. A dance style brought to the slave plantation by West Africans, marked by stomping and rhythmic slapping of the body (performed in place of rhythm-making instruments, which were denied the slaves by masters fearful of secret codes communicated via drumming); also known as the Juba Dance.
4. Inspired players ("cookers") of pianos or other stringed instruments ("box").
5. Reference to the jazz pianist, composer, and bandleader Duke Ellington (1899–1974), one of the creators of big-band jazz.
6. Reference to avant-garde or "free" jazz saxophonist John Coltrane (1926–1967), whose "sheets of sound" approach to improvisation was known for its speed and dexterity.

Call Me Bud Powell.[7] You wanna imitate this?
Listen. Spree dee deet sprree deee whee spredeee whee deee

My calling card. The dialectic of silence.
The Sound approach.   45
Life one day will be filled even further with we numbers we song
But primitive place now, we wailing be kept underground.

But keep it in mind. Call me something Dukish. Something Sassy.[8]
Call me by my real name.[9] When the world change
We wailing be in it, help make it, for real time.   50

Call Me. I call you. We call We.
Say, Hey Wailers. Hey, Wailers.
Hey hey hey, Wailers. Wail On!

                                                                1982

7. Influential jazz pianist of the mid-1940s   9. The opening line of Melville's *Moby-Dick* is
(1924–1966), composer of the Song "Wail" (1951).   "Call me Ishmael."
8. Title of a Duke Ellington composition.

SONIA SANCHEZ
b. 1934

Among the most varied and enduring writers who came of age during the Black
Arts era, Sonia Sanchez has stood at the crossroads of the many forces that lent
this period of African American cultural ferment its aura of contradiction and possibility. An early celebrant of Black Power as a strictly gendered movement, Sanchez
became a pioneering champion of black feminism alert to the bitter ironies of misogyny that often fueled the rhetoric of black "liberation." A onetime vociferous convert
to the Nation of Islam, she became a voice for spiritual evolution encompassing
ancestral African religiosity and Eastern modes of meditative discipline. A scholarly
master of Euro-American literary and philosophical traditions, her voice exploded off
the page with a vernacular gusto defiant of inherited conventions and expectations.
And yet at every phase of her remarkable career as poet, playwright, short story
writer, essayist, performer, political activist, and educator, Sanchez has remained a
consistent exemplar of creativity rooted in respect for black communal values and
insistent on self-transformation as foundation of collective realization.

Sanchez was born Wilsonia Benita Driver on September 9th 1934, in Birmingham,
Alabama to Wilson L. Driver and Lena Jones Driver. Having lost her mother as a
one-year-old, Sanchez spent her early years shuttling among different relatives as her
father sought the means to reunify the scattered Driver family, an experience of
domestic upheaval to which she would frequently return in her literary work. Those
disruptive origins were given their most troubling focus when, at the age of six, Sanchez's grandmother died. In reaction, she began to stutter, which led her to "turn into
myself and listen to those calling me." The heightened attention to speech, familial
loss, and displacement that characterized Sanchez's childhood ultimately opened into
the wide-ranging fluency, intimacy, and affirmation of her poetic voice.

When Sanchez was nine, her father moved the family to Harlem, New York in flight from the South: "I just came to New York to get my kids out of what was happening down there, school-wise and social-wise." Though still struggling with her speech impediment, Sanchez found her Harlem neighborhood an exhilarating environment of competing sights, sounds, smells, and appetites, being particularly attracted to the atmosphere of friendly challenge that characterized the male-dominated streets. It was to this environment of playful competition that she attributed the inspiration for exerting "sheer will power" through which she overcame her stuttering and began to excel in school. After obtaining a degree from Hunter College, Sanchez was selected to participate in a poetry workshop at New York University with Louise Bogan, whom she frequently credits as a crucial force in shaping her literary aspirations.

Sanchez emerged from these studies anxious to find her place in the "new wave" of contemporary black expression. In the 1960s, Sanchez published poetry and essays in numerous periodicals, including *The Liberator, Negro Digest,* and *Black Dialogue,* establishing her importance to the evolving "black aesthetic" program. These works display Sanchez as a political thinker bent on expressing social ideas in urgent and uncompromising terms. Fittingly, her first book, *Homecoming* (1969), was published by Broadside Press, a small black publishing venture that became a vehicle for many of the most powerful new voices of the Black Arts era.

Sanchez's importance to the Black Arts movement was not limited to her literary contributions. While figures like Amiri Baraka, Maulana Karenga, and Stokley Carmichael were building revolutionary organizations that aimed to supplant white power structures, Sanchez embedded herself in the mainstream education system with the intent of transforming its mission and identity. Joining other activists at San Francisco University, Sanchez became a leader in the effort to establish Black Studies, which not only provided a new platform for probing the history and meaning of race in global perspective but also issued a fundamental challenge to American universities as engines of class reproduction and racial domination. When Sanchez joined the Nation of Islam in 1972, what appeared to be a sudden swerve of purpose and affiliation could also be seen as a continuation of her quest for an institutional form of black solidarity based on promotion of alternative historical understanding and a deeply pedagogical practice. Serving as the Nation of Islam's Director of Culture, Sanchez rose to prominence as an NOI spokesperson, writing frequently about the black family for the organization's street newspaper *Muhammad Speaks.* By this time Sanchez was herself a mother, having had her daughter Anita with her first husband, Albert Sanchez, and then giving birth to twin sons, Morani Neusi and Mungu Neusi, with her second husband, poet Etheridge Knight. Sanchez's experience as a mother quickened in her a passion for understanding maternal sensibility as a link to ancestral power and conduit to revolutionary regeneration. The relation of mother and child emerges in the 1970s as a key motif of her poetry, colored by a "blues consciousness" strong enough to face searing trauma without falling into the stuttering disablement of despair.

After her marriage to Knight failed, Sanchez's work sought new ways to develop broad themes of social and spiritual struggle from the roots of personal anguish. In *A Blues Book for Blue Black Magical Women* (1974), for example, a semi-autobiographical narrative becomes Sanchez's vehicle for reflecting on the history of black women's suffering and endurance that takes on the sweep of mythic epic. At the same time, the teacherly impulse that activated her leadership in the Black Studies movement and characterized her work as Nation of Islam advocate fed her efforts to magnify her politics by passing to succeeding generations the lessons of struggle. Bringing youngsters into the communal circle of Black Arts literary experience, Sanchez wrote several children's books—*It's a New Day* (1971), *The Adventures of Fathead, Smallhead, and Squarehead* (1973), and *A Sound Investment* (1980)—that deploy popular idioms to imbue her narratives with practical and spiritual learning.

As Sanchez's poetry developed, this effort to merge intimate feeling and public implication led to innovative explorations of vernacular expression that helped define the "voice" of the Black Arts era. Defying conventions of standard verse form, and flouting decorum with bursts of profanity (often in slyly humorous ways), Sanchez insisted that feeling dictate the length of the poetic line and that enunciation take precedence over propriety in determining poetic meaning. The poems collected in *We a BaddDDD People* (1970) capture the intersection of militant assertion and street-wise articulation through which Sanchez achieved a partnership of public meaning and personal expression. And as with *Homecoming*, this second book of poems sought to activate in its audience an awakening to the social import of private experience: "My first books were about being aggressive and confrontational. They were books that said 'By golly by gee, I didn't know all this happened to us as a people. Now I'm going to put it right up in your face, and tell you what it's all about.'"

With its continued maturation, Sanchez's work expanded its allusive universe, encompassing aspects of African cosmology, Eastern religion, and Euro-American history into writing that never loses its grounding in the African American tradition. If the early work is powerful for its unrelenting disparagement of oppressive "witeness," it also bears in its punishing repetitions and relatively circumscribed imagery traces of the girlhood Sanchez seeking to release herself from the stammering hesitations of constrained consciousness. As her poetry becomes more thematically capacious, the stutter modulates into a fluent and varied voice, blending the confident tones of Swahili praise song with blues and gospel intonations into a newfound spiritual confidence. As early as *A Blues Book for Blue Black Magical Women*, Sanchez begins to cultivate a poetic and narrative stance that remains defiant and accusatory while reflecting a widening vision of how gender, race, class, place, history, and disposition shape the crucible in which individual and collective identities are forged. While locating new resources of lyric intimacy, increasingly her work also exerts a critical pressure on more narrow, especially misogynistic, features of Black Arts ideology and writing, inviting advocates of revolutionary black thought to admit the healing powers of African-derived wisdom into the framework of radical contemporary action. By the time of the long poem *Does Your House Have Lions?* (1997), an emotionally powerful account of her brother's fatal struggle with the AIDS virus, Sanchez has shaped the stuttering impulse into a means for speaking the unspeakable and facing tragedy with indomitable courage.

Sanchez's drama and prose have been as effective as her poetry in shaping this evolving vision. In such tightly designed plays as *Sister Son/ji* (1969), Sanchez challenges the masculinist ethos of much Black Arts era drama by fashioning women protagonists who, despite subjection to physical, mental, and economic violence, assert the primacy of their own "revolutionary" knowledge and desire. These plays champion the "blackness" of the everyday ghetto, finding there a radical spirit embodied in women struggling to survive the ravages of modern urban existence. That spirit of defiant survival likewise animates much of Sanchez's prose work, such as *homegirls and handgrenades* (1985), which offers a panoramic vision of a black woman's encounter with the full resources of black tradition.

No matter the poetic or narrative structure in which she is working, Sanchez is above all directed by the sound of words as they flit between the anchoring page and the activated voice. "When I write I always read my poems aloud," she has said. Famous for the dynamism of her public readings, Sanchez has long mastered the full range of African and African American vocal resources probed through study and tested by experience, moving effortlessly from exuberant chant or celebratory shout to anguished cry or whispered prayer. This sonic range has allowed her to bring to life a gallery of vivid personages, from the "badd" warrior sisters of her early poetry to the no less fiery, but also meditative maternal griots of more recent work. Having become now what she terms an "ordained stutterer," Sanchez offers her audiences the privileged practice of "speaking in tongues" as she continues to confront the possibilities of renewal within searing legacies of traumatic history.

homecoming

i have been a
way so long
once after college
i returned tourist
style to watch all   5
the niggers killing
themselves with
3 for oners[1]
with
needles   10
that
cd
not support
their
stutters.   15
                            now woman
i have returned
leaving behind me
all those hide and
seek[2] faces peeling   20
with freudian dreams.
this is for real.
                            black
                    niggers
                            my beauty.   25
baby.
i have learned it
ain't like they say
in the newspapers.

                                            1969

poem at thirty

it is midnight
no magical bewitching
hour for me
i know only that
i am here waiting   5
remembering that
once as a child
i walked two
miles in my sleep.
did i know   10
then where i
was going?

1. A method of selling heroin to new users; the discount is a means of expanding the market by creating new addicts.
2. Children's game in which players conceal themselves until tagged "it"; once tagged, a player calls out "Ollie Ollie oxen free," or "all outs, all in free."

traveling. i'm
always traveling.
i want to tell   15
you about me
about nights on a
brown couch when
i wrapped my
bones in lint and   20
refused to move.
no one touches
me anymore.
father do not
send me out   25
among strangers.
you you black man
stretching scraping
the mold from your body.
here is my hand.   30
i am not afraid
of the night.

1969

Summer Words of a Sistuh Addict

the first day i shot dope
was on a sunday.
         i had just come
home from church
         got mad at my motha   5
cuz she got mad at me. u dig?
         went out. shot up
behind a feelen against her.
         it felt good.
gooder than dooing it. yeah.   10
         it was nice.
i did it. uh huh. i did it.   uh. huh.
i want to do it again, it felt so gooooood.
        and as the sistuh
        sits in her silent /
        remembered / high   15
        someone leans for
        ward gently asks her:
        sistuh.
        did u   20
        finally
        learn how to hold yo / mother?
and the music of the day
        drifts in the room
to mingle with the sistuh's young tears.   25
  and we all sing.

1969

blk/ rhetoric

(for Killebrew, Keeby, Icewater,
Baker, Gary Adams and
Omar Shabazz)[1]

who's gonna make all
that beautiful blk / rhetoric
mean something.
          like
i mean   5
          who's gonna take
the words
              blk / is / beautiful
and make more of it
than blk / capitalism.   10
                u dig?
      i mean
            like who's gonna
take all the young / long / haired
natural / brothers and sisters   15
and let them
            grow till
                all that is
impt is them
            selves   20
                moving in straight /
revolutionary / lines
                toward the enemy
(and we know who that is)
                  like. man.   25
who's gonna give our young
blk / people new heroes
      (instead of catch / phrases)
      (instead of cad / ill / acs)
      (instead of pimps)   30
      (instead of wite / whores)
      (instead of drugs)
      (instead of new dances)
      (instead of chit / ter / lings)[2]
      (instead of a 35¢ bottle of ripple)[3]   35
      (instead of quick / fucks in the hall / way
        of wite / america's mind)
like. this. is an S O S[4]
me. calling. . . . .

1. Artists, poets, and community activists, several of whom (Carl Killebrew, Robert Keeby) were, like Sanchez, published in the 1960s by the Detroit-based Broadside Press, founded in 1965 by poet Dudley Randall (1914–2000) as a venue for hundreds of writers during the Black Arts movement.
2. Animal (usually hog) intestines, a feature of the African American culinary tradition originating in slavery, when masters provided slaves only the cheapest remains of slaughtered livestock.
3. Inexpensive brand of red wine (also known as "bum wine").
4. Reference to the poem "SOS" by Black Arts poet Amiri Baraka (1934–2014), which ends: "calling all black people, come in, black people, come / on in." (SOS) is an internationally recognized signal of distress in radio code.

calling. . . . .

some / one,   40

pleasereplysoon.

1969

Sister Son/ji

CHARACTER: SISTER SON/JI
*dressed in shapeless blk/burlap, blk/leotards & stockings; gray/natural wig—is
made to look in her fifties.*

SCENE: *The stage is dark except for a light directed on the middle of the stage
where there is a dressing/room/table with drawers/and chair—a noise is heard
off stage—more like a deep/guttural/laugh mixed with the sound of two/slow/
dragging feet—as a figure moves and stops, back to the audience, the stage
lightens.*

TIME: *Age and now and never again.*

SISTER SON/JI [*As she turns around, the faint sound of music is heard.*]   not
yet. turn off that god/damn music, this is not my music/day. i'll tell u
when to play music to soothe my savage sounds.[1] this is my quiet time,
my time for reading or thinking thoughts that shd be thought [*pause*]
now after all that talk, what deep thoughts shd i think today. Shall they
be deeper than the sounds of my blk/today or shall they be louder than
the sounds of my white/yesterdays. [*Moves to the dressing/table and sits
in the chair*] Standing is for young people. i ain't young no mo. My
young days have gone, they passed me by so fast that i didn't even have
a chance to see them. What did i do with them? What did i say to them?
do i still remember them? Shd I remember them? hold on Sister Son/
ji—today is tuesday. Wed. is yr/day for remembering. tuesday is for
reading and thinking thoughts of change.
    Hold on! hold on for what? am i not old? older than the mississippi
hills i settled near. Ain't time and i made a truce so that i am time
        a blk/version of past/ago & now/time.
    no, if i want to i shall remember.
    rememberings are for the old.
    What else is left them? My family is gone. all my beautiful children
are buried here in mississippi.
    Chausiku. Mtume. Baraka. Mungu.[2] brave warriors. DEAD.
    Yes. rememberings are for the near/dead/dying.
    for death is made up of past/actions/deeds and thoughts. [*Rises*]
    So. Fuck the hold/ons today. i shall be a remembered Sister Son/ji.
today i shall be what i was/shd have been and never can be again. today
i shall bring back yesterday as it can never be today.
    as it should be tomorrow. [*She drags her chair back to the dressing
table and opens the drawer—her movements are still slow-oldish—she
takes off her gray/wig and puts on a straightened blk/wig—stands and*

---

1. Reference to the opening line of the 1697 play
The Mourning Bride by English playwright William Congreve (1636?–1715): "Music has charms

to soothe a savage breast."
2. Swahili names: Chausiku (messenger); Mtume
(envoy); Baraka (blessing); Mungu (prophet).

puts on a wide belt, a long necklace and a bracelet on her right ankle. As she sits and begins to remove the make/up of old age from her face her movements quicken and become more active. A recording of Sammy Davis Jr. singing, "This is my beloved"[3] is heard and she joins in.]

SISTER SON/JI "strange spice from the south, honey from the dew drifting, imagine this in one perfect one and this is my beloved. And when he moves and when he talks to me, music—ah-ah-mystery—"

[*Hums the rest as she takes off all the make/up and puts on some lipstick. When she stands again she is young—a young/negro/woman of 18 or 19. She picks up a note/book and begins to run across the stage.*]

SISTER SON/JI i'm coming nesbitt. i'm coming. Hey. thought i'd never catch u—how are u? [*Looks down for she has that shyness of very young women who are unsure/uncertain of themselves and she stretches out her hand and begins to walk—a lover's walk.*] yeah, i'm glad today is friday too. that place is a mad/house, hunter college[4] indeed. do u know nesbitt that that ole/ bitch in my political theory course couldn't remember my name and there are only 12 of us in the class—only 3 negroes—as different as day and night and she called out Miss Jones, Miss Smith, Miss Thomas and each time she looked at the three of us and couldn't remember who was who. Ain't that a drag? But she remembered the ofays'[5] names/faces and they all look like honey. [*Turns and faces him*] you know what i did? u know what i did nesbitt? i stood up, picked up my note/book and headed for the door and u know she asked where i was going and i said out of here—away from u because u don't even know my name unless i raise my hand when u spit out three/blk/names—and she became that flustered/red/whiteness that ofays become, and said but u see it's just that—and i finished it for her—i sd it's just that we all look alike. yeah. well damn this class [I wanted to say fuck this class, honey, but she might have had a heart/attack/rt/there in class] i said damn this class. i'm a human being to be remembered just like all these other human beings in this class. and with that I walked out. [*Is smiling as she turns her head*] what did u say? am i going back? no honey. how/why shd i return? she showed me no respect. none of the negroes in that class was being respected as the individuals we are. just three/big/ blk/masses of blk/womanhood. that is not it. can't be. [*Stops walking*] Uh-huh. i'll lose the credit for that course but i'll appeal when i'm a senior and u know what i'll write on that paper. i'll write the reason i lost these three credits is due to discrimination, yes, that's what i'll say and . . . oh honey. yes. it might have been foolish but it was right. after all at some point a person's got to stand up for herself just a little and . . . oh. u have a surprise. what? there? that's yrs? boss. o it's boss.[6] [*Jumps up and down*] Nesbitt yr/father is the nicest man. what a beautiful car. now u can drive up from Howard[7] on weekends. yes. i'd like that. Let's go for a ride, u know upstate N.Y. is pretty this time of yr. where we headed for?

Yes i do love u nesbitt. i've told u so many times but i'm scared to do it because I might get pregnant; i'm scared of the act, i guess u're right in saying that i'm against it becuz it has not been sanctioned by church/ marriage and

3. "And This Is My Beloved," popular song from the 1953 musical *Kismet*, recorded by African American singer, dancer, and actor Sammy Davis Jr. (1925–1990) in 1955.
4. Sanchez's alma mater, an all-women's college in New York City from which she graduated in 1955.
5. Whites (derogatory slang).
6. The best (slang).
7. Howard University, a historically black institution located in Washington, D.C.

i'm trembling nesbitt.
i feel the cold air on my thighs. how shall I move my
    love; i keep missing the beat of yr/fast/movements.
is it time to go already? that's rt. we do have to go to
    yr/father's/dance. how do i look?
any different? i thought not. i'm ready to go.

[*Softly*] nesbitt do u think after a first love each succeeding love is a repetition? [*The stage darkens and* SON/JI *moves to the dressing table and sits. Then a tape of Malcolm's*[8] *voice is heard and* SON/JI *adds a long skirt, removes the straightened/wig and puts on large/hoop/earrings.*]

SISTER SON/JI   racist? brothers & sisters. he is not the racist here in white/america. he is a beautiful/blk/man who talks about separation cuz we must move there. no more fucking SIT/ins-toilet/ins-EAT/ins—just like he says—the time for ins is over and the time for outs is here. out of this sadistic/masochistic/society that screams its paleface over the world. the time for blk/nationhood is here. [*Gets up and moves forward.*]

Listen. listen. did u hear those blk/words of that
    beautiful/blk/warrior/prince—

Did u see his flashing eyes and did u hear his dagger/words. cuz if u did then u will know as i have come to know. u will change—u will pick up yr/roots and become yr/self again—u will come home to blk/ness for he has looked blk/people in the eye and said
    welcome home. yr/beautiful/blkness/awaits u. here's my hand brother/
    sister—welcome. Home. (*Stage lightens.*)
    brother Williams, this blk/power/conference is outa sight. i ain't never seen so many heavee[9]/blk/people together. i am learning too much. this morning i heard a sister talk about blk/women supporting their blk/men, listening to their men, sacrificing, working while blk/men take care of bizness, having warriors and young sisters. i shall leave this conference brother with her words on my lips. i will talk to sisters abt loving their blk/men and letting them move in tall/straight/lines toward our freedom. yes i will preach blk/love/respect between blk/men and women for that will be the core/basis of our future in white/america.
    But, why do u have to split man. u've been out all this week to meetings. can't we have some time together. the child is in bed. and i don't feel like reading. it's just 11P.M. can't we talk/touch. we hardly talk anymore. i'm afraid that one day we'll have nothing to say to each other.
    yes. i know u're tired. i know that the brothers are always on yr/case where u're organizing; and u need to unwind from the week but i want to unwind with u. i want to have a glass of wine with u and move into yr/arms; i want to feel u moving inside of me. we haven't made love in weeks man and my body feels dead, unalive. i want to talk abt our past/future—if we have one in this ass/hole country. Don't go. Stay home with me and let us start building true blk/lives—let our family be a family built on mutual love and respect. Don't leave me man. i've been by myself for weeks. we need time together. blk/people gots to spend all their spare time together or they'll fall into the same traps their fathers

8. Malcolm X (1925–1965), African American activist, Nation of Islam minister, and black nationalist known in part for his fiery oratory.
9. Or heavy: profound (slang).

and mothers fell into when they went their separate ways and one called it retaining their manhood while the other called it just plain/don't/care/about/family/hood. a man is a man in a house where a woman/children cry out for a man's presence—where young warriors can observe their fathers' ways and grow older in them—where young sisters can receive the smiles of their fathers and carry their smiles to their future husbands. Is there time for all this drinking—going from bar to bar. Shouldn't we be getting ourselves together—strengthening our minds, bodies and souls away from drugs, weed,[1] whiskey and going out on Saturday nites. alone. what is it all about or is the rhetoric apart from the actual being/doing? What is it all about if the doings do not match the words?

[*The stage becomes dark with only a spotlight on* SISTER SON/JI's *face and since she is constantly moving on the stage, sometimes she is not seen too clearly.*]

SISTER SON/JI [*Is crooning softly*]   hee. haa haa. THE HONKIES ARE COMING TO TOWN TODAY. HOORAY. HOORAY. HOORAY.
THE CRACKERS ARE COMING TO TOWN TODAY. TODAY. TODAY. HOORAY.[2]

where are u man? hee hee hee. the shadow knows.[3] we are our brother's keepers.[4] we must have an undying love for each other.

it's 5 A.M. in the morning.
i am scared of voices moving in my head.
ring-around-the-honkies-a-pocketful-of-
gunskerboomkerboomwehavenopains.[5]

the child is moving inside of me. where are you? Man yr/son moves against this silence. he kicks against my silence.
Aaaaaaah. Aaaaaaah. Aaaaaaah. oh, i must keep walking. man, come fast. come faster than the speed of bullets—[6]faster than the speed of lightning and when u come we'll see it's SUPER-BLOOD.[7] HEE HEE. HAA. FOOLED U DIDN'T IT? Ahh—go way. go way voices that send me spinning into nothingness. Ah. aah. aaah. aaaaah. Aaaaaah. aAaaAaah. Aaaaah. Aaaaaah. AaAaah. AaaaaaaaaaaaaaaaaaaaaaH. (SISTER SON/JI *falls on her knees and chants.*)

What is my name o blk/prince in what house do
I walk while i smell yr/distant smells
how have i come into this land
by what caravan did i cross the
desert of yr/blk/body?

1. Marijuana (slang).
2. Play on the civil war song "When Johnny Comes Marching Home," the lyrics of which were written in 1863 by Irish American bandleader Patrick Gilmore (1829–1892) to the tune of an Irish anti-war folksong, "Johnny I Hardly Knew Ye." "Honkies," "Crackers": white people (derogatory slang).
3. *The Shadow*, a popular 1930s radio drama about a crime-fighting vigilante, began each show with the lines: "Who knows what evil lurks in the hearts of men? The Shadow knows!"
4. In the biblical story in which Cain killed his brother Abel, God asked the killer, "Where is your brother, Abel?" Cain answered: "I know not: Am I my brother's keeper?" (Genesis 4.9).
5. Play on the medieval children's rhyme "Ring Around the Rosie / A Pocket Full of Posies," an allegory of the bubonic plague or "Black Death" that swept Europe in the 14th century.
6. The hero Superman was said to be "faster than a speeding bullet" in the radio drama of the 1940s and TV show of the 1950s.
7. "Blood": comrade or "brother" (African American vernacular).

[SISTER SON/JI *finally moves to dressing/table. Her walk is slower, almost oldish. She rests her head. Then the sound of drums is heard mixed with a Coltrane[8] sound.* SISTER SON/JI *puts her hands over her ears to drown out the sounds but they grow louder and she lifts her head, removes her jewelry, removes the long skirt, puts on a gun and belt, ties a kerchief around her head and puts a baby/carrier on her back. The music subsides.*]

SISTER SON/JI   do u think they will really attack us? what abt world opinion? no, i hadn't noticed that they had a new administration, newer and better fascist pigs.[9] So we must send all the children away. will i help take them? but will i have enough time to get back and help. good. Ahh—u think it'll be a long/drawn/out fight. are we well prepared, mume?—come children. Malika-Nakawa-Damisi, Mungu, Mjumbe,[1] Mtume, Baraka. come. the trucks are ready to take us on our trip. make sure u have yr/lunches and canteens. make sure u have yr/identification tags, where is our drummer?

Mwenge[2] play us yur/songs as we leave.

i shall return soon, mume.[3] i shall return soon. [*The sounds of guns/ helicopters are heard.*]

So the war is becoming unpopular, and many devils[4] are refusing to fight us. good. mume, can we trust the devils who have come to fight on our side? the women and I don't mind the male/devils here but the female/devils who have followed them. they shd not be allowed here. what happens to them when the one they are following is killed. It will become a problem if we don't send them packing rt away.

Ah, that sounds like a heavy attack. It is. women, sisters. Let us sing the killing/song for our men. let us scream the words of dying as we turn/move against the enemy.

[SISTER SON/JI *moves as she chants.*]

OOOOU-WAH
OOOOU-WAH
OOOU-OOOU-OOOU-WAH-WAH-WAH-
OOOU-OOOU-OOOU-WAH-WAH-WAH-
EEYE-YO
EEYE-YO
EEYE-EEYE-EEYE-YO-YO-
EEYE-EEYE-EEYE-YO-YO-

Is it true that Mungu is here? But, he is only thirteen. a child. He's still a child, mume. He's as tall as u mume but he's still a boy. send him back. all the other warriors are fifteen. are we—do we need soldiers that badly. Mume, please send him back. he's just a boy. he's just my little boy. he's not so tall stretched out on the ground. the bullets have taken away his height. Mungu, Mungu, Mungu. can u hear me? do my words go in and out yr/bullet/holes till they finally rest inside u? Mungu. Mungu. Mungu. My first warrior. i love u my little one even as u stare yr/death stare.

---

8. John Coltrane (1926–1967), avant-garde jazz musician whose experimental style was known as the "Coltrane sound."
9. Police (slang).
1. Swahili names: Maliki (king); Nakala (immaculate); Damisi (cheerful); Mjumbe (messenger).

2. Firebrand (Swahili).
3. Husband (Swahili).
4. Derogatory term for white people, used prominently in the writings and speeches of Nation of Islam leader Elijah Muhammad (1897–1975).

[*SCREAM—HEY—SCREAM—HEY.*]

Yes. u, death. i'm calling yr/name. why not me? Stay away from my family. i've given u one son—one warrior for yr/apprenticeship. git stepping death for our tomorrows will be full of life/living/births.

if he keeps the devil/woman then he shd be made to leave. Yes. he must go. Mume, tell me what are all these deaths for, with more likely to come? so he can feel sorry for a devil/woman and bring her whiteness among all this BLK/NESS.

he feels sorry for her. and what abt our teachings. have we forgotten so soon that we hate devils. that we are in a death/struggle with the beasts. if she's so good, so liberal, send her back to her own kind. Let her liberalize them. Let her become a camp follower[5] to the hatred that chokes white/america. yes I wd vote to send yr/partner to certain death if he tries to keep her.

these mississippi hills will not give up our dead. my son/our son did not die for integration. u must still remember those ago/yrs when we had our blk/white period. they died for the right of blk/children to run on their own land and let their bodies explode with the sheer joy of living. of being blk/and many children have died and these brown hills and red gullies[6] will not give up our dead. and neither will i. [*The sounds of guns, planes are heard. SISTER SON/JI moves slowly to the dressing/table. The war/sounds decrease and a sound like Coltrane mixed with drums begins slowly, tiredly. She puts on the gray/haired/wig, takes off the gun and baby carrier—and puts on the make/up of all the yrs she has gathered. Then she turns around in the chair and stares at the audience.*]

SISTER SON/JI   Death is a five o'clock door forever changing time. And wars end. Sometimes too late. i am here. still in mississippi. Near the graves of my past. We are at peace. the state supports me and others like me and i have all the time i want to do what all old/dying people do. Nothing. but I have my memories. [*Rises*] Yes. hee, hee. i have my sweet/astringent memories becuz we dared to pick up the day and shake its tail until it became evening. a time for us. blk/ness. blk/people. Anybody can grab the day and make it stop. can u my friends? or maybe it's better if i ask: WILL YOU?

1969

a/coltrane/poem[1]

my favorite things[2]
is u/blowen
yo/favorite/things.

stretchen the mind
till it bursts past the con/fines of   5

---

5. Civilian who follows an army unit to assist or exploit military personnel; here, a prostitute.
6. "Brown hills and red gullies": citation from 1968 poem "The Idea of Ancestry" by Etheridge Knight (1931–1991), Sanchez's husband at the time of the play's composition.
1. John Coltrane (1926–1967), jazz saxophonist of the 1960s "new wave" celebrated for his virtuosity, experimental zeal, and spiritual dedication.
2. "My Favorite Things": 1961 Coltrane composition that refers in its title and melody to a song by Richard Rodgers (1902–1976) and Oscar Hammerstein II (1895–1960) from their 1959 musical *The Sound of Music.*

solo/en melodies.

> to the many solos
of the
> mind/spirit.

> > are u sleepen   (to be   10
> > are u sleepen   sung
> > brotha john   softly)
> > brotha john[3]

> > where u have gone to.
> > no mornin bells[4]   15
> > are ringen here. only the quiet
aftermath of assassinations.[5]

> > but i saw yo/murder/
the massacre
> > of all blk/musicians. planned   20
in advance.

> > yrs befo u blew away our passsst
> and showed us our futureeeeee
screech   screeech   screeeeech   screeech
a/love/supreme.   alovesupreme a lovesupreme.[6]   25
> > A LOVE SUPREME
scrEEEccCHHHHH screeeeEEECHHHHHHH
sCReeeEEECHHHHHH SCREEEECCCCHHHH
SCREEEEEEEECCCHHHHHHHHHHHH
a lovesupremealovesupremealovesupreme[7] for our blk
people.   30
> > BRING IN THE WITE/MOTHA/fuckas
> ALL THE MILLIONAIRES/BANKERS/ol
MAIN/LINE/ASS/RISTOCRATS (ALL
THEM SO-CALLED BEAUTIFUL   35
PEOPLE)
> > WHO HAVE KILLED
> WILL CONTINUE TO
> > KILL US WITH
THEY CAPITALISM/18% OWNERSHIP   40
OF THE WORLD.
> > YEH. U RIGHT
THERE. U ROCKEFELLERS. MELLONS
VANDERBILTS
> > FORDS.[8]   45

3. English rendition of the French nursery melody "Frère Jacques," traditionally sung in a round.
4. With a pun on *mourning*.
5. Reference to the sequence of assassinations that marked the 1960s: John F. Kennedy (1917–1963), 35th president of the United States (1960–63); Malcolm X (1925–1965), black nationalist minister of the Nation of Islam and human rights activist; Martin Luther King Jr. (1929–1968), cofounder of the Southern Christian Leadership Conference and civil rights leader; and Robert F. Kennedy (1925–1968), U.S. attorney general (1961–64), New York senator (1964–68), and, at the time of his death, presidential aspirant.
6. "A Love Supreme": An elaborate, four-part Coltrane composition; written partly in celebration of his triumph over drug and alcohol addiction, this musical suite is organized as a kind of religious journey moving from "Acknowledgement" through "Resolution" and "Pursuance" to a concluding "Psalm."
7. In this and other passages of the poem, Sanchez evokes key features of Coltrane's style: the legato compression of notes played at breakneck speed, sometimes called "sheets of sound"; sustained, tonally varied wailings or "screeching"; and rapid alterations of length, pitch, and emphasis.
8. Prominent American families who amassed fortunes during the period of industrial expansion from the mid-19th to mid-20th centuries in oil production and banking (Rockefellers), steel production and banking (Mellons), railroads (Vanderbilts), and automobile manufacturing (Fords).

```
                    yeh.
GITem.
          PUSHem/PUNCHem/STOMPem. THEN
LIGHT A FIRE TO
                    THEY pilgrim asses.                    50
TEAROUT they eyes.
                    STRETCH they necks
till no mo
          raunchy sounds of MURDER/
POVERTY/STARVATION                                         55
                    come from they
throats.
screeeeeeeeeeeeeeeeeCHHHHHHHHHHH
SCREEEEEEEEEEEEEEECHHHHHHHHHHH
screeEEEEEEEEEEEEEEEEEEEEEEEEEEECCCCHHHHHHHH         60
SCREEEEEEEEEEEEEEEEEEEEEEEEEEEEEEEEE
     EEEEEECHHHHHHHHHHH
BRING IN THE WITE/LIBERALS ON THE SOLO SOUND
OF YO/FIGHT IS MY FIGHT
                    SAXOPHONE.                             65
                    TORTURE
THEM FIRST AS THEY HAVE
                    TORTURED US WITH
PROMISES/
          PROMISES. IN WITE/AMURICA. WHEN                  70
ALL THEY WUZ DOEN
                    WAS HAVEN FUN WITH THEY
ORGIASTIC DREAMS OF BLKNESS.
                    (JUST SOME MO
CRACKERS⁹ FUCKEN OVER OUR MINDS.)                          75
                    MAKE THEM
SCREEEEEEAM
          FORGIVE ME. IN SWAHILI.
DONT ACCEPT NO MEA CULPAS.¹
                    DON'T WANT TO HEAR                     80
BOUT NO EUROPEAN FOR/GIVE/NESS.
DEADDYINDEADDYINDEADDYINWITEWESTERN
          SHITTTTTT
(softly   da-dum-da da da da da da da da da/da-dum-da
till it   da da da da da da da da da                       85
builds              da-dum- da da da
up)       da-dum. da. da. da.   this is a part of my
          favorite things.
          da dum da da da da da da
          da da da da                                      90
          da dum da da da da da
          da da da da
```

9. White people (derogatory slang).
1. Formal acknowledgments of fault (from
Latin—*mea* "my," *culpa*: "guilt"); "Swahili":

Bantu language spoken by various ethnic groups
in East and Southeast Africa.

```
                da dum da da da da
                da dum da da da da— — — —
(to be    rise up blk/people                                          95
sung                de dum da da da da
slowly    move straight in yo/blkness
to tune             da dum da da da da
of my     step over the wite/ness
favorite  that is yesssss terrrrrr day                                100
things.)  weeeeeeee  are  tooooooooday.
(f        da dum
 a        da da da (stomp, stomp) da da da
 s        da dum
 t        da da da (stomp, stomp) da da da                            105
 e        da dum
 r)       da da da (stomp)   da da da dum (stomp)
          weeeeeeeee (stomp)
              areeeeeeeee (stomp)
                      areeeeeeeee (stomp, stomp)                      110
          tooooooday          (stomp.
                  day              stomp.
                  day                  stomp.
                  day                      stomp.
                  day                          stomp!)                115
(soft     rise up blk/people. rise up blk/people
chant)    RISE. & BE. what u can.
          MUST BE.BE.BE.BE.BE.BE.BE-E-E-E-
                      BE-E-E-E-E-
              yeh. john coltrane.                                     120
my favorite things is u.
                  showen us life/
                              liven.
a love supreme.
              for each                                               125
          other
     if we just
  lisssssSSSTEN.
```

1970

TCB[1]

```
wite/motha/fucka
wite/motha/fucka
wite/motha/fucka

                    whitey.
wite/motha/fucker                                                      5
wite/motha/fucker
wite/motha/fucker
```

---

1. Vernacular acronym for "Taking Care of Business" (to perform effectively or responsibly); in the 1960s, TCB also meant "Together Collected and Black."

ofay.

wite/mutha/fucka
wite/mutha/fucka   10
wite/mutha/fucka

devil.

wite/mutha/fucker
wite/mutha/fucker
wite/mutha/fucker   15

pig.

wite/mother/fucker
wite/mother/fucker
wite/mother/fucker

cracker.   20

wite/muther/fucka
wite/muther/fucka
wite/muther/fucka

honky.[2]

now. that it's all sed.   25
let's get to work.

1970

A poem for my brother[1]

(reflections on his death from AIDS: June 8, 1981)

1. death

The day you died
a fever starched my bones.
within the slurred
sheets, i hoarded my legs
while you rowed out among the boulevards   5
balancing your veins on sails.
easy the eye of hunger
as i peeled the sharp
sweat and swallowed wholesale molds.

2. recovery (a)

What comes after   10
is consciousness of the morning
of the licensed sun that subdues
immoderate elements.
there is a kindness in illness
the indulgence of discrepancies.   15

---

2. "Honky," "cracker," "devil," "ofay," "whitey":
derogatory terms for white person; "pig": derogatory slang for policeman.
1. Sanchez's half-brother Wilson Driver Jr., who

contracted acquired immunodeficiency syn-
drome (AIDS) a year or more before it was clinically discovered and named.

reduced to the ménage² of houses
and green drapes that puff their seasons
toward the face.
i wonder what to do now.
i am afraid   20
i remember a childhood that cried
after extinguished lights
when only the coated banners answered.

3. recovery (b)

There is a savior in these buds
look how the phallic stems distend   25
in welcome.
O copper flowerheads
confine my womb that i may dwell within.
i see these gardens, whom i love
i feel the sky's sweat on my face   30
now that these robes no longer bark
i praise abandonment.

4. wake

i have not come for summary.
must i renounce all babylons?³
here, without psalms,   35
these leaves grow white
and burn the bones with dance.
here, without surfs,
young panicles⁴ bloom on the clouds and fly
while myths tick grey as thunder.   40

5. burial

you in the crow's rain
rusting amid ribs
my mouth spills your birth
i have named you prince of boards
stretching with the tides.   45

you in the toad's tongue
peeling on nerves
look. look. the earth is running palms.

6. (on) (the) (road). again.⁵

somewhere a flower walks in mass
purchasing wholesale christs   50
sealing white-willow sacraments.

---

2. Household members (French).
3. The ancient city-state Babylon of Mesopotamia was known for its regal luxuriance, most
famously as the site of the Hanging Gardens,
one of the Seven Wonders of the World. Referred
to in the Bible as a doomed outpost of the Anti-
christ (Revelations 17–18), "Babylon" serves as a
generic term for a place of sensual excess, and
was often applied to New York in the 1970s.
4. Loosely branched cluster of flowers in pyra-
midal form.
5. "On the Road," a blues song recorded in 1928
by the Memphis Jug Band, served as inspiration
for the 1965 composition "On the Road Again"
by singer-songwriter Bob Dylan (b. 1941).

naked on steeples
where trappist[6] idioms sail
an atom peels the air.

O i will gather my pulse   55
muffled by sibilants[7]
and follow disposable dreams.

1987

6. Referring to the Order of Cistercians of the
Strict Observance, a Catholic religious order of
cloistered contemplative monastics established
in 1664.
7. Sounds such as the letter *s*, often having a
hissing effect.

ED BULLINS
b. 1935

One of the most prolific and influential playwrights, producers, essayists, and
short-story writers of the Black Arts movement, Ed Bullins was born in Philadelphia to Bertha Marie Queen and Edward Bullins. Shortly after quitting high
school, Bullins joined the navy but later returned to Philadelphia to complete his
secondary education. His writing career began in 1958 when he entered Los Angeles City College and began reading extensively and writing short fiction. However, it
was not until 1964, when Bullins enrolled in the creative writing program at San
Francisco State College, that he began to write the plays for which he is most
widely known.

Bullins was a key figure in San Francisco's articulation of the Black Arts and
Black Power movements, serving as minister of culture in the Black Panther Party
in the wake of having seen Amiri Baraka's transformational drama *Dutchman* in
1964. That experience established the foundation of Bullins's black nationalism,
which was unapologetically political and insistently cultural, displaying a disdain
for rhetorical flourish as a substitute for unvarnished action.

In the mid-1960s, unable to find anyone in San Francisco who was willing to
produce his plays, Bullins formed several theater companies and produced his work
himself, in lofts, coffeehouses, and bars. In 1967, after reading some of Bullins's
work, director Robert Macbeth invited the playwright to join the newly established
New Lafayette Theatre in Harlem. Bullins's first works, produced in 1968 at the
New Lafayette, *Three Plays by Ed Bullins* (*The Electronic Nigger*; *A Son, Come
Home*; and *Clara's Ole Man*), were quite successful with audiences and won him
the Vernon Rice Drama Desk Award. Bullins remained a central figure to the New
Lafayette until the company's demise in 1972. In 1973, Bullins served as the
playwright-in-residence at the American Place Theatre, also in New York City; and
for the next ten years, he was on staff at the Public Theatre's New York Shakespeare Festival.

Beginning in 1965 with his first short play, *How Do You Do?*, Bullins has written
more than fifty plays, over forty of which have been professionally produced. His
work has progressed through a book of short stories, *The Hungered One, Early
Writings* (1971); dozens of plays, including *In the Wine Time* (1969), *Goin'a Buffalo*
(1969), *In New England Winter* (1971), *The Fabulous Miss Marie* (1971), and the

Obie Award–winning *The Taking of Miss Janie* (1975); two children's plays, *I Am Lucy Terry* (1976) and *The Mystery of Phillis Wheatley* (1976); and the books for two musicals, *Sepia Star* (1977) and *Storyville* (1977). Bullins is the recipient of two Guggenheim fellowships, three Rockefeller grants, and an honorary doctorate from Columbia College in Chicago.

Clara's Ole Man works within the scenario characteristic of Bullins's drama, which explores the lives of urban black people whose hardscrabble existence seethes with a compelling blend of violence and untapped intelligence, sensitivity, and longing. In one sense, its milieu is the basic domestic scene of classic American theater, in which young and old struggle to define the terms of aspiration that preoccupy so much of the American drama. But this narrative is complicated in Bullins's work by the specific realities of black experience, whose energies have been at once diverted and intensified by the hovering injustice of what *Clara's Ole Man* depicts as a pervasive cultural madness. The play leaves us to ask whether the tension between dream and reality yields inevitable tragedy or whether some triumph of assertion breaks through the looming aura of repression and loss.

Clara's Ole Man

THE PEOPLE:

CLARA, *a light brown girl of 18, well-built with long, dark hair. A blond streak runs down the middle of her head, and she affects a pony tail. She is pensive, slow in speech but feline. Her eyes are heavy-lidded and brown; she smiles— rather, blushes—often.*

BIG GIRL, *a stocky woman wearing jeans and tennis shoes and a tight-fitting blouse which accents her prominent breasts. She is of an indeterminable age, due partly to her lack of makeup and plain hair style. She is anywhere from 25 to 40, and is loud and jolly, frequently breaking out in laughter from her own jokes.*

JACK, *20 years old, wears a corduroy Ivy League suit and vest. At first,* JACK'S *speech is modulated and too eloquent for the surroundings but as he drinks his words become slurred and mumbled.*

BABY GIRL, BIG GIRL'S *mentally retarded teenaged sister. The girl has the same hairdo as* CLARA. *Her face is made up with mascara, eye shadow, and she has black arching eyebrows penciled darkly, the same as* CLARA.

MISS FAMIE, *a drunken neighbor.*

STOOGIE, *a local street-fighter and gang leader. His hair is processed.*[1]

BAMA, *one of* STOOGIE'S *boys.*

HOSS, *another of* STOOGIE'S *boys.*

C.C., *a young wino.*

TIME: *Early spring, the mid-1950s.*

SCENE: *A slum kitchen on a rainy afternoon in South Philadelphia. The room is very clean, wax glosses the linoleum and old wooden furniture; a cheap but*

---

1. Straightened by application of chemicals.

clean red checkered oilcloth covers the table. If the room could speak it would say, "I'm cheap but clean."

A cheap AM radio plays rhythm 'n' blues music throughout the play. The furniture is made up of a wide kitchen table where a gallon jug of red wine sits. Also upon the table is an oatmeal box, cups, mugs, plates and spoons, ashtrays and packs of cigarettes. Four chairs circle the table, and two sit against the wall back-stage. An old-fashioned wood- and coal-burning stove takes up a corner of the room, and a gas range of 1935 vintage is backstage next to the door to the yard. A large, smoking frying pan is on one of the burners.

JACK and BIG GIRL are seated at opposite ends of the table; CLARA stands at the stove fanning the fumes toward the door. BABY GIRL plays upon the floor with a homemade toy.

CLARA [*fans, fumes*] Uummm uummm . . . well, there goes the lunch. I wonder how I was dumb enough to burn the bacon?

BIG GIRL Just comes natural with you, honey, all looks and no brains . . . now with me and my looks, anybody in South Philly can tell I'm a person that naturally takes care of business . . . hee hee . . . ain't that right, Clara?

CLARA Awww girl, go on. You's the worst messer-upper I knows. You didn't even go to work this morn'. What kind of business is that?

BIG GIRL It's all part of my master plan, baby. Don't you worry none . . . Big Girl knows what she's doin'. You better believe that!

CLARA Yeah, you may know what you're doin' but I'm the one who's got to call in for you and lie that you're sick.

BIG GIRL Well, it ain't a lie. You know I got this cough and stopped up feeling. [*Looking at JACK*] You believe that, don't you, young blood?[2]

JACK Most certainly. You could very well have a respiratory condition and also have all the appearances of a extremely capable person.

BIG GIRL [*slapping table*] HEE HEE . . . SEE CLARA? . . . SEE? Listen ta that, Clara. I told you anybody could tell it. Even ole hot lips here can tell.

CLARA [*pours out grease and wipes stove*] Awww . . . he just says that to be nice . . . he's always sayin' things like that.

BIG GIRL Is that how he talked when he met you the other day out to your aunt's house?

CLARA [*hesitating*] Nawh . . . nawh he didn't talk like that.

BIG GIRL Well, how did he talk, huh?

CLARA Awww . . . Big Girl. I don't know.

BIG GIRL Well, who else does? You know what kind of line a guy gives ya. You been pitched at enough times, haven't ya? By the looks of him I bet he gave ya the ole smooth college boy approach . . . [*To JACK.*] C'mon, man, drink up. We got a whole lot mo' ta kill. Don't you know this is my day off and I'm celebratin'?

JACK [*takes a drink*] Thanks . . . this is certainly nice of you to go to all this trouble for me. I never expected it.

BIG GIRL What did you expect, young blood?

JACK [*takes another sip*] Ohhh, well . . . I . . .

---

2. Comrade or "brother" (African American vernacular).

CLARA [*to* BABY GIRL *on floor*]   Don't put that dirty thing in your mouf, gal! *She walks around the table to* BABY GIRL *and tugs her arm.* Now, keep that out of your mouf!

BABY GIRL [*holds to toy sullenly*]   NO!

CLARA   You keep quiet, you hear, gal!

BABY GIRL   NO!

CLARA   If you keep tellin' me no I'm goin' ta take you upstairs ta Aunt Toohey.

BABY GIRL [*throws back head and drums feet on floor*]   NO! NO! SHIT! DAMN! NO! SHIT!

CLARA [*disturbed*]   NOW STOP THAT! We got company.

BIG GIRL [*laughs hard and leans elbows upon table*]   HAW HAW HAW . . . I guess she told you, Clara. Hee hee . . . that little dirty mouf bitch, [*pointing to* BABY GIRL *and becoming choked*] . . . that little . . . [*cough cough*] . . . hooeee boy!

CLARA   You shouldn't have taught her all them nasty words, Big Girl. Now we can't do anything with her. [*Turns to* JACK] What do you think of that?

JACK   Yes, it does seem a problem. But with proper guidance she'll more than likely be conditioned out of it when she gets into a learning situation among her peer group.

BIG GIRL [*takes a drink and scowls*]   BULLSHIT!

CLARA   Aww . . . B.G.

JACK   I beg your pardon, Miss?

BIG GIRL   I said bullshit! Whatta ya mean with proper guidance . . . *points.* I taught that little bitch myself . . . the best cuss words I know before she ever climbed out of her crib . . . whatta ya mean when she gets among her "peer" group?

JACK   I didn't exactly say that. I said when . . .

BIG GIRL [*cuts him off*]   Don't tell me what you said, boy. I got ears. I know all them big horseshit doctor words . . . tell him, Clara . . . tell him what I do. Where do I work. Clara?

CLARA   Awww . . . B.G., please.

BIG GIRL   Do like I say! Do like big wants you to!

CLARA [*surrenders*]   She works out at the state nut farm.

BIG GIRL [*triumphant*]   And tell mister smart and proper what I do.

CLARA [*automatically*]   She's a technician.

JACK   Oh, that's nice. I didn't mean to suggest there was anything wrong with how you raised your sister.

BIG GIRL [*jolly again*]   Haw haw haw . . . Nawh, ya didn't. I know you didn't even know what you were sayin', young blood. Do you know why I taught her to cuss?

JACK   Why no, I have no idea. Why did you?

BIG GIRL   Well, it was to give her freedom, ya know?

    [JACK *shakes his head.*]

Ya see, workin' in the hospital with all the nuts and fruits and crazies and weirdos I get ideas 'bout things. I saw how when they get these kids in who have cracked up and even with older people who come in out of their skulls they all mostly cuss. Mostly all of them, all the time they out of their heads, they cuss all the time and do other wild things, and boy do some of them really get into it and let out all of that filthy shit that's been stored up all them years. But when the docs start shockin' them puttin' them on insulin[3] they quiets down, that's when the docs think they're gettin' better, but really they ain't. They're just learn'n like before to hold it in . . . just like before, that's one reason most of them come back or are always on the verge afterwards of goin' psycho again.

JACK [*enthusiastic*]   Wow, I never thought of that! That ritual action of purging and catharsis[4] can open up new avenues in therapy and in learning theory and conditioning subjects . . .

BIG GIRL   Saaay whaaa . . . ? What did you have for breakfast, man?

CLARA [*struck*]   That sounds so wonderful . . .

JACK [*still excited*]   But I agree with you. You have an intuitive grasp of very abstract concepts!

BIG GIRL [*beaming*]   Yeah, yeah . . . I got a lot of it figured out . . . [*To* JACK] Here, fill up your glass again, man.

JACK [*to* CLARA]   Aren't you drinking with us?

CLARA   Later. Big Girl doesn't allow me to start in drinking too early.

JACK [*confused*]   She doesn't?

BIG GIRL [*cuts in*]   Well, in Baby Girl's case I said to myself that I'm teach'n her how in front and lettin' her use what she knows whenever it builds up inside. And it's really good for her, gives her spirit and everything.

CLARA   That's what probably warped her brain.

BIG GIRL   Hush up! You knows it was dat fuckin' disease. All the doctors said so.

CLARA   You don't believe no doctors 'bout nothin' else!

BIG GIRL [*glares at* CLARA]   Are you showin' out,[5] Clara? Are you showin' out to your little boyfriend?

CLARA   He ain't mah boyfriend.

JACK [*interrupts*]   How do you know she might not have spirit if she wasn't allowed to curse?

BIG GIRL [*sullen*]   I don't know anything, young blood. But I can take a look at myself and see the two of us. Look at me! [*Stares at* JACK] LOOK AT ME!

JACK   Yes, yes, I'm looking.

BIG GIRL   Well, what do you see?

CLARA   B.G. . . . PLEASE!

BIG GIRL [*ignores*]   Well, what do you see?

JACK [*worried*]   Well, I don't really know . . . I . . .

BIG GIRL   Well, let me tell you what you see. You see a fat bitch who's 20 pounds overweight and looks ten years older than she is. You want to know how I got this way and been this way most of my life and would be worse off if I didn't let off some steam drinkin' this rotgut[6] and speakin' my mind?

JACK [*to* BIG GIRL *who doesn't listen but drinks*]   Yes, I would like to hear.

---

3. Insulin shock therapy was a psychiatric treatment common in the 1940s and 1950s performed by injecting schizophrenic patients with large doses of insulin to induce comas.
4. In psychology, the process of reliving an event and releasing the emotions associated with it; in drama, the process of purifying emotions through the audience's vicarious experience of the characters' experience.
5. Showing off; flaunting oneself.
6. Cheap liquor.

[CLARA *finishes the stove and takes seat between the two.* BABY GIRL *goes to the yard door but does not go out into the rain; she sits down and looks out through the door at an angle.*]

BIG GIRL   Ya see, when I was a little runt of a kid my mother found out she couldn't keep me or Baby Girl any longer cause she had TB,[7] so I got shipped out somewheres and Baby Girl got shipped out somewheres else. People that Baby Girl went to exposed her to the disease. She was lucky, I ended up with some fuckin' Christians . . .

CLARA   Ohhh, B.G., you shouldn't say that!

BIG GIRL   Well, I sho as hell just did! . . . Damned kristers![8] I spent 12 years with those people, can you imagine? A dozen years in hell. Christians . . . HAAA . . . always preachin' 'bout some heaven over yonder and building a bigger hell here den any devil have imagination for.

CLARA   You shouldn't go round sayin' things like dat.

BIG GIRL   I shouldn't! Well what did you Christian mammy and pot-gutted pappy teach you? When I met you you didn't even know how to take a douche.

CLARA   YOU GOT NO RIGHT!!! [*She momentarily rises as if she's going to launch herself on* BIG GIRL.]

BIG GIRL [*condescending*]   Awww . . . forget it, sweetie . . . don't make no never mind, but you remember how you us'ta smell when you got ready fo bed . . . like a dead hoss[9] or a baby skunk . . . [*To* JACK, *explaining*] That damned Christian mamma and pappa of hers didn't tell her a thing 'bout herself . . . ha ha ha . . . thought if she ever found out her little thing was used fo anything else 'cept squattin' she'd fall backwards right up in it . . . ZaaaBOOM . . . STRAIGHT TA HELL . . . ha ha . . . didn't know that lil Clara had already found her heaven and on the same trail.

CLARA [*ashamed*]   Sometimes . . . sometimes . . . I just want to die for bein' here.

BIG GIRL [*enjoying herself*]   Ha ha ha . . . that wouldn't do no good. Would it? Just remember what shape you were in when I met you, kid. Ha ha ha. *To* JACK. Hey, boy, can you imagine this pretty little trick here had her stomach seven months in the wind,[1] waitin' on a dead baby who died from the same disease that Baby Girl had . . .

CLARA   He didn't have any nasty disease like Baby Girl!

BABY GIRL [*hears her name but looks out door*]   NO! NO! SHIT! DAMN! SHIT! SHIT!

BIG GIRL   HAW HAW HAW . . . now we got her started . . .
      [*She laughs for over a minute;* JACK *waits patiently, sipping;* CLARA *is grim.* BABY GIRL *has quieted.*]

BIG GIRL   She . . . she . . . ha ha . . . was walkin' round with a dead baby in her and had no place to go.

CLARA [*fills a glass*]   I just can't understand you, B.G. You know my baby died after he was born. Somedays you just get besides yourself.

BIG GIRL   I'm only helpin' ya entertain your guest.

CLARA   Awww . . . B.G. It wasn't his fault. I invited him.

JACK [*dismayed*]   Well, I asked really. If there's anything wrong I can go.

---

7. [T.B.] Tuberculosis, a potentially fatal infectious disease of the lungs.
8. Zealous or sanctimonious Christians.

9. Horse.
1. Seven months pregnant.

BIG GIRL   Take it easy, young blood. I'm just havin' a little fun. Now let's get back to the Clara Saga . . . ya hear that word, junior? . . . S-A-G-A, SUCKER! You college boys don't know it all. Yeah, her folks had kicked her out and the little punk she was big for what had tried to put her out on the block[2] and when that didn't work out . . . [*mocking and making pretended blushes*] . . . because our sweet little thing here was soooo modest and sedate . . . the nigger split! . . . HAW HAW HAW . . . HE MADE IT TO NEW YORK!

> [*She goes into a laughing, choking and crying fit.* BABY GIRL *rushes over to her and on tip toes pats her back.*]

BABY GIRL   Big Girl! Big Girl! Big Girl! [*A knocking sounds and* CLARA *exits to answer the door.*]

BIG GIRL   [*catches her breath*] Whatcha want, little sister?

BABY GIRL   The cat. The cat. Cat got kittens. Cat got kittens.

BIG GIRL   [*still coughing and choking*]   Awww, go on. You know there ain't no cat under there with no kittens. [*To* JACK] She's been makin' that story up for two months now about how some cat crawls up under the steps and has kittens. She can't fool me none. She just wants a cat but I ain't gonna get none.

JACK   Why not, cats aren't so bad. My mother has one and he's quite a pleasure to her.

BIG GIRL   For your mammy maybe, but all they mean round here . . . [*singsong*] . . . is fleas and mo mouths to feed. With an invalid aunt upstairs we don't need anymo expenses.

JACK   [*gestures toward* BABY GIRL]   It shows that she has a very vivid imagination to make up that story about the kittens.

BIG GIRL   Yeah, her big sister ain't the biggest liar in the family.

> [CLARA *returns with* MISS FAMIE *staggering behind her, a thin middle-aged woman in long seamen's raincoat, dripping wet, and wearing house slippers that are soaked and squish water about the kitchen floor.*]

BIG GIRL   Hi, Miss Famie. I see you're dressed in your rainy glad rags today.

MISS FAMIE   [*slurred speech of the drunk*]   Hello, B.G. Yeah, I couldn't pass up seein' Aunt Toohey, so I put on my weather coat. You know that don't a day pass that I don't stop up to see her.

BIG GIRL   Yeah, I know, Miss Famie. Every day you go up there with that quart of gin under your dress and you two ole lushes put it away.

MISS FAMIE   Why, B.G. You should know better than that.

CLARA   [*re-seated*]   B.G., you shouldn't say that . . .

BIG GIRL   Why shouldn't I? I'm payin' for over half of that juice and I don't git to see none of it 'cept the empty bottles.

BABY GIRL   CAT! CAT! CAT!

MISS FAMIE   Oh, the baby still sees them there cats.

CLARA   You should be ashamed to talk to Miss Famie like that.

BIG GIRL   [*to* JACK]   Why you so quiet? Can't you speak to folks when they come in?

JACK   I'm sorry. [*To* MISS FAMIE] Hello, mam.

MISS FAMIE   Why howdie, son.

CLARA   Would you like a glass of wine, Miss Famie?

MISS FAMIE   Don't mind if I do, sister.

---

2. "Put her out on the block": prostitute her.

BIG GIRL   Better watch it, Miss Famie. Wine and gin will rust your gizzard.[3]

CLARA   Ohh . . . [pours a glass of wine] . . . Here, Miss Famie.

BABY GIRL   CAT! CAT!

BIG GIRL [singsong, lifting her glass]   Mus' I tell . . . muscatel . . . jitterbug champagne.[4] [Reminisces] Remember, Clara, the first time I got you to take a drink? To MISS FAMIE. You should of seen her. Some of this same cheap rotgut here. She'd never had a drink before but she wanted to show me how game she was. She was a bright little smart thing, just out of high school and didn't know her butt from a doorknob.

MISS FAMIE   Yes, indeed, that was Clara all right.

BIG GIRL   She drank three water glasses down and got so damned sick I had to put my finger down her throat and make her heave it up . . . HAW HAW . . . babbled her fool head off all night . . . said she'd be my friend always . . . that we'd always be together . . .

MISS FAMIE [gulps down her drink]   Wine will make you do that the first time you get good'n high on it.

JACK [takes drink]   I don't know. You know . . . I've never really been wasted and I've been drinkin' for quite some time now.

BIG GIRL   Quite some time, huh? Six months?

JACK   Nawh. My mother used to let me drink at home. I've been drinkin' since 15. And I drank all the time I was in the service.

BIG GIRL   Just because you been slippin' some drinks out of ya mammy's bottle and you slipped a few under ya belt with the punks in the barracks don't make ya a drinker, boy!

CLARA   B.G. . . . do you have to?

[MISS FAMIE finishes her second drink as BIG GIRL and CLARA stare at each other.]

MISS FAMIE   Well, I guess I better get up and see Aunt Toohey. [She leaves]

JACK   Nice to have met you, mam.

MISS FAMIE   Well, good-bye, son.

BIG GIRL [before MISS FAMIE reaches top of stairs]   That ole ginhead tracked water all over your floor, Clara.

CLARA   Makes no never mind to me. This place stays so clean I like when someone comes so it gets a little messy so I have somethin' ta do.

BIG GIRL   Is that why Jackie boy is here? So he can do some messin' 'round?

CLARA   Nawh, B.G.

JACK [stands]   Well, I'll be going. I see that . . .

BIG GIRL [rises and tugs his sleeve]   Sit down an' drink up, young blood. [Pushes him back into his seat] There's wine here . . . [slow and suggestive] . . . there's a pretty girl here . . . you go for that, don't you?

JACK   It's not that . . .

BIG GIRL   You go for fine little Clara, don't you?

JACK   Well, yes, I do . . .

BIG GIRL   HAW HAW HAW . . . [slams the table and sloshes wine] . . . HAW HAW HAW . . . [slow and suggestive] . . . What I tell ya, Clara? You're a winner. First time I laid eyes on you I said to myself that you's a winner.

CLARA [takes a drink]   Drink up, B.G.

---

3. "Rust your gizzard": ruin your innards.   4. "Jitterbug champagne": cheap white wine.

BIG GIRL [*to* JACK]   You sho you like what you see, young blood?

JACK [*becomes bold.*]   Why sure. Do you think I'd come out on a day like this for anybody?

BIG GIRL   HAW HAW HAW . . . [*peels of laughter and more coughs*] . . .

JACK [*to* CLARA]   I was going to ask you to go to the matinee 'round Pep's[5] but I guess it's too late now.

CLARA [*hesitates*]   I never been.

BIG GIRL [*sobers*]   That's right. You never been to Pep's and it's only 'round the corner. What you mean it's too late, young blood? It don't start gettin' good till round four.

JACK   I thought she might have ta start gettin' supper.

BIG GIRL   She'd only burn it the fuck up too if she did. *To* CLARA. I'm goin' ta take you to Pep's this afternoon.

CLARA   You don't have ta, B.G.

BIG GIRL   It's my day off, ain't it?

CLARA   But it costs so much, don't it?

BIG GIRL   Nawh, not much . . . you'll like it. Soon as C.C. comes over ta watch Baby Girl we can go.

CLARA [*brightens*]   O.K.!

JACK   I don't know who's there now, but they always have a good show. Sometimes Ahmad Jamal[6] . . .

BABY GIRL [*cuts speech*]   CAT! CAT! CAT!

BIG GIRL   Let's toast to that . . . [*raising her glass* . . .] To Pep's on a rainy day!

JACK   HEAR! HEAR! [*He drains his glass. A tumbling sound is heard from the backyard as they drink and* BABY GIRL *claps hands as* STOOGIE, BAMA *and* HOSS *appear in yard doorway. The three boys are no more than 16. They are soaked but wear only thin jackets, caps and pants. Under* STOOGIE's *cap he wears a bandanna to keep his processed hair dry.*]

BIG GIRL   What the hell is this?

STOOGIE [*goes to* BIG GIRL *and pats her shoulder*]   The heat, B.G. The man was on our asses so we had to come on in out of the rain, baby, dig?

BIG GIRL   Well tell me somethin' I don't know, baby. Why you got to pick mah back door? I ain't never ready for any more heat than I gets already.

STOOGIE   It just happened that way, B.G. We didn't have any choice.

BAMA   That's right, Big Girl. You know we ain't lame 'nuf to be usin' yo pad for no highway.

HOSS   Yeah, baby, you know how it is when the man is there.

BIG GIRL   Well, that makes a difference. [*Smiles*] Hey, what'cha standin' there with your faces hangin' out for? Get yourselves a drink.

   [HOSS *goes to the sink to get glasses for the trio;* STOOGIE *looks* JACK *over and nods to* BAMA, *then turns to* CLARA.]

STOOGIE   How ya doin', Clara. Ya lookin' fine as ever.

CLARA   I'm okay, Stoogie. I don't have to ask 'bout you none. Bad news sho travels fast.

STOOGIE [*holds arms apart in innocence*]   What'cha mean, baby? What'cha been hearin' 'bout Poppa Stoogie?

CLARA   Just the regular. That your gang's fightin' the Peaceful Valley guys up in North Philly.

---

5. Philadelphia jazz club, popular in the 1960s.   6. African American jazz pianist (b. 1930).

STOOGIE   Awww . . . dat's old stuff. Sheet . . . you way behind, baby.

BAMA   Yeah, sweetcake, dat's over.

CLARA   Already?

HOSS   Yeah, we just finished sign'n a peace treaty with Peaceful Valley.

BAMA   Yeah, we out ta cool the War Lords now from ov'va on Powelton Avenue.

HOSS   Ole Stoogie here is settin' up the war council now; we got a pact with Peaceful Valley and, man, when we come down on those punk War Lords . . . baby . . . it's just gonna be all ov'va.

BIG GIRL   Yeah, it's always one thing ta another with you punks.

STOOGIE   Hey, B.G., cool it! We can't help it if people always spreadin' rumors 'bout us. Things just happen an' people talk and don' understand and get it all wrong, dat's all.

BIG GIRL   Yeah, all of it just happens, huh? It's just natural . . . you's growin' boys.

STOOGIE   That's what's happen'n, baby. Now take for instance Peaceful Valley. Las' week we went up there . . . ya know, only five of us in Crook's Buick.

CLARA   I guess ya was just lookin' at the scenery?

HOSS   Yeah, baby, dat's it. We was lookin' . . . fo' some jive half-ass niggers.

[*The boys laugh and giggle as* STOOGIE *enacts the story.*]

STOOGIE   Yeah, we spot Specs from off'a Jefferson and Gratz walkin' with them bad foots down Master . . . ha ha ha . . .

BAMA   Tell them what happened to Specs, man.

HOSS   Awww, man, ya ain't gonna drag mah man Bama again?

[*They laugh more, slapping and punching each other, taking off their caps and cracking each other with them, gulping their wine and performing for the girls and* JACK.]

[STOOGIE *has his hair exposed.*]

STOOGIE   Bama here . . . ha ha ha . . . Bama burnt dat four-eyed mathafukker in the leg.

HOSS   Baby, you should'a seen it!

CLARA   Yeah, that's what I heard.

STOOGIE   Yeah, but listen, baby. [*Points to* BAMA] He was holding the only heat[7] we had . . . ha ho ho . . . and dis jive sucker was aimin at Spec's bad foots . . . ha ha . . . while that blind mathafukker was blastin' from 'round the corner straight through the car window . . .

[*They become nearly hysterical with laughter and stagger and stumble around the table.*]

HOSS   Yeah . . . ha ha . . . mathafukkin' glass was flyin' all over us . . . ha ha . . . we almost got sliced ta death and dis stupid mathafukker was shootin' at the man's bad foots . . . ha ha . . .

BAMA [*scratching his head*]   Well, man. Well, man . . . I didn't know what kind of rumble[8] we was in.

[CLARA *and* BIG GIRL *laugh as they refill their glasses, nearly emptying the jug.* BIG GIRL *gets up and pulls another gallon out of the refrigerator as laughter subsides.*]

BIG GIRL [*sits down*]   What's the heat[9] doin' after ya?

---

7. Gun.
8. Gang fight.
9. Police.

STOOGIE   Nothin'.

CLARA   I bet!

STOOGIE [*sneer*]   That's right, baby. They just singled us out to make examples out of.

> [*This gets a laugh from his friends.*]

BIG GIRL   What did you get?

HOSS   Get?

BIG GIRL [*turns on him*]   You tryin' ta get wise, punk?

STOOGIE [*patronizing*]   Awww, B.G. You not goin' ta take us serious, are ya?

> [*Silence*]

Well, ya see. We were walkin' down Broad Street by the State Store,[1] see? And we see this old rumdum[2] come out and stagger down the street carryin' this heavy package . . .

CLARA   And?

STOOGIE   And he's stumblin', see. Like he's gonna fall. So good ole Hoss here says, "Why don't we help that pore man out?" So Bama walks up and helps the man carry his package, and do you know what?

BIG GIRL   Yeah, the mathafukker "slips" down and screams and some cops think you some wrong doin' studs . . . yeah, I know . . . of course you didn't have time to explain.

STOOGIE   That's right, B.G. So to get our breath so we could tell our side of it we just stepped in here, dig?

BIG GIRL   Yeah, I dig. [*Menacing*]   Where is it?

HOSS   Where's what?

> [*Silence*]

STOOGIE   If you had just give me another minute, B.G. [*Pulls out a quart of vodka*]   Well, no use savin' it anyway. Who wants some 100-proof tiger piss?

BAMA [*to* STOOGIE]   Hey, man, how much was in dat mathafukker's wallet?

STOOGIE [*nods toward* JACK]   Cool it, sucker.

HOSS [*to* STOOGIE]   But, man, you holdin' the watch and ring too!

STOOGIE [*advancing on them*]   What's wrong with you jive-ass mathafukkers?

BIG GIRL   Okay, cool it? There's only one person gets out of hand 'round here, ya understand?

STOOGIE   Okay, B.G. Let it slide . . .

BABY GIRL   CAT! CAT! CAT!

BAMA [*to* HOSS]   Hey, man, dis chick's still chasin' dose cats.[3]

STOOGIE [*to* JACK]   Drink up, man. Not everyday ya get dis stuff. [BAMA *picks up the beat of the music and begins a shuffling dance.* BABY GIRL *begins bouncing in time to the music.*]

HOSS   C'mon, Baby Girl; let me see ya do the slide.

BABY GIRL   NO! NO! [*She claps and bounces.*]

HOSS [*demonstrates his steps, trying to out-dance* BAMA]   C'mon, Baby Girl, shake that thing!

CLARA   No, stop that, Hoss. She don't know what she's doin!

BIG GIRL   That's okay, Clara. Go on, Baby Girl, do the thing.

---

1. Liquor store.
2. Drunkard.
3. Guys.

[STOOGIE *grabs salt from the table and shakes it upon the floor, under the feet of the dancers.*]

STOOGIE DO THE SLIDE,[4] MAN! SLIDE!

[BABY GIRL *lumbers up and begins a grotesque maneuver while grunting out strained sounds.*]

BABY GIRL Uuuhhh . . . sheeeee . . . waaa . . . uuhhh . . .

BIG GIRL [*standing, toasting*] DO THE THING, BABY!!!

CLARA Awww . . . B.G. Why don't you stop all dat?

STOOGIE [*to* JACK] C'mon, man, git with it.

[JACK *shakes his head and* STOOGIE *goes over to* CLARA *and holds out his hand.*]

STOOGIE Let's go, Baby.

CLARA Nawh . . . I don't dance no mo . . .

STOOGIE C'mon, pretty mamma . . . watch this step . . . [*He cuts a fancy step.*]

BIG GIRL Go on and dance, sister.

[STOOGIE *moves off and the three boys dance.*]

CLARA Nawh . . . B.G., you know I don't go for that kind of stuff no mo.

BIG GIRL Go on, baby!

CLARA No!

BIG GIRL I want you to dance, Clara.

CLARA Nawh . . . I just can't.

BIG GIRL DO LIKE I SAY! DO LIKE BIG WANTS!

[*The dancers stop momentarily but begin again when* CLARA *joins them.* BABY GIRL *halts and resumes her place upon the floor, fondling her toy. The others dance until the record stops.*]

STOOGIE [*to* JACK] Where you from, man?

JACK Oh, I live over in West Philly now, but I come from up around Master.

STOOGIE Oh? Do you know Hector?

JACK [*trying to capture an old voice and mannerism*] Yeah, man. I know the cat.

STOOGIE What's your name, man?

JACK Jack, man, maybe you know me by Tookie.

STOOGIE [*ritually*] Tookie . . . Tookie . . . yeah, man, I think I heard about you. You us'ta be in the ole Jet Cobras![5]

JACK Well, I us'ta know some of the guys then. I been away for a while.

BAMA [*matter-of-factly*] Where you been, man? Jail?

JACK I was in the Marines for three years.

STOOGIE Hey, man. That must'a been a gas.

JACK It was okay. I seen a lot . . . went a lot of places.

BIG GIRL Yeah, you must'a seen it all.

STOOGIE Did you get to go anywhere overseas, man?

JACK Yeah, I was aboard ship most of the time.

HOSS Wow, man. That sounds cool.

BAMA You really was overseas, man?

JACK Yeah. I went to Europe and North Africa and the Caribbean.

STOOGIE What kind of a boat were you on, man?

JACK A ship.

BIG GIRL A boat!

---

4. Popular 1960s dance.   5. Philadelphia street gang.

JACK No, a ship.

STOOGIE [*rising,* BAMA *and* HOSS *surrounding* JACK] Yeah, man, dat's what she said . . . a boat!

CLARA STOP IT!!!

BABY GIRL NO! NO! NO! SHIT! SHIT! SHIT! DAMN! SHIT!

MISS FAMIE [*voice from upstairs*] Your Aunt don't like all that noise.

BIG GIRL You and my aunt better mind ya fukkin' ginhead business or I'll come up there and ram those empty bottles up where it counts!

BAMA [*sniggling*] Oh, baby. We forgot your aunt was up dere sick.

STOOGIE Yeah, baby. Have another drink.

> [*He fills all glasses except* CLARA'*s. She pulls hers away.*]

CLARA Nawh, I don't want any more. Me and BIG GIRL are goin' out after a while.

BAMA Can I go too?

BIG GIRL There's always have to be one wise mathafukker.

BAMA I didn't mean nuttin', B.G., honest.

STOOGIE [*to* JACK] What did you do in the Army, man?

JACK [*feigns a dialect*] Ohhh, man. I told you already I was in the Marines!

HOSS [*to* CLARA] Where you goin'?

CLARA B.G.'s takin' me to Pep's.

BAMA Wow . . . dat's nice, baby.

BIG GIRL [*gesturing toward* JACK] Ole smoothie here suggesting takin' Clara but it seems he backed out, so I thought we might step around there anyway.

JACK [*annoyed*] I didn't back out!

STOOGIE [*to* JACK] Did you screw any of them foreign bitches when you were in Japan, man?

JACK Yeah, man. I couldn't help it. They was all over, ya know?

BIG GIRL He couldn't beat them off.

STOOGIE Yeah, man. I dig.

JACK Especially in France and Italy. Course, the Spanish girls are the best, but the ones in France and Italy ain't so bad either.

HOSS You mean those French girls ain't as good as those Spanish girls?

JACK Nawh, man, the Spanish girls are the best.

BAMA I never did dig no Mexican nor Rican spic bitches. Too tough, man.

JACK They ain't Mexican or Puerto Rican. They Spanish . . . from Spain . . . Spanish is different from Mexican. In Spain . . .

STOOGIE What'cha do now, man?

JACK Ohhh . . . I'm goin' ta college prep on the G.I. Bill[6] now . . . and workin' a little.

STOOGIE Is that why you sound like you got a load of shit in your mouth?

JACK What do you mean!

STOOGIE I thought you talked like you had shit in your mouth because you had been ta college, man.

JACK I don't understand what you're tryin' to say, man.

STOOGIE It's nothin', man. You just talk funny sometimes . . . ya know what I mean. Hey, man, where do you work?

JACK [*visibly feeling his drinks*] Nawh, man, I don't know what ya mean and I don't go to college, man, it's college prep.

---

6. 1944 law that provided military veterans financial assistance for education.

STOOGIE Thanks, man.

JACK And I work at the P.O.

BAMA Pee-who?

JACK The Post Office, man.

BAMA No shit, baby.

STOOGIE Thanks, George. I always like know things I don't know anything about. [*He turns back on* JACK.]

JACK [*to* BIG GIRL] Hey, what time ya goin' round to Pep's?

BIG GIRL Soon . . . are you in a hurry, young blood? You don't have to wait for us.

JACK [*now drunk*] That's okay . . . it's just gettin' late, ya know, man . . . and I was wonderin' what time Clara's ole man gets home . . .

BIG GIRL Clara's ole man? . . . Whad do you mean, man? . . . [*The trio begins snickering, holding their laughter back;* JACK *is too drunk to notice.*]

JACK Well, Clara said for me to come by today in the afternoon when her ole man would be at work . . . and I was wonderin' what time he got home . . .

> [BIG GIRL *stands, tilting over her chair to crash backwards on the floor. Her bust juts out; she is controlled but furious.*]

BIG GIRL Clara's ole man is home now . . .

> [*A noise is heard outside as C.C. comes in the front door. The trio are laughing louder but with restraint;* CLARA *looks stunned.*]

C. C. It's just Me . . . just ole C.C.

HOSS Shsss . . . shut up, man.

JACK [*starts up and feels drunk for the first time*] What . . . you mean he's been upstairs all this time?

BIG GIRL [*staring*] Nawh, man, I don't mean that!

JACK [*looks at* BIG GIRL, *then at the laughing boys and finally to* CLARA] Ohhh . . . jezzus! [*He staggers to the backyard door, past* BABY GIRL, *and becomes sick.*]

BIG GIRL [*to* CLARA] Didn't you tell him? Didn't you tell him a fukkin' thing?

> [C. C. *comes in. He is drunk and weaves and says nothing. He sees the wine, searches for a glass, bumps into one of the boys, is shoved into another, and gets booted in the rear before he reaches wine and seat.*]

BIG GIRL Didn't you tell him?

CLARA I only wanted to talk, B.G. I only wanted to talk to somebody. I don't have anybody to talk to . . . *crying* . . . I don't have anyone . . .

BIG GIRL It's time for the matinee. *To* STOOGIE. Before you go, escort my friend out, will ya?

CLARA Ohhh . . . B.G. I'll do anything but please . . . ohhh Big . . . I won't forget my promise.

BIG GIRL Let's go. We don't want to miss the show, do we?

CLARA Please, B.G., please. Not that. It's not his fault! Please!

BIG GIRL DO LIKE I SAY! DO LIKE I WANT YOU TO DO!

> [CLARA *drops her head and rises and exits stage right followed by* BIG GIRL. STOOGIE *and his boys finish their drinks, stalk and swagger about.* BAMA *opens the refrigerator and* HOSS *takes one long last guzzle.*]

BAMA Hey, Stoogie babe, what about the split?[7]

STOOGIE [*drunk*] Later, you square-ass, lame-ass mathafukker!

---

7. Division of stolen goods.

[HOSS *giggles*.]

BABY GIRL   CAT! CAT! CAT!

C.C. [*seated drinking*]   Shut up, Baby Girl. Ain't no cats out dere.

MISS FAMIE [*staggers from upstairs, calls back*] Good night Toohey. See ya tomorrow.

> [*With a nod from* STOOGIE, BAMA *and* HOSS *take* JACK's *arms and wrestle him into the yard. The sounds of* JACK's *beating are heard.* MISS FAMIE *wanders to the yard door, looks out but staggers back from what she sees and continues sprawling toward the exit, stage right.*]

BABY GIRL   CAT! CAT! CAT!

C.C.   SHUT UP! SHUT ON UP, BABY GIRL! I TOLE YA . . . DERE AIN'T NO CATS OUT DERE!!!

BABY GIRL   NO! DAMN! SHIT! SHIT! DAMN! NO! NO!

> [STOOGIE *looks over the scene and downs his drink, then saunters outside. Lights dim out until there is a single soft spot on* BABY GIRL's *head, turned wistfully toward the yard, then blackness. Curtain.*]

ELDRIDGE CLEAVER
1935–1998

B orn in Wabbeseka, Arkansas, to Thelma and Leroy Eldridge Cleaver, Eldridge Cleaver moved with his family first to Phoenix and then to Los Angeles, where, as a teenager, he became involved in petty crime. In 1954 he was convicted of drug possession. This began a long journey through the California prison system, beginning with a term at Soledad and, after conviction for rape and assault with the intent to commit murder, moving through Folsom and San Quentin prisons. Like Malcolm X, Cleaver converted to the Black Muslim faith while in prison and devoted much of his incarceration to self-education.

Upon his release from prison, Cleaver became a writer for *Ramparts* magazine, there publishing portions of an autobiographical novella titled *Black Moochie* (completed in exile in 1969). By 1967, he had become the minister of information and head of the international section of the Oakland-based Black Panther Party. His best-selling collection of essays, *Soul on Ice* (1968), made him one of the foremost revolutionary celebrities of the 1960s. Not unaware of the nature of American showmanship, Cleaver embraced the performative ethos of contemporary black culture, fusing politics and spectacle in a series of public stances that culminated with his candidacy for the presidency in 1968. Fleeing criminal charges from a shoot-out with the Oakland police, he spent much of the 1970s abroad, residing in Cuba, Algeria, and Europe. Upon his return to the United States, Cleaver announced his rebirth as a fundamentalist Christian.

The style, tone, and ideology of the writings in *Soul on Ice* were influential for aspiring young revolutionary writers of the Black Arts movement. Given the book's histrionic, even incendiary flair (Cleaver had renounced and critiqued his sexual violence, but did not repudiate its underlying psychological politics), Cleaver's contributions to what later would be termed critical race studies and postcolonial critique are easily overlooked. Though *Soul on Ice* foregrounds the racial politics of sexuality in developing its ideas about the history of American race relations, the book's most trenchant insights about servitude and sovereignty often arise in its extensive commentaries on music, dance, and other forms of cultural expression. In this respect, Cleaver's autobiographical essays, made equally of history, philosophy, and myth, represent one of the era's most suggestive archives of social analysis and imaginative criticism.

From Soul on Ice

Convalescence

> . . . just as in childhood I envied Negroes for what seemed to me their superior masculinity, so I envy them today for what seems to me their superior physical grace and beauty. I have come to value physical grace very highly, and I am now capable of aching with all my being when I watch a Negro couple on the dance floor, or a Negro playing baseball or basketball. *They are on the kind of terms with their own bodies that I should like to be on with mine, and for that precious quality they seem blessed to me.* [Italics added]
>
> —Norman Podhoretz,[1]
> "My Negro Problem—And Ours,"
> *Commentary*, February 1963

> Why envy the Negro his grace, his physical skills? Why not ask what it is that prevents grace and physical skill from becoming a general property of the young? Mr. Podhoretz speaks of middle-class, white respectability—what does this mean but being cut off from the labor process, the work process, the creative process, as such? *The solution is thus not the direct liquidation of the color line,*[2] *through the liquidation of color; but rather through a greater physical connectedness of the whites; and a greater intellective connectedness of the blacks . . .*" [Italics added]
> —Irving Louis Horowitz,[3] Chairman,
> Department of Sociology, Hobart and William Smith
> Colleges, Geneva, New York, *Commentary*, June 1963

If the separation of the black and white people in America along the color line had the effect, in terms of social imagery, of separating the Mind from the Body—the oppressor whites usurping sovereignty by monopolizing the Mind, abdicating the Body and becoming bodiless Omnipotent Administrators and Ultrafeminines; and the oppressed blacks, divested of sovereignty and therefore of Mind, manifesting the Body and becoming mindless Super-masculine Menials and Black Amazons[4]—if this is so, then the 1954 U.S. Supreme Court decision in the case of *Brown v. Board of Education,*[5] demolishing the principle of segregation of the races in public education

1. Conservative American political pundit (b. 1930), editor of *Commentary* magazine from 1960 to 1995.
2. "Color line": phrase referring to racial segregation that arose in the period of Reconstruction following the Civil War; first given public currency by ex-slave and political activist Frederick Douglass (1818–1895) in an 1881 essay of the same name, "the color line" gained broad popularity with its use in *The Souls of Black Folk* (1903) by African American sociologist and civil rights activist W. E. B. Du Bois (1868–1963).
3. American sociologist (1929–2012), founding editor of the journal *Society*.
4. Throughout *Soul on Ice*, Cleaver uses the term "Omnipotent Administrator" to refer to the archetype of slavemaster, who cedes embodiment to the laboring slave, or "Supermasculine Menial"; in this formulation, white women become sexually alluring but dependent "Ultrafeminines" and black women are described as self-reliant "Black Amazons."
5. Landmark U.S. Supreme Court case that overturned *Plessy v. Ferguson* (1896) and declared unconstitutional state laws establishing separate schools for white and black students.

and striking at the very root of the practice of segregation generally, was a major surgical operation performed by nine men in black robes on the racial Maginot Line[6] which is imbedded as deep as sex or the lust for lucre in the schismatic[7] American psyche. This piece of social surgery, if successful, performed without benefit of any anesthetic except God and the Constitution, in a land where God is dead and the Constitution has been in a coma for 180 years, is more marvelous than a successful heart transplant would be, for it was meant to graft the nation's Mind back onto its Body and vice versa.

If the foregoing is true, then the history of America in the years following the pivotal Supreme Court edict should be a record of the convalescence of the nation. And upon investigation we should be able to see the Omnipotent Administrators and Ultrafeminines grappling with their unfamiliar and alienated Bodies, and the Supermasculine Menials and Amazons attempting to acquire and assert *a mind of their own*. The record, I think, is clear and unequivocal. The bargain which seems to have been struck is that the whites have had to turn to the blacks for a clue on how to swing with the Body, while the blacks have had to turn to the whites for the secret of the Mind. It was Chubby Checker's[8] mission, bearing the Twist as *good news*, to teach the whites, whom history had taught to forget, how to shake their asses again. It is a skill they surely must once have possessed but which they abandoned for puritanical dreams of escaping the corruption of the flesh, by leaving the terrors of the Body to the blacks.

In the swift, fierce years since the 1954 school desegregation decision, a rash of seemingly unrelated mass phenomena has appeared on the American scene—deviating radically from the prevailing Hot-Dog-and-Malted-Milk norm of the bloodless, square,[9] superficial, faceless Sunday-Morning atmosphere that was suffocating the nation's soul. And all of this in a nation where the so-called molders of public opinion, the writers, politicians, teachers, and cab drivers, are willful, euphoric liars or zip-dam ostriches and owls,[1] a clique of undercover ghosts, a bunch of Walter Jenkinses,[2] a lot of coffee-drinking, cigarette-smoking, sly, suck-assing, status-seeking, cheating, nervous, dry-balled, tranquillizer-gulched, countdown-minded, out-of-style, slithering snakes. No wonder that many "innocent people," the manipulated and the stimulated, some of whom were game for a reasonable amount of mystery and even adventure, had their minds scrambled. These observers were not equipped to either *feel* or *know* that a radical break, a revolutionary leap out of their sight, had taken place in the secret parts of this nation's soul. It was as if a driverless vehicle were speeding through the American night down an unlighted street toward a stone wall and was boarded on the fly by a stealthy ghost with a drooling leer on his face, who, at the last detour before chaos and disaster, careened the vehicle down a smooth highway that leads to the future and life; and to ask these Americans

---

6. Defensive structure of concrete, tanks, and other weaponry dividing France and Germany, built by the French from 1930 to 1939; it failed to deter the German invasion of France during World War II.

7. Divisive, divided; "lucre": money.

8. African American singer (born Ernest Evans in 1941) who ignited the "twist" dance craze with his 1960 cover of Hank Ballard's rhythm-and-blues song "The Twist."

9. Conventional; unenlightened.

1. Owls: thought to be blind in daylight; "ostriches": thought to bury their heads in the sand (i.e., be oblivious to what's in plain sight). "Zip-dam": damn nothing; useless, worthless (southern vernacular).

2. Walter Jenkins (1918–1985), longtime aide to Lyndon B. Johnson (1908–1972), 36th president of the United States (1963–68), whose career ended in 1964 when he was charged with disorderly conduct with another man in a Washington, D.C., public restroom.

to understand that they were the passengers on this driverless vehicle and that the lascivious ghost was the Saturday-night crotchfunk of the Twist, or the "Yeah, Yeah, Yeah!"[3] which the Beatles high-jacked from Ray Charles, to ask these Calvinistic[4] profligates to see the logical and reciprocal links is more cruel than asking a hope-to-die Okie Music[5] buff to cop the sounds of John Coltrane.[6]

In the beginning of the era came a thief with a seven-year itch who knew that the ostriches and the owls had been bribed with a fix of Euphony,[7] which is their kick. The thief knew that he need not wait for the cover of night, that with impunity he could show his face in the marketplace in the full light of the sun, do his deed, scratch his dirt, sell his loot to the fence[8] while the ostriches and owls, coasting on Euphony, one with his head in a hole—any hole—and the other with his head in the clouds, would only cluck and whisper and hear-see-speak no evil.

So Elvis Presley[9] came, strumming a weird guitar and wagging his tail across the continent, ripping off fame and fortune as he scrunched his way, and, like a latter-day Johnny Appleseed,[1] sowing seeds of a new rhythm and style in the white souls of the white youth of America, whose inner hunger and need was no longer satisfied with the antiseptic white shoes and whiter songs of Pat Boone.[2] "You can do anything," sang Elvis to Pat Boone's white shoes, "but don't you step on my Blue Suede Shoes!"[3]

During this period of ferment and beginnings, at about the same time that the blacks of Montgomery, Alabama, began their historic bus boycott[4] (giving birth to the leadership of Martin Luther King, signifying to the nation that, with this initiative, this first affirmative step, somewhere in the universe a gear in the machinery had shifted), something, a target, came into focus. The tensions in the American psyche had torn a fissure in the racial Maginot Line and through this fissure, this tiny bridge between the Mind and Body, the black masses, who had been silent and somnolent since the '20s and '30s, were now making a break toward the dimly seen light that beckoned to them through the fissure. The fact that these blacks could now take such a step was perceived by the ostriches and owls as a sign of national decay, a sign that the System had caved in at that spot. And this gave birth to a fear, a fear that quickly became a focus for all the anxieties and exasperations in the Omnipotent Administrators' minds; and to embody this perceived decay and act as a lightning rod for the fear, the beatniks[5] bloomed onto the American scene.

3. Refrain from the Beatles's first popular song in America, "She Loves You" (1963).
4. After the theological system of French Protestant reformer John Calvin (1509–1564) whose teachings stressed God's strict power and humans' depravity. Ray Charles (1930–2004), African American singer-songwriter who fused blues, gospel, and rhythm-and-blues into an early version of "soul music" in the 1950s.
5. American "country music," in reference to its many prominent practitioners from Oklahoma.
6. Jazz saxophonist of the 1960s "new wave" celebrated for his virtuosity, experimental zeal, and spiritual dedication (1926–1967).
7. Pleasing, sweet sound.
8. Receiver of stolen goods ("loot").
9. American singer and actor (1935–1977), referred to as the "King of Rock and Roll" after becoming its most popular icon in the 1950s.
1. John Chapman (1774–1851), American pioneer who sowed apple seeds throughout Pennsyl-

vania, Ohio, Illinois, and Indiana, mainly for the production of alcohol.
2. White American singer of the 1950s (b. 1934) who popularized African American songs among white audiences; he was known for his white shoes.
3. "Blue Suede Shoes": rock-and-roll standard written in 1955 by Carl Perkins (1932–1998) and covered by Elvis Presley in 1956; the song became a signature piece of Presley's performances.
4. The Montgomery Bus Boycott (1955–56), a seminal event in the civil rights movement, began when Rosa Parks (1913–2005), an African American seamstress and civil rights activist, refused to obey a bus driver's order that she yield her seat to a white passenger and move to the "colored" section of the vehicle.
5. Popular nickname for the American literary and countercultural movement of the 1950s and early 1960s known as the "Beat Generation."

Like pioneers staking their claims in the no-man's land that lay along the racial Maginot Line, the beatniks, like Elvis Presley before them, dared to do in the light of day what America had long been doing in the sneak-thief anonymity of night—consorted on a human level with the blacks. Reviled, cursed, held in contempt by the "molders of public opinion," persecuted by the police, made into an epithet of derision by the deep-frozen geeks of the Hot-Dog-and-Malted-Milk set, the beatniks irreverently refused to go away. Allen Ginsberg and Jack Kerouac[6] ("the Suzuki rhythm boys," James Baldwin[7] called them, derisively, in a moment of panic, "tired of white ambitions" and "dragging themselves through the Negro street at dawn, looking for an angry fix";[8] "with," as Mailer put it, "the black man's code to fit their facts"). Bing Crosbyism, Perry Comoism, and Dinah Shoreism[9] had led to cancer, and the vanguard of the white youth knew it.

And as the spirit of revolt crept across the continent from that wayward bus in Montgomery, Alabama, seeping like new life into the cracks and nooks of the northern ghettos and sweeping in furious gales across the campuses of southern Negro colleges, erupting, finally, in the sit-ins and freedom rides[1]—as this swirling maelstrom of social change convulsed the nation, shocking an unsuspecting American public, folk music, speaking of fundamental verities, climbed slowly out of the grave; and the hip lobe of the national ear, twitching involuntarily at first, began to listen.

From the moment that Mrs. Rosa Parks, in that bus in Montgomery, Alabama, resisted the Omnipotent Administrator, contact, however fleeting, had been made with the lost sovereignty—the Body had made contact with its Mind—and the shock of that contact sent an electric current throughout this nation, traversing the racial Maginot Line and striking fire in the hearts of the whites. The wheels began to turn, the thaw set in, and though Emmett Till and Mack Parker[2] were dead, though Eisenhower sent troops to Little Rock,[3] though Autherine Lucy's token presence at the University of Alabama[4] was a mockery—notwithstanding this, it was already clear that the 1954 major surgical operation[5] had been successful and the patient would live. The challenge loomed on the horizon: Africa, black, enigmatic, and hard-driving, had begun to parade its newly freed nations into the UN; and the Islam of Elijah Muhammad,[6] amplified as it was fired in salvos

6. Jack Kerouac (1922–1966), writer of the Beat Generation, best known for his experimental novel *On the Road* (1957); Allen Ginsberg (1926–1997), poet of the Beat Generation, best known for his long poem "Howl" (1954).
7. In his essay "The Black Boy Looks at the White Boy" (1961), African American writer James Baldwin (1924–1987) responds to the essay "The White Negro: Superficial Reflections on the Hipster" (1957) by white American writer Norman Mailer (1923–2007).
8. Phrase from the opening of Ginsberg's poem "Howl."
9. Dinah Shore (1916–1994), Perry Como (1912–2002), Bing Crosby (1903–1977): white singers popular in the 1940s and 1950s.
1. Freedom Riders were interracial groups of civil rights activists who defied segregation laws by riding interstate buses into southern states in 1961.
2. Mack Charles Parker (1936–1959): African American man accused of lynching a white woman; Parker was kidnapped and lynched by a white mob in Pearl River County, Mississippi, before he could stand trial. Emmett Louis Till (1941–1955): African American youth murdered near Money, Mississippi, by white men for reportedly flirting with a white woman.
3. When nine African American students seeking to integrate a segregated Little Rock high school faced violence from white mobs, Dwight Eisenhower (1890–1969), 34th president of the United States (1952–60), sent U.S. Army troops to protect them.
4. Autherine Lucy (b. 1939) enrolled at the University of Alabama in 1956 as its first African American student.
5. I.e., the U.S. Supreme Court ruling in *Brown v. Board of Education*.
6. Elijah Muhammad (1897–1985), leader of the Nation of Islam, an African American religious organization popularly known as the Black Muslims.

from the piercing tongue of Malcolm X,[7] was racing through the Negro streets with Allen Ginsberg and Jack Kerouac.

Then, as the verbal revolt of the black masses soared to a cacophonous peak—the Body, the Black Amazons and Supermasculine Menials, becoming conscious, shouting, in a thousand different ways, *"I've got a Mind of my own!"*; and as the senator from Massachusetts[8] was saving the nation from the Strangelove grasp of Dirty Dick,[9] injecting, as he emerged victorious, a new and vivacious spirit into the people with the style of his smile and his wife's hairdo; then, as if a signal had been given, as if the Mind had shouted to the Body, "I'm ready!"—the Twist, superseding the Hula Hoop,[1] burst upon the scene like a nuclear explosion, sending its fallout of rhythm into the Minds and Bodies of the people. The fallout: the Hully Gully, the Mashed Potato, the Dog, the Smashed Banana, the Watusi, the Frug, the Swim.[2] The Twist was a guided missile, launched from the ghetto into the very heart of suburbia. The Twist succeeded, as politics, religion, and law could never do, in writing in the heart and soul what the Supreme Court could only write on the books. The Twist was a form of therapy for a convalescing nation. The Omnipotent Administrator and the Ultrafeminine responded so dramatically, in stampede fashion, to the Twist precisely because it afforded them the possibility of reclaiming their Bodies again after generations of alienated and disembodied existence.

The stiff, mechanical Omnipotent Administrators and Ultrafemines presented a startling spectacle as they entered in droves onto the dance floors to learn how to Twist. They came from every level of society, from top to bottom, writhing pitifully though gamely about the floor, feeling exhilarating and soothing new sensations, release from some unknown prison in which their Bodies had been encased, a sense of freedom they had never known before, a feeling of communion with some mystical root-source of life and vigor, from which sprang a new awareness and enjoyment of the flesh, a new appreciation of the possibilities of their Bodies. They were swinging and gyrating and shaking their dead little asses like petrified zombies trying to regain the warmth of life, rekindle the dead limbs, the cold ass, the stone heart, the stiff, mechanical, disused joints with the spark of life.

This spectacle truly startled many Negroes, because they perceived it as an intrusion by the Mind into the province of the Body, and this intimated chaos; because the Negroes knew, from the survival experience of their everyday lives, that the system within which they were imprisoned was based upon the racial Maginot Line and that the cardinal sin, crossing the line—which was, in their experience, usually initiated from the black side—was being committed, *en masse*, by the whites. The Omnipotent Administrators and Ultrafemines were storming the Maginot Line! A massive assault had been launched without parallel in American history,

---

7. Born Malcolm Little and later known as El-Hajj Malik El-Shabazz, Malcolm X (1925–1965) was an African American political and religious activist who came to prominence as a minister in the Nation of Islam.
8. I.e., John F. Kennedy (1917–1963), U.S. senator from Massachusetts (1952–60), and 35th president of the United States, serving from 1961 until his assassination in 1963.
9. Nickname for Richard M. Nixon (1913–

1994), 37th president of the United States (1968–74) and Kennedy's opponent in the 1960 presidential election. "Strangelove": reference to the 1964 film *Dr. Strangelove*, directed by Stanley Kubrick (1928–1999); the film's eponymous hero is a sometime Nazi nuclear scientist.
1. Plastic toy requiring circular movement of the hips, popular in the mid-1950s.
2. Popular dances of the early 1960s, all influenced by the Twist.

and to Negroes it was confusing. Sure, they had witnessed it on an individual scale: they had seen many ofays[3] destroy the Maginot Line in themselves. But this time it had all the appearances of a national movement. There were even rumors that President Kennedy and his Jackie[4] were doing the Twist secretly in the White House; that their Number One Boy[5] had been sent to the Peppermint Lounge[6] in disguise to learn how to Twist, and he in turn brought the trick back to the White House. These Negroes knew that something fundamental had changed.

"Man, what done got into them ofays?" one asked.

"They trying to get back," said another.

"Shit," said a young Negro who made his living by shoplifting. "If you ask me, I think it must be the end of the world."

"Oooo-weee!" said a Negro musician who had been playing at a dance and was now standing back checking the dancers. "Baby, I don't dig this action at all! Look here, baby, pull my coat to[7] what's going down! I mean, have I missed it somewhere? Where've I been? Baby, I been blowing[8] all my life and I ain't never dug no happenings like this. You know what, man, I'm gon' cut that fucking weed[9] aloose. Oooo-weee! Check that little bitch right there! What the fuck she trying to do? Is she trying to shake it or break it? Oooo-weee!"

A Negro girl said: "Take me home, I'm sick!"

Another one said: "No, let's stay! This is too much!"

And a bearded Negro cat,[1] who was not interested in learning how to Twist himself, who felt that if he was interested in doing it, he could get up from the table right now and start Twisting, he said, sitting at the table with a tinsel-minded female:[2] "It ain't nothing. They just trying to get back, that's all."

"Get back?" said the girl, arching her brows quizzically, "Get back from where?"

"From wherever they've been," said the cat, "where else?"

"Are they doing it in Mississippi is what I want to know," said a tall, deadly looking Negro who had a long razor line down his left cheek and who had left Mississippi in a hurry one night.

And the dancers: they were caught up in a whirl of ecstasy, swinging like pendulums, mechanical like metronomes or puppets on invisible strings being manipulated by a master with a sick sense of humor. "They look like Chinese doing communal exercise," said a Negro. "That's all they're doing, calisthenics!"

"Yeah," said his companion. "They're trying to get in shape."

But if at first it was funny and confusing, it was nonetheless a breakthrough. The Omnipotent Administrators and Ultrafeminines were discovering new aspects of the Body, new possibilities of rhythm, new ways to move. The Hula Hoop had been a false start, a mechanized, theatrical attempt by the Mind to supply to itself what only the Body can give. But,

3. Derogatory term for whites (slang).
4. Jacqueline Lee "Jackie" Bouvier Kennedy Onassis (1929–1994), wife of John F. Kennedy, known for her fashionable dress and hairstyles, and for her impeccable public bearing as First Lady.
5. Possibly Robert F. Kennedy (1925–1968), brother of the president who served as U.S. attorney general during the Kennedy administration.
6. Popular discotheque in New York City from 1958 to 1965 that helped launch the Twist as a dance craze; Jackie Kennedy arranged a temporary "Peppermint Lounge" in the White House.
7. I.e., inform me about (slang).
8. Playing a wind instrument (slang).
9. Marijuana (slang).
1. Black male; here, specifically a jazz aficionado.
2. Woman obsessed with jewelry and fashion.

with the Twist, at last they knew themselves to be swinging.[3] The forces acting upon the world stage in our era had created, in the collective psyche of the Omnipotent Administrators and Ultrafeminines, an irresistible urge—to just stand up and shake the ice and cancer out of their alienated white asses—and the Hula Hoop and Twist offered socially acceptable ways to do it.

Of course, not all the whites took part in these joyful experiments. For many, the more "suggestive" a dance became—i.e., the more it became pure Body and less Mind—the more scandalous it seemed to them; and their reaction in this sense was an index to the degree of their alienation from their Bodies. But what they condemned as a sign of degeneracy and moral decay was actually a sign of health, a sign of hope for full recovery. As Norman Mailer prophesied: ". . . the Negro's equality would tear a profound shift into the psychology, the sexuality, and the moral imagination of every white alive."[4] Precisely because the Mind will have united with the Body, theory will have merged with practice.

It is significant that the Twist and the Hula Hoop came into the scene in all their fury at the close of the Eisenhower and the dawn of the Kennedy era. It could be interpreted as a rebellion against the vacuous Eisenhower years. It could also be argued that the same collective urge that gave rise to the Twist also swept Kennedy into office. I shudder to think that, given the closeness of the final vote in 1960,[5] Richard Nixon might have won the election in a breeze if he had persuaded one of his Ultrafeminine daughters, not to mention Ultrapat,[6] to do the Twist in public. Not if Kennedy had stayed on the phone a week sympathizing with Mrs. Martin Luther King, Jr.,[7] over the fact that the cat was in jail, would he have won. Even as I am convinced that Luci Baines Johnson,[8] dancing the Watusi in public with Killer Joe Piro,[9] won more votes for her old man in 1964 than a whole boxcar full of his hog-calling speeches ever did.

When the Birmingham Revolt erupted in the summer of 1963[1] and President Kennedy stepped into the void and delivered his unprecedented speech to the nation on civil rights[2] and sent his bill to Congress, the foundation had been completed. Martin Luther King, Jr.,[3] giving voice to the needs of the Body, and President Kennedy, speaking out the needs of the Mind, made contact on that day. The Twisters, sporting their blue suede shoes, moved beyond the ghost in white shoes who ate a Hot Dog and sipped Malted Milk as he danced the mechanical jig of Satan on top of Medgar Evers'[4] tomb. In vain now would the murderers bomb that church and

3. Lively with pleasure and sophistication (slang).

4. Quotation from "The White Negro."

5. The Kennedy-Nixon election was the closest in modern history until 2000; many interpreters saw Kennedy's telegenic charm defeating the rigidity of Nixon's public persona.

6. I.e., Pat Nixon (1912–1993), wife of Richard Nixon.

7. I.e., Coretta Scott King (1927–2006).

8. Younger daughter of President Lyndon B. Johnson (b. 1947).

9. Frank "Killer Joe" Piro (1921–1989), high-society dance instructor who popularized such 1960s dances as the Twist and the Watusi among white celebrities.

1. I.e., the series of protests in Birmingham, Alabama, that were contributions to passage of the Civil Rights Act of 1964, which outlawed major forms of racial segregation.

2. On June 11, 1963, President Kennedy delivered his Civil Rights Address, in which he proposed what was to become the 1964 Civil Rights Act.

3. African American clergyman, civil rights leader, and co-founder of the Southern Christian Leadership Conference. King (1929–1968) congratulated Kennedy on his speech, calling it "one of the most eloquent, profound, and unequivocal pleas for justice and the freedom of all men ever made by any president."

4. Medgar Wiley Evers (1925–1963), African American civil rights activist involved in the integration of the University of Mississippi, was assassinated by a white supremacist just hours after Kennedy's speech.

slaughter grotesquely those four little black girls[5] (what did they hope to kill? were they striking at the black of the skin or the fire of the soul? at history? at the Body?). In vain also the assassins' bullets that crashed through the head of John Kennedy, taking a life, yes, but creating a larger-than-life and failing utterly to expunge from the record the March on Washington[6] and its truth: that this nation—bourgeois or not, imperialist or not, murderous or not, ugly or not—its people, somewhere in their butchered and hypocritical souls, still contained an epic potential of spirit which is its hope, a bottomless potential which fires the imaginations of its youth. It was all too late. It was too late because it was time for the blacks ("I've got a *Mind* of my own!") to riot, to sweep through the Harlem night like a wave of locusts, breaking, screaming, bleeding, laughing, crying, rejoicing, celebrating, in a jubilee of destruction, to regurgitate the white man's bullshit they'd been eating for four hundred years; smashing the windows of the white man's stores, throwing bricks they wished were bombs, running, leaping whirling like a cyclone through the white man's Mind, past his backlash, through the night streets of Rochester, New Jersey, Philadelphia.[7] And even though the opposition, gorging on Hot Dogs and Malted Milk, with blood now splattered over the white shoes, would still strike out in the dark against the manifestations of the turning, showing the protocol of Southern Hospitality reserved for Niggers and Nigger Lovers—SCHWERNER–CHANEY–GOODMAN[8]—it was still too late. For not only had Luci Baines Johnson danced the Watusi in public with Killer Joe, but the Beatles were on the scene,[9] injecting Negritude by the ton into the whites, in this post–Elvis Presley–beatnik era of ferment.

Before we toss the Beatles a homosexual kiss—saying, "If a man be ass enough to reach for the bitch in them, that man will kiss a man, and if a woman reaches for the stud in them, that woman will kiss a woman"[1]—let us marvel at the genius of their image, which comforts the owls and ostriches in the one spot where Elvis Presley bummed their kick: Elvis, with his *un*funky (yet mechanical, alienated) bumpgrinding,[2] was still too much Body (too soon) for the strained collapsing psyches of the Omnipotent Administrators and Ultrafeminines; whereas the Beatles, affecting the caucasoid[3] crown of femininity and ignoring the Body on the visual plane (while their music on the contrary being full of Body), assuaged the doubts of the owls and ostriches by presenting an incorporeal, cerebral image.

Song and dance are, perhaps, only a little less old than man himself. It is with his music and dance, the recreation through art of the rhythms suggested by and implicit in the tempo of his life and cultural environment,

---

5. Reference to the September 15, 1963, bombing of the 16th Street Baptist Church in Birmingham, Alabama, that killed four African American girls, a turning point in the civil rights movement that contributed to passage of the Civil Rights Act of 1964.
6. The March on Washington for Jobs and Freedom occurred on August 28, 1963, culminating in Martin Luther King Jr.'s "I Have a Dream" speech; on November 22 of that year, President Kennedy was assassinated in Dallas, Texas.
7. Racial rebellions (or "riots") took place in Harlem, Rochester, and Philadelphia in 1964, and in Newark, New Jersey, in 1967.
8. Andrew Goodman (1943–1964), Michael Schwerner (1939–1964), and James Earl Chaney (1943–1964) were civil rights workers murdered

during "Freedom Summer" of 1964 when helping African Americans in Philadelphia, Mississippi, register to vote. Goodman and Schwerner were white; Chaney was black.
9. "Beatlemania" began with the band's 1964 tour of the United States.
1. Possible play on Leviticus 20.13: "If a man also lies with a man, as he lies with a woman, both of them have committed an abomination: they shall surely be put to death; their blood shall be upon them."
2. Sexually suggestive dancing; "*un*funky": not soulful; "bummed their kick": saddened their pleasure (slang).
3. Characteristic of the white, so-called Caucasian race.

that man purges his soul of the tensions of daily strife and maintains his harmony in the universe. In the increasingly mechanized, automated, cybernated[4] environment of the modern world—a cold, bodiless world of wheels, smooth plastic surfaces, tubes, pushbuttons, transistors, computers, jet propulsion, rockets to the moon, atomic energy—man's need for affirmation of his biology has become that much more intense. He feels need for a clear definition of where his body ends and the machine begins, where man ends and the *extensions* of man begin. This great mass hunger, which transcends national or racial boundaries, recoils from the subtle subversions of the mechanical environment which modern technology is creating faster than man, with his present savage relationship to his fellow men, is able to receive and assimilate. This is the central contradiction of the twentieth century; and it is against this backdrop that America's attempt to unite its Mind with its Body, to save its soul, is taking place.

It is in this connection that the blacks, personifying the Body and thereby in closer communion with their biological roots than other Americans, provide the saving link, the bridge between man's biology and man's machines. In its purest form, as adjustment to the scientific and technological environment of our era, as purgative and lullaby-soother of man's soul, it is the jazz issuing from the friction and harmony of the American Negro with his environment that captured the beat and tempo of our times. And although modern science and technology are the same whether in New York, Paris, London, Accra, Cairo, Berlin, Moscow, Tokyo, Peking, or São Paulo, jazz is the only true international medium of communication current in the world today, capable of speaking creatively, with equal intensity and relevance, to the people in all those places.

The less sophisticated (but no less Body-based) popular music of urban Negroes—which was known as Rhythm and Blues before the whites appropriated and distilled it into a product they called Rock 'n' Roll—is the basic ingredient, the core, of the gaudy, cacophonous hymns with which the Beatles of Liverpool drive their hordes of Ultrafeminine fans into catatonia[5] and hysteria. For Beatle fans, having been alienated from their own Bodies so long and so deeply, the effect of these potent, erotic rhythms is electric. Into this music, the Negro projected—as it were, *drained off*, as pus from a sore—a powerful sensuality, his pain and lust, his love and his hate, his ambition and his despair. The Negro projected into his music his very Body. The Beatles, the four long-haired lads from Liverpool, are offering up as their gift the Negro's Body, and in so doing establish a rhythmic communication between the listener's own Mind and Body.

Enter the Beatles—soul by proxy, middlemen between the Mind and the Body. A long way from Pat Boone's White Shoes. A way station on a slow route traveled with all deliberate speed.[6]

1968

4. Computerized.
5. Trance-like state of rigidity.
6. Allusion to the 1955 Supreme Court ruling *Griffin v. County School Board of Prince Edward County*, which reinforced the 1954 *Brown v. Board of Education* decision by mandating that desegregation of the nation's schools proceed with "all deliberate speed."

A. B. SPELLMAN
b. 1935

I n keeping with James Stewart's claim that music for the Black Arts movement was the site of a revolutionary black aesthetic, for A. B. Spellman African American music is both a "weapon of survival" for black culture and a resource for artistic *and* social self-determination. In his essay "Not Just Whistling Dixie," Spellman suggests that slave music proved "it was possible to dance in chains." Accordingly, aesthetics and politics are always woven together for Spellman, providing the common thread uniting his multiple engagements with music, poetry, editing, sociology, education, and social activism.

Born in 1935 in Nixonton, a hamlet outside of Elizabeth City, North Carolina, Spellman was early introduced to art, performance, and teaching; both his parents were teachers and his father was also a painter. Traveling blues and jazz music troupes in his childhood initiated him into the experience of being an attentive audience for music and vernacular performance.

Spellman left these modest but nourishing origins for Howard University in 1952, where he met classmates LeRoi Jones (Amiri Baraka), dramatist Joseph Walker, and poet Lucille Clifton; he took theater courses with Owen Dodson and Arthur Davis, and numerous literature courses with Sterling Brown, with whom Spellman deepened his appreciation of the relation between literature, jazz, and cultural vision. He was also active in the Howard Players theater ensemble and led informal writing groups with Baraka and others.

In 1958 Spellman left Howard with a B.A. in political science and history, in addition to having begun courses in law; urged by Baraka, he made his way to New York City, where he joined the Beat community and later, also with Baraka, became increasingly engaged in black nationalist artistic projects. In 1963 he began reviewing music in *Kulchur*, the journal for which Baraka had just enlisted Frank O'Hara as art editor. O'Hara would later write the introduction to Spellman's single book of poetry, *The Beautiful Days* (1965), proclaiming that Spellman's poems were "lean, strong, sexy poems" that cut "through a lot of contemporary nonsense to what is actually happening to him." In the early 1960s Spellman also helped found the journal *Umbra* and, with Baraka and Larry Neal, worked on *Cricket*, a magazine dedicated to African American music and black nationalism.

In 1966 Spellman published his most influential work, *Four Lives in the Bebop Business*, a study that profiles jazz musicians Cecil Taylor, Ornette Coleman, Herbie Nicholas, and Jackie McLean in order to "tell what it means to be a black artist in America." As an exploration of the economic, social, and political entanglements of jazz and American culture it has few peers.

After moving to Atlanta, Spellman began teaching courses in poetry, creative writing, and African American literature and culture at Emory, Morehouse, and Atlanta University Center, and (later) at Rutgers and Harvard Universities. In 1968 he contributed poems and an essay to the energetic and radical collective manifesto of the Black Arts movement, *Black Fire: An Anthology of Afro-American Writing*, edited by Baraka and Neal. As he continued editing various experimental journals and writing reviews and poems in magazines (such as *Ebony*, *Jazz*, and *Downbeat*), he founded the Atlanta Center for the Black Arts, the first project in what would become a lifetime commitment to the social praxis of arts accessibility, appreciation, and pedagogy. Departing from Harvard in 1973, Spellman joined the National Endowment for the Arts, first as director of the Arts in Education study project and two years later in the NEA Expansion Arts Program, for which he worked tirelessly until his retirement in April 2005.

The best of Spellman's poetry is saturated by and continually interrogates the complex interactions of poetry, jazz, communal resistance, loss, and social transformation that Spellman acted out in his life. "Did John's Music Kill Him?"—a particularly challenging formulation of the Black Arts genre known as "the Coltrane poem"—imagines the loss of the saxophonist John Coltrane as also a loss of black communal presence. The poet seeks to recapture in Coltrane's absence an agency of expressive, assertive, and emancipatory black expression. In "Did John's Music Kill Him?" we witness Spellman speaking at the crossroads of poetic song text and musical performance, seeking a voice capable of articulating a communal aspiration from within a moment of personal struggle.

Did John's[1] Music Kill Him?

in the morning part
of evening he would stand
before his crowd. the voice
would call his name &
redlight fell around him.   5
jimmy'd bow a quarter hour
till Mccoy fed block chords[2]
to his stroke, elvin's[3] thunder
roll & eric's[4] scream. then john.

then john. *little old lady*   10
had a nasty mouth. *summertime*
when the war is. *africa*[5] ululating[6]
a line bunched up like itself
into knots paints beauty black.

trane's horn had words in it   15
i know when i sleep sober & dream
those dreams i duck in the world
of sun & shadow. yet even in the day john
& a little grass[7] put them on me clear
as tomorrow in a glass enclosure.   20

kill me john my life eats
life. The thing that beats out of
me happens in a vat enclosed
& fermenting & wanting to explode
like your song.   25

---

1. John Coltrane (1926–1967), avant-garde jazz saxophonist known as "Trane."
2. A series of unadorned chords, usually rich in dissonance, arranged in widely spaced intervals of equal length.
3. The members of Coltrane's quartet. Jimmy Garrison (1934–1976), double bass player. McCoy Tyner (b. 1938), pianist. Elvin Jones (b. 1927), drummer.

4. Eric Dolphy (1928–1964), jazz clarinetist, saxophonist, and flutist who sometimes played with Coltrane.
5. "Africa," "Summertime," "Little Old Lady": Coltrane compositions first released in 1961 on the albums *Africa/Brass, My Favorite Things*, and *Coltrane Jazz*, respectively.
6. Shrill, wordless wailing.
7. Marijuana (slang).

so beat john's death words down
on me in the darker part
of evening. the black light issued
from him in the pit he made
around us. worms came clear   30
to me where i thought i had been
brilliant. o john death will
not contain you death
will not contain you

1969

JUNE JORDAN
1936–2002

Like her life of multiple identities and commitments ("I am Black and I am female and I am a mother and I am bisexual and I am a nationalist and I am an anti-nationalist. And I mean to be fully and freely all that I am!"), June Jordan's writings consist of myriad voices that together rebuke injustice and violation, resist the reduction of identity to categories, affirm communal and personal self-determination, and yearn for liberation. These voices come to sing and to scream, to orchestrate lyrical encounters with sharp-edged realities, while simultaneously putting themselves into question, persistently negotiating the complex relations between self and other, poetic expression and political struggle, aesthetic possibility and communal confrontation.

Jordan was born in Harlem, New York, on July 9, 1936, to Granville and Mildred Jordan, Jamaican natives who had escaped a life of poverty by emigrating to the United States. Despite their pride in their new American identity, the Jordans also had to contend with the racial tensions of their new country. Jordan's upbringing as a first-generation American in the black urban ghetto had a distinct influence on her writings, as did her tumultuous home life. In her essays and poems, she details her turbulent relationship with her father, who referred to her as "he," projecting his desire for a son instead of a daughter. In *Soldier: A Poet's Childhood* (2001), Jordan vividly recalls the alternating volatility and tenderness of the first twelve years of her life, including the abuse she often suffered at the hands of her father: "Like a growling beast, the roll-away mahogany doors rumble open, and the light snaps on and a fist smashes into the side of my head and I am screaming awake: 'Daddy! What did I do?!'" But Jordan's father, an admirer of black nationalist Marcus Garvey, also instilled in her a passion for literature and awareness of racial politics that mirrored his own; as a child, she read religious verse, Shakespeare, Edgar Allan Poe, and Paul Laurence Dunbar.

Jordan was also profoundly influenced by the limits of her mother's life, especially her mother's thwarted desire to be an artist. In poems such as "Getting Down to Get Over" (1977) and in the essay "Many Rivers to Cross" (1985), Jordan places her mother's life and eventual suicide in the context of the long-neglected history of black women everywhere: "momma / help me / turn the face of history *to your face*." Throughout her career Jordan sought to redress that neglect, critiquing versions of Western feminism that do not adequately consider issues of race, class, or motherhood.

It was during the early 1960s that Jordan began publishing poems, stories, and essays (under the name June Meyer, having married Michael Meyer, a white anthropology student at Columbia University she met while earning her B.A. at Barnard) in *Esquire*, *The Nation*, *Evergreen Review*, *Partisan Review*, *Black World*, *Black Creation*, *Essence*, the *Village Voice*, the *New York Times*, and elsewhere. The Harlem Riot of 1964 was a turning point for Jordan's commitment to blending activism and art. After the riot, Jordan was "filled with hatred for everything and everyone white," further concretizing her commitment to the Black Arts and Black Power movements: "This is a battle I have attempted to help define, and forward as though my own life depended on its success. In truth, my life does depend on the outcome of our Black struggles for freedom to be ourselves, in self-respecting self-sufficiency." But learning to struggle without hatred is the source from which sprang the best of Jordan's early poetry: reflections on the Harlem Riot were the occasion, Jordan writes, when "I resolved not to run on hatred but, instead, to use what I loved, words, for the sake of the people I loved." That resolution, however, was itself always a struggle, since it bore—in the very (white English) language of its utterance—the wounds of rupture, loss, division, violence, and the consciousness of exile: "But as a Black poet and writer, I hate words that cancel my name and my history and the freedom of my future: I hate the words that condemn and refuse the language of my people in America."

Driven by this tension within the very words she employed as weapons against oppression, Jordan examined throughout her work the relationship between power and language, particularly the quality of resistance embodied in black English. Jordan championed black English in much of her writing, celebrating its beauty and its efficacy most notably in her first novel, *His Own Where* (1970), which was written entirely in black English twelve years before Alice Walker's better known novel *The Color Purple* (1982). In response to attacks on the language of *His Own Where*, Jordan published the incisive essay "White English / Black English: The Politics of Translation," declaring that any longing for black self-determination must disrupt the hegemony of "standard" (i.e., white) English and assert black English as the medium of autonomous blackness: "Language is political. That's why you and me, my Brother and my Sister, that's why we sposed to choke our natural self into the weird, lying, barbarous, unreal, white speech and writing habits that the school lay down like holy law. Because, in other words, the powerful don't play; they mean to keep that power, and those who are the powerless (you and me) better shape up— mimic/ape/suck—in the very image of the powerful, or the powerful will destroy you—you and our children." And yet she observes, too, that the resisting power of black language—"magical and basic and irresistible"—is also the possibility of loss, suffering, fragmentation; and thus language for Jordan becomes the embattled, scarred, and disfigured terrain of the confrontation between transcendental yearning and functional, material struggle, a continuous "process of translation"—in short, "a political process" in which rupture and redress, loss and love, privation and purpose perpetually mix.

Fittingly, then, descriptions of Jordan's life and writing emphasize her determination to defy easy categorization. The sentiment is exemplified in one of her most famous poems, "Poem about My Rights," with its defiant refrain: "I am not wrong: Wrong is not my name / My name is my own my own my own." Such clear-cut resistance to labeling, to any kind of censorship or limitation, is also central to Jordan's second essay collection, *On Call* (1985), which focuses on worldwide liberation struggles in places such as Palestine, Nicaragua, and South Africa. Jordan's courageous public stands on the causes she championed often incited controversy; in the early 1980s, for instance, major media outlets and her own publisher refused to print her work because she adamantly supported the Palestinian liberation movement.

Pivotal to Jordan's writing career was her commensurate role as an educator. From children's writing workshops in Brooklyn to her final post as professor of African American studies and women's studies at the University of California at Berkeley, the classroom served as a vital performative and pedagogical space for Jordan's political activism and literary inspiration. As founding director of Berkeley's successful Poetry for the People program, Jordan worked with undergraduates and high school students, encouraging them to use poetry as a tool for self-expression and self-empowerment.

From activism to teaching and to writing, all of June Jordan's endeavors were informed by her philosophical assertions that our lives are "an intimate face of universal struggle" and that "by declaring the truth, you create truth." At the same time, Jordan moved among positions of black nationalism; international feminism; gay, lesbian, and bi-sexual activism; and neo-Marxism, always trying to confound any perspective that would not take dynamic account of the ways in which power is inscribed within the complex relations of race, class, gender, and sexuality. Thus Jordan's writing moves constantly between subjective and objective experience, articulating differing claims in mutual implication: "You begin with your family and the kids on the block, and next you open your eyes to what you call your people and that leads you into land reform into Black English into Angola leads you back to your own bed where you lie by yourself, wondering if you deserve to be peaceful, or trusted or desired or left to the freedom of your own unfaltering heart." Both self-questioning and provocatively assertive, Jordan's narrative takes place in a language that is itself articulated in many accents and different dialects, in both "black" and "white" English, taking place in both local and global frameworks.

Even amid controversy and failing health, Jordan remained a strong, passionate, and vibrant presence in the literary world. She received numerous awards and honors for her work and activism throughout her lifetime, including a 1972 National Book Award nomination for *His Own Where*, the National Association of Black Journalists Award, and various fellowships from the Massachusetts Council of the Arts, the National Endowment for the Arts, and the New York Foundation for the Arts. She was also awarded the Distinguished Alumna Award from Barnard in 1997.

June Jordan died of breast cancer at her home in Berkeley on June 14, 2002. During one of her final public speaking engagements, at the thirtieth anniversary celebration of Barnard's Center for Research on Women in 2001, Jordan read from the title poem of her last book, *Some of Us Did Not Die* (2002). In the poem she invokes the image of a Nietzschean predatory hawk swooping over her dying body: "He makes that dive / to savage / me / and inches / from the blood flood lusty / beak / I roll away / I speak / I laugh out loud / Not yet / big bird of prey / not yet."

In Memoriam: Martin Luther King, Jr.[1]

I

honey people murder mercy U.S.A.
the milkland turn to monsters teach
to kill to violate pull down destroy
the weakly freedom growing fruit
from being born   5

America

tomorrow yesterday rip rape
exacerbate despoil disfigure

---

1. Co-founder of the Southern Christian Leadership Conference and civil rights leader (1929–1968); Jordan wrote this poem shortly after King's assassination in April 1968.

crazy running threat the
deadly thrall
appall belief dispel
the wildlife burn the breast
the onward tongue
the outward hand
deform the normal rainy
riot sunshine shelter wreck
of darkness derogate
delimit blank
explode deprive
assassinate and batten up
like bullets fatten up
the raving greed
reactivate a springtime
terrorizing

death by men by more
than you or I can

STOP

II

They sleep who know a regulated place
or pulse or tide or changing sky
according to some universal
stage direction obvious
like shorewashed shells

we share an afternoon of mourning
in between no next predictable
except for wild reversal hearse rehearsal
bleach the blacklong lunging
ritual of fright insanity and more
deplorable abortion
more and
more

1968

Gettin Down to Get Over

Dedicated to my mother

MOMMA MOMMA MOMMA
momma momma
mammy
nanny
granny
woman
mistress
sista

luv

blackgirl
slavegirl

gal

honeychile
sweetstuff
sugar
sweetheart
baby
Baby Baby

MOMMA MOMMA
Black Momma
Black bitch
Black pussy
piecea tail
nice piecea ass

hey daddy! hey
bro!
we walk together (an')
talk together (an')
dance and *do*
(together)
dance and do/hey!
daddy!
bro!
hey!
nina nikki nonni nommo nommo[1]
momma Black
Momma

Black Woman
Black
Female Head of Household
Black Matriarchal Matriarchy
Black Statistical
Lowlife Lowlevel Lowdown
Lowdown and *up*
to be Low-down
Black Statistical
Low Factor
Factotem
Factitious Fictitious
Figment Figuring in Lowdown Lyin
Annual Reports[2]

10

15

20

25

30

35

40

45

50

---

1. Originally referring to hermaphroditic ancestral spirits worshipped by the Dogon in Mali,
nommo came to denote the transformative power
of speech among African and African American

social movements of the 1960s and 1970s.
2. The references in this stanza are to
government-agency reports on low-income
citizens.

Black Woman/Black
Hallelujah Saintly
patient
smilin
humble   55
givin thanks
for
Annual Reports and
Monthly Dole[3]   60
and
Friday night
and
(*good* God!)
Monday mornin: Black and Female   65
martyr masochist
(A BIG WHITE LIE)
Momma Momma

What does Mothafuckin mean?
WHO'S THE MOTHAFUCKA   70
FUCKED MY MOMMA
messed yours over
and right now
be trippin on[4] my starveblack
female soul   75
a macktruck[5]
mothafuck
the first primordial
the paradig/digmatic
dogmatistic mothafucka who   80
is he?
hey!
momma momma

dry eyes on the
shy/dark/hidden/cryin Black   85
face
of the loneliness
the rape
the brokeup mailbox
an' no western union roses[6]   90
come inside the kitchen
and no poem
take you through the whole night
and no big
Black   95
burly
hand
be holdin yours

---

3. Government welfare.
4. "Trippin on": becoming angry at.
5. Anything large (after the Mack brand of commercial trucks).

6. The Western Union telegram company introduced gift telegrams with candy and flowers in the 1960s.

to have to hold onto
no   100
big Black burly hand
no nommo
no Black prince
come riding from the darkness
on a beautiful black horse   105
no bro
no daddy

"I was sixteen when I met my father.
In a bar.
In Baltimore.   110
He told me who he was
and what he does.
Paid for the drinks.
I looked.
I listened.   115
And I left him.
It was civil
perfectly
and absolute bull
shit.   120
The drinks was leakin waterweak
and never got down to my knees."

hey daddy
what they been and done to you
and what you been and done   125
to me
to momma
momma momma
hey
sugar daddy   130
big daddy
sweet daddy
Black Daddy
The Original Father Divine[7]
the everlovin   135
deep
tall
bad
buck[8]   140
jive[9]
cold
strut
bop[1]
split   145
tight

7. Reverend Major Jealous Divine (1876–1967),
African American spiritual leader.
8. Racial slur for black man, connoting an irredeemably violent, rude, lecherous rebel against
white authority.
9. Sly, clever, or deceitful (slang).
1. Rebellious (after the 1940s avant-garde jazz
form called "Bebop").

loose
close
hot
hot
hot   150
sweet SWEET DADDY
WHERE YOU BEEN AND
WHEN YOU COMIN BACK TO ME
HEY
WHEN YOU COMIN BACK   155
TO MOMMA
momma momma

And Suppose He Finally Say
"Look, Baby.
I Loves Me Some   160
Everything about You.
Let Me Be Your Man."
That reach around the hurtin
like a dream.
And I ain never wakin up   165
from that one.
momma momma
momma momma

                         II

Consider the Queen   170

hand on her hip
sweat restin from
the corn/bean/greens' field
steamy under the pale/sly
suffocatin sun   175

Consider the Queen

she fix the cufflinks
on his Sunday shirt
and fry some chicken
bake some cake
and tell the family   180
"Never mine about the bossman
don' know how a human
bein spozed to act. Jus'
never mind about him.
Wash your face.   185
Sit down. And let
the good Lord bless this table."

Consider the Queen

her babies pullin at the nipples   190
pullin at the momma milk

the infant fingers gingerly
approach caress the
soft/Black/swollen/momma breast

and there   195
inside the mommasoft
life-spillin treasure chest
the heart
breaks

rage by grief by sorrow   200
weary weary
breaks
breaks quiet
silently
the weary sorrow   205
quiet now the furious
the adamant the broken
busted beaten down and beaten up
the beaten beaten beaten
weary heart beats   210
tender-steady
and the babies suck/
the seed of blood
and love glows at the
soft/Black/swollen momma breast   215

Consider the Queen

she works when she works
in the laundry *in jail*
in the school house *in jail*
in the office *in jail*   220
on the soap box *in jail*
on the desk
on the floor
on the street
on the line[2]   225
at the door
lookin fine
at the head of the line
steppin sharp from behind
in the light   230
with a song
wearing boots
or a belt
and a gun
drinkin wine when it's time   235
when the long week is done
but she works when she works
in the laundry in jail
she works when she works

2. I.e., factory assembly line.

Consider the Queen 240

she sleeps when she sleeps
with the king in the kingdom
she
sleeps when she sleeps
with the wall 245
with whatever it is who happens
to call
with me and with you
(to survive you make
do/you explore more and more) 250
so she sleeps when she sleeps
a really deep sleep

Consider the Queen

a full/Black/glorious/a purple rose
aroused by the tiger breathin 255
beside her
a shell with the moanin
of ages inside her
a hungry one feedin the folk
what they need 260

Consider the Queen.

III

Blackman
let that white girl go
She know what you ought to know.
(By now.) 265

IV

MOMMA MOMMA
momma momma
family face
face of the family alive
momma 270
mammy
momma
woman
sista
baby 275
luv

the house on fire/
poison waters/
earthquake/
and the air a nightmare/ 280
turn

turn
turn around the
national gross product[3]
growin   285
really gross/turn
turn
turn the pestilence away
the miserable killers
and Canarsie   290
Alabama[4]
people beggin to be people
warfare on the welfare
of the folk/
hey   295
turn
turn away
the trickbag[5] university/the
trickbag propaganda/
trickbag   300
tricklins of prosperity/of
pseudo-"status"
lynchtree necklace
on the strong
round   305
neck of you
my momma
momma momma
turn away
the f.b.i./the state police/the cops/   310
the/everyone of the
infest/incestuous investigators
into you
and Daddy/into us
hey   315
turn
my mother
turn
the face of history
to your own   320
and please be smilin
if you can
be smilin
at the family

momma momma   325

let the funky[6] forecast
be the last
one we will ever
want to listen to

---

3. Gross National Product (GNP), the value of all labor and goods produced nationally each year.
4. The Canarsie subway line in Brooklyn emerges at Alabama Avenue.
5. Deceptively scheming.
6. Weird eccentric, pungent.

And Daddy see 330
the stars fall down
and burn a light
into the singin
darkness of your eyes
my Daddy 335
my Blackman
you take my body in
your arms/you use
the oil of coconuts/of trees and
flowers/fish and new fruits 340
from the new world
to enflame me in this otherwise
cold place
please

meanwhile 345
momma
momma momma
teach me how to kiss
the king within the kingdom
teach me how to t.c.b.[7]/to make do 350
and be
like you
teach me to survive my
momma
teach me how to hold a new life 355
momma
help me
turn the face of history
to your face.

1972

From The Talking Back of Miss Valentine Jones: *Poem # One*

well I wanted to braid my hair
bathe and bedeck my
self so fine
so fully aforethought for
your pleasure 5
see:
I wanted to travel and read
and runaround fantastic
into war and peace:
I wanted to 10
surf
dive
fly
climb
conquer 15
and be conquered

7. Take care of business.

THEN
I wanted to pickup the phone
and find you asking me
if I might possibly be alone   20
some night
(so I could answer cool
as the jewels I would wear
on bareskin for your
digmedaddy delectation[1]:)   25
"WHEN
you comin ova?"
But
I had to remember to write down
margarine on the list   30
and shoepolish and a can of
sliced pineapples in casea company
and a quarta skim milk cause Teresa's
gainin weight and don' nobody groove on[2]
that much   35
girl
and next I hadta sort for darks and lights before
the laundry hit the water which I had
to kind a keep a eye on be-
cause if the big hose jumps the sink again that   40
Mrs. Thompson gointa come upstairs
and brain me with a mop don' smell too
nice even though she hang
it headfirst out the winda
and I had to check   45
on William like to
burn hisself to death with fever
boy so thin be
callin all day "Momma! Sing to me?"
"Ma! Am I gone die?" and me not   50
wake enough to sit beside him longer than
to wipeaway the sweat or change the sheets/
his shirt and feed him orange
juice before I fall out sleep and
Sweet My Jesus ain but one can   55
left
and we not thru the afternoon
and now
you (temporarily) shownup with a thing
you say's a poem and you   60
call it
"Will The Real Miss Black America Standup?"[3]

                    guilty po' mouth[4]
                    about duty beauties of my

---

1. Delight; "digmedaddy": playful call for attention from a male lover.
2. Find pleasure in.
3. Parody of the signature line from the television game show "To Tell the Truth" (1956–2002),
in which a panel of celebrities attempted to guess
the identity or occupation of a "mystery guest."
4. To poor mouth: claim impoverishment, regardless of one's actual financial status.

headrag   65
boozedup doozies[5] about
never mind
cause love is blind

well
I can't use it headrag   70

and the very next bodacious[6] Blackman
call me queen
because my life ain shit
because (in any case) he ain been here to share it
with me headrag   75
(dish for dish and do for do and
dream for dream)
I'm gone scream him out my house
be-
cause what I wanted was headrag   80
to braid my hair/bathe and bedeck my
self so fully be-
cause what I wanted was
your love
not pity headrag   85
be-
cause what I wanted was
your love
your love

                                                    1976

Poem about Police Violence

Tell me something
what you think would happen if
everytime they kill a black boy
then we kill a cop
everytime they kill a black man
then we kill a cop   5

you think the accident rate would lower
subsequently?

sometimes the feeling like amaze me baby
comes back to my mouth and I am quiet   10
like Olympian pools[1] from the running the
mountainous snows under the sun

sometimes thinking about the 12th House of the Cosmos[2]
or the way your ear ensnares the tip

---

5. "Boozedup doozies": crazy drunkards.
6. Awesome (African American slang).
1. River pools on Mount Olympus, sacred summit of the gods in Greek mythology.

2. In astrology, the sphere of life associated with transition from dreams to reality, connected also with sacrifices, prisons, betrayals, and self-undoings.

of my tongue or signs that I have never seen   15
like DANGER WOMEN WORKING

I lose consciousness of ugly bestial rabid
and repetitive affront as when they tell me
18 cops in order to subdue one man
18 strangled him to death in the ensuing scuffle (don't   20
you idolize the diction of the powerful: *subdue* and
scuffle my oh my) and that the murder
that the killing of Arthur Miller on a Brooklyn
street was just a "justifiable accident" again[3]
(again)   25

People been having accidents all over the globe
so long like that I reckon that the only
suitable insurance is a gun
I'm saying war is not to understand or rerun
war is to be fought and won   30

sometimes the feeling like amaze me baby
blots it out/the bestial but
not too often

tell me something
what you think would happen if   35
everytime they kill a black boy
then we kill a cop
everytime they kill a black man
then we kill a cop

you think the accident rate would lower   40
subsequently?

                                                                      1978

Poem for South African Women

Commemoration of the 40,000 women and children who, August
9, 1956, presented themselves in bodily protest against the "dom-
pass" in the capital of apartheid.[1] Presented at the United Nations,
August 9, 1978.

Our own shadows disappear as the feet of thousands
by the tens of thousands pound the fallow land
into new dust that
rising like a marvelous pollen will be
fertile   5

3. The 1978 death by "pressure applied to the throat" of African American businessman Arthur Miller while intervening in a struggle between police and his brother, Samuel, after a traffic stop in the Crown Heights section of Brooklyn, one of a number of controversial killings of black citizens by white New York City police officers during the 1970s and 1980s.

1. The Woman's March on the Union Buildings of Pretoria, South Africa, was organized to protest the pass (or "dompas") laws that prevented people of non-European descent from entering "white" areas, one aspect of the system of enforced racial segregation known as apartheid.

even as the first woman[2] whispering
imagination to the trees around her made
for righteous fruit
from such deliberate defense of life
as no other still 10
will claim inferior to any other safety
in the world

The whispers too they
intimate to the inmost ear of every spirit
now aroused they 15
carousing in ferocious affirmation
of all peaceable and loving amplitude
sound a certainly unbounded heat
from a baptismal[3] smoke where yes
there will be fire 20

And the babies cease alarm as mothers
raising arms
and heart high as the stars so far unseen
nevertheless hurl into the universe
a moving force 25
irreversible as light years
traveling to the open
eye

And who will join this standing up
and the ones who stood without sweet company 30
will sing and sing
back into the mountains and
if necessary
even under the sea

we are the ones we have been waiting for 35

1978

Poem about My Rights

Even tonight and I need to take a walk and clear
my head about this poem about why I can't
go out without changing my clothes my shoes
my body posture my gender identity my age
my status as a woman alone in the evening / 5
alone on the streets / alone not being the point /
the point being that I can't do what I want
to do with my own body because I am the wrong
sex the wrong age the wrong skin and
suppose it was not here in the city but down on the beach / 10
or far into the woods and I wanted to go

---

2. The biblical Eve.   3. Ritually purified (usually by water).

there by myself thinking about God / or thinking
about children or thinking about the world / all of it
disclosed by the stars and the silence:
I could not go and I could not think and I could not   15
stay there
alone
as I need to be
alone because I can't do what I want to do with my own
body and   20
who in the hell set things up
like this
and in France they say if the guy penetrates
but does not ejaculate then he did not rape me
and if after stabbing him if after screams if   25
after begging the bastard and if even after smashing
a hammer to his head if even after that if he
and his buddies fuck me after that
then I consented and there was
no rape because finally you understand finally   30
they fucked me over because I was wrong I was
wrong again to be me being me where I was / wrong
to be who I am[1]
which is exactly like South Africa
penetrating into Namibia penetrating into   35
Angola and does that mean I mean how do you know if
Pretoria ejaculates what will the evidence look like the
proof of the monster jackboot ejaculation on Blackland
and if
after Namibia and if after Angola and if after Zimbabwe[2]   40
and if after all of my kinsmen and women resist even to
self-immolation of the villages and if after that
we lose nevertheless what will the big boys say will they
claim my consent:
Do You Follow Me: We are the wrong people of   45
the wrong skin on the wrong continent and what
in the hell is everybody being reasonable about
and according to the *Times* this week
back in 1966 the C.I.A. decided that they had this problem
and the problem was a man named Nkrumah[3] so they   50
killed him and before that it was Patrice Lumumba[4]
and before that it was my father on the campus
of my Ivy League school[5] and my father afraid
to walk into the cafeteria because he said he

1. Lines 23–30 draw upon an infamous case of rape in Aix-en-Provence on May 2–3, 1978, in which a group of young men took revenge on two female Belgian campers in the rocky inlet of Morgiou near Marseilles for refusing their advances.
2. The Republic of South Africa borders on Namibia, which in turn borders Angola, while Zimbabwe borders South Africa and Namibia. Pretoria is one of South Africa's three capital cities, serving as the executive capital. The language of violent invasion refers to the South African Border War (also called the "Angolan Bush War") of 1966–89.
3. Kwame Nkrumah (1909–1972), president of Ghana and its predecessor state, the Gold Coast, from 1951 to 1966, well known for his advocacy of Pan-Africanism. Nkrumah was overthrown by a military coup supported by the U.S. Central Intelligence Agency (CIA).
4. Patrice Emery Lumumba (1925–1961), prime minister of the Congo from 1960 until his assassination in 1961 after a coup possibly supported by the CIA. He was president of the Congolese National Movement against the colonial power of Belgium and is regarded as a martyr.
5. Jordan attended Barnard College, an experience she recounts in her book *Civil Wars* (1981).

was wrong the wrong age the wrong skin the wrong   55
gender identity and he was paying my tuition and
before that
it was my father saying I was wrong saying that
I should have been a boy because he wanted one / a
boy and that I should have been lighter skinned and   60
that I should have had straighter hair and that
I should not be so boy crazy but instead I should
just be one / a boy and before that
it was my mother pleading plastic surgery for
my nose and braces for my teeth and telling me   65
to let the books loose to let them loose in other
words
I am very familiar with the problems of the C.I.A.
and the problems of South Africa and the problems
of Exxon Corporation[6] and the problems of white   70
America in general and the problems of the teachers
and the preachers and the F.B.I. and the social
workers and my particular Mom and Dad / I am very
familiar with the problems because the problems
turn out to be   75
me
I am the history of rape
I am the history of the rejection of who I am
I am the history of the terrorized incarceration of
my self   80
I am the history of battery assault and limitless
armies against whatever I want to do with my mind
and my body and my soul and
whether it's about walking out at night
or whether it's about the love that I feel or   85
whether it's about the sanctity of my vagina or
the sanctity of my national boundaries
or the sanctity of my leaders or the sanctity
of each and every desire
that I know from my personal and idiosyncratic   90
and indisputably single and singular heart
I have been raped[7]
be-
cause I have been wrong the wrong sex the wrong age
the wrong skin the wrong nose the wrong hair the   95
wrong need the wrong dream the wrong geographic
the wrong sartorial[8] I
I have been the meaning of rape
I have been the problem everyone seeks to
eliminate by forced   100

---

6. Corporate oil producer and distributor, known since 1999 as ExxonMobil Corporation after a merger with Mobil Oil. The "problems" refer to the nationalization of Exxon holdings in Iraq shortly before the OPEC oil embargo of 1973.
7. In *Civil Wars*, Jordan writes: "We, women and Black and First World Peoples, have become accustomed to the concept of rape: our bodies, our coloring, the structure of our genes, the violated boundaries of our lands, the forced extinction of our leaders and our dreams, the derogation of our singular beauty, our singular art, the systematic suffering of our children, the social sterilization of our wombs; these testify to our familiarity with rape. . . . *I have been raped*."
8. Relating to tailoring or clothes.

penetration with or without the evidence of slime and /
but let this be unmistakable this poem
is not consent I do not consent
to my mother to my father to the teachers to
the F.B.I. to South Africa to Bedford-Stuy[9]   105
to Park Avenue to American Airlines to the hardon
idlers on the corners to the sneaky creeps in
cars
I am not wrong: Wrong is not my name
My name is my own my own my own   110
and I can't tell you who the hell set things up like this
but I can tell you that from now on my resistance
my simple and daily and nightly self-determination
may very well cost you your life

1980

9. Abbreviation for the section of Brooklyn called Bedford Stuyvesant, which has a large African American population.

JAYNE CORTEZ
1936–2012

The rich spectrum of Jayne Cortez's artistic and political concerns can be seen just by glancing at titles of her volumes of verse and music-backed poetry recordings. *Festivals and Funerals, Scarifications, Mouth on Paper, Firespitter, Coagulations*— these and other titles foreground the importance in Cortez's poetry of performance, ritual, invention, community, embodied assertion, and revolutionary experimentation. When asked about her creative process, Cortez has responded: "I use dreams, the subconscious and the real objects, I open up the body and use organs and I sink them into works, and I ritualize them and fuse them into events. I guess the poetry is like a festival. Everything can be transformed." Juxtaposing vision and desire, dreams and reality, ghostly encounters and political struggle, Cortez's poetry summons this power of collective transformation with distinctive thematic and lyrical force. Even the name of her band (The Firespitters), with which she has performed and recorded much of her poetry, reveals the import of communal struggle: Firespitter, or Kpo-nungo, is a mask from the African Ivory Coast, one said to embody an aggressive supernatural power that would combat any forces that might disrupt the well-being of the community. Hence festivals (carnivalesque transformations) and funerals (irrevocable losses) are bound to each other in Cortez's poetry, and scarification and coagulation constitute a dialectic of trauma and recovery that crystallizes in the ritual of Cortez's blues-laced, African-inspired praise-songs.

Jayne Cortez was born in Arizona on the Fort Huachuca army base where her father was stationed, the middle child between an older sister and younger brother. The public school system was segregated, and she attended a one-room schoolhouse composed mostly of black and Native American children. At age seven, Cortez moved with her family to San Diego for nearly a year to live with her maternal grandmother's family (noting her performative aspirations, Cortez's grandfather took her aside one day and said, "You want to be an actress like Lena Horne, or somebody") and then migrated to the Watts section of Los Angeles, which provided a community where Cortez encountered instruction in performance: "We played the Dozens, signified, told jokes, and performed for each other. It was an everyday ritual." Cortez also took advantage of the musical atmosphere of her parents' house, where she was exposed to Ella Fitzgerald, Billie Holiday, Lena Horne, Duke Ellington, Count Basie, and Jimmy Lunceford; she "fell in love" with Charlie Parker and Thelonious Monk. Cortez herself played piano, bass, and cello, and took courses in music theory and harmony while attending the Manual Arts High School, where she also studied drawing, painting, and design, and started writing at the age of fourteen.

After high school, Cortez attended Compton Junior College in hopes of becoming an actress, but left school at eighteen when she married jazz saxophonist Ornette Coleman, with whom she had a son named Denardo, who has come to play drums regularly with both his mother's and his father's bands. Nineteen sixty-three was an important year for Cortez's relation to the Civil Rights movement; she traveled to Mississippi to work with Fannie Lou Hamer, the great civil rights activist who challenged voting restrictions for blacks. (Cortez composed an elegy for Hamer in the late 1970s, "Big Fine Woman from Rueville.") By 1964, after a divorce from Coleman, Cortez had co-founded the Watts Repertory Theatre Company, for which she served as artistic director until 1970. Directing plays, acting, and reading poetry, Cortez developed her early poetry within this venue of communal performance; most of the pieces in her first volume of poetry, *Pissstained Stairs and the Monkey Man's Wares* (1969) were written for the Watts Repertory to perform, and in the mid-1960s she also began composing and recording her poems with music.

In 1972 Cortez formed her own publishing company, Bola Press. She was a teacher and writer-in-residence at Rutgers University from 1977 to 1983. Cortez has traveled and read her poetry throughout the Caribbean, Latin America, Africa, and Europe. She has produced stunning recordings of many of her works, among them *There It Is* (1982) and *Maintain Control* (1986). Her books of poetry include *Festivals and Funerals* (1971) and *On the Imperial Highway: New and Selected Poems* (2008). She has received numerous awards, including an American Book Award for *Mouth on Paper* (1980); a New York Foundation for the Arts Award (1987); and the Langston Hughes Medal (2001). Cortez formed, along with Ghana-born Zimbabwe resident Ama Ata Aidoo, the Organization of Women Writers of Africa (OWWA).

Wide-ranging in theme and form, Cortez's poems display a persistent ability to disturb convention, stir remembrance, and spark response that is at once political and spiritual. "How Long Has Trane Been Gone" subtly suggests the African American mode of call-and-response to cultivate the reader's participation in collective explorations of black identity. With Coltrane "gone," a "willed" remembrance is required of the audience members for the project of communal restoration after searing loss to begin. Positing Trane as the site of an essential being, the poem offers possibilities of communal liberation that are continually deferred ("How long / Have black people been gone") until the loss of Coltrane becomes a powerful instigation for shared innovation. If Coltrane is apotheosized into a spectral symbol of iconic nationalism, the poem warns, the potential of the community for engaged revitalization can be squandered. And yet what remains strong within this threat of miscast worship is the speaker's own summons to common voice—"Now tell me abut the good things / I'm telling / you about / John Coltrane"—the voice that Cortez kept strong through a lifetime of dazzling poetic performance.

How Long Has Trane Been Gone[1]

Tell me about the good things
you clappin & laughin

Will you remember
or will you forget

Forget about the good things   5
like Blues & Jazz being black
Yeah Black Music
all about you

And the musicians that
write & play about you   10
a black brother groanin
a black sister moanin
& beautiful black children
ragged . . . underfed laughin
not knowin   15

Will you remember their names
or do they have no names
no lives—only products
to be used when you wanna
dance fuck & cry   20

You takin—they givin
You livin—they
creating starving dying
trying to make a better tomorrow
Giving you & your children a history   25
But what do you care about
history—Black History
and John Coltrane

No
All you wanna do   30
is pat your foot
sip a drink & pretend
with your head bobbin up & down
What do you care about acoustics
bad microphones or out-of-tune pianos   35
& noise
You the club owners & disc jockeys
made a deal didn't you
a deal about Black Music
& you really don't give   40
a shit long as you take[2]

---

1. Cf. blues standard "How Long, How Long Blues" as performed in 1928 by American blues singer-songwriter Leroy Carr (1905–1935), which begins: "How long, baby how long / Has that eve- ning train been gone / How long, how long, baby how long." "Trane": John Coltrane (1926–1967), African American avant-garde jazz saxophonist.
2. I.e., take a profit.

        There was a time
when KGFJ[3] played all black music
from Bird to Johnny Ace[4]
on show after show   45
but what happened
I'll tell you what happened
they divided black music
doubled the money
& left us split again   50
is what happened

John Coltrane's dead & some
of you
have yet to hear him play
How long how long has that Trane been gone   55

and how many more Tranes will go
before you understand your life
John Coltrane who had the whole of
life wrapped up in B flat
John Coltrane like Malcolm[5]   60
True image of Black Masculinity

Now tell me about the good things
I'm telling you about
John Coltrane

A name that should ring   65
throughout the projects[6] mothers
Mothers with sons
who need John Coltrane
Need the warm arm of his music
like words from a Father   70
words of Comfort
words of Africa
words of Welcome
How long how long has that Trane been gone

John palpitating love notes   75
in a lost-found nation[7]
within a nation
His music resounding discovery
signed Always
John Coltrane   80

3. Radio station in Los Angeles dubbed a
"Negro-appeal" station in the 1920s and 1930s
when it began to employ black announcers and
play African American music; the station's call
letters stood for "Keeping Good Folks Joyful."
4. Born John Marshall Alexander Jr. (1929–
1954), Ace was an American rhythm-and-blues
singer in the early 1950s who shot himself while
playing Russian roulette backstage at a concert.
"Bird": Charles Parker Jr. (1920–1955), jazz saxophonist and composer, a founding figure of bebop
and a major influence on the next wave of avant-
garde jazz musicians, including Coltrane and

Cortez's first husband, saxophonist Ornette Coleman (b. 1930).
5. Malcolm X (1925–1965), powerful black leader
of the early 1960s, minister of the Nation of Islam
from 1952–1964 and later founder of the Organization of Afro-American Unity.
6. Public housing.
7. I.e., the African American religion known as
the Nation of Islam, founded by Wallace Fard
Muhammad (1877–?), author of Teaching for the
Lost Found Nation of Islam in a Mathematical
Way (c. 1932).

Rip those dead white people off
your walls Black People
black people whose walls
should be a hall
A Black Hall Of Fame   85
so our children will know
will know & be proud
Proud to say I'm from Parker City—Coltrane City—Ornette City
Pharoah City living on Holiday street next to
James Brown[8] park in the State of Malcolm   90

How Long
how long
will it take for you to understand
that Tranes been gone
riding in a portable radio   95
next to your son who's lonely
Who walks walks walks into nothing
no city no state no home no Nothing
how long
How long   100
Have black people been gone

                                                                1969

8. Popular soul singer (b. 1928). Ferrell "Pharoah" Sanders (b. 1940), tenor saxophonist who played in
Coltrane's quartet from 1965 to 1967. Billie Holiday (1915–1959), jazz singer.

LARRY NEAL
1937–1981

Poet, essayist, theorist, editor, playwright, literary and music critic, pianist and
flutist, filmmaker, screenwriter, folklorist, scholar, teacher, Larry Neal was the
intellectual leader of the Black Arts movement. One of the most subtle theorists of
the era's articulation of aesthetics and politics and a leading practitioner of its many
expressive forms, Neal is remembered especially for a series of incisive essays produced in the decade from the mid-1960s to the mid-1970s that not only gave the
Black Arts movement its name and aspects of its distinctive style, but also provided,
in sinewy prose, cogent declarations of its philosophical foundations, cultural conditions, and revolutionary aspirations.

The oldest of five sons, Lawrence Paul Neal was born on September 5, 1937, in
Atlanta, Georgia, to Woodie and Maggie Neal. Both parents were strong influences on Neal and nurtured him with a rich sense of cultural inheritance. In a
"personal note" attached to his second volume of poetry, *Hoodoo Hollerin' Bebop
Ghosts* (1971), Neal writes of his father as the first nationalist he ever knew, a man
who had less than a high school education but was exceptionally well-read, insistent on self-reliance and practicality, and "in the most memorable sense of the
term, say in the tradition of Walter White, Marcus Garvey, and A. J. Rodgers, a
'race man.'" If his father gave him a political and legal education (Woodie Neal,

after serving in WWII as a battleship pipe fitter and a switchman for the Reading Railroad, was also "a fugitive from the Georgia law of the thirties," Neal claimed), his mother "represents the aesthetic side of the family." A lover of music and poetry, Neal's mother would recite poetry by Paul Laurence Dunbar and Langston Hughes to her children and was committed to Neal's receiving an education in music and the arts.

The family moved to North Philadelphia when Neal was quite young, settling in the Johnson Housing Projects; it was there that his mother, determined to have her sons well educated, converted to Catholicism (at Saint Elizabeth's Church) so that they could enroll in a Catholic school. Neal graduated from Roman Catholic High School in Philadelphia in 1956 and then took a degree in English and history from Lincoln University in 1961. In 1963 Neal earned an M.A. from the University of Pennsylvania in folklore (a perpetual interest in Neal's poetry, prose, and drama) before moving to New York in 1964 and a year later marrying Evelyn Rodgers (a chemist originally from Fairfield, Alabama).

Larry and Evelyn settled into Harlem in a section then called Sugar Hill, where their brownstone became a hub of cultural energy until his untimely death of a heart attack in January of 1981. Harlem proved to be invigorating for Neal, a place full of important literary figures such as Ishmael Reed, Quincy Troupe, Askia Muhammad Touré, Stanley Crouch, Henry Dumas, and Amiri Baraka. Though his first job in Harlem was as a copy editor for John Wiley and Sons, he almost immediately became involved (whether as founder, editor, and/or contributor) in many of the progressive black "little magazines" of the 1960s—*Liberator, Soulbook,* the *Journal of Black Poetry, Black Theater,* and *Black World*—for which he variously wrote journalistic accounts of cultural events, conducted interviews with writers, artists, and musicians, and published his own creative and critical work. This period also marked Neal's increased involvement in the Black Liberation movement, which gradually shaped his writing and brought him closer especially with Baraka, with whom he shared a growing skepticism, inspired by Malcolm X, of Martin Luther King's nonviolent approach to black liberation.

Uncompromising yet deeply learned in his avowals of radical black politics, Neal found himself at the heart of black nationalist struggle. In a nearly emblematic event, Neal was wounded while leaving the Schomburg Center for Research in Black Culture in 1965 by someone who ostensibly loathed his politics. But such violence did not slow him down. In the mid-1960s he co-directed, with Baraka and Touré, the critically important and controversial Black Arts Repertory Theatre/School in Harlem, which produced works such as Baraka's *Jello* and *Dutchman* and provided a space for poetry readings and concerts focused on themes of revolutionary community. As Neal's involvement with theater increased, so did his subtlety in thinking about music and performance, both of which became increasingly central to his aesthetic theories and political practices. Neal continued to write important criticism on figures such as Ralph Ellison, Albert Murray, Baraka, and Archie Shepp while working out his own ideas and formulating new projects.

Published the same year as the movement's most important manifesto (the 1968 anthology of poetry and prose called *Black Fire,* which Neal edited with Baraka), Neal's eponymous essay "The Black Arts Movement" sounds one of the period's most definitive moments of expressive self-assertion. Indeed, declaring black art to be "the aesthetic and spiritual sister of the Black Power concept," "The Black Arts Movement" essay, like Neal's poetry, plays, and other prose, fundamentally addresses itself to "the Afro-American desire for self-determination and nationhood," opposing itself "to any concept of the artist that alienates him from his community." The nationalist turn from civil rights to black liberation was, in Neal's view, also a movement away from parochialism; black nationhood could not be truly imagined, let alone accomplished, without a revaluation of Western notions of aesthetics, agency, subjectivity, and tradition. Thus, for Neal the politics of the Black Power movement are inextricably tied to "a radical reordering of the nature and function of both art and the artist" and a "dissolution" of the Western focus on individual identity.

The late 1960s and early 1970s were a remarkably productive period for Neal, as he attempted to maintain a continuity with the Black Arts movement while refining his revisionary critical flair in ever subtler thinking about the relationships between aesthetics and politics, identity and community, and art and philosophy. In addition to numerous screenplays, scripts for television, and documentaries, Neal wrote and produced two major plays during his lifetime, *The Glorious Monster in the Bell of the Horn* (1976) and *In an Upstate Motel* (1981). One critic described *The Glorious Monster* as a "lyric drama, a poetic interpretation of the hopes and aspirations of black artists and the middle class on the eve of the dropping of the A-bomb on Hiroshima." Staged by the Negro Ensemble Company in the spring of 1981, *In an Upstate Motel* was existentially darker than *Glorious Monster*, offering a tense drama about the aftermath of a failed assassination attempt made by a black man and woman (cocaine addicts and sexual partners); in a contemporary *New York Times* review, Frank Rich wrote of Neal as having taken "a familiar premise—a gangland hit man and his woman on the lam—and infused it with Proustian ghosts, Pinteresque menace, even a dash of jazz."

At this time, Neal grew increasingly involved with the world of academia and formal cultural institutions, teaching at numerous universities and working as a consultant for a number of arts foundations. Neal held the Andrew W. Mellon chair in humanities at Howard University and received a Guggenheim Fellowship in 1971. He also served as executive director of the DC Commission on the Arts and Humanities from 1976 to 1979.

During this period, Neal continued to publish a prolific stream of poetry, prose, drama, TV, and film. The poems anthologized here offer just a sampling of the richly diverse traditions on which Neal drew. It is nearly impossible to separate the media in which Neal worked: music, performance, and poetry especially shared elements that Neal sought to bring together in what he calls (in the afterword to *Black Fire*) "new syntheses." Like many of the other writers of the Black Arts era, Neal focused on music as the quintessential art ("Our music has always been the most dominant manifestation of what we are and feel, literature was just an afterthought"); but he also incorporated music and performance into his poetics, seeking a language that didn't imitate music but that enacted its philosophical and formal imperatives. Indeed, Neal wrote, "the poet must become a performer, the way James Brown is a performer—loud, gaudy, and racy. He must take his work where his people are: Harlem, Watts, Philadelphia, Chicago, and the rural South. . . . Poets must learn to sing, dance, and chant their work, tearing into the substance of their individual and collective experiences. We must make literature move people to a deeper understanding of what this thing is all about, be a kind of priest, a black magician, working juju with the word on the world."

The poems included here—all from *Hoodoo Hollerin' Bebop Ghosts*—evince this artistic urgency and the formal inventiveness that gives that urgency structural clarity and thematic character. In an interview, Neal once described this volume as "a book full of ghosts' voices," a poetic attempt to "understand and manipulate the collective myths of the race" that themselves exert spectral energies of history, loss, and labor on the poet's task. This ghostly purpose roots Neal's voice in traditional idioms of hoodoo, slavery, and African and African American myth, while remaining startlingly fresh, not least on account of the rich re-imagining of inherited figures and images of a culture undergoing constant displacement and renewal. Continuity and revision, ritual and performance, music and style, spectrality and power—these, and many others, are the topics that constitute Neal's unique poetics, a poetics—whether somberly "bearing witness" or jubilantly "riffing"—that are as much concerned with transgressive critique ("So we pick up our axes and prepare / to blast the white dream"; "Don't Say Goodbye to the Porkpie Hat") as it is with confronting violation, death, love—the very elements of black experience that do not just contain but inspire Neal's hope for communal liberation.

Harlem Gallery: From the Inside

For Melvin Tolson[1]

The bars on Eighth Avenue in Harlem
glow real yellow, hard against formica
tables. They speak of wandering ghosts
and Harlem saints;[2] the words lay slick
on greasy floors: rain-wet butt in the junkie's[3]   5
mouth, damp notebook in the number runner's[4] hand.
no heads turn as the deal goes down—we wait.

Harlem rain explodes, flooding the avenues
rats float up out of the sewers.
Do we need the Miracles[5] or a miracle?   10

Listen baby, to the mean[6] scar-faced sister,
between you and her and me and you there are no
distances. short reach of the .38,[7] a sudden
migraine hammering where your brains used to be;
then it's over, no distance between the needle   15
and the rope, instant time, my man, history as
one quick fuck.

Uptight against these sounds, but everything ain't
all right,[8] the would-be
warriors of the nitty-gritty[9] snap fingers,   20
ghosts boogaloo[1] against this haze
Malcolm[2] eyes in the yellow glow;
blood on black hands,
compacted rooms of gloom;
Garvey's[3] flesh in the rat's teeth   25
Lady Day at 100 Centre Street[4]
Charlie Parker dead in the penthouse
of an aristocratic bitch.[5]
Carlos Cook

1. African American modernist poet (1898–
1966), author of the long poetic work entitled *Harlem Gallery*. Neal stated: "Tolson—whose poetry
I really like—is so contorted and strange in his
way. I wanted to write a counter-statement, not a
response. Mine was from the inside. I felt that
Tolson was from the outside. I thought I was closer
to what the gallery of Harlem was. I got that poem
walking up 8th Avenue one day in the summer."
2. Devout members of Harlem's storefront
churches.
3. Drug addict's.
4. Courier of bets made in a popular form of
street gambling.
5. Rhythm-and-blues group, led by singer William
"Smokey" Robinson Jr. (b. 1940), on the Motown
label, active from 1955 to 1983.
6. Formidable.
7. A .38-caliber revolver.
8. Play on "Uptight (Everything Is Alright),"
popular 1966 "soul" song by African American
singer-songwriter Stevie Wonder (born Stevland
Hardaway Judkins, 1950); "uptight" in the song
connotes a good feeling.
9. Unvarnished, basic facts.
1. Latino-influenced dance popular in the 1960s.
2. I.e., Malcolm X (1925–1965), black nationalist leader, minister of the Nation of Islam, and
human rights activist.
3. Marcus Mosiah Garvey (1887–1940), black
nationalist founder of the U.N.I.A. (Universal
Negro Improvement Association).
4. African American jazz and blues singer Billie
"Lady Day" Holiday (1915–1959), who was convicted on narcotics charges in 1947 after being
arraigned at the criminal branch of the New York
Supreme Court at 100 Centre Street, Manhattan.
5. Jazz saxophonist and composer (1920–1955),
who died in a suite at the Stanhope Hotel owned
by friend and patroness Baroness Pannonica
"Nica" de Koenigswarter (1913–1988), a British
jazz enthusiast and member of the prominent
Rothschild international financial dynasty.

Ras   30
Shine and Langston
the Barefoot Prophet
Ira Kemp
the Signifying Monkey
Bud Powell   35
Trane
Prez
Chano Pozo
Eloise Moore[6]—all
falling faces in the Harlem rain   40
asphalt memory of blood and pain.

1966

Don't Say Goodbye to the Porkpie Hat

Mingus, Bird, Prez, Langston,[1] and them

Don't say goodbye to the Porkpie Hat
that rolled along on padded shoulders,[2]
        that swang bebop[3] phrases
        in Minton's jelly roll[4] dreams
Don't say goodbye to hip hats tilted in the style of a soulful era;   5
the Porkpie Hat that Lester dug[5]
swirling in the sound of sax blown suns

6. Civil rights activist and black nationalist Audley Eloise Moore, known as "Queen Mother" Moore (1898–1996). Carlos Cook: i.e., Carlos A. Cooks (1913–1966), Dominican-born black nationalist founder of the African Nationalist Pioneer Movement (ANPM), considered the ideological heir to Marcus Garvey for his efforts to continue the work of the U.N.I.A. after Garvey's death; Cooks was known as a riveting street orator. Ras: allusion to Ras-the-Destroyer, character in *Invisible Man* (1952) by African American author Ralph Ellison (1914–1994), a charismatic black nationalist street orator based on the historical Ras DeKiller, founding member of the Harlem-based Ethiopian Pacific Movement. Shine: African American folk hero, most famously in the "toast" poem "The Titanic," which celebrates Shine's sexual prowess, physical strength, rebellious temper, and trickster capacity for survival. Langston: Langston Hughes, African American poet (1902–1967). Barefoot Prophet: reference to 1929 photograph by African American photographer James Van Der Zee (1886–1983) of Elder Clayhorn Martin, known as Prophet Martin or the Barefoot Prophet, a Harlem street preacher who delivered sermons barefoot, evoking the prophet Isaiah, who endured three years of barefoot walking to symbolize the imminent captivity of Israel (Isaiah 20.2). Ira Kemp: black nationalist Harlem street orator and head of the Harlem Labor Union (1900–1938). The Signifying Monkey: trickster figure in African American folklore, derived from African mythology, who defeats opponents through rhe-

torical mastery known as "signifying." Bud Powell: Earl Rudolph "Bud" Powell (1924–1966), jazz pianist and composer. Trane: John Coltrane (1926–1967), African American avant-garde jazz saxophonist. Prez: Lester "Prez" Young (1909–1959), African American jazz saxophonist and clarinetist. Chano Pozo: Cuban-born Latin-jazz percussionist and dancer (1915–1948).
1. Langston Hughes (1902–1967), African American poet, novelist, playwright, and journalist; Charles Mingus (1922–1979), African American jazz bassist, composer, and bandleader; Charlie "Bird" Parker Jr. (1920–1955), African American jazz saxophonist and composer; Lester "Prez" Young (1909–1959), African American jazz saxophonist and clarinetist, known also for his style in dress, which often included a zoot suit and the cylindrical, flat-topped hat known as the "porkpie." In 1959 Mingus wrote a musical elegy for Young called "Goodbye Pork Pie Hat" (later renamed "Theme for Lester Young").
2. Characteristic of the zoot suit.
3. Style of jazz developed in the 1940s, characterized by fast tempos and complex melodic improvisation.
4. Jelly Roll Morton (born Ferdinand Joseph LeMothe; 1890–1941), African American ragtime and jazz pianist, composer, and bandleader. Minton's Playhouse, established by Henry Minton in 1938, was a Harlem bar and nightclub that hosted improvisational performances by many jazz luminaries in the bebop era.
5. Enjoyed and understood.

phrase on phrase, repeating bluely
tripping in and under crashing
hi-hat cymbals,[6] a fickle girl   10
getting sassy on the rhythms.
Musicians heavy with memories
move in and out of this gloom;
the Porkpie Hat reigns supreme
smell of collard greens   15
and cotton madness
commingled in the nigger elegance of the style.
        The Porkpie Hat sees tonal memories
        of salt peanuts and hot house birds[7]
        the Porkpie Hat sees . . .   20
Cross riffing[8] square kingdoms, riding midnight Scottsboro
trains.[9] We are haunted by the lynched limbs.
On the road:
It would be some hoodoo[1] town
It would be some cracker place   25
you might meet redneck[2] lynchers
face to face
but mostly you meet mean horn blowers
running obscene riffs
Jelly Roll spoke of such places: 30
the man with the mojo hand[3]
the dyke with the .38[4]
the yaller[5] girls
and the knifings.

Stop-time Buddy and Creole Sydney[6]   35
wailed in here. Stop time.[7]
chorus repeats, stop and shuffle.
stop and stomp.
listen to the horns, ain't they mean[8]?
now ain't they mean   40
in blue
in blue
in blue streaks of mellow wisdom
blue notes

---

6. Pedal-operated pair of cymbals, part of the modern drum kit for percussionists in rhythm-and-blues and jazz bands.
7. "Hot House": jazz standard composed by Tadd Dameron (1917–1965) but made famous as a bebop tune played by jazz trumpeter Dizzy Gillespie (1917–1993) and Charlie "Bird" Parker in the early 1950s. "Salt Peanuts": bebop standard composed in 1943 by Gillespie.
8. Improvising with agility.
9. The "Scottsboro Boys" were nine black teenagers charged with assault and rape in Alabama in 1931 after hobos riding a freight train accused the young men of attacking white women on the train. The defendants were sentenced to death and subjected to threats of lynching by a white mob; their convictions were overturned on appeal when the women admitted to having concocted the story to avoid vagrancy and prostitution charges, though several of the defendants served years in prison.

1. African American folk magic, also called "conjure," developed from the syncretism of several African, American, and European traditions.
2. "Redneck," "cracker": pejorative terms for white people, usually from the rural South.
3. In hoodoo, a talisman carried for its supernatural power offering good luck or protection from harm.
4. A .38-caliber revolver; "dyke": lesbian.
5. Light-complected ("high yellow") African American.
6. Sydney Bechet (1897–1959), African American jazz saxophonist, clarinetist, and composer, one of jazz's first important soloists; Charles Joseph "Buddy" Bolden (1877–1931), African American cornetist, originator of a New Orleans style of early jazz known as "ragtime."
7. In tap dancing, jazz, and blues, accompaniment consisting of a regular pattern of sounds, separated by silences.
8. Gritty, honest, excellent.

coiling around 45
the Porkpie Hat
and ghosts of dead musicians drifting through
here on riffs that smack
of one-leg trumpet players
and daddy glory piano ticklers[9] 50
who
twisted arpeggios[1]
with diamond-flashed fingers.
There was Jelly Roll Morton, the sweet mackdaddy,[2]
hollering Waller, and Willie The Lion Smith—[3] 55
some mean showstoppers.

Ghosts of dead holy rollers ricocheted in the air funky[4]
with white lightnin'[5] and sweat.
Emerald bitches shot shit[6] in a kitchen smelling
of funerals and fried chicken. 60
Each city had a different sound:
there was Mambo, Rhega, Jeanne;
holy the voice of the righteous sisters.

Shape to shape, horn to horn
the Porkpie Hat resurrected himself 65
night to night, from note to note
skimming the horizons, flashing bluegreenyellow lights
and blowing black stars
and weird looneymoon changes;[7] chords coiled about him
and he was flying 70
fast
zipping
past
sound
into cosmic silences. 75
And yes
and caresses flowed from the voice in the horn in the blue
of the yellow whiskey room where bad hustlers with big
coats moved, digging the fly[8] sister, fingerpopping while
tearing at chicken and waffles. 80

The Porkpie Hat loomed specter like, a vision for the world;
shiny, the knob toe shoes,[9]
sporting hip camel coats
and righteous[1] pin stripes—
pants pressed razor shape; 85
and caressing his horn, baby like.

---

9. Many early and mid-20th-century jazz pianists in Harlem were called "piano ticklers."
1. Notes of a chord played in succession rather than simultaneously.
2. Slick womanizer.
3. Willie "the Lion" Smith (born William Henry Joseph Bonaparte Bertholoff Smith, 1893–1973), African American jazz pianist who, like jazz pianist and composer Fats Waller (born Thomas Wright Waller, 1904–1943), were "ticklers" associated with an improvised form of jazz music called "stride" that was developed in Harlem during the 1920s and 1930s.
4. Redolent; "holy rollers": fire-and-brimstone preachers or church members.
5. Moonshine liquor.
6. I.e., injected narcotics (usually poor-quality heroin).
7. In jazz, harmonic progressions; chord changes.
8. Brash and beautiful.
9. Zoot-style shoes.
1. Flashy; attractive and expensive.

So we pick up our axes[2] and prepare
to blast the white dream;
we pick up our axes
re-create ourselves and the universe,   90
sounds splintering the deepest regions
of spiritual space
crisp and moaning voices
leaping in the horns of destruction,
blowing death and doom to all who have no use for the   95
spirit.

So we cook out of sight[3]
into cascading motions of joy delight
shooflies the Bird lolligagging[4]
and laughing for days,   100
and the rhythms way up in there
wailing, sending scarlet rays, luminescent,
spattering bone and lie.
we go on cool lords
wailing on into star nights,   105
rocking whole worlds, unfurling song on song
into long stretches of green spectral shimmerings,
blasting on, fucking the moon with the blunt edge
of a lover's tune, out there now, joy riffing
for days and do   110
railriding and do
talking some lovely shit and do
to the Blues God who blesses us.

No, don't say goodbye to the Porkpie Hat—
he lives, oh yes.   115

Lester lives and leaps
Delancey's dilemma is over
Bird lives
Lady[5] lives
Eric[6] stands next to me   120
while I finger the Afro-horn
Bird lives
Lady lives
Lester leaps in[7] every night
Tad's delight[8]   125
is mine now
Dinah knows
Richie knows
that Bud is Buddha[9]

---

2. Horns, usually saxophones (jazz slang).
3. "Out of sight": exciting, revolutionary; "cook": in jazz, to play with great energy and inspiration.
4. Fooling around; making love. "Shooflies": chases playfully.
5. Jazz singer Billie "Lady Day" Holiday (1915–1959).
6. Jazz clarinetist and saxophonist Eric Dolphy (1928–1964).
7. "Lester Leaps In": Young composition, first recorded in 1930 with the Count Basie Band.
8. Song on the album *'Round About Midnight* (1957) by jazz trumpeter and composer Miles Davis (1926–1991), written by Tadd Dameron.
9. Earl Rudolph "Bud" Powell (1924–1966), jazz pianist and composer; Richie Powell (1931–1956), jazz pianist and brother of Bud Powell; Dinah Washington (born Ruth Lee Jones, 1924–1963), jazz, blues, and gospel singer.

that Jelly Roll dug juju[1]   130
and Lester lives
in Ornett's[2] leapings
the Blues God lives
we live
live   135
spirit lives
and sound lives
bluebird[3] lives
lives and leaps
dig the mellow voices   140
dig the Porkpie Hat
dig the spirit in Sun Ra's[4] sound
dig the cosmic Trane[5]
dig be
dig be   145
dig be
spirit lives in sound
dig be
sound lives in spirit
dig be   150
yeah!!!
spirit lives
spirit lives
spirit lives
SPIRIT!!!   155
SWHEEEEEEEEEEEEEEETTT!!!

take it again
this time from the top

                                                                    1967

Malcolm X—An Autobiography[1]

I am the Seventh Son of the son
who was also the seventh.[2]
I have drunk deep of the waters of my ancestors,
have traveled the soul's journey toward cosmic harmony—
the Seventh Son.   5

1. Magical power infused into an object, of West African origin; a style of music marked by complex polyrhythms, originating among the Yoruba people of Nigeria; or, marijuana.
2. Ornette Coleman (b. 1930), avant-garde jazz saxophonist and composer.
3. Bluebird Jazz, subsidiary of RCA records since the early 1930s, which recorded many important jazz musicians (including Fats Waller) and re-released recordings of many earlier jazz masters (including Jelly Roll Morton).
4. Born Herman Poole Blount (1914–1993), avant-garde saxophonist, composer, bandleader, and "cosmic philosopher."
5. John Coltrane (1926–1967), avant-garde jazz saxophonist, composer, and bandleader.

1. Malcolm X (born Malcolm Little and later known as El-Hajj Malik Shabazz, 1925–1965), black nationalist leader, minister of the Nation of Islam, human rights activist, and (with Alex Haley, 1921–1992) author of The Autobiography of Malcolm X (1965).
2. Malcolm X was his father's seventh child; according to some African cosmologies and European folk traditions, the seventh son is associated with a veiled birth and with mystical powers of healing and spiritual insight. In the chapter "Of Our Spiritual Strivings" in The Souls of Black Folk (1903), African American author W. E. B. Du Bois (1868–1963) wrote: "The Negro is a sort of seventh son, born with a veil, and gifted with second sight in this American world."

Have walked slick avenues
and seen grown men fall, to die in a blue doom
of death and ancestral agony;
have seen old men glide, shadowless, feet barely
touching the pavements.   10

I sprang out of the Midwestern plains
the bleak Michigan landscape,[3] the black blues of Kansas
City, these kiss-me-nights;
out of the bleak Michigan landscape wearing the slave name
Malcolm Little.[4]   15

Saw a brief vision in Lansing when I was seven, and in
my momma's womb heard the beast[5] cry death;
a landscape on which white robed figures[6] ride, and my
Garvey father[7] silhouetted against the night-fire
gun in hand,   20
form outlined against a panorama of violence.[8]

Out of the Midwestern bleakness, I sprang, pushed eastward,
past shack on country nigger shack, across the wilderness
of North America.[9]
I hustler. I pimp. I unfulfilled black man   25
bursting with destiny.
New York City Slim called me Big Red,[1]
and there was no escape, close nights of the smell of death.
Pimp. Hustler. The day fills these rooms.
I'm talking about New York, Harlem.   30
Talking about the neon madness.
Talking about ghetto eyes and nights
Talking about death protruding across the room
Talking about Small's Paradise.[2]
Talking about cigarette butts, and rooms smelly with white   35
sex-flesh,[3] and dank sheets, and being on the run.
Talking about cocaine illusions.
Talking about stealing and selling.
Talking about these New York cops who smell
of blood and money.   40
I am Big Red, tiger, vicious, Big Red, bad nigger, will kill.

But there is rhythm here
Its own special substance:

---

3. Much of Malcolm's early life was spent in Lansing, Michigan.
4. In his *Autobiography*, Malcolm wrote that he changed his surname to "X" in 1952 upon joining the Nation of Islam because "my 'X' replaced the white slavemaster name of 'Little' which some blue-eyed devil named Little had imposed on my paternal forebears." "X" signified the African name lost during the Middle Passage that would be restored upon complete emancipation.
5. Nation of Islam term for the white man.
6. I.e., the Black Legion, an offshoot of the Ku Klux Klan, a white supremacist terrorist group.
7. Reverend Earl Little (1890–1931) was a disciple of Marcus Garvey (1887–1940), black nationalist founder of the U.N.I.A. (Universal Negro Improvement Association).
8. This stanza describes the opening paragraphs of *The Autobiography of Malcolm X*.
9. Nation of Islam phrase commonly used by Malcolm X in speeches he made as its most prominent minister.
1. "It was, of course, because of him [Malcolm's white grandfather] that I got my reddish-brown 'mariny' color of skin, and my hair of the same color" (*The Autobiography of Malcolm X*), which led to his nicknames Big Red and Detroit Red.
2. Harlem restaurant and nightclub, popular from the 1920s to the 1940s.
3. Reference to young Malcolm's affair with a white prostitute, Sophia.

I hear Billie sing, no Good Man, and dig Prez,[4] wearing
the Zoot suit of life, the Porkpie hat tilted at the 45
correct angle; through the Harlem smoke of beer and
whiskey, I understand the mystery of the Signifying
Monkey;[5]
in a blue haze of inspiration
I reach for the totality of being. 50
I am at the center of a swirl of events.
War and death.
Rhythm.
Hot women.
I think life a commodity bargained 55
for across the bar in Small's.
I perceive the echoes of Bird[6]
and there is a gnawing in the maw[7]
of my emotions.

And then there is jail. 60
America is the world's greatest jailer,[8]
and we are all in jails
Holy spirits contained like magnificent
birds of wonder.
I now understand my father urged on by the ghost of Garvey, 65
and see a small brown man standing in a corner.[9]
The cell. Cold. Dank.
The light around him vibrates.
(Am I crazy?)
But to understand is to submit to a more perfect will, 70
a more perfect order.
To understand is to surrender the imperfect self
for a more perfect self.

Allah formed man, I follow
and shake within the very depth of my most interesting being; 75
and I bear witness to the Message of Allah
and I bear witness; all praise is due Allah.

1967

---

4. Lester "Prez" Young (1909–1959), African
American jazz saxophonist and clarinetist, known
also for his style in dress, which often included
the high-waisted, wide-shouldered "zoot suit"
fashionable among young black men in the 1940s
and the cylindrical, flat-topped hat known as the
"porkpie." Young received his nickname Prez (or
President) from jazz singer Billie Holiday (1915–
1959), one of whose most famous standards was
the song "No Good Man" (itself a pun on the
name of the white bandleader Benny Goodman
[1909–1986], with whom Holiday had her first
formal performance and recording sessions).
5. Trickster figure in African American folklore,
derived from African mythology, who defeats
opponents through rhetorical mastery known as
"signifying."
6. I.e., Charlie "Yardbird" Parker Jr. (1920–

1955), jazz saxophonist and composer known for
his development of the "bebop" style in the
1940s and 1950s.
7. Mouth, throat, or stomach: receptacle into
which food is taken by swallowing.
8. A common motif in Malcolm's speeches in
the early 1960s, most famously in "Message to
the Grass Roots": "Don't be shocked when I say I
was in prison. You're still in prison. That's what
America means: prison."
9. Reference to Malcolm's "pre-vision" of Nation
of Islam founder Wallace D. Fard (1877–?) while in
prison: ". . . as I lay on my bed, I suddenly, with a
start, became aware of a man sitting beside me in
my chair. . . . He wasn't black, and he wasn't white.
He was light-brown-skinned. . . . He just sat there.
Then, suddenly as he had come, he was gone."

The Black Arts Movement

I

The Black Arts Movement is radically opposed to any concept of the artist that alienates him from his community. Black Art is the aesthetic and spiritual sister of the Black Power concept. As such, it envisions an art that speaks directly to the needs and aspirations of Black America. In order to perform this task, the Black Arts Movement proposes a radical reordering of the western cultural aesthetic. It proposes a separate symbolism, mythology, critique, and iconology. The Black Arts and the Black Power concept both relate broadly to the Afro-American's desire for self-determination and nationhood. Both concepts are nationalistic. One is concerned with the relationship between art and politics; the other with the art of politics.

Recently, these two movements have begun to merge: the political values inherent in the Black Power concept are now finding concrete expression in the aesthetics of Afro-American dramatists, poets, choreographers, musicians, and novelists. A main tenet of Black Power is the necessity for Black people to define the world in their own terms. The Black artist has made the same point in the context of aesthetics. The two movements postulate that there are in fact and in spirit two Americas—one black, one white. The Black artist takes this to mean that his primary duty is to speak to the spiritual and cultural needs of Black people. Therefore, the main thrust of this new breed of contemporary writers is to confront the contradictions arising out of the Black man's experience in the racist West. Currently, these writers are re-evaluating western aesthetics, the traditional role of the writer, and the social function of art. Implicit in this re-evaluation is the need to develop a "black aesthetic." It is the opinion of many Black writers, I among them, that the Western aesthetic has run its course: it is impossible to construct anything meaningful within its decaying structure. We advocate a cultural revolution in art and ideas. The cultural values inherent in western history must either be radicalized or destroyed, and we will probably find that even radicalization is impossible. In fact, what is needed is a whole new system of ideas. Poet Don L. Lee[1] expresses it:

> . . . We must destroy Faulkner, dick, jane, and other perpetuators of evil. It's time for DuBois, Nat Turner, and Kwame Nkrumah. As Frantz Fanon[2] points out: destroy the culture and you destroy the people. This must not happen. Black artists are culture stabilizers; bringing back old values, and introducing new ones. Black Art will talk to the people and with the will of the people stop impending "protective custody."

The Black Arts Movement eschews "protest" literature. It speaks directly to Black people. Implicit in the concept of "protest" literature, as Brother Knight[3] has made clear, is an appeal to white morality:

1. African American poet and critic Lee (b. 1942) is now known as Haki Madhubuti; the remarks Neal cites below are from a symposium on the question "Should black writers direct their work toward black audiences?" published in *Negro Digest* in January 1968.
2. Martinican psychiatrist (1925–1961), author of several important critiques of racism and colonialism. William Faulkner (1897–1962), modern-

ist writer from Mississippi. W. E. B. Du Bois (1865–1963), scholar, editor of *Crisis* (1909–34), and co-founder of the NAACP. Turner (1800–1831), leader of an 1831 slave rebellion in Virginia. Nkrumah (1909–1972), first president of independent Ghana.
3. Etheridge Knight (1931–1985), poet. The remarks Neal cites are from the January 1968 *Negro Digest* symposium.

Now any Black man who masters the technique of his particular art form, who adheres to the white aesthetic, and who directs his work toward a white audience is, in one sense, protesting. And implicit in the act of protest is the belief that a change will be forthcoming once the masters are aware of the protestor's "grievance" (the very word connotes begging, supplications to the gods). Only when that belief has faded and protestings end, will Black art begin.

Brother Knight also has some interesting statements about the development of a "Black aesthetic":

> Unless the Black artist establishes a "Black aesthetic" he will have no future at all. To accept the white aesthetic is to accept and validate a society that will not allow him to live. The Black artist must create new forms and new values, sing new songs (or purify old ones); and along with other Black authorities, he must create a new history, new symbols, myths and legends (and purify old ones by fire). And the Black artist, in creating his own aesthetic, must be accountable for it only to the Black people. Further, he must hasten his own dissolution as an individual (in the Western sense)—painful though the process may be, having been breast-fed the poison of "individual experience."

When we speak of a "Black aesthetic" several things are meant. First, we assume that there is already in existence the basis for such an aesthetic. Essentially, it consists of an African-American cultural tradition. But this aesthetic is finally, by implication, broader than that tradition. It encompasses most of the useable elements of Third World culture. The motive behind the Black aesthetic is the destruction of the white thing, the destruction of white ideas, and white ways of looking at the world. The new aesthetic is mostly predicated on an Ethics which asks the question: whose vision of the world is finally more meaningful, ours or the white oppressors'? What is truth? Or more precisely, whose truth shall we express, that of the oppressed or of the oppressors? These are basic questions. Black intellectuals of previous decades failed to ask them. Further, national and international affairs demand that we appraise the world in terms of our own interests. It is clear that the question of human survival is at the core of contemporary experience. The Black artist must address himself to this reality in the strongest terms possible. In a context of world upheaval, ethics and aesthetics must interact positively and be consistent with the demands for a more spiritual world. Consequently, the Black Arts Movement is an ethical movement. Ethical, that is, from the viewpoint of the oppressed. And much of the oppression confronting the Third World and Black America is directly traceable to the Euro-American cultural sensibility. This sensibility, anti-human in nature, has, until recently, dominated the psyches of most Black artists and intellectuals; it must be destroyed before the Black creative artist can have a meaningful role in the transformation of society.

It is this natural reaction to an alien sensibility that informs the cultural attitudes of the Black Arts and the Black Power movement. It is a profound ethical sense that makes a Black artist question a society in which art is one thing and the actions of men another. The Black Arts Movement believes that your ethics and your aesthetics are one.[4] That the contradiction between ethics and aesthetics in western society is symptomatic of a dying culture.

The term "Black Arts" is of ancient origin, but it was first used in a positive sense by LeRoi Jones:

> We are unfair
> And unfair
> We are black magicians
> Black arts we make
> in black labs of the heart
>
> The fair are fair
> and deathly white
>
> The day will not save them
> And we own the night[5]

There is also a section of the poem "Black Dada Nihilismus" that carries the same motif. But a fuller amplification of the nature of the new aesthetics appears in the poem "Black Art":

> Poems are bullshit unless they are
> teeth or trees or lemons piled
> on a step. Or black ladies dying
> of men leaving nickel hearts
> beating them down. Fuck poems
> and they are useful, wd they shoot
> come at you, love what you are,
> breathe like wrestlers, or shudder
> strangely after pissing. We want live
> words of the hip world, live flesh &
> coursing blood. Hearts Brains
> Souls splintering fire. We want poems
> like fists beating niggers out of Jocks
> or dagger poems in the slimy bellies
> of the owner-jews . . .

Poetry is a concrete function, an action. No more abstractions. Poems are physical entities: fists, daggers, airplane poems, and poems that shoot guns. Poems are transformed from physical objects into personal forces:

> . . . Put it on him poem. Strip him naked
> to the world! Another bad poem cracking
> steel knuckles in a jewlady's mouth
> Poem scream poison gas on breasts in green berets . . .

Then the poem affirms the integral relationship between Black Art and Black people:

> . . . Let Black people understand
> that they are the lovers and the sons
> of lovers and warriors and sons

---

4. Reference to Austrian-British philosopher Ludwig Wittgenstein's *Tractatus Logico-Philosophicus* (1921), Proposition 6.

5. From Amiri Baraka's poem "In Memory of Malcolm" (1965).

of warriors Are poems & poets &
all the loveliness here in the world

It ends with the following lines, a central assertion in both the Black Arts Movement and the philosophy of Black Power:

We want a black poem. And a
Black World.
Let the world be a Black Poem
And let All Black People Speak This Poem
Silently
or LOUD

The poem comes to stand for the collective conscious and unconscious of Black America—the real impulse in back of the Black Power movement, which is the will toward self-determination and nationhood, a radical reordering of the nature and function of both art and the artist.

1968

Some Reflections on the Black Aesthetic

This outline below is a rough overview of some categories and elements that constituted a "Black Aesthetic"[1] outlook. All of these categories need further elaboration, so I am working on a larger essay that will tie them all together.

		1. RACE MEMORY[4] (Africa, Middle Passage)
Mythology	*formal manifestation*	Rhythm as an expression of race memory; rhythm as a
Spirit worship, Orishas, ancestors, African Gods. Syncretism/catholic voodoo, macumba,[2] Holy Ghost, Jesus as somebody you might know, like a personal deity. River spirits.	Samba, Calypso, Batucada, Cha-Cha, juba, gospel songs, jubilees, work song, spirituals.[3]	basic creative principle; rhythm as existence, creative force as vector of existence. Swinging[5]
		2. MIDDLE PASSAGE[6] (Diaspora) Race memory: terror, landlessness, claustrophobia: "America is a prison . . ." Malcolm X.[7]

1. Black Arts movement theorist Hoyt Fuller coined the term "black aesthetic" to denote what he called "a system of isolating and evaluating the artistic works of black people which reflects the special characteristics and imperatives of black experience" ("Towards a Black Aesthetic," 1968). In the wake of Fuller's manifesto, efforts to elaborate "a Black Aesthetic" were undertaken by such writers as Amiri Baraka, Addison Gayle, Stephen Henderson, Maulana Ron Karenga, and Neal.
2. Bantu religious practices in Afro-Brazilian communities; "Orishas": spirits of deities in the religious system of the Yoruba, a West African ethnic group; "Syncretism": the melding of beliefs and practices from different religious traditions; "voodoo": a syncretic religion that melds Dahomean voudon with Catholicism, practiced chiefly in Haiti.
3. "Gospel songs, jubilees, work song, spirituals": musical genres deriving from African American slave experience; "Samba, Calypso, Batucanda, Cha-Cha, juba": dances and musical traditions of Afro-Latino derivation.
4. In psychology, posited memories, feelings, and ideas inherited from one's ancestors.
5. Stylish, sophisticated, lively.
6. The forced voyage of African slaves to the Americas, leading to the scattering ("diaspora") of African peoples through the New World.
7. African American activist and black nationalist leader (1925–1965); Malcolm uttered the phrase "America is a prison" in many speeches, most famously in "Message to the Grass Roots" (1963).

Neo-Mythology
Shamans: Preachers, poets, blues singers, musicians, mackdaddies,[8] and politicians.

formal manifestation
All aspects of Black dance styles in the New World. Pelvic. Dress and walk.

3. TRANSMUTATION AND SYNTHESIS

Funky Butt, Stomps, Jump Jim Crow, Buck 'n' Wing, Jigs, Snake, Grind, slow drag, jitterbug, twist, Watusi, fish, swim, boogaloo, etc.[9] Dance to the *after* beat.[1] Dance as race memory; transmitted through the collective folk consciousness.

Neo-Mythology
Legba, Oshun, Yemaya, Urzulie,[2] Soul Momma, Evil women, Good loving women, woman as primarily need/ man as doer. Blues singer as poet and moral judge; bad man Earth centered, but directed cosmologically. Folk poet, philosopher, priest, priestess, conjurer,[3] preacher, teacher, hustler, seer, soothsayer[4] . . .

4. BLUES GOD/TONE AS MEANING AND MEMORY

Sound as racial memory, primeval. Life breath. Word is perceived as energy or force. Call and response Blues perceived as an emanation outside of man, but yet a manifestation of his being/reality. Same energy source as Gospel, field holler,[5] but delineated in narrative song. The African voice transplanted. This God must be the meanest and the strongest. He survives and persists Once perceived as an evil force: ". . . and I (Dude Botley)[6] got to thinking about how many thousands of people (Buddy) Bolden had made happy and all of them women who used to idolize him 'Where are they now?' I say to myself.

---

8. Conspicuously successful pimps (slang); "shamans": priests or priestesses who use magic to heal the sick or gain access to the spirit world.
9. "Funky Butt . . . boogaloo": African American dances of the 1940s, 1950s, and 1960s.
1. Reference to the syncopated rhythm characteristic of blues and jazz.
2. Or Oxun: orisha of sexual passion and fertility, a river deity; Legba: orisha of crossroads, doorways, and gates, a messenger and trickster deity; Oshun: orisha of love, beauty, wealth, and diplomacy; Yemaya: orisha of the moon, sea-mother.
3. In the African American syncretic religion

known as hoodoo, a person considered to have power over the spirit world.
4. Fortune-teller or oracle.
5. Form of vocal music originating in slavery, akin to the work song.
6. Apocryphal New Orleans musician, often cited as an eyewitness expert on the African American cornetist Charles Joseph "Buddy" Bolden (1877–1931), originator of a New Orleans style of early jazz known as ragtime. Neal quotes extensively here a passage from *Jazz Masters of New Orleans* (1967), by jazz historian Martin T. Williams (1924–1992).

Then I hear Bolden's cornet. I look through the crack and there he is, relaxed back in the chair, blowing that silver cornet softly, just above a whisper, and I see he's got his hat over the bell of the horn. I put my ear close to the keyhole. I thought I heard Bolden play the blues before, and play hymns at funerals, but what he is playing now is real strange and I listen carefully, because he's playing something that for a while sounds like the blues, then like a hymn. I cannot make out the tune, but after awhile I catch on. He is mixing up the blues with the hymns. He plays the blues real sad and the hymn sadder than the blues and then the blues sadder than the hymn. That is the first time that I had ever heard hymns and blues cooked up together. A strange cold feeling comes over me; I get sort of scared because I know the Lord don't like that mixing the Devil's music with his music. . . . It sounded like a battle between the Good Lord and the Devil. Something tells me to listen and see who wins. If Bolden stops on the hymn, the Good Lord wins; if he stops on the blues, the Devil wins."

5. BLACK ARTS MOVEMENT/BLACK ART AESTHETIC

Feeling/ contemporary and historical. Energy intensifies.

HISTORY AS UNITARY MYTH

Shango, Nat Turner, Denmark, Vesey, Brer' Rabbit, High John

HISTORY AS UNITARY MYTH (cont'd)

the Conqueror, Jack Johnson, Ray Robinson, Signifying Monkey, Malcolm X, Adam Clayton Powell, Garvey, DuBois, Hon. Elijah Muhammed, Martin L. King, Rap Brown, Rev. Franklin, Charlie Parker, Duke Ellington,[7] James Brown, Bessie Smith, Moms Mabley, King Pleasure, Raefilt Johnson. Son House. Louis Armstrong. . . .[1] Voodoo again/Ishmael Reed's Hoodoo. Islamic suffis.[2] Third World's destiny. The East as the Womb and the Tomb. Fanon's[3] Third World, Bandung Humanism.[4]

5. BLACK ARTS MOVEMENT/BLACK ART AESTHETIC (cont'd)

Non-matrixed art forms: Coltrane, Ornette, Sun Ra.[8] More concerned with the vibrations of the Word, than with the Word itself. Like signifying.[9] The Black Nation as Poem. Ethical stance as aesthetic. The synthesis of the above presented outline. The integral unity of culture, politics, and art. Spiritual. Despises alienation in the European sense. Art consciously committed; art addressed primarily to Black and Third World people. Black attempts to realize the world as art by making Man more

7. Edward Kennedy "Duke" Ellington (1899–1974), jazz pianist, composer, and band leader; Shango: orisha of fire, lightning, and thunder; Nat Turner (1800–1831) and Denmark Vesey (1767–1822), leaders of slave rebellions; Brer' Rabbit, High John the Conqueror, and Signifying Monkey: heroes of African American folk culture who defy authority through wit, magic, and deception, respectively; John Arthur "Jack" (1878–1946) and Sugar Ray Robinson (born Walter Smith Jr., 1921–1989): African American boxing champions; Malcolm X (born Malcolm Little, 1925–1965), black nationalist, minister of the Nation of Islam, and human rights activist; Adam Clayton Powell Sr. (1865–1953): pastor of Abyssinian Baptist Church, a large activist congregation in Harlem, whose son Adam Clayton Powell Jr. (1908–1972) was the first African American elected to Congress from New York City; Marcus Mosiah Garvey Jr. (1887–1940), Jamaican-born political leader, founder of the Universal Negro Improvement Association and advocate of the "Back to Africa" movement; W. E. B. Du Bois (1868–1963), African American sociologist, author, civil rights activist, and Pan-African political philosopher; Elijah Muhammad (born Elijah Robert Poole, 1897–1975), leader of the Nation of Islam from 1934 to 1975); Martin Luther King Jr. (1929–1968), African American civil rights leader and co-founder of the Southern Christian Leadership Conference; H. Rap Brown, later known as Jamil Abdullah Al-Amin (b. 1943), chairman of the Student Nonviolent Coordinating Committee (SNCC) and minister of justice for the Black Panther Party in the 1960s; Reverend C. L. Franklin (1915–1984), African American preacher and civil rights activist, father of the legendary soul and gospel singer Aretha Franklin (b. 1942); Charles "Charlie" Parker Jr. (1920–1955), African American jazz saxophonist and composer known

for advancing the "bebop" style of jazz.
8. Sun Ra (born Herman Poole Blount, 1914–1993); Ornette Coleman (b. 1930); John Coltrane (1926–1967): avant-garde jazz saxophonists and composers whose "non-matrixed" styles departed from conventional musical time signatures or measures.
9. Or signifyin': African American verbal strategy of indirection that exploits the gap between literal and metaphorical meaning.
1. African American jazz trumpeter, singer, and composer (1901–1971); James Brown (1933–2006): African American singer and songwriter known as the "King of Soul," an originator of funk music; Bessie Smith (1894–1927): African American singer; Jackie "Moms" Mabley (born Loretta Mary Aiken, 1894–1975): African American comedian and pioneer of the so-called Chitlin' Circuit of African American vaudeville; King Pleasure (born Clarence Beeks, 1922–1981), African American jazz vocalist; Eddie James "Son" House (1902–1988): African American blues singer-songwriter.
2. Followers of an Islamic form of mysticism. "Voodoo again/Ishmael Reed's hoodoo": African American writer Ishmael Reed (b. 1938), creator of a style of writing that blends aspects of the Haitian syncretic religion Voodoo, or Vodou, and hoodoo, an African American syncretic religious practice also known as "conjure."
3. Franz Fanon (1925–1961), Martinique-born French-Algerian philosopher, psychiatrist, and post-colonial writer.
4. Pan-African philosophical and political theory promoted by the Revolutionary Action Movement (RAM), led by Robert F. Williams (1925–1996). RAM's 1964 conference "The Black Revolution's Relationship to the Bandung World" evoked the first Asian-African Conference of newly independent African and Asian states that took place in the Indonesian city of Bandung in 1955.

Revolution is the operational mythology. Symbol change. Expanded metaphors as in the poetry of Curtis Lyle and Stanley Crouch; or L. Barrett's *Song For MuMu*[5] . . . Nigger styles and masks such as Rinehart in the *Invisible Man*.[6] Style as in James P. Johnson description of stride pianists in the twenties. Bobby Blue Bland wearing a dashiki[7] and a process. All of this links up with the transmutation of African styles and the revitalization of these styles in the West. compatible to it and it more compatible to Man. Styles itself from nigger rhythms to cosmic sensibility. Black love, conscious and affirmed. Change.

1972

Uncle Rufus Raps on the Squared Circle[1]

> Once I saw a prize fighter boxing a yokel. The fighter was swift and amazingly scientific. His body was one violent flow of rapid rhythmic action. He hit the yokel a hundred times while the yokel held up his arms in stunned surprise. But suddenly the yokel, rolling about in the gale of boxing gloves, struck one blow and knocked science, speed and footwork as cold as a well-digger's posterior. The smart money hit the canvas. The long shot got the nod. The yokel had simply stepped inside of his opponent's sense of time.
> —Ralph Ellison, *Invisible Man*

Sporting events, like beauty contests, horse shows, public assassinations—all forms of spectacle—have implicit within them a distinct metaphysical character, said Uncle Rufus while lighting his cigar. We had been talking about the Ali-Frazier fight.[2] He had once been a boxer. Then later he became a singer and dancer in a minstrel show.[3] Needless to say, Uncle Rufus is a most fascinating gentleman. Following our discussion, I discovered that he was

---

5. Carlto Lindsay Barrett (b. 1941), Jamaican writer and photographer, who published his first novel, *Song for MuMu*, in 1967; K. Curtis Lyle, African American poet and founder of the Watts Writers Workshop in Los Angeles; Stanley Crouch (b. 1945), African American poet, novelist, and critic.

6. Rinehart, an elusive character in the 1952 novel *Invisible Man* by Ralph Ellison (1914–1994), appears only by reputation of his multiple guises, including pimp, bookie, and preacher.

7. Loose-fitting pullover garment, usually colorful, common in West Africa and popular among African American men in the 1960s and 1970s; Robert Calvin "Bobby Blue" Bland (b. 1930), African American blues and soul singer.

1. "Squaring the circle," a mathematical conundrum originating among Babylonian geometers, is a metaphor for an impossible task such as proving rational truth for a transcendental rather than material reality. "Raps": expounds on orally, often in a long monologue (African American vernacular).

2. Also known as the "Fight of the Century," the fight between heavyweight champion Joe Frazier (1944–2011) and Muhammad Ali (born Cassius Marcellus Clay Jr., 1942) occurred on March 8, 1971, in New York City. After refusing to enter the U.S. Army in 1967 on grounds of religious conscientious objection, Ali had become a symbol of anti-establishment rebellion, while Frazier was taken as representative of a more conservative stance within the African American community; the fight was thus widely taken as symbolic of national tensions in the early 1970s.

3. American form of spectacle consisting of comic and musical acts performed by actors in blackface.

one of the prime sources for Melvin B. Tolson's extremely muscular masterpiece entitled *The Harlem Gallery*.[4] Further, Uncle Rufus staunchly maintains that he knew the real John Henry[5] who, by the way, was an excellent bare-knuckle fighter.

The day after the Ali-Frazier fight, I met him uptown at a little spot in Harlem called My Bar. The bar is a very hip joint.[6] It's run by a tall yellow[7] guy named Julian May. It's a good place to talk all kinds of sports. Julian's got himself a brand-new color TV in the back room. And there's a bartender there, Ray, who is a statistical and historical expert on all sports, especially the ones in which we dominate, or the ones in which we have determined the stylistic mode and strategy. But Ray would never speak in these terms; he absorbs his data on sports because he loves them and sees them as significant encounters with the unknowable nature of the world. Ray's attitude toward sports like boxing, football and basketball is a healthy blend of the mysterious and scientific.

I am sitting at the bar, discussing with Ray the function of energy in athletics when Uncle Rufus bops[8] into the door. He peacocks in a pearl gray homburg.[9] The coat is blue cashmere. He sports a golden-headed serpent cane;[1] the shoes, French, Shriner and Urner, contrast exquisitely with his spats[2] which are the same pearl gray color as the homburg.

I order him a Jack Daniels,[3] and introduce him to Ray. A discussion ensues concerning the geometry of basketball. I feel shut out of the conversation; and besides, I didn't invite my uncle here to talk about basketball. I was really getting irritated with the whole thing when some customers finally worked into the bar.

So now that I had Uncle Rufus to myself, I asked him his opinion of the Ali-Frazier fight. He began the discussion with some commentary on a few of the events that transpired in the aftermath of Jack Johnson's victory over Jim Jeffries back in Reno on July 4, 1910.[4]

"It was during the days of the steamboat, and after that famous bout," he said, "there was fighting going on between the blacks and whites. This happened because the whites were so infuriated by Jack's victory that they began beating up on the colored. A man got lynched in Cap Giradeau[5] when he tried to collect a bet he had made with a white farmer by the name of Cyrus Compton.

"I was working on a show called Stall's Minstrels. Now this show was out of Cairo, Illinois, which is smack on the Mississippi River. But we was working in a dance hall in Henderson, Kentucky. I think they called that

---

4. Melvin B. Tolson (1898–1966), African American poet, whose long poem "Harlem Gallery" (1965) uses jazz rhythms and modernist techniques to tell stories of African American life.
5. American folk hero whose extraordinary strength as a steel-driver were proven in a race against a steam-powered hammer.
6. Sophisticated place. My Bar: establishment frequented by Neal.
7. Light-complected African American.
8. Walk with exaggerated confidence.
9. Type of fedora hat popular in the mid-20th century; "peacocks": behaves or dresses flamboyantly.
1. In Greek mythology, the rod of Asclepius, god of medicine, is a serpent-entwined staff wielded by the deity as an instrument of his healing arts. That emblem passed into the tradition of Anglo-American medicine established by physician

John Radcliffe (1652–1714) in which a master physician carried a gold cane as sign of his authority, then passed that healing scepter to a disciple at the end of his career.
2. Cloth or leather gaiter covering the instep or ankle. French, Shriner, and Urner: maker of men's dress shoes based in Boston, Massachusetts.
3. Brand of American whiskey.
4. Johnson (1878–1946) was the first African American world heavyweight boxing champion, a position he maintained from 1908 to 1915. His fight against James J. "Jim" Jeffries (1875–1953), billed as "The Fight of the Century," became in the popular press and public imagination a symbolic contest between the white and black races.
5. Cape Girardeau, commonly referred to as "Cape," is a city in southeast Missouri.

hall The Stomp. All the great troupes had worked it. The Creole Show and Black Patti's Troubadours[6] had also been through there. And while I was in Henderson, I heard a splendid concert of operatic selections by Sissieretta Jones."

"Well, what about the fight?" I asked.

"Oh . . . the fight? Which fight?"

"It's hard to tell now; I asked you about the Ali-Frazier fight, and you started talking about Jack Johnson which, it seems to me, doesn't have much to do with this conversation."

"Let's put it this way, son: You order me another one of these Jack Daniels, and sit back patiently so you can learn something for once in your life."

"If you wasn't my Uncle Rufus, I would tell you to go and eat shit, talking to me that way."

"Never mind that . . . I want it on the rocks with water on the side."

I ordered the drink. Ray came over, poured his drink, then mine. I think I saw them exchange winks.

"Well, as I was trying to say, I was in Henderson, and I heard that they was fighting and all."

"Who was fighting and all?"

"The colored and white.

"They say, no sooner did Jack win the match than the fighting broke out. Well, I was in Henderson, and I heard that they was fighting in Evansville, Indiana. Evansville is right across the Ohio River from Henderson, so I went up there. Man, even with the fighting and all going on, them colored people was celebrating. But not like they was doing in '35 when Joe Louis won his match against Carnera.[7] No it was nothing compared to that. But it was still some celebration.

"The next day, after the all-night-long parties, some smartass little colored boy by the name of Open Mouth Rainey got shot to death in the Silver Dollar Bar and Grill. It seems this guy, Open Mouth, strolled into the restaurant and asked the owner for a cup of coffee as strong as Jack Johnson, and a steak beat up like Jim Jeffries. When he said that, the owner slapped him, reaching quickly for his six-shooter which was right under the counter. Open Mouth Rainey pulled his forty-four, but it was too late. The man had gotten the drop on[8] Open Mouth. He burned[9] him five times. Open Mouth barely had a chance. Let me tell you: Some of them crackers[1] was sure mad that a nigger was now the heavyweight champion of the world.

"But the colored knew that it was quite natural for there to be a black champion. Since we was the first boxers in this country anyway. You see, Larry, boxing started out in Virginia. There it was the custom for the sons of aristocratic families to go to England where they received a first-rate education in the humanities. Also, while there, they were supposed to acquire the finer virtues by circulating among and socializing with the English gentry. Now along with education of the mind went the education of the body.

6. Musical and acrobatic act that flourished from 1896 to 1915, founded by African American opera singer Matilda Sissieretta Joyner Jones (1868–1933). The Creole Show: Founded in 1890, famous as the first minstrel group to feature a female performer.

7. In June 1935, black boxing champion Joe Louis (1914–1981) beat former heavyweight champion Primo Carnera (1906–1967), an Italian American whom the press turned into a symbol of Italian Fascist leader Benito Mussolini; Louis's victory was read as an event with international significance, particularly by African Americans who sympathized with Ethiopia, which was colonized by Italy.

8. Succeed in getting the advantage (slang). "Forty-four": a .44-caliber hand gun.

9. Shot.

1. White people (pejorative slang).

Therefore, they were trained in the manly art of boxing. Now these scions of Southern aristocracy returned home from England with a good education and a knowledge of the rudiments of boxing. Back home, they started training some of the young slaves to be boxers. So they held contests among the slaves from different plantations.

"Pugilism, as it relates to us, son, got its formal start, however, with the career of one Tom Molyneaux.[2] Mr. Molyneaux was the first colored champion. He was born in Virginia, a slave; and when he was, through some mysterious process, granted his freedom, he traveled to New York. By then, he had beaten everybody around, both Negroes and whites. Then he went to England to fight Tom Cribb[3] who was then the world champion. This fight took place in December of 1810; I forget the exact date. But it was at Capthall Common in Sussex. These were the days before the Queensberry rules.[4] As I recall, it was a dreary day, the fight lasted forty rounds. Tom Cribb won, but a lots of folks, particularly a guy they called West Indian Charlie, protested that there was tricknology involved in Cribb's victory.[5] But be that as it may, that's how the colored got into boxing.

"All of the plantation owners, from all points, used to gather at their respective plantations to place wagers on one slave or the other. These men were all gentlemen, fine education, breeding, and plenty of money. So in many ways, they didn't care who really won the fight. It was all just considered good sport. They liked the way them niggers circled each other and doing them fancy steps, and dropping them bombs and do. Naturally, they got specially excited when one of them fellers drew blood. I once saw two slaves beat each other to death."

"It is late in the afternoon, sun swarming all over us. I am inside of a bull of a man named Silas. Amos swings a wild right at me. I block it easily, but he catches me with a left hook. It seems like all day we have been fighting like this. My arms and his arms are heavy, but we smash at each other and at the white blurry faces surrounding us. We go on like this until the sun begins going down. . . . The shouting and the rooting has died down now; now we lean on each other breathing hard and tied up in sweat like wrestlers. The contest has boiled down to grunts and awkward swings. . . . As darkness comes, we are both still standing. Judge Tate calls it a tie. They throw me in the buckboard, and carry me back to the plantation."

"You got the right idea, son. That's almost exactly how it was in those days. Yeah, that's just the way it went down. Them folks really liked the sports. And since they had lots of money, and not much to do, they just gambles all the time.

"Yes siree, them folks liked the sports and the sporting houses[6] too. And I'm sure you know that they had betting tables in them houses too. An ex-boxer by the name of Bill Richmond[7] ran one of the biggest whore houses in the city of New Orleans; but even though he himself was colored, he didn't allow no colored in there—'cept them girls he had working for him.

---

2. African American bare-knuckle boxer (1784–1818) who spent the majority of his career in Great Britain and Ireland. Born a slave, Molyneaux was granted his freedom after his master won large sums betting on his fights with other slaves.
3. English bare-knuckle boxer (1781–1848).
4. Guidelines meant to ensure courtesy and fairness in boxing matches, named after John Douglass, 9th Marquess of Queensberry.
5. Cribb won in the 35th round, after a dispute in the 19th round when Cribb appeared to some as having failed to resume fighting after a referee-ordered break.
6. I.e., houses of prostitution.
7. African American boxer (1763–1829), born a slave; a friend and coach of Molyneaux.

"I told you I used to be a boxer before I went to Stall's Minstrels. Woody Johnson was manager (may he rest in peace). I was swift and dancy, in the bantamweight class,[8] like Eligio Sardinas who was otherwise known as "Kid Chocolate."[9] I had me a pretty snappy jab, and my left hook was a monster. I got tired of the fight game though. And then I decided to go into show business? Why? 'Cause there was some very nice people in the business in those days, real educated and refined people like J. Rosamund Johnson.[1] And I wanted to be one of them. So I gave up the fight game, even though I was good. In my time, I was on good terms with boxers like Battling Siki, Tiger Flowers, Joe Gans, Sammy the Smasher and Sam Langford.[2] Me and Sam used to party a lot together. I'm not just name-dropping, son; I'm simply giving you my credentials so you will fully appreciate the facts I'm about to give you concerning the squared circle.

"A lots of black guys started hanging round the sporting events. In those days, we refered to these guys as the Sporting Crowd; or we called them Sports for short. Now all these sportsmens was fast livers. They dressed in the latest fashions, and wore finely tailored suits. Jelly Roll Morton[3] used to hang around with that bunch quite often. Jelly Roll was the real sporting type. He played a wicked piano, was a ladies' man, spoke French, and had him a diamond ring on every finger. He even had a diamond in his middle tooth. You was liable to see old Jelly Roll anywhere and with anybody. He was around boxers and jockeys as much as he was round musicians.

"Well, now that we're talking about Jelly Roll, this brings me to the part of my discussion about boxing in general, and the Ali-Frazier fight in particular. Did you know that there is a distinct connection between boxing and music? You say you didn't know that? Well, there is. You see it's like this: Boxing is just another kind of rhythm activity. Like all sports is based on rhythm. Dig:[4] If you ain't got no rhythm, you can't play no sports. Like jumping rope ain't nothing but dancing. Beating on the punching bag is the same as beating on drums. Everything connected with sports is connected with rhythm. You just think about it for a while. Every fighter has his own particular rhythmic style just the way musicians do. You ever notice that some fighters dance around a lot, doing fast rhythms; while some other guy is slower, likes to do the slow drag instead of the Lindy Hop or the jitterbug.[5] Yes, Larry, this is so with all of its possible variations.

"All sports are just expressions of a particular attitude toward rhythm. But boxing unlike many other sports confines the players to a very small area of confrontation. Boxers are contained within a square. And this makes for particular difficulties. But it also makes for the particular attraction to the sport. Most men can identify with the sport because most men, at one time or the other, have had to hold their hands up. But what about the square?

8. Division of boxing for fighters weighing no more than 118 pounds.
9. Eligio Sardiñas Montalvo (1910–1998), Cuban lightweight champion from 1931 to 1933, a celebrity in American high society of the 1930s.
1. John Rosamond Johnson (1873–1954), African American composer and singer during the Harlem Renaissance; brother of author and civil rights activist James Weldon Johnson (1871–1938).
2. Black Canadian boxer (1883–1956); Battling Siki: Louis Mbarick Fall (1897–1925), Senegalese light-heavyweight boxer; Tiger Flowers: Theodore Flowers (1895–1927), the first African American

middleweight boxing champion; Joe Gans: Joseph Gant (1874–1910), African American lightweight boxing champion from 1902 to 1908; Samuel Langford (1883–1956), black Canadian boxer who held the title of World Colored Heavyweight Champion from 1910 to 1918.
3. Ferdinand Joseph LaMothe (1884–1941), African American ragtime and jazz pianist, composer, and bandleader.
4. Understand; pay attention.
5. Jitterbug, Lindy Hop: fast-moving swing dances of the 1920s and 1930s; "slow drag": dance set to bluesy music that lags behind the beat.

What has it to do with the sport? Well, the square symbolizes a discrete universe. That is to say, it brings to bear upon the material universe a particular sense of order. All geometrical constructs do. For example, the triangle, the Trinity and other ternary[6] clusters seem to represent spiritual dynamism. The circle, on the other hand, represents some aspect of infinity. Perhaps oneness in God. The square, in its quaternary[7] aspect, appears to symbolize the material realm, or the rational intellect. There is a negative aspect to the square though. In some ways the square implies stasis, and even decadence. But regardless of all of these factors, the square is the context in which one fighter confronts another one.

"Here we are dealing with the underlying premises behind the sport. We could say something about ritual here, but that side of the street has already been covered in great detail by Mr. Jack Johnson in his autobiography.[8] Instead here, we are discussing the metaphysics of geometrical and dynamic modality.

"Now there are several things that determine the winner of a fight, or any sporting contest for that matter. But all of these things are essentially tied up with rhythm. Because even though there is an implied circle within the square (and naturally without the square), one rhythmically described by the fighters themselves, the square, in this connection, is the creation of a particular historical sensibility. This sensibility manifests itself in all spheres of life and art. We see it asserting itself in architecture, technology and sociopolitical theories. The circle, on the other hand, exists as an ever-evolving metaconstruct. The fighter's duty is to rhythmically discern the essential unity between the circle and the square.

"Take this Muhammad Ali, for example; he knows all about squares and circles 'cause he is a Muslim. And all of them folks knows all about things like that. Like 360°=Allah.[9] That kind of thing. He even know about rhythm. I hear he's a poet. Rhythm concerns the modality of space, sound, motion, and existence. Both space and motion can be manipulated rhythmically. Existence can also be manipulated in like manner; but we'll deal with that some other time when we are discussing contests that involve more than four persons. If we went into that now, we would have to discuss history, and that bitch is not the subject of my discussion.

"All fighters must understand the principles of rhythmic modality. The fighter who best understands these principles will most likely win the contest. Again, young man, rhythm here refers to the duration and the structure of the contest, its interlocking spatial and dynamic relationships, the manner in which one proceeds to handle the space dominated by his body, and the body of his opponent. It also refers to the artistic or technical manipulation of the space encompassed by the square which these fools erroneously call the "ring." By the use of a calculus, therefore, we arrive at the conclusion that the Ali-Frazier fight was, in fact, a contest of essentially different attitudes toward music.

"This was the secret wisdom that Jelly Roll Morton passed on to boxers of the twenties. This principle was orally transmitted through a long line of

6. Having three elements or parts. "Trinity": the Christian doctrine that defines God as a unity of three divine persons: the Father, the Son, and the Holy Spirit.
7. Having four elements or parts.
8. Refers to *Jack Johnson Is a Dandy: An Autobiography*, published in 1969.

9. At the time of the Muhammad, before his prophecies, 360 different gods were worshipped at the sacred site of the Kaaba in Mecca, the chief deity among them being "Allah." In Islam as in many other traditions, a full circle of 360 degrees represents wholeness, unity, and eternity.

boxers until it was momentarily obscured by Floyd Patterson,[1] who was the first Hamlet of the boxing profession.

"Now Ali understands these principles of rhythm and music. Theoretically, that's what's so sweet about him. You see, he believes in riffing.[2] He certainly has got the body, the legs, and the mouth for it. But Frazier is somewhere else in the musical universe. Frazier is stomp-down[3] blues, bacon, grits, and Sunday church. 'Course them Muslims is different. They don't be eating none of that hog. They say it ruin your brains. It didn't seem to do Frazier no harm though, 'cept he do seem a little slow with the rap sometimes. But Joe Louis, an Alabama boy, raised on blackstrap molasses, was slow with the rap too. And you know how mean he could be upon entering the squared circle. But Ali is body bebop,[4] while Frazier is slow brooding blues with a gospel bearing. Ali understands the mysteries of the circles and the squares, the same as Sufi[5] poets do. That is to say, Larry, the essential metaphysics of these forms, for him, a constant source of religious and intellectual meditation. Ali prays (does his salats[6]) in quiet meditation. But most likely, Frazier wants to shout in church. However, Ali, as a Muslim intellectual, has been forced to suppress his gospel impulse. But he can't suppress it totally. You can still hear it in his voice when he speaks, or when he tries to sing. But blues and gospel ain't his thing. Frazier can't sing, but he sings better than Ali. And that's why Frazier won the fight.

"I don't mean that he outsung Ali during the fight. I mean, instead, that he sang his particular song better than Ali sang his. Old slow-blues, pork-eating Frazier is moody and relentless. He got plenty killer in him. But bebop body, your man, is the urbanized philosopher of the would-be righteous, the future shaper in many respects. However, he is a blase singer, having a tendency to sound-down mammy-loving country boys who lack causes, and who are grateful for any desperate break they can get. Boys like Frazier envision purple suits, full-length Russian sable, beige Eldoradoes,[7] the perfumed cluster of female flesh, and triumphant kisses from the Sepia Queen.[8]

"Ali envisions a Nation full of intricate order, like an interlocking network of squares and rectangles. He dreams of kissing the black stone of Mecca.[9] No loose perfumed ladies there. Perhaps there, mosques fly as zones of ultimate righteousness. The Muslim women wear long dresses; they pursue long periods of silence as they sidestep sin, murmuring polite Koranic knowledge.

"Your problem, my boy, primarily concerns making both of them understand the implicit unity between the circle and the square. Using a variant of the calculus that we set up earlier, I would say, therefore, that Frazier needs Ali's squares, and Ali needs Frazier's circles. I can't see it no other way.

"The essential dynamics of the squared circle demand that each contestant really understand how he sings best. That he choreograph and orchestrate his game in terms of what he does best. Theoretically, everyone in the sporting game knows this. But the pragmatics or translation of this abstract

1. Heavyweight champion from the mid-1950s to early 1960s (1935–2006).
2. Heavy-footed, action-packed blues-inspired dance.
3. Nimble improvising.
4. Jazz style of the 1940s and 1950s characterized by fast tempo and melodic improvisation.
5. A mystical, inward-focused path in Islam.
6. The five daily prayers practiced by Muslims.

7. Luxury automobile produced by Cadillac from 1953 to 2002.
8. Lillian Goodner (1896–1994), African American blues singer billed as "Sister Lillian: Queen of the Sepias."
9. The eastern cornerstone of the Kaaba, located in the center of Mecca's Grand Mosque, one of the holiest sites in the Islamic world.

knowledge often eludes us. In the case of the particular spectacle under discussion, the fighters were very much evenly matched. They just simply manifested different choreographic styles. But given the pressure of the evening, its particular psychological atmosphere, its forced political overtone, the winner would be the one who most acutely understood the principles of spatial and psychic rhythm. Ali's science was winning until the first stunning blow caught him somewhere around the eighth round. (Note the quaternity of the number eight: 8.) But Ali also had not paced himself properly from the beginning of the match. He allowed himself to enter Frazier's system of deceptive choreography; a system full of treacherous memories that lay in the cut ready to pummel that bebopping body of his. The way to fight slow grinding powerhouses like Frazier is to not let them touch you at all—if it's humanly possible. Because, beneath that dull rap, there is a mad churning engine. And you have got to respect that kind of power." He looked at his watch.

"How about one for the road?" I said.

"That's all right with me, but it has got to be a quickie. I'm supposed to meet this chippie[1] in a little while."

When the next round of drinks came, I toasted him and thanked him for his time. "Wow! Uncle Rufus, all that time you was talking you never told me who you were pulling for."

He looked at me long and hard. Then his black face broke into a sarcastic smile. He reached down beneath the bar stool, and pulled his cane out. He held it up so that the golden-headed serpent would glitter as it caught the low amber light of the My Bar sign. He looked at the cane, and then at me. I could see now, looking at him full in the face, that he was really much older than he seemed. I saw the cane swiftly fly back. Before I had time to react, Uncle Rufus had whacked me hard across my arm.

"What was that about?" I whined, rubbing my aching arm.

"It's about you not learning to ask the right questions, especially after I done took all this time explaining things to you. Sheet! I really shouldn't give you no answer. But since you once told me you wanted to be a boxer, here it is: I was pulling for both of them. But this time, your old uncle put his money on slow blues. . . ."

1972

---

1. Promiscuous woman; prostitute.

ISHMAEL REED
b. 1938

L auded by musician Max Roach as the Charlie Parker of African American letters, but reviled by critics displeased by his controversial political assertions, Ishmael Reed has consistently provoked complex, often contradictory, reactions from readers and critics. Working in multiple media (from novels, poetry, and essays to dramas, songs, and collages), Reed insistently interrogates norms of literary genre and cultural belief. He conjures alchemies of narrative and poetic forms, combining fragments from a broad range of traditions, religions, and languages in order to challenge established modes of self-comportment that seem natural not only to the culture in which we live but also to the very language we speak—"I want a switch, a shift, a shift in syntax, a shift in structure, a change, a surprise!"

The son of Henry Lenoir (a fundraiser for the YMCA) and Thelma Coleman (a saleslady), Ishmael Reed was born February 22, 1938, in Chattanooga, Tennessee, taking the surname of his mother's second husband, Bennie Stephen Reed (an auto worker). Reed has a total of seven siblings in his two families. In 1942 Reed moved with his mother to Buffalo, New York, where she found work in a series of wartime industries. In the 1950s Reed attended several different schools—including Buffalo Technical High School and East High School—and eventually enrolled in evening classes at what was then called Millard Fillmore College (now part of SUNY Buffalo). He grew deeply interested in music, both classical and jazz, took up both the trombone and the violin, and performed for a brief stint with a string quartet. Working in the Buffalo public library by day and taking classes by night, Reed used what little other time he had to refine his developing craft as writer; it was ultimately a story called "Something Pure" that impressed one of his English professors so much that Reed was made a full-time student in the bachelor of arts program. "They signed a petition and got me into the day school," he has written, "and I was quite a celebrity in the English classes."

Though he applied himself avidly to his courses in English, American studies, and linguistics, Reed decided to withdraw from university in his junior year (1960), in part due to financial difficulty but also because he felt that he needed a new atmosphere in which to pursue his experiments with language. Reed reflects on his withdrawal from college with a mix of righteousness and cheeky regret: "This was the best thing that could have happened to me at the time because I was able to continue experimenting along the lines I wanted, influenced by [Nathanael] West and others. I just didn't want to be a slave to somebody else's reading lists. I kind of regret the decision now because I've gotten some of the most racist and horrible things said to me because of this."

Moving to "Buffalo's notorious Talbert Mall Project," Reed began working for a newspaper as a staff correspondent for the *Empire Star Weekly*, which he claims taught him discipline in writing. With his editor, Reed began to co-host a radio program on the station WVFO in 1961, "The Buffalo Community Roundtable." Pioneering and provocative, the show was canceled after Reed conducted a particularly incendiary on-air interview with Malcolm X. During the rest of his time in Buffalo, Reed wrote a play called *Ethan Booker* and acted in a number of dramatic productions of works by Edward Albee, Tennessee Williams, and Lorraine Hansberry. In September 1960 Reed married Priscilla Rose; their daughter, Timothy Brett Reed, was born two years later. In that same year, 1962, Reed moved to New York City, which he would make his home for about five years, separating himself from his new wife and family.

Arriving in New York with aspirations to be "a W. B. Yeats," Reed found work and peers that at once humbled and energized him: "New York taught me my voice and I developed my style further from contact with such people as Calvin Hernton, David Henderson, Joe Johnson, Steve Cannon, and Tom Dent." Distancing himself both from white New York avant-garde poets and from Black Arts writers like Amiri Baraka, Reed discovered some of his greatest artistic partners in musicians such as Cecil Tayler, Bill Dixon, Albert Ayler, and (especially) Sun Ra, determining that it was of utmost importance for black poets to "capture [the] rhythm and sound" of the myriad varieties of black life. He continued working as a journalist and writer, serving as editor in chief of *Advance*, a Newark, New Jersey, weekly, and he co-founded, along with his friend the painter Walter Bowart, the *East Village Other*, one of New York's first "underground" newspapers. At this time Reed also began work on his first full-length novel, *The Free-Lance Pallbearers*, while a participant in the Umbra Workshop, an association of young writers that was a galvanizing force in the emerging black aesthetic.

In 1967 Reed left New York for California, first settling in Berkeley and later in Oakland, where he married Carla Blank, a dancer and choreographer with whom Reed had a second daughter, Tennessee. Since his move to California Reed has taught at the University of California, Berkeley, and has held visiting positions at the Universities of Washington and Seattle, as well as SUNY Buffalo, Yale, and Dartmouth. During this period, Reed also became a cultural impresario, co-founding the Yardbird Publishing Company along with poets Steve Cannon and Al Young; establishing I. Reed Books; and forming with Victor H. Cruz the Before Columbus Foundation, a multiethnic organization dedicated to "promoting a pan-cultural view of America" largely by supporting innovative and neglected American writers of any race. Winner of numerous awards, including multiple nominations for National Book Awards in fiction and poetry, a Guggenheim fellowship, and a MacArthur Fellowship, Reed has been a powerful and prolific writer in multiple genres, having published to date nine novels, several books of nonfiction, plays both written and produced, and five books of poetry, not to mention a continuous stream of editorial and journalistic work.

Reed's literary hallmark is his pointed use of an unrelenting and unforgiving satire that frequently offends because its targets are Western conventionality and the African American literary canon. Inspired by a newspaper editorial about politicians who preside over dying cities, Reed's first novel, *The Free-Lance Pallbearers* (1967), also burlesques Ralph Ellison's novelistic masterpiece *Invisible Man* (1952). Two years later, Reed published his second novel, *Yellow Back Radio Broke-Down* (1969), a parody of the American Western that was critically lauded by black writers. Reed again garnered critical acclaim in 1972 with the release of *Mumbo Jumbo*, a novel that chronicles the progress of a metaphysical plague during the 1920s, and *Conjure: Selected Poems 1963–1970*, a volume that draws its inspiration from African religions and African American folk traditions. Both *Mumbo Jumbo* and *Conjure* were nominated for the National Book Award. During the remainder of the 1970s Reed also released a varied array of essay collections, fiction, and poetry: *Chattanooga: Poems* (1973), *The Last Days of Louisiana Red* (1974), *Flight to Canada* (1976), *A Secretary to the Spirits* (1978), and *Shrovetide in New Orleans* (1978).

By waging what he calls "guerilla warfare against the Historical Establishment," Reed seeks to dislocate our fashions of aesthetic, political, and social imagining, and the violence he enacts on ideas of story and solidarity has won him no small number of critics. In addition to his attacks on "Christianity, Western art and morality, the hypocrisy of democratic ideals, American history, and the tyrannical myths that shape the American mind," Reed is ruthlessly critical of the black middle class and has articulated acid critiques of black nationalists and "separatists," black "marxists and existentialists"—all objects of his derision and dismissal who often reciprocate in kind. Yet Reed's antagonisms seem outweighed by his large syncretic vision of myth and culture, which can hardly be considered as exclusionary as his polemics would sometimes imply. Whether drawing on Egyptology, Catholic ritual, Greek myth, Voodoo religion, the Western canon, colloquial vernacular, jazz music, or popular culture (from television programs to the most transient fads), Reed hopes to animate "the full diversity and richness and depth" of black American culture as at once embedded in and yet distinct from dominant American culture. Branding the black nationalism of the Black Arts movement "mono-cultural," Reed's aesthetic aspires to a kind of internationalism that challenges African American forms of expression even as it seeks more richly to illuminate and expand them.

Reed continued to court controversy during the 1980s and 1990s, especially with the publication of *Reckless Eyeballing* (1986), a satiric and unsettling narrative about 1980s feminism, the New York theater scene, and racial and sexual crimes committed in New York City. The novel was roundly criticized by white and black feminist theorists and by major literary reviewers. Contemporary American politics provides the inspiration for the three other parodic fictions Reed penned during this period:

The Terrible Twos (1982); *The Terrible Threes* (1989); and *Japanese by Spring* (1993), his most commercially successful novel.

Reed has declared that he largely considers himself as a "fetish-maker," his books and words "amulets" with magical powers of conjuration and provocation. Reed's radical deployment of the supernatural and surreal constitutes part of what he terms "neo-hoodoo aesthetics." If on the one hand this hybrid program seems to defamiliarize or parody even our most sacred cultural assumptions so that we might gain critical awareness of the interlacing of social idioms and political power in contemporary America, then, on the other hand, Reed hasn't so much abandoned realism as he has sought out new ways to represent the experience of African Americans. As he puts it in the essay "19 Necromancers from Now," "Sometimes I feel that the condition of the Afro-American writer in this country is so strange that one has to go to the supernatural for an analogy. . . . The Afro-American artist is similar to the Necromancer." Concerned in his resurrection of "ancient hoodoo epistemology" with the darker connections among historical destruction, slavery, the sorrow of exile, and survival, Reed cannot help but explore this traumatic territory in ways that make rambunctious heroes out of conjure men and trickster figures. His writing playfully explores the genealogies of different cultures' systems of belief, juxtaposing their dissonant tones and themes in order to generate new sounds and ideas. This aesthetic dynamism evokes the kind of competing voices that seem to make Reed both revolutionary and reactionary, a writer whose wide-ranging styles, influences, and effects offer a radically new yet tradition-infused gumbo of multiple existence, the destiny of which is perpetually yet to be determined.

The Ghost in Birmingham[1]

The only Holy Ghost in Birmingham is Denmark Vesey's[2] Holy Ghost, brooding, moving in and out of things. No one notices the figure in antique cloak of the last century, haunting the pool games, talking of the weather with a passerby, attending mass meetings, standing guard, coming up behind each wave of protest, reloading a pistol. No one notices the antique figure in shabby clothing, moving in and out of things—rallies of moonshine gatherings—who usurps a pulpit and preaches a fire sermon, plucking the plumage of a furious hawk,[3] a sparrow having passively died, moving in and out of chicken markets, watching sparrow habits become hawk habits, through bar stools and greenless parks, beauty salons, floating games,[4] going somewhere, haranguing the crowds, his sleeves rolled up like a steel worker's, hurling epithets at the pharoah's club-wielding brigade, under orders to hunt down the first born of each low lit hearth.[5]

1. Alabama city that was the site of key struggles in the civil rights movement; notable for the racially motivated bombing of the 16th Street Baptist Church that killed four African American girls in the year of the poem's composition.
2. Denmark Vesey (originally Telemanque, 1767–1822), African American slave, carpenter, church founder, and abolitionist activist who planned in Charleston, South Carolina, what would have been the largest slave rebellion in U.S. history; Vesey's plot was betrayed and he was hanged. "Holy Ghost": in Christian theology, the third person of the Holy Trinity.
3. "Furious hawk": reference to chapters 77 and 78 of the *Egyptian Book of the Dead*, which concern transformations of divinity (especially in the guise of Osiris, god of the underworld) into a golden hawk. "Fire sermon": in Theravada Buddhism, the Ādittapariyāya Sutta, or Fire Sermon, teaches that detachment from one's thoughts and senses leads to enlightenment.
4. "Floating games": i.e., gambling competitions that move from place to place to avoid the police.
5. In Exodus, the tenth plague visited upon the Egyptians for enslaving the Israelites called for the death of all Egyptian first-born males, a sanction that finally convinced Pharoah to submit and free the Hebrew slaves (Exodus 11.1–12.36). The Birmingham Civil Rights Campaign employed the Children's Crusade, organized by Martin Luther King Jr. (1929–1968), in which hundreds of schoolchildren were met by fire hoses and police dogs ordered to attack by the city's commissioner of public safety, Eugene "Bull" Connor (1897–1973).

There are no bulls in America in the sense of great symbols,[6] which preside over resuscitation of godheads, that shake the dead land green. Only the "bull" of Birmingham,[7] papier maché, ten dollars down monthly terms, carbon copy mock heroic American variety of bullhood, who told a crowded room of flashbulbs that there was an outsider moving in and out of things that night,[8] a spectre who flashed through the night like pentecost.[9]

He's right, there was.

Not the spook[1] of the Judaic mystery, the universal immersed in the particular. Not the outsider from unpopular mysteries, a monstrous dialectic waddling through the corridors of his brain, but the nebulous presence hidden by flash-bulbing events in Birmingham, Metempsychosis[2] stroking the air.

Pragma the bitch has a knight errant called Abbadon,[3] in the old texts the advocate of dreadful policies. The whore,[4] her abominations spilling over, her stinking after-births sliming their way towards a bay of pigs,[5] has a bland and well-groomed knight errant who said that "if we hand down a few more decisions, pile up paper, snap a few more pictures by Bachrach of famous people before grand rhetorical columns of the doric order, perhaps they will stop coming out into the streets in Raleigh, Greensboro, Jackson and Atlanta (sometimes called the Athens of the south).[6]

> Pragma's well-groomed and bland procurer is on long
>   distance manufacturing heroes,[7]
> Heroes who bray in sirens screaming in from Idlewild,[8] winging
>   in from points south,
> Their utterances cast into bronze by press-card-carrying
>   harpies,[9] those creatures of distorted reality.

6. While in Egyptian mythology, the bull-deity is venerated as an emblem of renewal-by-sacrifice, in America *bulls* is derogatory slang for the police.

7. I.e., Connor.

8. In the midst of the Birmingham campaign, Connor issued a statement to the press that asserted: "Ladies and gentlemen, for 42 days now the city of Birmingham has been under siege from outside agitators led by Martin Luther King."

9. The festival, fifty days after Easter and nine days after Ascension Thursday, commemorates the descent of the Holy Spirit upon the Apostles and the women followers of Jesus.

1. Ghost, with a pun on a derogatory term for a black person. "The spook of the Judaic mystery" refers to the Old Testament's Spirit of God, which appears first in Genesis:2.

2. The transmigration of the soul, a doctrine popular in many Eastern religions (e.g., Buddhism, Hinduism, and Jainism), though most often used in the contexts of Greek cultic religions such as Orphism and in Greek philosophical writing.

3. Destruction (Hebrew); in the Book of Revelation, the angel Abbadon is depicted as the king of an army of locusts released from a bottomless pit (Revelation 9.1–11). "Pragma": personification of the state (from the Greek word *pragmatikos*). "Knight errant": a figure of medieval romantic chivalric literature who wanders in search of adventures to prove his worthiness.

4. Reference to the Whore of Babylon, symbol of cultural degradation, described in the Book of Revelation as she who holds "a golden cup in her hand full of abominations and filthiness of her fornication" (Revelation 17.4).

5. "Bay of pigs": allusion to U.S.-sponsored invasion of Cuba in 1961 by Cuban exiles intending the overthrow of Communist leader Fidel Castro (b. 1926); the mission's failure was an embarrassment for the government of President John F. Kennedy (1917–1963).

6. The public outcry over Bull Connor's use of police dogs to attack the Children's Crusade convinced the reluctant Kennedy administration to propose sweeping reforms that became the Civil Rights Act of 1964. "Bachrach": Ernest Bachrach (1899–1990), Hollywood photographer, famous for his ennobling portraits of celebrities. "Doric order": one of the three organization systems of classical Greek architecture. "Raleigh, Greensboro, Jackson, and Atlanta": sites of important events in the civil rights movement.

7. During the 1960 presidential campaign, Kennedy and his brother, Robert F. Kennedy (1925–1968), made a series of calls to King's wife, Coretta Scott King (1927–2006), and government officials offering assistance in securing the release of King from jail after a civil rights protest in Atlanta. A similar series of calls from President Kennedy to Mrs. King occurred when King was jailed during the Birmingham campaign.

8. New York City airport (renamed John F. Kennedy Airport, or JFK, in December 1963, following Kennedy's assassination in November).

9. In Greek mythology, creatures, part woman and part bird, who snatch food from their victims.

O ebony-limbed Osiris,[1] what clown folk singer or acrobat
    shall I place the tin wreath upon?[2]
When will Osiris be scattered[3] over 100 ghettoes?   5

Heroes are ferried in by motorcycle escorts, their faces cast
    into by Pointillism,[4] by Artzybasheff,
Sculptor of Henry Luce's America.[5]

Introducing the King of Birmingham,[6] sometimes called the
    anointed one,
And receives the tin wreath across Americana banquet rooms,
His hands dripping with blood like a fanatical monk as
    rebellion squirms on the stake.   10

Introducing the Black Caligula,[7] who performs a strip tease of
    the psyche,
Between Tiffany ads and Vat 69,[8] giving up a little pussy for a
    well-groomed and bland knight errant.

O ebony-limbed Osiris, what knight club tap dancing charlatan
    shall I place the tin wreath upon?
All things are flowing said the poet when gods ambushed
    gods:[9]
    Khan follows Confucius[1]   15
    Light follows darkness
Tin wreathed heroes are followed by the figure in antique clothes,
    obscured by the flash-bulbing events in Birmingham.
Metempsychosis in the air.

                                              1963

---

1. Osiris is frequently depicted as having ebony skin, generally considered symbolic of his role as Lord of the Dead but also related to his African origin.
2. Echoes part III, stanza 7, of "E.P. Ode pour l'élection de son sepulchre" from the long poem *Hugh Selwyn Mauberly* (1920) by American poet Ezra Pound (1985–1972): "O bright Apollo, . . . What god, man or hero / Shall I place a tin wreath upon!"
3. In Egyptian mythology, when Set murdered his brother Osiris, in order to usurp his throne, Set dismembered the body and scattered its pieces across the land.
4. A technique of painting in which small colored dots are applied in patterns to make an image.
5. Boris Artzybasheff (1899–1965), Russian-born illustrator and painter active in America, notable for his surreal designs and anti-Nazi art in magazines such as *Fortune*, *Time*, and *Life*, whose publisher, Henry Robinson Luce (1898–1967) was called "the most influential private citizen in America of his day."
6. I.e., Martin Luther King Jr.
7. Gaius Julius Caesar Augustus Germanicus (12–41), 3rd Roman emperor (r. 37–41) and commonly known as Caligula, the first of the so-called Mad Emperors, was notorious for his despotism and cruelty.
8. Brand of scotch whiskey; "Tiffany": fine jewelry company.
9. An evocation of part III, stanza three, of Pound's "E.P. Ode pour l'élection de son sepulchre"—"All things are flowing / Sage Heracleitus says; / But a tawdry cheapness / Shall outlast our days." The pre-Socratic Greek philosopher Heraclitus of Epheseus (535–475 B.C.E.) is best known for his philosophy of constant change as expressed in the saying often misattributed to him, "Everything flows."
1. Mimics the second stanza of part III of "E.P. Ode pour l'election de son sepulchre": "Christ follows Dionysus, / Phallic and ambrosial / Made way for macerations; / Caliban casts out Ariel." Genghis Kahn (1162–1227), Mongol military leader who founded the Mongol Empire, the largest contiguous empire in world history (1206–1368); Confucius (c. 551–479 B.C.E.), Chinese teacher and philosopher. Pound's poem refers in turn to: Dionysus, Greek god of vegetation, wine, and ecstatic dance; Caliban, dark-skinned beast-man, offspring of the powerful witch Sycorax, a character in *The Tempest* (1611) by William Shakespeare (1564–1616); and Ariel, a spirit character in Shakespeare's play.

I am a cowboy in the boat of Ra

'The devil must be forced to reveal any such physical evil (potions, charms, fetishes, etc.) still outside the body and these must be burned.' (Rituale Romanum, published 1947, *endorsed by the coat-of-arms and introductory letter from Francis cardinal Spellman)*[1]

I am a cowboy in the boat of Ra,[2]
sidewinders[3] in the saloons of fools
bit my forehead   like   O[4]
the untrustworthiness of Egyptologists[5]
who do not know their trips.[6] Who was that   5
dog-faced man?[7] they asked, the day I rode
from town.

School marms with halitosis[8] cannot see
the Nefertiti[9] fake chipped on the run by slick
germans, the hawk behind Sonny Rollins'[1] head or   10
the ritual beard of his axe; a longhorn[2] winding
its bells thru the Field of Reeds.[3]

I am a cowboy in the boat of Ra. I bedded
down with Isis, Lady of the Boogaloo,[4] dove
down deep in her horny, stuck up her Wells-Far-ago[5]   15

1. Francis Joseph Spellman (1889–1967), cardinal and archbishop of the Roman Catholic diocese of New York, a steadfast social, theological, and political conservative. "Rituale Romanum": written under Pope Paul V in 1614, one of the official books of the Roman Rite, it contains the only formal rite of exorcism sanctioned by the Catholic Church. "Coat-of-arms": heraldric emblem denoting the bearer's rank and identity.
2. Ancient Egyptian sun god of Heliopolis; typically represented as a hawk-headed man; father of Osiris, Isis, and Set. As a creator who masters death, Ra travels to the Underworld in the night-boat called "meseket" and, while there, takes the form of a ram-headed god; in the morning, he sails above Egypt in a boat called "manjet."
3. A species of rattlesnake that inhabits the low-land deserts of the southern United States: used in the 19th century to denote a devious person and in the 1940s as a term for a thug (specifically, a gangster's bodyguard).
4. In the Haitian syncretic religion of Vodou, a *vévé* (or sacred design) symbolic of being. "Bit my forehead": in the ancient Egyptian mythology upon which Reed is drawing, Osiris's son Horus, who seeks vengeance against his uncle, Set, for the murder of his father, is bitten and stung by poisonous creatures.
5. Scholars specializing in the study of ancient Egypt, a discipline that arose alongside the early 19th-century European invasion of Egypt during which many Egyptian treasures were excavated and transported back to European countries.
6. Pun on slang for hallucinations and other effects induced by drugs.
7. Perhaps Anubus, the Egyptian god of the dead, shown typically as a jackal-headed man. An anticipation, too, of Loup Garou (line 36), a shapeshifting wolflike creature of folkloric ori-

gin. Cf. "Who was that masked man, anyway?"—a refrain from *The Lone Ranger,* popular radio and TV show from the 1930s to the 1950s.
8. Fetid breath.
9. Wife of Pharaoh Akenaten (c. 1375–1358 B.C.E.); a statue of her head was stolen by Germans and chipped in the early 20th century.
1. Theodore Walker Rollins (b. 1930), African American jazz saxophonist; his album *Sonny Meets Hawk* (1963) features him accompanied by (or in jazz parlance, playing "behind") African American jazz saxophonist Coleman Hawkins, nicknamed "Hawk" (1904–1969). Also relevant to Reed's poem is Rollins's 1957 album *Way Out West,* which contains a number of parodic versions of hokey Western songs such as "I'm an Old Cowhand."
2. Breed of cattle (with pun on the "long horn," or saxophone, played by Rollins); "ritual beard of his axe": Rollins was known for his elaborate beard that could be compared to the shape of his saxophone (or "axe" in jazz slang).
3. Egyptian afterworld, below the western horizon, a region of perpetual spring over which Osiris ruled and to which dead souls were carried in a magical boat. It was the dead souls' task to farm the fields. Relevant, too, is that the abandoned baby Moses was found among the reeds in a basket or small "ark" crafted of bulrushes along the Nile by Pharaoh's daughter (Exodus 2.3–6).
4. Latino-jazz musical and dance form popular in the 1960s. Isis: Egyptian nature goddess and patroness of the dead; sister and wife of Osiris, represented by a sun-disk between the horns of a cow.
5. Wells Fargo was a 19th-century overland stage company in the American West, with pun on *farrago* or hodgepodge (from the Latin *farrago,* mixed fodder for cattle).

in daring midday getaway. 'Start grabbing the
blue', I said from top of my double crown.[6]

I am a cowboy in the boat of Ra. Ezzard Charles[7]
of the Chisholm Trail.[8] Took up the bass but they
blew off my thumb. Alchemist in ringmanship[9] but a   20
sucker for the right cross.[1]

I am a cowboy in the boat of Ra. Vamoosed[2] from
the temple I bide my time. The price on the wanted
poster was a-going down, outlaw alias copped[3] my stance
and moody greenhorns[4] were making me dance;
    while my mouth's   25
shooting iron[5] got its chambers jammed.

I am a cowboy in the boat of Ra. Boning-up[6] in
the ol West I bide my time. You should see
me pick off these tin cans whippersnappers.[7] I
write the motown long plays[8] for the comeback of   30
Osiris.[9] Make them up when stars stare at sleeping
steer out here near the campfire. Women arrive
on the backs of goats and throw themselves on
my Bowie.[1]

I am a cowboy in the boat of Ra. Lord of the lash,   35
the Loup Garou Kid.[2] Half breed son of Pisces and
Aquarius. I hold the souls of men in my pot.[3] I do
the dirty boogie with scorpions. I make the bulls[4]
keep still and was the first swinger to grape the taste.[5]

6. Allusion to the combined crowns of the Egyptian cults of Ammon and Ra, which symbolized a unified Egypt. "Start grabbing the blue": hands up, with an allusion to the color of Egyptian royalty.
7. Ezzard Mack Charles (1921–1975), African American boxing champion, famous for making a rare successful comeback in the ring.
8. Most popular of the post–Civil War trails used to drive cattle from Texas to Kansas, where they were transported by train into midwestern markets.
9. I.e., boxing. "Alchemist": practitioner of the magic "art" of transmuting base metals into gold.
1. In boxing, a way of countering an opponent's blow by hitting back from the side.
2. Left quickly.
3. Stole, copied.
4. Novices.
5. Gun (with a sexual pun).
6. Studying (with a sexual pun).
7. "Tin cans whippersnappers": deceitful and insignificant persons.
8. "Motown long plays": long-playing gramophone records (or "33⅓"s) made for the Detroit-based rhythm-and-blues and soul recording label Motown.
9. The Egyptian judge of the dead. "Comeback" refers to Osiris's resurrection after his murder and dismemberment by his brother Set, Egyptian god of the setting sun.
1. Large knife created by James Bowie (1796–1836), used in the mid-19th century by miners, hunters, cowboys, and soldiers; it became a symbol of the American West.
2. Loup Garou: werewolf (French); in Haiti, the loup-garou is a sorcerer who can change into an animal, insect, tree, or inorganic object. In Reed's 1969 novel *Yellow Back radio Broke-Down*, the hero Loup Garou Kid is a "member of the divine family, a black cowboy who has existed at least since the ancient Egyptian civilization and who is being hunted by the Christian Goddess"; he is fitted with the "lash" of the whip, which he uses to flick guns from his opponents' hands.
3. "I hold the souls of men in my pot": reference to Khnum, Egyptian creator deity who molded men from clay on his potter's wheel (with a pun on slang for marijuana). "Half breed son of Pisces and Aquarius": image of a threshold or liminal condition. (E.g., Reed's birthday, February 22, falls between the eleventh zodiac sign, Aquarius, and the twelfth, Pisces, thus occupying a "cusp," an area of ambiguity or multiplicity in the symbolism of the zodiac.)
4. Police (slang); "scorpions": in Ancient Egyptian mythology, the scorpion was an emblem of ambivalence and duplicitous power; "dirty boogie": sexual intercourse (African American slang).
5. "Grape the taste": play on phrase connoting drinking of liquor; "swinger": person who leads an active, varied sexual life.

I am a cowboy in his boat. Pope Joan[6] of the   40
Ptah Ra.[7] C/mere a minute willya doll?
Be a good girl and
bring me my Buffalo horn of black powder
bring me my headdress of black feathers
bring me my bones of Ju-Ju snake[8]   45
go get[9] my eyelids of red paint.
Hand me my shadow[1]

I'm going into town after Set

I am a cowboy in the boat of Ra
look out Set   here I come Set   50
to get Set   to sunset Set
to unseat Set   to Set down Set

      usurper of the Royal couch
      imposter Radio of Moses' bush[2]
      party pooper O hater of dance   55
      vampire outlaw of the milky way

                                    1968

Beware: Do Not Read This Poem

tonite, *thriller*[1] was
abt an ol woman, so vain she
surrounded her self w/
    many mirrors

It got so bad that finally she   5
locked herself indoors & her
whole life became the
    mirrors

6. Apocryphal female pope, said to have ruled 855–58 C.E. The legend may derive from the true story of a woman who dressed as a man and entered the Roman Catholic administrative hierarchy to remain with her lover, ca. 850. "Pope Joan" is also the name of a "stop" card game in which the winner is the first to run out of cards.
7. Ptah was an Egyptian deity, chief god of Memphis and god of craftsmanship. Ra was the sun god. The two became Ptah-Ra when the city-states of Memphis and Heliopolis combined.
8. A fetish or magic charm, amulet, or spell used by tribal peoples of West Africa to counter evil spirits. In *Tell my Horse* (1938), African American novelist and folklorist Zora Neale Hurston (1891–1960) notes that a gourd strung with beads and snake bones is one of the sacred objects of Haitian Vodou ritual.
9. "Bring me . . . bring me . . . go get": cf. the

Preface to the prophetic epic *Milton* (1804–10) by British poet William Blake (1757–1827), which includes the lines: "Bring me my Bow of burning gold: / Bring me my Arrows of desire: / Bring me my Spear: O clouds unfold! / Bring me my Chariot of fire!"
1. The Ancient Egyptians regarded the shadow, the body, and the soul as three parts of the human being. "Shadow" is also late 19th-century derogatory slang for a black person.
2. Yahweh revealed himself to Moses as a burning bush while he was tending Jethro's herd in the desert of Horeb; he was then given divine commission to lead the Israelites out of slavery in Egypt (Exodus 1–10).
1. Popular television series (1960–62), hosted by Boris Karloff (an actor famous for his roles in horror films, the best known of which was in the 1931 James Whale film adaptation of *Frankenstein*.)

one day the villagers broke
into her house, but she was too   10
swift for them, she disappeared
    into a mirror
each tenant who bought the house
after that, lost a loved one to
    the ol woman in the mirror: 15
    first a little girl
    then a young woman
    then the young woman/s husband

the hunger of this poem is legendary
it has taken in many victims   20
back off from this poem
it has drawn in yr feet
back off from this poem
it has drawn in yr legs
back off from this poem   25
it is a greedy mirror
you are into[2] this poem. from
   the waist down
nobody can hear you can they?

this poem has had you up to here   30
    belch
this poem aint got no manners
you cant call out frm this poem
relax now & go w/ this poem
move & roll on to this poem   35

    do not resist this poem
    this poem has yr eyes
    this poem has his head
    this poem has his arms
    this poem has his fingers   40
    this poem has his fingertips

this poem is the reader & the
reader this poem

statistic: the us bureau of missing persons reports
    that in 1968 over 100,000 people disappeared   45
    leaving no solid clues
        nor trace   only
   a space   in the lives of their friends

                                          1968

2. Pun meaning both "absorbed by" and "obsessed with."

Neo-HooDoo[1] Manifesto

Neo-HooDoo is a "Lost American Church"[2] updated. Neo-HooDoo is the music of James Brown[3] without the lyrics and ads for Black Capitalism. Neo-HooDoo is the 8 basic dances of 19-century New Orleans' *Place Congo*—[4] the Calinda the Bamboula the Chacta the Babouille the Conjaille the Juba the Congo and the VooDoo[5]—modernized into the Philly Dog, the Hully Gully, the Funky Chicken, the Popcorn, the Boogaloo[6] and the dance of great American choreographer Buddy Bradley.[7]

Neo-HooDoos would rather "shake that thing"[8] than be stiff and erect. (There were more people performing a Neo-HooDoo sacred dance, the Boogaloo, at Woodstock than chanting Hare Krishna . . . Hare Hare!)[9] All so-called "Store Front Churches" and "Rock Festivals" receive their matrix in the HooDoo rites of Marie Laveau[1] conducted at New Orleans' Lake Pontchartrain, and Bayou St. John[2] in the 1880s. The power of HooDoo challenged the stability of civil authority in New Orleans and was driven underground where to this day it flourishes in the Black ghettos throughout the country. Thats why in Ralph Ellison's[3] modern novel *Invisible Man* New Orleans is described as "The Home of Mystery." "Everybody from New Orleans got that thing," Louis Armstrong[4] said once.

HooDoo is the strange and beautiful "fits" the Black slave Tituba[5] gave the children of Salem. (Notice the arm waving ecstatic females seemingly possessed at the "Pentecostal," "Baptist," and "Rock Festivals," [all fronts for Neo-HooDoo]). The reason that HooDoo isn't given the credit it deserves in influencing American Culture is because the students of that culture both "overground" and "underground" are uptight closet Jeho-vah[6] revisionists.

---

1. Hoodoo, also known as "conjure," is a form of African American folk magic or syncretic religion that blends European, Native American, and African traditions.
2. Allusion to the African American version of Islam known as the Nation of Islam, or the "Lost-Found Nation of Islam."
3. African American singer-songwriter, among the originators of soul and funk music (1933–2006).
4. French for Congo Square, an open space in New Orleans just north of the French Quarter notable for its history of African American music and dance dating to the slavery era of the 18th and 19th centuries.
5. VooDoo: associated with the African American spiritual practices of Louisiana or New Orleans Voodoo, a blend of Catholic and African religious forms. African American dance forms: "Calinda": created by Caribbean slaves in the 1720s; "Bamboula": named for type of drum brought to New Orleans by African slaves; "Chacta": blended from African and Native American influences; "Babouille": French-influenced creation of Louisiana slaves; "Conjaille": choreographed to heavily rhythmic music; "Juba": characterized by stomping and slapping, also known as the "hambone." Reed draws on the 1867 essay "The Dance in Place Congo" by white American novelist George Washington Cable (1844–1925), known for his portrayals of Creole life in New Orleans.
6. African American dances popular in the 1960s.
7. "Ghost" choreographer behind many famous dancers in the early to mid-20th century (1908–

1972). Because he was black, Bradley was never credited for his work in American theater and film.
8. Blues and jazz slang for dancing, the phrase appears as early as 1925 in a song recorded by African American bluesman Papa Charlie Jackson (1885–1938) called "Shake That Thing."
9. Sixteen-word Hindu mantra praising the one-ness of God. The Hare Krishnas (officially, the International Society for Krishna Consciousness, or ISKON) came to the United States in 1965 and soon became a staple of youth counter-culture in the 1960s and 1970s. "Woodstock": reference to the Woodstock Music and Art Fair, held in Bethel, New York, in August 1969 and attended by half a million people.
1. Also known as the "Witch Queen of New Orleans" (1794–1881), a practitioner of a form of New Orleans Voodoo followed by thousands of multiracial adherents.
2. New Orleans neighborhood.
3. African American novelist (1914–1994); the phrase from *Invisible Man* (1952) appears on a leaflet distributed by the elusive multifaced character Rinehart, billed as "Spiritual Technologist."
4. African American jazz trumpeter, composer, and singer (1901–1971).
5. Slave who was the first person accused of witchcraft during the Salem witchcraft trials of 1692–93.
6. Transliteration of the Ancient Hebraic name for God, whose enunciation is forbidden in the Old Testament.

They would assert the American and East Indian and Chinese thing before they would the Black thing. Their spiritual leaders Ezra Pound and T. S. Eliot[7] hated Africa and "Darkies." In Theodore Roszak's book *The Making of a Counter Culture*[8]—there is barely any mention of the Black influence on this culture even though its members dress like Blacks talk like Blacks walk like Blacks, gesture like Blacks wear Afros and indulge in Black music and dance (Neo-HooDoo).

Neo-HooDoo is sexual, sensual and digs the old "heathen" good good loving. An early American HooDoo song says:

> Now lady I ain't no mill man
> Just the mill man's son
> But I can do your grinding
> till the mill man comes[9]

Which doesnt mean that women are treated as "sexual toys" in Neo-HooDoo or as one slick Jeho-vah Revisionist recently said, "victims of a raging hormone imbalance." Neo-HooDoo claims many women philosophers and theoreticians which is more than ugh religions Christianity and its offspring Islam can claim. When our theoretician Zora Neale Hurston[1] asked a *Mambo* (a female priestess in the Haitian VooDoo) a definition of VooDoo the Mambo lifted her skirts and exhibited her Erzulie Seal, her Isis seal.[2] Neo-HooDoo identifies with Julia Jackson[3] who stripped HooDoo of its oppressive Catholic layer—Julia Jackson said when asked the origin of the amulets and talismans in her studio, "I make all my own stuff. It saves money and it's as good. People who has to buy their stuff ain't using their heads."

Neo-HooDoo is not a church for egotripping[4]—it takes its "organization" from Haitian VooDoo of which Milo Rigaud[5] wrote:

> Unlike other established religions, there is no hierarchy of bishops, archbishops, cardinals, or a pope in VooDoo. Each oum'phor is a law unto itself, following the traditions of VooDoo but modifying and changing the ceremonies and rituals in various ways. Secrets of VooDoo.

Neo-HooDoo believes that every man is an artist and every artist a priest. You can bring your own creative ideas to Neo-HooDoo. Charlie "Yardbird (Thoth)" Parker[6] is an example of the Neo-HooDoo artist as an innovator and improvisor.

---

7. T. S. Eliot (1888–1965), Ezra Pound (1885–1972): American modernist poets.
8. *The Making of a Counter Culture: Reflections on the Technocratic Society and its Youthful Opposition*, the first work to refer to the 1960s youth movement of war protestors, hippie dropouts, and social rebels as a "counterculture," was written by historian Roszak (1933–2011) in 1969.
9. From "Mill Man Blues," a 1928 recording by African American blues singer Billy Bird (b. unknown).
1. African American folklorist, anthropologist, and novelist (1891–1960).
2. Erzulie is a family of voodoo spirits, or *loa*, derived from the African Dahomey cosmological deity of love, beauty, and luxury, akin to the god-

dess Isis's role in Egyptian mythology. "Seal" serves here as a euphemism for female genitalia.
3. Practitioner of hoodoo spirits (b. unknown), made famous as "Queen Julia Jackson" by the Bayou bluesman and ethnographer Mac "Dr. John" Rebennack (b. 1940) in his song "Jump Sturdy," released on the 1969 album *Gris-Gris*.
4. Narcissistic indulgence.
5. Haitian anthropologist, lawyer, ethnologist, and author (1914–?); *Secrets of Voodoo* was published in 1969.
6. African American jazz saxophonist and composer (1920–1955). ("Thoth": in Egyptian mythology, god of writing, science, mediation between good and evil, and cosmic order.)

In Neo-HooDoo, Christ the landlord deity ("render unto Caesar")[7] is on probation. This includes "The Black Christ" and "The Hippie Christ." Neo-HooDoo tells Christ to get lost. (Judas Iscariot[8] holds an honorary degree from Neo-HooDoo.)

Whereas at the center of Christianity lies the graveyard the organ-drone[9] and the cross, the center of Neo-HooDoo is the drum the anhk[1] and the Dance. So Fine, Barefootin, Heard It Through the Grapevine,[2] are all Neo-HooDoos.

Neo-HooDoo has "seen a lot of things in this old world."[3]

Neo-HooDoo borrows from Ancient Egyptians (ritual accessories of Ancient Egypt are still sold in the House of Candles and Talismans on Stanton Street in New York, the Botanical Gardens in East Harlem, and Min and Mom on Haight Street in San Francisco, examples of underground centers found in ghettos throughout America).

Neo-HooDoo borrows from Haiti Africa and South America.
Neo-HooDoo comes in all styles and moods.

Louis Jordon Nellie Lutcher John Lee Hooker Ma Rainey Dinah Washington the Temptations Ike and Tina Turner Aretha Franklin Muddy Waters Otis Redding Sly and the Family Stone B.B. King Junior Wells Bessie Smith Jelly Roll Morton Ray Charles Jimi Hendrix Buddy Miles the 5th Dimension the Chambers Brothers Etta James[4] and acolytes Creedance Clearwater Revival the Flaming Embers Procol Harum[5] are all Neo-HooDoos. Neo-HooDoo never turns down pork. In fact Neo-HooDoo is the Bar-B-Cue of Amerika. The Neo-HooDoo cuisine is Geechee Gree Gree[6] Verta Mae's *Vibration Cooking*.[7] (Ortiz Walton's[8] Neo-HooDoo Jass Band performs at the Native Son Restaurant in Berkeley, California. Joe Overstreet's[9] Neo-

7. The beginning of a phrase attributed to Jesus, which reads in full: "Render unto Caesar the things which are Caesar's, and unto God the things which are God's" (Matthew 22.21), a saying taken in part to mean that Christians must submit to earthly authority in anticipation of spiritual redemption.
8. One of Christ's twelve disciples, who betrayed him to the Roman authorities (Matthew 26.47–48; Mark 14.42–43; Luke 22.47; John 18.1–2).
9. Sustained, sober sound produced by extended chords or note clusters; a musical style developed in various spiritual traditions, including European church music.
1. Egyptian hieroglyphic for "life," also known as the "key of life."
2. Popular rhythm-and-blues or soul songs of the 1960s. "So Fine": written by Johnny Otis (1921–2012), recorded by The Fiestas in 1959; "Barefootin'": recorded by Robert Parker (b. 1930) in 1966; "I Heard It Through the Grapevine": written by Norman Whitfield (1940–2008) and Barrett Strong (b. 1941), made famous by the 1968 recording of Marvin Gaye (1939–1984).
3. Line from the song "Signed, Sealed, and Delivered" by African American singer and composer Stevie Wonder (born Stevland Hardaway Judkins, 1950).

4. 20th-century African American singers and musicians.
5. Creedence Clearwater Revival, the Flaming Embers, Procol Harum: white rock bands influenced by black musical traditions, active in the 1960s and 1970s.
6. "Geechee": culture of the Gullah people, descendants of slaves from the Lowcountry region of Georgia and South Carolina (derived from the Ogeechee River near Savannah, Georgia). "Gree Gree" or gris-gris: a voodoo amulet that protects its wearer from evil; hence, an epithet of voodoo culture. "Amerika": a German spelling used in the counterculture 1960s, meant to evoke the Nazi fascism of the 1930s and 1940s.
7. Also known as *The Travel Notes of a Geechee Girl* (1970), an autobiographical cookbook emphasizing African American culinary arts as a source of cultural consciousness, by anthropologist and radio personality Vertamae Smart-Grosvenor (b. 1939).
8. Bass player and bandleader of the Neo-Hoodoo Jazz Band, Walton (1934–2010) was the first African American to be a member of a major American orchestra, the Boston Symphony Orchestra.
9. African American painter, sculptor, and conceptual artist (b. 1933).

HooDoo exhibit will happen at the Berkeley Gallery Sept. 1, 1970 in Berkeley.)

Neo-HooDoo ain't Negritude.[1] Neo-HooDoo never been to France. Neo-HooDoo is "your Mama" as Larry Neal[2] said. Neo-HooDoos Little Richard, and Chuck Berry[3] nearly succeeded in converting the Beatles. When the Beatles said they were more popular than Christ[4] they seemed astonished at the resulting outcry. This is because although they could feebly through amplification and technological sham 'mimic' (as if Little Richard and Chuck Berry were Loa [Spirits] practicing ventriloquism on their "Horses"[5]) the Beatles failed to realize that they were conjuring the music and ritual (although imitation) of a Forgotten Faith, a traditional enemy of Christianity which Christianity the Cop[6] Religion has had to drive underground each time they meet. Neo-HooDoo now demands a rematch, the referees were bribed and the adversary had resin on his gloves.[7]

The Vatican Forbids Jazz Masses in Italy
Rome, Aug. 6 (UPI)—The Vatican today barred jazz and popular music from masses in Italian churches and forbade young Roman Catholics to change prayers or readings used on Sundays and holy days.

It said such changes in worship were "eccentric and arbitrary."

A Vatican document distributed to all Italian bishops did not refer to similar experimental masses elsewhere in the world, although Pope Paul VI and other high-ranking churchmen are known to dislike the growing tendency to deviate from the accepted form of the mass.

Some Italian churches have permitted jazz masses played by combos while youthful worshipers sang such songs as "We Shall Overcome."[8]

Church leaders two years ago rebuked priests who permitted such experiments.[9] The New York Times, August 7, 1970.

Africa is the home of the loa (Spirits) of Neo-HooDoo although we are building our own American "pantheon." Thousands of "Spirits" (Ka) who would laugh at Jeho-vah's fury concerning "false idols" (translated everybody else's religion) or "fetishes." Moses, Jeho-vah's messenger and zombie[1] swiped the secrets of VooDoo from old Jethro[2] but nevertheless ended up

---

1. African black consciousness movement shaped in response to French colonialism and racism by Martiniquean poet and political leader Aimé Césaire (1913–2008), Guianan poet Léon-Gontran Damas (1912–1978), and Senegalese poet and first president (1960–1980) Léopold Sédar Senghor (1906–2001).
2. African American poet, playwright, and cultural theorist of the Black Arts movement (1937–1981).
3. Charles Edward Anderson "Chuck Berry" (b. 1926) and Little Richard (born Richard Wayne Penniman in 1932): African American rhythm-and-blues singer-songwriters and pioneers of rock 'n' roll music.
4. Beatles lead singer John Lennon's (1940–1980) remarks at a press conference, made at the height of "Beatlemania" hysteria, that the Beatles were "more popular than Jesus now," were initially published in the *London Evening Standard* in March 1966 and went all but unnoticed, but they incited anger in the United States when quoted in *Datebook* in August 1966.
5. The loa (spirits) of Haitian Voodoo arrive in the ritual space by "riding a horse," that is, by possessing a ritual priest or *Houngan*.
6. Police (with a pun on "copped," or stolen).
7. In boxing, the referee properly wipes boxers' gloves free of the resin used on shoes to prevent slipping on the canvas ring surface.
8. Popular anthem of the civil rights movement, derived from the gospel song "I'll Overcome Someday" by African American minister and composer Rev. Charles Albert Tindley (1851–1933).
9. In fact, under Pope Paul VI the Vatican issued edicts that approved the "new Order of the Mass," opening Roman Catholic liturgy to vernacular languages and various musical traditions.
1. In Haitian Voodoo, an animated corpse brought back to life by mystical means; "fetishes": inanimate objects believed to possess supernatural powers, first used by Portuguese colonists to refer to religious objects used in West African religious practices.
2. In the Book of Exodus, Moses's father-in-law, a priest of Midion.

with a curse. (Warning, many White "Black delineators" who practiced HooDoo VooDoo for gain and did not "feed"[3] the Black Spirits of HooDoo ended up tragically. Bix Beiderbecke and Irene Castle[4] (who exploited Black Dance in the 1920s and relished in dressing up as a Nun) are examples of this tragic tendency.

Moses had a near heart attack when he saw his sons dancing nude before the Black Bull God Apis.[5] They were dancing to a "heathen sound" that Moses had "heard before in Egypt" (probably a mixture of Sun Ra and Jimmy Reed[6] played in the nightclub district of ancient Egypt's "The Domain of Osiris"[7]—named after the god who enjoyed the fancy footwork of the pigmies[8]).

The continuing war between Moses and his "Sons" was recently acted out in Chicago in the guise of an American "trial."[9]

I have called Jeho-vah (most likely Set[1] the Egyptian Sat-on [a pun on the fiend's penalty] Satan) somewhere "a party-pooper and hater of dance." Neo-HooDoos are detectives of the metaphysical about to make a pinch.[2] We have issued warrants for a god arrest. If Jeho-vah reveals his real name he will be released on his own recognizance de-horned and put out to pasture.

A dangerous paranoid pain-in-the-neck a CopGod from the git-go, Jeho-vah was the successful law and order candidate in the mythological relay of the 4th century A.D. Jeho-vah is the God of punishment. The H-Bomb is a typical Jeho-vah "miracle." Jeho-vah is why we are in Vietnam. He told Moses to go out and "subdue" the world.[3]

> *There has never been in history another such culture as the Western civilization—a culture which has practiced the belief that the physical and social environment of man is subject to rational manipulation and that history is subject to the will and action of man; whereas central to the traditional cultures of the rivals of Western civilization, those of Africa and Asia, is a belief that it is environment that dominates man.* The Politics of Hysteria, *Edmund Stillman and William Pfaff.*[4]

"Political leaders" are merely altar boys from Jeho-vah. While the targets of some "revolutionaries" are laundramats and candy stores, Neo-HooDoo

3. In Voodoo practice, the loa are seen as hard-working powers who must be fed by those who serve them if they are to enter the ritual space when summoned.
4. American ballroom dancer (1893–1969), who, with her husband Vernon (1887–1918), invigorated early 20th-century popular dance by infusing it with the rhythms of ragtime and jazz. Leo Bismark "Bix" Beiderbecke (1903–1931): white American jazz cornetist and composer.
5. Deity worshipped in the Memphis region of Egypt, associated with the renewal of life.
6. Matthis James "Jimmy" Reed (1925–1976), African American blues guitarist and songwriter. Sun Ra (born Herman Poole Blount, 1914–1993): African American jazz experimentalist, band-leader, poet, and "cosmic philosopher."
7. Egyptian god of the underworld and the afterlife.
8. 19th-century anthropological name bestowed most notably on peoples of Central Africa such as the Aka, Eté, Baka, Twa, and Mbuti. Baka

Pygmies are renowned for eponymous ritual participatory dances.
9. Reference to the Chicago Eight trial of 1968, in which seven young white defendants were charged with inciting to riot during the 1968 Democratic National Convention. The eighth man, the charges against whom were eventually dropped, was Black Panther Bobby Seale (b. 1936).
1. Egyptian god of storms, darkness, and chaos; the brother and usurping murderer of Osiris.
2. Arrest.
3. Cf. Genesis 1.28: "And God blessed them, and God said unto them, Be fruitful, and multiply, and fill the earth, and subdue it: and have dominion over the fish of the sea, and over the fowl of the air, and over every living thing that moves upon the earth."
4. Political analysts Pfaff (b. 1928) and Stillman (1924–1981) argue in their 1964 book that the cold war mentality of mid 20th-century America constituted a condition of "mass hysteria."

targets are TV the museums the symphony halls and churches art music and literature departments in Christianizing (education I think they call it!) universities which propogate the Art of Jeho-vah—much Byzantine Middle Ages Renaissance painting of Jeho-vah's "500 years of civilization" as Nixon[5] put it are Jeho-vah propaganda. Many White revolutionaries can only get together with 3rd world people on the most mundane 'political' level because they are of Jeho-vah's party and don't know it.[6] How much Black music do so called revolutionary underground radio stations play. On the other hand how much Bach?[7]

Neo-HooDoos are Black Red (Black Hawk[8] an American Indian was an early philosopher of the HooDoo Church) and occasionally White (Madamemoiselle Charlotte[9] is a Haitian Loa [Spirit]).

Neo-HooDoo is a litany seeking its text
Neo-HooDoo is a Dance and Music closing in on its words
Neo-HooDoo is a Church finding its lyrics
Cecil Brown Al Young Calvin Hernton

David Henderson Steve Cannon Quincy Troupe
Ted Joans Victor Cruz N.H. Pritchard Ishmael Reed
Lennox Raphael Sarah Fabio Ron Welburn[1] are Neo-
HooDoo's "Manhattan Project"[2] of writing . . .

A Neo-HooDoo celebration will involve the dance music
and poetry of Neo-HooDoo and whatever ideas the
participating artists might add. A Neo-HooDoo seal
is the Face of an Old American Train.
Neo-HooDoo signs are everywhere!
Neo-HooDoo is the Now Locomotive swinging
up the Tracks of the American Soul.

Almost 100 years ago HooDoo was forced to say
Goodbye to America. Now HooDoo is
back as Neo-HooDoo
You can't keep a good church down![3]

1970

5. In his "Address to the Nation on the Situation in Southeast Asia" on April 30, 1970, President Richard M. Nixon (1913–1994) said: "My fellow Americans, we live in an age of anarchy, both abroad and at home. We see mindless attacks on all the great institutions which have been created by free civilizations in the last 500 years. Even here in the United States, great universities are being systematically destroyed."
6. An echo of lines from "The Marriage of Heaven and Hell" (1790) by English poet William Blake (1757–1827) regarding the epic *Paradise Lost* (1664) of John Milton (1608–1674): "The reason Milton wrote in fetters when he wrote of / Angels & God, and at liberty when of Devils & Hell, is because he / was a true Poet and of the Devil's party without knowing it."

7. Johann Sebastian Bach (1685–1750), German composer of the Baroque period.
8. Sauk leader who fought against U.S. forces in the War of 1812 (1767–1838).
9. A loa of European descent, generally believed to speak French and to enable priests to speak French.
1. A catalogue of African American poets and activists associated with the Black Arts movement and in several cases the literary collective Umbra, of which Reed himself was a member.
2. Secretive American research project (1942–46) that produced the first atomic bomb during World War II.
3. Play on the popular adage, "You can't keep a good man down."

From Mumbo Jumbo[1]

1

A True Sport, the Mayor of New Orleans, spiffy in his patent-leather brown and white shoes, his plaid suit, the Rudolph Valentino[2] parted-down-the-middle hair style, sits in his office. Sprawled upon his knees is Zuzu, local doo-wack-a-doo and voo-do-dee-odo fizgig. A slatternly floozy,[3] her green, sequined dress quivers.

Work has kept Your Honor late.

The Mayor passes the flask of bootlegged[4] gin to Zuzu. She takes a sip and continues to spread sprawl and behave skittishly. Loose. She is inhaling from a Chesterfield[5] cigarette in a shameless brazen fashion.

The telephone rings.

The Mayor removes his hand and picks up the receiver; he recognizes at once the voice of his poker pardner[6] on the phone.

Harry, you'd better get down here quick. What was once dormant is now a Creeping Thing.

The Mayor stands up and Zuzu lands on the floor. Her posture reveals a small flask stuck in her garter as well as some healthily endowed gams.[7]

What's wrong, Harry?

I gots to git down to the infirmary, Zuzu, something awful is happening, the Thing has stirred in its moorings. The Thing that my Grandfather Harry and his generation of Harrys had thought was nothing but a false alarm.

The Mayor, dragging the woman by the fox skins hanging from her neck, leaves city hall and jumps into his Stutz Bearcat[8] parked at the curb. They drive until they reach St. Louis Cathedral[9] where 19th-century HooDoo Queen Marie Laveau[1] was a frequent worshiper; its location was about 10 blocks from Place Congo. They walk up the steps and the door's Judas Eye[2] swings open.

---

1. At one time thought to be a god or spirit worshipped in West African religions, or an idol of such a spirit (of uncertain Mandingo origin, possibly *maamajomboo*, the name of a mask or masked dancer representing a cultic society and participating in religious ceremonies); by way of colloquial corruption, "mumbo jumbo" is now taken to mean obscure or meaningless speech.
2. Known as the "Latin lover," an Italian actor and early screen idol (1895–1926).
3. Promiscuous woman; "fizgig": a firework or whirling top that fizzes as it moves; hence, a flirtatious girl (1920s slang).
4. Refers to the illegal production, smuggling, or selling of liquor under Prohibition (1919–33).
5. Cigarette brand, popular in the 1920s and 1930s.
6. Partner.
7. Legs (slang).
8. American sports car of the pre– and post–World War I period.
9. Oldest continuously operating cathedral in the United States, the seat of the Roman Catholic archdiocese of New Orleans.
1. Also known as the "Witch Queen of New Orleans" (1794–1881), a practitioner of a form of syncretic religion known as New Orleans Voodoo followed by thousands of multiracial adherents.
2. Peephole. "Place Congo": French for Congo Square, an open space in New Orleans just north of the French Quarter, notable for its history of African American music and dance dating to the slavery era of the 18th and 19th centuries.

Joe Sent Me.[3]

What's going on, hon? Is this a speakeasy? Zuzu inquires in her cutesy-poo drawl.

The door opens to a main room of the church which has been converted into an infirmary. About 22 people lie on carts. Doctors are rushing back and forth; they wear surgeon's masks and white coats. Doors open and shut.

1 man approaches the Mayor who is walking from bed to bed examining the sleeping occupants, including the priest of the parish.

What's the situation report, doc? the Mayor asks.

We have 22 of them. The only thing that seems to anesthetize them is sleep.

When did it start?

This morning. We got reports from down here that people were doing "stupid sensual things," were in a state of "uncontrollable frenzy," were wriggling like fish, doing something called the "Eagle Rock" and the "Sassy Bump"; were cutting a mean "Mooche,"[4] and "lusting after relevance." We decoded this coon[5] mumbo jumbo. We knew that something was Jes Grewing just like the 1890s flair-up. We thought that the local infestation area was Place Congo so we put our antipathetic substances to work on it, to try to drive it out; but it started to play hide and seek with us, a case occurring in 1 neighborhood and picking up in another. It began to leapfrog all about us.

But can't you put it under 1 of them microscopes? Lock it in? Can't you protective-reaction[6] the dad-blamed thing? Look I got an election coming up—

To blazes with your election, man! Don't you understand, if this Jes Grew becomes pandemic it will mean the end of Civilization As We Know It?

That serious?

Yes. You see, it's not 1 of those germs that break bleed suck gnaw or devour. It's nothing we can bring into focus or categorize; once we call it 1 thing it forms into something else.

No man. This is a *psychic epidemic*, not a lesser germ like typhoid yellow fever or syphilis. We can handle those. This belongs under some ancient Demonic Theory of Disease.

3. Common password used to gain access to illegal liquor parlors, or "speakeasies," during Prohibition.
4. Mooche, Sassy Bump, Eagle Rock: dance moves associated with rural African Americans in the 1920s (all carry punning sexual innuendo).
5. Derogatory term for black person.
6. A phrase coined by British military strategist Basil Liddell Hart (1895–1970) in 1935 to describe the tactic of upsetting the enemy's equilibrium through preemptive attack. The term was used often by the administration of President Richard M. Nixon (1913–1994) as a euphemism for its bombing campaign against North Vietnam.

Well, what about the priest?

We tried him but it seized him too. He was shouting and carrying on like any old coon wench[7] with a bass drum.

What about the patients, did you ask any of them about how they knew it?

Yes, I, Harry. When we thought it was physical we examined his output, and drinking water to determine if we could find some normal germ. We asked him questions, like what he had seen.

What *did* he see?

He said he saw Nkulu Kulu of the Zulu[8], a locomotive with a red green and black python entwined in its face, Johnny Canoeing[9] up the tracks.

Well Clem, how about his feelings? How did he feel?

He said he felt like the gut heart and lungs of Africa's interior. He said he felt like the Kongo: "Land of the Panther."[1] He said he felt like "deserting his master," as the Kongo is "prone to do." He said he felt he could dance on a dime.

Well, his hearing, Clem. His hearing.

He said he was hearing shank bones, jew's harps,[2] bagpipes, flutes, conch horns, drums, banjos, kazoos.

Go on go on and then what did he say?

He started to speak in tongues.[3] There are no isolated cases in this thing. It knows no class no race no consciousness. It is self-propagating and you can never tell when it will hit.

Well doc, did you get other opinions?

Who do you think some of those other cases are? 6 of them are some of the most distinguished bacteriologists epidemologists and chemists from the University.

---

7. Lewd woman.

8. The amaZulu are an ethnic group in South Africa, made famous in Europe by their conflict with the British in the late 19th century. "Nkulu Kulu": each of these names refers to a type of bird in the isiZulu language.

9. Parading or dancing, in reference to the "Junkanoo" musical street parade marked by a dance form of West African origin that occurs in the Bahamas each Boxing Day (December 26). "Red green and black": flag colors for African nationalism as defined first by the "Declaration of Rights of the Negro People of the World" (1920) issued by the Universal Negro Improvement Association (U.N.I.A.) of black nationalist Marcus Garvey (1887–1940), an idea developed in response to the popular song "Every Race Has a Flag but the

Coon" (1900). "Python": a genus of constrictor snake found in Asia and Africa (where it is thought to signify authority, fertility, and rebirth).

1. The Congo is both a major river and a geographical area in western equatorial Africa along the Congo Basin; in Anglo-American literature, "Congo" often symbolizes the otherness of Africa. The panther appears on the coat of arms of the Democratic Republic of the Congo.

2. Musical instruments played by placing the reed in the performer's mouth and plucking it to produce a note. "Shank bones": a percussion instrument, often used to create dance rhythms.

3. Fluid vocalizing without any readily comprehensible meaning, associated with religious practices (particularly in Pentecostal and Charismatic Christianity); also known as "glossolalia."

There is a commotion outside. The Mayor rushes out to see Zuzu rejoicing. Slapping the attendants who are attempting to placate her. The people on carts suddenly leap up and do their individual numbers. The Mayor feels that uncomfortable sensation at the nape and soon he is doing something resembling the symptoms of Jes Grew, and the Doctor who rushes to his aid starts slipping dipping gliding on out of doors and into the streets. Shades of windows fly up. Lights flick on in buildings. And before you know it the whole quarter is in convulsions from Jes Grew's entrance into the Govi[4] of New Orleans; the charming city, the amalgam of Spanish French and African culture, is out-of-its-head. By morning there are 10,000 cases of Jes Grew.

*   *   *

The foolish Wallflower Order[5] hadn't learned a damned thing. They thought that by fumigating the Place Congo in the 1890s when people were doing the Bamboula the Chacta the Babouille the Counjaille the Juba[6] the Congo and the VooDoo that this would put an end to it. That it was merely a fad. But they did not understand that the Jes Grew epidemic was unlike physical plagues.

Actually Jes Grew was an anti-plague. Some plagues caused the body to waste away; Jes Grew enlivened the host. Other plagues were accompanied by bad air (malaria). Jes Grew victims said that the air was as clear as they had ever seen it and that there was the aroma of roses and perfumes which had never before enticed their nostrils. Some plagues arise from decomposing animals, but Jes Grew is electric as life and is characterized by ebullience and ecstasy. Terrible plagues were due to the wrath of God; but Jes Grew is the delight of the gods. So Jes Grew is seeking its words. Its text. For what good is a liturgy without a text? In the 1890s the text was not available and Jes Grew was out there all alone. Perhaps the 1920s will also be a false alarm and Jes Grew will evaporate as quickly as it appeared again broken-hearted and double-crossed (+ +)

*   *   *

Once the band starts, everybody starts swaying from one side of the street to the other, especially those who drop in and follow the ones who have been to the funeral. These people are known as "the second line" and they may be anyone passing along the street who wants to hear the music. *The spirit hits them and they follow*

(My italics)
Louis Armstrong[7]

Mumbo Jumbo

[Mandingo *mā-mā-gyo-mbō*, "magician who makes the troubled spirits of ancestors go away": *mā-mā*, grandmother + *gyo*, trouble + *mbō*, to leave.]

---

4. Cemetery ("govi" are soul jars or pots in the idiom of Hoodoo, a syncretic African American religious and magical practice also known as "conjure").

5. In *Mumbo Jumbo*, an international conspiracy dedicated to maintaining monotheism and repressing the impulse to dance, working in concert with the Knights Templar (a Christian military order famous for its campaigns during the medieval expeditionary religious wars known as the Crusades).

6. Slave dances. Reed draws on the 1867 essay "The Dance in Place Congo" by white American novelist George Washington Cable (1844–1925), known for his portrayals of Creole life in New Orleans.

7. African American jazz trumpeter, composer, and singer from New Orleans (1901–1971). The citation is from Armstrong's memoir, *Satchmo: My Life in New Orleans* (1954).

*The American Heritage Dictionary
of the English Language*

> Some *unknown natural phenomenon* occurs
> which cannot be explained,
> and a new local demigod is named.
> —Zora Neale Hurston on the origin of a new loa[8]

> The earliest Ragtime song, like Topsy,[9] "jes' grew."

> We appropriated about the last one of the "jes' grew" songs.
> It was a song which had been sung for years
> all through the South. The words were unprintable, but
> the tune was irresistible, and belonged to nobody.
> —James Weldon Johnson,[1]
> *The Book of American Negro Poetry*

2

With the astonishing rapidity of Booker T. Washington's Grapevine Tele-graph[2] Jes Grew spreads through America following a strange course. Pine Bluff and Magnolia Arkansas are hit; Natchez, Meridian and Greenwood Mississippi report cases. Sporadic outbreaks occur in Nashville and Knoxville Tennessee as well as St. Louis where the bumping and grinding cause the Gov to call up the Guard. A mighty influence, Jes Grew infects all that it touches.

1972

Epilogue

In the year 1909 ". . . it began as a flair-up. Localized in a few places, the South, the West and the Northeast. It knew neither class, race nor consciousness." An Atonist,[3] whose cover was editorial writer for the *Musical Courier*,[4] wrote in 1899:

> Society has decreed that ragtime and cakewalking[5] are the thing, and one reads with amazement and disgust of historical and aristocratic names joining in this sex dance, a milder edition of African orgies.

---

8. Spirits in the syncretic religion of Haitian Voodoo. Zora Neale Hurston: African American novelist, folklorist, and anthropologist (1891–1960). The citation is from Hurston's book *Tell My Horse: Voodoo and Life in Haiti and Jamaica* (1938).
9. Slave girl in the 1852 novel *Uncle Tom's Cabin* by American novelist Harriet Beecher Stowe (1811–1896). "Ragtime": musical genre, popular between the late 1890s and the end of World War I, distinguished by its syncopated, "ragged" rhythms; a progenitor of jazz.
1. African American author, diplomat, lawyer, and civil rights activist (1871–1938). *The Book of American Negro Poetry* was published in 1922.
2. Booker T. Washington (1856–1915), African American educator, orator, political advisor, and

ex-slave autobiographer, wrote in *Up from Slavery* (1903) that slaves in the South spread news of current events rapidly by "what was termed the 'grape-vine' telegraph."
3. A member of the Wallflower Order.
4. 19th- and 20th-century American music trade publication. The following paragraph is cited from an 1899 editorial in the journal.
5. Dance competition form, developed from "walk-arounds" performed at get-togethers of slaves on plantations, at the end of which the winning couple is awarded a huge cake; performed in minstrel shows until the 1890s, after which it was popular in African American communities for several decades.

Cakewalking and ragtime are symptoms of that X factor. The stumper of *Psychic Epidemologists*.[6] It was 11 years before Hinckle Von Vampton's message, to those in the know, that Sigmund Freud[7] was dispatched to America for the purpose of diagnosing this phenomenon. (Sigmund Freud as you will recall is the man who grew up in a town dominated by the 200-foot steeple belonging to a church named for the Virgin Mary. It affected him. He began to trace Man's "neurosis" to situations arising from this elemental relationship. The Mother and Son! [How many times do you hear of Electra?[8]]

Freud, whose real talent lies in the coinage of new terms for processes as old as the Ark.[9] He is as gifted as an American soap canvasser[1] at this. This is why perhaps he was better known here than in his own Vienna.

Freud drinks from a Dixie Cup as the party sails into New York harbor. He stands in awe before Niagara Falls. He then pushes into the hinterland of the American soul and here in this astral Bear country[2] he sees the festering packing Germ.

Freud faints. What he saw must have been unsettling to this man accustomed to the gay Waltzing circles of Austria, the respectable clean-cut family, the protocol, the formalities of "civilization." Smelling salts are administered to their teacher by followers who've not seen such an outburst since their teacher waxed all "paranoid" when someone awarded him a medal upon which was etched the Sphinx[3] being questioned by the traveler. Or on another occasion when Carl Jung confronted him with the fable of the fossilized corpses of peat moss.[4]

What did this man see? What did this clear-headed, rational, "prudish" and "chaste" man see? "The Black Tide of Mud," he was to call it. "We must make a dogma . . . an unshakable bulwark against the Black Tide of Mud,"[5] uttered this man who as a child returned from church and imitated the minister and repeated his sermons in a "self-righteous manner."

A tall, bespectacled man summons a news conference.

Q. What did the Doctor mean by "The Black Tide of Mud?"
A. He meant occultism.[6]
Q. Why, then, did he employ the language of the Churchman: "Dogma"?
A. It was merely a figure of speech.
Q. But according to his theories, don't figures of speech have latent significance?

---

6. Experts in the distribution of health-related events (especially disease).

7. Austrian neurologist, known as the "father of psychoanalysis" (1856–1939). Hinckle Von Vampton: main villain of *Mumbo Jumbo*, a member of the Knights Templar.

8. In Greek legend, daughter of Agamemnon and Clytemnestra who plotted with her brother Orestes the murder of their mother in revenge for her killing of their father. Hence, in the neo-Freudian psychology of Swiss psychotherapist Carl Gustav Jung (1875–1961), "the Electra complex" refers to a child's psychosexual competition with the mother for love of the father.

9. I.e., Noah's Ark, which allowed for the repopulation of the earth after the Flood recounted in Genesis 6–9.

1. Door-to-door seller of soap.

2. "Astral Bear country": pun from combination of Astral Bear or Ursa Major (a prominent constellation in the northern sky) and bear country, a backwoods or uncivilized area.

3. In Greek mythology, a creature with a lion's haunches, great bird's wings, and a woman's face. Part of the legend of the Greek character Oedipus—after whom Freud named the "complex" in which a child competes with his father for love of his mother—involves the hero's solving the "riddle of the Sphinx": What walks on four legs in the morning, two at noon, and three in the evening? (The correct answer is: man.)

4. Peat bogs, located mostly in coastal regions of northern Europe, provide highly acidic, cold saline conditions that have led to the mummification of corpses.

5. The anecdote is recounted by Jung in *Memories, Dreams, and Reflections*, published two years after Jung's death in 1963.

6. Belief in supernatural presences in everyday life.

... Please, Dr. Jung pleads. No more questions. I must return to the Doctor.

1 reporter insists on 1 more question.

Q. Before you leave, Doctor, can you give us Dr. Freud's impressions of America?

A. He considers it "a big mistake."[7]

Freud, who disliked prophecy, was in no position to make a diagnosis. He admitted once that he could not discover "this 'oceanic' feeling in myself."[8] Lacking harmony with the world, he was unable to see what it was.

Later Jung travels to Buffalo New York and at a dinner table discovers what Freud saw. Europeans living in America have undergone a transformation. Jung calls this process "going Black."[9] This chilly Swiss keeps it to himself however.

Strange. It seems that the most insightful pictures of America are done by Europeans or Blacks. Myrdal, Tocqueville, Jung, Trollope, Hernton, Clarence Major, Al Young, or Blacks who know both Europe and America: Wright, Baldwin, Chester Himes, John A. Williams, William Gardner Smith, Cecil Brown.[1] I once leafed through a photo book about the West. I was struck by how the Whites figured in the center of the photos and drawings while Blacks were centrifugally distant. The center was usually violent: gunfighting lynching murdering torturing. The Blacks were usually, if it were an interior, standing in the doorway. Digging the center.

The clock on the wall strikes 10:00 P.M. The lecture should have concluded an hour before. But when PaPa LaBas[2] gets started he doesn't stop. He's a Ghede.[3] Garrulous gluttonous satirical sardonic but unafraid to march up to the President's Palace and demand tribute.

What did Freud mean by The Black Tide of Mud? Why were there later to be assassinations of cultural heroes? In 1914 Scott Joplin,[4] who, after announcing that ragtime will "hypnotize this Nation," is taken to Ward Island[5] where they fritter away his powers with shock therapy. Scott Joplin has healed many with his ability to summon this X factor, the Thing that Freud saw, the indefinable quality that James Weldon Johnson called "Jes Grew."

7. In *The Life and Work of Sigmund Freud: Years of Maturity, 1901–1919* (1957), British neurologist and psychoanalyst Ernest Jones (1879–1958) cites Freud as having said: "America is a mistake, admittedly a gigantic mistake, but a mistake nevertheless."
8. "'Oceanic' feeling": term coined by French author Romain Rolland (1866–1944) and popularized by Freud to indicate a religious feeling of limitlessness or the sensation of eternity; the remark cited here appears in Freud's *Civilization and Its Discontents* (1930).
9. "The Complications of American Psychology," first published (1930) as "Your Negroid and Indian Behavior"—Carl G. Jung. [Author's note.] Reed is citing an actual article, which Jung published in 1930 as a reflection on his time in the United States.
1. American activist and legislator (1929–2006). K. Gunnar Myrdal (1898–1987): Swedish economist, author of *An American Dilemma: The Negro Problem and Modern Democracy* (1940); Alexis de Tocqueville (1805–1859): French historian, author of *Democracy in America* (1835–40); Frances Trollope (1779–1863): English novelist and author of *Domestic Manners of the*

Americans (1832); Calvin C. Hernton (1932–2001): African American poet and essayist; Clarence Major (b. 1936): African American poet, painter, and scholar; Al Young (b. 1939): African American poet and educator; Richard Wright (1908–1960): African American novelist and essayist; James Baldwin (1924–1987): African American novelist and essayist; Chester Himes (1909–1960): African American novelist; John A. Williams (b. 1925): African American novelist; William Gardner Smith (1927–1974): African American novelist and journalist.
2. Elderly Harlem detective and *houngan*, or Voodoo priest, the protagonist of Reed's novel.
3. That is, he was from the family of loa, or spirits in Haitian Voodoo, that embody the powers of death and fertility.
4. African American pianist known for his ragtime compositions (1867/8–1917).
5. Wards Island, in the East River of New York City, was home of the Manhattan State Hospital, the largest psychiatric institution in the world from 1899 until its downsizing in 1920. Joplin was hospitalized there in 1916 for schizophrenia aggravated by syphilis.

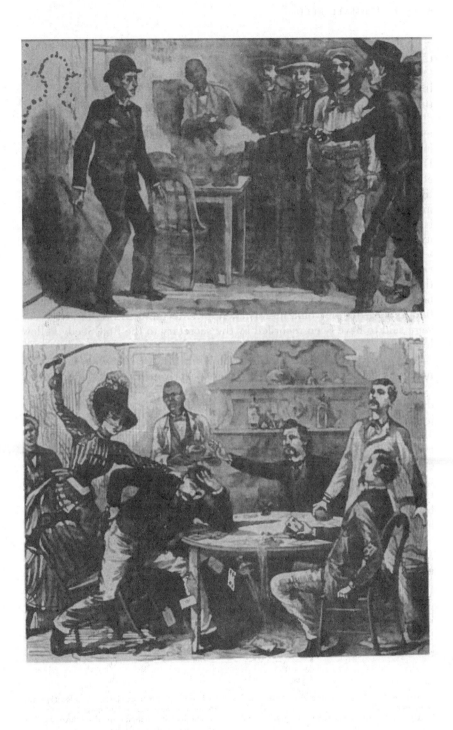

"It belonged to nobody," Johnson said. "Its words were unprintable but its tune irresistible." Jes Grew, the Something or Other that led Charlie Parker[6] to scale the Everests of the Chord. Riff fly skid dip soar and gave his Alto Godspeed. Jes Grew that touched John Coltrane's Tenor[7]; that tinged the voice of Otis Redding and compelled Black Herman[8] to write a dictionary to Dreams that Freud would have envied. Jes Grew was the manic in the artist who would rather do glossolalia than be "neat clean or lucid." Jes Grew, the despised enemy of the Atonist Path, those Left-Handed practitioners of the Petro Loa,[9] those too taut to spring from sharp edges, wiggle jiggle go all the way down and come up shaking. Jes Grew is the lost liturgy seeking its litany. Its words, chants held in bondage by the mysterious Order[1] "which saved the 2nd Crusade from annihilation by Islamic hordes." Those disgraced Knights. Jes Grew needed its words to tell its carriers what it was up to. Jes Grew was an influence which sought its text, and whenever it thought it knew the location of its words and Labanotations[2] it headed in that direction. There had been a sporadic episode in the 1890s and it was driven back into its Cell. Jes Grew was jumpy now because it was 1920 and something was going on. A Stirring. If it could not find its Text then it would be mistaken for entertainment. Its basic dances were said to have been recorded by the secretary to the first Seedy Fellow himself.

Jes Grew was going around in circles until the 1920s when it impregnated America's "hysteria." I was there, a private eye practicing in my Neo-HooDoo therapy center named by my critics Mumbo Jumbo Kathedral because I awarded the Asson to myself. Licensed myself. I was a jacklegged[3] detective of the metaphysical who was on the case; and in 1920 there was a crucial case. In 1920 Jes Grew swept through this country and whether they liked it or not Americans were confronted with the choices of whether to Eagle Rock or Buzzard Swoop,[4] whether to join the contagion or quarantine it, whether to go with Jes Grew or remain loyal to the Atonist Path protected by the Wallflower Order, its administrative backbone, composed of grumblers and sourpusses to whom no 1 ever asked:

"May I Have This 1?"

Papa LaBas notices that some of the students are leaving the hall. It is nearly 10:30 P.M.

I will end now . . . Are there any questions?

A woman, whose hair has been sprayed and sculpted into a huge soft black ball of cotton raises her hand.

Yes?

PaPa LaBas, how did you live to become 100 years old?

---

6. African American jazz alto saxophonist and composer (1920–1955).

7. African American jazz tenor saxophonist and composer (1926–1967).

8. Benjamin Rucker (1892–1934), African American stage magician and Voodoo doctor, author of *Secrets of Magic, Mystery, and Legerdemain* (1925); as a character in *Mumbo Jumbo*, he is an ally of Papa LaBas. Otis Redding (1941–1967): African American rhythm-and-blues and soul singer-songwriter.

9. Family of spirits in Haitian Voodoo typically thought to make malevolent magic.

1. The Knights Templar are also known as "The Mysterious Order of Malta."

2. Standardized system for recording and analyzing human motion, primarily used by choreographers.

3. Makeshift, amateur.

4. Dances associated with the "honky tonks" (music bars) of the early 20th century.

Serving my *Ka*,[5] daughter. Even a healthy body is useless unless the spirit is provided for with its own unique vitamins. There is a prescription for every soul here. The process has been developed from our ancient artificers until now.

You mean, the woman continues, that there are signs which determine our spiritual heritage?

Yes. In a superficial way it operates in a manner similar to the way natal astrology works: the notion that what happens in the heavens has an influence upon our lives on earth. Of course what is known as "natal astrology" has been corrupted by the Atonist scholars who've over 1000s of years brought their traditional prejudices to the art. We do not use the systems employed by the Egyptians Aztecs or Babylonians. Taurus[6] for example is described as—in his main qualities—reliable patient slow honest trustworthy. Sounds to me like the deft hand of the Atonist Path who've had it in for Taurus for 1000s of years; unable to resist any opportunity to emasculate this figure—and get this, his colors are pastels—they've created a weak Bull. Saks 5th Avenue[7] window dressing. Wonder does he play football and appear on talk shows?

Early tabloid editors as they were, they doctored the ancient texts at Heliopolis.[8] Who worked about a horseshoe-like table in this early center of Yellow Journalism[9] where they made their heroes look radiant, glowing; umbraging the heroes of others in this City Room of Hypocrisy.

Compare this description of Taurus with that of a Black loa, by the Haitian houngans who've maintained The Work largely uncorrupted. The Loa Agovi Minorie boasts when mounting a woman that his phallus is so hard that the brilliance of his organ's bulb resembles that of a mirror.

Houngans in Haiti as well as Priests of Africa and South America are able to identify any Spirit or God that possesses a person, an art the Greeks knew, taught to them by an aide to the Human Germ who went into exile after the Master was assassinated by the arch Atonist in Egypt.

The Greeks established temples to the Egyptian's Osiris and Isis[1] where people were allowed to go out of their minds so that spirits could enter their heads; all under the watchful eyes of trained priests who knew the knowledge that Dionysus[2] brought from Egypt. It is in this dictionary, which was committed to memory by the Human Germ's aides when they fled to the Sudan and Nubia[3] and brought to the Americas when the slaves came, that you will find something to fit your head. 1000s of loas some of whose qualities are modified when conjoined with certain rites just as those of the 12 Houses of Astrology are when matched with the planets. The rites, principally Rada and Petro,[4] are not inherently good or evil; it depends upon how they are used. The houngan practices the Rada rites with the Right Hand.

5. The soul or "vital essence," according to Egyptian mythology.
6. The second astrological sign in the Zodiac, symbolized by the bull.
7. Upscale department store based in New York City.
8. One of the oldest cities in ancient Egypt, Heliopolis was destroyed in the construction of medieval Cairo.
9. I.e., sensationalist journalism.
1. Egyptian goddess of magic and nature, sister and wife of Osiris, god of the underworld and afterlife; after Osiris was murdered and dismembered by his usurping brother, Set, the grieving Isis reassembled her husband's body so that he could be resurrected as patron of the dead.
2. Greek god of harvest, wine, and ritual ecstasy.
3. Region along the Nile river located in southern Egypt and northern Sudan.
4. Petro and Rada, the two main types of Voodoo ceremony, focus respectively on the "sweet" (or loving) and "bitter" (or ill-tempered) loa.

Cheap, evil *bokors*[5] practice the rites with the Left Hand. The Left Hand Work, Dirty Work has been frowned upon from the time of the ancient Egyptians until North America.

So wherever the untampered word exists the Atonists move in. They know that Jes Grew needs its words and steps, or else it becomes merely a flair-up. Without substance it never fully catches on. When the people defeat their religious arm they move in their secular troops, men good at confusing people by making up new words that would be palatable to the masses who confuse quackery with profundity. Exorcism becomes Psychoanalysis, Hex becomes Death Wish, Possession becomes Hysteria.

5. Hired voodoo sorcerers or priests who are said to "serve the loa with both hands," that is, through both dark and beneficial magic.

This explains why Holy Wars have been launched against Haiti under the cover of "bringing stability to the Caribbean." 1 such war lasted longer than Vietnam. But you don't hear much about it because the action was against niggers. From 1914 to 1934 Southern Marines "because they knew how to handle niggers" destroyed the government and ruined the economy in their attempt to kill Jes Grew's effluvia by fumigating its miasmatic source.[6] The Blues is a Jes Grew, as James Weldon Johnson surmised. Jazz was a Jes Grew which followed the Jes Grew of Ragtime. Slang is Jes Grew too.

The Black professor interrupts PaPa LaBas.

This is all we have time for, PaPa LaBas. Thank you very much for being with us tonight. PaPa LaBas is an eccentric old character from the 20s who thrills us with his tales about those golden times and his role in bringing about the holiday we are celebrating today.

The students smile at this old man accepting his inevitable envelope containing the honorarium. He loves to come to the university for his annual lecture on Jes Grew. All the students are wearing Jes Grew buttons of their own design.

Papa LaBas sprightly walks through the door of the classroom wearing his opera hat, the smoked glasses, carrying the cane, that familiar 1920s outfit— The Handsome Stranger of the 1919 Poster, by R. di Maga—fatal, skeptical—

PaPa LaBas?

---

6. Refers to the U.S. occupation of Haiti, 1915–34, part of American efforts to expand U.S. influence in the Caribbean and Latin America during the first part of the 20th century.

Someone is calling, a cracked old voice. He turns about. It is he. The old man who in his devotion to empirical method had washed out any prophecy for which his ancestors were famous. He had written derisively of it after the last flair-up when Jes Grew launched a trial balloon, sent out a feeler; he had sought to inoculate the populace by writing that it would have to imitate Crane and Twain[7] before it would amount to anything. That it was a fad like Flagpole Sitting and Goldfish Swallowing.[8] His imagery was about as contemporary as he was because the craft of Jes Grew put him into a tizzy. He didn't know what to make of it. In his last lucid interview he had regretted that he had opposed Hoffman Rubin Zimmerman the Beatles and the poet in the Balaam seat, Negro delineators in the tradition of Paul Whiteman, Dvorak, Fred Astaire, Sophie Tucker, Mae West, Dan Rice, George Gershwin. Singing the Blues.[9] Getting hot. Contacting Jes Grew Carriers so that some of it would rub off. Using the word Man as a fugitive part of speech. He had denounced their warped syntax composition and grammar; but now he wished he had bent a little. It was too late. The imitators were on the decline and the members were taking over. Jes Grew was latching onto its blood. After all Liverpool ain't Memphis and the Monterey Jazz Festival no Bucket of Blood.[1] Now the delineators were taking a backseat to the Jes Grew Carriers, those jockey-dressed amulets[2] on the Southern Lawn of America's consciousness. Those who made Sutter's Gold prospectors[3] jittery by their presence.

Those who would never be allowed at the Free Enterprise gaming wheels, blackjack tables and slots because of that Black gentleman there in the beret with the goatee and whiskers. He threw 7, 7 times. They called it HooDooing the dice. The Jes Grew factor.

The Carriers were learning too. As long as they were stagemen, like those clowns who were so adept in the art of rap they could recite the 1st 15 listings in the telephone book and still entice the masses. They were supplied with Town Hall, Carnegie,[4] the Grand Ballroom of the Hilton Hotel, but

---

7. Mark Twain, pen name of Samuel Clemens, American author and satirist (1835–1910); Stephen Crane (1871–1900), American novelist, poet, and journalist.
8. A fad among American college students in the 1920s. "Flagpole Sitting": fad of endurance during the 1920s and 1930s begun in 1924 by Alvin "Shipwreck" Kelly (1893–1952) as a Hollywood publicity stunt.
9. Popular song of 1927 recorded by jazz cornetist Leon Bismark "Bix" Beiderbecke (1903–1931) and saxophonist Orie "Frankie" Trumbauer (1901–1956). Abbie Hoffman (1938–1994) and Jerry Rubin (1936–1989), social and political activists who co-founded the Youth International Party, the "Yippies," in 1967; both were tried for conspiracy as members of the so-called Chicago Eight, charged with inciting violence at the 1968 Democratic Party National Convention in Chicago. Robert Zimmerman (b. 1941): better known as Bob Dylan, American singer-songwriter and counterculture icon. Balaam: Old Testament diviner who refused to give his support to an enemy of the Israelites (Numbers 22). Paul Whiteman (1890–1967): American bandleader popular in the 1920s. Antonin Leopold Dvorak (1841–1904): Czech composer who

blended folk idioms and Romantic symphonic conventions. Fred Astaire (1899–1987): American film and stage dancer, actor, and singer. Sophie Tucker (1886–1966): American singer and actress popular in the first half of the 20th century. Mae West (1893–1980): American film actress and sex idol, known for her bawdy wit. Dan Rice (1823–1900), American circus entertainer and clown, famous for his minstrel routines. George Gershwin (1898–1937): American songwriter and pianist, best known for compositions blending jazz and classical styles.
1. New Orleans "juke joint" or roadside blues bar, made famous in the song of the same name by blues guitarist Little Freddie King (born Fread Eugene Martin in 1940). Liverpool: hometown of the Beatles. Memphis: often called "the home of the blues." Monterey Jazz Festival: annual California jazz festival that debuted in 1958.
2. I.e., statuettes of black jockeys, often with minstrel-like features, used by middle-class whites as lawn ornaments.
3. The California Gold Rush began when gold was discovered at the mill operated by Swiss businessman Johann August Sutter (1803–1880) on the American River near Coloma, California.

when they went after the fetishes of the Atonist Path strange things happened. The mysteriously unfulfilled orders from the bookstores. The tapes turned up missing. The microphone in that innocent little box about 15 feet from where you're speaking. You know, what Atonists call "paranoid fantasies" began to occur.

It all came down to Kipling's[5] vision. They all, Left, Right, etc., wanted to wear their pith helmets[6] riding on their cultural elephants but Sabu[7] no longer wished to be their guide.

But now this pitiful creature who said something about "Black Studies so much blackeyed peas" had to stand on the soapbox as the Religious Atonist had before. Lecturing on Freud and Marx and all the old names. He resembled the embarrassed gargoyle[8] dismayed and condemned to watch his former worshipers pass him by as they went into the centers of Jes Grew. Pagan Mysteries.

Sometimes he would yammer on and on about his mother and dad in the garment district and how hard it was for them. Everyone should be sheltered, fed, there was no disagreement about the body. It was what to do about the head.

LaBas felt everybody should have their own head or the head of God which the Atonist's mundane "system" wouldn't admit. *Homo economicus*.[9] The well-fed the will-less robot who yields his head to the Sun King. The sad old creature wanted the Jes Grew Carriers to have his head. Cut out this Jes Grew that keeps a working man up to all hours of the night with its carryings on. The Ballyhoo of its Whoopie.[1] Its Cab Calloway hidihidiho.[2]

He wanted them to have *his* head. An Atonist head. While LaBas wanted them to have the heads their people had left for them or create new ones of their own. A library of stacks a 1000 miles long. Therefore he and PaPa LaBas disagreed about what to do with the head, not the body.

PaPa LaBas attempted to ignore this ideological tramp but wasn't able to; the man followed him out to the automobile parking lot.

LaBas, why do you mystify your past? These youngsters need something palpable. Not this bongo drumming[3] called Jes Grew.

Bongo drumming requires very intricate technique. A rhythmic vocabulary larger than French English or Spanish, the 1-time vernacular languages.

Come now, the old man smiles. Come now, PaPa LaBas.

4. Carnegie Hall in New York City, a prestigious concert venue. Town Hall: New York City performance space associated with activists and progressive artists.
5. Rudyard Kipling (1865–1936), English author known for children's tales and origin stories set in colonized India and Africa.
6. Light, hard hats worn for protection from the sun in hot climates, often associated with colonialists in the tropics.
7. Sabu Dastagir (1924–1963), film actor of Indian origin credited only by his first name, who played the main character, Mowgli, in the 1942 adaptation of Kipling's 1894 story collection *The Jungle Book*.
8. In architecture, an ornamental spout in the

form of a grotesque human or animal; hence, a weathered, absurd, and ugly person.
9. The economic human (Latin), a phrase designating the model of human activity as driven by rational decision and self-interested motivation.
1. A shout, associated with merrymaking; "Ballyhoo": clamor.
2. Cabell "Cab" Calloway III (1907–1994), African American jazz singer and bandleader; his trademark call "Hi-De-Ho" formed the chorus of his most famous song, "Minnie the Moocher" (1931), and was used as the title for his 1947 "race film," a musical with an all-black cast starring Calloway and his band.
3. Afro-Cuban percussive tradition originating in the eastern region of 19th-century Cuba.

The man stands next to the driver's window as PaPa LaBas climbs into his automobile. The man puffs on his pipe. The man's face is bloated. Sanguine.

Each year the students would invite PaPa LaBas to the campus to discuss the Harlem Renaissance.[4] After all, he had attended this "Negro Awakening." The Cabarets, the Speaks, and he knew the many painters, show people, film makers. He knew Park Ave. as well as those on Striver's Row.[5] He went to the celebrations at Irvington-on-Hudson as well as to the Chitterling Switches.[6] But the children seemed more interested in the fact that he was 100 years old than anything else.

PaPa LaBas begins the electric starter.[7] One of the gas lamps was broken. The beautiful interior furnishings faded. The French telephone removed long ago.

The man is still standing there. The strange wounded expression. Do aging anteaters smile?

PaPa LaBas, you must come clean with those students. They must have a firm background in the Classics. Serious works, the achievements of mankind which began in Greece and then sort of wiggled all over the place like a chicken with its neck wrung. (He had once written in a private interview that he didn't know whether to dismiss Jes Grew or go with it. His language reflected this indecision.)

PaPa LaBas continues to ignore the man. He wants to get home, they are having greens and hog's head[8] to celebrate the Holiday.

Will you please move over?

The car jolts forward. The 1914 Locomobile Town Coupe[9] has by this time developed a mind of its own. The man crashes to the pavement of the parking lot like a sandbag. His glasses are sprawled on the ground in front of him. He doesn't appear to be hurt because he lifts himself from the pavement and begins a ponderous trot in pursuit of the car. He stops and clutches his chest as if in pain.

PaPa LaBas watches him in his rear-view mirror as the man, a sad figure, turns and slowly walks toward the campus. He would sleep there under an elm until the next morning when he would climb on the soapbox and harangue about Freud Marx Youth, etc. etc. The man himself a relic from another age like the 1 letter in the neon sign that is off the blink. The poor frumpy, frowzy man. He wouldn't last long. Couldn't be more than 70–75. A mere youngster. PaPa LaBas steers the car over the bridge. He saw the lights of Manhattan. Chuckling to himself he thought of the lecture: the flights of fancy, the tangential excursions, a classroom that knew what he was talking about.

---

4. New York City–based African American cultural movement of the 1920s and 1930s, also called "the Negro Awakening" after an 1896 essay of that title by Booker T. Washington.
5. Three rows of townhouses in west Harlem associated with an emerging African American middle-class community in the early to mid-20th century. "Park Ave.": area of New York's East Side inhabited during this period by wealthy whites.
6. Small southern towns, a term adapted in the North during the 1920s by African Americans to designate a fund-raising party (early in *Mumbo*

Jumbo, such a party is held for an anti-lynching campaign). Irvington-on-Hudson: affluent suburb north of New York City.
7. First used in 1896, the most common device for starting an automobile's internal combustion engine.
8. "Greens and hog's head": food associated with African American cuisine.
9. Another designation for the Stutz Bearcat that Papa LaBas is described as driving in the novel's beginning; the Locomobile Company of America, founded in 1899, went out of business in 1929.

People in the 60s said they couldn't follow him. (In Santa Cruz the students walked out.) What's your point? they asked in Seattle whose central point, the Space Needle, is invisible from time to time. What are you driving at? they would say in Detroit in the 1950s. In the 40s he haunted the stacks of a ghost library. In the 30s he sought to recover his losses like everybody else. In the 20s they knew. And the 20s were back again. Better. Arna Bontemps[1] was correct in his new introduction to *Black Thunder*. Time is a pendulum. Not a river. More akin to what goes around comes around. (*Locomobile rear moving toward neoned Manhattan skyline. Skyscrapers gleam like magic trees. Freeze frame.*)

Jan. 31st, 1971 3:00 P.M.
Berkeley, California

1. African American poet, novelist, scholar, educator, and contributor to the Harlem Renaissance (1902–1973), whose introduction to the 1968 reissue of his 1936 neo–slave narrative novel *Black Thunder: Gabriel's Revolt: Virginia, 1800* begins with the words: "Time is not a river. Time is a pendulum."

MICHAEL S. HARPER
b. 1938

Born in 1938 in Brooklyn, New York, to Walter Warren Harper (a postal worker and supervisor) and Katherine Johnson Harper (a medical stenographer), Michael Steven Harper entered a family endowed with an artistic sensibility attuned especially to the poetic and musical traditions of twentieth-century African American culture. Most memorably for Harper, his parents had an impressive record collection—the only problem being that Harper was not allowed to use it, which of course only provoked him to play the records when they were out of the house. Thus feasting on the music of Bessie Smith, Count Basie, Louis Armstrong, Charlie Parker, Miles Davis, and Billie Holiday, Harper avers that he learned "to think in terms of music," a foundation that he has come to consider a necessity for a poet, since "musicians were always at the frontier of what we call 'parlance,' the way in which they express themselves to other people." While his mother was Episcopal and his father Catholic, Harper considered himself a Baptist "because of the great singing"; Harper writes, "Every Sunday I had to *hit the meter* (put money in the collection box), hit the holy water, and take the subway to 52nd Street to catch Bird play."

In 1951, when Harper was thirteen, his family moved to a predominantly white neighborhood in West Los Angeles, an area in which, Harper later recalled, "the homes of some black families were bombed in the early 1950s." Harper remembers the experience as a traumatic one, causing him to grapple with severe racial tensions in an alien environment. In Los Angeles Harper entered the Susan Miller Dorsey High School, where he was placed on a vocational track for industrial arts. Harper's father, however, went to the school "to straighten out a counselor" and was consequently able to get Michael enrolled in the academic program at the high school. Harper struggled in high school, in part because of racial animus, in part because of his serious asthma (inherited from his mother) that led to failing grades in his physical education classes, thus keeping him off the honor roll. During his high school years, Harper worked as a newspaper boy and explored the streets of Los Angeles.

Although Harper had a strong interest in poetry during high school, it was not until college that he began to write his own verse. Harper enrolled at Los Angeles City College in 1955, and then moved on to Los Angeles State College, which he attended until 1961. Harper had been encouraged to pursue medicine, and there was a significant precedent in his family to do so: his grandfather had delivered him at birth, and his great-grandfather, Dr. John Albert Johnson, a bishop in the African Methodist Episcopal Church, was a medical missionary to the dioceses of South Africa from 1907 to 1916. Harper initially pursued a premedical track in college, but found himself sitting in the back of classrooms writing poetry. Furthermore, a zoology professor in college, assuming that blacks could not make it to medical school, advised Harper to give up medicine: Harper remembers being told that he "should pick up a broom and forget the microscope." Though Harper's poems display a deep appreciation of and interest in medicine, the human body, suffering, and healing, a lack of enthusiasm and myriad obstacles deflected Harper from the premedical path, at which point he seriously began writing poetry and reading works—such as Ralph Ellison's *Invisible Man* and the letters of John Keats—that would prove to have a lasting influence on his life and work.

While in college, Harper, in addition to taking classes and writing poetry, worked full time as a postal worker, an experience he describes as marking "the real beginning of my life." He was surrounded by men like his father, black men who were well educated but "who couldn't get employment in the private sector; they were formidable people, witty, zany, and with spunk." After college, in the winter of 1961, Harper entered graduate school to study creative writing at the Iowa Writers Workshop, where he received a master's degree in English. Although a trying experience, one in which racial difference grew even more acutely complex for Harper due to the institutionalization of segregated student housing in Iowa City, Harper made friends with other writers and artists. Harper credits Iowa with helping him mature as an artist: "Among other things, Philip Roth accused me of writing a 'pornographic' novella." Whether that was meant as compliment or condemnation, he realized at Iowa that his work was substantively different from the work done by his white peers.

Despite the ambivalence toward academia generated by his Iowa experience, Harper returned to Los Angeles in 1962 to student-teach at Pasadena City College and spent the 1960s working in various West Coast colleges. During this time, Harper published poems in many journals, but it was with the publication of his first book of poetry, *Dear John, Dear Coltrane* (1970), which in 1971 received a nomination for a National Book Award (under the valuation of Gwendolyn Brooks, Robert Penn Warren, and Denise Levertov), that Harper became a well-known poet. That same year, Harper received an offer of a tenured appointment as an associate professor at Brown University, where since 1983 he has served as the Israel J. Kapstein Professor of English.

Dear John, Dear Coltrane not only pays homage to John Coltrane, the legendary jazz saxophonist and composer, but does so by translating Coltrane's musical style into poetic verse. Indeed, Harper's poetry, in this and subsequent volumes, is stunningly improvisational, rhythmic, and performative, most deeply felt when sung or recited aloud. Harper himself emphasizes the musicality of his poetry: "I'm trying to write a poem for the ear as well as the eye." He would release six more acclaimed collections during the 1970s: *History Is Your Own Heartbeat* (1971), which won the Poetry Award of the Black Academy of Arts and Letters; *Photographs: Negatives: History as Apple Tree* (1972); *Song: I Want a Witness* (1972); *Debridement* (1973); *Nightmare Begins Responsibility* (1975); and *Images of Kin: New and Selected Poems* (1977), which won the Melville-Cane Award and was a nominee for the National Book Award. Though Harper continued to write and publish poetry during the last two decades of the twentieth century, he did so at a somewhat slower pace. Volumes produced during this period include *Rhode Island: Eight Poems* (1981), *Healing Song for the Inner Ear* (1985), *Songlines: Mosaics* (1991), *Honorable Amendments* (1995), and *Songlines in Michaeltree: New and Collected Poems* (2000). In 1988, he was honored as the first poet laureate of Rhode Island.

Harper's careful attention to cultural process, to the ways meanings and values are legitimated and related, allows him to explore the poetic technique he inherits from Coltrane: modality. "My poems are rhythmic rather than metric; the pulse is jazz, the tradition generally oral; my major influences musical; my debts, mostly to the musicians . . . who taught me to see about experience, pain, and love, and who made it artful and archetypal." Modal form not only provides Harper a method for poetic composition and performance, but also serves as a paradigm for a new *vision* of perception and being. To use the idiom of the Black Arts movement, modality entwines aesthetic and political aspects of African American expression against the grain of Western conceptions of self and society, becoming itself a form in which a particular version of the black ethos might be more fully realized. As Harper puts it in an interview with Abraham Chapman, modes "are forces. . . . Modality is always about relationships; modality is also about energy, energy irreducible and true only unto itself." Modality thus bears within it a revolutionary potentiality, implying new relations between word and world that connect to a historical continuum preceding slavery.

Harper once noted, "Poetry, for me, is not a career; it's expiation and bondage. You don't choose." Yet it is precisely through this unchosen dialectic of atonement and strife that Harper has created verse which he has described as "fundamentally testamental," a poetic form of witness that bravely faces events of profound historical loss, both public and private. For Harper, this testamental poetry emerges as an attempt at locating himself in what he calls "this very strange terrain" of American history, which Harper considers to be a matter of voice. But this voice—its rhythms, timbre, contours, and propositions—always emerges not as an autobiographical quest, but as an attempt to articulate in poetry the anguished cries of those whose voices have gone unheard and unrecorded. In his modal poetics, Harper seeks to encounter historical trauma not simply to heal wounds, but in many cases to open up injuries that have been forgotten or become numb. Harper's poetry of "expiation and bondage" constitutes a poetics that perpetually confronts a history of betrayals, violations, and abject losses, thus seeking to tear open what Harper considers the closed myths of national fantasy. Experimenting with generic boundaries and rhythmic phrasings, Harper's poems function both as witness to trauma and as traumatization of language, for they seek to forge new relations among present, past, and future in a verse of bold intellectual intensity and rare emotional grittiness.

Dear John, Dear Coltrane[1]

a love supreme,[2] a love supreme
a love supreme, a love supreme

Sex fingers toes
in the marketplace
near your father's church   5
in Hamlet, North Carolina[3]—
witness to this love
in this calm fallow[4]
of these minds,
there is no substitute for pain: 10
genitals gone or going,
seed burned out,
you tuck the roots in the earth,

---

1. John Coltrane (1926–1967), avant-garde saxophonist and deeply influential jazz composer.
2. The title of a four-part piece (1964) that is one of Coltrane's most famous recordings.

3. Coltrane's birthplace.
4. Cultivated land allowed to lie idle during the growing season.

turn back, and move
by river through the swamps,   15
singing: *a love supreme, a love supreme;*
what does it all mean?
Loss, so great each black
woman expects your failure
in mute change, the seed gone.   20
You plod up into the electric city—
your song now crystal and
the blues. You pick up the horn
with some will and blow
into the freezing night: 25
a love supreme, a love supreme—

Dawn comes and you cook[5]
up the thick sin 'tween
impotence and death, fuel
the tenor sax cannibal   30
heart, genitals and sweat
that makes you clean[6]—
a love supreme, a love supreme—

Why you so black?
cause I am   35
why you so funky[7]?
cause I am
why you so black?
cause I am
why you so sweet?   40
cause I am
why you so black?
cause I am
a love supreme, a love supreme:

So sick   45
you couldn't play *Naima*,[8]
so flat[9] we ached
for song you'd concealed
with your own blood,
your diseased liver[1] gave   50
out its purity,
the inflated heart
pumps out, the tenor kiss,
tenor love:
a love supreme, a love supreme—   55
a love supreme, a love supreme—

1970

---

5. Play with inspiration (jazz idiom), with overtone of drug use (heroin is "cooked" to prepare it for injection).
6. In musical terms, to play with technical precision; also, free of drug addiction.
7. Soulful, gritty.

8. Another of Coltrane's compositions (Naima was his first wife's name), first recorded in 1959 on the album *Giant Steps*.
9. Pun on "flat" meaning both depressed and below the "proper" pitch in music, played or sung.
1. Coltrane died of liver cancer at the age of 40.

Trays[1]: A Portfolio

1

At the tray
she looks in the heart
of these negatives,[2]
her borning-room[3]
fireplace oven full of pitch,[4]   5
roasting the brick sidings,
her heart warmed
from the inside cradle
in a windowless bath.

2

Two African veils   10
on two sons
clothed in their isolettes[5]
burn in a hospital.

3

From a pan of chemicals
the images turn from black   15
to white flames as we
agitate the quart
tank developer:[6]
black men,
two sons stoppered   20
from isolette
to incinerator,
a child walks
under her apron
as film develops   25
in her black and white eyes;
she stoops over the boys
on the primed cut smock,
born, inflated, enlarged.

4

We grade paper from one to six   30
as our number of children;
little contrast to extreme contrast,
two to four the perfect negative

---

1. In the photographic dark room, the square, low-rimmed pans containing various chemical "baths" in which the development process takes place.
2. Images that reverse in tone the original photographic scene, becoming the "masters" from which copies can be made.
3. In old New England houses, a room desig-nated as a family infirmary, used especially for child birthing and nursing.
4. Dark, sticky, resinous substance, residue of smoke from wood fires.
5. Incubators used for premature infants.
6. Pan containing chemical solution into which exposed film is immersed in the developing process.

in our perfect family
enlarged as a light bulb   35
with a shade; we fight
the dirt on the negatives,
touch up with spotting liquid[7]
absorbed by numbered paper:
contact: print:[8]   40
blacken our negatives with light.

5

Pumpkin, squash, green
peppers, onions, carrots
squat in cellar piles;
I hear the gargle   45
of hot-water pipes
gushing through copper;
the mice spin between walls
eating paper under my drain;
the water pump whirs   50
iron rust in each drain
from artesian fields[9] underground.
From the cellar door
near the boarded well
is a concord grape arbor;   55
I walk by evergreen seedlings,
verbernum[1] bush
looking for cranberries
to harvest as drops of blood
on a weed-eaten farm.   60
In a clot of pines
my sons roll in their bog
in a pool of grass,
each step trundled,[2]
each laugh bedded with blood.   65

1972

History as Apple Tree

Cocumscussoc[1] is my village,
the western arm of Narragansett

---

7. Used to "touch up" or hide flaws in the photographic print.
8. A "contact print" is made by exposing photographic paper while it is held tightly against the
negative.
9. Areas in which water flows to the surface
naturally.
1. Species of shrub, notable for clusters of fragrant white flowers (more often spelled
"viburnum").

2. Moved as if on wheels; revolving.
1. Variously translated as "marshy meadows"
and "where there are sharpening stones," Con-
cumscussoc is the Narragansett tribe's name for
the part of their ancestral homeland in what is
now North Kingston, Rhode Island, a locale
that became the site of 17th-century European
trading posts and an 18th-century slaveholding
plantation.

Bay; Canonicus[2] chief sachem;
black men escape into his tribe.

How does patent not breed heresy?   5
Williams came to my chief
for his tract of land,
hunted by mad Puritans,
founded Providence Plantation;[3]
Seekonk[4] where he lost   10
first harvest, building, plant,
then the bay from these natives:
he set up trade.
With Winthrop[5] he bought
an island, *Prudence*;   15
two others, *Hope* and *Patience*[6]
he named, though small.
His trading post at the cove;
Smith's[7] at another close by.
We walk the Pequot[8] trail   20
as artery or spring.

Wampanoags, Cowesets,
Nipmucks, Niantics[9]
came by canoe for the games;
matted bats, a goal line,   25
a deerskin filled with moss:
lacrosse.[1] They danced;
we are told they gambled their souls.

In your apple orchard
legend conjures Williams' name;   30
he was an apple tree.[2]
Buried on his own lot
off Benefit Street
a giant apple tree grew;
two hundred years later,   35
when the grave was opened,
dust and root grew
in his human skeleton:
bones became apple tree.

2. Native American chief, or sachem, who ruled the Narragansett when the Pilgrims landed in New England. In 1636 he granted Rhode Island to Roger Williams (1603–1684), Anglo-American theologian, proponent of the separation of church and state, advocate for fair dealings with Native Americans, and founder of the city of Providence, Rhode Island.
3. Rhode Island was fully named "The Colony of Rhode Island and Providence Plantations" until the American Revolution.
4. Williams's first settlement—on the east bank of the Seekonk River—was abandoned soon after it was founded because it was officially within the borders of Plymouth Colony.
5. John Winthrop (1587/8–1649), governor of Massachusetts Bay Colony when Williams came to the colonies from England.
6. Islands purchased by Williams in 1637 that became part of the town of Portsmouth in 1664. Prudence: island whose Native American name was Chibacuwese, purchased by Williams in 1637.
7. Richard Smith (1596–1666), the first European settler in the Narragansett country.
8. Stretch of land named for the Pequot people, a Native American tribe that occupied much of what is now Connecticut in the 17th century.
9. Native American tribes that lived in what is now Rhode Island and Massachusetts.
1. Native American game consisting of up to 1,000 men on a field that stretched between 500 yards and several miles, played to settle tribal disputes, to toughen young men for combat, and to express spiritual devotion to "the Creator."
2. In 1860 Zachariah Allen sought to locate Williams's remains at the site of his burial; he found instead an apple tree root, which is now housed at the Rhode Island Historical Society in Providence.

As black man I steal away   40
in the night to the apple tree,
place my arm in the rich grave,
black sachem on a family plot,
take up a chunk of apple root,
let it become my skeleton,   45
become my own myth:
my arm the historical branch,
my name the bruised fruit,
black human photograph: apple tree.

1972

Psychophotos of Hampton[1]

... in all fairness to Washington we must recall that Armstrong,
in effect, gave Washington his career.
—Robert B. Stepto[2]

Dining at 8 and 6:30
with a lunchpail for noon,
I type out the echoes of artist
in the high studio of the tower,[3]
blackened in the image of Etienne,[4]   5
his cannibal ancestry sharpened
by the sloped Adirondacks[5] toward Montreal
where French/Indian alliances of beaver pelts[6]
end in burrows of buffalo on open plains,
another mountain range to cross, the salt lick   10
of lake claiming runaway bigamists,
and the great Sioux herds on the run to Cody,[7]
named for the diseased man who died in Denver,[8]
his widow offered forty grand to be buried near his name.

---

1. Hampton Normal and Agricultural Institute—now known as Hampton University—was founded in Hampton, Virginia, on the grounds of a former plantation in 1868 with support of former officers and soldiers in the Union Army as an industrial school for newly freed but still impoverished African Americans. In 1877, the principal, Samuel Chapman Armstrong, extended the program to incorporate Native Americans in the pedagogic "civilizing process." One of Armstrong's earliest students was Booker T. Washington (1856–1915), African American author, political advisor, and educator, who adopted features of Hampton's curriculum as the first leader of Alabama's Tuskegee Institute, a position he attained largely due to Armstrong's recommendation.
2. Professor of English and African American Studies at Yale University (b. 1945); Stepto's most extensive account of the Washington-Armstrong relationship is found in his 1979 book *From Behind the Veil: A Study of Afro-American Literature*.
3. The tower studio in the 19th-century mansion of the Yaddo estate in Saratoga Springs, New York, which was developed into an artist's colony by Spencer Trask (1844–1909) and his wife, Katrina (1853–1922) in 1881.

4. A figure described in Katrina Trask's posthumously printed *The Story of Yaddo* (1923): "He had been brought from Africa by a missionary who intended to train him for missionary service.... One night after midnight, I opened my door ... there, just outside the threshold, lay Etienne. He was the blackest black man that could be imagined ... the son of a cannibal, a carving knife in his hand, at my door! He learned very fast and had the most amazing opinions about life. Candour compels me to confess that, after having sharpened his wits at our American institutions, his missionary zeal failed to develop, and he went back to Africa as—a trader!"
5. Mountain range in the northeastern region of New York, where part of the French and Indian War (1754–63) occurred.
6. Common currency among French settlers and Native American tribes.
7. Cody, Wyoming, planned and developed by Colonel William Frederick ("Buffalo Bill") Cody (1846–1917), American soldier, bison hunter, and showman. Cody had a number of skirmishes with people of the Great Sioux Nation, a confederation of Native American tribes.
8. Cody is buried on Lookout Mountain, 20 miles west of Denver.

On a ride down 9W to Esopus, New York,   15
where Wiltwyck boys from five boroughs
came to the Roosevelt mansion-estate,[9] the volunteers
driving buses with Menonnite alms,[1] to home visits
of abandoned projects,[2] each welfare roll breaking
in fired windows, I take the granite sites   20
of General Armstrong into view, his great twin
burial rocks, Vermont granite, Sandwich lava[3]
entrancing the mausoleum of the great divide
of history, of railroad lands, of the *Dakotah*,[4]
Sandwich missions, the uplift of schoolmarms   25
tuning the pens of the Freedmen's Bureau[5] toward
the thin line of traintrack near Emancipation Tree.[6]

At $68/head,[7] the great Dakotah nation went to college,
from Black Hills to mosquitoed swamp near Fort Monroe,[8]
where the fevered zeal of the government   30
reimbursed each Indian with black suit,
haircut, and a class photograph:

I walk out over swampgrounds, campsites,
drumbeats of the great cemetery
surrounded by sane spirits of the great mansion   35
at Arlington where Robert E. Lee's[9] doorstep
sprouted with Union graves terraced from his veranda:

For Daniel Fire-Cloud, Sioux, South Dakotah
died September 3 1886, 14 years
Armstrong Firecloud, Sioux, born Hampton   40
died August 6 1886 infant
Virginia Medicine-Bull, Sioux, South Dakotah
died January 30 1886
Simon Mazakutte, Sioux, South Dakotah
died March 26 1884, 18 years   45
Benjamin Bear-Bird, Sioux, South Dakotah

9. The Wiltwyck School for Boys, in Esopus, New York, along route 9W on the opposite side of the Hudson River from the Roosevelt family mansion, opened in 1936 as a reform school for African American juvenile delinquents.
1. Charity from the Mennonites, a Christian Anabaptist denomination influenced by the teachings of Menno Simons (1496–1561), which emphasize nonviolence and pacifism.
2. Public housing units.
3. Armstrong, having declared his wish "to be buried in the school graveyard, among the students," was laid under a marker shaped at its head from a large fragment of volcanic rock brought from the Sandwich Islands (present-day Hawaii, site of his upbringing as a missionary's son) and at its feet by a quartz boulder hewn from the Berkshire Hills (the southern continuation of Vermont's Green Mountains).
4. The Sioux are divided three ways according to geography and dialect; in addition to the Nakota and Lakota, the Dakota include the easternmost group, situated near the confluence of the Mississippi and Missouri Rivers.
5. Popular name for the U.S. Bureau of Refugees, Freedmen, and Abandoned Lands, estab-lished after the Civil War by Congress to provide practical aid to four million newly emancipated African Americans. Armstrong was given his commission to found Hampton by the Bureau.
6. Located near the library on Hampton's campus, at which in 1863 the Emancipation Proclamation was read to people in Hampton for the first time.
7. Harper glosses this passage in another context: "*Psychophotos of Hampton* refers to a historical photobook about the early Hampton Institute. Depicted in this book are Plains Indians who perished of 'swamp fever' while wards of the Bureau of Indian Affairs at $68 a head, which was part of the national policy of the period."
8. Military installation in Hampton. Black Hills: small, isolated mountain range extending from South Dakota to Wyoming.
9. Arlington House, overlooking the Potomac River and Washington, D.C., once home to Confederate general Robert E. Lee (1807–1870), grounds of which were selected as the site of Arlington National Cemetery, in part to prevent Lee from returning to his home.

died August 4 1885, aged 2 years
Edith Yellow-Hair, Sioux, South Dakotah
died November 26 1885, aged 8 years
Emma Whips, Sioux, South Dakotah   50
died March 25 1885
Lora Bowed-Head Snow, Sioux, South Dakotah
died March 20 1885, aged 22 years
Mary Pretty-Hair, Sioux, South Dakotah
died January 6 1885, aged 14 years   55
Eva Good-Road, Sioux, South Dakotah
died January 4 1884, aged 17 years
Belany Sayon-Sululand, South Africa
died December 10 1884, aged 22 years
Edward Buck, Sioux, South Dakotah   60
died May 30 1884, aged 17 years
Croaking Wing, Mandan, North Dakotah
died April 21 1884, aged 17 years
Francesca Rios, Papago, Arizona
died August 21 1883, aged 15 years   65
Henry Kendall Acolehut, Yuma, Arizona
died August 13 1883, aged 22 years
Tasute White Back, Gros Ventre, North Dakotah
died January 24 1882, aged 15 years.[1]
I leave out fully anglicized names,[2]   70
some duplications among the Sioux (meaning dog)
for fear of repeat of the Dakotah.
Buried in graveyards of the great founding
academies, their souls finally saved
from highlands where they were born.   75
The great Lincoln train[3]
winds into great centennial avenues
where each kneeled slave has the great veil
lifted from his eyes,[4] his enlightened
face literate from heart to mind,   80
penciled in nightmare,
where the rainbow mansion,
tiered rose garden, Bearground Swamp[5]
vessels the dark interior
of this book I write of the Shadow,   85
Unjungian[6] and unsurveyed,

1. Inventory of figures buried in the Hampton University Cemetery.
2. I.e., changed from original Native American names as part of the "civilizing process."
3. I.e., the funeral train of President Abraham Lincoln (1809–1865), which traced a 1,650-mile route from Washington, D.C., to his longtime home in Springfield, Illinois.
4. Reference to the Booker T. Washington National Monument at Tuskegee University, a statue by American sculptor Charles Keck (1875–1951), dedicated in 1922, depicting Washington lifting "the veil of ignorance from his people," symbolized by a terrified crouching slave.
5. Bear Swamp, southeast of Yaddo's rose garden, was the location of the homestead of European settler Jacobus Barhyte (1762–1841), which was later owned by his former slaves Thomas and Nancy Campbell. "Rainbow mansion": Yaddo's main house is graced with a large Tiffany-designed stained-glass window.
6. Carl Gustav Jung (1875–1961), Swiss psychiatrist and founder of analytic psychology, referred to the unconscious as "the shadow" or "shadow aspect" of personality that was both "a reservoir of human darkness" and the "seat of creativity." "Yaddo" was itself a baby pronunciation by the Trasks' young children (all four of whom died in childhood) of "The Shadows," an inn that once stood where the Trask estate was erected, a site where American poet Edgar Allan Poe (1809–1849) wrote "The Raven," which ends with the lines: "And the lamplight o'er him streaming throws his shadow on the floor; / And my soul from out that shadow that lies floating on the floor / Shall be lifted—nevermore!"

in the cleaning of your first bedroom,[7]
over and over the coaldust you brought
under fingernails[8]
as you scratched toward the caning   90
which would take your exhibition,
your address of the great ship,
its crew calling for water,
clear-watered-buckets-scooping-downward
in five equally broken fingers.[9]   95

Separate as the limed hand
the five great Indian nations[1]
disappear along the trail
of tears, the common man of Andrew
Jackson[2] looking moonstruck in black regiments   100
for the Seminoles of Florida,
each Catholic outpost
St. Paul's reservation of Little Crow[3]
waiting for rations,
the St. Louis Fair   105
where Geronimo breathed the gas[4]
from the Ford caught in the mud
gatewayed in his western eyes,
to New Orleans, where the musicians
stomp all night to Buster's[5] for breakfast,   110
the buildings boarded up with slave anklets,
the militia protecting the war ships
of Toussaint[6] in Napoleon's gift to Jefferson.

7. Reference to Washington's account in his autobiography, *Up from Slavery* (1901), of his job while a student at Hampton of cleaning student rooms before the start of term; his diligent janitorial skills are presented as having gained him admission to the school.
8. Reference to an earlier job of Washington's, work in a coal mine, about which he wrote "it was very hard to get one's skin clean after the day's work was over"; it was while working in the mine that Washington overheard talk about "a great school for coloured people somewhere in Virginia."
9. These lines refer to a famous parable from Washington's "Atlanta Exposition Address" (1905), which concludes: "To those of my race who depend upon bettering their condition in a foreign land, or who understand the importance of cultivating friendly relations with the Southern white man who is their next-door neighbor, I would say: 'Cast down your bucket where you are'—cast down in making friends, in every manly way, of the people of all races by whom we are surrounded."
1. The Cherokee, Chickasaw, Choctaw, Creek, and Seminole—sometimes called by Anglo-European settlers the Five Civilized Tribes—who were uprooted from their homes east of the Mississippi River and forcibly moved to what was then called Indian Territory in what is now the eastern portion of Oklahoma. The most infamous of these removals was the Trail of Tears of 1838, in which President Martin Van Buren (1782–1862) enforced the highly contentious Treaty of New Echota (1835) with the Cherokee Nation, resulting in the deaths of 4,000 Cherokees.
2. Seventh president of the United States from 1829 to 1837 (1767–1845), a leading advocate of "Indian Removal."
3. Also known as Taoyateduta (1810?–1863), chief of the Mdewakanton Sioux tribe, who led the Sioux Uprising of 1862 when the U.S. government threatened forced removal of his people from east of the Minnesota River to the Dakotas.
4. The aged Geronimo (1829–1909), a prominent Native American leader of the Chiracahua Apache, signed autographs for ten cents each at the 1904 St. Louis World's Fair, officially known as the Louisiana Purchase Exposition, which commemorated the 1803 purchase of territory from the French government of Napoleon Bonaparte (1769–1821) by the government of President Thomas Jefferson (1743–1826), more than doubling the country's size.
5. New Orleans soul food restaurant. "Stomp": compete in jazz instrumental performance.
6. François-Dominique Toussaint L'Ouverture (1743–1803), leader of the Haitian Revolution against France (1791–1804) after having served under Napoleon; in 1801, Jefferson supported France in its plan to attack Toussaint and his ex-slave compatriots.

Your simplest image was the crab-barrel,[7]
each black hand pulling the escaping soul   115
back into the pit where the turpentine
gangs sang,[8] cutting their way through each
wilderness, each Indian amulet dropping
in cross-fires of settlers,
your great dining hall opening: 120
"I was born a slave,"[9]
countered by Aristotle's
"some men are natural born slaves,"[1]
in the boards of Wall Street,
where Melville[2] wrote the dark glimmerings   125
scrimshaw[3] tales, attached by the whale,
his bludgeoned knife raised in combat,
his sweat in the oiled battle with self,
where the nation stormed in fish beds
as laughing men and women dove   130
in triangular trade winds.[4]

The last view is the best,
from the terrace overhang,
with a toothbrush,
seeing rock gardens and roses   135
pool in cascading fountains:
the Renaissance built on slave trading,
Etienne proud of his lineage,
Booker T's bookings humbling his beginnings,[5]
the abstract masks giving off power,   140
its conjured being dynamized in my skin,
reminiscing at the founder's table
where the talk was of politics,
rhetoric, and the literature of the great
rainbowed swamp from the vision of the black tower.   145

                                                            1977

---

7. Washington was known to employ so-called crab stories in his speeches, as recounted in 1923 by black nationalist activist Marcus Garvey (1887–1940): "Most of the trouble I have had in advancing the cause of the race has come from negroes. Booker Washington aptly described the race in one of his lectures by stating that we were like crabs in a barrel, that none would allow the other to climb over, but on any such attempt all would continue to pull back into the barrel the one crab that would make the effort to climb out."
8. In Florida's turpentine camps, where black prisoners were often forced to work, songs were sung to the rhythms of their hard labor.
9. Opening words of *Up from Slavery*.
1. Cited from *Politics* (Book I, section II) by Greek philosopher Aristotle (384–322 B.C.E.).
2. American novelist and poet Herman Melville

(1819–1891), in whose *Moby-Dick: Or, The Whale* (1851) the narrator, Ishmael, declares in the opening chapter: "Who ain't a slave? Tell me that."
3. Scrollwork, engravings, and carvings done by whalers using the bones and teeth of marine mammals.
4. Reference to the Atlantic "triangle" trade, in which slaves, manufactured goods, and cash crops were exchanged among African, European, and New World states and companies.
5. Directly after telling the story of Etienne at Yaddo, Katrina Trask writes: "But I must return to the dinner-table where Booker Washington waits. . . . He had conquered: and yet the simplicity with which he spoke of his life, his frank assertion—'I was born a slave,' his absolute freedom from all pride in his accomplishment, his freedom from all bitterness . . . thrilled me."

TONI CADE BAMBARA
1939–1995

Toni Cade Bambara was an activist writer who championed African American communal traditions, especially the spoken language and storytelling patterns of black folk that she first encountered from "the speakers on Speaker's Corner in Harlem." Active in the Black Arts movement during the 1960s, she edited the anthology *The Black Woman* (1970), one of the pivotal texts in African American feminist writing. Her other anthology, *Tales and Stories for Black Folks* (1971), which she called "a part of our Great Kitchen Tradition," is directly addressed to African American youth. Celebrated as one of the finest African American short story writers, Bambara published two collections, *Gorilla, My Love* (1972) and *The Sea Birds Are Still Alive* (1977), as well as a futuristic revolutionary novel, *The Salt Eaters* (1980). Her second novel, *These Bones Are Not My Child* (written in 1987 and published posthumously in 2000), confronts with searing and imaginative power the Atlanta child murders of the 1970s.

Born Miltona Mirkin Cade in New York City on March 25, 1939, she and her brother were raised by their mother, Helen Brent Henderson Cade. Bambara's mother refused to distinguish "between how a girl should think and behave and how a boy should think and behave," expecting her children to cultivate their own judgment. She was also adamant that black history be taught accurately in any school her children attended. Bambara paid tribute to her mother's nurturance of her own imaginative development in the dedication to *The Salt Eaters*: "Mama, Helen Brent Henderson Cade Brehon, who in 1948, having come upon me day-dreaming in the middle of the kitchen floor, mopped around me." Bambara further honored her matrilineal tradition by adding Bambara to her name after she discovered that her grandmother had adopted it as part of her surname.

After graduating in 1959 from a joint undergraduate program in theater arts and English at Queens College, Bambara did graduate work in African fiction at the City College of New York, returning there to teach from 1965 to 1969. In the 1960s, while working as a social worker and as a recreational and occupational therapist, she began to publish short fiction in journals such as *Vendome, Massachusetts Review, The Liberator, Prairie Schooner,* and *Redbook.*

But it was not until 1970, after participating in some early women's consciousness groups and editing *The Black Woman*—one of the first major anthologies to feature the work of Nikki Giovanni, Audre Lorde, Alice Walker, Paule Marshall, and others—that Bambara began to take her literary talents seriously. In 1971 Bambara edited a second anthology, *Tales and Stories for Black Folks*, which combined work by established black writers such as Langston Hughes, Alice Walker, and Ernest Gaines with stories by several of her freshmen composition students at Livingston College. This collection contains some much-loved black fairy tales, such as Bambara's "Three Little Panthers," which demonstrates the richness of black English and the revolutionary values of the black folk tradition.

Also included in this anthology is Bambara's short story "Raymond's Run," which features a feisty black adolescent girl, as do many of the short stories included in her first collection, the highly acclaimed *Gorilla, My Love*. Written in rhythmic urban black English, these stories challenged the role of female victim in which much of early 1970s feminist literature indulged. *Gorilla, My Love* also announced Bambara's most persistent stylistic characteristic—the use of jazz improvisation as the basis of her storytelling. Bambara's second collection, *The Sea Birds Are Still*

Alive, which avoids the safety of conventional linear plots, shares with her first a focus on the sensibilities of black neighborhoods in big cities.

Bambara's use of jazz improvisation becomes still more complex in her first novel, *The Salt Eaters*, a multilayered narrative that explores the high emotional costs of sustained political struggle in the African American community and the extra psychological toll such activism takes on black women. In the novel, a community organizer named Velma Henry attempts suicide after years of battling to save a community center facing chronic funding problems and feuding among the constituencies it serves. Bambara's narrative plunges the reader into the community's attempts to heal Velma, from the chants of the female elders to "traditional folk remedies" and "modern medical techniques." The novel has been much admired by other African American writers, such as Toni Morrison, who oversaw its publication while working as an editor at Random House, and John Wideman, who compared the narrator's weaving of conversations, thoughts, and dreams to "concentric circles and the concepts of sacred space and sacred time of traditional African religion."

Bambara, like other artists of her generation, felt that a global political activism was an essential component of her contribution to the literary world. She traveled to Cuba in 1973 for the meeting of the Federation of Cuban Women and to Vietnam in 1975 to meet with the Women's Union. While living in the South in the late 1970s, she helped found the Southern Collective of African American Writers. She also wrote the introduction to the groundbreaking anthology about women of color titled *This Bridge Called My Back* (1981), edited by the Chicana writers and theorists Gloria Anzaldua and Cherrie Moraga. In addition, Bambara contributed to *Love Struggle and Change: Stories by Women* (1988), the West Coast anthology of work by Latinas, African Americans, and lesbian women.

In the 1980s and early 1990s, Bambara focused on film and video projects. Several of her short stories ("Gorilla, My Love," "Medley," "Witchbird," "The Johnson Girls," and "The Long Night") have been adapted to film. She helped create *The Bombing of Osage Avenue* (1986), a video about the attack on MOVE, the alternative black group bombed by the Philadelphia police in 1985. Bambara was also one of four writers who scripted Louis Messiah's monumental film biography of W. E. B. Du Bois.

In a 1982 interview, Bambara described her work as suffused with two defining characteristics: "the tremendous capacity for laughter, but also a tremendous capacity for rage." Until her death, Bambara honed those contradictory impulses in working to better her neighbors in Philadelphia, where she was intensely involved in community activism. She was thus an exemplary cultural worker of the Black Arts era, seeking to fuse ideas, words, and actions into a visionary vehicle for critical engagement and social transformation.

Gorilla, My Love

That was the year Hunca Bubba changed his name. Not a change up, but a change back, since Jefferson Winston Vale was the name in the first place. Which was news to me cause he'd been my Hunca Bubba my whole lifetime, since I couldn't manage Uncle to save my life. So far as I was concerned it was a change completely to somethin soundin very geographical weatherlike to me, like somethin you'd find in a almanac. Or somethin you'd run across when you sittin in the navigator seat with a wet thumb on the map crinkly in your lap, watchin the roads and signs so when Granddaddy Vale say "Which way, Scout," you got sense enough to say take the next exit or take a left or whatever it is. Not that Scout's my name. Just the name Granddaddy call whoever sittin in the navigator seat. Which is usually me cause I don't feature sittin in the back with the pecans. Now, you figure pecans all right to be sittin with. If you thinks so, that's your business. But they dusty sometime and make you cough. And they got a way of slidin around and dippin down sudden, like maybe a rat in the buckets. So if you scary like me, you sleep with the lights on and blame it on Baby Jason and, so as not to waste good electric, you study the maps. And that's how come I'm in the navigator seat most times and get to be called Scout.

So Hunca Bubba in the back with the pecans and Baby Jason, and he in love. And we got to hear all this stuff about this woman he in love with and all. Which really ain't enough to keep the mind alive, though Baby Jason got no better sense than to give his undivided attention and keep grabbin at the photograph which is just a picture of some skinny woman in a countrified dress with her hand shot up to her face like she shame fore cameras. But there's a movie house in the background which I ax about. Cause I am a movie freak from way back, even though it do get me in trouble sometime.

Like when me and Big Brood and Baby Jason was on our own last Easter and couldn't go to the Dorset cause we'd seen all the Three Stooges they was. And the RKO Hamilton[1] was closed readying up for the Easter Pageant that night. And the West End, the Regun and the Sunset[2] was too far, less we had grownups with us which we didn't. So we walk up Amsterdam Avenue to the Washington and *Gorilla, My Love* playin, they say, which suit me just fine, though the "my love" part kinda drag Big Brood some. As for Baby Jason, shoot, like Granddaddy say, he'd follow me into the fiery furnace if I say come on. So we go in and get three bags of Havmore potato chips which not only are the best potato chips but the best bags for blowin up and bustin real loud so the matron come trottin down the aisle with her chunky self, flashin that flashlight dead in your eye so you can give her some lip, and if she answer back and you already finish seein the show anyway, why then you just turn the place out. Which I love to do, no lie. With Baby Jason kickin at the seat in front, egging me on, and Big Brood mumblin bout what fiercesome things we goin do. Which means me. Like when the big boys come up on us talkin bout Lemme a nickel. It's me that hide the money. Or when the bad boys in the park take Big Brood's Spaudeen[3] way from him. It's me that jump on they back and fight awhile. And it's me that turns out the show if the matron get too salty.[4]

So the movie come on and right away it's this churchy music and clearly not about no gorilla. Bout Jesus. And I am ready to kill, not cause I got anything gainst Jesus. Just that when you fixed to watch a gorilla picture you don't wanna get messed around with Sunday School stuff. So I am mad. Besides, we see this raggedy old brown film *King of Kings*[5] every year and enough's enough. Grownups figure they can treat you just anyhow. Which burns me up. There I am, my feet up and my Havmore potato chips really salty and crispy and two jawbreakers in my lap and the money safe in my

1. RKO Hamilton and Dorset: old theaters in the Hamilton Heights section of New York City, a mostly African American neighborhood at the time of the story.
2. Old theaters in West Harlem, to the south of Hamilton Heights.
3. Spaulding Hi-Bounce ball, a pink rubber ball used in street games like handball and stickball.

4. In 1940s New York, children generally were not allowed to attend movies without a female supervisor, or matron, to control their behavior. "Salty": hostile.
5. 1927 silent movie epic about the life of Christ, directed by Cecil B. DeMille (1881–1959). "Raggedy": shabby, and "brown" because of its sepia-toned sequences.

shoe from the big boys, and here comes this Jesus stuff. So we all go wild. Yellin, booin, stompin and carryin on. Really to wake the man in the booth up there who musta went to sleep and put on the wrong reels. But no, cause he holler down to shut up and then he turn the sound up so we really gotta holler like crazy to even hear ourselves good. And the matron ropes off the children section and flashes her light all over the place and we yell some more and some kids slip under the rope and run up and down the aisle just to show it take more than some dusty ole velvet rope to tie us down. And I'm flingin the kid in front of me's popcorn. And Baby Jason kickin seats. And it's really somethin. Then here come the big and bad matron, the one they let out in case of emergency. And she totin that flashlight like she gonna use it on somebody. This here the colored matron Brandy and her friends call Thunderbuns. She do not play. She do not smile. So we shut up and watch the simple ass picture.

Which is not so simple as it is stupid. Cause I realize that just about anybody in my family is better than this god they always talkin about. My daddy wouldn't stand for nobody treatin any of us that way. My mama specially. And I can just see it now, Big Brood up there on the cross talkin bout Forgive them Daddy cause they don't know what they doin. And my Mama say Get on down from there you big fool, whatcha think this is, playtime? And my Daddy yellin to Granddaddy to get him a ladder cause Big Brood actin the fool, his mother side of the family showin up. And my mama and her sister Daisy jumpin on them Romans beatin them with they pocketbooks. And Hunca Bubba tellin them folks on they knees they better get out the way and go get some help or they goin to get trampled on. And Granddaddy Vale sayin Leave the boy alone, if that's what he wants to do with his life we ain't got nothin to say about it. Then Aunt Daisy givin him a taste of that pocketbook, fussin bout what a damn fool old man Granddaddy is. Then everybody jumpin in his chest like the time Uncle Clayton went in the army and come back with only one leg and Granddaddy say somethin stupid about that's life. And by this time Big Brood off the cross and in the park playin handball or skully[6] or somethin. And the family in the kitchen throwin dishes at each other, screamin bout if you hadn't done this I wouldn't had to do that. And me in the parlor trying to do my arithmetic yellin Shut it off.

Which is what I was yellin all by myself which make me a sittin target for Thunderbuns. But when I yell We want our money back, that gets everybody in chorus. And the movie windin up with this heavenly cloud music and the smart-ass up there in his hole in the wall turns up the sound again to drown us out. Then there comes Bugs Bunny which we already seen so we know we been had. No gorilla my nuthin. And Big Brood say Awwww sheeet, we goin to see the manager and get our money back. And I know from this we business. So I brush the potato chips out of my hair which is where Baby Jason like to put em, and I march myself up the aisle to deal with the manager who is a crook in the first place for lyin out there sayin *Gorilla, My Love* playin. And I never did like the man cause he oily and pasty at the same time like the bad guy in the serial, the one that got a hideout behind a push-button bookcase and play "Moonlight Sonata" with

---

6. Street game played with a ball on pavement with a chalked "board."

gloves on.[7] I knock on the door and I am furious. And I am alone, too. Cause Big Brood suddenly got to go so bad even though my mama told us bout goin in them nasty bathrooms. And I hear him sigh like he disgusted when he get to the door and see only a little kid there. And now I'm really furious cause I get so tired grownups messin over kids just cause they little and can't take em to court. What is it, he say to me like I lost my mittens or wet on myself or am somebody's retarded child. When in reality I am the smartest kid P.S. 186 ever had in its whole lifetime and you can ax anybody. Even them teachers that don't like me cause I won't sing them Southern songs or back off when they tell me my questions are out of order. And cause my Mama come up there in a minute when them teachers start playin the dozens[8] behind colored folks. She stalk in with her hat pulled down bad and that Persian lamb coat draped back over one hip on account of she got her fist planted there so she can talk that talk which gets us all hypnotized, and teacher be comin undone cause she know this could be her job and her behind cause Mama got pull with the Board and bad by her own self anyhow.

So I kick the door open wider and just walk right by him and sit down and tell the man about himself and that I want my money back and that goes for Baby Jason and Big Brood too. And he still trying to shuffle me out the door even though I'm sittin which shows him for the fool he is. Just like them teachers do fore they realize Mama like a stone on that spot and ain't backin up. So he ain't gettin up off the money. So I was forced to leave, takin the matches from under his ashtray, and set a fire under the candy stand, which closed the raggedy ole Washington down for a week. My Daddy had the suspect it was me cause Big Brood got a big mouth. But I explained right quick what the whole thing was about and I figured it was even-steven. Cause if you say Gorilla, My Love, you suppose to mean it. Just like when you say you goin to give me a party on my birthday, you gotta mean it. And if you say me and Baby Jason can go South pecan haulin with Granddaddy Vale, you better not be comin up with no stuff about the weather look uncertain or did you mop the bathroom or any other trickified business. I mean even gangsters in the movies say My word is my bond. So don't nobody get away with nothin far as I'm concerned. So Daddy put his belt back on. Cause that's the way I was raised. Like my Mama say in one of them situations when I won't back down, Okay Badbird, you right. Your point is well-taken. Not that Badbird my name, just what she say when she tired arguin and know I'm right. And Aunt Jo, who is the hardest head in the family and worse even than Aunt Daisy, she say, You absolutely right Miss Muffin, which also ain't my real name but the name she gave me one time when I got some medicine shot in my behind and wouldn't get up off her pillows for nothin. And even Granddaddy Vale—who got no memory to speak of, so sometime you can just plain lie to him, if you want to be like that—he say, Well if that's what I said, then that's it. But this name business was different they said. It wasn't like Hunca Bubba had gone back on his word or anything. Just that he was thinkin bout gettin married and was usin his real name now. Which ain't the way I saw it at all.

7. Reference to the 1945 film serial *Federal Operator 99*, in which George J. Lewis (1903–1995) played a sophisticated villain who plots crimes while playing the "Moonlight Sonata" by German composer Ludwig van Beethoven (1770–1827).

8. Verbal contest of ritual insult played in African American communities.

So there I am in the navigator seat. And I turn to him and just plain ole ax him. I mean I come right on out with it. No sense goin all around that barn the old folks talk about. And like my mama say, Hazel—which is my real name and what she remembers to call me when she bein serious— when you got somethin on your mind, speak up and let the chips fall where they may. And if anybody don't like it, tell em to come see your mama. And Daddy look up from the paper and say, You hear your mama good, Hazel. And tell em to come see me first. Like that. That's how I was raised.

So I turn clear round in the navigator seat and say, "Look here, Hunca Bubba or Jefferson Windsong Vale or whatever your name is, you gonna marry this girl?"

"Sure am," he say, all grins.

And I say, "Member that time you was baby-sittin me when we lived at four-o-nine and there was this big snow and Mama and Daddy got held up in the country so you had to stay for two days?"

And he say, "Sure do."

"Well. You remember how you told me I was the cutest thing that ever walked the earth?"

"Oh, you were real cute when you were little," he say, which is suppose to be funny. I am not laughin.

"Well. You remember what you said?"

And Grandaddy Vale squintin over the wheel and axin Which way, Scout. But Scout is busy and don't care if we all get lost for days.

"Watcha mean, Peaches?"

"My name is Hazel. And what I mean is you said you were going to marry *me* when I grew up. You were going to wait. That's what I mean, my dear Uncle Jefferson." And he don't say nuthin. Just look at me real strange like he never saw me before in life. Like he lost in some weird town in the middle of night and lookin for directions and there's no one to ask. Like it was me that messed up the maps and turned the road posts round. "Well, you said it, didn't you?" And Baby Jason lookin back and forth like we playin ping-pong. Only I ain't playin. I'm hurtin and I can hear that I am screamin. And Grandaddy Vale mumblin how we never gonna get to where we goin if I don't turn around and take my navigator job serious.

"Well, for cryin out loud, Hazel, you just a little girl. And I was just teasin."

"'And I was just teasin,'" I say back just how he said it so he can hear what a terrible thing it is. Then I don't say nuthin. And he don't say nuthin. And Baby Jason don't say nuthin nohow. Then Granddaddy Vale speak up. "Look here, Precious, it was Hunca Bubba what told you them things. This here, Jefferson Winston Vale." And Hunca Bubba say, "That's right. That was somebody else. I'm a new somebody."

"You a lyin dawg," I say, when I meant to say treacherous dog, but just couldn't get hold of the word. It slipped away from me. And I'm crying and crumplin down in the seat and just don't care. And Granddaddy say to hush and steps on the gas. And I'm losin my bearins and don't even know where to look on the map cause I can't see for cryin. And Baby Jason cryin too. Cause he is my blood brother and understands that we must stick together or be forever lost, what with grownups playin change-up and turnin you round every which way so bad. And don't even say they sorry.

1972

From The Salt Eaters

"Are you sure, sweetheart, that you want to be well?"

Velma Henry turned stiffly on the stool, the gown ties tight across her back, the knots hard. So taut for so long, she could not swivel. Neck, back, hip joints dry, stiff. Face frozen. She could not glower, suck her teeth, roll her eyes, do any of the Velma-things by way of answering Minnie Ransom, who sat before her humming lazily up and down the scales, making a big to-do of draping her silky shawl, handling it as though it were a cape she'd swirl any minute over Velma's head in a wipe-out veronica,[1] or as though it were a bath towel she was drying her back with in the privacy of her bathroom.

Minnie Ransom herself, the fabled healer of the district, her bright-red flouncy dress drawn in at the waist with two different strips of kenti cloth,[2] up to her elbows in a minor fortune of gold, brass and silver bangles, the silken fringe of the shawl shimmying at her armpits. Her head, wrapped in some juicy hot-pink gelee,[3] was tucked way back into her neck, eyes peering down her nose at Velma as though old-timey spectacles perched there were slipping down.

Velma blinked. Was ole Minnie trying to hypnotize her, mesmerize her? Minnie Ransom, the legendary spinster of Claybourne, Georgia, spinning out a song, drawing *her* of all people up. Velma the swift; Velma the elusive; Velma who had never mastered the kicks, punches and defense blocks, but who had down cold the art of being not there when the blow came. Velma caught, caught up, in the weave of the song Minnie was humming, of the shawl, of the threads, of the silvery tendrils that extended from the healer's neck and hands and disappeared into the sheen of the sunlight. The glistening bangles, the metallic threads, the dancing fringe, the humming like bees. And was the ole swamphag[4] actually sitting there dressed for days, legs crossed, one foot swinging gently against the table where she'd stacked the tapes and records? Sitting there flashing her bridgework and asking some stupid damn question like that, blind to Velma's exasperation, her pain, her humiliation?

Velma could see herself: hair matted and dusty, bandages unraveled and curled at the foot of the stool like a sleeping snake, the hospital gown huge in front, but tied up too tight in back, the breeze from the window billowing out the rough white muslin and widening the opening in the back. She could not focus enough to remember whether she had panties on or not. And Minnie Ransom perched on her stool actually waiting on an answer, drawling out her hummingsong, unconcerned that any minute she might strike the very note that could shatter Velma's bones.

"I like to caution folks, that's all," said Minnie, interrupting her own humming to sigh and say it, the song somehow buzzing right on. "No sense us wasting each other's time, sweetheart." The song running its own course up under the words, up under Velma's hospital gown, notes pressing against

---

1. In bullfighting, a *pase* or cape movement in which the cape is swung slowly away from the charging bull while the matador keeps his feet stationary.
2. Colorfully patterned woven fabric from Ghana and the Ivory Coast whose colors are associated with ritualistic meanings in Ashanti and Akan culture (called also *kente*).
3. Woman's headwrap (in Yoruba called *gele*).
4. Old and unattractive woman thought to have magical or manipulative powers.

her skin and Velma steeling herself against intrusion. "A lot of weight when you're well. Now, you just hold that thought."

Velma didn't know how she was to do that. She could barely manage to hold on to herself, hold on to the stingy stool, be there all of a piece and resist the buzzing bee tune coming at her. Now her whole purpose was surface, to go smooth, be sealed and inviolate.

She tried to withdraw as she'd been doing for weeks and weeks. Withdraw the self to a safe place where husband, lover, teacher, workers, no one could follow, probe. Withdraw her self and prop up a borderguard to negotiate with would-be intruders. She'd been a borderguard all her childhood, so she knew something about it. She was the one sent to the front door to stand off the landlord, the insurance man, the green-grocer, the fishpeddler, to insure Mama Mae one more bit of peace. And at her godmother's, it was Smitty who sent her to the front door to misdirect the posse. No, no one of that name lived here. No, this was not where the note from the principal should be delivered.

*   *   *

She is in the park around the bonfire singing. Minnie is there, M'Dear, Doc Serge and some older man she doesn't know by name, the face faintly familiar, but the green uniform throwing her off. And Obie is there, Mama Mae, Palma and Lil James called Jabari now and Marcus and. And someone or something hovering near daring her to look, to recognize. Not an old friend but someone she hasn't met but ought to know but dare not look at. A taboo glance, formidable, ancient, locking her jaws, her thighs, keeping her head down. Medusa, Lot's Wife, Eurydice, Noah,[5] she will not look. She keeps her eyes on her feet, swollen from stomping. They are all stomping, agitating the ground, agitating an idea, calling up something or someone, and the idea clusters in the image centers and settles there. She will not look at that either. It is taking all of her to concentrate on not looking.

She would not have cut Medusa's head off, she is thinking, watching the mud come up worms between her toes. She would simply have told the sister to go and comb her hair. Or gotten a stick to drive the serpents out. Serpents or snakes? She draws a line in the dirt with her big toe.

Different remedies for snakebite and the bite of the serpent, she'd been hearing for a lifetime. Daddy Dolphy had told her too in the woods that time. M'Dear had dropped her basket and slit his shirt with her shears before Velma knew what had happened. Had pushed him on the ground and taken his knife from him and slit open his shoulder before Velma could cry out. "Quick, salt." And she'd managed to find it in the gathering basket and knew somehow it was salt and not some other odd thing to be bringing

---

5. The hero of the biblical Flood story. In Genesis 9.22, Noah's son, Ham, happens upon his father asleep and naked. Instead of covering him, Ham informs his two brothers, Shem and Japheth, of what he has seen. The brothers walk backward into their father's tent, so their faces are turned away from his nakedness, and they cover him. When Noah awakens, he knows what Ham has done and puts a curse on him: "And he said, Cursed be Canaan; a servant of servants shall he be unto his brethren" (Genesis 9.25). In Greek mythology, Medusa is a Gorgon whose snake-haired head had the power of turning into stone all who looked upon it. In Genesis 19.26, Lot and his family are led by two angels out of the doomed city of Sodom and warned not to look back. Lot's wife rebels and looks back, and she is immediately transformed into a pillar of salt. In Greek mythology, Eurydice is the wife of Orpheus. Although she is killed by a snakebite, Hades, king of the underworld, agrees to return Eurydice to the world of the living, on one condition—that once the reunited couple leaves the land of death, they do not look back. As they climb up to the land of the living, Orpheus, upon seeing the sun again, turns back either in fear of losing Eurydice or to share his delight with her. In that moment, she disappears forever.

along to the woods. Daddy Dolphy had gulped some, held some in his mouth and was ripping off his sleeve when M'Dear snatched a fistful of leaves from a bush and packed a salt poultice into the wound and tied up his shoulder tightly with the sleeve tourniquet. "Helps neutralize the venom," M'Dear explained, her voice calm, as if certain the twisting of the sleeve would do the rest. "To neutralize the serpent's another matter," Daddy Dolphy had winked, taking deep breaths.

She thought she knew that. At some point in her life she was sure Douglass, Tubman, the slave narratives, the songs, the fables, Delaney, Ida Wells, Blyden, DuBois, Garvey, the singers, her parents, Malcolm, Coltrane,[6] the poets, her comrades, her godmother, her neighbors, had taught her that. Thought she knew how to build immunity to the sting of the serpent that turned would-be cells, could-be cadres into cargo cults.[7] Thought she knew how to build resistance, make the journey to the center of the circle, stay poised and centered in the work and not fly off, stay centered in the best of her people's traditions and not be available to madness, not become intoxicated by the heady brew of degrees and career and congratulations for nothing done, not become anesthetized by dazzling performances with somebody else's aesthetic, not go under. Thought the workers of the sixties had pulled the Family safely out of range of the serpent's fangs so the workers of the seventies could drain the poisons, repair damaged tissues, retrain the heartworks, realign the spine. Thought the vaccine offered by all the theorists and activists and clear thinkers and doers of the warrior clan would take. But amnesia had set in anyhow. Heart / brain / gut muscles atrophied anyhow. Time was running out anyhow. And the folks didn't even have a party, a consistent domestic and foreign policy much less a way to govern. Something crucial had been missing from the political / economic / social / cultural / aesthetic / military / psychosocial / psychosexual mix. And what could it be? And what should she do? She'd been asking it aloud one morning combing her hair, and the answer had almost come tumbling out of the mirror naked and tatooed with serrated teeth and hair alive, birds and insects peeping out at her from the mud-heavy hanks of the ancient mothers' hair. And she had fled feverish and agitated from the room, flopped languid and dissolved at Jamahl's, lest she be caught up and entrapped in glass, fled lest she be ensorceled,[8] fled finally into a sharp and piercing world, fled into the carbon cave.

---

6. John Coltrane (1926–1967), African American jazz saxophonist, bandleader, and composer who exerted an enormous influence on the jazz of the 1960s and 1970s, and became the most imitated of modern jazz musicians. Frederick Douglass (1817–1895), a runaway slave who became one of the foremost abolitionists and civil rights leaders in the United States during the 19th century. Harriet Tubman (1820?–1913), a runaway slave who became a leading abolitionist during the Civil War. She led many other African Americans to freedom in the North through the establishment of a secret network of safe houses known as the Underground Railroad. Martin Delaney (1812–1885), a freeborn African American from Virginia who is most typically portrayed as "The Malcolm X of the 19th century"; he was a recognized geographer, anthropologist, author, and lecturer, as well as the first black field-grade officer in the U.S. Army. Ida B. Wells (1862–1931), African American journalist and activist who led an anti-lynching crusade in the 1890s. Edward Wilmot Blyden (1832–1912), African American intellectual and activist whose lectures and sermons across the country emphasized Africanist ideas and black nationalist sentiments. W. E. B. Du Bois (1868–1963), African American editor, author, historian, sociologist, and leader of the civil rights movement in the United States. He helped found the NAACP. Marcus Garvey (1887–1940), fervent black nationalist leader who inspired among black people throughout the world a sense of pride in their African heritage. Malcolm X (1925–1965), militant African American leader who articulated concepts of race pride and black nationalism in the early 1960s.
7. Religious practices in which traditional, preindustrial societies, having come into contact with "advanced" cultures (often through colonialist occupation), seek to obtain material objects through magic.
8. Bewitched.

And now, standing there barefoot on the ground in the park, she still could not face up, would not lift her head to look at anything but her own swollen feet. She might steal a glance sideways at the woman next to her and study the elegant shoes, the red and gold and white sequined ruffles at the hem of the extravagant gown, the hands clasped with three wedding bands shining on the ring finger—before she wrenched her eyes back to the safety of her swollen feet. There might be an answer. But she would not look up from her feet.

1980

CAROLYN M. RODGERS
1940–2010

Bridge, conversion, transformation, breaking through, "gettin ovah": these are the touchstone terms through which Carolyn Rodgers conducted her struggle to burst through alienation and oppression and forge connections between self and other, present and past, oracular militancy and nurturing spirituality. For Rodgers, responding to a question posed by Mari Evans, literature "functions as a type of catharsis or amen arena," a site of firm pronouncement and shared purification. From her appropriations of the "masculinist" discourse of the Black Arts movement to her turn toward Christianity, Rodgers embraced a complex rhythm of demystification and reconstruction, seeking affirmative "love and joy" where injustice and pain once ruled. Whether embodied in the figure of her mother, music, or the "purity of mystical light" that she openly sought in her later years, Rodgers imagined her voice as a performative realization of an intricate selfhood: "I see myself as becoming. I am a has-been, would perhaps, going to be. Underneath, I'm a dot. With no i's."

Born on December 14, 1940, in Chicago to Clarence and Bazella Colding Rodgers, Carolyn Rodgers was raised in an environment where the arts (music especially) were seen as fundamental. Educated in the Chicago public school system, Rodgers played the guitar and developed an ambivalent relationship to both her parents, resenting her father's wishing that he had three sons and one daughter, instead of one son and three daughters, and becoming increasingly disillusioned with her mother's Christianity and seeming McCarthyism. In 1960 Rodgers enrolled at the University of Illinois at Chicago and there began writing "quasi seriously"; she was "frustrated along with the rest of [her] peers, and it seemed to be a natural, enjoyable, effective outlet." The following year, Rodgers transferred to Chicago's Roosevelt University. She earned a B.A. in 1965 and eventually earned an M.A. in English from the University of Chicago. After graduating, Rodgers went into one of the few fields of employment available to well-educated black women in the early 1960s: social work. She worked at the YMCA from 1963 to 1966, and became engaged with Chicago's antipoverty program from 1965 to 1968.

While continuing in social work, Rodgers also began to attend the Organization of Black African Culture (OBAC) Writers Workshops and the Gwendolyn Brooks Writers Workshop meetings, where she encountered poets like Don L. Lee (Haki Madhubuti), Johari Amini, Sterling Plumpp, Hoyt Fuller, and Gwendolyn Brooks herself. After a few years of refining her idiosyncratic vision of Black

Arts poetry, Rodgers co-founded Third World Press with Madhubuti and Amini, the press which published Rodgers's first three books of poetry. During this period of poetic growth Rodgers also took a number of academic positions, which began a lifelong love of teaching while working as a book reviewer and columnist and contributing essays and poetry to numerous journals, most notably *Black World*.

Rodgers's first three volumes of poetry, *Paper Soul* (1968), *Songs of a Blackbird* (1969), and *2 Love Raps* (1969), bear the mark of her commitment to the Black Arts movement and the politics of communal black struggle ("I will write about Black people repossessing this earth, a-men"). These volumes won Rodgers much acclaim, including the first Conrad Kent Rivers Memorial Fund Award, the Poet Laureate Award of the Society of Midland Authors, and a National Endowment for the Arts award. Hoyt Fuller, in his introduction to *Paper Soul*, sensed the combination of change, metaphor, and connectivity that would define Rodgers throughout her career: Rodgers's "perspective, both sharp and sweeping," he wrote, "encompasses the broad regions of what is and also the clear image of what might be. . . ." In both practice and theory, these first three volumes from Third World Press embody Rodgers's most militant embrace of the Black Arts movement; they were released along with her incisive neo-Marxist critiques of the "decadence" of so-called bourgeois art, her revaluations of the politics of form and language ("The [English] words are a *form* of the oppressor"), and her reconsiderations of poetic imitation as both self-empowering and self-disabling ("Like, most Black children can outdo James Brown in their imitations of him / The college student who left home talking mush mouth / African tonal, and returns talking 'better english,' becomes the tool of the system through the sounds he makes which are of an alien oppressive culture").

Yet what Fuller dubbed Rodgers's particular blend of rootedness in the materiality of the present and her clear but contingent image of transformation through reimagined loss did not always win her praise from fellow black artists. Madhubuti himself questioned Rodgers's ostensible mixing of Standard English and black idiomatic constructions. And many, Madhubuti included, were critical of what was referred to as the "excessive" obscenity of Rodgers's verse, though there were shrewder critics, like Stephen Henderson, who sensed "a kind of verbalized social dissonance" in her sometimes insistently obscene performances. Rodgers's response to such characterizations was two-fold, at once pugnacious and subversive: "The Last M.F." promises to cease using obscenity in an excess of compliance that is as bitingly ironic as it is traumatizing of expression. Even in such early poems, within the sacramental violence of revolutionary vision there exist tensions of a voice searching for its proper form. In *Songs of a Blackbird*, Rodgers is already attempting to work through and utilize what she calls, in the poem "Breakthrough," "tangled feelings" that frustrate and generate new experiments in poetic structure, style, and statement.

Soon after, in the early 1970s, Rodgers left the Third World Press for a more mainstream publisher and broke publicly with OBAC. By the time Rodgers put together her volume of new and selected poems in *how i got ovah* (1975), she had departed from her earlier skepticism towards her mother's Christianity and "crossed over," on the "sturdy Black bridge" of her mother's example, converting to Christianity and experiencing a "spiritual transformation" of self in "a root revival of love." In the author's note, Rodgers announces that she has altered or eliminated certain words (i.e., obscenities) in order to make her poetry more accessible to as many people as possible. The poetry that follows this volume in the 1970s and 1980s proclaims that it has gotten "through my mean period," and Rodgers became more concerned with issues of faith and femininity than with the vision of radical revolution that, spiced with vernacular wit and verbal ingenuity, make her among the most nuanced of the Black Arts poets.

Yet Rodgers's own view of her poetic development as a circular return within a process of perpetual transformation is confirmed by poems like "U Name This One" and "I Have Been Hungry," lyrical performances that imagine revolutionary change while still enacting the particularity of a woman's position within that change. "U Name This One" invokes revolution as radical alteration that offers the potential to negate rather than continuously repeat violence. Living itself is equated with "guerilla warfare," whether it is figured as the elegiac performance of blues musicians of a lost "state of peace," in the twice-weekly blood baptisms that take place on the streets of Chicago, or in the tragic death of poor Judy, who was kicked out of school for being pregnant and then died when trying to abort the pregnancy in order to regain her former place in the community. "I Have Been Hungry" asserts difference and desire as constitutive of a woman who seeks liberation for *both* self and community, and cannot take comfort in tales of individual liberation that end in alienation ("deep into / the wonderment of loneliness") rather than communal restitution. Demystification of a redemption in the present for past misdeeds—"nightmares and knowledge," the "tears" that cannot be erased—is juxtaposed with a potential future envisaged as something that "even i can not know," as an event towards which "*i*" must struggle and yearn within the multiplicity of identities proposed by the "craving[s]" of "love." Such poems bear the lasting features of Rodgers's distinct contribution to the Black Arts period as a voice at once humble and defiant, realistic and visionary.

For Sistuhs Wearin' Straight Hair

me?
i never could keep my edges and kitchen[1]
straight
even after
supercool / straighterPerm had burned   5
whiteness onto my scalp[2]
my edges and kitchen didn't
ever get the message that they
was not supposed to go back home.
oh yeah. edges and kitchens   10
will tell that they know where
they nat'chal home is at!

                                                            1969

The Last M.F.

they say,
that i should not use the word
muthafucka anymo
in my poetry or in any speech i give.
they say,   5
that i must and can only say it to myself
as the new Black Womanhood suggests
a softer self
a more reserved speaking self. they say,

---

1. Small hairs at the nape of the neck (black vernacular); edges: very small hairs at a woman's hairline.

2. Reference to the process of straightening curled hair through chemical applications.

that respect is hard won by a woman 10
who throws a word like muthafucka around
and so they say because we love you
throw that word away, Black Woman . . .
i say,
   that i only call muthafuckas, muthafuckas 15
so no one should be insulted. only
pigs and hunks[1] and negroes who try to divide and
destroy our moves toward liberation.
i say,
that i am soft, and you can subpoena my man, put him 20
on trial, and he will testify that i am
soft in the right places at the right times
and often we are so reserved, i have nothing to say
but they say that this new day
creates a new dawn woman, 25
one who will listen to Black Men
and so i say
this is the last poem i will write calling
all manner of wites, card-carrying muthafuckas
and all manner of Blacks (negroes too) sweet 30
muthafuckas, crazy muthafuckas, lowdown muthafuckas
cool muthafuckas, mad and revolutionary muthafuckas.
But anyhow you all know just like i do (whether i say
it or not), there's plenty of MEAN[2] muthafuckas out
here trying to do the struggle in and we all know 35
that none of us can relax until the last m.f.'s
been done in.

             1969

Poem for Some Black Women

i am lonely.
all the people i know
i know too well

there was comfort in that
at first but now 5
we know each others miseries
  too well.
we are
 lonely women, who spend time waiting for
  occasional flings 10

we live with fear,
we are lonely.
we are talented, dedicated, well read
  BLACK, COMMITTED,

we are lonely. 15

1. Hunkies, or honkies: whites (pejorative slang); "pigs": police officers. 2. Tough (black vernacular).

we understand the world problems
Black women's problems with Black men
          but all
we really understand is
          lonely.   20

when we laugh,
we are so happy to laugh
we cry when we laugh
    we are lonely.
we are busy people   25
always doing things
fearing getting trapped in rooms
loud with empty . . .
              yet
knowing the music of silence/hating it/hoarding it   30
loving it/treasuring it,
    it often birthing our creativity
          we   are   lonely

being soft and being hard
supporting our selves, earning our own bread   35
soft/hard/hard/soft/
knowing that need must not show
                        will frighten away
knowing that we must
walk back-wards nonchalantly on our tip-toesssss   40
    into
happiness,
    if only for stingy moments

we know too much
we learn to understand everything,   45
to make too much sense out
of the world,
of pain
      of lonely . . .

we buy clothes, we take trips,   50
we wish, we pray, we meditate, we curse, we crave, we coo, we caw,

          we need ourselves sick, we need, we need
we lonely we grow tired of tears we grow tired of fear
we grow tired but must al-ways be soft and not too serious . . .
          not too smart not too bitchy not too sapphire   55
       not too dumb not too not too not too
a little less a little more
                    add here detract there
                              .lonely.

                                                                  1971

U Name This One

let uh revolution come. uh
state of peace is not known to me
anyway
since i grew uhround in chi town[1]
where   5
howlin wolf howled in the tavern on 47th st.[2]
and muddy waters[3] made us cry the salty nigger blues,
    where pee wee cut lonnell fuh messin wid
    his sistuh and blood baptized the street
    at least twice ev'ry week and judy got   10
    kicked outa grammar school fuh bein pregnant
    and died tryin to ungrow the seed[4]
    we was all up in there and
        just living was guerilla warfare, yeah.

let uh revolution come.   15
couldn't be no action like what
i dun already seen.

                                  1975

I Have Been Hungry

Preface: This poem was written because I was asked to contribute to an anthology of black and white women, and the title of the anthology was *I Had Been Hungry All My Years.*[1]

1

and you white girl
shall i call you sister now?
can we share any secrets of sameness,
any singularity of goals. . . .
you, white girl with the head that   5
perpetually tosses over-rated curls
while i religiously toss my over-rated behind
you white girl
i am yet suspicious of/
for deep inside of me   10
there is the still belief that
i am
a road

1. Chicago.
2. Gerri's Palm Tavern, a magnet for African American blues and jazz musicians in the 1950s. Howlin Wolf: African American blues guitarist and singer (born Chester Arthur Burnett, 1910–1976); a statue of him was placed in a Chicago park afer his death.
3. Chicago blues guitarist and singer (born McKinley Morganfield, 1915–1983).
4. I.e., attempting to induce an abortion.
1. I.e., *I Had Been Hungry All the Years: An Anthology of Women's Poetry*, edited by Glenna Luschei and Del Marie Rogers (1975); the anthology's title refers to the poem "I Had Been Hungry, All the Years" by American poet Emily Dickinson (1830–1886).

you would travel
to my man.

15

2

and how could you, any of you
think that a few loud words and years
could erase the tears
blot out the nightmares and knowledge,
smother the breeded mistrust
and how could any of you think that i
after being empty for so long
could fill up on fancy fierce platitudes. . . .

20

some new/old knowledge has risen in me like yeast
but still old doubts deflate

25

am i—really—so beautiful
as i sweat and am black and oh so
greasy in the noonday sun

the most beauty that i am i am inside
and so few deign to touch
i am a forest of expectation.
the beauty that i will be is yet
to be defined

30

what i can be even i can not know.

3

and what does a woman want?[2]
what does any woman want
but a soft man to hold her hard
a sensitive man to help her fight off
the insensitive pangs of living.
and what is living to a woman
without the weight of some man
pulling her down/puffing her out

35

40

do not tell me
liberated tales of woman/woeman
who seek only to satisfy them selves
with them selves, all, by them selves
i will not believe you
i will call you a dry canyon
them, a wilderness
of wearying and failures

45

50

2. The founder of psychoanalysis, Austrian neurologist and psychologist Sigmund Freud (1856–1939), remarked to French author and psychoanalyst Marie Bonaparte (1882–1962), "The great question that has never been answered, and which I have not yet been able to answer, despite my thirty years of research into the feminine soul, is 'What does a woman want?'"

a fearing of hungerings from
and deep into
the wonderment of loneliness
and what makes any woman so.

4

as for me—   55
i am simple
a simple foolish woman.[3]
all that i have ever wanted
i have not had
and much of what i have had   60
i have not wanted.

   my father never wanted three girls
and only one son, one sun. . . .
God, how he wished his seeds
had transformed themselves into   65
three boys and only one girl—
for heaven's sake, only one good for nothing
wanting needing love and approval seeking bleeding
girl.
and so, i have spent my days   70
so many of my days seeking the approval
which was never there
craving the love
i never got
and what am i now,   75
no longer a simple girl
bringing lemonade and cookies
begging favor

   and what am i now
no longer a world-torn woman   80
showering my "luck" in a
cold bottle of cold duck[4]

and—who—am i now
but a
saved   85
sighing
singular thing. a woman. . . .
ah, here i am[5]
and
here have i been   90
i say,
i

---

3. Cf. Proverbs 9.13: "A foolish woman is clamorous: she is simple, and knoweth nothing."
4. Inexpensive sparkling wine made in the United States. (Cf. the end of Dickinson's opening stanza: "I, trembling, drew the table near / And touched the curious wine.")
5. Cf. 1 Samuel 3.4: "That the Lord called Samuel: and he answered, Here am I."

have been hungry,
ravenously hungry,
all   95
my
years

1975

HAKI R. MADHUBUTI
b. 1942

Poet, essayist, publisher, and educator, Haki Madhubuti (born Don Luther Lee) is one of the most widely read and anthologized writers of the Black Arts movement. A vociferous proponent of "black aesthetic" expression untainted by mainstream conventions and values, Madhubuti perhaps more than any Black Arts era artist fused theoretical ideas with literary and social practice. Rejecting aesthetic activity as an end in itself, Madhubuti argues instead that art serves the ends of the community from which the artist arises. In his own work and life, Madhubuti answered this demand by taking direct responsibility for the production and circulation of his own writing and that of many fellow black artists, giving substance to his claim that "black poetry comes out of a love of one's self, what is at bottom a love of one's people."

Born in Little Rock, Arkansas, in 1942, the son of James Lee and Maxine Graves Lee, Madhubuti moved at an early age to Detroit's "Black Bottom." With his father largely absent, Madhubuti's mother worked several jobs in order to sustain him and his sister in the barest of circumstances. Even amidst these dire conditions, Maxine Lee impressed upon her children the value of black culture and history. From his mother, Madhubuti gained vivid awareness of the intellectual and spiritual resources sustained by black people struggling for material survival. Her death from complications of alcoholism when Madhubuti was sixteen shattered his sense of wellbeing and transplanted him to Chicago, where he would ultimately become an iconic figure among the city's many black intellectuals and artists.

Madhubuti's journey to that position of cultural importance took him first through the Army and a series of clerical and retail jobs, which later fueled his early work's satirical anger at the commercial ambitions of middle-class America, white and black. And yet the discipline and financial training of that employment served him well, shaping the entrepreneurial genius that he displayed from his first efforts to establish his public reputation as a poet. Producing enough poems to fill a first volume, *Think Black* (1967), Madhubuti decided to avoid standard publishing outlets, printing his works on single sheets, binding them by hand, and selling them himself at barbershops, bus stops, and other gathering places in the African American community. "At first I didn't know *what* I was going to do with all these books." But his work sold briskly, not only convincing Madhubuti to make a lifetime of writing but affirming his vision of literary production as deriving from, addressing, and returning to the black community itself. His pronouncement that "black poets now are dedicated to building their own medium of communication" was one that he was proving could be literally enacted.

Madhubuti followed *Think Black* with two books of verse, *Black Pride* (1968) and *Don't Cry, Scream* (1969), which together established the hallmarks of a poetic style that reflected the central tenets of his evolving black aesthetic. Drawing his vocabulary and rhythms from the edgy, muscular timbres of the urban street, Madhubuti's verse constructs a performative syntax that treats the page as a platform for direct messages of pain, outrage, and hope. Madhubuti's sometimes rollickingly simple lines encourage the listener's pleasurable engagement with sound and wit, while his caustic denunciations of what he called the "con game of white society" invited his audience to face decisions about cultural and political allegiance. In an essay entitled "Black Poetics/ for the many to come," Madhubuti explains the reciprocity of poet and community that animates this didactic aim of artistic production: "There is *no* neutral blackart. Blackpoetry is and will continue to be an important factor in culture building."

Madhubuti thus sees the black poet as primarily a cultural preservationist and prophet, capable of restoring fundamental values and on that foundation erecting a new black nation. "Black poets are culture stabilizers: bring back old values, and introduce new ones. Black poetry will give the people a future." That simultaneously educative and visionary function required the African American poet in Madhubuti's view to make the poetry itself a material manifestation of the very community it would restore and renew. His pioneering role as a publisher of contemporary black literature is thus integral to his aesthetic and social ideals. In 1967, working out of a basement with fellow Chicago poets Carolyn Rodgers and Johari Amini, Madhubuti founded Third World Press, which quickly emerged as a leading vehicle of Black Arts movement writing, publishing such luminaries of the era as Gwendolyn Brooks (an early sponsor of Madhubuti's own poetic development), Amiri Baraka, and Sonia Sanchez. That same year, Madhubuti joined Rodgers, Sanchez, and other black artists in the formation of the Organization of Black American Culture (OBAC), which soon spurred an explosion in collective communal artistic production, including the first great "wall of respect" depicting great figures of African American culture and history in murals painted on the crumbling buildings of Chicago's Southside ghetto. Two years later, Madhubuti aimed more directly to affect the education of the black community by co-founding the Institute of Positive Education, which offers an Afrocentric curriculum designed to combat "the contradictory and anti-black implications of the educational system." That system, Madhubuti declared, "is set up largely to preserve that which *is,* not that which necessarily needs to be created, i.e., black nationalism or black consciousness. Some of the answers will have to be a surprise, but at least we know a surprise is coming."

This sense of a world at the precipice of being born animated Madhubuti's writings of the 1970s, most evidently in *We Walk the Way of the New World* (1970), *Directionscore* (1971), and *Book of Life* (1973). These books chart Madhubuti's effort to lend new lyricism to his view of the African American writer as an embodiment of community fully committed to building a new black nation. "Culture is the sustaining force of any nation," he wrote during this period, reformulating the conjunction of art and social experience in terms that would gradually widen his interest from black American experience to a concern with the international community of peoples of color. This shift can be seen in the intricate threads of historical reference that suffuse "Killing Memory," which extends his early focus on violence in African American history to an exploration of global oppression in the post-colonial world. Aptly, Madhubuti's poetic line changes pace to survey widening swaths of historical experience, though the energy characteristic of his early verse remains in force.

Unsurprisingly, Madhubuti's writing has polarized critics from its earliest appearance. Defiant of aesthetic and social norms, his work has been accused of "roughness" and "propagandism" for its unapologetic mixing of popular idioms and grand themes. At the same time, the underlying craft of these transgressions has captured the imagination of generations of readers, particularly among the very people for whom his work is intended as healing encouragement and revolutionary guide. This volatile contrast of censure and acceptance has made Madhubuti one of the most visible and influential writers of Black Arts era.

Introduction [to *Think Black*]

I was born into slavery in Feb. of 1942. In the spring of that same year 110,000 persons of Japanese descent were placed in protective custody by the white people of the United States.[1] Two out of every three of these were American citizens by birth; the other third were aliens forbidden by law to be citizens. No charges had been filed against these people nor had any hearing been held. The removal of these people was on racial or ancestral grounds only. World War II, the war against racism; yet no Germans or other enemy aliens were placed in protective custody. There should have been Japanese writers directing their writings toward Japanese audiences.

Black. Poet. Black poet am I. This should leave little doubt in the minds of anyone as to which is first. Black art is created from black forces that live within the body. These forces can be lost at any time as in the case of Louis Lomax, Frank Yerby and Ralph Ellison.[2] Direct and meaningful contact with black people will act as energizers for the black forces. Black art will elevate and enlighten our people and lead them toward an awareness of self, i.e., their blackness. It will show them mirrors. Beautiful symbols. And will aid in the destruction of anything nasty and detrimental to our advancement as a people. Black art is a reciprocal art. The black writer learns from his people and because of his insight and "know how" he is able to give back his knowledge to the people in a manner in which they can identify, learn and gain some type of mental satisfaction, e.g., rage or happiness. We must destroy Faulkner, dick, jane, and other perpetuators of evil. It's time for Du Bois, Nat Turner and Kwame Nkrumah. As Frantz Fanon[3] points out: destroy the culture and you destroy people. This must not happen. Black artists are culture stabilizers; bringing back old values, and introducing new ones. Black art will talk to the people and with the will of the people stop the impending "protective custody."

1. Reference to the relocation and internment by the U.S. government of Japanese Americans living along the country's Pacific coast in the wake of the attack on Pearl Harbor on December 7, 1941.
2. Ralph Waldo Ellison (1914–1994), African American novelist, scholar, and cultural critic; Louis E. Lomax (1922–1970), African American author, the first black American television journalist; Frank G. Yerby (1916–1991), African American historical novelist.
3. Frantz Fanon (1925–1961), Martinique-born French-Algerian psychoanalyst, philosopher, and postcolonial theorist; Kwame Nkrumah (1909–1972), African independence leader, first prime minister of Ghana (1957–1960); Nat Turner (1800–1831), American slave leader of a slave revolt in Virginia who was convicted of "conspiring to rebel and make insurrection" and executed; W. E. B. Du Bois (1868–1963), African American author, philosopher, and civil rights activist; William Faulkner (1897–1962), American novelist; "dick, jane": characters in books used to teach children to read in the mid-20th century, written mostly in the 1930s by American authors William S. Gray (1885–1960) and Zerna Addis Sharp (1889–1981).

America calling.
negroes.
can you dance?
play foot / baseball?
nanny?
cook?
needed now. negroes
who can entertain
ONLY.
others not
wanted.
(& are considered extremely dangerous.)

1967

Two Poems

(from "Sketches from a Black-Nappy-Headed Poet")

last week
my mother died/
& the most often asked question
at the funeral;
was not of her death   5
or of her life before death
                              but

why was i present
with/out
a   10
tie on.

i ain't seen no poems stop a .38,[1]
i ain't seen no stanzas break a honkie's[2] head,
i ain't seen no metaphors stop a tank,
i ain't seen no words kill
& if the word was mightier than the sword   5
pushkin[3] wouldn't be fertilizing russian soil/
& until my similes can protect me from a night stick[4]
i guess i'll keep my razor
& buy me some more bullets.

1968

1. I.e., a .38 caliber handgun.
2. White person's (pejorative slang).
3. Russian poet Alexander Pushkin (1799–1835), whose great grandfather Abram Petro-

vitch Gannibal (1696–1781) was an African brought to Russia as a gift for the czar Peter the Great (1672–1725).
4. Police truncheon or club.

Gwendolyn Brooks[1]

she doesn't wear
costume jewelry
& she knew that walt disney[2]
was/is making a fortune off
false-eyelashes and that time magazine[3] is the   5
authority on the knee/grow.
her makeup is total-real.

a negro english instructor called her:
    "a fine negro poet."
a whi-te critic said: 10
    "she's a credit to the negro race."
somebody else called her:
    "a pure negro writer."
johnnie mae, who's a senior in high school said:
    "she & langston[4] are the only negro poets we've   15
    read in school and i understand her."
pee wee used to carry one of her poems around in his
    back pocket;
        the one about being cool.[5] that was befo pee wee
        was cooled by a cop's warning shot.   20

into the sixties
a word was born . . . . BLACK
& with black came poets
& from the poet's ball points came:
black doubleblack purpleblack blueblack beenblack was   25
black daybeforeyesterday blackerthan ultrablack super
black blackblack yellowblack niggerblack blackwhi-te-man
blackerthanyoueverbes ¼ black unblack coldblack clear
black my momma's blackerthanyourmomma pimpleblack fall
black so black we can't even see you black on black in   30
black by black technically black mantanblack[6] winter
black coolblack 360degreesblack coalblack midnight
black black when it's convenient rustyblack moonblack
black starblack summerblack electronblack spaceman
black shoeshineblack jimshoeblack underwearblack ugly   35
black auntjimammablack, uncleben'srice[7] black williebest[8]
black blackisbeautifulblack i justdiscoveredblack negro
black unsubstanceblack.

1. African American poet and novelist (1917–2000).
2. American animator, film producer, director, and entrepreneur (1901–1966).
3. American weekly news journal, founded in 1923.
4. Langston Hughes, African American poet, novelist, playwright, and columnist (1902–1967).
5. Reference to Brooks's poem "We Real Cool" (1959).
6. Cf. Mantan Moorland (1902–1973), African American actor known for his minstrel-like roles in films of the 1930s and 1940s.
7. Uncle Ben's, a brand of rice associated with the image of an elderly black man dressed as a servant; Aunt Jemima, a brand of pancake mix associated with the image of a black female character from the minstrel tradition.
8. Better known by his Hollywood name, "Sleep'n'eat," Best (1916–1962) was an African American character actor who adopted the conventions of the minstrel tradition.

and everywhere the
lady "negro poet" 40
appeared the poets were there.
they listened & questioned
& went home feeling uncomfortable/unsound & so-untogether
they read/re-read/wrote & re-wrote
& came back the next time to tell the 45
lady "negro poet"
how beautiful she was/is & how she had helped them
& she came back with:
how necessary they were and how they've helped her.
the poets walked & as space filled the vacuum between 50
them & the
lady "negro poet"
u could hear one of the blackpoets say:
"bro, they been callin that sister by the wrong name."

1969

Don't Cry, Scream

(for John Coltrane[1]/ from a black poet/ in a basement apt. crying
dry tears of "you ain't gone.")

into the sixties
a trane
came/ out of the
fifties with a
golden boxcar 5
riding the rails
of novation.[2]
blowing
a-melodics[3]
screeching, 10
screaming,
blasting—
driving some away,
(those paper readers[4] who thought
manhood was something innate) 15

bring others in,
(the few who didn't believe that the
world existed around established whi
teness & leonard bernstein[5])
music that ached. 20
murdered our minds (we reborn)
born into a neoteric[6] aberration.

1. Avant-garde jazz saxophonist, composer, and bandleader (1926–1967).
2. Innovation or revolution.
3. Coltrane experimented with traditional melodic structures and melodies, revising standard songs through innovative musical techniques.
4. In mid-20th-century jazz slang, a pejorative term for a musician who plays music as written, not with interpretive or improvisational feeling.
5. American conductor and composer (1918–1990).
6. Modern (often pejorative, as in "newfangled," but here appreciative).

& suddenly
you envy the
BLIND man—   25
you know that he will
hear what you'll never
see.
                    your music is like
                    my head—nappy black/   30
                    a good nasty feel with
                    tangled songs of:
                            we-eeeeeeeeeee   sing
                            WE-EEEeeeeeeeeee   loud &
                            WE-EEEEEEE EEEEEEEEEE high   35
                                                     with
                                                     feeling

a people playing
the sound of me when
i combed it. combed at   40
it.

i cried for billy holiday.[7]
the blues. we ain't blue
the blues exhibited illusions of manhood.
destroyed by you. Ascension[8] into: 45

            scream-eeeeeeeeeeeeee-ing   sing
            SCREAM-EEEeeeeeeeeeee-ing   loud &
            SCREAM-EEEEEEEEEEE EEE-ing   long with
                                             feeling

we ain't blue, we are black.   50
we ain't blue, we are black.
                (all the blues did was
                make me cry)
soultrane[9] gone on a trip
he left man images   55
he was a life-style of
man-makers & annihilator
of attache case carriers.

Trane done went.
(got his hat & left me one)   60

naw brother,
i didn't cry,
i just—
        Scream-eeeeeeeeeeeeee e-ed   sing loud
        SCREAM-EEEEEEEEEEE EEEEEEE-ED   & high with   65
        we-eeeeeeeeeee eeeeeeeeee ee   feeling

---

7. Billie Holiday, African American jazz singer (1915–1959).
8. Title of a 1966 Coltrane album, used for its evocations of astronomy (the rising of a star above the horizon) and theology (the bodily rising of a soul after the body's death).
9. Title of 1958 Coltrane album.

WE-EEEEEEeeeeeeee EEEEEEE   letting
WE-EEEEEEEEEEEEEEEEEEEEEEEE   yr/voice
WHERE YOU DONE GONE, BROTHER? break

it hurts, grown babies   70
dying. born. done caught me
a trane. steel wheels broken
by popsicle sticks. i went out
& tried to buy a nickle bag[1]
with my standard oil card.[2]   75

    (swung on a faggot who politely
    scratched his ass in my presence.
    he smiled broken teeth stained from
    his over-used tongue. fisted-face.
    teeth dropped in tune with ray   80
    charles singing "yesterday."[3])

blonds had more fun[4]—
with snagga-tooth niggers
who saved pennies & pop bottles for week-ends
to play negro & other filthy inventions.   85
be-bop-en[5] to james brown's
cold sweat[6]—these niggers didn't sweat,
they perspired. & the blond's dye came out,
i ran. she did too, with his pennies, pop bottles
& his mind. tune in next week same time same station   90
for anti-self in one lesson.
to the negro cow-sissies
who did tchaikovsky[7] &
the beatles[8] & live in
split-level homes & had   95
split-level minds & babies.
who committed the act of
love with their clothes on.
    (who hid in the bathroom to read
    jet mag.,[9] who didn't read the chicago   100
    defender[1] because of the misspelled
    words & had shelves of books by
    europeans on display. untouched. who
    hid their little richard[2] & lightnin'
    slim[3] records & asked: "John who?"   105

1. Small amount of marijuana.
2. Credit card issued by a 1960s oil conglomerate.
3. 1965 song written by English singer-songwriter Paul McCartney (b. 1942) that first appeared on the Beatles' 1965 album *Help!* Some music historians believe that McCartney subconsciously patterned "Yesterday" on the 1960 recording of "Georgia on My Mind" by African American singer-songwriter Ray Charles (1930–2004), who himself covered "Yesterday" in 1967.
4. Play on 1950s and 1960s ad slogan for Lady Clairol hair coloring product, "Is it true blondes have more fun?"
5. Getting high, intoxicated.
6. 1967 album recorded by African American singer-songwriter James Brown (1933–2006); its eponymous opening track is considered one of the first appearances of "funk" music, a blend of soul, jazz, and rhythm-and-blues styles.
7. Pyotr Ilyich Tchaikovsky (1840–1893), Russian symphonic composer.
8. English rock band, active 1960–69.
9. Weekly African American magazine founded in 1951 by John H. Johnson (1918–2005).
1. Historically black-owned newspaper founded in 1905 by Robert Sengstack Abbott (1870–1940).
2. Born Richard Wayne Penniman (b. 1932), African American rock 'n' roll pioneer known for his high-energy performances and flamboyant persona.
3. Born Otis V. Hicks (1913–1974), blues singer known for his grainy but expressive voice.

instant hate.)
they didn't know any better,
brother, they were too busy getting
into debt, expressing humanity &
taking off color. 110

SCREAMMMM/we-eeeee/screech/teee   improvise
aheeeeeeeee/screeeeeee/theeee/ee   with
ahHHHHHHHHH/WEEEEEEEE/scrEEEEEEE feeling
we-eeeeeWE-EEEEEEEEWE-EE- EEEEE
the ofays[4] heard you & 115
were wiped out. spaced.
one clown asked me during,
my favorite things,[5] if
you were practicing.
i fired on the muthafucka & said, 120
"i'm practicing."

naw brother,
i didn't cry.
i got high off my thoughts—
they kept coming back, 125
back to destroy me.

& that BLIND man
i don't envy him anymore
i can see his hear
& hear his heard through my pores. 130
i can see my me. it was truth you gave,
like a daily shit
it had to come.
    can you scream—brother? very
    can you scream—brother? soft 135

i hear you.
i hear you.

and the Gods will too.

1969

Move Un-noticed to Be Noticed:
A Nationhood Poem

move, into our own, not theirs
into our.
they own it (for the moment): the unclean world, the
        polluted space, the un-censor-

---

4. Whites (pejorative slang).
5. Title of 1961 Coltrane album, whose eponymous track was a remake of the tune from the
1959 musical *The Sound of Music* by Richard
Rodgers (1902–1979) and Oscar Hammerstein II
(1895–1960).

ed air, yr / foot steps as they   5
run wildly in the wrong
direction.

move, into our own, not theirs
into our.
move, you can't buy own.   10
own is like yr/hair (if u let it live); a natural extension of ownself.
own is yr/ reflection, yr/ total-being; the way u walk, talk,
            dress and relate to each other is *own*.

own is you,
cannot be bought or sold: can u buy yr/ writing hand   15
            yr/ dancing feet, yr/ speech,
            yr/ woman (if she's real),
            yr/ manhood?

own is ours.
all we have to do is   *take it*,   20
take it the way u take from one another,
    the way u take artur rubenstein over thelonious monk,[1]
    the way u take eugene genovese over lerone bennett,[2]
    the way u take robert bly over imamu baraka,[3]
    the way u take picasso over charles white,[4]   25
    the way u take marianne moore over gwendolyn brooks,[5]
    the way u take *inaction* over *action*.
move. move to act.   act.
act into thinking and think into action.
try to think. think.   try to think think think.   30
try to think. think (like i said, into yr/ own) think.
try to think. don't hurt yourself, i know it's new.
try to act,
act into thinking and think into action.
can u do it, hunh? i say hunh, can u stop moving like a drunk gorilla?   35
            ha ha   che che
            ha ha   che che
            ha ha   che che
            ha ha   che che
move   40
what is u anyhow: a professional car watcher, a billboard for
    nothingness, a sane madman, a reincarnated clark gable[6]?
either you is or you ain't![7]

the deadliving
are the worldmakers,   45
the image breakers,
the rule takers: blackman can you stop a hurricane?

1. Theolonious Monk (1917–1982), African American modernist and bebop jazz pianist and composer; Arthur Rubenstein (1887–1982), Polish American classical pianist and composer.
2. Lerone Bennett Jr. (b. 1928), African American historian of race; Eugene Genovese (1930–2012), American historian of slavery.
3. Imamu Amiri Baraka (1934–2014), African American poet, playwright, novelist, and Black Arts movement activist; Robert Bly (b. 1926), American poet and leader of the "mythopoetic men's movement."
4. Charles Wilbert White (1918–1979), African American painter and muralist; Pablo Picasso (1881–1973), Spanish painter, sculptor, printmaker, and ceramicist.
5. Gwendolyn Brooks (1917–2000), African American poet and novelist; Marianne Moore (1887–1972), American poet.
6. Clark Gable (1901–1960), American film actor.
7. Cf. the 1944 jazz song "Is You Is or Is You Ain't My Baby" by African American songwriter and bandleader Louis Jordan (1908–1975).

"I remember back in 1954 or '55, in Chicago, when we had
13 days without a murder, that was before them colored
people started calling themselves *black*." 50
move.
move,
move to be moved,
move into yr / ownself, Clean.
Clean, u is the first black hippy i've ever met. 55
why u bes dressen so funny, anyhow, hunh?
i mean, is that u Clean?
why u bes dressen like an airplane, can u fly,
i mean,
will yr/ blue jim-shoes fly u, 60
& what about yr/ tailor made bell bottoms, Clean?
can they lift u above madness,
turn u into the right direction,
& that red & pink scarf around yr / neck what's that for Clean,
hunh?   will it help u fly, yeah, swing, swing ing swing 65
            swinging high above telephone wires with dreams
            of this & that and illusions of trying to take bar-b-q
            ice cream away from lion minded[8] niggers who
            didn't even know that *polish* is more than a
            sausage. 70
"clean as a tack,
rusty as a nail,
haven't had a bath
sence columbus sail."

when u goin be something real, Clean? 75
like yr/ own, yeah, when u goin be yr/ ownself?

the deadliving
are the worldmakers,
the image breakers,
the rule takers: blackman can u stop a hurricane, mississippi[9] couldn't. 80
blackman if u can't stop what mississippi couldn't, *be it. be it.*
blackman be the wind, be the win, the win, the win, win win:

        wooooooooooowe boom boom   wooooooooooowe bah
        wooooooooooowe boom boom   wooooooooooowe bah
if u can't stop a hurricane, be one. 85
        wooooooooooowe boom boom   wooooooooooowe bah
        wooooooooooowe boom boom   wooooooooooowe bah
be the baddddest hurricane that ever came, a black hurricane.
        wooooooooooowe boom boom   wooooooooooowe bah
        wooooooooooowe boom boom   wooooooooooowe bah 90
the badddest black hurricane that ever came, a black
            hurricane named Beulah,
go head Beulah, do the hurricane.
        wooooooooooowe boom boom   wooooooooooowe bah
        wooooooooooowe boom boom   wooooooooooowe bah 95

8. Allusion to the African American folk trickster the Signifying Monkey, who, while swinging
from tree to tree, uses verbal dexterity to fool his
nemesis, the Lion.
9. Reference to the devastating hurricane of
1967 named Beulah.

move
move to be moved from the un-moveable,
into our own, yr/ self is own, yrself is own, own yourself.
go where you/ we go, hear the unheard and do,
do the undone, do it, do it, do it *now*, Clean   100
and tomorrow your sons will
be alive to praise
you.

                      1970

Killing Memory

For Nelson and Winnie Mandela[1]

the soul and fire of windsongs must not be neutral
cannot be void of birth and dying
wasted life
locked
in the path of vicious horrors   5
masquerading
as progress and spheres of influence

what of mothers
without milk of willing love,
of fathers   10
whose eyes and vision
have been separated from feelings of earth and growth,
of children
whose thoughts dwell
on rest and food and   15
human kindness?

Tomorrow's future rains in
atrocious mediocrity and suffering deaths.

in america's america the excitement is over
a rock singer's glove and burning hair[2]   20
as serious combat rages over
prayer in schools,
the best diet plan,
and women
learning how to lift weights   25
to the rhythms of
"what's love got to do with it?"[3]

1. Nelson Rolihlahla Mandela (1918–2013), South African anti-apartheid leader of the African National Congress (ANC), jailed for his activism from 1964 to 1990; he was the nation's first post-apartheid president, from 1994 to 1999. Winnie Madikizela-Mandela (b. 1936), Mandela's wife from 1957 to 1996 and political activist who headed the ANC Women's League.

2. Reference to African American pop singer Michael Jackson (1958–2009), known for wearing a single glove while performing onstage; Jackson's hair accidentally caught fire while filming a 1984 commercial for Pepsi.
3. Title of 1984 song by African American singer Tina Turner (born Anna Mae Bullock in 1939).

ask the children,
always the children caught in the
absent spaces of adult juvenility   30
all
brake dancing and singing to
"everything is everything"[4] while
noise occupies the mind as
garbage feeds the brain.   35

in el Salvador mothers search for their sons[5]
and teach their daughters the way of the knife.

in south afrika mothers bury hearts without bodies
while pursuing the secrets of forgotten foreparents.

in afghanistan mothers claim bones and teeth from   40
mass graves and curse the silent world.

in lebanon the sons and daughters receive horror hourly
sacrificing childhood for the promise of land.

in ethiopia mothers separate wheat from the desert's dust
while the bones of their children cut through dried skin.   45

tomorrow's future
may not belong to the people,
may not belong to dance or music
where
getting physical is not an exercise[6] but   50
simply translates into people working,
people fighting,
people enduring insults and smiles,
enduring crippling histories and black pocket politics
wrapped in diseased blankets[7]   55
bearing AIDS markings in white,
destined for victims that do not question
gifts from strangers
do not question
love of enemy.   60

who owns the earth?
most certainly not the people,
not the hands that work the waterways,
nor the backs bending in the sun,
or the boned fingers soldering transistors,   65
not the legs walking the massive fields,

---

4. 1970 album by African American singer
Diana Ross (b. 1944).
5. Reference to the Comité de Madres Monsignor Romero (Spanish for Committee of the
Mothers Monsignor Romero), or Comadres, an
organization of women whose children were forcibly "disappeared" by the El Salvadoran government during the Salvadoran Civil War (1979–92)
because their parents opposed the military regime

then in power.
6. Reference to 1981 pop hit "Let's Get Physical," by Australian pop singer Olivia Newton-
John (b. 1948).
7. Reference to British captain Simeon Ecuyer's
ruse against Native American tribes during the
Siege of Fort Pitt (1763) of giving tribal representatives a gift of smallpox-infected blankets.

or the knees glued to pews of storefront or granite churches
or the eyes blinded by computer terminals,
not the bloated bellies on toothpick legs
all victims of decisions   70
made at the washington monument and lenin's tomb[8]
by aged actors viewing
red dawn and the *return of rambo part IX.*[9]

tomorrow
may not belong to the   75
women and men laboring,
hustling,
determined to avoid contributing
to the wealth
of gravediggers from foreign soil   80
& soul.
determined to stop the erosion
of indigenous music
of building values
of traditions.   85

memory is only precious if
you have it.

memory is only functional
if it works for you.

people   90
of colors and voices
are locked in multi-basement state buildings
stealing memories
more efficient
than vultures tearing flesh   95
from
decaying bodies.

the order is that the people are to
believe and believe
questioning or contemplating   100
the direction of the weather is
unpatriotic.

it is not that we distrust poets and politicians.

we fear the disintegration of thought,
we fear the cheapening of language,   105
we fear the history of victims and the loss of vision,

8. Lenin's Mausoleum, also known as Lenin's Tomb, located in Moscow's Red Square, is the resting place of Russian revolutionary Vladimir Lenin (1870–1924); the Washington Monument is an obelisk on the National Mall in Washington, D.C., built to commemorate the first U.S. president, George Washington (1732–1799).
9. Refers to the *Rambo* action film series starring American actor and director Sylvester Stallone (b. 1946), which follows the violent adventures of a psychologically troubled veteran of the Vietnam War. *Red Dawn*: 1984 film directed by John Milius (b. 1944) about a fictional war between the United States and the Soviet Union.

we fear writers whose answer to
maggots drinking from the open
wounds of babies
is
to cry genocide while demanding   110
ten cents per word and
university chairs.
we fear politicians
that sell coffins at a discount   115
and consider ideas blasphemy
as young people world over bleed from the teeth while
aligning themselves with whoever
brings the food.
whoever brings love.   120

who speaks the language of
bright memory?

who speaks the language of
necessary memory?

the face of poetry must be fire erupting volcanoes,   125
hot silk forging new histories,
poetry delivering light greater than barricades of silence,
poetry dancing, preparing seers, warriors, healers
and parents beyond the age of babies,
poetry delivering melodies that cure dumbness & stupidity   130
yes, poets uttering to the intellect and spirit,
screaming to the genes and environments,
revitalizing the primacy of the word and world,
poets must speak the language of the rain,
   decipher the message of the sun,   135
   play the rhythms of the earth,
   demand the cleaning of the atmosphere,
   carry the will and way of the word,
   feel the heart and questions of the people
   and be conditioned and ready   140
   to move.

to come
at midnight or noon

to run
against the monied hurricane in this   145
the hour of forgotten selves.
forgiven promises
and
frightening whispers
of rulers in heat.   150

1987

DAVID HENDERSON
b. 1942

B orn and raised in Harlem, David Henderson has enjoyed a varied career as teacher, educational experimentalist, cultural administrator, and music critic. In the early 1960s Henderson studied writing and religion at a number of New York City institutions, including Bronx Community College, Hunter College, and the New School for Social Research, as well as the East-West Institute in Cambridge, Massachusetts. But perhaps the most formative site for Henderson in his early years as a writer was the Umbra workshop, which he helped form on New York's Lower East Side with fellow African American writers Calvin Hernton, Tom Dent, Raymond Patterson, Ishmael Reed, and Ronald Snellings (now Askia Muhammad Touré). Joined by a common interest in welding avant-garde artistic practices to "racial and social awareness," the Umbra group declared itself to be in fierce opposition to the mainstream "commercial press and slick in-group journals" in order to forge "a whole and healthy society." While Umbra's inspiration soon burned out for many of its adherents, Henderson remained true to its forward-looking spirit, editing its final anthology in 1967 and remaining an Umbra impresario well into the twenty-first century.

Appropriately enough, Henderson has called himself one of his generation's "griots," that is, communal storytellers tasked with archiving shared experience by sustaining its living vitality. That sense of responsibility for sustaining tradition in the present so that it can inform the future marked his later work with the Free Southern Theatre in New Orleans, the Teachers and Writers Collaborative at Columbia University, Berkeley's University Without Walls, and the National Endowment for the Humanities. Likewise, in such projects as the funk opera *Ghetto Follies* (1978), his classic 1978 study of black rock icon Jimi Hendrix entitled *Jimi Hendrix: Voodoo Child of the Aquarian Age* (later reissued as *'Scuse Me While I Kiss the Sky*), and a 1991 radio documentary on African American beat poet Bob Kaufman, Henderson has displayed extraordinary erudition in order to champion what he has called African American expressive "eruptions" as the lifeblood of black cultural experience. He has often embodied those eruptions himself by performing his work with such experimental jazz masters as Ornette Coleman, Sun Ra, and David Murray.

At the core of Henderson's poetry is the desire to both memorialize and transform specific localities of black experience—especially the Harlem of his youth—in concert with the furious aspirations of the "new wave" of black expression. In his first two collections, *Felix of the Silent Forest* (1967) and *De Mayor of Harlem* (1970), Henderson's deep knowledge of jazz propels his poetic line across the page, animating Harlem as a blur of historical, personal, and mythic sounds and images. His heroes "walk the city hungry in every sense," buffeted by large historical forces but breaking free with the imaginative agility characteristic of jazz improvisation. These jazz-infused energies continue to define his work in later volumes like *The Low-East* (1980) and *Neo-California* (1998), while his thematic interests have become increasingly international in scope, even as his focus remains on "Third World America."

This mutual pressure of the immediate and the encompassing can be felt throughout the poem "Keep on Pushing," which takes its cue from a single event on a Harlem street that exploded into a conflagration which helped redefine the meaning of black life in the post-civil-rights era. Its combination of finely calibrated

detail and epic sweep exemplifies Henderson's ability to capture, in the words of
fellow African American Black Arts poet Amiri Baraka, "the emotional consciousness of a culture."

Keep on Pushing

(Harlem Rebellion, Summer 1964[1]—A Documentary)
The title and excerpts are taken from a hit recording
(summer, 1964) by the famous rhythm and blues trio—
Curtis Mayfield and the Impressions.[2]

I

Lenox Avenue[3] is a big street
The sidewalks are extra wide—three and four times
    the size of a regular Fifth Avenue or East 34th
    sidewalk—and must be so to contain the
    unemployed   5
vigiling[4] Negro males,
and police barricades.

The Police Commissioner can
muster five hundred cops in five minutes
He can summon extra   10
tear-gas bombs / guns / ammunition
within a single call
to a certain general alarm /
For Harlem
reinforcements come from the Bronx   15
just over the three-borough bridge /
    a shot   a cry   a rumor
can muster five hundred Negroes
from idle and strategic street corners
    bars   stoops   hallways   windows   20
Keep on pushing.

II

I walk Harlem
I see police eight to a corner
crude mathematics
eight to one   25
eight for one

---

1. During the summer of 1964, a fifteen-year-
old black youth named James Powell was shot in
the Yorkville section of New York City by white
off-duty police officer Thomas Gilligan, who,
when asked by Powell's grieving friend, "Why
did you shoot him?," took his police badge from
his pocket, pinned it on his shirt, and answered,
"This is why." Angry protests met by police violence followed in three days known journalisti-
cally as the New York Riot of 1964.
2. Curtis Lee Mayfield (1942–1999), rhythm-
and-blues, soul, and funk singer-songwriter,
composed anthemic music for the civil rights
movement, principally with the Impressions, an
African American soul group founded in 1958
with an evolving cast that included Mayfield
until his departure for a solo career in 1970.
3. The primary north-south avenue in Harlem
(renamed Malcolm X Boulevard), called "Harlem's
heartbeat" by African American poet Langston
Hughes (1902–1967).
4. Watching, wakeful.

I see the white storeowners and the white keepers
and I see the white police force
The white police in the white helmets
and the white proprietors in their white shirts   30
talk together and
look around.

I see black handymen put to work because of the riots
boarding up smashed storefronts
They use sparkling new nails   35
The boards are mostly fresh hewn pine
and smell rank fresh.
The pine boards are the nearest Lenox Avenue will
    ever have to trees.
        Phalanxes of police   40
march   up and down
They are   dispatched   and   gathered   helmet heads
Bobbing white black and blue
They walk around   squadroned and platooned
groups of   six   eight   twelve.   45
Even in a group
the sparse black cop walks alone
or with a singular
talkative
white buddy.   50
            Keep on pushing

III

I walk and the children playing frail street games seem
like no other children anywhere
they seem unpopular   foreign
as if in the midst of New York civilization existed
a cryptic and closed society.   55
    Am I in Korea?[5]
I keep expecting to see
companies of camouflage-khakied marines
the Eighth Army[6]
Red Crosses[7]—a giant convoy   60
Down the narrow peopled streets
jeeps with granite-face military men
marching grim champions of the Free World[8]
Trucks dispensing Hershey bars Pall   Malls[9]
medical equipment   65
nurses doctors drugs serums to treat
the diseased and the maimed

---

5. The Korean War (1950–53) pitted North and South Korea against each other, with the Communist-bloc nations of China and the Soviet Union supporting the North and the United States and its allies supporting the South.
6. The Eighth U.S. Army (EUSA) was assigned to guard the border between North and South Korea, and remained stationed in South Korea for decades after the war's end.

7. The American Red Cross, an organization that provides medical and emergency aid to disaster victims and military personnel.
8. Cold war–era term used by the United States and its allies to describe those countries outside the Communist sphere of influence.
9. Brand of American cigarettes, popular in the 1950s and 1960s.

and from the Harlem River[1]
blasting whistles horns
volleying firebombs[2] against the clouds   70
the 7th Fleet[3] . . .

> but the prowling Plymouths[4]
> and helmeted outlaws from Queens
> persist.
> > *Keep On A'Pushing*   75

IV

I see the plump pale butchers pose with their signs:
   "Hog maws[5] 4 pounds for 1 dollar"
   "Pigs ears 7 pounds for 1 dollar"
   "Neckbones   chitterlings[6] 6 pounds for 1"
   Nightclubs,   liquor stores   bars 3, 4, 5 to one block   80
3 & 4 shots for one dollar
I see police eight to one
   in its entirety Harlem's 2nd law of Thermodynamics[7]
      Helmet
         nightsticks[8] bullets to barehead   85
         black reinforced shoes to sneaker
Am I in Korea?

V

At night Harlem sings and dances
And as the newspapers say:
they also pour their whiskey on one another's heads.   90
They dog and slop[9] in the bars
The children monkey[1] in front of Zero's Records Chamber
on 116th and Lenox
They mash potatoes and madison[2] at the Dawn Casino,
Renaissance Ballroom, Rockland Palace, and the Fifth
   Avenue Armory[3]   95
on 141st and the Harlem River.[4]

—*Come out of your windows*

---

1. Waterway separating the boroughs of Manhattan and the Bronx in New York City.
2. Homemade incendiary weapon, nicknamed "the poor man's grenade" (also called a Molotov cocktail).
3. The Seventh Fleet is the U.S. Navy's permanent naval force deployed in the Pacific near Japan and South Korea.
4. American automobile brand used by many city police departments in the 1950s and 1960s.
5. Pig stomach, a specialty of African American cuisine (or "soul food").
6. Pig intestines (pronounced "chitlins"), likewise a "soul food" staple.
7. Newton's 2nd Law of Thermodynamics states that all physical processes move in only one direction, towards greater degradation of energy—that is, toward disorder or entropy.
8. Police batons or clubs.
9. Get drunk. "Dog": malinger or idle lazily.
1. Popular dance in the early 1960s.
2. Like the "mashed potato," a dance popular in the late 1950s and early 1960s.
3. Harlem landmarks built and active in the early and mid-20th century: Dawn Casino, Renaissance Ballroom, and Rockland Palace were known for their dances and jazz performances, especially in the 1930s and 1940s; the Armory is home to the 369th Infantry Regiment, nicknamed "the Harlem Hellfighters," the first African American regiment to see battle during World War I.
4. The boundaries of West Harlem, between 116th and 141st streets.

dancehalls, bars and grills   Monkey   Dog[5]   in the street
like Martha and the Vandellas[6]
Dog for NBC   100
The Daily News and *The New York Times*
Dog for Andrew Lyndon Johnson[7]
and shimmy[8] a bit
for "the boys upstate"[9]
and the ones in Mississippi   105

> *Cause you got soul*
> *Everybody knows . . .*
> *Keep on Pushin'*

VI

This twilight
I sit in Baron's Fish & Chip Shack   110
Alfonso (the counterman) talks of ammunition
The *Journal-American*[1] in my lap
headlines promise EXCLUSIVE BATTLE PHOTOS
by a daring young photographer they call Mel Finkelstein[2]
through him they insure "The Face of Violence—The Most
    Striking Close-ups"/   115
WWRL[3] the radio station that serves
the Negro community
tools along on its rhythm n blues vehicle
The colorful unison announcers
declare themselves "The most soulful station in the nation"   120
Then the lecture series on Democracy comes on
The broadcaster for this series doesn't sound soulful
    (eight to one he's white, representing management)
We Negroes are usually warned of the evils of Communism
and the fruits of Democracy / but this evening he tells us   125
that / in this troubled time we must keep our heads
and our Law
and our order (and he emphasizes order)
he says violence only hurts (and he emphasizes hurts)
    the cause of freedom and dignity /   He urges the troubled   130
restless residents of Harlem and Bedford-Stuyvesant[4] to stay in
their homes, mark an end to the tragic and senseless violence
a pause

---

5. Popular 1960s dance.
6. African American "Motown" or soul singing group known for their 1964 hit "Dancing in the Streets."
7. Conflation of two U.S. presidents: Andrew Johnson (1808–1875), 17th U.S. president (1865–69), who was inaugurated after the assassination of Abraham Lincoln (1809–1865) and failed to protect ex-slaves in the immediate aftermath of the Civil War; and Lyndon Baines Johnson (1903–1973), 36th U.S. president (1963–69), who was inaugurated after the assassination of John F. Kennedy (1917–1963) and sought to protect the rights of African Americans through passage of the Civil Rights Act of 1964 and the Voting Rights Act of 1965.
8. Dance move in which the body is held still but the shoulders are vibrated quickly; first popularized by the "flappers" of the 1920s.
9. Prison inmates (slang).
1. The New York *Journal-American*, published from 1937 to 1966, an afternoon publication owned by the Hearst Corporation, the largest newspaper chain in the United States during the 1950s and 1960s.
2. American photojournalist (1930–1992).
3. Radio station that featured rhythm-and-blues, soul, and funk music in the 1960s, along with lectures on culture and politics.
4. Brooklyn neighborhood, referred to in the 1960s as "Brooklyn's Little Harlem." The Harlem uprising of 1964 eventually spread to Bedford-Stuyvesant.

then he concludes
"Remember
    this is the land of the free"   135
and a rousing mixed chorus ends with the majestic harmony of
  "AND THE HOME OF THE BRAVE . . ."

Alfonso didn't acknowledge
he hears it every hour on the hour.
The Rhythm n Blues returns   140
a flaming bottle bursts on Seventh Avenue
and shimmies the fire across the white divider line
helmets
and faces white as the fluorescence of the streets   145
bob by
Prowl cars[5] speeding wilding wheeling
the loony turns of the modulating demodulating sirens
climb the tenements window by window
Harlem moves in an automatic platform   150
The red fish lights swirl the gleaming storefronts
there will be no Passover this night[6]
and then again the gunfire high
in the air   death static
           over everything . . .   155
ripped glass
shards   sirens   gunfire
down towards 116th
  as Jocko scenes[7] radio WWRL

late at night Jocko hustles[8] wine: Italian Swiss Colony Port   160
sherry and muscatel.   Gypsy Rose and Hombre "The
  Man's Adult Western Wine"[9]
but by day and evening
his raiment for Harlem's head is different
zealous Jocko coos forward   165
his baroque tongue
snakes like fire
           "Headache?
               . . . *take Aspirin*
            Tension?   170
               . . . *take Compōz!*"[1]

Keep on pushin'
Someway somehow
I know we can make it
With just a little bit of soul.   175

                                       1970

---

5. I.e., police cars used to cruise the streets.
6. The Jewish holiday Passover (from the Hebrew *pesach*, meaning protection) arises from the biblical story in which God instructed the Hebrews to protect themselves from the Pharaoh by smearing lamb's blood over their doorways so that the angel of death would "pass over" their homes (Exodus 12.1–20). Many of the businesses destroyed in the violence that engulfed Bedford-Stuyvesant were owned by Jewish merchants.

7. Enlivens, makes the scene (slang); "Jocko": Douglas Wendell Henderson Sr. (1918–2000), legendary African American disk jockey who worked at WWRL in the 1960s.
8. Sells aggressively.
9. Hombre, Gypsy Rose, Italian Swiss Colony: brands of cheap wine popular in the 1960s and 1970s.
1. "Headache? . . . Compōz": early 1960s advertising slogan for a popular sedative.

NIKKI GIOVANNI
b. 1943

B orn in Knoxville, Tennessee, and given the name Yolande Cornelia Giovanni Jr., Nikki Giovanni was one of the first Black Arts movement poets to achieve stardom. Her unabashed advocacy of violent militancy as a proper black response to white oppression brought her instant fame. She appeared on talk shows, received honorary degrees, and brushed off with consummate ease inquiries about incompatibility between her fame as a poet and her avowedly revolutionary intentions to destroy white America.

Giovanni was raised in the all-black neighborhood of Lincoln Heights, Cincinnati, Ohio, until the age of fourteen, when she moved back to Knoxville to live with her grandparents. Her grandmother, Emma Louvenia, who worked tirelessly for the black community as a member of the Gospel Church, alerted the young Giovanni to the problems of racism. In high school, Giovanni was introduced to the work of other African American writers, finding particular inspiration in the writing of Gwendolyn Brooks.

An exceptionally bright student, Giovanni entered the all-black Fisk University in 1960 at age seventeen. Strongly influenced by the civil rights movement, she led the reestablishment of Fisk's chapter of the Student Non-violent Coordinating Committee (SNCC) in 1964 after the university's previous banning of the group. Shortly after Giovanni's graduation in 1967, her grandmother passed away; grief-stricken, Giovanni turned to her work. While writing her own poetry, Giovanni also organized the first Cincinnati Black Arts Festival and attended the Detroit Conference of Unity and Art at which she met H. Rap Brown, who had replaced Stokely Carmichael as the head of SNCC. From then on, Giovanni began to associate with prominent leaders of the Black Arts and Black Power movements. She always insisted, however, that her poetry was an expression of her individual experience and not necessarily of the black community as a whole. Giovanni says, "I write what I see and I take responsibility for it. Why should thirty million people have to have me as a spokesman?" This tension between expansive collectivity and personal intimacy is the hallmark of such signal poems as "Nikki-Rosa" and "Ego Tripping."

After the assassination of Martin Luther King Jr. in 1968, Giovanni (who was living in Ohio at the time) moved to New York City, entering the MFA program at Columbia University on a National Foundation of the Arts Fellowship. Giovanni felt, however, that her teachers neither respected nor understood her work, and she soon left to pursue writing on her own. In rapid succession between 1967 and 1970, Giovanni produced three volumes of poetry that were avidly read by black audiences: *Black Feeling, Black Talk* (1967), *Black Judgment* (1968), and *Re: Creation* (1970). The boldness and accessibility of Giovanni's revolutionary proclamations quickly made her one of the leading figures of the Black Arts movement. She went on to record a recitation of her verse called *Truth Is on Its Way* (1971); backed by a New York religious choir, the album enacted Giovanni's claim that, in the African American tradition, poetry cannot be divorced from music, an aesthetic Giovanni continued to pursue in several more recordings of her poetry read in musical settings.

Throughout the 1970s Giovanni's popularity grew with audiences, both black and white, even as her peers among Black Arts poets grew skeptical of her commitment to revolutionary expression. Determined to support herself and her young son through writing, Giovanni worked tirelessly to promote her work, making speeches and reading her poetry all over the country in as many as 200 public appearances a year. She wrote prolifically; *Cotton Candy on a Rainy Day* (1978) was her twelfth book published in the decade since the appearance of *Black Feeling, Black Talk*. Giovanni was fulfilling the Black Arts aim of bringing the new black poetry to the people, yet she was often accused of compromising her integrity for the sake of fame, suffering particularly harsh criticism among fellow Black Arts writers for accepting a Woman of the Year Award from the *Ladies' Home Journal* in 1973. In reply, Giovanni insisted that her selection for the award by a white organization was an indication of progress in race relations.

But perhaps of greater significance was Giovanni's continued commitment to a poetics of intimacy, in which sharply observed features of personal experience bear the weight of larger social concern. Fittingly, in later decades she has devoted considerable time to writing for children and to teaching, having served since 1987 as distinguished professor at Virginia Tech University.

For Saundra

i wanted to write
a poem
that rhymes
but revolution doesn't lend
itself to be-bopping[1]   5

then my neighbor
who thinks i hate
asked—do you ever write
tree poems—i like trees
so i thought   10
i'll write a beautiful green tree poem
peeked from my window
to check the image
noticed the school yard was covered
with asphalt   15
no green—no trees grow
in manhattan

then, well, i thought the sky
i'll do a big blue sky poem
but all the clouds have winged   20
low since no-Dick[2] was elected

so i thought again
and it occurred to me
maybe i shouldn't write
at all   25
but clean my gun
and check my kerosene supply

---

1. Stylization (from a vernacular term describing a distinctive way of walking, so named in tribute to the experimental jazz movement of the 1940s known as "bebop," which put a premium on improvisational virtuosity).
2. I.e., Richard M. Nixon (1913–1994), 37th president of the United States (1969–74).

perhaps these are not poetic
times
at all   30

1968

Beautiful Black Men

(with compliments and apologies to all not mentioned by name)

i wanta say just gotta say something
bout those beautiful beautiful beautiful outasight[1]
black men
with they afros
walking down the street   5
is the same ol danger
but a brand new pleasure

sitting on stoops, in bars, going to offices
running numbers,[2] watching for their whores
preaching in churches, driving their hogs[3]   10
walking their dogs, winking at me
in their fire red, lime green, burnt orange
royal blue tight tight pants that hug
what i like to hug

jerry butler, wilson pickett, the impressions   15
temptations, mighty mighty sly[4]
don't have to do anything but walk
on stage
and i scream and stamp and shout
see new breed men[5] in breed alls   20
dashiki[6] suits with shirts that match
the lining that compliments the ties
that smile at the sandals
where dirty toes peek at me
and i scream and stamp and shout   25
for more beautiful beautiful beautiful
black men with outasight afros

1968

---

1. Incomparably "cool" (slang).
2. I.e., carrying betting slips in an illegal gambling operation.
3. Large, highly customized motorcycles.
4. Musical artists and groups popular in the 1960s. Butler (b. 1939), rhythm-and-blues singer. Pickett (1941–2006), soul singer. The Impressions were a soul group. The Temptations were a Motown group. Sly Stone (born Sylvester Stewart, 1944), lead singer of the soul, funk, and rock group Sly and the Family Stone.
5. "New Breed": term used to describe Black Consciousness writers and activists in the 1960s.
6. Brightly colored, loose-fitting pullover garment widely worn in West Africa, popular among African American men in the 1960s and 1970s.

Nikki-Rosa[1]

childhood remembrances are always a drag
if you're Black
you always remember things like living in Woodlawn[2]
with no inside toilet
and if you become famous or something   5
they never talk about how happy you were to have your mother
all to yourself and
how good the water felt when you got your bath from one of those
big tubs that folk in chicago barbecue in
and somehow when you talk about home   10
it never gets across how much you
understood their feelings
as the whole family attended meetings about Hollydale[3]
and even though you remember
your biographers never understand   15
your father's pain as he sells his stock
and another dream goes
and though you're poor it isn't poverty that
concerns you
and though they fought a lot   20
it isn't your father's drinking that makes any difference
but only that everybody is together and you
and your sister have happy birthdays and very good christmasses
and I really hope no white person ever has cause to write about me
because they never understand Black love is Black wealth and
     they'll   25
probably talk about my hard childhood and never understand that
all the while I was quite happy

                                                      1968

Revolutionary Music

you've just got to dig sly[1]
and the family stone
damn the words
you gonna be dancing to the music[2]
james brown[3] can go to   5
viet nam
or sing about whatever he
has to

---

1. Childhood nickname of the poet bestowed by her elder sister, Gary Ann.
2. Black suburb of Cincinnati.
3. All-black housing development outside of Cincinnati in which Giovanni's parents had hoped to build a home but could not because of discrimination in the housing loan industry.
1. Sly Stone (born Sylvester Stewart, 1944), lead singer of the soul, funk, and rock group Sly and the Family Stone.

2. Allusion to Sly and the Family Stone's 1968 "Dance to the Music."
3. African American soul and funk singer-songwriter (1933–2006). His 1968 performance for U.S. troops in South Vietnam of "America Is My Home," composed in response to criticism of the war by black leaders such as Stokely Carmichael (1941–1998) and Martin Luther King Jr. (1929–1968), drew criticism from Black Consciousness activists.

since   he already told
the honkie[4]   10
"although you happy you better try
to get along
money won't change you
but time is taking you on"[5]
not to mention   15
doing a whole
song they can't even snap
their fingers to
"good god! ugh!"[6]
talking bout   20
"i got the feeling baby i got the feeling"[7]
and "hey everybody let me tell you the news"[8]
martha and the vandellas dancing in the streets[9]
while shorty long is functioning at that junction[1]
yeah we hip to that   25
aretha[2] said they better
think
but she already said
"ain't no way to love you"[3]
(and you know she wasn't talking to us)   30
and dig the o'jays[4] asking "must i always be a stand in
for love"
i mean they say "i'm a fool for being myself"

While the mighty mighty impressions[5] have told the world
for once and for all   35
"We're a Winner"
even our names—le roi[6] has said—are together
impressions
temptations
                                                      supremes   40
                                                      delfonics
                                                        miracles
                                 intruders[7] (i mean intruders?)
                   not beatles and animals[8] and white bad things like
                                   young rascles[9] and shit   45

---

4. White man (pejorative slang).
5. Version of lyrics from Brown's 1966 song "Money Won't Change You."
6. Typical Brown exclamation.
7. Brown's funk song "I Got the Feelin'" was released in 1968.
8. Line from Brown's 1967 funk song "Let Yourself Go."
9. "Motown" or soul group Martha and the Vandellas released the song "Dancing in the Streets" in 1964.
1. African American soul singer-songwriter Frederick Earl "Shorty" Long released "Function at That Junction" in 1966.
2. Soul and gospel singer Aretha Franklin (b. 1942), whose 1968 song "Think" contains the chorus, "You better think (think) think (think) think (think) about what you're trying to do to me."
3. Franklin's 1968 song "Ain't No Way" appears

on her album *Lady Soul*.
4. Philadelphia-based soul group popular in the 1960s and 1970s; Giovanni paraphrases lines from their 1966 song "Stand In for Love."
5. African American soul group whose 1967 song "We're a Winner," written by Curtis Mayfield (1942–1999), was one of the most prominent anthems of black pride in 1960s popular music.
6. I.e., LeRoi Jones, or Amiri Baraka, African American author, black nationalist activist, and prominent theorist of the Black Arts movement (1934–2014).
7. Temptations . . . Intruders: African American soul groups popular in the 1960s.
8. Beatles, Animals: English rock 'n' roll bands of the 1960s.
9. The Young Rascals, American so-called blue-eyed (i.e., white) soul group active from 1965 to 1972.

we be digging all
our revolutionary music conciously or un
cause sam cooke said "a change is gonna come"[1]

1968

All I Gotta Do

all i gotta do
is sit and wait
sit and wait
and its gonna find
me   5
all i gotta do
is sit and wait
if i can learn
how

what i need to do   10
is sit and wait
cause i'm a woman[1]
sit and wait
what i gotta do
is sit and wait   15
cause i'm a woman
it'll find me

you get yours
and i'll get mine[2]
if i learn   20
to sit and wait
you got yours
i want mine
and i'm gonna get it
cause i gotta get it   25
cause i need to get it
if i learn how

thought about calling
for it on the phone
asked for a delivery   30
but they didn't have it
thought about going
to the store to get it
walked to the corner
but they didn't have it   35

1. "Change Is Gonna Come": 1964 rhythm-and-blues song by African American singer-songwriter Sam Cooke (born Samuel Cook, 1931–1964).
1. Play on 1962 song "I'm a Woman" by American pop and jazz singer Peggy Lee (1920–2002),
with its aggressive chorus: "'Cause I'm a woman / W-O-M-A-N / I'll say it again . . ."
2. Play on 1969 song "You Got Yours and I'll Get Mine" by Philadelphia-based soul group the Delfonics.

called your name
in my sleep
sitting and waiting
thought you would awake me
called your name   40
lying in my bed
but you didn't have it
offered to go get it
but you didn't have it
so i'm sitting   45

all i know
is sitting and waiting
waiting and sitting
cause i'm a woman
all i know   50
is sitting and waiting
cause i gotta wait
wait for it to find
me

1970

Ego Tripping[1] (there may be a reason why)

I was born in the congo[2]
I walked to the fertile crescent[3] and built the sphinx[4]
I designed a pyramid so tough that a star
        that only glows every one hundred years falls
        into the center giving divine perfect light[5]   5
I am bad[6]

I sat on the throne
        drinking nectar with allah[7]
I got hot and sent an ice age to europe
        to cool my thirst   10
My oldest daughter is nefertiti[8]
        the tears from my birth pains

1. Preening, with a glance at "tripping" induced by psychedelic drug use (1960s slang).
2. European designation for the Congo River basin, an area of Central Africa once dominated by Belgian, French, and Portuguese colonial powers; thought by many anthropologists to be the site of human origin several hundred thousand years ago.
3. Middle Eastern region historically encompassing ancient Egypt and Mesopotamia through which the Nile, Jordan, Euphrates, and Tigris rivers flow, connecting the eastern bank of the Mediterranean Sea to the Persian Gulf; it was home to several farming-based early civilizations.
4. Ancient Egyptian mythic figure with a lion's body, bird's wings, and woman's head, the largest and most famous of which was built on the Giza Plateau on the west bank of the Nile, adjacent to the Great Pyramids.
5. At midnight on the autumn equinox of 2170 B.C.E., accepted in mystical traditions as the year of the Great Pyramid's completion, Alcyone, the central star in the Pleiades group, stood exactly on the Pyramid's meridian; with allusion to the idea of God as a life-giving "perfect light" present in biblical, Gnostic, and Hindu writings.
6. That is, formidable (black vernacular).
7. God (Arabic).
8. Great Royal Wife (1370–1330 B.C.E.) of the ancient Egyptian pharaoh Amenhotep IV (later known as Akhenaten), who ruled from 1369 to 1322 B.C.E. Nefertiti ("her beauty has come") was legendary for her comeliness and religiosity.

created the nile
I am a beautiful woman

I gazed on the forest and burned   15
    out the sahara desert[9]
    with a packet of goat's meat
    and a change of clothes
I crossed it in two hours
I am a gazelle so swift   20
    so swift you can't catch me

    For a birthday present when he was three
I gave my son hannibal an elephant
    He gave me rome for mother's day[1]
My strength flows ever on   25

My son noah built new/ark[2] and
I stood proudly at the helm
    as we sailed on a soft summer day
I turned myself into myself and was
    jesus   30
    men intone my loving name
    All praises All praises
I am the one who would save

I sowed diamonds in my back yard
My bowels deliver uranium   35
    the filings from my fingernails are
    semi-precious jewels
    On a trip north
I caught a cold and blew
My nose giving oil to the arab world   40
I am so hip[3] even my errors are correct
I sailed west to reach east[4] and had to round off
    the earth as I went
    The hair from my head thinned and gold was laid
    across three continents   45

I am so perfect so divine so ethereal so surreal
I cannot be comprehended
    except by my permission

I mean . . . I . . . can fly
    like a bird in the sky . . .   50

1970

9. World's largest hot desert, stretching across northern Africa from the Red Sea to the outskirts of the Atlantic Ocean.
1. The Carthaginian politician and military leader Hannibal (247–182 B.C.E.) led a massive army (including 37 war elephants) across the Pyrenees and Alps into northern Italy to defeat the Romans during the Second Punic War (218–203 B.C.E.).
2. Blends allusion to the biblical Noah, who upon God's commandment built an ark that saved him and a remnant of living creatures from the Flood (Genesis 6–9), with Newark, New Jersey, which native African American poet and Black Arts movement leader Amiri Baraka (1934–2014) called "New Ark" in the wake of the Newark riots of 1967.
3. Sophisticated, knowing (black vernacular).
4. Allusion to Italian explorer Christopher Columbus (1451–1506), who reached the Caribbean on a voyage whose intended destination was Japan.

JAMES ALAN McPHERSON

b. 1943

One of the most gifted short story writers to emerge during the 1960s and 1970s, James Alan McPherson was born to James and Mabel McPherson in Savannah, Georgia. He briefly attended Morgan State University before receiving a B.A. degree from Morris Brown College in Atlanta. In 1965 McPherson was recruited by Harvard University Law School and during the same year his second short story, "Gold Coast," was awarded first prize in a fiction contest sponsored by the *Atlantic Monthly*. After completing his law degree and later earning an M.F.A. from the University of Iowa, he continued to produce prize-winning fiction. McPherson has been an instructor of creative writing and African American literature at the University of Iowa (1968–69), the University of California, Santa Cruz (1969), Morgan State University (1969–70), and the University of Virginia (1976–81).

Hue and Cry: Short Stories earned McPherson a National Institute of Arts and Letters grant in 1970, a Rockefeller grant that same year, and a Guggenheim fellowship two years later. McPherson later won a Pulitzer Prize for his collection *Elbow Room* and was awarded a MacArthur Foundation grant in 1981.

McPherson is largely known for his short stories in which a fine ear for the rhythms of black vernacular speech combines with a keen eye for nuanced character within the textures of daily African American experience. Many of McPherson's stories involve emblems of mobility, energy, and the clash of technology and embodied citizenship—such as cars and trains (which he was able to convey vividly, in part because he worked his way through college as a waiter aboard the Great Northern Railroad). At the heart of a McPherson tale is always a parable about possibility hidden beneath the surfaces of poverty, displacement, or interpersonal struggle; indeed, McPherson's stories abound with images of surfaces (of clothes, furniture, photographs, and other well-observed material objects of everyday life), which he subtly invites us either to read as ciphers of hidden aspiration or to read beyond for the gritty sensibility they materialize.

Although McPherson's stories deal intimately with issues of race and class, he always attempts to highlight the universality of his characters' predicaments. Of his own work, McPherson hopes that it can be read as "about people, all kinds of people. . . . As a matter of fact, certain of them happen to be white; but I have tried to keep the color part of most of them far in the background, where these things should be rightly kept."

Problems of Art

Seated rigidly on the red, plastic-covered sofa, waiting for Mrs. Farragot to return from her errand, Corliss Milford decided he did not feel comfortable inside the woman's apartment. Why this was he could not tell. The living room itself, as far as he could see around, reflected the imprint of a mind as meticulous as his own. Every item seemed in place; every detail meshed into an overriding suggestion of order. This neatness did no damage to the image of Mrs. Farragot he had assembled, even before visiting her at home.

Her first name was Mary, and she was thin and severe of manner. He recalled that her walnut-brown face betrayed few wrinkles; her large brown eyes were quick and direct without being forceful; her thin lips, during conversation, moved with precision and resolve. Even her blue summer dress, with pearl-white buttons up its front, advertized efficiency of character. The bare facts of her personal life, too, argued neatness and restraint; he had them down on paper, and the paper rested on his knee. Milford juggled his knee; the paper shifted, but did not fall. That too, he thought. It was part of why he felt uneasy. For a few seconds, he entertained the notion that the living room was no more than a sound stage on a movie lot. Somehow, it seemed too calculated.

Milford's suspicion of an undisclosed reality was heightened by the figure in the painting on the wall across the room. It was the portrait of a sad-eyed Jesus. Immaculate in white and blue robes, the figure held a pink hand just above the red, valentine-shaped heart painted at the center of its chest. Bright drops of red blood dripped from the valentine. Such pictures as this Milford had seen before in dimestores. Though it had a certain poignancy, he thought, it was . . . cheap. It conveyed a poverty of the artist's imagination and tended to undermine the sophistication of those who purchased such dimensionless renditions. Did not the Latin poor build great cathedrals? Even country Baptists wheeled their preachers about in Cadillacs. Why then, Milford asked himself, would a poor black woman compound an already bleak existence by worshipping before a dimestore rendition of a mystery? He recalled having heard someplace something about the function of such images, but could not recall exactly what he had heard. The plastic crinkled as he shifted on the sofa to review Mrs. Farragot's papers. She had been born in Virginia, but had lived for many years in Los Angeles. She was a widow, but received no compensation from her husband's social security. She had been arrested for driving under the influence of alcohol, although she insisted that she was a teetotaler. About the only consistent factual evidence about her that Milford knew was her insistence, over a period of two weeks, that no one but a white lawyer could represent her at the license revocation hearing. For her firm stand on this, she was now notorious in all the cubbyhole offices of Project Gratis.[1] Milford looked again at the portrait. Perhaps that explains it, he thought. Then he thought, perhaps it does not.

He leaned back on the sofa, impatient now for Mrs. Farragot to return. According to his watch it was 11:45 a.m. The hearing was scheduled for 1:30 p.m. The day was already humid and muggy, and would probably grow warmer as events developed in the afternoon. But Milford was used to it. For want of a better rationalization, he liked to call such occasions invigorating. Now he sighed and glanced again about the room, wondering just who would return with her to act as witness and corroborator. Since his mind was trained to focus on those areas where random facts formed a confluence of palpable reality, he became restless for easy details. His eyes swept over the brown coffee table; above the red, plastic-covered armchair across the room; past the tall glass china closet packed with jade-green and brandy-red and sunset-orange cut-glass ashtrays and knick-knacks whose scale-like patterns sparkled in the late morning sunlight streaming lazily

---

1. Free (Latin).

through the open window on bright particles of dust; beyond the china closet to the yellow-white door leading into the quiet, smell-less kitchen from which sounded the hum of a refrigerator; past the doorframe, quickly, and to the sofa's edge on his right to where a group of pictures in cheap aluminum frames stood grouped on a brown plywood end table. These he examined more closely. The larger one was of Mrs. Mary Farragot. It was a close-up of her face as it must have looked ten years ago. There were fewer wrinkles and no strains of gray in her ebony black hair. She was smiling contentedly. This, Milford thought, was not the face of an alcoholic. It reflected strength and motherly concern. Next to this picture was a small color print of two white children. Both were smiling. One, a blond boy seated in a blue high chair, grinned with his spoon raised above a yellow dish of cereal, as if about to strike. The little girl, with dark brown hair, posed extravagantly beside the chair, her skinny right arm raised in anticipation of the falling spoon. The picture was inscribed: "To Aunt Mary, Love, Tracy and Ken." Corliss Milford did not pause to examine their faces. Instead, his eyes were drawn to the third picture. This was a faded black and white enlargement of a very weak print. Behind the glass stood a robust black man in army uniform, saluting majestically. His grin was mischievous and arrogant; his nostrils flared. The thumb of his raised hand stood out prominently from his temple; a few inches above the hand the edge of an army private's cap hung casually over his forehead like an enlarged widow's peak.

This is a good picture, Milford decided. He picked it up and examined its details more closely. The man stood in what was obviously an exaggeration of attention. He saw that the man's left brogan[2] was hooked nonchalantly around his right ankle. In the background a flagpole whistled up some six or eight feet above the man's head. The flag was snapping briskly in what might have been the morning breeze, although the faded condition of the print obscured the true direction of the sun. Milford counted the number of stars in the flag. Then he peered deeper into the background, beyond the pole, and saw what might have been palm trees, and beyond these mountains. His eyes moved from the mountains back to the flagpole and down the pole past the saluting soldier to the bottom of the picture, where the grass was smooth as a billiard table. His eyes fastened on a detail he had missed before: a bugle stood upright on its mouth just at the soldier's feet; in fact, the man's left brogan was pointing slyly at the bugle. This was why the man was grinning. Near the bugle, at an angle, someone, probably the soldier, had written: "To Mary Dear, Lots of Love, 'Sweet Willie.'" There was a flowing line just below this inscription, as if the signer had taken sudden inspiration.

Corliss Milford shifted his eyes to the papers on the sofa beside him. Mrs. Farragot had reported that she was a widow. He had written that down. But now he recalled she had actually said "grass widow,"[3] which meant that Sweet Willie was still around. It also explained why she was not drawing social security. Perhaps, he thought, it also justified her frustration if indeed she had been drunk when arrested. There was no doubt that it accounted completely for the bitterness which had compelled her to request specifically the services of a white lawyer. From his picture, Milford

2. Heavy shoe commonly worn as part of a military or police uniform.

3. An abandoned wife or mistress.

concluded, Willie Farragot seemed to reek of irresponsibility. Perhaps all the men she knew were like him. This would account for the difficulty she seemed to be having in getting a witness to corroborate her story that she had not been drunk or driving when arrested.

Now he shifted his eyes to the print on the wall, but this time with more understanding. He had re-entered the living room on another level, and now he could sympathize. Still, he did not like the painting. A disturbing absence of nuance undermined the face: the small brown eyes were dimensionless, as if even they did not believe the message they had been calculated to convey. The pigeon nose had no special prominence, no irregularity suggestive of regality; even the lips, wafer-thin and pink, suggested only a glisten of determination. In the entire face, from forehead to chin, there was not the slightest hint of tragedy or transcendence. To appreciate it, Milford concluded, required of one an act of faith. The robes, though enamel white and royal blue, drooped without majesty from shoulders that were round and ordinary. And the larger-than-life valentine heart seemed to have been merely positioned at the center of the figure's chest. The entire image suffered badly from a lack of calculation. It did not draw one into it. Its total effect did no more than suggest that the image, at the complete mercy of a commercial artist, had resigned itself to being painted. The face reflected a nonchalant resignation to this fate. If the mouth was a little sad it was not from the weight of this world's sins but rather from an inability to comprehend the nature of sin itself.

Milford was beginning to draw contrasts between the figure and the picture of Sweet Willie when Mrs. Mary Farragot opened the door and stepped quickly into the room. A heavyset brownskinned man followed behind her. "May Francis Cripps wouldn't come," she announced in a quiet, matter of fact voice, "but Clarence was there too. He seen it all. Clarence Winfield, this here's Mr. Milford from that free law office round there."

Milford stepped to the center of the room and extended his hand.

"How do?" the man, named Winfield, boomed. He grasped Milford's hand and squeezed it firmly. "Everything Miss Mary told you, she told you the truth. I was there and I seen it all. Them cops had no call to arrest her. She warn't drunk, she warn't driving, and I know damn well she warn't going nowheres in that car." While saying this Winfield ran the thumb of his left hand around the inside of his belt, tucking his shirt more neatly into his trousers. "Like I say," he continued, dropping Milford's hand, "I was there and I seen the whole thing."

Corliss Milford stepped back and considered the man. He wore a light brown seersucker suit and a red shirt. A red silk handkerchief flowered from the pocket of his jacket. A red silk tie dangled in his left hand. He had obviously just finished shaving because the pungent scent of a cheap cologne wafted from his body each time he moved. There was something familiar about the cologne, Milford thought; he imagined he had smelled it before, but could not remember when or where. He turned and sat on the plastic-covered sofa, crossing his leg. "I'm from Project Gratis," Milford announced. "Did Mrs. Farragot tell you about my interest in her case?"

Clarence Winfield nodded. "When Miss Mary told me what happen I put on my business clothes and rush right on over here. I told her"—and here he threw a comforting glance at Mrs. Farragot who stood several feet behind him—"I told her, I say, 'Miss Mary, you don't have to beg May Francis and

Big Boy and them to testify for you.' Anyway, that nigger Big Boy couldn't hit a crooked lick with a straight stick."[4]

"Speak good English now, Clarence, for the Lord's sakes," Mrs. Farragot called. "We got to go downtown. And there's one thing I learnt about white people: if they don't understand what you saying they just ain't gonna hear it." She looked conspiratorially at Milford.

The lawyer did not say anything.

Clarence Winfield glanced again at Mrs. Farragot. "I knows good English," he said. "Don't you forget, I worked round white folks too. They hears what they wants to hear." Then he looked at Milford and said, "No offense intended."

The lawyer studied the two of them. Over Winfield's broad shoulder he saw Mrs. Farragot leaning against the chair, directly under the painting. With both hands placed firmly on her hips, she stood surveying the two men with something close to despair playing over her face. Milford noticed her high brown cheeks twitch slightly. Her lips were drawn and thin. She seemed about to say something to Winfield, but no words came from her mouth. The big, middle-aged black man remained standing in the middle of the room as if waiting for something to happen. The longer Milford studied him, the more he became convinced that it was not the smell of the cologne but something else, possibly something about his carriage, which made him seem so familiar. The man seemed eager to be in motion. He seemed self-conscious and awkward standing at attention. Corliss Milford took up the papers from the sofa. He flipped a page to the statement of facts he had typed before leaving the office. "Now Mr. Winfield," he said, "please tell me what you saw the night of August 7 of this year."

Clarence Winfield cleared his throat several times, then glanced once more at Mrs. Farragot. "That there's a night I remember well," he began slowly. "It was hot as a sonofabitch. I was setting on my porch with May Francis Cripps and Buster Williams. It warn't no more than eight-thirty 'cause the sun had just gone down and the sky up the street was settling in from pink to purple to black. I remember it well. We had us some beer and was shooting the shit and the only sound was the crickets scraping and a few kids up the block raising hell when all at once there come this loud honking. I look 'cross the street and seen Miss Mary here come running out her door and down the stairs. I knowed it was her 'cause she left the door open and the light from in here come out through the screen and spotlight her porch like a stage. Yeah, come to think of it, just like a stage. See, there was this car right behind hers that was park so close the headlights was burning right into Miss Mary's tail end, and right up close behind *him* was another car. Well, the guy was trap and couldn't get out. I don't know who was in that car, but that guy kept honking his horn 'cause he couldn't move without scratching against Miss Mary's car. I never found out who that guy was, but man he played Dixie[5] on that horn. See, he couldn't back back either 'cause that car behind had him squeezed in like a Maine sardine. That's the way it is round here in summertime. There's so many big cars park end to end it look like some big-time I-talian gangsters was having a convention. For folks poor as these round here, I don't know where in the *hell* all these here cars come from. Me, I drive . . ."

<hr />

4. Inversion of the saying "Hit a straight lick with a crooked stick," meaning to make an important statement in an oblique way.
5. I.e., made a lot of noise (colloquial).

"You see what I mean, Clarence?" Mrs. Farragot interrupted. She walked toward Winfield, her hands still on her hips. "The man didn't ask about no *gangsters!* All he want is the *facts!*" Then she threw up her hands, cast a look of exasperation at Milford, and dropped into the plastic-covered armchair beneath the painting.

"It's all right," Milford told the two of them. He set down his notes and watched Mrs. Farragot. She was sprawled in the armchair; her arms were folded, her legs were crossed, and there was great impatience in her face. Milford attempted to communicate to her, with a slight movement of his pencil, that he had no objection to the mode of Winfield's presentation.

For his own part, Clarence Winfield grinned bashfully. Then he said, "'Scuse me, Miss Mary; you right," Then he swallowed again and proceeded, this time pausing tentatively before each sentence. "Well, me and May Francis and Buster listen to all this racket and we seen Miss Mary here, plain as day, open up her car and start it up and cut on the headlights. Now *her* car was lighting up the taillights of the car in front of her, and it reflect back on her behind the wheel. I seen that. And I heard this guy steady honking on his horn. Well, just about then who should drive up the street in his new Buick but Big Boy Ralston. He lives up the block there, 'bout five houses down from me. Big Boy a security guard down to the bank and I guess he just naturally take his work serious. I mean he bring it home when he come. Anyway, he drives up just about even with this guy that's honking and he stops and calls out, 'Who that making all that motherfucking racket?' Well, this makes the other guy mad and then he *really* tore into that horn. By this time the street is all lit up like a department store. All three of 'em got they headlights and brakelights on so the street's all white and yellow and red and Big Boy car is fire engine red and the sky is black and purple now, with just a little bit of pink way over West yonder where the sun done gone down. But this guy is still playing Chopsticks on that horn. Big Boy holler, 'If you don't quit that racket I'ma put my foot up your ass as far as your nose!' Well, that there just shell old Buster's peanuts. He scream out, 'Stomp on his ass, Big Boy!' Big Boy lean out the window and look over at us setting on the porch. He holler, 'That go for you too, Buster. I'm tired of this shit every night. Ain't y'all got nothing else to do but set on them motherfucking steps selling wolf tickets?' But this guy is honking hard and strong now, and he don't pay Big Boy no mind. So Big Boy scream, 'You blowing your own funeral music, chump!' And he jerk open the door of his Buick. But right about then I seen Miss Mary pull out of her spot and go *fa*ward about three feet. I seen that, 'cause my eyes got pulled in that direction when her brake-light went off and the red in the back of her car went all yellow and white. Well, Big Boy leaves his motor running and he jumps out his car and slam the door. Old Buster laugh and say to me and May Francis, 'Watch old Big Boy *bogart*[6] this motherfucker. I ain't seen a Friday go by yet he don't floor somebody.' I think old Buster was right. When Big Boy round his car his shoulders was hunched like he was fixing to clean house. The light was shining on his brown uniform and that red Buick and I tell you the truth, you couldn't hardly tell the steel in that Buick from the steel in him. He moved round that car like six feet and three hundred

---

6. Punch (from the American film actor Humphrey Bogart, 1899–1957, known for his "tough guy" roles).

pounds of mad nigger in a *po*-lice uniform fixing to clean him somebody's *plow!*"[7]

Here Winfield paused to chuckle. "Lawd," he said, not looking at anyone in particular, "that there was a *night!* We just set and watch and drunk our beer. People run out they houses. Some look out they windows. Some of them bad kids round here commence to sic Big Boy on. Well, this guy in the car warn't no fool. He must of knowed he didn't have a snowball's chance in hell against Big Boy. He cut his wheels fast and scrunch out of that space like a flash. Fact is, he just miss swatting Big Boy as he wheeled round that Buick. Well, old Big Boy rush back round his front end to get in his car and go after the guy. But just then, who should I see but Miss Mary here come back backing up real slow-like into her old parking space. Well, just then *four* things happen, all at the same time. Them wild kids yell; Miss Mary's brakelights come on fast and red; there was a real loud *scrruunch!*; and Big Boy scream, 'Mother-*fuck!*' See, Miss Mary here done back back right into the side of his red Buick."

Milford sat transfixed. He leaned forward on the sofa, oblivious to anything but the big man in the brown seersucker suit standing quietly in the center of the room. He did not notice Mrs. Mary Farragot, seated in the armchair beneath the picture of Jesus, draw her crossed arms tighter about her breasts.

"*Now,*" Clarence Winfield continued, wetting his lips slowly, "now we come to the part *you* interested in. See, when Big Boy mad he don't have no respect for *nobody!* He run over to Miss Mary's car, pull open the door, and commence to give her hell. Buster Williams spit on the sidewalk and said to us, 'Oh shit! Now they go'n be some *real* trouble. The one thing *nobody* can do is mess with Big Boy Buick. Me, I seen the time he near kilt a guy for putting a dent in his *bumper,* so you know they's hell to pay now with the side all smash in. Somebody better run and call up the *po*-lice!' He nudge May Francis and she taken and run up to her place to call up the law. And just in time too. I heard Big Boy tell Miss Mary here, 'Woman, what the fuck you mean back backing into my car that way? If you was a man I'd kick your ass to kingdom come!' Lawd, he cuss this poor woman here something awful . . ."

"Please, Clarence," Mrs. Farragot called from behind him. "Just get the thing told." She looked at Milford while saying this. "This man ain't got all day."

Corliss Milford said nothing. Nor did he allow his eyes to respond to Mrs. Farragot's searching expression. Instead, he kept his face turned toward the big man standing before him and touched his pencil to the paper on his lap.

Clarence Winfield smiled, as if the gesture had reassured him. "Okay," he said, to no one in particular. "Me and Buster run on over before Big Boy could swing on Miss Mary here. Like I say, Big Boy don't much care *who* he swing on when he gets mad. Poor Miss Mary here just standing there in her peejays crying and carrying on, she so excited, and there was dogs barking and them wild kids was running round whooping and hollering in the floodlights of them two cars, and by this time the sky was all black and purple with no pink. I tell you, man, it was a sight. Buster, he run down the

---

7. "Fixing to clean him somebody's plow": intending to beat somebody up (slang).

corner for more beer and Miss Bessie Mayfair, up the block, lean out her window and scream, 'Fish sandwiches! Hot fresh fish sandwiches, just out the pan! Don't rush, they's plenty. Fifty cents!' Miss Bessie don't miss a chance to make a dollar. Anyway, long about then a squad car come screaming up with red and white lights flashing and it screech to a stop right longside Big Boy's red Buick and this white cop lean out the passenger window and holler, 'Stand back! Don't nobody touch the body. The law is here to take charge! Big Boy push me away from him and look at that cop. He stare him dead in the face and say, 'Drop dead yourself, cream-puff!' Hot damn! That's what I heard him say. That street was all lit up like a department store with red and white lights flashing on all them people in blue and brown and pink clothes. Lawd, it was a sight! But even in all them lights I saw this white cop turn red in the face; his own strobe lights made his face look like it was bleeding. I seen that. I seen the driver get out of the car. It was a colored fellow and he walk like he was ready to do somebody in. He walk up real close to Big Boy and look him dead in the eye. He say, real cool-like, 'What it is, feller?' and Big Boy say, 'Plenty! This here woman done *ruin* my new Buick Electra[8] with *push*-button drive and *black leather* bucket seats! There ain't a worser thing that could of happen to me.' So the colored cop begin to question Miss Mary. She was so mad and angry and crying so much I guess he thought she was drunk, 'cause he ask her to walk the line. He just walk over to the sidewalk and point the toe of his shoe to a crack. Well, Miss Mary here look at him and say, 'No. No, *sah. N. O. Naw!*' That's what I recollect she said. Then I heard him tell her the law was writ so that if she refuse she was bound to lose her license. Well, by this time there was so much commotion going on till I suspect Miss Mary here was too embarrassed to even *think* about walking no line. Folks was laughing, drinking beer, grabbing for fish sandwiches and raising so much hell till I reckon a private person like Miss Mary here would rather lose her license than walk the line in her *pee*jays. So she refuse. Well, them two cops put her in the car and taken her off to jail. Like I said, I seen it all, and I done told you the truth of all I seen. And I'm ready anytime to go down and tell the same thing to the judge."

Corliss Milford completed his notes. He had scribbled sporadically during the recitation. Now he looked up at Clarence Winfield, who shifted impatiently as though confirming his eagerness to be on his way downtown. Then he looked at Mrs. Mary Farragot, still seated in the armchair behind Winfield, her arms locked tightly across her breasts. "His story corroborates yours in all essential details," Milford called to her.

"Of course it do," Mrs. Farragot answered. "That ain't the problem." She shrugged. "The problem is how in the *hell* can I tell a white judge something like all that Clarence just said without being thrown out of court?" She paused and sighed, raising her head so that her hair almost touched the edge of the picture frame. "What I wanted me in the first place," Mrs. Farragot added slowly, "was a white boy that could make some *logic* out of all that."

Now both she and Winfield looked imploringly at Corliss Milford.

---

8. Luxury automobile built in a variety of models from 1959 to 1990.

II

At 1:45 p.m. the three of them sat waiting outside the hearing room of the Department of Motor Vehicles. During the drive downtown, Milford had attempted to think through the dimensions of the situation; now he decided that Mrs. Farragot had been right all along. Since this was not a jury case, there was no way a judge would allow Clarence Winfield to tell his version of the story. As Mrs. Farragot had anticipated, any defense she offered would have to be confined to the facts. Milford cast a sidewise glance at the woman, seated on the bench beside him, with new appreciation of her relative sophistication. In the car she had disclosed that she did domestic work for a suburban stockbroker; from listening in on conversations between the broker and his wife, she must have discerned how a bureaucracy, and the people who made it function, must of necessity be restricted to the facts. And as colorful as were the circumstances of her case, there was not the slightest possibility that any responsible lawyer could include them in her defense.

A pity, too, Milford thought, turning his gaze to Clarence Winfield. Despite the imprecision of his language, the man possessed a certain rough style. He watched Winfield pacing the waxed tile floor of the corridor. The black man had put on his tie now, but because of the excessive heat allowed it to hang loosely about his collar. At one point, with Milford looking on, Winfield lifted his right foot and polished the pointed toe of his shoe against the cloth of his left trouser leg. When he saw Milford watching, Winfield grinned. A pity, the lawyer concluded. Now he would have to restrict the man's statement to yes or no answers to specific questions. He motioned for Winfield to come over to the bench. "Now listen," Milford said, "when you talk to the hearing officer, restrict your statement to the *last* part of your story, the part about her *not* being drunk when she was arrested. You understand?"

Clarence Winfield nodded slyly.

"And don't volunteer anything, please. I'll ask all the questions."

Winfield nodded again.

"Do like he tell you now Clarence, hear?" Mrs. Farragot said, leaning sideways on the bench. "Don't mess up things for me in front of that man in there." Then she said to Milford, "Clarence one of them from downhome.[9] He tend to talk around a point."

"Ah hell!" Winfield said, and was about to say more when the door to the hearing room opened and a voice called, "Mary Farragot?"

It was a woman's voice.

Corliss Milford stood. "I'm representing Mrs. Farragot," he said. "I'm with Brown and Barlow's Project Gratis."

"Well, we're ready," the woman called, and she stepped out into the corridor. She was short and plump, but not unattractive in a dark green pantsuit. Her silver blond hair was cut short. Dark eyelashes, painted, Milford suspected, accentuated her pink face. "I'm Hearing Officer Harriet Wilson," she announced.

As she stood holding open the door, Milford noticed Mrs. Farragot staring intently at Hearing Officer Harriet Wilson. The expression on her face

---

9. I.e., from the rural South.

was one he had not seen before. Suddenly he remembered the photograph of Mrs. Farragot on her plywood end table, and the expression became more familiar. He touched her shoulder and whispered, "Let's go on in." They filed into the hearing room, Mrs. Farragot leading and Clarence Winfield bringing up the rear. Over his shoulder, Milford saw the hearing officer sniffing the air as she shut the door. The room was humid. Over on the window sill a single electric fan rotated wearily, blowing more humid air into the small room. They seated themselves in metal chairs around a dark brown hardwood table. Only Hearing Officer Harriet Wilson remained standing.

"Now," Hearing Officer Wilson said, "we're ready to begin." She smiled round the table pleasantly, her eyes coming to rest on the red silk handkerchief flowering out of Clarence Winfield's coat pocket. It seemed to fascinate her. "Now," she said again, moving her eyes slowly away from the handkerchief, "I'll get the complaining officer and we'll begin." She moved toward a glass door at the back of the room.

"Lawyer Milford," Mrs. Farragot whispered as the glass door opened and shut. She tugged his coat. "Lawyer Milford, I thought it was men that handled these hearings."

Milford shrugged. "Times change," he answered.

Mrs. Farragot considered this. She glanced at the glass door, then at Winfield seated on her right. "Tell you what, lawyer Milford," she said suddenly. "Actually, Clarence don't do too bad when he talk. Maybe you ought to let him tell his story after all."

"I thought we had already agreed on procedure," the lawyer muttered. He found himself irritated by the mysterious look which had again appeared in Mrs. Farragot's eyes. She looked vaguely amused. "We can't change now," he told her.

"Miss Mary," Winfield volunteered, "I can't tell it exactly like I did before."

"Clarence, that don't matter, long as you hit on the facts. Ain't that right?" she asked Milford.

He had no choice but to nod agreement.

"Good," Mrs. Farragot said. She straightened in her chair and brushed her hand lightly across her sweating forehead.

It seemed to Milford she was smiling openly now.

Hearing Officer Harriet Wilson re-entered the room. Behind her, carrying a bulky tape recorder, stepped the arresting officer. He was a tall, olive-brownskinned man who moved intently in a light gray summer suit. Cool dignity flashed in his dark brown eyes; his broad nose twitched, seeming to sniff the air. He placed the recorder on the table near Hearing Officer Wilson's chair, then seated himself at the head of the table. He crossed his leg casually. Then he gazed at the three seated on his right and said, "Officer Otis S. Smothers."

"How do?" Winfield called across the table.

Milford nodded curtly.

Mrs. Farragot said nothing. Her eyes were fixed on the tape recorder.

Hearing Officer Harriet Wilson noticed her staring and said, "This is not a jury matter, dear. At this hearing all we do is tape all relevant testimony and forward it on to the central officer at the state capital. The boys up there make the final decision."

Milford felt a knee press against his under the table. "I should of knowed," Mrs. Farragot whispered beside him. "Won't be long they gonna just give you a lie detector and railroad you that way."

Milford shushed her into silence.

From the head of the table Officer Smothers seemed to be studying them, quiet amusement tugging at the corners of his plump lips.

Officer Wilson placed a finger on the record button and looked round the table. Milford felt Mrs. Farragot tense beside him. A desperate warmth seemed to exude from her body. Officer Wilson smiled cheerily at Clarence Winfield, but sobered considerably as her eyes came to rest on Officer Smothers. She pressed the record button. After reciting the date and case record into the microphone, she swore in the parties. Then she motioned for Officer Smothers to make his statement. It seemed to Milford that Smothers, while taking his oath, had raised his right hand a bit higher than Mrs. Farragot and Winfield. Now he told his version of the story, presenting a minor masterpiece of exactness and economy. His vocabulary was precise, his delivery flawless. When he reached the part of his testimony concerning the sobriety test, he pulled a sheet of paper from his coat pocket and recited, ". . . suspect was informed of her legal obligation to submit to the test. Suspect's reply was . . ." and he touched a lean brown finger to the page ". . . 'I ain't go'n do *nothin'*!'" These words, delivered in comic imitation of a whine, stung Milford's ears. Even Mrs. Farragot, he noticed, winced at the sound. And Clarence Winfield, slouching in his chair, looked sheepish and threatened. To Milford the action seemed especially cruel when Smothers looked over at Hearing Officer Wilson and said in crisp, perfect English, "That's all I have to say," as though he intended to end the recital of facts without some account of his own response to the refusal. Milford watched Smothers as he leaned back in his chair, looking just a bit self-righteous.

"If you have no questions," Hearing Officer Harriet Wilson said to Milford. Her finger was already on the off button of the recorder.

"You *did* offer her a test, then?" Milford asked, stalling for time to reconsider his position.

"Of course," Smothers replied, his fingers meshed, his hands resting professionally on his knee.

"And you had already concluded there was probable cause to believe she was drunk?"

"Certainly."

"How?"

"Her breath, her heavy breathing, and her slurred speech."

"Could you have mistaken a Southern accent for slurred speech?"

"No, I couldn't have," Smothers answered nonchalantly. "I'm from the South myself."

Across the table Hearing Officer Harriet Wilson smiled to herself, her finger tapping the metal casing just above the off button on the recorder.

"Let me say something here," Clarence interrupted. "I was there. I seen the whole thing. It warn't like that at all."

Hearing Officer Wilson looked at Winfield out of the corner of her eye. "Do you want this witness to testify now?" she asked Milford.

But before the lawyer could answer he felt the pressure of Mrs. Farragot's hand on his shoulder. Looking up, he saw her standing over him. "Nome, thank you," he heard her say in a voice very much unlike her own. She was facing Hearing Officer Wilson but looking directly at the recorder. Her face was expressionless. Only her voice betrayed emotion. "I'm innocent," Mrs. Farragot began. "But who go'n believe me, who go'n take my word against the word of that officer? Both of us black, but he ain't bothering his self with that and I ain't concerning myself with it either. But I do say I'm innocent of the charges he done level against me. The night this thing happen I was inside my house in my pajamas minding my own business. I wasn't even *fixing* to drive no car . . ."

She told her side of the story.

While she talked, in a slow, precise tone, Milford watched the two officers. It was obvious that Hearing Officer Harriet Wilson was deeply moved; she kept her eyes lowered to the machine. But Officer Smothers seemed impervious to the woman's pleadings. His meshed fingers remained propped on his knee; his eyes wandered coolly about the room. At one point he lifted his left hand to rub the side of his nose.

When Mrs. Farragot had finished speaking she eased down into her chair. No one spoke for almost a minute; the only sounds in the room were the soft buzz of the recorder and the hum of the window fan. Then Clarence Winfield cleared his throat noisily. Officer Harriet Wilson jumped.

"Tell me something, Officer Smothers?" Milford said. "If you did offer a test, which one was it?"

"I asked her to walk the line, as both of us have already testified," Smothers answered.

"That was the only test you offered?"

"That's right," Smothers said in a tired voice.

"But doesn't the statute provide that a suspect has the right to choose one of *three* tests: *either* the breathalyzer, the blood or the urine? As I read the statute, there's nothing about walking the line."

"I suppose that's right," Officer Smothers said.

"Are you authorized to choose, arbitrarily, a test of your own devising?"

"My choice was *not* arbitrary!" Smothers protested. "The policy is to use that one on the scene. Usually, the others are used down at the station."

Now Milford relaxed. He smiled teasingly at the olive-skinned officer. "*Was* this lady offered one of the other tests down at the station before being booked?"

"I don't really know," the officer answered. "I didn't stay around after filing the report."

Milford turned to Mrs. Farragot, new confidence cooling his words. "*Were* you offered any other tests?"

"No, suh," she said quietly, her voice almost breaking. "They didn't offer me nothing in front of my house and they didn't offer me nothing down to the jail. They just taken me in a cell in my pajamas."

"We've had enough," Hearing Officer Harriet Wilson said. Her pink face seemed both sad and amused. She pressed the off button. "You'll hear from the board within thirty days," she called across the table to Mrs. Farragot. "In the meantime you can retain your license."

They all stood abruptly. Milford smiled openly at Officer Smothers, noting with considerable pleasure the man's hostile glare. Milford offered his hand. They barely touched palms. Then the lawyer took Mrs. Farragot's arm and steered her toward the door. Clarence Winfield came behind, tearing off his tie. Just before Winfield closed the door, Hearing Officer Harriet Wilson's voice came floating after them on the moist heat of the room: "Otis, tell the boys that in the future . . ."

Milford and Clarence Winfield waited by the bench while Mrs. Farragot rushed down the corridor toward the ladies' room. Winfield walked around, adjusting his trousers. Milford felt pleased with himself. He had taken command of a chaotic situation and forced it to a logical outcome. Absently, he followed Clarence Winfield over to the water fountain and waited while Winfield refreshed himself. "This meant a lot to her," Milford observed.

Winfield kept a stiff thumb on the metal button. The cold water splashed the side of his face as he turned his face upward and nodded agreement.

"All this sweat over one freak accident." Milford observed.

"Yeah," Winfield said. He straightened and wiped his face with the red silk handkerchief. "Many's the time I've told Miss Mary about that drinking."

"What's a beer on a hot night," Milford said, bending to drink.

Clarence Winfield chuckled. "Man, Miss Mary don't drink no *beer!*" He leaned close to Milford's ear. "She don't drink nothing but Maker's Mark."[1] He laughed again. "I thought you *knowed* that."

Turning his head, Milford saw Mrs. Farragot coming up the hall. Her blue dress swished gaily. It seemed to him that she was strutting. He observed for certain that she was smiling broadly, not unlike the picture of her next to Sweet Willie on the coffee table in her home.

Clarence Winfield nudged him, causing the cold water to splash into his eyes. "Don't you pay it no mind," Winfield was saying. "Between the two of us, why we ought to be able to straighten her out."

1975

1. Fashionable brand of bourbon whisky.

AMUS MOR
b. 1949?

One of the great enigmas of modern African American art, Amus Mor was a kind of spectral presence in the Black Arts movement, central to its aesthetic principles and achievement, yet peripheral to its recorded history. Little interested in publishing or preserving his works in textual form, Mor nevertheless imprinted himself in the consciousness of the era's titanic figures (such as Larry Neal and Amiri Baraka), who found in the riveting oral renderings of his densely textured, formally innovative poems an inspirational guide to the performative ethos of the "new wave" poetic practice. As Baraka once wrote, Mor was "missing in action," but the action left its traces upon the consciousness of his era's major authors and thinkers, for as Baraka went on to say, Mor "excited our whole generation with [his] use of The Music and the mytho-biographical narrative of person and place."

Born David Moore, Mor was an almost legendary figure in the dynamic Black Arts scene of Chicago's South Side in the mid-1960s, famous as much for his prodigious learning as for performing his poetry with a uniquely compelling repertoire of vocalizations translated from black vernacular forms such as the dozens, toasts, and the electrically sprung syncopations of bebop scatting. While he was occasionally sighted within the new organizations that emerged from Chicago's Black Arts effervescence (such as the Association for the Advancement of Creative Musicians and the Organization of Black American Culture), his fugitive spirit couldn't be held for long by any single group or cadre. Similarly, after a stint of teaching at Prairie State Junior College in Chicago Heights and at the University of Massachusetts, he left teaching altogether, having "decided that there was little possible relevant work that can be done inside the 'system.'" Appearing occasionally on recordings that combined avant-garde jazz musicians with Black Arts poets, such as Muhal Richard Abram's *Levels and Degrees of Light* (1967) and Woodie King's *Black Spirits: A Festival of New Black Poets in America* (1972), Mor has continued to remain outside the system of literary history that accounts for the presence of poems in anthologies, classrooms, and even the work of later poets.

Yet in poems such as "The Bird Song," "The Coming of John," and "We Are the Hip Men," Mor makes his claim as a creative force utterly integral to the Black Arts sensibility. These works crackle with implications that feel too volatile for the page, though the precision of his craft is evident in the way patterns of words and themes can be threaded across the page by our eyes, in visual imitation of their inflection by the strong, well-controlled voice that can be heard on Mor's recordings. In these scattered remnants of a lost-found poetic master, we find evidence of a figure who remains (to cite Baraka again) "an awesome example of the artistic and political power of the Black Arts Movement."

Poem to the Hip[1] Generation

(Who are we? Where are we going? What are we here for?)[2]

david dug genesis[3]
    did not dream
        heard the electric storm
           that was his intro
over the roof tops of grand blvd[4]   5
    in the soup line's hey-day[5]
        that lone wall of green
        and it must have been a kitchenette[6] april's
        holy week
                with a man before him   10
    fetus to a nation's first step
        he was david

he was ageless on that birth
    with its strangle-hold on the infinite
8 lb Louis or lion   15
    on the welfare's tables[7]

---

1. Sophisticated; knowing (black vernacular).
2. Play on name of the 1897 painting "Where Do We Come From? What Are We? Where Are We Going?" by French artist Eugène Henri Paul Gauguin (1848–1903); created at a time of great personal crisis, Gauguin's work depicts women at various stages of life pondering the fate of human existence.
3. Taken as slang, "dug" means appreciated or understood. Taken as Standard English, the line offers an allusion to the Jewish folktale of King David's inadvertently digging up the *Eben Sheti-yyah* ("foundation stone" in Hebrew) around which God built the earth, and which also served as the pedestal for the Ark of the Covenant (containing the stone tablets on which the Ten Commandments were inscribed). Notably, Mor's given name was David.
4. Grand Boulevard on Chicago's South Side, the heart of Chicago's African American population between the 1920s and 1940s.
5. I.e., the Great Depression during the decade preceding World War II, when large numbers of unemployed and their families stood in line for free meals.
6. Small apartment in mid-20th-century urban African American communities; African American author Richard Wright (1908–1960) called kitchenettes "our prison, our death sentence without trial."
7. I.e., the registry of people on public assistance.

live a decade's spell
    until that day
anno domino[8] decade
    and two years from explosion[9]   20

the home runs on the grass
    set sail in a trunk
        when the rains came to the backs of the project[1]
    units
    fred harris and the 12 kings blew gage[2] in a open   25
      truck
and black nat sang of america majic boy[3]
    so soon he was into the academy
of Lester the president[4]

deeyoodaaadayodeedaadeedaaa   30
waayoobeeyoudaadooyoodeedaa
weyouudeeyoodaa[5]

who are we
where are we going
what are we here for   35
      dadadoodaaleedaa
      datundoodadeedaa
not targets of the kelly boys[6]
    with their twenty rifles
      snipers[7] across may st   40
    two years from harry trumans great sin
    looking at the stone carvings on the buildings
under the ivy
      the wood lattices
      and the pidgeon stool on the window ledges   45
    we set men of tongues
and when they asked of us
    "will ford what are you doing in the lavatory this hour
on my period"
    and we answered them   50
    "am smoking some shit"
    those tricks[8] thought we spoke of dung
    and so walked away saying

---

8. I.e., *anno domini*, "year of our Lord" (Latin), abbreviated A.D.
9. I.e., 1943, two years before the U.S. atomic bombings of the Japanese cities of Hiroshima and Nagasaki, what the poem will later call "harry trumans great sin," referring to the decision of President Harry S. Truman (1884–1972) to use atomic weapons to end the Pacific campaign of World War II.
1. Public housing, usually large apartment buildings.
2. Smoked marijuana. "12 kings": Chicago street gang in the 1940s.
3. Reference to the song "Nature Boy," made famous by African American singer Nat King Cole (born Nathaniel Adams Coles, 1919–1965), which contains the lines, "And then one day / a magic day / he passed my way. . . ."

4. I.e., jazz saxophonist Lester Young (1909–1959), nicknamed "Prez" (for President of Tenor Saxophone); Young created his own slang language (such as "bread" for money) that he used with friends while observing which music critics "got it," and which didn't.
5. Mor "transcribes" here, in the style of vocal improvisation called "scat singing," Lester Young's 1944 solo on the composition "These Foolish Things."
6. I.e., Chicago police, under the direction of Mayor Edward Joseph Kelly (1876–1950).
7. The sniper rifle used by law enforcement was made standard in January 1943, "two years from harry trumans sin."
8. Prostitutes (derogatory slang term for women in general).

"we'll have none of that kind of language
                        here"   55
we copped[9] and knew
              we slept brown and frizzly headed
         against the base of test tubes
and they scolded
              "what are you doing sleep in my classroom   60
         wake up ford or get out"
but we didn't care
                   "cool" we answered
              and they thinking we spoke of the windows drafts
         walked away stiffly   65
    like the cinema monsters they almost were
         with their white smocks graying

we knocked the squares[1] they were
         stood hip in their forum
              ran hip in their bungalowed streets   70
         wrapped our girlfriends in our bears
    juiced[2] and were warm
         in these basements of 49
              we were always sister america
         beside you   75
              thats where i want to be forever
         i left my soullove in the river waiting for a helping
                   hand
         we are the hip men
         we are here to conquer   80
         we are going to heaven
         and hell shall happen to states of their bodies
AS IT WAS IN THE BEGINNING
AS IT WAS IN THE BEGINNING AND EVER SHALL BE WORLD
         WITH END AMEN[3]   85

         then pat was walking in that fine suede coat
    that francis turned her onto
         walking in white bucks[4]
              and a necks print scarf
    and we heard who we really were   90
         that saturday
under the shadows of el grids[5]
with six tray[6] under construction
         the men pulling up the green hornets tracks
    and the people of saturday getting coloreder   95
              as we went west
         into the furtile crescent[7]

9. Took drugs.
1. Conventional or "un-hip" people (black slang).
2. High on drugs or alcohol.
3. From Gloria Patri, a Christian statement of praise to God; translated from Latin, it reads, "Glory be to the Father, and to the Son, and to the Holy Spirit; as it was in the beginning, is now, and ever shall be, world without end. Amen."
4. Deerskin shoes, here symbolically "un-hip."
5. Refers to Chicago's public transportation sys-

tem known as the "El" or elevated railway.
6. I.e., the Sixty-Third Street train stop, then the boundary of Chicago's South Side black neighborhood.
7. Historically, a Middle Eastern region encompassing Ancient Egypt and Mesopotamia that spawned several early civilizations, "the fertile crescent" refers here to the African American neighborhoods of Chicago's South Side.

ingleside drexel maryland[8]
we dug our messiah and knew him that day
   in bright sun   100

and he shall come clouded in veils seen by none but a child[9]
   on the records speaker
     above little bruces shop
   dwee doot a leet boy dwee dootalee bop
       dweedootaleebaoohbaa[1]   105
bird sang massiahic
   clear at last
     doo yee dee daa
      there were objects of the late forties on the streets
  the buick with the dyna flow[2] holes   110
wopdaaaeeeeyaalaaadeebop
and i looked at the cashmere sweater

   with the stomachs hole
     and realized that i wouldnt be
     a 19 year old fat failure fullback   115
  and we being whom we were
    should never have said in english
"white pot   dark pot   mus i tell"
"bordeau   burgandy   mums baby"
"pernod[3] anyone"   120

so the songs led us
"hit that jive jack"[4]
led us
"voot nay on the voutnay"
   and we spoke in those years saying   125
"the ghost acapulco gold"[5]
"donde esta la mote"[6]
"bennydexiesaggie"
"morph man meth man"[7]
"knick and we trip"[8]   130
"Meth monster"
   and we laughed
   now we were so intelligent we spoke saying
"dialotte diaxoxen demarol"[9]
"crystal"[1] we had learned to say   135

8. Chicago streets leading to 63rd Street East, the end of the green line of the "El"; "green hornet": radio, television, and comic book vigilante hero of the 1930s–1960s.
9. Cf. Revelation 1.7: "Behold, he cometh with clouds; and every eye shall see him, and they also which pierced him: and all kindreds of the earth shall wail because of him."
1. Mor's scatting "transcribes" here and in the following lines the solo of jazz saxophonist Charlie "Bird" Parker (1920–1955) on the 1946 composition "Ornithology."
2. In 1947, Buick automobiles introduced an automatic transmission called the Dynaflow.
3. Anise-flavored liquor; "bordeau, burgandy, mums": French wines (Bordeaux, Burgundy, Mumms).
4. 1941 song by Nat King Cole.
5. Potent form of Mexican marijuana.
6. "Where is the *mote* [or black *mote*: honey-laced marijuana] (Spanish).
7. "Benny . . . meth": slang terms for various kinds of amphetamines (drugs).
8. Become intoxicated on drugs; "Knick": "knick knocking," the compulsive jerky movements suffered by methamphetamine addicts.
9. Pain-relieving drugs (or analgesics).
1. I.e., crystal meth (slang for methamphetamine).

and we were so religious
we repeated the alphabet
and so courageous
we took on the magic dragon[2]
then allah came over filthy processed streets   140
and layed outside the white boys window
he wasn't long for doom
and pointed the stranger his buildings of gold
then we were with malady in their infirmarys
they wrote stelezine prolixin[3] anti depressent   145
like dead potato plants we were drug
and they said
"six hun-zred liquid scorzine or hydro"[4]
the right said
"choke that basterd out"   150
but we spit at them
in the prisons our mothers loved
till our eyes gave blood
when they wrote electricity[5]
and we said   155
"No god" at last
danced like snow flake[6]
even said
"thank yo boss"
and took to the alleys   160
how could they know we had won it in our mecca[7]
now we have forgotten
the hypo points on reel cable tables[8] in san francisco
forgotten when we were super hip
and said   165
"lemme snort peter quill"[9]
and now there is a greenback disaster[1] almost here
and we have walked the south side in blue fezes[2]
like the muslims we are always
and if you hear us coming   170
but you never will[3]
until we 'make you out of stone'
this love
and if you hear us coming
baadaapbaadeebeeeyaadaa daaadaaatdaadeedeeeyaadaa   175
doobaaaooodaapdoooyadaa deedoopdaadeeedoooyabaaaa
AS IT WAS IN THE BEGINNING

---

2. I.e., marijuana.
3. I.e., anti-psychotic drug used in treatment of schizophrenia (as is Stelazine).
4. I.e., hydrocodone, an opioid derived from codeine.
5. I.e., electroconvulsive therapy, applied to psychiatric patients usually to treat depression or mania; the use of this technique in the United States peaked in the 1940s.
6. Fred "Snowflake" Toones (1906–1962), Hollywood film actor whose roles deployed the stereotyping conventions of minstrelsy.
7. Islamic pilgrimage destination, or generally the central place for a group or activity.

8. Tables made from large spools made to hold cables that haul cable cars up and down the inclines of San Francisco. "Hypo points": hypodermic syringe needles.
9. PCP ("Peter") or heroin ("quill"), which can both be snorted; Peter Quill was also the name of a radio detective series in the early 1940s whose eponymous hero was a scientific genius.
1. Economic crisis ("greenback": dollar bill).
2. Cone-shaped, flat-crowned, brimless hats commonly worn especially by men in the Middle East.
3. "If you hear us . . . never will": black revolutionary slogan of the 1960s.

AS IT WAS IN THE BEGINNING AND EVER SHALL BE WORLD
WITHOUT END AMEN

we are the hipmen   180
going into sun
stand up against us
mister gog[4] youre done
where are we going
into the sky   185
halt our boogie[5]
and a continent shy
we are the hipmen
singing like black doves
why were we sent here   190
only to love

1972

4. Gog and Magog are scriptural names, often used for the satanic enemies of God's people in apocalyptic texts (e.g., Ezekiel and Revelation).

5. Departure (after the jazz form boogie-woogie, and the energetic dance it spawned).

JAMES T. STEWART
?–1996

Painter, musician, poet, and cultural theorist, James T. Stewart exerted a powerful influence on the more visible architects of the Black Arts movement such as Larry Neal and Amiri Baraka. Through a series of essays seeking to define the philosophical basis of a "black revolutionary" vision, Stewart articulated the place of art in a post-civil-rights program of cultural transformation that would be at once analytical and soulful, experimental and populist. Though he gradually receded from view as others became more prominent advocates for Black Arts ideologies and institutions, Stewart's ideas were critical to the cogency of the movement's presiding aspirations, and he remained a vital force as mentor to generations of emerging black artists within Philadelphia's African American avant-garde culture.

Having immersed himself in radical thought while serving in the Air Force near Boston in the late 1940s, Stewart returned to his native Philadelphia in the late 1950s, where he played in the experimental "free form" jazz scene being defined by John Coltrane and, most importantly, participated in discussions among young black intellectuals and activists such as Neal, Charles Fuller, Verta Mae Grosvenor, and Maybelle Moor, who had formed a collective called Muntu. Named after German historian Janheinz Jahn's influential book *Muntu: The New African Culture*, the Muntu group developed a form of black nationalism that fused postcolonial politics, pan-African spiritualism, vernacular cultural resources, and revolutionary intention. As a simultaneously visual, musical, and literary practitioner, Stewart lent special expertise to this enterprise, especially insofar as Neal envisioned a new movement in which cultural and political revolution continuously challenged and fueled one another, moving the black community to ever-more powerful forms of self-realization. Stewart's work was among the earliest Black Arts speculations to give this vision conceptual depth as well as historical particularity.

"The Development of the Black Revolutionary Artist" opened Baraka and Neal's groundbreaking anthology *Black Fire* (1968), which assembled many of the most creative radical black poets and intellectuals of the era. Notwithstanding its cool scholarly tone and painstaking discursive craft, it took on the force of a manifesto, enjoying a consequential place within subsequent efforts to forge a "black aesthetic" for the Black Arts movement. With a lucidity that likewise defined Stewart's musical and artistic work, the essay sets forth the argument not only for a distinctive form of black expression, but more importantly for an identifiable sensibility underlying the cross-cultural experiences of non-white peoples. Thus, Stewart's "revolutionary artist" does not so much make as recover the elemental power of transformative creativity, which properly lies in the very community that the artist aims to help realize in its full potentiality.

The Development of the Black Revolutionary Artist

Cosmology is that branch of physics that studies the universe. It then proceeds to make certain assumptions, and from these, construct "models." If the model corresponds to reality, and certain factors are predictable, then it can be presumed to substantiate the observable phenomena in the universe. This essay is an attempt to construct a model: a particular way of looking at the world. This is necessary because existing white paradigms or models do not correspond to the realities of black existence. It is imperative that we construct models with different basic assumptions.

The dilemma of the "negro" artist is that he makes assumptions based on the wrong models. He makes assumptions based on white models. These assumptions are not only wrong, they are even antithetical to his existence. The black artist must construct models which correspond to his own reality. The models must be non-white. Our models must be consistent with a black style, our natural aesthetic styles, and our moral and spiritual styles. In doing so, we will be merely following the natural demands of our culture. These demands are suppressed in the larger (white) culture, but, nonetheless, are found in our music and in our spiritual and moral philosophy. Particularly in music, which happens to be the purest expression of the black man in America.

In Jahn Janheinz's *Muntu*,[1] he tells us about temples made of mud that vanish in the rainy seasons and are erected elsewhere. They are never made of much sturdier material. The buildings and the statues in them are always made of mud. And when the rains come the buildings and the statues are washed away. Likewise, most of the great Japanese artists of the eighteenth and nineteenth centuries did their exquisite drawings on rice paper with black ink and spit. These were then reproduced by master engravers on fragile newssheets that were distributed to the people for next to nothing. These sheets were often used for wrapping fish. They were a people's newssheet. Very much like the sheets circulated in our bars today.

My point is this: that in both of the examples just given, there is little concept of fixity. The work is fragile, destructible; in other words, there is a

---

1. German literary critic and historian Janheinz Jahn (1918–1973) influenced Black Arts movement theorists, principally through his books *Muntu: African Culture and the Western World* (1961) and *History of Neo-African Literature* (1966).

total disregard for the perpetuation of the product, the picture, the statue, and the temple. Is this ignorance? According to Western culture evaluations, we are led to believe so. The white researcher, the white scholar, would have us believe that he "rescues" these "valuable" pieces. He "saves" them from their creators, those "ignorant" colored peoples who would merely destroy them. Those people who do not know their value. What an audacious presumption!

The fact is that *these* people did know their value. But the premises and values of their creation are of another order, of another cosmology, constructed in terms agreeing with their own particular models of existence. Perpetuation, as the white culture understands it, simply does not exist in the black culture. We know, all non-whites know, that man can not create *a* forever; but he can create forever. But he can only create if he creates as change. Creation is itself perpetuation and change is being.

In this dialectical apprehension of reality it is the act of creation of a work as it comes into existence that is its only being. The operation of art is dialectical. Art goes. Art is not fixed. Art can not be fixed. Art is change, like music, poetry and writing are, when conceived. They must move (swing).[2] Not necessarily as physical properties, as music and poetry do; but intrinsically, by their very nature. But they must go spiritually, noumenally.[3] This is what makes those mud temples in Nigeria go. Those prints in Japan. This is what makes black culture go.

All white Western art forms, up to and including those of this century, were matrixed.[4] They all had a womb, the germinative idea out of which the work evolved, or as in the tactile forms (sculpture and painting, for instance), unifying factors that welded the work together, e.g., the plot of a play, the theme of a musical composition, and the figure. The trend in contemporary white forms is toward the elimination of the matrix, in the play "happenings,"[5] and in music, aleatory or random techniques. All of these are influenced by Eastern traditions. It is curious and sometimes amusing to see the directions that these forms take.

The music that black people in this country created was matrixed to some degree; but it was largely improvisational also, and that aspect of it was non-matrixed. And the most meaningful music being created today is non-matrixed. The music of Ornette Coleman.[6]

The sense in which "revolutionary" is understood is that a revolutionary is against the established order, regime, or culture. The bourgeoisie calls him a revolutionary because he threatens the established way of life—things as they are. They can not accept change, though change is inevitable. The revolutionary understands change. Change is what it is all about. He is not a revolutionary to his people, to his compatriots, to his comrades. He is, instead, a brother. He is a son. She is a sister, a daughter.

The dialectical method is the best instrument we have for comprehending physical and spiritual phenomena. It is the essential nature of being, existence; it is the property of being and the "feel" of being; it is the implicit *sense*

---

2. Move rhythmically (derived from swing music, a form of jazz developed in the 1930s).
3. I.e., posited or known independent of sense perception.
4. Characterized by bounded structure.
5. Term coined by American conceptual artist Allan Kaprow (1927–2006) to denote a perfor-

mance art form developed in the early 1960s that can arise anywhere, involving chance (or "aleatory") events and improvised audience participation.
6. African American jazz saxophonist and composer known for innovations in the 1960s "free jazz movement" (b. 1930).

of it. This sense, black people have. And the revolutionary artist must understand this sense of reality, this philosophy of reality which exists in all non-white cultures. We need our own conventions, a convention of procedural elements, a kind of stylization, a sort of insistency which leads inevitably to a certain kind of methodology—a methodology affirmed by the spirit.

That spirit is black.

That spirit is non-white.

That spirit is patois.[7]

That spirit is Samba.[8]

Voodoo.[9]

The black Baptist church in the South.

We are, in essence, the ingredients that will create the future. For this reason, we are misfits, estranged from the white cultural present. This is our position as black artists in these times. Historically and sociologically we are the rejected. Therefore, we must know that we are the building stones for the New Era. In our movement toward the future, "ineptitude" and "unfitness" will be an aspect of what we do. These are the words of the established order—the middle-class value judgments. We must turn these values in on themselves. Turn them inside out and make ineptitude and unfitness desirable, even mandatory. We must even, ultimately, be estranged from the dominant culture. This estrangement must be nurtured in order to generate and energize our black artists. This means that he can not be "successful" in any sense that has meaning in white critical evaluations. Nor can his work ever be called "good" in any context or meaning that could make sense to that traditional critique.

Revolution is fluidity. What are the criteria in times of social change? Whose criteria are they, in the first place? Are they ours or the oppressors'? If being is change, and the sense of change is the time of change—and what is, is about to end, or is over—where are the criteria?

History qualifies us to have this view. Not as some philosophical concept acting out of matter and movement—but as being. So, though the word "dialectic" is used, the meaning and sense of it more than the word, or what the word means, stand as postulated experience. Nothing can be postulated without fixing it in time—standing it still, so to speak. It can not be done. The white Westerner was on his way toward understanding this when he rejected the postulated systems of his philosophies; when he discarded methodology in favor of what has come to be called existentialism.[1] But inevitably, he postulated existence; or at least, it was attempted. Therefore, existentialism got hung up in just the same way as the philosophical systems from which it has extricated itself.

But we need not be bothered with that. We need merely to see how it fits; how the word *dialectic* fits; what change means; and what fluidity, movement and revolution mean. The purpose of writing is to enforce the sense we have of the future. The purpose of writing is to enforce the sense we have of responsibility—the responsibility of understanding our roles in the shaping of a new world. After all, experience is development; and development is destruction. The great Indian thinkers had this figured out centu-

7. Nonstandard language, used especially to refer to vernacular forms of English spoken in the Caribbean.
8. An Afro-Brazilian dance and musical genre.
9. A syncretic religion practiced chiefly in Haiti and Louisiana.
1. A philosophical account of human experience emphasizing the individual as solely responsible for giving meaning to life and for living "authentically."

ries ago. That is why, in the Hindu religion, the god Siva appears—Siva, the god of destruction.

All history is "tailored" to fit the needs of the particular people who write it. Thus, one of our "negro" writers failed to understand the historicity of the Nation of Islam.[2] He failed to understand. This was because his assumptions were based on white models and on a self-conscious "objectivity." This is the plight of the "negro" man of letters, the negro intellectual who needs to demonstrate a so-called academic impartiality to the white establishment.

Now, on the other hand, a dialectical interpretation of revolutionary black development rooted in the *Western* dialectic also will not do. However, inherent in the Western dialectical approach is the idea of imperceptible and gradual quantitative change; changes which give rise to a new state. This approach has also illustrated that there are no immutable social systems or eternal principles; and that there is only the inherency in things of contradictions—of opposing tendencies. It has also illustrated that the role of the "science of history"[3] is to help bring about a fruition of new aggregates. These were all good and canonical to the kind of dialectics that came out of Europe in the nineteenth century.

But contemporary art is rooted in a European convention. The standards whereby its products are judged are European. However, this is merely *one* convention. Black culture implies, indeed engenders, for the black artist another order, another way of looking at things. It is apparent in the music of Giuseppe Logan,[4] for example, that the references are not white or European. But it is jazz and it is firmly rooted in the experiences of black individuals in this country. These references are found also in the work of John Coltrane, Ornette Coleman, Grachan Moncur and Milford Graves.[5]

A revolutionary art is being expressed today. The anguish and aimlessness that attended our great artists of the 'forties and 'fifties and which drove most of them to early graves, to dissipation and dissolution, is over. Misguided by white cultural references (the models the culture set for its individuals), and the incongruity of these models with black reality, men like Bird[6] were driven to willful self-destruction. There was no program. And the reality-model was incongruous. It was a white reality-model. If Bird had had a black reality-model, it might have been different. But though Parker knew of the new development in the black culture, even helped to ferment it, he was hung up in an incompatible situation. They were contradictions both monstrous and unbelievable. They were contradictions about the nature of black and white culture, and what that had to mean to the black individual in this society. In Bird's case, there was a dichotomy between his genius and the society. But, that he couldn't find the adequate model of being was the tragic part of the whole thing. Otherwise, things could have been more meaningful and worthwhile.

2. A syncretic African American religion founded in Detroit by Wallace D. Fard Muhammad (1893–?) in 1930. "One of our 'negro' writers . . .": reference to C. Eric Lincoln (1924–2000), African American historian of religion and author of *Black Muslims in America* (1961).
3. Historiography, the study of the methodology and development of history as an academic discipline, began to become popular in the late 19th century.

4. Jazz pianist and percussionist active in the free jazz movement (b. 1935).
5. Experimental jazz percussionist (b. 1941); John Coltrane: avant-garde jazz saxophonist (1926–1967); Grachan Moncur: jazz trombonist active in the free jazz movement (b. 1937).
6. Charlie "Bird" Parker, jazz saxophonist associated with the bebop style of the 1940s (1920–1955).

The most persistent feature of all existence is change. In other words, it is this property which is a part of everything which exists in the world. As being, the world is change. And it is this very property that the white West denies. The West denies change, defies change . . . resists change. But change is the basic nature of everything that is. Society is. Culture is. Every-thing that is—in society—its people and their manner of being, and the way in which they make a living. But mainly the modes of what is material, and how the material is produced. What it looks like and what it means to those who produce it and those who accept it. And this is how philosophy, art, morality and certain other things are established. But all established things are temporary, and the nature of being is, like music, changing.

Art can not apologize out of existence the philosophical ethical position of the artist. After all, the artist is a man in society, and his social attitudes are just as relevant to his art as his aesthetic position. However, the white Western aesthetics is predicated on the idea of separating one from the other—a man's art from his actions. It is this duality that is the most distin-guishable feature of Western values.

Music is a social activity. Jazz music, in particular, is a social activity, participated in by artists collectively. Within a formal context or procedure, jazz affords the participants a collective form for individual group develop-ment in a way white musical forms never did. The symphony, for instance, is a dictatorship. There is a rigidity of form and craft-practice—a virtual enslavement of the individual to the autocratic conductor. Music is a social activity in a sense that writing, painting and other arts can never be. Music is made with another. It is indulged in with others. It is the most social of the art forms except, say, architecture. But music possesses, in its essence, a property none of the other forms possesses. This property of music is its ontological[7] procedures—the nature of which is dialectical. In other words, music possesses properties of being that come closest to the condition of life, of existence. And, in that sense, I say its procedures are ontological— which doesn't mean a thing, but that music comes closest to being. This is why music teaches. This is what music teaches.

The point of the whole thing is that we must emancipate our minds from Western values and standards. We must rid our minds of these values. Say-ing so will not be enough. We must try to shape the thinking of our people. We must goad our people by every means, remembering as Ossie Davis[8] stated: that the task of the Negro (sic, black) writer is revolutionary by defi-nition.[9] He must view his role vis-à-vis white Western civilization, and from this starting point in his estrangement begin to make new definitions founded on his own culture—on definite black values.

1968

---

7. Relating to being or existence.
8. African American actor, director, author, and social activist (born Raiford Chatman Davis, 1917–2005).

9. Quoted from Davis's contribution to a forum on "The Task of the Negro Writer as Artist" pub-lished in Negro Digest in April 1965.

The Contemporary Period

The fabled awakening in Harlem during the 1920s notwithstanding, one could argue that the true African American renaissance occurred during the last quarter of the twentieth century. The impact of African American artistic production on American and world culture had never been greater: in film and television, which made African American performers household names; in music, with the explosion of rap and gospel and the inclusion of jazz programming as a constituent of prestigious cultural institutions such as Carnegie Hall and Lincoln Center; in theater, where musicals and dramas by African Americans became staples on and off Broadway; and in the visual arts, as museums and private collectors purchased works by African American painters and sculptors in increasing numbers. Never before had so much distinguished writing been produced by black Americans. Toni Morrison became the first African American Nobel laureate in literature in 1993, by which time her novels had won a sheaf of awards as well as a secure place in the American literary canon. In 1990, August Wilson's *The Piano Lesson* won the playwright a second Pulitzer Prize for drama. Before his death in 2005, he completed a cycle of ten plays—one for each decade—that depicts his version of the variegated African American experience of the twentieth century. In sharp contrast to earlier periods when only one or two black writers could rise to prominence at a time, Morrison and Wilson did not stand alone. From Maya Angelou in autobiography to Pulitzer Prize–winners Rita Dove, Yusef Komunyakaa, Tracy K. Smith, and Natasha Trethewey in poetry to Charles Johnson and

President Barack Obama's inauguration in 2009, uniting generations of black Americans across class, region, and gender divides, affirmed feelings of national belonging and renewed hopes in the struggle for racial equality.

John Edgar Wideman in fiction to Ntozake Shange and Suzan-Lori Parks in theater to Alice Walker in the essay, dozens of writers garnered critical acclaim, large audiences, or both. The institutionalization of African American literature as a subject of academic inquiry ensured that these writers and their readers were keenly aware of the tradition in which they worked. Whether the writers embraced the tradition or resisted its premises, their work extended its contours.

Critical trends that distinguished African American literature during the contemporary period are (1) the acknowledgment of the multiplicity of African American identities; (2) a renewed interest in history, as writers imagine the psychological and spiritual lives of African Americans during slavery and segregation; (3) the emergence of a community of black women writing; (4) a continuing exploration of music and other forms of vernacular culture as springboards for literary innovation and theoretical analysis; (5) an openness to speculative or science fiction to inform poetry and prose; and (6) the influence of African American literary scholarship.

MOVEMENT LEGACIES

The historical conditions that enabled this literary and cultural renaissance were set in motion by the civil rights movement in the 1950s and 1960s. The movement initiated a national conversation about racism, labeling it as a moral wrong and identifying those who took action against it as moral agents. As the nightly television news documented, African Americans were in the vanguard of the movement, and their sense of who they were was forever changed. At the same time that they saw in themselves and their children the capacity for moral heroism, they identified with Africans who were waging a similar struggle against colonialism in Ghana, Nigeria, and Kenya. Black American leaders, including Martin Luther King Jr., Malcolm X, and Whitney Young, traveled to Africa, and their reports from the continent strengthened the sense of connection that blacks in the United States felt with its people. The change in consciousness was accompanied by a change in material conditions. By agitating for opportunities for equal education, better jobs, and decent housing, the civil rights movement created a substantial middle class among black Americans that would in turn constitute an audience to which black writers could appeal.

By the late 1960s the Black Power and antiwar movements had taken hold, especially among blacks on college campuses. For the latter, the goal was no longer integration, but separatism. The Vietnam War, in which blacks served in much greater numbers than were proportionate to their percentage of the population, was another political flash point that radicalized a significant segment of the community. Some effects of these political movements on artistic production were immediate; others were long term and far reaching. Manifestoes of the Black Arts movement, the designation assumed by cultural workers allied with Black Power activists, insisted on art that was functional, collective, and committed to revolution and change. The prescriptiveness that resulted proved too constricting, and the dictates of the Black Arts movement were soon discarded. But the movement heralded a shift toward art that was for and about the black community.

This inward turn revealed communities that had never been monolithic. As the literature increasingly reflected, African American communities differed according to geography and region, class, and ethnicity. The most celebrated poetic voices of the 1960s spoke in the brisk accents of northern cities. But many African Americans lived in the South, spoke in the slower cadences of the region, and drew from the well of political experience that was the civil rights movement. The decade of the 1960s that Alice Walker depicts in her poems and essays differs markedly from that of Amiri Baraka. In the North, Midwest, and West, black people lived in small towns as often as in big cities. John Washington, the protagonist of David Bradley's novel *The Chaneysville Incident*, returns home to rural Pennsylvania; Morrison's titular protagonist Sula returns to the Bottom, the black neighborhood in a small fictional Ohio city, and characters in Sherley Anne Williams's "Tell Martha Not to Moan" inhabit the farm towns of California's San Joaquin Valley. As the literature reflected the regional diversity of black communities, it revealed an increasing class stratification as well. Educational and professional opportunities that became available in the wake of the civil rights movement widened the gap between the middle class and the poor. Writers explored the tensions that ensued and the divide that opened even between members of the same family. Wideman's *Brothers and Keepers* is a poignant case in point. Far from monolithic, the black community was ethnically diverse. Paule Marshall's 1959 novel, *Brown Girl, Brownstones*, was among the first to focus on a character's coming-of-age in a neighborhood of West Indian immigrants who live with, yet apart from, the southern-born black migrants who are their neighbors. The novel's "Bajan" (Barbadian) characters bring with them to Brooklyn, along with their dreams and aspirations, a new vernacular as well as a different sense of "home." *Brown Girl* was a harbinger. The progressive movements around issues of race led to the amendments to the Immigration and Nationality Act in 1965 and 1990, which, respectively, ended quotas based on nationality and increased the overall number of immigrants allowed into the United States each year. Significant demographic changes occurred in the black population. By the turn of the century, stories of immigrants of African descent from throughout the Caribbean as well as Africa and Europe confirmed the impossibility of identifying a unified black experience.

Although the women's movement is popularly identified with the white middle class, several of its most visionary voices belonged to African American women. Toni Cade Bambara, June Jordan, and Audre Lorde analyzed the inextricability of sexism and racism. They protested racism in the women's movement and sexism in the Black Power movement and challenged activists in both to see the common roots of their oppression. Addressing those African Americans, both men and women, who saw feminism as a diversion from the struggle against racial oppression, Lorde insisted: "Black women have particular and legitimate issues which affect our lives as Black women, and addressing those issues does not make us less Black." Black feminists argued that the simultaneous oppressions of race, gender, and class defined the lives of many African American women. Any strategy for liberation would have to take these interlocking factors into account.

The movement for gay rights was the last of the progressive causes spawned by the struggle for civil rights. It protested discrimination on the basis of sexual preference. Lorde and Jordan became leaders in this effort, as did Essex Hemphill and Samuel Delany. The movement claimed James Baldwin as a forefather, although Baldwin did not always claim the movement. Those who did claim it fought to be accepted as "black" among gays

In "The Louisiana Project" (2003), Carrie Mae Weems incorporates photographs, narrative, and video to represent what she calls "the footnotes of history" in a work commemorating the bicentennial of the Louisiana Purchase. Weems, like her literary peers, reimagines slavery in her work. Here dressed as an antebellum woman, she gazes on the expanse of a plantation.

and as "gay" among blacks. Like the feminist movement, the gay rights movement was highly controversial among African Americans. It served as yet another reminder that the differences among black Americans were by many measures as great as the differences between them and white Americans. Multiple threads make up the weave of contemporary African American life and literature.

DETOURS THROUGH THE PAST

As college students joined the protest movements of the 1960s and 1970s, they also fought for a more inclusive curriculum on campus. Black studies departments were established around the country. Historians examined the past from a black perspective, and their scholarship soon sparked writers' imaginations. Two works by historian John Blassingame are cases in point. While slavery is among the most frequently studied topics in U.S. historiography, few historians documented the slaves' point of view before Blassingame's *The Slave Community: Plantation Life in the Ante-Bellum South*

(1972). Most historians argued that inadequate documentation existed, a situation Blassingame began to correct with his massive anthology, *Slave Testimony* (1977). Literary scholars began teaching slave narratives, which many now consider the foundation of the African American literary tradition. Nathan Huggins published the first history of the Harlem Renaissance in 1971, initiating the still-ongoing study of that important chapter in literary history. Historian Gerda Lerner edited *Black Women in White America* (1973), which further revised the understanding of African Americans' roles in U.S. history as both the victims of oppression and the agents of change. Toni Morrison, then an editor at Random House, was the guiding force behind *The Black Book* (1974), a folk history in the form of a scrapbook that collected posters and patents, bills of sale, spirituals and blues, family photographs, formulas for conjure, and interpretations of dreams. Like the academic histories, it did not highlight the accomplishments of notable men and women; it recovered the experiences of heretofore anonymous folk. Literary anthologies such as Houston Baker's *Black Literature in America* (1971), Stephen Henderson's *Understanding the New Black Poetry: Black Speech and Black Music as Poetic References* (1972), and Mary Helen Washington's *Black-Eyed Susans: Classic Stories By and About Black Women* (1975) recuperated poetry and prose that pointed to the existence of a black literary tradition. Building on this tradition, novelists began to invent new versions of the past. Ernest Gaines wrote a novel in the form of a fictional autobiography, *The Autobiography of Miss Jane Pittman* (1971), that reached a large audience—especially after it was adapted into a television movie. Alex Haley's *Roots* (1976) was turned into a television mini-series that became the talk of the nation, as U.S. households tuned in nightly to watch the journey of one family from freedom in Africa to slavery in America to freedom in the United States. Whether history, criticism, or fiction, this work may be understood in terms that scholar Stuart Hall describes in "The Dialogics of Identity": "Identity is never finished. It moves into the future by way of a constructive detour of the past."

Slavery, a long chapter in the American past, galvanized the imaginations of black writers. While many earlier writers saw only shame in slavery, writers in the contemporary period have seen it as a way of understanding the present. From one perspective, slavery represents a wound in the psyche of present-day African Americans that has not yet healed; from another, slavery is the moral blot on the nation's soul that must be confronted and cleansed. Without question, the history of slavery contains dramatic stories of physical courage and spiritual survival. Consequently, writers imagined the interior lives of enslaved individuals, the ties that bound them as families and communities, and the acts of will that were required for resistance and survival. Among the notable examples are David Bradley's *The Chaneysville Incident* (1981), Octavia Butler's *Kindred* (1979), Charles Johnson's *Oxherding Tale* (1982) and *Middle Passage* (1989), Edward P. Jones's *The Known World* (2003), Morrison's *Song of Solomon* (1977) and *Beloved* (1987), Naylor's *Mama Day* (1988), Caryl Phillips's *Cambridge* (1991) and *Crossing the River* (1993), Ishmael Reed's *Flight to Canada* (1976), and Sherley Anne Williams's *Dessa Rose* (1986). Poets Jay Wright in *Death as History* (1967) and Rita Dove in *Thomas and Beulah* (1986) were similarly determined to cure what Morrison deemed the "national amnesia" around the history of slavery, a history that began for African Americans in 1619 and lasted 250 years. The stories they told were, of course, as different as the writers were from one another. Bradley wrote about the Underground Railroad in western Pennsylvania, while in *Beloved* Morrison's characters escape from slavery in Kentucky to "freedom" in Ohio. Gayl Jones imagined a plantation in Brazil, while characters in *Crossing the River* and *Dessa Rose* trekked across the United States, seeking freedom in the West. Edward P. Jones depicted a black slaveholder. Naylor invented an all-black community in the Sea Islands where the legacy of slavery was self sufficiency, while Johnson tested Enlightenment ideas of freedom and citizenship. In studies such as Orlando Patterson's *Slavery and Social Death* (1982) and Paul Gilroy's *The Black Atlantic* (1993), scholars confirmed the insights of these fictions when they began to perceive slavery as a central element in the development of modernity.

Detours through the past did not necessarily reach back to the nineteenth century. In the 1970s many African Americans lost faith in the dream of integration; others were concerned lest they be assimilated into the dominant society without understanding or appreciating the segregated communities which they were now being allowed to leave. Many writers followed the direction of Albert Murray "south to a very old place," as he titled his memoir. Upon returning to his hometown of Mobile, Alabama, Murray wrote, "[T]he neighborhood that was the center of the world as you first knew it had been razed, completely industrialized, and enclosed in a chain-link fence by the Scott Paper Towel Company." In *Train Whistle Guitar*, Murray reinvents that world in fiction. Angelou's memoir likewise revisits a depression-era South and re-creates both the dignity of women like her grandmother Mama Henderson and teacher Mrs. Flowers and the randomness of attacks on their hard-earned sense of themselves. Surely the most lyrical evocation of the communities that once nurtured the souls of black folk is the opening passage of *Sula*; tellingly, here the Bottom, a name that was once widely applied to the black sections of southern towns, is located in the Midwest:

> In that place, where they tore the nightshade and blackberry patches from their roots to make room for the Medallion City Golf Course, there was once a neighborhood. It stood in the hills above the valley town of Medallion and spread all the way to the river. It is called the suburbs now, but when black people lived there it was called the Bottom.

As it unfolds, the novel elegizes the impromptu ceremonies of everyday life, the sassy talk, and the raunchy humor that characterized life in the Bottom. But the perspective is never sentimental or nostalgic. Racism is an invisible yet pervasive and disfiguring presence.

THE COMMUNITY OF BLACK WOMEN WRITING

The emergence of what Hortense Spillers calls "the community of black women writing" is one of the hallmarks of the contemporary period. Events in 1970 signaled its arrival. *The Black Woman*, an anthology edited by Toni Cade Bambara, heralded an effort by black women to define themselves. Another impetus was the recuperation of literary precursors Jessie Fauset, Nella Larsen, and Zora Neale Hurston, whose classic volume of folklore *Mules and Men* was reprinted in 1970. At that time, Hurston remained, in her biographer Robert Hemenway's words, "one of the most significant

The Sisterhood. Vertamae Grosvenor, Alice Walker, Lori Sharpe, Toni Morrison, June Jordan, Nana Maynard, Ntozake Shange, and Audrey Edwards met informally in New York during the 1970s.

unread authors in America." Her work would soon reach hundreds of thousands of readers; it would provide a touchstone for the writing of a new generation as well. The year 1970 saw the publication of extraordinary first novels by Morrison (*The Bluest Eye*) and Walker (*The Third Life of Grange Copeland*). Powerfully written and deeply unsettling in their exploration of family violence, sexual oppression and abuse, and the corrosive effects of racism and poverty, these novels ran counter to the then prevailing mood of righteous anger and triumphant struggle. Angelou's *I Know Why the Caged Bird Sings* partook more in that mood, but at its dramatic center—as in Morrison's novel—was the rape of a girl. In a society ordered by hierarchies of power based on race, class, and gender, no one is more powerless, hence more vulnerable, than a poor black girl. In these texts such characters anchor the critique of social ideology.

In a sharp departure from many of their male precursors, Morrison, Walker, and their female contemporaries did not focus on the traumatic encounters of blacks and whites across the color line. The interracial conflicts at the heart of narratives by black male writers from Frederick Douglass to Ralph Ellison to Amiri Baraka did not take center stage. Racism remained a major concern. But for these writers, the most painful consequences of racism were played out in the most intimate relationships. Making hitherto private traumas public soon proved controversial. Women writers were accused of bashing black men and, worse, of being disloyal to the race. For example, Shange's *for colored girls who have considered suicide/when the rainbow is enuf,* a "choreopoem" that was clearly indebted to Baraka and the Black Arts movement for its poetic technique, became the object of controversy when it was staged on Broadway in 1977. Critics focused on the image of black male characters, none of whom appeared on stage, rather than the female characters whose stories were being told.

"What did it mean for a black woman to be an artist in our grandmother's time? In our great-grandmothers' day?" asks Walker in her classic essay "In Search of Our Mothers' Gardens," which offers a theory of black female creativity and defines a tradition of black women's art. Despite believing that the answer to her question is "cruel enough to stop the blood," Walker imagines generations of black women artists who released their creativity in song and the crafts of quilt making, baking, and gardening, which Walker reevaluates as art. The portrait Walker draws of her mother gardening is the portrait of an artist "ordering the universe in her personal conception of Beauty." Many writers share Walker's impulse to recuperate the artistic legacy of their foremothers: Paule Marshall pays homage to the "poets in the kitchen" whose linguistic creativity inspires her own, while Naylor endows her protagonist Mama Day, a midwife and conjure woman, with the ability to quilt, bake, and garden superlatively. In *Sula* Morrison creates the "magnificent" Eva Peace, a character whose will to order the universe according to her own personal conception is both beautiful and sinister.

THE *INNER* CITY

Black male writers turned inward as well. In his "Homewood" trilogy (*Hiding Place, Damballah,* and *Sent for You Yesterday*), John Edgar Wideman maps both the Pittsburgh neighborhood in which his characters have lived for generations and the psychological terrain that defines them as individuals and as members of an extended family. Telling the history of that family in the language in which they lived it and summoning the spirits of their ancestors through memories and dreams, Wideman writes fiction that is innovative in both content and form. All but one of August Wilson's plays are also set in Pittsburgh, and their textured representations of African American culture as it evolved through the twentieth century are at the core of Wilson's art. As he states, "[T]he field of manners and rituals of social intercourse—the music, speech, rhythms, eating habits, religious beliefs, gestures, notions of common sense, attitudes toward sex, concepts of beauty and justice, and the responses to pleasure and pain—have enabled [African Americans] to survive the loss of our political will and the disruption of our history." If Wilson's drama is grounded in the everyday expressions of African Americans, his often soaring monologues reveal the capaciousness of their concerns, their heroic aspirations, their moral triumphs and defeats. For example, *Joe Turner's Come and Gone,* set in 1911, recounts the experiences of migrants newly arrived in the city, alienated from its ways and ultimately hopeful that they can make a future there. By the 1980s, the period in which Wilson's *King Hedley II* is set, despair is pervasive: "the people wandering all over the place. They got lost. They don't even know the story of how they got from tit to tat." Of course, this is precisely the story Wilson's dramas tell.

THE 1980s AND 1990s

The despair in *King Hedley II* reflected the mood in much of urban black America during the 1980s. The protagonist's sense of himself may be royal, but the reality of his prospects as he tries to move from a career of petty crime to one of entrepreneurship is grim. Shrinking employment opportunities and rising rates of drug abuse and violence took their toll on inner city black neighborhoods during the Reagan years, a time when such problems were low on the national agenda. While Martin Luther King Jr.'s birthday was made a national holiday in 1986, most initiatives put forward by civil rights organizations were rejected. Rather than the guarantor of civil rights, the federal government began to be viewed as antagonistic to the civil rights agenda—particularly to programs of affirmative action. In response, Jesse Jackson waged vigorous campaigns for the Democratic presidential nomination in 1984 and 1988; neither was successful but both led to significant increases in the number of registered black voters. More African Americans than ever before won elective office on the local and state levels: in 1989 Douglas Wilder was elected governor of Virginia, the first black governor of a state since Reconstruction. Overwhelmingly, black voters supported Democratic candidates. But a small group of black conservatives, among them essayists Stanley Crouch and Shelby Steele, drew notice. In 1991 President George H. Bush nominated Clarence Thomas to the Supreme Court. The nomination, already intensely controversial, became even more so when law professor Anita Hill accused Thomas of sexual harassment. After televised hearings and the Senate vote, Justice Thomas took his seat.

The Thomas-Hill hearings initiated a series of media spectacles that focused on African Americans in the 1990s. In 1991 Rodney King was beaten by Los Angeles police officers after a high-speed chase. When, despite the existence of an incriminating videotape, the officers were acquitted of all charges, violence erupted in Los Angeles that resulted in thirty-eight deaths, four thousand arrests, and damage estimated at more than $500 million. In 1995, O. J. Simpson, a former professional football player and sports commentator, was tried for the murder of his ex-wife and another man. Gavel-to-gavel television coverage made the trial one of the most watched in history. Reaction to Simpson's acquittal divided substantially along racial lines, as most whites denounced the verdict and most blacks applauded it. Issues of police misconduct were raised in Simpson's defense, issues that were set in bold relief again in 1999, when New York City police officers killed an unarmed West African immigrant, Amadou Diallo.

Some of the idealistic fervor of the 1960s was reignited, as the struggle against apartheid in South Africa gained momentum during the 1980s. On college campuses, in churches, in corporations, and in Congress, African Americans were in the forefront of the movement for sanctions against the apartheid regime. When Nelson Mandela toured the United States in 1990, after his release from twenty-seven years in prison, he received a hero's welcome. For blacks, his visit was the culmination of a growing identification, both political and cultural, with Africa. Human rights activists in the United States had long made common cause with anticolonialist activists. From the 1960s onward, black popular culture in this country assimilated African and pseudo-African elements, including names, hairstyles, dress, and the celebration of Kwanzaa, a holiday created in the United States by Ron Karenga. In the academy, Molefi Asante formulated the ideology of Afrocentrism, which called for scholarship based on Africa as the center of civilization. Although his ideas were not widely accepted by other scholars, Asante won a popular following.

Writers across a broad spectrum incorporated African images and belief systems into their work. Examples include Tina McElroy's *Baby of the Family*, Marshall's *Praisesong for the Widow*, Morrison's *Beloved*, Shange's *Sassafrass, Cypress, & Indigo*, Wideman's *Damballah*, and Wilson's *Joe Turner's Come and Gone*. African cosmologies and mythologies inform Harryette Mullen's poetry. The figure of the "ancestor" in writing by Lucille Clifton, Marshall, Morrison, and Naylor reflects a reconnection with African spiritual and cultural rituals. Johnson in *Middle Passage* and Walker in *The Color Purple* and *Possessing the Secret of Joy* invent African settings for their fiction. Many African American writers cite the influence on their work of African writers, notably Chinua Achebe, Ama Ata Aidoo, Ayi Kweh Armah, Buchi Emecheta, Bessie Head, Camara Laye, Ngugi wa Thiong'o, Sembene Ousmane, Flora Nwapa, and Wole Soyinka, the first African writer to receive the Nobel Prize for literature.

In *The Two Generations* (1991), Jamaican-born Albert Chong, an artist of African and Chinese descent, shows the history of migration and immigration and the roots tying diasporic subjects to the Caribbean with his inclusion of the passport, necklace, and tools.

REMAPPING AFRICAN AMERICAN LITERARY TERRAIN

A consciousness grew among some African Americans who saw themselves both as citizens of the United States and as members of a transnational community of people of African descent. This consciousness reflected both the increasing influence of African and Afro-Caribbean writers on the development of African American literature and the fact that a number of black writers in the United States were themselves immigrants. Jamaica Kincaid, who came to the United States from Antigua, "the small place" to which she often returns in her writing, is among the best known, although she resists being identified with any school. Kincaid's critique of colonialism is striking, as is her representation of the complicated relationship between mothers and daughters under a colonialist regime. Edwidge Danticat's characters fly back and forth between Haiti and Brooklyn in a circuit of travel that is typical of twenty-first-century immigrants. In its themes and images, Danticat's work, like Kincaid's, often resonates as well with that of the community of black women writing in the United States. Born in St. Kitts, in the British West Indies, and raised in the United Kingdom, Caryl Phillips, who now lives part of the time in New York City, has reimagined the history of Africans throughout the diaspora in his novels. Whether the Barbadian characters that Hilton Als draws in *The Women,* or the settings that shift between the United States and Jamaica in Michelle Cliff's fiction, or the interfacing of Afro-Caribbean and Asian-Caribbean cultures in Patricia Powell's novel *The Pagoda,* the terrain of African American literature is being re-mapped.

A NEW CENTURY

9/11 became the immediately recognizable shorthand for the terrorist attacks on September 11, 2001, that destroyed the World Trade Center in New York City, damaged the U.S. Pentagon in Washington, D.C., and downed a passenger plane in rural Pennsylvania. More than three thousand people were killed in the first foreign attack on the continental United States since the nation's founding. The effect was traumatic for Americans, who had felt themselves invulnerable to violence on such a massive scale. In the immediate aftermath of 9/11, Americans bonded together across lines of race, region, and political persuasion. However, the presidential election the year before had been so close that it was decided by the Supreme Court (*Bush v. Gore*). Politically, the nation was sharply divided. Economic uncertainty and fears of another attack deepened the national disequilibrium, especially as the nation entered two wars: in Afghanistan in 2001 and Iraq in 2003.

Katrina, the hurricane that hit the Gulf Coast in August 2005, wreaked havoc on New Orleans and the coastal regions of Alabama and Mississippi and caused almost a thousand deaths. Americans in the affected areas went without food and water for days, as they waited to be rescued by a federal government that seemed incompetent if not callous in its response. The televised faces of these Americans were mainly black and poor. Journalists who referred to them as "refugees" rather than citizens added insult to injury. In protest, one New Orleans resident wrapped herself in the American flag; others held up a flag with a hand-written sign that said, "We are Americans too." Inevitably scenes of children separated from their parents and dying elders evoked images of the historical traumas of slavery and segregation. Although most disagreed with rapper Kanye West when he declared that President George W. Bush "doesn't care about black people," many African Americans shared his exasperation. Katrina seemed like a return to a nightmare from which people thought they had awakened.

In January 2008, Barack Obama, an African American and the junior senator from Illinois, won the Iowa caucus in the campaign for the presidential nomination of the Democratic Party. Apart from a memorable keynote speech at the 2004 convention, Obama was little known in black America. But his victory in predominantly white Iowa changed that. African Americans who had supported Senator Hillary Clinton, front-runner for the nomination and wife of former president Bill Clinton, shifted their support to Obama. As John Lewis, a hero of the civil rights movement and a congressman from Georgia, expressed it, they did not want to be caught on the wrong side of history. To many older blacks, who had never imagined that in their lifetimes a black person could be elected president, the inconceivable became a possibility. Senator Obama, with his soaring oratory and promise of hope and change, soon came to represent the culmination of the struggle for racial equality. Hundreds of thousands of blacks, Latinos, and young people registered to vote for the first time. In September, a financial crisis hit Wall Street, and Obama's cool, measured response sealed his victory over Republican senator John McCain. When Obama's election was announced, dancing broke out in the streets of African American communities. Almost two million Americans, of every race, stood in the frigid cold of January 20, 2009, to witness his inauguration.

On his first day in office, the president signed the Lilly Ledbetter Fair Pay Act that made it easier for workers to file pay discrimination lawsuits. Despite implacable opposition from Republicans in Congress, including leaders' repeated threats to make him a one-term president, Obama achieved legislative victories. Chief among them was the Affordable Care Act which promised to extend health care to thirty million uninsured Americans. Opponents dubbed the act "Obamacare," a term intended to be derisive, but which the president eventually embraced as a sign of his success. On the international front, President Obama began to restore frayed relations with allies; an important step was the ending of the war in Iraq in 2009. He also ended the "don't ask, don't tell" policy that prohibited gays in the military from acknowledging their sexual preference, and in 2012 the president expressed his support for marriage equality.

That November President Obama was re-elected by a margin of almost five million votes over Republican rival Mitt Romney, former governor of Massachusetts. President Obama's second inauguration drew pointed attention to the historical significance of his tenure. Myrlie Evers Williams, the widow of civil rights martyr Medgar Evers, who was assassinated in the driveway of their Jackson, Mississippi home in 1963, gave the invocation. The gay Cuban American poet, Richard Blanco, composed the ceremonial poem "One Today." In his speech, the president invoked historical sites associated with struggles for equality: Seneca Falls (the New York town where a pioneering women's rights convention was held in 1848), Selma (the Alabama town where Reverend Martin Luther King, Jr. led the pivotal march for voting rights for blacks in 1965), and Stonewall (the bar in the

New York City neighborhood of Greenwich Village where demonstrations against a police raid in 1969 marked the beginning of the gay rights movement. The references marked the progress the nation has made, even as they suggested how much work remained to be done.

Historians and social critics will long debate the meaning of Barack Obama's election. Although it marked a turning point in U.S. history, it did not produce the postracial society that some had anticipated. The struggle for racial equality continues. Obama's presidency was quickly engulfed by a series of crises in the national and international economies, natural disasters, and global unrest in addition to political stalemate at home. Black unemployment continued to be twice that of whites. Some activists argued that one consequence of having a black president was the diminishment of the longstanding tradition of black protest. But almost 95 percent of African American voters supported the president's reelection in 2012. In the main, they endorsed his policies and embraced the sense of possibility for themselves and their children that he embodied. For African American literary historians, Barack Obama, whose memoir *Dreams from My Father: A Story of Race and Inheritance* (1995) became a bestseller, was significant for another reason: the president of the United States was an African American writer.

EXPERIMENTAL TEXTS/FUTURISTIC FICTIONS

Increasingly African American writers create fictions that imagine the future and poems and plays whose formal risk taking provides the pleasure of the text. Experimentalism in African American literature dates back at least to Jean Toomer's *Cane* (1923). It is significant that Toomer wrote drama as well as fiction and poetry. His expressionistic plays *Barlo* and *Natalie Mann* are precursors of Suzan-Lori Parks's *An American Play* and *Topdog/Underdog*, which won the Pulitzer Prize in 2002. Formally experimental, sharply satirical, and sometimes profanely funny, Parks's plays cast African American actors in the roles of the nation's founders to highlight the absence of blacks from conventional historical narratives. Identity is fluid, never fixed in these plays, which open themselves to diverse interpretations.

Elements of jazz performance—riffs and improvisation, sound and rhythm—partially inspire the poetic experiments of Yusef Komunyakaa, Nathaniel Mackey, and Harryette Mullen. Komunyakaa, who has co-edited three volumes of jazz poetry, pays homage to musicians—"painful gods jive talk through / bloodstained reeds & shiny brass"—as he tries to imagine how it feels "to scream for help through a horn." Working like a consummate jazzman, Mackey extends tradition, blends cross-cultural influences, and establishes a signature sound in his poetry and fiction. Describing the juxtaposition of influences on one of her poems, Mullen imagines it "as the place where Sappho meets the blues at the crossroads." Fragmented and densely allusive, postmodern black poetry challenges readers, especially those less fluent in the multiple literary traditions in which the authors work. But it rewards those readers who persevere.

Science fiction offers the possibility of inventing a world in which racial and gender categories no longer apply, which is perhaps one reason it appeals to African American writers. Poet Tracy Smith and novelist Colson Whitehead occasionally deploy techniques of science fiction in their poetry and prose. Octavia Butler and Samuel Delany are two of the genre's most respected practitioners. Doro, a four-thousand-year-old character who appears in several of Butler's novels, appropriates the bodies of others regardless of gender and race. One of Delany's novels, *Triton*, features more than forty different genders. Time travel, a key motif in Butler's popular *Kindred*, allows her to represent the past and present simultaneously, to highlight both how much has changed and how much has not. Delany, who invents entire civilizations in his fiction, is similarly unbound by constraints of time and place. Literary theorist Frederick Jameson deems Delany's Nevèrÿon series "a major and unclassifiable achievement in contemporary American literature." It is fitting that the first allusion in the work included here, an excerpt from Delany's *Atlantis: Model 1924*, is to Jean Toomer.

OLD GENRES/NEW TRENDS

At the turn of the twenty-first century, African American writers, in a resurgence of interest in autobiography as a genre, told new stories of growing up black. Barack Obama and Danzy Senna chronicle their coming of age in biracial families. June Jordan and Paule Marshall recount growing up in Brooklyn in families whose roots were in the Caribbean. Scholars Houston Baker, Jr., Henry Louis Gates, Jr., and Deborah McDowell pen haunting memoirs of life in the segregated South. This work reflects the recent and widespread popularity of the memoir as a genre, but it also harks back to the beginnings of the African American tradition. Performance poetry represents another variation on an old genre. Throughout African American literary history, some poets have created work to be heard rather than read and to take up immediate rather than long-range concerns. In the 1990s the poetry slam became popular in diverse venues: on campuses, in nightclubs, and on television. In 2002 *Def Poetry Jam* was produced on Broadway. Poets performed work inflected with the rhythms of rap and often accompanied by recordings of hip-hop, much as Langston Hughes had performed his poems to the accompaniment of the Fats Waller jazz band in the 1920s and The Last Poets had recorded their verse in the 1960s.

In 1996 talk-show personality Oprah Winfrey established a book club for her television audience that introduced fiction by Morrison and Ernest Gaines to a huge new audience that spanned the lines of race, class, and ethnicity; equally important, Oprah's Book Club highlighted work by emerging writers such as Pearl Cleage, Breena Clarke, and Danticat. As popular fiction by black authors such as E. Lynn Harris and Terry McMillan sold in the millions, the number of novels published by African Americans increased exponentially. Lines blurred between literary and commercial fiction; writers published in multiple genres, including detective fiction, mysteries, and romance novels. In the new century, urban fiction dominated the African American literary marketplace. Scholar Eve Dunbar describes these novels as the literary counterpart to hip-hop, in which women have a greater voice. In all of these genres, publishers discovered a large audience that craved fiction that reflected their actual lives or the "good life" to which they aspired. Eager to discuss what they read, readers organized book clubs, in an updated version of nineteenth-century literary societies. Oprah's Book Club was replicated in microcosm in communities across the nation. Book columns were featured in the popular magazines *Ebony* and *Essence,* while Internet sites provided readers endless opportunities to evaluate books for themselves.

Finally, scholarship about African American literature and by African American writers has flourished during the contemporary period. Indeed, literary scholars have documented, analyzed, and to an extent helped produce the renaissance among African American writers. At the same time, poets and writers have been among the most influential literary critics. By the 1980s scholarly studies had begun to appear in some number. Robert Stepto's *Behind the Veil: A Study of Afro-American Narrative* (1979), Houston Baker's *The Journey Back: Issues in Black Literature and Criticism* (1980), and Barbara Christian's *Black Women Novelists: The Development of a Tradition, 1892–1976* (1980) are examples of the variety of critical studies in this period. Anthologies of critical essays such as Roseann Bell, Bettye Fisher, and Beverley Guy Sheftall's *Sturdy Black Bridges: Visions of Black Women in Literature* (1979); Dexter Fisher and Robert Stepto's *Afro-American Literature: The Reconstruction of Instruction* (1979); Henry Louis Gates Jr.'s *Black Literature and Literary Theory* (1984); and Michael Harper and Robert Stepto's *Chants of Saints: A Gathering of Afro-American Literature, Art, and Scholarship* (1979) suggested different approaches to teaching and theorizing about black literatures.

Poets and novelists were major voices in this critical conversation. They organized themselves into groups such as Cave Canem and the Dark Room Collective to facilate the exchange of ideas. Practically every contemporary writer in *The Norton Anthology of African American Literature* has either written essays that recovered older writers, illuminated the relationship between the African American oral tradition and African American literatures, and/or crafted literary theories derived from his or her own literary practice. After writing perhaps the most influential reading of her own fiction in an essay titled "Unspeakable Things Unspoken," Toni Morrison published a widely cited volume of essays, *Playing in the Dark* (1992), articulating the theory that American literary classics such as Melville's *Moby-Dick* and Hawthorne's romances reflect the African presence in American life, even when race is not their subject. Morrison's critical intervention was one catalyst in moving American literary study to take greater account of race in the formation of all literary traditions in the United States.

Unlike their predecessors, the younger writers of the contemporary period studied African American literature in the classroom. For example, Naylor asserts that reading Morrison's *The Bluest Eye* as a college student gave her the authority to begin writing fiction herself. Her novels, especially *Linden Hills* and *Mama Day,* acknowledge her debt to Morrison, Hurston, and Walker as well as to Dante's *Inferno* and Shakespeare's *The Tempest.* Walker, who first found Hurston's name in a footnote as she was doing research for a short story, claimed her as a literary foremother, wrote essays about her, and described her own novel *The Color Purple* as a "love letter to Zora." Scholars, notably Henry Louis Gates Jr., have subsequently identified the pattern of shared themes and tropes in the two authors' texts. As Gates demonstrates in his critical study *The Signifying Monkey* (1988), black texts "talk" to other black texts and the art of signifying is simultaneously oral and literary. He asserts, moreover, that the African American literary tradition is "double-voiced"—that is, it reflects writers' reading of Western texts, but it "repeats with a difference, a black difference that manifests itself in specific language use." Theories of intertextuality have become central to African American literary study.

Hurston first defined *signifying* as a cultural practice in *Mules and Men.* Gates appropriated the term in his attempt "to locate and identify how the black tradition had theorized about itself." Much African American literary theory was similarly tethered to black vernacular tradition. Stepto's *Behind the Veil* employed call and response as a metaphor for intertexuality. In his influential *Blues, Ideology and Afro-American Literature,* Baker extrapolated "a vernacular theory" from the blues. Deborah McDowell posited *The Changing Same,* a figure borrowed from Baraka's study of black music, for intertexuality in black women's writing, while Mae Henderson fused poststructuralist and feminist theory in "Speaking in Tongues," a trope derived from the Bible by way of the black sanctified church. Even as they created theories that took into account the "signifyin(g) black difference," critics of African American literature engaged in readings from the wide range of perspectives that existed in the academy, such as formalism, Marxism, psychoanalysis, poststructuralism, and feminism. By the turn of the century scholars were producing biographies, critical monographs, anthologies, and works of literary theory in unprecedented quantity.

Their ideological investments were various, their methodologies were diverse, and so too were their conclusions. Feminist critics, for example, were skeptical of the concept of tradition, which as Mary Helen Washington noted, had often been used to "exclude or misrepresent women." Spillers asserted that "'tradition' for black women's writing community is a matrix of *discontinuities* that partially articulate various periods of consciousness in the history of an African-American people." Hazel Carby advocated that "black feminist criticism be regarded as a problem, not a solution, as a sign that should be interrogated, a locus of contradictions." Queer theorists including Robert Reid-Pharr and Charles Nero likewise challenged the assumptions underlying the concept of tradition and the metaphors of family that often accompanied it. In *The Practice of Diaspora* (2003), Brent Edwards argued that African American texts were part of a global circuit of art and ideas.

From its beginning as an academic subject, African American literary study has been interdisciplinary; Sterling Brown, to name one pioneer, was as interested in folklore and music as in formal literature. The literature is now taught in African American studies, ethnic studies, and women's studies departments as well as in English. In the 1980s and 1990s, this interdisciplinarity contributed to the development of cultural studies, a diverse interdisciplinary field that sees culture not as a static "canon" or "tradition" but as the emerging and dynamic product of a network of antagonistic power relations. It is not surprising that cultural studies has been profoundly concerned with African American culture. Acting on the premise that identity today is formulated through interaction with film, video, and mass-produced music as well as, if not more than, in relation to traditional social structures, African American cultural critics such as Daphne Brooks, Michael Eric Dyson, bell hooks, Wahneema Lubiano, Valerie Smith, Michele Wallace, and Cornel West have turned their critical attention to black popular culture. They also use the tools of textual analysis to clarify the meanings of media spectacles such as the Thomas-Hill hearings. African American literary and cultural scholarship has gained a strong foothold in the academy and a significant audience outside of it.

ALBERT MURRAY
1916–2013

Albert Murray's career as a writer was distinguished by his insistent drive to create, in fiction and nonfiction, the literary equivalents of blues and jazz. Murray the modernist undertook this project under the auspices of Eliot, Hemingway, Joyce, Faulkner, and especially Thomas Mann—all highly conscious writers who employ mythic patterns and a wide range of intellectual and artistic references to give their writing the peculiar weight and force that define a vital aspect of the modern. But Murray wore these influences lightly. In a voice unmistakably his own, he brought to life the little-explored aspect of African American experience that views the shortfalls and tragedies of life in much the way they are regarded in blues-idiom music, where trouble is taken for granted ("Trouble, trouble," one blues song says, "I've had it all my days") but where defeat is never conceded. Murray's heroes learn to regard their lives as fairy tales and romances in which, whether they receive official recognition or not, they achieve a style of living and loving and making art that transcends the bounds of officialdom. Ultimately, they achieve a way of life—even in the violent briar patches of segregated America—which, like the music of Louis Armstrong and Duke Ellington, is the envy of the world.

Born on May 12, 1916, in Nokomis, Alabama, Albert Lee Murray was adopted soon after birth by sharecropper, dockworker, railway crosstie cutter, and sawmill hand Hugh Murray and homemaker Mattie (James) Murray. Murray grew up in Magazine Point, outside of Mobile, where he discovered a world at once stiflingly provincial and open to possibility. At Mobile County Training School, Murray fell under the influence of the principal, Benjamin Francis Baker, who regarded him as part of the "Talented Tenth," whose goals involved loyalty to past and future generations of African Americans and the will to assume leadership on a broad scale. Murray received a scholarship to attend college and enrolled at Tuskegee Institute in 1935.

At Tuskegee, Murray pursued an intense program of literary studies, reading assigned texts along with unassigned new works by such critics as Edmund Wilson and Morton Zabel, which encouraged and enhanced his study of the literary moderns. He also tuned in to the national radio broadcasts of Duke Ellington, Earl Hines, and other jazz masters whose work was fast becoming a consuming passion. Though they did not become close friends until later, Murray the undergraduate was aware of another ambitious reader at Tuskegee, music major Ralph Ellison.

Murray pursued graduate study at the University of Michigan before returning to Tuskegee Institute (in 1942), where he taught English and directed theatrical productions. In 1943, he enlisted in the air force. He served through World War II and continued, in active and inactive service at home and abroad, until his retirement as a major in 1962. Between stints of active service, he received his master's degree from New York University (in 1948) and taught at Tuskegee. After retiring from the air force, Murray settled in New York City, where he worked as a writer and as an occasional visiting professor—at Colgate, Barnard, Columbia, Emory, the University of Massachusetts at Boston, Washington and Lee, and elsewhere.

In 1970, when Murray was fifty-four years old, he published his first book, *The Omni-Americans,* a compendium of essays and reviews that challenged the prevailing social-scientific view of Negro Americans as marginal victims of white racism by asserting the wholeness and the defiant stylishness of blacks who are, in Murray's formulation, in some ways *the* quintessentially representative American group: not just Afro- or African Americans but *Omni*-Americans. *South to a Very Old Place* (1971), the book that Murray speaks of as his favorite, is a novel-cum-travelog in which the author takes off from Harlem to retrace his southern roads and highways while investigating the state of race relations (including the art and rhetoric along the color line) after the civil rights revolution. *The Hero and the Blues* (1973) collects lectures on jazz, blues, and literature that Murray had delivered the previous year at the University of Missouri. *Stomping the Blues* (1976) was begun as a picture book on jazz and then expanded into a comprehensive aesthetic of the music in its "Saturday night" setting, where it drives the blues off the dance floor (to stomp the blues) and heralds the revelry that also defines blues-idiom music. *Good Morning, Blues* (1985), the autobiography of Count Basie as told to Murray, presents the story of "the boy from Red Bank" who became a piano sensation and then bandleader on the Kansas City Southwest circuit before his music and fame traveled around the world. In this book, as in the others, the emphasis is on heroic accomplishment in the face of what can appear to be unpromising odds.

The Blue Devils of Nada (1996) collects Murray's essays on Romare Bearden, Duke Ellington, and Ernest Hemingway and on the processes of writing the Basie book (that four-fisted piano collaboration). This book also studies riff-style artistic expression in a world infected with entropy (or meaningless randomness)—infested with "the blue devils of nada." (Of course the "blue devils" are, like blues music itself, ironically named insofar as they represent not only misery and wretchedness in blue but also the Blue Devil bomber-pilotlike warriors, ever on duty against the misery and wretchedness associated with blue moods.) According to this philosopher of the music, the best way to fight the blues is with the blues!

Sometime in the mid-1940s, Murray began a novel. Working on it off and on between other projects, he released part one as *Train Whistle Guitar* in 1974. *The Spyglass Tree* was published in 1991 and *The Seven League Boots* in 1996. This trilogy comprises an eloquent "lyrical reminiscence" by a highly intelligent and winning narrator whose nickname is Scooter.

In *Train Whistle Guitar,* Scooter remembers the Deep South of the 1920s not as a Gothic prison house but as an enthralling and at times bewildering scene of adventures. This first novel, and indeed the entire trilogy, concerns problems of history and memory in a culture where official schoolbook history is one thing (and a powerful thing it can be) while the versions of the past traded by adults in the barbershop and in the front room at home are something else again. Of course, Scooter, like his maker, will need both the "learned" and the vernacular traditions: good book training and the dirty dozens, both.

The Spyglass Tree takes Scooter to a college strongly resembling Tuskegee, where his dorm room replaces his hometown's chinaberry tree as a lookout post from which to gain perspective on the widening world. Perspective, along with history and memory, is a concern throughout the Scooter trilogy. *The Seven League Boots* retells, in riff choruslike recapitulations, stories narrated in the first two books as it pushes forward the saga of Scooter, now a recent college graduate, who is hired, during the Swing Era, as bass player in the band of the legendary itinerant jazz musician / composer Bossman, the "Emperor of Syncopation," who looks a lot like Duke Ellington.

Well into his eighties, Murray continued to burnish his reputation as a man of letters. With co-editor John Callahan, he published *Trading Twelves,* a selection of his correspondence with Ellison. In 2001, he published another collection of essays, speeches, and interviews, *From the Briarpatch File,* and a volume of poems, *Conjugations and Reiterations.*

In addition to his work as a writer, Murray was a major figure in the institutionalization of jazz through his work with the Smithsonian, in Washington, D.C., and especially with Lincoln Center, in New York City. Working with Wynton Marsalis, Rob Gibson, and Stanley Crouch, Murray has provided intellectual leadership to Lincoln Center's jazz department, championing against all doubters the idea that jazz is a fine art form whose values of resiliency, improvisation, and individuality, all within a group context, mark it as *the* quintessential American art form and *the* music of the twentieth century.

From Train Whistle Guitar

[HISTORY LESSONS]

It was as if you had been born hearing and knowing about trains and train whistles, and the same was also true of sawmills and sawmill whistles. I already knew how to mark the parts of the day by sawmill whistles long before I learned to read time as such from the face of a clock.

Sometimes, probably having heard the earliest morning sawmill whistles in my sleep as you sometimes hear neighborhood roosters crowing for day-break, I used to wake up and lie listening long enough to hear the first-shift hands passing by outside. That was when the daytime fireman relieved the night fireman, and it was also the time when you could hear the logging crews that came that way going to work on that part of Mobile River and Three Mile Creek. These were the putt-boat pilots and the raftmen, some of whom were also skiffboatmen. And there were also the boom men, who used to wear their turned down hip boots (which I also used to call magel-lan boots and isthmus of panama boots) to and from home, carrying their peavies and hook-and-jam poles angling across their shoulders as pike men did in story books and also as railroad crosstie cutters used to carry their crosscut saws and broadaxes to and from the timber woods.

It was the head day-shift fireman who always blew the next whistle, and that was when the main-shift hands would be coming by. So that was when what you heard passing was not only the log carriage experts like, say, old Sawmill Turner, for instance; but also the shed crews and the yard crews, including the timekeepers and tallymen. But I was usually asleep again by then, and when I woke up for good it would be time to get up and be ready before the first school bell rang.

It would be full daylight then, and by the time you finished breakfast, the first lumber trucks would be grinding their way up out of Sawdust Bottom. And when you heard the next gear shift, that meant they were finally up the hill and leveling off into our flat but somewhat sandy and rutty road to come whining by the gate. Then the next gearstroke meant that they were ready to pick up speed to fade on away because they had turned onto Buck-shaw Road, which was macadamized like Telegraph Road even before the Cochrane Bridge was built and they finally paved it with asphalt like the Chickasaw Highway and made it a part of US 90.

•

From September through the fall and winter and spring the next thing after the first lumber trucks was always the first school bell. So from then on it was as if you didn't really hear either the sawmills or train whistles (or even boat whistles) anymore until after three o'clock. Because during that part of every day except Saturday and Sunday, everything you did was part of the also and also that school bells and school bell times were all about. Such as singing in 70-degree Fahrenheit schoolroom unison: *Good morning to you good morning to you good morning dear teacher good morning to you.* With your scrubbed hands on the pencil tray desk for roll call and fingernail inspection, with your hair trimmed and combed and brushed and your head erect, your back straight, your shoulders square and your eyes on the exemplary pre-lesson neatness of the janitor-washed blackboard with its semi-permanent border design and theme of the month and motto of the month and chalk colored checkerboard calendar.

Good solo teacher talk morning dear children.

Good unison-pupil response-chant morning dear teacher.

A very good morning from toothpaste smiles and rainbow ribbons and oil-cloth book satchels and brown bag sandwich smells to you Miss So and Miss So and Miss So and So and Miss So-So and Miss So On and Miss So Forth to Miss Metcalf.

Then (when the first kitten mitten mornings of steaming breath and glittering wayside ponds were outside once more) also: *Old Jack Frost is a funny old fellow when the wind begins he begins to bellow. He bites little children on their nose. He bites little children on their toes. He makes little girls say Oh! Oh! Oh! And he makes little boys say Ouch! Ouch! Ouch! He makes little pointed-ats wring hands and blow fingers and say Oh! Oh! Oh! And he makes little nodded-and-smiled-ats shake fists and say Ouch! Ouch! Ouch! He makes little sugar and spice and everything nice girls say—!—!—! And he makes little frogs and snails and puppydogtail boys (but not Scooter and not Little Buddy Marshall and not old Cateye Gander Gallagher the Gallinipper) say—!—!—!*

But sometimes (especially during afternoon quiet sessions) you could still hear the syrup-green sawdust whine of the log carriage even from that far away, and I could hardly wait to get back home to my own play sawmill, which millwright that I already was I had built complete with boom, rafts, conveyer ramp, carriage, slab and sawdust pile, stacking yard, dry kiln and planer shed, long before the time came to go to school that first year. Because in the summertime in those days I almost always used to become a hard rolling sawmill man as soon as Buckshaw whistle used to blow for high noon no matter what else I was supposed to be at the time. Because that was when you could sit at the sawhorse table outside under the chinaberry tree stripped to the waist like a stacking yard hand, eating new corn and pole beans (or snap beans or string beans) plus new red-skinned potatoes; or butterbeans plus okra; or green (shelled) blackeye peas plus okra; or crowder peas plus okra; along with the very thinnest of all shortening-rich golden crusted corners of cornbread. Not to mention the yellow-flecked mellowness of the home churned buttermilk of those days. Or the homemade lemonade or fresh ice-tea. Especially when you could drink it from your very own quart-size fruit jar not only as if you had been stacking lumber all the morning but also as if all the good cooking in your napkin-covered slat basket had been prepared by your honey brown good-looking wife or woman, who had put on her frilly starched baby doll gingham dress and brought it to where she now sat beside you fanning away the flies in the stacking yard shade.

But all of that was before Miss Lexine Metcalf, and her blue and green and yellow globe revolving on its tilted axis with its North and South Poles, and its Eastern and Western Hemispheres, and its equator plus its Torrid

and North Temperate and South Temperate and Frigid Zones and its continents and its oceans and seas and gulfs and great lakes and rivers and
basins, and its mountain ranges and plains and deserts and oases, and its
islands and peninsulas and archipelagos and capes and horns and straits.

Because from then on (what with her sandtable igloos and wigwams and
thatched huts and mud huts and caravan tents and haciendas and chalets
and chinese paper houses with lanterns; and what with her bulletin board
costumes of many lands and her teacher's desk that could become the
Roundtable from which armor-clad knights errant set forth to do battle
with dragons and blackboard problems; what with her window box plants
that could become Robin Hood's forest and what with her magic pointer
that could change everyday Gasoline Point schoolgirls into Cinderellas and
Sleeping Beauties and you into Prince Charming or Roland or Siegfried or
Sinbad or Ulysses and your Buster Brown shoes or your Keds into Seven
League Boots) I was to become a schoolboy above and beyond everything
else, for all the absolutely indispensable times I was still to play hooky with
Little Buddy Marshall.

What with Miss Lexine Metcalf with whose teacher-pronunciation my
given name finally became the classroom equivalent not only of Scooter but
also of the other nickname Mama used to call me which was Man which
was to say Mama's Man which was to say Mama's Little Man which was to
say Mama's Big Man; because Miss Lexine Metcalf was the one who also
said it looking at you as if to let you know that she was also calling you what
Miss Tee had always called you, which was her mister. *My Mister. Hello My
Mister. This is My Mister. Show them My Mister.*

What with Miss Lexine Metcalf who came to be the one who was there
in the classroom. But what also with Miss Tee, from whom had already
come ABC blocks and ABC picture books and wax crayon coloring sets,
and was the one for whom you learned your first numbers, and who was
also the one who said: *This is My Mister who can write his name all by himself.
Show them My Mister. This is My Mister who can do addition and subtraction
all by himself. Show them My Mister. And show them how My Mister can also
recite from the Reader all by himself. The cat said not I. The dog said not I.
The little red hen said I will and she did. The little choo choo going up the hill
said I think I can I think I can I thought I could I thought I could. Because it
tried and it did.*

•

Sometimes a thin gray, ghost-whispering mid-winter drizzle would begin
while you were still at school, and not only would it settle in for the rest of
the mist-blurred, bungalow-huddled afternoon, but it would still be falling
after dark as if it would continue throughout the night; and even as you
realized that such was the easiest of all times to get your homework (even
when it was arithmetic) done (no matter what kind of schoolboy you were)
you also knew as who hasn't always known that it was also and also the very
best of all good times to be where grown folks were talking again, especially
when there were the kind of people visiting who always came because there
was somebody there from out of town and you could stay up listening
beyond your usual time to be in bed.

Their cane bottom chairs and hide bottom chairs and rocking chairs plus
stools always formed the same old family-cozy semi-circle before the huge
open hearth, and from your place in the chimney corner you could see the

play of the firelight against their faces and also watch their tale-time shadows moving against the newspaper wallpaper walls and the ceiling. Not even the best of all barbershops were ever to surpass the best of such nights at home.

They would be talking and rocking and smoking and sometimes drinking, and, aware of the roof sanding, tree-shivering night weather outside, I would be listening, and above us on the scalloped mantlepiece was the old fashioned pendulum clock, which was Papa's heirloom from that ancestral mansion of ante-bellum columns and gingham crisp kitchens in which his mulatto grandmother had herself been an inherited slave until Sherman's March to the Sea[1] but which I still remember as the Mother Goose clock; because it ticked and tocked and ticked and tocked and tocked and struck not only the hours but also the quarter-hours with the soft clanging sound you remember when you remember fairy tale steeples and the rainbow colors of nursery rhyme cobwebs; because it hickory dickory docked and clocked like a brass spoon metronome above the steel blue syncopation of guitar string memories; because it hockey-tock rocked to jangle like such honky tonk piano mallets as echo midnight freight train distances beyond patch-quilt horizons and bedside windowpanes.

Sometimes it would be obvious enough that they were only telling the tallest tales and the most outrageous lies they could either remember or fabricate, and sometimes you could be every bit as certain that their primary purpose was to spell out as precisely as possible the incontestable facts and most reliable figures involved in the circumstance under consideration. But when you listened through the meshes of the Mother Goose clock you already knew long before you came to recognize any necessity to understand (not to mention explain) that no matter which one they said or even believed they were doing they were almost always doing it at least a little of both. (Because even as the Mother Goose clock was measuring the hours and minutes of ordinary days and nights and time tables its tictoculation created that fabulous once upon a time spell under which you also knew that the Jacksonville of the section gang song for instance was really a make-believe place even though you could find it by moving your finger to the right from Pensacola and across Tallahassee on the map of Florida—just as you could find Kansas City by tracing left from St. Louis on the map of Missouri.)

Sometimes there would also be such winter-delicious things as papershell pecans and chinquapins and fresh roasted peanuts to pass around in Mama's pinestraw bowl-basket, and sometimes there was homemade blackberry wine or muscadine wine,[2] and sometimes when it was really a very very special occasion Miss Alzenia Nettleton, who was once a cook in the Governor's Mansion, would either send or bring one of her mouth-melting sweet potato pones. Sometimes when it was blizzard weather there would be a big cast-iron pot of lye hominy (which is something I didn't learn to like until later on), and on some of the best nights the main reason everybody was there in the first place was that it was hog-killing-time weather and somebody had brought Mama the makings of a feast of chitterlings and/or

---

1. General William Tecumseh Sherman's destructive march through Georgia, from Atlanta to Savannah in late 1864 divided the Confederacy in two and played a major role in its defeat.

2. Wine made from grapes of a vine common to the southeastern United States. "Chinquapins": nuts from a small tree related to the chestnut.

middlings,[3] but of course when that happened the best of the talking seldom if ever got started until the eating was almost over.

Uncle Jerome would always be there unless there was a fruit boat to be unloaded that night, clearing his throat even when he was not going to say anything, squinting his eyes and making a face and clearing again and swallowing and stretching and rolling his chin because he was a preacher. Because although he had been a longshoreman for the last twenty some odd years and a field hand for some thirty odd years before that, he was supposed to have the Call, although he had never been called by any congregation to be the pastor of any church.

Sometimes Mister Doc Donahue the Dock Hand would also be there. But they wouldn't be drinking just wine with him there. Because leather bellied stevedore[4] that he was he always said that wine was for women and children and Christmas morning fruitcake, and he would get up and get the longshoreman's knapsack he always carried along with his cargo hook and bring out a brown crockery jug of corn whiskey, which always made Papa look over at Mama and get just about tickled to death. They would be passing it around, pouring against the light of the fire, and there would be that aroma then, which I always used to enjoy as much as the smell of warm cigar ashes and freshly opened Prince Albert tobacco cans.

They would talk on and on, and then (when somebody mentioned something about the weather itself and somebody else said Yeah but talking about some weather) you could always tell you were going to hear about the great Juvember Storm again, and sometimes that would be what they spent the rest of the night telling about, each one telling it as he remembered it from where he was at the time, with Uncle Jerome telling his as if it all had been something happening in the Bible, although nobody, not even he, ever claimed that it had actually stormed for forty days and forty nights. But Uncle Jerome always pointed out that everything under the sun was in the Bible including automobiles, because old Ezekiel saw the wheel in the middle of the wheel, and what was an airship but a horseless chariot in the sky, and if somebody didn't cut in on him he would stand up and begin walking the floor and preaching another one of his sermons.

Everybody had his own way of telling about it, but no matter how many parts were added you always saw the main part the same way: rivers and creeks rising and overflowing the back country, washing houses off their foundations and sometimes completely away; bales of cotton and barrels of flour and molasses and cans of lard floating out of warehouses and scattering through the swamps; horses neighing and cows lowing and trying to swim but drowning because (so they used to say) their behinds sucked in so much water; people living in barns and hay lofts and paddling everywhere in skiff boats, people camping in lean-to tent cities in the hills like hobos. People camping on the bluffs like Indians, people camping on timber rafts like the early settlers; trains not running because not only were the tracks washed out but in some places whole spans of bridges had been swept loose. . . .

Then afterwards, there was the epidemic during which even more perished than during the storm itself. But all of that was always a part of the storm story also. And that was when Uncle Jerome always used to say God

---

3. Pork or bacon cut from between the shoulders of the hog. "Chitterlings": the small intestines of pigs cooked for food.
4. Loader and unloader of ship cargo.

was warning sinners that He could do it again although He had promised that it would be the fire next time, and he would get up and start clearing his throat and making faces and walking the floor again and then he would go on to show you how even in the almighty act of bringing the flood again God had also brought the fire next time after all. Because what so many many people had suffered and died from was the FEVER, which meant that they were being consumed in a fire more terrible than brimstone! Mess around with mortal man born in sin and shaped in inequity but Gentlemen Sir don't you never start trying to mess with God.

But Papa, whose given name was Whit probably for Whitley but maybe for Whitney and so was sometimes called Papa Whit and sometimes Unka Whit, who had not been inside a church except to attend somebody's funeral since he was baptized thirty some odd years ago, would then take another swallow from his whiskey glass and wipe his mouth and wink at Mister Doc the Dock Hand and look over at Mama because he knew good and well she was going to be scandalized to mortification and say Amen God sure did work a mysterious way His wonders or His blessings or which-ever it was to bestow because that was the same storm that had made more good paying jobs for our folks in that country than anything else till the war came.

What I always used to call Papa was Papoo and he used to call me his little gingerbrown papoose boy, which may have been why I called him Papoo in the first place. He himself was as white as any out and out white man I have ever seen in my life. And no wonder either, because not only was he said to be a whole lot more than just half white, it was also said quite accurately that he was acknowledged by most of his white blood relatives much more readily than he himself was ever willing to acknowledge any of them (except when it came to such legal matters as clearing titles to property inherited in com-mon). I myself once overheard Mama telling Aunt Callie the Cat Callahan that the main reason we had moved down into Mobile County when the war boom came was to get away from Papa's white kinfolks in the country. And another time I heard her telling Miss Sadie Womack about how red Papa's ears used to turn when the white people back in the country used to see him driving her into town in the buckboard[5] and pretend that they thought she was not his wife but only one of his black field hands.

Papa himself never talked about white people as such. But sometimes when they were talking about hard times, somebody would get him to tell about some of the things he had seen and done during those times when he had to go off somewhere and pass for white to get a job. That was something to hear about also, and one time when I was telling Little Buddy Marshall about it the next day, he said: Everybody say, don't care how much of his skin and his keen nose and his flat ass Mister Whit might have got from the whitefolks, he got his mother-wit from the getting place. That's how come you don't never catch nobody calling him no old shit-colored peckerwood behind his back.

There was also that time with that white man downtown by the marine store on Government Street. He and Papa knew each other and they were laughing and talking and I was having a good time looking in store win-dows, and I went looking all the way up to the sporting goods store, and

5. Four-wheeled open carriage.

when I came back they were talking about a job; and the man said something about something both of them had been doing somewhere, and that brought up something else, and I heard the man say Papa was a fool for being a durned ole niggie when he could be a wyat man. Hell Whit you as wyat as I am any durned day of the week be durned if you ain't, and Papa just shook his head and said You don't understand, Pete.

Midwinter nights around the fireplace was one of the times when Soldier Boy Crawford used to tell about crossing the Atlantic Ocean and about the mines and the torpedoes and the submarines, and then about the French places he had been to, and sometimes he would mix in a lot of French words with what he was saying such as bonjour come on tally voo and such as sand meal killing my trees easy to Paree and such as donay me unbootay cornyak silver plate and such as voo lay voo zig zig and so on, screwing up his face and narrowing his shoulders as well as his eyes and wiggling his fingers as if he were playing the words as notes on a musical instrument.

When you heard him talking about France in the barbershop he was usually telling either about the Argonne Forest or the Hindenburg Line[6] or about French women whom he called frog women. But what he used to talk mostly about at the fireside was the kind of farming country they had over there, especially the wine making country. And he would also tell about the mountain country and the churches which he said had the finest bells and the keenest steeples and the prettiest windows in the world: Talking about some stain glass church windows y'all ain't seen no stain glass church windows y'all ain't seen no church statues and I ain't talking about no wood I'm talking about natural stone nine hundred years old.

What he used to tell about Paris at such times was mostly about the buildings and the streets with the cafes on the sidewalk and the parks and the cabarets, and that was also when he used to tell about eating horse meat, snails and frogs legs (but not about the pissoirs and the bidets and best of all the poules[7] from whom came french kissing). He would always say Gay Paree was the best city in the world, and that was also when he would always say A man is a man over there and if somebody said as somebody as often as not did that a man ain't nothing but a man nowhere, you knew he was going to say Yeah but that ain't what I'm talking about, what I'm talking about is somewhere you can go anywhere you big enough to go and do anything you big enough to do and have yourself some of anything you got the money to pay for. That's what I'm talking about.

Soldier Boy Crawford, (who during blizzard weather also used to wear his woolen wraparound leggings along with his Army coat and overseas cap and who also had a steel helmet that looked like a wash basin but which he called his doughboy hat and who was said to have brought back a German Luger plus some hand grenades plus a bayonet, a musette bag[8] and a gas mask too because he for one was never going to let them catch him with his pants down if he could help it) was the main one who used to tell me and

6. Running from Lens in northern France to Rheims in the northeast, consolidated German forces stemmed Allied advances to the west during World War I. The Argonne Forest in northeastern France is a wooded region that was a major battleground during World War I.

7. Hens (French, literal trans.); here, prostitutes. "Pissoirs.": public urinals. "Bidets": French-style toilets.
8. Small leather or canvas shoulderbag used by soldiers or travelers.

Little Buddy Marshall about all of the things Luzana Cholly had done during the war. Because old Luze himself never did talk about any of that, not even when you asked him about it. Sometimes he used to say he was going to save it and tell us about it when we were old enough to understand it, and sometimes he would answer one or two questions about something, say, like how far Big Bertha could shoot, and how the Chau-Chau automatic rifle worked and things like that. But you could never get him to sit down and tell about the actual fighting like Soldier Boy Crawford did. Once you got Soldier Boy Crawford worked up he was subject to fight the whole war all over again.

The rain that was falling then would be crackling down on the shingles of the gabled roof of that house, and the fire in the hearth would sparkle as Papa poked it, and I would be in my same chair in my same place in the corner; and sometimes they would be telling about some of the same old notorious rounders and roustabouts that the guitar players and the piano players made up songs about. Especially if Mister Doc Donahue was there, because he was the one who could always remember something else about old John Henry, who went with blue steel sparks, and old John Hardy, who went with greased lightning. Once he held the floor all night just describing how old Stagolee shot and killed Billy Lyons, and what happened at that famous trial.

Mister Doc Donahue was also the one who used to tell about how old Robert Charles declared war on the city of New Orleans and fought the whole police force all by himself with his own special homemade bullets. But the best of all the old so-called outlaws he used to tell about was always the one from Alabama named Railroad Bill. Who was so mean when somebody crossed him and so tricky that most people believed that there was something supernatural about him. He was the one that no jail could hold overnight and no bloodhounds could track beyond a certain point. Because he worked a mojo[9] on them that nobody ever heard of before or since. And the last time he broke jail, they had the best bloodhounds in the whole state there to track him. But the next morning they found them all tied together in a fence corner near the edge of the swamp, not even barking anymore, just whining, and when they got them untangled they were ruined forever, couldn't scent a polecat and wouldn't even run a rabbit; and nobody ever saw or came near hide nor hair of old Railroad Bill from that time on.

Naturally the whitefolks claimed they caught him and lynched him; but everybody knew better. The whitefolks were always claiming something like that. They claimed that they had caught old Pancho Villa and hung him for what he had done out in New Mexico; and they claimed that they had hemmed up old Robert Charles in a steeple and burned him alive; and they also claimed that Jessie Willard had salivated old Jack Johnson[1] down in Havana that time! Well, they could go around bragging about how the great white hope had put the big black menace back in his place and proved white supremacy all they wanted to, but everybody knew that Jack Johnson who was married to a white woman had to trade his world championship in for his American citizenship, and thirty thousand dollars to get back in the USA and there was a picture in every barbershop which showed him letting

---

9. A spell; witchcraft.
1. American prizefighter (1878–1946), first black world heavyweight champion (1908–15).

himself be counted out, lying shading his eyes from the Cuban sun, lying with his legs propped like somebody lying on the front porch; and as for Jessie Willard, everybody knew he couldn't even stand up to Jack Dempsey,[2] who was the same Jack Dempsey who brought back old John L. Sullivan's color line because he didn't ever intend to get caught in the same ring with the likes of Jack Johnson, Sam Langford or even somebody like Harry Wills, not even with a submachine gun. Everybody knew that.

The whitefolks claimed that they had finally caught up with old Railroad Bill at some crossroads store somewhere and had slipped up on him while he was sitting in the middle of the floor sopping molasses with his gun lying off to one side, and they swore that they had blown the back of his head off with a double barrel charge of triple-ought buckshot. But in the first place Railroad Bill didn't eat molasses, and in the second place he didn't have to break into any store to get something to eat. Because folks kept him in plenty of rations everywhere he went by putting out buckets of it in certain special places for him mostly along the Railroad which was what his name was all about; and in the third place he must have broken into more than fifty stores by that time and he just plain didn't rob a store in the broad open daylight, not and then sit down in the middle of the floor and eat right there, and in the fourth place there was at least a dozen other mobs in at least a dozen other places all claiming that they had been the ones who laid him low, each one of them telling a completely different tale about how and when and where it all happened. Some claimed that they had hung him upside down on the drawbridge and then riddled him and left what was left of him there for the buzzards. But they never settled on which bridge.

I didn't know very much about history then. Which was what all that about Uncle Walt and the bloodhounds was all about too. Because I knew even while it was happening that it wasn't just happening then. I didn't know very much about historical cause and effect then, but I knew enough to realize that when something happened it was a part of something that had been going on before, and I wasn't surprised at all that time when I was awakened in the middle of the night and got up and saw Uncle Walt sitting by the fire in Papa's clothes talking about how he had made his way through Tombigbee Swamp. He slept in Uncle Jerome's bed and Uncle Jerome slept on a pallet in front of the fireplace. They put ointment on the bruises and rubbed his joints down in Sloan's Liniment, and he slept all day the next day and all the day after that too, telling about it again the second night by the fire with his feet soaking in a tub of hot salt water, and I could see it all and I was in it too, and it was me running through the swamps, hearing them barking, coming, and it was me who swam across the creek and was running wet and freezing in the soggy shoes all the next day. Hungry and cold but not stopping even when I didn't hear them anymore, and not hopping a freight either, because they would be looking for you to do that. It was me who made my way because I knew that country like the Indians knew it, and I knew the swamps and the streams like the old keelboat men and I knew the towns and villages like a post rider, and then it was me who was long gone like a Natchez Trace[3] bandit.

---

2. American prizefighter (1895–1983), heavyweight champion from 1919 to 1926.

3. An old road connecting Natchez, Mississippi,
with Nashville, Tennessee.

I saw Uncle Walt sitting there in the firelight not afraid but careful, talking about how he was going to make it across the Mason-Dixon,[4] and I didn't really know anything at all about whatever it was he had done or hadn't done, and I still don't know what it was, but I knew that whatever it was it was trouble, and I said It's like once upon a time back then. Because that's what Mama always said, who knew it from her grandfather, who was Uncle Walt's grandfather too, who knew it from his father when there was no hope of foot rest this side of Canada, which was also called Canaan, which was the Promised Land, and I also knew that all of that was about something called the Underground Railroad, which ran from the House of Bondage to the land of Jubilo.[5]

They were always talking about freedom and citizenship, and that was something else that Uncle Jerome used to start preaching about. He had all kinds of sermons ready for times like that. Sometimes he would be talking about children of Israel, and sometimes it would be the walls of Jericho, and sometimes it would be the big handwriting on the wall which was also the BIG HAND writing on the wall which was also the Big Hand writing on the WAR. That was when he used to say that the color of freedom was blue. The Union Army came dressed in blue. The big hand that signed the freedom papers signed them in blue ink which was also blood. The very sky itself was blue, limitless (*and gentlemen, sir, before I'd be a slave, I'll be buried in my grave*). And I said *My name is Jack the Rabbit and my home is in the briarpatch.*

Sometimes he would also say that the freedom road was a road through the wilderness and sometimes it wasn't any road at all because there never was any royal road to freedom for anybody (so don't you let nobody turn you round. And don't you let nobody know too much about your business either. And I said Call me Jack the Bear on my way somewhere).

Then it would be Education again. They didn't ever get tired of talking about that, the old folks telling about how they learned to spell and write back in the old days when they used to use slate tablets and the old Blueback Webster. The old days when they used to have to hold school whenever and wherever they could. Whenever they could spare the time from working the crops and wherever the teacher could find a place to shelter them. Whenever there was a teacher.

Then later on I was the one they meant when they said the young generation was the hope and glory. Because I had come that far in school by then; and sometimes it was Geography and sometimes it was History, and sometimes I had to tell about it, and sometimes I had to get the book and read it to them. Especially when it was about the Revolutionary War. Sometimes I had to read about Columbus too, and sometimes it would also be the explorers and the early settlers. But most of the time what they wanted to hear about was how the original thirteen colonies became the first thirteen states and who said what and who did what during that time and how the Constitution was made and who the first Presidents were and what they did.

That was also when I used to love to recite the Declaration of Independence, and the Gettysburg Address for them; and I could also recite the

---

4. Boundary between Pennsylvania and Maryland. Before the Civil War it was seen as the division between free and slave states.
5. The North; heaven. "Underground Railroad":

secret network that helped Southern slaves reach the North or Canada in the years before the Civil War.

Preamble to the Constitution and part of the Emancipation Proclamation; and I could also quote from the famous speeches of Patrick Henry and James Otis and Citizen Tom Paine; and I knew all kinds of sayings from *Poor Richard's Almanac.*

That boy can just about preach that thing right now, Mister Jeff Jefferson said one night after I had recited the William Lloyd Garrison and Frederick Douglass parts from the National Negro History Week pageant.

That boy can talk straight out of the dictionary when he want to, Mister Big Martin said looking at me but talking to everybody.

It just do you good to hear that kind of talk.

Whitefolks need to hear some talk like that.

The whitefolks the very one said all that, Jeff.

What kind of whitefolks talking like that?

Histry-book whitefolks.

What kind of histry-book whitefolks?

Whitefolks in that same book that child reading.

I ain't never heard no whitefolks believing nothing like that in all of my born days.

Whitefolks printed that book, didn't they?

I don't care who printed that book, that's *freedom* talk.

Well, the histry book whitefolks got up the Constitution, didn't they?

Yeah, and there was some histry book blackfolks in there somewhere too, you can just about bet on that. There was a jet-black roustabout right in there with old Christopher Columbus, and the very first one to try to climb that bunker hill was a mean black son-of-a-gun from Boston.[6] Ain't nothing never happened and wasn't some kind of a black hand mixed up in it somewhere. You just look at it close enough. The very first ones to come up with iron was them royal black Ethiopians.

You right about that, Mister Big Martin said, ain't nobody going to dispute you about that.

I know I'm right, Mister Jeff said, And I still say these whitefolks need to hear some of that kind of gospel. These ain't no histry book whitefolks around here and this ain't no histry. This ain't nothing but just a plain old everyday mess!

Trying to keep the black man down.

All whitefolks ain't like that, Phil.

Yeah, but them that is.

And some of us too, Jesus, Miss Minnie Ridley Stovall said, Lord the truth is the light, and some of us just ain't ready yet.

Amen, Mister Big Martin said.

Amen? Mister Phil Motley said. What you mean Amen?

That's what I want to know, Mister Jeff Jefferson said.

I mean the truth is the light just like Minnie say.

I done told you, Miss Minnie Ridley Stovall said.

Well ain't none of these peckerwoods around here ready for nothing neither, but just look at them. That's some truth for the light too.

Yeah but I still say some of us still ain't learned how to stick together yet.

Now Big'un, you know good and well that can get to be a horse of another color, Mister Doc Donahue said. I for one don't never intend to be sticking

---

6. Crispus Attucks (1723?–1770), former slave, among the first men to die in the Boston Massacre.

with any and everybody coming along because he say he one of us. You know better than that.

That's why I say *some* of us, Jesus, Miss Minnie Ridley Stovall said.

That's all right about all that, Mister Big Martin said. I'm talking about when you talking about going up against that stone wall. I want us to be ready. I'm talking about Stonewall Jackson. I'm talking about Jericho. That's what I'm talking about.

Well, we talking about the same thing then, Mister Phil Motley said.

That's all right about your Stonewall Jackson too, Mister Jeff Jefferson said, and your Vardaman and your Pitchfork Ben and all the rest of them. This child right here is getting old Stonewall Jackson's water ready.

They were all laughing then. Because everybody in Gasoline Point knew how Shorty Hollingsworth had met his waterloo and got the name Hot Water Shorty. His wife had come up behind him and dashed a pot of scalding lye water down the seat of his pants while he was sitting on the front steps cleaning his shotgun and bragging about what he was going to do if she didn't have his supper on the table in the next five minutes. He had yelled, dropped his shotgun and lit out across the barbwire fence and hadn't stopped until he was chin deep in Three Mile Creek. He had a new name from then on and he also had a new reputation: he could outrun a striped-assed ape.

Uncle Jerome said I was learning about verbs and adverbs and proverbs; and he preached his sermon on the dictionary that time, and he had his own special introduction to the principles of grammar: A noun is someone or something; a pronoun is anything or anybody; a verb is tells and does and is; an adverb is anyhow, anywhere, anytime; an adjective is number and nature; a preposition is relationship; and conjunction is membership; and interjection is the spirit of energy.

Then that time when Aunt Sue was visiting us from Atmore, old Mayfield Turner was there. Old Sawmill Turner, the log carriage expert, who Mama said had been trying to marry Aunt Sue for more than seventeen years, which meant that he had started before she married her first husband (she was visiting us because she had just separated from her fourth husband). Old Sawmill was wearing his blue pinstripe, tailor-made suit and his Edwin Clapp shoes and smelling like the barbershop and sitting cross-legged like Henry Ford; and every time he took a puff on his White Owl, he flashed his diamond ring like E. Berry Wall. Sometimes when they were talking about him behind his back they used to give him names like John D. Rockefeller Turner and J. P. Morgan Turner and Jay Gould Turner[7] because he also sported pearl gray kidskin gloves, and he was always talking about stocks and bonds and worrying about the National Debt.

I was reading about Valley Forge[8] that night, and I knew he was there just as I knew that Mister Lige and Miss Emma Tolliver and Bro Mark Simpkins and his wife, Miss Willeen were all there, because they were always the first ones to come by to see Aunt Sue when she was in town. But at first the only ones that I was really conscious of were Miss Lula Crayton

7. Appended to "Turner" are the names of American financial tycoons of the late 19th and early 20th centuries.
8. Southeastern Pennsylvania location of the Revolutionary Army headquarters from late 1777 to mid-1778; severe winter weather caused much suffering.

and Miss Liza Jefferson, because every time I paused Miss Lula Crayton
kept saying Tribulation tribulation trials and tribulation, and Miss Ida Jefferson would respond one time as if she were hearing some new gossip, and
the next time as if I were reading the Bible itself (saying Honey don't tell
me, saying Lord have mercy Jesus).

Then I happened to glance up and see old Sawmill again, and he had
stopped puffing on his cigar. He was leaning forward with his hand under
his chin, his eyes closed, his lips moving, repeating everything I was reading, word for word. He had forgotten all about Aunt Sue, for the time being
at least. I was reading about how the Redcoats were wining and dining and
dancing warm in Philadelphia while the ragtag bobtail Continental Army
was starving and freezing in makeshift huts and hovels, and about how
General George Washington himself had to get out and personally whip
slackers and stragglers and would-be deserters back into the ranks with the
flat of his sword. All of which was what Give me liberty or give me death
really meant, which was why whenever you talked about following in the
footsteps of our great American forefathers you were also talking about the
bloody tracks the half barefooted troops left in the snow that fateful winter.

Everytime I glanced up I could see old Sawmill Turner still leaning forward toward me, his lips still moving, the tip of his cigar gone to ash. Then
when I came to the end of the chapter and closed the book, he stood up and
stepped out; into the center of the semi-circle as Uncle Jerome always did.
I'm a histry scholar myself, he said. I been a histry scholar ever since I first
saw all of them seals and emblems down at the post office when I was a
little boy back in Lowdnes County. Then he ran his hand down into his
pocket and pulled out a fat roll of brand-new greenbacks, which he held
against his chest like a deck of gambling cards. He peeled off a crisp one-
dollar bill and held it up and said, Old George Washington is number one
because he was first in war and first in peace and first in the hearts of his
countrymen. He got it started.

And old Abe Lincoln. (*He held up a five-dollar bill.*) Came along later on
and had to save the Union. Old Alexander Hamilton didn't get to be the
President, but he was in there amongst them when they started talking
about how they were going to handle the money, and here he is. (*He pulled
off a ten-dollar bill.*) And here's old Tom Jefferson. (*Off came a twenty-dollar
bill.*) Now he was a educated man and he knowed exactly what to do with
his book learning. And then you come on up to old Ulysses S. Grant. (He
held up a fifty-dollar bill without even pausing.) He was the one old Abe
Lincoln himself had to send for when the going got tight, and later on they
made him the eighteenth President.

He held up the fifty-dollar bill long enough for everybody to see that it
really was a fifty-dollar bill and then he held up a hundred-dollar bill and
said, Old Ben Franklin didn't ever even want to be the President. But old
Ben Franklin left just as big a mark in histry as any of them. They didn't put
him up there on no one-hundred-dollar bill for nothing. Old Ben Franklin
was one of the smartest men they had back in them days, and everybody
give him his due respect. Old Ben Franklin told them a lot of good points
about how to put them clauses in the Constitution. He was just about the
first one they thought about when they had to send somebody across the
water to do some official business for the Government with them fast talking Frenchmen. And talking about being cunning, old Ben Franklin was the
one that took a kite and a Cocola bottle and stole naked lightning.

He came and stood in front of my chair then. This boy is worth more than one hundred shares of gilt-edged preferred, and the good part about it is we all going to be drawing down interest on him. Then he handed me a five-dollar bill as crisp as the one he had held up before, and told me to buy myself a fountain pen; and he told Mama he was going to be the one to stake me to all the ink and paper I needed as long as I stayed in school. All I had to do was show him my report card.

All I could do was say thank you, and I said I would always do my best. And Miss Lula Crayton said Amen. And Miss Liza Jefferson said God bless the lamb and God bless you Mayfield Turner. Then before anybody else could say anything he excused himself and Aunt Sue walked him to the door and he put on his alpaca topcoat, his black Homburg hat and his Wall Street gloves and was gone.

All Mama could do was wipe her eyes, and all Papa could do was look at the floor and shake his head and smile. But Uncle Jerome was on his feet again, saying he was talking about the word made manifest for Manifest Destiny;[9] and I knew he was going to take over where Sawmill Turner had left off and preach a whole sermon with me in it that night. And so did everybody else, and they were looking at me as if I really had become the Lamb or something. So I looked at the mantlepiece, and I heard the Mother Goose clock and outside there was the Valley Forge bitter wind in the turret-tall chinaberry tree.

1974

9. In the 19th century, a doctrine that the United States had both the right and the duty to expand across North America.

MAYA ANGELOU
b. 1928

In an interview with African American critic Claudia Tate, Maya Angelou proclaimed, "All my work is meant to say, 'You may encounter many defeats but you must not be defeated.' In fact, the encountering may be the very experience which creates the vitality and the power to endure."

The career of Maya Angelou is a testament both to her vitality and to her power to endure. Angelou has expressed her talents as a dancer, singer, producer, composer, journalist, actor, and teacher as well as a writer. Beginning with *I Know Why the Caged Bird Sings* (1970), which was nominated for a National Book Award, she has chronicled her various careers in four other autobiographical volumes. Angelou has also published five volumes of poetry: *Just Give Me a Cool Drink of Water 'for I Diiie* (1971), which was nominated for a Pulitzer Prize, *Oh Pray My Wings Are Gonna Fit Me Well* (1975), *And Still I Rise* (1978), *Shaker Why Don't You Sing* (1983), *Now Sheba Sings the Song* (1987), and *I Shall Not Be Moved* (1990). Chosen by President Bill Clinton to read at his inauguration on January 21, 1993, Angelou was both the first African American and the first woman poet to be so honored.

Born Marguerite Annie Johnson on April 4, 1928, in St. Louis, Angelou moved frequently as a child. Her divorced parents, Vivian Baxter and Bailey Johnson, sent her and her brother, Bailey, back and forth between St. Louis and Stamps, Arkansas, where her paternal grandmother lived, then finally to San Francisco to settle with their mother. It was her ten years in Arkansas that provided Angelou with the experiences that would be the core of her immensely popular autobiography, *I Know Why the Caged Bird Sings.*

In that volume Angelou describes what it meant to be a black girl in Arkansas during the Depression. One vivid example was the treatment she received from the ironically named dentist Dr. Lincoln, who refused to treat her seriously decayed teeth because she was black. Angelou reflects: "It seems terribly unfair to have a toothache and a headache and to have to bear at the same time the heavy burden of Blackness." However, the racism of the South was exceeded by the trauma of her being raped at age eight by her mother's boyfriend. After naming her assailant, Angelou had to endure the horror of the trial and the subsequent murder of her rapist by her uncles. Feeling that her words had the power to kill, she descended into silence for the next five years. The writer who was later to state, "I write for the Black voice and any ear which can hear it," spent many years unable to speak herself, but listening to and absorbing the voices around her.

Despite the difficulties of her early life, Angelou's autobiographies and poetry are full of references to the positive, life-affirming values, particularly courage, of the African American community in which she grew up. Her grandmother Annie Henderson, of Stamps, embodied for this injured child strength in the face of adversity. Through the Depression and despite racism and sexism, Henderson's ability to keep her general store solvent and her pride intact excited her granddaughter's admiration. Another resilient southern woman, Mrs. Flowers, the aristocrat of black Stamps, helped Angelou regain her voice through afternoons of reading and reciting literary classics.

These experiences in the South provided Angelou with the "power to endure" her adolescent years in California. *I Know Why the Caged Bird Sings* recounts her headlong rush into maturity as she became the first African American streetcar conductor in San Francisco and graduated from Mission High School at sixteen only to deliver a son one month later. Throughout the second volume of her autobiography, *Gather Together in My Name* (1974), Angelou weathers difficulties with men and with jobs, including a week's stint with prostitution and a flirtation with drugs.

In the third volume of her autobiography, *Singin' and Swingin' and Gettin' Merry Like Christmas* (1976), Angelou recounts her life as a dancer and member of the European touring cast of *Porgy and Bess*. In *The Heart of a Woman* (1981), Angelou relates her growing commitment to writing and her involvement in the civil rights movement of the 1960s. She moved to Brooklyn to learn the craft of writing from her friend John Oliver Killens, who introduced her to the Harlem Writers Guild and to writers such as Paule Marshall and James Baldwin. During this time, she met Martin Luther King Jr. and became the Southern Christian Leadership Conferences' northern coordinator. She also appeared as the White Queen in Jean Genet's play *The Blacks.*

Angelou's travels are the subject of her fifth autobiographical volume, *All God's Children Need Traveling Shoes* (1984). In this book she tells of her quest to understand Africa during a stay in Ghana and of her decision to return to the southern United States for the first time since her childhood. It is not surprising that her sojourn in Africa helped her understand herself both as an African and as an American. *A Song Flung Up to Heaven* (2002) recapitulates many experiences chronicled in the earlier volumes; she ends this record of her life as she prepares to write *Caged Bird.* Her first six autobiographies were reissued in *I Know Why the Caged Bird Sings: Collected Autobiographies of May Angelou* (2004). *Mom and Me and Mom* (2013) focuses on Angelou's relationship with her mother, Vivian Baxter.

Angelou is also a prolific poet, whose lyrics draw on African American oral traditions. Many of her poems explore the vicissitudes of love and the pleasures and difficulties of being an African American. Her *Collected Poems* was published in 1994, and *A Brave and Startling Truth* appeared in 1995. In 1993 President Bill Clinton invited Angelou to write a poem for his inauguration; the poem she recited, "On the Pulse of Morning," won the 1994 Grammy Award in the Best Spoken Word category. Angelou has also written for television—the PBS series *Black, Blues, Black* (1968) and a teleplay of *Caged Bird*—and for the screen—*Georgia, Georgia* (1971) and *Sister, Sister* (1979). She received a Tony nomination for best supporting actress in the television series *Roots*. Writing across a range of genres, including children's books, cookbooks, and inspirational volumes, Angelou continues to be among the most popular African American writers. As her audience has grown, her critical reputation has declined. *Caged Bird*, however, remains widely admired.

More than fifty colleges and universities have awarded Angelou honorary degrees, including Smith College, Mills College, and the University of Arkansas. In 1981 she accepted a lifetime appointment as the first Reynolds Professor of American Studies at Wake Forest University. In 2010 she was awarded the Presidential Medal of Freedom by President Barack Obama.

Still I Rise

You may write me down in history
With your bitter, twisted lies,
You may trod me in the very dirt
But still, like dust, I'll rise.

Does my sassiness upset you?   5
Why are you beset with gloom?
'Cause I walk like I've got oil wells
Pumping in my living room.

Just like moons and like suns,
With the certainty of tides,   10
Just like hopes springing high,
Still I'll rise.

Did you want to see me broken?
Bowed head and lowered eyes?
Shoulders falling down like teardrops,   15
Weakened by my soulful cries.

Does my haughtiness offend you?
Don't you take it awful hard
'Cause I laugh like I've got gold mines
Diggin' in my own back yard.   20

You may shoot me with your words,
You may cut me with your eyes,
You may kill me with your hatefulness,
But still, like air, I'll rise.

Does my sexiness upset you?   25
Does it come as a surprise

That I dance like I've got diamonds
At the meeting of my thighs?

Out of the huts of history's shame
I rise   30
Up from a past that's rooted in pain
I rise
I'm a black ocean, leaping and wide,
Welling and swelling I bear in the tide.
Leaving behind nights of terror and fear   35
I rise
Into a daybreak that's wondrously clear
I rise
Bringing the gifts that my ancestors gave,
I am the dream and the hope of the slave.   40
I rise
I rise
I rise.

1978

My Arkansas

There is a deep brooding
in Arkansas.
Old crimes like moss pend
from poplar trees.
The sullen earth   5
is much too
red for comfort.

Sunrise seems to hesitate
and in that second
lose its   10
incandescent aim, and
dusk no more shadows
than the noon.
The past is brighter yet.

Old hates and   15
ante-bellum[1] lace, are rent
but not discarded.
Today is yet to come
in Arkansas.
It writhes. It writhes in awful   20
waves of brooding.

1978

1. Existing before the Civil War.

From I Know Why the Caged Bird Sings

Chapter 15

[MRS. FLOWERS]

For nearly a year, I sopped around the house, the Store, the school and the church, like an old biscuit, dirty and inedible. Then I met, or rather got to know, the lady who threw me my first life line.

Mrs. Bertha Flowers was the aristocrat of Black Stamps. She had the grace of control to appear warm in the coldest weather, and on the Arkansas summer days it seemed she had a private breeze which swirled around, cooling her. She was thin without the taut look of wiry people, and her printed voile dresses and flowered hats were as right for her as denim overalls for a farmer. She was our side's answer to the richest white woman in town.

Her skin was a rich black that would have peeled like a plum if snagged, but then no one would have thought of getting close enough to Mrs. Flowers to ruffle her dress, let along snag her skin. She didn't encourage familiarity. She wore gloves too.

I don't think I ever saw Mrs. Flowers laugh, but she smiled often. A slow widening of her thin black lips to show even, small white teeth, then the slow effortless closing. When she chose to smile on me, I always wanted to thank her. The action was so graceful and inclusively benign.

She was one of the few gentlewomen I have ever known, and has remained throughout my life the measure of what a human being can be.

Momma[1] had a strange relationship with her. Most often when she passed on the road in front of the Store, she spoke to Momma in that soft yet carrying voice, "Good day, Mrs. Henderson." Momma responded with "How you, Sister Flowers?"

Mrs. Flowers didn't belong to our church, nor was she Momma's familiar.[2] Why on earth did she insist on calling her Sister Flowers? Shame made me want to hide my face. Mrs. Flowers deserved better than to be called Sister. Then, Momma left out the verb. Why not ask, "How *are* you, *Mrs. Flowers?*" With the unbalanced passion of the young, I hated her for showing her ignorance to Mrs. Flowers. It didn't occur to me for many years that they were as alike as sisters, separated only by formal education.

Although I was upset, neither of the women was in the least shaken by what I thought an unceremonious greeting. Mrs. Flowers would continue her easy gait up the hill to her little bungalow, and Momma kept on shelling peas or doing whatever had brought her to the front porch.

Occasionally, though, Mrs. Flowers would drift off the road and down to the Store and Momma would say to me, "Sister, you go on and play." As I left I would hear the beginning of an intimate conversation. Momma persistently using the wrong verb, or none at all.

"Brother and Sister Wilcox is sho'ly the meanest—" "Is," Momma? "Is"? Oh, please, not "is," Momma, for two or more. But they talked, and from the side of the building where I waited for the ground to open up and swallow me, I heard the soft-voiced Mrs. Flowers and the textured voice of my

1. I.e., Angelou's grandmother.
2. A member of one's family or someone as close as family.

grandmother merging and melting. They were interrupted from time to time by giggles that must have come from Mrs. Flowers (Momma never giggled in her life). Then she was gone.

She appealed to me because she was like people I had never met personally. Like women in English novels who walked the moors (whatever they were) with their loyal dogs racing at a respectful distance. Like the women who sat in front of roaring fireplaces, drinking tea incessantly from silver trays full of scones and crumpets. Women who walked over the "heath" and read morocco-bound[3] books and had two last names divided by a hyphen. It would be safe to say that she made me proud to be Negro, just by being herself.

She acted just as refined as whitefolks in the movies and books and she was more beautiful, for none of them could have come near that warm color without looking gray by comparison.

It was fortunate that I never saw her in the company of powhitefolks. For since they tend to think of their whiteness as an evenizer, I'm certain that I would have had to hear her spoken to commonly as Bertha, and my image of her would have been shattered like the unmendable Humpty-Dumpty.

One summer afternoon, sweet-milk[4] fresh in my memory, she stopped at the Store to buy provisions. Another Negro woman of her health and age would have been expected to carry the paper sacks home in one hand, but Momma said, "Sister Flowers, I'll send Bailey up to your house with these things."

She smiled that slow dragging smile, "Thank you, Mrs. Henderson. I'd prefer Marguerite, though." My name was beautiful when she said it. "I've been meaning to talk to her, anyway." They gave each other age-group looks.

Momma said, "Well, that's all right then. Sister, go and change your dress. You going to Sister Flowers's."

The chifforobe[5] was a maze. What on earth did one put on to go to Mrs. Flowers' house? I knew I shouldn't put on a Sunday dress. It might be sacrilegious. Certainly not a house dress, since I was already wearing a fresh one. I chose a school dress, naturally. It was formal without suggesting that going to Mrs. Flowers' house was equivalent to attending church.

I trusted myself back into the Store.

"Now, don't you look nice." I had chosen the right thing, for once.

"Mrs. Henderson, you make most of the children's clothes, don't you?"

"Yes, ma'am. Sure do. Store-bought clothes ain't hardly worth the thread it take to stitch them."

"I'll say you do a lovely job, though, so neat. That dress looks professional."

Momma was enjoying the seldom-received compliments. Since everyone we knew (except Mrs. Flowers, of course) could sew competently, praise was rarely handed out for the commonly practiced craft.

"I try, with the help of the Lord, Sister Flowers, to finish the inside just like I does the outside. Come here, Sister."

I had buttoned up the collar and tied the belt, apronlike, in back. Momma told me to turn around. With one hand she pulled the strings and the belt

3. Leather-bound.
4. Milk that has had sugar added to it.

5. Combination bureau and wardrobe.

fell free at both sides of my waist. Then her large hands were at my neck, opening the button loops. I was terrified. What was happening?

"Take it off, Sister." She had her hands on the hem of the dress.

"I don't need to see the inside, Mrs. Henderson, I can tell . . ." But the dress was over my head and my arms were stuck in the sleeves. Momma said, "That'll do. See here, Sister Flowers, I French-seams[6] around the arm-holes." Through the cloth film, I saw the shadow approach. "That makes it last longer. Children these days would bust out of sheet-metal clothes. They so rough."

"That is a very good job, Mrs. Henderson. You should be proud. You can put your dress back on, Marguerite."

"No ma'am. Pride is a sin. And 'cording to the Good Book, it goeth before a fall."

"That's right. So the Bible says. It's a good thing to keep in mind."

I wouldn't look at either of them. Momma hadn't thought that taking off my dress in front of Mrs. Flowers would kill me stone dead. If I had refused, she would have thought I was trying to be "womanish" and might have remembered St. Louis.[7] Mrs. Flowers had known that I would be embar-rassed and that was even worse. I picked up the groceries and went out to wait in the hot sunshine. It would be fitting if I got a sunstroke and died before they came outside. Just dropped dead on the slanting porch.

There was a little path beside the rocky road, and Mrs. Flowers walked in front swinging her arms and picking her way over the stones.

She said, without turning her head, to me, "I hear you're doing very good school work, Marguerite, but that it's all written. The teachers report that they have trouble getting you to talk in class." We passed the triangular farm on our left and the path widened to allow us to walk together. I hung back in the separate unasked and unanswerable questions.

"Come and walk along with me, Marguerite." I couldn't have refused even if I wanted to. She pronounced my name so nicely. Or more correctly, she spoke each word with such clarity that I was certain a foreigner who didn't understand English could have understood her.

"Now no one is going to make you talk—possibly no one can. But bear in mind, language is man's way of communicating with his fellow man and it is language alone which separates him from the lower animals." That was a totally new idea to me, and I would need time to think about it.

"Your grandmother says you read a lot. Every chance you get. That's good, but not good enough. Words mean more than what is set down on paper. It takes the human voice to infuse them with the shades of deeper meaning."

I memorized the part about the human voice infusing words. It seemed so valid and poetic.

She said she was going to give me some books and that I not only must read them, I must read them aloud. She suggested that I try to make a sen-tence sound in as many different ways as possible.

"I'll accept no excuse if you return a book to me that has been badly handled." My imagination boggled at the punishment I would deserve if in fact I did abuse a book of Mrs. Flowers'. Death would be too kind and brief.

---

6. Stitches the seam on both sides of the fabric so that no raw edges are exposed.

7. Angelou had been raped in St. Louis by her mother's boyfriend.

The odors in the house surprised me. Somehow I had never connected Mrs. Flowers with food or eating or any other common experience of common people. There must have been an outhouse, too, but my mind never recorded it.

The sweet scent of vanilla had met us as she opened the door.

"I made tea cookies this morning. You see, I had planned to invite you for cookies and lemonade so we could have this little chat. The lemonade is in the icebox."

It followed that Mrs. Flowers would have ice on an ordinary day, when most families in our town bought ice late on Saturdays only a few times during the summer to be used in the wooden ice-cream freezers.

She took the bags from me and disappeared through the kitchen door. I looked around the room that I had never in my wildest fantasies imagined I would see. Browned photographs leered or threatened from the walls and the white, freshly done curtains pushed against themselves and against the wind. I wanted to gobble up the room entire and take it to Bailey, who would help me analyze and enjoy it.

"Have a seat, Marguerite. Over there by the table." She carried a platter covered with a tea towel. Although she warned that she hadn't tried her hand at baking sweets for some time, I was certain that like everything else about her the cookies would be perfect.

They were flat round wafers, slightly browned on the edges and butter-yellow in the center. With the cold lemonade they were sufficient for childhood's lifelong diet. Remembering my manners, I took nice little lady-like bites off the edges. She said she had made them expressly for me and that she had a few in the kitchen that I could take home to my brother. So I jammed one whole cake in my mouth and the rough crumbs scratched the insides of my jaws, and if I hadn't had to swallow, it would have been a dream come true.

As I ate she began the first of what we later called "my lessons in living." She said that I must always be intolerant of ignorance but understanding of illiteracy. That some people, unable to go to school, were more educated and even more intelligent than college professors. She encouraged me to listen carefully to what country people called mother wit. That in those homely sayings was couched the collective wisdom of generations.

When I finished the cookies she brushed off the table and brought a thick, small book from the bookcase. I had read *A Tale of Two Cities*[8] and found it up to my standards as a romantic novel. She opened the first page and I heard poetry for the first time in my life.

"It was the best of times and the worst of times . . ." Her voice slid in and curved down through and over the words. She was nearly singing. I wanted to look at the pages. Were they the same that I had read? Or were there notes, music, lined on the pages, as in a hymn book? Her sounds began cascading gently. I knew from listening to a thousand preachers that she was nearing the end of her reading, and I hadn't really heard, heard to understand, a single word.

"How do you like that?"

It occurred to me that she expected a response. The sweet vanilla flavor was still on my tongue and her reading was a wonder in my ears. I had to speak.

---

8. A novel about the French Revolution, by English writer Charles Dickens (1812–1870).

I said, "Yes, ma'am." It was the least I could do, but it was the most also.

"There's one more thing. Take this book of poems and memorize one for me. Next time you pay me a visit, I want you to recite."

I have tried often to search behind the sophistication of years for the enchantment I so easily found in those gifts. The essence escapes but its aura remains. To be allowed, no, invited, into the private lives of strangers, and to share their joys and fears, was a chance to exchange the Southern bitter wormwood for a cup of mead with Beowulf or a hot cup of tea and milk with Oliver Twist.[9] When I said aloud, "It is a far, far better thing that I do, than I have ever done . . ." tears of love filled my eyes at my selflessness.

On that first day, I ran down the hill and into the road (few cars ever came along it) and had the good sense to stop running before I reached the Store.

I was liked, and what a difference it made. I was respected not as Mrs. Henderson's grandchild or Bailey's sister but for just being Marguerite Johnson.

Childhood's logic never asks to be proved (all conclusions are absolute). I didn't question why Mrs. Flowers had singled me out for attention, nor did it occur to me that Momma might have asked her to give me a little talking to. All I cared about was that she had made tea cookies for *me* and read to *me* from her favorite book. It was enough to prove that she liked me.

Momma and Bailey were waiting inside the Store. He said, "My, what did she give you?" He had seen the books, but I held the paper sack with his cookies in my arms shielded by the poems.

Momma said, "Sister, I know you acted like a little lady. That do my heart good to see settled people take to you all. I'm trying my best, the Lord knows, but these days . . ." Her voice trailed off. "Go on in and change your dress."

In the bedroom it was going to be a joy to see Bailey receive his cookies. I said, "By the way, Bailey, Mrs. Flowers sent you some tea cookies—"

Momma shouted, "What did you say, Sister? You, Sister, what did you say?" Hot anger was crackling in her voice.

Bailey said, "She said Mrs. Flowers sent me some—"

"I ain't talking to you, Ju." I heard the heavy feet walk across the floor toward our bedroom. "Sister, you heard me. What's that you said?" She swelled to fill the doorway.

Bailey said, "Momma." His pacifying voice—"Momma, she—"

"You shut up, Ju. I'm talking to your sister."

I didn't know what sacred cow I had bumped, but it was better to find out than to hang like a thread over an open fire. I repeated, "I said, 'Bailey, by the way, Mrs. Flowers sent you—'"

"That's what I thought you said. Go on and take off your dress. I'm going to get a switch."

At first I thought she was playing. Maybe some heavy joke that would end with "You sure she didn't send me something?" but in a minute she was back in the room with a long, ropy, peach-tree switch, the juice smelling bitter at having been torn loose. She said, "Get down on your knees. Bailey, Junior, you come on, too."

The three of us knelt as she began, "Our Father, you know the tribulations of your humble servant. I have with your help raised two grown boys. Many's the day I thought I wouldn't be able to go on, but you gave me the strength to see my way clear. Now, Lord, look down on this heavy heart today. I'm trying to raise my son's children in the way they should go, but, oh, Lord, the Devil try to hinder me on every hand. I never thought I'd live to hear cursing under this roof, what I try to keep dedicated to the glorification of God. And cursing out of the mouths of babes. But you said, in the last days brother would turn against brother, and children against their parents. That there would be a gnashing of teeth and a rendering of flesh. Father, forgive this child, I beg you, on bended knee."

I was crying loudly now. Momma's voice had risen to a shouting pitch, and I knew that whatever wrong I had committed was extremely serious. She had even left the Store untended to take up my case with God. When she finished we were all crying. She pulled me to her with one hand and hit me only a few times with the switch. The shock of my sin and the emotional release of her prayer had exhausted her.

Momma wouldn't talk right then, but later in the evening I found that my violation lay in using the phrase "by the way." Momma explained that "Jesus was the Way, the Truth and the Light," and anyone who says "by the way" is really saying, "by Jesus," or "by God" and the Lord's name would not be taken in vain in her house.

When Bailey tried to interpret the words with: "Whitefolks use 'by the way' to mean while we're on the subject," Momma reminded us that "whitefolks' mouths were most in general loose and their words were an abomination before Christ."

Chapter 16

["MAM"]

Recently a white woman from Texas, who would quickly describe herself as a liberal, asked me about my hometown. When I told her that in Stamps my grandmother had owned the only Negro general merchandise store since the turn of the century, she exclaimed, "Why, you were a debutante." Ridiculous and even ludicrous. But Negro girls in small Southern towns, whether poverty-stricken or just munching along on a few of life's necessities, were given as extensive and irrelevant preparations for adulthood as rich white girls shown in magazines. Admittedly the training was not the same. While white girls learned to waltz and sit gracefully with a tea cup balanced on their knees, we were lagging behind, learning the mid-Victorian values with very little money to indulge them. (Come and see Edna Lomax spending the money she made picking cotton on five balls of ecru tatting thread. Her fingers are bound to snag the work and she'll have to repeat the stitches time and time again. But she knows that when she buys the thread.)

We were required to embroider and I had trunkfuls of colorful dishtowels, pillowcases, runners and handkerchiefs to my credit. I mastered the art of crocheting and tatting, and there was a lifetime's supply of dainty doilies that would never be used in sacheted dresser drawers. It went without saying that all girls could iron and wash, but the finer touches around the home, like setting a table with real silver, baking roasts and cooking vegetables without meat, had to be learned elsewhere. Usually at the source of those habits. During my tenth year, a white woman's kitchen became my finishing school.

Mrs. Viola Cullinan was a plump woman who lived in a three-bedroom house somewhere behind the post office. She was singularly unattractive until she smiled, and then the lines around her eyes and mouth which made her look perpetually dirty disappeared, and her face looked like the mask of an impish elf. She usually rested her smile until late afternoon when her women friends dropped in and Miss Glory, the cook, served them cold drinks on the closed-in porch.

The exactness of her house was inhuman. This glass went here and only here. That cup had its place and it was an act of impudent rebellion to place it anywhere else. At twelve o'clock the table was set. At 12:15 Mrs. Cullinan sat down to dinner (whether her husband had arrived or not). At 12:16 Miss Glory brought out the food.

It took me a week to learn the difference between a salad plate, a bread plate and a dessert plate.

Mrs. Cullinan kept up the tradition of her wealthy parents. She was from Virginia. Miss Glory, who was a descendant of slaves that had worked for the Cullinans, told me her history. She had married beneath her (according to Miss Glory). Her husband's family hadn't had their money very long and what they had "didn't 'mount to much."

As ugly as she was, I thought privately, she was lucky to get a husband above or beneath her station. But Miss Glory wouldn't let me say a thing against her mistress. She was very patient with me, however, over the housework. She explained the dishware, silverware and servants' bells.

The large round bowl in which soup was served wasn't a soup bowl, it was a tureen. There were goblets, sherbet glasses, ice-cream glasses, wine glasses, green glass coffee cups with matching saucers, and water glasses. I had a glass to drink from, and it sat with Miss Glory's on a separate shelf from the others. Soup spoons, gravy boat, butter knives, salad forks and carving platter were additions to my vocabulary and in fact almost represented a new language. I was fascinated with the novelty, with the fluttering Mrs. Cullinan and her Alice-in-Wonderland house.

Her husband remains, in my memory, undefined. I lumped him with all the other white men that I had ever seen and tried not to see.

On our way home one evening, Miss Glory told me that Mrs. Cullinan couldn't have children. She said that she was too delicate-boned. It was hard to imagine bones at all under those layers of fat. Miss Glory went on to say that the doctor had taken out all her lady organs. I reasoned that a pig's organs included the lungs, heart and liver, so if Mrs. Cullinan was walking around without those essentials, it explained why she drank alcohol out of unmarked bottles. She was keeping herself embalmed.

When I spoke to Bailey about it, he agreed that I was right, but he also informed me that Mr. Cullinan had two daughters by a colored lady and that I knew them very well. He added that the girls were the spitting image of their father. I was unable to remember what he looked like, although I had just left him a few hours before, but I thought of the Coleman girls. They were very light-skinned and certainly didn't look very much like their mother (no one ever mentioned Mr. Coleman).

My pity for Mrs. Cullinan preceded me the next morning like the Cheshire cat's smile. Those girls, who could have been her daughters, were beautiful. They didn't have to straighten their hair. Even when they were caught in the rain, their braids still hung down straight like tamed snakes. Their mouths were pouty little cupid's bows. Mrs. Cullinan didn't know what she missed. Or maybe she did. Poor Mrs. Cullinan.

For weeks after, I arrived early, left late and tried very hard to make up for her barrenness. If she had had her own children, she wouldn't have had to ask me to run a thousand errands from her back door to the back door of her friends. Poor old Mrs. Cullinan.

Then one evening Miss Glory told me to serve the ladies on the porch. After I set the tray down and turned toward the kitchen, one of the women asked, "What's your name, girl?" It was the speckled-faced one. Mrs. Cullinan said, "She doesn't talk much. Her name's Margaret."

"Is she dumb?"

"No. As I understand it, she can talk when she wants to but she's usually quiet as a little mouse. Aren't you, Margaret?"

I smiled at her. Poor thing. No organs and couldn't even pronounce my name correctly.

"She's a sweet little thing, though."

"Well, that may be, but the name's too long. I'd never bother myself. I'd call her Mary if I was you."

I fumed into the kitchen. That horrible woman would never have the chance to call me Mary because if I was starving I'd never work for her. I decided I wouldn't pee on her if her heart was on fire. Giggles drifted in off the porch and into Miss Glory's pots. I wondered what they could be laughing about.

Whitefolks were so strange. Could they be talking about me? Everybody knew that they stuck together better than the Negroes did. It was possible that Mrs. Cullinan had friends in St. Louis who heard about a girl from Stamps being in court and wrote to tell her. Maybe she knew about Mr. Freeman.[1]

My lunch was in my mouth a second time and I went outside and relieved myself on the bed of four-o'clocks. Miss Glory thought I might be coming down with something and told me to go on home, that Momma would give me some herb tea, and she'd explain to her mistress.

I realized how foolish I was being before I reached the pond. Of course Mrs. Cullinan didn't know. Otherwise she wouldn't have given me the two nice dresses that Momma cut down, and she certainly wouldn't have called me a "sweet little thing." My stomach felt fine, and I didn't mention anything to Momma.

That evening I decided to write a poem on being white, fat, old and without children. It was going to be a tragic ballad. I would have to watch her carefully to capture the essence of her loneliness and pain.

The very next day, she called me by the wrong name. Miss Glory and I were washing up the lunch dishes when Mrs. Cullinan came to the doorway. "Mary?"

Miss Glory asked, "Who?"

---

1. A reference to Angelou's rape and the subsequent trial of Mr. Freeman.

Mrs. Cullinan, sagging a little, knew and I knew. "I want Mary to go down to Mrs. Randall's and take her some soup. She's not been feeling well for a few days."

Miss Glory's face was a wonder to see. "You mean Margaret, ma'am. Her name's Margaret."

"That's too long. She's Mary from now on. Heat that soup from last night and put it in the china tureen and, Mary, I want you to carry it carefully."

Every person I knew had a hellish horror of being "called out of his name." It was a dangerous practice to call a Negro anything that could be loosely construed as insulting because of the centuries of their having been called niggers, jigs, dinges, blackbirds, crows, boots and spooks.

Miss Glory had a fleeting second of feeling sorry for me. Then as she handed me the hot tureen she said, "Don't mind, don't pay that no mind. Sticks and stones may break your bones, but words . . . You know, I been working for her for twenty years."

She held the back door open for me. "Twenty years. I wasn't much older than you. My name used to be Hallelujah. That's what Ma named me, but my mistress give me 'Glory,' and it stuck. I likes it better too."

I was in the little path that ran behind the houses when Miss Glory shouted, "It's shorter too."

For a few seconds it was a tossup over whether I would laugh (imagine being named Hallelujah) or cry (imagine letting some white woman rename you for her convenience). My anger saved me from either outburst. I had to quit the job, but the problem was going to be how to do it. Momma wouldn't allow me to quit for just any reason.

"She's a peach. That woman is a real peach." Mrs. Randall's maid was talking as she took the soup from me, and I wondered what her name used to be and what she answered to now.

For a week I looked into Mrs. Cullinan's face as she called me Mary. She ignored my coming late and leaving early. Miss Glory was a little annoyed because I had begun to leave egg yolk on the dishes and wasn't putting much heart in polishing the silver. I hoped that she would complain to our boss, but she didn't.

Then Bailey solved my dilemma. He had me describe the contents of the cupboard and the particular plates she liked best. Her favorite piece was a casserole shaped like a fish and the green glass coffee cups. I kept his instructions in mind, so on the next day when Miss Glory was hanging out clothes and I had again been told to serve the old biddies on the porch, I dropped the empty serving tray. When I heard Mrs. Cullinan scream, "Mary!" I picked up the casserole and two of the green glass cups in readiness. As she rounded the kitchen door I let them fall on the tiled floor.

I could never absolutely describe to Bailey what happened next, because each time I got to the part where she fell on the floor and screwed up her ugly face to cry, we burst out laughing. She actually wobbled around on the floor and picked up shards of the cups and cried, "Oh, Momma. Oh, dear Gawd. It's Momma's china from Virginia. Oh, Momma, I sorry."

Miss Glory came running in from the yard and the women from the porch crowded around. Miss Glory was almost as broken up as her mistress. "You mean to say she broke our Virginia dishes? What we gone do?"

Mrs. Cullinan cried louder, "That clumsy nigger. Clumsy little black nigger."

Old speckled-face leaned down and asked, "Who did it, Viola? Was it Mary? Who did it?"

Everything was happening so fast I can't remember whether her action preceded her words, but I know that Mrs. Cullinan said, "Her name's Margaret, goddamn it, her name's Margaret." And she threw a wedge of the broken plate at me. It could have been the hysteria which put her aim off, but the flying crockery caught Miss Glory right over her ear and she started screaming.

I left the front door wide open so all the neighbors could hear.

Mrs. Cullinan was right about one thing. My name wasn't Mary.

1970

PAULE MARSHALL
b. 1929

Paule Marshall wrote the novel that most black feminist critics consider to be the beginning of contemporary African American women's writings. *Brown Girl, Brownstones* was published in 1959 to fine critical reviews but without much fanfare because most African American literature of the time focused mainly on black manhood. Since then *Brown Girl, Brownstones* has been claimed by well-known African American women writers such as Alice Walker and Ntozake Shange as important to their own literary development, because it centered black women's experience within the context of a specifically black culture. Marshall's fiction represents the complex intersection of race, gender, and class in women's lives, even as it maps the historical and contemporary journeys that produce African diasporic subjects in the twentieth and twenty-first centuries.

Born April 9 in Stuyvesant Heights (now Bedford Stuyvesant), New York, the daughter of Ada and Samuel Burke, Marshall grew up in an immigrant community confronted by racism and the challenge of maintaining a Caribbean identity while succeeding in the capitalist culture of the United States. It is not surprising that the themes of colonialism; immigration; the lure of American materialism; racism; African, Caribbean, and African American cultures; and the importance of women's voices in the intersection of these cultures are central to Marshall's works. These include five novels—*Brown Girl, Brownstones* (1959), *The Chosen Place, the Timeless People* (1969), *Praisesong for the Widow* (1983), *Daughters* (1991), and *The Fisher King* (2000)—as well as her collection of novellas, *Soul Clap Hands and Sing* (1961); her short stories; her memoir, *Triangular Road* (2009); and her much-quoted essay, "The Making of a Writer: From the Poets in the Kitchen" (1983). In "Poets in the Kitchen" Marshall traces the powerful influence that her mother and her friends had on her writing. By claiming these supposedly "ordinary" women as her primary literary mentors, Marshall emphasizes the artistry of the oral tradition, so much a part of Caribbean culture, as well as the African belief that the day-to-day rituals of life are the bases of art. Years before the discussions of black English with which we are familiar today, Marshall demonstrated how blacks in the diaspora imbued the King's English with their own values and aesthetics. In *Brown Girl, Brownstones*, Marshall dug into American stereotypes of gender and race through her complex characterizations of the apparently domineering Silla, the supposedly weak Deighton, and their brown daughter Selina. Written against the ideological position that the black family was deviant, the evolving position that West Indians were a model minority, and the 1950s American belief that women were to be submissive, Marshall's first novel questioned American concepts of womanhood and manhood.

In addition to her education in "the wordshop of the kitchen," Marshall read nineteenth- and early-twentieth-century novelists Charles Dickens, Thomas Mann, and Joseph Conrad and from them learned much about rendering characters, especially in relation to culture and setting. Although she graduated from Brooklyn College in 1953 with a degree in English, Marshall at that time had read only two African American writers: Paul Lawrence Dunbar and Richard Wright. During the 1950s, she was especially influenced by two other African American thinkers: Ralph Ellison, whose *Shadow and Act* (1964) she has called her "literary bible," and James Baldwin, whose essays were especially influential to her both as a writer and as a thinker. Like many other African American women she did not encounter earlier African American women writers until the late 1960s, when she read Zora Neale Hurston, Dorothy West, and Gwendolyn Brooks, whose *Maud Martha* (1953) she would call "the finest portrayal of an African American woman in the novel to date and one which had a decided influence on [my] work."

After completing college, Marshall sought work as a journalist, at a time when most professional black women were to be teachers or social workers. It was during her employment at a small black magazine, *Our World,* afraid that she might end up a hack writer, that she began writing *Brown Girl, Brownstones,* not so much for publication as to "unravel [her] own knots." The writing of that novel, which she called an "exhilarating experience," converted her into a fiction writer. But she did not anticipate the resistance to her becoming a writer from her first husband, Kenneth Marshall, whom she had married in 1950 and with whom she had a son. From that experience Marshall learned what other contemporary American women writers such as Tillie Olsen in *Silences* (1978) and Alice Walker in *One Child of One's Own* would later write about—that motherhood and authorship are often seen in this society as antithetical.

As a journalist, Marshall traveled to the Caribbean and South America, the settings of *Soul Clap Hands and Sing.* Comprising four novellas—*Barbados, Brooklyn, British Guiana,* and *Brazil*—this collection is the first to trace the connections among black cultures in various parts of the Western Hemisphere. In her second novel, Marshall continued her focus on the world outside the United States. Her monumental *The Chosen Place, the Timeless People* is primarily set in the Caribbean and was called by Jamaican poet Edward Braithwaite "a truly third world novel," for it explores the hidden complexities of the relationship between the supposedly underdeveloped world and the developed worlds.

Marshall's first two novels and her stories of the 1960s were ahead of their time in that they clearly focused on the variety of black communities, and on black women, at a time when black cultural nationalism fostered a monolithic view of blacks as urban African American and male. Although her novels received fine reviews, Marshall did not become well known. While she received many awards, including a Guggenheim fellowship and a National Endowment for the Arts fellowship, she had difficulty making a living as a writer. During the 1970s she taught creative writing at universities such as Yale and Columbia and remarried, living part of the time in Haiti and part of the time in the United States. Perhaps as a result of her complicated life, she did not publish her third novel, *Praisesong for the Widow,* until 1982.

Praisesong for the Widow features a very unlikely heroine, Avey Johnson, an African American, middle-class, middle-aged woman who has achieved the American Dream but feels her "dis-ease" with it. Marshall's portrayal of Avey's journey from dis-ease to health is a praise song, an African ritual. At the same time *Praisesong,* like

Marshall's other novels, is concerned with the ways in which American materialism threatens black cultural wholeness. *Praisesong* also completes a journey begun in *Brown Girl, Brownstones,* what critic Susan Willis calls "an arc of recovery," for Avey has to take a cultural journey back—a journey that Selina began—from the United States through the Caribbean, to an African communal past to regain her sense of wholeness.

In the early 1980s, the Feminist Press reissued Marshall's long out-of-print *Brown Girl, Brownstones* as well as some of her short fiction in *Reena and Other Stories* (1982), thus making her work available to a new generation. In 1991 Marshall published *Daughters,* a novel set in the United States and Triunion, a fictional nation in the West Indies. Through the ancestor figures Congo Jane and Will Cudjoe, comrades in the struggle against slavery, the late-twentieth-century characters in the novel understand their obligation to themselves and to each other. In Marshall's novel *The Fisher King* (2000), diverse characters—in Brooklyn and Paris, poor and middle class, of Caribbean and black southern parentage—are bound by the memory and the music that are the legacy of a deceased jazzman.

In 1992 Marshall received the MacArthur Award, a fitting tribute to her stature as one of the Western Hemisphere's major contemporary black women writers and as a pioneer in her own right.

Reena

Like most people with unpleasant childhoods, I am on constant guard against the past—the past being for me the people and places associated with the years I served out my girlhood in Brooklyn. The places no longer matter that much since most of them have vanished. The old grammar school, for instance, P.S. 35 ("Dirty 5's" we called it and with justification) has been replaced by a low, coldly functional arrangement of glass and Permastone which bears its name but has none of the feel of a school about it. The small, grudgingly lighted stores along Fulton Street, the soda parlor that was like a church with its stained-glass panels in the door and marble floor have given way to those impersonal emporiums, the supermarkets. Our house even, a brownstone relic whose halls smelled comfortingly of dust and lemon oil, the somnolent street upon which it stood, the tall, muscular trees which shaded it were leveled years ago to make way for a city housing project—a stark, graceless warren for the poor. So that now whenever I revisit that old section of Brooklyn and see these new and ugly forms, I feel nothing. I might as well be in a strange city.

But it is another matter with the people of my past, the faces that in their darkness were myriad reflections of mine. Whenever I encounter them at the funeral or wake, the wedding or christening—those ceremonies by which the past reaffirms its hold—my guard drops and memories banished to the rear of the mind rush forward to rout the present. I almost become the child again—anxious and angry, disgracefully diffident.

Reena was one of the people from that time, and a main contributor to my sense of ineffectualness then. She had not done this deliberately. It was just that whenever she talked about herself (and this was not as often as most people) she seemed to be talking about me also. She ruthlessly analyzed herself, sparing herself nothing. Her honesty was so absolute it was a kind of cruelty.

She had not changed, I was to discover in meeting her again after a separation of twenty years. Nor had I really. For although the years had altered our positions (she was no longer the lord and I the lackey) and I could even afford to forgive her now, she still had the ability to disturb me profoundly by dredging to the surface those aspects of myself that I kept buried. This time, as I listened to her talk over the stretch of one long night, she made vivid without knowing it what is perhaps the most critical fact of my existence—that definition of me, of her and millions like us, formulated by others to serve out their fantasies, a definition we have to combat at an unconscionable cost to the self and even use, at times, in order to survive; the cause of so much shame and rage as well as, oddly enough, a source of pride: simply, what it has meant, what it means, to be a black woman in America.

We met—Reena and myself—at the funeral of her aunt who had been my godmother and whom I had also called aunt, Aunt Vi, and loved, for she and her house had been, respectively, a source of understanding and a place of calm for me as a child. Reena entered the church where the funeral service was being held as though she, not the minister, were coming to officiate, sat down among the immediate family up front, and turned to inspect those behind her. I saw her face then.

It was a good copy of the original. The familiar mold was there, that is, and the configuration of bone beneath the skin was the same despite the slight fleshiness I had never seen there before; her features had even retained their distinctive touches: the positive set to her mouth, the assertive lift to her nose, the same insistent, unsettling eyes which when she was angry became as black as her skin—and this was total, unnerving, and very beautiful. Yet something had happened to her face. It was different despite its sameness. Aging even while it remained enviably young. Time had sketched in, very lightly, the evidence of the twenty years.

As soon as the funeral service was over, I left, hurrying out of the church into the early November night. The wind, already at its winter strength, brought with it the smell of dead leaves and the image of Aunt Vi there in the church, as dead as the leaves—as well as the thought of Reena, whom I would see later at the wake.

Her real name had been Doreen, a standard for girls among West Indians (her mother, like my parents, was from Barbados), but she had changed it to Reena on her twelfth birthday—"As a present to myself"—and had enforced the change on her family by refusing to answer to the old name. "Reena. With two e's!" she would say and imprint those e's on your mind with the indelible black of her eyes and a thin threatening finger that was like a quill.

She and I had not been friends through our own choice. Rather, our mothers, who had known each other since childhood, had forced the relationship. And from the beginning, I had been at a disadvantage. For Reena, as early as the age of twelve, had had a quality that was unique, superior, and therefore dangerous. She seemed defined, even then, all of a piece, the raw edges of her adolescence smoothed over; indeed, she seemed to have escaped adolescence altogether and made one dazzling leap from childhood into the very arena of adult life. At thirteen, for instance, she was reading Zola, Hauptmann, Steinbeck, while I was still in the thrall of the Little

Minister and Lorna Doone.[1] When I could only barely conceive of the world beyond Brooklyn, she was talking of the Civil War in Spain, lynchings in the South, Hitler in Poland[2]—and talking with the outrage and passion of a revolutionary. I would try, I remember, to console myself with the thought that she was really an adult masquerading as a child, which meant that I could not possibly be her match.

For her part, Reena put up with me and was, by turns, patronizing and impatient. I merely served as the audience before whom she rehearsed her ideas and the yardstick by which she measured her worldliness and knowledge.

"Do you realize that this stupid country supplied Japan with the scrap iron to make the weapons she's now using against it?" she had shouted at me once.

I had not known that.

Just as she overwhelmed me, she overwhelmed her family, with the result that despite a half dozen brothers and sisters who consumed quantities of bread and jam whenever they visited us, she behaved like an only child and got away with it. Her father, a gentle man with skin the color of dried tobacco and with the nose Reena had inherited jutting out like a crag from his nondescript face, had come from Georgia and was always making jokes about having married a foreigner—Reena's mother being from the West Indies. When not joking, he seemed slightly bewildered by his large family and so in awe of Reena that he avoided her. Reena's mother, a small, dry, formidably black woman, was less a person to me than the abstract principle of force, power, energy. She was alternately strict and indulgent with Reena and, despite the inconsistency, surprisingly effective.

They lived when I knew them in a cold-water railroad flat above a kosher butcher on Belmont Avenue in Brownsville,[3] some distance from us—and this in itself added to Reena's exotic quality. For it was a place where Sunday became Saturday, with all the stores open and pushcarts piled with vegetables and yard goods lined up along the curb, a crowded place where people hawked and spat freely in the streaming gutters and the men looked as if they had just stepped from the pages of the Old Testament with their profuse beards and long, black, satin coats.

When Reena was fifteen her family moved to Jamaica in Queens and since, in those days, Jamaica was considered too far away for visiting, our families lost contact and I did not see Reena again until we were both in college and then only once and not to speak to. . . .

I had walked some distance and by the time I got to the wake, which was being held at Aunt Vi's house, it was well under way. It was a good wake. Aunt Vi would have been pleased. There was plenty to drink, and more than enough to eat, including some Barbadian favorites: coconut bread, pone made with the cassava root, and the little crisp codfish cakes that are so hot with peppers they bring tears to the eyes as you bite into them.

---

1. Eponymous heroine of the historical romance by English novelist R. D. Blackmore (1825–1900). Emile Zola (1840–1902), French novelist, known primarily as an exemplar of literary naturalism. Gerhart Hauptmann (1862–1946), German dramatist, novelist, and poet. John Steinbeck (1902–1968), American writer, best known for *The Grapes of Wrath* (1939). The Little Minister is the eponymous hero of the popular sentimental novel by English writer James M. Barrie (1860–1837), who was also the author of *Peter Pan*.

2. Germany invaded Poland in 1939, thereby beginning World War II. Civil war raged in Spain from 1936 to 1939.

3. Section of Brooklyn.

I had missed the beginning, when everyone had probably sat around talking about Aunt Vi and recalling the few events that had distinguished her otherwise undistinguished life. (Someone, I'm sure, had told of the time she had missed the excursion boat to Atlantic City and had her own private picnic—complete with pigeon peas and rice and fricassee chicken—on the pier at 42nd Street.) By the time I arrived, though, it would have been indiscreet to mention her name, for by then the wake had become—and this would also have pleased her—a celebration of life.

I had had two drinks, one right after the other, and was well into my third when Reena, who must have been upstairs, entered the basement kitchen where I was. She saw me before I had quite seen her, and with a cry that alerted the entire room to her presence and charged the air with her special force, she rushed toward me.

"Hey, I'm the one who was supposed to be the writer, not you! Do you know, I still can't believe it," she said, stepping back, her blackness heightened by a white mocking smile. "I read both your books over and over again and I can't really believe it. My Little Paulie!"

I did not mind. For there was respect and even wonder behind the patronizing words and in her eyes. The old imbalance between us had ended and I was suddenly glad to see her.

I told her so and we both began talking at once, but Reena's voice overpowered mine, so that all I could do after a time was listen while she discussed my books, and dutifully answered her questions about my personal life.

"And what about you?" I said, almost brutally, at the first chance I got. "What've you been up to all this time?"

She got up abruptly. "Good Lord, in here's noisy as hell. Come on, let's go upstairs."

We got fresh drinks and went up to Aunt Vi's bedroom, where in the soft light from the lamps, the huge Victorian bed and the pink satin bedspread with roses of the same material strewn over its surface looked as if they had never been used. And, in a way, this was true. Aunt Vi had seldom slept in her bed or, for that matter, lived in her house, because in order to pay for it, she had had to work at a sleeping-in job which gave her only Thursdays and every other Sunday off.

Reena sat on the bed, crushing the roses, and I sat on one of the numerous trunks which crowded the room. They contained every dress, coat, hat, and shoe that Aunt Vi had worn since coming to the United States. I again asked Reena what she had been doing over the years.

"Do you want a blow by blow account?" she said. But despite the flippancy, she was suddenly serious. And when she began it was clear that she had written out the narrative in her mind many times. The words came too easily; the events, the incidents had been ordered in time, and the meaning of her behavior and of the people with whom she had been involved had been painstakingly analyzed. She talked willingly, with desperation almost. And the words by themselves weren't enough. She used her hands to give them form and urgency. I became totally involved with her and all that she said. So much so that as the night wore on I was not certain at times whether it was she or I speaking.

From the time her family moved to Jamaica until she was nineteen or so, Reena's life sounded, from what she told me in the beginning, as ordinary as mine and most of the girls we knew. After high school she had gone on to one of the free city colleges, where she had majored in journalism, worked part time in the school library, and, surprisingly enough, joined a houseplan. (Even I hadn't gone that far.) It was an all-Negro club, since there was a tacit understanding that Negro and white girls did not join each other's houseplans. "Integration, Northern style," she said, shrugging.

It seems that Reena had had a purpose and a plan in joining the group. "I thought," she said with a wry smile, "I could get those girls up off their complacent rumps and out doing something about social issues. . . . I couldn't get them to budge. I remember after the war when a Negro ex-soldier had his eyes gouged out by a bus driver down South I tried getting them to demonstrate on campus. I talked until I was hoarse, but to no avail. They were too busy planning the annual autumn frolic."

Her laugh was bitter but forgiving and it ended in a long, reflective silence. After which she said quietly, "It wasn't that they didn't give a damn. It was just, I suppose, that like most people they didn't want to get involved to the extent that they might have to stand up and be counted. If it ever came to that. Then another thing. They thought they were safe, special. After all, they had grown up in the North, most of them, and so had escaped the southern-style prejudice; their parents, like mine, were struggling to put them through college; they could look forward to being tidy little schoolteachers, social workers, and lab technicians. Oh, they were safe!" The sarcasm scored her voice and then abruptly gave way to pity. "Poor things, they weren't safe, you see, and would never be as long as millions like themselves in Harlem, on Chicago's South Side, down South, all over the place, were unsafe. I tried to tell them this—and they accused me of being oversensitive. They tried not to listen. But I would have held out and, I'm sure, even brought some of them around eventually if this other business with a silly boy hadn't happened at the same time. . . ."

Reena told me then about her first, brief, and apparently innocent affair with a boy she had met at one of the houseplan parties. It had ended, she said, when the boy's parents had met her. "That was it," she said and the flat of her hand cut into the air. "He was forbidden to see me. The reason? He couldn't bring himself to tell me, but I knew. I was too black.

"Naturally, it wasn't the first time something like that had happened. In fact, you might say that was the theme of my childhood. Because I was dark I was always being plastered with Vaseline so I wouldn't look ashy. Whenever I had my picture taken they would pile a whitish powder on my face and make the lights so bright I always came out looking ghostly. My mother stopped speaking to any number of people because they said I would have been pretty if I hadn't been so dark. Like nearly every little black girl, I had my share of dreams of waking up to find myself with long, blond curls, blue eyes, and skin like milk. So I should have been prepared. Besides, that boy's parents were really rejecting themselves in rejecting me.

"Take us"—and her hands, opening in front of my face as she suddenly leaned forward, seemed to offer me the whole of black humanity. "We live surrounded by white images, and white in this world is synonymous with the good, light, beauty, success, so that, despite ourselves sometimes, we run after that whiteness and deny our darkness, which has been made into the symbol of all that is evil and inferior. I wasn't a person to that boy's parents, but a symbol of the darkness they were in flight from, so that just as they—that boy, his parents, those silly girls in the houseplan—were running from me, I started running from them. . . ."

It must have been shortly after this happened when I saw Reena at a debate which was being held at my college. She did not see me, since she was one of the speakers and I was merely part of her audience in the crowded auditorium. The topic had something to do with intellectual freedom in the colleges (McCarthyism[4] was coming into vogue then) and aside from a Jewish boy from City College, Reena was the most effective—sharp, provocative, her position the most radical. The others on the panel seemed intimidated not only by the strength and cogency of her argument but by the sheer impact of her blackness in their white midst.

Her color might have been a weapon she used to dazzle and disarm her opponents. And she had highlighted it with the clothes she was wearing: a white dress patterned with large blocks of primary colors I remember (it looked Mexican) and a pair of intricately wrought silver earrings—long and with many little parts which clashed like muted cymbals over the microphone each time she moved her head. She wore her hair cropped short like a boy's and it was not straightened like mine and the other Negro girls' in the audience, but left in its coarse natural state: a small forest under which her face emerged in its intense and startling handsomeness. I remember she left the auditorium in triumph that day, surrounded by a noisy entourage from her college—all of them white.

"We were very serious," she said now, describing the left-wing group she had belonged to then—and there was a defensiveness in her voice which sought to protect them from all censure. "We believed—because we were young, I suppose, and had nothing as yet to risk—that we could do something about the injustices which everyone around us seemed to take for granted. So we picketed and demonstrated and bombarded Washington with our protests, only to have our names added to the Attorney General's list for all our trouble. We were always standing on street corners handing out leaflets or getting people to sign petitions. We always seemed to pick the coldest days to do that." Her smile held long after the words had died.

"I, we all, had such a sense of purpose then," she said softly, and a sadness lay aslant the smile now, darkening it. "We were forever holding meetings, having endless discussions, arguing, shouting, theorizing. And we had fun. Those parties! There was always somebody with a guitar. We were always singing. . . ." Suddenly, she began singing—and her voice was sure, militant, and faintly self-mocking,

> "But the banks are made of marble
> With a guard at every door
> And the vaults are stuffed with silver
> That the workers sweated for . . ."

When she spoke again the words were a sad coda to the song. "Well, as you probably know, things came to an ugly head with McCarthy reigning in Washington, and I was one of the people temporarily suspended from school."

She broke off and we both waited, the ice in our glasses melted and the drinks gone flat.

"At first, I didn't mind," she said finally. "After all, we were right. The fact that they suspended us proved it. Besides, I was in the middle of an affair,

4. I.e., the hunt for Communists in every sphere of American life, especially in government, academia, and show business. The hysteria was pro-   moted in the early 1950s by Wisconsin senator Joseph R. McCarthy (1908–1957).

a real one this time, and too busy with that to care about anything else." She paused again, frowning.

"He was white," she said quickly and glanced at me as though to surprise either shock or disapproval in my face. "We were very involved. At one point—I think just after we had been suspended and he started working—we even thought of getting married. Living in New York, moving in the crowd we did, we might have been able to manage it. But I couldn't. There were too many complex things going on beneath the surface," she said, her voice strained by the hopelessness she must have felt then, her hands shaping it in the air between us. "Neither one of us could really escape what our color had come to mean in this country. Let me explain. Bob was always, for some odd reason, talking about how much the Negro suffered, and although I would agree with him I would also try to get across that, you know, like all people we also had fun once in a while, loved our children, liked making love—that we were human beings, for God's sake. But he only wanted to hear about the suffering. It was as if this comforted him and eased his own suffering—and he did suffer because of any number of things: his own uncertainty, for one, his difficulties with his family, for another . . .

"Once, I remember, when his father came into New York, Bob insisted that I meet him. I don't know why I agreed to go with him. . . ." She took a deep breath and raised her head very high. "I'll never forget or forgive the look on that old man's face when he opened his hotel-room door and saw me. The horror. I might have been the personification of every evil in the world. His inability to believe that it was his son standing there holding my hand. His shock. I'm sure he never fully recovered. I know I never did. Nor can I forget Bob's laugh in the elevator afterwards, the way he kept repeating: 'Did you see his face when he saw you? Did you? . . .' He had used me, you see. I had been the means, the instrument of his revenge.

"And I wasn't any better. I used him. I took every opportunity to treat him shabbily, trying, you see, through him, to get at that white world which had not only denied me, but had turned my own against me." Her eyes closed. "I went numb all over when I understood what we were doing to, and with, each other. I stayed numb for a long time."

As Reena described the events which followed—the break with Bob, her gradual withdrawal from the left-wing group ("I had had it with them too. I got tired of being 'their Negro,' their pet. Besides, they were just all talk, really. All theories and abstractions. I doubt that, with all their elaborate plans for the Negro and for the workers of the world, any of them had ever been near a factory or up to Harlem")—as she spoke about her reinstatement in school, her voice suggested the numbness she had felt then. It only stirred into life again when she talked of her graduation.

"You should have seen my parents. It was really their day. My mother was so proud she complained about everything: her seat, the heat, the speaker; and my father just sat there long after everybody had left, too awed to move. God, it meant so much to them. It was as if I had made up for the generations his people had picked cotton in Georgia and my mother's family had cut cane in the West Indies. It frightened me."

I asked her after a long wait what she had done after graduating.

"How do you mean, what I did. Looked for a job. Tell me, have you ever looked for work in this man's city?"

"I know." I said, holding up my hand. "Don't tell me."

We both looked at my raised hand which sought to waive the discussion, then at each other and suddenly we laughed, a laugh so loud and violent with pain and outrage it brought tears.

"Girl," Reena said, the tears silver against her blackness. "You could put me blindfolded right now at the Times Building[5] on 42nd Street and I would be able to find my way to every newspaper office in town. But tell me, how come white folks is so *hard?*"

"Just bo'n hard."

We were laughing again and this time I nearly slid off the trunk and Reena fell back among the satin roses.

"I didn't know there were so many ways of saying 'no' without ever once using the word," she said, the laughter lodged in her throat, but her eyes had gone hard. "Sometimes I'd find myself in the elevator, on my way out, and smiling all over myself because I thought I had gotten the job, before it would hit me that they had really said no, not yes. Some of those people in personnel had so perfected their smiles they looked almost genuine. The ones who used to get me, though, were those who tried to make the interview into an intimate chat between friends. They'd put you in a comfortable chair, offer you a cigarette, and order coffee. How I hated that coffee. They didn't know it—or maybe they did—but it was like offering me hemlock. . . .

"You think Christ had it tough?" Her laughter rushed against the air which resisted it. "I was crucified five days a week and half-day on Saturday. I became almost paranoid. I began to think there might be something other than color wrong with me which everybody but me could see, some rare disease that had turned me into a monster.

"My parents suffered. And that bothered me most, because I felt I had failed them. My father didn't say anything but I knew because he avoided me more than usual. He was ashamed, I think, that he hadn't been able, as a man and as my father, to prevent this. My mother—well, you know her. In one breath she would try to comfort me by cursing them: 'But Gor blind them,'"—and Reena's voice captured her mother's aggressive accent—"'if you had come looking for a job mopping down their floors they would o' hire you, the brutes. But mark my words, their time goin' come, cause God don't love ugly and he ain't stuck on pretty . . .' And in the next breath she would curse me, 'Journalism! Journalism! Whoever heard of colored people taking up journalism. You must feel you's white or something so. The people is right to chuck you out their office. . . .' Poor thing, to make up for saying all that she would wash my white gloves every night and cook cereal for me in the morning as if I were a little girl again. Once she went out and bought me a suit she couldn't afford from Lord and Taylor's. I looked like a Smith girl[6] in blackface in it. . . . So guess where I ended up?"

"As a social investigator for the Welfare Department. Where else?"

We were helpless with laughter again.

"You too?"

"No" I said, "I taught, but that was just as bad."

"No," she said, sobering abruptly. "Nothing's as bad as working for Welfare. Do you know what they really mean by a social investigator? A spy.

5. I.e., the office building of the *New York Times,* in midtown Manhattan.
6. I.e., a student at Smith College, in Northamp-

ton, Massachusetts, then as now a member of the elite Seven Sisters group of women's schools.

Someone whose dirty job it is to snoop into the corners of the lives of the poor and make their poverty more vivid by taking from them the last shred of privacy. 'Mrs. Jones, is that a new dress you're wearing?' 'Mrs. Brown, this kerosene heater is not listed in the household items. Did you get an authorization for it?' 'Mrs. Smith, is that a telephone I hear ringing under the sofa?' I was utterly demoralized within a month.

"And another thing. I thought I knew about poverty. I mean, I remember, as a child, having to eat soup made with those white beans the government used to give out free for days running, sometimes, because there was nothing else. I had lived in Brownsville, among all the poor Jews and Poles and Irish there. But what I saw in Harlem, where I had my case load, was different somehow. Perhaps because it seemed so final. There didn't seem to be any way to escape from those dark hallways and dingy furnished rooms. . . . All that defeat." Closing her eyes, she finished the stale whiskey and soda in her glass.

"I remember a client of mine, a girl my age with three children already and no father for them and living in the expensive squalor of a rooming house. Her bewilderment. Her resignation. Her anger. She could have pulled herself out of the mess she was in? People say that, you know, including some Negroes. But this girl didn't have a chance. She had been trapped from the day she was born in some small town down South.

"She became my reference. From then on and even now, whenever I hear people and groups coming up with all kinds of solutions to the quote Negro problem, I ask one question. What are they really doing for that girl, to save her or to save the children? . . . The answer isn't very encouraging."

It was some time before she continued, and then she told me that after Welfare she had gone to work for a private social-work agency, in their publicity department, and had started on her master's in journalism at Columbia. She also left home around this time.

"I had to. My mother started putting the pressure on me to get married. The hints, the remarks—and you know my mother was never the subtle type—her anxiety, which made me anxious about getting married after a while. Besides, it was time for me to be on my own."

In contrast to the unmistakably radical character of her late adolescence (her membership in the left-wing group, the affair with Bob, her suspension from college), Reena's life of this period sounded ordinary, standard—and she admitted it with a slightly self-deprecating, apologetic smile. It was similar to that of any number of unmarried professional Negro women in New York or Los Angeles or Washington: the job teaching or doing social work which brought in a fairly decent salary, the small apartment with kitchenette which they sometimes shared with a roommate; a car, some of them; membership in various political and social action organizations for the militant few like Reena; the vacations in Mexico, Europe, the West Indies, and now Africa; the occasional date. "The interesting men were invariably married," Reena said and then mentioned having had one affair during that time. She had found out he was married and had thought of her only as the perfect mistress. "The bastard," she said, but her smile forgave him.

"Women alone!" she cried, laughing sadly, and her raised opened arms, the empty glass she held in one hand made eloquent their aloneness. "Alone and lonely, and indulging themselves while they wait. The girls of the house-plan have reached their majority only to find that all those years they spent accumulating their degrees and finding the well-paying jobs in the hope that this would raise their stock have, instead, put them at a disadvantage. For the few eligible men around—those who are their intellectual and professional peers, whom they can respect (and there are very few of them)— don't necessarily marry them, but younger women without the degrees and the fat jobs, who are no threat, or they don't marry at all because they are either queer or mother-ridden. Or they marry white women. Now, intellectually I accept this. In fact, some of my best friends are white women . . ." And again our laughter—that loud, searing burst which we used to cauterize our hurt mounted into the unaccepting silence of the room. "After all, our goal is a fully integrated society. And perhaps, as some people believe, the only solution to the race problem is miscegenation.[7] Besides, a man should be able to marry whomever he wishes. Emotionally, though, I am less kind and understanding, and I resent like hell the reasons some black men give for rejecting us for them."

"We're too middle-class-oriented," I said. "Conservative."

"Right. Even though, thank God, that doesn't apply to me."

"Too threatening . . . castrating . . ."

"Too independent and impatient with them for not being more ambitious . . . contemptuous . . ."

"Sexually inhibited and unimaginative . . ."

"And the old myth of the excessive sexuality of the black woman goes out the window," Reena cried.

"Not supportive, unwilling to submerge our interests for theirs . . ."

"Lacking in the subtle art of getting and keeping a man . . ."

We had recited the accusations in the form and tone of a litany, and in the silence which followed we shared a thin, hopeless smile.

"They condemn us," Reena said softly but with anger, "without taking history into account. We are still, most of us, the black woman who had to be almost frighteningly strong in order for us all to survive. For, after all, she was the one whom they left (and I don't hold this against them; I understand) with the children to raise, who had to *make* it somehow or the other. And we are still, so many of us, living that history.

"You would think that they would understand this, but few do. So it's up to us. We have got to understand them and save them for ourselves. How? By being, on one hand, persons in our own right and, on the other, fully the woman and the wife. . . . Christ, listen to who's talking! I had my chance. And I tried. Very hard. But it wasn't enough."

The festive sounds of the wake had died to a sober murmur beyond the bedroom. The crowd had gone, leaving only Reena and myself upstairs and the last of Aunt Vi's closest friends in the basement below. They were drinking coffee. I smelled it, felt its warmth and intimacy in the empty house, heard the distant tapping of the cups against the saucers and voices muted by grief. The wake had come full circle: they were again mourning Aunt Vi.

And Reena might have been mourning with them, sitting there amid the satin roses, framed by the massive headboard. Her hands lay as if they had been broken in her lap. Her eyes were like those of someone blind or dead. I got up to go and get some coffee for her.

"You met my husband," she said quickly, stopping me.

---

7. The mixing of races, especially marriage between a white person and a member of another race.

"Have I?" I said, sitting down again.

"Yes, before we were married even. At an autograph party for you. He was free-lancing—he's a photographer—and one of the Negro magazines had sent him to cover the party."

As she went on to describe him I remembered him vaguely, not his face, but his rather large body stretching and bending with a dancer's fluidity and grace as he took the pictures. I had heard him talking to a group of people about some issue on race relations very much in the news then and had been struck by his vehemence. For the moment I had found this almost odd, since he was so fair skinned he could have passed for white.

They had met, Reena told me now, at a benefit show for a Harlem day nursery given by one of the progressive groups she belonged to, and had married a month afterward. From all that she said they had had a full and exciting life for a long time. Her words were so vivid that I could almost see them: she with her startling blackness and extraordinary force and he with his near-white skin and a militancy which matched hers; both of them moving among the disaffected in New York, their stand on political and social issues equally uncompromising, the line of their allegiance reaching directly to all those trapped in Harlem. And they had lived the meaning of this allegiance, so that even when they could have afforded a life among the black bourgeoisie of St. Albans or Teaneck,[8] they had chosen to live if not in Harlem so close that there was no difference.

"I—we—were so happy I was frightened at times. Not that anything would change between us, but that someone or something in the world outside us would invade our private place and destroy us out of envy. Perhaps this is what did happen. . . ." She shrugged and even tried to smile but she could not manage it. "Something slipped in while we weren't looking and began its deadly work.

"Maybe it started when Dave took a job with a Negro magazine. I'm not sure. Anyway, in no time, he hated it: the routine, unimaginative pictures he had to take and the magazine itself, which dealt only in unrealities: the high-society world of the black bourgeoisie and the spectacular strides Negroes were making in all fields—you know the type. Yet Dave wouldn't leave. It wasn't the money, but a kind of safety which he had never experienced before which kept him there. He would talk about free-lancing again, about storming the gates of the white magazines downtown, of opening his own studio but he never acted on any one of these things. You see, despite his talent—and he was very talented—he had a diffidence that was fatal.

"When I understood this I literally forced him to open the studio—and perhaps I should have been more subtle and indirect, but that's not my nature. Besides, I was frightened and desperate to help. Nothing happened for a time. Dave's work was too experimental to be commercial. Gradually, though, his photographs started appearing in the prestige camera magazines and money from various awards and exhibits and an occasional assignment started coming in.

"This wasn't enough somehow. Dave also wanted the big, gaudy commercial success that would dazzle and confound that white world downtown and force it to *see* him. And yet, as I said before, he couldn't bring himself to try—and this contradiction began to get to him after awhile.

8. Section of Queens, New York, and a town in New Jersey, respectively, with solid middle-class black populations.

"It was then, I think, that I began to fail him. I didn't know how to help, you see. I had never felt so inadequate before. And this was very strange and disturbing for someone like me. I was being submerged in his problems—and I began fighting against this.

"I started working again (I had stopped after the second baby). And I was lucky because I got back my old job. And unlucky because Dave saw it as my way of pointing up his deficiencies. I couldn't convince him otherwise: that I had to do it for my own sanity. He would accuse me of wanting to see him fail, of trapping him in all kinds of responsibilities. . . . After a time we both got caught up in this thing, an ugliness came between us, and I began to answer his anger with anger and to trade him insult for insult.

"Things fell apart very quickly after that. I couldn't bear the pain of living with him—the insults, our mutual despair, his mocking, the silence. I couldn't subject the children to it any longer. The divorce didn't take long. And thank God, because of the children, we are pleasant when we have to see each other. He's making out very well, I hear."

She said nothing more, but simply bowed her head as though waiting for me to pass judgment on her. I don't know how long we remained like this; but when Reena finally raised her head, the darkness at the window had vanished and dawn was a still, gray smoke against the pane.

"Do you know," she said, and her eyes were clear and a smile had won out over pain, "I enjoy being alone. I don't tell people this because they'll accuse me of either lying or deluding myself. But I do. Perhaps, as my mother tells me, it's only temporary. I don't think so, though. I feel I don't ever want to be involved again. It's not that I've lost interest in men. I go out occasionally, but it's never anything serious. You see, I have all that I want for now."

Her children first of all, she told me, and from her description they sounded intelligent and capable. She was a friend as well as a mother to them, it seemed. They were planning, the four of them, to spend the summer touring Canada. "I will feel that I have done well by them if I give them, if nothing more, a sense of themselves and their worth and importance as black people. Everything I do with them, for them, is to this end. I don't want them ever to be confused about this. They must have their identifications straight from the beginning. No white dolls for them!"

Then her job. She was working now as a researcher for a small progressive news magazine with the promise that once she completed her master's in journalism (she was working on the thesis now) she might get a chance to do some minor reporting. And like most people, she hoped to write someday. "If I can ever stop talking away my substance," she said laughing.

And she was still active in any number of social action groups. In another week or so she would be heading a delegation of mothers down to City Hall "to give the mayor a little hell about conditions in the schools in Harlem." She had started an organization that was carrying on an almost door-to-door campaign in her neighborhood to expose, as she put it, "the blood suckers: all those slumlords and storekeepers with their fixed scales, the finance companies that never tell you the real price of a thing, the petty salesmen that leech off the poor. . . ." In May she was taking her two older girls on a nationwide pilgrimage to Washington to urge for a more rapid implementation of the school desegregation law.

"It's uncanny," she said, and the laugh which accompanied the words was warm, soft with wonder at herself, girlish even, and the air in the room which had refused her laughter before rushed to absorb this now. "Really uncanny. Here I am, practically middle-aged, with three children to raise by myself and with little or no money to do it, and yet I feel, strangely enough, as though life is just beginning—that it's new and fresh with all kinds of possibilities. Maybe it's because I've been through my purgatory and I can't ever be overwhelmed again. I don't know. Anyway, you should see me on evenings after I put the children to bed. I sit alone in the living room (I've repainted it and changed all the furniture since Dave's gone, so that it would at least look different)—I sit there making plans and all of them seem possible. The most important plan right now is Africa. I've already started saving the fare."

I asked her whether she was planning to live there permanently and she said simply, "I want to live and work there. For how long, for a lifetime, I can't say. All I know is that I have to. For myself and for my children. It is important that they see black people who have truly a place and history of their own and who are building for a new and, hopefully, more sensible world. And I must see it, get close to it, because I can never lose the sense of being a displaced person here in America because of my color. Oh, I know I should remain and fight not only for integration (even though, frankly, I question whether I want to be integrated into America as it stands now, with its complacency and materialism, its soullessness) but to help change the country into something better, sounder—if that is still possible. But I have to go to Africa. . . ."

"Poor Aunt Vi," she said after a long silence and straightened one of the roses she had crushed. "She never really got to enjoy her bed of roses what with only Thursdays and every other Sunday off. All that hard work. All her life. . . . Our lives have got to make more sense, if only for her."

We got up to leave shortly afterward. Reena was staying on to attend the burial, later in the morning, but I was taking the subway to Manhattan. We parted with the usual promise to get together and exchange telephone numbers. And Reena did phone a week or so later. I don't remember what we talked about though.

Some months later I invited her to a party I was giving before leaving the country. But she did not come.

1962

To Da-Duh, in Memoriam

> ". . . Oh Nana! all of you is not involved in this evil business
> Death, Nor all of us in life."
> —FROM "AT MY GRANDMOTHER'S GRAVE," BY LEBERT BETHUNE[1]

I did not see her at first I remember. For not only was it dark inside the crowded disembarkation shed in spite of the daylight flooding in from outside, but standing there waiting for her with my mother and sister I was still somewhat blinded from the sheen of tropical sunlight on the water of the bay which we had just crossed in the landing boat, leaving behind us the ship that had brought us from New York lying in the offing. Besides, being only nine years of age at the time and knowing nothing of islands I was

---

1. Jamaican-born poet (b. 1937).

busy attending to the alien sights and sounds of Barbados, the unfamiliar smells.

I did not see her, but I was alerted to her approach by my mother's hand which suddenly tightened around mine, and looking up I traced her gaze through the gloom in the shed until I finally made out the small, purposeful, painfully erect figure of the old woman headed our way.

Her face was drowned in the shadow of an ugly rolled-brim brown felt hat, but the details of her slight body and of the struggle taking place within it were clear enough—an intense, unrelenting struggle between her back which was beginning to bend ever so slightly under the weight of her eighty-odd years and the rest of her which sought to deny those years and hold that back straight, keep it in line. Moving swiftly toward us (so swiftly it seemed she did not intend stopping when she reached us but would sweep past us out the doorway which opened onto the sea and like Christ walk upon the water!), she was caught between the sunlight at her end of the building and the darkness inside—and for a moment she appeared to contain them both: the light in the long severe old-fashioned white dress she wore which brought the sense of a past that was still alive into our bustling present and in the snatch of white at her eye; the darkness in her black high-top shoes and in her face which was visible now that she was closer.

It was as stark and fleshless as a death mask, that face. The maggots might have already done their work, leaving only the framework of bone beneath the ruined skin and deep wells at the temple and jaw. But her eyes were alive, unnervingly so for one so old, with a sharp light that flicked out of the dim clouded depths like a lizard's tongue to snap up all in her view. Those eyes betrayed a child's curiosity about the world, and I wondered vaguely seeing them, and seeing the way the bodice of her ancient dress had collapsed in on her flat chest (what had happened to her breasts?), whether she might not be some kind of child at the same time that she was a woman, with fourteen children, my mother included, to prove it. Perhaps she was both, both child and woman, darkness and light, past and present, life and death—all the opposites contained and reconciled in her.

"My Da-duh," my mother said formally and stepped forward. The name sounded like thunder fading softly in the distance.

"Child," Da-duh said, and her tone, her quick scrutiny of my mother, the brief embrace in which they appeared to shy from each other rather than touch, wiped out the fifteen years my mother had been away and restored the old relationship. My mother, who was such a formidable figure in my eyes, had suddenly with a word been reduced to my status.

"Yes, God is good," Da-duh said with a nod that was like a tic. "He has spared me to see my child again."

We were led forward then, apologetically because not only did Da-duh prefer boys but she also liked her grandchildren to be "white," that is, fair-skinned; and we had, I was to discover, a number of cousins, the outside children of white estate managers and the like, who qualified. We, though, were as black as she.

My sister being the oldest was presented first. "This one takes after the father," my mother said and waited to be reproved.

Frowning, Da-duh tilted my sister's face toward the light. But her frown soon gave way to a grudging smile, for my sister with her large mild eyes and little broad winged nose, with our father's high-cheeked Barbadian cast to her face, was pretty.

"She's goin' be lucky," Da-duh said and patted her once on the cheek. "Any girl child that takes after the father does be lucky."

She turned then to me. But oddly enough she did not touch me. Instead leaning close, she peered hard at me, and then quickly drew back. I thought I saw her hand start up as though to shield her eyes. It was almost as if she saw not only me, a thin truculent child who it was said took after no one but myself, but something in me which for some reason she found disturbing, even threatening. We looked silently at each other for a long time there in the noisy shed, our gaze locked. She was the first to look away.

"But Adry," she said to my mother and her laugh was cracked, thin, apprehensive. "Where did you get this one here with this fierce look?"

"We don't know where she came out of, my Da-duh," my mother said, laughing also. Even I smiled to myself. After all I had won the encounter. Da-duh had recognized my small strength—and this was all I ever asked of the adults in my life then.

"Come, soul," Da-duh said and took my hand. "You must be one of those New York terrors you hear so much about."

She led us, me at her side and my sister and mother behind, out of the shed into the sunlight that was like a bright driving summer rain and over to a group of people clustered beside a decrepit lorry. They were our relatives, most of them from St. Andrews although Da-duh herself lived in St. Thomas,[2] the women wearing bright print dresses, the colors vivid against their darkness, the men rusty black suits that encased them like straitjackets. Da-duh, holding fast to my hand, became my anchor as they circled round us like a nervous sea, exclaiming, touching us with their calloused hands, embracing us shyly. They laughed in awed bursts: "But look Adry got big-big children! / "And see the nice things they wearing, wrist watch and all!" / "I tell you, Adry has done all right for sheself in New York. . . ."

Da-duh, ashamed at their wonder, embarrassed for them, admonished them the while. "But oh Christ," she said, "why you all got to get on like you never saw people from 'Away' before? You would think New York is the only place in the world to hear wunna. That's why I don't like to go anyplace with you St. Andrews people, you know. You all ain't been colonized."

We were in the back of the lorry finally, packed in among the barrels of ham, flour, cornmeal and rice and the trunks of clothes that my mother had brought as gifts. We made our way slowly through Bridgetown's[3] clogged streets, part of a funereal procession of cars and open-sided buses, bicycles and donkey carts. The dim little limestone shops and offices along the way marched with us, at the same mournful pace, toward the same grave ceremony—as did the people, the women balancing huge baskets on top their heads as if they were no more than hats they wore to shade them from the sun. Looking over the edge of the lorry I watched as their feet slurred the dust. I listened, and their voices, raw and loud and dissonant in the heat, seemed to be grappling with each other high overhead.

Da-duh sat on a trunk in our midst, a monarch amid her court. She still held my hand, but it was different now. I had suddenly become her anchor, for I felt her fear of the lorry with its asthmatic motor (a fear and distrust, I later learned, she held of all machines) beating like a pulse in her rough palm.

2. A parish in the Caribbean island-state of Barbados.　　3. Capital of Barbados.

As soon as we left Bridgetown behind though, she relaxed, and while the others around us talked she gazed at the canes standing tall on either side of the winding marl road. "C'dear," she said softly to herself after a time. "The canes this side are pretty enough."

They were too much for me. I thought of them as giant weeds that had overrun the island, leaving scarcely any room for the small tottering houses of sunbleached pine we passed or the people, dark streaks as our lorry hurtled by. I suddenly feared that we were journeying, unaware that we were, toward some dangerous place where the canes, grown as high and thick as a forest, would close in on us and run us through with their stiletto blades. I longed then for the familiar: for the street in Brooklyn where I lived, for my father who had refused to accompany us ("Blowing out good money on foolishness," he had said of the trip), for a game of tag with my friends under the chestnut tree outside our aging brownstone house.

"Yes, but wait till you see St. Thomas canes," Da-duh was saying to me. "They's canes father, bo," she gave a proud arrogant nod. "Tomorrow, God willing, I goin' take you out in the ground and show them to you."

True to her word Da-duh took me with her the following day out into the ground. It was a fairly large plot adjoining her weathered board and shingle house and consisting of a small orchard, a good-sized canepiece and behind the canes, where the land sloped abruptly down, a gully. She had purchased it with Panama money sent her by her eldest son, my uncle Joseph, who had died working on the canal. We entered the ground along a trail no wider than her body and as devious and complex as her reasons for showing me her land. Da-duh strode briskly ahead, her slight form filled out this morning by the layers of sacking petticoats she wore under her working dress to protect her against the damp. A fresh white cloth, elaborately arranged around her head, added to her height, and lent her a vain, almost roguish air.

Her pace slowed once we reached the orchard, and glancing back at me occasionally over her shoulder, she pointed out the various trees.

"This here is a breadfruit," she said. "That one yonder is a papaw. Here's a guava. This is a mango. I know you don't have anything like these in New York. Here's a sugar apple." (The fruit looked more like artichokes than apples to me.) "This one bears limes. . . ." She went on for some time, intoning the names of the trees as though they were those of her gods. Finally, turning to me, she said, "I know you don't have anything this nice where you come from." Then, as I hesitated: "I said I know you don't have anything this nice where you come from. . . ."

"No," I said and my world did seem suddenly lacking.

Da-duh nodded and passed on. The orchard ended and we were on the narrow cart road that led through the canepiece, the canes clashing like swords above my cowering head. Again she turned and her thin muscular arms spread wide, her dim gaze embracing the small field of canes, she said—and her voice almost broke under the weight of her pride, "Tell me, have you got anything like these in that place where you were born?"

"No."

"I din' think so. I bet you don't even know that these canes here and the sugar you eat is one and the same thing. That they does throw the canes into some damn machine at the factory and squeeze out all the little life in them to make sugar for you all so in New York to eat. I bet you don't know that."

"I've got two cavities and I'm not allowed to eat a lot of sugar."

But Da-duh didn't hear me. She had turned with an inexplicably angry motion and was making her way rapidly out of the canes and down the slope at the edge of the field which led to the gully below. Following her apprehensively down the incline amid a stand of banana plants whose leaves flapped like elephants ears in the wind, I found myself in the middle of a small tropical wood—a place dense and damp and gloomy and tremulous with the fitful play of light and shadow as the leaves high above moved against the sun that was almost hidden from view. It was a violent place, the tangled foliage fighting each other for a chance at the sunlight, the branches of the trees locked in what seemed an immemorial struggle, one both necessary and inevitable. But despite the violence, it was pleasant, almost peaceful in the gully, and beneath the thick undergrowth the earth smelled like spring.

This time Da-duh didn't even bother to ask her usual question, but simply turned and waited for me to speak.

"No," I said, my head bowed. "We don't have anything like this in New York."

"Ah," she cried, her triumph complete. "I din' think so. Why, I've heard that's a place where you can walk till you near drop and never see a tree."

"We've got a chestnut tree in front of our house," I said.

"Does it bear?" She waited. "I ask you, does it bear?"

"Not anymore," I muttered. "It used to, but not anymore."

She gave the nod that was like a nervous twitch. "You see," she said. "Nothing can bear there." Then, secure behind her scorn, she added, "But tell me, what's this snow like that you hear so much about?"

Looking up, I studied her closely, sensing my chance, and then I told her, describing at length and with as much drama as I could summon not only what snow in the city was like, but what it would be like here, in her perennial summer kingdom.

". . . And you see all these trees you got here," I said. "Well, they'd be bare. No leaves, no fruit, nothing. They'd be covered in snow. You see your canes. They'd be buried under tons of snow. The snow would be higher than your head, higher than your house, and you wouldn't be able to come down into this here gully because it would be snowed under. . . ."

She searched my face for the lie, still scornful but intrigued. "What a thing, huh?" she said finally, whispering it softly to herself.

"And when it snows you couldn't dress like you are now," I said. "Oh no, you'd freeze to death. You'd have to wear a hat and gloves and galoshes and ear muffs so your ears wouldn't freeze and drop off, and a heavy coat. I've got a Shirley Temple coat with fur on the collar. I can dance. You wanna see?"

Before she could answer I began, with a dance called the Truck which was popular back then in the 1930's. My right forefinger waving, I trucked around the nearby trees and around Da-duh's awed and rigid form. After the Truck I did the Suzy-Q, my lean hips swishing, my sneakers sidling zigzag over the ground. "I can sing," I said and did so, starting with "I'm Gonna Sit Right Down and Write Myself a Letter," then without pausing, "Tea For Two," and ending with "I Found a Million Dollar Baby in a Five and Ten Cent Store."

For long moments afterwards Da-duh stared at me as if I were a creature from Mars, an emissary from some world she did not know but which intrigued her and whose power she both felt and feared. Yet something about my performance must have pleased her, because bending down she slowly lifted her long skirt and then, one by one, the layers of petticoats until she came to a drawstring purse dangling at the end of a long strip of cloth tied round her waist. Opening the purse she handed me a penny. "Here," she said half-smiling against her will. "Take this to buy yourself a sweet at the shop up the road. There's nothing to be done with you, soul."

From then on, whenever I wasn't taken to visit relatives, I accompanied Da-duh out into the ground, and alone with her amid the canes or down in the gully I told her about New York. It always began with some slighting remark on her part: "I know they don't have anything this nice where you come from," or "Tell me, I hear those foolish people in New York does do such and such. . . ." But as I answered, recreating my towering world of steel and concrete and machines for her, building the city out of words, I would feel her give way. I came to know the signs of her surrender: the total stillness that would come over her little hard dry form, the probing gaze that like a surgeon's knife sought to cut through my skull to get at the images there, to see if I were lying; above all, her fear, a fear nameless and profound, the same one I had felt beating in the palm of her hand that day in the lorry.

Over the weeks I told her about refrigerators, radios, gas stoves, elevators, trolley cars, wringer washing machines, movies, airplanes, the cyclone at Coney Island, subways, toasters, electric lights: "At night, see, all you have to do is flip this little switch on the wall and all the lights in the house go on. Just like that. Like magic. It's like turning on the sun at night."

"But tell me," she said to me once with a faint mocking smile, "do the white people have all these things too or it's only the people looking like us?"

I laughed. "What d'ya mean," I said. "The white people have even better." Then: "I beat up a white girl in my class last term."

"Beating up white people!" Her tone was incredulous.

"How you mean!" I said, using an expression of hers. "She called me a name."

For some reason Da-duh could not quite get over this and repeated in the same hushed, shocked voice, "Beating up white people now! Oh, the lord, the world's changing up so I can scarce recognize it anymore."

One morning toward the end of our stay, Da-duh led me into a part of the gully that we had never visited before, an area darker and more thickly overgrown than the rest, almost impenetrable. There in a small clearing amid the dense bush, she stopped before an incredibly tall royal palm which rose cleanly out of the ground, and drawing the eye up with it, soared high above the trees around it into the sky. It appeared to be touching the blue dome of sky, to be flaunting its dark crown of fronds right in the blinding white face of the late morning sun.

Da-duh watched me a long time before she spoke, and then she said very quietly, "All right, now, tell me if you've got anything this tall in that place you're from."

I almost wished, seeing her face, that I could have said no. "Yes," I said. "We've got buildings hundreds of times this tall in New York. There's one called the Empire State Building that's the tallest in the world. My class visited it last year and I went all the way to the top. It's got over a hundred floors. I can't describe how tall it is. Wait a minute. What's the name of that hill I went to visit the other day, where they have the police station?"

"You mean Bissex?"

"Yes, Bissex. Well, the Empire State Building is way taller than that."

"You're lying now!" she shouted, trembling with rage. Her hand lifted to strike me.

"No, I'm not," I said. "It really is, if you don't believe me I'll send you a picture postcard of it soon as I get back home so you can see for yourself. But it's way taller than Bissex."

All the fight went out of her at that. The hand poised to strike me fell limp to her side, and as she stared at me, seeing not me but the building that was taller than the highest hill she knew, the small stubborn light in her eyes (it was the same amber as the flame in the kerosene lamp she lit at dusk) began to fail. Finally, with a vague gesture that even in the midst of her defeat still tried to dismiss me and my world, she turned and started back through the gully, walking slowly, her steps groping and uncertain, as if she were suddenly no longer sure of the way, while I followed triumphant yet strangely saddened behind.

The next morning I found her dressed for our morning walk but stretched out on the Berbice chair in the tiny drawing room where she sometimes napped during the afternoon heat, her face turned to the window beside her. She appeared thinner and suddenly indescribably old.

"My Da-duh," I said.

"Yes, nuh," she said. Her voice was listless and the face she slowly turned my way was, now that I think back on it, like a Benin mask, the features drawn and almost distorted by an ancient abstract sorrow.

"Don't you feel well?" I asked.

"Girl, I don't know."

"My Da-duh, I goin' boil you some bush tea," my aunt, Da-duh's youngest child, who lived with her, called from the shed roof kitchen.

"Who tell you I need bush tea?" she cried, her voice assuming for a moment its old authority. "You can't even rest nowadays without some malicious person looking for you to be dead. Come girl," she motioned me to a place beside her on the old-fashioned lounge chair, "give us a tune."

I sang for her until breakfast at eleven, all my brash irreverent Tin Pan Alley songs, and then just before noon we went out into the ground. But it was a short, dispirited walk. Da-duh didn't even notice that the mangoes were beginning to ripen and would have to be picked before the village boys got to them. And when she paused occasionally and looked out across the canes or up at her trees it wasn't as if she were seeing them but something else. Some huge, monolithic shape had imposed itself, it seemed, between her and the land, obstructing her vision. Returning to the house she slept the entire afternoon on the Berbice chair.

She remained like this until we left, languishing away the mornings on the chair at the window gazing out at the land as if it were already doomed; then, at noon, taking the brief stroll with me through the ground during which she seldom spoke, and afterwards returning home to sleep till almost dusk sometimes.

On the day of our departure she put on the austere, ankle length white dress, the black shoes and brown felt hat (her town clothes she called them), but she did not go with us to town. She saw us off on the road outside her house and in the midst of my mother's tearful protracted farewell, she leaned down and whispered in my ear, "Girl, you're not to forget now to send me the picture of that building, you hear."

By the time I mailed her the large colored picture postcard of the Empire State building she was dead. She died during the famous '37 strike[4] which began shortly after we left. On the day of her death England sent planes flying low over the island and in a show of force—so low, according to my aunt's letter, that the downdraft from them shook the ripened mangoes from the trees in Da-duh's orchard. Frightened, everyone in the village fled into the canes. Except Da-duh. She remained in the house at the window so my aunt said, watching as the planes came swooping and screaming like monstrous birds down over the village, over her house, rattling her trees and flattening the young canes in her field. It must have seemed to her lying there that they did not intend pulling out of their dive, but like the hardback beetles which hurled themselves with suicidal force against the walls of the house at night, those menacing silver shapes would hurl themselves in an ecstasy of self-immolation onto the land, destroying it utterly.

When the planes finally left and the villagers returned they found her dead on the Berbice chair at the window.

She died and I lived, but always, to this day even, within the shadow of her death. For a brief period after I was grown I went to live alone, like one doing penance, in a loft above a noisy factory in downtown New York and there painted seas of sugar-cane and huge swirling Van Gogh suns and palm trees striding like brightly-plumed Tutsi warriors across a tropical landscape, while the thunderous tread of the machines downstairs jarred the floor beneath my easel, mocking my efforts.

1967

The Making of a Writer: From the Poets in the Kitchen

Some years ago, when I was teaching a graduate seminar in fiction at Columbia University, a well known male novelist visited my class to speak on his development as a writer. In discussing his formative years, he didn't realize it but he seriously endangered his life by remarking that women writers are luckier than those of his sex because they usually spend so much time as children around their mothers and their mothers' friends in the kitchen.

What did he say that for? The women students immediately forgot about being in awe of him and began readying their attack for the question and answer period later on. Even I bristled. There again was that awful image of women locked away from the world in the kitchen with only each other to talk to, and their daughters locked in with them.

But my guest wasn't really being sexist or trying to be provocative or even spoiling for a fight. What he meant—when he got around to explaining himself more fully—was that, given the way children are (or were) raised in our society, with little girls kept closer to home and their mothers, the woman writer stands a better chance of being exposed, while growing up, to the kind of talk that goes on among women, more often than not in the kitchen; and that this experience gives her an edge over her male counterpart by instilling in her an appreciation for ordinary speech.

---

4. Labor riots in the Caribbean that precipitated the struggle for independence for many island-states.

It was clear that my guest lecturer attached great importance to this, which is understandable. Common speech and the plain, workaday words that make it up are, after all, the stock in trade of some of the best fiction writers. They are the principal means by which characters in a novel or story reveal themselves and give voice sometimes to profound feelings and complex ideas about themselves and the world. Perhaps the proper measure of a writer's talent is skill in rendering everyday speech—when it is appropriate to the story—as well as the ability to tap, to exploit, the beauty, poetry and wisdom it often contains.

"If you say what's on your mind in the language that comes to you from your parents and your street and friends you'll probably say something beautiful." Grace Paley[1] tells this, she says, to her students at the beginning of every writing course.

It's all a matter of exposure and a training of the ear for the would-be writer in those early years of apprenticeship. And, according to my guest lecturer, this training, the best of it, often takes place in as unglamorous a setting as the kitchen.

He didn't know it, but he was essentially describing my experience as a little girl. I grew up among poets. Now they didn't look like poets—whatever that breed is supposed to look like. Nothing about them suggested that poetry was their calling. They were just a group of ordinary housewives and mothers, my mother included, who dressed in a way (shapeless housedresses, dowdy felt hats and long, dark, solemn coats) that made it impossible for me to imagine they had ever been young.

Nor did they do what poets were supposed to do—spend their days in an attic room writing verses. They never put pen to paper except to write occasionally to their relatives in Barbados. "I take my pen in hand hoping these few lines will find you in health as they leave me fair for the time being," was the way their letters invariably began. Rather, their day was spent "scrubbing floor," as they described the work they did.

Several mornings a week these unknown bards would put an apron and a pair of old house shoes in a shopping bag and take the train or streetcar from our section of Brooklyn out to Flatbush.[2] There, those who didn't have steady jobs would wait on certain designated corners for the white housewives in the neighborhood to come along and bargain with them over pay for a day's work cleaning their houses. This was the ritual even in the winter.

Later, armed with the few dollars they had earned, which in their vocabulary became "a few raw-mouth pennies," they made their way back to our neighborhood, where they would sometimes stop off to have a cup of tea or cocoa together before going home to cook dinner for their husbands and children.

The basement kitchen of the brownstone house where my family lived was the usual gathering place. Once inside the warm safety of its walls the women threw off the drab coats and hats, seated themselves at the large center table, drank their cups of tea or cocoa, and talked. While my sister and I sat at a smaller table over in a corner doing our homework, they talked—endlessly, passionately, poetically, and with impressive range. No subject was beyond them. True, they would indulge in the usual gossip:

---

1. American short story writer (1922–2007).   2. A section of Brooklyn.

whose husband was running with whom, whose daughter looked slightly "in the way" (pregnant) under her bridal gown as she walked down the aisle. That sort of thing. But they also tackled the great issues of the time. They were always, for example, discussing the state of the economy. It was the mid and late 30's then, and the aftershock of the Depression, with its soup lines and suicides on Wall Street, was still being felt.

Some people, they declared, didn't know how to deal with adversity. They didn't know that you had to "tie up your belly" (hold in the pain, that is) when things got rough and go on with life. They took their image from the bellyband that is tied around the stomach of a newborn baby to keep the navel pressed in.

They talked politics. Roosevelt was their hero. He had come along and rescued the country with relief and jobs, and in gratitude they christened their sons Franklin and Delano and hoped they would live up to the names.

If F.D.R. was their hero, Marcus Garvey[3] was their God. The name of the fiery, Jamaican-born black nationalist of the 20's was constantly invoked around the table. For he had been their leader when they first came to the United States from the West Indies shortly after World War I. They had contributed to his organization, the United Negro Improvement Association (UNIA), out of their meager salaries, bought shares in his ill-fated Black Star Shipping Line, and at the height of the movement they had marched as members of his "nurses' brigade" in their white uniforms up Seventh Avenue in Harlem during the great Garvey Day parades. Garvey: He lived on through the power of their memories.

And their talk was of war and rumors of wars. They raged against World War II when it broke out in Europe, blaming it on the politicians. "It's these politicians. They're the ones always starting up all this lot of war. But what they care? It's the poor people got to suffer and mothers with their sons." If it was *their* sons, they swore they would keep them out of the Army by giving them soap to eat each day to make their hearts sound defective. Hitler? He was for them "the devil incarnate."

Then there was home. They reminisced often and at length about home. The old country. Barbados—or Bimshire, as they affectionately called it. The little Caribbean island in the sun they loved but had to leave. "Poor—poor but sweet" was the way they remembered it.

And naturally they discussed their adopted home. America came in for both good and bad marks. They lashed out at it for the racism they encountered. They took to task some of the people they worked for, especially those who gave them only a hard-boiled egg and a few spoonfuls of cottage cheese for lunch. "As if anybody can scrub floor on an egg and some cheese that don't have no taste to it!"

Yet although they caught H in "this man country," as they called America, it was nonetheless a place where "you could at least see your way to make a dollar." That much they acknowledged. They might even one day accumulate enough dollars, with both them and their husbands working, to buy the brownstone houses which, like my family, they were only leasing at that period. This was their consuming ambition: to "buy house" and to see the children through.

---

3. Founder of the Universal Negro Improvement Association (1887–1940).

There was no way for me to understand it at the time, but the talk that filled the kitchen those afternoons was highly functional. It served as therapy, the cheapest kind available to my mother and her friends. Not only did it help them recover from the long wait on the corner that morning and the bargaining over their labor, it restored them to a sense of themselves and reaffirmed their self-worth. Through language they were able to overcome the humiliations of the work-day.

But more than therapy, that freewheeling, wide-ranging, exuberant talk functioned as an outlet for the tremendous creative energy they possessed. They were women in whom the need for self-expression was strong, and since language was the only vehicle readily available to them they made of it an art form that—in keeping with the African tradition in which art and life are one—was an integral part of their lives.

And their talk was a refuge. They never really ceased being baffled and overwhelmed by America—its vastness, complexity and power. Its strange customs and laws. At a level beyond words they remained fearful and in awe. Their uneasiness and fear were even reflected in their attitude toward the children they had given birth to in this country. They referred to those like myself, the little Brooklyn-born Bajans (Barbadians), as "these New York children" and complained that they couldn't discipline us properly because of the laws here. "You can't beat these children as you would like, you know, because the authorities in this place will dash you in jail for them. After all, these is New York children." Not only were we different, American, we had, as they saw it, escaped their ultimate authority.

Confronted therefore by a world they could not encompass, which even limited their rights as parents, and at the same time finding themselves permanently separated from the world they had known, they took refuge in language. "Language is the only homeland," Czeslaw Milosz, the emigré Polish writer and Nobel Laureate, has said. This is what it became for the women at the kitchen table.

It served another purpose also, I suspect. My mother and her friends were after all the female counterpart of Ralph Ellison's invisible man.[4] Indeed, you might say they suffered a triple invisibility, being black, female and foreigners. They really didn't count in American society except as a source of cheap labor. But given the kind of women they were, they couldn't tolerate the fact of their invisibility, their powerlessness. And they fought back, using the only weapon at their command: the spoken word.

Those late afternoon conversations on a wide range of topics were a way for them to feel they exercised some measure of control over their lives and the events that shaped them. "Soully-gal, talk yuh talk!" they were always exhorting each other. "In this man world you got to take yuh mouth and make a gun!" They were in control, if only verbally and if only for the two hours or so that they remained in our house.

For me, sitting over in the corner, being seen but not heard, which was the rule for children in those days, it wasn't only what the women talked about—the content—but the way they put things—their style. The insight, irony, wit and humor they brought to their stories and discussions and their poet's inventiveness and daring with language—which of course I could only sense but not define back then.

4. Protagonist of Ellison's 1952 novel *Invisible Man*.

They had taken the standard English taught them in the primary schools of Barbados and transformed it into an idiom, an instrument that more adequately described them—changing around the syntax and imposing their own rhythm and accent so that the sentences were more pleasing to their ears. They added the few African sounds and words that had survived, such as the derisive suck-teeth sound and the word "yam," meaning to eat. And to make it more vivid, more in keeping with their expressive quality, they brought to bear a raft of metaphors, parables, Biblical quotations, sayings and the like:

"The sea ain' got no back door," they would say, meaning that it wasn't like a house where if there was a fire you could run out the back. Meaning that it was not to be trifled with. And meaning perhaps in a larger sense that man should treat all of nature with caution and respect.

"I has read hell by heart and called every generation blessed!" They sometimes went in for hyperbole.

A woman expecting a baby was never said to be pregnant. They never used that word. Rather, she was "in the way" or, better yet, "tumbling big." "Guess who I butt up on in the market the other day tumbling big again!"

And a woman with a reputation of being too free with her sexual favors was known in their book as a "thoroughfare"—the sense of men like a steady stream of cars moving up and down the road of her life. Or she might be dubbed "a free-bee," which was my favorite of the two. I liked the image it conjured up of a woman scandalous perhaps but independent, who flitted from one flower to another in a garden of male beauties, sampling their nectar, taking her pleasure at will, the roles reversed.

And nothing, no matter how beautiful, was ever described as simply beautiful. It was always "beautiful-ugly": the beautiful-ugly dress, the beautiful-ugly house, the beautiful-ugly car. Why the word "ugly," I used to wonder, when the thing they were referring to was beautiful, and they knew it. Why the antonym, the contradiction, the linking of opposites? It used to puzzle me greatly as a child.

There is the theory in linguistics which states that the idiom of a people, the way they use language, reflects not only the most fundamental views they hold of themselves and the world but their very conception of reality. Perhaps in using the term "beautiful-ugly" to describe nearly everything, my mother and her friends were expressing what they believed to be a fundamental dualism in life: the idea that a thing is at the same time its opposite, and that these opposites, these contradictions make up the whole. But theirs was not a Manichaean brand of dualism that sees matter, flesh, the body, as inherently evil, because they constantly addressed each other as "soully-gal"—soul: spirit; gal: the body, flesh, the visible self. And it was clear from their tone that they gave one as much weight and importance as the other. They had never heard of the mind/body split.

As for God, they summed up His essential attitude in a phrase. "God," they would say, "don' love ugly and He ain' stuck on pretty."

Using everyday speech, the simple commonplace words—but always with imagination and skill—they gave voice to the most complex ideas. Flannery O'Connor would have approved of how they made ordinary language work, as she put it, "doubletime," stretching, shading, deepening its meaning.

Like Joseph Conrad[5] they were always trying to infuse new life in the "old old words worn thin . . . by . . . careless usage." And the goals of their oral art were the same as his: "to make you hear, to make you feel . . . to make you *see*." This was their guiding esthetic.

By the time I was 8 or 9, I graduated from the corner of the kitchen to the neighborhood library, and thus from the spoken to the written word. The Macon Street Branch of the Brooklyn Public Library was an imposing half block long edifice of heavy gray masonry, with glass-paneled doors at the front and two tall metal torches symbolizing the light that comes of learning flanking the wide steps outside.

The inside was just as impressive. More steps—of pale marble with gleaming brass railings at the center and sides—led up to the circulation desk, and a great pendulum clock gazed down from the balcony stacks that faced the entrance. Usually stationed at the top of the steps like the guards outside Buckingham Palace[6] was the custodian, a stern-faced West Indian type who for years, until I was old enough to obtain an adult card, would immediately shoo me with one hand into the Children's Room and with the other threaten me into silence, a finger to his lips. You would have thought he was the chief librarian and not just someone whose job it was to keep the brass polished and the clock wound. I put him in a story called "Barbados" years later and had terrible things happen to him at the end.

I sheltered from the storm of adolescence in the Macon Street library, reading voraciously, indiscriminately, everything from Jane Austen to Zane Grey, but with a special passion for the long, full-blown, richly detailed 18th- and 19th-century picaresque tales: "Tom Jones," "Great Expectations," "Vanity Fair."[7]

But although I loved nearly everything I read and would enter fully into the lives of the characters—indeed, would cease being myself and become them—I sensed a lack after a time. Something I couldn't quite define was missing. And then one day, browsing in the poetry section, I came across a book by someone called Paul Laurence Dunbar,[8] and opening it I found the photograph of a wistful, sad-eyed poet who to my surprise was black. I turned to a poem at random. "Little brown-baby wif spa'klin' / eyes / Come to yo' pappy an' set on his knee." Although I had a little difficulty at first with the words in dialect, the poem spoke to me as nothing I had read before of the closeness, the special relationship I had had with my father, who by then had become an ardent believer in Father Divine[9] and gone to live in Father's "kingdom" in Harlem. Reading it helped to ease somewhat the tight knot of sorrow and longing I carried around in my chest that refused to go away. I read another poem. "'Lias! 'Lias! Bless de Lawd! / Don' you know de day's / erbroad? / Ef you don' get up, you scamp / Dey'll be

5. Polish-born writer of fiction (1857–1924). The following quotation is from the preface to *The Nigger of the "Narcissus."* O'Connor (1925–1964), American fiction writer who noted that the aim of the short story writer is "to make the concrete work double time" (*Mystery and Manners*, 1969).
6. London residence of the British sovereigns; its guards are the famous Beefeaters.
7. Novels by the English authors Henry Fielding (1707–1754), Charles Dickens (1812–1870), and William Thackeray (1811–1863), respectively. Austen (1775–1817), English novelist. Grey (1875–1939), American writer of westerns.
8. American poet (1872–1906).
9. Born George Baker (1880–1965), he became the most popular Harlem religious leader of the 1930s, gaining wealth and attracting many followers to his cultlike Peace Mission movement.

trouble in dis camp." I laughed. It reminded me of the way my mother sometimes yelled at my sister and me to get out of bed in the mornings.

And another: "Seen my lady home las' night / Jump back, honey, jump back. / Hel' huh han' an' sque'z it tight . . ." About love between a black man and a black woman. I had never seen that written about before and it roused in me all kinds of delicious feelings and hopes.

And I began to search then for books and stories and poems about "The Race" (as it was put back then), about my people. While not abandoning Thackeray, Fielding, Dickens and the others, I started asking the reference librarian, who was white, for books by Negro writers, although I must admit I did so at first with a feeling of shame—the shame I and many others used to experience in those days whenever the word "Negro" or "colored" came up.

No grade school literature teacher of mine had ever mentioned Dunbar or James Weldon Johnson or Langston Hughes.[1] I didn't know that Zora Neale Hurston[2] existed and was busy writing and being published during those years. Nor was I made aware of people like Frederick Douglass and Harriet Tubman[3]—their spirit and example—or the great 19th-century abolitionist and feminist Sojourner Truth. There wasn't even Negro History Week when I attended P.S. 35 on Decatur Street!

What I needed, what all the kids—West Indian and native black American alike—with whom I grew up needed, was an equivalent of the Jewish shul,[4] someplace where we could go after school—the schools that were shortchanging us—and read works by those like ourselves and learn about our history.

It was around that time also that I began harboring the dangerous thought of someday trying to write myself. Perhaps a poem about an apple tree, although I had never seen one. Or the story of a girl who could magically transplant herself to wherever she wanted to be in the world—such as Father Divine's kingdom in Harlem. Dunbar—his dark, eloquent face, his large volume of poems—permitted me to dream that I might someday write, and with something of the power with words my mother and her friends possessed.

When people at readings and writers' conferences ask me who my major influences were, they are sometimes a little disappointed when I don't immediately name the usual literary giants. True, I am indebted to those writers, white and black, whom I read during my formative years and still read for instruction and pleasure. But they were preceded in my life by another set of giants whom I always acknowledged before all others: the group of women around the table long ago. They taught me my first lessons in the narrative art. They trained my ear. They set a standard of excellence. This is why the best of my work must be attributed to them; it stands as testimony to the rich legacy of language and culture they so freely passed on to me in the wordshop of the kitchen.

1983

---

1. Author of poetry, fiction, and plays (1902–1967). Johnson (1871–1938), lyricist, writer, and civil rights activist who became secretary of the NAACP.
2. Writer and anthropologist (1891–1960).

3. A fugitive slave (1820?–1913) who rescued many other slaves. Douglass (1817–1896), orator, author, abolitionist, and supporter of women's rights.
4. School, synagogue (Yiddish).

TONI MORRISON
b. 1931

In 1993 Toni Morrison became the first African American author to win the Nobel Prize for literature; today she enjoys both critical acclaim and popular success on a scale rivaled by few other American writers. She has published ten novels—*The Bluest Eye* (1970), *Sula* (1973), *Song of Solomon* (1977), *Tar Baby* (1981), *Beloved* (1987), *Jazz* (1991), *Paradise* (1997), *Love* (2003), *A Mercy* (2008), and *Home* (2012)—as well as an influential critical volume, *Playing in the Dark* (1991). Rooted in the history and culture of African Americans, her novels evoke a past that is scarred by the violence both of slavery and its long aftermath and redeemed by the power of love and the grace of laughter. They are philosophically speculative yet vividly imagined and written in a prose that is by turns lyrical, elusive, colloquial, and transcendent. The best art, Morrison once asserted in a phrase that could be applied to her own, is "unquestionably political and irrevocably beautiful at the same time."

A storyteller with an abiding moral vision, Morrison confronts contemporary issues of racism, sexism, class exploitation, and imperialism by exploring her characters' emotional and psychological response to these structures of domination. Although she has written the libretto for the opera *Margaret Garner*, two plays, a short story, and substantial nonfiction, the novel is Morrison's chosen genre. In her essay "Rootedness: The Ancestor as Foundation," she argues that the novel has an urgent function in modern life, in part because "parents don't sit around and tell their children those classical, mythological archetypal stories that we heard years ago." Those stories and the cultural matrix from which they come shape her literary aesthetic. As she explains it, she does not

> regard Black literature as simply books *by* Black people, or simply as literature written *about* Black people or simply as literature that uses a certain mode of language in which you sort of drop g's. There is something very identifiable about it and it is my struggle to *find* that elusive but identifiable style in the books.

Born Chloe Anthony Wofford on February 18, 1931, in Lorain, Ohio, a steel town on the shores of Lake Erie, Morrison grew up in a region that in the nineteenth century had been a center of abolitionism. Her parents, George and Ramah Willis Wofford, were southerners who migrated to the North, bringing traditions of song and storytelling with them. The history of the region and of her family would find its way into her fiction and extend representations of the South/North geography traditionally mapped in African American literature. An excellent student, Morrison became the first member of her family to go to college. When she arrived at Howard University in Washington, D.C., she found that her classmates could not pronounce her name, so she became "Toni." An English major and a classics minor, she took courses with Alain Locke, one of the major figures of the Harlem Renaissance. But an important aspect of her education took place outside the classroom: her travels through the South as a member of the Howard Players, a theater troupe, taught her much about voice, pitch, and nuance. She graduated in 1953. After earning a master's degree at Cornell University, where she wrote a thesis on suicide in the works of William Faulkner and Virginia Woolf, she taught for two years at Texas Southern University and then for five years at Howard. In 1959 she married Harold Morrison, a Jamaican architect, with whom she had two sons, Harold Ford and Slade Kevin.

After her marriage ended in 1964, she moved with her children to Syracuse, New York, to take a job as a textbook editor. She subsequently became an editor at Random House in New York City, where, during an almost twenty-year career, she published many authors, including Toni Cade Bambara, Lucille Clifton, Leon Forrest, Gayl Jones, and June Jordan.

Morrison had joined a writers group in Washington and begun a story that eventually developed into *The Bluest Eye*. Set in Lorain, the novel distinguishes itself first by putting the experience of a poor black girl, who is invisible in the world and a victim at home, at its center. Unlike classic novels by black men, including Richard Wright's *Native Son* and Ralph Ellison's *Invisible Man*, which focus on interracial conflict, *The Bluest Eye* explores the black family and community as sites where the most painful consequences of racism are experienced. While the novel demonstrates Morrison's knowledge of classical mythology and popular American culture, of African American history and Western literary tradition, its language like its plot is fresh and original. By way of explanation, Morrison declared that she wrote the novel she had always wanted to read.

Sula elegizes the culture and communities that sustained African Americans from the Emancipation through the civil rights movement. It remembers life in the Bottom, a black neighborhood in the hills of the fictional city of Medallion, Ohio, that has been destroyed in the name of progress before the novel begins. From the images of destruction that introduce the text, through a series of deaths by fire and water, in rituals to stave off fear and to bury the dead, to the "circles of sorrow" that close it, *Sula* is suffused with sadness. Despite racism so unyielding that it seemed another force of nature, or perhaps because of it, the community's elders bonded together out of kinship and necessity. As the novel begins and ends, their legacy has been totally destroyed. The Bottom is home to Sula Peace and Nel Wright, the main characters, who, despite differences in class and personality, become fast friends and "use each other to grow on." Meeting again after a ten-year separation, Nel's "rapid soprano and Sula's dark sleepy chuckle make a duet." In its focus on female friendship, *Sula* breaks new ground. Not unlike blacks, who only belatedly recognized the value of the segregated communities that nurtured them for generations, Sula and Nel fail to recognize how valuable their friendship is until they have lost it. The recognition that their friendship is the most important thing in their lives comes only after Nel marries, has children, and leads a conventional life and after Sula dies, having improvised a life that defies convention.

While her first two novels won Morrison a small but devoted following, *Song of Solomon* earned her wide recognition, including the National Book Critics Award; it was the first book by a black author since *Native Son* to be a Book of the Month Club main selection. Layered with allusions to *The Odyssey*, the Old Testament, W. E. B. Du Bois's *The Souls of Black Folk*, Ralph Ellison's *Invisible Man*, William Faulkner's *Go Down, Moses*, and Gabriel Garcia Marquez's *One Hundred Years of Solitude*, the novel borrows many of its metaphors from African American folklore. Indeed, *Song* recounts a quest to uncover the history of black Americans that was never written but was preserved in fragments in the oral tradition: songs, stories, personal testimonies, jokes, and children's rhymes. The protagonist, Milkman Dead, is an indulged son of the bourgeoisie; the materialism that has meant spiritual death for his father threatens him as well.

Even as she re-creates the traditionally male quest narrative, Morrison revises the Western classics to give voice to women. When Milkman falters, only the intervention and piloting of his aunt, Pilate, allows him to continue his quest. Blues singer, bootlegger, and conjure woman, Pilate is a mythical outsider whose life-affirming ideology the novel endorses. It mourns the fate of its other female characters, Milkman's mother, Ruth; his sisters, Corinthians and Lena; and his cousin/lover, Hagar, whose fidelity to conventional gender roles constricts and constrains them. As a result of the novel's narrative strategies, the reader, like Milkman, becomes a participant in the journey who sorts out clues, follows false leads, becomes vulnerable, and eventually achieves the prize of greater self-knowledge.

Further expanding the symbolic geography of African American literature, *Tar Baby* moves from the Caribbean to New York City to rural Florida to Paris, as it charts the adventures of Jadine and Son, the two main characters whose love cannot overcome their cultural differences. They struggle to debate and define the usefulness of the past: as it continues in the static existence of Son's hometown of Eloe, Florida, or in the lives of Jadine's aunt and uncle, servants to a white candy magnate, or in the mythic stories of the blind horsemen of Iles de Chevalier. *Tar Baby* is arguably Morrison's most controversial work; some readers find its lush prose and explicit indictment of imperialism appealing, but others do not. Critics debate its gender politics and its representation of the West Indies.

By contrast, most critics agree that *Beloved* is Morrison's masterpiece. It builds on the foundation of slave narratives and engages its precursors in the American tradition, including Twain's *Adventures of Huckleberry Finn*, Faulkner's *Light in August*, and Harriet Beecher Stowe's *Uncle Tom's Cabin*. It draws on the extensive historiography of slavery. Most important, it depicts the interior lives of the men and women who were slaves, the spiritual strength it took for them to survive, and their struggle to love each other and themselves. The novel's seed was a newspaper clipping about Margaret Garner, an enslaved woman on trial in Cincinnati for killing her infant daughter to prevent her being returned to slavery. Morrison came across the clipping as she edited *The Black Book*, a scrapbook of folk history, at Random House. The novel begins eighteen years after the killing, and its protagonist, Sethe, works assiduously at "keeping the past at bay." But, when Paul D., one of the Sweet Home men with whom she had grown up in slavery, arrives at her door and disturbs the ghost of her dead child, subsequently called Beloved, Sethe is compelled to confront the worst experience of her life. Her surviving daughter, Denver, who has no recollection of slavery, must strive to understand the "unspeakable things unspoken" that constitute their history. In that history the shattered relationships between mothers and daughters are central.

The history that *Beloved* represents is both private and public, personal and collective. As Sethe's mother-in-law, Baby Suggs, reflects, "Not a house in the country ain't packed to its rafters with some dead Negro's grief." Sethe's tale may be the most chilling, but *Beloved* weaves together many stories of slavery: of resistance and defeat, victimization and villainy, courage and heroism. For readers, who are often as reluctant to confront slavery as the novel's characters are, Sethe and Denver model a way into the past and a way to move beyond it. Like the characters, readers may gain an understanding that history is communal and can be apprehended only through acts of empathy and imagination.

Structurally experimental, *Beloved* begins *in medias res*. "The reader is snatched, yanked, thrown into an environment completely foreign," Morrison remarks, "snatched just as the slaves were from one place to another, from any place to another, without preparation and without defense." The effect is to create "a shared experience" between the reader and the novel's characters. As the reader is drawn more deeply into the world of the novel, the experience can be disconcerting. In the end, however, this is a novel about survival—it begins after slavery has ended—and about the resilience of the human spirit. *Beloved* won the Pulitzer Prize, among other honors, and in 1999, Oprah Winfrey produced and starred in a film based on the novel. The movie received mixed reviews and failed at the box office. However, Winfrey's admiration for Morrison's fiction later led to the selection of several of her novels for Oprah's Book Club, which in turn made them best-sellers.

Jazz is set in a fictional version of 1920s Harlem. Rather than the famous figures of the Harlem Renaissance, its main characters are southern migrants caught up in a love triangle reminiscent of the blues. The catalyst for the plot was a photograph, taken by the famous African American photographer James Van Der Zee, of a young woman who died refusing to identify her lover as the person who shot her. Morrison is not as interested in the love triangle plot as she is in how the story is told. The blues theme goes through many variations; indeed, the novel's narrative strategies emulate the improvisational freedom of jazz itself.

In 1997 Morrison published *Paradise,* a novel that depicts the difficulty of achieving community, even when people act with courage and idealism. The main characters are descendants of the founders of the all-black town of Ruby, Oklahoma. They revel in the stories of their ancestors' deeds: "Testimonies to endurance, wit, skill, and strength. Tales of luck and courage. But why were there no stories to tell of themselves?" Unlike most of Morrison's fiction, *Paradise* emphasizes the limitations of history as a guide to the present. Some readers found its characters flatter and its prose less accessible than the characters and prose in the earlier novels. Others found *Paradise* to be her most transcendent work.

Love revisits the themes of female friendship, envy, and love, first broached in *Sula.* As Heed and Christine grow to adulthood, in a small town where the social upheavals of the late twentieth century echo dimly, their bond is threatened by jealousy and enmity sown by Bill Cosey, Heed's father and the owner of a resort that prospered under segregation. Class as well as race is an impediment to love. In addition to love between friends, the novel explores love in its various facets: parental, erotic, and spiritual. In this regard, it plays variations on one of Morrison's major themes.

The setting shifts dramatically again in *A Mercy* to seventeenth-century North America, before the nation was established and before racial categories were fixed. What did it mean to be black in this time and place? What were the initial encounters across lines of difference? *A Mercy* suggests that relationships were more malleable; trust could grow in situations where whites and blacks, thrown together under desperate conditions, depended on each other for small acts of mercy. The novel ponders how and why racial animus took root and how racial hierarchies came to be seen as signs of social progress.

Its spare prose and more elegiac tone distinguish *Home* from other novels in Morrison's corpus, although its central question is both familiar and profound. Can African Americans move beyond the dispossession that was the initial condition of their journey to the New World? Is it possible for them to claim a home? Is it possible for any of us? Frank Money, a Korean War veteran, from Lotus, Georgia, a barren backwater for which it is impossible to feel nostalgia, is the protagonist who must answer the question.

Critics continue to be drawn to Morrison's oeuvre, in part because her novels participate in multiple literary traditions. As befits a humanities professor, she draws frequently on seminal texts in the Western tradition. She insists on her identity as a black writer, and her work signifies on a range of African American texts. While asserting the importance of African writers, notably Chinua Achebe, Awi Kweh Armah, Bessie Head, and Camara Laye, to her work, she acknowledges an affinity with classic American writers. In "Unspeakable Things Unspoken: The Afro-American Presence in American Literature," Morrison examines "the ways in which the presence of Afro-Americans has shaped the choices, the language, the structure" of nineteenth-century canonical American literature. Rejecting the long-standing view that the authors of the American Renaissance chose not to write about slavery, Morrison argues that they could not ignore the "Africanist" presence in their midst. Her illustrative text is *Moby-Dick.* The essay is also notable for Morrison's brilliant readings of the opening passages of her first five novels. The highly influential critical volume *Playing in the Dark: Whiteness and the Literary Imagination* continues the analysis begun in this essay, extending it to interpret fiction by Edgar Allan Poe, Willa Cather, and Ernest Hemingway. For several weeks in 1991, *Jazz* and *Playing in the Dark* were simultaneously on the *New York Times* best-seller list.

Morrison has also been an influential teacher. In the 1970s she taught at the State University of New York at Purchase and also at Yale; in the 1980s, she taught at Bard College and then the State University of New York at Albany. From 1989 to 2006 she was the Robert F. Goheen Professor of Humanities at Princeton. Morrison's profile as a public intellectual has risen steadily as a result of numerous interviews and the book reviews and essays she has written on major events of the day. In 1992 she edited *Race-ing Justice, En-gendering Power: Essays on Anita Hill, Clarence Thomas, and the Construction of Social Reality*, a collection of essays on issues arising from the nomination of Clarence Thomas to the U.S. Supreme Court. The Thomas-Hill hearings were a watershed event in racial and gender politics in America. In 1997 Morrison co-edited with Claudia Brodsky-Lacour *Birth of a Nationhood: Gaze, Script, and Spectacle in the O. J. Simpson Case*, a volume interpreting the sensational murder trial of the former pro-football player that dominated the media in 1995.

In her speech accepting the Nobel Prize, Morrison proclaimed the value of the literary vocation: "word-work is sublime . . . because it is generative; it makes meaning that secures our difference, our human difference—the way in which we are like no other life." As her novels map experience across centuries and regions, they explore our humanity in all its dimensions. Triumph and tragedy, pettiness and heroism, the mundane and the transcendent are constantly in play. These themes are explored in prose that carries the unmistakable signature of its creator. Her moral vision and artistic command make Toni Morrison an indispensable writer for our time.

SULA

> "Nobody knew my rose of the world but me. . . . I had too much glory. They don't want glory like that in nobody's heart."
> —The Rose Tattoo[1]

Part One

In that place, where they tore the nightshade and blackberry patches from their roots to make room for the Medallion City Golf Course, there was once a neighborhood. It stood in the hills above the valley town of Medallion and spread all the way to the river. It is called the suburbs now, but when black people lived there it was called the Bottom. One road, shaded by beeches, oaks, maples and chestnuts, connected it to the valley. The beeches are gone now, and so are the pear trees where children sat and yelled down through the blossoms to passersby. Generous funds have been allotted to level the stripped and faded buildings that clutter the road from Medallion up to the golf course. They are going to raze the Time and a Half Pool Hall, where feet in long tan shoes once pointed down from chair rungs. A steel ball will knock to dust Irene's Palace of Cosmetology, where women used to lean their heads back on sink trays and doze while Irene lathered Nu Nile into their hair. Men in khaki work clothes will pry loose the slats of Reba's Grill, where the owner cooked in her hat because she couldn't remember the ingredients without it.

There will be nothing left of the Bottom (the footbridge that crossed the river is already gone), but perhaps it is just as well, since it wasn't a town anyway: just a neighborhood where on quiet days people in valley houses could hear singing sometimes, banjos sometimes, and, if a valley man

---

1. Play by American dramatist Tennessee Williams (1911–1983).

happened to have business up in those hills—collecting rent or insurance payments—he might see a dark woman in a flowered dress doing a bit of cakewalk, a bit of black bottom,[2] a bit of "messing around" to the lively notes of a mouth organ. Her bare feet would raise the saffron dust that floated down on the coveralls and bunion-split shoes of the man breathing music in and out of his harmonica. The black people watching her would laugh and rub their knees, and it would be easy for the valley man to hear the laughter and not notice the adult pain that rested somewhere under the eyelids, somewhere under their head rags and soft felt hats, somewhere in the palm of the hand, somewhere behind the frayed lapels, somewhere in the sinew's curve. He'd have to stand in the back of Greater Saint Matthew's and let the tenor's voice dress him in silk, or touch the hands of the spoon carvers (who had not worked in eight years) and let the fingers that danced on wood kiss his skin. Otherwise the pain would escape him even though the laughter was part of the pain.

A shucking, knee-slapping, wet-eyed laughter that could even describe and explain how they came to be where they were.

A joke. A nigger joke. That was the way it got started. Not the town, of course, but that part of town where the Negroes lived, the part they called the Bottom in spite of the fact that it was up in the hills. Just a nigger joke. The kind white folks tell when the mill closes down and they're looking for a little comfort somewhere. The kind colored folks tell on themselves when the rain doesn't come, or comes for weeks, and they're looking for a little comfort somehow.

A good white farmer promised freedom and a piece of bottom land to his slave if he would perform some very difficult chores. When the slave completed the work, he asked the farmer to keep his end of the bargain. Freedom was easy—the farmer had no objection to that. But he didn't want to give up any land. So he told the slave that he was very sorry that he had to give him valley land. He had hoped to give him a piece of the Bottom. The slave blinked and said he thought valley land was bottom land. The master said, "Oh, no! See those hills? That's bottom land, rich and fertile."

"But it's high up in the hills," said the slave.

"High up from us," said the master, "but when God looks down, it's the bottom. That's why we call it so. It's the bottom of heaven—best land there is."

So the slave pressed his master to try to get him some. He preferred it to the valley. And it was done. The nigger got the hilly land, where planting was backbreaking, where the soil slid down and washed away the seeds, and where the wind lingered all through the winter.

Which accounted for the fact that white people lived on the rich valley floor in that little river town in Ohio, and the blacks populated the hills above it, taking small consolation in the fact that every day they could literally look down on the white folks.

Still, it was lovely up in the Bottom. After the town grew and the farm land turned into a village and the village into a town and the streets of Medallion were hot and dusty with progress, those heavy trees that sheltered the shacks up in the Bottom were wonderful to see. And the hunters

---

2. A popular dance of the 1920s; some saw it as indecent. "Cakewalk": a stage dance developed by black entertainers.

who went there sometimes wondered in private if maybe the white farmer was right after all. Maybe it was the bottom of heaven.

The black people would have disagreed, but they had no time to think about it. They were mightily preoccupied with earthly things—and each other, wondering even as early as 1920 what Shadrack was all about, what that little girl Sula who grew into a woman in their town was all about, and what they themselves were all about, tucked up there in the Bottom.

1919

Except for World War II, nothing ever interfered with the celebration of National Suicide Day. It had taken place every January third since 1920, although Shadrack,[3] its founder, was for many years the only celebrant. Blasted and permanently astonished by the events of 1917, he had returned to Medallion handsome but ravaged, and even the most fastidious people in the town sometimes caught themselves dreaming of what he must have been like a few years back before he went off to war. A young man of hardly twenty, his head full of nothing and his mouth recalling the taste of lipstick, Shadrack had found himself in December, 1917, running with his comrades across a field in France. It was his first encounter with the enemy and he didn't know whether his company was running toward them or away. For several days they had been marching, keeping close to a stream that was frozen at its edges. At one point they crossed it, and no sooner had he stepped foot on the other side than the day was adangle with shouts and explosions. Shellfire was all around him, and though he knew that this was something called *it*, he could not muster up the proper feeling—the feeling that would accommodate *it*. He expected to be terrified or exhilarated—to feel *something* very strong. In fact, he felt only the bite of a nail in his boot, which pierced the ball of his foot whenever he came down on it. The day was cold enough to make his breath visible, and he wondered for a moment at the purity and whiteness of his own breath among the dirty, gray explosions surrounding him. He ran, bayonet fixed, deep in the great sweep of men flying across this field. Wincing at the pain in his foot, he turned his head a little to the right and saw the face of a soldier near him fly off. Before he could register shock, the rest of the soldier's head disappeared under the inverted soup bowl of his helmet. But stubbornly, taking no direction from the brain, the body of the headless soldier ran on, with energy and grace, ignoring altogether the drip and slide of brain tissue down its back.

When Shadrack opened his eyes he was propped up in a small bed. Before him on a tray was a large tin plate divided into three triangles. In one triangle was rice, in another meat, and in the third stewed tomatoes. A small round depression held a cup of whitish liquid. Shadrack stared at the soft colors that filled these triangles: the lumpy whiteness of rice, the quivering blood tomatoes, the grayish-brown meat. All their repugnance was contained in the neat balance of the triangles—a balance that soothed him, transferred some of its equilibrium to him. Thus reassured that the white,

3. The name given to a captive Judean by Nebuchadnezzar, king of the Babylonians (Daniel 1.1–7). Because they refuse to worship the golden image, Shadrack and his companions were thrown into the furnace, where they were not burned (Daniel 3.13–27).

the red and the brown would stay where they were—would not explode or burst forth from their restricted zones—he suddenly felt hungry and looked around for his hands. His glance was cautious at first, for he had to be very careful—anything could be anywhere. Then he noticed two lumps beneath the beige blanket on either side of his hips. With extreme care he lifted one arm and was relieved to find his hand attached to his wrist. He tried the other and found it also. Slowly he directed one hand toward the cup and, just as he was about to spread his fingers, they began to grow in higgledy-piggledy fashion like Jack's beanstalk all over the tray and the bed. With a shriek he closed his eyes and thrust his huge growing hands under the covers. Once out of sight they seemed to shrink back to their normal size. But the yell had brought a male nurse.

"Private? We're not going to have any trouble today, are we? Are we, Private?"

Shadrack looked up at a balding man dressed in a green-cotton jacket and trousers. His hair was parted low on the right side so that some twenty or thirty yellow hairs could discreetly cover the nakedness of his head.

"Come on. Pick up that spoon. Pick it up, Private. Nobody is going to feed you forever."

Sweat slid from Shadrack's armpits down his sides. He could not bear to see his hands grow again and he was frightened of the voice in the apple-green suit.

"Pick it up, I said. There's no point to this . . ." The nurse reached under the cover for Shadrack's wrist to pull out the monstrous hand. Shadrack jerked it back and overturned the tray. In panic he raised himself to his knees and tried to fling off and away his terrible fingers, but succeeded only in knocking the nurse into the next bed.

When they bound Shadrack into a straitjacket, he was both relieved and grateful, for his hands were at last hidden and confined to whatever size they had attained.

Laced and silent in his small bed, he tried to tie the loose cords in his mind. He wanted desperately to see his own face and connect it with the word "private"—the word the nurse (and the others who helped bind him) had called him. "Private" he thought was something secret, and he wondered why they looked at him and called him a secret. Still, if his hands behaved as they had done, what might he expect from his face? The fear and longing were too much for him, so he began to think of other things. That is, he let his mind slip into whatever cave mouths of memory it chose.

He saw a window that looked out on a river which he knew was full of fish. Someone was speaking softly just outside the door . . .

Shadrack's earlier violence had coincided with a memorandum from the hospital executive staff in reference to the distribution of patients in high-risk areas. There was clearly a demand for space. The priority or the violence earned Shadrack his release, $217 in cash, a full suit of clothes and copies of very official-looking papers.

When he stepped out of the hospital door the grounds overwhelmed him: the cropped shrubbery, the edged lawns, the undeviating walks. Shadrack looked at the cement stretches: each one leading clearheadedly to some presumably desirable destination. There were no fences, no warnings, no obstacles at all between concrete and green grass, so one could easily ignore the tidy sweep of stone and cut out in another direction—a direction of one's own.

Shadrack stood at the foot of the hospital steps watching the heads of trees tossing ruefully but harmlessly, since their trunks were rooted too deeply in the earth to threaten him. Only the walks made him uneasy. He shifted his weight, wondering how he could get to the gate without stepping on the concrete. While plotting his course—where he would have to leap, where to skirt a clump of bushes—a loud guffaw startled him. Two men were going up the steps. Then he noticed that there were many people about, and that he was just now seeing them, or else they had just materialized. They were thin slips, like paper dolls floating down the walks. Some were seated in chairs with wheels, propelled by other paper figures from behind. All seemed to be smoking, and their arms and legs curved in the breeze. A good high wind would pull them up and away and they would land perhaps among the tops of the trees.

Shadrack took the plunge. Four steps and he was on the grass heading for the gate. He kept his head down to avoid seeing the paper people swerving and bending here and there, and he lost his way. When he looked up, he was standing by a low red building separated from the main building by a covered walkway. From somewhere came a sweetish smell which reminded him of something painful. He looked around for the gate and saw that he had gone directly away from it in his complicated journey over the grass. Just to the left of the low building was a graveled driveway that appeared to lead outside the grounds. He trotted quickly to it and left, at last, a haven of more than a year, only eight days of which he fully recollected.

Once on the road, he headed west. The long stay in the hospital had left him weak—too weak to walk steadily on the gravel shoulders of the road. He shuffled, grew dizzy, stopped for breath, started again, stumbling and sweating but refusing to wipe his temples, still afraid to look at his hands. Passengers in dark, square cars shuttered their eyes at what they took to be a drunken man.

The sun was already directly over his head when he came to a town. A few blocks of shaded streets and he was already at its heart—a pretty, quietly regulated downtown.

Exhausted, his feet clotted with pain, he sat down at the curbside to take off his shoes. He closed his eyes to avoid seeing his hands and fumbled with the laces of the heavy high-topped shoes. The nurse had tied them into a double knot, the way one does for children, and Shadrack, long unaccustomed to the manipulation of intricate things, could not get them loose. Uncoordinated, his fingernails tore away at the knots. He fought a rising hysteria that was not merely anxiety to free his aching feet; his very life depended on the release of the knots. Suddenly without raising his eyelids, he began to cry. Twenty-two years old, weak, hot, frightened, not daring to acknowledge the fact that he didn't even know who or what he was . . . with no past, no language, no tribe, no source, no address book, no comb, no pencil, no clock, no pocket handkerchief, no rug, no bed, no can opener, no faded postcard, no soap, no key, no tobacco pouch, no soiled underwear and nothing nothing nothing to do . . . he was sure of one thing only: the unchecked monstrosity of his hands. He cried soundlessly at the curbside of a small Midwestern town wondering where the window was, and the river, and the soft voices just outside the door . . .

Through his tears he saw the fingers joining the laces, tentatively at first, then rapidly. The four fingers of each hand fused into the fabric, knotted themselves and zigzagged in and out of the tiny eyeholes.

By the time the police drove up, Shadrack was suffering from a blinding headache, which was not abated by the comfort he felt when the policemen pulled his hands away from what he thought was a permanent entanglement with his shoelaces. They took him to jail, booked him for vagrancy and intoxication, and locked him in a cell. Lying on a cot, Shadrack could only stare helplessly at the wall, so paralyzing was the pain in his head. He lay in this agony for a long while and then realized he was staring at the painted-over letters of a command to fuck himself. He studied the phrase as the pain in his head subsided.

Like moonlight stealing under a window shade an idea insinuated itself: his earlier desire to see his own face. He looked for a mirror; there was none. Finally, keeping his hands carefully behind his back he made his way to the toilet bowl and peeped in. The water was unevenly lit by the sun so he could make nothing out. Returning to his cot he took the blanket and covered his head, rendering the water dark enough to see his reflection. There in the toilet water he saw a grave black face. A black so definite, so unequivocal, it astonished him. He had been harboring a skittish apprehension that he was not real—that he didn't exist at all. But when the blackness greeted him with its indisputable presence, he wanted nothing more. In his joy he took the risk of letting one edge of the blanket drop and glanced at his hands. They were still. Courteously still.

Shadrack rose and returned to the cot, where he fell into the first sleep of his new life. A sleep deeper than the hospital drugs; deeper than the pits of plums, steadier than the condor's wing; more tranquil than the curve of eggs.

The sheriff looked through the bars at the young man with the matted hair. He had read through his prisoner's papers and hailed a farmer. When Shadrack awoke, the sheriff handed him back his papers and escorted him to the back of a wagon. Shadrack got in and in less than three hours he was back in Medallion, for he had been only twenty-two miles from his window, his river, and his soft voices just outside the door.

In the back of the wagon, supported by sacks of squash and hills of pumpkins, Shadrack began a struggle that was to last for twelve days, a struggle to order and focus experience. It had to do with making a place for fear as a way of controlling it. He knew the smell of death and was terrified of it, for he could not anticipate it. It was not death or dying that frightened him, but the unexpectedness of both. In sorting it all out, he hit on the notion that if one day a year were devoted to it, everybody could get it out of the way and the rest of the year would be safe and free. In this manner he instituted National Suicide Day.

On the third day of the new year, he walked through the Bottom down Carpenter's Road with a cowbell and a hangman's rope calling the people together. Telling them that this was their only chance to kill themselves or each other.

At first the people in the town were frightened; they knew Shadrack was crazy but that did not mean that he didn't have any sense or, even more important, that he had no power. His eyes were so wild, his hair so long and matted, his voice was so full of authority and thunder that he caused panic on the first, or Charter, National Suicide Day in 1920. The next one, in 1921, was less frightening but still worrisome. The people had seen him a year now in between. He lived in a shack on the riverbank that had once belonged to his grandfather long time dead. On Tuesday and Friday he sold the fish he had caught that morning, the rest of the week he was drunk, loud, obscene, funny and outrageous. But he never touched anybody, never fought, never caressed. Once the people understood the boundaries and nature of his madness, they could fit him, so to speak, into the scheme of things.

Then, on subsequent National Suicide Days, the grown people looked out from behind curtains as he rang his bell; a few stragglers increased their speed, and little children screamed and ran. The tetter heads tried goading him (although he was only four or five years older then they) but not for long, for his curses were stingingly personal.

As time went along, the people took less notice of these January thirds, or rather they thought they did, thought they had no attitudes or feelings one way or another about Shadrack's annual solitary parade. In fact they had simply stopped remarking on the holiday because they had absorbed it into their thoughts, into their language, into their lives.

Someone said to a friend, "You sure was a long time delivering that baby. How long was you in labor?"

And the friend answered, "'Bout three days. The pains started on Suicide Day and kept up till the following Sunday. Was borned on Sunday. All my boys is Sunday boys."

Some lover said to his bride-to-be, "Let's do it after New Years, 'stead of before. I get paid New Year's Eve."

And his sweetheart answered, "OK, but make sure it ain't on Suicide Day. I ain't 'bout to be listening to no cowbells whilst the weddin's going on."

Somebody's grandmother said her hens always started a laying of double yolks right after Suicide Day.

Then Reverend Deal took it up, saying the same folks who had sense enough to avoid Shadrack's call were the ones who insisted on drinking themselves to death or womanizing themselves to death. "May's well go on with Shad and save the Lamb the trouble of redemption."

Easily, quietly, Suicide Day became a part of the fabric of life up in the Bottom of Medallion, Ohio.

1920

It had to be as far away from the Sundown House as possible. And her grandmother's middle-aged nephew who lived in a Northern town called Medallion was the one chance she had to make sure it would be. The red shutters had haunted both Helene Sabat and her grandmother for sixteen years. Helene was born behind those shutters, daughter of a Creole[4] whore who worked there. The grandmother took Helene away from the soft lights and flowered carpets of the Sundown House and raised her under the dolesome eyes of a multicolored Virgin Mary, counseling her to be constantly on guard for any sign of her mother's wild blood.

---

4. A person of mixed French and black descent.

So when Wiley Wright came to visit his Great Aunt Cecile in New Orleans, his enchantment with the pretty Helene became a marriage proposal—under the pressure of both women. He was a seaman (or rather a lakeman, for he was a ship's cook on one of the Great Lakes lines), in port only three days out of every sixteen.

He took his bride to his home in Medallion and put her in a lovely house with a brick porch and real lace curtains at the window. His long absences were quite bearable for Helene Wright, especially when, after some nine years of marriage, her daughter was born.

Her daughter was more comfort and purpose than she had ever hoped to find in this life. She rose grandly to the occasion of motherhood—grateful, deep down in her heart, that the child had not inherited the great beauty that was hers: that her skin had dusk in it, that her lashes were substantial but not undignified in their length, that she had taken the broad flat nose of Wiley (although Helene expected to improve it somewhat) and his generous lips.

Under Helene's hand the girl became obedient and polite. Any enthusiasms that little Nel showed were calmed by the mother until she drove her daughter's imagination underground.

Helene Wright was an impressive woman, at least in Medallion she was. Heavy hair in a bun, dark eyes arched in a perpetual query about other people's manners. A woman who won all social battles with presence and a conviction of the legitimacy of her authority. Since there was no Catholic church in Medallion then, she joined the most conservative black church. And held sway. It was Helene who never turned her head in church when latecomers arrived; Helene who established the practice of seasonal altar flowers; Helene who introduced the giving of banquets of welcome to returning Negro veterans. She lost only one battle—the pronunciation of her name. The people in the Bottom refused to say Helene. They called her Helen Wright and left it at that.

All in all her life was a satisfactory one. She loved her house and enjoyed manipulating her daughter and her husband. She would sigh sometimes just before falling asleep, thinking that she had indeed come far enough away from the Sundown House.

So it was with extremely mixed emotions that she read a letter from Mr. Henri Martin describing the illness of her grandmother, and suggesting she come down right away. She didn't want to go, but could not bring herself to ignore the silent plea of the woman who had rescued her.

It was November. November, 1920. Even in Medallion there was a victorious swagger in the legs of white men and a dull-eyed excitement in the eyes of colored veterans.

Helene thought about the trip South with heavy misgiving but decided that she had the best protection: her manner and her bearing, to which she would add a beautiful dress. She bought some deep-brown wool and three-fourths of a yard of matching velvet. Out of this she made herself a heavy but elegant dress with velvet collar and pockets.

Nel watched her mother cutting the pattern from newspapers and moving her eyes rapidly from a magazine model to her own hands. She watched her turn up the kerosene lamp at sunset to sew far into the night.

The day they were ready, Helene cooked a smoked ham, left a note for her lake-bound husband, in case he docked early, and walked head high and arms stiff with luggage ahead of her daughter to the train depot.

It was a longer walk than she remembered, and they saw the train steaming up just as they turned the corner. They ran along the track looking for the coach pointed out to them by the colored porter. Even at that they made a mistake. Helene and her daughter entered a coach peopled by some twenty white men and women. Rather than go back and down the three wooden steps again, Helene decided to spare herself some embarrassment and walk on through to the colored car. She carried two pieces of luggage and a string purse; her daughter carried a covered basket of food.

As they opened the door marked COLORED ONLY, they saw a white conductor coming toward them. It was a chilly day but a light skim of sweat glistened on the woman's face as she and the little girl struggled to hold the door open, hang on to their luggage and enter all at once. The conductor let his eyes travel over the pale yellow woman and then stuck his little finger into his ear, jiggling it free of wax. "What you think you doin', gal?"

Helene looked up at him.

So soon. So soon. She hadn't even begun the trip back. Back to her grandmother's house in the city where the red shutters glowed, and already she had been called "gal." All the old vulnerabilities, all the old fears of being somehow flawed gathered in her stomach and made her hands tremble. She had heard only that one word; it dangled above her wide-brimmed hat, which had slipped, in her exertion, from its carefully leveled placement and was now tilted in a bit of a jaunt over her eye.

Thinking he wanted her tickets, she quickly dropped both the cowhide suitcase and the straw one in order to search for them in her purse. An eagerness to please and an apology for living met in her voice. "I have them. Right here somewhere, sir . . ."

The conductor looked at the bit of wax his fingernail had retrieved. "What was you doin' back in there? What was you doin' in that coach yonder?"

Helene licked her lips. "Oh . . . I . . ." Her glance moved beyond the white man's face to the passengers seated behind him. Four or five black faces were watching, two belonging to soldiers still in their shit-colored uniforms and peaked caps. She saw their closed faces, their locked eyes, and turned for compassion to the gray eyes of the conductor.

"We made a mistake, sir. You see, there wasn't no sign. We just got in the wrong car, that's all. Sir."

"We don't 'low no mistakes on this train. Now git your butt on in there."

He stood there staring at her until she realized that he wanted her to move aside. Pulling Nel by the arm, she pressed herself and her daughter into the foot space in front of a wooden seat. Then, for no earthly reason, at least no reason that anybody could understand, certainly no reason that Nel understood then or later, she smiled. Like a street pup that wags its tail at the very doorjamb of the butcher shop he has been kicked away from only moments before, Helene smiled. Smiled dazzlingly and coquettishly at the salmon-colored face of the conductor.

Nel looked away from the flash of pretty teeth to the other passengers. The two black soldiers, who had been watching the scene with what appeared to be indifference, now looked stricken. Behind Nel was the bright and blazing light of her mother's smile; before her the midnight eyes of the soldiers. She saw the muscles of their faces tighten, a movement under the skin from blood to marble. No change in the expression of the eyes, but a hard wetness that veiled them as they looked at the stretch of her mother's foolish smile.

As the door slammed on the conductor's exit, Helene walked down the aisle to a seat. She looked about for a second to see whether any of the men would help her put the suitcases in the overhead rack. Not a man moved. Helene sat down, fussily, her back toward the men. Nel sat opposite, facing both her mother and the soldiers, neither of whom she could look at. She felt both pleased and ashamed to sense that these men, unlike her father, who worshiped his graceful, beautiful wife, were bubbling with a hatred for her mother that had not been there in the beginning but had been born with the dazzling smile. In the silence that preceded the train's heave, she looked deeply at the folds of her mother's dress. There in the fall of the heavy brown wool she held her eyes. She could not risk letting them travel upward for fear of seeing that the hooks and eyes in the placket of the dress had come undone and exposed the custard-colored skin underneath. She stared at the hem, wanting to believe in its weight but knowing that custard was all that it hid. If this tall, proud woman, this woman who was very particular about her friends, who slipped into church with unequaled elegance, who could quell a roustabout[5] with a look, if *she* were really custard, then there was a chance that Nel was too.

It was on that train, shuffling toward Cincinnati, that she resolved to be on guard—always. She wanted to make certain that no man ever looked at her that way. That no midnight eyes or marbled flesh would ever accost her and turn her into jelly.

For two days they rode; two days of watching sleet turn to rain, turn to purple sunsets, and one night knotted on the wooden seats (their heads on folded coats), trying not to hear the snoring soldiers. When they changed trains in Birmingham for the last leg of the trip, they discovered what luxury they had been in through Kentucky and Tennessee, where the rest stops had all had colored toilets. After Birmingham there were none. Helene's face was drawn with the need to relieve herself, and so intense was her distress she finally brought herself to speak about her problem to a black woman with four children who had got on in Tuscaloosa.

"Is there somewhere we can go to use the restroom?"

The woman looked up at her and seemed not to understand. "Ma'am?" Her eyes fastened on the thick velvet collar, the fair skin, the high-tone voice.

"The restroom," Helene repeated. Then, in a whisper, "The toilet."

The woman pointed out the window and said, "Yes, ma'am. Yonder."

Helene looked out of the window halfway expecting to see a comfort station in the distance; instead she saw gray-green trees leaning over tangled grass. "Where?"

"Yonder," the woman said. "Meridian. We be pullin' in direc'lin." Then she smiled sympathetically and asked, "Kin you make it?"

Helene nodded and went back to her seat trying to think of other things—for the surest way to have an accident would be to remember her full bladder.

At Meridian the women got out with their children. While Helene looked about the tiny stationhouse for a door that said COLORED WOMEN, the other woman stalked off to a field of high grass on the far side of the track. Some white men were leaning on the railing in front of the stationhouse. It was

---

5. A longshoreman or an unskilled laborer.

not only their tongues curling around toothpicks that kept Helene from asking information of them. She looked around for the other woman and, seeing just the top of her head rag in the grass, slowly realized where "yonder" was. All of them, the fat woman and her four children, three boys and a girl, Helene and her daughter, squatted there in the four o'clock Meridian sun. They did it again in Ellisville, again in Hattiesburg, and by the time they reached Slidell, not too far from Lake Pontchartrain, Helene could not only fold leaves as well as the fat woman, she never felt a stir as she passed the muddy eyes of the men who stood like wrecked Dorics[6] under the station roofs of those towns.

The lift in spirit that such an accomplishment produced in her quickly disappeared when the train finally pulled into New Orleans.

Cecile Sabat's house leaned between two others just like it on Elysian Fields.[7] A Frenchified shotgun house, it sported a magnificent garden in the back and a tiny wrought-iron fence in the front. On the door hung a black crepe wreath with purple ribbon. They were too late. Helene reached up to touch the ribbon, hesitated, and knocked. A man in a collarless shirt opened the door. Helene identified herself and he said he was Henri Martin and that he was there for the settin'-up. They stepped into the house. The Virgin Mary clasped her hands in front of her neck three times in the front room and once in the bedroom where Cecile's body lay. The old woman had died without seeing or blessing her granddaughter.

No one other than Mr. Martin seemed to be in the house, but a sweet odor as of gardenias told them that someone else had been. Blotting her lashes with a white handkerchief, Helene walked through the kitchen to the back bedroom where she had slept for sixteen years. Nel trotted along behind, enchanted with the smell, the candles and the strangeness. When Helene bent to loosen the ribbons of Nel's hat, a woman in a yellow dress came out of the garden and onto the back porch that opened into the bedroom. The two women looked at each other. There was no recognition in the eyes of either. Then Helene said, "This is your . . . grandmother, Nel." Nel looked at her mother and then quickly back at the door they had just come out of.

"No. That was your great-grandmother. This is your grandmother. My . . . mother."

Before the child could think, her words were hanging in the gardenia air. "But she looks so young."

The woman in the canary-yellow dress laughed and said she was forty-eight, "an old forty-eight."

Then it was she who carried the gardenia smell. This tiny woman with the softness and glare of a canary. In that somber house that held four Virgin Marys, where death sighed in every corner and candles sputtered, the gardenia smell and canary-yellow dress emphasized the funeral atmosphere surrounding them.

The woman smiled, glanced in the mirror and said, throwing her voice toward Helene, "That your only one?"

"Yes," said Helene.

"Pretty. A lot like you."

---

6. I.e., like columns holding up the roofs.
7. In classic mythology, the home of the blessed after they die; here, a street in New Orleans.

"Yes. Well. She's ten now."

"Ten? Vrai?[8] Small for her age, no?"

Helene shrugged and looked at her daughter's questioning eyes. The woman in the yellow dress leaned forward. "Come. Come, chere."

Helene interrupted. "We have to get cleaned up. We been three days on the train with no chance to wash or . . ."

"Comment t'appelle?"

"She doesn't talk Creole."

"Then you ask her."

"She wants to know your name, honey."

With her head pressed into her mother's heavy brown dress, Nel told her and then asked, "What's yours?"

"Mine's Rochelle. Well. I must be going on." She moved closer to the mirror and stood there sweeping hair up from her neck back into its halo-like roll, and wetting with spit the ringlets that fell over her ears. "I been here, you know, most of the day. She pass on yesterday. The funeral tomorrow. Henri takin' care." She struck a match, blew it out and darkened her eyebrows with the burnt head. All the while Helene and Nel watched her. The one in a rage at the folded leaves she had endured, the wooden benches she had slept on, all to miss seeing her grandmother and seeing instead that painted canary who never said a word of greeting or affection or . . .

Rochelle continued. "I don't know what happen to de house. Long time paid for. You be thinkin' on it? Oui?" Her newly darkened eyebrows queried Helene.

"Oui."[9] Helene's voice was chilly. "I be thinkin' on it."

"Oh, well. Not for me to say . . ."

Suddenly she swept around and hugged Nel—a quick embrace tighter and harder than one would have imagined her thin soft arms capable of.

"'Voir![1] 'Voir!" and she was gone.

In the kitchen, being soaped head to toe by her mother, Nel ventured an observation. "She smelled so nice. And her skin was so soft."

Helene rinsed the cloth. "Much handled things are always soft."

"What does 'vwah' mean?"

"I don't know," her mother said. "I don't talk Creole." She gazed at her daughter's wet buttocks. "And neither do you."

When they got back to Medallion and into the quiet house they saw the note exactly where they had left it and the ham dried out in the icebox.

"Lord, I've never been so glad to see this place. But look at the dust. Get the rags, Nel. Oh, never mind. Let's breathe awhile first. Lord, I never thought I'd get back here safe and sound. Whoo. Well, it's over. Good and over. Praise His name. Look at that. I told that old fool not to deliver any milk and there's the can curdled to beat all. What gets into people? I told him not to. Well, I got other things to worry 'bout. Got to get a fire started. I left it ready so I wouldn't have to do nothin' but light it. Lord, it's cold. Don't just sit there, honey. You could be pulling your nose . . ."

Nel sat on the red-velvet sofa listening to her mother but remembering the smell and the tight, tight hug of the woman in yellow who rubbed burned matches over her eyes.

8. True (French).
9. Yes (French).
1. Good-bye (a contracted form of the French *au revoir*).

Late that night after the fire was made, the cold supper eaten, the surface dust removed, Nel lay in bed thinking of her trip. She remembered clearly the urine running down and into her stockings until she learned how to squat properly; the disgust on the face of the dead woman and the sound of the funeral drums. It had been an exhilarating trip but a fearful one. She had been frightened of the soldiers' eyes on the train, the black wreath on the door, the custard pudding she believed lurked under her mother's heavy dress, the feel of unknown streets and unknown people. But she had gone on a real trip, and now she was different. She got out of bed and lit the lamp to look in the mirror. There was her face, plain brown eyes, three braids and the nose her mother hated. She looked for a long time and suddenly a shiver ran through her.

"I'm me," she whispered. "Me."

Nel didn't know quite what she meant, but on the other hand she knew exactly what she meant.

"I'm me. I'm not their daughter. I'm not Nel. I'm me. Me."

Each time she said the word *me* there was a gathering in her like power, like joy, like fear. Back in bed with her discovery, she stared out the window at the dark leaves of the horse chestnut.

"Me," she murmured. And then, sinking deeper into the quilts, "I want . . . I want to be . . . wonderful. Oh, Jesus, make me wonderful."

The many experiences of her trip crowded in on her. She slept. It was the last as well as the first time she was ever to leave Medallion.

For days afterward she imagined other trips she would take, alone though, to faraway places. Contemplating them was delicious. Leaving Medallion would be her goal. But that was before she met Sula, the girl she had seen for five years at Garfield Primary but never played with, never knew, because her mother said that Sula's mother was sooty. The trip, perhaps, or her new found me-ness, gave her the strength to cultivate a friend in spite of her mother.

When Sula first visited the Wright house, Helene's curdled scorn turned to butter. Her daughter's friend seemed to have none of the mother's slackness. Nel, who regarded the oppressive neatness of her home with dread, felt comfortable in it with Sula, who loved it and would sit on the red-velvet sofa for ten to twenty minutes at a time—still as dawn. As for Nel, she preferred Sula's woolly house, where a pot of something was always cooking on the stove; where the mother, Hannah, never scolded or gave directions; where all sorts of people dropped in; where newspapers were stacked in the hallway, and dirty dishes left for hours at a time in the sink, and where a one-legged grandmother named Eva handed you goobers from deep inside her pockets or read you a dream.

1921

Sula Peace lived in a house of many rooms that had been built over a period of five years to the specifications of its owner, who kept on adding things: more stairways—there were three sets to the second floor—more rooms, doors and stoops. There were rooms that had three doors, others that opened out on the porch only and were inaccessible from any other part of the house; others that you could get to only by going through somebody's bedroom. The creator and sovereign of this enormous house with the four sickle-pear trees in the front yard and the single elm in the back yard was

Eva Peace, who sat in a wagon on the third floor directing the lives of her children, friends, strays, and a constant stream of boarders. Fewer than nine people in the town remembered when Eva had two legs, and her oldest child, Hannah, was not one of them. Unless Eva herself introduced the subject, no one ever spoke of her disability; they pretended to ignore it, unless, in some mood of fancy, she began some fearful story about it— generally to entertain children. How the leg got up by itself one day and walked on off. How she hobbled after it but it ran too fast. Or how she had a corn on her toe and it just grew and grew and grew until her whole foot was a corn and then it traveled on up her leg and wouldn't stop growing until she put a red rag at the top but by that time it was already at her knee.

Somebody said Eva stuck it under a train and made them pay off. Another said she sold it to a hospital for $10,000—at which Mr. Reed opened his eyes and asked, "Nigger gal legs goin' for $10,000 a *piece?*" as though he could understand $10,000 a *pair*—but for *one?*

Whatever the fate of her lost leg, the remaining one was magnificent. It was stockinged and shod at all times and in all weather. Once in a while she got a felt slipper for Christmas or her birthday, but they soon disappeared, for Eva always wore a black laced-up shoe that came well above her ankle. Nor did she wear overlong dresses to disguise the empty place on her left side. Her dresses were mid-calf so that her one glamorous leg was always in view as well as the long fall of space below her left thigh. One of her men friends had fashioned a kind of wheelchair for her: a rocking-chair top fitted into a large child's wagon. In this contraption she wheeled around the room, from bedside to dresser to the balcony that opened out the north side of her room or to the window that looked out on the back yard. The wagon was so low that children who spoke to her standing up were eye level with her, and adults, standing or sitting, had to look down at her. But they didn't know it. They all had the impression that they were looking up at her, up into the open distances of her eyes, up into the soft black of her nostrils and up at the crest of her chin.

Eva had married a man named BoyBoy and had three children: Hannah, the eldest, and Eva, whom she named after herself but called Pearl, and a son named Ralph, whom she called Plum.

After five years of a sad and disgruntled marriage BoyBoy took off. During the time they were together he was very much preoccupied with other women and not home much. He did whatever he could that he liked, and he liked womanizing best, drinking second, and abusing Eva third. When he left in November, Eva had $1.65, five eggs, three beets and no idea of what or how to feel. The children needed her; she needed money, and needed to get on with her life. But the demands of feeding her three children were so acute she had to postpone her anger for two years until she had both the time and the energy for it. She was confused and desperately hungry. There were very few black families in those low hills then. The Suggs, who lived two hundred yards down the road, brought her a warm bowl of peas, as soon as they found out, and a plate of cold bread. She thanked them and asked if they had a little milk for the older ones. They said no, but Mrs. Jackson, they knew, had a cow still giving. Eva took a bucket over and Mrs. Jackson told her to come back and fill it up in the morning, because the evening milking had already been done. In this way, things went on until near December. People were very willing to help, but Eva felt she would soon run her welcome out; winters were hard and her neighbors were not that much better off. She would lie in bed with the baby boy, the two girls wrapped in quilts on the floor, thinking. The oldest child, Hannah, was five and too young to take care of the baby alone, and any housework Eva could find would keep her away from them from five thirty or earlier in the morning until dark—way past eight. The white people in the valley weren't rich enough then to want maids; they were small farmers and tradesmen and wanted hard-labor help if anything. She thought also of returning to some of her people in Virginia, but to come home dragging three young ones would have to be a step one rung before death for Eva. She would have to scrounge around and beg through the winter, until her baby was at least nine months old, then she could plant and maybe hire herself out to valley farms to weed or sow or feed stock until something steadier came along at harvest time. She thought she had probably been a fool to let BoyBoy haul her away from her people, but it had seemed so right at the time. He worked for a white carpenter and toolsmith who insisted on BoyBoy's accompanying him when he went West and set up in a squinchy little town called Medallion. BoyBoy brought his new wife and built them a one-room cabin sixty feet back from the road that wound up out of the valley, on up into the hills and was named for the man he worked for. They lived there a year before they had an outhouse.

Sometime before the middle of December, the baby, Plum, stopped having bowel movements. Eva massaged his stomach and gave him warm water. Something must be wrong with my milk, she thought. Mrs. Suggs gave her castor oil, but even that didn't work. He cried and fought so they couldn't get much down his throat anyway. He seemed in great pain and his shrieks were pitched high in outrage and suffering. At one point, maddened by his own crying, he gagged, choked and looked as though he was strangling to death. Eva rushed to him and kicked over the earthen slop jar, washing a small area of the floor with the child's urine. She managed to soothe him, but when he took up the cry again late that night, she resolved to end his misery once and for all. She wrapped him in blankets, ran her finger around the crevices and sides of the lard can and stumbled to the outhouse with him. Deep in its darkness and freezing stench she squatted down, turned the baby over on her knees, exposed his buttocks and shoved the last bit of food she had in the world (besides three beets) up his ass. Softening the insertion with the dab of lard, she probed with her middle finger to loosen his bowels. Her fingernail snagged what felt like a pebble; she pulled it out and others followed. Plum stopped crying as the black hard stools ricocheted onto the frozen ground. And now that it was over, Eva squatted there wondering why she had come all the way out there to free his stools, and what was she doing down on her haunches with her beloved baby boy warmed by her body in the almost total darkness, her shins and teeth freezing, her nostrils assailed. She shook her head as though to juggle her brains around, then said aloud, "Uh uh. Nooo." Thereupon she returned to the house and her bed. As the grateful Plum slept, the silence allowed her to think.

Two days later she left all of her children with Mrs. Suggs, saying she would be back the next day.

Eighteen months later she swept down from a wagon with two crutches, a new black pocketbook, and one leg. First she reclaimed her children, next she gave the surprised Mrs. Suggs a ten-dollar bill, later she started building a house on Carpenter's Road, sixty feet from BoyBoy's one-room cabin, which she rented out.

When Plum was three years old, BoyBoy came back to town and paid her a visit. When Eva got the word that he was on his way, she made some lemonade. She had no idea what she would do or feel during that encounter. Would she cry, cut his throat, beg him to make love to her? She couldn't imagine. So she just waited to see. She stirred lemonade in a green pitcher and waited.

BoyBoy danced up the steps and knocked on the door.

"Come on in," she hollered.

He opened the door and stood smiling, a picture of prosperity and good will. His shoes were a shiny orange, and he had on a citified straw hat, a light-blue suit, and a cat's-head stickpin in his tie. Eva smiled and told him to sit himself down. He smiled too.

"How you been, girl?"

"Pretty fair. What you know good?" When she heard those words come out of her own mouth she knew that their conversation would start off polite. Although it remained to be seen whether she would still run the ice pick through the cat's-head pin.

"Have some lemonade."

"Don't mind if I do." He swept his hat off with a satisfied gesture. His nails were long and shiny. "Sho is hot, and I been runnin' around all day."

Eva looked out of the screen door and saw a woman in a pea-green dress leaning on the smallest pear tree. Glancing back at him, she was reminded of Plum's face when he managed to get the meat out of a walnut all by himself. Eva smiled again, and poured the lemonade.

Their conversation was easy: she catching him up on all the gossip, he asking about this one and that one, and like everybody else avoiding any reference to her leg. It was like talking to somebody's cousin who just stopped by to say howdy before getting on back to wherever he came from. BoyBoy didn't ask to see the children, and Eva didn't bring them into the conversation.

After a while he rose to go. Talking about his appointments and exuding an odor of new money and idleness, he danced down the steps and strutted toward the pea-green dress. Eva watched. She looked at the back of his neck and the set of his shoulders. Underneath all of that shine she saw defeat in the stalk of his neck and the curious tight way he held his shoulders. But still she was not sure what she felt. Then he leaned forward and whispered into the ear of the woman in the green dress. She was still for a moment and then threw back her head and laughed. A high-pitched big-city laugh that reminded Eva of Chicago. It hit her like a sledge hammer, and it was then that she knew what to feel. A liquid trail of hate flooded her chest.

Knowing that she would hate him long and well filled her with pleasant anticipation, like when you know you are going to fall in love with someone and you wait for the happy signs. Hating BoyBoy, she could get on with it, and have the safety, the thrill, the consistency of that hatred as long as she wanted or needed it to define and strengthen her or protect her from routine vulnerabilities. (Once when Hannah accused her of hating colored people, Eva said she only hated one, Hannah's father BoyBoy, and it was hating him that kept her alive and happy.)

Happy or not, after BoyBoy's visit she began her retreat to her bedroom, leaving the bottom of the house more and more to those who lived there: cousins who were passing through, stray folks, and the many, many newly married couples she let rooms to with housekeeping privileges, and after 1910 she didn't willingly set foot on the stairs but once and that was to light a fire, the smoke of which was in her hair for years.

Among the tenants in that big old house were the children Eva took in. Operating on a private scheme of preference and prejudice, she sent off for children she had seen from the balcony of her bedroom or whose circumstances she had heard about from the gossipy old men who came to play checkers or read the *Courier*, or write her number.[2] In 1921, when her granddaughter Sula was eleven, Eva had three such children. They came with woolen caps and names given to them by their mothers, or grandmothers, or somebody's best friend. Eva snatched the caps off their heads and ignored their names. She looked at the first child closely, his wrists, the shape of his head and the temperament that showed in his eyes and said, "Well. Look at Dewey. My my mymymy." When later that same year she sent for a child who kept falling down off the porch across the street, she said the same thing. Somebody said, "But, Miss Eva, you calls the other one Dewey."

"So? This here's another one."

When the third one was brought and Eva said "Dewey" again, everybody thought she had simply run out of names or that her faculties had finally softened.

"How is anybody going to tell them apart?" Hannah asked her.

"What you need to tell them apart for? They's all deweys."

When Hannah asked the question it didn't sound very bright, because each dewey was markedly different from the other two. Dewey one was a deeply black boy with a beautiful head and the golden eyes of chronic jaundice. Dewey two was light-skinned with freckles everywhere and a head of tight red hair. Dewey three was half Mexican with chocolate skin and black bangs. Besides, they were one and two years apart in age. It was Eva saying things like, "Send one of them deweys out to get me some Garret, if they don't have Garret, get Buttercup,"[3] or, "Tell them deweys to cut out that noise," or, "Come here, you dewey you," and, "Send me a dewey," that gave Hannah's question its weight.

Slowly each boy came out of whatever cocoon he was in at the time his mother or somebody gave him away, and accepted Eva's view, becoming in fact as well as in name a dewey—joining with the other two to become a trinity with a plural name . . . inseparable, loving nothing and no one but themselves. When the handle from the icebox fell off, all the deweys got whipped, and in dry-eyed silence watched their own feet as they turned their behinds high up into the air for the stroke. When the golden-eyed dewey was ready for school he would not go without the others. He was seven, freckled dewey was five, and Mexican dewey was only four. Eva solved the problem by having them all sent off together. Mr. Buckland Reed said, "But one of them's only four."

"How you know? They all come here the same year," Eva said.

<hr />

2. Eva played the numbers, an illegal lottery that involves betting on certain combinations of digits.

3. Brands of snuff.

"But that one there was one year old when he came, and that was three years ago."

"You don't know how old he was when he come here and neither do the teacher. Send 'em."

The teacher was startled but not unbelieving, for she had long ago given up trying to fathom the ways of the colored people in town. So when Mrs. Reed said that their names were Dewey King, that they were cousins, and all were six years old, the teacher gave only a tiny sigh and wrote them in the record book for the first grade. She too thought she would have no problem distinguishing among them, because they looked nothing alike, but like everyone else before her, she gradually found that she could not tell one from the other. The deweys would not allow it. They got all mixed up in her head, and finally she could not literally believe her eyes. They spoke with one voice, thought with one mind, and maintained an annoying privacy. Stouthearted, surly, and wholly unpredictable, the deweys remained a mystery not only during all of their lives in Medallion but after as well.

The deweys came in 1921, but the year before Eva had given a small room off the kitchen to Tar Baby, a beautiful, slight, quiet man who never spoke above a whisper. Most people said he was half white, but Eva said he was all white. That she knew blood when she saw it, and he didn't have none. When he first came to Medallion, the people called him Pretty Johnnie, but Eva looked at his milky skin and cornsilk hair and out of a mixture of fun and meanness called him Tar Baby. He was a mountain boy who stayed to himself, bothering no one, intent solely on drinking himself to death. At first he worked in a poultry market, and after wringing the necks of chickens all day, he came home and drank until he slept. Later he began to miss days at work and frequently did not have his rent money. When he lost his job altogether, he would go out in the morning, scrounge around for money doing odd jobs, bumming or whatever, and come home to drink. Because he was no bother, ate little, required nothing, and was a lover of cheap wine, no one found him a nuisance. Besides, he frequently went to Wednesday-night prayer meetings and sang with the sweetest hill voice imaginable "In the Sweet By-and-By." He sent the deweys out for his liquor and spent most of his time in a heap on the floor or sitting in a chair staring at the wall.

Hannah worried about him a little, but only a very little. For it soon became clear that he simply wanted a place to die privately but not quite alone. No one thought of suggesting to him that he pull himself together or see a doctor or anything. Even the women at prayer meeting who cried when he sang "In the Sweet By-and-By" never tried to get him to participate in the church activities. They just listened to him sing, wept and thought very graphically of their own imminent deaths. The people either accepted his own evaluation of his life, or were indifferent to it. There was, however, a measure of contempt in their indifference, for they had little patience with people who took themselves that seriously. Seriously enough to try to die. And it was natural that he, after all, became the first one to join Shadrack—Tar Baby and the deweys—on National Suicide Day.

Under Eva's distant eye, and prey to her idiosyncrasies, her own children grew up stealthily: Pearl married at fourteen and moved to Flint, Michigan, from where she posted frail letters to her mother with two dollars folded into the writing paper. Sad little nonsense letters about minor troubles, her husband's job and who the children favored. Hannah married a laughing man named Rekus who died when their daughter Sula was about three years old, at which time Hannah moved back into her mother's big house prepared to take care of it and her mother forever.

With the exception of BoyBoy, those Peace women loved all men. It was manlove that Eva bequeathed to her daughters. Probably, people said, because there were no men in the house, no men to run it. But actually that was not true. The Peace women simply loved maleness, for its own sake. Eva, old as she was, and with one leg, had a regular flock of gentleman callers, and although she did not participate in the act of love, there was a good deal of teasing and pecking and laughter. The men wanted to see her lovely calf, that neat shoe, and watch the focusing that sometimes swept down out of the distances in her eyes. They wanted to see the joy in her face as they settled down to play checkers, knowing that even when she beat them, as she almost always did, somehow, in her presence, it was they who had won something. They would read the newspaper aloud to her and make observations on its content, and Eva would listen feeling no obligation to agree and, in fact, would take them to task about their interpretation of events. But she argued with them with such an absence of bile, such a concentration of manlove, that they felt their convictions solidified by her disagreement.

With other people's affairs Eva was equally prejudiced about men. She fussed interminably with the brides of the newly wed couples for not getting their men's supper ready on time; about how to launder shirts, press them, etc. "Yo' man be here direc'lin. Ain't it 'bout time you got busy?"

"Aw, Miss Eva. It'll be ready. We just having spaghetti."

"Again?" Eva's eyebrows fluted up and the newlywed pressed her lips together in shame.

Hannah simply refused to live without the attentions of a man, and after Rekus' death had a steady sequence of lovers, mostly the husbands of her friends and neighbors. Her flirting was sweet, low and guileless. Without ever a pat of the hair, a rush to change clothes or a quick application of paint, with no gesture whatsoever, she rippled with sex. In her same old print wraparound, barefoot in the summer, in the winter her feet in a man's leather slippers with the backs flattened under her heels, she made men aware of her behind, her slim ankles, the dew-smooth skin and the incredible length of neck. Then the smile-eyes, the turn of the head—all so welcoming, light and playful. Her voice trailed, dipped and bowed; she gave a chord to the simplest words. Nobody, but nobody, could say "hey sugar" like Hannah. When he heard it, the man tipped his hat down a little over his eyes, hoisted his trousers and thought about the hollow place at the base of her neck. And all this without the slightest confusion about work and responsibilities. While Eva tested and argued with her men, leaving them feeling as though they had been in combat with a worthy, if amiable, foe, Hannah rubbed no edges, made no demands, made the man feel as though he were complete and wonderful just as he was—he didn't need fixing— and so he relaxed and swooned in the Hannah-light that shone on him simply because he was. If the man entered and Hannah was carrying a coal scuttle up from the basement, she handled it in such a way that it became a gesture of love. He made no move to help her with it simply because he wanted to see how her thighs looked when she bent to put it down, knowing that she wanted him to see them too.

But since in that crowded house there were no places for private and spontaneous lovemaking, Hannah would take the man down into the cellar in the summer where it was cool back behind the coal bin and the newspapers, or in the winter they would step into the pantry and stand up against the shelves she had filled with canned goods, or lie on the flour sack just under the rows of tiny green peppers. When those places were not available, she would slip into the seldom-used parlor, or even up to her bedroom. She liked the last place least, not because Sula slept in the room with her but because her love mate's tendency was always to fall asleep afterward and Hannah was fastidious about whom she slept with. She would fuck practically anything, but sleeping with someone implied for her a measure of trust and a definite commitment. So she ended up a daylight lover, and it was only once actually that Sula came home from school and found her mother in the bed, curled spoon in the arms of a man.

Seeing her step so easily into the pantry and emerge looking precisely as she did when she entered, only happier, taught Sula that sex was pleasant and frequent, but otherwise unremarkable. Outside the house, where children giggled about underwear, the message was different. So she watched her mother's face and the face of the men when they opened the pantry door and made up her own mind.

Hannah exasperated the women in the town—the "good" women, who said, "One thing I can't stand is a nasty woman"; the whores, who were hard put to find trade among black men anyway and who resented Hannah's generosity; the middling women, who had both husbands and affairs, because Hannah seemed too unlike them, having no passion attached to her relationships and being wholly incapable of jealousy. Hannah's friendships with women were, of course, seldom and short-lived, and the newly married couples whom her mother took in soon learned what a hazard she was. She could break up a marriage before it had even become one—she would make love to the new groom and wash his wife's dishes all in an afternoon. What she wanted, after Rekus died, and what she succeeded in having more often than not, was some touching every day.

The men, surprisingly, never gossiped about her. She was unquestionably a kind and generous woman and that, coupled with her extraordinary beauty and funky elegance of manner, made them defend her and protect her from any vitriol that newcomers or their wives might spill.

Eva's last child, Plum, to whom she hoped to bequeath everything, floated in a constant swaddle of love and affection, until 1917 when he went to war. He returned to the States in 1919 but did not get back to Medallion until 1920. He wrote letters from New York, Washington, D.C., and Chicago full of promises of homecomings, but there was obviously something wrong. Finally some two or three days after Christmas, he arrived with just the shadow of his old dip-down walk. His hair had been neither cut nor combed in months, his clothes were pointless and he had no socks. But he did have a black bag, a paper sack, and a sweet, sweet smile. Everybody welcomed him and gave him a warm room next to Tar Baby's and waited for him to tell them whatever it was he wanted them to know. They waited in vain for his telling but not long for the knowing. His habits were much like Tar Baby's but there were no bottles, and Plum was sometimes cheerful and animated. Hannah watched and Eva waited. Then he began to steal from them, take trips to Cincinnati and sleep for days in his room with the record player going. He got even thinner, since he ate only snatches of things at beginnings or endings of meals. It was Hannah who found the bent spoon black from steady cooking.[4]

So late one night in 1921, Eva got up from her bed and put on her clothes. Hoisting herself up on her crutches, she was amazed to find that she could still manage them, although the pain in her armpits was severe. She practiced a few steps around the room, and then opened the door. Slowly, she manipulated herself down the long flights of stairs, two crutches under her left arm, the right hand grasping the banister. The sound of her foot booming in comparison to the delicate pat of the crutch tip. On each landing she stopped for breath. Annoyed at her physical condition, she closed her eyes and removed the crutches from under her arms to relieve the unaccustomed pressure. At the foot of the stairs she redistributed her weight between the crutches and swooped on through the front room, to the dining room, to the kitchen, swinging and swooping like a giant heron, so graceful sailing about in its own habitat but awkward and comical when it folded its wings and tried to walk. With a swing and a swoop she arrived at Plum's door and pushed it open with the tip of one crutch. He was lying in bed barely visible in the light coming from a single bulb. Eva swung over to the bed and propped her crutches at its foot. She sat down and gathered Plum into her arms. He woke, but only slightly.

"Hey, man. Hey. You holdin' me, Mamma?" His voice was drowsy and amused. He chuckled as though he had heard some private joke. Eva held him closer and began to rock. Back and forth she rocked him, her eyes wandering around his room. There in the corner was a half-eaten store-bought cherry pie. Balled-up candy wrappers and empty pop bottles peeped from under the dresser. On the floor by her foot was a glass of strawberry crush and a *Liberty* magazine. Rocking, rocking, listening to Plum's occasional chuckles, Eva let her memory spin, loop and fall. Plum in the tub that time as she leaned over him. He reached up and dripped water into her bosom and laughed. She was angry, but not too, and laughed with him.

"Mamma, you so purty. You so purty, Mamma."

Eva lifted her tongue to the edge of her lip to stop the tears from running into her mouth. Rocking, rocking. Later she laid him down and looked at him a long time. Suddenly she was thirsty and reached for the glass of strawberry crush. She put it to her lips and discovered it was blood-tainted water and threw it to the floor. Plum woke up and said, "Hey, Mamma, whyn't you go on back to bed? I'm all right. Didn't I tell you? I'm all right. Go on, now."

"I'm going, Plum," she said. She shifted her weight and pulled her crutches toward her. Swinging and swooping, she left his room. She dragged herself to the kitchen and made grating noises.

Plum on the rim of a warm light sleep was still chuckling. Mamma. She sure was somethin'. He felt twilight. Now there seemed to be some kind of wet light traveling over his legs and stomach with a deeply attractive smell. It wound itself—this wet light—all about him, splashing and running into his skin. He opened his eyes and saw what he imagined was the great wing of an eagle pouring a wet lightness over him. Some kind of baptism, some kind of blessing, he thought. Everything is going to be all right, it said.

4. I.e., from heating and dissolving powdered heroin in water to make a solution for injection.

Knowing that it was so he closed his eyes and sank back into the bright hole of sleep.

Eva stepped back from the bed and let the crutches rest under her arms. She rolled a bit of newspaper into a tight stick about six inches long, lit it and threw it onto the bed where the kerosene-soaked Plum lay in snug delight. Quickly, as the *whoosh* of flames engulfed him, she shut the door and made her slow and painful journey back to the top of the house.

Just as she got to the third landing she could hear Hannah and some child's voice. She swung along, not even listening to the voices of alarm and the cries of the deweys. By the time she got to her bed someone was bounding up the stairs after her. Hannah opened the door. "Plum! Plum! He's burning, Mamma! We can't even open the door! Mamma!"

Eva looked into Hannah's eyes. "Is? My baby? Burning?" The two women did not speak, for the eyes of each were enough for the other. Then Hannah closed hers and ran toward the voices of neighbors calling for water.

1922

It was too cool for ice cream. A hill wind was blowing dust and empty Camels wrappers about their ankles. It pushed their dresses into the creases of their behinds, then lifted the hems to peek at their cotton underwear. They were on their way to Edna Finch's Mellow House, an ice-cream parlor catering to nice folks—where even children would feel comfortable, you know, even though it was right next to Reba's Grill and just one block down from the Time and a Half Pool Hall. It sat in the curve of Carpenter's Road, which, in four blocks, made up all the sporting life available in the Bottom. Old men and young ones draped themselves in front of the Elmira Theater, Irene's Palace of Cosmetology, the pool hall, the grill and the other sagging business enterprises that lined the street. On sills, on stoops, on crates and broken chairs they sat tasting their teeth and waiting for something to distract them. Every passerby, every motorcar, every alteration in stance caught their attention and was commented on. Particularly they watched women. When a woman approached, the older men tipped their hats; the younger ones opened and closed their thighs. But all of them, whatever their age, watched her retreating view with interest.

Nel and Sula walked through this valley of eyes chilled by the wind and heated by the embarrassment of appraising stares. The old men looked at their stalklike legs, dwelled on the cords in the backs of their knees and remembered old dance steps they had not done in twenty years. In their lust, which age had turned to kindness, they moved their lips as though to stir up the taste of young sweat on tight skin.

Pig meat. The words were in all their minds. And one of them, one of the young ones, said it aloud. Softly but definitively and there was no mistaking the compliment. His name was Ajax, a twenty-one-year-old pool haunt of sinister beauty. Graceful and economical in every movement, he held a place of envy with men of all ages for his magnificently foul mouth. In fact he seldom cursed, and the epithets he chose were dull, even harmless. His reputation was derived from the way he handled the words. When he said "hell" he hit the *h* with his lungs and the impact was greater than the achievement of the most imaginative foul mouth in the town. He could say "shit" with a nastiness impossible to imitate. So, when he said "pig meat" as Nel and Sula passed, they guarded their eyes lest someone see their delight.

It was not really Edna Finch's ice cream that made them brave the stretch of those panther eyes. Years later their own eyes would glaze as they cupped their chins in remembrance of the inchworm smiles, the squatting haunches, the track-rail legs straddling broken chairs. The cream-colored trousers marking with a mere seam the place where the mystery curled. Those smooth vanilla crotches invited them; those lemon-yellow gabardines beckoned to them.

They moved toward the ice-cream parlor like tightrope walkers, as thrilled by the possibility of a slip as by the maintenance of tension and balance. The least sideways glance, the merest toe stub, could pitch them into those creamy haunches spread wide with welcome. Somewhere beneath all of that daintiness, chambered in all that neatness, lay the thing that clotted their dreams.

Which was only fitting, for it was in dreams that the two girls had first met. Long before Edna Finch's Mellow House opened, even before they marched through the chocolate halls of Garfield Primary School out onto the playground and stood facing each other through the ropes of the one vacant swing ("Go on." "No. You go."), they had already made each other's acquaintance in the delirium of their noon dreams. They were solitary little girls whose loneliness was so profound it intoxicated them and sent them stumbling into Technicolored visions that always included a presence, a someone, who, quite like the dreamer, shared the delight of the dream. When Nel, an only child, sat on the steps of her back porch surrounded by the high silence of her mother's incredibly orderly house, feeling the neatness pointing at her back, she studied the poplars and fell easily into a picture of herself lying on a flowered bed, tangled in her own hair, waiting for some fiery prince. He approached but never quite arrived. But always, watching the dream along with her, were some smiling sympathetic eyes. Someone as interested as she herself in the flow of her imagined hair, the thickness of the mattress of flowers, the voile[5] sleeves that closed below her elbows in gold-threaded cuffs.

Similarly, Sula, also an only child, but wedged into a household of throbbing disorder constantly awry with things, people, voices and the slamming of doors, spent hours in the attic behind a roll of linoleum galloping through her own mind on a gray-and-white horse tasting sugar and smelling roses in full view of a someone who shared both the taste and the speed.

So when they met, first in those chocolate halls and next through the ropes of the swing, they felt the ease and comfort of old friends. Because each had discovered years before that they were neither white nor male, and that all freedom and triumph was forbidden to them, they had set about creating something else to be. Their meeting was fortunate, for it let them use each other to grow on. Daughters of distant mothers and incomprehensible fathers (Sula's because he was dead; Nel's because he wasn't), they found in each other's eyes the intimacy they were looking for.

Nel Wright and Sula Peace were both twelve in 1922, wishbone thin and easy-assed. Nel was the color of wet sandpaper—just dark enough to escape the blows of the pitch-black truebloods and the contempt of old women who worried about such things as bad blood mixtures and knew that the origins of a mule and a mulatto were one and the same.[6] Had she

5. A sheer, fine fabric.
6. Etymologically, "mulatto" (a person of mixed black and white descent) has the same derivation as "mule" (the sterile offspring of a donkey and a horse).

been any lighter-skinned she would have needed either her mother's protection on the way to school or a streak of mean to defend herself. Sula was a heavy brown with large quiet eyes, one of which featured a birthmark that spread from the middle of the lid toward the eyebrow, shaped something like a stemmed rose. It gave her otherwise plain face a broken excitement and blue-blade threat like the keloid scar[7] of the razored man who sometimes played checkers with her grandmother. The birthmark was to grow darker as the years passed, but now it was the same shade as her gold-flecked eyes, which, to the end, were as steady and clean as rain.

Their friendship was as intense as it was sudden. They found relief in each other's personality. Although both were unshaped, formless things, Nel seemed stronger and more consistent than Sula, who could hardly be counted on to sustain any emotion for more than three minutes. Yet there was one time when that was not true, when she held on to a mood for weeks, but even that was in defense of Nel.

Four white boys in their early teens, sons of some newly arrived Irish people, occasionally entertained themselves in the afternoon by harassing black schoolchildren. With shoes that pinched and woolen knickers that made red rings on their calves, they had come to this valley with their parents believing as they did that it was a promised land—green and shimmering with welcome. What they found was a strange accent, a pervasive fear of their religion and firm resistance to their attempts to find work. With one exception the older residents of Medallion scorned them. The one exception was the black community. Although some of the Negroes had been in Medallion before the Civil War (the town didn't even have a name then), if they had any hatred for these newcomers it didn't matter because it didn't show. As a matter of fact, baiting them was the one activity that the white Protestant residents concurred in. In part their place in this world was secured only when they echoed the old residents' attitude toward blacks.

These particular boys caught Nel once, and pushed her from hand to hand until they grew tired of the frightened helpless face. Because of that incident, Nel's route home from school became elaborate. She, and then Sula, managed to duck them for weeks until a chilly day in November when Sula said, "Let's us go on home the shortest way."

Nel blinked, but acquiesced. They walked up the street until they got to the bend of Carpenter's Road where the boys lounged on a disused well. Spotting their prey, the boys sauntered forward as though there were nothing in the world on their minds but the gray sky. Hardly able to control their grins, they stood like a gate blocking the path. When the girls were three feet in front of the boys, Sula reached into her coat pocket and pulled out Eva's paring knife. The boys stopped short, exchanged looks and dropped all pretense of innocence. This was going to be better than they thought. They were going to try and fight back, and with a knife. Maybe they could get an arm around one of their waists, or tear . . .

Sula squatted down in the dirt road and put everything down on the ground: her lunchpail, her reader, her mittens, her slate. Holding the knife in her right hand, she pulled the slate toward her and pressed her left forefinger down hard on its edge. Her aim was determined but inaccurate. She

7. Thick scar.

slashed off only the tip of her finger. The four boys stared open-mouthed at the wound and the scrap of flesh, like a button mushroom, curling in the cherry blood that ran into the corners of the slate.

Sula raised her eyes to them. Her voice was quiet. "If I can do that to myself, what you suppose I'll do to you?"

The shifting dirt was the only way Nel knew that they were moving away; she was looking at Sula's face, which seemed miles and miles away.

But toughness was not their quality—adventuresomeness was—and a mean determination to explore everything that interested them, from one-eyed chickens high-stepping in their penned yards to Mr. Buckland Reed's gold teeth, from the sound of sheets flapping in the wind to the labels on Tar Baby's wine bottles. And they had no priorities. They could be distracted from watching a fight with mean razors by the glorious smell of hot tar being poured by roadmen two hundred yards away.

In the safe harbor of each other's company they could afford to abandon the ways of other people and concentrate on their own perceptions of things. When Mrs. Wright reminded Nel to pull her nose, she would do it enthusiastically but without the least hope in the world.

"While you sittin' there, honey, go 'head and pull your nose."

"It hurts, Mamma."

"Don't you want a nice nose when you grow up?"

After she met Sula, Nel slid the clothespin under the blanket as soon as she got in the bed. And although there was still the hateful hot comb to suffer through each Saturday evening, its consequences—smooth hair—no longer interested her.

Joined in mutual admiration they watched each day as though it were a movie arranged for their amusement. The new theme they were now discovering was men. So they met regularly, without even planning it, to walk down the road to Edna Finch's Mellow House, even though it was too cool for ice cream.

Then summer came. A summer limp with the weight of blossomed things. Heavy sunflowers weeping over fences; iris curling and browning at the edges far away from their purple hearts; ears of corn letting their auburn hair wind down to their stalks. And the boys. The beautiful, beautiful boys who dotted the landscape like jewels, split the air with their shouts in the field, and thickened the river with their shining wet backs. Even their footsteps left a smell of smoke behind.

It was in that summer, the summer of their twelfth year, the summer of the beautiful black boys, that they became skittish, frightened and bold—all at the same time.

In that mercury mood in July, Sula and Nel wandered about the Bottom barefoot looking for mischief. They decided to go down by the river where the boys sometimes swam. Nel waited on the porch of 7 Carpenter's Road while Sula ran into the house to go to the toilet. On the way up the stairs, she passed the kitchen where Hannah sat with two friends, Patsy and Valentine. The two women were fanning themselves and watching Hannah put down some dough, all talking casually about one thing and another, and had gotten around, when Sula passed by, to the problems of child rearing.

"They a pain."

"Yeh. Wish I'd listened to mamma. She told me not to have 'em too soon."

"Any time atall is too soon for me."

"Oh, I don't know. My Rudy minds his daddy. He just wild with me. Be glad when he growed and gone."

Hannah smiled and said, "Shut your mouth. You love the ground he pee on."

"Sure I do. But he still a pain. Can't help loving your own child. No matter what they do."

"Well, Hester grown now and I can't say love is exactly what I feel."

"Sure you do. You love her, like I love Sula. I just don't like her. That's the difference."

"Guess so. Likin' them is another thing."

"Sure. They different people, you know . . ."

She only heard Hannah's words, and the pronouncement sent her flying up the stairs. In bewilderment, she stood at the window fingering the curtain edge, aware of a sting in her eye. Nel's call floated up and into the window, pulling her away from dark thoughts back into the bright, hot daylight.

They ran most of the way.

Heading toward the wide part of the river where trees grouped themselves in families darkening the earth below. They passed some boys swimming and clowning in the water, shrouding their words in laughter.

They ran in the sunlight, creating their own breeze, which pressed their dresses into their damp skin. Reaching a kind of square of four leaf-locked trees which promised cooling, they flung themselves into the four-cornered shade to taste their lip sweat and contemplate the wildness that had come upon them so suddenly. They lay in the grass, their foreheads almost touching, their bodies stretched away from each other at a 180-degree angle. Sula's head rested on her arm, an undone braid coiled around her wrist. Nel leaned on her elbows and worried long blades of grass with her fingers. Underneath their dresses flesh tightened and shivered in the high coolness, their small breasts just now beginning to create some pleasant discomfort when they were lying on their stomachs.

Sula lifted her head and joined Nel in the grass play. In concert, without ever meeting each other's eyes, they stroked the blades up and down, up and down. Nel found a thick twig and, with her thumbnail, pulled away its bark until it was stripped to a smooth, creamy innocence. Sula looked about and found one too. When both twigs were undressed Nel moved easily to the next stage and began tearing up rooted grass to make a bare spot of earth. When a generous clearing was made, Sula traced intricate patterns in it with her twig. At first Nel was content to do the same. But soon she grew impatient and poked her twig rhythmically and intensely into the earth, making a small neat hole that grew deeper and wider with the least manipulation of her twig. Sula copied her, and soon each had a hole the size of a cup. Nel began a more strenuous digging and, rising to her knee, was careful to scoop out the dirt as she made her hole deeper. Together they worked until the two holes were one and the same. When the depression was the size of a small dishpan, Nel's twig broke. With a gesture of disgust she threw the pieces into the hole they had made. Sula threw hers in too. Nel saw a bottle cap and tossed it in as well. Each then looked around for more debris to throw into the hole: paper, bits of glass, butts of cigarettes, until all of the small defiling things they could find were collected there. Carefully they replaced the soil and covered the entire grave with uprooted grass.

Neither one had spoken a word.

They stood up, stretched, then gazed out over the swift dull water as an unspeakable restlessness and agitation held them. At the same instant each girl heard footsteps in the grass. A little boy in too big knickers was coming up from the lower bank of the river. He stopped when he saw them and picked his nose.

"Your mamma tole you to stop eatin' snot, Chicken," Nel hollered at him through cupped hands.

"Shut up," he said, still picking.

"Come up here and say that."

"Leave him 'lone, Nel. Come here, Chicken. Lemme show you something."

"Naw."

"You scared we gone take your bugger away?"

"Leave him 'lone, I said. Come on, Chicken. Look. I'll help you climb a tree."

Chicken looked at the tree Sula was pointing to—a big double beech with low branches and lots of bends for sitting.

He moved slowly toward her.

"Come on, Chicken, I'll help you up."

Still picking his nose, his eyes wide, he came to where they were standing. Sula took him by the hand and coaxed him along. When they reached the base of the beech, she lifted him to the first branch, saying, "Go on. Go on. I got you." She followed the boy, steadying him, when he needed it, with her hand and her reassuring voice. When they were as high as they could go, Sula pointed to the far side of the river.

"See? Bet you never saw that far before, did you?"

"Uh uh."

"Now look down there." They both leaned a little and peered through the leaves at Nel standing below, squinting up at them. From their height she looked small and foreshortened.

Chicken Little laughed.

"Y'all better come on down before you break your neck," Nel hollered.

"I ain't never coming down," the boy hollered back.

"Yeah. We better. Come on, Chicken."

"Naw. Lemme go."

"Yeah, Chicken. Come on, now."

Sula pulled his leg gently.

"Lemme go."

"OK, I'm leavin' you." She started on.

"Wait!" he screamed.

Sula stopped and together they slowly worked their way down.

Chicken was still elated. "I was way up there, wasn't I? Wasn't I? I'm a tell my brovver."

Sula and Nel began to mimic him: "I'm a tell my brovver; I'm a tell my brovver."

Sula picked him up by his hands and swung him outward then around and around. His knickers ballooned and his shrieks of frightened joy startled the birds and the fat grasshoppers. When he slipped from her hands and sailed away out over the water they could still hear his bubbly laughter.

The water darkened and closed quickly over the place where Chicken Little sank. The pressure of his hard and tight little fingers was still in

Sula's palms as she stood looking at the closed place in the water. They expected him to come back up, laughing. Both girls stared at the water.

Nel spoke first. "Somebody saw." A figure appeared briefly on the opposite shore.

The only house over there was Shadrack's. Sula glanced at Nel. Terror widened her nostrils. Had he seen?

The water was so peaceful now. There was nothing but the baking sun and something newly missing. Sula cupped her face for an instant, then turned and ran up to the little plank bridge that crossed the river to Shadrack's house. There was no path. It was as though neither Shadrack nor anyone else ever came this way.

Her running was swift and determined, but when she was close to the three little steps that led to his porch, fear crawled into her stomach and only the something newly missing back there in the river made it possible for her to walk up the three steps and knock at the door.

No one answered. She started back, but thought again of the peace of the river. Shadrack would be inside, just behind the door ready to pounce on her. Still she could not go back. Ever so gently she pushed the door with the tips of her fingers and heard only the hinges weep. More. And then she was inside. Alone. The neatness, the order startled her, but more surprising was the restfulness. Everything was so tiny, so common, so unthreatening. Perhaps this was not the house of the Shad. The terrible Shad who walked about with his penis out, who peed in front of ladies and girl-children, the only black who could curse white people and get away with it, who drank in the road from the mouth of the bottle, who shouted and shook in the streets. This cottage? This sweet old cottage? With its made-up bed? With its rag rug and wooden table? Sula stood in the middle of the little room and in her wonder forgot what she had come for until a sound at the door made her jump. He was there in the doorway looking at her. She had not heard his coming and now he was looking at her.

More in embarrassment than terror she averted her glance. When she called up enough courage to look back at him, she saw his hand resting upon the door frame. His fingers, barely touching the wood, were arranged in a graceful arc. Relieved and encouraged (no one with hands like that, no one with fingers that curved around wood so tenderly could kill her), she walked past him out of the door, feeling his gaze turning, turning with her.

At the edge of the porch, gathering the wisps of courage that were fast leaving her, she turned once more to look at him, to ask him . . . had he . . . ?

He was smiling, a great smile, heavy with lust and time to come. He nodded his head as though answering a question, and said, in a pleasant conversational tone, a tone of cooled butter, "Always."

Sula fled down the steps, and shot through the greenness and the baking sun back to Nel and the dark closed place in the water. There she collapsed in tears.

Nel quieted her. "Sh, sh. Don't, don't. You didn't mean it. It ain't your fault. Sh. Sh. Come on, le's go, Sula. Come on, now. Was he there? Did he see? Where's the belt to your dress?"

Sula shook her head while she searched her waist for the belt.

Finally she stood up and allowed Nel to lead her away. "He said, 'Always. Always.'"

"What?"

Sula covered her mouth as they walked down the hill. Always. He had answered a question she had not asked, and its promise licked at her feet.

A bargeman, poling away from the shore, found Chicken late that afternoon stuck in some rocks and weeds, his knickers ballooning about his legs. He would have left him there but noticed that it was a child, not an old black man, as it first appeared, and he prodded the body loose, netted it and hauled it aboard. He shook his head in disgust at the kind of parents who would drown their own children. When, he wondered, will those people ever be anything but animals, fit for nothing but substitutes for mules, only mules didn't kill each other the way niggers did. He dumped Chicken Little into a burlap sack and tossed him next to some egg crates and boxes of wool cloth. Later, sitting down to smoke on an empty lard tin, still bemused by God's curse and the terrible burden his own kind had of elevating Ham's sons,[8] he suddenly became alarmed by the thought that the corpse in this heat would have a terrible odor, which might get into the fabric of his woolen cloth. He dragged the sack away and hooked it over the side, so that the Chicken's body was half in and half out of the water.

Wiping the sweat from his neck, he reported his find to the sheriff at Porter's Landing, who said they didn't have no niggers in their county, but that some lived in those hills 'cross the river, up above Medallion. The bargeman said he couldn't go all the way back there, it was every bit of two miles. The sheriff said whyn't he throw it on back into the water. The bargeman said he never shoulda taken it out in the first place. Finally they got the man who ran the ferry twice a day to agree to take it over in the morning.

That was why Chicken Little was missing for three days and didn't get to the embalmer's until the fourth day, by which time he was unrecognizable to almost everybody who once knew him, and even his mother wasn't deep down sure, except that it just had to be him since nobody could find him. When she saw his clothes lying on the table in the basement of the mortuary, her mouth snapped shut, and when she saw his body her mouth flew wide open again and it was seven hours before she was able to close it and make the first sound.

So the coffin was closed.

The Junior Choir, dressed in white, sang "Nearer My God to Thee" and "Precious Memories," their eyes fastened on the songbooks they did not need, for this was the first time their voices had presided at a real-life event.

Nel and Sula did not touch hands or look at each other during the funeral. There was a space, a separateness, between them. Nel's legs had turned to granite and she expected the sheriff or Reverend Deal's pointing finger at any moment. Although she knew she had "done nothing," she felt convicted and hanged right there in the pew—two rows down from her parents in the children's section.

Sula simply cried. Soundlessly and with no heaving and gasping for breath, she let the tears roll into her mouth and slide down her chin to dot the front of her dress.

---

8. Blacks. Ham, whose name means "swarthy" in Hebrew, was a son of Noah and was believed to be the ancestor of both the Egyptians and the Nubians.

As Reverend Deal moved into his sermon, the hands of the women unfolded like pairs of raven's wings and flew high above their hats in the air. They did not hear all of what he said; they heard the one word, or phrase, or inflection that was for them the connection between the event and themselves. For some it was the term "Sweet Jesus." And they saw the Lamb's eye and the truly innocent victim: themselves. They acknowledged the innocent child hiding in the corner of their hearts, holding a sugar-and-butter sandwich. That one. The one who lodged deep in their fat, thin, old, young skin, and was the one the world had hurt. Or they thought of their son newly killed and remembered his legs in short pants and wondered where the bullet went in. Or they remembered how dirty the room looked when their father left home and wondered if that is the way the slim, young Jew[9] felt, he who for them was both son and lover and in whose downy face they could see the sugar-and-butter sandwiches and feel the oldest and most devastating pain there is: not the pain of childhood, but the remembrance of it.

Then they left their pews. For with some emotions one has to stand. They spoke, for they were full and needed to say. They swayed, for the rivulets of grief or of ecstasy must be rocked. And when they thought of all that life and death locked into that little closed coffin they danced and screamed, not to protest God's will but to acknowledge it and confirm once more their conviction that the only way to avoid the Hand of God is to get in it.

In the colored part of the cemetery, they sank Chicken Little in between his grandfather and an aunt. Butterflies flew in and out of the bunches of field flowers now loosened from the top of the bier and lying in a small heap at the edge of the grave. The heat had gone, but there was still no breeze to lift the hair of the willows.

Nel and Sula stood some distance away from the grave, the space that had sat between them in the pews had dissolved. They held hands and knew that only the coffin would lie in the earth; the bubbly laughter and the press of fingers in the palm would stay aboveground forever. At first, as they stood there, their hands were clenched together. They relaxed slowly until during the walk back home their fingers were laced in as gentle a clasp as that of any two young girlfriends trotting up the road on a summer day wondering what happened to butterflies in the winter.

1923

The second strange thing was Hannah's coming into her mother's room with an empty bowl and a peck of Kentucky Wonders[1] and saying, "Mamma, did you ever love us?" She sang the words like a small child saying a piece at Easter, then knelt to spread a newspaper on the floor and set the basket on it; the bowl she tucked in the space between her legs. Eva, who was just sitting there fanning herself with the cardboard fan from Mr. Hodges' funeral parlor, listened to the silence that followed Hannah's words, then said, "Scat!" to the deweys who were playing chain gang near the window. With the shoelaces of each of them tied to the laces of the others, they stumbled and tumbled out of Eva's room.

---

9. I.e., Jesus.

1. A kind of string bean.

"Now," Eva looked up across from her wagon at her daughter. "Give me that again. Flat out to fit my head."

"I mean, did you? You know. When we was little."

Eva's hand moved snail-like down her thigh toward her stump, but stopped short of it to realign a pleat. "No. I don't reckon I did. Not the way you thinkin'."

"Oh, well. I was just wonderin'." Hannah appeared to be through with the subject.

"An evil wonderin' if I ever heard one." Eva was not through.

"I didn't mean nothing by it, Mamma."

"What you mean you didn't *mean* nothing by it? How you gone not mean something by it?"

Hannah pinched the tips off the Kentucky Wonders and snapped their long pods. What with the sound of the cracking and snapping and her swift-fingered movements, she seemed to be playing a complicated instrument. Eva watched her a moment and then said, "You gone can them?"

"No. They for tonight."

"Thought you was gone can some."

"Uncle Paul ain't brought me none yet. A peck ain't enough to can. He say he got two bushels for me."

"Triflin'."

"Oh, he all right."

"Sho he all right. Everybody all right. 'Cept Mamma. Mamma the only one ain't all right. Cause she didn't *love* us."

"Awww, Mamma."

"Awww, Mamma? Awww, Mamma? You settin' here with your healthy-ass self and ax me did I love you? Them big old eyes in your head would a been two holes full of maggots if I hadn't."

"I didn't mean that, Mamma. I know you fed us and all. I was talkin' 'bout something else. Like. Like. Playin' with us. Did you ever, you know, play with us?"

"Play? Wasn't nobody playin' in 1895. Just 'cause you got it good now you think it was always this good? 1895 was a killer, girl. Things was bad. Niggers was dying like flies. Stepping tall, ain't you? Uncle Paul gone bring me *two* bushels. Yeh. And they's a melon downstairs, ain't they? And I bake every Saturday, and Shad brings fish on Friday, and they's a pork barrel full of meal, and we float eggs in a crock of vinegar . . ."

"Mamma, what you talkin' 'bout?"

"I'm talkin' 'bout 18 and 95 when I set in that house five days with you and Pearl and Plum and three beets, you snake-eyed ungrateful hussy. What would I look like leapin' 'round that little old room playin' with youngins with three beets to my name?"

"I know 'bout them beets, Mamma. You told us that a million times."

"Yeah? Well? Don't that count? Ain't that love? You want me to tinkle you under the jaw and forget 'bout them sores in your mouth? Pearl was shittin' worms and I was supposed to play rang-around-the-rosie?"

"But Mamma, they had to be some time when you wasn't thinkin' 'bout . . ."

"No time. They wasn't no time. Not none. Soon as I got one day done here come a night. With you all coughin' and me watchin' so TB wouldn't take you off and if you was sleepin' quiet I thought, O Lord, they dead and put my hand over your mouth to feel if the breath was comin' what you talkin' 'bout did I love you girl I stayed alive for you can't you get that through your thick head or what is that between your ears, heifer?"

Hannah had enough beans now. With some tomatoes and hot bread, she thought, that would be enough for everybody, especially since the deweys didn't eat vegetables no how and Eva never made them and Tar Baby was living off air and music these days. She picked up the basket and stood with it and the bowl of beans over her mother. Eva's face was still asking her last question. Hannah looked into her mother's eyes.

"But what about Plum? What'd you kill Plum for, Mamma?"

It was a Wednesday in August and the ice wagon was coming and coming. You could hear bits of the driver's song. Now Mrs. Jackson would be tipping down her porch steps. "Jes a piece. You got a lil ole piece layin' 'round in there you could spare?" And as he had since the time of the pigeons, the iceman would hand her a lump of ice saying, "Watch it now, Mrs. Jackson. That straw'll tickle your pretty neck to death."

Eva listened to the wagon coming and thought about what it must be like in the icehouse. She leaned back a little and closed her eyes trying to see the insides of the icehouse. It was a dark, lovely picture in this heat, until it reminded her of that winter night in the outhouse holding her baby in the dark, her fingers searching for his asshole and the last bit of lard scooped from the sides of the can, held deliberately on the tip of her middle finger, the last bit of lard to keep from hurting him when she slid her finger in and all because she had broken the slop jar and the rags had frozen. The last food staple in the house she had rammed up her baby's behind to keep from hurting him too much when she opened up his bowels to pull the stools out. He had been screaming fit to kill, but when she found his hole at last and stuck her finger up in it, the shock was so great he was suddenly quiet. Even now on the hottest day anyone in Medallion could remember—a day so hot flies slept and cats were splaying their fur like quills, a day so hot pregnant wives leaned up against trees and cried, and women remembering some three-month-old hurt put ground glass in their lovers' food and the men looked at the food and wondered if there was glass in it and ate it anyway because it was too hot to resist eating it—even on this hottest of days in the hot spell, Eva shivered from the biting cold and stench of that outhouse.

Hannah was waiting. Watching her mother's eyelids. When Eva spoke at last it was with two voices. Like two people were talking at the same time, saying the same thing, one a fraction of a second behind the other.

"He give me such a time. Such a time. Look like he didn't even want to be born. But he come on out. Boys is hard to bear. You wouldn't know that but they is. It was such a carryin' on to get him born and to keep him alive. Just to keep his little heart beating and his little old lungs cleared and look like when he came back from that war he wanted to git back in. After all that carryin' on, just gettin' him out and keepin' him alive, he wanted to crawl back in my womb and well . . . I ain't got the room no more even if he could do it. There wasn't space for him in my womb. And he was crawlin' back. Being helpless and thinking baby thoughts and dreaming baby dreams and messing up his pants again and smiling all the time. I had room enough in my heart, but not in my womb, not no more. I birthed him once. I couldn't do it again. He was growed, a big old thing. Godhavemercy, I couldn't birth him twice. I'd be laying here at night and he be downstairs in that room, but when I closed my eyes I'd see him . . . six feet tall smilin' and crawlin' up the stairs quietlike so I wouldn't hear and opening the door soft so I wouldn't hear and he'd be creepin' to the bed trying to spread my legs trying to get back up in my womb. He was a man, girl, a big old growed-up man. I didn't have that much room. I kept on dreaming it. Dreaming it and I knowed it was true. One night it wouldn't be no dream. It'd be true and I would have done it, would have let him if I'd've had the room but a big man can't be a baby all wrapped up inside his mamma no more; he suffocate. I done everything I could to make him leave me and go on and live and be a man but he wouldn't and I had to keep him out so I just thought of a way he could die like a man not all scrunched up inside my womb, but like a man."

Eva couldn't see Hannah clearly for the tears, but she looked up at her anyway and said, by way of apology or explanation or perhaps just by way of neatness, "But I held him close first. Real close. Sweet Plum. My baby boy."

Long after Hannah turned and walked out of the room, Eva continued to call his name while her fingers lined up the pleats in her dress.

Hannah went off to the kitchen, her old man's slippers plopping down the stairs and over the hardwood floors. She turned the spigot on, letting water break up the tight knots of Kentucky Wonders and float them to the top of the bowl. She swirled them about with her fingers, poured the water off and repeated the process. Each time the green tubes rose to the surface she felt elated and collected whole handfuls at a time to drop in twos and threes back into the water.

Through the window over the sink she could see the deweys still playing chain gang; their ankles bound one to the other, they tumbled, struggled back to their feet and tried to walk single file. Hens strutted by with one suspicious eye on the deweys, another on the brick fireplace where sheets and mason jars[2] were boiled. Only the deweys could play in this heat. Hannah put the Kentucky Wonders over the fire and, struck by a sudden sleepiness, she went off to lie down in the front room. It was even hotter there, for the windows were shut to keep out the sunlight. Hannah straightened the shawl that draped the couch and lay down. She dreamed of a wedding in a red bridal gown until Sula came in and woke her.

But before the second strange thing, there had been the wind, which was the first. The very night before the day Hannah had asked Eva if she had ever loved them, the wind tore over the hills rattling roofs and loosening doors. Everything shook, and although the people were frightened they thought it meant rain and welcomed it. Windows fell out and trees lost arms. People waited up half the night for the first crack of lightning. Some had even uncovered barrels to catch the rain water, which they loved to drink and cook in. They waited in vain, for no lightning no thunder no rain came. The wind just swept through, took what dampness there was out of the air, messed up the yards, and went on. The hills of the Bottom, as always, protected the valley part of town where the white people lived, and the next morning all the people were grateful because there was a dryer heat. So they set about their work early, for it was canning time, and who knew but what the wind would come back this time with a cooling rain. The men who worked in the valley got up at four thirty in the morning and looked at the sky where the sun was already rising like a hot white bitch. They beat the brims of their hats against their legs before putting them on and trudged down the road like old promises nobody wanted kept.

2. Used for home canning.

On Thursday, when Hannah brought Eva her fried tomatoes and soft scrambled eggs with the white left out for good luck, she mentioned her dream of the wedding in the red dress. Neither one bothered to look it up for they both knew the number was 522.[3] Eva said she'd play it when Mr. Buckland Reed came by. Later she would remember it as the third strange thing. She had thought it odd even then, but the red in the dream confused her. But she wasn't certain that it was third or not because Sula was acting up, fretting the deweys and meddling the newly married couple. Because she was thirteen, everybody supposed her nature was coming down, but it was hard to put up with her sulking and irritation. The birthmark over her eye was getting darker and looked more and more like a stem and rose. She was dropping things and eating food that belonged to the newly married couple and started in to worrying everybody that the deweys needed a bath and she was going to give it to them. The deweys, who went wild at the thought of water, were crying and thundering all over the house like colts.

"We ain't got to, do we? Do we got to do what she says? It ain't Saturday." They even woke up Tar Baby, who came out of his room to look at them and then left the house in search of music.

Hannah ignored them and kept on bringing mason jars out of the cellar and washing them. Eva banged on the floor with her stick but nobody came. By noon it was quiet. The deweys had escaped, Sula was either in her room or gone off somewhere. The newly married couple, energized by their morning lovemaking, had gone to look for a day's work happily certain that they would find none.

The air all over the Bottom got heavy with peeled fruit and boiling vegetables. Fresh corn, tomatoes, string beans, melon rinds. The women, the children and the old men who had no jobs were putting up for a winter they understood so well. Peaches were stuffed into jars and black cherries (later, when it got cooler, they would put up jellies and preserves). The greedy canned as many as forty-two a day even though some of them, like Mrs. Jackson, who ate ice, had jars from 1920.

Before she trundled her wagon over to the dresser to get her comb, Eva looked out the window and saw Hannah bending to light the yard fire. And that was the fifth (or fourth, if you didn't count Sula's craziness) strange thing. She couldn't find her comb. Nobody moved stuff in Eva's room except to clean and then they put everything right back. But Eva couldn't find it anywhere. One hand pulling her braids loose, the other searching the dresser drawers, she had just begun to get irritated when she felt it in her blouse drawer. Then she trundled back to the window to catch a breeze, if one took a mind to come by, while she combed her hair. She rolled up to the window and it was then she saw Hannah burning. The flames from the yard fire were licking the blue cotton dress, making her dance. Eva knew there was time for nothing in this world other than the time it took to get there and cover her daughter's body with her own. She lifted her heavy frame up on her good leg, and with fists and arms smashed the windowpane. Using her stump as a support on the window sill, her good leg as a lever, she threw herself out of the window. Cut and bleeding she clawed the air trying to aim her body toward the flaming, dancing figure. She missed and came

3. I.e., in a dream book, which gives numbers to specific dreams (the corresponding number can then be played).

crashing down some twelve feet from Hannah's smoke. Stunned but still conscious, Eva dragged herself toward her firstborn, but Hannah, her senses lost, went flying out of the yard gesturing and bobbing like a sprung jack-in-the-box.

Mr. and Mrs. Suggs, who had set up their canning apparatus in their front yard, saw her running, dancing toward them. They whispered, "Jesus, Jesus," and together hoisted up their tub of water in which tight red tomatoes floated and threw it on the smoke-and-flame-bound woman. The water did put out the flames, but it also made steam, which seared to sealing all that was left of the beautiful Hannah Peace. She lay there on the wooden sidewalk planks, twitching lightly among the smashed tomatoes, her face a mask of agony so intense that for years the people who gathered 'round would shake their heads at the recollection of it.

Somebody covered her legs with a shirt. A woman unwrapped her head rag and placed it on Hannah's shoulder. Somebody else ran to Dick's Fresh Food and Sundries to call the ambulance. The rest stood there as helpless as sunflowers leaning on a fence. The deweys came and stepped in the tomatoes, their eyes raked with wonder. Two cats sidled through the legs of the crowd, sniffing the burned flesh. The vomiting of a young girl finally broke the profound silence and caused the women to talk to each other and to God. In the midst of calling Jesus they heard the hollow clang of the ambulance bell struggling up the hill, but not the "Help me, ya'll" that the dying woman whispered. Then somebody remembered to go and see about Eva. They found her on her stomach by the forsythia bushes calling Hannah's name and dragging her body through the sweet peas and clover that grew under the forsythia by the side of the house. Mother and daughter were placed on stretchers and carried to the ambulance. Eva was wide awake. The blood from her face cuts filled her eyes so she could not see, could only smell the familiar odor of cooked flesh.

Hannah died on the way to the hospital. Or so they said. In any case, she had already begun to bubble and blister so badly that the coffin had to be kept closed at the funeral and the women who washed the body and dressed it for death wept for her burned hair and wrinkled breasts as though they themselves had been her lovers.

When Eva got to the hospital they put her stretcher on the floor, so preoccupied with the hot and bubbling flesh of the other (some of them had never seen so extreme a burn case before) they forgot Eva, who would have bled to death except Old Willy Fields, the orderly, saw blood staining his just-mopped floors and went to find out where it was coming from. Recognizing Eva at once he shouted to a nurse, who came to see if the bloody one-legged black woman was alive or dead. From then on Willy boasted that he had saved Eva's life—an indisputable fact which she herself admitted and for which she cursed him every day for thirty-seven years thereafter and would have cursed him for the rest of her life except by then she was already ninety years old and forgot things.

Lying in the colored ward of the hospital, which was a screened corner of a larger ward, Eva mused over the perfection of the judgment against her. She remembered the wedding dream and recalled that weddings always meant death. And the red gown, well that was the fire, as she should have known. She remembered something else too, and try as she might to deny it, she knew that as she lay on the ground trying to drag herself through the sweet peas and clover to get to Hannah, she had seen Sula standing on the back porch just looking. When Eva, who was never one to hide the faults of her children, mentioned what she thought she'd seen to a few friends, they said it was natural. Sula was probably struck dumb, as anybody would be who saw her own mamma burn up. Eva said yes, but inside she disagreed and remained convinced that Sula had watched Hannah burn not because she was paralyzed, but because she was interested.

1927

Old people were dancing with little children. Young boys with their sisters, and the church women who frowned on any bodily expression of joy (except when the hand of God commanded it) tapped their feet. Somebody (the groom's father, everybody said) had poured a whole pint jar of cane liquor into the punch, so even the men who did not sneak out the back door to have a shot, as well as the women who let nothing stronger than Black Draught enter their blood, were tipsy. A small boy stood at the Victrola turning its handle and smiling at the sound of Bert Williams' "Save a Little Dram for Me."

Even Helene Wright had mellowed with the cane, waving away apologies for drinks spilled on her rug and paying no attention whatever to the chocolate cake lying on the arm of her red-velvet sofa. The tea roses above her left breast had slipped from the brooch that fastened them and were hanging heads down. When her husband called her attention to the children wrapping themselves into her curtains, she merely smiled and said, "Oh, let them be." She was not only a little drunk, she was weary and had been for weeks. Her only child's wedding—the culmination of all she had been, thought or done in this world—had dragged from her energy and stamina even she did not know she possessed. Her house had to be thoroughly cleaned, chickens had to be plucked, cakes and pies made, and for weeks she, her friends and her daughter had been sewing. Now it was all happening and it took only a little cane juice to snap the cords of fatigue and damn the white curtains that she had pinned on the stretcher only the morning before. Once this day was over she would have a lifetime to rattle around in that house and repair the damage.

A real wedding, in a church, with a real reception afterward, was rare among the people of the Bottom. Expensive for one thing, and most newly-weds just went to the courthouse if they were not particular, or had the preacher come in and say a few words if they were. The rest just "took up" with one another. No invitations were sent. There was no need for that formality. Folks just came, bringing a gift if they had one, none if they didn't. Except for those who worked in valley houses, most of them had never been to a big wedding; they simply assumed it was rather like a funeral except afterward you didn't have to walk all the way out to Beechnut Cemetery.

This wedding offered a special attraction, for the bridegroom was a handsome, well-liked man—the tenor of Mount Zion's Men's Quartet, who had an enviable reputation among the girls and a comfortable one among men. His name was Jude Greene, and with the pick of some eight or ten girls who came regularly to services to hear him sing, he had chosen Nel Wright.

He wasn't really aiming to get married. He was twenty then, and although his job as a waiter at the Hotel Medallion was a blessing to his parents and their seven other children, it wasn't nearly enough to support a wife. He had brought the subject up first on the day the word got out that the town was building a new road, tarmac, that would wind through Medallion on down to the river, where a great new bridge was to be built to connect Medallion to Porter's Landing, the town on the other side. The war over, a fake prosperity was still around. In a state of euphoria, with a hunger for more and more, the council of founders cast its eye toward a future that would certainly include trade from cross-river towns. Towns that needed more than a house raft to get to the merchants of Medallion. Work had already begun on the New River Road (the city had always meant to name it something else, something wonderful, but ten years later when the bridge idea was dropped for a tunnel it was still called the New River Road).

Along with a few other young black men, Jude had gone down to the shack where they were hiring. Three old colored men had already been hired, but not for the road work, just to do the picking up, food bringing and other small errands. These old men were close to feeble, not good for much else, and everybody was pleased they were taken on; still it was a shame to see those white men laughing with the grandfathers but shying away from the young black men who could tear that road up. The men like Jude who could do real work. Jude himself longed more than anybody else to be taken. Not just for the good money, more for the work itself. He wanted to swing the pick or kneel down with the string or shovel the gravel. His arms ached for something heavier than trays, for something dirtier than peelings; his feet wanted the heavy work shoes, not the thin-soled black shoes that the hotel required. More than anything he wanted the camaraderie of the road men: the lunch buckets, the hollering, the body movement that in the end produced something real, something he could point to. "I built that road," he could say. How much better sundown would be than the end of a day in the restaurant, where a good day's work was marked by the number of dirty plates and the weight of the garbage bin. "I built that road." People would walk over his sweat for years. Perhaps a sledge hammer would come crashing down on his foot, and when people asked him how come he limped, he could say, "Got that building the New Road."

It was while he was full of such dreams, his body already feeling the rough work clothes, his hands already curved to the pick handle, that he spoke to Nel about getting married. She seemed receptive but hardly anxious. It was after he stood in lines for six days running and saw the gang boss pick out thin-armed white boys from the Virginia hills and the bull-necked Greeks and Italians and heard over and over, "Nothing else today. Come back tomorrow," that he got the message. So it was rage, rage and a determination to take on a man's role anyhow that made him press Nel about settling down. He needed some of his appetites filled, some posture of adulthood recognized, but mostly he wanted someone to care about his hurt, to care very deeply. Deep enough to hold him, deep enough to rock him, deep enough to ask, "How you feel? You all right? Want some coffee?" And if he were to be a man, that someone could no longer be his mother. He chose the girl who had always been kind, who had never seemed hell-bent to marry, who made the whole venture seem like his idea, his conquest.

The more he thought about marriage, the more attractive it became. Whatever his fortune, whatever the cut of his garment, there would always be the hem—the tuck and fold that hid his raveling edges; a someone sweet, industrious and loyal to shore him up. And in return he would shelter her, love her, grow old with her. Without that someone he was a waiter hanging around a kitchen like a woman. With her he was head of a household pinned to an unsatisfactory job out of necessity. The two of them together would make one Jude.

His fears lest his burst dream of road building discourage her were never realized. Nel's indifference to his hints about marriage disappeared altogether when she discovered his pain. Jude could see himself taking shape in her eyes. She actually wanted to help, to soothe, and was it true what Ajax said in the Time and a Half Pool Hall? That "all they want, man, is they own misery. Ax em to die for you and they yours for life."

Whether he was accurate in general, Ajax was right about Nel. Except for an occasional leadership role with Sula, she had no aggression. Her parents had succeeded in rubbing down to a dull glow any sparkle or splutter she had. Only with Sula did that quality have free reign, but their friendship was so close, they themselves had difficulty distinguishing one's thoughts from the other's. During all of her girlhood the only respite Nel had had from her stern and undemonstrative parents was Sula. When Jude began to hover around, she was flattered—all the girls liked him—and Sula made the enjoyment of his attentions keener simply because she seemed always to want Nel to shine. They never quarreled, those two, the way some girlfriends did over boys, or competed against each other for them. In those days a compliment to one was a compliment to the other, and cruelty to one was a challenge to the other.

Nel's response to Jude's shame and anger selected her away from Sula. And greater than her friendship was this new feeling of being needed by someone who saw her singly. She didn't even know she had a neck until Jude remarked on it, or that her smile was anything but the spreading of her lips until he saw it as a small miracle.

Sula was no less excited about the wedding. She thought it was the perfect thing to do following their graduation from general school. She wanted to be the bridesmaid. No others. And she encouraged Mrs. Wright to go all out, even to borrowing Eva's punch bowl. In fact, she handled most of the details very efficiently, capitalizing on the fact that most people were anxious to please her since she had lost her mamma only a few years back and they still remembered the agony in Hannah's face and the blood on Eva's.

So they danced up in the Bottom on the second Saturday in June, danced at the wedding where everybody realized for the first time that except for their magnificent teeth, the deweys would never grow. They had been forty-eight inches tall for years now, and while their size was unusual it was not unheard of. The realization was based on the fact that they remained boys in mind. Mischievous, cunning, private and completely unhousebroken, their games and interests had not changed since Hannah had them all put into the first grade together.

Nel and Jude, who had been the stars all during the wedding, were forgotten finally as the reception melted into a dance, a feed, a gossip session, a playground and a love nest. For the first time that day they relaxed and looked at each other, and liked what they saw. They began to dance, pressed in among the others, and each one turned his thoughts to the night that was coming on fast. They had taken a housekeeping room with one of Jude's aunts (over the protest of Mrs. Wright, who had rooms to spare, but

Nel didn't want to make love to her husband in her mother's house) and were getting restless to go there.

As if reading her thoughts, Jude leaned down and whispered, "Me too." Nel smiled and rested her cheek on his shoulder. The veil she wore was too heavy to allow her to feel the core of the kiss he pressed on her head. When she raised her eyes to him for one more look of reassurance, she saw through the open door a slim figure in blue, gliding, with just a hint of a strut, down the path toward the road. One hand was pressed to the head to hold down the large hat against the warm June breeze. Even from the rear Nel could tell that it was Sula and that she was smiling; that something deep down in that litheness was amused. It would be ten years before they saw each other again, and their meeting would be thick with birds.

Part Two

1937

Accompanied by a plague of robins, Sula came back to Medallion. The little yam-breasted shuddering birds were everywhere, exciting very small children away from their usual welcome into a vicious stoning. Nobody knew why or from where they had come. What they did know was that you couldn't go anywhere without stepping in their pearly shit, and it was hard to hang up clothes, pull weeds or just sit on the front porch when robins were flying and dying all around you.

Although most of the people remembered the time when the sky was black for two hours with clouds and clouds of pigeons, and although they were accustomed to excesses in nature—too much heat, too much cold, too little rain, rain to flooding—they still dreaded the way a relatively trivial phenomenon could become sovereign in their lives and bend their minds to its will.

In spite of their fear, they reacted to an oppressive oddity, or what they called evil days, with an acceptance that bordered on welcome. Such evil must be avoided, they felt, and precautions must naturally be taken to protect themselves from it. But they let it run its course, fulfill itself, and never invented ways either to alter it, to annihilate it or to prevent its happening again. So also were they with people.

What was taken by outsiders to be slackness, slovenliness or even generosity was in fact a full recognition of the legitimacy of forces other than good ones. They did not believe doctors could heal—for them, none ever had done so. They did not believe death was accidental—life might be, but death was deliberate. They did not believe Nature was ever askew—only inconvenient. Plague and drought were as "natural" as springtime. If milk could curdle, God knows robins could fall. The purpose of evil was to survive it and they determined (without ever knowing they had made up their minds to do it) to survive floods, white people, tuberculosis, famine and ignorance. They knew anger well but not despair, and they didn't stone sinners for the same reason they didn't commit suicide—it was beneath them.

Sula stepped off the Cincinnati Flyer[4] into the robin shit and began the long climb up into the Bottom. She was dressed in a manner that was as

4. A train.

close to a movie star as anyone would ever see. A black crepe dress splashed with pink and yellow zinnias, foxtails, a black felt hat with the veil of net lowered over one eye. In her right hand was a black purse with a beaded clasp and in her left a red leather traveling case, so small, so charming—no one had seen anything like it ever before, including the mayor's wife and the music teacher, both of whom had been to Rome.

Walking up the hill toward Carpenter's Road, the heels and sides of her pumps edged with drying bird shit, she attracted the glances of old men sitting on stone benches in front of the courthouse, housewives throwing buckets of water on their sidewalks, and high school students on their way home for lunch. By the time she reached the Bottom, the news of her return had brought the black people out on their porches or to their windows. There were scattered hellos and nods but mostly stares. A little boy ran up to her saying, "Carry yo' bag, ma'am?" Before Sula could answer his mother had called him, "You, John. Get back in here."

At Eva's house there were four dead robins on the walk. Sula stopped and with her toe pushed them into the bordering grass.

Eva looked at Sula pretty much the same way she had looked at BoyBoy that time when he returned after he'd left her without a dime or a prospect of one. She was sitting in her wagon, her back to the window she had jumped out of (now all boarded up) setting fire to the hair she had combed out of her head. When Sula opened the door she raised her eyes and said, "I might have knowed them birds meant something. Where's your coat?"

Sula threw herself on Eva's bed. "The rest of my stuff will be on later."

"I should hope so. Them little old furry tails ain't going to do you no more good than they did the fox that was wearing them."

"Don't you say hello to nobody when you ain't seen them for ten years?"

"If folks let somebody know where they is and when they coming, then other folks can get ready for them. If they don't—if they just pop in all sudden like—then they got to take whatever mood they find."

"How you been doing, Big Mamma?"

"Gettin' by. Sweet of you to ask. You was quick enough when you wanted something. When you needed a little change or . . ."

"Don't talk to me about how much you gave me, Big Mamma, and how much I owe you or none of that."

"Oh? I ain't supposed to mention it?"

"OK. Mention it." Sula shrugged and turned over on her stomach, her buttocks toward Eva.

"You ain't been in this house ten seconds and already you starting something."

"Takes two, Big Mamma."

"Well, don't let your mouth start nothing that your ass can't stand. When you gone to get married? You need to have some babies. It'll settle you."

"I don't want to make somebody else. I want to make myself."

"Selfish. Ain't no woman got no business floatin' around without no man."

"You did."

"Not by choice."

"Mamma did."

"Not by choice, I said. It ain't right for you to want to stay off by yourself. You need . . . I'm a tell you what you need."

Sula sat up. "I need you to shut your mouth."

"Don't nobody talk to me like that. Don't nobody . . ."

"This body does. Just 'cause you was bad enough to cut off your own leg you think you got a right to kick everybody with the stump."

"Who said I cut off my leg?"

"Well, you stuck it under a train to collect insurance."

"Hold on, you lyin' heifer!"

"I aim to."

"Bible say honor thy father and thy mother that thy days may be long upon the land thy God giveth thee."

"Mamma must have skipped that part. Her days wasn't too long."

"Pus mouth! God's going to strike you!"

"Which God? The one watched you burn Plum?"

"Don't talk to me about no burning. You watched your own mamma. You crazy roach! You the one should have been burnt!"

"But I ain't. Got that? I ain't. Any more fires in this house, I'm lighting them!"

"Hellfire don't need lighting and it's already burning in you . . ."

"Whatever's burning in me is mine!"

"Amen!"

"And I'll split this town in two and everything in it before I'll let you put it out!"

"Pride goeth before a fall."

"What the hell do I care about falling?"

"Amazing Grace."

"You sold your life for twenty-three dollars a month."

"You throwed yours away."

"It's mine to throw."

"One day you gone need it."

"But not you. I ain't never going to need you. And you know what? Maybe one night when you dozing in that wagon flicking flies and swallowing spit, maybe I'll just tip on up here with some kerosene and—who knows—you may make the brightest flame of them all."

So Eva locked her door from then on. But it did no good. In April two men came with a stretcher and she didn't even have time to comb her hair before they strapped her to a piece of canvas.

When Mr. Buckland Reed came by to pick up the number, his mouth sagged at the sight of Eva being carried out and Sula holding some papers against the wall, at the bottom of which, just above the word "guardian," she very carefully wrote Miss Sula Mae Peace.

◎ ◎ ◎

Nel alone noticed the peculiar quality of the May that followed the leaving of the birds. It had a sheen, a glimmering as of green, rain-soaked Saturday nights (lit by the excitement of newly installed street lights); of lemon-yellow afternoons bright with iced drinks and splashes of daffodils. It showed in the damp faces of her children and the river-smoothness of their voices. Even her own body was not immune to the magic. She would sit on the floor to sew as she had done as a girl, fold her legs up under her or do a little dance that fitted some tune in her head. There were easy sun-washed days and purple dusks in which Tar Baby sang "Abide With Me" at prayer meetings, his lashes darkened by tears, his silhouette limp with regret against the whitewashed walls of Greater Saint Matthew's. Nel listened and was moved to smile. To smile at the sheer loveliness that pressed in from the windows and touched his grief, making it a pleasure to behold.

Although it was she alone who saw this magic, she did not wonder at it. She knew it was all due to Sula's return to the Bottom. It was like getting the use of an eye back, having a cataract removed. Her old friend had come home. Sula. Who made her laugh, who made her see old things with new eyes, in whose presence she felt clever, gentle and a little raunchy. Sula, whose past she had lived through and with whom the present was a constant sharing of perceptions. Talking to Sula had always been a conversation with herself. Was there anyone else before whom she could never be foolish? In whose view inadequacy was mere idiosyncrasy, a character trait rather than a deficiency? Anyone who left behind that aura of fun and complicity? Sula never competed; she simply helped others define themselves. Other people seemed to turn their volume on and up when Sula was in the room. More than any other thing, humor returned. She could listen to the crunch of sugar underfoot that the children had spilled without reaching for the switch; and she forgot the tear in the living-room window shade. Even Nel's love for Jude, which over the years had spun a steady gray web around her heart, became a bright and easy affection, a playfulness that was reflected in their lovemaking.

Sula would come by of an afternoon, walking along with her fluid stride, wearing a plain yellow dress the same way her mother, Hannah, had worn those too-big house dresses—with a distance, an absence of a relationship to clothes which emphasized everything the fabric covered. When she scratched the screen door, as in the old days, and stepped inside, the dishes piled in the sink looked as though they belonged there; the dust on the lamps sparkled; the hair brush lying on the "good" sofa in the living room did not have to be apologetically retrieved, and Nel's grimy intractable children looked like three wild things happily insouciant in the May shine.

"Hey, girl." The rose mark over Sula's eye gave her glance a suggestion of startled pleasure. It was darker than Nel remembered.

"Hey yourself. Come on in here."

"How you doin'?" Sula moved a pile of ironed diapers from a chair and sat down.

"Oh, I ain't strangled nobody yet so I guess I'm all right."

"Well, if you change your mind call me."

"Somebody need killin'?"

"Half this town need it."

"And the other half?"

"A drawn-out disease."

"Oh, come on. Is Medallion that bad?"

"Didn't nobody tell you?"

"You been gone too long, Sula."

"Not too long, but maybe too far."

"What's that supposed to mean?" Nel dipped her fingers into the bowl of water and sprinkled a diaper.

"Oh, I don't know."

"Want some cool tea?"

"Mmmm. Lots of ice, I'm burnin' up."

"Iceman don't come yet, but it's good and cold."

"That's fine."

"Hope I didn't speak too soon. Kids run in and out of here so much." Nel bent to open the icebox.

"You puttin' it on, Nel. Jude must be wore out."

"*Jude* must be wore out? You don't care nothin' 'bout my back, do you?"

"Is that where it's at, in your back?"

"Hah! Jude thinks it's everywhere."

"He's right, it is everywhere. Just be glad he found it, wherever it is. Remember John L.?"

"When Shirley said he got her down by the well and tried to stick it in her hip?" Nel giggled at the remembrance of that teen-time tale. "She should have been grateful. Have you seen her since you been back?"

"Mmm. Like a ox."

"That was one dumb nigger, John L."

"Maybe. Maybe he was just sanitary."

"Sanitary?"

"Well. Think about it. Suppose Shirley was all splayed out in front of you? Wouldn't you go for the hipbone instead?"

Nel lowered her head onto crossed arms while tears of laughter dripped into the warm diapers. Laughter that weakened her knees and pressed her bladder into action. Her rapid soprano and Sula's dark sleepy chuckle made a duet that frightened the cat and made the children run in from the back yard, puzzled at first by the wild free sounds, then delighted to see their mother stumbling merrily toward the bathroom, holding on to her stomach, fairly singing through the laughter: "Aw. Aw. Lord. Sula. Stop." And the other one, the one with the scary black thing over her eye, laughing softly and egging their mother on: "Neatness counts. You know what cleanliness is next to . . ."

"Hush." Nel's plea was clipped off by the slam of the bathroom door.

"What y'all laughing at?"

"Old time-y stuff. Long gone, old time-y stuff."

"Tell us."

"Tell *you?*" The black mark leaped.

"Uh huh. Tell us."

"What tickles us wouldn't tickle you."

"Uh huh, it would."

"Well, we was talking about some people we used to know when we was little."

"Was my mamma little?"

"Of course."

"What happened?"

"Well, some old boy we knew name John L. and a girl name . . ."

Damp-faced, Nel stepped back into the kitchen. She felt new, soft and new. It had been the longest time since she had had a rib-scraping laugh. She had forgotten how deep and down it could be. So different from the miscellaneous giggles and smiles she had learned to be content with these past few years.

"O Lord, Sula. You haven't changed none." She wiped her eyes. "What was all that about, anyway? All that scramblin' we did trying to do it and not do it at the same time?"

"Beats me. Such a simple thing."

"But we sure made a lot out of it, and the boys were dumber than we were."

"Couldn't nobody be dumber than I was."

"Stop lying. All of 'em liked you best."

"Yeah? Where are they?"

"They still here. You the one went off."

"Didn't I, though?"

"Tell me about it. The big city."

"Big is all it is. A big Medallion."

"No. I mean the life. The nightclubs, and parties . . ."

"I was in college, Nellie. No nightclubs on campus."

"Campus? That what they call it? Well. You wasn't in no college for—what—ten years now? And you didn't write to nobody. How come you never wrote?"

"You never did either."

"Where was I going to write to? All I knew was that you was in Nashville. I asked Miss Peace about you once or twice."

"What did *she* say?"

"I couldn't make much sense out of her. You know she been gettin' stranger and stranger after she come out the hospital. How is she anyway?"

"Same, I guess. Not so hot."

"No? Laura, I know, was doing her cooking and things. Is she still?"

"No. I put her out."

"Put her out? What for?"

"She made me nervous."

"But she was doing it for nothing, Sula."

"That's what you think. She was stealing right and left."

"Since when did you get froggy⁵ about folks' stealing?"

Sula smiled. "OK. I lied. You wanted a reason."

"Well, give me the real one."

"I don't know the real one. She just didn't belong in that house. Digging around in the cupboards, picking up pots and ice picks . . ."

"You sure have changed. That house was always full of people digging in cupboards and carrying on."

"That's the reason, then."

"Sula. Come on, now."

"You've changed too. I didn't used to have to explain everything to you."

Nel blushed. "Who's feeding the deweys and Tar Baby? You?"

"Sure me. Anyway Tar Baby don't eat and the deweys still crazy."

"I heard one of 'em's mamma came to take him back but didn't know which was hern."

"Don't nobody know."

"And Eva? You doing the work for her too?"

"Well, since you haven't heard it, let me tell you. Eva's real sick. I had her put where she could be watched and taken care of."

"Where would that be?"

"Out by Beechnut."

"You mean that home the white church run? Sula! That ain't no place for Eva. All them women is dirt poor with no people at all. Mrs. Wilkens and them. They got dropsy and can't hold their water—crazy as loons. Eva's odd, but she got sense. I don't think that's right, Sula."

---

5. Jumpy, nervous.

"I'm scared of her, Nellie. That's why . . ."

"Scared? Of Eva?"

"You don't know her. Did you know she burnt Plum?"

"Oh, I heard that years ago. But nobody put no stock in it."

"They should have. It's true. I saw it. And when I got back here she was planning to do it to me too."

"Eva? I can't hardly believe that. She almost died trying to get to your mother."

Sula leaned forward, her elbows on the table. "You ever known me to lie to you?"

"No. But you could be mistaken. Why would Eva . . ."

"All I know is I'm scared. And there's no place else for me to go. We all that's left, Eva and me. I guess I should have stayed gone. I didn't know what else to do. Maybe I should have talked to you about it first. You always had better sense than me. Whenever I was scared before, you knew just what to do."

The closed place in the water spread before them. Nel put the iron on the stove. The situation was clear to her now. Sula, like always, was incapable of making any but the most trivial decisions. When it came to matters of grave importance, she behaved emotionally and irresponsibly and left it to others to straighten out. And when fear struck her, she did unbelievable things. Like that time with her finger. Whatever those hunkies[6] did, it wouldn't have been as bad as what she did to herself. But Sula was so scared she had mutilated herself, to protect herself.

"What should I do, Nellie? Take her back and sleep with my door locked again?"

"No. I guess it's too late anyway. But let's work out a plan for taking care of her. So she won't be messed over."

"Anything you say."

"What about money? She got any?"

Sula shrugged. "The checks come still. It's not much, like it used to be. Should I have them made over to me?"

"Can you? Do it, then. We can arrange for her to have special comforts. That place is a mess, you know. A doctor don't never set foot in there. I ain't figured out yet how they stay alive in there as long as they do."

"Why don't I have the checks made over to you, Nellie? You better at this than I am."

"Oh no. People will say I'm scheming. You the one to do it. Was there insurance from Hannah?"

"Yes. Plum too. He had all that army insurance."

"Any of it left?"

"Well I went to college on some. Eva banked the rest. I'll look into it, though."

". . . and explain it all to the bank people."

"Will you go down with me?"

"Sure. It's going to be all right."

"I'm glad I talked to you 'bout this. It's been bothering me."

"Well, tongues will wag, but so long as we know the truth, it don't matter."

6. Disparaging term for Hungarians, but used often of any whites.

Just at that moment the children ran in announcing the entrance of their father. Jude opened the back door and walked into the kitchen. He was still a very good-looking man, and the only difference Sula could see was the thin pencil mustache under his nose, and a part in his hair.

"Hey, Jude. What you know good?"

"White man running it—nothing good."

Sula laughed while Nel, high-tuned to his moods, ignored her husband's smile saying, "Bad day, honey?"

"Same old stuff," he replied and told them a brief tale of some personal insult done him by a customer and his boss—a whiney tale that peaked somewhere between anger and a lapping desire for comfort. He ended it with the observation that a Negro man had a hard row to hoe in this world. He expected his story to dovetail into milkwarm commiseration, but before Nel could excrete it, Sula said she didn't know about that—it looked like a pretty good life to her.

"Say what?" Jude's temper flared just a bit as he looked at this friend of his wife's, this slight woman, not exactly plain, but not fine either, with a copperhead over her eye. As far as he could tell, she looked like a woman roaming the country trying to find some man to burden down with a lot of lip and a lot of mouths.

Sula was smiling. "I mean, I don't know what the fuss is about. I mean, everything in the world loves you. White men love you. They spend so much time worrying about your penis they forget their own. The only thing they want to do is cut off a nigger's privates. And if that ain't love and respect I don't know what is. And white women? They chase you all to every corner of the earth, feel for you under every bed. I knew a white woman wouldn't leave the house after 6 o'clock for fear one of you would snatch her. Now ain't that love? They think rape soon's they see you, and if they don't get the rape they looking for, they scream it anyway just so the search won't be in vain. Colored women worry themselves into bad health just trying to hang on to your cuffs. Even little children—white and black, boys and girls— spend all their childhood eating their hearts out 'cause they think you don't love them. And if that ain't enough, you love yourselves. Nothing in this world loves a black man more than another black man. You hear of solitary white men, but niggers? Can't stay away from one another a whole day. So. It looks to me like you the envy of the world."

Jude and Nel were laughing, he saying, "Well, if that's the only way they got to show it—cut off my balls and throw me in jail—I'd just as soon they left me alone." But thinking that Sula had an odd way of looking at things and that her wide smile took some of the sting from that rattlesnake over her eye. A funny woman, he thought, not that bad-looking. But he could see why she wasn't married; she stirred a man's mind maybe, but not his body.

⊙ ⊙ ⊙

He left his tie. The one with the scriggly yellow lines running lopsided across the dark-blue field. It hung over the top of the closet door pointing steadily downward while it waited with every confidence for Jude to return.

Could he be gone if his tie is still here? He will remember it and come back and then she would . . . uh. Then she could . . . tell him. Sit down quietly and tell him. "But Jude," she would say, "you *knew* me. All those days and years, Jude, you *knew* me. My ways and my hands and how my stomach folded and how we tried to get Mickey to nurse and how about that time when the landlord said . . . but you said . . . and I cried, Jude. You knew me and had listened to the things I said in the night, and heard me in the bathroom and laughed at my raggedy girdle and I laughed too because I knew you too, Jude. So how could you leave me when you knew me?"

But they had been down on all fours naked, not touching except their lips right down there on the floor where the tie is pointing to, on all fours like (uh huh, go on, say it) like dogs. Nibbling at each other, not even touching, not even looking at each other, just their lips, and when I opened the door they didn't even look for a minute and I thought the reason they are not looking up is because they are not doing that. So it's all right. I am just standing here. They are not doing that. I am just standing here and seeing it, but they are not really doing it. But then they did look up. Or you did. You did, Jude. And if only you had not looked at me the way the soldiers did on the train, the way you look at the children when they come in while you are listening to Gabriel Heatter[7] and break your train of thought—not focusing exactly but giving them an instant, a piece of time, to remember what they are doing, what they are interrupting, and to go on back to wherever they were and let you listen to Gabriel Heatter.And I did not know how to move my feet or fix my eyes or what. I just stood there seeing it and smiling, because maybe there was some explanation, something important that I did not know about that would have made it all right. I waited for Sula to look up at me any minute and say one of those lovely college words like *aesthetic* or *rapport*, which I never understood but which I loved because they sounded so comfortable and firm. And finally you just got up and started putting on your clothes and your privates were hanging down, so soft, and you buckled your pants belt but forgot to button the fly and she was sitting on the bed not even bothering to put on her clothes because actually she didn't need to because somehow she didn't look naked to me, only you did. Her chin was in her hand and she sat like a visitor from out of town waiting for the hosts to get some quarreling done and over with so the card game could continue and me wanting her to leave so I could tell you privately that you had forgotten to button your fly because I didn't want to say it in front of her, Jude. And even when you began to talk, I couldn't hear because I was worried about you not knowing that your fly was open and scared too because your eyes looked like the soldiers' that time on the train when my mother turned to custard.

Remember how big that bedroom was? Jude? How when we moved here we said, Well, at least we got us a real big bedroom, but it was small then, Jude, and so shambly, and maybe it was that way all along but it would have been better if I had gotten the dust out from under the bed because I was ashamed of it in that small room. And then you walked past me saying, "I'll be back for my things." And you did but you left your tie.

The clock was ticking. Nel looked at it and realized that it was two thirty, only forty-five minutes before the children would be home and she hadn't even felt anything right or sensible and now there was no time or wouldn't be until nighttime when they were asleep and she could get into bed and

7. Radio journalist (1890–1972).

maybe she could do it then. Think. But who could think in that bed where *they* had been and where they *also* had been and where only she was now?

She looked around for a place to be. A small place. The closet? No. Too dark. The bathroom. It was both small and bright, and she wanted to be in a very small, very bright place. Small enough to contain her grief. Bright enough to throw into relief the dark things that cluttered her. Once inside, she sank to the tile floor next to the toilet. On her knees, her hand on the cold rim of the bathtub, she waited for something to happen . . . inside. There was stirring, a movement of mud and dead leaves. She thought of the women at Chicken Little's funeral. The women who shrieked over the bier and at the lip of the open grave. What she had regarded since as unbecoming behavior seemed fitting to her now; they were screaming at the neck of God, his giant nape, the vast back-of-the-head that he had turned on them in death. But it seemed to her now that it was not a fist-shaking grief they were keening but rather a simple obligation to say something, do something, feel something about the dead. They could not let that heart-smashing event pass unrecorded, unidentified. It was poisonous, unnatural to let the dead go with a mere whimpering, a slight murmur, a rose bouquet of good taste. Good taste was out of place in the company of death, death itself was the essence of bad taste. And there must be much rage and saliva in its presence. The body must move and throw itself about, the eyes must roll, the hands should have no peace, and the throat should release all the yearning, despair and outrage that accompany the stupidity of loss.

"The real hell of Hell is that it is forever." Sula said that. She said doing anything forever and ever was hell. Nel didn't understand it then, but now in the bathroom, trying to feel, she thought, "If I could be sure that I could stay here in this small white room with the dirty tile and water gurgling in the pipes and my head on the cool rim of this bathtub and never have to go out the door, I would be happy. If I could be certain that I never had to get up and flush the toilet, go in the kitchen, watch my children grow up and die, see my food chewed on my plate . . . Sula was wrong. Hell ain't things lasting forever. Hell is change." Not only did men leave and children grow up and die, but even the misery didn't last. One day she wouldn't even have that. This very grief that had twisted her into a curve on the floor and flayed her would be gone. She would lose that too.

"Why, even in hate here I am thinking of what Sula said."

Hunched down in the small bright room Nel waited. Waited for the oldest cry. A scream not for others, not in sympathy for a burnt child, or a dead father, but a deeply personal cry for one's own pain. A loud, strident: "Why me?" She waited. The mud shifted, the leaves stirred, the smell of overripe green things enveloped her and announced the beginnings of her very own howl.

But it did not come.

The odor evaporated; the leaves were still, the mud settled. And finally there was nothing, just a flake of something dry and nasty in her throat. She stood up frightened. There was something just to the right of her, in the air, just out of view. She could not see it, but she knew exactly what it looked like. A gray ball hovering just there. Just there. To the right. Quiet, gray, dirty. A ball of muddy strings, but without weight, fluffy but terrible in its malevolence. She knew she could not look, so she closed her eyes and crept past it out of the bathroom, shutting the door behind her. Sweating with fear, she stepped to the kitchen door and onto the back porch. The lilac bushes preened at the railing, but there were no lilacs yet. Wasn't it time? Surely it was time. She looked over the fence to Mrs. Rayford's yard. Hers were not in bloom either. Was it too late? She fastened on this question with enthusiasm, all the time aware of something she was not thinking. It was the only way she could get her mind off the flake in her throat.

She spent a whole summer with the gray ball, the little ball of fur and string and hair always floating in the light near her but which she did not see because she never looked. But that was the terrible part, the effort it took not to look. But it was there anyhow, just to the right of her head and maybe further down by her shoulder, so when the children went to a monster movie at the Elmira Theater and came home and said, "Mamma, can you sleep with us tonight?" she said all right and got into bed with the two boys, who loved it, but the girl did not. For a long time she could not stop getting in the bed with her children and told herself each time that they might dream a dream about dragons and would need her to comfort them. It was so nice to think about their scary dreams and not about a ball of fur. She even hoped their dreams would rub off on her and give her the wonderful relief of a nightmare so she could stop going around scared to turn her head this way or that lest she see it. That was the scary part—seeing it. It was not coming at her; it never did that, or tried to pounce on her. It just floated there for the seeing, if she wanted to, and O my God for the touching if she wanted to. But she didn't want to see it, ever, for if she saw it, who could tell but what she might actually touch it, or want to, and then what would happen if she actually reached out her hand and touched it? Die probably, but no worse than that. Dying was OK because it was sleep and there wasn't no gray ball in death, was there? Was there? She would have to ask somebody about that, somebody she could confide in and who knew a lot of things, like Sula, for Sula would know or if she didn't she would say something funny that would make it all right. Ooo no, not Sula. Here she was in the midst of it, hating it, scared of it, and again she thought of Sula as though they were still friends and talked things over. That was too much. To lose Jude and not have Sula to talk to about it because it was Sula that he had left her for.

Now her thighs were really empty. And it was then that what those women said about never looking at another man made some sense to her, for the real point, the heart of what they said, was the word *looked*. Not to promise never to make love to another man, not to refuse to marry another man, but to promise and know that she could never afford to look again, to see and accept the way in which their heads cut the air or see moons and tree limbs framed by their necks and shoulders . . . never to look, for now she could not risk looking—and anyway, so what? For now her thighs were truly empty and dead too, and it was Sula who had taken the life from them and Jude who smashed her heart and the both of them who left her with no thighs and no heart just her brain raveling away.

And what am I supposed to do with these old thighs now, just walk up and down these rooms? What good are they, Jesus? They will never give me the peace I need to get from sunup to sundown, what good are they, are you trying to tell me that I am going to have to go all the way through these days all the way, O my god, to that box with four handles with never nobody settling down between my legs even if I sew up those old pillow cases and rinse down the porch and feed my children and beat the rugs and haul the coal up out of the bin even then nobody, O Jesus, I could be a mule or plow the furrows with my hands if need be or hold these rickety walls up with my back if need be if I knew that somewhere in this world in the pocket of some night I could open my legs to some cowboy lean hips but you are trying to tell me no and O my sweet Jesus what kind of cross is that?

1939

When the word got out about Eva being put in Sunnydale, the people in the Bottom shook their heads and said Sula was a roach. Later, when they saw how she took Jude, then ditched him for others, and heard how he bought a bus ticket to Detroit (where he bought but never mailed birthday cards to his sons), they forgot all about Hannah's easy ways (or their own) and said she was a bitch. Everybody remembered the plague of robins that announced her return, and the tale about her watching Hannah burn was stirred up again.

But it was the men who gave her the final label, who fingerprinted her for all time. They were the ones who said she was guilty of the unforgivable thing—the thing for which there was no understanding, no excuse, no compassion. The route from which there was no way back, the dirt that could not ever be washed away. They said that Sula slept with white men. It may not have been true, but it certainly could have been. She was obviously capable of it. In any case, all minds were closed to her when that word was passed around. It made the old women draw their lips together; made small children look away from her in shame; made young men fantasize elaborate torture for her—just to get the saliva back in their mouths when they saw her.

Every one of them imagined the scene, each according to his own predilections—Sula underneath some white man—and it filled them with choking disgust. There was nothing lower she could do, nothing filthier. The fact that their own skin color was proof that it had happened in their own families was no deterrent to their bile. Nor was the willingness of black men to lie in the beds of white women a consideration that might lead them toward tolerance. They insisted that all unions between white men and black women be rape; for a black woman to be willing was literally unthinkable. In that way, they regarded integration with precisely the same venom that white people did.

So they laid broomsticks across their doors at night and sprinkled salt on porch steps.[8] But aside from one or two unsuccessful efforts to collect the dust from her footsteps, they did nothing to harm her. As always the black people looked at evil stony-eyed and let it run.

Sula acknowledged none of their attempts at counter-conjure or their gossip and seemed to need the services of nobody. So they watched her far more closely than they watched any other roach or bitch in the town, and their alertness was gratified. Things began to happen.

First off, Teapot knocked on her door to see if she had any bottles. He was the five-year-old son of an indifferent mother, all of whose interests sat around the door of the Time and a Half Pool Hall. Her name was Betty but she was called Teapot's Mamma because being his mamma was precisely

---

8. Traditional methods of warding off witches.

her major failure. When Sula said no, the boy turned around and fell down the steps. He couldn't get up right away and Sula went to help him. His mother, just then tripping home, saw Sula bending over her son's pained face. She flew into a fit of concerned, if drunken, motherhood, and dragged Teapot home. She told everybody that Sula had pushed him, and talked so strongly about it she was forced to abide by the advice of her friends and take him to the county hospital. The two dollars she hated to release turned out to be well spent, for Teapot did have a fracture, although the doctor said poor diet had contributed substantially to the daintiness of his bones. Teapot's Mamma got a lot of attention anyway and immersed herself in a role she had shown no inclination for: motherhood. The very idea of a grown woman hurting her boy kept her teeth on edge. She became the most devoted mother: sober, clean and industrious. No more nickels for Teapot to go to Dick's for a breakfast of Mr. Goodbars and soda pop: no more long hours of him alone or wandering the roads while she was otherwise engaged. Her change was a distinct improvement, although little Teapot did miss those quiet times at Dick's.

Other things happened. Mr. Finley sat on his porch sucking chicken bones, as he had done for thirteen years, looked up, saw Sula, choked on a bone and died on the spot. That incident, and Teapot's Mamma, cleared up for everybody the meaning of the birthmark over her eye; it was not a stemmed rose, or a snake, it was Hannah's ashes marking her from the very beginning.

She came to their church suppers without underwear, bought their steaming platters of food and merely picked at it—relishing nothing, exclaiming over no one's ribs or cobbler. They believed that she was laughing at their God.

And the fury she created in the women of the town was incredible—for she would lay their husbands once and then no more. Hannah had been a nuisance, but she was complimenting the women, in a way, by wanting their husbands. Sula was trying them out and discarding them without any excuse the men could swallow. So the women, to justify their own judgment, cherished their men more, soothed the pride and vanity Sula had bruised.

Among the weighty evidence piling up was the fact that Sula did not look her age. She was near thirty and, unlike them, had lost no teeth, suffered no bruises, developed no ring of fat at the waist or pocket at the back of her neck. It was rumored that she had had no childhood diseases, was never known to have chicken pox, croup or even a runny nose. She had played rough as a child—where were the scars? Except for a funny-shaped finger and that evil birthmark, she was free of any normal signs of vulnerability. Some of the men, who as boys had dated her, remembered that on picnics neither gnats nor mosquitoes would settle on her. Patsy, Hannah's one-time friend, agreed and said not only that, but she had witnessed the fact that when Sula drank beer she never belched.

The most damning evidence, however, came from Dessie, who was a big Daughter Elk[9] and knew things. At one of the social meetings she revealed something to her friends.

---

9. I.e., she held an important office in the Elks, a fraternal organization.

"Yeh, well I noticed something long time ago. Ain't said nothing 'bout it 'cause I wasn't sure what it meant. Well . . . I did mention it to Ivy but not nobody else. I disremember how long ago. 'Bout a month or two I guess 'cause I hadn't put down my new linoleum yet. Did you see it, Cora? It's that kind we saw in the catalogue."

"Naw."

"Get on with it, Dessie."

"Well, Cora was with me when we looked in the catalogue . . ."

"We all know 'bout your linoleum. What we don't know is . . ."

"OK. Let me tell it, will you? Just before the linoleum come I was out front and seed Shadrack carryin' on as usual . . . up by the well . . . walkin' 'round it salutin' and carryin' on. You know how he does . . . hollerin' commands and . . ."

"Will you get on with it?"

"Who's tellin' this? Me or you?"

"You."

"Well, let me tell it then. Like I say, he was just cuttin' up as usual when Miss Sula Mae walks by on the other side of the road. And quick as that"—she snapped her fingers—"he stopped and cut on over 'cross the road, steppin' over to her like a tall turkey in short corn. And guess what? He tips his hat."

"Shadrack don't wear no hat."

"I know that but he tipped it anyway. You know what I mean. He acted like he had a hat and reached up for it and tipped it at her. Now you know Shadrack ain't civil to nobody!"

"Sure ain't."

"Even when you buyin' his fish he's cussin'. If you ain't got the right change he cussin' you. If you act like a fish ain't too fresh he snatch it out of your hand like he doin' you the favor."

"Well, everybody know he a reprobate."

"Yeh, so how come he tip his hat to Sula? How come he don't cuss her?"

"Two devils."

"Exactly!"

"What'd she do when he tipped it? Smile and give him a curtsey?"

"No, and that was the other thing. It was the first time I see her look anything but hateful. Like she smellin' you with her eyes and don't like your soap. When he tipped his hat she put her hand on her throat for a minute and cut out. Went runnin' on up the road to home. And him still standin' there tippin' away. And—this the point I was comin' to—when I went back in the house a big sty come on my eye. And I ain't never had no sty before. Never!"

"That's 'cause you saw it."

"Exactly."

"Devil all right."

"No two ways about it," Dessie said, and she popped the rubber band off the deck of cards to settle them down for a nice long game of bid whist.

Their conviction of Sula's evil changed them in accountable yet mysterious ways. Once the source of their personal misfortune was identified, they had leave to protect and love one another. They began to cherish their husbands and wives, protect their children, repair their homes and in general band together against the devil in their midst. In their world, aberrations were as much a part of nature as grace. It was not for them to expel or annihilate it. They would no more run Sula out of town than they would kill the robins that brought her back, for in their secret awareness of Him, He was not the God of three faces[1] they sang about. They knew quite well that He had four, and that the fourth explained Sula. They had lived with various forms of evil all their days, and it wasn't that they believed God would take care of them. It was rather that they knew God had a brother and that brother hadn't spared God's son, so why should he spare them?

There was no creature so ungodly as to make them destroy it. They could kill easily if provoked to anger, but not by design, which explained why they could not "mob kill" anyone. To do so was not only unnatural, it was undignified. The presence of evil was something to be first recognized, then dealt with, survived, outwitted, triumphed over.

Their evidence against Sula was contrived, but their conclusions about her were not. Sula was distinctly different. Eva's arrogance and Hannah's self-indulgence merged in her and, with a twist that was all her own imagination, she lived out her days exploring her own thoughts and emotions, giving them full reign, feeling no obligation to please anybody unless their pleasure pleased her. As willing to feel pain as to give pain, to feel pleasure as to give pleasure, hers was an experimental life—ever since her mother's remarks sent her flying up those stairs, ever since her one major feeling of responsibility had been exorcised on the bank of a river with a closed place in the middle. The first experience taught her there was no other that you could count on; the second that there was no self to count on either. She had no center, no speck around which to grow. In the midst of a pleasant conversation with someone she might say, "Why do you chew with your mouth open?" not because the answer interested her but because she wanted to see the person's face change rapidly. She was completely free of ambition, with no affection for money, property or things, no greed, no desire to command attention or compliments—no ego. For that reason she felt no compulsion to verify herself—be consistent with herself.

She had clung to Nel as the closest thing to both an other and a self, only to discover that she and Nel were not one and the same thing. She had no thought at all of causing Nel pain when she bedded down with Jude. They had always shared the affection of other people: compared how a boy kissed, what line he used with one and then the other. Marriage, apparently, had changed all that, but having had no intimate knowledge of marriage, having lived in a house with women who thought all men available, and selected from among them with a care only for their tastes, she was ill prepared for the possessiveness of the one person she felt close to. She knew well enough what other women said and felt, or said they felt. But she and Nel had always seen through them. They both knew that those women were not jealous of other women; that they were only afraid of losing their jobs. Afraid their husbands would discover that no uniqueness lay between their legs.

Nel was the one person who had wanted nothing from her, who had accepted all aspects of her. Now she wanted everything, and all because of *that*. Nel was the first person who had been real to her, whose name she knew, who had seen as she had the slant of life that made it possible to

---

1. I.e., the Christian Trinity: the Father, the Son, the Holy Spirit.

stretch it to its limits. Now Nel was one of *them*. One of the spiders whose only thought was the next rung of the web, who dangled in dark dry places suspended by their own spittle, more terrified of the free fall than the snake's breath below. Their, eyes so intent on the wayward stranger who trips into their net, they were blind to the cobalt on their own backs, the moonshine fighting to pierce their corners. If they were touched by the snake's breath, however fatal, they were merely victims and knew how to behave in that role (just as Nel knew how to behave as the wronged wife). But the free fall, oh no, that required—demanded—invention: a thing to do with the wings, a way of holding the legs and most of all a full surrender to the downward flight, if they wished to taste their tongues or stay alive. But alive was what they, and now Nel, did not want to be. Too dangerous. Now Nel belonged to the town and all of its ways. She had given herself over to them, and the flick of their tongues would drive her back into her little dry corner where she would cling to her spittle high above the breath of the snake and the fall.

It had surprised her a little and saddened her a good deal when Nel behaved the way the others would have. Nel was one of the reasons she had drifted back to Medallion, that and the boredom she found in Nashville, Detroit, New Orleans, New York, Philadelphia, Macon and San Diego. All those cities held the same people, working the same mouths, sweating the same sweat. The men who took her to one or another of those places had merged into one large personality: the same language of love, the same entertainments of love, the same cooling of love. Whenever she introduced her private thoughts into their rubbings or goings, they hooded their eyes. They taught her nothing but love tricks, shared nothing but worry, gave nothing but money. She had been looking all along for a friend, and it took her a while to discover that a lover was not a comrade and could never be— for a woman. And that no one would ever be that version of herself which she sought to reach out to and touch with an ungloved hand. There was only her own mood and whim, and if that was all there was, she decided to turn the naked hand toward it, discover it and let others become as intimate with their own selves as she was.

In a way, her strangeness, her naïveté, her craving for the other half of her equation was the consequence of an idle imagination. Had she paints, or clay, or knew the discipline of the dance, or strings; had she anything to engage her tremendous curiosity and her gift for metaphor, she might have exchanged the restlessness and preoccupation with whim for an activity that provided her with all she yearned for. And like any artist with no art form, she became dangerous.

She had lied only once in her life—to Nel about the reason for putting Eva out, and she could lie to her only because she cared about her. When she had come back home, social conversation was impossible for her because she could not lie. She could not say to those old acquaintances, "Hey, girl, you looking good," when she saw how the years had dusted their bronze with ash, the eyes that had once opened wide to the moon bent into grimy sickles of concern. The narrower their lives, the wider their hips. Those with husbands had folded themselves into starched coffins, their sides bursting with other people's skinned dreams and bony regrets. Those without men were like sour-tipped needles featuring one constant empty eye. Those with men had had the sweetness sucked from their breath by ovens and steam kettles. Their children were like distant but exposed wounds whose aches were no less intimate because separate from their flesh. They had looked at the world and back at their children, back at the world and back again at their children, and Sula knew that one clear young eye was all that kept the knife away from the throat's curve.

She was pariah, then, and knew it. Knew that they despised her and believed that they framed their hatred as disgust for the easy way she lay with men. Which was true. She went to bed with men as frequently as she could. It was the only place where she could find what she was looking for: misery and the ability to feel deep sorrow. She had not always been aware that it was sadness that she yearned for. Lovemaking seemed to her, at first, the creation of a special kind of joy. She thought she liked the sootiness of sex and its comedy; she laughed a great deal during the raucous beginnings, and rejected those lovers who regarded sex as healthy or beautiful. Sexual aesthetics bored her. Although she did not regard sex as ugly (ugliness was boring also), she liked to think of it as wicked. But as her experiences multiplied she realized that not only was it not wicked, it was not necessary for her to conjure up the idea of wickedness in order to participate fully. During the lovemaking she found and needed to find the cutting edge. When she left off cooperating with her body and began to assert herself in the act, particles of strength gathered in her like steel shavings drawn to a spacious magnetic center, forming a tight cluster that nothing, it seemed, could break. And there was utmost irony and outrage in lying under someone, in a position of surrender, feeling her own abiding strength and limitless power. But the cluster did break, fall apart, and in her panic to hold it together she leaped from the edge into soundlessness and went down howling, howling in a stinging awareness of the endings of things: an eye of sorrow in the midst of all that hurricane rage of joy. There, in the center of that silence was not eternity but the death of time and a loneliness so profound the word itself had no meaning. For loneliness assumed the absence of other people, and the solitude she found in that desperate terrain had never admitted the possibility of other people. She wept then. Tears for the deaths of the littlest things: the castaway shoes of children; broken stems of marsh grass battered and drowned by the sea; prom photographs of dead women she never knew; wedding rings in pawnshop windows; the tidy bodies of Cornish hens in a nest of rice.

When her partner disengaged himself, she looked up at him in wonder trying to recall his name; and he looked down at her, smiling with tender understanding of the state of tearful gratitude to which he believed he had brought her. She waiting impatiently for him to turn away and settle into a wet skim of satisfaction and light disgust, leaving her to the postcoital privateness in which she met herself, welcomed herself, and joined herself in matchless harmony.

At twenty-nine she knew it would be no other way for her, but she had not counted on the footsteps on the porch, and the beautiful black face that stared at her through the blue-glass window. Ajax.

Looking for all the world as he had seventeen years ago when he had called her pig meat. He was twenty-one then, she twelve. A universe of time between them. Now she was twenty-nine, he thirty-eight, and the lemon-yellow haunches seemed not so far away after all.

She opened the heavy door and saw him standing on the other side of the screen door with two quarts of milk tucked into his arms like marble statues. He smiled and said, "I been lookin' all over for you."

"Why?" she asked.

"To give you these," and he nodded toward one of the quarts of milk.

"I don't like milk," she said.

"But you like bottles don't you?" He held one up. "Ain't that pretty?"

And indeed it was. Hanging from his fingers, framed by a slick blue sky, it looked precious and clean and permanent. She had the distinct impression that he had done something dangerous to get them.

Sula ran her fingernails over the screen thoughtfully for a second and then, laughing, she opened the screen door.

Ajax came in and headed straight for the kitchen. Sula followed slowly. By the time she got to the door he had undone the complicated wire cap and was letting the cold milk run into his mouth.

Sula watched him—or rather the rhythm in his throat—with growing interest. When he had had enough, he poured the rest into the sink, rinsed the bottle out and presented it to her. She took the bottle with one hand and his wrist with the other and pulled him into the pantry. There was no need to go there, for not a soul was in the house, but the gesture came to Hannah's daughter naturally. There in the pantry, empty now of flour sacks, void of row upon row of canned goods, free forever of strings of tiny green peppers, holding the wet milk bottle tight in her arm she stood wide-legged against the wall and pulled from his track-lean hips all the pleasure her thighs could hold.

He came regularly then, bearing gifts: clusters of black berries still on their branches, four meal-fried porgies[2] wrapped in a salmon-colored sheet of the Pittsburgh *Courier*, a handful of jacks, two boxes of lime Jell-Well, a hunk of ice-wagon ice, a can of Old Dutch Cleanser with the bonneted woman chasing dirt with her stick; a page of Tillie the Toiler comics, and more gleaming white bottles of milk.

Contrary to what anybody would have suspected from just seeing him lounging around the pool hall, or shooting at Mr. Finley for beating his own dog, or calling filthy compliments to passing women, Ajax was very nice to women. His women, of course, knew it, and it provoked them into murderous battles over him in the streets, brawling thick-thighed women with knives disturbed many a Friday night with their bloodletting and attracted whooping crowds. On such occasions Ajax stood, along with the crowd, and viewed the fighters with the same golden-eyed indifference with which he watched old men playing checkers. Other than his mother, who sat in her shack with six younger sons working roots,[3] he had never met an interesting woman in his life.

His kindness to them in general was not due to a ritual of seduction (he had no need for it) but rather to the habit he acquired in dealing with his mother, who inspired thoughtfulness and generosity in all her sons.

She was an evil conjure woman, blessed with seven adoring children whose joy it was to bring her the plants, hair, underclothing, fingernail parings, white hens, blood, camphor, pictures, kerosene and footstep dust that she needed, as well as to order Van Van, High John the Conqueror, Little John to Chew, Devil's Shoe String, Chinese Wash, Mustard Seed and the Nine Herbs from Cincinnati.[4] She knew about the weather, omens, the living,

---

2. A type of fish.
3. Conjuring, performing witchcraft.

4. Powders and roots to be used in conjuring.

the dead, dreams and all illnesses and made a modest living with her skills. Had she any teeth or ever straightened her back, she would have been the most gorgeous thing alive, worthy of her sons' worship for her beauty alone, if not for the absolute freedom she allowed them (known in some quarters as neglect) and the weight of her hoary knowledge.

This woman Ajax loved, and after her—airplanes. There was nothing in between. And when he was not sitting enchanted listening to his mother's words, he thought of airplanes, and pilots, and the deep sky that held them both. People thought that those long trips he took to large cities in the state were for some sophisticated good times they could not imagine but only envy; actually he was leaning against the barbed wire of airports, or nosing around hangars just to hear the talk of the men who were fortunate enough to be in the trade. The rest of the time, the time he was not watching his mother's magic or thinking of airplanes, he spent in the idle pursuits of bachelors without work in small towns. He had heard all the stories about Sula, and they aroused his curiosity. Her elusiveness and indifference to established habits of behavior reminded him of his mother, who was as stubborn in her pursuits of the occult as the women of Greater Saint Matthew's were in the search for redeeming grace. So when his curiosity was high enough he picked two bottles of milk off the porch of some white family and went to see her, suspecting that this was perhaps the only other woman he knew whose life was her own, who could deal with life efficiently, and who was not interested in nailing him.

Sula, too, was curious. She knew nothing about him except the word he had called out to her years ago and the feeling he had excited in her then. She had grown quite accustomed to the clichés of other people's lives as well as her own increasing dissatisfaction with Medallion. If she could have thought of a place to go, she probably would have left, but that was before Ajax looked at her through the blue glass and held the milk aloft like a trophy.

But it was not the presents that made her wrap him up in her thighs. They were charming, of course (especially the jar of butterflies he let loose in the bedroom), but her real pleasure was the fact that he talked to her. They had genuine conversations. He did not speak down to her or at her, nor content himself with puerile questions about her life or monologues of his own activities. Thinking she was possibly brilliant, like his mother, he seemed to expect brilliance from her, and she delivered. And in all of it, he listened more than he spoke. His clear comfort at being in her presence, his lazy willingness to tell her all about fixes[5] and the powers of plants, his refusal to baby or protect her, his assumption that she was both tough and wise—all of that coupled with a wide generosity of spirit only occasionally erupting into vengeance sustained Sula's interest and enthusiasm.

His idea of bliss (on earth as opposed to bliss in the sky) was a long bath in piping-hot water—his head on the cool white rim, his eyes closed in reverie.

"Soaking in hot water give you a bad back." Sula stood in the doorway looking at his knees glistening just at the surface of the soap-gray water.

"Soaking in Sula give me a bad back."

"Worth it?"

5. Spells.

"Don't know yet. Go 'way."

"Airplanes?"

"Airplanes."

"Lindbergh know about you?"

"Go 'way."

She went and waited for him in Eva's high bed, her head turned to the boarded-up window. She was smiling, thinking how like Jude's was his craving to do the white man's work, when two deweys came in with their beautiful teeth and said, "We sick."

Sula turned her head slowly and murmured, "Get well."

"We need some medicine."

"Look in the bathroom."

"Ajax in there."

"Then wait."

"We sick now."

Sula leaned over the bed, picked up a shoe and threw it at them.

"Cocksucker!" they screamed, and she leaped out of the bed naked as a yard dog. She caught the redheaded dewey by his shirt and held him by the heels over the banister until he wet his pants. The other dewey was joined by the third, and they delved into their pockets for stones, which they threw at her. Sula, ducking and tottering with laughter, carried the wet dewey to the bedroom and when the other two followed her, deprived of all weapons except their teeth, Sula had dropped the first dewey on the bed and was fishing in her purse. She gave each of them a dollar bill which they snatched and then scooted off down the stairs to Dick's to buy the catarrh remedy they loved to drink.

Ajax came sopping wet into the room and lay down on the bed to let the air dry him. They were both still for a long time until he reached out and touched her arm.

He liked for her to mount him so he could see her towering above him and call soft obscenities up into her face. As she rocked there, swayed there, like a Georgia pine on its knees, high above the slipping, falling smile, high above the golden eyes and the velvet helmet of hair, rocking, swaying, she focused her thoughts to bar the creeping disorder that was flooding her hips. She looked down, down from what seemed an awful height at the head of the man whose lemon-yellow gabardines had been the first sexual excitement she'd known. Letting her thoughts dwell on his face in order to confine, for just a while longer, the drift of her flesh toward the high silence of orgasm.

If I take a chamois and rub real hard on the bone, right on the ledge of your cheek bone, some of the black will disappear. It will flake away into the chamois and underneath there will be gold leaf. I can see it shining through the black. I know it is there . . .

How high she was over his wand-lean body, how slippery was his sliding sliding smile.

And if I take a nail file or even Eva's old paring knife—that will do—and scrape away at the gold, it will fall away and there will be alabaster. The alabaster is what gives your face its planes, its curves. That is why your mouth smiling does not reach your eyes. Alabaster is giving it a gravity that resists a total smile.

The height and the swaying dizzied her, so she bent down and let her breasts graze his chest.

Then I can take a chisel and small tap hammer and tap away at the alabaster. It will crack then like ice under the pick, and through the breaks I will see the loam, fertile, free of pebbles and twigs. For it is the loam that is giving you that smell.

She slipped her hands under his armpits, for it seemed as though she would not be able to dam the spread of weakness she felt under her skin without holding on to something.

I will put my hand deep into your soil, lift it, sift it with my fingers, feel its warm surface and dewy chill below.

She put her head under his chin with no hope in the world of keeping anything at all at bay.

I will water your soil, keep it rich and moist. But how much? How much water to keep the loam moist? And how much loam will I need to keep my water still? And when do the two make mud?

He swallowed her mouth just as her thighs had swallowed his genitals, and the house was very, very quiet.

◎ ◎ ◎

Sula began to discover what possession was. Not love, perhaps, but possession or at least the desire for it. She was astounded by so new and alien a feeling. First there was the morning of the night before when she actually wondered if Ajax would come by that day. Then there was an afternoon when she stood before the mirror finger-tracing the laugh lines around her mouth and trying to decide whether she was good-looking or not. She ended this deep perusal by tying a green ribbon in her hair. The green silk made a rippling whisper as she slid it into her hair—a whisper that could easily have been Hannah's chuckle, a soft slow nasal hiss she used to emit when something amused her. Like women sitting for two hours under the marcelling irons[6] only to wonder two days later how soon they would need another appointment. The ribbon-tying was followed by other activity, and when Ajax came that evening, bringing her a reed whistle he had carved that morning, not only was the green ribbon still in her hair, but the bathroom was gleaming, the bed was made, and the table was set for two.

He gave her the reed whistle, unlaced his shoes and sat in the rocking chair in the kitchen.

Sula walked toward him and kissed his mouth. He ran his fingers along the nape of her neck.

"I bet you ain't even missed Tar Baby, have you?" he asked.

"Missed? No. Where is he?"

Ajax smiled at her delicious indifference. "Jail."

"Since when?"

"Last Saturday."

"Picked up for drunk?"

"Little bit more than that," he answered and went ahead to tell her about his own involvement in another of Tar Baby's misfortunes.

On Saturday afternoon Tar Baby had stumbled drunk into traffic on the New River Road. A woman driver swerved to avoid him and hit another car. When the police came, they recognized the woman as the mayor's niece and arrested Tar Baby. Later, after the word got out, Ajax and two other

6. Heated curling irons used for waving hair.

men went to the station to see about him. At first they wouldn't let them in. But they relented after Ajax and the other two just stood around for one hour and a half and repeated their request at regular intervals. When they finally got permission to go in and looked in at him in the cell, he was twisted up in a corner badly beaten and dressed in nothing but extremely soiled underwear. Ajax and the other men asked the officer why Tar Baby couldn't have back his clothes. "It ain't right," they said, "to let a grown man lay around in his own shit."

The policeman, obviously in agreement with Eva, who had always maintained that Tar Baby was white, said that if the prisoner didn't like to live in shit, he should come down out of those hills, and live like a decent white man.

More words were exchanged, hot words and dark, and the whole thing ended with the arraignment of the three black men, and an appointment to appear in civil court Thursday next.

Ajax didn't seem too bothered by any of it. More annoyed and inconvenienced than anything else. He had had several messes with the police, mostly in gambling raids, and regarded them as the natural hazards of Negro life.

But Sula, the green ribbon shining in her hair, was flooded with an awareness of the impact of the outside world on Ajax. She stood up and arranged herself on the arm of the rocking chair. Putting her fingers deep into the velvet of his hair, she murmured, "Come on. Lean on me."

Ajax blinked. Then he looked swiftly into her face. In her words, in her voice, was a sound he knew well. For the first time he saw the green ribbon. He looked around and saw the gleaming kitchen and the table set for two and detected the scent of the nest. Every hackle on his body rose, and he knew that very soon she would, like all of her sisters before her, put to him the death-knell question "Where you been?" His eyes dimmed with a mild and momentary regret.

He stood and mounted the stairs with her and entered the spotless bathroom where the dust had been swept from underneath the claw-foot tub. He was trying to remember the date of the air show in Dayton. As he came into the bedroom, he saw Sula lying on fresh white sheets, wrapped in the deadly odor of freshly applied cologne.

He dragged her under him and made love to her with the steadiness and the intensity of a man about to leave for Dayton.

Every now and then she looked around for tangible evidence of his having ever been there. Where were the butterflies? the blueberries? the whistling reed? She could find nothing, for he had left nothing but his stunning absence. An absence so decorative, so ornate, it was difficult for her to understand how she had ever endured, without falling dead or being consumed, his magnificent presence.

The mirror by the door was not a mirror by the door, it was an altar where he stood for only a moment to put on his cap before going out. The red rocking chair was a rocking of his own hips as he sat in the kitchen. Still, there was nothing of his—his own—that she could find. It was as if she were afraid she had hallucinated him and needed proof to the contrary. His absence was everywhere, stinging everything, giving the furnishings primary colors, sharp outlines to the corners of rooms and gold light to the dust collecting on table tops. When he was there he pulled everything toward himself. Not only her eyes and all her senses but also inanimate things seemed to exist because of him, backdrops to his presence. Now that he had gone, these things, so long subdued by his presence, were glamorized in his wake.

Then one day, burrowing in a dresser drawer, she found what she had been looking for: proof that he had been there, his driver's license. It contained just what she needed for verification—his vital statistics: Born 1901, height 5'11", weight 152 lbs., eyes brown, hair black, color black. Oh yes, skin black. Very black. So black that only a steady careful rubbing with steel wool would remove it, and as it was removed there was the glint of gold leaf and under the gold leaf the cold alabaster and deep, deep down under the cold alabaster more black only this time the black of warm loam.

But what was this? Albert Jacks? His name was Albert Jacks? A. Jacks. She had thought it was Ajax. All those years. Even from the time she walked by the pool hall and looked away from him sitting astride a wooden chair, looked away to keep from seeing the wide space of intolerable orderliness between his legs; the openness that held no sign, no sign at all, of the animal that lurked in his trousers; looked away from the insolent nostrils and the smile that kept slipping and falling, falling, falling so she wanted to reach out with her hand to catch it before it fell to the pavement and was sullied by the cigarette butts and bottle caps and spittle at his feet and the feet of other men who sat or stood around outside the pool hall, calling, singing out to her and Nel and grown women too with lyrics like *pig meat* and *brown sugar* and *jailbait* and *O Lord, what have I done to deserve the wrath*, and *Take me, Jesus, I have seen the promised land*, and *Do, Lord, remember me* in voices mellowed by hopeless passion into gentleness. Even then, when she and Nel were trying hard not to dream of him and not to think of him when they touched the softness in their underwear or undid their braids as soon as they left home to let the hair bump and wave around their ears, or wrapped the cotton binding around their chests so the nipples would not break through their blouses and give him cause to smile his slipping, falling smile, which brought the blood rushing to their skin. And even later, when for the first time in her life she had lain in bed with a man and said his name involuntarily or said it truly meaning *him*, the name she was screaming and saying was not his at all.

Sula stood with a worn slip of paper in her fingers and said aloud to no one, "I didn't even know his name. And if I didn't know his name, then there is nothing I did know and I have known nothing ever at all since the one thing I wanted was to know his name so how could he help but leave me since he was making love to a woman who didn't even know his name.

"When I was a little girl the heads of my paper dolls came off, and it was a long time before I discovered that my own head would not fall off if I bent my neck. I used to walk around holding it very stiff because I thought a strong wind or a heavy push would snap my neck. Nel was the one who told me the truth. But she was wrong. I did not hold my head stiff enough when I met him and so I lost it just like the dolls.

"It's just as well he left. Soon I would have torn the flesh from his face just to see if I was right about the gold and nobody would have understood that kind of curiosity. They would have believed that I wanted to hurt him just like the little boy who fell down the steps and broke his leg and the people think I pushed him just because I looked at it."

Holding the driver's license she crawled into bed and fell into a sleep full of dreams of cobalt blue.

When she awoke, there was a melody in her head she could not identify or recall ever hearing before. "Perhaps I made it up," she thought. Then it came to her—the name of the song and all its lyrics just as she had heard it many times before. She sat on the edge of the bed thinking, "There aren't any more new songs and I have sung all the ones there are. I have sung them all. I have sung all the songs there are." She lay down again on the bed and sang a little wandering tune made up of the words *I have sung all the songs all the songs I have sung all the songs there are* until, touched by her own lullaby, she grew drowsy, and in the hollow of near-sleep she tasted the acridness of gold, left the chill of alabaster and smelled the dark, sweet stench of loam.

1940

"I heard you was sick. Anything I can do for you?"

She had practiced not just the words but the tone, the pitch of her voice. It should be calm, matter-of-fact, but strong in sympathy—for the illness though, not for the patient.

The sound of her voice as she heard it in her head betrayed no curiosity, no pride, just the inflection of any good woman come to see about a sick person who, incidentally, had such visits from nobody else.

For the first time in three years she would be looking at the stemmed rose that hung over the eye of her enemy. Moreover, she would be doing it with the taste of Jude's exit in her mouth, with the resentment and shame that even yet pressed for release in her stomach. She would be facing the black rose that Jude had kissed and looking at the nostrils of the woman who had twisted her love for her own children into something so thick and monstrous she was afraid to show it lest it break loose and smother them with its heavy paw. A cumbersome bear-love that, given any rein, would suck their breath away in its crying need for honey.

Because Jude's leaving was so complete, the full responsibility of the household was Nel's. There were no more fifty dollars in brown envelopes to count on, so she took to cleaning rather than fret away the tiny seaman's pension her parents lived on. And just this past year she got a better job working as a chambermaid in the same hotel Jude had worked in. The tips were only fair, but the hours were good—she was home when the children got out of school.

At thirty her hot brown eyes had turned to agate, and her skin had taken on the sheen of maple struck down, split and sanded at the height of its green. Virtue, bleak and drawn, was her only mooring. It brought her to Number 7 Carpenter's Road and the door with the blue glass; it helped her to resist scratching the screen as in days gone by; it hid from her the true motives for her charity, and, finally, it gave her voice the timbre she wanted it to have: free of delight or a lip-smacking "I told you so" with which the news of Sula's illness had been received up in the Bottom—free of the least hint of retribution.

Now she stood in Eva's old bedroom, looking down at that dark rose, aware of the knife-thin arms sliding back and forth over the quilt and the boarded-up window Eva had jumped out of.

Sula looked up and without a second's pause followed Nel's example of leaving out the greeting when she spoke.

"As a matter of fact, there is. I got a prescription. Nathan usually goes for me but he . . . school don't let out till three. Could you run it over to the drugstore?"

"Where is it?" Nel was glad to have a concrete errand. Conversation would be difficult. (Trust Sula to pick up a relationship exactly where it lay.)

"Look in my bag. No. Over there."

Nel walked to the dresser and opened the purse with the beaded clasp. She saw only a watch and the folded prescription down inside. No wallet, no change purse. She turned to Sula: "Where's your . . ."

But Sula was looking at the boarded-up window. Something in her eye right there in the corner stopped Nel from completing her question. That and the slight flare of the nostrils—a shadow of a snarl. Nel took the piece of paper and picked up her own purse, saying, "OK. I'll be right back."

As soon as the door was shut, Sula breathed through her mouth. While Nel was in the room the pain had increased. Now that this new pain killer, the one she had been holding in reserve, was on the way her misery was manageable. She let a piece of her mind lay on Nel. It was funny, sending Nel off to that drugstore right away like that, after she had not seen her to speak to for years. The drugstore was where Edna Finch's Mellow House used to be years back when they were girls. Where they used to go, the two of them, hand in hand, for the 18-cent ice-cream sundaes, past the Time and a Half Pool Hall, where the sprawling men said "pig meat," and they sat in that cool room with the marble-top tables and ate the first ice-cream sundaes of their lives. Now Nel was going back there alone and Sula was waiting for the medicine the doctor said not to take until the pain got really bad. And she supposed "really bad" was now. Although you could never tell. She wondered for an instant what Nellie wanted; why she had come. Did she want to gloat? Make up? Following this line of thought required more concentration than she could muster. Pain was greedy; it demanded all of her attention. But it was good that this new medicine, the reserve, would be brought to her by her old friend. Nel, she remembered, always thrived on a crisis. The closed place in the water; Hannah's funeral. Nel was the best. When Sula imitated her, or tried to, those long years ago, it always ended up in some action noteworthy not for its coolness but mostly for its being bizarre. The one time she tried to protect Nel, she had cut off her own finger tip and earned not Nel's gratitude but her disgust. From then on she had let her emotions dictate her behavior.

She could hear Nel's footsteps long before she opened the door and put the medicine on the table near the bed.

As Sula poured the liquid into a sticky spoon, Nel began the sickroom conversation.

"You look fine, Sula."

"You lying, Nellie. I look bad." She gulped the medicine.

"No. I haven't seen you for a long time, but you look . . ."

"You don't have to do that, Nellie. It's going to be all right."

"What ails you? Have they said?"

Sula licked the corners of her lips. "You want to talk about that?"

Nel smiled, slightly, at the bluntness she had forgotten. "No. No, I don't, but you sure you should be staying up here alone?"

"Nathan comes by. The deweys sometimes, and Tar Baby . . ."

"That ain't help, Sula. You need to be with somebody grown. Somebody who can . . ."

"I'd rather be here, Nellie."

"You know you don't have to be proud with me."

"Proud?" Sula's laughter broke through the phlegm. "What you talking about? I like my own dirt, Nellie. I'm not proud. You sure have forgotten me."

"Maybe. Maybe not. But you a woman and you alone."

"And you? Ain't you alone?"

"I'm not sick. I work."

"Yes. Of course you do. Work's good for you, Nellie. It don't do nothing for me."

"You never *had* to."

"I never would."

"There's something to say for it, Sula. 'Specially if you don't want people to have to do for you."

"Neither one, Nellie. Neither one."

"You can't have it all, Sula." Nel was getting exasperated with her arrogance, with her lying at death's door still smart-talking.

"Why? I can do it all, why can't I have it all?"

"You *can't* do it all. You a woman and a colored woman at that. You can't act like a man. You can't be walking around all independent-like, doing whatever you like, taking what you want, leaving what you don't."

"You repeating yourself."

"How repeating myself?"

"You say I'm a woman and colored. Ain't that the same as being a man?"

"I don't think so and you wouldn't either if you had children."

"Then I really would act like what you call a man. Every man I ever knew left his children."

"Some were taken."

"Wrong, Nellie. The word is 'left.'"

"You still going to know everything, ain't you?"

"I don't know everything, I just do everything."

"Well, you don't do what I do."

"You think I don't know what your life is like just because I ain't living it? I know what every colored woman in this country is doing."

"What's that?"

"Dying. Just like me. But the difference is they dying like a stump. Me, I'm going down like one of those redwoods. I sure did live in this world."

"Really? What have you got to show for it?"

"Show? To who? Girl, I got my mind. And what goes on in it. Which is to say, I got me."

"Lonely, ain't it?"

"Yes. But my lonely is *mine*. Now your lonely is somebody else's. Made by somebody else and handed to you. Ain't that something? A secondhand lonely."

Nel sat back on the little wooden chair. Anger skipped but she realized that Sula was probably just showing off. No telling what shape she was really in, but there was no point in saying anything other than what was the truth. "I always understood how you could take a man. Now I understand why you can't keep none."

"Is that what I'm supposed to do? Spend my life keeping a man?"

"They worth keeping, Sula."

"They ain't worth more than me. And besides, I never loved no man because he was worth it. Worth didn't have nothing to do with it."

"What did?"

"My mind did. That's all."

"Well I guess that's it. You own the world and the rest of us is renting. You ride the pony and we shovel the shit. I didn't come up here for this kind of talk, Sula . . ."

"No?"

"No. I come to see about you. But now that you opened it up, I may as well close it." Nel's fingers closed around the brass rail of the bed. Now she would ask her. "How come you did it, Sula?"

There was a silence but Nel felt no obligation to fill it.

Sula stirred a little under the covers. She looked bored as she sucked her teeth. "Well, there was this space in front of me, behind me, in my head. Some space. And Jude filled it up. That's all. He just filled up the space."

"You mean you didn't even love him?" The feel of the brass was in Nel's mouth. "It wasn't even loving him?"

Sula looked toward the boarded-up window again. Her eyes fluttered as if she were about to fall off into sleep.

"But . . ." Nel held her stomach in. "But what about me? What about me? Why didn't you think about me? Didn't I count? I never hurt you. What did you take him for if you didn't love him and why didn't you think about me?" And then, "I was good to you, Sula, why don't that matter?"

Sula turned her head away from the boarded window. Her voice was quiet and the stemmed rose over her eye was very dark. "It matters, Nel, but only to you. Not to anybody else. Being good to somebody is just like being mean to somebody. Risky. You don't get nothing for it."

Nel took her hands from the brass railing. She was annoyed with herself. Finally when she had gotten the nerve to ask the question, the right question, it made no difference. Sula couldn't give her a sensible answer because she didn't know. Would be, in fact, the last to know. Talking to her about right and wrong was like talking to the deweys. She picked at the fringe on Sula's bedspread and said softly, "We were friends."

"Oh, yes. Good friends," Sula said.

"And you didn't love me enough to leave him alone. To let him love me. You had to take him away."

"What you mean take him away? I didn't kill him, I just fucked him. If we were such good friends, how come you couldn't get over it?"

"You laying there in that bed without a dime or a friend to your name having done all the dirt you did in this town and you still expect folks to love you?"

Sula raised herself up on her elbows. Her face glistened with the dew of fever. She opened her mouth as though to say something, then fell back on the pillows and sighed. "Oh, they'll love me all right. It will take time, but they'll love me." The sound of her voice was as soft and distant as the look in her eyes. "After all the old women have lain with the teen-agers; when all the young girls have slept with their old drunken uncles; after all the black men fuck all the white ones; when all the white women kiss all the black ones; when the guards have raped all the jailbirds and after all the whores make love to their grannies; after all the faggots get their mothers' trim;

when Lindbergh sleeps with Bessie Smith and Norma Shearer makes it with Stepin Fetchit;[7] after all the dogs have fucked all the cats and every weathervane on every barn flies off the roof to mount the hogs . . . then there'll be a little love left over for me. And I know just what it will feel like."

She closed her eyes then and thought of the wind pressing her dress between her legs as she ran up the bank of the river to four leaf-locked trees and the digging of holes in the earth.

Embarrassed, irritable and a little bit ashamed, Nel rose to go. "Goodbye, Sula. I don't reckon I'll be back."

She opened the door and heard Sula's low whisper. "Hey, girl." Nel paused and turned her head but not enough to see her.

"How you know?" Sula asked.

"Know what?" Nel still wouldn't look at her.

"About who was good. How you know it was you?"

"What you mean?"

"I mean maybe it wasn't you. Maybe it was me."

Nel took two steps out the door and closed it behind her. She walked down the hall and down the four flights of steps. The house billowed around her light then dark, full of presences without sounds. The deweys, Tar Baby, the newly married couples, Mr. Buckland Reed, Patsy, Valentine, and the beautiful Hannah Peace. Where were they? Eva out at the old folks' home, the deweys living anywhere, Tar Baby steeped in wine, and Sula upstairs in Eva's bed with a boarded-up window and an empty pocketbook on the dresser.

When Nel closed the door, Sula reached for more medicine. Then she turned the pillow over to its cool side and thought about her old friend. "So she will walk on down that road, her back so straight in that old green coat, the strap of her handbag pushed back all the way to the elbow, thinking how much I have cost her and never remember the days when we were two throats and one eye and we had no price."

Pictures drifted through her head as lightly as dandelion spores: the blue eagle that swallowed the E of the Sherman's Mellowe wine that Tar Baby drank; the pink underlid of Hannah's eye as she probed for a fleck of coal dust or a lash. She thought of looking out of the windows of all those trains and buses, looking at the feet and backs of all those people. Nothing was ever different. They were all the same. All of the words and all of the smiles, every tear and every gag just something to do.

"That's the same sun I looked at when I was twelve, the same pear trees. If I live a hundred years my urine will flow the same way, my armpits and breath will smell the same. My hair will grow from the same holes. I didn't mean anything. I never meant anything. I stood there watching her burn and was thrilled. I wanted her to keep on jerking like that, to keep on dancing."

Then she had the dream again. The Clabber Girl Baking Powder lady was smiling and beckoning to her, one hand under her apron. When Sula came near she disintegrated into white dust, which Sula was hurriedly trying to

7. Actor (1902–1985) who played stereotypical Hollywood blacks (grinning, lazy, and slow) in films from the 1920s through the 1950s. Charles Lindbergh (1902–1974), white aviator. Smith (1894?–1937), black blues singer. Shearer (1900–1983), white actress of the 1920s and 1930s.

stuff into the pockets of her blue-flannel housecoat. The disintegration was awful to see, but worse was the feel of the powder—its starchy slipperiness as she tried to collect it by handfuls. The more she scooped, the more it billowed. At last it covered her, filled her eyes, her nose, her throat, and she woke gagging and overwhelmed with the smell of smoke.

Pain took hold. First a fluttering as of doves in her stomach, then a kind of burning, followed by a spread of thin wires to other parts of her body. Once the wires of liquid pain were in place, they jelled and began to throb. She tried concentrating on the throbs, identifying them as waves, hammer strokes, razor edges or small explosions. Soon even the variety of the pain bored her and there was nothing to do, for it was joined by fatigue so great she could not make a fist or fight the taste of oil at the back of her tongue.

Several times she tried to cry out, but the fatigue barely let her open her lips, let alone take the deep breath necessary to scream. So she lay there wondering how soon she would gather enough strength to lift her arm and push the rough quilt away from her chin and whether she should turn her cheek to the cooler side of the pillow now or wait till her face was thoroughly soaked and the move would be more refreshing. But she was reluctant to move her face for another reason. If she turned her head, she would not be able to see the boarded-up window Eva jumped out of. And looking at those four wooden planks with the steel rod slanting across them was the only peace she had. The sealed window soothed her with its sturdy termination, its unassailable finality. It was as though for the first time she was completely alone—where she had always wanted to be—free of the possibility of distraction. It would be here, only here, held by this blind window high above the elm tree, that she might draw her legs up to her chest, close her eyes, put her thumb in her mouth and float over and down the tunnels, just missing the dark walls, down, down until she met a rain scent and would know the water was near, and she would curl into its heavy softness and it would envelop her, carry her, and wash her tired flesh always. Always. Who said that? She tried hard to think. Who was it that had promised her a sleep of water always? The effort to recall was too great; it loosened a knot in her chest that turned her thoughts again to the pain.

While in this state of weary anticipation, she noticed that she was not breathing, that her heart had stopped completely. A crease of fear touched her breast, for any second there was sure to be a violent explosion in her brain, a gasping for breath. Then she realized, or rather she sensed, that there was not going to be any pain. She was not breathing because she didn't have to. Her body did not need oxygen. She was dead.

Sula felt her face smiling. "Well, I'll be damned," she thought, "it didn't even hurt. Wait'll I tell Nel."

1941

The death of Sula Peace was the best news folks up in the Bottom had had since the promise of work at the tunnel. Of the few who were not afraid to witness the burial of a witch and who had gone to the cemetery, some had come just to verify her being put away but stayed to sing "Shall We Gather at the River" for politeness' sake, quite unaware of the bleak promise of their song. Others came to see that nothing went awry, that the shallow-minded and small-hearted kept their meanness at bay, and that the entire event be characterized by that abiding gentleness of spirit to which they themselves had arrived by the simple determination not to let anything—anything at all: not failed crops, not rednecks, lost jobs, sick children, rotten potatoes, broken pipes, bug-ridden flour, third-class coal, educated social workers, thieving insurance men, garlic-ridden hunkies, corrupt Catholics, racist Protestants, cowardly Jews, slaveholding Moslems, jackleg nigger preachers, squeamish Chinamen, cholera, dropsy or the Black Plague, let alone a strange woman—keep them from their God.

In any case, both the raw-spirited and the gentle who came—not to the white funeral parlor but to the colored part of the Beechnut Cemetery—felt that either *because* Sula was dead or just *after* she was dead a brighter day was dawning. There were signs. The rumor that the tunnel spanning the river would use Negro workers became an announcement. Planned, abandoned and replanned for years, this project had finally begun in 1937. For three years there were rumors that blacks would work it, and hope was high in spite of the fact that the River Road leading to the tunnel had encouraged similar hopes in 1927 but had ended up being built entirely by white labor—hillbillies and immigrants taking even the lowest jobs. But the tunnel itself was another matter. The craft work—no, they would not get that. But it was a major job, and the government seemed to favor opening up employment to black workers. It meant black men would not have to sweep Medallion to eat, or leave the town altogether for the steel mills in Akron and along Lake Erie.

The second sign was the construction begun on an old people's home. True, it was more renovation than construction, but the blacks were free, or so it was said, to occupy it. Some said that the very transfer of Eva from the ramshackle house that passed for a colored women's nursing home to the bright new one was a clear sign of the mystery of God's ways, His mighty thumb having been seen at Sula's throat.

So it was with a strong sense of hope that the people in the Bottom watched October close.

Then Medallion turned silver. It seemed sudden, but actually there had been days and days of no snow—just frost—when, late one afternoon, a rain fell and froze. Way down Carpenter's Road, where the concrete sidewalks started, children hurried to the sliding places before shopkeepers and old women sprinkled stove ashes, like ancient onyx, onto the new-minted silver. They hugged trees simply to hold for a moment all that life and largeness stilled in glass, and gazed at the sun pressed against the gray sky like a worn doubloon, wondering all the while if the world were coming to an end. Grass stood blade by blade, shocked into separateness by an ice that held for days.

Late-harvesting things were ruined, of course, and fowl died of both chill and rage. Cider turned to ice and split the jugs, forcing the men to drink their cane liquor too soon. It was better down in the valley, since, as always, the hills protected it, but up in the Bottom black folks suffered heavily in their thin houses and thinner clothes. The ice-cold wind bled what little heat they had through windowpanes and ill-fitting doors. For days on end they were virtually housebound, venturing out only to coal-bins or right next door for the trading of vital foodstuffs. Never to the stores. No deliveries were being made anyway, and when they were, the items were saved for better-paying white customers. Women could not make it down the icy slopes and therefore missed days of wages they sorely needed.

The consequence of all that ice was a wretched Thanksgiving of tiny tough birds, heavy pork cakes, and pithy sweet potatoes. By the time the ice began to melt and the first barge was seen shuddering through the ice skim on the river, everybody under fifteen had croup, or scarlet fever, and those over had chilblains, rheumatism, pleurisy,[8] earaches and a world of other ailments.

Still it was not those illnesses or even the ice that marked the beginning of the trouble, that self-fulfilled prophecy that Shadrack carried on his tongue. As soon as the silvering began, long before the cider cracked the jugs, there was something wrong. A falling away, a dislocation was taking place. Hard on the heels of the general relief that Sula's death brought a restless irritability took hold. Teapot, for example, went into the kitchen and asked his mother for some sugar-butter-bread. She got up to fix it and found that she had no butter, only oleomargarine. Too tired to mix the saffron-colored powder into the hard cake of oleo, she simply smeared the white stuff on the bread and sprinkled the sugar over it. Teapot tasted the difference and refused to eat it. This keenest of insults that a mother can feel, the rejection by a child of her food, bent her into fury and she beat him as she had not done since Sula knocked him down the steps. She was not alone. Other mothers who had defended their children from Sula's malevolence (or who had defended their positions as mothers from Sula's scorn for the role) now had nothing to rub up against. The tension was gone and so was the reason for the effort they had made. Without her mockery, affection for others sank into flaccid disrepair. Daughters who had complained bitterly about the responsibilities of taking care of their aged mothers-in-law had altered when Sula locked Eva away, and they began cleaning those old women's spittoons without a murmur. Now that Sula was dead and done with, they returned to a steeping resentment of the burdens of old people. Wives uncoddled their husbands; there seemed no further need to reinforce their vanity. And even those Negroes who had moved down from Canada to Medallion, who remarked every chance they got that they had never been slaves, felt a loosening of the reactionary compassion for Southern-born blacks Sula had inspired in them. They returned to their original claims of superiority.

The normal meanness that the winter brought was compounded by the small-spiritedness that hunger and scarlet fever produced. Even a definite and witnessed interview of four colored men (and the promise of more in the spring) at the tunnel site could not break the cold vise of that lean and bitter year's end.

Christmas came one morning and haggled everybody's nerves like a dull ax—too shabby to cut clean but too heavy to ignore. The children lay wall-eyed on creaking beds or pallets near the stove, sucking peppermint and oranges in between coughs while their mothers stomped the floors in rage at the cakes that did not rise because the stove fire had been so stingy; at the curled bodies of men who chose to sleep the day away rather than face the silence made by the absence of Lionel trains, drums, cry-baby dolls and rocking horses. Teen-agers sneaked into the Elmira Theater in the afternoon and let Tex Ritter[9] free them from the recollection of their fathers'

---

8. Inflammation around the lungs. "Croup": inflammation of the larynx. "Scarlet fever": contagious bacterial disease. Croup and scarlet fever were once common childhood illnesses.

"Chilblains": sores (usually on the hands or feet) caused by prolonged exposure to cold.
9. Country music pioneer and actor (1906–1974).

shoes, yawning in impotence under the bed. Some of them had a bottle of wine, which they drank at the feet of the glittering Mr. Ritter, making such a ruckus the manager had to put them out. The white people who came with Christmas bags of rock candy and old clothes were hard put to get a *Yes'm, thank you*, out of those sullen mouths.

Just as the ice lingered in October, so did the phlegm of December— which explained the enormous relief brought on by the first three days of 1941. It was as though the season had exhausted itself, for on January first the temperature shot up to sixty-one degrees and slushed the whiteness overnight. On January second drab patches of grass could be seen in the fields. On January third the sun came out—and so did Shadrack with his rope, his bell and his childish dirge.

He had spent the night before watching a tiny moon. The people, the voices that kept him company, were with him less and less. Now there were long periods when he heard nothing except the wind in the trees and the plop of buckeyes on the earth. In the winter, when the fish were too hard to get to, he did picking-up jobs for small businessmen (nobody would have him in or even near their homes), and thereby continued to have enough money for liquor. Yet the drunk times were becoming deeper but more seldom. It was as though he no longer needed to drink to forget whatever it was he could not remember. Now he could not remember that he had ever forgotten anything. Perhaps that was why for the first time after that cold day in France he was beginning to miss the presence of other people. Shadrack had improved enough to feel lonely. If he was lonely before, he didn't know it because the noise he kept up, the roaring, the busyness, protected him from knowing it. Now the compulsion to activity, to filling up the time when he was not happily fishing on the riverbank, had dwindled. He sometimes fell asleep before he got drunk; sometimes spent whole days looking at the river and the sky; and more and more he relinquished the military habits of cleanliness in his shack. Once a bird flew into his door—one of the robins during the time there was a plague of them. It stayed, looking for an exit, for the better part of an hour. When the bird found the window and flew away, Shadrack was grieved and actually waited and watched for its return. During those days of waiting, he did not make his bed, or sweep, or shake out the little rag-braid rug, and almost forgot to slash with his fish knife the passing day on his calendar. When he did return to housekeeping, it was not with the precision he had always insisted upon. The messier his house got, the lonelier he felt, and it was harder and harder to conjure up sergeants, and orderlies, and invading armies; harder and harder to hear the gunfire and keep the platoon marching in time. More frequently now he looked at and fondled the one piece of evidence that he once had a visitor in his house: a child's purple-and-white belt. The one the little girl left behind when she came to see him. Shadrack remembered the scene clearly. He had stepped into the door and there was a tear-stained face turning, turning toward him; eyes hurt and wondering; mouth parted in an effort to ask a question. She had wanted something—from him. Not fish, not work, but something only he could give. She had a tadpole over her eye (that was how he knew she was a friend—she had the mark of the fish he loved), and one of her braids had come undone. But when he looked at her face he had seen also the skull beneath, and thinking she saw it too—knew it was there and was afraid—he tried to think of something to say to comfort her, something to stop the hurt from spilling out of her eyes. So he had said "always," so she would not have to be afraid of the change—the falling away of skin, the drip and slide of blood, and the exposure of bone underneath. He had said "always" to convince her, assure her, of permanency.

It worked, for when he said it her face lit up and the hurt did leave. She ran then, carrying his knowledge, but her belt fell off and he kept it as a memento. It hung on a nail near his bed—unfrayed, unsullied after all those years, with only the permanent bend in the fabric made by its long life on a nail. It was pleasant living with that sign of a visitor, his only one. And after a while he was able to connect the belt with the face, the tadpole-over-the-eye-face that he sometimes saw up in the Bottom. His visitor, his company; his guest, his social life, his woman, his daughter, his friend—they all hung there on a nail near his bed.

Now he stared at the tiny moon floating high over the ice-choked river. His loneliness had dropped down somewhere around his ankles. Some other feeling possessed him. A feeling that touched his eyes and made him blink. He had seen her again months? weeks? ago. Raking leaves for Mr. Hodges, he had gone into the cellar for two bushel baskets to put them in. In the hallway he passed an open door leading to a small room. She lay on a table there. It was surely the same one. The same little-girl face, same tadpole over the eye. So he had been wrong. Terribly wrong. No "always" at all. Another dying away of someone whose face he knew.

It was then he began to suspect that all those years of rope hauling and bell ringing were never going to do any good. He might as well sit forever on his riverbank and stare out of the window at the moon.

By his day-slashed calendar he knew that tomorrow was the day. And for the first time he did not want to go. He wanted to stay with the purple-and-white belt. Not go. Not go.

Still, when the day broke in an incredible splash of sun, he gathered his things. In the early part of the afternoon, drenched in sunlight and certain that this would be the last time he would invite them to end their lives neatly and sweetly, he walked over the rickety bridge and on into the Bottom. But it was not heartfelt this time, not loving this time, for he no longer cared whether he helped them or not. His rope was improperly tied; his bell had a tinny unimpassioned sound. His visitor was dead and would come no more.

Years later people would quarrel about who had been the first to go. Most folks said it was the deweys, but one or two knew better, knew that Dessie and Ivy had been first. Said that Dessie had opened her door first and stood there shielding her eyes from the sun while watching Shadrack coming down the road. She laughed.

Maybe the sun; maybe the clots of green showing in the hills promising so much; maybe the contrast between Shadrack's doomy, gloomy bell glinting in all that sweet sunshine. Maybe just a brief moment, for once, of not feeling fear, of looking at death in the sunshine and being unafraid. She laughed.

Upstairs, Ivy heard her and looked to see what caused the thick music that rocked her neighbor's breasts. Then Ivy laughed too. Like the scarlet fever that had touched everybody and worn them down to gristle, their laughter infected Carpenter's Road. Soon children were jumping about giggling and men came to the porches to chuckle. By the time Shadrack reached the first house, he was facing a line of delighted faces.

Never before had they laughed. Always they had shut their doors, pulled down the shades and called their children out of the road. It frightened him, this glee, but he stuck to his habit—singing his song, ringing his bell and holding fast to his rope. The deweys with their magnificent teeth ran out from Number 7 and danced a little jig around the befuddled Shadrack, then cut into a wild aping of his walk, his song and his bell-ringing. By now women were holding their stomachs, and the men were slapping their knees. It was Mrs. Jackson, who ate ice, who tripped down off her porch and marched—actually marched—along behind him. The scene was so comic the people walked into the road to make sure they saw it all. In that way the parade started.

Everybody, Dessie, Tar Baby, Patsy, Mr. Buckland Reed, Teapot's Mamma, Valentine, the deweys, Mrs. Jackson, Irene, the proprietor of the Palace of Cosmetology, Reba, the Herrod brothers and flocks of teen-agers got into the mood and, laughing, dancing, calling to one another, formed a pied piper's band[1] behind Shadrack. As the initial group of about twenty people passed more houses, they called to the people standing in doors and leaning out of windows to join them; to help them open further this slit in the veil, this respite from anxiety, from dignity, from gravity, from the weight of that very adult pain that had undergirded them all those years before. Called to them to come out and play in the sunshine—as though the sunshine would last, as though there really was hope. The same hope that kept them picking beans for other farmers; kept them from finally leaving as they talked of doing; kept them knee-deep in other people's dirt; kept them excited about other people's wars; kept them solicitous of white people's children; kept them convinced that some magic "government" was going to lift them up, out and away from that dirt, those beans, those wars.

Some, of course, like Helene Wright, would not go. She watched the ruckus with characteristic scorn. Others, who understood the Spirit's touch which made them dance, who understood whole families bending their backs in a field while singing as from one throat, who understood the ecstasy of river baptisms under suns just like this one, did not understand this curious disorder, this headless display and so refused also to go.

Nevertheless, the sun splashed on a larger and larger crowd that strutted, skipped, marched, and shuffled down the road. When they got down to where the sidewalk started, some of them stopped and decided to turn back, too embarrassed to enter the white part of town whooping like banshees.[2] But except for three or four, the fainthearted were put to shame by the more aggressive and abandoned, and the parade danced down Main Street past Woolworth's and the old poultry house, turned right and moved on down the New River Road.

At the mouth of the tunnel excavation, in a fever pitch of excitement and joy, they saw the timber, the bricks, the steel ribs and the tacky wire gate that glittered under ice struck to diamond in the sun. It dazzled them, at first, and they were suddenly quiet. Their hooded eyes swept over the place where their hope had lain since 1927. There was the promise: leaf-dead. The teeth unrepaired, the coal credit cut off, the chest pains unattended, the school shoes unbought, the rush-stuffed mattresses, the broken toilets,

---

1. In the tale of the Pied Piper of Hamlin, the elders refused to pay the piper for freeing the town of rats, so he charmed the town's children into following him away forever.

2. Female spirits of Gaelic folklore; their wailing portends the coming of death.

the leaning porches, the slurred remarks and the staggering childish malevolence of their employers. All there in blazing sunlit ice rapidly becoming water.

Like antelopes they leaped over the little gate—a wire barricade that was never intended to bar anything but dogs, rabbits and stray children—and led by the tough, the enraged and the young they picked up the lengths of timber and thin steel ribs and smashed the bricks they would never fire in yawning kilns, split the sacks of limestone they had not mixed or even been allowed to haul; tore the wire mesh, tipped over wheelbarrows and rolled forepoles down the bank, where they sailed far out on the icebound river.

Old and young, women and children, lame and hearty, they killed, as best they could, the tunnel they were forbidden to build.

They didn't mean to go in, to actually go down into the lip of the tunnel, but in their need to kill it all, all of it, to wipe from the face of the earth the work of the thin-armed Virginia boys, the bull-necked Greeks and the knife-faced men who waved the leaf-dead promise, they went too deep, too far . . .

A lot of them died there. The earth, now warm, shifted; the first forepole slipped; loose rock fell from the face of the tunnel and caused a shield to give way. They found themselves in a chamber of water, deprived of the sun that had brought them there. With the first crack and whoosh of water, the clamber to get out was so fierce that others who were trying to help were pulled to their deaths. Pressed up against steel ribs and timber blocks young boys strangled when the oxygen left them to join the water. Outside, others watched in terror as ice split and earth shook beneath their feet. Mrs. Jackson, weighing less than 100 pounds, slid down the bank and met with an open mouth the ice she had craved all her life. Tar Baby, Dessie, Ivy, Valentine, the Herrod boys, some of Ajax's younger brothers and the deweys (at least it was supposed; their bodies were never found)—all died there. Mr. Buckland Reed escaped, so did Patsy and her two boys, as well as some fifteen or twenty who had not gotten close enough to fall, or whose timidity would not let them enter an unfinished tunnel.

And all the while Shadrack stood there. Having forgotten his song and his rope, he just stood there high up on the bank ringing, ringing his bell.

1965

Things were so much better in 1965. Or so it seemed. You could go downtown and see colored people working in the dime store behind the counters, even handling money with cash-register keys around their necks. And a colored man taught mathematics at the junior high school. The young people had a look about them that everybody said was new but which reminded Nel of the deweys, whom nobody had ever found. Maybe, she thought, they had gone off and seeded the land and growed up in these young people in the dime store with the cash-register keys around their necks.

They were so different, these young people. So different from the way she remembered them forty years ago.

Jesus, there were some beautiful boys in 1921! Look like the whole world was bursting at the seams with them. Thirteen, fourteen, fifteen years old. Jesus, they were fine. L. P., Paul Freeman and his brother Jake, Mrs. Scott's twins—and Ajax had a whole flock of younger brothers. They hung out of attic windows, rode on car fenders, delivered the coal, moved into Medallion and moved out, visited cousins, plowed, hoisted, lounged on the church steps, careened on the school playground. The sun heated them and the moon slid down their backs. God, the world was *full* of beautiful boys in 1921.

Nothing like these kids. Everything had changed. Even the whores were better then: tough, fat, laughing women with burns on their cheeks and wit married to their meanness: or widows couched in small houses in the woods with eight children to feed and no man. These modern-day whores were pale and dull before those women. These little clothes-crazy things were always embarrassed. Nasty but shamed. They didn't know what shameless was. They should have known those silvery widows in the woods who would get up from the dinner table and walk into the trees with a customer with as much embarrassment as a calving mare.

Lord, how time flies. She hardly recognized anybody in the town any more. Now there was another old people's home. Look like this town just kept on building homes for old people. Every time they built a road they built a old folks' home. You'd think folks was living longer, but the fact of it was, they was just being put out faster.

Nel hadn't seen the insides of this most recent one yet, but it was her turn in Circle Number 5 to visit some of the old women there. The pastor visited them regularly, but the circle thought private visits were nice too. There were just nine colored women out there, the same nine that had been in the other one. But a lot of white ones. White people didn't fret about putting their old ones away. It took a lot for black people to let them go, and even if somebody was old and alone, others did the dropping by, the floor washing, the cooking. Only when they got crazy and unmanageable were they let go. Unless it was somebody like Sula, who put Eva away out of meanness. It was true that Eva was foolish in the head, but not so bad as to need locking up.

Nel was more than a little curious to see her. She had been really active in church only a year or less, and that was because the children were grown now and took up less time and less space in her mind. For over twenty-five years since Jude walked out she had pinned herself into a tiny life. She spent a little time trying to marry again, but nobody wanted to take her on with three children, and she simply couldn't manage the business of keeping boyfriends. During the war she had had a rather long relationship with a sergeant stationed at the camp twenty miles down river from Medallion, but then he got called away and everything was reduced to a few letters— then nothing. Then there was a bartender at the hotel. But now she was fifty-five and hard put to remember what all that had been about.

It didn't take long, after Jude left, for her to see what the future would be. She had looked at her children and knew in her heart that that would be all. That they were all she would ever know of love. But it was a love that, like a pan of syrup kept too long on the stove, had cooked out, leaving only its odor and a hard, sweet sludge, impossible to scrape off. For the mouths of her children quickly forgot the taste of her nipples, and years ago they had begun to look past her face into the nearest stretch of sky.

In the meantime the Bottom had collapsed. Everybody who had made money during the war moved as close as they could to the valley, and the white people were buying down river, cross river, stretching Medallion like two strings on the banks. Nobody colored lived much up in the Bottom any more. White people were building towers for television stations up there and there was a rumor about a golf course or something. Anyway, hill land was more valuable now, and those black people who had moved down right after the war and in the fifties couldn't afford to come back even if they wanted to. Except for the few blacks still huddled by the river bend, and some undemolished houses on Carpenter's Road, only rich white folks were building homes in the hills. Just like that, they had changed their minds and instead of keeping the valley floor to themselves, now they wanted a hilltop house with a river view and a ring of elms. The black people, for all their new look, seemed awfully anxious to get to the valley, or leave town, and abandon the hills to whoever was interested. It was sad, because the Bottom had been a real place. These young ones kept talking about the community, but they left the hills to the poor, the old, the stubborn—and the rich white folks. Maybe it hadn't been a community, but it had been a place. Now there weren't any places left, just separate houses with separate televisions and separate telephones and less and less dropping by.

These were the same thoughts she always had when she walked down into the town. One of the last true pedestrians, Nel walked the shoulder road while cars slipped by. Laughed at by her children, she still walked wherever she wanted to go, allowing herself to accept rides only when the weather required it.

Now she went straight through the town and turned left at its farthest end, along a tree-lined walk that turned into a country road farther on and passed the cemetery, Beechnut Park.

When she got to Sunnydale, the home for the aged, it was already four o'clock and turning chill. She would be glad to sit down with those old birds and rest her feet.

A red-haired lady at the desk gave her a pass card and pointed to a door that opened onto a corridor of smaller doors. It looked like what she imagined a college dormitory to be. The lobby was luxurious—modern—but the rooms she peeped into were sterile green cages. There was too much light everywhere; it needed some shadows. The third door, down the hall, had a little name tag over it that read EVA PEACE. Nel twisted the knob and rapped a little on the door at the same time, then listened a moment before she opened it.

At first she couldn't believe it. She seemed so small, sitting at that table in a black-vinyl chair. All the heaviness had gone and the height. Her once beautiful leg had no stocking and the foot was in a slipper. Nel wanted to cry—not for Eva's milk-dull eyes or her floppy lips, but for the once proud foot accustomed for over a half century to a fine well-laced shoe, now stuffed gracelessly into a pink terrycloth slipper.

"Good evening, Miss Peace. I'm Nel Greene come to pay a call on you. You remember me, don't you?"

Eva was ironing and dreaming of stairwells. She had neither iron nor clothes but did not stop her fastidious lining up of pleats or pressing out of wrinkles even when she acknowledged Nel's greeting.

"Howdy. Sit down."

"Thank you." Nel sat on the edge of the little bed. "You've got a pretty room, a real pretty room, Miss Peace."

"You eat something funny today?"

"Ma'am?"

"Some chop suey? Think back."

"No, ma'am."

"No? Well, you gone be sick later on."

"But I didn't have no chop suey."

"You think I come all the way over here for you to tell me that? I can't make visits too often. You should have some respect for old people."

"But Miss Peace, I'm visiting *you*. This is *your* room." Nel smiled.

"What you say your name was?"

"Nel Greene."

"Wiley Wright's girl?"

"Uh huh. You do remember. That makes me feel good, Miss Peace. You remember me and my father."

"Tell me how you killed that little boy."

"What? What little boy?"

"The one you threw in the water. I got oranges. How did you get him to go in the water?"

"I didn't throw no little boy in the river. That was Sula."

"You. Sula. What's the difference? You was there. You watched, didn't you? Me, I never would've watched."

"You're confused, Miss Peace. I'm Nel. Sula's dead."

"It's awful cold in the water. Fire is warm. How did you get him in?" Eva wet her forefinger and tested the iron's heat.

"Who told you all these lies? Miss Peace? Who told you? Why are you telling lies on me?"

"I got oranges. I don't drink they old orange juice. They puts something in it."

"Why are you trying to make out like I did it?"

Eva stopped ironing and looked at Nel. For the first time her eyes looked sane.

"You think I'm guilty?" Nel was whispering.

Eva whispered back, "Who would know that better than you?"

"I want to know who you been talking to." Nel forced herself to speak normally.

"Plum. Sweet Plum. He tells me things." Eva laughed a light, tinkly giggle—girlish.

"I'll be going now, Miss Peace." Nel stood.

"You ain't answered me yet."

"I don't know what you're talking about."

"Just alike. Both of you. Never was no difference between you. Want some oranges? It's better for you than chop suey. Sula? I got oranges."

Nel walked hurriedly down the hall, Eva calling after her, "Sula?" Nel couldn't see the other women today. That woman had upset her. She handed her pass back to the lady, avoiding her look of surprise.

Outside she fastened her coat against the rising wind. The top button was missing so she covered her throat with her hand. A bright space opened in her head and memory seeped into it.

Standing on the riverbank in a purple-and-white dress, Sula swinging Chicken Little around and around. His laughter before the hand-slip and the water closing quickly over the place. What had she felt then, watching Sula going around and around and then the little boy swinging out over the water? Sula had cried and cried when she came back from Shadrack's house. But Nel had remained calm.

"Shouldn't we tell?"

"Did he see?"

"I don't know. No."

"Let's go. We can't bring him back."

What did old Eva mean by *you watched?* How could she help seeing it? She was right there. But Eva didn't say *see,* she said *watched.* "I did not watch it. I just saw it." But it was there anyway, as it had always been, the old feeling and the old question. The good feeling she had had when Chicken's hands slipped. She hadn't wondered about that in years. "Why didn't I feel bad when it happened? How come it felt so good to see him fall?"

All these years she had been secretly proud of her calm, controlled behavior when Sula was uncontrollable, her compassion for Sula's frightened and shamed eyes. Now it seemed that what she had thought was maturity, serenity and compassion was only the tranquillity that follows a joyful stimulation. Just as the water closed peacefully over the turbulence of Chicken Little's body, so had contentment washed over her enjoyment.

She was walking too fast. Not watching where she placed her feet, she got into the weeds by the side of the road. Running almost, she approached Beechnut Park. Just over there was the colored part of the cemetery. She went in. Sula was buried there along with Plum, Hannah and now Pearl. With the same disregard for name changes by marriage that the black people of Medallion always showed, each flat slab had one word carved on it. Together they read like a chant: PEACE 1895–1921, PEACE 1890–1923, PEACE 1910–1940, PEACE 1892–1959.

They were not dead people. They were words. Not even words. Wishes, longings.

All these years she had been harboring good feelings about Eva; sharing, she believed, her loneliness and unloved state as no one else could or did. She, after all, was the only one who really understood why Eva refused to attend Sula's funeral. The others thought they knew; thought the grandmother's reasons were the same as their own—that to pay respect to someone who had caused them so much pain was beneath them. Nel, who did go, believed Eva's refusal was not due to pride or vengeance but to a plain unwillingness to see the swallowing of her own flesh into the dirt, a determination not to let the eyes see what the heart could not hold.

Now, however, after the way Eva had just treated her, accused her, she wondered if the townspeople hadn't been right the first time. Eva *was* mean. Sula had even said so. There was no good reason for her to speak so. Feeble-minded or not. Old. Whatever. Eva knew what she was doing. Always had. She had stayed away from Sula's funeral and accused Nel of drowning Chicken Little for spite. The same spite that galloped all over the Bottom. That made every gesture an offense, every off-center smile a threat, so that even the bubbles of relief that broke in the chest of practically everybody when Sula died did not soften their spite and allow them to go to Mr. Hodges' funeral parlor or send flowers from the church or bake a yellow cake.

She thought about Nathan opening the bedroom door the day she had visited her, and finding the body. He said he knew she was dead right away not because her eyes were open but because her mouth was. It looked to him like a giant yawn that she never got to finish. He had run across the street to Teapot's Mamma, who, when she heard the news, said, "Ho!" like the conductor on the train when it was about to take off except louder, and then did a little dance. None of the women left their quilt patches in disarray to run to the house. Nobody left the clothes halfway through the wringer to run to the house. Even the men just said "uhn," when they heard. The day passed and no one came. The night slipped into another day and the body was still lying in Eva's bed gazing at the ceiling trying to complete a yawn. It was very strange, this stubbornness about Sula. For even when China, the most rambunctious whore in the town, died (whose black son and white son said, when they heard she was dying, "She ain't dead yet?"), even then everybody stopped what they were doing and turned out in numbers to put the fallen sister away.

It was Nel who finally called the hospital, then the mortuary, then the police, who were the ones to come. So the white people took over. They came in a police van and carried the body down the steps past the four pear trees and into the van for all the world as with Hannah. When the police asked questions nobody gave them any information. It took them hours to find out the dead woman's first name. The call was for a Miss Peace at 7 Carpenter's Road. So they left with that: a body, a name and an address. The white people had to wash her, dress her, prepare her and finally lower her. It was all done elegantly, for it was discovered that she had a substantial death policy. Nel went to the funeral parlor, but was so shocked by the closed coffin she stayed only a few minutes.

The following day Nel walked to the burying and found herself the only black person there, steeling her mind to the roses and pulleys. It was only when she turned to leave that she saw the cluster of black folk at the lip of the cemetery. Not coming in, not dressed for mourning, but there waiting. Not until the white folks left—the gravediggers, Mr. and Mrs. Hodges, and their young son who assisted them—did those black people from up in the Bottom enter with hooded hearts and filed eyes to sing "Shall We Gather at the River" over the curved earth that cut them off from the most magnificent hatred they had ever known. Their question clotted the October air, Shall We Gather at the River? The beautiful, the beautiful river? Perhaps Sula answered them even then, for it began to rain, and the women ran in tiny leaps through the grass for fear their straightened hair would beat them home.

Sadly, heavily, Nel left the colored part of the cemetery. Further along the road Shadrack passed her by. A little shaggier, a little older, still energetically mad, he looked at the woman hurrying along the road with the sunset in her face.

He stopped. Trying to remember where he had seen her before. The effort of recollection was too much for him and he moved on. He had to haul some trash out at Sunnydale and it would be good and dark before he got home. He hadn't sold fish in a long time now. The river had killed them all. No more silver-gray flashes, no more flat, wide, unhurried look. No more slowing down of gills. No more tremor on the line.

Shadrack and Nel moved in opposite directions, each thinking separate thoughts about the past. The distance between them increased as they both remembered gone things.

Suddenly Nel stopped. Her eye twitched and burned a little.

"Sula?" she whispered, gazing at the tops of trees. "Sula?"

Leaves stirred; mud shifted; there was the smell of overripe green things. A soft ball of fur broke and scattered like dandelion spores in the breeze.

"All that time, all that time, I thought I was missing Jude." And the loss pressed down on her chest and came up into her throat. "We was girls together," she said as though explaining something. "O Lord, Sula," she cried, "girl, girl, girlgirlgirl."

It was a fine cry—loud and long—but it had no bottom and it had no top, just circles and circles of sorrow.

1973

Rootedness: The Ancestor as Foundation

There is a conflict between public and private life, and it's a conflict that I think ought to remain a conflict. Not a problem, just a conflict. Because they are two modes of life that exist to exclude and annihilate each other. It's a conflict that should be maintained now more than ever because the social machinery of this country at this time doesn't permit harmony in a life that has both aspects. I am impressed with the story of—probably Jefferson, perhaps not, who walked home alone after the presidential inauguration. There must have been a time when an artist could be genuinely representative *of* the tribe and *in* it; when an artist could have a tribal or racial sensibility and an individual expression of it. There were spaces and places in which a single person could enter and behave as an individual within the context of the community. A small remnant of that you can see sometimes in Black churches where people shout. It is a very personal grief and a personal statement done among people you trust. Done within the context of the community, therefore safe. And while the shouter is performing some rite that is extremely subjective, the other people are performing as a community in protecting that person. So you have a public and a private expression going on at the same time. To transfer that is not possible. So I just do the obvious, which is to keep my life as private as possible; not because it is all that interesting, it's just important that it be private. And then, whatever I do that is public can be done seriously.

The autobiographical form is classic in Black American or Afro-American literature because it provided an instance in which a writer could be representative, could say, "My single solitary and individual life is like the lives of the tribe; it differs in these specific ways, but it is a balanced life because it is both solitary and representative." The contemporary autobiography tends to be 'how I got over—look at me—alone—let me show you how I did it.' It is inimical, I think, to some of the characteristics of Black artistic expression and influence.

The label "novel" is useful in technical terms because I write prose that is longer than a short story. My sense of the novel is that it has always functioned for the class or the group that wrote it. The history of the novel as a form began when there was a new class, a middle class, to read it; it was an art form that they needed. The lower classes didn't need novels at that time because they had an art form already: they had songs, and dances, and ceremony, and gossip, and celebrations. The aristocracy didn't need it because they had the art that they had patronized, they had their own pictures painted, their own houses built, and they made sure their art separated them from the rest of the world. But when the industrial revolution began, there emerged a new class of people who were neither peasants nor aristo-crats. In large measure they had no art form to tell them how to behave in this new situation. So they produced an art form: we call it the novel of manners, an art form designed to tell people something they didn't know. That is, how to behave in this new world, how to distinguish between the good guys and the bad guys. How to get married. What a good living was. What would happen if you strayed from the fold. So that early works such as *Pamela*, by Samuel Richardson, and the Jane Austen material provided social rules and explained behavior, identified outlaws, identified the people, habits, and customs that one should approve of. They were didactic in that sense. That, I think, is probably why the novel was not missed among the so-called peasant cultures. They didn't need it, because they were clear about what their responsibilities were and who and where was evil, and where was good.

But when the peasant class, or lower class, or what have you, confronts the middle class, the city, or the upper classes, they are thrown a little bit into disarray. For a long time, the art form that was healing for Black people was music. That music is no longer *exclusively* ours; we don't have exclusive rights to it. Other people sing it and play it; it is the mode of con-temporary music everywhere. So another form has to take that place, and it seems to me that the novel is needed by African-Americans now in a way that it was not needed before—and it is following along the lines of the function of novels everywhere. We don't live in places where we can hear those stories anymore; parents don't sit around and tell their children those classical, mythological archetypal stories that we heard years ago. But new information has got to get out, and there are several ways to do it. One is in the novel. I regard it as a way to accomplish certain very strong functions—one being the one I just described.

It should be beautiful, and powerful, but it should also *work*. It should have something in it that enlightens; something in it that opens the door and points the way. Something in it that suggests what the conflicts are, what the problems are. But it need not solve those problems because it is not a case study, it is not a recipe. There are things that I try to incorporate into my fiction that are directly and deliberately related to what I regard as the major characteristics of Black art, wherever it is. One of which is the ability to be both print and oral literature: to combine those two aspects so that the stories can be read in silence, of course, but one should be able to hear them as well. It should try deliberately to make you stand up and make you feel something profoundly in the same way that a Black preacher requires his congregation to speak, to join him in the sermon, to behave in a certain way, to stand up and to weep and to cry and to accede or to change and to modify—to expand on the sermon that is being delivered. In the same way that a musician's music is enhanced when there is a response from the audience. Now in a book, which closes, after all—it's of some importance to me to try to make that connection—to try to make that hap-pen also. And, having at my disposal only the letters of the alphabet and some punctuation, I have to provide the places and spaces so that the reader can participate. Because it is the affective and participatory relation-ship between the artist or the speaker and the audience that is of primary importance, as it is in these other art forms that I have described.

To make the story appear oral, meandering, effortless, spoken—to have the reader *feel* the narrator without *identifying* that narrator, or hearing him or her knock about, and to have the reader work *with* the author in the construction of the book—is what's important. What is left out is as important as what is there. To describe sexual scenes in such a way that they are not clinical, not even explicit—so that the reader brings his own sexuality to the scene and thereby participates in it in a very personal way. And owns it. To construct the dialogue so that it is heard. So that there are no adverbs attached to them: "loudly," "softly," "he said menacingly." The menace should be in the sentence. To use, even formally, a chorus. The real presence of a chorus. Meaning the community or the reader at large, commenting on the action as it goes ahead.

In the books that I have written, the chorus has changed but there has always been a choral note, whether it is the "I" narrator of *Bluest Eye*, or the town functioning as a character in *Sula*, or the neighborhood and the community that responds in the two parts of town in *Solomon*. Or, as extreme as I've gotten, all of nature thinking and feeling and watching and responding to the action going on in *Tar Baby*, so that they are in the story: the trees hurt, fish are afraid, clouds report, and the bees are alarmed. Those are the ways in which I try to incorporate, into that traditional genre the novel, unorthodox novelistic characteristics—so that it is, in my view, Black, because it uses the characteristics of Black art. I am not suggesting that some of these devices have not been used before and elsewhere—only the reason why I do. I employ them as well as I can. And those are just some; I wish there were ways in which such things could be talked about in the criticism. My general disappointment in some of the criticism that my work has received has nothing to do with approval. It has something to do with the vocabulary used in order to describe these things. I don't like to find my books condemned as bad or praised as good, when that condemnation or that praise is based on criteria from other paradigms. I would much prefer that they were dismissed or embraced based on the success of their accomplishment within the culture out of which I write.

I don't regard Black literature as simply books written *by* Black people, or simply as literature written *about* Black people, or simply as literature that uses a certain mode of language in which you just sort of drop g's. There is something very special and very identifiable about it and it is my struggle to *find* that elusive but identifiable style in the books. My joy is when I think that I have approached it; my misery is when I think I can't get there.

[There were times when I did.] I got there in several separate places when I knew it was exactly right. Most of the time in *Song of Solomon*, because of the construction of the book and the tone in which I could blend the acceptance of the supernatural and a profound rootedness in the real world at the same time with neither taking precedence over the other. It is indicative of the cosmology, the way in which Black people looked at the world. We are very practical people, very down-to-earth, even shrewd people. But within that practicality we also accepted what I suppose could be called superstition and magic, which is another way of knowing things. But to blend those two worlds together at the same time was enhancing, not limiting. And some of those things were "discredited knowledge" that Black people had; discredited only because Black people were discredited therefore what they *knew* was "discredited." And also because the press toward upward social mobility would mean to get as far away from that kind of knowledge as possible. That kind of knowledge has a very strong place in my work.

I have talked about function in that other question, and I touched a little bit on some of the other characteristics [or distinctive elements of African-American writing], one of which was oral quality, and the participation of the reader and the chorus. The only thing that I would add for this question is the presence of an ancestor; it seems to me interesting to evaluate Black literature on what the writer does with the presence of an ancestor. Which is to say a grandfather as in Ralph Ellison, or a grandmother as in Toni Cade Bambara, or a healer as in Bambara or Henry Dumas. There is always an elder there. And these ancestors are not just parents, they are sort of timeless people whose relationships to the characters are benevolent, instructive, and protective, and they provide a certain kind of wisdom.

How the Black writer responds to that presence interests me. Some of them, such as Richard Wright, had great difficulty with that ancestor. Some of them, like James Baldwin, were confounded and disturbed by the presence or absence of an ancestor. What struck me in looking at some contemporary fiction was that whether the novel took place in the city or in the country, the presence or absence of that figure determined the success or the happiness of the character. It was the absence of an ancestor that was frightening, that was threatening, and it caused huge destruction and disarray in the work itself. That the solace comes, not from the contemplation of serene nature as in a lot of mainstream white literature, nor from the regard in which the city was held as a kind of corrupt place to be. Whether the character was in Harlem or Arkansas, the point was there, this timelessness was there, this person who represented this ancestor. And it seemed to be one of those interesting aspects of the continuum in Black or African-American art, as well as some of the things I mentioned before: the deliberate effort, on the part of the artist, to get a visceral, emotional response as well as an intellectual response as he or she communicates with the audience.

The treatment of artists by the people for whom they speak is also of some interest. That is to say, when the writer is one of them, when the voice is not the separate, isolated ivory tower voice of a very different kind of person but an implied "we" in a narration. This is disturbing to people and critics who view the artist as the supreme individual. It is disturbing because there is a notion that that's what the artist is—always in confrontation with his own society, and you can see the differences in the way in which literature is interpreted. Whether or not Sula is nourished by that village depends on your view of it. I know people who believe that she was destroyed by it. My own special view is that there was no other place where she could live. She would have been destroyed by any other place; she was permitted to "be" only in that context, and no one stoned her or killed her or threw her out. Also it's difficult to see who the winners are if you are not looking at it from that point of view. When the hero returns to the fold— returns to the tribe—it is seen by certain white critics as a defeat, by others as a triumph, and that is a difference in what the *aims* of the art are.

In *Song of Solomon* Pilate is the ancestor. The difficulty that Hagar [youngest of the trio of women in that household] has is how far removed she is from the experience of her ancestor. Pilate had a dozen years of close, nurturing relationships with two males—her father and her brother. And that intimacy and support was in her and made her fierce and loving because she had that experience. Her daughter Reba had less of that and related to men in a very shallow way. Her daughter had even less of an association with men as a child, so that the progression is really a diminishing of their abilities because of the absence of men in a nourishing way in their lives. Pilate is the apogee of all that: of the best of that which is female and the best of that which is male, and that balance is disturbed if it is not nurtured, and if it is not counted on and if it is not reproduced. That is the disability we must be on guard against for the future—the female who reproduces the female who reproduces the female. You know there are a lot of people who talk about the position that men hold as of primary importance, but actually it is if we don't keep in touch with the ancestor that we are, in fact, lost.

The point of the books is that it is *our* job. When you kill the ancestor you kill yourself. I want to point out the dangers, to show that nice things don't always happen to the totally self-reliant if there is no conscious historical connection. To say, see—this is what will happen.

I don't have much to say about that [the necessity to develop a specific Black feminist model of critical inquiry] except that I think there is more danger in it than fruit, because any model of criticism or evaluation that excludes males from it is as hampered as any model of criticism of Black literature that excludes women from it. For critics, models have some function. They like to talk in terms of models and developments and so on, so maybe it's of some use to them, but I suggest that even for them there is some danger in it.

If anything I do, in the way of writing novels (or whatever I write) isn't about the village or the community or about you, then it is not about anything. I am not interested in indulging myself in some private, closed exercise of my imagination that fulfills only the obligation of my personal dreams—which is to say yes, the work must be political. It must have that as its thrust. That's a perjorative term in critical circles now: if a work of art has any political influence in it, somehow it's tainted. My feeling is just the opposite: if it has none, it is tainted.

The problem comes when you find harangue passing off as art. It seems to me that the best art is political and you ought to be able to make it unquestionably political and irrevocably beautiful at the same time.

1984

The Site of Memory

My inclusion in a series of talks on autobiography and memoir is not entirely a misalliance. Although it's probably true that a fiction writer thinks of his or her work as alien in that company, what I have to say may suggest why I'm not completely out of place here. For one thing, I might throw into relief the differences between self-recollection (memoir) and fiction, and also some of the similarities—the places where those two crafts embrace and where that embrace is symbiotic.

But the authenticity of my presence here lies in the fact that a very large part of my own literary heritage is the autobiography. In this country the print origins of black literature (as distinguished from the oral origins) were slave narratives. These book-length narratives (autobiographies, recollections, memoirs), of which well over a hundred were published, are familiar texts to historians and students of black history. They range from the adventure-packed life of Olaudah Equiano's *The Interesting Narrative of the Life of Olaudah Equiano, or Gustavus Vassa, the African, Written by Himself* (1769) to the quiet desperation of *Incidents in the Life of a Slave Girl: Written by Herself* (1861), in which Harriet Jacob ("Linda Brent") records hiding for seven years in a room too small to stand up in; from the political savvy of Frederick Douglass's *Narrative of the Life of Frederick Douglass, an American Slave, Written by Himself* (1845) to the subtlety and modesty of Henry Bibb, whose voice, in *Life and Adventures of Henry Bibb, an American Slave, Written by Himself* (1849), is surrounded by ("loaded with" is a better phrase) documents attesting to its authenticity. Bibb is careful to note that his formal schooling (three weeks) was short, but that he was "educated in the school of adversity, whips, and chains." Born in Kentucky, he put aside his plans to escape in order to marry. But when he learned that he was the father of a slave and watched the degradation of his wife and child, he reactivated those plans.

Whatever the style and circumstances of these narratives, they were written to say principally two things. One: "This is my historical life—my singular, special example that is personal, but that also represents the race." Two: "I write this text to persuade other people—you, the reader, who is probably not black—that we are human beings worthy of God's grace and the immediate abandonment of slavery." With these two missions in mind, the narratives were clearly pointed.

In Equiano's account, the purpose is quite up-front. Born in 1745 near the Niger River and captured at the age of ten, he survived the Middle Passage, American plantation slavery, wars in Canada and the Mediterranean; learned navigation and clerking from a Quaker named Robert King, and bought his freedom at twenty-one. He lived as a free servant, traveling widely and living most of his latter life in England. Here he is speaking to the British without equivocation: "I hope to have the satisfaction of seeing the renovation of liberty and justice resting on the British government. . . . I hope and expect the attention of gentlemen of power. . . . May the time come—at least the speculation is to me pleasing—when the sable people shall gratefully commemorate the auspicious era of extensive freedom." With typically eighteenth-century reticence he records his singular and representative life for one purpose: to change things. In fact, he and his co-authors *did* change things. Their works gave fuel to the fires that abolitionists were setting everywhere.

More difficult was getting the fair appraisal of literary critics. The writings of church martyrs and confessors are and were read for the eloquence of their message as well as their experience of redemption, but the American slaves' autobiographical narratives were frequently scorned as "biased," "inflammatory" and "improbable." These attacks are particularly difficult to understand in view of the fact that it was extremely important, as you can imagine, for the writers of these narratives to appear as objective as possible—not to offend the reader by being too angry, or by showing too much outrage, or by calling the reader names. As recently as 1966, Paul

Edwards, who edited and abridged Equiano's story, praises the narrative for its refusal to be "inflammatory."

"As a rule," Edwards writes, "he [Equiano] puts no emotional pressure on the reader other than that which the situation itself contains—his language does not strain after our sympathy, but expects it to be given naturally and at the proper time. This quiet avoidance of emotional display produces many of the best passages in the book." Similarly, an 1836 review of Charles Bell's *Life and Adventures of a Fugitive Slave*, which appeared in the "Quarterly Anti-Slavery Magazine," praised Bell's account for its objectivity. "We rejoice in the book the more, because it is not a partisan work. . . . It broaches no theory in regard to [slavery], nor proposes any mode or time of emancipation."

As determined as these black writers were to persuade the reader of the evil of slavery, they also complimented him by assuming his nobility of heart and his high-mindedness. They tried to summon up his finer nature in order to encourage him to employ it. They knew that their readers were the people who could make a difference in terminating slavery. Their stories—of brutality, adversity and deliverance—had great popularity in spite of critical hostility in many quarters and patronizing sympathy in others. There was a time when the hunger for "slave stories" was difficult to quiet, as sales figures show. Douglass's *Narrative* sold five thousand copies in four months; by 1847 it had sold eleven thousand copies. Equiano's book had thirty-six editions between 1789 and 1850. Moses Roper's book had ten editions from 1837 to 1856; William Wells Brown's was reprinted four times in its first year. Solomon Northrop's book sold twenty-seven thousand copies before two years had passed. A book by Josiah Henson (argued by some to be the model for the "Tom" of Harriet Beecher Stowe's *Uncle Tom's Cabin*) had a pre-publication sale of five thousand.

In addition to using their own lives to expose the horrors of slavery, they had a companion motive for their efforts. The prohibition against teaching a slave to read and write (which in many Southern states carried severe punishment) and against a slave's learning to read and write had to be scuttled at all costs. These writers knew that literacy was power. Voting, after all, was inextricably connected to the ability to read; literacy was a way of assuming and proving the "humanity" that the Constitution denied them. That is why the narratives carry the subtitle "written by himself," or "herself," and include introductions and prefaces by white sympathizers to authenticate them. Other narratives, "edited by" such well-known anti-slavery figures as Lydia Maria Child and John Greenleaf Whittier, contain prefaces to assure the reader how little editing was needed. A literate slave was supposed to be a contradiction in terms.

One has to remember that the climate in which they wrote reflected not only the Age of Enlightenment but its twin, born at the same time, the Age of Scientific Racism. David Hume, Immanuel Kant and Thomas Jefferson, to mention only a few, had documented their conclusions that blacks were incapable of intelligence. Frederick Douglass knew otherwise, and he wrote refutations of what Jefferson said in "Notes on the State of Virginia": "Never yet could I find that a black had uttered a thought above the level of plain narration, never see even an elementary trait of painting or sculpture." A sentence that I have always thought ought to be engraved at the door to the Rockefeller Collection of African Art. Hegel, in 1813, had said that Africans had no "history" and couldn't write in modern languages. Kant disregarded a perceptive observation by a black man by saying, "This fellow was quite black from head to foot, a clear proof that what he said was stupid."

Yet no slave society in the history of the world wrote more—or more thoughtfully—about its own enslavement. The milieu, however, dictated the purpose and the style. The narratives are instructive, moral and obviously representative. Some of them are patterned after the sentimental novel that was in vogue at the time. But whatever the level of eloquence or the form, popular taste discouraged the writers from dwelling too long or too carefully on the more sordid details of their experience. Whenever there was an unusually violent incident, or a scatological one, or something "excessive," one finds the writer taking refuge in the literary conventions of the day. "I was left in a state of distraction not to be described" (Equiano). "But let us now leave the rough usage of the field . . . and turn our attention to the less repulsive slave life as it existed in the house of my childhood" (Douglass). "I am not about to harrow the feelings of my readers by a terrific representation of the untold horrors of that fearful system of oppression. . . . It is not my purpose to descend deeply into the dark and noisome caverns of the hell of slavery" (Henry Box Brown).

Over and over, the writers pull the narrative up short with a phrase such as, "But let us drop a veil over these proceedings too terrible to relate." In shaping the experience to make it palatable to those who were in a position to alleviate it, they were silent about many things, and they "forgot" many other things. There was a careful selection of the instances that they would record and a careful rendering of those that they chose to describe. Lydia Maria Child identified the problem in her introduction to "Linda Brent's" tale of sexual abuse: "I am well aware that many will accuse me of indecorum for presenting these pages to the public; for the experiences of this intelligent and much-injured woman belong to a class which some call delicate subjects, and others indelicate. This peculiar phase of Slavery has generally been kept veiled; but the public ought to be made acquainted with its monstrous features, and I am willing to take the responsibility of presenting them with the veil drawn [aside]."

But most importantly—at least for me—there was no mention of their interior life.

For me—a writer in the last quarter of the twentieth century, not much more than a hundred years after Emancipation, a writer who is black and a woman—the exercise is very different. My job becomes how to rip that veil drawn over "proceedings too terrible to relate." The exercise is also critical for any person who is black, or who belongs to any marginalized category, for, historically, we were seldom invited to participate in the discourse even when we were its topic.

Moving that veil aside requires, therefore, certain things. First of all, I must trust my own recollections. I must also depend on the recollections of others. Thus memory weighs heavily in what I write, in how I begin and in what I find to be significant. Zora Neale Hurston said, "Like the dead-seeming cold rocks, I have memories within that came out of the material that went to make me." These "memories within" are the subsoil of my work. But memories and recollections won't give me total access to the unwritten interior life of these people. Only the act of the imagination can help me.

If writing is thinking and discovery and selection and order and meaning, it is also awe and reverence and mystery and magic. I suppose I could dispense with the last four if I were not so deadly serious about fidelity to the milieu out of which I write and in which my ancestors actually lived. Infidelity to that milieu—the absence of the interior life, the deliberate excising of it from the records that the slaves themselves told—is precisely the problem in the discourse that proceeded without us. How I gain access to that interior life is what drives me and is the part of this talk which both distinguishes my fiction from autobiographical strategies and which also embraces certain autobiographical strategies. It's a kind of literary archeology: on the basis of some information and a little bit of guesswork you journey to a site to see what remains were left behind and to reconstruct the world that these remains imply. What makes it fiction is the nature of the imaginative act: my reliance on the image—on the remains—in addition to recollection, to yield up a kind of a truth. By "image," of course, I don't mean "symbol"; I simply mean "picture" and the feelings that accompany the picture.

Fiction, by definition, is distinct from fact. Presumably it's the product of imagination—invention—and it claims the freedom to dispense with "what really happened," or where it really happened, or when it really happened, and nothing in it needs to be publicly verifiable, although much in it can be verified. By contrast, the scholarship of the biographer and the literary critic seems to us only trustworthy when the events of fiction can be traced to some publicly verifiable fact. It's the research of the "Oh, yes, this is where he or she got it from" school, which gets its own credibility from excavating the credibility of the sources of the imagination, not the nature of the imagination.

The work that I do frequently falls, in the minds of most people, into that realm of fiction called fantastic, or mythic, or magical, or unbelievable. I'm not comfortable with these labels. I consider that my single gravest responsibility (in spite of that magic) is not to lie. When I hear someone say, "Truth is stranger than fiction," I think that old chestnut is truer than we know, because it doesn't say that truth is truer than fiction; just that it's stranger, meaning that it's odd. It may be excessive, it may be more interesting, but the important thing is that it's random—and fiction is not random.

Therefore the crucial distinction for me is not the difference between fact and fiction, but the distinction between fact and truth. Because facts can exist without human intelligence, but truth cannot. So if I'm looking to find and expose a truth about the interior life of people who didn't write it (which doesn't mean that they didn't have it); if I'm trying to fill in the blanks that the slave narratives left—to part the veil that was so frequently drawn, to implement the stories that I heard—then the approach that's most productive and most trustworthy for me is the recollection that moves from the image to the text. Not from the text to the image.

Simone de Beauvoir, in *A Very Easy Death*, says, "I don't know why I was so shocked by my mother's death." When she heard her mother's name being called at the funeral by the priest, she says, "Emotion seized me by the throat. . . . 'Françoise de Beauvoir': the words brought her to life; they summed up her history, from birth to marriage to widowhood to the grave. Françoise de Beauvoir—that retiring woman, so rarely named, became an *important* person." The book becomes an exploration both into her own grief and into the images in which the grief lay buried.

Unlike Mme. de Beauvoir, Frederick Douglass asks the reader's patience for spending about half a page on the death of his grandmother—easily the most profound loss he had suffered—and he apologizes by saying, in effect, "it really was very important to me. I hope you aren't bored by my indulgence." He makes no attempt to explore that death: its images or its meaning. His narrative is as close to factual as he can make it, which leaves no room for subjective speculation. James Baldwin, on the other hand, in *Notes of a Native Son*, says, in recording his father's life and his own relationship to his father, "All of my father's Biblical texts and songs, which I had decided were meaningless, were ranged before me at his death like empty bottles, waiting to hold the meaning which life would give them for me." And then his text fills those bottles. Like Simone de Beauvoir, he moves from the event to the image that it left. My route is the reverse: the image comes first and tells me what the "memory" is about.

I can't tell you how I felt when my father died. But I was able to write *Song of Solomon* and imagine, not him, and not his specific interior life, but the world that he inhabited and the private or interior life of the people in it. And I can't tell you how I felt reading to my grandmother while she was turning over and over in her bed (because she was dying, and she was not comfortable), but I could try to reconstruct the world that she lived in. And I have suspected, more often than not, that I *know* more than she did, that I *know* more than my grandfather and my great-grandmother did, but I also know that I'm no wiser than they were. And whenever I have tried earnestly to diminish their vision and prove to myself that I know more, and when I have tried to speculate on their interior life and match it up with my own, I have been overwhelmed every time by the richness of theirs compared to my own. Like Frederick Douglass talking about his grandmother, and James Baldwin talking about his father, and Simone de Beauvoir talking about her mother, these people are my access to me; they are my entrance into my own interior life. Which is why the images that float around them—the remains, so to speak, at the archeological site—surface first, and they surface so vividly and so compellingly that I acknowledge them as my route to a reconstruction of a world, to an exploration of an interior life that was not written and to the revelation of a kind of truth.

So the nature of my research begins with something as ineffable and as flexible as a dimly recalled figure, the corner of a room, a voice. I began to write my second book, which was called *Sula*, because of my preoccupation with a picture of a woman and the way in which I heard her name pronounced. Her name was Hannah, and I think she was a friend of my mother's. I don't remember seeing her very much, but what I do remember is the color around her—a kind of violet, a suffusion of something violet—and her eyes, which appeared to be half closed. But what I remember most is how the women said her name: how they said "Hannah Peace" and smiled to themselves, and there was some secret about her that they knew, which they didn't talk about, at least not in my hearing, but it seemed *loaded* in the way in which they said her name. And I suspected that she was a little bit of an outlaw but that they approved in some way.

And then, thinking about their relationship to her and the way in which they talked about her, the way in which they articulated her name, made me think about friendship between women. What is it that they forgive each other for? And what is it that is unforgivable in the world of women? I don't want to know any more about Miss Hannah Peace, and I'm not going to ask my mother who she really was and what did she do and what were you laughing about and why were you smiling? Because my experience when I do this with my mother is so crushing: she will give you *the* most pedestrian information you ever heard, and I would like to keep all of my remains and my images intact in their mystery when I begin. Later I will get to the facts. That way I can explore two worlds—the actual and the possible.

What I want to do this evening is to track an image from picture to meaning to text—a journey which appears in the novel that I'm writing now, which is called *Beloved*.

I'm trying to write a particular kind of scene, and I see corn on the cob. To "see" corn on the cob doesn't mean that it suddenly hovers; it only means that it keeps coming back. And in trying to figure out "What is all this corn doing?" I discover what it *is* doing.

I see the house where I grew up in Lorain, Ohio. My parents had a garden some distance away from our house, and they didn't welcome me and my sister there, when we were young, because we were not able to distinguish between the things that they wanted to grow and the things that they didn't, so we were not able to hoe, or weed, until much later.

I see them walking, together, away from me. I'm looking at their backs and what they're carrying in their arms: their tools, and maybe a peck basket. Sometimes when they walk away from me they hold hands, and they go to this other place in the garden. They have to cross some railroad tracks to get there.

I also am aware that my mother and father sleep at odd hours because my father works many jobs and works at night. And these naps are times of pleasure for me and my sister because nobody's giving us chores, or telling us what to do, or nagging us in any way. In addition to which, there is some feeling of pleasure in them that I'm only vaguely aware of. They're very rested when they take these naps.

And later on in the summer we have an opportunity to eat corn, which is the one plant that I can distinguish from the others, and which is the harvest that I like the best; the others are the food that no child likes—the collards, the okra, the strong, violent vegetables that I would give a great deal for now. But I do like the corn because it's sweet, and because we all sit down to eat it, and it's finger food, and it's hot, and it's even good cold, and there are neighbors in, and there are uncles in, and it's easy, and it's nice.

The picture of the corn and the nimbus of emotion surrounding it became a powerful one in the manuscript I'm now completing.

Authors arrive at text and subtext in thousands of ways, learning each time they begin anew how to recognize a valuable idea and how to render the texture that accompanies, reveals or displays it to its best advantage. The process by which this is accomplished is endlessly fascinating to me. I have always thought that as an editor for twenty years I understood writers better than their most careful critics, because in examining the manuscript in each of its subsequent stages I knew the author's process, how his or her mind worked, what was effortless, what took time, where the "solution" to a problem came from. The end result—the book—was all that the critic had to go on.

Still, for me, that was the least important aspect of the work. Because, no matter how "fictional" the account of these writers, or how much it was a product of invention, the act of imagination is bound up with memory. You know, they straightened out the Mississippi River in places, to make room for houses and livable acreage. Occasionally the river floods these places. "Floods" is the word they use, but in fact it is not flooding; it is remembering. Remembering where it used to be. All water has a perfect memory and is forever trying to get back to where it was. Writers are like that: remembering where we were, what valley we ran through, what the banks were like, the light that was there and the route back to our original place. It is emotional memory—what the nerves and the skin remember as well as how it appeared. And a rush of imagination is our "flooding."

Along with personal recollection, the matrix of the work I do is the wish to extend, fill in and complement slave autobiographical narratives. But only the matrix. What comes of all that is dictated by other concerns, not least among them the novel's own integrity. Still, like water, I remember where I was before I was "straightened out."

1987

Unspeakable Things Unspoken: The Afro-American Presence in American Literature[1]

I

I planned to call this paper "Canon Fodder," because the terms put me in mind of a kind of trained muscular response that appears to be on display in some areas of the recent canon debate. But I changed my mind (so many have used the phrase) and hope to make clear the appropriateness of the title I settled on.

My purpose here is to observe the panoply of this most recent and most anxious series of questions concerning what should or does constitute a literary canon in order to suggest ways of addressing the Afro-American presence in American Literature that require neither slaughter nor reification—views that may spring the whole literature of an entire nation from the solitude into which it has been locked. There is something called American literature that, according to conventional wisdom, is certainly not Chicano literature, or Afro-American literature, or Asian-American, or Native American, or . . . It is somehow separate from them and they from it, and in spite of the efforts of recent literary histories, restructured curricula and anthologies, this separate confinement, be it breached or endorsed, is the subject of a large part of these debates. Although the terms used, like the vocabulary of earlier canon debates, refer to literary and/or humanistic value, aesthetic criteria, value-free or socially anchored readings, the contemporary battle plain is most often understood to be the claims of others against the white-male origins and definitions of those values; whether those definitions reflect an eternal, universal and transcending paradigm or

1. Presented as The Tanner Lecture on Human Values at the University of Michigan, October 7, 1988. [All notes are Morrison's—editor.]

whether they constitute a disguise for a temporal, political and culturally specific program.

Part of the history of this particular debate is located in the successful assault that the feminist scholarship of men and women (black and white) made and continues to make on traditional literary discourse. The male part of the whitemale equation is already deeply engaged, and no one believes the body of literature and its criticism will ever again be what it was in 1965: the protected preserve of the thoughts and works and analytical strategies of whitemen.

It is, however, the "white" part of the question that this paper focuses on, and it is to my great relief that such terms as "white" and "race" can enter serious discussion of literature. Although still a swift and swiftly obeyed call to arms, their use is no longer forbidden.[2] It may appear churlish to doubt the sincerity, or question the proclaimed well-intentioned self-lessness of a 900-year-old academy struggling through decades of chaos to "maintain standards." Yet of what use is it to go on about "quality" being the only criterion for greatness knowing that the definition of quality is itself the subject of much rage and is seldom universally agreed upon by everyone at all times? Is it to appropriate the term for reasons of state; to be in the position to distribute greatness or withhold it? Or to actively pursue the ways and places in which quality surfaces and stuns us into silence or into language worthy enough to describe it? What is possible is to try to recognize, identify and applaud the fight for and triumph of quality when it is revealed to us and to let go the notion that only the dominant culture or gender can make those judgments, identify that quality or produce it.

Those who claim the superiority of Western culture are entitled to that claim only when Western civilization is measured thoroughly against other civilizations and not found wanting, and when Western civilization owns up to its own sources in the cultures that preceded it.

A large part of the satisfaction I have always received from reading Greek tragedy, for example, is in its similarity to Afro-American communal structures (the function of song and chorus, the heroic struggle between the claims of community and individual hubris) and African religion and philosophy. In other words, that is part of the reason it has quality for me—I feel intellectually at home there. But that could hardly be so for those unfamiliar with my "home," and hardly a requisite for the pleasure they take. The point is, the form (Greek tragedy) makes available these varieties of provocative love because it is masterly—not because the civilization that is its referent was flawless or superior to all others.

One has the feeling that nights are becoming sleepless in some quarters, and it seems to me obvious that the recoil of traditional "humanists" and some post-modern theorists to this particular aspect of the debate, the "race" aspect, is as severe as it is because the claims for attention come from that segment of scholarly and artistic labor in which the mention of "race" is either inevitable or elaborately, painstakingly masked; and if all of the ramifications that the term demands are taken seriously, the bases of Western civilization will require re-thinking. Thus, in spite of its implicit and explicit acknowledgement, "race" is still a virtually unspeakable thing, as can be seen in the apologies, notes of "special use" and circumscribed

2. See "Race," Writing, and Difference, ed. Henry Louis Gates (University of Chicago Press, 1986).

definitions that accompany it[3]—not least of which is my own deference in surrounding it with quotation marks. Suddenly (for our purposes, suddenly) "race" does not exist. For three hundred years black Americans insisted that "race" was no usefully distinguishing factor in human relationships. During those same three centuries every academic discipline, including theology, history, and natural science, insisted "race" was *the* determining factor in human development. When blacks discovered they had shaped or become a culturally formed race, and that it had specific and revered difference, suddenly they were told there is no such thing as "race," biological or cultural, that matters and that genuinely intellectual exchange cannot accommodate it.[4] In trying to come to some terms about "race" and writing, I am tempted to throw my hands up. It always seemed to me that the people who invented the hierarchy of "race" when it was convenient for them ought not to be the ones to explain it away, now that it does not suit their purposes for it to exist. But there *is* culture and both gender and "race" inform and are informed by it. Afro-American culture exists and though it is clear (and becoming clearer) how it has responded to Western culture, the instances where and means by which it has shaped Western culture are poorly recognized or understood.

I want to address ways in which the presence of Afro-American literature and the awareness of its culture both resuscitate the study of literature in the United States and raise that study's standards. In pursuit of that goal, it will suit my purposes to contextualize the route canon debates have taken in Western literary criticism.

I do not believe this current anxiety can be attributed solely to the routine, even cyclical arguments within literary communities reflecting unpredictable yet inevitable shifts in taste, relevance or perception. Shifts in which an enthusiasm for and official endorsement of William Dean Howells, for example, withered; or in which the legalization of Mark Twain in critical court rose and fell like the fathoming of a sounding line (for which he may or may not have named himself); or even the slow, delayed but steady swell of attention and devotion on which Emily Dickinson soared to what is now, surely, a permanent crest of respect. No. Those were discoveries, reappraisals of individual artists. Serious but not destabilizing. Such accommodations were simple because the questions they posed were simple: Are there one hundred sterling examples of high literary art in American literature and no more? One hundred and six? If one or two fall into disrepute, is there space, then, for one or two others in the vestibule, waiting like girls for bells chimed by future husbands who alone can promise them security, legitimacy—and in whose hands alone rests the gift of critical longevity? Interesting questions, but, as I say, not endangering.

Nor is this detectable academic sleeplessness the consequence of a much more radical shift, such as the mid-nineteenth century one heralding the authenticity of American literature itself. Or an even earlier upheaval— receding now into the distant past—in which theology and thereby Latin, was displaced for the equally rigorous study of the classics and Greek to be followed by what was considered a strangely arrogant and upstart proposal:

---

3. Among many examples, *They Came Before Columbus, The African Presence in Ancient America* by Ivan van Sertima (New York: Random House, 1976), pp. xvi–xvii.

4. Tzvetan Todorov, "'Race.' Writing, and Culture," translated by Loulou Mack, in Gates, *op cit.* pp. 370–380.

that English literature was a suitable course of study for an aristocratic education, and not simply morally instructive fodder designed for the working classes. (The Chaucer Society was founded in 1848, four hundred years after Chaucer died.) No. This exchange seems unusual somehow, keener. It has a more strenuously argued (and felt) defense and a more vigorously insistent attack. And both defenses and attacks have spilled out of the academy into the popular press. Why? Resistance to displacement within or expansion of a canon is not, after all, surprising or unwarranted. That's what canonization is for. (And the question of whether there should be a canon or not seems disingenuous to me—there always is one whether there should be or not—for it is in the interests of the professional critical community to have one.) Certainly a sharp alertness as to *why* a work is or is not worthy of study is the legitimate occupation of the critic, the pedagogue and the artist. What is astonishing in the contemporary debate is not the resistance to displacement of works or to the expansion of genre within it, but the virulent passion that accompanies this resistance and, more importantly, the quality of its defense weaponry. The guns are very big; the trigger-fingers quick. But I am convinced the mechanism of the defenders of the flame is faulty. Not only may the hands of the gun-slinging cowboy-scholars be blown off, not only may the target be missed, but the subject of the conflagration (the sacred texts) is sacrificed, disfigured in the battle. This canon fodder may kill the canon. And I, at least, do not intend to live without Aeschylus or William Shakespeare, or James or Twain or Hawthorne, or Melville, etc., etc., etc. There must be some way to enhance canon readings without enshrining them.

When Milan Kundera, in *The Art of the Novel*, identified the historical territory of the novel by saying "The novel is Europe's creation" and that "The only context for grasping a novel's worth is the history of the European novel," the *New Yorker* reviewer stiffened. Kundera's "personal 'idea of the novel,'" he wrote, "is so profoundly Eurocentric that it's likely to seem exotic, even perverse, to American readers. . . . *The Art of the Novel* gives off the occasional (but pungent) whiff of cultural arrogance, and we may feel that Kundera's discourse . . . reveals an aspect of his character that we'd rather not have known about. . . . In order to become the artist he now is, the Czech novelist had to discover himself a second time, as a European. But what if that second, grander possibility hadn't been there to be discovered? What if Broch, Kafka, Musil—all that reading—had never been a part of his education, or had entered it only as exotic, alien presence? Kundera's polemical fervor in *The Art of the Novel* annoys us, as American readers, because we feel defensive, excluded from the transcendent 'idea of the novel' that for him seems simply to have been there for the taking. (If only he had cited, in his redeeming version of the novel's history, a few more heroes from the New World's culture.) Our novelists don't discover cultural values within themselves; they invent them."[5]

Kundera's views, obliterating American writers (with the exception of William Faulkner) from his own canon, are relegated to a "smugness" that Terrence Rafferty disassociates from Kundera's imaginative work and applies to the "sublime confidence" of his critical prose. The confidence of an exile who has the sentimental education of, and the choice to become, a European.

I was refreshed by Rafferty's comments. With the substitution of certain phrases, his observations and the justifiable umbrage he takes can be appropriated entirely by Afro-American writers regarding their own exclusion from the "transcendent 'idea of the novel.'"

For the present turbulence seems not to be about the flexibility of a canon, its range among and between Western countries, but about its miscegenation. The word is informative here and I do mean its use. A powerful ingredient in this debate concerns the incursion of third-world or so-called minority literature into a Eurocentric stronghold. When the topic of third world culture is raised, unlike the topic of Scandinavian culture, for example, a possible threat to and implicit criticism of the reigning equilibrium is seen to be raised as well. From the seventeenth century to the twentieth, the arguments resisting that incursion have marched in predictable sequence: 1) there is no Afro-American (or third world) art. 2) it exists but is inferior. 3) it exists and is superior when it measures up to the "universal" criteria of Western art. 4) it is not so much "art" as ore—rich ore—that requires a Western or Eurocentric smith to refine it from its "natural" state into an aesthetically complex form.

A few comments on a larger, older, but no less telling academic struggle—an extremely successful one—may be helpful here. It is telling because it sheds light on certain aspects of this current debate and may locate its sources. I made reference above to the radical upheaval in canon-building that took place at the inauguration of classical studies and Greek. This canonical re-routing from scholasticism to humanism was not merely radical, it must have been (may I say it?) savage. And it took some seventy years to accomplish. Seventy years to eliminate Egypt as the cradle of civilization *and* its model and replace it with Greece. The triumph of that process was that Greece lost its own origins and became itself original. A number of scholars in various disciplines (history, anthropology, ethnobotany, etc.) have put forward their research into cross-cultural and inter-cultural transmissions with varying degrees of success in the reception of their work. I am reminded of the curious publishing history of Ivan van Sertima's work, *They Came Before Columbus*, which researches the African presence in Ancient America. I am reminded of Edward Said's *Orientalism*, and especially the work of Martin Bernal, a linguist, trained in Chinese history, who has defined himself as an interloper in the field of classical civilization but who has offered, in *Black Athena*, a stunning investigation of the field. According to Bernal, there are two "models" of Greek history: one views Greece as Aryan or European (the Aryan Model); the other sees it as Levantine—absorbed by Egyptian and Semitic culture (the Ancient Model). "If I am right," writes Professor Bernal, "in urging the overthrow of the Aryan Model and its replacement by the Revised Ancient one, it will be necessary not only to rethink the fundamental bases of 'Western Civilization' but also to recognize the penetration of racism and 'continental chauvinism' into all our historiography, or philosophy of writing history. The Ancient Model had no major 'internal' deficiencies or weaknesses in explanatory power. It was overthrown for external reasons. For eighteenth and nineteenth century Romantics and racists it was simply intolerable for Greece, which was seen not merely as the epitome of Europe but also as its pure childhood, to have been the result of the mixture of native Europeans and *colonizing* Africans and Semites. Therefore the Ancient Model had to be overthrown and replaced by something more acceptable."[6]

It is difficult not to be persuaded by the weight of documentation Martin Bernal brings to his task and his rather dazzling analytical insights. What struck me in his analysis were the *process* of the fabrication of Ancient Greece and the *motives* for the fabrication. The latter (motive) involved the concept of purity, of progress. The former (process) required mis-reading, pre-determined selectivity of authentic sources, and—silence. From the Christian theological appropriation of Israel (the Levant), to the early nineteenth-century work of the prodigious Karl Müller, work that effectively dismissed the Greeks' own record of their influences and origins as their "Egyptomania," their tendency to be "wonderstruck" by Egyptian culture, a tendency "manifested in the 'delusion' that Egyptians and other non-European 'barbarians' had possessed superior cultures, from which the Greeks had borrowed massively,"[7] on through the Romantic response to the Enlightenment, and the decline into disfavor of the Phoenicians, "the essential force behind the rejection of the tradition of massive Phoenician influence on early Greece was the rise of racial—as opposed to religious— anti-semitism. This was because the Phoenicians were correctly perceived to have been culturally very close to the Jews."[8]

I have quoted at perhaps too great a length from Bernal's text because *motive*, so seldom an element brought to bear on the history of history, is located, delineated and confronted in Bernal's research, and has helped my own thinking about the process and motives of scholarly attention to and an appraisal of Afro-American presence in the literature of the United States.

Canon building is Empire building. Canon defense is national defense. Canon debate, whatever the terrain, nature and range (of criticism, of history, of the history of knowledge, of the definition of language, the universality of aesthetic principles, the sociology of art, the humanistic imagination), is the clash of cultures. And *all* of the interests are vested.

In such a melee as this one—a provocative, healthy, explosive melee— extraordinarily profound work is being done. Some of the controversy, however, has degenerated into *ad hominem* and unwarranted speculation on the personal habits of artists, specious and silly arguments about politics (the destabilizing forces are dismissed as merely political; the status quo sees itself as not—as though the term "*a*political" were only its prefix and not the most obviously political stance imaginable since one of the functions of political ideology is to pass itself off as immutable, natural and "innocent"), and covert expressions of critical inquiry designed to neutralize and disguise the political interests of the discourse. Yet much of the research and analysis has rendered speakable what was formerly unspoken and has made humanistic studies, once again, the place where one has to go to find out what's going on. Cultures, whether silenced or monologistic, whether repressed or repressing, seek meaning in the language and images available to them.

Silences are being broken, lost things have been found and at least two generations of scholars are disentangling received knowledge from the

6. Martin Bernal, *Black Athena: The Afroasiatic Roots of Classical Civilization, volume I: The Fabrication of Ancient Greece 1785–1985* (Rutgers University Press, 1987), p. 2.

7. *Ibid.*, p. 310.
8. *Ibid.*, p. 337.

apparatus of control, most notably those who are engaged in investigations of French and British Colonialist Literature, American slave narratives, and the delineation of the Afro-American literary tradition.

Now that Afro-American artistic presence has been "discovered" actually to exist, now that serious scholarship has moved from silencing the witnesses and erasing their meaningful place in and contribution to American culture, it is no longer acceptable merely to imagine us and imagine for us. We have always been imagining ourselves. We are not Isak Dinesen's "aspects of nature," nor Conrad's unspeaking. We are the subjects of our own narrative, witnesses to and participants in our own experience, and, in no way coincidentally, in the experience of those with whom we have come in contact. We are not, in fact, "other." We are choices. And to read imaginative literature by and about us is to choose to examine centers of the self and to have the opportunity to compare these centers with the "raceless" one with which we are, all of us, most familiar.

II

Recent approaches to the reading of Afro-American literature have come some distance; have addressed those arguments, mentioned earlier, (which are not arguments, but attitudes) that have, since the seventeenth century, effectively silenced the autonomy of that literature. As for the charge that "there is no Afro-American art," contemporary critical analysis of the literature and the recent surge of reprints and re-discoveries have buried it, and are pressing on to expand the traditional canon to include classic Afro-American works where generically and chronologically appropriate, and to devise strategies for reading and thinking about these texts.

As to the second silencing charge, "Afro-American art exists, but is inferior," again, close readings and careful research into the culture out of which the art is born have addressed and still address the labels that once passed for stringent analysis but can no more: that it is imitative, excessive, sensational, mimetic (merely), and unintellectual, though very often "moving," "passionate," "naturalistic," "realistic" or sociologically "revealing." These labels may be construed as compliments or pejoratives and if valid, and shown as such, so much the better. More often than not, however, they are the lazy, easy brand-name applications when the hard work of analysis is deemed too hard, or when the critic does not have access to the scope the work demands. Strategies designed to counter this lazy labeling include the application of recent literary theories to Afro-American literature so that non-canonical texts can be incorporated into existing and forming critical discourse.

The third charge, that "Afro-American art exists, but is superior only when it measures up to the 'universal' criteria of Western art," produces the most seductive form of analysis, for both writer and critic, because comparisons are a major form of knowledge and flattery. The risks, nevertheless, are twofold: 1) the gathering of a culture's difference into the skirts of the Queen is a neutralization designed and constituted to elevate and maintain hegemony. 2) circumscribing and limiting the literature to a mere reaction to or denial of the Queen, judging the work solely in terms of its referents to Eurocentric criteria, or its sociological accuracy, political correctness or its pretense of having no politics at all, cripple the literature and infantilize the serious work of imaginative writing. This response-oriented concept of Afro-American literature contains the seeds of the next (fourth) charge: that when Afro-American art is worthy, it is because it is "raw" and "rich," like ore, and like ore needs refining by Western intelligences. Finding or imposing Western influences in/on Afro-American literature has value, but when its sole purpose is to *place* value only where that influence is located it is pernicious.

My unease stems from the possible, probable, consequences these approaches may have upon the work itself. They can lead to an incipient orphanization of the work in order to issue its adoption papers. They can confine the discourse to the advocacy of diversification within the canon and/or a kind of benign co-existence near or within reach of the already sacred texts. Either of these two positions can quickly become another kind of silencing if permitted to ignore the indigenous created qualities of the writing. So many questions surface and irritate. What have these critiques made of the work's own canvas? Its paint, its frame, its framelessness, its spaces? Another list of approved subjects? Of approved treatments? More self-censoring, more exclusion of the specificity of the culture, the gender, the language? Is there perhaps an alternative utility in these studies? To advance power or locate its fissures? To oppose elitist interests in order to enthrone egalitarian effacement? Or is it merely to rank and grade the readable product as distinct from the writeable production? Can this criticism reveal ways in which the author combats and confronts received prejudices and even creates *other terms* in which to rethink one's attachment to or intolerance of the material of these works? What is important in all of this is that the critic not be engaged in laying claim on behalf of the text to his or her own dominance and power. Nor to exchange his or her professional anxieties for the imagined turbulence of the text. "The text should become a problem of passion, not a pretext for it."

There are at least three focuses that seem to me to be neither reactionary nor simple pluralism, nor the even simpler methods by which the study of Afro-American literature remains the helpful doorman into the halls of sociology. Each of them, however, requires wakefulness.

One is the development of a theory of literature that truly accommodates Afro-American literature: one that is based on its culture, its history, and the artistic strategies the works employ to negotiate the world it inhabits.

Another is the examination and re-interpretation of the American canon, the founding nineteenth-century works, for the "unspeakable things unspoken"; for the ways in which the presence of Afro-Americans has shaped the choices, the language, the structure—the meaning of so much American literature. A search, in other words, for the ghost in the machine.

A third is the examination of contemporary and/or non-canonical literature for this presence, regardless of its category as mainstream, minority, or what you will. I am always amazed by the resonances, the structural gear-shifts, and the *uses* to which Afro-American narrative, persona and idiom are put in contemporary "white" literature. And in Afro-American literature itself the question of difference, of essence, is critical. What makes a work "Black"? The most valuable point of entry into the question of cultural (or racial) distinction, the one most fraught, is its language—its unpoliced, seditious, confrontational, manipulative, inventive, disruptive, masked and unmasking language. Such a penetration will entail the most careful study, one in which the impact of Afro-American presence on modernity becomes clear and is no longer a well-kept secret.

I would like to touch, for just a moment, on focuses two and three.

We can agree, I think, that invisible things are not necessarily "not-there"; that a void may be empty, but is not a vacuum. In addition, certain absences are so stressed, so ornate, so planned, they call attention to themselves; arrest us with intentionality and purpose, like neighborhoods that are defined by the population held away from them. Looking at the scope of American literature, I can't help thinking that the question should never have been "Why am I, an Afro-American, absent from it?" It is not a particularly interesting query anyway. The spectacularly interesting question is "What intellectual feats had to be performed by the author or his critic to erase me from a society seething with my presence, and what effect has that performance had on the work?" What are the strategies of escape from knowledge? Of willful oblivion? I am not recommending an inquiry into the obvious impulse that overtakes a soldier sitting in a World War I trench to think of salmon fishing. That kind of pointed "turning from," deliberate escapism or transcendence may be life-saving in a circumstance of immediate duress. The exploration I am suggesting is, how does one sit in the audience observing, watching the performance of Young America, say, in the nineteenth century, say, and reconstruct the play, its director, its plot and its cast in such a manner that its very point never surfaces? Not why. How? Ten years after Tocqueville's prediction in 1840 that "'Finding no stuff for the ideal in what is real and true, poets would flee to imaginary regions . . .' in 1850 at the height of slavery and burgeoning abolitionism, American writers chose romance." Where, I wonder, in these romances is the shadow of the presence from which the text has fled? Where does it heighten, where does it dislocate, where does it necessitate novelistic invention; what does it release; what does it hobble?

The device (or arsenal) that serves the purpose of flight can be Romanticism versus verisimilitude; new criticism versus shabbily disguised and questionably sanctioned "moral uplift"; the "complex series of evasions," that is sometimes believed to be the essence of modernism; the perception of the evolution of art; the cultivation of irony, parody; the nostalgia for "literary language"; the rhetorically unconstrained textuality versus socially anchored textuality, and the undoing of textuality altogether. These critical strategies can (but need not) be put into service to reconstruct the historical world to suit specific cultural and political purposes. Many of these strategies have produced powerfully creative work. Whatever *uses* to which Romanticism is put, however suspicious its origins, it has produced an incontestably wonderful body of work. In other instances these strategies have succeeded in paralyzing both the work and its criticism. In still others they have led to a virtual infantilization of the writer's intellect, his sensibility, his craft. They have reduced the meditations on theory into a "power struggle among sects" reading unauthored and unauthorable material, rather than an outcome of reading *with* the author the text both construct.

In other words, the critical process has made wonderful work of some wonderful work, and recently the means of access to the old debates have altered. The problem now is putting the question. Is the nineteenth century flight from blackness, for example, successful in mainstream American literature? Beautiful? Artistically problematic? Is the text sabotaged by its own proclamations of "universality"? Are there ghosts in the machine? Active but unsummoned presences that can distort the workings of the machine and can also *make* it work? These kinds of questions have been consistently put by critics of Colonial Literature vis-à-vis Africa and India and other third world countries. American literature would benefit from similar critiques. I am made melancholy when I consider that the act of defending the Eurocentric Western posture in literature as not only "universal" but also "race-free" may have resulted in lobotomizing that literature, and in diminishing both the art and the artist. Like the surgical removal of legs so that the body can remain enthroned, immobile, static—under house arrest, so to speak. It may be, of course, that contemporary writers deliberately exclude from their conscious writerly world the subjective appraisal of groups perceived as "other," and whitemale writers frequently abjure and deny the excitement of framing or locating their literature in the political world. Nineteenth-century writers, however, would never have given it a thought. Mainstream writers in Young America understood their competition to be national, cultural, but only in relationship to the Old World, certainly not vis-à-vis an ancient race (whether Native American or African) that was stripped of articulateness and intellectual thought, rendered, in D. H. Lawrence's term, "uncreate." For these early American writers, how could there be competition with nations or peoples who were presumed unable to handle or uninterested in handling the written word? One could write about them, but there was never the danger of their "writing back." Just as one could speak to them without fear of their "talking back." One could even observe them, hold them in prolonged gaze, without encountering the risk of being observed, viewed, or judged in return. And if, on occasion, they were themselves viewed and judged, it was out of a political necessity and, for the purposes of art, could not matter. Or so thought Young America. It could never have occurred to Edgar Allan Poe in 1848 that I, for example, might read *The Gold Bug* and watch his efforts to render my grandfather's speech to something as close as braying as possible, an effort so intense you can see the perspiration—and the stupidity—when Jupiter says "I knows," and Mr. Poe spells the verb "nose."[9]

Yet in spite or because of this monologism there is a great, ornamental, prescribed absence in early American literature and, I submit, it is instructive. It only seems that the canon of American literature is "naturally" or "inevitably" "white." In fact it is studiously so. In fact these absences of vital presences in Young American literature may be the insistent fruit of the scholarship rather than the text. Perhaps some of these writers, although under current house arrest, have much more to say than has been realized. Perhaps some were not so much transcending politics, or escaping blackness, as they were transforming it into intelligible, accessible, yet artistic modes of discourse. To ignore this possibility by never questioning the strategies of transformation is to disenfranchise the writer, diminish the text and render the bulk of the literature aesthetically and historically incoherent—an exorbitant price for cultural (white-male) purity, and, I believe, a spendthrift one. The re-examination of founding literature of the United States for the unspeakable unspoken may reveal those texts to have

9. Older America is not always distinguishable from its infancy. We may pardon Edgar Allan Poe in 1848 but it should have occurred to Kenneth Lynn in 1986 that some young Native American might read his Hemingway biography and see herself described as "squaw" by this respected scholar, and that some young men might shudder reading the words "buck" and "half-breed" so casually included in his scholarly speculations.

deeper and other meanings, deeper and other power, deeper and other significances.

One such writer, in particular, it has been almost impossible to keep under lock and key is Herman Melville.

Among several astute scholars, Michael Rogin has done one of the most exhaustive studies of how deeply Melville's social thought is woven into his writing,[1] He calls our attention to the connection Melville made between American slavery and American freedom, how heightened the one rendered the other. And he has provided evidence of the impact on the work of Melville's family, milieu, and, most importantly, the raging, all-encompassing conflict of the time: slavery. He has reminded us that it was Melville's father-in-law who had, as judge, decided the case that made the Fugitive Slave Law law, and that "other evidence in *Moby Dick* also suggests the impact of Shaw's ruling on the climax of Melville's tale. Melville conceived the final confrontation between Ahab and the white whale some time in the first half of 1851. He may well have written his last chapters only after returning from a trip to New York in June. [Judge Shaw's decision was handed down in April, 1851]. When New York anti-slavery leaders William Seward and John van Buren wrote public letters protesting the *Sims* ruling, the New York *Herald* responded. Its attack on "The Anti-Slavery Agitators" began: "Did you ever see a whale? Did you ever see a mighty whale struggling?" . . . [2]

Rogin also traces the chronology of the whale from its "birth in a state of nature" to its final end as commodity.[3] Central to his argument is that Melville in *Moby Dick* was being allegorically and insistently political in his choice of the whale. But within his chronology, one singular whale transcends all others, goes beyond nature, adventure, politics and commodity to an abstraction. What is this abstraction? This "wicked idea"? Interpretation has been varied. It has been viewed as an allegory of the state in which Ahab is Calhoun, or Daniel Webster; an allegory of capitalism and corruption, God and man, the individual and fate, and most commonly, the single allegorical meaning of the white whale is understood to be brute, indifferent Nature, and Ahab the madman who challenges that Nature.

But let us consider, again, the principal actor, Ahab, created by an author who calls himself Typee, signed himself Tawney, identified himself as Ishmael, and who had written several books before *Moby Dick* criticizing missionary forays into various paradises.

Ahab loses sight of the commercial value of his ship's voyage, its point, and pursues an idea in order to destroy it. His intention, revenge, "an audacious, immitigable and supernatural revenge," develops stature—maturity—when we realize that he is not a man mourning his lost leg or a scar on his face. However intense and dislocating his fever and recovery had been after his encounter with the white whale, however satisfactorily "male" this vengeance is read, the vanity of it is almost adolescent. But if the whale is more than blind, indifferent Nature unsubduable by masculine aggression, if it is as much its adjective as it is its noun, we can consider the possibility that Melville's "truth" was his recognition of the moment in America when whiteness became ideology. And if the white whale is the ideology of race,

1. See Michael Paul Rogin, *Subversive Genealogy: The Politics and Art of Herman Melville* (University of California Press, 1985), p. 15.

2. *Ibid.,* pp. 107 and 142.
3. *Ibid.,* p. 112.

what Ahab has lost to it is personal dismemberment and family and society and his own place as a human in the world. The trauma of racism is, for the racist and the victim, the severe fragmentation of the self, and has always seemed to me a cause (not a symptom) of psychosis—strangely of no interest to psychiatry. Ahab, then, is navigating between an idea of civilization that he renounces and an idea of savagery he must annihilate, because the two cannot co-exist. The former is based on the latter. What is terrible in its complexity is that the idea of savagery is not the missionary one: it is white racial ideology that is savage and if, indeed, a white, nineteenth-century, American male took on not abolition, not the amelioration of racist institutions or their laws, but the very concept of whiteness as an inhuman idea, he would be very alone, very desperate, and very doomed. Madness would be the only appropriate description of such audacity, and "he heaves me," the most succinct and appropriate description of that obsession.

I would not like to be understood to argue that Melville was engaged in some simple and simple-minded black/white didacticism, or that he was satanizing white people. Nothing like that. What I am suggesting is that he was overwhelmed by the philosophical and metaphysical inconsistencies of an extraordinary and unprecedented idea that had its fullest manifestation in his own time in his own country, and that that idea was the successful assertion of whiteness as ideology.

On the *Pequod* the multiracial, mainly foreign, proletariat is at work to produce a commodity, but it is diverted and converted from that labor to Ahab's more significant intellectual quest. We leave whale as commerce and confront whale as metaphor. With that interpretation in place, two of the most famous chapters of the book become luminous in a completely new way. One is Chapter 9, The Sermon. In Father Mapple's thrilling rendition of Jonah's trials, emphasis is given to the purpose of Jonah's salvation. He is saved from the fish's belly for one single purpose, "To preach the Truth to the face of Falsehood! That was it!" Only then the reward "Delight"—which strongly calls to mind Ahab's lonely necessity. "Delight is to him . . . who against the proud gods and commodores of this earth, ever stand forth his own inexorable self. . . . Delight is to him whose strong arms yet support him, when the ship of this base treacherous world has gone down beneath him. Delight is to him who gives no quarter in the truth and kills, burns, and destroys all sin though he pluck it out from under the robes of Senators and Judges. Delight—top-gallant delight is to him who acknowledges no law or lord, but the Lord his God, and is only a *patriot to heaven*" [italics mine]. No one, I think, has denied that the sermon is designed to be prophetic, but it seems unremarked what the nature of the sin is—the sin that must be destroyed, regardless. Nature? A sin? The terms do not apply. Capitalism? Perhaps. Capitalism fed greed, lent itself inexorably to corruption, but probably was not in and of itself sinful to Melville. Sin suggests a moral outrage within the bounds of man to repair. The concept of racial superiority would fit seamlessly. It is difficult to read those words ("destruction of sin," "patriot to heaven") and not hear in them the description of a different Ahab. Not an adolescent male in adult clothing, a maniacal egocentric, or the "exotic plant" that V. S. Parrington thought Melville was. Not even a morally fine liberal voice adjusting, balancing, compromising with racial institutions. But another Ahab: the only white male American heroic enough to try to slay the monster that was devouring the world as he knew it.

Another chapter that seems freshly lit by this reading is Chapter 42, The Whiteness of the Whale. Melville points to the do-or-die significance of his effort to say something unsayable in this chapter. "I almost despair," he writes, "of putting it in a comprehensive form. It was the whiteness of the whale that above all things appalled me. But how can I hope to explain myself here; and yet in some dim, random way, explain myself I must, *else all these chapters might be naught*" [italics mine]. The language of this chapter ranges between benevolent, beautiful images of whiteness and whiteness as sinister and shocking. After dissecting the ineffable, he concludes: "Therefore . . . symbolize whatever grand or gracious he will by whiteness, no man can deny that in its profoundest *idealized significance* it calls up a peculiar apparition to the soul." I stress "idealized significance" to emphasize and make clear (if such clarity needs stating) that Melville is not exploring white *people,* but whiteness idealized. Then, after informing the reader of his "hope to light upon some chance clue to conduct us to the hidden course we seek," he tries to nail it. To provide the key to the "hidden course." His struggle to do so is gigantic. He cannot. Nor can we. But in nonfigurative language, he identifies the imaginative tools needed to solve the problem: "subtlety appeals to subtlety, and without imagination no man can follow another into these halls." And his final observation reverberates with personal trauma. "This visible [colored] world seems formed in love, the invisible [white] spheres were formed in fright." The necessity for whiteness as privileged "natural" state, the invention of it, was indeed formed in fright.

"Slavery," writes Rogin, "confirmed Melville's isolation, decisively established in *Moby Dick*, from the dominant consciousness of his time." I differ on this point and submit that Melville's hostility and repugnance for slavery would have found company. There were many white Americans of his acquaintance who felt repelled by slavery, wrote journalism about it, spoke about it, legislated on it and were active in abolishing it. His attitude to slavery alone would not have condemned him to the almost autistic separation visited upon him. And if he felt convinced that blacks were worthy of being treated like whites, or that capitalism was dangerous—he had company or could have found it. But to question the very notion of white progress, the very idea of racial superiority, of whiteness as privileged place in the evolutionary ladder of humankind, and to meditate on the fraudulent, self-destroying philosophy of that superiority, to "pluck it out from under the robes of Senators and Judges," to drag the "judge himself to the bar,"—that was dangerous, solitary, radical work. Especially then. Especially now. To be "only a patriot to heaven" is no mean aspiration in Young America for a writer—or the captain of a whaling ship.

A complex, heaving, disorderly, profound text is *Moby Dick*, and among its several meanings it seems to me this "unspeakable" one has remained the "hidden course," the "truth in the Face of Falsehood." To this day no novelist has so wrestled with its subject. To this day literary analyses of canonical texts have shied away from that perspective: the informing and determining Afro-American presence in traditional American literature. The chapters I have made reference to are only a fraction of the instances where the text surrenders such insights, and points a helpful finger toward the ways in which the ghost drives the machine.

Melville is not the only author whose works double their fascination and their power when scoured for this presence and the writerly strategies taken to address or deny it. Edgar Allan Poe will sustain such a reading. So will Nathaniel Hawthorne and Mark Twain; and in the twentieth century, Willa Cather, Ernest Hemingway, F. Scott Fitzgerald, and William Faulkner, to name a few. Canonical American literature is begging for such attention.

It seems to me a more than fruitful project to produce some cogent analysis showing instances where early American literature identifies itself, risks itself, to assert its antithesis to blackness. How its linguistic gestures prove the intimate relationship to what is being nulled by implying a full descriptive apparatus (identity) to a presence-that-is-assumed-not-to-exist. Afro-American critical inquiry can do this work.

I mentioned earlier that finding or imposing Western influences in/on Afro-American literature had value provided the valued process does not become self-anointing. There is an adjacent project to be undertaken—the third focus in my list: the examination of contemporary literature (both the sacred and the profane) for the impact Afro-American presence has had on the structure of the work, the linguistic practice, and fictional enterprise in which it is engaged. Like focus two, this critical process must also eschew the pernicious goal of equating the fact of that presence with the achievement of the work. A work does not get better because it is responsive to another culture; nor does it become automatically flawed because of that responsiveness. The point is to clarify, not to enlist. And it does not "go without saying" that a work written by an Afro-American is automatically subsumed by an enforcing Afro-American presence. There is a clear flight from blackness in a great deal of Afro-American literature. In others there is the duel with blackness, and in some cases, as they say, "You'd never know."

III

It is on this area, the impact of Afro-American culture on contemporary American literature, that I now wish to comment. I have already said that works by Afro-Americans can respond to this presence (just as non-black works do) in a number of ways. The question of what constitutes the art of a black writer, for whom that modifier is more search than fact, has some urgency. In other words, other than melanin and subject matter, what, in fact, may make me a black writer? Other than my own ethnicity—what is going on in my work that makes me believe it is demonstrably inseparable from a cultural specificity that is Afro-American?

Please forgive the use of my own work in these observations. I use it not because it provides the best example, but because I know it best, know what I did and why, and know how central these queries are to me. Writing is, *after* all, an act of language, its practice. But *first* of all it is an effort of the will to discover.

Let me suggest some of the ways in which I activate language and ways in which that language activates me. I will limit this perusal by calling attention only to the first sentences of the books I've written, and hope that in exploring the choices I made, prior points are illuminated.

The Bluest Eye begins "Quiet as it's kept, there were no marigolds in the fall of 1941." That sentence, like the ones that open each succeeding book, is simple, uncomplicated. Of all the sentences that begin all the books, only two of them have dependent clauses; the other three are simple sentences and two are stripped down to virtually subject, verb, modifier. Nothing fancy here. No words need looking up; they are ordinary, everyday words. Yet I hoped the simplicity was not simple-minded, but devious, even loaded. And that the process of selecting each word, for itself and its relationship to the others in the sentence, along with the rejection of others for their echoes, for what is determined and what is not determined, what is almost there and what must be gleaned, would not theatricalize itself, would not erect a proscenium—at least not a noticeable one. So important to me was this unstaging, that in this first novel I summarized the whole of the book on the first page. (In the first edition, it was printed in its entirety on the jacket.)

The opening phrase of this sentence, "Quiet as it's kept," had several attractions for me. First, it was a familiar phrase familiar to me as a child listening to adults; to black women conversing with one another; telling a story, an anecdote, gossip about some one or event within the circle, the family, the neighborhood. The words are conspiratorial. "Shh, don't tell anyone else," and "No one is allowed to know this." It is a secret between us and a secret that is being kept from us. The conspiracy is both held and withheld, exposed and sustained. In some sense it was precisely what the act of writing the book was: the public exposure of a private confidence. In order fully to comprehend the duality of that position, one needs to think of the immediate political climate in which the writing took place, 1965–1969, during great social upheaval in the life of black people. The publication (as opposed to the writing) involved the exposure; the writing was the disclosure of secrets, secrets "we" shared and those withheld from us by ourselves and by the world outside the community.

"Quiet as it's kept," is also a figure of speech that is written, in this instance, but clearly chosen for how speakerly it is, how it speaks and bespeaks a particular world and its ambience. Further, in addition to its "back fence" connotation, its suggestion of illicit gossip, of thrilling revelation, there is also, in the "whisper," the assumption (on the part of the reader) that the teller is on the inside, knows something others do not, and is going to be generous with this privileged information. The intimacy I was aiming for, the intimacy between the reader and the page, could start up immediately because the secret is being shared, at best, and eavesdropped upon, at the least. Sudden familiarity or instant intimacy seemed crucial to me then, writing my first novel. I did not want the reader to have time to wonder "What do I have to do, to give up, in order to read this? What defense do I need, what distance maintain?" Because I know (and the reader does not—he or she has to wait for the second sentence) that this is a terrible story about things one would rather not know anything about.

What, then, is the Big Secret about to be shared? The thing we (reader and I) are "in" on? A botanical aberration. Pollution, perhaps. A skip, perhaps, in the natural order of things: a September, an autumn, a fall without marigolds. Bright common, strong and sturdy marigolds. When? In 1941, and since that is a momentous year (the beginning of World War II for the United States), the "fall" of 1941, just before the declaration of war, has a "closet" innuendo. In the temperate zone where there is a season known as "fall" during which one expects marigolds to be at their peak, in the months before the beginning of U.S. participation in World War II, something grim is about to be divulged. The next sentence will make it clear that the sayer, the one who knows, is a child speaking, mimicking the adult black women on the porch or in the back yard. The opening phrase is an effort to be grownup about this shocking information. The point of view of a child alters the priority an adult would assign the information. "We thought it was because Pecola was having her father's baby that the marigolds did not grow" foregrounds the flowers, backgrounds illicit, traumatic, incomprehensible sex coming to its dreaded fruition. This foregrounding of "trivial" information and backgrounding of shocking knowledge secures the point of view but gives the reader pause about whether the voice of children can be trusted at all or is more trustworthy than an adult's. The reader is thereby protected from a confrontation too soon with the painful details, while simultaneously provoked into a desire to know them. The novelty, I thought, would be in having this story of female violation revealed from the vantage point of the victims or could-be victims of rape—the persons no one inquired of (certainly not in 1965)—the girls themselves. And since the victim does not have the vocabulary to understand the violence or its context, gullible, vulnerable girl friends, looking back as the knowing adults they pretended to be in the beginning, would have to do that for her, and would have to fill those silences with their own reflective lives. Thus, the opening provides the stroke that announces something more than a secret shared, but a silence broken, a void filled, an unspeakable thing spoken at last. And they draw the connection between a minor destabilization in seasonal flora with the insignificant destruction of a black girl. Of course "minor" and "insignificant" represent the outside world's view—for the girls both phenomena are earthshaking depositories of information they spend that whole year of childhood (and afterwards) trying to fathom, and cannot. If they have any success, it will be in transferring the problem of fathoming to the presumably adult reader, to the inner circle of listeners. At the least they have distributed the weight of these problematical questions to a larger constituency, and justified the public exposure of a privacy. If the conspiracy that the opening words announce is entered into by the reader, then the book can be seen to open with its close: a speculation on the disruption of "nature," as being a social disruption with tragic individual consequences in which the reader, as part of the population of the text, is implicated.

However a problem, unsolved, lies in the central chamber of the novel. The shattered world I built (to complement what is happening to Pecola), its pieces held together by seasons in childtime and commenting at every turn on the incompatible and barren white-family primer, does not in its present form handle effectively the silence at its center. The void that is Pecola's "unbeing." It should have had a shape—like the emptiness left by a boom or a cry. It required a sophistication unavailable to me, and some deft manipulation of the voices around her. She is not *seen* by herself until she hallucinates a self. And the fact of her hallucination becomes a point of outside-the-book conversation, but does not work in the reading process.

Also, although I was pressing for a female expressiveness (a challenge that re-surfaced in *Sula*), it eluded me for the most part, and I had to content myself with female personae because I was not able to secure throughout the work the feminine subtext that is present in the opening sentence (the women gossiping, eager and aghast in "Quiet as it's kept"). The shambles this struggle became is most evident in the section on Pauline Breedlove where I resorted to two voices, hers and the urging narrator's, both of which are extremely unsatisfactory to me. It is interesting to me now that where I thought I would have the most difficulty subverting the language to a feminine mode, I had the least: connecting Cholly's "rape" by the white-men to his own of his daughter. This most masculine act of aggression becomes feminized in my language, "passive," and, I think, more accurately repellent when deprived of the male "glamor of shame" rape is (or once was) routinely given.

The points I have tried to illustrate are that my choices of language (speakerly, aural, colloquial), my reliance for full comprehension on codes embedded in black culture, my effort to effect immediate co-conspiracy and intimacy (without any distancing, explanatory fabric), as well as my (failed) attempt to shape a silence while breaking it are attempts (many unsatisfactory) to transfigure the complexity and wealth of Afro-American culture into a language worthy of the culture.

In *Sula*, it's necessary to concentrate on *two* first sentences because what survives in print is not the one I had intended to be the first. Originally the book opened with "Except for World War II nothing ever interfered with National Suicide Day." With some encouragement, I recognized that it was a false beginning. *"In medias res"* with a vengeance, because there was no *res* to be in the middle of—no implied world in which to locate the specific-ity and the resonances in the sentence. More to the point, I knew I was writing a second novel, and that it too would be about people in a black community not just foregrounded but totally dominant; and that it was about black women—also foregrounded and dominant. In 1988, certainly, I would not need (or feel the need for) the sentence—the short section—that now opens *Sula*. The threshold between the reader and the black-topic text need not be the safe, welcoming lobby I persuaded myself it needed at that time. My preference was the demolition of the lobby altogether. As can be seen from *The Bluest Eye*, and in every other book I have written, only *Sula* has this "entrance." The others refuse the "presentation"; refuse the seduc-tive safe harbor; the line of demarcation between the sacred and the obscene, public and private, them and us. Refuse, in effect, to cater to the dimin-ished expectations of the reader, or his or her alarm heightened by the emotional luggage one carries into the black-topic text. (I should remind you that *Sula* was begun in 1969, while my first book was in proof, in a period of extraordinary political activity.)

Since I had become convinced that the effectiveness of the original beginning was only in my head, the job at hand became how to construct an alternate beginning that would not force the work to genuflect and would complement the outlaw quality in it. The problem presented itself this way: to fashion a door. Instead of having the text open wide the moment the cover is opened (or, as in *The Bluest Eye*, to have the book stand exposed before the cover is even touched, much less opened, by plac-ing the complete "plot" on the first page—and finally on the cover of the first edition), here I was to posit a door, turn its knob and beckon for some four or five pages. I had determined not to mention any characters in those pages, there would be no people in the lobby—but I did, rather heavy-handedly in my view, end the welcome aboard with the mention of Shadrack and Sula. It was a craven (to me, still) surrender to a worn-out technique of novel writing: the overt announcement to the reader whom to pay attention to. Yet the bulk of the opening I finally wrote is about the community, a view of it, and the view is not from within (this is a door, after all) but from the point of view of a stranger—the "valley man" who might happen to be there on some errand, but who obviously does not live there and to and for whom all this is mightily strange, even exotic. You can see why I despise much of this beginning. Yet I tried to place in the opening sentence the signature terms of loss: "There used to be a neighborhood here; not any more." That may not be the world's worst sentence, but it doesn't "play," as they say in the theater.

My new first sentence became "In that place, where they tore the night-shade and blackberry patches from their roots to make room for the Medallion City Golf Course, there was once a neighborhood." Instead of my original plan, here I am introducing an outside-the-circle reader into the circle. I am translating the anonymous into the specific, a "place" into a "neighborhood," and letting a stranger in through whose eyes it can be viewed. In between "place" and "neighborhood" I now have to squeeze the specificity and the *difference*; the nostalgia, the history, and the nostalgia for the history; the violence done to it and the consequences of that violence. (It took three months, those four pages, a whole summer of nights.) The nostalgia is sounded by "once"; the history and a longing for it is implied in the connotation of "neighborhood." The violence lurks in having something torn out by its roots—it will not, cannot grow again. Its consequences are that what has been destroyed is considered weeds, refuse necessarily removed in urban "development" by the unspecified but no less known "they" who do not, cannot, afford to differentiate what is displaced, and would not care that this is "refuse" of a certain kind. Both plants have darkness in them: "black" and "night." One is unusual (nightshade) and has two darkness words: "night" and "shade." The other (blackberry) is common. A familiar plant and an exotic one. A harmless one and a dangerous one. One produces a nourishing berry; one delivers toxic ones. But they both thrived there together, *in that place when it was a neighborhood*. Both are gone now, and the description that follows is of the other specific things, in this black community, destroyed in the wake of the golf course. Golf course conveys what it is not, in this context: not houses, or factories, or even a public park, and certainly not residents. It is a manicured place where the likelihood of the former residents showing up is almost nil.

I want to get back to those berries for a moment (to explain, perhaps, the length of time it took for the language of that section to arrive). I always thought of Sula as quintessentially black, metaphysically black, if you will, which is not melanin and certainly not unquestioning fidelity to the tribe. She is new world black and new world woman extracting choice from choicelessness, responding inventively to found things. Improvisational. Daring, disruptive, imaginative, modern, out-of-the-house, outlawed, unpolicing, uncontained and uncontainable. And dangerously female. In her final conversation with Nel she refers to herself as a special kind of black person woman, one with choices. Like a redwood, she says. (With all due respect to the dream landscape of Freud, trees have always seemed feminine to me.) In any case, my perception of Sula's double-dose of *chosen* blackness and *biological* blackness is in the presence of those two words of darkness in "nightshade" as well as in the uncommon quality of the vine itself. One variety is called "enchanter," and the other "bittersweet" because the berries taste bitter at first and then sweet. Also nightshade was thought to counteract witchcraft. All of this seemed a wonderful constellation of signs for Sula. And "blackberry patch" seemed equally appropriate for Nel:

nourishing, never needing to be tended or cultivated, once rooted and bearing. Reliably sweet but thorn-bound. Her process of becoming, heralded by the explosive dissolving of her fragilely-held-together ball of string and fur (when the thorns of her self-protection are removed by Eva), puts her back in touch with the complex, contradictory, evasive, independent, liquid modernity Sula insisted upon. A modernity which overturns pre-war definitions, ushers in the Jazz Age (an age *defined* by Afro-American art and culture), and requires new kinds of intelligences to define oneself.

The stage-setting of the first four pages is embarrassing to me now, but the pains I have taken to explain it may be helpful in identifying the strategies one can be forced to resort to in trying to accommodate the mere fact of writing about, for and out of black culture while accommodating and responding to mainstream "white" culture. The "valley man's" guidance into the territory was my compromise. Perhaps it "worked," but it was not the work I wanted to do.

Had I begun with Shadrack, I would have ignored the smiling welcome and put the reader into immediate confrontation with his wound and his scar. The difference my preferred (original) beginning would have made would be calling greater attention to the traumatic displacement this most wasteful capitalist war had on black people in particular, and throwing into relief the creative, if outlawed, determination to survive it whole. Sula as (feminine) solubility and Shadrack's (male) fixative are two extreme ways of dealing with displacement—a prevalent theme in the narrative of black people. In the final opening I replicated the demiurge of discriminatory, prosecutorial racial oppression in the loss to commercial "progress" of the village, but the references to the community's stability and creativeness (music, dancing, craft, religion, irony, wit all referred to in the "valley man's" presence) refract and subsume their pain while they are in the thick of it. It is a softer embrace than Shadrack's organized, public madness—his disruptive remembering presence which helps (for a while) to cement the community, until Sula challenges them.

"The North Carolina Mutual Life Insurance agent promised to fly from Mercy to the other side of Lake Superior at 3:00."

This declarative sentence is designed to mock a journalistic style; with a minor alteration it could be the opening of an item in a smalltown newspaper. It has the tone of an everyday event of minimal local interest. Yet I wanted it to contain (as does the scene that takes place when the agent fulfills his promise) the information that *Song of Solomon* both centers on and radiates from.

The name of the insurance company is real, a well known black-owned company dependent on black clients, and in its corporate name are "life" and "mutual;" *agent* being the necessary ingredient of what enables the relationship between them. The sentence also moves from North Carolina to Lake Superior—geographical locations, but with a sly implication that the move from North Carolina (the south) to Lake Superior (the north) might not actually involve progress to some "superior state"—which, of course it does not. The two other significant words are "fly," upon which the novel centers and "Mercy," the name of the place from which he is to fly. Both constitute the heartbeat of the narrative. Where is the insurance man flying to? The other side of Lake Superior is Canada, of course, the historic terminus of the escape route for black people looking for asylum. "Mercy," the other significant term, is the grace note; the earnest though, with one exception, unspoken wish of the narrative's population. Some grant it; some never find it; one, at least, makes it the text and cry of her extemporaneous sermon upon the death of her granddaughter. It touches, turns and returns to Guitar at the end of the book—he who is least deserving of it—and moves him to make it his own final gift. It is what one wishes for Hagar; what is unavailable to and unsought by Macon Dead, senior; what his wife learns to demand from him, and what can never come from the white world as is signified by the inversion of the name of the hospital from Mercy to "no-Mercy." It is only available from within. The center of the narrative is flight; the spring-board is mercy.

But the sentence turns, as all sentences do, on the verb: promised. The insurance agent does not declare, announce, or threaten his act. He promises, as though a contract is being executed—faithfully—between himself and others. Promises broken, or kept; the difficulty of ferreting out loyalties and ties that bind or bruise wend their way throughout the action and the shifting relationships. So the agent's flight, like that of the Solomon in the title, although toward asylum (Canada, or freedom, or home, or the company of the welcoming dead), and although it carries the possibility of failure and the certainty of danger, is toward change, an alternative way, a cessation of things-as-they-are. It should not be understood as a simple desperate act, the end of a fruitless life, a life without gesture, without examination, but as obedience to a deeper contract with his people. It is his commitment to them, regardless of whether, in all its details, they understand it. There is, however, in their response to his action, a tenderness, some contrition, and mounting respect ("They didn't know he had it in him") and an awareness that the gesture enclosed rather than repudiated themselves. The note he leaves asks for forgiveness. It is tacked on his door as a mild invitation to whomever might pass by, but it is not an advertisement. It is an almost Christian declaration of love as well as humility of one who was not able to do more.

There are several other flights in the work and they are motivationally different. Solomon's the most magical, the most theatrical and, for Milkman, the most satisfying. It is also the most problematic—to those he left behind. Milkman's flight binds these two elements of loyalty (Mr. Smith's) and abandon and self-interest (Solomon's) into a third thing: a merging of fealty and risk that suggests the "agency" for "mutual" "life," which he offers at the end and which is echoed in the hills behind him, and is the marriage of surrender and domination, acceptance and rule, commitment to a group *through* ultimate isolation. Guitar recognizes this marriage and recalls enough of how lost he himself is to put his weapon down.

The journalistic style at the beginning, its rhythm of a familiar, hand-me-down dignity is pulled along by an accretion of detail displayed in a meandering unremarkableness. Simple words, uncomplex sentence structures, persistent understatement, highly aural syntax—but the ordinariness of the language, its colloquial, vernacular, humorous and, upon occasion, parabolic quality sabotage expectations and mask judgments when it can no longer defer them. The composition of red, white and blue in the opening scene provides the national canvas/flag upon which the narrative works and against which the lives of these black people must be seen, but which must not overwhelm the enterprise the novel is engaged in. It is a composition of color that heralds Milkman's birth, protects his youth, hides its

1098 | TONI MORRISON

purpose and through which he must burst (through blue Buicks, red tulips in his waking dream, and his sisters' white stockings, ribbons and gloves) before discovering that the gold of his search is really Pilate's yellow orange and the glittering metal of the box in her ear.

These spaces, which I am filling in, and can fill in because they were planned, can conceivably be filled in with other significances. That is planned as well. The point is that into these spaces should fall the ruminations of the reader and his or her invented or recollected or misunderstood knowingness. The reader as narrator asks the questions the community asks, and both reader and "voice" stand among the crowd, within it, with privileged intimacy and contact, but without any more privileged information than the crowd has. That egalitarianism which places us all (reader, the novel's population, the narrator's voice) on the same footing reflected for me the force of flight and mercy, and the precious, imaginative yet realistic gaze of black people who (at one time, anyway) did not mythologize what or whom it mythologized. The "song" itself contains this unblinking evaluation of the miraculous and heroic flight of the legendary Solomon, an unblinking gaze which is lurking in the tender but amused choral-community response to the agent's flight. Sotto (but not completely) is my own giggle (in Afro-American terms) of the proto-myth of the journey to manhood. Whenever characters are cloaked in Western fable, they are in deep trouble; but the African myth is also contaminated. Unprogressive, unreconstructed, self-born Pilate is unimpressed by Solomon's flight and knocks Milkman down when, made new by his appropriation of his own family's fable, he returns to educate her with it. Upon hearing all he has to say, her only interest is filial. "Papa? . . . I've been carryin' Papa?" And her longing to hear the song, finally, is a longing for balm to die by, not a submissive obedience to history—anybody's.

The opening sentence of *Tar Baby*, "He believed he was safe," is the second version of itself. The first, "He thought he was safe," was discarded because "thought" did not contain the doubt I wanted to plant in the reader's mind about whether or not he really was—safe. "Thought" came to me at once because it was the verb my parents and grandparents used when describing what they had dreamed the night before. Not "I dreamt," or "It seemed" or even "I saw or did" this or that—but "I thought." It gave the dream narrative distance (a dream is not "real") and power (the control implied in *thinking* rather than *dreaming*). But to use "thought" seemed to undercut the faith of the character and the distrust I wanted to suggest to the reader. "Believe" was chosen to do the work properly. And the person who does the believing is, in a way, about to enter a dream world, and convinces himself, eventually, that he is in control of it. He believed; was convinced. And although the word suggests his conviction, it does not reassure the reader. If I had wanted the reader to trust this person's point of view I would have written "He was safe." Or, "Finally, he was safe." The unease about this view of safety is important because safety itself is the desire of each person in the novel. Locating it, creating it, losing it.

You may recall that I was interested in working out the mystery of a piece of lore, a folk tale, which is also about safety and danger and the skills needed to secure the one and recognize and avoid the other. I was not, of course, interested in re-telling the tale; I suppose that is an idea to pursue, but it is certainly not interesting enough to engage me for four years. I have said, elsewhere, that the exploration of the Tar Baby tale was like stroking a pet to see what the anatomy was like but not to disturb or distort its mystery. Folk lore may have begun as allegory for natural or social phenomena; it may have been employed as a retreat from contemporary issues in art, but folk lore can also contain myths that re-activate themselves endlessly through providers—the people who repeat, reshape, reconstitute and reinterpret them. The Tar Baby tale seemed to me to be about masks. Not masks as covering what is to be hidden, but how masks come to life, take life over, exercise the tensions between itself and what it covers. For Son, the most effective mask is none. For the others the construction is careful and delicately borne, but the masks they make have a life of their own and collide with those they come in contact with. The texture of the novel seemed to want leanness, architecture that was worn and ancient like a piece of mask sculpture: exaggerated, breathing, just athwart the representational life it displaced. Thus, the first and last sentences had to match, as the exterior planes match the interior, concave ones inside the mask. Therefore "He believed he was safe" would be the twin of "Lickety split, lickety split, lickety lickety split." This close is 1) the last sentence of the folk tale. 2) the action of the character. 3) the indeterminate ending that follows from the untrustworthy beginning. 4) the complimentary meter of its twin sister [u u / u u / with u u u / u u u /], and 5) the wide and marvelous space between the contradiction of those two images: from a dream of safety to the sound of running feet. The whole mediated world in between. This masked and unmasked; enchanted, disenchanted; wounded and wounding world is played out on and by the varieties of interpretation (Western and Afro-American) the Tar Baby myth has been (and continues to be) subjected to. Winging one's way through the vise and expulsion of history becomes possible in creative encounters with that history. Nothing, in those encounters, is safe, or should be. Safety is the foetus of power as well as protection from it, as the uses to which masks and myths are put in Afro-American culture remind us.

"124 was spiteful. Full of a baby's venom."

Beginning *Beloved* with numerals rather than spelled out numbers, it was my intention to give the house an identity separate from the street or even the city; to name it the way "Sweet Home" was named; the way plantations were named, but not with nouns or "proper" names—with numbers instead because numbers have no adjectives, no posture of coziness or grandeur or the haughty yearning of arrivistes and estate builders for the parallel beautifications of the nation they left behind, laying claim to instant history and legend. Numbers here constitute an address, a thrilling enough prospect for slaves who had owned nothing, least of all an address. And although the numbers, unlike words, can have no modifiers, I give these an adjective—spiteful (There are three others). The address is therefore personalized, but personalized by its own activity, not the pasted-on desire for personality.

Also there is something about numerals that makes them spoken, heard, in this context, because one expects words to read in a book, not numbers to say, or hear. And the sound of the novel, sometimes cacaphonous, sometimes harmonious, must be an inner ear sound or a sound just beyond hearing, infusing the text with a musical emphasis that words can do sometimes even better than music can. Thus the second sentence is not one: it is a phrase that properly, grammatically, belongs as a dependent clause with the first. Had I done that, however, (124 was spiteful, comma, full of a baby's venom, or 124 was full of a baby's venom) I could not have had the accent on *full* [/ u u / u / u pause / u u u u / u].

Whatever the risks of confronting the reader with what must be immediately incomprehensible in that simple, declarative authoritative sentence, the risk of unsettling him or her, I determined to take. Because the *in medias res* opening that I am so committed to is here excessively demanding. It is abrupt, and should appear so. No native informant here. The reader is snatched, yanked, thrown into an environment completely foreign, and I want it as the first stroke of the shared experience that might be possible between the reader and the novel's population. Snatched just as the slaves were from one place to another, from any place to another, without preparation and without defense. No lobby, no door, no entrance—a gangplank, perhaps (but a very short one). And the house into which this snatching—this kidnapping—propels one, changes from spiteful to loud to quiet, as the sounds in the body of the ship itself may have changed. A few words have to be read before it is clear that 124 refers to a house (in most of the early drafts "The women *in the house* knew it" was simply "The women knew it." "House" was not mentioned for seventeen lines), and a few more have to be read to discover why it is spiteful, or rather the source of the spite. By then it is clear, if not at once, that something is beyond control, but is not beyond understanding since it is not beyond accommodation by both the "women" and the "children." The fully realized presence of the haunting is both a major incumbent of the narrative and sleight of hand. One of its purposes is to keep the reader preoccupied with the nature of the incredible spirit world while being supplied a controlled diet of the incredible political world.

The subliminal, the underground life of a novel is the area most likely to link arms with the reader and facilitate making it one's own. Because one must, to get from the first sentence to the next, and the next and the next. The friendly observation post I was content to build and man in *Sula* (with the stranger in the midst), or the down-home journalism of *Song of Solomon* or the calculated mistrust of the point of view in *Tar Baby* would not serve here. Here I wanted the compelling confusion of being there as they (the characters) are; suddenly, without comfort or succor from the "author," with only imagination, intelligence, and necessity available for the journey. The painterly language of *Song of Solomon* was not useful to me in *Beloved*. There is practically no color whatsoever in its pages, and when there is, it is so stark and remarked upon, it is virtually raw. Color seen for the first time, without its history. No built architecture as in *Tar Baby*, no play with Western chronology as in *Sula*; no exchange between book life and "real" life discourse—with printed text units rubbing up against seasonal black child-time units as in *The Bluest Eye*. No compound of houses, no neighborhood, no sculpture, no paint, no time, especially no time because memory, prehistoric memory, has no time. There is just a little music, each other and the urgency of what is at stake. Which is all they had. For that work, the work of language is to get out of the way.

I hope you understand that in this explication of how I practice language is a search for and deliberate posture of vulnerability to those aspects of Afro-American culture that can inform and position my work. I sometimes know when the work works, when *nommo* has effectively summoned, by reading and listening to those who have entered the text. I learn nothing from those who resist it, except, of course, the sometimes fascinating display of their struggle. My expectations of and my gratitude to the critics who enter, are great. To those who talk about how as well as what; who identify the workings as well as the work; for whom the study of Afro-American literature is neither a crash course in neighborliness and tolerance, nor an infant to be carried, instructed or chastised or even whipped like a child, but the serious study of art forms that have much work to do, but are already legitimatized by their own cultural sources and predecessors—in or out of the canon—I owe much.

For an author, regarding canons, it is very simple: in fifty, a hundred or more years his or her work may be relished for its beauty or its insight or its power; or it may be condemned for its vacuousness and pretension—and junked. Or in fifty or a hundred years the critic (as canon builder) may be applauded for his or her intelligent scholarship and powers of critical inquiry. Or laughed at for ignorance and shabbily disguised assertions of power—and junked. It's possible that the reputations of both will thrive, or that both will decay. In any case, as far as the future is concerned, when one writes, as critic or as author, all necks are on the line.

1989

ERNEST J. GAINES
b. 1933

Ernest Gaines's childhood on a Louisiana plantation has been central to his development as a writer. A reservoir of the spoken wisdom and of the stories, historical settings, and drama of the several generations of Creole, Cajun, and African American country people who still populate southern Louisiana, Gaines's writing draws on his early memories, which he refreshes by taking frequent trips back to Pointe Coupee Parish.

Born to Manuel and Adrienne Gaines on January 15, 1933, in Oscar, Louisiana, young Ernest worked in the fields from an early age. His aunt Augusteen Jefferson was a powerful influence; she had no legs, but provided materially and spiritually for her nephew. She would become the model for the many inspiring older women in his fiction, especially the protagonist of his immensely popular *The Autobiography of Miss Jane Pittman* (1971) and Tante Lou in *A Lesson before Dying* (1993). Beginning with *Catherine Carmier* (1964), his first novel, and *Bloodline* (1968), his first collection of short stories, Gaines has dedicated himself to conveying the emotional and physical geographies of the twelve or fifteen plantations that once bound together the two parishes whose fictional center is Bayonne. The vivid sense of place, the attention to voice, as well as the ability to suggest complex moral dilemmas with the barest physical description makes Gaines's fiction very attractive to filmmakers. But he is decidedly a literary craftsman.

As a teenager Gaines moved to California, where his mother and stepfather believed he would find greater opportunities. In Vallejo he enrolled in junior college. He read widely, especially admiring the works of nineteenth-century Russian novelists such as Turgenev, Gogol, and Tolstoy, whose chronicles of the strains serfdom put on their society were especially resonant for a young man who had just left the rural and segregated South. In fact, Gaines has said that *Catherine Carmier*, while inspired by one of Lightning Hopkins's blues songs, was modeled on Turgenev's *Fathers and Sons*. The relationship between fathers and sons and the definition of manhood are central themes in Gaines's work: in the short stories of *Bloodline*—especially "The Sky Is Gray" and "Three Men"—as well as in his novels *In My Father's House* (1978), *A Gathering of Old Men* (1983) and *A Lesson before Dying*.

In interviews, Gaines has explained that he was not influenced by African American writers such as Richard Wright and Ralph Ellison, simply because black writers were not on the curriculum of his college. Wright, he points out, would not have been important to him because of his urban focus. Instead, Gaines said, "I learned much about dialogue from Faulkner, especially when we're dealing with southern dialects. I learned rhythms and things from Gertrude Stein." Critics have also noted the influence of Ernest Hemingway on Gaines's style. Like Hemingway, who was among the best-known Anglo-American modernists, Gaines has consistently attempted to capture in writing the speech of a particular region in America, in an understated yet vivid prose.

After a two-year stint in the army, Gaines attended San Francisco State College, graduating in 1957. Then, at the height of a literary renaissance triggered by the arrival in the mid-1950s of Beat writers such as Allen Ginsberg and Jack Kerouac, Gaines found himself living in San Francisco, an ideal place to begin a career as a writer. While in college, Gaines had begun publishing short stories in a campus publication called *Transfer*. Literary agent Dorothea Oppenheimer saw the stories and assisted Gaines in getting a Wallace Stegner fellowship at Stanford and a contract for a novel with Dial Press. As Gaines's career accelerated, so did his determination to keep the regional focus in his work.

"Knowing the place, knowing the people" is a project Gaines conceives of in the broadest possible terms. Understanding locale means being able to tap into a communal store of memories available through folklore and storytelling. Gaines has used a variety of strategies to achieve the "transfer" from oral lore to paper. Aware that he is capable, at best, of producing only an approximation of the actual speech each master storyteller uses, Gaines creates a heightened unifying voice "that compensate[s] . . . for not having the audience and the sound and the performance there." Early on, he realized that achieving "voice" meant giving the historical information back to the central characters. This is how Gaines describes the process, which he perfected in his first-person narrative *The Autobiography of Miss Jane Pittman*:

> I went to the Louisiana Room at the LSU library and I went through page after page . . . Then I said, OK, I've got all this information and now I must go back here, Miss Jane . . . I must in some way—and that's how we come back to the voice thing—give her all this information and let her tell this thing the way she would tell it, as an illiterate black woman a hundred years old talking about these things . . . I cannot just give her hunks of history and throw them to her, and have her describe, "It was Sunday at seven o'clock and Huey Long was going from New Orleans to such and such a place" . . . because she never would have spoken that way. . . . The historian would have been the one speaking that way.

The 108-year-old Miss Jane narrates her story, beginning with her girlhood on a slave plantation, through the violence of the Reconstruction era, the establishment of Jim Crow laws, the valiant protests of the early civil rights movements, and ending on the cusp of the desegregation of Bayonne. Gaines uses other characters to jolt Miss Jane's memory and to fill in details that she forgets. But her inimitable voice is the mainspring of the novel. In *A Gathering of Old Men*, Gaines uses the collective voices of fifteen elderly African American to tell a story of courageous resistance to racism. *A Lesson before Dying* is another popular novel; Oprah Winfrey selected it for her book club, and it was adapted for the stage and television. In the book itself, Gaines gives voice to the teenager Jefferson, who is awaiting execution for a murder he did not commit, by incorporating portions of his diary into the text. The teacher Grant Wiggins is the novel's first-person narrator; he, no less than Jefferson, learns the lesson in manhood to which the title refers. The plot of "The Sky Is Gray," printed here, is less dramatic; but much depends on the ability of the teenage protagonist to draw the appropriate conclusions from his experience.

Ernest Gaines lives and writes in San Francisco.

The Sky Is Gray

I

Go'n be coming in a few minutes. Coming round that bend down there full speed. And I'm go'n get out my handkerchief and wave it down, and we go'n get on it and go.

I keep on looking for it, but Mama don't look that way no more. She's looking down the road where we just come from. It's a long old road, and far's you can see you don't see nothing but gravel. You got dry weeds on both sides, and you got trees on both sides, and fences on both sides, too. And you got cows in the pastures and they standing close together. And when we was coming out here to catch the bus I seen the smoke coming out of the cows's noses.

I look at my mama and I know what she's thinking. I been with Mama so much, just me and her, I know what she's thinking all the time. Right now it's home—Auntie and them. She's thinking if they got enough wood—if she left enough there to keep them warm till we get back. She's thinking if it go'n rain and if any of them go'n have to go out in the rain. She's thinking 'bout the hog—if he go'n get out, and if Ty and Val be able to get him back in. She always worry like that when she leaves the house. She don't worry too much if she leave me there with the smaller ones, 'cause she know I'm go'n look after them and look after Auntie and everything else. I'm the oldest and she say I'm the man.

I look at my mama and I love my mama. She's wearing that black coat and that black hat and she's looking sad. I love my mama and I want put my arm round her and tell her. But I'm not supposed to do that. She say that's weakness and that's crybaby stuff, and she don't want no crybaby round her. She don't want you to be scared, either. 'Cause Ty's scared of ghosts and she's always whipping him. I'm scared of the dark, too, but I make 'tend I ain't. I make 'tend I ain't 'cause I'm the oldest, and I got to set a good sample for the rest. I can't ever be scared and I can't ever cry. And that's why I never said nothing 'bout my teeth. It's been hurting me and hurting me close to a month now, but I never said it. I didn't say it 'cause I didn't want act like a crybaby, and 'cause I know we didn't have enough money to go have it pulled. But, Lord, it been hurting me. And look like it wouldn't start till at night when you was trying to get yourself little sleep. Then soon's you shut your eyes—ummm-ummm, Lord, look like it go right down to your heartstring.

"Hurting, hanh?" Ty'd say.

I'd shake my head, but I wouldn't open my mouth for nothing. You open your mouth and let that wind in, and it almost kill you.

I'd just lay there and listen to them snore. Ty there, right 'side me, and Auntie and Val over by the fireplace. Val younger than me and Ty, and he sleeps with Auntie. Mama sleeps round the other side with Louis and Walker.

I'd just lay there and listen to them, and listen to that wind out there, and listen to that fire in the fireplace. Sometimes it'd stop long enough to let me get little rest. Sometimes it just hurt, hurt, hurt. Lord, have mercy.

2

Auntie knowed it was hurting me. I didn't tell nobody but Ty, 'cause we buddies and he ain't go'n tell nobody. But some kind of way Auntie found out. When she asked me, I told her no, nothing was wrong. But she knowed it all the time. She told me to mash up a piece of aspirin and wrap it in some cotton and jugg it down in that hole. I did it, but it didn't do no good. It stopped for a little while, and started right back again. Auntie wanted to tell Mama, but I told her, "Uh-uh." 'Cause I knowed we didn't have any money, and it just was go'n make her mad again. So Auntie told Monsieur Bayonne, and Monsieur Bayonne came over to the house and told me to kneel down 'side him on the fireplace. He put his finger in his mouth and made the Sign of the Cross on my jaw. The tip of Monsieur Bayonne's finger is some hard, 'cause he's always playing on that guitar. If we sit outside at night we can always hear Monsieur Bayonne playing on his guitar. Sometimes we leave him out there playing on the guitar.

Monsieur Bayonne made the Sign of the Cross over and over on my jaw, but that didn't do no good. Even when he prayed and told me to pray some, too, that tooth still hurt me.

"How you feeling?" he say.

"Same," I say.

He kept on praying and making the Sign of the Cross and I kept on praying, too.

"Still hurting?" he say.

"Yes, sir."

Monsieur Bayonne mashed harder and harder on my jaw. He mashed so hard he almost pushed me over on Ty. But then he stopped.

"What kind of prayers you praying, boy?" he say.

"Baptist," I say.

"Well, I'll be—no wonder that tooth still killing him. I'm going one way and he pulling the other. Boy, don't you know any Catholic prayers?"

"I know 'Hail Mary,'" I say.

"Then you better start saying it."

"Yes, sir."

He started mashing on my jaw again, and I could hear him praying at the same time. And, sure enough, after while it stopped hurting me.

Me and Ty went outside where Monsieur Bayonne's two hounds was and we started playing with them. "Let's go hunting," Ty say. "All right," I say; and we went on back in the pasture. Soon the hounds got on a trail, and me and Ty followed them all 'cross the pasture and then back in the woods, too. And then they cornered this little old rabbit and killed him, and me and Ty made them get back, and we picked up the rabbit and started on back home. But my tooth had started hurting me again. It was hurting me plenty now, but I wouldn't tell Monsieur Bayonne. That night I didn't sleep a bit, and first thing in the morning Auntie told me to go back and let Monsieur Bayonne pray over me some more. Monsieur Bayonne was in his kitchen making coffee when I got there. Soon's he seen me he knowed what was wrong.

"All right, kneel down there 'side that stove," he say. "And this time make sure you pray Catholic. I don't know nothing 'bout that Baptist, and I don't want know nothing 'bout him."

3

Last night Mama say, "Tomorrow we going to town."

"It ain't hurting me no more," I say. "I can eat anything on it."

"Tomorrow we going to town," she say.

And after she finished eating, she got up and went to bed. She always go to bed early now. 'Fore Daddy went in the Army, she used to stay up late. All of us sitting out on the gallery or round the fire. But now, look like soon's she finish eating she go to bed.

This morning when I woke up, her and Auntie was standing 'fore the fireplace. She say: "Enough to get there and get back. Dollar and a half to have it pulled. Twenty-five for me to go, twenty-five for him. Twenty-five for me to come back, twenty-five for him. Fifty cents left. Guess I get little piece of salt meat with that."

"Sure can use it," Auntie say. "White beans and no salt meat ain't white beans."

"I do the best I can," Mama say.

They was quiet after that, and I made 'tend I was still asleep.

"James, hit the floor," Auntie say.

I still made 'tend I was asleep. I didn't want them to know I was listening.

"All right," Auntie say, shaking me by the shoulder. "Come on. Today's the day."

I pushed the cover down to get out, and Ty grabbed it and pulled it back.

"You, too, Ty," Auntie say.

"I ain't getting no teef pulled," Ty say.

"Don't mean it ain't time to get up," Auntie say. "Hit it, Ty."

Ty got up grumbling.

"James, you hurry up and get in your clothes and eat your food," Auntie say. "What time y'all coming back?" she say to Mama.

"That 'leven o'clock bus," Mama say. "Got to get back in that field this evening."

"Get a move on you, James," Auntie say.

I went in the kitchen and washed my face, then I ate my breakfast. I was having bread and syrup. The bread was warm and hard and tasted good. And I tried to make it last a long time.

Ty came back there grumbling and mad at me.

"Got to get up," he say. "I ain't having no teefes pulled. What I got to be getting up for?"

Ty poured some syrup in his pan and got a piece of bread. He didn't wash his hands, neither his face, and I could see that white stuff in his eyes.

"You the one getting your teef pulled," he say. "What I got to get up for. I bet if I was getting a teef pulled, you wouldn't be getting up. Shucks; syrup again. I'm getting tired of this old syrup. Syrup, syrup, syrup. I'm go'n take with the sugar diabetes. I want me some bacon sometime."

"Go out in the field and work and you can have your bacon," Auntie say. She stood in the middle door looking at Ty. "You better be glad you got syrup. Some people ain't got that—hard 's time is."

"Shucks," Ty say. "How can I be strong."

"I don't know too much 'bout your strength," Auntie say; "but I know where you go'n be hot at, you keep that grumbling up. James, get a move on you; your mama waiting."

I ate my last piece of bread and went in the front room. Mama was standing 'fore the fireplace warming her hands. I put on my coat and my cap, and we left the house.

4

I look down there again, but it still ain't coming. I almost say, "It ain't coming yet," but I keep my mouth shut. 'Cause that's something else she don't like. She don't like for you to say something just for nothing. She can see it ain't coming, I can see it ain't coming, so why say it ain't coming. I don't say it, I turn and look at the river that's back of us. It's so cold the smoke's just raising up from the water. I see a bunch of pool-doos not too far out—just on the other side the lilies. I'm wondering if you can eat pool-doos. I ain't too sure, 'cause I ain't never ate none. But I done ate owls and blackbirds, and I done ate redbirds, too. I didn't want kill the redbirds, but she made me kill them. They had two of them back there. One in my trap, one in Ty's trap. Me and Ty was go'n play with them and let them go, but she made me kill them 'cause we needed the food.

"I can't," I say. "I can't."

"Here," she say. "Take it."

"I can't," I say. "I can't. I can't kill him, Mama, please."

"Here," she say. "Take this fork, James."

"Please, Mama, I can't kill him," I say.

I could tell she was go'n hit me. I jerked back, but I didn't jerk back soon enough.

"Take it," she say.

I took it and reached in for him, but he kept on hopping to the back.

"I can't, Mama," I say. The water just kept on running down my face. "I can't," I say.

"Get him out of there," she say.

I reached in for him and he kept on hopping to the back. Then I reached in farther, and he pecked me on the hand.

"I can't, Mama," I say.

She slapped me again.

I reached in again, but he kept on hopping out my way. Then he hopped to one side and I reached there. The fork got him on the leg and I heard his leg pop. I pulled my hand out 'cause I had hurt him.

"Give it here," she say, and jerked the fork out my hand.

She reached in and got the little bird right in the neck. I heard the fork go in his neck, and I heard it go in the ground. She brought him out and helt him right in front of me.

"That's one," she say. She shook him off and gived me the fork. "Get the other one."

"I can't, Mama," I say. "I'll do anything, but don't make me do that."

She went to the corner of the fence and broke the biggest switch over there she could find. I knelt 'side the trap, crying.

"Get him out of there," she say.

"I can't, Mama."

She started hitting me 'cross the back. I went down on the ground, crying.

"Get him," she say.

"Octavia?" Auntie say.

'Cause she had come out of the house and she was standing by the tree looking at us.

"Get him out of there," Mama say.

"Octavia," Auntie say, "explain to him. Explain to him. Just don't beat him. Explain to him."

But she hit me and hit me and hit me.

I'm still young—I ain't no more than eight; but I know now; I know why I had to do it. (They was so little, though. They was so little. I 'member how I picked the feathers off them and cleaned them and helt them over the fire. Then we all ate them. Ain't had but a little bitty piece each, but we all had a little bitty piece, and everybody just looked at me 'cause they was so proud.) Suppose she had to go away? That's why I had to do it. Suppose she had to go away like Daddy went away? Then who was go'n look after us? They had to be somebody left to carry on. I didn't know it then, but I know it now. Auntie and Monsieur Bayonne talked to me and made me see.

5

Time I see it I get out my handkerchief and start waving. It's still 'way down there, but I keep waving anyhow. Then it come up and stop and me and Mama get on. Mama tell me go sit in the back while she pay. I do like she say, and the people look at me. When I pass the little sign that say "White" and "Colored," I start looking for a seat. I just see one of them back there, but I don't take it, 'cause I want my mama to sit down herself. She comes in the back and sit down, and I lean on the seat. They got seats in the front, but I know I can't sit there, 'cause I have to sit back of the sign. Anyhow, I don't want sit there if my mama go'n sit back here.

They got a lady sitting 'side my mama and she looks at me and smiles little bit. I smile back, but I don't open my mouth, 'cause the wind'll get in and make that tooth ache. The lady take out a pack of gum and reach me a slice, but I shake my head. The lady just can't understand why a little boy'll turn down gum and she reach me a slice again. This time I point to my jaw. The lady understands and smiles little bit, and I smile little bit, but I don't open my mouth, though.

They got a girl sitting 'cross from me. She got on a red overcoat and her hair's plaited in one big plait. First, I make 'tend I don't see her over there, but then I start looking at her little bit. She make 'tend she don't see me, either, but I catch her looking that way. She got a cold, and every now and then she h'ist[1] that little handkerchief to her nose. She ought to blow it, but she don't. Must think she's too much a lady or something.

1. Hoist.

Every time she h'ist that little handkerchief, the lady 'side her say something in her ear. She shakes her head and lays her hands in her lap again. Then I catch her kind of looking where I'm at. I smile at her little bit. But think she'll smile back? Uh-uh. She just turn up her little old nose and turn her head. Well, I show her both of us can turn us head. I turn mine too and look out at the river.

The river is gray. The sky is gray. They have pool-doos on the water. The water is wavy, and the pool-doos go up and down. The bus go round a turn, and you got plenty trees hiding the river. Then the bus go round another turn, and I can see the river again.

I look toward the front where all the white people sitting. Then I look at that little old gal again. I don't look right at her, 'cause I don't want all them people to know I love her. I just look at her little bit, like I'm looking out that window over there. But she knows I'm looking that way, and she kind of look at me, too. The lady sitting 'side her catch her this time, and she leans over and says something in her ear.

"I don't love him nothing," that little old gal says out loud.

Everybody back there hear her mouth, and all of them look at us and laugh.

"I don't love you, either," I say. "So you don't have to turn up your nose, Miss."

"You the one looking," she say.

"I wasn't looking at you," I say. "I was looking out that window, there."

"Out that window, my foot," she say. "I seen you. Everytime I turned round you was looking at me."

"You must of been looking yourself if you seen me all them times," I say.

"Shucks," she say, "I got me all kind of boyfriends."

"I got girlfriends, too," I say.

"Well, I just don't want you getting your hopes up," she say.

I don't say no more to that little old gal 'cause I don't want have to bust her in the mouth. I lean on the seat where Mama sitting, and I don't even look that way no more. When we get to Bayonne, she jugg her little old tongue out at me. I make 'tend I'm go'n hit her, and she duck down 'side her mama. And all the people laugh at us again.

6

Me and Mama get off and start walking in town. Bayonne is a little bitty town. Baton Rouge is a hundred times bigger than Bayonne. I went to Baton Rouge once—me, Ty, Mama, and Daddy. But that was 'way back yonder, 'fore Daddy went in the Army. I wonder when we go'n see him again. I wonder when. Look like he ain't ever coming back home. . . . Even the pavement all cracked in Bayonne. Got grass shooting right out the sidewalk. Got weeds in the ditch, too; just like they got at home.

It's some cold in Bayonne. Look like it's colder than it is home. The wind blows in my face, and I feel that stuff running down my nose. I sniff. Mama says use that handkerchief. I blow my nose and put it back.

We pass a school and I see them white children playing in the yard. Big old red school, and them children just running and playing. Then we pass a café, and I see a bunch of people in there eating. I wish I was in there 'cause I'm cold. Mama tells me keep my eyes in front where they belong.

We pass stores that's got dummies, and we pass another café, and then we pass a shoe shop, and that bald-head man in there fixing on a shoe. I look at him and I butt into that white lady, and Mama jerks me in front and tells me stay there.

We come up to the courthouse, and I see the flag waving there. This flag ain't like the one we got at school. This one here ain't got but a handful of stars. One at school got a big pile of stars—one for every state. We pass it and we turn and there it is—the dentist office. Me and Mama go in, and they got people sitting everywhere you look. They even got a little boy in there younger than me.

Me and Mama sit on that bench, and a white lady come in there and ask me what my name is. Mama tells her and the white lady goes on back. Then I hear somebody hollering in there. Soon's that little boy hear him hollering, he starts hollering, too. His mama pats him and pats him, trying to make him hush up, but he ain't thinking 'bout his mama.

The man that was hollering in there comes out holding his jaw. He is a big old man and he's wearing overalls and a jumper.

"Got it, hanh?" another man asks him.

The man shakes his head—don't want open his mouth.

"Man, I thought they was killing you in there," the other man says. "Hollering like a pig under a gate."

The man don't say nothing. He just heads for the door, and the other man follows him.

"John Lee," the white lady says. "John Lee Williams."

The little boy juggs his head down in his mama's lap and holler more now. His mama tells him go with the nurse, but he ain't thinking 'bout his mama. His mama tells him again, but he don't even hear her. His mama picks him up and takes him in there, and even when the white lady shuts the door I can still hear little old John Lee.

"I often wonder why the Lord let a child like that suffer," a lady says to my mama. The lady's sitting right in front of us on another bench. She's got on a white dress and a black sweater. She must be a nurse or something herself, I reckon.

"Not us to question," a man says.

"Sometimes I don't know if we shouldn't," the lady says.

"I know definitely we shouldn't," the man says. The man looks like a preacher. He's big and fat and he's got on a black suit. He's got a gold chain, too.

"Why?" the lady says.

"Why anything?" the preacher says.

"Yes," the lady says. "Why anything?"

"Not us to question," the preacher says.

The lady looks at the preacher a little while and looks at Mama again.

"And look like it's the poor who suffers the most," she says. "I don't understand it."

"Best not to even try," the preacher says. "He works in mysterious ways—wonders to perform."

Right then little John Lee bust out hollering, and everybody turn they head to listen.

"He's not a good dentist," the lady says. "Dr. Robillard is much better. But more expensive. That's why most of the colored people come here. The white people go to Dr. Robillard. Y'all from Bayonne?"

"Down the river," my mama says. And that's all she go'n say, 'cause she don't talk much. But the lady keeps on looking at her, and so she says, "Near Morgan."

"I see," the lady says.

7

"That's the trouble with the black people in this country today," somebody else says. This one here's sitting on the same side me and Mama's sitting, and he is kind of sitting in front of that preacher. He looks like a teacher or somebody that goes to college. He's got on a suit, and he's got a book that he's been reading. "We don't question is exactly our problem," he says. "We should question and question and question—question everything."

The preacher just looks at him a long time. He done put a toothpick or something in his mouth, and he just keeps on turning it and turning it. You can see he don't like that boy with that book.

"Maybe you can explain what you mean," he says.

"I said what I meant," the boy says. "Question everything. Every stripe, every star, every word spoken. Everything."

"It 'pears to me that this young lady and I was talking 'bout God, young man," the preacher says.

"Question Him, too," the boy says.

"Wait," the preacher says. "Wait now."

"You heard me right," the boy says. "His existence as well as everything else. Everything."

The preacher just looks across the room at the boy. You can see he's getting madder and madder. But mad or no mad, the boy ain't thinking 'bout him. He looks at that preacher just's hard's the preacher looks at him.

"Is this what they coming to?" the preacher says. "Is this what we educating them for?"

"You're not educating me," the boy says. "I wash dishes at night so that I can go to school in the day. So even the words you spoke need questioning."

The preacher just looks at him and shakes his head.

"When I come in this room and seen you there with your book, I said to myself, 'There's an intelligent man.' How wrong a person can be."

"Show me one reason to believe in the existence of a God," the boy says.

"My heart tells me," the preacher says.

"'My heart tells me,'" the boy says. "'My heart tells me.' Sure, 'My heart tells me.' And as long as you listen to what your heart tells you, you will have only what the white man gives you and nothing more. Me, I don't listen to my heart. The purpose of the heart is to pump blood throughout the body, and nothing else."

"Who's your paw, boy?" the preacher says.

"Why?"

"Who is he?"

"He's dead."

"And your mom?"

"She's in Charity Hospital with pneumonia. Half killed herself, working for nothing."

"And 'cause he's dead and she's sick, you mad at the world?"

"I'm not mad at the world. I'm questioning the world. I'm questioning it with cold logic, sir. What do words like Freedom, Liberty, God, White, Colored mean? I want to know. That's why *you* are sending us to school, to read and to ask questions. And because we ask these questions, you call us mad. No sir, it is not us who are mad."

"You keep saying 'us'?"

"'Us.' Yes—us. I'm not alone."

The preacher just shakes his head. Then he looks at everybody in the room—everybody. Some of the people look down at the floor, keep from looking at him. I kind of look 'way myself, but soon 's I know he done turn his head, I look that way again.

"I'm sorry for you," he says to the boy.

"Why?" the boy says. "Why not be sorry for yourself? Why are you so much better off than I am? Why aren't you sorry for these other people in here? Why not be sorry for the lady who had to drag her child into the dentist office? Why not be sorry for the lady sitting on that bench over there? Be sorry for them. Not for me. Some way or the other I'm going to make it."

"No, I'm sorry for you," the preacher says.

"Of course, of course," the boy says, nodding his head. "You're sorry for me because I rock that pillar you're leaning on."

"You can't ever rock the pillar I'm leaning on, young man. It's stronger than anything man can ever do."

"You believe in God because a man told you to believe in God," the boy says. "A white man told you to believe in God. And why? To keep you ignorant so he can keep his feet on your neck."

"So now we the ignorant?" the preacher says.

"Yes," the boy says. "Yes." And he opens his book again.

The preacher just looks at him sitting there. The boy done forgot all about him. Everybody else make 'tend they done forgot the squabble, too.

Then I see that preacher getting up real slow. Preacher's a great big old man and he got to brace himself to get up. He comes over where the boy is sitting. He just stands there a little while looking down at him, but the boy don't raise his head.

"Get up, boy," preacher says.

The boy looks up at him, then he shuts his book real slow and stands up. Preacher just hauls back and hit him in the face. The boy falls back 'gainst the wall, but he straightens himself up and looks right back at that preacher.

"You forgot the other cheek," he says.

The preacher hauls back and hit him again on the other side. But this time the boy braces himself and don't fall.

"That hasn't changed a thing," he says.

The preacher just looks at the boy. The preacher's breathing real hard like he just run up a big hill. The boy sits down and opens his book again.

"I feel sorry for you," the preacher says. "I never felt so sorry for a man before."

The boy makes 'tend he don't even hear that preacher. He keeps on reading his book. The preacher goes back and gets his hat off the chair.

"Excuse me," he says to us. "I'll come back some other time. Y'all, please excuse me."

And he looks at the boy and goes out the room. The boy h'ist his hand up to his mouth one time to wipe 'way some blood. All the rest of the time he keeps on reading. And nobody else in there say a word.

8

Little John Lee and his mama come out the dentist office, and the nurse calls somebody else in. Then little bit later they come out, and the nurse calls another name. But fast 's she calls somebody in there, somebody else comes in the place where we sitting, and the room stays full.

The people coming in now, all of them wearing big coats. One of them says something 'bout sleeting, another one says he hope not. Another one says he think it ain't nothing but rain. 'Cause, he says, rain can get awful cold this time of year.

All round the room they talking. Some of them talking to people right by them, some of them talking to people clear 'cross the room, some of them talking to anybody'll listen. It's a little bitty room, no bigger than us kitchen, and I can see everybody in there. The little old room's full of smoke, 'cause you got two old men smoking pipes over by that side door. I think I feel my tooth thumping me some, and I hold my breath and wait. I wait and wait, but it don't thump me no more. Thank God for that.

I feel like going to sleep, and I lean back 'gainst the wall. But I'm scared to go to sleep. Scared 'cause the nurse might call my name and I won't hear her. And Mama might go to sleep, too, and she'll be mad if neither one of us heard the nurse.

I look up at Mama. I love my mama. I love my mama. And when cotton come I'm go'n get her a new coat. And I ain't go'n get a black one, either. I think I'm go'n get her a red one.

"They got some books over there," I say. "Want read one of them?"

Mama looks at the books, but she don't answer me.

"You got yourself a little man there," the lady says.

Mama don't say nothing to the lady, but she must've smiled, 'cause I seen the lady smiling back. The lady looks at me a little while, like she's feeling sorry for me.

"You sure got that preacher out here in a hurry," she says to that boy.

The boy looks up at her and looks in his book again. When I grow up I want be just like him. I want clothes like that and I want keep a book with me, too.

"You really don't believe in God?" the lady says.

"No," he says.

"But why?" the lady says.

"Because the wind is pink," he says.

"What?" the lady says.

The boy don't answer her no more. He just reads in his book.

"Talking 'bout the wind is pink," that old lady says. She's sitting on the same bench with the boy and she's trying to look in his face. The boy makes 'tend the old lady ain't even there. He just keeps on reading. "Wind is pink," she says again. "Eh, Lord, what children go'n be saying next?"

The lady 'cross from us bust out laughing.

"That's a good one," she says. "The wind is pink. Yes sir, that's a good one."

"Don't you believe the wind is pink?" the boys says. He keeps his head down in the book.

"Course I believe it, honey," the lady says. "Course I do." She looks at us and winks her eye. "And what color is grass, honey?"

"Grass? Grass is black."

She bust out laughing again. The boy looks at her.

"Don't you believe grass is black?" he says.

The lady quits her laughing and looks at him. Everybody else looking at him, too. The place quiet, quiet.

"Grass is green, honey," the lady says. "It was green yesterday, it's green today, and it's go'n be green tomorrow."

"How do you know it's green?"

"I know because I know."

"You don't know it's green," the boy says. "You believe it's green because someone told you it was green. If someone had told you it was black you'd believe it was black."

"It's green," the lady says. "I know green when I see green."

"Prove it's green," the boy says.

"Sure, now," the lady says. "Don't tell me it's coming to that."

"It's coming to just that," the boy says. "Words mean nothing. One means no more than the other."

"That's what it all coming to?" that old lady says. That old lady got on a turban and she got on two sweaters. She got a green sweater under a black sweater. I can see the green sweater 'cause some of the buttons on the other sweater's missing.

"Yes ma'am," the boy says. "Words mean nothing. Action is the only thing. Doing. That's the only thing."

"Other words, you want the Lord to come down here and show Hisself to you?" she says.

"Exactly, ma'am," he says.

"You don't mean that, I'm sure?" she says.

"I do, ma'am," he says.

"Done, Jesus," the old lady says, shaking her head.

"I didn't go 'long with that preacher at first," the other lady says; "but now—I don't know. When a person say the grass is black, he's either a lunatic or something's wrong."

"Prove to me that it's green," the boy says.

"It's green because the people say it's green."

"Those same people say we're citizens of these United States," the boy says.

"I think I'm a citizen," the lady says.

"Citizens have certain rights," the boy says. "Name me one right that you have. One right, granted by the Constitution, that you can exercise in Bayonne."

The lady don't answer him. She just looks at him like she don't know what he's talking 'bout. I know I don't.

"Things changing," she says.

"Things are changing because some black men have begun to think with their brains and not their hearts," the boy says.

"You trying to say these people don't believe in God?"

"I'm sure some of them do. Maybe most of them do. But they don't believe that God is going to touch these white people's hearts and change things tomorrow. Things change through action. By no other way."

Everybody sit quiet and look at the boy. Nobody says a thing. Then the lady 'cross the room from me and Mama just shakes her head.

"Let's hope that not all your generation feel the same way you do," she says.

"Think what you please, it doesn't matter," the boy says. "But it will be men who listen to their heads and not their hearts who will see that your children have a better chance than you had."

"Let's hope they ain't all like you, though," the old lady says. "Done forgot the heart absolutely."

"Yes ma'am, I hope they aren't all like me," the boy says. "Unfortunately, I was born too late to believe in your God. Let's hope that the ones who come after will have your faith—if not in your God, then in something else, something definitely that they can lean on. I haven't anything. For me, the wind is pink, the grass is black."

9

The nurse comes in the room where we all sitting and waiting and says the doctor won't take no more patients till one o'clock this evening. My mama jumps up off the bench and goes up to the white lady.

"Nurse, I have to go back in the field this evening," she says.

"The doctor is treating his last patient now," the nurse says. "One o'clock this evening."

"Can I at least speak to the doctor?" my mama asks.

"I'm his nurse," the lady says.

"My little boy's sick," my mama says. "Right now his tooth almost killing him."

The nurse looks at me. She's trying to make up her mind if to let me come in. I look at her real pitiful. The tooth ain't hurting me at all, but Mama say it is, so I make 'tend for her sake.

"This evening," the nurse says, and goes on back in the office.

"Don't feel 'jected, honey," the lady says to Mama. "I been round them a long time—they take you when they want to. If you was white, that's something else; but we the wrong color."

Mama don't say nothing to the lady, and me and her go outside and stand 'gainst the wall. It's cold out there. I can feel that wind going through my coat. Some of the other people come out of the room and go up the street. Me and Mama stand there a little while and we start walking. I don't know where we going. When we come to the other street we just stand there.

"You don't have to make water, do you?" Mama says.

"No, ma'am," I say.

We go on up the street. Walking real slow. I can tell Mama don't know where she's going. When we come to a store we stand there and look at the dummies. I look at a little boy wearing a brown overcoat. He's got on brown shoes, too. I look at my old shoes and look at his'n again. You wait till summer, I say.

Me and Mama walk away. We come up to another store and we stop and look at them dummies, too. Then we go on again. We pass a café where the white people in there eating. Mama tells me keep my eyes in front where they belong, but I can't help from seeing them people eat. My stomach starts growling 'cause I'm hungry. When I see people eating, I get hungry; when I see a coat, I get cold.

A man whistles at my mama when we go by a filling station. She makes 'tend she don't even see him. I look back and I feel like hitting him in the mouth. If I was bigger, I say; if I was bigger, you'd see.

We keep on going. I'm getting colder and colder, but I don't say nothing. I feel that stuff running down my nose and I sniff.

"That rag," Mama says.

I get it out and wipe my nose. I'm getting cold all over now—my face, my hands, my feet, everything. We pass another little café, but this'n for white people, too, and we can't go in there, either. So we just walk. I'm so cold now I'm 'bout ready to say it. If I knowed where we was going I wouldn't be so cold, but I don't know where we going. We go, we go, we go. We walk clean out of Bayonne. Then we cross the street and we come back. Same thing I seen when I got off the bus this morning. Same old trees, same old walk, same old weeds, same old cracked pave[2]—same old everything.

I sniff again.

"That rag," Mama says.

I wipe my nose real fast and jugg that handkerchief back in my pocket 'fore my hand gets too cold. I raise my head and I can see David's hardware store. When we come up to it, we go in. I don't know why, but I'm glad.

It's warm in there. It's so warm in there you don't ever want to leave. I look for the heater, and I see it over by them barrels. Three white men standing round the heater talking in Creole. One of them comes over to see what my mama want.

"Got any axe handles?" she says.

Me, Mama and the white man start to the back, but Mama stops me when we come up to the heater. She and the white man go on. I hold my hands over the heater and look at them. They go all the way to the back, and I see the white man pointing to the axe handles 'gainst the wall. Mama takes one of them and shakes it like she's trying to figure how much it weighs. Then she rubs her hand over it from one end to the other end. She turns it over and looks at the other side, then she shakes it again, and shakes her head and puts it back. She gets another one and she does it just like she did the first one, then she shakes her head. Then she gets a brown one and do it that, too. But she don't like this one, either. Then she gets another one, but 'fore she shakes it or anything, she looks at me. Look like she's trying to say something to me, but I don't know what it is. All I know is I done got warm now and I'm feeling right smart better. Mama shakes this axe handle just like she did the others, and shakes her head and says something to the white man. The white man just looks at his pile of axe handles, and when Mama pass him to come to the front, the white man just scratch his head and follows her. She tells me come on and we go on out and start walking again.

We walk and walk, and no time at all I'm cold again. Look like I'm colder now 'cause I can still remember how good it was back there. My stomach growls and I suck it in to keep Mama from hearing it. She's walking right 'side me, and it growls so loud you can hear it a mile. But Mama don't say a word.

10

When we come up to the courthouse, I look at the clock. It's got quarter to twelve. Mean we got another hour and a quarter to be out here in the cold.

2. I.e., pavement.

We go and stand 'side a building. Something hits my cap and I look up at the sky. Sleet's falling.

I look at Mama standing there. I want stand close 'side her, but she don't like that. She say that's crybaby stuff. She say you got to stand for yourself, by yourself.

"Let's go back to that office," she says.

We cross the street. When we get to the dentist office I try to open the door, but I can't. I twist and twist, but I can't. Mama pushes me to the side and she twist the knob, but she can't open the door, either. She turns 'way from the door. I look at her, but I don't move and I don't say nothing. I done seen her like this before and I'm scared of her.

"You hungry?" she says. She says it like she's mad at me, like I'm the cause of everything.

"No, ma'am," I say.

"You want eat and walk back, or you rather don't eat and ride?"

"I ain't hungry," I say.

I ain't just hungry, but I'm cold, too. I'm so hungry and cold I want to cry. And look like I'm getting colder and colder. My feet done got numb. I try to work my toes, but I don't even feel them. Look like I'm go'n die. Look like I'm go'n stand right here and freeze to death. I think 'bout home. I think 'bout Val and Auntie and Ty and Louis and Walker. It's 'bout twelve o'clock and I know they eating dinner now. I can hear Ty making jokes. He done forgot 'bout getting up early this morning and right now he's probably making jokes. Always trying to make somebody laugh. I wish I was right there listening to him. Give anything in the world if I was home round the fire.

"Come on," Mama says.

We start walking again. My feet so numb I can't hardly feel them. We turn the corner and go on back up the street. The clock on the courthouse starts hitting for twelve.

The sleet's coming down plenty now. They hit the pave and bounce like rice. Oh, Lord; oh, Lord, I pray. Don't let me die, don't let me die, don't let me die, Lord.

11

Now I know where we going. We going back of town where the colored people eat. I don't care if I don't eat. I been hungry before. I can stand it. But I can't stand the cold.

I can see we go'n have a long walk. It's 'bout a mile down there. But I don't mind. I know when I get there I'm go'n warm myself. I think I can hold out. My hands numb in my pockets and my feet numb, too, but if I keep moving I can hold out. Just don't stop no more, that's all.

The sky's gray. The sleet keeps on falling. Falling like rain now—plenty, plenty. You can hear it hitting the pave. You can see it bouncing. Sometimes it bounces two times 'fore it settles.

We keep on going. We don't say nothing. We just keep on going, keep on going.

I wonder what Mama's thinking. I hope she ain't mad at me. When summer come I'm go'n pick plenty cotton and get her a coat. I'm go'n get her a red one.

I hope they'd make it summer all the time. I'd be glad if it was summer all the time—but it ain't. We got to have winter, too. Lord, I hate the winter. I guess everybody hate the winter.

I don't sniff this time. I get out my handkerchief and wipe my nose. My hands's so cold I can hardly hold the handkerchief.

I think we getting close, but we ain't there yet. I wonder where everybody is. Can't see a soul but us. Look like we the only two people moving round today. Must be too cold for the rest of the people to move round in.

I can hear my teeth. I hope they don't knock together too hard and make that bad one hurt. Lord, that's all I need, for that bad one to start off.

I hear a church bell somewhere. But today ain't Sunday. They must be ringing for a funeral or something.

I wonder what they doing at home. They must be eating. Monsieur Bayonne might be there with his guitar. One day Ty played with Monsieur Bayonne's guitar and broke one of the strings. Monsieur Bayonne was some mad with Ty. He say Ty wasn't go'n ever 'mount to nothing. Ty can go just like Monsieur Bayonne when he ain't there. Ty can make everybody laugh when he starts to mocking Monsieur Bayonne.

I used to like to be with Mama and Daddy. We used to be happy. But they took him in the Army. Now, nobody happy no more. . . . I be glad when Daddy comes home.

Monsieur Bayonne say it wasn't fair for them to take Daddy and give Mama nothing and give us nothing. Auntie say, "Shhh, Etienne. Don't let them hear you talk like that." Monsieur Bayonne say, "It's God truth. What they giving his children? They have to walk three and a half miles to school hot or cold. That's anything to give for a paw? She's got to work in the field rain or shine just to make ends meet. That's anything to give for a husband?" Auntie say, "Shhh, Etienne, shhh." "Yes, you right," Monsieur Bayonne say. "Best don't say it in front of them now. But one day they go'n find out. One day." "Yes, I suppose so," Auntie say. "Then what, Rose Mary?" Monsieur Bayonne say. "I don't know, Etienne," Auntie say. "All we can do is us job, and leave everything else in His hand . . ."

We getting closer, now. We getting closer. I can even see the railroad tracks.

We cross the tracks, and now I see the café. Just to get in there, I say. Just to get in there. Already I'm starting to feel little better.

12

We go in. Ahh, it's good. I look for the heater; there 'gainst the wall. One of them little brown ones. I just stand there and hold my hands over it. I can't open my hands too wide 'cause they almost froze.

Mama's standing right 'side me. She done unbuttoned her coat. Smoke rises out of the coat, and the coat smells like a wet dog.

I move to the side so Mama can have more room. She opens out her hands and rubs them together. I rub mine together, too, 'cause this keep them from hurting. If you let them warm too fast, they hurt you sure. But if you let them warm just little bit at a time, and you keep rubbing them, they be all right every time.

They got just two more people in the café. A lady back of the counter, and a man on this side the counter. They been watching us ever since we come in.

Mama gets out the handkerchief and count up the money. Both of us know how much money she's got there. Three dollars. No, she ain't got three dollars, 'cause she had to pay us way up here. She ain't got but two dollars and a half left. Dollar and a half to get my tooth pulled, and fifty cents for us to go back on, and fifty cents worth of salt meat.

She stirs the money round with her finger. Most of the money is change 'cause I can hear it rubbing together. She stirs it and stirs it. Then she looks at the door. It's still sleeting. I can hear it hitting 'gainst the wall like rice.

"I ain't hungry, Mama," I say.

"Got to pay them something for they heat," she says.

She takes a quarter out the handkerchief and ties the handkerchief up again. She looks over her shoulder at the people, but she still don't move. I hope she don't spend the money. I don't want her spending it on me. I'm hungry, I'm almost starving I'm so hungry, but I don't want her spending the money on me.

She flips the quarter over like she's thinking. She's must be thinking 'bout us walking back home. Lord, I sure don't want walk home. If I thought it'd do any good to say something, I'd say it. But Mama makes up her own mind 'bout things.

She turns 'way from the heater right fast, like she better hurry up and spend the quarter 'fore she change her mind. I watch her go toward the counter. The man and the lady look at her, too. She tells the lady something and the lady walks away. The man keeps on looking at her. Her back's turned to the man, and she don't even know he's standing there.

The lady puts some cakes and a glass of milk on the counter. Then she pours up a cup of coffee and sets it 'side the other stuff. Mama pays her for the things and comes on back where I'm standing. She tells me sit down at the table 'gainst the wall.

The milk and the cakes's for me; the coffee's for Mama. I eat slow and I look at her. She's looking outside at the sleet. She's looking real sad. I say to myself, I'm go'n make all this up one day. You see, one day, I'm go'n make all this up. I want say it now; I want tell her how I feel right now; but Mama don't like for us to talk like that.

"I can't eat all this," I say.

They ain't got but just three little old cakes there. I'm so hungry right now, the Lord knows I can eat a hundred times three, but I want my mama to have one.

Mama don't even look my way. She knows I'm hungry, she knows I want it. I let it stay there a little while, then I get it and eat it. I eat just on my front teeth, though, 'cause if cake touch that back tooth I know what'll happen. Thank God it ain't hurt me at all today.

After I finish eating I see the man go to the juke box. He drops a nickel in it, then he just stand there a little while looking at the record. Mama tells me keep my eyes in front where they belong. I turn my head like she say, but then I hear the man coming toward us.

"Dance, pretty?" he says.

Mama gets up to dance with him. But 'fore you know it, she done grabbed the little man in the collar and done heaved him 'side the wall. He hit the wall so hard he stop the juke box from playing.

"Some pimp," the lady back of the counter says. "Some pimp."

The little man jumps up off the floor and starts toward my mama. 'Fore you know it, Mama done sprung open her knife and she's waiting for him.

"Come on," she says. "Come on. I'll gut you from your neighbo[3] to your throat. Come on."

3. Navel.

I go up to the little man to hit him, but Mama makes me come and stand 'side her. The little man looks at me and Mama and goes on back to the counter.

"Some pimp," the lady back of the counter says. "Some pimp." She starts laughing and pointing at the little man. "Yes sir, you a pimp, all right. Yes sir-ree."

13

"Fasten that coat, let's go," Mama says.

"You don't have to leave," the lady says.

Mama don't answer the lady, and we right out in the cold again. I'm warm right now—my hands, my ears, my feet—but I know this ain't go'n last too long. It done sleet so much now you got ice everywhere you look.

We cross the railroad tracks, and soon's we do, I get cold. That wind goes through this little old coat like it ain't even there. I got on a shirt and a sweater under the coat, but that wind don't pay them no mind. I look up and I can see we got a long way to go. I wonder if we go'n make it 'fore I get too cold.

We cross over to walk on the sidewalk. They got just one sidewalk back here, and it's over there.

After we go just a little piece, I smell bread cooking. I look, then I see a baker shop. When we get closer, I can smell it more better. I shut my eyes and make 'tend I'm eating. But I keep them shut too long and I butt up 'gainst a telephone post. Mama grabs me and see if I'm hurt. I ain't bleeding or nothing and she turns me loose.

I can feel I'm getting colder and colder, and I look up to see how far we still got to go. Uptown is 'way up yonder. A half mile more, I reckon. I try to think of something. They say think and you won't get cold. I think of that poem, "Annabel Lee."[4] I ain't been to school in so long—this bad weather—I reckon they done passed "Annabel Lee" by now. But passed it or not, I'm sure Miss Walker go'n make me recite it when I get there. That woman don't never forget nothing. I ain't never seen nobody like that in my life.

I'm still getting cold. "Annabel Lee" or no "Annabel Lee," I'm still getting cold. But I can see we getting closer. We getting there gradually.

Soon 's we turn the corner, I see a little old white lady up in front of us. She's the only lady on the street. She's all in black and she's got a long black rag over her head.

"Stop," she says.

Me and Mama stop and look at her. She must be crazy to be out in all this bad weather. Ain't got but a few other people out there, and all of them's men.

"Y'all done ate?" she says.

"Just finish," Mama says.

"Y'all must be cold then?" she says.

"We headed for the dentist," Mama says. "We'll warm up when we get there."

"What dentist?" the old lady says. "Mr. Bassett?"

"Yes, ma'am," Mama says.

"Come on in," the old lady says. "I'll telephone him and tell him y'all coming."

Me and Mama follow the old lady in the store. It's a little bitty store, and it don't have much in there. The old lady takes off her head rag and folds it up.

"Helena?" somebody calls from the back.

"Yes, Alnest?" the old lady says.

"Did you see them?"

"They're here. Standing beside me."

"Good. Now you can stay inside."

The old lady looks at Mama. Mama's waiting to hear what she brought us in here for. I'm waiting for that, too.

"I saw y'all each time you went by," she says. "I came out to catch you, but you were gone."

"We went back of town," Mama says.

"Did you eat?"

"Yes, ma'am."

The old lady looks at Mama a long time, like she's thinking Mama might be just saying that. Mama looks right back at her. The old lady looks at me to see what I have to say. I don't say nothing. I sure ain't going 'gainst my mama.

"There's food in the kitchen," she says to Mama. "I've been keeping it warm."

Mama turns right around and starts for the door.

"Just a minute," the old lady says. Mama stops. "The boy'll have to work for it. It isn't free."

"We don't take no handout," Mama says.

"I'm not handing out anything," the old lady says. "I need my garbage moved to the front. Ernest has a bad cold and can't go out there."

"James'll move it for you," Mama says.

"Not unless you eat," the old lady says. "I'm old, but I have my pride, too, you know."

Mama can see she ain't go'n beat this old lady down, so she just shakes her head.

"All right," the old lady says. "Come into the kitchen."

She leads the way with that rag in her hand. The kitchen is a little bitty little old thing, too. The table and the stove just 'bout fill it up. They got a little room to the side. Somebody in there laying 'cross the bed—'cause I can see one of his feet. Must be the person she was talking to: Ernest or Alnest—something like that.

"Sit down," the old lady says to Mama. "Not you," she says to me. "You have to move the cans."

"Helena?" the man says in the other room.

"Yes, Alnest?" the old lady says.

"Are you going out there again?"

"I must show the boy where the garbage is, Alnest," the old lady says.

"Keep that shawl over your head," the old man says.

"You don't have to remind me, Alnest. Come, boy," the old lady says.

We go out in the yard. Little old back yard ain't no bigger than the store or the kitchen. But it can sleet here just like it can sleet in any big back yard. And 'fore you know it, I'm trembling.

"There," the old lady says, pointing to the cans. I pick up one of the cans and set it right back down. The can's so light, I'm go'n see what's inside of it.

"Here," the old lady says. "Leave that can alone."

I look back at her standing there in the door. She's got that black rag wrapped round her shoulders, and she's pointing one of her little old fingers at me.

"Pick it up and carry it to the front," she says. I go by her with the can, and she's looking at me all the time. I'm sure the can's empty. I'm sure she could've carried it herself—maybe both of them at the same time. "Set it on the sidewalk by the door and come back for the other one," she says.

I go and come back, and Mama looks at me when I pass her. I get the other can and take it to the front. It don't feel a bit heavier than that first one. I tell myself I ain't go'n be nobody's fool, and I'm go'n look inside this can to see just what I been hauling. First, I look up the street, then down the street. Nobody coming. Then I look over my shoulder toward the door. That little old lady done slipped up there quiet 's mouse, watching me again. Look like she knowed what I was go'n do.

"Ehh, Lord," she says. "Children, children. Come in here, boy, and go wash your hands."

I follow her in the kitchen. She points toward the bathroom, and I go in there and wash up. Little bitty old bathroom, but it's clean, clean. I don't use any of her towels; I wipe my hands on my pants legs.

When I come back in the kitchen, the old lady done dished up the food. Rice, gravy, meat—and she even got some lettuce and tomato in a saucer. She even got a glass of milk and a piece of cake there, too. It looks so good, I almost start eating 'fore I say my blessing.

"Helena?" the old man says.

"Yes, Alnest?"

"Are they eating?"

"Yes," she says.

"Good," he says. "Now you'll stay inside."

The old lady goes in there where he is and I can hear them talking. I look at Mama. She's eating slow like she's thinking. I wonder what's the matter now. I reckon she's thinking 'bout home.

The old lady comes back in the kitchen.

"I talked to Dr. Bassett's nurse," she says. "Dr. Bassett will take you as soon as you get there."

"Thank you, ma'am," Mama says.

"Perfectly all right," the old lady says. "Which one is it?"

Mama nods toward me. The old lady looks at me real sad. I look sad, too.

"You're not afraid, are you?" she says.

"No, ma'am," I say.

"That's a good boy," the old lady says. "Nothing to be afraid of. Dr. Bassett will not hurt you."

When me and Mama get through eating, we thank the old lady again.

"Helena, are they leaving?" the old man says.

"Yes, Alnest."

"Tell them I say good-bye."

"They can hear you, Alnest."

"Good-bye both mother and son," the old man says. "And may God be with you."

Me and Mama tell the old man good-bye, and we follow the old lady in the front room. Mama opens the door to go out, but she stops and comes back in the store.

"You sell salt meat?" she says.

"Yes."

"Give me two bits worth."

"That isn't very much salt meat," the old lady says.

"That's all I have," Mama says.

The old lady goes back of the counter and cuts a big piece off the chunk. Then she wraps it up and puts it in a paper bag.

"Two bits," she says.

"That looks like awful lot of meat for a quarter," Mama says.

"Two bits," the old lady says. "I've been selling salt meat behind this counter twenty-five years. I think I know what I'm doing."

"You got a scale there," Mama says.

"What?" the old lady says.

"Weigh it," Mama says.

"What?" the old lady says. "Are you telling me how to run my business?"

"Thanks very much for the food," Mama says.

"Just a minute," the old lady says.

"James," Mama says to me. I move toward the door.

"Just one minute, I said," the old lady says.

Me and Mama stop again and look at her. The old lady takes the meat out of the bag and unwraps it and cuts 'bout half of it off. Then she wraps it up again and juggs it back in the bag and gives the bag to Mama. Mama lays the quarter on the counter.

"Your kindness will never be forgotten," she says. "James," she says to me.

We go out, and the old lady comes to the door to look at us. After we go a little piece I look back, and she's still there watching us.

The sleet's coming down heavy, heavy now, and I turn up my coat collar to keep my neck warm. My mama tells me turn it right back down.

"You not a bum," she says. "You a man."

1963

LUCILLE CLIFTON
1936–2010

66 To understand my poetry," Lucille Clifton told biographer Hilary Holladay, "I don't think approaching it simply intellectually will help. It has to be a balance, I think, between intellect and intuition." Too often readers rely too much on the latter, and see only the rich humor and celebratory spirit of poems like "good times" and ["in the inner city"]. In fact even in these popular poems, there is an undercurrent of sadness and anger. Frequently the mood of Clifton's poetry is elegiac, as it mourns people and communities that have passed away. Her poems are intellectually challenging as well. They reflect a profound understanding of African American history, a deep knowledge of multiple spiritual traditions—both Western and Eastern—and the courage to write honestly about her experience as an Ameri-

can, born poor, black, and female. Her poems depict the various passages in her life from girlhood, to marriage and motherhood, to the illnesses against which she struggled during her last decades. Loss or, more particularly, the ability to survive loss is one of her major themes. An award-winning poet, Clifton was also the author of a memoir, *Generations*, as well as almost twenty children's books.

Born June 27, 1936, in Depew, New York, to Samuel and Thelma Moore Sayles, Clifton grew up in a community of blacks who had migrated from the South and whites who had emigrated from Europe to work in the steel mills around Buffalo. Her father had a vibrant personality and a gift for storytelling. He carried with him the memory of his proud great-grandmother, Caroline Sale, who was born in Dahomey in 1822. The stories he told would find their way into Clifton's poetry and prose. So too would recollections of his adultery and abuse. Although Thelma Sayles, who suffered from epilepsy, was often depressed and withdrawn, she wrote poetry that while never published made an indelible impression on her daughter. From 1953 to 1955, Clifton attended Howard University, where she studied under Sterling Brown and Owen Dodson and alongside classmates Amiri Baraka, Roberta Flack, and Toni Morrison. Poor grades forced Clifton to drop out of Howard. She returned to Buffalo and enrolled at the State University of New York at Fredonia. The novelist Ishmael Reed, a childhood friend, introduced her to Fred Clifton, a philosophy student at the University of Buffalo, whom she married in 1958. The couple had six children, four daughters and two sons. In 1967, the Cliftons moved to Baltimore.

In 1969 Clifton published *Good Times*, which the *New York Times* named one of the best books of the year. Set in the inner city, the volume's poems emphasize spiritual survival amid material deprivation. Joy comes when the rent is paid and an uncle hits the number. Not everyone triumphs: "miss rosie," the homeless woman "wrapped up like garbage," is a haunting presence. Introducing a concern with family history that would thread throughout her corpus, a pair of poems evokes Clifton's parents: "my mother moved among the days" and "my father's fingers moved among the couplers." The last image refers to industrial machinery. In "Ca'line," the speaker intones, "remember the child / running across dahomey," and a series of poems depicts "Buffalo soldiers," whose battlefield is the streets. Although the lines do not rhyme, the use of alliteration, assonance, and repetition in Clifton's poems makes music. Moreover, the poems' short lines, lack of capitalization, and missing punctuation force readers to think about how space in poems creates meaning. Although critics frequently refer to Clifton's poetry as "deceptively simple," she preferred the term "clearly complex." What seems like clarity in her poems is often the representation of the complexity of human experience.

Like *Good Times*, *Good News about the Earth* (1972) and *An Ordinary Woman* (1974) were published by Random House, where Morrison was Clifton's editor. An interest in ecological themes characterizes the first, which also contains "some jesus," one of Clifton's first poetic sequences on religion, and a section on heroes that includes poems in honor of, among others, Malcolm X and Richard Penniman, the singer better known as Little Richard. Kali, the Hindu goddess, is the focus of a poetic sequence in *An Ordinary Woman*. From 1974 to 1979, Clifton was poet-in-residence at Coppin State College. From 1975 to 1985, she was poet laureate of the state of Maryland.

Dedicated to the memory of her father, Clifton's *Generations* (1976) recounts the events surrounding his death and becomes a meditation on the meaning of his life and the lives of the author's extended family. Published the year before Alex Haley's *Roots* and Toni Morrison's *Song of Solomon*, the memoir anticipates the intensifying desire among African American writers to reconnect with an African past. *Generations* maps the journey of her ancestor Caroline Sale from New Orleans to Virginia in 1830 alongside the narrator Lucille's journey from Baltimore to Buffalo to bury her father. That journey awakens her memories of her father's stories. Through her identification with her dead kin, enabled both by her father's remembered voice and by family pictures, beginning with the photograph of Sale and her son that is the memoir's frontispiece, Clifton memorializes her dead. Gradually, she comes to terms with their loss, a loss that finally has less to do with Africa than with an acutely personal grief. At the conclusion, grief gives way to acceptance, renewal, and no small measure of triumph.

With *Two-Headed Woman* (1980), Clifton began to make herself a primary subject of her poetry. "What the mirror said" and "homage to my hips" are testaments to a hard-won self-love. In "forgiving my father," Clifton alludes to the incest that she suffered. Rather than victim, she writes as an incest survivor. "Poem on my fortieth birthday to my mother who died young" honors her mother's legacy, while determining to avoid her fate; Thelma Sayles died at the age of forty-four. Rather than despairing, the poet celebrates "the light that came to lucille clifton"—that is, understanding derived from supernatural experience. The volume's title evokes the folk belief that some individuals are born with second sight; Clifton describes her own sense of difference that came from having been born with twelve fingers, and she begins to explore the etymology of her name, Lucille, which means light.

In 1969 the poet began a parallel career as the author of children's books. The first was *Some of the Days of Everett Anderson*, which initiated a series of eight books about a black boy and his family. Among her other titles are *The Black BCs*, *The Lucky Stone*, and *All of Us Come Across the Water*. In 1976, she received an Emmy award for co-writing the screenplay for *Free to Be You and Me*, a children's program hosted by Marlo Thomas. Clifton used the metaphors of windows and mirrors to explain her commitment to writing for children. All human beings need "mirrors through which you can see yourself and windows through which you can see the world. And minority children have not had mirrors." Her books provided them. In 1984, shortly after the death of her husband from cancer at the age of forty-nine, Clifton published *Everett Anderson's Goodbye*, about the five stages of grief the character experienced after the death of his father. It won the American Library Association's Coretta Scott King Award.

After Fred Clifton's death, Lucille taught at the University of California at Santa Cruz for four years. In 1987, she published *Next: New Poems* and *Good Woman: Poems and a Memoir*, which collected her first five books. Both volumes were nominated for the Pulitzer Prize for poetry, making Clifton the first poet ever to receive two nominations in the same year. In 1989, Clifton returned to Maryland and became Distinguished Professor of the Humanities at St. Mary's College, where she taught until her death. In this next stage of her career, she became an even more prolific and celebrated poet. Her poems continued to fuse her exploration of women's history with spiritual quests. In the title poem from *Quilting: Poems 1987–1990*, the speaker asks:

> how does this poem end?
>> do the daughters' daughters quilt?
>> do the alchemists practice their tables
>> do the worlds continue spinning
>> away from each other forever?

The volume, with sections named after traditional designs for quilts, includes poems in praise of womanhood, such as "poem to my uterus"; "to my last period"; and "wishes for sons," which begins "i wish them cramps / i wish them a strange town / and the last tampon. / i wish them no 7/11." It concludes with "blessing the boats," which became another one of Clifton's signature poems. *Quilting* was also nominated for the Pulitzer Prize.

At the height of her career, Clifton won numerous awards, including the Shelly Memorial Prize from the Poetry Society of America (1992), the Anisfield-Wolf Lifetime Achievement Award, and the Ruth Lilly Poetry Prize in 2007. In 1999 she was elected to the board of chancellors of the Academy of American Poets and named a fellow of the American Academy of Arts and Sciences. She gave a host of readings, usually to standing-room-only audiences, who responded to the infectious humor and thoughtful reflection that characterized these performances. In the words of poet Rita Dove, "Lucille's laugh is like her spirit—large and full, warm and open. And her poems, for all their surface compactness, burst at the seams with this generous spirit."

That generosity of spirit animates even the poems that deal with the most difficult subjects. Clifton had surgery for breast cancer in 1994. Her illness is the subject of many of the poems in *The Terrible Stories* (1996). The opening sequence, "a dream of foxes," allegorizes the fear and danger illness produced in Clifton, which she treats more explicitly in poems that depict her diagnosis, treatment, and recovery. Alongside these poems are accounts of family history and of African American history from the Middle Passage to the assassinations of civil rights heroes Medgar Evers and Martin Luther King. To complete this continuum of terrible stories that are autobiographical and historical, Clifton adds a sequence titled "from the Book of David" that connects the suffering of her people to all people. The questions the poet asks are profound. She has no answers, but determines to keep living until she does: "even when i am dancing now I am dancing / myself onto the tongue of heaven / hoping to move into some sure / answer from the Lord."

Clifton's health worsened, but her spirit remained strong. *Blessing the Boats: New and Selected Poems, 1988–2000* won the National Book Award when it was published in 2000. In poems like "study the masters," Clifton asked readers to consider how important the lives of "invisible" black women are and have been to the definition of the American nation. *Mercy* (2004) and *Voices* (2008) were the final volumes Clifton published. She died on February 13, 2010, at the age of seventy-three. Poet Elizabeth Alexander spoke for many when she reflected, "I do not think there is an American poet as beloved as Clifton, or one whose influence radiated as widely." Later that year, proof of that assertion came when seventy-three poets gathered at James Madison University to read seventy-three of Clifton's poems in her memory.

[in the inner city]

in the inner city
or
like we call it
home
we think a lot about uptown   5
and the silent nights
and the houses straight as
dead men
and the pastel lights
and we hang on to our no place   10
happy to be alive
and in the inner city
or
like we call it
home

Frank Stewart's *The Radio Players* (1978), bringing together young and old, rich and poor, depicts inner-city residents at a block party enjoying good times.

good times

my Daddy has paid the rent
and the insurance man is gone
and the lights is back on
and my uncle Brud has hit
for one dollar straight   5
and they is good times
good times
good times

my Mama has made bread
and Grampaw has come   10
and everybody is drunk
and dancing in the kitchen
and singing in the kitchen
oh these is good times
good times   15
good times

oh children think about the
good times

Malcolm

nobody mentioned war
but doors were closed
black women shaved their heads
black men rustled in the alleys like leaves
prophets were ambushed as they spoke   5
and from their holes black eagles flew
screaming through the streets

homage to my hips

these hips are big hips.
they need space to
move around in.
they don't fit into little
petty places, these hips   5
are free hips.
they don't like to be held back.
these hips have never been enslaved,
they go where they want to go
they do what they want to do.   10
these hips are mighty hips.
these hips are magic hips.
i have known them
to put a spell on a man and
spin him like a top!   15

what the mirror said

listen,
you a wonder.
you a city
of a woman.
you got a geography   5
of your own.
listen,
somebody need a map
to understand you.
somebody need directions   10
to move around you.
listen,
woman,
you not a noplace
anonymous   15
girl;
mister with his hands on you
he got his hands on

some
damn
body!   20

[the light that came to lucille clifton]

the light that came to lucille clifton
came in a shift of knowing
when even her fondest sureties
faded away, it was the summer
she understood that she had not understood   5
and was not mistress even
of her own off eye then
the man escaped throwing away his tie and
the children grew legs and started walking and
she could see the peril of an   10
unexamined life.
she closed her eyes, afraid to look for her
authenticity
but the light insists on itself in the world;
a voice from the nondead past started talking,   15
she closed her ears and it spelled out in her hand
"you might as well answer the door, my child,
the truth is furiously knocking."

blessing the boats

(at St. Mary's)

may the tide
that is entering even now
the lip of our understanding
carry you out
beyond the face of fear   5
may you kiss
the wind then turn from it
certain that it will
love your back   may you
open your eyes to water   10
water waving forever
and may you in your innocence
sail through this to that

study the masters

like my aunt timmie.
it was her iron,
or one like hers,

that smoothed the sheets
the master poet slept on.   5
home or hotel, what matters is
he lay himself down on her handiwork
and dreamed.   she dreamed too, words:
some cherokee, some masai and some
huge and particular as hope.   10
if you had heard her
chanting as she ironed
you would understand form and line
and discipline and order and
america.   15

JOHN EDGAR WIDEMAN
b. 1941

In his preface to *The Homewood Trilogy*, John Edgar Wideman writes about the night of his grandmother's funeral in Pittsburgh in 1974: "It became clear to me . . . that I needn't look any further than the place I was born and the people who'd loved me to find what was significant and lasting in literature. My university training had both thwarted and prepared this understanding." Wideman had already published two well-received novels. After 1974, however, he was to publish the works for which he is best known, works rooted in the terrain of his childhood neighborhood, Homewood. But for Wideman the road back to Homewood was a difficult one: "In America, especially if you're black, there is a temptation to buy a kind of upward mobility. One of the requirements is to forget. Eventually, I felt impoverished by that act."

John Wideman was born on June 14, 1941, in Washington, D.C., the oldest of five children of Edgar and Betty French Wideman. Shortly before his first birthday, the family moved to Homewood, a black neighborhood on the eastern side of Pittsburgh, Pennsylvania. Wideman was to spend the first ten years of his life there, where his great-great-great-grandmother, a fugitive slave, had found freedom in the mid-nineteenth century and where much of his extended family still lived. Wideman's father worked as a waiter, garbage man, and paperhanger. But although the family was poor, his parents, according to Wideman, "followed the traditional striving middle-class pattern." In 1951 the family moved to the predominantly white upper-middle-class neighborhood of Shadyside. There, Wideman attended Peabody High School, where he began to compartmentalize his life by associating with his white friends in the classroom and gym and his African American friends outside of school. Basketball star, senior class president, and valedictorian, Wideman won a Benjamin Franklin Scholarship to the University of Pennsylvania.

In college, Wideman played out what he has called a theatrical performance. As he described it later, in the autobiographical *Brothers and Keepers* (1984), "Just two choices as far as I could tell: either/or. Rich or poor. White or black. Win or lose. . . . To succeed in the man's world you must become like the man and the man sure didn't claim no bunch of nigger relatives in Pittsburgh." Wideman began with a major in psychology but switched to English when he discovered he was to study rats rather than psychoanalytic theory. He earned membership in Phi Beta Kappa, competed in track, and won all-Ivy status as a forward on the basketball team. In his senior year, he traded his dream of becoming an NBA star for that of becoming a writer. In 1963 John Wideman became only the second African American to win a Rhodes Scholarship (Alain Locke had been the first, fifty-five years earlier.) At Oxford University's New College, Wideman studied eighteenth-century literature. He also served as captain and coach of the university's basketball team, leading it to an amateur championship. In 1966 he was awarded a bachelor of philosophy degree and returned to the United States with Judith Ann Goldman, whom he had married in 1965.

From 1966 to 1967, as Kent Fellow at the University of Iowa's Writers' Workshop, Wideman completed his first novel, A Glance Away (1967). Choosing to support himself through teaching while he continued to write, Wideman taught at the University of Pennsylvania from 1967 to 1974. His second novel, Hurry Home, was published in 1970. Both these early novels deal with African American characters, but the questions Wideman poses in them are not so much racial as existential. A Glance Away depicts a day in the lives of Eddie Lawson, an African American and a recovering drug addict, and Robert Thurley, a gay white English professor, as each struggles to understand himself. Hurry Home tells the story of Cecil Braithwaite, an African American law school graduate who, at the time the novel opens, is working as a janitor and who decides to travel to Europe and then to Africa in an attempt to somehow merge the two cultures to which he is heir—an attempt at which he ultimately fails. In his use of flashbacks, varying points of view, journals, letters, dreams, and puns, Wideman creates what critic John Leonard called "a rich and complicated novel." Because of the formally complex nature of his work, critics located Wideman in the tradition of Joyce, Eliot, and Faulkner.

Wideman was, at this time, unconnected to the black literary tradition, conceding in a 1968 Negro Digest article that he was not familiar with "that school of black writers which seeks to establish the black aesthetic." When two of his undergraduate students at the University of Pennsylvania asked him to teach a course on African American literature in 1968, Wideman at first declined. Then, in a crucial turnabout, he decided to take on the challenge. The course eventually led to the university's first African American studies program and for Wideman personally "awakened in [him] a different sense of self-image and the whole notion of a third world."

That different sense influenced Wideman's third novel, The Lynchers (1973), in which race and setting loom large. The Lynchers tells the story of a failed conspiracy by a group of black men in a Philadelphia ghetto to lynch one representative white policeman as vengeance for the thousands of black lives lost to lynching. The novel explores themes that would be important in Wideman's later work: relationships between black men and the significance of history, for it begins with a chronicling of lynchings in the United States. For Wideman, the novel's emphasis on pain, degradation, and hopelessness led to an impasse in his writing career. In 1973, wanting "to get away from that Ivy League competitiveness, the pressure to be somebody," he accepted a teaching position at the University of Wyoming at Laramie and moved west with his wife and three children.

In Wyoming, Wideman continued to read nineteenth- and twentieth-century African American writers; to study history and linguistics; and, as he put it, "to forge a new language for talking about the places I'd been, the people important to me." That search for a new language, along with a personal event—his younger brother Robby was arrested, tried for murder, and sentenced to life in prison without parole—greatly affected his works of the 1980s and 1990s.

In nearly all of Wideman's subsequent work, he uses both the lyrical language he developed during these years and the technique, dream time, what critic Randall Kenan called Wideman's "own patented stream of consciousness, sliding easily through tense and point of view." Damballah (1981), Hiding Place (1981), and Sent for You Yesterday (1983) established Wideman's reputation as, according to Mel Watkins in the New York Times Book Review, "one of America's premier writers of fiction."

As Wideman notes in his preface to *The Homewood Trilogy*, "the tension of multiple traditions, European and Afro-American, the Academy and the Street, animates these texts." In an unusual move, Wideman decided to have each of his Homewood books published originally in paperback to reach more readers, particularly "the people and the world [he] was writing about." All three books revolve around the descendants of Sybela Owens, the great-great-great-grandmother who escaped slavery and settled in Homewood in the late 1850s with the help of her owner's son, who would later become her husband. *Damballah*, the first part of the trilogy, is a collection of twelve interrelated short stories spanning generations; the stories are imagined as "long overdue letters" to Wideman's brother Robby. *Hiding Place*, a novel, traces the life of Tommy, Sybela's great-great-great-grandson, who is wanted for a murder he didn't commit. Featuring the same characters, setting, and language, *Sent for You Yesterday*, the third part of the trilogy, travels back and forth from the 1920s to the 1970s to trace the lives of two Homewood families, the Frenches and the Tates. *Sent for You Yesterday* won the P.E.N./Faulkner Award in 1984.

Wideman's next work, the popular *Brothers and Keepers* (1984), draws inspiration from Homewood but is the author's first venture into nonfiction, as he comes to terms in this autobiographical work with the very different lives he and his younger brother Robby have led. Some reviewers found Wideman's indictment of white society unjustified—especially given his own escape from the ghetto. However, Jonathan Yardley, in the *Washington Post Book World*, observed that in his "effort to understand what happened, to confess and examine his own sense of guilt about his brother's fate (and his own)," Wideman has written "a depiction of the inexorably widening chasm that divides middle-class black Americans from the black underclass." Ironically, in 1986, Wideman's middle child, Jacob, confessed to the murder of his roommate at summer camp, and the eighteen-year-old was sentenced to life in prison.

Reuben, published in 1987, engages the judicial system through its portrayal of a lawyer to the poor and dispossessed black citizenry of Homewood. Though stark in its indictment of the judicial system, *Reuben* did not provoke critics as much as Wideman's next novel, *Philadelphia Fire* (1990), based on the 1985 bombing of the Philadelphia headquarters of MOVE, which was authorized by the city's first African American mayor and led to the deaths of eleven people and the destruction of much of the neighborhood. Against this background, Wideman sets the search by an African American writer named Cudjoe for a small boy reported to have escaped the flames. At the novel's climax, in what critic Rosemary L. Bray called an "act of almost unimaginable boldness," the young boy is transformed into Wideman's own son, Jacob.

Between these two novels, Wideman published his second collection of short stories, *Fever*. Although critics praised "Valaida," in which a Jewish Holocaust survivor tries to reach out to his African American cleaning woman, and "Little Brother," about the inability of whites and blacks to live together without mutual hurt, the title story, "Fever," was considered the prize of the collection. For this story Wideman drew on historical accounts of blacks and whites working side by side during the yellow fever epidemic that hit Philadelphia in 1793.

Wideman's *Fatheralong: A Meditation on Fathers and Sons, Race and Society* (1994) echoes the themes of *Brothers and Keepers*. At its center is a journey taken by the author and his father to the family's South Carolina home place. Renewing kinship ties and visiting the graves of his ancestors, Wideman reflects on the silent distance between generations. "Arrayed against the possibility of conversation between fathers and sons, is the country they inhabit, everywhere proclaiming the inadequacy of black fathers, their lack of manhood in almost every sense the term's understood." *Fatheralong* breaks the silence eloquently.

Always a prolific writer, Wideman continues to publish both fiction and nonfiction. *The Cattle Killing* (1997) takes its title from the Xhosa's people's ritual destruction of their herds in order to resist European domination and depicts events from eighteenth-century Philadelphia to the present; *Two Cities* (1998) is a present-day love story set in Pittsburgh and Philadelphia and told in rap-inflected prose. Different formal strategies characterize *Fanon* (2010), a novel-within-a-novel in which a contemporary African American novelist, Thomas, undertakes writing the life of Frantz Fanon. Born in Martinique, Fanon was a philosopher, psychiatrist, and anticolonialist freedom fighter, whose 1961 book *The Wretched of the Earth* became a bible for liberation movements around the globe. The novel is a meditation on Fanon's legacy in a post-9/11 world. *Briefs: Stories for the Palm of the Mind* (2010) is a collection of "micro-stories," each of which is described as a "single breath, to be caught, held, shared, and savored." As the title of Wideman's memoir suggests, *Hoop Roots: Basketball, Race, and Love* (2001) reiterates major themes in his work.

Early in his career Wideman won critical acclaim, and his subsequent accomplishments make him one of the most important writers of his generation. After an auspicious beginning that demonstrated his command of modernist literary techniques, he developed an aesthetic that incorporates elements of African American history, literature, and culture. He invented a new way of writing black English, experimented with fusions of memory and music, and represented historical events from the inside out, by exploring the inner lives of fictional and nonfictional characters with unflinching honesty.

The recipient of numerous awards, including the O. Henry Prize and the MacArthur Fellowship, popularly known as "the genius award," John Edgar Wideman was the first author to win the Pen/Faulkner Award for Fiction twice. He is professor of Africana studies and literary arts at Brown University.

From Brothers and Keepers

[ROBBY'S VERSION]

At about the time I was beginning to teach Afro-American literature at the University of Pennsylvania, back home on the streets of Pittsburgh Robby was living through the changes in black culture and consciousness I was reading about and discussing with my students in the quiet of the classroom. Not until we began talking together in prison did I learn about that side of his rebelliousness. *Black Fire*[1] was a book I used in my course. It was full of black rage and black dreams and black love. In the sixties when the book was published, young black men were walking the streets with, as one of the *Black Fire* writers put it, dynamite growing out of their skulls. I'd never associated Robby with the fires in Homewood and in cities across the land, never envisioned him bobbing in and out of the flames, a constant danger to himself, to everyone around him because "dynamite was growing out of his skull." His plaited naps hadn't looked like fuses to me. I was teaching, I was trying to discover words to explain what was happening to black people. That my brother might have something to say about these matters never occurred to me. The sad joke was, I never even spoke to Robby. Never knew until years later that he was the one who could have told me much of what I needed to hear.

It was a crazy summer. The summer of '68. We fought the cops in the streets. I mean sure nuff punch-out fighting like in them Wild West movies

---

1. *Black Fire: An Anthology of Afro-American Writing* (1968), edited by LeRoi Jones (Amiri Baraka) and Larry Neal.

and do. Shit. Everybody in Homewood up on Homewood Avenue duking with the cops. Even the little weeny kids was there, standing back throwing rocks. We fought that whole summer. Cop cars all over the place and they'd come jumping out with night sticks and fists balled up. They wore leather jackets and gloves and sometimes they be wearing them football helmets so you couldn't go upside they heads without hurting your hand. We was rolling. Steady fighting. All you need to be doing was walking down the avenue and here they come. Screeching the brakes. Pull up behind you and three or four cops come busting out the squad car ready to rumble. Me and some the fellas just minding our business walking down Homewood and this squad car pulls up. Hey, you. Hold it. Stop where you are, like he's talking to some silly kids or something. All up in my face. What you doing here, like I ain't got no right to be on Homewood Avenue, and I been walking on Homewood Avenue all my life an ain't no jive police gon get on my case just cause I'm walking down the avenue. Fuck you, pig. Ain't none your god-damn business, pig. Well, you know it's on then. Cop come running at Henry and Henry ducks down on one knee and jacks the motherfucker up. Throw him clean through that big window of Murphy's five-and-dime. You know where I mean. Where Murphy's used to be. Had that cop snatched up in the air and through that window before he knew what hit him. Then it's on for sure. We rolling right there in the middle of Homewood Avenue.

That's the way it was. Seem like we was fighting cops every day. Funny thing was, it was just fighting. Wasn't no shooting or nothing like that. Somebody musta put word out from Downtown. You can whip the niggers' heads but don't be shooting none of em. Yeah. Cause the cops would get out there and fight but they never used no guns. Might bust your skull with a nightstick but they wasn't gon shoot you. So the word must have been out. Cause you know if it was left to the cops they would have blowed us all away. Somebody said don't shoot and we figured that out so it was stone rock 'n' roll and punch-up time.

Sometimes I think the cops dug it too. You know like it was exercise or something. Two or three carloads roll up and it's time to get it on. They was looking for trouble. You could tell. You didn't have to yell pig or nothing. Just be minding your business and here they come piling out the car ready to go ten rounds. I got tired of fighting cops. And getting whipped on. We had some guys go up on the rooves. Brothers was gon waste the mother-fuckers from up there when they go riding down the street but shit, wasn't no sense bringing guns into it long as they wasn't shooting at us. Brothers didn't play in those days. We was organized. Cops jump somebody and in two minutes half of Homewood out there on them cops' ass. We was orga-nized and had our own weapons and shit. Rooftops and them old boarded-up houses was perfect for snipers. Dudes had pistols and rifles and shotguns. You name it. Wouldna believed what the brothers be firing if it come to that but it didn't come to that. Woulda been stone war in the streets. But the shit didn't come down that way. Maybe it woulda been better if it did. Get it all out in the open. Get the killing done wit. But the shit didn't hit the fan that summer. Least not that way.

Lemme see. I woulda been in eleventh grade. One more year of Westing-house left after the summer of '68. We was the ones started the strike. Right in the halls of good old Westinghouse High School. Like I said, we had this organization. There was lots of organizations and clubs and stuff like that back then but we had us a mean group. Like, if you was serious business you was wit us. Them other people was into a little bit of this and that, but we was in it all the way. We was gon change things or die trying. We was known as bad. Serious business, you know. If something was coming down they always wanted us wit them. See, if we was in it, it was some mean shit. Had to be. Cause we didn't play. What it was called was Together. Our group. We was so bad we was having a meeting once and one the brothers bust in. Hey youall. Did youall hear on the radio Martin Luther King[2] got killed? One the older guys running the meeting look up and say, We don't care nothing bout that ass-kissing nigger, we got important business to take care of. See, we just knew we was into something. Together was where it was at. Didn't nobody dig what King putting down. We wasn't about begging whitey for nothing and we sure wasn't taking no knots without giving a whole bunch back. After the dude come in hollering and breaking up the meeting we figured we better go on out in the street anyway cause we didn't want no bullshit. You know. Niggers running wild and tearing up behind Martin Luther King getting wasted. We was into planning. Into organization. When the shit went down we was gon be ready. No point in just flying around like chickens with they heads cut off. I mean like it ain't news that whitey is offing niggers. So we go out the meeting to cool things down. No sense nobody getting killed on no humbug.

Soon as we got outside you could see the smoke rising off Homewood Avenue. Wasn't that many people out and Homewood burning already, so we didn't really know what to do. Walked down to Hamilton and checked it out around in there and went up past the A & P. Say to anybody we see, Cool it. Cool it, brother. Our time will come. It ain't today, brother. Cool it. But we ain't really got no plan. Didn't know what to do, so me and Henry torched the Fruit Market and went on home.

Yeah. I was a stone mad militant. Didn't know what I was saying half the time and wasn't sure what I wanted, but I was out there screaming and hollering and waving my arms around and didn't take no shit from nobody. Mommy and them got all upset cause I was in the middle of the school strike. I remember sitting down and arguing with them many a time. All they could talk about was me messing up in school. You know. Get them good grades and keep your mouth shut and mind your own business. Trying to tell me white folks ain't all bad. Asking me where would niggers be if it wasn't for good white folks. They be arguing that mess at me and they wasn't about to hear nothing I had to say. What it all come down to was be a good nigger and the white folks take care of you. Now I really couldn't believe they was saying that. Mommy and Geral[3] got good sense. They ain't nobody's fools. How they talking that mess? Wasn't no point in arguing really, cause I was set in my ways and they sure was set in theirs. It was the white man's world and wasn't no way round it or over it or under it. Got to get down and dance to the tune the man be playing. You know I didn't want to hear nothing like that, so I kept on cutting classes and fucking up and doing my militant thing every chance I got.

2. African American clergyman and civil rights leader (1929–1968), advocate of nonviolent resistance.

3. Nickname for Geraldine, Robby's first wife.

I dug being a militant cause I was good. It was something I could do. Rap to people. Whip a righteous message on em. People knew my name. They'd listen. And I'd steady take care of business. This was when Rap Brown and Stokely and Bobby Seale and them on TV. I identified with those cats. Malcolm and Eldridge and George Jackson.[4] I read their books. They was Gods. That's who I thought I was when I got up on the stage and rapped at the people. It seemed like things was changing. Like no way they gon turn niggers round this time.

You could feel it everywhere. In the streets. On the corner. Even in jive Westinghouse High people wasn't going for all that old, tired bullshit they be laying on you all the time. We got together a list of demands. Stuff about the lunchroom and a black history course. Stuff like that and getting rid of the principal. We wasn't playing. I mean he was a mean nasty old dude. Hated niggers. No question about that. He wouldn't listen to nobody. Didn't care what was going on. Everybody hated him. We told them people from the school board his ass had to go first thing or we wasn't coming back to school. It was a strike, see. Started in Westinghouse, but by the end of the week it was all over the city. Langley and Perry and Fifth Avenue and Schenley. Sent messengers to all the schools, and by the end of the week all the brothers and sisters on strike. Shut the schools down all cross the city, so they knew we meant business. Knew they had to listen. The whole Board of Education came to Westinghouse and we told the principal to his face he had to go. The nasty old motherfucker was sitting right there and we told the board, He has to go. The man hates us and we hate him and his ass got to go. Said it right to his face and you ought to seen him turning purple and flopping round in his chair. Yeah. We got on his case. And the thing was they gave us everything we asked for. Yes . . . Yes . . . Yes. Everything we had on the list. Sat there just as nice and lied like dogs. Yes. We agree. Yes. You'll have a new principal. I couldn't believe it. Didn't even have to curse them out or nothing. Didn't even raise my voice cause it was yes to this and yes to that before the words out my mouth good.

We's so happy we left that room with the Board and ran over to the auditorium and in two minutes it was full and I'm up there screaming. We did it. We did it. People shouting back Right on and Work out and I gets that whole auditorium dancing in they seats. I could talk now. Yes, I could. And we all happy as could be, cause we thought we done something. We got the black history course and got us a new principal and, shit, wasn't nothing we couldn't do, wasn't nothing could stop us that day. Somebody yelled, Party, and I yelled back, Party, and then I told them, Everybody come on up to Westinghouse Park. We gon stone party. Wasn't no plan or nothing. It all just started in my head. Somebody shouted party and I yelled Party and the next thing I know we got this all-night jam going. We got bands and lights and we partied all night long. Ima tell you the truth now. Got more excited bout the party than anything else. Standing up there on the stage I could hear the music and see the niggers dancing and I'm thinking, Yeah. I'm

4. Leaders in the Black Power movement of the late 1960s. Brown (b. 1943), Southern Nonviolent Coordinating Committee (SNCC) leader. Stokely Carmichael (1941–1998), SNCC leader. Seale (b. 1937), member of the Black Panthers. Malcolm X (1925–1965), powerful political and religious leader, author of *The Autobiography of Malcolm X* (1965). Eldridge Cleaver (1935–1998), member of the Black Panthers, author of *Soul on Ice* (1968). Jackson (1941–1971), author of *Soledad Brother: The Prison Letters of George Jackson* (1970).

thinking bout getting high and tipping round, checking out the babes and grooving on the sounds. Got me a little reefer and sipping out somebody's jug of sweet wine and the park's full of bloods[5] and I'm in heaven. That's the way it was too. We partied all night long in Westinghouse Park. Cops like to shit, but wasn't nothing they could do. This was 1968. Wasn't nothing they could do but surround the park and sit out there in they cars while we partied. It was something else. Bands and bongos and niggers singing, *Oh bop she bop* everywhere in the park. Cops sat out in them squad cars and Black Marias, but wasn't nothing they could do. We was smoking and drinking and carrying on all night and they just watched us, just sat in the dark and didn't do a thing. We broke into the park building to get us some lectricity for the bands and shit. And get us some light. Broke in the door and took what we wanted, but them cops ain't moved an inch. It was our night and they knew it. Knew they better leave well enough alone. We owned Westinghouse Park that night. Thought we owned Homewood.

In a way the party was the end. School out pretty soon after that and nobody followed through. We come back to school in the fall and they got cops patrolling the halls and locks on every door. You couldn't go in or out the place without passing by a cop. They had our ass then. Turned the school into a prison. Wasn't no way to get in the auditorium. Wasn't no meetings or hanging out in the halls. They broke up all that shit. That's when having police in the schools really got started. When it got to be a regular everyday thing. They fixed us good. Yes, yes, yes, when we was sitting down with the Board, but when we come back to school in September everything got locks and chains on it.

We was just kids. Didn't really know what we wanted. Like I said. The party was the biggest thing to me. I liked to get up and rap. I was a little Stokely, a little Malcolm in my head but I didn't know shit. When I look back I got to admit it was mostly just fun and games. Looking for a way to get over. Nothing in my head. Nothing I could say I really wanted. Nothing I wanted to be. So they lied through their teeth. Gave us a party and we didn't know no better, didn't know we had to follow through, didn't know how to keep our foot in they ass.

Well, you know the rest. Nothing changed. Business as usual when we got back in the fall. Hey, hold on. What's this? Locks on the doors. Cops in the halls. Big cops with big guns. Hey, man, what's going down? But it was too late. The party was over and they wasn't about to give up nothing no more. We had a black history class, but wasn't nobody eligible to take it. Had a new principal, but nobody knew him. Nobody could get to him. And he didn't know us. Didn't know what we was about except we was trouble. Troublemakers; and he had something for that. Boot your ass out in a minute. Give your name to the cops and you couldn't get through the door cause everybody had to have an I.D. Yeah. That was a new one. Locks and I.D.'s and cops. Wasn't never our school. They made it worse instead of better. Had our chance, then they made sure we wouldn't have no more chances.

It was fun while it lasted. Some good times, but they was over in a minute and then things got worser and worser. Sixty-eight was when the dope came

---

5. Blacks, term of intimacy used by some African Americans.

in real heavy too. I mean you could always get dope but in '68 seems like they flooded Homewood. Easy as buying a quart of milk. Could cop your works in a drugstore. Dope was everywhere that summer. Cats ain't never touched the stuff before got into dope and dope got into them. A bitch, man. It come in like a flood.

Me. I start to using heavy that summer. Just like everybody else I knew. The shit was out there and it was good and cheap, so why not? What else we supposed to be doing? It was part of the fun. The good times. The party.

We lost it over the summer, but I still believe we did something hip for a bunch of kids. The strike was citywide. We shut the schools down. All the black kids was with us. The smart ones. The dumb ones. It was hip to be on strike. To show our asses. We had them honkies scared. Got the whole Board of Education over to Westinghouse High. We lost it, but we had them going, Bruh. And I was in the middle of it. Mommy and them didn't understand. They thought I was just in trouble again. The way I always was. Daddy said one his friends works Downtown told him they had my name down there. Had my name and the rest of the ringleaders'. He said they were watching me. They had my name Downtown and I better be cool. But I wasn't scared. Always in trouble, always doing wrong. But the strike was different. I was proud of that. Proud of getting it started, proud of being one the ringleaders. The mad militant. Didn't know exactly what I was doing, but I was steady doing it.

The week the strike started, think it was Tuesday, could have been Monday but I think it was Tuesday, cause the week before was when some the students went to the principal's office and said the student council or some damn committee or something wanted to talk to him about the lunchroom and he said he'd listen but he was busy till next week, so it could have been Monday, but I think it was Tuesday cause knowing him he'd put it off long as he could. Anyway, Mr. Lindsay sitting in the auditorium. Him and vice-principal Meers and the counselor, Miss Kwalik. They in the second or third row sitting back and the speakers is up on stage behind the mike but they ain't using it. Just talking to the air really, cause I slipped in one the side doors and I'm peeping what's going on. And ain't nothing going on. Most the time the principal whispering to Miss Kwalik and Mr. Meers. Lindsay got a tablet propped up on his knee and writes something down every now and then but he ain't really listening to the kids on stage. Probably just taking names cause he don't know nobody's name. Taking names and figuring how he's gon fuck over the ones doing the talking. You. You in the blue shirt, Come over here. Don't none them know your name less you always down in the office cause you in trouble or you one the kiss-ass, nicey-nice niggers they keep for flunkies and spies. So he's taking names or whatever, and every once in a while he says something like, Yes. That's enough now. Who's next? Waving the speakers on and off and the committee, or whatever the fuck they calling theyselves, they ain't got no better sense than to jump when he say jump. Half of them so scared they stuttering and shit. I know they glad when he wave them off the stage cause they done probably forgot what they up there for.

Well, I get sick of this jive real quick. Before I know it I'm up on the stage and I'm tapping the mike and can't get it turned on so I goes to shouting. Talking trash loud as I can. Damn this and damn that and Black Power and I'm somebody. Tell em ain't no masters and slaves no more and we want freedom and we want it now. I'm stone preaching. I'm chirping. Get on the teachers, get on the principal and everybody else I can think of. Called em zookeepers. Said they ran a zoo and wagged my finger at the chief zookeeper and his buddies sitting down there in the auditorium. Told the kids on the stage to go and get the students. You go here. You go there. Like I been giving orders all my life. Cleared the stage in a minute. Them chairs scraped and kids run off and it's just me up there all by my ownself. I runs out of breath. I'm shaking, but I'm not scared. Then it gets real quiet. Mr. Lindsay stands up. He's purple and shaking worse than me. Got his finger stabbing at me now. Shoe's on the other foot now. Up there all by myself now and he's doing the talking.

Are you finished? I hope you're finished cause your ass is grass. Come down from there this instant. You've gone too far this time, Wideman. Get down from there. I want you in my office immediately.

They's all three up now, Mr. Lindsay and Miss Kwalik and Meers, up and staring up at me like I'm stone crazy. Like I just pulled out my dick and peed on the stage or something. Like they don't believe it. And to tell the truth I don't hardly believe it myself. One minute I'm watching them kids making fools of theyselves, next minute I'm badmouthing everything about the school and giving orders and telling Mr. Lindsay to his face he ain't worth shit. Now the whiteys is up and staring at me like I'm a disease, like I'm Bad Breath or Okey Doke the damn fool and I'm looking round and it's just me up there. Don't know if the other kids is gone for the students like I told them or just run away cause they scared.

Ain't many times in life I felt so lonely. I'm thinking bout home. What they gon say when Mr. Lindsay calls and tells them he kicked my ass out for good. Cause I had talked myself in a real deep hole. Like, Burn, baby burn. We was gon run the school our way or burn the motherfucker down. Be our school or wasn't gon be no school. Yeah, I was yelling stuff like that and I was remembering it all. Cause it was real quiet in there. Could of heard a pin drop in the balcony. Remembering everything I said and then starting to figure how I was gon talk myself out this one. Steady scheming and just about ready to cop a plea. I's sorry boss. Didn't mean it, Boss. I was just kidding. Making a joke. Ha. Ha. I loves this school and loves you Mr. Lindsay. My head's spinning and I'm moving away from the mike but just at that very minute I hears the kids busting into the balcony. It's my people. It's sure nuff them. They bust into the balcony and I ain't by myself no more. I'm hollering again and shaking a power fist and I tells Mr. Lindsay:

You get out. You leave.

I'm king again. He don't say a word. Just splits with his flunkies. The mike starts working and that's when the strike begins.

Your brother was out there in the middle of it. I was good, too. Lot of the time I be thinking bout the party afterward, my heart skipping forward to the party, but I was willing to work. Be out front. Take the weight. Had the whole city watching us, Bruh.

1984

Damballah[1]

Orion[2] let the dead, gray cloth slide down his legs and stepped into the river. He picked his way over slippery stones till he stood calf deep. Dropping to one knee he splashed his groin, then scooped river to his chest, both hands scrubbing with quick, kneading spirals. When he stood again, he stared at the distant gray clouds. A hint of rain in the chill morning air, a faint, clean presence rising from the far side of the hills. The promise of rain coming to him as all things seemed to come these past few months, not through eyes or ears or nose but entering his black skin as if each pore had learned to feel and speak.

He watched the clear water race and ripple and pucker. Where the sun cut through the pine trees and slanted into the water he could see the bottom, see black stones, speckled stones, shining stones whose light came from within. Above a stump at the far edge of the river, clouds of insects hovered. The water was darker there, slower, appeared to stand in deep pools where tangles of root, bush and weed hung over the bank. Orion thought of the eldest priest chalking a design on the floor of the sacred *obi*.[3] Drawing the watery door no living hands could push open, the crossroads where the spirits passed between worlds. His skin was becoming like that in-between place the priest scratched in the dust. When he walked the cane rows and dirt paths of the plantation he could feel the air of this strange land wearing out his skin, rubbing it thinner and thinner until one day his skin would not be thick enough to separate what was inside from everything outside. Some days his skin whispered he was dying. But he was not afraid. The voices and faces of his fathers bursting through would not drown him. They would sweep him away, carry him home again.

In his village across the sea were men who hunted and fished with their voices. Men who could talk the fish up from their shadowy dwellings and into the woven baskets slung over the fishermen's shoulders. Orion knew the fish in this cold river had forgotten him, that they were darting in and out of his legs. If the whites had not stolen him, he would have learned the fishing magic. The proper words, the proper tones to please the fish. But here in this blood-soaked land everything was different. Though he felt their

1. In *The Homewood Trilogy* (1985), of which *Damballah* is a part, Wideman quotes from Maya Deren's *Divine Horsemen: The Voodoo Gods of Haiti:*

Damballah Wedo is the ancient, the venerable father; so ancient, so venerable, as of a world before the troubles began; and his children would keep him so; image of the benevolent, paternal innocence, the great father of whom one asks nothing save his blessing. . . . There is almost no precise communication with him, as if his wisdom were of such major cosmic scope and of such grand innocence that it could not perceive the minor anxieties of his human progeny, nor be transmuted to the petty precision of human speech. Yet it is this very detachment which comforts, and which is evidence, once more, of some original and primal vigor that has somehow remained inaccessible to whatever history, whatever immediacy might diminish it. Damballah's very presence, like the simple, even absent-minded caress of a father's hand, brings peace. . . . Damballah is himself unchanged by life, and so is at once the ancient past and the assurance of the future. . . .

Associated with Damballah as members of the Sky Pantheon, are Badessy, the wind, Sobo and Agarou Tonerre, the thunder. . . . They seem to belong to another period of history. Yet precisely because these divinities are, to a certain extent, vestigial, they give, like Damballah's detachment, a sense of historical extension, of the ancient origin of the race. To invoke them today is to stretch one's hand back to that time and to gather up all history into a solid, contemporary ground beneath one's feet.

One song invoking Damballah requests that he "Gather up the Family."

2. Hunter of Greek myth. Drunk, he raped Merope, to whom he was betrothed. Her father blinded him, but his vision was restored by the sun's rays. Upon his death, Artemis turned him into a constellation.

3. Or obeah, a form of witchcraft or magic practiced in Africa and also in parts of the South and in the West Indies.

slick bodies and saw the sudden dimples in the water where they were feeding, he understood that he would never speak the language of these fish. No more than he would ever speak again the words of the white people who had decided to kill him.

The boy was there again hiding behind the trees. He could be the one. This boy born so far from home. This boy who knew nothing but what the whites told him. This boy could learn the story and tell it again. Time was short but he could be the one.

"That Ryan, he a crazy nigger. One them wild African niggers act like he fresh off the boat. Kind you stay away from less you lookin for trouble." Aunt Lissy had stopped popping string beans and frowned into the boy's face. The pause in the steady drumming of beans into the iron pot, the way she scrunched up her face to look mean like one of the Master's pit bulls told him she had finished speaking on the subject and wished to hear no more about it from him. When the long green pods began to shuttle through her fingers again, it sounded like she was cracking her knuckles, and he expected something black to drop into the huge pot.

"Fixin to rain good. Heard them frogs last night just a singing at the clouds. Frog and all his brothers calling down the thunder. Don't rain soon them fields dry up and blow away." The boy thought of the men trudging each morning to the fields. Some were brown, some yellow, some had red in their skins and some white as the Master. Ryan black, but Aunt Lissy blacker. Fat, shiny blue-black like a crow's wing.

"Sure nuff crazy." Old woman always talking. Talking and telling silly stories. The boy wanted to hear something besides an old woman's mouth. He had heard about frogs and bears and rabbits too many times. He was almost grown now, almost ready to leave in the mornings with the men. What would they talk about? Would Orion's voice be like the hollers the boy heard early in the mornings when the men still sleepy and the sky still dark and you couldn't really see nobody but knew they were there when them cries and hollers came rising through the mist.

Pine needles crackled with each step he took, and the boy knew old Ryan knew somebody spying on him. Old nigger guess who it was, too. But if Ryan knew, Ryan didn't care. Just waded out in that water like he the only man in the world. Like maybe wasn't no world. Just him and that quiet place in the middle of the river. Must be fishing out there, some funny old African kind of fishing. Nobody never saw him touch victuals Master set out and he had to be eating something, even if he was half crazy, so the nigger must be fishing for his breakfast. Standing there like a stick in the water till the fish forgot him and he could snatch one from the water with his beaky fingers.

A skinny-legged, black waterbird in the purring river. The boy stopped chewing his stick of cane, let the sweet juice blend with his spit, a warm syrup then whose taste he prolonged by not swallowing, but letting it coat his tongue and the insides of his mouth, waiting patiently like the figure in the water waited, as the sweet taste seeped away. All the cane juice had trickled down his throat before he saw Orion move. After the stillness, the illusion that the man was a tree rooted in the rocks at the riverbed, when motion came, it was too swift to follow. Not so much a matter of seeing Orion move as it was feeling the man's eyes inside him, hooking him before he could crouch lower in the weeds. Orion's eyes on him and through him boring a hole in his chest and thrusting into that space one word *Damballah*. Then the hooded eyes were gone.

On a spoon you see the shape of a face is an egg. Or two eggs because you can change the shape from long oval to moons pinched together at the middle seam or any shape egg if you tilt and push the spoon closer or farther away. Nothing to think about. You go with Mistress to the chest in the root cellar. She guides you with a candle and you make a pouch of soft cloth and carefully lay in each spoon and careful it don't jangle as up and out of the darkness following her rustling dresses and petticoats up the earthen steps each one topped by a plank which squirms as you mount it. You are following the taper she holds and the strange smell she trails and leaves in rooms. Then shut up in a room all day with nothing to think about. With rags and pieces of silver. Slowly you rub away the tarnished spots; it is like finding something which surprises you though you knew all the time it was there. Spoons lying on the strip of indigo: perfect, gleaming fish you have coaxed from the black water.

Damballah was the word. Said it to Aunt Lissy and she went upside his head, harder than she had ever slapped him. Felt like crumpling right there in the dust of the yard it hurt so bad but he bit his lip and didn't cry out, held his ground and said the word again and again silently to himself, pretending nothing but a bug on his burning cheek and twitched and sent it flying. Damballah. Be strong as he needed to be. Nothing touch him if he don't want. Before long they'd cut him from the herd of pickaninnies. No more chasing flies from the table, no more silver spoons to get shiny, no fat, old woman telling him what to do. He'd go to the fields each morning with the men. Holler like they did before the sun rose to burn off the mist. Work like they did from can to caint. From first crack of light to dusk when the puddles of shadow deepened and spread so you couldn't see your hands or feet or the sharp tools hacking at the cane.

He was already taller than the others, a stork among the chicks scurrying behind Aunt Lissy. Soon he'd rise with the conch horn and do a man's share so he had let the fire rage on half his face and thought of the nothing always there to think of. In the spoon, his face long and thin as a finger. He looked for the print of Lissy's black hand on his cheek, but the image would not stay still. Dancing like his face reflected in the river. Damballah. "Don't you ever, you hear me, ever let me hear that heathen talk no more. You hear me, boy? You talk Merican, boy." Lissy's voice like chicken cackle. And his head a barn packed with animal noise and animal smell. His own head but he had to sneak round in it. Too many others crowded in there with him. His head so crowded and noisy lots of time don't hear his own voice with all them braying and cackling.

Orion squatted the way the boy had seen the other old men collapse on their haunches and go still as a stump. Their bony knees poking up and their backsides resting on their ankles. Looked like they could sit that way all day, legs folded under them like wings. Orion drew a cross in the dust. Damballah. When Orion passed his hands over the cross the air seemed to shimmer like it does above a flame or like it does when the sun so hot you can see waves of heat rising off the fields. Orion talked to the emptiness he shaped with his long black fingers. His eyes were closed. Orion wasn't speaking but sounds came from inside him the boy had never heard before, strange words, clicks, whistles and grunts. A singsong moan that rose and fell and floated like the old man's busy hands above the cross. Damballah like a drum beat in the chant. Damballah a place the boy could enter, a familiar sound he began to anticipate, a sound outside of him which slowly forced its way inside, a sound measuring his heartbeat then one with the pumping surge of his blood.

The boy heard part of what Lissy saying to Primus in the cooking shed: "Ryan he yell that heathen word right in the middle of Jim talking bout Sweet Jesus the Son of God. Jump up like he snake bit and scream that word so everybody hushed, even the white folks what came to hear Jim preach. Simple Ryan standing there at the back of the chapel like a knot poked out on somebody's forehead. Lookin like a nigger caught wid his hand in the chicken coop. Screeching like some crazy hoot owl while Preacher Jim praying the word of the Lord. They gon kill that simple nigger one day."

Dear Sir:

The nigger Orion which I purchased of you in good faith sight unseen on your promise that he was of sound constitution "a full grown and able-bodied house servant who can read, write, do sums and cipher" to recite the exact words of your letter dated April 17, 1852, has proved to be a burden, a deficit to the economy of my plantation rather than the asset I fully believed I was receiving when I agreed to pay the price you asked. Of the vaunted intelligence so rare in his kind, I have seen nothing. Not an English word has passed through his mouth since he arrived. Of his docility and tractability I have seen only the willingness with which he bares his leatherish back to receive the stripes constant misconduct earn him. He is a creature whose brutish habits would shame me were he quartered in my kennels. I find it odd that I should write at such length about any nigger, but seldom have I been so struck by the disparity between promise and performance. As I have accrued nothing but expense and inconvenience as a result of his presence, I think it only just that you return the full amount I paid for this flawed *piece of the Indies*.

You know me as an honest and fair man and my regard for those same qualities in you prompts me to write this letter. I am not a harsh master, I concern myself with the spiritual as well as the temporal needs of my slaves. My nigger Jim is renowned in this county as a preacher. Many say I am foolish, that the words of scripture are wasted on these savage blacks. I fear you have sent me a living argument to support the critics of my Christianizing project. Among other absences of truly human qualities I have observed in this Orion is the utter lack of a soul.

She said it time for Orion to die. Broke half the overseer's bones knocking him off his horse this morning and everybody thought Ryan done run away sure but Mistress come upon the crazy nigger at suppertime on the big house porch naked as the day he born and he just sat there staring into her eyes till Mistress screamed and run away. Aunt Lissy said Ryan ain't studying no women, ain't gone near to woman since he been here and she say his ain't the first black butt Mistress done seen all them nearly grown boys walkin round summer in the onliest shirt Master give em barely come down to they knees and niggers man nor woman don't get drawers the first. Mistress and

Master both seen plenty. Wasn't what she saw scared her less she see the ghost leaving out Ryan's body.

The ghost wouldn't steam out the top of Orion's head. The boy remembered the sweaty men come in from the fields at dusk when the nights start to cool early, remembered them with the drinking gourds in they hands scooping up water from the wooden barrel he filled, how they throw they heads back and the water trickles from the sides of they mouth and down they chin and they let it roll on down they chests, and the smoky steam curling off they shoulders. Orion's spirit would not rise up like that but wiggle out his skin and swim off up the river.

The boy knew many kinds of ghosts and learned the ways you get round their tricks. Some spirits almost good company and he filled the nothing with jingles and whistles and took roundabout paths and sang to them when he walked up on a crossroads and yoo-hooed at doors. No way you fool the haunts if a spell conjured strong on you, no way to miss a beating if it your day to get beat, but the ghosts had everything in they hands, even the white folks in they hands. You know they there, you know they floating up in the air watching and counting and remembering them strokes Ole Master laying cross your back.

They dragged Orion across the yard. He didn't buck or kick but it seemed as if the four men carrying him were struggling with a giant stone rather than a black bag of bones. His ashy nigger weight swung between the two pairs of white men like a lazy hammock but the faces of the men all red and twisted. They huffed and puffed and sweated through they clothes carrying Ryan's bones to the barn. The dry spell had layered the yard with a coat of dust. Little squalls of yellow spurted from under the men's boots. Trudging steps heavy as if each man carried seven Orions on his shoulders. Four grown men struggling with one string of black flesh. The boy had never seen so many white folks dealing with one nigger. Aunt Lissy had said it time to die and the boy wondered what Ryan's ghost would think dropping onto the dust surrounded by the scowling faces of the Master and his overseers.

One scream that night. Like a bull when they cut off his maleness. Couldn't tell who it was. A bull screaming once that night and torches burning in the barn and Master and the men coming out and no Ryan.

Mistress crying behind a locked door and Master messing with Patty down the quarters.

In the morning light the barn swelling and rising and teetering in the yellow dust, moving the way you could catch the ghost of something in a spoon and play with it, bending it, twisting it. That goldish ash on everybody's bare shins. Nobody talking. No cries nor hollers from the fields. The boy watched till his eyes hurt, waiting for a moment when he could slip unseen into the shivering barn. On his hands and knees hiding under a wagon, then edging sideways through the loose boards and wedge of space where the weathered door hung crooked on its hinge.

The interior of the barn lay in shadows. Once beyond the sliver of light coming in at the cracked door the boy stood still till his eyes adjusted to the darkness. First he could pick out the stacks of hay, the rough partitions dividing the animals. The smells, the choking heat there like always, but rising above these familiar sensations the buzz of flies, unnaturally loud, as if the barn breathing and each breath shook the wooden walls. Then the boy's eyes followed the sound to an open space at the center of the far wall. A black shape there. Orion there, floating in his own blood. The boy ran at the blanket of flies. When he stomped, some of the flies buzzed up from the carcass. Others too drunk on the shimmering blood ignored him except to join the ones hovering above the body in a sudden droning peal of annoyance. He could keep the flies stirring but they always returned from the recesses of the high ceiling, the dark corners of the building, to gather in a cloud above the body. The boy looked for something to throw. Heard his breath, heavy and threatening like the sound of the flies. He sank to the dirt floor, sitting cross-legged where he had stood. He moved only once, ten slow paces away from Orion and back again, near enough to be sure, to see again how the head had been cleaved from the rest of the body, to see how the ax and tongs, branding iron and other tools were scattered around the corpse, to see how one man's hat and another's shirt, a letter that must have come from someone's pocket lay about in a helter-skelter way as if the men had suddenly bolted before they had finished with Orion.

Forgive him, Father. I tried to the end of my patience to restore his lost soul. I made a mighty effort to bring him to the Ark of Salvation but he had walked in darkness too long. He mocked Your Grace. He denied Your Word. Have mercy on him and forgive his heathen ways as you forgive the soulless beasts of the fields and birds of the air.

She say Master still down slave row. She say everybody fraid to go down and get him. Everybody fraid to open the barn door. Overseer half dead and the Mistress still crying in her locked room and that barn starting to stink already with crazy Ryan and nobody gon get him.

And the boy knew his legs were moving and he knew they would carry him where they needed to go and he knew the legs belonged to him but he could not feel them, he had been sitting too long thinking on nothing for too long and he felt the sweat running on his body but his mind off somewhere cool and quiet and hard and he knew the space between his body and mind could not be crossed by anything, knew you mize well try to stick the head back on Ryan as try to cross that space. So he took what he needed out of the barn, unfolding, getting his gangly crane's legs together under him and shouldered open the creaking double doors and walked through the flame in the center where he had to go.

Damballah said it be a long way a ghost be going and Jordan chilly and wide and a new ghost take his time getting his wings together. Long way to go so you can sit and listen till the ghost ready to go on home. The boy wiped his wet hands on his knees and drew the cross and said the word and settled down and listened to Orion tell the stories again. Orion talked and he listened and couldn't stop listening till he saw Orion's eyes rise up through the back of the severed skull and lips rise up through the skull and the wings of the ghost measure out the rhythm of one last word.

Late afternoon and the river slept dark at its edges like it did in the mornings. The boy threw the head as far as he could and he knew the fish would hear it and swim to it and welcome it. He knew they had been waiting. He knew the ripples would touch him when he entered.

1985

SAMUEL R. DELANY
b. 1942

Samuel R. (Chip) Delany Jr., one of very few African American science fiction writers, is one of the most important authors in the genre. During a career that began in 1962, he has published over twenty novels and more than a dozen works of nonfiction and has repeatedly won the Hugo and Nebula awards, the most coveted prizes in science fiction. In 2002, he was inducted into the Science Fiction Hall of Fame. However, because science fiction is often characterized as marginal, Delany has had to defend the field in order to be seen as a serious writer. It is not surprising that both through the richness of his own science fiction and through his collections of essays about the genre, he has done so passionately, maintaining at times that "the science fictional enterprise is richer than the enterprise of mundane fiction." Critics have listened, comparing him to Kierkegaard, Kafka, and Joyce and hailing his contribution not just to science fiction but to contemporary American literature as a whole.

The son of Margaret and Samuel R. Delany Sr., Samuel R. Delany Jr. was born and raised in Harlem. His father, a prosperous funeral director, sent him to the progressive and white Dalton School. Delany's struggle with undiagnosed dyslexia, and possibly his shifting back and forth between the world of Harlem and the world of Dalton, resulted in his leading a tumultuous and difficult childhood. After Dalton, Delany went to the Bronx High School of Science, where he concentrated on math and physics. At the same time, he played the guitar, wrote a violin concerto, and studied acting and ballet. Between 1954 and 1961, he wrote several apprentice novels.

At the age of nineteen, in 1961, Delany married the poet Marilyn Hacker, who encouraged him to submit a manuscript to Ace Books, where she worked. This first book, *The Jewels of Aptor* (1962), explores themes of quest, of the capabilities of technology, and of the status of the artist, themes to which Delany would often return. Between 1962 and 1965, Delany published five novels. After a nervous breakdown in 1965, he slowed his pace and from 1966 to 1969 produced *Babel-17* (1966); *The Einstein Intersection* (1967), for which he won the Nebula award; and *Nova* (1969), the culmination of his traditional science fiction phase. For the next several years Delany lived in the Heavenly Breakfast commune in New York City, where he played in a rock band and published what some critics consider a pornographic novel, *The Tides of Lust* (1973), which also appears under the title *Equinox*. Delany and Hacker separated in 1975 and divorced in 1980.

In 1975 Delany published the novel that established him as a major American writer: *Dhalgren*. In an important 1977 essay on Delany, critic Peter Alterman notes that, within Delany's novels and especially within *Dhalgren*, "time, logic and point of view are cut loose from traditional literary positions, and function relativistically." Kid, *Dhalgren*'s narrator, is dyslexic and epileptic, and the narrative itself is somewhat disorienting. Nonetheless, in *Dhalgren*, as in Delany's later novels, time, logic, and point of view are rigidly controlled by the rules of a relativistic universe. Delany's vision, as Alterman points out, is both grounded in the concrete, sensual, "realistic" world and celebratory of the mythic, metaphoric elements of language. Such concern with language is central to all Delany's writing: the early, more traditional science fiction; the nonfiction; and the "postmodernist" novels of the 1970s and 1980s. Definitely it makes itself felt in *Atlantis: Model 1924* (1995), which by its abundance of wordplay and literary allusion weaves a dense but dancing network of humor, myth, and madness.

Delany's science fiction is notable too for its racially diverse characters, unusual in the genre, and for its bold, occasionally graphic explorations of sexuality. *Triton* (1976) features more than forty different sexes. Set in the 1980s, *The Mad Man* (1994, 2002) follows a black gay graduate student whose dissertation topic is a Korean American philosopher who was murdered outside a gay bar. The student begins to find his life imitating details of his subject's. The protagonist of *Dark Reflections* (2007) is a gay African American poet who lives most of his life in New York City. Starting with his experience in late middle age, the plot moves backward to his youth. *Through the Valley of the Nest of Spiders* (2012) departs from Delany's other fiction in that it is set in a tourist town on the Georgia coast. The novel centers on a black gay couple who maintain a relationship that is both committed and open. They work as garbagemen, run a movie theater that features pornographic films and promotes gay sex, and are handymen at a lesbian art colony. Like Delany's other fiction, the novel is by turns philosophical, sexually explicit, and lyrical.

Sexuality is a central theme in *The Motion of Light in Water* (1988), the critically acclaimed memoir that recounts Delany's development as a writer from 1959 to 1965. *Bread & Wine: An Erotic Tale of New York* (1988), an illustrated memoir on which Delany collaborated with writer/artist Mia Wolff, recounts Delany's relationship with his long-time partner, Dennis Ricketts. Delany's other nonfiction is also formally innovative. *Times Square Red, Times Square Blue* (1999) contains two long essays that explore sexuality, social interaction, and the politics of urban space, but one is written in narrative prose and the other in the discourse of critical theory. He has also published *1948: Selected Letters* (2000) and *Shorter Views: Queer Thoughts & the Politics of the Paraliterary*. In 1993, he received the William Whitehead Memorial Award for Lifetime Contributions to Lesbian and Gay Literature.

Delany has served on the faculties of the State University of New York at Buffalo, the University of Wisconsin at Milwaukee, and the University of Massachusetts at Amherst. Since January 2001, he has been professor of English and creative writing at Temple University. He is the subject of a film, *The Polymath, or, the Life and Opinions of Samuel R. Delaney, Gentleman*, whose title takes an apt measure of the man.

From Atlantis: Model 1924

d

> The One remains, the many change and pass;
> Heaven's light forever shines, Earth's shadows fly;
> Life, like a dome of many-coloured glass,
> Stains the white radiance of Eternity.
> —Percy Bysshe Shelley,[1] *Adonaïs*

> . . . plough through thrashing glister toward
> fata morgana's lucent melting shore,
> weave toward New World littorals that are
> mirage and myth and actual shore.
> —Robert Hayden,[2] "Middle Passage"

Sam turned on the bench, to see, standing behind him, the man he'd bumped when he'd been staring through the planks.

"Yes," Sam said. "That's right. I am."

---

1. English Romantic poet (1792–1822); his elegy *Adonais* was written in memory of fellow poet John Keats, who died of tuberculosis in 1821.

2. African American poet (1913–1980). "Middle Passage" (1945) depicts the famous mutiny on the slave ship *Amistad*.

"I know it's none of my business," the man said. "But I'd bet a lot of people meet you and think you're white."

Well, a lot of people up here did. "Some of them."

"The reason I suspected, I suppose, is that I have a colored friend—a writer. A marvelous writer. He writes stories, but they're much more like poems. You read them, and you can just *see* the sunlight on the fields and hear the sound of the Negro girls' laughter. His name is Jean—"

"—Toomer?"[3] Sam supplied.

"Now don't tell me you're related to him . . . ?" The man laughed. "Though you look somewhat like him. You know, Jean just ran off with the wife of my very good friend, Waldo—so I don't think I'm really *supposed* to like him right through here—it's the kind of thing you don't write your mother about. But I do—like him, that is. He's handsome, brilliant, talented. How could one help it? Maybe that's why I took a chance and spoke to you—because you do look something like him. New York is the biggest of cities, but the smallest of worlds. Everybody always turns out to know everyone else—"

"No," Sam said. "No. I'm not his relative. But he's a friend of my . . ." How did you explain about your brother's strange girlfriend—who was the one who *knew* everybody. "A friend of my brother's. Well, a friend of a girl my brother knows." Though Clarice had said he looked like Toomer, she hadn't mentioned the abscension. "She was the one who told me about him." He couldn't imagine Clarice approving of such carryings on.

"Oh, well, there—you see. You know, that man you were watching, in the boat—do you mind if I sit down?"

"No. Sure . . . !"

The young man stepped around the bench's end, flopped to the seat, and flung both arms along the back: "Lord, he was hung! Like a stallion! Pissed like a racehorse, too!" He looked over, grinning behind his glasses. "To see it from up here at all, someone's got to throw a stream as thick as a fire hose. It was something, 'ey?"

Sam was surprised—and found himself grinning at the ridiculousness of it. People didn't strip down to stand up and make water before all New York—but if someone did, even less did you talk about it. That both had happened within the hour seemed to overthrow the anxiety of the last minutes, and struck him as exorbitantly comic.

"But did you see what he did?" Sam asked. "Did you see?"

"I saw as much as you, I bet—maybe more, the way you ran off." The fellow hit him playfully on the shoulder with the back of his hand.

"I mean, he must have jumped in . . . for a swim. Or maybe—"

"No," the man said. "I don't think he'd have done that." He seemed suddenly pensive. "It's much too cold. The water's still on the nippy side, this early in spring."

"But he *must* have," Sam said. He'd stopped laughing. "I saw the boat, later on—over there." He pointed toward Brooklyn. "There was no one in it. I know it was the same boat. Because of the hat, and . . . because of his hat."

"No one in it?" The man seemed surprised.

"It was floating empty. He must have fallen overboard—or jumped in. Then he couldn't get back up. The boat was just drifting, turning in circles. Really—there was no one in it at all!"

3. African American poet and fiction writer (1894–1967); his experimental novel *Cane* (1923) was one of the major works of the Harlem Renaissance.

The man narrowed his eyes, then looked pensively out at the sky while a train's open-air trundle filled the space beneath them. Through the green v's of the beams supporting the rail, over the walkway's edge, Sam could see the car tops moving toward the city. Finally the man said: "No, I don't think that's what happened. He was probably one of the Italian fishermen living over there. I live over there, too—not too far from them. A clutch of Genovesi."[4] He too waved toward Brooklyn. "God, those guineas are magnificent animals! Swim like porpoises—at least the boys do. You can watch them, frisking about in the water just down from where I live. Fell in? Naw . . . !" He burlesqued the word, speaking it in an exaggerated tone of someone who didn't use it naturally. "It's a bold swimmer who jumps into the midst of his own pee. You think he went under in his own maelstrom, while your white aeroplane of Help soared overhead? Oh, no. The East River's not really a river, you know. It's a saltwater estuary—complete with tides. So even that whole herd of pissers from the Naval Shipyard, splattering off the concrete's edge every day, doesn't significantly change the taste. Jump? I'll tell you what's more likely. After he spilled his manly quarts, he lay down in the bottom and let his boat float, with the sunlight filling it up around him as if it were a tub and the light was a froth of suds. And when, finally, he drifts into the dago docks, he'll jump up, grab hold of it, and shake that long-skinned guinea pizzle for the little Genoese lassies out this afternoon to squeal over, go running to their mothers, and snigger at. No, suicidal or otherwise, his kind doesn't go in for drowning."

Sam started to repeat that the boat had been empty. But—well, *was* there a chance he'd missed the form stretched on the bottom? Sam said: "You live in Brooklyn?" because that was all he could think to say. (No. He remembered the oar. The boat had been empty, he was sure of it—almost.)

The man inclined his head: "Sebastian Melmoth, at your service. One-ten Columbia Heights, Apartment c33." The man took his glasses off, held them up to the sky, examining them for dust, then put them back on.

Sam said: "I think he fell over. Maybe he was drunk or crazy or . . . drunk. Maybe that's why he took his clothes off—?"

"—to piss in the river?" The man cocked his head, quizzical. "It's possible. Those guineas drink more than I do. A couple of quarts of dago red'll certainly make your spigot spout." He looked over at Sam, suddenly sober-faced. "My name isn't really Sebastian Melmoth. Do you know who Sebastian Melmoth was?"

Sam shook his head.

"That was the name Wilde used, after he got out of Reading and was staying incognito in France. Oscar Wilde[5]—you know, *The Ballad of Reading Gaol*—'each man kills the thing he loves'?"

"*The Importance of Being Earnest*," Sam answered.

"The importance of being earnest to be *sure!*" The man nodded deeply.

"They did that down on the school campus—the play—where I grew up."

"School?" The man raised an eyebrow.

"The college—it's a Negro college, in North Carolina. My father works there. My mama's Dean of Women. The students put it on, three years ago, I guess. We all went to see it."

---

4. Natives of Genoa, a seaport in northern Italy.
5. Irish poet, playwright, novelist, and critic

(1854–1900); imprisoned from 1895 to 1897 because of his homosexuality.

The man threw back his head and barked a single syllable of laughter. "I'm sorry—but the idea of *The Importance of Being Earnest* in blackface—well, not blackface. But as a minstrel—" The man's laughter fractured his own sentence. ". . . Really!" He bent forward, rocked back, recovering. "That's just awful of me. But maybe—" he turned, sincere questioning among his features nudging through the laugh's detritus—"they only used the lighter-skinned students for the—?"

"No," Sam said, suppressing the indignation from his voice. "No, they had students of *all* colors, playing whichever part they did best. They just had to be able to speak the lines."

"Really?" the man asked, incredulously.

Sam put his hands on his thighs, ready to stand and excuse himself. There seemed no need at all to continue this.

"You know," the man said, sitting back again, again looking at the sky. "I would have *loved* to have seen that production! Actually, it sounds quite exciting. More than exciting—it might even have been important. In fact, I wouldn't be surprised if it's the sort of thing that *all* white people should be made to see—Shakespeare and Wilde and Ibsen, with Negro actors of all colors, taking whichever parts. It would probably do us some good!"

Surprised once more, Sam took his hands from his thighs. His sister Jules, who had played Gwendolen Fairfax (and was as light as his mother), had said much the same thing after it was over—though the part of Cecily Cardew had been taken by pudgy little black-brown Milly Potts ("Memory, my dear Cecily, is the diary we all carry about with us . . ."), who'd jazzed up the lines unmercifully, strutting and flaunting every phrase as much as it could bear and then some, rolling her eyes, shooting her hands in the air, and making the whole audience, including Papa, rock in their seats, clutch their stomachs and howl (the women's cackles cutting over and continuing after the men's bellowings)—to the point where the other actors couldn't say their own lines, trying to hold their laughter. Later, a more serious Papa had said that though it was *supposed* to be funny, it *wasn't* supposed to be funny in the way Milly had made it so. But now it was hard to think of the play any other way.

The man said: "I don't live in Apartment c 33, actually. You know what that was? That was the cell number Wilde had at Reading. 'The brave man does it with a sword, the coward with a—'"

"What?" Sam asked.

"Kills the thing he loves," the man intoned. "I was going to put c 33 on my door, once. But then I thought better. It's a nice room, though. It's right in front of Roebling's old room."

"Roebling . . . ?"

"Washington Roebling. He's the man who made this bridge." The man raised his head, to take in caging cables. "Who hung these lines here? *He* took over the job from his father, John Augustus Roebling.[6] The Bridge killed his father, John, you know. He'd already completed the plans and was at the waterfront, surveying to start the work—when a runaway cart sliced open his foot. It became infected until, three weeks later, tetanus did him in—with spasms that near broke his bones, with crying out for water. So the son, Washington, took it up. The problem, you see, was to dig the foundations out for those great stone towers." The man gestured left, then right.

---

6. John Augustus (1806–1869) and Washington Roebling (1837–1926), designer and chief engineer, respectively, of the Brooklyn Bridge.

"How to excavate them, there in the water, the both of them, with those gigantic dredging machines. They had to dig out, beneath the river, two areas a hundred-seventy-two feet by a hundred-two—for each about a third the size of a football field. You know how they did it? They built two immense, upside-down iron and wooden boxes. The bottoms—or, better, the roofs—were made of five layers of foot-square pine timbers, bolted together. They caulked them within an inch of their lives, covered them over with sheet tin, then covered over the whole with wood again. Then they dropped those upside-down caissons into the drink, with the air still in them. They let the workers down through shafts that were pressurized to keep the air in and the water out. Working on the bottom, the poor bohunks and square-heads they had in there dredged out muck and mud till they hit bedrock—seventy-eight feet six inches below the high-tide line on the Manhattan side and forty-four feet six inches below on the Brooklyn side. The workers had a nine-foot high space to dig in, all propped up with six-by-six beams. The pressure was immense—and they used what they called clamshell buckets to haul out the dredgings. Right at the very beginning, young Roebling was down in the caissons inspecting—came up too fast and got the bends. He was a cripple for the rest of his life. So he stayed in the room at the back of where I live now, surveying the work through the window with a telescope and directing it through his wife—the bridge—who went down to the docks every day to bring his orders and take back her report: spying through his glass at the stanchions he'd raised—twin gnomons swinging their shadows around the face of the sound, insistently marking out his days, till new navigators remap those voyages to and beyond love's peripheries, till another alphabet, another hunt can reconfigure the word. There're twenty corpses down under those towers. When it was all done, they poured concrete through the air shafts into the work space, filled it up, sealed it down to the bedrock. Twenty corpses, at least—"

"They buried the men in the caissons?" Sam asked, surprised.

"I'm speaking figuratively. Some twenty workers died in the bridge's construction—and do you know, no one is really sure of their names? I like to think of those towers as their tombstones. This one falling from the top of some steam-powered boom derrick, that one hit in the head by a swinging beam. I see them, buried, all twenty, in those hypogea at the river bottom, while the stanchions' shadows sweep away the years between their deaths and the sea's mergence with the sun, while the noon signal sirens all the dead swimmers through the everyday . . . ." For a moment he was pensive. (Uncomfortable Sam thought again of the . . . Italian fisherman?) "Everybody always talks about John Augustus—a kraut, you see," the man went on. "There's nothing dumber than a dumb kraut, but there's nothing smarter than a smart one—we all know that. The war taught it to us if it taught us anything. John built bridges all over kingdom come: over the Allegheny, over the Monongahela, over Niagara Falls, the Ohio—each runs under a Roebling bridge. You'd think, sometimes, he was out to build a single bridge across the whole of the country. And the plans for this one were, yes, his. But I want to write the life of Washington. (Don't think it's an accident John named his son after our good first president!)" Again, he nodded deeply. "Roebling—Washington A. Roebling—*was* this bridge; this bridge was Washington Roebling. He was born into it, through his father: every rivet and cable you see around us sings of him. Write such a life? It shouldn't be too hard. To get the feel of it, all I have to do is to go into the back room, look out the window, and imagine . . . *this*, cable by cable, rising over the river."

When the man was quiet, Sam said with some enthusiasm: "The plaque says the bridge was opened to traffic in 1883. That's the year they started the first commercial electricity in New York City and Hartford, Connecticut!" because, along with and among his magic and tricks, Sam had lots of such informations—like the sixty stories of the Woolworth Building—and this was a man who might appreciate it.

"*Really*—?" the young man asked, conveying more surprise than was reasonable.

"That's right."

"In May it was—since you're being so particular—the very month we're in: on the twenty-fourth, that's when they started to roll and stroll across. Though your plaque doesn't say *that!* Nor does it say how, on the first day, when they opened the walkway here to the curious hordes, going down those steps there a woman tripped and screamed—and the crowds, thinking the whole structure was collapsing, stampeded. Twelve people were trampled to death. It's a strange bridge, a dangerous bridge in its way; things happen here. I mean things in your mind—" a wicked smile behind his glasses gave way to a warm one—"that you wouldn't ordinarily think of." The man held out his hand. "My name's Harold. Harold Hart.[7] People call me Hart. A few folks—especially in the family—call me Harry. But I'm becoming Hart more and more these days."

Sam seized the hand to shake—in his own hand with their nails like helmets curving the tops of the enlarged first joints, their forward rims like visors. "Sam." He shook vigorously—let go, and put his hands down beside him. "My name is Sam." No, the man was not particularly looking at them. "My birthday's just coming up—" he felt suddenly expansive—"and it happens during the transit of Mercury."

"Does it now? And the last year of construction on this bridge, here—in 1882—took place under the last transit of Venus! A fascinating man," the man said, leaving Sam for a moment confused. "When you live in the same room as someone, realize when you go to the bathroom, or leave by the front door, or simply stop to gaze out the window, you're doubtless doing exactly what he did, walking the same distances, seeing what he saw, feeling what he felt, it gives you an access to the bodily reality of a fellow you could never get at any other way—unless, of course, you went out in a boat on the river yourself, and, underneath, stood up, pulled down your pants, and let fly into the flood!" Playfully the man hit at Sam's shoulder once more, then turned to the water, sniggering.

At contact, realizing what the man was referring to, Sam felt the anxiety from the bridge's Brooklyn end flood back. Perhaps, he thought, he *should* excuse himself and go.

But the man said, snigger now a smile and face gone thoughtful: "Sam— now *that's* the name of a poet. There's the biography I should *really* write."

A tug pulled out from under the traffic way's edge—as the dinghy had floated out when Sam had been nearer Brooklyn.

"Pardon?"

---

7. Harold Hart Crane (1899–1932), American Modernist poet who in 1930 published a poem called *The Bridge*, which used the Brooklyn Bridge as its unifying figure.

"A marvelous, wonderful, immensely exciting poet—named Sam. Another kraut. Roebling—John Augustus—was born in Prussia—Mühlhausen!" He pronounced it with a crisp, German accent, like some vaudeville comic (Mr. Horstein?) taking off Kaiser Wilhelm.[8] "But Sam was born in Vienna. His parents brought him here when he was seven or eight. No grammar, no spelling, and scarcely any form, but a quality to his work that's unspeakably eerie—and the most convincing gusto. Still, by the time he was your age, Sam was as American as advertising or apple pie. He died about seven years ago—I never met him. But—do you know Woodstock?"

"Pardon?" Sam repeated.

"Amazing little town, in upstate New York—full of anarchists and artists and—" he leaned closer to whisper, the snigger back—"free lovers!" He sat back again. "It's full of all the things that make life really fine in this fatuous age. It's a place to learn the measurement of art and to what extent it's an imposition—a fulcrum of shifted energy! It's a town where, on Christmas Eve morning, leaves blow in a wailing, sunny wind, all about outside the house, over the snow patches. It's a good place to roast turkeys and dance till dawn. A good place to climb mountains, or to curl up with a volume of the *Bough*[9]—though you can get bored there, sweeping, drawing pictures, masturbating the cat . . . Well, that's where I spent this past winter. That's where I discovered Sam—somewhere between making heaps of apple sauce and cooking the turkey in front of an open fire in a cast-iron pig! I've been growing this mustache since about then. How do you think it looks?"

"It looks fine." It looked rather thin for all that time—certainly thinner than Hubert's. "You found Sam's books?"

"Alas, poor Sam never *had* a book. But I found his notebooks and his manuscripts—a friend of mine had them. He let me borrow them so I could copy some of them out."

"He lived in Woodstock?"

"Sam? No, he lived right here in the city—within walking distance of the bridge." This time he gestured toward Manhattan. "Oh, Sam was very much a city poet. He lived just on the Lower East Side, there. Went to P.S. One-sixty at Suffolk and Rivington Street. Worked in the sweatshops—stole what time he could to go to the Metropolitan Museum, take piano lessons. He played piano just beautifully—that's what my friend said. And drew his pictures; and wrote his poems. He wrote a poem once, right here, while he was walking across the bridge with his oldest brother, Daniel—there were eight boys in the family, I believe." Again the man spread his arms along the bench back; one hand went behind Sam's shoulder. "Late in November—just a month before Christmas—they were walking across, from Brooklyn, talking, like you and me, when Sam pulled out his notebook and started writing." He closed his eyes, lifted his chin: "'Is this the river "East", I heard? / Where the ferry's, tugs, and sailboats stirred / And the reaching wharves from the inner land / Outstretched like the harmless receiving hand . . . / But look! at the depths of the dripling tide / That dripples, re-ripples like locusts astride / As the boat turns upon the silvery spread / It leaves strange—a shadow—dead . . .'"

8. William II (1859–1941), emperor of Germany, king of Prussia, and aggressive Central Powers leader during World War I.

9. I.e., *The Golden Bough*, a twelve-volume study of myth and religion, written by James Frazer (1854–1941).

Through the cables, the dark, flat, and—yes—dead green spread behind the tug. Ripples crawled to the wake's rim, like silver beetles, to quiver and glitter at, though unable to cross, the widening borders.

"The river's very beautiful," Sam said, because beauty was the aspect of nature and poetry it seemed safest to speak of.

"Oh, not for Sam the poet. If anything, for him it was terrifying. He was to die, looking out at it, from a window of the Manhattan Hospital for the Destitute, up on Ward's Island. They keep the dying there—and the insane. It's only an island away from Brother's, where the *General Slocum* beached after it burned up a thousand krauts and drenched them till they drowned, back in 'aught-four—makes you wonder what we needed a war for. It was the dust and the airless walls of his brother Adolf's leather shop where he worked that first seated in the floor of Sam's breath that terrible, spiritual, stinking illness—have you ever visited anyone dying of TB?[1] They do stink, you know? Here in the city, you learn to recognize the stench—if you hang out in the slums. Nobody ever talks about that, but—*Lord!*—they smell. The lungs bleed and die and rot in their chests; and their breath and their bodies erupt with the putrefaction of it—in a way it's a purification too, I suppose. But before he was nineteen, Sam had already learned the rustle of nurses around his bed, like the husks of summer locusts. All the nuns—and he'd been reading Poe, the ghoul-haunted woodlands, that sort of stuff—once made our rogue tanton bolt St. Anthony's at Woodhaven, in terror for his life. That's where they first packed him off to die. For a while after that he stayed in New Jersey—Paterson—with Morris, another brother. But a few months later, he was back in another hospital—Sea View this time, on Staten Island." Without closing his eyes, again the man recited: "'And the silvery tinge that sparkles aloud / Like brilliant white demons, which a tide has towed / From the rays of the morning sun / Which it doth ceaselessly shine upon.' But that was written some years before, when he was well—walking across the bridge here with Daniel. Still: 'loud, brilliant white demons . . .'? He had a very excitable poetic apprehension—like any true poet would want to or—really—must have. Don't you think?"

By now Sam was feeling somewhat sulky there'd been no praise of his own eccentric bit of electrical information. He was not about to condone all this biography. "It doesn't sound all *that* good of a poem."

"Well, in a way, it's not. But it's what poetry—real poetry—is made of: '. . . The dripling tide that dripples, re-ripples . . .' Really, for any word-lover, that's quite wonderful! Words must create and tear down whole visions, cities, worlds!" (Sam was not sure if he was saying Sam—the other Sam—did this or didn't.) "And then, Sam was only a child when he died—twenty-three. I'm twenty-four now. A year older than Sammy. But I suppose he was too young, or too uneducated—too unformed to make *real* poems. But then, Keats, Rimbaud[2]—all that material: you can feel its sheer verbal excitement, can't you?" He chuckled, as if to himself. "Twenty-four? In a moment I'll sneeze—and be *older* than Keats!"

Sam looked at the face now looking past his; at first he'd put it at Hubert's age. But there was a dissoluteness to it—the skin was not as clear as it might be, the eyes were not as bright as they should be; and, of course, just

---

1. Tuberculosis.
2. Arthur Rimbaud (1854–1891), French Symbolist poet who wrote all his works between the ages of fifteen and twenty. John Keats (1795–1821), English Romantic poet.

the way he spoke—that made the man seem older than twenty-four. Sam asked: "Don't poems have to make sense, besides just sounding nice?" A teacher down in Raleigh had once explained to them why Edgar Poe was not really a good poet, even after they'd all applauded her recitation of "The Bells." Apparently Poe had not been a very good man—and people who were not good men, while they could write fun poems, simply *couldn't* write great ones.

"Oh, do they, now? But there're many interesting ways to seem not to be making sense while you're actually making very good sense indeed—using myths, symbols, poetic associations and rhetorical gestures. I never wrote my mother about Sam—just as I never wrote her about Jean's scooting off with Margy. I haven't written her about Emil yet, either—but I'll have to do that, soon. I wonder if I'll write her about you? Grace proffers the truth in a regular Sunday Delivery, and I send her back lies—of omission mostly. (Can you imagine, telling her about some wild afternoon I had at Sand Street, skulking down behind the piled-up planks and plates beside the Yard?) So I just assume they can be corrected later. I dare say it's all quite incoherent to you. But it's leading up to something—a bigger truth. I just have to get my gumption up to it. At any rate—" he chuckled—"Sam was not only a poet. He drew pictures. He played the piano beautifully, as I said—at least that's what my friend who'd known him told me. You see, it was a poetic sensibility in embryo, struggling to express itself in all the arts. Do you play an instrument?"

"The cornet." Playing the cornet, Sam had always figured, was like knowing about electricity in Hartford and the number of stories in the Woolworth Building. Or maybe a couple of magic tricks.

"Well, then, you see?" the man said. "You and little Sammy Greenberg are very much alike!"

"He was a jewboy!" Sam exclaimed—because till then, for all he'd been trying to withhold, he'd really begun to identify with his strange namesake who had once walked across the bridge and had seen, as had he, the water dripple, re-ripple . . .

"Yes, he was, my young, high-yellow, towering little whippersnapper!" The man laughed.

Once more Sam started, because, though he knew the term—high-yellow—, nobody had ever actually called him that before. (He'd been called "nigger" by both coloreds *and* whites and knew what to do when it happened. But this was a new insult, though it was given so jokingly, he wondered if it was worth taking offense.) Sam put his hands on his thighs again, then put them back on the bench, to arch his fingertips against the wood, catching his nails in weathered grain. Was *this* man, Sam wondered a moment, Jewish? Wasn't there something Semitic in his features? Sam asked: "Do you write poems, too?"

"Me?" The young man brought one hand back, the slender fingers splayed wide against the sweater he wore under his corduroy jacket. "Do I write poems? *Me?*" He took a breath. "I'm in advertising, actually. Ah, but I *should* be writing poems. I *will* be writing poems. Have I ever written poems?" He scowled, shook his head. "*Perhaps* I've written poems. Once I found a beautiful American word: 'findrinny.' But no American writer ever wrote it down save Melville. And since it never made it from *Moby-Dick* into any dictionary (I've looked in half a dozen), I've finally settled on 'spindrift.' Go look *it* up! It's equally lovely in the lilt and lay of what it means. Believe me, if I wrote a real poem, everyone would be talking about it—writing about it. When I write a poem—find its lymph and sinew, fix a poem that speaks with a tongue more mine than any you'll ever actually hear me talking with—you'll know it! Boni and Liveright did *Cane* last year, *Beyond the Pleasure Principle*[3] this year; I just wonder when they'll get to me. I can promise you—Crane," he said suddenly, sat forward, and scowled. "Isn't that endlessly ironic?" He shook his head. "Crane—that's whom they're all mad about now. Someone showed me the manuscript. And, dammit, some of them are actually good! They're planning to get endorsements from Benét[4] and Nunnally Johnson—he lives in Brooklyn, too."

"A poet? Named Crane?" Sam asked.

The man nodded, glancing over. "Nathalia Crane. She lives in Flatbush, out where it builds up again and Brooklyn starts to look at least like a town; and she's in love with the janitor's boy—some snub-nosed freckle-cheeked mick named Jones."

"In the heart of Brooklyn?" Sam said.

"If Brooklyn can be said to have a heart. I wonder why, no matter how hard I try to get away, I always end up working with sweets—Dad makes chocolates, you see. Well, I've lived off them long enough. Personally, I think Brooklyn, once you leave the Heights, is a heartless place. For heart, you go downtown into the Village. Really, the irony's just beyond me. She's supposed to be ten—or was, a couple of years ago. They go on about her like she was Hilda Conkling or Helen Adam.[5] And they actually gave me the thing for review! I mean, I told them—under no *circumstances* would I! Could you think of anything more absurd—*me* reviewing *that*? If I liked it, people would think I was joking. If I hated it, they'd think I was simply being malicious. *They* thought it would be fun. No—I said; I certainly wouldn't be trapped into *that* one. Poetry's more serious than—" Again he broke off and turned, to regard Sam with a fixity that, as the silence grew, grew uncomfortable with it. "I mean, any poem worth its majority must pell-mell through its stages of love, meditation, evocation, and beauty. It's got to hie through tragedy, war, recapitulation, ecstasy, and final declaration. But sometimes I think *she's* got more of the Great War in her poems than I do. I wonder if that makes the geeky girl a better poet? No, I'm not going to be able to take these engineering specifications, instruction manuals, and giant architectural catalogs much longer—Lord, they're real doorstoppers! Soon, I'm going to leave that job—the only question is, at my behest or theirs?"

"You're quitting your—?"

"*Nobody* can write poems and have a job at the same time. It's impossible!"

"You don't think so?" He wondered if he should mention that Clarice worked as a secretary to the principal in the school where Hubert taught—and seemed to turn out her share.

"Do you think I should quit my job because they—not the people I work for, but the people I sometimes write for—asked me to review that silly little girl's silly little book? Of poems?" He crossed his arms severely, hunched his shoulders as if it had suddenly grown chill. "And, of course, they're not silly. Really. They're quite good—a handful of them. But they're not as good as

3. A study in psychoanalysis by Sigmund Freud (1856–1939), first published in German in 1920. "Boni and Liveright": an innovative publishing company of the early 20th century.
4. William Benét (1886–1950), American poet, novelist, and editor, who was on the staff of the New York *Evening Post Literary Review* in the early 1920s.
5. Child prodigies, both poets, of the early 1920s.

poems I wrote when I was that age. (But doesn't every poet feel like that?) And they're certainly not as good as the poems I could write now!" He rocked a few times on the bench, then declared: "Now who do you think it was who wrote,

"Here's Crane with a seagull and Lola the Drudge,
With one pound of visions and one of Pa's fudge.

"Do you think there's that much fudge—and does anybody ever really notice? Fidge, perhaps? Well, Lowell[6] did in Poe . . ." He rocked a few more times, then began, softly, intensely, voiced, yes, but quiet as a whisper:

"And midway on that structure I would stand
One moment, not as diver, but with arms
That open to project a disk's resilience
Winding the sun and planets in its face.
Water should not stem that disk, nor weigh
What holds its speed in vantage of all things
That tarnish, creep, or wane; and in like laughter,
Mobile yet posited beyond even that time
The Pyramids shall falter, slough into sand,—
And smooth and fierce above the claim of wings,
And figured in that radiant field that rings
The Universe:—I'd have us hold one consonance
Kinetic to its poised and deathless dance."

He broke off, turning aside, then added: "No, wait a minute. What about this." Now the voice was louder:

"To be, Great Bridge, in vision bound of thee,
So widely belted, straight and banner-wound,
Multi-colored, river-harboured and upbourne
Through the bright drench and fabric of our veins,—
With white escarpments swinging into light,
Sustained in tears the cities are endowed
And justified, conclamant with the fields
Revolving through their harvests in sweet torment.

"And steady as the gaze incorporate
Of flesh affords, we turn, surmounting all
In keenest transience to that sear arch-head,—
Expansive center, purest moment and electron
That guards like eyes that must always look down
Through blinding cables to the ecstasy
That crashes manifoldly on us when we hear
The looms, the wheels, the whistles in concord
Teathered and antiphonal to a dawn
Whose feet are shuttles, silvery with speed
To tread upon and weave our answering world,
Recreate and resonantly risen in this dome."

Again the man sat back, relaxed his arms. "All right—tell me: is that the greatest—" he growled *greatest* in mock exaggeration—"poem you've ever heard? Or is it?"

---

6. James Russell Lowell (1819–1891), American poet. His *Fable for Critics* (1848) includes the lines "There comes Poe with his raven, like Barnaby Rudge, / Three-fifths of him genius and two-fifths sheer fudge."

Sam looked up, where arch ran into arch, along great cables. "What's it *about*?" he asked, looking back. "The bridge?"

"It's called . . . 'Finale'!" The man seemed, now, absolutely delighted, eyes bright behind his lenses.

"I get the parts about . . . the bridge, I think. But what's the dome?"

"Ah, that's Sam's 'starry splendor dome'—from a poem he wrote, called 'Words.' 'One sad scrutiny from my warm inner self / That age hath—but the pleasure of its own / And that which rises from my inner tomb / Is but the haste of the starry splendor dome / O though, the deep hath fear of thee. . . .' It goes on like that—and ends: '. . . Another morning must I wake to see— / That lovely pain, O that conquering script / cannot banish me.' Conquering script—I like that idea: that the pen is mightier; that writing conquers." His eyes had gone up to tangle in the harp of slant and vertical cables, rising toward the beige-stone doubled groin. "Yes, I think I'll use it, make that one mine—too."

"Can you do that?" Sam asked. "If you write your own poems, can you just take words and phrases from someone else's?"

The man looked down. "Did you ever see a poem by a man named Eliot[7]— read it in *The Dial* a couple of Novembers back? No, you probably didn't. But his poem is nothing *but* words and phrases borrowed from other writers: Shakespeare, Webster, Wagner[8]—all sorts of people."

"Taking other people's poems," Sam said, "that doesn't sound right to me."

"Then I'll link Sam's words to words of mine, engulf them, digest and transform them, *make* them words of my own. Really, it's all right. You said you grew up on a college campus?" Leaning forward, his face became a bit wolfish. "The word is . . . 'allusion'!"

"I grew up there," Sam said. "But I didn't go to school there."

"I see. But look what I've managed to call up! Go on—take a look there, now." The man nodded toward Manhattan. "What's that city, do you think?"

Sam turned, about to say . . . But the city had changed, astonishingly, while they'd been sitting. The sunlight, in lowering, had smelted its copper among the towers, to splash the windows of the southernmost skyscrapers, there the Pulitzer, in the distance the Fuller, there the Woolworth Building itself.

"Risen from the sea, just off the Pillars of Hercules—that's Atlantis,[9] boy—a truly wonder-filled city, far more so than any you've ever visited yet, or certainly ever lived in." Behind Sam the man lowered his voice: "I'm a kind of magician who makes things appear and disappear. But not just doves and handkerchiefs and coins. I'm one of O'Shaunessey's movers and shakers, an archæologist of evening. I call up from the impassive earth the whole of the world around you, Sam—stalking the wild nauga and bringing it all down to words, paired phalluses, bridge between man and man. I create and crumble worlds, cities, visions! No, friend! It is Atlantis that I sing. And poets have been singing it since Homer, son; still, it's amazing what, at any moment, might be flung up by the sea. So: *ecce* Atlantic Irrefragable, corymbulous of towers, each tower a gnomon[1] on the gold afternoon, flinging around it its

---

7. T. S. Eliot (1888–1965), Modernist poet. The work alluded to is *The Waste Land* (1922).
8. Richard Wagner (1813–1883), German composer, especially of large-scale operas. John Webster (1580–1625), English dramatist.
9. In Greek myth, Atlantis was a large island in the western sea. Plato described it as a utopia that was destroyed by earthquake. The Pillars of Hercules are two great rocks on either side of the

Strait of Gibraltar, supposedly placed by Hercules during one of his Twelve Labors.
1. Object whose shadow indicates the time of day, as the pointer on a sundial. "*Ecce*": behold (Latin). "Irrefragable": impossible to break. "Corymbulous": made up of several separate stalks all rising to the same height; usually used to describe a flower such as Queen Anne's lace.

metric shadow. And you should see it by moonlight—! They speak a wonder-filled language there, Sam: not like any tongue you've ever heard. My pop—C.A.—thinks poetry should be a pleasure taken up in the evening—but not so in Atlantis. No! There, Raphèl maì amècche zabì almi makes as lucid sense as mene, mene tekel upharsin[2] or Mon sa me el kirimoor—nor is it anywhere near as dire as Daniel. But we *need* Asia's, Africa's fables! In Atlantis, when I stand on the corner and howl my verses, no one looks at me and asks, 'Whadja say?' Because mine's the tongue they speak there. In Atlantis I'll get back my filched *Ulysses*[3] with the *proper* apology. I tell you, all twenty of those dead workers are up and dancing there with savage sea-girls, living high and healthy in garden-city splendor, their drinking late into the dawn putting out Liberty's light each morning. And the niggers and the jewboys, the wops and the krauts say hey, hi, and howdy—and quote Shakespeare and Adelaide Crapsey[4] all evening to each other. And even if I were to pull a Steve Brodie[5] this moment from the brink of the trolley lane there—watchman, what of the track?—, as long as that city's up, the river would float me, singing on my back, straight into its docks at a Sutton gone royal, no longer a dead end, and I'd walk its avenues in every sort of splendor. You say you saw the empty boat of our dark friend a-dribble over his gunwale? Well, if it was empty, it's because he's found safe harbor there. And he's happy, happy—oh, he's happy, Sam, as only a naked stallion (may St. Titus protect your foreskin in these heathen lands) prancing in the city can be!"

Sam said: "Wow . . . !" though his "Wow" was at the gilded stones, the burnished panes, the towers before him, rather than at the words that wove from behind through the woof of towers ahead. He glanced back at the man, then turned to the city again, where, in a building he couldn't name, copper light fell from one window—"Oh . . . !" Sam breathed—to the window below. "Wow . . ."

"Atlantis," the man repeated. "And the only way to get there is the bridge: the arched nave of this loom, the temple of this stranded warp, the pick of some epiphenomenal gull among them as it shuttles tower to tower, bobbin, spool, and spindle. The bridge—that's what brings us exhausted devils, in the still and tired evening, to Atlantis."

"That's . . . I mean—"

"Atlantis? There, you can see it, when the sun's like this—the city whose kings ordered this bridge be built. Better, the city grows, weaves, wavers from the bridge, boy—not the bridge from the city. For the bridge is a woob—orbly and woob are Sammy's words: a woob's something halfway between a womb and a web. Roebling's bridge, Stella's bridge, my bridge! Trust me—it wasn't gray, girder-grinding, grim and grumpy New York that wove out from this mill. Any dull, seamy era can throw up an Atlantis—Atlantis, I say: city of mirrors, City of Dreadful Night, there a-glittering in the sun! Vor cosma saga. Look at those towers—those molte alti torri, those executors of Mars,[6] like those 'round Montereggione. Vor shalmer raga.

2. Numbered, weighed divisions (Aramaic, literal trans.). From Daniel 5.26–28: "God hath numbered thy kingdom, and finished it. . . . Thou art weighed in the balances, and art found wanting. . . . Thy kingdom is divided."
3. Stream-of-consciousness novel by Irish writer James Joyce (1882–1941), published in 1922 but banned for obscenity in the United States until 1933.

4. Minor American poet (1878–1914), best known for developing a five-line form called a "cinquain."
5. I.e., jump off the bridge.
6. I.e., towers tall as the twin giants of Greek mythology, Otus and Ephialtes, who captured and chained up the god of war. "Molte alti-torri": very high towers (Italian).

Look at them, listen: O Jerusalem and Nineveh—among them you can hear Nimrod's[7] horn bleating and Ephialtes' chain a-rattle. Whose was the last funeral you tagged behind, when the bee drowsed with the bear? What primaveral prince, priest, pauper, Egyptian mummy was it, borne off to night, fire, and forever? What mother's son—or daughter—was it, boxed now and buried? *Per crucem ad lucem.* Everything living arcs to an end. Nabat. Kalit. The hour to suffer. It's a dangerous city, Sam. *Et in Arcadia ego.*[8] Anything can be stolen from you any moment. But all you get bringing up the rear of funerals in November is shattered by the sea—for death's as marvelous a mystery as either birth or madness. Go strolling in our city parks, Caina, Ptolomea, Judecca. (The only one I don't have to worry about getting frozen into, I guess, is Antenora—if only thanks to the change of season). *Li jorz iert clers e sanz grant vent.* Go on, ask: *'Maestro, di, che terra è questa?'*[9] No, not penitence, but song. I'm still not ready for repentance. See, I'm looking for Atlantis, too, Sam—sometimes I think the worst that can happen is that I'll be stuck with the opportunists in the vestibule—maybe even allowed to loll among the pages of the virtuous *Pagan.* But then I'm afraid you're more likely to find me running in circles on burning sand, under a slow fall of fire—that's if I don't just snap and end up in the trees, where harpies[1] peck the bleeding bark. Mine and Amfortas's wounds both could use us some of Achilles' rust—if not a little general ataraxy.[2] In Atlantis you spend *every* night carousing with Charlie Chaplin[3]—and celebrate each dawn with randy icemen at your knees. In Atlantis, you can strut between Jim Harris and the emperor every day, Mike Drayton squiring Goldilocks behind. In Atlantis, all poets wake up in the morning *real* advertising successes—and cheese unbinds, like figs. Step right up, sit down with your own Sammy, drink a glass of malmsey,[4] and share a long clay stem. When this Orlando is to his dark tower come[5] when I split my ivory horn in two, bleeding from lip and ear (you think my pop will be my Ganelon and finally pluck me from my santa gesta?[6]—will they hear me eight miles or thirty leagues away, the note borne by an angel? You're sensitive, boy—sensitive to beauty. I can tell from your 'Wow!'—it's a sensitive 'Wow!' So—Wow!—I know you know what I'm talking of. As well, you're a handsome boy—like Jean. Only *handsomer* than Jean; I'd say it if anyone asked me. But there—I *have* said it; and it's still true! That's the job of poets, you know—to speak the terrifying, simple truths, that, for most people, are so difficult they stick in the throat from embarrassment. I mean, what's poetry for, anyway? To write a reply on the back of a paper somebody slips you at the baths with their address on it whom you don't feel like fucking? To celebrate some black theft of goose, cigar, and perfume—rather than toss it out the window at Thompson's?"

Sam had been used to people down home saying, "The Bishop has some *fine* looking boys!" He'd even had two or three girls at the school get moony

7. Grandson of Noah and a noted hunter (Genesis 10.8–9). Jerusalem is a city in Israel, the holy land of the Jews, Christians, and Muslims. Nineveh was the ancient capital of Assyria (now Iraq).
8. And I too in Arcadia (Latin). Arcadia was a region of ancient Greece known for its pastoral tranquility.
9. Master, what land is this? (Italian).
1. Half bird, half woman creatures of Greek mythology.
2. A state of calmness, free from emotional distress.

3. Preeminent comedic star of early silent films (1889–1977).
4. Sweet Madeira wine.
5. From Shakespeare's *King Lear* 3.4.170–73: "Child Rowland to the dark tower came" is a line of nonsense verse quoted by Edgar pretending to be insane. Orlando is the Italian name for "Roland" (see n. 6, this page).
6. Godly achievements (Italian). Ganelon was a French warrior in the *Song of Roland*, who arranges for his stepson Roland's defeat and death in battle.

and giggly about him, fascinated with the silliest thing he'd say. But the notion of himself as *really* handsome . . . ? He pushed his fingertips over the green bench planks, beneath his thighs.

"Actually," the man said behind him (again Sam looked at the city), "I'm probably as good a poet as I am because I'm quite brave. I'm not some Jonathan Yankee nor yet, really, a Pierrot.[7] But I've trod far shadowier grounds than those Wordsworth[8] preluded his excursion to cover—precisely because they are *not* in the mind of man. Sure. I mean, here a logical fellow must ask: okay, what finally keeps me from it? We have the river's flow—instead of certainty. I could be any old priestess of Hesperus[9]—wrecked on whatever. Am I really going to sing three times? It's a pretty easy argument that, whether in Egypt or at the Dardanelles, with any two towns divided by water, one can always play Abydos to the other's Sestos: for every Hero somewhere there's a Leander, and every Hero has her Hellespont.[1] There's always hope as long as he remembers how to swim. I mean what are you going to do with Eve, La Gioconda, and Delilah[2]—replace the latter two with Magdalene or Mary? Do I covet the extinction of light in dark waters? Three Marys will rise up and calm the roar: sure—Mary Garden, Merry Andrews, and Mary Baker Eddy.[3]

"But we have the bridge.

"Oh, surely, it starts with your having a satori in the dentist chair, and the next you know you're at work on your hieros gamos and giggling over what Dol Common said to Sir Epicure.[4] There are some folks to whom the thunder speaks; but there are others who need poets to rend and read into it their own trap-clap. (I hope you're not sure, either, who that their own refers to.) It ends, however, here, with *me* talking to *you*—I certainly didn't *think* I would be, half an hour ago. Not when I first saw you. The ones who terrify me are always the short, muscular blonds—and the tall, dark, handsome ones. Like you. "Tall, dark, and handsome'? That's trite for terror. But it's true. I live with a short, muscular blond. We have a nice, six-dollar a week room. Only, I confess, it's the eight dollar room I lust after. *That's* Roebling's room. My blond's a sailor. His old man's the building owner. Now *he's* got the view—but he tells me I can come in and use it whenever I want. They're nice, that way. You can't imagine what it took, getting up nerve to speak to him—but I said, his name's Emil—to talk with him; and really talking with someone is different from simply speaking. I mean, you and I are speaking. But are we *talking* yet? Perhaps we ought to find out if we can. Still, suddenly, Emil and I—my handsome sailor, my golden wanderer, off after his *own* fleece—we were talking—telling each other how we felt. About one another. About the world. We talked till the sun came up; then he kissed my eyes with a speech entirely beyond words, and I've been able to do nothing but babble my happiness since. We decided it really would be terrible if we

---

7. A stock character of French pantomime, usually depicted as a clown dressed in white and black.
8. William Wordsworth (1770–1850), English Romantic poet.
9. The morning star. Also a reference to Henry Wadsworth Longfellow's poem "The Wreck of the Hesperus."
1. Or the Dardanelles, a strait separating Europe and Asia Minor. Hero and Leander were lovers who lived on either side of the water; every night Leander would swim from his town, Abydos, to Hero's town, Sestos, guided by the light of Hero's torch. He drowned one night when the torch blew out; Hero killed herself when she found his body.
2. Samson's mistress, who betrays him to his enemies (Judges 16.5). "La Gioconda": the cheerful woman (Italian); the title of Leonardo da Vinci's Mona Lisa.
3. Founder of the Christian Science Church (1821–1910). Garden (1877–1967), soprano opera star of the early 20th century.
4. A swindler and the greedy fool she dupes in Ben Jonson's satire *The Alchemist* (1610). "Satori": a state of sudden enlightenment.

ever left each other. So he asked me to move in with him. All life is a bridge, I told him. Even the whole world. He's like an older brother—it's like living with a brother. And once again I'm hearing things before dawn. I'm three years younger than he—and two inches taller! But sometimes, it's true, I feel like I'm the elder. His father can't imagine that anything could be going on that shouldn't be—if anything is going on at all." Sam *heard* him shrug . . . "It's a hoot. The last person to pick him up and suckle at his schlong was Lauritz Melchior. Now, because they both speak Danish, we get to lurk backstage at the Met,[5] about as regular as *The Brooklyn Eagle.* But it's very pure. Very severe, between us—Emil and me. But he *is* a sailor—and he goes on voyages. He's away, now—in South America. But in Atlantis, I live forever, in my room with my Victrola and my love. It makes my dark room light and light." Suddenly the man leaned forward again. (Sam could hear him, not see him, closer at his back.) "Tell me, Sam: Have you ever tried to kiss the sun? I mean, deep kiss it—French kiss it as they've just begun to say. Maul it with your lips and tongue? Flung your arms around it, pulled it down on top of you, till it seared your chest and toasted the white wafer cheek of love, poached the orbs in your skull, even while you thrust your mouth out and into its fires till the magma at its core blackened the wet muscle of all articulation? Well, Atlantis is the town in which everybody, man and woman, can kiss the sun and still have the moon smile down on them—not this stock, market culture of the stock market. And believe me, sometimes when the sun's away, you'll find yourself needs reaching for the moon. All I do is sweat with imagined jealousies while he's gone—Emil, I mean. But someday, he's going to come home, just while I'm in the throes of it, down on the daybed, with you or some guinea fisherman's randy brat—does it matter which? And . . ." The man sat back. Sam couldn't see him for the city—though he heard his fingers snap: "That'll be it! But that's not for today. That's for another time. Do you want to come back to the place with me—have a drink? We could be alone. I'm a good man to get soused with, if you like to get soused—and what self-respecting Negro doesn't? Come on, relax. Spend a little time—come with me, boy-oh-boy, and we'll get boozy and comfortable."

Was it the mention of the fisherman? Was it the mention of the moon? Suddenly Sam stood and turned around. "Look," he said. "I'm going to get a policeman."

The man frowned, put his head to the side.

"I'm going to get a *policeman.* This isn't right—" He thought: How do you explain to this fellow that the boat was really empty, that a man had *really* drowned?

"But you don't have to do—"

"I'm sorry! But I have tell *somebody!* Look, we just can't—"

The man was looking at Sam's hands—which, in his excitement, had come loose to wave all over the day.

"I know all about it—the force of the club in the hand of the working man. Really," the man added, with a worried look, "policemen are *so* dull. Laughter's what you want here. Celebration of the city. Beauty. Higher thoughts. Get yourself lost in that lattice of flame. Humor's the artist's only weapon against the proletariat—and, in this city, my friend, the police are as proletarian as they come. Hey, I'm not going to make you do anything you don't—I mean I only *asked* . . . only offered you a sociable drink—"

---

5. I.e., the Metropolitan Opera House.

"I'm going to get a policeman," Sam repeated. "Now." He added: "Maybe we'll be back—!" He started away. "In a few minutes."

From behind him the man called out, almost petulantly: "*That's* not the way to Atlantis!"

Sam glanced back.

"And you're a damned fool if you think I'm going to wait around for *you.*" The man stood now, one hand on the bench back, like someone poised to run. His final salvo: "Don't think you'll ever get to it calling the law on people like *me!*"

Sam started again. Really, the fellow was a fool! What in the world had made him sit there listening, letting the man drench him in his lurid monologue? Sam broke into a lope, into a run—turned and, practically dancing backwards, looked once more:

The man was hurrying off, into Brooklyn, into Flatbush, or wherever he'd said he lived, moving away almost as fast as Sam was moving toward the city. Sam turned ahead, in time to take the stairs down the Manhattan stanchion—two at a step. Three minutes later, he almost missed the narrow entrance down to Rose. He had to swing around the rail, come back, and, at the entrance, plunge in silence by gray stone.

He found a policeman coming along the black metal railing by City Hall Park, where tall buildings' shadows had already darkened the lower stories to gray— save when Sam passed an east-west street, gilded with sudden sun. He hurried up to the officer. "Excuse me, sir. Please." On the other side of the park's grass, light glinted on the edge of the sprawling trolley terminal's tin roof— where some of the green paint had come away . . . ? "But I think someone's drowned—in the river, sir. I was up walking across, into Brooklyn, and—"

"You saw someone do a Brodie off the bridge?" Below the midnight visor, webbed in forty-plus years' wrinkles, river-green eyes were perfectly serious.

"Someone jump, you mean? No. He was in a boat. I could see it, down in the water. And later on, I saw the boat again—and it was empty. A green rowboat—I think."

The policeman said: "Oh. You saw him go over?"

Sam watched the man's dull squint and his ordinary thumb laid up against the belly of his shirt between his jacket flaps, like something inevitable. He thought about putting his own hands in his pockets, but kept them hanging by force. "Well, no—not really. I mean, I didn't actually *see* it. But later—I saw the same boat. The oar was floating behind it. And there was nobody in it."

"Oh," the policeman said again. The ordinary thumb rose, and the officer scratched ash-blown blond, cap edge a-joggling on the walnuts of his knuckles. "And how long ago was this?"

"Just a few minutes," Sam said, trying to figure how long he'd been talking with the man on the bridge. "Maybe twenty, twenty-five minutes." Probably it was over thirty. Could it have been an hour? "But, well, you know. It takes some time to get all the way back over, to this side, from Brooklyn."

"It was on the Brooklyn side?"

"It was closer to the Brooklyn side than ours."

"Then why didn't you try to get some help over there?" The officer dropped his hand to put a fist on his bullet-belt.

"I didn't see anybody over there. And I was coming back this way, anyway—I mean, I don't think there's anything anybody could have done.

Not now. Even then. But I still thought I ought to tell somebody. An officer. That it happened—that it probably happened . . . I mean."

"Oh," the policeman said a third time. "I see."

Sam looked around, looked at the policeman, who seemed to be waiting for him to leave, and finally said a hurried, "I just wanted to tell you— Thank you, sir," and ducked around him, embarrassment reddening his cheeks, rouging his neck.

At the corner, Sam glanced back, hoping the officer would be marking it down on his pad—at least the time or the place or something—in case, later, it came up. (Above, incomplete construction marked the day with girders and derrick, flown against the clouds in sight of the sound; for a moment Sam recalled the white workers who, with saw and torch, would hang there, humming, through the week.) *Would* that white man remember? But the officer was walking on, crossing silver tracks in a fan of sunlight, one untroubled hand flipping his billyclub down, around, and up—now one way, now the other.

Starting purposefully uptown, Sam mulled, block after block, toward the twilight city, now on the disappearance of the fisherman, now on the ravings of the stranger on the bridge, now on the three girls coming down the steps when he'd arrived at the underpass, whose delicate descent had innocently initiated it all, now on the policeman who'd brought the afternoon to its inconclusive close. A knot had tied low in his throat—an anxious thing that wouldn't be swallowed, that kept him walking, kept him thinking, kept him rehearsing and revising bits of the day in their dialogue—till, stalking some greater understanding still eluding him, he got as far as Fifty-second Street.

Nestled in the grip of gilded tritons and swept round by cast nereids[6] metal drapes, up on the pediment of a bank, with its brazen disk, from arrow-tipped hands, down-cast, short one right and long one left (a wonderful water clock, he thought suddenly and absurdly, in which the water had all run out), Sam realized it was just after . . . twenty-five-to-five!

Along all four legs of the intersection, he looked with electric attention for a subway stop's green globes. He'd been due at Elsie and Corey's almost forty minutes ago!

1995

6. Sea nymphs

SHERLEY ANNE WILLIAMS
1944–1999

Short story writer, dramatist, critic, poet, and novelist Sherley Anne Williams combined in her work a keen sense of the tradition of black oral and Western literary forms with the concerns of class that are often camouflaged by race in contemporary American literature. Williams felt an affinity with "protest fiction" and claimed kin with Alice Walker, Sterling Brown, Langston Hughes, James Baldwin,

Zora Neale Hurston, Ernest Gaines, Amiri Baraka, and Toni Morrison, writers who render black life as significant in and of itself and not simply as an adjunct to the white experience or as an irritation in the history of the United States.

Williams was born, the third of four daughters, on August 25, in Bakersfield, California, to Fesse Winson and Lelia Marie (Silers) Williams. Her parents were laborers, and as a child Williams worked alongside them in the fruit and cotton fields. Her father died of tuberculosis when she was eight, and her mother when she was sixteen. Ruise, Sherley's older sister, then became her guardian. Encouraged by a high school science teacher, Williams studied at Fresno State. After earning a B.A. in history in 1966, she began to write short stories. In 1967, the *Massachusetts Review* published "Tell Martha Not to Moan."

Williams studied and taught as she wrote. Between 1966 and 1967 she did graduate work at Howard University; from 1970 to 1972 she worked as a community educator in Washington, D.C. In 1972 she taught in the black studies department at Brown University and earned her master's degree. That same year the manuscript she had worked on during her time at Howard and Brown was published as *Give Birth to Brightness: A Thematic Study in Neo-Black Literature*. In *Give Birth*, Williams contrasts Amiri Baraka's "Dutchman" and "The Slave" with James Baldwin's "Blues for Mister Charlie" and Ernest Gaines's "Of Love and Dust," arguing that while Baraka draws his characters from a Western tradition, Baldwin and Gaines find theirs in the life of the collective black community.

While researching the history and literature of African Americans and teaching at California State University at Fresno and then at the University of California at San Diego, Williams continued to write. Her first volume of poetry, *The Peacock Poems* (1975), which was nominated for the National Book Award, both draws on her childhood in Bakersfield and gives glimpses of her son, John Malcolm. Her second collection, *Some One Sweet Angel Chile* (1982), employs the point of view of women from different historical eras: nineteenth-century Hannah in "Letters from a New England Negro," twentieth-century blues singer Bessie Smith in "Regular Reefer," and her own past self in "The Iconography of Childhood."

In 1986 Williams published her novel *Dessa Rose,* which she had revised and expanded from a short story titled "Meditations on History" (1980). Like Williams's poetry, the novel reflects her deep knowledge of African American history as well as the musicality of its oral tradition. Williams based her story on two historical events: an 1829 slave uprising in Kentucky led by a pregnant black woman, which is discussed in Angela Davis's essay "Reflections on the Black Woman's Role in the Community of Slaves," and the giving of sanctuary to runaway slaves in North Carolina by a white woman living on an isolated farm in 1830, which Williams first read about in Davis's essay and then more deeply in Herbert Aptheker's *American Slave Revolts*. Although inspired by historical sources, *Dessa Rose* is not determined by them, for Williams has these two women, who challenge the stereotypes of African American slave women and antebellum southern white women, meet. *Dessa Rose* is also Williams's outraged response to William Styron's *Confessions of Nat Turner* (1967), which, Williams points out, in its limitations is an indication of how "African Americans remain at the mercy of literature and writing." In structuring her novel as if it were being told, so that we hear the difference between Dessa Rose's memory of her experience, her telling of it to a white man, and that man's interpretation of her story, Williams highlights an important aspect of the slave narrative tradition—that is, that these narratives were often told to whites who did not necessarily understand or sympathize with the slave's story but who, because they could write, became the transmitters of the slave experience. Called "artistically brilliant, emotionally affecting and totally unforgettable" in its uncompromising portrayal of American slavery by *New York Times* reviewer David Bradley, *Dessa Rose* was both a critical and a popular success, going into its third printing only a few months after publication.

Williams continued her own impressive literary efforts while teaching African American literature at the University of California at San Diego, until her death in 1999.

The Peacock Poems: 1

the trimming of the feathers

I wish I could still stay
down by the fire at the end of the row
and jes watch the baby but Daddy
say I'm a big girl now

not big enough to have my own sack   5
jes only to help pile the cotton
in the middle of the row fo Mamma to put
in her'n. I gots to keep my jacket button;

it's cold. Mamma say I move
mo faster I wouldn't be feelin it so much.   10
I can't do what her and Daddy do move
slow and fast togetha and get a bunch

of cotton and keep warm and watch
the baby, Le'rn. Maybe I get old
as Jesmarie even Ruise I can do a   15
hundred pounds a day hold

the baby—but she won't need no holdin
by then. Mamma sing Daddy hum.
He pickin the row side Ruise
and Jesmarie and they pickin side-a us. We come   20

early fo it's even light and Mamma
face be so dark under them white
head rags and by the end of the day
they be dirty wid sweat. It be gettin on to night

then. Us all be tired. I be thinkin bout   25
the beans Mamma cook. Jack
come wid the bus. Daddy take
the baby and Mamma drag the sack.

1975

I Want Aretha[1] to Set This to Music

I Want Aretha to Set
    This to Music:
        I surprise girlhood
        in your face; I know
        my own, have been a   5
        prisoner of my own

1. Aretha Franklin (b. 1942), African American singer known as the "Queen of Soul."

dark skin and fleshy
lips, walked that same high
butty strut despite
all this; rejected   10
the mask my mother
wore so stolidly
through womanhood and
wear it now myself.

I see the mask, sense   15
the girl and the woman
you became, wonder
if mask and woman
are one, if pain is
the sum of all your   20
knowing, victim the
only game you learned.

Old and in pain and
bearing up bearing up
and hurt and age These   25
are the signs of our
womanhood but I'll
make book Bessie[2] did
more than just endure.

                        •

          hear it?   30
          hear it?

Oh I'm lonesome now
    but I won't be lonesome long
Say I'm lonely now
    but I don't need to be lonesome long
You know it take a man wid some style and passion   35
    to make a single woman sing these lonely songs

          one-sided bed Blues

Never had a man talk to me
    to say the things he say
Never had a man talk like this, honey,   40
    say the things you say.
Man talk so strong
    till I can't tell Night from Day.

His voice be low words come slow   45
    and he be movin all the while
His voice be low words come slow
    and he be movin, Lawd! all the while.

---

2. Bessie Smith (1898?–1937), African American singer known as the "Empress of the Blues." "Make book": bet.

I'm his radio and he sho
    know how to tune my dial.   50

My bed one-sided from me
    sleepin alone all the time
My bed *wop*-sided from me
    sleepin alone so much of the time
And the fact that it empty   55
    show how this man is messin wid my mind.

•

what's out there knockin
Is what the world
don't get enough of

•

1982

Tell Martha Not to Moan

My mamma is a big woman, tall and stout, and men like her cause she soft and fluffy-looking. When she round them it all smiles and dimples and her mouth be looking like it couldn't never be fixed to say nothing but darling and honey.

They see her now, they sho see something different. I should not even come today. Since I had Larry things ain't been too good between us. But— that's my mamma and I know she gon be there when I need her. And sometime when I come, it okay. But this ain't gon be one a them times. Her eyes looking all ove me and I know it coming. She snort cause she want to say god damn but she don't cuss. "When it due, Martha?"

First I start to say, what. But I know it ain't no use. You can't fool old folks bout something like that, so I tell her.

"Last part of November."

"Who the daddy?"

"Time."

"That man what play piano at the Legion?"

"Yeah."

"What he gon do bout it?"

"Mamma, it ain't too much he can do, now is it? The baby on its way."

She don't say nothing for a long time. She sit looking at her hands. They all wet from where she been washing dishes and they all wrinkled like yo hand be when they been in water too long. She get up and get a dish cloth and dry em, then sit down at the table. "Where he at now?"

"Gone."

"Gone? Gone where?" I don't say nothing and she start cussing then. I get kinda scared cause mamma got to be real mad foe she cuss and I don't know who she cussing—me or Time. Then she start talking to me. "Martha, you just a fool. I told you that man wan't no good first time I seed him. A musician the worst kind of men you can get mixed up with. Look at you. You ain't even eighteen years old yet, Larry just barely two, and here you is pregnant again."

She go on like that for a while and I don't say nothing. Couldn't no way. By the time I get my mouth fixed to say something, she done raced on so far ahead that what I got to say don't have nothing to do with what she saying right then. Finally she stop and ask, "What you gon do now? You want to come back here?" She ain't never liked me living with Orine and when I say no, she ask, "Why not? It be easier for you."

I shake my head again. "If I here, Time won't know where to find me, and Time coming; he be back. He gon to make a place for us, you a see."

"Hump, you just played the fool again, Martha."

"No Mamma, that not it at all; Time want me."

"Is that what he say when he left?"

"No, but . . ."

Well, like the first night we met, he come over to me like he knowed me for a long time and like I been his for awmost that long. Yeah, I think that how it was. Cause I didn' even see him when we come in the Legion that first night.

Me and Orine, we just got our checks that day. We went downtown and Orine bought her some new dresses. But the dress she want to wear that night don't look right so we go racing back to town and change it. Then we had to hurry home and get dressed. It Friday night and the Legion crowded. You got to get there early on the weekend if you want a seat. And Orine don't want just any seat; she want one right up front. "Who gon see you way back there? Nobody. You don't dance, how you gon meet people? You don't meet people, what you doing out?" So we sit up front. Whole lots a people there that night. You can't even see the bandstand cross the dance floor. We sharing the table with some more people and Orine keep jabbing me, telling me to sit cool. And I try cause Orine say it a good thing to be cool.

The set end and people start leaving the dance floor. That when I see Time. He just getting up from the piano. I like him right off cause I like men what look like him. He kind of tall and slim. First time I ever seed a man wear his hair so long and nappy[1]—he tell me once it an African Bush—but he look good anyway and he know it. He look round all cool. He step down from the bandstand and start walking toward me. He come over to the table and just look. "You," he say, "you my Black queen." And he bow down most to the floor.

Ah shit! I mad cause I think he just trying to run a game. "What you trying to prove, fool?" I ask him.

"Ah man," he say and it like I cut him. That the way he say it. "Ah man. I call this woman my Black queen—tell her she can rule my life and she call me a fool."

"And sides what, nigga," I tell him then, "I ain't black." And I ain't, I don't care what Time say. I just a dark woman.

"What's the matter, you shamed of being Black? Ain't nobody told you Black is pretty?" He talk all loud and people start gathering round. Somebody say, "Yeah, you tell her bout it, soul." I embarrassed and I look over at Orine. But she just grinning, not saying nothing. I guess she waiting to see what I gon do so I stand up.

"Well if I is black, I is a fine black." And I walk over to the bar. I walk just like I don't know they watching my ass, and I hold my head up. Time follow me right on over to the bar and put his arm round my shoulder.

1. Kinky.

"You want a drink?" I start to say no cause I scared. Man not supposed to make you feel like he make me feel. Not just like doing it—but, oh, like it right for him to be there with me, touching me. So I say yes. "What's your name?" he ask then.

I smile and say, "They call me the player." Orine told a man that once in Berkeley and he didn't know what to say. Orine a smart woman.

"Well they call me Time and I know yo mamma done told you Time ain't nothing to play with." His smile cooler than mine. We don't say nothing for a long while. He just stand there with his arm round my shoulder looking at us in the mirror behind the bar. Finally he say, "Yeah, you gon be my Black queen." And he look down at me and laugh. I don't know what to do, don't know what to say neither, so I just smile.

"You gon tell me your name or not?"

"Martha."

He laugh. "That a good name for you."

"My mamma name me that so I be good. She name all us kids from the Bible,"[2] I tell him laughing.

"And is you good?"

I nod yes and no all at the same time and kind of mumble cause I don't know what to say. Mamma really did name all us kids from the Bible. She always saying, "My mamma name me Veronica[3] after the woman in the Bible and I a better woman for it. That why I name all my kids from the Bible. They got something to look up to." But mamma don't think I'm good, specially since I got Larry. Maybe Time ain't gon think I good neither. So I don't answer, just smile and move on back to the table. I hear him singing soft-like, "Oh Mary don't you weep, tell yo sister Martha not to moan." And I kind of glad cause most people don't even think bout that when I tell em my name. That make me know he really smart.

We went out for breakfast after the Legion close. Him and me and Orine and German, the drummer. Only places open is on the other side of town and at first Time don't want to go. But we finally swade him.

Time got funny eyes, you can't hardly see into em. You look and you look and you can't tell nothing from em. It make me feel funny when he look at me. I finally get used to it, but that night he just sit there looking and don't say nothing for a long time after we order.

"So you don't like Black?" he finally say.

"Do you?" I ask. I think I just ask him questions, then I don't have to talk so much. But I don't want him to talk bout that right then, so I smile and say, "Let's talk bout you."

"I am not what I am." He smiling and I smile back, but I feel funny cause I think I supposed to know what he mean.

"What kind of game you trying to run?" Orine ask. Then she laugh. "Just cause we from the country don't mean we ain't hip to niggas trying to be big-time. Ain't that right, Martha?"

I don't know what to say, but I know Time don't like that. I think he was going to cuss Orine out, but German put his arm round Orine and he laugh. "He just mean he ain't what he want to be. Don't pay no mind to that cat. He always trying to blow some shit." And he start talking that talk, rapping to Orine.

2. In the New Testament, Martha is the sister of Mary of Bethany; symbol of active religious service.

3. She gave Jesus a cloth with which to wipe his face on the way to the Crucifixion; legend held that his image was impressed on it.

I look at Time. "That what you mean?"

He all lounged back in the seat, his legs stretched way out under the table. He pour salt in a napkin and mix it up with his finger. "Yeah, that's what I mean. That's all about me. Black is pretty, Martha." He touch my face with one finger. "You let white people make you believe you ugly. I bet you don't even dream."

"I do too."

"What do you dream?"

"Huh?" I don't know what he talking bout. I kind of smile and look at him out the corner of my eye. "I dreams bout a man like you. Why, just last night, I dream—"

He start laughing. "That's all right. That's all right."

The food come then and we all start eating. Time act like he forgot all bout dreams. I never figure out how he think I can just sit there and tell him the dreams I have at night, just like that. It don't seem like what I dream bout at night mean as much as what I think bout during the day.

We leaving when Time trip over this white man's feet. That man's feet all out in the aisle but Time don't never be watching where he going no way. "Excuse me," he say kind of mean.

"Say, watch it buddy." That white man talk most as nasty as Time. He kind of old and maybe he drunk or an Okie.

"Man, I said excuse me. You the one got your feet in the aisle."

"You," that man say, starting to get up, "you better watch yourself boy."

And what he want to say that for? Time step back and say real quiet, "No, motherfucker. You the one. You better watch yourself and your daughter too. See how many babies she gon have by boys like me." That man get all red in the face, but the woman in the booth with him finally start pulling at him, telling him to sit down, shut up. Cause Time set to kill that man.

I touch Time's arm first, then put my arm round his waist. "Ain't no use getting messed behind somebody like that."

Time and that man just looking at each other, not wanting to back down. People was gon start wondering what going on in a few minutes. I tell him, "Got something for you, baby," and he look down at me and grin. Orine pick it up. We go out that place singing, "Good loving, good, good loving, make you feel so clean."

"You like to hear me play?" he ask when we in the car.

"This the first time they ever have anybody here that sound that good."

"Yeah," Orine say. "How come you all staying round a little jive-ass town like Ashley?"

"We going to New York pretty soon," Time say kind of snappy.

"Well, shit, baby, you—"

"When you going to New York?" I ask real quick. When Orine in a bad mood, can't nobody say nothing right.

"Couple of months." He lean back and put his arm round me. "They doing so many things with music back there. Up in the City, they doing one maybe two things. In L.A. they doing another one, two things. But, man, in New York, they doing everything. Person couldn't never get stuck in one groove there. So many things going on, you got to be hip, real hip to keep up. You always growing there. Shit, if you 'live and playing, you can't help but grow. Say, man," he reach and tap German on the shoulder, "let's leave right now."

We all crack up. Then I say, "I sorry but I can't go, got to take care of my baby."

He laugh, "Sugar, you got yo baby right here."

"Well, I must got two babies then."

We pull in front of the partment house then but don't no one move. Finally Time reach over and touch my hair. "You gon be my Black queen?"

I look straight ahead at the night. "Yeah," I say. "Yeah."

We go in and I check first on Larry cause sometimes that girl don't watch him good. When I come in some nights, he be all out the cover and shivering but too sleepy to get back under em. Time come in when I'm pulling the cover up on Orine two kids.

"Which one yours," he ask.

I go over to Larry bed. "This my baby," I tell him.

"What's his name?"

"Larry."

"Oh, I suppose you name him after his daddy?"

I don't like the way he say that, like I was wrong to name him after his daddy. "Who else I gon name him after?" He don't say nothing and I leave him standing there. I mad now and I go in the bedroom and start pulling off my clothes. I think, That nigga can stand up in the living room all night, for all I care; let Orine talk to German and him, too. But Time come in the bedroom and put his arms round me. He touch my hair and my face and my tittie, and it scare me. I try to pull away but he hold me too close. "Martha," he say, "Black Martha." Then he just stand there holding me, not saying nothing, with his hand covering one side on my face. I stand there trembling but he don't notice. I know a woman not supposed to feel the way I feel bout Time, not right away. But I do.

He tell me things nobody ever say to me before. And I want to tell him that I ain't never liked no man much as I like him. But sometime you tell a man that and he go cause he think you liking him a whole lot gon hang him up.

"You and me," he say after we in bed, "we can make it together real good." He laugh. "I used to think all I needed was that music, but it take a woman to make that music sing, I think. So now stead of the music and me, it be the music and me and you."

"You left out Larry," I tell him. I don't think he want to hear that. But Larry my baby.

"How come you couldn't be free," he say real low. Then, "How you going when I go if you got a baby?"

"When you going?"

He turn his back to me. "Oh, I don't know. You know what the song say, 'When a woman take the blues, She tuck her head and cry. But when a man catch the blues, he grab his shoes and slide.' Next time I get the blues," he laugh a little, "next time the man get too much for me, I leave here and go someplace else. He always chasing me. The god damn white man." He turn over and reach for me. "You feel good. He chasing me and I chasing dreams. You think I'm crazy, huh? But I'm not. I just got so many, many things going on inside me I don't know which one to let out first. They all want out so bad. When I play—I got to be better, Martha. You gon help me?"

"Yes, Time, I help you."

"You see," and he reach over and turn on the light and look down at me, "I'm not what I am. I up tight on the inside but I can't get it to show on the outside. I don't know how to make it come out. You ever hear Coltrane[4]

---

4. John Coltrane (1926–1967), African American jazz musician.

blow? That man is together. He showing on the outside what he got on the inside. When I can do that, then I be somewhere. But I can't go by myself. I need a woman. A Black woman. Them other women steal your soul and don't leave nothing. But a Black woman—" He laugh and pull me close. He want me and that all I care bout.

Mamma come over that next morning and come right on in the bedroom, just like she always do. I kind of shamed for her to see me like that, with a man and all, but she don't say nothing cept scuse me, then turn away. "I come to get Larry."

"He in the other bedroom," I say, starting to get up.

"That's okay; I get him." And she go out and close the door.

I start to get out the bed anyway. Time reach for his cigarettes and light one. "Your mamma don't believe in knocking, do she?"

I start to tell him not to talk so loud cause Mamma a hear him, but that might make him mad. "Well, it ain't usually nobody in here with me for her to walk in on." I standing by the bed buttoning my house coat and Time reach out and pull my arm, smiling.

"I know you ain't no tramp, Martha. Come on, get back in bed."

I pull my arm way and start out the door. "I got to get Larry's clothes together," I tell him. I do got to get them clothes together cause when Mamma come for Larry like that on Sadday morning, she want to keep him for the rest of the weekend. But—I don't know. It just don't seem right for me to be in the bed with a man and my mamma in the next room.

I think Orine and German still in the other bedroom. But I don't know; Orine don't too much like for her mens to stay all night. She say it make a bad impression on her kids. I glad the door close anyway. If Mamma gon start talking that "why don't you come home" talk the way she usually do, it best for Orine not to hear it.

Orine's two kids still sleep but Mamma got Larry on his bed tickling him and playing with him. He like that. "Boy, you sho happy for it to be so early in the morning," I tell him.

Mamma stop tickling him and he lay there breathing hard for a minute. "Big Mamma," he say laughing and pointing at her. I just laugh at him and go get his clothes.

"You gon marry this one?" Every man I been with since I had Larry, she ask that about.

"You think marrying gon save my soul, Mamma?" I sorry right away cause Mamma don't like me to make fun of God. But I swear I gets tired of all that. What I want to marry for anyway? Get somebody like Daddy always coming and going and every time he go leave a baby behind. Or get a man what stay round and beat me all the time and have my kids thinking they big shit just cause they got a daddy what stay with them, like them saddity kids at school. Shit, married or single they still doing the same thing when they goes to bed.

Mamma don't say nothing else bout it. She ask where he work. I tell her and then take Larry in the bathroom and wash him up.

"The older you get, the more foolish you get, Martha. Them musicians ain't got nothing for a woman. Lots sweet talk and babies, that's all. Welfare don't even want to give you nothing for the one you got now, how you gon—" I sorry but I just stop listening. Mamma run her mouth like a clatterbone on a goose ass sometime. I just go on and give her the baby and get the rest of his things ready.

"So your mamma don't like musicians, huh?" Time say when I get back in the bedroom. "Square-ass people. Everything they don't know about, they hate. Lord deliver me from a square-ass town with square-ass people." He turn over.

"You wasn't calling me square last night."

"I'm not calling you square now, Martha."

I get back in the bed then and he put his arm round me. "But they say what they want to say. Long as they don't mess with me things be okay. But that's impossible. Somebody always got to have their little say about your life. They want to tell you where to go, how to play, what to play, where to play it—shit, even who to fuck and how to fuck em. But when I get to New York—"

"Time, let's don't talk now."

He laugh then. "Martha, you so Black." I don't know what I should say so I don't say nothing, just get closer and we don't talk.

That how it is lots a time with me and him. It seem like all I got is lots little pitchers in my mind and can't tell nobody what they look like. Once I try to tell him bout that, bout the pitchers, and he just laugh. "Least your head ain't empty. Maybe now you got some pictures, you get some thoughts." That make me mad and I start cussing, but he laugh and kiss me and hold me. And that time, when we doing it, it all—all angry and like he want to hurt me. And I think bout that song he sing that first night bout having the blues. But that the only time he mean like that.

Time and German brung the piano a couple days after that. The piano small and all shiny black wood. Time cussed German when German knocked it against the front door getting it in the house. Time went to put it in the bedroom but I want him to be thinking bout me, not some damn piano when he in there. I tell him he put it in the living room or it don't come in the house. Orine don't want it in the house period, say it too damn noisy—that's what she tell me. She don't say nothing to Time. I think she halfway scared of him. He pretty good bout playing it though. He don't never play it when the babies is sleep or at least he don't play loud as he can. But all he thinking bout when he playing is that piano. You talk to him, he don't answer; you touch him, he don't look up. One time I say to him, "Pay me some tention," but he don't even hear. I hit his hand, not hard, just playing. He look at me but he don't stop playing. "Get out of here, Martha." First I start to tell him he can't tell me what to do in my own self's house, but he just looking at me. Looking at me and playing and not saying nothing. I leave.

His friends come over most evenings when he home, not playing. It like Time is the leader. Whatever he say go. They always telling him how good he is. "Out of sight, man, the way you play." "You ought to get out of this little town so somebody can hear you play." Most times, he just smile and don't say nothing, or he just say thanks. But I wonder if he really believe em. I tell him, sometime, that he sound better than lots a them men on records. He give me his little cool smile. But I feel he glad I tell him that.

When his friends come over, we sit round laughing and talking and drinking. Orine like that cause she be playing up to em all and they be telling her what a fine ass she got. They don't tell me nothing like that cause Time be sitting right there, but long as Time telling me, I don't care. It like when we go to the Legion, after Time and German started being with us. We all the time get in free and then get to sit at one a the big front tables. And Orine like that cause it make her think she big-time. But she still her same old picky self; all the time telling me to "sit cool, Martha," and "be cool, girl." Acting like cool the most important thing in the world. I finally just tell her, "Time like me just the way I am, cool or not." And it true; Time always saying that I be myself and I be fine.

Time and his friends, they talk mostly bout music, music and New York City and white people. Sometime I get so sick a listening to em. Always talking bout how they gon put something over on the white man, gon take something way from him, gon do this, gon do that. Ah shit! I tell em. But they don't pay me no mind.

German say, one night, "Man, this white man come asking if I want to play at his house for—"

"What you tell him, man, 'Put money in my purse'?" Time ask. They all crack up. Me and Orine sit there quiet. Orine all swole up cause Time and them running some kind of game and she don't know what going down.

"Hey, man, yo all member that time up in Frisco when we got fired from that gig and wan't none of our old ladies working?" That Brown, he play bass with em.

"Man," Time say, "all I remember is that I stayed high most of the time. But how'd I stay high if ain't nobody had no bread? Somebody was putting something in somebody's purse." He lean back laughing a little. "Verna's mamma must have been sending her some money till she got a job. Yeah, yeah man, that was it. You remember the first time her mamma sent that money and she gave it all to me to hold?"

"And what she wanna do that for? You went out and gambled half a it away and bought pot with most of the rest." German not laughing much as Time and Brown.

"Man, I was scared to tell her, cause you remember how easy it was for her to get her jaws tight. But she was cool, didn't say nothing. I told her I was going to get food with the rest of the money and asked her what she wanted, and—"

"And she say cigarettes," Brown break in laughing, "and this cat, man, this cat tell her, 'Woman, we ain't wasting this bread on no nonessentials!'" He doubled over laughing. They all laughing. But I don't think it that funny. Any woman can give a man money.

"I thought the babe was gon kill me, her jaws was so tight. But even with her jaws tight, Verna was still cool. She just say, 'Baby, you done fucked up fifty dollars on nonessentials; let me try thirty cents.'"

That really funny to em. They all cracking up but me. Time sit there smiling just a little and shaking his head. Then, he reach out and squeeze my knee and smile at me. And I know it like I say; any woman can give a man money.

German been twitching round in his chair and finally he say, "Yeah, man, this fay dude want me to play at his house for fifty cent." That German always got to hear hisself talk. "I tell him take his fifty cent and shove it up his ass—oh scuse me. I forgot that baby was here—but I told him what to do with it. When I play for honkies, I tell him, I don't play for less than two hundred dollars and he so foolish he gon pay it." They all laugh, but I know German lying. Anybody offer him ten cent let lone fifty, he play.

"It ain't the money, man," Time say. "They just don't know what the fuck going on." I tell him Larry sitting right there. I know he ain't gon pay me no mind, but I feel if German can respect my baby, Time can too. "Man they go out to some little school, learn a few chords, and they think they know it all.

Then, if you working for a white man, he fire you and hire him. No, man, I can't tie shit from no white man."

"That where you wrong," I tell him. "Somebody you don't like, you supposed to take em for everything they got. Take em and tell em to kiss yo butt."

"That another one of your pictures, I guess," Time say. And they all laugh cause he told em bout that, too, one time when he was mad with me.

"No, no," I say. "Listen, one day I walking downtown and this white man offer me a ride. I say okay and get in the car. He start talking and hinting round and finally he come on out and say it. I give you twenty dollars, he say. I say okay. We in Chinatown by then and at the next stop light he get out his wallet and give me a twenty-dollar bill. 'That what I like bout you colored women,' he say easing all back in his seat just like he already done got some and waiting to get some more. 'Yeah,' he say, 'you all so easy to get.' I put that money in my purse, open the door and tell him, 'Motherfucker, you ain't got shit here,' and slam the door."

"Watch your mouth," Time say, "Larry sitting here." We all crack up.

"What he do then?" Orine ask.

"What could he do? We in Chinatown and all them colored folks walking round. You know they ain't gon let no white man do nothing to me."

Time tell me after we go to bed that night that he kill me if he ever see me with a white man.

I laugh and kiss him. "What I want with a white man when I got you?" We both laugh and get in the bed. I lay stretched out waiting for him to reach for me. It funny, I think, how colored men don't never want no colored women messing with no white mens but the first chance he get, that colored man gon be right there in that white woman's bed. Yeah, colored men sho give colored womens a hard way to go. But I know if Time got to give a hard way to go, it ain't gon be for scaggy fay babe, and I kinda smile to myself.

"Martha—"

"Yeah, Time," I say turning to him.

"How old you—eighteen? What you want to do in life? What you want to be?"

What he mean? "I want to be with you," I tell him.

"No, I mean really. What you want?" Why he want to know, I wonder. Everytime he start talking serious-like, I think he must be hearing his sliding song.

"I don't want to have to ask nobody for nothing. I want to be able to take care of my own self." I won't be no weight on you, Time, I want to tell him. I won't be no trouble to you.

"Then what are you doing on the Welfare?"

"What else I gon do? Go out and scrub somebody else's toilets like my mamma did so Larry can run wild like I did? No. I stay on Welfare awhile, thank you."

"You see what the white man have done to us, is doing to us?"

"White man my ass," I tell him. "That was my no good daddy. If he'd gone out and worked, we woulda been better off."

"How he gon work if the man won't let him?"

"You just let the man turn you out. Yeah, that man got yo mind."

"What you mean?" he ask real quiet. But I don't pay no tention to him.

"You always talking bout music and New York City, New York City and the white man. Why don't you forget all that shit and get a job like other men? I hate that damn piano."

He grab my shoulder real tight. "What you mean, 'got my mind?' What you mean?" And he start shaking me. But I crying and thinking bout he gon leave.

"You laugh cause I say all I got in my mind is pitchers but least they better some old music. That all you ever think about, Time."

"What you mean? What you mean?"

Finally I scream. "You ain't gon no damn New York City and it ain't the white man what gon keep you. You just using him for a scuse cause you scared. Maybe you can't play." That the only time he ever hit me. And I cry cause I know he gon leave for sho. He hold me and say don't cry, say he sorry, but I can't stop. Orine bamming on the door and Time yelling at her to leave us lone and the babies crying and finally he start to pull away. I say, "Time . . ." He still for a long time, then he say, "Okay, Okay, Martha."

No, it not like he don't want me no more, he—

"Martha. Martha. You ain't been listening to a word I say."

"Mamma." I say it soft cause I don't want to hurt her. "Please leave me lone. You and Orine—and Time too, sometime—yo all treat me like I don't know nothing. But just cause it don't seem like to you that I know what I'm doing, that don't mean nothing. You can't see into my life."

"I see enough to know you just get into one mess after another." She shake her head and her voice come kinda slow. "Martha, I named you after that woman in the Bible cause I want you to be like her. Be good in the same way she is. Martha, that woman ain't never stopped believing. She humble and patient and the Lord make a place for her." She lean her hands on the table. Been in them dishes again, hands all wrinkled and shiny wet. "But that was the Bible. You ain't got the time to be patient, to be waiting for Time or no one else to make no place for you. That man ain't no good. I told you—"

Words coming faster and faster. She got the cow by the tail and gon on down shit creek. It don't matter though. She talk and I sit here thinking bout Time. "You feel good . . . You gon be my Black queen? . . . We can make it together . . . You feel good . . ." He be back.

1967

ALICE WALKER
b. 1944

Prolific and controversial, Alice Walker is one of the most important African American writers of her generation. She is perhaps best known because of the controversy generated by her Pulitzer Prize–winning *The Color Purple* (1982), the first novel by an African American woman to win this award. She has, however, published more than thirty books, including seven other novels, and numerous volumes of poetry and essays, children's books, and collections of short stories. But *The Color Purple* is a point of demarcation in Walker's oeuvre in that it is both the completion of the cycle of novels she announced in the early 1970s and the beginning of new emphases for her as a writer.

Fourteen years before *The Color Purple*, with the publication of *Once: Poems* (1968), written when she was barely twenty-three, Walker declared herself an African American woman writer committed to exploring the lives of black women. In a 1973 interview with critic Mary Helen Washington, Walker described the three types of black women characters she felt were missing from much of the literature of the United States. The first were those who were exploited both physically and emotionally, whose lives were narrow and confining, and who were driven sometimes to madness, such as Margaret and Mem Copeland in Walker's first novel, *The Third Life of Grange Copeland* (1970). The second were those who were victims not so much of physical violence as of psychic violence, women who are alienated from their own culture. The third type of black woman character, represented most effectively by Celie and Shug in *The Color Purple*, are those African American women who, despite the oppressions they suffer, achieve some wholeness and create spaces for other oppressed communities.

Walker was certainly aware of the ways in which southern black women had always been artists, even when that word was not applied to them. Born on February 9, 1944, to sharecroppers Minnie Lou Grant and Willie Lee Walker, she grew up in the small town of Eatonton, Georgia. Her mother, who worked as a domestic and made everything Alice and her seven siblings used, was known for the incredible gardens she grew, gardens her literary daughter commemorated in the classic essay "In Search of Our Mothers' Gardens: The Legacy of Southern Black Women" (1974). From her mother's artistry, Walker learned that African American women's experience and art are based on spirituality, especially as it relates to nature. Though not admitted to libraries or schools, and definitely lacking any rooms of their own, they expressed themselves in the media allowed to them: cooking, gardening, storytelling, quilting.

When Walker was eight, one of her brothers "accidentally" shot her with a gun he'd received for Christmas, resulting in the loss of one eye. Not only did this experience make Walker feel like an outcast but it also caused her to begin to notice relationships and to start recording her observations and feelings in a notebook. Her early experience of being different may be in some sense responsible for her tendency to pursue "forbidden" subjects in her writing, such as her protest of female genital circumcision, which she redefines as mutilation, in her fifth novel, *Possessing the Secret of Joy* (1992).

Walker left Eatonton in 1961 to go to college, first at Spelman, a black women's college in Atlanta, then two years later at Sarah Lawrence, in the suburbs of New York City. Both educational experiences had a lasting effect on her writing. Her years at Spelman coincided with the rise of the civil rights movement, the subject of many of her short stories, essays, and her second novel *Meridian* (1976). While at Sarah Lawrence, she became pregnant, at a time when abortion was illegal. Contemplating suicide because of the shame her family would feel and because of the powerlessness she felt, Walker instead began writing, and soon published her first book, *Once*.

The works Walker published during the 1970s had a decisive effect on the literary world. Her focus on southern African American women's voices helped galvanize an explosion of black women's creative and critical expressions. In *The Third Life of Grange Copeland*, she explored familial cruelty, especially as it is triggered by societal forces such as racism, unemployment, and sexism. She challenged the 1960s African American cultural nationalist position, which idealized "black manhood" and seldom acknowledged the oppression of women. In her second poetry collection, *Revolutionary Petunias* (1972) and in *In Love & Trouble: Stories of Black Women* (1973), Walker continued to represent the lives of southern black peasant women, detailing the heroic resistance of the supposedly backward Sammy Lou in the poem "Revolutionary Petunias" and Mrs. Johnson, the guardian of southern black culture, in the story "Everyday Use."

From 1965 to 1968 Walker was actively involved in the civil rights movement, including voter registration drives in Georgia and campaigns for welfare rights and children's programs in Mississippi. She also lived for a time on the Lower East Side of New York City, where she worked for the welfare department, an experience that inspired her story "Advancing Luna." In 1967 she married Melvyn Levanthal, a white civil rights lawyer. At a time when interracial marriage was illegal in Mississippi, Walker and Leventhal lived in that state and there had a daughter, Rebecca. Together they worked to desegregate the Mississippi schools. They divorced in 1977, at which time Walker moved first to New York City, then to northern California, and eventually to Mexico, where she still lives.

During the 1970s Walker published a series of remarkable essays, among them "Looking for Zora" (1975), "Saving the Life That Is Your Own: The Importance of Models in the Artist's Life" (1976), and "One Child of One's Own" (1979). The lucidity of her prose, the richness of her humor and irony, and the power of her passion made Walker an outstanding essayist; she is also one of the most widely read. In addition to her own writing, her recuperation of the legacy of Zora Neale Hurston was a signal contribution to literary history. In her essays and in the Hurston reader that she edited, *I Love Myself When I AM Laughing . . .* (1979), Walker championed her foremother's legacy. Years later, in a collection of essays titled *Anything You Love Can Be Saved* (1997), she took deserved pride in her accomplishment.

Unwavering in her commitment to exploring the lives and the work of other black women, Walker coined the term *womanism* early in her career. The word is derived from a black folk expression ("womanish"), and Walker prefers it to *feminism* because it honors a long-standing tradition of strength among black women. The title of her second collection of short stories, *You Can't Keep a Good Woman Down* (1991), reflects a womanist impulse. These stories take up topical and controversial themes, such as abortion and interracial relationships, and are a bridge between her earlier novels and *The Color Purple*.

Few works in the African American tradition have generated as much controversy as *The Color Purple*; arguably only Richard Wright's *Native Son* elicited similarly impassioned responses. On the one hand, the book's champions point to the unflinching honesty of the novel, its originality, and its command of black vernacular English. Walker renders the novel in the singular voice of her barely literate protagonist; no mediating narrator intervenes. The novel received the Pulitzer Prize, the National Book Award, and the American Book Award. None of this recognition allayed its detractors who censured the novel for its representation of incest and domestic abuse in African American families as well as for its depiction of lesbianism. Still others criticized the novel's representation of Africa, suggesting that it was historically inaccurate. The controversy intensified with the release of Steven Spielberg's film adaptation in 1985, which was attacked for its supposedly negative portrayal of black men; even some of the novel's admirers were put off by the film's Hollywood gloss. In Walker's view, however, the film made Celie's story accessible to those real-life women, who like her protagonist, do not read books. Walker records her response to the controversy in "The Same River Twice" (1996). *The Color Purple* took on another life as a Broadway musical in 2004.

Several of Walker's subsequent novels—*The Temple of My Familiar* (1989), *Possessing the Secret of Joy* (1992), and *By the Light of My Father's Smile* (1998)—are set in part outside of the United States; her characters have a global and spiritual consciousness that is similar to the one Walker articulates in her nonfiction. Walker's activism and art are of a piece. Her volume of poems *Horses Make a Landscape Look More Beautiful* and her essays in *Living by the Word* (1988) demonstrate her commitment to environmentalism as well as human rights. Walker's collected poems *Her Blue Body Everything We Know: Earthling Poems: 1965–1990*, appeared in 1991. In 2000 Walker published *The Way Forward Is with a Broken Heart* (2000), a collection of short stories that she acknowledges are "personal." *Sent by Earth: A Message from the Grandmother Spirit after the Attack on the World Trade Center and Pentagon*, a volume of political commentary and poetry, was published in 2001. In subsequent volumes, Walker addresses political controversies in Africa and the Middle East as well as in the United States. The title *We Are the Ones We Have Been Waiting For* (2006) encapsulates her sense of social obligation and her sense of optimism.

Alice Walker remains what she has been for more than forty years: a gifted and prolific writer, a bold thinker, and a woman who is determined to confront and embrace the contradictions of her life and the paradoxes of our time.

Women

They were women then
My mama's generation
Husky of voice—Stout of
Step
With fists as well as   5
Hands
How they battered down
Doors
And ironed
Starched white   10
Shirts
How they led
Armies
Headragged Generals
Across mined   15
Fields
Booby-trapped
Ditches
To discover books
Desks   20
A place for us
How they knew what we
Must know
Without knowing a page
Of it   25
Themselves.

1970

Outcast

for Julius Lester

Be nobody's darling;
Be an outcast.
Take the contradictions
Of your life
And wrap around   5
You like a shawl,
To parry stones
To keep you warm.

Watch the people succumb
To madness   10

With ample cheer;
Let them look askance at you
And you askance reply.

Be an outcast;
Be pleased to walk alone   15
(Uncool)
Or line the crowded
River beds
With other impetuous
Fools.   20

Make a merry gathering
On the bank
Where thousands perished
For brave hurt words
They said.   25

Be nobody's darling;
Be an outcast.
Qualified to live
Among your dead.

1973

"Good Night, Willie Lee, I'll See You in the Morning"

Looking down into my father's
dead face
for the last time
my mother said without
tears, without smiles   5
without regrets
but with *civility*
"Good night, Willie Lee, I'll see you
in the morning."
And it was then I knew that the healing   10
of all our wounds
is forgiveness
that permits a promise
of our return
at the end.   15

1979

In Search of Our Mothers' Gardens

I described her own nature and temperament. Told how they
needed a larger life for their expression. . . . I pointed out that in
lieu of proper channels, her emotions had overflowed into paths
that dissipated them. I talked, beautifully I thought, about an art

"In Search of Our Mothers' Gardens"

Honoring the Creativity

of the

Black Woman

~~In the early Twenties a young black poet named~~ Jean Toomer *when the poet*

walked through Georgia in ~~order to confront and defeat the~~ *the early twenties he discovered*
a curious thing:
~~fear he had of the land of his heritage and his birth. While~~ *black women unborn. It was*
~~there he came face to face with physical and~~ spiritual ~~beauty~~ *intense* ~~was~~

so ~~inexhaustible~~, so deep, so unconscious, that the ~~people~~ *women* who

possessed it were *themselves* unaware of the richness they held. They

stumbled ~~about~~ blindly through their lives, ~~like~~ creatures so

~~p~~dulled and confused by pain, so mutilated in ~~spirit~~ *body*, that they

thought too little of themselves even to hope. In the selfless

abstractions that their bodies became in the use of others, they
not mere women, but
~~were~~ they became, Saints.
Who were these "saints"? These crazy, loony, pitiful women?
These "Saints" were, partly, our grandmothers and our mothers.
Some of them, without a doubt, were our mothers + grandmothers
In the still heat of the Post-Reconstruction South this is *But not all.*

how they seemed to Jean Toomer: Exquisite butterflies trapped

in an evil honey, toiling away their lives in a time that barely

acknowledged them, except as the "mule of the world."

They dreamed dreams that no one knew - not even themselves,

in a coherent fashion - and saw visions no one could understand. *They wandered*
or set about the countryside crooning lullabies to ghosts, and painting
They moved to music no one ever heard. And they waited.

They waited for a day when the unknown, undefined thing

that was in them would be made known; and knew, somehow, that

their minds... to their bodies... desert their... sought to... real, like a faded... forbidding the red dust.

1

This manuscript page from "In Search of Our Mothers' Gardens" demonstrates not only Alice Walker's attention to detail and revision but also her effort to distinguish between the "bod[ies]" and "spirit[s]" of the black women who were denied the possibility of becoming writers and artists.

that would be born, an art that would open the way for women the likes of her. I asked her to hope, and build up an inner life against the coming of that day. . . . I sang, with a strange quiver in my voice, a promise song.

—JEAN TOOMER,[1] "AVEY," CANE

The poet speaking to a prostitute who falls asleep while he's talking—

1. A writer of the Harlem Renaissance (1894–1967). *Cane* is a mixture of narrative prose and lyric poetry.

When the poet Jean Toomer walked through the South in the early twenties, he discovered a curious thing: black women whose spirituality was so intense, so deep, so *unconscious*, that they were themselves unaware of the richness they held. They stumbled blindly through their lives: creatures so abused and mutilated in body, so dimmed and confused by pain, that they considered themselves unworthy even of hope. In the selfless abstractions their bodies became to the men who used them, they became more than "sexual objects," more even than mere women: they became "Saints." Instead of being perceived as whole persons, their bodies became shrines: what was thought to be their minds became temples suitable for worship. These crazy Saints stared out at the world, wildly, like lunatics—or quietly, like suicides; and the "God" that was in their gaze was as mute as a great stone.

Who were these Saints? These crazy, loony, pitiful women?

Some of them, without a doubt, were our mothers and grandmothers.

In the still heat of the post-Reconstruction South, this is how they seemed to Jean Toomer: exquisite butterflies trapped in an evil honey, toiling away their lives in an era, a century, that did not acknowledge them, except as "the *mule* of the world."[2] They dreamed dreams that no one knew—not even themselves, in any coherent fashion—and saw visions no one could understand. They wandered or sat about the countryside crooning lullabies to ghosts, and drawing the mother of Christ in charcoal on courthouse walls.

They forced their minds to desert their bodies and their striving spirits sought to rise, like frail whirlwinds from the hard red clay. And when those frail whirlwinds fell, in scattered particles, upon the ground, no one mourned. Instead, men lit candles to celebrate the emptiness that remained, as people do who enter a beautiful but vacant space to resurrect a God.

Our mothers and grandmothers, some of them: moving to music not yet written. And they waited.

They waited for a day when the unknown thing that was in them would be made known; but guessed, somehow in their darkness, that on the day of their revelation they would be long dead. Therefore to Toomer they walked, and even ran, in slow motion. For they were going nowhere immediate, and the future was not yet within their grasp. And men took our mothers and grandmothers, "but got no pleasure from it." So complex was their passion and their calm.

To Toomer, they lay vacant and fallow as autumn fields, with harvest time never in sight: and he saw them enter loveless marriages, without joy; and become prostitutes, without resistance; and become mothers of children, without fulfillment.

For these grandmothers and mothers of ours were not Saints, but Artists; driven to a numb and bleeding madness by the springs of creativity in them for which there was no release. They were Creators, who lived lives of spiritual waste, because they were so rich in spirituality—which is the basis of Art— that the strain of enduring their unused and unwanted talent drove them insane. Throwing away this spirituality was their pathetic attempt to lighten the soul to a weight their work-worn, sexually abused bodies could bear.

2. Allusion to a statement in Zora Neale Hurston's *Their Eyes Were Watching God* (1937): "De nigger woman is de mule uh de world." "Post-Reconstruction South": i.e., the South after home rule (and thus white supremacy) was restored following the Confederacy's social and political "reconstruction" (1865–77).

What did it mean for a black woman to be an artist in our grandmothers' time? In our great-grandmothers' day? It is a question with an answer cruel enough to stop the blood.

Did you have a genius of a great-great-grandmother who died under some ignorant and depraved white overseer's lash? Or was she required to bake biscuits for a lazy backwater tramp, when she cried out in her soul to paint watercolors of sunsets, or the rain falling on the green and peaceful pasture-lands? Or was her body broken and forced to bear children (who were more often than not sold away from her)—eight, ten, fifteen, twenty children—when her one joy was the thought of modeling heroic figures of rebellion, in stone or clay?

How was the creativity of the black woman kept alive, year after year and century after century, when for most of the years black people have been in America, it was a punishable crime for a black person to read or write? And the freedom to paint, to sculpt, to expand the mind with action did not exist. Consider, if you can bear to imagine it, what might have been the result if singing, too, had been forbidden by law. Listen to the voices of Bessie Smith, Billie Holiday, Nina Simone, Roberta Flack, and Aretha Franklin,[3] among others, and imagine those voices muzzled for life. Then you may begin to comprehend the lives of our "crazy," "Sainted" mothers and grandmothers. The agony of the lives of women who might have been Poets, Novelists, Essayists, and Short-Story Writers (over a period of centuries), who died with their real gifts stifled within them.

And, if this were the end of the story, we would have cause to cry out in my paraphrase of Okot p'Bitek's[4] great poem:

> O, my clanswomen
> Let us all cry together!
> Come,
> Let us mourn the death of our mother,
> The death of a Queen
> The ash that was produced
> By a great fire!
> O, this homestead is utterly dead
> Close the gates
> With *lacari* thorns,
> For our mother
> The creator of the Stool is lost!
> And all the young women
> Have perished in the wilderness!

But this is not the end of the story, for all the young women—our mothers and grandmothers, *ourselves*—have not perished in the wilderness. And if we ask ourselves why, and search for and find the answer, we will know beyond all efforts to erase it from our minds, just exactly who, and of what, we black American women are.

One example, perhaps the most pathetic, most misunderstood one, can provide a backdrop for our mothers' work: Phillis Wheatley,[5] a slave in the 1700s.

---

3. Black American female singers from the 1920s to the present.
4. African poet (b. 1931). Walker has changed the original masculine nouns in *Song of Lawino* (1966) to feminine equivalents.
5. Highly educated black slave (1753–1784) who wrote formal, neoclassical poems.

Virginia Woolf,[6] in her book *A Room of One's Own*, wrote that in order for a woman to write fiction she must have two things, certainly: a room of her own (with key and lock) and enough money to support herself.

What then are we to make of Phillis Wheatley, a slave, who owned not even herself? This sickly, frail black girl who required a servant of her own at times—her health was so precarious—and who, had she been white, would have been easily considered the intellectual superior of all the women and most of the men in the society of her day.

Virginia Woolf wrote further, speaking of course not of our Phillis, that "any woman born with a great gift in the sixteenth century [insert "eighteenth century," insert "black woman," insert "born or made a slave"] would certainly have gone crazed, shot herself, or ended her days in some lonely cottage outside the village, half witch, half wizard [insert "Saint"], feared and mocked at. For it needs little skill and psychology to be sure that a highly gifted girl who had tried to use her gift for poetry would have been so thwarted and hindered by contrary instincts [add "chains, guns, the lash, the ownership of one's body by someone else, submission to an alien religion"], that she must have lost her health and sanity to a certainty."

The key words, as they relate to Phillis, are "contrary instincts." For when we read the poetry of Phillis Wheatley—as when we read the novels of Nella Larsen[7] or the oddly false-sounding autobiography of that freest of all black women writers, Zora Hurston—evidence of "contrary instincts" is everywhere. Her loyalties were completely divided, as was, without question, her mind.

But how could this be otherwise? Captured at seven, a slave of wealthy, doting whites who instilled in her the "savagery" of the Africa they "rescued" her from . . . one wonders if she was even able to remember her homeland as she had known it, or as it really was.

Yet, because she did try to use her gift for poetry in a world that made her a slave, she was "so thwarted and hindered by . . . contrary instincts, that she . . . lost her health. . . ." In the last years of her brief life, burdened not only with the need to express her gift but also with a penniless, friendless "freedom" and several small children for whom she was forced to do strenuous work to feed, she lost her health, certainly. Suffering from malnutrition and neglect and who knows what mental agonies, Phillis Wheatley died.

So torn by "contrary instincts" was black, kidnapped, enslaved Phillis that her description of "the Goddess"—as she poetically called the Liberty she did not have—is ironically, cruelly humorous. And, in fact, has held Phillis up to ridicule for more than a century. It is usually read prior to hanging Phillis's memory as that of a fool. She wrote:

> The Goddess comes, she moves divinely fair,
> Olive and laurel binds her *golden* hair.
> Wherever shines this native of the skies,
> Unnumber'd charms and recent graces rise. [My italics][8]

It is obvious that Phillis, the slave, combed the "Goddess's" hair every morning; prior, perhaps, to bringing in the milk, or fixing her mistress's lunch. She took her imagery from the one thing she saw elevated above all others.

---

6. British novelist and essayist (1882–1941). *A Room of One's Own* was published in 1929.
7. Black woman novelist (1893–1964) of the Harlem Renaissance.
8. From Wheatley's "To His Excellency, General Washington" (1775).

With the benefit of hindsight we ask, "How could she?"

But at last, Phillis, we understand. No more snickering when your stiff, struggling, ambivalent lines are forced on us. We know now that you were not an idiot or a traitor; only a sickly little black girl, snatched from your home and country and made a slave; a woman who still struggled to sing the song that was your gift, although in a land of barbarians who praised you for your bewildered tongue. It is not so much what you sang, as that you kept alive, in so many of our ancestors, *the notion of song.*

Black women are called, in the folklore that so aptly identifies one's status in society, "the *mule* of the world," because we have been handed the burdens that everyone else—*everyone* else—refused to carry. We have also been called "Matriarchs," "Superwomen," and "Mean and Evil Bitches." Not to mention "Castraters" and "Sapphire's[9] Mama." When we have pleaded for understanding, our character has been distorted; when we have asked for simple caring, we have been handed empty inspirational appellations, then stuck in the farthest corner. When we have asked for love, we have been given children. In short, even our plainer gifts, our labors of fidelity and love, have been knocked down our throats. To be an artist and a black woman, even today, lowers our status in many respects, rather than raises it: and yet, artists we will be.

Therefore we must fearlessly pull out of ourselves and look at and identify with our lives the living creativity some of our great-grandmothers were not allowed to know. I stress *some* of them because it is well known that the majority of our great-grandmothers knew, even without "knowing" it, the reality of their spirituality, even if they didn't recognize it beyond what happened in the singing at church—and they never had any intention of giving it up.

How they did it—those millions of black women who were not Phillis Wheatley, or Lucy Terry or Frances Harper or Zora Hurston or Nella Larsen or Bessie Smith; or Elizabeth Catlett, or Katherine Dunham,[1] either—brings me to the title of this essay, "In Search of Our Mothers' Gardens," which is a personal account that is yet shared, in its theme and its meaning, by all of us. I found, while thinking about the far-reaching world of the creative black woman, that often the truest answer to a question that really matters can be found very close.

In the late 1920s my mother ran away from home to marry my father. Marriage, if not running away, was expected of seventeen-year-old girls. By the time she was twenty, she had two children and was pregnant with a third. Five children later, I was born. And this is how I came to know my mother: she seemed a large, soft, loving-eyed woman who was rarely impatient in our home. Her quick, violent temper was on view only a few times a year, when she battled with the white landlord who had the misfortune to suggest to her that her children did not need to go to school.

She made all the clothes we wore, even my brothers' overalls. She made all the towels and sheets we used. She spent the summers canning vegetables

9. Wife of "the Kingfish" in *Amos and Andy*, a popular early radio and television show.
1. Black American dancer and choreographer

(1909–2006). Terry (1730–1821), black poet. Harper (1825–1911), black poet and activist. Catlett (1915–2012), black educator and sculptor.

and fruits. She spent the winter evenings making quilts enough to cover all our beds.

During the "working" day, she labored beside—not behind—my father in the fields. Her day began before sunup, and did not end until late at night. There was never a moment for her to sit down, undisturbed, to unravel her own private thoughts; never a time free from interruption—by work or the noisy inquiries of her many children. And yet, it is to my mother—and all our mothers who were not famous—that I went in search of the secret of what has fed that muzzled and often mutilated, but vibrant, creative spirit that the black woman has inherited, and that pops out in wild and unlikely places to this day.

But when, you will ask, did my overworked mother have time to know or care about feeding the creative spirit?

The answer is so simple that many of us have spent years discovering it. We have constantly looked high, when we should have looked high—and low.

For example: in the Smithsonian Institution in Washington, D.C., there hangs a quilt unlike any other in the world. In fanciful, inspired, and yet simple and identifiable figures, it portrays the story of the Crucifixion. It is considered rare, beyond price. Though it follows no known pattern of quilt-making, and though it is made of bits and pieces of worthless rags, it is obviously the work of a person of powerful imagination and deep spiritual feeling. Below this quilt I saw a note that says it was made by "an anonymous Black woman in Alabama, a hundred years ago."

If we could locate this "anonymous" black woman from Alabama, she would turn out to be one of our grandmothers—an artist who left her mark in the only materials she could afford, and in the only medium her position in society allowed her to use.

As Virginia Woolf wrote further, in *A Room of One's Own*:

> Yet genius of a sort must have existed among women as it must have existed among the working class. [Change this to "slaves" and "the wives and daughters of sharecroppers."] Now and again an Emily Brontë or a Robert Burns [change this to "a Zora Hurston or a Richard Wright"[2]] blazes out and proves its presence. But certainly it never got itself on to paper. When, however, one reads of a witch being ducked, of a woman possessed by devils [or "Sainthood"], of a wise woman selling herbs [our root workers], or even a very remarkable man who had a mother, then I think we are on the track of a lost novelist, a suppressed poet, of some mute and inglorious Jane Austen. . . . Indeed, I would venture to guess that Anon, who wrote so many poems without signing them, was often a woman. . . .

And so our mothers and grandmothers have, more often than not anonymously, handed on the creative spark, the seed of the flower they themselves never hoped to see: or like a sealed letter they could not plainly read.

And so it is, certainly, with my own mother. Unlike "Ma" Rainey's[3] songs, which retained their creator's name even while blasting forth from Bessie Smith's mouth, no song or poem will bear my mother's name. Yet so many of the stories that I write, that we all write, are my mother's stories. Only recently

---

2. Black American novelist (1908–1960). Brontë (1819–1848), English novelist and poet. Burns (1759–1796), Scottish poet.

3. Gertrude Pridgett Rainey (1886–1939), black blues singer and songwriter.

did I fully realize this: that through years of listening to my mother's stories of her life, I have absorbed not only the stories themselves, but something of the manner in which she spoke, something of the urgency that involves the knowledge that her stories—like her life—must be recorded. It is probably for this reason that so much of what I have written is about characters whose counterparts in real life are so much older than I am.

But the telling of these stories, which came from my mother's lips as naturally as breathing, was not the only way my mother showed herself as an artist. For stories, too, were subject to being distracted, to dying without conclusion. Dinners must be started, and cotton must be gathered before the big rains. The artist that was and is my mother showed itself to me only after many years. This is what I finally noticed:

Like Mem, a character in *The Third Life of Grange Copeland*,[4] my mother adorned with flowers whatever shabby house we were forced to live in. And not just your typical straggly country stand of zinnias, either. She planted ambitious gardens—and still does—with over fifty different varieties of plants that bloom profusely from early March until late November. Before she left home for the fields, she watered her flowers, chopped up the grass, and laid out new beds. When she returned from the fields she might divide clumps of bulbs, dig a cold pit, uproot and replant roses, or prune branches from her taller bushes or trees—until night came and it was too dark to see.

Whatever she planted grew as if by magic, and her fame as a grower of flowers spread over three counties. Because of her creativity with her flowers, even my memories of poverty are seen through a screen of blooms—sunflowers, petunias, roses, dahlias, forsythia, spirea, delphiniums, verbena . . . and on and on.

And I remember people coming to my mother's yard to be given cuttings from her flowers; I hear again the praise showered on her because whatever rocky soil she landed on, she turned into a garden. A garden so brilliant with colors, so original in its design, so magnificent with life and creativity, that to this day people drive by our house in Georgia—perfect strangers and imperfect strangers—and ask to stand or walk among my mother's art.

I notice that it is only when my mother is working in her flowers that she is radiant, almost to the point of being invisible—except as Creator: hand and eye. She is involved in work her soul must have. Ordering the universe in the image of her personal conception of Beauty.

Her face, as she prepares the Art that is her gift, is a legacy of respect she leaves to me, for all that illuminates and cherishes life. She has handed down respect for the possibilities—and the will to grasp them.

For her, so hindered and intruded upon in so many ways, being an artist has still been a daily part of her life. This ability to hold on, even in very simple ways, is work black women have done for a very long time.

This poem is not enough, but it is something, for the woman who literally covered the holes in our walls with sunflowers:

> They were women then
> My mama's generation
> Husky of voice—Stout of
> Step
> With fists as well as

4. Walker's first novel.

Hands
How they battered down
Doors
And ironed
Starched white
Shirts
How they led
Armies
Headragged Generals
Across mined
Fields
Booby-trapped
Kitchens
To discover books
Desks
A place for us
How they knew what we
Must know
Without knowing a page
Of it
Themselves.

Guided by my heritage of a love of beauty and a respect for strength—in search of my mother's garden, I found my own.

And perhaps in Africa over two hundred years ago, there was just such a mother; perhaps she painted vivid and daring decorations in oranges and yellows and greens on the walls of her hut; perhaps she sang—in a voice like Roberta Flack's—*sweetly* over the compounds of her village; perhaps she wove the most stunning mats or told the most ingenious stories of all the village storytellers. Perhaps she was herself a poet—though only her daughter's name is signed to the poems that we know.

Perhaps Phillis Wheatley's mother was also an artist.

Perhaps in more than Phillis Wheatley's biological life is her mother's signature made clear.

1974

Everyday Use

for your grandmama

I will wait for her in the yard that Maggie and I made so clean and wavy yesterday afternoon. A yard like this is more comfortable than most people know. It is not just a yard. It is like an extended living room. When the hard clay is swept clean as a floor and the fine sand around the edges lined with tiny, irregular grooves, anyone can come and sit and look up into the elm tree and wait for the breezes that never come inside the house.

Maggie will be nervous until after her sister goes: she will stand hopelessly in corners, homely and ashamed of the burn scars down her arms and legs, eying her sister with a mixture of envy and awe. She thinks her sister has held life always in the palm of one hand, that "no" is a word the world never learned to say to her.

You've no doubt seen those TV shows where the child who has "made it" is confronted, as a surprise, by her own mother and father, tottering in weakly from backstage. (A pleasant surprise, of course: What would they do if parent and child came on the show only to curse out and insult each other?) On TV mother and child embrace and smile into each other's faces. Sometimes the mother and father weep, the child wraps them in her arms and leans across the table to tell how she would not have made it without their help. I have seen these programs.

Sometimes I dream a dream in which Dee and I are suddenly brought together on a TV program of this sort. Out of a dark and soft-seated limousine I am ushered into a bright room filled with many people. There I meet a smiling, gray, sporty man like Johnny Carson who shakes my hand and tells me what a fine girl I have. Then we are on the stage and Dee is embracing me with tears in her eyes. She pins on my dress a large orchid, even though she has told me once that she thinks orchids are tacky flowers.

In real life I am a large, big-boned woman with rough, man-working hands. In the winter I wear flannel nightgowns to bed and overalls during the day. I can kill and clean a hog as mercilessly as a man. My fat keeps me hot in zero weather. I can work outside all day, breaking ice to get water for washing; I can eat pork liver cooked over the open fire minutes after it comes steaming from the hog. One winter I knocked a bull calf straight in the brain between the eyes with a sledge hammer and had the meat hung up to chill before nightfall. But of course all this does not show on television. I am the way my daughter would want me to be: a hundred pounds lighter, my skin like an uncooked barley pancake. My hair glistens in the hot bright lights. Johnny Carson has much to do to keep up with my quick and witty tongue.

But that is a mistake. I know even before I wake up. Who ever knew a Johnson with a quick tongue? Who can even imagine me looking a strange white man in the eye? It seems to me I have talked to them always with one foot raised in flight, with my head turned in whichever way is farthest from them. Dee, though. She would always look anyone in the eye. Hesitation was no part of her nature.

"How do I look, Mama?" Maggie says, showing just enough of her thin body enveloped in pink skirt and red blouse for me to know she's there, almost hidden by the door.

"Come out into the yard," I say.

Have you ever seen a lame animal, perhaps a dog run over by some careless person rich enough to own a car, sidle up to someone who is ignorant enough to be kind to him? That is the way my Maggie walks. She has been like this, chin on chest, eyes on ground, feet in shuffle, ever since the fire that burned the other house to the ground.

Dee is lighter than Maggie, with nicer hair and a fuller figure. She's a woman now, though sometimes I forget. How long ago was it that the other house burned? Ten, twelve years? Sometimes I can still hear the flames and feel Maggie's arms sticking to me, her hair smoking and her dress falling off her in little black papery flakes. Her eyes seemed stretched open, blazed open by the flames reflected in them. And Dee. I see her standing off under the sweet gum tree she used to dig gum out of; a look of concentration on her face as she watched the last dingy gray board of the house fall in toward the red-hot brick chimney. Why don't you do a dance around the ashes? I'd wanted to ask her. She had hated the house that much.

I used to think she hated Maggie, too. But that was before we raised the money, the church and me, to send her to Augusta to school. She used to read to us without pity; forcing words, lies, other folks' habits, whole lives upon us two, sitting trapped and ignorant underneath her voice. She washed us in a river of make-believe, burned us with a lot of knowledge we didn't necessarily need to know. Pressed us to her with the serious way she read, to shove us away at just the moment, like dimwits, we seemed about to understand.

Dee wanted nice things. A yellow organdy dress to wear to her graduation from high school; black pumps to match a green suit she'd made from an old suit somebody gave me. She was determined to stare down any disaster in her efforts. Her eyelids would not flicker for minutes at a time. Often I fought off the temptation to shake her. At sixteen she had a style of her own: and knew what style was.

I never had an education myself. After second grade the school was closed down. Don't ask me why: in 1927 colored asked fewer questions than they do now. Sometimes Maggie reads to me. She stumbles along good-naturedly but can't see well. She knows she is not bright. Like good looks and money, quickness passed her by. She will marry John Thomas (who has mossy teeth in an earnest face) and then I'll be free to sit here and I guess just sing church songs to myself. Although I never was a good singer. Never could carry a tune. I was always better at a man's job. I used to love to milk till I was hooked in the side in '49. Cows are soothing and slow and don't bother you, unless you try to milk them the wrong way.

I have deliberately turned my back on the house. It is three rooms, just like the one that burned, except the roof is tin; they don't make shingle roofs any more. There are no real windows, just some holes cut in the sides, like the portholes in a ship, but not round and not square, with rawhide holding the shutters up on the outside. This house is in a pasture, too, like the other one. No doubt when Dee sees it she will want to tear it down. She wrote me once that no matter where we "choose" to live, she will manage to come see us. But she will never bring her friends. Maggie and I thought about this and Maggie asked me, "Mama, when did Dee ever *have* any friends?"

She had a few. Furtive boys in pink shirts hanging about on washday after school. Nervous girls who never laughed. Impressed with her they worshiped the well-turned phrase, the cute shape, the scalding humor that erupted like bubbles in lye. She read to them.

When she was courting Jimmy T she didn't have much time to pay to us, but turned all her faultfinding power on him. He *flew* to marry a cheap city girl from a family of ignorant flashy people. She hardly had time to recompose herself.

When she comes I will meet—but there they are!

Maggie attempts to make a dash for the house, in her shuffling way, but I stay her with my hand. "Come back here," I say. And she stops and tries to dig a well in the sand with her toe.

It is hard to see them clearly through the strong sun. But even the first glimpse of leg out of the car tells me it is Dee. Her feet were always neat-looking, as if God himself had shaped them with a certain style. From the other side of the car comes a short, stocky man. Hair is all over his head a foot long and hanging from his chin like a kinky mule tail. I hear Maggie suck in her breath. "Uhnnnh," is what it sounds like. Like when you see the wriggling end of a snake just in front of your foot on the road. "Uhnnnh."

Dee next. A dress down to the ground, in this hot weather. A dress so loud it hurts my eyes. There are yellows and oranges enough to throw back the light of the sun. I feel my whole face warming from the heat waves it throws out. Earrings gold, too, and hanging down to her shoulders. Bracelets dangling and making noises when she moves her arm up to shake the folds of the dress out of her armpits. The dress is loose and flows, and as she walks closer, I like it. I hear Maggie go "Uhnnnh" again. It is her sister's hair. It stands straight up like the wool on a sheep. It is black as night and around the edges are two long pigtails that rope about like small lizards disappearing behind her ears.

"Wa-su-zo-Tean-o!" she says, coming on in that gliding way the dress makes her move. The short stocky fellow with the hair to his navel is all grinning and he follows up with "Asalamalakim, my mother and sister!" He moves to hug Maggie but she falls back, right up against the back of my chair. I feel her trembling there and when I look up I see the perspiration falling off her chin.

"Don't get up," says Dee. Since I am stout it takes something of a push. You can see me trying to move a second or two before I make it. She turns, showing white heels through her sandals, and goes back to the car. Out she peeks next with a Polaroid. She stoops down quickly and lines up picture after picture of me sitting there in front of the house with Maggie cowering behind me. She never takes a shot without making sure the house is included. When a cow comes nibbling around the edge of the yard she snaps it and me and Maggie *and* the house. Then she puts the Polaroid in the back seat of the car, and comes up and kisses me on the forehead.

Meanwhile Asalamalakim is going through motions with Maggie's hand. Maggie's hand is as limp as a fish, and probably as cold, despite the sweat, and she keeps trying to pull it back. It looks like Asalamalakim wants to shake hands but wants to do it fancy. Or maybe he don't know how people shake hands. Anyhow, he soon gives up on Maggie.

"Well," I say. "Dee."

"No, Mama," she says. "Not 'Dee,' Wangero Leewanika Kemanjo!"

"What happened to 'Dee'?" I wanted to know.

"She's dead," Wangero said. "I couldn't bear it any longer, being named after the people who oppress me."

"You know as well as me you was named after your aunt Dicie," I said. Dicie is my sister. She named Dee. We called her "Big Dee" after Dee was born.

"But who was *she* named after?" asked Wangero.

"I guess after Grandma Dee," I said.

"And who was she named after?" asked Wangero.

"Her mother," I said, and saw Wangero was getting tired. "That's about as far back as I can trace it," I said. Though, in fact, I probably could have carried it back beyond the Civil War through the branches.

"Well," said Asalamalakim, "there you are."

"Uhnnnh," I heard Maggie say.

"There I was not," I said, "before 'Dicie' cropped up in our family, so why should I try to trace it that far back?"

He just stood there grinning, looking down on me like somebody inspecting a Model A car. Every once in a while he and Wangero sent eye signals over my head.

"How do you pronounce this name?" I asked.

"You don't have to call me by it if you don't want to," said Wangero.

"Why shouldn't I?" I asked. "If that's what you want us to call you, we'll call you."

"I know it might sound awkward at first," said Wangero.

"I'll get used to it," I said. "Ream it out again."

Well, soon we got the name out of the way. Asalamalakim had a name twice as long and three times as hard. After I tripped over it two or three times he told me to just call him Hakim-a-barber. I wanted to ask him was he a barber, but I didn't really think he was, so I didn't ask.

"You must belong to those beef-cattle peoples down the road," I said. They said "Asalamalakim" when they met you, too, but they didn't shake hands. Always too busy: feeding the cattle, fixing the fences, putting up salt-lick shelters, throwing down hay. When the white folks poisoned some of the herd the men stayed up all night with rifles in their hands. I walked a mile and a half just to see the sight.

Hakim-a-barber said, "I accept some of their doctrines, but farming and raising cattle is not my style." (They didn't tell me, and I didn't ask, whether Wangero (Dee) had really gone and married him.)

We sat down to eat and right away he said he didn't eat collards and pork was unclean. Wangero, though, went on through the chitlins and corn bread, the greens and everything else. She talked a blue streak over the sweet potatoes. Everything delighted her. Even the fact that we still used the benches her daddy made for the table when we couldn't afford to buy chairs.

"Oh, Mama!" she cried. Then turned to Hakim-a-barber. "I never knew how lovely these benches are. You can feel the rump prints," she said, running her hands underneath her and along the bench. Then she gave a sigh and her hand closed over Grandma Dee's butter dish. "That's it!" she said. "I knew there was something I wanted to ask you if I could have." She jumped up from the table and went over in the corner where the churn stood, the milk in it clabber by now. She looked at the churn and looked at it.

"This churn top is what I need," she said. "Didn't Uncle Buddy whittle it out of a tree you all used to have?"

"Yes," I said.

"Uh huh," she said happily. "And I want the dasher, too."

"Uncle Buddy whittle that, too?" asked the barber.

Dee (Wangero) looked up at me.

"Aunt Dee's first husband whittled the dash," said Maggie so low you almost couldn't hear her. "His name was Henry, but they called him Stash."

"Maggie's brain is like an elephant's," Wangero said, laughing. "I can use the churn top as a centerpiece for the alcove table," she said, sliding a plate over the churn, "and I'll think of something artistic to do with the dasher."

When she finished wrapping the dasher the handle stuck out. I took it for a moment in my hands. You didn't even have to look close to see where hands pushing the dasher up and down to make butter had left a kind of sink in the wood. In fact, there were a lot of small sinks; you could see where thumbs and fingers had sunk into the wood. It was beautiful light yellow wood, from a tree that grew in the yard where Big Dee and Stash had lived.

After dinner Dee (Wangero) went to the trunk at the foot of my bed and started rifling through it. Maggie hung back in the kitchen over the dishpan. Out came Wangero with two quilts. They had been pieced by Grandma Dee and then Big Dee and me had hung them on the quilt frames on the front porch and quilted them. One was in the Lone Star pattern. The other was Walk Around the Mountain. In both of them were scraps of dresses Grandma Dee had worn fifty and more years ago. Bits and pieces of Grandpa Jarrell's Paisley shirts. And one teeny faded blue piece, about the size of a penny matchbox, that was from Great Grandpa Ezra's uniform that he wore in the Civil War.

"Mama," Wangero said sweet as a bird. "Can I have these old quilts?"

I heard something fall in the kitchen, and a minute later the kitchen door slammed.

"Why don't you take one or two of the others?" I asked. "These old things was just done by me and Big Dee from some tops your grandma pieced before she died."

"No," said Wangero. "I don't want those. They are stitched around the borders by machine."

"That'll make them last better," I said.

"That's not the point," said Wangero. "These are all pieces of dresses Grandma used to wear. She did all this stitching by hand. Imagine!" She held the quilts securely in her arms, stroking them.

"Some of the pieces, like those lavender ones, come from old clothes her mother handed down to her," I said, moving up to touch the quilts. Dee (Wangero) moved back just enough so that I couldn't reach the quilts. They already belonged to her.

"Imagine!" she breathed again, clutching them closely to her bosom.

"The truth is," I said, "I promised to give them quilts to Maggie, for when she marries John Thomas."

She gasped like a bee had stung her.

"Maggie can't appreciate these quilts!" she said. "She'd probably be backward enough to put them to everyday use."

"I reckon she would," I said. "God knows I been saving 'em for long enough with nobody using 'em. I hope she will!" I didn't want to bring up how I had offered Dee (Wangero) a quilt when she went away to college. Then she had told me they were old-fashioned, out of style.

"But they're *priceless*!" she was saying now, furiously; for she has a temper. "Maggie would put them on the bed and in five years they'd be in rags. Less than that!"

"She can always make some more," I said. "Maggie knows how to quilt."

Dee (Wangero) looked at me with hatred. "You just will not understand. The point is these quilts, *these* quilts!"

"Well," I said, stumped. "What would *you* do with them?"

"Hang them," she said. As if that was the only thing you *could* do with quilts.

Maggie by now was standing in the door. I could almost hear the sound her feet made as they scraped over each other.

"She can have them, Mama," she said, like somebody used to never winning anything, or having anything reserved for her. "I can 'member Grandma Dee without the quilts."

I looked at her hard. She had filled her bottom lip with checkerberry snuff and it gave her face a kind of dopey, hangdog look. It was Grandma Dee and Big Dee who taught her how to quilt herself. She stood there with her scarred hands hidden in the folds of her skirt. She looked at her sister with something like fear but she wasn't mad at her. This was Maggie's portion. This was the way she knew God to work.

When I looked at her like that something hit me in the top of my head and ran down to the soles of my feet. Just like when I'm in church and the spirit of God touches me and I get happy and shout. I did something I never had done before: hugged Maggie to me, then dragged her on into the room, snatched the quilts out of Miss Wangero's hands and dumped them into Maggie's lap. Maggie just sat there on my bed with her mouth open.

"Take one or two of the others," I said to Dee.

But she turned without a word and went out to Hakim-a-barber.

"You just don't understand," she said, as Maggie and I came out to the car.

"What don't I understand?" I wanted to know.

"Your heritage," she said. And then she turned to Maggie, kissed her, and said, "You ought to try to make something of yourself, too, Maggie. It's really a new day for us. But from the way you and Mama still live you'd never know it."

She put on some sunglasses that hid everything above the tip of her nose and her chin.

Maggie smiled; maybe at the sunglasses. But a real smile, not scared. After we watched the car dust settle I asked Maggie to bring me a dip of snuff. And then the two of us sat there just enjoying, until it was time to go in the house and go to bed.

1973

Advancing Luna—and Ida B. Wells[1]

I met Luna the summer of 1965 in Atlanta where we both attended a political conference and rally. It was designed to give us the courage, as temporary civil rights workers, to penetrate the small hamlets farther south. I had taken a bus from Sarah Lawrence[2] in New York and gone back to Georgia, my home state, to try my hand at registering voters. It had become obvious from the high spirits and sense of almost divine purpose exhibited by black people that a revolution was going on, and I did not intend to miss it. Especially not this summer, student-studded version of it. And I thought it would be fun to spend some time on my own in the South.

Luna was sitting on the back of a pickup truck, waiting for someone to take her from Faith Baptist, where the rally was held, to whatever gracious black Negro home awaited her. I remember because someone who assumed I would also be traveling by pickup introduced us. I remember her face when I said, "No, no more back of pickup trucks for me. I know Atlanta well enough, I'll walk." She assumed of course (I guess) that I did not wish to ride beside her because she was white, and I was not curious enough about what she might have thought to explain it to her. And yet I was struck by her passivity, her *patience* as she sat on the truck alone and ignored, because someone had told her to wait there quietly until it was time to go.

This look of passively waiting for something changed very little over the years I knew her. It was only four or five years in all that I did. It seems

1. African American journalist and activist (1862–1931). Her "Red Report" (1895), which proved that the lynching of black men in the South was not related to the rape of white women, helped initiate the antilynching campaigns of the 1890s.

2. College in Bronxville, New York, a suburb of New York City.

longer, perhaps because we met at such an optimistic time in our lives. John Kennedy and Malcolm X had already been assassinated, but King had not been and Bobby Kennedy had not been. Then too, the lethal, bizarre elimination by death of this militant or that, exiles, flights to Cuba, shoot-outs between former Movement friends sundered forever by lies planted by the FBI, the gunning down of Mrs. Martin Luther King, Sr., as she played the Lord's Prayer on the piano in her church (was her name Alberta?), were still in the happily unfathomable future.

We believed we could change America because we were young and bright and held ourselves *responsible* for changing it. We did not believe we would fail. That is what lent fervor (revivalist fervor, in fact; we would *revive* America!) to our songs, and lent sweetness to our friendships (in the beginning almost all interracial), and gave a wonderful fillip to our sex (which, too, in the beginning, was almost always interracial).

What first struck me about Luna when we later lived together was that she did not own a bra. This was curious to me, I suppose, because she also did not need one. Her chest was practically flat, her breasts like those of a child. Her face was round, and she suffered from acne. She carried with her always a tube of that "skin-colored" (if one's skin is pink or eggshell) medication designed to dry up pimples. At the oddest times—waiting for a light to change, listening to voter registration instructions, talking about her father's new girlfriend, she would apply the stuff, holding in her other hand a small brass mirror the size of her thumb, which she also carried for just this purpose.

We were assigned to work together in a small, rigidly segregated South Georgia town that the city fathers, incongruously and years ago, had named Freehold. Luna was slightly asthmatic and when overheated or nervous she breathed through her mouth. She wore her shoulder-length black hair with bangs to her eyebrows and the rest brushed behind her ears. Her eyes were brown and rather small. She was attractive, but just barely and with effort. Had she been the slightest bit overweight, for instance, she would have gone completely unnoticed, and would have faded into the background where, even in a revolution, fat people seem destined to go. I have a photograph of her sitting on the steps of a house in South Georgia. She is wearing tiny pearl earrings, a dark sleeveless shirt with Peter Pan collar, Bermuda shorts, and a pair of those East Indian sandals that seem to adhere to nothing but a big toe.

The summer of '65 was as hot as any other in that part of the South. There was an abundance of flies and mosquitoes. Everyone complained about the heat and the flies and the hard work, but Luna complained less than the rest of us. She walked ten miles a day with me up and down those straight Georgia highways, stopping at every house that looked black (one could always tell in 1965) and asking whether anyone needed help with learning how to vote. The simple mechanics: writing one's name, or making one's "X" in the proper column. And then, though we were required to walk, everywhere, we were empowered to offer prospective registrants a car in which they might safely ride down to the county courthouse. And later to the polling places. Luna, almost overcome by the heat, breathing through her mouth like a dog, her hair plastered with sweat to her head, kept looking straight ahead, and walking as if the walking itself was her reward.

I don't know if we accomplished much that summer. In retrospect, it seems not only minor, but irrelevant. A bunch of us, black and white, lived together. The black people who took us in were unfailingly hospitable and kind. I took them for granted in a way that now amazes me. I realize that at each and every house we visited I *assumed* hospitality, I *assumed* kindness. Luna was often startled by my "boldness." If we walked up to a secluded farmhouse and half a dozen dogs ran up barking around our heels and a large black man with a shotgun could be seen whistling to himself under a tree, she would become nervous. I, on the other hand, felt free to yell at this stranger's dogs, slap a couple of them on the nose, and call over to him about his hunting.

That month with Luna of approaching new black people every day taught me something about myself I had always suspected: I thought black people superior people. Not simply superior to white people, because even without thinking about it much, I assumed almost everyone was superior to them; but to everyone. Only white people, after all, would blow up a Sunday-school class and grin for television over their "victory," *i.e.,* the death of four small black girls. Any atrocity, at any time, was expected from them. On the other hand, it never occurred to me that black people *could* treat Luna and me with anything but warmth and concern. Even their curiosity about the sudden influx into their midst of rather ignorant white and black Northerners was restrained and courteous. I was treated as a relative, Luna as a much welcomed guest.

Luna and I were taken in by a middle-aged couple and their young school-age daughter. The mother worked outside the house in a local canning factory, the father worked in the paper plant in nearby Augusta. Never did they speak of the danger they were in of losing their jobs over keeping us, and never did their small daughter show any fear that her house might be attacked by racists because we were there. Again, I did not expect this family to complain, no matter what happened to them because of us. Having understood the danger, they had assumed the risk. I did not think them particularly brave, merely typical.

I think Luna liked the smallness—only four rooms—of the house. It was in this house that she ridiculed her mother's lack of taste. Her yellow-and-mauve house in Cleveland, the eleven rooms, the heated garage, the new car every year, her father's inability to remain faithful to her mother, their divorce, the fight over the property, even more bitter than over the children. Her mother kept the house and the children. Her father kept the car and his new girlfriend, whom he wanted Luna to meet and "approve." I could hardly imagine anyone disliking her mother so much. Everything Luna hated in her she summed up in three words: *"yellow and mauve."*

I have a second photograph of Luna and a group of us being bullied by a Georgia state trooper. This member of Georgia's finest had followed us out into the deserted countryside to lecture us on how misplaced—in the South— was our energy, when "the Lord knew" the North (where he thought all of us lived, expressing disbelief that most of us were Georgians) was just as bad. (He had a point that I recognized even then, but it did not seem the point where we were.) Luna is looking up at him, her mouth slightly open as always, a somewhat dazed look on her face. I cannot detect fear on any of our faces, though we were all afraid. After all, 1965 was only a year after 1964 when three civil rights workers had been taken deep into a Mississippi forest by local officials and sadistically tortured and murdered. Luna almost always carried a flat black shoulder bag. She is standing with it against her side, her thumb in the strap.

At night we slept in the same bed. We talked about our schools, lovers, girlfriends we didn't understand or missed. She dreamed, she said, of going to Goa. I dreamed of going to Africa. My dream came true earlier than hers: an offer of a grant from an unsuspected source reached me one day as I was writing poems under a tree. I left Freehold, Georgia, in the middle of summer, without regrets, and flew from New York to London, to Cairo, to Kenya, and, finally, to Uganda, where I settled among black people with the same assumptions of welcome and kindness I had taken for granted in Georgia. I was taken on rides down the Nile as a matter of course, and accepted all invitations to dinner, where the best local dishes were superbly prepared in my honor. I became, in fact, a lost relative of the people, whose ancestors had foolishly strayed, long ago, to America.

I wrote to Luna at once.

But I did not see her again for almost a year. I had graduated from college, moved into a borrowed apartment in Brooklyn Heights, and was being evicted after a month. Luna, living then in a tenement on East 9th Street, invited me to share her two-bedroom apartment. If I had seen the apartment before the day I moved in I might never have agreed to do so. Her building was between Avenues B and C and did not have a front door. Junkies, winos, and others often wandered in during the night (and occasionally during the day) to sleep underneath the stairs or to relieve themselves at the back of the first-floor hall.

Luna's apartment was on the third floor. Everything in it was painted white. The contrast between her three rooms and kitchen (with its red bathtub) and the grungy stairway was stunning. Her furniture consisted of two large brass beds inherited from a previous tenant and stripped of paint by Luna, and a long, high-backed church pew which she had managed somehow to bring up from the South. There was a simplicity about the small apartment that I liked. I also liked the notion of extreme contrast, and I do to this day. Outside our front window was the decaying neighborhood, as ugly and ill-lit as a battleground. (And allegedly as hostile, though somehow we were never threatened with bodily harm by the Hispanics who were our neighbors, and who seemed, more than anything, *bewildered* by the darkness and filth of their surroundings.) Inside was the church pew, as straight and spare as Abe Lincoln lying down, the white walls as spotless as a monastery's, and a small, unutterably pure patch of blue sky through the window of the back bedroom. (Luna did not believe in curtains, or couldn't afford them, and so we always undressed and bathed with the lights off and the rooms lit with candles, causing rather nun-shaped shadows to be cast on the walls by the long-sleeved high-necked nightgowns we both wore to bed.)

Over a period of weeks, our relationship, always marked by mutual respect, evolved into a warm and comfortable friendship which provided a stability and comfort we both needed at that time. I had taken a job at the Welfare Department during the day, and set up my typewriter permanently in the tiny living room for work after I got home. Luna worked in a kindergarten, and in the evenings taught herself Portuguese.

It was while we lived on East 9th Street that she told me she had been raped during her summer in the South. It is hard for me, even now, to relate my feeling of horror and incredulity. This was some time before Eldridge Cleaver wrote of being a rapist/revolutionary; of "practicing" on black women before moving on to white. It was also, unless I'm mistaken, before LeRoi Jones (as he was then known; now of course Imamu Baraka,[3] which has an even

---

3. African American poet, playwright, and essayist (1934–2014); one of the major figures of the Black Arts movement of the 1960s. Cleaver (1935– 1998), ex–Black Panther leader and author of *Soul on Ice* (1968).

more presumptuous meaning than "the King") wrote his advice to young black male insurrectionaries (women were not told what to do with *their* rebelliousness): "Rape the white girls. Rape their fathers." It was clear that he meant this literally and also as: to rape a white girl *is* to rape her father. It was the misogynous cruelty of this latter meaning that was habitually lost on black men (on men in general, actually), but nearly always perceived and rejected by women of whatever color.

"Details?" I asked.

She shrugged. Gave his name. A name recently in the news, though in very small print.

He was not a Movement star or anyone you would know. We had met once, briefly. I had not liked him because he was coarse and spoke of black women as "our" women. (In the early Movement, it was pleasant to think of black men wanting to own us as a group; later it became clear that owning us meant exactly *that* to them.) He was physically unattractive, I had thought, with something of the hoodlum about him: a swaggering, unnecessarily mobile walk, small eyes, rough skin, a mouthful of wandering or absent teeth. He was, ironically, among the first persons to shout the slogan everyone later attributed solely to Stokeley Carmichael—Black Power! Stokeley was chosen as the originator of this idea by the media, because he was physically beautiful and photogenic and articulate. Even the name—Freddie Pye—was diminutive, I thought, in an age of giants.

"What did you do?"

"Nothing that required making a noise."

"Why didn't you scream?" I felt I would have screamed my head off.

"You know why."

I did. I had seen a photograph of Emmett Till's[4] body just after it was pulled from the river. I had seen photographs of white folks standing in a circle roasting something that had talked to them in their own language before they tore out its tongue. I knew why, all right.

"What was he trying to prove?"

"I don't know. Do you?"

"Maybe you filled him with unendurable lust," I said.

"I don't think so," she said.

Suddenly I was embarrassed. Then angry. Very, very angry. *How dare she tell me this!* I thought.

Who knows what the black woman thinks of rape? Who has asked her? Who *cares*? Who has even properly acknowledged that *she* and not the white woman in this story is the most likely victim of rape? Whenever interracial rape is mentioned, a black woman's first thought is to protect the lives of her brothers, her father, her sons, her lover. A history of lynching has bred this reflex in her. I feel it as strongly as anyone. While writing a fictional account of such a rape in a novel, I read Ida B. Wells's autobiography three times, as a means of praying to her spirit to forgive me.

My prayer, as I turned the pages, went like this: *"Please forgive me. I am a writer."* (This self-revealing statement alone often seems to me sufficient reason to require perpetual forgiveness; since the writer is guilty not only of

---

4. Thirteen-year-old African American who was killed in Mississippi in 1955, supposedly because he whistled at a white woman. His death became symbolic of the racial injustices of the South. His killers were acquitted.

always wanting to know—like Eve—but also of trying—again like Eve—to find out.) *"I cannot write contrary to what life reveals to me. I wish to malign no one. But I must struggle to understand at least my own tangled emotions about interracial rape. I know, Ida B. Wells, you spent your whole life protecting, and trying to protect, black men accused of raping white women, who were lynched by white mobs, or threatened with it. You know, better than I ever will, what it means for a whole people to live under the terror of lynching. Under the slander that their men, where white women are concerned, are creatures of uncontrollable sexual lust. You made it so clear that the black men accused of rape in the past were innocent victims of white criminals that I grew up believing black men literally did not rape white women. At all. Ever. Now it would appear that some of them, the very twisted, the terribly ill, do. What would you have me write about them?"*

Her answer was: *"Write nothing. Nothing at all. It will be used against black men and therefore against all of us. Eldridge Cleaver and LeRoi Jones don't know who they're dealing with. But you remember. You are dealing with people who brought their children to witness the murder of black human beings, falsely accused of rape. People who handed out, as trophies, black fingers and toes. Deny! Deny! Deny!"*

And yet, I have pursued it: *"Some black men themselves do not seem to know what the meaning of raping someone is. Some have admitted rape in order to denounce it, but others have accepted rape as a part of rebellion, of 'paying whitey back.' They have gloried in it."*

"They know nothing of America," she says. *"And neither, apparently, do you. No matter what you think you know, no matter what you feel about it, say nothing. And to your dying breath!"*

Which, to my mind, is virtually useless advice to give to a writer.

Freddie Pye was the kind of man I would not have looked at then, not even once. (Throughout that year I was more or less into exotica: white ethnics who knew languages were a peculiar weakness; a half-white hippie singer; also a large Chinese mathematician who was a marvelous dancer and who taught me to waltz.) There was no question of belief.

But, in retrospect, there was a momentary *suspension* of belief, a kind of *hope* that perhaps it had not really happened; that Luna had made up the rape, "as white women have been wont to do." I soon realized this was unlikely. I was the only person she had told.

She looked at me as if to say: "I'm glad *that* part of my life is over." We continued our usual routine. We saw every interminable, foreign, depressing, and poorly illuminated film ever made. We learned to eat brown rice and yogurt and to tolerate kasha and odd-tasting teas. My half-black hippie singer friend (now a well-known reggae singer who says he is from "de I-lands" and not Sheepshead Bay) was "into" tea and kasha and Chinese vegetables.

And yet the rape, the knowledge of the rape, out in the open, admitted, pondered over, was now between us. (And I began to think that perhaps— whether Luna had been raped or not—it had always been so; that her power over my life was exactly the power *her word on rape* had over the lives of black men, over *all* black men, whether they were guilty or not, and therefore over my whole people.)

Before she told me about the rape, I think we had assumed a lifelong friendship. The kind of friendship one dreams of having with a person one has known in adversity; under heat and mosquitoes and immaturity and the threat of death. We would each travel, we would write to each other from the three edges of the world.

We would continue to have an "international list" of lovers whose amorous talents or lack of talents we would continue (giggling into our dotage) to compare. Our friendship would survive everything, be truer than everything, endure even our respective marriages, children, husbands—assuming we *did*, out of desperation and boredom someday, marry, which did not seem a probability, exactly, but more in the area of an amusing idea.

But now there was a cooling off of our affection for each other. Luna was becoming mildly interested in drugs, because everyone we knew was. I was envious of the open-endedness of her life. The financial backing to it. When she left her job at the kindergarten because she was tired of working, her errant father immediately materialized. He took her to dine on scampi at an expensive restaurant, scolded her for living on East 9th Street, and looked at me as if to say: "Living in a slum of this magnitude must surely have been your idea." As a cullud, of course.

For me there was the welfare department every day, attempting to get the necessary food and shelter to people who would always live amid the dirty streets I knew I must soon leave. I was, after all, a Sarah Lawrence girl "with talent." It would be absurd to rot away in a building that had no front door.

I slept late one Sunday morning with a painter I had met at the Welfare Department. A man who looked for all the world like Gene Autry,[5] the singing cowboy, but who painted wonderful surrealist pictures of birds and ghouls and fruit with *teeth*. The night before, three of us—me, the painter, and "an old Navy buddy" who looked like his twin and who had just arrived in town—had got high on wine and grass.

That morning the Navy buddy snored outside the bedrooms like a puppy waiting for its master. Luna got up early, made an immense racket getting breakfast, scowled at me as I emerged from my room, and left the apartment, slamming the door so hard she damaged the lock. (Luna had made it a rule to date black men almost exclusively. My insistence on dating, as she termed it, "anyone" was incomprehensible to her, since in a politically diseased society to "sleep with the enemy" was to become "infected" with the enemy's "political germs." There is more than a grain of truth in this, of course, but I was having too much fun to stare at it for long. Still, coming from Luna it was amusing, since she never took into account the risk her own black lovers ran by sleeping with "the white woman," and she had apparently been convinced that a summer of relatively innocuous political work in the South had cured her of any racial, economic, or sexual political disease.)

Luna never told me what irked her so that Sunday morning, yet I remember it as the end of our relationship. It was not, as I at first feared, that she thought my bringing the two men to the apartment was inconsiderate. The way we lived allowed us to *be* inconsiderate from time to time. Our friends were varied, vital, and often strange. Her friends especially were deeper than they should have been into drugs.

The distance between us continued to grow. She talked more of going to Goa.[6] My guilt over my dissolute if pleasurable existence coupled with my mounting hatred of welfare work, propelled me in two directions: south and

---

5. Singing cowboy film star of the 1930s through the 1950s.

6. Coastal region of southwestern India, formerly a Portuguese colony.

to West Africa. When the time came to choose, I discovered that *my* summer in the South had infected me with the need to return, to try to understand, and write about, the people I'd merely lived with before.

We never discussed the rape again. We never discussed, really, Freddie Pye or Luna's remaining feelings about what had happened. One night, the last month we lived together, I noticed a man's blue denim jacket thrown across the church pew. The next morning, out of Luna's bedroom walked Freddie Pye. He barely spoke to me—possibly because as a black woman I was expected to be hostile toward his presence in a white woman's bedroom. I was too surprised to exhibit hostility, however, which was only a part of what I felt, after all. He left.

Luna and I did not discuss this. It is odd, I think now, that we didn't. It was as if he was never there, as if he and Luna had not shared the bedroom that night. A month later, Luna went alone to Goa, in her solitary way. She lived on an island and slept, she wrote, on the beach. She mentioned she'd found a lover there who protected her from the local beachcombers and pests.

Several years later, she came to visit me in the South and brought a lovely piece of pottery which my daughter much later dropped and broke, but which I glued back together in such a way that the flaw improves the beauty and fragility of the design.

Afterwords, Afterwards Second Thoughts

That is the "story." It has an "unresolved" ending. That is because Freddie Pye and Luna are still alive, as am I. However, one evening while talking to a friend, I heard myself say that I had, in fact, written *two* endings. One, which follows, I considered appropriate for such a story published in a country truly committed to justice, and the one above, which is the best I can afford to offer a society in which lynching is still reserved, at least subconsciously, as a means of racial control.

I said that if we in fact lived in a society committed to the establishment of justice for everyone ("justice" in this case encompassing equal housing, education, access to work, adequate dental care, et cetera), thereby placing Luna and Freddie Pye in their correct relationship to each other, *i.e.*, that of brother and sister, *compañeros*, then the two of them would be required to struggle together over what his rape of her had meant.

Since my friend is a black man whom I love and who loves me, we spent a considerable amount of time discussing what this particular rape meant to us. Morally wrong, we said, and not to be excused. Shameful; politically corrupt. Yet, as we thought of what might have happened to an indiscriminate number of innocent young black men in Freehold, Georgia, had Luna screamed, it became clear that more than a little of Ida B. Wells's fear of probing the rape issue was running through us, too. The implications of this fear would not let me rest, so that months and years went by with most of the story written but with me incapable, or at least unwilling, to finish or to publish it.

In thinking about it over a period of years, there occurred a number of small changes, refinements, puzzles, in angle. Would these shed a wider light on the continuing subject? I do not know. In any case, I returned to my notes, hereto appended for the use of the reader.

LUNA: IDA B. WELLS—DISCARDED NOTES

Additional characteristics of Luna: At a time when many in and out of the Movement considered "nigger" and "black" synonymous, and indulged in a sincere attempt to fake Southern "hip" speech, Luna resisted. She was the kind of WASP who could not easily imitate another's ethnic style, nor could she even exaggerate her own. She was what she was. A very straight, clear-eyed, coolly observant young woman with no talent for existing outside her own skin.

IMAGINARY KNOWLEDGE

Luna explained the visit from Freddie Pye in this way:

"He called that evening, said he was in town, and did I know the Movement was coming north? I replied that I did know that."

When could he see her? he wanted to know.

"Never," she replied.

He had burst into tears, or something that sounded like tears, over the phone. He was stranded at wherever the evening's fund-raising event had been held. Not in the place itself, but outside, in the street. The "stars" had left, everyone had left. He was alone. He knew no one else in the city. Had found her number in the phone book. And had no money, no place to stay.

Could he, he asked, crash? He was tired, hungry, broke—and even in the South had had no job, other than the Movement, for months. Et cetera.

When he arrived, she had placed our only steak knife in the waistband of her jeans.

He had asked for a drink of water. She gave him orange juice, some cheese, and a couple of slices of bread. She had told him he might sleep on the church pew and he had lain down with his head on his rolled-up denim jacket. She had retired to her room, locked the door, and tried to sleep. She was amazed to discover herself worrying that the church pew was both too narrow and too hard.

At first he muttered, groaned, and cursed in his sleep. Then he fell off the narrow church pew. He kept rolling off. At two in the morning she unlocked her door, showed him her knife, and invited him to share her bed.

Nothing whatever happened except they talked. At first, only he talked. Not about the rape, but about his life.

"He was a small person physically, remember?" Luna asked me. (She was right. Over the years he had grown big and, yes, burly, in my imagination, and I'm sure in hers.) "That night he seemed tiny. A child. He was still fully dressed, except for the jacket and he, literally, hugged his side of the bed. I hugged mine. The whole bed, in fact, was between us. We were merely hanging to its edges."

At the fund-raiser—on Fifth Avenue and 71st Street, as it turned out—his leaders had introduced him as the unskilled, barely literate, former Southern fieldworker that he was. They had pushed him at the rich people gathered there as an example of what "the system" did to "the little people" in the South. They asked him to tell about the thirty-seven times he had been jailed. The thirty-five times he had been beaten. The one time he had lost consciousness in the "hot" box. They told him not to worry about his grammar. "Which, as you may recall," said Luna, "was horrible." Even so, he had tried to censor his "ain'ts" and his "us'es" He had been painfully aware that he was on exhibit, like Frederick Douglass had been for the Abolitionists. But unlike Douglass he had no oratorical gift, no passionate language, no silver tongue. He knew the rich people and his own leaders perceived he was nothing: a broken man, unschooled, unskilled at anything . . .

Yet he had spoken, trembling before so large a crowd of rich, white Northerners—who clearly thought their section of the country would never have the South's racial problems—begging, with the painful stories of his wretched life, for their money.

At the end, all of them—the black leaders, too—had gone. They left him watching the taillights of their cars, recalling the faces of the friends come to pick them up: the women dressed in African print that shone, with elaborately arranged hair, their jewelry sparkling, their perfume exotic. They were so beautiful, yet so strange. He could not imagine that one of them could comprehend his life. He did not ask for a ride, because of that, but also because he had no place to go. Then he had remembered Luna.

Soon Luna would be required to talk. She would mention her confusion over whether, in a black community surrounded by whites with a history of lynching blacks, she had a right to scream as Freddie Pye was raping her. For her, this was the crux of the matter.

And so they would continue talking through the night.

This is another ending, created from whole cloth. If I believed Luna's story about the rape, and I did (had she told anyone else I might have dismissed it), then this reconstruction of what might have happened is as probable an accounting as any is liable to be. Two people have now become "characters."

I have forced them to talk until they reached the stumbling block of the rape, *which they must remove themselves,* before proceeding to a place from which it will be possible to insist on a society in which Luna's word alone on rape can never be used to intimidate an entire people, and in which an innocent black man's protestation of innocence of rape is unprejudicially heard. Until such a society is created, relationships of affection between black men and white women will always be poisoned—from within as from without—by historical fear and the threat of violence, and solidarity among black and white women is only rarely likely to exist.

Postscript: Havana, Cuba, November 1976

I am in Havana with a group of other black American artists. We have spent the morning apart from our Cuban hosts bringing each other up to date on the kind of work (there are no apolitical artists among us) we are doing in the United States. I have read "Luna."

High above the beautiful city of Havana I sit in the Havana Libre pavilion with the muralist/photographer in our group. He is in his mid-thirties, a handsome, brown, erect individual whom I have known casually for a number of years. During the sixties he designed and painted street murals for both SNCC[7] and the Black Panthers, and in an earlier discussion with Cuban artists he showed impatience with their explanation of why we had seen no murals covering some of the city's rather dingy walls: Cuba, they had said, unlike Mexico, has no mural tradition. "But the point of a revolution," insisted Our Muralist, "is to make new traditions!" And he had pressed

---

7. Southern Nonviolent Coordinating Committee. One of the major civil rights organizations, it launched the voter registration drives in the South in the early 1960s.

his argument with such passion for the *usefulness*, for revolutionary communication, of his craft, that the Cubans were both exasperated and impressed. They drove us around the city for a tour of their huge billboards, all advancing socialist thought and the heroism of men like Lenin, Camilo, and Che Guevara, and said, "These, *these* are our 'murals'!"

While we ate lunch, I asked Our Muralist what he'd thought of "Luna." Especially the appended section.

"Not much," was his reply. "Your view of human weakness is too biblical," he said. "You are unable to conceive of the man without conscience. The man who cares nothing about the state of his soul because he's long since sold it. In short," he said, "you do not understand that some people are simply evil, a disease on the lives of other people, and that to remove the disease altogether is preferable to trying to interpret, contain, or forgive it. Your 'Freddie Pye,'" and he laughed, "was probably raping white women on the instructions of his government."

Oh ho, I thought. Because, of course, for a second, during which I stalled my verbal reply, this comment made both very little and very much sense.

"I *am* sometimes naive and sentimental," I offered. I am sometimes both, though frequently by design. Admission in this way is tactical, a stimulant to conversation.

"And shocked at what I've said," he said, and laughed again. "Even though," he continued, "you know by now that blacks could be hired to blow up other blacks, and could be hired *by someone* to shoot down Brother Malcolm, and hired *by someone* to provide a diagram of Fred Hampton's[8] bedroom so the pigs could shoot him easily while he slept, you find it hard to believe a black man could be hired *by someone* to rape white women. But think a minute, and you will see why it is the perfect disruptive act. Enough blacks raping or accused of raping enough white women and any political movement that cuts across racial lines is doomed.

"Larger forces are at work than your story would indicate," he continued. "You're still thinking of lust and rage, moving slowly into aggression and purely racial hatred. But you should be considering money—which the rapist would get, probably from your very own tax dollars, in fact—and a maintaining of the status quo; which those hiring the rapist would achieve. I know all this," he said, "because when I was broke and hungry and selling my blood to buy the food and the paint that allowed me to work, I was offered such 'other work.'"

"But you did not take it."

He frowned. "There you go again. How do you know I didn't take it? It paid, and I was starving."

"You didn't take it," I repeated.

"No," he said. "A black and white 'team' made the offer. I had enough energy left to threaten to throw them out of the room."

"But even if Freddie Pye *had been* hired *by someone* to rape Luna, that still would not explain his second visit."

"Probably nothing will explain that," said Our Muralist. "But assuming Freddie Pye *was* paid to disrupt—by raping a white woman—the black struggle in the South, he may have wised up enough later to comprehend the significance of Luna's decision not to scream."

---

8. Black Panther thought to have been murdered by the Chicago police.

"So you are saying he *did have* a conscience?" I asked.

"Maybe," he said, but his look clearly implied I would never understand anything about evil, power, or corrupted human beings in the modern world.

But of course he is wrong.

1981

AUGUST WILSON
1945–2005

ugust Wilson was "theater's poet of black America," according to his obituary in the *New York Times*. His death from cancer in 2005 came swiftly, but not before he completed his master work, the epic cycle of ten plays that represent and reimagine the history of African Americans during the twentieth century. Chronologically in terms of setting, the plays begin with *Gem of the Ocean*, set in 1904, just as blacks begin to migrate from the rural South to the nation's cities, and end with *Radio Golf*, set in 1997, as gentrification threatens to displace blacks from the communities they have struggled to build. All ten plays showcase Wilson's gift for distilling the poetry of African American expression, his commitment to recovering the unwritten history of African American communities, and his political consciousness. They produce a powerful theatrical experience that continues to win praise from audiences and critics alike.

One of only seven American dramatists ever to win two Pulitzer Prizes (one for *Fences* and one for *The Piano Lesson*), Wilson was also the first African American ever to have two plays (*Fences* and *Joe Turner's Come and Gone*) running simultaneously on Broadway. Among other accolades, he won a Tony Award for *Fences* and seven New York Drama Critics' Circle Awards during his career. In 2005 he became the first African American to have a Broadway theater named in his honor. Tony Kushner, another acclaimed playwright, called Wilson "a giant figure in the American theater. Heroic is not a word one uses often without embarrassment to describe a writer or playwright, but the diligence and ferocity of effort behind the creation of his body of work is really an epic story."

By Wilson's own account in the preface to *Three Plays* (1991), the story began in 1965 with "a typewritten yellow-labeled record titled 'Nobody in Town Can Bake a Sweet Jellyroll Like Mine' by someone named Bessie Smith. . . . It was the beginning of my consciousness that I was representative of a culture and the carrier of some very valuable antecedents." Wilson evoked that memory in his first big hit, *Ma Rainey's Black Bottom*, set in Chicago in the 1920s. Blues are a touchstone in the subsequent plays, all set in the Hill District of Pittsburgh: *Fences*, set in the 1950s; *The Piano Lesson*, set in the 1930s; *Two Trains Running*, set in the 1960s; *Seven Guitars*, set in the 1940s; *King Hedley II*, set in the 1980s; and *Jitney*, written before *Ma Rainey* and set in the 1970s. Bookending the century, *Gem of the Ocean* and *Radio Golf* were the last plays Wilson wrote.

Wilson was born Frederick August Kittel in Pittsburgh in 1945, the fourth of six children and the namesake of his German American father. When he became a writer, Wilson honored his African American mother, Daisy Wilson, by legally adopting her name. As a young child, he lived in the poor, racially mixed Hill District. After his parents' divorce and his mother's remarriage to an African American named David Belford, the family moved to a largely white suburb, where Wilson experienced the harshness of racism. Bricks were thrown at the family home. In school where he was the only black student in his class, Wilson later told an interviewer, "There was a note on my desk every single day. It said, 'Go home, nigger.'" After a teacher accused him of plagiarism, he quit school. At the age of fifteen, he embarked on a plan to educate himself, spending his days at the local library and reading books by the dozen.

Along with his reading, he began to absorb the oral traditions passed down from one generation of black men to the next. At the age of twenty-one, he remembered following an old man into Pat's Place, a cigar store in Pittsburgh, where "these guys would stand around every day and I would stand around in the background and listen to them. . . . Little did I know that many years later . . . I would make use of them in my plays." In the late 1960s, Wilson became involved in the Black Power movement and began writing poetry and short stories, publishing his work in local black journals. With a group of fellow poets, he founded the Black Horizons on the Hill Theater, where he worked as an actor and director. But not until he moved to St. Paul, Minnesota, in 1978, did he launch himself as a playwright. It is not surprising that his first play, *Jitney*, set in a taxi stand in the Hill, conjured the voices he remembered from Pat's Place. They form a choral backdrop to the drama of a father and son whose relationship is defined by a furious mixture of anger and love.

In 1982, the year that *Jitney* was produced in Pittsburgh, *Ma Rainey's Black Bottom* was accepted at the Eugene O'Neill Playwrights Conference headed by Lloyd Richards. There Wilson began one of his most important professional relationships. Richards, the first African American director to work on Broadway (he directed the debut of Lorraine Hansberry's *A Raisin in the Sun*), was the dean of the Yale School of Drama and the artistic director of the Yale Repertory Theatre; he became a fervent champion of Wilson's work. Under his direction, *Ma Rainey* was produced on Broadway in 1984 and was a commercial and critical success, running for 275 performances and winning the New York Drama Critics' Circle Award as well as several Tony nominations. Critic Frank Rich hailed Wilson as "a major find for the American theater" and praised him for writing "with compassion, raucous humor and penetrating wisdom." Despite its title, the play did not focus on the great blues singer but on the rivalries within her band and the racism that shadowed their careers. As was his custom, Wilson was telling "a history that had never been told."

In a 1999 interview in *The Paris Review*, Wilson cited his major influences as being the "the four B's": the blues was the primary influence, followed by Jorge Luis Borges, Amiri Baraka, and the painter Romare Bearden. He explained what he had learned from each: "From Borges, those wonderful gaucho stories from which I learned that you can be specific as to a time and place and culture and still have the work resonate with the universal themes of love, honor, duty, betrayal, etc. From Amiri Baraka, I learned that all art is political, although I don't write political plays. From Romare Bearden, I learned that the fullness and richness of everyday life can be rendered without compromise or sentimentality." At some point in his career, Wilson determined to write a play for every decade of the twentieth century. They would be set in the specific place of the Hill District and explore universal themes within that particular context. Rather than historical figures, they would focus on the everyday lives of ordinary African Americans.

Fences is the story of sanitation worker Troy Maxson and his son, Cory, who has ambitions that his father is sure will be thwarted by racism. Consequently, Troy strives to instill a sense of duty in Cory, even as he withholds affection. As he tells his son, "I done give you everything I had to give you. I gave you your life! . . . And liking your black ass wasn't part of the bargain." After four years of polishing and productions at several venues, *Fences* opened in New York in 1987. Starring James Earl Jones as Troy and Mary Alice as his long suffering wife, Rose, the play was a tremendous critical success, winning the New York Drama Critics' Circle Award, four Tony Awards (including Best Play), and the Pulitzer Prize for drama. When the play was revived on Broadway in 2010, Denzel Washington and Viola Davis won

Tony Awards for their leading roles. According to the *Village Voice*'s Michael Fein-gold, the play established Wilson's reputation as "a mythmaker who sees his basically naturalistic panorama plays as stages in an allegorical history of black America."

Wilson's next play, *Joe Turner's Come and Gone*, was lauded by Frank Rich as "a spiritual allegory" that "will give a lasting voice to a generation of uprooted black Americans." Many critics consider it Wilson's supreme achievement. Set in a board-ing house in Pittsburgh in 1911, *Joe Turner's Come and Gone* explores the lives of characters in danger of being cut off from their African and southern roots by their migration to the North. Loomis, the main character and the most alienated, searches for his wife, who has been abducted by the bounty hunter Joe Turner, a legendary figure in the blues. After ten years on a chain gang, Loomis is "a man who done for-got his song, forgot how to sing it." Over the course of the drama, he remembers, and the song becomes, in Wilson's words, "both a wail and a whelp of joy." The center-piece of the play is the juba, a dance with origins in Africa, which becomes the ritual of remembrance for Loomis and for the play's other displaced characters.

In his customary fashion, while *Joe Turner* wended its way to Broadway, Wilson wrote his next play, *The Piano Lesson*, which premiered at the Yale Repertory The-atre in 1987, opened on Broadway in 1990, and won the Pulitzer Prize. Set in 1937, *The Piano Lesson* revolves around the conflict between a brother and a sister, Boy Willie and Berniece, and their relationship to a piano, which comes to symbolize the "choice between revering symbols of African ancestry and converting them to functional use." Some critics noted the scarcity of complicated female characters in the play. Others praised the "music of the dialogue" and how "phrase by phrase and speech by speech, Wilson is as sheerly listenable as Handel."

Wilson's next play in his cycle, *Two Trains Running*, opened on Broadway in April 1992. The play is again set in a luncheonette in the late 1960s. Although the charac-ters are not directly involved in the turbulent events of the period, one critic noted that the play "embodies the entire black political dialectic from that time to this—isolation vs. assimilation, hostility toward vs. cooperation with whites, clinging to bitter memory vs. moving on into a better world." Critic Cheryl McCourtie of the *Crisis* noted how the play resonated with her own life experience: "Sitting in on *Two Trains Running* about the workers and 'regulars' in a Pittsburgh restaurant in 1969 is like eavesdropping on a group of family members." That sense of familiarity spoke both to the audience's experiences and to the pattern of kinship that emerged among Wilson's characters. The protagonist of *King Hedley II* is the son of a character in *Seven Guitars*. He wears his name and royal sense of himself proudly, but the reality of his prospects is grim. The 1980s as Wilson's drama depicts the decade was a period of despair. In the words of one character, "The people wandering all over the place. They got lost. They don't even know the story of how they got from tit to tat."

Wilson's last two plays recall that story and show the consequences of forgetting it. *Gem of the Ocean* (2004) is peopled with characters for whom slavery is a living memory. The play explores the possibilities of a newly won freedom. Aunt Ester, the 280-year-old presiding spirit of the play, is well known for her healing gifts, which Citizen Barlow, weighed down with the burden of guilt along with the unrealized hopes inscribed in his name, comes seeking. Bedraggled and eloquent, Solly Two Kings, a former conductor on the Underground Railroad, assists in the healing ritual that is performed. If Solly Two Kings is eager to embrace the pain and heroism of the past, Caesar, the entrepreneur and constable, is eager to cash in on the materialism of the present. As always with Wilson's plays, the journey to the future requires a detour through the past. In a theatrical masterstroke, the play enacts the Middle Passage through a fusion of voices and light. *Radio Golf* (2005) completes the cycle of plays on a pessimistic note. In the 1990s, middle-class black Americans are on the cusp of achieving material and political success far beyond their ancestors' imagin-ings. Harmond Wilks, the play's protagonist, is a candidate for mayor of Pittsburgh; his wife, Mame, holds a prominent position in the governor's office. The Hill is now ripe for gentrification, and the development plans require the demolition of the house at 1839 Wiley, the home of Aunt Ester. Her spiritual legatees, Sterling Johnson

This 1940 picture of two men walking alongside a North Carolina road heading north evokes the alienation and uncertain future that Herald Loomis faces in *Joe Turner's Come and Gone*.

and Elder Joseph Barlow, the grandson of the character in *Gem of the Ocean*, raise their objections in an eloquent fury. Harmond is torn, but the vapid values of the era have sapped his soul.

August Wilson wrote other plays, but these ten dramas, sometimes called the Pittsburgh cycle, constitute his signal contribution to African American letters. With their rich eloquence, blues-tinged humor, tragic ironies, and sharp political critiques, these plays earned Wilson the title "theater's poet of black America."

Joe Turner's Come and Gone

Characters

SETH HOLLY, *owner of the boardinghouse*
BERTHA HOLLY, *his wife*
BYNUM WALKER, *a rootworker*
RUTHERFORD SELIG, *a peddler*
JEREMY FURLOW, *a resident*
HERALD LOOMIS, *a resident*
ZONIA LOOMIS, *his daughter*
MATTIE CAMPBELL, *a resident*
REUBEN SCOTT, *boy who lives next door*
MOLLY CUNNINGHAM, *a resident*
MARTHA LOOMIS, *Herald Loomis's wife*

SETTING

August, 1911. A boardinghouse in Pittsburgh. At right is a kitchen. Two doors open off the kitchen. One leads to the outhouse and SETH *'s workshop. The other to* SETH*'s and* BERTHA*'s bedroom. At left is a parlor. The front door opens into the parlor, which gives access to the stairs leading to the upstairs rooms. There is a small outside playing area.*

THE PLAY

It is August in Pittsburgh, 1911. The sun falls out of heaven like a stone. The fires of the steel mill rage with a combined sense of industry and progress. Barges loaded with coal and iron ore trudge up the river to the mill towns that dot the Monongahela[1] and return with fresh, hard, gleaming steel. The city flexes its muscles. Men throw countless bridges across the rivers, lay roads and carve tunnels through the hills sprouting with houses.

From the deep and the near South the sons and daughters of newly freed African slaves wander into the city. Isolated, cut off from memory, having forgotten the names of the gods and only guessing at their faces, they arrive dazed and stunned, their heart kicking in their chest with a song worth singing. They arrive carrying Bibles and guitars, their pockets lined with dust and fresh hope, marked men and women seeking to scrape from the narrow, crooked cobbles and the fiery blasts of the coke furnace a way of bludgeoning and shaping the malleable parts of themselves into a new identity as free men of definite and sincere worth.

Foreigners in a strange land, they carry as part and parcel of their baggage a long line of separation and dispersement which informs their sensibilities and marks their conduct as they search for ways to reconnect, to reassemble, to give clear and luminous meaning to the song which is both a wail and a whelp of joy.

Act 1

SCENE ONE

The lights come up on the kitchen. BERTHA *busies herself with breakfast preparations.* SETH *stands looking out the window at* BYNUM *in the yard.* SETH *is in his early fifties. Born of Northern free parents, a skilled craftsman, and owner of the boardinghouse, he has a stability that none of the other characters have.* BERTHA *is five years his junior. Married for over twenty-five years, she has learned how to negotiate around* SETH *'s apparent orneriness.*

SETH [*At the window, laughing.*]   If that ain't the damndest thing I seen. Look here, Bertha.
BERTHA   I done seen Bynum out there with them pigeons before.
SETH   Naw . . . naw . . . look at this. That pigeon flopped out of Bynum's hand and he about to have a fit.
     [BERTHA *crosses over to the window.*]
     He down there on his hands and knees behind that bush looking all over for that pigeon and it on the other side of the yard. See it over there?
BERTHA   Come on and get your breakfast and leave that man alone.

1. River in Pennsylvania.

SETH   Look at him . . . he still looking. He ain't seen it yet. All that old mumbo jumbo nonsense. I don't know why I put up with it.

BERTHA   You don't say nothing when he bless the house.

SETH   I just go along with that 'cause of you. You around here sprinkling salt all over the place . . . got pennies lined up across the threshold . . . all that heebie-jeebie stuff. I just put up with that 'cause of you. I don't pay that kind of stuff no mind. And you going down there to the church and wanna come come home and sprinkle salt all over the place.

BERTHA   It don't hurt none. I can't say if it help . . . but it don't hurt none.

SETH   Look at him. He done found that pigeon and now he's talking to it.

BERTHA   These biscuits be ready in a minute.

SETH   He done drew a big circle with that stick and now he's dancing around. I know he'd better not . . .

[SETH *bolts from the window and rushes to the back door.*]

Hey, Bynum! Don't be hopping around stepping in my vegetables.

Hey, Bynum . . . Watch where you stepping!

BERTHA   Seth, leave that man alone.

SETH [*Coming back into the house.*]   I don't care how much he be dancing around . . . just don't be stepping in my vegetables. Man got my garden all messed up now . . . planting them weeds out there . . . burying them pigeons and whatnot.

BERTHA   Bynum don't bother nobody. He ain't even thinking about your vegetables.

SETH   I know he ain't! That's why he out there stepping on them.

BERTHA   What Mr. Johnson say down there?

SETH   I told him if I had the tools I could go out here and find me four or five fellows and open up my own shop instead of working for Mr. Olowski. Get me four or five fellows and teach them how to make pots and pans. One man making ten pots is five men making fifty. He told me he'd think about it.

BERTHA   Well, maybe he'll come to see it your way.

SETH   He wanted me to sign over the house to him. You know what I thought of that idea.

BERTHA   He'll come to see you're right.

SETH   I'm going up and talk to Sam Green. There's more than one way to skin a cat. I'm going up and talk to him. See if he got more sense than Mr. Johnson. I can't get nowhere working for Mr. Olowski and selling Selig five or six pots on the side. I'm going up and see Sam Green. See if he loan me the money.

[SETH *crosses back to the window.*]

Now he got that cup. He done killed that pigeon and now he's putting its blood in that little cup. I believe he drink that blood.

BERTHA   Seth Holly, what is wrong with you this morning? Come on and get your breakfast so you can go to bed. You know Bynum don't be drinking no pigeon blood.

SETH   I don't know what he do.

BERTHA   Well, watch him, then. He's gonna dig a little hole and bury that pigeon. Then he's gonna pray over that blood . . . pour it on top . . . mark out his circle and come on into the house.

SETH   That's what he doing . . . he pouring that blood on top.

BERTHA   When they gonna put you back working daytime? Told me two months ago he was gonna put you back working daytime.

SETH   That's what Mr. Olowski told me. I got to wait till he say when. He tell me what to do. I don't tell him. Drive me crazy to speculate on the man's wishes when he don't know what he want to do himself.

BERTHA   Well, I wish he go ahead and put you back working daytime. This working all hours of the night don't make no sense.

SETH   It don't make no sense for that boy to run out of here and get drunk so they lock him up either.

BERTHA   Who? Who they got locked up for being drunk?

SETH   That boy that's staying upstairs . . . Jeremy. I stopped down there on Logan Street on my way home from work and one of the fellows told me about it. Say he seen it when they arrested him.

BERTHA   I was wondering why I ain't seen him this morning.

SETH   You know I don't put up with that. I told him when he came . . .

[BYNUM *enters from the yard carrying some plants. He is a short, round man in his early sixties. A conjure man, or rootworker,*[2] *he gives the impression of always being in control of everything. Nothing ever bothers him. He seems to be lost in a world of his own making and to swallow any adversity or interference with his grand design.*]

What you doing bringing them weeds in my house? Out there stepping on my vegetables and now wanna carry them weeds in my house.

BYNUM   Morning, Seth. Morning, Sister Bertha.

SETH   Messing up my garden growing them things out there. I ought to go out there and pull up all them weeds.

BERTHA   Some gal was by here to see you this morning, Bynum. You was out there in the yard . . . I told her to come back later.

BYNUM   [*To* SETH]   You look sick. What's the matter, you ain't eating right?

SETH   What if I was sick? You ain't getting near me with none of that stuff.

[BERTHA *sets a plate of biscuits on the table.*]

BYNUM   My . . . my . . . Bertha, your biscuits getting fatter and fatter.

[BYNUM *takes a biscuit and begins to eat.*]

Where Jeremy? I don't see him around this morning. He usually be around riffing and raffing on Saturday morning.

SETH   I know where he at. I know just where he at. They got him down there in the jail. Getting drunk and acting a fool. He down there where he belong with all that foolishness.

BYNUM   Mr. Piney's boys got him, huh? They ain't gonna do nothing but hold on to him for a little while. He's gonna be back here hungrier than a mule directly.

SETH   I don't go for all that carrying on and such. This is a respectable house. I don't have no drunkards or fools around here.

BYNUM   That boy got a lot of country in him. He ain't been up here but two weeks. It's gonna take a while before he can work that country out of him.

SETH   These niggers coming up here with that old backward country style of living. It's hard enough now without all that ignorant kind of acting. Ever since slavery got over with there ain't been nothing but foolish-acting niggers. Word get out they need men to work in the mill and put in these roads . . . and niggers drop everything and head North looking for freedom. They don't know the white fellows looking too. White fellows coming from all over the world. White fellow come over and in six months got more than what I got. But these niggers keep on

2. Adherent of African American spiritual beliefs derived from Africa.

coming. Walking . . . riding . . . carrying their Bibles. That boy done carried a guitar all the way from North Carolina. What he gonna find out? What he gonna do with that guitar? This the city.

[*There is a knock on the door.*]

Niggers coming up here from the backwoods . . . coming up here from the country carrying Bibles and guitars looking for freedom. They got a rude awakening.

[SETH *goes to answer the door.* RUTHERFORD SELIG *enters. About* SETH's *age, he is a thin white man with greasy hair. A peddler, he supplies* SETH *with the raw materials to make pots and pans which he then peddles door to door in the mill towns along the river. He keeps a list of his customers as they move about and is known in the various communities as the People Finder. He carries squares of sheet metal under his arm.*]

Ho! Forgot you was coming today. Come on in.

BYNUM If it ain't Rutherford Selig . . . the People Finder himself.

SELIG What say there, Bynum?

BYNUM I say about my shiny man. You got to tell me something. I done give you my dollar . . . I'm looking to get a report.

SELIG I got eight here, Seth.

SETH [*Taking the sheet metal.*] What is this? What you giving me here? What I'm gonna do with this?

SELIG I need some dustpans. Everybody asking me about dustpans.

SETH Gonna cost you fifteen cents apiece. And ten cents to put a handle on them.

SELIG I'll give you twenty cents apiece with the handles.

SETH Alright. But I ain't gonna give you but fifteen cents for the sheet metal.

SELIG It's twenty-five cents apiece for the metal. That's what we agreed on.

SETH This low-grade sheet metal. They ain't worth but a dime. I'm doing you a favor giving you fifteen cents. You know this metal ain't worth no twenty-five cents. Don't come talking that twenty-five cent stuff to me over no low-grade sheet metal.

SELIG Alright, fifteen cents apiece. Just make me some dustpans out of them.

[SETH *exits with the sheet metal out the back door.*]

BERTHA Sit on down there, Selig. Get you a cup of coffee and a biscuit.

BYNUM Where you coming from this time?

SELIG I been upriver. All along the Monongahela. Past Rankin and all up around Little Washington.[3]

BYNUM Did you find anybody?

SELIG I found Sadie Jackson up in Braddock. Her mother's staying down there in Scotchbottom[4] say she hadn't heard from her and she didn't know where she was at. I found her up in Braddock on Enoch Street. She bought a frying pan from me.

BYNUM You around here finding everybody how come you ain't found my shiny man?

SELIG The only shiny man I saw was the Nigras working on the road gang with the sweat glistening on them.

BYNUM Naw, you'd be able to tell this fellow. He shine like new money.

---

3. Here and throughout there are numerous references to towns and cities in Pennsylvania.

4. Now called Hazelwood.

SELIG   Well, I done told you I can't find nobody without a name.

BERTHA   Here go one of these hot biscuits, Selig.

BYNUM   This fellow don't have no name. I call him John 'cause it was up around Johnstown where I seen him. I ain't even so sure he's one special fellow. That shine could pass on to anybody. He could be anybody shining.

SELIG   Well, what's he look like besides being shiny? There's lots of shiny Nigras.

BYNUM   He's just a man I seen out on the road. He ain't had no special look. Just a man walking toward me on the road. He come up and asked me which way the road went. I told him everything I knew about the road, where it went and all, and he asked me did I have anything to eat 'cause he was hungry. Say he ain't had nothing to eat in three days. Well, I never be out there on the road without a piece of dried meat. Or an orange or an apple. So I give this fellow an orange. He take and eat that orange and told me to come and go along the road a little ways with him, that he had something he wanted to show me. He had a look about him made me wanna go with him, see what he gonna show me.

   We walked on a bit and it's getting kind of far from where I met him when it come up on me all of a sudden, we wasn't going the way he had come from, we was going back my way. Since he said he ain't knew nothing about the road, I asked him about this. He say he had a voice inside him telling him which way to go and if I come and go along with him he was gonna show me the Secret of Life. Quite naturally I followed him. A fellow that's gonna show you the Secret of Life ain't to be taken lightly. We get near this bend in the road . . .

   [SETH enters with an assortment of pots.]

SETH   I got six here, Selig.

SELIG   Wait a minute, Seth. Bynum's telling me about the secret of life. Go ahead, Bynum. I wanna hear this.

   [SETH sets the pots down and exits out the back.]

BYNUM   We get near this bend in the road and he told me to hold out my hands. Then he rubbed them together with his and I looked down and see they got blood on them. Told me to take and rub it all over me . . . say that was a way of cleaning myself. Then we went around the bend in that road. Got around that bend and it seem like all of a sudden we ain't in the same place. Turn around that bend and everything look like it was twice as big as it was. The trees and everything bigger than life! Sparrows big as eagles! I turned around to look at this fellow and he had this light coming out of him. I had to cover up my eyes to keep from being blinded. He shining like new money with that light. He shined until all the light seemed like it seeped out of him and then he was gone and I was by myself in this strange place where everything was bigger than life.

   I wandered around there looking for that road, trying to find my way back from this big place . . . and I looked over and seen my daddy standing there. He was the same size he always was, except for his hands and his mouth. He had a great big old mouth that look like it took up his whole face and his hands were as big as hams. Look like they was too big to carry around. My daddy called me to him. Said he had been thinking about me and it grieved him to see me in the world carrying other people's songs and not having one of my own. Told me he was gonna show me how to find my song. Then he carried me further into this big place until we come to this ocean. Then he showed me something I ain't got words to tell you. But if you stand to witness it, you done seen something there. I stayed in that place awhile and my daddy taught me the meaning of this thing that I had seen and showed me how to find my song. I asked him about the shiny man and he told me he was the One Who Goes Before and Shows the Way. Said there was lots of shiny men and if I ever saw one again before I died then I would know that my song had been accepted and worked its full power in the world and I could lay down and die a happy man. A man who done left his mark on life. On the way people cling to each other out of the truth they find in themselves. Then he showed me how to get back to the road. I came out to where everything was its own size and I had my song. I had the Binding Song. I choose that song because that's what I seen most when I was traveling . . . people walking away and leaving one another. So I takes the power of my song and binds them together.

[SETH *enters from the yard carrying cabbages and tomatoes.*]

Been binding people ever since. That's why they call me Bynum. Just like glue I sticks people together.

SETH   Maybe they ain't supposed to be stuck sometimes. You ever think of that?

BYNUM   Oh, I don't do it lightly. It cost me a piece of myself every time I do. I'm a Binder of What Clings. You got to find out if they cling first. You can't bind what don't cling.

SELIG   Well, how is that the Secret of Life? I thought you said he was gonna show you the secret of life. That's what I'm waiting to find out.

BYNUM   Oh, he showed me alright. But you still got to figure it out. Can't nobody figure it out for you. You got to come to it on your own. That's why I'm looking for the shiny man.

SELIG   Well, I'll keep my eye out for him. What you got there, Seth?

SETH   Here go some cabbage and tomatoes. I got some green beans coming in real nice. I'm gonna take and start me a grapevine out there next year. Butera says he gonna give me a piece of his vine and I'm gonna start that out there.

SELIG   How many of them pots you got?

SETH   I got six. That's six dollars minus eight on top of fifteen for the sheet metal come to a dollar twenty out the six dollars leave me four dollars and eighty cents.

SELIG   [*Counting out the money.*]   There's four dollars and . . . eighty cents.

SETH   How many of them dustpans you want?

SELIG   As many as you can make out them sheets.

SETH   You can use that many? I get to cutting on them sheets figuring how to make them dustpans . . . ain't no telling how many I'm liable to come up with.

SELIG   I can use them and you can make me some more next time.

SETH   Alright, I'm gonna hold you to that, now.

SELIG   Thanks for the biscuit, Bertha.

BERTHA   You know you welcome anytime, Selig.

SETH   Which way you heading?

SELIG   Going down to Wheeling. All through West Virginia there. I'll be back Saturday. They putting in new roads down that way. Makes traveling easier.

SETH That's what I hear. All up around here too. Got a fellow staying here working on that road by the Brady Street Bridge.[5]

SELIG Yeah, it's gonna make traveling real nice. Thanks for the cabbage, Seth. I'll see you on Saturday.

    [SELIG *exits.*]

SETH [*To* BYNUM] Why you wanna start all that nonsense talk with that man? All that shiny man nonsense.

BYNUM You know it ain't no nonsense. Bertha know it ain't no nonsense. I don't know if Selig know or not.

BERTHA Seth, when you get to making them dustpans make me a coffeepot.

SETH What's the matter with your coffee? Ain't nothing wrong with your coffee. Don't she make some good coffee, Bynum?

BYNUM I ain't worried about the coffee. I know she makes some good biscuits.

SETH I ain't studying no coffeepot, woman. You heard me tell the man I was gonna cut as many dustpans as them sheets will make . . . and all of a sudden you want a coffeepot.

BERTHA Man, hush up and go on and make me that coffeepot.

    [JEREMY *enters the front door. About twenty-five, he gives the impression that he has the world in his hand, that he can meet life's challenges head on. He smiles a lot. He is a proficient guitar player, though his spirit has yet to be molded into song.*]

BYNUM I hear Mr. Piney's boys had you.

JEREMY Fined me two dollars for nothing! Ain't done nothing.

SETH I told you when you come on here everybody know my house. Know these is respectable quarters. I don't put up with no foolishness. Everybody know Seth Holly keep a good house. Was my daddy's house. This house been a decent house for a long time.

JEREMY I ain't done nothing, Mr. Seth. I stopped by the Workmen's Club and got me a bottle. Me and Roper Lee from Alabama. Had us a half pint. We was fixing to cut that half in two when they came up on us. Asked us if we was working. We told them we was putting in the road over yonder and that it was our payday. They snatched hold of us to get that two dollars. Me and Roper Lee ain't even had a chance to take a drink when they grabbed us.

SETH I don't go for all that kind of carrying on.

BERTHA Leave the boy alone, Seth. You know the police do that. Figure there's too many people out on the street they take some of them off. You know that.

SETH I ain't gonna have folks talking.

BERTHA Ain't nobody talking nothing. That's all in your head. You want some grits and biscuits, Jeremy?

JEREMY Thank you, Miss Bertha. They didn't give us a thing to eat last night. I'll take one of them big bowls if you don't mind.

    [*There is a knock at the door.* SETH *goes to answer it. Enter* HERALD LOOMIS *and his eleven-year-old daughter,* ZONIA. HERALD LOOMIS *is thirty-two years old. He is at times possessed. A man driven not by the hellhounds that seemingly bay at his heels, but by his search for a world that speaks to something about himself. He is unable to harmonize the*]

---

5. A bridge in Pittsburgh across the Monongahela River.

forces that swirl around him, and seeks to recreate the world into one that contains his image. He wears a hat and a long wool coat.]

LOOMIS Me and my daughter looking for a place to stay, mister. You got a sign say you got rooms.

[SETH *stares at* LOOMIS, *sizing him up.*]

Mister, if you ain't got no rooms we can go somewhere else.

SETH How long you plan on staying?

LOOMIS Don't know. Two weeks or more maybe.

SETH It's two dollars a week for the room. We serve meals twice a day. It's two dollars for room and board. Pay up in advance.

[LOOMIS *reaches into his pocket.*]

It's a dollar extra for the girl.

LOOMIS The girl sleep in the same room.

SETH Well, do she eat off the same plate? We serve meals twice a day. That's a dollar extra for food.

LOOMIS Ain't got no extra dollar. I was planning on asking your missus if she could help out with the cooking and cleaning and whatnot.

SETH Her helping out don't put no food on the table. I need that dollar to buy some food.

LOOMIS I'll give you fifty cents extra. She don't eat much.

SETH Okay . . . but fifty cents don't buy but half a portion.

BERTHA Seth, she can help me out. Let her help me out. I can use some help.

SETH Well, that's two dollars for the week. Pay up in advance. Saturday to Saturday. You wanna stay on then it's two more come Saturday.

[LOOMIS *pays* SETH *the money.*]

BERTHA My name's Bertha. This my husband, Seth. You got Bynum and Jeremy over there.

LOOMIS Ain't nobody else live here?

BERTHA They the only ones live here now. People come and go. They the only ones here now. You want a cup of coffee and a biscuit?

LOOMIS We done ate this morning.

BYNUM Where you coming from, Mister . . . I didn't get your name.

LOOMIS Name's Herald Loomis. This my daughter, Zonia.

BYNUM Where you coming from?

LOOMIS Come from all over. Whicheverway the road take us that's the way we go.

JEREMY If you looking for a job, I'm working putting in that road down there by the bridge. They can't get enough mens. Always looking to take somebody on.

LOOMIS I'm looking for a woman named Martha Loomis. That's my wife. Got married legal with the papers and all.

SETH I don't know nobody named Loomis. I know some Marthas but I don't know no Loomis.

BYNUM You got to see Rutherford Selig if you wanna find somebody. Selig's the People Finder. Rutherford Selig's a first-class People Finder.

JEREMY What she look like? Maybe I seen her.

LOOMIS She a brownskin woman. Got long pretty hair. About five feet from the ground.

JEREMY I don't know. I might have seen her.

BYNUM You got to see Rutherford Selig. You give him one dollar to get her name on his list . . . and after she get her name on his list Rutherford

Selig will go right on out there and find her. I got him looking for somebody for me.

LOOMIS You say he find people. How you find him?

BYNUM You just missed him. He's gone downriver now. You got to wait till Saturday. He's gone downriver with his pots and pans. He come to see Seth on Saturdays. You got to wait till then.

SETH Come on, I'll show you to your room.

[SETH, LOOMIS, and ZONIA exit up the stairs.]

JEREMY Miss Bertha, I'll take that biscuit you was gonna give that fellow, if you don't mind. Say, Mr. Bynum, they got somebody like that around here sure enough? Somebody that find people?

BYNUM Rutherford Selig. He go around selling pots and pans and every house he come to he write down the name and address of whoever lives there. So if you looking for somebody, quite naturally you go and see him . . . 'cause he's the only one who know where everybody live at.

JEREMY I ought to have him look for this old gal I used to know. It be nice to see her again.

BERTHA [Giving JEREMY a biscuit.] Jeremy, today's the day for you to pull them sheets off the bed and set them outside your door. I'll set you out some clean ones.

BYNUM Mr. Piney's boys done ruined your good time last night, Jeremy . . . what you planning for tonight?

JEREMY They got me scared to go out, Mr. Bynum. They might grab me again.

BYNUM You ought to take your guitar and go down to Seefus. Seefus got a gambling place down there on Wylie Avenue.[6] You ought to take your guitar and go down there. They got guitar contest down there.

JEREMY I don't play no contest, Mr. Bynum. Had one of them white fellows cure me of that. I ain't been nowhere near a contest since.

BYNUM White fellow beat you playing guitar?

JEREMY Naw, he ain't beat me. I was sitting at home just fixing to sit down and eat when somebody come up to my house and got me. Told me there's a white fellow say he was gonna give a prize to the best guitar player he could find. I take up my guitar and go down there and somebody had gone up and got Bobo Smith and brought him down there. Him and another fellow called Hooter. Old Hooter couldn't play no guitar, he do more hollering than playing, but Bobo could go at it awhile.

This fellow standing there say he the one that was gonna give the prize and me and Bobo started playing for him. Bobo play something and then I'd try to play something better than what he played. Old Hooter, he just holler and bang at the guitar. Man was the worst guitar player I ever seen. So me and Bobo played and after a while I seen where he was getting the attention of this white fellow. He'd play something and while he was playing it he be slapping on the side of the guitar, and that made it sound like he was playing more than he was. So I started doing it too. White fellow ain't knew no difference. He ain't knew as much about guitar playing as Hooter did. After we play awhile, the white fellow called us to him and said he couldn't make up his mind, say all three of us was the best guitar player and we'd have to split the prize between us. Then he give us twenty-five cents. That's eight cents apiece and a penny on the side. That cured me of playing contest to this day.

BYNUM   Seefus ain't like that. Seefus give a whole dollar and a drink of whiskey.

JEREMY   What night they be down there?

BYNUM   Be down there every night. Music don't know no certain night.

BERTHA   You go down to Seefus with them people and you liable to end up in a raid and go to jail sure enough. I don't know why Bynum tell you that.

BYNUM   That's where the music at. That's where the people at. The people down there making music and enjoying themselves. Some things is worth taking the chance going to jail about.

BERTHA   Jeremy ain't got no business going down there.

JEREMY   They got some women down there, Mr. Bynum?

BYNUM   Oh, they got women down there, sure. They got women everywhere. Women be where the men is so they can find each other.

JEREMY   Some of them old gals come out there where we be putting in that road. Hanging around there trying to snatch somebody.

BYNUM   How come some of them ain't snatched hold of you?

JEREMY   I don't want them kind. Them desperate kind. Ain't nothing worse than a desperate woman. Tell them you gonna leave them and they get to crying and carrying on. That just make you want to get away quicker. They get to cutting up your clothes and things trying to keep you staying. Desperate women ain't nothing but trouble for a man.

[SETH enters from the stairs.]

SETH   Something ain't setting right with that fellow.

BERTHA   What's wrong with him? What he say?

SETH   I take him up there and try to talk to him and he ain't for no talking. Say he been traveling . . . coming over from Ohio. Say he a deacon[7] in the church. Say he looking for Martha Pentecost. Talking about that's his wife.

BERTHA   How you know it's the same Martha? Could be talking about anybody. Lots of people named Martha.

SETH   You see that little girl? I didn't hook it up till he said it, but that little girl look just like her. Ask Bynum. [To BYNUM] Bynum. Don't that little girl look just like Martha Pentecost?

BERTHA   I still say he could be talking about anybody.

SETH   The way he described her wasn't no doubt about who he was talking about. Described her right down to her toes.

BERTHA   What did you tell him?

SETH   I ain't told him nothing. The way that fellow look I wasn't gonna tell him nothing. I don't know what he looking for her for.

BERTHA   What else he have to say?

SETH   I told you he wasn't for no talking. I told him where the outhouse was and to keep that gal off the front porch and out of my garden. He asked if you'd mind setting a hot tub for the gal and that was about the gist of it.

BERTHA   Well, I wouldn't let it worry me if I was you. Come on get your sleep.

BYNUM   He says he looking for Martha and he a deacon in the church.

SETH   That's what he say. Do he look like a deacon to you?

BERTHA   He might be, you don't know. Bynum ain't got no special say on whether he a deacon or not.

7. Church officer.

SETH   Well, if he the deacon I'd sure like to see the preacher.

BERTHA   Come on get your sleep. Jeremy, don't forget to set them sheets outside the door like I told you.

[BERTHA *exits into the bedroom.*]

SETH   Something ain't setting right with that fellow, Bynum. He's one of them mean-looking niggers look like he done killed somebody gambling over a quarter.

BYNUM   He ain't no gambler. Gamblers wear nice shoes. This fellow got on clodhoppers.[8] He been out there walking up and down them roads.

[ZONIA *enters from the stairs and looks around.*]

BYNUM   You looking for the back door, sugar? There it is. You can go out there and play. It's alright.

SETH   [*Showing her the door.*] You can go out there and play. Just don't get in my garden. And don't go messing around in my workshed.

[SETH *exits into the bedroom. There is a knock on the door.*]

JEREMY   Somebody at the door.

[JEREMY *goes to answer the door. Enter* MATTIE CAMPBELL. *She is a young woman of twenty-six whose attractiveness is hidden under the weight and concerns of a dissatisfied life. She is a woman in an honest search for love and companionship. She had suffered many defeats in her search, and though not always uncompromising, still believes in the possibility of love.*]

MATTIE   I'm looking for a man named Bynum. Lady told me to come back later.

JEREMY   Sure, he here. Mr. Bynum, somebody here to see you.

BYNUM   Come to see me, huh?

MATTIE   Are you the man they call Bynum? The man folks say can fix things?

BYNUM   Depend on what need fixing. I can't make no promises. But I got a powerful song in some matters.

MATTIE   Can you fix it so my man come back to me?

BYNUM   Come on in . . . have a sit down.

MATTIE   You got to help me. I don't know what else to do.

BYNUM   Depend on how all the circumstances of the thing come together. How all the pieces fit.

MATTIE   I done everything I knowed how to do. You got to make him come back to me.

BYNUM   It ain't nothing to make somebody come back. I can fix it so he can't stand to be away from you. I got my roots and powders, I can fix it so wherever he's at this thing will come up on him and he won't be able to sleep for seeing your face. Won't be able to eat for thinking of you.

MATTIE   That's what I want. Make him come back.

BYNUM   The roots is a powerful thing. I can fix it so one day he'll walk out his front door . . . won't be thinking of nothing. He won't know what it is. All he knows is that a powerful dissatisfaction done set in his bones and can't nothing he do make him feel satisfied. He'll set his foot down on the road and the wind in the trees be talking to him and everywhere he step on the road, that road'll give back your name and something will pull him right up to your doorstep. Now, I can do that. I can take my roots and fix that easy. But maybe he ain't supposed to come back. And if he ain't supposed to come back . . . then he'll be in your bed one

8. Country shoes; boots.

morning and it'll come up on him that he's in the wrong place. That he's lost outside of time from his place that he's supposed to be in. Then both of you be lost and trapped outside of life and ain't no way for you to get back into it. 'Cause you lost from yourselves and where the places come together, where you're supposed to be alive, your heart kicking in your chest with a song worth singing.

MATTIE Make him come back to me. Make his feet say my name on the road. I don't care what happens. Make him come back.

BYNUM What's your man's name?

MATTIE He go by Jack Carper. He was born in Alabama then he come to West Texas and find me and we come here. Been here three years before he left. Say I had a curse prayer on me and he started walking down the road and ain't never come back. Somebody told me, say you can fix things like that.

BYNUM He just got up one day, set his feet on the road, and walked away?

MATTIE You got to make him come back, mister.

BYNUM Did he say goodbye?

MATTIE Ain't said nothing. Just started walking. I could see where he disappeared. Didn't look back. Just keep walking. Can't you fix it so he come back? I ain't got no curse prayer on me. I know I ain't.

BYNUM What made him say you had a curse prayer on you?

MATTIE 'Cause the babies died. Me and Jack had two babies. Two little babies that ain't lived two months before they died. He say it's because somebody cursed me not to have babies.

BYNUM He ain't bound to you if the babies died. Look like somebody trying to keep you from being bound up and he's gone on back to whoever it is 'cause he's already bound up to her. Ain't nothing to be done. Somebody else done got a powerful hand in it and ain't nothing to be done to break it. You got to let him go find where he's supposed to be in the world.

MATTIE Jack done gone off and you telling me to forget about him. All my life I been looking for somebody to stop and stay with me. I done already got too many things to forget about. I take Jack Carper's hand and it feel so rough and strong. Seem like he's the strongest man in the world the way he hold me. Like he's bigger than the whole world and can't nothing bad get to me. Even when he act mean sometimes he still make everything seem okay with the world. Like there's part of it that belongs just to you. Now you telling me to forget about him?

BYNUM Jack Carper gone off to where he belong. There's somebody searching for your doorstep right now. Ain't no need you fretting over Jack Carper. Right now he's a strong thought in your mind. But every time you catch yourself fretting over Jack Carper you push that thought away. You push it out your mind and that thought will get weaker and weaker till you wake up one morning and you won't even be able to call him up on your mind.

[BYNUM *gives her a small cloth packet.*]

Take this and sleep with it under your pillow and it'll bring good luck to you. Draw it to you like a magnet. It won't be long before you forget all about Jack Carper.

MATTIE How much . . . do I owe you?

BYNUM Whatever you got there . . . that'll be alright.

[MATTIE *hands* BYNUM *two quarters. She crosses to the door.*]

You sleep with that under your pillow and you'll be alright.

[MATTIE *opens the door to exit and* JEREMY *crosses over to her.* BYNUM *overhears the first part of their conversation, then exits out the back.*]

JEREMY   I overheard what you told Mr. Bynum. Had me an old gal did that to me. Woke up one morning and she was gone. Just took off to parts unknown. I woke up that morning and the only thing I could do was look around for my shoes. I woke up and got out of there. Found my shoes and took off. That's the only thing I could think of to do.

MATTIE   She ain't said nothing?

JEREMY   I just looked around for my shoes and got out of there.

MATTIE   Jack ain't said nothing either. He just walked off.

JEREMY   Some mens do that. Womens too. I ain't gone off looking for her. I just let her go. Figure she had a time to come to herself. Wasn't no use of me standing in the way. Where you from?

MATTIE   Texas. I was born in Georgia but I went to Texas with my mama. She dead now. Was picking peaches and fell dead away. I come up here with Jack Carper.

JEREMY   I'm from North Carolina. Down around Raleigh where they got all that tobacco. Been up here about two weeks. I likes it fine except I still got to find me a woman. You got a nice look to you. Look like you have mens standing in your door. Is you got mens standing in your door to get a look at you?

MATTIE   I ain't got nobody since Jack left.

JEREMY   A woman like you need a man. Maybe you let me be your man. I got a nice way with the women. That's what they tell me.

MATTIE   I don't know. Maybe Jack's coming back.

JEREMY   I'll be your man till he come. A woman can't be by her lonesome. Let me be your man till he come.

MATTIE   I just can't go through life piecing myself out to different mens. I need a man who wants to stay with me.

JEREMY   I can't say what's gonna happen. Maybe I'll be the man. I don't know. You wanna go along the road a little ways with me?

MATTIE   I don't know. Seem like life say it's gonna be one thing and end up being another. I'm tired of going from man to man.

JEREMY   Life is like you got to take a chance. Everybody got to take a chance. Can't nobody say what's gonna be. Come on . . . take a chance with me and see what the year bring. Maybe you let me come and see you. Where you staying?

MATTIE   I got me a room up on Bedford. Me and Jack had a room together.

JEREMY   What's the address? I'll come by and get you tonight and we can go down to Seefus. I'm going down there and play my guitar.

MATTIE   You play guitar?

JEREMY   I play guitar like I'm born to it.

MATTIE   I live at 1727 Bedford Avenue. I'm gonna find out if you can play guitar like you say.

JEREMY   I plays it sugar, and that ain't all I do. I got a ten-pound hammer and I knows how to drive it down. Good god . . . you ought to hear my hammer ring!

MATTIE   Go on with that kind of talk, now. If you gonna come by and get me I got to get home and straighten up for you.

JEREMY   I'll be by at eight o'clock. How's eight o'clock? I'm gonna make you forget all about Jack Carper.

MATTIE   Go on, now. I got to get home and fix up for you.

JEREMY Eight o'clock, sugar.

[*The lights go down in the parlor and come up on the yard outside.*
ZONIA *is singing and playing a game.*]

ZONIA

>I went downtown
>To get my grip
>I came back home
>Just a pullin' the skiff[9]
>
>I went upstairs
>To make my bed
>I made a mistake
>And I bumped my head
>Just a pullin' the skiff
>
>I went downstairs
>To milk the cow
>I made a mistake
>And I milked the sow
>Just a pullin' the skiff
>
>Tomorrow, tomorrow
>Tomorrow never comes
>The marrow the marrow
>The marrow in the bone.

[REUBEN *enters.*]

REUBEN Hi.

ZONIA Hi.

REUBEN What's your name?

ZONIA Zonia.

REUBEN What kind of name is that?

ZONIA It's what my daddy named me.

REUBEN My name's Reuben. You staying in Mr. Seth's house?

ZONIA Yeah.

REUBEN That your daddy I seen you with this morning?

ZONIA I don't know. Who you see me with?

REUBEN I saw you with some man had on a great big old coat. And you
was walking up to Mr. Seth's house. Had on a hat too.

ZONIA Yeah, that's my daddy.

REUBEN You like Mr. Seth?

ZONIA I ain't see him much.

REUBEN My grandpap say he a great big old windbag. How come you living in Mr. Seth's house? Don't you have no house?

ZONIA We going to find my mother.

REUBEN Where she at?

ZONIA I don't know. We got to find her. We just go all over.

REUBEN Why you got to find her? What happened to her?

ZONIA She ran away.

REUBEN Why she run away?

ZONIA I don't know. My daddy say some man named Joe Turner did
something bad to him once and that made her run away.

9. African American game song.

REUBEN   Maybe she coming back and you don't have to go looking for her.

ZONIA   We ain't there no more.

REUBEN   She could have come back when you wasn't there.

ZONIA   My daddy said she ran off and left us so we going looking for her.

REUBEN   What he gonna do when he find her?

ZONIA   He didn't say. He just say he got to find her.

REUBEN   Your daddy say how long you staying in Mr. Seth's house?

ZONIA   He don't say much. But he never stay too long nowhere. He say we got to keep moving till we find her.

REUBEN   Ain't no kids hardly live around here. I had me a friend but he died. He was the best friend I ever had. Me and Eugene used to keep secrets. I still got his pigeons. He told me to let them go when he died. He say, "Reuben, promise me when I die you'll let my pigeons go." But I keep them to remember him by. I ain't never gonna let them go. Even when I get to be grown up. I'm just always gonna have Eugene's pigeons.
[*Pause.*]
Mr. Bynum a conjure man. My grandpap scared of him. He don't like me to come over here too much. I'm scared of him too. My grandpap told me not to let him get close enough to where he can reach out his hand and touch me.

ZONIA   He don't seem scary to me.

REUBEN   He buys pigeons from me . . . and if you get up early in the morning you can see him out in the yard doing something with them pigeons. My grandpap say he kill them. I sold him one yesterday. I don't know what he do with it. I just hope he don't spook me up.[1]

ZONIA   Why you sell him pigeons if he's gonna spook you up?

REUBEN   I just do like Eugene do. He used to sell Mr. Bynum pigeons. That's how he got to collecting them to sell to Mr. Bynum. Sometime he give me a nickel and sometime he give me a whole dime.
[LOOMIS *enters from the house.*]

LOOMIS   Zonia!

ZONIA   Sir?

LOOMIS   What you doing?

ZONIA   Nothing.

LOOMIS   You stay around this house, you hear? I don't want you wandering off nowhere.

ZONIA   I ain't wandering off nowhere.

LOOMIS   Miss Bertha set that hot tub and you getting a good scrubbing. Get scrubbed up good. You ain't been scrubbing.

ZONIA   I been scrubbing.

LOOMIS   Look at you. You growing too fast. Your bones getting bigger everyday. I don't want you getting grown on me. Don't you get grown on me too soon. We gonna find your mamma. She around here somewhere. I can smell her. You stay on around this house now. Don't you go nowhere.

ZONIA   Yes, sir.
[LOOMIS *exits into the house.*]

REUBEN   Wow, your daddy's scary!

ZONIA   He is not! I don't know what you talking about.

REUBEN   He got them mean-looking eyes!

---

1. I.e., work conjure against or put a curse on.

ZONIA   My daddy ain't got no mean-looking eyes!

REUBEN   Aw, girl, I was just messing with you. You wanna go see Eugene's pigeons? Got a great big coop out the back of my house. Come on, I'll show you.

[RUEBEN *and* ZONIA *exit as the lights go down.*]

SCENE TWO

It is Saturday morning, one week later. The lights come up on the kitchen. BERTHA *is at the stove preparing breakfast while* SETH *sits at the table.*

SETH   Something ain't right about that fellow. I been watching him all week. Something ain't right, I'm telling you.

BERTHA   Seth Holly, why don't you hush up about that man this morning?

SETH   I don't like the way he stare at everybody. Don't look at you natural like. He just be staring at you. Like he trying to figure out something about you. Did you see him when he come back in here?

BERTHA   That man ain't thinking about you.

SETH   He don't work nowhere. Just go out and come back. Go out and come back.

BERTHA   As long as you get your boarding money it ain't your cause about what he do. He don't bother nobody.

SETH   Just go out and come back. Going around asking everybody about Martha. Like Henry Allen seen him down at the church last night.

BERTHA   The man's allowed to go to church if he want. He say he a deacon. Ain't nothing wrong about him going to church.

SETH   I ain't talking about him going to church. I'm talking about him hanging around *outside* the church.

BERTHA   Henry Allen say that?

SETH   Say he be standing around outside the church. Like he be watching it.

BERTHA   What on earth he wanna be watching the church for, I wonder?

SETH   That's what I'm trying to figure out. Looks like he fixing to rob it.

BERTHA   Seth, now do he look like the kind that would rob the church?

SETH   I ain't saying that. I ain't saying how he look. It's how he do. Anybody liable to do anything as far as I'm concerned. I ain't never thought about how no church robbers look . . . but now that you mention it, I don't see where they look no different than how he look.

BERTHA   Herald Loomis ain't the kind of man who would rob no church.

SETH   I ain't even so sure that's his name.

BERTHA   Why the man got to lie about his name?

SETH   Anybody can tell anybody anything about what their name is. That's what you call him . . . Herald Loomis. His name is liable to be anything.

BERTHA   Well, until he tell me different that's what I'm gonna call him. You just getting yourself all worked up about the man for nothing.

SETH   Talking about Loomis: Martha's name wasn't no Loomis nothing. Martha's name is Pentecost.

BERTHA   How you so sure that's her right name? Maybe she changed it.

SETH   Martha's a good Christian woman. This fellow here look like he owe the devil a day's work and he's trying to figure out how he gonna pay him. Martha ain't had a speck of distrust about her the whole time she was living here. They moved the church out there to Rankin and I was sorry to see her go.

BERTHA   That's why he be hanging around the church. He looking for her.

SETH   If he looking for her, why don't he go inside and ask? What he doing hanging around outside the church acting sneakly like?

[BYNUM *enters from the yard.*]

BYNUM   Morning, Seth. Morning, Sister Bertha.

[BYNUM *continues through the kitchen and exits up the stairs.*]

BERTHA   That's who you should be asking the questions. He been out there in that yard all morning. He was out there before the sun come up. He didn't even come in for breakfast. I don't know what he's doing. He had three of them pigeons line up out there. He dance around till he get tired. He sit down awhile then get up and dance some more. He come through here a little while ago looking like he was mad at the world.

SETH   I don't pay Bynum no mind. He don't spook me up with all that stuff.

BERTHA   That's how Martha come to be living here. She come to see Bynum. She come to see him when she first left from down South.

SETH   Martha was living here before Bynum. She ain't come on here when she first left from down there. She come on here after she went back to get her little girl. That's when she come on here.

BERTHA   Well, where was Bynum? He was here when she came.

SETH   Bynum ain't come till after her. That boy Hiram was staying up there in Bynum's room.

BERTHA   Well, how long Bynum been here?

SETH   Bynum ain't been here no longer than three years. That's what I'm trying to tell you. Martha was staying up there and sewing and cleaning for Doc Goldblum when Bynum came. This the longest he ever been in one place.

BERTHA   How you know how long the man been in one place?

SETH   I know Bynum. Bynum ain't no mystery to me. I done seen a hundred niggers like him. He's one of them fellows never could stay in one place. He was wandering all around the country till he got old and settled here. The only thing different about Bynum is he bring all this heebie-geebie stuff with him.

BERTHA   I still say he was staying here when she came. That's why she came . . . to see him.

SETH   You can say what you want. I know the facts of it. She come on here four years ago all heartbroken 'cause she couldn't find her little girl. And Bynum wasn't nowhere around. She got mixed up in that old heebie-geebie nonsense with him after he came.

BERTHA   Well, if she came on before Bynum I don't know where she stayed. Cause she stayed up there in Hiram's room. Hiram couldn't get along with Bynum and left out of here owing you two dollars. Now, I know you ain't forgot about that!

SETH   Sure did! You know Hiram ain't paid me that two dollars yet. So that's why he be ducking and hiding when he see me down on Logan Street. You right. Martha did come on after Bynum. I forgot that's why Hiram left.

BERTHA   Him and Bynum never could see eye to eye. They always rubbed each other the wrong way. Hiram got to thinking that Bynum was trying to put a fix on him and he moved out. Martha came to see Bynum and ended up taking Hiram's room. Now, I know what I'm talking about. She stayed on here three years till they moved the church.

SETH   She out there in Rankin now. I know where she at. I know where they moved the church to. She right out there in Rankin in that place used to be shoe store. Used to be Wolf's shoe store. They moved to a bigger place and they put that church in there. I know where she at. I know just where she at.

BERTHA Why don't you tell the man? You see he looking for her.

SETH I ain't gonna tell that man where that woman is! What I wanna do that for? I don't know nothing about that man. I don't know why he looking for her. He might wanna do her a harm. I ain't gonna carry that on my hands. He looking for her, he gonna have to find her for himself. I ain't gonna help him. Now, if he had come and presented himself as a gentleman—the way Martha Pentecost's husband would have done— then I would have told him. But I ain't gonna tell this old wild-eyed mean-looking nigger nothing!

BERTHA Well, why don't you get a ride with Selig and go up there and tell her where he is? See if she wanna see him. If that's her little girl . . . you say Martha was looking for her.

SETH You know me, Bertha. I don't get mixed up in nobody's business.

[BYNUM enters from the stairs.]

BYNUM Morning, Seth. Morning, Bertha. Can I still get some breakfast? Mr. Loomis been down here this morning?

SETH He done gone out and come back. He up there now. Left out of here early this morning wearing that coat. Hot as it is, the man wanna walk around wearing a big old heavy coat. He come back in here paid me for another week, sat down there waiting on Selig. Got tired of waiting and went on back upstairs.

BYNUM Where's the little girl?

SETH She out there in the front. Had to chase her and that Reuben off the front porch. She out there somewhere.

BYNUM Look like if Martha was around here he would have found her by now. My guess is she ain't in the city.

SETH She ain't! I know where she at. I know just where she at. But I ain't gonna tell him. Not the way he look.

BERTHA Here go your coffee, Bynum.

BYNUM He says he gonna get Selig to find her for him.

SETH Selig can't find her. He talk all that . . . but unless he get lucky and knock on her door he can't find her. That's the only way he find anybody. He got to get lucky. But I know just where she at.

BERTHA Here go some biscuits, Bynum.

BYNUM What else you got over there, Sister Bertha? You got some grits and gravy over there? I could go for some of that this morning.

BERTHA [Sets a bowl on the table.] Seth, come on and help me turn this mattress over. Come on.

SETH Something ain't right with that fellow, Bynum. I don't like the way he stare at everybody.

BYNUM Mr. Loomis alright, Seth. He just a man got something on his mind. He just got a straightforward mind, that's all.

SETH What's that fellow that they had around here? Moses, that's Moses Houser. Man went crazy and jumped off the Brady Street Bridge. I told you when I seen him something wasn't right about him. And I'm telling you about this fellow now.

[There is a knock on the door. SETH goes to answer it. Enter RUTHERFORD SELIG.]

Ho! Come on in, Selig.

BYNUM   If it ain't the People Finder himself.

SELIG   Bynum, before you start . . . I ain't seen no shiny man now.

BYNUM   Who said anything about that? I ain't said nothing about that. I just called you a first-class People Finder.

SELIG   How many dustpans you get out of that sheet metal, Seth?

SETH   You walked by them on your way in. They sitting out there on the porch. Got twenty-eight. Got four out of each sheet and made Bertha a coffeepot out the other one. They a little small but they got nice handles.

SELIG   That was twenty cents apiece, right? That's what we agreed on.

SETH   That's five dollars and sixty cents. Twenty on top of twenty-eight. How many sheets you bring me?

SELIG   I got eight out there. That's a dollar twenty makes me owe you . . .

SETH   Four dollars and forty cents.

SELIG   [*Paying him.*]   Go on and make me some dustpans. I can use all you can make.

   [LOOMIS *enters from the stairs.*]

LOOMIS   I been watching for you. He say you find people.

BYNUM   Mr. Loomis here wants you to find his wife.

LOOMIS   He say you find people. Find her for me.

SELIG   Well, let see here . . . find somebody, is it?

   [SELIG *rummages through his pockets. He has several notebooks and he is searching for the right one.*]

   Alright now . . . what's the name?

LOOMIS   Martha Loomis. She my wife. Got married legal with the paper and all.

SELIG   [*Writing.*]   Martha . . . Loomis. How tall is she?

LOOMIS   She five feet from the ground.

SELIG   Five feet . . . tall. Young or old?

LOOMIS   She a young woman. Got long pretty hair.

SELIG   Young . . . long . . . pretty . . . hair. Where did you last see her?

LOOMIS   Tennessee. Nearby Memphis.

SELIG   When was that?

LOOMIS   Nineteen hundred and one.

SELIG   Nineteen . . . hundred and one. I'll tell you, mister . . . you better off without them. Now you take me . . . old Rutherford Selig could tell you a thing or two about these women. I ain't met one yet I could understand. Now, you take Sally out there. That's all a man needs is a good horse. I say giddup and she go. Say whoa and she stop. I feed her some oats and she carry me wherever I want to go. Ain't had a speck of trouble out of her since I had her. Now, I been married. A long time ago down in Kentucky. I got up one morning and I saw this look on my wife's face. Like way down deep inside her she was wishing I was dead. I walked around that morning and every time I looked at her she had that look on her face. It seem like she knew I could see it on her. Every time I looked at her I got smaller and smaller. Well, I wasn't gonna stay around there and just shrink away. I walked out on the porch and closed the door behind me. When I closed the door she locked it. I went out and bought me a horse. And I ain't been without one since! Martha Loomis, huh? Well, now I'll do the best I can do. That's one dollar.

LOOMIS   [*Holding out dollar suspiciously.*]   How you find her?

SELIG   Well now, it ain't no easy job like you think. You can't just go out there and find them like that. There's a lot of little tricks to it. It's not an easy job keeping up with you Nigras the way you move about so. Now you take this woman you looking for . . . this Martha Loomis. She could be anywhere. Time I find her, if you don't keep your eye on her, she'll be gone off someplace else. You'll be thinking she over here and she'll be over there. But like I say there's a lot of little tricks to it.

LOOMIS   You say you find her.

SELIG   I can't promise anything but we been finders in my family for a long time. Bringers and finders. My great-granddaddy used to bring Nigras across the ocean on ships. That's wasn't no easy job either. Sometimes the winds would blow so hard you'd think the hand of God was set against the sails. But it set him well in pay and he settled in this new land and found him a wife of good Christian charity with a mind for kids and the like and well . . . here I am, Rutherford Selig. You're in good hands, mister. Me and my daddy have found plenty Nigras. My daddy, rest his soul, used to find runaway slaves for the plantation bosses. He was the best there was at it. Jonas B. Selig. Had him a reputation stretched clean across the country. After Abraham Lincoln give you all Nigras your freedom papers and with you all looking all over for each other . . . we started finding Nigras for Nigras. Of course, it don't pay as much. But the People Finding business ain't so bad.

LOOMIS   [Hands him the dollar.]   Find her. Martha Loomis. Find her for me.

SELIG   Like I say, I can't promise you anything. I'm going back upriver, and if she's around in them parts I'll find her for you. But I can't promise you anything.

LOOMIS   When you coming back?

SELIG   I'll be back on Saturday. I come and see Seth to pick up my order on Saturday.

BYNUM   You going upriver, huh? You going up around my way. I used to go all up through there. Blawknox . . . Clairton. Used to go up to Rankin and take that first righthand road. I wore many a pair of shoes out walking around that way. You'd have thought I was a missionary spreading the gospel the way I wandered all around them parts.

SELIG   Okay, Bynum. See you on Saturday.

SETH   Here, let me walk out with you. Help you with them dustpans.

   [SETH and SELIG exit out the back. BERTHA enters from the stairs carrying a bundle of sheets.]

BYNUM   Herald Loomis got the People Finder looking for Martha.

BERTHA   You can call him a People Finder if you want to. I know Rutherford Selig carries people away too. He done carried a whole bunch of them away from here. Folks plan on leaving plan by Selig's timing. They wait till he get ready to go, then they hitch a ride on his wagon. Then he charge folks a dollar to tell them where he took them. Now, that's the truth of Rutherford Selig. This old People Finding business is for the birds. He ain't never found nobody he ain't took away. Herald Loomis, you just wasted your dollar.

   [BERTHA exits into the bedroom.]

LOOMIS   He say he find her. He say he find her by Saturday. I'm gonna wait till Saturday.

   [The lights fade to black.]

SCENE THREE

It is Sunday morning, the next day. The lights come up on the kitchen. SETH *sits talking to* BYNUM *The breakfast dishes have been cleared away.*

SETH They can't see that. Neither one of them can see that. Now, how much sense it take to see that? All you got to do is be able to count. One man making ten pots is five men making fifty pots. But they can't see that. Asked where I'm gonna get my five men. Hell, I can teach anybody how to make a pot. I can teach you. I can take you out there and get you started right now. Inside of two weeks you'd know how to make a pot. All you got to do is want to do it. I can get five men. I ain't worried about getting no five men.

BERTHA [*Calls from the bedroom.*] Seth. Come on and get ready now. Reverend Gates ain't gonna be holding up his sermon 'cause you sitting out there talking.

SETH Now, you take the boy, Jeremy. What he gonna do after he put in that road? He can't do nothing but go put in another one somewhere. Now, if he let me show him how to make some pots and pans . . . then he'd have something can't nobody take away from him. After a while he could get his own tools and go off somewhere and make his own pots and pans. Find him somebody to sell them to. Now, Selig can't make no pots and pans. He can sell them but he can't make them. I get me five men with some tools and we'd make him so many pots and pans he'd have to open up a store somewhere. But they can't see that. Neither Mr. Cohen nor Sam Green.

BERTHA [*Calls from the bedroom.*] Seth . . . time be wasting. Best be getting on.

SETH I'm coming, woman! [*To* BYNUM] Want me to sign over the house to borrow five hundred dollars. I ain't that big a fool. That's all I got. Sign it over to them and then I won't have nothing.

[JEREMY *enters waving a dollar and carrying his guitar.*]

JEREMY Look here, Mr. Bynum . . . won me another dollar last night down at Seefus! Me and that Mattie Campbell went down there again and I played contest. Ain't no guitar players down there. Wasn't even no contest. Say, Mr. Seth, I asked Mattie Campbell if she wanna come by and have Sunday dinner with us. Get some fried chicken.

SETH It's gonna cost you twenty-five cents.

JEREMY That's alright. I got a whole dollar here. Say Mr. Seth . . . me and Mattie Campbell talked it over last night and she gonna move in with me. If that's alright with you.

SETH Your business is your business . . . but it's gonna cost her a dollar a week for her board. I can't be feeding nobody for free.

JEREMY Oh, she know that, Mr. Seth. That's what I told her, say she'd have to pay for her meals.

SETH You say you got a whole dollar there . . . turn loose that twenty-five cents.

JEREMY Suppose she move in today, then that make seventy-five cents more, so I'll give you the whole dollar for her now till she gets here.

[SETH *pockets the money and exits into the bedroom.*]

BYNUM So you and that Mattie Campbell gonna take up together?

JEREMY   I told her she don't need to be by her lonesome, Mr. Bynum. Don't make no sense for both of us to be by our lonesome. So she gonna move in with me.

BYNUM   Sometimes you got to be where you supposed to be. Sometimes you can get all mixed up in life and come to the wrong place.

JEREMY   That's just what I told her, Mr. Bynum. It don't make no sense for her to be all mixed up and lonesome. May as well come here and be with me. She a fine woman too. Got them long legs. Knows how to treat a fellow too. Treat you like you wanna be treated.

BYNUM   You just can't look at it like that. You got to look at the whole thing. Now, you take a fellow go out there, grab hold to a woman and think he got something 'cause she sweet and soft to the touch. Alright. Touching's part of life. It's in the world like everything else. Touching's nice. It feels good. But you can lay your hand upside a horse or a cat, and that feels good too. What's the difference? When you grab hold to a woman, you got something there. You got a whole world there. You got a way of life kicking up under your hand. That woman can take and make you feel like something. I ain't just talking about in the way of jumping off into bed together and rolling around with each other. Anybody can do that. When you grab hold to that woman and look at the whole thing and see what you got . . . why, she can take and make something out of you. Your mother was a woman. That's enough right there to show you what a woman is. Enough to show you what she can do. She made something out of you. Taught you converse, and all about how to take care of yourself, how to see where you at and where you going tomorrow, how to look out to see what's coming in the way of eating, and what to do with yourself when you get lonesome. That's a mighty thing she did. But you just can't look at a woman to jump off into bed with her. That's a foolish thing to ignore a woman like that.

JEREMY   Oh, I ain't ignoring her, Mr. Bynum. It's hard to ignore a woman got legs like she got.

BYNUM   Alright. Let's try it this way. Now, you take a ship. Be out there on the water traveling about. You out there on that ship sailing to and from. And then you see some land. Just like you see a woman walking down the street. You see that land and it don't look like nothing but a line out there on the horizon. That's all it is when you first see it. A line that cross your path out there on the horizon. Now, a smart man know when he see that land, it ain't just a line setting out there. He know that if you get off the water to go take a good look . . . why, there's a whole world right there. A whole world with everything imaginable under the sun. Anything you can think of you can find on that land. Same with a woman. A woman is everything a man need. To a smart man she water and berries. And that's all a man need. That's all he need to live on. You give me some water and berries and if there ain't nothing else I can live a hundred years. See, you just like a man looking at the horizon from a ship. You just seeing a part of it. But it's a blessing when you learn to look at a woman and see in maybe just a few strands of her hair, the way her cheek curves . . . to see in that everything there is out of life to be gotten. It's a blessing to see that. You know you done right and proud by your mother to see that. But you got to learn it. My telling you ain't gonna mean nothing. You got to learn how to come to your own time and place with a woman.

JEREMY What about your woman, Mr. Bynum? I know you done had some woman.

BYNUM Oh, I got them in memory time. That lasts longer than any of them ever stayed with me.

JEREMY I had me an old gal one time . . .

[*There is a knock on the door.* JEREMY *goes to answer it. Enter* MOLLY CUNNINGHAM. *She is about twenty-six, the kind of woman that "could break in on a dollar anywhere she goes." She carries a small cardboard suitcase, and wears a colorful dress of the fashion of the day.* JEREMY's *heart jumps out of his chest when he sees her.*]

MOLLY You got any rooms here? I'm looking for a room.

JEREMY Yeah . . . Mr. Seth got rooms. Sure . . . wait till I get Mr. Seth. [*Calls.*] Mr. Seth! Somebody here to see you! [*To* MOLLY] Yeah, Mr. Seth got some rooms. Got one right next to me. This a nice place to stay, too. My name's Jeremy. What's yours?

[SETH *enters dressed in his Sunday clothes.*]

SETH Ho!

JEREMY This here woman looking for a place to stay. She say you got any rooms.

MOLLY Mister, you got any rooms? I seen your sign say you got rooms.

SETH How long you plan to staying?

MOLLY I ain't gonna be here long. I ain't looking for no home or nothing. I'd be in Cincinnati if I hadn't missed my train.

SETH Rooms cost two dollars a week.

MOLLY Two dollars!

SETH That includes meals. We serve two meals a day. That's breakfast and dinner.

MOLLY I hope it ain't on the third floor.

SETH That's the only one I got. Third floor to the left. That's pay up in advance week to week.

MOLLY [*Going into her bosom.*] I'm gonna pay you for one week. My name's Molly. Molly Cunningham.

SETH I'm Seth Holly. My wife's name is Bertha. She do the cooking and taking care of around here. She got sheets on the bed. Towels twenty-five cents a week extra if you ain't got none. You get breakfast and dinner. We got fried chicken on Sundays.

MOLLY That sounds good. Here's two dollars and twenty-five cents. Look here, Mister . . . ?

SETH Holy. Seth Holly.

MOLLY Look here, Mr. Holly. I forgot to tell you. I likes me some company from time to time. I don't like being by myself.

SETH Your business is your business. I don't meddle in nobody's business. But this is a respectable house. I don't have no riffraff around here. And I don't have no women hauling no men up to their rooms to be making their living. As long as we understand each other then we'll be alright with each other.

MOLLY Where's the outhouse?

SETH Straight through the door over yonder.

MOLLY I get my own key to the front door?

SETH Everybody get their own key. If you come in late just don't be making no whole lot of noise and carrying on. Don't allow no fussing and fighting around here.

MOLLY You ain't got to worry about that, mister. Which way you say that outhouse was again?

SETH Straight through that door over yonder.

[MOLLY *exits out the back door.* JEREMY *crosses to watch her.*]

JEREMY Mr. Bynum, you know what? I think I know what you was talking about now.

[*The lights go down on the scene*]

SCENE FOUR

The lights come up on the kitchen. It is later the same evening. MATTIE *and all the residents of the house, except* LOOMIS, *sit around the table. They have finished eating and most of the dishes have been cleared.*

MOLLY That sure was some good chicken.

JEREMY That's what I'm talking about. Miss Bertha, you sure can fry some chicken. I thought my mama could fry some chicken. But she can't do half as good as you.

SETH I know it. That's why I married her. She don't know that, though. She think I married her for something else.

BERTHA I ain't studying you, Seth. Did you get your things moved in alright, Mattie?

MATTIE I ain't had that much. Jeremy helped me with what I did have.

BERTHA You'll get to know your way around here. If you have any questions about anything just ask me. You and Molly both. I get along with everybody. You'll find I ain't no trouble to get along with.

MATTIE You need some help with the dishes?

BERTHA I got me a helper. Ain't I, Zonia? Got me a good helper.

ZONIA Yes, ma'am.

SETH Look at Bynum sitting over there with his belly all poked out. Ain't saying nothing. Sitting over there half asleep. Ho, Bynum!

BERTHA If Bynum ain't saying nothing what you wanna start him up for?

SETH Ho, Bynum!

BYNUM What you hollering at me for? I ain't doing nothing.

SETH Come on, we gonna Juba.[2]

BYNUM You know me, I'm always ready to Juba.

SETH Well, come on, then.

[SETH *pulls out a harmonica and blows a few notes.*]
Come on there, Jeremy. Where's your guitar? Go get your guitar. Bynum say he's ready to Juba.

JEREMY Don't need no guitar to Juba. Ain't you never Juba without a guitar?

[JEREMY *begins to drum on the table.*]

SETH It ain't that. I ain't never Juba with one! Figured to try it and see how it worked.

BYNUM [*Drumming on the table.*] You don't need no guitar. Look at Molly sitting over there. She don't know we Juba on Sunday. We gonna show you something tonight. You and Mattie Campbell both. Ain't that right, Seth?

SETH You said it! Come on, Bertha, leave them dishes be for a while. We gonna Juba.

BYNUM Alright. Let's Juba down!

---

2. Dance a circle dance, which was one of the earliest forms of African American secular music and performance.

[*The Juba is reminiscent of the Ring Shouts of the African slaves. It is a call and response dance.* BYNUM *sits at the table and drums. He calls the dance as others clap hands, shuffle and stomp around the table. It should be as African as possible, with the performers working themselves up into a near frenzy. The words can be improvised, but should include some mention of the Holy Ghost. In the middle of the dance* HERALD LOOMIS *enters.*]

LOOMIS [*In a rage.*]   Stop it! Stop!

[*They stop and turn to look at him.*]

You all sitting up here singing about the Holy Ghost. What's so holy about the Holy Ghost? You singing and singing. You think the Holy Ghost coming? You singing for the Holy Ghost to come? What he gonna do, huh? He gonna come with tongues of fire to burn up your woolly heads? You gonna tie onto the Holy Ghost and get burned up? What you got then? Why God got to be so big? Why he got to be bigger than me? How much big is there? How much big do you want?

[LOOMIS *starts to unzip his pants.*]

SETH   Nigger, you crazy!

LOOMIS   How much big you want?

SETH   You done plumb lost your mind!

[LOOMIS *begins to speak in tongues and dance around the kitchen.* SETH *starts after him.*]

BERTHA   Leave him alone, Seth. He ain't in his right mind.

LOOMIS [*Stops suddenly.*]   You all don't know nothing about me. You don't know what I done seen. Herald Loomis done seen some things he ain't got words to tell you.

[LOOMIS *starts to walk out the front door and is thrown back and collapses, terror-stricken by his vision.* BYNUM *crawls to him.*]

BYNUM   What you done seen, Herald Loomis?

LOOMIS   I done seen bones rise up out the water. Rise up and walk across the water. Bones walking on top of the water.

BYNUM   Tell me about them bones, Herald Loomis. Tell me what you seen.

LOOMIS   I come to this place . . . to this water that was bigger than the whole world. And I looked out . . . and I seen these bones rise up out the water. Rise up and begin to walk on top of it.

BYNUM   Wasn't nothing but bones and they walking on top of the water.

LOOMIS   Walking without sinking down. Walking on top of the water.

BYNUM   Just marching in a line.

LOOMIS   A whole heap of them. They come up out the water and started marching.

BYNUM   Wasn't nothing but bones and they walking on top of the water.

LOOMIS   One after the other. They just come up out the water and start to walking.

BYNUM   They walking on the water without sinking down. They just walking and walking. And then . . . what happened, Herald Loomis?

LOOMIS   They just walking across the water.

BYNUM   What happened, Herald Loomis? What happened to the bones?

LOOMIS   They just walking across the water . . . and then . . . they sunk down.

BYNUM   The bones sunk into the water. They all sunk down.

LOOMIS   All at one time! They just all fell in the water at one time.

BYNUM   Sunk down like anybody else.

LOOMIS   When they sink down they made a big splash and this here wave come up . . .

BYNUM   A big wave, Herald Loomis. A big wave washed over the land.

LOOMIS   It washed them out of the water and up on the land. Only . . . only . . .

BYNUM   Only they ain't bones no more.

LOOMIS   They got flesh on them! Just like you and me!

BYNUM   Everywhere you look the waves is washing them up on the land right on top of one another.

LOOMIS   They black. Just like you and me. Ain't no difference.

BYNUM   Then what happened, Herald Loomis?

LOOMIS   They ain't moved or nothing. They just laying there.

BYNUM   You just laying there. What you waiting on, Herald Loomis?

LOOMIS   I'm laying there . . . waiting.

BYNUM   What you waiting on, Herald Loomis?

LOOMIS   I'm waiting on the breath to get into my body.

BYNUM   The breath coming into you, Herald Loomis. What you gonna do now?

LOOMIS   The wind's blowing the breath into my body. I can feel it. I'm starting to breathe again.

BYNUM   What you gonna do, Herald Loomis?

LOOMIS   I'm gonna stand up. I got to stand up. I can't lay here no more. All the breath coming into my body and I got to stand up.

BYNUM   Everybody's standing up at the same time.

LOOMIS   The ground's starting to shake. There's a great shaking. The world's busting half in two. The sky's splitting open. I got to stand up.

[LOOMIS *attempts to stand up.*]

My legs . . . my legs won't stand up!

BYNUM   Everybody's standing and walking toward the road. What you gonna do, Herald Loomis?

LOOMIS   My legs won't stand up.

BYNUM   They shaking hands and saying goodbye to each other and walking every whichaway down the road.

LOOMIS   I got to stand up!

BYNUM   They walking around here now. Mens. Just like you and me. Come right up out the water.

LOOMIS   Got to stand up.

BYNUM   They walking, Herald Loomis. They walking around here now.

LOOMIS   I got to stand up. Get up on the road.

BYNUM   Come on, Herald Loomis.

[LOOMIS *tries to stand up.*]

LOOMIS   My legs won't stand up! My legs won't stand up!

[LOOMIS *collapses on the floor as the lights go down to black.*]

Act 2

SCENE ONE

The lights come up on the kitchen. BERTHA *busies herself with breakfast preparations.* SETH *sits at the table.*

SETH   I don't care what his problem is! He's leaving here!

BERTHA You can't put the man out and he got that little girl. Where they gonna go then?

SETH I don't care where he go. Let him go back where he was before he come here. I ain't asked him to come here. I knew when I first looked at him something wasn't right with him. Dragging that little girl around with him. Looking like he be sleeping in the woods somewhere. I knew all along he wasn't right.

BERTHA A fellow get a little drunk he's liable to say or do anything. He ain't done no big harm.

SETH I just don't have all that carrying on in my house. When he come down here I'm gonna tell him. He got to leave here. My daddy wouldn't stand for it and I ain't gonna stand for it either.

BERTHA Well, if you put him out you have to put Bynum out too. Bynum right there with him.

SETH If it wasn't for Bynum ain't no telling what would have happened. Bynum talked to that fellow just as nice and calmed him down. If he wasn't here ain't no telling what would have happened. Bynum ain't done nothing but talk to him and kept him calm. Man acting all crazy with that foolishness. Naw, he's leaving here.

BERTHA What you gonna tell him? How you gonna tell him to leave?

SETH I'm gonna tell him straight out. Keep it nice and simple. Mister, you got to leave here!

[MOLLY enters from the stairs.]

MOLLY Morning.

BERTHA Did you sleep alright in that bed?

MOLLY Tired as I was I could have slept anywhere. It's a real nice room, though. This is a nice place.

SETH I'm sorry you had to put up with all that carrying on last night.

MOLLY It don't bother me none. I done seen that kind of stuff before.

SETH You won't have to see it around here no more.

[BYNUM is heard singing offstage.]

I don't put up with all that stuff. When that fellow come down here I'm gonna tell him.

BYNUM [Singing.]

Soon my work will all be done
Soon my work will all be done
Soon my work will all be done

I'm going to see the king.

BYNUM [Enters.] Morning, Seth. Morning, Sister Bertha. I see we got Molly Cunningham down here at breakfast.

SETH Bynum, I wanna thank you for talking to that fellow last night and calming him down. If you hadn't been here ain't no telling what might have happened.

BYNUM Mr. Loomis alright, Seth. He just got a little excited.

SETH Well, he can get excited somewhere else 'cause he leaving here.

[MATTIE enters from the stairs.]

BYNUM Well, there's Mattie Campbell.

MATTIE Good morning.

BERTHA Sit on down there, Mattie. I got some biscuits be ready in a minute. The coffee's hot.

MATTIE Jeremy gone already?

BYNUM   Yeah, he leave out of here early. He got to be there when the sun come up. Most working men got to be there when the sun come up. Everybody but Seth. Seth work at night. Mr. Olowski so busy in his shop he got fellows working at night.

[LOOMIS *enters from the stairs.*]

SETH   Mr. Loomis, now . . . I don't want no trouble. I keeps me a respectable house here. I don't have no carrying on like what went on last night. This has been a respectable house for a long time. I'm gonna have to ask you to leave.

LOOMIS   You got my two dollars. That two dollars say we stay till Saturday.

[LOOMIS *and* SETH *glare at each other.*]

SETH   Alright. Fair enough. You stay till Saturday. But come Saturday you got to leave here.

LOOMIS [*Continues to glare at* SETH. *He goes to the door and calls.*]   Zonia. You stay around this house, you hear? Don't you go anywhere.

[LOOMIS *exits out the front door.*]

SETH   I knew it when I first seen him. I knew something wasn't right with him.

BERTHA   Seth, leave the people alone to eat their breakfast. They don't want to hear that. Go on out there and make some pots and pans. That's the only time you satisfied is when you out there. Go on out there and make some pots and pans and leave them people alone.

SETH   I ain't bothering anybody. I'm just stating the facts. I told you, Bynum.

[BERTHA *shoos* SETH *out the back door and exits into the bedroom.*]

MOLLY [*To* BYNUM]   You one of them voo-doo people?

BYNUM   I got a power to bind folks if that what you talking about.

MOLLY   I thought so. The way you talked to that man when he started all that spooky stuff. What you say you had the power to do to people? You ain't the cause of him acting like that, is you?

BYNUM   I binds them together. Sometimes I help them find each other.

MOLLY   How do you do that?

BYNUM   With a song. My daddy taught me how to do it.

MOLLY   That's what they say. Most folks be what they daddy is. I wouldn't want to be like my daddy. Nothing ever set right with him. He tried to make the world over. Carry it around with him everywhere he go. I don't want to be like that. I just take life as it come. I don't be trying to make it over.

[*Pause.*]

Your daddy used to do that too, huh? Make people stay together?

BYNUM   My daddy used to heal people. He had the Healing Song. I got the Binding Song.

MOLLY   My mama used to believe in all that stuff. If she got sick she would have gone and saw your daddy. As long as he didn't make her drink nothing. She wouldn't drink nothing nobody give her. She was always afraid somebody was gonna poison her. How your daddy heal people?

BYNUM   With a song. He healed people by singing over them. I seen him do it. He sung over this little white girl when she was sick. They made a big to-do about it. They carried the girl's bed out in the yard and had all her kinfolk standing around. The little girl laying up there in the bed. Doctors standing around can't do nothing to help her. And they had my daddy come up and sing his song. It didn't sound no different than any other song. It was just somebody singing. But the song was its own thing and it come out and took upon this little girl with its power and it healed her.

MOLLY   That's sure something else. I don't understand that kind of thing. I guess if the doctor couldn't make me well I'd try it. But otherwise I don't wanna be bothered with that kind of thing. It's too spooky.

BYNUM   Well, let me get on out here and get to work.

[BYNUM *gets up and heads out the back door.*]

MOLLY   I ain't meant to offend you or nothing. What's your name . . . Bynum? I ain't meant to say nothing to make you feel bad now.

[BYNUM *exits out the back door.*]

[*To* MATTIE] I hope he don't feel bad. He's a nice man. I don't wanna hurt nobody's feelings or nothing.

MATTIE   I got to go on up to Doc Goldblum's and finish this ironing.

MOLLY   Now, that's something I don't never wanna do. Iron no clothes. Especially somebody else's. That's what I believe killed my mama. Always ironing and working, doing somebody's else's work. Not Molly Cunningham.

MATTIE   It's the only job I got. I got to make it someway to fend for myself.

MOLLY   I thought Jeremy was your man. Ain't he working?

MATTIE   We just be keeping company till maybe Jack come back.

MOLLY   I don't trust none of these men. Jack or nobody else. These men liable to do anything. They wait just until they get one woman tied and locked up with them . . . then they look around to see if they can get another one. Molly don't pay them no mind. One's just as good as the other if you ask me. I ain't never met one that meant nobody no good. You got any babies?

MATTIE   I had two for my man, Jack Carper. But they both died.

MOLLY   That be the best. These men make all these babies, then run off and leave you to take care of them. Talking about they wanna see what's on the other side of the hill. I make sure I don't get no babies. My mama taught me how to do that.

MATTIE   Don't make me no mind. That be nice to be a mother.

MOLLY   Yeah? Well, you go on, then. Molly Cunningham ain't gonna be tied down with no babies. Had me a man one time who I thought had some love in him. Come home one day and he was packing his trunk. Told me the time come when even the best of friends must part. Say he was gonna send me a Special Delivery some old day. I watched him out the window when he carried that trunk out and down to the train station. Said if he was gonna send me a Special Delivery I wasn't gonna be there to get it. I done found out the harder you try to hold onto them, the easier it is for some gal to pull them away. Molly done learned that. That's why I don't trust nobody but the good Lord above, and I don't love nobody but my mama.

MATTIE   I got to get on. Doc Goldblum gonna be waiting.

[MATTIE *exits out the front door.* SETH *enters from his workshop with his apron, gloves, goggles, etc. He carries a bucket and crosses to the sink for water.*]

SETH   Everybody gone but you, huh?

MOLLY   That little shack out there by the outhouse . . . that's where you make them pots and pans and stuff?

SETH   Yeah, that's my workshed. I go out there . . . take these hands and make something out of nothing. Take that metal and bend and twist it whatever way I want. My daddy taught me that. He used to make pots and pans. That's how I learned it.

MOLLY   I never knew nobody made no pots and pans. My uncle used to shoe horses.

[JEREMY *enters at the front door.*]

SETH   I thought you was working? Ain't you working today?

JEREMY   Naw, they fired me. White fellow come by told me to give him fifty cents if I wanted to keep working. Going around to all the colored making them give him fifty cents to keep hold to their jobs. Them other fellows, they was giving it to him. I kept hold to mine and they fired me.

SETH   Boy, what kind of sense that make? What kind of sense it make to get fired from a job where you making eight dollars a week and all it cost you is fifty cents. That's seven dollars and fifty cents profit! This way you ain't got nothing.

JEREMY   It didn't make no sense to me. I don't make but eight dollars. Why I got to give him fifty cents of it? He go around to all the colored and he got ten dollars extra. That's more than I make for a whole week.

SETH   I see you gonna learn the hard way. You just looking at the facts of it. See, right now, without the job, you ain't got nothing. What you gonna do when you can't keep a roof over your head? Right now, come Saturday, unless you come up with another two dollars, you gonna be out there in the streets. Down up under one of them bridges trying to put some food in your belly and wishing you had given that fellow that fifty cents.

JEREMY   Don't make me no difference. There's a big road out there. I can get my guitar and always find me another place to stay. I ain't planning on staying in one place for too long noway.

SETH   We gonna see if you feel like that come Saturday!

[SETH *exits out the back.* JEREMY *sees* MOLLY.]

JEREMY   Molly Cunningham. How you doing today, sugar?

MOLLY   You can go on back down there tomorrow and go back to work if you want. They won't even know who you is. Won't even know it's you. I had me a fellow did that one time. They just went ahead and signed him up like they never seen him before.

JEREMY   I'm tired of working anyway. I'm glad they fired me. You sure look pretty today.

MOLLY   Don't come telling me all that pretty stuff. Beauty wanna come in and sit down at your table asking to be fed. I ain't hardly got enough for me.

JEREMY   You know you pretty. Ain't no sense in you saying nothing about that. Why don't you come on and go away with me?

MOLLY   You tied up with that Mattie Campbell. Now you talking about running away with me.

JEREMY   I was just keeping her company 'cause she lonely. You ain't the lonely kind. You the kind that know what she want and how to get it. I need a woman like you to travel around with. Don't you wanna travel around and look at some places with Jeremy? With a woman like you beside him, a man can make it nice in the world.

MOLLY   Moll can make it nice by herself too. Molly don't need nobody leave her cold in hand. The world rough enough as it is.

JEREMY   We can make it better together. I got my guitar and I can play. Won me another dollar last night playing guitar. We can go around and I can play at the dances and we can just enjoy life. You can make it by yourself alright, I agrees with that. A woman like you can make it anywhere she go. But you can make it better if you got a man to protect you.

MOLLY   What places you wanna go around and look at?

JEREMY All of them! I don't want to miss nothing. I wanna go everywhere and do everything there is to be got out of life. With a woman like you it's like having water and berries. A man got everything he need.

MOLLY You got to be doing more than playing that guitar. A dollar a day ain't hardly what Molly got in mind.

JEREMY I gambles real good. I got a hand for it.

MOLLY Molly don't work. And Molly ain't up for sale.

JEREMY Sure, baby. You ain't got to work with Jeremy.

MOLLY There's one more thing.

JEREMY What's that, sugar?

MOLLY Molly ain't going South.
[*The lights go down on the scene.*]

SCENE TWO

The lights come up on the parlor. SETH *and* BYNUM *sit playing a game of dominoes.* BYNUM *sings to himself.*

BYNUM [*Singing.*]

> They tell me Joe Turner's come and gone
> Ohhh Lordy
> They tell me Joe Turner's come and gone
> Ohhh Lordy
> Got my man and gone
>
> Come with forty links of chain
> Ohhh Lordy
> Come with forty links of chain
> Ohhh Lordy
> Got my man and gone

SETH Come on and play if you gonna play.

BYNUM I'm gonna play. Soon as I figure out what to do.

SETH You can't figure out if you wanna play or you wanna sing.

BYNUM Well sir, I'm gonna do a little bit of both.
[*Playing.*]
There. What you gonna do now?
[*Singing.*]

> They tell me Joe Turner's come and gone
> Ohhh Lordy
> They tell me Joe Turner's come and gone
> Ohhh Lordy

SETH Why don't you hush up that noise.

BYNUM That's a song the women sing down around Memphis. The women down there made up that song. I picked it up down there about fifteen years ago.
[LOOMIS *enters from the front door.*]

BYNUM Evening, Mr. Loomis.

SETH Today's Monday, Mr. Loomis. Come Saturday your time is up. We done ate already. My wife roasted up some yams. She got your plate sitting in there on the table. [*To* BYNUM] Whose play is it?

BYNUM Ain't you keeping up with the game? I thought you was a domino player. I just played so it got to be your turn.

[LOOMIS *goes into the kitchen, where a plate of yams is covered and set on the table. He sits down and begins to eat with his hands.*]

SETH [*Plays.*]   Twenty! Give me twenty! You didn't know I had that ace five. You was trying to play around that. You didn't know I had that lying there for you.

BYNUM   You ain't done nothing. I let you have that to get mine.

SETH   Come on and play. You ain't doing nothing but talking. I got a hundred and forty points to your eighty. You ain't doing nothing but talking. Come on and play.

BYNUM [*Singing.*]

> They tell me Joe Turner's come and gone
> Ohhh Lordy
> They tell me Joe Turner's come and gone
> Ohhh Lordy
> Got my man and gone
>
> He come with forty links of chain
> Ohhh Lordy

LOOMIS   Why you singing that song? Why you singing about Joe Turner?

BYNUM   I'm just singing to entertain myself.

SETH   You trying to distract me. That's what you trying to do.

BYNUM [*Singing.*]

> Come with forty links of chain
> Ohhh Lordy
> Come with forty links of chain
> Ohhh Lordy

LOOMIS   I don't like you singing that song, mister!

SETH   Now, I ain't gonna have no more disturbance around here, Herald Loomis. You start any more disturbance and you leavin' here, Saturday or no Saturday.

BYNUM   The man ain't causing no disturbance, Seth. He just say he don't like the song.

SETH   Well, we all friendly folk. All neighborly like. Don't have no squabbling around here. Don't have no disturbance. You gonna have to take that someplace else.

BYNUM   He just say he don't like the song. I done sung a whole lot of songs people don't like. I respect everybody. He here in the house too. If he don't like the song, I'll sing something else. I know lots of songs. You got "I Belong to the Band," "Don't You Leave Me Here." You got "Praying on the Old Campground," "Keep Your Lamp Trimmed and Burning" . . . I know lots of songs.

[*Sings.*]

> Boys, I'll be so glad when payday come
> Captain, Captain, when payday comes
> Gonna catch that Illinois Central
> Going to Kankakee

SETH   Why don't you hush up that hollering and come on and play dominoes.

BYNUM   You ever been to Johnstown, Herald Loomis? You look like a fellow I seen around there.

LOOMIS I don't know no place with that name.

BYNUM That's around where I seen my shiny man. See, you looking for this woman. I'm looking for a shiny man. Seem like everybody looking for something.

SETH I'm looking for you to come and play these dominoes. That's what I'm looking for.

BYNUM You a farming man, Herald Loomis? You look like you done some farming.

LOOMIS Same as everybody. I done farmed some, yeah.

BYNUM I used to work at farming . . . picking cotton. I reckon everybody done picked some cotton.

SETH I ain't! I ain't never picked no cotton. I was born up here in the North. My daddy was a freedman. I ain't never even seen no cotton!

BYNUM Mr. Loomis done picked some cotton. Ain't you, Herald Loomis? You done picked a bunch of cotton.

LOOMIS How you know so much about me? How you know what I done? How much cotton I picked?

BYNUM I can tell from looking at you. My daddy taught me how to do that. Say when you look at a fellow, if you taught yourself to look for it, you can see his song written on him. Tell you what kind of man he is in the world. Now, I can look at you, Mr. Loomis, and see you a man who done forgot his song. Forgot how to sing it. A fellow forget that and he forget who he is. Forget how he's supposed to mark down life. Now, I used to travel all up and down this road and that . . . looking here and there. Searching. Just like you, Mr. Loomis. I didn't know what I was searching for. The only thing I knew was something was keeping me dissatisfied. Something wasn't making my heart smooth and easy. Then one day my daddy gave me a song. That song had a weight to it that was hard to handle. That song was hard to carry. I fought against it. Didn't want to accept that song. I tried to find my daddy to give him back the song. But I found out it wasn't his song. It was my song. It had come from way deep inside me. I looked long back in memory and gathered up pieces and snatches of things to make that song. I was making it up out of myself. And that song helped me on the road. Made it smooth to where my footsteps didn't bite back at me. All the time that song getting bigger and bigger. That song growing with each step of the road. It got so I used all of myself up in the making of that song. Then I was the song in search of itself. That song rattling in my throat and I'm looking for it. See, Mr. Loomis, when a man forgets his song he goes off in search of it . . . till he find out he's got it with him all the time. That's why I can tell you one of Joe Turner's niggers. 'Cause you forgot how to sing your song.

LOOMIS You lie! How you see that? I got a mark on me? Joe Turner done marked me to where you can see it? You telling me I'm a marked man. What kind of mark you got on you?

[BYNUM *begins singing.*]

BYNUM

> They tell me Joe Turner's come and gone
> Ohhh Lordy
> They tell me Joe Turner's come and gone
> Ohhh Lordy
> Got my man and gone

LOOMIS   Had a whole mess of men he catched. Just go out hunting regular like you go out hunting possum. He catch you and go home to his wife and family. Ain't thought about you going home to yours. Joe Turner catched me when my little girl was just born. Wasn't nothing but a little baby sucking on her mama's titty when he catched me. Joe Turner catched me in nineteen hundred and one. Kept me seven years until nineteen hundred and eight. Kept everybody seven years. He'd go out hunting and bring back forty men at a time. And keep them seven years.

I was walking down this road in this little town outside of Memphis. Come up on these fellows gambling. I was a deacon in the Abundant Life Church. I stopped to preach to these fellows to see if maybe I could turn some of them from their sinning when Joe Turner, brother of the Governor of the great sovereign state of Tennessee, swooped down on us and grabbed everybody there. Kept us all seven years.

My wife Martha gone from me after Joe Turner catched me. Got out from under Joe Turner on his birthday. Me and forty other men put in our seven years and he let us go on his birthday. I made it back to Henry Thompson's place where me and Martha was sharecropping and Martha's gone. She taken my little girl and left her with her mama and took off North. We been looking for her ever since. That's been going on four years now we been looking. That's the only thing I know to do. I just wanna see her face so I can get me a starting place in the world. The world got to start somewhere. That's what I been looking for. I been wandering a long time in somebody else's world. When I find my wife that be the making of my own.

BYNUM   Joe Turner tell why he caught you? You ever asked him that?

LOOMIS   I ain't never seen Joe Turner. Seen him to where I could touch him. I asked one of them fellows one time why he catch niggers. Asked him what I got he want? Why don't he keep on to himself? Why he got to catch me going down the road by my lonesome? He told me I was worthless. Worthless is something you throw away. Something you don't bother with. I ain't seen him throw me away. Wouldn't even let me stay away when I was by my lonesome. I ain't tried to catch him when he going down the road. So I must got something he want. What I got?

SETH   He just want you to do his work for him. That's all.

LOOMIS   I can look at him and see where he big and strong enough to do his own work. So it can't be that. He must want something he ain't got.

BYNUM   That ain't hard to figure out. What he wanted was your song. He wanted to have that song to be his. He thought by catching you he could learn that song. Every nigger he catch he's looking for the one he can learn that song from. Now he's got you bound up to where you can't sing your own song. Couldn't sing it them seven years 'cause you was afraid he would snatch it from under you. But you still got it. You just forget how to sing it.

LOOMIS [To BYNUM]   I know who you are. You one of them bones people.

[The lights go down to black.]

SCENE THREE

The lights come up on the kitchen. It is the following morning. MATTIE *and* BYNUM *sit at the table.* BERTHA *busies herself at the stove.*

BYNUM   Good luck don't know no special time to come. You sleep with that up under your pillow and good luck can't help but come to you. Sometimes it come and go and you don't even know it's been there.

BERTHA   Bynum, why don't you leave that gal alone? She don't wanna be hearing all that. Why don't you go on and get out the way and leave her alone?

BYNUM [*Getting up.*]   Alright, alright. But you mark what I'm saying. It'll draw it to you just like a magnet.

[BYNUM *exits up the stairs ad* LOOMIS *enters.*]

BERTHA   I got some grits here, Mr. Loomis.

[BERTHA *sets a bowl on the table.*]

If I was you, Mattie, I wouldn't go getting all tied up with Bynum in that stuff. That kind of stuff, even if it do work for a while, it don't last. That just get people more mixed up than they is already. And I wouldn't waste my time fretting over Jeremy either. I seen it coming. I seen it when she first come here. She that kind of woman run off with the first man got a dollar to spend on her. Jeremy just young. He don't know what he getting into. That gal don't mean him no good. She's just using him to keep from being by herself. That's the worst use of a man you can have. You ought to be glad to wash him out of your hair. I done seen all kind of men. I done seen them come and go through here. Jeremy ain't had enough to him for you. You need a man who's got some understanding and who willing to work with that understanding to come to the best he can. You got your time coming. You just tries too hard and can't understand why it don't work for you. Trying to figure it out don't do nothing but give you a troubled mind. Don't no man want a woman with a troubled mind.

   You get all that trouble off your mind and just when it look like you ain't never gonna find what you want . . . you look up and it's standing right there. That's how I met my Seth. You gonna look up one day and find everything you want standing right in front of you. Been twenty-seven years now since that happened to me. But life ain't no happy-go-lucky time where everything be just like you want it. You got your time coming. You watch what Bertha's saying.

[SETH *enters.*]

SETH   Ho!

BERTHA   What you doing come in here so late?

SETH   I was standing down there on Logan Street talking with the fellows. Henry Allen tried to sell me that old piece of horse he got.

[*He sees* LOOMIS.]

Today's Tuesday, Mr. Loomis.

BERTHA [*Pulling him toward the bedroom.*]   Come on in here and leave that man alone to eat his breakfast.

SETH   I ain't bothering nobody. I'm just reminding him what day it is.

[SETH *and* BERTHA *exit into the bedroom.*]

LOOMIS   That dress got a color to it.

MATTIE   Did you really see them things like you said? Them people come up out the ocean?

LOOMIS   It happened just like that, yeah.

MATTIE   I hope you find your wife. It be good for your little girl for you to find her.

LOOMIS   Got to find her for myself. Find my starting place in the world. Find me a world I can fit in.

MATTIE   I ain't never found no place for me to fit. Seem like all I do is start over. It ain't nothing to find no starting place in the world. You just start from where you find yourself.

LOOMIS   Got to find my wife. That be my starting place.

MATTIE   What if you don't find her? What you gonna do then if you don't find her?

LOOMIS   She out there somewhere. Ain't no such thing as not finding her.

MATTIE   How she got lost from you? Jack just walked away from me.

LOOMIS   Joe Turner split us up. Joe Turner turned the world upside-down. He bound me on to him for seven years.

MATTIE   I hope you find her. It be good for you to find her.

LOOMIS   I been watching you. I been watching you watch me.

MATTIE   I was just trying to figure out if you seen things like you said.

LOOMIS [Getting up.]   Come here and let me touch you. I been watching you. You a full woman. A man needs a full woman. Come on and be with me.

MATTIE   I ain't got enough for you. You'd use me up too fast.

LOOMIS   Herald Loomis got a mind seem like you a part of it since I first seen you. It's been a long time since I seen a full woman. I can smell you from here. I know you got Herald Loomis on your mind, can't keep him apart from it. Come on and be with Herald Loomis.

[LOOMIS has crossed to MATTIE. He touches her awkwardly, gently, tenderly. Inside he howls like a lost wolf pup whose hunger is deep. He goes to touch her but finds he cannot.]

I done forgot how to touch.

[The lights fade to black.]

SCENE FOUR

It is early the next morning. The lights come up on ZONIA *and* REUBEN *in the yard.*

REUBEN   Something spookly going on around here. Last night Mr. Bynum was out in the yard singing and talking to the wind . . . and the wind it just be talking back to him. Did you hear it?

ZONIA   I heard it. I was scared to get up and look. I thought it was a storm.

REUBEN   That wasn't no storm. That was Mr. Bynum. First he say something . . . and the wind it say back to him.

ZONIA   I heard it. Was you scared? I was scared.

REUBEN   And then this morning . . . I seen Miss Mabel!

ZONIA   Who Miss Mabel?

REUBEN   Mr. Seth's mother. He got her picture hanging up in the house. She been dead.

ZONIA   How you seen her if she been dead?

REUBEN   Zonia . . . if I tell you something you promise you won't tell anybody?

ZONIA   I promise.

REUBEN   It was early this morning . . . I went out to the coop to feed the pigeons. I was down on the ground like this to open up the door to the coop . . . when all of a sudden I seen some feets in front of me. I looked up . . . and there was Miss Mabel standing there.

ZONIA   Reuben, you better stop telling that! You ain't seen nobody!

REUBEN   Naw, it's the truth. I swear! I seen her just like I see you. Look . . . you can see where she hit me with her cane.

ZONIA   Hit you? What she hit you for?

REUBEN   She says, "Didn't you promise Eugene something?" Then she hit me with her cane. She say, "Let them pigeons go." Then she hit me again. That's what made them marks.

ZONIA   Jeez man . . . get away from me. You done see a haunt!

REUBEN   Shhhh. You promised, Zonia!

ZONIA   You sure it wasn't Miss Bertha come over there and hit you with her hoe?

REUBEN   It wasn't no Miss Bertha. I told you it was Miss Mabel. She was standing right there by the coop. She had this light coming out of her and then she just melted away.

ZONIA   What she had on?

REUBEN   A white dress. Ain't even had no shoes or nothing. Just had on that white dress and them big hands . . . and that cane she hit me with.

ZONIA   How you reckon she knew about the pigeons? You reckon Eugene told her?

REUBEN   I don't know. I sure ain't asked her none. She say Eugene was waiting on them pigeons. Say he couldn't go back home till I let them go. I couldn't get the door to the coop open fast enough.

ZONIA   Maybe she an angel? From the way you say she look with that white dress. Maybe she an angel.

REUBEN   Mean as she was . . . how she gonna be an angel? She used to chase us out her yard and frown up and look evil all the time.

ZONIA   That don't mean she can't be no angel 'cause of how she looked and 'cause she wouldn't let no kids play in her yard. It go by if you got any spots on your heart and if you pray and go to church.

REUBEN   What about she hit me with her cane? An angel wouldn't hit me with her cane.

ZONIA   I don't know. She might. I still say she was an angel.

REUBEN   You reckon Eugene the one who sent old Miss Mabel?

ZONIA   Why he send her? Why he don't come himself?

REUBEN   Figured if he send her maybe that'll make me listen. 'Cause she old.

ZONIA   What you think it feel like?

REUBEN   What?

ZONIA   Being dead.

REUBEN   Like being sleep only you don't know nothing and can't move no more.

ZONIA   If Miss Mabel can come back . . . then maybe Eugene can come back too.

REUBEN   We can go down to the hideout like we used to! He could come back everyday! It be just like he ain't dead.

ZONIA   Maybe that ain't right for him to come back. Feel kinda funny to be playing games with a haunt.

REUBEN   Yeah . . . what if everybody came back? What if Miss Mabel came back just like she ain't dead? Where you and your daddy gonna sleep then?

ZONIA   Maybe they go back at night and don't need no place to sleep.

REUBEN   It still don't seem right. I'm sure gonna miss Eugene. He's the bestest friend anybody ever had.

ZONIA   My daddy say if you miss somebody too much it can kill you. Say he missed me till it liked to killed him.

REUBEN   What if your mama's already dead and all the time you looking for her?

ZONIA   Naw, she ain't dead. My daddy say he can smell her.

REUBEN   You can't smell nobody that ain't here. Maybe he smelling old Miss Bertha. Maybe Miss Bertha your mama?

ZONIA   Naw, she ain't. My mamma got long pretty hair and she five feet from the ground!

REUBEN   Your daddy say when you leaving?

[ZONIA *doesn't respond.*]

Maybe you gonna stay in Mr. Seth's house and don't go looking for your mama no more.

ZONIA   He say we got to leave on Saturday.

REUBEN   Dag! You just only been here for a little while. Don't seem like nothing ever stay the same.

ZONIA   He say he got to find her. Find him a place in the world.

REUBEN   He could find him a place in Mr. Seth's house.

ZONIA   It don't look like we never gonna find her.

REUBEN   Maybe he find her by Saturday then you don't have to go.

ZONIA   I don't know.

REUBEN   You look like a spider!

ZONIA   I ain't no spider!

REUBEN   Got them long skinny arms and legs. You look like one of them Black Widows.

ZONIA   I ain't no Black Window nothing! My name is Zonia!

REUBEN   That's what I'm gonna call you . . . Spider.

ZONIA   You can call me that, but I don't have to answer.

REUBEN   You know what? I think maybe I be your husband when I grow up.

ZONIA   How you know?

REUBEN   I ask my grandpap how you know and he say when the moon falls into a girl's eyes that how you know.

ZONIA   Did it fall into my eyes?

REUBEN   Not that I can tell. Maybe I ain't old enough. Maybe you ain't old enough.

ZONIA   So there! I don't know why you telling me that lie!

REUBEN   That don't mean nothing 'cause I can't see it. I know it's there. Just the way you look at me sometimes look like the moon might have been in your eyes.

ZONIA   That don't mean nothing if you can't see it. You supposed to see it.

REUBEN   Shucks, I see it good enough for me. You ever let anybody kiss you?

ZONIA   Just my daddy. He kiss me on the cheek.

REUBEN   It's better on the lips. Can I kiss you on the lips?

ZONIA   I don't know. You ever kiss anybody before?

REUBEN   I had a cousin let me kiss her on the lips one time. Can I kiss you?

ZONIA   Okay.

[REUBEN *kisses her and lays his head against her chest.*]

What you doing?

REUBEN   Listening. Your heart singing!

ZONIA   It is not.

REUBEN   Just beating like a drum. Let's kiss again.

[*They kiss again.*]

Now you mine, Spider. You my girl, okay?

ZONIA   Okay.

REUBEN   When I get grown, I come looking for you.

ZONIA   Okay.

[*The lights fade to black.*]

SCENE FIVE

The lights come up on the kitchen. It is Saturday. BYNUM, LOOMIS, *and* ZONIA *sit at the table.* BERTHA *prepares breakfast.* ZONIA *has on a white dress.*

BYNUM   With all this rain we been having he might have ran into some washed-out roads. If that wagon got stuck in the mud he's liable to be still upriver somewhere. If he's upriver then he ain't coming until tomorrow.

LOOMIS   Today's Saturday. He say he be here on Saturday.

BERTHA   Zonia, you gonna eat your breakfast this morning.

ZONIA   Yes, ma'am.

BERTHA   I don't know how you expect to get any bigger if you don't eat. I ain't never seen a child that didn't eat. You about as skinny as a bean pole.
   [*Pause.*]
   Mr. Loomis, there's a place down on Wylie. Zeke Mayweather got a house down there. You ought to see if he got any rooms.
   [LOOMIS *doesn't respond.*]
   Well, you're welcome to some breakfast before you move on.
   [MATTIE *enters from the stairs.*]

MATTIE   Good morning.

BERTHA   Morning, Mattie. Sit on down there and get you some breakfast.

BYNUM   Well, Mattie Campbell, you been sleeping with that up under your pillow like I told you?

BERTHA   Bynum, I told you to leave that gal alone with all that stuff. You around here meddling in other people's lives. She don't want to hear all that. You ain't doing nothing but confusing her with that stuff.

MATTIE   [*To* LOOMIS]   You all fixing to move on?

LOOMIS   Today's Saturday. I'm paid up till Saturday.

MATTIE   Where you going to?

LOOMIS   Gonna find my wife.

MATTIE   You going off to another city?

LOOMIS   We gonna see where the road take us. Ain't no telling where we wind up.

MATTIE   Eleven years is a long time. Your wife . . . she might have taken up with someone else. People do that when they get lost from each other.

LOOMIS   Zonia. Come on, we gonna find your mama.
   [LOOMIS *and* ZONIA *cross to the door.*]

MATTIE   [*To* ZONIA]   Zonia, Mattie got a ribbon here match your dress. Want Mattie to fix your hair with her ribbon?
   [ZONIA *nods.* MATTIE *ties the ribbon in her hair.*]
   There . . . it got a color just like your dress. [*To* LOOMIS] I hope you find her. I hope you be happy.

LOOMIS   A man looking for a woman be lucky to find you.
   You a good woman, Mattie. Keep a good heart.
   [LOOMIS *and* ZONIA *exit.*]

BERTHA   I been watching that man for two weeks . . . and that's the closest I come to seeing him act civilized. I don't know what's between you all, Mattie . . . but the only thing that man needs is somebody to make him laugh. That's all you need in the world is love and laughter. That's all anybody needs. To have love in one hand and laughter in the other.

[BERTHA *moves about the kitchen as though blessing it and chasing away the huge sadness that seems to envelop it. It is a dance and demonstration of her own magic, her own remedy that is centuries old and to which she is connected by the muscles of her heart and the blood's memory.*]

You hear me, Mattie? I'm talking about laughing. The kind of laugh that comes from way deep inside. To just stand and laugh and let life flow right through you. Just laugh to let yourself know you're alive.

[*She begins to laugh. It is a near-hysterical laughter that is a celebration of life, both its pain and its blessing.* MATTIE *and* BYNUM *join in the laughter.* SETH *enters from the front door.*]

SETH   Well, I see you all having fun.

[SETH *begins to laugh with them.*]

That Loomis fellow standing up there on the corner watching the house. He standing right up there on Manila Street.

BERTHA   Don't you get started on him. The man done left out of here and that's the last I wanna hear of it. You about to drive me crazy with that man.

SETH   I just say he standing up there on the corner. Acting sneaky like he always do. He can stand up there all he want. As long as he don't come back in here.

[*There is a knock on the door.* SETH *goes to answer it. Enter* MARTHA LOOMIS [PENTECOST]. *She is a young woman about twenty-eight. She is dressed as befitting a member of an Evangelist church.* RUTHERFORD SELIG *follows.*]

SETH   Look here, Bertha. It's Martha Pentecost. Come on in, Martha. Who that with you? Oh . . . that's Selig. Come on in, Selig.

BERTHA   Come on in, Martha. It's sure good to see you.

BYNUM   Rutherford Selig, you a sure enough first-class People Finder!

SELIG   She was right out there in Rankin. You take that first righthand road . . . right there at that church on Wooster Street. I started to go right past and something told me to stop at the church and see if they needed any dustpans.

SETH   Don't she look good, Bertha.

BERTHA   Look all nice and healthy.

MARTHA   Mr. Bynum . . . Selig told me my little girl was here.

SETH   There's some fellow around here say he your husband. Say his name is Loomis. Say you his wife.

MARTHA   Is my little girl with him?

SETH   Yeah, he got a little girl with him. I wasn't gonna tell him where you was. Not the way this fellow look. So he got Selig to find you.

MARTHA   Where they at? They upstairs?

SETH   He was standing right up there on Manila Street. I had to ask him to leave 'cause of how he was carrying on. He come in here one night—

[*The door opens and* LOOMIS, *and* ZONIA *enter.* MARTHA *and* LOOMIS *stare at each other.*]

LOOMIS   Hello, Martha.

MARTHA   Herald . . . Zonia?

LOOMIS   You ain't waited for me, Martha. I got out the place looking to see your face. Seven years I waited to see your face.

MARTHA   Herald, I been looking for you. I wasn't but two months behind you when you went to my mama's and got Zonia. I been looking for you ever since.

LOOMIS   Joe Turner let me loose and I felt all turned around inside. I just wanted to see your face to know that the world was still there. Make sure everything still in its place so I could reconnect myself together. I got there and you was gone, Martha.

MARTHA   Herald . . .

LOOMIS   Left my little girl motherless in the world.

MARTHA   I didn't leave her motherless, Herald. Reverend Tolliver wanted to move the church up North 'cause of all the trouble the colored folks was having down there. Nobody knew what was gonna happen traveling them roads. We didn't even know if we was gonna make it up here or not. I left her with my mama so she be safe. That was better than dragging her out on the road having to duck and hide from people. Wasn't no telling what was gonna happen to us. I didn't leave her motherless in the world. I been looking for you.

LOOMIS   I come up on Henry Thompson's place after seven years of living in hell, and all I'm looking to do is see your face.

MARTHA   Herald, I didn't know if you was ever coming back. They told me Joe Turner had you and my whole world split half in two. My whole life shattered. It was like I had poured it in a cracked jar and it all leaked out the bottom. When it go like that there ain't nothing you can do put it back together. You talking about Henry Thompson's place like I'm still gonna be working the land by myself. How I'm gonna do that? You wasn't gone but two months and Henry Thompson kicked me off his land and I ain't had no place to go but to my mama's. I stayed and waited there for five years before I woke up one morning and decided that you was dead. Even if you weren't, you was dead to me. I wasn't gonna carry you with me no more. So I killed you in my heart. I buried you. I mourned you. And then I picked up what was left and went on to make life without you. I was a young woman with life at my beckon. I couldn't drag you behind me like a sack of cotton.

LOOMIS   I just been waiting to look on your face to say my goodbye. That goodbye got so big at times, seem like it was gonna swallow me up. Like Jonah[3] in the whale's belly I sat up in that goodbye for three years. That goodbye kept me out on the road searching. Not looking on women in their houses. It kept me bound up to the road. All the time that goodbye swelling up in my chest till I'm about to bust. Now that I see your face I can say my goodbye and make my own world.

[LOOMIS *takes* ZONIA*'s hand and presents her to* MARTHA.]

Martha . . . here go your daughter. I tried to take care of her. See that she had something to eat. See that she was out of the elements. Whatever I know I tried to teach her. Now she need to learn from her mother whatever you got to teach her. That way she won't be no one-sided person.

[LOOMIS *stoops to* ZONIA.]

Zonia, you go live with your mama. She a good woman. You go on with her and listen to her good. You my daughter and I love you like a daughter. I hope to see you again in the world somewhere. I'll never forget you.

ZONIA [*Throws her arms around* LOOMIS *in a panic.*]   I won't get no bigger! My bones won't get no bigger! They won't! I promise! Take me with you till we keep searching and never finding. I won't get no bigger! I promise!

LOOMIS   Go on and do what I told you now.

---

3. Biblical figure swallowed by a whale after disobeying God's commandment.

MARTHA [*Goes to* ZONIA *and comforts her.*]   It's alright, baby. Mama's here. Mama's here. Don't worry. Don't cry.
   [MARTHA *turns to* BYNUM.]
   Mr. Bynum, I don't know how much to thank you. God bless you.

LOOMIS   It was you! All the time it was you that bind me up! You bound me to the road!

BYNUM   I ain't bind you, Herald Loomis. You can't bind what don't cling.

LOOMIS   Everywhere I go people wanna bind me up. Joe Turner wanna bind me up! Reverend Tolliver wanna bind me up. You wanna bind me up. Everybody wanna bind me up. Well, Joe Turner's come and gone and Herald Loomis ain't for no binding. I ain't gonna let nobody bind me up!
   [LOOMIS *pulls out a knife.*]

BYNUM   It wasn't you, Herald Loomis. I ain't bound you. I bound the little girl to her mother. That's who I bound. You binding yourself. You bound onto your song. All you got to do is stand up and sing it, Herald Loomis. It's right there kicking at your throat. All you got to do is sing it. Then you be free.

MARTHA   Herald . . . look at yourself! Standing there with a knife in your hand. You done gone over to the devil. Come on . . . put down the knife. You got to look to Jesus. Even if you done fell away from the church you can be saved again. The Bible say, "The Lord is my shepherd I shall not want. He maketh me to lie down in green pastures. He leads me beside the still water. He restoreth my soul. He leads me in the path of righteousness for His name's sake. Even though I walk through the shadow of death—"

LOOMIS   That's just where I be walking!

MARTHA   "I shall fear no evil. For Thou art with me. Thy rod and thy staff, they comfort me."

LOOMIS   You can't tell me nothing about no valleys. I done been all across the valleys and the hills and the mountains and the oceans.

MARTHA   "Thou preparest a table for me in the presence of my enemies."

LOOMIS   And all I seen was a bunch of niggers dazed out of their woolly heads. And Mr. Jesus Christ standing there in the middle of them, grinning.

MARTHA   "Thou annointest my head with oil, my cup runneth over."

LOOMIS   He grin that big old grin . . . and niggers wallowing at his feet.

MARTHA   "Surely goodness and mercy shall follow me all the days of my life, and I shall dwell in the house of the Lord forever."

LOOMIS   Great big old white man . . . your Mr. Jesus Christ. Standing there with a whip in one hand and tote board in another, and them niggers swimming in a sea of cotton. And he counting. He tallying up the cotton. "Well, Jeremiah . . . what's the matter, you ain't picked but two hundred pounds of cotton today? Got to put you on half rations." And Jeremiah go back and lay up there on his half rations and talk about what a nice man Mr. Jesus Christ is 'cause he give him salvation after he die. Something wrong here. Something don't fit right!

MARTHA   You got to open up your heart and have faith, Herald. This world is just a trial for the next. Jesus offers you salvation.

LOOMIS   I been wading in the water. I been walking all over the River Jordan.[4] But what it get me, huh? I done been baptized with blood of the

---

4. River in which John the Baptist baptized Jesus Christ (Matthew 3.13–17).

lamb and the fire of the Holy Ghost. But what I got, huh? I got salvation? My enemies all around me picking the flesh from my bones. I'm choking on my own blood and all you got to give me is salvation?

MARTHA You got to be clean, Herald. You got to be washed with the blood of the lamb.

LOOMIS Blood make you clean? You clean with blood?

MARTHA Jesus bled for you. He's the Lamb of God who takest away the sins of the world.

LOOMIS I don't need nobody to bleed for me! I can bleed for myself.

MARTHA You got to be something, Herald. You just can't be alive. Life don't mean nothing unless it got a meaning.

LOOMIS What kind of meaning you got? What kind of clean you got, woman? You want blood? Blood make you clean? You clean with blood?

[LOOMIS *slashes himself across the chest. He rubs the blood over his face and comes to a realization.*]

I'm standing! I'm standing. My legs stood up! I'm standing now!

[*Having found his song, the song of self-sufficiency, fully resurrected, cleansed and given breath, free from any encumbrance other than the workings of his own heart and the bonds of the flesh, having accepted the responsibility for his own presence in the world, he is free to soar above the environs that weighed and pushed his spirit into terrifying contractions.*]

Goodbye, Martha.

[LOOMIS *turns and exits, the knife still in his hands.* MATTIE *looks about the room and rushes out after him.*]

BYNUM Herald Loomis, you shining! You shining like new money!

[*The lights go down to* BLACK.]

1988

OCTAVIA BUTLER
1947–2006

O ctavia Butler described herself in a 1999 interview as "comfortably asocial—a hermit in the middle of Seattle—a pessimist if I'm not careful, a feminist, a Black, a former Baptist, an oil-and-water combination of ambition, laziness, insecurity, certainty, and drive." The contradictions in her personality and the keen self-consciousness with which she could analyze them helped make her a distinctive writer. One of a handful of African Americans to publish science fiction, Octavia Butler shaped the genre to reflect her black feminist perspectives and as a result attracted black women readers to the genre. But her writing won readers across the spectrum. Indeed, when asked if he could be any author in the world in 2012, Pulitzer Prize–winning author Junot Díaz replied that he would be Octavia Butler, who he claimed has written nine perfect novels.

Born in Pasadena, California, on June 22, 1947, and raised by her mother and grandmother (her father died shortly after her birth), Butler, an introspective only child in a strict Baptist household, was drawn early to magazines such as *Amazing, Fantasy and Science Fiction,* and *Galaxy* and soon began reading all the science fiction classics. She was particularly impressed by Ursula Le Guin's *Dispossessed* and the first of Frank Herbert's Dune series. California, with its highly fluid, ethnically mixed population, has long been a congenial birthplace for science fiction about imaginative mixes of societies, time periods, and races, producing some of the genre's finest writers, including A. E. van Vogt, Philip K. Dick, and Harlan Ellison, who discovered Butler through the Open Door Workshop of the Writers Guild of America. After a short time writing "terrible stories about thirty-year-old men who drank and smoked too much," Butler began composing early versions of what would become the Patternist series.

The series, which consists of *Patternmaster* (1976), *Mind of My Mind* (1977), *Survivor* (1978), *Wild Seed* (1980), and *Clay's Ark* (1984), immerses the reader in a fully rendered universe whose central figure is a four-thousand-year-old immortal named Doro. Able to move at will, from body to body and across time periods, Doro sustains himself by appropriating the bodies of others, regardless of gender or race, although he prefers to inhabit black males. A powerful Nubian patriarch who maintains his supremacy by using his exceptional psychic powers and physical strength, Doro has fathered enough descendants to build a dynasty known as "the Pattern." Butler also created Mary, one of Doro's daughters, an exceptionally gifted telepath, as well as Emma, who adopts Mary and is a strong, elegant female figure, in many ways a prototypical feminist science fiction character.

Butler's best-known book, *Kindred* (1988), was originally intended to be a Patternist novel but was too realistic to fit into the series' futurist frame. In *Kindred*, Dana, a twenty-six-year-old black woman, is transported from the Los Angeles suburb where she lives with her white husband in 1976, the nation's bicentennial, to a Maryland plantation in the antebellum South; there she finds herself the property of a family whose eldest son, Rufus, has summoned her to save him. Throughout this fantasy, Butler describes how the imprint of slavery is carried not only in the minds but also on the bodies of all African Americans, as symbolized in the novel by Dana's loss of an arm during her ordeal.

Dawn (1987) initiated a trilogy that includes *Adulthood Rites* (1988) and *Imago* (1989). Retitled *Lilith's Brood* in 2000, the series features Lilith and her genetically altered children, who are saved by extraterrestrials, called the Oankali, after the earth is destroyed. The Oankali, a group with three genders, are biological traders who are driven to share genes with other intelligent species. In these novels, Butler uses genetic science, especially the discovery of mitochondrial DNA, to critique racial essentialism.

Parable of the Sower (1993) was the first of Butler's Parable novels, which focus on the twentieth-century ills afflicting the African American community, notably drug addiction. To combat the resulting spiritual deterioration and cultural chaos, the novel invents a multicultural family led by Lauren Olamina, an "empath," a figure crippled by the pain of others. She becomes the prophet of a new faith, Earthseed, that carries the promise of redemption for a world on the brink of destruction. The second installment, *Parable of the Talents* (1999) won the Nebula Award given to the year's best science fiction novel. Further confirmation of Butler's talent came with the MacArthur Fellowship, known as the "genius award," she received in 1999. In 2000 she received the PEN Center West Lifetime Achievement Award.

Overcoming what she described as writer's block, Butler published a final novel, *Fledgling*, in 2005. In a departure from her earlier fiction, this novel's conflict pitted two bands of zombies against each other. However, in its themes of racial and gender equality, *Fledgling* is consistent with Butler's longstanding concerns; it seemed to signal a renewed engagement with her writing. Sadly, that promise ended with Butler's sudden death at her Seattle home in 2006.

Although Butler wrote short fiction infrequently, "Bloodchild," reprinted here, is one of her most powerful, well-crafted efforts. As do her novels, Butler's story challenges our contemporary ideas about gender and race in a futuristic way that few African American writers have attempted.

Bloodchild

My last night of childhood began with a visit home. T'Gatoi's sisters had given us two sterile eggs. T'Gatoi gave one to my mother, brother, and sisters. She insisted that I eat the other one alone. It didn't matter. There was still enough to leave everyone feeling good. Almost everyone. My mother wouldn't take any. She sat, watching everyone drifting and dreaming without her. Most of the time she watched me.

I lay against T'Gatoi's long, velvet underside, sipping from my egg now and then, wondering why my mother denied herself such a harmless pleasure. Less of her hair would be gray if she indulged now and then. The eggs prolonged life, prolonged vigor. My father, who had never refused one in his life, had lived more than twice as long as he should have. And toward the end of his life, when he should have been slowing down, he had married my mother and fathered four children.

But my mother seemed content to age before she had to. I saw her turn away as several of T'Gatoi's limbs secured me closer. T'Gatoi liked our body heat, and took advantage of it whenever she could. When I was little and at home more, my mother used to try to tell me how to behave with T'Gatoi—how to be respectful and always obedient because T'Gatoi was the Tlic government official in charge of the Preserve, and thus the most important of her kind to deal directly with Terrans. It was an honor, my mother said, that such a person had chosen to come into the family. My mother was at her most formal and severe when she was lying.

I had no idea why she was lying, or even what she was lying about. It *was* an honor to have T'Gatoi in the family, but it was hardly a novelty. T'Gatoi and my mother had been friends all my mother's life, and T'Gatoi was not interested in being honored in the house she considered her second home. She simply came in, climbed onto one of her special couches and called me over to keep her warm. It was impossible to be formal with her while lying against her and hearing her complain as usual that I was too skinny.

"You're better," she said this time, probing me with six or seven of her limbs. "You're gaining weight finally. Thinness is dangerous." The probing changed subtly, became a series of caresses.

"He's still too thin," my mother said sharply.

T'Gatoi lifted her head and perhaps a meter of her body off the couch as though she were sitting up. She looked at my mother, and my mother, her face lined and old-looking, turned away.

"Lien, I would like you to have what's left of Gan's egg."

"The eggs are for the children," my mother said.

"They are for the family. Please take it."

Unwillingly obedient, my mother took it from me and put it to her mouth. There were only a few drops left in the now-shrunken, elastic shell, but she squeezed them out, swallowed them, and after a few moments some of the lines of tension began to smooth from her face.

"It's good," she whispered. "Sometimes I forget how good it is."

"You should take more," T'Gatoi said. "Why are you in such a hurry to be old?"

My mother said nothing.

"I like being able to come here," T'Gatoi said. "This place is a refuge because of you, yet you won't take care of yourself."

T'Gatoi was hounded on the outside. Her people wanted more of us made available. Only she and her political faction stood between us and the hordes who did not understand why there was a Preserve—why any Terran could not be courted, paid, drafted, in some way made available to them. Or they did understand, but in their desperation, they did not care. She parceled us out to the desperate and sold us to the rich and powerful for their political support. Thus, we were necessities, status symbols, and an independent people. She oversaw the joining of families, putting an end to the final remnants of the earlier system of breaking up Terran families to suit impatient Tlic. I had lived outside with her. I had seen the desperate eagerness in the way some people looked at me. It was a little frightening to know that only she stood between us and that desperation that could so easily swallow us. My mother would look at her sometimes and say to me, "Take care of her." And I would remember that she too had been outside, had seen.

Now T'Gatoi used four of her limbs to push me away from her onto the floor. "Go on, Gan," she said. "Sit down there with your sisters and enjoy not being sober. You had most of the egg. Lien, come warm me."

My mother hesitated for no reason that I could see. One of my earliest memories is of my mother stretched alongside T'Gatoi, talking about things I could not understand, picking me up from the floor and laughing as she sat me on one of T'Gatoi's segments. She ate her share of eggs then. I wondered when she had stopped and why.

She lay down now against T'Gatoi, and the whole left row of T'Gatoi's limbs closed around her, holding her loosely, but securely. I had always found it comfortable to lie that way but, except for my older sister, no one else in the family liked it. They said it made them feel caged.

T'Gatoi meant to cage my mother. Once she had, she moved her tail slightly, then spoke. "Not enough egg, Lien. You should have taken it when it was passed to you. You need it badly now."

T'Gatoi's tail moved once more, its whip motion so swift I wouldn't have seen it if I hadn't been watching for it. Her sting drew only a single drop of blood from my mother's bare leg.

My mother cried out—probably in surprise. Being stung doesn't hurt. Then she sighed and I could see her body relax. She moved languidly into a more comfortable position within the cage of T'Gatoi's limbs. "Why did you do that?" she asked, sounding half asleep.

"I could not watch you sitting and suffering any longer."

My mother managed to move her shoulders in a small shrug. "Tomorrow," she said.

"Yes. Tomorrow you will resume your suffering—if you must. But for now, just for now, lie here and warm me and let me ease your way a little."

"He's still mine, you know," my mother said suddenly. "Nothing can buy him from me." Sober, she would not have permitted herself to refer to such things.

"Nothing," T'Gatoi agreed, humoring her.

"Did you think I would sell him for eggs? For long life? My son?"

"Not for anything," T'Gatoi said stroking my mother's shoulders, toying with her long, graying hair.

I would like to have touched my mother, shared that moment with her. She would take my hand if I touched her now. Freed by the egg and the sting, she would smile and perhaps say things long held in. But tomorrow, she would remember all this as a humiliation. I did not want to be part of a remembered humiliation. Best just to be still and know she loved me under all the duty and pride and pain.

"Xuan Hoa, take off her shoes," T'Gatoi said. "In a little while I'll sting her again and she can sleep."

My older sister obeyed, swaying drunkenly as she stood up. When she had finished, she sat down beside me and took my hand. We had always been a unit, she and I.

My mother put the back of her head against T'Gatoi's underside and tried from that impossible angle to look up into the broad, round face. "You're going to sting me again?"

"Yes, Lien."

"I'll sleep until tomorrow noon."

"Good. You need it. When did you sleep last?"

My mother made a wordless sound of annoyance. "I should have stepped on you when you were small enough," she muttered.

It was an old joke between them. They had grown up together, sort of, though T'Gatoi had not, in my mother's lifetime, been small enough for any Terran to step on. She was nearly three times my mother's present age, yet would still be young when my mother died of age. But T'Gatoi and my mother had met as T'Gatoi was coming into a period of rapid development—a kind of Tlic adolescence. My mother was only a child, but for a while they developed at the same rate and had no better friends than each other.

T'Gatoi had even introduced my mother to the man who became my father. My parents, pleased with each other in spite of their very different ages, married as T'Gatoi was going into her family's business—politics. She and my mother saw each other less. But sometime before my older sister was born, my mother promised T'Gatoi one of her children. She would have to give one of us to someone, and she preferred T'Gatoi to some stranger.

Years passed. T'Gatoi traveled and increased her influence. The Preserve was hers by the time she came back to my mother to collect what she probably saw as her just reward for her hard work. My older sister took an instant liking to her and wanted to be chosen, but my mother was just coming to term with me and T'Gatoi liked the idea of choosing an infant and watching and taking part in all the phases of development. I'm told I was first caged within T'Gatoi's many limbs only three minutes after my birth. A few days later, I was given my first taste of egg. I tell Terrans that when they ask whether I was ever afraid of her. And I tell it to Tlic when T'Gatoi suggests a young Terran child for them and they, anxious and ignorant, demand an adolescent. Even my brother who had somehow grown up to fear and distrust the Tlic could probably have gone smoothly into one of their families if he had been adopted early enough. Sometimes, I think for his sake he should have been. I looked at him, stretched out on the floor across the room, his eyes open, but glazed as he dreamed his egg dream. No matter what he felt toward the Tlic, he always demanded his share of egg.

"Lien, can you stand up?" T'Gatoi asked suddenly.

"Stand?" my mother said. "I thought I was going to sleep."

"Later. Something sounds wrong outside." The cage was abruptly gone.

"What?"

"Up, Lien!"

My mother recognized her tone and got up just in time to avoid being dumped on the floor. T'Gatoi whipped her three meters of body off her couch, toward the door, and out at full speed. She had bones—ribs, a long spine, a skull, four sets of limbbones per segment. But when she moved that way, twisting, hurling herself into controlled falls, landing running, she seemed not only boneless, but aquatic—something swimming through the air as though it were water. I loved watching her move.

I left my sister and started to follow her out the door, though I wasn't very steady on my own feet. It would have been better to sit and dream, better yet to find a girl and share a waking dream with her. Back when the Tlic saw us as not much more than convenient big warm-blooded animals, they would pen several of us together, male and female, and feed us only eggs. That way they could be sure of getting another generation of us no matter how we tried to hold out. We were lucky that didn't go on long. A few generations of it and we would have *been* little more than convenient big animals.

"Hold the door open, Gan," T'Gatoi said. "And tell the family to stay back."

"What is it?" I asked.

"N'Tlic."[1]

I shrank back against the door. "Here? Alone?"

"He was trying to reach a call box, I suppose." She carried the man past me, unconscious, folded like a coat over some of her limbs. He looked young—my brother's age perhaps—and he was thinner than he should have been. What T'Gatoi would have called dangerously thin.

"Gan, go to the call box," she said. She put the man on the floor and began stripping off his clothing.

I did not move.

After a moment, she looked up at me, her sudden stillness a sign of deep impatience.

"Send Qui," I told her. "I'll stay here. Maybe I can help."

She let her limbs begin to move again, lifting the man and pulling his shirt over his head. "You don't want to see this," she said. "It will be hard. I can't help this man the way his Tlic could."

"I know. But send Qui. He won't want to be of any help here. I'm at least willing to try."

She looked at my brother—older, bigger, stronger, certainly more able to help her here. He was sitting up now, braced against the wall, staring at the man on the floor with undisguised fear and revulsion. Even she could see that he would be useless.

"Qui, go!" she said.

He didn't argue. He stood up, swayed briefly, then steadied, frightened sober.

"This man's name is Bram Lomas," she told him, reading from the man's arm band. I fingered my own arm band in sympathy. "He needs T'Khotgif Teh. Do you hear?"

"Bram Lomas, T'Khotgif Teh," my brother said. "I'm going." He edged around Lomas and ran out the door.

Lomas began to regain consciousness. He only moaned at first and clutched spasmodically at a pair of T'Gatoi's limbs. My younger sister, finally awake from her egg dream, came close to look at him, until my mother pulled her back.

---

1. Presumably, without a Tlic guardian or protector.

T'Gatoi removed the man's shoes, then his pants, all the while leaving him two of her limbs to grip. Except for the final few, all her limbs were equally dexterous. "I want no argument from you this time, Gan," she said.

I straightened. "What shall I do?"

"Go out and slaughter an animal that is at least half your size."

"Slaughter? But I've never—"

She knocked me across the room. Her tail was an efficient weapon whether she exposed the sting or not.

I got up, feeling stupid for having ignored her warning, and went into the kitchen. Maybe I could kill something with a knife or an ax. My mother raised a few Terran animals for the table and several thousand local ones for their fur. T'Gatoi would probably prefer something local. An achti, perhaps. Some of those were the right size, though they had about three times as many teeth as I did and a real love of using them. My mother, Hoa, and Qui could kill them with knives. I had never killed one at all, had never slaughtered any animal. I had spent most of my time with T'Gatoi while my brother and sisters were learning the family business. T'Gatoi had been right. I should have been the one to go to the call box. At least I could do that.

I went to the corner cabinet where my mother kept her larger house and garden tools. At the back of the cabinet there was a pipe that carried off waste water from the kitchen—except that it didn't any more. My father had rerouted the waste water before I was born. Now the pipe could be turned so that one half slid around the other and a rifle could be stored inside. This wasn't our only gun, but it was our most easily accessible one. I would have to use it to shoot one of the biggest of the achti. Then T'Gatoi would probably confiscate it. Firearms were illegal in the Preserve. There had been incidents right after the Preserve was established—Terrans shooting Tlic, shooting N'Tlic. This was before the joining of families began, before everyone had a personal stake in keeping the peace. No one had shot a Tlic in my lifetime or my mother's, but the law still stood—for our protection, we were told. There were stories of whole Terran families wiped out in reprisal back during the assassinations.

I went out to the cages and shot the biggest achti I could find. It was a handsome breeding male and my mother would not be pleased to see me bring it in. But it was the right size, and I was in a hurry.

I put the achti's long, warm body over my shoulder—glad that some of the weight I'd gained was muscle—and took it to the kitchen. There, I put the gun back in its hiding place. If T'Gatoi noticed the achti's wounds and demanded the gun, I would give it to her. Otherwise, let it stay where my father wanted it.

I turned to take the achti to her, then hesitated. For several seconds, I stood in front of the closed door wondering why I was suddenly afraid. I knew what was going to happen. I hadn't seen it before but T'Gatoi had shown me diagrams, and drawings. She had made sure I knew the truth as soon as I was old enough to understand it.

Yet I did not want to go into that room. I wasted a little time choosing a knife from the carved, wooden box in which my mother kept them. T'Gatoi might want one, I told myself, for the tough, heavily furred hide of the achti.

"Gan!" T'Gatoi called, her voice harsh with urgency.

I swallowed. I had not imagined a simple moving of the feet could be so difficult. I realized I was trembling and that shamed me. Shame impelled me through the door.

I put the achti down near T'Gatoi and saw that Lomas was unconscious again. She, Lomas, and I were alone in the room, my mother and sisters probably sent out so they would not have to watch. I envied them.

But my mother came back into the room as T'Gatoi seized the achti. Ignoring the knife I offered her, she extended claws from several of her limbs and slit the achti from throat to anus. She looked at me, her yellow eyes intent. "Hold this man's shoulders, Gan."

I stared at Lomas in panic, realizing that I did not want to touch him, let alone hold him. This would not be like shooting an animal. Not as quick, not as merciful, and, I hoped, not as final, but there was nothing I wanted less than to be part of it.

My mother came forward. "Gan, you hold his right side," she said. "I'll hold his left." And if he came to, he would throw her off without realizing he had done it. She was a tiny woman. She often wondered aloud how she had produced, as she said, such "huge" children.

"Never mind," I told her, taking the man's shoulders. "I'll do it."

She hovered nearby.

"Don't worry," I said. "I won't shame you. You don't have to stay and watch."

She looked at me uncertainly, then touched my face in a rare caress. Finally, she went back to her bedroom.

T'Gatoi lowered her head in relief. "Thank you, Gan," she said with courtesy more Terran than Tlic. "That one . . . she is always finding new ways for me to make her suffer."

Lomas began to groan and make choked sounds. I had hoped he would stay unconscious. T'Gatoi put her face near his so that he focused on her.

"I've stung you as much as I dare for now," she told him. "When this is over, I'll sting you to sleep and you won't hurt any more."

"Please," the man begged. "Wait . . ."

"There's no more time, Bram. I'll sting you as soon as it's over. When T'Khotgif arrives she'll give you eggs to help you heal. It will be over soon."

"T'Khotgif!" the man shouted, straining against my hands.

"Soon, Bram." T'Gatoi glanced at me, then placed a claw against his abdomen slightly to the right of the middle, just below the last rib. There was movement on the right side—tiny, seemingly random pulsations moving his brown flesh, creating a concavity here, a convexity there, over and over until I could see the rhythm of it and knew where the next pulse would be.

Lomas's entire body stiffened under T'Gatoi's claw, though she merely rested it against him as she wound the rear section of her body around his legs. He might break my grip, but he would not break hers. He wept helplessly as she used his pants to tie his hands, then pushed his hands above his head so that I could kneel on the cloth between them and pin them in place. She rolled up his shirt and gave it to him to bite down on.

And she opened him.

His body convulsed with the first cut. He almost tore himself away from me. The sounds he made . . . I had never heard such sounds come from anything human. T'Gatoi seemed to pay no attention as she lengthened and deepened the cut, now and then pausing to lick away blood. His blood vessels contracted, reacting to the chemistry of her saliva, and the bleeding slowed.

I felt as though I were helping her torture him, helping her consume him. I knew I would vomit soon, didn't know why I hadn't already. I couldn't possibly last until she was finished.

She found the first grub. It was fat and deep red with his blood—both inside and out. It had already eaten its own egg case, but apparently had not yet begun to eat its host. At this stage, it would eat any flesh except its mother's. Let alone, it would have gone on excreting the poisons that had both sickened and alerted Lomas. Eventually it would have begun to eat. By the time it ate its way out of Lomas's flesh, Lomas would be dead or dying—and unable to take revenge on the thing that was killing him. There was always a grace period between the time the host sickened and the time the grubs began to eat him.

T'Gatoi picked up the writhing grub carefully, and looked at it, somehow ignoring the terrible groans of the man.

Abruptly, the man lost consciousness.

"Good," T'Gatoi looked down at him. "I wish you Terrans could do that at will." She felt nothing. And the thing she held . . .

It was limbless and boneless at this stage, perhaps fifteen centimeters long and two thick, blind and slimy with blood. It was like a large worm. T'Gatoi put it into the belly of the achti, and it began at once to burrow. It would stay there and eat as long as there was anything to eat.

Probing through Lomas's flesh, she found two more, one of them smaller and more vigorous. "A male!" she said happily. He would be dead before I would. He would be through his metamorphosis and screwing everything that would hold still before his sisters even had limbs. He was the only one to make a serious effort to bite T'Gatoi as she placed him in the achti.

Paler worms oozed to visibility in Lomas's flesh. I closed my eyes. It was worse than finding something dead, rotting, and filled with tiny animal grubs. And it was far worse than any drawing or diagram.

"Ah, there are more," T'Gatoi said, plucking out two long, thick grubs. You may have to kill another animal, Gan. Everything lives inside you Terrans."

I had been told all my life that this was a good and necessary thing Tlic and Terran did together—a kind of birth. I had believed it until now. I knew birth was painful and bloody, no matter what. But this was something else, something worse. And I wasn't ready to see it. Maybe I never would be. Yet I couldn't *not* see it. Closing my eyes didn't help.

T'Gatoi found a grub still eating its egg case. The remains of the case were still wired into a blood vessel by their own little tube or hook or whatever. That was the way the grubs were anchored and the way they fed. They took only blood until they were ready to emerge. Then they ate their stretched, elastic egg cases. Then they ate their hosts.

T'Gatoi bit away the egg case, licked away the blood. Did she like the taste? Did childhood habits die hard—or not die at all?

The whole procedure was wrong, alien. I wouldn't have thought anything about her could seem alien to me.

"One more, I think," she said. "Perhaps two. A good family. In a host animal these days, we would be happy to find one or two alive." She glanced at me. "Go outside, Gan, and empty your stomach. Go now while the man is unconscious."

I staggered out, barely made it. Beneath the tree just beyond the front door, I vomited until there was nothing left to bring up. Finally, I stood shaking, tears streaming down my face. I did not know why I was crying, but I could not stop. I went farther from the house to avoid being seen. Every time I closed my eyes I saw red worms crawling over redder human flesh.

There was a car coming toward the house. Since Terrans were forbidden motorized vehicles except for certain farm equipment, I knew this must be Lomas's Tlic with Qui and perhaps a Terran doctor. I wiped my face on my shirt, struggled for control.

"Gan," Qui called as the car stopped. "What happened?" He crawled out of the low, round, Tlic-convenient car door. Another Terran crawled out the other side and went into the house without speaking to me. The doctor. With his help and a few eggs, Lomas might make it.

"T'Khotgif Teh?" I said.

The Tlic driver surged out of her car, reared up half her length before me. She was paler and smaller than T'Gatoi—probably born from the body of an animal. Tlic from Terran bodies were always larger as well as more numerous.

"Six young," I told her. "Maybe seven, all alive. At least one male."

"Lomas?" she said harshly. I liked her for the question and the concern in her voice when she asked it. The last coherent thing he had said was her name.

"He's alive," I said.

She surged away to the house without another word.

"She's been sick," my brother said, watching her go. "When I called, I could hear people telling her she wasn't well enough to go out even for this."

I said nothing. I had extended courtesy to the Tlic. Now I didn't want to talk to anyone. I hoped he would go in—out of curiosity, if nothing else.

"Finally found out more than you wanted to know, eh?"

I looked at him.

"Don't give me one of *her* looks," he said. "You're not her. You're just her property."

One of her looks. Had I picked up even an ability to imitate her expressions?

"What'd you do, puke?" He sniffed the air. "So now you know what you're in for."

I walked away from him. He and I had been close when we were kids. He would let me follow him around when I was home and sometimes T'Gatoi would let me bring him along when she took me into the city. But something had happened when he reached adolescence. I never knew what. He began keeping out of T'Gatoi's way. Then he began running away—until he realized there was no "away." Not in the Preserve. Certainly not outside. After that he concentrated on getting his share of every egg that came into the house, and on looking out for me in a way that made me all but hate him—a way that clearly said, as long as I was all right, he was safe from the Tlic.

"How was it, really?" he demanded, following me.

"I killed an achti. The young ate it."

"You didn't run out of the house and puke because they ate an achti."

"I had . . . never seen a person cut open before." That was true and enough for him to know. I couldn't talk about the other. Not with him.

"Oh," he said. He glanced at me as though he wanted to say more, but he kept quiet.

We walked, not really headed anywhere. Toward the back, toward the cages, toward the fields.

"Did he say anything?" Qui asked. "Lomas, I mean."

Who else would he mean? "He said 'T'Khotgif.'"

Qui shuddered. "If she had done that to me, she'd be the last person I'd call for."

"You'd call for her. Her sting would ease your pain without killing the grubs in you."

"You think I'd care if they died?"

No. Of course he wouldn't. Would I?

"Shit!" He drew a deep breath. "I've seen what they do. You think this thing with Lomas was bad? It was nothing."

I didn't argue. He didn't know what he was talking about.

"I saw them eat a man," he said.

I turned to face him. "You're lying!"

"I saw them eat a man." He paused. "It was when I was little. I had been to the Hartmund house and I was on my way home. Halfway here, I saw a man and a Tlic and the man was N'Tlic. The ground was hilly. I was able to hide from them and watch. The Tlic wouldn't open the man because she had nothing to feed the grubs. The man couldn't go any farther and there were no houses around. He was in so much pain he told her to kill him. He begged her to kill him. Finally, she did. She cut his throat. One swipe of one claw. I saw the grubs eat their way out, then burrow in again, still eating."

His words made me see Lomas's flesh again, parasitized, crawling. "Why didn't you tell me that?" I whispered.

He looked startled, as though he'd forgotten I was listening. "I don't know."

"You started to run away not long after that, didn't you?"

"Yeah. Stupid. Running inside the Preserve. Running in a cage."

I shook my head, said what I should have said to him long ago. "She wouldn't take you, Qui. You don't have to worry."

"She would . . . if anything happened to you."

"No. She'd take Xuan Hoa. Hoa . . . wants it." She wouldn't if she had stayed to watch Lomas.

"They don't take women," he said with contempt.

"They do sometimes." I glanced at him. "Actually, they prefer women. You should be around them when they talk among themselves. They say women have more body fat to protect the grubs. But they usually take men to leave the women free to bear their own young."

"To provide the next generation of host animals," he said, switching from contempt to bitterness.

"It's more than that!" I countered. Was it?

"If it were going to happen to me, I'd want to believe it was more, too."

"It *is* more!" I felt like a kid. Stupid argument.

"Did you think so while T'Gatoi was picking worms out of that guy's guts?"

"It's not supposed to happen that way."

"Sure it is. You weren't supposed to see it, that's all. And his Tlic was supposed to do it. She could sting him unconscious and the operation wouldn't have been as painful. But she'd still open him, pick out the grubs, and if she missed even one, it would poison him and eat him from the inside out."

There was actually a time when my mother told me to show respect for Qui because he was my older brother. I walked away hating him. In his way, he was gloating. He was safe and I wasn't. I could have hit him, but I didn't think I would be able to stand it when he refused to hit back, when he looked at me with contempt and pity.

He wouldn't let me get away. Longer-legged, he swung ahead of me and made me feel as though I were following him.

"I'm sorry," he said.

I strode on, sick and furious.

"Look, it probably won't be that bad with you. T'Gatoi likes you. She'll be careful."

I turned back toward the house, almost running from him.

"Has she done it to you yet?" he asked, keeping up easily. "I mean, you're about the right age for implantation. Has she—"

I hit him. I didn't know I was going to do it, but I think I meant to kill him. If he hadn't been bigger and stronger, I think I would have.

He tried to hold me off, but in the end, had to defend himself. He only hit me a couple of times. That was plenty. I don't remember going down, but when I came to, he was gone. It was worth the pain to be rid of him.

I got up and walked slowly toward the house. The back was dark. No one was in the kitchen. My mother and sisters were sleeping in their bedrooms—or pretending to.

Once I was in the kitchen, I could hear voices—Tlic and Terran from the next room. I couldn't make out what they were saying—didn't want to make it out.

I sat down at my mother's table, waiting for quiet. The table was smooth and worn, heavy and well-crafted. My father had made it for her just before he died. I remembered hanging around underfoot when he built it. He didn't mind. Now I sat leaning on it, missing him. I could have talked to him. He had done it three times in his long life. Three clutches of eggs, three times being opened and sewed up. How had he done it? How did any-one do it?

I got up, took the rifle from its hiding place, and sat down again with it. It needed cleaning, oiling.

All I did was load it.

"Gan?"

She made a lot of little clicking sounds when she walked on bare floor, each limb clicking in succession as it touched down. Waves of little clicks.

She came to the table, raised the front half of her body above it, and surged onto it. Sometimes she moved so smoothly she seemed to flow like water itself. She coiled herself into a small hill in the middle of the table and looked at me.

"That was bad," she said softly. "You should not have seen it. It need not be that way."

"I know."

"T'Khotgif—Ch'Khotgif now—she will die of her disease. She will not live to raise her children. But her sister will provide for them, and for Bram Lomas." Sterile sister. One fertile female in every lot. One to keep the fam-ily going. That sister owed Lomas more than she could ever repay.

"He'll live then?"

"Yes."

"I wonder if he would do it again."

"No one would ask him to do that again."

I looked into the yellow eyes, wondering how much I saw and understood there, and how much I only imagined. "No one ever asks us," I said. "You never asked me."

She moved her head slightly. "What's the matter with your face?"

"Nothing. Nothing important." Human eyes probably wouldn't have noticed the swelling in the darkness. The only light was from one of the moons, shining through a window across the room.

"Did you use the rifle to shoot the achti?"

"Yes."

"And do you mean to use it to shoot me?"

I stared at her, outlined in moonlight—coiled, graceful body. "What does Terran blood taste like to you?"

She said nothing.

"What are you?" I whispered. "What are we to you?"

She lay still, rested her head on her topmost coil. "You know me as no other does," she said softly. "You must decide."

"That's what happened to my face," I told her.

"What?"

"Qui goaded me into deciding to do something. It didn't turn out very well." I moved the gun slightly, brought the barrel up diagonally under my own chin. "At least it was a decision I made."

"As this will be."

"Ask me, Gatoi."

"For my children's lives?"

She would say something like that. She knew how to manipulate people, Terran and Tlic. But not this time.

"I don't want to be a host animal," I said. "Not even yours."

It took her a long time to answer. "We use almost no host animals these days," she said. "You know that."

"You use us."

"We do. We wait long years for you and teach you and join our families to yours." She moved restlessly. "You know you aren't animals to us."

I stared at her, saying nothing.

"The animals we once used began killing most of our eggs after implantation long before your ancestors arrived," she said softly. "You know these things, Gan. Because your people arrived, we are relearning what it means to be a healthy, thriving people. And your ancestors, fleeing from their home-world, from their own kind who would have killed or enslaved them— they survived because of us. We saw them as people and gave them the Preserve when they still tried to kill us as worms."

At the word "Worms" I jumped. I couldn't help it, and she couldn't help noticing it.

"I see," she said quietly. "Would you really rather die than bear my young, Gan?"

I didn't answer.

"Shall I go to Xuan Hoa?"

"Yes!" Hoa wanted it. Let her have it. She hadn't had to watch Lomas. She'd be proud. . . . Not terrified.

T'Gatoi flowed off the table onto the floor, startling me almost too much.

"I'll sleep in Hoa's room tonight," she said. "And sometime tonight or in the morning, I'll tell her."

This was going too fast. My sister. Hoa had had almost as much to do with raising me as my mother. I was still close to her—not like Qui. She could want T'Gatoi and still love me.

"Wait! Gatoi!"

She looked back, then raised nearly half her length off the floor and turned it to face me. "These are adult things, Gan. This is my life, my family!"

"But she's . . . my sister."

"I have done what you demanded. I have asked you!"

"But—"

"It will be easier for Hoa. She has always expected to carry other lives inside her."

Human lives. Human young who would someday drink at her breasts, not at her veins.

I shook my head. "Don't do it to her, Gatoi." I was not Qui. It seemed I could become him, though, with no effort at all. I could make Xuan Hoa my shield. Would it be easier to know that red worms were growing in her flesh instead of mine?

"Don't do it to Hoa," I repeated.

She stared at me, utterly still.

I looked away, then back at her. "Do it to me."

I lowered the gun from my throat and she leaned forward to take it.

"No," I told her.

"It's the law," she said.

"Leave it for the family. One of them might use it to save my life someday."

She grasped the rifle barrel, but I wouldn't let go. I was pulled into a standing position over her.

"Leave it here!" I repeated. "If we're not your animals, if these are adult things, accept the risk. There is risk, Gatoi, in dealing with a partner."

It was clearly hard for her to let go of the rifle. A shudder went through her and she made a hissing sound of distress. It occurred to me that she was afraid. She was old enough to have seen what guns could do to people. Now her young and this gun would be together in the same house. She did not know about our other guns. In this dispute, they did not matter.

"I will implant the first egg tonight," she said as I put the gun away. "Do you hear, Gan?"

Why else had I been given a whole egg to eat while the rest of the family was left to share one? Why else had my mother kept looking at me as though I were going away from her, going where she could not follow? Did T'Gatoi imagine I hadn't known?

"I hear."

"Now!" I let her push me out of the kitchen, then walked ahead of her toward my bedroom. The sudden urgency in her voice sounded real. "You would have done it to Hoa tonight!" I accused.

"I must do it to someone tonight."

I stopped in spite of her urgency and stood in her way. "Don't you care who?"

She flowed around me and into my bedroom. I found her waiting on the couch we shared. There was nothing in Hoa's room that she could have used. She would have done it to Hoa on the floor. The thought of her doing it to Hoa at all disturbed me in a different way now, and I was suddenly angry.

Yet I undressed and lay down beside her. I knew what to do, what to expect. I had been told all my life. I felt the familiar sting, narcotic, mildly pleasant. Then the blind probing of her ovipositor.[2] The puncture was painless, easy.

---

2. A pointed tubular organ with which a female insect deposits her eggs.

So easy going in. She undulated slowly against me, her muscles forcing the egg from her body into mine. I held on to a pair of her limbs until I remembered Lomas holding her that way. Then I let go, moved inadvertently, and hurt her. She gave a low cry of pain and I expected to be caged at once within her limbs. When I wasn't, I held on to her again, feeling oddly ashamed.

"I'm sorry," I whispered.

She rubbed my shoulders with four of her limbs.

"Do you care?" I asked. "Do you care that it's me?"

She did not answer for some time. Finally, "You were the one making choices tonight, Gan. I made mine long ago."

"Would you have gone to Hoa?"

"Yes. How could I put my children into the care of one who hates them?"

"It wasn't . . . hate."

"I know what it was."

"I was afraid."

Silence.

"I still am." I could admit it to her here, now.

"But you came to me . . . to save Hoa."

"Yes." I leaned my forehead against her. She was cool velvet, deceptively soft. "And to keep you for myself," I said. It was so. I didn't understand it, but it was so.

She made a soft hum of contentment. "I couldn't believe I had made such a mistake with you," she said. "I chose you. I believed you had grown to choose me."

"I had, but . . ."

"Lomas."

"Yes."

"I have never known a Terran to see a birth and take it well. Qui has seen one, hasn't he?"

"Yes."

"Terrans should be protected from seeing."

I didn't like the sound of that—and I doubted that it was possible. "Not protected," I said. "Shown. Shown when we're young kids, and shown more than once. Gatoi, no Terran ever sees a birth that goes right. All we see is N'Tlic—pain and terror and maybe death."

She looked down at me. "It is a private thing. It has always been a private thing."

Her tone kept me from insisting—that and the knowledge that if she changed her mind, I might be the first public example. But I had planted the thought in her mind. Chances were it would grow, and eventually she would experiment.

"You won't see it again," she said. "I don't want you thinking any more about shooting me."

The small amount of fluid that came into me with her egg relaxed me as completely as a sterile egg would have, so that I could remember the rifle in my hands and my feelings of fear and revulsion, anger and despair. I could remember the feelings without reviving them. I could talk about them.

"I wouldn't have shot you," I said. "Not you." She had been taken from my father's flesh when he was my age.

"You could have," she insisted.

"Not you." She stood between us and her own people, protecting, interweaving.

"Would you have destroyed yourself?"

I moved carefully, uncomfortably. "I could have done that. I nearly did. That's Qui's 'away.' I wonder if he knows."

"What?"

I did not answer.

"You will live now."

"Yes." *Take care of her*, my mother used to say. Yes.

"I'm healthy and young," she said. "I won't leave you as Lomas was left—alone, N'Tlic. I'll take care of you."

1984

YUSEF KOMUNYAKAA
b. 1947

"Poetry is a kind of distilled insinuation," asserts Yusef Komunyakaa. "It's a way of expanding and talking around an idea or question. Sometimes, more actually gets said through such a technique than a full frontal assault." Komunyakaa's fifteen volumes of poetry tell readers much about life in Bogalusa, Louisiana, where he grew up during the civil rights movement; about the Vietnam War, during which Komunyakaa served as a soldier and war correspondent; and about life in Australia, where he spent a year. Whatever the setting, the poems explore the moral challenges of modern life. Usually composed of short lines of colloquial English, his poems reflect a philosophical turn of mind as well as a jazz influence. "Jazz has space, and space equals freedom," he comments. Like jazz his poems create "a place where a certain kind of meditation can take place."

Born April 29, 1947, in Bogalusa, a town not far from New Orleans, Komunyakaa observed the craftsmanship of his father, James William Brown, a carpenter, for whom he was named. As an adult he reclaimed the name Komunyakaa, which his grandfather had lost upon immigrating to the United States from Trinidad. He served in the U.S. Army from 1968 until 1971, spending a year in South Vietnam as a soldier and a second year as a correspondent; he was awarded a Bronze Star. Later he would draw on these experiences in the volume *Dien Cai Dau*, a title that means "crazy" in Vietnamese. Returning to the United States, he enrolled in the University of Colorado Springs; he later earned an M.A. and M.F.A. in creative writing from Colorado State University and the University of California at Irvine, respectively. During his graduate student years, he published his first books, *Dedication & Other Darkhorses* (1977) and *Lost in the Bonewheel Factory* (1979). Like his father, he is a craftsman, but his medium is the word.

With the publication of *Copacetic* (1984), Komunyakaa began to receive wide recognition. The title, a word frequently associated with jazz musicians, means everything is in excellent order. It anticipates the poetic diction, a fusion of colloquial speech and jazz talk, that Komunyakaa deploys in the volume. The poems represent his childhood and youth. He first heard jazz on the radio in Louisiana; he remembers a Louis Armstrong trumpet solo and a Dinah Washington ballad. As he told an interviewer, "Song lyrics brought me to the power of words . . . the songs taught me to listen." Musical metaphors are woven throughout his poetry, as are tributes to jazz musicians. In "February in Sydney," he pays homage to Bud Powell, Lester Young,

Ben Webster, and Coleman Hawkins: "Painful gods jive talk through / bloodstained reeds & shiny brass," as he tries to imagine how it feels "to scream for help through a horn." Continuing his engagement with the music, Komunyakaa has co-edited several volumes of jazz poetry with Sascha Feinstein, engaged in collaborations with musicians, and written song lyrics and librettos.

Neon Vernacular: Selected and New Poems (1994) earned Komunyakaa the Pulitzer Prize along with the Kingsley Tuft Poetry Award. The poems bring together his experience in the U.S. South and in Vietnam, the dilemma of being black in a white world, the chaos of urban life, and the compensations of music. Deeply personal references are juxtaposed with social observations; they are all filtered through the poet's deceptively simple style. Subsequent volumes, including Thieves of Paradise (1998), Warhorses (2008), and The Chameleon Couch (2011), have burnished his reputation. Elected a chancellor of the American Academy of Poets in 1999, Komunyakaa has won prestigious awards, including the 2011 Wallace Stevens Award and the William Faulkner Award from the Université de Rennes. Poet Toi Derricotte aptly describes Komunyakaa's poems as "razor-sharp pieces that tell us more about our culture than any news broadcast."

February in Sydney[1]

Dexter Gordon's[2] tenor sax
plays "April in Paris"
inside my head all the way back
on the bus from Double Bay.
Round Midnight,[3] the '50's,   5
cool cobblestone streets
resound footsteps of Bebop[4]
musicians with whiskey-laced voices
from a boundless dream in French.
Bud, Prez, Webster & The Hawk,[5]   10
their names run together
like mellifluous riffs.
Painful gods jive talk through
bloodstained reeds & shiny brass
where music is an anesthetic.   15
Unreadable faces from the human void
float like torn pages across the bus
windows. An old anger drips into my throat,
& I try thinking something good,
letting the precious bad   20
settle to the salty bottom.
Another scene keeps repeating itself:
I emerge from the dark theatre,
passing a woman who grabs her red purse
& hugs it to her like a heart attack.   25
Tremolo. Dexter comes back to rest
behind my eyelids. A loneliness

1. City in southeastern Australia.
2. American jazz musician.
3. French film (1986), directed by Bertrand Tavernien, about the friendship between a young Parisian jazz devotee and an aging jazz musician.
4. Jazz characterized by complex melodies and harmonies and shifting accents; often played very fast.
5. American jazz musicians. Bud Powell, Lester Young, Ben Webster, and Coleman Hawkins, respectively.

lingers like a silver needle
under my black skin,
as I try to feel how it is
to scream for help through a horn.   30

1989

Facing It

My black face fades,
hiding inside the black granite.
I said I wouldn't,
dammit: No tears.
I'm stone. I'm flesh.   5
My clouded reflection eyes me
like a bird of prey, the profile of night
slanted against morning. I turn
this way—the stone lets me go.
I turn that way—I'm inside   10
the Vietnam Veterans Memorial[1]
again, depending on the light
to make a difference.
I go down the 58,022 names,
half-expecting to find   15
my own in letters like smoke.
I touch the name Andrew Johnson;
I see the booby trap's white flash.
Names shimmer on a woman's blouse
but when she walks away   20
the names stay on the wall.
Brushstrokes flash, a red bird's
wings cutting across my stare.
The sky. A plane in the sky.
A white vet's image floats   25
closer to me, then his pale eyes
look through mine. I'm a window.
He's lost his right arm
inside the stone. In the black mirror
a woman's trying to erase names: 30
No, she's brushing a boy's hair.

1988

Sunday Afternoons

They'd latch the screendoors
& pull venetian blinds,
Telling us not to leave the yard.

---

1. In Washington, D.C.

But we always got lost
Among mayhaw & crabapple.   5

Juice spilled from our mouths,
& soon we were drunk & brave
As birds diving through saw vines.
Each nest held three or four
Speckled eggs, blue as rage.   10

Where did we learn to be unkind,
There in the power of holding each egg
While watching dogs in June
Dust & heat, or when we followed
The hawk's slow, deliberate arc?   15

In the yard, we heard cries
Fused with gospel on the radio,
Loud as shattered glass
In a Saturday-night argument
About trust & money.   20

We were born between Oh Yeah
& Goddammit. I knew life
Began where I stood in the dark,
Looking out into the light,
& that sometimes I could see   25

Everything through nothing.
The backyard trees breathed
Like a man running from himself
As my brothers backed away
From the screendoor. I knew   30

If I held my right hand above my eyes
Like a gambler's visor, I could see
How their bedroom door halved
The dresser mirror like a moon
Held prisoner in the house.   35

                                                   1992

Banking Potatoes

Daddy would drop purple-veined vines
Along rows of dark loam
& I'd march behind him
Like a peg-legged soldier,
Pushing down the stick   5
With a V cut into its tip.

Three weeks before the first frost
I'd follow his horse-drawn plow

That opened up the soil & left
Sweet potatoes sticky with sap,
Like flesh-colored stones along a riverbed
Or diminished souls beside a mass grave.

They lay all day under the sun's
Invisible weight, & by twilight
We'd bury them under pine needles
& then shovel in two feet of dirt.
Nighthawks scalloped the sweaty air,
Their wings spread wide

As plowshares. But soon the wind
Knocked on doors & windows
Like a frightened stranger,
& by mid-winter we had tunneled
Back into the tomb of straw,
Unable to divide love from hunger.

1992

Birds on a Powerline

Mama Mary's counting them
Again. Eleven black. A single
Red one like a drop of blood

Against the sky. She's convinced
They've been there two weeks.
I bring her another cup of coffee

& a Fig Newton. I sit here reading
Frances Harper[1] at the enamel table
Where I ate teacakes as a boy,

My head clear of voices brought back.
The green smell of the low land returns,
Stealing the taste of nitrate.

The deep-winter eyes of the birds
Shine in summer light like agate,
As if they could love the heart

Out of any wild thing. I stop,
With my finger on a word, listening.
They're on the powerline, a luminous

Message trailing a phantom
Goodyear blimp. I hear her say
Jesus, I promised you. Now

1. African American writer and activist (1825–1911), particularly involved in the abolitionist movement.

He's home safe, I'm ready.
My travelling shoes on. My teeth
In. I got on clean underwear.

1993

NATHANIEL MACKEY
b. 1947

One might think of Nathaniel Mackey as a jazz musician whose instrument is the word. In a 1995 interview in *Callaloo*, Mackey suggested some of the reasons music is central to his writing: "Music includes so much: it's social, it's religious, it's metaphysical, it's aesthetic, it's expressive, it's creative, it's destructive. It just covers so much." So does Mackey's multigeneric oeuvre. He has written four book-length volumes of poetry (*Eroding Witness; Song of Udhra; Whatsaid Serif* and *Splay Anthem*, which won the National Book Award for poetry in 2006), as well as several chapbooks, three works of fiction (*Bedouin Hornbook, Djbot Baghostus's Run,* and *Atet A.D.*), and two books of literary criticism (*Discrepant Engagement: Dissonance, Cross-Culturality and Experimental Writing* and *Gassire's Lute*). He has co-edited a jazz poetry anthology, founded the literary journal *Hambone,* and recorded an album (*Strick: Song of the Andoumboulou 16–25*). Like a consummate jazz player, Mackey's work extends tradition, blends cross-cultural influences, and establishes a signature sound.

Mackey was born in 1947 in Miami to Sadie Jane Wilcox and Alexander Obadiah Mackey. When Mackey was four, his parents separated, and he moved with his mother to California. In his teens he began listening to bebop, then to free jazz. Simultaneously he discovered the poetry of William Carlos Williams and Amiri Baraka and as a student at Princeton read Donald Allen's *The New American Poetry,* which included the Black Mountain "projectivist" poets Charles Olson, Robert Creeley, and Robert Duncan. Avant-garde poetry as well as post-bop jazz would inform Mackey's aesthetic. After graduating from college, Mackey taught mathematics for a year, then earned a Ph.D. in English and American literature at Stanford. He published his first chapbook, *Four for Trane,* in 1978.

From the beginning Mackey's work was characterized as postmodern, an adjective that is apt in that his poetry resists conventional literary categories and insists on a wide range of reference. His work challenges readers, but it is not abstruse. Mackey has said that he writes for the eye as well as for the ear; his poetry is meant to be both read and heard. Critic Paul Naylor, who edited an issue of *Callaloo* devoted to Mackey in 2000, calls "the cultural mix found in his work . . . astonishing." It includes references to Haitian *vodun* and Cuban *santeria*; Andalusian music; the Koran and Islamic writers; Dogon philosophy; Caribbean fiction, especially the work of the Guyanese novelist Wilson Harris; and African American music and literature. One indication of Mackey's experimentalism is that his four books of poems (published in 1985, 1993, 1998, and 2006) may be read as a single serial poem.

"I think of fiction in an open, genre-blending sense," Mackey states, confirming that his approach to fiction is also unconventional. "26.IX.81" was first published as an installment in *From a Broken Bottle Traces of Perfume Still Emanate,* a series of letters written by N., a jazz musician and member of a band called the Mystic Horn Society, to the mysterious Angel of Dust, a figure who appears throughout Mackey's writing. Each letter responds to a rehearsal or performance by the band. This letter later became part of *Djbot Baghostus's Run*. Its reflections are aesthetic, social, and metaphysical. In other words, it is as meaningful as music.

A teacher and a scholar, Mackey has taught at the University of Wisconsin; the University of Southern California; the University of California at Santa Cruz; and Duke University, where he is professor of English. He was also chancellor of the Academy of American Poets.

Falso Brilhante[1]

for Elis Regina[2]

I wake up chasing my breath, my
dead lungs undone by alcohol and cocaine,
   a rope of dust at my throat . . .
Raw thread of a dirge woven into the
wind, all night I wonder
           what   5
but unruliness ranges the heart . . .

                    A blunt featherless
    bird hovering close to my chest as
I wake up, what but ennui that I'd even   10
   wonder, what but a whim, the clouded rum
     I drink   drains me of light
I dream I hang from, dangling,
                   draped
as in rags, white fractured sky from which   15
                       I fall . . .
   White sky made blue by the blackness
beyond it, withered light, wind says *Better*
                  not
  to have been born.   20
          Breath caught in
a cloud, I cross myself, *So be it,*
               my self-embrace
   a rickety crib I serenade
            myself   25
              inside . . .
And I'm singing all the songs that made me a
  star, my arms like wings as though
they were not quite my own anymore . . .

                   Leaned   30
on by a ghost, I launch a prayer to Iansã, Ogum[3]
   at my back, my torn voice haloed

---

1. False brilliance (Portuguese).
2. Popular Brazilian singer who died in the early 1980s from respiratory problems after drinking rum.

3. Or Ogoun, the Yoruba god of hunters and blacksmiths. Iansã, the Yoruba goddess of the river Niger, is often associated with St. Barbara and was the patron saint of Elis Regina.

by an orbiting chorus as it bleeds,
hand on my heart as if I were taking an
               oath,   35
                   a faint, fading
   spark, the seeds of this parting planted
who knows how far back . . .

     A see-thru lid on the coffin I rest in.
See-thru exit, see-thru sign of the times . . .   40
   Weepers fill the streets of São Paulo,[4]
 I wake up gasping,   chasing my breath,
                     another
snuffed-out star.   Prophetic wingtip skimming
the water . . .   45
     A crystalline cut color makes
                in time . . .
   In every crack the same suffocating sweat,
                       this
   world with its arrows . . .   50
            Its rosary of worms, its
    neon angels, its megatons . . .

                       One eye with
God, the other eye with Satan, I watch the
   empty-eyed, pipe-smoking saints . . .   55

The keepers of bread do with the world as they
                  will,
   whose cards collapse . . .
               The way the
   wind has of having its way   60
           with a falling
             leaf

                   1985

Song of the Andoumboulou:[1] 8

—maitresse erzulie[2]—

One hand on her hip, one hand
   arranging her hair,
        blue heaven's
   bride. Her beaded hat she hangs
from a nail on the danceroom   5
          wall . . .

   As though an angel sought
   me out in my sleep or I sat up

---

4. A city in Brazil.
1. Funeral prayer of the Dogon, a West African people.

2. Mistress erzulie (French creole). Erzulie is the Haitian vodoun (goddess) of love; flirtatious and sensuous, she is often called "mistress."

sleepless, eyes like rocks,

night   10

like so many such nights I've known.

Not yet asleep I'm no longer

awake,   lie awaiting what

stalks the unanswered air,

still   15

awaiting what blunts the running

flood

or what carries, all Our Mistress's

whispers,

thrust   20

of a crosscut saw . . .

Who sits at her feet fills his

head with wings, oils his

mouth

with rum, readies her way   25

with perfume . . .

From whatever glimpse

of her I get I take heart, I hear them

say,

By whatever bit of her I touch

I take   30

hold

1994

From Djbot Baghostus's Run

26.IX.81

Dear Angel of Dust,

Thank you for your letter. It arrived yesterday. I'm glad to hear you're doing well and that the various demands on your time that you mention have eased up. I'd begun to wonder why I hadn't heard from you for so long. Things here have been busy as well. We've had a number of gigs recently and we've all been doing a fair amount of writing—which means we've also been putting in more rehearsal time. No, we haven't (to answer your question) found a drummer yet. We've been too busy to really apply ourselves to the search. Furthermore, the drum-dreams we had a few weeks back, I've begun to feel, did more to confuse than to clarify matters. Whether it's a drummer named Penny or a drummer named Djeannine we should be looking for we've been unable to reach an agreement on.

I have, however, given some thought to the second letter you wrote me in July, the one regarding my after-the-fact lecture/libretto. The questions you posed have stayed with me—most of all the big one you dropped on me, "Why opera?" I must admit I'm not a fan of opera. Nor do I especially know anything about it. But since anything, it seems, can be an opera nowadays, I could easily answer by asking, "Why not?" The roots of either "why," I suspect, have to do with certain suppositions regarding social and artistic arrival and/or elevation—antithetically to do with a Eurocentric ladder whose "axiomaticness" makes one ask with no real hope of ascertaining why. The roots of either "why" and of my reasons why, in other words, concern opera's aura more than anything else.

It goes back to a movie I saw as a kid in the early fifties, my first exposure to "opera," *Carmen Jones*.[1] Dorothy Dandridge and Harry Belafonte starred in it. Max Roach and Pearl Bailey[2] were in it as well and on one of his recordings of "What Is This Thing Called Love?" Bird[3] throws in a quote from the score. My older brother took me to see it and what I remember most is that it struck us as funny, that whenever someone burst into song we broke out laughing. At one point we laughed so loud and so long an usher came over to quiet us down. We laughed loudest at the end of the movie. When Belafonte choked Carmen to death and then started singing my brother and I thought we'd die.

What made us laugh was the incongruity—the unreality and the inappropriateness of singing, the gap between song and circumstance. That gap, that incongruity, obeyed a principle of non-equivalence, an upfront absence of adequation I've since made a case for regarding as apt. Such a case calls non-equivalence post-equivalence. That is, the post-equivalent slide of a pointedly unsecured address makes for an apt, operatic inappropriateness—an accusative, therefore apt incongruity. Call it fiddling while Rome burns. This is largely, though not entirely, what I'm up to.

It was exactly this I was thinking about the other night when an uncanny coincidence occurred. The notion of operatic incongruity, of an elevated, broken vessel the sound of whose shattering antithetically rings true, was much on my mind as I got up to turn the television on. I pushed in the knob and what came on was the tail-end of a Memorex commercial: Ella Fitzgerald[4] hitting an extremely high note while in the foreground a wine glass shattered. I could hardly believe it. I immediately thought of two things: 1) Rahsaan's[5] piece "Rip, Rig and Panic," whose opening section ends with the sound of breaking glass, and 2) Aunt Nancy's phrase "an eye made of opera glass."

The coincidence turned out to be catalytic. The sense of a straining see-thru mode which telescopes its own demise immediately had me under its spell. Turning away from the TV set, I sat down and began a new after-the-fact lecture / libretto, the first paragraph of which came so effortlessly it seemed to be writing itself:

> Jarred Bottle's I made of opera glass dropped out. Orb and vessel both (i.e., glass eye, reading glass and wine glass rolled into one), it dropped out, fell to the floor and shattered, having turned lower-case and taken the place of Aunt Nancy's u. An apostrophe had already pried the n and the t apart, opening the door thru which Ain't Nancy had come in and which remained ajar, a concrete epigraph endorsed in namesake fashion by a Platonic / Pythagorean pun. Jarred Bottle had begun his lecture by reading a quote: "Some clever fellow, making a play with words,

---

1. Famous musical film of the 1950s with African American characters based on French composer Georges Bizet's opera *Carmen*.
2. African American singer and actor (1918–1990). Dandridge (1922–1963), first African American woman to become a major film star in the United States. Belafonte (b. 1927), one of the first African American men to become a major film star in the United States. Roach (1925–2007), jazz drummer.

3. Charlie "Bird" Parker (1920–1955), one of the greatest bebop musicians.
4. Jazz singer (1918–1993). A reference to a television commercial in which Fitzgerald's voice recorded on a Memorex-brand cassette tape was clear enough to break a wineglass.
5. Rahsaan Roland Kirk (1936–1977), saxophonist, clarinetist, and flutist, famous for playing three horns at once.

called the soul a jar, because it can easily be jarred by persuasive words into believing this or that."

I quickly found myself at a loss as to where to go from there. Not only did words no longer come effortlessly but now they didn't come at all. I found myself put off by and caught up in qualms about the patness of the "shattered I," its apparent endorsement of currently fashionable notions of a nonexistent self, a dead subject and such. My own effortless recourse to some such implication turned me off. That the self gets all the more talked about by way of its widely insisted-upon disappearance turns out to be an irony I'm evidently not able to get beyond.

Thus the paragraph turned out to be no more than a heuristic wedge, an impromptu foot-in-the-door whose playing back of imprints availed itself of a suspect effortlessness which could now be and had to be parted with, put aside. It was a possible music I now turned my attention to. Abandoning paper and pen, I turned off the TV, took out my alto and began working on a solo which would hopefully both allude to and bridge Bird's *Carmen Jones* quote and Rahsaan's "Rip, Rig and Panic." (Rahsaan, by the way, alludes to Bird's quote in the course of his solo on "Wham Bam Thank You Ma'am" on Mingus's[6] album *Oh Yeah*.) The solo would be a part of my antithetical opera.

The working out of it went pretty well. I came up with a number of combinations and transitions, the more complex and oblique of which built upon a sensation of spindly support, a Platonic rapport between panicky stritch and impromptu aria somewhat like impishness and trauma holding hands. My playing grew possessed of a geometric high, a Pythagorean dismay (almost outrage at points) before incommensurables—but only in order not to console "Pythagorean" expectations, only in order to acknowledge or arouse a sense of aliquant excess, an elegant post-equivalent drift. I took out staff paper and as I went along wrote out the passages I felt I might not otherwise remember.

There were some wrinkles which at first refused to be ironed out. I tinkered, fine-tuned and tested for quite a while, working out most of them though a few went on getting the best of me. I arrived at a point where putting it all aside for a while seemed to be the best thing to do, so I set the horn in the stand on the floor and got up and turned the TV back on. There was a Peter Lorre[7] movie on the Late Show and I sat back down to watch it, my mind still mainly on the impasse I'd reached in my impromptu post-equivalent solo.

Not long after sitting back down I fell asleep. I must've slept for quite some time. By the time I woke up, that is, there was a test pattern on the TV screen. What woke me up was the sound of an alto playing a familiar tune, a tune whose name was on the tip of my tongue though as I slept I couldn't for the life of me recall what it was. The effort to do so woke me up.

I awoke, rubbed the sleep from my eyes and looked around, noticing the test pattern on the TV screen and the fact that the sound I'd heard was no dream but was coming from my alto sitting on the floor. I rubbed my eyes again and shook my head as if to clear it of cobwebs, taken aback by the sight of the horn apparently playing itself. I looked on in disbelief as keys

6. Charles Mingus (1922–1979), jazz bassist and composer.

7. Film star of the 1930s and 1940s who often played villains (1904–1964).

were pressed and let go, the horn fingered by invisible hands. The tune, I realized after a while, was "The Inflated Tear," Rahsaan's lament recalling a nurse's mistake which had left him blind.

I sat glued to my chair, the horn's captive. There was a lush but alarmed quality to its tone, a namesake fluidity which not only bordered on but clearly crossed over into effortlessness. Indeed, the horn was possessed of a virtuosity which amounted to the ultimate in effortlessness: automatism. I sat entranced by its utter fluency, the utter finesse with which it held forth on the emotional flood to which it owed itself. Automatic alto spoke of a blind Atlantean[8] reservoir of feeling, an inordinate rush and/or capacity from which it ever so lightly held back, all the more insistent, all the more extrapolatively brought into being by its doing so. Automatic alto (effortless alto) spoke eloquently as well as at length of operatic inflation and of its related, residual theme of aliquant excess, the very theme which had been so much on my mind.

Every now and then, however, automatic alto tripped itself up, critiqued its own effortlessness by deliberately having a beginner's difficulty with fourth-line D. By resorting to a beginner's unsuccessful effort to avoid the "break" in using the octave key automatic alto not only brought the issue of human agency to the fore but brought me more actively into the picture. I found I couldn't, that is, help trying to correct automatic alto's lapses into awkwardness. With each problematic D I lent it a bit of body English, gesturing as though I were holding it and playing it, correctly coordinating my left thumb's roll with the appropriate changes in lip and tongue pressure. In doing so I contracted a host of automatic stigmata. I could actually feel the weight of the horn pull the strap against the back of my neck, feel the reed against my lower lip, feel the octave key underneath my thumb and so forth. It was as though automatic alto were playing me, as if I were its axe, its instrument. Even so, its voice broke like that of a boy entering puberty. I could do nothing, body English notwithstanding, to assist it.

But the more automatic alto faltered the more deeply it had me under its spell. I was its axe, its instrument, no "as if" about it. With each "break" it indicated its own suspect effortlessness, but in doing so it implicated a fallible human hand, a broken vessel—namely, in this instance, me. The more it faltered the more I lent it support. But the more support I lent it—the more I gestured, the more body English I resorted to—the more inept its non-avoidance of the "break" became. With each lapse into awkwardness it brought me abreast of my own ineffectuality, seemed intent on teaching me humility—which, in a sense, it very effectively did. Automatic alto (awkward alto) clearly had a mind of its own.

What awkward alto seemed intent on saying was that I was the problem, not the solution, that aliquant excess provided not a see-thru advance but a before-the-fact Atlantean collapse. This, of course, I'd long suspected and, in that sense, already knew, but the way in which awkward alto went on to both base itself upon and embroider a blend of precipitous forethought and residual truth not only renewed but ever so expertly strengthened its hold on me. Residual truth turned into precipitous afterthought. I couldn't help noting that even though I was its axe awkward alto (aliquant[9] alto) had apparently gotten me under its skin. I was a ghost, a grain of salt in

8. Symbol of high civilization as used in Plato and W. E. B. Du Bois.

9. Designating a part of a number that divides the number evenly and leaves no remainder.

the machine. Mine was the salt- or sand-anointed voice, the unavoided "break."

After the last of these non-avoidances "The Inflated Tear" gave way to "L'oiseau rebelle,"[1] a quote of Rahsaan's quote of Bird's quote of *Carmen Jones*'s quote of *Carmen*. Aliquant alto might as well have meant aliquant elevation, aliquant/operatic aura come home to roost. It belabored the fact that what it quoted was already a quote of a quote of a quote, as though in so doing it thumbed a long since remaindered book. This accounted for the "break," the inept employment of the octave key, the lack of the appropriate tongue and lip coordination. Aliquant alto, it invited one to say, was "all thumb."

Having made its joke and having tossed out its quote of a quote of a quote of a quote, aliquant alto again took up "The Inflated Tear," playing it now without the slightest lapse into awkwardness. The finesse and facility with which it now played almost blew me away. I sat entranced as it ran the gamut from a velvety calm reminiscent of Johnny Hodges to a nervous, on-the-edge intensity worthy of Jimmy Lyons,[2] a nervous, pistol-pointed-at-one's-head sense of emergency.

Automatic alto had now come full circle, clearly come to be the host of a circuitous muse. In attempting to sidestep or critique its own technical finesse, it was now willing to admit, it had simply replaced what it took to be artificial wholeness, artificial health, with artificial breakage, artificial debris. This was a dilemma one couldn't help addressing, it went on to announce, in a period haunted by (hemmed in by) artifice, operatic reflex. Was there no way to be genuinely broken it rhetorically asked by way of a distraught, strangled, bittersweet cry, a Braxtonian[3] mix confronting form with flight. Was there no way to be genuinely whole it rhetorically asked by way of a smooth, unhurried blaze of ballad warmth, ballad hearth, ballad health.

I was now even more deeply entranced as automatic alto came full circle by playing the tune straight. Its unhurried blaze of ballad warmth brought Benny Carter[4] to mind, causing me to see that "The Inflated Tear" was the watery, post-equivalent bridge I'd been after, the sunken, lush, dreamless Atlantean drift I'd been looking for.

Automatic alto's Carteresque ballad warmth gradually gave way to a benedictory aubade which made one think of Carlos Ward (more specifically, the edge he puts on "Desireless" on Don Cherry's[5] *Relativity Suite*). It was on this note of salt-inflected fluidity—with its related sense of endless flotation and a requisite regard for longstanding limbo—that automatic alto brought its recital to a close.

Everything was now silent except for the hum of the TV set. I sat riveted to my seat, mulling over the implications of the upstart serenade the horn had treated me to. Automatic alto (upstart alto) had overcome the impasse I'd arrived at in my impromptu post-equivalent solo, ironed out the wrinkles I'd been unable to correct. Exactly how it'd done so I now sat trying to figure out.

---

1. Rebellious bird (French); here, the title of an aria from *Carmen* and a song from *Carmen Jones*. Also a reference to Parker's nickname.
2. Alto saxophonist who played in Cecil Taylor's demanding jazz orchestra. Hodges (1906–1970), alto saxophonist in Duke Ellington's orchestra.
3. From Anthony Braxton (b. 1945), avant-garde

African American composer.
4. Great arranger, composer, and multitalented brass jazz musician (1907–2003).
5. Jazz and avant-garde composer and trumpet player (1936–1996). Ward (b. 1947), Panamanian alto saxophonist.

It took me a while but I eventually figured it out—the result of which please give a listen to on the cassette you'll find enclosed: "Robotic Aria for Prepared and Unprepared Alto." As you'll hear, I've availed myself not only of automatic alto's technical solutions but of its theme of built-in obstruction as well. The aria consists of two parts, "prepared" and "unprepared." For the former I taped a sawed-off popsicle stick under the octave key. The latter begins, as you can hear, with the sound of me peeling off the tape and the popsicle stick falling to the floor.

I find the aria notable, even if I do say so myself, for the head-on hedging mixed with head-on address it carries off, its dredging up of a watery precipitate (post-equivalent bridge and post-equivalent debris rolled into one).

As always, I look forward to your response.

Yours,

N.

1986

CHARLES JOHNSON
b. 1948

Winner of the 1990 National Book Award for the novel *Middle Passage*, only the second African American man to receive this honor, Charles Johnson is concerned that the complexity of African American truths has yet to be told. In his critical study *"Being and Race"* (1988), he argues that African American authors have been too narrow in their description of New World black life, that instead of presenting its multiplicities and its underlying philosopical concerns, they have repeated the limited observations of sociologists and historians. As a result, Johnson has contended, many African American writers have participated in their own stereotyping. Johnson's writing is dedicated to breaking those stereotypes and exploring the philosophical traditions that African Americans have both used and transformed. He has created revisionary fables of traditional African American narratives and related them to a variety of philosophical constructs: Western philosophies such as phenomenology, Eastern philosophies such as Buddhism, and African cosmologies that have not been given their full due as philosophies.

Johnson was born in Evanston, Illinois, in 1948. His father came from a large, poor family and had only a second-grade education, but his mother finished high school and maintained a devotion to books throughout her life. She introduced Johnson to literature and art, which fueled his desire to become a visual artist. Johnson was also inspired by his father, a practical, resourceful person, and his uncle, who built many houses in Evanston. Because of the strengths of his family, Johnson understood, despite national rhetoric about blacks as underprivileged, that his own folk had contributed to the development of the United States.

When his father objected to a career in art because he was worried about how Johnson would make a living, Charles majored in journalism but enrolled in a mail-order cartooning course and after two years began publishing drawings in various publications. Upon entering Southern Illinois University in 1967, Johnson went directly to the college newspaper with his political sketches. By the time he gradu-ated, Johnson had published a book of cartoons, called *Black Humor* (1970).

At twenty-two, just after his marriage, an idea for a novel occurred to him. For the next few years, while a graduate student in philosophy at Southern Illinois Uni-versity, Johnson wrote seven novels, none of which he published. It was his explora-tion of Western philosophy and his relationship with author John Gardner that helped him draw the connection between the African American historical experi-ence and various philosophical traditions. *Faith and the Good Thing* (1974), his first published novel, was written under Gardner's tutelage and reflects Johnson's con-cern with philosophical traditions as a source of imaginative writing.

While working on his Ph.D., Johnson found himself slowly molding a novel in which he would break new artistic ground, a novel that would have been impossible without the scholarship on African American history and literature that was inspired by the movements of the 1960s. Later Johnson would say about the origins of *The Oxherding Tale* (1974) that

> it became increasingly clear to me as I read criticism, that one of the most indigenous native forms of literature that we have in this country is the slave narrative. And I wanted to take the slave narrative and do something philo-sophical with it.

Oxherding Tale is one of the first African American novels to explore American slav-ery from the point of view of the different epistemologies embodied in his charac-ters' conceptions of knowledge and reality. As the result of a practical joke between master and slave, Andrew Hawkins, the narrator, is "accidentally" conceived. His mother is the mistress of the plantation and his father is a house slave doomed to be an oxherder after Andrew's conception and birth. Johnson's narrative reminds us that U.S. slaveowners read the philosophers of their day. Thus when Andrew turns five and his father decides to educate him, he engages as his teachers Ezekiel, an anarchist-transcendalist-mystic, as well as the European philosopher Karl Marx, who is visiting America. Johnson also explores gender politics by having Andrew become sexually enslaved to Flou Hatfield, a widow who owns a cotton plantation; from her he learns variations of sexual pleasure, another way of knowing. The ten-sion between Horace Bannon, the Soulcatcher in the novel, who uses his intuition to detect the feelings and consciousness of the escaped slaves he sets out to capture, and the philosophically aware Andrew is the basis of a unique African American philosophical mystery. *Oxherding Tale* was not an easy book to sell, for it did not fit the publishing trends in African American literature of the day. It went to more than twenty publishers before it was accepted by Indiana University Press.

While Johnson wrote *Oxherding Tale,* he taught writing at the University of Washington in Seattle. He had become a Buddhist and an active martial arts devo-tee. The title story of *The Sorcerer's Apprentice* (1986) contains a main character from the Allmuseri tribe of Africa, the origin of Mingo in "The Education of Mingo" as well as a central element in *Middle Passage* (1990).

Middle Passage tells the story of an educated, recently emancipated slave from Indiana who ends up in New Orleans and who, as a result of his attempt to escape from the clutches of a black schoolmarm, ends up as a stowaway on the ironically named illegal slave ship *The Republic*. Without question, Rutherford is a rogue, a trickster, a long-standing character type in African American literature. His experi-ences as a "black" with the forty members of the Allmuseri who are captured and destined to become slaves, but who rebel on the ship, changes his view of himself and possible modes of existence. The novel probes the underlying concepts of phi-losophy in the West, especially those that resulted in the peculiar institution of slavery. At the same time, it confronts the philosophically advanced but perhaps overly refined cosmology of the Allmuseri. *Middle Passage* was a best-seller and won the 1990 National Book Award.

In *Dreamer* (1998), a detailed and dramatic evocation of the civil rights move-ment, Johnson pays homage to Martin Luther King, Jr., by taking him seriously both as an activist and as a thinker. He invents as King's stand-in Chaym Smith, whose physical resemblance, dissimilar experience, and Buddhist beliefs highlight the leader's spiritual uniqueness and the ambiguities inherent in his leadership. *Dreamer* is set in Chicago, where the historical King faced a series of tough political challenges and defeats in his last years. The primary challenge the novel's King confronts is sustaining the idealism that motivates his work, shapes his rhetoric, and shores up his courage.

Turning the Wheel: Essay on Buddhism and Writing (2003) offers a context for understanding the role Buddhism plays in Johnson's fiction and his life. "Were it not for the Buddhadharma," he writes, "I'm convinced that, as a black American, and as an artist, I would not have been able to successfully negotiate my last half century of life in this country. Or at least not with a high level of creative productivity." In this explication of fundamental Buddhist practices, Johnson argues that Buddhism and creativity are linked.

Johnson describes his fiction aptly as a place "where fiction and philosophy meet." There one encounters Eastern and Western philosophies as well as a reimagined African American past. In his view, the lessons of that past, especially when they are inflected with philosophical insights, are urgently needed, if the future is to be secured.

The Education of Mingo

Once, when Moses Green took his one-horse rig into town on auction day, he returned to his farm with a bondsman[1] named Mingo. He came early in a homespun suit, stayed through the sale of fifteen slaves, and paid for Mingo in Mexican coin. A monkeylike old man, never married, with tangled hair, ginger-colored whiskers like broomstraw, and a narrow knot of a face, Moses, without children, without kinfolk, who seldom washed because he lived alone on sixty acres in southern Illinois, felt the need for a field hand and helpmate—a friend, to speak the truth plainly.

Riding home over sumps and mudholes into backcountry imprecise yet startlingly vivid in spots as though he were hurtling headlong into a rigid New Testament parable, Moses chewed tobacco on that side of his mouth that still had good teeth and kept his eyes on the road and ears of the Appaloosa[2] in front of his rig; he chattered mechanically to the boy, who wore tow-linen trousers a size too small, a straw hat, no shirt, and shoes repaired with wire. Moses judged him to be twenty. He was the youngest son of the reigning king of the Allmuseri, a tribe of wizards, according to the auctioneer, but they lied anyways, or so thought Moses, like abolitionists and Red Indians; in fact, for Moses Green's money nearly everybody in the New World from Anabaptists to Whigs[3] was an outrageous liar and twisted the truth (as Moses saw it) until nothing was clear anymore. He was a dark boy. A wild, marshy-looking boy. His breastbone was broad as a barrel; he had thick hands that fell away from his wrists like weights and, on his sharp cheeks, a crescent motif. "Mingo," Moses said in a voice like gravel scrunching under a shoe, "you like rabbit? That's what I fixed for tonight. Fresh

---

1. Slave.
2. North American horse with white or solid-colored coat covered with small spots. "Sumps": marshy pits or swamps.
3. A dominant political party in early 19th-

century America. "Allmuseri": an African people. "Anabaptists": 16th-century European Christian sect that held that only true believers should be baptized.

rabbit, sweet taters, and cornbread. Got hominy[4] made from Indian corn on the fire, too. Good eatings, eh?" Then he remembered that Mingo spoke no English, and he gave the boy a friendly thump on his thigh. "'S all right. I'm going to school you myself. Teach you everything I know, son, which ain't so joe-fired much—just common sense—but it's better'n not knowing nothing, ain't it?" Moses laughed till he shook; he liked to laugh and let his hair down whenever he could. Mingo, seeing his strangely unfiled teeth, laughed, too, but his sounded like barking. It made Moses jump a foot. He swung 'round his head and squinted. "Reckon I'd better teach you how to laugh, too. That half grunt, half whinny you just made'll give a body heart failure, son." He screwed up his lips. "You sure got a lot to learn."

Now Moses Green was not a man for doing things halfway. Education, as he dimly understood it, was as serious as a heart attack. You had to have a model, a good Christian gentleman like Moses himself, to wash a Moor[5] white in a single generation. As he taught Mingo farming and table etiquette, ciphering with knotted string, and how to cook ashcakes,[6] Moses constantly revised himself. He tried not to cuss, although any mention of Martin Van Buren or Free-Soilers[7] made his stomach chew itself; or sop cornbread in his coffee; or pick his nose at public market. Moses, policing all his gestures, standing the boy behind his eyes, even took to drinking gin from a paper sack so Mingo couldn't see it. He felt, late at night when he looked down at Mingo snoring loudly on his corn-shuck mattress, now like a father, now like an artist fingering something fine and noble from a rude chump of foreign clay. It was like aiming a shotgun at the whole world through the African, blasting away all that Moses, according to his lights, tagged evil, and cultivating the good; like standing, you might say, on the sixth day, feet planted wide, trousers hitched, and remaking the world so it looked more familiar. But sometimes it scared him. He had to make sense of things for Mingo's sake. Suppose there was lightning dithering in dark clouds overhead? Did that mean rain? Or the Devil whaling his wife? Or— you couldn't waffle on a thing like that. "Rain," said Moses, solemn, scratching his neck. "For sure, it's a storm. Electri-city, Mingo." He made it a point to despoil meanings with care, choosing the ones that made the most common sense.

Slowly, Mingo got the hang of farm life, as Moses saw it—patience, grit, hard work, and prayerful silence, which wasn't easy, Moses knew, because *every*thing about him and the African was as different as night and day, even what idealistic philosophers of his time called structures of intentional consciousness[8] (not that Moses Green called it that, being a man for whom nothing was more absolute than an ax handle, or the weight of a plow in his hands, but he knew sure enough they didn't see things quite the same way). Mingo's education, to put it plainly, involved the evaporation of one coherent, consistent, complete universe and the embracing of another one alien, contradictory, strange.

Slowly, Mingo conquered knife and spoon, then language. He picked up the old man's family name. Gradually, he learned—soaking them up like a

---

4. Hulled corn kernels cooked into a pudding.
5. I.e., a black African.
6. Cornmeal cakes baked in hot ashes.
7. Members of a U.S. political party formed in 1847–48 to oppose the extension of slavery into territories gained from Mexico. It ran Martin

Van Buren (1782–1862) for president, but he was defeated by Zachary Taylor. Van Buren had already served as president from 1837 to 1841.
8. A reference to the rationalism of Enlightenment philosophy, which Johnson often parodies.

sponge—Moses's gestures and idiosyncratic body language. (Maybe too well, for Moses Green had a milk leg[9] that needed lancing and hobbled, favoring his right knee; so did Mingo, though he was strong as an ox. His *t*'s had a reedy twang like the quiver of a ukulele string; so did Mingo's.) That African, Moses saw inside a year, was exactly the product of his own way of seeing, as much one of his products and judgments as his choice of tobacco; was, in a sense that both pleased and bum-squabbled the crusty old man, himself: a homunculus,[1] or a distorted shadow, or—as Moses put it to his lady friend Harriet Bridgewater—his own spitting image.

"How you talk, Moses Green!" Harriet sat in a Sleepy Hollow chair on the Sunday afternoons Moses, in his one-button sack coat and Mackinaw hat,[2] visited her after church services. She had two chins, wore a blue dress with a flounce of gauze and an apron of buff satin, above which her bosom slogged back and forth as she chattered and knitted. There were cracks in old Harriet Bridgewater's once well-stocked mind (she had been a teacher, had traveled to places Moses knew he'd never see), into which she fell during conversations, and from which she crawled with memories and facts that, Moses suspected, Harriet had spun from thin air. She was the sort of woman who, if you told her of a beautiful sunset you'd just seen, would, like as not, laugh—a squashing sound in her nose—and say, "Why, Moses, that's not beautiful at all!" And then she'd sing a sunset more beautiful— like the good Lord coming in a cloud—in some faraway place like Crete or Brazil, which you'd probably never see. That sort of woman: haughty, worldly, so clever at times he couldn't stand it. Why Moses Green visited her . . .

Even he didn't rightly know why. She wasn't exactly pretty, what with her gull's nose, great heaps of red-gold hair, and frizzy down on her arms, but she had a certain silvery beauty intangible, elusive, inside. It was comforting after Reverend Raleigh Liverspoon's orbicular[3] sermons to sit a spell with Harriet in her religiously quiet, plank-roofed common room. He put one hand in his pocket and scratched. She knew things, that shrewd Harriet Bridgewater, like the meaning of Liverspoon's gnomic[4] sermon on property, which Moses couldn't untangle to save his life until Harriet spelled out how being and having were sorta the same thing: "You kick a man's mule, for example, and isn't it just like ramming a boot heel in that man's belly? Or suppose," she said, wagging a knitting needle at him, "you don't fix those chancy steps of yours and somebody breaks his head—his relatives have a right to sue you into the poorhouse, Moses Green." This was said in a speech he understood, but usually she spoke properly in a light, musical voice, such that her language, as Moses listened, was like song. Her dog, Ruben—a dog so small he couldn't mount the bitches during rutting season and, crazed, jumped Harriet's chickens instead—ran like a fleck of light around her chair. Then there was Harriet's three-decked stove, its sheet-iron stovepipe turned at a right angle, and her large wooden cupboard—all this, in comparison to his own rude, whitewashed cabin, and Harriet's endless chatter, now that her husband, Henry, was dead (when eating fish, he had breathed when he should have swallowed, then swallowed when he

---

9. A leg painfully swollen by inflammation of and clotting in the veins.
1. Miniature adult.
2. A hat made of heavy wool, often plaid.

3. Circular.
4. Full of aphorisms, or short statements of principles or truths.

should have breathed), gave Moses, as he sat in his Go-to-meeting clothes nibbling egg bread (his palm under his chin to catch crumbs), a lazy feeling of warmth, well-being, and wonder. Was he sweet on Harriet Bridgewater? His mind weathervaned—yes, no; yes, no—when he thought about it. She was awesome to him. But he didn't exactly like her opinions about his education of young Mingo. Example: "There's only *so* much he can learn, being a salt-water African and all, don't-chooknow?"

"So?"

"You know he'll never completely adjust."

"So?" he said.

"You know everything here's strange to him."

"So?" he said again.

"And it'll *always* be a little strange—like seeing the world through a fun house mirror?"

Moses knocked dottle[5] from his churchwarden pipe, banging the bowl on the hard wooden arm of his chair until Harriet, annoyed, gave him a tight look. "You oughta see him, though. I mean, he's right smart—r'ally. It's like I just shot out another arm and that's Mingo. Can do anything I do, like today—he's gonna he'p Isaiah Jenson fix some windows and watchermercallems"—he scratched his head—"fences, over at his place." Chuckling, Moses struck a friction match on his boot heel. "Only thing Mingo won't do is kill chicken hawks; he feeds 'em like they was his best friends, even calls 'em Sir." Lightly, the old man laughed again. He put his left ankle on his right knee and cradled it. "But otherwise, Mingo says just what I says. Feels what I feels."

"Well!" Harriet said with violence. Her nose wrinkled—she rather hated his raw-smelling pipe tobacco—and testily laid down a general principle. "Slaves are tools with life in them, Moses, and tools are lifeless slaves."

The old man asked, "Says who?"

"Says Aristotle." She said this arrogantly, the way some people quote Scripture. "He owned thirteen slaves (they were then called *banausos*), sage Plato,[6] fifteen, and neither felt the need to elevate their bondsmen. The institution is old, Moses, old, and you're asking for a peck of trouble if you keep playing God and get too close to that wild African. If he turns turtle on you, what then?" Quotations followed from David Hume,[7] who, Harriet said, once called a preposterous liar one New World friend who informed him of a bondsman who could play any piece on the piano after hearing it only once.

"P'raps," hemmed Moses, rocking his head. "I reckon you're right."

"I know I'm right, Moses Green." She smiled.

"Harriet—"

The old woman answered, "Yes?"

"You gets me confused sometimes. Abaht my feelings. Half the time I can't rightly hear what you say, 'cause I'm all taken in by the way you say it." He struggled, shaking saliva from the stem of his pipe. "Harriet, your Henry, d'ya miss him much? I mean, abaht now you should be getting married

5. Unburned or partially burned tobacco.
6. In ancient Greece, during the time of Plato and Aristotle, slavery was common. "*Banausos*": artisan (Greek); the word also has to do with things utilitarian or with money making.
7. Scottish philosopher and historian (1711–1776) who, as a radical skeptic, denied the possibility of certain knowledge.

again, don't you think? You get along okay by yourself, but I been thinking I . . . Sometimes you make me feel—"

"Yes?" She brightened. "Go on."

He didn't explain how he felt.

Moses, later on the narrow, root-covered road leading to Isaiah Jenson's cabin, thought Harriet Bridgewater wrong about Mingo and, strange to say, felt closer to the black African than to Harriet. So close, in fact, that when he pulled his rig up to Isaiah's house, he considered giving Mingo his farm when he died, God willing, as well as his knowledge, beliefs, and prejudices. Then again, maybe that was overdoing things. The boy was all Moses wanted him to be, his own emanation, but still, he thought, himself. Different enough from Moses so that he could step back and admire him.

Swinging his feet off the buckboard,[8] he called, "Isaiah!" and, hearing no reply, hobbled, bent forward at his hips, toward the front door—"H'lo?"— which was halfway open. Why could he see no one? "Jehoshaphat!" blurted Moses. From his lower stomach a loamy feeling crawled up to his throat. "Y'all heah? Hey!" The door opened with a burst at his fingertips. Snatching off his hat, ducking his head, he stepped inside. It was dark as a poor man's pocket in there. Air within had the smell of boiled potatoes and cornbread. He saw the boy seated big as life at Isaiah's table, struggling with a big lead-colored spoon and a bowl of hominy. "You two finished al-raid-y, eh?" Moses laughed, throwing his jaw forward, full of pride, as Mingo fought mightily, his head hung over his bowl, to get food to his mouth. "Whar's that fool Isaiah?" The African pointed over his shoulder, and Moses's eyes, squinting in the weak light, followed his wagging finger to a stream of sticky black fluid like the gelatinous trail of a snail flowing from where Isaiah Jenson, cold as stone, lay crumpled next to his stove, the image of Mingo imprisoned on the retina of his eyes. Frail moonlight funneled through cracks in the roof. The whole cabin was unreal. Simply unreal. The old man's knees knocked together. His stomach jerked. Buried deep in Isaiah's forehead was a meat cleaver that exactly split his face and disconnected his features.

"Oh, my Lord!" croaked Moses. He did a little dance, half juba,[9] half jig, on his good leg toward Isaiah, whooped, "Mingo, what'd you *do*?" Then, knowing full well what he'd done, he boxed the boy behind his ears, and shook all six feet of him until Moses's teeth, not Mingo's, rattled. The old man sat down at the table; his knees felt rubbery, and he groaned: "Lord, *Lord, Lord!*" He blew out breath, blenched, his lips skinned back over his tobacco-browned teeth, and looked square at the African. "Isaiah's daid! You understand that?"

Mingo understood that; he said so.

"And you're responsible!" He stood up, but sat down again, coughing, then pulled out his handkerchief and spit into it. "Daid! You know what daid means?" Again, he hawked and spit. "Responsible—you know what *that* means?"

He did not; he said, "Nossuh, don't know as I know that one, suh. Not Mingo, boss. Nossuh!"

---

8. Four-wheeled carriage with a floor made of long boards.

9. Southern plantation dance that includes clapping the hands and slapping the knees and thighs.

Moses sprang up suddenly like a steel spring going off and slapped the boy till his palm stung. Briefly, the old man went bananas, pounding the boy's chest with his fists. He sat down again. Jumping up so quick made his head spin and legs wobble. Mingo protested his innocence, and it did not dawn on Moses why he seemed so indifferent until he thought back to what he'd told him about chicken hawks. Months ago, maybe five, he'd taught Mingo to kill chicken hawks and be courteous to strangers, but it got all turned around in the African's mind (how was he to know New World customs?), so he was courteous to chicken hawks (Moses groaned, full of gloom) and killed strangers. "You idjit!" hooted Moses. His jaw clamped shut. He wept hoarsely for a few minutes like a steer with the strangles[1] "Isaiah Jenson and me was friends, and—" He checked himself; what'd he said was a lie. They weren't friends at all. In fact, he thought Isaiah Jenson was a pigheaded fool and only tolerated the little yimp in a neighborly way. Into his eye a fly bounded. Moses shook his head wildly. He'd even sworn to Harriet, weeks earlier, that Jenson was so troublesome, always borrowing tools and keeping them, he hoped he'd go to Ballyhack[2] on a red-hot rail. In his throat a knot tightened. One of his eyelids jittered up, still itchy from the fly; he forced it down with his finger, then gave a slow look at the African. "Great Peter," he mumbled. "You couldn'ta known that."

"Go home now?" Mingo stretched out the stiffness in his spine. "Powerful tired, boss."

Not because he wanted to go home did Moses leave, but because he was afraid of Isaiah's body and needed time to think things through. Dry the air, dry the evening down the road that led them home. As if to himself, the old man grumped, "I gave you thought and tongue, and look at what you done with it—they gonna catch and kill you, boy, just as sure as I'm sitting heah."

"Mingo?" The African shook his long head, sly; he touched his chest with one finger. "Me? Nossuh."

"Why the hell you keep saying that?" Moses threw his jaw forward so violently muscles in his neck stood out. "You kilt a man, and they gonna burn you crisper than an ear of corn. Ay, God, Mingo," moaned the old man, "you gotta act responsible, son!" At the thought of what they'd do to Mingo, Moses scrooched the stalk of his head into his stiff collar. He drilled his gaze at the smooth-faced African, careful not to look him in the eye, and barked, "What're you thinking now??"

"What Mingo know, Massa Green know. Bees like what Mingo sees or don't see is only what Massa Green taught him to see or don't see. Like Mingo lives through Massa Green, right?"

Moses waited, suspicious, smelling a trap. "Yeah, all that's true."

"Massa Green, he owns Mingo, right?"

"Right," snorted Moses. He rubbed the knob of his red, porous nose. "Paid good money—"

"So when Mingo works, it bees Massa Green workin', right? Bees Massa Green workin', thinkin', doin' through Mingo—ain't that so?"

Nobody's fool, Moses Green could latch onto a notion with no trouble at all; he turned violently off the road leading to his cabin, and plowed on toward Harriet's, pouring sweat, remembering two night visions he'd had,

1. Infectious disease of horses and cattle, marked by inflammation of mucous membranes.   2. Hell (slang).

recurrent, where he and Mingo were wired together like say two ventrilo-quist's dummies, one black, one white, and there was somebody—who he didn't know, yanking their arm and leg strings simultaneously—how he couldn't figure, but he and Mingo said the same thing together until his liver-spotted hands, the knuckles tight and shriveled like old carrot skin, flew up to his face and, shrieking, he started hauling hips across a cold black countryside. But so did Mingo, *his* hands on *his* face, pumping his knees right alongside Moses, shrieking, their voice inflections identical; and then the hazy dream doorwayed luxuriously into another where he was greaved[3] on one half of a thrip—a coin halfway between a nickel and a dime—and on the reverse side was Mingo. Shaking, Moses pulled his rig into Harriet Bridgewater's yard. His bowels, burning, felt like boiling tar. She was standing on her porch in a checkered Indian shawl, staring at them, her book still open, when Moses scrambled, tripping, skinning his knees, up her steps. He shouted, "Harriet, this boy done kilt Isaiah Jenson in cold blood." She lost color and wilted back into her doorway. Her hair was swinging in her eyes. Hands flying, he stammered in a flurry of anxiety, "But it wasn't altogether Mingo's fault—he didn't know what he was doin'."

"Isaiah? You mean Izay-yah? He didn't kill Izay-yah?"

"Yeah, aw no! Not really—" His mind stuttered to a stop.

"Whose fault is it then?" Harriet gawked at the African picking his nose in the wagon (Moses had, it's true, not policed himself as well as he'd wanted). A shiver quaked slowly up her left side. She sloughed off her con-fusion, and flashed, "I can tell you whose fault it is, Moses. Yours! Didn't I say not to bring that wild African here? Huh? Huh? Huh? You both should be—put to sleep."

"Aw, woman! Hesh up!" Moses threw down his hat and stomped it out of shape. "You just all upsetted." Truth to tell, he was not the portrait of com-posure himself. There were rims of dirt in his nails. His trouser legs had blood splattered on them. Moses stamped his feet to shake road powder off his boots. "You got any spirits in the house? I need your he'p to untangle this thing, but I ain't hardly touched a drop since I bought Mingo, and my throat's pretty dr—"

"You'll just have to get it yourself—on the top shelf of the cupboard." She touched her face, fingers spread, with a dazed gesture. There was suddenly in her features the intensity found in the look of people who have a year, a month, a minute only to live. "I think I'd better sit down." Lowering herself onto her rocker, she cradled on her lap a volume by one M. Shelley, a recent tale of monstrosity and existential horror,[4] then she demurely settled her breasts. "It's just like you, Moses Green, to bring all your bewilderments to me."

The old man's face splashed into a huge, foamy smile. He kissed her gen-tly on both eyes, and Harriet, in return, rubbed her cheek like a cat against his gristly jaw. Moses felt lighter than a feather. "Got to have somebody, don't I?"

In the common room, Moses rifled through the cupboard, came up with a bottle of luke-warm bourbon and, hands trembling, poured himself three fingers' worth in a glass. Then, because he figured he deserved it, he refilled his glass and, draining it slowly, sloshing it around in his mouth, considered

3. Engraved.
4. I.e., *Frankenstein* (1818), by the English writer Mary Shelley (1797–1851).

his options. He could turn Mingo over to the law and let it go at that, but damned if he couldn't shake loose the idea that killing the boy somehow wouldn't put things to rights; it would be like they were killing Moses himself, destroying a part of his soul. Besides, whatever the African'd done, it was what he'd learned through Moses, who was not the most reliable lens for looking at things. You couldn't rightly call a man responsible if, in some utterly alien place, he was without power, without privilege, without property—was, in fact, property—if he had no position, had nothing, or virtually next to nothing, and nothing was his product or judgment. "Be damned!" Moses spit. It was a bitter thing to siphon your being from someone else. He knew that now. It was like, on another level, what Liverspoon had once tried to deny about God and man: *If* God was (and now Moses wasn't all that sure), and *if* He made the world, then a man didn't have to answer for anything. Rape or murder, it all referred back to who-or-whatever was responsible for that world's make-up. Chest fallen, he tossed away his glass, lifted the bottle to his lips, then nervously lit his pipe. Maybe . . . maybe they could run, if it came to that, and start all over again in Missouri, where he'd teach Mingo the difference between chicken hawks and strangers. But, sure as day, he'd do it again. He couldn't change. What was *was.* They'd be running forever, across all space, all time—so he imagined—like fugitives with no fingers, no toes, like two thieves or yokefellows, each with some God-awful secret that could annihilate the other. Naw! Moses thought. His blood beat up. The deep, powerful stroke of his heart made him wince. His tobacco maybe. Too strong. He sent more whiskey crashing down his throat. *Naw!* You couldn't have nothing and just go as you pleased. How strange that owner and owned magically dissolved into each other like two crossing shafts of light (or, if he'd known this, which he did not, particles, subatomic, interconnected in a complex skein of relatedness). Shoot him maybe, reabsorb Mingo, was that more merciful? *Naw!* He was fast; fast. Then manumit[5] the African? Noble gesture, that. But how in blazes could he disengage himself when Mingo shored up, sustained, *let be* Moses's world with all its sores and blemishes every time he opened his oily black eyes? Thanks to the trouble he took cementing Mingo to his own mind, he could not, by thunder, do without him now. Giving him his freedom, handing it to him like a rasher of bacon, would shackle Mingo to him even more. There seemed, just then, no solution.

Undecided, but mercifully drunk now, his pipebowl too hot to hold any longer, Moses, who could not speak his mind to Harriet Bridgewater unless he'd tied one on, called out: "I come to a decision. Not about Mingo, but you'n' me." It was then seven o'clock. He shambled, feet shuffling, toward the door. "Y'know, I was gonna ask you to marry me this morning"—he laughed; whiskey made his scalp tingle—"but I figured living alone was better when I thought how married folks—and sometimes wimmin with dogs—got to favoring each other . . . like they was wax candles flowing tergether. Hee-hee." He stepped gingerly, holding the bottle high, his ears brick red, face streaky from wind-dried sweat, back onto the quiet porch. He heard a moan. It was distinctly a moan. "Harriet? Harriet, I ain't put it too well, but I'm asking you now." On the porch her rocker slid back, forth, squeaking on the floorboards. Moses's bottle fell—*bip!*—down the stairs,

---

5. Release from slavery.

bounced out into the yard, rolled, and bumped into Harriet Bridgewater. Naw, he thought. Aw, naw. By the wagon, by a chopping block near a pile of split faggots, by the ruin of an old handpump caked with rust, she lay on her side, the back fastenings of her dress burst open, her mouth a perfect O. The sight so wounded him he wept like a child. It was then seven-fifteen.

October 7 of the year of grace 1855.

Midnight found Moses Green still staring down at her. He felt sick and crippled and dead inside. Every shadowed object thinging in the yard beyond, wrenched up from its roots, hazed like shapes in a hallucination, was a sermon on vanity; every time he moved his eyes he stared into a grim homily on the deadly upas[6] of race and relatedness. Now he had no place to stand. Now he was undone. "Mingo . . . come ovah heah." He was very quiet.

"Suh?" The lanky African jumped down from the wagon, faintly innocent, faintly diabolical. Removed from the setting of Moses's farm, the boy looked strangely elemental; his skin had the texture of plant life, the stones of his eyes an odd, glossy quality like those of a spider, which cannot be read. "Talky old hen daid now, boss."

The old man's face shattered. "I was gonna marry that woman!"

"Naw." Mingo frowned. From out of his frown a huge grin flowered. "You say—I'm quoting you now, suh—a man needs a quiet, patient, uncomplaining woman, right?"

Moses croaked, "When did I say that?"

"Yesstiday." Mingo yawned. He looked sleepy. "Go home now, boss?"

"Not just yet." Moses Green, making an effort to pull himself to his full height, failed. "You lie face down—heah me?—with your hands ovah your head till I come back." With Mingo hugging the front steps, Moses took the stairs back inside, found the flintlock[7] Harriet kept in her cupboard on account of slaves who swore to die in the skin of freemen, primed it, and stepped back, so slowly, to the yard. Outside, the air seemed thinner. Bending forward, perspiring at his upper lip, Moses tucked the cold barrel into the back of Mingo's neck, cushioning it in a small socket of flesh above the African's broad shoulders. With his thumb he pulled the hammer back. Springs in the flintlock whined. Deep inside his throat, as if he were speaking through his stomach, he talked to the dark poll of the boy's back-slanting head.

"You ain't never gonna understand why I gotta do this. You a saddle across my neck, always will be, even though it ain't rightly all your fault. Mingo, you more me than I am myself. Me planed away to the bone! Ya understand?" He coughed and went on miserably: "All the wrong, all the good you do, now or tomorrow—it's me indirectly doing it, but without the lies and excuses, without the feeling what's its foundation, with all the polite make-up and apologies removed. It's an empty gesture, like the swing of a shadow's arm. You can't never see things exactly the way I do. I'm guilty. It was me set the gears in motion. Me . . ." Away in the octopoid darkness a wild bird—a night-hawk maybe—screeched. It shot noisily away with blurred wings askirring when the sound of hoofs and wagons rumbled closer. Eyes narrowed to slits, Moses said—a dry whisper—"Get up, you damned fool." He let his round shoulders slump. Mingo let his broad

---

6. Harmful or poisonous influence or institution.   7. A type of gun.

shoulders slump. "Take the horses," Moses said; he pulled himself up to his rig, then sat, his knees together beside the boy. Mingo's knees drew together. Moses's voice changed. It began to rasp and wheeze; so did Mingo's. "Missouri," said the old man, not to Mingo but to the dusty floor of the buckboard, "if I don't misremember, is off thataway somewheres in the west."

1986

NTOZAKE SHANGE
b. 1948

I n a 1976 interview in *Time* magazine, Ntozake Shange recalled the circumstances that prompted the writing of "A Nite with Beau Willie," one of the most powerful poems in the work for which she is best known, *for colored girls who have considered suicide / when the rainbow is enuf*:

> It was hot. I was broke. I didn't have enough money for a subway token. I was miserable. The man in the next room was beating up his old lady. It went on for hours and hours. She was screaming. He was laughing. Every time he hit her I would think, yeah, man, well that has already happened to me. So I sat down and wrote "Beau Willie." All my anger came out.

Shange's young adult experiences while living in a Harlem boardinghouse were a far cry from her "rich and somewhat protected" childhood. She was born Paulette Williams on October 18, 1948, in Trenton, New Jersey, the daughter of Eloise Williams, a psychiatric social worker and educator, and Paul T. Williams, a surgeon, for whom she was named. When she was eight, her family moved to St. Louis, Missouri. Shange remembers the difficulties she encountered when she was bused to a formerly segregated German-American school: "I was not prepared for it. . . . I was being harrassed and chased around by these white kids. My parents were busy being proud."

The family moved back to Trenton when she was thirteen, and the adolescent Shange began a period of intense reading, devouring the works of Dostoevsky, Melville, Carson McCullers, Edna St. Vincent Millay, Simone de Beauvoir, and Jean Genet, among others. In addition, Shange's artistic development was nourished by her parents' friendships with prominent performers such as Josephine Baker, Dizzy Gillespie, Chuck Berry, Charlie Parker, and Miles Davis. W. E. B. Du Bois was also a visitor in her family's home. Shange enrolled at Barnard College, in New York City, in 1966. Despite emotional upheaval, marked by a series of suicide attempts and a difficult separation from her law-student husband, she graduated with honors in 1970. In 1971, while studying for a master's degree in African American studies at the University of California at Los Angeles, she took an African name. *Ntozake* translates as "she who comes with her own things," and *Shange* as "who walks like a lion."

From 1972 to 1975 Shange taught humanities, women's studies, and African American studies at various colleges in California. At the same time, she was reciting poetry and dancing with West Coast performance groups, including her own company, For Colored Girls Who Have Considered Suicide. She moved to New York in 1975 during the Public Theater's production of her choreopoem—poems that are performed much like the movements of a dramatic dance sequence—*for colored girls who have considered suicide / when the rainbow is enuf.* The play went on to become the second by an African American woman to reach Broadway (Hansberry's *Raisin in the Sun* opened on Broadway in 1958). In addition to tremendous popular success, the play won Obie and Outer Critics Circle awards and was nominated for the Emmy, Grammy, and Tony awards.

Janet League (left) and Ntozake Shange (right), perform in a 1976 production of *for colored girls who have considered suicide when the rainbow is enuf.*

for colored girls is a mesh of poetry, music, dancing, and light. Seven women, dressed in the colors of the rainbow plus brown, the color of the earth and the body, perform twenty poems, without any set or props. In her introduction to the piece, Shange writes that *for colored girls* is about "our struggle to become all that is forbidden, all that is forfeited by our gender, all that we have forgotten." Tracing the women's emotions from youth to maturity, the piece focuses on the lack of communication between men and women and on the misunderstanding of women, exploring particularly the theme of unrequited love. Although many of the poems center on the physical, psychological, and emotional pain experienced by its characters, the piece also asserts the possibility of surviving and developing self-esteem with the support of other women. Many critics praised *for colored girls* as witty and unpredictable; others faulted it for undeveloped characterizations and especially for a lack of sympathetic male figures. It is not surprising that it sparked much debate in African American intellectual circles.

After *for colored girls*, Shange went on to publish a novella, *Sassafrass* (1977); three novels, *Sassafrass, Cypress, and Indigo* (1982), *Betsey Brown* (1985), and *Liliane: Resurrection of the Daughter* (1994); the historical novel *Some Sing, Some Cry* (2012), co-authored with her sister Ifa Bayeza; and several volumes of poetry, including *Nappy Edges* (1978), *Ridin' the Moon in Texas: Word Paintings* (1987), and *The Love Space Demands* (1991), in which her resistance to conventional grammar and spelling reflect a rejection of the hierarchies inherent in standard English as well as a connection with the African American oral tradition. Two of her plays were produced by Joseph Papp's New York Shakespeare Festival (*Spell #7* and *A Photograph: Lovers-in-Motion*), and in 1980 she won a second Obie, for her adaptation of Brecht's *Mother Courage*, which featured a black family during the American Civil War. Her nonfiction books *See No Evil: Prefaces, Essays and Accounts, 1976–1983* (1984), *if I can cook you know God can* (1975), and *lost in language & sound: or how I found my way to the arts* (2011) as well as two visually beautiful children's books, *i live in music* (1994), with illustrations by Romare Bearden, and *ellington was not a street* (2004).

Throughout her innovative, productive career, Ntozake Shange's work has been foremost a celebration of language. As she told a *New Yorker* interviewer in 1976, "I listen to words, and when people can't say what they mean they are in trouble."

From for colored girls who have considered suicide / when the rainbow is enuf

* * *

 lady in green
somebody almost walked off wid alla my stuff
not my poems or a dance i gave up in the street
but somebody almost walked off wid alla my stuff
like a kleptomaniac workin hard & forgettin while stealin
this is mine / this aint yr stuff /   5
now why dont you put me back & let me hang out in my own self
somebody almost walked off wid alla my stuff
& didnt care enuf to send a note home saying
i waz late for my solo conversation
or two sizes too small for my own tacky skirts   10
what can anybody do wit somethin of no value on
a open market / did you getta dime for my things /
hey man / where are you goin wid alla my stuff /
this is a woman's trip & i need my stuff /
to ohh & ahh abt / daddy / i gotta mainline number 15
from my own shit / now wontchu put me back / & let
me play this duet / wit this silver ring in my nose /
honest to god / somebody almost run off wit alla my stuff /
& i didnt bring anythin but the kick & sway of it
the perfect ass for my man & none of it is theirs 20
this is mine / ntozake[1] "her own things" / that's my name /
now give me my stuff / i see ya hidin my laugh / & how i
sit wif my legs open sometimes / to give my crotch
some sunlight / & there goes my love my toes my chewed
up finger nails / niggah / wif the curls in yr hair / 25
mr. louisiana hot link / i want my stuff back /
my rhythms & my voice / open my mouth / & let me talk ya
outta / throwin my shit in the sewar / this is some delicate
leg & whimsical kiss / i gotta have to give to my choice /
without you runnin off wit alla my shit /   30
now you cant have me less i give me away / & i waz
doin all that / til ya run off on a good thing /
who is this you left me wit / some simple bitch
widda bad attitude / i wants my things /
i want my arm wit the hot iron scar / & my leg wit the 35
flea bite / i want my calloused feet & quik language back
in my mouth / fried plantains / pineapple pear juice /
sun-ra & joseph & jules[2] / i want my own things / how i lived them /
& give me my memories / how i waz when i waz there /
you cant have them or do nothin wit them /   40
stealin my shit from me / dont make it yrs / makes it stolen /
somebody almost run off wit alla my stuff / & i waz standin
there / lookin at myself / the whole time

---

1. She who comes with her own things (Xhosa).
2. Perhaps a reference to Shange's friends Joseph Jarmin, member of the Chicago Art Ensemble, and Jules Allen, photographer. Sun Ra (1914?–1993), African American jazz musician and composer.

& it waznt a spirit took my stuff / waz a man whose
ego walked round like Rodan's[3] shadow / waz a man faster   45
n my innocence / waz a lover / i made too much
room for / almost run off wit alla my stuff /
& i didn't know i'd give it up so quik / & the one running wit it /
dont know he got it / & i'm shoutin this is mine / & he dont
know he got it / my stuff is the anonymous ripped off treasure   50
of the year / did you know somebody almost got away with me /
me in a plastic bag under their arm / me
danglin on a string of personal carelessness / i'm spattered wit
mud & city rain / & no i didnt get a chance to take a douche /
hey man / this is not your perogative / i gotta have me in my   55
pocket / to get round like a good woman shd / & make the poem
in the pot or the chicken in the dance / what i got to do /
i gotta have my stuff to do it to /
why dont ya find yr own things / & leave this package
of me for my destiny / what ya got to get from me /   60
i'll give it to ya / yeh / i'll give it to ya /
round 5:00 in the winter / when the sky is blue-red /
& Dew City is gettin pressed / if it's really my stuff /
ya gotta give it to me / if ya really want it / i'm
the only one / can handle it   65

    lady in blue
that niggah will be back tomorrow, sayin 'i'm sorry'

    lady in yellow
get this, last week my ol man came in sayin, 'i don't know
how she got yr number baby, i'm sorry'

                                                     1977

Nappy Edges*

*the roots of your hair / what
turns back when we sweat, run,
make love, dance, get afraid, get
happy: the tell-tale sign of living /
nappy edges (a cross country sojourn)   5

   st. louis / such a colored town / a whiskey
black space of history & neighborhood / forever ours /
   to lawrenceville[1] / where the only road open
to me / waz cleared by colonial slaves / whose children never
moved / never seems like / mended the torments of the Depression   10
the stains of demented spittle / dropped from lips of crystal women /
still makin independence flags /

---

3. Perhaps a reference to Rodan, a winged
Godzilla-like monster of a 1950s Japanese science
fiction film.

1. An Illinois town, south of St. Louis.

from st. louis / on a halloween's eve to the veiled prophet /
usurpin the mystery of mardi gras / made it mine tho the queen
waz always fair / that parade / of pagan floats & tambourines /   15
commemoratin me / unlike the lonely walks wit liberal trick or
treaters / back to my front door / bag half empty /
   my face enuf to scare anyone i passed / a colored kid /
whatta gas

     1) here   20
       a tree
       wonderin the horizon
       dipped in blues &
       untended bones
       usedta hugs drawls   25
       rhythm & decency
       here a tree
       waitin to be hanged

     sumner[2] high school / squat & pale on the corner / like
our vision / waz to be vague / our memory   30
of the war / that made us free to be forgotten
becomin paler / a linear movement from south carolina
to missouri / freedmen / landin in jackie wilson's[3] yelp / daughters of
the manumitted swimmin in tina turner's[4] grinds / this is chuck
berry's town / disavowin misega-nation[5] / in any situation / & they let   35
us be / electric blues & bo diddley's[6] cant / rockin pneumonia &
boogie-woogie flu / the slop & short-fried heads / runnin always to
the river
     / from chambersbourg[7] / lil italy / i passed everyday
at the sweet shoppe / & waz afraid / the cops raided truants /   40
regularly / after dark i wd not be seen / wit any other colored /
sane / lovin my life /
     in the 'bourg / seriously expectin to be gnarled /
hey niggah / over here /
     & behind the truck lay five hands claspin chains /   45
round the trees / 4 more sucklin steel /
                hey niggah / over here
this is the borderline /
a territorial dispute /
                hey / niggah /   50
over here /
     cars loaded wit families / fellas from the factory / one or two
practical nurses / black / become our trenches / some dig into cement
wit elbows / under engines / do not be seen / in yr hometown / after
sunset we suck up our shadows /   55

     2) i will sit here
       my shoulders brace an enormous oak
       dreams waddle in my lap

2. A town in southeastern Illinois.
3. African American singer and boxer
(1934–1984).
4. African American soul and pop singer (b.
1939). "Manumitted": freed from slavery.
5. A play on the word *miscegenation*, which

means sexual relations between a man and a
woman of different races. Berry (b. 1926), African
American rock guitarist, songwriter, and singer.
6. African American blues singer and musician
(1928–2008).
7. Illinois town.

round to miz bertha's where lil richard[8]
gets his process   60
run backwards to the rosebushes / a drunk man / lyin
down the block to the nuns in pink habits
prayin in a pink chapel
my dreams run to meet aunt marie
my dreams draw blood from ol sores   65
    these stains & scars are mine
        this is my space
           i am not movin

                    1978

Bocas:[1] A Daughter's Geography

i have a daughter / mozambique
i have a son / angola[2]
our twins
salvador & johannesburg[3] / cannot speak
the same language   5
but we fight the same old men / in the new world

we are so hungry for the morning
we're trying to feed our children the sun
but a long time ago / we boarded ships / locked in
depths of seas our spirits / kisst the earth   10
on the atlantic side of nicaragua costa rica
our lips traced the edges of cuba puerto rico
charleston & savannah / in haiti[4]
we embraced &
made children of the new world   15
but old men spit on us / shackled our limbs
but for a minute
our cries are the panama canal / the yucatan[5]
we poured thru more sea / more ships / to manila[6]
ah ha we're back again   20
everybody in manila awreaddy speaks spanish

the old men sent for the archbishop of canterbury[7]
"can whole continents be excommunicated?"
"what wd happen to the children?"
"wd their allegiance slip over the edge?"   25

8. African American singer, songwriter (b. 1932), known for his sleek, wavy ("processed") hairdo.
1. Mouths (Spanish).
2. Mozambique and Angola are African nations long torn by civil war.
3. South African city near the black township of Soweto, the site of much poverty and racial unrest. Salvador, a city in Brazil, saw a tremendous influx of slaves to work its sugar plantations, which accounts for its strong African heritage.
4. Countries and towns that were ports of entry or places of labor for African slaves brought to the Western Hemisphere.
5. A peninsula in southeastern Mexico. The Panama Canal is perhaps a reference to the part blacks played in its construction.
6. Capital city of the Philippines. African slaves were brought to the Philippines by the Spanish during their rule over the islands.
7. Head of the Church of England.

"dont worry bout lumumba[8] don't even think bout
ho chi minh[9] / the dead cant procreate"
so say the old men

but i have a daughter / la habana[1]
i have a son / guyana[2]   30
our twins
santiago & brixton[3] / cannot speak
the same language
yet we fight the same old men

the ones who think helicopters rhyme with hunger   35
who think patrol boats can confiscate a people
the ones whose dreams are full of none of our
children
they see mae west & harlow[4] in whittled white cafes
near managua[5] / listening to primitive rhythms in   40
jungles near pétionville[6]
with bejeweled benign natives
ice skating in abidjan[7]
unaware of the rest of us in chicago
all the dark urchins   45
rounding out the globe / primitively whispering
the earth is not flat old men

there is no edge
no end to the new world
cuz i have a daughter / trinidad[8]
i have a son / san juan[9]   50
our twins
capetown & palestine[1] / cannot speak the same
language / but we fight the same old men
the same men who thought the earth waz flat
go on over the edge / go on over the edge old men   55
you'll see us in luanda.[2] or the rest of us
in chicago
rounding out the morning /
we are feeding our children the sun   60

1983

---

8. Patrice Lumumba (1925–1961), first prime minister of the Congo (now Democratic Republic of the Congo); ousted by Joseph Kasavubu, he died under mysterious circumstances.
9. Vietnamese nationalist leader (1890–1969) who was the first president of North Vietnam (1954–69).
1. Or Havana; the capital of Cuba.
2. A country in northeast South America, much of whose population is descended from African slaves.
3. A poor, racially mixed section of London. Santiago is the capital of Chile.
4. Mae West (1892?–1980) and Jean Harlow (1911–1937), American film stars known for

their sultry personas and spicy wit.
5. Capital of Nicaragua.
6. City in Haiti.
7. Former capital of the Ivory Coast, a country in west Africa.
8. One of the islands of the Caribbean nation of Trinidad and Tobago.
9. The capital of Puerto Rico.
1. Historically, a region comprising parts of modern Israel, Egypt, and Jordan; also the nation of the Palestinian people. Capetown is the capital of South Africa.
2. The capital of Angola; in the 16th to the 19th centuries, it was the center of slave trade to Brazil.

GAYL JONES
b. 1949

ayl Jones once told her mentor, poet Michael Harper, "I used to say that I learned to write by listening to people talk. I still feel that the best of my writing comes from having *heard* rather than having read." Her frequent use of first-person narrators magnifies the sense that one is hearing the stories; their voices carry the accents and idiom of Jones's Kentucky childhood. Yet their invention is a measure of her literary achievement. She identifies a wide range of influences on her work, from *The Canterbury Tales* to *Don Quixote* to *Finnegans Wake* to contemporary novels by Latin Americans, Native Americans, and African Americans. A critic as well as a fiction writer, Jones argues in her study "Liberating Voices: Oral Tradition in African American Literature" that when black writers in the United States "began to trust the literary possibilities of their own verbal and musical creations and to employ self-inspired techniques, they began to transform (their literary models) and to gain artistic sovereignty."

Born in Lexington, Kentucky, to Franklin and Lucille Jones, she was raised in a family of storytellers; both her mother and her grandmother wrote their stories down. By grade school, Jones was writing stories of her own. Success came early: she began winning prizes for her work while an undergraduate at Connecticut College, where she studied with poet Robert Hayden and earned a B.A. in 1971. She later earned an M.A. (1973) and a D.A. (1975) in creative writing from Brown University, where she studied with Harper. She began teaching at Wellesley College. In 1975 she published her first novel, *Corregidora*, set partly in Kentucky and partly in Brazil. *Corregidora* depicted a family in which generations of women confront slavery's legacy—a legacy of sexual subjugation and abuse—which continued to destroy the possibility of love between black men and women long into the twentieth century. Toni Morrison, then an editor at Random House, shepherded the novel into print.

Jones was prolific, publishing a second novel, *Eva's Man* (1977), and a collection of short stories, *White Rat* (1978), in quick succession. Several of her plays were also produced, notably *Chile Woman* (1974). She continued to depict violent relationships in her fiction and drew characters, often victims of incest and sexual abuse, whose anguish pushed them to the edge of madness. She found an analog for her concerns in the blues, a genre that has long provided public expression for private pain and that shaped the form as well as the content of her fiction. However, her use of first-person narrators prompted some of her critics to confuse Jones with her characters. Attacks on her work grew more personal. Perhaps in response, Jones turned her hand to poetry. She published three volumes, including *Song for Anninho* (1981), *The Hermit Woman* (1983), and *Xarque and Other Poems* (1985). The first, a book-length poem, portrays enslaved lovers in Brazil who escape to the maroon settlement of Palmares.

With her literary achievements came an appointment to the faculty of the University of Michigan. While at Michigan she married Robert Higgins, whose arrest for assault in 1983 prompted her resignation from the university and their flight into exile. After five years in Europe, the couple returned to the United States in 1988 and lived reclusively in Lexington. She continued to write steadily. When *The Healing* appeared in 1998, twenty years after her last novel had been published, the *New York Times* called it "a stunning literary return"; it was selected as a finalist for the National Book Award. Written in the first person, *The Healing* demonstrates an extensive knowledge of U.S. popular culture at the close of the century. After its protagonist, the former manager of a rock singer, discovers that she has a gift for healing, the novel wends its way to a happy ending. The press attention it garnered yielded a different result. It brought Robert Higgins to the attention of the police. When the authorities arrived at the couple's home to serve an outstanding warrant, Higgins committed suicide. Jones herself was briefly institutionalized. News reports tended again to blur the line between Jones's art and her life. She has remained silent about the latter. In *Mosquito* (2000), an African American female truck driver offers a picaresque account of her adventures with the "new underground railroad," which gives sanctuary to Mexican immigrants.

When asked decades earlier why Brazil figures so prominently in *Corregidora* and elsewhere in her writing, Jones noted that exploring Brazilian history and landscape helped her writing by "getting away from things that some readers consider 'autobiographical' or 'private obsessions' rather than literary inventions." In the selection printed here, a great-grandmother speaks through the protagonist Ursa's memory to describe acts of resistance in colonial Brazil. These acts in turn inspire Ursa's to fashion her own act of resistance and to free herself from the burden of history.

From Corregidora

* * *

"Ursa."

"What, Mama?"

"I know about those other things you would never let me know."

I said nothing. She was telling me she knew about my own private memory.

"Do you want me to talk?"

"Sometime when you're back here and feel you have to."

"Awright."

She pulled her shawl around her tighter. I fingered my trade beads.[1]

"You see all these colors in them, these formations?" I asked.

She looked at my neck, and touched them. We stopped walking for a moment.

"They form naturally," I said. "They just form naturally that way. No one paints them on."

"Those stripes too?"

"Yes."

She looked like she couldn't believe it, but I knew she did. She kept touching them for a time and then we started walking. We walked slowly.

"You didn't ask where your father is now, Ursa."

"Do you want to tell me?"

"No. I mean, I don't know."

We kept walking. We walked so slow it was almost like we weren't really walking. We had left early enough for me not to miss the bus, though, as if she had wanted to stand down there with me as long as possible before I had to get up on the bus, and she had to turn around and go back up to that house. The only thing that had changed in it was the kitchen, the old iron

1. Glass beads made in Europe and used for trading gold, ivory, palm oil, and slaves in Africa.

coal stove replaced with a gas one—the kind you used bottle gas from a tank outside the house, like people do in the country where there are no gas lines—and the old icebox replaced by a Frigidaire. She had moved the icebox into a corner and used it for storage space. And the old iron stove was still rusting in the backyard. The one they used to empty ashes from, lifting out those big iron rings in the top. That stove had always frighted me. When I was older, though, they'd make me take the tray out, and empty the ashes against the side of the road. The big bed was still in the middle room, except she had moved the trundle bed[2] out of the front room, and put it in there too. I didn't know whether she slept in the big bed or the trundle one, and that wasn't something I felt I could ask her. It would have seemed ridiculous to an outsider, but to us I think it would have been a kind of prying she didn't want, or need. *They'd slept there before I did.* And in the front room that ageless china cabinet. The big one with all the good dishes and the silverware that was never taken out. I could never remember its ever having come out, even on holidays. The only time it was opened was to be dusted or polished. I'd never looked, but I think it had been imported from Brazil, or I used to think so. It was an expensive dark-mahogany thing, the best thing we had in the house. Great Gram used to be in charge of it at first, and then Grandmama, and now I guess Mama was. When I had gone through the house, it was still sparkling.

After a while, she began speaking again, hugging her shawl to her. It sounded almost as if she were speaking in pieces, instead of telling one long thing.

"After he come, they didn't talk to me about making generations anymore or about anything that happened with Corregidora, but Martin and me could hear them in there talking between theyselves. We'd be in the front room, and they'd be back in there in the bedroom, Great Gram telling Mama how Corregidora wouldn't let her see some man because he was too black." Mama kept talking until it wasn't her that was talking, but Great Gram. I stared at her because she wasn't Mama now, she was Great Gram talking: "He wouldn't let me see him, cause he said he was too black for me. He liked his womens black, but he didn't wont us with no black mens. It wasn't color cause he didn't even wont us with no light black mens, cause there was a man down there as light as he was, but he didn't even wont us with him, cause there was one girl he caught with him, and had her beat, and sold the man over to another plantation, cause I think he just wont to get rid of him anyway. Cause Corregidora himself was looking like a Indian—if I said that to him I have my ass off—so that this light black man looked more like a white man than he did, so I just think he wont any excuse to get rid of him. I don't even know how he got him. He didn't buy him himself, I think he just come in with a load of other mens they wont to work out in the fields, cause he had cane, you know. But anyway he wouldn't let me see him, cause he said a black man wasn't nothing but a waste of pussy, and wear me out when it came to the other mens. He didn't send nothing but the rich mens in there to me, cause he said I was his little gold pussy, his little gold piece, and it didn't take some of them old rich mens no time, and then I still be fresh for him. But he said he didn't wont no waste on nothing black. Some of them womens he had just laying naked, and just sent trash into them. But some of us he called hisself cultivating us, and then didn't send nothing but cultivated mens to us, and we had these private rooms, you know. But some of these others, they had to been three or four or five whores fucking in the same room. But then if we did something he didn't like he might put us in there and send trash into us, and then we be catching everything then. So after that, first time he just talked to me real hard, said he didn't wont no black bastard fucking me, he didn't wont no black bastard fucking all in his piece. He was real mad. He grab hold of me down between my legs and said he didn't wont nothing black down there. He said if he just catch me fucking something black, they wouldn't have no pussy, and he wouldn't have none neither. And then he was squeezing me all up on my pussy and then digging his hands up in there. We was up in his room. That's where he always bring me when he wont to scold me about something, or fuck with me. Him and his wife was living in separated rooms then. Then he was just digging all up in me till he got me where he wonted me and then he just laid me down on that big bed of his and started fucking me . . .

"Any of them, even them he had out in the fields, if he wonted them, he just ship their own husbands out of bed, and get in there with them, but didn't nothing happen like what happened over on that other plantation, cause I guess that other plantation served as a warning, cause they might wont your pussy, but if you do anything to get back at them, it'll be your life they be wonting, and then they make even that some kind of a sex show, all them beatings and killings wasn't nothing but sex circuses, and all them white peoples, mens, womens, and childrens crowding around to see . . .

"Naw, he said he wouldn't've been nothing but a waste of my pussy, cause he said my pussy bring gold. But what was funny after that they kept claiming he did something. Not Corregidora, but this black man. I was only talking to him once, all Corregidora did was seen us talking, and I guess he figure the next step was we be down in the grass or something. I don't know, but they said he did something, and they were goin to beat him real bad. He was young too, young man, so he run away. When somebody run away, it almost mean you can do whatever you wont to with them. I think he woulda run away anyway, cause he had this dream, you know, of running away and joining up with them renegade slaves up in Palmares,[3] you know. I kept telling him that was way back before his time, but he wouldn't believe me, he said he was going to join up with some black mens that had some dignity. You know, Palmares, where these black mens had started their own town, escaped and banded together. I said the white men had killed all of them off but he wouldn't believe me. He said that was what his big dream was, to go up there and join all these other black mens up there, and have him a woman, and then come back and get his woman and take her up there, but he had to find his way first, and know exactly where he was going. I said he couldn't know where he was going because Palmares was way back two hundred years ago, but he said Palmares was now. But they claimed he did something, and he had to leave before he planned to. Wasn't nothing but seventeen or eighteen. This ole man said he told him to rub garlic on his feet so the hounds wouldn't smell him, but he said the boy must've forgot

---

3. State in Brazil founded during the 17th century by runaway slaves.

to. We was all praying for him, though. They sent this whole mob of mens out after him. You know, they didn't need no mob for just one person. Mob and hounds. So they can have the hounds to smell out nigger blood, cause they trained them to do that. But it was only because Corregidora thought he'd been fooling with me when he hadn't, or that we'd been fooling with each other, cause all that was all uncalled-for. Sometimes I would be a little bold with him, little bolder than the others, cause I know I was the piece he wonted the most, so I said, 'He wasn't after my pussy. He ain't been after my pussy. He even too young to know I got one.' 'Ain't no nigger on this place too young to know you got one, way I got them trained,' he said. He moved away from me, then he moved back toward me. He must've been fucking me while they was chasing after *him*. But maybe he did the right thing to run anyway, because maybe if he had stayed there, the way Corregidora was looking when he seen us talking he might've had him beat dead. I ain't never seen him look like that, cause when he send them white mens in there to me he didn't look like that, cause he be nodding and saying what a fine piece I was, said I was a fine speciment of a woman, finest speciment of a woman he ever seen in his life, said he had tested me out hisself, and then they would be laughing, you know, when they come in there to me. Cause tha's all they do to you, was feel up on you down between your legs see what kind of genitals you had, either so you could breed well, or make a good whore. Fuck each other or fuck them. Tha's the first thing they would think about, cause if you had somebody who was a good fucker you have plenty to send out in the field, and then you could also make you plenty money on the side, or inside. But he was up there fucking me while they was out chasing *him*. 'Don't let no black man fool with you, do you hear? I don't wont nothing black fucking with my pussy.' I kept saying I wouldn't. 'I don't wont nothing black trying to fuck you, do you hear that?' 'Yes, I hear.' Let his own color mess with me all they wont to. Sometimes I used to think he even wonted to be in there watching, but out of respect for them, not me, he wouldn't. Yes, tha's just how I was feeling, while he was up there jumping up and down between my legs they was out there with them hounds after that boy. Wasn't nothing but seventeen. Couldn't've been more than seventeen or eighteen. And he had this dream he told me about. That was all he wanted me for, was to tell me about this dream. He must've trusted me a lot, though, cause I could've been one of them to run back to Corregidora with it. But I wouldn't. It was because he seen us out there talking. I wouldn't even go tell him, cause I would've been seen telling him. And I kept feeling all that time he was running, he kept thinking I'd told something when I didn't. And then there I was kept crying out, and ole Corregidora thinking it was because he was fucking so good I was crying. 'Ain't nobody do it to you like this, is it?' I said, 'Naw.' I just kept saying Naw, and he just kept squeezing on my ass and fucking. And then somehow it got in my mind that each time he kept going down in me would be that boy's feets running. And then when he come, it meant they caught him . . .

"When they come back, they said they lost the boy at the river. They said they got to the river they didn't see him no more. We was all glad. We didn't show it, but the rest of us was all glad and rejoicing inside. But you know what happened? Three days after that somebody seen him floating on the water. What happened was they chased him as far as the river and he just jumped in and got drownded. Cause they didn't know nothing till three days after that when he rose . . .

"Corregidora must've done some rejoicing then. He didn't show it but he must've had it all inside. Ole man kept telling me if the boy had just remembered to rub garlic on his feet, the bloodhounds wouldn't've been able to follow. I asked him if he ever tried it. He said, Naw, but he heard of folks that did. I asked him where was they. He said they was gone. He didn't know where to, but they must've made it, cause didn't nobody bring them back."

She quit talking, and looked over at me suddenly, Mama again: "They just go on like that, and then get in to talking about the importance of passing things like that down. I've heard that so much it's like I've learned it off by heart. But then with him there they figured they didn't have to tell me no more, but then what they didn't realize was they was telling Martin too . . ."

It was as if she had *more* than learned it off by heart, though. It was as if their memory, the memory of all the Corregidora women, was her memory too, as strong with her as her own private memory, or almost as strong. But now she was Mama again.

"One day after we'd been married, I don't know, maybe six months. (He had come into the house to live, you know. Not on account of hisself but me. I kept saying I couldn't not help them out, and if we didn't live there, I couldn't help us and them too. He said he'd help us, all I had to do was worry about them. I said something about how little he was making. Naw, it was almost like he moved in that house out of anger, not for me, but for anger.) Well, he had gone fishing one day, but when he came back, though, instead of coming around to the front where I was, he went around the back to the kitchen and put them in a big pan of water, and then he was gonna come around to the front and have me cut them up and fry them. Well, what happened is he must've started through their room and there she was, sitting on that bed in there powdering up under her breasts. I don't know if she seen him or not—this was your grandmama—but she just kept powdering and humming, cause when I started through there, there she was powdering, and looking down at her breasts, and lifting them up and powdering under them, and there he was just standing in the door with his arms spread up over the door, and sweat showing through his shirt, just watching her. I don't know what kind of expression he had on his face. His lips was kind of smiling, but his eyes wasn't. He seen me and he just kept standing there. I was looking at Mama and then looking up at him, and after he seen me the first time he just kept looking at her. She was acting like she didn't know we was there, but I know she had to know. He was just standing there like he was hypnotized or something. I know she knew. She knew it, cause they both knew he wasn't getting what he wanted from me. Cause you know with them in there, I couldn't. I'd let him rub me down there. I kept telling him it was because they were in there that I wouldn't. But . . . even if they hadn't been. There she was just sitting there lifting up her breasts. I don't know when it was she decided she'd let him know she seen him, but then all a sudden she set the box of powder down and looked up. Her eyes got real hateful. First she looked at me, then she looked at him. 'You black bastard, watching me. What you doing watching me, you black bastard?' She still had her breasts all showing and just cussing at him. He started over there where she was, but I got between them. 'Martin, don't.' He just kept looking at me, like it was me he was hating, but it was her he was calling a half-white heifer. Her powder and him sweating all up under his arms, and me holding him. She kept calling him a nasty black bastard, and he kept calling her a half-white heifer.

"'Messing with my girl, you ain't had no right messing with my girl.'

"'I'ma come over there and mess with your ass the next time you show it,' he said, but then I got him in the kitchen, and there was them fish in that pan a water he had waiting for me to clean. He pushed me away from him, and grabbed them fish and started cutting them up hisself. 'What do we have to do, go up under the house?' he kept asking me. 'What do we have to do, go up under the house?'

"'Please, Martin.'

"He just kept grabbing those fish and cutting them up.

"When I came back through the house, Mama rolled her eyes at me. 'Messing with my girl, he ain't had no bit of right.'

"After that, whenever Martin wanted to get from one part of the house to the next, he'd go around the house . . . But she just kept acting like she didn't even know he was there."

She was quiet again, and then she said, "They had us sleeping in the narrow old trundle bed in the front room, the one you was sleeping in afterwards. I kept telling him it was because they were in there I wouldn't, but then that time they weren't there he wanted to take me in *their* bed . . ."

I didn't ask her whether she had let him. That was something she didn't have to tell me.

When we got to the highway, Mama took my arm.

"I think what really made them dislike Martin was because he had the nerve to ask them what I never had the nerve to ask."

"What was that?"

"How much was hate for Corregidora and how much was love."

I said nothing. She squeezed my arm. "I'll try to pretend you're okay until you tell me different," she said.

"I'm okay, Mama."

She kept looking at me. I didn't like the way she was looking. I wanted to ask what about her now, how lonely was *she*. She'd told me about *then*, but what about *now*. Shortly after Grandmama died, she had written me a letter saying that Mr. Floyd had started to get sweet on her, talking about how he wanted to court her, but she said she hadn't let him. She said he could just stay across that road, cause all he really wanted to do was to move out of that trailer, and into *her* house, and probably bring his mama with him. I hadn't known whether to believe her or not, because I knew too many of my own excuses when men came to the piano, and then Logan—the man Max hired to see to it that men don't bother me—was my best excuse. I could just give him that "he's bothering me" look, and he'd put the man out.

After a while, Mama squeezed my arm again. She kept hold of it until the bus came and she put me on. "Do you know me any better now?" she asked. I only smiled at her. She stayed standing there until the bus pulled off. She didn't let me see her walk back to the house.

I leaned back against the seat and closed my eyes. Then suddenly it was like I was remembering something out of a long past. I was a child, drowsy, thinking I was sleeping or dreaming. It was a woman and a man's voice, both whispering.

"No."

"Why don't you come?"

"No."

"What are you afraid of?"

"I'm not. I'm just not going with you."

"Why do you keep fighting me? Or is it yourself you keep fighting?"

I drifted back into sleep. I never heard that man's voice again.

I was thinking that now that Mama had gotten it all out, her own memory—at least to me anyway—maybe she and *some man* . . . But then, I was thinking, what had I done about my *own* life?

1975

JAMAICA KINCAID
b. 1949

Born Elaine Potter Richardson on May 25, 1949, in St. John's, Antigua, in the British West Indies, Jamaica Kincaid remembers life in that former British colony as a series of ongoing tensions between appearance and reality: "I was always being told I should be something, and then my whole upbringing was something I was not: English." The evocation of that sense of dislocation and an intense exploration of the mother–daughter relationship are the major elements of Kincaid's much-celebrated works. She has published *At the Bottom of the River* (1983), a densely poetic prose work; *Annie John* (1985), short stories that became a novel; *A Small Place* (1988), a critique of colonialism in Antigua; *Lucy* (1990), a sparse, beautifully precise novel that evokes what critic and writer Thulani Davis calls "the psychological space between leaving and arriving"; *An Autobiography of My Mother* (1996), praised by critics for its hypnotic yet disturbing language; and the novel *Mr. Potter* (2002). She has written a book in memoriam to her brother; a book on one of her most important avocations, titled *My Garden Book* (1999); and a travel book, *Among Flowers: A Walk in the Himalaya* (2005).

Kincaid has portrayed life for an immigrant from the West Indies to the United States in styles—the metaphoric quality of *Annie John*, the minimalism of *Lucy*—that reflect modernist influences. Certainly her work does feel indebted to the modernist writings of Virginia Woolf and James Joyce. In an interview with Selvyn Cudjoe, she recalls reading stories by French *nouveau roman* writer Alain Robbe-Grillet for the first time:

> I cannot describe them except that they broke every rule. When I read them, the top of my head came off and I thought, "This is really living!" And I knew that whatever I did, I would not be interested in realism.

Although her work has been praised by critics for its feminist investigation of the mother–daughter relationship in a third world and immigrant context, Kincaid herself views her writing as much more of an individual phenomenon:

> I don't really want to be placed in that category. I don't mind if people put me in it, but I don't claim to be in it. But that's just me as an individual. I mean, I always see myself as alone. I can't bear to be in a group of any kind, or in the school of anything.

A precocious child, Jamaica Kincaid, then Elaine Richardson, won scholarships to colonial schools in Antigua, including the much-hated Princess Margaret School, where she has said her education was so "Empire" that she "thought all the great writing had been done before 1900." At sixteen she came to New York as an au pair, eventually intending to become a nurse—an experience that is the basis for her second novel, *Lucy*. Instead, Kincaid studied photography and wrote for various magazines, including an early breakthrough interview with Gloria Steinem for the magazine *Ingenue*. Changing her name from Elaine Potterson to Jamaica Kincaid, she graduated to the *New Yorker*, which published sections of *At the Bottom of the River* and *Annie John*.

At the Bottom of the River is a collection of short stories, dreams, and reflections, which won the Morton Dauwen Zabel Award from the American Academy and Institute of Arts and Letters. While critics such as novelist Anne Tyler noted "its almost insultingly obscure quality," they also praised its poetic exploration of two themes: "the wonderful terrible strength of a loving mother" and "the mysteriousness of ordinary life." Those two themes are also central to Kincaid's first novel, *Annie John*.

Annie John is the work of Kincaid's that is most often assumed to be autobiographical. The story chronicles, in richly detailed prose, the childhood of a young girl in Antigua who gradually becomes estranged from her mother. When asked in a 1985 interview about its correspondence to her own childhood, Kincaid answered, "The feelings in it are autobiographical, yes. I didn't want to say it was autobiographical because I felt that would be somehow admitting something about myself, but it is, and so that's that."

Perhaps her most analytical work, her third published book, *A Small Place*, is an essay addressed to a tourist from North America or Europe, traveling in Antigua, that in stark sentences describes the destructive effects of colonialism. Some reviewers were upset by its rage, while others, especially in Europe, praised its powerful critique of imperialism. The critique grounds the documentary film *Love and Debt* (2001), which focuses on the nation of Jamaica.

In 1990, Kincaid published *Lucy*, in many ways complementary to her first novel. *Lucy* is a young Antiguan woman who comes to New York to work as an au pair for a young white couple with four children and feels estranged from the mother she left, even as she cannot connect with her life in New York. Kincaid's *The Autobiography of My Mother* also focuses on the theme of motherhood. Xuela Claudette Richardson, the daughter of a Carib mother and a half-Scottish, half-African father, delivers a book-length monologue that powerfully evokes the loss of the mother she never knew.

Jamaica Kincaid is recognized as a talented, unique stylist. She teaches at Claremont McKenna College in Southern California.

From Annie John

Chapter Two

THE CIRCLING HAND

During my holidays from school, I was allowed to stay in bed until long after my father had gone to work. He left our house every weekday at the stroke of seven by the Anglican[1] church bell. I would lie in bed awake, and I could hear all the sounds my parents made as they prepared for the day ahead. As my mother made my father his breakfast, my father would shave, using his shaving brush that had an ivory handle and a razor that matched; then he would step outside to the little shed he had built for us as a bathroom, to quickly bathe in water that he had instructed my mother to leave outside overnight in the dew. That way, the water would be very cold, and he believed that cold water strengthened his back. If I had been a boy, I

---

1. Of the Episcopal Church of England.

would have gotten the same treatment, but since I was a girl, and on top of that went to school only with other girls, my mother would always add some hot water to my bathwater to take off the chill. On Sunday afternoons, while I was in Sunday school, my father took a hot bath; the tub was half filled with plain water, and then my mother would add a large caldronful of water in which she had just boiled some bark and leaves from a bay-leaf tree. The bark and leaves were there for no reason other than that he liked the smell. He would then spend hours lying in this bath, studying his pool coupons or drawing examples of pieces of furniture he planned to make. When I came home from Sunday school, we would sit down to our Sunday dinner.

My mother and I often took a bath together. Sometimes it was just a plain bath, which didn't take very long. Other times, it was a special bath in which the barks and flowers of many different trees, together with all sorts of oils, were boiled in the same large caldron. We would then sit in this bath in a darkened room with a strange-smelling candle burning away. As we sat in this bath, my mother would bathe different parts of my body; then she would do the same to herself. We took these baths after my mother had consulted with her obeah[2] woman, and with her mother and a trusted friend, and all three of them had confirmed that from the look of things around our house—the way a small scratch on my instep had turned into a small sore, then a large sore, and how long it had taken to heal; the way a dog she knew, and a friendly dog at that, suddenly turned and bit her; how a porcelain bowl she had carried from one eternity and hoped to carry into the next suddenly slipped out of her capable hands and broke into pieces the size of grains of sand; how words she spoke in jest to a friend had been completely misunderstood—one of the many women my father had loved, had never married, but with whom he had had children was trying to harm my mother and me by setting bad spirits on us.

When I got up, I placed my bedclothes and my nightie in the sun to air out, brushed my teeth, and washed and dressed myself. My mother would then give me my breakfast, but since, during my holidays, I was not going to school, I wasn't forced to eat an enormous breakfast of porridge, eggs, an orange or half a grapefruit, bread and butter, and cheese. I could get away with just some bread and butter and cheese and porridge and cocoa. I spent the day following my mother around and observing the way she did every-thing. When we went to the grocer's, she would point out to me the reason she bought each thing. I was shown a loaf of bread or a pound of butter from at least ten different angles. When we went to market, if that day she wanted to buy some crabs she would inquire from the person selling them if they came from near Parham, and if the person said yes my mother did not buy the crabs. In Parham was the leper colony, and my mother was con-vinced that the crabs ate nothing but the food from the lepers' own plates. If we were then to eat the crabs, it wouldn't be long before we were lepers ourselves and living unhappily in the leper colony.

How important I felt to be with my mother. For many people, their wares and provisions laid out in front of them, would brighten up when they saw her coming and would try hard to get her attention. They would dive under-neath their stalls and bring out goods even better than what they had on

---

2. Religious ritual practiced in Africa and in parts of the American South and the West Indies.

display. They were disappointed when she held something up in the air, looked at it, turning it this way and that, and then, screwing up her face, said, "I don't think so," and turned and walked away—off to another stall to see if someone who only last week had sold her some delicious christo-phine[3] had something that was just as good. They would call out after her turned back that next week they expected to have eddoes or dasheen[4] or whatever, and my mother would say, "We'll see," in a very disbelieving tone of voice. If then we went to Mr. Kenneth, it would be only for a few min-utes, for he knew exactly what my mother wanted and always had it ready for her. Mr. Kenneth had known me since I was a small child, and he would always remind me of little things I had done then as he fed me a piece of raw liver he had set aside for me. It was one of the few things I liked to eat, and, to boot, it pleased my mother to see me eat something that was so good for me, and she would tell me in great detail the effect the raw liver would have on my red blood corpuscles.

We walked home in the hot midmorning sun mostly without event. When I was much smaller, quite a few times while I was walking with my mother she would suddenly grab me and wrap me up in her skirt and drag me along with her as if in a great hurry. I would hear an angry voice saying angry things, and then, after we had passed the angry voice, my mother would release me. Neither my mother nor my father ever came straight out and told me anything, but I had put two and two together and I knew that it was one of the women that my father had loved and with whom he had had a child or children, and who never forgave him for marrying my mother and having me. It was one of those women who were always trying to harm my mother and me, and they must have loved my father very much, for not once did any of them ever try to hurt him, and whenever he passed them on the street it was as if he and these women had never met.

When we got home, my mother started to prepare our lunch (pumpkin soup with droppers, banana fritters with salt fish stewed in antroba and tomatoes, fungie with salt fish stewed in antroba and tomatoes, or pepper pot,[5] all depending on what my mother had found at market that day). As my mother went about from pot to pot, stirring one, adding something to the other, I was ever in her wake. As she dipped into a pot of boiling some-thing or other to taste for correct seasoning, she would give me a taste of it also, asking me what I thought. Not that she really wanted to know what I thought, for she had told me many times that my taste buds were not quite developed yet, but it was just to include me in everything. While she made our lunch, she would also keep an eye on her washing. If it was a Tuesday and the colored clothes had been starched, as she placed them on the line I would follow, carrying a basket of clothespins for her. While the starched colored clothes were being dried on the line, the white clothes were being whitened on the stone heap. It was a beautiful stone heap that my father had made for her: an enormous circle of stones, about six inches high, in the middle of our yard. On it the soapy white clothes were spread out; as the sun dried them, bleaching out all stains, they had to be made wet again by dousing them with buckets of water. On my holidays, I did this for my mother. As I watered the clothes, she would come up behind me, instructing

3. Chayote, a pear-shaped vegetable native to the Americas.

4. Tropical plants whose roots are edible.
5. A West Indian stew.

me to get the clothes thoroughly wet, showing me a shirt that I should turn over so that the sleeves were exposed.

Over our lunch, my mother and father talked to each other about the houses my father had to build; how disgusted he had become with one of his apprentices, or with Mr. Oatie; what they thought of my schooling so far; what they thought of the noises Mr. Jarvis and his friends made for so many days when they locked themselves up inside Mr. Jarvis's house and drank rum and ate fish they had caught themselves and danced to the music of an accordion that they took turns playing. On and on they talked. As they talked, my head would move from side to side, looking at them. When my eyes rested on my father, I didn't think very much of the way he looked. But when my eyes rested on my mother, I found her beautiful. Her head looked as if it should be on a sixpence. What a beautiful long neck, and long plaited hair, which she pinned up around the crown of her head because when her hair hung down it made her too hot. Her nose was the shape of a flower on the brink of opening. Her mouth, moving up and down as she ate and talked at the same time, was such a beautiful mouth I could have looked at it forever if I had to and not mind. Her lips were wide and almost thin, and when she said certain words I could see small parts of big white teeth—so big, and pearly, like some nice buttons on one of my dresses. I didn't much care about what she said when she was in this mood with my father. She made him laugh so. She could hardly say a word before he would burst out laughing. We ate our food, I cleared the table, we said goodbye to my father as he went back to work, I helped my mother with the dishes, and then we settled into the afternoon.

When my mother, at sixteen, after quarreling with her father, left his house on Dominica and came to Antigua,[6] she packed all her things in an enormous wooden trunk that she had bought in Roseau for almost six shillings. She painted the trunk yellow and green outside, and she lined the inside with wallpaper that had a cream background with pink roses printed all over it. Two days after she left her father's house, she boarded a boat and sailed for Antigua. It was a small boat, and the trip would have taken a day and a half ordinarily, but a hurricane blew up and the boat was lost at sea for almost five days. By the time it got to Antigua, the boat was practically in splinters, and though two or three of the passengers were lost overboard, along with some of the cargo, my mother and her trunk were safe. Now, twenty-four years later, this trunk was kept under my bed, and in it were things that had belonged to me, starting from just before I was born. There was the chemise, made of white cotton, with scallop edging around the sleeves, neck, and hem, and white flowers embroidered on the front—the first garment I wore after being born. My mother had made that herself, and once, when we were passing by, I was even shown the tree under which she sat as she made this garment. There were some of my diapers, with their handkerchief hemstitch that she had also done herself; there was a pair of white wool booties with matching jacket and hat; there was a blanket in white wool and a blanket in white flannel cotton; there was a plain white linen hat with lace trimming; there was my christening outfit; there were two of my baby bottles: one in the shape of a normal baby bottle, and the other shaped like a boat, with a nipple on either end; there was a thermos

---

6. Both Antigua and Dominica are islands in the British West Indies.

in which my mother had kept a tea that was supposed to have a soothing effect on me; there was the dress I wore on my first birthday: a yellow cotton with green smocking on the front; there was the dress I wore on my second birthday: pink cotton with green smocking on the front; there was also a photograph of me on my second birthday wearing my pink dress and my first pair of earrings, a chain around my neck, and a pair of bracelets, all specially made of gold from British Guiana; there was the first pair of shoes I grew out of after I knew how to walk; there was the dress I wore when I first went to school, and the first notebook in which I wrote; there were the sheets for my crib and the sheets for my first bed; there was my first straw hat, my first straw basket—decorated with flowers—my grandmother had sent me from Dominica; there were my report cards, my certificates of merit from school, and my certificates of merit from Sunday school.

From time to time, my mother would fix on a certain place in our house and give it a good cleaning. If I was at home when she happened to do this, I was at her side, as usual. When she did this with the trunk, it was a tremendous pleasure, for after she had removed all the things from the trunk, and aired them out, and changed the camphor balls,[7] and then refolded the things and put them back in their places in the trunk, as she held each thing in her hand she would tell me a story about myself. Sometimes I knew the story first hand, for I could remember the incident quite well; sometimes what she told me had happened when I was too young to know anything; and sometimes it happened before I was even born. Whichever way, I knew exactly what she would say, for I had heard it so many times before, but I never got tired of it. For instance, the flowers on the chemise, the first garment I wore after being born, were not put on correctly, and that is because when my mother was embroidering them I kicked so much that her hand was unsteady. My mother said that usually when I kicked around in her stomach and she told me to stop I would, but on that day I paid no attention at all. When she told me this story, she would smile at me and say, "You see, even then you were hard to manage." It pleased me to think that, before she could see my face, my mother spoke to me in the same way she did now. On and on my mother would go. No small part of my life was so unimportant that she hadn't made a note of it, and now she would tell it to me over and over again. I would sit next to her and she would show me the very dress I wore on the day I bit another child my age with whom I was playing. "Your biting phase," she called it. Or the day she warned me not to play around the coal pot, because I liked to sing to myself and dance around the fire. Two seconds later, I fell into the hot coals, burning my elbows. My mother cried when she saw that it wasn't serious, and now, as she told me about it, she would kiss the little black patches of scars on my elbows.

As she told me the stories, I sometimes sat at her side, leaning against her, or I would crouch on my knees behind her back and lean over her shoulder. As I did this, I would occasionally sniff at her neck, or behind her ears, or at her hair. She smelled sometimes of lemons, sometimes of sage, sometimes of roses, sometimes of bay leaf. At times I would no longer hear what it was she was saying; I just liked to look at her mouth as it opened and closed over words, or as she laughed. How terrible it must be for all the

---

7. Used to keep insects out of storage places.

people who had no one to love them so and no one whom they loved so, I thought. My father, for instance. When he was a little boy, his parents, after kissing him goodbye and leaving him with his grandmother, boarded a boat and sailed to South America. He never saw them again, though they wrote to him and sent him presents—packages of clothes on his birthday and at Christmas. He then grew to love his grandmother, and she loved him, for she took care of him and worked hard at keeping him well fed and clothed. From the beginning, they slept in the same bed, and as he became a young man they continued to do so. When he was no longer in school and had started working, every night, after he and his grandmother had eaten their dinner, my father would go off to visit his friends. He would then return home at around midnight and fall asleep next to his grandmother. In the morning, his grandmother would awake at half past five or so, a half hour before my father, and prepare his bath and breakfast and make everything proper and ready for him, so that at seven o'clock sharp he stepped out the door off to work. One morning, though, he overslept, because his grandmother didn't wake him up. When he awoke, she was still lying next to him. When he tried to wake her, he couldn't. She had died lying next to him sometime during the night. Even though he was overcome with grief, he built her coffin and made sure she had a nice funeral. He never slept in that bed again, and shortly afterward he moved out of that house. He was eighteen years old then.

When my father first told me this story, I threw myself at him at the end of it, and we both started to cry—he just a little, I quite a lot. It was a Sunday afternoon; he and my mother and I had gone for a walk in the botanical gardens. My mother had wandered off to look at some strange kind of thistle, and we could see her as she bent over the bushes to get a closer look and reach out to touch the leaves of the plant. When she returned to us and saw that we had both been crying, she started to get quite worked up, but my father quickly told her what had happened and she laughed at us and called us her little fools. But then she took me in her arms and kissed me, and she said that I needn't worry about such a thing as her sailing off or dying and leaving me all alone in the world. But if ever after that I saw my father sitting alone with a faraway look on his face, I was filled with pity for him. He had been alone in the world all that time, what with his mother sailing off on a boat with his father and his never seeing her again, and then his grandmother dying while lying next to him in the middle of the night. It was more than anyone should have to bear. I loved him so and wished that I had a mother to give him, for, no matter how much my own mother loved him, it could never be the same.

When my mother got through with the trunk, and I had heard again and again just what I had been like and who had said what to me at what point in my life, I was given my tea—a cup of cocoa and a buttered bun. My father by then would return home from work, and he was given his tea. As my mother went around preparing our supper, picking up clothes from the stone heap, or taking clothes off the clothesline, I would sit in a corner of our yard and watch her. She never stood still. Her powerful legs carried her from one part of the yard to the other, and in and out of the house. Sometimes she might call out to me to go and get some thyme or basil or some other herb for her, for she grew all her herbs in little pots that she kept in a corner of our little garden. Sometimes when I gave her the herbs, she might stoop down and kiss me on my lips and then on my neck. It was in such a paradise that I lived.

The summer of the year I turned twelve, I could see that I had grown taller; most of my clothes no longer fit. When I could get a dress over my head, the waist then came up to just below my chest. My legs had become more spindlelike, the hair on my head even more unruly than usual, small tufts of hair had appeared under my arms, and when I perspired the smell was strange, as if I had turned into a strange animal. I didn't say anything about it, and my mother and father didn't seem to notice, for they didn't say anything, either. Up to then, my mother and I had many dresses made out of the same cloth, though hers had a different, more grownup style, a boat neck or a sweetheart neckline, and a pleated or gored skirt, while my dresses had high necks with collars, a deep hemline, and, of course, a sash that tied in the back. One day, my mother and I had gone to get some material for new dresses to celebrate her birthday (the usual gift from my father), when I came upon a piece of cloth—a yellow background, with figures of men, dressed in a long-ago fashion, seated at pianos that they were playing, and all around them musical notes flying off into the air. I immediately said how much I loved this piece of cloth and how nice I thought it would look on us both, but my mother replied, "Oh, no. You are getting too old for that. It's time you had your own clothes. You just cannot go around the rest of your life looking like a little me." To say that I felt the earth swept away from under me would not be going too far. It wasn't just what she said, it was the way she said it. No accompanying little laugh. No bending over and kissing my little wet forehead (for suddenly I turned hot, then cold, and all my pores must have opened up, for fluids just flowed out of me). In the end, I got my dress with the men playing their pianos, and my mother got a dress with red and yellow overgrown hibiscus, but I was never able to wear my own dress or see my mother in hers without feeling bitterness and hatred, directed not so much toward my mother as toward, I suppose, life in general.

As if that were not enough, my mother informed me that I was on the verge of becoming a young lady, so there were quite a few things I would have to do differently. She didn't say exactly just what it was that made me on the verge of becoming a young lady, and I was so glad of that, because I didn't want to know. Behind a closed door, I stood naked in front of a mirror and looked at myself from head to toe. I was so long and bony that I more than filled up the mirror, and my small ribs pressed out against my skin. I tried to push my unruly hair down against my head so that it would lie flat, but as soon as I let it go it bounced up again. I could see the small tufts of hair under my arms. And then I got a good look at my nose. It had suddenly spread across my face, almost blotting out my cheeks, taking up my whole face, so that if I didn't know I was me standing there I would have wondered about that strange girl—and to think that only so recently my nose had been a small thing, the size of a rosebud. But what could I do? I thought of begging my mother to ask my father if he could build for me a set of clamps into which I could screw myself at night before I went to sleep and which would surely cut back on my growing. I was about to ask her this when I remembered that a few days earlier I had asked in my most pleasing, winning way for a look through the trunk. A person I did not recognize answered in a voice I did not recognize, "Absolutely not! You and I don't have time for that anymore." Again, did the ground wash out from under me? Again, the answer would have to be yes, and I wouldn't be going too far.

Because of this young-lady business, instead of days spent in perfect harmony with my mother, I trailing in her footsteps, she showering down on me her kisses and affection and attention, I was now sent off to learn one thing and another. I was sent to someone who knew all about manners and how to meet and greet important people in the world. This woman soon asked me not to come again, since I could not resist making farting-like noises each time I had to practice a curtsy, it made the other girls laugh so. I was sent for piano lessons. The piano teacher, a shriveled-up old spinster from Lancashire, England, soon asked me not to come back, since I seemed unable to resist eating from the bowl of plums she had placed on the piano purely for decoration. In the first case, I told my mother a lie—I told her that the manners teacher had found that my manners needed no improvement, so I needn't come anymore. This made her very pleased. In the second case, there was no getting around it—she had to find out. When the piano teacher told her of my misdeed, she turned and walked away from me, and I wasn't sure that if she had been asked who I was she wouldn't have said, "I don't know," right then and there. What a new thing this was for me: my mother's back turned on me in disgust. It was true that I didn't spend all my days at my mother's side before this, that I spent most of my days at school, but before this young-lady business I could sit and think of my mother, see her doing one thing or another, and always her face bore a smile for me. Now I often saw her with the corners of her mouth turned down in disapproval of me. And why was my mother carrying my new state so far? She took to pointing out that one day I would have my own house and I might want it to be a different house from the one she kept. Once, when showing me a way to store linen, she patted the folded sheets in place and said, "Of course, in your own house you might choose another way." That the day might actually come when we would live apart I had never believed. My throat hurt from the tears I held bottled up tight inside. Sometimes we would both forget the new order of things and would slip into our old ways. But that didn't last very long.

In the middle of all these new things, I had forgotten that I was to enter a new school that September. I had then a set of things to do, preparing for school. I had to go to the seamstress to be measured for new uniforms, since my body now made a mockery of the old measurements. I had to get shoes, a new school hat, and lots of new books. In my new school, I needed a different exercise book for each subject, and in addition to the usual—English, arithmetic, and so on—I now had to take Latin and French, and attend classes in a brand-new science building. I began to look forward to my new school. I hoped that everyone there would be new, that there would be no one I had ever met before. That way, I could put on a new set of airs; I could say I was something that I was not, and no one would ever know the difference.

On the Sunday before the Monday I started at my new school, my mother became cross over the way I had made my bed. In the center of my bedspread, my mother had embroidered a bowl overflowing with flowers and two lovebirds on either side of the bowl. I had placed the bedspread on my bed in a lopsided way so that the embroidery was not in the center of my bed, the way it should have been. My mother made a fuss about it, and I could see that she was right and I regretted very much not doing that one little thing that would have pleased her. I had lately become careless, she said, and I could only silently agree with her.

I came home from church, and my mother still seemed to hold the bedspread against me, so I kept out of her way. At half past two in the afternoon, I went off to Sunday school. At Sunday school, I was given a certificate for best student in my study-of-the-Bible group. It was a surprise that I would receive the certificate on that day, though we had known about the results of a test weeks before. I rushed home with my certificate in hand, feeling that with this prize I would reconquer my mother—a chance for her to smile on me again.

When I got to our house, I rushed into the yard and called out to her, but no answer came. I then walked into the house. At first, I didn't hear anything. Then I heard sounds coming from the direction of my parents' room. My mother must be in there, I thought. When I got to the door, I could see that my mother and father were lying in their bed. It didn't interest me what they were doing—only that my mother's hand was on the small of my father's back and that it was making a circular motion. But her hand! It was white and bony, as if it had long been dead and had been left out in the elements. It seemed not to be her hand, and yet it could only be her hand, so well did I know it. It went around and around in the same circular motion, and I looked at it as if I would never see anything else in my life again. If I were to forget everything else in the world, I could not forget her hand as it looked then. I could also make out that the sounds I had heard were her kissing my father's ears and his mouth and his face. I looked at them for I don't know how long.

When I next saw my mother, I was standing at the dinner table that I had just set, having made a tremendous commotion with knives and forks as I got them out of their drawer, letting my parents know that I was home. I had set the table and was now half standing near my chair, half draped over the table, staring at nothing in particular and trying to ignore my mother's presence. Though I couldn't remember our eyes having met, I was quite sure that she had seen me in the bedroom, and I didn't know what I would say if she mentioned it. Instead, she said in a voice that was sort of cross and sort of something else, "Are you going to just stand there doing nothing all day?" The something else was new; I had never heard it in her voice before. I couldn't say exactly what it was, but I know that it caused me to reply, "And what if I do?" and at the same time to stare at her directly in the eyes. It must have been a shock to her, the way I spoke. I had never talked back to her before. She looked at me, and then, instead of saying some squelching thing that would put me back in my place, she dropped her eyes and walked away. From the back, she looked small and funny. She carried her hands limp at her sides. I was sure I could never let those hands touch me again; I was sure I could never let her kiss me again. All that was finished.

I was amazed that I could eat my food, for all of it reminded me of things that had taken place between my mother and me. A long time ago, when I wouldn't eat my beef, complaining that it involved too much chewing, my mother would first chew up pieces of meat in her own mouth and then feed it to me. When I had hated carrots so much that even the sight of them would send me into a fit of tears, my mother would try to find all sorts of ways to make them palatable for me. All that was finished now. I didn't think that I would ever think of any of it again with fondness. I looked at my parents. My father was just the same, eating his food in the same old way, his two rows of false teeth clop-clopping like a horse being driven off to market. He was regaling us with another one of his stories about when he was a young man and played cricket on one island or the other. What he said now must have been funny, for my mother couldn't stop laughing. He didn't seem to notice that I was not entertained.

My father and I then went for our customary Sunday-afternoon walk. My mother did not come with us. I don't know what she stayed home to do. On our walk, my father tried to hold my hand, but I pulled myself away from him, doing it in such a way that he would think I felt too big for that now.

That Monday, I went to my new school. I was placed in a class with girls I had never seen before. Some of them had heard about me, though, for I was the youngest among them and was said to be very bright. I liked a girl named Albertine, and I liked a girl named Gweneth. At the end of the day, Gwen and I were in love, and so we walked home arm in arm together.

When I got home, my mother greeted me with the customary kiss and inquiries. I told her about my day, going out of my way to provide pleasing details, leaving out, of course, any mention at all of Gwen and my overpowering feelings for her.

1985

GLORIA NAYLOR
b. 1950

When Gloria Naylor read Toni Morrison's *The Bluest Eye* as a twenty-seven-year-old sophomore at Brooklyn College in 1978, she felt that she had been given "the authority . . . to enter this forbidden terrain" of prose. Assured by Morrison's work that "not only is your story worth telling but it can be told in words so painstakingly eloquent that it becomes a song," Naylor wrote her first novel, *The Women of Brewster Place* (1982). Immensely successful, that work was followed by four others: *Linden Hills* (1985), *Mama Day* (1988), *Bailey's Cafe* (1992), and *The Men of Brewster Place* (1998). Naylor has said that her first four novels constitute a quartet intended to appeal to readers black and white. One of the first African American women writers who has studied both her African ancestors and the European tradition, Naylor consciously draws on Western sources even as her writings reflect the complexity of the African American female experience.

Gloria Naylor was born on January 25, 1950, in New York City because her mother, Alberta (McAlpin) Naylor, had made her husband, Roosevelt Naylor, promise that none of their children would be born in Mississippi. A dedicated reader in a state that segregated access to libraries, Naylor's mother passed on to her eldest daughter a respect for education and the written word. Although Naylor's potential was recognized early on, she joined the Jehovah's Witnesses after graduating from high school and from 1968 to 1975 served as a missionary in New York,

North Carolina, and Florida. After becoming disenchanted with the Witnesses, she moved to New York, where she briefly studied nursing and then enrolled in Brooklyn College. Her B.A. in English was followed by a master's degree from Yale, a partial fulfillment of which was the writing of her second novel, *Linden Hills.*

With the publication of *The Women of Brewster Place* in 1982, Naylor was quickly recognized as an important new voice in American fiction at a time when other African American women writers, Toni Morrison and Alice Walker among them, were receiving much attention. Praised for the richness of its prose and the intense humaneness of its vision, *Brewster Place* won the 1983 American Book Award. Some faulted it, however, along with Walker's *The Color Purple* (1982), for what was seen as a conscious effort to portray males negatively and to repeatedly cast women as the victims of male violence, both physical and emotional. Such criticism extended even to Naylor's portrayal of Lorraine and Theresa, the lesbians of "The Two." Notwithstanding these caveats, the novel continues to be seen as a paean to the diversity of the African American experience, and it was made into a television movie by Oprah Winfrey.

Naylor's second novel, *Linden Hills,* moves from the ghetto to a middle-class black suburb. Set in the 1980s, the novel traces the journey of Willie Mason, a young African American poet, as he travels with a fellow poet through the exclusive black neighborhood looking for odd jobs and meeting the inhabitants. Like Amiri Baraka's *The System of Dante's Hell* (1965), *Linden Hills* is, among other things, an ambitious rewriting of the *Inferno.* In its sharing a general geography with *Brewster Place,* as well as some characters, *Linden Hills* signaled the almost Faulknerian importance of place to Naylor. *Mama Day,* Naylor's third novel, moves away from the inner city and the suburb to Willow Springs, an island off the southeastern coast of the United States that has been owned by Mama Day's family since before the Civil War. Just as *Linden Hills* reminds us that the black middle class is at least a hundred years old, *Mama Day* reiterates the existence of a three-hundred-year-old African American folk tradition. The last of Naylor's quartet is *Bailey's Cafe,* which is written in the form of a jazz suite. Set in a 1948 Brooklyn neighborhood, the novel explores the disruption of lives by sexual abuse and violence. In 1998 Naylor revisited characters from her first book to tell their stories from a male perspective.

Gloria Naylor has taught at George Washington University, Princeton, the University of Pennsylvania, New York University, Boston University, Brandeis, Cornell, and Brooklyn College. She has received both a National Endowment for the Arts fellowship and a Guggenheim fellowship. With these awards and her five novels, she demonstrates her authority over the literary terrain.

From The Women of Brewster Place

The Two

At first they seemed like such nice girls. No one could remember exactly when they had moved into Brewster. It was earlier in the year before Ben was killed—of course, it had to be before Ben's death. But no one remembered if it was in the winter or spring of that year that the two had come. People often came and went on Brewster Place like a restless night's dream, moving in and out in the dark to avoid eviction notices or neighborhood bulletins about the dilapidated condition of their furnishings. So it wasn't until the two were clocked leaving in the mornings and returning in the evenings at regular intervals that it was quietly absorbed that they now claimed Brewster as home. And Brewster waited, cautiously prepared to claim them, because you never knew about young women, and obviously single at that. But when no wild music or drunken friends careened out of the corner building on weekends, and especially, when no slightly eager husbands were encouraged to linger around that first-floor apartment and run errands for them, a suspended sigh of relief floated around the two when they dumped their garbage, did their shopping, and headed for the morning bus.

The women of Brewster had readily accepted the lighter, skinny one. There wasn't much threat in her timid mincing walk and the slightly protruding teeth she seemed so eager to show everyone in her bell-like good mornings and evenings. Breaths were held a little longer in the direction of the short dark one—too pretty, and too much behind. And she insisted on wearing those thin Qiana[1] dresses that the summer breeze molded against the maddening rhythm of the twenty pounds of rounded flesh that she swung steadily down the street. Through slitted eyes, the women watched their men watching her pass, knowing the bastards were praying for a wind. But since she seemed oblivious to whether these supplications went answered, their sighs settled around her shoulders too. Nice girls.

And so no one even cared to remember exactly when they had moved into Brewster Place, until the rumor started. It had first spread through the block like a sour odor that's only faintly perceptible and easily ignored until it starts growing in strength from the dozen mouths it had been lying in, among clammy gums and scum-coated teeth. And then it was everywhere—lining the mouths and whitening the lips of everyone as they wrinkled up their noses at its pervading smell, unable to pinpoint the source or time of its initial arrival. Sophie could—she had been there.

It wasn't that the rumor had actually begun with Sophie. A rumor needs no true parent. It only needs a willing carrier, and it found one in Sophie. She had been there—on one of those August evenings when the sun's absence is a mockery because the heat leaves the air so heavy it presses the naked skin down on your body, to the point that a sheet becomes unbearable and sleep impossible. So most of Brewster was outside that night when the two had come in together, probably from one of those air-conditioned movies downtown, and had greeted the ones who were loitering around their building. And they had started up the steps when the skinny one tripped over a child's ball and the darker one had grabbed her by the arm and around the waist to break her fall. "Careful, don't wanna lose you now." And the two of them had laughed into each other's eyes and went into the building.

The smell had begun there. It outlined the image of the stumbling woman and the one who had broken her fall. Sophie and a few other women sniffed at the spot and then, perplexed, silently looked at each other. Where had they seen that before? They had often laughed and touched each other—held each other in joy or its dark twin—but where had they seen *that* before? It came to them as the scent drifted down the steps and entered their nostrils on the way to their inner mouths. They had seen that—done that—with their men. That shared moment of invisible communion reserved for two and hidden from the rest of the world behind laughter or tears or a touch. In the days before babies, miscarriages, and other broken dreams, after stolen caresses in barn stalls and cotton houses, after intimate walks from church and secret kisses with boys who were now long forgotten or

1. Nylon.

permanently fixed in their lives—that was where. They could almost feel the odor moving about in their mouths, and they slowly knitted themselves together and let it out into the air like a yellow mist that began to cling to the bricks on Brewster.

So it got around that the two in 312 were *that* way. And they had seemed like such nice girls. Their regular exits and entrances to the block were viewed with a jaundiced eye. The quiet that rested around their door on the weekends hinted of all sorts of secret rituals, and their friendly indifference to the men on the street was an insult to the women as a brazen flaunting of unnatural ways.

Since Sophie's apartment windows faced theirs from across the air shaft, she became the official watchman for the block, and her opinions were deferred to whenever the two came up in conversation. Sophie took her position seriously and was constantly alert for any telltale signs that might creep out around their drawn shades, across from which she kept a religious vigil. An entire week of drawn shades was evidence enough to send her flying around with reports that as soon as it got dark they pulled their shades down and put on the lights. Heads nodded in knowing unison—a definite sign. If doubt was voiced with a "But I pull my shades down at night too," a whispered "Yeah, but you're not *that* way" was argument enough to win them over.

Sophie watched the lighter one dumping their garbage, and she went outside and opened the lid. Her eyes darted over the crushed tin cans, vegetable peelings, and empty chocolate chip cookie boxes. What do they do with all them chocolate chip cookies? It was surely a sign, but it would take some time to figure that one out. She saw Ben go into their apartment, and she waited and blocked his path as he came out, carrying his toolbox.

"What ya see?" She grabbed his arm and whispered wetly in his face.

Ben stared at her squinted eyes and drooping lips and shook his head slowly. "Uh, uh, uh, it was terrible."

"Yeah?" She moved in a little closer.

"Worst busted faucet I seen in my whole life." He shook her hand off his arm and left her standing in the middle of the block.

"You old sop bucket," she muttered, as she went back up on her stoop. A broken faucet, huh? Why did they need to use so much water?

Sophie had plenty to report that day. Ben had said it was terrible in there. No, she didn't know exactly what he had seen, but you can imagine—and they did. Confronted with the difference that had been thrust into their predictable world, they reached into their imaginations and, using an ancient pattern, weaved themselves a reason for its existence. Out of necessity they stitched all of their secret fears and lingering childhood nightmares into this existence, because even though it was deceptive enough to try and look as they looked, talk as they talked, and do as they did, it had to have some hidden stain to invalidate it—it was impossible for them both to be right. So they leaned back, supported by the sheer weight of their numbers and comforted by the woven barrier that kept them protected from the yellow mist that enshrouded the two as they came and went on Brewster Place.

Lorraine was the first to notice the change in the people on Brewster Place. She was a shy but naturally friendly woman who got up early, and had read the morning paper and done fifty sit-ups before it was time to leave for work. She came out of her apartment eager to start her day by greeting any of her neighbors who were outside. But she noticed that some of the people who had spoken to her before made a point of having something else to do with their eyes when she passed, although she could almost feel them staring at her back as she moved on. The ones who still spoke only did so after an uncomfortable pause, in which they seemed to be peering through her before they begrudged her a good morning or evening. She wondered if it was all in her mind and she thought about mentioning it to Theresa, but she didn't want to be accused of being too sensitive again. And how would Tee even notice anything like that anyway? She had a lousy attitude and hardly ever spoke to people. She stayed in that bed until the last moment and rushed out of the house fogged-up and grumpy, and she was used to being stared at—by men at least—because of her body.

Lorraine thought about these things as she came up the block from work, carrying a large paper bag. The group of women on her stoop parted silently and let her pass.

"Good evening," she said, as she climbed the steps.

Sophie was standing on the top step and tried to peek into the bag. "You been shopping, huh? What ya buy?" It was almost an accusation.

"Groceries." Lorraine shielded the top of the bag from view and squeezed past her with a confused frown. She saw Sophie throw a knowing glance to the others at the bottom of the stoop. What was wrong with this old woman? Was she crazy or something?

Lorraine went into her apartment. Theresa was sitting by the window, reading a copy of *Mademoiselle*. She glanced up from her magazine. "Did you get my chocolate chip cookies?"

"Why good evening to you, too, Tee. And how was my day? Just wonderful." She sat the bag down on the couch. "The little Baxter boy brought in a puppy for show-and-tell, and the damn thing pissed all over the floor and then proceeded to chew the heel off my shoe, but, yes, I managed to hobble to the store and bring you your chocolate chip cookies."

Oh, Jesus, Theresa thought, she's got a bug up her ass tonight.

"Well, you should speak to Mrs. Baxter. She ought to train her kid better than that." She didn't wait for Lorraine to stop laughing before she tried to stretch her good mood. "Here, I'll put those things away. Want me to make dinner so you can rest? I only worked half a day, and the most tragic thing that went down was a broken fingernail and that got caught in my typewriter."

Lorraine followed Theresa into the kitchen. "No, I'm not really tired, and fair's fair, you cooked last night. I didn't mean to tick off like that; it's just that . . . well, Tee, have you noticed that people aren't as nice as they used to be?"

Theresa stiffened. Oh, God, here she goes again. "What people, Lorraine? Nice in what way?"

"Well, the people in this building and on the street. No one hardly speaks anymore. I mean, I'll come in and say good evening—and just silence. It wasn't like that when we first moved in. I don't know, it just makes you wonder; that's all. What are they thinking?"

"I personally don't give a shit what they're thinking. And their good evenings don't put any bread on my table."

"Yeah, but you didn't see the way that woman looked at me out there. They must feel something or know something. They probably—"

"They, they, they!" Theresa exploded. "You know, I'm not starting up with this again, Lorraine. Who in the hell are they? And where in the hell are we? Living in some dump of a building in this God-forsaken part of town around a bunch of ignorant niggers with the cotton still under their fingernails because of you and your theys. They knew something in Linden Hills, so I gave up an apartment for you that I'd been in for the last four years. And then they knew in Park Heights, and you made me so miserable there we had to leave. Now these mysterious theys are on Brewster Place. Well, look out that window, kid. There's a big wall down that block, and this is the end of the line for me. I'm not moving anymore, so if that's what you're working yourself up to—save it!"

When Theresa became angry she was like a lump of smoldering coal, and her fierce bursts of temper always unsettled Lorraine.

"You see, that's why I didn't want to mention it." Lorraine began to pull at her fingers nervously. "You're always flying up and jumping to conclusions—no one said anything about moving. And I didn't know your life has been so miserable since you met me. I'm sorry about that," she finished tearfully.

Theresa looked at Lorraine, standing in the kitchen door like a wilted leaf, and she wanted to throw something at her. Why didn't she ever fight back? The very softness that had first attracted her to Lorraine was now a frequent cause for irritation. Smoked honey. That's what Lorraine had reminded her of, sitting in her office clutching that application. Dry autumn days in Georgia woods, thick bloated smoke under a beehive, and the first glimpse of amber honey just faintly darkened about the edges by the burning twigs. She had flowed just that heavily into Theresa's mind and had stuck there with a persistent sweetness.

But Theresa hadn't known then that this softness filled Lorraine up to the very middle and that she would bend at the slightest pressure, would be constantly seeking to surround herself with the comfort of everyone's goodwill, and would shrivel up at the least touch of disapproval. It was becoming a drain to be continually called upon for this nurturing and support that she just didn't understand. She had supplied it at first out of love for Lorraine, hoping that she would harden eventually, even as honey does when exposed to the cold. Theresa was growing tired of being clung to—of being the one who was leaned on. She didn't want a child—she wanted someone who could stand toe to toe with her and be willing to slug it out at times. If they practiced that way with each other, then they could turn back to back and beat the hell out of the world for trying to invade their territory. But she had found no such sparring partner in Lorraine, and the strain of fighting alone was beginning to show on her.

"Well, if it was that miserable, I would have been gone a long time ago," she said, watching her words refresh Lorraine like a gentle shower.

"I guess you think I'm some sort of a sick paranoid, but I can't afford to have people calling my job or writing letters to my principal. You know I've already lost a position like that in Detroit. And teaching is my whole life, Tee."

"I know," she sighed, not really knowing at all. There was no danger of that ever happening on Brewster Place. Lorraine taught too far from this neighborhood for anyone here to recognize her in that school. No, it wasn't her job she feared losing this time, but their approval. She wanted to stand out there and chat and trade makeup secrets and cake recipes. She wanted to be secretary of their block association and be asked to mind their kids while they ran to the store. And none of that was going to happen if they couldn't even bring themselves to accept her good evenings.

Theresa silently finished unpacking the groceries. "Why did you buy cottage cheese? Who eats that stuff?"

"Well, I thought we should go on a diet."

"If *we* go on a diet, then you'll disappear. You've got nothing to lose but your hair."

"Oh, I don't know. I thought that we might want to try and reduce our hips or something." Lorraine shrugged playfully.

"No, thank you. We are very happy with our hips the way they are," Theresa said, as she shoved the cottage cheese to the back of the refrigerator. "And even when I lose weight, it never comes off there. My chest and arms just get smaller, and I start looking like a bottle of salad dressing."

The two women laughed, and Theresa sat down to watch Lorraine fix dinner. "You know, this behind has always been my downfall. When I was coming up in Georgia with my grandmother, the boys used to promise me penny candy if I would let them pat my behind. And I used to love those jawbreakers—you know, the kind that lasted all day and kept changing colors in your mouth. So I was glad to oblige them, because in one afternoon I could collect a whole week's worth of jawbreakers."

"Really. That's funny to you? Having some boy feeling all over you."

Theresa sucked her teeth. "We were only kids, Lorraine. You know, you remind me of my grandmother. That was one straight-laced old lady. She had a fit when my brother told her what I was doing. She called me into the smokehouse and told me in this real scary whisper that I could get pregnant from letting little boys pat my butt and that I'd end up like my cousin Willa. But Willa and I had been thick as fleas, and she had already given me a step-by-step summary of how she'd gotten into her predicament. But I sneaked around to her house that night just to double-check her story, since that old lady had seemed so earnest. 'Willa, are you sure?' I whispered through her bedroom window. 'I'm tellin' ya, Tee,' she said. 'Just keep both feet on the ground and you home free.' Much later I learned that advice wasn't too biologically sound, but it worked in Georgia because those country boys didn't have much imagination."

Theresa's laughter bounced off of Lorraine's silent, rigid back and died in her throat. She angrily tore open a pack of the chocolate chip cookies. "Yeah," she said, staring at Lorraine's back and biting down hard into the cookie, "it wasn't until I came up north to college that I found out there's a whole lot of things that a dude with a little imagination can do to you even with both feet on the ground. You see, Willa forgot to tell me not to bend over or squat or—"

"Must you!" Lorraine turned around from the stove with her teeth clenched tightly together.

"Must I what, Lorraine? Must I talk about things that are as much a part of life as eating or breathing or growing old? Why are you always so uptight about sex or men?"

"I'm not uptight about anything. I just think it's disgusting when you go on and on about—"

"There's nothing disgusting about it, Lorraine. You've never been with a man, but I've been with quite a few—some better than others. There were a couple who I still hope to this day will die a slow, painful death, but then there were some who were good to me—in and out of bed."

"If they were so great, then why are you with me?" Lorraine's lips were trembling.

"Because—" Theresa looked steadily into her eyes and then down at the cookie she was twirling on the table. "Because," she continued slowly, "you can take a chocolate chip cookie and put holes in it and attach it to your ears and call it an earring, or hang it around your neck on a silver chain and pretend it's a necklace—but it's still a cookie. See—you can toss it in the air and call it a Frisbee or even a flying saucer, if the mood hits you, and it's still just a cookie. Send it spinning on a table—like this—until it's a wonderful blur of amber and brown light that you can imagine to be a topaz or rusted gold or old crystal, but the law of gravity has got to come into play, sometime, and it's got to come to rest—sometime. Then all the spinning and pretending and hoopla is over with. And you know what you got?"

"A chocolate chip cookie," Lorraine said.

"Uh-uh." Theresa put the cookie in her mouth and winked. "A lesbian." She got up from the table. "Call me when dinner's ready, I'm going back to read." She stopped at the kitchen door. "Now, why are you putting gravy on that chicken, Lorraine? You know it's fattening."

The Brewster Place Block Association was meeting in Kiswana's apartment. People were squeezed on the sofa and coffee table and sitting on the floor. Kiswana had hung a red banner across the wall, "Today Brewster—Tomorrow America!" but few understood what that meant and even fewer cared. They were there because this girl had said that something could be done about the holes in their walls and the lack of heat that kept their children with congested lungs in the winter. Kiswana had given up trying to be heard above the voices that were competing with each other in volume and length of complaints against the landlord. This was the first time in their lives that they felt someone was taking them seriously, so all of the would-be-if-they-could-be lawyers, politicians, and Broadway actors were taking advantage of this rare opportunity to display their talents. It didn't matter if they often repeated what had been said or if their monologues held no relevance to the issues; each one fought for the space to outshine the other.

"Ben ain't got no reason to be here. He works for the landlord."

A few scattered yeahs came from around the room.

"I lives in this here block just like y'all," Ben said slowly. "And when you ain't got no heat, I ain't either. It's not my fault 'cause the man won't deliver no oil."

"But you stay so zooted[2] all the time, you never cold no way."

"Ya know, a lot of things ain't the landlord's fault. The landlord don't throw garbage in the air shaft or break the glass in them doors."

"Yeah, and what about all them kids that be runnin' up and down the halls."

"Don't be talking 'bout my kids!" Cora Lee jumped up. "Lot of y'all got kids, too, and they no saints."

"Why you so touchy—who mentioned you?"

"But if the shoe fits, steal it from Thom McAn's."

"Wait, please." Kiswana held up her hands. "This is getting us nowhere. What we should be discussing today is staging a rent strike and taking the landlord to court."

2. Drunk.

"What we should be discussin'," Sophie leaned over and said to Mattie and Etta, "is that bad element that done moved in this block amongst decent people."

"Well, I done called the police at least a dozen times about C. C. Baker and them boys hanging in that alley, smoking them reefers, and robbing folks," Mattie said.

"I ain't talkin' 'bout them kids—I'm talkin' 'bout those two livin' 'cross from me in 312."

"What about 'em?"

"Oh, you know, Mattie," Etta said, staring straight at Sophie. "Those two girls who mind their business and never have a harsh word to say 'bout nobody—them the two you mean, right, Sophie?"

"What they doin'—livin' there like that—is wrong, and you know it." She turned to appeal to Mattie. "Now, you a Christian woman. The Good Book say that them things is an abomination against the Lord. We shouldn't be havin' that here on Brewster and the association should do something about it."

"My Bible also says in First Peter not to be a busybody in other people's matters, Sophie. And the way I see it, if they ain't botherin' with what goes on in my place, why should I bother 'bout what goes on in theirs?"

"They sinning against the Lord!" Sophie's eyes were bright and wet.

"Then let the Lord take care of it," Etta snapped. "Who appointed you?"

"That don't surprise me comin' from *you*. No, not one bit!" Sophie glared at Etta and got up to move around the room to more receptive ears.

Etta started to go after her, but Mattie held her arm. "Let that woman be. We're not here to cause no row over some of her stupidness."

"The old prune pit," Etta spit out. "She oughta be glad them two girls are that way. That's one less bed she gotta worry 'bout pullin' Jess out of this year. I didn't see her thumpin' no Bible when she beat up that woman from Mobile she caught him with last spring."

"Etta, I'd never mention it in front of Sophie 'cause I hate the way she loves to drag other people's business in the street, but I can't help feelin' that what they're doing ain't quite right. How do you get that way? Is it from birth?"

"I couldn't tell you, Mattie. But I seen a lot of it in my time and the places I've been. They say they just love each other—who knows?"

Mattie was thinking deeply. "Well, I've loved women, too. There was Miss Eva and Ciel, and even as ornery as you can get, I've loved you practically all my life."

"Yeah, but it's different with them."

"Different how?"

"Well . . ." Etta was beginning to feel uncomfortable. "They love each other like you'd love a man or a man would love you—I guess."

"But I've loved some women deeper than I ever loved any man," Mattie was pondering. "And there been some women who loved me more and did more for me than any man ever did."

"Yeah." Etta thought for a moment. "I can second that, but it's still different, Mattie. I can't exactly put my finger on it, but . . ."

"Maybe it's not so different," Mattie said, almost to herself. "Maybe that's why some women get so riled up about it, 'cause they know deep down it's not so different after all." She looked at Etta. "It kinda gives you a funny feeling when you think about it that way, though."

"Yeah, it does," Etta said, unable to meet Mattie's eyes.

Lorraine was climbing the dark narrow stairway up to Kiswana's apartment. She had tried to get Theresa to come, but she had wanted no part of it. "A tenants' meeting for what? The damn street needs to be condemned." She knew Tee blamed her for having to live in a place like Brewster, but she could at least try to make the best of things and get involved with the community. That was the problem with so many black people—they just sat back and complained while the whole world tumbled down around their heads. And grabbing an attitude and thinking you were better than these people just because a lot of them were poor and uneducated wouldn't help, either. It just made you seem standoffish, and Lorraine wanted to be liked by the people around her. She couldn't live the way Tee did, with her head stuck in a book all the time. Tee didn't seem to need anyone. Lorraine often wondered if she even needed her.

But if you kept to yourself all the time, people started to wonder, and then they talked. She couldn't afford to have people talking about her, Tee should understand that—she knew from the way they had met. Understand. It was funny because that was the first thing she had felt about her when she handed Tee her application. She had said to herself, I feel that I can talk to this woman, I can tell her why I lost my job in Detroit, and she will understand. And she had understood, but then slowly all that had stopped. Now Lorraine was made to feel awkward and stupid about her fears and thoughts. Maybe Tee was right and she was too sensitive, but there was a big difference between being personnel director for the Board of Education and a first-grade teacher. Tee didn't threaten their files and payroll accounts but, somehow, she, Lorraine, threatened their children. Her heart tightened when she thought about that. The worst thing she had ever wanted to do to a child was to slap the spit out of the little Baxter boy for pouring glue in her hair, and even that had only been for a fleeting moment. Didn't Tee understand that if she lost this job, she wouldn't be so lucky the next time? No, she didn't understand that or anything else about her. She never wanted to bother with anyone except those weirdos at that club she went to, and Lorraine hated them. They were coarse and bitter, and made fun of people who weren't like them. Well, she wasn't like them either. Why should she feel different from the people she lived around? Black people were all in the same boat—she'd come to realize this even more since they had moved to Brewster—and if they didn't row together, they would sink together.

Lorraine finally reached the top floor; the door to Kiswana's apartment was open but she knocked before she went in. Kiswana was trying to break up an argument between a short light-skinned man and some woman who had picked up a potted plant and was threatening to hit him in the mouth. Most of the other tenants were so busy rooting for one or the other that hardly anyone noticed Lorraine when she entered. She went over and stood by Ben.

"I see there's been a slight difference of opinion here," she smiled.

"Just nigger mess, miss. Roscoe there claim that Betina ain't got no right being secretary 'cause she owe three months' rent, and she say he owe more than that and it's none of his never mind. Don't know how we got into all this. Ain't what we was talkin' 'bout, no way. Was talkin' 'bout havin' a block party to raise money for a housing lawyer."

Kiswana had rescued her Boston Fern from the woman and the two people were being pulled to opposite sides of the room. Betina pushed her way out of the door, leaving behind very loud advice about where they could put their secretary's job along with the block association, if they could find the space in that small an opening in their bodies.

Kiswana sat back down, flushed and out of breath. "Now we need someone else to take the minutes."

"Do they come with the rest of the watch?" Laughter and another series of monologues about Betina's bad-natured exit followed for the next five minutes.

Lorraine saw that Kiswana looked as if she wanted to cry. The one-step-forward-two-steps-backwards progression of the meeting was beginning to show on her face. Lorraine swallowed her shyness and raised her hand. "I'll take the minutes for you."

"Oh, thank you." Kiswana hurriedly gathered the scattered and crumpled papers and handed them to her. "Now we can get back down to business."

The room was now aware of Lorraine's presence, and there were soft murmurs from the corners, accompanied by furtive glances while a few like Sophie stared at her openly. She attempted to smile into the eyes of the people watching her, but they would look away the moment she glanced in their direction. After a couple of vain attempts her smile died, and she buried it uneasily in the papers in her hand. Lorraine tried to cover her trembling fingers by pretending to decipher Betina's smudged and misspelled notes.

"All right," Kiswana said, "now who had promised to get a stereo hooked up for the party?"

"Ain't we supposed to vote on who we wants for secretary?" Sophie's voice rose heavily in the room, and its weight smothered the other noise. All of the faces turned silently toward hers with either mild surprise or coveted satisfaction over what they knew was coming. "I mean, can anybody just waltz in here and get shoved down our throats and we don't have a say about it?"

"Look, I can just go," Lorraine said. "I just wanted to help, I—"

"No, wait." Kiswana was confused. "What vote? Nobody else wanted to do it. Did you want to take the notes?"

"She can't do it," Etta cut in, "unless we was sitting here reciting the ABC's, and we better not do that too fast. So let's just get on with the meeting."

Scattered approval came from sections of the room.

"Listen here!" Sophie jumped up to regain lost ground. "Why should a decent woman get insulted and y'll take sides with the likes of them?" Her finger shot out like a pistol, which she swung between Etta and Lorraine.

Etta rose from her seat. "Who do you think you're talkin' to, you old hen's ass? I'm as decent as you are, and I'll come over there and lam you in the mouth to prove it!"

Etta tried to step across the coffee table, but Mattie caught her by the back of the dress; Etta turned, tried to shake her off, and tripped over the people in front of her. Sophie picked up a statue and backed up into the wall with it slung over her shoulder like a baseball bat. Kiswana put her head in her hands and groaned. Etta had taken off her high-heeled shoe and was waving the spiked end at Sophie over the shoulders of the people who were holding her back.

"That's right! That's right!" Sophie screamed. "Pick on me! Sure, I'm the one who goes around doin' them filthy, unnatural things right under your noses. Every one of you knows it; everybody done talked about it, not just me!" Her head moved around the room like a trapped animal's. "And any woman—any woman who defends that kind of thing just better be watched. That's all I gotta say—where there's smoke, there's fire, Etta Johnson!"

Etta stopped struggling against the arms that were holding her, and her chest was heaving in rapid spasms as she threw Sophie a look of wilting hate, but she remained silent. And no other woman in the room dared to speak as they moved an extra breath away from each other. Sophie turned toward Lorraine, who had twisted the meeting's notes into a mass of shredded paper. Lorraine kept her back straight, but her hands and mouth were moving with a will of their own. She stood like a fading spirit before the ebony statue that Sophie pointed at her like a crucifix.

"Movin' into our block causin' a disturbance with your nasty ways. You ain't wanted here!"

"What have any of you ever seen me do except leave my house and go to work like the rest of you? Is it disgusting for me to speak to each one of you that I meet in the street, even when you don't answer me back? Is that my crime?" Lorraine's voice sank like a silver dagger into their consciences, and there was an uneasy stirring in the room.

"Don't stand there like you a Miss Innocent," Sophie whispered hoarsely. "I'll tell ya what I seen!"

Her eyes leered around the room as they waited with a courtroom hush for her next words.

"I wasn't gonna mention something so filthy, but you forcin' me." She ran her tongue over her parched lips and narrowed her eyes at Lorraine. "You forgot to close your shades last night, and I saw the two of you!"

The silence in the room tightened into a half-gasp.

"There you was, standin' in the bathroom door, drippin' wet and as naked and shameless as you please . . ."

It had become so quiet it was now painful.

"Calling to the other one to put down her book and get you a clean towel. Standin' in that bathroom door with your naked behind. I saw it—I did!"

Their chests were beginning to burn from a lack of air as they waited for Lorraine's answer, but before the girl could open her mouth, Ben's voice snaked from behind her like a lazy breeze.

"Guess *you* get out the tub with your clothes on, Sophie. Must make it mighty easy on Jess's eyes."

The laughter that burst out of their lungs was such a relief that eyes were watery. The room laid its head back and howled in gratitude to Ben for allowing it to breathe again. Sophie's rantings could not be heard above the wheezing, coughing, and backslapping that now went on.

Lorraine left the apartment and grasped the stairway railing, trying to keep the bile from rising into her throat. Ben followed her outside and gently touched her shoulder.

"Miss, you all right?"

She pressed her lips tightly together and nodded her head. The lightness of his touch brought tears to her eyes, and she squeezed them shut.

"You sure? You look 'bout ready to keel over."

Lorraine shook her head jerkily and sank her nails deeply into her palm as she brought her hand to her mouth. I mustn't speak, she thought. If I open my mouth, I'll scream. Oh, God, I'll scream or I'll throw up, right here, in front of this nice old man. The thought of the churned up bits of her breakfast and lunch pouring out of her mouth and splattering on Ben's trouser legs suddenly struck her as funny, and she fought an overwhelming desire to laugh. She trembled violently as the creeping laughter tried to deceive her into parting her lips.

Ben's face clouded over as he watched the frail body that was so bravely struggling for control. "Come on now, I'll take you home." And he tried to lead her down the steps.

She shook her head in a panic. She couldn't let Tee see her like this. If she says anything smart to me now, I'll kill her, Lorraine thought. I'll pick up a butcher knife and plunge it into her face, and then I'll kill myself and let them find us there. The thought of all those people in Kiswana's apartment standing over their bleeding bodies was strangely comforting, and she began to breathe more easily.

"Come on now," Ben urged quietly, and edged her toward the steps.

"I can't go home." She barely whispered.

"It's all right, you ain't gotta—come on."

And she let him guide her down the stairs and out into the late September evening. He took her to the building that was nearest to the wall on Brewster Place and then down the outside steps to a door with a broken dirty screen. Ben unlocked the door and led her into his damp underground rooms.

He turned on the single light bulb that was hanging from the ceiling by a thick black cord and pulled out a chair for her at the kitchen table, which was propped up against the wall. Lorraine sat down, grateful to be able to take the weight off of her shaky knees. She didn't acknowledge his apologies as he took the half-empty wine bottle and cracked cup from the table. He brushed off the crumbs while two fat brown roaches raced away from the wet cloth.

"I'm makin' tea," he said, without asking her if she wanted any. He placed a blackened pot of water on the hot plate at the edge of the counter, then found two cups in the cabinet that still had their handles intact. Ben put the strong black tea he had brewed in front of her and brought her a spoon and a crumpled pound bag of sugar. Lorraine took three heaping teaspoons of sugar and stirred the tea, holding her face over the steam. Ben waited for her face to register the effects of the hot sweet liquid.

"I liked you from first off," he said shyly, and seeing her smile, he continued. "You remind me lots of my little girl." Ben reached into his hip pocket and took out a frayed billfold and handed her a tiny snapshot.

Lorraine tilted the picture toward the light. The face stamped on the celluloid paper bore absolutely no resemblance to her at all. His daughter's face was oval and dark, and she had a large flat nose and a tiny rounded mouth. She handed the picture back to Ben and tried to cover her confusion.

"I know what you thinkin'," Ben said, looking at the face in his hands. "But she had a limp—my little girl. Was a breech baby, and the midwife broke her foot when she was birthed and it never came back right. Always kinda cripped along—but a sweet child." He frowned deeply into the picture and paused, then looked up at Lorraine. "When I seen you—the way you'd walk up the street all timid-like and tryin' to be nice to these-here folks and the look on your face when some of 'em was just downright rude—you kinda broke up in here." He motioned toward his chest. "And you just sorta limped along inside. That's when I thought of my baby."

Lorraine gripped the teacup with both hands, but the tears still squeezed through the compressed muscles in her eyes. They slowly rolled down her face but she wouldn't release the cup to wipe them away.

"My father," she said, staring into the brown liquid, "kicked me out of the house when I was seventeen years old. He found a letter one of my girlfriends had written me, and when I wouldn't lie about what it meant, he told me to get out and leave behind everything that he had ever bought me. He said he wanted to burn them." She looked up to see the expression on Ben's face, but it kept swimming under the tears in her eyes. "So I walked out of his home with only the clothes on my back. I moved in with one of my cousins, and I worked at night in a bakery to put myself through college. I would send him a birthday card each year, and he always returned them unopened. After a while I stopped putting my return address on the envelopes so he couldn't send them back. I guess he burned those too." She sniffed the mucus up into her nose. "I still send those cards like that—without a return address. That way I can believe that, maybe, one year before he dies, he'll open them."

Ben got up and gave her a piece of toilet paper to blow her nose in.

"Where's your daughter now, Mr. Ben?"

"For me?" Ben sighed deeply. "Just like you—livin' in a world with no address."

They finished their tea in silence and Lorraine got up to go.

"There's no way to thank you, so I won't try."

"I'd be right hurt if you did." Ben patted her arm. "Now come back anytime you got a mind to. I got nothing, but you welcome to all of that. Now how many folks is that generous?"

Lorraine smiled, leaned over, and kissed him on the cheek. Ben's face lit up the walls of the dingy basement. He closed the door behind her, and at first her "Good night, Mr. Ben" tinkled like crystal bells in his mind. Crystal bells that grew larger and louder, until their sound was distorted in his ears and he almost believed that she had said "Good night, Daddy Ben"—no—"Mornin' Daddy Ben, mornin' Daddy Ben, mornin' . . ." Ben's saliva began to taste like sweating tin, and he ran a trembling hand over his stubbled face and rushed to the corner where he had shoved the wine bottle. The bells had begun almost to deafen him and he shook his head to relieve the drumming pain inside of his ears. He knew what was coming next, and he didn't dare waste time by pouring the wine into a cup. He lifted the bottle up to his mouth and sucked at it greedily, but it was too late. *Swing low, sweet chariot.* The song had started—the whistling had begun.

It started low, from the end of his gut, and shrilled its way up into his ears and shattered the bells, sending glass shards flying into a heart that should have been so scarred from old piercings that there was no flesh left to bleed. But the glass splinters found some minute, untouched place—as they always did—and tore the heart and let the whistling in. And now Ben would have to drink faster and longer, because the melody would now ride on his body's blood like a cancer and poison everywhere it touched. *Swing low, sweet chariot.* It mustn't get to his brain. He had a few more seconds before it got to his brain and killed him. He had to be drunk before the poison crept up his neck muscles, past his mouth, on the way to his brain. If he was drunk, then he could let it out—sing it out into the air before it touched his brain, caused him to remember. *Swing low, sweet chariot.* He couldn't die there under the ground like some animal. Oh, God, please make him drunk. And he promised—he'd never go that long without a drink again. It was just the meeting and then that girl that had kept him from it this long, but he swore it would never happen again—just please, God, make him drunk.

The alcohol began to warm Ben's body, and he felt his head begin to get numb and heavy. He almost sobbed out his thanks for this redeeming answer to his prayers, because the whistling had just reached his throat and he was able to open his mouth and slobber the words out into the room. The saliva was dripping from the corners of his mouth because he had to take huge gulps of wine between breaths, but he sang on—drooling and humming—because to sing was salvation, to sing was to empty the tune from his blood, to sing was to unremember Elvira, and his daughter's "Mornin', Daddy Ben" as she dragged her twisted foot up his front porch with that song hitting her in the back.

Swing low

"Mornin', Ben. Mornin', Elvira."

Sweet chariot

The red pick-up truck stopped in front of Ben's yard.

Comin' for to carry me home

His daughter got out of the passenger side and began to limp toward the house.

Swing low

Elvira grinned into the creviced face of the white man sitting in the truck with tobacco stains in the corner of his mouth. "Mornin', Mr. Clyde. Right nice day, ain't it, sir?"

Sweet chariot

Ben watched his daughter come through the gate with her eyes on the ground, and she slowly climbed up on the porch. She took each step at a time, and her shoes grated against the rough boards. She finally turned her beaten eyes into his face, and what was left of his soul to crush was taken care of by the bell-like voice that greeted them. "Mornin', Daddy Ben. Mornin', Mama."

"Mornin', baby," Ben mumbled with his jaws tight.

Swing low

"How's things up at the house?" Elvira asked. "My little girl do a good job for you yesterday?"

Sweet chariot

"Right fine, Elvira. Got that place clean as a skinned rat. How's y'all's crops comin'?"

"Just fine, Mr. Clyde, sir. Just fine. We sure appreciate that extra land you done rented us. We bringin' in more than enough to break even. Yes, sir, just fine."

The man laughed, showing the huge gaps between his tobacco-rotted teeth. "Glad to do it. Y'all some of my best tenants. I likes keepin' my people happy. If you needs somethin', let me know."

"Sure will, Mr. Clyde, sir."

"Aw right, see y'all next week. Be by the regular time to pick up the gal."

"She be ready, sir."

The man started up the motor on the truck, and the tune that he whistled as he drove off remained in the air long after the dust had returned to the ground. Elvira grinned and waved until the red of the truck had disappeared over the horizon. Then she simultaneously dropped her arm and smile and turned toward her daughter. "Don't just stand there gawkin'. Get in the house—your breakfast been ready."

"Yes, Mama."

When the screen door had slammed shut, Elvira snapped her head around to Ben. "Nigger, what is wrong with you? Ain't you heard Mr. Clyde talkin' to you, and you standin' there like a hunk of stone. You better get some sense in you head 'fore I knock some in you!"

Ben stood with his hands in his pockets, staring at the tracks in the dirt where the truck had been. He kept balling his fists up in his overalls until his nails dug into his palms.

"It ain't right, Elvira. It just ain't right and you know it."

"What ain't right?" The woman stuck her face into his and he backed up a few steps. "That that gal work and earn her keep like the rest of us? She can't go to the fields, but she can clean house, and she'll do it! I see it's better you keep your mouth shut 'cause when it's open, ain't nothin' but stupidness comin' out." She turned her head and brushed him off as she would a fly, then headed toward the door of the house.

"She came to us, Elvira." There was a leaden sadness in Ben's voice. "She came to us a long time ago."

The thin woman spun around with her face twisted into an airless knot. "She came to us with a bunch of lies 'bout Mr. Clyde 'cause she's too damn lazy to work. Why would a decent widow man want to mess with a little black nothin' like her? No, anything to get out of work—just like you."

"Why she gotta spend the night then?" Ben turned his head slowly toward her. "Why he always make her spend the night up there alone with him?"

"Why should he make an extra trip just to bring her tail home when he pass this way every Saturday mornin' on the way to town? If she wasn't lame, she could walk it herself after she finish work. But the man nice enough to drop her home, and you want to bad-mouth him along with that lyin' hussy."

"After she came to us, you remember I borrowed Tommy Boy's wagon and went to get her that Friday night. I told ya what Mr. Clyde told me. 'She ain't finished yet, Ben.' Just like that—'She ain't finished yet.' And then standin' there whistlin' while I went out the back gate." Ben's nails dug deeper into his palms.

"So!" Elvira's voice was shrill. "So it's a big house. It ain't like this shit you got us livin' in. It take her longer to do things than most folks. You know that, so why stand there carryin' on like it mean more than that?"

"She ain't finished yet, Ben." Ben shook his head slowly. "If I was half a man I woulda—"

Elvira came across the porch and sneered into his face. "If you was half a man, you coulda given me more babies and we woulda had some help workin' this land instead of a half-grown woman we gotta carry the load for. And if you was even quarter a man, we wouldn't be a bunch of miserable sharecroppers on someone else's land—but we is, Ben. And I'll be damned if I see the little bit we got taken away 'cause you believe that gal's lowdown lies! So when Mr. Clyde come by here, you speak—hear me? And you act as grateful as your pitiful ass should be for the favors he done us."

Ben felt a slight dampness in his hands because his fingernails had broken through the skin of his palms and the blood was seeping around his cuticles. He looked at Elvira's dark braided head and wondered why he didn't take his hands out of his pockets and stop the bleeding by pressing them around it. Just lock his elbows on her shoulders and place one hand on each side of her temples and then in toward each other until the blood stopped. His big calloused hands on the bones of her skull pressing in and in, like you would with a piece of dark cloth to cover the wounds on your body and clot the blood. Or he could simply go into the house and take his shotgun and press his palms around the trigger and handle, emptying the bullets into her sagging breasts just long enough—just pressing hard enough—to stop his palms from bleeding.

But the gram of truth in her words was heavy enough to weigh his hands down in his pockets and keep his feet nailed to the wooden planks in the porch, and the wounds healed over by themselves. Ben discovered that if he sat up drinking all night Friday, he could stand on the porch Saturday morning and smile at the man who whistled as he dropped his lame daughter home. And he could look into her beaten eyes and believe that she had lied.

The girl disappeared one day, leaving behind a note saying that she loved them very much, but she knew that she had been a burden and she understood why they had made her keep working at Mr. Clyde's house. But she felt that if she had to earn her keep that way, she might as well go to Memphis where the money was better.

Elvira ran and bragged to the neighbors that their daughter was now working in a rich house in Memphis. And she was making out awful well because she always sent plenty of money home. Ben would stare at the envelopes with no return address, and he found that if he drank enough every time a letter came, he could silence the bell-like voice that came chiming out of the open envelope—"Mornin' Daddy Ben, mornin' Daddy Ben, mornin' . . ." And then if he drank enough every day he could bear the touch of Elvira's body in the bed beside him at night and not have his sleep stolen by the image of her lying there with her head caved in or her chest ripped apart by shotgun shells.

But even after they lost the sharecropping contract and Elvira left him for a man who farmed near the levee and Ben went north and took a job on Brewster, he still drank—long after he could remember why. He just knew that whenever he saw a mailman, the crystal bells would start, and then that strange whistling that could shatter them, sending them on that deadly journey toward his heart.

He never dreamed it would happen on a Sunday. The mailman didn't run on Sundays, so he had felt safe. He hadn't counted on that girl sounding so much like the bells when she left his place tonight. But it was okay, he had gotten drunk in time, and he would never take such a big chance again. No, Lord, you pulled me through this time, and I ain't pressin' your mercy no more. Ben stumbled around his shadowy damp rooms, singing now at the top of his voice. The low, trembling melody of "Swing Low, Sweet Chariot" passed through his greasy windows and up into the late summer air.

Lorraine had walked home slowly, thinking about the old man and the daughter who limped. When she came to her stoop, she brushed past her neighbors with her head up and didn't bother to speak.

Theresa got off the uptown bus and turned the corner into Brewster Place. She was always irritable on Friday evenings because they had to do payroll inventories at the office. Her neck ached from bending over endless lists of computer printouts. What did that damn Board of Education think— someone in accounting was going to sneak one of their relatives on the payroll? The biggies had been doing that for years, but they lay awake at night, thinking of ways to keep the little guys from cashing in on it too. There was something else that had been turning uncomfortably in her mind for the last few weeks, and just today it had lain still long enough for her to pinpoint it—Lorraine was changing. It wasn't exactly anything that she had said or done, but Theresa sensed a firmness in her spirit that hadn't been there before. She was speaking up more—yes, that was it—whether the subject was the evening news or bus schedules or the proper way to hem a dress. Lorraine wasn't deferring to her anymore. And she wasn't apologizing for seeing things differently from Theresa.

Why did that bother her? Didn't she want Lorraine to start standing up for herself? To stop all that sniveling and hand-wringing every time Theresa raised her voice? Weren't things the way she had wanted them to be for the last five years? What nagged at Theresa more than the change was the fact that she was worrying about it. She had actually thought about picking a fight just to see how far she could push her—push her into what? Oh, God, I must be sick, she thought. No, it was that old man—that's what it was. Why was Lorraine spending so much time with that drunk? They didn't have a damn thing in common. What could he be telling her, doing for her, that was causing this? She had tried—she truly had—to get Lorraine to show some backbone. And now some ignorant country winehead was doing in a few weeks what she couldn't do for the last five years.

Theresa was mulling this over when a little girl sped past her on skates, hit a crack in the sidewalk, and fell. She went to walk around the child, who looked up with tears in her eyes and stated simply, "Miss, I hurt myself." She said it with such a tone of wonder and disappointment that Theresa smiled. Kids lived in such an insulated world, where the smallest disturbance was met with cries of protest. Oh, sweetheart, she thought, just live on and you'll wish many a day that the biggest problem in your life would be a scraped knee. But she was still just a little girl, and right now she wanted an audience for her struggle with this uninvited disaster.

Theresa bent down beside her and clucked her teeth loudly. "Oh, you did? Let's see." She helped her off the ground and made an exaggerated fuss over the scraped knee.

"It's bleeding!" The child's voice rose in horror.

Theresa looked at the tiny specks of blood that were beading up on the grimy knee. "Why, it sure is." She tried to match the note of seriousness in the child's tone. "But I think we have a little time before you have to worry about a transfusion." She opened her pocketbook and took out a clean tissue. "Let's see if we can fix it up. Now, I want you to spit on this for me and I'll wipe your knee."

The girl spit on the tissue. "Is it gonna hurt?"

"No, it won't hurt. You know what my grandma used to call spit? God's iodine. Said it was the best thing for patching anything up—except maybe a broken leg."

She steadied the girl's leg and gently dabbed at the dirty knee. "See, it's all coming off. I guess you're gonna live." She smiled.

The child looked at her knee with a solemn face. "I think it needs a Band-Aid."

Theresa laughed. "Well, you're out of luck with me. But you go on home and see if your mama has one for you—if you can remember which knee it was by then."

"What are you doing to her?" The voice pierced the air between the child and Theresa. She looked up and saw a woman rushing toward them. The woman grabbed the child to her side. "What's going on here?" Her voice was just half an octave too high.

Theresa stood up and held out the dirty and bloody tissue. "She scraped her knee." The words fell like dead weights. "What in the hell did you think I was doing?" She refused to let the woman avoid her eyes, enjoying every minute of her cringing embarrassment.

"Mama, I need a Band-Aid, you got a Band-Aid?" The child tugged on her arm.

"Yes, yes, honey, right away." The woman was glad to have an excuse to look down. "Thank you very much," she said, as she hurried the child away. "She's always so clumsy. I've told her a million times to be careful on those skates, but you know . . ."

"Yeah, right," Theresa said, watching them go. "I know." She balled the tissue in her hand and quickly walked into the building. She slammed the apartment door open and heard Lorraine running water in the bathroom.

"Is that you, Tee?"

"Yeah," she called out, and then thought, No, it's not me. It's not me at all. Theresa paced between the kitchen and living room and then realized that she still had the tissue. She threw it into the kitchen garbage and turned on the faucet to its fullest pressure and started washing her hands. She kept lathering and rinsing them, but they still felt unclean. Son-of-a-bitch, she thought, son-of-a-fucking-bitch! She roughly dried her hands with some paper towels and fought the impulse to wash them again by starting dinner early. She kept her hands moving quickly, chopping more onions, celery, and green peppers than she really needed. She vigorously seasoned the ground beef, jabbing the wooden spoon repeatedly into the red meat.

When she stopped to catch her breath and glanced toward the kitchen window, a pair of squinty black eyes were peering at her from the corner of a shade across the air shaft. "What the hell . . . ?" She threw down her spoon and ran over to the window.

"You wanna see what I'm doing?" The shade was pulled up with such force it went spinning on its rollers at the top of the window. The eyes disappeared from the corner of the shade across the air shaft.

"Here!" Theresa slammed the window up into its casing. "I'll even raise this so you can hear better. I'm making meat loaf, you old bat! Meat loaf!" She stuck her head out of the window. "The same way other people make it! Here, I'll show you!"

She ran back to the table and took up a handful of chopped onions and threw them at Sophie's window. "See, that's the onions. And here, here's the chopped peppers!" The diced vegetables hit against the windowpane. "Oh, yeah, I use eggs!" Two eggs flew out of the window and splattered against Sophie's panes.

Lorraine came out of the bathroom, toweling her hair. "What's all the shouting for? Who are you talking to?" She saw Theresa running back and forth across the kitchen, throwing their dinner out of the window. "Have you lost your mind?"

Theresa picked up a jar of olives. "Now, here's something *freaky* for you— olives! I put olives in my meat loaf! So run up and down the street and tell that!" The jar of olives crashed against the opposite building, barely missing Sophie's window.

"Tee, stop it!"

Theresa put her head back out the window. "Now olives are definitely weird, but you gotta take that one up with my grandmother because it's her recipe! Wait! I forgot the meat—can't have you think I would try to make meat loaf without meat." She ran back to the table and grabbed up the bowl.

"Theresa!" Lorraine rushed into the kitchen.

"No, can't have you thinking that!" Theresa yelled as she swung back her arm to throw the bowl through Sophie's window. "You might feel I'm a *pervert* or something—someone you can't trust your damn children around!"

Lorraine caught her arm just as she went to hurl the bowl out of the window. She grabbed the bowl and shoved Theresa against the wall.

"Look," Lorraine said, pressing against the struggling woman, "I know you're pissed off, but ground sirloin is almost three dollars a pound!"

The look of sincere horror on Lorraine's face as she cradled the bowl of meat in her arm made Theresa giggle, and then slowly she started laughing and Lorraine nodded her head and laughed with her. Theresa laid her head back against the wall, and her plump throat vibrated from the full sounds passing through it. Lorraine let her go and put the bowl on the table. Theresa's sides were starting to ache from laughing, and she sat down in one of the kitchen chairs. Lorraine pushed the bowl a little further down the table from her, and this set them off again. Theresa laughed and rocked in the chair until tears were rolling down her cheeks. Then she crossed that fine line between laughter and tears and started to sob. Lorraine went over to her, cradled her head in her chest, and stroked her shoulders. She had no idea what had brought on all of this, but it didn't matter. It felt good to be the one who could now comfort.

The shade across the air shaft moved a fraction of an inch, and Sophie pressed one eye against her smeared and dripping windowpane. She looked at the two women holding each other and shook her head. "Um, um, um."

The next day Lorraine was on her way back from the supermarket, and she ran into Kiswana, who was coming out of their building, carrying an armful of books.

"Hi," she greeted Lorraine, "you sure have a full load there."

"Well, we ran out of vegetables last night." Lorraine smiled. "So I picked up a little extra today."

"You know, we haven't seen you at the meetings lately. Things are really picking up. There's going to be a block party next weekend, and we can use all the help we can get."

Lorraine stopped smiling. "Did you really think I'd come back after what happened?"

The blood rushed to Kiswana's face and she stared uncomfortably at the top of her books. "You know, I'm really sorry about that. I should have said something—after all, it was my house—but things just sort of got out of hand so quickly, I'm sorry, I . . ."

"Hey, look, I'm not blaming you or even that woman who made such a fuss. She's just a very sick lady, that's all. Her life must be very unhappy if she has to run around and try to hurt people who haven't done anything to her. But I just didn't want any more trouble, so I felt I ought to stay away."

"But the association is for all of us," Kiswana insisted, "and everyone doesn't feel the way she did. What you do is your own business, not that you're doing anything, anyway. I mean, well, two women or two guys can't live together without people talking. She could be your cousin or sister or something."

"We're not related," Lorraine said quietly.

"Well, good friends then," Kiswana stammered. "Why can't good friends just live together and people mind their own business. And even if you're not friends, even . . . well, whatever." She went on miserably, "It was my house and I'm sorry, I . . ."

Lorraine was kind enough to change the subject for her. "I see you have an armful yourself. You're heading toward the library?"

"No." Kiswana gave her a grateful smile. "I'm taking a few classes on the weekends. My old lady is always on my back about going back to school, so I enrolled at the community college." She was almost apologetic. "But I'm only studying black history and the science of revolution, and I let her know that. But it's enough to keep her quiet."

"I think that's great. You know, I took quite a few courses in black history when I went to school in Detroit."

"Yeah, which ones?"

While they were talking, C. C. Baker and his friends loped up the block. These young men always moved in a pack, or never without two or three. They needed the others continually near to verify their existence. When they stood with their black skin, ninth-grade diplomas, and fifty-word vocabularies in front of the mirror that the world had erected and saw nothing, those other pairs of tight jeans, suede sneakers, and tinted sunglasses imaged nearby proved that they were alive. And if there was life, there could be dreams of that miracle that would one day propel them into the heaven populated by their gods—Shaft and Superfly.[3] While they grew old awaiting that transformation they moved through the streets, insuring that they could at least be heard, if not seen, by blasting their portable cassette players and talking loudly. They continually surnamed each other Man and clutched at their crotches, readying the equipment they deemed necessary to be summoned at any moment into Superfly heaven.

The boys recognized Kiswana because her boyfriend, Abshu, was director of the community center, and Lorraine had been pointed out to them by parents or some other adult who had helped to spread the yellow mist. They spotted the two women talking to each other, and on a cue from C. C., they all slowed as they passed the stoop. C. C. Baker was greatly disturbed by the thought of a Lorraine. He knew of only one way to deal with women other than his mother. Before he had learned exactly how women gave birth, he knew how to please or punish or extract favors from them by the execution of what lay curled behind his fly. It was his lifeline to that part of his being that sheltered his self-respect. And the thought of any woman who lay beyond the length of its power was a threat.

"Hey, Swana, better watch it talkin' to that dyke—she might try to grab a tit!" C. C. called out.

"Yeah, Butch, why don't ya join the WACS[4] and really have a field day."

Lorraine's arms tightened around her packages, and she tried to push past Kiswana and go into the building. "I'll see you later."

3. Larger-than-life heroes of 1970s black action films.   4. Women's Army Corps.

"No, wait." Kiswana blocked her path. "Don't let them talk to you like that. They're nothing but a bunch of punks." She called out to the leader, "C. C., why don't you just take your little dusty behind and get out of here. No one was talking to you."

The muscular tan boy spit out his cigarette and squared his shoulders. "I ain't got to do nothin'! And I'm gonna tell Abshu you need a good spankin' for taking up with a lesbo." He looked around at his reflections and preened himself in their approval. "Why don't ya come over here and I'll show ya what a real man can do." He cupped his crotch.

Kiswana's face reddened with anger. "From what I heard about you, C. C., I wouldn't even feel it."

His friends broke up with laughter, and when he turned around to them, all he could see mirrored was respect for the girl who had beat him at the dozens.[5] Lorraine smiled at the absolutely lost look on his face. He curled his lips back into a snarl and tried to regain lost ground by attacking what instinct told him was the weaker of the two.

"Ya laughing at me, huh, freak? I oughta come over there and stick my fist in your cunt-eatin' mouth!"

"You'll have to come through me first, so just try it." Kiswana put her books on the stoop.

"Aw, Man, come on. Don't waste your time." His friends pulled at his arm. "She ain't nothing but a woman."

"I oughta go over there and slap that bitch in her face and teach her a lesson."

"Hey, Man, lay light, lay light," one whispered in his ear. "That's Abshu's woman, and that big dude don't mind kickin' ass."

C. C. did an excellent job of allowing himself to be reluctantly pulled away from Kiswana, but she wasn't fooled and had already turned to pick up her books. He made several jerky motions with his fist and forefinger at Lorraine.

"I'm gonna remember this, Butch!"

Theresa had watched the entire scene out of the window and had been ready to run out and help Kiswana if the boy had come up on the stoop. That was just like Lorraine to stand there and let someone else take up for her. Well, maybe she'd finally learned her lesson about these ignorant nothings on Brewster Place. They weren't ever going to be accepted by these people, and there was no point in trying.

Theresa left the window and sat on the couch, pretending to be solving a crossword puzzle when Lorraine came in.

"You look a little pale. Were the prices that bad at the store today?"

"No, this heat just drains me. It's hard to believe that we're in the beginning of October." She headed straight for the kitchen.

"Yeah," Theresa said, watching her back intently. "Indian Summer and all that."

"Mmm." Lorraine dumped the bags on the table. "I'm too tired to put these away now. There's nothing perishable in there. I think I'll take some aspirin and lay down."

---

5. Informal but serious game of mutual insult, the playing of which offers the possibility of proving one's verbal superiority over an opponent.

"Do that," Theresa said, and followed her into the bedroom. "Then you'll be rested for later. Saddle called—he and Byron are throwing a birthday party at the club, and they want us to come over."

Lorraine was looking through the top dresser drawer for her aspirin. "I'm not going over there tonight. I hate those parties."

"You never hated them before." Theresa crossed her arms in the door and stared at Lorraine. "What's so different now?"

"I've always hated them." Lorraine closed the drawer and started searching in the other one. "I just went because you wanted to. They make me sick with all their prancing and phoniness. They're nothing but a couple of fags."

"And we're just a couple of dykes." She spit the words into the air.

Lorraine started as if she'd been slapped. "That's a filthy thing to say, Tee. You can call yourself that if you want to, but I'm not like that. Do you hear me? I'm not!" She slammed the drawer shut.

So she can turn on me but she wouldn't say a word to that scum in the streets, Theresa thought. She narrowed her eyes slowly at Lorraine. "Well, since my friends aren't good enough for the Duchess from Detroit," she said aloud, "I guess you'll go spend another evening with your boyfriend. But I can tell you right now I saw him pass the window just before you came up the block, and he's already stewed to the gills and just singing away. What do you two do down there in that basement—harmonize? It must get kinda boring for you, he only knows one song."

"Well, at least he's not a sarcastic bitch like some people."

Theresa looked at Lorraine as if she were a stranger.

"And I'll tell you what we do down there. We talk, Theresa—we really, really talk."

"So you and I don't talk?" Theresa's astonishment was turning into hurt. "After five years, you're going to stand there and say that you can talk to some dried-up wino better than you can to me?"

"You and I don't talk, Tee. You talk—Lorraine listens. You lecture—Lorraine takes notes about how to dress and act and have fun. If I don't see things your way, then you shout—Lorraine cries. You seem to get a kick out of making me feel like a clumsy fool."

"That's unfair, Lorraine, and you know it. I can't count the times I've told you to stop running behind people, sniveling to be their friends while they just hurt you. I've always wanted you to show some guts and be independent."

"That's just it, Tee! You wanted me to be independent of other people and look to you for the way I should feel about myself, cut myself off from the world, and join you in some crazy idea about being different. When I'm with Ben, I don't feel any different from anybody else in the world."

"Then he's doing you an injustice," Theresa snapped, "because we are different. And the sooner you learn that, the better off you'll be."

"See, there you go again. Tee the teacher and Lorraine the student, who just can't get the lesson right. Lorraine, who just wants to be a human being—a lousy human being who's somebody's daughter or somebody's friend or even somebody's enemy. But they make me feel like a freak out there, and you try to make me feel like one in here. The only place I've found some peace, Tee, is in that damp ugly basement, where I'm not different."

"Lorraine." Theresa shook her head slowly. "You're a lesbian—do you understand that word?—a butch, a dyke, a lesbo, all those things that kid was shouting. Yes, I heard him! And you can run in all the basements in the world, and it won't change that, so why don't you accept it?"

"I have accepted it!" Lorraine shouted. "I've accepted it all my life, and it's nothing I'm ashamed of. I lost a father because I refused to be ashamed of it—but it doesn't make me any *different* from anyone else in the world."

"It makes you damned different!"

"No!" She jerked open the bottom drawer of her dresser and took out a handful of her underwear. "Do you see this? There are two things that have been a constant in my life since I was sixteen years old—beige bras and oatmeal. The day before I first fell in love with a woman, I got up, had oatmeal for breakfast, put on a beige bra, and went to school. The day after I fell in love with that woman, I got up, had oatmeal for breakfast, and put on a beige bra. I was no different the day before or after that happened, Tee."

"And what did you do when you went to school that next day, Lorraine? Did you stand around the gym locker and swap stories with the other girls about this new love in your life, huh? While they were bragging about their boyfriends and the fifty dozen ways they had lost their virginity, did you jump in and say, 'Oh, but you should have seen the one I gave it up to last night?' Huh? Did you? Did you?"

Theresa was standing in front of her and shouting. She saw Lorraine's face crumple, but she still kept pushing her.

"You with your beige bras and oatmeal!" She grabbed the clothes from Lorraine's hand and shook them at her. "Why didn't you stand in that locker room and pass around a picture of this great love in your life? Why didn't you take her to the senior prom? Huh? Why? Answer me!"

"Because they wouldn't have understood," Lorraine whispered, and her shoulders hunched over.

"That's right! There go your precious 'theys' again. They wouldn't understand—not in Detroit, not on Brewster Place, not anywhere! And as long as they own the whole damn world, it's them and us, Sister—them and us. And that spells different!"

Lorraine sat down on the bed with her head in her hands, and heavy spasms shook her shoulders and slender back. Theresa stood over her and clenched her hands to keep herself from reaching out and comforting her. Let her cry. She had to smarten up. She couldn't spend the rest of her life in basements, talking to winos and building cardboard worlds that were just going to come crashing down around her ears.

Theresa left the bedroom and sat in the chair by the living room window. She watched the autumn sky darken and evening crystallize over the tops of the buildings while she sat there with the smugness of those who could amply justify their methods by the proof of their victorious ends. But even after seven cigarettes, she couldn't expel the sour taste in her mouth. She heard Lorraine move around in the bedroom and then go into the shower. She finally joined her in the living room, freshly clothed. She had been almost successful in covering the puffiness around her eyes with makeup.

"I'm ready to go to the party. Shouldn't you start getting dressed?"

Theresa looked at the black pumps and the green dress with black print. Something about the way it hung off of Lorraine's body made her feel guilty.

"I've changed my mind. I don't feel up to it tonight." She turned her head back toward the evening sky, as if the answer to their tangled lives lay in its dark face.

"Then I'm going without you." The tone of Lorraine's voice pulled her face unwillingly from the window.

"You won't last ten minutes there alone, so why don't you just sit down and stop it."

"I have to go, Tee." The urgency in her words startled Theresa, and she made a poor attempt of hiding it.

"If I can't walk out of this house without you tonight, there'll be nothing left in me to love you. And I'm trying, Theresa; I'm trying so hard to hold on to that."

Theresa would live to be a very old woman and would replay those words in her mind a thousand times and then invent a thousand different things she could have said or done to keep the tall yellow woman in the green and black dress from walking out of that door for the last time in her life. But tonight she was a young woman and still in search of answers, and she made the fatal mistake that many young women do of believing that what never existed was just cleverly hidden beyond her reach. So Theresa said nothing to Lorraine that night, because she had already sadly turned her face back to the evening sky in a mute appeal for guidance.

Lorraine left the smoky and noisy club and decided to walk home to stretch the time. She had been ready to leave from the moment she had arrived, especially after she saw the disappointment on everyone's face when she came in without Theresa. Theresa was the one who loved to dance and joke and banter with them and could keep a party going. Lorraine sat in a corner, holding one drink all night and looking so intimidated by the people who approached her that she killed even the most persistent attempts at conversation. She sensed a mood of quiet hysteria and self-mockery in that club, and she fled from it, refusing to see any possible connection with her own existence.

She had stuck it out for an hour, but that wasn't long enough. Tee would still be up, probably waiting at that window, so certain that she would be returning soon. She thought about taking a bus downtown to a movie, but she really didn't want to be alone. If she only had some friends in this city. It was then that she thought about Ben. She could come up the street in back of Brewster Place and cut through the alley to his apartment. Even if Tee was still in that window, she couldn't see that far down the block. She would just tap lightly on his door, and if he wasn't too drunk to hear her, then he wouldn't be too far gone to listen tonight. And she had such a need to talk to someone, it ached within her.

Lorraine smelled the claw-edged sweetness of the marijuana in the shadowy alley before she had gone more than fifty feet in. She stopped and peered through the leaden darkness toward the end and saw no one. She took a few more cautious steps and stopped to look again. There was still no one. She knew she would never reach Brewster like this; each time she stopped her senseless fears would multiply, until it would be impossible to get through them to the other side. There was no one there, and she would just have to walk through quickly to prove this to her pounding heart.

When she heard the first pair of soft thuds behind her, she willed herself not to stop and look back because there was no one there. Another thud and she started walking a little faster to reassure herself of this. The fourth thud started her to running, and then a dark body that had been pressed against the shadowy building swung into her path so suddenly she couldn't stop in time, and she bumped into it and bounced back a few inches.

"Can't you say excuse me, dyke?" C. C. Baker snarled into her face.

Lorraine saw a pair of suede sneakers flying down behind the face in front of hers and they hit the cement with a dead thump. Her bladder began to loosen, and bile worked its way up into the tightening throat as she realized what she must have heard before. They had been hiding up on the wall, watching her come up that back street, and they had waited. The face pushed itself so close to hers that she could look into the flared nostrils and smell the decomposing food caught in its teeth.

"Ain't you got no manners? Stepping on my foot and not saying you sorry?"

She slowly backed away from the advancing face, her throat working convulsively. She turned to run in the direction of the formless thuds behind her. She hadn't really seen them so they weren't there. The four bodies that now linked themselves across the alley hit her conscious mind like a fist, and she cried out, startled. A hand shot itself around her mouth, and her neck was jerked back while a hoarse voice whispered in her ear.

"You ain't got nothing to say now, huh? Thought you was real funny laughing at me in the streets today? Let's see if you gonna laugh now, dyke!" C. C. forced her down on her knees while the other five boys began to close in silently.

She had stepped into the thin strip of earth that they claimed as their own. Bound by the last building on Brewster and a brick wall, they reigned in that unlit alley like dwarfed warrior-kings. Born with the appendages of power, circumcised by a guillotine, and baptized with the steam from a million non-reflective mirrors, these young men wouldn't be called upon to thrust a bayonet into an Asian farmer, target a torpedo, scatter their iron seed from a B-52 into the wound of the earth, point a finger to move a nation, or stick a pole into the moon—and they knew it. They only had that three-hundred-foot alley to serve them as stateroom, armored tank, and executioner's chamber. So Lorraine found herself, on her knees, surrounded by the most dangerous species in existence—human males with an erection to validate in a world that was only six feet wide.

"I'm gonna show you somethin' I bet you never seen before." C. C. took the back of her head, pressed it into the crotch of his jeans, and jerkily rubbed it back and forth while his friends laughed. "Yeah, now don't that feel good? See, that's what you need. Bet after we get through with you, you ain't never gonna wanna kiss no more pussy."

He slammed his kneecap into her spine and her body arched up, causing his nails to cut into the side of her mouth to stifle her cry. He pushed her arched body down onto the cement. Two of the boys pinned her arms, two wrenched open her legs, while C. C. knelt between them and pushed up her dress and tore at the top of her pantyhose. Lorraine's body was twisting in convulsions of fear that they mistook for resistance, and C. C. brought his fist down into her stomach.

"Better lay the fuck still, cunt, or I'll rip open your guts."

The impact of his fist forced air into her constricted throat, and she worked her sore mouth, trying to form the one word that had been clawing inside of her—"Please." It squeezed through her paralyzed vocal cords and fell lifelessly at their feet. Lorraine clamped her eyes shut and, using all of the strength left within her, willed it to rise again.

"Please."

The sixth boy took a dirty paper bag lying on the ground and stuffed it into her mouth. She felt a weight drop on her spread body. Then she opened her eyes and they screamed and screamed into the face above hers—the face that was pushing this tearing pain inside of her body. The screams tried to break through her corneas out into the air, but the tough rubbery flesh sent them vibrating back into her brain, first shaking lifeless the cells that nurtured her memory. Then the cells went that contained her powers of taste and smell. The last that were screamed to death were those that supplied her with the ability to love—or hate.

Lorraine was no longer conscious of the pain in her spine or stomach. She couldn't feel the skin that was rubbing off of her arms from being pressed against the rough cement. What was left of her mind was centered around the pounding motion that was ripping her insides apart. She couldn't tell when they changed places and the second weight, then the third and fourth, dropped on her—it was all one continuous hacksawing of torment that kept her eyes screaming the only word she was fated to utter again and again for the rest of her life. Please.

Her thighs and stomach had become so slimy from her blood and their semen that the last two boys didn't want to touch her, so they turned her over, propped her head and shoulders against the wall, and took her from behind. When they had finished and stopped holding her up, her body fell over like an unstringed puppet. She didn't feel her split rectum or the patches in her skull where her hair had been torn off by grating against the bricks. Lorraine lay in that alley only screaming at the moving pain inside of her that refused to come to rest.

"Hey, C. C., what if she remembers that it was us?"

"Man, how she gonna prove it? Your dick ain't got no fingerprints." They laughed and stepped over her and ran out of the alley.

Lorraine lay pushed up against the wall on the cold ground with her eyes staring straight up into the sky. When the sun began to warm the air and the horizon brightened, she still lay there, her mouth crammed with paper bag, her dress pushed up under her breasts, her bloody pantyhose hanging from her thighs. She would have stayed there forever and have simply died from starvation or exposure if nothing around her had moved. There was no wind that morning, so the tin cans, soda bottles, and loose papers were still. There wasn't even a stray cat or dog rummaging in the garbage cans for scraps. There was nothing moving that early October morning—except Ben.

Ben had come out of the basement and was sitting in his usual place on an old garbage can he had pushed up against the wall. And he was singing and swaying while taking small sips from the pint bottle he kept in his back pocket. Lorraine looked up the alley and saw the movement by the wall. Side to side. Side to side. Almost in perfect unison with the sawing pain that kept moving inside of her. She crept up on her knees, making small grunting sounds like a wounded animal. As she crawled along the alley, her hand brushed a loose brick, and she clawed her fingers around it and dragged it along the ground toward the movement on Brewster Place. Side to side. Side to side.

Mattie left her bed, went to the bathroom, and then put on her tea kettle. She always got up early, for no reason other than habit. The timing mechanism that had been embedded in her on the farm wasn't aware that she now lived in a city. While her coffee water was heating up, she filled a pitcher to water her plants. When she leaned over the plants at the side of the apartment, she saw the body crawling up the alley. She raised the window and leaned out just to be sure the morning light wasn't playing tricks with her eyes. "Merciful Jesus!" She threw a coat over her nightgown, slipped on a pair of shoes, and tried to make her arthritic legs hurry down the steps.

Lorraine was getting closer to the movement. She raised herself up on her bruised and stiffened knees, and the paper bag fell out of her mouth. She supported herself by sliding against the wall, limping up the alley toward the movement while clawing her brick and mouthing her silent word. Side to side. Side to side. Lorraine finally reached the motion on top of the garbage can. Ben slowly started to focus her through his burgundy fog, and just as he opened his lips to voice the words that had formed in his brain—"My God, child, what happened to you?"—the brick smashed down into his mouth. His teeth crumbled into his throat and his body swung back against the wall. Lorraine brought the brick down again to stop the moving head, and blood shot out of his ears, splattering against the can and bottom of the wall. Mattie's screams went ricocheting in Lorraine's head, and she joined them with her own as she brought the brick down again, splitting his forehead and crushing his temple, rendering his brains just a bit more useless than hers were now.

Arms grabbed her around the waist, and the brick was knocked from her hand. The movement was everywhere. Lorraine screamed and clawed at the motions that were running and shouting from every direction in the universe. A tall yellow woman in a bloody green and black dress, scraping at the air, crying, "Please. Please."

1982

EDWARD P. JONES
b. 1951

Edward P. Jones acknowledges that he was thinking of James Joyce "and what he had done with Dublin when I began thinking of my own stories." Set in his birthplace of Washington, D.C., *Lost in the City* (1992) and *Aunt Hagar's Children* (2006) are volumes of interrelated stories that, like Joyce's *Dubliners*, limn insular communities with distinctive customs and rituals. Black migrants from the rural South populate Jones's mid-twentieth-century Washington, a city within blocks of the national government but invisible to it. Jones maps his city meticulously, even including street addresses, and draws equally detailed portraits of its residents, who, despite the struggles against poverty and racism, find sources of hope in their lives. Each volume has fourteen carefully arranged stories. For example, the first story in *Lost in the City*, "The Girl Who Raised Pigeons," features the youngest protagonist, while the last, "Marie," features the oldest. The pattern is reversed in *Aunt Hagar's Children*, where some of the minor characters from the first volume reappear. As a result readers enter fully imagined, richly textured fictive communities, which they experience as comprehensive wholes.

Growing up in Washington, in a family that moved eighteen times in eighteen years, Jones came to know its neighborhoods well. Jeanette Jones was a single mother who worked menial jobs to support herself and her three children. A scholarship to the College of the Holy Cross in Massachusetts meant a way out to Edward, who subsequently earned an M.F.A. in creative writing at the University of Virginia. He returned to Washington, where he worked for years as a business writer. Then in 2003, he published the novel *The Known World*, which won the Pulitzer Prize. Unlike the short stories, it is set in Manchester County, Virginia, a place that Jones invents, in the nineteenth century. It builds on a little-noted historical fact: a few hundred blacks were slaveholders. The novel opens with the death of Henry Townsend, a former slave who, with the aid of a powerful white mentor, has purchased slaves of his own; his widow, Caldonia, disappoints the slaves on their plantation when she decides not to free them. The moral complexities multiply, even in the minor transactions between the novel's carefully drawn characters. Widely praised, *The Known World* earned Jones a raft of honors. In 2005, he received the MacArthur Fellowship, popularly referred to as the "genius award."

Although the stories evoke the world in which Jones grew up, they are not autobiographical. As he told an interviewer about "The Girl Who Raised Pigeons":

> I named that tough little girl Betsy Ann, the name of a girl I knew in childhood. That first girl was not tough, was picked on and had a terrible stutter. The best that I could do for her, in my world, was name a no nonsense girl for her. Give her something she never had in real life. The fictional girl overcomes all the way until, at the end, she is ready to take on the world.

Jones understands the transformative power of fiction. His careful attention to the material and emotional specificities of his characters' lives enables him to enact the transformation.

The Girl Who Raised Pigeons

Her father would say years later that she had dreamed that part of it, that she had never gone out through the kitchen window at two or three in the morning to visit the birds. By that time in his life he would have so many notions about himself set in concrete. And having always believed that he slept lightly, he would not want to think that a girl of nine or ten could walk by him at such an hour in the night without his waking and asking of the dark, Who is it? What's the matter?

But the night visits were not dreams, and they remained forever as vivid to her as the memory of the way the pigeons' iridescent necklaces flirted with light. The visits would begin not with any compulsion in her sleeping mind to visit, but with the simple need to pee or to get a drink of water. In the dark, she went barefoot out of her room, past her father in the front room conversing in his sleep, across the kitchen and through the kitchen window, out over the roof a few steps to the coop. It could be winter, it could be summer, but the most she ever got was something she called pigeon silence. Sometimes she had the urge to unlatch the door and go into the coop, or, at the very least, to try to reach through the wire and the wooden slats to stroke a wing or a breast, to share whatever the silence seemed to conceal. But she always kept her hands to herself, and after a few minutes, as if relieved, she would go back to her bed and visit the birds again in sleep.

What Betsy Ann Morgan and her father Robert did agree on was that the pigeons began with the barber Miles Patterson. Her father had known Miles long before the girl was born, before the thought to marry her mother had even crossed his mind. The barber lived in a gingerbread brown house with his old parents only a few doors down from the barbershop he owned on the corner of 3rd and L streets, Northwest. On some Sundays, after Betsy Ann had come back from church with Miss Jenny, Robert, as he believed his wife would have done, would take his daughter out to visit with relatives and friends in the neighborhoods just beyond Myrtle Street, Northeast, where father and daughter lived.

One Sunday, when Betsy Ann was eight years old, the barber asked her again if she wanted to see his pigeons, "my children." He had first asked her some three years before. The girl had been eager to see them then, imagining she would see the same frightened creatures who waddled and flew away whenever she chased them on sidewalks and in parks. The men and the girl had gone into the backyard, and the pigeons, in a furious greeting, had flown up and about the barber. "Oh, my babies," he said, making kissing sounds. "Daddy's here." In an instant, Miles's head was surrounded by a colorful flutter of pigeon life. The birds settled on his head and his shoulders and along his thick, extended arms, and some of the birds looked down meanly at her. Betsy Ann screamed, sending the birds back into a flutter, which made her scream even louder. And still screaming, she ran back into the house. The men found her in the kitchen, her head buried in the lap of Miles's mother, her arms tight around the waist of the old woman, who had been sitting at the table having Sunday lunch with her husband.

"Buster," Miles's mother said to him, "you shouldn't scare your company like this. This child's bout to have a heart attack."

Three years later Betsy Ann said yes again to seeing the birds. In the backyard, there was again the same fluttering chaos, but this time the sight of the wings and bodies settling about Miles intrigued her and she drew closer until she was a foot or so away, looking up at them and stretching out her arm as she saw Miles doing. "Oh, my babies," the barber said. "Your daddy's here." One of the birds landed on Betsy Ann's shoulder and another in the palm of her hand. The gray one in her hand looked dead at Betsy Ann, blinked, then swiveled his head and gave the girl a different view of a radiant black necklace. "They tickle," she said to her father, who stood back.

For weeks and weeks after that Sunday, Betsy Ann pestered her father about getting pigeons for her. And the more he told her no, that it was impossible, the more she wanted them. He warned her that he would not do anything to help her care for them, he warned her that all the bird-work meant she would not ever again have time to play with her friends, he warned her about all the do-do the pigeons would let loose. But she remained a bulldog about it, and he knew that she was not often a bulldog about anything. In the end he retreated to the fact that they were only renters in Jenny and Walter Creed's house.

"Miss Jenny likes birds," the girl said. "Mr. Creed likes birds, too."

"People may like birds, but nobody in the world likes pigeons."

"Cept Mr. Miles," she said.

"Don't make judgments bout things with what you know bout Miles."

Miles Patterson, a bachelor and, some women said, a virgin, was fifty-six years old and for the most part knew no more about the world than what he could experience in newspapers or on the radio and in his own neighborhood, beyond which he rarely ventured. "There's ain't nothing out there in the great beyond for me," Miles would say to people who talked with excitement about visiting such and such a place.

It was not difficult for the girl to convince Miss Jenny, though the old woman made it known that "pigeons carry all them diseases, child." But there were few things Jenny Creed would deny Betsy Ann. The girl was known by all the world to be a good and obedient child. And in Miss Jenny's eyes, a child's good reputation amounted to an assent from God on most things.

For years after he relented, Robert Morgan would rise every morning before his daughter, go out onto the roof, and peer into the coop he had constructed for her, looking for dead pigeons. At such a time in the morning, there would be only fragments of first light, falling in long, hopeful slivers over the birds and their house. Sometimes he would stare absently into the coop for a long time, because being half-asleep, his mind would forget why he was there. The murmuring pigeons, as they did with most of the world, would stare back, with looks more of curiosity than of fear or anticipation or welcome. He thought that by getting there in the morning before his daughter, he could spare her the sight and pain of any dead birds. His plan had always been to put any dead birds he found into a burlap sack, take them down to his taxicab, and dispose of them on his way to work. He never intended to tell her about such birds, and it never occurred to him that she would know every pigeon in the coop and would wonder, perhaps even worry, about a missing bird.

They lived in the apartment Jenny and Walter Creed had made out of the upstairs in their Myrtle Street house. Miss Jenny had known Clara, Robert's wife, practically all of Clara's life. But their relationship had become little more than hellos and good-byes as they passed in the street before Miss Jenny came upon Clara and Robert one rainy Saturday in the library park at Mt. Vernon Square. Miss Jenny had come out of Hahn's shoe store, crossed New York Avenue, and was going up 7th Street. At first, Miss Jenny thought the young man and woman, soaked through to the skin, sitting on the park bench under a blue umbrella, were feebleminded or straightout crazy. As she came closer, she could hear them laughing, and the young man was swinging the umbrella back and forth over their heads, so that the rain would fall first upon her and then upon himself.

"Ain't you William and Alice Hobson baby girl?" Miss Jenny asked Clara.

"Yes, ma'am." She stood and Robert stood as well, now holding the umbrella fully over Clara's head.

"Is everything all right, child?" Miss Jenny's glasses were spotted with mist, and she took them off and stepped closer, keeping safely to the side where Clara was.

"Yes, ma'am. He—" She pushed Robert and began to laugh. "We came out of Peoples and he wouldn't let me have none a the umbrella. He let me get wet, so I took the umbrella and let him have some of his own medicine."

Robert said nothing. He was standing out of the range of the umbrella and he was getting soaked all over again.

"We gonna get married, Miss Jenny," she said, as if that explained everything, and she stuck out her hand with her ring. "From Castleberg's," she said. Miss Jenny took Clara's hand and held it close to her face.

"Oh oh," she said again and again, pulling Clara's hand still closer.

"This Robert," Clara said. "My"—and she turned to look at him—"fiancé." She uttered the word with a certain crispness: It was clear that before Robert Morgan, *fiancé* was a word she had perhaps never uttered in her life.

Robert and Miss Jenny shook hands. "You gonna give her double pneumonia even before she take your name," she said.

The couple learned the next week that the place above Miss Jenny was vacant and the following Sunday, Clara and Robert, dressed as if they had just come from church, were at her front door, inquiring about the apartment.

That was one of the last days in the park for them. Robert came to believe later that the tumor that would consume his wife's brain had been growing even on that rainy day. And it was there all those times he made love to her, and the thought that it was there, perhaps at first no bigger than a grain of salt, made him feel that he had somehow used her, taken from her even as she was moving toward death. He would not remember until much, much later the times she told him he gave her pleasure, when she whispered into his ear that she was glad she had found him, raised her head in that bed as she lay under him. And when he did remember, he would have to take out her photograph from the small box of valuables he kept in the dresser's top drawer, for he could not remember her face any other way.

Clara spent most of the first months of her pregnancy in bed, propped up, reading movie magazines and listening to the radio, waiting for Robert to come home from work. Her once pretty face slowly began to collapse in on itself like fruit too long in the sun, eaten away by the rot that despoiled from the inside out. The last month or so she spent in the bed on the third floor at Gallinger Hospital. One morning, toward four o'clock, they cut open her stomach and pulled out the child only moments after Clara died, mother and daughter passing each other as if along a corridor, one into death, the other into life.

The weeks after her death Robert and the infant were attended to by family and friends. They catered to him and to the baby to such an extent that sometimes in those weeks when he heard her cry, he would look about at the people in a room, momentarily confused about what was making the sound. But as all the people returned to their lives in other parts of Washington or in other cities, he was left with the ever-increasing vastness of the small apartment and with a being who hadn't the power to ask, yet seemed to demand everything.

"I don't think I can do this," he confessed to Miss Jenny one Friday evening when the baby was about a month old. "I know I can't do this." Robert's father had been the last to leave him, and Robert had just returned from taking the old man to Union Station a few blocks away. "If my daddy had just said the word, I'da been on that train with him." He and Miss Jenny were sitting at his kitchen table, and the child, sleeping, was in her cradle beside Miss Jenny. Miss Jenny watched him and said not a word. "Woulda followed him all the way back home. . . . I never looked down the line and saw bein by myself like this."

"It's all right," Miss Jenny said finally. "I know how it is. You a young man. You got a whole life in front a you," and the stone on his heart grew lighter. "The city people can help out with this."

"The city?" He looked through the fluttering curtain onto the roof, at the oak tree, at the backs of houses on K Street.

"Yes, yes." She turned around in her chair to face him fully. "My niece works for the city, and she say they can take care of chirren like this who don't have parents. They have homes, good homes, for chirren like her. Bring em up real good. Feed em, clothe em, give em good schoolin. Give em everything they need." She stood, as if the matter were settled. "The city people care. Call my niece tomorra and find out what you need to do. A young man like you shouldn't have to worry yourself like this." She was at the door, and he stood up too, not wanting her to go. "Try to put all the worries out your mind." Before he could say anything, she closed the door quietly behind her.

She did not come back up, as he had hoped, and he spent his first night alone with the child. Each time he managed to get the baby back to sleep after he fed her or changed her diaper, he would place her in the crib in the front room and sit without light at the kitchen table listening to the trains coming and going just beyond his window. He was nineteen years old. There was a song about trains that kept rumbling in his head as the night wore on, a song his mother would sing when he was a boy.

The next morning, Saturday, he shaved and washed up while Betsy Ann was still sleeping, and after she woke and he had fed her again, he clothed her with a yellow outfit and its yellow bonnet that Wilma Ellis, the schoolteacher next door, had given Betsy Ann. He carried the carriage downstairs first, leaving the baby on a pallet of blankets. On the sidewalk he covered her with a light green blanket that Dr. Oscar Jackson and his family up the street had given the baby. The shades were down at Miss Jenny's windows, and he heard no sound, not even the dog's barking, as he came and went. At the child's kicking feet in the carriage he placed enough diapers and powdered formula to last an expedition to Baltimore. Beside her, he placed a blue rattle from the janitor Jake Horton across the street.

He was the only moving object within her sight and she watched him intently, which made him uncomfortable. She seemed the most helpless thing he had ever known. It occurred to him perversely, as he settled her in, that if he decided to walk away forever from her and the carriage and all her stuff, to walk but a few yards and make his way up or down 1st Street for no place in particular, there was not a damn thing in the world she could do about it. The carriage was facing 1st Street Northeast, and with some effort—because one of the wheels refused to turn with the others—he maneuvered it around, pointing toward North Capitol Street.

In those days, before the community was obliterated, a warm Myrtle Street Saturday morning filled both sidewalks and the narrow street itself with playing children oblivious to everything but their own merriment. A grownup's course was generally not an easy one, but that morning, as he made his way with the soundless wheels of the carriage, the children made way for Robert Morgan, for he was the man whose wife had passed away. At her wake, some of them had been held up by grownups so they could look down on Clara laid out in her pink casket in Miss Jenny's parlor. And though death and its rituals did not mean much beyond the wavering understanding that they would never see someone again, they knew from what their parents said and did that a clear path to the corner was perhaps the very least a widow man deserved.

Some of the children called to their parents still in their houses and apartments that Robert was passing with Clara's baby. The few grownups on porches came down to the sidewalk and made a fuss over Betsy Ann.

More than midway down the block, Janet Gordon, who had been one of Clara's best friends, came out and picked up the baby. It was too nice a day to have that blanket over her, she told Robert. You expectin to go all the way to Baltimore with all them diapers? she said. It would be Janet who would teach him—practicing on string and a discarded blond-haired doll—how to part and plait a girl's hair.

He did not linger on Myrtle Street; he planned to make the visits there on his way back that evening. Janet's boys, Carlos and Carleton, walked on either side of him up Myrtle to North Capitol, then to the corner of K Street. There they knew to turn back. Carlos, seven years old, told him to take it easy. Carleton, younger by two years, did not want to repeat what his brother had said, so he repeated one of the things his grandfather, who was losing his mind, always told him: "Don't get lost in the city."

Robert nodded as if he understood and the boys turned back. He took off his tie and put it in his pocket and unbuttoned his suit coat and the top two buttons of his shirt. Then he adjusted his hat and placed the rattle nearer the baby, who paid it no mind. And when the light changed, he maneuvered the carriage down off the sidewalk and crossed North Capitol into Northwest.

Miles the barber gave Betsy Ann two pigeons, yearlings, a dull-white female with black spots and a sparkling red male. For several weeks, in the morning, soon after she had dutifully gone in to fill the feed dish and replace the water, and after they had fortified themselves, the pigeons took to the air and returned to Miles. The forlorn sound of their flapping wings echoed in her head as she stood watching them disappear into the colors of the morning, often still holding the old broom she used to sweep out their coop.

So in those first weeks, she went first to Miles's after school to retrieve the pigeons, usually bringing along Ralph Holley, her cousin. Miles would put the birds in the two pigeon baskets Robert would bring over each morning before he took to the street in his taxicab.

"They don't like me," Betsy Ann said to Miles one day in the second week. "They just gonna keep on flyin away. They hate me."

Miles laughed, the same way he laughed when she asked him the first day how he knew one was a girl pigeon and the other was a boy pigeon.

"I don't think that they even got to the place of likin or not likin you," Miles said. She handed her books to Ralph, and Miles gave her the two baskets.

"Well, they keep runnin away."

"Thas all they know to do," which was what he had told her the week before. "Right now, this is all the home they know for sure. It ain't got nothin to do with you, child. They just know to fly back here."

His explanations about everything, when he could manage an explanation, rarely satisfied her. He had been raising pigeons all his life, and whatever knowledge he had accumulated in those years was now such an inseparable part of his being that he could no more explain the birds than he could explain what went into the act of walking. He only knew that they did all that birds did and not something else, as he only knew that he walked and did not fall.

"You might try lockin em in for while," he said. "Maybe two, three days, however long it take em to get use to the new home. Let em know you the boss and you ain't gonna stand for none a this runnin away stuff."

She considered a moment, then shook her head. She watched her cousin peering into Miles's coop, his face hard against the wire. "I guess if I gotta lock em up there ain't no use havin em."

"Why you wanna mess with gotdamn pigeons anyway?" Ralph said as they walked to her home that day.

"Because," she said.

"Because what?" he said.

"Because, thas all," she said. "Just because."

"You oughta get a puppy like I'm gonna get," Ralph said. "A puppy never run away."

"A puppy never fly either. So what?" she said. "You been talking bout gettin a gotdamn puppy for a million years, but I never see you gettin one." Though Ralph was a year older and a head taller than his cousin, she often bullied him.

"You wait. You wait. You'll see," Ralph said.

"I ain't waitin. You the one waitin. When you get it, just let me know and I'll throw you a big party."

At her place, he handed over her books and went home. She considered following her cousin back to his house after she took the pigeons up to the coop, for the idea of being on the roof with birds who wanted to fly away to be with someone else pained her. At Ralph's L Street house, there were cookies almost as big as her face, and Aunt Thelma, Clara's oldest sister, who was, in fact, the very image of Clara. The girl had never had an overwhelming curiosity about her mother, but it fascinated her to see the face of the lady in all the pictures on a woman who moved and laughed and did mother things.

She put the pigeons back in the coop and put fresh water in the bath bowls. Then she stood back, outside the coop, its door open. At such moments they often seemed contented, hopping in and out of cubicles, inspecting the feed and water, all of which riled her. She would have preferred—and understood—agitation, some sign that they were unhappy and ready to fly to Miles again. But they merely pecked about, strutted, heads bobbing happily, oblivious of her. Pretending everything was all right.

"You shitheads!" she hissed, aware that Miss Jenny was downstairs within earshot. "You gotdamn stupid shitheads!"

That was the fall of 1957.

Myrtle Street was only one long block, running east to west. To the east, preventing the street from going any farther, was a high, medieval-like wall of stone across 1st Street, Northeast, and beyond the wall were the railroad tracks. To the west, across North Capitol, preventing Myrtle Street from going any farther in that direction, was the high school Gonzaga, where white boys were taught by white priests. When the colored people and their homes were gone, the wall and the tracks remained, and so did the high school, with the same boys being taught by the same priests.

It was late spring when Betsy Ann first noticed the nest, some two feet up from the coop's floor in one of the twelve cubicles that made up the entire structure. The nest was nothing special, a crude, ill-formed thing of straw and dead leaves and other, uncertain material she later figured only her hapless birds could manage to find. They had not flown back to Miles in a long time, but she had never stopped thinking that it was on their minds each time they took to the air. So the nest was the first solid indication that the pigeons would stay forever, would go but would always return.

About three weeks later, on an afternoon when she was about to begin the weekly job of thoroughly cleaning the entire coop, she saw the two eggs. She thought them a trick of the light at first—two small and perfect wonders alone in that wonderless nest without any hallelujahs from the world. She put off the cleaning and stood looking at the male bird, who had moved off the nest for only a few seconds, rearrange himself on the nest and look at her from time to time in that bored way he had. The female bird was atop the coop, dozing. Betsy Ann got a chair from the kitchen and continued watching the male bird and the nest through the wire. "Tell me bout this," she said to them.

As it happened, Robert discovered the newly hatched squabs when he went to look for dead birds before going to work. About six that morning he peered into the coop and shivered to find two hideous, bug-eyed balls of movement. They were a dirty orange and looked like baby vultures. He looked about as if there might be someone responsible for it all. This was, he knew now, a point of no return for his child. He went back in to have his first cup of coffee of the day.

He drank without enjoyment and listened to the chirping, unsettling, demanding. He would not wake his daughter just to let her know about the hatchlings. Two little monsters had changed the predictable world he was trying to create for his child and he was suddenly afraid for her. He turned on the radio and played it real low, but he soon shut it off, because the man on WOOK was telling him to go in and kill the hatchlings.

It turned out that the first pigeon to die was a stranger, and Robert never knew anything about it. The bird appeared out of nowhere and was dead less than a week later. By then, a year or so after Miles gave her the yearlings, she had eight birds of various ages, resulting from hatches in her coop and from trades with the barber ("for variety's sake," he told her) and with a family in Anacostia. One morning before going to school, she noticed the stranger perched in one of the lower cubicles, a few inches up from the floor, and though he seemed submissive enough, she sensed that he would peck with all he had if she tried to move him out. His entire body, what little there was left of it, was a witness to misery. One ragged cream-colored tail feather stuck straight up, as if with resignation. His bill was pitted as if it had been sprayed with minute pellets, and his left eye was covered with a patch of dried blood and dirt and decaying flesh.

She placed additional straw to either side of him in the cubicle and small bowls of water and feed in front of the cubicle. Then she began to worry that he had brought in some disease that would ultimately devastate her flock.

Days later, home for lunch with Ralph, she found the pigeon dead near the water tray, his wings spread out full as if he had been preparing for flight.

"Whatcha gonna do with him?" Ralph asked, kneeling down beside Betsy Ann and poking the dead bird with a pencil.

"Bury him. What else, stupid?" She snatched the pencil from him. "You don't think any a them gonna do it, do you?" and she pointed to the few stay-at-home pigeons who were not out flying about the city. The birds looked down uninterestedly at them from various places around the coop. She dumped the dead bird in a pillowcase and took it across 1st Street to the grassy spot of ground near the Esso filling station in front of the medieval wall. With a large tablespoon, she dug two feet or so into the earth and dropped the sack in.

"Beaver would say something over his grave," Ralph said.

"What?"

"Beaver. The boy on TV."

She gave him a cut-eye look and stood up. "You do it, preacher man," she said. "I gotta get back to school."

After school she said to Miss Jenny, "Don't tell Daddy bout that dead pigeon. You know how he is: He'll think it's the end of the world or somethin."

The two were in Miss Jenny's kitchen, and Miss Jenny was preparing supper while Betsy Ann did her homework.

"You know what he do in the mornin?" Betsy Ann said. "He go out and look at them pigeons."

"Oh?" Miss Jenny, who knew what Robert had been doing, did not turn around from the stove. "Wants to say good mornin to em, hunh?"

"I don't think so. I ain't figured out what he doin," the girl said. She was sitting at Miss Jenny's kitchen table. The dog, Bosco, was beside her and one of her shoes was off and her foot was rubbing the dog's back. "I was sleepin one time and this cold air hit me and I woke up. I couldn't get back to sleep cause I was cold, so I got up to see what window was open. Daddy wasn't in the bed and he wasn't in the kitchen or the bathroom. I thought he was downstairs' warmin up the cab or somethin, but when I went to close the kitchen window, I could see him, peekin in the coop from the side with a flashlight. He scared me cause I didn't know who he was at first."

"You ask him what he was doin?"

"No. He wouldn't told me anyway, Miss Jenny. I just went back to my room and closed the door. If I'da asked him straight out, he would just make up something or say maybe I was dreamin. So now when I feel that cold air, I just look out to see if he in bed and then I shut my door."

Sometimes, when the weather allowed, the girl would sit on the roof plaiting her hair or reading the funny papers before school, or sit doing her homework in the late afternoon before going down to Miss Jenny's or out to play. She got pleasure just from the mere presence of the pigeons, a pleasure that was akin to what she felt when she followed her Aunt Thelma about her house, or when she jumped double dutch for so long she had to drop to the ground to catch her breath. In the morning, the new sun rising higher, she would place her chair at the roof's edge. She could look down at tail-wagging Bosco looking up at her, down through the thick rope fence around the roof that Robert had put up when she was a year old. She would hum or sing some nonsense song she'd made up, as the birds strutted and pecked and preened and flapped about in the bath water. And in the evening she watched the pigeons return home, first landing in the oak tree, then over to the coop's landing board. A few of them, generally the males, would settle on her book or on her head and shoulders. Stroking the breast of one, she would be rewarded with a cooing that was as pleasurable as music, and when the bird edged nearer so that it was less than an inch away, she smelled what seemed a mixture of dirt and rainy air and heard a heart that seemed to be hurling itself against the wall of the bird's breast.

She turned ten. She turned eleven.

In the early summer of 1960, there began a rumor among the children of Betsy Ann's age that the railroad people were planning to take all the land around Myrtle Street, perhaps up to L Street and down to H Street. This rumor—unlike the summer rumor among Washington's Negro children that Richard Nixon, if he were elected president, would make all the children go to school on Saturday from nine to twelve and cut their summer vacations in half—this rumor had a long life. And as the boys scraped their knuckles on the ground playing Poison, as the girls jumped rope until their bouncing plaits came loose, as the boys filled the neighborhood with the sounds of amateur hammering as they built skating trucks, as the girls made up talk for dolls with names they would one day bestow on their children, their conversations were flavored with lighthearted speculation about how far the railroad would go. When one child fell out with another, it became standard to try to hurt the other with the "true fact" that the railroad was going to take his or her home. "It's a true fact, they called my daddy at his work and told him we could stay, but yall gotta go. Yall gotta." And then the tormentor would stick out his or her tongue as far as it would go.

There were only two other girls on Myrtle Street who were comfortable around pigeons, and both of them moved away within a month of each other. One, LaDeidre Gordon, was a cousin of the brothers Carlos and Carleton. LaDeidre believed that the pigeons spoke a secret language among themselves, and that if she listened long enough and hard enough she could understand what they were saying and, ultimately, could communicate with them. For this, the world lovingly nicknamed her "Coo-Coo." After LaDeidre and the second girl moved, Betsy Ann would take the long way around to avoid passing where they had lived. And in those weeks she found a comfort of sorts at Thelma and Ralph's, for their house and everything else on the other side of North Capitol Street, the rumor went, would be spared by the railroad people.

Thelma Holley, her husband, and Ralph lived in a small house on L Street, Northwest, two doors from Mt. Airy Baptist Church, just across North Capitol Street. Thelma had suffered six miscarriages before God, as she put it, "took pity on my womb" and she had Ralph. But even then, she felt God had given with one hand and taken with the other, for the boy suffered with asthma. Thelma had waited until the seventh month of her pregnancy before she felt secure enough to begin loving him. And from then on, having given her heart, she thought nothing of giving him the world after he was born.

Ralph was the first colored child anyone knew to have his own television. In his house there had been three bedrooms, but Thelma persuaded her husband that an asthmatic child needed more space. Her husband knocked down the walls between the two back bedrooms and Ralph then had a bedroom that was nearly twice as large as that of his parents. And in that enormous room, she put as much of the world as she and her husband could afford.

Aside from watching Thelma, what Betsy Ann enjoyed most in that house was the electric train set, which dominated the center of Ralph's room. Over an area of more than four square feet, running on three levels, the trains moved through a marvelous and complete world Ralph's father had constructed. In that world, there were no simple plastic figures waving beside the tracks. Rather, it was populated with such people as a hand-carved woman of wood, in a floppy hat and gardener's outfit of real cloth, a woman who had nearly microscopic beads of sweat on her brow as she knelt down with concentration in her flower garden; several inches away, hand-carved schoolchildren romped about in the playground. One group of children was playing tag, and on one boy's face was absolute surprise as he was being tagged by a girl whose cheek was lightly smudged with dirt. A foot or so away, in a small field, two hand-carved farmers of wood were arguing, one with his finger in the other's face and the other with his fist heading toward the chest of the first. The world also included a goat-populated mountain with a tunnel large enough for the trains to go through, and a stream made of light blue glass. The stream covered several tiny fish of many colors which had almost invisible pins holding them suspended from the bottom up to give the impression that the fish were swimming.

What Thelma would not put in her son's enormous room, despite years of pleadings from him, was a dog, for she had learned in childhood that all animals had the power to suck the life out of asthmatics. "What you need with some ole puppy?" she would tease sometimes when he asked. "You'll be my little puppy dog forever and forever." And then she would grab and hug him until he wiggled out of her arms.

By the time he was six, the boy had learned that he could sometimes stay all day in the room and have Thelma minister to him by pretending he could barely breathe. He hoped that over time he could get out of her a promise for a dog. But his pretending to be at death's door only made her worry more, and by the middle of 1961, she had quit her part-time, GS-4 clerk-typist position at the Interior Department, because by then he was home two or three times a week.

Gradually, as more people moved out of Myrtle Street, the room became less attractive for Betsy Ann to visit, for Ralph grew difficult and would be mean and impatient with her and other visiting children. "You stupid, thas all! You just the stupidest person in the whole wide world," he would say to anyone who did not do what he wanted as fast as he wanted. Some children cried when he lit into them, and others wanted to fight him.

In time, the boy Betsy Ann once bullied disappeared altogether, and so when she took him assignments from school, she tried to stay only the amount of time necessary to show politeness. Then, too, the girl sensed that Thelma, with her increasing coldness, felt her son's problem was partly the result of visits from children who weren't altogether clean and from a niece who lived her life in what Thelma called "pigeon air" and "pigeon dust."

When he found out, the details of it did not matter to Robert Morgan: He only knew that his daughter had been somewhere doing bad while he was out doing the best he could. It didn't matter that it was Darlene Greenley who got Betsy Ann to go far away to 7th and Massachusetts and steal candy bars from Peoples Drug, candy she didn't even like, to go away the farthest she had ever been without her father or Miss Jenny or some other adult.

She knew Darlene, fast Darlene, from going to Ralph's ("You watch and see," Darlene would whisper to her, "I'm gonna make him my boyfriend"), but they had never gone off together before the Saturday that Thelma, for the last time, expelled all the children from her house. "Got any money?" Darlene said on the sidewalk after Thelma had thrown them out. She was stretching her bubble gum between her teeth and fingers and twirling the stuff the way she would a jump rope. When Betsy Ann shook her head, Darlene said she knew this Peoples that kinda like y'know gave children candy just for stopping by, and Betsy Ann believed her.

The assistant manager caught the girls before they were out of the candy and toy aisle and right away Darlene started to cry. "That didn't work the last time I told you to stay outa here," the woman said, taking the candy out of their dress pockets, "and it ain't gonna work now." Darlene handed her candy over, and Betsy Ann did the same. Darlene continued to cry. "Oh, just shut up, you little hussy, before I give you somethin to really cry about."

The assistant manager handed the candy to a clerk and was about to drag the girls into a back room when Etta O'Connell came up the aisle. "Yo daddy know you this far from home, Betsy Ann?" Miss Etta said, tapping Betsy Ann in the chest with her walking stick. She was, at ninety-two, the oldest person on Myrtle Street. It surprised Betsy Ann that she even knew her name, because the old woman, as far as Betsy Ann could remember, had never once spoken a word to her.

"You know these criminals?" the assistant manager said.

"Knowed this one since the day she born," Miss Etta said. The top of her stick had the head of an animal that no one had been able to identify, and the animal, perched a foot or so higher than Miss Etta's head, looked down at Betsy Ann with a better-you-than-me look. The old woman uncurled the fingers of the assistant manager's hand from around Betsy Ann's arm. "Child, whatcha done in this lady's sto?"

In the end, the assistant manager accepted Miss Etta's word that Betsy Ann would never again step foot in the store, that her father would know what she had done the minute he got home. Outside, standing at the corner, Miss Etta raised her stick and pointed to K Street. "You don't go straight home with no stoppin, I'll know," she said to Betsy Ann, and the girl sprinted off, never once looking back. Miss Etta and Darlene continued standing at the corner. "I think that old lady gave me the evil eye," Darlene told Betsy Ann the next time they met. "She done took all my good luck away. Yall got ghosties and shit on yo street." And thereafter, she avoided Betsy Ann.

Robert tanned her hide, as Miss Jenny called it, and then withheld her fifty-cents-a-week allowance for two months. For some three weeks he said very little to her, and when he did, it was almost always the same words: "You should be here, takin care a them damn birds! That's where you should be, not out there robbin somebody's grocery store!" She stopped correcting him about what kind of store it was after the first few times, because each time she did he would say, "Who the grownup here? You startin to sound like you runnin the show."

The candy episode killed something between them, and more and more he began checking up on her. He would show up at the house when she thought he was out working. She would come out of the coop with a bag of feed or the broom in her hand and a bird sitting on her head and she would find him standing at the kitchen window watching her. And several times a day he would call Miss Jenny. "Yo daddy wanna know if you up there," Miss Jenny would holler out her back window. Robert called the school so much that the principal herself wrote a letter telling him to stop.

He had been seeing Janet Gordon for two years, and about three or four times a month, they would take in a movie or a show at the Howard and then spend the night at a tourist home. But after the incident at Peoples, he saw Janet only once or twice a month. Then he began taking his daughter with him in the cab on most Saturdays. He tried to make it seem as if it were a good way to see the city.

Despite his reasons for taking her along, she enjoyed riding with him at first. She asked him for one of his old maps, and, with a blue crayon, she would chart the streets of Washington she had been on. Her father spent most of his time in Southeast and in Anacostia, but sometimes he went as far away as Virginia and Maryland, and she charted streets in those places as well. She also enjoyed watching him at work, seeing a part of him she had never known: The way he made deliberate notations in his log. Patted his thigh in time to music in his head until he noticed her looking at him. Raised his hat any time a woman entered or left the cab.

But the more she realized that being with him was just his way of keeping his eye on her, the more the travels began losing something for her. When she used the bathroom at some filling station during her travels, she found him waiting for her outside the bathroom door, his nail-bitten hands down at his sides, his hat sitting perfectly on his head, and a look on his face that said Nothin. Nothin's wrong. Before the autumn of 1961 had settled in, she only wanted to be left at home, and because the incident at Peoples was far behind them, he allowed it. But he went back to the old ways of checking up on her. "Tell him yes," she would say when Miss Jenny called out her back window. "Tell him a million times yes, I'm home."

Little by little that spring and summer of 1961 Myrtle Street emptied of people, of families who had known no other place in their lives. Robert dreaded coming home each evening and seeing the signs of still another abandoned house free to be picked clean by rogues coming in from other neighborhoods: old curtains flapping out of screenless windows, the street with every kind of litter, windows so naked he could see clean through to the backyard. For the first time since he had been knowing her, Miss Jenny did not plant her garden that year, and that small patch of ground, with alien growth tall as a man, reverted to the wild.

He vowed that until he could find a good place for himself and his child, he would try to make life as normal as possible for her. He had never stopped rising each morning before Betsy Ann and going out to the coop to see what pigeons might have died in the night. And that was what he did that last morning in midautumn. He touched down onto the roof and discovered it had snowed during the night. A light, nuisance powder, not thick enough to cover the world completely and make things beautiful the way he liked. Though there was enough sunlight, he did not at first notice the tiny tracks, with even tinier, intermittent spots of blood, leading from the coop, across his roof and over to the roof of the house next door, the schoolteacher's house that had been empty for more than four months. He did, however, hear the birds squawking before he reached the coop, but this meant nothing to him, because one pigeon sound was more or less like another to him.

The night before there had been sixteen pigeons of various ages, but when he reached the coop, five were already dead and three were in their last moments, dragging themselves crazily about the floor or from side to side in the lower cubicles. Six of them he would kill with his own hands. Though there were bodies with holes so deep he saw white flesh, essence, it was the sight of dozens of detached feathers that caused his body to shake, because the scattered feathers, more than the wrecked bodies, spoke to him of helplessness. He closed his eyes as tight as he could and began to pray, and when he opened them, the morning was even brighter.

He looked back at the window, for something had whispered that Betsy Ann was watching. But he was alone and he went into the coop. He took up one dead bird whose left wing and legs had been chewed off; he shook the bird gently, and gently he blew into its face. He prayed once more. The pigeons that were able had moved to the farthest corner of the coop and they watched him, quivering. He knew now that the squawking was the sound of pain and it drove him out of their house.

When he saw the tracks, he realized immediately that they had been made by rats. He bent down, and some logical piece of his mind was surprised that there was a kind of orderliness to the trail, even with its ragged bits of pigeon life, a fragment of feather here, a spot of blood there.

He did not knock at Walter and Miss Jenny's door and wait to go in, as he had done each morning for some thirteen years. He found them at the breakfast table, and because they had been used to thirteen years of knocking, they looked up at him, amazed. Most of his words were garbled, but they followed him back upstairs. Betsy Ann had heard the noise of her father coming through the kitchen window and bounded down the stairs. She stood barefoot in the doorway leading from the front room to the kitchen, blinking herself awake.

"Go back to bed!" Robert shouted at her.

When she asked what was the matter, the three only told her to go back to bed. From the kitchen closet, Robert took two burlap sacks. Walter followed him out onto the roof and Betsy Ann made her way around Miss Jenny to the window.

Her father shouted at her to go to her room and Miss Jenny tried to grab her, but she managed to get onto the roof, where Walter held her. From inside, she had heard the squawking, a brand new sound for her. Even with Walter holding her, she got a few feet from the coop. And when Robert told her to go back inside, she gave him the only no of their lives. He looked but once at her and then began to wring the necks of the birds injured beyond all hope. Strangely, when he reached for them, the pigeons did not peck, did not resist. He placed all of the bodies in the sacks, and when he was all done and stood covered in blood and viscera and feathers, he began to cry.

Betsy Ann and her father noticed almost simultaneously that there were two birds completely unharmed, huddled in an upper corner of the coop. After he tied the mouths of the sacks, the two birds, as if of one mind, flew together to the landing board and from there to the oak tree in Miss Jenny's yard. Then they were gone. The girl buried her face in Walter's side, and when the old man saw that she was barefoot, he picked her up.

She missed them more than she ever thought she would. In school, her mind would wander and she would doodle so many pigeons on the backs of her hands and along her arms that teachers called her Nasty, nasty girl. In the bathtub at night, she would cry to have to wash them off. And as she slept, missing them would take shape and lean down over her bed and wake her just enough to get her to understand a whisper that told her all over again how much she missed them. And when she raged in her sleep, Robert would come in and hold her until she returned to peace. He would sit in a chair beside her bed for the rest of the night, for her rages usually came about four in the morning and with the night so near morning, he saw no use in going back to bed.

She roamed the city at will, and Robert said nothing. She came to know the city so well that had she been blindfolded and taken to practically any place in Washington, even as far away as Anacostia or Georgetown, she could have taken off the blindfold and walked home without a moment's trouble. Her favorite place became the library park at Mount Vernon Square, the same park where Miss Jenny had first seen Robert and Clara together, across the street from the Peoples where Betsy Ann had been caught stealing. And there on some warm days Robert would find her, sitting on a bench, or lying on the grass, eyes to the sky.

For many weeks, well into winter, one of the birds that had not been harmed would come to the ledge of a back window of an abandoned house that faced K Street. The bird, a typical gray, would stand on the ledge and appear to look across the backyards in the direction of Betsy Ann's roof, now an empty space because the coop had been dismantled for use as firewood in Miss Jenny's kitchen stove. When the girl first noticed him and realized who he was, she said nothing, but after a few days, she began to call to him, beseech him to come to her. She came to the very edge of the roof, for now the rope fence was gone and nothing held her back. When the bird would not come to her, she cursed him. After as much as an hour it would fly away and return the next morning.

On what turned out to be the last day, a very cold morning in February, she stepped out onto the roof to drink the last of her cocoa. At first she sipped, then she took one final swallow, and in the time it took her to raise the cup to her lips and lower it, the pigeon had taken a step and dropped from the ledge. He caught an upwind that took him nearly as high as the tops of the empty K Street houses. He flew farther into Northeast, into the colors and sounds of the city's morning. She did nothing, aside from following him, with her eyes, with her heart, as far as she could.

1992

RITA DOVE
b. 1952

Rita Dove was the first African American and the youngest person to be named poet laureate of the United States, an office in which she served from 1993 to 1995, as well as the first African American since Gwendolyn Brooks to be awarded the Pulitzer Prize for poetry. At the beginning of her career Dove rejected what she perceived to be the narrowness of the 1960s Black Arts movement in favor of a more inclusive sensibility. In a 1991 interview published in *Callaloo,* she asserted her intention to present characters who are seen as individuals, "as persons who have their very individual lives, and whose histories make them react to the world in different ways." In the opinion of *Callaloo* editor, Charles Rowell, Dove's decision helped change the direction of African American poetry. Even as it would continue to respond to social injustice, it would explore personal, rather than collective histories and take a more lyrical turn.

Dove was born in 1952 in Akron, Ohio, to parents who greatly valued education. Her father, Ray A. Dove, was the only sibling among ten children to go to college. Despite being at the top of his class when he received his master's degree, Ray Dove had to work as an elevator operator at Goodyear for a number of years before becoming the first black chemist in the tire and rubber industry. While shielding their children from such discrimination, Ray and Elvira (Hurd) Dove retained their faith in education. Their daughter Rita began writing plays and stories at an early age and became interested in writing as a career when a high-school teacher took her to a local writers conference.

The first national recognition of Dove's talent came in 1970 with her invitation to the White House as a Presidential Scholar, an award given to the top one hundred high school seniors each year. A National Achievement Scholar, she enrolled in Miami University in Oxford, Ohio. Following her graduation in 1973, Dove received a Fulbright scholarship to study at Tubingen University in West Germany, a locale that would influence her work. Later she did graduate work at the University of Iowa's Writers Workshop. As early as 1974 her poetry began to appear in major periodicals. In addition to four chapbooks, Dove has published eleven volumes of poems; a book of short stories, *Fifth Sunday* (1985); a novel, *Through the Ivory Gate* (1992); a play, *The Darker Face of Earth* (1996); and a collection of essays, *The Poet's World* (1995). Her third volume of poems, *Thomas and Beulah* (1986), was awarded the Pulitzer Prize in poetry, solidifying her reputation and furthering critical interest in her work.

Dove's earliest published volumes were the chapbooks *Ten Poems* (1977) and *The Only Dark Spot in the Sky* (1980), both of which contain poems later reprinted in *The Yellow House on the Corner* (1980). Although some critics saw *The Yellow House* as overly autobiographical, others noted its tight control and discipline. While the volume is concerned with the movement from girlhood to womanhood, Dove avoids a mundane treatment of this topic by her unusual use of biblical imagery, as she imagines the laying on of hands to be a healing through sexuality. Further, in *The Yellow House,* monumental events of history merge with everyday events so that the reader feels the continuity between the private moment and the public happening. Dove's second major volume, *Museum* (1983), mixes autobiographical poems with those that cross cultures. Such poems as "My Father's Telescope" and "Why I Turned Vegetarian" provide family snapshots, while others, especially the travel poems, contrast the personal and the historical. Dove's gathering together of European women as well as women from other parts of the world is distinctive.

In *Thomas and Beulah,* Dove returned to her own history to present, in narrative verse, the saga of her family. Based loosely on the lives of her maternal grandparents, Thomas and Beulah Hurd, who lived in Akron, Ohio, *Thomas and Beulah* gracefully compresses personal and social history into two sections: "Mandolin," which contains twenty-three poems and is told from Thomas's perspective, and "Canary in Bloom," which consists of twenty-one poems and is told from Beulah's perspective. Helpful to the reader in interpreting the poems is a chronology, giving a dated guide to the family's myths. In explaining her use of this guide, Dove notes that

> In a certain way it's also a parody on history because private dates are put on equal footing with dates of publicly important happenings. But significant

events in the private sphere are rarely written up in history books, although they make up the life-sustaining fabric of humanity.

Further undercutting a monolithic construct of history are Thomas's and Beulah's differing versions of the same events. Nonetheless, the lasting impression of *Thomas and Beulah* is that both parents manage to maintain their goodness despite the struggles they undergo, and that both are able to pass on to their children the value of dignity and the power of the imagination. *Thomas and Beulah* received great praise, with many critics noting Dove's economy of style and the way in which she artfully wedded biography and lyric.

That economy of style is further exhibited in her chapbook *The Other Side of the House* (1988) and in *Grace Notes* (1989). In *Mother Love* (1995), Dove takes her explorations of relationships into the realm of Greek myth. In a series of sonnets, she examines the mother-daughter love between Demeter and Persephone. Greek myth and American history are the dual sources of her verse drama *The Darker Face of the Earth*. On the Bus with Rosa Parks* (1999) opens with a cycle of poems about a working-class couple, Pearl and Joe, and ends with the heroism of civil rights legend Rosa Parks ("How she sat there, / the time right inside a place / so wrong it was ready"). With understatement and precision, these poems marvel at the extraordinariness of ordinary peoples' lives.

Dove retains the capacity to make poetry out of the events of her own life. After a fire destroyed their home in 1998, she and her husband, Fred Viebahn, took up ballroom dancing as a way to relieve stress and renew the joy in their lives. It also inspired a book of poetry, *American Smooth* (2004). According to Dove, the title refers to the "jazzier American version of fox trots, tangos, and waltzes." She found more meaning in the term:

> it seemed representative of so much that is quintessentially American. By "quintessentially American" I mean more African American, the way we kind of riff on things and make them our own. And that became the overlying metaphor for the entire book, the idea of taking whatever you're handed—whether it's history's ironies or a dance style—and making it your own.

The title poem captures a moment of transcendence through dance. But the phrase *American Smooth* has broader application; it informs the experience of African American artists like orchestra leader James Reese Europe and movie actor Hattie McDaniel, who are the subjects of poems anthologized here.

Herself an accomplished musician, Dove was inspired to write *Sonata Mulattica: A Life in Five Movements* (2009) in order to recover the life and legacy of George Augustus Polgreen Bridgetower, a violin prodigy who performed with Ludwig van Beethoven. Beethoven dedicated a composition, *Sonata Mulattica*, to Bridgewater. After they quarreled, Beethoven renamed the composition, which today is known as the *Kreutzer Sonata*. The once-celebrated Bridgetower, the son of a Polish-German mother and an Afro-Caribbean father, became a historical footnote. Dove's poems, which imagine lives for Beethoven and Joseph Haydn as well as Bridgetower, restore her subject to his place in the pantheon of classical musicians and also consider the fleeting nature of fame.

A prolific writer, Dove has taught creative writing at various universities, including Arizona State, Tuskegee, and the University of Virginia, where she is the Commonwealth Professor of English. She has edited important volumes, including *The Best American Poetry 2000* and *The Penguin Anthology of 20th Century American Poetry* (2011). Her literary contributions have won her election to the most prestigious intellectual organizations in the United States, including the American Philosophical Society, the American Academy of Arts and Sciences, and the American Academy of Arts and Letters. The recipient of many honors, she has received a Guggenheim fellowship, a Walt Whitman award, the National Medal in the Humanities, and the National Medal of Arts; she is the only poet to have received both medals. The citation for the latter praised her advocacy of the arts as well as her creation of works "that are equal parts beauty, lyricism, critique, and politics."

David Walker[1] (1785–1830)

Free to travel, he still couldn't be shown how lucky
he was: *They strip and beat and drag us about*
like rattlesnakes. Home on Brattle Street, he took in the sign
on the door of the slop shop. All day at the counter—
white caps, ale-stained pea coats. Compass: needles,   5
eloquent as tuning forks, shivered, pointing north.
Evenings, the ceiling fan sputtered like a second pulse.
Oh Heaven! I am full!! I can hardly move my pen!!!

On the faith of an eve-wink, pamphlets were stuffed
into trouser pockets. Pamphlets transported   10
in the coat linings of itinerant seamen, jackets
ringwormed with salt traded drunkenly to pursers
in the Carolinas, pamphlets ripped out, read aloud:
Men of colour, who are also of sense.
Outrage. Incredulity. Uproar in state legislatures.   15

We are the most wretched, degraded and abject set
of beings that ever lived since the world began.
The jewelled canaries in the lecture halls tittered,
pressed his dark hand between their gloves.
Every half-step was no step at all.   20
Every morning, the man on the corner strung a fresh
bunch of boots from his shoulders. "I'm happy!" he said.
"I never want to live any better or happier than
when I can get a-plenty of boots and shoes to clean!"

A second edition. A third.   25
The abolitionist press is *perfectly appalled.*
Humanity, kindness and the fear of the Lord
does not consist in protecting devils. A month—
his person (is that all?) found face-down
in the doorway at Brattle Street,   30
his frame slighter than friends remembered.

1980

---

1. A Boston dealer in old clothes and a militant abolitionist. His *Appeal in Four Articles* (1829) urged blacks the world over to revolt against their oppressors; when he died mysteriously in June 1830, it was rumored that he had been poisoned.

Parsley[1]

1. The Cane[2] Fields

There is a parrot imitating spring
in the palace, its feathers parsley green.
Out of the swamp the cane appears

to haunt us, and we cut it down. El General
searches for a word; he is all the world   5
there is. Like a parrot imitating spring,

we lie down screaming as rain punches through
and we come up green. We cannot speak an R—
out of the swamp, the cane appears

and then the mountain we call in whispers *Katalina*.[3]   10
The children gnaw their teeth to arrowheads.
There is a parrot imitating spring.

El General has found his word: *perejil.*
Who says it, lives. He laughs, teeth shining
out of the swamp. The cane appears   15

in our dreams, lashed by wind and streaming.
And we lie down. For every drop of blood
there is a parrot imitating spring.
Out of the swamp the cane appears.

2. The Palace

The word the general's chosen is parsley.   20
It is fall, when thoughts turn
to love and death; the general thinks
of his mother, how she died in the fall
and he planted her walking cane at the grave
and it flowered, each spring stolidly forming   25
four-star blossoms. The general

pulls on his boots, he stomps to
her room in the palace, the one without
curtains, the one with a parrot
in a brass ring. As he paces he wonders   30
Who can I kill today. And for a moment
the little knot of screams
is still. The parrot, who has traveled

all the way from Australia in an ivory
cage, is, coy as a widow, practising   35

---

1. On October 2, 1937, Rafael Trujillo (1891–
1961), dictator of the Dominican Republic,
ordered 20,000 blacks killed because they could
not pronounce the letter "r" in *perejil,* the Spanish word for parsley [Dove's note].
2. I.e., sugar cane.
3. Katarina (because "We cannot speak an R").

spring. Ever since the morning
his mother collapsed in the kitchen
while baking skull-shaped candies
for the Day of the Dead,[4] the general
has hated sweets. He orders pastries   40
brought up for the bird; they arrive

dusted with sugar on a bed of lace.
The knot in his throat starts to twitch;
he sees his boots the first day in battle
splashed with mud and urine   45
as a soldier falls at his feet amazed—
how stupid he looked!—at the sound
of artillery. *I never thought it would sing*
the soldier said, and died. Now

the general sees the fields of sugar   50
cane, lashed by rain and streaming.
He sees his mother's smile, the teeth
gnawed to arrowheads. He hears
the Haitians sing without R's
as they swing the great machetes: 55
Katalina, they sing, *Katalina*,

mi madle, mi amol en muelte.[5] God knows
his mother was no stupid woman; she
could roll an R like a queen. Even
a parrot can roll an R! In the bare room   60
the bright feathers arch in a parody
of greenery, as the last pale crumbs
disappear under the blackened tongue. Someone

calls out his name in a voice
so like his mother's, a startled tear   65
splashes the tip of his right boot.
My mother, my love in death.
The general remembers the tiny green sprigs
men of his village wore in their capes
to honor the birth of a son. He will   70
order many, this time, to be killed

for a single, beautiful word.

1983

4. All Soul's Day, November 2. An Aztec festival for the spirits of the dead that coincides with the Catholic calendar. In Latin America and the Caribbean, friends and relatives of the dead move in procession to cemeteries, bearing candles, flowers, and food, all of which may be shaped to resemble symbols of death, such as skulls or coffins.
5. I.e., *mi madre, mi amor en muerte:* "my mother, my love in death" (Spanish).

Receiving the Stigmata[1]

There is a way to enter a field
empty-handed, your shoulder
behind you and air tightening.

The kite comes by itself,
a spirit on a fluttering string.   5

Back when people died for
the smallest reasons, there was
always a field to walk into.
Simple men fell to their knees
below the radiant crucifix   10
and held out their palms

in relief. Go into the field
and it will reward. Grace

is a string growing straight
from the hand. Is   15
the hatchet's shadow on the
rippling green.

                                                        1983

FROM THOMAS AND BEULAH[1]

The Event

Ever since they'd left the Tennessee ridge
with nothing to boast of
but good looks and a mandolin,

the two Negroes leaning
on the rail of a riverboat
were inseparable: Lem plucked   5

to Thomas' silver falsetto.
But the night was hot and they were drunk.
They spat where the wheel

---

1. Wounds or marks on a person that resemble
the five wounds received by Jesus Christ at the
Crucifixion.
1. The story in this sequence of poems begins
with Thomas making his way north to Akron,
Ohio. He loses his best friend, who, on a
drunken dare from Thomas, drowns, leaving
behind his mandolin. Thomas carries the instrument with him and eventually hangs it on his
parlor wall. He and Beulah (Hebrew for "married

one" or "possessed"; in the Bible it refers to the
Promised Land) marry and have four daughters.
Thomas works at the Good-year Zeppelin factory
(a zeppelin is a cylindrical airship kept aloft by
gas). The Depression puts him out of work, so he
cleans offices for a living until Goodyear rehires
him at the start of World War II. Beulah works
in a dress shop and later makes hats. Thomas
dies at sixty-three from a heart attack; Beulah
dies six years later.

churned mud and moonlight,
they called to the tarantulas
down among the bananas   10

to come out and dance.
*You're so fine and mighty; let's see
what you can do,* said Thomas, pointing   15

to a tree-capped island.
Lem stripped, spoke easy: *Them's chestnuts,
I believe.* Dove

quick as a gasp. Thomas, dry
on deck, saw the green crown shake   20
as the island slipped

under, dissolved
in the thickening stream.
At his feet

a stinking circle of rags,   25
the half-shell mandolin.
Where the wheel turned the water

gently shirred.[2]

                  1986

Motherhood

She dreams the baby's so small she keeps
misplacing it—it rolls from the hutch
and the mouse carries it home, it disappears
with his shirt in the wash.
Then she drops it and it explodes   5
like a watermelon, eyes spitting.

Finally they get to the countryside;
Thomas has it in a sling.
He's strewing rice along the road
while the trees chitter with tiny birds.   10
In the meadow to their right three men
are playing rough with a white wolf. She calls

warning but the wolf breaks free
and she runs, the rattle
rolls into the gully, then she's   15
there and tossing the baby behind her,

2. Drew together.

listening for its cry as she straddles
the wolf and circles its throat, counting
until her thumbs push through to the earth.
White fur seeps red. She is hardly breathing   20
The small wild eyes
go opaque with confusion and shame, like a child's.

1986

Daystar

She wanted a little room for thinking:
but she saw diapers steaming on the line,
a doll slumped behind the door.

So she lugged a chair behind the garage
to sit out the children's naps.   5

Sometimes there were things to watch—
the pinched armor of a vanished cricket,
a floating maple leaf. Other days
she stared until she was assured
when she closed her eyes   10
she'd see only her own vivid blood.

She had an hour, at best, before Liza appeared
pouting from the top of the stairs.
And just *what* was mother doing
out back with the field mice? Why,   15
building a palace. Later
that night when Thomas rolled over and
lurched into her, she would open her eyes
and think of the place that was hers
for an hour—where   20
she was nothing,
pure nothing, in the middle of the day.

1986

The Oriental Ballerina

twirls on the tips of a carnation
while the radio scratches out a morning hymn.
Daylight has not ventured as far

as the windows—the walls are still dark,
shadowed with the ghosts   5
of oversized gardenias. The ballerina

pirouettes to the wheeze of the old
rugged cross, she lifts
her shoulders past the edge

of the jewelbox lid. Two pink slippers   10
touch the ragged petals, no one
should have feet that small! In China

they do everything upside down:
this ballerina has not risen but drilled
a tunnel straight to America   15

where the bedrooms of the poor
are papered in vulgar flowers
on a background the color of grease, of

teabags, of cracked imitation walnut veneer.
On the other side of the world   20
they are shedding robes sprigged with

roses, roses drifting with a hiss
to the floor by the bed
as, here, the sun finally strikes the windows

suddenly opaque,   25
noncommital as shields. In this room
is a bed where the sun has gone

walking. Where a straw nods over
the lip of its glass and a hand
reaches for a tissue, crumpling it to a flower.   30

The ballerina had been drilling all night!
She flaunts her skirts like sails,
whirling in a disk so bright,

so rapidly she is standing still.
The sun walks the bed to the pillow   35
and pauses for breath (in the Orient,

breath floats like mist
in the fields), hesitating
at a knotted handkerchief that has slid

on its string and has lodged beneath   40
the right ear which discerns
the most fragile music

where there is none. The ballerina dances
at the end of a tunnel of light,
she spins on her impossible toes—   45

the rest is shadow.
The head on the pillow sees nothing
else, though it feels the sun warming

its cheeks. *There is no China;*
no cross, just the papery kiss
of a kleenex above the stink of camphor,
the walls exploding with shabby tutus. . . .

50

1986

Pastoral

Like an otter, but warm,
she latched onto the shadowy tip
and I watched, diminished
by those amazing gulps. Finished
she let her head loll, eyes
unfocused and large: milk-drunk.

5

I liked afterwards best, lying
outside on a quilt, her new skin
spread out like meringue. I felt then
what a young man must feel
with his first love asleep on his breast:
desire, and the freedom to imagine it.

10

1989

American Smooth

We were dancing—it must have
been a foxtrot or a waltz,
something romantic but
requiring restraint,
rise and fall, precise
execution as we moved
into the next song without
stopping, two chests heaving
above a seven-league
stride—such perfect agony
one learns to smile through,
ecstatic mimicry
being the *sine qua non*
of American Smooth.
And because I was distracted
by the effort of
keeping my frame
(the leftward lean, head turned
just enough to gaze out
past your ear and always
smiling, smiling),
I didn't notice

5

10

15

20

how still you'd become until
we had done it
(for two measures?
four?)—achieved flight,   25
that swift and serene
magnificence,
before the earth
remembered who we were   30
and brought us down.

2004

The Return of Lieutenant James Reese Europe

(Victory Parade, New York City, February 1919.)

We trained in the streets: the streets where we came from.
We drilled with sticks, boys darting between bushes, shouting—
that's all you thought we were good for. We trained anyway.
In camp we had no plates or forks. First to sail, first to
    join the French,   5
first to see combat with the shortest training time.

My, the sun is looking fine today.

We toured devastation, American good will
in a forty-four piece band. Dignitaries smiled; the wounded
settled back to dream. That old woman in St. Nazaire   10
who tucked up her skirts so she could "walk the dog."[1]
German prisoners tapping their feet as we went by.

Miss Flatiron with your tall cool self: How do.

You didn't want us when we left but we went.
You didn't want us coming back but here we are,   15
stepping right up white-faced Fifth Avenue in a phalanx
(*no prancing, no showing of teeth, no swank*)
past the Library lions, eyes forward, tin hats aligned—

a massive, upheld human shield.

No jazz for you: We'll play a brisk French march   20
and show our ribbons, flash our *Croix de Guerre*[2]
(yes, we learned French, too) all the way
until we reach 110th Street and yes! take our turn
onto Lenox Avenue and all those brown faces and then—

Baby, Here Comes Your Daddy Now!   25

2004

---

1. Popular dance accompanying the 1916 blues song "Walkin' the Dog" by Shelton Brooks.

2. French military decoration awarded to individual soldiers and units for valor in combat.

Hattie McDaniel Arrives at the Coconut Grove[1]

late, in aqua and ermine, gardenias
scaling her left sleeve in a spasm of scent,
her gloves white, her smile chastened, purse giddy
with stars and rhinestones clipped to her brilliantined hair,
on her free arm that fine Negro,   5
Mr. Wonderful Smith.[2]

It's the day that isn't, February 29th,
at the end of the shortest month of the year—
and the shittiest, too, everywhere
except Hollywood, California,   10
where the maid can wear mink and still be a maid,
bobbing her bandaged head and cursing
the white folks under her breath as she smiles
and shoos their silly daughters
in from the night dew . . . what can she be   15
thinking of, striding into the ballroom
where no black face has ever showed itself
except above a serving tray?

Hi-Hat Hattie, Mama Mac, Her Haughtiness,
the "little lady" from Showboat[3] whose name   20
Bing[4] forgot, Beulah & Bertha & Malena
& Carrie & Violet & Cynthia & Fidelia,
one half of the Dark Barrymores[5]—
dear Mammy we can't help but hug you crawl into
your generous lap tease you   25
with arch innuendo so we can feel that
much more wicked and youthful
and sleek but oh what

we forgot: the four husbands, the phantom
pregnancy, your famous parties, your celebrated   30
ice box cake. Your giggle above the red petticoat's rustle,
black girl and white girl walking hand in hand
down the railroad tracks
in Kansas City, six years old.
The man who advised you, now   35
that you were famous, to "begin eliminating"
your more "common" acquaintances
and your reply (catching him square
in the eye): "That's a good idea.
I'll start right now by eliminating you."   40

Is she or isn't she? Three million dishes,
a truckload of aprons and headrags later, and here
you are: poised, between husbands
and factions, no corset wide enough
to hold you in, your huge face a dark moon split   45
by that spontaneous smile—your trademark,
your curse. No matter, Hattie: It's a long, beautiful walk
into that flower-smothered standing ovation,
so go on
and make them wait.   50

2004

WALTER MOSLEY
b. 1952

Within a decade of publishing his first book, Walter Mosley entered into the company of contemporary American novelists whose work is expected to last. Even more striking than the speed of his literary arrival, though, was his chosen vehicle: a series of mystery novels set in postwar Los Angeles featuring a reluctant black investigator, Easy Rawlins. In American literary history only three other crime writers—Edgar Allan Poe, inventor of the detective story; Dashiell Hammett, creator of detectives Sam Spade and the Continental Op; and Raymond Chandler, whose classic hard-boiled private eye novels featuring Philip Marlowe are frequently cited as precursors to Mosley's work—have received similar critical scrutiny as serious (as opposed to pure genre) figures. There does exist a somewhat submerged genre of black crime writing, stretching from Rudolph Fisher's Harlem-based voodoo novel *The Conjure Man Dies* (1932) to Chester Himes's Coffin Ed and Gravedigger Jones police procedurals in the 1960s, but Mosley's books are the first to capture mainstream attention, including appearances on best-seller lists, film adaptations, and even the enthusiastic endorsement of a U.S. president, Bill Clinton. In short order Mosley single-handedly integrated a formerly white literary genre, in the process lending it a new level of moral complexity and a hard-headed racial realism. He has gone on to write more than three dozen books in multiple genres, including literary fiction, science fiction, political monographs, and a young adult novel.

Walter Mosley was born on January 12, 1952, in the South Central section of Los Angeles, where he attended both a private black elementary school, which taught classes in black history, and the local public schools. An only child, Mosley remembers "an emptiness to my childhood that I filled up with fantasies." His mother, Ella Slatkin Mosley, a Bronx-born Jewish schoolteacher, gave him books. His African American father, a school custodian and gifted storyteller, originally from South Texas, bequeathed to him both the language and the tales of his southern background. There are obvious parallels between Leroy Mosley and Easy Rawlins: both grew up in Houston's black Fifth Ward, both were combat veterans of World War II, and both were (or are) mesmerizing narrators. Three of Walter Mosley's novels are dedicated to his father.

Mosley lived a somewhat knockabout existence after graduation from Johnson State College in Vermont in 1977, working as a potter, a caterer, and a computer programmer. He began writing in earnest in the mid-1980s, first poetry, and then fiction at the City College of New York. His first completed novel, *Gone Fishin'*, which is narrated by Easy Rawlins, did not find a publisher. But when he placed Easy in a classic hard-boiled mystery in *Devil in a Blue Dress* (1990), critical and commercial success was quick in coming—as were succeeding volumes—*A Red Death* (1991), *White Butterfly* (1992), *Black Betty* (1994), *A Little Yellow Dog* (1996), *Bad Boy Brawly Brown* (2002), *Six Easy Pieces* (2003), *Little Scarlet* (2004), *Cinnamon Kiss* (2005), and *Blonde Faith* (2007).

The Easy Rawlins novels are unique in American crime fiction in a number of respects. For one thing, they unfold in real historical time: *Devil in a Blue Dress* being set in the postwar Los Angeles of 1948, *A Little Yellow Dog* taking place just before the assassination of John F. Kennedy in 1963. The critic R. W. B. Lewis noted that the novels are less a series than a *saga*, one that recalls William Faulkner's Yoknapatawpha novels in the density with which it peoples and animates its home around South Central L.A. They are also unique in the candor with which they confront racism in American life; when Mosley's black characters collide with white Los Angeles police officers, echoes of the 1992 Rodney King beating are impossible to ignore. In no sense, though, are these protest novels; the teeming and vibrant community that Mosley creates is full of autonomous and unpredictable characters, not typecast victims. Their real uniqueness, though—and most lasting literary value— resides in the figure of Easy Rawlins, a man of quicksilver sensibility who must wrestle with his own demons as well as the villains, white and black, whom he encounters in his perambulations around Los Angeles. Mosley has said that his conception of Easy owes much to the novels of Albert Camus, and there is something distinctly existential in the way this black man must work out his private conceptions of morality by acting in an often absurd, white-controlled world where justice can be—and usually is—denied to him.

Mosley has created three other popular and critically acclaimed series named for their memorable protagonists. Fearless Jones, like Rawlins, is a World War II veteran with a penchant for trouble. Leonid McGill is an ex-boxer, hard drinker, and private investigator whose beat is New York City. Finally, there is Socrates Fortlow, the protagonist of the cycle of stories *Always Outnumbered, Always Outgunned*

Black masculinity is the subject of this Budd Williams photograph and of Walter Mosley's story, *Equal Opportunity*. The gestures of the men in the photo belie their stoic faces.

(1997); the volume was the basis of a film starring Laurence Fishburne. An ex-convict scrambling to make a living on the outside, Socrates struggles with questions of good and evil with the seriousness suggested by his name. Subsequent volumes in this series include *Walking the Dog* (1999) and *The Right Mistake* (2008). Like Mosley's other crime fiction, these books stand out for their narrative mastery, vernacular humor, and engagement with moral questions.

Although Mosley's reputation rests mainly on his crime fiction, he has published widely in other genres. *RL's Dream* (1995) was his first work of literary fiction; the protagonist Soupspoon Wise, a blues singer in New York City, faces a decision reminiscent of the legendary deal with the devil made by blues singer Robert Johnson. *The Last Days of Ptolemy Grey* (2010) marks another departure for Mosley, as it imagines a character that is given a second chance at life, but at the price of a hastened death. According to novelist Edwidge Danticat, *Last Days* "is a beautiful meditation on love, frailty and old age." In the science fiction genre Mosley has published *Blue Light* (1999), *Futureland: Nine Stories of an Imminent World* (2001), *The Wave* (2005), and *Gift of Fire/The Head of a Pin* (2012). Mosley's political commitments inspire the publication of several works, including *What Next: An African American Initiative Toward World Peace* (2003) and *Twelve Steps Toward Political Revelation* (2011).

Despite his commercial success, in 1996 Moseley decided to forgo an advance and publish *Gone Fishin'* with a small black-owned press. This gesture of solidarity earned him the respect of the community of African American writers and publishers. Mosley also enjoys an international reputation; his books have been translated into more than twenty languages. Prolific, popular, and critically acclaimed, Mosley is a writer who defies categorization.

Equal Opportunity

1

Bounty Supermarket was on Venice Boulevard,[1] miles and miles from Socrates' home. He gaped at the glittering palace as he strode across the hot asphalt parking lot. The front wall was made from immense glass panes with steel framing to hold them in place. Through the big windows he could see long lines of customers with baskets full of food. He imagined apples and T-bone steaks, fat hams and the extra-large boxes of cereal that they only sold in supermarkets.

The checkers were all young women, some of them girls. Most were black. Black women, black girls—taking money and talking back and forth between themselves as they worked; running the packages of food over the computer eye that rang in the price and added it to the total without them having to think a thing.

In between the checkout counters black boys and brown ones loaded up bags for the customers.

Socrates walked up to the double glass doors and they slid open moaning some deep machine blues. He came into the cool air and cocked his ear to that peculiar music of supermarkets; steel carts wheeling around, crashing together, resounding with the thuds of heavy packages. Children squealing and yelling. The footsteps and occasional conversation blended together until they made a murmuring sound that lulled the ex-convict.

There was a definite religious feel to being in the great store. The lofty ceilings, the abundance, the wealth.

1. Major thoroughfare in Los Angeles.

Dozens of tens and twenties, in between credit cards and bank cards, went back and forth over the counters. Very few customers used coupons. The cash seemed to be endless. How much money passed over those counters every day?

And what would they think if they knew that the man watching them had spent twenty-seven years doing hard time in prison? Socrates barked out a single-syllable laugh. They didn't have to worry about him. He wasn't a thief. Or, if he was, the only thing he ever took was life.

"Sir, can I help you?" Anton Crier asked.

Socrates knew the name because it was right there, on a big badge on his chest. ANTON CRIER ASST. MGR. He wore tan pants and a blue blazer with the supermarket insignia over the badge.

"I came for an application," Socrates said. It was a line that he had spent a whole day thinking about; a week practicing. *I came for an application.* For a couple days he had practiced saying *job application,* but after a while he dropped the word *job* to make his request sound more sure. But when he went to Stony Wile and told him that he planned to say "I came for a application," Stony said that you had to say *an application.*

"If you got a word that starts with *a, e, i, o,* or *u* then you got to say *an* instead of *a,*" Stony had said.

Anton Crier's brow knitted and he stalled a moment before asking, "An application for what?"

"A job." There, he'd said it. It was less than a minute and this short white man, just a boy really, had already made him beg.

"Oh," said Anton Crier, nodding like a wise elder. "Uh. How old are you, sir?"

"Ain't that against the law?" Like many other convicts Socrates was a student of the law.

"Huh?"

"Askin' me my age. That's against the law. You cain't discriminate against color or sex or religion or infirmity or against age. That's the law."

"Uh, well, yes, of course it is. I know that. I'm not discriminating against you. It's just that we don't have any openings right now. Why don't you come in the fall when the kids are back at school?"

Anton leaned to the side, intending to leave Socrates standing there.

"Hold on," Socrates said. He held up his hands, loosely as fists, in a nonchalant sort of boxing stance.

Anton looked, and waited.

"I came for an application," Socrates repeated.

"But I told you . . ."

"I know what you said. But first you looked at my clothes and at my bald head. First yo' eyes said that this is some kinda old hobo and what do he want here when it ain't bottle redemption time."

"I did not . . ."

"It don't matter," Socrates said quickly. He knew better than to let a white man in uniform finish a sentence. "You got to give me a application. That's the law too."

"Wait here," young Mr. Crier said. He turned and strode away toward an elevated office that looked down along the line of cash registers.

Socrates watched him go. So did the checkers and bag boys. He was their boss and they knew when he was unhappy. They stole worried glances at Socrates.

Socrates stared back. He wondered if any of those young black women would stand up for him. Would they understand how far he'd come to get there?

He'd traveled more than fourteen miles from his little apartment down in Watts.[2] They didn't have any supermarkets or jobs in his neighborhood. And all the stores along Crenshaw and Washington[3] knew him as a bum who collected bottles and cans for a living.

They wouldn't hire him.

Socrates hadn't held a real job in over thirty-seven years. He'd been unemployed for twenty-five months before the party with Shep, Fogel, and Muriel.

They'd been out carousing. Three young people, blind drunk.

Back at Shep's, Muriel gave Socrates the eye. He danced with her until Shep broke it up. But then Shep fell asleep. When he awoke to find them rolling on the floor the fight broke out in earnest.

Socrates knocked Shep back to the floor and then he finished his business with Muriel even though she was worried about her man. But when she started to scream and she hit Socrates with that chair he hit her back.

It wasn't until the next morning, when he woke up, that he realized that his friends were dead.

Then he'd spent twenty-seven years in prison. Now, eight years free, fifty-eight years old, he was starting life over again.

Not one of those girls, nor Anton Crier, was alive when he started his journey. If they were lucky they wouldn't understand him.

2

There was a large electric clock above the office. The sweep hand reared back and then battered up against each second, counting every one like a drummer beating out time on a slave galley.

Socrates could see the young assistant manager through the window under the clock. He was saying something to an older white woman sitting there. The woman looked down at Socrates and then swiveled in her chair to a file cabinet. She took out a piece of paper and held it while lecturing Anton. He reached for the paper a couple of times but the woman kept it away from him and continued talking. Finally she said something and Crier nodded. He took the paper from her and left the office, coming down the external stairs at a fast clip. Walking past the checkers he managed not to look at Socrates before he was standing there in front of him.

"Here," he said, handing the single-sheet application form to Socrates. Crier never stopped moving. As soon as Socrates had the form between his fingers the younger man was walking away.

Socrates touched the passing elbow and asked, "You got a pencil?"

"What?"

"I need a pencil to fill out this form."

"You, you, you can just send it in."

"I didn't come all this way for a piece'a paper, man. I come to apply for a job."

Anton Crier stormed over to one of the checkers, demanded her pencil, then rushed back to Socrates.

"Here," he said.

Socrates answered, "Thank you," but the assistant manager was already on his way back to the elevated office.

Half an hour later Socrates was standing at the foot of the stairs leading up to Anton and his boss. He stood there waiting for one of them to come down. They could see him through the window.

They knew he was there.

So Socrates waited, holding the application in one hand and the borrowed pencil in the other.

After twenty minutes he was wondering if a brick could break the wall of windows at the front of the store.

After thirty minutes he decided that it might take a shotgun blast.

Thirty-nine minutes had gone by when the woman, who had bottled red hair, came down to meet him. Anton Crier shadowed her. Socrates saw the anger in the boy's face.

"Yes? Can I help you?" Halley Grimes asked. She had a jailhouse smile— insincere and crooked.

"I wanted to ask a couple of things about my application."

"All the information is right there at the top of the sheet."

"But I had some questions."

"We're very busy, sir." Ms. Grimes broadened her smile to show that she had a heart, even for the aged and confused. "What do you need to know?"

"It asks here if I got a car or a regular ride to work."

"Yes," beamed Ms. Grimes. "What is it exactly that you don't understand?"

"I understand what it *says* but I just don't get what it means."

The look of confusion came into Halley Grimes's face. Socrates welcomed a real emotion.

He answered her unasked question. "What I mean is that I don't have a car or a ride but I can take a bus to work."

The store manager took his application form and fingered the address.

"Where is this street?" she asked.

"Down Watts."

"That's pretty far to go by bus, isn't it? There are stores closer than this one, you know."

"But I could get here." Socrates noticed that his head wanted to move as if to the rhythm of a song. Then he heard it: "Baby Love," by Diana Ross and the Supremes.[4] It was being played softly over the loudspeaker. "I could get here."

"Well." Ms. Grimes seemed to brighten. "We'll send this in to the main office and, if it's clear with them, we'll put it in our files. When there's an opening we'll give you a call."

"A what?"

"A call. We'll call you if you're qualified and if a job opens up."

"Uh, well, we got to figure somethin' else than that out. You see, I don't have no phone."

---

4. Popular 1960s singing group.

"Oh, well then." Ms. Grimes held up her hands in a gesture of helplessness. "I don't see that there's anything we can do. The main office demands a phone number. That's how they check on your address. They call."

"How do they know that they got my address just 'cause'a some phone they call? Wouldn't it be better if they wrote me?"

"I'm very busy, sir. I've told you that we need a phone number to process this application." Halley Grimes held out the form toward Socrates. "Without that there really isn't anything I can do."

Socrates kept his big hands down. He didn't want to take the application back—partly because he didn't want to break the pudgy white woman's fingers.

"Do me a favor and send it in," he said.

"I told you . . ."

"Just send it in, okay? Send it in. I'll be back to find out what they said."

"You don't . . ."

"Just send it in." There was violence in this last request.

Halley Grimes pulled the application away from his face and said, "All right. But it won't make any difference."

3

Socrates had to transfer on three buses to get back to his apartment.

And he was especially tired that day. Talking to Crier and Grimes had worn him out.

He boiled potatoes and eggs in a saucepan on his single hot plate and then cut them together in the pot with two knives, adding mustard and sweet pickle relish. After the meal he had two shots of whiskey and one Camel cigarette.

He was asleep by nine o'clock.

His dream blared until dawn.

It was a realistic sort of dream; no magic, no impossible wish. It was just Socrates in a nine-foot cell with a flickering fluorescent light from the walkway keeping him from sleeping and reading, giving him a headache, hurting his eyes.

"Mr. Bennett," the sleeping Socrates called out from his broad sofa. He shouted so loudly that a mouse in the kitchen jumped up and out of the potato pan pinging his tail against the thin tin as he went.

Socrates heard the sound in his sleep. He turned but then slipped back into the flickering, painful dream.

"What you want?" the guard asked. He was big and black and meaner than anyone Socrates had ever known.

"I cain't read. I cain't sleep. That light been like that for three days now."

"Put the pillow on your head," the big guard said.

"I cain't breathe like that," Socrates answered sensibly.

"Then don't," Mr. Bennett replied.

As the guard walked away, Socrates knew, for the first time really, why they kept him in that jail. He would have killed Bennett if he could have right then; put his fingers around that fat neck and squeezed until the veins swelled and cartilage popped and snapped. He was so mad that he balled his fists in his sleep twenty-five years after the fact.

He was a sleeping man wishing that he could sleep. And he was mad, killing mad. He couldn't rest because of the crackling, buzzing light, and the more it shone the angrier he became. And the angrier he got the more scared he was. Scared that he'd kill Bennett the first chance he got.

The anger built for days in that dream. The sound of grinding teeth could be heard throughout Socrates' two rooms.

Finally, when he couldn't stand it anymore, he took his rubber squeeze ball in his left hand and slipped his right hand through the bars. He passed the ball through to his right hand and gauged its weight in the basket of his fingers. He blinked back at the angry light, felt the weight of his hard rubber ball. The violent jerk started from his belly button, traveled up through his chest and shoulder, and down until his fingers tensed like steel. The ball flew in a straight line that shattered the light, broke it into blackness.

And in the jet night he heard Bennett say, "That's the last light you get from the state of Indiana."

Socrates woke up in the morning knowing that he had cried. He could feel the strain in the muscles of his throat. He got out of bed thinking about Anton Crier and Halley Grimes.

4

"You what?" asked Stony Wile. He'd run into Socrates getting off a bus on Central and offered to buy his friend a beer. They went to Moody's bar on 109th Street.

"I been down there ev'ry day for five days. An ev'ry day I go in there I ask'em if they got my okay from the head office yet."

"An' what they say about that?"

"Well, the first day that boy, that Anton Crier, just said no. So I left. Next day he told me that I had to leave. But I said that I wanted to talk to his boss. She come down an' tell me that she done already said how I cain't work there if I don't have no phone."

"Yeah," asked Stony Wile. "Then what'd you do?"

"I told'em that they should call downtown and get some kinda answer on me because I was gonna come back ev'ryday till I get some kinda answer." There was a finality in Socrates' voice that opened Stony's eyes wide.

"You don't wanna do sumpin' dumb now, Socco," he said.

"An' what would that be?"

"They could get you into all kindsa trouble, arrest you for trespassin' if you keep it up."

"Maybe they could. Shit. Cops could come in here an' blow my head off too, but you think I should kiss they ass?"

"But that's different. You got to stand up for yo' pride, yo' manhood. But I don't see it wit' this supermarket thing."

"Well," Socrates said. "On Thursday Ms. Grimes told me that the office had faxed her to say I wasn't qualified for the position. She said that she had called the cops and said that I'd been down there harassin' them. She said that they said that if I ever come over there again that they would come arrest me. Arrest me! Just for tryin' t'get my rights."

"That was the fourth day?" Stony asked to make sure that he was counting right.

"Uh-huh. That was day number four. I asked her could I see that fax paper but she said that she didn't have it, that she threw it out. You ever hear'a anything like that? White woman workin' for a white corporation throwin' out paperwork?"

Stony was once a shipbuilder but now worked on a fishing day boat out of San Pedro.[5] He'd been in trouble before but never in jail. He'd never thought about the thousands of papers he'd signed over his life; never wondered where they went.

"Why wouldn't they throw them away?" Stony asked.

"Because they keep ev'ry scrap'a paper they got just as long as it make they case in court."

Stony nodded. Maybe he understood.

"So I called Bounty's head office," Socrates said. "Over in Torrence."

"You lyin'."

"An' why not? I applied for that job, Stony. I should get my hearin' wit' them."

"What'd they say?"

"That they ain't never heard'a me."

"You lyin'," Stony said again.

"Grimes an' Crier the liars. An' you know I went down there today t'tell'em so. I was up in Anton's face when he told me that Ms. Grimes was out. I told him that they lied and that I had the right to get me a job."

"An' what he say?"

"He was scared. He thought I mighta hit'im. And I mighta too except Ms. Grimes comes on down."

"She was there?"

"Said that she was on a lunch break; said that she was gonna call the cops on me. Shit. I called her a liar right to her face. I said that she was a liar and that I had a right to be submitted to the main office." Socrates jabbed his finger at Stony as if he were the one holding the job hostage. "I told'er that I'd be back on Monday and that I expected some kinda fair treatment."

"Well that sounds right," Stony said. "It ain't up to her who could apply an' who couldn't. She got to be fair."

"Yeah," Socrates answered. "She said that the cops would be waitin' for me on Monday. Maybe Monday night you could come see me in jail."

5

On Saturday Socrates took his canvas cart full of cans to the Boys Market on Adams. He waited three hours behind Calico, an older black woman who prowled the same streets he did, and two younger black men who worked as a team.

Calico and DJ and Bernard were having a good time waiting. DJ was from Oakland and had come down to L.A. to stay with his grandmother when he was fifteen. She died a year later so he had to live on the streets since then. But DJ didn't complain. He talked about how good life was and how much he was able to collect on the streets.

5. Here and throughout are references to cities and towns in the Los Angeles area and elsewhere in California.

"Man," DJ said. "I wish they would let me up there in Beverly Hills just one week. Gimme one week with a pickup an' I could live for a year offa the good trash they got up there. They th'ow out stuff that still work up there."

"How the fuck you know, man?" Bernard said. "When you ever been up Beverly Hills?"

"When I was doin' day work. I helped a dude build a cinder-block fence up on Hollandale. I saw what they th'owed out. I picked me up a portable TV right out the trash an' I swear that sucker get ev'ry channel."

"I bet it don't get cable," Bernard said.

"It would if I'da had a cable to hook it up wit'."

They talked like that for three hours. Calico cooed and laughed with them, happy to be in the company of young men.

But Socrates was just mad.

Why the hell did he have to wait for hours? Who were they in that supermarket to make full-grown men and women wait like they were children?

At two o'clock he got up and walked away from his canvas wagon.

"Hey," Bernard called. "You want us t'watch yo' basket?"

"You could keep it," Socrates said. "I ain't never gonna use the goddam thing again."

Calico let out a whoop at Socrates' back.

On Sunday Socrates sharpened his pocket knife on a graphite stone. He didn't keep a gun. If the cops caught him with a gun he would spend the rest of his life in jail. But there was no law against a knife blade three inches or less; and three inches was all a man who knew how to use a knife needed.

Socrates sharpened his knife but he didn't know why exactly. Grimes and Crier weren't going to harm him, at least not with violence. And if they called the cops a knife wouldn't be any use anyway. If the cops even thought that he had a knife they could shoot him and make a good claim for self-defense.

But Socrates still practiced whipping out the knife and slashing with the blade sticking out of the back end of his fist.

"Hah!" he yelled.

6

He left the knife on the orange crate by his sofa bed the next morning before leaving for Bounty Supermarket. The RTD[6] bus came right on time and he made his connections quickly, one after the other.

In forty-five minutes he was back in that parking lot. It was a big building, he thought, but not as big as the penitentiary had been.

A smart man would have turned around and tried some other store, Socrates knew that. It didn't take a hero to make a fool out of himself.

It was before nine-thirty and the air still had the hint of a morning chill. The sky was a pearl gray and the parking lot was almost empty.

Socrates counted seven breaths and then walked toward the door with no knife in his hand. He cursed himself softly under his breath because he had no woman at home to tell him that he was a fool.

---

6. Rapid Transit District; public transportation.

Nobody met him at the door. There was only one checker on duty while the rest of the workers went up and down the aisles restocking and straightening the shelves.

With nowhere else to go, Socrates went toward the elevated office. He was half the way there when he saw Halley Grimes coming down the stairs. Seeing him she turned and went, ran actually, back up to the office.

Socrates was sure that she meant to call the police. He wanted to run but couldn't. All he could do was take one step after the other; the way he'd done in his cell sometimes, sometimes the way he did at home.

Two men appeared at the high door when Socrates reached the stairs. Salt and pepper, white and black. The older one, a white man, wore a tan wash-and-wear suit with a cheap maroon tie. The Negro had on black jeans, a black jacket, and a white turtleneck shirt. He was very light-skinned but his nose and lips would always give him away.

The men came down to meet him. They were followed by Grimes and Crier.

"Mr. Fortlow?" the white man inquired.

Socrates nodded and looked him in the eye.

"My name is Parker," he continued. "And this is Mr. Weems."

"Uh-huh," Socrates answered.

The two men formed a wall behind which the manager and assistant manager slipped away.

"We work for Bounty," Mr. Weems said. "Would you like to come upstairs for a moment?"

"What for?" Socrates wanted to know.

"We'd like to talk," Parker answered.

The platform office was smaller than it looked from the outside. The two cluttered desks that sat back to back took up most of the space. Three sides were windows that gave a full panorama of the store. The back wall had a big blackboard on it with the chalked-in time schedules of everyone who worked there. Beneath the blackboard was a safe door.

"Have a seat, Mr. Fortlow." Parker gestured toward one of the two chairs. He sat in the other chair while Weems perched on a desk.

"Coffee?" asked Parker.

"What's this all about, man?" Socrates asked.

Smiling, Parker said, "We want to know what your problem is with Ms. Grimes. She called the head office on Friday and told us that she was calling the police because she was afraid of you."

"I don't have no problem with Ms. Grimes or Anton Crier or Bounty Supermarket. I need a job and I wanted to make a application. That's all."

"But she told you that you had to have a phone number in order to complete your file," said Weems.

"So? Just 'cause I don't have no phone then I cain't work? That don't make no sense at all. If I don't work I cain't afford no phone. If I don't have no phone then I cain't work. You might as well just put me in the ground."

"It's not Bounty's problem that you don't have a phone." Parker's face was placid but the threat was in his tone.

"All I want is to make a job application. All I want is to work," Socrates said. Really he wanted to fight. He wanted his knife at close quarters with those private cops. But instead he went on, "I ain't threatened nobody. I ain't said I was gonna do a thing. All I did was to come back ev'ry day an' ask if they had my okay from you guys yet. That's all. On the job application they asked if I had a car or a ride to work—to see if I could get here. Well, I come in ev'ry day for a week at nine-thirty or before. I come in an' asked if I been cleared yet. I didn't do nuthin' wrong. An' if that woman is scared it must be 'cause she knows she ain't been right by me. But I didn't do nuthin'."

There was no immediate answer to Socrates' complaint. The men looked at him but kept silent. There was the hum of machinery coming from somewhere but Socrates couldn't figure out where. He concentrated on keeping his hands on his knees, on keeping them open.

"But how do you expect to get a job when you come in every day and treat the people who will be your bosses like they're doing something wrong?" Weems seemed really to want to know.

"If I didn't come in they woulda th'owed out my application, prob'ly did anyway. I ain't no kid. I'm fifty-eight years old. I'm unemployed an' nowhere near benefits. If I don't find me some way t'get some money I'll starve. So, you see, I had to come. I couldn't let these people say that I cain't even apply. If I did that then I might as well die."

Parker sighed. Weems scratched the top of his head and then rubbed his nose.

"You can't work here," Parker said at last. "If we tried to push you off on Ms. Grimes she'd go crazy. She really thought that you were going to come in here guns blazing."

"So 'cause she thought that I was a killer then I cain't have no job?" Socrates knew the irony of his words but he also knew their truth. He didn't care about a job just then. He was happy to talk, happy to say what he felt. Because he knew that he was telling the truth and that those men believed him.

"What about Rodriguez?" Weems asked of no one in particular.

"Who's that?" Socrates asked.

"He's the manager of one of our stores up on Santa Monica,"[7] Weems replied.

"I don't know," Parker said.

"Yeah, sure, Connie Rodriguez." Weems was getting to like the idea. "He's always talking about giving guys a chance. We could give him a chance to back it up with Mr. Fortlow here."

Parker chewed on his lower lip until it reddened. Weems grinned. It seemed to Socrates that some kind of joke was being played on this Connie Rodriguez. Parker hesitated but he liked the idea.

Parker reached down under the desk and came out with a briefcase. From this he brought out a sheet of paper; Socrates' application form.

"There's just one question," Parker said.

7

"What he wanna know?" Stony Wile asked at Iula's grill. They were there with Right Burke, Markham Peal, and Howard Shakur. Iula gave Socrates a party when she heard that he got a job as a general food packager and food delivery person at Bounty Supermarket on Santa Monica Boulevard. She made the food and his friends brought the liquor.

---

7. A boulevard in Los Angeles.

"He wanted to know why I had left one of the boxes blank."

"What box?"

"The one that asks if I'd ever been arrested for or convicted of a felony."

"Damn. What you say?"

"That I musta overlooked it."

"An' then you lied?"

"Damn straight. But he knew I was lyin'. He was a cop before he went to work for Bounty. Both of 'em was. He asked me that if they put through a check on me would it come up bad? An' I told him that he didn't need to put through no checks."

"Mmm!" Stony hummed, shaking his head. "That's always gonna be over your head, man. Always."

Socrates laughed and grabbed his friend by the back of his neck.

He hugged Stony and then held him by the shoulders. "I done had a lot worse hangin' over me, brother. At least I get a paycheck till they find out what I am."

1998

HARRYETTE MULLEN
b. 1953

Taking issue with critics who argue that her poems "skirt the edge of meaning," Harryette Mullen insists that she intends them to be meaningful: "to allow, or suggest, or open up, or insinuate possible meanings, even in those places where the poem drifts between intentional utterance and improvisational wordplay, between comprehensible statements and the pleasures of sound itself." In seven volumes of poetry, she explores the meanings of race and gender identity, the pervasiveness and the politics of commodity culture, and the varied textures of American language. A lyric poet, she weaves her words from black folklore and Western poetic tradition, from pop culture and the literary avant-garde, from critical theory and colloquial speech.

Mullen was born in Florence, Alabama, and grew up in Fort Worth, Texas, a cultural environment that was partly southern, partly southwestern. As a child at the end of the Jim Crow era, Mullen lived in a world that was segregated from whites; it existed alongside a Mexican American culture whose language fascinated her, even though she could not understand it. She was somewhat distanced from the black community, because her family had emigrated to Texas from Pennsylvania. Of necessity, she became an avid student of both vernacular black speech and Spanish. At the University of Texas she earned a B.A. in English, going on to earn an M.A. and Ph.D. in literature from the University of California at Santa Cruz. She has been on the faculty of Cornell and the University of California at Los Angeles, where she currently teaches literature and creative writing. She describes her own writing as "multi-voiced" texts that "express the actual diversity of my own experience."

That diversity is only partly reflected in *Tree Tall Woman* (1981), a volume whose speakers are mainly southern-born African Americans whose concept of identity is striking but univocal. Her second book, *Trimmings* (1991), focuses on gender as much as race; in its linguistic play and experimentation, it creates a dialogue with Gertrude Stein's *Tender Buttons* (1914), though unlike Stein's prose work, *Trimmings* is also a work of social and political commentary. The title, *S*PeRM**K*T* (1992), Mullen explains, "is the word 'supermarket' with some letters missing and asterisks replace the missing letters. The missing letters just happen to be U-A-R-E, so it's like 'you are what you eat.'" The poem's witty riffs on brand-name foods and advertisements critique the ways capitalism structures every aspect of people's lives. The formal innovations of these two books burnished Mullen's reputation in the postmodern avant-garde. But she was concerned that they distanced her work from African American readers. Naming Gwendolyn Brooks, Amiri Baraka, Bob Kaufman, and Melvin Tolson among her influences, Mullen locates herself in the African American tradition. She strove to create a poem that would speak to her various audiences.

Muse & Drudge (1995) is a series of quatrains that are rich in allusions to literature, culture, history, and the poet's private experience. The title evokes Zora Neale Hurston's volume *Mules and Men;* like Hurston, Mullen explores the identities blacks assume apart from the polarities that the dominant culture imagines. She is a master of wordplay; the poem is in the tradition of the oral performances Hurston documents. One couplet quotes *Mules* directly: "now I'm standing in my tracks / stepping back on my abstract," an image that affirms the sense that the speaker is living in her own language. But Mullen is not transcribing folk speech. Hers is a postmodern mélange that reflects the multiple traditions in which she works. She remembers "thinking of this poem as the place where Sappho meets the blues at the crossroads, I imagined Sappho becoming Sapphire and singing the blues." The poem blends diverse sources—blues lyrics, the Bible, Egyptian mythology, African American history, Hollywood movies, and colloquial speech—often juxtaposing them in startling combination: "ain't cut drylongso / her songs so many-hued / hum some blues in technicolor / pick a violet guitar." The figure of the blues woman, a symbol of female creativity in much late-twentieth-century African American writing, is the force field in which these images are aligned. *Muse & Drudge* distills the complex and diverse kinds of knowledge that Mullen and her readers possess. No one reader will likely decode all of the poem's allusions. Read aloud, though, the poem makes music that is both dizzying and beautiful.

Sleeping with the Dictionary (2002) was a finalist for the National Book Award. Its title evokes Mullen's continued fascination with language—its elusive meanings and endless permutations. The title reflects as well her on-going interest in automatic writing, a process that relies on the workings of the unconscious. Such experimentalism is at the core of her poetry, but so too is the consciousness of African American tradition. Consequently, her poetry reflects crisscrossed influences and diverse poetic strategies. *Sleeping with the Dictionary* is both challenging and playful. It led reviewer Hoke S. Glover to conclude: "This is her art: to reconstruct, redefine and create out of splicing and stitching back together the pieces of meaning in language."

From Muse & Drudge

[Sapphire's lyre styles]

Sapphire's lyre[1] styles
plucked eyebrows

---

1. Stringed musical instrument.

bow lips and legs
whose lives are lonely too

my last nerve's lucid music   5
sure chewed up the juicy fruit
you must don't like my peaches
there's some left on the tree

you've had my thrills
a reefer a tub of gin   10
don't mess with me I'm evil
I'm in your sin

clipped bird eclipsed moon
soon no memory of you
no drive or desire survives   15
you flutter invisible still

                                                        1995

[country clothes hung on her all and sundry]

country clothes hung on her all and sundry
bolt of blue have mercy ink perfume
that snapping turtle pussy
won't let go until thunder comes

call me pessimistic   5
but I fall for sour pickles
sweets for the heat
awrr reet peteet patootie

shadows crossed her face
distanced by the medium   10
riffing through it
too poor to pay attention

sepia bronze mahogany
say froggy jump salty
jelly in a vise   15
buttered up broke ice

                                                        1995

[odds meeting on a bus]

odds meeting on a bus
the wrecked cognition
calling baby sister
what sounds like abuse

you have the girl you paid for   5
now lie on her
rocky garden
I build my church

a world for itself
where music comes to itself   10
three thirds of heaven
sure to be raining

on her own jive
player and instrument
all the way live   15
the way a woman might use it

1995

[why these blues come from us]

why these blues come from us
threadbare material soils
the original colored
pregnant with heavenly spirit

stop running from the gift   5
slow down to catch up with it
knots mend the string quilt
of kente[1] stripped when kin split

white covers of black material
dense fabric that obeys its own logic   10
shadows pieced together tears and all
unfurling sheets of bluish music

burning cloth in a public place
a crime against the state
raised the cost of free expression   15
smoke rose to offer a blessing

1995

[go on sister sing your song]

go on sister sing your song
lady redbone señora rubia[1]
took all day long
shampooing her nubia[2]

---

1. Banded material fabric, originally from Ghana.
1. Spanish equivalent of "lady redbone"; a woman with a reddish complexion.

2. Allusion to the historical region encompassing present-day southern Egypt and northern Sudan that was the site of an early "black" civilization.

she gets to the getting place   5
without or with him
must I holler when
you're giving me rhythm

members don't get weary
add some practice to your theory   10
she wants to know is it a men thing
or a him thing

wishing him luck
she gave him lemons to suck
told him please dear   15
improve your embouchure[3]

1995

[tomboy girl with cowboy boots]

tomboy girl with cowboy boots
takes coy bow in prom gown
your orange California suits
you riding into sundown

lifeguard at apartheid[1] park   5
rough, dirty, a little bit hard
broken blossom, poke a possum
park your quark in a hard aardvark

a wave goodbye, a girl
bred on the Queen Mary[2]   10
big legged gal
how come you so contrary

let the birds pick her
make a nest of her hair
let the rootman conjure   15
her to stare and stir air

1995

[sauce squandering sassy cook]

sauce squandering sassy cook
took a gander bumped a pinch of goose

3. The adjustment of a player's mouth to the mouthpiece of a wind instrument necessary to produce a musical tone.
1. The South African system of segregation of African peoples from people of European descent;
abolished in 1991. The term is also applied to other forms of racial separation.
2. The luxury cruise ship that made its maiden voyage in 1936 from Great Britain to the United States.

skinned squadroon cotillion[1] filled
uptown ballroom with squalid quadrille[2]

don't eat no crow, don't you know   5
ain't studying about taking low
if I do not care for chitterlings[3]
'tain't nobody's pidgin[4]

Hawkins[5] was talking
while I kept on walking   10
now I'm standing in my tracks
stepping back on my abstract

if not a don't at least a before
skin of a rubber chicken
these days I ignore   15
I'm less interested in

1995

[marry at a hotel, annul 'em]

marry at a hotel, annul 'em
nary hep male rose sullen
let alley roam, yell melon
dull normal fellow hammers omelette

divine sunrises   5
Osiris's irises
his splendid mistress
is his sis Isis[1]

creole[2] cocoa loca
crayon gumbo[3] boca   10
crayfish crayola
jumbo mocha-cola

warp maid fresh
fetish coquettish
a voyeur leers   15
at x-rated reels

1995

---

1. Formal ball, such as a coming-out dance.
2. Square dance, of French origin, usually performed by four couples.
3. A part of the small intestine of swine, usually served fried or in a sauce; considered by some a soul food delicacy.
4. Auxiliary language resulting from contact with two different languages that is primarily a simplified form of one of them.

5. Cold weather (black vernacular). The Hawk is the wind.
1. Goddess of fertility and nature in Egyptian mythology, who was sister and wife (or consort) of Osiris, god of the underworld.
2. French patois; blend of languages.
3. Okra plant or pods (Bantu); also a stew or thick soup, usually containing okra and chicken or seafood.

[precious cargo up crooked alleys]

precious cargo up crooked alleys
mules and drugs
blood on the lilies
of the fields

drive by lightning   5
let Mississippi rip
catch some sense
if you get my drift

watch out for the wrecking crew
they'll knock you into the dirt   10
your attic will be in your basement
and you'll know how it feels to be hurt

a planet struck by fragments
of a shattered comet
tell it after the break   15
save it for the next segment

                                                    1995

[with all that rope they gave us]

with all that rope they gave us
we pulled a mule out of the mud
dragging backwoods along
in our strong blackward progress

she just laughs   5
at weak-kneed scarecrow
as rainbow crow flies
over those ornery cornrows[1]

everlasting arms
too short for boxers   10
leaning meaning
signifying say what

Ethiopian breakdown
underbelly tussle
lose the facts just keep the hustle   15
leave your fine-tooth comb at home

                                                    1995

1. Braided hairstyle.

[the royal yellow sovereign]

the royal yellow sovereign
a fragile grass stained widow
black veins hammered gold
folded hands applaud above a budding

flat back green and easy   5
stacked for salt meat seasoning
some fat on that rack
might make her more tasty

a frayed one way slave's
sassy fast sashay   10
fastens her smashing essay
sad to say yes unless

your only tongue turns
me loose excuse my French
native speaker's opening act   15
a tight clench in the dark theater

[tom-tom can't catch]

tom-tom can't catch
a green cabin
ginger hebben[1] as
ancestor dances in Ashanti[2]

history written with whitening   5
darkened reels and jigs[3]
perform a mix of wiggle
slouch fright and essence of enigma

a tanned Miss Ann[4] startles
as the slaver screen's   10
queen of denial a bottle
brown as toast Egyptian

today's dread would awe
Topsy[5] undead her missionary
exposition in what Liberia[6]   15
could she find freedom to study her story

1995

---

1. Heaven.
2. A people of Ghana in West Africa.
3. Plantation dances; here used in a pejorative reference to African Americans.
4. White woman.

5. Young black female character in Harriet Beecher Stowe's *Uncle Tom's Cabin* (1852).
6. Nation in West Africa, founded by former slaves from the United States.

[massa had a yeller]

massa[1] had a yeller
macaroon a fetter
in his claptrap
of couth that shrub rat

sole driver rode   5
work hard on demand
he's the man
just as long as he can

outside MOMA[2]
on the sidewalk   10
Brancusi's[3] blonde
sells ersatz Benin[4] bronzes

Joe Moore never
worked for me—oh moaner
you shall be free   15
by degrees and pedigrees

1995

[cough drops prick thick]

cough drops prick thick
orange ink remover inside
people eating tuna fish
treat the architecture to pesticides

elaborate trash   5
disparaged rags
if I had my rage
I'd tear the blueprint up

chained thus together
voice held me hostage   10
divided our separate ways
with a knife against my throat

black dream you came
sleep chilled stuttering spirit
drunk on apple ripple   15
still in my dark unmarked grave

1995

---

1. I.e., master; a term used by slaves to refer to their male owners.
2. The Museum of Modern Art, located in New York City.
3. Reference to the sculpture *La Negresse Blonde* by Romanian abstract sculptor Constantin Brancusi (1876–1957).
4. Imitations of highly prized bronze sculptures from the African kingdom of Benin.

[ain't cut drylongso]

ain't cut drylongso[1]
her songs so many-hued
hum some blues in technicolor
pick a violet guitar

emblems of motion   5
muted amused mulish
there's more to love
where that came from

heavy model chevy of yore
old time religion   10
low down get real down
get right with Godzilla[2]

write on the vagina
of virgin lamb paper
mother times mirror   15
divided by daughter

1995

[soulless divaism]

soulless divaism
incog iconicism
a dead straight head
the spectrum wasted

dicty kickpleat[1]   5
beats deadbeats
hussified dozens
womanish like you groan

belly to belly
iron pot and cauldron   10
close to home
the core was melting

head maid in made out
house of swank kickback
placage conquer bind   15
lemon melon melange

1995

---

1. Ordinary or everyday (black vernacular).
2. Monster from the movies.

1. Fold of cloth in a woman's straight skirt.
"Dicty": bourgeois, stuck-up person.

[moon, whoever knew you]

moon, whoever knew you
had a high IQ until tonight
so high and mighty bright
poets salute you with haiku[1]

fixing her lips to sing   5
hip strutters ditty bop[2]
hand-me-down dance of ample
style stance and substance

black-eyed pearl
around the world girl   10
somebody's anybody's
yo-yo fulani[3]

occult iconic crow
solo mysterioso[4]
flying way out   15
on the other side of far

                                                    1995

1. Form of Japanese poetry, usually consisting of seventeen syllables.
2. To display hip mannerisms that are out of key with one's personality.
3. Play on words. The Fulani are a nomadic people in West Africa.
4. Title of a tune by jazz pianist Thelonious Monk (1917–1982).

ESSEX HEMPHILL
1957–1995

I n his poetry and prose collection *Ceremonies* (1992), Essex Hemphill wrote of the double alienation that occurs when a man tries to assert his identity as both a homosexual and an African American. His short essay "Loyalty" rejects the notion that he has sinned against "nature and the race" and renounces the silence that has been imposed on black gays with the following declaration:

> I speak for thousands, perhaps hundreds of thousands of men who live and die in the shadows of secrets, unable to speak of the love that helps them endure and contribute to the race. Their ordinary kisses, stolen or shared behind facades of heroic achievement, their kisses of sweet spit and loyalty are scrubbed away by the propaganda makers of the race, the "Talented Tenth" who would just as soon have us believe Black people can fly, rather than reveal that Black men have been longing to kiss one another, and have done so, for centuries.

By aggressively insisting on the truth, Hemphill forced awareness of a presence that a homophobic society would rather ignore. Although he was known primarily as a poet, his compelling prose as well as his poetry gained him increasing recognition and popularity in the early 1990s.

Born on April 16, 1957, in Chicago, Hemphill was reared in a southeast Washington, D.C., neighborhood, which he described as "a ghetto that had not yet suffered the fatal wounds and injuries caused by drugs and Black-on-Black crime." After graduating from high school in 1975, Hemphill pursued his interests in English and journalism at the University of Maryland. Later, he studied English at the University of the District of Columbia.

Hemphill's *Earth Life,* a chapbook, was published in 1985, with *Conditions,* his second collection, following in 1986. He edited and contributed to *Brother to Brother: New Writings by Black Gay Men* (1991), an anthology initiated by the late Joseph Fairchild Beam; the volume won the American Library Association's 1993 Gay and Lesbian Book Award. During the early 1990s, Hemphill participated in several gay black film projects, including *Looking for Langston, Out of the Shadows,* and *Tongues Untied. Ceremonies* was his first large collection and included both new work and pieces that had been seen in anthologies such as *In the Life, Men & Intimacy,* and *Gay and Lesbian Poetry in Our Time.*

Fueling Hemphill's work was his scorn for "watered-down versions of Black life in America." Instead, Hemphill confronted his reader with "the ass-splitting truth," thereby hoping to reestablish, uncloseted, his connection to the larger community. Although his style in both poetry and prose can be blunt, verging on the violent, Hemphill's intent was not to sever ties with the straight world but rather to come home to a world where the mothers of gay men understand this lesson: "Do not feel shame for how I live / I chose this tribe / of warriors and outlaws." His powerful language and images construct an alternative to the sad, doomed stereotype of gay life. In Hemphill's new, erotic world, men transform old institutions to fit their needs, as in "American Wedding," where "Everytime we kiss / we confirm the new world coming."

In recognition of his achievements, Hemphill became an artist in residence at the Getty Museum in Los Angeles in 1993. That same year, he won the Gregory Kolovakos award for AIDS writing.

Essex Hemphill died on November 4, 1995. To recognize his accomplishments, members of the Gay Men of African Descent (GMAD) and Black Nations / Queer Nations declared December 10, 1995, as the National Day of Remembrance. Memorials were held throughout the United States acknowledging Hemphill as a pioneer in the literary arts as they related to gay and lesbian peoples throughout the world.

FROM CONDITIONS

XXI

You judge a woman
by the length of her skirt,
by the way she walks,
talks, looks, and acts;
by the color of her skin you judge   5
and will call her "bitch!"
"Black bitch!"
if she doesn't answer your:
"Hey baby, whatcha gonna say
to a man."   10

You judge a woman
by the job she holds,
by the number of children she's had,
by the number of digits on her check;
by the many men she may have lain with   15
and wonder what jive murphy[1]
you'll run on her this time.

You tell a woman
every poetic love line
you can think of,   20
then like the desperate needle
of a strung out junkie
you plunge into her veins,
travel wild through her blood,
confuse her mind, make her hate   25
and be cold to the men to come,
destroying the thread of calm
she held.

You judge a woman
by what she can do for you alone   30
but there's no need
for slaves to have slaves.

You judge a woman
by impressions you think you've made.
Ask and she gives,   35
take without asking,
beat on her and she'll obey,
throw her name up and down the streets
like some loose whistle—
knowing her neighbors will talk.   40
Her friends will chew her name.
Her family's blood will run loose
like a broken creek.
And when you're gone,
a woman is left   45
healing her wounds alone.
But we so called men,
we so called brothers
wonder why it's so hard
to love *our* women   50
when we're about loving them
the way america
loves us.

1986

---

1. Pick-up lines (slang), specifically used to talk someone into a sexual encounter.

XXII

If there were seven blind men
one of them unable to hear
would be father.
He would be the one
promising to deliver   5
what never arrives.
He is the bridge
which on one side
I stand feeling doomed
to never forgive him   10
for the violence in our past,
while on the other side
he vigorously waves to me
to cross over,
but he doesn't know   15
the bridge has fallen through.

If there were seven blind men
the deaf one would be father.
The mute, his son.

                                                    1986

XXIV

In america
I place my ring
on your cock
where it belongs.
No horsemen   5
bearing terror,
no soldiers of doom
will swoop in
and sweep us apart.
They're too busy   10
looting the land
to watch us.
They don't know
we need each other
critically.   15
They expect us to call in sick,
watch television all night,
die by our own hands.
They don't know
we are becoming powerful.   20
Everytime we kiss
we confirm the new world coming.

What the rose whispers
before blooming

I vow to you.   25
I give you my heart,
a safe house.
I give you promises other than
milk, honey, liberty.
I assume you will always   30
be a free man with a dream.
In america,
place your ring
on my cock
where it belongs.   35
Long may we live
to free this dream.

1986

CARYL PHILLIPS
b. 1958

Informed by the fragmented histories of Africans in the Caribbean, Europe, the United States, and on the African continent, Caryl Phillips's novels chart journeys in the past and present across what he calls "the Atlantic Sound." Those journeys produce complex linguistic and cultural negotiations: multiple voices speak through his texts; parents and children embrace conflicting traditions. Phillips's novels take on innovative forms that approximate the ruptures and disjunctures inherent in the histories they reimagine. Yet part of the pleasure of his writing is its investment in character. If, he says, the idea for a piece comes first, "it remains merely an idea until I've got a character. When I have a character, then it becomes the reality." What makes his mappings of the transatlantic passages—from Africa to the Caribbean to Europe and back to the Caribbean and the United States—so memorable is the reader's intimate knowledge of the travelers.

Born on the West Indian island of St. Kitts, Phillips was taken as an infant to Great Britain, where his parents settled in the northern industrial city of Leeds. Only as a student at Oxford did Phillips become aware of Caribbean culture and the African diaspora that spawned it. In 1976 racial unrest swept Britain, as the children of immigrants challenged their marginal position in British society. Phillips began to read African American literature as voraciously as he had been reading Russian writing. He changed his major from psychology to English. Among the influences he cites are Richard Wright, James Baldwin, Toni Morrison, Henrik Ibsen, William Faulkner, Kamau Braithwaite, and Derek Walcott. Initially drawn to the theater, Phillips wrote plays and scripts for radio and television before embarking on a remarkably successful literary career. He has subsequently lived in London and St. Kitts. Since 1998 he has lived in New York City; he now teaches at Yale University.

Phillips describes his first two novels, *The Final Passage* (1985) and *A State of Independence* (1986), as having been "written out of a sense of elation at having 'rediscovered' the Caribbean" after identifying himself culturally as a Briton. In between his novels, Phillips published *The European Tribe* (1987), a travel narrative in which he offered commentary on European societies with a decided lack of deference. His third novel, *Higher Ground* (1989), is set partly in Africa. Already well respected in Britain, Phillips came to the attention of U.S. audiences with the publication of *Cambridge* (1991). The novel chronicles the story of Emily, a nineteenth-century English woman who escapes an arranged marriage by traveling to her father's West Indian plantation, where she crosses paths with Cambridge, a slave on trial for killing the plantation overseer. The text adheres to the conventions of the Victorian novel: it combines entries from Emily's diary and Cambridge's first-person narrative recounting his own extensive travels to tell its story. The novel re-creates the historically correct tone and syntax for their voices as it creates a hybrid that could have been produced only in the late twentieth century.

In *Crossing the River* (1993), Phillips states, he "wanted to make a connection between the African world which was left behind and the diasporan world which people had entered once they crossed the water." He "wanted to make an affirmative connection, not a connection based upon exploitation or suffering or misery, but a connection based upon a kind of survival." The novel begins with the desperate decision of an African father to sell his three children into slavery. Encompassing 250 years of history, *Crossing the River* narrates the separate experiences of the children and their descendants. *The Nature of Blood* (1997) continues the pattern of juxtaposing narratives, this time between Jews in fifteenth-century and twentieth-century Europe. In *The Atlantic Sound* (2000), a travel narrative, Phillips retraces the journey his parents made by ship to England, then reenacts the Middle Passage of his ancestors. He draws sharp vignettes of people he meets in Liverpool, Charleston, and Accra and writes tellingly of the histories that shaped their present.

In the collection of essays *A New World Order* (2001), Phillips considers how Caribbean immigrants have redefined the national identity of the United Kingdom. This idea takes fictional form in the novel *In the Falling Snow* (2009), which centers on the conflict between an immigrant father and his black British son. *Dancing in the Dark* (2005) fictionalizes the lives of early twentieth-century performers George Walker and Bert Williams, whose plays *Abyssinia* and *In Dahomey* were produced on Broadway. A Caribbean immigrant, Williams perfected the persona of the "stage darky." The novel invents interior lives for these figures and explores themes of ethnic, racial, and sexual identity.

In the section of *Crossing the River* printed here, the daughter who was sold to traders in Africa reaches the end of her life's journey. She has planned to travel to California; as yet she has made her way only as far as the Colorado Territory. The setting is unusual for Phillips, but the themes of homelessness, separation, and longing are typical. Through the character of Martha, he pays homage to Morrison by evoking Sethe, the unforgettable protagonist of *Beloved*.

From Crossing the River

II. West

Curling herself into a tight fist against the cold, Martha huddled in the doorway and wondered if tonight she might see snow. Beautiful. Lifting her eyes without lifting up her head, she stared at the wide black sky that would once more be her companion. White snow, come quickly. A tall man in a long overcoat, and with a freshly trimmed beard, chin tucked into his chest, looked down at her as he walked by. For a moment she worried that he might spit, but he did not. So this was Colorado Territory, a place she had crossed prairie and desert to reach. Hoping to pass through it quickly, not believing that she would fall over foolish like a lame mule. Old woman. They had set her down and continued on to California. She hacked violently. Through some atavistic mist, Martha peered back east, beyond Kansas, back beyond her motherhood, her teen years, her arrival in Virginia, to a smooth white beach where a trembling girl waited with two boys and a man. Standing off, a ship. Her journey had been a long one. But now the sun had set. Her course was run. *Father, why hast thou forsaken me?*[1]

Lucy would be waiting for her in California, for it was she who had persuaded Martha Randolph that there were colored folks living on both sides of the mountains now. Living. According to Lucy, colored folks of all ages and backgrounds, of all classes and colors, were looking to the coast. Lucy's man had told her, and Lucy in turn had told Martha. Girl, you sure? Apparently, these days colored folks were not heading west prospecting for no gold, they were just prospecting for a new life without having to pay no heed to the white man and his ways. Prospecting for a place where things were a little better than bad, and where you weren't always looking over your shoulder and wondering when somebody was going to do you wrong. Prospecting for a place where your name wasn't 'boy' or 'aunty', and where you could be a part of this country without feeling like you wasn't really a part. Lucy had left behind a letter for her long-time friend, practically begging her to come out west and join her and her man in San Francisco. It would make the both of us happy. And although Martha still had some trouble figuring out words and such, she could make out the sense in Lucy's letter, and she reckoned that's just what she was going to do. Pioneer. She was going to stop her scrubbing and washing. Age was getting the better of her now, and arthritis had a stern hand on all parts of her body. She would pioneer west. Martha pulled her knees up towards her and stretched out a hand to adjust the rags around her feet. She blocked up the holes where the wind was whistling through. Stop. The doorway protected her on three sides, and she felt sure that she should be able to sleep here without disturbing anyone. Just leave me be. But she felt strangely beyond sleep. As though her body were sliding carelessly towards a kind of sleep. Like when she lost Eliza Mae. Moma. Moma.

Martha unglued her eyes and stared up into the woman's face. 'Do you have any folks?' It had started to snow now. Early snow, huge, soft snowflakes spinning down out of the clear, black sky. 'You must be cold.' It was dark and, the woman aside, there was nobody else in sight. When they had set her down here, they had told her that this was Main Street, as though this information freed them of any responsibility. But she did not blame them. A few saloons, a restaurant, a blacksmith, a rooming house or two, indeed this was Main Street. 'I have a small cabin where you can stay the night.' Martha looked again at the woman who stood before her in a black coat, with a thick shawl thrown idly across her shoulders and a hat fastened tightly to her head. Perhaps this woman had bought her daughter? Was Eliza Mae living here in Colorado Territory? There was no reason to go clear to California if Eliza Mae were here in Colorado Territory. Eliza Mae returned to her? 'Can you get up?' The woman stretched out her gloved hand and Martha stared hard at it. Eliza Mae was gone. This hand could no more lead her back to her daughter than it could lead Martha back to her own youthful self. A small cabin. This woman was offering her some place with a roof,

---

1. Last words spoken by Christ on the Cross (Matthew 27.46).

and maybe even a little heating. Martha closed her eyes. After countless years of journeying, the hand was both insult and salvation, but the woman was not to know this. 'Please, take my hand. I'm not here to harm you. I just want to help. Truly.' Martha uncurled her fingers and set them against the woman's hide-bound hand. The woman felt neither warm nor cold. 'Can you stand by yourself?' Inside of herself, Martha laughed. Can this woman not see that they abandoned me? At least they had shown some charity and not discarded her upon the plains. But stand by herself? Martha Randolph. Squatting like a filthy bag of bones. Watching the snow. Don't know nobody in these parts. Barely recognizing herself. No ma'am, she thought. I doubt if I'll ever be able to stand by myself again. But no matter. I done enough standing by myself to last most folks three or four lifetimes. Ain't nothing shameful in resting now. No ma'am, nothing shameful at all. She squeezed. The woman's hand squeezed back. 'Can you stand by yourself?' Martha shook her head.

I look into his eyes, but his stare is constant and frightens me. He shows no emotion. 'Lucas?' He turns from me and scrapes the wooden chair across the floor. He sits heavily upon it. He lifts his hands to his head and buries his face in his cupped and calloused palms. Eliza Mae runs to me and clutches the hem of my dress. The light in the lamp jumps and the room sways, first one way and then the next. I pull Eliza Mae towards me and hide her small body in the folds of my dress. Lucas looks up. He opens his mouth to speak. His face is tired, older than his thirty-five years. The weight of yet another day in the field sits heavily upon him. But not just this. I run my hand across Eliza Mae's matted hair. On Sunday I will pull the comb through the knots and she will scream. Outside, I can hear the crickets, their shrill voices snapping, like twigs being broken from a tree. 'Master dead.' Eliza Mae looks from me to her father, then back to me. Poor child, she does not understand. 'Lucas, we going to be sold?' Lucas lowers his eyes.

The sun is at its highest point. The overseer is looking across at me, so again I bend down and start to pick. Already I have the hands of a woman twice my age, the skin beaten, bloodied and bruised, like worn-out leather. The overseer rides his horse towards me, its legs stepping high, prancing, almost dancing. He looks down at me, the sun behind him, framing his head, forming a halo. He raises his whip and brings it down on my arm. I don't hear the words that fall from his mouth. I simply think, Master dead. What now? I bend down and again I start to pick. I can still feel his eyes upon me. And the sun. And now the horse is turning. It dances away from me.

I stand with the rest of the Virginia property. Master's nephew, a banker from Washington, is now our new master. He has no interest in plantation life. He holds a handkerchief to his face and looks on with detachment. Everything must be sold. The lawyer grabs the iron-throated bell and summons the people to attention. Then the auctioneer slaps his gavel against a block of wood. I fall to my knees and take Eliza Mae in my arms. I did not suckle this child at the breast, nor did I cradle her in my arms and shower her with what love I have, to see her taken away from me. As the auctioneer begins to bellow, I look into Eliza Mae's face. He is calling out the date, the place, the time. Master would never have sold any of us. I tell this to my terrified child. Slaves. Farm animals. Household furniture. Farm tools. We are to be sold in this order. I watch as Lucas soaks a cloth in cold water. He comforts me and places it first on my forehead, and then on that of his child. Last night he came to me, his eyes grown red with drink. He confessed that death would be easier. This way we are always going to be wondering. Always worrying. His voice broke and he choked back the remaining words. Then he took me in the circle of his arms and laid me down. Until the old horn blew to mark the start of a new day.

Farmers have come from all over the county. A fun-seeking crowd, ready for haggling, but amongst them I see the lean-faced men. The traders, with their trigger-happy minds, their mouths tight and bitter. I try not to look into anybody's eyes. The auctioneer is dressed formally. Dark vest, colorful cutaway coat.[2] He continues to yell. Now, as he does so, he motions towards us with his gavel. Then he slaps this instrument against the wooden block with a thud. Now again he gestures towards us. My throat is dry. Eliza Mae moves restlessly, so I take her hand. She cries. I pinch her to quiet her. I am sorry, but it is for her own good. The auctioneer beckons forward the traders. They look firstly at the men. A trader prods Lucas's biceps with a stick. If a trader buys a man, it is down the river. To die. That much we all know. The families in need of domestics, or the farmers in need of breeding wenches, they look across at us and wait their turn. I am too old for breeding. They do not know that I would also disappoint. My Eliza Mae holds on to me, but it will be to no avail. She will be a prime purchase. And on her own she stands a better chance of a fine family. I want to tell her this, to encourage her to let go, but I have not the heart. I look on. The auctioneer cries to the heavens. A band strikes up. A troupe of minstrels begins to dance. Soon the bidding will begin. 'Moma.' Eliza Mae whispers the word over and over again, as though this were the only word she possessed. This one word. This word only.

Martha leaned against the woman and peered into the small, dark room. Still cold. Through the half-light, she saw the single bed, the mattress rolled back and revealing an ugly grid of rusty wire. Then she felt the woman's gentle touch guiding her across the room and into a hard-backed wooden chair. Like a child. Martha sat and watched as the woman first lit the lamp and then quickly made up the bed, stretching a clean sheet tight like a drumskin across its length and breadth. Having done so, she helped Martha the two paces across the room and set her down to rest upon the corner of the bed. Martha's right eye was clouding over, but she could make out the woman's motions as she now attempted to fire some life into the pot-bellied stove. She failed, and bestowed a sad smile upon Martha. Girl, don't worry. Don't worry yourself. The woman reached for the pitcher and poured a glass of water. 'Here, take it and drink. Are you cold?' Martha dragged her tongue around her swollen lips. Then she took the water and held the glass between both hands. She swallowed deeply, and as she did so the woman knelt and began to remove the wet rags that swaddled Martha's feet. No. Please. Martha closed her eyes.

She could only once remember being this cold. That was on that miserable December day that she had crossed the Missouri, riding in the back of the Hoffmans' open wagon. When they arrived on the western shore, Martha, by now gaunt and tired, having travelled clear from Virginia with only the briefest of stops, stepped down into the iciness that was a Kansas winter. Did they buy me to kill me? All her belongings dangled in a bundle that she held in one hand. She no longer possessed either a husband or a daughter, but her memory of their loss was clear. She remembered the disdainful posture of Master's nephew, and the booming voice of the auctioneer. She remembered the southern ladies in their white cotton sun bonnets and long-sleeved dresses, and the poorer farmers who hoped to find a bargain, their bony mules hitched to lame carriages. The trader who had prodded Lucas with a stick bought him for a princely sum. But Martha held on to some hope, for Lucas was a man who never failed to make friends with dogs. He charmed them with his dark, gentle voice. Lucas was not a man to let his body fetch up in flinty, lonely ground. Eliza Mae was sold after Martha. The Hoffmans could no doubt detect in their purchase a powerful feeling towards this girl, so they had bundled Martha into their wagon and left quickly. They had made their transaction, and the festivities would run their natural course without them. Goodbye, everybody. Once they had passed out of sight, the woman offered Martha a lace handkerchief, which Martha ignored.

Within the year, the Hoffmans had decided to sell up and leave Virginia. They had decided to settle outside of the city of Kansas, in a part of the country which was young and promising for pioneers. Good roads provided easy access to the back country, and new arrivants were permitted to purchase land from the United States government at a cost of two dollars an acre. Mr Eugene Hoffman intended to do a little farming on his five-acre homestead, and he had ambitions of building up a herd of forty cattle and a dozen or so hogs. Cleo Hoffman, her training having prepared her for a life of teaching music, mainly the piano, was equally optimistic. Deeply religious people, they were sadly without children. In this Kansas, Martha sometimes heard voices. Perhaps there was a God. Perhaps not. She found herself assaulted by loneliness, and drifting into middle age without a family. Voices from the past. Some she recognized. Some she did not. But, nevertheless, she listened. Recognizing her despair, Mr and Mrs Hoffman took Martha with them to a four-day revival by the river, where a dedicated young circuit rider named Wilson attempted to cast light in on Martha's dark soul. Satan be gone. The young evangelist preached with all his might, but Martha could find no solace in religion, and was unable to sympathize with the sufferings of the son of God when set against her own private misery. She stared at the Kansas sky. The shield of the moon shone brightly. Still she heard voices. Never again would the Hoffmans mention their God to Martha.

And then one morning, Mr Hoffman called the graying Martha to him. She knew this would eventually happen, for the crops were not selling, and once again the cattle had come back from market. A merciful market where nothing would sell. Martha had overheard them arguing with each other at the dinner table. Mr Hoffman looked at Martha, and then down at his hands which were folded in front of him. 'We have to go west, Martha. To where there is work for us. Kansas is still too young.' He paused. 'We are going to California, but we shall have to sell you back across the river in order that we can make this journey.' Martha's heart fell like a stone. No. 'We shall do all that we can to ensure that you are rewarded with good Christian owners.' No. He continued to speak, but Martha did not hear a word he uttered. Across the river to Hell. Eventually she asked, 'When?' She was unable to tell whether she had cut him off by speaking. Mr Hoffman cleared his throat. 'Next week, Martha.' He paused and looked up at her. 'I'm sorry.' This appeared to be his way of apologizing and dismissing her at the same time. It was possible that he was sorry. For himself. Martha was not sure if she should or could leave. Then Mr Hoffman climbed to his feet. 'You can leave, Martha.'

That night, Martha packed her bundle and left the house. For where, she was not sure (don't care where), being concerned only with heading west (going west), away from the big river (away from Hell), and avoiding nigger traders who would gladly sell her back over the border and into Missouri. The dark night spread before her, but behind the drifting clouds she knew the sky was heavy with stars. (Feeling good.) And then Martha heard the barking of dogs, and she tumbled into a ditch. (Lord, give me Lucas's voice.) She waited but heard nothing, only silence. (Thank you.) Eventually, Martha climbed to her feet and began to run. (Like the wind, girl.) Never again would she stand on an auction block. (Never.) Never again would she be renamed. (Never.) Never again would she belong to anybody. (No sir, never.) Martha looked over her shoulders as she ran. (Like the wind, girl.) And then, later, she saw dawn announcing its bold self, and a breathless Martha stopped to rest beneath a huge willow tree. (Don't nobody own me now.) She looked up, and through the thicket of branches she saw the morning star throbbing in the sky. As though recklessly attempting to preserve its life into the heart of a new day.

The woman poured Martha another glass of water, which Martha held tightly, as though trying to pull some heat from the wet glass. Still cold. She stared at Martha, who noticed now that this woman had the defensive, watchful eyes of a person who had never lost control of herself. The woman loosened her shawl, revealing a gold necklace at her throat. Still cold. 'Should I leave you now?' Beneath the hat, Martha could detect a shock of gray hair, but she was unclear as to whether or not the woman was trying to conceal it. Then somebody moved outside, their shadow darkening the line of light at the bottom of the closed door, their weight firing the floorboards. No. Martha's breath ran backwards into her body. For a moment, she was unsure if she would ever have the power to expel it and then, against her will, she burst in a quiet sigh. Eliza Mae. Come back for her? 'Shall I leave you now?' 'No.' Martha released the word, without quite understanding why she had done so. Then, as the woman sat on the edge of the mattress, and Martha felt the bed lurch beneath her, she regretted the generosity of her invitation. The woman was making herself at home.

I put down the plates in front of these men and stand back. They do not take their eyes from me. 'Thank you, ma'am.' The one with the blue eyes speaks quietly. The other two are in his shadow. They all dress alike in fancy attire; silver spurs, buckskin pants, and hats trimmed with rattlesnake skin. These three unshaven men, who sit uncomfortably in my restaurant. My other customers have left. They have driven away my customers. The truth is, there was only one other customer. These days, I am lucky to set eyes on more than six or seven a day. Colored men don't appear to be riding the trail like they used to. Coming in here with their kidneys and lungs all ruined, spitting blood, arms and legs broken over and over. Even the toughest of them lasted only a few years, but now it looks like their day is done. 'Anything else I can get you?' They still haven't touched their food.

'When's he due back, ma'am?' I run my hands down the front of my dress. They are more worn than ever, not just from the cooking, but from the washing and cleaning. It is almost ten years now since I arrived in Dodge[3] and set up laundering clothes, then cooking some, then doing both when Lucy agreed to come in and help me out. 'He'll be back at dusk.' My mind turns to Lucy in the back. Waiting for me. Needing my help. We have a large order of washing needs finishing up before morning. 'Dusk?' He lets the word fall gently from his lips, as though he were the first man to coin such a term. I nod.

There used to be four of them when they last came up the trail. I don't remember the fourth man, but I know that there used to be a fourth. They arrived as four, but left as three. This time they have arrived as three and will leave as three. They tried to cheat Chester while playing poker in the saloon bar, but Chester, in his gentle manner, sneaked a little piece of chewing tobacco into his mouth and pointed up their ways. According to the sheriff, the fourth man, the scoundrel amongst them, he drew the first gun. The sheriff let Chester go. Gunplay is second nature to Chester. Their food is getting cold. One man picks up his fork and chases the potatoes through the gravy and around the plate a little. I know he wants to eat. He is waiting for the signal with mounting hunger. I tell the man that I have to go out back now, but he simply stares at me with those blue eyes. I tell him that I have clothes to wash. I offer him this information almost as a gift. He looks across at his friends, who can barely restrain themselves. They want to eat. He waves a dismissive hand in my face. Then, as though it is not important, he reaches into his pocket and throws a few bills on to the table top. He tells me that they will leave when they have finished. That they will wait out front for Chester.

I lift the dripping pile of clothes out of the boiler and drop them into the tub. I feel Lucy's eyes upon me, but I will not turn to face her. I am hot. I wipe my brow with the sleeve of my dress, and then again I bend over and try to squeeze more water from the shirts. She puts her hand on my shoulder, this woman who has been both friend and sister to me. She puts her hand on my shoulder and presses. She says nothing, and I still do not turn around. I continue to knead the clothes between my tired fingers. 'Martha,' she begins. 'Martha, child.' I turn to look at her. I drop the clothes and wrap my wet arms around her, and she pulls me close. I begin to sob. She says, 'You must go to Chester and warn him.' I listen to her, but we both know that it is too late. Even as she insists that I should leave now, she clasps me tighter.

I stand in the street. I see him in the distance, the dust clouding slowly around him as his horse, frame bent, head low, ambles out of the sunset and into the shadow that marks the beginning of the street. And they see him too. All three of them. They jump down from the rail. Lucy stands in the open doorway and looks on. I had only been in Dodge a few weeks when he came to me with his clothes to be laundered. He came back every Tuesday afternoon, as regular as sunset, but he barely spoke. Tipped his hat, always called me 'ma'am', never asked me for no money, or no credit, or no nothing. And then one day he told me that his name was Chester, that he was a wrangler on a ranch just outside of Dodge, that nobody could *top off*

---

3. Dodge City, Kansas, frontier town founded in 1871.

a bad horse like him, that he could smell loneliness like a buffalo could smell water. I told him, I didn't need no help, I just needed some companionship, that's all. He looked at me with a broad, knowing look, a look that could charm the gold out of a man's teeth, and asked if I wanted to move in with him into his store. I asked him what he sold, and he told me that he didn't sell a 'damn thing', but, there was plenty of room if I wanted to open up a business. He said that if we were going to prospect for happiness together, then he figured we ought to try and make a little money too. I told Chester that I didn't think I could make him no babies no more. He smiled and said, 'I got babies some place that I ain't been no kind of father to. Figure it's best if I don't bother with no more baby-making.' He paused. 'I guess you noticed I ain't one to dress to impress the local belles.' Then he laughed some, till the tears streamed down his sweet chocolate face. That same afternoon, I pulled off my apron, pulled on a clean, calico dress, pinned down my hair with a bandana, and moved everything to Chester's place, which turned out to be a proper store. Chester said he won it in a card game from a storekeeper who had headed south to Mexico with everything he owned in his pockets. He claimed that, to begin with, some folks didn't take to the idea of a colored owning decent property, but by and by people let him be. He sat amongst the lumber stores, merchants, watchmakers, carpenters, blacksmiths, mechanics, medical men and lawyers, trading nothing.

I soon set up in business concocting stews and soups for weary, half-starved colored men who had long since spent their trail rations. Vegetables and livestock, grown and raised in and around Dodge, appeared on the market. Beans, potatoes and onions at twenty-five cents a pound, beef at quarter the price, and large, plump turkeys at less than two dollars a piece. War came and war went and, almost unnoticed, the Union toppled. For a week or so, all lines were forgotten as Dodge toasted the victors in liquor until most folks could no longer hold a glass. I was free now, but it was difficult to tell what difference being free was making to my life. I was just doing the same things like before, only I was more contented, not on account of no emancipation proclamation, but on account of my Chester. I look down the street and see him coming yet closer, his shoulders square, his head held high. For ten long years, this man has made me happy. For ten long years, this man has made me forget—and that's a gift from above. I never thought anybody could give me so much love, even without trying, without appearing to make any effort, without raising no dust about it. Just steering and roping, and whatever manner of business he felt like seeing to in the days, watching the sunset at dusk, and a little whiskey and cards at night. Always there when I needed him. I glance at Lucy, whose face is a picture of fear. I want to tell her, 'Don't worry, Lucy.' And then the shots ring out and Chester slumps from the saddle, but his foot gets caught up in the stirrup. His horse stops and lets Chester fall respectfully to the ground. Three brave men with pistols smoking, and Lucy screaming.

Lucy brings the candle to my room and sits on a wicker chair. She has not yet stopped crying. I have not begun. 'We can go up to Leavenworth,[4] she says. 'I hear that the colored troops in the Fort are always looking for somebody to wash and clean for them. And plenty of colored folks still figuring

4. I.e., Fort Leavenworth, Kansas; an army post.

to come across the Missouri and into Kansas.' I stare back at her, but say nothing. 'We can't stay here, Martha.' I know this. I know that I will never again be happy in fast-loving, high-speeding Dodge. Not without Chester. And the restaurant. 'We can take our business to Leavenworth, establish a laundry.' I nod in agreement. Then I ask her. 'Lucy,' I say, 'did I ever tell you that I had a daughter?' She looks back at me in astonishment.

Again she asked Martha if she was cold, and this time Martha could not hold back the sad confession that, despite this woman's efforts, her body remained numb. Too late. The woman smiled, then stood and stoked at the stove, but her gesture was one of idle hope. Too late. On top of the stove sat a great iron kettle which reminded Martha of the one back east, twenty-five years ago, in Virginia, which rang like a bell when you struck it. And if you put the tips of your fingers against it, you could feel the black metal still humming long after the kettle had ceased its song. Martha used to catch rainwater in it, the same rainwater with which she would wash Eliza Mae's matted hair. Keep still, girl. Such misery in one life. She looked at the palms of her hands where the darker skin had now bled into the lighter, and she wondered if freedom was more important than love, and indeed if love was at all possible without somebody taking it from her. Her tired mind swelled and surged with these difficult thoughts, until it pained her to think. The woman finally stopped her stoking. Martha could feel the tears welling up behind her eyes. 'Can I help?' No, you must go. 'Are you all right?' No. Please go. 'I'm sorry about the stove.' No. No. No. Martha stifled a sob.

It seemed another age now, although in truth it was only two months ago that Lucy, her hair in a wrap, had come to her in the small, two-roomed cabin that they shared, and broken the news of her impending marriage. It had been a dark night, the solitary light from a candle teasing the two friends with the twin possibilities of both warmth and security. Not that Lucy's news came as any surprise to Martha, for she had long been aware of her friend's feelings for the colored man from the dry goods store. Tubs and boilers no longer had a hold on Lucy's mind, and now she would be escaping them by marrying this man who had built himself a storey and a half house from the profits of selling that boom-town, sure-fire money-maker at a dollar a pound: nails. Martha took Lucy's hands in her own, and told her that she was pleased, and that Lucy must not, under any circumstances, worry over her. With this said, she encouraged Lucy to begin packing if she was going to leave, as planned, in the morning. Lucy levered herself out of her chair and began to address herself to the tasks at hand, while an ailing Martha sat basking in the glow of the candle and watched her. These days, Martha's old body was overburdened, and seldom did she pass an afternoon without a few cat-naps. By evening her feet and ankles were so swollen that she had to use both hands to pull off her shoes, and her undergarments now grew strangely tight during the days, her underskirt band often cutting into her waist. She desperately needed to rest, but she had determined that Lucy must never see the evidence of her malaise. And certainly not now. Lucy was to leave with a clear conscience, but not before Martha had herded her into the picture-making man's studio and ordered her to sit still. She watched her friend as she continued to gather up her few belongings, and Martha began to laugh quietly to herself.

A week later, the man came into the cabin outhouse, his arms burdened down with a bundle of heavy flannel shirts and coarse pants that needed laundering. Such visits were becoming less common, for either men seemed to be getting accustomed to giving their own garments the soap and water treatment, or Martha had serious competition from some place that she had not, as yet, heard about. The conversation that he struck up with Martha was a generous one, in that he desired to know if she could possibly manage this load by herself. Well, excuse me, mister. Was there anybody else in town to whom he might turn? Feigning ignorance of what he might be implying, Martha took the clothes and assured him that they would be ready for him whenever he needed them. This was just as well, he said, for he would soon be leaving for California with a group of colored pioneers. He informed her of this fact as though it were something that one ought to be proud of, and with this announcement delivered, he tipped his hat and wished her good day. After he left, Martha thought long and hard about her own prospects. The many years of her life with Lucy in this two-roomed cabin were now at an end, and although this Leavenworth had suited her, despite its numerous saloons, billiard parlors and houses of joy, Martha felt that she must leave. Not that Leavenworth was either violent or dangerous. In fact, the townsmen had established a liking for law and order, and introduced codes that were rigidly enforced by deputies and marshals, which meant that in this town the fast gun was not the law. But although Leavenworth was free of the turbulence of Dodge, and in spite of the fact that her years here had been peaceful, if somewhat lonely, Martha had a strange notion that she, too, must become a part of the colored exodus that was heading west. Lucy had left behind a letter, not so much inviting Martha to come out and join her and her future husband in San Francisco, but begging her to do so. Martha unfolded the square of paper and decided to look it over one more time. Then, when she had finished, she blew out the lamp and sat quietly in the dark. Eliza Mae was once again back in her mind, not that her lost child had ever truly vanished. Perhaps her girl-child had pioneered west?

When, some days later, the man returned for his clean and well-ironed garments, Martha eyeballed him directly and announced that she, too, would be coming along. She deliberately did not ask, but he, with equal deliberation, did not respond. So once again, Martha informed him of her decision, and only now did he put down the clothes and begin to explain why this would not be possible. He advised Martha that this was to be a long and difficult journey, with at least twenty wagons, and they would have to cope with what the Indians called 'crazy weather', both blizzards and heat. Martha simply stared back at the man, forcing him to continue. 'We'll be following stream beds most of the way, but you never know.' He shrugged his shoulders. 'And we'll likely be called upon to walk, for the wagons will use every ounce of space for food, water, tools, and so on.' Martha found herself borrowing courage from this conversation, the way she had seen some men do from tequila. 'My role will be to cook for you,' she said. 'I won't be a burden, but I don't have no savings.' She went on, assuring him that she knew about wild and dangerous country, and had many times seen horses and oxen shot that had broken their legs, and watched as the trailriders made soup out of their hides and bones. She claimed that she had been aboard wagons that had fallen clean apart, that she knew sagebrush and sidewinders[5] like they were her kin, and the shifting sands and whirling dust of the

5. Small desert rattlesnakes.

cactus-shrouded world would suit her just dandy. 'I'm afraid of nothing,' said Martha, 'least of all Indians or hard times. Colored folks generally got to be obligated to white folks to get clear to California, but you colored pioneers are offering me a chance. You let me work my fare out and I'll cook, wash clothes, and powerfully nurse to the sick and ailing. And I ain't fussy about sleeping on no bare ground. I done it plenty of times before, had the beaten hardness of the earth for a bed and the sky for covering.' The man looked blankly at her, but Martha, anxious that she should not be fooled, pressed on and asked after him when they proposed leaving. 'The day after tomorrow,' he said, his voice low, his expression now one of confusion. 'I'll be ready,' said Martha, tearing at her apron. 'And you just tell your people that you done found a cook.' He smiled weakly, then turned and left, his arms laden with clean laundry. My daughter. The energy of youth once more stirred within her. I know I'm going to find my child in California.

But the woman who now stood above Martha, casting pitiful glances, was not her daughter. Eliza Mae? 'I'll leave you now,' she said. 'But you must expect to receive me in the morning.' You must expect to receive me? Did she mean by this to suggest that Martha had some choice over their arrangement? That she could, if she so wished, choose not to receive her in the morning? Martha watched the woman back slowly out of the cold room. Thank you. She left Martha alone. Sickness had descended upon her and she was unable to respond. Martha felt the sadness of not possessing a faith that could reassure her that, having served her apportioned span, she would now be ushered to a place of reunion. She looked through the cracked window-pane. Dawn was some hours off, back east, approaching slowly. To be reunited. The town of Denver was mantled in a deep snow, the arms of the trees sheathed in a thin frost, the same thin frost that enveloped Martha's faithless heart.

The evening sky is streaked with red and yellow. I watch as the sun prepares to go down beneath the horizon. To my left, there is panic. Voices begin to climb. A pioneer has broken an ox by driving it too hard. It has to be slaughtered, but at least there will be fresh meat. He ignores this commotion and stands before me with frustration written across his face. I know that I have slowed down their progress. It is this that he wishes to talk with me about. He rolls a cigarette, his fingers clammy and stiff, and then he gestures me to rest upon the hide-bottom chair. He is a man who speaks as much with his hands as his voice. I had noticed this when he first came in with his bundle of flannel shirts and coarse pants. 'Well?' This is his beginning. I know what will follow. I look beyond him. A storm is working its way across the land. My old ears can still hear the dull rumbling of thunder.

Six weeks ago we set out across the open prairie, dust clouds rising, the noonday sun at full strength, a party of seventy colored people walking to the side of our wagons. The wagons were drawn by six oxen trained to work in pairs, animals which have a tendency to skittishness, and as such they initially frightened me. The first and rear wagons were attended to by experienced drivers, but the rest were handled by we pioneers. The idea was that I should cook for all those without family, mainly bullwhackers,[6] all men,

---

6. Wagon drivers.

and this I tried to do, rustling up bacon and salt pork and any game or beast that the men might happen to shoot along the way. I made sure each wagon had ample amounts of flour, sugar, coffee and rice, and a plentiful supply of ten-gallon water kegs. Other provisions and equipment in my charge included vinegar, soap, matches, cooking utensils and field stoves. But it was never easy. Before dawn, the freezing wind ripped through our clothing and right into the marrow. At noon, and early in the afternoon, the sun often caused us serious discomforts, made worse by the type of clothing that we wore. Heavy pants and flannel shirts for the men, and high-necked, long-sleeved, dark dresses that wouldn't show the dirt for the women. At night, we drew the wagons into a circle, and camp fires were built, meals cooked, and tales told of white expeditions where cruelties were often inflicted upon colored men and women.

The wagon train soon settled into a routine where one difficult day seemed much like the next, and where there was no discernible change to the uniform landscape. However, I felt myself growing weaker, and I tried in vain to diguise my ailments. Some days we covered ten miles across the dry grass, some days twelve or fifteen, depending upon repairs or the weather. We saw Indians, and I felt some sympathy with them, but the Indian bands kept their distance and watched, choosing not to make anything of their encounters with the dark white men. Except on one occasion, when a column of a dozen warriors, at their head a chief, rode out towards the train. Behind them came the squaws, some with papooses slung across their backs, and all around them yapped pitiful-looking dogs who would in time become food. The chief halted, as did the wagon train, and he dismounted. By means of facial expressions and gestures, he made it known that we could pass in peace. I watched as our leader rewarded him with sugar and tobacco, and he in turn was rewarded with grunts of approval. Our only other visitors were the dark, shaggy buffalo who moved at such a slow pace that it was difficult to make out their progress. Our leader forbade the men, who were tiring of my pork, to stalk and hunt these monsters, informing them that should they be *spooked* and stampede, they would happily trample all before them. The occasional deer or game bird was the only alternative to that which we carried aboard the wagons.

Ten days ago, the river source began to dwindle to a mere trickle, and water was severely rationed. I watched the oxen pulling the enormous loads with heroism, and I witnessed the equally impressive bravery of the pioneers who, dehydrated as they were, energy flowing back and forth, still managed to pursue the torture. My own state became perilous, racked as I was with exhaustion, but still I managed to keep my misery to myself. Until yesterday. When it became clear that I was unable to prepare any more meals. I had long since been relieved of laundry duties, owing to the water rationing, and I had occasionally begged a ride on a wagon while all others walked. But then, this final humiliation. Yesterday morning, under the dazzling, intense blue of the Colorado sky, the foothills of the Rockies in the distance, this frustrated man sat before me with a stern face and shared with me his water ration. Suddenly, and without warning, his face softened and he spoke. 'Today and tomorrow you will rest, Martha. Ride in Jacob's wagon on the flour sacks. Tomorrow evening we shall speak again.' He took my hand with what I imagined to be real affection.

'Well?' This is his beginning. I know what will follow. 'You must find some shelter, for you will never survive the journey to California.' I say nothing. The sun finally disappears beneath the horizon. I look across to the large fire where they are preparing the evening meal. Six weeks ago, I was one of them. But times have changed. Still, I cherish these brave people—these colored pioneers—among whom I travel. They took upon themselves this old, colored woman and chose not to put her down like a useless load. Until now. 'Tomorrow, Martha.' I nod, unable to find the words to convince him that he must not feel guilty. None of them should. I am grateful. That is all. I am simply grateful. I smile at this man who is young enough to be my son. 'Thank you,' he says. He turns away before one of us discovers words that are best left undisturbed.

At dawn, they bear me like a slaughtered hog up and into the back of a wagon. But first they have cleared out some supplies to make room for me. Other wagons will bear the burden of carrying these provisions. He approaches and tells me that I will be taken to Denver, which lies some miles off their course. If I leave now, I may reach by sunset, which will give the wagon a chance to rejoin the group within two days. It is still cold. He offers me an extra blanket, which I take. We are to peel off from the main group, myself and two men, and strike out alone. He tells me that I have nothing to be afraid of. God willing, he hopes one day to find me in California. I thank him. All about me the pioneers stir. Sunken-eyed, still tired. I nursed and fed many of them through the first trying days, forcing food and water down their throats, and rallying them to their feet in order that they might trudge ten more miles towards their beloved California. Once there, they all dream of tasting true freedom, of learning important skills, of establishing themselves as a sober and respectable class of people. This is their dream. My weakness will delay them no longer. I hear the snap of a whip, and the driver yelling a sharp, impatient phrase to his oxen. As we move off, the tears begin to course down my old face.

We pass into a town on whose outskirts stand log cabins, some finished, some unfinished, but clearly being attended to. The town is growing. As we journey on, I see stores, rooming houses and saloons. But I see only two people. Indians. I remember the day the colored troops of Leavenworth paraded Indian scalps, fingers with rings attached, and ears that had been pulled clean off. They behaved like the men whose uniforms they wore. And now the Indians disappear from view. Up here in the Rockies, my breath is short and I gasp for air. I lie back down, but cannot rediscover my previous position. And then the wagon shudders to a halt, and one of my fellow pioneers appears before me. 'This is Main Street, Miss Martha.' I look at him as he pulls his collar tight up under his chin. Behind him the wind is rising, and the sky is beginning to darken. 'We're under instructions to set you down right here and high-tail it back to the others.'

In the pre-dawn hours of an icy February morning, Martha opened her eyes. Outside it was still dark, and the snow continued to spin. A dream began to wash through her mind. Martha dreamed that she had travelled on west to California, by herself, and clutching her bundle of clothing. Once there she was met by Eliza Mae, who was now a tall, sturdy colored woman of some social standing. Together, they tip-toed their way through the mire of the streets to Eliza Mae's residence, which stood on a fine, broad avenue. They were greeted by Eliza Mae's schoolteacher husband and the three children, who were all dressed in their Sunday best, even though this was not Sunday. A dumbstruck Martha touched their faces. Eliza Mae insisted that her mother should stay and live with them, but Martha was reluctant. All was not right. There was still no news of Lucas, and her Eliza Mae now called herself Cleo. Martha refused to call her daughter by this name, and insisted on calling her a name that her children and husband found puzzling. Soon it was time for Martha to leave, but her daughter simply forbade her mother to return east. Martha, feeling old and tired, sat down and wept openly, and in front of her grandchildren. She would not be going any place. She would never again head east. To Kansas. To Virginia. Or to beyond. She had a westward soul which had found its natural-born home in the bosom of her daughter.

Martha Randolph won't be taking any washing today. No tubs, no ironing. No cooking, either. Martha will simply sleep through the day. The woman, her cold body wrapped in her black coat, left the Denver streets which were now clad in thick snow. She opened the door and looked in upon the small colored woman, who stared back at her with wide eyes. The unsuccessful fire in the pot-bellied stove was dead. The woman gently closed in the door. Martha won't be taking any washing today. And the woman wondered who or what this woman was. They would have to choose a name for her if she was going to receive a Christian burial.

1993

BARACK OBAMA
b. 1961

The forty-fourth president of the United States, Barack Obama, was the first African American elected to that office. His historic election in 2008 came less than fifty years after the Voting Rights Act ensured the franchise for blacks in the South. By any measure a watershed in U.S. history, it signaled for some the realization of the promise of the Declaration of Independence and the dawning of a postracial society. For others, African Americans in particular, his election marked a triumph in a continuing struggle for equal rights. More than two million people attended the president's inauguration in January 2009. Outsized hopes soon collided with outsize challenges: economic crises, partisan political conflict, and global unrest. Obama's presidency proved as eventful and controversial as it was historic.

Born in Honolulu, Hawaii, to Stanley Ann Dunham, a white woman from Kansas, and Barack Obama Sr., an exchange student from Kenya, Barack Obama achieved national prominence as the keynote speaker at the 2004 Democratic Party convention, where he declared that his story could have happened only in the United States. He grew up mainly in Hawaii, although he lived for a time in Indonesia, the homeland of his mother's second husband. Returning to Hawaii, he attended the exclusive Punahou School, where he was more dedicated to basketball than to his studies. Outside of school, he began to read African American literature in his quest to understand his identity. He spent two years at Occidental College in

Los Angeles, before transferring to Columbia University in New York City. After graduation, Obama moved to Chicago, where he worked as a community organizer. He entered Harvard Law School, where he became the first African American elected president of the prestigious law review. Returning to Chicago, he practiced law briefly before launching his political career. He served in the Illinois State Senate from 1997 to 2004, during which time he also taught at the University of Chicago Law School. In 2004 he was elected to the U.S. Senate, where he served until his election to the presidency. In 2009 he was awarded the Nobel Peace Prize.

On his first day in office, the president signed the Lilly Ledbetter Fair Pay Act, which made it easier for workers to file pay discrimination lawsuits. Despite implacable opposition from Republicans in Congress, including leaders' repeated threats to make him a one-term president, Obama achieved legislative victories. Chief among them was the Affordable Care Act, which promised to extend health care to thirty million uninsured Americans. Opponents dubbed the act "Obamacare," a term intended to be derisive, but which the president eventually embraced as a sign of his success. On the international front, President Obama began to restore frayed relations with allies; an important step was ending the war in Iraq in 2009. He also ended the "don't ask, don't tell" policy, which prohibited gays in the military from acknowledging their sexual preference, and in 2012 the president expressed his support for marriage equality.

That November President Obama was re-elected by a margin of almost five million votes over Republican rival Mitt Romney, former governor of Massachusetts. Obama's second inauguration drew pointed attention to the historical significance of his tenure. Myrlie Evers-Williams, the widow of civil rights martyr Medgar Evers, who was assassinated in the driveway of their Jackson, Mississippi, home in 1963, gave the invocation. The gay Cuban American poet Richard Blanco composed and read the ceremonial poem, "One Today." In his speech, the president invoked sites associated with historical struggles for equality: Seneca Falls (the New York town where a pioneering women's rights convention was held in 1848), Selma (the Alabama town where Reverend Martin Luther King, Jr., led the pivotal march for voting rights for blacks in 1965), and Stonewall (the bar in the New York City neighborhood of Greenwich Village where demonstrations against a police raid in 1969 marked the beginning of the gay rights movement). These references marked the progress the nation had made, even as they suggested how much work remained to be done.

Significantly, President Obama is a man of words as well as deeds. His first book, *Dreams from My Father: A Story of Race and Inheritance* (1995) is a coming-of-age narrative in the tradition of *Narrative of the Life of Frederick Douglass*, Richard Wright's *Black Boy*, and James Baldwin's *Notes of a Native Son*. In the opinion of literary scholar Robert Stepto, "Obama's narrative is a marvel in many ways; these include the ways it refreshes our readings and recollections of the whole of African American literature." Obama is also the author of *The Audacity of Hope: Thoughts on Reclaiming the American Dream* (2006) and a children's book, *Of Thee I Sing: A Letter to My Daughters* (2010). A master orator, Obama riveted throngs of admirers on the campaign trail in 2008 and 2012. Given at a moment when his first presidential campaign was threatened by controversy sparked by comments made by his former pastor, Reverend Jeremiah Wright, "A More Perfect Union" helped stem the furor. But its importance transcends the circumstances that occasioned it. Delivered on March 18, 2008, at Constitution Hall in Philadelphia, it is an important statement on the history of race in the United States, as it reflects on the progress that has been made, the issues that remain unresolved, and the different implications they have for blacks and whites.

A More Perfect Union

"We the people, in order to form a more perfect union."

Two hundred and twenty-one years ago, in a hall that still stands across the street, a group of men gathered and, with these simple words, launched America's improbable experiment in democracy. Farmers and scholars, statesmen and patriots who had traveled across an ocean to escape tyranny and persecution finally made real their declaration of independence at a Philadelphia convention that lasted through the spring of 1787.

The document they produced was eventually signed but ultimately unfinished. It was stained by this nation's original sin of slavery, a question that divided the colonies and brought the convention to a stalemate until the founders chose to allow the slave trade to continue for at least twenty more years, and to leave any final resolution to future generations.

Of course, the answer to the slavery question was already embedded within our Constitution—a Constitution that had at its very core the ideal of equal citizenship under the law; a Constitution that promised its people liberty, and justice, and a union that could be and should be perfected over time.

And yet words on a parchment would not be enough to deliver slaves from bondage, or provide men and women of every color and creed their full rights and obligations as citizens of the United States. What would be needed were Americans in successive generations who were willing to do their part—through protests and struggle, on the streets and in the courts, through a civil war and civil disobedience and always at great risk—to narrow that gap between the promise of our ideals and the reality of their time.

This was one of the tasks we set forth at the beginning of this campaign—to continue the long march of those who came before us, a march for a more just, more equal, more free, more caring and more prosperous America. I chose to run for the presidency at this moment in history because I believe deeply that we cannot solve the challenges of our time unless we solve them together—unless we perfect our union by understanding that we may have different stories, but we hold common hopes; that we may not look the same and we may not have come from the same place, but we all want to move in the same direction—towards a better future for of children and our grandchildren.

This belief comes from my unyielding faith in the decency and generosity of the American people. But it also comes from my own American story.

I am the son of a black man from Kenya and a white woman from Kansas. I was raised with the help of a white grandfather who survived a depression to serve in Patton's army during World War II and a white grandmother who worked on a bomber assembly line at Fort Leavenworth while he was overseas. I've gone to some of the best schools in America and lived in one of the world's poorest nations. I am married to a black American who carries within her the blood of slaves and slaveowners—an inheritance we pass on to our two precious daughters. I have brothers, sisters, nieces, nephews, uncles and cousins, of every race and every hue, scattered across three continents, and for as long as I live, I will never forget that in no other country on Earth is my story even possible.

It's a story that hasn't made me the most conventional candidate. But it is a story that has seared into my genetic makeup the idea that this nation is more than the sum of its parts—that out of many, we are truly one.

Throughout the first year of this campaign, against all predictions to the contrary, we saw how hungry the American people were for this message of unity. Despite the temptation to view my candidacy through a purely racial lens, we won commanding victories in states with some of the whitest populations in the country. In South Carolina, where the Confederate flag still flies, we built a powerful coalition of African Americans and white Americans.

This is not to say that race has not been an issue in the campaign. At various stages in the campaign, some commentators have deemed me either "too black" or "not black enough." We saw racial tensions bubble to the surface during the week before the South Carolina primary. The press has scoured every exit poll for the latest evidence of racial polarization, not just in terms of white and black, but black and brown as well.

And yet, it has only been in the last couple of weeks that the discussion of race in this campaign has taken a particularly divisive turn.

On one end of the spectrum, we've heard the implication that my candidacy is somehow an exercise in affirmative action; that it's based solely on the desire of wide-eyed liberals to purchase racial reconciliation on the cheap. On the other end, we've heard my former pastor, Reverend Jeremiah Wright, use incendiary language to express views that have the potential not only to widen the racial divide, but views that denigrate both the greatness and the goodness of our nation; that rightly offend white and black alike.

I have already condemned, in unequivocal terms, the statements of Reverend Wright that have caused such controversy. For some, nagging questions remain. Did I know him to be an occasionally fierce critic of American domestic and foreign policy? Of course. Did I ever hear him make remarks that could be considered controversial while I sat in church? Yes. Did I strongly disagree with many of his political views? Absolutely—just as I'm sure many of you have heard remarks from your pastors, priests, or rabbis with which you strongly disagreed.

But the remarks that have caused this recent firestorm weren't simply controversial. They weren't simply a religious leader's effort to speak out against perceived injustice. Instead, they expressed a profoundly distorted view of this country—a view that sees white racism as endemic, and that elevates what is wrong with America above all that we know is right with America; a view that sees the conflicts in the Middle East as rooted primarily in the actions of stalwart allies like Israel, instead of emanating from the perverse and hateful ideologies of radical Islam.

As such, Reverend Wright's comments were not only wrong but divisive, divisive at a time when we need unity; racially charged at a time when we need to come together to solve a set of monumental problems—two wars, a terrorist threat, a falling economy, a chronic health care crisis and potentially devastating climate change; problems that are neither black or white or Latino or Asian, but rather problems that confront us all.

Given my background, my politics, and my professed values and ideals, there will no doubt be those for whom my statements of condemnation are not enough. Why associate myself with Reverend Wright in the first place, they may ask? Why not join another church? And I confess that if all that I knew of Reverend Wright were the snippets of those sermons that have run in an endless loop on the television and YouTube, or if Trinity United Church of Christ conformed to the caricatures being peddled by some commentators, there is no doubt that I would react in much the same way.

But the truth is, that isn't all that I know of the man. The man I met more than twenty years ago is a man who helped introduce me to my Christian faith, a man who spoke to me about our obligations to love one another, to care for the sick and lift up the poor. He is a man who served his country as a U.S. Marine, who has studied and lectured at some of the finest universities and seminaries in the country, and who for over thirty years led a church that serves the community by doing God's work here on Earth—by housing the homeless, ministering to the needy, providing day care services and scholarships and prison ministries, and reaching out to those suffering from HIV/AIDS.

In my first book, *Dreams From My Father*, I described the experience of my first service at Trinity:

> People began to shout, to rise from their seats and clap and cry out, a forceful wind carrying the reverend's voice up into the rafters. . . . And in that single note—hope!—I heard something else; at the foot of that cross, inside the thousands of churches across the city, I imagined the stories of ordinary black people merging with the stories of David and Goliath, Moses and Pharaoh, the Christians in the lion's den, Ezekiel's field of dry bones. Those stories—of survival, and freedom, and hope—became our story, my story; the blood that had spilled was our blood, the tears our tears; until this black church, on this bright day, seemed once more a vessel carrying the story of a people into future generations and into a larger world. Our trials and triumphs became at once unique and universal, black and more than black; in chronicling our journey, the stories and songs gave us a means to reclaim memories that we didn't need to feel shame about . . . memories that all people might study and cherish—and with which we could start to rebuild.

That has been my experience at Trinity. Like other predominantly black churches across the country, Trinity embodies the black community in its entirety—the doctor and the welfare mom, the model student and the former gangbanger. Like other black churches, Trinity's services are full of raucous laughter and sometimes bawdy humor. They are full of dancing, clapping, screaming and shouting that may seem jarring to the untrained ear. The church contains in full the kindness and cruelty, the fierce intelligence and the shocking ignorance, the struggles and successes, the love and yes, the bitterness and bias that make up the black experience in America.

And this helps explain, perhaps, my relationship with Reverend Wright. As imperfect as he may be, he has been like family to me. He strengthened my faith, officiated at my wedding, and baptized my children. Not once in my conversations with him have I heard him talk about any ethnic group in derogatory terms, or treat whites with whom he interacted with anything but courtesy and respect. He contains within him the contradictions—the good and the bad—of the community that he has served diligently for so many years.

I can no more disown him than I can disown the black community. I can no more disown him than I can my white grandmother—a woman who helped raise me, a woman who sacrificed again and again for me, a woman who loves me as much as she loves anything in this world, but a woman who once confessed her fear of black men who passed by her on the street, and who on more than one occasion has uttered racial or ethnic stereotypes that made me cringe.

These people are a part of me. And they are a part of America, this country that I love.

Some will see this as an attempt to justify or excuse comments that are simply inexcusable. I can assure you it is not. I suppose the politically safe thing would be to move on from this episode and just hope that it fades into the woodwork. We can dismiss Reverend Wright as a crank or a demagogue, just as some have dismissed Geraldine Ferraro,[1] in the aftermath of her recent statements, as harboring some deep-seated racial bias.

But race is an issue that I believe this nation cannot afford to ignore right now. We would be making the same mistake that Reverend Wright made in his offending sermons about America—to simplify and stereotype and amplify the negative to the point that it distorts reality.

The fact is that the comments that have been made and the issues that have surfaced over the last few weeks reflect the complexities of race in this country that we've never really worked through—a part of our union that we have yet to perfect. And if we walk away now, if we simply retreat into our respective corners, we will never be able to come together and solve challenges like health care, or education, or the need to find good jobs for every American.

Understanding this reality requires a reminder of how we arrived at this point. As William Faulkner once wrote, "The past isn't dead and buried. In fact, it isn't even past." We do not need to recite here the history of racial injustice in this country. But we do need to remind ourselves that so many of the disparities that exist in the African-American community today can be directly traced to inequalities passed on from an earlier generation that suffered under the brutal legacy of slavery and Jim Crow.

Segregated schools were, and are, inferior schools; we still haven't fixed them, fifty years after *Brown v. Board of Education*, and the inferior education they provided, then and now, helps explain the pervasive achievement gap between today's black and white students.

Legalized discrimination—where blacks were prevented, often through violence, from owning property, or loans were not granted to African-American business owners, or black homeowners could not access FHA mortgages, or blacks were excluded from unions, or the police force, or fire departments—meant that black families could not amass any meaningful wealth to bequeath to future generations. That history helps explain the wealth and income gap between black and white, and the concentrated pockets of poverty that persist in so many of today's urban and rural communities.

---

1. Ferraro (1935–2011) was a congresswoman, the first female candidate for U.S. vice president nominated by a major party, and a Hillary Clinton supporter in 2008.

A lack of economic opportunity among black men, and the shame and frustration that came from not being able to provide for one's family, contributed to the erosion of black families—a problem that welfare policies for many years may have worsened. And the lack of basic services in so many urban black neighborhoods—parks for kids to play in, police walking the beat, regular garbage pick-up and building code enforcement—all helped create a cycle of violence, blight and neglect that continues to haunt us.

This is the reality in which Reverend Wright and other African Americans of his generation grew up. They came of age in the late fifties and early sixties, a time when segregation was still the law of the land and opportunity was systematically constricted. What's remarkable is not how many failed in the face of discrimination, but rather how many men and women overcame the odds; how many were able to make a way out of no way for those like me who would come after them.

But for all those who scratched and clawed their way to get a piece of the American Dream, there were many who didn't make it—those who were ultimately defeated, in one way or another, by discrimination. That legacy of defeat was passed on to future generations—those young men and increasingly young women who we see standing on street corners or languishing in our prisons, without hope or prospects for the future. Even for those blacks who did make it, questions of race, and racism, continue to define their worldview in fundamental ways. For the men and women of Reverend Wright's generation, the memories of humiliation and doubt and fear have not gone away; nor have the anger and the bitterness of those years. That anger may not get expressed in public, in front of white co-workers or white friends. But it does find voice in the barbershop or around the kitchen table. At times, that anger is exploited by politicians, to gin up votes along racial lines, or to make up for a politician's own failings.

And occasionally it finds voice in the church on Sunday morning, in the pulpit and in the pews. The fact that so many people are surprised to hear that anger in some of Reverend Wright's sermons simply reminds us of the old truism that the most segregated hour in American life occurs on Sunday morning. That anger is not always productive; indeed, all too often it distracts attention from solving real problems; it keeps us from squarely facing our own complicity in our condition, and prevents the African-American community from forging the alliances it needs to bring about real change. But the anger is real; it is powerful; and to simply wish it away, to condemn it without understanding its roots, only serves to widen the chasm of misunderstanding that exists between the races.

In fact, a similar anger exists within segments of the white community. Most working- and middle-class white Americans don't feel that they have been particularly privileged by their race. Their experience is the immigrant experience—as far as they're concerned, no one's handed them anything, they've built it from scratch. They've worked hard all their lives, many times only to see their jobs shipped overseas or their pension dumped after a lifetime of labor. They are anxious about their futures, and feel their dreams slipping away; in an era of stagnant wages and global competition, opportunity comes to be seen as a zero sum game, in which your dreams come at my expense. So when they are told to bus their children to a school across town; when they hear that an African American is getting an advantage in landing a good job or a spot in a good college because of an injustice that they themselves never committed; when they're told that their fears about crime in urban neighborhoods are somehow prejudiced, resentment builds over time.

Like the anger within the black community, these resentments aren't always expressed in polite company. But they have helped shape the political landscape for at least a generation. Anger over welfare and affirmative action helped forge the Reagan Coalition. Politicians routinely exploited fears of crime for their own electoral ends. Talk show hosts and conservative commentators built entire careers unmasking bogus claims of racism while dismissing legitimate discussions of racial injustice and inequality as mere political correctness or reverse racism.

Just as black anger often proved counterproductive, so have these white resentments distracted attention from the real culprits of the middle-class squeeze—a corporate culture rife with inside dealing, questionable accounting practices, and short-term greed; a Washington dominated by lobbyists and special interests; economic policies that favor the few over the many. And yet, to wish away the resentments of white Americans, to label them as misguided or even racist, without recognizing they are grounded in legitimate concerns—this too widens the racial divide, and blocks the path to understanding.

This is where we are right now. It's a racial stalemate we've been stuck in for years. Contrary to the claims of some of my critics, black and white, I have never been so naïve as to believe that we can get beyond our racial divisions in a single election cycle, or with a single candidacy—particularly a candidacy as imperfect as my own.

But I have asserted a firm conviction—a conviction rooted in my faith in God and my faith in the American people—that working together we can move beyond some of our old racial wounds, and that in fact we have no choice is we are to continue on the path of a more perfect union.

For the African-American community, that path means embracing the burdens of our past without becoming victims of our past. It means continuing to insist on a full measure of justice in every aspect of American life. But it also means binding our particular grievances—for better health care, and better schools, and better jobs—to the larger aspirations of all Americans—the white woman struggling to break the glass ceiling, the white man who's been laid off, the immigrant trying to feed his family. And it means taking full responsibility for our own lives—by demanding more from our fathers, and spending more time with our children, and reading to them, and teaching them that while they may face challenges and discrimination in their own lives, they must never succumb to despair or cynicism; they must always believe that they can write their own destiny.

Ironically, this quintessentially American—and yes, conservative— notion of self-help found frequent expression in Reverend Wright's sermons. But what my former pastor too often failed to understand is that embarking on a program of self-help also requires a belief that society can change.

The profound mistake of Reverend Wright's sermons is not that he spoke about racism in our society. It's that he spoke as if our society was static; as if no progress has been made; as if this country—a country that has made it possible for one of his own members to run for the highest office in the land and build a coalition of white and black, Latino and Asian, rich and poor, young and old—is still irrevocably bound to a tragic past. But what we know—what we have seen—is that America can change. That is true genius of this nation. What we have already achieved gives us hope—the audacity to hope—for what we can and must achieve tomorrow.

In the white community, the path to a more perfect union means acknowledging that what ails the African-American community does not just exist in the minds of black people; that the legacy of discrimination—and current incidents of discrimination, while less overt than in the past—are real and must be addressed. Not just with words, but with deeds—by investing in our schools and our communities; by enforcing our civil rights laws and ensuring fairness in our criminal justice system; by providing this generation with ladders of opportunity that were unavailable for previous generations. It requires all Americans to realize that your dreams do not have to come at the expense of my dreams; that investing in the health, welfare, and education of black and brown and white children will ultimately help all of America prosper.

In the end, then, what is called for is nothing more, and nothing less, than what all the world's great religions demand—that we do unto others as we would have them do unto us. Let us be our brother's keeper, Scripture tells us. Let us be our sister's keeper. Let us find that common stake we all have in one another, and let our politics reflect that spirit as well.

For we have a choice in this country. We can accept a politics that breeds division, and conflict, and cynicism. We can tackle race only as spectacle—as we did in the OJ trial—or in the wake of tragedy, as we did in the aftermath of Katrina—or as fodder for the nightly news. We can play Reverend Wright's sermons on every channel, every day, and talk about them from now until the election, and make the only question in this campaign whether or not the American people think that I somehow believe or sympathize with his most offensive words. We can pounce on some gaffe by a Hillary supporter as evidence that she's playing the race card, or we can speculate on whether white men will all flock to John McCain in the general election regardless of his policies.

We can do that.

But if we do, I can tell you that in the next election, we'll be talking about some other distraction. And then another one. And then another one. And nothing will change.

That is one option. Or, at this moment, in this election, we can come together and say, "Not this time." This time we want to talk about the crumbling schools that are stealing the future of black children and white children and Asian children and Hispanic children and Native American children. This time we want to reject the cynicism that tells us that these kids can't learn, that those kids who don't look like us are somebody else's problem. The children of America are not those kids, they are our kids, and we will not let them fall behind in a twenty-first-century economy. Not this time.

This time we want to talk about how the lines in the emergency room are filled with whites and blacks and Hispanics who do not have health care; who don't have the power on their own to overcome the special interests in Washington, but who can take them on if we do it together.

This time we want to talk about the shuttered mills that once provided a decent life for men and women of every race, and the homes for sale that once belonged to Americans from every religion, every region, every walk of life. This time we want to talk about the fact that the real problem is not that someone who doesn't look like you might take your job; it's that the corporation you work for will ship it overseas for nothing more than a profit.

This time we want to talk about the men and women of every color and creed who serve together, and fight together, and bleed together under the same proud flag. We want to talk about how to bring them home from a war that never should have been authorized and never should have been waged, and we want to talk about how we'll show our patriotism by caring for them, and their families, and giving them the benefits they have earned.

I would not be running for president if I didn't believe with all my heart that this is what the vast majority of Americans want for this country. This union may never be perfect, but generation after generation has shown that it can always be perfected. And today, whenever I find myself feeling doubtful or cynical about this possibility, what gives me the most hope is the next generation—the young people whose attitudes and beliefs and openness to change have already made history in this election.

There is one story in particular that I'd like to leave you with today—a story I told when I had the great honor of speaking on Dr. King's birthday at his home church, Ebenezer Baptist, in Atlanta.

There is a young, twenty-three-year-old white woman named Ashley Baia who organized for our campaign in Florence, South Carolina. She had been working to organize a mostly African-American community since the beginning of this campaign, and one day she was at a roundtable discussion where everyone went around telling their story and why they were there.

And Ashley said that when she was nine years old, her mother got cancer. And because she had to miss days of work, she was let go and lost her health care. They had to file for bankruptcy, and that's when Ashley decided that she had to do something to help her mom.

She knew that food was one of their most expensive costs, and so Ashley convinced her mother that what she really liked and really wanted to eat more than anything else was mustard and relish sandwiches. Because that was the cheapest way to eat.

She did this for a year until her mom got better, and she told everyone at the roundtable that the reason she joined our campaign was so that she could help the millions of other children in the country who want and need to help their parents too.

Now Ashley might have made a different choice. Perhaps somebody told her along the way that the source of her mother's problems were blacks who were on welfare and too lazy to work, or Hispanics who were coming into the country illegally. But she didn't. She sought out allies in her fight against injustice.

Anyway, Ashley finishes her story and then goes around the room and asks everyone else why they're supporting the campaign. They all have different stories and reasons. Many bring up a specific issue. And finally they come to this elderly black man who's been sitting there quietly the entire time. And Ashley asks him why he's there. And he does not bring up a specific issue. He does not say health care or the economy. He does not say education or the war. He does not say that he was there because of Barack Obama. He simply says to everyone in the room, "I am here because of Ashley."

"I'm here because of Ashley." By itself, that single moment of recognition between that young white girl and that old black man is not enough. It is not enough to give health care to the sick, or jobs to the jobless, or education to our children.

But it is where we start. It is where our union grows stronger. And as so many generations have come to realize over the course of the two hundred and twenty-one years since a band of patriots signed that document in Philadelphia, that is where the perfection begins.

2008

ELIZABETH ALEXANDER
b. 1962

Elizabeth Alexander's poetry and prose explores "the black interior," which she defines as "black life and creativity behind the public face of stereotype and limited imagination." When her poems represent historical figures, such as Marcus Garvey, Nat Turner, and the participants in the Amistad revolt, Alexander invents an interior life for them. In a sequence of poems, "The Venus Hottentot," she gives voice to Saartjie Baartman, the South African woman, whose body became the object of public fascination in early-nineteenth-century London. Another poem cycle chronicles the life of boxer Muhammad Ali. Alexander's own life becomes a subject as well: she writes about haircuts and house parties, marriage, and motherhood. In these poems, Alexander discovers the extraordinary in the everyday. She quotes Sterling Brown in "Ars Poetica 100," one of her series of poems on the art of poetry: "every 'I' is a dramatic 'I.'" It is not surprising that she also identifies Gwendolyn Brooks and Walt Whitman as precursors. Like Brooks, Alexander has a fascination with wordplay and poetic form (she writes sonnets and villanelles as well as narrative poems in free verse). Like Whitman, Alexander is a profoundly democratic poet. The spirits of Brooks and Whitman animate "Praise Song for the Day," the poem that Alexander wrote for the inauguration of President Barack Obama in January 2009.

Born in New York City and raised in Washington, D.C., Alexander invokes the specific black cultural histories of both places in her work, depicting landmarks, such as the Schomburg Center for Research in Black Culture and Dunbar High School, as well as people walking down the street, who are themselves repositories of history. As the daughter of an activist, Clifford Alexander, and a professor, Adele Logan Alexander, she honors their legacy of "race work." But she describes her own vocation as "culture work." Inspired by musicians, painters, and performers, she remarks, "the study of African American history and culture has been a great gift to my work because the font of rich stories and characters appear limitless." Her essays, collected in The Black Interior (2004) and Power and Possibility (2007), focus on that history and culture. Alexander has also edited Love's Instruments:

Poems by Melvin Dixon (1995) and The Essential Gwendolyn Brooks (2005). She admires these poets not only for their craft but also for their ability to break free of what she calls "mainstream constructions of blackness" that titillate audiences while veiling black people from themselves. Her own poetry strives to pierce the veils and deconstruct the stereotypes. A scholar as well as a poet, Alexander is chair of the Department of African American Studies at Yale University.

The Venus Hottentot[1]

(1825)

1. Cuvier[2]

Science, science, science!
Everything is beautiful

blown up beneath my glass.
Colors dazzle insect wings.

A drop of water swirls   5
like marble. Ordinary

crumbs become stalactites
set in perfect angles

of geometry I'd thought
impossible. Few will   10

ever see what I see
through this microscope.

Cranial measurements
crowd my notebook pages,

and I am moving closer,   15
close to how these numbers

signify aspects of
national character.

Her genitalia
will float inside a labeled   20

pickling jar in the Musée
de l'Homme on a shelf

---

1. Saartije Baartman (1790–1815), an enslaved South African considered remarkable because of her large breasts and buttocks, was exhibited in circuses and private shows across 19th-century Europe.

2. French surgeon, naturalist, and zoologist (1769–1832) who, after Baartman's death, made a plaster cast of her body and studied her skeleton, brain, and genitals. These remains were placed on display at the Musée de l'Homme.

above Broca's brain:[3]
"The Venus Hottentot."

Elegant facts await me.   25
Small things in this world are mine.

2.

There is unexpected sun today
in London, and the clouds that
most days sift into this cage
where I am working have dispersed.   30
I am a black cutout against
a captive blue sky, pivoting
nude so the paying audience
can view my naked buttocks.

I am called "Venus Hottentot."   35
I left Capetown with a promise
of revenue: half the profits
and my passage home: A boon!
Master's brother proposed the trip;
the magistrate granted me leave.   40
I would return to my family
a duchess, with watered-silk

dresses and money to grow food,
rouge and powders in glass pots,
silver scissors, a lorgnette,   45
voile and tulle instead of flax,
cerulean blue instead
of indigo. My brother would
devour sugar-studded non-
pareils, pale taffy, damask plums.   50

That was years ago. London's
circuses are florid and filthy,
swarming with cabbage-smelling
citizens who stare and query,
"Is it muscle? bone? or fat?"   55
My neighbor to the left is
The Sapient Pig, "The Only
Scholar of His Race." He plays

at cards, tells time and fortunes
by scraping his hooves. Behind   60
me is Prince Kar-mi, who arches
like a rubber tree and stares back
at the crowd from under the crook
of his knee. A professional

---

3. An anatomical specimen showing Broca's area, a region of the brain responsible for speech and discovered by Pierre Paul Broca in 1861.

animal trainer shouts my cues.   65
There are singing mice here.

"The Ball of Duchess DuBarry":
In the engraving I lurch
toward the *belles dames*, mad-eyed, and
they swoon. Men in capes and pince-nez   70
shield them. Tassels dance at my hips.
In this newspaper lithograph
my buttocks are shown swollen
and luminous as a planet.

Monsieur Cuvier investigates   75
between my legs, poking, prodding,
sure of his hypothesis.
I half expect him to pull silk
scarves from inside me, paper poppies,
then a rabbit! He complains   80
at my scent and does not think
I comprehend, but I speak

English. I speak Dutch. I speak
a little French as well, and
languages Monsieur Cuvier   85
will never know have names.
Now I am bitter and now
I am sick. I eat brown bread,
drink rancid broth. I miss good sun,
miss Mother's *sadza*. My stomach   90

is frequently queasy from mutton
chops, pale potatoes, blood sausage.
I was certain that this would be
better than farm life. I am
the family entrepreneur!   95
But there are hours in every day
to conjur my imaginary
daughters, in banana skirts

and ostrich-feather fans.[4]
Since my own genitals are public   100
I have made other parts private.
In my silence I possess
mouth, larynx, brain, in a single
gesture. I rub my hair
with lanolin, and pose in profile   105
like a painted Nubian

archer, imagining gold leaf
woven through my hair, and diamonds.
Observe the wordless Odalisque.
I have not forgotten my Xhosa   110

---

4. A reference to African American dancer, singer, and actress Josephine Baker (1906–1975) and her famous costumes in her vaudeville act.

clicks. My flexible tongue
and healthy mouth bewilder
this man with his rotting teeth.
If he were to let me rise up

from this table, I'd spirit   115
his knives and cut out his black heart,
seal it with science fluid inside
a bell jar, place it on a low
shelf in a white man's museum
so the whole world could see   120
it was shriveled and hard,
geometric, deformed, unnatural.

                                                          1990

When

In the early 1980s, the black men
were divine, spoke French, had read everything,
made filet mignon with green peppercorn sauce,
listened artfully to boyfriend troubles,
operatically declaimed boyfriend troubles,   5
had been to Bamako and Bahia,
knew how to clear bad humours from a house,
had been to Baldwin's villa in Saint-Paul,[1]
drank espresso with Soyinka and Senghor,[2]
kissed hello on both cheeks, quoted Baraka's   10
"Black Art": "Fuck poems/and they are useful,"
tore up the disco dance floor, were gold lit,
photographed well, did not smoke, said "Ciao,"

then all the men's faces were spotted.[3]

                                                          2005

Ars Poetica #100: I Believe

Poetry, I tell my students,
is idiosyncratic. Poetry

is where we are ourselves
(though Sterling Brown[1] said

---

1. Home in Saint-Paul de Vence of American novelist, essayist, playwright, poet, and social critic James Baldwin (1924–1987), who in his writing highlighted the intersection of homosexual, black, and masculine identities.
2. Senegalese poet, politician, and cultural theorist (1906–2001). Soyinka (b. 1934), Nigerian poet and winner of the 1986 Nobel Prize in literature.

3. Lesions caused by the rare skin cancer Kaposi sarcoma are a symptom of AIDS, which became associated with the gay community when first clinically observed in 1981.
1. Poet, literary critic, and professor of African American literature (1901–1989).

"Every 'I' is a dramatic 'I'"),   5
digging in the clam flats

for the shell that snaps,
emptying the proverbial pocketbook.

Poetry is what you find
in the dirt in the corner,   10

overhear on the bus, God
in the details, the only way

to get from here to there.
Poetry (and now my voice is rising)

is not all love, love, love,   15
and I'm sorry the dog died.

Poetry (here I hear myself loudest)
is the human voice,

and are we not of interest to each other?

2005

SUZAN-LORI PARKS
b. 1963

A s an undergraduate Suzan-Lori Parks took a creative writing course from James Baldwin, who encouraged her to write plays. At the end of the year, he called her "an utterly astounding and beautiful creature who may become one of the most valuable artists of our time." That is what she became. Her formally experimental, sharply satirical, and sometimes profanely funny plays revise our understanding of history by filling what Parks calls the "fabricated absence" of black people. The absence is intentional, and Parks determines to fill the "holes" that are left. That requires writing beyond realism and beyond the three-act structure of the well-made play. For example, the "Foundling Father" in *The American Play* is played by a black actor, whose presence challenges the idea of Founding Father, even as it suggests that the nation is somehow an historical orphan. While Parks offers a genealogy, she resists the idea that one can derive fixed meanings from her plays. They open themselves instead to diverse *readings*, or interpretations. As audiences meet the challenges of producing those readings, they develop new, complex, and inclusive understandings of the nation's past.

Widely produced and critically celebrated, Parks's plays have won numerous awards, including the Pulitzer Prize for drama for *Topdog/Underdog* in 2002. Parks was the first black woman to receive this honor; in 2001, she was awarded the MacArthur Fellowship, popularly known as the "genius award." Selected titles of her plays are a measure of the breadth of her interests and imaginative reach:

Suzan-Lori Parks's *Topdog/Underdog* depicts the relationship between two brothers, Booth (Mos Def) and Lincoln (Jeffrey Wright). This photograph by Michael Daniel shows the set of the run-down boarding-house room used in the Broadway production at the Ambassador Theater and hints at the resentments and tensions between the two brothers.

Imperceptible Mutabilities in the Third Kingdom (1990); *The Death of the Last Black Man in the Whole Entire World* (1992); *The America Play* (1994); *Venus* (1995), inspired by the life of Saartjie Baartman, a South African woman whose body became the object of public fascination in nineteenth-century London and Paris; *In the Blood* and *Fucking A* (2000), two riffs on Nathaniel Hawthorne's *The Scarlet Letter*; *Father Comes Home from the Wars (Parts 1, 8 & 9)* (2009); and *The Book of Grace* (2010). In 2007 her *365 Plays/365 Days*, was produced in over seven hundred theaters worldwide, creating one of the largest grassroots collaborations in theater history. In 2011, she wrote a new libretto for George Gershwin's classic opera *Porgy and Bess,* presented on Broadway to critical acclaim.

Born in Fort Knox, Kentucky, to a military family, Parks relocated first to Texas and then to Germany, where she became fluent in the language and learned "what it feels like to be neither white nor black, but simply foreign." She graduated from Mount Holyoke College. In addition to theater, she has written for film: notably the screenplays for *Girl 6* and *The Great Debaters,* as well as the television adaptation of Zora Neale Hurston's *Their Eyes Were Watching God.* Parks's novel, *Getting Mother's Body,* set in the west Texas of her childhood, appeared in 2003.

Her most popular play, *Topdog/Underdog,* features two brothers, Booth and Lincoln, named for two of the most consequential figures in United States history—Abraham Lincoln, the sixteenth president of the United States, and John Wilkes Booth, his assassin. The play's characters, by contrast, are anonymous men, whose twentieth-century lives seem desperate and degraded. Their blackness highlights the brothers' complex relationship to the national history, even as their rivalry connects them to a long line of literary precursors, including Cain and Abel, the first biblical brothers, and Romulus and Remus, the twins who, according to myth, founded Rome. Dexterous wordplay, plot twists, and visceral humor characterize the play. Parks describes the experience of writing *Topdog/Underdog* as "quicksilver," a reference to the process by which the back of glass is coated with tin to give it a reflecting power. The phrase seems appropriate to the experience of reading it as well, as *Top/Dog* reflects dimensions of U.S. history that readers have not heretofore imagined.

Topdog/Underdog

THE PLAYERS

LINCOLN the topdog
BOOTH (aka 3-Card), the underdog

PLACE

here

TIME

now

AUTHOR'S NOTES: FROM THE "ELEMENTS OF STYLE"

I'm continuing the use of my slightly unconventional theatrical elements. Here's a road map.

- *(Rest)*
  Take a little time, a pause, a breather; make a transition.

- A Spell
  An elongated and heightened *(Rest)*. Denoted by repetition of figures' names with no dialogue. Has sort of an architectural look:

LINCOLN
BOOTH
LINCOLN
BOOTH

This is a place where the figures experience their pure true simple state. While no action or stage business is necessary, directors should fill this moment as they best see fit.

- [Brackets in the text indicate optional cuts for production.]

- (Parentheses around dialogue indicate softly spoken passages (asides; sotto voce)).

I am God in nature;
I am a weed by the wall.
—Ralph Waldo Emerson
From "Circles"
Essays: First Series (1841)

Scene One

[*Thursday evening. A seedily furnished rooming house room. A bed, a reclining chair, a small wooden chair, some other stuff but not much else.* BOOTH, *a black man in his early 30s, practices his 3-card monte scam on the classic setup: 3 playing cards and the cardboard playing board atop 2 mismatched milk crates. His moves and accompanying patter are, for the most part, studied and awkward.*]

BOOTH   Watch me close watch me close now: who-see-thuh-red-card-who-see-thuh-red-card? I-see-thuh-red-card. Thuh-red-card-is-thuh-winner. Pick-thuh-red-card-you-pick-uh-winner. Pick-uh-black-card-you-pick-uh-loser. Theres-thuh-loser, yeah, theres-thuh-black-card, theres-thuh-other-loser-and-theres-thuh-red-card, thuh-winner.

(*Rest*)

Watch me close watch me close now: 3-Card-throws-thuh-cards-lightning-fast. 3-Card-thats-me-and-Ima-last. Watch-me-throw-cause-here-I-go. One-good-pickll-get-you-in, 2-good-picks-and-you-gone-win. See-thuh-red-card-see-thuh-red-card-who-see-thuh-red-card?

(*Rest*)

Dont touch my cards, man, just point to thuh one you want. You-pick-that-card-you-pick-a-loser, yeah, that-cards-a-loser. You-pick-that-card-thats-thuh-other-loser. You-pick-that-card-you-pick-a-winner. Follow that card. You gotta chase that card. You-pick-thuh-dark-deuce-thats-a-loser-other-dark-deuces-thuh-other-loser, red-deuce, thuh-deuce-of-heartsll-win-it-all. Follow thuh red card.

(*Rest*)

Ima show you thuh cards: 2 black cards but only one heart. Now watch me now. Who-sees-thuh-red-card-who-knows-where-its-at? Go on, man, point to thuh card. Put yr money down cause you aint no clown. No? Ah you had thuh card, but you didnt have thuh heart.

(*Rest*)

You wanna bet? 500 dollars? Shoot. You musta been watching 3-Card real close. Ok. Lay the cash in my hand cause 3-Cards thuh man. Thank you, mister. This card you say?

(*Rest*)

Wrong! Sucker! Fool! Asshole! Bastard! I bet yr daddy heard how stupid you was and drank himself to death just cause he didnt wanna have nothing to do witchu! I bet yr mama seen you when you was born and she wished she was dead, sucker! Ha Ha Ha! And 3-Card, once again, wins all thuh money!!

(*Rest*)

What? Cops looking my way? Fold up thuh game, and walk away. Sneak outa sight. Set up on another corner.

(*Rest*)

Yeah.

(*Rest*)

[*Having won the imaginary loot and dodged the imaginary cops,* BOOTH *sets up his equipment and starts practicing his scam all over again.* LINCOLN *comes in quietly. He is a black man in his later 30s. He is dressed in an antique frock coat and wears a top hat and fake beard, that is, he is dressed to look like Abraham Lincoln. He surreptitiously walks into the room to stand right behind* BOOTH, *who, engrossed in his cards, does not notice* LINCOLN *right away.*]

BOOTH Watch me close watch me close now: who-see-thuh-red-card-who-see-thuh-red-card? I-see-thuh-red-card. Thuh-red-card-is-thuh-winner. Pick-thuh-red-card-you-pick-uh-winner. Pick-uh-black-card-you-pick-uh-loser. Theres-thuh-loser-yeah-theres-thuh-black-card, theres-thuh-other-loser-and-theres-thuh-red-card, thuh-winner. Don't touch my cards, man, don't—
(Rest)
Dont do that shit. Dont do that shit. Dont do that shit!
  [BOOTH, *sensing someone behind him, whirls around, pulling a gun from his pants. While the presence of* LINCOLN *doesnt surprise him, the* LINCOLN *costume does.*]
BOOTH And woah, man dont *ever* be doing that shit! Who thuh fuck you think you is coming in my shit all spooked out and shit. You pull that one more time I'll shoot you!
LINCOLN I only had a minute to make the bus.
BOOTH Bullshit.
LINCON Not completely. I mean, its either bull or shit, but not a complete lie so it aint bullshit, right?
(Rest)
Put yr gun away.
BOOTH Take off the damn hat at least.
  [LINCOLN *takes off the stovepipe hat.* BOOTH *puts his gun away.*]
LINCOLN Its cold out there. This thing kept my head warm.
BOOTH I dont like you wearing that bullshit, that shit that bull that disguise that getup that motherdisfuckinguise anywhere in the daddy-dicksticking vicinity of my humble abode.
  [LINCOLN *takes off the beard.*]
LINCOLN Better?
BOOTH Take off the damn coat too. Damn, man. Bad enough you got to wear that shit all day you come up in here wearing it. What my women gonna say?
LINCOLN What women?
BOOTH I got a date with Grace tomorrow. Shes in love with me again but she dont know it yet. Aint no man can love her the way I can. She sees you in that getup its gonna reflect bad on me. She coulda seen you coming down the street. Shit. Could be standing outside right now taking her ring off and throwing it on the sidewalk.
  [BOOTH *takes a peek out the window.*]
BOOTH I got her this ring today. Diamond. Well, diamond-esque, but it looks just as good as the real thing. Asked her what size she wore. She say 7 so I go boost a size 6 and a half, right? Show it to her and she loves it and I shove it on her finger and its a tight fit right, so she cant just take it off on a whim, like she did the last one I gave her. Smooth, right?
  [BOOTH *takes another peek out the window.*]
LINCOLN She out there?
BOOTH Nope. Coast is clear.
LINCOLN You boosted a ring?
BOOTH Yeah. I thought about spending my inheritance on it but—take off that damn coat, man, you make me nervous standing there looking like a spook, and that damn face paint, take it off. You should take all of it off at work and leave it there.
LINCOLN I dont bring it home someone might steal it.

BOOTH   At least *take it off* there, then.

LINCOLN   Yeah.

   (Rest)

   [LINCOLN *takes off the frock coat and applies cold cream, removing the whiteface.*]

LINCOLN   I was riding the bus. Really I only had a minute to make my bus and I was sitting in the arcade thinking, should I change into my street clothes or should I make the bus? Nobody was in there today anyway. Middle of the week middle of winter. Not like on weekends. Weekends the place is packed. So Im riding the bus home. And this kid asked me for my autograph. I pretended I didnt hear him at first. I'd had a long day. But he kept asking. Theyd just done Lincoln in history class and he knew all about him, he'd been to the arcade but, I dunno, for some reason he was tripping cause there was Honest Abe right beside him on the bus. I wanted to tell him to go fuck hisself. But then I got a look at him. A little rich kid. Born on easy street, you know the type. So I waited until I could tell he really wanted it, the autograph, and I told him he could have it for 10 bucks. I was gonna say 5, cause of the Lincoln connection but something in me made me ask for 10.

BOOTH   But he didnt have a 10. All he had was a penny. So you took the penny.

LINCOLN   All he had was a 20. So I took the 20 and told him to meet me on the bus tomorrow and Honest Abe would give him the change.

BOOTH   Shit.

LINCOLN   Shit is right.

   (Rest)

BOOTH   Whatd you do with thuh 20?

LINCOLN   Bought drinks at Luckys. A round for everybody. They got a kick out of the getup.

BOOTH   You shoulda called me down.

LINCOLN   Next time, bro.

   (Rest)

   You making bookshelves? With the milk crates, you making bookshelves?

BOOTH   Yeah, big bro, Im making bookshelves.

LINCOLN   Whats the cardboard part for?

BOOTH   Versatility.

LINCOLN   Oh.

BOOTH   I was thinking we dont got no bookshelves we dont got no dining room table so Im making a sorta modular unit you put the books in the bottom and the table top on top. We can eat and store our books. We could put the photo album in there.

   [BOOTH *gets the raggedy family photo album and puts it in the milk crate.*]

BOOTH   Youd sit there, I'd sit on the edge of the bed. Gathered around the dinner table. Like old times.

LINCOLN   We just gotta get some books but thats great, Booth, thats real great.

BOOTH   Dont be calling me Booth no more, K?

LINCOLN   You changing yr name?

BOOTH   Maybe.

LINCOLN

BOOTH

LINCOLN   What to?

BOOTH   Im not ready to reveal it yet.

LINCOLN   You already decided on something?

BOOTH   Maybe.

LINCOLN   You gonna call yrself something african? That be cool. Only pick
something thats easy to spell and pronounce, man, cause you know, some
of them african names, I mean, ok, Im down with the power to the people
thing, but, no ones gonna hire you if they cant say yr name. And some
of them fellas who got they african names, no one can say they names
and they cant say they names neither. I mean, you dont want yr new
handle to obstruct yr employment possibilities.

BOOTH

LINCOLN

BOOTH   You bring dinner?

LINCOLN   "Shango" would be a good name. The name of the thunder god.
If you aint decided already Im just throwing it in the pot. I brought
chinese.

BOOTH   Lets try the table out.

LINCOLN   Cool.

> [*They both sit at the new table. The food is far away near the door.*]

LINCOLN

BOOTH

LINCOLN   I buy it you set it up. Thats the deal. Thats the deal, right?

BOOTH   You like this place?

LINCOLN   Ssallright.

BOOTH   But a little cramped sometimes, right?

LINCOLN   You dont hear me complain. Although that recliner sometimes
Booth, man—no Booth, right—man, Im too old to be sleeping in that
chair.

BOOTH   Its my place. You dont got a place. Cookie, she threw you out.
And you cant seem to get another woman. Yr lucky I let you stay.

LINCOLN   Every Friday you say *mi casa es su casa*.

BOOTH   Every Friday you come home with yr paycheck. Today is Thursday and I tell you brother, its a long way from Friday to Friday. All kinds
of things can happen. All kinds of bad feelings can surface and erupt
while yr little brother waits for you to bring in yr share.

(Rest)

I got my Thursday head on, Link. Go get the food.

> [LINCOLN *doesnt budge.*]

LINCOLN   You dont got no running water in here, man.

BOOTH   So?

LINCOLN   You dont got no toilet you dont got no sink.

BOOTH   Bathrooms down the hall.

LINCOLN   You living in thuh Third World, fool! Hey, I'll get thuh food.

> [LINCOLN *goes to get the food. He sees a stray card on the floor and exam-*
> *ines it without touching it. He brings the food over, putting it nicely on*
> *the table.*]

LINCOLN   You been playing cards?

BOOTH   Yeah.

LINCOLN   Solitaire?

BOOTH   Thats right. Im getting pretty good at it.

LINCOLN   Thats soup and thats sauce. I got you the meat and I got me the skrimps.

BOOTH   I wanted the skrimps.

LINCOLN   You said you wanted the meat. This morning when I left you said you wanted the meat.

(Rest)

Here man, take the skrimps. No sweat.

[They eat. Chinese food from styrofoam containers, cans of soda, fortune cookies. LINCOLN eats slowly and carefully, BOOTH eats ravenously.]

LINCOLN   Yr getting good at solitaire?

BOOTH   Yeah. How about we play a hand after eating?

LINCOLN   Solitaire?

BOOTH   Poker or rummy or something.

LINCOLN   You know I dont touch thuh cards, man.

BOOTH   Just for fun.

LINCOLN   I dont touch thuh cards.

BOOTH   How about for money?

LINCOLN   You dont got no money. All the money you got I bring in here.

BOOTH   I got my inheritance.

LINCOLN   Thats like saying you dont got no money cause you aint never gonna do nothing with it so its like you dont got it.

BOOTH   At least I still got mines. You blew yrs.

LINCOLN

BOOTH

LINCOLN   You like the skrimps?

BOOTH   Ssallright.

LINCOLN   Whats yr fortune?

BOOTH   "Waste not want not." Whats yrs?

LINCOLN   "Your luck will change!"

[BOOTH finishes eating. He turns his back to LINCOLN and fiddles around with the cards, keeping them on the bed, just out of LINCOLNs sight. He mutters the 3-card patter under his breath. His moves are still clumsy. Every once and a while he darts a look over at LINCOLN who does his best to ignore BOOTH.]

BOOTH   ((((Watch me close watch me close now: who-see-thuh-red-card-who-see-thuh-red-card? I-see-thuh-red-card. Thuh-red-card-is-thuh -winner. Pick-thuh-red-card-you-pick-uh-winner. Pick-uh-black-card-and-you-pick-uh-loser. Theres-thuh-loser, yeah, theres-thuh-black-card, theres-thuh-other-loser-and-theres-thuh-red-card, thuh-winner! Cop C, Stick, Cop C! Go on—))))

LINCOLN   ((Shit.))

BOOTH   (((((((One-good-pickll-get-you-in, 2-good-picks-and-you-gone-win. Dont touch my cards, man, just point to thuh one you want. You-pick-that-card-you-pick-uh-loser, yeah, that-cards-uh-loser. You-pick-that-card-thats-thuh-other-loser. You-pick-that-card-you-pick-uh-winner. Follow-that-card. You-gotta-chase-that-card!)))))))

LINCOLN   You wanna hustle 3-card monte, you gotta do it right, you gotta break it down. Practice it in smaller bits. Yr trying to do the whole thing at once thats why you keep fucking it up.

BOOTH   Show me.

LINCOLN   No. Im just saying you wanna do it you gotta do it right and if you gonna do it right you gotta work on it in smaller bits, thatsall.

BOOTH   You and me could team up and do it together. We'd clean up, Link.

LINCOLN   I'll clean up—bro.

[LINCOLN *cleans up. As he clears the food,* BOOTH *goes back to using the "table" for its original purpose.*]

BOOTH   My new names 3-Card. 3-Card, got it? You wanted to know it so now you know it. 3-card monte by 3-Card. Call me 3-Card from here on out.

LINCOLN   3-Card. Shit.

BOOTH   Im getting everybody to call me 3-Card. Grace likes 3-Card better than Booth. She says 3-Cards got something to it. Anybody not calling me 3-Card gets a bullet.

LINCOLN   Yr too much, man.

BOOTH   Im making a point.

LINCOLN   Point made, 3-Card. Point made.

[LINCOLN *picks up his guitar. Plays at it.*]

BOOTH   Oh, come on, man, we could make money you and me. Throwing down the cards. 3-Card and Link: look out! We could clean up you and me. You would throw the cards and I'd be yr Stickman. The one in the crowd who looks like just an innocent passerby, who looks like just another player, like just another customer, but who gots intimate connections with you, the Dealer, the one throwing the cards, the main man. I'd be the one who brings in the crowd, I'd be the one who makes them want to put they money down, you do yr moves and I do mines. You turn yr head and I turn the card—

LINCOLN   It aint as easy as all that. Theres—

BOOTH   We could be a team, man. Rake in the money! Sure thered be some cats out there with fast eyes, some brothers and sisters who would watch real close and pick the right card, and so thered be some days when we would lose money, but most of the days we would come out on top! Pockets bulging, plenty of cash! And the ladies would be thrilling! You could afford to get laid! Grace would be all over me again.

LINCOLN   I thought you said she was all over you.

BOOTH   She is she is. Im seeing her tomorrow but today we gotta solidify the shit twixt you and me. Big brother Link and little brother Booth—

LINCOLN   3-Card.

BOOTH   Yeah. Scheming and dreaming. No one throws the cards like you, Link. And with yr moves and my magic, and we get Grace and a girl for you to round out the posse. We'd be golden, bro! Am I right?

LINCOLN

LINCOLN

BOOTH   Am I right?

LINCOLN   I dont touch thuh cards, 3-Card. I dont touch thuh cards no more.

LINCOLN

BOOTH

LINCOLN

BOOTH

BOOTH   You know what Mom told me when she was packing to leave? You was at school motherfucker you was at school. You got up that morning and sat down in yr regular place and read the cereal box while Dad read the sports section and Mom brought you yr dick toast and then you got on the damn school bus cause you didnt have the sense to do nothing else you was so into yr own shit that you didnt have the sense to feel nothing else going on. I had the sense to go back cause I was feeling something going on man, I was feeling something changing. So I—

LINCOLN Cut school that day like you did almost every day—

BOOTH She was putting her stuff in bags. She had all them nice suitcases but she was putting her stuff in bags.

(Rest)

Packing up her shit. She told me to look out for you. I told her I was the little brother and the big brother should look out after the little brother. She just said it again. That I should look out for you. Yeah. So who gonna look out for me. Not like you care. Here I am interested in an economic opportunity, willing to work hard, willing to take risks and all you can say you shiteating motherfucking pathetic limpdick uncle tom, all you can tell me is how you dont do no more what I be wanting to do. Here I am trying to earn a living and you standing in my way. YOU STANDING IN MY WAY, LINK!

LINCOLN Im sorry.

BOOTH Yeah, you sorry all right.

LINCOLN I cant be hustling no more, bro.

BOOTH What you do all day aint no hustle?

LINCOLN Its honest work.

BOOTH Dressing up like some crackerass white man, some dead president and letting people shoot at you sounds like a hustle to me.

LINCOLN People know the real deal. When people know the real deal it aint a hustle.

BOOTH We do the card game people will know the real deal. Sometimes we will win sometimes they will win. They fast they win, we faster we win.

LINCOLN I aint going back to that, bro. I aint going back.

BOOTH You play Honest Abe. You aint going back but you going all the way back. Back to way back then when folks was slaves and shit.

LINCOLN Dont push me.

BOOTH

LINCOLN

BOOTH You gonna have to leave.

LINCOLN I'll be gone tomorrow.

BOOTH Good. Cause this was only supposed to be a temporary arrangement.

LINCOLN I will be gone tomorrow.

BOOTH Good.

[BOOTH *sits on his bed.* LINCOLN, *sitting in his easy chair with his guitar, plays and sings.*]

LINCOLN

My dear mother left me, my fathers gone away
My dear mother left me and my fathers gone away
I dont got no money, I dont got no place to stay.

My best girl, she threw me out into the street
My favorite horse, they ground him into meat
Im feeling cold from my head down to my feet.

My luck was bad but now it turned to worse
My luck was bad but now it turned to worse
Dont call me up a doctor, just call me up a hearse.

BOOTH You just made that up?

LINCOLN I had it in my head for a few days.

BOOTH Sounds good.

LINCOLN Thanks.

(Rest)

Daddy told me once why we got the names we do.

BOOTH Yeah?

LINCOLN Yeah.

(Rest)

He was drunk when he told me, or maybe I was drunk when he told me. Anyway he told me, may not be true, but he told me. Why he named us both. Lincoln and Booth.

BOOTH How come. How come, man?

LINCOLN It was his idea of a joke.

[Both men relax back as the lights fade.]

Scene Two

[Friday evening. The very next day. BOOTH comes in looking like he is bundled up, against the cold. He makes sure his brother isnt home, then stands in the middle of the room. From his big coat sleeves he pulls out one new shoe then another, from another sleeve come two more shoes. He then slithers out a belt from each sleeve. He removes his coat. Underneath he wears a very nice new suit. He removes the jacket and pants revealing another new suit underneath. The suits still have the price tags on them. He takes two neckties from his pockets and two folded shirts from the back of his pants. He pulls a magazine from the front of his pants. Hes clearly had a busy day of shoplifting. He lays one suit out on LINCOLNS easy chair. The other he lays out on his own bed. He goes out into the hall returning with a folding screen which he sets up between the bed and the recliner creating 2 separate spaces. He takes out a bottle of whiskey and two glasses, setting them on the two stacked milk crates. He hears footsteps and sits down in the small wooden chair reading the magazine. LINCOLN, dressed in street clothes, comes in.]

LINCOLN Taaaaadaaaaaaaa!

BOOTH Lordamighty, Pa, I smells money!

LINCOLN Sho nuff, Ma. Poppas brung home thuh bacon.

BOOTH Bringitherebringitherebringithere.

[With a series of very elaborate moves LINCOLN brings the money over to BOOTH.]

BOOTH Put it in my hands, Pa!

LINCOLN I want ya tuh smells it first, Ma!

BOOTH Put it neath my nose then, Pa!

LINCOLN Take yrself a good long whiff of them greenbacks.

BOOTH Oh lordamighty Ima faint, Pa! Get me muh med-sin!

[LINCOLN quickly pours two large glasses of whiskey.]

LINCOLN Dont die on me, Ma!

BOOTH Im fading fast, Pa!

LINCOLN Thinka thuh children, Ma! Thinka thuh farm!

BOOTH 1-2-3.

[Both men gulp down their drinks simultaneously.]

LINCOLN and BOOTH AAAAAAAAAAAAAAAAAAAAAAH!

[*Lots of laughing and slapping on the backs.*]

LINCOLN   Budget it out man budget it out.

BOOTH   You in a hurry?

LINCOLN   Yeah. I wanna see how much we got for the week.

BOOTH   You rush in here and dont even look around. Could be a fucking A-bomb in the middle of the floor you wouldnt notice. Yr wife, Cookie—

LINCOLN   X-wife—

BOOTH   —could be in my bed you wouldnt notice—

LINCOLN   She was once—

BOOTH   Look the fuck around please.

[LINCOLN *looks around and sees the new suit on his chair.*]

LINCOLN   Wow.

BOOTH   Its yrs.

LINCOLN   Shit.

BOOTH   Got myself one too.

LINCOLN   Boosted?

BOOTH   Yeah, I boosted em. Theys stole from a big-ass department store. That store takes in more money in one day than we will in our whole life. I stole and I stole generously. I got one for me and I got one for you. Shoes belts shirts ties socks in the shoes and everything. Got that screen too.

LINCOLN   You all right, man.

BOOTH   Just cause I aint good as you at cards dont mean I cant do nothing.

LINCOLN   Lets try em on.

[*They stand in their separate sleeping spaces,* BOOTH *near his bed,* LINCOLN *near his recliner, and try on their new clothes.*]

BOOTH   Ima wear mine tonight. Gracell see me in this and *she* gonna ask me tuh marry *her.*

(*Rest*)

I got you the blue and I got me the brown. I walked in there and walked out and they didnt as much as bat an eye. Thats how smooth lil bro be, Link.

LINCOLN   You did good. You did real good, 3-Card.

BOOTH   All in a days work.

LINCOLN   They say the clothes make the man. All day long I wear that getup. But that dont make me who I am. Old black coat not even real old just fake old. Its got worn spots on the elbows, little raggedy places thatll break through into holes before the winters out. Shiny strips around the cuffs and the collar. Dust from the cap guns on the left shoulder where they shoot him, where they shoot me I should say but I never feel like they shooting me. The fella who had the gig before I had it wore the same coat. When I got the job they had the getup hanging there waiting for me. Said thuh fella before me just took it off one day and never came back.

(*Rest*)

Remember how Dads clothes used to hang in the closet?

BOOTH   Until you took em outside and burned em.

(*Rest*)

He had some nice stuff. What he didnt spend on booze he spent on women. What he didnt spend on them two he spent on clothes. He had some nice stuff. I would look at his stuff and calculate thuh how long it would take till I was big enough to fit it. Then you went and burned it all up.

LINCOLN   I got tired of looking at em without him in em.

(Rest)

They said thuh fella before me—he took off the getup one day, hung it up real nice, and never came back. And as they offered me thuh job, saying of course I would have to wear a little makeup and accept less than what they would offer a—another guy—

BOOTH   Go on, say it. "White." Theyd pay you less than theyd pay a white guy.

LINCOLN   I said to myself thats exactly what I would do: wear it out and then leave it hanging there and not come back. But until then, I would make a living at it. But it dont make me. Worn suit coat, not even worn by the fool that Im supposed to be playing, but making fools out of all those folks who come crowding in for they chance to play at something great. Fake beard. Top hat. Dont make me into no Lincoln. I was Lincoln on my own before any of that.

[The men finish dressing. They style and profile.]

BOOTH   Sharp, huh?

LINCOLN   Very sharp.

BOOTH   You look sharp too, man. You look like the real you. Most of the time you walking around all bedraggled and shit. You look good. Like you used to look back in thuh day when you had Cookie in love with you and all the women in the world was eating out of yr hand.

LINCOLN   This is real nice, man. I dont know where Im gonna wear it but its real nice.

BOOTH   Just wear it around. Itll make you feel good and when you feel good yll meet someone nice. Me I aint interested in meeting no one nice, I mean, I only got eyes for Grace. You think she'll go for me in this?

LINCOLN   I think thuh tie you gave me'll go better with what you got on.

BOOTH   Yeah?

LINCOLN   Grace likes bright colors dont she? My ties bright, yrs is too subdued.

BOOTH   Yeah. Gimmie yr tie.

LINCOLN   You gonna take back a gift?

BOOTH   I stole the damn thing didnt I? Gimmie yrs! I'll give you mines.

[They switch neckties. BOOTH is pleased. LINCOLN is more pleased.]

LINCOLN   Do thuh budget.

BOOTH   Right. Ok lets see: we got 314 dollars. We put 100 aside for the rent. 100 a week times 4 weeks makes the rent and—

LINCOLN and BOOTH   —we dont want thuh rent spent.

BOOTH   That leaves 214. We put aside 30 for the electric leaving 184. We put aside 50 for thuh phone leaving 134.

LINCOLN   We dont got a phone.

BOOTH   We pay our bill theyll turn it back on.

LINCOLN   We dont need no phone.

BOOTH   How you gonna get a woman if you dont got a phone? Women these days are more cautious, more whaddacallit, more circumspect. You go into a club looking like a fast daddy, you get a filly to give you her numerophono and gone is the days when she just gives you her number and dont ask for yrs.

LINCOLN   Like a woman is gonna call me.

BOOTH   She dont wanna call you she just doing a preliminary survey of the property. Shit, Link, you dont know nothin no more.

(Rest)

She gives you her number and she asks for yrs. You give her yr number. The phone number of yr home. Thereby telling her 3 things: 1) you got a home, that is, you aint no smooth talking smooth dressing *homeless* joe; 2) that you is in possession of a telephone and a working telephone number which is to say that you got thuh cash and thuh wherewithal to acquire for yr self the worlds most revolutionary communication apparatus and you together enough to pay yr bills!

LINCOLN   Whats 3?

BOOTH   You give her yr number you telling her that its cool to call if she should so please, that is, that you aint got no wife or wife approximation on the premises.

(Rest)

50 for the phone leaving 134. We put aside 40 for "med-sin."

LINCOLN   The price went up. 2 bucks more a bottle.

BOOTH   We'll put aside 50, then. That covers the bills. We got 84 left. 40 for meals together during the week leaving 44. 30 for me 14 for you. I got a woman I gotta impress tonight.

LINCOLN   You didnt take out for the phone last week.

BOOTH   Last week I was depressed. This week things is looking up. For both of us.

LINCOLN   Theyre talking about cutbacks at the arcade. I only been there 8 months, so—

BOOTH   Dont sweat it man, we'll find something else.

LINCOLN   Not nothing like this. I like the job. This is sit down, you know, easy work. I just gotta sit there all day. Folks come in kill phony Honest Abe with the phony pistol. I can sit there and let my mind travel.

BOOTH   Think of women.

LINCOLN   Sometimes.

(Rest)

All around the whole arcade is buzzing and popping. Thuh whirring of thuh duckshoot, baseballs smacking the back wall when someone misses the stack of cans, some woman getting happy cause her fella just won the ring toss. The Boss playing the barker talking up the fake freaks. The smell of the ocean and cotton candy and rat shit. And in thuh middle of all that, I can just sit and let my head go quiet. Make up songs, make plans. Forget.

(Rest)

You should come down again.

BOOTH   Once was plenty, but thanks.

(Rest)

Yr Best Customer, he come in today?

LINCOLN   Oh, yeah, he was there.

BOOTH   He shoot you?

LINCOLN   He shot Honest Abe, yeah.

BOOTH   He talk to you?

LINCOLN   In a whisper. Shoots on the left whispers on the right.

BOOTH   Whatd he say this time?

LINCOLN "Does thuh show stop when no ones watching or does thuh show go on?"

BOOTH Hes getting deep.

LINCOLN Yeah.

BOOTH Whatd he say, that one time? "Yr only yrself—"

LINCOLN "—when no ones watching," yeah.

BOOTH Thats deep shit.

(Rest)

Hes a brother, right?

LINCOLN I think so.

BOOTH He know yr a brother?

LINCOLN I dunno.

BOOTH Hes a *deep* black brother.

LINCOLN Yeah. He makes the day interesting.

BOOTH (Rest)

Thats a fucked-up job you got.

LINCOLN Its a living.

BOOTH But you aint living.

LINCOLN Im alive aint I?

(Rest)

One day I was throwing the cards. Next day Lonny died. Somebody shot him. I knew I was next, so I quit. I saved my life.

(Rest)

The arcade gig is the first lucky break Ive ever had. And Ive actually grown to like the work. And now theyre talking about cutting me.

BOOTH You was lucky with thuh cards.

LINCOLN Lucky? Aint nothing lucky about cards. Cards aint luck. Cards is work. Cards is skill. Aint never nothing lucky about cards.

(Rest)

I dont wanna lose my job.

BOOTH Then you gotta jazz up yr act. Elaborate yr moves, you know. You was always too stiff with it. You cant just sit there! Maybe, when they shoot you, you know, leap up flail yr arms then fall down and wiggle around and shit so they gotta shoot you more than once. Blam Blam Blam! Blam!

LINCOLN Help me practice. I'll sit here like I do at work and you be like one of the tourists.

BOOTH No thanks.

LINCOLN My paychecks on the line, man.

BOOTH I got a date. Practice on yr own.

(Rest)

I got a rendezvous with Grace. Shit she so sweet she makes my teeth hurt.

(Rest)

Link, uh, howbout slipping me an extra 5 spot. Its the biggest night of my life.

LINCOLN

BOOTH

[LINCOLN *gives* BOOTH *a* 5er]

BOOTH Thanks.

LINCOLN No sweat.

BOOTH   Howabout I run through it with you when I get back. Put on yr getup and practice till then.

LINCOLN   Sure.

> [BOOTH *leaves.* LINCOLN *stands there alone. He takes off his shoes, giving them a shine. He takes off his socks and his fancy suit, hanging it neatly over the little wooden chair. He takes his getup out of his shopping bag. He puts it on, slowly, like an actor preparing for a great role: frock coat, pants, beard, top hat, necktie. He leaves his feet bare. The top hat has an elastic band which he positions securely underneath his chin. He picks up the white pancake makeup but decides against it. He sits. He pretends to get shot, flings himself on the floor and thrashes around. He gets up, considers giving the new moves another try, but instead pours himself a big glass of whiskey and sits there drinking.*]

Scene Three

> [*Much later that same Friday evening. The recliner is reclined to its maximum horizontal position and* LINCOLN *lies there asleep. He wakes with a start. He is horrific, bleary eyed and hungover, in his full* LINCOLN *regalia. He takes a deep breath, realizes where he is and reclines again, going back to sleep.* BOOTH *comes in full of swagger. He slams the door trying to wake his brother who is dead to the world. He opens the door and slams it again. This time* LINCOLN *wakes up, as hungover and horrid as before.* BOOTH *swaggers about, his moves are exaggerated, rooster-like. He walks round and round* LINCOLN *making sure his brother sees him.*]

LINCOLN   You hurt yrself?

BOOTH   I had me "an evening to remember."

LINCOLN   You look like you hurt yrself.

BOOTH   Grace Grace Grace. *Grace.* She wants me back. She wants me back so bad she wiped her hand over the past where we wasnt together just so she could say we aint never been apart. She wiped her hand over our breakup. She wiped her hand over her childhood, her teenage years, her first boyfriend, just so she could say that she been mine since the dawn of time.

LINCOLN   Thats great, man.

BOOTH   And all the shit I put her through: she wiped it clean. And the women I saw while I was seeing her—

LINCOLN   Wiped clean too?

BOOTH   Mister Clean, Mister, Mister Clean!

LINCOLN   Whered you take her?

BOOTH   We was over at her place. I brought thuh food. Stopped at the best place I could find and stuffed my coat with only the best. We had the music we had the candlelight we had—

LINCOLN   She let you do it?

BOOTH   Course she let me do it.

LINCOLN   She let you do it without a rubber?

BOOTH   —Yeah.

LINCOLN   Bullshit.

BOOTH   I put my foot down—and she *melted.* And she was—huh—she was something else. I dont wanna get you jealous, though.

LINCOLN   Go head, I dont mind.

BOOTH   *(Rest)*
Well, you know what she looks like.

LINCOLN   She walks on by and the emergency room fills up cause all the guys get whiplash from lookin at her.

BOOTH   Thats right thats right. Well—she comes to the door wearing nothing but her little nightie, eats up the food I'd brought like there was no tomorrow and then goes and eats on me.

(Rest)

LINCOLN   Go on.

BOOTH   I dont wanna make you feel bad, man.

LINCOLN   Ssallright. Go on.

BOOTH   *(Rest)*

Well, uh, you know what shes like. Wild. Goodlooking. So sweet my teeth hurt.

LINCOLN   A sexmachine.

BOOTH   Yeah.

LINCOLN   A hotsy-totsy.

BOOTH   Yeah.

LINCOLN   Amazing Grace.

BOOTH   Amazing Grace! Yeah. Thats right. She let me do her how I wanted. And no rubber.

(Rest)

LINCOLN   Go on.

BOOTH   You dont wanna hear the mushy shit.

LINCOLN   Sure I do.

BOOTH   You hate mushy shit. You always hated thuh mushy shit.

LINCOLN   Ive changed. Go head. You had "an evening to remember," remember? I was just here alone sitting here. Drinking. Go head. Tell Link thuh stink.

(Rest)

Howd ya do her?

BOOTH   Dogstyle.

LINCOLN   Amazing Grace.

BOOTH   In front of a mirror.

LINCOLN   So you could see her. Her face her breasts her back her ass. Graces got a great ass.

BOOTH   Its all right.

LINCOLN   Amazing Grace!

[BOOTH *goes into his bed area and takes off his suit, tossing the clothes on the floor.*]

BOOTH   She said next time Ima have to use a rubber. She let me have my way this time but she said that next time I'd have to put my boots on.

LINCOLN   Im sure you can talk her out of it.

BOOTH   Yeah.

(Rest)

What kind of rubbers you use, I mean, when you was with Cookie.

LINCOLN   We didnt use rubbers. We was married, man.

BOOTH   Right. But you had other women on the side. What kind you use when you was with them?

LINCOLN   Magnums.

BOOTH   Thats thuh kind I picked up. For next time. Grace was real strict about it. Magnums.

[While BOOTH *sits on his bed fiddling with his box of condoms,* LINCOLN *sits in his chair and resumes drinking.*]

LINCOLN   Theyre for "the larger man."

BOOTH   Right. Right.

[LINCOLN *keeps drinking as* BOOTH, *sitting in the privacy of his bedroom, fiddles with the condoms, perhaps trying to put one on.*]

LINCOLN   Thats right.

BOOTH   Graces real different from them fly-by-night gals I was making do with. Shes in school. Making something of herself. Studying cosmetology. You should see what she can do with a womans hair and nails.

LINCOLN   Too bad you aint a woman.

BOOTH   What?

LINCOLN   You could get yrs done for free, I mean.

BOOTH   Yeah. She got this way of sitting. Of talking. That. Everything she does is. Shes just so hot.

(*Rest*)

We was together 2 years. Then we broke up. I had my little employment difficulty and she needed time to think.

LINCOLN   And shes through thinking now.

BOOTH   Thats right.

LINCOLN

BOOTH

LINCOLN   Whatcha doing back there?

BOOTH   Resting. That girl wore me out.

LINCOLN   You want some med-sin?

BOOTH   No thanks.

LINCOLN   Come practice my moves with me, then.

BOOTH   Lets hit it tomorrow, K?

LINCOLN   I been waiting. I got all dressed up and you said if I waited up—come on, man, they gonna replace me with a wax dummy.

BOOTH   No shit.

LINCOLN   Thats what theyre talking about. Probably just talk, but—come on, man, I even lent you 5 bucks.

BOOTH   Im tired.

LINCOLN   You didnt get shit tonight.

BOOTH   You jealous, man. You just jail-us.

LINCOLN   You laying over there yr balls blue as my boosted suit. Laying over there waiting for me to go back to sleep or black out so I wont hear you rustling thuh pages of yr fuck book.

BOOTH   Fuck you, man.

LINCOLN   I was over there looking for something the other week and theres like 100 fuck books under yr bed and theyre matted together like a bad fro, bro, cause you spunked in the pages and didnt wipe them off.

BOOTH   Im hot. I need constant sexual release. If I wasnt taking care of myself by myself I would be out there running around on thuh town which costs cash that I dont have so I would be doing worse: I'd be out there doing who knows what, shooting people and shit. Out of a need for unresolved sexual release. I'm a hot man. I aint apologizing for it. When I dont got a woman, I gotta make do. Not like you, Link. When you dont got a woman you just sit there. Letting yr shit fester. Yr dick, if it aint failed off yet, is hanging there between yr legs, little whiteface shriveled-up blank-shooting grub worm. As goes thuh man so goes thuh mans dick. Thats what I say. Least my shits intact.

(*Rest*)

You a limp dick jealous whiteface motherfucker whose wife dumped him cause he couldnt get it up and she told me so. Came crawling to me cause she needed a man.

(*Rest*)

I gave it to Grace good tonight. So goodnight.

LINCOLN   (*Rest*)

Goodnight.

LINCOLN

BOOTH

LINCOLN

BOOTH

LINCOLN

BOOTH

> [LINCOLN *sitting in his chair.* BOOTH *lying in bed. Time passes.* BOOTH *peeks out to see if* LINCOLN *is asleep.* LINCOLN *is watching for him.*]

LINCOLN   You can hustle 3-card monte without me you know.

BOOTH   Im planning to.

LINCOLN   I could contact my old crew. You could work with them. Lonny aint around no more but theres the rest of them. Theyre good.

BOOTH   I can get my own crew. I dont need yr crew. Buncha has-beens. I can get my own crew.

LINCOLN   My crews experienced. We usedta pull down a thousand a day. Thats 7 G a week. That was years ago. They probably do twice, 3 times that now.

BOOTH   I got my own connections, thank you.

LINCOLN   Theyd take you on in a heartbeat. With my say. My say still counts with them. They know you from before, when you tried to hang with us but—wernt ready yet. They know you from then, but I'd talk you up. I'd say yr my bro, which they know, and I'd say youd been working the west coast. Little towns. Mexican border. Taking tourists. I'd tell them you got moves like I dreamed of having. Meanwhile youd be working out yr shit right here, right in this room, getting good and getting better every day so when I did do the reintroductions youd have some marketable skills. Youd be passable.

BOOTH   I'd be more than passable, I'd be the be all end all.

LINCOLN   Youd be the be all end all. And youd have my say. If yr interested.

BOOTH   Could do.

LINCOLN   Youd have to get a piece. They all pack pistols, bro.

BOOTH   I *got* a piece.

LINCOLN   Youd have to be packing something more substantial than that pop gun, 3-Card. These hustlers is upper echelon hustlers they pack upper echelon heat, not no Saturday night shit, now.

BOOTH   Whata you know of heat? You aint hung with those guys for 6, 7 years. You swore off em. Threw yr heat in thuh river and you "Dont touch thuh cards." I know more about heat than you know about heat.

LINCOLN   Im around guns every day. At the arcade. Theyve all been reworked so they only fire caps but I see guns every day. Lots of guns.

BOOTH   What kinds?

LINCOLN   You been there, you seen them. Shiny deadly metal each with their own deadly personality.

BOOTH Maybe I *could* visit you over there. I'd boost one of them guns and rework it to make it shoot for real again. What kind you think would best suit my personality?

LINCOLN You aint stealing nothing from the arcade.

BOOTH I go in there and steal if I want to go in there and steal I go in there and steal.

LINCOLN It aint worth it. They dont shoot nothing but blanks.

BOOTH Yeah, like you. Shooting blanks.

(Rest)

(Rest)

You ever wonder if someones gonna come in there with a real gun? A real gun with real slugs? Someone with uh axe tuh grind or something?

LINCOLN No.

BOOTH Someone who hates you come in there and guns you down and gets gone before anybody finds out.

LINCOLN I dont got no enemies.

BOOTH Yr X.

LINCOLN Cookie dont hate me.

BOOTH Yr Best Customer? Some miscellaneous stranger?

LINCOLN I cant be worrying about the actions of miscellaneous strangers.

BOOTH But there they come day in day out for a chance to shoot Honest Abe.

(Rest)

Who are they mostly?

LINCOLN I dont really look.

BOOTH You must see something.

LINCOLN Im supposed to be staring straight ahead. Watching a play, like Abe was.

BOOTH All day goes by and you never ever take a sneak peek at who be pulling the trigger.

[*Pulled in by his own curiosity,* BOOTH *has come out of his bed area to stand on the dividing line between the two spaces.*]

LINCOLN Its pretty dark. To keep thuh illusion of thuh whole thing.

(Rest)

But on thuh wall opposite where I sit theres a little electrical box, like a fuse box. Silver metal. Its got uh dent in it like somebody hit it with they fist. Big old dent so everything reflected in it gets reflected upside down. Like yr looking in uh spoon. And thats where I can see em. The assassins.

(Rest)

Not behind me yet but I can hear him coming. Coming in with his gun in hand, thuh gun he already picked out up front when he paid his fare. Coming on in. But not behind me yet. His dress shoes making too much noise on the carpet, the carpets too thin, Boss should get a new one but hes cheap. Not behind me yet. Not behind me yet Cheap lightbulb just above my head.

(Rest)

And there he is. Standing behind me. Standing in position. Standing upside down. Theres some feet shapes on the floor so he knows just where he oughta stand. So he wont miss. Thuh gun is always cold. Winter or summer thuh gun is always cold. And when the gun touches me he can feel that Im warm and he knows Im alive. And if Im alive then he can shoot me dead. And for a minute, with him hanging back there behind me, its real. Me looking at him upside down and him looking at me looking like Lincoln. Then he shoots.

(Rest)

I slump down and close my eyes. And he goes out thuh other way. More come in. Uh whole day full. Bunches of kids, little good for nothings, in they school uniforms. Businessmen smelling like two for one martinis. Tourists in they theme park t-shirts trying to catch it on film. Housewives with they mouths closed tight, shooting more than once.

(Rest)

They all get so into it. I do my best for them. And now they talking bout cutting me, replacing me with uh wax dummy.

BOOTH   You just gotta show yr boss that you can do things a wax dummy cant do. You too dry with it. You gotta add spicy shit.

LINCOLN   Like what.

BOOTH   Like when they shoot you, I dunno, scream or something.

LINCOLN   Scream?

   [*Booth plays the killer without using his gun.*]

BOOTH   Try it. I'll be the killer. Bang!

LINCOLN   Aaaah!

BOOTH   Thats good.

LINCOLN   A wax dummy can scream. They can put a voicebox in it and make it like its screaming.

BOOTH   You can curse. Try it. Bang!

LINCOLN   Motherfucking cocksucker!

BOOTH   Thats good, man.

LINCOLN   They aint going for that, though.

BOOTH   You practice rolling and wiggling on the floor?

LINCOLN   A little.

BOOTH   Lemmie see. Bang!

   [LINCOLN *slumps down, falls on the floor and silently wiggles around.*]

BOOTH   You look more like a worm on the sidewalk. Move yr arms. Good. Now scream or something.

LINCOLN   Aaaah! Aaaaah! Aaaah!

BOOTH   A little tougher than that, you sound like yr fucking.

LINCOLN   Aaaaaah!

BOOTH   Hold yr head or something, where I shotcha. Good. And look at me! I am the assassin! *I am Booth!!* Come on man this is life and death! Go all out!

   [LINCOLN *goes all out.*]

BOOTH   Cool, man thats cool. Thats enough.

LINCOLN   Whatdoyathink?

BOOTH   I dunno, man. Something about it. I dunno. It was looking too real or something.

LINCOLN   Goddamn you! They dont want it looking too real. I'd scare the customers. Then I'd be out for sure. Yr trying to get me fired.

BOOTH   Im trying to help. Cross my heart.

LINCOLN   People are funny about they Lincoln shit. Its historical. People like they historical shit in a certain way. They like it to unfold the way they folded it up. Neatly like a book. Not raggedy and bloody and screaming. You trying to get me fired.

(*Rest*)

I am uh brother playing Lincoln. Its uh stretch for anyones imagination. And it aint easy for me neither. Every day I put on that shit, I leave my own shit at the door and I put on that shit and I go out there and I make it work. I make it look easy but its hard. That shit is hard. But it works. Cause I work it. And you trying to get me fired.

(*Rest*)

I swore off them cards. Took nowhere jobs. Drank. Then Cookie threw me out. What thuh fuck was I gonna do? I seen that "Help Wanted" sign and I went up in there and I looked good in the getup and agreed to the whiteface and they really dug it that me and Honest Abe got the same name.

(*Rest*)

Its a sit down job. With benefits. I dont wanna get fired. They wont give me a good reference if I get fired.

BOOTH   Iffen you was tuh get fired, then, well—then you and me could—hustle the cards together. We'd have to support ourselves somehow.

(*Rest*)

Just show me how to do the hook part of the card hustle, man. The part where the Dealer looks away but somehow he sees—

LINCOLN   I couldnt remember if I wanted to.

BOOTH   Sure you could.

LINCOLN   No.

(*Rest*)

Night, man.

BOOTH   Yeah.

> [LINCOLN *stretches out in his recliner.* BOOTH *stands over him waiting for him to get up, to change his mind. But* LINCOLN *is fast asleep.* BOOTH *covers him with a blanket then goes to his bed, turning off the lights as he goes. He quietly rummages underneath his bed for a girlie magazine which, as the lights fade, he reads with great interest.*]

Scene Four

> [*Saturday. Just before dawn.* LINCOLN *gets up. Looks around.* BOOTH *is fast asleep, dead to the world.*]

LINCOLN   No fucking running water.

> [*He stumbles around the room looking for something which he finally finds: a plastic cup, which he uses as a urinal. He finishes peeing and finds an out of the way place to stow the cup. He claws at his* LINCOLN *getup, removing it and tearing it in the process. He strips down to his t-shirt and shorts.*]

LINCOLN   Hate falling asleep in this damn shit. Shit. Ripped the beard. I can just hear em tomorrow. Busiest day of the week. They looking me over to make sure Im presentable. They got a slew of guys working but Im the only one they look over every day. "Yr beards ripped, pal. Sure, we'll getcha new one but its gonna be coming outa yr pay." Shit. I should quit right then and there. I'd yank off the beard, throw it on the ground and stomp it, then go strangle the fucking boss. Thatd be good. My hands around his neck and his bug eyes bugging out. You been ripping me off since I took this job and now Im gonna have to take it outa *yr* pay, motherfucker. Shit.

(*Rest*)

Sit down job. With benefits.

(Rest)

Hustling. Shit, I was good. I was great. Hell I was the be all end all. I was throwing cards like throwing cards was made for me. Made for me and me alone. I was the best anyone ever seen. Coast to coast. Everybody said so. And I never lost. Not once. Not one time. Not never. Thats how much them cards was mines. I was the be all end all. I was that good.

(Rest)

Then you woke up one day and you didnt have the taste for it no more. Like something in you knew—. Like something in you knew it was time to quit. Quit while you was still ahead. Something in you was telling you—. But hells no. Not Link thuh stink. So I went out there and threw one more time. What thuh fuck. And Lonny died.

(Rest)

Got yrself a good job. And when the arcade lets you go yll get another good job. I dont gotta spend my whole life hustling. Theres more to Link than that. More to me than some cheap hustle. More to life than cheating some idiot out of his paycheck or his life savings.

(Rest)

Like that joker and his wife from out of town. Always wanted to see the big city. I said you could see the bigger end of the big city with a little more cash. And if they was fast enough, faster than me, and here I slowed down my moves I slowed em way down and my Lonny, my right hand, my Stickman, Lonny could draw a customer in like nothing else, Lonny could draw a fly from fresh shit, he could draw Adam outa Eve just with that look he had, Lonny always got folks playing.

(Rest)

Somebody shot him. They dont know who. Nobody knows nobody cares.

(Rest)

We took that man and his wife for hundreds. No, thousands. We took them for everything they had and everything they ever wanted to have. We took a father for the money he was gonna get his kids new bike with and he cried in the street while we vanished. We took a mothers welfare check, she pulled a knife on us and we ran. She threw it but her aim werent shit. People shopping. Greedy. Thinking they could take me and they got took instead.

(Rest)

Swore off thuh cards. Something inside me telling me—. But I was good.

LINCOLN

LINCOLN

> [*He sees a packet of cards. He studies them like an alcoholic would study a drink. Then he reaches for them, delicately picking them up and choosing 3 cards.*]

LINCOLN   Still got my moves. Still got my touch. Still got my chops. Thuh feel of it. And I aint hurting no one, God. Link is just here hustling hisself.

(Rest)

Lets see whatcha got.

> [*He stands over the monte setup. Then he bends over it placing the cards down and moving them around. Slowly at first, aimlessly, as if*

hes just making little ripples in water. But then the game draws him in. Unlike BOOTH, LINCOLNS *patter and moves are deft, dangerous, electric.]*

LINCOLN   (((Lean in close and watch me now: who see thuh black card who see thuh black card I see thuh black card black cards thuh winner pick thuh black card thats thuh winner pick thuh red card thats thuh loser pick thuh other red card thats thuh other loser pick thuh black card you pick thuh winner. Watch me as I throw thuh cards. Here we go.)))

(Rest)

(((Who see thuh black card who see thuh black card? You pick thuh red card you pick a loser you pick that red card you pick a loser you pick thuh black card thuh deuce of spades you pick a winner who sees thuh deuce of spades thuh one who sees it never fades watch me now as I throw thuh cards. Red losers black winner follow thuh deuce of spades chase thuh black deuce. Dark deuce will get you thuh win.)))

> *[Even though* LINCOLN *speaks softly,* BOOTH *wakes and, unbeknownst to Lincoln, listens intently.]*

(Rest)

LINCOLN   ((10 will get you 20, 20 will get you 40.))

(Rest)

((Ima show you thuh cards: 2 red cards but only one spade. Dark winner in thuh center and thuh red losers on thuh sides. Pick uh red card you got a loser pick thuh other red card you got a loser pick thuh black card you got a winner. One good pickll get you in, 2 good picks and you gone win. Watch me come on watch me now.))

(Rest)

((Who sees thuh winner who knows where its at? You do? You sure? Go on then, put yr money where yr mouth is. Put yr money down you aint no clown. No? Ah, you had thuh card but you didnt have thuh heart.))

(Rest)

((Watch me now as I throw thuh cards watch me real close. Ok, man, you know which card is the deuce of spades? Was you watching Links lighting fast express? Was you watching Link cause he the best? So you sure, huh? Point it out first, then place yr bet and Linkll show you yr winner.))

(Rest)

((500 dollars? You thuh man of thuh hour you thuh man with thuh power. You musta been watching Link real close. You must be thuh man who know thuh most. Ok. Lay the cash in my hand cause Link the man. Thank you, mister. This card you say?))

(Rest)

((Wrong! Ha!))

(Rest)

((Thats thuh show. We gotta go.))

> *[Lincoln puts the cards down. He moves away from the monte setup. He sits on the edge of his easy chair, but he can't take his eyes off the cards.]*
>
> *[Intermission]*

Scene Five

[*Several days have passed. Its now Wednesday night.* BOOTH *is sitting in his brand-new suit. The monte setup is nowhere in sight. In its place is a table with two nice chairs. The table is covered with a lovely tablecloth and there are nice plates, silverware, champagne glasses and candles. All the makings of a very romantic dinner for two. The whole apartment in fact takes its cue from the table. Its been cleaned up considerably. New curtains on the windows, a doily-like object on the recliner.* BOOTH *sits at the table darting his eyes around, making sure everything is looking good.*]

BOOTH   Shit.

[*He notices some of his girlie magazines visible from underneath his bed. He goes over and nudges them out of sight. He sits back down. He notices that theyre still visible. He goes over and nudges them some more, kicking at them finally. Then he takes the spread from his bed and pulls it down, hiding them. He sits back down. He gets up. Checks the champagne on much melted ice. Checks the food.*]

BOOTH   Foods getting cold, Grace!! Dont worry man, she'll get here, she'll get here.

[*He sits back down. He goes over to the bed. Checks it for springiness. Smoothes down the bedspread. Double-checks 2 matching silk dressing gowns, very expensive, marked "His" and "Hers." Lays the dressing gowns across the bed again. He sits back down. He cant help but notice the visibility of the girlie magazines again. He goes to the bed, kicks them fiercely, then on his hands and knees shoves them. Then he begins to get under the bed to push them, but he remembers his nice clothing and takes off his jacket. After a beat he removes his pants and, in this half-dressed way, he crawls under the bed to give those telltale magazines a good and final shove.* LINCOLN *comes in. At first* BOOTH, *still stripped down to his underwear, thinks its his date. When he realizes its his brother, he does his best to keep* LINCOLN *from entering the apartment.* LINCOLN *wears his frock coat and carries the rest of his getup in a plastic bag.*]

LINCOLN   You in the middle of it?

BOOTH   What the hell you doing here?

LINCOLN   It yr in thuh middle of it I can go. Or I can just be real quiet and just—sing a song in my head or something.

BOOTH   The casas off limits to you tonight.

LINCOLN   You know when we lived in that 2-room place with the cement backyard and the frontyard with nothing but trash in it, Mom and Pops would do it in the middle of the night and I would always hear them but I would sing in my head, cause, I dunno, I couldnt bear to listen.

BOOTH   You gotta get out of here.

LINCOLN   I would make up all kinds of songs. Oh, sorry, yr all up in it. No sweat, bro. No sweat. Hey, Grace, howyadoing?!

BOOTH   She aint here yet, man. Shes running late. And its a good thing too cause I aint all dressed yet. Yr gonna spend thuh night with friends?

LINCOLN   Yeah.

[BOOTH *waits for* LINCOLN *to leave.* LINCOLN *stands his ground.*]

LINCOLN   I lost my job.

BOOTH   Hunh.

LINCOLN   I come in there right on time like I do every day and that motherfucker gives me some song and dance about cutbacks and too many folks complaining.

BOOTH   Hunh.

LINCOLN   Showd me thuh wax dummy—hes buying it right out of a catalog.
(*Rest*)
I walked out still wearing my getup.
(*Rest*)
I could go back in tomorrow. I could tell him I'll take another pay cut. Thatll get him to take me back.

BOOTH   Link. Yr free. Dont go crawling back. Yr free at last! Now you can do anything you want. Yr not tied down by that job. You can—you can do something else. Something that pays better maybe.

LINCOLN   You mean Hustle.

BOOTH   Maybe. Hey, Graces on her way. You gotta go.
[LINCOLN *flops into his chair.* BOOTH *is waiting for him to move.* LINCOLN *doesnt budge.*]

LINCOLN   I'll stay until she gets here. I'll act nice. I wont embarrass you.

BOOTH   You gotta go.

LINCOLN   What time she coming?

BOOTH   Shes late. She could be here any second.

LINCOLN   I'll meet her. I met her years ago. I'll meet her again.
(*Rest*)
How late is she?

BOOTH   She was supposed to be here at 8.

LINCOLN   Its after 2 a.m. Shes—shes late.
(*Rest*)
Maybe when she comes you could put the blanket over me and I'll just pretend like Im not here.
(*Rest*)
I'll wait. And when she comes I'll go. I need to sit down. I been walking around all day.

BOOTH

LINCOLN
[BOOTH *goes to his bed and dresses hurriedly.*]

BOOTH   Pretty nice, right? The china thuh silver thuh crystal.

LINCOLN   Its great.
(*Rest*)
Boosted?

BOOTH   Yeah.

LINCOLN   Thought you went and spent yr inheritance for a minute, you had me going I was thinking shit, BOOTH—3-Card—that 3-Cards gone and spent his inheritance and the gal is—late.

BOOTH   Its boosted. Every bit of it.
(*Rest*)
Fuck this waiting bullshit.

LINCOLN   She'll be here in a minute. Dont sweat it.

BOOTH   Right.
[BOOTH *comes to the table. Sits. Relaxes as best he can.*]

BOOTH   How come I got a hand for boosting and I dont got a hand for throwing cards? Its sorta the same thing—you gotta be quick—and slick. Maybe yll show me yr moves sometime.

LINCOLN

BOOTH

LINCOLN

BOOTH

LINCOLN   Look out the window. When you see Grace coming, I'll go.

BOOTH   Cool. Cause youd jinx it, youd really jinx it. Maybe you being here has jinxed it already. Naw. Shes just a little late. You aint jinxed nothing.

> [BOOTH sits by the window, glancing out, watching for his date. LINCOLN sits in his recliner. He finds the whiskey bottle, sips from it. He then rummages around, finding the raggedy photo album. He looks through it.]

LINCOLN   There we are at that house. Remember when we moved in?

BOOTH   No.

LINCOLN   You were 2 or 3.

BOOTH   I was 4.

LINCOLN   I was 9. We all thought it was the best fucking house in the world.

BOOTH   Cement backyard and a frontyard full of trash, yeah, dont be going down memory lane man, yll jinx thuh vibe I got going in here. Gracell be walking in here and wrinkling up her nose cause you done jinxed up thuh joint with yr raggedy recollections.

LINCOLN   We had some great times in that house, bro. Selling lemonade on thuh corner, thuh treehouse out back, summers spent lying in thuh grass and looking at thuh stars.

BOOTH   We never did none of that shit.

LINCOLN   But we had us some good times. That row of nails I got you to line up behind Dads car so when he backed out the driveway to work—

BOOTH   He came back that night, only time I ever seen his face go red, 4 flat tires and yelling bout how thuh white man done sabotaged him again.

LINCOLN   And neither of us flinched. Neither of us let on that itd been us.

BOOTH   It was at dinner, right? What were we eating?

LINCOLN   Food.

BOOTH   We was eating pork chops, mashed potatoes and peas. I remember cause I had to look at them peas real hard to keep from letting on. And I would glance over at you, not really glancing not actually turning my head, but I was looking at you out thuh corner of my eye. I was sure he was gonna find us out and then he woulda whipped us good. But I kept glancing at you and you was cool, man. Like nothing was going on. You was cooooool.

(Rest)

What time is it?

LINCOLN   After 3.

(Rest)

You should call her. Something mighta happened.

BOOTH   No man, Im cool. She'll be here in a minute. Patience is a virtue. She'll be here.

LINCOLN   You look sad.

BOOTH   Nope. Im just, you know, Im just—

LINCOLN   Cool.

BOOTH   Yeah. Cool.

> [BOOTH comes over, takes the bottle of whiskey and pours himself a big glassful. He returns to the window looking out and drinking.]

BOOTH   They give you a severance package, at thuh job?

LINCOLN   A weeks pay.

BOOTH   Great.

LINCOLN   I blew it. Spent it all.

BOOTH   On what?

LINCOLN   —. Just spent it.

(Rest)

It felt good, spending it. Felt really good. Like back in thuh day when I was really making money. Throwing thuh cards all day and strutting and rutting all night. Didnt have to take no shit from no fool, didnt have to worry about getting fired in favor of some damn wax dummy. I was thuh shit and they was my fools.

(Rest)

Back in thuh day.

(Rest)

(Rest)

Why you think they left us, man?

BOOTH   Mom and Pops? I dont think about it too much.

LINCOLN   I dont think they liked us.

BOOTH   Naw. That aint it.

LINCOLN   I think there was something out there that they liked more than they liked us and for years they was struggling against moving towards that more liked something. Each of them had a special something that they was struggling against. Moms had hers. Pops had his. And they was struggling. We moved out of that nasty apartment into a house. A whole house. It wernt perfect but it was a house and theyd bought it and they brought us there and everything we owned, figuring we could be a family in that house and them things, them two separate things each of them was struggling against, would just leave them be. Them things would see thuh house and be impressed and just leave them be. Would see thuh job Pops had and how he shined his shoes every night before he went to bed, shining them shoes whether they needed it or not, and thuh thing he was struggling against would see all that and just let him be, and thuh thing Moms was struggling against, it would see the food on the table every night and listen to her voice when she'd read to us sometimes, the clean clothes, the buttons sewed on all right and it would just let her be. Just let us all be, just regular people living in a house. That wernt too much to ask.

BOOTH   Least we was grown when they split.

LINCOLN   16 and 11 aint grown.

BOOTH   16s grown. Almost. And I was ok cause you were there.

(Rest)

Shit man, it aint like they both one day both, together packed all they shit up and left us so they could have fun in thuh sun on some tropical island and you and me would have to grub in thuh dirt forever. They didnt leave together. That makes it different. She left. 2 years go by. Then he left. Like neither of them couldnt handle it no more. She split then he split. Like thuh whole family mortgage bills going to work thing was just too much. And I dont blame them. You dont see me holding down a steady job. Cause its bullshit and I know it. I seen how it cracked them up and I aint going there.

(Rest)

It aint right me trying to make myself into a one woman man just because she wants me like that. One woman rubber-wearing mother-fucker. Shit. Not me. She gonna walk in here looking all hot and shit trying to see how much she can get me to sweat, how much she can get me to give her before she gives me mines. Shit.

LINCOLN

BOOTH

LINCOLN   Moms told me I shouldnt never get married.

BOOTH   She told me thuh same thing.

LINCOLN   They gave us each 500 bucks then they cut out.

BOOTH   Thats what Im gonna do. Give my kids 500 bucks then cut out. Thats thuh way to do it.

LINCOLN   You dont got no kids.

BOOTH   Im gonna have kids then Im gonna cut out.

LINCOLN   Leaving each of yr offspring 500 bucks as yr splitting.

BOOTH   Yeah.

(Rest)

Just goes to show Mom and Pops had some agreement between them.

LINCOLN   How so.

BOOTH   Theyd stopped talking to eachother. Theyd stopped *screwing* eachother. But they had an agreement. Somewhere in there when it looked like all they had was hate they sat down and did thuh "split" budget.

(Rest)

When Moms splits she gives me 5 hundred-dollar bills rolled up and tied up tight in one of her nylon stockings. She tells me to put it in a safe place, to spend it only in case of an emergency, and not to tell nobody I got it, not even you. 2 years later Pops splits and before he goes—

LINCOLN   He slips me 10 fifties in a clean handkerchief: "Hide this some-wheres good, dont go blowing it, dont tell no one you got it, especially that Booth."

BOOTH   Theyd been scheming together all along. They left separately but they was in agreement. Maybe they arrived at the same place at the same time, maybe they renewed they wedding vows, maybe they got another family.

LINCOLN   Maybe they got 2 new kids. 2 boys. Different than us, though. Better.

BOOTH   Maybe.

[*Their glasses are empty. The whiskey bottle is empty too.* BOOTH *takes the champagne bottle from the ice tub. He pops the cork and pours drinks for his brother and himself.*]

BOOTH   I didnt mind them leaving cause you was there. Thats why Im hooked on us working together. If we could work together it would be like old times. They split and we got that room downtown. You was done with school and I stopped going. And we had to run around doing odd jobs just to keep the lights on and the heat going and thuh child protec-tion bitch off our backs. It was you and me against thuh world, Link. It could be like that again.

LINCOLN

BOOTH

LINCOLN

BOOTH

LINCOLN   Throwing thuh cards aint as easy as it looks.

BOOTH   I aint stupid.

LINCOLN   When you hung with us back then, you was just on thuh side-lines. Thuh perspective from thuh sidelines is thuh perspective of a customer. There was all kinds of things you didnt know nothing about.

BOOTH   Lonny would entice folks into thuh game as they walked by. Thuh 2 folks on either side of ya looked like they was playing but they was only pretending tuh play. Just tuh generate excitement. You was moving thuh cards as fast as you could hoping that yr hands would be faster than yr customers eyes. Sometimes you won sometimes you lost what else is there to know?

LINCOLN   Thuh customer is actually called the "Mark." You know why?

BOOTH   Cause hes thuh one you got yr eye on. You mark him with yr eye.

LINCOLN

LINCOLN

BOOTH   Im right, right?

LINCOLN   Lemmie show you a few moves. If you pick up these yll have a chance.

BOOTH   Yr playing.

LINCOLN   Get thuh cards and set it up.

BOOTH   No shit.

LINCOLN   Set it up set it up.

> [*In a flash,* BOOTH *clears away the romantic table setting by gathering it all up in the tablecloth and tossing it aside. As he does so he reveals the "table" underneath: the 2 stacked monte milk crates and the cardboard playing surface.* LINCOLN *lays out the cards. The brothers are ready.* LINCOLN *begins to teach* BOOTH *in earnest.*]

LINCOLN   Thuh deuce of spades is thuh card tuh watch.

BOOTH   I work with thuh deuce of hearts. But spades is cool.

LINCOLN   Theres thuh Dealer, thuh Stickman, thuh Sides, thuh Lookout and thuh Mark. I'll be thuh Dealer.

BOOTH   I'll be thuh Lookout. Lemmie be thuh Lookout, right? I'll keep an eye for thuh cops. I got my piece in my pants.

LINCOLN   You got it on you right now?

BOOTH   I always carry it.

LINCOLN   Even on a date? In yr own home?

BOOTH   You never know, man.

(*Rest*)

So Im thuh Lookout.

LINCOLN   Gimmie yr piece.

> [BOOTH *gives* LINCOLN *his gun.* LINCOLN *moves the little wooden chair to face right in front of the setup. He then puts the gun on the chair.*]

LINCOLN   We dont need nobody standing on the corner watching for cops cause there aint none. Thatll be the lookout.

BOOTH   I'll be thuh Stickman, then.

LINCOLN   Stickman knows the game inside out. You aint there yet. But you will be. You wanna learn good, be my Sideman. Playing along with the Dealer, moving the Mark to lay his money down. You wanna learn, right?

BOOTH   I'll be thuh Side.

LINCOLN   Good.

(Rest)

First thing you learn is what is. Next thing you learn is what aint. You dont know what is you dont know what aint, you dont know shit.

BOOTH Right.

LINCOLN

BOOTH

BOOTH Whatchu looking at?

LINCOLN Im sizing you up.

BOOTH Oh yeah?!

LINCOLN Dealer always sizes up thuh crowd.

BOOTH Im yr Side, Link, Im on yr team, you dont go sizing up yr own team. You save looks like that for yr Mark.

LINCOLN Dealer always sizes up thuh crowd. Everybody out there is part of the crowd. His crew is part of the crowd, he himself is part of the crowd. Dealer always sizes up thuh crowd.

> [LINCOLN *looks* BOOTH *over some more then looks around at an imaginary crowd.*]

BOOTH Then what then what?

LINCOLN Dealer dont wanna play.

BOOTH Bullshit man! Come on you promised!

LINCOLN Thats thuh Dealers attitude. He *acts* like he dont wanna play. He holds back and thuh crowd, with their eagerness to see his skill and their willingness to take a chance, and their greediness to win his cash, the larceny in their hearts, all goad him on and push him to throw his cards, although of course the Dealer has been wanting to throw his cards all along. Only he dont never show it.

BOOTH Thats some sneaky shit, Link.

LINCOLN It sets thuh mood. You wanna have them in yr hand before you deal a hand, K?

BOOTH Cool. —K.

LINCOLN Right.

LINCOLN

BOOTH

BOOTH You sizing me up again?

LINCOLN Theres 2 parts to throwing thuh cards. Both parts are fairly complicated. Thuh moves and thuh grooves, thuh talk and thuh walk, thuh patter and thuh pitter pat, thuh flap and thuh rap: what yr doing with yr mouth and what yr doing with yr hands.

BOOTH I got thuh words down pretty good.

LINCOLN You need to work on both.

BOOTH K.

LINCOLN A goodlooking walk and a dynamite talk captivates their entire attention. The Mark focuses with 2 organs primarily: his eyes and his ears. Leave one out you lose yr shirt. Captivate both, yr golden.

BOOTH So them times I seen you lose, them times I seen thuh Mark best you, that was a time when yr hands werent fast enough or yr patter werent right.

LINCOLN You could say that.

BOOTH So, there was plenty of times—

> [LINCOLN *moves the cards around.*]

LINCOLN You see what Im doing? Dont look at my hands, man, look at my eyes. Know what is and know what aint.

BOOTH What is?

LINCOLN My eyes.

BOOTH What aint?

LINCOLN My hands. Look at my eyes not my hands. And you standing there thinking how thuh fuck I gonna learn how tuh throw thuh cards if I be looking in his eyes? Look into my eyes and get yr focus. Dont think about learning how tuh throw thuh cards. Dont think about nothing. Just look into my eyes. Get yr focus.

BOOTH Theyre red.

LINCOLN Look into my eyes.

BOOTH You been crying?

LINCOLN Just look into my eyes, fool. Now. Look down at thuh cards. I been moving and moving and moving them around. Ready?

BOOTH Yeah.

LINCOLN Ok, Sideman, thuh Marks got his eye on you. Yr gonna show him its easy.

BOOTH K.

LINCOLN Pick out thuh deuce of spades. Dont pick it up just point to it.

BOOTH This one, right?

LINCOLN Dont ask thuh Dealer if yr right, man, point to yr card with confidence.

> [BOOTH *points*.]

BOOTH That one.

> (*Rest*)

Flip it over, man.

> [LINCOLN *flips over the card. It is in fact the deuce of spades.* BOOTH *struts around gloating like a rooster.* LINCOLN *is mildly crestfallen.*]

BOOTH Am I right or am I right?! Make room for 3-Card! Here comes thuh champ!

LINCOLN Cool. Stay focused. Now we gonna add the second element. Listen.

> [LINCOLN *moves the cards and speaks in a low hypnotic voice.*]

LINCOLN Lean in close and watch me now: who see thuh black card who see thuh black card I see thuh black card black cards thuh winner pick thuh black card thats thuh winner pick thuh red card thats thuh loser pick thuh other red card thats thuh other loser pick thuh black card you pick thuh winner. Watch me as I throw thuh cards. Here we go.

> (*Rest*)

Who see thuh black card who see thuh black card? You pick thuh red card you pick a loser you pick that red card you pick a loser you pick thuh black card thuh deuce of spades you pick a winner who sees thuh deuce of spades thuh one who sees it never fades watch me now as I throw thuh cards. Red losers black winner follow thuh deuce of spades chase thuh black deuce. Dark deuce will get you thuh win. One good pickll get you in 2 good picks you gone win. 10 will get you 20, 20 will get you 40.

> (*Rest*)

Ima show you thuh cards: 2 red cards but only one spade. Dark winner in thuh center and thuh red losers on thuh sides. Pick uh red card you got a loser pick thuh other red card you got a loser pick thuh black card you got a winner. Watch me watch me watch me now.

> (*Rest*)

Ok, 3-Card, you know which cards thuh deuce of spades?

BOOTH   Yeah.

LINCOLN   You sure? Yeah? You sure you sure or you just think you sure? Oh you sure you sure huh? Was you watching Links lighting fast express? Was you watching Link cause he the best? So you sure, huh? Point it out. Now, place yr bet and Linkll turn over yr card.

BOOTH   What should I bet?

LINCOLN   Dont bet nothing man, we just playing. Slap me 5 and point out thuh deuce.

> [BOOTH *slaps* LINCOLN 5, *then points out a card which* LINCOLN *flips over. It is in fact again the deuce of spades.*]

BOOTH   Yeah, baby! 3-Card got thuh moves! You didnt know lil bro had thuh stuff, huh? Think again, Link, think again.

LINCOLN   You wanna learn or you wanna run yr mouth?

BOOTH   Thought you had fast hands. Wassup? What happened tuh "Links Lightning Fast Express"? Turned into uh local train looks like tuh me.

LINCOLN   Thats yr whole motherfucking problem. Yr so busy running yr mouth you aint never gonna learn nothing! You think you something but you aint shit.

BOOTH   I aint shit, I am *The* Shit. Shit. Wheres thuh dark deuce? Right there! Yes, baby!

LINCOLN   Ok, 3-Card. Cool. Lets switch. Take thuh cards and show me whatcha got. Go on. Dont touch thuh cards too heavy just—its a light touch. Like yr touching Graces skin. Or, whatever, man, just a light touch. Like uh whisper.

BOOTH   Like uh whisper.

> [BOOTH *moves the cards around, in an awkward imitation of his brother.*]

LINCOLN   Good.

BOOTH   Yeah. All right. Look into my eyes.

> [BOOTHS *speech is loud and his movements are jerky. He is doing worse than when he threw the cards at the top of the play.*]

BOOTH   Watch-me-close-watch-me-close-now: who-see-thuh-black-card- who-see-thuh-black-card? I-see-thuh-black-card. Here-it-is. Thuh- black-card-is-thuh-winner. Pick-thuh-black-card-and-you-pick-uh-winner. Pick-uh-red-card-and-you-pick-uh-loser. Theres-thuh-loser-yeah-theres- thuh-red-card, theres-thuh-other-loser-and-theres-thuh-black-card, thuh- winner. Watch-me-close-watch-me-close-now: 3-Card-throws-thuh-cards -lightning-fast. 3-Card-thats-me-and-Ima-last. Watch-me-throw-cause- here-I-go. See thuh black card? Yeah? Who see I see you see thuh black card?

LINCOLN   Hahahahhahahahahahahah!

> [LINCOLN *doubles over laughing.* BOOTH *puts on his coat and pockets his gun.*]

BOOTH   What?

LINCOLN   Nothing, man, nothing.

BOOTH   *What?!*

LINCOLN   Yr just, yr just a little wild with it. You talk like that on thuh street cards or no cards and theyll lock you up, man. Shit. Reminds me of that time when you hung with us and we let you try being thuh Stick cause you wanted to so bad. Thuh hustle was so simple. Remember? I told you that when I put my hand in my left pocket you was to get thuh Mark tuh pick thuh card on that side. You got to thinking something like Links left means my left some dyslexic shit and turned thuh wrong card. There was 800 bucks on the line and you fucked it up.

(Rest)

But it was cool, little bro, cause we made the money back. It worked out cool.

(Rest)

So, yeah, I said a light touch, little bro. Throw thuh cards light. Like uh whisper.

BOOTH Like Graces skin.

LINCOLN Like Graces skin.

BOOTH What time is it?

[LINCOLN *holds up his watch.* BOOTH *takes a look.*]

BOOTH Bitch. *Bitch!* She said she was gonna show up around 8. 8-a-fucking-clock.

LINCOLN Maybe she meant 8 *a.m.*

BOOTH Yeah. She gonna come all up in my place talking bout how she *love* me. How she cant stop *thinking* bout me. Nother mans shit up in her nother mans thing in her nother mans dick on her breath.

LINCOLN Maybe something happened to her.

BOOTH Something happened to her all right. She trying to make a chump outa me. I aint her chump. I aint nobodys chump.

LINCOLN Sit. I'll go to the payphone on the corner. I'll—

BOOTH Thuh world puts its foot in yr face and you dont move. You tell thuh world tuh keep on stepping. But Im my own man, Link. I aint you.

[BOOTH *goes out, slamming the door behind him.*]

LINCOLN You got that right.

[*After a moment* LINCOLN *picks up the cards. He moves them around fast, faster, faster.*]

Scene Six

[*Thursday night. The room looks empty, as if neither brother is home.* LINCOLN *comes in. Hes high on liquor. He strides in, leaving the door slightly ajar.*]

LINCOLN Taaadaaaa!

(Rest)

(Rest)

Taadaa, motherfucker. Taadaa!

(Rest)

Booth—uh, 3-Card—you here? Nope. Good. Just as well.

Ha Ha *Ha Ha Ha!*

[*He pulls an enormous wad of money from his pocket. He counts it, slowly and luxuriously, arranging and smoothing the bills and sounding the amounts under his breath. He neatly rolls up the money, secures it with a rubber band and puts it back in his pocket. He relaxes in his chair. Then he takes the money out again, counting it all over again, but this time quickly, with the touch of an expert hustler.*]

LINCOLN You didnt go back, Link, you got back, you got it back you got yr shit back in thuh saddle, man, you got back in business. Walking in Luckys and you seen how they was looking at you? Lucky starts pouring for you when you walk in. And the women. You see how they was look-ing at you? Bought drinks for everybody. Bought drinks for Lucky. Bought drinks for Luckys damn dog. Shit. And thuh women be hanging on me and purring. And I be feeling that old call of thuh wild calling. I got more phone numbers in my pockets between thuh time I walked out that door and thuh time I walked back in than I got in my whole life. Cause my shit is *back*. And back better than it was when it left too. Shoot. Who thuh man? Link. Thats right. Purrrrring all up on me and letting me touch them and promise them shit. 3 of them sweethearts in thuh restroom on my dick all at once and I was *there* my shit was there. And Cookie just went out of my mind which is cool which is very cool. 3 of them. Fighting over it. Shit. Cause they knew I'd been throwing thuh cards. Theyd seen me on thuh corner with thuh old crew or if they aint seed me with they own eyes theyd heard word. Links thuh stink! Theyd heard word and they seed uh sad face on some poor sucker or a tear in thuh eye of some stupid fucking tourist and they figured it was me whod just took thuh suckers last dime, it was me who had all thuh suckers loot. They knew. They knew.

> [BOOTH *appears in the room. He was standing behind the screen, unseen all this time. He goes to the door, soundlessly, just stands there.*]

LINCOLN   And they was all in Luckys. Shit. And they was waiting for me to come in from my last throw. Cant take too many fools in one day, its bad luck, Link, so they was all waiting in there for me to come in thuh door and let thuh liquor start flowing and thuh music start going and let thuh boys who dont have thuh balls to get nothing but a regular job and uh weekly paycheck, let them crowd around and get in somehow on thuh excitement, and make way for thuh ladies, so they can run they hands on my clothes and feel thuh magic and imagine thuh man, with plenty to go around, living and breathing underneath.

(Rest)

They all thought I was down and out! They all thought I was some NoCount HasBeen LostCause motherfucker. But I got my shit back. Thats right. They stepped on me and kept right on stepping. Not no more. Who thuh man?! Goddamnit, who thuh—

> [BOOTH *closes the door.*]

LINCOLN

BOOTH   *(Rest)*

LINCOLN   Another evening to remember, huh?

BOOTH   *(Rest)*

Uh—yeah, man, yeah. Thats right, thats right.

LINCOLN   Had me a memorable evening myself.

BOOTH   I got news.

(Rest)

What you been up to?

LINCOLN   Yr news first.

BOOTH   Its good.

LINCOLN   Yeah?

BOOTH   Yeah.

LINCOLN   Go head then.

BOOTH   *(Rest)*

Grace got down on her knees. Down on her knees, man. Asked *me* tuh marry *her*.

LINCOLN   Shit.

BOOTH   Amazing Grace!

LINCOLN   Lucky you, man.

BOOTH And guess where she was, I mean, while I was here waiting for her. She was over at her house watching tv. I'd told her come over Thursday and I got it all wrong and was thinking I said Wednesday and here I was sitting waiting my ass off and all she was doing was over at her house just watching tv.

LINCOLN Howboutthat.

BOOTH She wants to get married right away. Shes tired of waiting. Feels her clock ticking and shit. Wants to have my baby. But dont look so glum man, we gonna have a boy and we gonna name it after you.

LINCOLN Thats great, man. Thats really great.

BOOTH

LINCOLN

BOOTH Whats yr news?

LINCOLN (Rest)
Nothing.

BOOTH Mines good news, huh?

LINCOLN Yeah. Real good news, bro.

BOOTH Bad news is—well, shes real set on us living together. And she always did like this place.
(Rest)
Yr gonna have to leave. Sorry.

LINCOLN No sweat.

LINCOLN This was only a temporary situation anyhow.

LINCOLN No sweat man. You got a new life opening up for you, no sweat. Graces moving in today? I can leave right now.

BOOTH I dont mean to put you out.

LINCOLN No sweat. I'll just pack up.
[LINCOLN *rummages around finding a suitcase and begins to pack his things.*]

BOOTH Just like that, huh? "No sweat"?! Yesterday you lost yr damn job. You dont got no cash. You dont got no friends, no nothing, but you clearing out just like that and its "no sweat"?!

LINCOLN Youve been real generous and you and Grace need me gone and its time I found my own place.

BOOTH No sweat.

LINCOLN No sweat.
(Rest)
K. I'll spill it. I got another job, so getting my own place aint gonna be so bad.

BOOTH You got a new job! Doing what?

LINCOLN Security guard.

BOOTH (Rest)
Security guard. Howaboutthat.
[LINCOLN *continues packing the few things he has. He picks up a whiskey bottle.*]

BOOTH Go head, take thuh med-sin, bro. You gonna need it more than me. I got, you know, I got my love to keep me warm and shit.

LINCOLN You gonna have to get some kind of work, or are you gonna let Grace support you?

BOOTH I got plans.

LINCOLN She might want you now but she wont want you for long if you dont get some kind of job. Shes a smart chick. And she cares about you.

But she aint gonna let you treat her like some pack mule while shes out working her ass off and yr laying up in here scheming and dreaming to cover up thuh fact that you dont got no skills.

BOOTH   Grace is very cool with who I am and where Im at, thank you.

LINCOLN   It was just some advice. But, hey, yr doing great just like yr doing.

LINCOLN

BOOTH

LINCOLN

BOOTH

BOOTH   When Pops left he didnt take nothing with him. I always thought that was fucked-up.

LINCOLN   He was a drunk. Everything he did was always half regular and half fucked-up.

BOOTH   Whyd he leave his clothes though? Even drunks gotta wear clothes.

LINCOLN   Whyd he leave his clothes whyd he leave us? He was uh drunk, bro. He—whatever, right? I mean, you aint gonna figure it out by thinking about it. Just call it one of thuh great unsolved mysteries of existence.

BOOTH   Moms had a man on thuh side.

LINCOLN   Yeah? Pops had side shit going on too. More than one. He would take me with him when he went to visit them. Yeah.

(Rest)

Sometimes he'd let me meet the ladies. They was all very nice. Very polite. Most of them real pretty. Sometimes he'd let me watch. Most of thuh time I was just outside on thuh porch or in thuh lobby or in thuh car waiting for him but sometimes he'd let me watch.

BOOTH   What was it like?

LINCOLN   Nothing. It wasnt like nothing. He made it seem like it was this big deal this great thing he was letting me witness but it wasnt like nothing.

(Rest)

One of his ladies liked me, so I would do her after he'd done her. On thuh sly though. He'd be laying there, spent and sleeping and snoring and her and me would be sneaking it.

BOOTH   Shit.

LINCOLN   It was alright.

BOOTH

LINCOLN

[LINCOLN *takes his crumpled Abe Lincoln getup from the closet. Isnt sure what to do with it.*]

BOOTH   Im gonna miss you—coming home in that getup. I dont even got a picture of you in it for the album.

LINCOLN   *(Rest)*

Hell, I'll put it on. Get thuh camera get thuh camera.

BOOTH   Yeah?

LINCOLN   What thuh fuck, right?

BOOTH   Yeah, what thuh fuck.

[BOOTH *scrambles around the apartment and finds the camera.* LINCOLN *quickly puts on the getup, including 2 thin smears of white pancake makeup, more like war paint than whiteface.*]

LINCOLN   They didnt fire me cause I wasnt no good. They fired me cause
they was cutting back. Me getting dismissed didnt have no reflection on
my performance. And I was a damn good Honest Abe considering.

BOOTH   Yeah. You look great man, really great. Fix yr hat. Get in thuh
light. Smile.

LINCOLN   Lincoln didnt never smile.

BOOTH   Sure he smiled.

LINCOLN   No he didnt, man, you seen thuh pictures of him. In all his
pictures he was real serious.

BOOTH   You got a new job, yr having a good day, right?

LINCOLN   Yeah.

BOOTH   So smile.

LINCOLN   Snapshots gonna look pretty stupid with me—
   [BOOTH *takes a picture.*]

BOOTH   Thisll look great in thuh album.

LINCOLN   Lets take one together, you and me.

BOOTH   No thanks. Save the film for the wedding.

LINCOLN   This wasnt a bad job. I just outgrew it. I could put in a word for
you down there, maybe when business picks up again theyd hire you.

BOOTH   No thanks. That shit aint for me. I aint into pretending Im someone else all day.

LINCOLN   I was just sitting there in thuh getup. I wasnt pretending
nothing.

BOOTH   What was going on in yr head?

LINCOLN   I would make up songs and shit.

BOOTH   And think about women.

LINCOLN   Sometimes.

BOOTH   Cookie.

LINCOLN   Sometimes.

BOOTH   And how she came over here one night looking for you.

LINCOLN   I was at Luckys.

BOOTH   She didnt know that.

LINCOLN   I was drinking.

BOOTH   All she knew was you couldnt get it up. You couldnt get it up with
her so in her head you was tired of her and had gone out to screw somebody new and this time maybe werent never coming back.
(Rest)
She had me pour her a drink or 2. I didnt want to. She wanted to get
back at you by having some fun of her own and when I told her to go out
and have it, she said she wanted to have her fun right here. With me.
(Rest)
And then, just like that, she changed her mind.
(Rest)
But she'd hooked me. That bad part of me that I fight down everyday. You
beat yrs down and it stays there dead but mine keeps coming up for
another round. And the bad part of me took her clothing off and carried
her into thuh bed and had her, Link, yr Cookie. It wasnt just thuh bad part
of me it was all of me, man, I had her. Yr damn wife. Right in that bed.

LINCOLN   I used to think about her all thuh time but I dont think about
her no more.

BOOTH   I told her if she dumped you I'd marry her but I changed my
mind.

LINCOLN I don't think about her no more.

BOOTH You dont go back.

LINCOLN Nope.

BOOTH Cause you cant. No matter what you do you cant get back to being who you was. Best you can do is just pretend to be yr old self.

LINCOLN Yr outa yr mind.

BOOTH Least Im still me!

LINCOLN Least I work. You never did like to work. You better come up with some kinda way to bring home the bacon or Gracell drop you like a hot rock.

BOOTH I got plans!

LINCOLN Yeah, you gonna throw thuh cards, right?

BOOTH Thats right!

LINCOLN You a double left-handed motherfucker who dont stand a chance in all get out out there throwing no cards.

BOOTH You scared. You scared I got yr shit.

LINCOLN You aint never gonna do nothing.

BOOTH You scared you gonna throw and Ima kick yr ass—like yr boss kicked yr ass like yr wife kicked yr ass—then Ima go out there and do thuh cards like you do and Ima be thuh man and you aint gonna be shit.

(Rest)

Ima set it up. And you gonna throw. Or are you scared?

LINCOLN Im gone.

> [LINCOLN *goes to leave.*]

BOOTH Fuck that!

LINCOLN

BOOTH

LINCOLN Damn. I didnt know it went so deep for you lil bro. Set up the cards.

BOOTH Thought you was gone.

LINCOLN Set it up.

BOOTH Ima kick yr ass.

LINCOLN Set it up!

> [BOOTH *hurriedly sets up the milk crates and cardboard top.* LINCOLN *throws the cards.*]

LINCOLN Lean in close and watch me now: who see thuh black card who see thuh black card I see thuh black card black cards thuh winner pick thuh black card thats thuh winner pick thuh red card thats thuh loser pick thuh other red card thats thuh other loser pick thuh black card you pick thuh winner. Who see thuh black card who see thuh black card? You pick thuh red card you pick a loser you pick that red card you pick a loser you pick thuh black card thuh deuce of spades you pick a winner who sees thuh deuce of spades thuh one who sees it never fades watch me now as I throw thuh cards. Red losers black winner follow thuh deuce of spades chase thuh black deuce. Dark deuce will get you thuh win. 10 will get you 20, 20 will get you 40. One good pickll get you in 2 good picks and you gone win.

(Rest)

Ok, man, wheres thuh black deuce?

> [BOOTH *points to a card.* LINCOLN *flips it over.* It is the deuce of spades.]

BOOTH Who thuh man?!

[LINCOLN *turns over the other 2 cards, looking at them confusedly.*]

LINCOLN Hhhhh.

BOOTH Who thuh man, Link?! Huh? Who thuh man, Link?!?!

LINCOLN You thuh man, man.

BOOTH I got yr shit down.

LINCOLN Right.

BOOTH "Right"? All you saying is "right"?

(*Rest*)

You was out on the street throwing. Just today. Werent you? You wasnt gonna tell me.

LINCOLN Tell you what?

BOOTH That you was out throwing.

LINCOLN I was gonna tell you, sure. Cant go and leave my little bro out thuh loop, can I? Didnt say nothing cause I thought you heard. Did all right today but Im still rusty, I guess. But hey—yr getting good.

BOOTH But I'll get out there on thuh street and still fuck up, wont I?

LINCOLN You seem pretty good, bro.

BOOTH You gotta do it for real, man.

LINCOLN I am doing it for real. And yr getting good.

BOOTH I dunno. It didnt feel real. Kinda felt—well it didnt feel real.

LINCOLN We're missing the essential elements. The crowd, the street, thuh traffic sounds, all that.

BOOTH We missing something else too, thuh thing thatll really make it real.

LINCOLN Whassat, bro?

BOOTH Thuh cash. Its just bullshit without thuh money. Put some money down on thuh table then itd be real, then youd do it for real, then I'd win it for real.

(*Rest*)

And dont be looking all glum like that I know you got money. A whole pocketful. Put it down.

LINCOLN

BOOTH

BOOTH You scared of losing it to thuh man, chump? Put it down, less you think thuh kid who got two left hands is gonna give you uh left hook. Put it down, bro, put it down.

[LINCOLN *takes the roll of bills from his pocket and places it on the table.*]

BOOTH How much you got there?

LINCOLN 500 bucks.

BOOTH Cool.

(*Rest*)

Ready?

LINCOLN Does it feel real?

BOOTH Yeah. Clean slate. Take it from the top. "One good pickll get you in 2 good picks and you gone win."

(*Rest*)

Go head.

LINCOLN Watch me now:

BOOTH Woah, man, woah.

(*Rest*)

You think Ima chump.

LINCOLN   No I dont.

BOOTH   You aint going full out.

LINCOLN   I was just getting started.

BOOTH   But when you got good and started you wasnt gonna go full out. You wasnt gonna go all out You was gonna do thuh pussy shit, not thuh real shit.

LINCOLN   I put my money down. Money makes it real.

BOOTH   But not if I dont put no money down tuh match it.

LINCOLN   You dont got no money.

BOOTH   I got money!

LINCOLN   You aint worked in years. You dont got shit.

BOOTH   I got money.

LINCOLN   Whatcha been doing, skimming off my weekly paycheck and squirreling it away?

BOOTH   I got money.

(Rest)

> [*They stand there sizing eachother up.* BOOTH *breaks away, going over to his hiding place from which he gets an old nylon stocking with money in the toe, a knot holding the money secure.*]

LINCOLN

BOOTH

BOOTH   You know she was putting her stuff in plastic bags? She was just putting her stuff in plastic bags not putting but shoving. She was shoving her stuff in plastic bags and I was standing in thuh doorway watching her and she was so busy shoving thuh shit she didnt see me. "I aint made of money," thats what he always saying. The guy she had on the side. I would catch them together sometimes. Thuh first time I cut school I got tired of hanging out so I goes home—figured I could tell Mom I was sick and cover my ass. Come in thuh house real slow cause Im sick and moving slow and quiet. He had her bent over. They both had all they clothes on like they was about to do something like go out dancing cause they was dressed to thuh 9s but at thuh last minute his pants had fallen down and her dress had flown up and theyd ended up doing something else.

(Rest)

They didnt see me come in, they didnt see me watching them, they didnt see me going out. That was uh Thursday. Something told me tuh cut school thuh next Thursday and sure enough—. He was her Thursday man. Every Thursday. Yeah. And Thursday nights she was always all cleaned up and fresh and smelling nice. Serving up dinner. And Pops would grab her cause she was all bright and she would look at me, like she didnt know that I knew but she was asking me not to tell nohow. She was asking me to—oh who knows.

(Rest)

She was talking with him one day, her sideman, her Thursday dude, her backdoor man, she needed some money for something, thered been some kind of problem some kind of mistake had been made some kind of mistake that needed cleaning up and she was asking Mr. Thursday for some money to take care of it. "I aint made of money," he says. He was putting his foot down. And then there she was 2 months later not showing yet, maybe she'd got rid of it maybe she hadnt maybe she'd stuffed it along with all her other things in them plastic bags while he waited outside in thuh car with thuh motor running. She musta known I was gonna walk in on her this time cause she had my payoff—my *inheritance*—she had it all ready for me. 500 dollars in a nylon stocking. Huh.

[*He places the stuffed nylon stocking on the table across from* LINCOLNS *money roll.*]

BOOTH Now its real.

LINCOLN Dont put that down.

BOOTH Throw thuh cards.

LINCOLN I dont want to play.

BOOTH Throw thuh fucking cards, man!!

LINCOLN (*Rest*)

2 red cards but only one black. Pick thuh black you pick thuh winner. All thuh cards are face down you point out thuh cards and then you move them around. Now watch me now, now watch me real close. Put thuh winning deuce down in the center put thuh loser reds on either side then you just move thuh cards around. Move them slow or move them fast, Links thuh king he gonna last.

(*Rest*)

Wheres thuh deuce of spades?

[BOOTH *chooses a card and chooses correctly.*]

BOOTH HA!

LINCOLN One good pickll get you in 2 good picks and you gone win.

BOOTH I know man I know.

LINCOLN Im just doing thuh talk.

BOOTH Throw thuh fucking cards!

[LINCOLN *throws the cards.*]

LINCOLN Lean in close and watch me now: who see thuh black card who see thuh black card I see thuh black card black cards thuh winner pick thuh black card thats thuh winner pick thuh red card thats thuh loser pick thuh other red card thats thuh other loser pick thuh black card you pick thuh winner. Watch me as I throw thuh cards. Here we go.

(*Rest*)

Ima show you thuh cards: 2 red cards but only one spade. Dark winner in thuh center and thuh red losers on thuh sides. Pick uh red card you got a loser pick thuh other red card you got a loser pick thuh black card you got a winner. Watch me watch me watch me now.

(*Rest*)

Who see thuh black card who see thuh black card? You pick thuh red card you pick a loser you pick that red card you pick a loser you pick thuh black card thuh deuce of spades you pick a winner who sees thuh deuce of spades thuh one who sees it never fades watch me now as I throw thuh cards. Red losers black winner follow thuh deuce of spades chase thuh black deuce. Dark deuce will get you thuh win.

(*Rest*)

Ok, 3-Card, you know which cards thuh deuce of spades? This is for real now, man. You pick wrong Im in yr wad and I keep mines.

BOOTH I pick right I got yr shit.

LINCOLN Yeah.

BOOTH Plus I beat you for real.

LINCOLN Yeah.

(Rest)
You think we're really brothers?

BOOTH   Huh?

LINCOLN   I know we *brothers*, but is we really brothers, you know, blood brothers or not, you and me, whatduhyathink?

BOOTH   I think we're brothers.

BOOTH

LINCOLN

BOOTH

LINCOLN

BOOTH

LINCOLN

LINCOLN   Go head man, wheres thuh deuce?
   [*In a flash* BOOTH *points out a card.*]

LINCOLN   You sure?

BOOTH   Im sure!

LINCOLN   Yeah? Dont touch thuh cards, now.

BOOTH   Im sure.
   [*The 2 brothers lock eyes.* LINCOLN *turns over the card that* BOOTH *selected and* BOOTH, *in a desperate break of concentration, glances down to see that he has chosen the wrong card.*]

LINCOLN   Deuce of hearts, bro. Im sorry. Thuh deuce of spades was this one.
   (Rest)
I guess all this is mines.
   [*He slides the money toward himself.*]

LINCOLN   You were almost right. Better luck next time.
   (Rest)
Aint yr fault if yr eyes aint fast. And you cant help it if you got 2 left hands, right? Throwing cards aint thuh whole world. You got other shit going for you. You got Grace.

BOOTH   Right.

LINCOLN   Whassamatter?

BOOTH   Mm.

LINCOLN   Whatsup?

BOOTH   Nothing.

LINCOLN   *(Rest)*
It takes a certain kind of understanding to be able to play this game.
   (Rest)
I still got thuh moves, dont I?

BOOTH   Yeah you still got thuh moves.
   [LINCOLN *cant help himself. He chuckles.*]

LINCOLN   I aint laughing at you, bro, Im just laughing. Shit there is so much to this game. This game is—there is just so much to it.
   [LINCOLN, *still chuckling, flops down in the easy chair. He takes up the nylon stocking and fiddles with the knot.*]

LINCOLN   Woah, she sure did tie this up tight, didnt she?

BOOTH   Yeah. I aint opened it since she gived it to me.

LINCOLN   Yr kidding. 500 and you aint never opened it? Shit. Sure is tied tight. She said heres 500 bucks and you didnt undo thuh knot to get a look at the cash? You aint needed to take a peek in all these years? Shit. I woulda opened it right away. Just a little peek.

BOOTH   I been saving it.

(*Rest*)

Oh, dont open it, man.

LINCOLN   How come?

BOOTH   You won it man, you dont gotta go opening it.

LINCOLN   We gotta see whats in it.

BOOTH   We *know* whats in it. Dont open it.

LINCOLN   You are a chump, bro. There could be millions in here! There could be nothing! I'll open it.

BOOTH   Dont.

LINCOLN

BOOTH   (*Rest*)

LINCOLN   Shit this knot aint coming out. I could cut it, but that would spoil the whole effect, wouldnt it? Shit. Sorry. I aint laughing at you Im just laughing. Theres so much about those cards. You think you can learn them just by watching and just by playing but there is more to them cards than that. And—. Tell me something, Mr. 3-Card, she handed you this stocking and she said there was money in it and then she split and you say you didnt open it. Howd you know she was for real?

BOOTH   She was for real.

LINCOLN   How you know? She coulda been jiving you, bro. Jiving you that there really *was* money in this thing. Jiving you big time. Its like thuh cards. And ooooh you certainly was persistent. But you was in such a hurry to learn thuh last move that you didnt bother learning thuh first one. That was yr mistake. Cause its thuh first move that separates thuh Player from thuh Played. And thuh first move is to know that there aint no winning. Taadaaa! It may look like you got a chance but the only time you pick right is when thuh man lets you. And when its thuh real deal, when its thuh real fucking deal, bro, and thuh moneys on thuh line, thats when thuh man wont want you picking right. He will want you picking wrong so he will make you pick wrong. Wrong wrong wrong. Ooooh, you thought you was finally happening, didnt you? You thought yr ship had come in or some shit, huh? Thought you was uh Player. But I played you, bro.

BOOTH   Fuck you. Fuck you FUCK YOU *FUCK YOU*!!

LINCOLN   Whatever, man. Damn this knot is tough. Ima cut it.

[LINCOLN *reaches in his boot, pulling out a knife. He chuckles all the while.*]

LINCOLN   Im not laughing at you, bro, Im just laughing.

[BOOTH *chuckles with him.* LINCOLN *holds the knife high, ready to cut the stocking.*]

LINCOLN   Turn yr head. You may not wanna look.

[BOOTH *turns away slightly. They both continue laughing.* LINCOLN *brings the knife down to cut the stocking.*]

BOOTH   I popped her.

LINCOLN   Huh?

BOOTH   Grace. I popped her. Grace.

(*Rest*)

Who thuh fuck she think she is doing me like she done? Telling me I dont got nothing going on. I showed her what I got going on. Popped her good. Twice. 3 times. Whatever.

(*Rest*)

She aint dead.

(Rest)

She werent wearing my ring I gived her. Said it was too small. Fuck that. Said it hurt her. Fuck that. Said she was into bigger things. *Fuck* that. Shes alive not to worry, she aint going out that easy, shes alive shes shes—.

LINCOLN   Dead. Shes—

BOOTH   Dead.

LINCOLN   Ima give you back yr stocking, man. Here, bro—

BOOTH   Only so long I can stand that little brother shit. Can only take it so long. Im telling you—

LINCOLN   Take it back, man—

BOOTH   That little bro shit had to go—

LINCOLN   Cool—

BOOTH   Like Booth went—

LINCOLN   Here, 3-Card—

BOOTH   That Booth shit is over. 3-Cards thuh man now—

LINCOLN   Ima give you yr stocking back, 3-Card—

BOOTH   Who thuh man now, huh? Who thuh man now?! Think you can fuck with me, motherfucker think again motherfucker think again! Think you can take me like Im just some chump some two lefthanded pussy dickbreath chump who you can take and then go laugh at. Aint laughing at me you was just laughing bunch uh bullshit and you know it.

LINCOLN   Here. Take it.

BOOTH   I aint gonna be needing it. Go on. You won it you open it.

LINCOLN   No thanks.

BOOTH   Open it open it open it open it. *OPEN IT!!!*

(Rest)

Open it up, bro.

LINCOLN

BOOTH

>   [LINCOLN *brings the knife down to cut the stocking. In a flash,* BOOTH *grabs* LINCOLN *from behind. He pulls his gun and thrusts it into the left side of* LINCOLNS *neck. They stop there poised.*]

LINCOLN   Dont.

>   [BOOTH *shoots* LINCOLN. LINCOLN *slumps forward, falling out of his chair and onto the floor. He lies there dead.* BOOTH *paces back and forth, like a panther in a cage, holding his gun.*]

2001

NATASHA TRETHEWEY
b. 1966

Named poet laureate of the United States in 2012, Natasha Trethewey explores the space where personal memory and official history meet and often diverge, "to create a public record of people who are excluded from the public record."

Consequently, she writes about maids, washerwomen, and factory workers; black soldiers in the Civil War; mixed-race servants in eighteenth-century Mexico and Spain; mixed-race prostitutes in early-twentieth-century New Orleans; and Gulf Coast residents whose lives were devastated by Hurricane Katrina. Her award-winning poems bring visibility and give voice to these people. The interplay of image and text is important in her work, as she is often inspired by photographs and paintings whose silent subjects are enabled to speak through her poems.

When Trethewey was born in Gulfport to a black mother and white father, her parents' marriage was a crime in Mississippi. Her birth date marked the hundredth anniversary of Confederate Memorial Day. Given that coincidence, she contends that she could not have "escaped learning about the Civil War and what it represented." Her biography inspires some of her themes, but so does her extensive study of history in general and of the Deep South in particular. She earned a B.A. at the University of Georgia, an M.A. at Hollins University, and an M.F.A. in poetry at the University of Massachusetts at Amherst. She is the Charles Howard Candler Professor of English and Creative Writing at Emory University.

Trethewey's poetry moves through history and across genres, from free verse to sonnets and villanelles. Her first book, *Domestic Work* (2000), includes a series of poems based on the life of her maternal grandmother; they depict the jobs she held and the ways she continuously defined herself. The volume expands its title's meaning from physical labor to "the everyday work that we do as humans to live with and without people that we've lost, of memory and forgetting, and of self-discovery." The opening poem, "Gesture of a Woman-in-Process," inspired by a photograph of a domestic worker who refused to stand still for the camera, sets the tone. *Bellocq's Ophelia* (2002) is an epistolary novella-in-verse that invents a life for one of the mixed-race prostitutes photographed in New Orleans by E. J. Bellocq. *Native Guard*, awarded the Pulitzer Prize for poetry in 2007, includes a poetic sequence that represents the Louisiana Native Guard, composed mainly of former slaves who were assigned to guard Confederate prisoners of war. Trethewey dedicates the volume to

Hurricane Katrina's path of destruction included Gulfport, Mississippi, hometown of Natasha Trethewey and subject of her nonfiction book *Beyond Katrina: A Meditation on the Mississippi Gulf Coast*. Photograph by John Cancalosi.

her mother, who was murdered by her second husband while her daughter was in college. Dedicated to her father, also a poet, *Thrall* (2012) maps the terrain of a difficult relationship between father and daughter. In "Enlightenment," the pair stands before a portrait of Thomas Jefferson at Monticello, arguing about his relationship with his slave mistress, Sally Hemings. Other poems imagine lives for subjects of Mexican paintings as well as for the slave of the famous Spanish painter Velázquez.

Beyond Katrina: A Meditation on the Mississippi Gulf Coast (2010) is a book of nonfiction interspersed with poems. Although most of the media attention after Hurricane Katrina focused on New Orleans, Trethewey, in the poems included here, turns her attention to the less visible suffering of her neighbors and kin.

Liturgy

To the security guard staring at the Gulf
thinking of bodies washed away from the coast,
   plugging her ears
against the bells and sirens—sound of alarm—
   the gaming floor   5
on the coast;

To Billy Scarpetta, waiting tables on the coast,
   staring at the Gulf
thinking of water rising, thinking of New Orleans,
   thinking of cleansing   10
the coast;

To the woman dreaming of returning to the coast,
   thinking of water rising,
her daughter's grave, my mother's grave—underwater—
   on the coast;   15

To Miss Mary, somewhere;

To the displaced, living in trailers along the coast,
   beside the highway,
in vacant lots and open fields; to everyone who stayed
   on the coast,   20
who came back—or cannot—to the coast;

To those who died on the coast.

This is a memory of the coast: to each his own
recollections, her reclamations, their
restorations, the return of the coast.   25

This is a time capsule for the coast: words of the people
—*don't forget us*—
the sound of wind, waves, the silence of graves,
the muffled voice of history, bulldozed and buried
under sand poured on the eroding coast,   30
the concrete slabs of rebuilding the coast.

This is a love letter to the Gulf Coast, a praise song, a dirge,
invocation and benediction, a requiem for the Gulf Coast.

This cannot rebuild the coast; it is an indictment,
   a complaint, 35
my *logos*—argument and discourse—with the coast.

This is my *nostos*—my pilgrimage to the coast, my memory,
   my reckoning—

native daughter: I am the Gulf Coast.

Nine months after Katrina, I went home for the first time. Driving down
Highway 49, after passing my grandmother's house, I went straight to the
cemetery where my mother is buried. It was more ragged than usual—the
sandy plots overgrown with weeds. The fence around it was still up, so I
counted the entrances until I reached the fourth one, which opened onto
the gravel road where I knew I'd find her. I searched first for the large, mis-
shapen shrub that had always showed me to her grave, and found it gone.
My own negligence had revisited me, and I stood there foolishly, a woman
who'd never erected a monument on her mother's grave. I walked in circles,
stooping to push back grass and weeds until I found the concrete border
that marked the plots of my ancestors. It was nearly overtaken, nearly
sunken beneath the dirt and grass. How foolish of me to think of monu-
ments and memory, of inscribing the landscape with narratives of remembrance, as I stood looking at my mother's near-vanished grave in the
post-Katrina landscape to which I'd brought my heavy bag of nostalgia. I
see now that remembrance is an individual duty as well—a duty native to
us as citizens, as daughters and sons. Private liturgy: I vow to put a stone
here, emblazoned with her name.
   Not far from the cemetery, I wandered the vacant lot where a church had
been. Debris still littered the grass. Everywhere, there were pages torn from
hymnals, Bibles, psalms pressed into the grass as if they were cemented
there. I bent close, trying to read one; to someone driving by along the
beach, I must have looked like a woman praying.

                                               2010

1. Witness

       Here is North Gulfport—
       its liquor stores and car washes,
       trailers and shotgun shacks
       propped at the road's edge;
       its brick houses hunkered 5
       against the weather, anchored
       to neat, clipped yards;
       its streets named for states
       and presidents—each corner
       a crossroads of memory, 10
       marked with a white obelisk;
       its phalanx of church houses—
       a congregation of bunkers

and masonry brick, chorus
of marquees: *God is not*   15
the author of fear; Without faith
we is victims; Sooner or later
everybody comes by here.

2. *Tower*

This week they are painting
the North Gulfport water tower.

Every day it grows whiter
until it is the color of clouds,

and the clouds in the heavy sky   5
seem whiter still. To paint the tower

the workmen have erected
a scaffolding around the tank,

a radius of poles from which to hang
the ropes that pull them up.   10

From a distance, the scaffolding
is a diadem, the crown

on a monument—a glory
wreath. That is what I saw

as I drove the flat land—down   15
Highway 49—toward home.

Up close now, beneath it, I see
what I had not: a circle of thorns.

3. *Watcher*

AFTER KATRINA, 2005

At first, there was nothing to do but watch.
For days, before the trucks arrived, before the work
of cleanup, my brother sat on the stoop and watched.

He watched the ambulances speed by, the police cars;
watched for the looters who'd come each day   5
to siphon gas from the car, take away the generator,

the air conditioner, whatever there was to be had.
He watched his phone for a signal, watched the sky
for signs of a storm, for rain so he could wash:

At the church, handing out diapers and water,   10
he watched the people line up, watched their faces
as they watched his. And when at last there was work,

he got a job, on the beach, as a *watcher*.
Behind safety goggles, he watched the sand for bones,
searched for debris that clogged the great machines.   15

Riding the prow of the cleaners, or walking ahead,
he watched for carcasses—chickens mostly, maybe
some cats or dogs. No one said *remains*. No one

had to. It was a kind of faith, that watching:
my brother trained his eyes to bear   20
the sharp erasure of sand and glass, prayed

there'd be nothing more to see.

4. Believer

FOR TAMARA JONES

The house is in need of repair, but is—
for now, she says—still hers. After the storm,
she laid hands on what she could reclaim:
the iron table and chairs etched with rust,
the dresser laced with mold. Four years gone,   5
she's still rebuilding the shed out back
and sorting through boxes in the kitchen—
a lifetime of bills and receipts, deeds
and warranties, notices spread on the table,
a barrage of red ink: PAST DUE. Now,   10
the house is a museum of everything

she can't let go: a pile of photographs—
fused and peeling—water stains blurring
the handwritten names of people she can't recall;
a drawer crowded with funeral programs   15
and church fans, rubber bands and paper sleeves
for pennies, nickels, and dimes. What stops me
is the stack of tithing envelopes. Reading my face,
she must know I can't see why—even now—
she tithes, why she keeps giving to the church.   20
First seek the kingdom of God, she tells me,
and the rest will follow—says it twice

as if to make a talisman of her words.

6. Prodigal

I.

Once, I was a daughter of this place:
daughter of Gwen, granddaughter
of Leretta, great of Eugenia McGee.

I was baptized in the church
my great-aunt founded, behind   5
the drapes my grandmother sewed.

As a child, I dozed in the pews
and woke to chant the *Lord's Prayer*—
mouthing the lines I did not learn.

Still a girl, I put down the red flower   10
and wore a white bloom pinned to my chest—
the mark of loss: a motherless child. All

the elders knew who I was, recalled me
each time I came home and spoke
my ancestors' names—Sugar, Son Dixon—   15

a native tongue. What is home but a cradle
of the past? Too long gone, I've found
my key in the lock of the old house

will not turn—a narrative of rust;
and everywhere the lacuna of vacant lots,   20
For Sale signs, a notice reading *Condemned*.

II.

I wanted to say I have come home
to bear witness, to read the sign
emblazoned on the church marquee—
Believe the report of the Lord—   25
and trust that this is noble work, that
which must be done. I wanted to say *I see*,
not *I watch*. I wanted my seeing to be
a sanctuary, but what I saw was this
in my rearview mirror, the marquee's   30
other side—*Face the things that confront you.*

My first day back, a pilgrim, I traveled
the old neighborhood, windows up,
steering the car down streets I hadn't seen
in years. It was Sunday. At the rebuilt church   35
across from my grandmother's house,
I stepped into the vestibule and found
not a solid wall as years before but
a new wall, glass through which I could see
the sanctuary. And so, I did not go in;   40
I stood there, my face against the glass,

watching. I could barely hear the organ;
the hymn they sang, but when the congregation rose,
filing out of the pews, I knew it was the call
to altar. And still, I did not enter. Outside,   45
as I'd lingered at the car, a man had said
You got to come in. You can't miss the word.
I got as far as the vestibule—neither in,
nor out. The service went on. I did nothing
but watch, my face against the glass—until   50
someone turned, looked back: saw me.

2010

EDWIDGE DANTICAT
b. 1969

" I wanted to raise the voice of a lot of the people that I knew growing up . . . poor people who had extraordinary dreams but also very amazing obstacles." Many of the people referred to in this quotation from Edwidge Danticat were Haitians or Haitian Americans who dreamed in Creole as well as in French and English and whose material poverty was offset by a rich cultural heritage and a storied history. Chronicling their experience in the Caribbean and their migration to the United States, Danticat's fiction won instant acclaim for its distinctive lyrical voice and for its sensitive depiction of what is gained and what is lost as people travel between cultures and translate their experiences into new languages.

Danticat spent the first twelve years of her life in Haiti, where she was raised by her Baptist minister uncle and his wife; then she immigrated to the United States to join her parents, who had preceded her there. The early separation from her parents, particularly her mother, would become a theme in Danticat's fiction. She spent her adolescence in Brooklyn, a section of New York City that was home to tens of thousands of Caribbean immigrants. After earning a degree in French from Barnard College, Danticat earned an M.F.A. at Brown University. Her thesis was a version of *Breath, Eyes, Memory*, the debut novel she published in 1994. The next year she published *Krik? Krak!*, a prize-winning collection of stories that takes it title from the Haitian tradition of the storyteller calling out *Krik?* and the audience responding *Krak*. In 1998 she published *The Farming of Bones*, a historical novel that depicts the 1937 massacre of Haitian workers in the Dominican Republic, the Spanish-speaking nation that shares the island of Hispaniola with French-speaking Haiti. The novel depicts the rituals of remembrance the survivors enact, as the text itself becomes a site of memory. While Danticat's work earned critical recognition and a sizable readership from the beginning of her career, when *Breath, Eyes, Memory* became an Oprah's Book Club selection in 1998, her audience multiplied several times over. She has used her increased visibility to promote both Haitian American literature and contemporary writing in general, by editing *The Butterfly's Way: Voices from the Haitian Diaspora in the United States* (2001) and *The Beacon Best of 2000: Great Writing by Women and Men of All Colors and Cultures*. In 2002 she published *After the Dance: A Walk through Carnival in Jacmel, Haiti* (2002), an account of her travels in Haiti and her first experience of carnival, a cultural ritual that her uncle had forbidden her on religious grounds.

In her own writing, Danticat continues to grapple with the ways that the traumas of the past shadow the present. *The Dew Breaker* (2004) introduces a mild-mannered Haitian American, a devoted husband and father living in Brooklyn, who has served in the Tonton Macoute, an army of torturers in Haiti. His daughter, an artist, must reconcile the man she loves with the man her father has been. Arguably Danticat's most poignant volume is the memoir *Brother, I'm Dying* (2007), which won the National Book Award. When the uncle who raised her comes to the United States, he is placed in detention in Miami, where he dies. Danticat's intervention cannot save him, but the situation compels her to reconsider the sacrifices tendered by both her uncle and her parents.

When she first arrived in the United States, Danticat observes, she was "completely between languages." Not sufficiently fluent in French to write in that language and never having been taught to write Haitian Creole, the language she spoke at home, she recalls that "my writing in English was as much an act of personal translation as it was an act of creative collaboration with the new place I was in." That sense of personal translation carries over to *Breath, Eyes, Memory*, the novel that remains Danticat's best-known work. Written in imagistic and lyrical prose, *Breath, Eyes, Memory* follows its protagonist as she moves between her Haitian homeland, where she is steeped in the storytelling of her maternal kin, and her new home in Brooklyn, from which she looks back at the culture she has left with a loving but critical eye. This fusion of celebration and critique is familiar in writing by African American women, including Zora Neale Hurston, Toni Morrison, and Alice Walker. Sophie, the protagonist of *Breath, Eyes, Memory*, is the child of rape who feels abandoned by her mother's decision to move to the United States and leave her in her grandmother's care. Sophie's consciousness is shaped by the stories the old woman tells, but the grandmother also adheres to the tradition of "testing," a means of confirming a young woman's virginity, that Sophie rejects as cruelly sexist. Coming of age in the United States, fluent in English but partial to the Creole that is her mother tongue, Sophie pieces together the disparate lessons of her life. The last chapter of the novel, included here, recounts Sophie's return to Haiti to bury her mother, Martine, whose immigrant dreams were not fulfilled. In an act of defiance and love, Sophie chooses to dress her mother in red for burial. By so doing, she identifies her defeated mother with the powerful Vodun goddess Erzulie and the freedom she symbolizes. Sophie reunites with her grandmother and aunt and reassesses her ties to Haiti. But she has returned only temporarily. Her infant daughter, Brigitte, calls her home to America.

From Breath, Eyes, Memory

Chapter 1

A flattened and drying daffodil was dangling off the little card that I had made my aunt Atie for Mother's Day. I pressed my palm over the flower and squashed it against the plain beige cardboard. When I turned the corner near the house, I saw her sitting in an old rocker in the yard, staring at a group of children crushing dried yellow leaves into the ground. The leaves had been left in the sun to dry. They would be burned that night at the *konbit*[1] potluck dinner.

I put the card back in my pocket before I got to the yard. When Tante[2] Atie saw me, she raised the piece of white cloth she was embroidering and waved it at me. When I stood in front of her, she opened her arms just wide enough for my body to fit into them.

"How was school?" she asked, with a big smile.

She bent down and kissed my forehead, then pulled me down onto her lap.

"School was all right," I said. "I like everything but those reading classes they let parents come to in the afternoon. Everybody's parents come except you. I never have anyone to read with, so Monsieur Augustin always pairs me off with an old lady who wants to learn her letters, but does not have children at the school."

"I do not want a pack of children teaching me how to read," she said. "The young should learn from the old. Not the other way. Besides, I have to rest my back when you have your class. I have work."

A blush of embarrassment rose to her brown cheeks.

---

1. Gathering (Kreyol, or Haitian creole).   2. Aunt (French).

"At one time, I would have given anything to be in school. But not at my age. My time is gone. Cooking and cleaning, looking after others, that's my school now. That schoolhouse is *your* school. Cutting cane was the only thing for a young one to do when I was your age. That's why I never want to hear you complain about your school." She adjusted a pink head rag wrapped tightly around her head and dashed off a quick smile revealing two missing side teeth. "As long as you do not have to work in the fields, it does not matter that I will never learn to read that ragged old Bible under my pillow."

Whenever she was sad, Tante Atie would talk about the sugar cane fields, where she and my mother practically lived when they were children. They saw people die there from sunstroke every day. Tante Atie said that, one day while they were all working together, her father—my grandfather—stopped to wipe his forehead, leaned forward, and died. My grandmother took the body in her arms and tried to scream the life back into it. They all kept screaming and hollering, as my grandmother's tears bathed the corpse's face. Nothing would bring my grandfather back.

The *bòlèt* man was coming up the road. He was tall and yellow like an amber roach. The children across the road lined up by the fence to watch him, clutching one another as he whistled and strolled past them.

This albino,[3] whose name was Chabin, was the biggest lottery agent in the village. He was thought to have certain gifts that had nothing to do with the lottery, but which Tante Atie believed put the spirits on his side. For example, if anyone was chasing him, he could turn into a snake with one flip of his tongue. Sometimes, he could see the future by looking into your eyes, unless you closed your soul to him by thinking of a religious song and prayer while in his presence.

I could tell that Tante Atie was thinking of one of her favorite verses as he approached. *Death is the shepherd of man and in the final dawn, good will be the master of evil.*

"*Honneur, mes belles,*[4] Atie, Sophie."

Chabin winked at us from the front gate. He had no eyelashes—or seemed to have none. His eyebrows were tawny and fine like corn silk, but he had a thick head of dirty red hair.

"How are you today?" he asked.

"Today, we are fine," Tante Atie said. "We do not know about tomorrow."

"*Ki niméro* today?" he asked. "What numbers you playing?"

"Today, we play my sister Martine's age," Tante Atie said. "Sophie's mother's age. Thirty-one. Perhaps it will bring me luck."

"Thirty-one will cost you fifty cents," he said.

Tante Atie reached into her bra and pulled out one *gourde.*[5]

"We will play the number twice," she said.

Even though Tante Atie played faithfully, she had never won at the *bòlèt*. Not even a small amount, not even once.

She said the lottery was like love. Providence was not with her, but she was patient.

The albino wrote us a receipt with the numbers and the amount Tante Atie had given him.

---

3. Person without pigmentation.
4. A pleasure, my ladies (French); used as a greeting or salutation.
5. The unit of currency in Haiti.

The children cringed behind the gate as he went on his way. Tante Atie raised her receipt towards the sun to see it better.

"There, he wrote your name," I said pointing to the letters, "and there, he wrote the number thirty-one."

She ran her fingers over the numbers as though they were quilted on the paper.

"Would it not be wonderful to read?" I said for what must have been the hundredth time.

"I tell you, my time is passed. School is not for people my age."

The children across the street were piling up the leaves in Madame Augustin's yard. The bigger ones waited on line as the smaller ones dropped onto the pile, bouncing to their feet, shrieking and laughing. They called one another's names: Foi, Hope, Faith, Espérance, Beloved, God-Given, My Joy, First Born, Last Born, Aséfi, Enough-Girls, Enough-Boys, Deliverance, Small Misery, Big Misery, No Misery. Names as bright and colorful as the giant poincianas in Madame Augustin's garden.

They grabbed one another and fell to the ground, rejoicing as though they had flown past the towering flame trees[6] that shielded the yard from the hot Haitian sun.

"You think these children would be kind to their mothers and clean up those leaves," Tante Atie said. "Instead, they are making a bigger mess."

"They should know better," I said, secretly wishing that I too could swim in their sea of dry leaves.

Tante Atie threw her arms around me and squeezed me so hard that the lemon-scented perfume, which she dabbed across her chest each morning, began to tickle my nose.

"Sunday is Mother's Day, *non?*" she said, loudly sucking her teeth. "The young ones, they should show their mothers they want to help them. What you see in your children today, it tells you about what they will do for you when you are close to the grave."

I appreciated Tante Atie, but maybe I did not show it enough. Maybe she wanted to be a real mother, have a real daughter to wear matching clothes with, hold hands and learn to read with.

"Mother's Day will make you sad, won't it, Tante Atie?"

"Why do you say that?" she asked.

"You look like someone who is going to be sad."

"You were always wise beyond your years, just like your mother."

She gently held my waist as I climbed down from her lap. Then she cupped her face in both palms, her elbows digging into the pleats of her pink skirt.

I was going to sneak the card under her pillow Saturday night so that she would find it as she was making the bed on Sunday morning. But the way her face drooped into her palms made me want to give it to her right then.

I dug into my pocket, and handed it to her. Inside was a poem that I had written for her.

She took the card from my hand. The flower nearly fell off. She pressed the tape against the short stem, forced the baby daffodil back in its place, and handed the card back to me. She did not even look inside.

"Not this year," she said.

---

6. Also known as royal poinciana or flamboyant trees; their bright reddish orange blossoms give the appearance of being in flames.

"Why not this year?"

"Sophie, it is not mine. It is your mother's. We must send it to your mother."

I only knew my mother from the picture on the night table by Tante Atie's pillow. She waved from inside the frame with a wide grin on her face and a large flower in her hair. She witnessed everything that went on in the bougainvillea,[7] each step, each stumble, each hug and kiss. She saw us when we got up, when we went to sleep, when we laughed, when we got upset at each other. Her expression never changed. Her grin never went away.

I sometimes saw my mother in my dreams. She would chase me through a field of wildflowers as tall as the sky. When she caught me, she would try to squeeze me into the small frame so I could be in the picture with her. I would scream and scream until my voice gave out, then Tante Atie would come and save me from her grasp.

I slipped the card back in my pocket and got up to go inside. Tante Atie lowered her head and covered her face with her hands. Her fingers muffled her voice as she spoke.

"When I am done feeling bad, I will come in and we will find you a very nice envelope for your card. Maybe it will get to your mother after the fact, but she will welcome it because it will come directly from you."

"It is your card," I insisted.

"It is for a mother, your mother." She motioned me away with a wave of her hand. "When it is Aunt's Day, you can make me one."

"Will you let me read it to you?"

"It is not for me to hear, my angel. It is for your mother."

I put the card back in my pocket, plucked out the flower, and dropped it under my shoes.

Across the road, the children were yelling each other's names, inviting passing friends to join them. They sat in a circle and shot the crackling leaves high above their heads. The leaves landed on their faces and clung to their hair. It was almost as though they were caught in a rain of daffodils.

I continued to watch the children as Tante Atie prepared what she was bringing to the potluck. She put the last touches on a large tray of sweet potato pudding that filled the whole house with its molasses scent.

As soon as the sun set, lamps were lit all over our quarter. The smaller children sat playing marbles near whatever light they could find. The older boys huddled in small groups near the school yard fence as they chatted over their books. The girls formed circles around their grandmothers' feet, learning to sew.

Tante Atie had promised that in another year or so she would teach me how to sew.

"You should not stare," she said as we passed a nearsighted old woman whispering mystical secrets of needle and thread to a little girl. The girl was squinting as her eyes dashed back and forth to keep up with the movements of her grandmother's old fingers.

"Can I start sewing soon?" I asked Tante Atie.

"Soon as I have a little time," she said.

She put her hand on my shoulder and bent down to kiss my cheek.

"Is something troubling you?" I asked.

"Don't let my troubles upset you," she said.

---

7. Tropical plants with large ornamental flowers.

"When I made the card, I thought it would make you happy. I did not mean to make you sad."

"You have never done anything to make me sad," she said. "That is why this whole thing is going to be so hard."

A cool evening breeze circled the dust around our feet.

"You should put on your blouse with the long sleeves," she said. "So you don't catch cold."

I wanted to ask her what was going to be so hard, but she pressed her finger over my lips and pointed towards the house.

She said "Go" and so I went.

One by one the men began to file out of their houses. Some carried plantains, others large Negro yams,[8] which made your body itch if you touched them raw. There were no men in Tante Atie's and my house so we carried the food ourselves to the yard where the children had been playing.

The women entered the yard with tins of steaming ginger tea and baskets of cassava[9] bread. Tante Atie and I sat near the gate, she behind the women and me behind the girls.

Monsieur Augustin stacked some twigs with a rusty pitchfork and dropped his ripe plantains and husked corn on the pile. He lit a long match and dropped it on the top of the heap. The flame spread from twig to twig, until they all blended into a large smoky fire.

Monsieur Augustin's wife began to pass around large cups of ginger tea. The men broke down into small groups and strolled down the garden path, smoking their pipes. Old *tantes*—aunties—and grandmothers swayed cooing babies on their laps. The teenage boys and girls drifted to dark corners, hidden by the shadows of rustling banana leaves.

Tante Atie said that the way these potlucks started was really a long time ago in the hills. Back then, a whole village would get together and clear a field for planting. The group would take turns clearing each person's land, until all the land in the village was cleared and planted. The women would cook large amounts of food while the men worked. Then at sunset, when the work was done, everyone would gather together and enjoy a feast of eating, dancing, and laughter.

Here in Croix-des-Rosets,[1] most of the people were city workers who labored in baseball or clothing factories and lived in small cramped houses to support their families back in the provinces. Tante Atie said that we were lucky to live in a house as big as ours, with a living room to receive our guests, *plus* a room for the two of us to sleep in. Tante Atie said that only people living on New York money or people with professions, like Monsieur Augustin, could afford to live in a house where they did not have to share a yard with a pack of other people. The others had to live in huts, shacks, or one-room houses that, sometimes, they had to build themselves.

In spite of where they might live, this potluck was open to everybody who wanted to come. There was no field to plant, but the workers used their friendships in the factories or their grouping in the common yards as a reason to get together, eat, and celebrate life.

8. Root vegetable; also known as white yams or African yams.

9. Edible root.

1. Village in Haiti.

Tante Atie kept looking at Madame Augustin as she passed the tea to each person in the women's circle around us.

"How is Martine?" Madame Augustin handed Tante Atie a cup of steaming tea. Tante Atie's hand jerked and the tea sprinkled the back of Madame Augustin's hand.

"I saw the *facteur*[2] bring you something big yesterday." Madame Augustin blew into her tea as she spoke. "Did your sister send you a gift?"

Tante Atie tried to ignore the question.

"Was it a gift?" insisted Madame Augustin. "It is not the child's birthday again, is it. She was just twelve, no less than two months ago."

I wondered why Tante Atie had not showed me the big package. Usually, my mother would send us two cassettes with our regular money allowance. One cassette would be for me and Tante Atie, the other for my grandmother. Usually, Tante Atie and I would listen to our cassette together. Maybe she was saving it for later.

I tried to listen without looking directly at the women's faces. That would have been disrespectful, as bad as speaking without being spoken to.

"How is Martine doing over there?" asked Stéphane, the albino's wife. She was a sequins piece worker, who made herself hats from leftover factory sequins. That night she was wearing a gold bonnet that made her look like a star had landed on her head.

"My sister is fine, thank you," Tante Atie finally answered.

Madame Augustin took a sip of her tea and looked over at me. She gave me a reprimanding look that said: Why aren't you playing with the other children? I quickly lowered my eyes, pretending to be studying some random pebbles on the ground.

"I would wager that it is very nice over there in New York," Madame Augustin said.

"I suppose it could be," said Tante Atie.

"Why have you never gone?" asked Madame Augustin.

"Perhaps it is not yet the time," said Tante Atie.

"Perhaps it is," corrected Madame Augustin.

She leaned over Tante Atie's shoulder and whispered in a not so low voice, "When are you going to tell us, Atie, when the car comes to take you to the airplane?"

"Is Martine sending for you?" asked the albino's wife.

Suddenly, all the women began to buzz with questions.

"When are you leaving?"

"Can it really be as sudden as that?"

"Will you marry there?"

"Will you remember us?"

"I am not going anywhere," Tante Atie interrupted.

"I have it on good information that it was a plane ticket that you received the other day," said Madame Augustin. "If you are not going, then who was the plane ticket for?"

All their eyes fell on me at the same time.

"Is the mother sending for the child?" asked the albino's wife.

"I saw the delivery," said Madame Augustin

"Then she is sending for the child," they concluded.

Suddenly a large hand was patting my shoulder.

2. Mailman (French).

"This is very good news," said the accompanying voice. "It is the best thing that is ever going to happen to you."

I could not eat the bowl of food that Tante Atie laid in front of me. I only kept wishing that everyone would disappear so I could go back home.

The night very slowly slipped into the early hours of the morning. Soon everyone began to drift towards their homes. On Saturdays there was the house to clear and water to fetch from long distances and the clothes to wash and iron for the Mother's Day Mass.

After everyone was gone, Monsieur Augustin walked Tante Atie and me home. When we got to our door he moved closer to Tante Atie as though he wanted to whisper something in her ear. She looked up at him and smiled, then quickly covered her lip with her fingers, as though she suddenly remembered her missing teeth and did not want him to see them.

He turned around to look across the street. His wife was carrying some of the pots back inside the house. He squeezed Tante Atie's hand and pressed his cheek against hers.

"It is good news, Atie" he said. "Neither you nor Sophie should be sad. A child belongs with her mother, and a mother with her child."

His wife was now sitting on the steps in front of their bougainvillea, waiting for him.

"I did not think you would tell your wife before I had a chance to tell the child," said Tante Atie to Monsieur Augustin.

"You must be brave," he said. "It is some very wonderful news for this child."

The night had grown a bit cool, but we both stood and watched as Monsieur Augustin crossed the street, took the pails from his wife's hand and bent down to kiss her forehead. He put his arms around her and closed the front door behind them.

"When you tell someone something and you call it a secret, they should know not to tell others," Tante Atie mumbled to herself.

She kept her eyes on the Augustins' house. The main light in their bedroom was lit. Their bodies were silhouetted on the ruffled curtains blowing in the night breeze. Monsieur Augustin sat in a rocking chair by the window. His wife sat on his lap as she unlaced her long braid of black hair. Monsieur Augustin brushed the hair draped like a silk blanket down Madame Augustin's back. When he was done, Monsieur Augustin got up to undress. Then slowly, Madame Augustin took off her day clothes and slipped into a long-sleeved night gown. Their laughter rose in the night as they began a tickling fight. The light flickered off and they tumbled into bed.

Tante Atie kept looking at the window even after all signs of the Augustins had faded into the night.

A tear rolled down her cheek as she unbolted the door to go inside. I immediately started walking towards our bedroom. She raced after me and tried to catch up. When she did, she pressed her hand down on my shoulder and tried to turn my body around, to face her.

"Do you know why I always wished I could read?"

Her teary eyes gazed directly into mine.

"I don't know why." I tried to answer as politely as I could.

"It was always my dream to read," she said, "so I could read that old Bible under my pillow and find the answers to everything right there between those pages. What do you think that old Bible would have us do right now, about this moment?"

"I don't know," I said.

"How can you not know?" she asked. "You try to tell me there is all wisdom in reading but at a time like this you disappoint me."

"You lied!" I shouted.

She grabbed both my ears and twisted them until they burned.

I stomped my feet and walked away. As I rushed to bed, I began to take off my clothes so quickly that I almost tore them off my body.

The smell of lemon perfume stung my nose as I pulled the sheet over my head.

"I did not lie," she said, "I kept a secret, which is different. I wanted to tell you. I needed time to reconcile myself, to accept it. It was very sudden, just a cassette from Martine saying, 'I want my daughter,' and then as fast as you can put two fingers together to snap, she sends me a plane ticket with a date on it. I am not even certain that she is doing this properly. All she tells me is that she arranged it with a woman who works on the airplane."

"Was I ever going to know?" I asked.

"I was going to put you to sleep, put you in a suitcase, and send you to her. One day you would wake up there and you would feel like your whole life here with me was a dream." She tried to force a laugh, but it didn't make it past her throat. "I had this plan, you see. I thought it was a good plan. I was going to tell you this, that in one week you would be going to see your mother. As far as you would know, it would just be a visit. I felt it in my heart and took it on Monsieur Augustin's advice that, once you got there, you would love it so much that you would beg your mother to let you stay. You have heard with your own two ears what everyone has said. We have no right to be sad."

I sunk deeper and deeper into the bed and lost my body in the darkness, in the folds of the sheets.

The bed creaked loudly as Tante Atie climbed up on her side.

"Don't you ever tell anyone that I cry when I watch Donald and his wife getting ready for bed," she said, sobbing.

I groped for my clothes in the dark and found the Mother's Day card I had made her. I tucked it under her pillow as I listened to her mumble some final words in her sleep.

Chapter 35

Joseph was on the couch, rocking the baby, when I came home. She was sleeping in his arms, with her index and middle fingers in her mouth. Joseph took her to our room and put her down without saying a word. He came back and pulled me down on the sofa. He picked up the answering machine and played me a message from Marc.

"Sophie, *je t'en prie*,[3] call me. It's about your mother."

Marc's voice was quivering, yet cold. It seemed as though he was purposely forcing himself to be casual.

I grabbed Joseph's collar, almost choking him.

---

3. Please (French).

"Let's not jump to any wild conclusions," he said.

"I am wondering why she is not calling me herself," I said.

"Maybe she's had a complication with the pregnancy."

"She was going to have an abortion today."

"Keep calm and dial."

The phone rang endlessly. Finally her answering machine picked up. "*S'il vous plait, laissez-moi un message.* Please leave me a message." Impeccable French and English, both painfully mastered, so that her voice would never betray the fact that she grew up without a father, that her mother was merely a peasant, that she was *from the hills.*

We sat by the phone all night, alternating between dialing and waiting.

Finally at six in the morning, Marc called.

His voice was laden with pain.

"Sophie. *Je t'en prie.* I am sorry."

He was sobbing.

"What is it?" I asked.

"*Calme-toi.*[4] Listen to me."

"Listen to what?"

"I am sorry," he said.

"Put my mother on the phone. What did you do?"

"It's not me."

"Please, Marc. Put my mother on the phone. Where is she? Is she in the hospital?"

He was sobbing. Joseph pressed his face against mine. He was trying to listen.

"Is my mother in the hospital?"

"*Non.* She is rather in the morgue."

I admired the elegance in the way he said it. Now he would have to say it to my grandmother, who had lost her daughter, and to my Tante Atie, who had lost her only sister.

"Am I hearing you right?" I asked.

"She is gone."

Joseph pressed harder against me.

"What happened?" I was shouting at Marc.

"I woke up in the middle of the night. Sometimes, I wake up and she's not there, so I was not worried. Two hours passed and I woke up again, I went to the bathroom and she was lying there."

"Lying there? Lying where? Talk faster, will you?"

"In blood. She was lying there in blood."

"Did she slip and fall?"

"It was very hard to see."

"What was very hard to see?"

"She had a mountain of sheets on the floor. She had prepared this."

"What?"

"She stabbed her stomach with an old rusty knife. I counted, and they counted again in the hospital. Seventeen times."

"Are you sure?"

"It was seventeen times."

"How could you sleep?" I shouted.

---

4. Relax, or calm yourself (French).

"She was still breathing when I found her," he said. "She even said something in the ambulance. She died there in the ambulance."

"What did she say in the ambulance?"

"*Mwin pa kapab enkò*. She could not carry the baby. She said that to the ambulance people."

"How could you sleep?" I was screaming at him.

"I did the best I could," he said. "I tried to save her. Don't you know how I wanted this child?"

"Why did you give her a child? Didn't you know about the nightmares?" I asked.

"You knew better about the nightmares," he said, "but where were you?"

I crashed into Joseph's arms when I hung up the phone.

It was as if the world started whirling after that, as though I had no control over anything. Everything raced by like a speeding train and I, breathlessly, sprang after it, trying to keep up.

I grabbed my suitcase from the closet and threw a few things inside.

"I am going with you," Joseph said.

"What about Brigitte? Who will look after her? I can't take her into this."

"Let's sit down and think of some way."

I didn't have time to sit and think.

"You stay. I go. It's that simple."

He didn't insist anymore. He helped me pack my bag. We woke up the baby and he drove me to the bus station.

We held each other until the bus was about to pull out.

I gave Brigitte a kiss on the forehead.

"Mommy will bring you a treat from the market."

She began to cry as I boarded the bus. Joseph took her away quickly, not looking back.

Marc was waiting in the house in Brooklyn when I got there. Somehow I expected there to be detectives, and flashing cameras, but this was New York after all. People killed themselves every day. Besides, he was a lawyer. He knew people in power. He simply had to tell them that my mother was crazy.

There was a trail of dried blood, down from the stairs to the living room and out to the street where they must have loaded her into the ambulance. The bathroom floor was spotless, however, except for the pile of bloody sheets stuffed in trash bags in the corner.

"Sophie, will you sit down?" Marc said, following me as I raced in and out of every room in the house. "I need to tell you how things will proceed."

I rushed into my mother's room. It was spotless and her bed was properly made. In her closet, everything was in some shade of red, her favorite color since she'd left Haiti.

"I was cleared beyond any doubt in your mother's *accident*. I have used what influence I have to make this very expeditious for all of us. I have contacted a funeral home. They will get her from the morgue and they will ship her to a funeral home in Dame Marie."[5]

If I died mute, I would never speak to him again. I would never open my mouth and address a word to him.

5. Village in Haiti.

"We can see her in the funeral home," he said. "They will ship her tomorrow night. That's the earliest possible. They have a service. They notify the family. I have already had your family notified."

How dare he? How could he? To send news that could kill my grandmother, by telegram.

"You can sleep at my house until the flight tomorrow night."

I had no intention of going to his house. I was going to spend the night right there, in my mother's house.

He did not leave me. He stayed in the living room and ate Chinese food while I crouched in the fetal position in the large bed in my mother's room.

Joseph let me listen to Brigitte's giggles when I called home. I heard a voice say Mama, but I knew it was his. She was still saying Dada, even though I knew he had tried to coach her.

"One day we'll all take a trip together," he said.

"This trip I must make alone."

"We are waiting for you," he said, "we love you very much. Don't stay there too long."

I lay in my mother's bed all night fighting evil thoughts: It is your fault that she killed herself in the first place. Your face took her back again. You should have stayed with her. If you were here, she would not have gotten pregnant.

When I woke up the next day, Marc was asleep on the sofa.

"Would you pick something for your mother to be buried in?" he asked.

He spoke to me the way older men addressed orphan children, with pity in his voice. If we had been in Haiti, he might have given me a penny to ease my pain.

I picked out the most crimson of all my mother's clothes, a bright red, two-piece suit that she was too afraid to wear to the Pentecostal services.

It was too loud a color for a burial. I knew it. She would look like a Jezebel, hot-blooded Erzulie[6] who feared no men, but rather made them her slaves, raped *them*, and killed *them*. She was the only woman with that power. It was too bright a red for burial. If we had an open coffin at the funeral home, people would talk. It was too loud a color for burial, but I chose it. There would be no ostentation, no viewing, neither pomp nor circumstance. It would be simple like she had wanted, a simple prayer at the grave site and some words of remembrance.

"Saint Peter won't allow your mother into Heaven in that," he said.

"She is going to Guinea," I said, "or she is going to be a star. She's going to be a butterfly or a lark in a tree. She's going to be free."

He looked at me as though he thought me as insane as my mother.

At my mother's dressing, in the Nostrand Avenue[7] funeral home, her face was a permanent blue. Her eyelids were stretched over her eyes as though they had been sewn shut.

I called Joseph one last time before we got on the plane. He put the baby on the phone to wish me *Bon Voyage*. This time she said *Manman*. When I said good-bye, she began to cry.

"She feels your absence," Joseph said.

"Does she sleep?" I asked.

"Less now," he said.

---

6. Virgin goddess of the moon, a Vodun deity. Jezebel was the wife of Ahab, a biblical king, and was associated with wickedness.

7. Major thoroughfare in Brooklyn, New York.

My mother was the heavy luggage that went under the plane. I did not sit next to Marc on the plane. There were enough seats so that I did not have to. There were not many people going to Haiti, only those who were in the same circumstances as we were, going to weddings or funerals.

At the airport in Port-au-Prince,[8] he spun his head around to look at everything. It had been years since he had left. He was observing, watching for changes: In the way the customs people said *Merci* and *au revoir* when you bribed them not to search your bags. The way the beggars clanked the pennies in their tin cans. The way the van drivers nearly killed one another on the airport sidewalk to reach you. The way young girls dashed forward and offered their bodies.

He had been told by the funeral home that my mother's body would follow us to the Cathedral Chapel in Dame Marie. A funeral home driver would pick her up. As soon as she got there, we could claim her and bury her, that same day, if that's what we wanted. The chauffeur arrived promptly and gave us a ride, in the hearse, to Dame Marie.

I felt my body stiffen as we walked through the *maché*[9] in Dame Marie. Marc had his eyes wide open, watching. He looked frightened of the *Macoutes*,[1] one of whom was sitting in Louise's stand selling her last colas.

People greeted me with waves and smiles on the way to my grandmother's house. It was as though I had lived there all my life.

Marc was straining to take in the sights. We walked silently. Louise's shack looked hollow and empty when we went by. In the cane fields, the men were singing about a mermaid who married a fisherman and became human.

My grandmother was sitting on the porch with her eyes on the road. I wondered how long she had been sitting there. For hours, through the night, since she had heard? We ran to each other. I told her everything. What I knew from him, where I blamed myself, and where he had blamed me.

She knew, she said, she knew even before she was told. When you let your salt lay in the sun, you are always looking out for rain. She even knew that my mother was pregnant. Remember, all of us have the gift of the unseen. Tante Atie was sitting on the steps with a black scarf around her head. She was clinging to the porch rail, now with two souls to grieve for.

Marc introduced himself to my grandmother reciting his whole name.

"Dreams move the wind," said my grandmother. "I knew, but she never spoke of you."

We decided to have the funeral the next morning, just among ourselves. That night we made a large pot of tea, which we shared with only Eliab and the other wandering boys. We did not call it a wake, but we played cards and drank ginger tea, and strung my wedding ring along a thread while singing a festive wake song: *Ring sways to Mother. Ring stays with Mother. Pass it. Pass it along. Pass me. Pass me along.*

Listening to the song, I realized that it was neither my mother nor my Tante Atie who had given all the mother-and-daughter motifs to all the stories they told and all the songs they sang. It was something that was essen-

---

8. Capital city of Haiti.
9. Market (Kreyol, or Haitian creole).
1. Originally the *Tonton Macoutes*, personal police force of Haitian dictator François (Papa Doc) Duvalier (1907–1971). Jean Claude (Baby Doc) Duvalier (b. 1951) changed the name of the force from *Macoutes*, which means "bogeymen," but the terror continued for several years after he was overthrown in 1986.

tially Haitian. Somehow, early on, our song makers and tale weavers had decided that we were all daughters of this land.

Marc slept in Tante Atie's room while Tante Atie slept in my grandmother's bed with her. They allowed me the courtesy of having my mother's bed all to myself.

The next day, we went together to claim my mother's body. My grandmother was wearing a crisp new black dress. She would surely wear black to her grave now. Tante Atie was wearing a purple frock. I wore a plain white dress, with a purple ribbon for my daughter. We sat on the plush velvet in the funeral chapel, waiting for them to bring her out. Tante Atie was numb and silent. My grandmother was watching for the black priest, the one they call Lavalas, to come through the door. The priest was the last missing pebble in the stream. Then we could take my mother to the hills.

Marc got up and walked around, impatiently waiting for them to wheel out her coffin. The velvet curtains parted and a tall mulatto[2] man theatrically pushed the coffin forward.

Marc raised the olive green steel lid and felt the gold satin lining. My mother was lying there with a very calm look on her face. I reached over to brush off some of the melting rouge, leaving just enough to accentuate her dress.

She didn't feel as cold as I expected. She looked as though she was dressed for a fancy affair and we were all keeping her from going on her way. Marc was weeping into his handkerchief. He reached into his vest pocket and pulled out a small Bible. He reached in and folded her hands over it. My grandmother dropped in a few threadless needles and Tante Atie, one copper penny.

My grandmother did not look directly at my mother's face, but at the red gloves on her hands and the matching shoes on her feet. My grandmother looked as though she was going to fall down, in shock.

We pulled her away and led her back to her seat. The priest came in and sprinkled holy water on my mother's forehead. He was short and thin, a tiny man with bulging eyes. He leaned forward and kissed my grandmother's hands. He crossed himself and held my grandmother's shoulder. Tante Atie fell on the ground; her body convulsing. Marc grabbed her and held her up. Her body slowly stilled but the tears never stopped flowing down her face.

"Let us take her home," said my grandmother.

They took her coffin up the hill in a cart. My grandmother walked in front with the driver and Tante Atie and I walked behind with the priest. As we went through the market, a crowd of curious observers gathered behind us.

We soon collected a small procession, people who recognized my grandmother and wanted to share her grief. The vendors ran and dropped their baskets at friends' houses, washed their feet and put on their clean clothes to follow my mother. School children trailed us in a long line. And in the cane fields, the men went home for their shirts and then joined in.

The ground was ready for my mother. Somehow the hole seemed endless, like a bottomless pit. The priest started off with a funeral song and the whole crowd sang the refrain.

2. Person with one white and one black parent.

Good-bye, brother. Good-bye, sister.
Pray to God for us.
On earth we see you nevermore
In heaven we unite.

People with gourd rattles and talking drums joined in. Others chimed in with cow horns and conch shells. My grandmother looked down at the grave, her eyes avoiding the coffin. Some of the old vendors held Tante Atie, keeping her body still.

My grandmother threw the first handful of dirt on the coffin as it was lowered into the ground. Then Tante Atie, and then me. I threw another handful for my daughter who was not there, but was part of this circle of women from whose gravestones our names had been chosen.

From the top of the hill, I saw our house, between the hills and the cane field.

I couldn't bear to see them shoveling dirt over my mother. I turned around and ran down the hill, ahead of the others. I felt my dress tearing as I ran faster and faster down the hill.

There were only a few men working in the cane fields. I ran through the field, attacking the cane. I took off my shoes and began to beat a cane stalk. I pounded it until it began to lean over. I pushed over the cane stalk. It snapped back, striking my shoulder. I pulled at it, yanking it from the ground. My palm was bleeding.

The cane cutters stared at me as though I was possessed. The funeral crowd was now standing between the stalks, watching me beat and pound the cane. My grandmother held back the priest as he tried to come for me.

From where she was standing, my grandmother shouted like the women from the market place, "Ou libéré?" Are you free?

Tante Atie echoed her cry, her voice quivering with her sobs.

"Ou libéré!"

There is always a place where women live near trees that, blowing in the wind, sound like music. These women tell stories to their children both to frighten and delight them. These women, they are fluttering lanterns on the hills, the fireflies in the night, the faces that loom over you and recreate the same unspeakable acts that they themselves lived through. There is always a place where nightmares are passed on through generations like heirlooms. Where women like cardinal birds return to look at their own faces in stagnant bodies of water.

I come from a place where breath, eyes, and memory are one, a place from which you carry your past like the hair on your head. Where women return to their children as butterflies or as tears in the eyes of the statues that their daughters pray to. My mother was as brave as stars at dawn. She too was from this place. My mother was like that woman who could never bleed and then could never stop bleeding, the one who gave in to her pain, to live as a butterfly. Yes, my mother was like me.

From the thick of the cane fields, I tried my best to tell her, but the words would not roll off my tongue. My grandmother walked over and put her hand on my shoulder.

"Listen. Listen before it passes. Paròl gin pié zèl. The words can give wings to your feet. There is so much to say, but time has failed you," she said. "There is a place where women are buried in clothes the color of flames, where we drop coffee on the ground for those who went ahead, where the daughter is never fully a woman until her mother has passed on before her. There is always a place where, if you listen closely in the night, you will hear your mother telling a story and at the end of the tale, she will ask you this question: *'Ou libéré?'* Are you free, my daughter?"

My grandmother quickly pressed her fingers over my lips.

"Now," she said, "you will know how to answer."

1994

COLSON WHITEHEAD
b. 1969

Born and raised in New York City, Whitehead graduated from Harvard College, where he was *not* accepted into a creative writing course. Within a decade, he had proven his doubters wrong. His journalism had appeared in the *New York Times*, *Salon*, and the *Village Voice*, for which he wrote a column on television. His first novel, *The Intuitionist* (1999), the mordantly inventive story of Lila Mae Watson, an elevator inspector, impressed reviewers for its ideas as well as its style and wit. They compared its author to Ralph Ellison and Toni Morrison, Don DeLillo and Thomas Pynchon. Employing the conventions of detective fiction, Whitehead creates a mystery about epistemology and racial identity. Writing with a deep knowledge of African American literary history, Whitehead locates *The Intuitionist* in the tradition of the black intellectual novel that he traces back to Jean Toomer's *Cane*, but his influences are diverse, including the postmodernist novel, science fiction, and popular culture.

Whitehead's second novel, *John Henry Days* (2001), won an array of prizes, and in 2002 Whitehead received a MacArthur Foundation fellowship, known popularly as the genius grant. *John Henry Days* is set in the West Virginia town, where, according to legend and the classic American folk song, the heroic steel driver died in a contest with a steam drill. The time is the present, and the occasion is the ceremony introducing a postage stamp in honor of John Henry. The novel's protagonist, J. Sutter, a young black journalist with an ironic sensibility, is part of the press junket sent to cover the event. In the chapters printed here, the novel satirizes the characters—local politicians and merchants, postal service administrators, stamp collectors, aspiring entertainers, and reporters—who have all bought into the public relations bonanza the event has become. The laughs in the scene are at their expense. But the novel also poses serious questions about the possibility of heroism in the postmodern age and of the relation of young, privileged African Americans to their history.

In his subsequent books, Whitehead demonstrates an impressive ability to move among genres with vision and verve. *The Colossus of New York* collects his essays about the city in the aftermath of 9/11. *Apex Hides the Hurt* (2006) is a comic tour de force that engages issues of history, marketing, and naming. The novel begins when a software millionaire decides that his town needs a new name; the local aristocracy is happy with the current name, while the mayor wants to reinstate the name chosen by the founding black settlers. A young black nomenclature consultant is hired to solve the problem. Whitehead's fourth novel, *Sag Harbor*, is his most autobiographical: the coming-of-age story is set in a resort favored by upper-middle-class African Americans. *Zone One* (2011) is a zombie novel that imagines post-apocalyptic life in New York City. With Whitehead's characteristic mixture of humor and rumination, the novel challenges readers to think about how we dehumanize others, how society tramples and consumes individuals, and how vulnerable we all are.

From John Henry[1] Days

1

This inveigler of invites and slayer of crudités, this drink ticket fondler and slim tipper, open bar opportunist, master of vouchers, queue-jumping wrangler of receipts, goes by the name of J. Sutter, views the facade of the Millhouse Inn through reptilian eyes.

Is he supposed to take this place seriously? The walls of the rustic hotel and restaurant are obviously some factory concoction, J. sees that from yards away, the ridges and pocks identical from stone to stone. He can't figure out what style its designers tried to effect, colonial flourishes abut antebellum[2] wood columns, modern double-pane windows nestle in artificially weathered frames of molting paint. Nice attempt by the toddler ivy along the walls, but hell, he discerns the wire firming it in place. But the water wheel is the biggest atrocity. The fountain jets force water over slats that do not move, the spray energetic and process of no natural movement, splashing into a cement pool lousy with plastic lily pads floating moronically, congregating near the drainage grate. Snug up against a hill, this establishment totally new, intended to service the legions of tourists who will flock here now for John Henry Days. They hope. A hipster kid with more hooks in his face than some ancient, uncatchable fish, strutting down Soho[3] in seventies' bellbottoms, has more period authenticity than this place. What is he doing here? He is going for the record, his works gurgling with slow, heavy fluids.

First things first when they hit the Social Room. Objective One: find a base of operations. Most of the tables had already been colonized by the other factions, but there is Frenchie tracking ahead, wading between chairs before the rest of them have finished taking stock of the room, on point, surveying, dithering a little between two tables to the far left of the podium before dropping his bag on one and motioning the other junketeers[4] over. He nods to himself, second-guessing his choice, but no, this is it, this table is definitely it. As J. and the rest march to join him, they progress to Objective Two, libations, scanning the joint as they advance on their seats. Two bartenders barely out of their teens work their alchemy in a corner under ferns. John Henry Days employment largesse stealing labor from the fast food outlets, J. surmises. The junketeers take their seats and dispatch Tiny and Dave for drinks. A few citizens of Talcott and Hinton hover around the

---

1. A historical black steel driver who died outracing a machine designed to replace him. In the folk story, he narrowly defeats a steam drill in a contest to drive steel through a mountain to make way for a railroad.
2. The period in the United States before the Civil War.

3. Neighborhood in downtown Manhattan, south of Houston Street.
4. Reporters assigned to cover events and media personnel; here, the John Henry Days Festival, held annually in July at the Great Bend Tunnel, near Talcott, a town in Summers County, West Virginia.

bar, but there is an opening on the left flank, a chink where Tiny or Dave might weasel in and dominate.

"I don't see a cash register," One Eye comments, sipping water.

"Me either," J. seconds.

These are some real white people, J. thinks, looking around. These people go into hair salons armed with pictures of stars on CBS television shows and demand. He is out of his element. He discovers the food table on the other side of the room. Looks like salad to start. His stomach grumbles again but he decides he can wait until the boys come back with the drinks. Bit of a line anyway. J. notices that the woman in the van has chosen a different table. Probably a good choice to keep her distance.

The drinks arrive, dock, find berth in waiting palms. Frenchie sniffs, asks, "This Gordon's or what?"

Tiny shakes his head. "No, tonight they're breaking out the good stuff. I asked the guy if he had any moonshine and he just looked at me. Was that un-p.c. of me?"

"Obviously you haven't heard of the great Talcott Moonshine War of Thirty-three," One Eye says over the rim of his glass. "You're stirring up old wounds."

J. has forgotten that afternoon's vomit incident but then he smells the gin. Bubbles break against his nose. He figures the ham sandwich he discovered in his suitcase has settled his stomach a bit. "Cheers," he says. Everybody's already drinking.

One Eye nods to the right, to an efficient-looking lady with a strong stride approaching their table, clipboard against her chest like armor. The handler. Can spot a handler a mile away, just as easily as she identified them. She introduces herself as Arlene. "I hope you had an easy trip out here," she says, smiling.

Nods all around. Tiny belches. J. thinks she is smiling at him more than the others. "I left some brochures with the press packets at the hotel," she says. "You should see what the county has to offer. Maybe you could include a little about the New River[5] in your articles."

"Articles?" Tiny says under his breath.

"I saw them," Dave says, ever the appeaser when it came to the game. "Sounds like there's a lot of nice things in these parts."

In these parts. One Eye and J. look at each other: Dave is shameless.

"You should check it out if you get a chance," Arlene advises, retreating from the table. "Well, you enjoy yourselves tonight; tomorrow is a big day. I see you've already made yourselves at home. If you have any questions, or if you'd like to talk to the mayor or one of the event planners, feel free to grab me at any time." She departs, but not before smiling at J. again. Why was she smiling like that. Some kind of overcompensation for slavery or what? He leaves his seat to nab some salad, passing Lawrence on the way, who raises two fingers in greeting without breaking eye contact with the fellow he is talking to. The man is a pro.

It is a cafeteria salad, a Vegas all-you-can-eat salad, but J. doesn't mind. He has a good feeling about the main course. He swipes a brown wooden bowl and tries to ration himself, judging the length of the buffet versus the capacity of the bowl (always this necessary consideration of cubic space), he

5. A river in West Virginia.

catches a glimpse of celery up ahead and makes a note to save precious room.

"Haven't these people ever heard of arugula?" Frenchie complains when he returns, looking a bit reticently at the fixings.

"Iceberg lettuce contains many important minerals," J. says.

The conversation in the room cuts out and at the podium Arlene asks for everyone's attention. She introduces Mayor Cliff and relinquishes the mike to a tall man with jagged gray hair and wolverine eyebrows. The skin of his face rough and sunken, eroded. Descended from railroad people, J. decides, he has timetable worry and collision fret in his genes. None of the other junketeers pay Cliff any mind; Dave is in the middle of an elaborate joke about a one-armed hooker.

The mayor says, "I'm glad you all came out here tonight to celebrate what our two towns have achieved in the past and what we will accomplish with this weekend." Feedback curses the air and a chubby teenager scrambles to minister to the p.a.[6] system. When the screech ends, Cliff thanks him and continues. "We've all been working hard these last few weeks and months, and I know I'm not the only one who's glad that the day is finally here. My wife is very happy, I can tell you that. Charlotte—will you stand up? See that big grin on her face? That means no more 3 A.M. phone calls from Angel about her latest flower brainstorm. No more waking up to find Martin asleep on our doorstep with a report on the latest disaster." A good part of the room chuckles in recognition. J. sighs. "Now it's all paid off. So drink up, get some food and enjoy yourselves—you've earned it!"

Cliff takes a sip of water. "Some of you may have already heard that Ben Vereen[7] will not be joining us tonight. I talked to his manager on the phone a few hours ago and he explained that while Mr. Vereen was very excited about coming down to Talcott, he was suffering from laryngitis and couldn't possibly perform." J. nibbles on a carrot and shakes his head. Laryngitis—probably resting after the vigorous and well-deserved ass-kicking he delivered upon his patently insane manager. "While this is a great blow—Mr. Vereen is an amazing performer loved the world over—we've arranged for some homegrown talent to appear after dinner. I won't reveal his identity right now, but I know that some of you have heard him before and know he will not disappoint." J. decides to tune him out. He doesn't need to listen to this homespun rubbish; he has all weekend to gather material, what little he needs. Will he have to do actual research? Who is he kidding. But he could always use a quote or two to round things out. Nine hundred to twelve hundred words—the website editor said they hadn't determined the average attention span of a web surfer, so they might trim his article if the next round of market research dictated. Twelve hundred words—he can excrete that modest sum in two hours no sweat, but a nice quote would spice it up. There is no need to listen tonight; he has two more days to badger some unsuspecting festival-goer into a colorful quote.

Cliff departed; in his stead ambles up some guy from the Post Office. Maybe ask that sister from the van her thoughts. She has something to say, J. figures. He sees her at the next table, listening to the Post Office guy, surrounded by the natives. Just as he is. J. looks around the room and confirms that they are the only black people in the joint. Honoring a black hero and them the only folks in the room. John Henry the American. He finishes off the last of the salad and looks over to see what is going on in the food area and he sees the red light.

He sees the red light and understands.

The red light at the head of a buffet table signifies one thing and one thing only: prime rib. J. has been waiting for this confirmation all day. In the airport he had glimpsed it in a vision and now it has come to pass. He sees himself cutting into the soft red meat, slicing first through the milky rind of fat, then gaining the meat and watching the blood extrude through dead pores at the loving, sedulous pressure of his cutting. J. sees the red light of the heating lamp at the far shore of the buffet table and immediately conjures mashed potatoes softening in essence of beef, the blood tinting the fluffy potato pink and refining it even purer, softer. This vision is the sublime distillation of all the buffets he's known, the one and true spirit summoned by caterly prayer. He waits for them to wheel out dinner, he waits to be fulfilled.

2

What makes him tick, this collector of stamps? He doesn't know himself. Alphonse Miggs sits in the Social Room of the Millhouse Inn, he sits on his hands at a table of eight, with seven folks he doesn't know. At the start of the evening his knuckles brushed against a lump in his jacket pocket. He withdrew a mothball and, supremely embarrassed, thrust it back where it came. He wasn't sure if anyone noticed his mark of shame. For the rest of the night he feels cursed with invisible pockets and all at the dinner can see his shame, the great pearl of naphthalene clinging to his person, smell the fumes of social incompetence emanating from it. Scoring their nostrils. The woman next to him, are her nostrils curling as she addresses him, is she sniffing him? She is about fifty years old, with a jubilant round face and well-pruned hedge of red hair. Noticing that he does not speak, noticing that he is one of two visitors from out of town at their table and not the black one, she introduces herself as the owner of the flower shop in Hinton.[8] Her name is Angel and she smiles at Alphonse, exposing lips swabbed by red lipstick. Her accent elasticizes her words, jaw-jutting, sweet-sounding. She gestures at the glad ring of rainbow flowers around the podium, the looping green garlands dipping along the walls, and informs him that she spent hours devising pleasant arrangements for this weekend. Is she sniffing him? He nods at the vase in the center of the table, at the halfhearted burst of drooping tulips. He says they are very elegant. She thanks him and introduces him to her husband, a skinny man with a sun-cragged face who smiles a greeting at him before turning back to his conversation with the man next to him. She is in charge of all the floral arrangements, Angel explains, from tonight's dinner to Saturday's afternoon steeldriving exhibition and dinner, even the grand finale on Sunday, the stamp ceremony in town. As she recounts the preparations for each event her face seems to recapitulate the satellite emotions of each endeavor, the daisy hassle of Saturday's lunch, the gladiolus hell of the steeldriving match. It is the biggest job she has ever done, her distributor downright apoplectic at the size of her shipment, the shifting orders and delivery

8. County seat of Summers County, West Virginia.

dates. She has never commanded so many flowers before, it is a science, she could write a book about it, she jokes, but it all turned out fine in the end as anyone could plainly see and she got the name of her flower shop in the program. Which is good publicity. And where is Mr. Miggs from?

The drive from Silver Spring[9] had been pleasant. It didn't matter where you lived, Alphonse believed, you go five minutes in any direction from your house and become a stranger in your own neighborhood. Windows, drapes, doorsteps, doors, each one harboring a stranger and not a neighbor, one of the great number that make up the rest of the world. All it takes is five minutes in any direction to find yourself in the nation. Drive six hours and what do you find?

In the Talcott Motor Lodge Alphonse had undressed, folding his driving clothes neatly and separately on the bedspread. Driving clothes, as if he were tooling around in a reconditioned Model T, white scarf trailing from his neck, but Alphonse Miggs has names and categories for his world, subsets and sub-subsets. The inventory eases navigation through the breakwater of his days. He then removed his black suit from the garment bag and hooked it on the bathroom door to let the steam soothe wrinkles. Stepping into the shower, he felt cleanser residue scrape his feet. He ran a fingernail along the surface of the tub, across the pattern of raised traction grooves arrayed in a flower pattern, and contemplated the white dust there. The packaged soap had no scent and did not foam. He used up the whole bar searching for lather.

He was the first to arrive. In general Alphonse prefers to be early; he sympathizes with movie mobsters who have run afoul of the organization and arrive at key meetings in public locations before the appointed time to test the vibe, but in this case he had merely misremembered the start of dinner. He was an hour early. Alphonse entered the Social Room and took a few awkward steps inside. No one paid him any mind. A blond woman steered her clipboard around the room, directing the staff by remote control, tapping her pen. Two bartenders with black bow ties arranged liquor bottles on their stand, swiveling the labels forward and crunching beer bottles into buckets of ice. Alphonse picked out a table that was neither too close to the podium nor too close to the wall. He wanted to fade, but he also wanted to see the proceedings. He sat in one chair, tried on the angle, and moved two chairs over. Baleful wail from the microphones. Everyone winced and stared at the teenager monkeying with the amp, the boy's hands skittered over knobs to tame the shriek. Silence then for a moment and the people returned to their tasks. Occasionally Alphonse caught the eye of one of them and they looked away quickly; it wasn't their job to figure out why he was sitting there so early. A teenage girl attacked his table, straightening the napkins and silverware, tickling the flowers into a pert attention. She skipped Alphonse's placement. He looked up at her and strained a smile from his face. She moved on to the next table. Alphonse turned his attention to the garden outside the French doors. Everything green and lush and orderly out there, darker greens coming to the fore, shadows brooding under leaves as a nearby mountain somewhere ate the sun.

A large man with a chef's hat rolled out serving tables through the kitchen door.

9. Town in Maryland, a suburb of Washington, D.C.

His philately newsletter announced the John Henry stamp that spring, reprinting word for word the USPS's[1] release. A 113 million run in panes of twenty. Used to be commemorative stamps were something special, their limited runs hypothesizing scarcity down the line, bloating value. But there were so many now, issued so frequently that their significance dwindled. Alphonse Miggs collected railroad stamps.

He watched the people arrive. The preparations trickled to last-minute adjustments, an errand of tonic water, discipline of curtains and the other guests arrived. Five men in light summer-weight suits appeared at the door and the woman with the clipboard descended on them, introducing herself and gesticulating. The men looked city. Alphonse figured they were agents from the glorious USPS. They took measure of the room, looked down at the terra-cotta tile on the floor, the light blue trim of the moldings. The woman gestured at the tables, at the bar: sit anywhere you like, help yourself to the refreshments. The postal men chose a table up front. One man took his jacket off and draped it over the seatback, but seeing that his comrades did not join him, replaced his jacket on his shoulders. They proceeded to the bar one by one for seltzer water and a slice of lemon.

Natives of Talcott in exuberant summer clothes sallied forth, exchanging greetings for the second or third time that day. Alphonse watched the clipboard woman wave hello to them. They all knew each other. Perhaps he'd spoken to this woman on the phone, Arlene. The John Henry announcement drew him in and he called for more information, although he couldn't possibly think what more he could have needed; the press release had been quite thorough. The USPS under Runyon[2] was very receptive to the public, maintained a line to answer questions, keep the dialogue open. The man who answered his call, after a not overlong and entirely decent wait on hold, informed him that if the gentleman was that interested in the Folk Heroes series, he might want to visit the town of Talcott, West Virginia, for their festival. He gave Alphonse a contact number and asked if he could help him with anything else. Civil servants get a bad rap, Alphonse thought. He called Arlene at the Visitors Center and she was delighted at his interest, the flowing signature scribbled on the business card enclosed with the information packet described a conscientious and caring nature. He made reservations.

Some later arrivals had no choice but to sit with the man. Guests staked claims for their parties, planting flags of purses and jackets, saving seats, savoring or ruing their place in the pecking order, made the best of things. Two couples sat down at Alphonse's table on the other side of the globe, as far from him as the rim would allow. One of the men nodded at Alphonse, and, not waiting for a response, looked into his lap as he slowly unfolded his napkin. Alphonse wondered if the table would fill up or if he'd remain out there on the ice cap. He made minute adjustments to the placement of his knife and fork. Contemplation of tines. Another local couple sat down between him and the other people, they greeted their friends, closing up the circle except for the seat to Alphonse's right. Alphonse sat on his hands.

An excited breeze teased the napes of all in the room: the salad table was open for business. The vanguard left their seats, heads darted toward, seats

---

1. U.S. Postal Service. "Philately": related to the collection and study of postage stamps.

2. Marvin T. Runyon (b. 1924), U.S. Postmaster General (1992–98).

emptied in twos and threes. Alphonse hustled up to beat the queue. He garnered a fine spot in the top third and they heaved forward, reading and deciphering the feet before them. A shoulder dipped and this was taken for a sign. So tight together they must smell him. Were those beets he saw, that burgundy jelly ahead? Alphonse glimpsed a man at the podium looking over his papers. The man whispered into the microphone, hello, hello. The line bristled. They were going to miss the introduction, trapped by mixed greens on the other side of the room. The man walked away from the podium, merely testing sound, but the line hurried anyway. Iceberg lettuce, shavings of carrot, chickpeas, and a nice portion of beets.

When he returned to his table, the final empty seat had been filled by a young black woman, alone. He realized he hadn't seen a lot of black people so far, and since the others at the table did not acknowledge her, he assumed she was a visitor like him. She looked down at his bowl and walked to the salad bar. He had dolloped too much blue cheese dressing. Black people are African Americans now. Alphonse recalled again, he pondered the fact repeatedly, that the first commemorative stamp in the world had also been a railroad stamp, issued by Peru in 1871 to celebrate the twentieth anniversary of the South American railroad. (It is a sign.) And now John Henry, a railroad hero up there with Casey Jones, was getting his due in a commemorative stamp. Alphonse thought about the bustle of the room and the itinerary of the next few days. What he had come there to do. The woman on his left introduced herself as the owner of a flower shop. He listens and sits on his hands.

The table behind Alphonse is rambunctious and distracting. He turns around and sees five men, obviously not from Talcott: their revels are hermetic, and have nothing to do with what is going on in the room, the occasion. They drink heavily; one of their number, a gaudily dressed man with an eyepatch, returns from the bar pinching glasses together with professional poise, bearing refills for him and his friends before they have drained the drinks already in front of them. Angel tilts her head and clucks. The black woman on his right catches Alphonse's eyes and says they are a bunch of loud journalists from New York City. She says her name is Pamela.

Before they can speak further, the woman with the clipboard taps on the microphone for attention, her lacquered fingernails clawing at the air. Salad forks are set aside. She introduces herself as Arlene from the Visitors Center, and thanks everyone in the room for attending. Alphonse feels like an impostor, of course. He has been invited to this function, but most of the people in the room are locals, have worked directly on planning the weekend. His purpose swiftly comforts him. He is undercover. The mayor of Talcott replaces Arlene at the microphone and makes a few remarks. The other people at Alphonse's table laugh at an inside joke, a nugget of Talcott lore. Mayor Cliff is tall and gaunt. Thick gray curly hair writhes on his head, soft against the sharp ridges of his cheekbones. Alphonse isn't listening. Tonight is the warm-up, he thinks. Tomorrow the tourists and the rest of the town, the others beside the town luminaries getting fed in the Social Room. Tomorrow the celebration is open to the public, John Henry activities and John Henry barbecues, Sunday's trumpets-and-drums unveiling and the official release of the panes to the public on Monday. Bigger and bigger stages for the stamp. He will take his place and respond to his cue. Alphonse's local post office had recently outfitted the teller windows with bulletproof glass.

Alphonse sits up at the mention of the man from the Post Office, Parker Smith. He watches the man leave his comrades at the Post Office table (Alphonse's assessment had been correct) and shake hands with the mayor. Two perfect squares of gray perch in his black hair above his ears, almost the size of stamps, which amuses Alphonse slightly. Smith smiles and the emissary from the government addresses the people. "On behalf of Marvin Runyon, Postmaster General, and all of us at the United States Postal Service," he says, teeth twinkling, "I'd like to thank the good people of Talcott and Hinton for inviting us down for this wonderful occasion. I know you must be hungry and eager for the great food and musical entertainment the good people at the Chamber of Commerce have lined up for y'all, so I'll be brief. Did I say *y'all*? I'm sorry, I meant to say you all. Must be my Southern roots acting up. Haven't had so much Southern hospitality since I was a youngster visiting my grandparents in North Carolina."

Like a pro he waits for the chuckles to subside. People are so vain, Alphonse thinks. He watches Smith's face twitch into earnestness. "I was talking about this with some of my colleagues just a bit earlier—how you can't help but get caught up in the great history of this region. Talcott was instrumental in a great moment of our nation's growth—the forging of a national railroad, an effort unrivaled in human history. It was not without cost, as I'm sure you good people know only too well. How many of the folks who take Amtrak,[3] or receive products shipped by CXS Transportation on the very railroad tracks just a few miles away, take the time to think about the good people of Talcott and Hinton whose grandparents and great-grandparents toiled under adverse conditions to bring this country together?" He takes faces in the crowd one by one with his eyes. "How often does one of those passengers on the train think about all the blood and sweat that made their journey possible? Part of what we at the Post Office hope to achieve by our issue of the Folk Heroes commemorative is to create awareness of the trials of men like John Henry, to invite Americans to walk in his shoes. That each time they use one of our Folk Heroes stamps, they think about the men who died to get us where we are today."

Is this man talking about a stamp or taking the beach at Normandy?[4] Smith rallies for his final push: "But you all here today know much more about the sacrifices of railroad workers than I do," humble now, "it's your history. You don't need to hear me go on about it—your families have lived it. I just hope that this stamp, and the celebrations this weekend, can help tell the story of the sacrifices of men. John Henry was an Afro-American, born into slavery and freed by Mr. Lincoln's famous proclamation. But more importantly, he was an American. He helped build this nation into what it is today, and his great competition with the steam drill is a testament to the strength of the human spirit. The USPS is proud to honor such an American. Thank you."

A few minutes later, Alphonse finds himself in the food line next to Pamela. They stand next to each other and do not speak and both know a little bit of token conversation is appropriate. They are seated at the same table and the night is already half over. But perhaps he is past the minuet of

---

3. U.S. passenger railroad system.
4. Reference to the Allied invasion of Normandy during World War II. On June 6, 1944, Allied forces, including the United States and Great Britain, stormed the beaches at Normandy and liberated France from the control of Nazi Germany.

social graces. Alphonse decides to play his part, however—they can sift in vain through the clues later—and asks the woman what brought her to Talcott. Her face stiffens a bit and she says that her father collected John Henry memorabilia. That's interesting, Alphonse offers, because he is a collector as well, a collector of railroad stamps. Then her expression. He has seen the expression on her face before. It is the uncomprehending, loose shape faces adopt when he tells people he collects stamps. He informs her of the coincidence of the first commemorative being a railroad stamp, and here they are today. She looks puzzled and grabs a plate. The fumes of naphthalene swirl around him.

The old joke: what did the young lady say to her stamp-collecting suitor?

Philately will get you nowhere.

Pamela and Alphonse forage from the heated trays and do not speak again until the end of the night, after the commotion at the journalists' table has come to an end.

3

Applause, hands sliding toward slanted forks, as the Post Office man leaves the podium and Arlene announces that dinner will be ready presently. Not presently enough for J. He looks up at the thin, meek man with the polka-dot bow tie standing over their table. A press laminate hangs around his neck, abject and ridiculous. J. feels embarrassed for him; wearing a press laminate is so gauche. After waiting in vain for Frenchie to finish his story or for one of them to acknowledge his presence, the man finally clears his throat and says, "Arlene said you were some writers from New York City."

"That's right," Tiny says, "We thought we'd git ourselves down yonder for this shindig."

"My name is Broderick Honnicut," he declares, tapping the press laminate. "I'm a staff writer for the *Hinton Owl*. Thought I'd come over and say hello."

"Staff writer for the *Hinton Owl*," Frenchie considers, raising his eyebrows at his colleagues. "Well, well. I think I've seen your byline."

"You broke the story on the chicken rustling ring, I do believe," Tiny says.

"Chicken rustling . . . ?" Honnicut utters.

"The chicken-choking scandal," Tiny corrects himself.

"Turned out the cover-up went to the highest levels of government," Frenchie breaks in, taking the baton. "The town barber was implicated, according to a high-level source."

"The alderman got caught with his hand in the cookie jar," Tiny says.

No need to mess with this guy, J. thinks. He just came over to be friendly and he gets this. It is going to be a long night if the boys are this cantankerous early on. He twists in his seat to ponder the red light.

"Allegedly, Tiny," Dave admonishes, "always remember allegedly." He turns to Honnicut, smiling. J. knows he is about to set the guy up. "They're just joking with you. Say, tell me: What's the *Hinton Owl*'s motto?"

"I don't know what you mean," Honnicut says, growing flustered.

"You know what I'm talking about," Dave explains. "Every paper has a motto. The *New York Times* has 'All the News That's Fit to Print,' every great newspaper has to have a motto. Beneath your logo, there's a motto, right? What does it say?"

"It says," Honnicut stumbles, "it says, 'A Hoot and a Holler: The *Hinton Owl* Sees All.'"

Dave smiles. "That's catchy."

"'A hoot and a snoot will keep you up all night,'" Frenchie says, and J. lights out for the food table. Because the red light is calling him. At the terminus of the buffet lies the sacred preserve of the Happy Hunting Grounds. Set above the cutting plate like a divine illumination, the red heating lamps warm the sweet meat. The red light is a beacon to the lost wayfarer, it is a tavern lamp after hours of wilderness black. J. experiences an involuntary physical response to the red light and begins to salivate. Sometimes he feels this in movie theaters, salivating at the glimpse of the red Exit sign. What a warm world it would be, he ponders, if we all slept under a red light at night.

When he returns, plate tottering, a sodden Babel[5] of flavor, J. notes that Honnicut has departed. J. is grateful—he couldn't take much more of that. He looks around for One Eye, but can't see him anywhere, not even in the food line. No matter. J. has important business. The potatoes have declined his invitation, but J. still savors the pliable tang of overcooked heads of broccoli, carrots in star shapes, decobbed corn in pearly water. And the prime rib, the prime rib, aloft in its own juice, mottled with tiny globules of luscious melted fat. He showers the meat with salt, as if there could be anything greater in the universe than beef drenched heartily with salt. He possesses teeth sharpened by evolution for the gnashing of meat, a digestive system engineered for the disintegration of meat, and he means to utilize the gifts of nature to their fullest expression.

"This may be the New South, but they haven't caught up to everything, thank God," Tiny says. "This ain't no vegetarian menu."

"Amen to that," J. says.

"Ben Vereen was coming here?" Frenchie asks, incredulous. His plate is immured by empty glasses, mutilated limes groaning at their bottoms.

"It's a living," J. says. He gobbles prime rib and winces with pleasure, fighting telltale paroxysm. He needs the meat to pile on the liquor.

"How are they going to pay for all this?"

"Emptying the town coffers."

"No new basketball uniforms for the high school varsity team."

"Not the basketball uniforms!"

"Any of you actually writing this thing up?" Tiny asks, a yellow liquid glistening in his beard. He has filled twin plates with buffet mounds of horrific symmetry.

"I'm doing it for this travel site Time Warner is putting up on the web," J. informs him.

"Those guys are just throwing money away," Frenchie opined. "Fine with me."

"I got some outfit called *West Virginia Life* on the hook," Dave begins, "a monthly job they put out down here. But before I placed it I had been thinking about making it a New South piece. No one thinks about West Virginia. Throw in a few lines about the national parks and the white rafting stuff they got around here. It would have been a nice change of pace to do a trend thing after all these movie things I've been doing."

"Seems like a good peg," Frenchie says. "Though if I were writing it up, I could see focusing on the industrial age–information age angle. John Henry's

---

5. Allusion to the biblical story of the Tower of Babel (Genesis 11.1–9); here meaning a variety.

man-against-machineness. That's still current, people can empathize with his struggle and get into it and all that shit."

"So you're going with Bob is Hip?" Tiny demands of Dave, his voice rising.

"Why not?"

"Are you sure it's not Bob's Alive!?" Tiny hisses.

It is an old argument. Freddie "the Bull" McGinty, before his unfortunate heart attack, had identified three elemental varieties of puff pieces, and over time the freelancer community had accepted his Anatomy of Puff. An early junketeer, the Bull (so named for his huge and cavernous nostrils) observed the nature of the List over time and posited that while all puff is tied by a golden cord to a subject, be it animal, vegetable or mineral, the pop expression of that subject can be reduced to three discrete schools of puff. For the sake of clarity, the Bull christened the archetypal subject Bob, and named the three essential manifestations of Bob as follows: Bob's Debut, Bob Returns, and Bob's Comeback. Each manifestation commanded its own distinct stock phrases and hyperbolic rhetoric.

Bob's Debut is obvious. Like lightning, Bob, the talented newcomer or long-struggling obscure artist, scorches the earth, his emergence charged by the profound electromagnetics of pre-Debut publicity and sometimes genuine merit. Such a glorious Debut deserves to be heralded in the glossy chambers of media. The out-of-nowhere record by the young lad from Leeds, the searching and surprisingly articulate second-person voice of the crab fisherman's roman à clef, the visionary directorial outing channeling the zeitgeist—all these works can be attributed to Bob, and Bob's Debut is a reliable story, the struggling talent is recognized, the indomitable vision championed. It makes good copy. This is the first manifestation of Bob.

Then comes Bob's Return. His sophomore record, aimless electronic noodling in some cuts, fame has gone to his head, but still listenable; the second novel, recapitulating some of the first's themes, somehow lacking, emboldened by success he tries to tackle too much; guaranteed by contract final-cut approval, the director esteems his instincts out of proportion, the special effects intrude and he can't trim it down to under two and a half hours. Bob's Return is well chronicled, he is a known quantity naturally pitched to editors, but not without hazards. He may have fallen out of favor among his initial champions and the long lead times of monthlies make cover stories a risky proposition. No editor wants to look at the cover of their magazine and see that they've showcased the profile of a celeb whose return had flopped miserably the week before. Editors guess, sniff the culture, and commit to Bob's Return, fingers crossed that the opening weekend box office will not be cursed, that the goddamned critics have not panned Bob's Return vehicle irredeemably to the mephitic baths of perdition. Weeklies and Sunday sections of major dailies have a leg up on the monthlies; if something magical happens, they can hitch a ride. This is the second manifestation of Bob.

Bob's Comeback is miraculous. It can occur two years after the doomed or mediocre Return, or twenty years. Many things could have happened in the intervening time to make Bob's Comeback printworthy: five crafty but overlooked novels consigned him to the twilight of midlist; three big-budget flops, two straight to video movies, one sitcom and a couple softcore thrillers fit only for the dingier cable outlets made a character actor of Bob; five very strange albums anointed Bob a critics' darling but a radio pariah. The long unchecked skid into obscurity. But then the comeback. Something shifts in pop. It helps if they have overcome a drug problem. Test screenings positive, publishing industry buzz a-flowing, advance radio airplay of the first single augurs good things. The publicity blows fire out of the cave, scaring the townsfolk, scaly thighs scraping in preparation for a rampage through the village. All the bad things the critics said are forgotten, the industry insiders rally around Bob, the author of the where-are-they-now? article is tendered his kill fee. Bob's Comeback makes covers. Equipped with a new look, a new agent, a new deal, Bob is back on top. Everybody loves an underdog, a redemption story. This is the third manifestation of Bob.

The Bull's musings were well received by his freelancing brethren. It brought order to their lives. Spat upon by editors, insulted by neophyte publicity minions, the junketeers embraced the woeful clarity of the trinity. By the time J. made the List, another variety had been identified and sanctioned by the junketeers. The trend piece. The phenomenon of the trend piece was brought to the table by a British music writer named Nigel Buttons, who had journeyed into the lounges and clubs of London, cozied up to DJs and promoters of tiny establishments situated at the bottoms of stairwells accessible only by alley, the garrets of demimonde, and decided that the three traditional categories could be expanded to include a new one: Bob Is Hip. By the addition of Bob Is Hip, Bob's other manifestations could be infused with new life by situating Bob in a scene or cultural eddy. Say Bob is a ukulele-playing gent who wears sunglasses on stage. If the evidence warrants, and even if it doesn't, Bob the ukulele-playing sunglasses-wearing gent can be insinuated within a burgeoning scene of ukulele-playing sunglasses-wearers—they have a culture and slang, they all sleep together, the romantic entanglements internecine. It is an exotic subculture that begs further exploration. Bob, blessed by a multirecord or multibook or multipicture deal, spotted by well-paid talent scouts with special acumen, takes an early lead on his cohorts and is now the glorious exponent of an underground movement. Depending on the circumstances, his Hip Debut promises a spectacular earthshaking realignment of pop; he finds his true voice in his Hip Return; the maundering and general getting-his-shit-together years of his decline are justified by the Hipness of his Comeback. The Bob Is Hip variation met with some initial protest until its endorsers suggested that creating novel catch phrases from "the new" or "post-" or devising witty neologisms for the nascent movement could ensure one's fame. A subculture is an amino acid soup out of which book deals crawl. More important, Bob Is Hip has broad applications. A manufacturer of blue jeans bruits its new tapered leg line. A junketeer attends and feasts at the event, but has no real peg to pitch the story. Armed with "The Neo Taper" and a broad manifesto, the blue jeans are a bona fide trend, no matter how short-lived, no matter how isolated. Presently, Bob Is Hip was a viable form of puff. Some junketeers jockeyed to grab credit for creating the quintessential Bob Is Hip piece, flailing their clippings in the air, neologisms underlined and backed up by concrete examples of their passage into conventional usage, but there were many contenders and the issue was never settled. Bob's manifestations had become four.

Tiny started the argument in the Social Room because of a recent disturbance among the junketeers. Since the days of Gutenberg, an ambient hype wafted the world, throbbing and palpitating. From time to time, some of that material cooled, forming bodies of dense publicity. Recently this phenomenon occurred more frequently. Everyone felt this change, it was tactile and insistent. They found themselves in abstract rooms at events of no obvious purpose. Certainly there was a person/artifact/idea on display being promoted, but there was no peg, no impending release that it could be traced to. Without a peg, the subjects in question were hard to sell to the editors of newspapers and magazines. And yet the articles ran, the expenses were reimbursed, payroll cut the checks. The public liked them. Updates on well-known public entities who were doing nothing at all, a computer marvel far from implementation, musicians in coffee shops years from demos. The undiscovered hired flacks before they needed them; the established but quiescent or loafing celeb retained publicity apparatus to remind the people of their mere presence. Hence the new, hotly debated variety called Bob's Alive! or Simply Bob. The golden cord had been severed and puff pieces roamed the newsstands, unmoored to any release date. Simply Bob. Gossip columnists had engaged in Simply Bob activities for years, some argued. A sighting at a club or restaurant, walking the shar-pei[6] on Fifth Avenue, cruising a downtown haberdashery: these engagements were memorialized by bold type in the daily gossip columns. With junketeers munching and noshing at the tables of nonevent more frequently these days, and finding their reportage published, some sort of addition to the now-ossified varieties of Bob seemed imminent.

J. doesn't have an opinion either way. While accustomed to thinking of four varieties of Bob, his work will not change if Bob's Alive! is ratified and passed by the body of junketeers. He will weather the rough seas of the polemic. Puff is puff; it is puff. Observing the debate from the sidelines, he will wait for the smoke to clear, and continue to perform his function as he has for many years now. J. saws off a corner of prime rib and sticks it in his mouth. One piece left. He decides to finish off the limp broccoli and save the final bit of beef for the end.

Tiny rails against Bob's Alive! "I was against Bob Is Hip, too," he reminds them with a snarl. "I never thought we should have gone that way. It's too diffuse—this is a prime example."

"I remember your whining," Frenchie recalls.

"And now you want to go and bring in this Bob's Alive! thing. Is Talcott Alive?"

"I said New South," Dave corrects. "That's a trend piece. I can bring in improved race relations. It's Bob's Hip. Talcott is hip, they have a black hero. I can bring in Atlanta. I can bring in lots of stuff. Houston—Houston is hot now, it's attracting a lot of diversity."

"I'd go for Debut personally," Frenchie says.

"Debut?" Dave asks. "John Henry has been around for years, this town is a physical thing that has a history. I don't personally care to know what that history is, but it surely exists. I think trend is perfectly appropriate."

"See what I'm talking about?" Tiny thunders, spraying droplets of a substance from his beard like a dog shaking off rain. "You could make a case for Talcott as Debut, Comeback or Return or Hip. It's all jumbled up now. I'm accustomed to four varieties of puff and I like it like that. Four elements, four humors, four seasons, four varieties of puff. Otherwise why have categories at all? Why not make everything a category. A puff for every little thing."

6. A breed of dog.

"We already have that," One Eye interjects. "We call them magazines." One Eye has been quiet all night, and after his comment he looks back down at his food and prods corn. J. asks him if anything is wrong.

"Just thinking is all," One Eye says.

"Thinking about your secret mission?"

"What?"

"You said in the van. A mission that could change the course of human events."

One Eye's one eye narrows. He had forgotten he mentioned it. Dave, Tiny and Frenchie continue their argument. One Eye leans over to J. and whispers, "I'm taking my name off the List. Permanently."

"You renounce Satan and all his works? How do you intend to do that?"

"I have been plotting and planning, my friend, plotting and planning." His face illegible. "I've had this event circled in my filofax[7] for some time now."

Before he can question One Eye further, J. sees Arlene go up to the podium. The musical entertainment. The red light beckons. Deciding he better get seconds on the prime rib before they close the food down, he throws his napkin on the seat and hustles. No hick is going to gyp him of his bounty. He removes himself and scurries over to the red light. One Eye looks disappointed, but J. figures he can pick up the conversation later. Arlene describes the singing prowess of one of the sons of Talcott, a boy who will go on to great things. This time J. doesn't take any vegetables. He asks for five proud slabs of prime rib. A young man departs one of the tables near the podium, a burly teenager with a soft balloon face. His baby fat has never gone away; it has chased the teenager's growth inch for inch, keeping in step, swelling proportionally. At the boy's table are an older man and woman—his mother and father, J. gathers. He hadn't noticed them before. That makes five black folks in the room. Who says integration can't work, he asks himself.

J. returns to the table, plate before him, the raja's rubies on a velvet bed. Dave and the others are watching the boy get himself together at the podium. He wears a black church suit and a brazen red tie clenched by a clumsy fat knot. His eyes and mouth, tiny things, disappear into his soft face like the buttons of a plush couch. The boy looks a little nervous, but then he starts to sing, and from the depths of him rouses a gorgeous baritone—it reels from the amplifiers like a flock of dazzling birds. The boy sings the "Ballad of John Henry." The boy sings,

> John Henry was just a baby,
> When he fell on his mammy's knee;
> He picked up a hammer and a little piece of steel,
> Said, "This hammer will be the death of me, Lord, Lord,
> This hammer will be the death of me."
>
> John Henry was a very small boy
> Sitting on his father's knee,
> Said, "The Big Bend Tunnel on the C&O road[8]
> Is gonna be the death of me, Lord, Lord,
> Is gonna be the death of me."

---

7. Brand name of a personal organizer system.　　8. Chesapeake and Ohio Railroad company.

John Henry went upon a mountain
And came down on the side;
The mountain was so tall, John Henry was so small,
That he laid down his hammer and he cried, "Lord, Lord,"
That he laid down his hammer and he cried.

The rude talk that pestered the earlier speakers disperses. Lord, Lord: He hacks at primal truth and splinters off words and the men and women ache. Enraptured, all of them, openmouthed in beatitude and slack in delight at the nimble phrasings of the boy. Except for J. J. attacks the prime rib. He has not had his fill. He cuts off a piece ringed by a crust of blackened fat and sticks it in his mouth. It is a big piece, a hearty plug of meat, he doesn't know what time he'll eat tomorrow and he needs the meat. He rends tendrils of meat with his teeth, repositions them with his tongue, rends them further. He swallows quickly, another piece already impaled on his merciless tines, and the plug catches in his throat. He can't breathe.

The boy sings.

John Henry told his captain,
"Captain go to town
And bring me back two twenty-pound hammers,
And I'll sure beat your steam drill down. Lord, Lord,
And I'll sure beat your steam drill down."

John Henry told his people,
"You know that I'm a man.
I can beat all the traps that have ever been made,
Or I'll die with my hammer in my band, Lord, Lord,
Or I'll die with my hammer in my hand."

The steam drill set on the right-hand side,
John Henry was on the left.
He said, "I will beat that steam drill down
Or hammer my fool self to death, Lord, Lord,
Or hammer my fool self to death."

It won't go down. He tries to swallow again but the plug will not oblige him. It is a stern and vengeful plug of meat. He tries to swallow again, panic trebling. Surely he isn't choking. It won't go down. He's going to die on a junket? This is some far-out shit, this is a fucking ironic way to go. Is he using ironic incorrectly? The copy editors are going to kill him. They are really cracking down on the misuse of the word ironic, it's like this global cabal of comma checkers and run-on sentences and fragments. Roaring in his ears. Why won't it go down? He finds it inconceivable that no one knows what is going on with him. They are looking at the boy and listening to his words. He has a problem asking for help. He does not want to look weak. And it might not be an emergency. Surely it will pass. The meat is just fucking with him. He could jump up, slam the table, knock over their free drinks, that would get their attention. But he's sitting there choking, quietly choking. Is this his pattern? That sounds like a diagnosis. And if he can self-diagnose, he can self-medicate. He has practice in that area. But you can't do that when your throat is stopped. Seduced by a red illumination. Bang, whimper, what the fuck.

The boy sings,

John Henry dropped the ten-pound hammer,
And picked up the twenty-pound sledge;
Every time his hammer went down,
You could see that steel going through, Lord, Lord,
You could see that steel going through.

John Henry was just getting started,
Steam drill was half way down;
John Henry said, "You're ahead right now,
But I'll beat you on the last go-around, Lord, Lord,
I'll beat you on the last go-around."

What's this guy singing? He's choking on the stubborn plug of meat. John Henry, John Henry. He works on the C&O Railroad. He pushes puff, he is going for the record. His muscles must be jumping out of his skin. It won't move, it sits like a bullet in his throat. No oxygen for me, thanks, I've had enough. Luke Cage the Marvel Comics superhero had bulletproof skin. At one point he had a sticker book where he kept stickers of Marvel Comics superheroes, they jumped out of the page, dynamic, Avengers Assemble and all that, muscles on full ripple, Luke Cage the jive-talking ex-con. This is what we get. Your whole life is supposed to flash before your eyes and this is what I get. Step into the light. Red light? What was up with that yellow shirt he wore anyway, some sleazy guy in a disco laying lines on the ladies, Luke Cage. He finds it incredible that in this crushing and collapsing time, he has the time to think these thoughts. But they say your life flashes before your eyes. I'm a sophisticated black man from New York City and I'm going to die down here. With cicadas, they got cicadas down here, don't they. I want roaches, real crumb-eating fucks from out of the drain.

The boy sings,

John Henry told his shaker,
"Big boy, you better pray
For if I miss this six-foot steel,
To-morrow will be your burying day, Lord, Lord,
To-morrow will be your burying day."

The men that made that steam drill
Thought it was mighty fine;
John Henry drove his fourteen feet,
While the steam drill only made nine, Lord, Lord,
While the steam drill only made nine.

John Henry went home to his good little woman,
Said, "Polly Ann, fix my bed,
I want to lay down and get some rest,
I've an awful roaring in my head, Lord, Lord,
I've an awful roaring in my head."

Isn't there something he is supposed to do? He feels like he is falling from a height. He can't think of it. He can excrete twelve hundred words in two hours and yet he can't think of any last words. How about an epitaph? He can't get farther than his name and the pertinent bookend dates. He slaps the table to get their attention. Their drinks jump. He sees a restaurant sign, yellow and deep blue, on the wall of a restaurant, on the walls of infinite restaurants. Who wants to be the guy in the picture turning blue? Black folks turn blue? Look for the telltale signs. Pictographs. Certainly public service announcements, like road signs and airport signs, need a simple language. Simple message, simple expression. Is that a journalistic axiom? He can't remember, and yet it sounds so official. Nobody notices his death. Sensation of falling. Who wants to be the blue guy in the choking picture on the wall of a cheap restaurant? Where is this place's sign? There must be laws about the placement of the signs, eating establishments must post them in convenient places. Federal law, but then maybe they vary from state to state. States' rights! States' rights, these people love their states' rights, signs on fountains, back of the bus, Rosa Parks. This place will fucking kill him. He should have known better. A black man has no business here, there's too much rough shit, too much history gone down here. The Northern flight, right: we wanted to get the fuck out. That's what they want, they want us dead. It's like the song says.

The boy sings,

> John Henry told his woman,
> "Never wear black, wear blue."
> She said, "John, don't never look back,
> For, honey, I've been good to you, Lord, Lord,
> For, honey, I've been good to you."
>
> John Henry was a steeldriving man,
> He drove in many a crew;
> He has now gone back to the head of the line
> To drive the heading on through, Lord, Lord,
> To drive the heading on through.

He stops falling. His body bursts and he is jerked up out of his seat. Involuntary Physical Response: the signs people keep on their lawns to repel burglars? He jumps out of his seat. My eyes must be popping out my head like some coon cartoon. His hands point to his throat. Can't these people see what's going on? The boy keeps singing. The pain is in his throat, around his throat and he would like them to make it stop. All these crackers looking up at me, looking up at the tree. Nobody doing nothing, just staring. They know how to watch a nigger die.

2001

KEVIN YOUNG
b. 1970

" How to forge an ancestry, both literal & literary" is the challenge Kevin Young sets for himself as poet, editor, curator, and critic. As poet, he imagines scenes from his family history and from the collective history of African Americans. He pays homage to his literary precursors from Langston Hughes to

Robert Lowell in volumes such as *Jelly Roll: A Blues* (2003) and *For the Confederate Dead* (2007). Diverse poetic forms reflect his multiracial, multigeneric literary ancestry. As editor, he has published collections of blues and jazz poems, *The Art of Losing: Poems of Grief and Healing* and *John Berryman: Selected Poems*; Berryman like Lowell pioneered the twentieth-century genre of "confessional poetry." Young's major critical work, *The Grey Album: On the Blackness of Blackness* (2012), is a meditation on African American art, literature, and music and the relationship of black American culture to American culture. In the tradition of Zora Neale Hurston and Ralph Ellison, he continues the practice of "lying"—defined as telling tales, improvising, and "storying"—that have enabled the survival of a peoples' spirit. With encyclopedic knowledge, cunning insight, and great humor, he shows how lying has shaped African Americans' art as well as their everyday lives.

Born in Lincoln, Nebraska, and educated at Harvard and Stanford universities, Young traces his family history to Louisiana. Recollections of real and fictive kin animate his work, beginning with "Reward," a poem evoking an advertisement for the capture of a fugitive slave named Elizabeth Young, in *Most Ways Home* (1995). Other poems invent a personal perspective on historical events including the Great Migration and the Vietnam War. Inspired by the painter Jean-Michel Basquiat, *To Repel Ghosts: Five Sides in B Minor* (2001) explores the meteoric career of an artist who broke the color line in postmodernist art; the poems echo Basquiat's formal techniques, as they place him in a genealogy of African American geniuses from bluesman Robert Johnson to jazz singer Billie Holiday. A devotee of popular culture, Young draws on Hollywood movies for *Black Maria* (2005), a volume that earns the praise "compulsively readable" from reviewers. Other volumes of poems are *Dear Darkness* (2010) and *Ardency: A Chronicle of the* Amistad *Rebels* (2012).

An astute reader and compiler of poetry, Young has co-edited the definitive collection of poems by Lucille Clifton and edited several anthologies, organized thematically, as, for example, *Giant Steps: The New Generation of African American Writers* (2000) and *The Hungry Ear: Poems of Food and Drink* (2012). He is the curator of literary collections and the Raymond Danowski Poetry Library at Emory University, where he is also the Atticus Haygood Professor of Creative Writing and English. In his work as editor and curator, Young helps define the landscape of contemporary American poetry.

66. Langston Hughes

LANGSTON HUGHES
LANGSTON HUGHES
   O come now
   & sang
them weary blues—   5

Been tired here
feelin low down
   Real
   tired here
since you quit town   10

Our ears no longer trumpets
Our mouths no more bells
   FAMOUS POET©—
   Busboy—Do tell
us of hell—   15

Mr Shakespeare in Harlem
Mr Theme for English B
    Preach on
    kind sir
of death, if it please—   20

We got no more promise
We only got ain't
    Let us in
    on how
you 'came a saint   25

LANGSTON
LANGSTON
    LANGSTON HUGHES
    Won't you send
all heaven's news   30

                    1999

Jook

    You have me
    to you quite addicted

    dear—my hands
    in your mouth—

    my wet-   5
    nurse, succor,

    cure. That old
    booze

    of you's
    what I want—   10

    dry gin, new
    world, Old Crow.

                    2003

Anthem

God, you are gorgeous—
& gone—

left no trace
among the trees

that line this lawn—   5
rain-fed

& -worn. I am warning
myself—take

no prisoners, hold on
not at all—   10

yet even without
a guard the chain gang

breaks rocks out
of habit—*hunh*—does not

look up to see   15
one man—*hunh*—chains

trailing—*hunh*—broken
as the jailbird's

wing, fleeing the field—
back stripes—*hunh*—stars   20

2003

Exodus[1]

Gabriel, Escalastio, Desiderio,[2]—in the seas beneath
the States, names new & Christian fell around you
like the lash. Before slavery, ten suns from water open
as a wound, you say you belonged to nothing
but home. Your back bore only spirit's teeth, scars   5
that meant manhood. Such rites of passage
protected little:—with in one moon you fared

no better than a slaver's shifting cargo of looking
glasses, olives. Out of boredom or freedom
of movement, the crew took a poker from under bitter   10
plaintains,—carved Captain's F into Cabin Boy's shoulder.
Parched as you were, would you have sipped the rum
& gunpowder smeared in that wound to make sure
it would brand? A few mad, swollen tongues caught

---

1. The biblical book that chronicles Moses leading the Israelites out of slavery in Egypt to Mount
Sinai, where they receive the word of God, accept
his sovereignty and laws, and receive the promise
of the land of Canaan.
2. The New World names given to some of the
African men who were kidnapped, enslaved, and
placed aboard a Spanish slave ship to Cuba in
January 1839. On a journey to another port in
Cuba, on the slave ship the *Amistad*, the captive
men rebelled, killing most of the crew but leaving
alive their purchasers, Don Jose Ruiz and Don
Pedro Montez, to sail the ship back to Africa.
Ruiz and Montez attempted to sail the ship
secretly back to Cuba but ended up in Long
Island, New York. The revolt sparked a court
case that would become a major fight for U.S.
abolitionists. The court ruled in the enslaved
men's favor, recognizing that they were illegally
transported from Africa, and ordered their
emancipation.

the saltwater Cabin Boy's good arm tossed. Was it 15
sanity drove cousin Fu-li to edge over the casket
of fresh water, lend it his own throat? Catching
him wet-lipped, Captain's men fed home
the whip:—even now you can hear his skin part,
can tell how much his body was water, how much 20
spine was book, just asking to be opened, read.

2011

TRACY K. SMITH
b. 1972

"When a poem can lead you into an unfamiliar place where you must watch and listen closely, think and associate quickly, and find your footing from scratch, it is imparting a set of skills that are yours to keep." Tracy Smith's poems offer readers just such a pathway and give them skills with which they can explore other writings. Born in northern California, raised in Massachusetts, and educated at Harvard, Columbia, and Stanford, Smith is currently assistant professor of creative writing at Princeton. While an undergraduate, she joined the Dark Room Collective, an organization of black writers in Cambridge, Massachusetts, that included Natasha Trethewey and Kevin Young among its members; she belongs to Cave Canem, an association of African American poets. Drawn to a wide range of subjects, from the Mexican migration to the United States to the exploitation of girls in East Africa and the U.S. war in Iraq, Smith is not adverse to writing political poetry. Her lyrical gift and probing intellect enable her to write effectively about current events and abstract ideas as well as the challenges and triumphs of her own life. *The Body's Question* (2003), written after her mother's death, explores the body as a site of discovery and joy. *Duende* (2007) takes its title from the creative force that inspires flamenco; Smith appropriates the term to apply to her own artistic production.

For *Life on Mars* (2011), which was awarded the Pulitzer Prize for poetry, Smith turns to the technique of science fiction, which, she observes, "allows us to extrapolate from the moment to where we will be in the future." The volume contains elegies for her father, an engineer who worked on the Hubble Space Telescope. Smith's poetry juxtaposes domestic detail, as she recollects her father's response to his father's death, and scientific metaphor, as she imagines an afterlife. Shifting registers, it also invokes rock star David Bowie and his extraterrestrial alter ego, Ziggy Stardust. Art, like science and religion, offers ways of understanding the universe. Smith draws on all three to think through philosophical questions and personal grief.

Sci-Fi

There will be no edges, but curves.
Clean lines pointing only forward.

History, with its hard spine & dog-eared
Corners, will be replaced with nuance,

Just like the dinosaurs gave way   5
To mounds and mounds of ice.

Women will still be women, but
The distinction will be empty. Sex,

Having outlived every threat, will gratify
Only the mind, which is where it will exist.   10

For kicks, we'll dance for ourselves
Before mirrors studded with golden bulbs.

The oldest among us will recognize that glow—
But the word *sun* will have been re-assigned

To a Standard Uranium-Neutralizing device   15
Found in households and nursing homes.

And yes, we'll live to be much older, thanks
To popular consensus. Weightless, unhinged,

Eons from even our own moon, we'll drift
In the haze of space, which will be, once   20

And for all, scrutable and safe.

2011

My God, It's Full of Stars

1.

We like to think of it as parallel to what we know,
Only bigger. One man against the authorities.
Or one man against a city of zombies. One man

Who is not, in fact, a man, sent to understand
The caravan of men now chasing him like red ants   5
Let loose down the pants of America. Man on the run.

Man with a ship to catch, a payload to drop,
This message going out to all of space. . . . Though
Maybe it's more like life below the sea: silent,

Buoyant, bizarrely benign. Relics   10
Of an outmoded design. Some like to imagine
A cosmic mother watching through a spray of stars,

Mouthing *yes, yes* as we toddle toward the light,
Biting her lip if we teeter at some ledge. Longing
To sweep us to her breast, she hopes for the best   15

While the father storms through adjacent rooms
Ranting with the force of Kingdom Come,
Not caring anymore what might snap us in its jaw.

Sometimes, what I see is a library in a rural community.
All the tall shelves in the big open room. And the pencils   20
In a cup at Circulation, gnawed on by the entire population.

The books have lived here all along, belonging
For weeks at a time to one or another in the brief sequence
Of family names, speaking (at night mostly) to a face,

A pair of eyes. The most remarkable lies.   25

2.

Charlton Heston[1] is waiting to be let in. He asked once politely.
A second time with force from the diaphragm. The third time,
He did it like Moses: arms raised high, face an apocryphal white.

Shirt crisp, suit trim, he stoops a little coming in,
Then grows tall. He scans the room. He stands until I gesture,   30
Then he sits. Birds commence their evening chatter. Someone fires

Charcoals out below. He'll take a whiskey if I have it. Water if I don't.
I ask him to start from the beginning, but he goes only halfway back.
That was the future once, he says. *Before the world went upside down.*

Hero, survivor, God's right hand man, I know he sees the blank   35
Surface of the moon where I see a language built from brick and bone.
He sits straight in his seat, takes a long, slow high-thespian breath,

Then lets it go. *For all I know, I was the last true man on this earth.* And:
May I smoke? The voices outside soften. Planes jet past heading off or back.
Someone cries that she does not want to go to bed. Footsteps overhead.   40

A fountain in the neighbor's yard babbles to itself, and the night air
Lifts the sound indoors. *It was another time*, he says, picking up again.
We were pioneers. Will you fight to stay alive here, riding the earth

Toward God-knows-where? I think of Atlantis buried under ice, gone
One day from sight, the shore from which it rose now glacial and stark.   45
Our eyes adjust to the dark.

3.

Perhaps the great error is believing we're alone,
That the others have come and gone—a momentary blip—
When all along, space might be choc-full of traffic,
Bursting at the seams with energy we neither feel   50

---

1. American actor (1923–2008) known for his heroic roles and, referenced in the poem, his portrayal of Moses in the popular film *The Ten Commandments* (1956).

Nor see, flush against us, living, dying, deciding,
Setting solid feet down on planets everywhere,
Bowing to the great stars that command, pitching stones
At whatever are their moons. They live wondering
If they are the only ones, knowing only the wish to know,   55
And the great black distance they—we—flicker in.

Maybe the dead know, their eyes widening at last,
Seeing the high beams of a million galaxies flick on
At twilight. Hearing the engines flare, the horns
Not letting up, the frenzy of being. I want it to be   60
One notch below bedlam, like a radio without a dial.
Wide open, so everything floods in at once.
And sealed tight, so nothing escapes. Not even time,
Which should curl in on itself and loop around like smoke.
So that I might be sitting now beside my father   65
As he raises a lit match to the bowl of his pipe
For the first time in the winter of 1959.

4.

In those last scenes of Kubrick's 2001[2]
When Dave is whisked into the center of space,
Which unfurls in an aurora of orgasmic light   70
Before opening wide, like a jungle orchid
For a love-struck bee, then goes liquid,
Paint-in-water, and then gauze wafting out and off,
Before, finally, the night tide, luminescent
And vague, swirls in, and on and on. . . .   75

In those last scenes, as he floats
Above Jupiter's vast canyons and seas,
Over the lava strewn plains and mountains
Packed in ice, that whole time, he doesn't blink.
In his little ship, blind to what he rides, whisked   80
Across the wide-screen of unparceled time,
Who knows what blazes through his mind?
Is it still his life he moves through, or does
That end at the end of what he can name?

On set, it's shot after shot till Kubrick is happy,   85
Then the costumes go back on their racks
And the great gleaming set goes black.

5.

When my father worked on the Hubble Telescope, he said
They operated like surgeons: scrubbed and sheathed
In papery green, the room a clean cold, and bright white.   90

2. A 1968 science fiction film directed by Stanley Kubrick thematically centered around human evolution, the development of technology, and extraterrestrial life.

He'd read Larry Niven[3] at home, and drink scotch on the rocks,
His eyes exhausted and pink. These were the Reagan years,
When we lived with our finger on The Button and struggled

To view our enemies as children. My father spent whole seasons
Bowing before the oracle-eye, hungry for what it would find.   95
His face lit-up whenever anyone asked, and his arms would rise

As if he were weightless, perfectly at ease in the never-ending
Night of space. On the ground, we tied postcards to balloons
For peace. Prince Charles married Lady Di.[4] Rock Hudson[5] died.

We learned new words for things. The decade changed.   100

The first few pictures came back blurred, and I felt ashamed
For all the cheerful engineers, my father and his tribe. The second time,
The optics jibed. We saw to the edge of all there is—

So brutal and alive it seemed to comprehend us back.

                                                                    2011

3. American science fiction author (b. 1938).
4. Charles, Prince of Wales and heir apparent of
Queen Elizabeth II, and Lady Diana Spencer
married in 1981. Their televised wedding
attracted a worldwide audience of more than 750
million.
5. American film and television actor
(1925–1985).

Timeline

AFRICAN AMERICAN LITERATURE IN CONTEXT

1492–1775

1492 Pedro Alonzo Nino, traditionally considered the first of many New World explorers of African descent, sails with Christopher Columbus

1526 First African slaves brought to what is now the United States by the Spanish

1619 Twenty Africans brought to Jamestown, Virginia, on Dutch ship and sold as indentured servants

1623 William Tucker, in Jamestown, is the first black child born in the English North American colonies

1641 Massachusetts becomes the first colony to legally recognize slavery

1645 First American slave ships sail, from Boston; triangular trade route brings African slaves to West Indies in exchange for sugar, tobacco, and wine, which are then sold for manufactured goods in Massachusetts

1646 John Wham and his wife are freed, becoming first recorded free blacks in New England

1652 Rhode Island passes first North American law against slavery

1662 Virginia is the first colony to declare that mother's status determines whether a child is born free or into slavery

1663 Major conspiracy by black and white indentured servants in Virginia is betrayed by servant

1688 Pennsylvania Quakers sign first official written protest against slavery in North America

1712 New York City slave revolt is quelled by militia • Pennsylvania becomes first colony to outlaw slave trade

1734 "Great Awakening" religious revival begins; Methodist and Baptist churches attract blacks by offering "Christianity for all"

1739 South Carolina slaves launch Stono Rebellion, killing 30 whites

1740 In response to the Stono Rebellion, South Carolina outlaws teaching slaves to write

1746 Lucy Terry writes "**Bars Fight**," the first poem extant written by an African American (not published until 1895)

1756–63 African Americans fight in French and Indian War

1757 Phillis Wheatley purchased in Boston

1758 First black Baptist church in colonies is erected on plantation in Virginia

1760 Jupiter Hammon, "**An Evening Thought: Salvation by Christ with Penitential Cries**," printed as a broadside, the first poetry published by an African American

1773 Phillis Wheatley, *Poems on Various Subjects, Religious and Moral*, published in London, first book published by an African American and second book published by an American woman • Slaves in Massachusetts petition legislature for freedom for first time

1774 Continental Congress prohibits importation of slaves after December 1, 1774

1775–83 American Revolutionary War; battles fought by African Americans include Bunker Hill, Lexington, and Concord

1775 First antislavery society organized by Philadelphia Quakers • Royal governor of Virginia offers freedom to any slave joining British army; 800 respond to form "Ethiopian Regiment" • Second Continental Congress resolves against importation of slaves

1776–1820

1776 Declaration of Independence adopted without antislavery statement proposed by Thomas Jefferson

1777 Vermont is one of the first states to abolish slavery in state constitution • New York is the first state to extend vote to black males, but limits voting in 1815 and 1821 with permit, property, and residency requirements

1780 Pennsylvania becomes the first state to allow interracial marriage • Free blacks in Massachusetts protest "taxation without representation" and petition for exemption from taxes

1783 Massachusetts Supreme Court grants black taxpayers suffrage

1786 Free blacks join in Shay's Rebellion, protesting the lack of concern over harsh conditions of farmers by Massachusetts government

1787 Constitution ratified, classifying one slave as three-fifths of one person for congressional apportionment, postponing prohibition of slave importation until 1808, and demanding return of fugitive slaves to masters • Congress passes Northwest Ordinance, banning slavery in Northwest Territories and all land north of Ohio River • Absalom Jones and Richard Allen organize Philadelphia Free African Society • Rhode Island free blacks establish African Union Society to promote repatriation to Africa, a position opposed by Philadelphia Free African Society

1789 Olaudah Equiano, *The Interesting Narrative of the Life of Olaudah Equiano, or Gustavus Vassa, the African*

1790 Pennsylvania abolitionists submit first antislavery petitions to U.S. Congress

1793 U.S. Congress passes first Fugitive Slave Law • Invention of cotton gin increases demand for slaves in South

1794 U.S. Congress prohibits slave trade with foreign countries • French National Convention abolishes slavery in French territories (ban will be repealed by Napoleon in 1802) • Richard Allen founds first African Methodist Episcopal church (AME), in Philadelphia

1796 Lucy Terry Prince becomes first woman to argue before Supreme Court, successfully defending against a white man trying to steal her family's land • Joshua Johnson, first black portrait painter to gain recognition in the United States, opens studio in Baltimore

1798 Georgia is last state to abolish slave trade • Venture Smith, *A Narrative of the Life and Adventures of Venture, A Native of Africa*

1800 U.S. citizens are prohibited from exporting slaves • Pennsylvania free blacks petition U.S. Congress to outlaw slavery • Gabriel Prosser and Jack Bowler organize 1,000 fellow slaves to seize Richmond, but plan is quelled by militia and leaders are executed along with many others

1802 Haitians force French government to end slavery in Haiti; François-Dominique Toussaint-Louverture is made governor

1803 Louisiana Purchase doubles size of the United States

1804 York, a slave, serves as guide for Lewis and Clark expedition to Pacific • Ohio sets precedent with passage of first "Black Laws" restricting rights and movements of free blacks in North

1807 United States outlaws importation of new slaves after January 1, 1808, but law is widely ignored • Britain abolishes slave trade

1811 Slave revolt in Louisiana led by Charles Deslandres ends with over 100 slaves killed or executed by U.S. troops

1812 Slaves and free blacks fight in War of 1812

1815 Quaker Levi Coffin establishes Underground Railroad to help slaves escape to Canada

1816–18 First Seminole War, involving runaway slaves and Native Americans fighting U.S. federal government in Florida

1816 American Colonization Society formed in Washington, D.C., to promote African repatriation of freed slaves to ease U.S. race problems; the society is supported by leading white congressmen

1817 Over 3,000 free blacks in Philadelphia meet to oppose American Colonization Society

1818 President given power to use armed vessels in Africa to halt illegal slave trade • U.S. Congress allots $100,000 to transport illegally imported slaves back to Africa

1820 Missouri Compromise reached, allowing Maine into Union as free state, Missouri as slave state in 1821, and outlawing slavery in all new Northern Plains states • American Colonization Society sends expedition to begin establishment of Liberia, a black republic

1820–1852

in West Africa; first repatriation ship, *Mayflower of Liberia,* leaves from New York City with 86 blacks

1821 African Grove Theatre, first all-black U.S. acting troupe, begins performances in New York City

1822 Denmark Vesey organizes slave revolt to take over Charleston, South Carolina, but is betrayed by a servant • Liberia formally founded by African American colonizers

1823 Alexander L. Twilight graduates from Middlebury College, Vermont, becoming first African American college graduate

1826 First U.S. colony for free blacks, Nashoba, established near Memphis, Tennessee

1828 "Theresa: A Haytien Tale" published in *Freedom's Journal.* This is quite possibly the first published work of African American fiction.

1829 David Walker, *David Walker's Appeal* • George Moses Horton, *The Hope of Liberty* • Three-day race riot breaks out in Cincinnati; more than 1,000 blacks flee to Canada after whites attack them and burn their homes

1830 First National Negro Convention convenes in Philadelphia

1831 Maria W. Stewart, **"Religion and the Pure Principles of Morality, the Sure Foundation on Which We Must Build"** • Nat Turner leads slave uprising in Southampton County, Virginia; at least 57 whites are killed; 3,000 soldiers and Virginia militiamen react by killing blacks indiscriminately; Turner is captured and hanged

1832 Maria W. Stewart, first American woman to engage in public political debates, begins speaking tour in Boston

1833 Oberlin College is founded as first coeducational U.S. college and is integrated from its inception

1834 Henry Blair, inventor of corn planter, is first recorded African American to receive patent • Antiabolitionist riots in Philadelphia and New York • British Parliament abolishes slavery in British Empire

1835–42 Second Seminole War

1836 U.S. House of Representatives passes first "gag rule," preventing any antislavery petition or bill from being introduced, read, or discussed

1837 Victor Séjour, **"The Mulatto"**

1838 Frederick Douglass escapes from slavery • Joshua Giddings of Ohio is first abolitionist elected to U.S. Congress

1839 Cinque leads successful slave revolt on Spanish ship *Amistad* • U.S. State Department rejects passport application by Philadelphia black man on basis that African Americans are not citizens

1840 Pope Gregory XVI states opposition to slave trade and slavery

1841 Quintuple Treaty signed by England, France, Russia, Austria, and Prussia, allowing mutual search of vessels on high seas to halt slave trade • Frederick Douglass makes his first antislavery speech, in Nantucket, Massachusetts

1843 Henry Highland Garnet delivers **"An Address to the Slaves of the United States"** at National Negro Convention, Buffalo, New York • Vermont and Massachusetts defy 1793 Fugitive Slave Act

1845 Frederick Douglass, *Narrative of the Life of Frederick Douglass, an American Slave, Written by Himself*

1847 William Wells Brown, *Narrative of William W. Brown* • Liberia declares independence and becomes first African republic

1848 Frederick Douglass speaks at first Women's Rights Convention in Seneca Falls, New York • Ohio reverses "Black Laws"

1849 Harriet Tubman escapes from slavery and begins work with Underground Railroad • Massachusetts Supreme Court upholds "separate but equal" ruling in first U.S. integration suit

1850 Clay Compromise strengthens 1793 Fugitive Slave Act, outlaws slave trade in Washington, D.C., admits California as free state, and admits Utah and New Mexico as either slave or free • Lucy Session becomes first recorded African American woman college graduate, receiving her degree from Oberlin College, in Ohio

1851 Sojourner Truth delivers **"Ar'n't I a Woman?"** at Women's Rights Conference in Akron, Ohio

1852 Harriet Beecher Stowe, *Uncle Tom's Cabin* • Martin R. Delany, *The Condition, Elevation, Emigration, and Destiny of the Colored People of the United States*

1853–1893

1853 Brown, *Clotel* • J. M. Whitfield, *America and Other Poems*

1854–64, 1885–89 Charlotte Forten Grimké writes **journals**

1854 Frances E. W. Harper, *Poems on Miscellaneous Subjects* • Kansas-Nebraska Act repeals Missouri Compromise of 1820 • Republican Party founded to oppose extension of slavery

1855 Douglass, *My Bondage and My Freedom* • "Bleeding Kansas" fighting begins as antislavery and proslavery settlers hold separate state conventions • John Mercer Langston is elected clerk of Brownhelm Township. Ohio, becoming first African American elected to political office

1857 Supreme Court declares African Americans are not citizens in *Dred Scott* decision

1859 Harriet Adams Wilson, *Our Nig,* first novel published in America by an African American • John Brown leads abolitionist raid in Harpers Ferry, West Virginia • Last U.S. slave ship lands in Alabama

1860 William Craft, *Running a Thousand Miles for Freedom* • South Carolina is first state to secede from Union

1861–65 American Civil War

1861 Harriet Jacobs, *Incidents in the Life of a Slave Girl* • Harper's "The Two Offers" is first short story published by an African American woman

1862 Congress bans slavery in District of Columbia and U.S. territories • President Lincoln issues Emancipation Proclamation, effective January 1, 1863, freeing slaves in rebel states • U.S. recognizes Liberia as free nation

1863 Slavery abolished in all Dutch colonies

1864 Fugitive Slave Laws repealed

1865 General Sherman orders up to 40 acres given to each black family, but President Johnson later reverses policy • Slavery outlawed by 13th Amendment • Freedmen's Bureau established • "Black Codes" issued in former Confederate states, severely limiting rights of freed women and men • President Lincoln assassinated • Ku Klux Klan founded in Tennessee

1866 Congress passes first Civil Rights Act declaring freed blacks U.S. citizens and nullifying black codes • Edward G.

Walker and Charles L. Mitchel are first blacks elected to state legislature

1867 Congress passes First Reconstruction Act, granting suffrage to black males in rebel states, among other rights • Nicholas Said, "A Native of Bornoo," published in the *Atlantic Monthly*

1868 Congress passes 14th Amendment, granting blacks equal citizenship and civil rights • Elizabeth Keckley, *Behind the Scenes; or, Thirty Years a Slave, and Four Years in the White House*

1869 National Women's Suffrage Association formed • Wyoming Territory is first to grant women suffrage in the United States

1870 Congress passes 15th Amendment, guaranteeing suffrage to all male U.S. citizens • Congress passes Enforcement Acts to control Ku Klax Klan and to federally guarantee civil and political rights • Rev. Hiram R. Revels of Mississippi is first black U.S. senator • Joseph H. Rainey is seated as first black U.S. representative; 5 other black men are also elected to U.S. House of Representatives • Richard T. Greener is first African American graduate of Harvard College

1871 Congress passes second Ku Klux Klan Act to enforce 14th Amendment

1874 Women's Christian Temperance Union founded in Ohio

1875 Congress passes Civil Rights Act of 1875, giving equal treatment in public places and access to jury duty

1877 Federal troops withdraw from South, officially ending Reconstruction

1881 Booker T. Washington founds Tuskegee Institute

1883 Supreme Court overturns Civil Rights Act of 1875

1884 Moses Fleetwood Walker plays baseball for Toledo Blue Stockings as one of first black major leaguers

1889 Charles Chesnutt, "**Dave's Neckliss**"

1890 Oklahoma admitted as first state with women's suffrage • Mississippi limits black suffrage through "understanding" test, setting precedent for other southern states

1892 Anna Julia Cooper, *A Voice from the South* • Harper, *Iola Leroy*

1893 Paul Laurence Dunbar, *Oak and Ivy*

1894–1926

1894 *The Woman's Era*, later to become the official organ of the National Association of Colored Women, begins publication

1895 Booker T. Washington delivers **"Atlanta Exposition Address"** • Alice Moore Dunbar Nelson, *Violets and Other Tales* • Ida B. Wells-Barnett, *A Red Record* • Dunbar, *Majors and Minors*

1896 Supreme Court approves segregation with "separate but equal" ruling in *Plessy v. Ferguson* • National League of Colored Women and National Federation of Afro-American Women merge to form National Association of Colored Women with Mary Church Terrell as president

1898 Spanish-American War

1899 Charles W. Chesnutt, *The Conjure Woman, The Wife of His Youth and Other Stories of the Color Line*

1900 Washington, *Up from Slavery* • Pauline E. Hopkins, *Contending Forces*.

1901 Pauline E. Hopkins, **"Bro'r Abr'm Jimson's Wedding"**

1902 James D. Corrothers, *The Black Cat Club*

1903 W. E. B. Du Bois, *The Souls of Black Folk*

1904 William Stanley Braithwaite, *Lyrics of Life and Love* • AME Church Review calls for a "New Negro Renaissance"

1905 Niagara Movement, dedicated to "aggressive action" for equal rights, is founded by Du Bois and others

1906 Madame C. J. Walker opens hair-care business, eventually becoming one of the first female American millionaires

1907 Alain Locke is first African American Rhodes Scholar

1908 Braithwaite, *The House of Falling Leaves with Other Poems* • Jack Johnson becomes first African American heavyweight champion of the world

1909 National Association for the Advancement of Colored People (NAACP) founded by Du Bois

1910–30 Great Migration of over 1 million southern blacks to northern cities

1912 James Weldon Johnson, *The Autobiography of an Ex-Colored Man* • Claude McKay, *Songs of Jamaica* and *Constab Ballads*

1913 Fenton Johnson, *A Little Dreaming*

1914–18 World War I

1916 Angelina Weld Grimke's *Rachel* is performed in Washington, D.C., the first full-length play written, performed, and produced by African Americans in the twentieth century • Marcus Garvey comes to the United States from Jamaica and begins "Back to Africa" movement with establishment of Universal Negro Improvement Association • Margaret Sanger opens first birth control clinic in the United States

1917 United States enters World War I • Thousands of blacks in "Silent Protest Parade" march down Fifth Avenue in New York City to protest racial inequalities • Claude McKay, **"The Harlem Dancer"** • Hubert Harrison, **"The East Louisville Horror"**

1918 Georgia Douglas Johnson, **"The Heart of a Woman"** • Marcus Garvey establishes the newspaper *Negro World*

1919 Du Bois organizes first Pan-African Congress in Paris • 83 lynchings recorded during "Red Summer of Hate" • American Communist Party organized • Hubert Harrison, **"Two Negro Radicalisms"**

1920 Du Bois, *Darkwater* • Ratification of 19th Amendment, granting suffrage to women

1921 René Maran, *Batouala*

1922–33 Harlem Renaissance

1922 Johnson, *The Book of American Negro Poetry* • McKay, **"Harlem Shadows"** • Dyer Anti-Lynching bill passes U.S. House of Representatives but fails in Senate

1923–25 Marcus Garvey, *The Philosophy and Opinions of Marcus Garvey*

1923 Jean Toomer, *Cane* • Oklahoma declares martial law to curb KKK

1925–27 Annual literary contests sponsored by *Crisis* and *Opportunity* magazines

1925 Alain Locke, **"The New Negro"** • Countee Cullen, *Color* • 40,000 KKK members parade in Washington, D.C. • Josephine Baker becomes sensation in Paris through *La Revue Negre*

1926 Eric Walrond, *Tropic Death* • Langston Hughes, **"The Weary Blues"** • Richard Bruce Nugent, **"Smoke, Lilies, and Jade"**

1927–1955

1927 Charles S. Johnson's anthology *Ebony and Topaz* • Cullen's anthology of black poetry *Caroling the Dusk* • *The Jazz Singer* is first "talkie" motion picture, with white actor Al Jolson as black-faced minstrel singer • Sterling Brown, **"When de Saints go Ma'ching Home"**

1928 McKay, *Home to Harlem* • Marita Bonner, *The Purple Flower* • Nella Larsen, *Quicksand* and *Passing* • Langston Hughes, **"Johannesburg Mines"**

1929 Jessie Fauset, *Plum Bun* • Wallace Thurman, *The Blacker the Berry* • Stock Market Crash ushers in Great Depression • Claude McKay, *Banjo*

1930 W. D. Fard founds Nation of Islam

1931 Arna Bontemps, *God Sends Sunday* • "Scotsboro boys" unjustly convicted of raping two white women in Alabama, prompting nationwide protest • George Samuel Schuyler, *Black No More* • Nicolás Guillén, *Sóngoro Consogo*

1932 Sterling A. Brown, **"Southern Road"** • Thurman, *Infants of the Spring*

1933 President Roosevelt pushes "New Deal" through Congress

1934 Nancy Cunard, *Negro, An Anthology* • Paul Robeson, **"I Want to Be African"** • Langston Hughes, **"Cubes"**

1935 Zora Neale Hurston, *Mules and Men* • National Council of Negro Women founded

1936 Bontemps, *Black Thunder* • Jesse Owens wins four gold medals at "Nazi Olympics" in Berlin

1937 Hurston, *Their Eyes Were Watching God* • Joe Louis becomes boxing's world heavyweight champion

1938 Richard Wright, *Uncle Tom's Children* • Crystal Bird Fauset elected to Pennsylvania House of Representatives, becoming first African American woman state legislator • Sterling Brown, **"Break of Day"**

1939–45 World War II

1939 Contralto Marian Anderson sings at Lincoln Memorial for 75,000 after her concert at Constitution Hall was prevented by Daughters of American Revolution

1940 Wright, *Native Son* • Hughes, *The Big Sea* • Robert Hayden, *Heart-Shape in the Dust*

1941 United States enters war after Japanese attack on Pearl Harbor • A. Philip Randolph of the Brotherhood of Sleeping Car Porters organizes march on Washington to protest segregation in the military and employment discrimination; President Roosevelt issues executive order forbidding racial and religious discrimination in government training programs and defense industries; Randolph calls off march

1942 Hurston, *Dust Tracks on a Road* • Margaret Walker, **"For My People"**

1943 First successful "sit-in" demonstration staged by Congress of Racial Equality (CORE) • Over 40 killed in race riots in Detroit and Harlem

1944 Melvin B. Tolson, *Rendezvous with America* • Chester Himes, **"Cotton Gonna Kill Me Yet"**

1945 Wright, *Black Boy* • Gwendolyn Brooks, *A Street in Bronzeville*

1946 Ann Petry, *The Street*

1947 Tolson named Poet Laureate of Liberia

1948 Dorothy West, *The Living Is Easy* • President Truman approves desegregation of the military and creates Fair Employment Board

1949 Langston Hughes, **"Bop"**

1950–53 Korean War

1950 Brooks wins Pulitzer Prize for *Annie Allen* (1949), the first African American to win Pulitzer Prize in any category • Ralph J. Bunche is first African American to receive Nobel Peace Prize

1951 Hughes, *Montage of a Dream Deferred*

1952 Ralph Ellison, *Invisible Man*

1953 Tolson, *Libretto for the Republic of Liberia* • Brooks, *Maud Martha* • James Baldwin, *Go Tell It on the Mountain* • Wright, *The Outsider*

1954 In *Brown v. Board of Education*, Supreme Court declares segregated schools unconstitutional, overturning *Plessy v. Ferguson* (1896)

1955 Baldwin, *Notes of a Native Son* • Rosa Parks arrested for refusing to give seat on bus to white man, setting off bus boycott led by Dr. Martin Luther King Jr. • 14-year-old Emmett Till lynched in Mississippi • Supreme Court orders speedy integration of schools • Interstate Commerce Commission orders integration of buses, trains, and waiting rooms for

1955–1968

interstate travel • Alice Childress, *Trouble in Mind*

1956 101 southern congressmen sign "Southern Manifesto" against school desegregation

1957 Congress approves Civil Rights Act of 1957 • Federal troops sent to Alabama to enforce school desegregation • Ghana is first African nation to gain independence from colonial rule • James Baldwin, "Princes and Powers"

1959 Lorraine Hansberry's *A Raisin in the Sun* is first Broadway play by an African American woman • Paule Marshall, *Brown Girl, Brownstones*

1960 Sit-in staged by four black students at Woolworth's lunch counter in North Carolina • Student Non-violent Coordinating Committee (SNCC) founded • Congress passes Civil Rights Act of 1960 • Gwendolyn Brooks, "A Bronzeville Mother Loiters in Mississippi . . ."

1961 Hughes, *The Best of Simple* • Hoyt Fuller revives *Negro Digest* • LeRoi Jones (Amiri Baraka), "Preface to a Twenty Volume Suicide Note" • Baraka, *Dutchman* • 13 "freedom riders" sponsored by CORE take bus trip across South to force integration of terminals

1962 Hayden, "Ballad of Remembrance" • Baldwin, *Another Country* • Riots break out after Supreme Court orders University of Mississippi to accept James Meredith as first black student; 12,000 federal troops are employed to restore order and ensure Meredith's admission

1963 Martin Luther King writes "Letter from Birmingham Jail" • National support for civil rights roused after police attack Alabama demonstration led by King • Civil rights March on Washington attracts over 200,000 demonstrators; King delivers "I Have a Dream" speech • President Kennedy assassinated

1964 Tolson, *Harlem Gallery* • Ellison, *Shadow and Act* • Baraka's *Dutchman* wins Obie Award • Malcolm X founds Organization of Afro-American Unity, officially splitting with Elijah Muhammad and the Black Muslims • 3 civil rights workers murdered in Mississippi by white segregationists, setting off Mississippi "Freedom Summer" • King wins Nobel Peace Prize • 24th Amendment ratified, outlawing poll tax used to limit black suffrage • Congress passes Civil Rights Act of 1964 and Economic Opportunity Act •

Sidney Poitier wins Academy Award for *Lilies of the Field* • Cassius Clay wins world heavyweight boxing championship, subsequently converts to Islam and changes name to Muhammad Ali • Adrienne Kennedy, *Funnyhouse of a Negro* • Amiri Baraka, "A Poem for Willie Best," "Black Dada Nihilismus," *The Slave* • Mari Evans, "Vive Noir!"

1965–73 Vietnam War

1965 Malcolm X, *The Autobiography of Malcolm X* • A. B. Spellman, *The Beautiful Days* • King leads march from Selma to Montgomery, Alabama • Malcolm X assassinated in New York City • Watts riot is most serious single racial disturbance in U.S. history • Black Arts Movement started by Amiri Baraka in Harlem • David Henderson, "Keep on Pushing" • Daniel Patrick Moynihan authors *The Negro Family: The Case For National Action*, a controversial report that shapes policy in the late 1960s

1966 Black Panther Party founded • National Organization for Women founded • Senator Edward W. Brooke (R-MA) becomes first elected black senator since Reconstruction • "Black Power" concept is adopted by CORE and SNCC

1967 Haki R. Madhubuti, *Think Black* • Jay Wright, *Death as History* • Ishmael Reed, "The Free-Lance Pallbearers" • King announces opposition to Vietnam War • Worst race riot in U.S. history in Detroit kills 43; major riots in Newark and Chicago • Thurgood Marshall becomes first black U.S. Supreme Court justice • Supreme Court overturns law against interracial marriage • Calvin Hernton, "Jitterbugging in the Streets" • Amiri Baraka, *Slave Ship*

1968 Etheridge Knight, *Poems from Prison* • Nikki Giovanni, *Black Feeling* • Eldridge Cleaver, *Soul on Ice* • Quincy Troupe's anthology *Watts Poets: A Book of New Poetry and Essays* • Carolyn Rodgers, *Paper Soul* • Earnest Gaines, *Bloodline* • Audre Lorde, *The First Cities* • June Jordan, *Who Look at Me* • Alice Walker, *Once: Poems* • King assassinated in Memphis • Senator Robert F. Kennedy assassinated in Los Angeles • Shirley Chisholm becomes first black woman elected to U.S. Congress • Amiri Baraka and Larry Neal edit *Black Fire*, a major collection of Black Arts poetry, prose, and drama including Stewart's "The Development of the Black Revolutionary Artist" • Amus Mor, "Poem to the Hip Generation"

1969–1988

1969   Sonia Sanchez, **"homecoming"** • Jayne Cortez, *Pisstained Stairs and the Monkey Man's Wares* • Lucille Clifton, *Good Times* • Al Young, *Dancing: Poems* • Major antiwar demonstrations in Washington • Raymond Patterson, *Twenty-Six Ways of Looking at a Blackman and Other Poems* Amiri Baraka, **"Ka 'Ba"** • Sonia Sanchez, *Sister Son/ji; Homecoming* • Haki Madhubuti, *Don't Cry, Scream*

1970   Charles Gordon wins Pulitzer Prize for *No Place to Be Somebody* (1969) • Maya Angelou, *I Know Why the Caged Bird Sings* • Toni Morrison, *The Bluest Eye* • Michael S. Harper, **"Dear John, Dear Coltrane"** • Toni Cade Bambara edits *The Black Woman* • Amiri Baraka, **"It's Nation Time"** • Sonia Sanchez, *We a BaddDDD People* • Henry Dumas, *Ark of Bones and Other Stories* • Nikki Giovanni, *Black Feeling, Black Talk/Black Judgment*

1971   Addison Gayle, **"The Black Aesthetic"** • Angelou, *Just Give Me A Cool Drink of Water 'fore I Diiie* • Gaines, *Autobiography of Miss Jane Pittman* • Supreme Court approves busing as method of desegregation • Supreme Court rules closing of Mississippi swimming pools to avoid desegregation is constitutional • Larry Neal, *Hoodoo Hollerin Bebop Ghosts*

1972   Reed, *Mumbo Jumbo* • Congress passes Equal Rights Amendment, which goes to states for ratification • Chisholm is first black woman to run for U.S. president • Toni Cade Bambara, *Gorilla My Love* • Michael S. Harper, *Song: I Want a Witness*

1973   Knight, *Belly Song and Other Poems* • Morrison, *Sula* • Supreme Court prohibits state restrictions on abortions in *Roe v. Wade*

1974   Charles Johnson, *Oxherding Tale* • Albert Murray, *Train Whistle Guitar* • Henry Dumas, *Play Ebony, Play Ivory*

1975   Ntozake Shange's *for colored girls who have considered suicide/when the rainbow is enuf* is second play by an African American woman to reach Broadway • Sherley Anne Williams, *Peacock Poems* • Gayl Jones, *Corregidora* • Carolyn M. Rodgers, *how I got ovah*

1976   Alex Haley awarded special Pulitzer Prize for *Roots* • Kennedy, *A Movie Star Has to Star in Black and White* • Octavia Butler, *Patternmaster* • Audre Lorde, *Coal*

1977   Toni Morrison, *Song of Solomon* • Wanda Coleman, *Art in the Court of the*

Blue Fag • Rita Dove, *Ten Poems* • TV miniseries based on Alex Haley's *Roots* attracts more viewers than any television program in history • Michael S. Harper, *Images of Kin: New and Selected Poems*

1978   James Alan McPherson wins Pulitzer Prize for his 1977 *Elbow Room* • Shange, **"Nappy Edges"** • Supreme Court disallows quotas for college admissions but gives limited approval to affirmative action programs • Audre Lorde, *The Black Unicorn*

1979   Walker edits *I Love Myself When I Am Laughing: A Zora Neale Hurston Reader* • Butler, *Kindred*

1980   Bambara, *The Salt Eaters* • Liberian president William Tolbert ousted by Staff Sargeant Samuel K. Doe, ending over 130 years of Americo-Liberian rule over indigenous Africans • June Jordan, *Passion: New Poems, 1977–1980*

1981   David Bradley, *The Chaneysville Incident*

1982   Charles Fuller wins Pulitzer Prize for his 1981 *A Soldier's Play* • Marshall, *Reena and Other Stories* • Lorde, *Zami: a new spelling of my name* • Gloria Naylor, *The Women of Brewster Place* • Equal Rights Amendment fails after 10 years, 3 states short of ratification

1983   Alice Walker wins Pulitzer Prize for her 1982 *The Color Purple*

1984   John Wideman, *Brothers and Keepers* • August Wilson's *Ma Rainey's Black Bottom* opens on Broadway • Rev. Jesse Jackson is first serious black contender for the U.S. presidency, winning 17 percent of popular vote in democratic primary • Vanessa Williams crowned first black Miss America

1985   Wideman, *The Homewood Trilogy* • Michelle Cliff, *The Land of Look Behind* • Jamaica Kincaid, *Annie John*

1986   Williams, *Dessa Rose* • Essex Hemphill, **"Conditions"** • Martin Luther King's birthday officially celebrated as federal holiday • Wole Soyinka of Nigeria is first person of African descent to win Nobel Prize for Literature • Etheridge Knight, "Ilu, the Talking Drum"

1987   Wilson wins Pulitzer Prize for Broadway play *Fences* (1986) • Dove wins Pulitzer Prize for *Thomas and Beulah* (1986) • Lucille Clifton, *Next*

1988   Morrison wins Pulitzer Prize for *Beloved* (1987) • Young, *Seduction by Light*

1988–2003

• Naylor, *Mama Day* • Wilson, *Joe Turner's Come and Gone*

1989   500,000 march in Washington for prochoice rally • L. Douglas Wilder of Virginia is first elected black governor • General Colin Powell becomes first black Chief of Staff for U.S. Armed Forces • Supreme Court approves state limits on abortion

1990   Wilson wins Pulitzer Prize for *The Piano Lesson* • Johnson's *Middle Passage* wins National Book Award • Cliff, *Bodies of Water* • Kincaid, *Lucy* • Walter Mosley, *Devil in a Blue Dress* • Elizabeth Alexander, *The Venus Hottentot*

1991   Clarence Thomas confirmed Supreme Court justice, despite Anita Hill's sexual harassment testimony

1992   Jordan, *Technical Difficulties* • Dove, *Through the Ivory Gate* • Terry McMillan, *Waiting to Exhale* • Police acquitted of beating Rodney King, setting off riots in Los Angeles • Carol Moseley Braun of Illinois becomes first African American woman elected to the U.S. Senate • Supreme Court rules against state bans of "hate speech" • Derek Walcott is first West Indian to win Nobel Prize for Literature • Edward P. Jones, *Lost in the City*

1993   Yusef Komunyakaa wins Pulitzer Prize for *Neon Vernacular* • Caryl Phillips, *Crossing the River* • Cornel West, *Race Matters* • Sarah and A. Elizabeth Delany, *Having Our Say: The Delany Sisters' First 100 Years* • Toni Morrison is first African American to win Nobel Prize for Literature • Maya Angelou reads "On the Pulse of Morning" at Clinton inauguration, becoming the first black poet to participate in a U.S. presidential inauguration • Supreme Court disallows congressional districts drawn to increase black representation

1994   Henry Louis Gates Jr., *Colored People* • Edwidge Danticat, *Breath, Eyes, Memory* • Nathan McCall, *Makes Me Wanna Holler: A Young Black Man in America* • Brent Staples, *Parallel Time: Growing Up in Black and White* • Rita Dove named U.S. Poet Laureate • David Levering Lewis wins Pulitzer Prize in Biography for *W. E. B. Du Bois: Biography of a Race, 1868–1919* • O. J. Simpson accused of murdering ex-wife and her friend; ensuing trial grips nation

1995   Dorothy West, *The Wedding* • Jamaica Kincaid, *The Autobiography of My Mother* • Rita Dove, *Mother Love* • Harryette Mullen, *Muse & Drudge* • O. J. Simpson acquitted of murder charges • Million Man March in Washington organized by Nation of Islam minister Louis Farrakhan • Colin Powell considered as a presidential candidate of the Republican Party • Barack Obama, *Dreams from My Father*

1996   Walter Mosley, *A Little Yellow Dog* • Terry McMillan, *How Stella Got Her Groove Back* • August Wilson, *Seven Guitars*, on Broadway

1997   California passes state ban on all forms of affirmative action (Proposition 209) • Randall Kennedy's *Race, Crime, and The Law* tracks discrimination in the criminal justice system

1998   Washington State abolishes all state affirmative action • Unexpurgated edition of Chester Himes's *Yesterday Will Make You Cry*

1999   Ralph Ellison's second novel, *Juneteenth*, published posthumously

2000   One month after contested presidential election results, the Supreme Court rules against recounts in Florida and effectively declares George W. Bush president with 271 electoral votes • Lucille Clifton, *Blessing the Boats* (wins National Book Award)

2001   Colson Whitehead, *John Henry Days* • President Bush appoints General Colin L. Powell Secretary of State and Condoleezza Rice National Security Advisor • Halle Berry first African American woman to win Academy Award for Best Actress • Lewis wins second Pulitzer Prize in Biography for *W. E. B. Du Bois: The Fight for Equality and the American Century, 1919–1963* • On September 11, terrorists hijack four commercial jetliners; two crash into World Trade Center in New York, one into Pentagon, and one into a field in Pennsylvania • Kevin Young, *To Repel Ghosts*

2002   University of Michigan Law School's affirmative action policy ruled constitutional • Suzan-Lori Parks wins Pulitzer in Drama for *Topdog/Underdog* • Hannah Crafts, *The Bondswoman's Narrative*, the first African American novel (written before 1861), is published

2003   Illinois governor George Ryan grants clemency to all 160 death-row inmates after his 2002 blue-ribbon Commission on Capital Punishment finds

2003–2013

systemic failures • President Bush orders U.S. Justice Department to file briefs urging Supreme Court to rule as unconstitutional University of Michigan's affirmative action policies in undergraduate and law school admissions • Edward P. Jones, *The Known World* (wins Pulitzer Prize for fiction) • Kevin Young, *Jelly Roll* • *Forbes* reveals Oprah Winfrey as the first African American woman to become a billionaire

2004   Rita Dove, *American Smooth* • Edwidge Danticat, *The Dew Breaker* • Barack Obama elected as U.S. senator from Illinois

2005   Condoleeza Rice named first female African American secretary of state under President George W. Bush • Hurricane Katrina hits the American southeast, crippling New Orleans, Louisiana, and the Gulf Coast of Mississippi and Alabama • Elizabeth Alexander, *American Sublime II* • August Wilson completes *Radio Golf*, the final play in his century cycle, only months before his death

2006   Edward P. Jones, *Aunt Hagar's Children*

2007   300 Tuskegee Airmen and their widows given Congressional Gold Medal for their service in World War II • Edwidge Danticat, *Brother, I'm Dying* • Natasha

Trethewey, *Native Guard* (wins the Pulitzer Prize for poetry)

2008   Barack Obama elected as the first African American president of the United States

2009   Barack Obama wins the Nobel Peace Prize • Eric Holder becomes the first African American to serve as United States Attorney General II • Colson Whitehead, *Sag Harbor*

2010   An earthquake measuring 7.0 on the Richter Scale shakes Haiti, killing over 100,000 • Natasha Trethewey, *Beyond Katrina* • Terrance Hayes, *Lighthead* (wins National Book Award for poetry)

2011   Tracy K. Smith, *Life on Mars* (wins Pulitzer Prize for poetry) • Kevin Young, *Ardency* • Following a 2003 invasion and years of occupation, American combat forces leave Iraq • Amidst widespread protests, Troy Anthony Davis is executed after being convicted of murdering a police officer in 1989

2012   Barack Obama reelected to serve his second term as president • Natasha Trethewey named Poet Laureate of the United States

2013   George Zimmerman, tried for the murder of African American teenager Trayvon Martin, acquitted of second degree murder and manslaughter.

Selected Bibliographies

SUGGESTED GENERAL READINGS

Political, Social, and Cultural History
In the twentieth century African American history moved from a footnote shaped by its status as "the Negro Problem" to a rich and complex textual independence informed by both national and international perspectives. For a sense of the profound changes in the study of race in history, see August Meier and Elliott Rudwick's *Black History and the Historical Profession 1915–1980* (1986) and John Hope Franklin's *Race and History: Selected Essays 1938–1988* (1989). An excellent resource for students is *The Harvard Guide to African-American History* (2001), edited by Evelyn Brooks Higginbotham et al., which comes with a CD-ROM with more than fifteen thousand bibliography entries available for searching. Historical studies include John Hope Franklin's *From Slavery to Freedom: A History of Negro Americans* (1947); Herbert Aptheker's *To Be Free: Studies in American Negro History* (1948); *The Making of Black America: Essays in Negro Life and History* (1969), edited by August Meier and Elliott Rudwick; Philip Foner's *Essays in Afro-American History* (1978); Bettina Aptheker's *Woman's Legacy: Essays on Race, Sex, and Class in American History* (1982); *The Southern Enigma: Essays on Race, Class, and Folk Culture* (1983), edited by Walter J. Fraser Jr. and Winfred B. Moore Jr.; *History and Tradition in Afro-American Culture* (1984), edited by Günter H. Lenz; Paula Giddings's *When and Where I Enter: The Impact of Black Women on Race and Sex in America* (1984); *In Resistance: Studies in African, Caribbean, and Afro-American History* (1986), edited by Gary Y. Okihiro; Benjamin Quarles's *The Negro in the Making of America* (1987); and Ira Berlin's *Many Thousands Gone: The First Two Centuries of Slavery in America* (1998). Several reference works on history and culture are *The Afro-American Encyclopedia* (1974), edited by Martin Rywell and Charles H. Wesley; *The Encyclopedia of African-American Culture and History* (1993), edited by Jack Salzman, David

Lionel Smith, and Cornel West; *The African American Century: How Black Americans Have Shaped Our Country* (2000), edited by Henry Louis Gates Jr. and Cornel West; and *African American Lives*, edited by Henry Louis Gates, Jr. and Evelyn Brooks Higginbotham (2004). For Pan-African perspectives, see *Africa and the Afro-American Experience: Eight Essays* (1977), edited by Lorraine A. Williams; Gregory U. Rigsby's *Alexander Crummell: Pioneer in Nineteenth-Century Pan-African Thought* (1987); Paul Gilroy's *the Black Atlantic: Modernity and Double-Consciousness* (1993); and John Cullen Gruesser's *Black on Black: Twentieth-Century African American Writing about Africa* (2000). Reference works include *The Dictionary of Global Culture* (1997), edited by Kwame Anthony Appiah, Henry Louis Gates Jr., and Michael Colin Vazquez; and *Africana: The Encyclopedia of African and African American Experience* (1999), edited by Kwame Anthony Appiah and Henry Louis Gates Jr. New technologies have brought two rich resources: Microsoft's multimedia encyclopedia *Encarta Africana* (2000), edited by Kwame Anthony Appiah and Henry Louis Gates Jr.; and the rich, continuously updated Web site www.africana.com.

Colonial and Antebellum Years
Studies of African American history of the colonial and antebellum periods include Lorenzo Johnston Greene's *The Negro in Colonial New England* (1969); A. Leon Higginbotham's *In the Matter of Color: The Colonial Period* (1978); Daniel F. Littlefield's *Africans and Creeks: From the Colonial Period to the Civil War* (1979); *Slavery and Freedom in the Age of the American Revolution* (1983), edited by Ira Berlin and Ronald Hoffman; William Dillion Piersen's *Black Yankees: The Development of an Afro-American Subculture in Eighteenth-Century New England* (1988); Jean Fagin Yellin's *Women and Sisters: The Antislavery Feminists in American Culture*

(1989); Peter Michael Voelz's *Slave and Soldier: The Military Impact of Blacks in the Colonial Americas* (1993); Joseph Douglas Deal's *Race and Class in Colonial Virginia: Indians, Englishmen, and Africans on the Eastern Shore during the Seventeenth Century* (1993); Donald R. Wright's *African Americans in the Colonial Era: From African Origins Through the American Revolution* (2000); Barbara A. Faggins's *Africans and Indians: An Afrocentric Analysis of Contacts between Africans and Indians in Colonial Virginia* (2001); *Another's Country: Archaeological and Historical Perspectives on Cultural Interactions in the Southern Colonies* (2002), edited by J. W. Joseph and Martha Zierden; and John Ernest's *Liberation Historiography: African American Writes and the Challenge of History, 1794–1861* (2004) and *A Nation within a Nation: Organizing African-American Communities before the Civil War* (2011). See also *Witness for Freedom: African American Voices on Race, Slavery, and Emancipation* (1993), edited by C. Peter Ripley.

Nineteenth Century: Slavery and Freedom
Studies of slave culture include Herbert Aptheker's *American Negro Slave Revolts* (1963); Eugene D. Genovese's *Roll, Jordan, Roll: The World the Slaves Made* (1976); Albert J. Raboteau's *Slave Religion: The "Invisible Institution" in the Antebellum South* (1978); John Blassingame's *The Slave Community* (1979); Orlando Patterson's *Slavery and Social Death: A Comparative Study* (1982); Sterling Stuckey's *Slave Culture* (1987); Wilma King's *Stolen Childhood: Slave Youth in Nineteenth-Century America* (1995); and *Slave Cultures and the Cultures of Slavery* (1995), edited by Stephan Palmié. Nineteenth-century studies include *The Black Man in America Since Reconstruction* (1970), edited by David M. Reimers; Dorothy Sterling's *We Are Your Sisters: Black Women in the Nineteenth Century* (1984); R. J. M. Blackett's *Beating against the Barriers: Biographical Essays in Nineteenth-Century Afro-American History* (1986); Hazel Carby's *Reconstructing Womanhood* (1987); *The African American Family in the South, 1861–1900* (1994), edited by Donald G. Nieman; Martha Elizabeth Hodes's *White Women, Black Men: Illicit Sex in the Nineteenth-Century South* (1997); James Oliver and Lois E. Horton's *In Hope of Liberty: Culture, Community, and Protest among Northern Free Blacks, 1700–1860* (1997); Saidiya V. Hartman's *Scenes of Subjection: Terror, Slavery, and Self-Making in Nineteenth-Century America* (1997); Chungchan Gao's *African Americans in the Reconstruction Era* (1999); Katherine Clay Bassard's *Spiritual Interrogations: Culture, Gender, and Community in Early African American Women's Writing* (1999); Eddie S. Glaude's *Exodus!: Religion, Race, and Nation in Early Nineteenth-Century Black America* (2000); John Stauffer's *The Black Hearts of* *Men: Radical Abolitionists and the Transformation of Race* (2002); and Jerrold M. Packard's *American Nightmare: The History of Jim Crow* (2002).

Twentieth Century
Crucial texts for twentieth-century political and social history include Gunnar Myrdal's *An American Dilemma: The Negro Problem and Modern Democracy* (1944); E. Franklin Frazier's *Black Bourgeoisie: The Rise of a New Middle-Class in the United States* (1962); Gilbert Osofsky's *Harlem: The Making of a Ghetto* (1963); William Van DeBurg's *New Day in Babylon: The Black Power Movement and American Culture, 1965–1975* (1992); Michael Omi and Howard Winant's *Racial Formation in the United States: From the 1960s to the 1990s* (1994); and Rayford Whittingham Logan's *The Betrayal of the Negro: From Rutherford Hayes to Woodrow Wilson* (1997). The March 2000 issue of *Sage*, edited by Elijah Anderson and Tukufu Zuberi, revisits the philosophy of Du Bois in *The Study of African American Problems: W. E. B. Du Bois's Agenda, Then and Now*. See also *Negro Protest Thought in the Twentieth Century* (1971), edited by August Meier, Elliott Rudwick, and Francis L. Broderick; Kevin Kelly Gaines's *Uplifting the Race: Black Leadership, Politics, and Culture in the Twentieth Century* (1996); *The House That Race Built: Black Americans, U.S. Terrain* (1997), edited by Wahneema Lubiano; *African Americans and Jews in the Twentieth Century: Studies in Convergence and Conflict* (1998), edited by V. P. Franklin et al; *Black American Intellectualism and Culture: A Social Study of African American Social and Political Thought* (1999), edited by James L. Conyer Jr.; Mary L. Dudziak's *Cold War Civil Rights: Race and the Image of American Democracy* (2000); and Anthony Dawahare's *Nationalism, Marxism, and African American Literature between the Wars: A New Pandora's Box* (2003). Studies of contemporary history include Andrew Billingsley's *Climbing Jacob's Ladder: The Enduring Legacy of African American Families* (1992) and *Against the Odds: Scholars Who Challenged Racism in the Twentieth Century* (2002), edited by Benjamin P. Bowser, Louis Kushnick, and Paul Grant. For women's history, see the collection of tapes and transcripts *Black Women Oral History Project Interviews* (1976–81) at Schlesinger Library, Radcliffe College; *Black Women in United States History* (1990–95), edited by Darlene Clark Hine; *"We specialize in the wholly impossible": A Reader in Black Women's History* (1995), edited by Darlene Clark Hine, Wilma King, and Linda Reed; Darlene Clark Hine and Kathleen Thompson's *A Shining Thread of Hope: The History of Black Women in America* (1998); and *A Companion to American Women's History* (2002), edited by Nancy A.

Hewitt, 2002. See also *Unequal Sisters: A Multicultural Reader in U.S. Women's History* (2000), edited by Vicki L. Ruiz and Ellen Carol DuBois.

Critical studies of the impact of migration on African Americans include Spencer R. Crew's *Field to Factory: Afro-American Migration, 1915–1940* (1987); E. Marvin Goodwin's *Black Migration in America from 1915 to 1960: An Uneasy Exodus* (1990); and *Black Exodus: The Great Migration from the American South* (1991), edited by Alferdteen Harrison. Studies of the twentieth century include Bruce Michael Tyler's *From Harlem to Hollywood: The Struggle for Racial and Cultural Democracy, 1920–1943* (1992) and *Radical Revisions: Rereading 1930s Culture* (1996), edited by Bill Mullen and Sherry Lee Linkon. See also Beth Tompkins Bates's *Pullman Porters and the Rise of Protest Politics in Black America, 1925–1945* (2001) and Zhang Aimin's *The Origins of the African American Civil Rights Movement, 1865–1956* (2002). On the 1960s, see *In Black America, 1968: The Year of Awakening* (1969), edited by Patricia W. Romero; *Race, Politics, and Culture: Critical Essays on the Radicalism of the 1960's* (1986), edited by Adolph Reed Jr.; Jennifer B. Smith's *An International History of the Black Panther Party* (1999); and James C. Hall's *Mercy, Mercy Me: African American Culture and the American Sixties* (2001).

Historical studies that focus on the economic system of the United States are numerous. For a history of African American labor, see the eight-volume study *The Black Worker: A Documentary History from Colonial Times to the Present* (1978), edited by Philip S. Foner and Ronald L. Lewis. Studies of work and economics include Jacqueline Jones's *The Dispossessed: America's Underclasses from the Civil War to the Present* (1992) and *American Work: Four Centuries of Black and White Labor* (1998); Julius Wilson's *When Work Disappears: The World of the New Urban Poor* (1997); Robert E. Weems's *Desegregating the Dollar: African American Consumerism in the Twentieth Century* (1998); Paul R. Mullins's *Race and Affluence: An Archaeology of African America and Consumer Culture* (1999); and Bruce Nelson's *Divided We Stand: American Workers and the Struggle for Black Equality* (2001). On the role of law in African American history, see Mary Frances Berry's *Black Resistance/White Law: A History of Constitutional Racism in America* (1971); C. Vann Woodward's *The Strange Career of Jim Crow* (1974); Eric Foner's *Reconstruction: America's Unfinished Revolution, 1863–1877* (1988); *The Black Abolitionist Papers* (1985–92), edited by C. Peter Ripley et al.; *African Americans and the Living Constitution* (1995), edited by John Hope Franklin and Genna Rae McNeil; A. Leon Higginbotham's *Shades of Freedom: Racial Politics and Presumptions of the American Legal Process* (1996); *Plessy v. Ferguson: A Brief History with Documents* (1997), edited by Brook Thomas; Gail Williams O'Brien's *The Color of the Law: Race, Violence, and Justice in the Post-World War II South* (1999); and *Local Matters: Race, Crime, and Justice in the Nineteenth-Century South* (2001), edited by Christopher Waldrep and Donald G. Nieman. See also *Interracialism: Black-White Intermarriage in American History, Literature, and Law* (2000), edited by Werner Sollors.

For studies of African American culture, see *African American Culture* (1996), edited by Sandra Adell, Thomas L. Morgan, and Patrick Roney; George E. Kent's *Blackness and the Adventure of Western Culture* (1972); *The Greatest Taboo: Homosexuality in Black Communities* (2001), edited by Deloy Constantine-Simms; *Sports Matters: Race, Recreation, and Culture* (2002), edited by John Bloom and Michael Nevin Willard; and Frances Smith Foster's *'Til Death or Distance Do Us Part: Love and Marriage in African America* (2010). Magazines, newspapers, religion, music, and art shape culture as well. For the role of periodicals in African American culture, see *The Negro and His Folklore in Nineteenth-Century Periodicals* (1977), edited by Bruce Jackson; *The Black Press in the Middle West, 1865–1985* (1996), edited by Henry Lewis Suggs; and *African-American Newspapers and Periodicals: A National Bibliography* (1998), edited by James P. Danky and Maureen E. Hady. See also Suggs's *P. B. Young, Newspaperman: Race, Politics, and Journalism in the New South, 1910–1962* (1988); Abby Arthur Johnson and Ronald Maberry Johnson's *Propaganda and Aesthetics: The Literary Politics of African-American Magazines in the Twentieth Century* (1991); and Eric Gardner's *Unexpected Places: Relocating Nineteenth-Century African American Literature* (2009).

Religion and the arts play crucial roles in cultural history. For an assessment of the various roles of religion in African American history, see Hans A. Baer and Merrill Singer's *African-American Religion in the Twentieth Century: Varieties of Protest and Accommodation* (1992); Evelyn Brooks Higginbotham's *Righteous Discontent: The Women's Movement in the Black Baptist Church, 1880–1920* (1993); and *African-American Religion: Interpretive Essays in History and Culture* (1997), edited by Timothy E. Fulop and Albert J. Raboteau. See also *Religion and American Culture: A Reader* (1995), edited by David G. Hackett. Several studies examine African American music and art including *Chant of Saints: A Gathering of Afro-American Literature, Art, and Scholarship* (1979), edited by Michael S. Harper and Robert B. Stepto. Two classic studies of African American music are Maud Cuney-Hare's *Negro Musicians and Their Music* (1996) and Eileen Southern's *The Music of Black Americans* (1997). For resources on music, see the bibliography for "The Vernacular

Tradition." For African American art, see Albert Boime's *The Art of Exclusion: Representing Blacks in the Nineteenth Century* (1990); Gus C. McElroy's *Facing History: The Black Image in American Art, 1710–1940* (1990); Sharon F. Patton's *African-American Art* (1998); and Michael D. Harris's *Colored Pictures: Race & Visual Representation* (2003). Richard Powell produced several studies: the essays collected in *Harlem Renaissance: Art of Black America* (1987) and *Rhapsodies in Black: Art of the Harlem Renaissance* (1997), for an exhibition devised and selected with David A. Bailey for London's Hayward Gallery. See also his *Black Art and Culture in the Twentieth Century* (1997). Studies of performance include *African Dance: An Artistic, Historical, and Philosophical Inquiry* (1996), edited by Kariamu Welsh Asante; John O. Perpener's *African-American Concert Dance: The Harlem Renaissance and Beyond* (2001); and Arthur Knight's *Disintegrating the Musical: Black Performance and American Musical Film* (2002). See the bibliography for "Drama and Performance" for more literary studies.

The Study of Literature

As the twentieth century came to a close, literary scholars continued to debate whether the literary designations known as genres can hold up to scrutiny. Students of literature do well to remember that authors of earlier times considered genre and poetic forms as writing models, even as they violated the rules of those models, and that poetry and prose use language in quite different ways. Many handbooks and glossaries are available to guide the student of literature through genre, theme, periodization, theory, and criticism that form the heart of many debates. For information on the distinguishing features of prose and poetry and their genres, *The New Princeton Encyclopedia of Poetry and Poetics* (1993), edited by Alex Preminger and T. V. F. Brogan, and *The Encyclopedia of Literature and Criticism* (1991), edited by Martin Coyle et al., are excellent general reference works. Excellent technical resources for the student of literature include *A Glossary of Literary Terms* (1981), edited by M. H. Abrams; *A Handbook to Literature* (2006), edited by William Harmon and C. Hugh Holman; and *Critical Terms for Literary Study* (1995), edited by Frank Lentricchia and Thomas McLaughlin. Students of prose can find guidance in the collection of essays gathered in *Essentials of the Theory of Fiction* (1988), edited by Michael Hoffman and Patrick Murphy; students of poetry will find John Hollander's *Rhyme Reason: A Guide to English Verse* (1981) a valuable introduction.

Genre Studies

For studies of the vernacular tradition, see J. Mason Brewer's *American Negro Folklore* (1968); Lawrence Levine's *Black Culture and Black Consciousness: Afro-American Folk Thought from Slavery to Freedom* (1977); Mary F. Berry and John Blassingame's *Long Memory: The Black Experience in America* (1982); Dolan Hubbard's *The Sermon and the African American Literary Imagination* (1994); and Bertram D. Ashe's *From within the Frame: Storytelling in African-American Fiction* (2002). See also the bibliography for "Vernacular Tradition."

Studies of African American poetry include Sterling A. Brown's *Outline for the Study of Poetry of American Negroes* (1931) and *Negro Poetry and Drama* (1937); J. Saunders Redding's *To Make a Poet Black* (1939); William H. Robinson's *Early Black American Poets* (1969); Jean Wagner's *Black Poets of the United States* (1973); Stephen Henderson's *Understanding the New Black Poetry: Black Speech and Black Music as Poetic References* (1973); *Black Sister: Poetry by Black American Women, 1746–1980* (1981), edited by Erlene Stetson; Mari Evans's *Black Women Writers, 1950–1980: A Critical Evaluation* (1984); D. H. Melham's *Heroism in the New Black Poetry: The Will and the Spirit* (1990); Fahamisha Patricia Brown's *Performing the Word: African-American Poetry as Vernacular Culture* (1999); *The Furious Flowering of African American Poetry* (1999), edited by Joanne V. Gabbin; *Reading Race in American Poetry: An Area of Act* (2000), edited by Aldon Lynn Nielsen; Lorenzo Thomas's *Extraordinary Measures: Afrocentric Modernism and Twentieth-Century American Poetry* (2000). Cheyl Clarke's *"After Mecca": Women Poets of the Black Arts Movement* (2005); and Lauri Ramey's *Slave Songs and the Birth of African American Poetry* (2008). Poetry has been collected in several anthologies and critical editions. Important studies include Joan R. Sherman's *Invisible Poets: Afro-Americans of the Nineteenth Century* (1989); *Collected Black Women's Poetry* (1988) in *The Schomburg Library of Nineteenth-Century Black Women Writers*; and *African-American Poetry of the Nineteenth Century: An Anthology* (1992). See also *The Garden Thrives: Twentieth-Century African-American Poetry* (1996), edited by Clarence Major.

For critical studies of drama and performance, see *The Theater of Black Americans: A Collection of Critical Essays* (1987), edited by Errol Hill; Leslie Catherine Sanders's *The Development of Black Theater in America: From Shadows to Selves* (1988); *Black Theatre and Performance: A Pan-African Bibliography* (1990), compiled by John Gray; Geneviève Fabre's *Drumbeats, Masks, and Metaphors: Contemporary Afro-American Theatre* (1993); Dana A. Williams's *Contemporary African American Female Playwrights: An Annotated Bibliography* (1998); *A Sourcebook of African-American Performance: Plays, People, Movements* (1999), edited by Annemarie Bean; Kimberly W. Benston's *Performing Blackness: Enactments of African-American Modernism*

(2000); and *African-American Performance and Theater History: A Critical Reader* (2001), edited by Harry J. Elam Jr. On drama from specific periods, see Daphne A. Brooks's *Bodies in Dissent: Spectacular Performances of Race and Freedom, 1850–1910* (2006); David Krasner's *A Beautiful Pageant: African American Theatre, Drama, and Performance in the Harlem Renaissance, 1910–1927* (2002); David Savran's *Highbrow/Lowbrow: Theater, Jazz, and the Making of the New Middle Class* (2010); *Black Theatre: Ritual Performance in the African Diaspora* (2002), edited by Paul Carter Harrison; Mance Williams's *Black Theatre in the 1960s and 1970s: A Historical-Critical Analysis of the Movement* (1985); and *Contemporary Black Men's Fiction and Drama* (2001), edited by Keith Clark; and Soyica Diggs Colbert's *The African American Theatrical Body: Reception, Performance, and the Stage* (2011).

Prose genres include the narrative, the novel, the short story, and the essay. Foremost in the narrative form are the slave narrative and the autobiography. For an understanding of the slave narrative and its place in the literary tradition, see *Great Slave Narratives* (1969), edited by Arna Wendell Bontemps; Robert B. Stepto's *From behind the Veil: A Study of Afro-American Narrative* (1979); Frances Smith Foster's *Witnessing Slavery: The Development of Ante-bellum Slave Narratives* (1994); *The Art of Slave Narrative: Original Essays in Criticism and Theory* (1982), edited by John Sekora and Darwin T. Turner; *The Slave's Narrative* (1990), edited by Charles T. Davis and Henry Louis Gates Jr.; *The Classic Slave Narratives* (1987), edited by Henry Louis Gates Jr.; *Pioneers of the Black Atlantic: Five Slave Narratives from the Enlightenment, 1772–1815* (1998), edited by Henry Louis Gates Jr. and William L. Andrews; *The Civitas Anthology of African American Slave Narratives* (1999), edited by William L. Andrews and Henry Louis Gates Jr.; Ashraf H. A. Rushdy's *Neo-slave Narratives: Studies in the Social Logic of a Literary Form* (1999); *Black Imagination and the Middle Passage* (1999), edited by Maria Diedrich, Henry Louis Gates Jr., and Carl Pedersen; *Incidents in the Life of a Slave Girl by Harriet Jacobs: Contexts and Criticism* (2001), edited by Nellie Y. McKay and Frances Smith Foster; *The Cambridge Companion to the African American Slave Narrative* (2007), edited by Audrey Fisch; and *Slave Narratives after Slavery* (2011), edited by William L. Andrews. On the development of the autobiographical tradition, see Stephen Butterfield's *Black Autobiography in America* (1974); William L. Andrews's *To Tell a Free Story: The First Century of Afro-American Autobiography, 1760–1865* (1986); *Sisters of the Spirit: Three Black Women's Autobiographies of the Nineteenth Century* (1986), edited by William L. Andrews; Mary Helen Washington's *Invented Lives* (1988); Joanne M. Braxton's *Black Women Writing Autobiography* (1989); *African American Autobiography: A Collection of Critical Essays* (1993), edited by William L. Andrews; and Frances Smith Foster's *Written by Herself: Literary Production of Early African American Women Writers* (1993). On the narrative tradition, see also *Journeys in New Worlds: Early American Women's Narratives* (1990), edited by William L. Andrews et al.; Joycelyn Moody's *Sentimental Confessions: Spiritual Narratives of Nineteenth-Century African American Women* (2001); Yolanda Pierce's *Hell without Fires: Slavery, Christianity, and the Antebellum Spiritual Narrative* (2005); and P. Gabrielle Foreman's *Activist Sentiments: Reading Black Women in the Nineteenth Century* (2009).

Studies of the African American novel include Vernon Loggins's *The Negro Author* (1931); Nick Aaron Ford's *The Contemporary Negro Novel: A Study in Race Relations* (1936); Sterling A. Brown's *The Negro in American Fiction* (1937); Hugh Gloster's *Negro Voices in American Fiction* (1948); Robert Bone's *The Negro Novel in America* (1965); Noel Schraufnagel's *From Apology to Protest: The Black American Novel* (1973); Bernard W. Bell's *The Afro-American Novel and Its Tradition* (1987); Thomas H. Nigel's *From Folklore to Fiction: A Study of Folk Heroes and Rituals in the Black American Novel* (1988); John Callahan's *In the African-American Grain: The Pursuit of Voice in Twentieth-Century Black Fiction* (1990); Farah Jasmine Griffin's *"Who Set You Flowin'?" The African-American Migration Narrative* (1995); J. Lee Greene's *Blacks in Eden: The African American Novel's First Century* (1996); Claudia Tate's *Psychoanalysis and Black Novels: Desire and the Protocols of Race* (1998); Lawrence R. Rodgers's *Canaan Bound: The African-American Great Migration Novel* (1997); and J. Lee Greene, *The Diasporan Self: Unbreaking the Circle in Western Black Novels* (2008). For the tradition in women's literature, see Barbara Christian's *Black Women Novelists* (1980); Hazel Carby's *Reconstructing Womanhood* (1987); Susan Willis's *Specifying: Black Women Writing the American Experience* (1987); Michael Awkward's *Inspiriting Influences: Tradition, Revision, and Afro-American Women's Novels* (1989); Karla F. C. Holloway's *Moorings and Metaphors: Figures of Culture and Gender in Black Women's Literature* (1992); and *The Schomburg Library of Nineteenth-Century Black Women Writers* (1988–91), edited by Henry Louis Gates Jr. et al. Madhu Dubey's *Black Women Novelists and the Nationalist Aesthetic* (1994); and Cheryl A. Wall's *Worrying the Line: Black Women Writers, Lineage, and Literary Tradition* (2005).

The shorter forms of prose include the short story and the essay. Studies in the short story are *The Black American Short Story in the 20th Century: A Collection of Critical*

Essays (1977), edited by Peter Bruck; Robert Bone's *Down Home: Origins of the Afro-American Short Story* (1988); and *The African American Short Story, 1970 to 1990: A Collection of Critical Essays* (1993), edited by Wolfgang Karrer and Barbara Puschmann-Nalenz. For the essay form, see Cheryl B. Butler's *The Art of the Black Essay: From Meditation to Transcendence* (2003). For the tradition in oratory, see *With Pen and Voice: A Critical Anthology of Nineteenth-Century African-American Women* (1995), edited by Shirley Wilson Logan.

Literary History

Guides to the literature include Blyden Jackson's *A History of Afro-American Literature* (1989); *The Oxford Companion to African American Literature* (1997), edited by William L. Andrews, Frances Smith Foster, and Trudier Harris, and their *The Concise Oxford Companion to African American Literature* (2001); and Dickson D. Bruce's *The Origins of African American Literature, 1680–1865* (2001). For critical issues affecting literary history, see Houston A. Baker's *Long Black Song: Essays in Black American Literature and Culture* (1972); Charles T. Davis's *Black Is the Color of the Cosmos: Essays on Afro-American Literature and Culture, 1942–1981* (1982), edited by Henry Louis Gates Jr.; *Redefining American Literary History* (1990), edited by LaVonne Brown Ruoff and Jerry W. Ward Jr.; Dickson D. Bruce's *Black American Writing from the Nadir: The Evolution of a Literary Tradition, 1877–1915* (1989); *The Black Columbiad: Defining Moments in African American Literature and Culture* (1994), edited by Werner Sollors and Maria Dietrich; and *Genius in Bondage: Literature of the Early Black Atlantic* (2001), edited by Vincent Carretta and Philip Gould. Excellent resources on authors and literary movements can also be found in the volumes edited by Trudier Harris and Thadious M. Davis in The Dictionary of Literary Biography series: *Afro-American Writers before the Harlem Renaissance*; *Afro-American Writers from the Harlem Renaissance to 1940*; *Afro-American Writers after 1955: Dramatists and Prose Writers*; and *Afro-American Poets since 1955*. See also *Black American Poets between Worlds, 1940–1960* (1986), edited by R. Baxter Miller; Lorraine Elena Roses and Ruth Elizabeth Randolph's *Harlem Renaissance and Beyond: Literary Biographies of 100 Black Women Writers, 1900–1945* (1990); Michel Fabre's *From Harlem to Paris: Black American Writers in France, 1840–1980* (1991); Elizabeth McHenry's *Forgotten Readers: Recovering the Lost History of African-American Literary Societies* (2002); and John Ernest's *Chaotic Justice: Rethinking African American Literary History* (2009).

Literary Theory and Criticism

An excellent overview of theory can be found in *African American Literary Theory: A Reader* (2000), edited by Winston Napier. For individual texts, see *Black Literature and Literary Theory* (1984), edited by Henry Louis Gates Jr.; Houston A. Baker Jr.'s *Blues, Ideology, and Afro-American Literature: A Vernacular Theory* (1984); *"Race," Writing, and Difference* (1986), edited by Henry Louis Gates Jr.; Henry Louis Gates Jr.'s *Figures in Black: Words, Signs, and the "Racial" Self* (1987) *The Signifying Monkey: A Theory of Afro-American Literary Criticism* (1988); and *Changing Our Own Words: Essays on Criticism, Theory, and Writing by Black Women* (1989), edited by Cheryl A. Wall; Sandra Adell's *Double-Consciousness/Double Bind: Theoretical Issues in Twentieth-Century Black Literature* (1994); and Hortense Spillers's *Black, White, and in Color: Essays on American Literature and Culture* (2003). Important texts for feminist criticism and theory include Barbara Smith's *Toward a Black Feminist Criticism* (1977); *Conjuring: Black Women, Fiction, and Literary Tradition* (1985), edited by Marjorie Pryse and Hortense J. Spillers; *Black Feminist Criticism and Critical Theory* (1989), edited by Joe Weixlmann and Houston A. Baker; *Reading Black, Reading Feminist: A Critical Anthology* (1990), edited by Henry Louis Gates Jr.; Houston A. Baker's *Workings of the Spirit: The Poetics of Afro-American Women's Writing* (1991); *Theorizing Black Feminisms: The Visionary Pragmatism of Black Women* (1993), edited by Stanlie M. James and Abena P. A. Busia; Deborah E. McDowell's *"The Changing Same": Black Women's Literature, Criticism, and Theory* (1995); Joyce Ann Joyce's *Warriors, Conjurers and Priests: Defining African-Centered Literary Criticism* (1994); Barbara Christian's *Black Feminist Criticism: Perspectives on Black Women Writers* (1997); *Female Subjects in Black and White: Race, Psychoanalysis, Feminism* (1997), edited by Elizabeth Abel, Barbara Christian, and Helene Moglen; *African American Literary Criticism, 1773 to 2000* (1999), edited by Hazel Arnett Ervin; *The Black Feminist Reader* (2000), edited by Joy James and T. Denean Sharpley-Whiting; Gina Wisker's *Post-Colonial and African American Women's Writing: A Critical Introduction* (2000); and *Black Feminist Cultural Criticism* (2001), edited by Jacqueline Bobo.

A wide range of critical approaches to African American literature and culture can be found in the numerous critical texts and collections of essays of recent decades. Excellent collections include *Within the Circle: An Anthology of African American Literary Criticism from the Harlem Renaissance to the Present* (1994), edited by Angelyn Mitchell; *Literary Influence and African-American Writers: Collected Essays* (1996), edited by Tracy Mishkin; Ross Posnock's *Color & Culture: Black Writers and the Making of the Modern Intellectual* (1998); and Robert E. Washington's *The Ideologies of African American Lit-*

erature from the Harlem Renaissance to the Black Nationalist Revolt: A Sociology of Literature Perspective (2001). For critical studies of nineteenth-century literature, see Slavery and the Literary Imagination (1989), edited by Deborah E. McDowell and Arnold Rampersad; Houston A. Baker's Long Black Song: Essays in Black American Literature and Culture (1990); Claudia Tate's Domestic Allegories of Political Desire: The Black Heroine's Text at the Turn of the Century (1992); The Culture of Sentiment: Race, Gender, and Sentimentality in Nineteenth-Century America (1992), edited by Shirley Samuels; Eric J. Sundquist's To Wake the Nations: Race in the Making of American Literature (1993); and John Ernest's Resistance and Reformation in Nineteenth-Century African-American Literature (1995).

The literary period popularly known as the Harlem Renaissance has generated tremendous scholarly interest, as the sheer volume of critical work attests. For a sense of the culture and politics of the period, see James Weldon Johnson's Black Manhattan (1930); Claude McKay's Harlem: Negro Metropolis (1940); The Harlem Renaissance Remembered: Essays (1984), edited by Arna Bontemps; David Levering Lewis's When Harlem Was in Vogue (1997); and George Hutchinson's The Harlem Renaissance in Black and White (1985). See as well Steven Watson's Circles of the Twentieth Century: The Harlem Renaissance (1995); Cary D. Winty's Black Culture and the Harlem Renaissance (1988); Carole Marks and Diana Edkins's The Power of Pride: Stylemakers and Rulebreakers of the Harlem Renaissance (1999); and Remember Me to Harlem: The Letters of Langston Hughes and Carl Van Vechten, 1925–1964 (2001), edited by Emily Bernard. The anthology The New Negro: Readings on Race, Representation, and African American Culture, 1892–1938 (2007) edited by Henry Louis Gates and Gene Andrew Jarrett, provides a history of the key metaphor of the period. Jonathan Gill's Harlem: The Four Hundred Year History from Dutch Village to Capital of Black America (2012) is an invaluable general history. For the central place Harlem holds in African American culture, see Harlem on My Mind: Cultural Capital of Black America, 1900–1968 (1995), edited by Allon Schoener, from the 1968 Metropolitan Museum of Art exhibition, and Sharifa Rhodes-Pitts's Harlem is Nowhere: A Journey to the Mecca of Black America (2011).

There is a large body of work on political currents in Harlem during the period. On the flourishing of radicalism, especially among Caribbean migrants, see Winston James's Holding Aloft the Banner of Ethiopia: Caribbean Radicalism in Early Twentieth Century America (1999); Joyce Moore Turner's Caribbean Crusaders and the Harlem Renaissance

(2005); Theodore Kornweibel's No Crystal Stair: Black Life and the "Messenger," 1917–1928 (1976); William J. Maxwell's New Negro, Old Left: African American Writing and Communism between the Wars (1999); James Smethurst's The New Red Negro: The Literary Left and African American Poetry, 1930–1946 (1999); and Barbara Foley's Spectres of 1919: Class and Nation in the Making of the New Negro (2008). Anthologies of political writing from the period include Voices of a Black Nation: Political Journalism in the Harlem Renaissance (1990), edited by Theodore G. Vincent; and African Fundamentalism: A Literary and Cultural Anthology of Garvey's Harlem Renaissance (1991), edited by Tony Martin.

As many historians have pointed out, the cultural forces of the period were not restricted to New York; work extending to other locations includes Davarian L. Baldwin's Chicago's New Negroes: Modernity, the Great Migration, and Black Urban Life (2007); The Muse in Bronzeville: African American Creative Expression in Chicago, 1932–1950 (2011) by Robert Bone and Richard A. Courage; The Black Chicago Renaissance, edited by Darlene Clark Hine and John McCluskey Jr. (2012); Adam McKible's edition of a serialized novel from the 1920s written by Edward Christopher Williams, When Washington Was in Vogue: A Lost Novel of the Harlem Renaissance (2005); and The Harlem Renaissance in the American West (2011), edited by Cary D. Wintz and Bruce A. Glasrud. Considerations of the international contours of the Harlem Renaissance include Kate A. Baldwin's Beyond the Color Line and the Iron Curtain: Reading Encounters between Black and Red, 1922–1963 (2002); Brent Hayes Edwards's The Practice of Diaspora: Literature, Translation, and the Rise of Black Internationalism (2003); and Michelle Ann Stephens's Black Empire: The Masculine Global Imaginary of Caribbean Intellectuals in the United States, 1914–1962 (2005). There is a great deal of work on links and parallels between the Harlem Renaissance and the Caribbean in particular, such as "Look for Me All Around You": Anglophone Caribbean Immigrants in the Harlem Renaissance, edited by Louis J. Parascandola (2005); Jennifer M. Wilks's Race, Gender, & Comparative Black Modernism: Suzanne Lacascade, Marita Bonner, Suzanne Césaire, Dorothy West (2008); Frank Andre Guridy's Forging Diaspora: Afro-Cubans and African Americans in a World of Empire and Jim Crow (2010); Antonio Lopez's Unbecoming Blackness: The Diaspora Cultures of Afro-Cuban America (2012); and Vera M. Kutzinski's The Worlds of Langston Hughes: Modernism and Translation in the Americas (2012).

Studies of popular culture, sexuality, and performance during the Harlem Renaissance include Jayna Brown's Babylon Girls: Black Women Performers and the Shaping of the Modern (2008); Shane Vogel's The Scene of

Harlem Cabaret: Race, Sexuality, Performance (2009); Erin D. Chapman's Prove It On Me: New Negroes, Sex, and Popular Culture in the 1920s (2012); and James F. Wilson's Bulldaggers, Pansies, and Chocolate Babies: Performance, Race, and Sexuality in the Harlem Renaissance (2011). As for African American visual art during the period, one should consult the important exhibition catalogues Harlem Renaissance: Art of Black America (1987); and Rhapsodies in Black: Art of the Harlem Renaissance (1997), ed. Richard J. Powell and David A. Bailey; as well as monographs such as Amy Helene Kirschke's Aaron Douglas: Art, Race, and the Harlem Renaissance (1995); Theresa A. Leininger-Miller's New Negro Artists in Paris: African American Painters and Sculptors in the City of Light, 1922–1934 (2001); Kirschke's Art in Crisis: W. E. B. Du Bois and the Struggle for African American Identity and Memory (2007); and Caroline Goeser's Picturing the New Negro: Harlem Renaissance Print Culture and Modern Black Identity (2007).

For retrospective critical assessments of the period, the 1996 volumes edited by Cary D. Wintz are excellent: Remembering the Harlem Renaissance; The Emergence of the Harlem Renaissance; The Politics and Aesthetics of "New Negro" Literature; The Critics and the Harlem Renaissance; Black Writers Interpret the Harlem Renaissance; Analysis and Assessment, 1940–1979; and Analysis and Assessment, 1980–1994. See also Houston A. Baker's Modernism and the Harlem Renaissance (1987) and Afro-American Poetics: Revisions of Harlem and the Black Aesthetic (1988); The Harlem Renaissance: Revaluations (1989), edited by Amritjit Singh, William S. Shiver, and Stanley Brodwin; James De Jongh's Vicious Modernism: Black Harlem and the Literary Imagination (1990); Craig Hansen Werner's Playing the Changes: From Afro-Modernism to the Jazz Impulses (1994); Harlem Renaissance Re-Examined (1997), edited by Victor A. Kramer and Robert A. Russ; Temples for Tomorrow: Looking Back at the Harlem Renaissance (2001), edited by Geneviève Fabre and Michel Feith; The Cambridge Companion to the Harlem Renaissance, edited by George Hutchinson (2007); and The Harlem Renaissance Revisited, edited by Jeffrey O. G. Debar (2010).

On the Harlem Renaissance writers, reference works include Margaret Perry's The Harlem Renaissance: An Annotated Bibliography and Commentary (1982); Afro-American Writers from the Harlem Renaissance to 1940 (1987), edited by Trudier Harris; the Dictionary of Literary Biography series; and Marie E. Rodgers's The Harlem Renaissance: An Annotated Reference Guide for Student Research (1998). An invaluable resource for all things Harlem is The Harlem Renaissance: A Historical Dictionary for the Era (1984), edited by Bruce Kellner. See also Charles Scruggs's The Sage in Harlem: H. L. Mencken and the Black Writers of the 1920s (1984); John Earl Bassett's Harlem in Review: Critical Reactions to Black American Writers, 1917–1939 (1992); Black American Prose Writers of the Harlem Renaissance (1994) and Black American Poets and Dramatists of the Harlem Renaissance (1995), both edited by Harold Bloom; Cheryl A. Wall's Women of the Harlem Renaissance (1995); Harlem's Glory: Black Women Writing, 1900–1950 (1996), edited by Lorraine Elena Roses and Ruth Elizabeth Randolph; and Melvin Beaunorus Tolson's The Harlem Group of Negro Writers (2001), edited by Edward J. Muller.

Important studies of Harlem Renaissance writers include Gloria T. Hull's Color, Sex and Poetry: Three Women Writers of the Harlem Renaissance (1987); Jon Woodson's To Make a New Race: Gurdjieff, Toomer, and the Harlem Renaissance (1999); Steven C. Tracy's Langston Hughes & the Blues (2001); and Sharon L. Jones's Rereading the Harlem Renaissance: Race, Class, and Gender in the Fiction of Jessie Fauset, Zora Neale Hurston, and Dorothy West (2002). See also Arnold Rampersad's The Art and Imagination of W. E. B. Du Bois (1990). Harlem Renaissance anthologies include Shadowed Dreams: Women's Poetry of the Harlem Renaissance (1989), edited by Maureen Honey; The Sleeper Wakes: Harlem Renaissance Stories by Women (1993), edited by Marcy Knopf; Classic Fiction of the Harlem Renaissance (1994), edited by William L. Andrews; Voices from the Harlem Renaissance (1994), edited by Nathan Irvin Huggins; The Portable Harlem Renaissance Reader (1995), edited by David Levering Lewis; "Double-Take": A Revisionist Harlem Renaissance Anthology (2001), edited by Venetria K. Patton and Maureen Honey; Lost Plays of the Harlem Renaissance, 1920–1940 (1996), edited by James V. Hatch and Leo Hamalian; and Gay Voices of the Harlem Renaissance (2003), edited by A. B. Christa Schwarz.

Important critical issues in literature are examined in several works. For conjunctions of identities, see Comparative American Identities: Race, Sex, and Nationality in the Modern Text, (1991), edited by Hortense J. Spillers; Subjects and Citizens: Nation, Race, and Gender from Oroonoko to Anita Hill (1995), edited by Michael Moon and Cathy N. Davidson; Werner Sollors's Neither Black nor White yet Both: Thematic Explorations of Interracial Literature (1999); Separate Spheres No More: Gender Convergence in American Literature, 1830–1930 (2000), edited by Monika M. Elbert; Mia Bay's The White Image in the Black Mind (2000); and Race and the Archaeology of Identity (2001), edited by Charles E. Orser Jr. Cultural history is examined in Afro-American Literary Study in the 1990s (1989), edited by Houston A. Baker Jr. and Patricia Redmond; History and Memory in African-

American Culture (1994), edited by Geneviève Fabre and Robert O'Meally; and The African Diaspora: African Origins and New World Identities (1999), edited by Isidore Okpewho, Carole Boyce Davies, and Ali A. Mazrui. Critical studies of literary history include several works by Houston A. Baker Jr.: The Journey Back: Issues in Black Literature and Criticism (1980); Afro-American Poetics: Revisions of Harlem and the Black Aesthetic (1988); Turn-

ing South Again: Re-Thinking Modernism/Re-Reading Booker T. (2001); and Critical Memory: Public Spheres, African American Writing, and Black Fathers and Sons in America (2001). See also Recovering the Black Female Body: Self-Representations by African American Women (2001), edited by Michael Bennett and Vanessa D. Dickerson; and Trudier Harris-Lopez's South of Tradition: Essays on African American Literature (2002).

THE VERNACULAR TRADITION

Studies of the African American vernacular have been many and varied; most refer to this area either as "folklore" or as "popular culture." (This anthology prefers "vernacular" because it is relatively free of the baggage associated with other terms, and because certain vernacular forms, such as jazz, should not be categorized as "folk" expression.) Some of the most outstanding general studies of the field are Alan Dundes, ed., Mother Wit from the Laughing Barrel: Readings in the Interpretation of Afro-American Folklore (1977); Lawrence Levine, Black Culture and Black Consciousness (1977); Roger Abrahams and John Szwed, eds., After Africa (1983); Sterling Stuckey, Slave Culture: Nationalist Theory and the Foundations of Black America (1987); and Roger Abrahams, Singing the Master (1992). For a general introduction to the meaning of vernacular materials, see also Melville Herskovitz's The Myth of the Negro Past (1941); Robert F. Thompson's Flash of the Spirit: African and Afro-American Art and Philosophy (1983); John Michael Vlatch's The Afro-American Tradition in Decorative Arts (1990); Nathaniel Mackey's Discrepant Engagement: Dissonance, Cross-Culturality, and Experimental Writing (1993); Ralph Ellison's The Collected Essays of Ralph Ellison (1995); Jacqui Malone's Steppin' on the Blues: The Visible Rhythms of African American Dance (1996); A Son's Return: Selected Essays of Sterling A. Brown (1996); Robin D.G. Kelley's Yo' Mama's Disfunktional !: Fighting the Culture Wars in Urban America (1998), Brent Edwards's The Practice of Diaspora: Literature, Translation and the Rise of Black Internationalism (2003), and Guthrie P. Ramsey's Race Music: Black Cultures from Bebop to Hip-Hop (Music of the African Diaspora) (2004). Useful reference books for tracking down data concerning the vernacular include John Szwed and Roger Abrahams, eds., Afro-American Folk Culture: An Annotated Bibliography (1978); William R. Ferris Jr., ed., Encyclopedia of Southern Culture (1989); and Jack Salzman, Cornel West, and David L. Smith, eds., Encyclopedia of African American History and Culture (1995).

For information concerning spirituals and gospel music, James Weldon Johnson and J. Rosamond Johnson's Book of American Negro Spirituals (1925–26) is indispensable. Also important are W. E. B. Du Bois's Souls of Black Folk (1903), particularly the chapter "The Sorrow Songs"; Howard W. Odum and Guy B. Johnson's The Negro and His Songs (1925); Bernard Katz's The Social Implications of Early Negro Music in the United States (1969); Tony Heilbut's Gospel Sound (1971); John Lovell's The Forge and the Flame (1972); James Cone's Spirituals and the Blues (1972); Howard Thurman's Deep River and the Negro Spiritual Speaks of Life and Death (1975); Eileen Southern's Music of Black Americans (3rd ed., 1997); and Willis James's Stars in de Elements: A Study of Negro Folk Music (1995). Michael W. Harris's Rise of Gospel Blues: The Music of Thomas Andrew Dorsey (1992) is an extremely useful study of this music and one of its major composers. Charles Molesworth's edition of The Works of Alain Locke (2012) also should be consulted. A key both for musical examples and for analysis is Bernice Johnson Reagon's 4-CD set called Wade in the Water (1997)

For an overview of jazz, consult Marshall W. Stearns's Story of Jazz (1956); Gunther Schuller's Early Jazz (1968) and The Swing Era (1989); Jazz 101: A Complete Guide to Learning and Loving Jazz (2000); and Jazz, by Gary Giddins and Scott DeVeaux (2009). The most reliable books on the meaning of the music are Amiri Baraka (LeRoi Jones)'s Blues People (1963); Albert Murray's Stomping the Blues (1976); Martin Williams's Jazz Tradition (1983); Robert G. O'Meally's The Jazz Cadence of American Culture (1998); Living With Music: Ralph Ellison's Jazz Writings (2002); and Brent Hayes Edwards, Farah Jasmine Griffin, and Robert G. O'Meally, Uptown Conversation: The New Jazz Studies, (2004). Consult also these autobiographies: Billie Holiday's Lady Sings the Blues (1956), Sidney Bechet's Treat it Gentle (1964), Willie "the Lion" Smith's Music on My Mind (1964), Duke Ellington's Music Is My Mistress (1973), and Dizzy Gillespie's To Be or Not to Bop (1979). See also John F. Szwed's

Space is the Place: The Lives of Sun Ra (1997), Salim Washington and Farah Jasmine Griffin's *Miles Davis, John Coltrane, and the Greatest Jazz Collaboration Ever* (2008), Robin D.G. Kelley's *Thelonious Monk: The Life and Times of an American Original* (2009), George Lewis's *A Power Stronger Than Itself: The AACM and American Experimental Music* (2009), and *African Rhythms: The Autobiography of Randy Weston* (2010).

Students of rhythm and blues should consult Nelson George's *The Death of Rhythm and Blues* (1988); Philip Ennis's *The Seventh Stream: The Emergence of Rock 'n' roll in American Popular Music* (1992); and Jacqui Malone's *Class Act: The Jazz Life of Choreographer Cholly Atkins* (2003)

The best studies of hip hop culture are Tricia Rose's *Black Noise* (1993); Bakari Kitwana's *Hip Hop Generation: Young Blacks and the Crisis in African-American Culture* (2002), Jeff Chang's *Can't Stop Won't Stop: A History of the Hip-Hop Generation* (2005); Adam Bradley's *Book of Rhymes: The Poetics of Hip-Hop*; Sujatha Fernandes's *Close to the Edge: In Search of the Global Hip Hop Generation* (2011), and Jay-Z's *Decoded* (2011). See also Michael E. Veal's *Dub: Soundscapes & Shattered Songs in Jamaican Reggae* (2007)

For studies of black sermons and prayers, consult James Weldon Johnson's *God's Trombones* (1927), Zora Neale Hurston's *Sanctified Church* (1983), Gerald L. Davis's *I Got the Word in Me and I Can Sing It, You Know* (1985), and James Melvin Washington's *Conversations with God* (1994). See also Charles V. Hamilton's *Black Preacher in America* (1972).

REALISM, NATURALISM, MODERNISM, 1940–1960

James Baldwin

Baldwin's novels are *Go Tell It on the Mountain* (1953), *Giovanni's Room* (1956), *Another Country* (1962), *Tell Me How Long the Train's Been Gone* (1968), *If Beale Street Could Talk* (1974), and *Just above My Head* (1979). Baldwin published a short story collection, *Going to Meet the Man* (1965). His essays and other nonfiction are collected in *The Price of the Ticket* (1985). He wrote two plays: *Blues for Mr. Charlie* (1964) and *The Amen Corner* (1968).

James Campbell's *Talking at the Gates: A Life of James Baldwin* (1991) is a recent biography. Critical treatments of Baldwin include Fern Maria Eckman's *The Furious Passage of James Baldwin* (1966); Horace A. Porter's *Stealing the Fire: The Art and Protest of James Baldwin* (1989); Quincy Troupe's *James Baldwin: The Legacy* (1989); Tracey Sherard's "Sonny's Bebop: Baldwin's 'Blues Text' as Intracultural Critique," *African American Review* 32 (1998); Katharine Larence Balfour's *The Evidence of Things Not Said: James Baldwin and the Promise of American Democracy* (2001), and Magdalena J. Zaborowska's *James Baldwin's Turkish Decade: Erotics of Exile* (2008). Collections of critical essays are Harold Bloom, ed., *James Baldwin* (1986); Fred L. Stanley and Nancy V. Burt, eds., *Critical Essays on James Baldwin* (1988); Jakob Kollhofer, ed., *James Baldwin: His Place in American Literary History and His Reception in Europe* (1991); Dwight A. McBride, ed., *James Baldwin Now* (1999); and D. Quentin Miller, ed., *Re-viewing James Baldwin: Things Not Seen* (2000); and Cora Kaplan and Bill Schwarz (eds.), *James Baldwin: America and Beyond* (2011).

Gwendolyn Brooks

Volumes of poetry by Brooks include *A Street in Bronzeville* (1945), *Annie Allen* (1949), *Bronzeville Boys and Girls* (1956), *The Bean Eaters* (1960), *Selected Poems* (1963), *In the Mecca* (1968), *Family Pictures* (1970), *Riot* (1970), *Aloneness* (1971), *Beckonings* (1975), *Primer for Blacks* (1981), and *To Disembark* (1981). Brooks's prose works include *Maud Martha* (1953, 1974); the autobiographical *Report from Part One* (1972); and *Report from Part Two* (1996); "Keziah," *TriQuarterly* 75 (1989); and "45 Years in Culture and Creative Writing; Many Talented New Voices Have Emerged to Comment on Our Complex Turbulent Times," *Ebony* 46 (1990). *The World of Gwendolyn Brooks* (1971) and *Blacks* (1987, 1991) are collections of her poetry and prose. Brooks edited *A Broadside Treasury* (1971), *Jump Bad: A New Chicago Anthology* (1971), and *A Capsule Course in Black Poetry Writing* (1975) as well as the short-lived journal *The Black Position* in 1971.

General critical and biographical information on Brooks can be found in R. Baxter Miller's *Langston Hughes and Gwendolyn Brooks: A Reference Guide* (1978); Harry B. Shaw's *Gwendolyn Brooks* (1980); Brian Lanker and Maya Angelou's "I Dream a World," *National Geographic* 176 (1989); and Martha Satch's "Honest Reporting: An Interview with Gwendolyn Brooks," *Southwest Review* 74 (1989).

Recent critical considerations of Brooks's work include Mary Helen Washington's "Taming All That Anger Down: Rage and Silence in Gwendolyn Brooks' Maud Martha," *Massachusetts Review* 24 (1983); Hortense J. Spillers's "'An Order of Constancy': Notes on Brooks and the Feminine," *The Centennial Review* 29 (1985); Charles Whitaker's "Gwendolyn Brooks—A Poet for All Ages," *Ebony* 42 (1987); John C. Gruesser's "Afro-American Travel Literature and Africanist Discourse," *Black American Literature Forum* 24 (1990);

Ann Folwell Stanford's "Dialectics of Desire: War and the Resistive Voice in Gwendolyn Brooks's 'Negro Hero' and 'Gay Chaps at the Bar,'" *African American Review* 26 (1992); Henry Taylor's "Gwendolyn Brooks: An Essential Sanity," *The Kenyon Review* 13 (1991); Ann Folwell Stanford's "'Like narrow banners for some gathering war': Readers, Aesthetics, and Gwendolyn Brooks's 'The Sundays of Satin-Legs Smith,'" *College Literature* 17 (1990); Gertrude Reif Hughes's "Making It Really New: Hilda Doolittle, Gwendolyn Brooks, and the Feminist Potential of Modern Poetry," *American Quarterly* 42 (1990); Malin Lavon Walther's "Re-Wrighting *Native Son*: Gwendolyn Brooks's Domestic Aesthetic in *Maud Martha*," *Tulsa Studies in Women's Literature* 13 (1994); Brooke Kenton Horvath's "The Satisfactions of What's Difficult in Gwendolyn Brooks's Poetry," *American Literature* 62 (1990); and Richard Flynn's "'The Kindergarten of New Consciousness': Gwendolyn Brooks and the Social Construction of Childhood," *African American Review* 34 (2000).

Book-length considerations of Brooks's work include Maria K. Mootry and Gary Smith's *A Life Distilled: Gwendolyn Brooks, Her Poetry and Fiction* (1987), D. H. Melhem's *Gwendolyn Brooks: Poetry and the Heroic Voice* (1987), George E. Kent's *A Life of Gwendolyn Brooks* (1990), Susan Marie Schweik's *A Gulf So Deeply Cut: American Women Poets and the Second World War* (1991), and Barbara Jean Bolden's *Urban Rage in Bronzeville: Social Commentary in the Poetry of Gwendolyn Brooks, 1945–1960* (1999). See also Stephen Caldwell Wright, ed., *On Gwendolyn Brooks: Reliant Contemplation* (2001).

Alice Childress

Higashada, Cheryl. *Black International Feminism: Women Writers of the Black Left, 1994–1995*. Urbana: University of Illinois, 2011. Perkins, Kathy. ed. *Selected Plays of Alice Childress*. Evanston, Illinois: Northwestern University Press. Washington, Mary Helen. "Alice Childress, Lorraine Hansberry, and Claudia Jones: Black Women Write the Popular Front" in James Smethurst, ed. *Left of the Color Line: Race, Radicalism, and Twentieth Century Literature of the United States*. Chapel Hill: University of North Carolina Press, 2012.

Ralph Ellison

Ellison's works include *Invisible Man* (1952); *Flying Home* (1990); *Juneteenth* (1999); and two collections of essays, *Shadow and Act* (1964) and *Going to the Territory* (1986).

Biographies of Ellison include Lawrence Jackson's *Ralph Ellison: Emergence of Genius* (2002) and Arnold Rampersad's *Ralph Ellison: A Biography* (2007). Book-length treatments of Ellison's work include Robert G. O'Meally's *The Craft of Ralph Ellison* (1980), Robert N. List's *Dedalus in Harlem: The Joyce-Ellison Connection* (1982), Alan Nadel's *Invisible Criticism: Ralph Ellison and the American Canon* (1988), Kerry McSweeney's *Invisible Man: Race and Identity* (1988), Jerry Gafio Watts's *The Black Intellectual: Ralph Ellison, Politics, and Afro-American Intellectual Life* (1994). John F. Callahan's *Ellison's Invisible Man* (2001), and Jerry Gafio Watts's *Heroism and the Black Intellectual: Ralph Ellison, Politics, and Afro-American Intellectual Life* (1994). Some collections of essays are John Hersey, ed., *Ralph Ellison: A Collection of Critical Essays* (1974); Harold Bloom, ed., *Ralph Ellison: Modern Critical Views* (1986); John M. Reilly, ed., *Twentieth Century Interpretations of* Invisible Man (1970); Robert G. O'Meally, ed., *New Essays on* Invisible Man (1988), Kimberly W. Benston, ed., *Speaking for You: The Vision of Ralph Ellison* (1987), and Robert J. Butler, ed., *The Critical Response to Ralph Ellison* (2002).

Lorraine Hansberry

A Raisin in the Sun (1959) and *The Sign in Sidney Brustein's Window* (1965) are available in a paperback edited by Robert Nemiroff. Also edited by Nemiroff is *Lorraine Hansberry: The Collected Last Plays* (1983), which contains *Les Blancs, The Drinking Gourd*, and *What Use Are Flowers?* Hansberry wrote the text for a photohistory, *The Movement: Documentary of a Struggle for Equality* (1964); notable among her essays is "The Negro Writer and His Roots," *Black Scholar* 12 (1981).

To Be Young, Gifted and Black: Lorraine Hansberry in Her Own Words (1969), edited by Nemiroff, contains biographical material; Nemiroff produced a play with this title. Elizabeth C. Phillips's, *The Works of Lorraine Hansberry* appeared in 1973. Anne Cheney's *Lorraine Hansberry* (1984) is a worthwhile biography. Critical discussions include Harold Cruse's *The Crisis of the Negro Intellectual* (1967), Steven R. Carter's *Hansberry's Drama: Commitment Amid Complexity* (1991), and Lloyd W. Brown's "Lorraine Hansberry as Ironist," *Journal of Black Studies* 4 (1974). Important essays by James Baldwin, Nikki Giovanni, Alex Haley, Adrienne Rich, and Margaret B. Wilkerson appear in *Lorraine Hansberry: Art of Thunder, Vision of Light*, a special issue of *Freedomways* 4 (1979), edited by Jean Carey Bond. More recent essays are Steven R. Carter's "Commitment amid Complexity: Lorraine Hansberry's Life-in-Action," *MELUS* 7 (1980), and "Images of Men in Lorraine Hansberry's Writing," *Black American Literature Forum* 19 (1985); Joy L. Abell's "African/American: Lorraine Hansberry's *Les Blancs* and the American Civil Rights Movement," *African American Review* 35 (2001); and Thelma J. Shinn's "Living the Answer: The Emergence of African American Feminist Drama," *Studies in the Humanities* 17 (1990). Dean Peerman's "*A Raisin in the Sun*: The Uncut Version," *The Christian Century* 25

(1989), discusses material cut from the original production of the play. See also Margaret Wilkerson's "*A Raisin in the Sun:* Anniversary of an American Classic," *Theatre Journal* 38 (1986), and Richard M. Leeson's *Lorraine Hansberry: A Research and Production Sourcebook* (1997).

Robert Hayden

The standard collection of Hayden's poetry is *Collected Poems* (1985), edited by Frederick Glaysher. A large collection of Hayden's poems that reprinted works from earlier volumes, *A Ballad of Remembrance* (1962), was revised and published in 1966 as *Selected Poems.* Individual volumes of poetry include *Heart-Shape in the Dust: Poems* (1940), *The Lion and the Archer: Poems* (1948), *Figure of Time* (1955), *Words in the Mourning Time: Poems* (1970), *The Night-Blooming Cereus* (1972), *Angle of Ascent: New and Selected Poems* (1975), and *American Journal* (1978, 1982). His prose is collected in *Collected Prose: Poets on Poetry* (1984). Among the numerous anthologies Hayden edited are *Kaleidoscope: Poems by American Negro Poets* (1967); *Afro-American Literature: An Introduction* (1971), edited with David J. Burrows and Frederick Lapides; *American Models: A Collection of Modern Stories* (1973), edited with James E. Miller Jr. and Robert O'Neal; *Person, Place and Point of View: Factual Prose for Interpretation and Extension* (1974); and *The Human Condition: Literature Written in the English Language* (1974). Hayden published two surveys of American poetry in the 1970s: "A Portfolio of Recent American Poems," *World Order* 5 (1971), and "Recent American Poetry—Portfolio II," *World Order* 9 (1975). He also wrote the introduction to the *Counterpoise Series* (1948) and the preface to the 1968 edition of Alain Locke's *The New Negro.*

Biographical information on Hayden can be found in Fred M. Fetrow's *Robert Hayden* (1984). Critical consideration of Hayden's work includes Xavier Nicholas's "Robert Hayden: Some Introductory Notes," *Michigan Quarterly Review* 31 (1992); Ann M. Gallagher's "Hayden's 'Those Winter Sundays,'" *The Explicator* 51 (1993); Alan Shapiro's "In Praise of the Impure: Narrative Consciousness in Poetry," *TriQuarterly* 81 (1991); Fred M. Fetrow's "Minority Reporting and Psychic Distancing in the Poetry of Robert Hayden," *CLA Journal* 33 (1989); Michael Collins's "On the Track of the Universal: 'Middle Passage' and America," *Parnassus: Poetry in Review* 17 (1992); Xavier Nicholas's "Robert Hayden and Michael Harper: A Literary Friendship," *Callaloo* 17 (1994); Brian Conniff's "Answering 'The Waste Land': Robert Hayden and the Rise of the African American Poetic Sequence," *African American Review* 33 (1999); and Frank Rashid's "Robert Hayden's Detroit Blues Elegies," *Callaloo* 24 (2001). Book-length treatments of Hayden's work include John Hatcher's

From the Auroral Darkness: The Life and Poetry of Robert Hayden (1984), Pontheolla T. Williams's *Robert Hayden: A Critical Analysis of His Poetry* (1987); see also Laurence Goldstein and Robert Chrisman, eds., *Robert Hayden: Essays on the Poetry* (2001).

Chester B. Himes

Himes wrote fifteen novels, among them *If He Hollers Let Him Go* (1945), *Lonely Crusade* (1947), *Third Generation* (1954), *The Primitive* (1955), *Cast the First Stone* (1955), *For Love of Imabelle* (1957), *Pinktoes* (1961), and *Cotton Comes to Harlem* (1965). His autobiographies, *The Quality of Hurt* and *My Life of Absurdity*, were published in 1972 and 1976, respectively.

Recent biographies include Michel Fabre and Edward Margolies's *The Several Lives of Chester Himes* (1997), and James Sallis's *Chester Himes: A Life* (2000); see also Michel Fabre and Robert E. Skinner, eds., *Conversations with Chester Himes* (1995). Critical discussions include Stephen F. Milliken's *Chester Himes: A Critical Appraisal* (1976); Edward Margolies's "The Thrillers of Chester Himes," *Studies in Black Literature* 1 (1970); David Ikard's "Love Jones: A Black Male Feminist Critique of Chester Himes's *If He Hollers Let Him Go* Source," *African American Review* 36 (2002); and Charles L. P. Silet's edited *The Critical Response to Chester Himes* (1999). Very informative is a chapter on Himes in Michel Fabre's *From Harlem to Paris: Black American Writers in Paris* (1991).

Bob Kaufman

Kaufman's work includes the broadside "Abomunisto Manifesto" (1959) and the books *Solitudes Crowded with Loneliness* (1965), *Golden Sardine* (1967), and *The Ancient Rain: Poems 1956–1978* (1981). Mel Clay's *Jazz—Jail and God: Bob Kaufman: An Impressionistic Biography* (1987) is a worthwhile biography. Critical studies include Kathryne V. Lindberg's "Bob Kaufman, Sir Real, and His Rather Surreal Self-Presentation," *Talisman* 11 (1993); Barbara Christian's "Whatever Happened to Bob Kaufman?" in *Beats: Essays in Criticism* (1981), edited by Lee Bartlett; Kush's "The Duende of Bob Kaufman," *Third Rail* 8 (1987); Maria Damon's edited "Bob Kaufman: A Special Section," *Callaloo* 25.1 (2002); and Lorenzo Thomas's "'Communicating by Horns': Jazz and Redemption in the Poetry of the Beats and the Black Arts Movement," *African American Review* 26 (1992).

Ann Petry

Petry's novels are *The Street* (1946), *Country Place* (1947), and *The Narrows* (1953). She's also published *Miss Muriel and Other Stories* (1971) as well as four children's books: *The Drugstore Cat* (1949), *Harriet Tubman: Conductor of the Underground Railway* (1955), *Tituba of Salem Village* (1988), and *Legends of the Saints* (1964).

Hilary Holladay's *Ann Petry* (1996) is a worthwhile biography. Critical discussion of Petry includes George R. Adams's "Riot as Ritual: Ann Petry's *In Darkness and Confusion,*" *Negro Literature Forum* 6 (1968); Vernon E. Lattin's "Ann Petry and the American Dream," *Black American Literature Forum* 12 (1978); Margaret McDowell's "*The Narrows:* A Fuller View of Ann Petry," *Black American Literature Forum* 14 (1980); Thelma Shinn's "Women in the Novels of Ann Petry," *Critique* 16 (1984); Gladys J. Washington's "A World Made Cunningly: A Closer Look at Ann Petry's Fiction," *CLA Journal* 30 (1986); Sybil Weir's "*The Narrows:* A Black New England Novel," *Studies in American Fiction* 15 (1987); Lindon Barrett's "(Further) Figures of Violence: The Street in the U.S. Landscape," in his *Blackness and Value: Seeing Double* (1999); Keith Clark's "A Distaff Dream Defered? Ann Petry and the Art of Subversion," *African American Review* 26 (1992); Carol E. Henderson's "The 'Walking Wounded': Rethinking Black Women's Identity in Ann Petry's *The Street,*" *Modern Fiction Studies* 46 (2000); and Richard Yarborough's "The Quest for the American Dream in Three Afro-American Novels: *If He Hollers Let Him Go, The Street,* and *Invisible Man,*" *MELUS* 8 (1981).

Melvin B. Tolson

Tolson's poetry includes *Libretto for the Republic of Liberia* (1953), *Harlem Gallery: Book I, The Curator* (1965), and *A Gallery of Harlem Portraits* (1979). His other major works are *Rendezvous with America* (1944), and *Caviar and Cabbage: Selected Columns by Melvin B. Tolson from the* Washington Tribune (1982).

Biographical information on Tolson can be found in Joy Flasch's *Melvin B. Tolson* (1972). More recent critical considerations of Tolson's work include Michael Bérubé's "Masks, Margins, and African American Modernism: Melvin Tolson's *Harlem Gallery,*" *PMLA* 105 (1990); Melvin B. Tolson Jr.'s "The Poetry of Melvin B. Tolson," *World Literature Today* 64 (1990); Craig Werner's "Blues for T. S. Eliot and Langston Hughes: The Afro-Modernist Aesthetic of *Harlem Gallery,*" *Black American Literature Forum* 24 (1990); Maria K. Mootry's "'The Step of Iron Feet': Creative Practice in the War Sonnets of Melvin B. Tolson and Gwendolyn Brooks," in *Reading Race in American Poetry: "An Area of Act"* (2000), edited by Aldon Lynn Nielsen; Mariann B. Russell's "Evolution of Style in the Poetry of Melvin B. Tolson" and Jon Woodson's "Melvin Tolson and the Art of Being Difficult," both in *Black American Poets between Worlds, 1940–1960* (1986), edited by Baxter R. Miller; and Aldon L. Nielsen's "Melvin B. Tolson and the De-Territorialization of Modernism," *African American Summer Review* 26 (1992). Book-length treatments of Tolson's work include Mariann Russell's *Melvin B. Tolson's* Harlem

Gallery: *A Literary Analysis* (1980), Robert M. Farnsworth's *Melvin B. Tolson, 1898–1966: Plain Talk and Poetic Prophecy* (1984), and Bérubé's *Marginal Forces/Cultural Centers: Tolson, Pynchon, and the Politics of the Canon* (1992).

Margaret Walker

Walker's poetry is collected in *This Is My Century: New and Collected Poems* (1988). Her individual volumes are *For My People* (1942), *Prophets for a New Day* (1970), and *October Journey* (1973). She has also published the novel *Jubilee* (1966) as well as *How I Wrote "Jubilee"* (1972), *A Poetic Equation: Conversations between Nikki Giovanni and Margaret Walker* (1974), *For Farish Street Green* (1988), and a work on fellow author and friend Wright: *Richard Wright, Daemonic Genius: A Portrait of the Man, a Critical Look at His Work* (1988). Maryemma Graham has edited two books of Walker's essays: *How I Wrote Jubilee and Other Essays on Life and Literature* (1990) and *On Being Female, Black, and Free: Essays by Margaret Walker, 1932–1992* (1997). Her articles include "New Poets," in *Black Expressions* (1969), edited by Addison Gayle Jr.; "Willing to Pay the Price," in *Many Shades of Black* (1969), edited by Stanley Wormley and Louis H. Fenderson; "Richard Wright," in *Richard Wright: Impressions and Perspectives* (1973), edited by David Ray and Robert Farnsworth; and "On Being Female, Black and Free," in *The Writer on Her Work* (1980), edited by Janet Sternburg.

Critical essays and biographical material for Walker include Eugenia Collier's "Fields and Watered Blood: Myth and Ritual in the Poetry of Margaret Walker," in *Black Women Writers (1950–1980): A Critical Evaluation* (1984), edited by Mari Evans; Gloria Hull's "Black Women Poets from Wheatley to Walker," *Negro American Literature Forum* 9 (1975); John Griffin Jones's "Margaret Walker Alexander," in his *Mississippi Writers Talking,* vol. II (1983); Nancy Berke's *Women Poets on the Left: Lola Ridge, Genevieve Taggard, Margaret Walker* (2001); Maryemma Graham's edited *Fields Watered with Blood: Critical Essays on Margaret Walker* (2001); Jacqueline Miller Carmichael's *Trumpeting a Fiery Sound: History and Folklore in Margaret Walker's* Jubilee (1998); and Charles Rowell's "Poetry, History and Humanism: An Interview with Margaret Walker," *Black World* 25 (1975).

Dorothy West

West's novels are *The Living Is Easy* (1948) and *The Wedding* (1995). Among her short stories are "The Typewriter" (1926); "An Unimportant Man" (1928); "The Richer, the Poorer," reprinted in *The Best Short Stories by Negro Writers* (1967), edited by Langston Hughes; and "Jack in the Pot," reprinted in *Harlem: Voices from the Soul of Black America* (1970), edited by John Henrik Clarke. She has also published a collection of works in *The Richer, the Poorer: Stories, Sketches, and Reminiscences* (1995). James and Renae Nadine Shackelford and Robert Saunders have compiled many of her writings in *The Dorothy West Martha's Vineyard: Stories, Essays, and Reminiscences by Dorothy West Writing in the Vineyard Gazette* (2001).

Biographical sources for West include her interviews for *The Black Women Oral History Project* (1991), edited by Ruth Edmonds Hill; *As I Remember It: A Portrait of Dorothy West* (1991), a film produced by Mekuria Productions in association with WGBH; and West's *Papers, 1914–1985*, at the Schlesinger Library. Critical work on West began with the reissue of *The Living Is Easy* in 1982 and includes Dorothy A. Clark's "Rediscovering Dorothy West," *American Visions* 8 (1993); Lawrence R. Rodgers's "Dorothy West's *The Living Is Easy* and the Ideal of Southern Folk Community," *African American Review* 26 (1992); Mary Helen Washington's "I Sign My Mother's Name: Alice Walker, Dorothy West, Paule Marshall" in *Mothering the Mind: Twelve Studies of Writers and Their Silent Partners* (1984), edited by Ruth Perry and Martine Watson Brownley; and Mary Helen Washington's "I Sign My Mother's Name: Maternal Power in Dorothy West's Novel *The Living Is Easy*," in her *Invented Lives: Narratives of Black Women (1860–1960)* (1987).

Richard Wright
Wright's fiction includes *Uncle Tom's Children* (1938), *Native Son* (1940), *The Outsider* (1953), *The Long Dream* (1958), *Eight Men* (1961), and *Lawd Today* (1963). *Black Boy*, his autobiography, was published in 1945; and a second installment, titled *American Hunger*, was published posthumously in 1977. Wright's essay "Tradition and Industrialization: The Plight of the Tragic Elite in Africa," originally appeared in *Presence Africaine* (June–November 1956). Wright's account of his experience in the Communist Party is included in *The God That Failed* by Richard Crossman (1959). The two-volume Library of America edition, prepared by

Arnold Rampersad, presents Wright's major works in unrevised and unabbreviated form, based on Wright's original typescripts and proofs.

Biographies of Wright include Constance Webb's *Richard Wright: A Biography* (1968); Michel Fabre's *The Unfinished Quest of Richard Wright* (1973), translated from the French by Isabel Barzun; Margaret Walker's *Richard Wright: Daemonic Genius* (1968); and Hazel Rowley's *Richard Wright: The Life and Times* (2001). Critical essays on Wright include James Baldwin's "Everybody's Protest Novel" and "Many Thousands Gone" in his *Notes of a Native Son* (1955); Irving Howe's "Black Boys and Native Sons" in *A World More Attractive* (1963); Ralph Ellison's response to Howe in "The World and the Jug" in *Shadow and Act* (1964). See also Ellison's "Richard Wright's Blues" in *Shadow and Act* and "Remembering Richard Wright" in *Going to the Territory* (1986). More recent criticism of Wright includes Robert Stepto's "I Thought I Knew These People: Richard Wright and the Afro-American Literary Tradition" in *Chant of Saints* (1979), edited by Michel S. Harper and Robert B. Stepto; Sherley Ann Williams's "Papa Dick and Sister-Woman: Reflections on Women in the Fiction of Richard Wright" in *American Novelists Revisited: Essays in Feminist Criticism* (1982), edited by Fritz Fleischmann; Houston Baker's *Blues, Ideology, and Afro-American Literature: A Vernacular Theory* (1984); Joyce Ann Joyce's *Richard Wright: Art of Tragedy* (1986); and Yoshinobu Hakutani's *Richard Wright and Racial Discourse* (1996). See also Kenneth Kinnamon, ed., *New Essays on Native Son* (1990); Yoshinobu Hakutani, ed., *Critical Essays on Richard Wright* (1982); Henry L. Gates Jr. and K. A. Appiah, eds., *Richard Wright: Critical Perspectives Past and Present* (1993); Arnold Rampersad, with Bruce Simon and Jeffrey Tucker, eds., *Richard Wright: A Collection of Critical Essays* (1995); and Harold Bloom, ed., *Richard Wright: Modern Critical Views* (1987).

THE BLACK ARTS ERA, 1960–1975

Toni Cade Bambara
Bambara published two collections of short stories, *Gorilla, My Love: Short Stories* (1972) and *The Sea Birds Are Still Alive: Collected Stories* (1977), and a novel, *The Salt Eaters* (1980). She also made a documentary film, *The Bombing of Osage Avenue* (1986). She edited two anthologies: *The Black Woman: An Anthology* (1970) and *Tales and Stories for Black Folks* (1971). Bambara also had two posthumous publications, an anthology of work titled *Deep Sightings and Rescue Missions: Fiction, Essays, and Conversations* (1996), edited by Toni Morrison, and a novel, *Those Bones are Not My*

Child (1999). Other published works are "Black Theater," in *Black Expressions: Essays by and about Black Americans in the Creative Arts* (1969), edited by Addison Gayle Jr.; "Toni Cade Bambara," in *The Writer and Her Work* (1980), edited by Janet Sternberg; "Programming with 'School Daze,'" in *Five for Five: The Films of Spike Lee* (1991), edited by Spike Lee; "Deep Sight & Rescue Missions," in *Lure and Loathing: Race, Identity, Assimilation* (1993), edited by Gerald Early; and "Julie Dash and the Black Independent Film Movement, Black Cinema," in *Black Cinema* (1993), edited by Mantia Diawara. Interviews can be found in *Conversa-*

tions with Toni Cade Bambara (2012), edited by Thabiti Lewis.

A bibliography on Bambara's work up to 1984 is Martha Vertreace's "Toni Cade Bambara: The Dance of Character and Community," in *American Women Writing Fiction: Memory, Identity, Family Space* (1989), edited by Mickey Pearlman. Post-1984 essays and books about Bambara include Susan Willis's *Specifying: Black Women Writing the American Experience* (1987); Elliot Butler-Evans's *Race, Gender and Desire: Narrative Strategies in the Fiction of Toni Cade Bambara, Toni Morrison and Alice Walker* (1989); Wendy K. Komar's "Dialectics of Connectedness: Supernatural Elements in Novels by Bambara, Cisneros, Grahn and Erdich," in *Haunting the House of Fiction* (1991); Nancy Porter's "Women's Interracial Friendships and Visions in *Meridian, The Salt Eaters, Civil Wars,* and *Dessa Rose,*" in *Traditions and the Talents of Women* (1991); Mary Comfort's "Liberating Figures in Toni Cade Bambara's *Gorilla, My Love,*" in *Studies in American Humor 3* (1998); *Contemporary African American Novelists: A Bio-Bibliographical Critical Sourcebook* (1999), edited by Emmanuel S. Nelson and Deborah G. Plant; Gloria Hull's "What It Is I Think She's Doing Anyhow: A Reading of Toni Cade Bambara's *The Salt Eaters*" in *Home Girls: A Black Feminist Anthology* (2000), edited by Barbara Smith; Margo Perkins's "Getting Basic: Bambara's Re-Visioning of Black Aesthetic," in *Race and Racism in Theory and Practice* (2000), edited by Berel Lang; Elizabeth Muther's "Bambara's Feisty Girls: Resistance Narratives in *Gorilla, My Love,* in *African American Review* 36 (2002); *Savoring the Salt: The Legacy of Toni Cade Bambara* (2007), edited by Linda Holmes and Cheryl A. Wall; Carter A. Mathes's "Scratching the Threshold: Textual Sound and Political Form in Toni Cade Bambara's *The Salt Eaters,*" in *Contemporary Literature* 50 (2009); and Sheila Smith McKoy's "The Future Perfect: Reframing Ancient Spirituality in Toni Cade Bambara's *The Salt Eaters,*" in *Journal of Ethnic Literature* 1 (2011).

Amiri Baraka

Baraka's *Selected Poetry* and *Selected Plays and Prose* appeared in 1979. His other volumes include *Preface to a Twenty Volume Suicide Note* (1962), *The Dead Lecturer* (1965), *Black Art* (1966), *Black Magic: Poetry 1961–1967* (1969), *In Our Terribleness* (1970), *It's Nation Time* (1970), *Spirit Reach* (1972), *Afrikan Revolution* (1973), *Hard Facts* (1976), *Reggae or Not!* (1982), *Transbluesency: The Selected Poetry of Amiri Baraka/Leroi Jones 1961–1995* (1995), *Wise Why's Y's: The Griot's Tale* (1995), *Funk Lore: New Poems 1984–1995* (1996), *Somebody Blew up America, & Other Poems* (2003), and *Un Poco Low Coups* (2004). Baraka wrote several important and well-received plays, among them *Dutchman* and *The Slave* (1964), *The Baptism* and *The Toilet* (1967), *Four Black Revolutionary Plays* (1969), *Jello* (1970), and *"The Motion of History" and Other Plays* (1972). His prose fiction includes *The System of Dante's Hell* (1965), *Tales* (1967), *The Fiction of Leroi Jones/Amiri Baraka* (2000), and *Tales of the Out & Gone: Short Stories* (2007). Nonfiction writings include *Blues People* (1963); *Home: Social Essays* (1966); *Black Music* (1967); *Raise Race Rays Raze* (1972); *Kawaida Studies: The New Nationalism* (1972); *Daggers and Javelins: Essays 1974–1979* (1984); *The Autobiography of LeRoi Jones* (1984); *The Music: Reflections on Jazz and Blues* (1987); *Conversations with Amiri Baraka* (1994), edited by Charlie Reilly; *Eulogies* (1996), edited by Michael Schwartz; *Jesse Jackson & Black People* (1996); *Bushwaacked!: A Counterfeit President for a Fake Democracy: A Collection of Essays on the 2000 National Elections* (2001); *The Essence of Reparation: Afro-American Self-Determination & Revolutionary Democratic Struggle in the United States of America* (2003); *Malcolm X as Ideology* (2008); *Digging: The Afro-American Soul of American Classical Music* (2009); and *Razor: Revolutionary Art for Cultural Revolution* (2012). Baraka also co-edited *Black Fire: An Anthology of Afro American Writing* (1968), with Larry Neal; *Confirmation: An Anthology of African-American Women* (1983), with Amina Baraka; and *Eyeminded: Living and Writing Contemporary Art* (2011), with Hettie Jones, Kellie Jones, Lisa Jones, and Guthrie P. Ramsey, Jr.

Critical studies include Theodore Hudson's *From Leroi Jones to Amiri Baraka: The Literary Works* (1973); Kimberly Benston's *Baraka: The Renegade and the Mask* (1976); Werner Sollors's *Amiri Baraka/LeRoi Jones: The Quest for a 'Populist Modernism'* (1978); Lloyd Brown's *Amiri Baraka* (1980); William J. Harris's *Poetry and Poetics of Amiri Baraka: The Jazz Aesthetic* (1985); Harry J. Elam Jr.'s *Taking it to the Street: The Social Protest Theater of Luis Valdez and Amiri Baraka* (1997); Nilgun Anadolu-Okur's *Contemporary African-American Theater: Afrocentricity in the Works of Larry Neal, Amiri Baraka, and Charles Fuller* (1997); Komozi Woodard's *A Nation Within a Nation: Amiri Baraka (LeRoi Jones) and Black Power Politics* (1999); Phillip U. Effiong's *In Search of a Model for African-American Drama: A Study of Selected Plays by Lorraine Hansberry, Amiri Baraka, and Ntozake Shange* (2000); Jerry Gafio Watts's *Amiri Baraka: The Politics and Art of a Black Intellectual* (2001); essays edited by Kalamu ya Salaam in *African American Review* 37 (2003); Daniel Matlin's "Lift up ur self!": Reinterpreting Amiri Baraka (LeRoi Jones), Black Power, and the Uplift Tradition," in *Journal of American History* (2006); and Kathy Lou Schultz's "Amiri Baraka's *Wise Why's Y's:* Lineages of the Afro-Modernist epic," in *Journal of Modern Literature* 35 (2012).

Ed Bullins

Among Bullins's many writings are *Electronic Nigger* (1969), *The Gentleman Caller* (1969), *Goin'a Buffalo* (1969), *In the Wine Time* (1969), *Death List* (1970), *The Devil Catchers* (1970), *It Bees Dat Way* (1970), *Night of the Beast: A Screenplay* (1970), *The Fabulous Miss Marie* (1971), *The Hungered One: Early Writings* (1971), *In New England Winter* (1971), *Next Time* (1972), *The Reluctant Rapist* (1973), *The Taking of Miss Janie* (1975), *I Am Lucy Terry* (1976), *The Mystery of Phyllis Wheatley* (1976), *Storyville* (1977), *C'mon Back to Heavenly House* (1978), *Steve and Velma* (1980), *Blacklist: A New Play of the Eighties* (1982), *New-Lost Plays by Ed Bullins* (1994), *Boy X Man* (1995), and *Ed Bullins: Twelve Plays and Selected Writings* (2006). Critical works include Lance Jeffers's "Bullins, Baraka, and Elder: The Dawn of Grandeur in Black Drama," in *CLA Journal* 16 (1972); Geneva Smitherman's "Ed Bullins/Stage One: Everybody Wants to Know Why I Sing the Blues," in *Black World* 23 (1976); Leslie Sanders's "'Dialect Determinism': Ed Bullins's Critique of the Rhetoric of the Black Power Movement," in *Belief vs. Theory in Black American Literary Criticism* (1986), edited by Chester J. Fontenot and Joe Weixlmann; Nathan Grant's "The Frustrated Project of Soul in the Drama of Ed Bullins," in *Language, Rhythm, and Sound: Black Popular Cultures into the Twenty-First Century* (1997), edited by Adrianne R. Andrews and Joseph K. Adjaye; Samuel Hay's *Ed Bullins: A Literary Biography* (1997); and Mike Sell's "Bullins as Editorial Performer: Textual Power and the Limits of Performance in the Black Arts Movement," in *Theatre Journal* 53 (2001).

Eldridge Cleaver

Cleaver's *Soul on Ice* was published in 1968. Some of his speeches and essays are collected in *Post-Prison Writings and Speeches* (1969), *Black Panther Leaders Speak: Huey P. Newton, Bobby Seale, Eldridge Cleaver and Company Speak Out through the Black Panther Party's Official Newspaper* (1976), edited by G. Louis Heath; *Revolution in the Congo* (1971), and *Target Zero: A Life in Writing* (2006), edited by Kathleen Cleaver. Cleaver published *Soul on Fire* in 1978, and a series of poetry chapbooks in 1984 entitled *Gangster Cigarettes, Toxic Waste and Acid Raid, Idi and the Sultan, A Hit Squad of Chinks, Natasha,* and *For the Princess.* His recordings include *Soul on Wax—Dig* (1968).

Critical studies include Lee Lockwood's *Conversations with Eldridge Cleaver* (1970); Henry Louis Gates, Jr.'s "Cuban Experience: Eldridge Cleaver on Ice," in *Transition* 9 (1975); John A. Oliver's *Eldridge Cleaver Reborn* (1977); Kathleen Rout's *Eldridge Cleaver* (1991); Kathryne V. Lindberg's "Cleaver, Newton, and David: Re-reading Panther Lyrics," in *Talisman* 23–26 (2001); Marvin X's *Eldridge Cleaver, My Friend the Devil: A Memoir* (2009); Douglas

Taylor's "Three Lean Cuts in a Hall of Mirrors: James Baldwin, Norman Mailer, and Eldridge Cleaver on Race and Masculinity," in *Texas Studies in Literature and Language* 52 (2010); and Nathaniel Mills's "Cleaver/Baldwin Revisited," in *Studies in American Naturalism* 7 (2012).

Jayne Cortez

Cortez's publications include *Pissstained Stairs and the Monkey Man's Wares* (1969), *Festivals and Funerals* (1971), *Scarifications* (1973), *Mouth on Paper* (1977), *Firespitter* (1982), *Merveilleux Coup de Foudre: Poetry of Jayne Cortez and Ted Joans* (1982), *Coagulations: New and Selected Poems* (1984), *Poetic Magnetic* (1991), *Somewhere in Advance of Nowhere* (1997), *Jazz Fan Looks Back* (2002), *The Beautiful Book* (2007), and *On the Imperial Highway: New and Selected Poems* (2009). Among her recordings are *Celebrations and Solitudes: The Poetry of Jayne Cortez* (1975), *Unsubmissive Blues* (1980), *There It Is* (1983), and *Maintain Control* (1986). Cortez has also released a number of recordings, many with her band, The Firespitters, including *Mountain Control* (1986), *Everywhere Drums* (1991), *Cheerful & Optimistic* (1994), *Taking the Blues Back Home* (1997), and *Borders of Disorderly Time: Poetry and Music* (2003). Her films include *Poetry in Motion* (1982) and *War on War* (1982), and among her video productions are *Jayne Cortez in Concert 1* (1982) and *Life and Influences of Jayne Cortez* (1987), produced in Sao Paolo by Museu da Literatura in 1987.

Cortez's poems have been included in numerous anthologies, among them *We Speak as Liberators: Young Black Poets* (1970), edited by Orde Coombs; *A Rock against the Wind: Black Love Poems* (1973), edited by Lindsay Patterson; *Black Sister: Poetry by Black American Women, 1746–1980* (1981), edited by Erlene Stetson; and *Confirmations: An Anthology of African American Women* (1983), edited by Amina Baraka and Amiri Baraka; *Moment's Notice: Jazz Poetry & Prose* (1993), edited by Art Lange and Nathaniel Mackey; *Every Eye Ain't Asleep: An Anthology of Poetry by African Americans Since 1945* (1994), edited by Michael S. Harper and Anthony Walton; and *Innovative Women Poets: An Anthology of Innovative Poetry by African Americans* (2006), edited by Aldon Lynn Nielsen and Lauri Ramey.

Critical works include Jayne Bolden's "All the Birds Sing Bass: The Revolutionary Blues of Jayne Cortez," *African American Review* 35 (2001); Kimberly Brown's "Of Poststructuralist Fallout, Scarification, and Blood Poems," in *Other Sisterhoods: Literary Theory and U.S. Women of Color* (1998), edited by Stanley Kumamoto; D. H. Melhem's "A MELUS Profile and Interview: Jayne Cortez," *MELUS* 21 (1996); Tony Bolden's "Taking the Blues Back Home: The Incarnation of Secular Priesthood in the Poetry of Jayne Cortez," in his *Afro-Blue: Improvisations in African American Poetry and Culture* (2004); T.J. Anderson III's "Hot House: Jayne Cortez and the Music of Illumination," in his *Notes to Make the Sound Come Right: Four Innovators of Jazz Poetry* (2004); Aldon Lynn Nielsen's "Capillary Currents: Jayne Cortez," in his *Integral Music: Languages of African American Innovation* (2004); Tom Lavazzi's "Echoes of DuBois: The Crisis Writings of Jayne Cortez," in his *Dialogism and Lyric Self-Fashioning: Bakhtin and the Voices of a Genre* (2008); Kevin Meehan's "Red Pepper Poetry: Jayne Cortez and Cross-Cultural Saturation," in his *People Get Ready: African Amerian and Caribbean Cultural Exchange* (2009); and Kimberly Nichele Brown's "Return to the Flesh: The Revolutionary Ideology Behind the Poetry of Jayne Cortez," in her *Writing the Black Revolutionary Diva: Women's Subjectivity and Decolonizing the Text* (2010).

Henry Dumas
Dumas's work can be found in the volumes *Ark of Bones and Other Stories* (1970); *Poetry for My People* (1970), reissued as *Play Ebony, Play Ivory in 1974*; *Jonah and the Green Stone* (1976); *Rope of Wind and Other Stories* (1979); *Goodbye Sweetwater: New & Selected Stories* (1988); *Knees of a Natural Man: The Selected Poetry of Henry Dumas* (1989); and *Echo Tree: The Collected Short Fiction of Henry Dumas* (2003). Critical considerations include the special issue of *Black American Literature Forum* 22 (1988), edited by Eugene B. Redmond; Dana A. Williams's "Making the Bones Live Again: A Look at the 'Bones People' in August Wilson's *Joe Turner's Come and Gone* and Henry Dumas's 'Ark of Bones,'" in *CLA Journal* 42 (1999); Patricia Schultheis's "Henry Dumas: Truths, Poetry, and Memory," in *Chattahoochee Review* 25 (2005); Salim Washington's "The Avenging Angel of Creation/Destruction: Black Music and the Afro-Technological in Science Fiction of Henry Dumas and Samuel R. Delaney," in *Journal of the Society for American Music* 2 (2008); Anissa Janine Wardi's "Currents of Memory: Ancestral Waters in Henry Dumas's 'Ark of Bones' and August Wilson's *Gem of the Ocean*," in *ISLE* 16 (2009); and Nathan Ragain's "A 'Reconcepted Am': Language, Nature, and Collectivity in Sun Ra and Henry Dumas," in *Criticism* 54 (2012).

Mari Evans
Evans's collections of poetry are *Where is All the Music?* (1968), *I Am a Black Woman* (1970), *Nightstar, 1973–1978* (1981), *A Dark and Splendid Mass* (1992), *How We Speak* (2002), and *Continuum: New and Selected Poems* (2007). Evan's literary criticism includes *Black Women Writers, 1950–1980: A Critical Evaluation* (1984) and *Clarity as Concept: A Poet's Perspective—A Collection of* Essays (2006).

Among her children's books are *JD* (1973), *I Look at Me!* (1974), *Singing Black: Alternative Nursery Rhymes for Children* (1976), *Jim Flying High* (1979), *Dear Corinne: Tell Somebody! Love, Annie: A Book about Secrets* (1999), and *'I'm Late': The Story of LaNeese and Moonlight and Alisha Who Didn't Have Anyone of Her Own* (2006). Evans has also written playscripts, including *River of My Song* (1973) and an adaptation of Zora Neale Hurston's *Their Eyes Were Watching God* entitled *Eyes* (1979). See also Evans's essay "Ethos and Creativity: The Impulse as Malleable," in *Where We Live: Essays about Indiana* (1989), edited by David Hoppe. Critical treatments include Robert P. Sedlack's "Mari Evans: Consciousness and Craft," in *CLA Journal* 15 (1972); David Dorsey's "The Art of Mari Evans" and Solomon Edwards's "Affirmation in the Works of Mari Evans," both in *Black Women Writers, 1950–1980*, edited by Mari Evans (1984); Robert L. Douglas, Sr.'s *Resistance, Insurgence, and Identity: The Art of Mari Evans, Nelson Stevens, and the Black Arts Movement* (2008); and Dana A. Williams's "Mari Evans's Blackness: A Definition," in *Langston Hughes Review* 22 (2008).

Nikki Giovanni
Among Giovanni's most noted collections of poetry are *Black Feeling, Black Talk* (1967), *Ego Tripping and Other Poems for Young People* (1974), *My House: Poems* (1972), *The Women and the Men* (1975), and *Cotton Candy on a Rainy Day* (1978), *The Selected Poems of Nikki Giovanni* (1996), *Love Poems* (1997), *Blues: For All the Changes: New Poems* (1999), and *Quilting the Black-Eyed Pea: Poems and Not Quite Poems* (2002). Her most recent collections include *The Collected Poetry of Nikki Giovanni, 1968–1998* (2003), *Acolytes* (2007), *Bicycles: Love Poems* (2009), and *Chasing Utopia* (2013). Her autobiographical work is *Gemini: An Extended Autobiographical Statement on My First Twenty-Five Years of Being a Black Poet* (1974). Giovanni has also published two edited volumes, *Shimmy Shimmy Shimmy Like My Sister Kate: Looking at the Harlem Renaissance through Poems* (1996) and *Grandmothers: Poems, Reminiscences, and Short Stories about the Keepers of our Traditions* (1994), as well as children's stories, such as *The Genie in the Jar* (1996), *Knoxville, Tennessee* (1994), *The Girl in the Circle* (2004), *On My Journey Now: Looking at African-American History through the Spirituals* (2007), and *Lincoln and Douglass: An American Friendship* (2008). Other work includes the collections *Re: Creation* (1970); *Dialogue* (1973), with James Baldwin; *A Poetic Equation: Conversations between Nikki Giovanni and Margaret Walker* (1974); *Conversations with Nikki Giovanni* (1992), edited by Virginia Fowler; and *Racism 101* (1994). For critical treatments, see Roderick R. Palmer's "The Poetry of Three Revolutionists: Don L. Lee, Sonia Sanchez, and Nikki Giovanni," in

CLA Journal 15 (1971); Martha Cook's "Nikki Giovanni: Place and Sense of Place in Her Poetry," in *Southern Women Writers* (1990), edited by Tonette Bond; Virginia C. Fowler's *Nikki Giovanni* (1992); and Rochelle A. Odon's "'To Fight the Fight I'm Fighting': The Voice of Nikki Giovanni and the Black Arts Movement," in *Langston Hughes Review* 22 (2008).

Michael S. Harper
Harper's poetry collections include *Dear John, Dear Coltrane* (1970), *History Is Your Own Heartbeat* (1971), *Photographs: Negatives: History as Apple Tree* (1972), *Song: I Want a Witness* (1972), *Debridement* (1973), *Nightmare Begins Responsibility* (1975), *Images of Kin: New and Selected Poems* (1977), *Rhode Island: Eight Poems* (1981), *Healing Song for the Inner Ear* (1985), *Honorable Amendments: Poems* (1995), *Songlines in Michaeltree: New and Collected Poems* (2000), *Selected Poems* (2002), and *Use Trouble: Poems* (2009). He authored, with Larry Kart and Al Young, "Jazz and Letters: A Colloquy," *TriQuarterly* (1986). Harper has also served as editor of *The Collected Poems of Sterling A. Brown* (1980) and as co-editor with Robert B. Stepto of *Chant of Saints: A Gathering of Afro-American Literature, Art and Scholarship* (1979), with John Wright for "A Ralph Ellison Festival," *Carlton Miscellany* (1980), and with Anthony Walton for *Every Shut Eye Ain't Asleep: An Anthology of Poetry by Americans Since 1945* (1994).

Critical treatments include Robert B. Stepto's "Michael S. Harper, Poet as Kinsman: The Family Sequences," in *Massachusetts Review* 17 (1976); Joseph Brown's "Their Long Scars Touch Ours: A Reflection on the Poetry of Michael Harper," in *Callaloo* 9 (1986); John F. Callahan's "'Close Roads': The Friendship Songs of Michael Harper" and Niccolo N. Donzella's "The Rage of Michael Harper," both in *Callaloo* 13 (1990); Kyle Grimes's "The Entropics of Discourse: Michael Harper's *Debridement* and the Myth of the Hero," in *Black American Literature Forum* 24 (1990); Elizabeth Dodd's "The Great Rainbowed Swamp: History as Moral Ecology in the Poetry of Michael S. Harper," in *ISLE* 7 (2000); *To Cut is to Heal: A Critical Companion to "Debridement"* (200), edited by Ben Lerner; and Meta Schettler's "Going to the Territory with Jay Wright and Michael Harper: Explorations of Black History and Culture," in *Obsidian* 7 (2006). General critical and biographical information can be found in David Lloyd's "Interview with Michael S. Harper," *TriQuarterly* 65 (1986); Michael Antonucci's "The Map on the Territory: An Interview with Michael S. Harper," *African American Review* 34 (2000); and in Heather Treseler's "Office Hours: A Memoir and An Interview with Michael S. Harper," in *Iowa Review* 39 (2009).

David Henderson
Henderson's poetry and prose can be found in *Felix of the Silent Forest* (1967), *De Mayor of Harlem* (1970), *Ghetto Follies* (1978), *The Low-East* (1980), *Neo-California* (1998), and *Jimi Hendrix: Voodoo Child of the Aquarian Age* (1978; reissued as *'Scuse Me While I Kiss the Sky* in 2009). He edited two volumes of work by the Umbra group, *Umbra Anthology 1967–1968* (1968) and *Umbra/Latin Soul 1974–1975* (1975). Critical considerations include Diana Middlebrook's "David Henderson's Holy Mission," in *Saturday Review* (1972) and Jean-Philippe Marcoux's "Move On Up: Free Jazz and Rhythm and Blues Performativities as Creative Acts of Cultural Re-inscription in David Hender's *De Mayor of Harlem*," in his *Jazz Griots: Music as History in the 1960s African American Poem* (2012).

Calvin Hernton
Hernton's volumes of poetry include *Glad to Be Dead* (1958), *Flame* (1958), *The Coming of Chronos to the House of Nightsong: An Epical Narrative of the South* (1964), *The Place* (1972), *Medicine Man* (1976), and *The Red Crag Gang and Black River Poems*, with Carla Bank (1999). His novel *Scarecrow* was published in 1974, and his plays include *Glad to Be Dead* (1958), *Flame* (1958), and *The Place* (1972). Hernton's nonfiction works include *Sex and Racism in America* (1965), *White Papers for White Americans* (1966), *Coming Together: Black Power, White Hatred, and Sexual Hang-ups* (1971), *The Cannabis Experience: An Interpretive Study of the Effects of Marijuana and Hashish*, with Joseph Berke (1977), and *The Sexual Mountain and Black Women Writers: Adventures in Sex, Literature, and Real Life* (1987).

For critical treatments of Hernton see Michel Oren's "The Enigmatic Career of Hernton's Scarecrow," in *Callaloo* 29 (2006) and Lauri Ramey's "Calvin C. Hernton: Portrait of a Poet," in *The Heritage Series of Black Poetry, 1962–1975: A Research Compendium*, edited by Paul Breman and Lauri Ramey (2007).

June Jordan
Jordan's collections of poetry include *Who Look at Me* (1969), *New Days: Poems of Exile and Return* (1974), *Things That I Do in the Dark: Selected Poetry* (1977), *Passion: New Poems* (1980), *Some Changes* (1981), *Living Room: New Poems* (1985), *Lyrical Campaigns: Selected Poems* (1989), *Naming Our Destiny: New and Selected Poems* (1989), *Haruko/Love Poems* (1993), *Kissing God Goodbye* (1997), and *Directed by Desire: The Collected Poems of June Jordan* (2005). Collections of essays are *Civil Wars* (1981), *On Call: Political Essays* (1985), *Moving Towards Home: Political Essays* (1989), *Technical Difficulties: African American Notes on the State of the Union* (1992), *June Jordan's Poetry for the People: A Revolutionary Blueprint* (1995), edited by Lauren Muller, *Affirmative*

Acts: Political Essays (1998), and *Some of Us Did Not Die: New and Selected Essays of June Jordan* (2002). Her children's books are *His Own Where* (1971), *Dry Victories* (1972), *Fannie Lou Hamer* (1972), *New Life: New Room* (1975), and *Kimako's Story* (1981). She has also edited *Soulscript: Afro-American Poetry* (1970); *The Voices of the Children* (1970), with Terri Bush; and *Some Changes* (1971). Jordan has also written the plays *In the Spirit of Sojourner Truth* (1979) and *The Issue* (1985), and the libretto and lyrics for the opera *I Was Looking at the Ceiling and Then I Saw the Sky: Earthquake/Romance* (1995), music composed by John Adams. Jordan also published a memoir, *Soldier: A Poet's Childhood* (2001).

Critical and biographical information can be found in *Diverse Voices: Essays on Twentieth-Century Women Writers in English* (1991), edited by Harriet Devine Jump; *The Woman That I Am: The Literature and Culture of Contemporary Women of Color* (1994), edited by D. S. Madison; Peter Erickson's "The Love Poetry of June Jordan," *Callaloo* 9 (1986); Jacqueline Vaught Brogan's "From Warrior to Womanist: The Development of June Jordan's Poetry," in *Speaking the Other Self: American Women Writers* (1997), edited by Jeanne Campbell Reesman; Margret Grebowicz and Valerie Kinloch's *Still Seeking an Attitude: Critical Reflections on the Work of June Jordan* (2004); Valerie Kinloch's *June Jordan: Her Life and Letters* (2006); Elizabeth Alexander's "Black Alive and Looking Straight at You: The Legacy of June Jordan," in her *Power and Possibility: Essays, Reviews, Interviews* (2007); Philip Metres's "June Jordan's Righteous Certainty: Poetic Address in Resistance Poetry," in his *Behind the Lines: War Resistance Poetry on the American Homefront Since 1941* (2007); and Brian Norman's "June Jordan and the Transnational American Protest," in his *The American Protest Essay and National Belonging: Addressing Division* (2007).

Adrienne Kennedy

Kennedy's work includes *Funnyhouse of a Negro* (1964); *Cities in Bezique: Two One-Act Plays* (1969); *People Who Led to My Plays* (1987); *Adrienne Kennedy: In One Act* (1988); *Deadly Triplets: A Theatre Mystery and Journal* (1990); *She Talks to Beethoven* (1990); *The Alexander Plays* (1992); *Jane and Jean in Concert* (1995); *Sleep Deprivation Chamber: A Theatre Piece* (1996); *A Movie Start Has to Star in Black and White* (2007); *Mom, How Did you Meet the Beatles?* (2008); *Ohio State Murders* (2009); and the memoir *People Who Led to My Plays* (1997). She also co-authored, with John Lennon and Victor Spinetti, *The Lennon Play: In His Own Write* (1968). Kennedy has also written, with Margaret B. Wilkerson, "Adrienne Kennedy: Reflections," *City Arts Monthly* (Feb. 1982). *The Adrienne Kennedy Reader*, edited by Werner Sollors, was published in 2001.

Her work has been given critical attention in Paul Carter Harrison's *The Drama of Nommo* (1972); Linda Kintz's *The Subject's Tragedy: Political Poetics, Feminist Theory and Drama* (1992); Paul K. Bryant-Jackson and Lois More Overbeck's edited *Intersecting Boundaries: The Theatre of Adrienne Kennedy* (1992); Elin Diamond's *Unmaking Mimesis* (1997); Elaine Aston's "Imag(in)ing A Life: Adrienne Kennedy's *People Who Led To My Plays* and *Deadly Triplets*," in *Auto/Biography and Identity: Women, Theatre and Performance* (2004), edited by Maggie B. Gale and Viv Gardner; Claudia Barrett's "'An Evasion of Ontology': Being Adrienne Kennedy," in *TDR: The Drama Review* 3 (2005); Philip C. Kolin's *Understanding Adrienne Kennedy* (2005); Sudarsan Sahoo's *Locating the Self: Fragmentation and Reconnection in the Plays of Adrienne Kennedy and August Wilson* (2011); "Personal Perspectives on Adrienne Kennedy" by various contemporary writers in *Modern Drama* 55 (2012); and Asmaa Kashef's *The Burst of the Suffocated Voices of African American Women: Adrienne Kennedy, Ntozake Shange, Aishah Rahman, Alexis De Veaux* (2103).

Martin Luther King Jr.

King's works include *Stride toward Freedom: The Montgomery Story* (1959); *Strength to Love* (1963); *Why We Can't Wait* (1964); *Where Do We Go from Here?* (1967); *Trumpet of Conscience* (1968); *The Papers of Martin Luther King, Jr.*, Volumes 1–6 (1992–2007); *All Labor Has Dignity* (2011), edited by Michael K. Honey; *A Gift of Love: Sermons from Strength to Love and Other Preachings* (2012); *"Thou, Dear God": Prayers that Open Hearts and Spirit* (2012), edited by Lewis V. Baldwin; and *"In A Single Garment of Destiny: A Global Vision of Justice* (2012), edited by Lewis V. Baldwin. See also James M. Washington's *A Testament of Hope: The Essential Writings of Martin Luther King* (1986) and James Cone's *Martin and Malcolm and America: A Dream or a Nightmare* (1991). Also valuable is Keith D. Miller's *Voice of Deliverance: The Language of Martin Luther King, Jr., and Its Sources* (1992), *The Autobiography of Martin Luther King, Jr.* (1998), edited by Clayborne Carson, and the audio CD *A Call to Conscience: The Landmark Speeches of Dr. Martin Luther King, Jr.* (2001), edited by Clayborne Carson and Kris Shepard. Critical considerations of King include Sanford Pinsker's "He Had a Dream, and It Shot Him: What Happened to Visions of Racial Harmony, and Why," *Virginia Quarterly Review* 72 (1996); Anita Patterson's *From Emerson to King: Democracy, Race, and the Politics of Protest* (1997); Keith Miller's "Epistemology of a Drum Major: Martin Luther King Jr. and the Black Folk Pulpit," *Rhetoric Society* 18 (1988); Nick Sharman's "'Remaining Awake through a Great Revolution': The

Rhetorical Strategies of Martin Luther King, Jr.," *Social Semiotics* 9 (1999); Bradford T. Stull's *Amid the Fall, Dreaming of Eden: DuBois, King, Malcolm X, and Emancipatory Composition* (1999); David A. Bobbitt's *The Rhetoric of Redemption: Kenneth Burke's Redemption Drama and Martin Luther King's "I Have a Dream" Speech* (2004); David Howard-Pitney's *Martin Luther King, Jr., Malcolm X, and the Civil Rights Struggle of the 1950s and 1960s: A Brief History with Documents* (2004); Michael K. Honey's *Going Down Jericho Road: The Memphis Strike, Martin Luther King's Last Campaign* (2007); Michael Eric Dyson's *April 4, 1968: Martin Luther King, Jr.'s Death and How it Changed America* (2008); Gary Selby's *Martin Luther King and the Rhetoric of Freedom: The Exodus Narrative in America's Struggle for Civil Rights* (2008); Jonathan Rieder's *The Word of the Lord is Upon Me: The Righteous Performance of Martin Luther King, Jr.* (2008); Eric Sundquist's *King's Dream* (2009); Ann Bausum's *Marching to the Mountaintop: How Poverty, Labor Fights, and Civil Rights Set the Stage for Martin Luther King, Jr.'s Final Hours* (2012); and Taylor Branch's multi-volume historical biography: *Parting the Waters: America in the King Years, 1954–63* (1988); *Pillar of Fire: America in the King Years, 1963–65* (1998); *At Canaan's Edge: America in the King Years, 1965–68* (2006), and *The King Years: Historic Moments in the Civil Rights Movement* (2013).

Etheridge Knight
Knight's collections include *Poems from Prison* (1968), *A Poem for Brother/man* (1972), *Belly Song and Other Poems* (1973), *Born of a Woman: New and Selected Poems* (1980), and *The Essential Etheridge Knight* (1986). Along with other inmates of Indiana State Prison, Knight wrote and edited *Black Voices from Prison* (1970). For critical discussions of Knight and his work, see Stephen Henderson's *Understanding the New Black Poetry: Black Speech and Black Music as Poetic References* (1973); Patricia L. Hill's "'The Violent Space': An Interpretation of the Function of the New Black Aesthetic as Seen in Etheridge Knight's Poetry," *Black American Literature Forum* 14 (1980), and "'Blues for a Mississippi Black Boy': Etheridge Knight's Craft in the Black Oral Tradition," *Mississippi Quarterly* 36 (1982–83); Craig Werner's "The Poet, the Poem, the People: Etheridge Knight's Aesthetic," in *Obsidian* 7 (1981); Sanford Pinsker's "A Conversation with Etheridge Knight," *Black American Literature Forum* 18 (1984); Haki Madbubuti's "Etheridge Knight: Making Up Poems," *Worcester Review* 19 (1998); David Tod Lawrene's "Talk Like a Man: Internal Dissonance and the Performance of Masculinity in Etheridge Knight's *Poems from Prison*," in *Griot* 27 (2008); David Kieran's "Lynching, Embodiment, and Post-1960 African American Poetry," in *Demands

of the Dead: Executions, Storytelling, and Activism in the United States* (2012), edited by Katy Ryan; and Michael S. Collins's *Understanding Etheridge Knight* (20112). For general biographical information, see Charles Rowell's "An Interview with Etheridge Knight," *Callaloo* 19 (1996).

Audre Lorde
Lorde's books of poetry are *The First Cities* (1968), *Cables to Rage* (1970), *From a Land Where Other People Live* (1973), *New York Head Shop and Museum* (1974), *Between Ourselves* (1976), *Coal* (1976), *The Black Unicorn* (1978), *Chosen Poems: Old and New* (1982), *Our Dead behind Us* (1986), *Undersong: Chosen Poems Old and New* (1992), *The Marvellous Arithmetic of Difference* (1993), and *The Collected Poems of Audre Lorde* (1997). Her nonfiction and theoretical works are *The Cancer Journals* (1980); her biomythobiography, *Zami: A New Spelling of My Name* (1982); *Sister Outsider* (1984); *I Am Your Sister: Black Women Organizing across Sexualities* (1985); *A Burst of Light* (1988); *The Audre Lorde Compendium: Essays, Speeches, and Journals* (1966); *Conversations with Audre Lorde* (2004), edited by Joan Wylie Hall, and *I Am Your Sister: Collected and Unpublished Writings of Audre Lorde* (2009), edited by Rudolph P. Byrd, Johnnetta Betsch Cole, and Beverly Guy-Sheftall.

A critical biography of Lorde is Alexis De Veaux's *Warrior Poet: A Biography of Audre Lorde* (2006). Critical treatments of her work include Mary DeShazer's chapter on Lorde, in her *Imagining the Muse* (1987); Gloria T. Hull's "Living on the Line: Audre Lorde and *Our Dead behind Us*," in *Changing Our Own Words* (1990), edited by Cheryl A. Wall; Barbara Smith's "'The Truth That Never Hurts': Black Lesbians in Fiction in the 1980s," in *Feminism: An Anthology of Literary Theory and Criticism* (1997), edited by Robyn R. Warhol and Diane Price Herndl; Kara Provost's "Becoming Afrekete: The Trickster in the Work of Audre Lorde," in *MELUS* 20 (1995); AnaLouise Keating's *Women Reading Women Writing: Self-Invention in Paula Gunn Allen, Gloria Anzaldúa, and Audre Lorde* (1996); Lynda Hall's "Passion(ate) Plays 'Wherever We Found Space': Lorde and Gomez Queer(y)ing Boundaries and Acting In," *Callaloo* 23 (2000); Cassie Premo Steele's *We Heal from Memory: Sexton, Lorde, Analdúa, and the Poetry of Witness* (2000); Zofia Burr's *Of Women, Poetry, and Power: Strategies of Address in Dickinson, Miles, Brooks, Lorde, and Angelou* (2002); Cheryl Clarke's "Transferences and Confluences: Black Arts and Black Lesbian-Feminism in Audre Lorde's *The Black Unicorn*," in her *"After Mecca": Women Poets and the Black Arts Movement* (2005); and Stella Bolaki's "'New Living the Old in a New Way': Home and Queer Migrations in Audre Lorde's *Zami*," in *Textual Practice* 25 (2011).

James Alan McPherson

McPherson's writings include *Hue and Cry* (1969); *Railroad* (1976); *Elbow Room* (1977); *Crabcakes: A Memoir* (1999); and *A Region Not Home: Reflections from Exile* (2001). With DeWitt Henry, he has edited three volumes: *Ploughshares Fall 1985* (1985); *Ploughshares Fall 1990: Confronting Racial Difference* (1990); and *Fathering Daughters: Reflections by Men* (1999). McPherson also anthologized the work of the late D'J Pancake in *The Stories of Breece D'J Pancake* (1983). His essays include "Indivisible Man" (with Ralph Ellison), *The Atlantic* (1970), "On Becoming an American Writer," *Topic* 126 (1980), and the collection of essays *A Region Not Home: Reflections from Exile* (2001). Critical works include Wahneema Lubiano's "Shuckin' Off the African-American Native Other: What's 'Po-Mo' Got to Do with It?," *Cultural-Critique* 18 (1991); Jon Wallace's *The Politics of Style: Language as Theme in the Fiction of Berger, McGuane, and McPherson* (1992); Herman Beavers's *Wrestling Angels into Song: The Fictions of Ernest J. Gaines and James Alan McPherson* (1995), Trent Masiki's "The Burden of Insight: Dramatic Irony and the Rhetoric of Illumination in Selections from *Elbow Room*," in *Short Story* 9 (2001); and DeWitt Henry's "About James Alan McPherson: A Profile," in *Ploughshares* 34 (2008).

Haki Madhubuti

Madhubuti's poetry collections include *Black Pride Poems* (1968), *Think Black* (1969), *Don't Cry Scream* (1969), *Directionscore: Selected and New Poems* (1971), *Book of Life* (1973), *GroundWork: New and Selected Poems from 1966–1996* (1996), *Heart Love: Wedding & Love Poems* (1998), *Run Toward Fear: New Poems and a Poet's Handbook* (2004), and *Liberation Narratives: New and Collected Poems 1966–2009* (2009). He has also edited various anthologies of poems and essays, including *Dynamite Voices 1: Black Poets of the 1960s* (1971); *To Gwen with Love: An Anthology Dedicated to Gwendolyn Brooks* (1971); *Enemies: The Clash of Races* (1978); *Earthquakes and Sunrise Missions: Poetry and Essays of Black Renewal, 1973–1983* (1984); *Say That the River Turns: The Impact of Gwendolyn Brooks* (1987); *Confusion by Any Other Name: Essays Exploring the Negative Impact of "The Black Man's Guide to Understanding Women"* (1990); *Why L.A. Happened: Implications of the '92 Los Angeles Rebellion* (1993); *Claiming Earth: Race Rage, Rape, Redemption: Blacks Seeking a Culture of Enlightened Empowerment* (1994); *Million Man March/Day of Absence: A Commemorative Anthology* (1996), with Maulana Karenga; *Tough Notes: Letters to Young Black Men* (2002). Other works include *Killing Memory, Seeking Ancestors* (1987); *Black Men, Obsolete, Single, Dangerous* (1988); *Life Studies: The Need for Afrikan Minds and Institutions* (1992); and *African Centered Education:*

Its Value, Importance, and Necessity in the Development of Black Children (1998), with Safisha Madhubuti. His most recent works include *YellowBlack: The First Twenty-One Years of a Poet's Life: A Memoir* (2005); *Honoring Genius: Gwendolyn Brooks: The Narrative of Craft, Art, Kindness, and Justice* (2011); and *Freedom to Self-Destruct: Much Easier to Believe Than Think: New and Collected Essays* (2011).

Critical treatments can be found in Paula Giddings's "From a Black Perspective: The Poetry of Don L. Lee," *Amistad: Writings on Black History and Culture* 19 (1971); Marlene Mosher and Arthur P. Davis's *New Directions from Don L. Lee* (1975); and Julie E. Thompson's "The Public Response to Haki R. Madhubuti, 1968–1988," *The Literary Griot: International Journal of Black Expressive Cultural Studies* 4 (1992); Rolland Murray's "How the Conjure-Man Gets Busy: Cultural Nationalism, Masculinity, and Performativity," in *Yale Journal of Criticism* 18 (2005); Regina Jennings's *Malcolm X and the Poetics of Haki Madhubuti* (2006); and Lita Hooper's *Art of Work: The Art and Life of Haki R. Madhubuti* (2007).

Malcolm X

The Autobiography of Malcolm X was co-authored with Alex Haley and published posthumously in 1965. Malcolm X's speeches and statements have been published in several collections, including *Malcolm X Speaks* (1965), *The Speeches of Malcolm X at Harvard* (1968), *By Any Means Necessary: Speeches, Interviews and a Letter* (1970), *Malcolm X: The Last Speeches* (1989), and *The Portable Malcolm X Reader* (2013), edited by Garrett Felber and Manning Marable. For general background, see Clifton E. Marsh's *From Black Muslims to Muslims: The Transition from Separatism to Islam, 1930–1980* (1984). See also George Breitman's *The Last Year of Malcolm X* (1968), Peter Goldman's *The Death and Life of Malcolm X* (1973), James Cone's *Martin and Malcolm and America: A Dream or a Nightmare* (1991), Bruce Perry's *Malcolm* (1991), Clayborne Carson's *Malcolm X: The FBI File* (1991), and Michael Eric Dyson's *Making Malcolm: The Myth and Meaning of Malcolm X* (1995). Also of interest is the collection *Malcolm X: In Our Own Image* (1992), edited by Joe Wood. More recent critical considerations of Malcolm X include Maulana Karenga's "The Oppositional Logic of Malcolm X: Differentiation, Engagement and Resistance," *Western Journal of Black Studies* 17 (1993); Michael Eric Dyson's *Making Malcolm: The Myth and Meaning of Malcolm X* (1996); Louis A. DeCaro, Jr.'s *Malcolm and the Cross: The Nation of Islam, Malcolm X, and Christianity* (1998); Bradford T. Stull's *Amid the Fall, Dreaming of Eden: DuBois, and Emancipatory Composition* (1999); Kenneth Mostern's *Autobiography and Black*

Identity Politics: Racialization in Twentieth-Century America (1999); Robert Terrill's *Malcolm X: Inventing Radical Judgment* (2004); David Howard-Pitney's *Martin Luther King, Malcolm X, and the Civil Rights Struggle of the 1950s and 1960s: A Brief History with Documents* (2004); James A. Tyner's *The Geography of Malcolm X: Black Radicalism and the Remaking of American Space* (2006); *Alex Haley's "The Autobiography of Malcolm X"* (2008), edited by Harold Bloom; Amiri Baraka's *Malcolm X As Ideology* (2008); Manning Marable's *Malcolm X: A Life of Reinvention* (2010); *By Any Means Necessary: Malcolm X—Real, Not Reinvented: Critical Conversations on Manning Marable's Biography of Malcolm X* (2012), edited by Herb Boyd, Ron Daniel, Maulana Karenda, and Haki R. Madhubuti; Peter Goldman's *The Death and Life of Malcolm X* (2013); and Graeme Aberneth's *The Iconography of Malcolm X* (2013). Useful source books are *The Malcolm X Encyclopedia* (2002), edited by Robert L. Jenkins and Mfanya Donald Tryman, and *The Cambridge Companion to Malcolm X* (2010), edited by Robert Terrill.

Amus Mor

Mor's poems appear in the anthologies *Black Spirits*, edited by Woodie King (1972) and *The Second Set: The Jazz Poetry Anthology, Vol. 2*, edited by Yusef Komunyakaa and Sascha Feinstein (1996). He can be heard reading his work on the albums *Levels and Degrees of Light*, by Muhal Richard Abrams (1967), *Young at Heart, Wise in Time*, by Muhal Richard Abrams (1969), and *Black Spirits: A Festival of New Black Poets in America*, by Woodie King (1972).

Critical and biographical discussions of Mor can be found in Amiri Baraka's *The Autobiography of Leroi Jones/Amiri Baraka* (1984); Ronald Michael Radano's *New Musical Figurations: Anthony Braxton's Cultural Critique* (1993), James Edward Smethurst's *The Black Arts Movement: Literary Nationalism in the 1960s and 1970s* (2005), and Margo Natalie Crawford's "The Poetics of Chant and Inner/Outer Space: The Black Arts Movement," in *The Cambridge Companion to American Poetry Since 1945*, edited by Jennifer Ashton (2013).

Larry Neal

Neal's books include *Black Boogaloo: Notes on Black Liberation* (1969); *Hoodoo Hollerin' Bebop Ghosts* (1974); and the posthumous collection, *Visions of a Liberated Future: Black Arts Movement Writings* (1989), edited by Michael Schwartz. With Amiri Baraka and A. B. Spellman, he wrote *Trippin': A Need for Change* (1969), Neal's plays are *The Glorious Monster in the Bell of the Horn* (1976) and *In an Upstate Motel* (1981). With Baraka, he edited *Black Fire: An Anthology of Afro-American Writing* (1968). Neal's critical essays were published in many journals; among them are "The

Negro in the Theater," *Drama Critique* (1964); "Cultural Front," *Liberator* (1965); "Black Writer's Views on Literary Lions and Values," *Negro Digest* (1968); and "The Black Arts Movement," *Drama Review* (1968).

For selected criticism, see the various interviews, critical essays, and bibliographies found in *Callaloo's Larry Neal: A Special Issue* 8 (1985), edited by Kimberly W. Benston; George D. Yancy's "Larry Neal: Phenomenological Facets," in *CLA Journal* 36 (1992); Nigun Anadolu-Okur's *Contemporary African-American Theater: Afrocentricity in the Works of Larry Neal, Amiri Baraka, and Charles Fuller* (1997); James Spady's *Larry Neal: Liberated Black Philly Poet with a Blues Streak of Mellow Wisdom* (1989); Christopher Funkhouser's "LeRoi Jones, Larry Neal, and the Cricket: Jazz and Poets' Black Fire," in *African American Review* 37 (2003); Erick King Watts's "The Ethos of a Black Aesthetic: An Exploration of Larry Neal's *Visions of a Liberated Future*," in *The Ethos of Rhetoric* (2004), edited by Michael J. Hyde.

Raymond Patterson

There are four volumes of Patterson verse: *26 Ways of Looking at a Black Man and Other Poems* (1969); *For K.L.* (1980); *Elemental Blues: Poems 1981–1982* (1983); and *Three Patterson Lyrics: For Soprano and Piano* (1986); he also issued two broadsides: *I've Got a Home in That Rock* (1977) and *At That Moment: A Legend of Malcolm X* (1967). His work also appears in numerous anthologies, including *Every Eye Ain't Asleep: An Anthology of Poetry by African-Americans Since 1945* (1991) and *The Vintage Book of African American Poetry* (2000), both edited by Michael S. Harper and Anthony Walton; *Soulscript: A Collection of Classic African American Poetry* (2004), edited by June Jordan; and *Words of Protest, Words of Freedom: Poetry in the American Civil Rights Movement and Era: An Anthology* (2012), edited by Lamar Coleman. Patterson's essays include: "What's Happening in Black Poetry?," in *A Gift of Tongues: Critical Challenges in Contemporary American Poetry* (1987), edited by Kathleen Aguero and Marie Harris; "'like we in hell': Henry Dumas's Harlem," in *Black American Literature Forum* 22 (1988); and "African American Epic Poetry: The Long Foreshadowing," in *The Furious Flowering of African American Poetry* (1999), edited by Joanne V. Gabbin.

Critical and biographical discussions of Patterson can be found in Aaron Kramer's "First Collection of Genuine New Voice," in *Freedomways* 10 (1970; Eugene B. Redmon's *Drumvoices: The Mission of Afro-American Poetry: A Critical History* (1976); James De Jongh's *Vicious Modernism: Black Harlem and the Literary Imagination* (1990); Molefi K. Asanta and Mark T. Mattson's *The African American Atlas: Black History and Culture—An Illustrated Ref-*

erence (1998); and Raoul Abdul's "Souls of Black Folk," in the *New York Amsterdam News* 94 (2003).

Ishmael Reed

Reed's novels include *The Free-Lance Pallbearers* (1967), *Yellow Back Radio Broke-Down* (1969), *Mumbo Jumbo* (1972), *The Last Days of Louisiana Red* (1974), *Flight to Canada* (1976), *The Terrible Twos* (1982), *Reckless Eyeballing* (1986), *The Terrible Threes* (1989), and *Japanese by Spring* (1993), and *Juice: A Novel* (2011). His plays are collected in *Ishmael Reed: The Plays* (2009), and his poems are collected in *New and Collected Poems* (1988) and *New and Collected Poems, 1964–2006* (2006). Among his book-length prose works are the essay collections *Shrovetide in Old New Orleans: Essays* (1978), *God Made Alaska for the Indians: Selected Essays* (1982), *Writing Is Fighting: Thirty-Seven Years of Boxing on Paper* (1988), *Airing Dirty Laundry* (1993), *Conversations with Ishmael Reed* (1995), *Another Day at the Front: Dispatches from the Race War* (2003), *Blues City: A Walk in Oakland* (2003), *Mixing It Up: Taking on the Media Bullies and Other Reflections* (2008), *Bigger Than Boxing: Muhammad Ali* (2008), *Barak Obama and the Jim Crow Media: The Return of the Nigger Breakers* (2010), and *Going Too Far: Essays about America's Nervous Breakdown* (2012). *The Reed Reader* was issued in 2000. Reed has edited numerous works, among them *19 Necromancers from Now* (1970), *Califia: The California Poetry* (1979), *The Before Columbus Foundation Fiction Anthology* (1992), *The Before Columbus Foundation Poetry Anthology* (1992), *From Totems to Hip-Hop* (2003), and *Pow Wow: Charting the Fault Lines in the American Experience: Short Fiction from Then to Now* (2009). Reed has also written several journal articles, including "Larry Neal: A Remembrance," *Callaloo* (1985), and "Henry Dumas: The Poet of Resurrection," *Black American Literature Forum* 22 (1988). He also wrote the introduction to Richard Negler's *Oakland Rhapsody: The Secret Soul of a Downtown* (1995).

A bibliography of Reed's work up to 1982 is Elizabeth A. Settle's *Ishmael Reed: A Primary and Secondary Bibliography* (1982). Book-length critical treatments are Robert Elliot Fox's *Conscientious Sorcerers: The Black Postmodernist Fiction of LeRoi Jones (Amiri Baraka), Ishmael Reed, and Samuel Delany* (1987); Reginald Martin's *Ishmael Reed and the New Black Aesthetic Critics* (1988); Jay Boyer's *Ishmael Reed* (1993); Sämi Ludwig's *Concrete Language: Intercultural Communication in Maxine Hong Kingston's "The Woman Warrior" and Ishmael Reed's "Mumbo Jumbo"* (1996); Patrick McGee's *Ishmael Reed and the Ends of Race* (1997); *The Critical Response to Ishmael Reed* (1999), edited by Bruce Allen Dick; A *Casebook Study of Ishmael Reed's "Yel-*

low Back Radio Broke-Down" (2003), edited by Pierre-Damien Mvuyekure; Jeffrey Ebbesen's *Postmodernism and Its Others: The Fiction of Ishmael Reed, Kathy Acker, and Don DeLillo* (2006); *African American Humor, Irony and Satire: Ishmael Reed, Satirically Speaking* (2007), edited by Dana A. Williams; and *On the Aesthetic Legacy of Ishmael Reed: Contemporary Assessments* (2013), edited by Sämi Ludwig.

Helpful and interesting journal articles are Robert Fox, "Blacking the Zero: Towards a Semiotics of Neo-Hoodoo," *Black American Literature Forum* 18 (1984); Michael Boccia, "Form of the Mystery: Ishmael Reed's *Mumbo Jumbo*," *Journal of Popular Literature* 3 (1987); Theodore Mason, "Performance, History, and Myth: The Problem of Ishmael Reed's *Mumbo Jumbo*," *Modern Fiction Studies* 34 (1988); Henry Louis Gates, Jr.'s "On 'The Blackness of Blackness': Ishmael Reed and a Critique of Sign," in his *The Signifying Monkey: A Theory of African-American Literary Criticism* (1989); Richard Hardack's "Swing to the White, Back to the Black: Writing and 'Sourcery' in Ishmael Reed's *Mumbo Jumbo*," in *Arizona Quarterly* 49 (1993); Richard Swope's "Crossing Western Space, or the HooDoo Detective on the Boundary in Ishmael Reed's *Mumbo Jumbo*," in *African American Review* 36 (2002); Lawrence W. Hogue's "Postmodernism, Traditional Cultural Forms, and the African American Narrative: Major's *Reflex*, Morrison's *Jazz*, and Reed's *Mumbo Jumbo*,' in *Novel* 35 (2002); Michael A. Chaney's "Slave Cyborgs and the Black Infovirus: Ishmael reed's Cybernetic Aesthetics," in *MFS: Modern Fiction Studies* 49 (2003); Glenda R. Carpio's "Conjuring the Mysteries of Slavery: Voodoo, Fetishism, and Stereotype in Ishmael Reed's *Flight to Canada*," in *American Literature* 77 (2005); and Anthony Zias's "Jew Grew, the Holy Grail, and the Desire for a Metanarrative to Believe: Reading Ishmael Reed's *Mumbo Jumbo* as a Historical Thriller," in *Genre* 42 (2009).

Carolyn M. Rodgers

Rodgers published several chapbooks and collections of poetry, including *Paper Soul* (1968), *Songs of a Black Bird* (1969), *2 Love Raps* (1969), *how i got ovah: New and Selected Poems* (1975), *The Heart as Ever Green* (1978), *Eden and Other Poems* (1983), *A Little Lower than Angels* (1984), *Echoes from a Circle Called Earth* (1984), *Finite Forms* (1985), *Morning Glory: Poems* (1989), and *We Are Only Human: Poems* (1996). Her work has been included in numerous anthologies, including *Black Sister: Poetry by Black American Women, 1746–1980* (1981), edited by Erlene Stetson. In addition to poetry, Rodgers also published numerous short stories, such as "Blackbird in a Cage" (1967), "A Statistic, Trying to Make It Home" (1969), and "One Time" (1975).

Critical considerations of Rodgers's work include Estella M. Sales's "Contradictions in

Black Life: Recognized and Reconciled in 'How I Got Ovah'," in *CLA Journal* 25 (1981); Bettye Parker-Smith's "Running Wild in Her Soul: The Poetry of Carolyn Rodgers" and Angelene Jamison's "Imagery in the Women Poems: The Art of Carolyn Rodgers," both in *Black Womern Writers: Arguments and Interviews* (1984), edited by Mari Evans; and Carmen L. Phelps's "Muddying Clear Waters: Carolyn Rodgers's Black Art," in her *Visionary Women of Chicago's Black Arts Movement* (2012).

Sonia Sanchez

Among Sanchez's poetry collections are *home coming* (1969), *We a Baddddd People* (1970), *It's a New Day: Poems for Young Brothas and Sistuhs* (1971), *Love Poems* (1973), *Blues Book for Blue Black Magical Women* (1974), *Selected Poems, 1974* (1975), *homegirls & handgrenades* (1984), *I've Been a Woman: New and Selected Poems* (1985), *Generations: Poetry, 1969–1985* (1986), *Under a Soprano Sky* (1987), *Wounded in the House of a Friend* (1995), *Does Your House Have Lions?* (1997), *Like the Singing Coming off the Drums: Love Poems* (1998), *Shake Loose My Skin: New and Selected Poems* (2000), and *Morning Haiku* (2010). Among recorded releases of her poetry are *We A BaddDDDD People* (1969), *Sonia Sanchez: A Sun Woman for All Seasons Reads her Poetry* (1971), *Sonia Sanchez: Selected Poems* (1974), *Sonia Sanchez with Attica Prison* (1979), *Sonia Sanchez Reading at SFSU* (1986), *The Full Moon of Sonia Sanchez* (1994), *All That and a Bag of Words* (1995), and *Dead Prez: U R Ripping Us Apart!!/Sonia Sanchez: When URE Heart Turns Cold* (2000). Sanchez has edited *Three Hundred Sixty Degrees of Blackness Comin' at You* (1971); *We Be Word Sorcerers: 25 Stories by Black Americans* (1973); and *Bum Rush the Page: A Def Poetry Jam*, with Tony Medina and Louis Reyes Rivera (2001). "Crisis and Culture: The Poet as a Creator of Social Values" (1983) is a critical essay by Sanchez. Sanchez's collections of children's stories are *The Adventures of Fathead, Smallhead, and Squarehead* (1973) and *A Sound Investment: Short Stories for Young Readers* (1980). Her published plays include *Sister Son/ji* (1969), *The Bronx is Next* (1970), *Dirty Hearts '72* (1973), *Uh Huh: But How Do It Free Us?* (1974), *Malcolm Man/Don't Live Here No Mo'* (1979), *Black Cats Back and Uneasy Landings* (1995), and *I'm Black When I'm Singing, I'm Blue When I Ain't and Other Plays* (1982), edited by Janqueline Wood. A collection of interviews is *Conversations with Sonia Sanchez* (2007), edited by Joyce A. Joyce.

For critical considerations see Houston A. Baker Jr.'s "Our Lady: Sonia Sanchez and the Writing of a Black Renaissance," in *Black Feminist Criticism and Critical Theory* (1988), edited by Joe Weixlmann and Baker; D. H. Melham's *Heroism in the New Black Poetry:*

The Will and the Spirit (1990); Joan V. Gabbin's "The Southern Imagination of Sonia Sanchez," in *Southern Women Writers: The New Generation* (1990), edited by Tonette Bond Inge and Doris Betts; Regina B. Jennings's "The Blue/Black Poetics of Sonia Sanchez," in *Language and Literature in the African American Imagination* (1992), edited by Carol Blackshire; Joyce A. Joyce's *Ijala: Sonia Sanchez and the African Poetic Tradition* (1998); Susan Kelly's "Discipline and Craft: An Interview with Sonia Sanchez," *African American Review* 34 (2000); Jacqueline Wood's "'To Wash My Ego in the Needs . . . of My People': Militant Womanist Rhetoric in the Drama of Sonia Sanchez," in *CLA Journal* 48 (2004); Yoshinobu Hakutani's "Cross-Cultural Poetics: Sonia Sanchez's *Like the Singing Coming off the Drums*," in his *Haiku and Modernist Poetics* (2009); Evie Shockley's "Expanding the Subject: Sonia Sanchez's *Does Your House Have Lions?*," in her *Renegade Poetry: Black Aesthetics and Formal Innovation in African-American Poetry* (2011); and Jean-Philippe Marcous's "Sister in the Struggle: Jazz Linguistics and the Feminized Quest for a Communicative 'Sound' in Sonia Sanchez's *Home Coming* and *We a BaddDDD People*," in his *Jazz Griots: Music as History in 1960s African American Poetry* (2011). Numerous articles on Sanchez's work can also be found in *BMa: The Sonia Sanchez Literary Review*, published 1994–2005.

A. B. Spellman

Spellman's poetry includes the collections *The Beautiful Days* (1965) and *Things I Must Have Known: Poetry* (2008). As well as publishing essays and reviews in numerous magazines and journals, he has also written *Four Lives in the Bebop Business* (1966), later revised as *Four Jazz Lives* (2004); and with Amiri Baraka and Larry Neal, *Trippin': A Need for Change* (1969). Critical and biographical treatments include Aaron Steinberg's "A Life in the Bebop Biz: A.B. Spellman Looks to His Future in Jazz," *JazzTimes* 35 (2005) and Sascha Feinstein's "Don't Give Up: An Interview with A.B. Spellman," in *Brilliant Corners* 13 (2009).

James T. Stewart

Along with his essay "The Development of the Black Revolutionary Artist," Stewart's poetry appears in the anthology *Black Fire* (1968), edited by Amiri Baraka/LeRoi Jones and Larry Neal. Other published essays include "Revolutionary Nationalism and the Black Artist" appears in the third issue of *Black Dialogue* (1966), "Just Intonation and the New Black Evolutionary Music," in *The Cricket* 2 (1968); "Position Paper: Revolutionary Black Music in the Total Context of Black Distension," in *The Cricket* 3 (1969), "A Consideration of the Art of Ornette Coleman," in *The Cricket* 4 (1969); and "Introduction to Black Aesthetics in

Music," in *The Black Aesthetic* (1971), edited by Addison Gayle, Jr. Discussions of Stewart's work can be found in Christopher Funkhouser's "LeRoi Jones, Larry Neal, and *The Cricket*: Jazz and Poet's Black Fire," in *African American Review* 37 (2003); James Edward Smethurst's *The Black Arts Movement: Literary Nationalism in the 1960s and 1970s* (2005); *New Thoughts on the Black Arts Movement* (2006), edited by Margo Crawford and Lisa Gail Collins; and Amy Abugo Ongiri's *Spectacular Blackness: The Cultural Politics of the Black Power Movement and the Search for a Black Aesthetic* (2010).

John Alfred Williams
Williams's publications include *Angry Ones* (1960), *Night Song* (1961), *Sissie* (1963), *The Man Who Cried I Am* (1967), *Sons of Darkness, Sons of Light, A Novel of Some Probability* (1969), *One for New York* (1969), *The Most Native of Sons: A Biography of Richard Wright* (1970), *Captain Blackman* (1972), *Mothersill and the Foxes* (1975), *The Junior Bachelor Society* (1976), *Click Song* (1982), *Berhama Account* (1985), *Jacob's Ladder* (1987), *Safari West* (1998), and *Clifford's Blues* (1999). In addition, he has edited *Angry Black* (1962); *Beyond the Angry Black* (1966); and *Bridges: Literature across Cultures* (1994), with Gilbert H. Muller. See also his *Africa: Her History, Lands and People* (1963); *This is My Country Too* (1965); *The Most Native of Sons: A Biogra-*

phy of Richard Wright (1970); *The King God Didn't Save: Reflections on the Life and Death of Martin Luther King, Jr.* (1971); *Flashbacks: A Twenty-Year Diary of Article Writing* (1973); *If I Stop, I'll Die: The Comedy and Tragedy of Richard Pryor* (1990), with Dennis A. Williams; and *Dear Chester, Dear John: Letters Between Chester Himes and John A. Williams* (2008).

Critical considerations include Langston Hughes's "Problems of the Negro Writer," *Saturday Review* (1963); Ronald Walcott's "The Man Who Cried I Am: Crying in the Dark," in *Studies in Black Literature* 3 (1972); Lynn C. Munro's "Culture and Quest in the Fiction of John A. Williams," in *CLA Journal* 22 (1978); John M. Reilly's "Thinking History in *The Man Who Cried I Am*," in *Black American Literature* Forum 21 (1987); Alan Nadel's "My Country Too: Time, Place, and African American Identity in the Work of John A. Williams," in his *Containment Culture: American Narratives, Postmodernism, and the Atomic Age* (1995); Virginia Smith's "Sorcery, Double-Consciousness, and Warring Souls: An Intertextual Reading of Middle Passage and Captain Blackman" in *African American Review* 30 (1996); and Jerry H. Bryant's "John A. Williams and the Realist's Dilemma," in his *Victims and Heroes: Racial Violence in the African American Novel* (1997). For biographical and general information, see Dennis Williams's "An Interview with John A. Williams," *Forkroads* (1995).

THE CONTEMPORARY PERIOD

Elizabeth Alexander
Alexander has published six books of poems: *The Venus Hottentot* (1990), *Body of Life* (1996), *Antebellum Dream Book* (2001), *American Sublime* (2005), *Miss Crandall's School for Young Ladies and Little Misses of Color* (2008), a collection of young adult poems written with Marilyn Nelson, and *Crave Radiance: New and Selected Poems 1990–2010* (2010). She has also authored, with Lyrae Van-Clief Stefanon, the chapbook *Poems in Conversation and a Conversation* (2008). Her poem "Praise Song for the Day: A Poem for Barack Obama's Presidential Inauguration" (2009) has been published in two chapbook editions. Alexander has also published two collections of essays, *Power and Possibility: Essays, Interviews, Reviews* (2007) and *The Black Interior* (2003). She is also editor of *The Essential Gwendolyn Brooks* (2005) and *Love's Instruments: Poems by Melvin Dixon* (1995). Alexander is also the author of several critical essays, including, "'We're Gonna Deconstruct Your Life!': The Making and Un-Making of the Black Bourgeois Patriarch in *Ricochet*," in *Representing Black Men* (1996), edited by Marcellus Blount and George P. Cunningham, "Meditations on

'Mecca': Gwendolyn Brooks and the Responsibilities of the Black Poet," in *By Herself, Women Reclaim Poetry* (2000), edited by Molly McQuade, "Dunbar Lives!" *African American Review* 41(2007), "The Negro Digs Up Her Past," *SAQ* (2005), and "Ripping out the Seams: New Thoughts on Black Experimental Poetry," *Michigan Quarterly Review* (2011). Interviews with Alexander include Christine Phillip's "An Interview with Elizabeth Alexander" in *Callaloo* 19 (2006) and Natasha Trethewey's "Natasha Trethewey Interviews Elizabeth Alexander" in *Southern Spaces* (2009). Critical considerations of her work include Malin Pereira's "'The Poet in the World, the World in the Poet': Cyrus Cassells's and Elizabeth Alexander's Versions of Post-Soul Cosmopolitanism," *African American Review* 41 (2007) and Wendy Walters's "Elizabeth Alexander's Amistad: Reading the Black History Poem through the Archive," *Callaloo* 33 (2010).

Maya Angelou
Angelou's six autobiographies have been collected in *I Know Why the Caged Bird Sings: The Collected Autobiographies of Maya*

Angelou (2004). Her poetry up to 1994 has
been collected in *The Complete Collected
Poems of Maya Angelou* (1994). Uncollected
books of poetry include *A Brave and Startling
Truth* (1995), *Phenomenal Woman: Four
Poems Celebrating Women* (1995), and *Amazing Peace* (2005). She has also written several
children's books, including: *Mrs. Flowers: A
Moment of Friendship* (1986), *Life Doesn't
Frighten Me* (1993), *Soul Looks Back in Wonder* (1993), *My Painted House, My Friendly
Chicken, and Me* (1994), *Kofi and His Magic*
(1996), *Angelina of Italy* (2004), *Izak of Lapland* (2004), *Renie Marie of France* (2004),
and *Mikale of Hawaii* (2004). Her essays
include *Lessons in Living* (1993), *Wouldn't
Take Nothing for My Journey Now* (1993), *Even
the Stars Look Lonesome* (1997), *Hallelujah!
The Welcome Table* (2004), *Mother: A Cradle
to Hold Me* (2006), and *Letter to My Daughter*
(2008). For more biographical information,
see *Conversations with Maya Angelou* (1989),
edited by Jeffrey M. Elliot. A book-length critical work on Angelou's autobiographies is Dolly
Aimee McPherson's *Order Out of Chaos: The
Autobiographical Works of Maya Angelou*
(1990). For critical analysis of her work, see
the following casebooks and chapters in
monographs: Harold Bloom's *Maya Angelou's
I Know Why the Caged Bird Sings* (1995);
Lyman B. Hagen's *Heart of a Woman, Mind of
a Writer, and Soul of a Poet: A Critical Analysis
of the Writings of Maya Angelou* (1997); *Maya
Angelou's I Know Why the Caged Bird Sings: a
Casebook* (1999), edited by Joanne M. Braxton; Barbara Bennett Woodhouse's, *Hidden
in Plain Sight: The Tragedy of Children's Rights
from Ben Franklin to Lionel Tate* (2008);
Cheryl Higashida's *Black Internationalist
Feminism: Women Writers of the Black Left,
1955–1995* (2011); and a special issue of the
Langston Hughes Review (2005) devoted to
her work.

Octavia Butler
Butler's works of fiction include three series:
the Patternist series, which includes *Patternmaster* (1976), *Mind of My Mind* (1977), *Survivor* (1978), *Wild Seed* (1980), and *Clay's Ark*
(1984); *Lilith's Brood*, which includes *Dawn*
(1987), *Adulthood Rites* (1988), and *Imago*
(1989); and *Parable*, which includes *Parable
of the Sower* (1993) and *Parable of the Talents*
(1998). Her stand-alone novels include *Kindred* (1979) and *Fledgling* (2005). She has also
published a collection of short stories, *Bloodchild and Other Stories* (1995); a second edition (2006) contains additional stories. For
biographical information and interviews, see
Joe Weixlmann's "An Octavia E. Butler Bibliography," *Black American Literature Forum*
(1984) and Larry McCaffery's *Across the
Wounded Galaxies: Interviews with Contemporary American Science Fiction Writers* (1990),
and *Conversations with Octavia Butler* (2010),

edited by Consuela Francis. The first full-length study of Butler's works is Gregory
Jerome Hampton's *Changing Bodies in the Fiction of Octavia Butler: Slaves, Aliens, and Vampires* (2010). Critical engagements with her
work include special issues devoted to her
work, *Science Fiction Studies* 36 (2010) and
Utopian Studies 19 (2008) and select chapters
in the monographs of John Blair Gamber, *Positive Pollutions and Cultural Toxins: Waste and
Contamination in Contemporary U.S. Ethnic
Literatures* (2012), and Timothy Spaulding, *Reforming the Pat: History, the Fantastic, and the
Postmodern Slave Narrative* (2005). Earlier
critical essays on Butler's work include Thelma
J. Shinn's "The Wise Witches: Black Women
Mentors in the Fiction of Octavia E. Butler," in
*Conjuring: Black Women, Fiction and Literary
Tradition* (1985), edited by Hortense Spillers
and Marjorie Pryse, and Dorothy Allison's
"The Future of the Female: Octavia Butler's
Mother Lode," in *Reading Black, Reading Feminist* (1990), edited by Henry Louis Gates Jr.

Lucille Clifton
Clifton is the author of thirteen collections of
poetry: *Good Times* (1969), *Good News About
the Earth* (1972), *An Ordinary Woman* (1974),
Two-Headed Woman (1980), *Good Woman:
Poems and a Memoir: 1969–1980* (1987),
Next: New Poems (1987), *Ten Oxherding Pictures* (1988), *Quilting: Poems 1987–1990*
(1991), *The Book of Light* (1993), *The Terrible
Stories* (1996), *Blessing The Boats: New and
Collected Poems 1988–2000* (2000), *Mercy*
(2004), and *Voices* (2008). Her poems have
recently been published in *The Collected
Poems of Lucille Clifton* (2012), edited by
Kevin Young with an introduction by Toni
Morrison. She is also the author of several
children's books, *The Black BCs* (1970), *Good,
Says Jerome* (1973), *All Us Come 'cross the
Water* (1973), *Don't Your Remember?* (1973),
The Boy Who Didn't Believe in Spring (1973),
The Times They Used to Be (1974), *My Brother
Fine with Me* (1975), *Three Wishes* (1976),
Amifika (1977), *The Lucky Stone* (1986), *My
Friend Jacob* (1980), *Sonora Beautiful* (1981),
and *Dear Creator: A Week of Poems for Young
People and Their Teachers* (1997). She is also
the author of the Everett Anderson series, children's books written in verse, which include:
Some of the Days of Everett Anderson (1970),
Everett Anderson's Christmas Coming (1971),
Everett Anderson's Year (1974), *Everett Anderson's Friend* (1976), *Everett Anderson's 1-2-3*
(1977), *Everett Anderson's Nine Month Long*
(1978), *Everett Anderson's Goodbye* (1983),
and *One of the Problems of Everett Anderson*
(2001).

For an extended biography of Clifton, see
Mary Jane Lupton's *Lucille Clifton: Her Life
and Letters* (2006). Critical engagements with
her work include: Alicia Ostriker's "Kin and
Kin: The Poetry of Lucille Clifton," *American*

Poetry Review 22 (1993); Gloria Hull's "Channeling the Ancestral Muse: Lucille Clifton and Dolores Kendrick," in *Female Subjects in Black and White: Race, Psychoanalysis, Feminism* (1997), edited by Elizabeth Abel et al.; Ajuan Maria Mance's "Re-Locating the Black Female Subject: The Landscape of the Body in the Poems of Lucille Clifton" in *Recovering the Black Female Body: Self-Representations by African American Women* (2001), edited by Michael Bennett et al.; Hilary Holladay's *Wild Blessings: The Poetry of Lucille Clifton* (2004); Cheryl A. Wall's *Worrying the Line: Black Women Writers, Lineage, and Literary Tradition* (2005); and a special issue of the *Langston Hughes Review* 22 (2008) devoted to her work. Articles published after Clifton's death include Carme Manuel Cuenca's "Quilting Sculptural Knots: Lucille Clifton's Revisionary Rewriting" in Silvia Pilar Castro-Borrego's *The Search for Wholeness and Diaspora Literacy in Contemporary African American Literature* (2011) and Mandolin Brassaw's article "The Light That Came to Lucille Clifton: Beyond Lucille and Lucifer," *MELUS: Multi-Ethnic Literature of the U.S.* 37 (2012).

Edwidge Danticat

Danticat is author of *Breath, Eyes, Memory* (1994), *Krik? Krak!* (1996), *The Farming of Bones* (1998), *Behind the Mountains* (2002), the travel book *After the Dance: A Walk Through Carnival in Jacmel, Haiti* (2002), *The Dew Breaker* (2004), *Anacaona: Golden Flower, Haiti, 1490* (2005), the memoir *Brother, I'm Dying* (2007), the children's book *Eight Days: A Story of Haiti* (2010), and the collection of essays *Create Dangerously: The Immigrant Artist at Work* (2011). She has also written "Claire of the Sea Light" in *Haiti Noir* (2010), of which she edited. She is also editor of *The Butterfly's Way: Voices from the Haitian Dyaspora in the United States* (2003) and *The Best American Essays 2011* (2011) with Robert Atwan. Interviews with Danticat include "The Dangerous Job of Edwidge Danticat: An Interview" in *Callaloo* 19 (1996), "An Interview with Edwidge Danticat" in *Contemporary Literature* 44 (2003), "Dyasporic Appetites and Longings: An Interview with Edwidge Danticat" in *Callaloo* 30 (2007), and "Up Close and Personal: Edwidge Danticat on Haitian Identity and the Writer's Life" in *African American Review* 43 (2009). Critical engagements with her work include Caine Mardorossian's *Reclaiming Difference: Caribbean Women Rewrite Postcolonialism* (2005), Meredith Gadsby's *Sucking Salt: Caribbean Women Writers, Migration, and Survival* (2006), and *Edwidge Danticat: a Reader's Guide* (2010), edited by Martin Munro.

Samuel R. Delany

Delaney's novels are *The Jewels of Aptor* (1962); *Captives of the Flame* (1963, rev. as *Out of the Dead City*, 1968); *The Towers of Toron* (1964, rev. 1968); *The Ballad of Beta-2* (1965); *City of a Thousand Suns* (1965, rev. 1969); *Babel-17* (1966); *Empire Star* (1966); *The Einstein Intersection* (1967, corr. ed. 1968); *Nova* (1968); *The Fall of the Towers* (1970), which was published as three earlier novels, *Captives of the Flame*, *The Towers of Toron*, and *City of a Thousand Suns*; *The Tides of Lust* (1973); *Dhalgren* (1975); *Triton* (1976); *Empire* (with Howard V. Chaykin, 1978); *Distant Stars* (1981); *Neveryona, or The Tale of Signs and Cities* (1983); *Stars in My Pocket Like Grains of Sand* (1984); *Flight from Neveryon* (1985); *The Bridge of Lost Desire* (1987); *They Fly at Ciron* (1993); *The Mad Man* (1994); *Hogg* (1994); and *Atlantis: Three Tales* (1995), *Dark Reflections* (2007), and *Through the Valley of the Nest of Spiders* (2012). He has also published the novellas *Time Considered as a Helix of Semi-Precious Stones*, in *World's Best Science Fiction* (1969) and *Phallos* (2004). He is also author of the *Return to Nevèrÿon* series, which includes *Tales of Nevèrÿon* (1979), *Neveryóna* (1983), *Flight from Nevèrÿon* (1985), and *The Bridge of Lost Desire* (1987). The most complete collection of his short stories is *Driftglass/Starshards* (1993). Uncollected short stories include "Empire Star" (1996), "Atlantis: Model 1924" in *Atlantis: Three Tales* (1995), "Tapestry" in *Aye and Gomorrah* (2003), "The Desert of Time" in *Omni* (1992), and "In The Valley of the Nest of Spiders" in *Black Clock* (2007). His memoirs and letters include *Heavenly Breakfast* (1979), *The Motion of Light in Water* (1988), *Times Square Red, Times Square Blue* (1999), *Bread & Wine: An Erotic Tale of New York* (1999), *1984: Selected Letters* (2000). His critical works include *The Jewel-hinged Jaw: Notes on the Language of Science Fiction* (1977); *The American Shore: Meditations on a Tale of Science Fiction* (1978); *Starboard Wine: More Notes on the Language of Science Fiction* (1984); *Wagner/Artaud: A Play of 19th and 20th Century Critical Fictions* (1988); *The Straits of Messina* (1989); *Silent Interviews* (1995); *Longer Views* (1996); *Shorter Views* (1999); *About Writing* (2005).

A biography is Seth McEvoy's *Samuel R. Delany* (1984). For interviews and more biographical information, see *Conversations with Samuel R. Delany* (2009). Critical engagements with his work include *Ash of Stars: On the Writing of Samuel R. Delany* (1996), edited by James Sallis, and Jeffrey Tucker's *A Sense of Wonder: Samuel R. Delany, Race, Identity, and Difference* (2004). Earlier critical interpretations of his work are found in Robert Elliot Fox's *Conscientious Sorcerers: The Black Postmodernist Fiction of LeRoi Jones/Amiri Baraka, Ishmael Reed, and Samuel R. Delany* (1987) and Jane Branhan Weedman's *Samuel R. Delany* (1982). The most recent bibliography is Michael W. Peplow and Robert S. Bravard's *Samuel R. Delany: A Selective Primary and Secondary Bibliography, 1979–1983*, in *Black*

American Literature Forum 18 (1984), a special issue devoted to Delany's writings.

Rita Dove

Dove's collections of poetry include: *The Yellow House on the Corner* (1980), *Museum* (1983), *Thomas and Beulah* (1986), *The Other Side of the House* (1988), with photographs by Tamarra Kaida, *Grace Notes* (1989), *Selected Poems* (1993), *Lady Freedom among Us* (1993), *Mother Love: Poems* (1995), *On the Bus with Rosa Parks: Poems* (1999), *American Smooth* (2004), and *Sonata Mulattica: Poems* (2009). Her chapbooks are *Ten Poems* (1977), *The Only Dark Spot in the Sky* (1980), *Mandolin* (1982), and *Evening Primrose* (1998). Her prose includes a collection of short stories, *Fifth Sunday* (1985), the novel *Through the Ivory Gate* (1992), and the collection of essays, *The Poet's World* (1995). Dove has also written *The Darker Face of the Earth: A Play* (1996). She has also edited *The Best American Poetry 2000* (2000) and *The Penguin Anthology of 20th Century American Poetry* (2011).

For biographical information and interviews, see *Conversations with Rita Dove* (2003), edited by Earl G. Ingersoll, and Camille Dungy's "Interview with Rita Dove," *Callaloo* 28 (2005). Critical engagements with her work include John Shoptaw's "Segregated Lives: Rita Dove's *Thomas and Beulah*" in *Reading Black, Reading Feminist* (1990), edited by Henry Louis Gates, Jr. and Theodora Carlisle's "Reading the Scars: Rita Dove's *The Darker Face of the Earth*," *African American Review* 34 (2000). Full-length studies include Therese Steffen's *Crossing Color: Transcultural Space and Place in Rita Dove's Poetry, Fiction, and Drama* (2001), Malin Pereira's *Rita Dove's Cosmopolitanism* (2003), and Pat Righelato's *Understanding Rita Dove* (2006). The most recent bibliography of Dove's works is Fred Viebahn's "Rita Dove: a Selective Bibliography" included in a special issue devoted to her work of *Callaloo* 31 (2008).

Ernest Gaines

Gaines is the author of *Catherine Carmier* (1964), *Of Love and Dust* (1967), *Bloodline* (1968), *The Autobiography of Miss Jane Pittman* (1971), *A Long Day in November* (1971), *In My Father's House* (1978), *A Gathering of Old Men* (1983), *A Lesson Before Dying* (1993), and *Mozart and Leadbelly: Stories and Essays* (2005). His short stories include the collection *Bloodline* (1968), "The Turtles" (1956), "Boy in the Double-Breasted Suit" (1957), "Mary Louis" (1960), and "My Grandpa and the Haint" (1966). He also published two short works, "Home: A Photo Essay" and "Miss Jane and I," both in *Callaloo* (May 1978).

For biographical information and interviews, see Marcia Gaudet and Carl Wooton's *Porch Talk with Ernest Gaines: Conversations on the Writer's Craft* (1990), Anne K. Simpson's *A Gathering of Gaines: The Man and the Writer* (1991), and John Lowe's *Conversations with Ernest Gaines* (1995). Book-length studies on Gaines include Valerie Babb's *Ernest Gaines* (1991), David C. Estes's *Critical Reflections on the Fiction of Ernest J. Gaines* (1994), Herman Beavers's *Wrestling Angels into Song: The Fictions of Ernest J. Gaines and James Alan McPherson* (1995), Philip Augur's *Native Sons in No Man's Land: Rewriting Afro-American Manhood in the Novels of Baldwin, Walker, Wideman, and Gaines* (2000), and Keith Clark's *Black Manhood in James Baldwin, Ernest J. Gaines, and August Wilson* (2002). For more recent critical engagements with Gaines's work, see chapters in the following monographs and critical essay collections: Keith Byerman's *Remembering the Past in Contemporary African American Fiction* (2005); *Contemporary African American Fiction: New Critical Essays* (2009), edited by Dana A. Williams; Michael Bibler's *Cotton's Queer Relations: Same-Sex Intimacy and the Literature of the Southern Plantation, 1936–1968* (2009); and Thadious Davis's *Southscapes: Geographies of Race, Region, & Literature* (2011). The most recent bibliography of Gaines's work is Frank Shelton's "Ernest J. Gaines," in *Fifty Southern Writers after 1900: A Biographical Sourcebook* (1987).

Essex Hemphill

Collections of Hemphill's poetry include *Earth Life* (1985), *Conditions* (1986), and, including prose as well, *Ceremonies* (1992). With Joseph Fairchild Beam, he edited *Brother to Brother: New Writings by Black Gay Men* (1991). His work is included in *In the Life: A Black Gay Anthology* (1985), edited by Martin Humphries; *New Men, New Minds: Breaking Male Tradition* (1987), edited by Franklin Abbott; and *Gay and Lesbian Poetry in Our Time* (1988), edited by Joan Larkin and Carl Morse. Critical engagements with his work include Melissa Fran Zeiger's *Beyond Consolation: Death, Sexuality, and the Changing Shapes of Elegy* (1997), Robert Reid-Pharr's *Black Gay Man: Essays* (2001), and Roger Sneed's *Representations of Homosexuality: A Black Liberation Theology and Cultural Criticism* (2010).

Charles Johnson

Johnson is the author of *Black Humor* (1970), *Half-Past Nation Time* (1972), *Faith and the Good Thing* (1974), *Oxherding Tale* (1982), *The Sorcerer's Apprentice: Tales and Conjurations* (1986), *Being and Race: Black Writing Since 1970* (1988), *Middle Passage* (1990), *Dreamer* (1998), *I Call Myself an Artist: Writings By and About Charles Johnson* (1999), edited by Rudolph P. Byrd, *King: The Photobiography of Martin Luther King, Jr.* (2000), *Soulcatcher: And Other Stories* (2001), *Turning the Wheel* (2003), and *Dr. King's Refriger-*

ator: And Other Bedtime Stories (2005). He has also edited *Black Men Speaking* (1997) with John McCluskey Jr. For interviews, see *Passing the Three Gates: Interviews with Charles Johnson* (2004), edited by Jim McWilliams. Critical engagements with his work include Jonathan Little's *Charles Johnson's Spiritual Imagination* (1997), *I Call Myself an Artist: Writings By and About Charles Johnson* (1999), edited by Rudolph Byrd, William Nash's *Charles Johnson's Fiction* (2003), Gary Storhoff's *Understanding Charles Johnson* (2004), Rudolph Byrd's *Charles Johnson's Novels: Writing the American Palimpsest* (2005), and Linda Selzer's *Charles Johnson in Context* (2009).

Edward P. Jones

Jones is the author of two collections of short stories, *Lost in the City* (1992) and *All Aunt Hagar's Children* (2006) and the novel *The Known World* (2003). For interviews and biographical information, consider Lawrence P. Jackson's "An Interview with Edward P. Jones" *African American Review* 34 (2000) and Maryemma Graham's "An Interview with Edward P. Jones" *African American Review* 42 (2008). Critical treatments of Jones's work include Katherine Clay Bassard's article "Imagining Other Worlds: Race, Gender, and the 'Power Line' in Edward P. Jones's *The Known World*," *African American Review* 42 (2008); Susan V. Donaldson's "Telling Forgotten Stories of Slavery in the Postmodern South," *Southern Literary Journal* 40 (2008); Carolyn Berman's "The Known World in World Literature: Bakhtin, Glissant, and Edward P. Jones," *Novel: A Forum on Fiction* 42 (2009); Sarah Mahurin Mutter's "'Such a Poor Word for a Wondrous Thing': Thingness and the Recovery of the Human in *The Known World*," *Southern Literary Journal* 43 (2011); and David Ikard's "White Supremacy under Fire: The Unrewarded Perspective in Edward P. Jones's *The Known World*," *MELUS: The Journal of the Society for the Study of the Multi-Ethnic Literature of the United States* 36 (2011).

Gayl Jones

Jones's novels include *Corregidora* (1975), *Eva's Man* (1977), *The Healing* (1998), and *Mosquito* (2000). The play *Chile Woman* was published in 1974 and a collection of stories, *White Rat*, was published in 1978. Her volumes of poetry include *Song for Anninho* (1981), *The Hermit Woman* (1983), and *Xarque and Other Poems* (1985). Though written earlier, Jones's critical study *Liberating Voices: Oral Tradition in African American Literature* was published in 1991. Important interviews include: Michael Harper's "Gayl Jones: An Interview" in *Chant of Saints* (1979), edited by Harper and Robert Stepto; Charles Rowell's "An Interview with Gayl Jones," *Callaloo* (1982); and Claudia Tate's *Black Women Writ-*

ers at Work (1983). Critical engagements with Jones's work can be found in the following monographs: Keith Byerman's *Fingering the Jagged Grain: Tradition and Form in Recent Black Fiction* (1985), Melvin Dixon's *Ride Out the Wilderness: Geography and Identity in Afro-American Literature* (1987), Madhu Dubey's *Black Women Novelists and the Nationalist Aesthetic* (1994), Ann du Cille's *Skin Trade* (1996), Venetria Patton's *Women in Chains: The Legacy of Slavery in Black Women's Fiction* (2000), Ashraf Rushdy's *Remembering Generations: Race and Family in Contemporary African American Fiction* (2001), Bernard W. Bell's *The Contemporary African American Novel: Its Folk Roots and Modern Literary Branches* (2005), Cheryl Wall's *Worrying the Line: Black Women Writers, Lineage, and Literary Tradition* (2005), Jennifer L. Griffiths's *Traumatic Possessions: The Body and Memory in African American Women's Writing and Performance* (2009), Christina Sharpe's *Monstrous Intimacies: Making Post-Slavery Subjects* (2010), and Stephanie Li's *Something Akin to Freedom: The Choice of Bondage in Narratives by African American Women* (2010).

Jamaica Kincaid

Kincaid is the author of *At the Bottom of the River* (1983), *Annie John* (1985), *A Small Place* (1988), *Annie, Gwen, Lilly, Pam, and Tulip* (1989), *Lucy* (1990), *Biography of a Dress* (1990), *The Autobiography of My Mother* (1995), *My Brother* (1997), *My Garden* (1999), *Talk Stories* (2001), *Mr. Potter* (2002), and *Among Flowers: A Walk in the Himalayas* (2005). She also edited *My Favorite Plant: Writers and Gardeners on the Plants They Love* (1998). Critical engagements with her work include Moira Ferguson's *Jamaica Kincaid: Where the Land Meets the Body* (1994), *Jamaica Kincaid* (first edition 2001), edited by Harold Bloom, Simone Alexander's *Mother Imagery in the Novels of Afro-Caribbean Women* (2001), J. Brooks Bouson's *Jamaica Kincaid: Writing Memory, Writing Back to the Mother* (2005), *Jamaica Kincaid and Caribbean Double Crossings* (2006), edited by Linda Lang-Peralta, Justin D. Edwards's *Understanding Jamaica Kincaid* (2007), and Jana Braziel's *Caribbean Genesis: Jamaica Kincaid and the Writing of New Worlds* (2009).

Yusef Komunyakaa

Komunyakaa is author of fifteen books of poetry: *Dedications and Other Darkhorses* (1977), *Lost in the Bone Wheel Factory* (1979), *Copacetic* (1984), *I Apologize for the Eyes in My Head* (1986), *Toys in a Field* (1986), *Dien Cai Dau* (1988), *Magic City* (1992), *Neon Vernacular* (1993), *Thieves of Paradise* (1998), *Pleasure Dome* (2001), *Talking Dirty to the Gods* (2001), *Taboo* (2004), *Gilgamesh* (2006), *Warhorses* (2008), and *The Chameleon Couch* (2011). He has also written two dramatic works, the libretto *Slip Knot* (2003) and *Gilgamesh: A Verse Play* (2006). He also published *Blues Notes: Essays, Interviews, and Commentaries* (2000), edited by Radiclani Clytus. Komuyakka has also co-edited with Sascha Feinstein *The Jazz Poetry Anthology* (1991) and *The Second Set: The Jazz Poetry Anthology. Volume 2* (1996) and served as guest editor for *The Best of American Poetry 2003*. Treatments of his work can be found in a special issue of *Callaloo* 28 (2005) devoted to his work, Trudier Harris's *The Scary Mason-Dixon Line: African American Writers and the South* (2009), and Daniel Cross Turner's *Southern Crossings: Poetry, Memory, and the Transcultural South* (2012). His work has also received critical attention in the following essays: Vince Gotera's "Killer Imagination," *Callaloo* (1990), Toi Derricotte's "The Tension between Memory and Forgetting in the Poetry of Yusef Komunyakaa," *Kenyon Review* (1993), Marilyn Nelson Waniek's "The Gender of Grief," *Southern Review* (1993).

Nathaniel Mackey

Mackey has published four chapbooks of poetry: *Four for Trane* (1978), *Septet for the End of Time* (1983), *Outlandish* (1992), and *Song of the Andoumboulou: 18–20* (1994). He has published five collections of poems: *Eroding Witness* (1985), *School of Udhra* (1993), *Whatsaid Serif* (1998), *Splay Anthem* (2006), and *Nod House* (2011). He has also released a compact disc recording of poems with musical accompaniment, *Strick: Song of the Andoumboulou 16–25* (1995). Mackey is also the author of an ongoing prose fiction project, *From a Broken Bottle Traces of Perfume Still Emanate*, currently consisting of four volumes: *Bedouin Hornbook* (1986), *Djbot Baghostus's Run* (1993), *Atet A. D.* (2001), and *Bass Cathedral* (2008). He has written three critical works, *Discrepant Engagement: Dissonance, Cross-Culturality, and Experimental Writing* (1993), *Gassire's Lute* (2001), and *Paracritical Hinge: Essays, Talks, Notes, Interviews* (2004). He is the editor of the literary magazine *Hambone* and co-edited *Moment's Notice: Jazz in Poetry and Prose* (1993) with Art Lange. Critical engagements with Mackey's work include: Meta DuEwa Jones's *The Muse is Music: Jazz Poetry from the Harlem Renaissance to Spoken Word* (2011), J. Edward Mallot's "Sacrificial Limbs, Lambs, Iambs, and I Ams: Nathaniel Mackey's Mythology of Loss," *Contemporary Literature* 45 (2004), *Conversations with Nathaniel Mackey* (1999), edited by Kamau Brathwaite, and special issues of *Talisman: A Journal of Contemporary Poetry and Poetics* 9 (1992) and *Callaloo* 23 (2000).

Paule Marshall

Marshall's published novels are *Brown Girl, Brownstones* (1959), *The Chosen Place, the Timeless People* (1969), *Praisesong for the Widow* (1983), *Daughters* (1991), and *The Fisher King* (2000). She has published a collection of novellas, *Soul Clap Hands and Sing* (1961), and a collection of novellas and short stories, *Reena and Other Stories* (1983), which includes the oft-cited essay "From the Poets in the Kitchen," and *Triangular Road: A Memoir* (2009) For biographical information and interviews, see *Conversations with Paule Marshall* (2010), edited by James C. Hall and Heather Hathaway. Critical engagements with Marshall's work include Dorothy Denniston's *The Fiction of Paule Marshall: Reconstructions of History, Culture, and Gender* (1995), Joyce Pettis's *Toward Wholeness in Paule Marshall's Fiction* (1995), Eugenia DeLamotte's *Places of Silence, Journeys of Freedom* (1998), Bernhard Melchior's *Re/Visioning the Self: Autobiographical and Cross-Cultural Dimensions in the Work of Paule Marshall* (1998), Heather Hathaway's *Caribbean Waves: Relocating Claude McKay and Paule Marshall* (1999), Catherine A. John's *Clear Word and Third Sight: Folk Groundings and Diasporic Consciousness*, Cheryl A. Wall's *Worrying the Line: Black Women Writers, Lineage, and Literary Tradition* (2005), and Meredith Gadsby's *Sucking Salt: Caribbean Women Writers, Migration, and Survival* (2006). Important essays in books are Barbara T. Christian's "Sculpture and Space: The Interdependency of Character and Culture in the Novels of Paule Marshall," in her *Black Women Novelists* (1980); Hortense Spillers's "The Chosen Place, the Timeless People: Some Figurations in the New World," in *Conjuring: Black Women: Fiction and Literary Tradition*, (1985), edited by Marjorie Pryse and Hortense Spillers; Susan Willis's "Describing Arcs of Recovery: Paule Marshall's Relationship to Afro-American Culture," in her *Specifying: Black Women Writing the American Experience* (1987); and Abena Busia's "What Is Your Nation?: Reconnecting Africa and Her Diaspora through Paule Marshall's Praisesong for the Widow," in *Changing Our Own Words: Essays on Criticism, Theory, and Writing by Black Women* (1989), edited by Cheryl Wall.

Toni Morrison

Morrison's novels include *The Bluest Eye* (1973), *Sula* (1974), *Song of Solomon* (1977), *Tar Baby* (1981), *Beloved* (1987), *Jazz* (1992), *Paradise* (1998), *Love* (2003), *A Mercy* (2008), and *Home* (2012). Her plays, performed but unpublished, include *Dreaming Emmett* (1986) and *Desdemona* (2011). She has also published the short story "Recitatif" in *Confirmation: An Anthology of African American Women* (1983), edited by Amiri Baraka and Amina Baraka. Her works for children, co-authored with her son, Slade Morrison, include *The Big Box* (1999), *The Book of Mean People* (2002), The *Who's Got Game Series*, which includes *The Ant and the Grasshopper?* (2003), *The Lion or the Mouse?* (2003), *The*

Poppy or the Snake? (2004), The Mirror or the Glass? (2005), and Peeny Butter Fudge (2009). She is also the sole author of Remember: The Journey to School Integration (2004). Morrison has also written several works of nonfiction, many of which have been collected in Playing in the Dark: Essays on Whiteness and the Literary Imagination (1992), and What Moves at the Margin: Selected Nonfiction (2008), edited by Carolyn C. Denard. Essays not collected include "Cooking Out," New York Times Book Review (June 10, 1971); "City Limits, Village Values: Concepts of the Neighborhood in Black Fiction," in Black Literature and the Urban Experience (1981), edited by Michale C. Jaye and Ann Chalmers Watts; "Memory, Creation and Writing," Thought (Dec. 1984). Her speeches given when she accepted the Nobel Prize (1993) and the National Book Foundation Medal for Distinguished Contribution to American Letters, The Dancing Mind (1996), have also been published separately. She is also the editor of The Black Book (1974), Race-ing Justice, En-Gendering Power: Essays on Anita Hill, Clarence Thomas, and the Construction of Social Reality (1992), Birth of a Nation'hood: Gaze, Script, and Spectacle in the O.J. Simpson Case (1997) with Claudia Brodsky Lacour, and Burn This Book: PEN Writers Speak Out on the Power of the Word (2009).

Toni Morrison: Conversations (2008), edited by Carolyn C. Denard, collects interviews with Morrison from 1976 to 2005. Full-length studies of her work include Terry Otten's The Crime of Innocence in the Fiction of Toni Morrison (1989), Doreatha D. Mbalia's Toni Morrison's Developing Class Consciousness (1991), Barbara Hill Rigney's The Voices of Toni Morrison (1991), Patrick Bjork's The Novels of Toni Morrison: The Search for Self and Place within the Community (1992), Karen Carmean's Toni Morrison's World of Fiction (1993), Trudier Harris's Fiction and Folklore: The Novels of Toni Morrison (1991), Lucille P. Fultz 's Toni Morrison: Playing with Difference (2003), Andrea O'Reilly's Toni Morrison and Motherhood: A Politics of the Heart (2004), Susan Neal Mayberry's Can't I Love What I Criticize?: The Masculine and Morrison (2007), and Evelyn Jaffe Schreiber's Race, Trauma, and Home in the Novels of Toni Morrison (2010). Collections of essays discussing Morrison's work include Toni Morrison: Critical Perspectives, Past and Present (1991), edited by Henry Louis Gates, Jr. and Anthony Appiah, New Essays on Song of Solomon (1995), edited by Valerie Smith, Approaches to Teaching the Novels of Toni Morrison (1997), edited by Nellie McKay and Kathryn Earle, Toni Morrison's Beloved: A Casebook (1999), edited by William L. Andrews and Nellie Y. McKay, Toni Morrison's Song of Solomon: A Casebook (2003), edited by Jan Furman, and The Cambridge Companion to Toni Morrison (2007), edited by Justine Tally. Special issues devoted to her work include special sections in Callaloo 13 (1990) and African American Review 26 (1992) and 35 (2001), Modern Fiction Studies 52 (2006), and MELUS: Multi-Ethnic Literature of the U.S. 36 (2011). The most recent published bibliography of Morrison's works is Debbie Mix's "Toni Morrison: A Selected Bibliography," MFS Modern Fiction Studies 39 (1993). The Toni Morrison Society maintains a bibliography of Morrison's primary texts and scholarship devoted to her work on its website.

Walter Mosley

Mosley's stand-alone novels include RL's Dream (1995), The Man in My Basement (2004), Walking the Line (2005), a novella in the Transgressions series, Fortunate Son (2006), The Tempest Tales (2008), and The Last Days of Ptolemy Grey (2010). He has also written a graphic novel with Stan Lee and Jack Kirby, Maximum Fantastic Four (2005). He is the author of several series, the Easy Rawlins mysteries, which include: Devil in a Blue Dress (1990), A Red Death (1991), White Butterfly (1992), Black Betty (1994), A Little Yellow Dog (1996), Gone Fishin' (1997), Bad Boy Brawly Brown (2002), Six Easy Pieces (2003), Little Scarlet (2004), Cinnamon Kiss (2005), and Blonde Faith (2007); the Fearless Jones mysteries, which include: Fearless Jones (2001), Fear Itself (2003), and Fear of the Dark (2006); the Leonid McGill Mysteries, which include: The Long Fall (2009), Known to Evil (2010), When the Thrill Is Gone (2011), and All I Did Was Shoot My Man (2012). He is also author of the Socrates Fortlow books, which include Always Outnumbered, Always Outgunned (1997), Walkin' the Dog (1999), and The Right Mistake (2008). His works of science fiction include Blue Light (1998), Futureland: Nine Stories of an Imminent World (2001), The Wave (2005), and The Gift of Fire / On the Head of a Pin (2012) and the Crosstown to Oblivion series, which includes two novellas published together, Merge/ Disciple (2012). Mosley has published two works of erotica, Killing Johnny Fry: A Sexistential Novel (2006) and Diablerie (2007). He has also written 47 (2005) for young adults. His nonfiction includes Workin' on the Chain Gang: Shaking off the Dead Hand of History (2000), What Next: An African American Initiative Toward World Peace (2003), Life Out of Context: Which Includes a Proposal for the Non-violent Takeover of the House of Representatives (2006), This Year You Write Your Novel (2007), and Twelve Steps Toward Political Revelation (2011). For biographical information and interviews, see Conversations with Walter Mosley, edited by Owen E. Brady. For critical engagements with his work, see Walter Mosley: A Critical Companion (2003), edited by Charles E. Wilson, Jr. and Finding a Way Home: A Critical Assessment of Walter Mosley's Fiction, edited by Owen E. Brady and Derek C. Maus.

Harryette Mullen
Mullen is author of *Tree Tall Woman* (1981), *Trimmings* (1991), *S*PeRM**K*T* (1992), *Muse and Drudge* (1995), *Blues Baby: Early Poems* (2002), which brings together *Tree Tall Woman* with uncollected poems from early in her work, *Sleeping with the Dictionary* (2002). *Trimmings*, *S*PeRM**K*T*, *Muse and Drudge* have also been collected in *Recyclopedia: Trimmings, S*PeRM**K*T, and Muse and Drudge* (2006). She is also author of *The Cracks Between What We Are and What We Are Supposed to Be: Essays and Interviews* (2012). Her critical essays include "Runaway Tongue: Resistant Orality in *Uncle Tom's Cabin*, *Incidents in the Life of a Slave Girl*, *Our Nig*, and *Beloved*" in *The Culture of Sentiment* (1992), edited by Shirley Samuels, "Optic White: Blackness and the Production of Whiteness" in *Diacritics* (1994), "'A Silence Between Us Like a Language': The Untranslatability of Experience in Sandra Cisneros' *Woman Hollering Creek*," *MELUS Journal* (1996), "African Signs and Spirit Writing," *Callaloo* (1996), "'Apple Pie with Oreo Crust': Fran Ross's Recipe for an Idiosyncratic American Novel," *MELUS Journal* (2002), and "'Artistic Expression was Flowing Everywhere': Alison Mills and Ntozake Shange, Black Bohemian Feminists in the 1970s," *Meridians* (2004). Interviews with Mullen include Elisabeth A. Frost's "An Interview with Harryette Mullen," *Contemporary Literature* 41 (2000); Kyle G. Dargan's "Everything We Can Imagine: An Interview with Harryette Mullen," *Callaloo* 30 (2008); Benjamin R. Lempert's "Harryette Mullen and the Contemporary Jazz Voice," *Callaloo* 33 (2010), and Barbara Henning's *Looking Up Harryette Mullen: Interviews on Sleeping With the Dictionary and Other Works* (2011). For critical analysis of her work, see chapters in Deborah Mix's *Vocabulary of Thinking: Gertrude Stein and Contemporary North American Women's Innovative Writing* (2007), Jennifer Ryan's *Post-jazz Poetics: a Social History* (2010), and Evie Shockley's *Renegade Poetics: Black Aesthetics and Formal Innovation in African American Poetry* (2011).

Albert Murray
Murray's novels are *South to a Very Old Place* (1971), *Train Whistle Guitar* (1974), *The Spyglass Tree* (1991), and *The Seven League Boots* (1996). He has also written *The Omni-Americans: Black Experience and American Culture* (1970) and *Stomping the Blues* (1976). In addition, he has published essay-and-lecture collections *The Hero and the Blues* (1973), *The Blue Devils of Nada* (1996), and *From the Briarpatch File: On Context, Procedure, and American Identity* (2001), as well as a book of poems, *Conjugations and Reiterations* (2001). *Good Morning, Blues* (1985) is the autobiography of Count Basie as told to Murray. He has also published correspondence between Ralph Elli-

son and himself in *Trading Twelves: The Selected Letters of Ralph Ellison and Albert Murray* (2000), edited by Murray and John F. Calhoun. For biographical information see *Conversations with Albert Murray*, a collection of interviews spanning from 1972 to 1996 edited by Roberta S. Maguire. For critical engagements with his work, see Warren Carson's "Albert Murray: Literary Reconstruction of the Vernacular Community," *African American Review* 27 (1993), Roberta Maguire's "Walker Percy and Albert Murray: The Story of Two 'part Anglo-Saxon Alabamians,'" *Southern Quarterly* 41 (2002), Michael Borshuk's *Swinging the Vernacular: Jazz and African American Modernist Literature* (2006), and *Albert Murray and the Aesthetic Imagination of a Nation* (2010), edited by Barbara A. Baker. Two early interesting articles on Murray are James Alan McPherson's "The View from the Chinaberry Tree," *Atlantic* (Dec. 1974) and John Wideman's "Stomping the Blues: Ritual in Black Music and Speech," *American Poetry Review* (1978).

Gloria Naylor
Naylor's novels are *The Women of Brewster Place* (1982), *Linden Hills* (1985), *Mama Day* (1988), *Bailey's Cafe* (1992), and *The Men of Brewster Place* (1999), and *1996* (2005). Her short fiction includes "A Life on Beekman Place," *Essence* (Mar. 1980) and "When Mama Comes to Call," *Essence* (Aug. 1982). She has also written the critical essays "Until Death Do Us Part . . . ," *Essence* (May 1985); "The Myth of the Matriarch," *Life* (1988); and "Love and Sex in the Afro-American Novel," *Yale Review* (1988). She also edited *Children of the Night: The Best Short Stories by Black Writers, 1967 to the Present* (1991). Her conversation with Toni Morrison, which was published in *Southern Review* (1985), illuminates both writers. For more interviews and biographical information, see *Conversations with Gloria Naylor* (2004), edited by Maxine Montgomery. A variety of critical points of view are featured in Henry Louis Gates Jr. and Anthony Appiah, eds., *Gloria Naylor: Critical Perspectives, Past and Present* (1993). Full-length studies of her work include Margaret Whitt's *Understanding Gloria Naylor* (1999), *Gloria Naylor's Early Novels* (1999), edited by Margot Anne Kelley, *Gloria Naylor: Strategy and Technique, Magic and Myth* (2001), edited by Shirley Stave, and Maxine Montgomery's *The Fiction of Gloria Naylor: Houses and Spaces of Resistance* (2010).

Barack Obama
Barack Obama has authored two nonfiction books, *Dreams from My Father: A Story of Race and Inheritance* (1995, revised and republished in 2004) and *The Audacity of Hope: Thoughts on Reclaiming the American Dream* (2006), and the children's book *Of Thee I Sing: A Letter to My Daughters* (2010). For critical engagements with his work, see Robert B. Stepto's *A Home*

Elsewhere: Reading African American Literature in the Age of Obama (2010) and Gene Andrew Jarrett's *Representing the Race: A New Political History of African American Literature* (2011).

Suzan-Lori Parks

Parks's plays include *The Sinner's Place* (1984), *Imperceptible Mutabilities in the Third Kingdom* (1989), *Betting on the Dust Commander* (1990), *The Death of the Last Black Man in the Whole Entire World* (1990), *Devotees in the Garden of Love* (1992), *The America Play* (1994), *Venus* (1996), *In the Blood* (1999), *Fucking A* (2000), *Topdog/Underdog* (2001), *365 Days/ 365 Plays* (2006), *Ray Charles Live!* (2007), *Father Comes Home from the Wars (Parts 1, 8 9)* (2009), *The Book of Grace* (2010), and a musical adaptation of *Porgy and Bess* (2011) with Diedre L. Murray. The radio plays *Pickling* (1990), *Third Kingdom* (1990), and *Locomotive* (1991). She is also author of the essay "New Black Math" in *Theatre Journal* 57 (2005) and *Getting Mother's Body: A Novel* (2003). An article written about her work include Brian Norman's "The Historical Uncanny: Segregation Signs in Getting Mother's Body, a Post-Civil Rights American Novel," *African American Review* 43 (2009) and major critical treatments include *Suzan-Lori Parks: A Casebook* (2007), edited by Kevin J. Wetmore, Jr. and Alycia Smith-Howard, and Philip C. Kolin's edited volume *Suzan-Lori Parks: Essays on the Plays and Other Works* (2010).

Caryl Phillips

Phillips is the author of *The Final Passage* (1985), *A State of Independence* (1986), *Higher Ground* (1989), *Cambridge* (1991), *Crossing the River* (1993), *The Nature of Blood* (1997), *A Distant Shore* (2003), *Dancing in the Dark* (2005), and *In the Falling Snow* (2009). His nonfiction includes *The European Tribe* (1987), *The Atlantic Sound* (2000), *A New World Order* (2001), *Foreigners* (2007), and *Colour Me English* (2011). He has also written the stage plays *Strange Fruit* (1981), *Where There is Darkness* (1982), *The Shelter* (1984), and *Rough Crossings* (2007). He is also editor of *Extravagant Strangers: A Literature of Belonging* (1997) and *The Right Set: A Tennis Anthology* (1999).

For biographical information and interviews, see *Conversations with Caryl Phillips* (2009). Critical engagements with his work include Gail Low's "A Chorus of Common Memory: Slavery and Redemption in Caryl Phillips's *Cambridge* and *Crossing the River*," in *Research in African Literatures* (1998), Claude Julien's "Surviving through a Pattern of Timeless Moments: A Reading of *Crossing the River*," in *Black Imagination and the Middle Passage* (1999), edited by Maria Diedrich and Henry Louis Gates, Jr., María Ropero's "Travel Writing and Postcoloniality: Caryl Phillips's *The Atlantic Sound*," *Atlantis* 25 (2003), Elena Saez's "Postcoloniality, Atlantic Orders, and

the Migrant Male in the Writings of Caryl Phillips," *Small Axe: A Caribbean Journal of Criticism* 9 (2005). His works are also discussed in chapters in the following books: Wendy Walters's *At Home in Diaspora: Black International Writing* (2005), Stephen Clingman's *The Grammar of Identity: Transnational Fiction and the Nature of the Boundary* (2009), Yogita Goyal's *Romance, Diaspora, and Black Atlantic Literature* (2010), Abigail Ward's *Caryl Phillips, David Dabydeen and Fred D'Aguiar: Representations of Slavery* (2011), and Akinwumi Adesokan's *Postcolonial Artists and Global Aesthetics* (2011).

Ntozake Shange

Shange is the author of the following plays: *For Colored Girls Who Have Considered Suicide/When the Rainbow Is Enuf: A Choreopoem*, (1975); *A Photograph: A Study of Cruelty* (1981); *Where the Mississippi Meets the Amazon* (1977), with Thulani Nkabinde and Jessica Hagedorn; *From Okra to Greens: A Different Kinda Love Story; A Play with Music and Dance* (1975, with a revised edition published in 1981); *Boogie Woogie Landscapes* (1978); *Spell No.7: A Geechee Quick Magic Trance Manual* (1979), published as *Spell No.7: A Theatre Piece in Two Acts* (1981); *Three Pieces: Spell No.7; A Photograph: Lovers in Motion; Boogie Woogie Landscapes* (1981); *It Has Not Always Been This Way: A Choreopoem*, (1981), a revision of *From Okra to Greens: A Different Kinda Love Story*, in collaboration with the *Sounds in Motion Dance Company*, Symphony Space Theater; *Three for a Full Moon* [and] *Bocas* (1982), *Three Views of Mt. Fuji* (1987); *Betsey Brown: A Rhythm and Blues Musical* (1989); *The Love Space Demands: A Continuing Saga* (1993). She has also adapted Bertolt Brecht's *Mother Courage and Her Children* (1980) and Willy Russell's *Educating Rita* (1982). Her novels include *Sassafrass, Cypress, and Indigo* (1982), *Betsey Brown* (1985), *Liliane: Resurrection of the Daughter* (1994), and *Some Sing, Some Cry* (2010), co-written with Ifa Bayeza. Shange's works of poetry include *Melissa and Smith* (1976); *Natural Disasters and Other Festive Occasions*, contains both prose and poems (1977); *A Photograph: Lovers in Motion: A Drama* (1977); *Nappy Edges* (1978) ; *Some Men* (1981); *A Daughter's Geography* (1983); *From Okra to Greens* (1984); *Ridin' the Moon in Texas: Word Paintings* (1987), responses to art in prose and poetry; *The Love Space Demands: A Continuing Saga* (1991); *Three Pieces* (1992); *The Sweet Breath of Life: A Poetic Narrative of the African-American Family* (2004), with photographs by the Kamoinge Workshop. Her prose includes *See No Evil: Prefaces, Essays and Accounts, 1976–1983*, (1984), *Plays, One* (1992), *If I Can Cook You Know God Can* (1999). She also edited *The Beacon Best of 1999: Creative Writing by Women and Men of All Colors* (1999). She has also written several works for children, including: *I Live in Music* (1994), illustrated by Romare Bearden, *Whitewash* (1997), *Float Like a Butterfly: Muhammad Ali, the Man Who Could Float Like a Butterfly and Sting Like a Bee* (2002), *Ellington Was Not a Street* (2003), and *Daddy Says* (2003).

Critical books on Shange include Neal Lester's *Ntozake Shange: A Critical Study of the Plays* (1995), Tejumola Olaniyan's *Scars of Conquest/Masks of Resistance: The Invention of Cultural Identities in African, African-American and Caribbean Drama* (1995), Lester's *Ntozake Shange: A Critical Study of the Plays* (1995), Kimberly Benston's *Performing Blackness* (2001), and Teresa N. Washington's *Our Mothers, Our Powers, Our Texts: Manifestations of Ajé in Africana Literature* (2005).

Tracy K. Smith

Smith has published three collections of poetry: *The Body's Question* (2003), *Duende* (2007), and *Life on Mars* (2011). She has contributed "My Next Great Poem" to *Poets on Teaching: A Sourcebook* (2010), edited by Joshua Marie Wilkinson. Her work is also included in *Gathering Ground: A Reader Celebrating Cave Canem's First Decade* (2006). Interviews with Smith can be found in *Callaloo* 27 (2004) and information regarding her membership in the Dark Room Collective can be found in Brian Reed's "The Dark Room Collective and Post-Soul Poetics" in *African American Review* 41 (2007).

Natasha Trethewey

In addition to the nonfiction book *Beyond Katrina: A Meditation on the Mississippi Gulf Coast* (2010), Trethewey's collections of poetry include *Domestic Work* (2000), *Bellocq's Ophelia* (2002), *Native Guard* (2006), and *Thrall* (2012). Trethewey also edited of *Best New Poets 2007* (2007) with Jeb Livengood. Critical discussions of her work include: Annette Debo's "Ophelia Speaks: Resurrecting Still Lives in Natasha Trethewey's Bellocq's Ophelia," *African American Review* 42 (2008), Brian Reed's "The Dark Room Collective and Post-Soul Poetics," in *African American Review* 41 (2007), and chapters in Katherine Henninger's *Ordering the Façade: Photography and Contemporary Southern Women's Writing* (2007), and Thadious M. Davis's monograph *Southscapes: Geographies of Race, Region, & Literature* (2011).

Alice Walker

Walker's works of fiction include *The Third Life of Grange Copeland* (1970), *In Love and Trouble: Stories of Black Women* (1973), *Meridian* (1976), *You Can't Keep a Good Woman Down* (1981), a collection of short stories, *The Color Purple* (1982), *The Temple of My Familiar* (1989), *Possessing the Secret of Joy* (1992), *Everyday Use* (1994), edited by Barbara Christian, *By the Light of My Father's Smile* (1998), *The Way Forward Is With a Broken Heart* (2000), *Now Is*

the Time to Open Your Heart: A Novel (2004). She has edited *I Love Myself When I'm Laughing . . . and Then Again When I Am Looking Mean and Impressive: A Zora Neale Hurston Reader* and written *The Same River Twice: Honoring the Difficult; A Meditation of Life, Spirit, Art, and the Making of the Film "The Color Purple," Ten Years Later* (1996). Her works of poetry from 1965 to 1990 have been collected in *Her Blue Body Everything We Know: Earthling Poems, 1965–1990 Complete* (1991). Collections published after 1990 include: *A Poem Traveled Down My Arm: Poem and Drawings* (2002), *Absolute Trust in the Goodness of the Earth: New Poems* (2003), and *Hard Times Require Furious Dancing: New Poems* (2010). Her nonfiction includes *In Search of Our Mother's Gardens: Womanist Prose* (1983), *Living by the Word: Selected Writings, 1973–1987*, *Warrior Marks: Female Genital Mutilation and the Sexual Blinding of Women* (1993), with Pratibha Parmar, *Alice Walker Banned* (1996), *Anything We Love Can Be Saved: A Writer's Activism* (1997), *Sent By Earth: A Message from the Grandmother Spirit after the Attacks on the World Trade Center and Pentagon* (2002), *We Are the Ones We Have Been Waiting For: Inner Light in a Time of Darkness: Meditations* (2006), *Overcoming Speechlessness: a Poet Encounters the Horror in Rwanda, Eastern Congo, and Palestine/Israel* (2010), *The Chicken Chronicles: Sitting with the Angels Who Have Returned with My Memories: Glorious, Rufus, Gertrude Stein, Splendor, Hortensia, Agnes of God, The Gladyses, & Babe: a Memoir* (2011), and *A Child's View from Gaza: Palestinian Children's Art and the Fight Against Censorship* (2012). She has also written works for children, including, *Langston Hughes: American Poet* (1973), *To Hell with Dying* (1988), *There is a Flower at the Tip of My Nose Smelling Me* (2008), *Finding the Green Stone* (1991), *Why War is Never a Good Idea* (2007).

For more biographical information, see Evelyn C. White's *Alice Walker: A Life* (2004) and *The World Has Changed: Conversations with Alice Walker* (2010), edited by Rudolph P. Byrd. Bibliographies are Louis and Darnell Pratt's *Alice Malsenior Walker: An Annotated Bibliography, 1968–1986* (1988), and Erma D. Banks and Keither Byerman's *Alice Walker: An Annotated Bibliography* (1989). Significant book-length critical studies published since these bibliographies include Elliot Butler-Evans's *Race, Gender and Desire: Narrative Strategies in the Fiction of Toni Cade Bambara, Toni Morrison and Alice Walker* (1989); Molly Hite's *The Other Side of the Story: Structures and Strategies of Contemporary Feminist Narrative* (1989); Donna Haisty Winchell's *Alice Walker* (1992); Henry Louis Gates Jr. and Anthony Appiah's *Alice Walker: Critical Perspectives Past and Present*; Lillie P. Howard's *Alice Walker and Zora Neale Hurston: The Common Bond* (1993); and Barbara T. Christian's *"Everyday Use" by Alice Walker: A Casebook* (1994). Treatments of her work can also be found in Trudier Harris's *South of Tradition: Essays on African American Literature* (2002), Jeff Abernathy's *To Hell and Back: Race and Betrayal in the Southern Novel* (2003), Gerri Bates's *Alice Walker: A Critical Companion* (2005), Brian Norman's *Neo-Segregation Narratives: Jim Crow in Post-Civil Rights American Literature* (2010), Channette Romero's *Activism and the American Novel: Religion and Resistance in Fiction by Women of Color* (2012), and Bernard W. Bell's *Bearing Witness to African American Literature: Validating and Valorizing Its Authority* (2012).

Colson Whitehead

Whitehead's novels include *The Intuitionist* (1999), *John Henry Days* (2001), *Apex Hides the Hurt* (2006), *Sag Harbor* (2009), and *Zone One: A Novel* (2011). He has also written a collection of essays, *The Colossus of New York* (2003). Critical considerations of Whitehead's work include Saundra Liggins's "The Urban Gothic Vision of Colson Whitehead's *The Intuitionist* (1999)," *African American Review* 40 (2006), Michele Elam's "Passing in the Post-Race Era: Danzy Senna, Philip Roth, and Colson Whitehead," *African American Review* 41 (2007), Howard Rambsy II's "The Rise of Colson Whitehead: Hi-Tech Narratives and Literary Ascent," in *New Essays on the African American Novel: From Hurston and Ellison to Morrison and Whitehead* (2008), edited by Lovalerie King and Linda F. Selzer. Whitehead is also discussed in Isiah Lavender III's *Race in American Science Fiction* (2011).

John Edgar Wideman

Wideman's novels include *A Glance Away* (1967), *Hurry Home* (1970), *The Lynchers* (1973), *Hiding Place* (1981), *Sent for You Yesterday* (1983), *Reuben* (1987), *Philadelphia Fire* (1990), *The Cattle Killing* (1996), *Two Cities* (1998), and *Fanon* (2008). His collections of short stories are *Damballah* (1981), *Fever* (1989), *The Stories of John Edgar Wideman* (1992), published as *All Stories Are True* in 1993, *God's Gym* (2005), and *Briefs* (2010). His nonfiction works include the memoirs *Brothers and Keepers* (1984) and *Hoop Roots: Basketball, Race, and Love* (2001) as well as *Fatheralong: A Meditation on Fathers and Sons, Race and Society* (1994). Wideman is also the author of the travel memoir *The Island: Martinique* (2003). He has also edited *My Soul Has Grown Deep: Classics of Early African-American Literature* (2001) and *The Best of the Drue Heinz Literature Prize* (2001). For interviews and more biographical information, see *Conversations with John Edgar Wideman* (1998), edited by TuSmith. Full-length studies of his work include James Coleman's *Blackness and Modernism: The Literary Career of John Edgar Wideman* (1989) and *Writing Blackness: John Edgar

Wideman's Art and Experimentation (2010), Keith Byerman's *John Edgar Wideman: A Study of the Short Fiction* (1998) and Tracie Guzzio's *All Stories Are True: History, Myth, and Trauma in the Work of John Edgar Wideman* (2011). For a collection of critical essays, see *Critical Essays on John Edgar Wideman* (2006), edited by Bonnie TuSmith and Byerman.

Sherley Anne Williams

Williams's poetry is collected in *The Peacock Poems* (1975; under Shirley Williams) and *Some One Sweet Angel Chile* (1982). Her fiction includes the short stories "Tell Martha Not to Moan," anthologized here, and "The Lawd Don't Like Ugly," in *Between Mothers and Daughters: Stories across Generations* (1985), edited by Susan Koppelman; the novel *Dessa Rose* (1986); and the children's book *Working Cotton* (1992). Her critical works include *Give Birth to Brightness: A Thematic Study in Neo-Black Literature* (1972); "The Blues Roots of Contemporary Afro-American Poetry," *Massachusetts Review* (1977); "Anonymous in America," *Boundary* (1978); "Meditations on History," in *Midnight Birds, Black-Eyed Susans* (1980), edited by Mary Helen Washington; and "Some Implications of Womanist Theory," in *Reading Black, Reading Feminist* (1990), edited by Henry Louis Gates Jr. Her play *Letters from a New England Negro* was published in *Callaloo* 5 (1979). Critical engagements with her work include chapters in the following monographs: Ashraf Rushdy's *Neo-slave Narratives: Studies in the Social Logic of a Literary Form* (1999), Angelyn Mitchell's *The Freedom to Remember: Narrative, Slavery, and Gender in Contemporary Black Women's Fiction* (2002), Jennifer Griffiths's *Traumatic Possessions: the Body and Memory in African American Women's Writing and Performance* (2009) and Jennifer Ryan's *Post-jazz Poetics a Social History* (2010). Important earlier essays discussing her work include Deborah McDowell's "Negotiating between Tennessees: Witnessing Slavery Father Freedom: *Dessa Rose*," in *Slavery and the Literary Imagination* (1989), edited by McDowell and Arnold Rampersand and Barbara Christian's "Somebody Forgot to Tell Somebody Something: African American Women's Historical Novels," in *Wild Women in the Whirlwind* (1990), Mae Henderson's *Speaking in Tongues*," in *Reading Black, Reading Feminist* (1990), edited by Gates; and Melissa Walker's *Down from the Mountaintop: Black Women's Novels in the Wake of the Civil Rights Movement, 1966–1989* (1991).

August Wilson

Wilson's plays include *Recycle* (1973), *Black Bart and the Sacred Hills* (1977), *Fullerton Street* (1980), *Jitney* (1982), *Ma Rainey's Black Bottom* (1984), *The Homecoming* (1989), *Fences* (198), *Joe Turner's Come and Gone* (1984), *The Coldest Day of the Year* (1989), *The Piano Les-*

son (1990), *Two Trains Running* (1991), *Seven Guitars* (1995), *King Hedley II* (1999), *How I Leaned What I Learned* (2002), *Gem of the Ocean* (2003), and *Radio Golf* (2005). His poetry has appeared in several periodicals as well as in *The Poetry of Black Americans: Anthology of the Twentieth Century* (1973), edited by Arnold Adoff. Several collections of essays discussing his work have been published, including: *August Wilson: A Casebook* (1994), edited by Marilyn Elkins, *May All Your Fences Have Gates: Essays on the Drama of August Wilson* (1994), edited by Alan Nadel, *August Wilson and Black Aesthetics* (2004), edited by Dana A. Williams and Sandra G. Shannon, *The Cambridge Companion to August Wilson* (2007). Full-length considerations of his work include Kim Pereira's *August Wilson and the African-American Odyssey* (1995), Sandra Garrett Shannon's *The Dramatic Vision of August Wilson* (1995), Joan Herrington's *I Ain't Sorry for Nothin' I Done: August Wilson's Process of Playwriting* (1998), Harry Elam's *The Past as Present in the Drama of August Wilson* (2004), Alan Nadel's *August Wilson: Completing the Twentieth-Century Cycle* (2010), and Mary Bogumil's *Understanding August Wilson* (2011). Those interested might also consider chapters in Keith Clark's *Black Manhood in Baldwin, Gaines, and Wilson* (2002) and Soyica Diggs Colbert's *The African American Theatrical Body: Reception, Performance* (2011). For collected interviews, see *Conversations with August Wilson* (2006).

Kevin Young
Young's collections of poetry include *Most Way Home* (1995), *To Repel Ghosts: Five Sides in B Minor* (2001), *Jelly Roll* (2003), *To Repel Ghosts: the Remix* (2005), *Black Maria* (2005), *For the Confederate Dead* (2007), *Dear Darkness* (2008), and *Ardency: a Chronicle of the Amistad Rebels* (2011). Young is also the author of the nonfiction book *The Grey Album: the Blackness of Blackness* (2012). Young has edited *The Collected Poems of Lucille Clifton 1965–2010* (2012) and several anthologies, including: *Giant Steps: the New Generation of African-American Writers* (2000), *Blues Poems* (2003), *Selected Poems: John Berryman* (2004), *Jazz Poems* (2006), *The Art of Losing: Poems of Grief and Healing* (2010), *The Best American Poetry* (2011), and *The Hungry Ear: Poems of Food and Drink* (2012). Interviews with Young and biographical information can be found in *Callaloo* (1998) and *Ploughshares 32* (2006). Critical treatments of Young's work include: Jennifer Drake's "African American Literature and the Post-Soul Aesthetic: Teaching the Poetry of Kevin Young and Elizabeth Alexander" in *Engaging Tradition, Making It New: Essays on Teaching Recent African American Literature* (2008), edited by Stephanie Brown and Éva Tettenborn, and Rick Benjamin's "Mixed-Up Medium: Kevin Young's Turn-of-the-Century American Tryptych" in *American Poets in the 21st Century: the New Poetics* (2007), edited by Claudia Rankine and Lisa Sewell.

PERMISSIONS ACKNOWLEDGMENTS

Edward C.L. Adams, "God" from TALES OF THE CONGAREE by Robert G. O'Meally and Edward C.L. Adams. Copyright © 1987 by the University of North Carolina Press. Used by permission of the publisher.

Elizabeth Alexander, "When" and "Ars Poetica #100: I Believe" from AMERICAN SUBLIME. Copyright © 2005 by Elizabeth Alexander. "The Venus Hottentot" from THE VENUS HOTTENTOT. Copyright © 1990 by the Rector and Visitors of the University of Virginia. Reprinted with the permission of The Permissions Company, Inc. on behalf of Graywolf Press, Minneapolis, Minnesota, www.graywolfpress.org

Lewis Allan [Abel Meeropol], "Strange Fruit" words and music by Lewis Allan. Copyright © 1939 (Renewed) by Music Sales Corporation (ASCAP). All Rights for the United States Controlled by Music Sales Corporation (ASCAP). International Copyright Secured. All Rights Reserved. Used by permission of Music Sales Corporation and Edward B. Marks Music Company c/o Carlin America, Inc.

Maya Angelou, "My Arkansas," copyright © 1978 by Maya Angelou and "Still I Rise," copyright © 1978 by Maya Angelou, from AND STILL I RISE. From I KNOW WHY THE CAGED BIRD SINGS, copyright © 1969 and renewed 1997 by Maya Angelou. Used by permission of Random House, Inc. Any third party use of this material, outside of this publication, is prohibited. Interested parties must apply directly to Random House, Inc. for permission.

James Baldwin, "Princes and Powers," copyright © 1957 by James Baldwin, was originally published in *Encounter*. Copyright renewed. Collected in NOBODY KNOWS MY NAME published by Vintage Books. "Sonny's Blues," copyright © 1957 by James Baldwin was originally published in Partisan Review. Collected in GOING TO MEET THE MAN published by Vintage Books. "Going to Meet the Man," copyright © 1965 by James Baldwin. Copyright renewed. Collected in GOING TO MEET THE MAN. Used by arrangement with the James Baldwin Estate. From NOTES OF A NATIVE SON, copyright © 1983 by James Baldwin. Reprinted by permission of Beacon Press, Boston.

Toni Cade Bambara, "Gorilla, My Love" from GORILLA, MY LOVE, copyright © 1960, 1963, 1964, 1965, 1968, 1970, 1971, 1972 by Toni Cade Bambara, from THE SALT EATERS, copyright © 1980 by Toni Cade Bambara. Used by permission of Random House, Inc. Any third party use of this material, outside of this publication, is prohibited. Interested parties must apply directly to Random House, Inc. for permission.

Amiri Baraka, "Preface to a Twenty Volume Suicide Note," "A Poem for Black Hearts," "Black Art," "The Revolutionary Theatre," "Dutchman," "Wailers," "Notes for a Speech," "A Poem for Willie Best," "Black Dada Nihilismus," "Ka'Ba," "Prologue to 'The Slave,'" and "Slave Ship." Reprinted by permission of SLL/Sterling Lord Literistic, Inc. Copyright by Amiri Baraka. From IT'S NATION TIME (Third World Press 1970). Reprinted by permission of Chris Calhoun Agency. Copyright © by Amiri Baraka.

Eric Barrier and William Griffin, "I Ain't No Joke," words and music by Eric Barrier and William Griffin. Copyright © 1987 UNIVERSAL-SONGS OF POLYGRAM INTERNATIONAL, INC. and ROBERT HILL MUSIC. All Rights Controlled and Administered by UNIVERSAL-SONGS OF POLYGRAM INTERNATIONAL, INC. All Rights Reserved. Used by permission. Reprinted by permission of Hal Leonard Corporation.

Eric Barrier, William Griffin, Chris E. Martin, and Nasir Jones, "New York State of Mind," words and music by Eric Barrier, William Griffin, Chris E. Martin and Nasir Jones. Copyright © 1994 EMI APRIL MUSIC INC., GIFTED PEARL MUSIC, UNIVERSAL MUSIC-Z SONGS and SKEMATICS MUSIC, INC. All Rights for GIFTED PEARL MUSIC Controlled and Administered by UNIVERSAL MUSIC-Z TUNES LLC. All Rights Reserved. International Copyright Secured. Used by permission. Contains elements of "Mahogany" by Eric Barrier and William Griffin. Reprinted by permission of Hal Leonard Corporation.

Gwendolyn Brooks, ""kitchenette building," "the mother," "a song in the front yard," "Sadie and Maud," "the vacant lot," "the preacher: ruminates behind the sermon," "The Sundays of Satin-Legs Smith," "The Rites for Cousin Vit," "The Children of the Poor," "The Lovers of the Poor," "We Real Cool," "The Chicago Defender Sends a Man to Little Rock," "Malcolm X," "Riot," and "Maud Martha." Reprinted by permission of Gwendolyn Brooks. "A Bronzeville Mother Loiters in Mississippi. Meanwhile a Mississippi Mother Burns Bacon" is reprinted by consent of Brooks Permissions.

Ed Bullins, "Clara's Ole Man" from FIVE PLAYS by Ed Bullins is reprinted with the permission of Scribner, a Division of Simon & Schuster, Inc. Copyright © 1968 by Ed Bullins. All rights reserved.

Octavia Butler, "Bloodchild" from BLOODCHILD AND OTHER STORIES. Originally published in *Isaac Asimov's Science Fiction Magazine* (June 1984). Copyright © 1984 by Octavia E. Butler. Reprinted with the permission of The Permissions Company, Inc., on behalf of Seven Stories Press, www.sevenstories.com

Shawn Carter, Douglas Gibbs, R. Johnson, and Justin Gregory Smith, "Song Cry," words and music by Shawn Carter, Douglas Gibbs, R. Johnson, and Justin Gregory Smith. Copyright © 2001 EMI BLACKWOOD MUSIC INC., LIL LULU PUBLISHING and HEAVY HARMONY MUSIC. All Rights for LIL LULU PUBLISHING Controlled and Administered by EMI BLACKWOOD MUSIC INC. All Rights Reserved. International Copyright Secured. Used by permission. Reprinted by permission of Hal Leonard Corporation and Heavy Harmony Music. Ralph Johnson, Extraslick Music (ASCAP) administered by Heavy Harmony Music. Douglas Gibbs, Chitty Chitty Music (ASCAP) administered by Heavy Harmony Music. Includes a sample of "Sounds Like A Love Song" by Ralph Johnson and Douglas Gibbs

Alice Childress, "Trouble in Mind" copyright © 1956, renewed by Alice Childress in 1984. Used by permission of Flora Roberts, Inc.

Eldridge Cleaver, "Convalescence" from SOUL ON ICE, copyright © 1968, 1996 by Eldridge Cleaver. Reprinted by permission of The McGraw-Hill Companies, Inc. Excerpt from "My Negro Problem-And Ours" by Norman Podhoretz from *Commentary*, Feb. 1963, is reprinted by permission of the author. Excerpt from a letter by Irving Louis Horowitz from Commentary, June 1963, is reprinted by permission of the publisher.

Lucille Clifton, "in the inner city," "good times," "malcolm," "study the masters," and "blessing the boats" from THE COLLECTED POEMS OF LUCILLE CLIFTON. Copyright © 1987, 1991, 2000 by Lucille Clifton. Reprinted with permission of The Permissions Company, Inc. on behalf of BOA Editions, Ltd. www.boaeditions.org. "homage to my hips," "what the mirror said," and "the light that came to lucille clifton from *two-headed woman* published by The University of Massacusetts Press (1980). Copyright © 1980 by Lucille Clifton. Now appears in *good woman: poems and a memoir, 1969–1980*, published by BOA Editions. Reprinted by permission of Curtis Brown Ltd.

from AMERICAN HUNGER by Richard Wright. Copyright 1944 by Richard Wright. Copyright © 1977 by Ellen Wright. Reprinted by permission of HarperCollins Publishers. "Blueprint for Negro Writing" published in *The New Challenge Magazine*. Copyright © 1937 by Richard Wright. Reprinted by permission of John Hawkins & Associates, Inc. and the Estate of Richard Wright.

Kevin Young, "Exodus" from ARDENCY: A CHRONICLE OF THE AMISTAD REBELS. Copyright © 2011 by Kevin Young. "Jook" and "Anthem" from JELLY ROLL. Copyright © 2003 by Kevin Young. Used by permission of Alfred A. Knopf, a division of Random House, Inc. Any third party use of this material, outside of this publication, is prohibited. Interested parties must apply directly to Random House, Inc. for permission. "Langston Hughes" from TO REPEL GHOSTS (2001) Is reprinted by permission of the publisher, Zoland Books.

IMAGES

2–3: Photograph by Michael P. Smith © The Historic New Orleans Collection; 5: CBS /Landov; 6: © Chuck Stewart; 24: © Ted Williams/CORBIS; 28: © Michael Ochs Archives/Corbis; 57: photo by Frank Stewart-Kamoinge Inc.; 92–93: © Bettmann/CORBIS; 95: Farm Security Administration; 96: Troy, Adrian. Frontispiece. Cavalcade of the American Negro. Illinois Writers' Program, comp. Chicago: Diamond Jubilee Exposition Authority, 1940; 100: The Granger Collection, New York / The Granger Collection; 122 (top): Library of Congress; The Crowley; 122 (bottom): Library of Congress; 246: Art © Catlett Mora Family Trust / Licensed by VAGA, New York, NY / CityParks Foundation; 390: Photo by Carl Van Vechten, courtesy Yale Collection of American Literature, Beinecke Rare Book and Manuscript Library, Yale University; 472: © Bettmann/CORBIS; 532–533: Moorland-Spingarn Research Center, Howard University; 537: AP IMAGES; 538: © Bettmann/CORBIS; 539: © Bruce Davidson/Magnum Photos; 540: AP Photo; 541: AP Photo; 545: Bettmann/CORBIS; 546: Getty Images; 547: © Bettmann/CORBIS; 548: AP Photo; 549: AP Photo; 556: © Bettmann/CORBIS; 559: © Bettmann/CORBIS; 560: Collection of University of California, Berkley Art Museum; purchased with the aid of funds from the National Endowment for the Arts (selected by The Committee for the Acquisition of Afro-American Art). Courtesy of Michael Rosenfeld Gallery, LLC, New York, NY. Photograph by Joshua Nefsky; 561: © Bettmann/Corbis / AP Images; 912–913: MSgt Cecilio Ricardo, U.S. Air Force. / Defense Imagery; 916: © Carrie Mae Weems. Courtesy of the artist and Jack Shainman Gallery, New York; 919: Schlesinger Library, Radcliffe Institute, Harvard University; 922: Albert Chong; 1126: photo by Frank Stewart-Kamoinge Inc.; 1181: Manuscript, Archives, and Rare Book Library, Robert W. Woodruff Library; 1208: Library of Congress; 1291: © Bettmann/CORBIS; 1370: photo by Budd Williams-Kamoinge Inc.; 1426: Michal Daniel; 1469: AP Photo/Eric Gay.

Index